HANDBOOK OF RESEARCH
ON TEACHING LITERACY THROUGH
THE COMMUNICATIVE AND VISUAL ARTS

HANDBOOK OF RESEARCH ON TEACHING LITERACY THROUGH THE COMMUNICATIVE AND VISUAL ARTS

EDITED BY

James Flood
Shirley Brice Heath
Diane Lapp

 A PROJECT OF THE INTERNATIONAL READING ASSOCIATION

MACMILLAN LIBRARY REFERENCE USA

Simon & Schuster Macmillan

New York

Prentice Hall International

London Mexico City New Delhi Singapore Sydney Toronto

Macmillan Library Reference USA
Simon & Schuster Macmillan
1633 Broadway
New York, NY 10019
Library of Congress Catalog Card Number: 96-31706
ISBN: 0-02-897182-5
Printed in the United States of America
Printing Number
1   2   3   4   5   6   7   8   9   10

Library of Congress Cataloging-in-Publication Data
Handbook of research on teaching literacy through the communicative and
visual arts / James Flood,
    Shirley Brice Heath, and Diane Lapp, editors.
        p.   cm.
    Includes index.
    ISBN: 0-02-897182-5 (alk. paper)
    1. Communication—Study and teaching—Research—Handbooks, manuals,
etc.   I. Flood, James.   II. Heath, Shirley Brice.   III. Lapp, Diane.
P91.3.H36   1996
302.2'07—dc20   96-31706
                                                                      CIP

This paper meets the requirements of ANSI/NISO Z39.48-1992 (Permanence
of Paper).

The Publisher gratefully acknowledges permission to reprint material from the
following sources:

Chapter 59A, "Like Happy Dreams—Integrating Visual Arts, Writing, and
Reading," by Anne Alejandro, Language Arts, January 1994. Copyright 1994 by
the National Council of Teachers of English. Reprinted with permission.

Chapter 60A, "The Eye and the Ear" by Jane Yolen. First appeared in Touch
Magic. Reprinted by permission of Curtis Brown, Ltd. Copyright © 1981 by
Jane Yolen.

In chapter 63A, portions of the Nov.–Dec. 1994 issue of Storyworks magazine
have been reprinted by permission of Scholastic Magazines.

CONTENTS

Part I

THEORETICAL BASES FOR COMMUNICATIVE AND VISUAL ARTS TEACHING

Linda Labbo
    University of Georgia and the National
    Reading Research Center

Michael McKenna
    Georgia Southern University and the
    National Reading Research Center

Part
II
METHODS OF INQUIRY IN COMMUNICATIVE AND VISUAL ARTS TEACHING

Part
III
RESEARCH ON LANGUAGE LEARNERS IN FAMILIES, COMMUNITIES, AND CLASSROOMS

Part V

EXPANDING INSTRUCTIONAL ENVIRONMENTS: TEACHING, LEARNING, AND ASSESSING THE COMMUNICATIVE AND VISUAL ARTS

Part VI

RESEARCH PERSPECTIVES ON CURRICULAR, EXTRACURRICULAR, AND POLICY PERSPECTIVES

Part
VII
VOICES FROM THE FIELD

PREFACE

The contributors of this handbook eagerly anticipate the next century of literacy education and research. In doing so, we have taken an optimistic look at how the concept of literacy is rapidly evolving by focusing on the myriad ways that learners gain knowledge and skills, rather than on the ways in which they do not. We realize that abandoning our irrational loyalty to a constrained perception of literacy is somewhat ironic: this myopic view has defined much of the research we have spent decades conducting. The innovations discussed in several of the handbook's chapters, for example, threaten the very notion of disseminating information by way of a typographic text such as this one. But we are too impressed by the instructional advances offered by embracing an expanded view of literacy to cling jealously to the past; we look hopefully to the future.

Around the world, learners in complex societies take in information visually, imitating practices of skills and attitudes they see demonstrated by others. These visual sources of information, from cave paintings forward, have supplemented oral communication. The art and forms of mediation for visual and verbal messages have developed in coordination with societal stratification and with institutions of support and education for particular segments of these arts. Technology, which has ranged from chunks of charcoal to the latest in electronic video and sound transmission, has mediated the visual and communicative arts and provided socialization into ways of using and appreciating these.

The move to an information economy has been serendipitous for the field of literacy education. The force of computers and other technologies in industry will continue, so that receiving an apprenticeship in a traditional field such as carpentry requires more than five years of education (while a college education usually takes only four). Automobile mechanics now must have multiple levels of certification in electronic engineering, and everyone from file clerks to professors must know how to manage electronic mail and combinations of video, audio, and print representations through their computers. If schools are to continue to see themselves as linked to the world of work and leisure in any way, their means of literacy education must reflect these worlds.

However, institutions of education have established hierarchies of acceptability for the visual and communicative arts that often conflict with the rankings at work within economic and commercial sectors of the current information-based economy. The education systems of modern complex societies typically stress limited ranges of the visual and communicative arts as appropriate display forms, giving highest status to the printed word—notably to students' handwritten verbal representations of their knowledge. This designation of supreme status increasingly contrasts with the pragmatic roles that visual arts and oral language play in everyday bureaucratic interactions and workplaces of all types, including professional occupations. Commingled forms of representation mark every successful sales encounter, city commission presentation, and reporting of the news, whether on television or in newsprint. Similarly, combinations of pictures, words, graphs and charts, music, sound effects, smells, and animation characterize advertising, newspapers, the World Wide Web, MTV, and the evening news on local television channels. Everywhere outside of school, layering of information and multiple types of skills, as well as simultaneous transmission through different art forms, predominates.

From a very early age, children watch images shifting approximately every seven seconds on the television screen with the background "noise" of musical and verbal messages. Whether or not very young children understand all that is happening in rapid-fire media presentations matters far less than the fact that they come to expect these features of presentation to accompany information. Often before they can speak, children can dance, grimace, and make singing noises sufficient to allow adults to recognize these gestures as imitative of a particular advertisement or cartoon. As children grow older, they are increasingly able to comprehend the multiply layered visual and verbal information from television or computer screens while talking with a friend on the telephone or doing their homework.

Teachers dedicate considerable efforts to teaching young readers to scan primary and secondary written texts. Yet their instructional design often ignores the reality that in their spare time, these same students effortlessly "surf" television channels, often catching only a few seconds of "what's going on" before settling on a program they may watch for a few minutes. Even after selecting, young people often watch two or three programs simultaneously, flipping back and forth among them. In viewing television, arcade games, or computer screens, youngsters manipulate controls so as to move rapidly from one type of program or activity to another, often while listening to music or carrying on conversations with friends. Despite the various sources of stimuli, in-depth viewing or engagement with computer technology follows personal interest and requires that the medium offer a continuing challenge. Computer games attract youth only so long as they are challenging; once youngsters have "cracked the system," or figured out how to win most of the time, they want to move on to another game. There is much to learn from this feature of the visual arts for teachers. Interests matter now more than ever for youth; and they offer the surest bridge between the simplex challenges and the success we envision for students—in and out of the classroom.

Throughout this volume such lessons, along with thoughtful pointers from the visual and communicative arts, appear often. The attempt here is to bring the visual arts into a central place in literacy and language education, along with the more established communicative arts of speaking and writing. Visual arts encompass everything from dramatic performances to comic books, television, and video arcade games; the communicative arts, such as reading, writing, and speaking, exist both independently and as integral elements of the visual arts. The role of the visual arts in the leisure activities of young people enables their extensive practice in essential skills, such as self-presentation, role-shifting, empathy-building, sense of plot development, and ability to focus on several things simultaneously. Yet these skills too rarely receive notice in classrooms.

In large part, ignorance of these skills for teachers and parents comes from an irrational loyalty to reading and writing—the expected communicative arts of school. The best reason many adults can give for not allowing more visual arts into the classroom is the fear that the time spent with such media forms will be taken away from the communicative arts. This view denies the layered forms that information takes on in the everyday world and reflects the usual adult views of the media as mutually exclusive. Yet in extra-classroom reality, visual arts motivate and serve as the overwhelmingly preferred companion to the communicative arts, so the mutually exclusive perception has no foundation in life outside the classroom. Moreover, all learners, young and old, constantly demonstrate our ability to attend to more than one thing at a time. (Consider, for example, the ways in which we can hold a telephone conversation in a phone booth while reading billboards and listening to two youngsters talking nearby.) Unless educators can move toward layering both information and forms of display, schools will grow increasingly further away from the learning skills and foundations of factual knowledge that adults in our society need. Acknowledging the responsibility to bring about such alterations in literacy education requires that we undertake numerous changes in attitudes and actions.

Picture books and artistically illustrated children's literature seem fine for very young children, but as we grow older and move through the educational system, we are expected to gain most from "grown-up books," whose every page is filled exclusively with words. In the United States, art books and published collections of illustrations receive the dubious title of "coffee table books," reinforcing their marginal status and association with leisure as distinct from serious work. Mixtures of words and pictures, such as those characteristic of comic books, magazines, and newspapers seem to move the genre lower on the scale of educational acceptability. Teachers can help debunk the notions behind this bias by using informational nonfiction texts, maps, charts, board diagrams, and pictures in classrooms and by encouraging students to do the same in their projects. Numerous teachers, especially in elementary, English as a second language, and adult education already incorporate a broad range of visual and communicative arts into their teaching. The voices of many such teachers appear in this handbook. But much more work needs to be done to carry these trends through secondary schools and into colleges and universities.

Aside from persuasion by anecdotal observations and an array of articles addressing questions of the relative merit or harm of the media (especially television), scholars in psychology and other disciplines linked to education have paid little attention to issues such as cognitive processing across media and its appropriateness within different content areas. Only in the 1970s did the communicative arts transcend the locked focus on learning to read and begin to receive considerable attention from scholars, primarily sociolinguists and anthropologists. In the subsequent decades, volumes on literacy, language learning, early literacy, writing, bilingualism, and language education have come in increasing numbers each year not only from researchers but teachers and student writers as well. Much of that work is reviewed by contributors in this handbook. But the sum of their conclusions constitutes a mandate: this work must be supplemented with substantial study of the cognitive and affective dimensions of the visual arts and their links with linguistic processing.

With this volume, we hope to have started this effort. We want to break the trend of literacy educators' exclusive focus on learning as reading and writing, and urge intense consideration of all the ways that visual arts impact learners' preparation and practices of learning in formal classrooms. We hope to inspire more research on visual arts and the integration of visual representations of knowledge with verbal means. Such inquiries must evolve simply from reporting the pleasure that learners take in drawing or illustrating their narratives to analyzing how different kinds of visual arts promote the cognitive developments rarely fostered by exclusively verbal displays.

Certain teases already appear in the literature. For example, language teachers may be more inclined to consider using drama in their classrooms when they learn that at an early age, children from societies where verbal teasing is prevalent have more developed language repertoires than their counterparts in societies where such teasing is rare. The characteristic of teasing that allows this phenomenon is the encouragement of creative role-playing and thus taking on of other voices. Nonnative English speakers engaged in dramatic role-playing display competencies with English that could never emerge from pencil-and-paper testing or classroom dialogues. Similarly, students reluctant to engage in science or social studies come alive with hypertext discovering ample oral collaborative opportunities to teach or tutor others about their knowledge. Video productions, photographic projects, and artistic creations of graphs, diagrams, and charts provide the chance for differential abilities of students to stand out, so that the hesitant writer receives praise as the superb illustrator.

This is not to suggest, however, that chances for displays of knowledge in multiple media should involve only those areas of students' personal preference or talent. Instead, the goal is to applaud the diverse talents that are hiding in our classrooms and thereby motivate learners to see themselves as learners and even experts in some areas while encouraging them to extend themselves in areas where they may have felt reluctant to go—such as writing or drawing.

Teachers already using visual and communicative arts in their literacy education need evidence from research to support their innovative creativity. They need to be able to comment in workshops with other teachers and in parent conferences on questions such as: What happens to retention and transfer of information and skills within active demonstration, as distinct from essay answers? Does active involvement with texts through drama or video production enable students to receive more information from such forms than when they simply view them? Can we achieve a more accurate rendering of a student's capabilities by tapping into multiple forms of demonstrating knowledge?

Only teachers and students themselves can best answer the question of the appropriateness of multiple forms of visual and communicative arts for all content or subject areas. They will ultimately discover, for example, whether or not musical demonstrations and practice will enable a deeper grasp of fractions. They will discover to what extent the learning of biochemistry or physics is enhanced by experience with computer simulations and laboratory manuals filled with illustrations. They will determine to what extent the preparation of graphs and charts to accompany an oral presentation on toxins in the air enhances the conceptual understanding of an English as a Second Language adult learner who wants to work in an environmental engineering firm. The context of classrooms and the insider perspectives of teachers and students must be sought out to provide answers to such questions. Otherwise, we will find ourselves at the end of another decade armed only with primarily programmatic statements, and scarcely any hard data to show the gains, losses, and trends that would come with serious consideration by literacy educators of both the visual and communicative arts.

The handbook editors and contributors have knowingly broached what they see as the likely direction of future literacy education. They do so with an admitted bias of hope. We would not be true to the purpose of this volume if we did not address these matters directly. Most educators conceive it as their exclusive task to teach reading and writing and to stress stable performance of such skills through response to school-given tasks and tests. They do much of their teaching through uniform sequences with extensive use of commercially prepared materials and curricular directives. These are obviously essential parts of providing a learning environment

that will enable learners to move through the formal educational system. But within literacy education, we feel there is special room for emphasizing the multiplicity and creative chaos of the visual and communicative arts adventure. We feel it essential to stress the uniqueness of each of the visual arts and their connections to many of the communicative arts. We urge serious consideration of this combination and the other classroom changes that follow from such consideration; among them, cross-age learning through production and reception of visual and verbal information and presentation, collaboration among students to prepare for presentation of learning activities for other students as well as for teachers and other authentic observers—even from outside the classroom.

We stand against the reducing of human learning to the representation of knowledge and skills primarily by written means. Teaching and learning are best when they represent the realm of freedom and creativity, as well as the stretching capacities of learners who know well how to adapt to being called upon to display knowledge under varying circumstances. The importance of granting somewhat equivalent rights of entry in classrooms to the visual *and* communicative arts appears particularly appropriate at the end of the twentieth century. Sociopolitical realities may well push harder than they have in the past on the vested interests of the standard approaches to literacy education that are typically represented in textbooks, standardized tests, teacher education, and curricular materials. We believe that combining presentation of materials and requests for displays of conceptual, discrete informational, and technical knowledge will enable all of us—students, teachers, teacher educators, and education researchers—to learn more.

We know of human beings that their changes in beliefs, attitudes, and theories come most easily after they have been entrained by certain actions; hence, ideology and belief often follow from rather than precede action. Teachers and students who already use and know the visual arts, whether through electronic technology or personal artistic talent represent the vanguard of a new paradigm. But they can take responsibility for bringing colleagues and students into action with the visual arts, so that changes in beliefs and motivations can follow from these actions. It is primarily by linking students, teachers, teacher educators, and researchers into communities of practice and inquiry that we can put to work a passion for what is possible and turn the next historical corner in a way that combines the best of the old and the new.

Finally, we would like to express our sincere thanks to every author and reviewer who participated in the development of this handbook. A special thanks is owed to the section editors without whose contributions this book would never have become a reality. We would also like to thank Dr. Linda Lungren, Michelle LeTourneau, Kelly Goss, Joan Irwin, Lloyd Chilton, Andrew Ambraziejus, Catherine Carter, and Ari Kast for their tremendous help with the production of this handbook.

James Flood
Shirley Brice Heath
Diane Lapp

CONTRIBUTORS

EDITORS

James Flood is a Professor of Reading and Language Education at San Diego State University. Dr. Flood was a Fulbright scholar in Portugal and Past President of the National Reading Conference. A noted researcher, teacher, and author of books and articles on literacy issues and a member of the California Reading Hall of Fame, he is the cochair of the International Reading Association's Visual Literacy Committee.

Shirley Brice Heath is a Professor of English and Linguistics, with courtesy appointments in Anthropology and Education, at Stanford University. Recipient of awards from NCTE and the International Reading Association, Dr. Heath is consulting editor for major journals in human development, literacy studies, and cultural anthropology.

Diane Lapp is a Professor of Reading and Language Education at San Diego State University. A widely respected teacher, she is the recipient of the International Reading Association's Outstanding Teacher Educator Award and a member of the California Reading Hall of Fame. Dr. Lapp, a noted researcher and author of many literacy books and articles, is also the cochair of the International Reading Association's Visual Literacy Committee.

SECTION EDITORS

Donna E. Alvermann is Research Professor of Reading at the University of Georgia and Codirector of the National Reading Research Center (NRRC), in collaboration with the University of Maryland. A widely published author, her research focuses on the role of classroom dialogue in content literacy instruction. She is particularly interested in alternative methodologies and their application for literacy research.

Victoria Chou is Professor of Reading, Writing, and Literacy and Acting Dean of the College of Education at the University of Illinois at Chicago. She studies variables that affect intercultural communication between teachers and students. She and Dr. Karen Sakash codirect Project 29, a DeWitt Wallace-Reader's Digest Pathways to Teaching Careers program that supports cohorts of provisionally certified bilingual (Spanish-English) teachers in Chicago public schools.

Bernice E. Cullinan, Professor of Reading at New York University, is a Past President of the International Reading Association and a member of the IRA Hall of Fame. She is coauthor of *Literature and the Child, Fourth Edition*, with Lee Galda and *Language, Literacy and the Child, Second Edition*, with Galda and Dorothy Strickland. She serves on the Advisory Board of WGBH for the Arthur series.

Lee Galda, a Professor of Language Education at the University of Georgia, is coauthor of *Language, Literacy and the Child, Second Edition*, with Bernice Cullinan and Dorothy Strickland and coauthor of *Literature and the Child, Fourth Edition*, with Cullinan. She studies children's engagement with literature and the influences of home and school on literacy learning.

Paul Messaris is an Associate Professor at the Annenberg School for Communication, University of Pennsylvania, in Philadelphia, Pennsylvania. His book *Visual "Literacy": Image, Mind, and Reality* (Boulder, CO: Westview Press, 1994) received the Diamond Anniversary Book Award from the Speech Communication Association in 1996. His most recent text is *Visual Persuasion: The Role of Images in Advertising* (Thousand Oaks, CA: Sage Publications).

Nancy L. Roser is a Professor of Language and Literacy Studies and the Priscilla Flawn Regents Professor of Early Childhood Education at the University of Texas at Austin. She is also Project Director of the Texas Center for Reading and Language Arts and Codirector of the project producing Texas standards for the English Language Arts. A widely published author, she is also on the editorial board of several journals and a member of IRA's Visual Literacy Committee.

James R. Squire is a retired publisher and professor of English education. A lecturer at Harvard Graduate School of Education and Senior Research Associate at Boston University, he is the former Executive Secretary of NCTE. Past President of the NCRE, chair of the School Division of the Association of American Publishers, and Past President of the International

Reading Association Hall of Fame, he has received lifetime contribution awards from NCRE, NCTE, and AAP.

Dorothy S. Strickland is the State of New Jersey Professor of Reading at Rutgers University. A former classroom teacher, she is a Past President of the International Reading Association. She received IRA's Outstanding Teacher Educator of Reading Award, and she was elected to the IRA Reading Hall of Fame. Author of numerous publications, she was the 1994 recipient of the Rewey Belle Inglis Award for Outstanding Woman in the Teaching of English from NCTE.

AUTHORS

Hal Adams is president of the Neighborhood Writing Alliance and faculty member in the College of Education at the University of Illinois at Chicago. Hal conducts adult writing workshops in neighborhood branch libraries, public housing residences, and public schools (with parents) in Chicago. He publishes writing from the workshops in the *Journal of Ordinary Thought*.

Ann Alejandro is an experienced classroom teacher in the Rio Grande River Valley in South Texas. She has published articles in *Language Arts*, a journal of the National Council of Teachers of English. She attempts to expand the literacy of her students through experiences in art, which is the core of her language arts curriculum and writings.

JoBeth Allen is a Professor of Language Education at the University of Georgia. She has been involved with collaborative action research for the past 15 years and is the coauthor of three books reporting action research in whole language classrooms. She studies university / public school collaborations and the effect of such on the literacy development of students, teachers, and teacher educators.

Richard L. Allington is Professor of Education and Chair of the Department of Reading at the State University of New York at Albany. He has served as President of the National Reading Conference and as a member of the board of directors of the International Reading Association. His most recent book, *Schools That Work: All Children Read and Write* (Longmans), was coauthored with Pat Cunningham.

Claire L. Asam, a native Hawaiian educator, is the curriculum and assessment coordinator for the Kamehameha Elementary School in Honolulu, Hawaii. She is a doctoral student in educational administration at the University of Hawaii. Throughout her career she has focused on improving the educational success of Hawaiian students. Toward this end, she has been a research and demonstration teacher, language arts consultant, and program director.

Steven Z. Athanases is Research Associate in the School of Education at Stanford University where he directs a research project on classroom assessment in educational reform. A former high school speech and English teacher, he received NCTE's Promising Research Award in English

Education for his study of classroom discourse about literature and diversity.

Kathryn H. Au, Associate Professor in the College of Education at the University of Hawaii in Honolulu, is the coordinator of a teacher education program designed to increase the number of native Hawaiian teachers. She has been elected president of the NRC and a vice president of AERA. Her research interest is the school literacy development of students of diverse cultural and linguistic backgrounds. Her latest textbook is *Literacy Instruction in Multicultural Settings*.

Lawrence Baines is an Assistant Professor in the English Education program at Florida State University in Tallahassee, Florida. Baines also writes prose, screenplays, and music. He studies the interrelationships among film, video, and books and their roles in literacy learning and teaching.

Carolyn D. Baker is an Associate Professor in the Graduate School of Education at the University of Queensland, Brisbane, Australia. In her research she has applied ethnomethodological and conversation analytic approaches to the analysis of texts and talk, primarily in the field of education. She has published widely on early literacy materials and "talk around text" in classrooms.

Barbara Holland Baskin is a Professor at the State University of New York at Stonybrook and Director of Child and Family Studies. Her research and publication interests relate to educational computer games and programs as effective instructional tools that will enhance literacy development.

James F. Baumann is a Professor of Reading Education at the University of Georgia. During the 1994–95 academic year, while on leave from the university, he engaged in teacher research on communication and literacy while teaching second grade full-time at Fowler Drive Elementary School in Athens, Georgia. He is a member of the board of directors of the International Reading Association.

Debra L. Bayles is an Assistant Professor of Reading and Language Arts at San Diego State University. Her current research interests center on the exploration of alternative ways of knowing—especially as related to teacher preparation, writing development, and reading comprehension. She also writes musical and dramatic presentations and performs with various musical and artistic groups.

Vikram Bhagat is currently a senior at Stanford University where he is majoring in economics. In addition to his studies, he is extremely interested in the multiple formats, roles, and definitions of literacy and these relationships to the leisure activities of young people.

Eleanor Binstock is Assistant Professor of Education in the Interdisciplinary Studies Department of National-Louis University in Chicago, Illinois. She has produced and directed documentary films for the Chicago Council on Fine Arts, and developed and taught film workshops and video-based curricula in the Alternative Schools Network in Chicago. Before that, she was an elementary school teacher in Montreal, Canada.

Betty Shockley Bisplinghoff is a classroom teacher in Athens, Georgia. She is a teacher researcher working on her doctorate in Language Education at the University of Georgia. She served as Director of the National Reading Research Center's School Research Consortium from 1993 to 1996 and is coauthor of two books reporting teacher research, *Engaging Children* and *Engaging Families*.

David Bloome is Professor of Education in the Department of Teaching and Learning at Peabody College of Vanderbilt University. He is the coeditor of *Linguistics and Education: An International Research Journal*, and author of numerous articles and books on social and cultural dimensions of language and literacy. His research has focused on classroom and community settings of literacy education.

Marc Brown, a noted author and illustrator, created the popular Arthur television series, which appears on WGBH, an educational television station in Boston. He is interested in supporting the literacy efforts of the classroom through television and other multimedia.

Bertram C. Bruce, a former senior researcher at Bolt, Berenak and Newman, is a Professor in the Department of Curriculum and Instruction at the University of Illinois. A well-known researcher and author, he studies issues related to many aspects of technology's role in education. He is a member of the International Reading Association's Visual Literacy Committee.

Beverly Bruneau is an Associate Professor in Teaching, Leadership, and Curriculum Studies at Kent State University. Her current research interests center on the development of constructivist preservice and continuing education programs, work with partnership primary schools, and the development of literacy teaching for kindergarten and primary children.

Wayne M. Butler serves as Acting Director of the University of Michigan's English Composition Board where he teaches writing on the Internet and works on university / public school on-line outreach projects. He has served on NCTE's Instructional Technology Committee, codeveloped the award-winning Daedalus Integrated Writing Environment, and is coauthor of *Writing the Information Superhighway* (Allyn and Bacon, 1997).

Robert Calfee is a Professor in the School of Education at Stanford University. A cognitive psychologist, his research interests include acquisition of early literacy and the influence of curricular and school context factors on the learning of young children. He is a member of the International Reading Association Hall of Fame.

John Carey is Managing Director of Greystone Communications, a telecommunications research and planning firm that he founded in 1980. He conducts research about new communi-

cations systems. Dr. Carey is also an Affiliated Research Fellow at Columbia University's Institute for Tele-Information and a consultant to the Freedom Forum Technology Studies Program.

Gen Ling Chang-Wells is a classroom teacher with the Toronto Board of Education. She is interested in the social constructivist model of learning and teaching and its relationship to helping children develop literacy strategies and an understanding of the meaning of historical time.

Joy Chu is a nationally recognized book designer and is frequently invited to serve as a judge in graphic arts shows. She is intricately involved in the many stages of book design. She is very interested in enhancing reading comprehension through the use of picture graphics.

Michelle Carey Clark is a third-grade teacher at Deerfield School in Short Hills, New Jersey. Through her integrated language arts instruction she helps students recognize the meaning of symbols and images as language cues, which, she believes, is a primary component of one's visual literacy experiences.

Marie M. Clay is Professor of Education Emeritus at the University of Auckland. She is a Past President of the International Reading Association and the author of numerous books and research studies on early childhood education and reading recovery. A widely respected scholar / educator, she is a member of the International Reading Association Hall of Fame.

Dwight Conquergood is Chair of Performance Studies at Northwestern University, and Faculty Associate at the Joint Center for Poverty Research, Northwestern University and University of Chicago. In addition to print publications, he has coproduced two award-winning documentaries based on his urban ethnographic research in Chicago: *Between Two Worlds: The Hmong Shaman in America* and *The Heart Broken in Half*.

Colette Daiute is Professor of Developmental Psychology at the City University of New York Graduate School. Dr. Daiute conducts research on the role of oral, written, and visual discourse in the development of knowledge and identity and its effect on literacy learning for all children.

Roger Desmond is Professor of Communication at the University of Hartford. A noted author, his most recent research has involved the creation and evaluation of print and video materials designed to teach young children about media and how they work. His most recent published research is an investigation of the role of media in the emotional states and moods of university undergraduates.

Anne Haas Dyson is a Professor at the Graduate School of Education, University of California, Berkeley. Her publications include *Multiple Worlds of Child Writers: Friends Learning to Write* (1989), *The Social Worlds of Children Learning to Write in an Urban Primary School* (1993), which won NCTE's 1994 David Russell Award for Distinguished Research, and *Writing Superheroes: Contemporary Childhood, Popular Culture, and Classroom Literacy* (1997).

Brian Edmiston is an Assistant Professor in the School of Teaching and Learning at Ohio State University. His research interests are in inquiry through drama, situated learning, dramatic play, learning to be ethical, and teacher research. Dr. Edmiston is the author, with Jeffrey Wilhelm, of *Imagining to Learn: Inquiry, Reading, Ethics, and Integration through Drama*.

Warwick Elley is Professor of Education at the University of Canterbury in New Zealand. A widely acclaimed researcher, scholar, and educator, he has conducted numerous studies on cross-national issues and their effect on the development and assessment of student literacy.

Patricia Enciso is an Assistant Professor in the School of Teaching and Learning at Ohio State University. She is currently a National Academy of Education Spencer Postdoctoral Fellow. Dr. Enciso has authored articles and chapters in *Language Arts*, *Reading and Writing Quarterly*, and *Reading Across Cultures: Teaching Literature in a Diverse Society* (edited by T. Rogers and A. Soter).

Roger Farr is a Chancellor's Professor at Indiana University. A Past President of the International Reading Association, he is currently the Director of the Center for Reading and Language Studies at Indiana University. Dr. Farr has written numerous standardized and performance assessments. His latest book, coauthored with Bruce Tone, is entitled *Portfolio and Performance Assessment: Helping Students Evaluate Their Progress as Readers and Writers*.

Linda Flower is Professor of Rhetoric and Director of the Center for University Outreach at Carnegie Mellon. From 1985 to 1995 she was Codirector of the National Center for the Study of Writing and Literacy at Berkeley and Carnegie Mellon. She is the author of *The Construction of Negotiated Meaning: A Social Cognitive Theory of Writing and of Problem-Solving Strategies for Writing in College and Community*.

Sarah Warshauer Freedman is a Professor of Education in the Graduate School of Education at University of California, Berkeley. She was the Director of the former National Center for the Study of Writing and Literacy. Her research interests include multicultural education and teacher research. Her most recent publication is "Exchanging Writing, Exchanging Cultures."

Vivian L. Gadsden is Associate Professor of Education and Director of the National Center on Fathers and Families at the University of Pennsylvania. Her work in visual and communicative literacy focuses on oral, reading, and written discourses across two and three generations within African-American, Latino, and white families. She also examines the implications of these discourses and interactions for children and adults learning in school, home, and community contexts.

Irene W. Gaskins is founder and director of the Benchmark School in Media, Pennsylvania. A widely recognized researcher and teacher, she studies issues related to reading and writing acquisition and development. Her findings have become the foundation of many effective instructional strategies.

Phillip C. Gonzales is the Senior Project Director of GOALS 2000 Preservice Partnership Program in the Los Angeles County Office of Education and Professor in the Teacher Education Department at California State University, Dominguez Hills. His most recent publication, *ESL / Bilingual Framework for the States of Washington, Oregon, Idaho, Montana, Wyoming, South Dakota, and Colorado*, is published in each state by the Bilingual Education Division of the State Departments of Education.

Judith L. Green, Professor of Education in the Graduate School of Education at the University of California, Santa Barbara, teaches in language and literacy ethnographic research and classroom discourse. She is a founding member of the Santa Barbara Classroom Discourse Group, an ethnographic research community composed of teachers, students, and university-based researchers. Her research focuses on literacy and social construction of knowledge in classrooms.

Jan Greenberg, writer and art educator, directed the Aesthetic Education program at Webster University. She is author of *The Painter's Eye: Learning to Look at Contemporary American Art* and numerous other books. She believes that art is a primary means of enhancing literacy.

Michael Griffin is currently on the faculty of the School of Journalism and Mass Communication at the University of Minnesota. He has published numerous articles on media literacy and visual communication in the mass media; his forthcoming book is titled *Re-Visualizing Media: The Force of the Image in Mass Communication*. Griffin was recently honored with a prestigious Annenberg Scholars Program Fellowship for his work on the visual rhetoric of television news imagery.

Pamela L. Grossman is the Boeing Professor of Teacher Education at the University of Washington, Seattle. Her work has focused on the preparation of secondary English teachers and how student teachers use and modify conceptual and pedagogical tools in their classrooms. In addition, she is working on a new model of professional development that builds a community of learners among high school English and social studies teachers at a school site.

Mel Grubb is Consultant-in-Charge, Reading / Language Arts Unit, Division of Curriculum, Instruction, and Assessment in the Los Angeles County Office of Education. Dr. Grubb is responsible for the training of hundreds of Los Angeles English / language arts teachers to conduct staff development training. These teachers are actively responsible for much of the inservice conducted in the region's schools.

Sherry Guice, Director of Educational Outreach at the National Research Center on English Learning and Achievement, teaches graduate reading courses in the Reading Department at the State University of New York at Albany. She is interested in children's responses to literature and how teachers organize situations where children learn to read and write. Her publications have appeared in *The Journal of Reading Behavior* and *The New Advocate*.

John T. Guthrie is a Professor of Human Development at the University of Maryland at College Park and Codirector of the National Reading Research Center. The former Director of Research for IRA, he is a Fellow in the American Psychological Association, American Psychological Society, and the National Council of Research in English. His many awards include the NRC Oscar Causey award for outstanding contributions to reading research and membership in the IRA Reading Hall of Fame.

Frederick L. Hamel is a doctoral student in curriculum and instruction at the University of Washington and a secondary English teacher at Bremerton High School. He received his M.A.T. in English education from the University of Chicago where he focused on methods for teaching writing. His current research interests include teacher learning and collegiality, student understanding of literature, and rhetorical theories of communication.

Violet J. Harris is an Associate Professor in the Department of Curriculum and Instruction at the University of Illinois at Urbana-Champaign. She is a University Scholar and recipient of awards and honors for her research on the historic development of literacy among African-Americans and multicultural children's literature.

John R. Hayes is Professor of Psychology and Director of the Center for Innovation in Learning at Carnegie Mellon University. He is a pioneer in studying writing as a problem-solving process and, with Linda Flower, created the first cognitive model of writers' composing processes. He has authored numerous books and articles, including a guide to research methods in writing, and studies of the evaluation of student writing.

Renee Hobbs, prominent authority on media literacy, is an Associate Professor of Communication at Babson College in Wellesley, Massachusetts, and Director of the Media Literacy Project at Clark University in Worcester, Massachusetts. Among other distinctions, she received the Golden Cable ACE Award (the cable industry's highest award) in 1995 for KNOW TV, a public-service media-literacy initiative.

Ana Huerta-Macias is currently an Assistant Professor and Coordinator of the TESOL Program in the Department of Curriculum and Instruction at New Mexico State University. Her research interests and publications are in the areas of bilingual education, sociolinguistics, family literacy, and teaching english to speakers of other languages. Most recently, she coedited *The Schooling of Latino Students: A Guide to Successful Practice*, Volumes I and II.

Glynda Hull is Associate Professor of Education and Director of the College Writing Programs at the University of California, Berkeley. Her recent research has focused on literacy and work, and she has written as well about remediation, writing instruction, and technology. She is the author, with James Paul Gee and Colin Lankshear, of *The New Work Order* (Westview, 1996), and the editor of *Changing Work, Changing Workers* (SUNY, 1997).

C. Jane Hydrick, a 30-year classroom teacher, is Past President of the NCTE and a Director of the National Board for Professional Teaching Standards. She was named Tempe Woman of the Year in 1985, received the 1989 Excellence in Language Arts Teaching Award, and has written many journal articles as well as editing and authoring several books, her most recent of which is *Parent's Guide to Literacy in the 21st Century*.

Cynthia R. Hynd is Associate Professor of Developmental Studies at the University of Georgia and a principal investigator with the National Reading Research Center. Her eight years of public school teaching included service as a remedial reading specialist and special education teacher. Dr. Hynd's research focuses on the cognitive aspects of learning from text.

Roselmina Indrisano is Professor of Education and Chair of the Department of Educational Studies at Boston University. She is a Past President of the International Reading Association and Past President and member of its Reading Hall of Fame. A widely recognized scholar and educator, she studies many issues related to literacy development and enhancement of struggling readers and their families.

Eugene Jongsma is Director of Educational Assessment for Harcourt Brace School Publishers where he has developed a variety of assessment products, supervised the development of customized state assessments, and provided professional development in alternative assessments. Prior to joining Harcourt Brace, Dr. Jongsma served on the faculties of the University of New Orleans and Southern Methodist University.

Richard M. Kerper is Professor of Education at Millersville University of Pennsylvania where he specializes in children's literature and language arts. He studies the many ways children do and could use illustrations to enhance comprehension of informational books.

Barbara Kiefer is a Professor of Education at Teachers College, Columbia University, where she teaches children's, reading, and language arts. She is coauthor of *Children's Literature in the Elementary School*, *Sixth Edition*, with Charlotte Huck, Janet Hickman, and Susan Hepler.

Mara Krechevsky is an educational researcher at Project Zero at Harvard University. She has developed and tested innovative means of assessment and curriculum techniques that recognize multiple avenues for demonstrating intelligence. She has consulted with many schools across the country on the practical application of multiple intelligences theory.

Linda Labbo is an Assistant Professor of Education at the University of Georgia in the Department of Reading Education.

She has also served as a principal investigator with the National Reading Research Center and has published in scholarly journals such as *Journal of Literacy Research*, *Reading Research Quarterly*, and *Language Arts*. Her research interests focus on the role of technology in young children's emergent literacy development.

Carol D. Lee is an Associate Professor of Education and Social Policy at Northwestern University. Her research centers around ways of drawing on the cultural capital that African-American and other diverse students bring from their home and community experiences to promote academic literacy.

Twila C. Liggett is Executive Director of the renowned educational program Reading Rainbow. In addition, she is Project Administrator and Developer of the Nebraska Educational TV Project, University of Nebraska. She continually creates innovative ways to develop visual literacy.

Anthony (Tony) Lucki, Senior Vice President and Publisher, Harcourt Brace School Publishers, guides the development and design of media programs for teaching literacy across all curriculum areas. He is interested in the role of the text and multimedia in literacy development.

Ulla C. Malkus teaches Development and Psychology in the Psychology Department at Wheelock College in Boston, Massachusetts. Her expertise, which is in the area of the assessment of emergent literacy, has been developed while looking through the lenses of kindergarten teachers.

Ann Dacey McCann is an elementary school teacher for Howard County, Maryland, Public Schools. Prior to that she was a graduate research assistant for the National Reading Research Center. Her research interests include designing and evaluating learning contexts that foster literacy engagement through interdisciplinary teaching.

Michael C. McKenna is Professor of Reading Education at Georgia Southern University. His research into beginning readers' use of electronic (talking) books has included studies sponsored by the National Reading Research Center. He has written widely on various aspects of electronic literacy as well as issues related to the use of technology in literacy assessment.

Richard Peter Mesa ("Pete") is currently a Distinguished Visiting Professor at Mills College in Oakland, California. Prior to coming to Mills College, he taught at several other universities. In addition, in a career of 34 years, he has served at every level of the school system as an English teacher, high school principal, urban and suburban school superintendent, and as California's Chief Deputy Superintendent of Public Instruction.

Lesley Mandel Morrow is a professor at Rutgers University Graduate School of Education. She has published extensively in journals, book chapters, and her own books. She is a member of the board of directors of the International Reading Association, was the recipient of the Association's Outstanding

Teachers Educator of Reading Award, and Fordham University's Alumni Award for Outstanding Achievement.

Lorri Neilsen is Associate Professor of Literacy at Mount Saint Vincent University in Halifax, Nova Scotia. A former teacher of art, drama, and English, she now teaches courses in literacy, gender, and feminist inquiry. A writer of books and articles on literacy learning and teaching, she is also a poet and essayist.

Susan B. Neuman is an Associate Professor of Reading and Language Arts at Temple University. Her research focuses on the effects of television viewing and reading, as well as parent involvement and early literacy. She is the author of *Literacy in the Television Age: The Myth of the TV Effect* (Ablex, 1995, second edition), and numerous articles that explore the relationship among media.

Jim Nicholson is a writer with the Philadelphia Daily News and a former investigative reporter. His more than 30 years' experience in the news business has netted him numerous awards, including the Best Writing Award from the American Society of Newspaper Editors and the Knight-Ridder Editorial Excellence Award.

W. Nikola-Lisa is an Associate Professor of Education at National-Louis University where he teaches courses in literacy development. A well-known author and recipient of an Ezra Jack Keats Fellowship, he is author of *Bein' with You This Way*, *Night Is Coming*, and *Storm*.

Janet L. Olson is an Associate Professor of Visual Arts at Boston University's School for the Arts and Chair of the Department of Art Education. She has written extensively on the relationship between visual and verbal forms of expression as it relates to education. Her current research continues to explore the intriguing and natural partnership of drawing and writing.

Sharon O'Neal is Director of Language Arts for the Texas Education Agency. A former classroom teacher, she is very interested in language arts curriculum and assessment issues that affect the literacy development of first and second language English students. She has also been very involved in the development of professional literacy standards for Texas educators.

Georgette Comuntzis Page, a specialist in children's visual literacy, has conducted research on the relationship between children's cognitive development and their interpretations of various forms of visual media. She has worked at Children's Television Workshop as coordinator of formative research for Sesame Street and has been on the faculties of Westminster College in Salt Lake City and West Virginia University.

Christine C. Pappas is a Professor of the Reading, Writing, and Literacy and Curriculum Design Programs at the University of Illinois at Chicago. Her current research involves working collaboratively with teacher researchers who are transforming literacy teaching-learning to develop culturally responsive pedagogy in urban schools.

Jeanne R. Paratore is an Associate Professor of Literacy, Language, and Cultural Studies at Boston University School of Education. A former classroom teacher who is very involved in field-based education, she is currently conducting research in three areas: family literacy, performance-based assessment, and peer discourse.

Katherine Paterson, an outstanding novelist, received the John Newbery Award in 1978 for Bridge to Terabithia and again in 1981 for Jacob Have I Loved. Her many books, which are loved by readers of all ages, are the basis of theatrical and media productions.

P. David Pearson is currently the John A. Hannah Distinguished Professor of Education at Michigan State University. He pursues research related to reading instruction and assessment. Past President of the National Reading Conference and the National Conference of Research in English, he was presented the NRC Oscar Causey Award for outstanding contributions to reading research and the IRA William S. Gray Citation of Merit for his contributions to theory, research, and practice.

Anthony D. Pellegrini is a Professor of Early Childhood Education at the University of Georgia. He studies children's early literacy and play. He has two recent books: Observing Children in the Natural World: A Methodological Primer (Erlbaum, 1996) and The Development of School-Based Literacy: A Social Ecological Study (in press with Lee Galda, Routledge).

Charles W. Peters, a secondary English language arts consultant for Oakland Intermediate School District in Waterford, Michigan, has authored many articles and book chapters and coedited two books. His most recent publication, "Language Arts and Curriculum Content: The Key to Aligning Instruction and Assessment in Literature-Based Approaches," will appear in Literature-Based Instruction: Present Issues, Future Directions, edited by Kathryn H. Au and Taffy E. Raphael.

Gary Pharness works in corporate settings around the issues of literacy and diversity. His expertise in communicative literacy is in bringing different stakeholders within a company together to build a culture of literacy that acknowledges all employees as having the capacity to think and to express their personal voice.

Gay Su Pinnell is Professor of Education at Ohio State University and has recently worked extensively in the area of Reading Recovery. A former classroom teacher and a well-established researcher and author, she is very interested in many factors that affect children's literacy acquisition and development. Her most recent text, Guided Reading, which was coauthored with Irene Fountas, is published by Heinemann.

Sheila A. Potter is an English Language Arts Specialist with the Michigan Department of Education and Codirector of the Michigan English Language Arts Framework (MELAF) Project. She serves on the boards of directors for the Michigan Reading Association and the Michigan Council of Teachers of English. Among her many publications is a handbook on student literacy portfolios entitled "Portrait with Wings," which was distributed to all Michigan school districts.

Claire L. Ramsey is an Assistant Research Scientist at the University of California, San Diego, and a lecturer in the Teacher Education Program at University of California, San Diego. A hearing signer of ASL, she has worked as an interpreter, instructional assistant, and researcher in classrooms with deaf children and their deaf and hearing teachers at elementary, middle school, and college levels.

David Reinking is Professor of Education at the University of Georgia where he serves as head of the Department of Reading Education. He is also a principal investigator with the National Reading Research Center and is Editor of the Journal of Literacy Research, a journal published by the National Reading Conference. Professor Reinking's primary research interest is in the connection between technology and literacy.

Laurel Richardson is Visiting Professor in the Cultural Studies Program in the School of Educational Policy and Leadership and Professor of Sociology at Ohio State University. She has written social science as narrative poetry, lyric poetry, drama, and responsive readings. Her most recent book, Fields of Play: Constructing an Academic Life, is available through Rutgers University Press.

John Richmond is a British specialist on curriculum and instruction and is currently developing television programs for teachers and students. He is a member of the faculty of the University of Nottingham where he studies many areas of literacy development.

Roger R. Rogalin is the Senior Vice President and Publisher of Macmillan / McGraw-Hill's School Division where he supervises the design and development of print and nonprint media for school textbooks. A well-respected scholar, he is interested in the connections between media and text and their influences on literacy development. He is also the past president of the Association of American Publishers.

Tamara Hanneman Rubin, Editorial Director of Scholastic Magazine, oversees the creation and design of several Scholastic print and visual media products. She is interested in the role of display graphics, design, and color as sources that promote reading motivation.

Marilyn C. Scala is a special education teacher at Munsey Park Elementary School in Manhasset, New York. She is a participant in the Lincoln Center Institute, a partnership between Lincoln Center for the Performing Arts and school districts to provide aesthetic education programs for teachers and students. She has coauthored a book, Three Voices: An Invitation to Poetry Across the Curriculum (Stenhouse, 1995).

Virginia C. Schroder is the Elementary Curriculum and Staff Development Specialist for the Manhasset Public Schools, Manhasset, New York. She is coauthor of *Three Voices: An Invitation to Poetry Across the Curriculum* (Stenhouse, 1995) and writes regularly for *Creative Classroom*, the Children's Television Workshop magazine. Ms. Schroder is also a participant in the Lincoln Center for the Performing Arts Institute, a collaborative workshop for aesthetic education in the schools.

Dona Schwartz is an Associate Professor at the School of Journalism and Mass Communication at the University of Minnesota. Her research in visual communication involves interrelated areas of historical and institutional influences shaping visual media, its forms and contents, and audiences' interpretive processes. Her writing includes *Waucoma Twilight: Generations of the Farm* (Smithsonian Institution Press, 1992) and *Contesting the Super Bowl* (Routledge, 1997).

Robert E. Shafer is Professor of Education Emeritus at Arizona State University. A widely published researcher and author, he is a past chair of the International Consortium of English Associations and has studied language teaching in many English-speaking countries.

Joan M. Shiring coordinates the Secondary English Education program at the University of Texas at Austin. She currently teaches a variety of graduate and undergraduate courses, codirects the Austin Writing Project, and has contributed articles to the *English Journal*, *Language Arts*, *The Journal of Teacher Education*, and *English in Texas*.

Elaine R. Silliman is on the faculty of the University of South Florida. She studies the goal and purpose of communication in classroom functioning and school reform. Her research and writing reflects her belief that being literate transcends the oral and written media of communication.

Susanne L. Singleton is a freelance writer. She is a former English and social studies teacher and former Vice President of Macmillan / McGraw-Hill School Publishing. She is very interested in the relationships among and the teaching of the language arts, the visual arts, and literacy.

Steve Stahl is a Professor of Reading Education at the University of Georgia and a principal investigator at the National Reading Research Center. He was formerly at the Center for the Study of Reading at the University of Illinois. A former elementary school teacher, his research interests are centered around issues in reading instruction at the primary grades and the relationship between vocabulary knowledge and reading comprehension.

Carol Susann Stavropoulos is an Assistant Professor of Art at the University of Georgia. She has served as technical consultant and researcher for the Ohio Partnership for the Visual Arts, sponsored by the Getty Center for Education on the Arts. Dr. Stavropoulos is the chair of the Arts and Learning Special Interest Group of the American Educational Research Association.

Thomas G. Sticht, President of Applied Behavioral and Cognitive Sciences, Inc., and Project Coordinator for the San Diego Consortium for Workforce Education and Lifelong Learning, is a recipient of IRA's Albert J. Harris Award, a member of its Reading Hall of Fame, UNESCO's International Literacy Prize Jury, and the National Governor's Association's Advisory Group for National Education Goal 6 (adult literacy). He has also chaired the California State Legislature's Workforce Literacy Task Force.

Susan Strecker is a doctoral student in Language and Literacy Studies at the University of Texas at Austin and Early Childhood Education instructor at Texas Lutheran University. A former Texas Teacher of the Year, she is particularly interested in literacy acquisition and public policy.

Michael R. Strickland, who teaches at Jersey City State College, is a poet. His many books include *Families: Poems Celebrating the African American Experience* (with Dorothy Strickland), *Poems that Sing to You*, *African American Poets*, and *Another Haircut at Sleepy Sam's*.

Anne P. Sweet is a Senior Research Associate in the National Institute on Student Achievement, Curriculum and Assessment, Office of Educational Research and Improvement, U.S. Department of Education. She is the National Institute's team leader for humanities, language arts, and social sciences, and the U.S. Department's scientific and technical expert on research in reading and K–12 literacy. Her research interests include arts-based approaches to literacy learning.

Robert (Rob) J. Tierney is Professor of Language, Literacy and Culture at Ohio State University and Director of the School of Teaching and Learning. Former editor of the *Reading Research Quarterly*, Past President of the National Reading Conference, and past chair of National Council of Teachers of English Research Assembly, he has worked collaboratively with students, teachers, and groups such as Apple Computer's Classroom of Tomorrow, Children's Television Workshop, and others.

Josefina (Josie) Villamil Tinajero is Assistant Dean of the College of Education and Professor of Bilingual Education at the University of Texas at El Paso where she also directs the nationally acclaimed Mother-Daughter / Father-Son Programs. She is the president of TABE—the Texas Association for Bilingual Education. Her most recent publication is *The Power of Two Languages: Literacy and Biliteracy for Spanish Speaking Children* (Macmillan / McGraw-Hill).

Steven Tozer, Associate Professor in the College of Education at the University of Illinois at Chicago, studies the social foundations of education. His book, *School and Society*, devotes a chapter (with Arlette Willis) to analysis of literacy in ideological context.

Diane H. Tracey is an Assistant Professor of Reading at Kean College of New Jersey where she teaches graduate and undergraduate courses in reading and literacy education. Her primary research interests include family literacy and the affective dimension of literacy learning.

JoAnne L. Vacca is a Professor of Curriculum and Instruction at Kent State University, Kent, Ohio. She was Chair of the Department of Teaching, Leadership and Curriculum Studies for ten years. A coauthor of *Content Area Reading* and *Reading and Learning to Read*, Dr. Vacca is Chair of the International Reading Association's Teacher Educator Award Committee.

Richard T. Vacca is a Professor of Teaching Leadership and Curriculum Studies at Kent State University, Kent, Ohio. A widely published author and a respected teacher, he is a recipient of the College Reading Association's 1989 A. B. Herr Award for Outstanding Contributions to Reading Education. Dr. Vacca served as the 42nd president of the International Reading Association in 1996–97.

Sheila W. Valencia is Associate Professor of Curriculum and Instruction at the University of Washington, Seattle. Her teaching and research focus on literacy instruction and assessment, with a special emphasis on classroom-based assessment. Dr. Valencia has served on the advisory boards of several national, state, and professional assessment projects including the National Academy of Education, National Task Force on Assessment, and the Joint Committee on Assessment of NCTE and IRA.

Richard L. Venezky is Unidel Professor of Educational Studies and Professor of Computer and Information Sciences and of Linguistics at the University of Delaware. He is also the National Research Director for the U.S. Secretary of Education's Initiative on Reading and Writing, President of the Reading Hall of Fame (1996–97), and director of computing for the Dictionary of Old English at the University of Toronto. His research interests include human information processing and literacy.

Kathy Waugh is Senior Editor at the Boston-based National Public Television station, WGBH. She directed the creation and development of the *Arthur* television series, which is broadcast nationally. She is interested in the role of television as a medium that will promote an expanded definition of what it means to be literate.

Lee Weinstein currently works in literacy and community development for organizations in the Downtown Eastside of Vancouver, designing literacy projects that reflect the lives of learners and their community. In addition to founding the Invergarry Learning Center in Surrey, B.C., he is the cofounder (with G. Pharness and others) of *Voices* magazine.

Gordon Wells is a Professor of Education in the Ontario Institute for Studies in Education in the University of Toronto. Dr. Wells' teaching is in the areas of language, literacy, and learning across the curriculum. His research is conducted collaboratively with teachers in the "Developing Inquiring Communities in Education Project," in which they are exploring the roles of spoken and written discourse in classroom activities.

Louise C. Wilkinson is Dean of the Graduate School of Education at Rutgers University. An elected Fellow of the American Psychological Association, she was appointed to National Review Panels for the U.S. Department of Education and the National Science Foundation. She has also served as a United States delegate to international education fora sponsored by the Organization for Economic Cooperation and Development, and the Organization for Asian Pacific Economic Cooperation.

Arlette Ingram Willis is an Assistant Professor with the Language and Literacy faculty in the Department of Curriculum and Instruction at the University of Illinois at Urbana-Champaign. Her current research and scholarly interests focus on preparing teachers to teach literacy in a diverse society, multicultural literature for grades 6–12, and historic barriers to literacy acquisition in the United States.

Michael Willmorth is a communication researcher at Boise State University in Idaho. He has conducted and published several studies on language and communication and has investigated the relationship between regional speech patterns and the mass media.

Karen K. Wixson is a Professor of Education and Associate Dean for Graduate Studies in the School of Education at the University of Michigan. She is currently studying the impact of the professional development component of the Michigan English Language Arts Framework (MELAF) project on teacher and district practices. She and others involved with this project recently published language arts articles discussing living and working with these standards.

Lauren L. Wohl is Director of Marketing and Publicist at Disney and Hyperion Books. She works with authors and film directors to coordinate books and films. She is very interested in unifying the multiple forms of communication in an attempt to strengthen children's literacy.

Jennifer Lynn Wolf has been a teacher of drama and English in secondary schools in California for the past ten years. Currently she teaches in the Cotati-Rhonert Park Unified School District in Sonoma County, California, where she attempts to expand student literacy through the use of multimedia.

Shelby A. Wolf is an Assistant Professor of Literacy Education at the University of Colorado at Boulder. Currently a National Academy of Education Spencer Postdoctoral Fellow, she is working on a study of preservice teachers' understandings of literacy. She is the coauthor of *The Braid of Literature: Children's Worlds of Reading* (Harvard University Press, 1992) and is working on a drama book with Dr. Heath entitled *A Different Stage: Multiple Selves in Community Youth Theatre*.

Karen D. Wood is a Professor of Reading Education at the University of North Carolina at Charlotte. A former middle school teacher and K–12 instructional coordinator, she is the author of numerous articles, chapters, and books relating current research and theory to classroom practice. Her current research interests involve strategies for improving students' viewing abilities, meeting the needs of diverse learners in the classroom, and integrating flexible grouping across the curriculum.

Philip Yenawine is a partner in Development Through Art, an educationally based company. Formerly he served as director of art education at the Metropolitan Museum of Art. He is interested in the viewer's perception of art as a medium that expands one's literacy.

Jane Yolen, noted author, has won numerous awards: *Owl Moon* won the Caldecott Award in 1988; *The Emperor and the Kite* was a Caldecott Honor Book; *The Devil's Arithmetic* won the Jewish Book Council Award, Commander Toad in Space won the Garden State Children's Book Award; *Piggins* won the Nebraska and New York State Children's Book Awards.

Josephine Peyton Young is a Graduate Research Assistant at the University of Georgia. She participates in the work of the National Reading Research Center. A former classroom teacher and musician, she examines images created in song as a means to motivate literacy learning for all children.

REVIEWERS

Arthur N. Applebee – Professor, State University of New York at Albany

Walter L. Buster – Teacher, Cotati-Rohnert Park Unified School District,California

Elizabeth Chiseri-Strater – Professor, University of North Carolina at Greensboro

Michelle Commeyras – Professor, The University of Georgia

Joan Curry – Professor, San Diego State University

Carol Dixon – Professor, University of California, Santa Barbara

Janet Emig – Emeritus Professor, Rutgers University

Nancy Farnan – Professor, San Diego State University

Sherri Furqueron – Director of Reading / Language Arts, Lightspan

James Paul Gee – Professor, Clark University

Celia Genishi – Professor, Teachers College, Columbia University

Kelly M. Goss – Teacher, San Diego Unified School District

Judith L. Green – Professor, University of California, Santa Barbara

Madeleine Grumet – Professor, City University of New York, Brooklyn College

John T. Guthrie – Professor, University of Maryland, College Park

Barbara Kapinus – Council of State School Officers, Maryland

Laurie Katz – Professor, Vanderbilt University

Judith Smith Koroscik – Professor, Ohio State University

Michelle M. LeTourneau – Teacher, San Diego Unified School District

Beverly Whitaker Long – Professor, University of North Carolina at Chapel Hill

Linda Lungren – Magnet Coordinator, San Diego Unified School District

Judith A. Meagher – Professor, University of Connecticut

Juel A. Moore – Principal, San Diego Unified School District

Elyse Pineau – Professor, Southern Illinois University, Carbondale

Georgiana Short – Professor, Ohio State University

Michael Smith – Professor, Rutgers University

John Stewig – Professor, University of Milwaukee

Lynne Thrope – Director, The Reading Room, El Cajon, California

Janice VanDyke – Instructor, San Diego State University

Grant Wiggins – Center on Learning Assessment and School Structure, Princeton, New Jersey

Susan Witten – State of Ohio Department of Education

THEORETICAL BASES FOR COMMUNICATIVE AND VISUAL ARTS TEACHING

INTRODUCTION

Paul Messaris

ANNENBERG SCHOOL FOR COMMUNICATION
UNIVERSITY OF PENNSYLVANIA

In recent years the term "literacy" has undergone a notable transformation. In its original sense the term signified the ability to read and write—in other words, the cognitive skills associated with the use of written language. Nowadays, however, one frequently comes across references to "visual literacy," "computer literacy," "television literacy," and the like. This extension of the literacy concept beyond the domain of verbal language is the result of a parallel change in conceptions of the proper scope of education. As the applications of image-based media in both homes and workplaces continue to expand, there is a growing realization that our educational system needs to do more in the way of preparing young people to deal effectively with nonverbal modes of communication—not at the expense of verbal language learning, but as a necessary complement to it. It is this broadening of educational focus that is reflected in the concept of multiple literacies.

The 10 chapters in this part of the handbook offer a theoretical basis for thinking about the integration of the multiple-literacies concept into the educational curriculum. In these chapters, as well as in the broader public discourse on these matters, the term literacy is used in two relatively distinct senses: on the one hand, it may be viewed positively, as an instrument for achieving intellectual growth. On the other hand, however, literacy is sometimes seen in a more negative light, as a means of defense against the potentially damaging influences of mass media. Although both of these aspects of literacy are important, the primary focus here is on the positive side of the phenomenon. In other words, literacy is treated mainly as a foundation for creative engagement with one's social and physical environment.

In Chapter 1, "Literacy for the Information Age," Renee Hobbs gives a more detailed account of the issues introduced above. Hobbs begins by pointing out that educators have traditionally taught *with* television and other media, as audiovisual aids, but not *about* these media. She then argues that the increasing importance of media messages in the lives of young people calls for a redefinition of the term "literacy," encompassing all forms of messages and including critical evaluation in addition to the skills of production and comprehension. Hobbs connects this expanded definition to five ideas which she considers essential components of any program in media literacy: all messages are the result of selection and choice among a variety of options; all messages are reflections of a particular view of social reality; the meanings of messages arise in the act of interpretation by individual receivers; the interpretation of messages is enhanced by an understanding of their economic, political, social, and aesthetic purposes; effective communication depends on an appreciation of the unique characteristics of each medium, format, and genre. According to Hobbs, this way of looking at literacy has significant implications for a wide variety of issues facing educators today, and she concludes by discussing several of these issues, including the relationship between schools and communities, multicultural education; ESL / bilingual education, the integration among various subject areas, and the development of new tools of assessment.

David Reinking, Linda Labbo and Michael McKenna reiterate the growing necessity for an expanded view of literacy. Their chapter "Navigating the Changing Landscape of Literacy: Current Theory and Research in Computer-Based Reading and Writing," confronts the narrow perceptions which underlie a stagnant concept of literacy, focusing on the computer as a powerful impetus for growth. Their review of the computer's profound influence on modern life serves as a compelling suggestion that literacy researchers begin to anticipate the inevitable rise of computer-based innovations, such as electronic text. They argue that the dominant role that electronic text will play in the near future requires that literacy researchers abandon their bias toward the printed text … and that refusing to acknowledge it dooms them to obsolescence.

The paradigm shift that must precede optimal integration of computers into literacy programs necessitates the development of comprehensive pedagogical theories. The authors identify new research avenues, emphasizing the need for a broad base of theoretical perspectives. A critical element of the requisite research on the sociocultural and instructional implications of electronic text is an inquiry into the qualities which are unique to electronic text. These distinguishing characteristics are: the interactivity and malleability of electronic texts, their organic inclusion of multimedia, or audiovisual effects, their flexible parameters of freedom and control, the richly varied textual structures they enable, and the new pragmatics and sociopolitical dimensions they contribute to the established literacy tradition.

In addition to the differences between electronic and printed texts, careful consideration of the generalizations that have emerged from classroom-based research will inform pedagogical theories about the computer's role in literacy development. Interestingly, these findings, which will inspire and guide future inquiry, are not always consistent with the assumptions on which much of the instructional use of computers is currently based.

The chapter closes with a discussion of the contemporary and past issues and trends in research on computer-based instruction. The authors note the promising shift from a constrained perspective on the computer's role within our established agenda to a fuller understanding of how it may substantially alter our notions of "reader," "writer," and "text."

The implications of an expanded definition of literacy are also addressed explicitly by Roger Desmond, in his chapter, "TV Viewing, Reading and Media Literacy." Desmond observes that the application of the literacy label to pictorial media has led to objections by writers who argue that video and print are not only logical opposites but also antagonistic to each other. Much of Desmond's chapter is devoted to a careful examination of one facet of this relationship, namely, the possibility that TV viewing has a negative impact on students' reading ability. In reviewing the research evidence on this topic, Desmond finds that there is indeed a recurring negative association between reading skills and viewing, but that the reasons for this association are not clear, since there is only mixed support for the most obvious explanation, that of simple displacement of one activity by the other. The likelihood that television is harmful to reading and school performance may be one reason for the fact that many media-literacy programs tend to emphasize the defensive side of the literacy concept. In noting this tendency, Desmond discusses the need to supplement it with an exploration of the ways in which media literacy can improve a viewer's capacity to use media as sources of information and insight. More specifically, he lists two components of this latter form of visual literacy: first, a viewer's ability to optimize the mental effort invested in the interpretation of any particular type of program; second, the ability to relate previous media experience and real-world knowledge to newly encountered content.

Susan Neuman also considers television's potential contribution to literacy development in her chapter, "Television as a Learning Environment: A Theory of Synergy." She demonstrates the qualitative differences among the various media, arguing that each of these distinct variations stimulates different cognitive processes. Accordingly, in order to develop the broadest range of processing skills, we must explore the ways in which the media can complement each other. Her "Theory of Synergy" derives from and complements this notion. The theory suggests that the effects of combining media will exceed the sum of their individual merits; that is, coordinating media will amplify the cognitive benefits offered by each individually.

Neuman goes on to outline several variables which affect the phenomenon of media synergy: environmental influence, accord between learner interests and literacy-related media, and the skills necessary for effective media use. Having acknowledged the necessity of future exploration of these factors, she proceeds to discuss the implications of the theory with respect to television. She focuses on the roles of parents and educators in integrating this medium into literacy development programs. The examples cited here clearly illustrate the possibilities offered by the most readily accessible media options.

The theme of using television for purposeful instruction is also taken up by Michael Willmorth in his chapter, "Television and Language Learning." While Neuman and Desmond were concerned about students' skills in dealing with written language, Willmorth's focus is primarily on speech. As in the case of reading ability, there is some evidence suggesting a negative relationship between TV viewing and the development of spoken language. However, as Willmorth demonstrates, the interpretation of these findings is open to question, and the more commonly accepted view in this area of scholarship has tended to be that television experience makes little or no difference to a child's developing mastery of speech. This view is derived from the belief that the acquisition of spoken-language skills depends on the active give-and-take of interpersonal interaction, something that television cannot supply. Willmorth challenges this view in two ways: first, he points out that children's TV viewing often does entail interpersonal interaction, not with the set but with parents, siblings, or other coviewers; second, he argues that, at least as far as vocabulary building is concerned, there are both theoretical and empirical reasons for assuming that active interaction may not be as crucial to language learning as previously supposed. With these considerations in mind, Willmorth goes on to discuss the application of television in the language classroom, with special emphasis on the use of TV materials that were not originally designed for instructional purposes. The discussion brings to a close this section's examination of the connection between media literacy and language.

In the next chapter attention shifts to visual matters. Under the rubric, "Visual Communication Skills and Media Literacy," Michael Griffin and Dona Schwartz develop a set of prescriptions for the types of visual knowledge that young people need in order to become competent participants in an increasingly visual culture. More than anything else, the authors argue that young people need to learn the distinction between pictures and reality. That is, they need to learn that photographic images are not simply direct records of the world around us. This learning entails an appreciation of the implications of framing and of other ways in which picture makers select what the viewer will see. It also entails the capacity to think about images in terms of their creators' intentions, as well as the conventions through which those intentions are expressed. Educators concerned about such matters have often advocated training young people in media production as a method for encouraging their acquisition of these forms of knowledge. Both Schwartz and Griffin have conducted research on the consequences of this sort of visual training, and they report that it can indeed have the desired effect, although in its initial stages it often seems to result primarily in the unreflective copying of mass media conventions. With the aim of contextualizing the knowledge that comes from production experience, the authors suggest that students should also be taught the theory and social history of visual practices.

The visual aspects of media literacy are examined further in the next two chapters of Part I. Both chapters explore the broader cognitive ramifications of learning about visual media. In his discussion of "Visual Intelligence and Analogical Thinking," the author takes as his starting point the fact that visual imagery has historically played an important role in the advancement of science and technology. This fact suggests that there may be significant cognitive commonalties between scientific and artistic creativity. One kind of intellectual process that these two areas appear to share is analogical thinking: the ability to notice underlying similarities between objects or events that are superficially different from each other, and to use those similarities productively as vehicles for deeper understanding and more effective communication. After illustrating how this intellectual process works in scientific discovery and technical communication, the author gives a detailed description of the ways in which analogical connections operate in visual representations. These considerations lead to the conclusion that skill in dealing with visual media may productively be thought of as part of a more encompassing artistic/scientific intelligence.

A similar view of visual literacy motivates Georgette Page's chapter, "Visual Intelligence and Spatial Aptitudes." The latter term refers to a person's ability to form accurate mental models of two- and three-dimensional spatial relationships, and to envision how those relationships would appear from varying points of view. Fluency in this mode of thought is considered a crucial requirement of such occupations as architecture, whose domains of activity or reference are physical structures. Spatial aptitude may also be a prerequisite for some of the cognitive processes that a viewer must be able to perform in the course of interpreting the content of visual media. It is this possibility that Page is particularly concerned with in this chapter. Page has done a substantial amount of research on children's responses to visual media, and this chapter presents data from three of her studies. The aim of these studies was to investigate the relationship between children's spatial skills and their ability to comprehend the composition and the editing in various video clips. In all three studies, this relationship turned out to be positive: children who performed better on tests of spatial aptitude also had higher comprehension scores. Page compares these results with the findings of other researchers, and she concludes that

while her studies treated spatial aptitude as the causal variable, its relationship to visual literacy may well be one of mutual reinforcement.

With the foregoing discussions of television and other visual media as a backdrop, the next chapter takes a look at the future. In the years ahead, literacy educators will face a rapidly changing media environment. The aim of John Carey's chapter, "Exploring Future Media," is to provide an overview of some of the challenges the environment will pose. After giving a detailed description of major technological developments that are expected to drive the evolution of new media forms, Carey offers a speculative account of potential implications of future media. Among other things, he predicts that new technologies may create greater opportunities for decentralized production and distribution of media materials; that a proliferation of available sources of media content may be accompanied by a narrower targeting of that content to specific audiences; that enhanced image quality and the integration of video and computers may lead to innovations in the "language" of visual media; and that novel forms of advertising may increasingly blur the distinction between commercial messages and program content. Adapting to such developments will be a demanding task, not only for students but also for their teachers.

The need for teachers to be open to new sources of knowledge, both inside and outside of the classroom, is a major concern of the chapter, "Balancing Act: Using Drama to Even the Exchange of Information in the Classroom." The author, Jennifer Lynn Massen, has extensive experience as a drama teacher, and she supports her argument with a wealth of examples drawn from this experience and from additional research. Using drama teaching as a paradigm for education in the communicative arts, Massen discusses a variety of ways in which drama in the classroom can be used to promote a reciprocal flow of information between students and teachers. To begin with, she points out that original productions can act as vehicles for introducing information from students' own lives and experiences into classes and youth groups. She argues further that the capacity to empathize with another person's point of view is central to good acting, and that drama is therefore a way of encouraging both teachers and students to acquire an understanding of multiple truths and perspectives. Another point Massen makes is that the inherently collaborative nature of theater promotes a healthy interdependence among participants—an outcome that is especially likely in contemporary youth drama groups, which typically eschew traditional distinctions between stars and supporting parts. Finally, Massen notes that the experience of producing drama gives the participants the satisfaction of genuine achievement. All these points could be adapted to the more general requirements of teaching about other communicative arts and media. Massen's discussion thus brings a reminder that a vital ingredient in the success of new literacy programs will be the interpersonal environment in which those programs are implemented.

1

LITERACY FOR THE INFORMATION AGE

Renee Hobbs

BABSON COLLEGE

For citizens living in the United States at the end of the 20th century, it hardly seems necessary to state the evidence which shows the dominance of film, television, and other mass media products on the lives of Americans (see Alton-Lee, Huthall, & Patrick, 1993; Howe, 1983; Kubey, & Csikszentmihalyi, 1990 for examples of recent evidence). There are few educators still in the practice of teaching who hold the same level of animosity toward television as the generation of teachers in the 1950s and 1960s, many of whom viewed television as their professional nemesis. Many teachers are increasingly using mass media "texts" to enrich their subject areas, comfortably moving between the textbook, the trade book, the newspaper, the film and the videotape in their efforts to bring rich ideas into the classroom.

As for the study of images and mass media in elementary and secondary schools, there has been increasing momentum among language arts and social studies teachers to include media analysis and production activities in the classroom. However, since the word "media" has become entrenched in the educational community as the province of librarians, and media technologies and messages conceived of as merely a delivery system to transfer messages, images have been relegated to the margins, taken for granted to serve as mere decoration. In a society where media use is the central leisure activity for most of its citizens and the dominant source of information about the world, the study of the mass media has been neglected in schools. Students have had little instructional support analyzing and thinking about media messages. Educators often mistakenly believe that they are engaged in expanding the concept of literacy when they use television to teach *with*, and few understand that media literacy consists of teaching *about* media as well.

So the problem is clear: our students are growing up in a world saturated with media messages, messages that fill the bulk of their leisure time and provide them with information about who to vote for and what consumer decisions to make. Yet students receive little to no training in the skills of analyzing or evaluating these messages, many of which make use of language, moving images, music, sound effects, special visual effects and other techniques that powerfully affect our emotional responses.

Educators' exclusive focus on language is a legacy of the historical context of the past, when cultural survival depended upon the mastery of the printed word. While these skills are even more important today, language is only one of a number of symbol systems which humans use to express and share meaning. Changes in communication technologies over the past 100 years have created a cultural environment that has extended and reshaped the role of language and the written word. Language must be appreciated as it exists in relationship to other forms of symbolic expression — including images, sound, music and electronic forms of communication. Scholars and educators are coming to recognize that literacy is not simply a matter of acquiring decontextualized decoding, comprehension and production skills, but that the concept of literacy must be connected with the culture and the contexts in which reading and writing are used (Cook-Gumperz, 1986).

This chapter urges educators to consider this new definition of literacy, a definition adapted by the author based on the work of educators who identify themselves with the "media literacy" movement (Firestone, 1993):

> Literacy is the ability to access, analyze, evaluate and communicate messages in a variety of forms.

Embedded in this definition are both a process for learning and an expansion of the concept of "text" to include messages of all sorts. This view of literacy posits the student as being actively engaged in the process of analyzing and creating messages, and as a result this definition reflects some basic principles of school reform, which generally include:

- inquiry based education
- student-centered learning

- problem solving in cooperative teams
- alternatives to standardized testing
- integrated curriculum

BASIC PROCESSES OF LITERACY: ACCESS, ANALYZE, EVALUATE AND COMMUNICATE

The four processes which constitute the new vision of literacy provide a powerful frame in which to consider how people develop skills in using language and other forms of symbolic expression. For example, the ability to *access* messages connects with those enabling skills that include decoding symbols and building broad vocabularies. It also involves those skills related to the locating, organizing and retrieving of information from a variety of sources. Additionally, access requires the ability to use the tools of technology, including video technology, computers and various on-line services. Access skills are often labeled as information literacy, or more recently, "driver training for the information superhighway."

The ability to *analyze* messages connects with those interpretive comprehension skills that include the ability to make use of categories, concepts or ideas; determine the genre of a work; make inferences about cause and effect; consider the specific strategies and techniques which are used to construct the work; and identify the author's purpose and point of view. At the secondary level, the ability to analyze messages may also include a recognition of the historical, political, economic or aesthetic contexts in which messages are created and consumed.

The ability to *evaluate* messages concerns those judgments about the relevance and value of the meaning of messages for the reader, including making use of prior knowledge to interpret a work; predicting a further outcome or a logical conclusion; identifying values in a message; and appreciating the aesthetic quality of a work. Although the skills of analysis and evaluation are frequently conflated by practitioners of media literacy, it is important to recognize that analysis skills depend upon the ability to grasp and make effective use of conceptual knowledge that is outside the student's own perspective, while evaluation skills make use of the student's existing world view, knowledge, attitudes and values.

The ability to *communicate* messages is at the heart of the traditional meaning of literacy, and the skills of writing and speaking have been highly valued by educators. In the last 20 years, writing has come to approach the primacy that reading has held in the language arts hierarchy. Communication skills are diverse and, to some extent, media-specific. General skills include: the ability to understand the audience with whom one is communicating; the effective use of symbols to convey meaning; the ability to organize a sequence of ideas, and the ability to capture and hold the attention and interest of the message receiver. Media-specific production skills for video include: learning to make effective choices in framing and point of view; learning to use visual and auditory symbolism; and learning how to manipulate time and space effectively through editing.

Expanding the Concept of "Text"

While the four concepts provide a new frame for thinking about the processes involved when people create and share messages, what makes the new vision of literacy so powerful is the application of these skills to *messages in a variety of forms.* At present, reading / language arts educators focus on literature as the core of the K–12 curriculum: the short story, poetry, drama and nonfiction are claimed to be ideal because they "motivate learning with appeal to universal feelings and needs ... classic literature speaks most eloquently to readers and writers" (California State Board of Education, 1986, p. 7).

But they also may seem disconnected and remote from the experiences of students, who have been "escorted across the globe even before they have permission to cross the street" (Meyrowitz, 1985, p. 238) by the television. Critics have claimed that, too often, a literature-based reading / language arts program "ignores the life experience, the history and the language practice of students" (Freire, & Macedo, 1987, p. 146), and that when literary materials are used primarily as vehicles for exercises in comprehension and vocabulary development, students may become alienated from the processes of reading and writing in a range of contexts.

In the past, educators have been comfortable to disenfranchise and overlook present-day cultural products, especially television, even though many works of literature which are now considered classic or traditional began their life as popular works designed for mass audiences (Beach, 1992). But just as scholars and critics have engaged in heated controversy over what texts are appropriate study objects to be included in the canon of essential literary works (Gless, & Herrnstein Smith, 1992), these debates are filtering into changes in the curriculum.

Many educators have discovered that the analysis of contemporary media can build skills that transfer to students' work with the written word. When educators permit and encourage the study of contemporary media products in classrooms, students develop skills that alter and reshape their relationship to media products. Nehamas (1992) explains that "[s]erious watching ... disarms many of the criticisms commonly raised about television." More important, analysis of media texts helps students gain interest in writing and speaking, and helps nurture students' natural curiosity and motivation. Consider a story presented by Lauren Axelrod (cited in White, 1993a), a high school teacher in Houston, Texas:

> I used media literacy concepts to get my low-achievement students to tackle Conrad's *Heart of Darkness* and T.S. Eliot's *The Wasteland.* I started with an extensive analysis of the Francis Ford Coppola film, *Apocalypse Now,* and we discussed the film's narrative structure, mood, point of view, rhythm and character development. Then a team of students read Conrad while another team read Eliot. We then applied the same concepts to the short story and poem in group discussion and writing exercises. Finally, students created a videotape which compared and contrasted the three works with each other. I saw students turn on to literature in a way I never saw them engage with anything in the classroom.

Media education exists as an increasingly vital component of elementary education in Great Britain, Canada, Australia,

Spain and other nations. In Great Britain the mandate includes media education as a strand within the National Standards developed in English, which requires students to study the ways in which media products convey meanings in a range of media texts (Alvarado, & Boyd-Barrett, 1992; Bazalgette, 1992; Brown, 1991; Buckingham, 1991; Lusted, 1991; Masterman, 1985). While still controversial among those who favor a more traditional and narrow view of 'culture,' scholarly work in media pedagogy has grown widely, and consensus is growing about the set of concepts, skills and learning environments that best help strengthen students' ability to access, analyze, evaluate and communicate messages in many forms.

The New Vision: Key Analytic Concepts

Current approaches to reading / language arts often make use of a laundry list of concepts that inform the work of teachers and students in a classroom. Such lists are the result of adding new paradigms for learning upon older models. Layer by layer, the models now used in reading / language arts have become cumbersome and unwieldy (Hawthorne, 1992). Hawthorne writes, "The scope of English heightens the individuality of curricular patterns. ... Teachers are left to weave the various components into a coherent pattern for themselves and their students" (p. 116). But a simple and powerful new definition of literacy, as proposed in this report, makes it possible to identify the most important processes, concepts and skills for K–12 instruction and makes use of these with a wide variety of message forms, from folktales to commercials, from historical fiction to newspaper photography.

Media literacy incorporates the theoretical traditions of semiotics, literary criticism, communication theory, research on arts education and language development. Although the conceptual principles of the new vision of literacy have taken many forms for various curriculum writers in Great Britain, Canada, Australia and the United States, the following ideas are critical components of all programs.

All messages are constructions. Print messages are created by an author who selects the ideas and words to convey meanings. Images are created by a photographer who makes similar selections, and television programs are created by a group of people, led by a producer, who make choices about each image and word used from many possible options. The construction of messages requires careful thinking, creativity and organizational skills. Knowing how messages are constructed helps the reader to appreciate the artistry involved and to better interpret the meaning of a work.

Messages are representations of social reality. Messages have a relationship with the lived experiences of individuals in many cultures. Even when a message is imaginary, hypothetical or fantastic, it represents social reality, which is defined as the perceptions about the contemporary world that are shared among individuals. Messages also represent the social realities of times and places far removed, and help us make sense of the past, present and future. People need the ability to judge the accuracy of particular messages that may or may not reflect social reality.

Individuals negotiate meaning by interacting with messages. The meaning of a message is found in the act of inter-pretation. Each reader or viewer uses prior knowledge and experience in the process of reading or critical viewing. A skill-ful reader or viewer examines many different stylistic features of the text and pays careful attention to the context in which the message occurs in the process of interpretation. Different individuals can find quality and beauty in various texts.

Messages have economic, political, social and aesthetic purposes. People create and share messages for many reasons, but in modern culture making money is one of the most important. Many messages produced in our culture have an economic purpose of some sort. When authors have political purposes, they use a message to gain power or authority over others. When their agenda is social, they use a message to present ideas about how people could or should behave, think or feel. When authors have an aesthetic motive, they use a message to experiment with different kinds of symbolic forms and ideas. Understanding how messages operate in terms of their economic, political, social and aesthetic purposes helps readers better understand the context of a work.

Each form of communication has unique characteristics. An author makes choices about which kinds of media are most appropriate to convey a particular message. Television news has characteristics that favor messages that are immediate and visual, while news photographs have characteristics that favor messages with an emotional component. When writing, an author must carefully choose the most effective genre in which to work, since an essay, a memo, a short story or a poem can all be effective forms, depending on the purpose, audience and content of the message. Being a good communicator means knowing which formats, genres and media to use in a wide variety of situations.

It is clear that the most dynamic concepts of current practice in reading / language arts instruction are wholly consistent with these key concepts. But when educators include the analysis and creation of film, photographs, newspapers, radio and television, new concepts are required to enable students to ask critical questions about these contemporary forms. Some of these concepts may be unfamiliar to reading / language arts teachers, particularly at the elementary level. For example, teachers in some communities have sometimes been reluctant to include the analysis of how messages have political or economic purposes. While it may be argued that analysis of the economics of literature is not of central value for young students, analysis of the economics of media messages is essential to help middle school and high school students understand the nature of communicative messages in contemporary culture. It would be irresponsible to include the study of film, television, newspapers or other mass media without providing students in grades 4 and up with a paradigm to help them understand the ways in which messages have value in the marketplace.

Media Literacy and Critical Thinking Skills

As glossily packaged and presented film, video and advertiser-supported materials enter the school classroom, teachers often consider video materials valuable because everyone in a classroom is presumed to be able to decode the messages on the screen. But the new vision of literacy presented in this chapter is not just aimed at cultivating the relatively simple process of decoding messages—it is the sophisticated analysis, evaluation and the active creation of messages that are the most significant, complex and vital skills needed for survival in an information age. These take a lifetime to master fully.

Even very young students can engage in conceptual analysis and evaluation of media messages, at a time when they are still beginning to master the decoding and comprehension skills required for print. According to Resnick (1987, p. 31):

> The most important single message of modern research on the nature of thinking is that the kinds of activities traditionally associated with thinking are not limited to advanced levels of development. Instead these activities are an intimate part of even elementary levels of reading … when learning is proceeding well.

When teachers make use of a full range of messages in developing children's literacy, higher-order cognitive skills can be integrated into the activities of very young children using media messages as study objects. This helps motivate students to master the basic accessing skills to crack the code of the printed word. These analytic concepts, already familiar to students in their work with media artifacts, can then be applied to print forms. Elementary teachers who have used this approach find that "much of the language used to view television critically is transferable to other media—noticing camera angles in photography, understanding differences between reality and fantasy. … There are also many connections to teaching verbal and written skills" (Lacy, 1993, pp. 11, 12).

What happens, according to British educators, is that when students critically examine a wide range of texts in both print and visual media, they develop more complex expectations about everything they read and see. "Media education is often seen as a way of defending children from television. It ought to be seen as a way of giving them high expectations of television, of all media, and of themselves" (Bazalgette, 1992, p. 45). Such views represent the potential of expanded literacy in reshaping the character of our nation's near limitless appetite for mass media products and in doing so, helping citizens reconnect to the rich storehouse of literary treasures from many cultures, past and present. If media literacy skills help young people develop an appetite for reading, we would judge it a stunning success. If media literacy skills help young people develop an appetite for the stimulating, complex and provocative kinds of television programming increasingly more available as a result of cable television, then in time, we would expect media industries to begin increasing the quality of programming. Such goals have yet to be examined among researchers because, as yet, there are so few community or school-based laboratories where media literacy is being implemented at a system-wide level. (The author is aware of only three districts in the United States which have attempted media literacy initiatives designed to reach all students in the school district: Billerica, Massachusetts; Cold Spring, Minnesota; and Dennis-Yarmouth, Massachusetts.)

THE CONSEQUENCES OF EXPANDING THE CONCEPT OF LITERACY

The new vision of literacy has consequences for some of the most important issues which face American educators today. As developed in the following pages, this chapter outlines how the new vision of literacy helps restore the important connection between the school and the culture, making education more relevant to the communities to which students belong. It also outlines how the new vision of literacy reflects the kind of authentic learning which occurs when reading and writing occur in contexts where "process, product and content are all interrelated" (Edelsky, Altwerger, & Flores, 1991, p. 9) and where language skills and language learning are conceived of as being inherently social processes, requiring direct engagement and experience tied to meaningful activity.

Building Relevance Between the Classroom and the Community

The claims by now are depressingly familiar: many students actively resist the process of learning in school, and while they can decode language, they cannot infer meaning; the school curriculum is fragmented and decontextualized, promoting indifference and intellectual dependency (Diaz, 1992; Hirsch, 1989). Fortunately, elementary educators have already begun to respond to these criticisms by making changes in their methods of instruction: moving away from a curriculum which emphasizes facts and isolated skills and toward an emphasis on collaborative, active learning which involves complex thought and interpretation.

Multicultural education is education that values human diversity and acknowledges that "alternative experiences and viewpoints are part of the growing process" (Grant, 1993). The new vision of literacy proposed in this report is fueled by this philosophy. It promotes cultural pluralism and social equality by making changes in the processes and content of school curriculum; in doing so, it is centered on "building meaningful relationships between curriculum and life" (Pang, 1992, p. 67).

Carlos Cortes argues that media literacy is essential to multicultural education, noting that media literacy strengthens students' knowledge about various media forms, helps develop analytic and creative skills in responding to media, and helps students become skilled in using print, images, sounds and other tools to express and share ideas. Cortes (1991, p. 153) writes, "Media can be used to stimulate students to consider multiple perspectives on current and historical multicultural dilemmas." Clearly, both multicultural education and the new vision of literacy proposed here share the goal of opening up the canon to expand the range of works which are studied in the classroom.

Not unexpectedly, much of the criticism that has developed about the inclusion of works by Hispanic Americans, Native Americans, African Americans and others can be directed at the new vision of literacy as well, which would include works from popular culture which some critics have labeled "trash." Educators who believe that "good literature" is a "salve one can apply to children from the wrong side of the tracks to heal them of their background" (Beach, 1992, p. 554) are likely to resist any effort which attempts to make the canon more responsive to the lives of students and their communities. But John Beach recognizes that the time is ripe to examine the variety of definitions of "good literature" and suggests that instead of viewing literature as a pyramid which places classic works at the top and works of popular culture at the bottom, it should be considered "like a tree with many branches; the 'best' can be found at the tip of each branch."

ESL / Bilingual Education. How might the new vision of literacy affect students who come to school speaking other languages besides English? According to bilingual / educators, the instructional methods which are most effective in ESL / bilingual education are identical with the active learner-centered model which the new vision of literacy promotes. Techniques which make use of drama, songs, objects and audiovisual materials to help convey meaning and content are highly effective.

In Portland, Maine, media artist Huey (also known as James Coleman) developed a media education program for ESL students speaking 27 languages, where students make film and video using animation and live-action techniques. Portland elementary teachers "have found that Huey's approach offers their students a creative way to improve their English, their public speaking and their communication skills in general. ... and it breaks down walls between schools and communities through cable TV and closed circuit screenings and student research within the community" (White, 1993b).

Writing for the College Board, Hirsch (1989, p. 60) notes:

> Over and over again, teachers in ESL and bilingual classrooms have realized the power of authentic tasks to motivate communication and language learning. ... In searching for authentic tasks and materials, many ESL and proficiency teachers are looking beyond traditional textbooks to primary sources in the language they are teaching, including newspapers, television commercials, menus, hotel receipts, children's books, and journalism and fiction.

Parent Education. In some communities, parents are active and supportive players in the day-to-day life of the school. In too many communities, however, parents are disenfranchised partners in the educational process. In considering the relationship between the new vision of literacy and the home--school connection, it is necessary to identify the high level of ambivalence and concern that many citizens have with the ways film, television and other mass media have shaped public discourse. Many adults believe that television has damaged the process we use to elect public officials, that mass media organizations disrupt the private lives of individuals unnecessarily; that violence in film and television programming desensitizes people and alters their conceptions of the

social world; and that the values of sensationalism have reshaped culture and the arts (Bianculli, 1993).

The new vision of literacy proposed in this chapter is based on a fundamental truism about the purpose of democracy: in order for citizens to be engaged in self-governance, they must critically analyze and evaluate information and resources. This work is essential if citizens are to take meaningful action and make meaningful decisions on issues of concern to the community. But in a culture in which citizens see themselves as spectators and consumers, democracy is threatened. When citizens do not employ their skills of analysis and evaluation to information and entertainment products, apathy and cynicism reign.

The new vision of literacy could help encourage parents to more fully embrace their responsibilities to help their children interpret the meanings of the complex messages which bombard them everyday. Too often, parents feel intimidated by the activity of the classroom, by routines that are established by educators who may unintentionally disempower parents from embracing their own authority as interpreters of textual materials. While some parents may hesitate to voice their interpretations of a literary work, parents often feel quite comfortable discussing their interpretations of a film, a situation comedy, a dramatic series, a documentary or an op-ed article. The new vision of literacy creates opportunities for parents and their children to engage with the complex task of sorting out the meanings of the messages in the environment.

Making Classrooms Centers for Authentic Learning

Educators have been discussing how to make learning more authentic since the 19th century, when John Dewey first began outlining how children's own activity, their work, could be a vehicle for learning. When learning is authentic, the content of classroom discourse is meaningful and relevant to students; language skills are not taught in isolation; connections between subject areas are emphasized. According to Sizer (1984), in authentic learning environments, students learn through direct experience with tasks they themselves value, with intellectual stimulation from teachers who ask thoughtful questions and provide supportive coaching.

The new vision of literacy helps nurture new relationships between teachers and students, helping rebind the current contrast that "exists between *paidia* (play) and *paideia* (education)" (Gallagher, 1992), based on the recognition that the aim of the reading / language arts teacher is to cultivate a learning environment where students bring their own naturally energetic exploration to the study of new ideas. Rather than considering language development as a series of isolated and fragmented skills, the new vision of literacy puts students at the center of the processes of accessing, analyzing, evaluating and communicating messages. Most important, the new vision of literacy is centered around empowerment, defined as the "process through which students learn to critically appropriate knowledge existing outside their immediate experience in order to broaden their understanding of themselves, the world and the possibilities for transforming the taken-for-granted assumptions about the way we live" McLaren, 1989, p. 186).

Integration with other subject areas. As is clearly evident, the new vision of literacy provides a simple, process-based model that makes connections between reading / language arts, the visual and performing arts, social studies and science. Shepard (1993, p. 35) explains how the new vision of literacy is an ideal tool for subject integration at the elementary level:

> If media literacy is presented to [teachers] as just another add-on, there will be little hope for its adoption. If, however, media literacy is presented not just as something that meets students' needs, but something that will meet the teacher's need to integrate the disparate elements of a broad curriculum, then it stands a good chance of becoming an important part of the curriculum. In fact, media literacy functions so well as an integrator that it would be worth using even if it were not as intrinsically important as it is.

Since mass media artifacts are relevant to science, social studies, the visual and performing arts as well as reading / language arts, teachers can easily make connections that stretch across subject areas by teaching with media and teaching about media.

In some communities teachers across the core subject areas are being trained in how to integrate media literacy concepts into many curriculum areas. In Billerica, Massachusetts, teachers in language arts, social studies, health education, science and the visual and performing arts are discovering the synergy which results from team-developed initiatives. For example, in the spring of 1994, teachers collaborated on a district-wide program to help students critically analyze tobacco advertising as part of the health curriculum. Students examined the historical, political and economic dimensions of tobacco advertising; they reviewed, categorized and analyzed a huge volume of persuasive materials designed to make smoking look attractive; and they made their own public service messages, targeted at their own community, to persuade them against smoking. More than 2,000 students in grades K–12 participated in the project by designing slogans, writing newspaper editorials, designing billboards, bumper stickers, posters, radio ads and videotape public service announcements. Teachers persuaded the local billboard company to put up one student's billboard design on the major highway of the town, giving thousands of citizens the opportunity to read a child's message, and creating a powerful message for students. Such examples emphasize the ways in which media literacy activities bring a renewed sense of relevance between the worlds of the classroom and the world of contemporary culture.

Using new tools of assessment. When assessment is authentic, it has as its central purpose the goal of providing feedback to a child and his or her parents about the quality of the learning experience. When assessment is authentic, it mirrors the ways in which standards of quality are evaluated in the world outside of the classroom: through close examination of products and performances.

For more than a century, assessment in the United States has been shaped by the needs of scholars and academics to standardize and quantify learning experiences (Gould, 1981). This has led to an atomized, fragmented view of the learning process, one conducive to "data reduction." Now, educators are coming to recognize the need to reclaim the assessment process, and as a result, diverse new forms of assessment are being used in schools.

The new vision of literacy provides simple and direct opportunities to observe, monitor and evaluate the processes of accessing, analyzing, evaluating and communicating messages in a range of informal and formal settings. Since the creation of messages is central to the new vision of literacy, portfolio-based models of assessment are consistent with the new vision. Indeed, the premise of the new vision is based on the idea that the processes of accessing, analyzing and evaluating messages all contribute to the creation and communication of messages, so that students can make direct connections between their reading and their writing, their viewing and analysis of images, and the process of creating messages using language, images, sounds, music, graphics and video.

The Toronto Board of Education's Benchmark Program has been using an assessment model designed to demystify educational goals and illuminate the nature of good performance (Larter, & Donnelly, 1993). By combining authentic performance activities with systematic observation and holistic evaluation, teachers can assess student skills in a way which most closely matches the broad general skills that are at the core of reading / language arts instruction. For example, in one benchmark of students' ability to comprehend nonprint information and their oral communication skills, grade 3 students in Toronto are asked to watch a videotape on owls and explain the major ideas in their own words. Students were found to generally lack strong skills in the comprehension of informative video, perhaps because their expectations about television shape their level of motivation and effort in decoding (Salomon, 1979). Such evidence reminds us of the lessons of the reading comprehension scholars—how important it is not to assume that our students understand what they see just because they see it.

The development of standards, tied to authentic performances, that allow educators to assess the quality of students' writing, speaking, listening and thinking skills is consistent with the new vision of literacy. The province of Ontario was the first in Canada to mandate that media literacy instruction be at least 30% of the reading / language arts program in grades 7–12. The performance of younger students from the Toronto Board of Education results suggests that students lack basic comprehension skills of information presented in video formats, pointing clearly to the necessity of direct instruction to help students in grades K–8 learn to comprehend, interpret and analyze a wide range of texts, including messages from television and the mass media.

Staff development issues. Teachers are just as ambivalent about media culture as the rest of the citizenry. As discussed earlier, teachers have a wide range of attitudes about the value and consequences of broadening the concept of literacy to include new materials, especially popular music, film, television and music videos. However, teachers who have attempted to incorporate these materials into their classroom realize that students have a tremendous amount of knowledge and interest in these messages, and teachers and students can share together in the learning process.

It is not difficult for teachers to move from teaching exclusively with media to addressing media as study objects. Some teachers have described the process as similar to the process of "consciousness raising" about gender and race which many educators experienced in the 1970s. "It's like putting on a new pair of glasses—you see the same things [in media culture], but now I approach these messages differently," wrote one teacher in a program of teacher education at the Harvard Institute on Media Education, a staff development program in media literacy that was conducted by the author in 1993 and 1994 that attracted educators from across the nation.

But German educator Dichanz (1992) writes plainly about what it takes to make the new vision of literacy a reality in schools: "It is the staff that has to translate tasks ... into practical work, and it is that staff that has to be provided with the theoretical background for this new approach..." For U.S. educators, this means that the work of staff development is best accomplished, not by individual teachers acting independently, but through coordinated and sustained efforts, using resources and tools which help them gain access to new ideas and practice new strategies of managing classroom activity. Such work is well underway at the state, district and local levels. For example, the State of New Mexico has mandated that all students complete a media literacy course before high school graduation, and begun a process of teacher training so that media literacy will be integrated into the curriculum at all grade levels. And in the community of Billerica, Massachusetts, after 3 years of study, 26 teachers have completed the first Master's Degree in Media Literacy, supported by Merrimack Education Center and Fitchburg State College, in order to implement a new vision of literacy in grades K–12 integrated within existing subject areas. Teachers graduating from this program are beginning to teach additional teachers in the New England area.

If media literacy is to emerge as a new vision of literacy for the information age, then a high degree of coordination will be required from among a range of shareholders: the scholarly community, educators in K–12 environments, parents, the publishing and media production industries, and the standardized testing industry. Given the decentralized nature of American schools, it is unlikely that such coordination will receive the support it needs, and more likely that media literacy initiatives will develop as a result of innovation and experimentation in the diverse "labs" of individual districts, schools and classrooms. For an institution which has historically clung to the concept of literacy as the central organizing force of education, we must respect the time it will take educators and scholars to promote the type of sustained and meaningful change that is needed for our schools.

References

Alton-Lee, A., Huthall, G., & Patrick, J. (1993). Reframing classroom research: A lesson from the private world of children. *Harvard Educational Review, 63,* 50–84.

Alvarado, M., & Boyd-Barrett, O. (Eds.). (1992). *Media education: An introduction.* London: British Film Institute.

Bazalgette, C. (1992). *Media education: Teaching English in the national curriculum series.* London: Hodder and Stoughton.

Beach, J. A. (1992). New trends in perspective: Literature's place in language arts education. *Language Arts, 69,* 550–556.

Bianculli, D. (1993). *Teleliteracy.* New York: Pantheon.

Brown, J. (1991). *Critical viewing skills education.* Hillsdale, NJ: Erlbaum.

Buckingham, D. (Ed.). (1991). *Watching media learning.* London: Routledge.

California State Board of Education. (1986). *English language frameworks for California public schools, K–12.* Sacramento, CA.

Cook-Gumperz, J. (Ed.). (1986). *The social construction of literacy.* Cambridge: Cambridge University Press.

Cortes, C. (1991). Empowerment through media literacy. In C. Sleeter (Ed.), *Empowerment though multicultural education.* Albany, NY: State University of New York Press.

Diaz, C. (Ed.). (1992). *Multicultural education for the 21st century.* Washington, DC: National Education Association.

Dichanz, H. (1992). Media in the teachers' professional and personal environment. In *Media Competency: A Challenge to School and Education.* Conference proceedings, Bertelsmann Foundation.

Edelsky, C., Altwerger, B., & Flores, B. (1991). *Whole language: What's the difference?* Portsmouth, NH: Heinemann.

Firestone, C. (1993). The Aspen Institute Communications and Society Program, *Media literacy: A report of the national leadership conference on media literacy.* Washington, DC.

Freire, P., & Macedo, D. (1987). *Literacy: Reading the word and the world.* South Hadley, MA: Bergin & Garvey.

Gallagher, S. (1992). *Hermenuetics and education.* Albany, NY: State University of New York Press.

Gless, D. J., & Herrnstein Smith, B. (Eds). (1992). *The politics of liberal education.* Durham, NC: Duke University Press.

Gould, S. J. (1981). *The mismeasure of man.* New York: W. W. Norton.

Grant, C. (1993). Cultural connections. *New dimensions in the world of reading* (Vol. 1). Needham, MA: Silver Burdett Ginn.

Hawthorne, R. C. (1992). *Curriculum in the making: Teacher choice and the classroom experience.* New York: Teachers' College Press.

Hirsch, B. (1989). *Languages of thought: Thinking, reading and foreign languages.* New York: The College Board.

Howe, M. (1983). *Learning from television: Psychological and educational research.* London: Academic Press.

Kubey, R., & Csikszentmihalyi, M. (1990). *Television and the quality of life: How viewing shapes everyday experience.* Hillsdale, N.J.: Erlbaum.

Lacy, L. (1993, May) Media Literacy ABC's. *Cable in the classroom,* pp. 11-12.

Larter, S., & Donnelly, J. (1993). Toronto's benchmark program. *Educational Leadership, 50,* 59-62.

Lusted, D. (Ed.). (1991). *The media studies book: A guide for teachers.* London: Routledge.

Masterman, L. (1985). *Teaching the media.* London: Routledge.

McLaren. P. (1989). *Life in schools.* New York: Longman.

Meyrowitz, J. (1985). *No sense of place: The impact of electronic media on behavior.* New York: Oxford University Press.

Nehamas, A. (1992). Serious watching. In D. J. Gless & B. Herrnstein Smith (Eds.), *The politics of liberal education.* Durham, NC: Duke University Press.

Pang, V. A. (1992). Institutional climate: Developing an effective multicultural school community. *Multicultural education for the 21st century.* Washington, DC: National Education Association.

Resnick, L. (1987). *Education and learning to think.* Washington, DC: National Academy Press.

Salomon, G. (1979). *Interaction of media, cognition and learning.* San Fransisco: Jossey-Bass.

Shepard, R. (1993). Elementary media education: The perfect curriculum. *English Quarterly, 25,* 35.

Sizer, T. (1984). *Horace's compromise.* New York: Houghton Mifflin.

White, R. (1993a). Forming a media arts department. *The Independent, 16,* 41,42.

White, R. (1993b). Video as a second language: Multilingual program. *The Independent, 16,* 47.

2

TELEVISION AS A LEARNING ENVIRONMENT: A THEORY OF SYNERGY

Susan B. Neuman

TEMPLE UNIVERSITY

Television usurps so much of our children's time. Surely it must influence their reading growth and developing reading interests. Its lack of intellectual substance, its rapid pacing, its cluttered mixture of visual movement and sound—television's role in the precipitous decline in achievement scores and school standards seems so plausible, so blatant. Why, then, have not researchers found a stronger relationship between television and its deleterious effects on literacy?

Two schools of thought have emerged to answer this question. One claims that there simply are no effects. While viewing may relate to reading achievement, its impact may be just too minor to be considered (Cook, Curtin, Ettema, Miller, & Van Camp, 1986). On the other hand, the second view suggests that effects may be masked due to flawed research designs (Hornik, 1981). Weak, or unreliable measures of viewing behavior, lack of statistical controls, nonrepresentative samples all may have led to ambiguous results and limited progress in the field.

This chapter will maintain that neither school of thought adequately explains the nature of the relationship between television, reading and other media. Rather, it will be argued that a better explanation lies in a theory of synergy: namely, in contrast to one medium (like television) displacing another (like reading), children often engage in a spirited interplay between media (Neuman, 1995). As interests are established, children are likely to alternate between video-based and print-related experiences on the basis of their accessibility, and their capacity to make optimal use of the particular medium. These activities appear to be guided by children's rather consistent patterns of interest, instead of specific medium presentation.

A theory of synergy is based on two propositions: (a) that there are qualitative differences in the content of each medium's messages; and (b) that the skills acquired from media act conjointly in helping children construct meaning and generate inferences in new contexts. This chapter will explore both propositions, then suggest implications for using television as a learning environment.

QUALITATIVE DIFFERENCES IN MEDIA

The premise that media convey information in qualitatively different forms is a legacy of Marshall McLuhan's elliptical phrase "the medium is the message" (McLuhan, 1964). Prior to McLuhan, there was an emphasis on a medium's content; following McLuhan, an emphasis on its form. In *The Gutenberg Galaxy* (1962) and *Understanding Media* (1964), McLuhan described every medium of communication as possessing a logic or grammar that constituted a set of devices for organizing experiences. Each medium employs specific symbols to tell a story and structures how individuals process and acquire information. A storybook, for example, uses print and illustrations to convey its message. Television uses both the integration of sound and visual images through movement to tell a story.

The distinctiveness of media derives from other critical aspects as well. Among these differences are the particular rules and conventions various media use in their treatment of material, the kinds of content they make available, their historical legacy, and the particular critical mass audience required by the economics of the industry to stay viable in the marketplace. All these factors suggest that while different media may convey similar material, each will do so in a qualitatively different form.

Media Comparison Studies. Intriguing insights by McLuhan led to a research tradition focusing on the distinctive cognitive consequences of media. Meringoff and her colleagues at

TABLE 2–1. Comparing Media

Study	Media compared	Results
Banker, & Meringoff (1982)	Film	Used various bases for substantiating inferences
		Conveyed appropriate character affect
	Silent film	Made comments of how film was made
	Descriptive aural version of film	Used more words in retellings
		Conveyed appropriate character affect
	Recorded story	Used more words in retelling
		Rarely used inferences other than those provided.
Beagles-Roos, & Gat (1983)	TV	Students scored higher in picture sorting.
		More uses of vague references in retellings
		Cited more details
		Justifications in references tied to story actions
	Radio	More expressive language
		Inferences drawn from verbal content and prior knowledge
Char, & Meringoff (1982)	TV	Produced most complete narratives
		Higher comprehension of vocabulary
	Storybook reading	Higher vocabulary
	Radio	Showed less comprehension of story
		Less comprehension of vocabulary
Hayes, Kelly, & Mandel (1986)	TV	Children's retention of action sequences greater
		Better comprehension
	Radio	More errors in summarizing
		Retention of dialogue not critical to story
Hoffner, Cantor, & Thorson (1988)	Audio only	Younger children had more difficulty under-
	Visual only	standing a narrative presented in an exclu-
	Audiovisual	sively visual form than either audio only or audiovisual.
Meringoff (1980)	TV	Cited more character actions
		More physical gesturing
		Relied on visual content for inferences
	Storybook	Recalled more figurative language
		Based inferences on textual content and out-side story information.
Neuman (1989)	TV	No significant differences in expressive language, retellings of story events and infer-ences
	Storybook	

Note. From Neuman, 1995.

Harvard's Project Zero (Meringoff et al., 1983) were among the first to investigate these distinctive features of learning from television and other media. One study (Meringoff, 1980), for example, analyzed children's apprehension of an African folktale presented in either an animated televised form or read aloud from a picture storybook. Verbal retellings indicated that children in the television group used character actions and visual cues to describe the story content, while the read-aloud group responded to aural cues or information not given in the story at all. These findings indicated that the specific details of content—the more subtle skills of drawing on one's prior knowledge—may vary according to the medium.

A large number of studies examining cross-media compari-sons followed this initial research. Beagles-Roos and Gat (1983), for example, analyzed cross-media comparisons of television and radio on first and fourth graders' story compre-hension. Children retold the story equivalently with radio and television presentations. However, there were striking differ-ences across media *in the way* they told the story. The radio version induced children to go beyond explicit and implicit story content to substantiate their inferences, much like the storybook treatment in Meringoff's study. Students, viewing the televised presentation, once again based their inferences on story actions. In a more recent study, Greenfield and Beagles-Roos (1988) found greater imaginative responses to

TABLE 2–2. Differences in Processing Media

Differences relate to	Proposed by	Perceived relationship
AIME	Salmon (1984)	Some media require a different level of effort expenditure than others
Pacing	Singer (1980) Singer, & Singer (1983)	Invariant pacing leads to different level of processing than learner controlled media
Interactivity	Winn (1977) Bagley, & Hunter (1992)	One-way media trains children to learn by observing and imitating; interactive media is constructive

story information when listening to radio than in an animated film format. Other studies, listed in Table 2–1, describe well how different media may influence children's interpretations of stories.

Some researchers following in this tradition have gone so far as to argue that repeated exposure to a particular medium may actually "cultivate" specific cognitive skills (Gerbner, Gross, Morgan, & Signorielli, 1982; Salomon, 1979). In a series of studies measuring children's ability to internalize film-like codes, Salomon reported that students deficient in cue-attending were able to internalize the "zooming" of a camera lens into a stimulus field, increasing their cue-attending skills (Salomon, 1979). Similarly, he found that students could transfer metacognitive modes of representation learned through computer activities to new situations, suggesting that media codes could be internalized, schematized, and then applied to new circumstances (Salomon, 1986). These studies demonstrate an important insight relevant to educators of literacy: different media presentations (television, storybooks, radio, film) do elicit slightly different interpretations of a story which are based on the medium's attributes like sound, moving pictures, and print.

Differences in Processing. Symbol systems are but one aspect of the differences among media. Other attributes, such as the psychological energy needed to process information, the pacing of information, and level of interactivity can influence how and how much children learn from the media (Bagley, & Hunter, 1992; Salomon, 1984; Singer & Singer, 1983).

To focus specifically on processing differences, Salomon introduced the construct of *amount of invested mental effort* (AIME) (Salomon, 1984). According to this model, AIME reflects the level of processing or mental energy needed to be expended to comprehend a medium. Television, with its format and pictures, is regarded by most as an easy medium, requiring little effort to learn. As a result, he argues, children tend to view the medium rather mindlessly, missing valuable opportunities to learn from it. Print, on the other hand, is perceived as "tough," requiring more AIME, leading to greater in-depth processing. Reporting on the invested mental effort in reading a narrative story or a televised version, Salomon found that sixth graders invested more effort in reading, and made more correct inferences than when viewing the tele-

vised version. Further, children in both versions made more correct inferences the more effort they reported investing.

The concept of AIME, however, has been criticized for failing to reflect differences in effort expenditure that may be due to context and purpose: Television viewing in schools, for example, may reflect a very different AIME than viewing television at home before bedtime. Further, a recent study reported that children's mental-effort expenditure may also vary as a function of viewer age, type of program, and reading level (expert readers vs. novice, Bordeaux, & Lange, 1991). Still, Salomon's concept of AIME highlights a potentially important difference among media: children view certain media more efficaciously than others which may influence their ability to learn from them.

Another difference between media is their pacing. Some researchers (Singer, & Singer, 1983) have argued that the pacing of certain media like television or radio may influence how children process information. Singer (1980), for example, suggests that the invariant pacing of television makes it difficult to efficiently retrieve information from memory. The emphasis on visual images in television is thought to favor a holistic interpretation of events, rather than a careful and deeper analysis. Radio, too, requires the listener to react to its pacing. Reading, on the other hand, is slower-paced—by its very deliberation, it seems to provide an opportunity for greater integration of the material with patterns of memory, wishes, and intentions.

Closely related to the pacing of the medium is its level of interactivity (Bagley, & Hunter, 1992). As currently defined, television, radio, and film offer only a one-way mode of communication. Although in some cases audience members may interact with these media, it is only at a superficial level (home shopping networks; call-in shows). Reading and new technologies like CD-ROM, however, are thought to more actively involve the child in the construction of meaning. Reading challenges children to become participants in their own learning. Consequently, these variations among media, described in Table 2–2, suggest that children will engage and use different strategies in interpreting information from them.

A large number of critics, unfortunately, have described these differences in such a way as to suggest that one medium is "good" and another "bad." Such self-declared experts including salesmen (Mander, 1978), journalists (Winn, 1977), and even a hypnotist (Moody, 1980) have claimed that television "dulls the senses," "trains right brain synapses," and "controls," while reading "develops the powers of imagination and inner visualization." A counterthesis, described below, is that the skills and information children acquire from their many experiences with media provide them with knowledge and strategies which may ultimately contribute to their literacy learning.

THE COMPLEMENTARITY OF MEDIA

Suggesting there are distinctive features of media that may influence the way children interpret stories leads to a second premise: children enjoy and learn from many different media.

In the process of interacting with media, children use a wide range of physical, perceptual, and cognitive skills. As they engage in each activity, they acquire not only domain-specific information, but strategic knowledge regarding the medium's strengths and limitations. In some cases, for example, visually presented moving images may instill insight and understanding far better than verbal descriptions. Other times, learning may require a motoric response, like learning to drive or to fix a car. Consequently, learning requires knowledge transformations from many different types of experiences, media-related and others.

Observing children's everyday activity in their home environments clearly demonstrates the complementarity of media. To examine these issues, I observed children's uses of media in a year-long ethnography of three families (Neuman, 1995). In contrast to one medium displacing another, I found that media often served complementary needs. In these family contexts, there was not a one-way but a *reciprocal,* ongoing relationship between television viewing, video, records, radio, toys, and print. Children's interests often crossed media lines as they looked for opportunities to spend time with their favorite characters and stories. For example, a child's love of a particular character or set of characters like the Brady Bunch would find expression through many different media: records, books, video, television, toys, even lunch boxes and bedsheets. One of the mothers, for example, described her daughter's current interest this way:

> Jennifer's just in love with Charlotte's Web right now. She tries to read a chapter when she wakes up in the morning. Then we got the video and I thought, "Oh dear"—here she was reading the book. But the video helped her get back into the book again, which surprised me. It brought her back to the book.
>
> She just loves Templeton. The video makes it so funny. And she laughs about that. And then when she gets in the book, she laughs because she knows what's going to happen. Whereas, I could never get into Templeton—he was the terrible one. So I think the video has given her a new angle on Templeton.

In this case, Jennifer's interest in *Charlotte's Web* first began with her teacher reading the book at school. At other times, however, Jennifer became interested in reading as a result of watching television. For example, having seen *Rainbow Brite* on TV, she bought a little golden book that she learned to read independently. Later, with her mother's help, she used these resources to write and illustrate her own book. Such similar cross-media patterns occurred with *Winnie-the-Pooh, The Cat and the Hat,* as well as *The Carebears,* which Jennifer described in a message to her mother: "Carebear my fafrit movie the carebear storybook."

For another family, the Clarkes, television was occasionally used to directly encourage reading. Scanning the Disney Channel guide each week, the mother would videotape a number of classics, including *The Lion, the Witch and the Wardrobe,* and *The Lord of the Rings* that she wanted the children to eventually read. The videos were used as a way of helping children get into the story, which she later read during their evening storyhour.

Cross-media connections were also evident in the home of single parent Mary-Alice Conley, where television or video often substituted for the children's storybook hour. Mary Alice rarely had time to read to the children. However, favorite books on video were a common feature in this household. I would often see the children watch stories like *The Velveteen Rabbit,* or *Green Eggs and Ham,* bought through the school book club. With no one to read the story to him, Alex repeatedly watched the video with intense interest, waiting for his favorite scene, "when all the toys get fired."

In this home, television was often used explicitly by Mary Alice as a catalyst for the children's literacy interactions. Linkages between Alex's interests in Sesame Street and print, for example, were seen in a calendar in his room, a primary vocabulary (and picture) learning game, an alphabet videotape, a Big Bird jigsaw puzzle, a subscription to the Sesame Street magazine and a Big Bird Cookbook. Similarly, Mary Alice joined another Book Club with many TV tie-ins for Stacey, who was just beginning to read on her own.

Television, film, and book characters all became embedded in children's pretend activities as well. For example, Jennifer incorporated the character of Heidi in a family play theme after watching on a few minutes of a Disney cartoon; Alex, who was 2½ years old, pretended to be "Big Bird" who was "always afraid," or "Snuffle-upagus" who always seemed to get into trouble. These characters were used in such common play themes as good versus evil, marriage and family, and fear of monsters. In fact, it was not uncommon for the children to invite particular friends over to play a mutually shared favorite of Rainbow Brite or Carebears. On some occasions, the older children invited their younger brother or sister to join in, but only if they were able to follow the story structure. When they did not, play was interrupted, as in the case when Jennifer yelled to her sister, "C'mon Leah, remember in Rainbowland you have to have a problem!" Such awareness of the implicit rules of the narrative was probably learned through multiple exposures to both video and print experiences.

The sheer variety of connections between television and print suggested that children's interests tended not to remain medium-specific. Seeking time beyond the immediate television or reading experience, children pursued their favorite stories and characters through multiple exposures with different media. In fact, the distinctions between media became increasingly blurred, as the children moved freely back and forth from visually oriented media (i.e., television, videotapes, movies) to print-oriented media (books, toy books, advertising circulars). Thus, contrary to displacing worthwhile activities, these observations indicated that television often served as a resource for children's emerging interests. Rather than conflict, there was a complementarity between children's media activities; children were the active agents in choosing leisure activities. Their media uses were guided by their interests and their practical assessment of attractive alternatives.

A THEORY OF SYNERGY

Synergy, however, goes beyond the assumption of complementarity. It assumes that the whole is greater than the sum of its parts. Considering their distinctive characteristics, a theory of synergy suggests that each medium's physical features, its structure, its method of handling material, may add a new dimension to children's knowledge and the means they employ to attain new knowledge. Thus, rather than detract from literacy, some moderate amounts of television, video, and other media may expose children to an additional set of processing tools, which in combination with others, contributes to their ability to interpret events. Since children apparently engage in inferencing strategies while viewing (Neuman, 1992), it is possible that these cognitive abilities are refined through practice and enhanced through their application in another medium. For example, in examining third graders' recall and inferential abilities, I found that the students who were given multimedia exposures of a similar story recalled more story structural elements than those students receiving repeated exposures through one medium alone (Neuman, 1989).

Consequently, there may be a spiraling effect. A greater facility to process information may enhance children's capability to acquire new information. Such an analysis might account for the replicated finding that a modest amount of viewing appears to be positively related to young children's reading scores (Neuman, 1988; Williams, Haertel, Haertel, & Walberg, 1982). Children in the elementary years and below, who watch between 2 and 3 hours of television per day achieve higher reading proficiency scores than those watching less than 1 hour.

Although the concept of synergy requires further hypothesis testing, this area of research suggests several important implications in using media to foster learning (Neuman, 1995). First, whether or not, or to what extent, a medium like televison may become a learning environment or remain "the vast wasteland," is subject to environmental influence. What children take away from the medium, how they use it, and how literate they become as viewers is shaped to a large extent by the way it is mediated by those in their environment. For example, though differing in pattern, each of the families that I observed in homes exercised controls over the amount and type of their children's television viewing. Television did not consume an inordinate amount of time in any of these families' daily lives, but was balanced with other interests and activities.

Second, the educative potential of a medium is mediated through linking children's interests directly with literacy-related materials. On numerous occasions, it was evident in home environments that cross-media connections were made intentionally to spark reading interests. In this respect, parents took seriously children's interests, which were shaped and transformed to reflect the educational priorities established by their families. Thus, in contexts where the mediational influences reinforce literacy practices, children's experiences with visual media may serve to support and enhance their emerging conceptions of print.

Third, there are skills involved in using media effectively. Cues provided by the medium itself, as in the case of television, which direct and guide viewers in their watching, can be informally taught through conversations by teachers, parents and children. For example, in several cases in the homes I

observed, children were made aware of some of the diverse technical elements of television and were encouraged to ask questions and to critically evaluate the explicit and implicit values in content. Acquiring this set of skills is an important process in orienting children to the language and grammar of television, and this process enables children to come to understand and anticipate story events.

While the virtue of books is widely accepted, few have acknowledged that television, radio, and other media can be used constructively for learning. Just as children are exposed to a diverse diet of genres and levels of reality and fantasy in reading, so too, can they learn about stories in a variety of media presentations. Such experiences may enrich children's understanding of stories and events, thus extending their engagement in literacy practices.

Implications of a Theory of Synergy for Television as a Learning Environment

In contrast to its critics, the bulk of the research evidence now suggests that television is intrinsically neither good nor "bad." Rather, it is a resource which like any other may be used or abused. Unfortunately, those who have condemned the TV set as a "mechanical" rival, prescribing to do away with it altogether, have failed to weigh its strengths and weaknesses. In doing so, they have ignored the possibilities of television as a means of extending children's interests and knowledge. These critics have also created an unnecessarily adverse distinction between what has traditionally been defined as "entertainment" and what is classified as "education"—a relationship that, in fact, may be more complementary than conflicting.

It is true that by design, television is not an instrument of teaching; yet the medium may have much to offer in educational value. For example, television is a remarkable disseminator of information. It has undoubtedly contributed to the public's knowledge and understanding of current social and political events. Similarly, television is a primary medium through which many children today are introduced to a wide variety of stories and genres. These opportunities could be used more fruitfully to help children see the important connections between their traditional school subjects and the different facets of our culture.

Too often many adults, particularly those in the educational community, have chosen to ignore television or even worse, have virulently attacked all uses of the medium. Articulating this perception in a public address, Jankowski (1986) reported:

> It is a source of constant amazement to me that the television set, an inert, immobile appliance that does not eat, drink or smoke, buy or sell anything, can't vote, doesn't have a job, can't think, can't turn itself on or off, and is used only at our option, can be seen as the cause of so much of society's ills by so many people in education.

Unfortunately, the assumption that media draw children's attention away from learning, has fostered a rather narrowly defined view of how literacy develops and how learning is thought to occur. Reading graded materials, such as basal readers, has often been considered the sine qua non in schools, sometimes at the cost of equally important hands-on experiences or activities involving other forms of symbolic representation. However, if children's ability to acquire literacy is said to be based on their prior knowledge, their conceptual understanding of language, and their uses of a variety of strategies, then there might be many paths to that goal, some of which may actually lie outside the printed page. For example, background knowledge derived from television, radio, and other sources, surely contributes to an individual's understanding and critical thinking when reading about similar events in newspapers and texts.

Indeed, children's interests in stories are often enhanced by their presentation in more than one medium. Cooper (1984), for example, found that after watching a televised version of a popular children's story, even the youngest children wanted to discuss its meaning, to explore the fiction further, to mull it over, and to go back to the book. We need to appreciate the special qualities inherent in each medium, to expose children to multiple genres and media presentations, and to build important connections between them.

Many children today are watching a great deal of televised fare that is inappropriate for their age and sophistication level. This concern raises two possible courses of action. If we take the position of technology determinist Neil Postman (1985) that "it is pointless to spend time or energy deploring television or even making proposals to improve it," then the only response is to lock the TV set up, or do whatever is necessary to keep it away from the innocent eyes of children. But if we believe that television can offer the potential to complement and enliven children's literacy experiences, it is imperative that greater efforts be made both to improve the quality of programming, and children's viewing habits. These efforts should involve all those concerned with children in our society. As Schramm, Lyle, and Parker (1961) found:

> We have a resource in children and a resource in television. We are concerned that television should strengthen, not debilitate, the human resource. This end can be accomplished most easily not by unilateral activity on the part of the TV industry, or by parents or schools, but rather by mobilizing all the chief forces in society which bear on the television-child relationship. It must be a shared effort to meet a shared responsibility. (p. 188)

Television has the potential to extend learning and literacy well beyond the classroom walls. It requires, however, the guidance and supervision of parents, and the skills and vision of educators building linkages between home and school learning.

The Role of Parents. Since television viewing behaviors tend to be developed at an early age, parents have a critical role in shaping the medium as a learning environment. Parents' own television behaviors, for one, influence their children's viewing habits; simply put, those who view excessively can expect to have children who do likewise. In our reading clinic, for example, we found that one of our children was being kept up every night until 2:00 or 3:00 a.m. to watch television with his mother. The young boy arrived in school generally around 1:00 p.m. and very often fell asleep shortly after. We found that it was impossible to influence his viewing habits until we

attempted to modify his mother's. Even though young children and early teens may fail at the time to internalize their parents' behaviors, these models are likely to be manifested later in adulthood. Himmelweit and Swift's 20-year follow-up study, for example, suggests a remarkable similarity between the pattern of media preferences and behaviors that occurred among parents and their children as older adults (Himmelweit, & Swift, 1976).

Thus, if the television set is on continuously, and parents themselves watch indiscriminately, discouraging children from asking questions because they might interrupt the program or challenge its content, then their children will most likely view equally unselectively and unthoughtfully. Likewise, if parents selectively watch programs from a range of news-related and entertainment fare, discuss and encourage their children to explore new ideas without fear of reprisal, then their children are far more likely to view more of this type of content and use it more wisely as well.

Similarly, parents who themselves spend time reading, who read to their children and provide them with a wide variety of print-related materials are sending a powerful message about the functions and pleasures of reading. Like television viewing, these models might not immediately influence the time and effort children devote to reading in their free time. Rather, children tend to internalize these parental examples which serve an inestimable role in laying the foundation for later successful reading. When parents take a special interest in children's literature, share their own favorite childhood stories with their youngsters, help them relate their reading of newspapers, magazines and books to everyday events—all these activities develop and nurture reading as an integral part in children's lives.

Parents can also encourage greater connections with print media. Research suggests that although television often stimulates children's interests, these interests rarely lead to action because of the lack of accessibility to further activities or materials. Parents can help maintain these interests by linking television directly with other print-related activities. For example, there are many cross-media connections between children's favorite television characters, books, and films, with popular Reading Rainbow stories being among the favorite books selected by children. A great number of popular books are selected and written for screen adaptation; similarly, books based on television-related characters and events, known as TV tie-ins, tend to flood the juvenile marketplace. Available through supermarkets, bookstores, and book clubs in schools, these materials add a dimension to children's viewing experiences, not only by directly linking them to print, but by allowing them to experience their favorite characters and events in a different contextual setting. In addition, many libraries today offer a wide variety of videotaped renditions of popular books, including such favorites as *The Velveteen Rabbit, Charlotte's Web*, and *Curious George* adventures. Encouraging children to borrow these tapes is useful on a number of accounts: (1) it generates interest in visiting the library, (2) it allows parents to more carefully control the content of what children are viewing on television, and (3) it gives children the opportunity to view the content repeatedly until they have mastered the story. Just like rereadings of favorite storybooks, children's comprehension of a televised story is enhanced by repeated presentations. Further, they often enjoy returning to the book after watching filmed versions of their favorite stories.

The Role of Educators. Today, teachers have many opportunities to use a wide variety of media materials in the classroom to enhance children's interests in stories. By experiencing similar stories across different media, children may become aware of the unique characteristics of each medium, as well as how the subtle distinctions within each contribute to differing adaptations and, occasionally, interpretations of characters and events in their favorite stories. Within the context of viewing, teachers may effectively highlight critical television viewing skills (Anderson, 1983) to encourage students to form purposes for viewing, to evaluate the plots of favorite stories, to judge the veracity of news stories or opinions, and apply the rules of logic and critical thinking to its content. Like other media, there are visual literacy skills, syntax and grammar skills to viewing television which may enhance students' learning from it.

In addition, other media, like newspapers and magazines tend to be an underutilized resource in linking children's interests in television and print. Magazines offer a diversity of content at children's reading levels in a brief, yet highly interesting format. Many of their favorite television characters, jokes from popular shows, and themes are featured in articles from such popular magazines as *Dynamite, Penny Power, 3-2-1 Contact,* and *National Geographic World,* and newspapers. These media are also an excellent resource for inclusion in classroom libraries, particularly for those students who are reluctant to read book-length materials.

PROMISING DIRECTIONS

Television is a unique mass medium, capable of transferring information and experiences, widely, quickly, and vividly with a realism and immediacy hardly matched by other mass media. We have not adequately explored its potential uses. In contrast, our focus to date has been on 'saving' children through either harnessing, eliminating, and discouraging television use. In only a few unique instances have we actually tapped the power of the medium to serve educational purposes. Surely our conceptions of its capacity to enhance children's learning and literacy have reflected the narrowness of our thinking rather than our broad vision.

Young children today possess a far more sophisticated knowledge of political and social events, richer vocabularies, and a greater familiarity of story genres, all of which have been influenced by the vast array of informational resources available to them. These sources of information need not compete with one another. Instead, they must join together to provide greater opportunities for learning and knowledge acquisition for an increasingly pluralistic society. Indeed, rather than banish new technologies, we must rejoice in the marvel of expanding knowledge bases, and explore ways of using this larger network of information to enrich children's lives and further their understanding of what it means to be truly literate.

References

Anderson, J. A. (1983). Television literacy and the critical viewer. In J. Bryant & D. Anderson (Ed.), *Children's understanding of television: Research on attention and comprehension* (pp. 297–330). New York: Academic Press.

Bagley, C., & Hunter, B. (1992). Restructuring, constructivism, and technology: Forging a new relationship. *Educational Technology, 32,* 22–27.

Banker, G. S., & Meringoff, L. (1982). *Without words: The meaning children derive from a non-verbal film story* (Tech. Rep. No. 26). Cambridge, MA: Harvard University, Project Zero.

Beagles-Roos, J., & Gat, I. (1983). Specific impact of radio and television on children's story comprehension. *Journal of Educational Psychology, 75,* 128–137.

Bordeaux, B. R., & Lange, G. (1991). Children's reported investment of mental effort when viewing television. *Communication Research, 18,* 617–635.

Char, C., & Meringoff, L. (1982). *Stories through sound: Children's comprehension of radio stories and the role of sound effects and music in story comprehension.* (Tech. Rep. No. 22). Cambridge, MA: Harvard University, Project Zero.

Cook, T., Curtin, T., Ettema, J., Miller, P., & Van Camp, K. (1986, November). *Television in the life of schools.* Paper presented at the Conference on Assessing Television's Impact on Children's Education, Washington, DC.

Cooper, M. (1984). Televised books and their effects on children's reading. *Uses of English, 35,* 41–49.

Gerbner, G., Gross, L., Morgan, M., & Signorielli, N. (1982). The "mainstreaming" of America: Violence profile No. 11. *Journal of Communication, 30,* 10–29.

Greenfield, P., & Beagles-Roos, J. (1988). Radio vs. television: Their cognitive impact on children of different socioeconomic and ethic groups. *Journal of Communication, 38,* 71–92.

Hayes, D. S., Kelly, S. B., & Mandel, M. (1986). Media differences in children's story synopses: Radio and television contrasted. *Journal of Educational Psychology, 78,* 341–346.

Himmelweit, B., & Swift, P. (1976). Continuities and discontinuities in media usage and taste: A longitudinal study. *Journal of Social Issues, 32,* 133–156.

Hoffner, C., Cantor, J., & Thorson, E. (1988). Children's understanding of a televised narrative. *Communication Research, 8,* 3–37.

Hornik, R. (1981). Out-of-school television and schooling: Hypotheses and methods. *Review of Educational Research, 51,* 193–214.

Jankowski, G. (1986). *Television and teachers: Educating each other.* (ERIC Document Reproduction Service No. ED 268 600).

Mander, J. (1978). *Four arguments for the elimination of television.* New York: William Morrow.

McLuhan, M. (1962). *The Gutenberg galaxy.* Toronto: University of Toronto Press.

McLuhan, M. (1964). *Understanding media.* New York: Signet Books.

Meringoff, L. (1980). A story a story: The influence of the medium on children's comprehension of stories. *Journal of Educational Psychology, 72,* 240–244.

Meringoff, L., Vibbert, M., Char, C., Fernie, D., Banker, G., & Gardner, H. (1983). How is children's learning from television distinctive? Exploiting the medium methodologically. In J. Bryant & D. Anderson (Eds.), *Children's understanding of television: Research on attention and comprehension* (pp. 151–180). New York: Academic Press.

Moody, K. (1980). *Growing up on television: The TV effect.* New York: Times Books.

Neuman, S. B. (1988). The displacement effect: Assessing the relation between television viewing and reading performance. *Reading Research Quarterly, 23,* 414–440.

Neuman, S. B. (1989). The impact of different media on children's story comprehension. *Reading Research and Instruction, 28,* 38–47.

Neuman, S. B. (1992). Is learning from media distinctive? Examining children's inferencing strategies. *American Educational Research Journal, 29,* 119–140.

Neuman, S. B. (1995). *Literacy in the television age: The myth of the TV effect* (2nd ed.). Norwood, NJ: Ablex.

Postman, N. (1985). *Amusing ourselves to death.* New York: Viking.

Salomon, G. (1979). *Interaction of media, cognition, and learning.* San Francisco: Jossey-Bass.

Salomon, G. (1984). Television is "easy" and print is "tough": The differential investment of mental effort as a function of perceptions and attributions. *Journal of Educational Psychology, 76,* 647–658.

Salomon, G. (1986). The computer as educator: Lessons from television research. *Educational Researcher, 15,* 13–19.

Schramm, W., Lyle, J., & Parker, E. (1961). *Television in the lives of our children.* Stanford, CA: Stanford University Press.

Singer, J. L. (1980). The power and limitations of television: A cognitive affective analysis. In P. H. Tannenbaum (Ed.), *The entertainment function of television* (pp. 31–65). Hillsdale, NJ: Erlbaum.

Singer, J. L., & Singer, D. (1983). Implications of childhood television viewing for cognition, imagination and emotion. In J. Bryant & D. Anderson (Eds.), *Children's understanding of television: Research on attention and comprehension* (pp. 265–296). New York: Academic Press.

Williams, P. A., Haertel, E. H., Haertel, G. D., & Walberg, H. J. (1982). The impact of leisure-time television on school learning: A research synthesis. *American Educational Research Journal, 19,* 19–50.

Winn, M. (1977). *The plug-in drug.* New York: Viking.

3

TV VIEWING, READING AND MEDIA LITERACY

Roger Desmond
UNIVERSITY OF HARTFORD

Speaking of media literacy, network producer and documentary host Linda Ellerbee remarks, "It ought to be taught in elementary school—how to watch television. Teach them what a commercial is really selling them" (Bianculli, 1992, p. 158). Ellerbee articulates a perspective that elicits fierce opposition; skeptics argue that perceiving and understanding the audio and video collage of television is nothing like the cognitive activities involved in reading. Joshua Meyrowitz (1985) states flatly, "Understanding visual symbols has nothing to do with literacy". To underscore the ease of accessibility of television, he offers evidence from ratings demonstrating that adult programs are enjoyed by children and vice versa. It is important to note that Meyrowitz uses the term "visual literacy" somewhat interchangeably with media literacy, as do others (Messaris, 1994).

Those critics who argue that media literacy is not the same as literacy are correct in their rejection of the implied metaphoric correspondence; the elusive first time viewer, upon first confronting an action–adventure program has no linguistic symbols to decode, no letters to recognize, no grammatical rules to master in order to recognize that someone is chasing or being chased. One of the consequences of applying the literacy label is an automatic invocation of print as the logical opposite of video; the opposition emanates from a belief (to be examined in detail later) that video experiences displace reading. Regardless of the validity of the claim, there is accumulating evidence of interdependence among media in the construction of narratives by viewers and readers. Marsha Kinder (1990) makes a strong argument for interdependence in her study of intertextual relationships among books, television, video games and film in the construction of the *Teenage Mutant Ninja Turtle* narrative. Another author suggests that this intertextuality is facilitated by the growing tendency of cross-ownership of media: the comic, the movie and the toy are all made and marketed by the same media agglomerate (Turow, 1992). We can acknowledge differences among media without rejecting the notion of media literacy. If the metaphor has substance, it will emerge in its explanatory power and the extent to which people recognize the problems which gave rise to the metaphor.

WHAT DOES IT MEAN TO BE MEDIA LITERATE?

There are two components of the definition implicit in the opinions cited earlier: teaching people to be critical consumers of entertainment and advertising fare, and teaching them to gain more insight and information from what they watch. In terms of the former position, a recently developed curriculum for high school students lists at least three general components of television literacy: (a) awareness of one's own relationship with the medium, including awareness of viewing habits and the categories of programming, (b) understanding the television industry and the conventions of television production, and (c) the critical-function, including awareness of the stereotypic distortion exhibited by many entertainment programs and the ways in which programming shapes our social customs and attitudes (Singer, & Singer, 1992). In a recent survey an evaluation of 26 critical viewing intervention and research programs for school children across the world, virtually every effort described embodies one or more of these three dimensions (Brown, 1991). Television is seen as a powerful force that needs counteracting with special training; to be a "critical" viewer is to be well trained in a kind of Deweyan skepticism.

Much less developed is the latter view of media literacy: improving the skills of viewers to extract more from the

Roger Desmond is Professor of Communication at University of Hartford. This article was written while he was a fellow at the Annenberg School for Communication at the University of Pennsylvania. He wishes to thank Kathleen Hall Jamieson and Elihu Katz for their support and encouragement of this project.

content than they typically do. While there has been some recent activity in this realm, the focus has been on viewers with some type of cognitive impairment, such as learning disabilities or emotional disturbance (Sprafkin, Gadow, & Kant, 1988; Sprafkin, Watkins, & Gadow, 1990). One study of the impact of viewing instructions on retarded adolescents and nonretarded fourth graders found that forewarning them that they would be tested after viewing produced no effects, but for both populations, instructions to watch "for fun" resulted in fewer propositions learned from the program than for all other conditions (Raynolds, 1991). While the majority of critical viewing programs has been conducted with children of preschool or elementary school ages, one educator provided "ideological decoding" training for adults and concluded that a program of how to "read between the lines" of television portrayals of politics, news events, and social issues was successful in elevating critical viewing skills in college students, but his evidence is entirely anecdotal (Brookfield, 1986). In a more formal investigation employing a lecture approach, seventh graders demonstrated more extensive learning of content from educational television programs than did controls (Von Kolnitz, 1986). The effect was particularly pronounced for students with high intellectual abilities (teacher designated).

Taken together, what these studies demonstrate is that it is *possible* to increase the amount and kind of information that people extract from the medium of television; whether these changes transfer to the everyday viewing context and whether they can overcome family patterns resistant to effortful viewing remain as unsolved problems for future research. In this context the work of Gavriel Salomon and the concept of AIME (amount of invested mental effort) is relevant; although there is convincing evidence that young viewers' and readers' investment of mental effort mediates what and how much they learn from television or print, there is need to clarify the role of mental effort for a definition of video literacy (Salomon, 1984). The conclusions of several studies suggest that television is often seen by viewers as inherently easier to decipher than print, which is why they invest less effort in viewing, but as one critic points out, observers globalize "television," ignoring the vast differences among formats and programs that they would acknowledge with respect to reading (Neuman, 1991). The literate viewer allocates AIME in the necessary amount for the appropriate category of program and learning goal, just as a reader allocates more AIME for a textbook than for a comic. Along with the critical function, then, we must include the concept of efficiency in a definition of media literacy; the literate viewer is one who can derive an adequate amount of information from each opportunity.

An additional dimension that has not been included in the goals of existing theory and research in the area is the set of skills involved in applying prior knowledge to the content of a television presentation, and the related skills of applying the fruits of media literacy to the world. In this regard there are several similarities among readers and viewers: both must be able to apply prior knowledge to a text or to a program to acquire new meanings, resolve ambiguities and account for missing information (Neuman, 1991). In the case of a young viewer, prior knowledge of a "cops n' robbers" script for

television programs will determine the amount of novel information that can be acquired (Collins, 1983). In terms of applying television or reading-derived information to social situations, a kind of "editor" must be part of the literacy equation or the cultivation of media-distorted information can occur (Signorielli, & Morgan, 1990). For the heavy viewer of many entertainment programs, the world is exaggerated in numerous ways; a literate viewer knows the difference between a satire like *The Simpsons* and a documentary about family life. In the majority of families and school reading programs, the distinction between fiction and reality is applied much more diligently to books than to television.

At this point, our definition of media literacy includes at least five dimensions: (l) awareness of one's own relationship with media, (2) knowledge of how media organizations shape their fare, and the conventions of production for each, (3) a critical-ideological awareness, (4) the role of effortfulness, and (5) relationships among prior knowledge, media comprehension and the "real" world. As Brown's (1991) survey illustrates, critical viewing research programs designed for children have concentrated much more on the first three than on the last two. In light of these dimensions, it is important to examine the rationale for efforts to increase media literacy. Primary among these has been the frequently voiced concern about the impact of television viewing on early readers. Media literacy programs, especially those that incorporate the first dimension of increasing awareness of media consumption patterns, have as one goal the reduction of television viewing and the increase of reading.

TELEVISION AND READING

Prior to the 1980s, the dominant conclusion of the majority of investigations of television's impact on reading was a simple, significant and straightforward negative association. More recent research has added complexity and some clarity to the elusive relationships among school achievement, reading comprehension, and extracurricular television viewing. One of the more frequently investigated hypotheses is displacement: Does TV viewing negatively affect the development of reading by taking the place of other activities? The question breaks down into two components: (a) Is there evidence that indicates that if children were not watching TV they would be reading or be engaged in other scholastically beneficial pursuits? and (b) Is there evidence that displacement results in the erosion of reading ability?

In terms of the first question, there is little evidence in support of a direct displacement effect, and some indirect evidence against it. Neuman (1988) examined the school performance data and self-reports of leisure time activities for over 2 million school children from 8 states, and found no impact of television on either school-related or leisure reading. She concludes that TV viewing is tied to a different set of gratifications than leisure reading, sports or time with friends. In a two-wave survey of high school students, Gaddy found weak displacement effects, and even weaker negative relationships between viewing and reading (Gaddy, 1986). In explaining his finding of small but consistently negative associations he concludes that if television displaces as little as 15 minutes per day of homework, its negative impact on school achievement would be large, over time. He also found TV viewing to be the smallest predictor of academic achievement among all those that were measured.

With respect to whether displacement, when it does occur, results in decreased reading performance, Williams (1986) found, as have other investigators, that the introduction of television into the social system resulted in an initial displacement of traditional activities. During this early introductory period, there was evidence for decreased school achievement, with a relatively rapid recovery and an accommodation of the medium into other leisure activities. More recently, Mutz, Roberts, and van Vuuren (1993) found evidence for functional reorganization of time in an 8-year panel study of fifth graders following the introduction of television in South Africa. Initially, television displaced movie attendance and radio listening, with no subsequent return to previous levels of these activities over the long term. There was no evidence of displacement of academically important activities from both individual and aggregate analyses. In these few studies, there is mixed evidence of displacement, and when it has been observed, long term impact on reading ability is highly dependent upon subgroups and amount of viewing.

Direct Effects

Although she did not find a global displacement effect of television, Neuman (1988) did find a pronounced curvilinear relationship between time spent with television and several measures of reading comprehension and vocabulary. Elementary school children who watched TV between 2 and 4 hours per day exhibited no great differences in reading ability; those who watched 4 or more hours per day showed a steady decline in reading and vocabulary. The effect is not as dramatic for high school students, since they watch less television than their younger counterparts. The only published meta-analysis of the literature regarding TV viewing and reading (23 articles, 274 correlations) concludes that while the overall correlation of TV watching and achievement is negative but small, the effect of viewing is increasingly deleterious up to a level of 40 hours (Williams, Haertel, Haertel, & Walberg, 1982). A review of 30 years of research reveals a similar trend across a number of studies, and concludes that 3 hours per day of viewing may be the critical peak in the decline of reading ability (Reinking, & Wu, 1990). Apart from hours of viewing, the review posits home environment, types of programs watched, and several other variables as mediators in the observed relationships.

Another extensive literature review examines five research approaches that have been used in previous studies and concludes that those most vulnerable to "reading inhibition" are the heavy viewers, socially advantaged and more intelligent viewers (Beentjies, & van der Voort, 1992). They present evidence that suggests that children higher in s.e.s. are vulnerable to deleterious effects because they *would* spend time in intellectually stimulating activities if they were not watching television, whereas lower s.e.s. children would not. The authors make a similar argument for IQ, citing two investigations that controlled for intelligence, and found a negative relationship between reading achievement and TV viewing only in more intelligent children. A panel study (one of the few in this area) found an initial high negative correlation between reading achievement and TV viewing which remained stable across 3 years, indicating no evidence for increasing levels of TV viewing as a causal factor in the reading–viewing equation (Ritchie, Price, & Roberts, 1987). The authors concede that although the relationships remained stable over time, and no increased displacement of reading by television was found, there is a clear possibility that the relationship between reading and television may be most critical prior to grade 3, when reading is described by Chall's (1983) second stage of reading. In terms of major conclusions from all of the research just reviewed, there are no individual investigations which support a "no effects" model regarding the impact of television viewing on reading achievement. The studies support models of either moderate or strong effects for children in specific categories, with heavy viewing as the most consistent mediator of the relationship between television viewing and reading achievement.

Toward Explanation of Relationships

If displacement alone is not the mechanism that explains the negative association between reading and TV watching, what other process might account for the recurring finding of negative correlations between reading and viewing television? One position which may help reveal a pattern throughout the research has been designated "concentration deprivation" (Beentjies, & van der Voort, 1991). They argue that television viewing, especially heavy viewing, may operate to decrease attention focusing, increase impulsiveness, and discourage task persistence in young viewers. In terms of attention, no research has directly investigated decreased attention span as a result of TV viewing, although educators often mention it as a probable outcome. If anything, research on attention to television suggests an alternating active-to-passive selective monitoring of the medium, with no evidence of a cognitive "drain" on other activities (Anderson, & Collins, 1988). Anderson and his colleagues have repeatedly found a cyclical attention sampling pattern when young children watch television, with more efficient sampling as children age (as children approach school age, for example, they pay more attention to regular television content than they do to commercials). In an investigation of attention to reading, Imai, Anderson, Wilkinson, and Yi (1992) find that first and third graders in reading lessons exhibit patterns of attention that bear some similarity to TV watching: they stop allocating attention when content becomes incomprehensible, just as children do when watching television. As Anderson (1992) summarized the lack of evidence for a negative impact of television on reading, " It is likely that attending to television does not constitute useful practice for developing the internal control necessary for sustaining active attention to difficult (and probably boring) academic content."

Impulsiveness and persistence have been studied in an experimental manipulation where 6-year-olds' viewing time was reduced by half over a 6-week period. Greater impulsivity and more reading and coloring book activity were observed in those children who watched their usual amounts, while impulsivity was decreased in the television restricted group (Gadberry, 1980). When second graders watched *Sesame Street* for 8 days in school, they showed significantly less task perseverance for a school task than did controls (Salomon, 1984). Children's ability to wait quietly, a variable related to task accomplishment and persistence, has been found to be negatively associated with heavy viewing, particularly when viewing was not mediated by parents discussions (Desmond, Hirsch, & Nicol, 1988; Singer, Singer, Desmond, Hirsch, & Nicol, 1985).

As is apparent from even a cursory examination of this domain, what is lacking is an adequate theoretical framework to organize results and to stimulate further research. The term "concentration deprivation" is frustrating, in that it connotes a general mindlessness resulting from prolonged exposure to television, for which there is scant evidence. There is evidence that people allocate less mental effort to television than they do to reading, but there is also evidence that this can be modified by instruction (Kubey, & Czikszentmihalyi, 1990; Salomon, 1984). In terms of young children, one of the most disturbing aspects of the research to date is that few investigations have concentrated on children in the first and second grades, where reading begins. A critical period alluded to earlier may be the time when heavy viewing does the most damage to young readers. Only one study has examined the relationship in viewers of this age group, and concluded that kindergarteners and first graders who were heavy viewers of television were less capable initial readers 1 year later than were their lighter-viewing counterparts (Singer et al., 1988). In this study, as in most others where IQ was measured, there are correlations among viewing, IQ, and reading-related skills that are difficult to unpack in a manner that provides a causal explanation, but as was alluded to earlier, when IQ is controlled for, the negative association between viewing and reading remains. When IQ is a predictor, it is the more intelligent viewers who exhibit the strongest negative effects of viewing. What might occur during this formative time that renders the heavy viewer a less capable reader in later years? One component that may suffer is the child's ability to visualize characters and events in a written or spoken story in a manner that allows for memory, reflection, and internalization. In other words, the child begins to "frame" narratives in a television-like manner, where events are more important than motives or the inner states of characters in stories. An ongoing study of childrens' story comprehension suggests that 6-year-olds who saw audiovisually presented stories based more inferences about the story on characters' appearance and actions than did those who read stories (Brown, 1991). It is clear that the possibility of "narrative deprivation" needs further investigation. A large part of reading comprehension is the ability to reflect on the events and inner states of actors in a story, and as Singer has suggested, the pace of television does not allow much time for reflection (Singer, 1976). There is also evidence of a tendency for "scripted" television viewing to interfere with comprehension of viewing (Collins, 1983). Finally, in a 3-year panel study of children aged 6–9, the heaviest viewers of television comprehended less of a program immediately after viewing than did lighter viewers, and this effect continued throughout the second year of the study (Singer et al., 1988). Taken together, these results suggest that heavy viewing during the hypothesized critical period may have negative implications for both television and reading story comprehension.

Until there is more research directed at the early reader-viewer, the bulk of evidence points to television viewing as one of several factors in the decline of reading comprehension in the past decade. As has been argued for viewing and aggression, it is also important to consider the aspects of these relationships that may be masked in the aggregation of results and debates over effect sizes; one disruptive child in a classroom may produce a chain reaction of tremendous import for the entire class (R. Kubey, personal communication, November 20, 1992). Similarly, one poor reader may demand inordinate amounts of time from a teacher at the expense of other students. Comstock and Paik's (1991) exhaustive analysis of the recurring negative correlation among viewing, reading and other concomitants of scholastic achievement concludes that, "There is no question that the amount of time spent viewing television by American children and teenagers is negatively associated with their academic performance" (p. 86). They, however, do not posit displacement as the only, or even the major contributor to the association: "The evidence supports a three-factor process in which large amounts of viewing not only (a) displace skill acquisition but also (b) interfere with further practice, or skill development and maintenance, and (c) lower the quality or value by decreased capacity of practice done in conjunction with television" (p. 136). In analyzing nine large-scale multivariate studies of the relationships among extracurricular factors and several indicators of academic achievement (including math and grades), they find that when the other predictors (s.e.s., ability, parents' education, special academic programs, etc.) are controlled for the negative association with television survives in six studies, and where it does not, the relationships are negative but not statistically significant. They argue for a "modest but important" causal relationship and an independent contribution to lowered achievement by television viewing. With respect to "practice in conjunction with television," Armstrong and Greenberg's (1990) finding of deficits in college students' performance of cognitive tasks done with a television on in the room is supportive of the relevance of the factor; the evidence points to a suppression of cognitive capacity, as opposed to distraction or heightened arousal. It is reasonable to assume that if adult cognitive task performance is hampered by an operating television set, children with developing cognitive capacity will be diminished more severely; homework done in front of a television will suffer. When relationships among homework, television viewing and parental influence were measured in a large national sample of high school students, homework had a direct impact upon achievement (positive) and television was negatively associated, though smaller in influence (Keith, Reimers, Fehrmann, Pottebaum, & Aubey, 1986). Results of causal modeling indicated that there was no evidence that homework displaced television viewing but that the obverse was true; as in other studies cited earlier, the effects of television were most pronounced for high achievers. There was no evidence of parental involvement in encouraging homework or in decreasing television viewing; the authors point out that such involvement would have more impact with younger children.

In adult college students there is evidence that reading leads to increased vocabulary learning, while television exposure does not (West, & Stanovich, 1991). When intellectual ability (measured by S.A.T. scores) was controlled, casual reading by college students predicted vocabulary and cultural literacy, while television predicted only cultural literacy. Vocabulary, spelling ability, and verbal fluency have all been associated with print exposure, even when reading comprehension is controlled (Stanovich, & Cunningham, 1992). Why does experience in reading increase our linguistic knowledge base when experience with electronic media does not? An investigation of the linguistic complexity of media reveals that the majority of television programs employs a 4th-grade vocabulary; novel words are present in many categories of print (Hayes, & Ahrens, 1988). Neuman argues that the idea that leisure reading is better for children than leisure viewing may be a reflection of a "literacy bias" on the part of educators and caregivers (Neuman, 1991). The evidence suggests that reading leads to information gain that is relevant to scholastic achievement; television does not.

Based on the hypothesized critical period for television-related deficiencies, the research reviewed above suggests that those critical viewing programs designed to repair deficiencies in concentration, narrative comprehension, and other subskills associated with school performance will be most effective with children in grades K–2; programs specifically targeted at reducing displacement of reading for older children are likely to be ineffective; the magnitude of displacement effects is small, and existing programs have not demonstrated their effectiveness. In light of the consistency of the viewing–achievement relationship and the fact that sheer consistency in multivariate studies is only one indicator of viewing-to-achievement causality, the impact of leisure viewing on these processes remains as the rationale for critical viewing programs at the elementary school level.

Other Dimensions of the Concept

As the previous review suggests there is more to the concept of media literacy than critical viewing, and there is more to critical viewing than the improvement of reading. Although the primary rationale for American intervention programs has been television's potential impact on learning and achievement, there are other areas where the dual-edged sword of criticism and enhancement of learning have been applied. Aggression is one candidate for modification of television effects; the majority of critical viewing programs has attempted to heighten children's awareness of the unreality and inherent danger of televised aggression. One intervention that has been praised because of its focus on media-depicted aggression and its consequences for imitation is Huesmann's program, but even in light of his success, he warns about the intractability of aggressive media content (Huesmann, Eron, Klein, & Fischer, 1986). Other areas where arguments for

effective intervention have been advanced include gender and ethnic stereotyping, and advertising. Virtually all critical viewing programs in Brown's (1991) survey address gender and race issues but, again, from a critical or protectionist perspective. In the case of both gender and ethnicity, we can say that virtually every intervention program reviewed has demonstrated gains in awareness of television stereotypes and stereotypic and inaccurate portrayals. As is also the case with every program, we cannot say whether these gains persist beyond the few days, hours or weeks in their evaluation periods, or whether children transfer these lessons to everyday viewing. The same conclusion is true of advertising, but there have been many more programs with similar results: impressive but short-term gains.

Moving beyond the American model, Canada and Australia have implemented large-scale programs of media education that encompass all the goals of the American system but with the additional dimension that was earlier designated critical-ideological. In Australia these programs have been in place, and recent evaluation data suggest that they have merit in terms of attaining some long-term goals (McMahon, & Quin, 1992). Their successful implementation is one factor in the development of a media literacy movement in the United States, led primarily by educators with some support by television networks and cable operators and moderate support by PBS affiliates in the larger cities. The major difference between the path to implementation in the United States and other countries is that in the United States there is far less consensus among the scholarly community for a *need* for media literacy intervention, and paradoxically, there is a greater reliance on the academic community for approval of such programs. The result is that grant proposal approvals and endorsements *for* the activists *from* the research community have not been forthcoming. One important reason for this tension is that media educational activists have focused on the deficit model, promoting their programs as prophylactics for a host of diseases that have not been supported by existing media research. There is no doubt, however, that media literacy as an educational movement is "in the air." In 1992 alone there were five international conferences on the topic; two at the Annenberg School for Communication at the University of Pennsylvania, and one each at the Aspen Institute in Maryland, in Guelph, Canada and in Bitburg, Germany.

What is clear from the interactions of researchers and activists at these meetings is that the goals of the groups have been so different, and their educations have differed so much that necessary dialogue among them will be a long time coming. One issue that has the potential to unite them is the temporary abandonment of the deficit model, and a shift toward an acquisition model.

One problem inherent in such a shift is that the deficit model gets good press; media literacy activists are the first to admit that public fear of negative media effects is a politically correct entry into program acceptance by school administrators and parents (Davis, 1992). Ultimately, an acquisition model would provide a framework for questions regarding issues such as (a) transfer—how lessons from entertainment and in-school viewing are, are not or could be applied to other domains of learning, (b) mental effort—how can viewers, listeners or users of CD-ROM, electronic games and so forth be stimulated to allocate more effort and attention to important content? and (c) can visual media production synthesize knowledge from other forms, for example, scriptwriting elicits research elicits reading skill and practice? These and other issues related to skill and information acquisition have the potential to unite the concerns of researchers, educators, and activists in ways that may prove fruitful for both producers and consumers of education.

What Research is Necessary?

The controversy surrounding the deficit model makes it a central priority for further research. The summary of work in the area cited earlier suggests that what we specifically do not need are more cross-sectional, correlational studies of relationships among leisure TV viewing, reading, and virtually every other indicator of scholastic achievement. Those data are in. What are necessary are some investigations that can assess the size of these relationships for significant population subgroups, and most important, nail down or at least disambiguate causality. A beginning step would be some longitudinal work. Earlier in this chapter a hypothesized critical period was invoked in an attempt to resolve some consistent lines of investigation into the relationships among media use and task persistence, practice in reading, math and other areas which may result in lowered abilities at later ages, where most of the current research is concentrated. If, as Anderson (1992) speculates, "It is possible that because young children find TV viewing easier than reading, that TV viewing displaces small but crucial amounts of leisure reading at the most critical ages" (p. 9), it is imperative that a time-series design with data points across the preschool years into grade 3 be employed. The work of Gadberry (1980) demonstrates the possibility that this work can be done, but her interrupted time-series analysis focused on only a few weeks of restricted viewing. Huesmann and Eron's (1986) investigation (over 20 years between measurements) of early viewing and aggression demonstrates the "payoff" of a longitudinal approach, but what is needed to resolve the causal role of early TV viewing is more frequent measurement of a difficult-to-measure population in the most formative years.

A second area of research concerns the entire notion of passivity; as Anderson (1992) points out, we lack a conceptual definition of this state, therefore pioneering efforts at conceptualization and operationalization are necessary. Passive viewing is one of the key elements of the deficit model in lay circles and popular writing; as such, it has been used to justify a need for media literacy. Even as a fuzzy concept, it is integrally linked with a number of important issues in cognition. It is possible that ultimately, a psychophysiological approach could yield a proxy, but early efforts have not paid off.

Among other gaps in our knowledge about television's relationship to education that were discussed earlier in the context of established knowledge is the issue of amount of viewing. It has seldom been adequately measured, but even with differential measures, it has traditionally been an independent variable. As such, its use has yielded a number of qualifiers of negative effects based on heavy viewing; even skeptics such as Neuman (1991) allow that it is heavy viewers who suffer the greatest deficit. If one of the goals of media literacy is to reduce the deficit, it is imperative that research designs examine the impact of viewer training on the amount and kind of viewing. There is an implicit assumption in the media literacy movement that critical viewing can alter everyday patterns of viewing, but little evidence for or against the assumption exists. Previous work suggests that the context most amenable to viewing modification is the family (Bryant, 1990). The role of the family in mediating television comprehension and enjoyment has long been investigated in the traditions of effects research, phenomenological and cultural studies but is seldom discussed with respect to media literacy. Since the viewing done at home is the major concern of the deficit arguments, the role of the family context in reinforcing and originating media education is crucial. What are needed are methods of providing systems models of media education, and theoretically sound evaluations of those methods.

The research agenda for the acquisition model is far less certain. As noted earlier, the issue of transfer is salient for educators and researchers: transfer of insights and information *from* television to other domains of knowledge, transfer of world knowledge *to* television, and transfer of media education from schools *to* everyday viewing. An important initial effort might examine the benefits of television scriptwriting as an exercise and as a measure of learning. Are scripts generated by the media-educated richer, more complex, more informative, more "visually literate" than those written by untrained writers? With respect to education issues, would a term paper be written and researched with more quality and thoroughness if it were assigned as a documentary script? One of the important issues in transfer is the perspective taking that is required of a scriptwriter; how can this information be presented in a manner that elicits attention, yet instructs? It is also important to examine some of the cognitive subskills that may underlie educational achievement. One author has suggested spatial perception and visual–verbal associational ability as areas that may benefit from visual literacy (Messaris, 1994). Adoption of an acquisition model as a research agenda does not mean that theoretical work becomes evaluation research. Inquiry into the maximization of media education potential has implications for a broader spectrum of emotion and cognition than has been addressed by the deficit model. We may explore the connections among thought, form and content in a brand new arena.

What Media Education Might Become

The majority of forecasts regarding the future of media in the past few decades has fared miserably, primarily because it was made in the economic "blue sky" of the 1950s and 1960s when all things were possible (Jassem, & Desmond, 1986). In the harsher light of the current global economy, poorly designed and administered programs of media literacy will go the way of marching bands and instruction in the arts—"extras" quickly and easily sliced from school budgets. Those that survive will require hard data on effectiveness from the research community, a difficult requirement in light of schisms between researchers and educator-advocates presented earlier. A great deal depends upon whether some good research is forthcoming; earlier suggestions represent a few possibilities, but theory building of the amount and kind witnessed in the search for connections between television and aggression or advertising and social behavior are necessary. In the past 20 years a number of models of the processes were developed, competition among them was partially resolved, new branches of the effects framework emerged, and just recently, recommendations have been heeded to some extent as evidenced by the Children's Television Act of 1990. If the same sort of concentrated labor is exhibited by investigators of media literacy, the necessary funds, coordination of efforts and concomitant publicity may enliven our research and enlighten our children.

References

Anderson, D. R. (1992, May). *Television, children and education: Issues for research.* Keynote address to the Annenberg Conference on Television and Education, Philadelphia.

Anderson, D. R., & Collins, P. A. (1988). *The influence on children's education: The effects of television on cognitive development.* Washington, DC: U.S. Department of Education.

Armstrong, G. B., & Greenberg, B. S. (1990). Background television as an inhibitor of cognitive processing. *Human Communication Research, 16*(3), 355–386.

Beentjies, J. W., & van der Voort, T. H. (1991). Children's written accounts of televised and written stories. *Educational Research and Development, 39*(3), 15–26.

Bianculli, D. (1992). *Teleliteracy: Taking television seriously.* Los Angeles: Continuum.

Brookfield, S. (1986). Media power and the development of media literacy: An adult educational interpretation. *Harvard Educational Review, 56*(2), 151–170.

Brown, J. A. (1991). *Television critical viewing skills education.* Hillsdale, NJ: Erlbaum.

Bryant, J. (Ed.). (1990). *Television and the American family.* Hillsdale, NJ: Erlbaum.

Chall, J. S. (1983). *Stages of reading development.* New York: McGraw-Hill.

Collins, W. A. (1983). Interpretation and inference in childrens' television viewing. In J. Bryant & D. R. Anderson (Eds.), *Childrens' understanding of television* (pp. 125–150). New York: Academic Press.

Comstock, G., & Paik, H. (1991). *Television and the American child.* Los Angeles: Academic Press.

Davis, J. (1992). *Media literacy: From activism to exploration.* Paper presented at the National Leadership Conference on Media Literacy, Aspen Institute, Queenstown, MD.

Desmond, Hirsch, & Nicol, (Summer, 1985). Family mediation patterns and television viewing—young children's use and grasp of the medium. *Human Communication Research, 11*(4), 461–480

Gadberry, S. (1980). Effects of restricting first graders' TV viewing on leisure time, i.q. change and cognitive style. *Journal of Applied Developmental Psychology, 1,* 161–176.

Gaddy, G. D. (1986). Television's impact on high school achievement. *Public Opinion Quarterly, 50,* 340–349.

Hayes, D. P., & Ahrens, M. (1988). Vocabulary simplifications for children: A special case of "motherese". *Journal of Child Language, 15,* 395–411.

Huesmann, L. R., & Eron, L. D. (1986). *Television and the aggressive child: A cross-cultural perspective.* Hillsdale, NJ: Erlbaum.

Huesmann, L. R., Eron, L. D., Klein, R., & Fischer, P. (1986). Mitigating the imitation of aggressive behaviors by changing children's attitudes about media violence. *Journal of Personality and Social Psychology, 44*(5), 899–910.

Imai, M., Anderson, R. C., Wilkinson, I. A. G., & Yi, H. (1992). Properties of attention during reading lessons. *Journal of Educationl Psychology, 84,* 160–173.

Jassem, H., & Desmond, R. J. (1986). Mass communication theory and new media. In B. Ruben (Ed.), *Information and behavior* (pp. 90–112). New Brunswick, NJ: Transaction.

Keith, T. Z., Reimers, T. M., Fehrmann, P. G., Pottebaum, S. M., & Aubey, L. W. (1986). Parental involvement, homework and TV time: Direct and indirect effects on high school achievement. *Journal of Educational Psychology, 78*(5), 373–380.

Kinder, M. (1990). *Playing with power in movies, television, and video games.* Berkeley, CA: University of California Press.

Kubey, R. W., & Czikszentmihalyi, M. (1990). *Television and the quality of life: How viewing shapes experience.* Hillsdale, NJ: Erlbaum.

McMahon, M., & Quin, R. (1992). Knowledge power and pleasure: Directions in media education. *Proceedings of the Second North American Conference on Media Education,* Guelph, Ontario.

Messaris, P. (1994). *Visual "literacy". Image, mind, and reality.* Boulder, CO: Westview Press.

Meyrowitz, J. (1985). *No sense of place.* New York: Academic Press.

Mutz, D., Roberts, D., & van Vuuren, D. (1993). Reconsidering the displacement hypothesis: Television's influence on children's time use. *Communication Research, 20*(1), 51–76.

Neuman, S. (1988). The displacement effect: Assessing the relation between television viewing and reading performance. *Reading Research Quarterly, 23*(4), 414–440.

Neuman, S. (1991). *Literacy in the television age: The myth of the tv effect.* Norwood, NJ: Ablex.

Raynolds, C. T. (1991). *The effects of viewing instructions on the recall of a television story by mildly retarded and nonretarded individuals.* E.D.D. dissertation, Columbia University.

Reinking, D., & Wu, J. H. (1990). Reexamining the research on television and reading. *Reading Research Quarterly, 29*(2), 30–43.

Ritchie, D., Price, V., & Roberts, D. (1987). Television, reading, and reading achievement: A reappraisal. *Communication Research, 14,* 292–315.

Salomon, G. (1984). TV is easy and print is tough: The role of perceptions and attributions in the processing of material. *Journal of Educational Psychology, 76,* 647–658.

Signorielli, N., & Morgan, M. (1990). *Cultivation analysis: New directions in media effects research.* Newbury Park, CA: Sage.

Singer, D. G., & Singer, J. L. (1992). *Creating critical viewers.* Denver, CO: Pacific Mountain Network.

Singer, J. L. (1976). Can TV stimulate imaginative play? *Journal of Communication, 26,* 76–80.

Singer, J. L., Singer, D. G., Desmond, R. J., Hirsch, B., & Nicol, A. (1988). Family mediation and childrens' comprehension of television: A longitudinal study. *Journal of Applied Developmental Psychology, 9.*

Sprafkin, J., Gadow, K., & Kant, L. (1988). Teaching emotionally disturbed children to discriminate reality from fantasy on television. *Journal of Special Education, 21,* 99–107.

Sprafkin, J., Watkins, L., & Gadow, K. (1990). Efficacy of a television curriculum for emotionally disturbed and learning disabled children. *Journal of Applied Developmental Psychology, 11,* 225–244.

Stanovich, K. E., & Cunningham, A. E. (1992). Studying the consequences of literacy: The cognitive correlates of print exposure. *Memory and Cognition, 20*(1), 51-68.

Turow, J. (1992). *Story telling in the age of media synergy.* Paper presented at the Second International Media Ecology Conference, Mainz, Germany.

Von Kolnitz, D. (1986). *The effect of critical television on the performance of seventh grade students.* Ph.D. dissertation, University of South Carolina.

West, R. F., & Stanovich, K. E. (1991). The incidental acquisition of information from reading. *Psychological Science, 2,* 325–330.

Williams, T. M. (1986). *The impact of television:* A natural experiment in three communities, New York: Academic Press.

·4·

TELEVISION AND LANGUAGE LEARNING

Michael Willmorth

BOISE STATE UNIVERSITY

Since the advent of audio(-visual) mass media—the phonograph, then radio, sound cinema, and finally television—hopes and fears have been expressed about their potential effects on the language used in the communities they serve. On the one hand, if good speech were used uniformly in the media, the pronunciation, vocabulary, and grammar used in everyday interpersonal interaction might be improved, should listeners take media speakers as behavioral models (Franklin, 1929, p. 315). On the other hand, if the speech heard in these media were not kept to sufficiently high standards, the language of the speech community might be degraded (Parsons, 1936, p. 27). Both positions generally assumed that, because the same linguistic messages would be heard by all media consumers regardless of regional and social differences in local speech varieties, there would, over time, be a leveling of these differences with each new generation of speakers.

This double-edged potential for influencing the language of a community is still believed to be one of the powers of television. Some teachers point to television as a source of models that speakers of nonstandard varieties might emulate to enhance career opportunities (Robbins, 1988). Others (and perhaps some of the same educators) have lamented that television provides numerous examples of "bad" language spoken by popular media figures, which are taken up by viewers and incorporated into subsequent face-to-face communication (Vann, 1991; "Mouths of babes," 1992).

Predictions about these wide-ranging effects of television on language seem to inform common folk beliefs about language learning (Schieffelin, & Eisenberg, 1984, p. 390) in contemporary, technologically developed societies. A study of Chinese immigrant children to the United States by Ikeda (1992) found that, even though the children did not watch television with the goal of learning to speak and understand English, they believed they might gain some such knowledge in passing; their mothers, however, were sure that their children's TV viewing behavior would strongly affect their development of English language skills.

Anecdotal evidence, too, seems to support beliefs about the efficacy of television as an aid to language learning. In one case, an unusually bright boy—he graduated from college at the age of ten—claimed that he learned to speak by the time he was 10 months old, "in part by repeating what he heard on TV game shows. As for reading, the youngster, whose IQ was measured at 180-plus, said, 'Some of my first words were from *TV Guide*'" (*TV Guide*, 1994, June 25). Another article profiled four immigrants to the United States who claimed to have learned about the English language and American culture in part while watching TV in the low-anxiety language-learning environment of their homes. At first they sought out easy-to-understand programs, which provided relatively simple verbal messages and significant amounts of redundant visual information to assist comprehension. As their skills with English improved, they sought out programs with more sophisticated language (Littwin, 1988).

In spite of these stories, however, most language researchers have credited television with very little, if any, influence on the language acquired and used by viewers. The apparent absence of the general leveling of linguistic variation in speech communities predicted in early speculation on the effects of mass media, already noted in 1938 by W. Cabell Greet (pp. 69, 70), is frequently offered as proof of TV's impotence. Most researchers in language acquisition have historically focused on speech in interpersonal interaction rather than in the media. Among these investigators, a consensus appears to have formed that if television does anything more to influence language than speed the diffusion of a limited number of vocabulary items across dialect regions (Trudgill, 1983, p. 61), it is perhaps merely to provide fodder for conversation around water coolers and at cocktail parties. However, a growing number of studies focusing on language in the media and on language learning processes indicate that TV may have some pervasive and profound effects.

31

CRITIQUE OF TELEVISION'S ROLE IN LANGUAGE LEARNING

As research into language learning has been carried out primarily in the fields of linguistics and psychology, most findings have reflected their theoretical and methodological frames. Scientific responses to folk beliefs about the power of television in language learning have stressed the intra- and interpersonal processes that are of primary interest in these disciplines. Since the give-and-take nature of interpersonal interaction and the use of simplified codes by adults to speak to children, for example, are usually considered fundamental for the development of normal communicative competence, they have been used as criteria for dismissing the possibility that television can have a significant role to play (Rice, 1984, pp. 170, 171; Sachs, Bard, & Johnson, 1981). Also, since the relationships between mass media and interpersonal communication processes have not been widely explored in these research traditions, it is not surprising that most language acquisition experts have not found television to be particularly relevant.

The argument usually made to support this position contrasts the apparently passive nature of a child viewing television with the activity of the child in face-to-face interaction with an adult (Trudgill, 1983, p. 61). The time spent watching television is time not spent practicing conversational skills, therefore the language learner is linguistically deprived in relation to others who do engage in activities that promote or require speaking (Winn, 1985, p. 11). The viewer may even regress into an earlier, lower level of competence due to reliance on the visual elements in TV messages for comprehension (pp. 54, 55).

Other critics focus on the nature of the linguistic messages on television, suggesting that they are too complex, too rapidly deployed, or too removed from the here-and-now of the viewer's physical environment to engage or even be comprehensible to a language learner (Clark, & Clark, 1977, p. 330). A third reason offered for the inability of television to facilitate language acquisition is that mere exposure to language in use is insufficient; the language learner must actively use the code in order to internalize new words and grammatical rules (Hoff-Ginsberg, & Schatz, 1982, pp. 22, 23). Even if children do take linguistic material from TV and imitate it, they are probably dealing with it as meaningless sound constructions, not as words (Ervin-Tripp, 1971, pp. 198, 199).

These assessments seem to be confirmed in the equivocal or negative findings of some of the initial studies that attempted to test whether and how television might be related to language learning. Nelson (1973, pp. 63–65), for example, found a negative correlation between the amount of TV viewing and the progress of language development at the age of 18 months. Selnow and Bettinghaus (1982) found a similar result for preschool children:

1. Children who watched more television displayed less sophisticated language,
2. Children who displayed less sophisticated language tended to view more language-poor programs, and
3. Children who used more sophisticated language tended to view programs that modeled more sophisticated language (p. 477).

These studies seemed to indicate that, in general, more TV viewing is associated with less well-developed language skills. However, both studies have raised questions about this interpretation of the results. It may have been that the children either acquired the language level of the programs they watched or that they sought out programs according to their existing language levels.

Other research from the fields of mass communication and social and cognitive psychology has challenged three of the traditional assumptions about language acquisition: (a) the necessity of interpersonal interaction, (b) the incomprehensibility of linguistic messages on TV, and (c) the ineffectiveness of social learning. Work in these disciplines suggests other ways of conceptualizing the relationship of television to language learning.

LANGUAGE IN THE TELEVISION MESSAGE SYSTEM

Rice and Wartella (1981) criticize the notion that "television-viewing is not interactive, that the child is a captive audience who can only passively receive what is presented. Just as the model oversimplifies face-to-face interchanges, it also does not capture the subtleties inherent in television-viewing" (p. 370). Television messages are composed from three different codes: (1) iconic, (2) media-specific, and (3) generic. The iconic aspects include pictorial representations, which, if realistic, are fairly easily understood by any viewer regardless of language competence. Media-specific codes are those exclusive to the "grammar" of television messages, including fade-outs and cuts to indicate transitions of some sort; viewers become familiar with these conventions without much time or effort. Generic codes are used both within and outside of watching TV; one of the most important of these is language. A viewer must use knowledge of language in everyday interpersonal experience to understand linguistic messages on television (p. 370).

There are significant differences between engaging in interpersonal linguistic interaction and attending to the verbal messages of a television program (Olson, 1987). Hollenbeck and Slaby (1979) note that:

> Infants learn to use contingent looking and vocalizing to elicit responses from adults. Yet, the high level of social control that infants typically attain with their caretakers stands in marked contrast to the complete lack of direct control that infants may achieve over the "social" stimulation produced by television. The same looking and vocalizing behaviors that serve infants so well while interacting with caretakers are responded to by television's characters, images, and sounds in a completely noncontingent way. (p. 45)

Nevertheless, young children can understand from TV pictures and sounds that a talking person is represented and may try to interpret such images with the same communicative strategies that they would employ in interpersonal situations. One researcher reported the behavior of her 3-year-old son as he watched her appearance in a TV interview. The boy tried to engage her image by signaling both verbally and nonverbally, and when she did not respond, he believed that she was ignoring him and broke off his TV viewing session angrily and left the room (Greenfield, 1984, p. 53).

Selnow and Bettinghaus (1982) believe that there are some benefits in the differences between child–parent and child–TV language experiences:

> Parents can interact with children and provide immediate feedback and reinforcement; television cannot. Parents can direct their messages to the interests of an individual child, whereas television, a mass medium, does not have this capacity. But television does offer messages pitched with a keen appeal to young viewers which engage them in the content. Furthermore, television can provide an assortment of language models and so display a greater variety of language styles than can be offered by parents. Beyond all this, television is always there, and is always available to a child at the touch of a button when parents may be preoccupied. (p. 471)

Thus, what the language learner loses in interaction is perhaps compensated to an extent by gaining access to varied and engaging material on demand.

INTERACTION IN TELEVISION VIEWING

The stereotypic image of the solitary TV-viewing child as a zombie mesmerized by the visual and sonic stimuli emanating from the set is in fact not confirmed by numerous studies of the lively activity that occurs among viewers. Far from suppressing interaction, it may stimulate it (Messaris, 1983, p. 293; Messaris, & Kerr, 1983). Young children are often praised by caregivers for mere mimicry of material from TV (Halpern, 1975, p. 66), but language learners also appropriate materials from TV to their own utterances in meaningful ways. Also, the use of the TV-viewing context as an occasion for verbal interaction may or may not be focused at any given moment on the TV message at hand.

Lemish (1987) carried out a study of 16 families with infants and toddlers to examine how TV viewing related to social interaction among the members of the household and to the acquisition of language skills by the young children. Toddlers walked up and touched the television set, talked back to *Sesame Street* characters, asked to have the set turned on, reiterated (outside of the viewing context) language they heard from television, and imitated TV action. Parents would call the attention of their children to objects on TV and would label or request a verbal label for objects familiar to the children. After the first birthday, the children practiced newly acquired words from TV with their parents as they watched (p. 42). The television-viewing activity was so closely linked with verbal interaction that it appeared to be integrated into the language-learning process for these children.

Lemish and Rice (1986) conducted a participant observation study of early TV experiences in the natural home environment. They found a strong relationship between TV viewing and language development in expanding vocabulary and practicing discourse. The way in which television is used

by mothers and their babies to explore and learn language is in many ways similar to the use of picture books in joint reading activities (Heath, & Branscomb, 1986).

Television provides occasions for verbal interaction among viewers of all ages. Some of the parent–child conversation involves interpretation and explanation of aspects of the TV message, including language itself (Winick, & Winick, 1979, p. 164). In a study focused on how children interact with others in the TV-viewing situation during commercials, Reid and Frazer (1980a) found that:

1. Commercials were used to draw others into conversations and activities related or unrelated to message content;
2. Attempts were made to gain information from parents or siblings in order to resolve ambiguities or complex message presentations; and
3. Commercials were used to avoid the demands and requests of others, especially those made by parents (p. 156).

At other times television may provide raw material for language play among children (James, & McCain, 1982, pp. 787, 788; Reid & Frazer, 1980b; Watson-Gegeo, & Boggs, 1977), an important activity in the development of linguistic skills. This practice of incorporating spoken material from TV into interpersonal interaction for playful or humorous purposes continues into adulthood. Alperstein (1990) describes how catch phrases from commercials are integrated and transformed into conversations among adults, where they may in turn be adopted indirectly by people who are not TV viewers. This practice may serve to facilitate social integration among people who do not know each other well but for whom TV images represent very familiar shared cultural knowledge.

COMPREHENSIBILITY OF TV SPEECH AS INPUT FOR LANGUAGE LEARNING

Certainly while much of the speech on television is incomprehensible for the beginning language learner, some programs are more incomprehensible than others, and many of them can be comprehended at different levels according to viewers' varying abilities. Huston and Wright (1983) note that the educational program *Sesame Street* contains a good deal of verbal humor and parody that children (the primary audience) would not be expected to understand. In fact, these elements apparently serve to make the program more appealing to older viewers, and so might promote joint viewing of the program by children and adults and reinforcement of the learning from TV through face-to-face interaction during viewing.

In spite of not getting the full range of meanings from the show, children may still understand enough of a television message to enjoy it and continue watching. Preverbal children may be fascinated by some programs and comprehend the activity represented in them going mainly by the visual elements on screen rather than by the verbal content (Huston, & Wright, p. 57). The visual elements of television may even serve to instill such linguistic knowledge as vocabulary by providing more easily interpreted and redundant iconic information along with the verbal message (Rice, Huston, Truglio, & Wright, 1990, p. 427).

Even among children's programs there is a good deal of variation in the difficulty of the language used. Rice, Huston, and Wright (1982) described the linguistic features of five children's television programs and discovered that many of Clark and Clark's (1977) generalizations about television language were inaccurate:

> The majority of comments in four of the programs were ones in which the speaker talked about things immediately accessible to view. Also, the stream of speech was not always rapid. In fact, the main characters of some programs had speaking styles consisting of a moderate, deliberate rate combined with a judicious use of pauses that distinctly marked linguistic units. Furthermore, there was considerable evidence of explicit attempts to adjust verbal messages to correspond to children's linguistic processing abilities, including various means of highlighting key linguistic messages. Another facilitative factor was the manner in which linguistic messages were combined with nonlinguistic production values. (Rice, 1984, p. 176)

Thus, some children's programs do not present overly complex verbal messages that are difficult to interpret; instead, they seem to be designed to match the linguistic capacities of their intended preschool audience.

Rice and Haight (1986) compared the nature of the speech used in two shows popular among very young viewers—*Sesame Street* and *Mr. Rogers' Neighborhood*—to the "motherese" of face-to-face communication. These programs seem to be addressing an audience of very young language learners, who, through their familiarity with these less complex utterances, may better comprehend the TV message. The speaking style in both these programs may share function as well as form with the similarly uncomplicated linguistic constructions adults may use with very young children in interpersonal interaction to facilitate language acquisition.

LANGUAGE ACQUISITION THROUGH OBSERVATIONAL LEARNING

While the primary focus in language acquisition research has traditionally been on interaction between language teachers and language learners, there have been a number of studies which provide evidence for the importance of observational learning. One argument is that because, on the average, children learn to comprehend over 14,000 words by the age of 6 (nine words per day), explicit tutoring for each word is not—indeed cannot be—required. It has been proposed that children utilize a "fast mapping" ability which allows them to "draw upon the linguistic and nonlinguistic context for a quick, initial, partial understanding of the word's meaning" as they overhear them used in the conversations of others (Rice, Buhr, & Nemeth, 1990, p. 33).

In general, personal participation in verbal activities is not required to gain an understanding of how particular verbal features are associated with aspects of the social situations in which language is used. It may be sufficient to be exposed to the ways in which language is used by certain sorts of people in certain contexts to learn those associations (Schieffelin, & Ochs, 1986, p. 167). Rice (1984) points out that:

> In the world that surrounds him, adults talk to other adults; children talk with other children, and there is a wide range of animate and inanimate actions, events, and interchanges that occur without regard to the presence of a youngster. The young language learner has ample opportunity to attend to, observe, and try to interpret the abundant and diverse real-world happenings that surround him. (pp. 171, 172)

In fact, Rice suggests that most of a child's language-learning opportunities are observational rather than participatory.

A study by Schiff (1979, cited in Rice, 1984, p. 173) found that, contrary to the results of similar research, hearing children raised by deaf parents and with relatively little exposure to hearing adults (and even less direct interaction with them) nevertheless learned oral language normally. As the children had been watching about 2 hours of TV each day, Rice (1984) believed it was "reasonable to suppose that the children's indirect, observational learning experiences (overhearing adult-to-adult conversations and observing patterns of verbal communication presented on TV) were also contributing significantly to their language learning" (p. 173).

Social learning theory provides an account of how it is that children acquire knowledge of the rules by which they can produce utterances that they have never heard or spoken before, one of the hallmarks of human language:

> In this approach to the language learning process, the child induces, from observation of a model, a set of abstract rules governing the language produced by that model. Evidence of learning can be found in the application of these rules to the child's production of language from stimuli not duplicative of the modeling sequence. It is the generalization of these rule governed responses in novel circumstances which suggests that a learning process, and not mere mimicking, is in operation. (Selnow, & Bettinghaus, 1982, p. 470)

The theory does not discount the importance of direct tutoring in gaining knowledge of linguistic rules, where differential reinforcement of grammatical and ungrammatical utterances would occur (Bandura, & Harris, 1966, pp. 342, 343). As Wood (1981, p. 257) suggests, these two processes work together in language acquisition.

Early work in Albert Bandura's development of social learning theory tested the effectiveness of modeling for imparting the rules of verbal syntax to language learners. In a number of these studies, observational learning proved to be, at least in the short term, a very effective means for acquiring the rules for producing unfamiliar grammatical constructions (Bandura, & Harris, 1966; Carroll, Rosenthal, & Brysh, 1972; Odom, Liebert, & Hill, 1968; Rosenthal, & Carroll, 1972). Social learning can take place through watching modeled behavior on TV as well as in interpersonal interaction (Bandura, 1967). Without much in the way of incentives or need for practice, viewers may acquire a very wide range of behaviors, expectations, attitudes, and concepts without being particularly aware that they are in fact learning anything.

INCIDENTAL LANGUAGE LEARNING FROM TELEVISION

Rice (1984) believes that TV is "an important part of a child's everyday language-learning laboratory, along with all the other rich and varied communicative interactions he observes in the world around him" (p. 177). Given that children in the United States expose themselves so much to television programs, Selnow and Bettinghaus (1982) ask:

> If the child speaks as his parents speak because he is frequently exposed to their language models, will it follow that greater exposure to television will lead to the development of language heavily influenced by television language models? (p. 471)

The few studies that have actually investigated language learning from television have focused mainly on the acquisition of vocabulary items.

In an experimental study on the ability of preschoolers to learn words from TV, Rice and Woodsmall (1988) found that learning of certain classes of words did indeed take place, and that fast mapping appeared to explain the accuracy with which the new vocabulary items were acquired. Five-year-olds were more accurate than 3-year-olds and gained relatively more words as well, suggesting that more advanced cognitive development or greater experience with observational learning also played a role. These findings were replicated by Rice et al. (1990), and Rice, Huston, et al. (1990) found that, from the ages of 3 to 5, naturalistic home viewing of *Sesame Street* led to the learning of new vocabulary items. Vocabulary improvement declined for older children in the study, which indicated the importance of age-appropriate verbal complexity in TV programs.

INCIDENTAL LANGUAGE SOCIALIZATION FROM TELEVISION

The socialization of an individual is usually considered as occurring through interpersonal interaction, but television also plays an important role in this process. It "bombards all classes, groups, and ages with the same perspectives at the same time" and is unique in "its ability to standardize, streamline, amplify, and share with virtually all members of society common cultural norms that had been local, parochial, and selective cultural patterns" (Gross, & Morgan, 1985, p. 222). In this regard, TV may be the most influential of all mass media because "unlike print media, television does not require literacy from its audience. Unlike the movies, television runs continuously. Unlike radio, television can show as well as tell" (p. 224). Dramatic entertainment on TV is educational in the way it presents lessons about the social world, and children are the most vulnerable class of viewers because they are less liable to clearly distinguish the fictive nature of television drama.

Corder-Bolz (1980) has described television as a secondary socializing agent. Like primary social agents, such as parents, teachers, and peers, TV provides information about social expectations; but unlike them, TV cannot act to enforce compliance. However, in those domains in which television serves an individual as the sole or most credible source of information about social expectations, TV can become a powerful socializing agent (p. 116).

As a secondary socializing agent, television may supplement a viewer's sociolinguistic knowledge with stereotypes of how people outside the viewer's everyday local experience use language differently, and how to think about these differences.

> Although they may never actually visit a courtroom, ranch, or spaceship, they may have TV-inspired ideas about the role of judges, ranch hands, and captains of spaceships, including the patterns of communication associated with each role. These examples could enhance children's awareness of such sociolinguistic variables as dialect differences, status indicators, styles of formal language, and conversational rules. (Rice, 1984, p. 177)

Hudson (1980) also names television as an important influence in language socialization in which "the child must become aware of a range of speech forms, although they may affect his own normal speech only peripherally, if at all" (pp. 16, 17). Thus television is implicated in the socialization of cultural knowledge, beliefs, and values about the world of language behavior.

The speech used in television dramatic entertainment is scripted, and therefore very likely to differ from the unrehearsed utterances produced by speakers in face-to-face interaction (cf. Ulrich, 1986). For example, a study of hesitation phenomena in three genres (documentary, family drama, and soap opera) by Johnson and Davis (1979) found that, contrary to expectations, unrealistic hesitations are characteristic of both scripted and unscripted TV dialogue. But the TV convention of naturalistic realism would lead one to expect that scripted or unscripted television dialogue not be so stylized, that viewers would not be able to understand such speech by applying the interpretive strategies for comprehending the speech they hear in interpersonal communication. Watching television may even contribute to the socialization of viewers toward the sorts of speech they do encounter in everyday interaction.

In the United States numerous distinct regional and social dialects of English are spoken, and television storytelling conveys messages about these varieties. Dillard (1985) observes that the mass media "have had a great deal of influence in determining what the American population in general has thought about dialects" (p. 205). Surveying one week of prime time entertainment programming, Willmorth (1988) found that northern U.S. dialects are overrepresented; such other regional dialects that do appear are leveled, often assigned to comedic characters or programs, and associated with relatively negative qualities in the characters that use them. Similarly, Rosenberg (1991) notes that regional dialects are hard to find on TV and are generally "rejected as unsuitable for national consumption" (p. F32).

One important social dialect of American English whose use in TV drama has received some attention is black English. To the extent it appears at all, it is generally homogenized and has served to stereotype characters into such categories as "power assertive," "comedian," and "victim" (Fine, & Anderson, 1980; Holland, 1986). Asante (1980, pp. 186, 187) suggests that the lack of authentic ways of speaking for black characters on TV may produce identity confusion in black children. Dillard (1985) likewise believes that, "Representations of dialect and argot on television are so patently stereotyped, where they are not so reduced as to be completely washed out, that not even preteens can find much to identify with" (p. 204). Authentic black dialect is also restricted outside TV drama; while southern accents are permitted for white sportscasters, blacks are not permitted to use black dialect (Chad, 1989; Dillard, 1985, pp. 220, 221).

Television drama also presents viewers with images of how males and females speak differently and what consequences apply to characters who use these styles. Mulac, Bradac, and Mann (1985) found clear sex-role stereotyping of linguistic elements in both educational and entertainment programs for children. Young viewers apparently use their knowledge of these speech stereotypes to make attributions about the sexual orientations of characters (Edelsky, 1977). McCorkle's (1982) analysis of Saturday morning children's dramatic programs uncovered equivocal messages about the efficacy of appropriate verbal strategies— associated mainly with female characters—for resolving conflicts. Skewed representations of male and female speech are also found in programs for adults: although the same-sex relationships portrayed in soap operas are similar to those in everyday life, the preponderance of male–female relationships and the intimacy of those conversations seem unlike the daily patterns of social interaction (Fine, 1981).

Finally, television drama carries messages about the relationship between speaking style and social class. Goldsen (1975) found that, just as in everyday interaction, address forms in various genres of TV drama contain sociolinguistic cues about the relative statuses of characters. A study by Ellis and Armstrong (1989) on TV sitcom dialogue indicated that middle-class TV characters, particularly males, used more elaborated speech than lower-class characters and than female characters generally. Male lower-class characters, however, were the most stigmatized linguistically: they used the greatest number of nonstandard American English features (p. 157). Ellis and Armstrong suggest that these TV speech stereotypes "provide role models for viewers and implicit messages about how people of different sexes and social class communicate" (p. 167).

SUMMARY OF RESEARCH FINDINGS

Current research gives a more complex view of the relationship between TV and language learning than the oversimplified notions of, on the one hand, a powerful blanket effect, and, on the other, a complete lack of influence. The assumptions on which these assessments are based are faulty. First, not all aspects of productive language competence seem to be easily learned from television. Existing research confirms only the acquisition of vocabulary, which can be learned quickly and without tutoring through "fast mapping," as positively related to TV viewing. This does not mean, however, that

television may not also be found to promote the acquisition of other aspects of speaking that are perhaps more difficult to observe, such as grammar or accent, should sufficiently sensitive research methods be used.

Second, there is no single way of speaking that characterizes all TV programs. Different programs have different target audiences and the nature of the speech in those programs is designed accordingly (cf. Bell, 1984). Some programs are better suited to less experienced language users, while others contain more sophisticated linguistic messages for mature speakers. Within programs, too, different characters may use different speaking styles. It is precisely in this context that TV can imbue certain ways of speaking with relative values according to the types of characters who use them, and thus it may contribute to language socialization. Milroy and Milroy (1985), for example, believe that TV may play a large role in teaching comprehension of the leveled (standard) dialect and in promoting attitudes toward different ways of speaking and language varieties in the speech community (pp. 29–31). These attitudes may cause some speakers to seek to adopt more prestigious ways of speaking, as modeled on TV, for use in certain situations (cf. "Losing an accent," 1979; Walton, 1992).

Third, not all listeners will take TV to be a credible source of information on the use of speech styles in face-to-face interaction; for these viewers, television will, most likely, not serve as an effective socializing agent. One might hypothesize that heavier viewers and viewers with weak influences from the local primary socializing agents, including parents and peers, may be more influenced. But in the multistep flow of influence and information from the mass media to light viewers via face-to-face communication with heavier viewers, the reach of TV messages about language may extend beyond actual viewers (Kimball, & Joy, 1987).

Finally, it is necessary to acknowledge the interaction of interpersonal communication with TV viewing, not simply television viewing in and of itself, to understand the role that watching television has in language acquisition and socialization. It is in face-to-face interaction that much of the work is accomplished that instills communicative competence and where opportunities for practice with newly acquired language skills are provided. If TV influences language learning in a speech community, it is only in conjunction with the reinforcing function of interpersonal interaction in observational learning. This view finds some agreement with earlier assessments of ineffectiveness of TV in the absence of interpersonal interaction (Ervin-Tripp, 1971, p. 195; Snow et al., 1976, p. 2). Considering the research presented in this chapter, however, it appears that television does indeed function alongside face-to-face communication in speech communities to influence language learning.

TELEVISION AND LANGUAGE TEACHING

The responses of educators to the relationship of television with language learning can be grouped into at least three categories. Those who focus on the apparently negative consequences of TV viewing for language learners stress the importance of reducing exposure to television (e.g., Winn, 1985). Others have taken TV viewing outside the classroom as a fact of modern life and have attempted to adapt traditional language-skills pedagogy accordingly. A third approach has involved bringing video into the language arts curriculum, both actual "off-the-air" programs and materials specially designed by educators to mimic many of the conventions of entertainment TV, but which function more efficiently as teaching aids.

Rather than complain about the possible deleterious effects of TV viewing on language skills, Becker (1973) adopted the approach that, "If you can't beat 'em, join 'em." Becker's monograph provides numerous examples of ways in which students' extracurricular exposure to television can be incorporated into language arts teaching strategies. Listening skills may be practiced by directing students to focus their attention on vocabulary and phrases, story comprehension, dialect and regional accent, figurative language, and accuracy of TV content. Speaking exercises might include oral class reports on viewed programs, using TV images as stimuli for verbalization, having students portray TV characters in role-play, and engaging students in vocabulary drills which use a game show format. Reading assignments may include books on TV personalities and behind-the-scenes descriptions of how TV programs are produced. Finally, teachers may have students write TV star biographies, compose letters to sponsors of TV shows or fan letters, write a different ending to a TV show viewed in class, and play critic by reviewing a TV show. Far from discouraging TV viewing, Becker even proposes that teachers assign programs to be watched as homework for subsequent in-class work.

Foreign language pedagogy has in recent years seen a great deal of attention paid to the use of "authentic" TV materials—those not originally designed as language teaching material. In many parts of the United States, foreign language TV stations and services provide news reports, commercials, and dramatic entertainment programming that can be used for in-class exercises (Berry-Bravo, 1991). News reports have timely and relevant content and a predictable format; they offer opportunities for practice with rapidly spoken numbers in sports and weather reports. News reports often repeat a limited number of vocabulary items and may help students acquire important general cultural knowledge about the places where the foreign language is spoken. Interviews on TV show body language and give examples of the filler words and transition phrases needed to maintain spontaneous dialogue; students can see and listen to a wide variety of interesting people, including Hispanic personalities speaking their native language. Television commercials contain intelligible native speech with idiomatic constructions and, like news stories, can reflect cultural assumptions; as teaching materials they have the virtue of short duration and often humorous tone.

Berry-Bravo stresses that using authentic materials requires greater preparation time than canned instructional materials, such as leading discussions before and after viewing. Background information on geography, history, and politics may be required, as well as making transcripts and vocabulary glossaries, giving repeated viewings, and developing tests for comprehension of the viewed material. However, using authentic materials does increase student motivation, provides sustained exposure to a limited set of topics, and improves retention of vocabulary and awareness of cultural concepts.

Just as the format of *Sesame Street* was designed to take advantage of the attractiveness of TV commercials for young viewers to teach vocabulary (among other cognitive skills) (White, 1980, p. 210), a recent college-level Spanish language course, *Destinos*, is based on the very popular *telenovelas* (soap operas) of Latin American television. The creators of this telecourse believe that if "a language cannot be separated from culture, then television is a most appropriate medium for providing a dramatized, cultural context for language instruction" and that "television can take you to places in a way that even the most dedicated and excellent of instructors, with a plethora of visual props and aids, cannot" (VanPatten, Marks, & Teschner, 1992, p. 3). The series revolves around the travels of a private detective throughout the Spanish-speaking world in order to unravel a mystery, and along the way students are exposed to the numerous varieties of the language as well as cultural differences among the communities where they are spoken. Students are drawn in by the story, and are motivated to learn the language in order to follow it to its conclusion. Unlike "authentic" foreign language material, *Destinos* is constructed to assist gradual language learning, with later episodes containing more complex and more rapidly spoken Spanish.

There is no simple way to regard the relationship of television to language learning, and teachers of language skills have not achieved a consensus in thinking about television as enemy or friend. Attitudes range from considering television as having very negative effects, to having no appreciable effect, to having very positive effects on language learning. Considering what is known from current research into this issue, it seems most appropriate to recommend that language skills educators come to an understanding of how TV may play a role in their students' language learning processes and whether it can be applied positively in particular situations to achieve desired pedagogical goals.

References

Alperstein, N. M. (1990). The verbal content of TV advertising and its circulation in everyday life. *Journal of Advertising, 19*(2), 15–22.

Asante, M. K. (1980). Television's impact on black children's language: An exploration. In M. K. Asante & A. S. Vandi (Eds.), *Contemporary black thought: Alternative analyses in social and behavioral science* (pp. 181–194). Beverly Hills, CA: Sage.

Bandura, A. (1967). The role of modeling processes in personality development. In W. W. Hartup & N. Smothergill (Eds.), *The young child* (pp. 42–57). Washington, DC: National Association for the Education of Young Children.

Bandura, A., & Harris, M. B. (1966). Modification of syntactic style. *Journal of Experimental Child Psychology, 4,* 341–352.

Becker, G. J. (1973). *Television and the classroom reading program: If you can't beat 'em, join 'em.* Newark, DE: International Reading Association.

Bell, A. (1984). Language style as audience design. *Language in Society, 13*(2), 145–204.

Berry-Bravo, J. (1991). Tuning in to live Spanish-language broadcasts. *Hispania, 74*(1), 199–201.

Carroll, W. R., Rosenthal, T. L., & Brysh, C. G. (1972). Social transmission of grammatical parameters. *Journal of Educational Psychology, 63*(6), 589–596.

Chad, N. (1989, June 22). Blacks say the sound of the city not a beautiful noise to network officials. *The Washington Post,* p. B11.

Clark, H., & Clark, E. (1977). *Psychology and language.* New York: Harcourt, Brace and Jovanovich.

Corder-Bolz, C. (1980). Mediation: The role of significant others. *Journal of Communication, 30*(3), 106–118.

Dillard, J. L. (1985). *Toward a social history of American English.* New York: Mouton.

Edelsky, C. (1977). Acquisition of an aspect of communicative competence: Learning what it means to be a lady. In S. Ervin-Tripp & C. Mitchell-Kernan (Eds.), *Child discourse* (pp. 225–243). New York: Academic Press.

Ellis, D. G., & Armstrong, G. B. (1989). Class, gender, and code on prime-time television. *Communication Quarterly, 37*(3), 157–169.

Ervin-Tripp, S. (1971). An overview of theories of grammatical development. In D. I. Slobin (Ed.), *The ontogenesis of grammar: A theoretical symposium* (pp. 189–212). New York: Academic Press.

Fine, M. G. (1981). Soap opera conversations: The talk that binds. *Journal of Communication, 31*(3), 97–107.

Fine, M. G., & Anderson, C. (1980). Dialectical features of black characters in situation comedies on television. *Phylon, 41*(4), 396–409 .

Franklin, H. B. (1929). *Sound motion pictures.* Garden City, NY: Doubleday.

Goldsen, R. K. (1975). Television's modes of address. *Journal of Communication, 25*(2), 44–49.

Greenfield, P. M. (1984). *Mind and media: The effects of television, videogames and computers.* Cambridge, MA: Harvard University Press.

Greet, W. C. (1938). A standard American language? *The New Republic, 95,* 68–70.

Gross, L., & Morgan, M. (1985). Television and enculturation. In J. R. Dominick & J. Fletcher (Eds.), *Broadcasting research methods* (pp. 221–234). Boston: Allyn & Bacon.

Halpern, W. I. (1975). Turned-on toddlers. *Journal of Communication, 25*(4), 66–70.

Heath, S. B., & Branscomb, A. (1986). The book as narrative prop in language acquisition. In B. B. Schieffelin & P. Gilmore (Eds.), *The acquisition of literacy: Ethnographic perspectives* (pp. 16–34). Norwood, NJ: Ablex.

Hoff-Ginsberg, E., & Schatz, M. (1982). Linguistic input and the child's acquisition of language. *Psychological Bulletin, 92*(1), 3–26.

Holland, I. E. (1986, May 22–26). *Nonstandard English on television: A content analysis.* Paper presented at the 36th annual meeting of the International Communication Association, Chicago. (ERIC Document Reproduction Service No. ED 277 071)

Hollenbeck, A. R., & Slaby, R. G. (1979). Infant visual and vocal responses to television. *Child Development, 50*(1), 41–45.

Hudson, R. A. (1980). *Sociolinguistics.* Cambridge: Cambridge University Press.

Huston, A. C., & Wright, J. C. (1983). Children's processing of television: The informative functions of formal features. In J. Bryant & D. R. Anderson (Eds.), *Children's understanding of television: Research on attention and comprehension* (pp. 35–68). New York: Academic Press.

Ikeda, R. (1992, April 4). *Analysis of TV use by Chinese immigrant children: An exploratory study.* Paper presented at the annual Sooner Communication Conference, Norman, OK. (ERIC Document Reproduction Service No. ED 345 312)

James, N. C., & McCain, T. A. (1982). Television games preschool children play: Patterns, themes and uses. *Journal of Broadcasting, 26*(4), 783–800.

Johnson, F. L., & Davis, L. K. (1979). Hesitation phenomena in televised family conversations in the U.S.A. *International Journal of Psycholinguistics, 6*(1), 29–45.

Kimball, M. M., & Joy, L. A. (1987). Television violence: Does it promote aggressive behavior? In M. E. Manley-Casimir & C. Luke (Eds.), *Children and television: A challenge for education* (pp. 49–75). New York: Praeger.

Lemish, D. (1987). Viewers in diapers: The early development of television viewing. In T. R. Lindlof (Ed), *Natural audiences: Qualitative research of media uses and effects* (pp. 33–57). Norwood, NJ: Ablex.

Lemish, D., & Rice, M. L. (1986). Television as a talking picture book: A prop for language acquisition. *Journal of Communication, 13,* 251–274.

Littwin, S. (1988, April 9). How TV Americanizes immigrants… for better or worse. *TV Guide,* pp. 4–8, 10.

Losing an accent, gaining—what? (1979, January 9). *The New York Times,* p. C12.

McCorkle, S. (1982). An analysis of verbal language in Saturday morning children's programs. *Communication Quarterly, 30*(3), 210–216.

Messaris, P. (1983). Family conversations about television. *Journal of Family Issues, 4*(2), 293–308.

Messaris, P., & Kerr, D. (1983). Mothers' comments about TV: Relation to family communication patterns. *Communication Research, 10*(2), 175–194.

Milroy, J., & Milroy, L. (1985). *Authority in language: Investigating language prescription and standardisation.* London: Routledge.

The mouths of babes. (1992, July 28). *The Christian Science Monitor,* p. 20.

Mulac, A., Bradac, J. J., & Mann, S. K. (1985). Male/female language differences and attributional consequences in children's television. *Human Communication Research, 11*(4), 481–506.

Nelson, K. (1973). Structure and strategy in learning to talk. *Monographs of the Society for Research in Child Development, 58*(1–2, Serial No. 149).

Odom, R. D., Liebert, R. M., & Hill, J. (1968). The effects of modeling cues, reward, and attentional set on the production of grammatical and ungrammatical syntactic constructions. *Journal of Experimental Child Psychology, 6*(1), 131–140.

Olson, D. R. (1987). Television and literacy. In M. E. Manley-Casimir & C. Luke (Eds.), *Children and television: A challenge for education* (p. 145–152). New York: Praeger.

Parsons, K. (1936, January 11). Announcers' English. *Scholastic*, pp. 13, 27.

Reid, L. N., & Frazer, C. F. (1980a). Children's use of television commercials to initiate social interaction in family viewing situations. *Journal of Broadcasting, 24*(2), 149–158.

Reid, L. N., & Frazer, C. F. (1980b). Television at play. *Journal of Communication, 30*(4), 66–73.

Rice, M. (1984). Cognitive aspects of communicative competence. In R. L. Schiefelbusch & J. Pickar (Eds.), *The acquisition of communicative competence* (pp. 141–189). Baltimore: University Park Press.

Rice, M. L., Buhr, J. C., & Nemeth, M. (1990). Fast mapping word-learning abilities of language-delayed preschoolers. *Journal of Speech and Hearing Disorders, 55*(1), 33–42.

Rice, M. L., & Haight, P. L. (1986). "Motherese" of Mr. Rogers: A description of the dialogue of educational television programs. *Journal of Speech and Hearing Disorders, 51*(3), 282–287.

Rice, M. L., Huston, A. C., Truglio, R., & Wright, J. C. (1990). Words from "Sesame Street": Learning vocabulary while viewing. *Developmental Psychology, 26*(3), 421–428.

Rice, M. L., Huston, A. C., & Wright, J. C. (1982). The forms of television: Effects on children's attention, comprehension, and social behavior. In D. Pearl, L. Bouthilet & J. Lazar (Eds.), *Television and behavior: Ten years of scientific progress and implications for the eighties: Volume 2: Technical reviews* (pp. 24–38). Rockville, MD: National Institute of Mental Health.

Rice, M., & Wartella, E. (1981). Television as a medium of communication: Implications for how to regard the child viewer. *Journal of Broadcasting, 25*(4), 365–372.

Rice, M. L., & Woodsmall, L. (1988). Lessons from television: Children's word learning when viewing. *Child Development, 59*(2), 420–429.

Robbins, J. F. (1988). Employers' language expectations and non-standard dialect speakers. *English Journal, 77*(6), 22–24.

Rosenberg, H. (1991, December 27). Let's hear it for dialects on television. *Los Angeles Times,* pp. F1, F32.

Rosenthal, T. L., & Carroll, W. R. (1972). Factors in vicarious modification of complex grammatical parameters. *Journal of Educational Psychology, 63*(2), 174–178.

Sachs, J., Bard, B., & Johnson, M. L. (1981). Language learning with restricted input: Case studies of two hearing children of deaf parents. *Applied Psycholinguistics (Journal of Child Language), 2*(1), 33–54.

Schieffelin, B. B., & Eisenberg, A. R. (1984). Cultural variations in children's conversations. In R. L. Schiefelbusch & J. Pickar (Eds.), *The acquisition of communicative competence* (pp. 377–420). Baltimore: University Park Press.

Schieffelin, B. B., & Ochs, E. (1986). Language socialization. *Annual Review of Anthropology, 15,* 163–191.

Selnow, G. W., & Bettinghaus, E. P. (1982). Television exposure and language development. *Journal of Broadcasting, 26*(1), 469–479.

Snow, C. E., Arlman-Rupp, A., Hassing, Y., Jobse, J., Joosten, J., & Vorster, J. (1976). Mothers' speech in three social classes. *Journal of Psycholinguistic Research, 5*(1), 1–20.

Trudgill, P. (1983). *On dialect: Social and geographical perspectives.* New York: New York University Press.

TV Guide. (1994, June 25), p. 6.

Ulrich, W. (1986). The use of fiction as a source of information about interpersonal communication: A critical view. *Communication Quarterly, 34*(2), 143–153.

Vann, A. S. (1991, April 9). Bad language moves from movie screen to principal's office. *The Christian Science Monitor,* p. 19.

VanPatten, B., Marks, M., & Teschner, R. V. (1992). *Faculty guide to accompany Destinos: An Introduction to Spanish.* New York: McGraw-Hill.

Walton, M. (1992, January 26). Say it again, Tom. *The Philadelphia Inquirer Magazine,* pp. 13–15, 22, 23, 31.

Watson-Gegeo, K. A., & Boggs, S. T. (1977). From verbal play to talk story: The role of routines in speech events. In S. Ervin-Tripp & C. Mitchell-Kernan (Eds.), *Child discourse* (pp. 67–90). New York: Academic Press.

White, P. B. (1980). *Sesame Street:* The packaging of a curriculum. *Journal of Educational Thought, 14*(3), 209–219.

Willmorth, M. J. (1988). *The representation of American English dialects in prime time network television dramatic programs.* Doctoral dissertation, University of Pennsylvania.

Winick, M. P., & Winick, C. (1979). *The television experience: What children see.* Beverly Hills, CA: Sage.

Winn, M. (1985). *The plug-in drug* (Rev. ed.). New York: Viking.

Wood, B. S. (1981). *Children and communication: Verbal and nonverbal language development* (2nd ed.). Englewood Cliffs, NJ: Prentice-Hall.

5

VISUAL COMMUNICATION SKILLS AND MEDIA LITERACY

Michael Griffin and Dona Schwartz

UNIVERSITY OF MINNESOTA

After an actor was elected to the White House in 1980, there was a great deal written about Ronald Reagan as the first consummate TV president. Young people who had reached voting age during the 1970s voted for Reagan in surprisingly large numbers, and political commentators quickly pointed out that Reagan's strongest support was among 18–29 year-olds, the first generation to grow up completely in the television age. Journalists increasingly took for granted that television was the new kingmaker, especially after Reagan's landslide over Mondale in 1984, and the American voter became routinely characterized as a viewer of campaign images rather than an interpreter of campaign issues.

By the mid-1980s the notion that images are more potent than words, and that given a lack of congruence between visual and verbal information the visual will win out, had been repeated often enough to become accepted wisdom. The most frequently cited anecdote is a story by CBS correspondent Lesley Stahl concerning her coverage of the Reagan presidential campaign in 1984. As related in Martin Schramm's *The Great American Video Game* (1987, pp. 23–26, 33–36), Bill Moyers' PBS special *The Public Mind: Illusions of News* (1989), and Kiku Adatto's *Picture Perfect: The Art and Artifice of Public Image Making* (1993, pp. 58–60), Stahl did a piece for the CBS Evening News that she considered sharply critical of the television photo opportunities set up by the Reagan camp during the campaign. In the report she specifically pointed out the contradictions between photo opportunities staged by the White House (e.g., his ribbon-cutting at the opening of a new senior citizen center) and actual administration policies (e.g., pushing for cuts in aid for the disabled and elderly). To her surprise, however, she received a call from the White House praising the report for its wonderful visuals. "They don't listen to you if you are contradicting great pictures," a presidential aide told her.

In interviews and his own memoirs, Reagan media adviser Michael Deaver has confirmed that the White House "loved Stahl's story," and that in their view the nearly 5 minutes of visual imagery (time spent rebroadcasting photo opportunities coordinated by the Reagan staff) was fortuitous free publicity, a series of positive images of the President that easily overwhelmed the critical commentary contained in Stahl's voice over (Adatto, 1993, pp. 58–60; Deaver, 1987; Moyers, 1989).

The degree to which images inevitably overpower words remains an open question. In the case of the Lesley Stahl report, her words may not have effectively countered the images primarily because her commentary was not really very critical. A review of the videotape of the Stahl report suggests that her criticism was voiced diplomatically and counterbalanced by her open praise for Reagan's "brilliant" use of television. Recent research on television news imagery suggests that pictures are most often produced and edited to serve the news script, rather than the other way around, and though the relevance of news images to the verbal report may often be tenuous there is still insufficient evidence to indicate that television visuals communicate a separate and more powerful message than the spoken text (Griffin, 1992).

What does seem clear is that for some time now the public has encountered increasingly image-conscious mass media with increasingly sophisticated image-production technology. Expanding forms of television—from CNN satellite news coverage to MTV—epitomize this development. And each new genre of image-conscious media—the tabloid infotainment shows that purport to take viewers behind the scenes of each new scandal, the "reality-based" crime and rescue dramas that construct an eyewitness experience for those tuning in, the frenetic and overdesigned "zines" attempting to invent the "look" of urban-electronic America, or the ever more entertainment-oriented local news programs striving to create "what viewers want to see"—provides innumerable examples of the artifice of image making and the disparity between pictures and reality.

Neil Postman (1985) argues eloquently that linguistic literacy does not provide adequate tools for the evaluation of this new "television-based epistemology." Television shows us images rather than tells us about things, he says, and all "ways of knowing" in the modern world have come to be filtered through the "show business" paradigm of TV (pp. 78–80). Yet one does not even need to take the argument this far to recognize that television has become a predominant medium of communication in our society and that its audiovisual nature exhibits a syntax and structure quite different from books and newspapers. It is no longer tenable to think that verbal skills alone will equip today's citizens for the audiovisual media environment they live in.

This chapter explores some of the factors involved in conceptualizing contemporary media literacy. What is required for basic media literacy at the end of the 20th century? To what extent does media literacy depend upon visual literacy and the teaching of visual communication skills? What is involved in training students to recognize and understand media forms, and in what contexts should these skills be taught?

UNDERSTANDING THE NATURE OF VISUAL REPRESENTATION

While young people today may be less inclined to read and thus less verbally literate than the previous generations, it has become a cliche that they are more visually facile and skilled. This increased "visual literacy" is attributed to children's copious exposure to and experience with television, video games, and computers. But the nature of this presumed visual acumen has not been rigorously examined, and anecdotal accounts of teaching visual media production and analysis at the university level suggest that students often fail to manifest even rudimentary visual acuity, especially with regard to the properties of mass media images.

The most fundamental and persistent problem one encounters in teaching visual communication is the routine confusion of pictures and reality, the naive view that images produced by photographic media (i.e., most of the images we encounter) are simply direct mechanical records of the world around us. This confusion takes place on multiple levels: at the level of single, photographically "recorded" still images, at the level of selected and ordered sequences of "recorded" action, and at the level of conventional formats and structures for audiovisual storytelling and exposition.

The most basic misconception is that cameras replicate the processes of human vision, reproducing a sensory record that mimics the way we see. As Messaris (1994) convincingly argues, pictorial comprehension relies heavily on the presence in pictures of "the same kinds of informational cues that viewers employ in making sense of real-world vision" (p. 167). However, the common belief that the camera is simply an extension of the eye and that pictures allow us to "look in" on real-world figures, places, and events as "eyewitnesses" is an enduring and influential myth. Of course, the myth is zealously promoted by a photographic industry eager to market the mechanical devices and supplies needed for "capturing reality" and by a television news industry invested in the conceit that they offer the viewer a "window on the world." Educators hoping to develop more critical media viewing skills among their students fight an uphill battle against the preconceptions cultivated by the media themselves.

Seeing the Picture Frame

In introductory photography and visual communication courses an initial challenge for students is simply to recognize the existence and implications of the picture frame. The activity of "framing" as a conscious process of abstraction seems totally unfamiliar to the overwhelming majority of college students. Unlike our normal semicircular field of vision in which we rapidly change our point of focus across an otherwise low-resolution background, pictures frame an abstracted moment in time, a preselected field of view. Training photography students to see the entire frame (realizing that peripheral elements will appear in the picture as clearly as central ones) is a struggle, running counter as it does to normal visual scanning and selective focus. It takes conscious effort and substantial practice for students to finally eliminate the trees and lampposts growing out of subjects' heads, and to notice and relate details from various areas of the frame, producing the kind of coherent, unified, and sharply demarcated image that we do not experience in natural vision.

Recognizing that the image frame encloses a purposeful abstraction from space and time does not make students immune to thinking about pictures as mechanical records, but it does give them the potential to recognize divergences between pictures and everyday visual experience. Awareness of the frame may be the most elementary building block in developing a consciousness of media selection and presentation, that is, media abstraction.

An understanding of pictures as abstractions paves the way for teaching about the psychological concepts of closure and gestalt, relating picture making to our desire to find resolution, coherence, and unity in the sensory surround (Arnheim, 1966, pp. 58–70; Gregory, 1970, pp. 11–31; Kohler, 1929; Zettl, 1990, pp. 114–119). The formally limited structure of pictures is very different from the fluid and ever-shifting processes of human vision, but the more condensed representation of pictures is a natural product of the human tendency toward simplification and resolution. Pictorial construction, then, seems to more closely parallel the mental processes of abstraction and categorization than the immediate sensory experiences of perception.

Interpreting Media Forms

The confusion of media and reality, that is, the failure to recognize the processes of mediation, involves more than the confusion of picture and subject. It is also encouraged by the naturalization of historically specific conventions of staging, camera movement, editing, image manipulation, narrative construction, documentary exposition, and news reporting. Thus, sophisticated media viewing demands an awareness of media presentations as intentionally articulated. Since no form of visual media simply reproduces reality, yet nearly all forms represent selected facets of real things, the pertinent issue for viewers and producers alike is how images are being constructed and presented to convey a particular view. Discerning that view requires a sense of what producers are up to, the ability to recognize order, structure, and artifice—the application of what Worth and Gross (1974) call an "inferential interpretational strategy."

In Worth and Gross' heuristic, interpretational encounters with symbolic events are classified as "attributional" or "inferential." Readers/viewers employ a strategy of attribution when they simply treat the symbolic representation of an event as evidence of the event's existence, drawing from their own real-world experience to evaluate or respond to it. The concept of attribution is particularly applicable to photographic media, the iconicity of which encourages viewers to respond as if the representation were real, reacting empathetically toward actions on a movie screen or accepting the existence of a videotape as irrefutable evidence of a crime.

Readers/viewers employ a strategy of inference when they recognize that the symbolic event is created or structured by some controlling consciousness. In this case they assume that the event is selected and ordered with some intention in mind and attempt to discern the implications of the symbolic structure. The assumption of intention suggests an articulator who "means to imply" and an interpreter who "means to infer." A movie viewer employing an inferential strategy would attend to cinematic techniques such as lighting, camera angle, and editing and infer their implications for character identification and narrative development.

In the Worth and Gross model, attribution and inference are not mutually exclusive, nor do they represent a rigid hierarchy in which viewers graduate from one to the other. But strategies of inference do depend upon an awareness and recognition of communicative structure. Those who can recognize the purposeful structuring of media representations have a much greater potential for moving between attribution and inference (or employing both in some proportion), while those who fail to do so must inevitably remain confined to attributional understandings and misunderstandings.

In terms of the attribution-inference model, teaching media literacy involves helping students attain a fuller range of interpretive skills. With regard to visual media, this entails moving beyond the naive acceptance of pictures as mere records of existence and building an understanding of how pictures are made and the nature of their complex relationship with reality. Media literacy, as it is defined here, involves knowledge of varying modes and styles of visual representation, not only an awareness of the selective abstraction inherent in picture making but a familiarity with the forms of symbolization that appear as proxies for reality. The predominant use of metonymy in film and television (the use of associated details or fragments to represent larger, unelaborated ideas, actions and events), together with the use of conventionalized editing formulas for constructing screen space and advancing narrative or expository progression,

produce recurrent syntactic patterns that make "literacy" a fitting analogy for these interpretive skills.

For example, characters in television dramas move from one scene to the next by means of routine elliptical editing. When "cops" in a police drama are called to the scene of a crime, they are often shown heading for the precinct door, or getting into a squad car, and then arriving in the next shot at some distant location. The details and duration of the trip are not represented. This metonymic compression of events, what Monaco calls "cinematic shorthand" in *How To Read a Film* (1981), involves predictable formulaic editing: actors walk away from the camera toward the door, the perspective cuts to a camera set-up outside on the street that pictures the actors emerging from the door and descending the steps to the sidewalk, the perspective cuts again to a camera set-up near the squad car and the camera pans with the actors as they get into the car, a cut to a more distant camera position gives us a brief shot of the car as it pulls away down the street, there is a cut to a shot of the squad car approaching the camera in a different setting, and finally, a closer shot of the officers jumping out of their car at the crime scene.

This quick series of six or seven shots normally lasts less than 10 seconds on the screen, yet will involve multiple takes from multiple camera set-ups to construct what appears to be a natural and seamless narrative event. Each apparently realistic scene in film and television is pieced together from a variety of shots and camera angles that compress, expand, shift, and alter perspective, time, and space. One of the ironies of film and television is the high degree of manipulation involved in constructing and maintaining the "natural" appearance of dramatic action. Perceptions of filmic realism seem to rely, in fact, on the consistency and familiarity of editing strategies.

Recognizing the presence or absence of these representational strategies, not to mention comprehending their function or impact, requires a conscious awareness of the symbolic system. When viewers watch characters from Murphy Brown engaged in comic banter around the coffee counter on their "news set," do they respond to the scene as a realistic representation of a work environment and identify with the employee camaraderie and needling depicted? Or do they recognize the coffee counter as a stage prop, strategically placed to provide a location for the actors to gather and exchange their lines? Do they see the habitual appearance of the coffee counter in each episode simply as a reflection of the "reality" of coffee-break rituals in the workplace? Or do they recognize it as a dramatic arena in which performers' relationships are displayed, entrances and exits are orchestrated, and a context for humorous one-liners is established?

These different interpretive strategies have significant implications for the way in which viewers respond to television content, as evidenced by the controversy surrounding Dan Quayle's criticism of Murphy Brown when she became a single mother. In news reports and talk show discussions the issue was framed as a debate between the Vice President of the United States and Murphy Brown, as if Murphy Brown was a real mother rather than a fictional television character. This kind of confusion over the status of media representations has been recounted in numerous anecdotes, from reports of fans at Star Trek conventions behaving as though Leonard Nimoy is really Mr. Spock, to accounts of the actor Robert Young receiving 5,000 requests for medical and emotional advice a week when he played the role of TV's Dr. Marcus Welby (Real, 1977, p. 121).

Many aspects of pictorial apprehension are a natural extension of unmediated visual perception (Messaris, 1994); therefore, it is not surprising to find cases in which viewers assume the existence of what they see in pictures. But what viewers of visual media most commonly see are metonymic "shorthands" for imagined realities that remain obscure or ambiguous. Much of the "live" coverage of the air war in the Persian Gulf consisted of reporter stand-ups in front of the blue cabanas of the Dhahran Hilton. Momentary streaks of light in the sky were touted as eye-witness evidence of Patriot missiles intercepting incoming Scuds (a belief which was later shown to be mistaken). Broadcast repeatedly, a brief excerpt of the Rodney King videotape became a synecdoche for police brutality everywhere, and a handful of images—flaming buildings, looters running in and out of storefronts, Reginald Denny being assaulted with a brick— were packaged together to present a simplistic symbol of the Los Angeles uprising.

Understanding the conventionalized nuances of a media system such as television requires a knowledge of how various genres of television programming are produced, the technical and structural choices available to producers, and the range of content selections and aesthetic decisions made by scriptwriters, photographers, set and graphics designers, and film and video editors. Since pictures tend to encourage attributional interpretation, critical viewing requires a heightened awareness of distinctions between fiction and nonfiction, reality and simulation. In order to engender critical viewing skills educators must develop and convey an appreciation of the multiple factors shaping the production and reception of media images of all kinds. The remainder of the chapter outlines factors to be considered in teaching about visual media, the role of aesthetics in media evaluations, and the place of media production in curricula designed to improve visual media literacy.

AESTHETICS AND VISUAL MEDIA

Aesthetic education is an important prerequisite for the recognition of visual media forms discussed above. The methods by which the subject matter of images is shaped and styled to meet the needs and practices of newspapers, magazines, film and television production, build upon a history of picture-making aesthetics that reaches back to ancient painting (Barnhurst, 1994). The relevance of aesthetics for this discussion does not revolve around philosophical notions of beauty as much as notions of appropriate and established forms and a recognition of differences in style. The pictorial style of most nature and calendar photography, picture postcards, tourism publicity, and Eastman Kodak brochures, for example, is directly descended from a tradition of photography that became established in photo societies of the 19th century (Griffin, 1995). In *Reading National Geographic* (1993), Catherine Lutz and Jane Collins provide a full historical exege-

sis of the way in which this same pictorialist style has been employed on the pages of *National Geographic* to present a pleasant and photogenic vision of the "cultural other." A consciousness of continuities of style links such studies of modern media to the study of aesthetics and art history (Berger, 1972).

The capacity to discriminate stylistic difference and understand its implications is an essential component of visual media literacy. Awareness of the aesthetic possibilities in pictorial representation encourages a sensitivity to the modes and styles of representation in various media, including news and documentary, media in which the aesthetic dimension is often denied or ignored. In *Representing Reality* (1991), Bill Nichols analyzes the aesthetics of documentary film to classify the predominant styles of documentary representation, specifying the shifting relationships between the camera and its subjects, and the viewer and the world. By focusing his attention on aesthetics rather than content, Nichols explores the documentary as a system of address. Instead of explaining the content or meaning of a specific film presentation, he illuminates the "language" of documentary, offering the reader a taxonomy of analytic categories with which to evaluate the status of documentary claims.

For instance, Nichols identifies four "modes of documentary representation": expository, observational, interactive, and reflexive (1991, pp. 32–68). The expository film takes the form of a report or persuasive essay. It addresses the viewer directly, using titles or a narrator to describe or comment upon what is happening on-screen. The voice-over narration helps advance the argument made by the film. Educational films, the type that students seem to associate most often with "documentary," tend to be expository in style. Propaganda films also favor the expository mode of address.

The observational mode refers to films that eschew narration and editing in favor of simply following and "observing" subjects and events with the camera. In the history of American documentary film this style is routinely referred to as "direct cinema." Although virtually every film and video employs some editing, and it can be argued that the mere presence of the camera inevitably affects the people and actions around it, "the observational mode stresses the nonintervention of the filmmaker" (Nichols, 1991, p. 38). The absence of voice-over narration often heightens perceptions of objectivity because, as students frequently claim, there is no omniscient voice "telling me what to think." However, despite appearances to the contrary, all filmmakers embed a point of view in their films through the decisions they make in the production process.

The interactive mode describes films in which the filmmaker *does* intervene to address and interact with the film's subjects. Interviewing is commonly a central part of interactive documentary style, although various forms of verbal exchange or testimony, and even monologue can characterize the filmmaker's encounters with subjects. Nichols describes cases in which filmmakers interject themselves into the visual presentation implicitly as interviewers, explicitly as participants, and boldly as provocateurs. Images demonstrating the validity (or incredibility) of statements made on-camera are often integrated into the unfolding argument of the film.

While interactive documentaries give the impression of allowing interviewees to "speak for themselves," the kinds of interactions elicited and their sequencing offer yet another vehicle for the filmmaker's own voice.

The reflexive mode integrates some examination of the process of representation itself into the film's argument. This is a more complicated mode of address and it is the least commonly chosen. Reflexive films or videos examine *how* we depict and describe the world. Rather than revolving around relationships between filmmakers and subjects, they tend to be concerned with the link between filmmakers (or the film text) and viewers. Built upon skepticism about the ability of media to provide objective representations of real life, they attempt to encourage a heightened critical consciousness among their own viewers. These films raise epistemological questions about media images and at the same time they offer their own representations of the world.

Concepts such as Nichols' "modes of representation" provide tools for evaluating the status and validity of media presentations. Once students can discern variations in visual modes of address they can begin to consider the implications of differing styles. Making an assessment of "reality-based" TV shows such as *Cops*, *Top Cops*, or *Rescue 911*, for example, might involve identifying the mix of observational and interactional modes of representation that characterize these programs. A viewer who is aware of the significance of the visual form would be likely to notice the way that the subjective positioning of the camera within police and emergency vehicles identifies the viewer with the main "characters" of these programs and frequently places the viewer in a seemingly interactive relationship with the victims and criminals that the protagonists encounter. At the same time, however, a skilled viewer would see that segments of apparent interaction are embedded into an overarching observational strategy, with the camera pulling back to a more objective (or third person) perspective that lends an impression of distance and dispassionate reporting. By routinely mixing the two modes within the program structure the "reality-based shows" combine the drama and emotional attraction of fictional entertainment with the aura and legitimacy of documentary or news. A better understanding of how this is accomplished leaves the viewer less susceptible to easy manipulation.

Similarly, research on TV news has begun to move beyond content coding to analyses of the "visual grammar" of TV news and the implications of that grammar for the scope and nature of news reporting (Ericson, Baranek, & Chan, 1987; Griffin, 1992; Gruneau & Hackett, 1990; Hartley, 1992a, 1992b). One of the developments evident in all of this work is the abandonment of the presumption that journalistic images represent an attempt to convey objective reality. As Hartley (1992b) notes, journalism has become "the art of televisualization" (p. 140). Ericson et al. write, "Using their sources, journalists offer accounts of reality, their own version of events as they think they are most appropriately visualized. The object of their accounts is rarely presented for the viewer, listener, or reader to contemplate directly. This holds true even in television news, where pictures most often show the reporter and his sources giving a 'talking head' account. Rarely shown are the documents, behaviors, or other objects discussed. When they

are shown, it is usually to represent indexically or symbolically, rather than iconically" (p. 4).

In other words, rather than bringing us images of actual news events as they occur (something TV newscasts can rarely deliver) television news operations construct visual proxies and present symbols of information (shots of the White House to suggest presidential deliberations, images of youths on the street corner to symbolize crime, a graphic of a microscope to represent medical research). In fact, the main activity of TV news operations is the creation and interjection of these kinds of symbolic emblems to provide a continuous semblance of the "eyewitness coverage" that is not there. Thus, TV news must be seen not as a daily visual record of ongoing events, but as a set of "plausible stories" visualized by symbolic and fictional devices. As Hartley (1992b) has observed, "The ideology of eyewitness authenticity is much stronger than the actuality of newsgathering practices" (p. 144). Consequently, even in the case of news it is a consciousness of aesthetic constructions that opens the way to a valid appraisal of media performance.

PRODUCTION TRAINING AS A VEHICLE FOR AESTHETIC EDUCATION

One logical way of helping students explore the role and influence of aesthetic skills is to educate them in visual media production. Studies of children's art classes (Schwartz, 1979) and children's filmmaking (Griffin, 1985) suggest that kids at very young ages can learn to practice established conventions of image making. But the skills they acquire most readily are those that mimic popular media forms. With increased production experience, some children are able to expand their aesthetic awareness and media skills but this requires continued involvement with and practice of visual production.

Among a sample group of sixth graders enrolled in Philadelphia public school art classes (Schwartz, 1979), boys who had adopted comic book models as templates displayed remarkable self-confidence and derived significant pleasure from drawing. Acutely aware of their inadequacy, most of the other children avoided drawing altogether. Although comic books were not the teachers' preferred examples of artistry, they provided simple, schematic blueprints that offered success and immediate social reinforcement. During several months of classroom observation many students continued to reproduce the same comic book characters with little change. Those who demonstrated enthusiasm for drawing and received positive feedback from teachers and classmates displayed a wider variety of forms and types of pictures. The extra attention and practice yielded improved manual skills and aesthetic sophistication.

Similarly, a study of child filmmakers in the New York Young Filmmakers Program (Griffin, 1985) found that a large number integrated television content and formats in their own films. Films such as *The Bionic Woman* and the *Six Million Dollar Kid* were typical. Nearly all of the children between ages 7 and 14 continued to duplicate television content and TV editing formats through several successive film productions. But some of the 13- or 14-year-old children who had been with the program long enough to complete four to six films, began to experiment with breaking the TV formulas and making more personal and aesthetically idiosyncratic films. As with the children's drawing, it seemed that initial experience led to the adoption of the most prevalently available models, but continuing experience and interest encouraged experimentation with a broader set of potential forms.

In university teaching as well, students often begin with the desire to learn only the most common industrial and technical formulas. Often, this desire is linked to the notion that reproducing industry norms is the surest path to successful employment. As their media experience grows, however, students often take an interest in pursuing a wider range of aesthetic possibilities. And it is most often these students who begin to exhibit a keener sense of differing media environments and practices, who, in effect, begin to develop the capacity to "code-switch" among them. This "code-switching" depends upon an understanding of the symbolic nature of visual images and their role in context-specific image systems.

Certainly, sophisticated interpretive abilities can be developed by students without extensive media production experience. At the same time, working professionals who produce visual media products on a daily basis may reveal little consciousness of the codes they employ, or the broader implications and possibilities of their work. Yet, hands-on experience with the production and manipulation of imagery seems to be a potentially effective means of cultivating a heightened awareness of style and an expanded range of aesthetic possibilities. As Gross (1974) suggests, such experience enhances "communicative competence."

THE HISTORY AND SOCIOLOGY OF VISUAL PRACTICES

The integration of hands-on training with theoretical and historical study of visual media further extends visual literacy skills. The processes of learning to control and manipulate framing, lighting, point of view, juxtaposition, and composition in the service of a specific goal can then be considered within the larger context of the history of art and media. Familiarity with the history of picture making inevitably leads to the recognition of a diversity of forms, contents, and expressive possibilities. It also reveals the relationship between particular aesthetic styles and genres and the institutional contexts from which they emerge.

Rosenblum (1978) makes the argument that aesthetic style must be viewed as a social process, studied as part of the larger social dynamic of which it is a part. To illustrate her point, Rosenblum describes the ways in which three stylistically distinct genres of photography—fine art, advertising, and photojournalism—are inextricably tied to the work routines, professional norms, and economic structures that shape these media production activities.

Helping students to understand that visual representations are both historically and socially situated deters them from deterministic assumptions that lead to complacent viewing. Students often claim that representations derive their form and content from inherent qualities possessed by the medium or the genre itself: "News broadcasts appear the way they do because that's what a news broadcast *is*." Familiarity with the historical and social forces contributing to the evolution of contemporary American media allows viewers to regard media images as symbolic and communicative rather than as natural, commonsense occurrences. Seen within a comparative framework, the cultural specificity of American media becomes even more salient.

Understanding style as a product of distinct social worlds of media practice also provides a powerful corrective to the myth that pictures simply reproduce reality. Studies by Christopherson (1974), Tuchman (1978), Rosenblum (1978), Becker (1982), Schwartz (1986), Schwartz and Griffin (1987), and Griffin (1995) illuminate the nature of the social worlds of image production by examining such dynamics as: the ways in which industry imperatives constrain expressive potentialities, the identification of particular aesthetic styles with members of specific social groups, and the ways in which institutional reward structures shape the processes of representation. Finally, studying the historical and social contexts of image production produces an impression of the overarching symbolic environment within which media images of all kinds jostle and interact. Students not only need to be introduced to the distinct worlds of image production that characterize different media, different social groups, differing professional, industrial, and amateur spheres of activity, but also need to consider how all these modes of representation relate to mass produced forms of popular culture. Confronting both the diversity and the homogenization of symbolic output cannot help but challenge the passivity with which pictures are routinely encountered.

CONCLUSION

This chapter has argued that communication media in the late 20th century increasingly deliver information, advertising, and entertainment through complex arrangements of pictorial images and symbols, increasingly making issues of media literacy issues of visual communication. Thus, a sophisticated understanding of the nature of visual communication is essential to critical media consumption. Such heightened awareness involves moving beyond the naive treatment of pictures as simple records of reality to a recognition of the symbolic and metonymic quality of images within systems of conventionalized media representation. This, in turn, requires experience with the ways in which visual media presentations are created and packaged, experience gained through training in visual analysis and media production.

The education needed by a critical media viewer parallels that needed by a skillful media producer. Both require an appreciation of the aesthetic factors that structure media representations. Both require enough familiarity with picture making to avoid the pitfalls of naive attribution. Media viewers need sophisticated interpretive skills in order to assess the plausibility, validity, and value of visual images, the preeminent vehicles of the information age. Media producers need interpretive skills sophisticated enough to allow effective, accurate message production that targets the intended audience.

Therefore, if media literacy is to become a goal of our educational system, teaching visual aesthetics and visual media production must become a routine part of elementary, secondary, and postsecondary curricula. Students must have regular opportunities to view and experiment with differing "modes of representation" (Nichols, 1991), and they must be encouraged to consider the implications of various production strategies for different "ways of seeing" (Berger, 1972). Historically, different styles of picturing the world have been linked to particular philosophical and socioeconomic systems. In the 20th century, industrial organizations for the mass production of images make this link more literal than ever. Only by critically examining the output of the commercial and noncommercial media around them, and by discovering through firsthand experience that alternative possibilities for pictorial production exist, can students become more aware of the production formulas of industrial media systems and the patterns of representation that result.

It is important that the interpretive skills of viewers not be limited to the most obvious levels of manifest content or the most conventional formulas of narrative exposition. The ability to consider new and unconventional media presentations, like the ability to read difficult material or solve unfamiliar problems, is a skill that separates the educationally privileged from those who are less advantaged. As technology and society continue to change at an accelerating pace, the ability to grapple with ambiguity and unfamiliar form will become increasingly valuable, and viewers limited by static conceptions and inadequate skills will continue to fall farther behind.

Thus, the acquisition of visual literacy skills, often confused with the simple preference for images or the talent for video games that many kids exhibit, is a crucial issue for educators. Far from visually literate, children (and university students) demonstrably lack sophistication about aesthetic forms, pictorial artifice, and visual manipulation. The logical way to attack the problem is to renew the teaching of visual media analysis and production from the earliest grades. Art classes, once required of all students as a core part of the curriculum, have been cut back or eliminated in many schools, competing for a part of students' time with other "elective courses." Teachers must reassert the importance of art and its role in basic education alongside language, mathematics, social studies and reading. As we enter the 21st century and new media technologies blur distinctions between written and visual modes of address, visual literacy can no longer be taken for granted as a natural byproduct of television viewing and computer games.

References

Adatto, K. (1993). *Picture perfect: The art and artifice of public image making.* New York: Basic Books.

Arnheim, R. (1966). *Toward a psychology of art.* Berkeley, CA: University of California Press.

Barnhurst, K. (1994). *Seeing the newspaper.* New York: St. Martin Press.

Becker, H. S. (1982). *Art worlds.* Berkeley, CA: University of California Press.

Berger, J. (1972). *Ways of seeing.* New York: Penguin.

Christopherson, R. W. (1974). From folk art to fine art: A transformation in the meaning of photographic work. *Urban Life and Culture, 3*(2), 123–157.

Deaver, M. (1987). *Behind the scenes.* New York: William Morrow.

Ericson, R. V., Baranek, P. M., & Chan, J. B. L., (1987). *Visualizing deviance: A study of news organizations.* Toronto: Toronto University Press.

Gregory, R. L. (1970). *The intelligent eye.* New York: McGraw-Hill.

Griffin, M. (1985). What young filmmakers learn from television: A study of structure in films made by children. *Journal of Broadcasting and Electronic Media, 29*(1), 79–92.

Griffin, M. (1992). Looking at TV news: Strategies for research. *Communication, 13*(2), 121–141.

Griffin, M. (1995). Amateur photography: Between art and industry. In L. Gross (Ed.), *On the margins of art worlds* (pp. 183–205). Boulder, CO: Westview Press.

Gross, L. (1974). Modes of communication and the acquisition of symbolic competence. In D. R. Olson (Ed.), *Media and symbols: The forms of expression, communication, and education,* (pp. 56-80). Seventy third yearbook of the National Society for the Study of Education. Chicago: University of Chicago Press.

Gruneau, R., & Hackett, R. A. (1990). The production of TV news. In J. Downing, A. Mohammadi, & A. Sreberny-Mohammadi (Eds.), *Questioning the media: A critical introduction* (pp. 281–295). Newbury Park, CA: Sage.

Hartley, J. (1992a). *Tele-ology: Studies in television.* New York: Routledge.

Hartley, J. (1992b). *The politics of pictures.* New York: Routledge.

Kohler, W. (1929). *Gestalt psychology.* New York: Liveright.

Lutz, C. A., & Collins, J. L. (1993). *Reading National Geographic.* Chicago: University of Chicago Press.

Messaris, P. (1994). *Visual literacy: Image, mind, reality.* Boulder, CO: Westview Press.

Monaco, J. (1981). *How to read a film: The art, technology, language, history, and theory of film and media.* New York: Oxford University Press.

Moyers, B. (1989). *The public mind: Illusions of news.* PBS special.

Nichols, B. (1991). *Representing reality.* Bloomington, IN: Indiana University Press.

Postman, N. (1985). *Amusing ourselves to death: Public discourse in the age of show business.* New York: Penguin.

Real, M. R. (1977). *Mass-mediated culture.* Englewood Cliffs, NJ: Prentice-Hall.

Rosenblum, B. (1978). *Photographers at work: A sociology of photographic styles.* New York: Holmes and Meier.

Schramm, M. (1987). *The great American video game.* New York: William Morrow.

Schwartz, D. (1979). *Towards a developmental sociology of art.* Unpublished masters thesis, Annenberg School for Communications, University of Pennsylvania, Philadelphia.

Schwartz, D. (1986). Camera clubs and fine art photography: The social construction of an elite code. *Urban Life Journal of Contemporary Ethnography, 15*(2), 165–195.

Schwartz, D., & Griffin, M. (1987). Amateur photography: The organizational maintenance of an aesthetic code. In T. R. Lindlof (Ed.), *Natural audiences: Qualitative research of media uses and effects* (pp. 198–224). Norwood, NJ: Ablex.

Tuchman, G. (1978). *Making news: A study in the construction of reality.* New York: Free Press.

Worth, S., & Gross, L. (1974). Symbolic strategies. *Journal of Communication, 24,* 27–39.

Zettl, H. (1990). *Sight sound motion: Applied media aesthetics* (2nd ed.). Belmont, CA: Wadsworth.

6

VISUAL INTELLIGENCE AND ANALOGICAL THINKING

Paul Messaris

ANNENBERG SCHOOL FOR COMMUNICATION
UNIVERSITY OF PENNSYLVANIA

One of the most famous stories of scientific creativity concerns the chemist Friedrich von Kekule, who worked in the latter half of the 19th century. In 1865, Kekule was attempting to infer the internal structure of the benzene molecule. He knew that it was composed of six carbon atoms and six hydrogen atoms, but he was finding it very difficult to visualize how these atoms were arranged. His working assumption, that the atoms were lined up in rows, was incompatible with other known facts about carbon and hydrogen. One evening, after much puzzling over this problem, Kekule sat in a chair by his fireplace and dozed. Strings of atoms appeared before his eyes, and they began to twine and twist like snakes. And then, suddenly, one of the snakes reared back and seized on its own tail. At that instant, Kekule awoke with the solution to his problem immediately clear: as subsequent research confirmed, the structure of benzene is based on a string of six carbon atoms arranged in a circle (Findlay, 1965, p. 39).

This story has often been used as an illustration of the crucial role that visual images have played in the development of human knowledge. In Kekule's case, the images were purely internal, products of his "mind's eye." However, as a growing body of scholarship has demonstrated, the advance of science and technology has also been affected critically by the various visual media that people have used for recording the appearance of external reality. This point is the principal conclusion of William Ivins' (1953) influential history of woodcuts, engravings, and other early techniques for the exact reproduction of pictures. According to Ivins, the development of these techniques acted as a stimulus for several fields of knowledge, such as botany, whose progress had been impeded by the lack of means for the exact transmission of visual information. Similarly, in a recent detailed examination of the interplay between art and science in the Renaissance, Edgerton (1991) argues that both architecture and engineering were affected profoundly by the 15th-century invention of linear perspective, which made it possible to create accurately scaled previsualizations of the appearance of three-dimensional structures. Indeed, as Edgerton had demonstrated in an earlier study, the first person to use linear perspective in a picture was most likely an architect, Filippo Brunelleschi (Edgerton, 1975).

Both Ivins and Edgerton, as well as other writers who have dealt with these matters, make a further point that is particularly relevant to the concerns of educators. They argue that, in addition to serving the purposes of specific scientific or technical tasks, visual media also contribute to the development of human intellect by enhancing their users' mental skills. This idea has become familiar to many educators through the well-known writings of Howard Gardner (1983, 1993), who has made the more general point that there are several distinct forms of intelligence, each of them related to particular modes of human communication. Gardner's discussion of visual media focuses on their connection to spatial intelligence, a set of mental skills having to do with the perception and comprehension of two- or three-dimensional shapes, objects, and relationships. Spatial intelligence is also the focus of Edgerton's and Ivins' writings. However, there is at least one other type of intellectual aptitude that has been associated with visual media, namely, analogical thinking (Hargittai, & Hargittai, 1994; Whittock, 1990). This aspect of visual intelligence will be the focus of the present chapter.

THE NATURE OF ANALOGICAL THINKING

Analogical thinking is the type of mental process illustrated by Kekule's vision of the snake biting its tail. In a detailed discussion of this story, Margaret Boden (1991, pp. 100, 101) pinpoints the essential features of that process: the ability to discern some structural similarity between two different objects, events, or situations, and to get a better understanding of one of them on the basis of the characteristics of the other. In Kekule's case the image of the snake twisting itself into a circle gave him the idea that the line of carbon atoms in the benzene molecule could also twist itself into a closed loop. As Boden demonstrates, similar leaps of mind are central components of creative thinking not only in the sciences but also in the arts. The role of analogical reasoning in scientific discoveries has also been documented by John-Steiner (1985) and Mitchell (1993, p. 7), while Vosniadou and Ortony (1989, p. 1) have argued that analogy is "one of the most fundamental aspects of human cognition." A related belief in the significance of analogical thinking for educational attainment is reflected in the inclusion of analogy items in such standardized tests as the GRE (Bejar, Chaffin, & Embretson, 1991).

The important role that analogy can play in visual media is perhaps most evident in the case of informational displays. Boden (1991, p. 101) notes that maps, diagrams, scale models, and family trees are all instances of analogical representation. Detailed demonstrations aimed partly at visual educators of the informational uses of visual analogy have been provided by Edward Tufte (1983, 1990). For example, Tufte discusses a classic chart that he says "may well be the best statistical graphic ever drawn" (1983, p. 40). Created in 1861 by the French engineer Charles Joseph Minard, this chart displays the fate of Napoleon's army during its disastrous invasion of Russia in 1812–13. The line that plots the army's direction of travel across a map of Poland and Russia starts out thick and then gets progressively thinner as Napoleon's men begin to die off. When the line reverses direction and traces the path of Napoleon's retreat, it becomes linked to a scale indicating the plummeting temperatures that reduced the army's size even further. All of the correspondences between this chart and the reality that it represents—the thickness of the line and the size of the army, the line's path across the page and the army's direction of travel, the downward-pointing scale and the falling temperatures—are examples of analogical representation.

Although the analogical aspects of visual media may be particularly clear in the case of informational displays, analogy is also a significant feature of the more purely artistic uses of visual images. An illustration of visual analogy in an artistic context is provided by Rudolf Arnheim (1969, pp. 120–129) in a discussion of a class exercise requiring students to draw abstract pictures of a good marriage and a bad marriage. One of Arnheim's students drew two circular figures, the first one consisting of smoothly curving lines, the second of spikes. Another student drew a pair of interlocking yin-yang figures and contrasted that with a pair of figures separated by some distance. In other words, both students' drawings are based on implicit analogies between the properties of visual shapes—smoothness versus roughness; closeness versus distance—and the abstract characteristics of human activities or relationships. Arnheim suggests that such connections are at the heart of the process by which abstract visual designs are able to evoke meaning. Furthermore, it can be argued that similar connections account for a significant part of the meaning of representational art as well (e.g., see Arnheim, 1954,

pp. 425–443; Messaris, 1994, pp. 40–44; Zettl, 1990). The following pages contain a closer look at these aspects of visual analogy. The discussion begins with an examination of the composition of individual images and then goes on to consider the consequences of juxtaposing two or more images, either in movie sequences or in complex static displays.

VISUAL COMPOSITION

As indicated above, the analogical basis of visual composition has been explored by several writers. For pedagogical purposes, a particularly useful introduction to the topic is provided by Molly Bang (1991) in a book which is ostensibly aimed at young children but nevertheless contains a systematic theoretical treatment of its subject. Drawing on her professional background as a prominent illustrator of children's books, Bang frames her presentation as a step-by-step examination of the stylistic decisions involved in the creation of a single picture, Little Red Riding Hood stalked by the wolf in the forest. This discussion entails such simple questions as whether the wolf's features should be pointed or curved and whether its eyes should be red or mauve, but the discussion's culmination is a set of general principles accounting for the meanings of individual design elements (shapes, sizes, colors, etc.) and the relationships among them. The central premise underlying all these principles is that viewers respond to the abstract features of visual composition on the basis of unconsciously perceived analogies to elements of real-world experience. As Bang puts it:

> This word *associate* is the key to the whole process of how picture structure affects our emotions. … We associate pointed shapes with real pointed objects. We associate red with real blood and fire. Specific elements such as points or color or size seem to call up the emotions we felt when we experienced actual sharp points or colors or noticeably large or small things. (p. 102)

Similar assumptions about the meaning of visual composition can be found in the work of other practicing artists. Among painters in the Western fine-arts tradition, an especially noteworthy investigator of these matters was Georges Seurat, who eventually developed an explicit theory that parallels Bang's in its essential details (Homer, 1964; Lee, 1990). For instance, he believed that a wedge-like shape pointing toward the top of a canvas would evoke both dynamism—because of the association with the properties of knives or other sharp-edged objects—and buoyancy—because of the association with upward movement in general. Consequently, in his rendition of scenes in which these qualities were an appropriate part of the tone he was trying to convey, Seurat would incorporate upward-pointing wedge shapes in the composition even when that meant sacrificing some of the naturalistic appearance of the image. As Homer (pp. 220–234) has noted, this practice is evident in such paintings as "Le Cirque" (1891) and "Le Chahut" (1890), in which upward-pointing tapers are added to the facial features of a circus acrobat, in the former case, and a line of high-stepping dances, in the latter.

In recent years, the assumptions underlying practices of this sort have been tested experimentally by such researchers as Hartmut Espe, whose work deals with advertising and industrial design. In Espe's experiments, viewers are shown pictures of abstract two- or three-dimensional objects and asked to indicate what meanings these objects express. One of Espe's studies investigated viewers' responses to three kinds of shapes: angular (triangle, star), orthogonal (square, rectangle), and curved (circle, ellipse). Viewers were asked to rate these shapes on two dimensions of meaning: how powerful and how active they appeared. Espe's assumption about the angular shapes was very much the same as Bang's and Seurat's: by analogy to the properties of real-world angular objects (wedges, knives, etc.), he expected these shapes to be seen as both powerful and active. For reasons that should be equally apparent, he expected the orthogonal shapes to be rated powerful but inactive, and the curved shapes to be rated neither powerful nor active. All these expectations were confirmed by the experimental results, which can therefore be seen as providing empirical support for the theoretical approach represented by Bang, Seurat, and scholars like Arnheim. Espe has also found, however, that the role of analogy in visual interpretation can be affected critically by context. For example, when viewers are shown a circle in a context that makes it appear three-dimensional instead of flat, the ratings of activity and power go up, perhaps because it is now seen as analogous to a ball, with connotations of sports.

The kinds of visual analogies investigated by Espe and illustrated in the examples from Bang and Seurat are relatively simple in the sense that they involve actual physical similarities between elements of a visual design and objects in the real world. For educational purposes, examples such as these may be the most convenient means for introducing the concepts of analogical representation to students. It would be a mistake, however, to assume that the analogical meanings in real works of art can always, or even frequently, be accounted for in such direct terms. A crucial feature of analogical thinking in art is its capacity to evoke meaning on the basis of purely conceptual parallels between the formal properties of a picture and the structural characteristics of some aspect of real-world experience. This was the case in the examples cited earlier from Arnheim, whose students were able to give visual form to the emotional qualities of marital relationships. The connection between visual education and the enhancement of intelligence seems especially clear in such instances.

The use of visual analogy for the sorts of complex purposes illustrated by Arnheim has been examined cross-culturally in a series of related studies. This body of research began with an investigation by Fischer (1961), an anthropologist concerned with the art of traditional, preindustrial cultures. Fischer was interested in the possibility that there might be an analogical connection between the stylistic features of a society's visual arts and the broader cultural values of that society. More specifically, he assumed that the relationships among design elements in a society's artworks might mirror the society's prevailing patterns of social relationship. For example, equality in a society's interpersonal relationships might be reflected by symmetrical compositions in a society's art, while the presence of rigid distinctions among the members of a society might be reflected in its art by distinct boundaries around the compositional elements. Fischer tested these assumptions with a sample of some 30 traditional cultures, such as the Ashanti, Balinese, and Navajo, from various parts of the world. The results of these tests strongly supported his theory. Furthermore, similar findings have since been reported by researchers working with other cultures (e.g., Dressler, & Robbins, 1975; Hatcher, 1988; Pocius, 1979). Taken together, these findings suggest that educating students about visual analogy in art may also give them a new window into other people's cultural values.

POINT OF VIEW IN VISUAL ART

The aspects of composition that have been examined up to this point have to do with the arrangement of design elements on the surface of the image. The time has now come to turn to a different type of compositional device in which analogical connections also play a major role. This device has to do with the point of view from which the image is presented to the viewer. In other words, what is at stake with this device is the viewer's placement relative to the people or places in a picture: close-up or more distant, eye-level or at an angle, and so on. The analogical basis of point of view has been analyzed in detail by Meyrowitz (1986), who argues that people respond to this device by analogy to the ways in which they respond to interpersonal distance and orientation in real-world social relationships. For example, since proximity in real life is related to intimacy and involvement, a close-up in an image should elicit relatively greater engagement from the viewer. Similarly, since bigger people are often stronger than smaller ones, a view from below may make the person in an image appear more powerful in the eyes of the spectator.

Point of view is an important compositional device in drawing, painting, and photography, as well as film and video camerawork. Indeed, in fictional movies the distance between the camera and the subject is one of the principal visual means for such effects as heightening the intensity of a scene as it moves towards its climax, maintaining the viewer's sympathy with the hero and emotional distance from secondary characters, or releasing the tension of the movie following the resolution of the action. Nevertheless, despite its importance in these and other situations, the potential uses of point of view often seem to be overlooked when nonprofessionals make pictures. Studies of amateur filmmakers and of young people learning to make movies find that both groups tend to record the action from a single, unvarying perspective (Chalfen, 1982; Griffin, 1985). It appears, therefore, that there is considerable scope for visual education in this area. Moreover, in view of the analogical connection between everyday social interactions and the uses of point of view in the visual media, it is conceivable that learning how to employ this compositional device effectively may have the additional consequence of strengthening students' real-world perspective-taking skills.

Yet another reason why visual educators might want to focus on point of view has to do with the political and advertising applications of this device. There is considerable evidence that manipulations of point of view can be effective instruments of visual persuasion in commercial advertisements and in political imagery. At the same time, though, there is reason to believe that viewers tend to overlook these manipulations. Consequently, drawing students' attention to point of view could contribute to the development of informed, critical attitudes toward potential influences of the visual media. Some indication of the need for this form of visual education comes from an experiment by Mandell and Shaw (1973) concerning the use of low camera angles in political imagery. This convention has a long history, especially—though by no means exclusively—in totalitarian political regimes. In Mandell and Shaw's study, college students were asked to make judgments about a political figure appearing in a newscast. There were three versions of this person's image: one taken at eye-level, the others at angles of 12 degrees below and above his eyes. Each student saw only one of these three versions. As the authors had predicted, judgments of how powerful the person looked were significantly higher among the students who saw the low-angle version. However, most of the students did not seem conscious of the influence of angle of view. At the conclusion of the study, they were asked directly to comment about camera angles used in the newscast. Out of a total of 78 students who saw either the high- or the low-angle versions, only 13 showed some awareness of this convention in their responses (Mandell, & Shaw, 1973, p. 362). Since similar findings have been reported from a second study of college students' responses to point of view, it would appear that this device is a particularly suitable object for the attention of visual educators.

THE JUXTAPOSITION OF IMAGES

In addition to operating at the level of the individual image, analogical relationships can also be present in the meanings created by bringing two or more images together, either in static displays such as print ads and billboards or in movie sequences. A relatively simple form of analogy is often encountered in film and television editing, whenever the duration of the shots is varied in order to suggest a mood or an emotional tone. Common examples of this practice include the use of fast-paced editing to generate excitement and impart a sense of dynamism to the events in a movie, or slow editing as a means of making things seem more tranquil. These uses of editing rhythm have been tested systematically by Kraft (1986) and Penn (1971), in experiments involving multiple versions of film clips, edited at speeds ranging from relatively high to relatively low. Viewers were asked to rate the activity level of these film clips; as expected, those who saw the versions with faster editing tended to see the clips as more active, while slower versions appeared calmer and more passive. These findings seem readily predictable, and the analogical connections that account for them are probably too obvious to need much explanation. Presumably, viewers' reactions to the pace of the editing are reflections of the way in which people respond to speed and slowness in the events of everyday reality.

A revealing elaboration of this editing principle has been investigated by Welch, Huston-Stein, Wright, and Plehal (1979) in a well-known study of television commercials aimed at children. Aside from the rhythm or pace of editing, this study was also concerned with the nature of editing transitions. In particular, the authors made a distinction between straight cuts, which create an instantaneous transition from one shot to the next, and dissolves or fades, both of which entail a more gradual replacement of one shot by another. The study was based on the assumption that the editing styles of children's commercials would differ according to the gender of the children they were aimed at. An analysis of a sample of Saturday-morning TV ads found support for that view. Commercials aimed at boys were characterized by faster editing and greater use of straight cuts, while girls' commercials had a slower editing pace and were more likely to employ fades or dissolves. The authors interpret these stylistic characteristics as "subtle sex-role cues." In other words, the commercials' editing styles appear to be analogical representations of conventional conceptions of masculinity and femininity: on the one hand speed and abruptness, on the other a more measured and gentle way of being.

An obvious question raised by the Welch study is whether children are actually sensitive to these stylistic evocations of gender. This question was explored in an ingenious follow-up experiment by Huston, Greer, Wright, Welch, and Ross (1984), in which identical commercials were edited in two different ways, corresponding to the two stylistic tendencies observed in the previous study. Children were shown these commercials and asked to guess whether they were intended for girls or for boys. The results showed that the children did indeed seem to have an intuitive grasp of the meaning of these stylistic manipulations. To be sure, this finding does not necessarily mean that the children were able to employ analogical thinking, even implicitly, in making the connection between style and gender. It is possible that they simply recognized the meaning of the editing on the basis of their past experience as viewers of TV commercials. However, if their responses were based even partly on analogical thought processes, this finding is an impressive indicator of young children's capacity for analogical thinking at a relatively high level of abstraction.

VISUAL SIMILE AND METAPHOR

In the editing conventions discussed above, it is the timing of the images, rather than their actual content, that exhibits analogical characteristics. There is, however, a very different form of analogical editing in which the content itself is the key to the analogy. This form of editing has a long history and is often thought of as having originated in the films of Sergei Eisenstein and other directors working in the early years of Soviet cinema. A clear example occurs in a scene from Eisenstein's "Strike" (1925), in which striking workers are massacred by government troops: at the climax of the massacre, Eisenstein edits into the scene a number of shots of animals being butchered in a slaughterhouse. This crosscutting between the two sets of images can be seen as the equivalent of a simile. It explicitly juxtaposes two events and implies an analogical connection between them.

Analogical cross-cutting figures prominently in certain films of Eisenstein and his contemporaries in the then USSR. For several years, this device was also popular in Hollywood, where Charlie Chaplin's notorious comparison between factory workers and sheep ("Modern Times," 1936) was one of many direct imitations of Soviet-style editing. Eventually, though, these kinds of juxtapositions became a rarity in fictional movies. As film critic Andre Bazin (1967) argued, the interruption of a movie's story line by the insertion of an extraneous image may have been incompatible with Hollywood cinema's increasing tendency toward unobtrusive narration. Consequently, when such an interruption is encountered in more recent movies—as in Howard Hawks' juxtaposition of kissing lovers and colliding trains in "Man's Favorite Sport?" (1964)—it is almost invariably a deliberate parody.

At the same time when this earlier style of cross-cutting has declined, however, other varieties of visual simile have taken its place. A relatively subtle example of this development occurs in Kon Ichikawa's "The Makioka Sisters," a Japanese film made in 1983. Toward the end of this film there is a scene in which an unmarried woman, who has endured a series of disappointing attempts at third-party matchmaking, finally meets a man she finds attractive. As she faces him for the first time, Ichikawa's camera goes from a shot of her to a shot of wind-ruffled foliage—with red colors prominent—in the window behind her. To a certain extent, this transition is similar to Hawks' pairing of a kiss and a crash. Yet there is also an important difference between them. Hawks' colliding trains appear out of nowhere, in a location that has no spatial relationship to anything else in the movie. In Ichikawa's case, on the other hand, the camera never strays from the space or time of the story's unfolding action. In that sense, Ichikawa's analogy may be considered less obtrusive. It could be argued, therefore, that a viewer has to be somewhat more discerning to spot such an analogy, and that a filmmaker may need to be more resourceful in creating it (Clifton, 1983).

Even less obtrusive visual similes can occur when the two images that are being juxtaposed appear together in a single shot, or when an analogical juxtaposition also serves as a narrative transition. The former possibility is discussed at length by Whittock (1990, pp. 43ff.) in connection with a shot from John Ford's "The Searchers" (1956): the hero of the film (played by John Wayne), riding through a desert landscape, shares the frame with the towering form of an isolated, rugged butte. Citing an earlier analysis by John F. Scott, Whittock observes that, while the analogical connection between rider and background seems compelling once it has been pointed out, the lack of a cut or other deliberate device for highlighting the juxtaposition makes it very easy to miss. Even when there is a cut, though, a visual simile can still be unobtrusive if the cut also serves a narrative purpose, which may monopolize the viewer's attention. The classic example of this latter possibility occurs in Stanley Kubrick's "2001: A Space Odyssey" (1968): a protohuman primate who has just learned how to use a bone as an ax tosses it high into the air, where its spinning is replaced by the movement of a space station in orbit above the Earth. This is a profound juxtaposition, comprising a wealth of analogical links, but the dramatic narrative leap with which these links coincide can deflect the viewer's attention away from nonnarrative levels of meaning.

Viewers' interpretations of a visual simile embedded in narrative editing have been investigated by Messaris (1981) in a study of college-students' responses to a 10-minute fiction film. In one of the scenes of this film, the protagonist, a fashionably dressed woman, walks into a clothing store; as she passes through the door, there is a cut to the interior of a church, and the same woman appears at the entrance. When the study was being planned, it had seemed to the author highly unlikely that any viewer would miss the analogical implications of the transition between store and church. It emerged, however, that only students with actual experience in filmmaking were particularly sensitive to that aspect of the transition's meaning. The study had been designed as a deliberate comparison among viewers with varying degrees of film-related experience. Students who had made films themselves exhibited a high level of awareness of the store/church analogy. As one of these students put it: "At that point I thought there was a … over-obvious … metaphor of fashionable store—church, you know, I thought kind of unsubtle" (pauses in original). And yet, despite this "over-obviousness," among the students without any filmmaking experience the most frequent interpretation of this sequence was purely narrative—that is, the store/church transition was interpreted only as a scene change from one location to another.

These results provide some indication of the potential value of film education for students' capacity to think analogically in contexts where they might not ordinarily be inclined to do so. However, the editing of fiction films is by no means the only source of examples of visual similes. While editing that is based only on analogy, without a narrative component, is now quite rare in mainstream fiction film and television, it appears to be gaining popularity in some forms of advertising and has become a staple of political ads and videos (see Morreale, 1991; Prince, 1990). Juxtaposition based on visual or conceptual analogy between two images is also very common in print advertising. For example, automotive advertisers have featured their products in association with lions (a Toyota ad emphasizing power and dominance over the competition), ice skaters (an Oldsmobile ad emphasizing smooth performance and elegant styling), jet airplanes (a Dodge ad emphasizing speed and power), eagles (a GM ad emphasizing speed and ease of travel), and tigers (the well-known Exxon series). Furthermore, there is another, related category of print advertising that also makes use of visual analogy but presents it in a distinctly different form. A case in point is a National Dairy board ad in which a glass of milk emerges out of a peeled banana. The object is to suggest nutritional equivalence, but this analogy is suggested through a merging or blending of the two foods, rather than a side-by-side pairing. As Kaplan (1990, 1992) has suggested, this kind of blending of the two terms of the analogy may appropriately be thought of as a visual metaphor.

How well do viewers cope with visual similes and metaphors? What role do visual experience and education play in equipping a viewer for the analogical thinking required in such cases? These questions have been addressed by the present author in a study conducted with Karen Nielsen (see Messaris, 1994, pp. 111–112). This study explored viewers' responses to two instances of analogical editing used for advertising purposes: Ronald Reagan's 1984 reelection campaign film, in which images of Reagan's first-term inauguration are intercut with images of people from various walks of life going to work in the morning (a visual expression of the campaign theme, "Morning in America"); and a TV commercial for fruit preserves in which the picture of the product is juxtaposed with images of nature and life on the farm, presumably as a way of suggesting purity and wholesomeness. These ads were shown to viewers from a variety of backgrounds, including people professionally occupied in TV production.

The central question pursued in the study was whether viewers would see any analogical element in the editing structures of the ads—for example, a comparison between Ronald Reagan and his fellow citizens getting ready to do their respective jobs, or an implied similarity between the qualities of the preserves and those of pristine nature. The results of this study indicated that awareness of such analogical links was higher among TV professionals than among other viewers. For example, while 87% of the former referred to some kind of analogical connection in their interpretation of the Reagan campaign film, the corresponding figure for other college-educated viewers was 59%. In addition to illustrating yet another way in which visual expertise may lead to enhanced analogical thinking, these findings also suggest that teaching students about visual similes and metaphors could contribute to their skills as interpreters of visual advertising.

CONCLUSIONS

The main lessons that emerge from what has been said so far are two: first, that analogical linkages play a major role in a wide variety of visual conventions; second, that the capacity for analogical thought is an important component of intelligence, in science as well as in art. More specifically, the presence of analogical relationships between image and meaning, or between one image and another, has been illustrated in connection with scientific or informational graphics; pictorial composition, the artistic and persuasive uses of point of view, editing rhythm, and visual similes or metaphors in advertising and in narrative cinema. It was noted that, aside from increasing students' fluency in analogical thinking, education about the uses of visual analogy might also improve perspective-taking skills (in the case of point-of-view conventions), as well as students' abilities to think critically about persuasive uses of visual media.

How might educators best respond to these opportunities? The various examples of visual analogy described in this chapter are partly intended as sources on which educators could draw in designing a visual curriculum. Students could be taught to recognize similar devices in artworks and in the mass media and to incorporate this recognition in their critical responses. Perhaps more important, such devices could also serve as models for students' own creative efforts in visual media. Not surprisingly, there is reason to believe that enhancement of visual intelligence is especially likely to occur when students have the opportunity to produce film or other media themselves (see Messaris, 1981; Tidhar, 1984), although there is some evidence that even the experience of viewing can serve as an effective cognitive stimulus in certain circumstances (see Salomon, 1979). Beyond encouraging their students to develop as visual thinkers, educators can also make important contributions to the ongoing task of assessment of aptitudes and achievements in this area. While sophisticated methods have already been developed for the measurement of some forms of visual skills—most notably, spatial intelligence (see Page's chapter in this volume)—there is much less precedent for the assessment of analogical thinking in visual matters. As Gardner (1993) has noted, there is a need for context-sensitive evaluation that measures visual skills as part of students' overall interactions with visual media, rather than through isolated tests. Educators who work directly with students in the classroom are particularly well-placed to respond to this need.

References

Arnheim, R. (1954). *Art and visual perception: A psychology of the creative eye.* Berkeley, CA: University of California Press.

Arnheim, R. (1969). *Visual thinking.* Berkeley, CA: University of California Press.

Bang, M. (1991). *Picture this: Perception and composition.* Boston: Bulfinch Press.

Bazin, A. (1967). *What is cinema?* (Vol. 1). (H. Gray, Trans). Berkeley, CA: University of California Press.

Bejar, I. I., Chaffin, R., & Embretson, S. (1991). *Cognitive and psychometric analysis of analogical problem solving.* New York: Springer.

Boden, M. A. (1991). *The creative mind: Myths and mechanisms.* New York: Basic Books.

Chalfen, R. (1982). Home movies as cultural documents. In S. Thomas (Ed.), *Film/culture: Explorations of cinema in its social context* (pp. 126–138). Metuchen, NJ: Scarecrow.

Clifton, N. R. (1983). *The figure in film.* Newark, DE: University of Delaware Press.

Dressler, W. W., & Robbins, M. C. (1975). Art styles, social stratification, and cognition: An analysis of Greek vase painting. *American Ethnologist, 2*(3), 427–434.

Edgerton, S. Y., Jr. (1975). *The renaissance rediscovery of linear perspective.* New York: Icon Editions.

Edgerton, S. Y., Jr. (1991). *The heritage of Giotto's geometry: Art and science on the eve of the scientific revolution.* Ithaca, NY: Cornell University Press.

Findlay, A. (1965). *A hundred years of chemistry* (3rd ed.) London: Duckworth.

Fischer, J. L. (1961). Art styles as cultural cognitive maps. *American Anthropologist, 63*(1), 79–93.

Gardner, H. (1983). *Frames of mind: The theory of multiple intelligences.* New York: Basic Books.

Gardner, H. (1993). *Multiple intelligences: The theory in practice.* New York: Basic Books.

Griffin, M. (1985). What young filmmakers learn from television: A study of structure in films made by children. *Journal of Broadcasting & Electronic Media, 29*(1), 79–92.

Hargittai, I., & Hargittai, M. (1994). The use of artistic analogies in chemical research and education. *Leonardo, 27*(1), 223–226.

Hatcher, E. P. (1988). *Visual metaphors: A methodological study in visual communication.* Albuquerque, NM: University of New Mexico Press.

Homer, W. I. (1964). *Seurat and the science of painting.* Cambridge, MA: MIT Press.

Huston, A., Greer, D., Wright, J., Welch, R., & Ross, R. (1984). Children's comprehension of televised formal features with masculine and feminine connotations. *Developmental Psychology, 20*(4), 706–716.

Ivins, W. M., Jr. (1953). *Prints and visual communication.* Cambridge, MA: MIT Press.

John-Steiner, V. (1985). *Notebooks of the mind: Explorations of thinking.* Albuquerque, NM: University of New Mexico Press.

Kaplan, S. J. (1990). Visual metaphors in the representation of communication technology. *Critical Studies in Mass Communication, 7*(1), 37–47.

Kaplan, S. J. (1992). A conceptual analysis of form and content in visual metaphors. *Communication, 13*(3), 197–209.

Kraft, R. N. (1986). The role of cutting in the evaluation and retention of film. *Journal of Experimental Psychology: Learning, Memory, and Cognition, 12,* 155–163.

Lee, E. W. (1990). *Seurat at Gravelines: The last landscapes.* Bloomington, IN: Indiana University Press.

Mandell, L. M., & Shaw, D. L. (1973). Judging people in the news—unconsciously: Effect of camera angle and bodily activity. *Journal of Broadcasting, 17*(3), 353–362.

Messaris, P. (1981). The film audience's awareness of the production process. *Journal of the University Film Association, 33*(4), 53–56.

Messaris, P. (1994). *Visual "literacy": Image, mind, and reality.* Boulder, CO: Westview Press.

Meyrowitz, J. (1986). Television and interpersonal behaviour: Codes of perception and response. In G. Gumpert & R. Cathcart (Eds.), *Inter/media: Interpersonal communication in a media world* (3rd ed., pp. 253–272). New York: Oxford University Press.

Mitchell, M. (1993). *Analogy-making as perception: A computer model.* Cambridge, MA: MIT Press.

Morreale, J. (1991). *A new beginning: A textual frame analysis of the political campaign film.* Albany, NY: State University of New York Press.

Penn, R. (1971). Effects of motion and cutting rates in motion pictures. *AV Communication Review, 19*(1), 29–50.

Pocius, G. L. (1979). Hooked rugs in Newfoundland: The representation of social structure in design. *Journal of American Folklore, 92,* 273–284.

Prince, S. (1990). Are the Bolsheviks in your breakfast cereal? In S. Thomas & W. A. Evans (Eds.), *Communication and culture: Language, performance, technology, and media* (pp. 180–184). Norwood, NJ: Ablex.

Salomon, G. (1979). *Interaction of media, cognition, and learning: An exploration of how symbolic forms cultivate mental skills and affect knowledge acquisition.* San Francisco: Jossey-Bass.

Tidhar, C. (1984). Children communicating in cinematic codes: Effects on cognitive skills. *Journal of Educational Psychology, 76*(5), 957–965.

Tufte, E. R. (1983). *The visual display of quantitative information.* Cheshire, CT: Graphics Press.

Tufte, E. R. (1990). *Envisioning information.* Cheshire, CT: Graphics Press.

Vosniadou, S., & Ortony, A. (1989). *Similarity and analogical reasoning.* Cambridge: Cambridge University Press.

Welch, R. L., Huston-Stein, A., Wright, J. C., & Plehal, R. (1979). Subtle sex-role cues in children's commercials. *Journal of Communication, 29*(3), 202–209.

Whittock, T. (1990). *Metaphor and Film.* New York: Cambridge University Press.

Zettl, H. (1990). *Sight sound motion: Applied media aesthetics* (2nd ed.). Belmont, CA: Wadsworth.

·7·

VISUAL INTELLIGENCE AND SPATIAL APTITUDES

Georgette Page
WEST VIRGINIA UNIVERSITY

Over time, developmentalists have taken many different perspectives in examining how children learn about their worlds. The theory of the great developmentalist Jean Piaget stresses the importance of interactions between children and their environment as they become more able to think logically and hypothetically (see Boden, 1979). Howard Gardner is another theorist who has looked at the interaction between child and environment; however, Gardner takes a broader stance and argues that, while Piaget thought he was including all intelligences in his theory, Piaget's theory only concerns the development of logical-mathematical knowledge (Gardner, 1993).

After examining a number of different populations such as prodigies, gifted, brain-injured, experts in different fields, and individuals from various cultures, Gardner (1983) became convinced that there are at least seven intelligences. Logical–mathematical intelligence is what the name indicates and is the ability to think logically, mathematically, and scientifically. Linguistic intelligence is shown in the works of novelists, poets, and others who use verbal language effectively. Spatial intelligence is the ability to form and transform mental images of three-dimensional reality and is evident in people such as sailors, painters, sculptors, engineers. Musical intelligence is obvious in master musicians such as Beethoven and Ellington. Bodily-kinesthetic intelligence is exemplified by dancers, athletes, and others who use all or part of their body in efficient ways. Finally, Gardner's theory suggests two forms of personal intelligence: interpersonal, involving skill in understanding other people, and intrapersonal, or the ability to know about oneself and use that knowledge to function competently in the world. This chapter concentrates on spatial intelligence and describes how children's abilities within that area of knowledge interact with visual literacy.

SPATIAL INTELLIGENCE

An important relationship exists between visual media and spatial intelligence even though visual media may also exercise several other areas of cognition, depending upon what type of material is presented (e.g., understanding words, interpersonal relationships, or bodily movements). In interpreting a film or a television program, viewers need to make sense of visual conventions such as cuts, zooms, dollying, split screens, and mats. These features may particularly challenge young viewers since they are not always isomorphic with naturally occurring phenomena, yet viewers who are skilled within the spatial realm of intelligence are more likely to understand them. Also, the more skilled they are in understanding these elements of visual media, the more likely they are to be competent within the spatial realm of intelligence.

Children's responses to the formal features of television have been examined in several studies by developmentalists and others (e.g., Calvert, Huston, Watkins, & Wright, 1982; Singer, & Singer, 1981; Smith, Anderson, & Fischer, 1985; Wright, & Huston, 1983). In this body of research, age is the factor which has been used to explain viewers' varied understandings. Other studies by visual communication scholars have addressed more specifically the individual characteristics of young children as they interpret certain conventions. For example, Acker and Tiemens (1981) tested elementary school children's perceptions of the changes in size of a televised image (a candy bar). Children watched a videotape in which a split screen showed two people, one on the left side of the screen and the other on the right, each holding a candy bar. The image on the right was identical to the one on the left. As the children watched the videotape, they saw the size of the candy bar on each side of the screen change. On one side, the camera cut to a close-up of the candy; on the other side, the camera zoomed in to a close-up of the candy. When the children were asked which candy bar had more to eat, they pointed to the one in which the zoom was used. The authors based this finding on a characteristic of Piaget's preoperational stage of development in which children are unable to conserve—namely, recognize that an object depicted in another way is still the same object. Preoperational children have trouble keeping in mind the qualities that are unchanging even though the object may appear to be different. In this video task, they had difficulty in conserving the fact that the candy bar was the same regardless of how it was portrayed on the two screens. When the camera cut to the close-up, they thought that it was not as big as the candy bar that "grew" as the camera zoomed in to the close-up (p. 341).

Although this study and others done by developmentalists and communication scholars illustrate that children interpret visual messages differently from adults, the researchers do not address spatial intelligence in any significant way to explain differences in comprehension. According to Gardner (1983), being competent within the spatial realm of intelligence involves several abilities, which concentrate on perceiving objects and their transformations in space. For instance, a person who has acquired spatial knowledge recognizes qualities of an object, perceives changes in that object, mentally rotates the object in space, and reproduces it by drawings, paintings, and other graphic depictions (p.173). A good example of spatial intelligence is illustrated by watching expert chess players.

Many of the abilities within the spatial realm pertain to perspectives or viewpoints and manipulation of objects in space. Visual media tap these skills when, for instance, producers depict characters simultaneously in two different spaces through matted images or split screens, cut from one shot to another within the same scene, or have cameras dolly around objects in a scene. Do young viewers use their spatial knowledge to help them make sense of these conventions? If so, how? This question has been explored in several studies by Comuntzis.

POINT OF VIEW: STUDY 1

The researcher examined children's comprehension of different viewpoints on television to see how it related to spatial knowledge in the real world. A positive relationship was found between young children's scores on a perspective-taking task—namely, children determined different viewpoints of characters in a three-dimensional display—and their level of skill in interpreting successive changing points of view in a short videotaped scene.

Method

Ninety-three children, 3 to 6 years of age, watched a videotape in which viewpoints of two girls playing a game of checkers changed by long shots (LS), over-the-shoulder shots (OS), and close-ups (CU). The sequence of shots is used conventionally in dialogue scenes (Monaco, 1977). The producer takes an establishing shot (LS) of the entire place of action, then cuts to an OS, which shows the partial back of one character and the front of another, then cuts to a CU of the face of the actor whose back was seen in the OS, and finally ends with a cut to a CU of the other actor. Watching this sequence of shots, the children answered questions about the various points of view.

Children viewed the videotape individually, and the researcher stopped the tape at each different shot to ask the child questions about the two characters' points of view. (Figure 7–1 illustrates these different shots). The actors in the televised scene were facing each other and saw different objects: a clock and picture were hung on the two walls behind them so that one could see the clock; the other, the picture. The questions posed to the children required "yes" or "no" answers; for instance, "Does Terry see the clock on the wall?" or "Does Annie see the picture on the wall?" "Does Terry see the side of Annie's face that you see?" Questions tapped the child's perspective-taking ability when viewing a televised dialogue scene. That is, the children revealed, by their answers, how skilled they were in understanding the points of view in each of the shots—LS, OS, and CU—in the scene.

Long Shot

Over-the-shoulder

Close-up (Annie)

Close-up (Terry)

FIGURE 7–1   Sequence of shots in video task

Scoring

Answers to the questions enabled the experimenter to categorize children into levels of perspective-taking ability. Developmental literature on perspective taking in real-world situations provided the basis for establishing the criteria for the different levels of ability (e.g., Flavell, Flavell, Green, & Wilcox, 1981; Gzesh, & Surber, 1985; Schachter, & Gollin, 1979). Initially, perspective taking was examined by Piaget and Inhelder (1956) in their seminal "three mountain study." They found that preoperational children (around the ages of 2 to 7 years) were unable to understand that their view of a visual display was different from someone else situated in a different viewing position. Since then, others have studied perspective taking and shown that children as young as 3 and 4 years perform well (e.g., Borke, 1975; Cox, 1975; Light, & Nix, 1983; Pillow, & Flavell, 1986).

Within the literature, there are two basic levels of perspective-taking ability beyond having no perspective-taking ability (Level 0). Children who have no perspective-taking skill discern what they see and assume that everyone else, regardless of viewing position, sees the same thing. At Level I, the child knows that a person standing in one position does not see the same thing as one who is in another viewing position. At Level II, the child knows that the person may see the same object but not the same parts of the object as someone with a different view. The child progresses from knowing *what* to understanding *how* visual perspectives may be different.

In the study, two more levels were established to accommodate advanced skills of perspective taking which might be relevant to the interpretation of visual media. Level III is demonstrated by the viewer knowing the viewpoint of the actor whose back is to the audience in the OS. Level IV specifically pertains to the viewer's ability to understand the subjective viewpoint in a CU—namely, the CU of one actor is the implied viewpoint of the other actor even though the actor is not visible.

Performances on the video task were compared to children's skill levels in a three-dimensional perspective-taking task. Figure 7–2 illustrates the "table task," in which dolls were situated around small blocks. On each side of the blocks were pictures (stickers) of familiar objects. The children were asked "yes" and "no" questions about what objects the dolls could see (e.g., "Does He-man see the heart?"). After they answered, they were placed at a level of ability. Score of children on performances in the table task was similar to that of the video task. The child who demonstrated knowledge of the visual perspectives at the first level understood what objects each character could see (e.g., He-man could see the elephant; Captain America could not see the flower). At the second level, children knew that each character saw the same object, but that they each saw different parts of the object. The highest level on the table task has been suggested in a study by Gzesh and Surber (1985) where children were asked to imagine, without actually seeing, a different perspective. At this highest level, the children accurately interpreted the *imagined* points of view of characters. For example, they correctly answered questions such as, "Pretend that Captain America is high up in the air over that block, and he's flying like Superman. Does he see the elephant's back?"

Results

Discriminant analyses were used in order to show how much the variables—table task performance, age, and sex—contributed to skill in comprehending the different changes in viewpoint on video. Age, followed by table task performance, contributed the most to performances on the video task. The average age for perspective takers (Levels I–IV) was 5 years 2

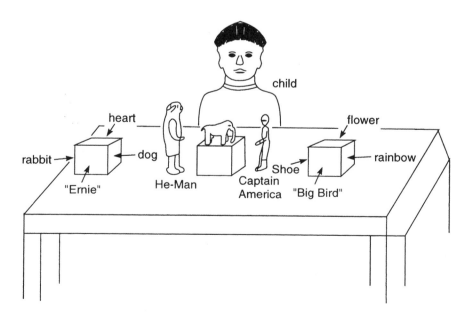

FIGURE 7–2 Three-dimensional display for table task

months; the average age of nonperspective takers (Level 0) was 4 years 3 months.

Experience with the medium of television did not influence the performances on the video task of this study. The children's parents were asked to record the number of hours their children watched TV in 1 week. Approximately one third of the sample responded to the task, and no relationship was found between these children's performances on the video task and the number of hours of television that they watched during a week.

The most important finding in the study supported the researcher's proposition that spatial intelligence is related to comprehension of the convention of changing viewpoints in television. Children who did well on the table perspective-taking task also performed at higher levels on the video task (i.e., Levels II–IV). These higher levels of ability in video perspective taking were demonstrated by children who could understand the more complicated shots in the televised scene. Thus, the argument may be made that in order for children to be skilled in following the changing viewpoints which occur in two-dimensional visual media such as film and television, they must first demonstrate competency as perspective takers in three-dimensional, actual situations. The data also suggest that spatial knowledge may be influenced by the viewer's understanding of changing perspectives on television.

POINT OF VIEW: STUDY 2

In a 1991 study on viewpoints by Comuntzis–Page, the LS and CU were examined in a segment of *Sesame Street* in which Bert and Ernie go to the movies. No OS shots were used in the segment, which makes the focus slightly different from the first study. The researcher questioned how young children interpreted the changes in points of view from shots of the muppets in the theater to shots of the film which the muppets are watching. For instance, could viewers understand that the muppets, not seen in the shots of the film, were indeed watching the screen? Did they understand that the muppets were watching a "movie"? How did the viewer interpret the CUs of the actors in the film?

Method

Thirty preschool-age children (mean age, 58.5 months) watched a videotaped segment of *Sesame Street* in which Bert and Ernie go to the cinema and join other muppets in the movie theater to watch a "Charlie Chaplin" film in which he has a romantic picnic with his female friend. The *Sesame Street* producer uses LSs and CUs to cut from shots of the muppets watching the movie to shots of the actors on the screen. The only connection with the audience in the theater during the shots of the movie screen occurs in Bert and Ernie's voice-over commentary. No over-the-shoulder shots, for instance, link the audience visually with the movie.

The experimenter paused the tape during various shots to assess whether children understood the different viewpoints from theater to movie screen. Questions such as, "Do you see the back of Bert's head?" "Does Ernie see Bert's nose?" were asked in the LS of the muppets in the theater . In the CUs of the actors in the film, viewers answered questions such as, "Does the man see the woman?" "Does Ernie see the woman?"

Scoring

As in the first study, children were classified according to their ability to understand various viewpoints on the videotape. The levels of ability were slightly modified in this study since there were no OS depictions in the segment. The three levels of ability included: Level I—The viewer determined that an actor in the shot may or may not have the same viewpoint as the viewer. Level II—The viewer understood that the actor saw things which the viewer did not see. For instance, children at Level II knew that Bert could see the back of the muppet who sat in front of Bert in the theater even though those children were not able to see the muppet's back. Level III—The viewer understood the point of view of an actor not at all visible in the CU. Children's performances on the table task (used in the first study), their age, and sex were used as independent variables in this study.

Results

Several variables distinguished those children who were at Levels I—III on the video task from those who had no understanding of different perspectives (Level 0). Again, age was a significant factor, with the average age being 5 years 5 months for Levels I—III and 3 years 8 months for Level 0. The average age of the children at Level I in the video task in this study was the same as that found in the first study—4 years 9 months.

The table task in the study was also an important factor in video task performance. Children who performed at higher levels in the video task also had a clear understanding of differences in perspectives in the table task. For those who were classified within the three levels of perspective taking on the video task, the average performance level in the table task was 2.8, almost at the third level, whereas the average level for those children who did not understand the televised points of view (Level 0) was 0.44 in the table task. Moreover, the performances of children at the first and second levels on the video task were not as strongly related to their age. Rather, those children at Levels I and II, who were able to understand the different perspectives of the actors in the videotaped scene, also performed at high levels on the table task. Thus, a relationship once again was found between visual literacy, demonstrated in this study by skill in determining different points of view of characters in a videotaped scene, and spatial knowledge within the three-dimensional, real world.

The findings from both this study and the previous one agree with Gardner's theory of multiple intelligences to the extent that perspective taking in real-world situations is a spatial skill that is related to changing viewpoints depicted in two-dimensional visual media. A third study by the present author examined another skill within the spatial realm—block building—to see if it, too, is relevant to young children's interpretations of visual media.

Developmental literature points to stages of block building, which advance, for the most part, by the experience a child (or adult) has with blocks and not so much by age. These stages are recognized by the qualities of constructions. Inexperienced block builders become more elaborate in their constructions as they progress through the stages. Seven stages have been described in elaborate detail by Johnson (1984); however, for the purposes of this study, three general levels were used: (l) blocks are put in simple patterns horizontally and/or stacked vertically; (2) blocks bridge and/or enclose spaces; and (3) blocks are placed in elaborate patterns, representations, and symbolizations (Isenberg, & Jalongo, 1984).

UNDERSTANDING THE SPACE OF MR. ROGERS' NEIGHBORHOOD

This study was the result of a comment heard in a PBS documentary by one of the producers of *Mr. Rogers' Neighborhood*. He said that little was known to them about how children make sense of the Neighborhood of Make-believe, a place where viewers are taken at some time during the program and where Mr. Rogers is the puppeteer for several puppets who interact with live actors. The researcher's purpose of the study was to look at how young children interpret the sequence of shots used to "transport" them from Mr. Rogers' living room to the Neighborhood of Make-believe and back to his living room. As in the previous two studies, a relationship was found between children's spatial intelligence, measured in this study by their block-building ability, and comprehension of the visuals depicted on television.

Method

Thirty-five 3- to 6-year-olds (average age, 59.6 months) participated in the study. Individually, they were interviewed by the researcher and her "Buddy, " a teddy bear. The children were asked to play for a while and show "Buddy" what they could do with the blocks in the room. After 5 minutes of block play, the researcher showed a segment of Mr. Rogers' show in which the trolley, in medium shots, goes from his living room, through what is presumably a tunnel, into the Neighborhood of Make-believe and back through the tunnel at the end of the segment.

After seeing the tape, the children were asked to reconstruct for "Buddy," who was not watching the tape, the scene of the trolley going from one space to another (i.e., to and from Mr. Rogers' living room and the Neighborhood of Make-believe). The researcher handed the child props that represented objects and actors in the segment and asked the child to place them on a table in the same way they were seen in the television. Slides were taken of the children's constructions of blocks and props to record what they did and to determine if a relationship existed between the two tasks.

Scoring

Children scored according to how accurately they reconstructed the spatial layout of Mr. Rogers' two neighborhoods. If they showed that they were only guessing or had no idea as to what was shown on the segment, the children scored nothing. They were categorized at the first level (Level I) for representing the space with two or more mistakes. If they made only one error in the placement of props, they were placed at Level II and if they made no mistakes, they were at Level III. Children's stage of block building, age, and sex were compared with their scores on the video task.

Results

Results from *t* tests revealed that the most important variable that contributed to the accurate reconstruction of Mr. Rogers' set was block-building stage. Children who performed well in putting each prop in the correct place to represent the spatial layout of Mr. Rogers' living room and Neighborhood of Make-believe were also at advanced stages of block building. Particularly, children performing at Levels I and II in the reconstruction task also were at higher stages of block building.

Age also contributed to the subjects' skills in representing the placement of objects in the televised space. Children at Levels I–III on the reconstruction task were considerably older (average age, 61.6 months) than those who were unable to understand anything about the spatial layout of Mr. Rogers' show (average age, 44.5 months).

Discussion

The study of Mr. Rogers' Neighborhood was a preliminary attempt to investigate the factors that may influence children's comprehension of the spatial layout of a televised scene. The results show that a relationship exists between visual literacy and block building. Since block building is an important skill within the spatial realm, the findings from this study lend support to the notion once again that processing visual information that is depicted in visual media is closely related to children's spatial knowledge in the real world.

THE INFLUENCE OF VISUAL LITERACY ON SPATIAL INTELLIGENCE

Studies on perspective taking and reconstruction of space in relation to comprehension of some of the forms and conventions of television have attempted to explain the effects of spatial intelligence on visual literacy. The reverse may also be true: Spatial intelligence may be affected by a person being more or less visually literate. Paul Messaris (1994) suggests, "… enhanced literacy in visual media might entail a reciprocal enhancement of spatial intelligence" (p. 125). Studies by Gavriel Salomon have explored this possibility.

Salomon's work is concerned with how and why formal features of media affect mental processes as they do. He carried out three experiments in which eighth graders were shown a painting by Brueghel. Sections of the painting were depicted by zooming in and out or by cutting, a method similar to that of the candy bar study by Acker and Tiemens (1981). The findings revealed that with the zoom, the children improved their recall of elements in the painting (Salomon, 1972). Salomon concluded that the children in these experiments used the conventions of media to help them understand more fully the visual information present in the painting. The study shows how a camera technique (zoom) can enhance a viewer's perception of a painting's elements. Thus, Salomon showed that, within the visual-spatial realm, experience with techniques used in one medium (film) may affect the comprehension of another medium (painting).

In another study, 76 ten- to eleven-year-olds viewed four different versions of an 8-minute televised film consisting of shots from various angles. Close-ups interchanged with long shots and zooms (Salomon, & Cohen, 1977). Children were more able to gather details when the zoom was used. The CU required them to glean information in bits and pieces and apply that information to the whole concept. On the other hand, the zoom enabled the children to see, without interruption, all the information as it related to the entire idea or object.

Salomon (1979) designed another investigation, reminiscent of the POV studies of Comuntzis, in which he hypothesized that the same improvements in spatial ability observed in his other studies could be repeated when he used the technique of changing viewpoints. His study, based on Piaget's "three mountain study," investigated what type of camera technique used for depicting different viewpoints would improve 7-year-olds' capacity to comprehend differences in perspectives.

Children in the study were assigned to one of four groups. The first condition was called "modeling" since it repeated the experience most viewers have in real-world situations—namely, they see the details of objects by walking around them and looking at them in one continuous motion. Modeling consisted of a film in which each of three familiar objects (a cup, a shoe, and an orange) was seen on a table in front of the viewer. A "smiley" face was placed behind each of the objects. A camera slowly moved around the table to where the face was and depicted "smiley's" viewpoint of each object.

A second condition was named "short-circuiting" because it jumped from one view of the object to another view. This condition was the same as the first except that instead of the camera's gradual movement, the 7-year-olds saw a slide of the initial position and a second slide of the final position of each rotation, which is similar to a cut used in film and television. The third condition was labeled "activation" since the viewers had to determine, without seeing, the various points of view. Activation consisted of slides of only the initial position; the viewers had to fill in the rest. The fourth condition had no treatment, only pretests and posttests which measured children's ability to change viewpoints in a three-dimensional display.

Results from this POV study by Salomon indicated that the activation and modeling groups did significantly better than the short-circuiting group, which, in turn, did better than the control group. The researcher also concluded that the effects of the treatment condition were related to mental capabilities: the activation condition enhanced performances of the already skillful; the modeling condition aided performances of the initially less skilled; and the short-circuiting only slightly supported the abilities of the more advanced children. Salomon suggested that a proper way to use these conventions to cultivate skills is first by modeling and later by activation (1979, p. 154).

Visual literacy, as the studies by Salomon show, involves various cognitive skills of the viewer and can be used to improve children's spatial intelligence. This proposition is also supported in a study by Chava Tidhar (1984) on the effects of filmmaking on children's cognitive skills. The author's purpose was to investigate the effects of the filmmaking experience on real-world spatial skills.

Eighty-seven fifth graders who participated in the study were placed into four different groups that learned to use photography, photography plus scenario design, photography plus editing, or the inclusion of all three activities. A fifth group was a control group that engaged in recreational activities unrelated to film or television. Pre- and posttests revealed that the 55-hour course had a significant effect on improving the spatial aptitudes of the students.

Tidhar concluded that "mastery of these skills is important for the development of literate consumers to the visual media" (p. 963). The researcher also suggested that other areas of knowledge might be supported and improved by learning these cinematic skills. Referring to the previous work by Lavin and Silver (1979), she cited evidence suggesting that when children who suffered from language deficits participated in art activities, their readiness for studying language, mathematics, and abstract thinking improved. Thus, being visually literate has an impact on spatial as well as other intelligences.

CONCLUSION

This chapter has shown how spatial intelligence relates to young viewers' knowledge of visual media. Given the predominance of television in our society, children everywhere are exposed to its many different forms and conventions. Therefore, the question of whether the experience with visual media influences their understandings of various mediated codes is a complicated one. What emerges from the findings, nevertheless, is that children's interpretation of these visual forms depends in large part on their individual abilities within the spatial realm. Those who know and operate comfortably in this area are apt to comprehend televised conventions better than those who are not as competent within the spatial realm.

The impact that visual literacy has on spatial capabilities is evident as well. This proposition may seem contradictory, given the argument that spatial intelligence may help create visual literacy. However, the relationship is reciprocal and spiraling: First, children develop basic skills in spatial intelligence; then, they become more literate in their comprehension of visual media which, in turn, contributes to improving their spatial capacities. Educators and others whose work centers around children should note the evidence of the investigations cited in this chapter and honor the important dance that takes place between spatial intelligence and visual literacy.

References

Acker, S., & Tiemens, R. (1981). Children's perception of changes in size of televised images. *Human Communication Research, 7*(4), 340–346.

Boden, M. (1979). *Jean Piaget.* New York: Viking.

Borke, H. (1975). Piaget's mountains revisited: Changes in the egocentric landscape. *Developmental Psychology, 11*(2), 240–243.

Calvert, S., Huston, A., Watkins, A., & Wright, J. (1982). The relation between selective attention to television forms and children's comprehension of content. *Child Development, 53,* 601–610.

Cox, M. (1975). The other observer in a perspective task. *British Journal of Educational Psychology, 45,* 83–85.

Flavell, J., Flavell, E., Green, F., & Wilcox, S. (1981). The development of three spatial perspective-taking rules. *Child Development, 52,* 356–358.

Gardner, H., (1983). *Frames of mind.* New York: Basic Books.

Gardner, H., (1993). *Multiple intelligences: The theory in practice.* New York: Basic Books.

Gzesh, S., & Surber, C. (1985). Visual perspective-taking skills in children. *Child Development, 56,* 1204–1213.

Isenberg, J., & Jalongo, M. (1984). *Creative expression and play in the early childhood curriculum.* New York: Macmillan.

Johnson, H. (1984). The art of block building. In E. Hirsh (Ed.), *The block book* (pp. 8–23). Washington, DC: NAEYC.

Lavin, C., & Silver, R. (1979). *Developing cognitive skills in handicapped children through art.* Paper presented at the annual interdisciplinary Conference on Piagetian Theory and its Implications for the Helping Professions (University Affiliated Program), University of Southern California, Los Angeles.

Light, P., & Nix, C. (1983). "Own view" versus "good view" in a perspective taking task. *Child Development, 54*(2), 480–483.

Messaris, P. (1994). *Visual "literacy." Image. mind and reality.* Boulder, CO: Westview Press.

Monaco, J. (1977). *How to read a film.* New York: Oxford University Press.

Piaget, J., & Inhelder, B. (1956). The child's conception of space (F. Langdon & J. Lunzen, Trans.). London: Routledge.

Pillow, B., & Flavell, J. (1986). Young children's knowledge of visual perception: Projective size and image. *Child Development, 57,* 125–135.

Salomon, G. (1972). Can we affect cognitive skills through media? An hypothesis and findings. *AVCR, 20*(4), 401–422.

Salomon, G. (1979). Shape, not only content. In E. Wartella (Ed.), *Children communicating: Media and development of thought, speech, and understanding* (pp. 53–82). Beverly Hills, CA: Sage.

Salomon, G., & Cohen, A. (1977). Television formats, mastery of mental skills and the acquisition of knowledge. *Journal of Educational Psychology, 69*(45), 612–619.

Schachter, D., & Gollin, E. (1979). Spatial perspective taking in young children. *Journal of Experimental Child Psychology, 27,* 467–478.

Singer, D., & Singer, J. (1981). Television and the developing imagination of the child. *Journal of Broadcasting, 25*(4), 373–387.

Smith, R., Anderson, D., & Fischer, C. (1985). Young children's comprehension on montage. *Child Development, 56*(4), 962–971.

Tidhar, C. (1984). Children communicating in cinematic codes: Effects on cognitive skills. *Journal of Educational Psychology, 76*(5), 957–965.

Wright, J., & Huston, A. (1983). A matter of form: Potentials of television for young viewers. *American Psychologist, 38,* 835–843.

·8·

EXPLORING FUTURE MEDIA

John Carey
GREYSTONE COMMUNICATIONS

What will the communication landscape look like 10 or 20 years into the future? Will it resemble a Buck Rogers or Star Trek world with tele-transportation, hologram telephones and other science fiction gadgets or will it resemble everyday life today? It appears that there will be many changes in the media landscape, for example, large-screen, high resolution TV sets; personal computers with audio, video and high resolution graphics capabilities; new forms of mobile communications; and many new interactive technologies. Further, some of these changes may have important political and social implications. For example, high definition TV may boost the prospects for politicians with a different personality/beauty quotient than the current generation of politicians. However, the media landscape in the next 10 to 20 years is not likely to fulfill the dreams of today's science fiction writers.

How can we get a handle on future media and the implications they may have for those who teach about media? It is difficult if not impossible to accurately predict future media development and adoption. No attempt will be made to predict the future in this chapter. An alternative approach to understanding future media is to analyze technology developments and media usage patterns that are already at work and assess the implications if these trends continue in the marketplace. This approach assumes that the not-too-distant future is staring us in the face if we will just take time to examine it.

This chapter examines some current technological developments and reviews possible effects associated with them. The technological developments include higher resolution images for television sets and personal computer display monitors; increased bandwidth in telephone and cable television systems; new networks linking personal computers and portable communication terminals; multimedia or the addition of new media channels such as audio and video to technologies that previously did not have such capabilities; and interactive media. Some of the issues associated with these technological developments include: changes in the production and design of content for new media; new possibilities for expressive communication in channels with greater bandwidth; adaptation of advertising to the new media environment; and changing characteristics of audience interactions with media.

TECHNOLOGICAL TRENDS

The telecommunications infrastructure in the United States is being upgraded at a very rapid pace (Kraushaar, 1994, pp. 1–5). This includes fiber-optic transmission, electronic digital switches, video servers and other components that increase the bandwidth or transmission capacity to schools, homes and businesses. Increased bandwidth linked with digital compression means that cable TV systems can have many more channels, telephone systems can carry video signals, and higher resolution images can be transmitted to TV sets, personal computer monitors and other display terminals. Higher resolution images include not only high-definition television (HDTV), which has been standardized, but also a broad spectrum of resolution enhancements that are possible in digital environments. In the future, a personal computer may display different types of visual information (e.g., text, graphics and video) with different degrees of resolution. Also, people may pay different prices for movies over fiber-optic cable based upon the resolution of the visual images, that is, movies delivered with higher resolution will require more bandwidth and therefore cost more.

At the same time, many new networks are coming into place. These include commercial on-line services and public networks such as the Internet. They also include private networks operated by state agencies and local area networks that link terminals in a school building or university campus. In addition, many of the new networks carry video via satellite or fiber-optic transmission for use in schools and businesses. The new networks link groups or communities of interest that are often geographically dispersed. Indeed, many of these communities were formed on the networks and would not have come into place without them.

With rapid technological change, it has also become more difficult to define media. The term multimedia has come into common usage to indicate a device that has some new capability. For example, a personal computer with a sound card or CD-ROM drive is often called a multimedia computer. The term multimedia implies that a device uses more than one medium to transmit or display information. In the past we gave such devices individualized names such as a television set. However, the evolution and upgrading of technology has been so rapid that there may be a reluctance to rename devices such as computers each year. The general trend captured by the term multimedia is nonetheless significant: commonplace technologies such as computers, telephones, radios and TVs are being upgraded to transmit or display additional media channels. For example, many radios and telephones can display text on small LED screens and many TVs can display a second channel superimposed as a window over the primary channel.

These technological developments are not taking place in the isolation of experimental laboratories. Many are moving quickly into homes, school and the work environment (Electronic Industries Association, 1994, pp. 5–35). The most important of the technologies entering these environments is undoubtedly the personal computer which can serve as a terminal for many present and future services. Indeed, the computer may become a household utility to provide a broad range of services much as a household stove is a utility for cooking many different types of meals.

Accompanying the diffusion of new technology, there has been a pattern of adopting multiple units of existing technologies. For example, the average U.S. home has two televisions, six radios and three telephones. Multiple units of a technology in homes support more individualized use of content. The old image of a family gathered around a television console in the living room has given way to family members spread throughout the house, each using personalized media. Similarly, in school environments, the number of personal computers per student has affected how they are used. With a very low computer-to-student ratio, the computer is largely a display device for teachers; with a moderate computer-to-student ratio, it becomes a time-shared work station; and with a high computer-to-student ratio, it becomes a personal tool of the student. The computer-to-student ratio increased steadily from the mid-1980s through the mid-1990s, thereby enhancing the computer's role as a personal tool of the student. However, poorer school districts still lag behind wealthier school districts in the number of computers available for instructional use, and many students still lack access to a personal computer (U.S. Department of Commerce, 1994, p. 169).

Interactive Media

Interactive media represent one of the most interesting technological developments. However, the term "interactive media" is used loosely and often inappropriately. It has become a popular term in advertisements for new technology and, like other catch phrases (e.g., "user friendly"), its relevance to a given technology can strain credibility. At the same time, it may be premature to set down a rigid definition, since the characteristics of many technologies are evolving rapidly. For discussion purposes, it may be argued that interactive media include technologies that provide:

- person-to-person communication mediated by a telecommunications channel, for example, a telephone call, fax, or e-mail;
- group communications mediated by a telecommunication channel, for example, audio, video and computer conferences;
- person-to-machine interactions that simulate an interpersonal communication exchange, for example, a student using a personal computer software package that simulates a student-teacher dialogue or a bank customer using an automated teller machine (ATM) that simulates a transaction with a teller; and,
- person-to-machine interactions with multiple action-response sequences, for example, playing a video game.

In addition, a traditional one-way medium such as broadcast radio or television can make use of an adjunct technology to provide an interactive component to programming. Radio call-in programs and automated voting by television viewers who call a special 900 telephone number are two examples. In California, one company has employed a specially transmitted data signal to provide an interactive component for television programs. A subscriber to this service uses a special terminal to play along with game shows and predict the action on sports programming.

The excitement and interest in interactive media appear to stem from several sources. First, many of the advances in technology over the past decade (along with lower costs and widespread adoption of some technologies) have provided a base for the development of new interactive services. Second, there is a reasonably good track record and a very strong economic carrot for interactive services in business, including interactive videodisc-based training, on-line information services, videoconferencing, e-mail and faxes, among other services. Third, there is considerable activity in the development of new interactive services for education (e.g., interactive television via satellite and pc-based multimedia) and many needs (e.g., rural education services and higher education courses for working adults) that can be addressed through interactive media (Carey, 1991, p. 11). Finally, in spite of a shaky start in the 1980s for interactive consumer services such as videotex, the on-line industry has developed a reasonably large consumer market and the Internet has grown dramatically.

Beyond these incentives for new services to address specific needs and generate revenue, there appear to be some important social motivations and communication values underlying our fascination with interactive media. Some interactive media offer an opportunity for more individuals to create communications: many individuals creating content for many other individuals. This may appeal to a democratic value for broad participation in public discussion about social and political events. In addition, interactive media often require users to participate actively in the selection and processing of information that is made available to them. Presumably, one cannot be a passive couch potato while using interactive media. Further, interactive media offer some opportunities to package and distribute information to highly specific groups of users. There are well-publicized examples of small software producers creating highly successful interactive services in basements or garages to the chagrin of large publishers and software producers. This may encourage us that the "little guy" can compete against large corporate entities in the interactive media arena (Thalhimer, 1994, p. 26).

Collectively, these values reflect a reaction against the forces that we associate with mass communication: large complex organizations creating public content that is distributed one-way to mass audiences. In this sense, the fascination with interactive media may represent a hope that they will enable us to break the control of one-way mass media on information and entertainment for the public.

IMPLICATIONS OF FUTURE MEDIA

The future media environment will affect many traditional media in terms of production, content and audience segmentation. For example, the reach of communication services will change. Among traditional mass media, some services have been targeting smaller audiences. In the next decade or two, other mass media services are likely to become more global, for example, some direct broadcast satellite services may be available in every country and some global newspapers may mix international, satellite-fed content with local content (all of which is printed locally). At the same time, some forms of interpersonal communication are expanding into wide-area group communication, for example, many e-mail systems have developed bulletin boards or conferences on topics. This information may be shared by a small group or hundreds of individuals spread across a wide region.

These trends suggest that over the next decade, the spectrum of information services is likely to be quite complex and the traditional communication taxonomies that the 20th century scholars have developed will have to be altered or replaced. A new classification system will have to include the reach of media (e.g., global, wide area, narrow area); access (e.g., public or private); characteristics of the audience (e.g., general or targeted); and direction of the information flow (e.g., one-way or interactive), among other characteristics and features.

Who Will Create Content?

Some of the most interesting questions about communication services in the future concern who will create them. Some academics and policy makers believe that the new technologies will help democratize media: they will break the traditional mass media model of information services in which a relatively small number of large institutions creates content for a mass audience. Presumably, desktop publishing and broadband switched networks will allow *many* groups to create information services for *many* distinct audiences. While this has occurred on the level of small-scale publishing,

it remains unclear whether traditional economic and marketplace forces will constrain such efforts on a larger scale. This is not to argue that small scale publishing of print or other materials will not have a powerful impact. It has been used to create and support revolutions; for example, Ayatollah Khomeini's use of audiocassettes to foment a revolution in Iran and Chinese students' use of fax to support their failed revolution in China. Further, desktop publishing has empowered many teachers to foment learning revolutions in the classroom.

In the future, more groups will be able to create and distribute information through private networks using new technologies and more groups will be able to create information for distribution on public networks such as the Internet. In the latter case, groups will create video press releases, packaged video segments for news programs, graphics and charts for newspapers, and so forth. This occurs now at a moderate level. In the future, it may flourish as technology empowers more groups to create such content. As a consequence, local producers of content such as teachers will have somewhat greater power relative to large publishers. At the same time, in other areas such as news production, the accuracy and reliability of diverse information sources may become a very contentious issue.

The broad public may also create content for news and other programming through their use of new technologies. A fiber-optic video network early in the next century may allow everyone watching a news program to respond instantly to questions posed by a reporter as well as vote at electronic town meetings. Prototype versions of such news programs and town meetings were tested in the 1970s, with mixed results (Becker, 1987, p. 120). Today, touchtone telephone can be used to obtain feedback from the public, but there is usually a delay of several hours or a day in receiving and tabulating the responses. In the future, instantaneous interactive formats will be available through fiber-optic technology. Even if the format is successful, it may prove to be a mixed blessing. The goal of soliciting broad public input to public affairs questions can be subsumed by media needs to entertain or political desires to manipulate public opinion.

At the other end of the scale, it is tempting to speculate about mergers among large media institutions and the convergence of mass media organizations with nonmedia organizations through their shared uses of communication technologies. What if news content were created not by traditional news organizations but rather by the Walt Disney Company, Bell Atlantic or a major international bank? This could occur in a few ways. First, major telecommunications organizations are developing large, multipurpose networks for consumers and, depending upon the regulatory climate, may produce news content for the networks. Such networks are likely to compete with traditional news organizations. Second, as major entertainment companies such as Walt Disney purchase broadcast networks and other companies with significant news operations, the traditional role of journalism may change. In an attempt to adapt to new technology environments such as DBS or fiber optics, the old guard of journalists in the news divisions might be swept aside and replaced by a new management team that would integrate news operations with other divisions in the parent organization. A company like Walt Disney may not want their brand image associated with "bad news." Third, a major bank or stock broker might develop specialized, private information services for their clients which, over time, could evolve into a general news operation in order to enhance the appeal of the service: the bank would serve "all your financial and information needs."

Within education, there have also been some attempts to merge entertainment and education content under the control of media conglomerates, for example, Whittle Communications' Channel One. While the results of early efforts have been mixed from economic, pedagogical and policy perspectives, the carrot for schools of gaining free services and equipment as well as the profit incentive for businesses will undoubtedly lead to many additional efforts.

One way or the other, industry convergence and new information services are likely to lead to some form of challenge to independent journalism over the next few decades along with challenges to public, nonprofit control over education services.

Narrow Audience Content

It appears likely that many current trends in how people use media will not only continue but flourish over the next few decades. These include multiple units of technologies in households, a greater number of choices for information and entertainment, and more portable media. Accompanying these trends, content will become more personalized or targeted for specific audiences. This is often called narrowcasting or, in an advertising context, direct marketing. However, there are economic constraints on some forms of narrowcasting (Neuman, 1991, pp. 145–163). The high costs associated with producing and distributing television programs are likely to constrain the number of cable channels that can be supported in the marketplace. Similarly, rising postal rates may inhibit some forms of direct marketing.

In an electronic information environment, for example, an on-line service or the Internet, there are fewer constraints in targeting information at the level of an individual user. Moreover, developments in artificial intelligence will assist in processing specific content for specific individuals: systems will grow in their knowledge about individuals over time, by analyzing records of a consumer's usage patterns, and present desired content or advertising that is targeted for specific types of users. Indeed, the use of artificial intelligence to process information requests, develop profiles of users and present targeted information to consumers may become a significant component in the media environment over the next two decades.

The Effects of Technology on Information Formats and Style

The shape of content (format, style, length, etc.) is influenced by the characteristics of the technology employed to communicate it. Television news formats differ from newspaper content, in part, because television can present powerful moving images but relatively few words while newspapers can present more words about a given story but limited visual images. What characteristics of communication technologies in the decades ahead are likely to shape future content? A technological infrastructure with fiber to the home and HDTV display screens will support highly detailed graphics and more data on the screen than is possible now. For this reason, the current trend of using more graphics and statistics in news, especially sports news, may flourish in the future technology environment. Fiber-optic technology will also support interactive services (e.g., live audience responses to questions posed in news programs) and on-demand services (e.g., ordering a specific movie to be delivered on a fiber-optic channel).

In addition, the use of personal computer memory to store text and video monitors to display text information has led to a number of important but subtle effects on information formats and style. For example, in an electronic text environment, the screen is a unit of content, just as a paragraph is a unit of content in a newspaper story. Similarly, the flow of information from one screen to another (e.g., tree and branching structure vs. hypercard stacks) affects the attention given to content items as well as the perceived relationship between different items. Indeed, an on-line text system is a distinct new medium and requires a different writing style as well as organization of content. Relatively few educators have begun to teach writing for screen-based text and relatively little research has addressed how students process information retrieved from data bases. For example, do students apply a critical perspective to information retrieved from data bases or do they accept it as true and accurate merely because it is stored in a computer?

One of the more dramatic features of HDTV has received relatively little attention—it displays skin tones and minor facial movements that are not readily captured on NTSC, even during a close-up shot. Minor changes in skin coloration can signal anger, excitement and other emotions. Minor facial movements convey a wide range of information and often provide clues concerning how a speaker feels about what he or she is saying. It remains unclear how program directors will use these screen characteristics or how viewers will interpret the new visual information.

Similarly, future large screens and wide screens with high resolution will offer an opportunity for our eyes to function as they do in face-to-face settings. That is, the screen will be able to display a large, high resolution panorama and each participant will be able to focus on large or small areas within the screen. Further, in a video windows environment, it may be possible to employ different resolutions for different visual elements on the screen; for example, the face of a speaker might be in one window with a very high resolution while the background screen might show other participants at a lower resolution.

The manipulation of time and space—through editing, slow motion, speeded up motion, etc.—can control how viewers perceive objects and actions. A viewer can see patterns that would not be perceived in everyday viewing of an object or action. Editing can also present multiple stories for a viewer and move the viewer instantly into the past or the future. When rendered creatively, these features can communicate or evoke exhilaration, surprise and fascination. These characteristics of motion video have been available to designers for a long time through film and videotape. The new opportunity in the emerging multimedia environment will be to add user interaction as a design element. That is, a user can choose options about what to see and control the speed of the action. A user could also maneuver through content and edit together a story or gain a unique perspective about the stored content.

Enhancements to screen size and screen resolution as well as the possibility of utilizing multiple screens or multiple windows within a single screen will provide new tools for educators in designing audiovisual materials for the classroom. In distance learning, for example, teachers and students will be able to see details that were difficult to display in earlier media. Further, it will be possible to create a virtual classroom in which viewers' eyes move freely across a field of vision where previously the camera had to move as a surrogate for the eye.

Associated with these developments are many questions about the "language" of new visual media. For example, some of the new multimedia systems use icons and virtual space to represent categories of content and guide users to the programming. How do people interpret icons and determine how to move through virtual space? Further, how does the cognitive processing of new visual media relate to the ways people interpret and process traditional still pictures, film and television (Messaris, 1994, pp. 41–112)?

Content for Interactive Television

In the commercial world of interactive television developers, there has been much discussion about potential "killer applications"—services or content that will be very attractive to consumers and will drive interactive television into millions of homes. Movies-on-demand and interactive games are two candidate killer applications. However, it may be the case that there are no killer applications and that a critical mass of services will be required to attract large numbers of households. Historically, some media have benefited from so-called killer applications (e.g., pay movie channels helped cable grow during the great expansion period of the 1970s) while other media have required a critical mass of titles or applications (e.g., compact disc players and VCRs).

It is also useful to ask if anyone would be able to recognize a new and original killer application if one were to be created. As Marshall McLuhan noted a few decades ago, we tend to fill new media with content from earlier media (McLuhan, 1964, pp. 259–268). Thus, early radio was filled with vaudeville acts and early television was filled with radio shows that had been converted to a television format. Virtually every proposed service for interactive television is a modified version of content or a service that already exists: movies-on-demand is really a videocassette rental service directly to the home; most of the proposed interactive home shopping channels are variations on existing shopping channels or a video rendition

of catalogue shopping; and interactive games between households will allow two people to play a game together in different locations instead of in the same room. These are enhancements to existing services, and they may be very attractive. But they are not bold new applications for a new medium. If history repeats itself, genuinely new applications will not emerge for a few years and they will not be recognized as creative innovations for an even longer period of time.

Advertising

Advertising may play a crucial role in the development of interactive television. Interactive television commercials can provide many new features for advertisers and consumers alike. For example, consumers could choose which commercial they wish to watch or which version of a commercial to watch. Commercials can offer contests in which a viewer might learn instantly if she or he has won a prize. Also, consumers can instantly request additional information or actually make a purchase during a commercial. These features may make commercials more appealing to viewers and potentially reduce channel switching behavior during commercials.

It is intriguing to ask what radical new forms of advertising might emerge in an interactive television environment? British Airways has developed a novel interactive commercial for theatres in the UK. On screen, a couple is walking through a park in Paris. Suddenly, a woman in the theatre shouts, "That's my boyfriend. That's Nigel." The onscreen boyfriend turns to the camera and says, "Michelle, I can explain everything." The interaction then continues between the boyfriend on screen and the woman who was planted in the theatre. This novel and creative commercial requires considerable logistical support in a theatre environment. However, the concept lends itself quite well to an interactive television environment, that is, speaking to narrow audience segments (in the near term) and potentially to each individual viewer (in the long term). More important, the commercial provides an example of a radical departure from the norm.

Other trends in advertising involve mixing commercials and content on the same screen (e.g., the commercial appears in a window over programming) as a way to reduce channel surfing; superimposing commercial messages or symbols within content (e.g., digitally inserting a Coca Cola logo onto a basketball court at selected points during a game); and dispensing coupons during commercials via printers attached to TV sets. For students and media researchers alike these trends raise several questions. What impact will these techniques have upon the acceptance, believability and influence of commercials? Will the distinction between commercial messages and program content be further blurred for viewers? Are people more likely to be affected by a commercial if they participate in it?

The Consumer of Interactive Media

Do consumers want to interact with television? Interactive television appears to fly in the face of the so-called "couch potato" stereotype for television viewers. If television viewers are so passive, what interest would they have in interacting with television programs? Of course, the stereotype of a passive, helpless viewer is a disputed concept (Neuman, 1991, pp. 80–85). Some researchers argue that TV viewers have always responded, directly or indirectly, to what they view. Further, there are many examples of viewers responding in large numbers to interactive telephone response polls in news programming and after major political speeches. In addition, the well-documented channel changing behavior of many viewers may be considered a simple form of interacting with television.

Nonetheless, the basic question of mass consumer appetite for interactive television remains unanswered. Further, what differences will we find among demographic groups? Will interactive television appeal more to males, as have on-line services and video games? Will usage skew toward younger audiences? A related question concerns the ability to maneuver through interactive systems. Will viewers who have experience with personal computers and automated teller machines find interactive television easier to use than those who do not have experience with other interactive technologies?

CONCLUSIONS

The adoption and use of future media technologies may provide us with an opportunity to study many important components of mediated communication. There is a large body of research that has examined mass media behavior and production conventions. However, an examination of consumer behavior and production conventions for interactive television and other new media is just beginning. A few of the issues that are likely to be addressed include: the growing sophistication of graphics in interactive systems and the reliance on them to convey meaning that was previously conveyed in text; the development of user behaviors in situations where there is/is not training or instructions on how to use a system; borrowing of conventions from older media in new multimedia systems; and, efficiency mechanisms (i.e., ways in which conventionalized messages can, over time, be communicated more quickly or simply).

For those who study the theoretical components of visual literacy, the new media will provide a rich laboratory for examining fundamental issues. For example, research scholars have devoted a great deal of energy to the exploration of visual communication processes that were at work in the early days of film and television. Through this research, they have tried to understand what components of visual literacy are based upon cognition and which components are learned (Messaris, 1994, pp. 14–21). With interactive visual media and other forms of multimedia, there will be an opportunity to study these issues in new contexts.

In the commercial marketplace, prospects for the future media environment are strong. There has been a growth in penetration of technologies (in homes, schools, and businesses) that will enable many to use interactive services, an improved telecommunications infrastructure to support the delivery of interactive services, and more experience in the design and marketing of interactive services. However, optimism must be tempered by the mixed track record of previous interactive technologies and uncertainty about current appetites for the new services that will be offered. In addition, some of the hopes and promises that are linked to the new media environment may not be realized. For example, the hope that new interactive media will lead to more information sources and greater diversity in content may fall short as traditional economic and institutional forces work upon the new multimedia environment.

From a teaching perspective, future media present many opportunities. There are both an opportunity and a strong need to train students about interactive media: what are the characteristics of these media; how does one write or design content for them; and, what social effects are associated with them; among other issues? In addition, the professional goals that teachers set for students and students set for themselves may change. While it is likely that many journalism and communication students will eventually create interactive multimedia services for great metropolitan newspapers or broadcast networks, it is just as likely that many students will create such services for telephone companies, computer software companies and noncommunication corporations such as banks or insurance companies.

References

Becker, L. (1987). A decade of research on interactive cable. In W. Dutton, J. Blumer, & K. Kraemer (Eds.), *Wired cities: Shaping the future of communications*. Boston: GK Hall.

Carey, J. (1991). Plato at the keyboard: Telecommunications technology and education policy. *The Annals of the American Academy of Political and Social Science, 514,* 11–21.

Electronic Industries Association (1994). *Electronic market data book*. Washington, DC: Electronic Industries Association.

Kraushaar, J. (1994). *Fiber deployment update*. Washington, DC: FCC Common Carrier Bureau.

McLuhan, M. (1964). *Understanding media: The extensions of man*. New York: McGraw Hill.

Messaris, P. (1994). *Visual "literacy" image, mind and reality*. Boulder, CO: Westview Press.

Neuman, W. R. (1991). *The future of the mass audience*. New York: Cambridge University Press.

Thalhimer, M. (1994). On-line on the internet. *Separating fact from fiction on the information superhighway*. New York: Freedom Forum Media Studies Center at Columbia University.

U.S. Department of Commerce (1994). *Statistical abstract of the United States*. Washington, DC: Bureau of the Census.

·9·

BALANCING ACT: USING DRAMA TO EVEN THE EXCHANGE OF INFORMATION IN THE CLASSROOM

Jennifer Lynn Wolf

COTATI-RHONERT PARK UNIFIED SCHOOL DISTRICT, SONOMA COUNTY, CALIFORNIA

Do you think that to believe in the imaginative fiction of another person, and bring it to life, is a trifle? That is what we do to the work of the dramatist; we bring to life what is hidden under the words; we put our own thoughts into the author's lines, and we establish our own relationships to other characters in the play, and the conditions of their lives; we filter through ourselves all the materials that we receive from the author and the director; we work over them, supplementing them out of our own imagination. The material becomes part of us, spiritually, and even physically; our emotions are sincere, and as a final result we have truly productive activity. (Constantin Stanislavski, 1936, p. 52)

The exchange of knowledge in our classrooms too often flows in one direction only, dispersed unidirectionally from the teacher to the student. As a result, students may have little opportunity to "bring to life what is hidden under the words" or to filter themselves through the information given them. The result is too often work that is not "truly productive." Recent classroom research has suggested innovative and imaginative ways of rerouting the flow of information in the classroom by asking students to take on the responsibility for teaching one another, through cooperative learning (Kagan, 1990), peer editing (Reif, 1992), reciprocal learning (Campione, Rutherford, Gordon, Walker, & Brown, in press) and peer tutoring (Heath, & Mangiola, 1992). Teachers and their partners in education have also been exploring successful ways for students to gather information from primary sources outside of the classroom: elders who know history from a unique perspective; professionals who mentor students in school-arranged jobs; members of ethnic communities who add multi-cultural information to the curriculum; guest artists who can assist students in the creative process. These approaches relieve the teacher from the burden of being the sole source of knowledge; instead, she becomes a kind of academic coach, designing and coordinating lessons within school curricula, facilitating new learning partnerships, providing supplementary information, observing, assisting, and evaluating student learners on an individual and as-needed basis.

In addition to dispensing knowledge to students and coaching students' gathering of knowledge, the teacher can also turn to students as a source of knowledge. In other words, the classroom can be structured so that information flows equally, or nearly equally, between the students and the teacher, so that the students and teacher share the responsibility of educating one another, each providing information that the other needs but does not have. As Stanislavski's words suggest, drama is an artistic process dependent upon such a reciprocal flow of information between its participants. Each brings knowledge and abilities that the others need in order to create a successful production. The playwright brings the language of the play's characters; the actors, the "sincere emotions" and imagination with which to bring the characters' words to life; and the director, the "materials" to fuse the relationships on stage into a polished performance.

Drama, then, with its plural emphases on reading, writing, speaking, and creating is a communicative art well-suited to increasing student literacy while at the same time improving the pedagogy that teaches it. This chapter argues that drama promotes the reciprocal exchange of information between students and teacher in four identifiable, and often overlapping, ways. Drama in the classroom: (1) brings missing information to the curriculum; (2) encourages understanding of multiple points of view and truths; (3) promotes creative problem solving through healthy interdependence; and (4) offers the satisfaction of genuine achievement.

Each of these four reasons for teaching drama is explored from two perspectives, that of drama theory and that of contemporary drama practice in classrooms and youth groups. The classical drama theory describes a type of drama that is most often about producing scripted three-act plays containing a protagonist, antagonist, conflict, and climax, that is character-based, that has been influenced by Method Acting, and that assumes a formal relationship with the audience. This is the kind of drama most often produced on American stages and taught in universities and theater academies. The contemporary drama projects described in this chapter have been observed as part of the research project *Learning for Anything Everyday*, which is looking at successful neighborhood-based, inner-city youth groups (Heath, & McLaughlin, 1993; McLaughlin, Irby, & Langman, 1994), and in the course of the author's experiences while teaching drama in an inner-city high school. While each contemporary theater group and class observed is unique, their work hangs together on recognizably common elements: the young actors perform their own original work, they perform their work as an ensemble, and their work is often experience-based; their work is about communicating the messages of their own lives to community audiences, with whom they often also discuss their work directly after the performance is completed. Although the contemporary drama groups cited and described here clearly reveal a knowledge and use of the elements of classical drama theory, they also reveal a unique theater aesthetic. These drama groups have selected what they need from an existing theory and improvised on it to forge a new art form that better suits their needs. They provide us with excellent examples of learning through drama as well as fine examples of students who can regulate the flow of information around them, taking in teachers' ideas and providing in exchange new ideas of their own.

BRINGING MISSING INFORMATION INTO THE CURRICULUM

Drama, perhaps more than any other art form, is about bringing new voices to an audience, about publishing others' words in performance. It is about communication—among characters, within the community of plays and playwrights, from the artists to the audience. In coming to a performance, the audience is expected to carefully observe and seriously consider new voices and new ideas. Kathleen George (1994) advises beginning playwrights to start the process by communicating among themselves so that they will be better prepared to communicate with others. Her list of prewriting "key questions":

What makes you angriest?
What makes you happiest?
What is your definition of a good life?
What is your concept of a spiritual dilemma?
What do you care about?
What would you risk your life for?
What makes you laugh? (p. xiii)

This list reinforces the notion of dramatic art as a responsibility to bring one's unique knowledge into the larger conversation.

When used as a lens through which to view plays of today's stage, George's questions focus attention on drama as an artistic tool for broadening conversations with audiences to include a wide range of new, controversial, and old ideas. Recent Pulitzer prize winning plays reveal as well as any drama's ability to serve nontraditional issues inside traditional ones to an audience. August Wilson's trilogy of generation plays—*Joe Turner, Ma Rainey's Black Bottom*, and *Fences*—is the beginning of "a cycle of plays designed to resurrect black voices from every decade of this century" (Moyers, 1989, p. 167). *The Kentucky Cycle* explores how the "settling" of European Americans in the Midwest was also the "unsettling" of the Native Americans. And Tony Kushner's *Angels in America* plays ask their audiences to simultaneously see people with AIDS as victims of a hard disease and as the best hope for defeating it.

Powerful plays like these also illustrate that drama communicates its new ideas through characters; characters who are like us in some ways, and also noticeably different from ourselves, thereby creating an interest in watching the play. Voices which speak compellingly to us from the stage may well be ones we would not listen to were we not sitting in seats facing a staged performance: *The Zoo Story's* insistent, homeless man in Central Park; *'Night Mother's* reclusive, suicidal epileptic; *The Woman Warrior's* young Chinese American who relinquishes her ability to speak in the confusion of her dual-cultural existence. Playwright Kathleen Betsko speaks clearly in her own, unique voice about the responsibility she feels to bring to audiences the stories of the working-class coal mining women who would otherwise be isolated from the conversations of the theater:

> I ended up as a playwright so that I can carry my old buddies around in three-D, have them talk to me on stage, pee my pants laughing with them as I used to. Many of them were as talented as me or more so. But they had too many problems, or Brown Lung, or a pack of kids at their knees, or unemployed husbands they couldn't leave to race off and get an education. But they gave me their vital language, their down-to-earth philosophies, and I hope I carry it all on. (Betsko, & Koenig, 1987, p. 56)

For August Wilson, characters demand that he represent them, that he give voice to their ideas that have so long been excluded from the conversation of the mainstream. His description of the play writing process acknowledges that acting as the bearer of missing information requires courage as you fuse your own self with the others who have been excluded:

> I crawl up inside the material, and I get so immersed in it that as I'm inventing this world, I'm also becoming part of it. You discover that you're walking down this landscape of the self, and you have to be willing to confront whatever it is that you discover there. The idea is to emerge at the end of the landscape with something larger than what you had when you went in—something that is part of the illumination of the truth. (Moyers, 1989, p. 178)

That drama is about the responsibility to bring new and excluded voices to the stage offers hope to educators. Teachers who teach ethnically, linguistically, religiously, sexually, and economically diverse classes know first hand that the stories, histories and dramas of their students' lives are all too often missing from the textbooks, reading lists, standardized tests, library catalogues and curricula which they are assigned to use. Even after a school or district realizes that a gap of missing information exists in the curriculum, there is most often substantial lag time between acknowledging the gap and providing the missing information in a useful, respectful way.

Teachers who know that they have already waited too long for the information that is missing from their curriculum, have a primary source of information available for immediate use inside their classrooms. Communicative arts teachers can use drama to invite students to bring the knowledge of their lives into the classroom in exchange for the knowledge that the teacher brings, and together they can create a more complete curriculum. In youth groups and classes in which the goal is to produce an original dramatic production, young performers become responsible for examining their own lives, opinions, and values in pursuit of an idea for a play, for creating characters and plots which bring their information to life in a compelling way, and for examining and rehearsing their ideas until they are worthy of formal presentation before others. In urban and inner-city areas across the United States, young people are learning that their unique knowledge is worthy of production.

In the last 3 years a group of Hmong teenagers in the Twin Cities of Minnesota have gathered together with a former teacher to produce ensemble plays about their experiences while immigrating to a new land and their memories of their first land (Hmong Theater Project, 1994; Hmong Youth Cultural Awareness Project, 1994). Each of the shows which they have written and performed has begun with the director asking the teen actors the question "What do you want to say?" Their most recent production is a dramatic collage of Hmong folktales which the students collected by interviewing community elders. Centered around the story of an orphan boy who is blessed with a dragon Princess for a wife until he takes her for granted, the play examines universal themes of trickery, greed, regret, and family love from a distinctly Hmong-American perspective. The actors are dressed in Hmong clothing and Birkenstock sandals, speak their lines in a combination of Hmong and English, play music on a makeshift orchestra of clay garden pots inspired by the gamelan orchestras of Southeast Asia, and perform to entertain an audience of both Hmong Americans and European Americans. After each performance, the Hmong players sit informally on the stage, inviting audience members to ask questions and adding to the information that they have just presented dramatically. They are careful to point out what they see as the most unique feature of their play—that they have scripted it. The students take pride in having not only collected their culture's stories, but also translated them to the permanence of the written word, an especially unusual act in a culture that for the majority of its existence has relied solely on oral language. As far as they know, their script is the only one of its kind, and the Hmong players clearly feel a responsibility as brokers of its cultural information.

A deaf teen actor and member of Central Touring Theater, an acting company which operates out of an urban high school in Minnesota, has taken on a similar responsibility of authoring a one-woman one-act play for her company's play writing festival. Typed in the same abbreviated language that the playwright uses to talk on her TTD phone system, her play *Sounds of Silence* (Hogue, 1994) begins with her protagonist taking pity on the audience for being deaf—deaf to her sign language. When she realizes that the audience cannot understand her signing of the lyrics to the Simon and Garfunkel song, she turns on a tape of the song to accompany her signing and asks the audience "Is that better?" This method of forcing an audience to take on a role other than their own (here the role of a deaf person) is a theatrically sophisticated means of bringing forth a message which the playwright feels has too long been kept from the general understanding: that the experience of being deaf is something from which hearing people could benefit. To illustrate her point, her opening monologue tells the story of the monarch butterflies which migrate over two thousand miles to the high mountain forests of Mexico. Once the butterflies arrive, the sound of their many wings beating back and forth in the trees where they land to recuperate is both the sound of silence and a sound which communicates.

Later in the play the protagonist takes on those who accuse her of being "not deaf enough" because she attends a hearing school, and those who ask her in ignorance how she can memorize her lines and drive a car, always coming back to the point that her deafness is only a handicap in the eyes of those who do not possess enough knowledge to see otherwise, those who have not known how to understand the silence of deaf communication.

Theater endeavors such as these offer fine examples of student artists offering new information to their audiences as well as exchanging information collaboratively with their adult directors. The Hmong players look to their director for the beginning question which provides the framework for considering the unique information they possess, as he then looks to them for their answers as the basis for the play.

ENCOURAGING UNDERSTANDING OF MULTIPLE TRUTHS AND POINTS OF VIEW

In the words of drama educator Dorothy Heathcote (1984, p. 79), "We begin this practice of playing [drama] at an early age because we realize that identifying with others is a human act of which we are capable." What Heathcote sees as instinctive human behavior—the desire to understand others by comparing and contrasting them to ourselves—Stanislavski pointed to as the basis of drama. He extended a curiosity about others into "a prime requirement for an actor," titled it "Characterization," and described it as "reincarnation" and "a real transformation—of body and soul" (Stanislavski, 1924, p. 33). A Russian acting teacher in the early 1900s, he observed and interviewed the greatest actors of his day, gathering methods that his students could use to convince audiences that they were someone other than themselves.

Actors today still subscribe to his method of acting for the guidance it offers in using the experiences and memories of one's life as an entry point into living the life of another on stage.

This is a fundamental challenge of acting—locating the place at which the actor and the character can meet and begin the process of creation. Regardless of the method of training the actor uses, the development of convincing real and imaginary others is a rigorous artistic challenge, one that draws on detailed observation, authentic research, and laborious repetition. The well-used textbook *Acting is Believing* (McGaw, 1980) establishes observation as the first step of characterization. One of its beginning exercises (p. 76) assigns students to "visit a busy railway station, hotel lobby or some other place where you will have opportunity to observe different people." Observation of others provides the actor with the raw material with which to build a character who is more than just a series of actions: "Practice reproducing the observed details until you can do them accurately, until you feel you have captured some of the inner quality of the person." The expectation is that observation and repetition will lead the actor to the construction of a complete other person—one the actor knows so well as to be able to predict his or her behaviors and decisions: "Prepare a short scene for which you supply circumstances leading to action that you believe would be true of the character you create."

Northwestern University acting professor Bud Beyer begins his students on the journey of characterization by sending them to the zoo (Mekler, 1987). Here they are instructed, over a period of several visits, to chose an animal with which they feel a particular affiliation, and take notes on every detail they can possibly observe—"qualities of the spine, fluidity or rigidity, explosiveness of movement, the center of gravity, the breathing rhythms, the sensory alignment, the primary sense that the animal uses" (p. 318). Students are even encouraged to interview and observe the zoo keepers. When students finally present their animals in class, Beyer challenges them by interacting with them in unexpected ways that force them to improvise and raise the question—do they respond as the animal or themselves? In other words, how well do they understand the (animal) other they have been observing? A second other is created in the final stage of Beyer's exercise, when he asks his students "without much forewarning … to begin to move out of the animal into a human form, carrying with them as many qualities of the animal as they can" (p. 318). This exercise demands a layering of points of view, finding an animal that has a bit of the actor in it, then creating an animal in which the actor is not visible, and then creating a third person who is something of the two previous characters and again something unique. The point of the exercise, says Beyer, "is to demonstrate the capacity of transformation that is possible by careful work" (p. 319).

Acting professor, playwright, and actor Anna Devere Smith (1993) warns that actors who do not work carefully enough at characterization fall into the trap of forcing the "character to walk in the *actor's shoes*." For Devere Smith "the spirit of acting is the *travel* from the self to the other," and she is interested in exploring with her students what prevents them from making this journey of characterization successfully. She asks how inhibitions affect our ability to empathize.

> If I have an inhibition about acting like a man, it may also point to an inhibition I have about seeing a man or hearing a man. To develop a voice one must develop an ear. To complete an action, one must develop a clear vision. (p. xxvii)

South American theater activist and teacher Augusto Boal (1992) urges his students to progress beyond "the starting point" of feeling the character's emotions to a more complete kind of empathy. "Exercises must be done," he says, only with "the aim of 'understanding' the experience, not simply feeling it. [Actors] must know why a person is moved, what is the nature of this emotion, what its causes are—not limit [them] selves simply to the how" (p. 44).

Understanding, empathy and a clear vision are qualities that mark successful teachers and students as well as actors. Teachers who listen carefully and take the time to observe their students as individuals gather the information they need to design lessons and present information in ways that are appealing and logically connected to the students' lives. Students who understand what is important to the teacher and how she approaches information are better able to ask questions that get answers and present what they have learned in a way that can be appreciated. And in the classroom that contains a diversity of perspectives, the ability to accept multiple points of view is essential for both students and teachers if everyone is to be welcomed equally into the learning process.

At the same time, however, numerous scholars and critics have pointed out how understanding of multiple truths (Gardner, 1991; Rose, 1989; Witherall, & Noddings, 1991) is stifled by the structure of our classrooms. Curricula with strictly defined "scope and sequence" imply that knowledge is attained by traveling down a single path; standardized tests send a clear message that problems have one right answer; textbooks too often present single methods of explanation for complex situations; and our grading system reduces student achievements to a single, quantifiable mark. While our jobs, relationships, and daily lives present us with problems which require an understanding of multiple points of view to arrive at solutions, our classrooms do not.

Students in classrooms and youth groups where drama is used are not only offered an abundance of situations in which to practice understanding multiple points of view, but are also given the responsibility of presenting a variety of perspectives on stage. In a beginning drama class in Central High School in St. Paul, Minnesota, teacher Jan Mandell assigns students the task of developing and performing a short play that communicates to the audience some of their views on life. Through the process of improvisation and group discussion, the class discovers that they can not come to agreement on how they view the life that they are supposed to present on stage. Some students are frustrated with the violence, anger, and racism, which they see as increasing in their lives; others feel a responsibility to actively seek out the positive components of their lives and learn from them. What are the consequences, they wonder, of accepting and presenting a truth that is too negative? Too positive? How can they include both points of view?

Their discussions ultimately lead to a group-authored, one-act play entitled *Judgment Day* (Central Touring Theater, 1994) in which a group of omniscient beings comes to earth to decide whether humanity should be destroyed for its flaws or preserved for its good qualities. Their task is to collect instances of human behavior that support either argument and present them to a head "Watcher" who makes a final decision at the end of the play. This framework requires the students in the drama class to become Watchers themselves, collecting the events in their own lives which can be seen from two different perspectives. A fight in the hallway shows how violent and selfish adolescents can be, until the scene is extended to reveal conflict resolution through the use of a peer counselor. Healthy families are contrasted with unhealthy families; violence in a football game is contrasted with violence on the streets; the energy gang members spend destroying a neighborhood is juxtaposed against the energy a church puts into saving its community. All student actors are required to take on a number of roles within the play, to experience acting as human beings at their best and at their worst. In addition, the actors take on the role of Watcher, a characterization which results in judging their own behavior from a third perspective. Their decision at the end of the play? One that allows for multiple truths to coexist:

> TOP WATCHER: I am very pleased with the savers and the destroyers of this case. I have come to a decision. I have decided to save and destroy America. We will come down, freeze dry America and turn it into a museum so that future generations can continue to learn from their mistakes.

The notion that drama is an art of multiple perspectives is also illustrated by a play submitted to the UC Berkeley New Plays Projects. Young playwright Joseph Brouillete not only wanted to bring to the stage information that has long been excluded from it, but was also determined to present the information from a variety of viewpoints. The result is his original one-act play, *20 Questions* (1994), which tells the story of coming out as a gay man interspliced and woven together with twenty monologues of gay men telling their own coming out stories. In his program notes the playwright is careful to explain that the play contains perspectives other than his own, that the monologues, instead of being of his own devising, come from interviews he conducted. Not all the men cast in the play are gay, and not all the gay men cast in the play are cast to deliver monologues which reflect their own experiences of coming out. Instead, each is required to find the elements within himself that allow him to relate to his character and use this as a basis for taking on the traits of another.

In San Francisco a small youth group of eight girls, directed by the author of this chapter, has taken on the task of creating a play which will show others what it is like to go to school in the inner city. The Director's Notes from their play program, describing how the play came about, reveal the girls' overriding concern for multiple truths:

> In talking the girls came to three conclusions about their play-to-be:
> 1. They wanted to balance the good and the bad of going to school in the city, to be realistic while breaking down stereotypes;

> 2. They wanted to protect people's privacy—to tell the stories of going to school in the city, rather than the story of one person who goes to school in the city;
> 3. They wanted to tell their story by their own book—in their own words and in their own style, not by someone else's formula or expectations.

The result of their concerns is a one-act ensemble play examining six different aspects of school life from a multitude of viewpoints. In the first scene, each actor describes how she gets to school in the morning. The monologues illustrate as much about each girl as they do about methods of transportation:

> A1: To get to school I catch the 44 at Hudson and Ingles. There's cockroaches on the bus. When they crawl outta them vents everyone yells, "Oooh! Step on em! Step on em!" but I just step outta the way cause I hate the way they crunch.

> A2: I walk 8 blocks up to 18th Street to Castro and Market where I take the empty 37 at 7:30 AM. The fog makes it a clean and quiet time of day.

> A3: I catch the 44 at 9th and Lawton at 7:45 or sometimes later. If there's ever a seat I might sit down and study for English. Otherwise I just stand up and hold on and try not to fall on anyone.

In the play's second scene, "Tardy," the girls take on the additional challenge of portraying the points of view of others they see and know at school. The girls explore the pervasive problem of students coming late to class at their school. They want to show that there are both legitimate reasons for coming to school late—"This girl got jumped on the 44—they cut off some of her hair with a switchblade. Then the cops came and made us all get off the bus;" "I'm sorry. I'm having an asthma attack;" "I had to take my little sister to school"— and reasons which do not deserve sympathy—"I just got here!;" "I had to go to the store ... Want one?" (offers a chip); "Didn't you see the fight on the second floor?" While short, each line underwent considerable debate between the actors and their director until it was agreed upon as accurate enough to be presented on stage. Looking at the first draft of the script, they immediately noticed an absence of references to drug use, something they saw as an unavoidable element of school life. At their school, "stoners" are known to cut class and walk the short distance to a canyon off school property to use and deal drugs, as well as hang out. The actors debated how, most realistically, to bring this information to their audience:

> A1: A canyon excuse ... Let's see ... um ...
> D: What would a stoner say, about being in the canyon?
> A2: I was playing down at the rope swing.
> A1: No, no. I was—
> A3: (in slow, slurred speech) I got all the way down there and I got so stoned I couldn't find my way back!
> A4: Oohh—somebody has to *be* a stoner?
> A5: Yeah! (laughter)
> A1: Let's see ... I don't know.
> D: What would a stoner say, what would Jake (a student whom they all know to come to class high regularly) say if he came to class late?
> A3: I couldn't find my way back.
> A6: He'd be like "Dude—

A2: He'd say "I was in the canyon smoking dope and I—
A7: The "Dude!" He would definitely say "Dude."
A1: Wait, wait. OK. "Dude I was in the canyon and I couldn't find my way out." (Lots of laughter and agreement—Yeah, Yeah!)
A4: And you have to be completely stoned, like "Wha-at?"
D: OK. She'll have to do the line like she's stoned?
A1: Yeah, slow and stoned.

Though the actors are enjoying working at getting the line right and are laughing during this interaction, they are not celebrating drug use or condoning Jake's behavior. While they like Jake as a person and a classmate, they also know that he is failing his classes because of his drug problem. They want to represent him accurately on stage so that their audience can in turn consider the multiple truths of his situation: that he is both clever, and wasting his intellect on drugs; that he is presenting a blatantly unacceptable excuse for his tardiness, and in doing so is also asking for help with a serious problem. To present the story of their school, the actors realize the need to present the many others who make up the diverse student body. And to present these others, they have to observe and consider them carefully, to experiment with their language and motivations and actions until they can actually become them for a short time. And in becoming these characters they are accepting that there is more than one way to look at life, that each way brings with it its own set of consequences, and that nothing is simple or clear cut.

PROMOTING CREATIVE PROBLEM SOLVING THROUGH HEALTHY INTERDEPENDENCE

Theater is a truly collaborative art. Either artists working in different roles—playwright, actor, director, set designer, stage manager, etc.—pool their resources toward the collective effort of producing a play for an audience, or each member of the company agrees to work at each of the tasks required. Either way, drama is not a solo art. Even the rare one-person show requires a relationship between at least two parties—the actor and the audience. As a play does not come with a set of lock-step instructions, theater demands a flexible, complex form of cooperation of its participants—a simple doling out of tasks will not satisfy. Each individual member of a company is responsible for, not only bringing his or her expertise to the project, but also listening to the ideas of others and incorporating them into one's own to construct a creative whole greater than the sum of its parts.

Theater, then, is a discipline of both individual and collaborative responsibility. New York actress and acting teacher Uta Hagen warns actors in her text *Respect for Acting* (1973) to observe carefully delineated responsibilities.

No director can help you with your substitutions since he has not been a part of your life experience. He will help you with the character elements he is after, dictate the pace, the surroundings, the given circumstances, and define your relationship to the other characters in the play, but how you make these things real to yourself, how you make them exist is totally private work (p. 37).

Strasberg-trained acting teacher Sandy Meisner warns actors that they cannot embark upon the task of creating a role by themselves. "What you do," he tells his students, "doesn't depend on you, but what the other actor does to you. You can't do anything unless the other actor does something to make you do it" (cited in Mekler, 1987, p. 24). And so the drama artist is constantly negotiating between the responsibility of her individual talents and her responsibility to respond to fellow artists. Viola Spolin (1985) perceives this negotiation as a matter of "timing" in actors, a balance between several factors of "both self-awareness and the ability to attune to the scene, the other players and the audience" (p. 55) .

In developing his increasingly well-known Theater of the Oppressed, theater teacher Augusto Boal (1985) expanded the traditional notion of theater ensemble to include the audience. He developed his new format amid the military coups and harsh dictatorships of Brazil of the mid 1960s. Designed for audiences of peasants and workers, his Forum Theater was designed to exceed the goal of entertaining an audience.

[Forum Theater] gave spectators themselves opportunity to discover their own solutions to their collective problems. Through storytelling techniques, Boal worked with groups to create a scene in which a protagonist is failing to achieve what s / he needs or desires. Audience members stop the dramatic action at any moment they feel the protagonist has an option s / he is not exercising. They then physically replace the protagonist in the scene and improvise their alternative action, thus rehearsing for social change. (Schutzman, & Cohen-Cruz, 1994, p. 2)

Boal's work draws a direct link between the traditional drama principles of ensemble work and creative problem solving. All those involved must allow for each other to the greatest extent possible: the playwrights by writing scripts that paradoxically encourage them to be changed; the actors on stage by acting convincingly enough so that those watching are drawn into participating, and the audience by watching carefully and critically enough so that they can suggest and act on alternatives not yet presented.

Since "drama consists of multiple attempts and multiple strategies to solve the problems confronting characters" (George, 1994, p. 10), it offers teachers and students a venue for creative problem solving through a healthy interdependence. When a group takes on the challenge of creating and performing its own dramatic piece, it is taking on a series of open ended artistic and management questions more complex than anything that a single individual would handle. Just as our school instruction has suffered from promoting the unrealistic notions of single points of view and exclusive truths, it does a disservice to students by suggesting that problems are best solved in a single, prescribed method. "There is a tendency in technologically oriented cultures," Elliot Eisner (1992) points out in his critique of education, "to conceive of rationality as a method of tightly linking means and ends" (p. 594). Youth and youth group leaders who work on drama know that means often lead to ends in unpredictable ways, and that the improvised qualities of interdependent collaboration can be an excellent method of creating solutions.

A feature common to contemporary youth drama groups performing original work is their insistence on the necessity of ensemble, eschewing traditional notions of star parts and minor roles, opting instead for making everyone equally responsible for the success of the show. Directors of contemporary youth drama spend significant amounts of their early rehearsal time engaged in exercises that build and strengthen their actors into an ensemble. A student in a high school advanced acting class describes how an exercise designed by their teacher to strengthen their ensemble brought with it unexpected benefits.

> One time we had two people. One person writes the poem and the other person goes off and makes up a dance. And you put it together. That takes a lot of trust. To read a poem—and you don't know what the dance is about because you haven't seen it—and to come together and put it together. And we were so amazed about how everything just worked out … it's all about building trust.

Once rehearsal periods move from exercises to preparation of a production piece, actors are expected to hold on to the notion of ensemble even in the lure of the spotlight. When ensemble actors are not performing lines they are expected to collaborate and contribute to the strength of the dramatic message they are presenting, as this excerpt from one youth group director's end-of-rehearsal critique makes clear:

> When someone's talking look at them! Don't talk to the person next to you. It doesn't mean that you're not on stage anymore. It means you are now a SUPPORTING character, instead of the lead right at that moment. So you watch what's going on. Throw your focus to the action of the play. When someone's talking look right at them and hear them! And REACT. And it's OK to react. As long as you are reacting TRUTHFULLY, that's fine. You know you're not into this play, you know, to make a joke? You're not here to show off for somebody who you want to impress? OK? Right? You're supporting what the play is saying.

In addition to the goal of working as an ensemble, the contemporary youth theater groups presented here share in common the goal of creating original material to perform. Each group observed has devised its own unique method of creating plays based on the talents of its ensemble members. One group begins by sitting around a tape recorder and discussing questions raised by their director, who then takes the tapes home, transcribes them, and brings them back the next day for use in devising a script centered around a theme that they identify as emerging from their conversation. Another group begins by brainstorming topics that interest them as problematic and then improvising scenes that move towards solutions. The director, in addition to structuring the initial improvisation exercises, works to join together what has been improvised into a sequential play, which the actors then rehearse to memorization. A third group chooses a theme important to them and then looks back into the immediate past of their lives and collects writings of all genres—school essays, journal entries, yearbook notes, newspaper articles, letters—related to their chosen theme. The director fashions the various writings into a draft of a script, which the group then rewrites through the rehearsal process. A fourth group, meeting daily, begins each morning by responding to writing prompts offered by the director, who then takes the writings home and arranges them into a first draft of a script, taking care to switch lines between actors and writers, so that privacy is maintained and the challenge of characterization still exists. Each of these methods proves that an even exchange of information between the youths and adults is both possible and profitable. In these instances the young actors bring to the process their ideas, opinions, and questions to be used as themes for their plays. The adult directors bring their abilities to collect, edit, and oversee as a means of structuring the play. Both skills are necessary, and neither could complete a play without the other.

Perhaps not surprisingly, the brief play resulting from the fourth group, as its title All-4-1 (FreeStreet Programs) suggests, brings the theme of working together to the stage. Their opening scene debates the definition and role of an ensemble on stage as well as in their lives in the tough inner city.

> ALL: All for one!
> A1: All for me—
> (group reacts)
> A2: No — all for me—
> A1: No — all for one — and that one is me —
> (group reacts)
> A3: Hey if you want me to be for you — you better be for me too—
> A4: If you want me to be for you — you better be for yourself
> A5: What do you mean for myself
> A6: How do you expect me to care about you if you don't care about yourself—
> A1: You better not be talking about me—
> A7: Why are you always trying to fight somebody—
> A1: Because I take care of myself I don't let anyone talk about me—
> A7: If you know the truth about yourself, you don't have to fight anyone on account of what they say.

THE SATISFACTION OF GENUINE ACHIEVEMENT

Uta Hagen's (1973) memories of how she came to love and respect the theater highlight the accomplishments available to those who pursue the art of drama: discipline, self-confidence, meaningful communication, the knowledge that you are contributing to the betterment of the community in which you live and work.

> In my parents' home, creative instincts and expression were considered worthy and noble. Talent went along with a responsibility to it. I was taught that concentrated work was a thing of joy in itself.… They showed me that love of work is not dependent upon outward success… that the theater should contribute to the spiritual life of a nation (Hagen, p. 7).

Putting up a dramatic production demands an honest revelation of the self, the repetition of rehearsal, the compromise of collaboration and the risk of taking on new challenges and then making them public before others for their critique. When playwrights, actors, technical designers, and directors set out to work on a play, they know that they will not see the results of their effort on stage for a delayed period of time.

Furthermore, the commitment they make to such a long-term project does not carry with it a guarantee of a successful outcome.

Art educator Judith Hanna (1992) argues for a closer connection between performance art (in her case, dance) and education in language that translates nicely into the achievements we want for our students in and beyond the classroom: "To create—and thus 'own'—a [production] is a badge of independence that shows publicly the result of motivation, hard work, perseverance, self-reliance, and responsibility" (p. 606). As Hanna's words of advocacy suggest, schools need to offer students ample opportunity for genuine achievement. Students need to take on challenges which last longer than a 50-minute class or even a 4-month semester; they need to be offered the opportunity not only to fail but to learn from their failures how to succeed. They also need to be offered the opportunity to present their achievements to a public larger than a single teacher—to experience community acceptance, and rejection of their efforts.

The Young Playwrights Festival in New York provides such an opportunity every year with its nationwide contest (Lamb, 1992). Writers younger than 18 are invited to submit original play scripts to the contest's panel of theater professionals for evaluation. Every play received is returned to the playwright with substantive typed comments and suggestions, written under the assumption that the young playwrights will continue to rewrite their pieces. The prize is an on-Broadway production of their play, complete with professional actors and directors. The student playwrights are flown to New York to participate in the rehearsal process as well as for opening night. One winner from the 1989 contest describes why embarking on the dramatic process is a risk, and why it is a risk worth taking:

> Watching a play you've written be staged is similar to putting your new born baby on display in the window at Macy's and having to stand there and watching as people crowd around and begin to critique your child. In short it's nerve-racking, frightening, horrifying, exhilarating, and wonderful. Only when the curtain is finally closed can you breathe a sigh of relief. "I'm still alive, and I think I heard someone clapping." (Allard, 1991, p. 129)

It is easy to imagine that for the student accustomed to receiving praise in the form of a letter grade or brief written comments, standing on a stage and listening to people applaud could be a heady experience. Another defining feature of the young contemporary drama groups presented here is that after the traditional curtain call, the actors are expected to come back to the stage as themselves and answer questions from their audience about the work they have just performed.

Such postplay discussions serve a number of purposes: to remind the students that their responsibility to the play extends beyond accepting applause, to bring the audience to life for the actors, to allow yet further points of view into the dramatic discussion their play has begun, to allow the audience a chance to disagree with what they have seen or to find out more about it, and to give student actors ideas for new productions. In a postplay interview, a high school junior considered how speaking with the audience provides evidence of a genuine achievement:

> I've felt people impacted by our work. I've had people come up to us and tell us that we made them think. And made them analyze and think about what they're doing in society and what society's doing to us. And that's a lot of proof in a lot of different ways.

A LOT OF PROOF IN A LOT OF DIFFERENT WAYS

> It is in the spirit of the acceptor of what children bring to the situation—always the receiver, the curious one, the playwright, the creator of tensions and occasionally the director and actor— that I have to function. (Heathcote, 1980, p. 15)

It is no coincidence that educator Dorothy Heathcote turns to the words of drama to explain what she has learned about successful education—that it requires a teacher who is looking for ways to even the exchange of information in her classroom between her students and herself. For the teacher who is ready to evaluate her success in the classroom by asking the question "Am I learning as much from my students as they are learning from me?" drama offers a valuable tool. By bringing missing information to the curriculum, encouraging multiple points of view, promoting creative problem solving, and offering the satisfaction of genuine achievement, drama not only offers teachers techniques for evenly exchanging information with their students but also models what such a successful education can look like. It can look like young people writing, rehearsing, and reviewing the performance of their own lives; it can look like students and teachers using one another as valuable and necessary learning resources; it can look like Augusto Boal's fantasy of the best possible kind of magic education through drama:

> I think this is how magicians should be: first they should do their magic to enchant us, then they should teach us their tricks. This is also how artists should be—we should be creators and also teach the public how to be creators, how to make art, so that we may all use that art together. (Boal, 1992, p. 29)

References

Allard, J. (1989) Painted rain. In W. Lamb (Ed.), *Hey Little Walter and other prize-winning plays from the 1989 and 1990 Young playwrights festivals.* New York: Dell Publishing.

Betsko, K., & Koenig, R. (Eds.). (1987). *Interviews with contemporary women playwrights.* New York: Beech Tree Press.

Boal, A. (1985). *Theater of the oppressed.* New York: Theater Communications Group.

Boal, A. (1992). *Games for actors and non-actors* (A. Jackson, Trans.). New York: Routledge.

Brouillette, J. (1994). *20 questions.* Unpublished play, University of California at Berkeley, New Plays Project, Berkeley, CA.

Campione, J. C., Rutherford, M., Gordon, A., Walker, J., & Brown, A.L. (in press). "Now I'm a real boy": Zones of proximal development for those at risk. In N. Jordon & J. Goldsmith-Phillips (Eds.). *Learning disabilities: New directions for assessment and intervention.*

Central Touring Theater. (1994). *Judgment day.* Unpublished play, Central Touring Theater, Central High School, St. Paul, MN.

Eisner, E. (1992). The misunderstood role of the arts in human development. *Phi Delta Kappan, 7,* 591–595.

FreeStreet Programs. (1994). Learning to breathe in a box. Unpublished play, FreeStreet programs, Chicago, IL.

Gardner, H. (1991). *The unschooled mind: How children think and how schools should teach.* New York: Basic Books.

George, K. G. (1994). *Playwriting: The first workshop.* Boston: Focal Press.

Hagen, U. (1973). *Respect for acting.* New York: Macmillan.

Hanna, J. L. (1992, April). Connections: Art, academics, and productive citizens. *Phil Delta Kappan, 7,* 601–607.

Heath, S. B., & Mangiola, L. (1992, March 10). Share the wisdom of youth through cross-age tutoring. *Education Monitor,* p. 5.

Heah, S. B., & McLaughlin, M. W. (Eds.). (1993). *Identity and inner-city youth: Beyond ethnicity and gender.* New York: Teachers College Press.

Heathcote, D. (1980). From the universal to the particular. In Robinson (Ed.), *Exploring theater and education* (pp. 5–70). London: Heinemann.

Heathcote, D. (1984). Drama as education. In N. McCaslin (Ed.), *Children and drama* (2nd ed.) (pp. 78–90). New York: Longman.

Hmong Theater Project. (1994). *Tub ntsuag thiab nkauj zaj: The orphan boy & the Dragon Princess.* Unpublished play, Hmong Theater Project, Minneapolis, MN.

Hmong Youth Cultural Awareness Program. (1994). *A free people: Our stories, our voices, our dreams.* Minneapolis, MN: Author.

Hogue, S. (1994). *Sounds of silence.* Unpublished play, Central Touring Theater, Central High School, St. Paul, MN.

Kagan, S. (1990). *Cooperative learning: Resources for teachers.* San Juan Capistrano, CA: Resources for Teachers.

Lamb, W. (Ed.). (1992). *Ten out of ten: 10 winning plays selected from the Young Playwrights Festival 1982–1991.* New York: Delacorte Press.

Living Women, (1994). *By our own book.* Unpublished play, Living Women, Corte Madera, CA.

McGaw, C., (1985). *Acting is believing: A basic method* (4th ed.). New York: Holt, Rinehart & Winston.

McLaughlin, M.W., Irby, M. Langman, J. (1994). *Urban sanctuaries: Neighborhood organizations in the lives and futures of inner-city youth.* San Francisco: Jossey-Bass.

Mekler, E. (1987). *The new generation of acting teachers.* New York: Penguin Books.

Moyers, B. (1989). *A world of ideas: Conversations with thoughtful men and women about American life today and the ideas shaping our future.* New York: Doubleday.

Reif, L. (1992). *Seeking diversity.* Portsmith, NH: Heinemann Boynton Cook.

Rose, M. (1989). *Lives on the boundary: A moving account of the struggles and achievements of America's educational underclass.* New York: Penguin Books.

Schutzman, M., & Cohen-Cruz, J. (Ed.). (1994). *Playing Boal: Theater, therapy, activism.* New York: Routledge.

Smith, A. D. (1993). *Fires in the mirror.* New York: Doubleday.

Spolin, V. (1985). *Theater games for rehearsal: A director's handbook.* Evanston IL: Northwestern University Press.

Stanislavski, C. (1924). *An actor's handbook.* New York: Theater Arts Books.

Stanislavski, C. (1936). *An actor prepares.* New York: Theater Arts Books.

Witherall, C., & Noddings, N. (Eds.). (1991). *Stories lives tell: Narrative and dialogue in education.* New York: Teachers College Press.

·10·

NAVIGATING THE CHANGING LANDSCAPE OF LITERACY: CURRENT THEORY AND RESEARCH IN COMPUTER-BASED READING AND WRITING

David Reinking and Linda Labbo
UNIVERSITY OF GEORGIA AND THE NATIONAL READING RESEARCH CENTER

Michael McKenna
GEORGIA SOUTHERN UNIVERSITY AND THE NATIONAL READING RESEARCH CENTER

A statistic from 1994 supports the assertion that the computer is the most important technological development of our time. In that year for the first time, the number of computers sold in the United States exceeded the number of televisions sold. The phenomenal rise in the sales of personal computer hardware and software from a modest start in the late 1970s is but one indication that the computer is central to how we define our world today as well as how we imagine our future. Given the proliferation of computer-based innovations across diverse everyday activities, it takes little imagination to see that advances in computer technology have become a catalyst for social and cultural change, much as television did almost a generation ago. But, the potential consequences of becoming digital, as one writer has put it (Negroponte, 1995), are likely to exceed exponentially the influence of television. Like television, computer technology promises to effect changes in popular culture; but unlike television, it is likely to effect profound changes in our intellectual lives as well (Lanham, 1993). Most important for the topic of this chapter, electronic forms of reading and writing will both contribute to and support those changes.

In fact, the brief history of the computer's influence on reading and writing is perhaps the best example of how broad and deep its influence has been on contemporary life. The technology of writing changed substantially with the introduction of word processing, which quickly became the most common application used by those who purchased personal microcomputers beginning in the late 1970s. Word process-

ing continues to evolve from its original use as a typographic tool for creating printed documents (see Bolter, 1991) to its increasing use as a digital tool for creating electronic multimedia documents. Another current example is the burgeoning use of the Internet for personal communication through e-mail and for disseminating information through on-line services and browser programs such as Mosaic and Netscape. The rise of the Internet is a major literacy event with indisputable, if not precisely discernible, societal and cultural implications in diverse areas such as education, advertising, mass communication, entertainment, and the political arena.

The pace at which the literate world is shifting from printed to digital forms of reading and writing has accelerated steadily since the introduction of the microcomputer. This trend can be seen at a number of levels. For more than a decade auto parts stores and bowling alleys have exchanged printed catalogs and score sheets for computer displays. More recently, we sign for deliveries using a stylus on an electronic tablet; hospital personnel use the same technology to record patients' medication and vital signs, which are transmitted electronically to a physician's office computer. More electronic encyclopedias are being sold today than their printed counterparts. Students at major universities such as Stanford, UCLA, and MIT, where many dorms have direct Internet connections, are using computers to register for courses, to research topics in libraries around the world, to submit their work to instructors, and to find out who in their dorm wants to chip in for a pizza. At the same time, the number of printed books and journals purchased by research libraries has steadily declined since 1985, while the number of electronic journals has risen from around 100 in 1991 to more than 400 by late 1994 (Stix, 1994). National Public Radio reported recently that newspaper circulation worldwide has been declining between one and two percent each year since 1991. Increasingly scholars are bypassing conventional journal publication to share their research and ideas electronically as is evidenced by the inclusion of formats for electronic citations in the most recent edition of the APA style manual.

These developments suggest that we have moved beyond a threshold of debate about whether computers will have any long-lasting effect on conceptions of literacy, conceptions that there had been no need to examine when the dominance of print was unquestioned. Our position in this chapter is that we are riding a juggernaut of change that implies a fundamental examination of how we are to conceptualize literacy in a digital, posttypographic world (see Reinking, 1995). Technology can no longer be marginalized as only one among many focal points that capture the attention of educators and scholars interested in literacy. Instead, events dictate that technology move to the center of every research and educational agenda related to literacy. Not to do so, we would argue, will not only relegate much of the past and present literacy research base to obsolescence but will create a vacuum of careful thought based on systematic research. If that happens, literacy researchers will lose the opportunity to influence constructively the changes that seem to be inevitable and to assist educators and students adjust to those changes.

To prevent our efforts from becoming obsolete and to contribute useful understandings, it will be necessary first, for literacy educators and researchers, to acknowledge that important changes are occurring in the way that we read and write and likewise to contemplate the implications of these changes. We have found that doing so is not always easy because of the tendency to view electronic texts as only printed texts displayed on a computer screen. Much as the first automobiles were referred to as 'horseless carriages' a text on a computer screen is sometimes referred to (and made to resemble) a 'page' of text. The distinction between page and screen may seem inconsequential until one has fully considered the important practical and theoretical implications of displaying text electronically. Later in this chapter we elaborate on the critical differences between printed and electronic texts that we believe are useful in understanding the relevance of emerging forms of electronic texts, conceptualizing new ones, and generating questions for research.

Another reason why moving technology to the center of literacy research may be difficult is that doing so often negates the relevance or importance of previous research based on reading and writing printed materials. For example, of what practical significance is current research in teaching children strategies to comprehend printed texts if electronic texts change not only what strategies make sense but also the options for modeling and supporting those strategies? Also, how useful are theoretical constructs such as reader response and intertextuality when the distinction between readers and writers becomes less clear in electronic documents such as

hypertexts and when thousands of formerly disjoint texts can be displayed immediately and seamlessly on a single computer screen?

Literacy researchers, individually and collectively, may understandably be reluctant to embrace technology when it threatens their substantial investment in print-based research. Nonetheless, the changes that are occurring, almost daily, around us make it increasingly difficult to ignore the current and potential implications of electronic forms of reading and writing. But to navigate through a changing literacy landscape, many researchers will need a map that orients them not only to what is happening and its potential consequences but also to how their interests centered in conventional print might be transformed in a world of electronic reading and writing. That is our aim in this chapter.

We have divided this chapter into two main parts. The first part focuses on theoretical perspectives and research aimed at identifying the fundamental differences between printed and electronic texts. The second part identifies several generalizations and supporting research concerning the computer's role in the acquisition of literacy. We believe these latter generalizations may help researchers develop pedagogical theories for integrating computers into literacy instruction and to generate useful research questions aimed at studying the effects of electronic reading and writing in classrooms. However, we wish to emphasize that there is considerable overlap between the content of these two sections and they are separated only for the sake of an orderly presentation. That is, understanding the differences between printed and electronic texts has implications for pedagogy, and studying the use of computer technology in classrooms is enriched by understanding the uniqueness of electronic texts. Ironically, our limited ability to deal with this overlap is an artifact of the fact that we must conform to the linear and hierarchical structures expected by readers of a printed text. As we discuss subsequently, hypertext, an electronic text based on associational networks, would easily accommodate a more realistic representation of this overlap.

THEORETICAL PERSPECTIVES AND RELATED RESEARCH

Establishing well-defined theoretical perspectives is a mark of maturity in the study of any phenomenon or in efforts to demarcate a domain of research. Striving for such maturity, according to Thomas Kuhn's often-cited argument, is a defining characteristic of research when there is a major shift in scientific paradigms or world views. Given current trends, we do not think it is an overstatement to suggest that emerging forms of electronic reading and writing require a paradigmatic shift in traditional conceptions of literacy. If so, seeking useful theoretical perspectives can be a gateway to greater understanding of the changes that are occurring and consequently what research is most needed.

We wish to emphasize that citing Kuhn and mentioning theory in the context of scientific paradigms does not mean that we think theoretical speculation about electronic forms of reading and writing should be limited to positivistic epistemologies, experimental designs, and quantitative methods. Indeed, a set of theoretical perspectives that is broad enough to encompass the pervasive effects of electronic reading and writing cannot be restricted to a single approach to research. For example, long before qualitative approaches had achieved widespread acceptance among educational researchers, Venezky (1983) proposed that computer-based instructional programs aimed at improving literacy could not be credibly evaluated exclusively through pre- and posttest designs with control groups. He argued that such approaches must be supplemented with data from questionnaires, interviews, and participant observations.

Likewise, we believe that useful theoretical perspectives must be broad enough to generate research questions across a wide range of literacy contexts and purposes. Researchers need to consider how digital texts affect literacy and learning in classrooms and schools as well as in the workplace. They also need to consider the sociocultural implications of electronic reading and writing for accomplishing work-related goals as well as for social and recreational purposes. The early and frequently atheoretical focus on using computers to dispense instruction for the purpose of accomplishing the goals of conventional print-based literacy (Reinking, & Bridwell-Bowles, 1991) must be replaced by a focus on determining the inherent characteristics of electronic reading and writing and how those differences might affect and effect classroom instruction and learning. In short, the most useful theoretical perspectives will help shape a new conception of literacy that accommodates electronic forms of reading and writing and will inform efforts to translate that new conception into a coherent agenda for research.

Differences Between Printed and Electronic Texts

Underlying an argument that new conceptions of literacy are needed is the assumption that electronic texts are substantially different from printed texts. Such differences, as we have noted at the outset of this chapter, may not be intuitively clear because of a natural inclination to conceptualize electronic texts in terms of the more familiar printed texts. Thus, it becomes especially important to identify, as precisely as possible, the new characteristics and capabilities of electronic texts that may be most basic to changing conceptions of literacy. We highlight those differences here although they have been more fully elaborated elsewhere (see Reinking, 1992, 1994, 1995; Reinking, & Chanlin, 1994). Also, we cite existing or potential research that illustrates the kinds of questions that an awareness of each difference might generate.

For the most part, this research is aimed at investigating the effects of electronic forms of reading and how the unique characteristics of electronic texts might be used purposefully to enhance comprehension and reading ability. By comparison, the empirical research related to electronic forms of writing remains relatively narrow, focusing predominantly on how word processing affects the writing of conventional printed texts (see the review by Reinking, & Bridwell-Bowles, 1991). Nonetheless, there has been increasing theoretical speculation about how unique electronic forms of writing, specifically hypertexts, suggest new areas of empirical investigation (see Hawisher, & Selfe, 1991; Selfe, & Hilligoss, 1994).

Interactivity and Malleability. A major characteristic of electronic texts is that they are interactive because they are so malleable. As stated aptly by Kaplan (1991), "In the digitized world, texts are intrinsically fluid, malleable, protean. ...And, it is no longer possible—even for the naive, atheoretical reader—to understand or even to approach them as fixed, stable, linear objects" (p. 19). The frequent description of reading as an interactive process, which preceded any serious attention to electronic texts by more than a decade, has had a metaphorical meaning when applied to printed texts because printed texts are inert, fixed, entities that challenge readers to make sense of them. Using the terms *interaction* or *transaction,* in the case of printed texts, is meant to emphasize that comprehension is the result of factors within texts and within readers and that readers must be cognitively active in relating textual information to their own knowledge. Electronic texts, however, can effect a literal interaction between readers, writers, and texts because texts presented digitally are by nature dynamic entities easily capable of being modified in response to the contingencies of a particular situation or the needs and wishes of individual readers or writers.

The term *interaction* when applied to electronic texts, therefore, can be much more like the give and take of a dialogue (Reinking, 1987). An electronic text, for example, can be programmed to monitor a particular reader's actions and evolving knowledge during reading, and it can adjust the textual presentation accordingly. An early study conducted by L'Allier (1980) illustrates how an awareness of this characteristic might generate research on new types of reading. In that study he adjusted expository texts using a complex algorithm that monitored individual student's reading rate, comprehension accuracy, and response times. In this adaptive reading condition, high school students who were identified as low achieving readers comprehended as much as their high achieving peers. Such an application suggests interesting pedagogical options for increasing learning from texts.

Since this early example, several other researchers have studied the effects of applications aimed at making reading more interactive (Blohm, 1982, 1987; MacGregor, 1988a, 1988b; Reinking, 1988; Reinking, & Rickman, 1990; Reinking, & Schreiner, 1985; Salomon, Globerson, & Guterman, 1989; Tobias, 1987, 1988). The conceptual basis for these applications has been the realization that computers make it possible to offer various forms of assistance to readers while they are reading. Cumulatively, the research on these applications suggests that providing such on-line assistance produces superior levels of understanding when compared to conventional printed texts (see Feldmann, & Fish, 1991 for an exception). For example, Reinking and Rickman (1990) had middle-grade students read several science texts presented either in a printed version accompanied by a conventional glossary or in an electronic version that provided on-line access to meanings of difficult words in the text. When reading the electronic version, students investigated the meanings of more words, recognized the meanings of more difficult terms used in the passage, and demonstrated greater comprehension of the scientific principles discussed.

A study by Salomon et al. (1989) illustrates how existing theoretical perspectives related to printed texts can apply to a consideration of electronic texts' interactivity and malleability and how such a perspective might lead to theory-based instructional applications. In that study the researchers designed a computer application they described as a "reading partner" aimed at simulating the interactions between a reader and an "intellectual, pedagogical partner" (p. 621). Vygotsky's (1978) sociodevelopmental theory and his idea of learning within a zone of proximal development guided the development of the application and the experimental hypotheses. Results indicated improvements in 7th-grade students' reading and writing due to the expenditure of more mental effort and metacognitive activity in the computer-based reading condition when compared to conventional reading of printed texts.

Other perspectives that emphasize the interactivity of electronic texts have been drawn from literary theory. In fact, we believe that as researchers interested in literacy attend more to the differences between printed and electronic texts, they will be drawn increasingly toward literary theory as helpful in conceptualizing the nature and implications of these differences. Also, literary theorists and classicists have become interested in the literary and cultural implications of electronic reading and writing (e.g., Bolter, 1991; Edwards, 1991; Landow, 1992; Lanham, 1993; Moulthrop, & Kaplan, 1994). Landow, for example, uses Roland Barthes' theoretical distinction between a "readerly" and "writerly" texts which becomes an objective reality in electronic texts, where interactivity may be employed to blur the distinction between readers and writers. For example, in *Marble Springs* (Larson, 1993), an electronic fiction written as a hypertext, readers not only explore flexibly the lives of people who live in an imaginary frontier town, but they are invited to create new characters by adding prose and poetry to the original text and to create new links among the original textual nodes. As this example also illustrates, considering interactivity from the perspective of literary theory provides perspectives that have as much to do with writing as reading. However, there is irony in turning to literary theory to expand understanding of electronic reading and writing. As Bolter (1991) has pointed out, electronic texts make moot many of the debates among literary theorists. For example, arguing for a deconstructionist point of view hardly seems necessary when, as in the case of a hypertext, there is no single text to deconstruct and where readers are creating unique meanings by virtue of their idiosyncratic navigation through flexibly structured textual nodes.

Audiovisual Effects. Displaying texts electronically on a computer screen provides unprecedented opportunities to combine a wide range of audiovisual effects with written prose. Such effects include digital graphics, animations, movies, and speech. Thus, multimedia is a term (along with the newer term *hypermedia*) that can increasingly be applied to electronic reading and writing. Although it is possible to combine printed materials with various other media such as film or tape recordings, the computer allows the capabilities of these and related media to be merged seamlessly with written prose and to be displayed, often simultaneously, by a single device. Also furthering the advantage of electronic texts in this regard is that a variety of audiovisual information is increasingly becoming available in digital forms (Negroponte, 1995). Once in digital form, such information can be easily and inexpensively incorporated into electronic texts. Also, the capability to create highly refined multimedia texts is becoming possible without highly specialized expertise, hardware, or software.

Thus, electronic texts have the potential to move written prose away from the center of textual meaning. When print is the only reasonable choice to disseminate texts widely, the alphabetic code is clearly one of the most efficient means of communicating information, especially abstract information. Although pictorial information such as illustrations, maps, and graphs, is often valued in printed texts, such information is typically viewed as ancillary to written prose. In electronic texts, on the other hand, it is conceivable that images and sound might play a much more central role in conveying meaning.

Several writers from various theoretical perspectives have highlighted the potential importance of electronic media in moving textual meaning away from the alphabetic code. Walter Ong's (1982) seminal work on the relation between orality and literacy is a frequently cited example in the current literature. Although he was writing at a time when microcomputers were a relatively new phenomenon, he predicted that the computer would play a role in furthering a "second orality" in which modern communication technology would restore some of the social and psychological orientations characteristic of primary oral cultures. More recently, writers such as Bolter (1991) have pointed out that electronic forms of reading and writing are reminiscent of primitive picture writing. Also, Lanham (1993) has pointed out that digital texts tend to draw a reader's attention to their visual characteristics as opposed to printed texts, which are typically designed to be transparent representations of meaning. In other words, we look more *at* the visual representation of electronic texts to derive meaning, not just *through* the visual representation of letters and words, as is the case in conventional printed texts. He has argued that this difference moves digital texts into a rhetorical position and away from the philosophical position occupied by conventional printed texts. Another example is Lemke (1994) who has pointed out the special relevance of semiotic theories in expanding conceptions of literacy to include multimedia documents.

Some existing theoretical perspectives that have been developed with conventional printed texts in mind remain relevant when applied to electronic texts. For example, Paivio's (1986) dual encoding hypothesis argues that textual information is more memorable when it is encoded both visually and linguistically. In fact, given the expanded possibilities of integrating visual (as well as auditory) material with written prose in electronic texts, it is likely that such a theory may be especially useful in guiding future research involving electronic reading and writing. Salomon's (1979; Salomon, Perkins, & Globerson, 1991) theoretical approach to defining media, based on the interaction of technologies and symbol systems in effecting cognition and learning, is applicable to electronic texts. Using that theory, Reinking (1987) argued that printed and electronic texts can be defined as different media from a cognitive perspective. It might be argued from current trends that electronic texts are becoming different media in a sociocultural sense as well.

There is relatively little research examining the multimedia capabilities of electronic texts, and the existing research has several limitations (see Reinking, & Chanlin, 1994 for a comprehensive review of the literature and an extended discussion of these limitations). One limitation is that much of the research is atheoretical and aimed at investigating whether displaying essentially identical texts on paper or screen produces differences in reading performance. Such studies have produced little evidence that relatively superficial differences in the visual display produce any notable differences in reading performance, especially in areas such as comprehension and recall (Reinking, 1992). Another limitation, at least from the standpoint of literacy researchers, is that much of the available research focuses on comparing various types of graphical representations displayed on a computer screen without considering their relation to written prose. For example, there have been several studies comparing the effects of learning from static graphics in printed texts and animated graphical representations in a comparable electronic text (e.g., Rieber, 1990). These studies have found advantages for computer animations only under highly constrained conditions, and then only inconsistently. However, in these studies the relation of the animated graphics to the written text has not been carefully considered. A more useful approach can be found in a series of studies reported by Hegarty, Carpenter, and Just (1991) in which sophisticated eye movement equipment was used to monitor readers' attention to static and animated graphics showing the operation of a machine. They also systematically varied how the accompanying text related to each of the graphical representations. A finding that points to the potential value of this type of research is that participants in the experiment who had low mechanical ability benefited more when the accompanying text was coordinated with the animated graphical representation.

The audiovisual capabilities of electronic texts also suggest new possibilities for enhancing literacy instruction. For many years there has been ongoing research addressing such possibilities using synthesized or digitized speech (McConkie, 1983; Olson, Foltz, & Wise, 1986; Olson, & Wise, 1987; Reitsma, 1988; Roth, & Beck, 1987; Wise, 1992). For example, Reitsma used a computer to assist 6- and 7-year-old children with the pronunciation of unfamiliar words during independent reading. He found that this condition effectively increased reading rate and reduced reading errors when compared to oral reading guided by a teacher and reading while listening to a tape-recorded version of the experimental texts. In our own current work we are investigating the effects of providing early readers with phonic analogies under various conditions while they read computerized versions of children's books (McKenna, 1994). Much more research is needed to investigate how audiovisual effects might be used with written prose in electronic texts.

Expanded Boundaries of Freedom and Control. Conventional printed texts exist within relatively limited boundaries of freedom, in terms of a reader's options for obtaining access to a particular text upon demand, and of control, in terms of a writer's options for restricting a reader's access to textual information during independent reading. For example, in the first case, if one is reading a text that alludes briefly to a particular automobile engine about which one wishes more information, it may be tedious, at best, to obtain another text that provides the desired elaboration (e.g., a trip to the library). On the other hand, in the second case, many teachers have experienced the frustration of admonishing students to note a particular feature of a text (e.g., a table) at a particular point as they read an assignment knowing that many students will choose to ignore that admonition. Both of these limitations, in one case the lack of unencumbered access to text and in the other limited ability to exert control over what readers attend to during independent reading, can be removed by electronic texts. As illustrated by the burgeoning use of the Internet, electronic texts expand the boundaries of freedom to flexibly access many texts in many geographical locations upon demand. Perhaps less obvious, and often less welcome or appreciated by many (see Reinking, 1994), is the fact that electronic texts provide the opportunity to exercise unprecedented control over what a particular reader may attend to during independent reading. And, that control can be exercised contingently for different readers reading the 'same' text.

More freedom and more control in accessing texts when they are available electronically create a need for new theoretical perspectives that suggest ways in which such capabilities might affect literate activities. Some authors have attempted to do so, although most of the speculation and research available has focused on the ability to limit access to text. For example, Wilkinson (1983) pointed out that texts displayed on a computer screen were viewed as if through a window providing the capability to limit readers' access to various units of text. Daniel and Reinking (1987) pointed out that the capability to limit readers' access to texts during independent reading allowed writers to make decisions about the placement of text in three dimensions. In addition to arranging texts on the two-dimensional space of the printed page, writers of electronic texts have available a third dimension: time; that is, they can make decisions about when a reader can view a particular portion of a text. Interestingly, this capability has been used as a literary tool by serious writers of hypertextual fiction (see Coover, 1993), which is ironic in the sense that hypertexts have typically been cited as an example of how readers have more freedom when reading electronically. A review of Stuart Moulthrop's *Victory Garden* (Bolter, Joyce, Smith, & Bernstein, 1993) points out how Moulthroup occasionally uses "guard fields" as a literary device in this example of hypertextual fiction. Guard fields are a mechanism in hypertextual writing by which an author can ensure that specified textual nodes are unavailable to readers until other specified nodes have been selected.

One straightforward example of research using the capability of the computer to control readers' access to text is the work of Tobias (1987, 1988). He investigated the effects of inserting questions in electronic texts that mandated review of relevant textual information when a reader answered a question incorrectly. That is, readers were not able to access subsequent portions of a text until they had reviewed an earlier portion of the text and corrected their response. Under such conditions he found that information related to the questions was better recalled in a posttest but that unrelated-information was not recalled as well by readers who read the text and answered the questions without mandatory review, thus exacerbating a problem found in previous studies of inserted questions in printed texts. He hypothesized that readers who were required to review attended only to portions of the text containing information relevant to the question. Testing that hypothesis, Reinking, Pickle, and Tao (1996) found that readers did spend more time on paragraphs containing relevant information but the researchers also were able to use the capabilities of the computer to change that strategy by providing readers with a new question after mandatory review.

There has been relatively little theoretical speculation and research about the computer's capability to expand readers' freedom to access texts. Some literary theorists (e.g., Bolter, 1991; Landow, 1992; Lanham, 1993) have speculated broadly about the potential societal implications of this capability, but there has been no systematic theoretical speculation about how this capability might affect the reading of particular texts or the teaching of literacy in schools. Clearly, however, there are implications for accessing multiple texts in reading and writing and for helping students acquire strategies for locating and using information from diverse sources, which may require creative use of key word searches using Boolean principles of inclusion, exclusion, and overlap. Existing research derived from the concept of intertextuality, such as the work of Spivey and King (1989), is not clearly applicable to electronic reading and writing because that research is based on a conception of distinctly separate and disjoint texts that are written with the assumption that they will be read in relative isolation from other texts.

A recent study by Stahl, Hynd, Britton, McNish, and Bosquet (in press) illustrates the type of research that might be conducted to address the possibilities for teaching and learning created by the computer's capability to expand teachers' and student's freedom to access textual information. They used the computer to provide high school students with a wide array of historical documents and commentaries concerning the Gulf of Tonkin incident leading to the U.S. entry into the Vietnam War. They hypothesized that providing easy access to these source documents might lead students to approach this historical event more analytically like historians as opposed to focusing only on factual information. Although they found some evidence supporting this hypothesis, they concluded that students may need more exposure to this type of reading activity and perhaps instruction that helps them compare and contrast critically information from various sources.

The increased control that electronic texts allow has brought to the surface previously subtle ethical and philosophical issues related to the appropriateness of limiting readers' access to texts. Reinking (1994) has argued that such control is exercised with printed texts but is often not obvious. For example, financial expediency frequently dictates that teachers only acquire what they consider to be a limited number of 'good' books for children to read in the classroom, thus limiting their choices by default. On the other hand, setting up what have been called "fire walls" to prevent children from accessing certain information on the Internet is an explicit act of control. Relevant to such considerations is the pragmatic perspective in literacy research provided by Cherryholmes (1993), who states that "It is often useful to accede power to texts because texts, in turn enhance the readers' power in other situations . . . " (p. 13). Such issues merit more discussion among researchers and educators who are attempting to understand more fully the implications of electronic reading and writing.

Alternative Textual Structures. A defining attribute of printed texts is that they have linear, hierarchical organizational structures. At the most basic level identifying some writing as a text has meant that it has a beginning, middle, and end. In addition to being linear, texts typically have implicit or explicit markers that indicate hierarchical relations among various elements or ideas contained in the text. In a narrative there are protagonists, major and minor characters, key events that advance the plot, and events of lesser importance that may be little more than interesting diversions. Most expository texts are radically hierarchical with many visual features such as headings to indicate explicitly the difference between super- and subordinate ideas and facts. Beginning writers and readers are explicitly taught to be aware of the linear, hierarchical characteristics of printed texts and to use that awareness as a guide to their own writing and reading. It is not required, of course, that conventional printed texts be written or read sequentially, or that readers or writers organize textual information hierarchically, but not to do so typically requires working against rather than in concert with the technology of print. An index or concordance is an example of how print-based texts acknowledge the legitimacy of nonlinear, nonhierarchical access to textual information, but such tools are post hoc constructions; no writer would consider starting the writing of a book by creating an index or concordance. Also, readers who begin an extended reading of a book with the index or concordance would soon find their task tedious and frustrating.

The technological capabilities and characteristics of electronic texts, on the other hand, do not demand linear and hierarchical structures; in fact, they invite more flexible organizational structures. It has been argued that a heterarchy is the most natural structure for electronic texts (Duchastel, 1986). An obvious example is that most informational computer programs are menu driven. Menu driven programs invite a reader to explore the information in idiosyncratic sequences, and the writers of such programs typically provide efficient tools for a reader to locate diverse information flexibly across the various menu options.

The best example of how electronic texts have the potential to reduce the dominance of linear, hierarchical structures in texts is a genre of electronic texts referred to as hypertext. Hypertext has existed as a relatively obscure concept since the early 1940s and as a term since the 1960s, but it has recently become an increasingly familiar concept inside and outside of the academic community. The most common defining attribute of hypertexts is that they are not linear and hierarchical. In hypertexts separate but related segments of texts are connected, or linked, in associational networks (Jonassen, 1986) not strictly organized into hierarchical outlines. A graphical representation of several hypertexts is shown in Figure 10–1a–c. Each labeled box in the figure is a

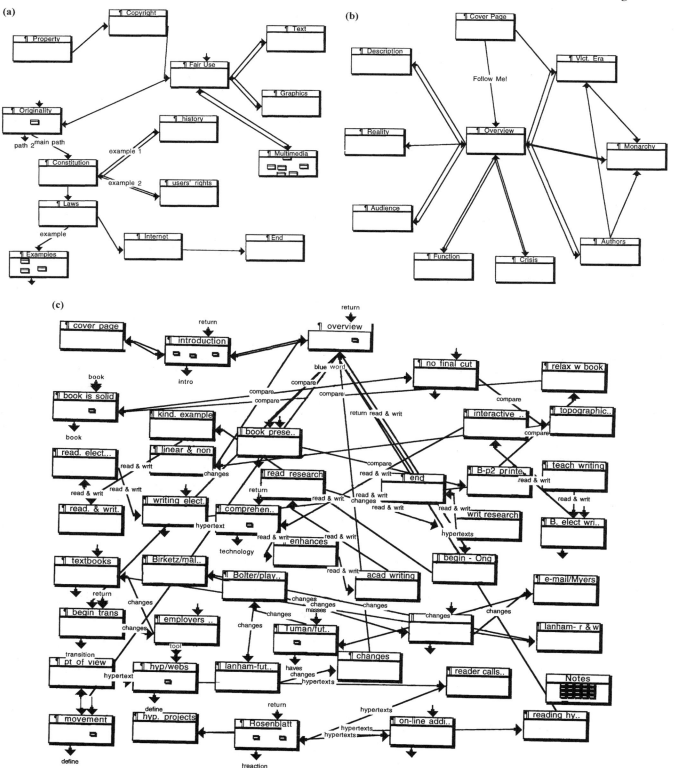

FIGURE 10–1a, 1b & 1c Graphical representation of several hypertexts

textual node containing a segment of text, typically a single or several paragraphs in length. The lines indicate links created by the author allowing readers to move from one node to another. As can be noted by comparing the three examples, the associational networks can be simple, and thus more restrictive to a reader who has fewer options, or they can be more complex, and thus less restrictive to a reader who has many options for moving through the network. Smaller boxes within larger boxes indicate textual information subsumed by a superordinate text, thus demonstrating that hypertexts need not abandon hierarchical, and sometimes linear, structures entirely.

Several writers have presented theoretical perspectives that characterize the organizational structures of hypertexts and what effect they have on literacy. For example, Duchastel (1986) suggested that printed texts can be semantically structured or format structured. A linear, hierarchically structured text, such as a psychology textbook is semantically structured because any particular portion of the text is dependent to some degree on what comes before or after it. On the other hand, an airline schedule is format structured because it is designed to facilitate individualized searches for specific information. He argues that electronic texts, when compared to printed texts, enable a wider range of written materials (e.g., the psychology text) to be presented as format structured texts that are more individualized.

Bolter (1991), on the other hand, has focused on how structure can be viewed in terms of the dominant writing space, which he defines as the "physical and visual field defined by a particular technology of writing" (p. 11). Writing spaces produce what he calls the hard structures associated with the tangible materials of writing such as pages and the soft structures which emerge from them. Soft structures like hard structures may also be manifest visually, but they are more likely to become psychological elements used by readers and writers. In the case of print, a paragraph would be an example of a soft structure that has a visual representation on the printed page but that is also a psychological representation for organizing meaning. Bolter proceeds to discuss the possible hard and soft structures that may be associated with hypertext. For example, the computer screen is a hard structure that dictates to some degree the structure of electronic writing (as noted in the previous section where we discussed how it provides opportunities for controlling access to texts), and a link between hypertextual nodes might become a soft structure that could influence how writers and readers organize textual information.

Other writers such as Lanham (1993; see also Landow, 1992) tend to view structural differences between printed and electronic texts in literary terms. For example, he argues that the structure of electronic texts, particularly their ability to draw attention to their visual appearance, makes them a more rhetorical medium when compared to printed texts, which are inherently more philosophical and somber. Similarly, Bolter (1991) points out that the logic of philosophical arguments and the mental discipline necessary to present them are subverted by hypertexts because hypertexts provide a mechanism for presenting ideas in a format more consistent

with the divergent and often circuitous routes characteristic of uninhibited thinking.

Some researchers are beginning to study the effects of hypertext on reading and writing. For example, Spiro, Coulson, Feltovich, and Anderson (1988) have found evidence that medical students recall less factual information but are better able to apply the content of medical texts when it is presented in a hypertext instead of a conventional printed text (see also Mannes, & Kintsch, 1987). Leu and Hillinger (1994) and Horney (1994) have studied readers' strategies in using hypertextual information, especially when they have access to a variety of on-line assistance. Other researchers have focused on the navigational aids that may be needed to help readers orient themselves with complex mazes of hypertextual information (e.g., Beasley, & Lister, 1992; Gay, Trumbull, & Mazur, 1991). More research is needed to investigate the effects of hypertexts on writing, reading, and learning .

The New Pragmatics and the Sociopolitical Dimensions of Literacy. Becoming literate has always included learning about the pragmatics of reading and writing, which includes an awareness of the social and political aspects of literate activity. Included in this domain are awarenesses as diverse as knowing that a comic book and a Dickens novel carry entirely different cultural connotations, knowing when a handwritten letter may be more appropriate than a typed one, and understanding the capabilities, motives, and potential effects that influence a newspaper's decision to print some stories and reject others. This dimension of literacy, typically learned informally, is emphasized by Brandt (1990) when she states, "Learning to read and write is not learning how texts stick together but how people stick together through literate means" (p. 42).

It is becoming increasingly clear that electronic reading and writing are affecting the pragmatics of literacy. The most prominent example is the widespread use of e-mail for communicating with individuals and with various groups whose members share some common interests. The evolution of accepted forms, contents, and practices related to e-mail communication is not complete and these issues are eventually addressed by the members of virtually any e-mail discussion group. Such groups focus on questions such as: Who should be included or excluded from the group? What types of content are appropriate to post to the whole group? When is it acceptable to forward a message to someone without permission of the original sender? Are there guidelines for when it is better to reply to an individual rather than to the entire group? Should one be allowed to publicize a product or service in which one has some financial interest?

Beyond establishing practical conventions of appropriateness related to these questions (often referred to as *netiquette*), e-mail leads to other questions that are beginning to attract the attention of literacy researchers. For example, what are the characteristics of e-mail that promote what seems to be a greater degree of informality and openness in writing? Do writers who resist expressing themselves in printed forms do so more readily in e-mail? Does e-mail encourage candidness, imperiousness, confrontational rudeness (often referred to as *flames*), and so forth. If so, why and what effects does participation in e-mail writing and reading produce on individual readers and writers? Fey (1994) has conducted research addressing the latter question using a feminist perspective to examine the interchanges among participants in an on-line college course. Is e-mail a catalyst for subverting established hierarchies of authority and decision making? Some studies suggest that it does in corporations (Kiesler, 1986) and in high schools (Neilsen, in press). How might e-mail be used to enhance the instruction of preservice teachers (e.g., Gallego, 1992; McIntyre, 1992; Myers, 1993)?

More studies are needed to address these and similar questions because the rise of e-mail and other forms of electronic texts is a major literacy event with far-reaching societal implications. For example, Rheingold (1993) has reflected extensively on his long-standing involvement with what he calls "virtual communities" on the Internet. He believes that electronic communities are analogous to the agora of ancient Greece "where citizens met to talk, gossip, argue, size each other up, [and] find the weak spots in political ideas by debating about them" (p. 14). And, as a free forum for expression he sees it as a powerful tool for extending democratic ideals. At the same time e-mail threatens some firmly entrenched notions about literacy. For example, the conversational informality of e-mail de-emphasizes the importance of accurate spelling and other mechanical aspects of writing. At another level, e-mail and other electronic forms of communication call into question the utility of current conceptions of copyright, plagiarism, and fair use. Also, it is beginning to undermine the utility of printed scholarly journals as the most efficient ways to disseminate and advance research (see Stix, 1994). Indeed, electronic texts advance postmodern views of literacy (Murphy, 1988) and have the potential to undermine the literary canon in the humanities (Bolter, 1991; Landow, 1992; Lanham, 1993). Issues of interest to the general public such as children's access to pornography on the Internet must also be addressed.

These developments and potential outcomes suggest that literacy research in a posttypographic world must gravitate even more toward a consideration of pragmatics particularly with regard to the social and political issues related to electronic reading and writing. Issues of policy must be carefully considered and researchers must seek to address questions that inform these discussions. In schools too we need to integrate a consideration of electronic literacy into the language arts curriculum (Reinking, 1994). Finally, in addressing issues related to pragmatics with regard to a changing literacy, we will benefit from taking an historical-analytic perspective (e.g., see Kaufer, & Carley, 1993), a perspective that has been less crucial when print was the only dominant form of reading and writing. By understanding more clearly the historical reasons that account for our conceptions of print-based literacy it will be easier to conceptualize and understand the transformations in literacy that we are currently experiencing.

GENERALIZATIONS CONCERNING LITERACY ACQUISITION AND CLASSROOM-BASED RESEARCH

During the 1980s most of the studies investigating instructional uses of computers for reading and writing were ad hoc comparisons of individual computer applications and conventional reading and writing activities. Focusing primarily on skill-based outcomes or specific products, these studies were not typically driven by any explicit psychological, social, or pedagogical theory (Reinking, & Bridwell-Bowles, 1991). However, more recent studies have followed the turn in literacy research toward conducting contextualized investigations of instruction taking into account the dynamic factors that shape teaching and learning in classrooms. Researchers interested in investigating the role of computer technology in shaping literacy in classrooms have begun to realize the inadequacy of limiting their investigations to conventional experimental designs (Baumann, Dillon, Shockley, Alvermann, & Reinking, 1996; Reinking, & Pickle, 1993). We believe that a few tentative generalizations can be made on the basis of this emerging research and that they can be useful in generating questions for research as well as in formulating a pedagogical theory for using computers in literacy instruction. In this section we present several representative generalizations along with examples of research that relate to them; however, we wish to emphasize that our list of generalizations is not exhaustive.

The effects of using computers for instruction are dependent upon a teacher's instructional philosophy and goals as much as upon the characteristics of the computer application or activity. Much of the interest in using computer technology in schools is based on the belief that it has the potential to expand instructional options and to transform positively the standard modes of teaching and learning in schools (Cuban, 1986; Newman, 1990; Papert, 1993; Sheingold, 1991). Yet, many writers have cautioned that there is nothing intrinsic to computer technology that will bring about educational reform (Cochran-Smith, Kahn, & Paris, 1990; Greenleaf, 1994; Mehan, 1989; Weir, 1989; Zorfass, & Remz, 1992). Indeed, a review of the literature examining the effects of using technology across the curriculum clearly indicates that simply introducing computer-based applications or activities into classrooms is not enough to achieve that potential (Means et al., 1993).

This conclusion holds when focusing exclusively on the language arts curriculum. The most extensively researched example is Bruce's long-term investigations of QUILL, a comprehensive application emphasizing process writing and reading for meaningful purposes in the middle grades (see Bruce, & Rubin, 1993 for an extensive summary). Across several years and many classrooms, Bruce and his colleagues concluded that teachers shaped the QUILL activities to fit their own views of reading and writing, sometimes subverting the specific intent of the program. They state that "rather than the new technology radically reshaping the learning environment, the computers themselves were shaped to fit the already established patterns" (Michaels, & Bruce, 1989,

p. 12) and that "... no innovation, no matter how well conceived, and ... how well intended or executed, can in and of [itself] be assured of achieving positive change in instruction" (p. 35). Yet, reflecting on their many years of experience Bruce and Rubin state that their "detailed, self-critical appraisal of the evidence [about QUILL] yields surprises and reveals a richness in what students and teachers do that belies both optimistic and pessimistic visions of technology in relation to educational change" (p. 1).

Bruce's conclusions are supported by several other studies examining diverse computer programs across the elementary grades. For example, Miller and Olson (1994) found that a 1st-grade teacher who was enthusiastic about integrating technology into her language arts curriculum advanced her own pedagogical goals for writing when implementing various story writing software into her classroom. Over time, the researchers documented how her use of the software enhanced her instruction but did not move her in new directions despite the possibilities offered by the software. Similarly, our own work (Labbo, Murray, & Phillips, 1995–96) documents how one primary grade teacher was guided by her literature-based philosophy of literacy instruction in creating computer-based writing centers. Likewise, Dickinson (1986) found that the classroom writing system a teacher had already established fashioned how students used word processing software.

On the other hand, there is evidence that under certain circumstances, usually over an extended period of time, appropriate software or computer-based activities can effect changes in the modes of teaching and learning in classrooms. For example, Cooper and Selfe (1990) report that computer conferencing in college courses gives students authority to resist an academic agenda that does not meet their needs or values. Landow (1992) also describes how replacing a conventional textbook in an undergraduate course on Victorian Literature with a hypertext that mingles texts created by faculty and graduate and undergraduate students radically reconfigures modes of teaching, learning, and assessment. Again, in our own work (Reinking, & Watkins, in press), we have found that over an entire school year introducing multimedia book reviews into middle-grade classrooms as an alternative to the conventional book report tended to disrupt conventional modes of instruction in ways that were often pleasant and appealing to teachers and students. We observed that for some teachers the various activities associated with this project led them to consider new instructional activities as extensions of the multimedia book reviews.

Integrating computers into reading and writing activities in the classroom can foster increases in collaboration and thus has potential to change the social organization of classrooms. A popular concern is that computers will create individuals who work in isolation and who prefer to interact with the computer rather than with people. There is no evidence to support this concern. Furthermore, we believe that the opposite conclusion is more accurate in classrooms. Computers, whether used to link people worldwide over the Internet or to engage students in classroom reading and writing activities, promote interaction and collaboration. In making this generalization we are drawing heavily on our own

research experiences in classrooms, but other studies too lend support to our position.

Several studies have highlighted the increases in social interaction that occur when word processing activities are introduced into classrooms. For example, Dickinson (1986) found that children who worked with a classroom writing buddy (often necessitated by virtue of the fact that few classrooms and labs have had enough computers for every student) discussed plans for their writing and reacted to each other's writing when they worked at the computer. Bruce, Michaels, and Watson-Gegeo (1985) found that computers encourage students to write in a variety of ways that include collaborations involving sharing notes, writing articles for the class newspaper, and reviewing books or plays. Heap's (1986) ethnographic study of 1st-grade students' writing provides evidence that the computer brought together peers of almost equal ability leading to interactions that allowed one or both to work within Vygotsky's (1978) zone of proximal development. Mehan (1989) noted that when 2nd- through 6th-grade students were allowed to work together on word processing, they were able to work out ideas collaboratively and were frequently made aware of points of view that differed from their own.

In our own work (Reinking, & Watkins, in press) we found that engaging students and teachers in learning Hypercard (a relatively simple but powerful authoring tool for creating computer presentations) and using it to create multimedia book reviews had noticeable effects on the social interaction and organization, at least during the times that students were engaged in that activity. For example, the ratio of student-to-teacher talk was greater during the activity, and teachers seemed to enjoy the fact that students often had more expertise than they did. Lower-ability students frequently took on a different persona when working on computer-based activities, frequently exhibiting more confidence and leadership when interacting with their high achieving peers. We also found that student-to-student interactions related to learning about the technology and meeting the challenges of programming their book reviews led to incidental sharing of information about enjoyable books. These findings are consistent with other studies that have found increases in social interaction when computers are integrated into various other areas of the curriculum (Friedman, 1990; McGee, 1987; Riel, 1989; Turner, & Depinto, 1992).

We believe that collaborative forms of reading and writing are likely to increase as electronic texts become more common in schools. As we have mentioned in a previous section, electronic texts blur the distinction between reader and writer by inviting readers to adapt and modify the texts of the original author, a possibility that could make writing and reading literally a socially constructed dialogue. Hypertexts in particular lend themselves to collaborative writing as Shirk (1991) has predicted; she states that "Writers will no longer create in solitary environments; they will become contributing members of hypertextual development teams" (p. 198). Classrooms may come to reflect what Landow (1992), in writing about the potential societal effects of electronic reading and writing, calls "a society of conversations in which no one conversation, no one discipline or ideology, dominates or founds the others" (p. 70). More research is needed to investigate these possibilities in classrooms.

Computers can promote the integration of reading and writing activities for purposeful communication. Research has confirmed the intuitive belief that students write and read better when they are engaged in personally meaningful and purposeful tasks (Kirby, & Kirby, 1985). However, during the 1980s the use of computers in classrooms too often worked against this principle. Many writers (e.g., Smith, 1984) pointed out how commercial software dominated computer-based reading and writing activities in classrooms and how most of that software focused on teaching, drilling, practicing, and assessing isolated skills.

That criticism is less valid today for diverse reasons including the increased sophistication and availability of hardware and software as well as an increased technological astuteness among teachers and students. For example, more than 10 years ago a project using computers to link students in two schools, one in California and one in Alaska, was noteworthy; today such links are commonplace as is evidenced by a recent report that found that in 1994 more than 35% of the nation's schools had at least one Internet connection (Heaviside, Malitz, & Carpenter, 1995). Due to such developments more attention is being paid to how a variety of engaging computer-based activities can serve as a springboard to meaningful reading and writing across the curriculum. There are even preliminary indications that the dominance of the conventional textbook is being seriously threatened. For example, it has already been several years since the state of Texas qualified computer-based science programs as alternatives to textbooks on a state textbook adoption list.

There has been relatively little research focusing on how computers can promote integrated and meaningful reading and writing activities but a few examples can be cited. Labbo, Field, and Watkins (1995) reported preliminary findings from an ongoing study investigating the opportunities for literacy development that occur when the Internet is used to connect 3rd-grade students in two schools, one in the Southern United States and one in Taiwan. The children in both schools were motivated to interact frequently through e-mail which is more immediate, affordable, and accessible than letters or telephone calls. In their interchanges they raised questions about their counterparts' culture and they wrote descriptive reports in a hypertext format about family life, school life, cultural activities, and forms of government. The available technology allowed them to scan photographs of their families and to include transcripts and audio segments of interviews with their school principal and teacher. They also wrote journal entries about typical daily activities. Another example is a study by Turner and Depinto (1992) which found that students who composed hypermedia documents were motivated to think about how to present information that made sense to their peers. Such computer-based reading and writing has all the characteristics of meaningful, authentic reading and writing tasks that are currently being promoted among literacy educators, and they stand in stark contrast to both early uses of the computer in classrooms and to conventional academic tasks. More research is needed to guide continued expansion of these types of activities in classrooms.

Computers can facilitate students' reading and writing by providing individualized assistance and by reducing the drudgery associated with some aspects of reading and writing. Salomon's (1979) theory of instructional media postulates that a critical attribute separating various instructional media is the degree to which a particular medium can supplant processes and skills necessary to acquire information from that medium or to perform a task with that medium. For example, motion pictures have an advantage over photographs because zoom and closeup shots can focus a viewer's attention to important details that might not be noticed by the viewer of a photograph. Using this theoretical position Reinking (1987) argued that printed and electronic texts should be considered different media because electronic texts provide many more opportunities for individual help and guidance during independent reading and writing. The examples of computer applications and research cited in earlier sections of this chapter devoted to the malleability of electronic texts and their capability to expand the boundaries of freedom and control in accessing textual information support this position. However, we provide additional examples here to highlight how these capabilities might figure in classroom instruction.

For example, in our own work (McKenna, 1994) we are investigating the effects of providing beginning readers with pronunciations of unfamiliar words sometimes accompanied by phonetically related words while reading popular children's books presented by a computer. We believe that electronic texts might provide options for innocuous and individualized phonics instruction without detracting from the enjoyment of children's literature. We believe that computer technology offers a variety of new instructional options for assisting students in learning fundamental but often mundane aspects of reading and writing and that such instruction can be accomplished in engaging ways that free teachers to concentrate on less transient aspects of literacy acquisition. We are also interested in related questions such as how far children might choose to read above their instructional level when they have access to supports that reduce the obstacles to successful reading. Our work extends several other rigorous, theory-based studies aimed at providing individualized assistance that reduces the difficulties facing some early readers. For example, Olson and his colleagues (Olson et al., 1986; Olson, & Wise, 1987) have experimented with various types of speech feedback; Reitsma (1988) has investigated how reading with computer-based speech feedback compares to teacher guided reading; and Roth and Beck (1987) have compared the effects of two theory-based computer word games with speech feedback on word recognition and comprehension.

Some of the research investigating the effects of word processing has focused on how it may assist young children overcome the limitations inherent in writing with conventional tools. For example Chang and Osguthorpe (1990) and Green (1984) have investigated how word processing supports emerging writers by providing visual, auditory, and motor help and by removing the often tedious aspects of early writing such as forming letters with a pencil. Also, Phenix and Hannan (1984) suggest that word processors bolster young children's efforts to revise, reread, and rewrite narratives because they can focus more on the content of their message and less on penmanship and spelling. In a case study of a kindergarten student, Cochran-Smith et al. (1990) conclude that the effectiveness of word processing activities for children's writing development is dependent on the writing task, the child's literacy development, the instructional context, and features of the word processing software.

We believe more research is needed to explore such factors and how they relate to the computer's ability to individualize assistance and to reduce the need for less engaging aspects of reading and writing processes. Studies are needed to investigate how instructional activities derived from such awarenesses can be implemented in classrooms and what their effects are on teaching and learning. We need to determine what Salomon et al. (1991) have called effects *with* and *of* media. That is, what are the immediate consequences of reading or writing a particular text *with* a computer and what are the long-term effects *of* the computer on the way students approach reading and writing in general?

ISSUES AND TRENDS: PAST, PRESENT AND FUTURE

Researchers' interest in computer technology and literacy spans almost 30 years, beginning with Richard Atkinson's research on a computer-based initial reading program at Stanford University (Atkinson, & Hansen, 1966). However, except for a few large projects such as Atkinson's at Stanford, which were typically supported by large grants, most of the research involving computers has occurred since microcomputers were introduced in the late 1970s. During the intervening 15 years, the perspectives and questions motivating interest in computers and literacy have evolved as computer technology and knowledge of its use has become more sophisticated, as the availability and use of computers have increased in and out of schools, and as educators and researchers have come to understand more fully the computer's potential to alter traditional conceptions of schooling and literacy. There has been an increasing, although sometimes reluctant, acceptance of the idea that electronic forms of reading and writing are moving closer to the mainstream of literacy. The early conception of computers as instructional devices that provided novel opportunities for accomplishing the goals of the conventional language arts curriculum has gradually given way to a realization that computers may precipitate fundamental changes in how we read and write. This shift represents a maturing of the technology and our understanding and use of it. Also, given the almost daily expansion of opportunities for electronic reading and writing, there is no reason to think that this trend will abate. We expect to see even more dramatic changes over the next 15–30 years. In this concluding section we identify some specific current and emerging issues and trends that we believe to be noteworthy for literacy researchers.

The trend away from simple, atheoretical studies comparing the effects of literacy activities with and without a computer, which we noted in an earlier section of this chapter, can be cited here again. Early studies frequently lacked theoretical justification and methodological rigor, and they provided specious answers to wrong questions (e.g., see a critique of the extensive research on IBM's writing-to-read program by Krendl, & Williams, 1990). Such studies mirror the unproductive approach used to study a variety of earlier media such as instructional television, and leaving such research behind is a positive development indicating that an interest in computers and literacy is not as transient as has been the interest in other instructional media. Also, unlike early studies, recent research has focused more on conceptual factors that separate printed and electronic texts such as those we have highlighted in this chapter as opposed to visual factors, such as the optimal amount of text to display on a single screen. Relatively minor variations in the visual display of texts on computer screens have not produced robust effects on the most valued aspects of literacy such as reading comprehension (Reinking, 1992; Reinking, & Chanlin, 1994); thus, we see the decreasing interest in such factors as a positive development. We also see a shift from inter- to intramedia comparisons (a distinction first alluded to by Wright, 1987). Early studies focused on comparing electronic and printed texts usually with the tacit assumption that printed texts were the standard against which electronic texts must compare favorably to be of any value. Now we are seeing more studies content to investigate how differences in computer-based reading and writing activities might be improved without comparisons to ostensibly parallel print-based activities. Indeed, as printed and electronic texts continue to diverge, such comparisons make less sense intuitively and practically. For example, why should researchers compare writing with a word processor to writing with conventional materials when no one would seriously propose abandoning word processing? Likewise, most word processors now include means to incorporate video and sound into written documents, which take them beyond the realm of print.

Another notable trend is that research devoted to investigating the relation between computer technology and literacy has benefited from and contributed to the broader interest in contextualized research in classrooms. Researchers today are conducting investigations consistent with Weir's (1989) point of view when she states, "The kind of teaching and learning I am concerned with treats the computer as an adjunct to socially mediated learning, as part of a context, a constellation of children with children at the computer, of teachers with children with computers" (p. 61). Such a perspective is consistent with recent trends in educational research that emphasize what Salomon (1991) has called systemic, as opposed to analytic research. That is, researchers are looking more globally at the effects of introducing computer-based literacy activities into classrooms and schools. To do so they are using conventional qualitative approaches such as action research (e.g., Labbo et al. 1995–96). Notably, they are at the vanguard of efforts to develop new approaches to classroom research. For example, in our own work we have extended Newman's (1990) concept of a formative experiment as a means to determine how computer-based activities can best accomplish specific literacy goals in classrooms (Baumann et al., 1996; Reinking, & Pickle, 1993; Reinking, & Watkins, in press). Also, Bruce and Rubin (1993) have introduced an approach to classroom research they call situated evaluation to study the effects of innovative reading and writing activities in classrooms.

Furthering the move toward classroom research is an increasing confidence that computer-based activities are not only likely to remain a part of classroom life but that they are moving steadily toward the mainstream of instruction. This point of view is reflected in calls for systematic instructional responses to the new skills and awarenesses that are necessary for readers and writers in a world where much reading and writing will take place electronically (Reinking, 1994). It is also reflected in the development of pedagogical theories centered in computer technology. For example, The Cognition and Technology Group at Vanderbilt University (1994) has developed a wide range of computer-based instructional activities centered in the concept of anchored instruction. In brief, anchored instruction postulates that students learn more when a variety of instructional activities, typically that include reading and writing, is related to a rich, shared experience presented as multimedia using a computer. More research is also investigating how young readers and writers experience emergent literacy when they have regular opportunities to engage in reading and writing activities involving computers. For example, in our own work (Labbo, 1994, 1995; Labbo, Reinking, & McKenna, 1995) we have examined kindergarten students' and teachers' extensive use of a word processing and drawing program as part of school and home activities. Our ethnographic data suggest that children take a variety of approaches in exploring software tools that allow them to express themselves symbolically. We found that children view the screen as a landscape to be explored, as canvas to be painted, as a page to be written upon, as a playground, and as a stage to narrate dynamic, spontaneous plays. Other mainstream researchers have also begun to conduct research into how computers figure into emergent literacy. For example, Sulzby (1994) has compared how literacy emerges in young children who have or have not had opportunities to use computers.

Another recent trend is the rise of perspectives on literacy that would have been unthinkable only a few years ago. More writers are not only questioning definitions of literacy based solely on print but are also beginning to identify explicitly the limitations of printed materials when compared to electronic forms of communication. The focus of this volume is a case in point. Another example is the topics of two plenary speeches presented at the 1994 meeting of the National Reading Conference (Flood, & Lapp, 1995; Reinking, 1995), a leading professional organization for literacy researchers. These talks focused, respectively, on the need to expand definitions of literacy to include visual literacy and on the need for literacy researchers to completely reorient their research agenda in light of the increasing prominence of electronic reading and writing. Also, members of The Cognition and Technology Group at Vanderbilt University (1994) have proposed the term 'representational literacy,' which is the ability to communicate ideas flexibly using multimedia. Other writers are seriously questioning whether our conventional bias for prose over other verbal and nonverbal modes of communication is justified (Bolter, 1991; Edwards, 1991; Landow, 1992; Lanham, 1989, 1993; Lemke, 1994; Tuman, 1992a, 1992b). Tuman (1992a) goes so far as to suggest that teachers of writing.

> must confront the possibility that the sustained, detailed crafting of written language is too difficult a task, too removed from normal, informal, sporadic uses of language, to be the normative impulse driving the truly language arts curriculum... [because in doing so] we doom many students to be labeled as failures. (p. 124)

These broadened perspectives point to a heightened consciousness about aspects of literacy that have been either transparent or foreign when printed materials were the only reasonable standard for reading and writing. These perspectives also highlight the need to examine the changing landscape of literacy by opening up interdisciplinary dialogues among scholars in areas as diverse as sociology, history, communication, literary criticism, and education. We understand that to be a primary goal of this volume and hope that our perspective on current theory and research contributes to the dialogue.

References

Atkinson, R. C., & Hansen, D. N. (1966). Computer-assisted instruction in initial reading: The Stanford project. *Reading Research Quarterly, 2,* 5–26.

Baumann, J. F., Dillon, D. R., Shockley, B. B., Alvermann, D. E., & Reinking, D. (1996). Perspectives in literacy research. In L. Baker, P. P. Afflerbach, & D. Reinking (Eds.), *Developing engaged readers in school and home communities* (pp. 217–246). Hillsdale, NJ: Erlbaum.

Beasley, R. E., & Lister, K. B. (1992). Application report: User orientation in a hypertext glossary. *Journal of Computer-Based Instruction, 19,* 115–118.

Blohm, P. J. (1982). Computer-aided glossing and facilitated learning in prose recall. In J. A. Niles & L. A. Harris (Eds.), *New inquiries in reading research and instruction* (pp. 24–28). Thirty-first Yearbook of the National Reading Conference. Rochester, NY: National Reading Conference.

Blohm, P. J. (1987). Effect on [sic] lookup aids on mature readers' recall of technical text. *Reading Research and Instruction, 26,* 77–88.

Bolter, J. D. (1991). *Writing space: The computer, hypertext, and the history of writing,* Hillsdale, NJ: Erlbaum. Also available as hypertext computer program.

Bolter, J. D., Joyce, M., Smith, J. B., & Bernstein, M. (1993). *Storyspace* [Computer program]. Cambridge, MA: Eastgate Systems.

Brandt, D. (1990). *Literacy as involvement: The acts of writers, readers, and texts.* Carbondale, IL: Southern Illinois Press.

Bruce, B., Michaels, S., & Watson-Gegeo, K. (1985). How computers can change the writing process. *Language Arts, 62,* 143–149.

Bruce, B. C., & Rubin, A. (1993). *Electronic quills: A situated evaluation of using computers for writing in classrooms.* Hillsdale, NJ: Erlbaum.

Chang, L., & Osguthorpe, R. (1990). The effects of computerized picture-word processing on kindergartner's language development. *Journal of Research in Childhood Education, 5*(1), 73–84.

Cherryholmes, C. H. (1993). Reading research. *Journal of Curriculum Studies, 25,* 1–32.

Cochran-Smith, M., Kahn, J., & Paris, C. (1990). Writing with a felicitous tool. *Theory into Practice, 29,* 235–245.

The Cognition and Technology Group at Vanderbilt University (1994). Multimedia environments for developing literacy in at-risk students. In B. Means (Ed.), *Technology and education reform: The reality behind the promise* (pp. 23–56). San Francisco: Jossey-Bass.

Cooper, M. M., & Selfe, C. L. (1990). Computer conferences and learning: Authority, resistance, and internally persuasive discourse. *College English, 52,* 847–869.

Coover, R. (1993, August 29). Hyperfiction: Novels for the computer. *The New York Times Book Review.*

Cuban, L. (1986). *Teachers and Machines.* New York: Teachers College Press.

Daniel, D. B., & Reinking, D. (1987). The construct of legibility in electronic reading environments. In D. Reinking (Ed.), *Reading and computers: Issues for theory and practice* (pp. 24–39). New York: Teachers College Press.

Dickinson, D. K. (1986). Cooperation, collaboration, and a computer: Integrating a computer into a first-second grade writing program. *Research in the Teaching of English, 20,* 357–378.

Duchastel, P. (1986). Computer text access. *Computer Education, 10,* 403–409.

Edwards, B. L. (1991). How computers change things: Literacy and the digitized word. *Writing Instructor, 10*(2), 68–76.

Feldmann, S. C., & Fish, M. C. (1991). Use of computer-mediated reading supports to enhance reading comprehension of high school students. *Journal of Educational Computing Research, 7,* 25–36.

Fey, M. H. (1994). Finding voice through computer communication: A new venue for collaboration. *Journal of Advanced Composition, 14*(1), 221–238.

Flood, J., & Lapp, D. (1995). Broadening the lens: Toward an expanded conceptualization of literacy. In K. A. Hinchman, D. J. Leu, & C. K. Kinzer (Eds.), *Perspectives on literacy research and practice: 44th Yearbook of the National Reading Conference* (pp. 1–16). Chicago: National Reading Conference.

Friedman. B. (1990, April). *Societal issues and school practices: An ethnographic investigation of the social context of school computer use.* Paper presented at the meeting of the American Educational Research Association, Boston.

Gallego, M. A. (1992, December). *Telecommunications: Beyond the dialogue journal.* Paper presented at the meeting of the National Reading Conference, San Antonio, TX.

Gay, G., Trumbull, D., & Mazur, J. (1991). Designing and testing navigational strategies and guidance tools for a hypermedia program. *Journal of Educational Computing Research, 7,* 189–202.

Green, J. O. (1984). New ways for special ed kids to communicate. *Classroom Computer Learning, 5*(3), 24–29.

Greenleaf, C. (1994). Technological indeterminacy: The role of classroom writing practices and pedagogy in shaping student use of the computer. *Written Communication, 11*(1), 85–130.

Hawisher, G. E., & Selfe, C. L. (Eds.). (1991). *Evolving perspectives on computers and composition studies.* Urbana, IL: National Council of Teachers of English.

Heap, J. L. (1986). *Collaborative practices during computer writing in a first grade classroom* (Report No. 143). Toronto: Ontario Department of Education. (ERIC Document Reproduction Service No. ED 273 979)

Heaviside, S., Malitz, G., & Carpenter, J. (1995). *Advanced telecommunications in US schools, K–12.* (Doc. No. NCES 95–731). Washington, DC: National Center for Education Statistics, U.S. Department of Education, Office of Educational Research and Improvement.

Hegarty, M., Carpenter, P. A., & Just, M. A. (1991). Diagrams in the comprehension of scientific texts. In R. Barr, M. L. Kamil, P. Mosenthal, & P. D. Pearson (Eds.), *Handbook of reading, research, Vol. 2* (pp. 641–668). New York: Longman.

Horney, M. (1994, December). *Project literacy: Hypermedia for hearing-impaired readers.* Paper presented at the meeting of the National Reading Conference, San Diego, CA.

Jonassen, D. H. (1986). Hypertext principles for text and courseware design. *Educational Psychologist, 21,* 269–292.

Kaplan, N. (1991). Ideology, technology, and the future of writing instruction. In G. E. Hawisher & C. L. Selfe (Eds.), *Evolving perspectives on computers and composition studies* (pp. 11–42). Urbana, IL: National Council of Teachers of English.

Kaufer. D. S., & Carley, K. M. (1993). *Communication at a distance: The influence of print on sociocultural organization and change.* Hillsdale, NJ: Erlbaum.

Kiesler, S. (1986). The hidden messages in computer networks. *Harvard Business Review.*

Kirby, D. R., & Kirby, K. (1985). The reading-writing connection. In L. W. Searfoss & J. E. Readence (Eds.), *Helping children learn to read* (pp. 338–353). Englewood Cliffs, NJ: Prentice-Hall.

Krendl, K. A., & Williams, R. B. (1990). The importance of being rigorous: Research on writing to read. *Journal of Computer-Based Instruction, 17,* 81–86.

Labbo, L. (1994, December). *Examining the influence of computers on young children's opportunities for literacy development.* Paper presented at the 44th meeting of the National Reading Conference, San Diego, CA.

Labbo, L. (1995, May). *Classroom, computer lab, and living room: Case studies of kindergartners' home and school computer-related experiences. A report of findings related to NRRC funded research.* Paper presented at the meeting of the International Reading Association, Anaheim, CA.

Labbo, L., Field, S., & Watkins J. (1995). Narrative as action research: One teacher's story. *Proceedings of the Qualitative Research Interest Group Conference for January 3–5, 1995.* Athens, GA.

Labbo, L., Murray, B. A., & Phillips, M. (1995–96). Writing to read: From inheritance to innovation and invitation. *The Reading Teacher, 49,* 314–321.

Labbo, L., Reinking, D., & McKenna, M. (1995). Examining teachers roles in incorporating a computer as an informal literacy tool in classrooms of young children. In K. A. Hinchman, D. J. Leu, & C. K. Kinzer (Eds.), *Perspectives on literacy research and practice: 44th Yearbook of the National Reading Conference* (pp. 459–465). Chicago: National Reading Conference.

L'Allier, J. J. (1980). *An evaluation study of a computer-based lesson that adjusts reading level by monitoring on task reader characteristics.* Unpublished doctoral dissertation, University of Minnesota, Minneapolis, MN.

Landow, G. (1992). *Hypertext: The convergence of contemporary critical theory and technology.* Baltimore: Johns Hopkins University Press.

Lanham, R. A. (1989). The electronic word: Literary study and the digital revolution. *New Literary History, 20*(2), 265–290.

Lanham, R. A. (1993). *The electronic word: Democracy, technology, and the arts.* Chicago: University of Chicago Press.

Larson, D. (1993). *Marble Springs.* [Computer software]. Cambridge, MA: Eastgate Systems.

Lemke, J. L. (1994, April). *Multiplying meaning: Composing multimedia text.* Paper presented at the meeting of the American Educational Research Association, New Orleans, LA.

Leu, D., & Hillinger, M. (1994, December). *Reading comprehension in hypermedia: Supporting changes to children's conceptions of a scientific principle.* Paper presented at the meeting of the National Reading Conference, San Diego, CA.

MacGregor, S. K. (1988a). Instructional design for computer-mediated text systems: Effects of motivation, learner control, and collaboration on reading performance. *Journal of Experimental Education, 56,* 142–147.

MacGregor, S. K. (1988b). Use of self-questioning with a computer-mediated text system and measures of reading performance. *Journal of Reading Behavior, 20,* 131–148.

Mannes, S. M., & Kintsch, W. (1987). Knowledge organization and text organization. *Cognition and Instruction, 4,* 91–115.

McConkie, G. W. (1983, December). *Computer-aided reading: A help for illiterate adults.* Paper presented at the meeting of the National Reading Conference, Austin, TX.

McIntyre, S. R. (1992, December). *Computer-mediated discourse: Electronic journaling and effective practice.* Paper presented at the meeting of the National Reading Conference, San Antonio, TX.

McKenna, M. (1994, December). *Effects of a program of computer-mediated books on the progress of beginning readers.* Paper presented at the 44th meeting of the National Reading Conference, San Diego, CA.

McGee, G. W. (1987). Social context variables affecting the implementation of microcomputers. *Journal of Educational Computing*

Research, 3, 189–206.

Means, B., Blando, J., Olson, K., Morocco, C. C., Remz, A. R., & Zorfass, J. (1993). *Using technology to support educational reform.* Washington, DC: U.S. Department of Education.

Mehan. H. (1989). Microcomputers in classrooms: Educational technology and social practice. *Anthropology & Education Quarterly, 20,* 4–21.

Michaels, S., & Bruce, B. (1989). *Classroom contexts and literacy development: How writing systems shape the teaching and learning of composition* (Tech. Rep. No. 476). Urbana-Campaign, IL: Center for the Study of Reading.

Miller, L., & Olson, J. (1994). Putting the computer in its place: A study of teaching with technology. *Journal of Curriculum Studies, 26*(2), 121–141.

Moulthrop, S., & Kaplan, N. (1994). They became what they beheld: The futility of resistance in the space of electronic writing. In C. L. Selfe & S. Hilligoss (Eds.), *Literacy and computers: The complications of teaching and learning with technology* (pp. 220–237). New York: The Modern Language Association.

Murphy, J. W. (1988). Computerization, postmodern epistemology, and reading in the postmodern era. *Educational Theory, 38*(2), 175–182.

Myers, J. (1993). Constructing community and intertextuality in electronic mail. In D. J. Leu & C. K. Kinzer (Eds.), *Examining central issues in literacy research, theory, and practice: 42nd Yearbook of the National Reading Conference* (pp. 251–262). Chicago: National Reading Conference.

Negroponte, N. (1995). *Being digital.* New York: Knopf.

Neilsen, L. (in press). Coding the light. In L. Neilsen & J. Willinsky (Eds.), *Coding the light: Gender, generation, and technologies of metamorphoses.* New York: Teachers College Press.

Newman, D. (1990). Opportunities for research on the organizational impact of school computers. *Educational Researcher, 19,* 8–13.

Olson, R. K., Foltz, G., & Wise, B. W. (1986). Reading instruction and remediation with the aid of computer speech. *Behavior Research Methods, Instruments, and Computers, 18,* 93–99.

Olson, R. K., & Wise, B. W. (1987). Computer speech in reading instruction. In D. Reinking (Ed.), *Reading and computers: Issues for theory and practice* (pp. 156–177). New York: Teachers College Press.

Ong, W. (1982). *Orality and literacy: The technologizing of the word.* New York: Methuen.

Paivio, A. (1986). *Mental representation: A dual coding approach.* New York: Oxford University Press.

Papert, S. (1993). *The children's machine: Rethinking school in the age of the computer.* New York: Basic Books.

Phenix, J., & Hannan, E. (1984). Word processing in the grade one classroom. *Language Arts, 8,* 804–812.

Reinking, D. (1987). Computers, reading, and a new technology of print. In D. Reinking (Ed.), *Reading and computers: Issues for theory and practice* (pp. 3–23). New York: Teachers College Press.

Reinking, D. (1988). Computer-mediated text and comprehension differences: The role of reading time, reader preference, and estimation of learning. *Reading Research Quarterly, 23,* 484–498.

Reinking, D. (1992). Differences between electronic and printed texts: An agenda for research. *Journal of Educational Multimedia and Hypermedia, 1*(1), 11–24.

Reinking, D. (1994). *Electronic literacy.* (Perspective in Reading Research No. 4). University of Georgia, University of Maryland: National Reading Research Center.

Reinking, D. (1995). Reading and writing with computers: Literacy research in a post-typographic world. In K. A. Hinchman, D. J. Leu & C. K. Kinzer (Eds.), *Perspectives on literacy research and practice: 44th Yearbook of the National Reading Conference* (pp. 17–33). Chicago: National Reading Conference.

Reinking, D., & Bridwell-Bowles, L. (1991). Computers in reading and writing. In R. Barr, M. L. Kamil, P. Mosenthal & P. D. Pearson (Eds.), *Handbook of reading research, Vol. 2* (pp. 310–340). New York: Longman.

Reinking, D., & Chanlin, L. J. (1994). Graphic aids in electronic texts. *Reading Research and Instruction, 33,* 207–232.

Reinking, D., & Pickle, J. M. (1993). Using a formative experiment to study how computers affect reading and writing in classrooms. In D. J. Leu & C. K. Kinzer (Eds.), *Examining central issues in literacy research, theory, and practice, The 42nd Yearbook of the National Reading Conference* (pp. 263–270). Chicago: National Reading Conference.

Reinking, D., Pickle, M., & Tao, L. (1996). *The effects of inserted questions and mandatory review in computer-mediated texts* (Research Report No. 50). The University of Georgia and the University of Maryland: National Reading Research Center.

Reinking, D., & Rickman, S. S. (1990). The effects of computer-mediated texts on the vocabulary learning and comprehension of intermediate-grade readers. *Journal of Reading Behavior, 22,* 395–411.

Reinking, D., & Schreiner, R. (1985). The effects of computer-mediated text on measures of reading comprehension and reading behavior. *Reading Research Quarterly, 20,* 536–552.

Reinking, D., & Watkins, J. (in press). *A formative experiment investigating the use of multimedia book reviews to increase elementary students' independent reading* (Research Report). University of Georgia, University of Maryland: National Reading Research Center.

Reitsma, P. (1988). Reading practice for beginners: Effects of guided reading, reading-while-listening, and independent reading with computer-based speech feedback. *Reading Research Quarterly, 23,* 219–235.

Rheingold, H. (1993). *The virtual community: Homesteading on the electronic frontier.* Reading, MA: Addison-Wesley.

Rieber, L. P. (1990). Using computer animated graphics in science instruction with children. *Journal of Educational Psychology, 82,* 135–140.

Riel, M. (1989). The impact of computers in classrooms. *Journal of Research on Computing in Education, 22,* 180–189.

Roth, S. F., & Beck, I. L. (1987). Theoretical and instructional implications of assessment of two microcomputer word recognition programs. *Reading Research Quarterly, 22,* 197–218.

Salomon, G. (1979). *Interaction of media, cognition, and learning,* San Francisco: Jossey-Bass.

Salomon, G. (1991). Transcending the qualitative-quantitative debate: The analytic and systemic approaches to educational research. *Educational Researcher, 20*(6), 10–18.

Salomon, G., Globerson, T., & Guterman, E. (1989). The computer as a zone of proximal development: Internalizing reading-related metacognitions from a reading partner. *Journal of Educational Psychology, 81,* 620–627.

Salomon, G., Perkins, D. N., & Globerson, T. (1991). Partners in cognition: Extending human intelligence with intelligent technologies. *Educational Researcher, 20*(3), 2–9.

Selfe, C. L., & Hilligoss, S. (Eds.). (1994). *Literacy and computers: The complications of teaching and learning technology.* New York: The Modern Language Association.

Sheingold, K. (1991). Restructuring for learning with technology: The potential for synergy. *Phi Delta Kappan, 73*(1), 17–27.

Shirk, H. N. (1991). Hypertext and composition studies. In G. E. Hawisher & C. L. Selfe (Eds.), *Evolving perspectives on computers and composition studies* (pp. 177–202). Urbana, IL: National Council of Teachers of English.

Smith, F. (1984). *The promise and threat of microcomputers in language education.* Victoria, BC: Abel Press.

Spiro, R. J., Coulson, R. L., Feltovich, P. J., & Anderson, D. K. (1988). *Cognitive flexibility theory: Advanced knowledge acquisition in ill-structured domains* (Tech. Rep. No. 441). Urbana-Campaign, IL: University of Illinois, Center for the Study of Reading.

Spivey, N. N., & King, J. R. (1989). Readers as writers composing from sources. *Reading Research Quarterly, 24,* 7–26.

Stahl, S. A., Hynd, C. R., Britton, B. K., McNish, M. M., & Bosquet, D. (in press). What happens when students read multiple source documents in history? *Reading Research Quarterly.*

Stix, G. (1994). The speed of write. *Scientific American, 271*(6), 106-111.

Sulzby, E. (1994, December). *Emergent writing on and off the computer: A final report on project CIEL (computers in early literacy).* Paper presented at the meeting of the National Reading Conference, San Diego, CA.

Tobias, S. (1987). Mandatory text review and interaction with student characteristics. *Journal of Educational Psychology, 79,* 154–161.

Tobias, S. (1988). Teaching strategic text review by computer and interaction with student characteristics. *Computers in Human Behavior, 4,* 299–310.

Tuman, M. C. (1992a). *Word perfect: Literacy in the computer age.* London: Falmer Press.

Tuman, M. C. (Ed.) (1992b). *Literacy online: The promise (and peril) of reading and writing with computers.* Pittsburgh, PA: University of Pittsburgh Press.

Turner, S. V., & Depinto, V. M. (1992). Students as hypermedia authors: Themes emerging from a qualitative study. *Journal of Research on Computing in Education, 25,* 187–199.

Venezky, R. L. (1983). Evaluating computer-assisted instruction on its own terms. In A. C. Wilkinson (Ed.), *Classroom computers and cognitive science* (pp. 31–49). New York: Academic Press.

Vygotsky, L. S. (1978). *Mind and society: The development of higher psychological processes.* Cambridge, MA: Harvard University Press.

Weir, S. (1989). The computer in schools: Machine as humanizer. *Harvard Educational Review, 59,* 61–73.

Wilkinson, A. C. (1983). Learning to read in real time. In A. C. Wilkinson (Ed.), *Classroom computers and cognitive science* (pp. 183–199). New York: Academic Press.

Wise, B.W. (1992). Whole words and decoding for short-term learning: Comparisons on a "talking-computer" system. *Journal of Experimental Child Psychology, 54,* 147–167.

Wright, P. (1987). Reading and writing for electronic journals. In B. K. Britton & S. M. Glynn (Eds.), *Executive control processes in reading* (pp. 23–55). Hillsdale, NJ: Erlbaum.

Zorfass, J., & Remz, A. R. (1992). Successful technology integration: The role of communication and collaboration. *Middle School Journal, 23*(5), 39–43.

METHODS OF INQUIRY IN COMMUNICATIVE AND VISUAL ARTS TEACHING

INTRODUCTION: EXPLORATIONS IN CROSSING BOUNDARIES

Donna E. Alvermann

UNIVERSITY OF GEORGIA

We shall not cease from exploration.
And the end of all our exploring
Will be to arrive where we started
And know the place for the first time.

—T.S. Eliot

The chapters in this part of the handbook are a diverse lot, bound together by their common focus on explorations into methodological inquiry in literacy. Because these chapters cross boundaries blurred by the ever expanding visions of literacy described in Part I of the handbook, they offer endless opportunities to explore new ways of representing data. They also offer openings into understanding familiar forms of inquiry— ethnographies, case studies, teacher research, university/school collaborations, alternative assessments—in new ways made possible by a heightened sensitivity to multiple literacies.

The authors of the chapters share at length how their explorations in crossing methodological boundaries have afforded them opportunities to push their own thinking about the role of the communicative and visual arts in literacy research. They do this in a number of ways. Some demonstrate how their broadened view of literacy—one that includes a variety of sign systems—has enabled them to capture the nuances of poetry, metaphors, computers, videos, performances, and works of art in developing finely tuned methods of inquiry. Others describe how exploring the intellectual sites of ethnographies and case studies has brought a new level of awareness to their own thinking about what constitutes literacy research. Still others address policy issues that affect how multiple literacies play themselves out in theory, research, and practice.

In the chapters that lead into this part on "Methods of Inquiry in Communicative and Visual Arts Teaching," the authors disclose how they have chosen to represent findings from their interests in areas as diverse as sociology, educa-

tion, and the multimedia. For example, Laurel Richardson in her chapter, "Poetic Representation," transforms an in-depth interview into a five-page narrative poem. In so doing she transgresses standard representational practices; as Richardson notes, prose may not be the most valid way to record people's talk. Claiming that the form in which researchers write shapes the content of their findings, Richardson shows how issues of validity go unnoticed in writing up interviews in standard prose. She also demonstrates with nine lyric poems how a researcher can reduce the distance between "self" and "Other"—a feat that normative ethnographic writing cannot replicate.

A second chapter that deals with issues of representation is Lorri Neilsen's "Remaking Sense, Reshaping Inquiry: Feminist Metaphors and a Literacy of the Possible." Rejecting metaphors spawned by research that treats literacy as something to think about and do rather than live, Neilsen advocates exploring methods of inquiry that demystify research, make use of multiple sign systems, value multiple ways of knowing, and promote "response-ability" to sensory-rich literacy experiences. For her feminist sensibilities, no single metaphor will do to represent the living inquiry she espouses. Rather, what Neilsen is calling for are complexly situated metaphors that connect lives to words.

The chapter, "Learning with Multiple Symbol Systems: Possibilities, Realities, Paradigm Shifts and Developmental Considerations," by Robert Tierney explores new methods of representing the dynamics of teaching and learning in nonverbocentric ways through multilayered text. Tierney develops the thesis that multimedia environments can serve as tools to transform how learners process and represent information. He does this by drawing on three examples from his own observations and research on how multiple symbol systems, when enlisted as vehicles for criss-crossing a variety of concepts, can support different ways of knowing and being known. In another chapter, "Transcription and Representation in Literacy Research," Carolyn Baker treats the process of transcribing talk and nonverbal activity as a method of inquiry. Claiming that this process is by no means neutral in terms of the decisions researchers make, Baker advances three themes about transcription practices as representations: they are forms of thinking and communicating that reflect cultural membership; they count as literacy practices in themselves; and they assign social and moral order to what is recorded. She also describes how description, layout, and formatting decisions leave traces of the theoretical and analytical work that went into producing them.

The next clustering of chapters includes three that were written to initiate and extend conversations about theoretical and practical applications of ethnographic and case study methodologies. The chapter "Ethnography and Ethnographers of and in Education: A Situated Perspective," by Judith Green and David Bloome, is an exploration of the influence of different intellectual sites on the relationship between theory and method. Green and Bloome trace some of the changes that have occurred in this relationship as members of various communities—social scientists, educational researchers, teachers, students, and ordinary citizens— engage in the practice of ethnography and ethnographic research. Their goal is to make visible a range of issues associated with the situatedness of this method of inquiry.

Steven Athanases extends the conversation begun by Green and Bloome. In his chapter, "Ethnography for the Study of Performance in the Classroom," Athanases explores why ethnography is well suited for studying performance. He identifies specific sites of learning (e.g., student planning time, rehearsals, performances, and reflections) that occurred in an ethnography he conducted of 10th-graders' performances of poetry. He also describes the different ways performance is used in K–12 classrooms and the potential of ethnography for studying such performance, including a brief overview of the key functions, features, and challenges of ethnographic methods.

In "Children Out of Bounds: The Power of Case Studies in Expanding Visions of Literacy Development," Anne Haas Dyson moves the conversation away from ethnography and into the realm of intense study of individual experience. She presents three cases written over a 15-year period to illustrate how her own changing frames for viewing those cases shaped their construction. Like the preceding authors in this cluster of chapters, Dyson deftly illustrates the methodological dynamics of her chosen line of inquiry. She also articulates how the dialogic process involved in constructing cases of young children's literacies can destabilize conceptual boundaries and cause one to cross over them.

Teacher research and collaborative inquiry between school- and university-based researchers constitute the next set of chapters in this part of the handbook. In the chapter, "Methodology in Teacher Research: Three Cases," James Baumann, JoBeth Allen, and Betty Shockley Bisplinghoff explore issues related to the tradition of teacher inquiry, including whether or not there is anything methodologically distinct about this form of research. Next they present three cases, each of which is representative of the diversity within the domain of teacher research and involves them as the inquir-

ers. The first two cases chronicle literacy acquisition in the primary grades, while the third explores the methodological diversity within the National Reading Research Center's teacher research community.

The theme of exploring methodological issues surrounding teacher inquiry is taken up with a different view in Christine Pappas' chapter, "Making 'Collaboration' Problematic in Collaborative School–University Research: Studying *with* Urban Teacher Researchers to Transform Literacy Curriculum Genres." Pappas argues that many of the uncertainties associated with school- and university-based collaborations are largely due to new conceptualizations about power/participant structures and the nature of knowledge, which, in turn, require changes in research methodologies. She asserts that because of these changes, collaboration itself must be made problematic.

In the last clustering of chapters in this part, Anne Sweet leads off with "A National Policy Perspective on Research Intersections Between Literacy and the Visual/Communicative Arts." She describes the national legislative arena and its role in creating a niche for the arts in an expanded view of literacy. She highlights the arts education research agenda, its interface with literacy education research, and the issues related to this interface. For example, Sweet addresses the problems encountered in designing interdisciplinary assessments in dance, music, theater, design, media, and visual arts. She closes with a look to the future and the prominence of problem-centered research with its emphasis on knowledge integration as opposed to the present focus on domain specific research.

Picking up on one of the issues addressed in Chapter 20, Carol Stavropoulos describes the steps taken to develop and test the quality of an instrument for assessing written statements about works of art. In this chapter, "Alternative Methodology for Diagnostic Assessment of Written and Verbal Responses to Works of Art," Stavropoulos uses Marc Chagall's *The Birthday* to explore the knowledge base and knowledge-seeking strategies an individual would need to respond to the Diagnostic Profile. Grounded in cognitive learning theory, the Diagnostic Profile assesses students' understandings of their own work as well as a range of art reproductions.

The implications of blurred boundaries and boundary crossings, which are integral to the whole notion of an expanded print literacy, are never more apparent than in Robert Calfee's chapter on "Assessing Development and Learning Over Time." As Calfee points out, one of the first challenges in developing a valid assessment of any kind is the ability to identify the construct that is to be assessed. Calfee tackles this challenge and other issues, such as measuring growth and validity, in his attempt to explore ways of linking conceptual analysis to the practical aspects of classroom assessment.

In summary, this part of the handbook, which describes methods of inquiry in communicative and visual arts teaching, contains numerous examples of border crossings—some more visible than others—but all within a view of the world that sees knowledge as connected, yet historically situated and partial. This world view is indispensable to understanding an expanded print literacy.

11

ETHNOGRAPHY FOR THE STUDY OF PERFORMANCE IN THE CLASSROOM

Steven Z. Athanases

STANFORD UNIVERSITY

Twenty-three fifth graders, stuck in a giant vat of imaginary taffy, move in slow motion, then following their teacher's coaching, freeze before moving again, now feeling their bodies grow light and bouncy on huge trampoline-like pillows. As the physical warm-ups end, the children listen as their teacher identifies the problem for today's improvisation workshop: How to dramatize challenges facing any one of the endangered species they have studied in science.

An 11th-grade U.S. History class quiets so that the first group can perform their original scripted dramatization of conflicts during the Civil Rights and Anti-War movements of the sixties, based on oral histories that the students audiotaped during fieldwork in the community. To introduce their scene, one group member performs a published poem thematically linked to these social movements.

In an undergraduate education course on literature for the high school, four students have selected key lines from Ibsen's *Ghosts* all spoken to Mrs. Alving, the protagonist, lines that speak society's narrow definitions of a woman's duty as wife and mother. The students encircle the class-as-Mrs. Alving, delivering the lines aggressively as if theirs are society's voices dictating duty, overlapping one another rapid-fire, then chanting the lines in a Greek chorus. Two students then move to the front of the room and assume the role of Mrs. Alving herself, one delivering some of her lines from the play, another speaking the inner thoughts Mrs. Alving may have felt the need to repress because of her socially inscribed roles.

These three classroom scenes are a small sample of the kinds of performance activities in which I have been engaged for over 20 years—as student, teacher, observer, and researcher. The scenes also suggest the range of ways in which performance activities occur in classrooms from kindergarten through university, including imagination exercises and improvisations, original narratives and dramas constructed from oral history interviews, performances of poems and plays, and symbolic enactments of literary, historical, and sociological themes. Whether teachers use performance as an occasional instructional strategy or as the foundation of their curriculum, their use of performance typically invites students to assume roles of other real people and literary characters; to enact, embody, and usually voice people's stories, dilemmas, insights; to interpret and critique texts; or to dialogue or argue with others. Through the use of performance, a teacher vivifies how history tells stories of real people's struggles, how literature holds accounts of characters' lives, how a curriculum can live as students imagine themselves walking a mile in another's moccasins. In these ways, the teacher, in asking students to perform, moves well beyond a transmission model of teaching with passive learners, inviting students to imagine, act, embody, shape, and feel their way into a deep knowing of the course content.

While these experiences of classroom performance are relatively rare in U.S. schools, their use holds rich potential for student learning, particularly when coupled with a range of literacy activities that help students plan, rehearse, and reflect on their own and their peers' performances. Such activities, with the act of performance itself, may support, among other things, subject-matter learning, language growth, self-esteem building, and affective and cognitive gains. Little research, however, has documented what such performances and accompanying activities yield for student learning.

This chapter explores the use of ethnography as a research method well suited to the study of classrooms in which such acts of performance play a prominent role. I begin with a brief

The 10th-grade performance study used as illustration in this chapter was funded by a postdoctoral fellowship from the James S. McDonnell Foundation Program in Cognititive Studies for Educational Practice.

survey of the ways in which performance is used primarily in K–12 classrooms and described in reports and textbooks. This survey includes arguments offered on behalf of performance as a learning strategy and, when results of studies of classroom performance are available, these are included. I then argue the need for research into classroom performance and describe ways in which ethnography is well suited to this task. For readers who are not experienced ethnographers, a brief overview of ethnography follows, highlighting its key functions, features, and challenges. Finally, the chapter identifies the ways in which ethnographic methods can document student learning through performance and related activities. These methods are illustrated by data from a recent study on the performance of poetry that I conducted with a class of 10th-grade students.

KINDS OF CLASSROOM PERFORMANCE

In a report on the state of performance studies, Strine, Long, and HopKins (1990) described ways in which the field, originally conceived as a means of studying literature, now embraces much more—other subject areas, other genres, other purposes. Their chronicle of historical change in production and scholarship in performance also provides a way of understanding changes in classroom uses of performance. I begin with a survey of performance of literature in classrooms— since historically this has been the most common focus of performance in schools—then briefly review some other recent forms of classroom performance.

Classroom Performance of Literature

Oral reading and creative drama have long held important places in some elementary school classrooms because these activities include, among other things, a sense of play, use of the imagination, narrative understanding, the body, the senses—elements and values often considered relevant to young children. At universities also, the study of oral interpretation of literature has long held a place in many departments of speech communication and communication studies. At the high school level, however, while some teachers have for many years used drama and other kinds of performance in their teaching, these instances in U.S. schools have been few overall, particularly in contrast to schools in the U.K. (Freedman, 1994; Squire & Applebee, 1968, 1969). Electives flourished in U.S. schools in the late 1960s and early 1970s in, for example, areas of theater and speech communication such as public speaking, oral communication, persuasion, acting, debate, drama and stagecraft, and oral interpretation. Universities graduated Speech Education majors to teach these courses and to direct related extracurricular activities.

By the early 1980s, however, high schools stripped electives from their programs, in many cases returning to only yearlong comprehensive English courses, in part because of general budget cuts in education, and because the graduation of the last post World War II baby boomers brought a sharp enrollment decline and difficulty in sustaining small elective

classes. Also, frequent press coverage of a decline in students' basic skills and of falling national test scores ushered in "accountability" in education and the perceived need to narrow English curricula to reading and writing, with speech and drama courses often perceived as unnecessary. Universities graduated fewer speech education majors since few school positions called for such preparation, and at some universities these degrees were eliminated altogether. In recent decades, if high schools offered students in-class speech and drama opportunities, it has been generally because English teachers have built them into their curricula, tying them closely to reading and writing instruction.

One result of the dearth of performance experience in middle schools and secondary schools is that, stripped of its origins in song, the poem and much other literature that students encounter have become merely printed text that students must read and study quietly and privately. This image of literature is far from that conceived by aesthetics and performance scholars such as William Craig Forrest who argued, "As with the musical score, the poem is a set of directions for performance" (1969a, p. 298). Seldom perceived in schools as a musical score or as material for dramatization or other forms of performance, literature has journeyed far from the stories of folklore and the oral narratives once widely spoken and sung to lute, lyre, and drum. In relatively rare cases, however, teachers use classroom performance for varied purposes, among these to engage students' thinking, emotions, voices, bodies, and communication skills in explorations into literature.

In a yearlong ethnography (Athanases, 1993), I studied two 10th-grade English classes in which the teachers diversified their literature curricula to include more works by authors of color, fostered response-centered instruction, and facilitated classroom discussions that featured student thinking. While discussions proved central to students' literary understanding and appreciation, they were subsets of rich oral language environments that included, among many forms of classroom communication, performances of literature. Table 11–1 shows the teachers' varied uses of performance events over

TABLE 11–1. Performance Events in Literature Study in Two 10th-Grade Classes During One School Year[a]

1. Full-class oral reading of dramatic literature in the study of *Oedipus, Lysistrata, Antigone,* and *Othello*
2. Videotaped Renaissance newscasts using *Othello* as data source
3. Solo performance of soliloquies from *Othello*
4. Performances of scenes from original modern-day tragedies written in small groups—to parallel themes from tragedies written by the Greeks and by Shakespeare
5. Small group oral read-arounds of poetry
6. Solo performances of original poems thematically linked to poems in a unit on literature of discrimination
7. Scripted solo performances of thematically-linked poetry programs
8. Small group performances of scripted scenes adapted from *Black Boy*
9. Small group scripted dramatic scenes in project presentations on group novels, in which characters from various literary works meet

[a] From Athanases (1993)

the course of the year. While the uses of performance of literature in classrooms vary, exemplified in Table 11–1, in K–12 classrooms they tend to fall within five categories.

Storytelling. Some teachers use storytelling as a way into literature and for an understanding of story and performance. In my own teaching of tenth graders, I preceded the study of Harper Lee's *To Kill a Mockingbird* with sessions of legend telling in a circle, lights off, curtains drawn (Athanases, 1984). After swapping local legends, we discussed what the legends shared, why we tell them, what keeps them alive—all as a set-up for the legend of Boo Radley which the students would encounter in Lee's novel. Fine (1990) described the swapping of folklore and performing "everyday" tales from students' own oral traditions as both a means of introducing students to performance and a way of understanding the nature of performance, its defining features, and its power.

Spontaneous Oral Readings. Teachers frequently invite students to read aloud from literary works in class and, in the case of dramatic works, occasionally invite students to read characters' parts so that the dialogue and conflicts of the drama can be heard. These are generally initial soundings, first encounters with literary works. Such readings can stimulate discussion and deepen student comprehension as the drama of the literature is heard. Thoughtful teachers know that students raised on media such as television, film, videos, and even CD-ROM need at least occasionally to have print voiced.

Dramatic Improvisations. Many published descriptive accounts of classroom performance concern the use of improvisational activities, particularly in the elementary grades but occasionally ranging up through even college-level courses. Authors of such works claim that improvisation can develop the child's understanding of the world (Heathcote, 1981), foster empathy (Wagner, 1990), clarify what students already know (Edmiston, Enciso, & King, 1987), enhance literary engagement and understanding (Rogers & O'Neill, 1993), and develop students' interpretive skills, including attention to textual details (Krondorfer & Bates, 1994). Many advocates of improvisation cite Dorothy Heathcote (whose teaching is described in Wagner, 1976), as an expert in leading classroom improvisation. Generally, advocates of this work value the process of learning to enact over performance as a theatrical product. In this vein, Stewig and Buege (1994) described ways to integrate "spontaneous drama" in whole language classrooms in the elementary grades, arguing that it is a language art that enables children to embody characters and situations, to explore nonverbal communication, and most important, to develop oral language proficiency.

Wagner (1990) identified two forms of improvisation. In *story drama*, students enact scenes related to literature under study. She described a set of activities she and a teacher conducted with seventh graders in the study of *Johnny Tremain* by Esther Forbes. Students participated in guided improvisations, followed by written reflections in diary entries that the fictive characters might have kept. In another activity, students clustered in written form traits and mental associations related to Johnny and Dove, the key characters in

conflict, enacted in pairs an imaginary scene of the two characters meeting, then wrote diary reflections after the conflict. In an extended illustration of *theme-oriented drama*, Wagner described how Dorothy Heathcote took her 6- to 8-year-old students through activities over a few days to help them understand differences between medical care of modern times and of the times of George Washington. Through coaching from their teacher and from other adult volunteers who played the roles of patients to the students' health care workers, students read and used the signs their teacher had prepared, prepared lists of health care problems and the supplies needed, wrote down directions for healing maladies, kept pencils behind their ears to maintain records of each patient's progress and detailed records for use by those on duty after the doctor or nurse would leave. Students engaged in historical imagining and empathy work, and practiced the use of more sophisticated language through their roles. In both forms of improvisation, teachers used purposeful designs to engage students in a range of literacy activities and acts of thinking. While the story drama form is more relevant to literature study, the wide range of literacy events built into both forms illustrates the learning potential of improvisation.

Similarly featuring this potential of story drama improvisation, Rogers and O'Neill (1993) identified four strategies that can help build bridges between literature and drama: the teacher assumes a role that asks the students to explore understanding; students conduct interviews in pairs from relevant imaginary perspectives; groups construct tableaux or still images of significant moments or abstract representations of textual elements; and a class conducts an inquiry, reflecting on literary events by putting a character on trial. In their work with one 9th-grade class, the authors found that writing-in-role following improvisations demonstrated literary engagement and understanding. With much older students in college level literature study, Krondorfer and Bates (1994) used improvisations in the form of "ritual enactment" in which a facilitator coached students through interviews, dialogues, and living sculptures that explored relationships among characters and events in the literary work and that brought to body and life students' responses to the literature, whether consciously or not.

Scripted Group Performance Based on Literary Works. Group performance of nondramatic literature has long held a place in theatres and classrooms, generally defined as the scripting of full literary works, portions of works, or compiled scripts of several short or excerpted works (Coger & White, 1973; Kleinau & McHughes, 1980; Long, Hudson, & Jeffrey, 1977; Maclay, 1971). These performances, often called readers theatre, feature conflicts, tensions, characterization, thematic connections across collections of short works, and other literary elements. Chamber theatre (Breen, 1978), one form of readers theatre, features the staging of prose fiction, in which the performance preserves the narration by staging the narrator's relationship to the tale, as well as staging some form of the tale itself. A chamber theatre production of Ken Kesey's *One Flew Over the Cuckoo's Nest*, for example, would stage Chief Bromden's narration of the story, including his dramatic visions of Nurse Ratched's monstrous treatment of patients in the psychiatric ward and his tale of the fog machine being turned on in the wards to blur the patients' thinking. In contrast, the motion picture of Kesey's novel gave viewers the action firsthand, rather than through the lens of Bromden's imagination.

For dramatic literature itself, Doyle (1993) advocated teaching students to ask critical questions of the literature and to enact scenes generated by those questions and issues, fostering a critical examination of culture. At the lower grade levels too, some teachers ask students to construct and perform short scripted dramatizations that feature key conflicts or themes from literary works, either as reconstructions of the works themselves or as original dramas borrowing themes and storylines from published works. In an account of group performances of literature in "classroom theatre," Wolf (1994) studied a class of 17 third- and fourth-grade predominantly special needs students, 11 of whom had been detained at some point in the primary grades and most of whom suffered from reading problems. In over ten sessions of classroom theatre led by a guest actor/director, students learned drama techniques, practiced warm-up exercises, and worked with basal reader selections and trade books on collaborative interpretation of text through script preparation, rehearsal, performance, and follow-up commentary. Wolf studied students' evolving notions of drama and their growth in dramatic interpretation.

First, students learned thoughtfully to consider multiple interpretations, drawing particularly on real-life experiences to sort through interpretive possibilities. They engaged in problem solving as they collaboratively constructed scripted scenes, negotiating plausible interpretations. In addition, the students engaged in a great deal of perspective taking, prompted by reflective writing tasks that asked "what-if" questions and by the director, teacher, and researcher who persistently asked such questions. Students gained a critical stance about their interpretive and performative choices, talking more and eventually initiating more criticism without the prodding of adults as they prepared final performance scripts. Wolf amply documented how "Undergirding an abbreviated line of spoken talk … is an analytic foundation of thought" (p. 35). Here group performance served aesthetic concerns but likewise triggered thinking and learning that could transfer to other situations and texts.

Solo Performance of Literature or of Excerpts From Literary Works. Some teachers have long emphasized the oral reading and memorization of dramatic monologues and soliloquies. Such acts of performance have provided students with opportunities to sound poetry and to speak the often heightened language of poets. In the case of texts with challenging language, such as Greek tragedies or Shakespeare's works, teachers often accompany oral work with written paraphrasing to foster students' comprehension of text. Seldom, however, do these events move beyond written paraphrasing and memorization of language to the performance interpretation of literature. This latter feature, however, has long been the focus of the field of oral interpretation, now more commonly referred to by speech communication scholars as performance studies.

Lee and Gura (1982) defined oral interpretation as "the art of communicating to an audience a work of literary art in its intellectual, emotional, and aesthetic entirety" (p. 3). It is the "aesthetic entirety" feature that particularly challenges the solo performer. Through the performance of an excerpt from a prose or dramatic work, the student is not merely an actor embodying a single role as part of a full play. Instead, the solo performer attempts to embody and convey a sense of the *full* scene or even full work of multiple characters, of action, of conflict. In the case of a collection of poems, the performer brings life to individual poems *and* may engage in literary teaching by selecting and sequencing poems to feature thematic and linguistic links—and then attempt to embody these features in performance.

Expanded Genres and Uses of Classroom Performance

Performance is used sometimes as an instructional strategy in varied subject areas in K–12 classes. In addition, the field of performance studies explores the nature of performance itself as it occurs in many genres in varied community settings and has embraced multiple genres and purposes for classroom performance, generally featuring college and university classes. For example, to link classroom learning with the world outside and to bring history alive, some teachers use the performance of oral history, in which students gather oral texts through fieldwork, then perform these histories as a means of understanding individuals, history, and culture (Stucky, 1995). Students conduct and tape a field interview, produce an interview transcript, construct a story from the transcript, and rehearse and perform that story. Fuoss and Hill (1992) described three kinds of assignments they use for teaching a university course in social movements: *unscripted* assignments that generally invite role-playing or improvisations, such as invented debates in which students argue from the perspectives of the social and historical figures they have studied; *scripted* assignments for which students perform extant texts (speeches, manifestos, poems, essays, letters); and *scripting* assignments, involving the original production of texts (e.g., an imaginary journal written by a social leader, an original narrative, or a manuscript constructed from several speeches, poems, or other texts). Students in a performance studies course at Northwestern University explored performance as dialogue between the lives of students at the university and survivors of the devastating 1972 Buffalo Creek flood in Appalachia (Olsen, 1992). Students staged an event to create a disruption real for audience members in the way that the flood disrupted the lives of Buffalo Creek residents; the director then interviewed audience members regarding their responses to the performance.

Park-Fuller and Pelias (1995) provided a catalogue of recent alternative performance genres in order to aid our understanding of this expanding field. In addition to *improvisation* in both writing and performing plays, the authors identified three other categories. *Storymaking* includes the construction of a script based on oral history interviews, and also includes the performance of personal narrative; conversational storytelling (a kind of staged swapping of tales); and fictive monologue, a scripted imaginary monologue of a fictional character. The *replication of life performances* includes conversational replication, based on transcripts of conversations and interviews (such as Anna Deavere Smith's recent productions), and restored performances (notated scripts of prior live performances so that performers can reenact what others have done). Finally, *performance art* uses a postmodern sensibility in, among other things, breaking norms of unity and completeness, inviting audience members to collaborate in meaning making. These works use strategies such as juxtaposition, which places images and symbols above narrative; psychic display, through which performers reveal their often fragmented psyches and selves in unpredictable and often shocking ways; and intertextuality, which gives centrality in performance to the intersection of texts and genres.

STUDYING WHAT PERFORMANCE YIELDS

The teacher or researcher interested in investigating the learning that any one of these many forms of performance yields might ask any number of questions. The educational writers I have surveyed have tapped classroom experiences from their roles as teachers and researchers to make claims based on anecdotal evidence and, in some cases, on empirical study. Their many claims I have cataloged, when not supported by empirical work, could be tested through study. A whole range of questions could drive such work. How, for example, might performing Chief Seattle's speech on the destruction of the American land shape, alter, deepen a student's understanding of and appreciation for the environmental history of the United States or the Native American view of land? What impact does interviewing African-American veterans of the Vietnam War and performing their oral histories for peers have on students' understanding of that war, of the ways in which racism figured in the armed forces in the sixties? What kinds of cultural understanding and language opportunities does role-playing children in other societies enable young children to have? What do students learn about the language of poetry through speaking it, rehearsing it, singing it? In classrooms where performance plays a central role, what kinds of things occur in students' use of language, behavior, attitudes, and values? If classroom experiences with performance appear to have an impact on students, to what can we attribute this impact? What features of a performance-rich learning environment shape what kinds of student learning? In what ways? With which students? These are just a sampling of the many questions that thoughtful teachers and researchers might ask about the potential values of performance for students.

In addition to educational writers, scholars from fields as varied as literary criticism, performance studies, rhetoric, and aesthetics have argued, in varied ways, the merits of performance that can be tested through structured inquiry. Geiger (1973) argued that performance, more deeply than silent reading, aids the knowing and "realization" of experiences and thoughts suggested by a text. Berleant (1980) pushed it perhaps one step further: performance creates an experience that enables us to become one with the work.

Forrest (1969b) foregrounded the embodiment that performance fosters, citing how it creates the direct kinesthetic sensation of the speaking body (how the speech sounds and feels to the body), vital to language experience. Related to this, Conquergood (1991) has discussed the body as a site of knowing. Bacon (1972) attended to the felt level of literary experience. Performance, he argued, demonstrates not just what a poem says, but also how it feels: "in performance, with the matching of the body of the poem with the body of the reader, we have the poem incarnate" (p. 6). One poet supported this claim by testifying that at a performance of her own works, the performance "took me back to the pain of the poem's birthing."

In the often challenging arena of contemporary U.S. classrooms, performance can breathe life into the study of literature that students find so often unstimulating and even stifling (Cameron, 1981). Performance can provide the necessary component of active learning to the curriculum (Duke, 1974) and in this way fits neatly with Reader Response theory that features the readers' active meaning-making processes in transactions with literature (e.g., Bleich, 1978; Fish, 1980; Rosenblatt, 1978). Also, performance can help recover the orality of texts and a view of literature as a dynamic event, valuable for students who too often see texts merely as artifacts (Fine, 1990). Fine argued that curricula must counter the stifling effects of print:

> Unless students understand that literature is a record of verbal performances, a translation of them into the print medium, and unless they learn how to restore the printed record to a live performance, then they will be cheated out of a full and rich experience with literature and the life it contains. (pp. 179, 180)

In addition, writers claim that performance fosters intimate encounters with heightened language, providing verbal models for students in language study. Others claim that learning to project to others meanings and feelings through performed language aids communicative competence. Finally, in the upper grades and college classrooms, making space for performance can rescue literature from the deadening effects of criticism, the overly analytical dismantling of texts that strips them of the lifeforce that inspired their creation (Shattuck, 1980). These are but a sampling of the arguments that have been offered in support of performance.

The Need for Research into Classroom Uses of Performance

Despite a great deal of advocacy literature and testimonials regarding the values and practices of classroom performance, relatively little research has examined the process and the impact of such activity in classrooms. In the field of speech communication, for example, despite calls for measurement to discover more about the interpreter's response and the impact of performance on readers and performers (e.g., Klyn, 1965; Long, 1973; Strine et al., 1990), little research has tested the various theories and claims regarding the power of performance in theaters and especially in classrooms. Herndon (1973) argued that the result suggested

> an inexplicable mystical experience culminating in artistic expression. ... The uncertainty about what is referred to when interpreters use the phrase, 'the reader experiences the literature,' prevents one from asking pertinent questions and setting relevant problems for research. This phrase and other similar phrases suggest vague and mystical concepts, and they deserve the skeptical treatment they usually get from scholars in more factual fields.

In her review of research on the effects of drama on the language arts, Wagner (1988) too noted that research on classroom drama has been relatively sparse. Some studies, she noted, had found significant correlations or effects, such as work conducted by Pellegrini (1980), in which students' involvement in dramatic play enhanced story comprehension and understanding of syntactic structure; Pellegrini (1984), in which drama correlated with kindergartners' word-writing fluency; and Wagner (1986), where role-playing strengthened students' persuasive writing in grades 4 and 8. Wagner noted, however, that the mode of research up to this point had been almost exclusively studies comparing the differential effects of teaching strategies (such as role-playing and drama) on written products. Lacking in research literature on drama in education, however, was qualitative research providing richly detailed observations of drama in the classroom, "descriptions that capture the immediacy and power of the child's struggle to make meaning" (p. 52). What, in the process of drama, proves particularly powerful for children's learning? In what ways? With which children? What do features of drama and other forms of performance enable students to do?

The dearth of research into classroom performance of literature can be attributed, in part, to little evidence that performance of literature has been systematically integrated into K–12 classrooms. Second, views of performance as mere child's play, as a nonacademic, often messy curricular frill, have relegated performance to the curricular margins, seldom viewed as an instructional method with cognitive power. In addition, some view performance from purely an aesthetic view and believe that one cannot empirically examine artistic experience. This view reinforces the notion that performance is some mystical activity that cannot be taught or investigated.

Even if researchers are committed to documenting and examining performance, however, the daunting challenge of studying performance as it occurs in schools also helps explain the dearth of such research. For example, planning, rehearsal, and performance events can be so complex and interrelated that they elude easy investigation. Also, the logistics of tracking planning and rehearsal sessions can be staggering since they often occur in different groups simultaneously in single classrooms, in other school spaces teachers find for students' rehearsals, and in out-of-school settings. Finally, rehearsals and performances are fleeting and difficult to describe, let alone to evaluate.

Why Ethnography Is Well Suited for Studying Classroom Performance

Ethnography holds potential for investigations of classroom performance for various reasons. First, ethnography's reliance on long-term participation and observation as a primary method of data collection can enable the investigator to track the students' unfolding learning over time and during multiple phases of often rather long-term rehearsal periods or performance units. Ethnographic work can situate student performances in the context of the sweep of a school year, embedded in a full set of curricular activities. Teachers who use classroom activities dealing with performance frequently plan these for various times over the course of the school year. Ethnographic work can capture how things students learn in some domains get internalized and picked up in others.

Second, because it requires immersion into a culture, ethnography can enable a researcher to examine students' performance learning in multiple classroom and out-of-class contexts, and can prove particularly appropriate for investigating the development of a "performance culture" in classrooms where performance holds a central role in curriculum and instruction. The researcher can investigate cultural patterns related to learning: How do students learn in this environment to do what they learn to do? How does a class of students get socialized into the acts of performance? What kinds of student responses and learning occur during units in which performance holds a key place?

Third, ethnography requires attention to the contexts of the school, including homes from which learners come and the community locations to which students go when they leave the building. How does performance figure in these out-of-the-classroom settings where students spend time? This attention to context can help frame an understanding of cultural patterns that occur in classrooms.

Finally, as my survey of kinds of classroom performance has demonstrated, in addition to the act of performance itself, teachers often include many learning-rich activities surrounding performance. It might be recalled that in Wagner's study (1990), children produced written clusters of characters' traits and mental associations, enacted an imaginary conflict of two characters meeting, then wrote diary reflections on the conflict. Heathcote's students (Wagner, 1990) prepared lists of health care problems and wrote detailed records of patients' progress as they played the roles of health care workers. Students in Wolf's study (1994) practiced warm-up exercises, planned and wrote scripts, and engaged in reflective writing in response to "what-if" questions. When these literacy activities are foregrounded and the learning made concrete and visible, a window into the world of learning through performance is opened. Such an approach moves the focus from merely the culminating act of performance to encompass more broadly the cognitive, kinesthetic, aesthetic, and communicative processes that students exercise during performance study. All these processes invite examination. Here, again, ethnography is well suited to the task. Using multiple data collection tools, an ethnography provides rich documentation of learning as it unfolds and varies over time, describing the varied processes and products of student learning.

PRINCIPLES FOR CONDUCTING ETHNOGRAPHY

Often, research considered "qualitative" in nature is referred to as ethnographic, even though it lacks the fundamental features of the disciplinary base of cultural anthropology. Principles for conducting anthropological research can guide ethnographic language studies in classrooms (e.g., Atkinson & Hammersley, 1993; Ellen, 1984; Goetz & LeCompte, 1984; Heath, 1982; Sanjek, 1990; Saville-Troike, 1982; Sperber, 1982). These principles are no doubt familiar to, and routinely shaping, the work of experienced ethnographers. For the less experienced in conducting ethnographic research, I provide an overview of the key purposes, features, and challenges of this method.

The central goal of ethnography is generally held to be the discovery of cultural patterns achieved through long-term fieldwork of participant observation. The researcher becomes immersed in the culture, using a relativistic view in which cultural norms are examined on their own terms, rather than through a deficit lens. The researcher situates the study of the culture firmly within contexts and intertwining social systems. In addition, extensive complementary scholarly study helps

TABLE 11–2. Principles in Conducting Classroom-Based Ethnographies of Literacy Learning[a]

Focus	Principle
Launching the study	Select sites thoughtfully and clarify selection process
	Negotiate entry and build rapport carefully
	Seek support to deal with costs
Early stages	Decide locus for study
	Locate key informants
	Beware of the role of authority and power
	Build rapport and trust, then take notes
Data collection	Observe rigorously
	Capture teacher wisdom
	Interview multiple informants
	Account for the complexity of context
	Balance tight order with the evolving nature of the research process
Analysis	Engage in ongoing preliminary analysis
	Decide what to analyze fully
	Test multiple analytic frames
Writing	Clarify how assumptions drove procedures
	Decide how to report
	Insure credibility and rigor by considering issues of validity and reliability
Reciprocation	Make contributions to community members

Adapted from Talbert (1973) and from Athanases and Heath (1995)

frame emerging cultural patterns. A set of principles, shown in Table 11–2, can guide the work of the ethnographer studying classroom performance, language, and learning. These principles are detailed in various writings, including Talbert (1973) and Athanases and Heath (1995). In the latter work, Shirley Brice Heath and I provide an historical background to ethnography, then feature dilemmas the ethnographer faces, using an extended illustration of a yearlong study I conducted and the ways in which I attempted to solve methodological problems. While many of the principles identified in Table 11–2 may seem self-explanatory, some warrant elaboration.

Launching the Study

Because of the long-term nature of ethnography and the need to become intimately involved in the community studied, the researcher is wise to thoughtfully select sites in which productive study can occur over an extended period of time and to articulate criteria for the selection process so that readers can understand how to place a study within larger bodies of related work. What features of the sites will allow findings from this study to be compared with those of other research? Once sites have been selected and entry has been negotiated, researchers new to a setting need to pay particular care to building rapport with key informants, generally the teachers and students there. Researchers from universities are wise to pay special attention to this need, since they are members of an hierarchically structured educational system in which they generally hold higher status in positions removed from the daily demands and often harsh circumstances of teaching children. A nonjudgmental stance is essential. The ethnographer must try to view, describe, and frame a culture through new eyes. In addition, members of the culture who feel judged by an outsider may withhold valuable insights, leaving the study significantly less powerful in capturing insiders' perspectives.

Ethnography can be an expensive enterprise because it requires large time commitments as the researcher becomes immersed in the culture. Beyond time, other costs can include the purchase of materials and purchase or rental of recording equipment during data collection, support services to handle data maintenance and organization, and research assistance to deal with extensive data analysis. Researchers planning ethnographic work are wise to seek release time from other duties in order to accommodate the extensive demands of fieldwork and to apply for grant support to defray costs. In addition, building ethnographic teams makes sense for sharing responsibilities of data collection and extensive analyses of qualitative data.

Data Collection

As the ethnographer becomes a frequent observer and perhaps participant in a culture, rigorously taking field notes, key informants from varied groups within the system can be consulted and interviewed for their perspectives on events. Various factors shape how cultural members perceive events, including membership in groups defined by gender and ethnicity and level of power within the culture. To frame an understanding of a class or school activity, an ethnographer may wish to consult people from various levels of power within the school, as well as parents and informed community members. Triangulation of data from varied sources can aid validity of claims in the study. Within the class, then, the ethnographer may wish to seek, through student surveys and interviews, balanced perspectives on relevant issues from, for example, more vocal and less vocal students, more and less academically prepared students, key actors in focal events and those who are observers. Finally, the ethnographer may wish to tap the teacher's wisdom of practice (Shulman, 1987) through acts of reflection that reveal thinking (Schon, 1983). In brief discussions before and after class, in extended interviews, or in written or audiotaped logs, the teacher can provide insights into classroom events and student motivations, purposes for class behavior, and reasons behind spontaneous adaptations of lessons during class sessions.

To understand the conditions that have shaped what occurs in the setting, the ethnographer collects data on the multiple layers of context within which the setting is situated. This portion of the project can be daunting in its complexity. In a national study, McLaughlin and Talbert (1993) provided a helpful framework for examining the embedded contexts that matter for secondary school teaching. Data on how context shapes classroom culture can be collected and categorized at levels, beginning from the broadest: national context (reform initiatives, national schooling norms), professional contexts (associations, collaboratives, teacher education programs), higher education standards (university entrance requirements that drive secondary school curricula), parents/local community, school system, school organization, subject area/department, and the classroom (subject and students).

Maintaining a precise trail of data collection purposes and procedures can aid the reliability of an ethnography. Also, keeping data filed and labeled can prevent the sensation of being overwhelmed by the large and varied bodies of data often collected during ethnographic fieldwork, such as field notes, lesson handouts and copies of board notes, student work samples, audiotapes of conversations, and interview transcripts. In addition, ongoing analysis through early review and coding of such data can enable the researcher to use emerging cultural patterns and insights to shape further survey and interview questions and to begin to track evidence for early claims and evidence that counters those claims.

Analysis and Writing

Deciding which data to analyze in what ways proves one of the most challenging tasks for the ethnographer. Examining different slices of data in different ways will yield different portraits; the ethnographer may wish to explore various organizing systems and analytic schemes to determine what they will yield (Talbert, 1973). Holding in focus key research questions that have driven the study and that have emerged

from early analysis can guide the researcher in the selection of analyses to conduct fully.

Ethnographic writing can never be objective, never pure representation through good field notes and mere writing up of results (e.g., Clifford, 1986; Pratt, 1986). The ethnographer sees through a frame (Goffman, 1974) and is responsible for identifying that frame. How have theoretical assumptions, philosophical and political biases, and practical considerations shaped decisions in the study? A clear explication of these in report writing enables the reader to understand the study's construction. Balancing numbers with stories is another challenge that the ethnographer faces in report writing. Numbers can help structure a whole: how large a place did a kind of event occupy in a given lesson, week, unit of instruction, marking period, or school year? Such a framing can help the reader understand the typicality or anomaly of stories the ethnographer details and the degree to which the stories capture the logic of actual life in the culture (Geertz, 1973). How oral discourse is transcribed is a matter of both theory and practicality and this system should be clarified. Stretches of transcribed discourse, often lengthy in print, need to be carefully selected as illustrations of events and phenomena analyzed.

To establish credibility in the reporting of ethnography, the researcher may want to clarify data collection and analytic procedures that aid the validity and reliability of claims (cf. Goetz & LeCompte, 1984). For example, in the clarification of validity, the researcher may want to consider questions such as these (from Athanases & Heath, 1995): Do survey and interview questions feature issues relevant to concerns of teachers and students? Are they relevant to the theoretical framing of the study? Have data been sampled repeatedly to warrant claims of patterns? Have multiple data sources been sampled and triangulated to warrant claims? Have data and claims from varied groups been examined and triangulated to substantiate analysis?

The report might include ways for the reader to trust that the research record is sufficiently reliable that some replication of portions of the study could be conducted. In addition to clarification of how theoretical assumptions have shaped procedures, other aids to reliability are the following: a precise trail of research moves; some consistency in interview questions across informants; preservation of primary data (such as exact language of informants) in reporting; internal reliability checks in the form of participants' own comments on discourse; perspectives balanced by groups of informants; independent coding of interviews, artifacts, and discourse data; and reports of emerging patterns reviewed and critiqued by outsiders and insiders (e.g., teachers in the study) (Athanases & Heath, 1995).

Ethnographer Reciprocation

A long-standing principle guiding anthropological fieldwork is the obligation to demonstrate reciprocity to a community in which the researcher has benefited from the time and close study of community members. The ethnographer in a school setting can do this in many ways, determined by a match of the needs of community members and the skills and re-sources of the researcher. Among these acts are providing resources for use in the site, assistance in lesson planning, reviews of student work, tutorial assistance, and clerical sup-port in the form of filing, organizing, and constructing class-room exhibits.

ETHNOGRAPHIC TOOLS FOR THE STUDY OF CLASSROOM PERFORMANCE

A study that examines classroom performance in the context of a full literacy program might employ a range of data collection tools to capture student learning in the assortment of classroom activities that occur. For example, I recently conducted a study in a 10th-grade English class in which the teacher and I taught a unit on the performance of poetry and investigated how students came to understand the performance concepts taught and how students worked on interpreting poetry through performance. For one por-tion of the unit, each student worked with a single poem over an 8-day period. The setting was an urban public school serving primarily children of middle- to low-income families. The class was heterogeneously grouped and ethnically

diverse: more than one third of the students were African American, and the rest were Chinese American, Latino, Filipino, and European American. I refer to this study simply as the 10th-grade performance study.

Table 11–3 shows data collected during just the focal unit of the 10th-grade performance study. Other ethnographic data were collected during the school year, such as teacher interviews, observation field notes of class sessions, instruc-tional artifacts, student work samples, and data on context.

The following discussion highlights some of the tools of Table 11–3 and explores ways in which the ethnographer might investigate student learning in the context of classroom performance. Some of these methods are most relevant to studies in which the researcher is also the classroom teacher or, as in the case of the 10th-grade performance study, works collaboratively with a teacher to design tools both to foster and to reveal student thinking and learning through the performance process. The data collection methods described address one very particular kind of classroom performance of literature (solo performance of individual poems). Principles and data collection tools are described, however, to provide ideas for ethnographers investigating many other forms of classroom performance.

Documenting Instruction and Its Impact

Due to its relative rarity in classrooms, performance of litera-ture is often a new classroom practice for students. For this reason, documentation of instruction in performance can help frame an investigation into how students learn about performance and become socialized into classroom environ-ments that foster certain kinds of performance. For the 10th-grade performance study, students' initial understandings of literature and performance were sampled before documenta-tion of instruction on performance. Table 11–3 shows that data for investigating these initial understandings were col-lected using some conventional tools of ethnography: field notes, surveys, interviews, and taping. The student surveys were designed to capture students' varied perceptions of performance and its purposes, students' past experiences with performance, and their notions of literary interpretation (an area that may well be affected by students' involvement in the performance of literature). Student work samples and other data on student performance (including field notes and audiotapes of classroom interactions) provided profiles of students' practices in literary understanding before classroom initiation into the performance experience. The final item in this first category of data, however, shows an attempt to gather baseline data on students' responses to a single pub-lished poem that featured a dramatic situation described in challenging language.

Once instruction began, data for this portion of the 10th-grade performance study included field notes, supported by instructional artifacts and selected audiotapes or videotapes of teaching, which helped track the instruction students re-ceived. In addition, teacher and student postclass debriefings and longer interviews provided information on class partici-pants' reflections on the instructional process and the content being taught. Similarly, in her study of elementary school

TABLE 11–3. Data from 10th-Grade Study of Solo Performance of Poetry

Focus	Data Collected
Students' initial understandings	Teacher reports: class community, student performance Observation field notes Audiotaped class sessions Survey: understandings, experiences with performance Written response to a single performed poem
Instruction on performance	Audiotaped whole-class instruction and discussions Observation field notes Instructional artifacts Interviews and debriefings with teachers, researcher Student interviews
Performance planning	Packets of written responses and planning notes
Rehearsals	Audiotaped small-group work sessions, discussions Student journal entries
Performances	Audiotaped performances in small groups Selected videotaped performances for full class Audiotaped assessment conferences: teacher and researcher Students' written reflections on their own and other students' performances
End of unit reflections	Student interviews Postwrite on same poem from beginning of unit Survey Class discussion

students' experiences of 10 weeks of classroom theatre, Wolf (1994) collected baseline data on students' notions of drama, then tracked the instruction conducted by a guest drama director and interviewed students regarding their notions of classroom drama and the sources of that understanding. She was able to learn from these data sources how students moved from a sense of drama as uncontrolled action with no limits and imitative of action films, to a deeper understanding of drama and what she called its rules, roles, and resources. Students reported certain features of instruction and classroom practice that shaped these new understandings.

Documenting Performance Planning and Learning

For group performances of various kinds, group planning sessions can be observed and taped to track how students construct scripts and performances and how they learn about literature, characters, and interpretation. Field notes and tapes of these planning sessions can be supported by copies of student planning notes. Particularly in the upper grades, when students plan solo performances of literature, copies of written work can enable student, teacher, and researcher to understand the student's evolving interpretations. The packet of written responses and planning notes identified in Table 11–3 as data on performance planning drew on activities Long and HopKins (1982) have described for cultivating the performer's resources and fostering application of performance understanding to multiple texts and performance experiences. In these activities, students engaged in a whole range of literacy events (reading, writing, imagining, researching, discussing, and speaking) as they planned for the rehearsal and performance process.

For example, in the activity Long and HopKins (1982) call "making plain sense," students do detective work with the literary text, noting and looking up unfamiliar references and challenging vocabulary so that they can make the language of the poem sufficiently comfortable for performance. One student in the 10th-grade performance study listed a set of 11 words and phrases that she needed to decode in her planning for a performance of Gwendolyn Brooks' "the mother" (1963), a poem in which the speaker reflects on the experience of apparently having more than one abortion. In these notes on just 2 of the 11 words from her planning packet, the student defines the difficult words and works through an understanding of how they apply to the drama of the poem:

> pulp: A soft, moist mass of matter.
> In the first stanza third line pulp means the baby is soft and moist.
> luscious: pleasant and sweet to taste.
> In the first stanza ninth line luscious means that the lady feels like eating her child and she sighs to taste him because he is sweet and pleasant.

Later in the packet, this student identifies the action of the lines, naming verbs for what the poem's speaker *does* in each line (Long & HopKins, 1982). Along the left margin of a copy of Brooks' poem, the student has listed 14 verbs. For example, as the speaker describes in the second stanza of the poem how she hears the voices of "my dim killed children" and begins to talk to these lost ones, the student has written these verbs:

hears, regrets, begs, and blames. These are just a sampling of an array of activities students completed for their packets of planning notes.

Documenting Learning from Rehearsals

Early Stages. As Rosenblatt (1978) has demonstrated, a reader's perceptions of a literary work evolve over time and with new influences. In the case of students' performances of whole or excerpted literary works, one valuable source of data is students' evolving transactions with the literary work, starting with their earliest perceptions. Students can record their first or earliest silent encounters with or soundings of the work. These responses can be handled through written journal entries or through cassette tapes, becoming a record of the student's earliest responses as they unfold.

After the earliest readings and soundings, the student might write some responses in a performance journal. An example of what one student in the 10th-grade performance study wrote to try to work out the meaning of a challenging portion of his selected poem, Herbert Martin's "A Negro Soldier's Viet Nam Diary" (1973), follows:

> I don't understand the meanings of these lines. At first the poem talked about how he discovered a mother and a child in a river. Then all of a sudden he throws in those lines. For ex. "Death hangs on the rice." What rice is he talking about? Also "The land bears no fruit" and "Grass is an amenity." I don't understand what that has to do with the rest of the poem. I guess he is saying that everything is a luxury. That we don't need these stuff except life.

Other prompts for these early performance encounters with a text might be those explored by Roloff (1973) in his meditation stage: What happened to me in this initial experience? What is this piece of literature all about?

Tracking the Rehearsals. With the rehearsal situated at the center of the learning experience, the performance journal can become a place for recording reflections in and out of class, during and after each rehearsal, from in-class small group "rough draft performance" sessions involving peer critiques and suggestions, to solo rehearsals in and out of class. Journal prompts can be general or focused, depending on student needs and on the focus of research. General prompts might build on Bleich's questions (1975) that trigger affective and associative responses: What do you *feel* when you rehearse this literary selection? What does the experience of performing the work remind you of?

Two oral interpretation textbooks provide more focused prompts. Gamble and Gamble (1977) suggest the following: (1) What types of feelings did the preceding passage evoke in you? (2) Can you point to specific phrases in the passage that you find particularly effective? (3) Why do you believe these phrases affect you as they do? Long and HopKins (1982) encourage students to talk back to the literary work, asking the author questions, an approach they model using one student's journal responses to a single poem. Journal entries such as these that explore new knowledge, new sense, new problems with a work prove particularly valuable for tracking evolving interpretations.

Documenting Performances

Table 11–3 shows that for the 10th-grade performance study, taped records of performances served as key data. The last piece of data on performances, however, features students' reflections. For example, before students performed for their peers, they wrote about their rehearsal process, responding to selected questions and suggestions such as: What problem or challenge did you find in performing this work? Why did this problem arise? How have you attempted to resolve it? Discuss something you came to realize, understand, or feel about the literary work through rehearsing it or an excerpt from it. Discuss something you especially want to convey in your performance. How have you attempted to do that in rehearsal? Discuss any risky performance choice you have made and why.

The student performing "A Negro Soldier's Viet Nam Diary" stated in his entry, "My character feels sick in the beginning. I want to show how he feels sorry and sick in the beginning, then gets angrier as the poem goes on." The following is an excerpt from another student's journal entry for this series of prompts. The student had rehearsed "Chase Henry" from Edgar Lee Masters' *Spoon River Anthology* (1982):

> I especially wanted to convey the sense that Chase Henry was more than just "the town drunkard," that inside he was a thinking, feeling, perhaps even an intelligent drunkard. I did not want to simply play the stereotype of a town drunk.

Other sources of data for students' reflections on their performances are in-class discussions and workshops that invite students to explore as fully as possible how their interpretations of literary works compare with the interpretations that other readers bring to the same works (for example, when listeners ask questions of the performer and make concrete suggestions so that the performer may revise the performance). This process of "checking out" a reading in relation to that of others provides data for investigation and can yield various potential benefits for the student: self-enlightenment (Bleich, 1975), understanding of how one has or has not been alive to all the cues of a text (Rosenblatt, 1976, 1978), and practice in persuasion (Fish, 1980).

Documenting Reflections

Table 11–3 shows that for the final focus category of end of unit reflections, students were surveyed and interviewed and wrote on the same poem they had written about two months earlier. In cases where students have engaged in multiple performance experiences over the course of a semester or school year, students will have collected a great deal of data from their performance process, from perhaps taped protocols of responses and written or taped journal entries through various stages of the planning, rehearsal, and performance process. All of these data can serve as material for the student's investigation into his or her performance process, culminating in a short reflective journal entry or even a case

study analyzing a theme emerging from the data—something that pulls together the ongoing reflections from the many stages and experiences of the performance process.

CONCLUSION

For various reasons this chapter has identified, classroom performance of literature and performance in other subject areas in K–12 classrooms has not occupied central places in curricula in the United States. Many writers, however, have advocated the use of performance as a valuable tool for learning, particularly in literature study. When such performance does occur, it can assume many forms in literature study: storytelling, spontaneous oral readings, dramatic improvisations on literary texts, scripted and rehearsed solo and group performances of all or parts of literary works, and original dialogues, group projects, and video presentations using scripts built from or paralleling scenes in literature. In addition, classroom performance arises in other subject areas and in other genres, such as oral history, invented debates between historical figures, performances based on transcripts of conversations, and various kinds of performance art, to name just a few.

Despite the advocacy literature on performance, little research has provided thick descriptions of what occurs when students engage in performance processes. For the researcher interested in conducting investigations resulting in such descriptions, ethnography holds possibilities that this chapter has discussed. The ethnographer can investigate performance in the context of larger literacy curricula and can document the complexities of students' planning, rehearsals, performances, and reflections as essential sites for learning.

Conducting a rigorous ethnographic study, however, remains an extremely costly and demanding undertaking. The time commitment is great for developing an intimate knowledge of a community and culture, even when that community is one small class of students. Resources are generally needed to fund the time and materials for data collection and analysis. The large amount of data generally collected for an ethnography can overwhelm the researcher during both the collection and analysis of data. For the researcher committed to ethnography and able to secure the necessary resources, anthropological guidelines can help shape a careful study. This chapter has overviewed these guidelines and identified some of the key problem areas the ethnographer will need to address.

Finally, an ethnography of classroom performance can draw on a wide array of data collection tools to capture the learning students do in such work. This chapter has outlined a variety of such tools. In addition, brief illustrations have been provided from a recent study conducted in a 10th-grade English class, in order to make concrete the data collection tools described. Perhaps these research guidelines, data collection tools, and illustrations can help serve the cause of good research and can help advance the knowledge base on the power of classroom performance for student learning in literature, in other subject areas, and in classes that study performance itself.

References

Athanases, S. Z. (1984). It's a sin to kill *Mockingbird*. In *Literature—News that stays news: Fresh approaches to the classics*. Urbana, IL: National Council of Teachers of English.

Athanases, S. Z. (1993). *Discourse about literature and diversity: A study of two urban tenth-grade classes*. Unpublished doctoral dissertation, Stanford University.

Athanases, S. Z., & Heath, S. B. (1995). Ethnography and the study of the teaching and learning of English. *Research in the Teaching of English, 29*(3), 263–287.

Atkinson, P., & Hammersley, M. (1993). Ethnography and participant observation. In N. K. Denzin & Y. S. Lincoln (Eds.), *Handbook of qualitative research*. Thousand Oaks, CA: Sage.

Bacon, W. A. (1972). The act of interpretation. *Oral English, 2,* 1–10.

Berleant, A. (1980). *Performance as knowing: Cognitive and non-cognitive dimensions*. Pre-Convention Conference on Interpretation, Speech Communication Association Annual Convention, New York City.

Bleich, D. (1975). *Readings and feelings: An introduction to subjective criticism*. Urbana, IL: National Council of Teachers of English.

Bleich, D. (1978). *Subjective criticism*. Baltimore: Johns Hopkins University Press.

Breen, R. S. (1978). *Chamber theatre*. Englewood Cliffs, NJ: Prentice-Hall.

Brooks, G. (1963). the mother. In *Selected poems*. New York: Harper & Row.

Cameron, J. C. (1981). Accessibility to literature through oral performance. *English Education, 13,* 3–9.

Clifford, J. (1986). Introduction: Partial truths. In J. Clifford & G. E. Marcus (Eds.), *Writing culture: The poetics and politics of ethnography* (pp. 1–26). Berkeley, CA: University of California Press.

Coger, L. I., & White, M. (1973). *Readers theatre handbook: A dramatic approach to literature* (Rev. ed.). Glenview, IL: Scott, Foresman.

Conquergood, D. (1991). Rethinking ethnography: Towards a critical cultural politics. *Communication Monographs, 58,* 179–194.

Doyle, C. (1993). *Raising curtains on education: Drama as a site for critical pedagogy*. Westport, CN: Bergin & Garvey.

Duke, C. R. (1974). *Creative dramatics and English teaching*. Urbana, IL: National Council of Teachers of English.

Edmiston, S., Enciso, P., & King, M. L. (1987). Empowering readers and writers through drama: Narrative theater. *Language Arts, 64*(2), 219–228.

Ellen, R. F. (Ed.). (1984). *Ethnographic research: A guide to general conduct*. New York: Harcourt, Brace and Jovanovich.

Fine, E. C. (1990). Student performance of literature. In S. Hynds & D. L. Rubin (Eds.), *Perspectives on talk and learning* (pp. 179–194). Urbana, IL: National Council of Teachers of English.

Fish, S. E. (1980). *Is there a text in this class?* Cambridge, MA: Harvard University Press.

Forrest, W. C. (1969a). The poem as a summons to performance. *British Journal of Aesthetics, IX*(July), 298–305.

Forrest, W. C. (1969b). Literature as aesthetic object: The kinesthetic stratum. *Journal of Aesthetics and Art Criticism, 27,* 455–459.

Freedman, S. W. (1994). *Exchanging writing, exchanging cultures: Lessons in school reform from the United States and Great Britain*. Cambridge, MA: Harvard University Press.

Fuoss, K. W., & Hill, R. T. (1992). A performance-centered approach for teaching a course in social movements. *Communication Education, 41*(1), 77–88.

Gamble, T., & Gamble, M. (1977). *Oral interpretation: The meeting of self and literature*. Skokie, IL: The National Textbook.

Geertz, C. (1973). *The interpretation of cultures*. New York: Basic Books.

Geiger, D. (1973). Poetic realizing as knowing. *Quarterly Journal of Speech, LIX,* 311.

Goetz, J. P., & LeCompte, M. D. (1984). *Ethnography and qualitative design in educational research*. New York: Harcourt, Brace and Jovanovich.

Goffman, E. (1974). *Frame analysis: An essay on the organization of experience*. New York: Harper & Row.

Heath, S. (1982). Ethnography in education: Defining the essentials. In P. Gilmore & A. A. Glatthorn (Eds.), *Children in and out of school: Ethnography and education*. Washington, DC: Center for Applied Linguistics.

Heathcote, D. (1981). Drama as education. In N. McCaslin (Ed.), *Children as drama* (2nd ed., pp. 78–90). New York: Longman.

Herndon, R. T. (1973). *A symbolic interactionist theory of reader-poetry encounter: A process description of the reader's interaction with new poetry*. Unpublished dissertation, Southern Illinois University.

Kleinau, M. L., & McHughes, J. L. (1980). *Theatres for literature*. Sherman Oaks, CA: Alfred Publishing.

Klyn, M. S. (1965). Potentials for research in oral interpretation. *Western Speech, 29*(2), 108–114.

Krondorfer, B., & Bates, R. (1994). Ritually enacting the reading experience: A dramatic way to teach literature. *English Education, 26*(4), 236–248.

Lee, C., & Gura, T. (1982). *Oral interpretation* (6th ed.). Boston: Houghton Mifflin.

Long, B. W. (1973). Research directions in the performance of literature. *Speech Monographs, 40*(August), 240.

Long, B. W., & HopKins, M. F. (1982). *Performing literature: An introduction to oral interpretation*. Englewood Cliffs, NJ: Prentice-Hall.

Long, B. W., Hudson, L., & Jeffrey, P. R. (1977). *Group performance of literature*. Englewood Cliffs, NJ: Prentice-Hall.

Maclay, J. H. (1971). *Readers theatre: Toward a grammar of practice*. New York: Random House.

Martin, H. (1973). A Negro soldier's Viet Nam diary. In *The poetry of Black America: Anthology of the 20th century*. New York: Harper & Row.

Masters, E. L. (1962). *Spoon river anthology*. New York: Collier MacMillan.

McLaughlin, M. W., & Talbert, J. E. (1993). *Contexts that matter for teaching and learning: Strategic opportunities for meeting the nation's educational goals*. Stanford, CA: Center for Research on the Context of Secondary School Teaching.

Olsen, D. (1992). Floods and church secretaries, Buffalo Creek and Northwestern: Struggling with the seams between. *Text and Performance Quarterly, 12*(4), 329–348.

Park-Fuller, L. M., & Pelias, R. (1995). Charting alternative performance and evaluative practices. *Communication Education, 44*(2), 126–139.

Pellegrini, A. D. (1980). The relationship between kindergartners' play and achievement in prereading, language, and writing. *Psychology in the Schools, 17,* 530–535.

Pellegrini, A. D. (1984). Symbolic functioning and children's early writing: The relations between kindergartners' play and isolated word-writing fluency. In R. Beach & L. Bridwell (Eds.), *New directions in composition research* (pp. 274–284). New York: Guilford.

Pratt, M. L. (1986). Fieldwork in common places. In J. Clifford & G. E. Marcus (Eds.), *Writing culture: The poetics and politics of ethnography* (pp. 27–50). Berkeley, CA: University of California Press.

Rogers, T., & O'Neill, C. (1993). Creating multiple worlds: Drama, language, and literary response. In G. E. Newell & R. K. Durst (Eds.), *Exploring texts: The role of discussion and writing in the teaching and learning of literature* (pp. 69–90). Norwood, MA: Christopher-Gordon.

Roloff, L. H. (1973). *The perception and evocation of literature.* Glenview, IL: Scott, Foresman.

Rosenblatt, L. (1976). *Literature as exploration.* New York: Noble and Noble.

Rosenblatt, L. (1978). *The reader, the text, the poem.* Carbondale, IL: Southern Illinois University Press.

Sanjek, R. (Ed.). (1990). *Fieldnotes: The makings of anthropology.* Ithaca, NY: Cornell University Press.

Saville-Troike, M. (1982). *The ethnography of communication: An introduction.* Oxford: Basil Blackwell.

Schon, D. (1983). *The reflective practitioner: How professionals think in action.* New York: Basic Books.

Shattuck, R. (1980). How to rescue literature. *The New York Review of Books, 27,* 29–35.

Shulman. L. S. (1987). Knowledge and teaching: Foundations of the new reform. *Harvard Educational Review, 57*(1), 1–22.

Sperber, D. (1982). *On anthropological knowledge.* Cambridge, MA: Cambridge University Press.

Squire, J. R., & Applebee, R. K. (1968). *High school English instruction today.* New York: Appleton-Century-Crofts.

Squire, J. R., & Applebee, R. K. (1969). *Teaching English in the United Kingdom.* Urbana, IL: National Council of Teachers of English.

Stewig, J. W., & Buege, C. (1994). *Dramatizing literature in whole language classrooms* (2nd ed.). New York: Teachers College Press.

Strine, M. S., Long, B. W., & HopKins, M. F. (1990). Research in interpretation: Trends, issues, priorities. In G. M. Phillips & J. T. Wood (Eds.), *Speech communication: Essays to commemorate the 75th anniversary of the Speech Communication Association* (pp. 181–204). Carbondale, IL: Southern Illinois University Press.

Stucky, N. (1995). Performing oral history: Storytelling and pedagogy. *Communication Education, 44*(1), 1–14.

Talbert, C. (1973). Anthropological research models. *Research in the Teaching of English, 7,* 190–211.

Wagner, B. J. (1976). *Dorothy Heathcote: Drama as a learning medium.* Washington, DC: National Education Association.

Wagner, B. J. (1986). *The effects of role playing on written persuasion: An age and channel comparison of fourth and eighth graders.* Unpublished doctoral dissertation, University of Illinois at Chicago. (University Microfilms No. 870516).

Wagner, B. J. (1988). Research currents: Does classroom drama affect the arts of language? *Language Arts, 65*(1), 46–55.

Wagner, B. J. (1990). Dramatic improvisation in the classroom. In S. Hynds & D. L. Rubin (Eds.), *Perspectives on talk and learning* (pp. 195–212). Urbana, IL: National Council of Teachers of English.

Wolf, S. (1994). Learning to act/acting to learn: Children as actors, critics, and characters in classroom theatre. *Research in the Teaching of English, 28*(1), 7–44.

12

TRANSCRIPTION AND REPRESENTATION IN LITERACY RESEARCH

Carolyn D. Baker
UNIVERSITY OF QUEENSLAND

MAKING AND USING TRANSCRIPTS IN LITERACY RESEARCH

The use of transcripts of talk and activity recorded in naturally occurring, routine classroom events and other settings such as homes and workplaces has become an important empirical and analytical resource in recent literacy research. This reflects the interests of many researchers in working from the data of everyday events as a basis for describing, explaining or theorizing how literacy activities are observably organized and accomplished by participants. Working with transcripts allows for claims and counterclaims about activities and practices to be referred to a permanent set of reanalyzable records. The analyses and theoretical claims that are produced on the basis of recordings and their associated transcripts are accountable to what other readers, viewers or listeners can see or hear for themselves in these records. Further, recordings and transcripts have the potential to generate multiple and possibly competing analyses and thus to make possible resistance to singular interpretations.

Transcripts from recordings are made in part because academic communications are organized primarily through print. For ethical reasons also, many research recordings cannot themselves be distributed. Representations of them need to be made. Talk and action have to be put on paper, or onto disk and screen, made into text. But the making of a transcript also has benefits interior to the study of recorded events. Transcription allows for more detailed and careful analysis than is possible with a witnessed but unrecorded scene. The making of a transcript "slows down" the talk and action for the analyst so that the detailed work of representing words and actions can be done. At any point in the transcription process the transcription-so-far "fixes" the talk and action onto paper. This allows for the notation, inspection and reinspection of what can be seen and heard to be occurring in the audio- or videotape. Transcription (the process) is a method of inquiry, involving analysis from the beginning. The transcript (the product) reflects that inquiry. As a number of researchers have observed, transcription is more than a merely technical matter; the transcription process and its outcomes are by no means neutral.

In this chapter I will review published literature on the making of transcripts and their consequences in educational research. This literature is relatively consistent in pointing out the nonneutrality of transcription practices. I will connect and extend a number of these observations to advance the themes, (1) that the practices of transcription are forms of reasoning and writing that reflect cultural membership, (2) that practices of transcription are literacy practices in themselves: how do we put words and actions on paper? how do we write and draw our transcript characters? and (3) most important, that transcription practices assemble transcript characters in particular ways and assign social and moral order to the literacy scenes observed. Transcription is in all these senses a form of representation in social science (see as a comparison Lynch & Woolgar, 1990). In the second part of the chapter I review some specific issues in transcription to illustrate how aspects of description, layout and formatting amount to a form of educational ethnography that is consequential for how we represent and understand language and meaning, students and texts, teachers and authority.

TRANSCRIPTION AS THEORY AND PRACTICE

Beginning with the work of Ochs (1979) the process of transcription has been studied in terms of the choices transcribers need to make and the effects of these choices on the form and content of the transcript. These are discussed in terms of the problems of selective observation that occur during transcription: "transcription is a selective process reflecting theoretical goals and definitions" (p. 44). As expressed in Green, Weade, and Graham (1988, pp. 17, 18):

> The completed transcript reflects a set of theoretical assumptions about the nature of the work accomplished through face-to-face conversations, the roles and relationships of participants, and the nature of instructional conversation. ...transcription ... is a heuristic device and not a literal record.

Ochs also states (p. 44) that "the transcriptions are the researcher's data." This holds true in that the transcript, once produced, becomes the text from which the formal, written analysis is launched. The transcripts are certainly the reader's data, because what appears in the transcript is a selection and a reduction of what was potentially available to the transcriber to indicate on paper.

Ochs details a number of alternative representational devices in transcripts involving child language. In addition to discussing transcribers' theoretical interests, Ochs demonstrates how cultural assumptions enter into the making of transcripts. For example:

> the perceived dominance of the adult may lead a transcriber or researcher to locate adult talk to the left of the child's talk on the transcript. This location, in turn, becomes a "natural" candidate for an interactional starting point." (1979, p. 51)

Transcription choices, then, may prereflectively evidence cultural assumptions, even aspects of social organization, in the way in which the transcript characters are visibly arranged in relation to each other, and other aspects of the interactional scene depicted. In this sense culture and implicit knowledge of social structure enter directly into the making of a transcript. They are captured in the texture of the transcript.

More recently Psathas and Anderson (1990), writing about the practices of transcription in conversation analysis, explain the work and the orientations to recorded interactions that are involved in following the Jeffersonian transcription system. In this approach "transcription, which of necessity entails repeated listenings to a tape, becomes an integral part of the analytic process" (p. 77). Regarding the issue of neutrality in transcription, Psathas and Anderson state (p. 75):

> there is not, and cannot be, a 'neutral' transcription system. The presumably 'neutral' presentation of the details of produced speech/action would be the actual embodied and situated original spoken production.

In conversation analysis, the transcript is treated as an aid to interpretation of the recording, which remains the primary resource for analytic work. On the status of the transcript they comment (p. 77):

> ...the status of the transcript remains that of being 'merely' being a representation of the actual interaction—i.e., it is not the interaction and it is not the 'data'. ... The original recordings, which ... are not in and of themselves 'neutral' or 'objective' renderings of what actually occurred, and which we will henceforth nevertheless refer to as 'the data', remain unaltered. Any transcription made of these data can serve as a *version* of the data for particular analytic purposes.

For conversation analysis, according to Psathas and Anderson, repeated direct listening to the recording is the arbiter of the fidelity and adequacy of the transcription: reliability is essentially a practical matter (pp. 77, 97). Psathas and Anderson discuss various "seemingly 'innocent' decisions of format and presentation [that] can and do have substantial implications for the analysis" (p. 85). Some of these decisions and their consequences will be sketched later in this chapter.

Mishler (1991) begins his discussion of transcription with an analogy to photography, cautioning against naive realism and against supposing an "innocent relationship between photographer and scene" (pp. 258, 259): "the meaning of a representation is problematic and dependent on variations in craft and context." He discusses transcription as an interpretive practice of "entextualisation" that involves a number of procedural and methodological decisions. He draws attention not only to the crafting of the image but also its location amid other textual material. He says of photographs (p. 258):

> What we assume to have been "really" there, and how the photographer selected and framed the event, and how the photograph is presented and located within the flow of other information, including other images ... along with the text that serves as its caption, all influence our understanding.

Applied to transcription in literacy research, this means that the presentation of transcript material (speech and action) in words, in particular formats or layouts, and/or in illustrations is read as part of a larger text. The photography analogy also supports Mishler's preference for a position in which objects and their representations are interconnected. This perspective places the interpretational and representational onus on the audio or video recording, on the transcribing, and on making the connection between image and reality (i.e., reading the image). The work of producing the transcript and its interpretation is seen to be cultural rather than merely technical.

Mishler is critical of Psathas and Anderson's privileging of the original recording as "the data"—as the reference against which the fidelity of the transcript can be determined (1991, p. 277). This privileging is done in conversation analysis along with the recognition that the recording is not ultimately the data (see quotation above). In practical terms transcribers have to work as if the recording represented the event or some significant aspects of it, even if that particular representation was just one of many other possibilities. At the same time it is instructive to consider the proposition put forward by Paoletti (1990) in a study of classroom interaction: it is not that the classroom produces the description, but that the description produces the classroom. Similarly, it is not that the speech or activity produces the transcription, but the transcription produces the character of the speech or activity for all practical purposes.

In addition to reviewing procedural and methodological decisions involved in making transcripts, Mishler comments on the effects of different transcription practices (1991, p. 270):

> Transcriptions of speech, like other forms of representation in science, reflexively document and affirm theoretical positions about relations between language and meaning. Different

transcripts are constructions of different worlds, each designed to fit our particular theoretical assumptions and allows us to explore their implications. And … they have a rhetorical function that locates them within a larger political and ideological context.

Mishler also notes (p. 277) that "the form of representation we use serves theoretical and rhetorical functions, and perhaps aesthetic ones as well." He presents different forms of transcription of the same recorded events to illustrate these points, drawing in part on the work of Michaels and Gee.

In a review of discourse analysis, Gee, Michaels and O'Connor (1992, p. 239ff.) include discussion of "transcription as an interpretive lens." Considerations of "how to display the talk or writing on a page" include representing the texture of the talk or writing through choices of format and speech delivery detail included or excluded. They illustrate that forms of transcription are consequential for what can be seen in the text/transcript by displaying two forms of a transcript of a "sharing time" story told by a student in a 2nd-grade classroom. The first version is organized by turns at talk, it includes questions interjected by the teacher during the delivery, and shows tone groupings, false starts, hesitations and the like. The second version organizes the student's story into lines and stanzas, adds headings, removes teacher turns, speech repairs and the like, and presents an "ideal" representation of the story. This second version allows one to see various aspects of structure and patterning in the story; it assigns a different order of competence to the student. This order of competence is brought out in the analysis of the second version of the transcript. Gee et al. (p. 240) point out that

> In educational research, we are often dealing with students whose ways of speaking, writing, and reasoning diverge from those of the teacher (and researcher). In these cases, it is especially important to be mindful that the transcript will inevitably leave out some information or, by its display, make certain features more salient than others.

The speech and writing of students with different literacy practices from those of teachers may in some transcription formats appear confused or incompetent while in other formats designed to extract their previously invisible linguistic and cultural strengths appear to be competent practitioners of different literacies than those recognized in formal schooling. For transcribers, a consequence of these observations is that the selection of formats for transcription involves ethical as well as technical considerations.

A collection of papers on transcription (Edwards & Lampert, 1993) provides further comment on theoretical as well as technical and procedural aspects of transcription using different systems. Du Bois, Schuetze-Coburn, Cumming, and Paolino (1993) present a detailed account of how transcription is done using particular symbols to indicate discourse features. Similarly, Gumperz and Berenz (1993, p. 91ff.) explain the workings of transcription from "within a sociolinguistic and functional perspective." They begin with statements of their theoretical position and associated statement of intent of the transcription system (p. 91f.).

We assume … that talk is basically interactive. … What we seek to account for is the ongoing, cooperative process of conversing. … Conversing in turn rests on speakers' and listeners' interpretation of verbal and nonverbal signs or contextualisation conventions. …

Our transcription system attempts to set down on paper all those perceptual cues that past research and ongoing analyses show participants rely on in their online processing of conversational management signs. … What is emphasized in our approach is the rhetorical impact these signs have in affecting the situated interpretations on which the conduct and outcome of the exchange depends. Transcription, when seen from this basically functional perspective, is an integral part of the analysis of inferential processes.

In this description of a transcription system it is clear that the system is designed to find and represent those discourse features that have been theorized as important to the organization of speaking and listening. Also, in presenting this theoretical perspective as a basis for describing the transcription system, the character of conversing, and thus the activities of conversationalists, have been represented already. This is evidence of the necessary reflection in any system of transcription of a theory of social action or a theory of social order.

These observations can be taken somewhat further. The work of transcription involves methods of organizing and formatting detail from the recording. It involves methods of making the heard or viewed event "orderly." In this sense transcription *assigns* a social, political, or moral order to the scene being transcribed. This point is crucially related to the place of transcription (and other forms of "representation") in ethnography. Woolgar's (1988) paper, "Reflexivity is the Ethnographer of the Text," discusses the relation between texts and the worlds they purportedly describe. He states (pp., 28, 29) that the conventions which structure the text

> impose order upon a fluid (pre-textual) realm of actants and entities; they produce an ordered structure of categories, objects and subjects; they define distances and relationships between these entities; the moral order of rights and obligations—which of these entities can say and do what about whom.

Woolgar did not refer to educational research in making these points, or in calling the text itself "a species of social/cultural activity" that constructs its own subjects. But the parallel is clear. The philosophical problems encountered in imaging, framing, even captioning in an anthropological account are identical to those involved in educational research. "It is in and through textual representation that the character of the other is achieved"—in this case the character of the literacy scene, its members, their activities, their practices. According to Woolgar, "we need continually to interrogate and find strange the process of representation as we engage in it. This kind of reflexivity is the ethnographer of the text" (pp. 28, 29). This reflexivity is demonstrated in the analyses presented by Gee et al. (1992) in showing how the "character of the other"—in their case the competence of the student who speaks black English—is achieved textually (see also Ochs, 1979, pp. 70, 71 on showing the grammatical competence of the child).

Woolgar's reference to a "pre-textual" realm has a parallel in Dorothy Smith's (1990, p. 151ff.) discussion of "encoding lived actualities." In her formulation of this process, texts (which may be taken to include transcripts) are accounts. Smith provides a statement concerning the misconstrued problem of capturing reality in a text:

> In a sense, a lived actuality never happens, for it is always lived; what is, happens, or has happened arises only at the point where a recording is made, a story is told, a picture is taken. The ontological problem of correspondence between descriptive terms and objects or events is bypassed, as indeed it should be, in that "what actually happened/what is" arises only at that moment of reflection where experience is intended by an account or encoding aiming at an account. (p. 151)

What went into the production of the account (transcript), and its articulation to social relations, are often lost to readers of the text:

> This is often a matter we don't attend to because in the social relation in which our own work is embedded we confront the text as our object. The text arises as an object in this relation of working. Its character as an object of that work becomes thematic in our consciousness. It does not appear before us in its active transactional being, as a moment in a sequence of practices concerted as a social relation. Our gaze, oriented toward the enterprise of inquiry, is not self-regarding. We do not in the orientation of our work recognize how at this moment, too, the text is taking on a distinctive character in the context of the social relations of our work and that this relation organises what we bring to bear upon the text as interpretive practices. (Smith, 1990, p. 154)

These discussions of the nonneutrality of transcription practices recognize that the analyst's practices of hearing and seeing, of interpreting and making sense of the scene, are always present in the text (transcript). The transcript is a product of the analyst's interpretive practices whether the notations used are innovated or whether they are conventionalized (as in the Jefferson transcription system: see Atkinson & Heritage 1984; Psathas & Anderson, 1990; or as in systems described in Edwards & Lampert, 1993). These practices are not individual: methods of hearing and seeing events are aspects of culture and are shared within language communities. Their sources are social as well as their effects in the representation, the transcript. It follows also that the process of transcription is itself a literacy practice. What transcribers do is to turn the spoken into the written in a way that is readable by other members of the research community. In attempting to preserve something of the aural and visual quality of the spoken or performed event, transcribers also attempt to transcribe so that a sequence of talk and interaction can be (imaginatively) heard as well as seen (Schenkein, 1978, p. xi; Mishler, 1991, p. 277).

TRANSCRIPTION AS TEXTUAL REPRESENTATION: AN ILLUSTRATION

Illustration of many of these points can be made with reference to a study in early literacy in which it was observed that beginning school reading books contain considerable amounts of speech written down in the form of text characters

talking to one another. This textual device could be designed to assist young students in the transition from oral to written language competence. In a study of the texts of beginning school reading books, Baker and Freebody (1989, pp. 75, 76) have shown some of the many ways in which "talk" can be reported on paper, each way itself characterizing the speakers in the "original" scene, the writer's relation to the heard talk, and the writer's implicit characterization of the interests of the reader of the text. The texts used here are fictional. There is no audio or video record of an "original" scene. This set of texts together serves a heuristic purpose for making points about how spoken language can be represented in writing, but they do not exhaust the possibilities.

Version One

> Jill complained that her doll Bumpity had bumped into the toy-box. She inquired of Jack if he could assist her in opening it. After a little consideration and after examining the box, Jack declared that he was unable to open it, whereupon Jill suggested that her father would know how, since it has been his, and that they should take it downstairs to him.

Version Two

> "Oh, dear!" said Jill
> "Bumpity bumped into the toy-box,
> and I cannot get it open.
> Jack, can you help me?"
> Jack looked at the toy-box.
> "I cannot open it," he said.
> "This is an old toy-box".
> "Let's take it down to father,"
> said Jill.
> "It is his old toy-box.
> He will know what to do with it".

Version Three

> Jill   Oh, de:ar—Bumpity bumped into the toy-box and I can't get it open Jack—can you help me? ((frustrated)) (3.0)
> Jack   I can't open it—this is an [old toy-box
> Jill   [Let's take it down to father-- it's his old toy-box—he'll know what to do with it.

In version one we have a highly "literate" characterization that on the one hand dispenses with an interest in actual words spoken while on the other hand uses various speech act verbs that characterize literate discourse (Olson & Astington, 1990). This particular usage makes the text characters, Jack and Jill, into literate, purposeful, logical, and methodical interactants. The text is written as if the narrator/reporter could know what is going on inside the heads and intentions of the speakers, as in much literary fiction. Note that as readers of the report we are heavily dependent on the narrator's characterization of who said what and how it was said. The use of indirect speech to characterize the gist of what went on, verbally, is akin to everyday descriptions of past events in which the actual words spoken are not accented through quotation marks.

In version two, the characters do their own speaking, and the narrator's metatextual voice is less visible/audible. The preferred verb of description is "said," which is less implicative of motive, purpose or effect than the verbs employed in version one. If Jill and Jack are still purposeful, logical and methodical interactants, this is accomplished here primarily through the grammatical and cooperative quality of their speeches, as conveyed in the reported talk. Version two should be recognizable as a segment from a basal reading series. It illustrates one way in which the written "representation" of oral events is presented in early reading materials (see also Baker & Freebody, 1986). Baker and Freebody surmised that this form of "representing" oral conversation is an implicit model for how children should talk in classrooms—in complete, correct sentences, one at a time. In comparison with version three, it is both idealized and undernotated, containing the straightforward reporting of what was said and done, in what order, and little else.

Several points can be made in relation to version three in light of transcription issues. In this version, the actual words and their sequential placement, an overlap, a prolonged vowel, and other devices indicate some of the auditory qualities of the speakers' interactions. The narrator disappears, replaced by a hypothetical transcriber. Note that in this version, the talk is represented in an ever-present tense, while in the previous two versions, the descriptions assign these events to history. This form of representation assists the convention used in most analyses of transcripts to comment on the talking and doing in the transcript in the present or present progressive tense (e.g., "Carol looks down at the book" or "teacher is pointing to the text"). In this way, analyses treat stretches of text as "as-they-happen" exemplars of what could occur again, rather than as historical records of unique events. This textual device helps construct the ordinariness, the routine character, and the replicability of events, and is part of the authentication process by which transcripts are assigned to an ever-present reality.

But in other respects, and inevitably, the auditory has been imbued with the character of writing. Ochs (1979, p. 61) raised the issue of whether people's speech should be represented phonetically or in terms of strictly standard orthography, resolving in favor of the modified orthography used in version three (see also Gumperz & Berenz, 1993, pp. 96, 97). A criticism of using modified orthography is that we can effectively construct our speakers as ungrammatical. Gumperz and Berenz (p. 97) warn about "diagnosis of participant categorization" through orthography choices, "especially in cases of stylistic mismatch among participants." Another issue arises in transcribing across accents: for example, American pronunciations are effectively captured in many conversation analysis transcripts. What is "said," what is "heard" and what is "written down" are not necessarily the same auditory phenomenon. Some auditory phenomena are difficult to represent: different kinds of laughter, for example (Jefferson, 1985; see also Du Bois et al., 1993, pp. 71, 72). Other points made by Heap (1982) are that people do not speak in upper- and lower-case letters. Similarly, they do not speak "in" a right-hand column.

In version three above, the transcriber has described Jill as speaking in a frustrated voice but no parallel characterization of how Jack speaks is given. Hence the quality of Jill's speech is marked, while Jack's is left unmarked, as if he were speaking neutrally or normally. The marking of Jill's utterance in this way documents a course of reasoning and action that calls on the transcriber's knowledge of when and how a given utterance qualifies for marking against the backdrop of 'normal' or 'neutral' speech.

Aspects of the physical layout and the conventions of transcription systems—for example alignments of overlaps, putting question marks wherever there are rising intonations and not necessarily at the end of questions—are often initially counterintuitive practices for literate transcribers. A literate bias in transcription might produce representations of talk in ideal-literate form, as in version two, where we find *tidied-up* textbook versions of how people should speak. This literate bias might include transcribing grammatically, in phrases, sentences and clauses, with grammatically correct commas and full stops, even if the cadence of the speech can later be heard to violate these literate rules. Transcriptions of classroom talk often show student answers delivered with rising intonation at the end, indicated through question marks. Du Bois et al. (1993, pp. 55, 56) call this an "appeal" in which a speaker "seeks a validating response from a listener." These notations help construct textual portraits of students as seekers of validation from teachers: the analysis begins in the notation.

A transcript made with sequential organization (or some other characteristic) foregrounded, when studied closely, provides the transcriber and the subsequent reader with a particular way of hearing oral conversation, for example, in the Jefferson system as a finely tuned sequence of turns, rather than as parallel sets of statements or as a series of random sentences. In comparison, representations of talk-on-paper that separate different speakers' talk into different columns, for instance, structure a distance between speakers and/or their activities which can inform subsequent reading/hearing practices. Edwards (1993, p. 3), citing Ochs, comments that

> arranging speaker turns one above the other gives the impression of symmetry and mutual interdependence between speakers, whereas arranging them in columns, one for each speaker, can give the impression of an asymmetry between them, with the leftmost being the most dominant.

A comparison of these versions of a fictional interactional scene shows the kinds of reading practices that are called upon from very young readers in making sense of talk-on-paper: one of the earliest literacy practices encountered in school. The comparison of these versions also highlights some of the issues involved in transcription in terms of (1) the prereflective use of cultural knowledge in making practical decisions such as when speech warrants being marked as different from normal or neutral; (2) the use of formatting as a way of assigning qualities and relationships to text characters; and (3) the production of an interested, constitutive representation of an interactional scene. Baker and Freebody (1986, 1989) argued that methods of representing talk in beginning school reading books were central to the constitution of childhood in early literacy materials.

ISSUES IN MAKING TRANSCRIPTS

Issues in transcription signaled by the preceding commentary include matters of description, matters of format and layout, and matters of depiction. Drawing on material from the literature reviewed and some additional illustrative cases, this section will address some of the practical matters involved in deciding how to characterize or represent people, their talk, their (inter)actions and the settings in which they interact.

Du Bois et al. (1993, pp. 45, 46) describe "broad" and "narrow" transcriptions:

> …a fairly broad transcription… includes the most basic transcription information: the words and who they were spoken by, the division of the stream of speech into turns and intonation units, the truncation of intonation units and words, intonation contours, medium and long pauses, laughter, and uncertain hearings or indecipherable words. In a more detailed, "narrow' transcription, the transcriber would also include notation of, among other things, accent, tone, prosodic lengthening, and breathing or other vocal noises.

One practical consideration in making any transcript is how much notation to assign to the talk or action. This is normally decided in terms of what order of analysis is to be sustained with the transcript. Some aspects of formatting and speech delivery notation were introduced in the previous section. In the sections which follow, it is primarily other aspects of "broad" transcription that will be dealt with. The sources cited contain detail regarding the transcription of finer details of speech delivery.

The Indefinite Extendability of Description

The issue of the indefinite extendability of description is raised in a useful way by Schegloff (1988, p. 2), who makes the point that "'describing' is not only a feature, it is also a topic of social science inquiry." That is, how people do "describing" is a social activity that can be studied as a topic. This is because descriptions are the result of the reasoning practices that are used to decide how to describe something. This applies both to everyday, "vernacular" describing and also to description in social science. The problem is that because there is no limit to the ways in which any event, person, social (inter)action and so forth can be described, we need to decide some "selection principles" to guide how we describe what it is we study.

Ochs raised this problem by considering such matters as how much detail should go into a transcript, whether and how much the nonverbal should be notated, whether inflections should be included, and so on. Among the selection principles mentioned in her chapter are accuracy; economy (too much notation would make it difficult for a researcher to "sort out the forest from the trees") (1979, p. 50); prior knowledge of children, language and so forth, and the purposes of the research. Schegloff's (1988, pp. 21, 22) selection

principle is different. He claims that "[t]here is a line of response to the problem of multiple description which offers an alternative to the type of solution which finds the inexorable presence of value, presupposition or ideology."

> …The crucial warrant that needs to be established for these descriptions is that they address aspects of the talk and other conduct which catch what is relevant for the participants.

The difference turns on whether we describe according to the displayed relevances of the participants in the scene or whether we describe according to the relevances of the researcher. Schegloff's ethnomethodological solution has not been applied consistently in literacy research. Descriptions are not always or necessarily connected to what the participants take themselves to be doing, or more precisely, how they characterize what they are doing in the course of doing it. Participants in everyday interaction do description and analysis no less than do researchers of those interactional scenes, thus providing researchers as well as each other with indications of the local relevancies in the setting (see also Baker, 1992).

Speaker Identification and Membership Categorization

The questions of how speakers in an interactional scene are identified, how they are characterized as speaking, and what they are characterized as doing, connect the issue of how the talk is heard by the transcriber/analyst with the issue of description, and through that how the procedures of transcription textually produce versions of social order.

Speier (1972) raised the problem of "speaker identification" as a general problem for conversational analysis. He wondered how transcribers/analysts could arrive at an appropriate characterization of the identities of the speakers in a conversational site. To what "membership categories" should they be assigned? The principled solution to the problem of who are these interactants speaking as, on any occasion, is found in identifying the self-characterizing work and scenic practices of the speakers themselves. Within an informal conversation, we can formulate our speaking as, say, educator, or parent, or woman, or friend. (This does not guarantee how we are heard as speaking, which is a problem inter alia of gender politics.) As Zimmerman (1992, p. 50) has described, "participants exhibit for one another (and for the analyst) their appreciation of who, situationally speaking, they are, and what, situationally speaking, they are up to." A further problem is that the identities adopted by speakers within a sequence of talk, or those attributed to them, can change.

Transcribers of classroom talk would normally take it that the interactional site 'naturally' contains the positions and identities of teachers and students, or in the case of early schooling, the relevant category-pair is often taken to be "teacher–children", which assigns a generational relevance to what is said and done. Having determined that classrooms contain the category-pair "teacher–student" as the essential frame for the analysis, this frame then informs the hearings that are made as well as the physical presentation of the transcript. This is a commonsense hearing of what kind of setting this is, and whatever the identifiers, classroom talk is often immediately recognizable as just that kind of talk (Heritage, 1984, 280–290).

But it may not be warranted to treat the entire recording as a record of people speaking as teacher and students. An example from classroom talk will show the problem. This segment is drawn from a transcription of a 7th-grade lesson on sex roles in the middle ages and sex roles now, that was video recorded in a coeducational secondary school in New South Wales (see Baker & Davies, 1989). The relevant segment is a stretch of "teacher–student" talk about "poor women" in the middle ages:

60	C	Cooked the meals for their husbands?
61	T	All right. What sort of stove did they have Charlie?
62	C	One ( )
63	T	Pardon?
64	C	Just an open fire ( ) fire ( ) hot.
65	T	(Don't Keith). What would that have meant; when they're cooking meals what would they need to have done before they could cook their meals.
66	C	Prepare it
67	T	Good—like doing what
68	C	Um
69	T	Pardon?
70	C	Um—starting the fire
71	T	Good. So. Getting all the wood—hmm. Martin?
72	M	They didn't have much meat so they had to get the water to boil the vegetables in.
73	T	Great, where did they get all the water from, John?
74	J	Um
75	T	Turn on the tap?
76	J	No, go down to the river or the moat or whatever.
77	T	or to the well. Yeah and draw the water. Good. ((writes on the board for five seconds)) Right. That'll do. Go across to the men. Oh, ho, what do *we* do in the old day, Penny?
78	P	The rich men would—um—rule? Or make sure the servants are doing their work.
79	T	Good. Right. We were the *rulers*—yes—give *orders*. We've changed since then haven't we? Do we give orders now? Stand up, Penny! No. Of course we don't. What else do rich men do, Diana? ((During the course of this delivery, the camera is on the face of a girl sitting in front of Penny. First there is a look of puzzlement, then a smile (of relief?)))
80	D	Go hunting?

It seems that for most of this segment, the participants are speaking as teacher (of "history") and students (of this same "history"). At line 77, what we noticed was a shift in self-assigned identity, in that at this point the teacher calls into relevance his identity *as a male*, and in doing so calls into relevance for what follows the gender identities of all the participants. It can be noticed that all those who have spoken on the topic up to this point have been boys. If the shift occurs from speaking as a teacher to speaking as a male on this occasion, similar shifts can occur in multiple ways. Gender can be used as topic and resource in talk. This shift by the teacher raises the problem whether it is plausible to describe all the preceding talk as gendered talk, even before any speaker has called one's gender into relevance. Is it appropriate to describe the whole preceding segment, (1) as talk "by boys" (an analyst's category), (2) as talk by "some of the students" (another analyst's category), or (3) as talk "as boys"? To describe the participants as talking "as boys" is a stronger formulation that may not be warranted upon inspection of how the speakers themselves formulate who they are, doing what. To describe them talking "as boys" holds the student speakers "accountable by gender" for what they say. This problem is endemic to studies of gender in interaction where talk is gendered by the analyst (boy(s) said/did x, girl(s) said/did y) without reference to the membership categories being claimed by the speakers themselves.

To extend this problem into the visual accompaniments to this talk: the visual scene of the "joke" in line 79 assists in our hearing of and analysis of the latter part of this sequence. The teacher's "joke" was aimed at Penny, presumably to create a "funny" confusion of whether she was a target of "rich men giving orders" in the middle ages or a student target of a teacher in the here-and-now, or a female target of a male order-giver in the here-and-now. The analysis is made more complicated (and, alternatively, assisted) by the fact that the video recording does not show Penny's face during this speech by the teacher, but shows the face of another girl sitting in front of Penny. This girl's face looks blank for the first part of the speech, then puzzled / slightly frowning, then relaxes into a smile. It took a while for the "joke" to be understood *as a joke*: that Penny was not expected to obey the order to "stand up." That we saw some doubt in the girl's face and that we then saw (what we think is) relief, is part of our work of characterizing this classroom lesson as presenting to students both a formal lesson message—that men and women should be equal—and an interactional subtext that simultaneously undermines that message. We also commented at various points on the teacher's use of his friendly, affectionate relationship with the students to effectively silence the girls. This is also a moral commentary. The analysis, then, was concerned with the politics of gender-talk in this particular lesson. In the course of analyzing lesson-knowledge and gender-talk, we produced an account of the politics and the moral ordering of this mixed-sex classroom, in which account the transcript was a central prop.

The question of who is speaking how to whom is related to the Quinean problem of opaque and transparent contexts of reference and attribution discussed by Coulter (1989, p. 47): an "opaque" description is one that is faithful to how the participant could have heard or seen some object or event while a "transparent" description can be provided by the analyst independent of how the participant could have seen it. We constructed the teacher as playing gender-games—addressing Penny "as a girl"—although there is no guarantee that he did. Moral implications of this problem of transparent and opaque descriptions have been identified by Jayussi (1984), showing how a reporter's categories of identification are part of the moral ordering involved in describing *any* social scene.

The Format and Layout of the Transcript

Ochs (1979) provides a detailed discussion of the textual effect of alternative transcript layouts. Transcript layout is one aspect of the broader issue of mapping conversations (Green & Wallatt, 1981). Ochs mentions the literacy-related point that the material presented to the left is given primacy in he reading of a transcript and that choice about where to place nonverbal descriptions accentuates or demotes the importance of these. Hence the repetition of layouts such as:

T	Why did the farmer wear the boots, Jason?
Ja	'Cause 'cause he needed to walk through the mud to get to the barn? ((quietly, head down))

produces a reading and a characterization that is different from the repetition of layouts such as:

T	Why did the farmer wear the boots, Jason?
Ja	((quietly, head down)) 'Cause 'cause he needed to walk through the mud to get to the barn?

Similarly, if some speaker identifications are placed to the left of others or if multiple columns are used, some speakers are in effect given the initiative by coming first on the left of the page (cf. Ochs, 1979, p. 51).

T		Why did the farmer wear the boots, Jason?
	Ja	'Cause, 'cause he needed...
T		Good. He needed them.

Rather than repeat all of the pertinent points that Ochs makes about layout, only some points from her work will be extended here. One point is that transcribers give a speaker interactional priority through layout, influenced by cultural assumptions. This in turn influences possible readings of the transcript. In this way the transcript can easily reproduce a social organization of age relations in which adults are given priority. Second, Ochs' claim (1979, p. 49) that "the researcher may be quite subtly influenced by an adult's status as caretaker or competent speaker in *letting* this figure assume the predominant location on the page of description" (my emphasis), should not be taken to mean that no work is involved in the decision. That work is precisely an example of the use of a course of practical reasoning within a culture in which adults are 'naturally' seen to be in control. In fact, this idea, "let the adult go on the left" is a perfect analogy to formulations like "let ABC define the angle x" in a mathematical proof. The third point is that Ochs suggests that in transcription we can counter cultural biases with deliberate transcription choices, for example, by prioritizing the utterances of the student or child. That in itself would be another case of the use of a course of practical reasoning and action that, in this case, is sensitive to the social effects of writing the transcript one way or the other. That is, transcription is a form of social practice, a form of textual action and activity that reproduces, modifies or challenges relations among categories of people.

Another aspect of layout that is significant for how a transcript is read is the division of speech into analytic units. Du Bois et al. (1993) discuss intonation units and turns as fundamental divisions. In their system of transcription, each intonation unit is a "stretch of speech uttered under a single coherent intonation contour" and "each intonation unit appears on a separate line" (pp. 46, 47). Speaker identifications show turn beginnings, and within these turns at talk successive intonation units are presented on subsequent lines of text according to intonation contours. Similarly, Gumperz and Berenz (1993, p. 95, 96) attempt to capture the "rhythmic organization of the turn" through division of turns into "informational phrases." Green et al. (1988), and Bloome and Theodorou (1988) use "message units" of teacher talk to organize transcription from videotape, with nonverbal and other contextual information put in a right-hand column.

Psathas and Anderson (1990) also draw attention to transcription issues, including numbering and denoting turns and utterances, denoting silences and deciding on where to assign pauses. Among the points they make about details of silences (p. 89):

The 'location' of a silence has considerable significance in interaction. That is, a half-second pause occurring in the middle of someone's turn while, say, they are involved in a 'word-search' (a *within* turn silence) is a far different interactional matter from a half-second pause following the production of the first part of an adjacency pair, such as a 'question' or a 'request' (a *between* turn silence). While this is frequently a straightforward matter, occasions do arise where the 'ownership' of a spate of silence is in question, and can be central in the analysis.

A segment from a kindergarten literacy lesson illustrates this question of whose silence the pause is made out to be:

6	T	Smarty pants, right. And *who is* Smarty Pants, do you think? Just by having a look at him on the front cover. Who do you think he is, Rachel?
7	R	A clown
8	T	A cu-lown right. Well turn over the front cover until we come to the *first page*. What can you see on that page what is he doing Linda? (3.0)
9	T	What is he doing? (2.0) Is he standing up like we stand up? His two feet? What's he doing, Sally Fraser?
10	S	He's he's he's standing upside down.

This transcript was made from an audiotape. If the 3.0 second pause were attributed to Linda, this would make it her hesitation, calling into question her competence to answer. The audiotape cannot indicate the local circumstances of the silence, which could have included any number of matters concerning attention, gaze, or other situational factors. Transcribing the pause as a silence in the sequence of turns does not entirely vindicate Linda, given the placement of the pause and given readers' knowledge about classroom questioning routines. However, it is less implicative than transcribing it as Linda's pause (see also Edwards, 1993, p. 24; Gumperz & Berenz, 1993, pp. 93, 102, on the significance of assigning pauses). Atkinson and Drew (1979) show the significance in courtroom hearings of the assignment of pauses, hesitations or silences to speakers. The character or competence of the witness (e.g. Linda) can be at stake.

Depicting the Nonverbal

These observations on the production of transcripts also apply to making written/graphic records of nonverbal activity. With the increased use of videotapes even more selection decisions are encountered. As Bloom (1993, p.155) describes,

The amount of detail that is preserved on video tape is, quite literally, enormous, even though the information present in the original event is necessarily reduced. ... This detail can be overwhelming to the researcher in trying to decide what to include and what to leave out of the transcription. In the effort to preserve a description rather than an interpretation, we could easily be engulfed by the details.

Bloom's suggestion here is that transcribers of videotaped material see themselves not as describing the scene, but necessarily as interpreting. As indicated before, this resolves the issue from the start that any transcription is an interested representation of some of the possible features of the scene.

Ochs (1979) provides an extensive discussion of the representation of the relation between the verbal and nonverbal in transcripts. Descriptions of nonverbal features of literacy scenes involve additional and different kinds of attention, and these descriptions are also strongly informed by a researcher's analytic point or purpose.

Among the decisions Ochs reviews (1979, p. 52ff.) concerning the relation of verbal to nonverbal in the recorded video scene are whether the nonverbal should be placed to the left or right of or above the verbal material; whether the verbal and nonverbal should be separated into columns, thus creating two discrete streams of action; and whether the nonverbal should be bracketed, thus making the verbal the primary stream of action.

Ochs points out (1979, p. 56ff.) that since in the case of young children's talk, features of the immediate physical setting are important props in the organization of talk, these are fully part of the communicative scene and necessary to understanding the scene. In the following example (p. 56f.) the child had been indicating the relevancies in the scene:

> This description [of talk, action and items in the child's reach] indicates the amount of nonverbal data that needs to be recorded to assess the nature of reference and other speech acts carried out by the child. For example, without indicating accompanying nonverbal behavior, we would not know if *steamroller* and *car* named the same referent, and we would not know the referents for the deictic terms *here's*, *here* and *that's*. The detailed recording of accompanying movements and eye gaze is, then, not superfluous to an analysis of communicative competence.

The problem of describing the nonverbal aspects of an interactional scene can expressed as the problem of 'capturing' some theoretically, organizationally and locally pertinent details of the scene. The challenge is to produce a selective but theoretically useful *depiction* of the scene, which is partly analogous to the problem of captioning a photograph (cf. Woolgar, 1988) or headlining a newspaper report (McHoul, 1982, p. 118ff.). The problems of nonverbal depiction are ones in which the technical and theoretical problems of transcribing talk are potentially multiplied. At the same time the interplay of verbal and visual depiction can become reciprocal resources in making a theoretical point, or in finding new interests in the material.

Transcribing practices are also enabled and constrained by the kinds of recording that have been made. In classroom studies, for example, researchers using only a single video

camera will have to privilege some activities over others. Bloome and Theodorou (1988) used a videotape in which the camera stayed on a group of students; the teacher could be heard on the tape. In transcribing the videotape, the teacher's verbal communications were entered into a left-hand column. The right-hand column in which the students' actions and interactions were represented is far more elaborate, including stick figures depicting positions, postures and actions of the three girls. This is consistent with the intent of the study. The stick figures are powerful indicators of how little the girls were physically oriented to the teacher during the 5-minute segment recorded. In the transcript, the teacher appears as a disembodied voice off stage and to the left.

TRANSCRIPTION AS A COMMUNICATIVE AND VISUAL ART

In Davies and Munro's (1987) analysis of "order in apparent disorder: a classroom scene observed," the videotaped "scene observed" was/is apparently (on first or commonsense viewing) "disorderly." A student was initially viewed as intensely disruptive, quite out of control. Upon close analysis of moment to moment talk, action and interaction, and drawing on particular theoretical resources, the authors showed him to be acting rationally inside the moral organization of that classroom scene. This interpretive feat was accomplished with the aid of illustrations to accompany descriptions of verbal and nonverbal aspects of the scene.

The Picasso-like sketches made from tracing over video stills depict just those elements—no fewer and no more—of the postures and movements of the classroom participants that the analysis depends on. These sketches, following Livingston's (1987) discussion of proof-accounts in geometry, are potentially better than, and more elegant than, a photograph or a video still. They "capture," not the scene itself in some essential way, but what the researchers have attended to and found pertinent in the course of observing the relation of talk and action.

The transcript and the representation of the visual scene observed are interpreted with the surrounding text: the discussion. It is in the discussion that features of the transcript are highlighted and a particular story is told about the talk and action. Thus the transcript, as indicated by Mishler (1991) is part of a rhetoric and part of an aesthetic. "Cultural values and political ideologies provide additional interpretive vantage points to locate the social, cognitive or affective relevance of, for example, unfamiliar-looking persons or activities as exotic, sympathetic or dangerous" (p. 258).

In another classroom study using videotaped sequences, Paoletti (1990) examined the fine detail of the coordination of teacher's talk and action and students' talk and action. This study was framed by the idea that a classroom is produced through participants' descriptions and actions in the everyday course of their interactions, and that the classroom is produced differently by different participants. The study was written to resist singular interpretations of the classroom, and to use recorded data to open out different interpretations which would lead to different possible subsequent courses of action. The published study included a number of transcribed classroom scenes with intervening discussion and analysis. Each of these transcriptions included verbal and accompanying nonverbal activity. These included "the year six girls" who were constructed as a group by the researcher on the basis of categorization done by the participants (teacher and students) themselves. The researcher presents the following scene in illustration of her witnessing this group's relationship with the teacher (pp. 130, 131):

Teacher	Move one of those desks over there and have a group of five girls. ((desk is moved))
Teacher	Jessica ( ) paint
Jessica	((Jessica whispers something to the teacher))
Teacher	You just said you want to paint! (Go and sit there please.) ((annoyed expression)) ((Jessica sits down, head on hand; the teacher stands near Kate's desk and says, looking at Kate:))
Teacher	Why is she upset?
Kate	I don't know. ((Kate answers the teacher looking at her and keeping eye contact with her.))
Sarah	She just doesn't want to sit next to us.
Teacher	Yeah, why?
Sarah	(I don't know,) you ask her. ((The teacher looks at them and then turns left and walks towards another group of desks.))

Paoletti (p. 131) states in relation to this scene: "The coldness, distance, awkwardness, and discomfort in this relationship became increasingly evident to me as observer, but was very subtly conveyed." This summary statement is similar to a caption to a photograph. The transcription attends considerably to eye contact as this had been identified in situ as an indicator of a problematic relationship between the teacher and these girls. Other groups of students were described in terms of their habits of distance or closeness in relation to the teacher.

In her account of the teacher's and students' collaborative work in constructing classroom order, Paoletti (1990, p. 132) offers the following demonstration from videotape:

| Teacher | ((To the class)) Right, by now everyone should be finished drawing and you should be up to the coloring and it doesn't have to be a marvellous decoration to hang on the wall, one colour is fine, and coloring very quickly is also fine, so you have to find out what to do next. |
| | ((At the word "drawing" all the children stop talking. After the teacher stops talking, for 10 seconds, the children keep silent, then a child starts to talk and others join in and, in about another 10 seconds, the level of noise is back at the situation before the teacher began to speak. The teacher keeps going around the desks.)) |

This coordination of timing of teacher talk and student silence is shown to be repeated. The transcript is presented to show the precision with which the students hear and respond to the teacher's organizational talk and their level of cooperation with her. Once the phenomenon had been noticed in viewing and reviewing the videotape, a stopwatch was used to calculate the synchrony. The precision of the timing indicated in the commentary represents the precision of the timing in the classroom. In this way the students as transcript characters are assigned a highly tuned attention to the teacher's organizational talk.

The transcription of videotaped scenes provides for the development of unique and creative responses to the challenges outlined in this chapter. In this sense transcription could be taken itself to be a species of "visual and communicative art."

THE TRANSCRIPT AS AN ACCOUNT OF THE PRACTICAL REASONING THAT PRODUCED IT

In his analyses of the proving of a Euclidean theorem, Livingston (1987) has traced the relation between the "lived work" of producing a proof, and the proof account (the text, the written proof that is given as a record of what was done). Each comprises half of the proof. The proof account (that which is written down in the course of proving) is a "guide to the practical action and practical reasoning that it is seen retrospectively to summarise and describe" (p. 100). Not all the reasoning and the choices and conventions that go into the work of proving appear in the proof account, although the proof account describes the kind of work that went into its own production. Livingston states that the proof "has its own texture of necessary and relevant—or identifying—detail" (p. 111). Like the proof account, a transcript is "a description of its own lived work" (p. 112). In reading a transcript we can recover how it was that this transcript could have been arrived at, and we can find the logic that went into its production. Paoletti's transcripts and commentaries provide well for this recovery.

This point about reading the "text" of a literacy event as an account is also informed by Smith's (1990, p. 153) interest in how texts are written and read:

> In the process of writing, making corrections, in thinking again about how to address a topic, in thinking through a topic so that it can be first thought, then expressed, adequately, clearly, and well, a text is developed that depends upon and intends the interpretative schema that has entered normatively into its creation. In the production of the text the same circular process is at work as that which arises between text and reader. Hence the text can be said to intend interpretive procedures as those practices and methods of reading which will read it for the sense intended.

Transcripts, then, are accounts of the theoretical and analytical work that went into producing them. Making transcripts is part of the work of making sense of what is observed in recorded sounds and images. Making sense of events seen and heard involves characterizing them in some way, assigning some kind of order to them. The transcription process imposes structure and order on events in the "pre-textual" realm of everyday life. What structure, order, meaning, rationality or morality those events are made to have are products of the work of transcription. Transcription, in this sense, is a process of theorizing and demonstrating social order; the transcript is an account of that theory of social order.

References

Atkinson, J. M., & Drew, P. (1979). *Order in court: The organization of verbal interaction in judicial settings.* London: Macmillan.

Atkinson, J. M., & Heritage, J. (1984). *Structures of social action: Studies in conversation analysis.* Cambridge: Cambridge University Press.

Baker, C. D., & Davies, B. (1989). A lesson on sex roles. *Gender and Education, 1*(1), 59–76.

Baker, C. D. (1992). Description and analysis in classroom talk and interaction. *Journal of Classroom Interaction, 27*(2), 9–14.

Baker, C. D., & Freebody, P. (1986). Representations of questioning and answering in children's first school books. *Language in Society, 15*(4), 451–484.

Baker, C. D., & Freebody, P. (1989). *Children's first school books: Introductions to the culture of literacy.* Oxford: Basil Blackwell.

Bloome, D., & Theodorou, E. (1988). Analyzing teacher–student and student–student discourse. In J. L. Green & J. O. Harker (Eds.), *Multiple perspective analyses of classroom discourse.* Norwood, NJ: Ablex.

Bloom, L., (1993). Transcription and coding for child language research: The parts are more than the whole. In J. A. Edwards & M. D. Lampert (Eds.), *Talking data: Transcription and coding in discourse research.* Hillsdale, NJ: Erlbaum.

Coulter, J. (1989). *Mind in action.* Cambridge & Oxford: Polity Press/Basil Blackwell.

Davies, B., & Munro, K. (1987). The perception of order in apparent disorder: A classroom scene observed. *Journal of Education for Teaching, 13*(2), 117–131.

Du Bois, J. W., Schuetze-Coburn, S., Cumming, S. & Paolino, D. (1993). Outline of discourse transcription. In J. A. Edwards & M. D. Lampert (Eds.), *Talking data: Transcription and coding in discourse research.* Hillsdale, NJ: Erlbaum.

Edwards, J. A. (1993). Principles and contrasting systems of discourse transcription. In J. A. Edwards & M. D. Lampert (Eds.), *Talking data: Transcription and coding in discourse research.* Hillsdale, NJ: Erlbaum.

Edwards, J. A., & Lampert, M. D. (Eds.). (1993). *Talking data: Transcription and coding in discourse research.* Hillsdale, NJ: Erlbaum.

Gee, J. P., Michaels, S., & O'Connor, M. C. (1992). Discourse analysis. In M. D. Lecompte, W. L. Millroy, & J. Preissle (Eds.), *The handbook of qualitative research in education.* San Diego: Academic Press.

Green, J. L., & Wallatt, C. (1981). Mapping instructional conversations—A sociolinguistic ethnography. In J. L. Green & C. Wallatt (Eds.), *Ethnography and language in educational settings.* Norwood, NJ: Ablex.

Green, J. L., Weade, R., & Graham, K. (1988). Lesson construction and student participation: A sociolinguistic analysis. In J. L. Green & J. O. Harker (Eds.), *Multiple perspective analyses of classroom discourse.* Norwood, NJ: Ablex.

Gumperz, J. J., & Berenz, N. (1993). Transcribing conversational exchanges. In J. A. Edwards & M. D. Lampert (Eds.), *Talking data: Transcription and coding in discourse research.* Hillsdale, NJ: Erlbaum.

Heap, J. L. (1982). Understanding classroom events: A critique of Durkin, with an alternative. *Journal of Reading Behavior, 14,* 391–411.

Heritage, J. (1984). *Garfinkel and ethnomethodology.* Cambridge & Oxford: Polity Press/Basil Blackwell.

Jayussi, L. (1984). *Categorization and the moral order.* London: Routledge.

Jefferson, G. (1985). An exercise in the transcription and analysis of laughter. In T. A. Van Dijk (Ed.), *Handbook of discourse analysis, Vol. 3: Discourse and dialogue.* London: Academic Press.

Livingston, E. (1987). *Making sense of ethnomethodology.* London: Routledge.

Lynch, M. & Woolgar, S. (Eds.). (1990). *Representation in scientific practice.* Cambridge, MA: MIT Press.

McHoul, A. W. (1982). *Telling how texts talk: Essays on reading and ethnomethodology.* London: Routledge.

Mishler, E. G. (1991). Representing discourse: The rhetoric of transcription. *Journal of Narrative and Life History, 1*(4), 255–280.

Ochs, E. (1979). Transcription as theory. In E. Ochs & B. Schieffelin (Eds.), *Developmental pragmatics.* New York: Academic Press.

Olson, D. R., & Astington, J. (1990). Talk about text: How literacy contributes to thought. *Journal of Pragmatics, 14,* 705–721.

Paoletti, I. (1990). Interpreting classroom climate: A study in a year five and six class. *International Journal of Qualitative Research in Education, 3*(2) 113–137.

Psathas, G., & Anderson, W. T. (1990). The 'practices' of transcription in conversation analysis. *Semiotica, 78*(12), 75–99.

Schegloff, E. A. (1988). Description in the social sciences I: Talk-in-interaction. *IPrA Papers in Pragmatics, 2*(1/2), 1–24.

Schenkein, J. (Ed.). (1978). *Studies in the organization of conversational interaction.* New York: Academic Press.

Smith, D. E. (1990). *The conceptual practices of power.* Boston: Northeastern University Press.

Speier, M. (1972). Some conversational problems for interactional analysis. In D. Sudnow (Ed.), *Studies in social interaction.* New York: Free Press.

Woolgar, S. (1988). Reflexivity is the ethnographer of the text. In S. Woolgar (Ed.), *Knowledge and reflexivity.* London: Sage.

Zimmerman, D. H. (1992). Achieving context: Openings in emergency calls. In G. Watson & R. Seiler (Eds.), *Text in context: Contributions to ethnomethodology.* Newbury Park, CA: Sage.

·13·

METHODOLOGY IN TEACHER RESEARCH:
THREE CASES

James F. Baumann, Betty Shockley Bisplinghoff, JoBeth Allen
UNIVERSITY OF GEORGIA

We found the prospect of becoming teacher researchers intriguing but also somewhat daunting. We imagined all research to be a tangle of experimental groups and control groups, double-tailed *t*-tests and analyses of variance. We doubted our competence and questioned our willingness to commit ourselves to the effort we knew such a project would require. We did, nevertheless, commit ourselves, because we felt it was important for teachers to take advantage of every opportunity to speak and be heard, to develop a voice, and to establish their credibility concerning educational issues....

[W]e came to believe that classroom research certainly could be done by teachers and that it was not necessarily a statistical analysis of a treatment applied to an experimental group. Our best insights came from observing and documenting our daily process. One team member commented:

> You have a question, you're willing to document the process you go through [to answer it], and you're willing to share it in the end. That's what we need—people who will share their stories.... It's important that this kind of work comes from us, comes from teachers who are really teaching children and know. (Keffer et al., 1995, pp. 2, 4)

Keffer and her colleagues are teacher researchers in the School Research Consortium (SRC), a teacher-research community affiliated with the University of Georgia site of the National Reading Research Center (NRRC) (Baumann, Allen, & Shockley, 1994). Their reflection on the process of becoming teacher researchers is similar to that of other teacher researchers within the SRC (Allen, Shockley, & Baumann, 1995). Most initially doubted their ability to conduct research, feeling overwhelmed by the technical aspects of conventional research methods. However, with a commitment to classroom inquiry founded upon the desire to improve their own teaching and supported by committed colleagues struggling with the same issues, SRC members sought out, adapted, and sometimes created research methods for teacher inquiry (Baumann et al., 1995). A desire to understand the complexities of their classrooms, to improve their effectiveness as teachers, and to share their knowledge with others through stories provide SRC members the impetus to engage in research.

But what is teacher research, and what are the methods of teacher inquiry? Is there consensus about the characteristics of teacher research? Is teacher research an adapted or hybridized form of existing educational research paradigms, or is it a distinct research genre? Do teacher researchers simply borrow methods from established forms of disciplined inquiry, or is there something methodologically distinct about teacher research? Do teacher researchers tend to use similar methods, or does teacher research represent a wide array of methods and analyses? In this chapter, we address these and other questions relating to methodology in teacher research.

We do so by first surveying the tradition of teacher inquiry and the methods that have been recommended or employed, highlighting the historical and contemporary diversity of teacher-research methods and opinions about them. Next we

The research described in this chapter, as well as the writing of the chapter itself, was supported by the National Reading Research Center of the University of Georgia and the University of Maryland. The NRRC is supported under the Educational Research and Development Center's Program (PR/Award No. 117A20007) as administered by the Office of Educational Research and Improvement, U.S. Department of Education. The findings and opinions expressed here do not necessarily reflect the position or policies of the NRRC, the OERI, or the U.S. Department of Education.

We thank Dr. Dera Weaver, an English teacher at Athens Academy, and Dr. James McLaughlin, a professor of Elementary Education at the University of Georgia, for their thoughtful, detailed, and constructive comments on earlier versions of this chapter.

present three cases of teacher inquiry and associated methods. We describe cases that range from a solitary classroom inquiry to a teacher-research community. Case one, told by Jim Baumann, involves his experience as a solo teacher researcher in the year he left the university to teach second grade full time, during which he explored the journey he and his students took toward literacy. Case two, told by JoBeth Allen, is a methodological story of collaborative inquiry in which Betty Shockley Bisplinghoff, a 1st-grade teacher, Barbara Michalove, a 2nd-grade teacher, and JoBeth, a university researcher, worked together on a multiyear investigation of literacy acquisition by low-income, diverse elementary school children and their families. The third case, told by Betty Shockley Bisplinghoff as Coordinator of the SRC, explores the methodological diversity within the NRRC's teacher-research community. We conclude the chapter with our collective thoughts and reflections on methods for classroom-based inquiry.

We present these cases not as comprehensive of the range of teacher-research perspectives, nor even as being representative of those we describe (all our stories are unique in their own ways). Rather, the cases reflect the diversity within the domain of teacher research, a major theme of this chapter. By necessity, we focus on teachers rather than students because it is teachers who are in search of appropriate and useful methodology. However, we acknowledge that although professional growth and development are essential features of teacher inquiry, the ultimate purpose of the enterprise is to promote the educational, social, and emotional well-being of the students we teach in classrooms.

METHODOLOGY SURVEY

In this section, we provide a short historical review of teacher research, followed by a discussion of the fundamental principles that constitute teacher research. We then examine the diversity within teacher research perspectives and conclude with thoughts on the paradigmatic identity of teacher research.

A Brief History of a Long Tradition

Historical treatments of teacher research recount a long and robust past, with notable periods of interest and disinterest in the movement. McFarland and Stansell (1993) trace the roots of teacher research from 17th- and 18th-century theologians and philosophers, such as Commenius and Rousseau who advocated observation as a foundation for child development and learning, to 19th-century European educators such as Pestalozzi and Herbart who developed and used naturalistic methods of observation for studying teaching and learning. Olson (1990b) presents Francis Parker's and John Dewey's experimental schools in the United States and Lowry's (1908) involvement of teachers in research efforts as evidence of inquiry-based teaching at the close of the 19th century. Lytle and Cochran-Smith (1994) cite Dewey's (1904) promotion of teachers' reflection on their work as a critical milestone in the history of teacher research. With the advent of psychological

testing in the 1920s and 1930s, however, the prominence of teacher as inquirer diminished in relation to the rise of experimental investigations (Olson, 1990b), with interest not to resurface in earnest until after World War II.

All those who examine the history of teacher research (e.g., Lytle & Cochran-Smith, 1994; McFarland & Stansell, 1993; Olson, 1990b) point to the action research movement of the 1950s as evidence of the resurgence of classroom-based inquiry. Corey's *Action Research to Improve School Practices* (1953) was representative of a large body of work (e.g., Corey, 1954; Shumsky, 1958; Wann, 1952; see a review by Wallace, 1987) that promoted teachers' examination of their practice as a means to improve their teaching. Interest in action research diminished again in the late 1950s (see Olson, 1990b) due considerably to the criticism that research of this nature lacked scientific rigor (Corman, 1957; Hodgkinson, 1957). Nevertheless, some interest in action research continued through the 1960s and 1970s in the United States (e.g., Odell, 1976; Rainey, 1973) and to an even greater extent in Great Britain (e.g., Clark, 1972; Winter, 1982).

The significant British action research movement paralleled events in the United States, beginning in the late 1940s (Olson, 1990b) and blossoming in the late 1960s and early 1970s. It was led by Lawrence Stenhouse (1973, 1975, 1980; see Rudduck & Hopkins, 1985, for a collection of Stenhouse's writings), who formalized the action research movement with the creation of the Center for Applied Research in Education at the University of East Anglia. Through this center, Stenhouse promoted teacher research, often in collaboration with university faculty, as a means to engage in reflective action within classrooms and to promote teachers' status and professionalism. Stenhouse's colleague John Elliott (1991, 1993; Elliott & MacDonald, 1975) continued this work through the Cambridge Institute of Education, a teacher-research consortium whose members focused on locating and creating methods appropriate and useful for classroom research projects.

Since the early 1980s, there has been a virtual explosion of interest in, conducting and reporting of, and writing about teacher research. Current literature is filled with stories of teachers who turned to reflective, action-oriented teaching as a professional way of life (e.g., Bissex & Bullock, 1987; Cochran-Smith & Lytle, 1993; Goswami & Stillman, 1987). Over the last decade, teacher research has become an integral presence at professional conferences (e.g., numerous teacher-research presentations at the annual conventions of the International Reading Association and the National Council of Teachers of English) and within education periodicals (e.g., D'Alessandro et al., 1992; Dillon, 1988; Llorens, 1994; Teale, 1995; the initiation of *Teacher Research: A Journal of Classroom Inquiry* in 1993). Further, there has been a steady stream of published collections of teacher-research investigations (e.g., Allen, Cary, & Delgado, 1995; Daiker & Morenberg, 1990; Hansen, Newkirk, & Graves, 1985; Mohr & Maclean, 1987; Olson, 1990a; Patterson, Santa, Short, & Smith, 1993; Patterson, Stansell, & Lee, 1990; Pinnell & Matlin, 1989; Wells, 1994).

The prevalence of classroom inquiry as a methodological orientation for educational research by and with teachers has not been reflected so widely in collections of research syntheses and perspectives. For example, as Cochran-Smith and Lytle (1990) note, the *Handbook of Research on Teaching* (Wittrock, 1986) fails to include reviews written by teachers and virtually ignores published teacher-researcher investigations (an exception being the methodology chapter by Erickson, who points to the power and promise of teacher researchers). Similarly, the first and second volumes of the *Handbook of Reading Research* (Pearson, 1984; Barr, Kamil, Mosenthal, & Pearson, 1991) have no chapters on, about, or by teacher researchers. The American Educational Research Association-sponsored *Complementary Methods for Research in Education* (Jaeger, 1988) fails to acknowledge teacher research as a method, and the National Conference on Research in English / National Council of Teachers of English-sponsored *Multidisciplinary Perspectives on Literacy Research* (Beach, Green, Kamil, & Shanahan, 1992) omits teacher research as a distinct perspective (although Moll, 1992, describes collaborative research with teachers in his chapter).

More recent volumes may indicate that teacher research has achieved some status within the established educational research community. For example, there is a chapter by Burton on teacher research within the International Reading Association / National Council of Teachers of English-sponsored *Handbook of Research on Teaching the English Language Arts* (Flood, Jensen, Lapp, & Squire, 1991); there is a "Teacher research in English" entry by Lytle and Cochran-Smith in the National Council of Teachers of English-sponsored *Encyclopedia of English Studies and Language Arts* (Purves, 1994); and, of course, there is the present chapter in this handbook.

In spite of the absence or delayed acceptance of teacher research within the realm of educational compendia, many individual writers have dealt with methodological issues. Buckingham's (1926) *Research for Teachers* may have been the first teacher-research "methods" text, and one of the few volumes available for many years, but a plethora of works is currently available (e.g., Brause & Mayher, 1991; Calhoun, 1994; Goswami & Stillman, 1987; Hopkins, 1993; Hubbard & Power, 1993; Kincheloe, 1991; Mohr & Maclean, 1987; Myers, 1985; Nixon, 1981; Oja & Smulyan, 1989; Sagor, 1992). But what are teacher-research methodologists reporting? What consensus or diversity is there under the broad umbrella of methods suggested and used in action and teacher research?

Principles and Consensus

In spite of considerable philosophical and methodological diversity within the teacher-research movement, there are several important common principles. One involves the perspective and process of classroom inquiry. Virtually all accounts refer to a teacher researcher's unique perspective, that is, a teacher's daily presence and intimate relationship with the research situation and participants. This insider, or emic, perspective (Cochran-Smith & Lytle, 1993, p. 43) enables a teacher to live the research experience in a

manner an outside (e.g., university) researcher cannot. Atwell (1993, p. ix) argues that the emic perspective brings power and insight to the research process: "My admittedly subjective role as provider for and teacher of these students, which I was careful to describe, did not negate my findings. My role as teacher made my findings possible, it made them specific and context rich, and it made them valuable to many of the teachers who read about them." Erickson (1986, p. 157), however, suggests that the emic nature of teacher research may simultaneously be a limitation: "In some ways the teacher's very closeness to practice, and the complexity of the classroom as a stimulus-rich environment, are liabilities for reflection."

A principle related to the insider perspective of teacher research is the interrelatedness of theory and practice and the critical reflection on them, that is, the notion of praxis (Cochran-Smith & Lytle, 1993; Kincheloe, 1991; Lather, 1986). Mayher and Brause (1991) see this process as theory building and fundamental to teacher research. They maintain that teaching practice stems from teachers' beliefs, or their theory of teaching. Therefore, a change in practice implies a change in personal theory. The process of theory / belief change involves "reflection-in-action of one's current practice; understanding and transforming research findings and theories so they can form the basis of practice; and sharing problems and reflections with colleagues both locally and nationally" (p. 23).

Another area of general consensus involves the fundamental elements of teacher research. Bissex (1987) states that a teacher researcher is an observer, a questioner, and a learner, all roles that result in a more complete teacher. Patterson and Shannon (1993) acknowledge differences among teacher researchers but describe similar fundamental qualities: "Diversity is a powerful characteristic of teacher research, but all researching teachers share a common process of reflecting on their practice, inquiring about it, and taking action" (p. 10). Burton (1991) also cites action and reflection as activities that teachers perform in classroom inquiry, but adds the element of reciprocity, that is, reflection leading to action and vice versa. Wells (1994, p. 26) takes these qualities and places them in an "action research cycle," which consists of four recursive components: observation, interpretation, planning for change, and action. Wells adds to these components the pervasive element that he calls the "practitioner's personal theory," which guides the research cycle. It is by making connections between practice and theory, Wells argues, that teachers create reflectiveness, the hallmark of teacher research.

Reflection and action alone, however, do not constitute teacher research. Although such qualities are necessary for teacher research and are likely to make one a better teacher, they are not sufficient for the process to occur. Teacher research must be a consciously initiated process that is implemented with a plan for data gathering and analysis. Patterson and Shannon (1993) state that "methods of inquiry need not be sophisticated, but they must be systematic" (p. 9). Cochran-Smith and Lytle (1990, p. 3) define teacher research as "systematic and intentional inquiry carried out by teachers." They elaborate as follows:

Systematic refers primarily to ways of gathering and recording information, documenting experiences inside and outside of classrooms, and making some kind of written record. *Systematic* also refers to ordered ways of collecting, rethinking, and analyzing classroom events for which there may be only partial or unwritten records. *Intentional* signals that teacher research is an activity that is planned rather than spontaneous. (Lytle & Cochran-Smith, 1994, p. 1154)

On the other hand, there is a fluid aspect to classroom inquiry. Hubbard and Power (1993) note that teacher-research methods might be "complicated and messy," and "you cannot divide the process into neat linear steps" (p. xvii). Patterson and Shannon (1993) concur that teacher research is "organic, sometimes messy, unpredictable, and generative—just like the teachers' lives in and out of school" (p. 9). In spite of this necessary flexibility and fluidity, teacher research is not amorphous. There is a structure to it as in other forms of disciplined inquiry (Shulman, 1988). The methodological structure of teacher research, as we will demonstrate in the following cases, involves organized documentation and data collection, systematic analyses, and thoughtful interpretations of results.

Epistemological Diversity

One characteristic in which teacher-research perspectives differ is in the manner in which knowledge is viewed and acquired. Cochran-Smith and Lytle (1993) offer a four-part structure of views of knowing through teacher research: "an approximation of university-based research; a more grassroots phenomenon that has its own internal standards of logic, consistency, and clarity; a reflective or reflexive process that is for the benefit of the individual; or a dialectical process of action and reflection aimed at social change" (p. 9). Drawing from this framework, we conceptualize the epistemological focus of teacher research as being established, pragmatic, or radical.

As Lytle and Cochran-Smith (1994) argue, some teacher researchers (e.g., Myers, 1985) take a fairly *established* approach, primarily viewing classroom inquiry as a means to replicate traditional, university-based methodology. This view of teacher research is much like the early iterations of action research, involving modification of extant educational research paradigms and tools to address hypothesis-testing types of teacher questions. Our conception of an established approach, however, goes beyond this quasi-positivistic view of teacher research to include teacher researchers who draw from existing research traditions, be they quantitative, qualitative, historical, philosophical, or others.

The *pragmatic* approach involves selecting or creating methodological tools and procedures appropriate for addressing teachers' classroom-based research questions. Such tools are typically those employed in qualitative or interpretive research, but not always. Sagor's (1992) five-step methodological process illustrates this pragmatic view: "The process of collaborative action research has five sequential steps: (1) problem formulation, (2) data collection, (3) data analysis, (4) reporting of results, [and] (5) action planning" (p. 10). Hubbard and Power (1993) represent the pragmatic perspective by offering various "research designs" (see chap. 3 and Appendix A) that teachers employed in their classroom studies. These designs typically involve question generation, selecting and collecting relevant data, data analysis, and reflection.

Teacher research, viewed from a *radical* epistemological orientation, is a means to free teachers from ideological constraints imposed by economic, social, and cultural conditions that impact education and teaching and learning in schools (e.g., Carr & Kemmis, 1986; Gitlin et al., 1992). For example, Berlin (1990, p. 14) likens teacher research to a militant exercise that involves a "long revolution." Kincheloe (1991, p. 19) describes teacher research as "critically grounded action research" that presupposes, among other things, the rejection of positivistic perspectives and the underlying assumption that all in education is political in nature. Shannon (1990) urges teacher researchers to move away from action and naturalistic research toward critical research so that they can examine the politics of reading instruction and move toward the restructuring of the organization, goals, and procedures in literacy programs.

We place no relative value on these perspectives and readily admit that they are intellectual constructs to describe retrospectively the inquiry that teachers have done. Each perspective, with its differing assumptions about how to learn and know about classroom events, leads to different questions and thus different methods for addressing them. These multiple epistemologies support the emerging theme in this review that teacher research is defined and described by and through its diversity.

Paradigmatic Identity

We are left with the question of whether teacher research represents its own, unique methodological paradigm, or whether it is an evolutionary hybrid on the educational research family tree. Many teacher researchers and theorists (e.g., Bissex & Bullock, 1987; Mohr & Maclean, 1987) argue for its uniqueness, with Atwell (1993, p. viii) referring to a "new research paradigm." We agree.

Cochran-Smith and Lytle (1993) assert that comparing teacher research with institutionalized (university) forms of research limits our understanding of classroom inquiry by teachers. Rather, they argue that "it is more useful to consider teacher research as its own genre, not entirely different from other types of systematic inquiry into teaching yet with some quite distinctive features" (p. 10). The variable features of teacher research, as Cochran-Smith and Lytle (figure on pp. 12, 13) describe, involve the ownership of teacher research, the nature and source of teachers' research questions, the theoretical frames teachers bring to inquiry, and the generalizability and utility of what is learned. For example, with regard to research questions, Cochran-Smith and Lytle describe university-initiated research questions as "generally emerging from study of a discipline...and/or analysis of theoretical and empirical literatures," as opposed to teacher-research questions "generally emerging from problems of practice" (p. 12). Our research on the evolution of teachers' questions within the SRC (Baumann et al., 1994) supports the notion that the immediate, day-to-day realities of classroom life, not esoteric theoretical or empirical constructs, guide teachers in their inquiry.

As we attempt to demonstrate in the following cases, although distinctive from institutionalized education research, teacher research does not represent a routinized, prescriptive paradigm, nor do we believe it should. Rather, teacher research is an evolving philosophical orientation toward practical theory. Teacher-researchers wonder about the interrelated aspects of their work—who their children and care givers are, what their social and cultural experiences are, and what that means for teaching; they wonder what the curriculum shouts and whispers; they wonder what the political context of school and schooling says and hides. In short, they wonder how to do the work as best as they can.

Teacher research critics and skeptics may view this paradigm as lacking in structure and rules. That is not so as we have tried to demonstrate. Teacher research is not haphazard; it has definitive characteristics and principles of application. Indeed there is variety in how such principles are applied in the doing of teacher research, as each of us has experienced and as we shall demonstrate in the following cases. Therefore, we present these cases, not as comprehensive of the range of teacher-research perspectives, nor even as being representative of those we describe. The cases reflect the diversity within the domain of teacher research. Nevertheless, we believe that within this diversity emerge the essential qualities of the teacher-research genre: reflection and action through systematic, intentional inquiry about classroom life.

CASE ONE—INDIVIDUAL TEACHER RESEARCH: JIM'S EXPERIENCE

During the 1994–95 school year, I returned to teach elementary school full time after a 17-year hiatus, during which I had attended graduate school and worked as a university education professor. In the year back in the classroom, I conducted two teacher-research studies. The following narrative describes this experience and the methodological soul-searching involved in identifying and employing research perspectives appropriate for my teacher-researcher role. It is important that the reader realizes that, at the time of writing this (August 1995), I was only 2 months away from the classroom, and my studies were still underway (some data gathering continued and much analysis was before me). Therefore, my exploration of teacher-research methods continues, and this story does not yet have an ending.

Background

In 1994–95, I taught second grade at Fowler Drive Elementary School in Athens, Georgia. My position came about through a job exchange with Betty Shockley Bisplinghoff. Betty took leave from her teaching position at Fowler, where she had taught for 11 years, to come to the University of Georgia and pursue a doctoral degree in Language Education. At the

university, Betty taught my undergraduate Reading Education courses, while continuing to serve as Coordinator of the School Research Consortium.

I was assigned a 2nd-grade teaching position at Fowler. I prepared to teach by obtaining a Georgia teaching license, which required me to take a university course in exceptional children and pass a state-mandated teacher certification test; later I set up my classroom, designed my curriculum, and participated in new-teacher in-service. The first day of school was August 19, 1994, and from that point on, I taught all day, everyday for 180 school days, from 7:20 a.m. bus duty to after-school faculty meetings, Parent-Teacher Organization meetings, and evening homework and planning. I received no special privileges due to my university affiliation; rather, my duties and responsibilities were just like those of every other teacher at Fowler and in the district. My year in second grade was wonderful, exceeding my expectations with regard to the richness of my experience, what I learned, and what the children taught me (Baumann, 1995a, 1995b). An integral part of my teaching experience was to engage in yearlong, classroom-based inquiries through the NRRC's School Research Consortium.

In this case, I address methodological issues associated with classroom inquiry from the perspective of an individual teacher researcher. As noted in our introduction, each of these cases is unique and not intended to represent the experience of other individual or groups of teacher researchers. For example, my history as a university researcher, no doubt, influenced how I approached teacher research, and my research was supported by the NRRC. Further, I acknowledge that I was a novice teacher researcher when I began my year in second grade and, at this point, remained an apprentice at best. Nevertheless, I did teach full time while simultaneously studying teaching and learning in my classroom, and therefore was a teacher researcher in the fullest sense.

Methodological History

I have engaged in educational research for over 15 years. My doctoral program in the late 1970s involved learning how to conduct educational research within the quantitative, experimental tradition. I followed the experimental research path through much of my career, primarily conducting classroom-based intervention studies exploring the efficacy of various reading comprehension strategies and methods (e.g., Baumann, 1984, 1986; Baumann & Bergeron, 1993; Baumann, Seifert-Kessell, & Jones, 1992), although the manner in which I employed quantitative methods changed across these studies, primarily by increasing the external or ecological validity (Bronfenbrenner, 1976) through design modifications. I acknowledge the limits of quantitative, experimental research (see Baumann section in Baumann, Dillon, Shockley, Alvermann, & Reinking, 1996), but I continue to see value in research of this nature and may conduct additional experimental studies in the future.

In the past several years, however, I have expanded my repertoire of research methods in relation to questions that have not been readily answerable through the kind of experimental / control group studies I conducted in the past. For example, during the 1993–94 school year, two 5th-grade teachers, Helene Hooten and Pat White, and I explored how to integrate planned, teacher-led instruction within a literature-based reading program framework (Baumann, Hooten, & White, 1996). Our purpose in this study was not to determine *whether* strategies could be infused within a literature-based framework; we felt confident that they could on the basis of extant research and our own experiences. Rather, we desired to find out *how* such a program of instruction could be designed, created, and modified to be as effective as possible. To answer this question, we selected an evolving research framework called *formative experiment* (Newman, 1990), which involves evaluating the factors that enhance or inhibit an instructional intervention's effectiveness and how the intervention might be adapted to achieve its educational goal (see Reinking section of Baumann et al., 1996).

This methodological structure worked well given our question. We spent a year teaching students reading strategies in conjunction with trade book reading while we gathered data on the successes and failures of our instruction and how we modified it on the basis of what we were learning. This methodological change from controlled experimental studies to the more "on-line" experimentation within the formative experiment framework paved the way for further growth as I sought methods compatible with my teacher-research questions.

Second-Grade Teacher-Research Studies

I conducted two studies during my year in second grade. One study was a self-examination of the impact that returning to teach had on me as a classroom teacher, a college instructor, and a researcher and writer (Baumann, 1995a). The second study, which built upon the collaborative 5th-grade study with Helene and Pat, examined how a teacher might integrate reading strategy instruction in word identification and comprehension into a literature-based framework across an entire school year (Baumann & Ivey, in press). Each study demanded its own methodology.

Impact of Returning to Teach. Clearly, given the introspective, personal nature of my return-to-teaching study, neither a conventional quantitative nor a formative experimental paradigm was appropriate. During the summer of 1993, while seeking an epistemological orientation for my self-study, JoBeth Allen introduced me to several important literatures that helped me make my initial methodological plans. One perspective came from the action research tradition (e.g., Corey, 1953; Wann, 1952, 1953), and, in particular, the *educative research* framework described and employed by Gitlin et al. (1992). According to Gitlin and colleagues, educative research "challenge[s] the creation of hierarchical differences within the educational community between teachers and academics" (p. 6). Educative research provides a mechanism for teachers' voices to be heard and respected and for them to take action on the basis of what they have learned. Further,

educative research recognizes the "importance of reciprocity and equity" and "brings individuals together in such a fashion that all participants have a say in setting the agenda or topic and all have the potential to benefit and learn from the experience" (p. 7). This perspective was appealing to me because I was going to be a teacher myself, and I anticipated having the voices of colleagues, parents, and the children themselves guide me in my inquiry.

The second perspective JoBeth introduced me to was *hermeneutic phenomenology,* the interpreted descriptions of lived experiences. Max van Manen's *Researching Lived Experience: Human Science for an Action Sensitive Pedagogy* (1990) seemed to be particularly relevant to my methodological needs. van Manen states that "hermeneutic phenomenological research edifies the personal insight (Rorty, 1979), contributing to one's thoughtfulness and one's ability to act toward others, children or adults, with tact or tactfulness" (p. 7). A phenomenological approach involves asking a "what is it like?" question. In my case the question was, "What is it like to return to teach elementary school after a 17-year hiatus?"

van Manen (1990) argues that the methodological structure for research from this perspective involves a "dynamic interplay" among the following activities, all of which seemed to characterize the study I conceived: "(1) turning to a phenomenon which seriously interests us and commits us to the world; (2) investigating experience as we live it rather than as we conceptualize it; (3) reflecting on the central themes that characterize the phenomenon; (4) describing the phenomenon through the art of writing and rewriting; (5) maintaining a strong and oriented pedagogical relation to the phenomenon; (6) balancing the research context by considering part and whole" (pp. 30, 31). The appeal of the hermeneutic phenomenological perspective was that it provided a framework for engaging in a self-study of my everyday lived experience (Dilthey, 1985) as a teacher. Critical elements of both educative and phenomenological research include personal histories, school histories, peer observation and commentary, and artifact collection and analysis—just the kinds of data that I anticipated collecting.

Teaching Reading Strategies Through Literature. In my second study, I wanted to examine carefully the process of implementing a reading strategy instructional program within a literature-based framework, but to do so from the teacher's perspective and developmentally across an entire school year. As this study was similar to the one Helene, Pat, and I had done in fifth grade, which employed a formative experiment structure and which suited our needs quite well, I decided to use this paradigm again. Therefore, my plan was to document the ongoing effectiveness of incorporating word identification, vocabulary, comprehension, literary, and writing strategies into the literature we were experiencing in the classroom. I would accomplish this by collecting data as I progressed throughout the year, analyzing the efficacy of my developing instructional model, and modifying it as appropriate given ongoing results. Thus, as school began in August 1994, I felt well equipped methodologically to conduct the two studies I had planned.

Epistemological Evolution

Cathy Fleischer (1994) described her 14-year (and still ongoing) development as a teacher researcher as a "research odyssey" (p. 86), in which she simultaneously conducted classroom-based inquiry and read extensively about teacher research and literacy. This odyssey resulted in "connections and disconnections between my practice and my reading," leading her "around bends, across barriers, toward a place and a stance teachers and researchers are surveying and may perhaps even occupy" (p. 7). Although my odyssey has been much less than 14 years (but is still ongoing), I too found, after teaching a class of 7- and 8-year-olds full days while trying to do research, that there are indeed bends and barriers in the road (Baumann, in press). Being the teacher while simultaneously trying to be a researcher is not the same as being an outside researcher working with one or more teachers (e.g., even though I taught classes of students regularly as part of the 5th-grade formative experiment, that experience was very different from being the classroom teacher who is there all day, everyday and is ultimately responsible for the children's learning and well being).

In a conversation with JoBeth Allen (personal communication, August 10, 1995) about some of the salient characteristics of teacher research, she suggested a short list of three: (a) Teacher research must be doable, given everything else that is going on in a teacher's life before, during, and after school. (b) Teacher research must be true to the intent behind it (reflective and action-oriented) and responsive to the students and their families. (c) Teacher research must be second to students; though not discrete from teaching and certainly capable of enhancing instruction, teacher research must never interfere with or detract from a teacher's primary responsibility to help students learn and grow. In retrospect, my research perspective and methods have indeed evolved over my year in the classroom due to issues of doability, trueness and responsiveness, and the primacy of students. This fluidity, by necessity, was true for both the studies I conducted in my classroom.

Responsive and Unresponsive Methods. My back-to-teaching inquiry, as it evolved throughout the school year, became a more solitary study than I had anticipated. As a result, I found the collaborative educative research framework (Gitlin et al., 1992) not as responsive as I had expected. For example, a cornerstone of educative research is horizontal evaluation, which involves dialogue among those involved in the research: "Horizontal Evaluation is a process in which teachers collaboratively analyze the relationship between their teaching intentions and their practices" (p. 52). I had originally planned on achieving this collaboration by conferring regularly with my "trading-places" partner, Betty Shockley Bisplinghoff, as well as by having other elementary classroom teachers within the School Research Consortium observe my teaching and then discuss with me what they observed. Given the demands of teaching and the challenges I faced as a retro-novice (I viewed myself as a beginning teacher all over again), finding time to meet with Betty and having classroom visitors regularly was not a high priority. (And,

honestly, having guests in my classroom was not something I relished early in the year, as the blemishes exceeded the beauty in my teaching. In retrospect, this involved the issue of "studying up" versus "studying down" [see Allen, Buchanan, Edelsky, & Norton, 1992; Harding, 1987], as I realized that I would be the "subject" of someone else's study [up] by having others in my classroom observing me. In short, I was threatened by the notion of visitors critiquing my teaching, which engendered strong emotions and taught me an important lesson about power relationships in research.) As a result, educative research as an epistemological framework essentially fell by the wayside during the school year; this implies no criticism of the method, only a mismatch between my goals and methods.

The hermeneutic phenomenology framework (van Manen, 1990) proved to be more resilient and responsive to my needs as a researcher. Although I continue to explore and learn about this perspective as I analyze data and write about my experience (I am no expert in "human science research"), the notion of a methodological approach that embraces the lived experience and is dependent upon anecdotal narrative felt right throughout the school year and still does. In fact, the notion of personal narrative as a primary method (e.g., Carter, 1993; Connelly & Clandinin, 1990; Krall, 1988) became more salient and integral to my research as the year progressed. My journal was narration, audio and video recordings of class events were stories in live action, and the interviews I conducted with children, parents, and others were first-person accounts.

Not all my data however, were "continuous narrative descriptions" (Erickson, 1986). Children's writing, class artwork and other artifacts, numerous school documents, classroom photographs, and the like also were fodder for my analyses. I even found quantitative data—numbers, at least—feeding into my self-study. For example, the informal reading inventories that I conducted at the beginning, middle, and end of the school year provided estimates of students' instructional reading levels, and these estimates proved to be instructive data for assessing children's growth in reading ability across the school year (Baumann, 1995b). I also took a look, albeit a skeptical one, at the results from the March-administered standardized tests, in relation to more authentic measures of students' growth and learning.

Formative Misfit. I also experienced methodological change in the reading strategies study, moving away from the formative experimental framework as the school year progressed. This occurred because the study, as conceived, was not doable and potentially jeopardized my teaching effectiveness. Formative experimentation requires that a researcher gather evaluative data in an ongoing manner to assess the impact of the instructional intervention, in this case my efforts to integrate strategies into literature-based instruction. I was able to do this the year before as a guest in Helene's and Pat's 5th-grade classrooms, but it did not work so well when I was the classroom teacher. Although I was preparing and teaching strategy lessons that conformed to the goals of the study, I was unable to gather the necessary ongoing, evaluative data (e.g., videotaping lessons, interviewing children, having others observe my strategy lessons). As noted previously, this was because I was consumed with relearning how to teach youngsters: developing rapport with the children and their care givers; understanding their abilities, experiences, and environments; organizing my classroom and my days for effective instruction; preparing appropriate lessons; creating a management program that was comfortable and workable; and so forth. In short, for about the first half of the school year, I needed to devote my energy and time primarily to doing what it took to be the best teacher I could for my children and their families, and if that meant letting some planned data gathering slide, so be it.

All through this period and throughout the entire year, however, I did faithfully gather and create narrative data and continued daily to make lengthy journal entries in which I reflected on my work and its impact on me, my students, and their families. I also took numerous photographs, I continued to conduct informal reading inventories (IRI), and I saved almost everything: my detailed daily lesson plans, letters and notes to parents, originals or copies of just about everything the children produced in the way of written work and artwork, and so forth.

In early spring, I used NRRC project funds to employ Gay Ivey, then a doctoral student at the university, to assist in data collection for the strategies project. We reviewed the formative experimental frame and alternatives. In looking at the data gathered thus far, we decided that a qualitative, interpretive case study (Merriam, 1988) would be an appropriate means to address our research questions, which now were: What do children learn about reading and writing within a literature-based instructional environment? and How can reading and writing strategies be taught explicitly, efficiently, and with transfer? We chose a case study because it enabled us to engage in "an intensive, holistic description and analysis of a single entity, phenomenon, or social unit" (p. 16), in this instance second graders' literacy strategy development within a literature-based environment.

Given the modified research plan, Gay and I focused on data collection for the strategies study during the spring. She videotaped lessons I taught, and she kept a journal in which she documented the instruction, the students' reaction to it, and her evaluation of the instructional environment. I focused more on strategy instruction in my daily journal entries. Gay interacted with the children during strategy lessons (e.g., joining me during assisted reading times). She also conducted one-on-one, videotaped interviews with all the children, during which they read for her and demonstrated their strategy knowledge while she queried them about their reading habits, attitudes, skills, and knowledge of literature.

In sum, research methods evolved during the process of teaching in relation to doability, trueness and responsiveness, and my instructional responsibilities. Thus, the methods coming out of the teacher-research studies were not the same ones that I planned going into the experience. I believe that the flexibility I afforded myself as a teacher researcher to modify research methods resulted in studies that were more responsive to the questions I had posed. This flexibility and responsiveness is extending into data analyses.

Flexible Data Analyses

Even though I may not have been conscious of it at the time, I did engage in data analysis throughout the school year. This occurred as I reread my daily journal; examined prior lesson plans while making new ones; compared results of one IRI with results from prior administrations; reviewed photographs; examined children's writing folders and reading journals for progress; and looked back at report card narrative comments while writing new ones. Nevertheless, these ongoing data analyses, a phase that is just commencing, were not systematic. And given the methodologically evolutionary nature of these investigations, my analysis plans are likely to be modified further as analyses proceed.

Data Sources. Data that fed into both of my investigations include, but are not limited to, the following sources:

- My personal journal, which spanned the two and one-half year process of planning for, implementing, and reflecting on my teaching experience, including daily entries for the 180 school days in second grade.

- Daily lesson plans, which detailed all instructional activities and materials.

- Originals or copies of the children's work, including their writing folders, published class books, reading response journals, content subject projects, bulletin board displays, and artwork.

- Numerous still photographs of the children working in the classroom and playing on the playground, as well as photos of special events (e.g., a 2nd-grade operetta) and displays (e.g., bulletin boards, art displays).

- Letters and correspondence I wrote to parents and care givers and notes I received from them.

- Video recordings of classroom events, including our Reading Strategies period, DEAR (drop-everything-and-read) time, Reading / Writing Buddies time (each of my students read and wrote weekly with a 5th-grade student), daily Class Meeting, and the individual literacy interviews Gay Ivey conducted with each student.

- Gay Ivey's journal, which focused on children's growth in literacy strategies and literary knowledge.

- Various school and district documents (e.g., new teacher orientation packet, faculty meeting notes, after-school workshop materials, PTO materials).

- Informal Reading Inventories on all students, conducted three times (August, January, and May).

- Narrative statements I wrote about each child's academic and social progress.

- Post-school-year interviews with Betty Shockley Bisplinghoff, my "trading-places" partner; Patricia Brown and Kim Lord, the principal and assistant principal, respectively, at Fowler Drive; Sally Hudson-Ross, a colleague at the university who returned to teach high school on a similar job exchange the year prior to my experience; and Veda McClain, a graduate student at the university who had two children attending Fowler Drive.

• Audiotape transcripts or notes from post-school-year conversations I had with several of my students and their parents or care givers; these conversations occurred in the children's homes and involved the children's and parents' assessments of and feelings about their 2nd-grade experiences.

Return-to-Teaching Study Analysis. I am engaging in hermeneutic phenomenological reflection and writing (van Manen, 1990, chaps. 4, 5). This involves the process of thematic analysis, in which one uncovers the "structures of experience" within the "lifeworld" one is exploring. In my case, thematic analysis involves extracting and understanding the essence of what it means to return to the lifeworld of a classroom teacher. All data sources are feeding into thematic analysis, particularly the narrative elements (e.g., my journal, the interviews, home visit transcripts and accounts, Gay's journal). Visual and artistic sources (e.g., school photographs, children's work, video images) are also important data in phenomenological analysis.

Thematic analysis proceeds by isolating thematic statements within the data, interpreting emerging themes, and extracting essential themes. Hermeneutic phenomenological research is fueled by writing, which is not viewed as an end product but essential to the process of thematic analysis. As van Manen (1990, p. 124) states, "Writing is our method." Therefore, the texts I have created through my journal writing, anecdotal record keeping, interviews, and so forth constitute ongoing analysis, and they provide grist for subsequent writing, revising, and analysis.

As the first step in thematic analysis, I am organizing, preparing, and previewing all relevant data. For example, I am currently rereading my personal journal while simultaneously correcting errors in transcription. I have secured a qualitative text analysis computer program, which I may use for retrieval and analysis of journal textual information. I am also rereading and correcting transcription errors of the interviews with colleagues, as well as the records of the home visits (some of which were audio recorded and transcribed and others for which I took notes and wrote descriptions from them afterward). Gay Ivey has transcribed all videotapes. I will read them and view the tapes, looking for the essential themes in my teaching. I am reviewing all the photographs of the school year and inventorying them for content. These data, as well as the other sources noted above, are being entered into the thematic analysis process so that the essence of my lived experience in second grade can be identified and understood.

Strategies Study Analysis. For the qualitative, interpretive case study paradigm (Merriam, 1988), Gay and I identified categories and properties through the process of content analysis (Lincoln & Guba, 1985). Content analysis made sense because it would permit analysis following data collection at the end of the school year. We also decided on the comprehensive selection of participants (LeCompte, Preissle, & Tesh, 1993, p. 72) to ensure adequate representation of the classroom population, including in the population children who were in my class 7 or more months of the school year.

Prior to data analysis, Gay and I constructed two sets of files, which constituted the case study data base (Yin, 1984) or case record (Patton, 1980). The first set included separate files for each of the students, comprising relevant data sources for individual children, including response journals, writing folders, informal notes, artwork, informal reading inventories and other assessments, progress reports, word study notebooks, language experience stories, transcripts of individual interviews, and portions of Gay's journal in which specific children were mentioned. The second set of files included general data sources, such as Jim's daily plan book and personal journal, letters sent to parents, a still photo collection showing students and the classroom across the year, the research video library, and a collection of information on school- and district-wide policies and activities. Data analysis proceeded in four phases.

In Phase 1, we scheduled a series of conferences to study the data we had collected for each second grader. During each session, we individually examined a student's case folder and jointly viewed the videotape of Gay's interview with that student. We also examined relevant information from the general data files. Next, we discussed in-depth the different kinds of knowledge about reading and writing demonstrated by each student, as evidenced by various data sources. We audiotaped these meetings, and Gay converted the tapes to written form by reviewing the entire recording and writing in narrative form the significant points and descriptions about an individual students' literacy learning contained on the tape.

In Phase 2, we read each of these summaries, noting instances in which we had described students demonstrating both general and specific knowledge about reading and writing. We individually made lists of literacy learnings for each student, and then shared our lists with each other and discussed them. Jim then consolidated these individual lists into a comprehensive list of literacy learnings for each student.

Phase 3 of analysis involved looking across all the cases to find recurring patterns among the data. We individually created codes for the descriptors and examples of students' learning generated in Phase 2. Patterns of literacy learning were examined according to substance and frequency, and similar patterns were collapsed under common codes. We then compared the patterns we had generated independently and reached consensus on those we considered most pervasive. The patterns that emerged represented what students learned about reading and writing in second grade.

From these patterns, we induced and defined categories and properties. For example, one of our emerging patterns was students' enjoyment and knowledge of books and stories in a variety of literacy activities. We labeled this category "Engagement With Literacy." Within this category, we noticed that students demonstrated specific knowledge about books, authors, and illustrators. We also noticed that students had opinions about books and literature and expressed them freely in their reading and writing. Because these two observations were salient features of this category, they became defining properties of the category. We followed this same procedure to induce and define four other categories and their defining properties.

In order to ensure a match between these categories and properties and the data, we conducted a negative-case analysis, which constituted Phase 4. In this analysis, we revisited each student's case folder and other data sources, including videotapes and Jim's journal and daily plan book, to study the fit between each category and property and the data. When categories and properties did not adequately explain specific cases, we refined them to account for this mismatch. We proceeded through each case in this manner until we could account for all negative cases. The result was a group of categories and properties that were comprehensive in the sense that they identified specific conditions under which the findings occurred. As a final step in analysis, we conducted an audit check, inviting a person unfamiliar with our inquiry to revisit our analysis process to determine if the same categories and properties emerge (Baumann & Ivey, in press).

Methodological Musings

What has my experience taught me about teacher research and methods for it? I have learned that conducting classroom inquiry while being the teacher responsible for the class represents a research situation different from any other I have experienced (Baumann, in press). This uniqueness is attributed to a teacher researcher's emic position and total affinity with the research environment. While employing or borrowing from extant research traditions, particularly interpretive ones (Erickson, 1986), teacher research is more than an ethnographic approach to classroom research, and teacher research goes beyond participant observation. The teacher researcher is a doer-evaluator, the person who does the job while concurrently examining the work and its impact. This is akin to the reflective practitioner notion (Schon, 1983) but extends it to include the systematic collection, reflection, and analysis required for disciplined inquiry (Shulman, 1988). In short, the teacher researcher systematically studies her or his work with the objective of doing it better as a result. This is simultaneously a simple, powerful, and daunting goal.

The environmental affinity involved with teacher research accrues both benefits and costs. As a teacher researcher, there are many benefits: You are there all the time to see and experience the multiple dimensions of academic and social learning across an extended time period; you can act upon what you see and learn firsthand, evaluate the impact of your actions, and then initiate new actions; you have paradigmatic flexibility in selecting methods that match your research questions; your teacher-research efforts are professionally fulfilling, and your voice is credible when sharing what you learned.

On the cost side, teacher research is time-consuming, hard work that adds a layer to an already hectic professional work schedule (it did not become "organic" for me, as it has for others; see the following cases); you must guard against having the research interfere with or detract from your primary instructional responsibility; and you must be sensitive to elitism that might arise among individuals or groups of teacher researchers. In spite of its potential costs, I have no doubt that my year would have failed to be as rich and significant as it was had I not systematically reflected on and acted upon my teaching. Although researching while teaching may not be for everyone (and maybe not an every-school-year event for those who do value it), I can attest that it does provide a teacher a powerful opportunity to learn, understand, and grow, both professionally and personally.

CASE TWO—COLLABORATIVE RESEARCH TEAM: BETTY, BARBARA AND JOBETH'S EXPERIENCE

In 1988, Betty Shockley Bisplinghoff was teaching first grade and Barbara Michalove (not an author on this chapter, Barbara Michalove is the third member of our research team) was teaching second grade at Fowler Drive Elementary, a school that was examining the effectiveness of its literacy instruction for students who struggled in school. The school invited JoBeth Allen, a local university teacher, into a long-term partnership to develop whole language instructional approaches and to study their influence on the children teachers worried about most, those who found learning to read and write difficult.

Several teachers were a part of the school's research group that first year, conducting case studies in their classrooms. However, Betty and Barbara collaborated closely with JoBeth, and a team was born which continues to the present. Our first study, a 4-year, multiple-case study culminated in *Engaging Children: Community and Chaos in the Lives of Young Literacy Learners* (Allen, Michalove, & Shockley, 1993); our second study was a 2-year study of home-school connections reported in *Engaging Families: Connecting Home and School Literacy Communities* (Shockley, Michalove, & Allen, 1995). We currently work together within the SRC.

Creating Responsive Methods

Over the course of these studies, we have created ways of gathering information and learning from it. Our research methods grew out of the realities of classroom life, which changed not only from year to year but from day to day. As each group of students was unique, opportunities for data collection were different. Since analysis was ongoing, we designed methods responsive to what we were (and were not) seeing and hearing.

Responsive data collection included (a) observational notes from both insider and outsider perspectives, focusing on individual learners; (b) observations of children and interviews with teachers and other adults outside the classroom setting; (c) ongoing records of student progress such as reading inventories, logs of one-to-one reading and writing conferences; (d) full-day observations of each classroom to record a fuller context than more focused reading and writing observations; and (e) interviews that JoBeth initially conducted outside of the classroom but that became more effective when Barbara conducted them within the instructional context of the classroom. Responsive data analysis included weekly reviews of all data sources on a focal child, the writing and sharing of research narratives, and interpretive dialogue techniques.

We learned to research by engaging in the research process. We created, adapted, reflected on, and revised methods predominantly from qualitative research. Flexibility and invention are fundamental to many qualitative traditions according to LeCompte et al. (1993):

> Sources and types of data are limited only by the creativity and energy of the researcher. ... Data, then, are any kind of information which researchers can identify and accumulate to facilitate answers to their queries. ... [A]s ethnographers negotiate initial relationships with participants ... they discover other possibilities for and limitations to acquiring data. (pp. 158, 159)

For *Engaging Children,* we began studying six children from Betty's and Barbara's classrooms, following their school experiences and literacy development for 3 years. Many of our methods grew out of our weekly data-analysis discussions. In the beginning, Barbara and Betty worried that to be considered "real researchers" they should be taking the kind of detailed observational notes JoBeth wrote. They even tried it—briefly. The result was intense frustration, sending them in search of methods that could be readily incorporated into their teaching lives. They came up with individual ways of detailing their decision making as teachers and documenting students' literacy development. This took time, however, and constant experimentation.

Betty harkened back to high school and college "research" experiences and found only the *Cliff Notes,* encyclopedia, and index card models. That first year she organized anecdotal notes by topics on index cards. Her next strategy, "read to learn," proved more fruitful. She read other teacher researchers like Nancie Atwell (1991) and Vivian Paley (1981, 1990) to learn how they integrated research with teaching. She began to identify links between thought and action, claiming her teaching journal as a legitimate and lasting record of experience. She used student conference logs and reading inventories as substantive accounts of individual and collective change over time. She cultivated the habit of dating work samples and anecdotal comments. She became the teacher with the notebook, recording direct quotes and descriptions as primary data sources.

The key came for Betty and Barbara when they made research a natural aspect of each day instead of one more thing to add on. Eventually, record keeping became an organic part of classroom routines (even though the records took many forms, from sticky notes to memos during telephone calls late at night). Both teachers developed forms of documentation that highlighted classroom experiences, a body of data that over time informed both daily practice and long-term research interests. JoBeth added the critical second pair of hands and eyes in each class; she focused on one child per visit, recorded conversations and other peer interactions, and documented the processes of text writing and reading. We were learning what each of us had to contribute to the collaboration and discussing on a weekly basis the kinds of information that were valuable.

From these discussions, we expanded our data collection from observational notes and teaching journals. We wanted more of the child's perspective, so we applied Almy and Genishi's (1979) guidelines:

- we asked children about themselves (in quarterly interviews);
- we observed children in various settings (individual, pairs, small groups, whole class);
- we studied children through others at school (we interviewed the media specialist, art, music, PE, and especially Chapter 1 and special education teachers) and in their lives outside of school (we interviewed the Boys Club director and made home visits); and
- we assessed development (daily writing, notes on classroom reading, and quarterly miscue and retelling analyses).

In addition, we set up weekly pen pal letters with JoBeth's undergraduate classes, through which we learned from the written dialogue as well as from the analyses of the preparatory teachers. JoBeth kept a research journal by tape-recording each day as she left the school. This provided a record of research decision points (Alvermann, 1988), that is, the development, modification, or abandonment of data collection or analysis strategies. Finally, in order to provide a richer context for readers, we stepped back from the living of classroom life and recorded and reflected on it in "a day in the life" of each classroom. These detailed, full-day transcripts of each classroom from JoBeth's observational vantage point, in combination with lesson plans and teaching journals, became Betty's and Barbara's teaching stories that laid the foundation for *Engaging Children.*

In our second study, we examined connections between home and school that Betty fostered with a set of "parallel practices" she had developed in first grade (home–school literacy journals; oral and written family stories; parent, child, teacher reflections). Barbara continued with the same children and families in second grade. By this time, Betty had come to view her classroom as "data world," a place where remarkable things happen everyday to gather, ponder, and interpret in relation to future teaching decisions. Consequently, she collected a great deal of information and asked parental permission to share what they were learning together with others, even though the first year was not designed as a research study. During the second year of the study, we were systematic in our data collection of the same sources of information and some additional ones. Table 13–1 shows the data collected and when we collected it.

Together we constructed and redesigned these methods, keeping them responsive to the children and to our ongoing analysis. For example, in the first study when a data analysis session focusing on the quarterly interviews JoBeth did with each child revealed that at least one child was "putting her on," Barbara suggested that she, as the teacher, should take over the interviewing, incorporating the questions into her daily reading and writing conferences. Barbara knew the children better and was able to embed questions in a logical

TABLE 13–1. Data Sources and Collection Time for *Engaging Families* Study

Information source	Collection
Tell Me About Your Child (letters from parents)	beginning of each year
Home Interest Inventory (by parents and children)	1st grade, beginning of year
Clay's Word Writing Assessment	1st, beg / mid / end
Standard Topic Writing	1st & 2nd, beg / mid / end
Informal Reading Inventory	1st & 2nd, beg / mid / end
Samples of Daily Writing	1st & 2nd, weekly
Houghton Mifflin Periodic Reading Survey	2nd, quarterly
Home-School Reading Journals (dialogue among families, children, and teacher)	1st & 2nd, all year
Family Stories (written by adult family members)	1st & 2nd, varied
Parent Reflections & Expectations Survey	1st & 2nd, end of year
Student Reflections & Expectations Survey	1st & 2nd, end of year
Anecdotal Notes	1st & 2nd, throughout
Parent Meetings (notes)	2nd, monthly

Note. In addition, Betty occasionally tape-recorded oral storytelling and videotaped a family storybook reading partly in her classroom. Barbara photographed classroom interactions and a family picnic at the park.

instructional framework and interpret responses in the full context of the classroom.

The study had built-in triangulation not only of data sources, as seen in Table 13–1, but also of perspectives. Betty and Barbara taught the children during different years, and JoBeth was an outsider. Frequently at data analysis sessions, especially in year two of both studies, Barbara discussed a child's current literacy and classroom life, Betty related that to the previous year, and JoBeth asked clarifying questions. At times these discussions led to the collection of new data or to the redesign of a current strategy. Thus, ongoing data analysis was critical to the design of responsive methods. It was also critical to building an interpretation of what we were living.

Interpretive Dialogue

Throughout our collaboration, we have discovered the power of talk to reflect on lived experience, to challenge interpretations, to generate assumptions, and to examine biases (e.g., JoBeth became worried that she was ignoring a child in the first study when she dreamed she had killed him). We created time to talk within a variety of structures, depending on the phase and focus of the project. These included a paid substitute teacher for weekly during-school data analysis sessions, weekly or biweekly work sessions at good restaurants, and week-long writing sessions at inspiring settings each summer (see the Appendix in Shockley et al., 1995).

In his chapter on qualitative methods in research on teaching in the 1986 handbook, Erickson wrote:

As Hymes notes (1982b), interpretive research methods are intrinsically democratic; one does not need special training to be able to understand the results of such research, nor does one need arcane skills in order to conduct it. Fieldwork research requires skills of observation, comparison, contrast, and reflection that all humans possess. In order to get through life we must all do interpretive fieldwork. What professional interpretive researchers do is to make use of ordinary skills of observation and reflection in espe-

cially systematic and deliberate ways. Classroom teachers can do this as well, by reflecting on their own practice. Their role is not that of the participant observer who comes from the outside world to visit, but that of an unusually observant participant who deliberates inside the scene of action. (1982, p. 157)

How did we deliberate on our observations? What forum allowed the comparison, contrast, and reflection necessary for interpretive research? We developed a process we call *interpretive dialogue,* carefully recorded analytic conversations about data that often served as oral drafts. Whether we were talking about one child and one week's data on that child at weekly Shockley Bisplinghoff / Allen or Michalove / Allen analysis meetings or a whole year's interactions with a family, we taped or hand-recorded our insights, both mundane and inspired. We also had frequent role dialogues concerning writing and authorship, discussing each writer's time, interest, strengths, weaknesses, and professional goals. We "listened" to and discussed other writing voices, novel research (e.g., *Praying for Sheetrock,* Green, 1991) as well as well-researched novels (e.g., *A Lesson Before Dying,* Gaines, 1993), and tried to honor our individual voices either by identifying section authors or writing in the lead author's voice.

As part of a larger school team in the first study, we wrote occasional research narratives, one- or two-page written interpretations of phenomena that interested, bothered, or puzzled us. This was a data-analysis strategy from the work of Jane Hansen, Donald Graves, Ruth Hubbard and colleagues (Hubbard & Stratton, 1985). Few people felt comfortable or had the time to write for each meeting (or even most of the meetings). However, we would come back to research narratives several years later and use them as a primary data analysis strategy in *Engaging Families.* We had a wide variety of information on each child / family / teacher relationship we were studying (see Table 13–1) which we analyzed individually (e.g., one week each of us would read all the data on Adrian); wrote a narrative interpretation of the issues, themes, and questions that resulted from the analysis; and then met to read and compare our narratives on that focal child.

Although the key to data analysis for us has been interpretive dialogue, we did not discover how important it was until we tried another approach. JoBeth had been studying grounded theory (Glaser & Strauss, 1967) and suggested that we try the fine-grained coding of the constant comparative method. We spent several full days reading about the methodology, coding four sets of transcripts together, and generating an extensive code list. We agreed to code the other sets on our own and to come together weekly to compare our analyses. A short segment of the lengthy code sheet follows:

TQ	teacher question
/Y / N	yes / no (type TQ)
/auth	author focus
/lrn	learning focus
/lks	likes of reader
/gnr	genre focus (silly books)
/prc	process (is C reading book?)
/eval	evaluation (of reading process, development)

Using the emerging codes, we coded a fourth journal set together, adding and clarifying subcategories. Our retreat over, we agreed to meet once a week having each "coded" the same set of data (one family / child) independently.

A funny thing happened at the first weekly meeting: We decided that we did not like our analysis process. Betty, as principal investigator, crystallized the misgivings we were all feeling. She said, "I'm worried that we're missing the forest for the trees. We're breaking this rich interaction down into little codes that become almost meaningless." We discussed what is unique about teacher research. When JoBeth typed out the code sheet, the analysis became more mechanistic than insightful. We stopped talking about children and families and talked instead of matching, modifying, or adding codes. The agenda Betty had written for our meeting included the following quote from Nancie Atwell (1991):

> I worry about attempts to package teacher research as another formula to be followed, shutting down the possibility of surprise through a slavish adherence to the conventions of experimental inquiry. ... It's [classroom research's] power lies in thinking side by side with others—our students among them—who care as much about writing, literature, and learning as we do. (p. xvi)

We decided that we were more interested in informing and affecting educational practice than in generating theories about it. We wanted to look closely at an experience that seemed meaningful to all participants and ask, What made this meaningful? What meanings did different people create from it? What difference for families, children, and teachers did the experience make?

Betty proposed a plan that we used the rest of the year:

1. Each researcher read through the original home–school journal to note illustrations, format, and so forth (we were missing a great deal by merely reading typed transcriptions). The visual display of data was more illuminating than the reduced transcripts.

2. Each researcher read the child's cumulative notebook Betty and Barbara had assembled, which included all data sources, making analytic memos as we read (journal transcripts had 3" right margins).

3. Each researcher wrote a 1–2 page narrative that included patterns of response and pivotal point of change, questions for further exploration, telling excerpts, and so forth.

4. At dinner meetings, we read the narratives aloud to each other, comparing insights, generating new questions, proposing issues and categories.

5. We made a three-column (one for each of us) chart of key insights, points of agreement and difference, and questions. We talked about the children, their families, and ourselves from our unique perspectives.

6. We continued to study the practices of other researchers.

We felt much truer to ourselves and to our data through our approach of written narratives and interpretive dialogue. The dread we had been feeling about line-by-line coding was replaced with an eagerness to read, write, ponder, discuss, and construct a meaningful interpretation. One reason we feel the process worked so well was that we had both the "insider's view" that teachers bring to school-based research, and an "outsider's view" (Erickson, 1986). Betty was the teacher who had generated the first year's data; she had a yearlong relationship with the children and families through which to interpret journals, reflections, and so forth. Barbara was the teacher who currently taught the children and interacted with the families; she was able to update the previous year's data with current information about how the child was developing, what pattern the 2nd-grade journal was taking, and so forth. JoBeth was the outsider, who did not know the children or their families; she asked questions that led us beyond the "taken for granted" and helped make the familiar strange for Betty and Barbara. Through interpretive dialogue in our weekly analysis sessions, and even more intensively during our summer writing sessions, we asked "From your perspective...?" questions of each other, aware that it was not consensus we were after but multiple perspectives.

At several points in our data analysis, we stepped back from the individual children and families and generated broad, working assumptions about ourselves, the children, and their families. We asked ourselves. What are we learning? We generated assumptions, which we continuously modified by rereading the data. The following are a few examples:

Assumptions About Ourselves as Teachers

- When we learn from parents, we make more informed decisions on behalf of kids.
- When we listened to and read family stories and journal entries, we developed "funds of knowledge for teaching" (Moll, Amanti, Neff, & Gonzales, 1992).

Assumptions About Parents

- All these parents care about their kids just like we care about ours.
- The journal process supported and developed many

parents' sense of efficacy, both as parents and as teachers.

- Family members often provided very explicit literacy instruction. Many had a repertoire of literacy support strategies; they would nudge, back off, press, and encourage children to feel successful. Occasionally the interactions became stressful, but the journal often served as a way of changing to more enjoyable interactions.

Assumptions About Children

- Children grew in their ways of responding to literature, and they grew in their literary conversations, both oral and written.
- Children saw the adults closest to them—their parents and teachers—as readers and writers.

Just as in the first study (Allen et al., 1993) we had broadened the dialogue by interviewing many people inside and outside of the school, in the second study (Shockley et al., 1995) we invited families to participate in the dialogue that helped us learn why and in what unique ways they had interpreted the experiences. These "member checks" occurred in a variety of ways. We took notes at monthly parent meetings during which Betty and Barbara frequently asked parents for their perceptions. For example, at one meeting, we asked parents how they would describe the school, saying we felt giving the demographics was inadequate. At another, Betty read a draft of an article about our shared home–school experience and asked for feedback (Shockley, 1993). We occasionally called parents to clarify or interpret events. We included three Family Portraits in *Engaging Families* (Shockley et al., 1995); during the revision stage, we gave each family a draft of its portrait, the section we had written about them, and again asked for written or verbal feedback. We were delighted by the serious and helpful responses.

Finally, the interpretive dialogue was impetus for and integral to countless rounds of drafting, responding, and revising. There was a constant interplay between written and oral composition. Each summer we gathered all our data, notes from our weekly analyses (including research narratives), boxes of professional references related to our study, three computers, and literary fiction that provided models of effective writing. We retreated for a week to a lake, ocean, or mountainside sanctuary and wrote for two 3-hour blocks each day; in the evening we each read aloud what we had written that day, gave each other feedback, and made revision notes.

Research for us is a communicative art, an evolving lesson in constructing meaning. We talked to understand the children, each other, and ourselves. We wrote to talk and talked to write. We read to write, sharing and discussing the works of favorite fiction writers as well as professional educators. Through our collaboration, we grew professionally in ways that became fundamental to our definitions of ourselves as teachers. We wanted to share the power and joy of our experience with other teachers. Out of that desire we created a plan for a broad network of teacher researchers, the School Research Consortium. The next section details their methodological evolution and insights.

CASE THREE—TEACHER-RESEARCH COMMUNITY: THE SCHOOL RESEARCH CONSORTIUM EXPERIENCE

It is a research day. Teachers who work together as researchers within the School Research Consortium (SRC) knew time was what they needed, time away from their teaching duties and school sites periodically to review their research needs. This reserved time for research was divided into two parts: The first half of each research day was used by individuals and teams to talk and plan while the second half found us reunited as a whole community for additional discussions and updates. In the following dialogue, Buddy Wiltcher, Beth Tatum, Barbara Jarrard, Mindy Rhoades, and Patti McWhorter are meeting at Beth's house to discuss their research progress and plans.

Patti: It takes so long to write because we all feel like we need to tell our stories first.... That seems to be part of our research process when you live your research like that and like we're doing.

Mindy: Part of it is, it's your life.... You don't go and you don't just measure things.... It's not like chemistry.

Barbara: There's no right or wrong answer.

Patti: That may be part of the phenomena.

Buddy: The story's the background.

Patti: Right.... The story's the context.

Mindy: [Without it] It's like giving people a novel and saying, "Read Chapter 14!"

Stories of teacher research are contributing to a rich and varied legacy of lives and learnings within the context of classrooms. Such stories help build a tradition among and between teachers that can be resurrected and revised as others engage in similar adventures. Each story is a unique tale of successes, confusions, and disappointments. Though plotted in different ways, they remain true to an emerging genre defined by setting and character, that is, classrooms and students.

The SRC is a community of researchers who share their stories of research with one another and with a broader community of educators through oral and written retellings. The SRC is supported by the University of Georgia site of the NRRC. From its conception, the NRRC has viewed school-based research as central to its mission and has worked to support research agendas that teachers have identified as critical. The first SRC studies were initiated at the beginning of the 1993–94 school year. As a long-time teacher researcher in the local school district, I (Betty) have felt membership in this community beyond my role as SRC Coordinator. I write to give some order to the many stories embedded in the individual efforts to bring self-initiated research to practice.

The combined stories of the researchers within the SRC talk of a developing methodology that is both varied in adaptations and unified in purpose. By developing and documenting their particular pathways to understanding, teacher researchers capture a record of growth and change that too often has been lost to the profession.

TABLE 13–2. SRC Project Titles and Descriptions

Title	Description
Middle School Student's Favorite Books and Factors Affecting What They Choose to Read	As media specialists, Shu-Hsien Chen and Barbara Davis wanted to know more about students' book choices. They worried about the students they saw leaving the media center empty-handed and complaining, "I can't find a good book," so they designed a study that would be sensitive to the voices of the students and the teachers in their middle school. Using interviews and surveys, they identified favorite reading materials and the factors that affected the choice of those materials.
Literacy Education for a Democratic Society (LEADS)	JoBeth Allen and Barbara Michalove, along with a group of teachers from a variety of school systems in the Atlanta/Athens area, were interested in exploring issues of activism within the teaching profession. Currently the group is spending time discussing readings related to education for democracy in preparation for implementing and studying Literacy for a Democratic Society in its various classroom manifestations during the coming school year.
Bridging Picture Books and Chapter Books: The Reading Challenge Project for Third-grade Students	Nancy Baumann, Christine Fuentes, and Jane Holman shared a concern about the difficult transition many children seemed to have from reading picture books to reading chapter books. Their study aimed to find ways to better support students in making this literate leap.
Computer Journals	This was Tina Allen's first attempt at combining research with teaching. She was eager to build research into her Chapter 1 program as she worked to facilitate the writing development of two of her students through dialogic computer journals. But she found research to be an on-again, off-again process of adjustments.
Teachers as Writers: Focusing on the Classroom	Ann Keffer, Debby Wood, Shelley Carr, Leah Mattison, Barbara Lanier, and Randi Stanulis worked together for two years to understand how thinking of themselves as writers and actually experiencing the process within a community of teachers who write might help them better understand the issues their students faced as writers. They associated their first year of work together as a "magical" experience but then in a second year went through a period of serious concern about the demands of their combined roles as teachers and researchers.
Active Learning, Interactive Classrooms, and Literacy Instruction	Patti McWhorter, Barbara Jarrard, Mindi Rhoades, and Buddy Wiltcher have been working together for two years to coordinate and document the changes that take place for teachers and their students when their high school classrooms become more student-centered. In their view, "It is on this sharing of control, the subsequent shifting of roles and responsibilities, and the resulting effect on literacy instruction that our study is focused."
A Parallel Journey: The Role of Memoir and Personal Narrative in the Construction of Literate Relationships	Karen Hankins began her first year of study with a project designed to help her better support the three students in her kindergarten class who had been identified as being fetal-alcohol syndrome or crack babies. In her self-study, an extension of the first year's work with the students, she recorded and examined through memoir writing her life episodes that either enhanced or discouraged the potential for interactions and connections with these three children and their families. She also claimed that "by combining case study and memoir, I will be generating a method for reflective qualitative analysis."
Exploring How Elementary and Middle School Partnerships Encourage Students' Engagement in Literate Activities	Georgiana Sumner and Johni Mathis are sisters with a shared concern for finding ways to motivate students to read. Georgiana taught second grade and Johni taught eighth. They have worked together as researchers within the SRC for two years. Their second year experience gave rise to troubling concerns regarding the value of doing research that does not turn out to be an exciting proclamation of success with all students all the time.

Our stories have beginnings but not endings. We are still much immersed in our processes of becoming teachers who research. For purposes of this condensed version of our storytellings, only 8 of the 17 projects initiated by the 40 SRC members will be highlighted. These story segments are taken from written reflections by the teacher researchers who were present at our last group meeting of the 1994–95 school year. Each teacher was asked to outline specific methodologies used in her / his project and to briefly isolate and elaborate their data analysis procedures. The title, authors, and a highlight of their research stories are included in Table 13–2 to provide a sort of book-jacket look at the many concerns SRC researchers consider worthy of their time and study.

Learning by Doing

Much is new and unresolved for us as a community of teachers who also research our beliefs and practices. Sylvia Ashton-Warner (1963) in her book *Teacher* announced, "I know all this because I've done it" (p. 34). This kind of claiming to know by doing is the emerging hallmark of the SRC. As teachers, we often feel privileged by special insights that are possible because of our unique positioning within classrooms with students on a daily basis. As members of the SRC, we accept and celebrate this unique perspective. Instead of being educated ahead of time in a particular research tradition, we choose to start from our own beginning places, to develop methods that work for us. We are learning to adjust and adapt, and invent our research practices as we work to achieve better understandings. We are in the process of doing it for ourselves. Whatever has gone before will certainly serve us well in this endeavor, but nothing influences us more strongly than our own unique responses to researching as teachers.

Reducing our sense of professional isolation through our work together in the SRC has been a first step toward the construction of a professional identity that is grounded in our own developing research traditions. It helps us move beyond a profession of technicians who are judged by how well we are able to repeat the performances of others to what Seymour Papert (1993) termed an "epistemological pluralism" (p. 6). This view encourages a variety of responses and accepts the influences of multiple contexts and personalities. Papert further encourages this perspective with, "The problem for society is to give teachers the same pluralist support that the best of them give their students. Individuals at different places need support to move from where they are. ... The practical consequence is that change cannot come about except pluralistically" (p. 75). The SRC acknowledges multiple perspectives through its support for varied and evolving methods and welcomes the particularity of response inherent in each teaching / researching situation.

In the following sections we outline aspects of evolving context-specific research methods—methods teachers are learning by doing. Teachers are beginning to trust themselves to be sensitive and systematic in developing their own research designs. As we share what we are learning about methods that work for us, we become what Nancie Atwell (1991) described as "adult[s] who learned in public" (p. 8). We risk this published reflection not only to offer ideas to other teacher researchers but also to enhance our learning-by-doing cycle of action and reflection. In Papert's (1993) words, "In education, the highest mark of success is not having imitators but inspiring others to do something else" (p. 78). Teacher researchers need to know that there is room for their independent creations within what should be a constantly evolving research perspective.

Balancing Reactions

Achieving the Balance Between Teaching and Research. Bartoli (1995) in *Unequal Opportunity: Learning to Read in the U.S.A.* wrote, "I think the uses to which we put our research are every bit as important as the purity of the methodology—possibly more so" (p. xvi). This concept works well for what we have come to view as a central feature of our researching processes: the fit between teacher needs and student needs in the research process. The alignment of research to particular teacher and student needs is a key to unlocking passions for the process and principles for research design. Each new school year and each new group of students bring with them a revised set of challenges and opportunities. Being sensitive and responsible to this concept is unique to the research of teachers. Vivian Paley (1990), a long-time teacher researcher, adds credence to this kind of wisdom. She, too, has come to know by doing and recalls, "Such is the way life in the classroom reinterprets the research. Whatever else I may choose to watch and record, my subjects draw me into deeper concerns and more vivid visions of their world" (p. 19).

We are teachers and researchers on a day-to-day basis. Keeping our balance between these two dimensions of our professionalism is a new challenge. Many SRC members have experienced a kind of seesaw effect when the daily demands of teaching outweighed the more long-term commitment to studying it. This weight shifting has been most evident in the SRC when teachers change grade levels or when system responsibilities such as national testing or standards evaluations are imposed on an already full workload.

The Teachers as Writers group really felt the impact of these kinds of changes on their attitudes toward research during the 1994–95 school year. After a highly motivating and successful first year as teachers researching their own involvement with writing, they proceeded to what seemed a logical next step—documenting ways in which their personal insights and experiences with writing might prove helpful for supporting their students as writers. What originally seemed so simple and straightforward turned into a year overburdened by the presence of research. Members of the group reported feeling "guilty" all year because they kept putting off focusing on their research issues due to more pressing systemic demands. Debby said, "Our community changed, people changing grade levels. I hadn't had a homeroom in five years; that's real different for me." Shelly agreed and added, "Ann was our glue. She was the only one who didn't have change." It was also the year their school had to do their 5-year standards accreditation review which required many more work hours.

This rising or sinking feeling can also be related to the group dynamics present with each new class of students. Listening closely to students may be one of the most important ways of gathering information for teacher researchers, but it is also one that keeps the teacher researcher off balance, unable to lay out a careful methodology in advance. Barbara Jarrard learned, "I really have to listen carefully to different groups of students." Ann Keffer arrived at a similar understanding: "As important as it is to ask ourselves what questions we most want to answer through our research, it is just as important to ask ourselves what questions a particular group of children are peculiarly suited to help us answer. ... This year I've been stunned by how much my students can tell me if I just *listen*." Barbara Jarrard has also learned to capitalize on this knowledge source. She wrote, "I ask my students to help cover the parts of data collection I know I am not very good at by building in reflective pieces in their projects." Many SRC researchers are coming to agree with Nancie Atwell (1991): "When teachers conduct research in [their] classrooms, [they] learn that kids' knowledge counts—and the kids do too" (p.13). We seem to listen to our students more intentionally when we are involved as researchers. Communication between and among students and teachers can be facilitated when research finds a home in our schools.

Tina Allen identified student interviews as her most helpful data source. This talking-to-understand process was used successfully by most of the SRC researchers. Finding ways to accent connections with students through research can lead to heightened respect and awareness for both students and teachers. Linda Rief (1992), another teacher researcher explained:

> I have to be a learner in and out of my classroom so I won't lose sight of what it's like for my students—so I will continue to hear their voices. I don't ever want to set myself up in the front of that classroom again sitting on a stool with all the answers. Like Byrd Baylor in her book *The Other Way to Listen (Baylor & Parnall, 1978),* I want always to remember, "If you think you're better than a horned toad you'll never hear its voice—even if you sit there in the sun forever." (p. 17)

Creating Methods That Help Keep the Balance. When our community first banded together, there were many discussions at SRC meetings about "What are data?" It was not an easy process deciding what to count as data sources and how to go about managing them. Teaching journals are probably the most often suggested form of documentation offered to teacher researchers. Several of the teachers in the SRC reported initial attempts to remain true to such a procedure only to feel troubled by it over time. Many tried to blend its use into practice but reported frustration with their attempts, as Barbara Jarrard's experience demonstrates:

> I started out trying to keep notes in a writing journal but after a fairly good start at keeping up with it, it was always somewhere else when I wanted to jot something down, so I started writing on scraps of paper which sometimes got to the journal and sometimes didn't. As I realized this wasn't working very well for me, I began to jot notes at the end of my lesson plan in my plan book which gave me very limited space. Although this wasn't a perfect solution, it did teach me that writing a little was better than nothing and in many ways better than a lot. I can almost always find time for a little when sometimes I would not start to write a lot of information. At first I really felt everything I wrote down had to be perfect and complete and this compulsion was causing me to spend time I didn't have on what should have been just notes.

Karen Hankins too had her story of learning to cope with the many options and issues related to data collection

in school settings. She had journals and writing folders for each child but worried that her records could easily become incomplete when one of the journals was lost and when one of her students hid pieces of her writing. Her school copy-machine budget did not allow her to make ongoing copies of these materials either. She did develop a helpful habit of using yellow sticky notes as cues for future evaluation, placing them directly on collected data sources. She had a tape recorder running in her classroom on some days so she could listen to it at night. She found her own voice to be overly intrusive and described the experience as "so painful I just didn't do it as often as I should have." She also interviewed her students and their parents. In an honest reflection of "This is really how it is!", Karen remembered:

> I jotted notes on everything from napkins at lunch to wrapping paper. I keep a journal but it is never with me when I need it! I don't carry it with me but sit and write when I am alone. I really wish I had the things I had written on. The best was a piece of laminating film that had dropped to the floor as we were trimming the edges of the laminated stage decorations while we watched the music teacher put the kids through a play practice. As I trimmed those edges, I was observing Nat.... It may give a person who keeps neat field notes a migraine thinking about it. But that piece of recycled school minutiae was a story in itself. It needed no date ... dress rehearsal day. It needed no context to give me a clue of where and what I was doing when I made the observation ... cutting the edges off stage decorations. It held in its lightweight transparency the weight of a teacher's cloudy thinking on those last days of school when she's trying to do three things at once....

Patti McWhorter's comments also illustrate this evolving process of data collection:

> I discovered early in this process of becoming a teacher researcher that I could quickly go overboard in data collection. Saving all student work was impractical. ... Copying was out; the budget was not large enough—nor was there enough time for me to do this. Audio and video taping was a good idea, but again, I had to decide what to tape. I think it all came down to predicting what would support, address, answer our research questions. Even then, things could take place spontaneously in class when I least expected it. At those points, I had to make myself jot notes in my journal or somewhere, so I could remember and describe those important moments.
>
> My plan book, in the second year of my classroom research, became a research log. I adapted my daily planning sheet to accommodate daily observations and notes. Since my plan book became a research journal, it worked for me. The plan book was always there—open—ready for me to jot notes. It was efficient. I liked it. Since I have always been a teacher who does a lot of notes about "next time I teach this" in my plan book and folders, this method fit more naturally into my routine while teaching than a separate journal. I use a separate journal for more intense reflection— less quick jotting—when I really need to process something about my teaching or my professional life.

Debby Wood's honesty with respect to the trials of data collection is another indication of just how disconcerting dealing with data collection can seem:

We had such a hard time finding methods that we thought were practical and feasible. To this day, I have not been able to master the use of a teaching journal. The idea of being videotaped gives me hives. I don't know if it was because we were so exhausted from the first year or what ... but none of the traditional methods of collecting data were inviting to me ... I don't think I spent a lot of time reflecting on what type of data would best serve the project ... I thought of what strategies I could fit into my existing classroom structure and what wouldn't drive me insane.

Data collection methods were closely related to the issues of balancing research and teaching. As noted in the two previous cases, teachers had to create methods that were doable, that helped them integrate research and teaching, and that were responsive to students. Most of us would agree with Karen: "The data I collected was more what than why, more process than product, more pain than procedure."

Shu-Hsien Chen and Barbara Davis also told of having to modify their original research plan to better accommodate the demands of school life and how this worked to their advantage. Originally, Barbara was going to interview teachers and students during the school day. According to Shu-Hsien and Barbara:

The problem with interviewing the students during the school day was that the teacher's free time did not correlate with the students' free, less-restrictive time. As for the teacher interviews, the schedule during the course of the school day fell through. Consequently, it became necessary to do all interviews at the end of the day, after the children had been dismissed. Time restraints also necessitated that group interviews, rather than individual ones, be done. We were, however, surprised and happy with the results of these interviews and feel that the students and teachers spoke much more freely in group situations than they might have done in one-on-one interviews.

Finding that balance between plans and realities helped Shu-Hsien and Barbara insure not only a sense of success with the process but also a research surprise that will prove helpful to others in the SRC. Group interviews outside the demands and pressures of a school day created a fit between research needs and student needs, and it provided better data. Becoming sensitive to shifts and changes in situations and feeling free to adjust research designs accordingly can be a teacher researcher's friend or foe, depending on the level of frustration she or he is experiencing at the time.

There was one method that everybody seemed to designate as essential—the importance of talk. Patti went so far as to declare, "At the university there's time to talk. That time is a source of power. Until we acknowledge that, they keep and have the power and we have none." This reaction to the isolation many teachers feel as they work behind their classroom doors everyday expresses the need for more frequent and open participation opportunities for teachers. Rarely do they feel that their voices are being recognized in public discourses on teaching and learning. Debby Wood said matter-of-factly, "Conversation was our data." This power of talk was not only a method used for establishing relationships with data but also contributed greatly when interpreting data. We include a discussion of this most simple but essential methodological feature in the following description of data analysis.

Balancing the Effort. According to the Teachers as Writers group, "Talk *is* data" as well as data analysis. "We had our personal writing, but it was the talk about the writing that was important to us and led us to the insights we gained." In fact, talk was so important that Georgiana recommended that next year the SRC provides "two day release time ... one day to talk it all out. Day two ready to sit down to writing."

Joint interpretation of data seems critical to SRC researchers. This aspect of the process helps reduce feelings of professional isolation and develops broader understandings among researchers within the SRC community. Christine Fuentes found "that discussions among ourselves were the best motivators and clarifiers for the project and modifications that needed to be made." Shelley Carr wrote essentially the same thing: "Discussing methods with my partners and other researchers was the best help. ... All of our analysis happened during group meetings. ... Many of our findings seemed to just appear from our conversations." Debby Wood elaborated on the process, explaining: "We would read the transcripts individually and would highlight parts that struck us as important. Then, as a group, we would share and discuss these themes."

Talk with a trusted outsider was also an element of the process for several teacher researchers. Georgiana and Johni valued the participation of university researcher Michelle Commeyras. As a "distant observer," Michelle offered someone "to talk with" that was "supportive" and "nonjudgmental" who could add "a different perspective [that was] not bogged down with classroom details." Ann Keffer recognized much the same effect when she wrote, "Our own group meetings always re-energized us, but talks with Betty [Coordinator of the SRC] helped the most. I found it exciting and helpful when NRRC folks started sending me articles that might bear on our research."

Several members of the community noted a variation of the talking-to-learn feature, the importance of preparing public presentations. Speaking to others created self-imposed deadlines and, as Ann mentioned, helped in "organizing our thoughts." Patti extended this line of thinking:

I have slowly come to realize that preparing for conference presentations or workshops has pushed us to analyze what we know.... Somehow the live audience was the pressure we needed to get out of the "starting box" in data analysis. For me, this goes back to my need to talk out what I know, what I am learning in my research.

There is a necessary interaction of oral and written talk that can be used effectively by teacher researchers. Based on her years of experience as a teacher researcher, Barbara Michalove advocated "bringing written reflections" to group meetings because "they made me analyze and reflect throughout the year." She thinks that sharing these written reflections with a "committed group of teachers" helps maintain the connections between ongoing research and instructional decision making. Patti also discussed the significance of such interactions:

The most helpful data analysis I have done is that which takes place when our small department research team meets on release days. Time to talk and write together is crucial, and we have developed an established routine. We work separately on our writing for the first few hours of the morning, then come together at lunch time to share what we have completed, moving on to the larger SRC meeting later in the day.

And finally, Debby provided the following summary of her data analysis insights:

I think it was important that we participated in this process [data analysis] throughout the year as opposed to waiting until summer. There would have been entirely too much data to analyze. The day-long retreats were by far the most beneficial type of support the SRC gave to me. The retreats enabled us to meet away from school and to focus on what we wanted to accomplish. There were no interruptions (from students, parents, or principals) and we thrived in this setting. We love the job we do with children ... but every once in a while it was such fun to have an "adult" day.

Learning From a Distance

As we stepped back from our deep commitment and involvement with our research community in order to compose this section, we created an opportunity to see anew, to relive experiences of the past 2 years. This distance allows us to find some peace in what often feels like almost too dynamic a process. Many outside of the education community believe that all teachers have to do is teach. They do not recognize or understand that their days are crowded with complex professional responsibilities that too often rest on the verge of toppling the apple cart. Adding research to the balance may not be for all teachers all the time, but, as we have learned in the SRC, once teachers bite from the research apple, many find that their sense of professionalism demands that they continue to pursue this opportunity. As Seymour Papert (1993) wrote, "Knowing that one can exercise choice in shaping and reshaping one's intellectual identity may be the most empowering idea one can ever achieve" (p. 125).

I believe that teacher researchers in the SRC may agree with Papert, but they recognize that this kind of professional fulfillment comes with a price. Adapting plan books as research records, learning to count on students as knowers, coming to value talk and writing as methods for knowing, and giving ourselves time to look back and review from a distance are helping us find our balance as teachers who also research. I believe Vivian Gussin Paley (1990) would concur as she once wrote, "Until I had my own questions to ask, my own set of events to watch, and my own ways of combining all of these with teaching, I did not learn very much at all" (p. 16). And as Ann points out so well,

Part of the story, too, is of our growing understanding of our roles as teacher researchers. After two years, we know that classroom research is not something one gets through with. Instead, it is a different approach to teaching in which theory informs practice and *practice informs theory* continually and immediately right in the classroom. If classroom research is to be an organic part of teaching, then it needs to be allowed to shape itself to the natural rhythms of a school year. The intensity with which we pursue our research needs to be allowed to ebb and flow to accommodate other demands on us and our students.

Barbara Jarrard discovered that "the material (data) I had collected the year before began to make more sense at a distance." Georgiana and Johni also found that relooking at data during the summer gave them information that was not apparent during the school year, noting that "your perceptions may not be what the facts are." Time to look back and not just forward is a difficult balance to achieve for teachers who always feel the encroaching demands of tomorrow before today is even finished. The new understandings that can emerge for teachers who research and who acquire the habits of data analysis as ongoing aspects of practice will know they have enriched their professional lives. When they share their stories with others, they give this understanding a life of its own that can travel through time from teacher to teacher, as Debby Wood was coming to recognize when she wrote,

[The first year of our study] was not child-focused so it didn't directly impact my instruction. But I was definitely affected personally and professionally. The interaction with my peers and the involvement with the SRC invigorated me and caused me to become excited about my profession and the possibility that I could possibly make a contribution to the profession as a whole. I'm sure this only made me better in my own classroom. We talk so much about self-esteem for our kids. Self-esteem isn't finite. I am still developing as a person and as a teacher. Becoming a teacher researcher helped me value myself as a teacher in a new and important way.

In *Seeing for Ourselves,* Glenda L. Bissex (1987) went so far as to say, "If teacher research had been on the horizon ten years ago, I might still be in a classroom myself rather than having been driven to choose between knowing and doing" (p. 5). Teacher researchers in the SRC are knowing and growing by doing.

CONCLUSION

What do our three teacher research cases say about methods for classroom-based inquiry? As in any collection of cases, they simultaneously represent uniqueness and commonality. A case is unique in that it is an "instance" or "example" of an event or situation (*Webster's,* 1980, p. 170). Our cases are unique because the experiences we have had are particular, and the voices we use to convey them are personal. Therefore, Jim makes no claim that his account of an individual teacher researcher is the same as others who have engaged in solitary classroom inquiry. JoBeth does not maintain that her description of their teacher / university researcher collaboration replicates the work of other such teams. Betty does not suggest that her unfinished story of the SRC duplicates the experience of other teacher-research communities. We have argued that teacher research is defined partly by its diversity, and we are confident that our cases support this assertion.

However, a case is "a set of circumstances or conditions" that contains "evidence supporting a conclusion or judgment" (*Webster's,* 1980, p. 170). Therefore, in spite of the diversity among our cases (and our acknowledgment that there are infinite other cases of teacher research, told and untold), our stories beg for a look across them to discover their commonalities. Thus, we structure our conclusion by looking at differences and similarities in teacher research methodology.

Uniqueness

Teacher-research efforts differ not only in researcher configuration, as our cases demonstrate (e.g., single researcher, collaborative inquiry, community of researchers), but also in the purpose behind a study. Purposes become manifest in research questions, which we have found to vary in source and substance (Baumann et al., 1994). Teachers engage in research to explore various questions that range from micro- to macrolevel in foci; for example, how to help one child develop comprehension-monitoring ability to how to improve school- or system-wide comprehension strategies instruction. Whatever the question, however, pedagogy remains central; that is, how to do the work of teaching better.

Teacher research differs in epistemological orientation. Jim's single-classroom inquiry and the teacher / university researcher collaboration JoBeth described fit best within our "pragmatic" epistemological category (i.e., selecting or creating appropriate methodological tools). However, we have seen within the SRC "established" studies (i.e., replicating university-based methodology), particularly within the first year of the community, as some teachers worked from their prior understandings of what counted as research. We also have "radical" SRC studies (i.e., having educational policy or political change as a research goal), for example, the Allen / Michalove examination of literacy in a democratic society (see Table 13–2). Teachers do research from various philosophical and political perspectives, and we believe that these multiple ways of viewing the world add to the richness of the genre.

Teacher-research studies differ dramatically in the types of data collected and used. Personal narrative has proved to be a powerful data source in many SRC studies. Observations and interviews were essential data sources in the Michalove / Allen / Shockley Bisplinghoff research, as well as in several SRC studies. Like many teacher-researchers, Jim is finding his extensive daily journal as a rich, primary record of his experience; in contrast, several SRC researchers found alternatives to teaching journals more effective for documenting classroom events and reflecting on them. Betty's "data world" view of classrooms leads each teacher-researcher to collect and examine a unique assemblage of sources of information.

Also, data analysis procedures vary from study to study. As Betty has documented, SRC researchers have used verbal interpretations among and between research team members as viable and powerful mechanisms for examining and understanding data from their studies. In contrast, Jim has borrowed from extant methodological traditions to ground his analyses, although he has had to adjust methods according to their doability, responsiveness, and impact on his instructional responsibilities. Teacher researchers also create analysis methods, as evidenced by the interpretive dialogue procedure JoBeth described in their collaborative inquiry.

Thus, as our cases demonstrate, no two teacher-research studies are alike in form or function. However, each is driven by several basic tenets common to this developing form.

Commonality

As noted in our review, most descriptions of teacher research include the processes of action and reflection. As teacher researchers ourselves, we concurrently did the work of teaching while standing back and examining it. The seemingly paradoxical task of simultaneous doing and reflecting underscores the tension and exhilaration inherent in teacher research.

The emic view teachers have with respect to research is a distinguishing mark of classroom inquiry. Insider status provides a unique vantage point for a researching teacher's reflective actions, and distinguishing what constitutes teaching and what constitutes researching becomes difficult and unimportant. As the teacher researchers cited in Betty's SRC story so eloquently stated, theory and practice become blended, if not blurred, in teacher research. Practical theories and theoretical practices are inescapable outcomes of teachers studying their work.

Methodological evolution is an inevitable characteristic of teacher research. Jim's choice of methods, as sensible as they seemed prior to day 1 in second grade, was only temporary. As soon as he got into the classroom and began to wrestle with the realities of researching while teaching, he found that methods needed to be adapted or scrapped. Teacher researchers are thoughtful in the methods they choose, but they cannot adhere to them slavishly. Methods are no more than tools of the trade that may and must be modified to achieve the goals underlying the inquiry.

A corollary to the preceding is the necessity of pragmatism in methodology. Methods must work in an efficient and effective manner for teacher researchers. JoBeth's, Betty's, and Barbara's frustrating venture into constant comparison and grounded theory led them back to their interpretive dialogue method. Why? Because it brought them back to the real purpose of their inquiry. It kept the experience whole rather than fragmented; as a result, they again enjoyed, rather than dreaded, data analysis sessions. The SRC researchers failed to find research journals as easy to keep and useful as reported by other teacher researchers in the published studies they were reading. Instead, they found ingenious ways to make daily records of their research experiences, be they addenda to daily plans, a hybrid plan book / research journal, or literally notes on transparency scraps. If it worked methodologically, its use persisted; if it did not, it atrophied or was thrown away.

As Betty documents, SRC researchers found the opportunity to have professional conversations a powerful methodological tool in teacher research. Having the time to discuss what was going on in classrooms and in students' lives released them from the isolation and anonymity of teaching-as-usual. The professionalism, esprit de corps, and simple self-esteem engendered by focused conversations with colleagues deepened their interest in, commitment to, and need for teacher inquiry. JoBeth described talk among team members and with the children and their parents as integral to their collaborative research. Even Jim, who studied himself and his classroom mostly in isolation throughout the school year, found post-school-year recorded conversations with colleagues, administrators, parents, and children extraordinarily illuminating.

We close by responding to the framing questions we posed at the beginning of this chapter. Teacher research is an evolving philosophical orientation toward practical theory; it is not simply an adapted or a hybridized conglomerate of existing educational research methods. It is true that teacher researchers adopt or adapt methodological tools from extant research traditions for data collection and analysis; this is in keeping with the pragmatic nature of much teacher research. As we have shown, however, teacher researchers also invent or create their own methods. But methods do not equate to methodology, and it is not the source of the methodological tools themselves that distinguishes teacher research. Instead, it is the unique and common characteristics we have discussed that define teacher research as its own genre. Therefore, we maintain that teacher research is a distinct, communicative art, a self-perpetuating lesson on constructing meaning. The diversity within this changing, reflective, action-oriented research pedagogy makes it vibrant and fulfilling for those who engage in it and, we believe, enlightening and thought provoking for those who read, use, learn, and benefit from it.

References

Allen, J., Buchanan, J., Edelsky, C., & Norton, G. (1992). Teachers as "they" at NRC: An invitation to enter the dialogue on the ethics of collaborative and non-collaborative classroom research. In C. K. Kinzer & D. J. Leu (Eds.), *Literacy research, theory, and practice: Views from many perspectives* (pp. 357–365). Chicago: National Reading Conference.

Allen, J., Cary, M., & Delgado, L. (Coordinators for the Kingsbridge Road Research Team). (1995). *Exploring blue highways: Literacy reform, school change, and the creation of learning communities.* New York: Teachers College Press.

Allen, J., Michalove, B., & Shockley, B. (1993). *Engaging children: Community and chaos in the lives of young Literacy learners.* Portsmouth, NH: Heinemann.

Allen, J., Shockley, B., & Baumann, J. F. (1995). Gathering 'round the kitchen table: Teacher inquiry in the NRRC school research consortium. *The Reading Teacher, 48,* 526–529.

Almy, M., & Genishi, C. (1979). *Ways of studying children.* New York: Teachers College Press.

Alvermann, D. (1988, January). *Data reduction and data display: Decisions facing the qualitative researcher.* Paper presented at Qualitative Research in Education Conference, Athens, GA.

Ashton-Warner, S. (1963). *Teacher.* New York: Simon & Schuster.

Atwell, N. (1991). *Side by side: Essays on teaching to learn.* Portsmouth, NH: Heinemann.

Atwell, N. (1993). Foreword. In L. Patterson, C. M. Santa, K. G. Short, & K. Smith (Eds.), *Teachers are researchers: Reflection and action* (pp. vii-xii). Newark, DE: International Reading Association.

Barr, R., Kamil, M. L., Mosenthal, P., & Pearson, P. D. (Eds.). (1991). *Handbook of reading research, Vol. II.* New York: Heinemann.

Bartoli, J. S. (1995). *Unequal opportunity: Learning to read in the U.S.A.* New York: Teachers College Press.

Baumann, J. F. (1984). The effectiveness of a direct instruction paradigm for teaching main idea comprehension. *Reading Research Quarterly, 20,* 95–115 .

Baumann, J. F. (1986). Teaching third-grade students to comprehend anaphoric relationships: The application of a direct instruction model. *Reading Research Quarterly, 21,* 70–90.

Baumann, J. F. (1995a). Sabbatical in second-grade: Reflecting on the lived experience. In C. K. Kinzer, K. Hinchman & D. J. Leu (Eds.), *Perspectives on literacy research and practice: Forty-fourth yearbook of the National Reading Conference* (pp. 390–399). Chicago: National Reading Conference.

Baumann, J. F. (1995b, September). 180 days in second grade: Knowing and growing together. *National Reading Research Center NEWS,* 1–3.

Baumann, J. F. (in press). The inside and outside of teacher research. In C. K. Kinzer, D. J. Leu & K. Hinchman (Eds.), *Forty-fifth yearbook of the National Reading Conference.* Chicago: National Reading Conference.

Baumann, J. F., Allen, J., & Shockley, B. (1994). Questions teachers ask: A report from the National Reading Research Center School Research Consortium. In D. J. Leu & C. K. Kinzer (Eds.), *Multidimensional aspects of literacy research, theory, and practice: Forty-third yearbook of the National Reading Conference* (pp. 474–484). Chicago: National Reading Conference.

Baumann, J. F., & Bergeron, B. S. (1993). Story map instruction using children's literature: Effects on first graders' comprehension of central story elements. *Journal of Reading Behavior, 25,* 407–437.

Baumann, J. F., Dillon, D. R., Shockley, B. B., Alvermann, D. A., & Reinking, D. (1996). Perspectives for literacy research. In L. Baker, P. P. Afflerbach & D. Reinking (Eds.), *Developing engaged readers in school and home communities* (pp. 217–246). Hillsdale, NJ: Erlbaum.

Baumann, J. F., Hooten, H., & White, P. (1996). Teaching skills and strategies with literature. In J. Baltas & S. Shafer (Eds.), *Balanced reading: Grades 3–6* (pp. 60–72). New York: Scholastic Professional Books.

Baumann, J. F., & Ivey, G. (in press). Delicate balances: striving for curricular and instructional equilibrium in a second-grade literature / strategy-based classroom, *Reading Research Quarterly.*

Baumann, J. F., Seifert-Kessell, N., & Jones, L. A. (1992). Effect of think-aloud instruction on elementary students' comprehension monitoring abilities. *Journal of Reading Behavior, 24,* 143–172.

Baumann, J. F., Shockley, B., Allen, J., Keffer, A., Carr, S., Lanier, B., Mattison, L., Wood, D., & Stanulis, R. (1995). Questions from within. *Reading Today, 13*(2), 23.

Baylor, B., & Parnall, P. (1978) *The other way to listen.* New York: Scribner.

Beach, R., Green, J. L., Kamil, M. L., & Shanahan, T. (Eds.). (1992). *Multidisciplinary perspectives on literacy research.* Urbana, IL: National Conference on Research in English / National Council of Teachers of English.

Berlin, J. A. (1990). The teacher as researcher: Democracy, dialogue, and power. In D. A. Daiker & M. Morenberg (Eds.), *The writing teacher as researcher: Essays in the theory and practice of class-*

based research (pp. 3–14). Portsmouth, NH: Boynton / Cook.

Bissex, G. L. (1987). What is a teacher-researcher? In G. L. Bissex & R. H. Bullock (Eds.), *Seeing for ourselves: Case-study research by teachers of writing* (pp. 3–5). Portsmouth, NH: Heinemann.

Bissex, G. L., & Bullock, R. H. (Eds.). (1987). *Seeing for ourselves: Case-study research by teachers of writing.* Portsmouth, NH: Heinemann.

Brause, R. S., & Mayher, J. S. (Eds.). (1991). *Search and re-search: What the inquiring teacher needs to know.* London: Falmer Press.

Bronfenbrenner, U. (1976). The experimental ecology of education. *Educational Researcher, 5,* 5–15.

Buckingham, B. R. (1926). *Research for teachers.* New York: Silver, Burdett.

Burton, F. R. (1991). Teacher-researcher projects: An elementary school teacher's perspective. In J. Flood, J. M. Jensen, D. Lapp & J. R. Squire (Eds.), *Handbook of research on teaching the English language arts* (pp. 226–230). New York: Macmillan.

Calhoun, E. F. (1994). *How to use action research in the self-renewing school.* Alexandria, VA: Association for Supervision and Curriculum Development.

Carr, W., & Kemmis, S. (1986). *Becoming critical.* London: Falmer Press.

Carter, K. (1993). The place of story in the study of teaching and teacher education. *Educational Researcher, 22*(1), 5–12.

Clark, P. A. (1972). *Action research and organizational change.* London: Harper & Row.

Cochran-Smith, M., & Lytle, S. L. (1990). Research on teaching and teacher research: The issues that divide us. *Educational Researcher, 19*(2), 2–11.

Cochran-Smith, M., & Lytle, S. L. (Eds.). (1993). *Inside / outside: Teacher research and knowledge.* New York: Teachers College Press.

Connelly, F. M., & Clandinin, D. J. (1990). Stories of experience and narrative inquiry. *Educational Researcher, 19*(5), 2–14.

Corey, S. M. (1953). *Action research to improve school practices.* New York: Teachers College Bureau of Publications, Columbia University.

Corey, S. M. (1954). Action research in education. *Journal of Educational Research, 47,* 375–380.

Corman, B. R. (1957). Action research: A teaching or a research method? *Review of Educational Research, 27,* 545–547.

Daiker, D. A., & Morenberg, M. (Eds.). (1990). *The writing teacher as researcher: Essays in the theory and practice of class-based research.* Portsmouth, NH: Boynton / Cook.

D'Alessandro, M., Diakiw, J. Y., Fuhler, C. J., O'Masta, G. M., Pils, L. J., Trachtenburg, P., & Wolf, J. (1992). Writing for publication: Voices from the classroom. *The Reading Teacher, 45,* 408–414.

Dewey, J. (1904). The relation of theory to practice in education. *Third yearbook of the National Society for the Study of Education, Part 1.* Chicago: University of Chicago Press.

Dillon, D. (Ed.). (1988). The reflective practitioner [Issue theme]. *Language Arts, 65*(7).

Dilthey, W. (1985). *Poetry and experience.* Princeton, NJ: Princeton University Press.

Elliott, J. (1991). *Action research for educational change.* Milton Keynes, England: Open University Press.

Elliott, J. (Ed.). (1993). *Reconstructing teacher education.* London: Falmer Press.

Elliott, J., & MacDonald, B. (1975). *People in classrooms* (Occasional Paper No. 2). Norwich, England: University of East Anglia / Center for Applied Research in Education.

Erickson, F. (1986). Qualitative methods in research on teaching. In M. C. Wittrock (Ed.), *Handbook of research on teaching* (3rd ed., pp. 119–161). New York: Macmillan.

Fleischer, C. (1994). Researching teacher-research: A practitioner's retrospective. *English Education, 26,* 86–124.

Flood, J., Jensen, J. M., Lapp, D., & Squire, J. R. (Eds.). (1991). *Handbook of research on teaching the English language arts.* New York: Macmillan.

Gaines, E. (1993). *A lesson before dying.* New York: Vintage.

Gitlin, A., Bringhurst, K., Burns, M., Cooley, V., Myers, B., Price, K., Russell, R., & Tiess, P. (1992). *Teachers' voices for school change: An introduction to educative research.* New York: Teachers College Press.

Glaser, B. C., & Strauss, A. L. (1967). *The discovery of grounded theory.* Chicago: Aldine.

Goswami, D., & Stillman, P. (Eds.). (1987). Reclaiming the classroom: *Teacher-research as an agency for change.* Upper Montclaire, NJ: Boynton / Cook.

Green, M. F. (1991). *Praying for sheetrock: A work of nonfiction.* Reading, MA: Addison-Wesley.

Hansen, J., Newkirk, T., & Graves, D. (Eds.). (1985). *Breaking ground: Teachers relate reading and writing in the elementary school.* Portsmouth, NH: Heinemann.

Harding, S. (1987). Introduction: Is there a feminist method? In S. Harding (Ed.), *Feminism & methodology* (pp. 1–14). Bloomington, IN: Indiana University Press.

Hodgkinson, H. L. (1957). Action research: A critique. *The Journal of Educational Sociology, 31*(4), 137–153.

Hopkins, D. (1993). *A teacher's guide to classroom research* (2nd ed.). Buckingham, England: Open University Press.

Hubbard, R., & Stratton, D. (Eds.). (1985). *Teachers and learners and other narratives of the Mast Way Research Project.* Durham, NH: Writing Process Lab.

Hubbard, R. S., & Power, B. M. (1993). *The art of classroom inquiry: A handbook for teacher-researchers.* Portsmouth, NH: Heinemann.

Hymes, D. (1982). Ethnographic monitoring. In H. T. Treuba, G. T. Guthrie & K. H. Au (Eds.), *Culture in the bilingual classroom.* Rowley, MA: Newbury House.

Jaeger, R. M. (Ed.). (1988). *Complementary methods for research in education.* Washington, DC: American Educational Research Association.

Keffer, A., Carr, S., Lanier, B., Mattison, L., Wood, D., & Stanulis, R. (1995). *Teacher-researchers discover magic in forming an adult writing workshop* (Perspective in Reading Research No. 9). Athens, GA: National Reading Research Center, Universities of Georgia and Maryland.

Kincheloe, J. L. (1991). *Teachers as researchers: Qualitative inquiry as a path to empowerment.* London: Falmer Press.

Krall, F. R. (1988). From the inside out—personal history as educational research. *Educational Theory, 38,* 467–479.

Lather, P. (1986). Research as praxis. *Harvard Educational Review, 56,* 257–277.

LeCompte, M. D., Preissle, J. P., & Tesh, R. (1993). *Ethnography and qualitative design in educational research* (2nd ed.). San Diego, CA: Academic Press.

Lincoln, Y. S., & Guba, E. G. (1985). *Naturalists inquiry.* Newbury Park, CA: Sage.

Llorens, M. B. (Ed.). (1994). Action research [Issue theme]. *The Elementary School Journal, 95*(1).

Lowry, C. D. (1908). The relation of superintendents and principals to the training and professional improvement of their teachers. *Seventh Yearbook of the National Society for the Study of Education, Part 1.* Chicago: University of Chicago Press.

Lytle, S. L., & Cochran-Smith, M. (1994). Teacher-research in English. In A. C. Purves (Ed.), *Encyclopedia of English studies and language arts* (pp. 1153–1155). New York: Scholastic.

Mayher, J. S., & Brause, R. S. (1991). The never-ending cycle of teacher growth. In R. S. Brause & J. S. Mayher (Eds.), *Search and* re-search: What the inquiring teacher needs to know (pp. 23–42). London: Falmer.

McFarland, K. P., & Stansell, J. C. (1993). Historical perspectives. In L. Patterson, C. M. Santa, K. G. Short & K. Smith, (Eds.), Teachers are researchers: Reflection and action (pp. 12–18). Newark, DE: International Reading Association.

Merriam, S. B. (1988). Case study research in education: A qualitative approach. San Francisco: Jossey-Bass.

Mohr, M., & Maclean, M. (1987). Working together: A guide for teacher-researchers. Urbana, IL: National Council of Teachers of English.

Moll, L. C. (1992). Literacy research in community and classrooms: A sociocultural approach. In R. Beach, J. L. Green, M. L. Kamil & T. Shanahan (Eds.), Multidisciplinary perspectives on literacy research (pp. 211–244). Urbana, IL: National Conference on Research in English / National Council of Teachers of English.

Moll, L., Amanti, C., Neff., & Gonzales, N. (1992). Funds of knowledge for teaching: Using a qualitative approach to connect homes and classrooms. Theory into Practice, 31(2), 132–141.

Myers, M. (1985). The teacher-researcher: How to study writing in the classroom. Urbana, IL: National Council of Teachers of English.

Newman, D. (1990). Opportunities for research on the organizational impact of school computers. Educational Researcher, 19(3), 8–13.

Nixon, J. (1981). A teacher's guide to action research. London: Grant McIntyre.

Odell, L. (1976). The classroom teacher as researcher. English Journal, 9(1), 106–111.

Oja, S., & Smulyan, L. (1989). Collaborative action research: A developmental perspective. London: Falmer Press.

Olson, M. W. (Ed.). (1990a). Opening the door to classroom research. Newark, DE: International Reading Association.

Olson, M. W. (1990b). The teacher as researcher: A historical perspective. In M. W. Olson (Ed.), Opening the door to classroom research (pp. 1–20). Newark, DE: International Reading Association.

Paley, V. G. (1981). Wally's stories. Cambridge, MA: Harvard University Press.

Paley, V. G. (1990). The boy who would be a helicopter: The uses of storytelling in the classroom. Cambridge, MA: Harvard University Press.

Papert, S. (1993). The children's machine: Rethinking school in the age of the computer. New York: Harper Collins.

Patterson, L., Santa, C. M., Short, K. G., & Smith, K. (Eds.). (1993). Teachers are researchers: Reflection and action. Newark, DE: International Reading Association.

Patterson, L., & Shannon, P. (1993). Reflection, inquiry, action. In L. Patterson, C. M. Santa, K. G. Short & K. Smith (Eds.), Teachers are researchers: Reflection and action (pp. 7–11). Newark, DE: International Reading Association.

Patterson, L. A., Stansell, J. C., & Lee, S. C. (1990). Teacher research: From promise to power. Katonah, NY: Richard C. Owen.

Patton, M. Q. (1980). Qualitative evaluation methods. Newbury Park, CA: Sage.

Pearson, P. D. (Ed.). (1984). Handbook of reading research. New York: Longman.

Pinnell, G. S., & Matlin, M. L. (Eds.). (1989). Teachers and research: Language learning in the classroom. Newark, DE: International Reading Association.

Purves, A. S. (Ed). (1994). Encyclopedia of English studies and language arts. New York: Scholastic.

Rainey, B. G. (1973). Action research. The Clearing House, 47, 371–375.

Rief, L. (1992). Seeking diversity: Language arts with adolescents. Portsmouth, NH: Heinemann.

Rorty, R. (1979). Philosophy and the mirror of nature. Princeton, NJ: Princeton University Press.

Rudduck J., & Hopkins, D. (1985). Research as a basis for teaching: Readings from the work of Lawrence Stenhouse. London: Heinemann.

Sagor, R. (1992). How to conduct collaborative action research. Alexandria, VA: Association for Supervision and Curriculum Development.

Schon, D. A. (1983). The reflective practitioner: How professionals think in action. New York: Basic Books.

Shannon, P. (1990). Commentary: Teachers are researchers. In M. W. Olson (Ed.), Opening the door to classroom research (pp. 141–154). Newark, DE: International Reading Association.

Shockley, B. (1993). Extending the literate community: Reading and writing with families. The New Advocate, 6(1), 11–24.

Shockley, B., Michalove, B., & Allen, J. (1995). Engaging families: Connecting home and school literacy communities. Portsmouth, NH: Heinemann.

Shulman, L. S. (1988). Disciplines of inquiry in education: An overview. In R. M. Jaeger (Ed.), Complementary methods for research in education (pp. 3–20). Washington, DC: American Educational Research Association.

Shumsky, A. (1958). The action research way of learning: An approach to in-service education. New York: Teachers College Bureau of Publications, Columbia University.

Stenhouse, L. (1973). The humanistic curriculum project. In H. Butcher & H. Pont (Eds.), Educational research in Britain 3. London: University of London Press.

Stenhouse, L. (1975). An introduction to curriculum research and development. London: Heinemann.

Stenhouse, L. (Ed.). (1980). Curriculum research and development in action. London: Heinemann.

Teale, W. H. (Ed.). (1995). Teachers as learners [Issue theme]. Language Arts, 72(4).

van Manen, M. (1990). Researching lived experience: Human science for an action sensitive pedagogy. London, Ontario: State University of New York.

Wallace, M. (1987). A historical review of action research: Some implications for the education of teachers and their managerial role. Journal of Education for Teaching, 13(2), 97–115.

Wann, D. (1952). Teachers as researchers. Educational Leadership, 9, 489–495.

Wann, D. (1953). Action research in schools. Review of Educational Research, 23, 337–345.

Webster's New Collegiate Dictionary. (1980). Springfield, MA: G. & C. Merriam.

Wells, G. (Ed.). (1994). Changing schools from within: Creating communities of inquiry. Toronto: Oise Press.

Winter, R. (1982). Dilemma analysis: A contribution to methodology for action research. Cambridge Journal of Education, 12, 161–174.

Wittrock, M. C. (Ed.). (1986). Handbook of research on teaching (3rd ed.). New York: Macmillan.

Yin, R. K. (1984). Case study research: Design and methods. Newbury Park, CA: Sage.

·14·

ASSESSING DEVELOPMENT AND
LEARNING OVER TIME

Robert Calfee

STANFORD UNIVERSITY

Not too many decades ago, *literacy* meant mastery of basic reading skills. *Evaluation* relied on reading speed and accuracy, behavioral objectives, and standardized test scores. *Measurement* was directly linked to "countable" indices. *Growth* meant changes in scale scores and grade-level equivalents. *Validity* was indexed by predictive and concurrent correlations. Quantitative methods ruled the roost.

Things have changed. Qualitative methods are ascendant. Definitions of *literacy* are much different. Print literacy is still important, and the "great debate" continues to rage (Chall, 1967, 1983, 1992). But the concept of literacy for tomorrow's graduates reflects computer technologies and the information highway, and a shift from a factory society to a communication world. Today, educators have good reasons for incorporating communicative and visual arts into the literacy domain. The key word for *evaluation* is now assessment, the label for an emerging paradigm that is the antithesis of testing, a paradigm in which teachers employ portfolios and performances to judge complex performances by qualitative methods. *Measurement* now entails subjective ratings of student productions; "scoring" and "rubrics" are hot topics. *Growth* remains a puzzle. A purported advantage of the new assessments is that student progress is more obvious, but it is difficult to pin down the exact meaning of this claim. Finally, no other assessment topic has provoked as much discussion as the meaning of *validity* in the new paradigm. The dialogue arises partly because of the paradigm shift but also because of continued rethinking of the basic concept. Scholars have proposed radical changes in the definition of validity and its operationalization. Some suggest that validity inheres not in a particular instrument or method, but in interpretations and consequences. For test publishers and users accustomed to straightforward "validity coefficients," the proposal is both revolutionary and disconcerting.

These four elements are the foundation for this chapter. The framework partly reflects my background and the charge by the Part editor, but also consideration of the topics covered by other writers on *Methods of inquiry,* who describe qualitative methods for understanding literacy in a variety of contexts and genres, but do not touch on the last three topics in my framework. My brief introductory discussion of literacy sets the stage, but I will rely on other Parts, especially Part I, for a more complete account.

Given the changes sketched above, all springing up within the past decade or two, covering the title would be a challenge under the best of circumstances. Advocates of quantitative and qualitative methods still live in largely different worlds, despite efforts at bridge building. Two of the topics—measurement and growth—have been largely disregarded in recent years, although the issues go back a long way (Calfee, 1993). The primary goal of this chapter is to present a conceptual framework linking these four elements. The second aim is to link this conceptual analysis to the practical aspects of classroom assessment, where the primary clients are teachers, students, parents, local administrators, while exploring how information from classrooms can serve external audiences.

As background for this chapter, I have relied on other handbooks (Barr, Kamil, Mosenthal, & Pearson, 1991; Belanoff, & Dickson, 1991; Berliner, & Calfee, in press; Bloom, Hastings, & Madaus, 1971; Bloom, Madaus, & Hastings, 1981; Flood, Jensen, Lapp, & Squire, 1991; Jackson, 1992; Linn, 1989; Pearson, 1984; Wittrock, 1986), selected journals (*Educational Measurement: Issues and Practice; Applied Measurement in Education; Review of Research in Education; Educational Assessment*), and several seminal volumes and articles (Baker, O'Neil, & Linn, 1993; Calfee, & Perfumo, 1996; Harlen, 1994; Kane, & Mitchell, in press; Linn, 1994; Moss, 1992, 1994a; OTA, 1992; Wiggins, 1993). I did not conduct an ERIC search, and have undoubtedly overlooked some nuggets. I have not extracted all the "goodies" from the aforementioned sources; in particular, I have neglected the OTA and Harlen citations, which I might have referenced continuously to do full credit. Nor have I attempted to portray the domain of visual and communicative arts for literacy educators, other than to suggest the importance of such a portrayal for purposes of construct definition, and to offer a few thoughts about how I might attempt such a task. The coverage is more contemporary than historical; although we can learn many lessons from history, I had to choose among competing priorities.

The prevailing theme throughout the chapter is the notion that adequate assessment of complex learning and achievement requires informed professional judgment. I will return repeatedly to the classroom as a touchstone for playing out this theme. Now let me look in turn at each of the four basic elements: (a) building an explicit definition of communicative and visual literacy as a foundation for professional evaluation, (b) assessment as the assigning of value to performance, (c) measuring growth, and (d) establishing validity.

Literacy Constructs and Curriculum: Foundation for Professional Assessment

Assessment requires a purpose, an audience, a method, a report, but above all an object or event—a "something" (Herman, Aschbacher, & Winters, 1992). For literacy, that "something" is a construct encompassing a set of concepts and practices that describe skills and knowledge about language and print, as well as the course of study for supporting the development of these skills and knowledge. Literacy does not occur naturally but is the result of tutelage, most often through schooling. Not every reader will agree with this statement, but the evidence appears overwhelming (Honig, 1996; Pressley, & Rankin, 1994).

The Construct of Critical Literacy. A "construct" implies something that is constructed, and several edifices have arisen under the literacy banner. Basic print literacy, for instance, covers the skills of decoding, spelling, literal comprehension, and the rudiments of writing. The minimum competency tests mandated in the 1970s aimed to ensure that every high school graduate could demonstrate competence in these skills. Scarcely was the ink dry on these policies than the nation began to realize the limited value of these mandates.

The alternative to basic print literacy is less easily defined. Some authorities emphasize exposure to content (print literacy plus cultural literacy; Hirsch, 1987). Others emphasize higher-level thinking, which seems clearly preferable to lower-level thinking (Resnick, 1987). Within print literacy, reading and writing might seem complementary, but in fact the two domains are separated by a broad chasm conceptually, organizationally, and practically (Clifford-Jonich, 1987).

For present purposes I will employ the construct of *critical literacy* (Brown, 1991; Calfee, 1994; Calfee, & Patrick, 1995) as a starting point, recognizing the need to extend the idea to include the other domains emphasized in this handbook. Ten years ago, with communicative and visual literacy barely on the horizon, it made sense to me to define critical

literacy as "the capacity to use language in all forms—listening, speaking, reading, and writing—to think, to solve problems, and to communicate." The inclusion of communication was innocuous; it ruffled no feathers, but neither did it arouse much attention. But today's world includes the power of technology to expand exponentially our definition of communication, and to extend print to include other representational modes. *USA Today* illustrates the potency of combining print and picture; the personal computer offers opportunities to create visualizations of incredible power and complexity; classrooms sprout with "webs," "story graphs," and other graphic organizers (Nowak, & Gowin, 1984). I therefore propose a variation on the original definition—"the capacity to use language *and other media for representing ideas* to think, to solve problems, and to communicate"—recognizing the slimness of this proposal. Olson (1995) offers a similar recommendation—"Perhaps it is time that we further relax our definition of writing to include … any graphic form used to convey information" (p. 292). He also presents the idea that becoming print literate entails more than "getting meaning;" it also entails "an understanding of how a text works" (p. 294).

Extending this reasoning to the visual and communicative domains, let me suggest that fully literate individuals appreciate how visual and communicative technologies operate; they can dissect a graphic and analyze a discussion. Witte and his colleagues (Witte, & Flach, 1994; Witte, Flach, Greenwood, & Wilson, 1995) emphasize the communicative aspects of all symbol systems. "…Engaging in symbolization processes such as reading and writing appears to force one to reflect, sometimes consciously and sometimes not, on both what and how one knows as he or she judges the potential meaning signaled by a given text, whether one being read or one being written, against his or her internal representation of the world. [These critical thinking] functions … point to a third function embedded in communicative acts, namely, problem solving [which] itself is a meaning-constructive process that entails problem representation, reflecting on what one knows, and using strategies to orchestrate" (pp. 222, 223). Mislevy, Yamamoto, and Anacker (1991) make a similar point: "Learners become more competent not simply by learning more facts and skills, but by reconfiguring their knowledge, by 'chunking' information to reduce memory loads, and by developing strategies and models that help them discern when and how facts and skills are important" (p. 10). Moreover, fully literate persons are capable of self-assessment. They are able to monitor their performance, to check how they are doing, to use self-reflection for corrective feedback. Sizer (1995) expresses this idea with characteristic force: "Good schools not only frequently tell their students how they are doing, but get the students into the habit of asking the question for themselves. The expectation of illuminating feedback—indeed, aggressively searching it out—is one of the universal characteristics of an educated person" (p. vi).

Curriculum Constructs. It is tempting to pursue these issues further, but other chapters in this handbook must serve this purpose. I turn now to another matter: defining the curriculum of critical literacy. Once the characteristics of a fully literate person are specified, the next question is how to build a road that helps a young child move from "here to there." This task is complicated by the fact that today's children spring from dramatically different backgrounds, and aspire toward dramatically different outcomes than those of previous eras. Commonalities exist. Sixth graders do not aim to go on welfare; they want to finish college and make a good living. On the other hand, not everyone aspires to become an algebraist, although top-lane mathematics is the entry point to the college track. Not everyone is enchanted by *Moby Dick*, although book reports can be the key to advanced placement.

One strategy for curriculum construction is to build a linear path, a scope-and-sequence chart, in which detailed objectives are taught at specific time points. A stage-based literacy curriculum (Chall, 1983, 1992) exemplifies this approach. The strategy works well for education as selection; much like sorting apples, a student's place in the social hierarchy depends on the slot through which he or she falls. In this model, achievement uses the average as a standard; students who do not fulfill the norm for their cohort are "below average," no matter how well or poorly they may do in absolute terms.

A second strategy views the learning as a natural matter. The "readiness" perspective falls within this category; when a child is ready to read, that is the time for instruction. The Whole Language philosophy reflects this assumption (Goodman, 1986). The curriculum emerges as individual students are immersed in literary works. A modicum of guidance by the teacher, and literacy will ensue.

A third strategy assumes that, to ensure that every student achieves his or her full potential, what is needed is an explicit but adaptable course of study—a developmental curriculum (Barr, 1984; Juel, 1991). The early years are critical, especially for those children from backgrounds that do not prepare them for the school regimen. The integrated primary model illustrates the possibilities of a flexible curriculum during the primary grades (Mason, 1984; McGee, & Richgels, 1990; Sulzby, & Teale, 1991). During the late elementary and middle school years, students must learn to apply the literacy skills that are the focus of this handbook. While we have models for the primary grades, the middle years pose a challenge to curriculum design, which call for a move from developmental growth toward subject matter competence. After leaving middle school, the high school student cannot expect to encounter an adaptable curriculum, however desirable that might be. High schools expect students to have mastered the fundamentals; teachers emphasize content over development.

Returning to the elementary and middle grades, what are the underlying principles of a developmental curriculum? The *Handbook of Research on Curriculum* (Jackson, 1992) offers interesting insights and analyses into this question but is mostly philosophical. The only reference to development is a brief commentary on possible implications of Piaget's theory of stages for curriculum design. Gehrke, Knapp, and Sirotnik (1992), "In search of the school curriculum," comment that dozens of images exist, none especially compelling: "Only a limited amount of research has focused on the state of the curriculum … [In language arts] oral language is the stepchild" (p. 69).

A comprehensive description of a developmental curriculum for print literacy is found in Moffett and Wagner (1992; also see Calfee, & Patrick, 1995; Paris, Wasik, & Turner, 1991), who lay out a course of study shaped around the changing capabilities of students from kindergarten through high school. This curriculum, which integrates reading, writing, and oral language, presents an ordered sequence of learning goals, but without the "linearity" of scope-and-sequence charts. The curriculum, built on a language experience philosophy (Allen, & Allen, 1982), relies on teachers as professionals who can adapt developmental concepts to different contexts. The surface events in a Moffett-Wagner curriculum may vary widely from one situation to another, but the underlying curriculum constructs will remain constant to the knowledgeable observer. It is not the constancy of the scope-and-sequence chart, nor the idiosyncrasy of the whole-language philosophy, but a design unlike either of these strategies.

How might a developmental curriculum incorporate the concepts of communicative and visual-graphic competence? At the outset, the construct of critical literacy sketched earlier is inherently communicative; one of the primary purposes of literacy learning is to provide individuals with tools that enhance interactions with one another. The integration of visual and graphic elements with other forms of print literacy is the challenge. Two recent innovations seem particularly noteworthy: (a) the use of graphic organizers as instructional strategies, and (b) the power of the personal computer for displaying rich and dynamic visual-graphic-print information, and as a tool for students (and teachers) to create their own visual-graphic-print products. Research has paid little attention to these elements until recently (Bromley, 1991; Heimlich, & Pittelman, 1986; Jonassen, 1985; Wright, Lickorish, Hull, & Ummelen, 1995), and the assumption seems to be that students can "naturally" learn how to process visual information. The expressive potential of this technology expands daily, and competence in multimedia comprehending and composing will certainly be highly valued in the years to come. The educational system is still largely in the dark ages when it comes to the resources, technological and human, needed to build a curriculum in this domain, but we need to think about the possibilities.

In the remaining sections of this chapter, the task of defining the construct and the curriculum will reemerge as fundamentally important. Evaluation is stymied when the thing to be appraised is ill-defined and evaluation becomes idiosyncratic. Psychological measurement turns out to be relatively straightforward for simple constructs, more difficult with complex constructs, and impossible when the construct is indeterminate. A substantial literature exists on models of learning and development, but these can be brought into play only if we know what is being learned and how it is being learned. Finally, whatever one's views of validity, construct definition is central to the validation process.

This section thus ends with a challenge rather than a conclusion. Extending the construct of print literacy to include communicative and graphic features moves the concept into the future. But if schools are to realize the potential of this advance and if assessment policy is to support the effort, then a significant task is the defining of a construct that lays out the curriculum from the early years of school onward describing what students need to learn and how teachers need to guide this learning within this domain.

In the remainder of the chapter I will rely for purposes of illustration on a definition for the domain of print literacy based on four strands (Calfee, & Drum, 1986): concept development, narrative comprehension and composition, expository comprehension and composition, and decoding-spelling. Each of these strands is separable, in the sense that different concepts and terminology apply, and that different curriculum paths are required. Any "real" literacy task may call on some or all of these domains; when I drive from Palo Alto to San Francisco, I operate my automobile as a "whole;" if it breaks down along the way, it helps to be able to trace the problem to one of a handful of independent systems. What I have not attempted to think through is the handful of additional components needed for a broader view of literacy that encompasses print, but also incorporates graphics and other communicative media.

Neither does this chapter attend to the instructional support needed to promote a curriculum. Surveys suggest that instruction in the elementary and middle grades still follows an assembly-line transmission model. Teacher talk dominates, and students are individually reinforced as they respond with correct answers. Visions of the classroom as a social-cognitive environment appear here and there: "Classroom instruction should provide an environment in which students are able to externalize their thoughts… [so that] the writer is able to step away from personal, abbreviated inner speech to external social speech" (Everson, 1991, p. 10). This allusion to Vygotskian learning offers an intriguing perspective but is far removed from present realities. Curriculum, instruction, assessment—coherence in the C-I-A troika—is probably critical for genuine educational reform.

The previous discussion has laid the foundation for considering different strategies for evaluation of visual and communicative literacy. Evaluation of student achievement has been a centerpiece of educational research for more than a century. Prior to the 1940s, studies of grading were commonplace. Beginning in the 1950s, research on standardized tests dominated the literature. The psychometric tradition discussed in the next section is well established, and I will assume that readers are familiar with this tradition, including both norm-referenced and criterion-referenced methods for assessing student achievement and program effectiveness (Linn, 1994).

Testing Psychometrics and Assessment. The foundation for the psychometric tradition is the notion of a trait "score," defined operationally by a test. The trait may encompass a broad domain like vocabulary or comprehension, or focus on a more closely specified objective like "long-short vowels." In either event, the starting point is the total score, the number of correct answers to 12 questions selected to sample the domain. The aim of psychometric analysis is to establish the reliability and validity of the total score. Reliability means that the set of questions—items or minitasks—contribute consistently to the total score. Validity means that the total score

correlates with other indices designed to tap the same domain.

Building on this foundation, psychometricians have moved the field to a high level of technical sophistication. In its simplest form, reliability is determined by the correlation of each item to the score. If a particular item rank-orders students differently than the total score, then the item undermines reliability. For practical purposes, psychometric reliability is the average correlation between individual items and the total scores. If every test item ranks students in the same order, then the total test score is reliable. To the degree that different items give different ranks, the test is unreliable.

Generalizability, a major extension of reliability (Cronbach, Gleser, Nanda, & Rajaratnam, 1972; Cronbach, Linn, Brennan, & Haertel, 1995; Shavelson, & Webb, 1991), advances the original ideas and methods in fundamentally important ways. Not only items, but all factors influencing the total score, can be included within a single coherent generalizability design. For example, suppose that some items on a vocabulary test require knowledge of Anglo-Saxon words while others are from Romance origins, and that some testees are English-only, while others come from a Spanish-language background. The test might appear unreliable because of differences in the rank-ordering of students and items from these two dimensions. Generalizability allows the psychometrician to identify different facets in the data structure, and to explore the reliability of total scores as well as profiles. For instance, the total scores might have limited reliability on first glance, but generalizability analysis might reveal that English-only students perform consistently better on Anglo-Saxon items while Spanish-background students do relatively better on Romance words. The potential of generalizability methods for establishing the reliability and validity of innovative assessments has yet to be fully realized; I will explore this matter more fully in the final section on validity.

Traditional testing has provoked critiques for more than a half-century (Gould, 1981; Haney, & Madaus, 1989; Hill, 1994). In the 1980s, scholars and practitioners began to propose a new strategy, *assessment,* as a complement if not a complete replacement for testing and psychometrics (for reviews, see Gipps, 1994; Glaser, 1981; Mitchell, 1992; Wiggins, 1993). Most discussions fall on the endpoints of the continuum in Table 14–1. Supporters of testing-psychometrics point to the trustworthiness and efficiency of traditional methods, and the perils of unproven methods (Hambleton, & Murphy, 1992; Mehrens, 1992). Advocates of innovative assessments typically meld their proposals into a total package that includes a social-cognitive curriculum, student-centered instruction, and professionalization of teaching (Mitchell, 1992; Wiggins, 1993). Researchers see assessment as an extension of qualitative methods and postmodernist philosophies, a counterpoint to quantitative methods and positivist philosophies. Practitioners view assessment as a way to empower the classroom teacher, while testing is a "time-clock" relic of the factory model of education.

While one can find early precursors of the current debate [e.g., Tyler (1934, 1989) in the 1930s; Bloom et al., 1981], a paradigm shift also seems brewing. Critical questions center

TABLE 14–1. Contrasts Between Externally Mandated Standardized Testing and Self-initiated Professional Assessment.

	Testing	Assessment
Purpose	External accountability	Classroom instructional decisions
Audiences	Policy makers Administrators General public	Teachers Students Parents
Methods	On-demand Multiple-choice Standardized conditions Objective scoring Psychometrics	Continuous performance Observation / "kid-watching" Less-than-fully-standardized Subjective rating Interpretive / hermeneutic
Dependability	Reliability based on interitem consistency Validity based on predictive correlations	Interrater and intertask consistency Trustworthiness based on moderation
Interpretation	Statistical indices Mastery of objectives Rank ordering of students Attainment of standards	Narrative descriptions Developmental progress Individual achievement Attainment of goals
Reporting	Statistical summaries and graphics Focus on total scores Demographic breakdowns Administrative unit breakdowns Official summary	Qualitative summaries and "stories" Emphasis on profiles Individual accounts School "report cards" Parent–student conference

around assessment concepts and methods, but equally important are (a) the match of assessment with curriculum outcomes, and (b) the role of the teacher as a professional assessor. Testing is seen as a match to a linear-behavioral curriculum, while assessment is better suited to dynamic-cognitive learning (Shepard, 1995). Testing places the teacher in the role of civil servant while assessment calls forth professional judgments. The choice of descriptive labels captures essential features of the debate.

Testing is typically connected with the multiple-choice format and behavioral objectives while assessment is linked to performance. Baker et al. (1993) provide one of the clearest conceptualizations of this idea, happily without beating any dead horses. Performance-based assessment uses open-ended tasks (directed toward production more than recognition), lays out complex tasks, offers students choice about the content and context for demonstrating competence, and situates the assessment in a setting where multiple skills are required, adequate time is allowed, and resources are available. The student can refer to books, notes, the library, other students—even the teacher! Baker et al. discuss the implications of this assessment strategy for various purposes and applications, and offer a balanced perspective on the advantages for improving the character and quality of instruction, which they weigh against a variety of risks.

A particularly significant issue is the feasibility of classroom-based assessment for large-scale accountability. Given the continuing pressure for public information about the public schools, the issue is not whether students will be "tested" (and programs evaluated), but how and by whom?

One strategy relies on externally mandated tests, the other on internally determined assessments. Many observers see the two as incompatible strategies (e.g., Cole, 1988; Gipps, 1994; Harp, 1991; Mehrens, 1992; Tierney, Carter, & Desai, 1991; Wixon, Valencia, & Lipson, 1994). Cost-efficient standardized testing is essential to ensure dependability and to avoid corruption. Assessment is a "teacher thing," and standardizing it destroys the idiosyncrasies that make it valuable in the local contexts.

One can find variations on these themes. Proponents of measurement-driven instruction (Popham, 1993) value tests as a policy lever for prescribing classroom practice. Others suggest that assessment systems may be valuable for their influence on classroom practice even when they are not trustworthy by psychometric standards (Gipps, 1994; Wiggins, 1993), but the data are not always supportive of this position (Martin-Kneip, Thornburg, & Cookson, 1994). The U.S. perspective on these issues, of course, reflects our history. While I cannot pursue the matter here, let me suggest that an examination of these issues in other settings might enlighten the current debate; the recent tensions in Great Britain between internally and externally mandated assessments of student achievement casts a different light on the meaning of accountability and the professional roles and responsibilities of teachers (Daugherty, 1995; Gipps, 1994; Harlen, 1994).

Following on this point, a central question in this chapter centers around the classroom teacher's role in the assessment of student progress through a complex developmental curriculum for purposes of internal (local) and external (public) accountability. A key question centers on the potential for professional judgments of student achievement to attain the same status as the objective psychometric methods that have evolved during the past half century. As suggested in the previous section, professional judgments must be grounded in a clearly explicated curriculum construct. But in addition, other building blocks include extensions of psychometric concepts, developments in qualitative methodology, practical experience with professional discourse or "moderation" as a way of calibrating teacher judgments, and studies of the influence of organizational factors on the professionalization of teachers (Linn, & Baker, 1996; McLaughlin, & Shepard, in press).

Professional Judgments of Complex Performances. Can teachers, given appropriate conditions, produce from a rich and situated body of classroom evidence the formative and summative judgments that document students' progress and accomplishments—judgments that are trustworthy and that carry added value beyond what can be learned from less expensive and more efficient alternatives? Human beings are certainly capable of performing such tasks. Reviewers of journal manuscripts (and handbook chapters) provide editors with written assessments that are complex, that are highly valued, and that are significant in high-stakes decisions—even though reviewers often disagree with one another. Physicians' medical notes may seem cryptic to the uninitiated, but they provide the basis within the professional community for diagnosis and treatment. Travel guides and wine reviews rely on words to convey images and communicate appraisals. *Consumer Reports* offer pages of richly descriptive information about products and services. Professors grade undergraduates and certify doctoral candidates.

In these instances and others, the value and trustworthiness of the information builds on a dialogic process, where multiple sources of information receive careful reading and intense exchanges among the parties. Can we rely on subjective judgments? The answer is that we do, with great regularity. The key is the creation of communities within which focused discussions are the standard. Multiple reviews and second opinions are routine; when uncertain, the policy is to ask for further clarification. Above all, the user of the information must be able to "think about it;" passive acceptance of a judgment is a poor practice, even when the judge is held in high esteem. Esteem is an important element in the process; whether or not the reputation is justified, used-car salespeople are seldom viewed as trustworthy sources of information about automobiles.

Subjective judgments are valued when the judge is viewed as a professional, when the client lacks knowledge about the domain, when the judgment carries the weight of a community of experts, and when there is an aura of competence and confidence. These conditions are not commonplace for elementary and middle-grade teachers. They are isolated, they lack a professional language, and they do not feel that they are trusted (Fraatz, 1987). These descriptors apply to U.S. teachers; the situation may be different in other cultures.

Judgments and Ratings. Descriptions can be and often are the basis for numerical judgments. Journal reviewers fill out rating scales, physicians estimate the success of a treatment, travel guides and wine books grant "stars," Olympic judges of diving and skating hold up number cards, and *Consumers Union* offers a plethora of ratings. The numbers allow analyses not possible from the descriptions. In the Olympics, some events are inherently numerical; the person with the shortest time in the 100-meter dash or the longest throw in the javelin toss wins even if the commentator finds the style less than elegant. Other events—diving, gymnastics, ice skating—are assessed by qualitative appraisals of performance, assessments that lead to quantitative ratings. Consistency is a matter of immediate public record. When the judges raise their cards, the audience sees immediately the extent of agreement, and can appraise the meaning of disagreement ("It looks like Country X favors its athletes and dings those from Country Y"). The point is that human beings can perform complex assessment tasks with sufficient consistency and credibility to serve for significant decisions. Their numerical judgments are treated as "real numbers;" they are used to rank order candidates (and judges), they are averaged, they are used to calculate consistency, and so on.

The conditions for trustworthy assessments based on teacher judgments, whether qualitative or quantitative, are fairly well established, the most convincing examples springing from the British experiences (e.g., Black, 1994; Daugherty, 1995; Harlen, 1994; Mitchell, 1992), but also from American experiences with large-scale assessments of complex performances (e.g., Gearhart, Herman, Novak, Wolf, & Abdi, 1994; Koretz, Stecher, Klein, & McCaffrey, 1994). Teacher organizations in the United States, in collaboration with the National Council on Measurement in Education, have prepared standards for teacher assessment of students (AFT, NCME, NEA, 1990), but these are largely exhortations to handle problems that challenge current thought and practice in the area (e.g., "Teachers should be skilled in using assessment results when making decisions about individual students, planning teaching, developing curriculum, and school improvement" p. 32).

The starting point for trustworthy judgments is a well-defined construct: for a diving judge, the schema for an ideal diving performance; for an elementary teacher of children's literature, the schema for a student's analysis of the narrative genre (e.g., Wolf, & Gearhart, 1994). The construct is explicit for performers and judges, and for the audience as well. Next comes the creation of a task environment for performance. The situation often combines standardized and nonstandardized elements, the required and the free-form. But all participants know what counts and what does not, what can be done and what cannot.

Finally, the judges operate as individuals within a community. They are expected to justify their ratings, and may be dismissed (or disregarded) if they cannot sustain standards of consistency and explanation. The key is an ongoing dialogue among members of the entire community, but especially among the judges, to clarify and explicate the construct and the process. Again, the British experience with *moderation* demonstrates the practicality of this idea within the context of the teaching profession (Harlen, 1994; also LeMahieu, Gitomer, & Eresh, 1995; Mitchell, 1992, p. 161ff.). Unfortunately, it appears that these conditions are seldom achieved in the lives of American teachers, for whom assessment is too often one more task piled on top of an impossible collection of mandates and responsibilities, a task for which they receive little professional preparation (for troubling examples, see Cizek, Rachor, & Fitzgerald, in press; Gearhart, 1994; Koretz et al., 1994; Moss et al., 1992; Stiggins, & Conklin, 1992; Valencia, Hiebert, & Afflerbach, 1994, especially the review by Wolf, 1994).

The Assessment of Literacy. Wines, cars, diving performance—these examples from the previous section pose a variety of challenges to judgment, but nothing compared to the assessment of literacy as defined in this section. The task can be trivialized—keep a record of pronunciation mistakes during oral reading, measure reading speed, count the number of details recalled from a passage. A behavioral curriculum, much like a 100-meter dash, may proceed by counting, "How many objectives has the student completed this month?" Gauging a student's growth in the use of language to think and communicate, however, requires an analysis by the teacher that is inherently descriptive, qualitative, and narrative in character. A social-cognitive curriculum looks at both outcome and process, at individual work and team activities, at surface performance and deeper reasoning, at activities completed and at tasks attempted. None of these is inherently countable; at least what counts is generally not what can be counted. Student movement through a developmental curriculum is generally more narrative than linear: flashbacks, digressions, asides. The teacher is in a position to tell the story, to explore motivation, to recount the episodes, to identify critical events. These are idealizations, to be sure, and a barrier to reform of classroom assessment is the mind-set established by years of experience with a linear behavioral literacy curriculum. Tittle (1994) describes the importance for the teacher of establishing an epistemology that links *substance* (curriculum, teaching and learning, development and change), *assessment methodology* (task format, conditions, collection and analysis of evidence), and *interpretation* (critical evaluation, reporting methods). These facets open the way for developing a "psychology of the assessor," but the job remains to be done.

A missing element in most literacy assessments is the link between student performance and curriculum benchmarks. Ideally, the teacher traces not a random or indeterminate "story," but rather the student's movement along the strands of the literacy curriculum. Qualitative assessments allow the teacher to adapt instruction for the class as a whole and for individual students, not through "individualization" but by shaping the environment for the entire "learning community." The story, when well told, provides feedback to students and to parents, not as a "Johnny is doing well, but has a problem here," but as a travelogue—"Johnny started here in September, here is where he is in March and how he got there, and here is where he needs to be in June and how we plan the rest of the trip" (e.g., Klimenkoff, & LaPick, 1996). It means reflecting on progress and successes, but also on challenges and failures. Mitchell (1992) observes that "[students saw] the portfolio as an opportunity to display success, [but] were reluctant to understand it as a record of development…, which necessarily includes failure, a truth difficult for students to accept." Other observers have noted teachers' "success orientation," the inclination to celebrate victories and ignore defeats (Cizek et al., in press). Complete stories can be told only against the framework of a clearly explicated developmental curriculum path, one where goals and standards are clearly explicated. As Gipps (1994) notes, "teachers cannot assess well a subject matter that they do not understand…, [They] need to understand the constructs they are assessing" (pp. 160, 161, also p. 138ff.).

Two contrasts serve as important themes for these stories: *profiles* versus *scores,* and *progress* versus *accomplishment.* As noted earlier, testing typically generates total scores, indicators of overall performance that summarize presumably complex performances. Even when test subscores are available, these are typically highly correlated, making it pointless to report subscore information (Davis, 1968; Thorndike, 1973). The implication seems to be that literacy is a unitary or "whole" construct.

An alternative interpretation starts with the notion of "unclean tests," where situational demands unrelated to the construct influence overall performance. The "real test bias" (Hill, 1994; Mehrens, 1992), according to this interpretation, may reflect the impact on the student of a high-pressure, time-bound, decontextualized, and depersonalized situation lacking purpose, guidance, and audience. As Wiggins (1993) puts it, "Answer *my* question, *my* way. You have one try…, you cannot rethink your answer…, you get no feedback" (p. 130). Under these conditions, which challenge some students more than others, subtests are correlated because of common (and irrelevant) demands that have nothing to do with what is being assessed .

Haertel and Wiley (in press) address the same issue when they discuss the *intents* versus the *ancillaries* of a test design; a clean test (Calfee, & Drum, 1979; Calfee, & Venezky, 1969) is one in which the ancillary demands are minimized. The classroom teacher is uniquely positioned for this strategy—given that he or she has a clear idea of the strands that comprise the literacy curriculum. Numerous studies suggest that teachers in the elementary grades judge student's reading by oral reading fluency (Allington, 1989), and that writing depends on mechanical features like spelling and grammatical conventions (Freedman, 1982). Oral language facility—listening comprehension and "story-telling" ability—tends to be disregarded, leading again to a one-dimensional characterization of student achievement.

If students' strengths and weaknesses are to stand out in an assessment, the first requirement is that a few distinctive performance strands must be identified; the second requirement is that ancillary requirements be minimized. The reason for emphasizing profiles as a complement to or replacement for an overall indicator is that instructional decision making, as well as feedback to students and parents, is better guided by specific patterns. A few assessment systems incorporate this strategy (e.g., Barrs, Ellis, Hester, & Thomas, 1988; Barr, & Hallam, *California Learning, Record;* Barrs, Ellis, Hester, & Thomas, *The Primary Language Record;* Darling-Hammond, & Godwin, 1993), but most classroom-based systems tend to merge performance into a holistic summary (Goodman, Goodman, & Hood, 1989; Harp, 1991).

Informative profiles are more likely to emerge from classroom assessment because the teacher can adapt the conditions of assessment to eliminate irrelevant barriers, but patterns are likely to appear only when the teacher has a clear conception of the distinctive features of each strand, and if the number of distinctive strands is relatively small—4 to 8 elements. The multitude of objectives typical of behavioral programs quickly exceeds the teacher's grasp. Research and practice on profiles in the literacy field is modest at best. The volume by Cronbach and Gleser (1965) is the classic work, but has seen little extension into practice. A few studies have shown that trustworthy profiles do exist for writing (cf. Freedman, 1983 and Roid, 1994, for example). In print literacy, teachers know about the third grader with rich oral language but impoverished decoding and spelling skills. In graphic literacy, I recall vividly a demonstration lesson—an analysis of *Puss in boots*—during which a 4th-grade boy at a front desk just to my left showed little interest in the story. He participated not at all, but proceeded to sketch all of the major characters as the class discussion proceeded. My informal assessment led me to conclude that he understood the story, and had the talent to express his understanding, but not in the ways that are commonly accepted in the classroom.

The second distinction contrasts accomplishment and progress. In textbook approaches to literacy, these two come down to the same thing. Tests certify that a student has "mastered" behavioral objectives by passing 80% of the items on a prescribed test; the student may then move ahead to the next section of the textbook. This strategy rests on two assumptions. One is that learning is well represented by the progression of objectives. The other is that expertise is appropriately assessed by the tests and the 80% standard. Both of these assumptions are inadequate when literacy is defined by capability in using language to think and to communicate. The progression is not a matter of detailed objectives, nor is mastery akin to collecting scout badges.

Wiggins (1993, Chap. 2) distinguishes between growth—movement over time—and accomplishment, which he describes as "progress toward a goal." Cizek (in press) offers a similar contrast between learning and achievement. Mislevy (1995) lays out a cogent argument about the distinctions between *trait / behavioral* and *cognitive / developmental* assessment; his language is demanding, but the analysis of the issues is penetrating. Johnny's story, stated earlier, illustrates the idea. Gauged against a developmental curriculum, the teacher's assessment may show that a fourth grader's expository compositions have moved from a level expected in 2nd-grade to a 3rd-grade level. The student has achieved a year's growth. On the other hand, the student has yet to accomplish the level expected of a fourth grader, and so has work ahead. Another facet of both growth and accomplishment is the quality of the performance; a composition may exhibit features of 3rd-grade work, but be rather shoddy. Greene (1991) describes the "process of making value judgments in accord with norms or principles or conceptions of the good made visible" (p. 13). The progression is not always linear. The student masters a strategy that applies to one set of tasks, and

then moves to a different level of challenge. "Learning is not always a matter of doing better" (Masters, & Mislevy, 1993); "Learners become more competent not simply by acquiring more facts and skills, but by reconfiguring their knowledge, by 'chunking' information to reduce memory loads, and by developing strategies and models that help them discern when and how facts are important" (Mislevy et al., 1991, p. 10).

Wiggins (1993, p. 171ff.) describes how the relative weighting of growth and accomplishment changes over the grades. In the early years of schooling, growth is more important, but as the student approaches certain critical mileposts (e.g., graduation from elementary and middle school, and perhaps the transition from third to fourth grade), then the level and quality of accomplishment become critical considerations. The teacher is in a position to establish the conditions of assessment: to set the same demanding tasks for all students, but offer more scaffolding for some students, to gauge the level of accomplishment relative to the difficulty of the task, to document the opportunity for students to learn and to perform.

At some point *standards* of achievement enter the discussion (Myers, 1994). While the politics of educational standards are relative newcomers, the pragmatics have been around for a long time. The most basic standard ranks candidates relative to one another on more or less explicit criteria. In the Olympics, only one person can receive a gold medal. In college admissions, only a fixed number of applicants can be admitted to top-ranked universities. The standard is relative to the cohort. Recent discussions—ranging from the 1970's minimum competency tests to the 1990's national standards—attempt to establish absolute standards. The assignment of grades, largely ignored in current discussions, offers an historical perspective on many of these issues. In surveys of grading practices (Brookhart, 1994), for instance, teachers express the tensions they confront in combining their impressions of developmental progress, attainment of expected level of performance, quality of the final product, effort and potential. The teacher's role vacillates between support and criticism; "Where teacher assessment is used for summative purposes then the relation between teacher and pupil can become strained, the teacher being seen as judge rather than facilitator" (Mitchell, 1992, p. 127).

Assessment strategies sensitive to these tensions clearly require informed professional judgment. The relevant evidence is difficult to standardize, the artifacts are complex, information is based not only on products but on observations over time about the process, and on discourse about the process. The teacher's role in this setting resembles that of an applied researcher (Cizek, in press; Hiebert, & Calfee, 1992; Sheingold, Heller, & Paulunknis, 1995), calling for conceptualization of the assessment question, the design of an assessment procedure, collection and analysis of data, interpretation and reporting, and a decision about how to proceed next. The assessment task must balance the collective and the individual; the teacher's observations of the class as a whole is often the soundest basis for major decisions, with attention to individuals for fine-tuning. A "testing" strategy typically focuses on individuals and downplays observations.

In practice, teachers often collect time-consuming test data that are uninformative and unused. For the entering kindergartner, as an example, knowledge of the alphabet is a trustworthy indicator of overall experience with print. The child who can name six letters in the middle of the alphabet is likely to come from a different background than the student who cannot name the letters. The teacher can administer lengthy batteries of other tests, but the additional information is likely to be negligible; far better to spend time investigating children's interests, styles, behavioral characteristics, and social preferences. Assessment that is algorithmic and routine is seldom informative; assessment that is incidental and unguided by clear purposes and questions is equally useless.

Human beings are clearly capable of complex judgments. Such judgments, whether qualitative or quantitative, require ongoing interaction within a professional community. They are most likely to be informative when guided by a clearly articulated purpose, audience, method, and plans for collection, analysis, interpretation, and reporting. For local purposes, qualitative-narrative accounts of student achievement are adequate. But other purposes call for numerical judgments. As Mitchell (1992) notes: "Judging is a teacher's professional responsibility. Whether this essay is a 3 or a 4, whether this answer has enough in it to make it acceptable or not, are questions demanding judgment informed by expertise, understanding of the reasons for the assessment, and knowledge of the use that will be made of the results. Numbers constitute the external sign that a judgment has been made according to a value system.... Purists will object that those who use educational evaluation should learn to read narrative assessments, but that does not work, for both practical and psychological reasons" (p. 137). It is to numbers that I turn next.

The Measurement of Achievement

Measurement is not a comfortable topic for elementary teachers, nor for those in high school English and Language arts. They are uneasy with mathematics in general, and they generally dislike the task of ranking and grading students. "Imagine using the word 'assess'... to describe children's growth and needs! If I interpret the definition correctly, it means deciding the value of things numerically... I shudder at these terms...," this from Suzanne Glazer (1994) as president of the International Reading Association. The reaction is understandable, although distressing. Mathematics instruction, despite recent developments, is ineffective for many students, including those who become teachers.

Why Measure Achievement? Advocates of qualitative assessment pose this question quite earnestly, and it deserves a serious response. One answer is that clients of the public schools deserve feedback, both relative ("How are we doing compared with others?") and absolute ("How are we doing compared with a preestablished standard of performance?"). At the local level, parents often want to know how their students are doing in general (understandable) and in comparison with other students (less understandable). On occasion, students also wonder about how they are coming along.

The typical response to these needs is to issue grades, with all of the tensions that this entails (Brookhart, 1994).

Measured achievement also serves for accountability. We live in a world where schools receive high-stakes grades (real estate agencies use the information for clients), where districts and even states are judged by the numbers, where the entire public school system is portrayed as succeeding or failing its responsibilities based on shifts of a few points on scales understood by a handful of exotic experts. One answer to "Why measure," therefore, is the pressure from various audiences for information about how well the schools are educating our children. If good indicators are not available, then bad ones will fill the gap. The information has to be simple, and simple is not easy. Some educators recommend that we rely on anecdotes (e.g., Gipps, 1994, p. 15ff.; Moss et al., 1992; Wixon et al., 1994), and argue against aggregate data. Unfortunately, stories can easily misrepresent typicality. So can statistics, to be sure, but our techniques for identifying lies in statistics are more advanced than those for challenging tall tales.

A second reason for measuring achievement is that the information has the potential to clearly document the growth and accomplishment of students both individually and collectively. Teachers frequently report that portfolio assessment helps them "see" student growth (Calfee, & Perfumo, 1996), and yet they are hard put to articulate what they mean by these statements. Growing children mark their heights monthly on the door frame; we can see that they are growing, but the marks change perceptions into indicators that open the way for greater precision and clearer communication. The argument is not that perceptions are better than ratings, nor that measures of growth are better than narratives of achievement. As noted earlier, the two are different in character and serve different purposes.

How Does Measurement Work? Measurement is assignment of numbers to objects or events according to a rule or operation—this adage from philosophy of science springs from the physical and natural sciences. A growing youngster compares the most recent mark and "counts" another inch of growth during the past 3 months; he is now only two inches shorter than his big sister. A variety of sophisticated mathematical operations spring forth within this simple context, operations that we take for granted outside of math classes.

Educational and psychological measurements pose more of a challenge than gauging height. *Educational measurement,* typically identified with psychometrics, has focused by and large on total test scores, where measurement begins by counting the number of correct answers on a norm- or criterion-referenced multiple-choice test (Linn, 1994). Complications arise in deciding what to measure and what it means, questions for the final section of this chapter. But testing is objective; computers can count the scores with little or no human intervention. *Psychological measurement,* in contrast, addresses the inherently subjective activity that takes place when human beings assign numbers to objects or events (Aftanas, 1988, 1994; Luce, & Krumhansl, 1988; Narens, & Luce, 1986). The earlier examples from Olympic events illustrate the concept, but it is far more widespread than may be appreciated. Poker players estimate the odds. Drivers guess whether to pass another car on a two-lane road. These are relatively simple situations, to be sure, and other judgments are more complex (Anderson, 1991; Tversky, & Fox, 1995; Tversky, & Kahneman, 1982). For instance, college admissions officers routinely combine complex portrayals to rank order applicants, and prospective students do the same in deciding which college to attend.

Although much is known about how human beings measure and are measured, these two fields are separated by a deep chasm, which seems not to have narrowed in recent years (Cronbach, 1975; Shepard, 1992). I assume that most readers are already familiar with the psychometric tradition, and so this section will focus on psychological measurement, which may prove critical for understanding the assessment of student growth and achievement. Current discussions of teacher ratings have been dominated by psychometrics, and the psychology of the task has not yet been explored (Tittle, 1994; also Messick, 1984).

This section is organized around four issues: (a) categories of psychological measurement, (b) psychological strategies for measurement, (c) context effects in measurement, and (d) applications of psychological measurement to assessments of student performance. Stevens (1951) is the classical reference for the first topic. He studied the esoteric field of psychophysics, research by 19th-century German and American psychologists on sensory and perceptual systems. Why does one light seem twice as bright as another? Why is one smell twice as intense as another? Stevens described four *measurement categories.* Numbers can be assigned *nominally,* like those on the backs of football players, on Social Security cards, or on student records. *Ordinal* measurement is typified by street addresses or "next in line" slips; the distance between objects and events is not reflected in the numbers, nor is your "wait time." In *interval* measurement, like temperature readings or the distances between houses in a tract, equal distances are reflected in equal numeric intervals. Stevens' fourth category was *ratio* measurement, where "0" actually means zero; we depend on this scale when we measure fence boards or children's heights—no fair standing on a stool. Beyond Stevens is the *relative* scale, typically associated with the dreaded logarithm. If a cat gains a pound, the owner says "She's getting fat!"; if a horse gains a pound, the owner disregards it—increments are judged relative to the magnitude of the object (Calfee, 1975). Each of these five scales has specifiable properties and attributes. For instance, it does not make sense to average the numbers on the backs of football players. Nor do bricklayers, watchmakers, and astronomers use the same measurement systems in dealing with distance and weight.

Stevens' major achievement was to show that human beings could operate with remarkable fidelity in all of these categories, given appropriate preparation. He showed that psychological measurement depended on the conditions of assessment. Presented a set of objects to arrange on a scale from large to small, a person's judgments depended on the scale and the collection. Was the scale open or closed; was the question "large-small" or "larger-smaller?" Were the endpoints of the scale clearly defined? Were the objects all clustered within a narrow range or spread more broadly? Was the distribution bell-shaped or skewed in one direction or another? Were the objects familiar or unusual?

Other researchers have investigated *strategies for judgments* of more complex objects and ratings. In these situations, subjective assessments of multidimensional objects or events are transformed into quantitative ratings. Odors vary in intensity, but also in pleasantness or disagreeability. Compositions vary in technical quality, but also in creativity or mundaneness. Research on psychological measurement has provided insight into these issues. For instance, Anderson's (1991) studies of impression formation illuminate the teacher's task in judging student achievements, especially the rendering of a summative judgment. Anderson's basic proposition is that human beings, confronted by a complex judgment, identify a small number of relevant dimensions, make independent judgments on each of these, and then "average" the judgments. The theory seems overly simple, but hundreds of studies offer support for the basic model (in education, cf. Freedman, 1993; Rotzel, 1974, for examples in writing and social studies).

The failures of the model are especially informative; they are generally situations when one particular feature of a situation is so compelling that it outweighs all others—a contextual effect. Most studies in this area have investigated intuitive assessments in laboratory settings and do not answer the question of how a trained judge might perform given clearly defined features and priorities. As in the instance of the psychometrist's total score, complications arise when the informant is being asked to give an overall impression based on competing subimpressions. Should the overall impression be an average of the components, a choice of the "best or worse," or a compensation (facet A is pretty bad, but B and C make up for it). A student portfolio contains five pieces, all of which are rough-drafts with poor spelling and grammar, miserable handwriting, one of which is simply too bad to believe, three of moderate quality as compositions, and then a personal narrative that is deep and compelling. How is the teacher to render an overall impression of this collection? Perhaps the best answer is that this is the wrong poor question, especially when the judgment is to be applied to a work (the student) in progress.

People's judgments are affected by *context.* Every measuring instrument is influenced by context, but the effects are often negligible. A yardstick, especially if it is made of aluminum, changes length with variations in temperature. Measurements of length in the Sahara and the Antarctic will differ slightly. People are also sensitive to particularities: the bombings of Dresden, Sarajevo, and the Oklahoma Federal building are more than memories of total tonnage and lives lost, more than the sum of the dreadful parts. Judgments depend on the situation (Parducci, 1995): some sailing days are better than others, and some tax returns are worse than others; billionaires have "bad hair days," and homeless children have moments of joy. These examples apply to teacher judgments of student achievement. Consider the assignment of grades, especially "grading on the curve." Assessment advocates tend to eschew grading. As a practical matter, teachers are often required to give grades, in which case, whatever the evidence and the constraints (e.g., grading on the curve), the judgments will reflect the context. Teachers accustomed to higher levels of performance will center their judgment scale at a higher point than teachers whose students typically perform at lower levels. Teachers whose experience encompasses a broad spectrum of student achievements will establish a different range than those with more limited experience. Memory records experience, and assessment depends on experience. The benefit of professional moderation is that it transcends the individual.

How do these ideas apply to the *measurement* of student achievement? To the best of my knowledge, no effort has been made to link the psychology of measurement to the pragmatics of teacher judgments of student achievement. Instead, technical discussions of teacher ratings have been dominated by the psychometrics of interrater and intertask consistency, topics for the final section of the chapter. When teachers assign a number to a student performance, what are the characteristics of the measurement scale? It is presumably more than a nominal assignment. Is the difference between a "3" and a "4" the same as that between a "4 and a 5?" Does a rating of "4" mean that the performance is twice as good as a "2" rating?

Such questions focus attention on the system of rubrics and benchmarks that are typically employed in teacher judgments of student achievements. Despite the label of "authentic measurement" (Hambleton, & Murphy, 1992), most rating systems are crude efforts at measurement. They typically include four to six categories, each with a "rubric" description, and sometimes one or more benchmark examples (Calfee, & Masuda, in press). In practice, raters tend to avoid the highest and lowest categories, and so the ratings often cover only two to four categories. The resulting numbers convey little more than a general impression, so that the earlier questions about measurement quality seldom apply.

A further complication arises with holistic ratings. Student performances are usually multidimensional, and so a summary measurement requires combining information about several facets of the work sample. Consumers' Union (CU) faces a similar challenge in rating products. Automobiles are complicated, and "measuring" overall quality is not a simple task. The CU proceeds by identifying a number of dimensions (appearance, handling, gas mileage, reliability), some of which can be assessed objectively, others requiring subjective judgments. The dimensions are clearly laid out, as are the weightings. Each dimension is independently measured, and then overall (holistic) measurements are generated by combining the various facets. The entire process is laid out explicitly for the audience, who can then make their own judgments about the final ratings.

To be sure, gauging student achievement is more complex than ranking automobiles. In addition to the "work product," the teacher, especially in the early grades, must juggle quality, effort, and growth. Assessing an on-demand snapshot of student performance is difficult enough. For the classroom teacher, there is the additional task of placing the current achievement within a social temporal framework. Taylor (1994) describes the perils of approaching this task from a "bean-counter" perspective, and addresses measurement as a psychometric rather than psychological issue. Delandshere and Petrosky (1994) inquire about the "measurement of complex performances," and argue against "assigning a number to a complex performance." They are undoubtedly correct when they advise against "translating complex interpretive statements into single ratings to provide data for statistical manipulation and evidence of reliability and validity." This advice, while sound, overlooks the measurement processes and possibilities—and the practical fact that student achievements (and school accomplishments) will be measured for accountability purposes. This task will either be done well or poorly; research on psychological measurement offers ways to dramatically improve current practice.

Assessing Progress and Accomplishment

Earlier, Chapter 1 distinguished between the assessment of progress (a motion picture) and accomplishment (a snapshot). Assessing progress is the greater challenge. *Development*—growth, learning, and progress—is a complex word with shades of meaning, "To expand or realize the possibilities of; to bring gradually to a fuller, greater, or better state" (American Heritage). Assessing growth in literacy as conceptualized in this volume requires informed judgment, and hence must be grounded in qualitative description. But inherent in the concept of development is the notion of measurement: "fuller, greater, or better." For many of today's educational audiences, descriptions of growth do not suffice. Narratives may be a starting point for assessment, and may serve needs of local audiences—students and parents—but demands for summative aggregation come quickly to the fore when we move beyond these groups to the policy arena. Given that a teacher or other evaluator has created a narrative of student progress, how can the story be translated by "assigning numbers to objects and events?"

How to Measure Growth? The answer to this question is a critical "missing link" in current discussions of assessment methods. Tests address this issue—inadequately, in my judgment—by normative and statistical methods. Students read better, on average, as they move through the grades; operationally, they can answer more demanding questions about more complex passages. Average scores of students at the beginning and the end of third grade become the norm for those levels of schooling, and expected growth during third grade is estimated by statistical extrapolation from these averages and associated variabilities. If a student scores at the average test levels during both at the beginning and the end of third grade, then he or she has made a year's progress. If the student is at average at the beginning but above average at the end, this represents more than a year's growth, and so on.

Stories of student achievement yield neither numbers nor averages, and so a different strategy is needed for measuring growth. The construct of a developmental curriculum offers a strategy grounded not in norms (what happens to be) but in standards (what should be). In telling the story, the teacher's task is to describe the student's progress along the route. By analogy, driving from New York to Chicago offers the traveler several choices, each with a different array of events. A northern route goes through Buffalo and Detroit, Niagara Falls and Motor City. A southern alternative crosses the Appalachians, Pittsburgh and Gary, Indiana. One can still ask "How far have we gone today?" and "How far do we have to go?" Road maps serve for measurement. In applying the metaphor to assessment of student achievement, the foundation is a clearly drawn road map—a developmental curriculum with standards and benchmarks. One strategy is represented by textbooks and scope-and-sequence charts, listing objectives to be mastered at specific grades. Much like an assembly line, the schedule specifies when each curriculum segment is to be attached.

In an alternative strategy, grade-in-school plays a role, but with significant differences. First, the criterion for grade-level mileposts rests not on statistical averages but on professional judgment, not on "what is" but "what should be." Second, standards of accomplishment are established for the *end* of the course of study "What should the fifth grader be able to do," and then these serve as goals for earlier years of schooling. A student's performance is judged not by performance relative to others in the grade cohort, but to his or her level of achievement on the curriculum map.

Developmental indicators can serve a variety of purposes. The individual student's achievement can be compared with classmates' achievements. Growth can be gauged by progress on the developmental map throughout the school year. As students approach critical mileposts in their school careers, it becomes increasingly important to attend to the distance between current achievement levels and the milepost levels. Nor does the final milepost in a series mark the end of the trail. For the traveler, attaining one goal can become a jumping-off spot for future achievements. Chicago is the gateway to the Rockies, the Sierra Nevada, and San Francisco. Reaching the final milepost does not mean completion of the journey but attainment of a standard, and an opportunity for further progress.

Providing a developmental road map places a different light on the concept of achievement standards. Some literacy programs, for instance, encourage students to compete in the number of books they read during a school year. Quantity does not ensure quality, however, and reading many books does not lead automatically to understanding and appreciation. Likewise, acceleration does not ensure depth of learning or mastery of skills.

Today's efforts to set literacy standards confuse several issues rather badly. Development, growth, progress toward accomplishment, and quality of performance are seldom separated. Rubric and benchmark systems are an amalgam of scales of excellence with a thin overlay of developmental progress (Calfee, & Masuda, in press). The primary criterion is "How good is the performance," followed by the secondary question "What is the developmental level of achievement?" This confounding leaves the assessment audience unclear about how to interpret the data. Should students be encouraged to give greater care to their present work, or should they move quickly to the next level? These tensions are heightened because the easiest targets for literacy assessment are often

surface features: for print literacy, the recounting of the literal features of a text, and for writing the conventions of vocabulary, spelling, punctuation, grammar, and handwriting. As long as purpose, audience, organization, and other deep-structure features of literacy are poorly operationalized, standards will reflect acquisition of basic skills, regardless of the rhetoric. When the dimensions of visual and communicative literacy are added to the mix, the challenge for assessment design becomes even greater, because the curriculum strands remain to be established in theory and in practice. The early sections of the handbook offer some clarity in this regard, but much work remains ahead to build a foundation for assessment.

Models of Growth. Another facet to the task of assessing development centers around the processes of learning and growth. In testing, a straight-line model of learning is either assumed (e.g., by calculating grade-level equivalents) or constructed (e.g., NAEP's standard scores). Percentile scores use a different approach; "growth" is defined as constant relative standing. The student who maintains the same rank over time is presumably learning at the same rate as his or her peers. A student who scores at the 50th percentile both at the beginning and ending third grade has made a year's progress relative to classmates. The student who starts at the 25th percentile in third grade and is still there at the end of the year has made no progress toward reaching the expected or 50th percentile.

How do individual students actually progress over time? Neither the psychometric models sketched above nor proposals by qualitative theorists have addressed this question. What should be measured? One answer appears in simple performance indicators like reading speed, number of books read, and length of a composition. Such indicators are scant images of the construct of literacy proposed in this volume.

Assuming that we can define a set of trustworthy indicators, there remains the task of assessing growth. The field of learning theory has been dormant in recent decades, but an important lesson from the 1950s and 1960s is that average trends can be misleading (Bower, & Hilgard, 1981, Chap. 12; also Rogosa, 1983). Figure 14–1 illustrates this point by contrasting patterns of individual learning with the average. The left-hand panel of Figure 14–1 compares individual and average trends for *linear* straight-line learning patterns over a three-point span. Average learning is identical in both the upper and lower plots. In the upper plot, however, rates of development are the same for every student, and the variability among individuals is slight. In the lower plot, students are similar at the beginning of the process, but variations in learning rates lead to large differences as time progresses. This "fanning," which appears in numerous achievement studies (e.g., Cole-man, 1966; Stanovich, 1986), has been labeled the Matthew effect—the rich become richer and the poor become poorer.

The right-hand panel in Figure 14–1 shows how qualitatively distinctive learning models can generate similar average learning patterns. In the upper plot, Student A accelerates early in learning and then slows down, while Student C is slow at the start and then speeds up. Only Student B progresses in

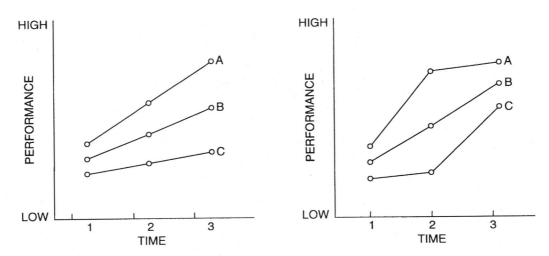

FIGURE 14–1 Examples of different learning patterns for individual students.

the steady fashion suggested by the average. The lower panel portrays a variation on the same theme. Student A "gets it" during Time 1, Student C is lost until Time 3, while Student B proceeds in two equal increments. Steady or incremental learning is typical of instructional programs that rely on practice to promote growth, while insightful "all-or-none" learning results from instruction that emphasizes strategic learning. At the level of individual students, "stage" models like those proposed by Piaget and his colleagues predict jumps in performance, while behavioral models based on reinforcement concepts are more compatible with continuous growth. Another issue, almost as long lost as learning, is transfer (Foertsch, 1995). If education is to move beyond the transmission model, then whatever is taught is valuable not for whether it is learned, but for whether it provides the student with strategies for handling new situations.

As an aside, I should note the paucity of data for exploring the acquisition of reading and writing over extended periods of time. Tierney (1991) reviews the handful of studies available, noting that most of these are case studies in the primary grades, with relatively little information about the instructional context.

Profiles of Performance. While investigations of standardized achievement generally yield single-factor descriptions of reading (e.g., Davis, 1968), qualitative assessments offer promise for distinguishing a student's relative strengths and weaknesses in various curriculum strands (Calfee, 1988; Calfee, & Masuda, in press). The earlier section on assessment introduced the concept of developmental *profiles* of student achievement. This idea is especially critical for understanding learning. The student who is enamored with baseball may excel in comprehending and composing expository passages, even though he or she is less capable at handling more literary works. Third graders with rich oral language may struggle with decoding and spelling. At any given grade level, a student's achievement level and progress toward milepost goals can be represented by a profile rather than a single score. Likewise, one can imagine that different learning mod-

els and patterns of individual differences apply to different curriculum strands. As typically taught, for example, decoding and spelling skills are likely to progress incrementally, while awareness of plot and character may occur through insightful leaps. But any discussion of profile assessment must be related to what is being taught, how it is being taught, and the goals of instruction.

Relatively little work is available on the psychometrics of achievement profiles (however, cf. Cronbach, & Gleser, 1965), perhaps because of the insensitivity of standardized tests to the "intents" of achievement. For instance, something seems awry when standardized reading and mathematics are as highly correlated as subtests within reading and mathematics. A potential advantage of a qualitative approach to assessment—narrative descriptions correlated with developmental curriculum strands—is that the intuitions frequently voiced by classroom teachers can be transformed into indicators that inform both practice and accountability. California reading test scores appeared to decline in the 1990s, leading immediately to the call for a shift from a literature-based approach in reading instruction back to an emphasis on phonics (Honig, 1996). In fact, the California scores were holistic judgments, and could be explained equally well by low skill levels, poorly designed reading instruction, changes in student demographics, or large class sizes. The availability of longitudinal and qualitative profiles might have shifted the debate from politics toward an analysis of student profiles. If California had reviewed the assessment data to distinguish between the quality of students' comprehension and composition *and* the level of basic skills in reading and writing, the State would have been in a stronger position to establish policy initiatives focused on an analysis of statewide strengths and weaknesses. Incidentally, profile analysis applies with equal force to individual students and to aggregate summaries.

But the individual student is the most important locus for action. Assessing development entails the measurement of growth. At one level, telling the story of a student's progress is a starting point, and may serve immediate needs. On the other hand, if a teacher is to make a persuasive argument about a student's growth, at least three criteria must be met. First, the "story of growth" must be translated into an explicit metric. This task is difficult under the best of circumstances, and teachers are generally neither prepared nor inclined to take on this job. The construct of a developmental curriculum offers a method for this translation with a substantial educational rationale, one that meshes well with the teacher's professional responsibilities and inclinations.

A second task centers around the concept of individual learning models. Substantial work, conceptual and practical, remains in this area. The scope-and-sequence charts of past decades are a poor match with a developmental approach toward social-cognitive learning: checklists of mastered objectives are no more adequate for this activity than appraising a painter's progress on an artwork by the amount of canvas covered with paint.

Finally, the tracking of profiles needs to be aimed toward curriculum-in-practice and overall accountability. The strengths and areas for improvement in one situation may be quite different from other situations. These judgments need to be contextualized by considerations of progress and accomplishment, of attainments and quality of performance.

Validating Teacher Assessments

The classical psychometric criteria for gauging the quality of an assessment are *reliability* and *validity*, the degree to which an assessment is consistent and means what it purports to mean. If one friend highly recommends movie X while a second pans it, then you should question the assessment process. If both friends agree that the movie is great but you find that you are horrified by the violence, you realize that you should have rephrased your question.

Note that the preceding summary of these two constructs did not use numbers, neither for the assessment nor for the appraisal of reliability and validity. Conventional psychometrics (e.g., Linn, 1989; Linn, 1994) typically begins with measurement: how reliable and valid are the *scores* for Text X? Reliability is measurable in this tradition; the correlation between the scores for two forms of the test, one index of reliability, yields a number that quantifies consistency and provides an index of the stability of individual scores. The most commonly employed indices of validity, *concurrent* and *predictive*, also employ correlations of the test score with other scores to measure validity.

These traditional methods are the foundations for the science (and pragmatics) of the assessment of human aptitudes and achievements. The *Standards for Educational and Psychological Measurement* (AERA, APA, & NEA, 1985), currently under revision, will undoubtedly take a somewhat different stance toward these concepts. It is unlikely, however, that the foundations will change substantially (e.g., Linn, 1994). These concepts and associated methods have their limitations, and have been the target of criticism in recent decades, but they remain fundamentally sound. Moreover, they have undergone substantial advances in recent decades. Messick (1995) captures the essence of these changes when he writes that "the term *score* is used generically in its broad-

est sense to mean any coding or summarization of observed consistencies or performance regularities on a test, questionnaire, observation procedure, or other assessment devices such as work samples, portfolios, and realistic problem simulations. [It] subsumes qualitative as well as quantitative summaries. ... Validity assumes both a scientific and a political role that can by no means be fulfilled by a simple correlation coefficient..." (pp. 741, 742). Critics of contemporary psychometrics seldom note that current testing practice takes limited advantage of recent advances. Psychometric principles apply equally to testing and assessment (Herman et al., 1992), and some of the more interesting explorations of the fundamentals have appeared in explorations of the potential of performance-based assessment for large-scale accountability (Baker et al., 1993; Freedman, 1993; Linn, & Baker, 1996; Shepard, 1989). The bottom line is that methods exist for reliable assessment, a fact that advocates of alternative methods must face.

Reliability and Generalizability. Reliability began with the idea of gauging consistency by the correlation between alternate forms of a test, or split-half scores of the same test. A specialization of this idea—each item on a multi-item test should correlate with the subtotal of other items—is now the basis for the various coefficients used in commercial tests. When a test publisher reports a high reliability coefficient, it means that all of the items rank students in the same order. Consistency is undercut by interactions between persons and items; if different items lead to different orderings of persons, then the total score is not trustworthy. Reliability, item correlations and person–item interactions are all indices of total score consistency; if reliability is high then item correlations are large and interactions small, and vice versa.

The stability of the total score depends directly on reliability (Cronbach et al., 1995). The *standard error of measurement* is an index of stability based on reliability. If the reliability coefficient is high for a test, then the standard error will be small; this means that if the same test or a different form of the test is readministered at a later time, then the person will receive the same score within a small margin of error. Low reliabilities mean high standard errors and wide variability over different administrations. Large standard errors are especially problematic for high-stakes decisions. The student placed in a remedial program or the school chosen for statewide honor may only reflect the luck of the draw when scores are unstable. In the field of standardized multiple-choice tests, publishers have learned how to construct tests with high reliability and stability. Administrators are understandably attracted by this feature of standardized tests—they seldom have to deal with surprises. The decision to retain a student or award a school based on standardized results is likely to hold up under reassessment. To be sure, the "meaning" of the assessment may be questioned, but that is seldom a critical matter for busy administrators.

Generalizability theory (Cronbach et al., 1972; Shavelson, & Webb, 1991; also Linn, 1989), actually a method rather than a theory, offers a sophisticated extension of the basic principles of item consistency for incorporating any number of facets in a test design. Imagine an open-ended test with multiple tasks, multiple administrations over time, multiple contexts, and multiple judges. The assessment goal is to determine students' overall competence in constructing exhibitions to certify their language arts accomplishments for high school graduation. A generalizability design might include variations in genre (a personal narrative, an expository essay, and a dramatic presentation), completed at different times during the senior year, spanning a variety of tasks (written papers, oral declamations, dramatic performances), sometimes individually and sometimes as part of a team, each activity assessed by a team of three teachers against a variety of rubrics. The genius of the generalizability method is that it gauges the trustworthiness of the student's overall performance relative to each facet (and combination of facets) in the assessment design.

Suppose the aim is to assess students' language arts achievement. A generalizability design based on the earlier example might include data from 200 seniors, each of whom writes a personal narrative, composes an essay on "Advice to the junior class," and delivers a dramatic monologue of their choosing, each composition to be judged by three teachers on the dimensions of substance, style, and technical adequacy. Generalizability analysis provides indicators similar to the familiar reliability coefficient for each facet of the design. Based on research to be described below, it is likely that (a) teachers will agree on students' relative standing for each performance, but that (b) students will line up differently for the narrative, essay, and monologue. Under these conditions, it makes no sense to average the three ratings; a mid-range average could mean that a student does middling well on all three tasks, or excels in some but not others. Averaging the ratings obscures information about student strengths and weaknesses, and about areas for program improvement.

This example shows again the centrality of construct definition for assessing student achievements. A "simple" theory views literacy as a unitary entity; just as children can line up from short to tall, students can be also arranged in order from least to most literate. But suppose we ask students to line up from small to big; now at least two constructs are at work—height and weight. We can expect disagreements in the ordering depending on whether a judge gives more weight to one or the other dimension. Likewise, consider an assessment system in which third graders are asked to make a book, and the teacher assesses several facets of performance during the process: students' interest in the project, creativity in approaching the task, technical skill in revising the final product, and use of artistic elements in the work. My classroom visits suggest that students respond differently to these facets; initial interest can make a big difference, but creativity may not follow interest, and the best spellers and grammarians are not necessarily the most talented artists.

Applications of generalizability have yielded important findings in the area of performance-based assessment. For example, we know that, given adequate preparation and clear-cut criteria, teachers can render consistent judgments of complex student performances; task variation, however, leads to inconsistent ratings (Dunbar, Koretz, & Hoover,

1991; Nystrand, Cohen, & Dowling, 1993; Saner, McCaffrey, Stecher, Klein, & Bell, 1994). Different writing prompts yield different rankings of students, as do many other assignment variations. Although this result has been in the literature for a long time (Linn, 1994, remarks that "Ralph Tyler was onto the 'task' issue in 1934"), educators have yet to develop a "theory of tasks." The usual response is to view this facet as a nuisance, and to ask how many tasks must be administered in order to achieve a stable estimate of overall performance; the answer is typically four to eight tasks, an imposing demand given the time and costs of the typical performance-based exercise (Linn, & Burton, 1994).

A different strategy searches for systematic facets that might influence student performance. As suggested above, a "simple" construct may be more complex than is typically assumed. "Writing," for instance, may actually comprise separable dimensions, not all of which are equally important over tasks. At one level, it is fairly clear that students vary in their ability to handle the mechanics and the organizational requirements in composing papers. Asking judges to provide holistic scores across these dimensions is probably one source of interjudge variability. But I have a different idea in mind. Looking back at the earlier example, it seems quite possible that different talents and interests are called forth in creating a personal narrative, an expository essay, and a dramatic monologue. Moreover, different students may have experienced quite different instructional opportunities for handling these different forms. This line of reasoning need not lead to "situated anarchy," the belief that every writing experience is unique, but it does suggest that the literacy curriculum should identify a small number of distinctive strands, that instruction should cover these domains, and that assessment tasks should connect with specific subconstructs (Calfee, & Drum, 1979). This idea connects to the earlier discussion of profiles, but from a different vantage point.

The Varieties of Validity. Given some level of reliability, what about validity? Does the indicator assess what it purports to assess? Reliability and validity are typically viewed as quite distinctive, but certain statistical features of validity can be handled, in part at least, by generalizability methods. *Predictive validity* focuses on the question, to what degree does indicator A predict indicator B, where both indicators are supposed to tap the same construct? *Concurrent validity* asks, to what degree do several indicators, all presumably measuring the same construct and assessed at the same time, rank students in the same order. Time (predictive validity) and tasks and judges (concurrent validity), from the generalizability perspective, are simply design facets. If student scores are stable over one or more of these facets, then the assessment satisfies the requirements of statistical validity.

Construct validity, as noted at the beginning of the chapter, is the centerpiece of contemporary validity theory. Generalizability methods can also serve in evaluating construct validation. The formulation of a construct requires substantive thinking more than a methodological algorithm. But once a construct has reached some degree of clarity, then a generalizability design offers a way to appraise the definition. The design presumably includes facets (e.g., topics, tasks, times, contexts, judges, rubrics) that operationalize the construct. To the degree that generalizability analysis reveals substantial inconsistencies associated with one or more facets of an assessment system, the overall score is of questionable trustworthiness. One conclusion from such findings is to distrust the assessment system (e.g., Koretz et al., 1994). Another approach is to search for consistent sources of the inconsistencies.

A central tenet of construct validity is the importance of bringing multiple sources of evidence to bear (Cronbach, & Meehl, 1955); an assessment must yield consistent evidence from different methods to ensure validity of the construct. When multiple sources are included in an assessment system—for example, the tasks in the narrative-essay-drama illustration—inconsistency may arise because different constructs are being tapped by different tasks. When generalizability analysis shows that performance varies across tasks, rather than fret about unreliability, educators might better reflect on the possibility that the tasks are linked to different talents. Portrayal of literacy as a holistic and naturalistic competence flies in the face of the rhetorical tradition, which suggests instead that different genres call forth different talents and interests. As the domain of literacy expands to include other dimensions—communicative and visual facets—we can expect to see the emergence of other constructs. The student who is facile with computer graphics as a mode of expression may not excel in the creation of printed texts, and it makes little sense to "average" performance over these domains. When teachers assess performance on different constructs without distinguishing among them, disagreement is predictable. Several studies of classroom grading have revealed just such idiosyncrasies in dimensions and criteria (Gearhart, 1994; Gearhart, Herman, Baker, & Whittaker, 1992; Moss et al., 1992; Valencia et al., 1994). Turning from emphasis on "total score" toward evaluation of performance profiles may significantly enlighten our conceptions of literacy and enhance the pragmatics of assessment.

While current views of validity agree on the centrality of *construct* validity, alternative proposals have emerged in recent years. Three of these developments are particularly relevant for present purposes: validity as *interpretative,* as *consequential,* and as *hermeneutic* (Shepard, 1993). All three take as a starting point the importance of establishing construct validity. All three complement technical methods of construct validation (e.g., generalizability) with qualitative strategies for "moderating" judgments. All three attempt to embrace a broad array of assessment policies, including standardized tests along with alternative methods. Finally, all three emphasize the policy aspects of assessment.

Given these commonalities, the three perspectives cast different lenses on the nature of validity, and on appropriate techniques for validation. Messick (1989) and Cronbach (1988) have offered lucid discussions of *validity as interpretation.* At its core, the theme is that an assessment—quantitative or qualitative—is not valid until the case is successfully argued. Student A scores at the 64th percentile in reading comprehension on the Iowa Test of Basic Skills; School B falls within the "comparison band" on the Maryland writing assessment; California is next to last on the list of states for the National Assessment of Educational Progress. The validity of these *statements* depends on the meaning attributed to each, and to the strength of counterarguments against plausible alternative interpretations. Consider this set of possible meanings, each of which casts the information in a new light: Student A is in trouble, because she was at the 87th percentile last year; School B, which serves a poor neighborhood in Baltimore, is doing fine, because the comparison band predicts that students should be among the poorest writers in Maryland; California is actually in pretty good shape, given that its class size is highest in the nation.

An assessment, from the interpretive perspective, offers evidence as the starting point for a debate. The trustworthiness of the evidence must be substantiated as part of the argument, but the connection between the evidence and the interpretive claim must also be established. For instance, the teacher of Student A argues that the current score is invalid because a family tragedy occurred just before the test. The argument aims not at the technical features of the assessment instrument and process, but at the particularities of the situation. The Baltimore school board may see the school assessment as valid—even encouraging—but parents may not be satisfied with this conclusion. And California State Department of Education apologists may receive letters about the inconclusive research on the relation of class size to achievement, and asked by the legislature to come up with other explanations.

The point in these examples is that validation entails more than calculating a numerical index of consistency or correlation. Taken to the extreme, to be sure, the interpretive perspective can lead to a *reductio ad absurdum;* no assessment can ever be validated in the sense that it can withstand all counterarguments. A more sensible position proceeds in stages, much like a trial. The first challenge is the establishment of construct validity, demonstrating empirically that an assessment system captures a definable entity. The second challenge is to defend particular interpretations against competing explanations. This second task is more rhetorical than technical in character.

The debate hinges on the clarity of the construct, and it is against this backdrop that technical issues reenter the picture. Messick (1995) emphasizes two major threats to construct validity: *under-representation* and *irrelevant variance.* An assessment may be undercut because it focuses on narrow features of the construct domain; compositions are judged on surface features like spelling and punctuation, leading to the counterargument that the scores say little about more substantial features of writing competence. A comprehension test requires first graders to decode difficult and unfamiliar words; decoding is an ancillary demand that leads to variance irrelevant to the students' ability to comprehend. Probably the greatest source of irrelevant variance for interpreting measures of student achievement centers around the issue of what they have been taught. The *Standards* (AERA, APA, & NEA, 1985) require that "When a test is used to make decisions about student promotion or graduation, there should be evidence that the test covers only the specific or generalized knowledge, skills and abilities that students have had an opportunity to learn" (p. 53). Interpretation of student achievement is clouded whenever the instructional record is not part of the evidence.

Messick (1989) has also been the flag bearer for the concept of *consequential validity*. Here the argument goes beyond "What does the assessment mean?" to "What should we do—and what will happen if we do it?" The issues are particularistic, and raise matters of equity and opportunity. Of the hundreds of thousands of literacy assessments conducted yearly, most are inconsequential. Printouts of standardized test scores are forwarded to practitioners who file them in a closet; portfolios are assembled and then discarded at the year-end. Local newspapers report yearly test scores for local schools; few surprises for real estate agents, who clip the articles to show clients.

But consequences sometimes entail high-stakes decisions. A student is retained in grade; a school or district is taken over by a higher authority; an election for State Superintendent of Schools centers on trends in student achievement. Consequential validity builds on the foundations, but then poses cost-benefit questions for decision makers. Given that an indicator system possesses construct validity, and given that the interpretive argument is sound, then what courses of action are available, and what are the merits of each? Some observers (e.g., Haertel, & Wiley, in press) are concerned that defining validity to encompass a broad spectrum renders the concept virtually impossible to operationalize, and recommend a return to the essentials of construct validity and on psychometric methods for validating specific instruments or collections of instruments. These concerns have merit, and it may make sense, especially for complex constructs, to separate the issues of instrument validity, interpretive validity, and consequential validity. On the other hand, it seems important to keep consequences in view as the technical process moves along.

The *hermeneutic definition of validity* springs from the work of Moss (1994b, 1995) in the area of qualitative assessment. The term comes from the Greek, meaning "the art of interpretation," but carries connotations that go beyond the interpretive dimension discussed earlier to encompass the notion of a community of interpretation. "A hermeneutic approach to assessment involves holistic, integrative interpretations of collected performances that seek to understand the whole in light of its parts, that privilege readers who are most knowledgeable about the context in which the assessment occurs, and that ground those interpretations... in a rational debate among the community of interpreters" (1994b, p. 7).

At a practical level, Moss' work brings to mind the British tradition of *moderation* (Daugherty, 1995; Gipps, 1994, p. 75ff., 140ff.; Harlen, 1994). British teachers, especially those in the elementary grades, rely on practitioner judgments to gauge student progress. Several other countries employ similar techniques, but often to calibrate teacher judgments with external criteria. In moderation, the teaching community is responsible for defining criteria and standards through an ongoing process of discussion and debate. The aim in moderation is not to ensure that teacher judgments of complex performances toe the line with an external indicator, but

rather to engage teachers in an ongoing dialogue about the dimensions and characteristics of development and achievement.

A major barrier to hermeneutic validation in the American context is the autonomy and isolation of the individual classroom teacher. The "decoupled" character of U.S. schools has been well documented both in general and in the specific area of assessment and grading practices (Rosenholz, 1989). A second barrier is that U.S. teachers are less secure in their professional knowledge of subject matter and curriculum strategies. Several studies have documented the difficulty teachers experience in reaching agreement about portfolio assessment in local settings (e.g., Moss et al., 1992; Shepard, 1995; also Koretz et al., 1994).

Validity: Quo Vadis? An underlying theme in these discussions is the proper role of numbers and measurement for establishing the reliability and validity of teacher assessments of complex achievements. From one perspective, because we know how to define and quantify reliability, then it easily assumes priority. The counterargument holds that validity is more central than reliability, and that numerical indices of reliability are replaceable by qualitative judgments of dependability and trustworthiness (Gipps, 1994; Moss, 1994b; Wiggins, 1993). From this perspective, numbers—measurement, ratings, grades, coefficients, and so on—are not required for assessment, and may actually be inimicable with assessment policy and practice. The reply is that if student progress is to be assessed by teachers, and if these assessments are to become part of public discussions of school accountability, then numbers will almost certainly have to be part of the process. I agree with Wiggins that "schools would be instantly more accountable if we worried less about... tests and more about making the teacher's daily work public and giving the student performer a more powerful voice" (p. 264). Accomplishing this goal will probably require a balance between quantitative and qualitative indicators, between numbers and anecdotes. Teachers may be uneasy with mathematics, but they can learn to make consistent judgments even in today's complex contexts. Olympic judges do not have advanced degrees in probability theory. What is needed for the professional assessment of literacy achievement is greater clarity about the construct, more explicit rubrics and benchmarks, and improvements in the assessment process.

An important insight from this debate is the realization that validation requires more than numbers. Argumentation is essential (Cronbach, 1988; Kane, 1992), as is a research-oriented mind-set (Cizek, in press; Hiebert, & Calfee, 1992). Both competencies may actually pose greater challenges in the professional preparation of teachers than skill in handling numbers. Interestingly, most discussions of number-free validation seem inevitably to return to quantification, especially when the mandate is external and the stakes are high.

Reliability is another matter. As noted above, one opinion holds that reliability is irrelevant; if an assessment is valid, that matters most. While this proposition has been attractively framed, the counterargument seems overwhelming. If an assessment is not trustworthy, if a judgment—no matter how arrived at or how complex in nature—reflects a particular set of circumstances, tasks, and assessors, then it cannot serve as a foundation for making a decision; Moss (1994a) argues that "reliability..., consistency, quantitatively defined, among measures that are intended as *interchangeable...*, is necessary to support inferences from particular samples of work evaluated by particular readers to the broader capabilities the assessments are intended to tap" (p. 111). It is easy to attack the claim that "validity depends on reliability." Both concepts have been defined at times by operations too lean and limited. Recent developments suggest that the fundamental principles still have merit, but require a different rendering: an assessment must be trustworthy as a basis for sound interpretation. But trustworthiness can be operationalized—quantitatively—in a variety of ways. Cronbach et al. (1995) argue that, especially in domains where the stakes are high and public accountability is involved, we should make the best possible use of existing techniques to quantify trustworthiness through generalizability methods. Decisions at the classroom and school levels may not be typically considered high stakes, but are nonetheless highly consequential for individual students and teachers. A challenge for the future is the translation of contemporary insights about reliability and validity into a form that is accessible to practitioners and their clients—teachers and students, but also principals and parents—for application in the classroom and at the school level.

Connecting the Pieces

Rousseau (1762 / 1979) made it sound easy; the class-size in *Emile* was one, student and teacher were both motivated, and the critical issues (as reflected in the book's index) were not assessment and accountability, but amour propre, anger, arts, and atheism. As narrative, this description of education can be compelling, but today's teachers and students live in a different time and play on a different stage. Today's conundrum is how to capture the essential richness of Rousseau in classrooms where teachers confront thirty-plus students with other matters on their MTV minds, while policy wonks and evaluators stand on the sidelines tapping out op-ed pieces on their laptop computers about the sad state of schools. A handbook is a serious document, but one can imagine the reaction of a classroom teacher to the previous material— "Give me a break!" In this section I will attempt to draw the pieces of this complex puzzle into a focused conclusion, one that connects research with practice.

The Main Argument. The purpose of this chapter is to address a practical need and offer a conceptual framework for action. The key words are *development, literacy, qualitative,* and *assessment.* We are emerging from an era when development meant mastery of objectives, when literacy was defined as a basic skill, when "qualitative" was neither defined nor valued, and when assessment was operationalized as testing. The underlying theme in earlier times was a factory model of schooling where teachers performed as civil servants, carrying out the orders of superiors, following the instructions in teacher manuals. In tomorrow's world, the headline is the move from an industrial society to an information age. The challenge is—on the fly—to transform schools into institutions where development is a key word, literacy is a high-level competence, qualitative portrayals are valued, and professional assessments are the foundation for accountability.

The starting point is a vision of what students should be able to "do" at the end of the course of study, and an image of the paths by which they may attain this achievement. This vision, the focus of other chapters in this handbook, constitutes the *construct* upon which the rest of the argument hinges.

The second element in the argument is the essentiality of informed professional judgment about literacy. When literacy is defined as mastery of basic skills, then assessment can be mechanized. The construct of critical literacy cannot be so easily gauged. Nonetheless, if schooling is to support the development of genuinely literate students, then professional preparation must ensure the internalization of the basic construct, along with methods of applied research that serve as the foundation for assessment in place of routine administration of standardized tests (Darling-Hammond, & Godwin, 1993; for specific recommendations about how teachers might conceptualize assessment, see Winograd, 1994). Part of the job in the United States is to construct a foundation for professional judgment in a policy context that asks for reform and improvement at the same time that demands on schools are increasing and resources are decreasing. Assessment practices and policies are important policy levers, and very public events for public schools. The result is that efforts at innovative assessment (e.g., in California, Kentucky, and Vermont) quickly attract attention. Special interest groups attack assessments for their own purposes, and technical panels challenge the adequacy of admittedly untested innovations. The resulting whiplash has understandable consequences; innovative programs are scuttled, and practitioners retreat to traditional ways.

The next two parts of the argument are tougher to expound. First is the tension between quantitative and qualitative assessment, which is palpable in contemporary discussions. If teachers are to gauge student achievement in ways that engage the public—students, parents, administrators, and the community—then measurement comes to the fore. A "gauge" is a "standard or scale of measurement, an instrument for measuring or testing." Teachers face severe tensions when asked to gauge progress, level of accomplishment, and quality of performance (Gipps, 1994, p. 127). As noted earlier, they operate from a "success orientation;" their primary role is to support student learning, and they are uncomfortable with mixed messages—"You're doing better, but not good enough." They do not like to give low grades. If forced to do so, they will, but they are seldom required to justify their judgments.

Then there is the question of what it means to assess. Large-scale testing programs, in contrast to grades, must meet technical standards of reliability and validity. Until recently, these requirements were defined by psychometricians; practically speaking, test publishers produced standardized tests that met administrative requirements even if teachers found the instruments somewhat mysterious and often irrelevant. Now teachers are invited or mandated to assess student achievements in complex domains for high-stakes decisions, and are challenged as individuals to meet psychometric criteria of reliability and validity. One response to this development is to ensure that teachers know more about these criteria (Stiggins, 1994). Another response is to reject the criteria. Neither response seems on target.

This chapter suggests that the key issues are *what* to assess and *how* to assess it. The touchstone for *what* is a coherent explication of a developmental literacy curriculum—what should students learn to become fully literate? The touchstone for *how* centers around the teacher's role as an applied researcher—not a transmitter of the canon, but a student of students.

Ancillary Issues. Several background matters remain unsettled at both conceptual and practical levels. First, techniques for the assessment of profiles and growth patterns of individual students are critical if teacher-based assessment is to go beyond narrative portrayal to a form adequate for public accountability. Unfortunately, the psychometrics of profile and growth models remain in a primitive state. Norm-referenced indices are routinely used to measure growth by standardized tests, but both grade-level and standardized scores have been subjected to serious criticism—this for the simple domain of standardized tests. Profile assessment remains largely an unexplored territory.

Another set of questions centers around the validity of less-than-fully-standardized student performances (Calfee, & Kapinus, in preparation). Consider the student writing portfolios now serving for assessment in many places. What should go into the portfolio? How much support should student receive in preparing and selecting entries for a portfolio? Should students be allowed to collaborate with one another in preparing entries? Should parents be allowed to help their children with portfolios? Should word processors and other technologies be allowed, and if so to what effect? (Powers, 1994). For assessors, how should they deal with portfolios that vary widely in the contents and the evidence of support? The tension is clear-cut. The argument can be made that decontextualized performance is invalid because it does not reflect a student's potential achievement. The complementary question is posed with equal clarity: "Whose work is it?" When students cooperate in completing an assignment, a student's achievement reflects not only his or her present capacity, but also the contribution of the group (Webb, 1993, 1995). Gearhart and Herman (1995), and Webb (1995) have laid out with extraordinary clarity the range of issues falling into this category. Data from portfolios and performance-based tasks are complex packages. How should the assessor weight the various contributions? Throw out the lowest score? Average everything? Make a holistic judgment? We are in the early stages of working out rationales and frameworks.

Finally comes the issue of equity (Garcia, & Pearson, 1994; Howe, 1994; Nettles, & Nettles, 1995). Students from homes that support the work of the school tend to do better on virtually any kind of assessment than children from less supportive backgrounds. Some assessment advocates suggest that students from at-risk backgrounds will have a better chance to reveal their potential through authentic performances, but the scant evidence on this point points in the opposite direction (Badger, 1995; Darling-Hammond, 1994). Schools and teachers differ in the quantity and quality of instruction, in the opportunity to learn and the opportunity to perform. Assessments, unlike tests, can document opportunity to learn, but educators have discussed this potential only in passing, the practical implementation of the idea remains to be worked out, and legislative bodies have explicitly rejected the policy. As noted earlier, opportunity to learn is a standard for assessment, and at least one study suggests that it matters (LeMahieu et al., 1995). Opportunity to perform is another matter. Opponents rightly criticize the unfairness of decontextualized conditions typical in most testing. These criticisms do not guarantee that authentic assessment is any fairer.

One of the original virtues attributed to standardized tests was a degree of objectivity that eliminated teacher bias. This virtue remains the object of considerable debate, to be sure, but largely missing from the discussion of alternative strategies for assessing student achievements is the possibility that subjective judgments will be biased. I have not located any article that addresses bias in teacher-based assessment.

A Bottom Line. Bridging the gap between classroom-level assessment and externally-mandated testing remains a fundamental tension in American schools. The annual PDK-Gallup polls (Elam, Rose, & Gallup, 1993) have shown for decades that parents trust their local schools (and presumably local teachers), but that this trust declines precipitously when citizens judge schools outside of their neighborhoods. The external accountability movement that emerged with *A Nation at Risk* now takes shape as a national testing program, an idea could scarcely have been envisaged at mid-century. The fact is that, since the emergence of standardized tests and basal textbooks after World War II, we have had a national curriculum. The future of National Standards program is unpredictable at present, but if it becomes a reality, classroom teachers are likely to see it as another mandate rather than a professional opportunity. If so, the program is likely to undercut the aspirations described in this chapter. Bryk and Hermanson (1993) distinguish between assessment indicators that monitor and that enlighten: "The ultimate test of an indicator system is not whether we are better informed but whether we act more prudently" (p. 476).

But there is reason for some optimism. This handbook envisions a literacy that moves beyond print to encompass the emerging opportunities of new technologies that enhance communication across a broad range of media. The representation of speech by print amplified the potential of human minds both individually and collectively. A quarter-century ago, *Small Talk* emerged at the Xerox Research Park as the prototype for today's Macintosh and Windows environments. Small Talk was supported by some of the most powerful computing resources available at the time.

Today, you can purchase a personal computer orders of magnitude more powerful for the price of a 1970 Volkswagen bug. The information highway has redefined communication. The fundamental question seems clear: what literacy curriculum should we provide our children to ensure that they move into the next century prepared to deal with these opportunities, and the barriers to achieving this goal? Assessment of student progress and accomplishments in this curriculum must be grounded in the answer to this question.

References

Aftanas, M. S. (1988). Theories, models, and standard systems of measurement. *Applied Psychological Measurement, 12,* 325–338.

Aftanas, M. S. (1994). On revitalizing the measurement curriculum. *American Psychologist, 47,* 889–890.

Allen, R. V., & Allen, C. (1982). *Language experience activities* (2nd ed.). Boston: Houghton Mifflin.

Allington, R. L. (1989). School response to reading failure: Chapter 1 and special education students in grades 2, 4, and 8. *Elementary School Journal, 89,* 529–542.

American Educational Research Association, American Psychological Association, & National Education Association. (1985). *Standards for educational and psychological testing.* Washington, DC: Author.

American Federation of Teachers, National Council on Measurement in Education, & National Education Association. (1990). Standards for teacher competence in educational assessment of students. *Educational Measurement: Issues and Practice, 9*(4), 30–32.

Anderson, N. H. (Ed.) (1991). *Contributions to information integration theory* (Vols. 1, 2). Hillsdale, NJ: Erlbaum.

Badger, E. (1995). The effect of expectations on achieving equity in state-wide testing: Lessons from Massachusetts. In M. T. Nettles & A. L. Nettles (Eds.), *Equity and excellence in educational testing and assessment* (pp. 289–308). Boston: Kluwer.

Baker, E. L., O'Neil, H. F., Jr., & Linn, R. L. (1993). Policy and validity prospects for performance-based assessment. *American Psychologist, 48,* 1210–1218.

Barr, M. A., & Hallam, P. J. (1996). Teacher parity in assessment with the California Learning Record. In R. C. Calfee & P. Perfumo (Eds.), *Writing Portfolios: Policy and practice.* Hillsdale, NJ: Erlbaum.

Barr, R. (1984). Beginning reading instruction from debate to reformation. In P. D. Pearson, *Handbook of reading research* (pp. 545–581). New York: Longman.

Barr, R., Kamil, M. L., Mosenthal, P. B., & Pearson, P. D. (Eds.). (1991). *Handbook of reading research* (Vol. 2). New York: Longman.

Barrs, M., Ellis, S., Hester, H., & Thomas, A. (1988). *The primary language record.* London: ILEA/Centre for Language in Primary Education.

Belanoff, P., & Dickson, M. (Eds.). (1991). *Portfolios: Process and product.* Portsmouth, NH: Boynton / Cook.

Berliner, D. A., & Calfee, R. C. (Eds.). (in press). *Handbook of educational psychology.* New York: Macmillan.

Black, P. J. (1994). Performance assessment and accountability: The experience in England and Wales. *Education Evaluation and Policy Analysis, 16,* 191–203.

Bloom, B. S., Hastings, J. T., & Madaus, G. F. (1971). *Handbook of formative and summative evaluation of student learning.* New York: McGraw-Hill.

Bloom, B. S., Madaus, G. F., & Hastings, J. T. (1981). *Evaluation to improve learning.* New York: McGraw-Hill.

Bower, G. H., & Hilgard, E. R. (1981). *Theories of learning,* (5th ed.). Englewood Cliffs, NJ: Prentice-Hall.

Bromley, K. D. (1991). *Webbing with literature.* Boston: Allyn & Bacon.

Brookhart, S. M. (1994). Teachers' grading: Practice and theory. *Applied Measurement in Education, 7,* 279–301.

Brown. R. G. (1991). *Schools of thought.* San Francisco: Jossey-Bass.

Bryk, A. S., & Hermanson, K. M. (1993). Educational indicator systems: Observations on their structure, interpretation, and use. *Review of Educational Research, 19,* 451–484.

Calfee, R. C. (1975). *Human experimental psychology.* New York: Holt, Rinehart and Winston.

Calfee, R. C. (1988). *Indicators of literacy: A monograph for the Center for Policy Research in Education.* Santa Monica, CA: Rand.

Calfee, R. C. (1993). Assessment, testing, measurement: What's the difference? *Educational Assessment, 1,* 1–7

Calfee, R. C. (1994). Critical literacy: Reading and writing for a new millennium. In N. J. Ellsworth, C. N. Hedley, & A. N. Baratta (Eds.), *Literacy: A redefinition* (pp. 19–38). Hillsdale, NJ: Erlbaum.

Calfee, R. C., & Drum, P. (1979). How the researcher can help the reading teacher with classroom assessment. In L. B. Resnick & P. A. Weaver (Eds.), *Theory and practice of early reading* (pp. 173–205). Hillsdale, NJ: Erlbaum.

Calfee, R. C., & Drum., P. A. (1986). Research on teaching reading. In M. C. Wittrock (Ed.), *Handbook of research on teaching* (3rd ed., pp. 804–849). New York: Macmillan.

Calfee, R. C., & Kapinus, B. (in preparation). *Validation practice and policy in the use of less-than-fully-standardized methods for large-scale assessment.* Washington, DC: Council of Chief State School Officers.

Calfee, R. C., & Masuda, W. V. (in press). *Rubrics and benchmarks in the assessment of writing.* Berkeley, CA: Center for the Study of Literacy and Writing, University of California.

Calfee, R. C., & Patrick, C. P. (1995). *Teach our children well.* Stanford, CA: Stanford Alumni Association.

Calfee, R. C., & Perfumo, P. (Eds.) (1996). *Writing portfolios: Policy and practice.* Hillsdale, NJ: Erlbaum.

Calfee, R. C., & Venezky, R. L. (1969). Component skills in beginning reading. In K. S. Goodman & J. T. Fleming (Eds.), *Psycholinguistics and the teaching of reading* (pp. 41–50). Newark, DE: International Reading Association.

Chall, J. S. (1967, 1983). *Learning to read: The great debate* (updated, 1983). New York: McGraw-Hill.

Chall, J. S. (1983). *Stages of reading development.* New York: McGraw-Hill.

Chall, J. S. (1992). The new reading debates: Evidence from science, art and ideology. *Teachers College Record, 94,* 315–328.

Cizek, G. J. (in press). Learning, achievement, and assessment: Constructs at a crossroad. In G. D. Phye (Ed.), *Handbook of classroom assessment.* Orlando, FL: Academic Press.

Cizek, G. J., Rachor, R. E., & Fitzgerald, S. M. (in press). Teachers' assessment practices: Preparation, isolation, and the kitchen sink. *Educational Assessment.*

Clifford-Jonich, G. J. (1987). *A Sisyphean task: Historical perspectives on the relationship between writing and reading instruction.* Berkeley, CA: Center for the Study of Writing, University of California.

Cole, N. (1988). A realist's appraisal of the prospects for unifying instruction and assessment. In C. V. Bunderson (Ed.), *Assessment in the service of learning* (pp. 103–117). Princeton, NJ: Educational Testing Service.

Coleman, J. S. (1966). *Equality of educational opportunity.* Washington, DC: Department of Health, Education, and Welfare.

Cronbach, L. J. (1975). Beyond the two disciplines of scientific psychology. *American Psychologist, 30,* 116–127.

Cronbach, L. J. (1988). Five perspectives on the validity argument. In H. Wainer & H. Braun (Eds.), *Test validity* (pp. 3–17). Hillsdale, NJ: Erlbaum.

Cronbach, L. J., & Gleser, G. C. (1965). *Personnel tests and personnel decisions.* Urbana, IL: University of Illinois Press.

Cronbach, L. J., Gleser, G. C., Nanda, H., & Rajaratnam, N. (1972). *The dependability of behavioral measurements.* New York: Wiley.

Cronbach, L. J., Linn, R. L., Brennan, R. L., & Haertel E. H. (1995). *Generalizability analysis for educational assessments* (Evaluation Comment, Summer, pp. 1–29). Los Angeles: UCLA / CRESST.

Cronbach, L. J., & Meehl, P. E. (1955). Construct validity in psychological tests. *Psychological Bulletin, 52,* 281–302.

Darling-Hammond, L. (1994). Performance-based assessment and educational equity. *Harvard Educational Review, 64,* 5–30.

Darling-Hammond, L., & Godwin, A. L. (1993). Progress toward professionalism in teaching. In G. Cawelti (Ed.), *Challenges and achievements in American education* (pp. 19–52). Alexandria, VA: Association for Supervision and Curriculum Development.

Daugherty, R. (1995). *National curriculum assessment: A review of policy 1987–1994.* London: Falmer Press.

Davis, F. B. (1968). Research in comprehension in reading. *Reading Research Quarterly, 3,* 499–545.

Delandshere, G., & Petrosky, A. (1994). Do the fundamental assumptions of education measurement hold for the assessment of complex performances? Paper presented at the meeting of the American Educational Research Association, San Francisco.

Dunbar, S. B., Koretz, D. M., & Hoover, H. D. (1991). Quality control in the development and use of performance assessments. *Applied Measurement in Education, 4,* 289–303.

Elam, S., Rose, L. C., & Gallup, A. M. (1993). The 25th Annual Phi Delta Kappa / Gallup poll of the public's attitudes toward the public schools. *Phi Delta Kappan, 75,* 137–152.

Everson, B. J. (1991). Vygotsky and the teaching of writing. *CSW Quarterly, 13*(3), 8–11.

Flood, J., Jensen, J. M., Lapp, D., & Squire, J. R. (Eds.). (1991). *Handbook of research in teaching the English language arts.* New York: Macmillan.

Foertsch, J. (1995). Where cognitive psychology applies: How theories about memory and transfer can influence composition pedagogy. *Written Communication, 12,* 360–383.

Fraatz, J. M. B. (1987). *The politics of reading.* New York: Teachers College Press.

Freedman, S. W. (1982). Some reasons for the grades we give compositions. *English Journal, 71,* 86–89.

Freedman, S. W. (1983). Student characteristics and essay test writing performance. *Research in the Teaching of English, 17,* 313–324.

Freedman, S. W. (1993). Linking large-scale testing and classroom portfolio assessments of student writing. *Educational Assessment, 1,* 27–52.

Garcia, G. E., & Pearson, P. D. (1994). Assessment and diversity. In L. Darling-Hammond (Ed.), *Review of research in education,* (Vol. 20, pp. 337–391). Washington, DC: American Educational Research Association.

Gearhart, M. (1994). *Issues in portfolio assessment* (Tech. Rep.). Los Angeles: UCLA / CRESST.

Gearhart, M., & Herman, J. L. (1995). *Portfolio assessment: Whose work is it?* (*Evaluation Comment,* Winter, pp. 1–16). Los Angeles: UCLA/CRESST.

Gearhart, M., Herman, J. L., Baker, E. L., & Whittaker, A. K. (1992). *Writing portfolios at the elementary level: A study of methods for writing assessment* (Tech. Rep. 337). Los Angeles: UCLA / CRESST.

Gearhart, M., Herman, J. L., Novak, J. R., Wolf, S. A., & Abdi, J. (1994). *Toward the instructional utility of large-scale writing assessment: Validation of a new narrative rubric.* (Tech. Rep.). Los Angeles: UCLA / CRESST.

Gehrke, N. J., Knapp, M. S., & Sirotnik, K. A. (1992). In search of the school curriculum. In G. Grant (Ed.), *Review of research in education* (Vol. 18, pp. 51–110). Washington, DC: American Educational Research Association.

Gipps, C. V. (1994). *Beyond testing: Towards a theory of educational assessment.* London: Falmer Press.

Glaser, R. (1981). The future of testing: A research agenda for cognitive psychology and psychometrics. *American Psychologist, 36,* 923–936.

Glazer, S. M. (1994). Authentic assessment, evaluation, portfolios: What do these terms really mean anyway? *Reading TODAY, 11*(7), 3, 4.

Goodman, K. S. (1986). *What's whole in whole language.* Portsmouth, NH: Heineman.

Goodman, K. S., Goodman, Y. M., & Hood, W. J. (1989). *The whole language evaluation book.* Portsmouth, NH: Heineman.

Gould, S. J. (1981). *The mismeasure of man.* New York: Norton.

Greene, M. (1991). Evaluation and dignity. *CSW Quarterly, 14*(1), 10–13.

Haertel, E. H., & Wiley, D. E. (in press). In M. S. Kane & R. Mitchell (Eds.), *Extended assessment tasks: Purposes, definitions, scoring, and accuracy.* Hillsdale, NJ: Erlbaum.

Hambleton, R. E., & Murphy, E. (1992). A psychometric perspective on authentic measurement. *Applied Measurement in Education, 5,* 1–16.

Haney, W., & Madaus, G. (1989). Searching for alternatives to standardized tests: Whys, whats, and whithers. *Phi Delta Kappan, 70,* 683–687.

Harlen, W. (Ed.). (1994). *Enhancing quality in assessment.* London: Paul Chapman.

Harp, B. (1991). *Assessment and evaluation in whole language programs.* Norwood, MA: Christopher-Gordon.

Heimlich, J. E., & Pittelman, S. D. (1986). *Semantic mapping: Classroom applications.* Newark, DE: International Reading Association.

Herman, J. L., Aschbacher, P. R., & Winters, L. (1992). *A practical guide to alternative assessment.* Alexandria, VA: Association for Supervision and Curriculum Development.

Hiebert, E. H., & Calfee, R. C. (1992). Assessment of literacy: From standardized tests to performances and portfolios. In A. E. Farstrup & S. J. Samuels (Eds.), *What research says about reading instruction* (pp. 70–100). Newark, DE: International Reading Association.

Hill, C. (1994) Testing and assessment: An applied linguistics perspective. *Educational Assessment, 2,* 179–212.

Hirsch, E. D., Jr. (1987). *Cultural literacy: What every American needs to know.* Boston: Houghton Mifflin.

Honig, B. (1996). *Every child a reader.* Thousand Oaks, CA: Corwin Press.

Howe, K. R. (1994). Standards, assessment, and equality of educational opportunity. *Educational Researcher, 23,* 27–33.

Jackson, P. W. (Ed.). (1992). *Handbook of research on curriculum.* New York: Macmillan.

Jonassen, D. H. (Ed.) (1985). *The technology of text: Principles for structuring, designing, and displaying text* (Vol. 2). Englewood Cliffs, NJ: Educational Technology Publications.

Juel, C. (1991). Beginning reading. In R. Barr, M. L. Kamil, P. B. Mosenthal & P. D. Pearson (Eds.), *Handbook of reading research* (Vol. 2, pp. 759–788). New York: Longman.

Kane, M. S. (1992). An argument-based approach to validity. *Psychological Bulletin, 112*, 527–535.

Kane, M. S., & Mitchell, R. (Eds.). (in press). *Implementing performance assessment: Promises, problems, and challenges.* Hillsdale, NJ: Erlbaum.

Klimenkoff, M., & LaPick, N. (1996). Promoting student self-assessment through portfolios, student-facilitated conferences, and cross-age interaction. In R. C. Calfee & P. Perfumo (Eds.), *Writing portfolios: Policy and practice.* Hillsdale, NJ: Erlbaum.

Koretz, D., Stecher, B., Klein, S., & McCaffrey, D. (1994). The Vermont portfolio assessment program: Findings and implications. *Educational Measurement: Issues and Practice, 13*(2), 3–16.

LeMahieu, P. G., Gitomer, D. H., & Eresh, J. T. (1995). Portfolios in large-scale assessment: Difficult but not impossible. *Educational Measurement: Issues and Practice, 14*(3), 11–16, 25–28.

Linn, R. L. (Ed.) (1989). *Educational measurement* (3rd ed.). New York: Macmillan.

Linn, R. L. (1994). Performance assessment: Policy promises and technical measurement standards. *Educational Researcher, 23*, 4–14.

Linn, R. L., & Baker E. L. (1996). Can performance-based student assessments be psychometrically sound? In J. B. Baron & D. P. Wolf (Eds.), *Performance-based student assessment: Toward access, capacity, and coherence* (pp. 84–103). Chicago: National Society for the Study of Education.

Linn, R. L., & Burton, E. (1994). Performance-based assessment: Implications of task specificity. *Educational Measurement: Issues and Practice, 13*(1), 5–8.

Luce, R. D., & Krumhansl, C. L. (1988). Measurement, scaling, and psychophysics. In R. C. Atkinson, R. J. Herrnstein, G. Lindzey, & R. D. Luce (Eds.), *Stevens' handbook of experimental psychology* (Vol. 1). New York: Wiley.

Martin-Kneip, G. O., Thornburg, D. G., & Cookson, P. W., Jr. (1994). The politics of assessment: Local, state, and national perspectives. *Educational Policy, 8*, 107–244. (Special issue).

Mason, J. M. (1984). Early reading from a developmental perspective. In P. D. Pearson (Ed.), *Handbook of reading research* (Vol. 1, pp. 505–543). New York: Longman.

Masters, G. N., & Mislevy, R. J. (1993). New views of student learning: Implications for educational measurement. In N. Frederiksen, R. J. Mislevy, & I. I. Bejar (Eds.), *Test theory for a new generation of tests* (pp. 219–242). Hillsdale, NJ: Erlbaum.

McGee, L. M., & Richgels, D. J. (1990). *Literacy's beginnings: Supporting young readers and writers.* Boston: Allyn & Bacon.

McLaughlin, M. W., & Shepard, L. A. (with O'Day, J. A.) (in press). *Improving education through standards-based reform.* Stanford, CA: National Academy of Education.

Mehrens, W. A. (1992). Using performance assessment for accountability purposes. *Educational Measurement: Issues and Practice, 11*(1), 3–9.

Messick, S. (1984). The psychology of educational measurement. *Journal of Educational Measurement, 21*, 215–237.

Messick, S. (1989). Validity. In R. L. Linn (Ed.), *Educational measurement* (3rd ed., pp. 13–104). New York: Macmillan.

Messick, S. (1995). Validity of psychological assessment: Validation of inferences from persons' responses and performances as scientific inquiry into score meaning. *American Psychologist, 50*, 741–749.

Mislevy, R. J. (1995). *On inferential issues arising in the California Learning Assessment System* (Tech. Rep.). Princeton, NJ: Educational Testing Service.

Mislevy, R. J., Yamamoto, K., & Anacker, S. (1991). *Toward a test theory for assessing student understanding* (Research Report RR-91-32-ONR). Princeton, NJ: Educational Testing Service.

Mitchell, R. (1992). *Testing for learning: How new approaches to evaluation can improve American schools.* New York: Free Press.

Moffett, J., & Wagner, B. J. (1992). *Student-centered language arts* (4th ed.). Portsmouth, NH: Boynton/Cook.

Moss, P. A. (1992). Portfolios, accountability, and an interpretive approach to validity. *Educational Measurement: Issues and Practice, 11*(3), 12–21.

Moss, P. A. (1994a). Validity in high stakes writing assessment: Problems and possibilities. *Assessing Writing, 1*, 109–128.

Moss, P. A. (1994b). Can there be validity without reliability? *Educational Researcher, 23*, 5–12.

Moss, P. A. (1995). Themes and variations in validity theory. *Educational Measurement: Issues and Practice, 14*(2), 5–13.

Moss, P. A., Beck, J. S., Ebbs, C., Matson, B., Muchmore, J., Steele, D., Taylor, C., & Herter, R. (1992). Portfolios, accountability, and an interpretive approach to validity. *Educational Measurement: Issues and Practice, 11*(3), 12–21.

Myers, M. (1994). Problems and issues facing the National Standards Project in English. *Education and Urban Society, 26*, 141–157.

Narens, L., & Luce, R. D. (1986). Measurement: The theory of numerical assignments. *Psychological Bulletin, 99*, 166–180.

Nettles, M. T., & Nettles, A. L. (Eds.). (1995). *Equity and excellence in educational testing and assessment.* Boston: Kluwer.

Nowak, J. D., & Gowin, D. B. (1984). *Learning how to learn.* New York: Cambridge University Press.

Nystrand, M., Cohen, A. S., & Dowling, N. M. (1993). Addressing reliability problems in the assessment of college writing. *Educational Assessment, 1*, 53–70.

Olson, D. R. (1995). Conceptualizing the written word: An intellectual biography. *Written Communication, 12*, 277–298.

OTA (Office of Technology Assessment). (1992). *Testing in American schools: Asking the right questions.* (OTA-SET-519). Washington, DC: U.S. Government Printing Office.

Parducci, A. (1995). *Happiness, pleasure, and judgment.* Hillsdale, NJ: Erlbaum.

Paris, S. G., Wasik, B. A., & Turner, J. C. (1991). The development of strategic readers. In R. Barr, M. L. Kamil, P. B. Mosenthal & P. D. Pearson (Eds.), *Handbook of reading research* (Vol. 2, pp. 609–640). New York: Longman.

Pearson, P. D. (Ed.). (1984). *Handbook of reading research* (Vol. 1). New York: Longman.

Popham, W. J. (1993). Educational testing in America: What's right, what's wrong? A criterion-referenced perspective. *Educational Measurement: Issues and Practice, 12*(1), 11–14.

Powers, D. E. (1994). Will they think less of my handwritten essay if others word process theirs? *Journal of Educational Measurement, 31*, 220–233.

Pressley, M. S., & Rankin, J. (1994). More about whole language methods of reading instruction for students at risk for early reading failure. *Learning Disabilities Research and Practice, 9*, 157–168.

Resnick, L. B. (1987). *Education and learning to think.* Washington, DC: National Academy Press.

Rogosa, D. R. (1983). Demonstrating the reliability of the difference score in the measurement of change. *Journal of Educational Measurement, 20*, 335–343.

Roid, G. H. (1994). Patterns of writing skills derived from cluster analysis of direct-writing assessments. *Applied Measurement in Education, 7*, 159–170.

Rosenholz, S. J. (1989). *Teachers' workplace.* White Plains, NY: Longman.

Rotzel, A. W. (1974). *Information processing theory in attitude change applied to social studies textbook materials.* Unpublished dissertation. Stanford, CA: School of Education.

Rousseau, J. J. (1762 / 1979). *Emile: On education* (Introduction, translation, and notes, A. Bloom). New York: Basic Books.

Saner, H., McCaffrey, D., Stecher, B., Klein, S., & Bell, R. (1994). *Educational Assessment, 2,* 325–340.

Shavelson, R. J., & Webb, N. M. (1991). *Generalizability theory: A primer.* Newbury Park, CA: Sage.

Sheingold, K., Heller, J. I., & Paulunknis S. T. (1995). *Actively seeking evidence: Teacher change through assessment development* (Tech. Rep.). Princeton, NJ: Educational Testing Service.

Shepard, L. A. (1989). Why we need better assessments. *Educational Leadership, 46*(7), 4–9.

Shepard, L. A. (1992). What policy makers who mandate tests should know about the new psychology of intellectual ability and learning. In B. R. Gifford & M. C. O'Connor (Eds.), *Changing assessments: Alternative views of aptitude, achievement, and instruction.* Boston: Kluwer.

Shepard, L. A. (1993). Evaluating test validity. In L. Darling-Hammond (Ed.), *Review of research in education* (Vol. 19, pp. 405–450). Washington, DC: American Educational Research Association.

Shepard, L. A. (1995). Using assessment to improve learning. *Educational Leadership, 52*(5), 38–43.

Sizer, T. R. (1995). Foreword: How'm I doing? In L. Darling-Hammond, J. Ancess & B. Falk (Eds.), *Authentic assessment in action* (pp. vii–xi). New York: Teachers College Press.

Stanovich, K. E. (1986). Matthew effects in reading: Some consequences of individual differences in the acquisition of reading. *Reading Research Quarterly, 21,* 360–406.

Stevens, S. S. (1951). Mathematics, measurement, and psychophysics. In S. S. Stevens (Ed.), *Handbook of experimental psychology* (pp. 1–49). New York: Wiley.

Stiggins, R. J. (1994). *Student-centered classroom assessment.* New York: Merrill.

Stiggins, R. J., & Conklin, N. F. (1992). *In teachers' hands: Investigating the practices of classroom assessment.* Albany, NY: State University of New York Press.

Sulzby, E., & Teale, W. (1991). Emergent literacy. In R. Barr, M. L. Kamil, P. B. Mosenthal & P. D. Pearson, (Eds.). *Handbook of reading research* (Vol. 2, pp. 727–757). New York: Longman.

Taylor, C. (1994). Assessment for measurement or standards: The peril and promise of large-scale assessment reform. *American Educational Research Journal, 31,* 231–262.

Thorndike, R. L. (1973). *Reading comprehension education in fifteen countries.* New York: Wiley.

Tierney, R. J. (1991). Studies of reading and writing growth: Longitudinal research on literacy development. In J. Flood, J. M. Jensen, D. Lapp & J. R. Squire (Eds.), *Handbook of research on teaching the English language arts* (pp. 176–194). New York: Macmillan.

Tierney R. J., Carter, M. A., & Desai, L. E. (1991). *Portfolio assessment in the reading-writing classroom.* Norwood, MA: Christopher-Gordon.

Tittle, C. K. (1994). Toward an educational psychology of assessment for teaching and learning: Theories, contexts, and validation arguments. *Educational Psychologist, 29,* 149–162.

Tversky, A., & Fox, C. R. (1995). Weighing risk and uncertainty. *Psychological Review, 102,* 269–283.

Tversky, A., & Kahneman, D. (1982). The framing of decisions and the psychology of choice. *Science, 211,* 453–458.

Tyler, R. W. (1934). *Constructing achievement tests.* Columbus, OH: Ohio State University.

Tyler, R. W. (1989). *Educational evaluation.* Boston: Kluwer.

Valencia, S. W., Hiebert, E. H., & Afflerbach, P. P. (Eds.). (1994). *Authentic reading assessment: Practices and possibilities.* Newark, DE: International Reading Association.

Webb, N. M. (1993). Collaborative group versus individual assessment in mathematics: Processes and outcomes. *Educational Assessment, 1,* 131–152.

Webb, N. M. (1995). Group collaboration in assessment: Competing objectives, processes, and outcomes. *Educational Evaluation and Policy Analysis, 17,* 239–261.

Wiggins, G. P. (1993). *Assessing student performance.* San Francisco: Jossey-Bass.

Winograd, P. (1994). Developing alternative assessments: Six problems worth solving. *Reading Teacher, 47,* 420–423.

Witte, S. P., & Flach J. (1994). Notes toward an assessment of advanced ability to communicate. *Assessing Writing, 1,* 207–246.

Witte, S. P., Flach, J., Greenwood, C., & Wilson, K. E. (1995). More notes toward an assessment of advanced ability to communicate. *Assessing Writing, 2,* 21–65.

Wittrock, M. C. (Ed.). (1986). *Handbook of research on teaching* (3rd ed.). New York: Macmillan.

Wixon, K. K., Valencia, S. W., & Lipson, M. Y. (1994). Issues in literacy assessment: Facing the realities of internal and external assessment. *Journal of Reading Behavior, 26,* 315–335.

Wolf, K. (1994). Commentary. In S. W. Valencia, E. H. Hiebert & P. P. Afflerbach (Eds.), *Authentic reading assessment: Practices and possibilities* (pp. 157–166). Newark, DE: International Reading Association.

Wolf, S. A., & Gearhart, M. (1994). Writing what you read: Narrative assessment as a learning event. *Language Arts, 71,* 425–444.

Wright, P., Lickorish, A., Hull, A., & Ummelen, N. (1995). Graphics in written directions: Appreciated by readers but not writers. *Applied Cognitive Psychology, 9,* 41–59.

15

CHILDREN OUT OF BOUNDS: THE POWER OF CASE STUDIES IN EXPANDING VISIONS OF LITERACY DEVELOPMENT

Anne Haas Dyson

UNIVERSITY OF CALIFORNIA, BERKELEY

"You're not supposed to leave the underworld," screams Liliana (alias Venus) at Sammy (alias Pluto). The third graders are playing Greek gods. They have named the boundaries of the relevant worlds, and Sammy is clearly out of bounds. He is supposed to be on the sand by the climbing structure, not on the grass by the fence.

"But I'm good now," he pleads, trying to redefine himself. He is tired of the lonely and hot underworld and longing for the more sociable and tree-shaded space guarded by the firm Liliana.

Out on the playground, children claim and define spaces, be their game Greek gods or kickball, cops-'n-robbers or hopscotch. And, of course, who's "in" and who's "out" is often a matter of contention. In many ways, this same task of establishing and maintaining boundaries faces adults who construct case studies, that is, studies of "bounded systems" in all their dynamic complexity (Stake, 1988, p. 256). The case might be a particular community, group, or, of particular interest in this chapter, individual. Whatever the unit, however, the "case" has a way of going out of bounds, forcing the observer to reconsider the designated spaces.

Consider, for example, another scene involving 8-year-old Sammy, a "case" in an ongoing qualitative study; the "bounded system", the particular human experience being studied, is that of learning to write.

Sammy is sitting with bowed head and, I expect, bowed heart as well. He had looked forward all morning to Author's Theater, when his classmates would act out his story. But all had not gone well, especially with Michael. Sammy had written the death of a superhero—an untenable text, according to Michael. Unable to ignore Sammy's misery, I tell him that just because Michael didn't like his story doesn't mean Michael doesn't like him. But Sammy is not buying this—and neither is his peer Makeda sitting beside him.

Makeda: But a story is kinda like *your* life. It's like it's kinda like it's what you're doing and they're doing. ... [to Sammy] Just say, "Oh yeah, I'm gonna get you. I'm not gonna be your friend no more. If you don't like my story, I don't like your story either." But *ignore* them when they're talking to you. That's what I do. Like Lettrice say, "I don't like your story." I say, "I don't like your story either. And I'm not your friend any more. And I'm going to ignore you next time." So she never did mess with me. (pause) She saw my big brother, she never did mess with me. She tried to get her whole gang on me, so I got my big brother. So that's what happened.

And Sammy and Makeda go to lunch.

I had begun by observing one child's writing but, soon, was enmeshed in a complex social drama featuring many children and the wider classroom and societal contexts in which their acts, and their writing, gained meaning. Moreover, I was attending to symbols other than the written marks on the page; as Sammy's story was enacted, discussed, argued about, and literally cried over, its personal and public meaning was mediated through many symbolic forms—spoken words as well as written ones, dramatic movement and expressive

Support for this work was provided by the Spencer Foundation and by the Educational Research and Development Center Program (Grant No. R117G10036 for the National Center for the Study of Writing) as administered by the Office of Educational Research and Improvement (OERI), U.S. Department of Education. The findings and opinions expressed in this report do not reflect the position or policies of the Spencer Foundation, the OERI, or the U.S. Department of Education.

gestures, and, potentially, illustrative drawings and decorative book designs.

Understanding Sammy's evolving history as a "writer" has demanded, therefore, that the conceptual boundaries—or definitions—of writing and of development be drawn in ways that accommodate his complex experience. And that experience forces me as an observer to attend to children other than Sammy, to symbols other than written ones. In this chapter, I explore the way in which the intense study of individual experience can destabilize, not physical playground boundaries, but *conceptual* ones and thereby allow new perspectives. Constructing or writing a case is a dialogic process, one that involves defining and redefining one's understandings. Moreover, this process may be enacted on a broader level when completed cases enter the public dialogue of professional gatherings and published accounts.

In the following sections, I first elaborate on the process of constructing a case and, second, the particular process of constructing cases of children learning written language. I highlight the use of interpretive methodology to construct cases (Geertz, 1973; Erickson, 1986); this methodology probes how specific people, in specific social circumstances, interpret or make sense of their everyday interactions. I then offer the case of three cases written successively over a 15-year period; collectively, these cases illustrate the methodological dynamics of case studies, the ways in which they may force an observer both to articulate conceptual boundaries and to go beyond them, to go out of bounds, as it were. Finally, in the concluding section, I consider the potential of case studies for crossing another kind of boundary, one that separates the diverse professionals concerned with children's lives (Florio-Ruane, 1991; Genishi, 1992)—and I also consider the limits imposed on that potential when such studies become prescriptive or normative guides.

In recent years, startling statistics have proclaimed the challenges facing our schools, especially schools like Sammy's, schools serving poor children in urban and rural settings. In its annual yearbooks, The Children's Defense Fund (e.g., 1994) presents the shameful statistics: the number of children living in poverty, labeled as "unready" for school, as "academically behind," and, eventually, as "dropouts." Of what importance, then, are the experiences of one child? Of what worth the hours, months, and, indeed, years that may be spent constructing a small number of cases? These, ultimately, are the questions addressed herein.

CONSTRUCTING A CASE: THE WORK OF DEFINITIONS AND DETAILS

Insight into the nature and the value of case construction comes, interestingly, from a biologist, Barbara McClintock. She was, wrote Stephen Gould (1987), committed to "following the peculiarities of individuals, not the mass properties of millions," (p. 167) and to tracing their complex interactions with each other and their environment—a commitment all the more intriguing because McClintock followed stalks of corn. In her own words, spoken to her biographer Evelyn Keller, one must understand

> how it [each plant] grows, understand its parts, understand when something is going wrong with it. [An organism] isn't just a piece of plastic, it's something that is constantly being affected by the environment, constantly showing attributes or disabilities in its growth... No two plants are exactly alike. ... I start with the seedling and I don't want to leave it. I don't feel I really know the story if I don't watch the plant all the way along. So I know every plant in the field. I know them intimately and I find it a great pleasure to know them. (cited in Gould, 1987, pp. 167, 168)

McClintock was interested in the ways information is passed on through genes, not through language, and in biological actions and reactions—processes microscopically removed from the interpretive processes of most people's everyday lives. Still, her words and her concerns are relevant here, for they speak of the importance of theoretical definitions and empirical details.

Negotiating Theoretical Boundaries

McClintock followed the narrative thread of an individual, intent on understanding a phenomenon—the workings of biological inheritance and development. Her story disputed the notion of a simplistic, one-way flow of information, from genome, to RNA, to DNA; and it revealed a fluid and mobile process, one filled with "hierarchical systems of regulation and control" and surprising reversals, including information entering the genome from the outside environment (as it does in AIDS) (Gould, 1987, p. 159). A single organism reverberates in an environment and, in the process, reveals the complexity within and without and highlights potentially critical points of contact (of, to stretch a word, negotiation) with that environment.

McClintock, then, speaks about respect for bounded complexity, about attention to its unfolding story, and, thus, about cases. The singular defining feature of any case is, in fact, its boundedness (Geertz, 1973; Stake, 1988). Some unit of integrity (a person, a group, a community) is both outlined and contained by a researcher, who is studying, not the case itself, but a case of *something*, some phenomenon (e.g., not maize, but biological inheritance). Thus, the researcher is constantly making decisions about what is, or is not, within the constructed bounds, what is, or is not, relevant to such a case.

Inherent in this process of bounding is one critical challenge—and strength—of case study analysis: the need, in the midst of the flow of unbounded experience, to make decisions about basic definitions of what exactly is being bound. Writing of anthropological cases of communities, Clifford Geertz grapples with the same strength and challenge:

> The locus of study is not the object of study. ... You can study different things in different places, and some things ... you can best study in confined localities. ... It is with the kind of material produced by ... almost obsessively fine-comb field study ... that the mega-concepts with which contemporary social science is afflicted—legitimacy, modernization, integration, conflict ... meaning—can be given the sort of sensible actuality that makes it possible to think not only realistically and concretely *about* them, but, what is more important, creatively and imaginatively *with* them. (1973, p. 23)

In interpretive research, one aims to understand some aspect of human experience and, given its complexity and, indeed, its abstractness, one needs to situate that experience within people's actions and reactions to the materiality, the local specificity, of their everyday worlds.

Working definitions in any one study *are* influenced by previous studies, where concepts were defined and elaborated. But the focus of the moment (i.e., the learning child in the viewing frame) exerts an influence as well. For the definitions arrived at must seem sensible (given the child's actions and reactions), just as McClintock's definitions had to allow for the actions and reactions of the maize. Thus, case studies have the potential to contribute new understandings of the concepts under study. In this chapter, the experience to be understood, to be conceived and reconceived, is that of learning to write.

Detailing Lived Experience

Implicit in the textual construction of a human actor is a second strength and challenge, one that highlights intentional *mind*, not genetic matter—the need to enter into, and try to understand, another's consciousness, another's world. And those "others" may be persons whose agency, whose actions and reactions, are often lost in a collective word that distances and dismisses (like "the masses" of the so-called Third World [Sahni, 1994] and "the at-risk" of the affluent one) or, in contrast, in a singular word that homogenizes and diminishes (like "the child" [Thorne, 1987]).

This strength, however, contains within it a potential weakness, the possibility of looking, not to understand, but to confirm what is "known," research reduced to illustrative anecdote of truths already held. Researchers, after all, are not ventriloquists (Geertz, 1988). They do not speak for others. They are writers who construct others' lives. Researchers' own life experiences and social positioning—their age, gender, ethnicity, indeed, their very status as outsider, "both enable and inhibit particular kinds of insight" (Rosaldo, 1989, p. 19).

But, as writers, they *can* work to make another's life world more perceptible, more accessible, by respecting the details of that world, the recurring themes and rhythms of the other's life scenes. Such respect entails time and presence—and painstaking reliving, as scrawled field notes are typed out, voice-packed audiotapes transcribed, and crumpled child papers are smoothed over again and again. And it also entails depicting the other's actions in descriptive words, rather than glossing them with abstractions like "competent," or not, "cooperative," or not, "motivated," or not; observers attend to the contextual specifics—the who's, what's, where's, and when's—of others' actions, attempting to grasp *their* value judgments, their interpretations (Bogdan, & Biklen, 1992).

Observers do, of course, have their own feelings about and reactions to the observed. Indeed, for both observing researchers (Ottenberg, 1990) and teachers (Almy, & Genishi, 1979; Florio-Ruane, 1989), those reactions and feelings are a potentially rich source of hypotheses about the other. It is this need to acknowledge but interrogate—literally bracket in one's notes—such responses that accounts, at least in part, for

the self-knowledge that may accompany attempts to understand others. For example, one might ask, who do I (and other participants in the scene) assume is competent or not? on the basis of what kinds of actions in what settings, using language to accomplish what purposes in what ways? What does this concept, *competence,* mean here?

Through such a dialogic process of considering and reconsidering the taken-for-granted, researchers seek a "textual connection," as Geertz (1988, p. 144) writes, a "common ground between the Written At and the Written About." That is, they use the limits of their own life experiences to understand another's. Thus, like its aesthetic cousin the literary text, the interpretive case has the potential to reveal "dimensions of . . . experience that are ordinarily invisible," to "hear aspects of it ordinarily lost in silence" (Greene, 1988, p. 19). This potential for seeing new dimensions of experience connects this second challenge with the first, the potential to go beyond old assumptions and conceptual boundaries, through, in McClintock's words, "the pleasure of know[ing] another."

STUDYING YOUNG WRITERS: THE BASICS OF LITERACY AND GROWTH

In studying literacy development, researchers face very basic definitional questions. Most important, perhaps, is: What is "it" that develops? What is reading, writing, or literacy? Where does one look for "it"? What boundaries should be drawn around "it"?

In the opening anecdote about Sammy, for example, is his writing in the *graphics* (e.g., Clay, 1975), in the exact words he formed on the page? Or is it in the *orthographics* (e.g., Read, 1971), in the linking of graphic signifier with signified in systematic ways? Or, maybe it is in Sammy's *process* (e.g., Graves, 1975), his planning of a message and his monitoring and revising of its objectified form. Yet another possibility: writing could be his *discourse* or *genre form* (e.g., Newkirk, 1987), his story—or, maybe, it's a *functional tool* at work in a particular *cultural event* (e.g., Heath, 1983), one involving the specifics of who, to whom, with what message and form, in what place and time, and, of course, for what reason. Or maybe writing is in the ideology of the society as a whole, its *societal discourse* (e.g., Gilbert, 1994); Sammy and Michael have different expectations about what can and cannot be written in the context of a superhero story—and Makeda has clear notions about what can or cannot be said about another's story (or at least about the stories of authors with big brothers).

In other words, should an observer attend primarily to the writing on the paper? the behavioral evidence of individual mind at work? the enactment of writing as social happening and cultural activity? or, perhaps, the textual constituents of ideological beliefs about what can or cannot be said by whom? Moreover, these questions can be asked from different perspectives. Sammy, Sammy's friends and family, his teacher, and his adult friend (the researcher) may all have different ways of defining what it means to write.

And as if these issues were not challenging enough, there are basic issues to be addressed about "development" as well. Again, what and where is it? Moreover, what sort of developmental pathway should one prepare to follow? Is growth a linear unfolding? a zigzagging phenomenon? a moving away from social supports? a gradual integration into social life?

Perhaps, to construct a case of Sammy's development, one should focus on outer signs of his internal concepts of "writing," looking for evidence of his mental grappling with unexpected information and unintended consequences (e.g., Ferreiro, 1978). Or, maybe one builds a case around collaborative encounters between Sammy and his teacher or more skilled peers, examining ways in which relative experts provide guidance (e.g., Snow, 1983). Or perhaps one should not assume singular teachers but make space for multiple co-participants in his writing activities and for changes in his way of participating with those others (e.g., Dyson, 1993a).

Over the last 25 years, researchers have conceptualized differently the mechanisms or processes of development, the desirable end goals, and the nature of expected pathways. Thus they have looked in different places for writing, both on and off the page. Reviews of expanding definitions of literacy (e.g., Nystrand, Greene, & Wiemelt, 1993) and of development (e.g., Bruner, & Haste, 1987) can be found elsewhere. The point herein is that it is these sorts of definitions that undergird researchers' ways of drawing boundaries around, and paying attention to, children; such definitions influence what is foregrounded and what is left in the background, what is carefully detailed and what is glossed over. Conversely, it is the details—the descriptions of children's "dailyness" (Polakow, 1992)—that in turn may challenge the viewing frame itself.

In writing cases, researchers must deal with the dangling threads—the child actions and reactions that cannot be understood, that suggest the need to refocus, to clarify and, sometimes, to redefine. Indeed, one theoretical perspective portrays the act of writing itself as a struggle with given words (like "literacy" and "development"). Writing is dialogic, argues Bakhtin (1981, 1986); it not only mediates interactions between writers and their audiences, but also mediates between writers' minds and the collective mind of the discourse community that has given them their words. Thus, in constructing cases, writers negotiate with available words, stretching them, rethinking them, aiming to make them "fit" their data. Then, through publications like this handbook, they participate in the process of figuring out what can legitimately be said about "writing" and "development" within the circle of people concerned about children and literacy.

UNRAVELING CASES

To illustrate the methodological dynamics of case study construction, I present abbreviated forms of three cases: those of Rachel, Jake, and Tina. The cases were all constructed from transcripts, collected products, and observational notes and, within each, child use of imaginative narrative discourse is highlighted. The children themselves were from similar sociocultural backgrounds (i.e., urban children whose heritage was predominantly African-American, and whose socioeconomic circumstance was primarily working class); they were all given to imaginative storytelling, all had complex relationships with peers—and all were singularly complex people.

The children are of different ages: Rachel was just 5, Jake was 6, and Tina (a classmate of Sammy's) was 7. The point of this analysis, however, is not to trace developmental patterns from child to child; rather, it is to examine the definitions, the viewing frame, that shaped each construction—and how that frame was complicated by the case itself. I chose these three from a larger set of 30, because they engendered clear and distinctive conceptual shifts. Tina, the most recent case, is presented most fully, but her case is set within the context of the preceding two.

For each case, I provide situational context, an edited sample of the case, details of analysis tools, and, finally, the conceptual understandings *and* puzzles yielded by the completed study. Collectively, the cases illustrate the boundary negotiation—and the theoretical re-envisioning—possible through sustained attention to the unfolding stories of children's lives.

Rachel: Writing as Symbol System

The research focus on the first of these cases, that of Rachel, was very close, the viewing boundaries very tightly set. A pictorial metaphor for the case study of Rachel might be this picture by Rachel herself: the single child in the viewing frame (see Figure 15–1).

Rachel may well be halfway through college now, but I met her in the kindergarten. She was one of five focal children in a study of young children's writing (Dyson, 1981, 1983). There was no child writing in her classroom, which had been designated my site by the school district. Therefore, I set up a classroom writing center and invited the children simply to come and write, however and whatever they wanted.

The center was not organized by any particular classroom social structure (other than as an optional individual choice during "free" activity time); there were no classroom expectations guiding what was produced, nor any social forums through which ways of talking about writing might become

FIGURE 15–1 Framing Rachel

routinized. As individual choice, a dominant purpose for most children at the center was to explore the medium itself. The children would arrange and rearrange known letters and letter-like forms on their papers, asking me if they would quite done "it" yet (i.e., written anything that could be read); and they also spent quite a bit of time writing known (or guessed at) names of important people in their lives. Most important, the children talked a great deal, to themselves, to me, and to each other. As a researcher, I was drawn to this talk and, thus, the specific question guiding the project became, What role does children's *oral* language play in their early *written* efforts?

Of all the regular child visitors to the center, Rachel stood out for her people-oriented personality; she was a mover and a shaker in the kindergarten scene. Relative to her peers, she was much more likely to use the writing center for the production of dramatic adventures. Now I would think of her as a performer in search of an audience (and I was convenient). Then I approached her primarily as a child writer; I asked what, how, and why she wrote and what role her talking—and Rachel was a talker—had in her efforts.

The Drama—and the Dramas of—Rachel. The following event is representative of how Rachel wrote a story and, also, of how I narrated the case of Rachel:

> Rachel is composing an elaborate story about 2 feuding sisters, one in a series of stories about sisters who are always together but always at odds (just as Rachel describes her own relationship with her 7-year-old sister Julie). Rachel's dominant composing media are pictures and dramatic dialogue and gesture. As her picture takes shape, she acts out a scene in which one sister has just locked the other out of the house.
>
> Rachel: "Sister, open up the door. [Rachel knocks twice on the table.] You dummy. Sister, you better come and open this door or else I'm gonna' throw this pumpkin shell on your head—"
>
> Quite suddenly, Rachel has a plan:
>
> That's what it's gonna be saying!

Rachel now writes the "teeny tiny" print-like markings, all in a line, in the uppermost left-hand side of her paper (see Figure 15–2). The writing, though small, stands for the loud orders and threats of the sister on the outs:

FIGURE 15–2 Rachel's feuding sisters

> It says, "Open the door, Sister. Open, open, open, else I'm gonna' throw this pumpkin shell right on your head."
>
> Later, Rachel explains to me (her so-called observer but, in this event, her audience) that she wrote little "'cuz I wanted you to try to guess."

Rachel did not always use such unconventional writing. Sometimes, her intention involved the more limited writing of names (e.g., a "note" or "letter," containing a picture and the addressee's name, or a list for "mommy so she'll know all of the my friends' names that was over here"). In those cases, her letters were legible and her words quite readable. For elaborate stories, though, pictures, dramatic talk, and "teeny tiny" writing were the favored media.

Defining the Viewing Frame: Analytic Tools. From much observing and taping of events like the story of the feuding sisters, file boxes began to fill with observational notes, transcripts, and child products. Using such diverse materials to construct a case requires a vocabulary or coding system, a way of describing the dimensions of the "bounded system" (e.g., the child's experience of writing); in this project, it required a means for describing how the children went about writing and the role of talk in that writing.

The nature of such a vocabulary is dependent upon those basic questions earlier discussed, including, What is writing? Where, in the mass of data, is it located? In the academic dialogue of the late 1970s, researchers emphasized the graphic and orthographic features of early writing (e.g., Bissex, 1980; Clay, 1975; Read, 1975) and the decision-making processes involved in crafting information on paper (e.g., Graves, 1975).

These definitions suggest that a researcher should focus on a child's ways of shaping (i.e., of planning, encoding, and monitoring) inner meanings in written forms and, also, the nature of the resulting forms. Thus, I constructed Rachel's case—and that of four other children—by describing her actions as she crafted meanings on paper. To do so, I developed an analytic vocabulary or category system that included four "components" of a child's writing process: *formulating a message, encoding the message, mechanically formulating letters or letter-like forms on paper, and decoding [or rereading] the message.* Accompanying each component was a list of "properties" or qualities that captured child variation in ways of enacting these components.

For example, in Rachel's feuding sisters story, the formulated message was *specific* (i.e., Rachel did not simply say "This is gonna say something about my sister.") and *coherent* (i.e., related to the other graphic marks, including the drawing, on the page). Her encoding was not *systematic* (e.g., Rachel was not using any evident orthographic system); and her forms were not *conventional*, although they were *linearly* arranged. In rereading, Rachel did not *segment her written message* (i.e., match portions of her oral message to her written one). On the other hand, in writing her lists, Rachel's specific message was systematically encoded (based on visual recall, however, rather than any sound/symbol matching), and her forms conventional.

In addition to writing process components, the category system included descriptors for the *functions* of children's talk. For example, in Rachel's feuding sister story, talk served primarily to *represent* or narrate the story, although it also served to *evaluate* (i.e., to express Rachel's attitude toward the world, particularly the obnoxious behavior of sisters) and to *interact* (e.g., to ask me to attend to her story). It served minimally to help her *encode* (e.g., to help transfer oral symbols to written ones through "sounding out") or to *seek information* (e.g., to seek spellings).

Uneasy Answers: Rachel Pushes the Boundaries. Analyses of all children's visits to the center, and fine-grained analyses of the focal children's writing and talking, led to tentative conclusions. Talk, it seemed, was initially something young children do *about* writing (i.e., "This is my mama's name"), rather than something young children encode *in* their writing. Over time, children's speech becomes both writing's raw material and its guiding tool—young children use speech to monitor and encode their ideas. Thus, their writing becomes more able to stand on its own, independent of any accompanying talk.

This suggested developmental pattern fit with the then dominant definition of development (i.e., development is an orderly transformation of child behavior, reflecting underlying changes in conceptual systems [Piaget, & Inhelder, 1969]). Moreover, it was also compatible with the dominant view of writing development. That development was a moving apart, a child learning to articulate and manipulate meaning without support from the immediate material and social context (Olson, 1977). The sense of such a portrayal was dependent upon the viewing frame, upon those tight boundaries drawn around individual children and their writing processes.

But such narrow tight boundaries could not quite contain the lively Rachel. As composer, Rachel did much more than write—she also drew and dramatized. The roots of her eventual accomplishments as a storywriter could not be in that line of teeny tiny writing alone. Moreover, her composing processes, like that of all children, were highly variable but related to her end goal. Her action on the page could not be understood separately from her intention in the world.

Finally, those narrowly drawn boundaries were also at odds with the project's methodology. Such boundaries implied a telescopic perspective on children, an attempt to make sense of their behavior from the faraway viewpoint of the adult world. But *interpretive* methodology aims to situate child behavior within the meaningful webs of present aims and social connections. The next case, that of Jake, continued to fray the edges of the existent conceptual boundaries.

Jake: Writing as Mediational Tool

The project involving Jake aimed to examine one of the dangling threads from the study described above—the drawing, storytelling, and dramatic gestures that seemed to serve as the developmental roots of conventional writing, at least as much as if not more so than lines of child mock writing (Dyson, 1989). The project initially focused on eight focal children's use of multiple media in their composing and how their use of these media changed over time. But the situ-

ational context of this project was quite different from that of Rachel's, and its local particulars helped shape the unfolding project in general—and the unfolding story of Jake in particular.

Jake's school was a small magnet school of 80 children, kindergartners through third graders. All the children had the same language arts teacher (Margaret), and they all participated in a daily journal time. As part of that journal time, the children shared their written texts, and Margaret led the children in appreciatory talk about individuals' accomplishments as artists and composers. Thus, individual children's ways of writing were shaped by—and were shaping—the literacy life of the school as a whole; my own role as instigator and interactional partner during writing time was minimal. For example, the children did not ask me, "What did I write?", to quote Clay (1975); very quickly, most of the youngest children began to emulate the storywriting of the oldest ones.

During the first year of this 2-year project, Jake was a first grader—a talkative, outgoing one. Despite his own sense of being "slow" in learning to read and write, he was highly engaged during journal time. Like Rachel, he composed dramatic stories, primarily by drawing and talking. His stories, though, were not about relationships but about fast-paced adventures, often involving speedy vehicles, and clashes between the good guys and bad guys. Moreover, the stories were not used to gain the attention of an adult interested in children's writing; they were used to gain the attention of his peers, especially his "straight man," so to speak, the calm, quiet, and artistic Manuel.

The Drama—and the Dramas—of Jake. The following event illustrates Jake's propensity toward wild adventures, his playfulness, and, most especially, his delight in teasing his friend Manuel. The event centers on the drawing in Figure 15–3.

Jake has just drawn the ground and the sky and—
Jake: Now I'm gonna make a mechanical man.

Manuel, sensible and calm, seeks some clarification:

Manuel: A mechanical man? You mean a robot man?
Jake: Yeah, I'm gonna make a robot man. You got it, Manuel.

FIGURE 15–3 Jake's robot man and flying earthling

Jake begins to elaborate in his talk and in his picture:

Jake: Here's a bomb head. It's gonna explode. It hasn't even exploded yet. When it does—

Manuel's a bit concerned:

Manuel: I hope it explodes in the next century.
Jake: Here comes the bomb explosion! There is the fire, a little smoke. (makes quick back-and-forth motions with his marker) . . . [omitted data] It's gonna explode in the next few days.
Manuel: I hope it happens on the weekend and then I won't be around.
Jake: Not for long this school will be around.

          . . .

          (adds another figure) I'm gonna make a flying earthling!

Jake's dynamic narratives were woven with talk and drawing; but his writing was neither dynamic nor narrative. Jake struggled with encoding, and, for support, he "copied offa" his pictures, capturing only its static, flat surface. For his robot man story, he wrote:

Once upon a time there were two men. One was flying up in to the clouds. The other man was staying on the ground. The and. . .

Over the 2 years of the project, Jake's social nature and flair for the dramatic did not change—but his composing changed. As a second grader, Jake's drawings often were sequenced to reveal key moments in his story; further, his playful interactions with peers could now occur *during* writing. To give a flavor of these changes, I provide another sample of Jake in action one year after the "robot man" event.

As is his custom, Jake is sitting beside Manuel. While Manuel works on the story of a snowman who comes to life, Jake has other plans:

Jake: (to Manuel) I'm deadly. I'm deadly. I'm gonna put your name in this story and you are gonna be deadly too. I'm gonna make sure you get blown to pieces. (laughs)
Manuel: Blown to pieces. (softly and a bit awed)
Jake: Yes sir. You won't be able to see your mommy ever again.

Jake writes, *Once there was a boy that is named Manuel.* Manuel playfully retaliates:

Manuel: In my story, you're going to meet a magician who's going to turn *you* into a snowman.
Jake: Well, actually, guess wha—
Manuel: And melt you flat.

Jake seems to back down:

Jake: Actually, um, I I'm, I—we're gonna, I'm writing about um us flying the fastest jet in the world.
          ⋮
          None of us—both of us are—isn't gonna get blown to pieces because it's the fastest jet—it can outrun any bullet.
Manuel: Oh wow! I like that.
Jake: And it's as bullet-proof as it can get.

But later:

Jake: Watch out Manuel! (writes *blow up*)
Manuel: Just at the very end when they're just so happy, it's

almost—they're just so happy and they read the entire story and they loved it, I get blown up.
Jake: Yeah.
Manuel: And they cry and cry and cry and cry—it's so dramatic.

Later, Jake reads his story to Manuel:

Once there was a boy that is named Manuel. Manuel is going to fly the fastest jet and I am going to fly the jet too. But Manuel's headquarters is going to blow up But I am OK. But I don't know about Manuel but I am going to find Manuel. But when I find him I like him. But I think I see him. He is in the jet. Manuel are you OK? yes I am OK. you are being attacked. I will shoot the bad guys out of the universe. OK yet shoot them now. The end.

In this event, as in others in the second grade, Jake played with Manuel, not only around his writing, but through the writing itself.

Defining the Viewing Frame: Analytic Tools. The case record of Jake was filled with the taped voices, written records, and collected products of the many children whose school lives were interwoven with his own. To make sense of Jake's data set—and that of 7 of his peers—I took from the literacy dialogue of the mid-1980s a definition of writing as a mediational tool used to participate in social events (Basso, 1974; Heath, 1983): Writing is not only a means of representing an individual's meaning; it also serves to mediate relationships between writers and others. Written forms do social work in the world. This definition of writing—this conceptual boundary—would frame both child writer and coparticipants in the observed event. Moreover, it would situate any particular event in a larger cultural world within which that event had some function and had gained some meaning.

Accompanying new views of literacy were new perspectives on development as well, most notably those inspired by the sociocultural theory of Vygotsky (1962, 1978). These perspectives also would draw a larger boundary around individual children, for those children would be seen as "grow[ing] *into* the intellectual life of those around them" (Vygotsky, 1978, p. 77; emphasis added). Vygotskian theory highlighted how children learned through interaction with others, and it emphasized language as the key learning tool; it was language that provided the cultural and cognitive link between child and adult mind and allowed the child to learn the ways of thinking—and the ways of reading and writing—of their society.

In Jake's case, however, the boundaries that "fit" the data were not those of child apprentices to adult-governed worlds (e.g., Heath, 1983; Ninio, & Bruner, 1978). The data were gathered through close observation of children, not through close observation of adult / child encounters. Those children had attended mainly to each other; adults had faded in and out of the viewing frame. Thus, in dialogue with both theory and data, I drew my analytic boundaries around children engaged with other children—children brought together and guided by adults in official worlds but children who organized their own life spaces in response to those worlds (Cook-Gumperz, 1981; Corsaro, 1985). Within such boundaries, it seemed possible to gain insight into the sociocultural dynamics of learning to write, that is, of developing control over a mediational tool in the social world of school children.

The research question, then, became, how did writing come to be a useful tool within the social lives and the symbolic repertoire of Jake and his peers? In Jake's case in particular, composing served to mediate his relationship with Manuel, a regular coparticipant in his events. For both boys, writing had meaning in a larger school world in which child stories were tools for both immediate engagement and later appreciation ("Just at the very end … they read the entire story … I get blown up"). The picture in Figure 15–4, by Jake himself, is a kind of pictorial metaphor for Jake's case. It depicts the linked fates of Jake and Manuel: Manuel, who wanted to be an artist, is drawing a picture of Jake, who wanted to be a pilot.

To answer the project question, I developed coding categories to describe how children used talk, pictures, and written texts to create and to enter into their own and others' composed worlds. One set of categories referred to the functions of the children's language, for example to *represent* aspects of real and imaginary situations, to *interact* with others, and to *evaluate* or express their feelings and attitudes. Another set examined the *meaning elements* represented in children's interwoven talk, drawing, and writing, including, for example, objects, actors, actions, placement in space and time (past, present, future) and sensorimotor qualities (direction, force, speed, volume). It was this vocabulary that revealed, for example, that, as a first grader, Jake's narrative talk during drawing moved through time, but his written language was stuck within the static space / time dimensions of his completed picture frame.

Jake Pushes Boundaries. As the 2 years of the study passed, Jake and his peers both clarified and complicated the guiding definitions of writing and development. Like Rachel, Jake was a child who used stories to express his feelings about— his evaluations of—the world. But this use was not seen simply as an attribute of Jake or as a reflection of his experienced world, nor was his composing seen as a direct reflection of placement along a linear evolution of writing behavior. Rather, Jake's

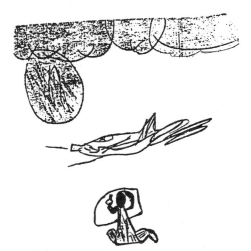

FIGURE 15–4 Framing Jake and Manuel

ways of composing, like those of his peers, were seen as shaped at the intersection of his symbolic resources and social intentions, which were themselves influenced by the social structure and interactional possibilities of his classroom, and, more broadly, the culture of his school.

Initially, Jake and his peers used the familiar tools of drawing and talk to participate in journal time. But, gradually, functional shifts occurred: writing itself began to assume more of the social and intellectual work of composing. Thus, a 2nd-grade Jake interacted with—teased—his good friend Manuel through writing as well as through talk. He manipulated the words on the page in order to manipulate Manuel. Moreover, he used evaluative techniques (Labov, & Waletsky, 1967), like suspending narrative action at critical points (e.g., "I am OK but I don't know about Manuel"), to express his feelings about his world (especially his consistent theme of friends threatened but saved, by him of course).

But Jake's talk did not become less important; for Jake and his peers, as for academics, texts became the center of— embedded in—social interactions and intellectual debates. In fact, it was this embedding that fueled and guided his writing. Jake *was not moving away from the social world;* he was learning new ways of engaging with it.

As the preceding analysis of Jake's writing and development suggests, my interpretive methodology and my guiding definitions of writing—as mediational tool in sociocultural events—were more compatible than they had been in the cases of Rachel and her peers. Still, these new boundaries around Jake and his classmates began to fray even as they took form. One reason simply was time. It is different to spend 2 years with a child, rather than a few months, as with Rachel. Jake was not just a child writer; he was a complex character— a peer among children, a sometimes struggling student, and, he hoped, a "tough" and "slick" kid. His choices of topic, characters, and plot events, his way of interacting with others about his texts— all said something about Jake's relationship to his social world and, perhaps, to the ideological one also (e.g., to being a boy, a vulnerable child in what he regarded as the tough and "crazy part" of the city).

Yet, the specifics of content choices and, more broadly, of sociocultural identity did not figure in any prominent way in Jake's case. But this changed in Tina's school.

Tina: Writing as Social and Ideological Dialogue

In Geertz's (1973, p. 23) words, one can "study different things in different places"—and Tina's school was a place in which issues of identity became strikingly visible. Her urban K–3 school served primarily two neighborhoods, one an African-American, low-income and working-class community, where Tina lived, and the other, an integrated but primarily European-American working- and middle-class community. At the preceding school, Jake's close friends had included children from diverse ethnic backgrounds, most of whom lived in his integrated working-class neighborhood. Tina's close friends were also from her neighborhood, but it was not integrated. Tina, like most of her peers, interacted with those from across the economic divide primarily in official school activities.

Thus, studying child literacy in the context of child social relationships brought into the viewing frame the interrelated issues of race, class, gender, and culture. Indeed, in my first study at this site, I examined how young child composers made use of diverse cultural resources—the discourse traditions of their home community, those of the popular media, and those stressed in school (Dyson, 1993a).

The second project at the site (Dyson, 1995) began with an informal visit to Tina's second grade classroom during writing time, when I noticed the pervasiveness of superheroes, figures like teenage ninjas (both the human and the "mutant turtle" variety) and X-men (a team of mutant humans, both women and men, with great powers). These superheroes were especially visible during an optional practice named "Author's Theater" by the children's teacher, Kristin; in this practice, the children chose classmates to act out their written stories.

Given that popular media stories appeal to children's ideologically informed desires as members of particular gender and age groups and, less directly, of particular ethnicities and socioeconomic circumstances (Kline, 1993), I wondered how such stories figured into the social and literacy life of Kristin's children (e.g., who wrote such stories, to be enacted by whom, with what sort of changes over time in textual content and structure). Although superhero stories were written primarily by boys, some girls did evidence interest—all working class girls, among them, Tina.

A tiny child with large glasses, Tina was a complex character, one who voiced a strong sense of identity as an African American, as a caring person who "love[d] the world," and as a "tough" kid. "She thinks just because I'm small," that "I can't beat her up," said Tina one day in the midst of a verbal (or rather chillingly silent) fight with her good friend Makeda, "But I'll show her." The complexity of Tina—and her intense reaction to being excluded from anybody's story world—is evident in the summarized drama below.

The Drama—and Dramas—of Tina. For weeks, the boys in Tina's 2nd-grade class had been writing stories for Author's Theater about ninjas, ninja turtles, and X-men—and, for weeks, Tina had been begging for a part to play, with no luck at all. The only boy who regularly included girls in superhero dramas was Sammy, and he, like other boys, picked only Melissa or Sarah, two slender, middle-class, and outgoing white girls—just as were the ninja's "foxy babes" in the popular media stories.

In actuality, neither Melissa nor Sarah campaigned for these roles; indeed, they were not allowed to watch such movies and cartoons. In this classroom, evidenced knowledge of popular media superheroes was related to both gender and class. That is, working class girls, like Tina, generally could carry on informed discussions about these characters, even though they did not write about them. Yet, despite their knowledge and, in some cases, their active campaigning for roles, they were regularly excluded.

Tina had had it. Usually, when she wrote in her journal (entitled "The Peace Book"), she wrote brief texts expressing her love of family and friends. But on this day, Tina enticed her best friend Holly to write a superhero story with her. "And no boys," she said firmly, "'cause the boys doesn't let us play."

Sitting side by side, Tina and Holly began playfully to plan an X-men story. (X-men stories were particularly appealing, since the X-men superhero team includes "strong" and "tough" girls, including girls of color.) When the children began, Tina planned to be the X-men character Rogue. But she quickly became "the toughest guy in the world. ... We're all Blobs!" (Blobs are huge, fleshy mutant humans, virtually indestructible and very bad guys.) "'Cause if somebody threw a metal ball at me, the energy go right through me and I would never know. And we're sisters robbing the world. ... And we'll never get sick. And we'll never die."

The sisters evolved, Tina becoming Uncle Blob, Holly niece Blob. As the girls became more and more animated, they moved to the classroom rug, deep in play. In the drama, Uncle Blob Tina captured the female X-men character Rogue, cutting off her long hair. Uncle Blob drank that hair, absorbing its fiery power, giving just a small bit to his begging niece Holly Blob. "The only thing you can do," he tells the girl, "is just shoot out fire at them [the X-men] and then just call me." (There are shades here of the ninja stories and of the girls who call for help.)

Class composing time ended before the children had put pencil to paper. The next day Tina was absent, and so each girl eventually authored her own X-men story. However, given the intensity of peer pressure, each girl also found it impossible to write the planned drama. For example, on the day Tina attempted to write her X-men story, both girls and boys begged for powerful good-guy roles—and expressed great unhappiness with the unapologetic bad guys Tina had in mind. This pressure resulted in a story without the Blob family but, also, a story without the usual good-guys-defeat-the-bad-guys encounter. Following is an edited excerpt from Tina's story:

> Once there were 4 X-men [Storm, Rogue, Jean Gray, and Archangel].
> And the X-men fought others.
> One X-men died.
> And the rest of them were
> sad. They cried.

This was an unusual superhero story for her class: there was a predominance of women, enacted primarily by girls of color; there was also a death among the good guys; and, most strikingly, a good cry by the superheroes. During the peer enactment of her story, Tina reinforced the disruption of the usual gendered order:

Tina: (reading) "One of the X-men *died*... And the rest were very sad. They cried." Everybody [all of the child actors] cry now, even the *boys*.

As a third grader, Tina temporarily abandoned her interest in X-men stories—"too boyish," she explained; indeed, she even wrote a superhero story featuring a female victim ("Batman will save us girls," she wrote, "Hurry Batman hurry."). Yet, she consistently campaigned for roles in boys' superhero stories, roles in which sometimes "the girls win."

Moreover, in February of her 3rd-grade year, she began once again writing (and once again involving classmates in) stories that displayed diverse gender relations, among them lovers or spouses, perpetrators / rescuers / victims, disciplinarian / disciplined, nurturer / nurtured, and teammates, with males and females in varied role combinations. As in the second grade, Tina's stories were linked to ongoing class issues and particular interpersonal engagements.

For example, in the last month of school, Tina wrote a superhero story that included diverse female / male roles. Moreover, it included both superhero themes from the popular media and information from a class unit on the superheroes of ancient Greece. In that unit, Tina chose Venus, goddess of beauty, as her project topic, as did her friend Makeda. Sitting side by side, Tina and Makeda initially drew Venus as fair-haired and white. Lena, also at their table, drew her goddess Black, but commented that she was sure it was "wrong," because "people from Greece are not Black."

"Yes, they can be," countered Tina. When Makeda reiterated that her Venus was white, Tina commented, "Well, maybe she's white to you, but not to me." And Tina (and later Makeda) drew a Black goddess as well. Moreover, Tina wrote the piece excerpted below, in which Venus, whose middle name is Tina, saves the world for both boys and girls:

> Once there was a boy and girl in the park and two men was walking by the park and the men saw the two kids. So the two men started to run after them. And the kids ran. One man chased the girl the other ran after the boy. The boy name was Aloyse [a classmate] and the [girl] name was Asia [her sister]. So when Venus Tina heard about this she was mad. So she came down ... and picked the kids up on her magical flying horse named Makeda. It was a girl horse and she took the two kids ... in the sky. There was a big park on a cloud. There was a lot of kids play[ing] on flying horses. It was kids from [Tina's] school. ... Then she took them home. They said what about those two mean men. Venus Tina made them nice. And on earth was fun again. She made parks safe for us kids of the world. By Tina. Love Tina.

Defining the Viewing Frame: Analytic Tools. In Tina's case study, the child in the viewing frame was interacting with others in the local situation but, at the same time, that local interaction was substantiating—and, in some ways, challenging— interactions that took place beyond the classroom walls. Understanding such complexity required a perspective on literacy that made explicit provision for the ideological dimension of language use.

Thus, I appropriated the language of Bakhtin's dialogism (1981, 1986; Volosinov, 1973), a theoretical perspective gaining increased visibility in the literacy dialogue of the 1990s. From a Bakhtinian vantage point, the conceptual boundary around Tina would include her interactional partners in the immediate social scene, just as it had in Jake's case. But the voices within that context would have ideological echoes. That is, from a dialogic perspective, writers not only use words in particular situations to interact with others; they also adopt or resist the expected words, the words available to them in those situations as women or men, as people of varied ages and heritages, of different roles, statuses and dispositions.

Moreover, this vantage point also suggested new visions of development. In these visions, children were not unproblematically "growing into the intellectual life of those around them" (Vygotsky, 1978, p. 77). Rather, they were also growing into, or in some way against, the existent social order through which that life was enacted. Social identification and social conflict—not only internal psycholinguistic conflicts and interactional guidance—influence the direction of learning (Dyson, 1995; Goodnow, 1990). Thus, my research question became, what is the nature of the interplay between the changing interactional and ideological dynamics of individual children's classroom lives and the changing nature of their writing processes and products?

A pictorial metaphor for Tina's case in particular, might be the product in Figure 15–5, which Tina drew during her 3rd-grade lapse in social activism. Tina juxtaposed symbolic material: the words *no no X-men* ("too boyish," she had said) and, underneath, large, colorful depictions of Aladdin and Princess Jasmine, the romantic pair from a popular fantasy movie. Tina's product was clearly rooted in the social world of her classroom *and* in the ideological world as well.

To construct Tina's case, I used ethnographic analysis of all class members' official and unofficial discussions of gender, race, and power (i.e., strength) *and* case study analysis of the content and structure of the writing and talking of the focal children, including Tina.

Just as in the cases of Rachel and Jake, many children in Tina's room initially made minimal use of actual print. Indeed, their written texts functioned primarily as *props* for (or, more accurately, as "tickets" to) the theater: their texts were largely invisible; they stood up and pretended to read texts that were not actually written. And, as in Jake's case, over time children's texts became more central to their social life in this classroom. In this project, however, I aimed to detail the children's social goals and the precise ways in which texts mediate those goals.

Thus, I constructed a category system to describe the children's social goals (e.g., affiliating with others, resisting

FIGURE 15–5 Framing Tina's social and ideological world

them, or, more equitably, negotiating with them) and, also, the way in which the written texts served those goals. For example, their texts could serve as *representations of valued characters and actions*, as *reinforcers of their authority as authors*, their right to say how the world is, and as *dialogic mediators* between themselves and others, as ways of anticipating and responding to others' reactions to their stories.

Tina Pushes Boundaries. The data analysis for this project is ongoing as of this writing. Still, the initial construction of Tina's case has further clarified and complicated perspectives on writing and its development and, moreover, on the potential use of case study methodology itself. To construct the case of Rachel, a child's writing was set against the backdrop of a developmental scheme of child literacy. To construct the case of Jake, a child's writing was first situated within the interactional dynamics of his daily school life. To construct the case of Tina, a case informed by Bakhtinian theory, that writing was also set within the *ideological* dynamics of her classroom community; and those dynamics sometimes foregrounded gender, race, or class.

The goal of the ongoing project is not to compare individual cases that represent particular categories (e.g., to compare a representative boy to a representative girl, or a representative black child to a representative white child). Rather, the goal is to examine how individuals (like Tina) participate in the classroom context as a whole and the interplay between the interactional and ideological dynamics of that classroom life and the particulars of their ways of writing. Gender, race, and class are included in the analysis when they are foregrounded in those dynamics, that is, when they are underscored in the social conversation being furthered through writing. (Such a perspective on gender, race, and class is consistent with poststructuralist theory, which emphasizes the fluid nature of sociocultural identity; see, for example, Williams, 1991.)

In Tina's case, her ways of writing were interrelated with the micropolitics of the classroom. Thus, social conflicts— not only social interactions—helped make salient for her new kinds of writing choices, newly imagined ways of depicting human relationships. What I as an adult might label an ideological critique did not originate from teacher-led critical discussions, but from child-initiated and teacher-supported objections to perceptions of unfair play. That is, Tina did not initiate criticisms of textual representations in and of themselves (e.g., she did not object to women being "sexual objects" in media stories); she reacted to exclusion. For example, she raised the issue of race when she felt excluded from being a "goddess," of gender when excluded from being a "good guy."

In both the first and the second grade, Tina's ways of developing her texts (e.g., the characters she included, the elaborations of basic descriptions and actions she added) were linked, in part, to ongoing class discussions about issues of gender, which were interrelated in complex ways with those of race, and, in the third grade, sexual orientation. In Bakhtin's sense, Tina had something important to "say" in the ongoing class conversation. For example, in her Venus story, Tina notes that both the boy and the girl were subject to the same fate (i.e., being chased by the mean men), and she explicitly marks the flying horse as a girl horse, as Makeda.

Further, Tina was not only developing her own text. She was a key player in the classroom collective; she "talked back" (hooks, 1990), raising issues that reverberated in the class and caused others to rethink—not in grand moments of collective classroom revolution, but in small moments of shifting positions. For instance, urged on by the resistance of her tough friend Tina (and encouraged by her approving teacher Kristin), Makeda imagined a Black Venus, despite the classroom books filled exclusively with fair-haired and light-skinned goddesses.

Just as Tina stretched the meaning of "Venus" in the local culture of her classroom to include her, so too the construction of her case has involved stretching definitions of literacy and of development to include the complexity of her experiences. Thus, like Rachel and Jake, Tina's case is providing material to think with, particularly, material to consider the interrelated ideological and interpersonal dynamics of learning to write. To use Geertz's words, Tina's case does not move from "already proven theorems to newly proven ones," but rather "plung[es]" more deeply into the same thing, that is, into the experience of learning to write (1973, p. 25).

SHIFTING CONTEXTS: THE ROLE OF CASES IN PROFESSIONAL DIALOGUE

What, then, is the role of case studies in the repertoire of scholarly ways of studying literacy? What professional contribution can be made through close observation of small numbers of children, given the thousands of children in our schools?

To answer that question, one might turn it on itself and ask, what *can* be done with thousands of children *but* count them? In mass, children—and the challenges they present—are faceless, nameless, and overwhelming. But these massive numbers of children are not isolated individuals; they are social participants included, or so we hope, in particular classrooms and schools, in particular institutions and communities.

Through interpretive case studies, researchers offer educators in these places no specific laws of causation, no precise predictions of the outcomes of one teaching strategy or another. But they do offer, through the richness of singular experiences, opportunities to consider the complexities of teaching and learning by embedding them within the details of everyday life in school. It is precisely those details that account for the tremendous potential of case studies to *both* further and stifle professional dialogue.

Providing a Basis for Dialogue

In its careful grounding of important abstractions in mundane particulars, case study research offers diverse professionals a means for identifying and talking about the dimensions and dynamics of living and learning in classrooms (and other settings as well). As Hymes (1972, p. xiv) noted in his discussion of educational ethnography, careful studies of particular classrooms and communities make available

> helpful perspectives and insights but for them to be effective in a classroom, they must be articulated in terms of the features of that classroom and its community context. The participants in the situation must themselves in effect be ethnographers of their own situation. [For them, research] can suggest new things to notice, reflect upon, and do... [But] in the last analysis, it is the understanding and insight of those in the concrete situation that will determine the outcome.

The illustrative cases in this chapter all focused on the dimensions and dynamics of learning to write. In each case, children's engagement with literacy—and the observer's visions of child literacy—were shaped by the social situations in which they found themselves. Those situations were interpreted differently by children from different sociocultural backgrounds and, indeed, by children with different personal dispositions, interests, and styles. Thus, the cases yielded, not prescriptions for practice, but material for reflection about particular aspects of the situated nature of learning to write.

For example, the cases illustrated ways in which the symbolic resources available to children matter. Educators in diverse settings might ask: is it possible for children to, and do particular children choose to, accompany their writing with drawing or drama, with collaborative talk? What challenges do such media present (e.g., the challenge of transforming dramatic sound effects to black and white squiggles, static pictures to dynamic narratives)?

Further, the cases illustrated ways in which official and unofficial social dynamics matter to classroom learning. Children's social goals influence their ways of writing, as do their social partners, including those they write with and those they write for. Moreover, the sorts of public forums available for public sharing and community building are worthy of consideration. Educators might consider, what sort of public participation is possible? with what sort of assumed purpose and expected response? If purpose or response is altered, do and how do patterns of participation change?

Finally, classroom texts (both child- and adult-authored) generate their own set of possibilities and constraints. Educators might consider if, and how, the literate culture (i.e., the dominant topics, themes, genres) figures into the ideological and interpersonal dynamic of the class. Are there points of tension? of children written out (or written in) by others in ways that are uncomfortable for them? How is—could—such discomfort be evidenced?

Just as important as such potential points of reflection anticipated by a researcher are those that are unanticipated. Teachers and other professionals in diverse roles bring their own concerns and vantage points to the details of specific cases (Florio-Ruane, 1991). As Genishi (1992) notes, teachers in particular, are interventionists who construct "theories of practice" (p. 198) that will help them take action to support the individuals in their classrooms. Their particular perspectives may cause them to foreground different research details or data, to identify different dynamics. For example, Florio-Ruane discusses how teachers responded to data gathered in their own classrooms by raising unanticipated issues about "contextual constraints that arise from outside the classroom" (p. 252), issues involving parents, administrators, textbook publishers, and politicians, among others.

Differing vantage points on the particularities of classroom life could be remarkably productive for all concerned. Indeed, they might contribute to the envisioned democratic participation in educational knowledge-creation discussed by Hymes (1972). As he notes, outside researchers can offer new perspectives, connecting local circumstances to overarching issues and to nonlocal but relevant experiences. But insiders by virtue of being insiders have access to the possibilities and problems of particular situations, access denied those whose participation is structured, at least in part, by theoretical and methodological demands. Yet, the very details that may contribute to dialogic encounters may also contribute to the rigidity of conceptual and professional boundaries.

Constructing Rigid Boundaries

When case study research yields texts of "classroom implications," details of behavior may be separated from the social and cultural circumstance that made those details locally sensible, and they may be separated as well from the conceptual issues that make those details nonlocally useful as material for reflection. Thus made anemic, case studies may give rise to illegal prescriptions, to suspect normative guides. Indeed, the very nature of researchers' written reports may infuse them with the artificial prescriptive authority of the distanced expert (Florio-Ruane, 1991).

For example, the "emergent literacy" behaviors of selected young children in particular settings have been represented as set "stages," as behaviors to be expected from other children in other contexts, children with different resources and end goals, children who may follow different developmental paths (for critiques, see Dyson, 1993b; Sahni, 1994). Interpretive methodology *is* used to ask basic developmental questions about changes over time in children's ways of participating in the everyday activities of family, peer, and community life (e.g., Corsaro, & Miller, 1992; Heath, 1983; Schieffelin, 1990). But exactly what sorts of child responses are universal, at what level of specificity, are questions, not taken-for-granted assumptions (Gaskins, Miller, & Corsaro, 1992).

Such caution is necessary, because people learn to read and write at different ages, with different guiding intentions and available materials, with the support of varied coparticipants, cultural resources, and symbolic tools (Farr, 1994; Sahni, 1994). First-grader Jake, for example, differed markedly from other portraits of beginning writers: he did not view writing as play (cf. Graves, 1983); he did not make extensive use of "invented" spellings (cf. Bissex, 1980); nor did he have any particular interest in writing personal narratives (cf. Sowers, 1985). The purpose of interpretive case studies is not to contribute to rigid developmental portraits. Rather, it is to gain insight into the complexity of literacy learning; any proposed universals must come from comparisons of cases carefully situated within diverse social circumstances.

This potential weakness—this use of detail, not to think with, but to prescribe from—also can occur in reference to teacher, rather than child, behavior. The specific procedures of specific teachers in specific school settings may become suggested "methods," instructional scripts, which are then transferred to other settings and other participants with different human and material resources, and different curricular possibilities (e.g., Bartolome, 1994; Reyes, 1992). Case studies may thus become ideological tools that help transform human variety into human deficiency.

Such a use of case study details—with its accompanying dismissal of situational complexity and theoretical depth—is antithetical to the very nature of case studies. Indeed, it is precisely because such a use *is* inappropriate that case study methodology has the potential to further true professional dialogue. To return to Hymes' (1972) insights, case studies may yield new ways of paying attention to, and potentially intervening in, the dimensions and dynamics of child learning in classrooms; but the transformation of new perspectives into specific interventions depends on the professional judgment of professional educators in particular circumstances.

Talking across Boundaries

In the introduction of this paper, Makeda said that a story was "kinda like *your* life," and, in a very fundamental sense, she was right. Stories, including those we tell about other people, are also about ourselves, written from our particular vantage points. In interaction, each speaker or writer infuses given words like literacy and development with new accents, new dimensions, because each is positioned differently in the social and ideological ground. Crossing conceptual boundaries is thus linked with crossing human ones: when we, with our diverse experiences and our common concerns, converse, we push each other out of bounds, we help each other attend to the world a bit differently.

Such ongoing conversations about children, teaching, and schooling are critical. Even in one school district teachers work in an amazing array of classroom situations, greeting children who bring to school diverse language and cultural resources, varied histories and relationships with literacy and, moreover, with educational and societal institutions. Rigid curricula and rigid teaching based on narrow visions of children's lives will not help teachers in their work. Moreover, not only is there present diversity, chronologically, the contextual ground of education is always shifting; our ways of thinking and talking about children and education are grounded in particular historical, intellectual, and cultural conditions (Cherryholmes, 1988).

Promoting conversation will require changes in institutional organization and epistemological visions beyond the focus of this chapter. But surely, one possible means for bringing adults out of their own distinctive professional boundaries and into common conversation is a mutual interest in, appreciation of, and pleasure in knowing the young. When studied indepth, individual children emerge from the shadows, as Sammy did from the underworld, potentially enriching the ongoing conversation about literacy, development, and schooling.

References

Almy, M., & Genishi, C. (1979). *Ways of studying children.* New York: Teachers College Press.

Bakhtin, M. (1981). Discourse in the novel. In C. Emerson & M. Holquist (Eds.), *The dialogic imagination: Four essays by M. Bakhtin* (pp. 259–422). Austin, TX: University of Texas Press.

Bakhtin, M. (1986). *Speech genres and other late essays.* Austin, TX: University of Texas Press.

Bartolome, L. I. (1994). Beyond the methods fetish: Toward a humanizing pedagogy. *Harvard Educational Review, 64,* 173–194.

Basso, K. (1974). The ethnography of writing. In R. Bauman & J. Sherzer (Eds.), *Explorations in the ethnography of speaking.* Cambridge: Cambridge University Press.

Bissex, G. (1980). *Gyns at wrk: A child learns to read and write.* Cambridge, MA: Harvard University Press.

Bogdan, R., & Biklen, S. (1992). *Qualitative research for education* (2nd ed.). Needham Heights, MA: Allyn & Bacon.

Bruner, J., & Haste, H. (Eds.) (1987). *Making sense: The child's construction of the world.* New York: Methuen.

Cherryholmes, C. H. (1988). *Power and criticism: Poststructural investigations in education.* New York: Teachers College Press.

Children's Defense Fund. (1994). *The state of America's children.* Washington, DC: Children's Defense Fund.

Clay, M. (1975). *What did I write?* Auckland: Heinemann.

Cook-Gumperz, J. (1981). Persuasive talk: The social organization of children's talk. In J. Greene & C. Wallat (Eds.), *Ethnography and language in educational settings* (pp. 25–50). Norwood, NJ: Ablex.

Corsaro, W. (1985). *Friendship and peer culture in the early years.* Norwood, NJ: Ablex.

Corsaro, W., & Miller, P. (Eds.). (1992). *Interpretive approaches to children's socialization.* San Francisco: Jossey-Bass.

Dyson, A. H. (1981). *A case study examination of the role of oral language in the writing processes of kindergartners.* Unpublished doctoral dissertation, University of Texas, Austin.

Dyson, A. H. (1983). The role of oral language in early writing processes. *Research in the Teaching of English, 17,* 1–30.

Dyson, A. H. (1989). *Multiple worlds of child writers: Friends learning to write.* New York: Teachers College Press.

Dyson, A. H. (1993a). *The social worlds of children learning to write in an urban primary school.* New York: Teachers College Press.

Dyson, A. H. (1993b). From invention to social action in early childhood literacy: A reconceptualization through dialogue about difference. *Early Childhood Research Quarterly, 8,* 409–426.

Dyson, A. H. (1995). Writing children: Reinventing the development of childhood literacy. *Written Communication, 12,* 3–46.

Erickson, F. (1986). Qualitative methods in research on teaching. In M. C. Wittrock (Ed.), *Handbook of research on teaching* (pp. 119–161). New York: Macmillan.

Farr, M. (1994). En los dos idiomas: Literacy practices among Chicano Mexicanos. In B. Moss (Ed.), *Literacy across communities* (pp. 9–48). Cresskill, NJ: Hampton Press.

Ferreiro, E. (1978). What is written in a written sentence? A developmental answer. *Journal of Education, 160,* 25–39.

Florio-Ruane, S. (1989). Social organization of classes and schools. In M. Reynolds (Ed.), *Knowledge base for the beginning teacher* (pp. 163–177). Oxford: Pergamon Press.

Florio-Ruane, S. (1991). Conversation and narrative in collaborative research: An ethnography of the written literacy forum. In C. Witherell & N. Noddings (Eds.), *Stories lives tell: Narrative and dialogue in education* (pp. 234–256). New York: Teachers College Press.

Gaskins, S. Miller, P., & Corsaro, W. (1992). Theoretical and methodological perspectives on the interpretive study of children. In W. Corsaro & P. Miller (Eds.), *Interpretive approaches to children's socialization* (pp. 5–24). San Francisco: Jossey-Bass.

Geertz, C. (1973). *The interpretation of cultures.* New York: Basic Books.

Geertz, C. (1988). *Works and lives: The anthropologist as author.* Stanford, CA: Stanford University Press.

Genishi, C. (1992). Looking forward: Toward stories of theory and practice. In C. Genishi (Ed.), *Ways of assessing children and curriculum: Stories of early childhood practice* (pp. 191–208). New York: Teachers College Press.

Gilbert, P. (1994). And they lived happily ever after: Cultural storylines and the construction of gender. In A. H. Dyson & C. Genishi (Eds.), *The need for story: Cultural diversity in classroom and community* (pp. 124–144). Urbana, IL: National Council of Teachers of English.

Goodnow, J. (1990). Using sociology to extend psychological accounts of cognitive development. *Human Development, 33,* 81–107.

Gould, S. (1987). *An urchin in the storm: Essays about books and ideas.* New York: W. W. Norton.

Graves, D. H. (1975). An examination of the writing processes of seven-year-old children. *Research in the Teaching of English, 9,* 227–41.

Graves, D. H. (1983). *Writing: Teachers and children at work.* Portsmouth, NH: Heinemann.

Greene, M. (1988). *The dialectic of freedom.* New York: Teachers College Press.

Heath, S.B. (1983). *Ways with words: Language, life and work in communities and classrooms.* Cambridge: Cambridge University Press.

hooks, b. (1990). Talking back. In R. Ferguson, M. Gever, T. Minh-ha, & C. West (Eds.), *Out there: Marginalization and contemporary cultures* (pp. 331–340). New York: The New Museum of Contemporary Art and Cambridge, MA: MIT Press.

Hymes, D. (1972). Introduction. In C. Cazden, V. John, & D. Hymes (Eds.), *Functions of language in the classroom* (pp. xi–xvii). New York: Teachers College Press.

Kline, S. (1993). *Out of the garden: Toys, TV, and children's culture in the age of marketing.* London: Verso.

Labov W., & Waletsky, J. (1967). Narrative analysis: Oral versions of personal experience. In *Essays on the verbal and visual arts, proceedings of the 1966 spring meeting of the American Ethnological Society* (pp. 12–44). Seattle: University of Washington Press.

Newkirk, T. (1987). The non-narrative writing of young children. *Research in the Teaching of English, 21,* 121–145.

Ninio, A., & Bruner, J. (1978). The achievement and antecedents of labeling. *Journal of Child Language, 5,* 1–15.

Nystrand, M., Greene, S., & Wiemelt, J. (1993). Where did composition studies come from? An intellectual history. *Written Communication, 10,* 267–333.

Olson, D. (1977). From utterance to text. *Harvard Educational Review, 47,* 247–279.

Ottenberg, S. (1990). Thirty years of fieldnotes: Changing relationships to the text. In R. Sanjek (Ed.), *Fieldnotes: The makings of anthropology* (pp. 139–160). Ithaca, NY: Cornell University Press.

Piaget, J., & Inhelder, B. (1969). *The psychology of the child.* New York: Basic Books.

Polakow, V. (1992). Deconstructing the discourse of care: Young children in the shadows of democracy. In S. Kessler & B. B. Swadener (Eds.), *Reconceptualizing the early childhood curriculum: Beginning the dialogue* (pp. 123–148). New York: Teachers College Press.

Read, C. (1975). Pre-school children's knowledge of English phonology. *Harvard Educational Review, 41,* 1–34.

Reyes, M. de la Luz. (1992). Challenging venerable assumptions: Literacy instruction for linguistically different students. *Harvard Educational Review, 62,* 427–446.

Rosaldo, R. (1989). *Culture and truth: The remaking of social analysis.* Boston: Beacon Press.

Sahni, U. (1994). *Building circles of mutuality: A sociocultural analysis of literacy in a rural classroom in India.* Unpublished doctoral dissertation, University of California, Berkeley.

Schieffelin, B. (1990). *The give and take of everyday life: Language socialization of Kaluli children.* Cambridge: Cambridge University Press.

Snow, C. (1983). Literacy and language: Relationships during the preschool years. *Harvard Educational Review, 53*(2), 165–189.

Sowers, S. (1985). Learning to write in a classroom workshop: A study in grades one through four. In M.F. Whiteman (Ed.), *Advances in writing research: Vol. 1. Children's early writing development* (pp. 297–342). Norwood, NJ: Ablex.

Stake, R. (1988). Case study methods in educational research: Seeking sweet water. In R. M. Jaeger (Ed.), *Complementary methods for research in education.* Washington, DC: American Educational Research Association.

Thorne, B. (1987). Re-visioning women and social change: Where are the children? *Gender & Society, 1,* 85–109.

Volosinov, V. N. (1973). *Marxism and the philosophy of language* (L. Matejka & I. R. Titunik, Trans.). New York: Seminar Press.

Vygotsky, L. (1962). *Thought and language.* Cambridge, MA: MIT Press.

Vygotsky, L. (1978). *Mind in society.* Cambridge, MA: Harvard University Press.

Williams, P. J. (1991). *The alchemy of race and rights.* Cambridge, MA: Harvard University Press.

16

ETHNOGRAPHY AND ETHNOGRAPHERS OF AND IN EDUCATION: A SITUATED PERSPECTIVE

Judith Green
UNIVERSITY OF CALIFORNIA, SANTA BARBARA

David Bloome
VANDERBILT UNIVERSITY

In this chapter, we explore sites of ethnography, not physical sites of people studied but intellectual sites that frame how ethnography is being undertaken in particular ways. The approach we have taken complements recent discussions of ethnography and ethnographic research in the social sciences and education emphasizing the scope of topics, research designs, methods, and theoretical traditions as well as differences from other qualitative and quantitative approaches to research (e.g., Duranti, & Goodwin, 1992; Egan-Robertson, & Willett, in press; Guthrie, & Hall, 1984; Hammersley, 1990; Spindler, & Spindler, 1987; Zaharlick, & Green, 1991). Yet, at the same time, our approach intends to provide another way of looking at ethnography and ethnographic research. As Brian Street's (1993b) review of Martyn Hammersley's (1992) book, *What's Wrong With Ethnography?* makes clear, ethnographic research has evolved and changed over the past 3 decades. Not only has the use of ethnography and ethnographic research become more sophisticated and researchers more aware of the complexities and issues involved, there have been important changes in what counts as ethnography and ethnographic research, who conducts such research, where and how the research agenda being pursued, and how such research contributes to evolving knowledge bases in education and the social sciences. These changes have led to enhanced understandings about how such research can be used to contribute to changes in various social institutions.

As a process of inquiry, ethnography has become a resource for a broad range of people including social scientists, teachers, students, and everyday members of society. Our discussion of ethnography as a process of inquiry differs from discussions of ethnography as primarily an act of writing (e.g., Clifford, & Marcus, 1986; van Maanen, 1988). We acknowledge that ethnography often involves writing about the culture of others (or as is more recently the case writing about the culture of one's own cultural group or subgroup) and that the writing process may influence the nature and meaning of inquiry. It is important to examine how writing is implicated in the meaning of ethnography (Atkinson, 1990). However, by emphasizing the inquiry process as the point of departure for discussing ethnography, rather than the writing as the point of departure, we emphasize ethnography as a way (or more accurately, as a set of ways) of exploring, knowing, and acting in and on the world neither subsumed by writing nor owned exclusively by academics. Through our analysis and discussion of various intellectual sites of ethnography, we make visible how the site shapes what counts as ethnography and how an ethnographic perspective and related practices inform the study of the social and cultural practices within and across social groups. As part of this discussion, we present the argument that ethnographic research, guided by social and cultural theories, provides a basis for the creation of a discipline within the field of education. This discipline has a set of methods, theories, questions, goals

The authors would like to thank Carol Dixon, University of California, Santa Barbara and Laurie Katz, Vanderbilt University for their editorial comments.

and practices that define what counts as ethnography-in-Education and as knowledge needed to engage in this form of ethnography.

To construct this argument and to examine relationships between site and the practice of ethnography, we approached the task of defining what counts as ethnography in a manner that parallels the ways in which ethnographers, grounded in cultural anthropology, enter a social group to examine the practices that members need to know, understand, produce and predict to participate in socially and culturally appropriate ways (cf. Goodenough, 1981; Heath, 1982). In describing our approach to this task, we are providing the reader with information about our own framework of the study of everyday practices. This information is needed to understand what we have included in our discussion and how our theoretical and methodological perspectives shaped the presentation about ethnography. We began by applying an ethnographic perspective and asking ethnographic questions derived, in this case, from cultural anthropology as a way of making visible what those who engage in ethnography mean by this term:

Where and by whom is ethnography being undertaken?
What questions about ethnography are being asked?
Who is doing the asking, when, for what reasons, and under what conditions?
What significance(s) do the questions have?

To present the issues identified, we integrate the voices of the ethnographers and others with our own to illustrate a range of issues about ethnography across sites raised over the past 3 decades. We selected the last 3 decades as a focus since this period parallels the beginnings of formal areas of study using ethnography in education. The Council on Anthropology and Education was formed in 1968 and the National Institute of Education established a panel to frame ethnographic studies of teaching as a linguistic process in 1974. This panel's report led a federal grant program that funded more than 2 million dollars in grants on this topic in 1978 (see Green, 1983a, for a synthesis of this group of studies). In making visible the issues raised across sites, we show that the arguments are not unique to one site. Rather, they are general ones that cross sites. This approach provides a basis for constructing a grounded view of ethnography as the practice of researchers within particular fields and disciplines. Our goal in taking this approach is to help readers construct an understanding of the range of issues involved in taking up ethnography as a theoretically driven, situated approach, not to synthesize ethnographic research or to reproduce discussions of field methods that already exists. For readers interested in additional discussions about ethnography across disciplines, we recommend the following as illustrative of discussions in, anthropology: Agar (1980), Ellen (1984), Geertz (1973, 1983), Gumperz and Hymes (1972), Pelto and Pelto (1978); in sociology: Denzin (1989), Denzin and Lincoln, (1994a), Hammersley and Atkinson (1983), van Maanen (1988); and education: Erickson (1986), Gumperz (1986), Graddol, Maybin and Stierer (1994), Heath (1982), Hymes (1982), Spindler (1982), Wolcott (1975, 1982, 1987), Zaharlick and Green (1991). For a historical analysis of ethnography, see Ellen (1984), Clifford (1988), Gilmore

and Smith, (1982), Harrington (1982), and Vidich and Lyman (1994).

The discussion of what counts as ethnography is presented in three sections. In the first section, we examine ethnography within social science. Through this discussion, we identify issues and directions in ethnography as practiced by social scientists across the disciplines of anthropology and sociology. We begin the second section by making a heuristic distinction between ethnography-*of*-education (e.g., anthropologists or sociologists studying education) and ethnography-*in*-education (e.g., educational researchers, teacher educators, teachers, and students employing ethnographic research to study education). In this section, we focus on ethnography-*in*-education to show how ethnography has become both a research approach for and a resource used by university-based researchers, teachers and students in preschools, elementary, secondary and higher education to collaborate in the study of everyday life in and out of schools. As part of this section, we illustrate how students and teachers have taken up the role of social scientists and adopted ethnographic perspectives and practices in order to explore their own communities. In the third section, we describe how ordinary people take up ethnography and ethnographic writing by describing the Mass Observation Project in the UK. Through the Mass Observation Project, ordinary people have become ethnographers of everyday life in Britain and their written contributions provide both a 'people's ethnography' and an archive that is being used by university-based researchers and others. In discussing the Mass Observation Project, we raise issues about the writing and reading of ethnography and ethnographic research that are applicable across sites of ethnographic research.

SOCIAL SCIENCE AS SITES OF ETHNOGRAPHY

In a recently published dialogue between American ethnographer Louis Smith (1990) and British ethnographer Martyn Hammersley, Smith asks whether, "Ethnography is ethnography is ethnography???" (p. 1). He answers his own question by arguing that:

> Ethnography as a social science is fractured along national lines (e.g., USA, UK, and the Commonwealth), disciplines (e.g., education, sociology and anthropology), substantive interests (e.g., classroom analysis, innovation and evaluation), smaller interpersonal University groups (e.g., Stanford, Manchester, East Anglia, etc.), paradigmatic perspectives (e.g., neo-positivists, interpretivists and critical theorists) and commitment to action and reform (action researchers versus more academic interpreters and analysts). (pp. 1, 2)

For Smith, what counts as ethnography varies with different sites and actors: national sites, university groups, conceptual and theoretical perspectives (i.e., philosophical positions, and purposes for doing ethnography). See Atkinson, Delamont, and Hammersley (1988) for a discussion of the differences between British and U.S. ethnographic research; see Corenstein (1992) for a description of ethnographic research in education in Mexico. Viewed in this way, there is no single place to go to define what counts as ethnography, only local sites inhabited by particular groups. Smith sees the differences as problematic, as fracturing the field, but he also argues that if we understand these differences, we can construct a productive dialogue among perspectives.

If we take Smith's challenge seriously, then the first task facing those of us who want to participate in such dialogues, engage in ethnographic research or use ethnographic research is to construct understandings of issues that shape what counts as ethnography in and across sites. However, as we illustrate in this section, defining what counts as ethnography is a complex and, at times, problematic task given the scope of issues, perspectives, and practices that come under the rubric of "ethnography" or "ethnographic."

Ethnography as Logics-in-Use

Ellen (1984) captured the variation suggested by Brian Street (1993a) and Louis Smith (1990) more than a decade ago in his book, *Ethnographic Research,* suggesting that concern over what counts as ethnography is not a new topic of discussion. In researching the history of ethnography for this textbook, he examined the ways in which the term ethnography was used across the academic fields of anthropology and sociology in the United States and the UK. His historical analysis showed that the term ethnography has been used to refer to a wide variety of phenomena and that there is a lack of common definition:

> Consider, for example, the word "ethnography". This word is used regularly to refer to empirical accounts of the culture and social organization of particular human populations (as in "an ethnographic monograph", "an ethnography"). The implication is that of a completed record, a product. But then the sense alters somewhat if we speak of "ethnography" as opposed to "theory", or of "an ethnographic account" (meaning living people) as opposed to an historical or archaeological account. Different again from all of these is the use of the term to indicate a set of research procedures, usually indicating intensive qualitative study of small groups through "participant-observation". ... Finally, "ethnography" may refer to an academic subject, a discipline in the wider sense involving the comparative study of ethnic groups. ... Thus, ethnography is something you may do, study, use, read, or write. The various uses reflect ways in which different scholars have appropriated the term, often for perfectly sound conceptual reasons. We would not wish to suggest that the word be employed in one sense only, even if it were possible to effectively dictate that this should be so. However, it is important to know that the differences, often subtle, exist. (pp. 7, 8)

As indicated in this quotation, the definition of ethnography as a process, a product, an area of study, or a way of constructing knowledge of the world depends on the context of use. Rather than seek a single point of view, which Ellen suggests may not be possible or desirable, we should seek understandings of the differences, often subtle, among the different uses within and across sites.

At the same time that Ellen reported this state of affairs, we found a similar pattern in discussion of criteria for an adequate ethnography (Green, & Bloome, 1983). In reviewing criteria for ethnography framed within anthropology to in-

form its use within Education, we found little agreement about criteria for assessing what counts as ethnography. Analysis of criteria for ethnography and research claiming an ethnographic perspective led us to draw a distinction among three approaches to ethnography in traditional social sciences as well as in Education: doing ethnography, adopting an ethnographic perspective, and using ethnographic tools. We argued, then, and continue to argue here, that *doing ethnography* involves the framing, conceptualizing, conducting, interpreting, writing, and reporting associated with a broad, in-depth, and long-term study of a social or cultural group, meeting the criteria for doing ethnography as framed within a discipline or field. (For example in anthropology, see discussions of criteria by Sanday, 1976; Spindler, 1982; Wolcott, 1975. For a complementary argument and a set of criteria for qualitative research in general see Denzin, & Lincoln, 1994b; Howe, & Eisenhart, 1990.)

By adopting an *ethnographic perspective,* we mean that it is possible to take a more focused approach (i.e., do less than a comprehensive ethnography) to study particular aspects of everyday life and cultural practices of a social group. Central to an ethnographic perspective is the use of theories of culture and inquiry practices derived from anthropology or sociology to guide the research. The final distinction, *using ethnographic tools,* refers to the use of methods and techniques usually associated with fieldwork. These methods may or may not be guided by cultural theories or questions about the social life of group members.

Having established the historical and complex nature of exploring what counts as ethnography, we now consider factors that contribute to the differences within and across disciplines and academic fields to help readers examine what difference the differences make. For heuristic purposes, we distinguish between a field and a discipline within a field. We use field to refer to an academic area of study that serves to bound a body of knowledge, sets of questions and practices of members. We view sociology, anthropology and education as fields. When we refer to the area as a field we use a capital letter. A discipline is a subarea within a field that has a particular point of view or approach to the study of issues and phenomena of concern within the field. For example, cultural anthropology is a discipline within a field. A cognitive approach within cultural anthropology is a subdiscipline within a broader area of study. This heuristic approach examines how differences in naming elements of an academic tradition provide a basis for examining variation within a field as well as variation across fields. While social scientists agree that historically ethnography has its roots within anthropology, they also acknowledge that it has since become an approach used by anthropologists, sociologists, educational researchers, and others, to study particular questions and issues of interest to their respective disciplines and academic fields. Viewed in this way, ethnographers are members of different disciplinary traditions within particular academic fields who are trained in particular theories and methods of their traditions to ask and explore particular questions for particular purposes (Ellen, 1984; Heath, 1982; Vidich, & Lyman, 1994; Zaharlick, & Green, 1991). Three examples, two from Anthropology and one from Sociology, make visible some of the issues involved in this way of viewing ethnography as situated practice.

In a special issue of the *Anthropology & Education Quarterly* on teaching fieldwork to educational researchers, George Spindler and Louise Spindler (1983) described the situated nature of ethnography as intellectual sites located in disciplinary traditions within an academic field:

> …we teach our students to do anthroethnography, meaning that the major concepts, models, techniques and purposes of "our" ethnography issue from the discipline and theory of cultural anthropology. (p. 191)

The term anthroethnography locates the work of the Spindlers in the field of anthropology (for a similar discussion see Hymes, 1982). The choice of cultural anthropology further locates their work in a discipline within anthropology. This difference shapes the meaning of the concepts used, the models selected, the purposes of the research and the techniques used. Thus, the decision to frame their approach in Cultural Anthropology has consequences for each step of the inquiry and interpretation processes.

Arthur Vidich and Sanford Lyman (1994) make a similar distinction from a sociological perspective. In their chapter, "Qualitative Methods: Their History in Sociology and Anthropology," they define a set of issues and perspectives related to understanding ethnography as situated in a disciplinary site, an academic field. They situate ethnography in sociology and describe how a sociological "attitude" grounds what counts as ethnography:

> Qualitative ethnographic social research, then, entails an attitude of detachment toward society that permits the sociologist to observe the conduct of self and others, to understand the mechanisms of social processes, and to comprehend and explain why both actors and processes are as they are. The existence of this sociological attitude is presupposed in any meaningful discussion of methods appropriate to ethnographic investigations. (p. 23)

Writing a decade apart, both sets of authors acknowledge the way in which disciplinary knowledge frames the "doing" of ethnography. For Vidich and Lyman (1994), the difference is in the development of a situated "attitude" framed by sociology. While they overview the historical roots of ethnography in anthropology, in the introduction to their chapter they also frame the current state of ethnography from a sociological perspective without providing a similar view of an anthropological attitude.

To help frame an anthropological attitude and to show the variation within an academic field, we represent an argument by Charles Harrington (1982). He argues that within anthropology, there is no common definition of ethnography. Rather, anthropology is, itself, a field with branches or disciplines including psychological, social, cultural, linguistic, visual anthropology among others. Within each site, branch or discipline, ethnographers engage in "ethnography" differently and the methodological practices used are themselves shaped by these differences. Through a discussion of participant observation, he shows that what counts as doing ethnog-

raphy as well as ethnographic methods, are situationally defined:

> Cultural, social, psychological, and other branches of anthropology … all share a dedication to the efficacy of a variety of techniques subsumed under the label "participant observation." By participant observation we mean not one technique, but rather a mélange of strategies aimed at producing an accurate model of the behaviors of particular people (including the related problems of how people justify their behaviors to themselves and how they describe them to others). … Participant observation is usually carried out in explicit or implicit combination with other strategies designed to elicit different sorts of data. Various subgroups of anthropology have developed their own ancillary methods in response to the specific problems that each has chosen to solve. For example, psychological anthropology has emphasized the importance of the systematic observation and recording of data, the collection of life and family histories, the use of adaptations of psychologist's assessment techniques, and so on. (pp. 327, 328).

The anthropological attitude indicated in this description contrasts with the sociological one framed by Vidich and Lyman (1994). As Harrington (1982) states, anthropologists' goals are "aimed at producing an accurate model of the behaviors of particular people (including the related problems of how people justify their behaviors to themselves and how they describe them to others)." An anthropologist, therefore, seeks insider (emic) knowledge about how members understand, view and interpret the patterns of everyday life. This approach requires the anthropologist to seek understandings of what it means to be a member of the particular group, and to use the models they construct to participate in the events and practices of everyday life (Sanday, 1976), reducing the distance between those within the group and the anthropologist. Thus, the difference in relationship between the anthropologist and sociologist and the groups they study is a distinguishing feature across academic fields.

The distinctions within and across sites (fields and disciplines within a field) framed above reflect differences in theory–method relationships and, point of view and inquiry practices. These distinctions point to ways that such differences influence all aspects of the ethnographic approach including the questions asked and the ways methods and techniques are used. A more extensive discussion of theory–method-question relationships can be found in Zaharlick and Green (1991). They show the difference between ethnographers interested in ethnography of communication and those who adopt a cultural ecology point of view. Ellen (1984) provides a distinction between theory, method and technique that is useful in understanding the relationships among different dimensions of an ethnography:

> Without claiming to provide the "correct" definitions, and while both recognizing that any definitions are (up to a point) arbitrary and that content of each category profoundly affects the others, we propose the following: (a) "theory": a supposition or body of suppositions designed to explain phenomena or data. (b) "methodology": the systematic study of the principles guiding anthropological investigation and the ways in which theory finds its application; an articulated, theoretically informed approach to the production of data, e.g., "Marxist methodology",

"ethnomethodology". (c) "method": a general mode of yielding data, e.g., interviewing. (d) "technique": a specific means of making particular methods effective, e.g., questionnaires, shorthand, kinship notations. "Methods" and "techniques" together constitute research procedures.

Thus, to understand what counts as ethnography in social science, readers must examine not only how ethnography is being undertaken but also the theories, purposes and questions of the disciplinary *and* academic field for the ethnography. Ethnography, thus, can be viewed as a logic-in-use (Pelto, & Pelto, 1978) within and across sites, and not as a unitary perspective with a single set of criteria for use.

The need to understand ethnography as a "logic-in-use" is not new. Almost two decades ago Ray Birdwhistell (1977) described the need for such an understanding in a response he gave to his students when they questioned about whether Margaret Mead and Gregory Bateson had a methodology:

> I tried to make clear what was involved in the use of the phrase "a methodology" when talking about ethnography. I tried to clarify the idea that methodology, at least as taught and practiced by the ethnographers I have known best, is not merely a technique for eliciting information related to closed and immutable questions. Nor is it a bundle of techniques; some kind of handydandy tool kit prepacked for field use. ... I have come to the conclusion that the past twenty-five years have seen a separation of theory from methods of research procedure. This tendency becomes manifest in the choice and analysis of import of problem, in the location of observational site, in the preliminary isolation of data, in the development of relevant, consistent and explicit techniques of observation, in the recording and storage of data, in the orientation of rules of evidence, and, finally, in the methods of data and evidence assessment and presentation that permit and assist in ordering reexamination, and research. (p. 104, 105)

As Birdwhistell argues, knowledge of the theory–method relationships is central to understanding as well as engaging in all aspects of ethnography. Each decision contributes to the coherence of the logic-in-use. Without such understandings, researchers may separate theory and method in favor of focusing on one or the other dimension. He writes:

> The interdependence of theory and methodology can be hidden by exclusive focus upon either philosophy or technique. Once separated, only the most sophisticated can reconstitute them into investigatory practice. ... There seems to have been a growing tendency, particularly among those disciplines concerned with what is termed "direct observation," for a number of investigators to reject the use of theory except as a device for the *interpretation* of data. (p. 104)

Shirley Heath (1982) illustrates the consequences of focusing on method or technique without considering theory–method relationships. In discussing the essentials of ethnography, she characterizes the early state of ethnography in education as involving some problematic elements. As part of this argument, she also draws distinctions between ethnography and other qualitative approaches.

> Recently, researchers in the field of education have been particularly prone to use the terms *ethnography* or *ethnographic* to describe studies using participant observation, naturalistic inquiry, and open-ended research designs. ... Thus ethnography in education has become a set of techniques in search of a discipline within the social sciences. A variety of researchers, many nonanthropologists, either "do ethnography" or critique ethnographic methods without reflecting the historical, methodological, and theoretical links of ethnography to cultural anthropology. Numerous methods and approaches, described as qualitative, naturalistic, ecological, and holistic, are identified as *ethnographic*, characteristics of or having the form of ethnography. Though it is not necessary to claim that only anthropologists can do ethnographic research, it is important to recognize that many of the methods, rationales for open-ended research techniques, and theoretical guides to interpretation of data gathered by these means derive in large part from anthropology. (p. 33)

Her argument does not claim ethnography for a particular group. She argues, however, that to avoid misappellation or misattribution, it is necessary to understand the historical roots of ethnography, to do more than adhere to the form of ethnography or use field methods, and to distinguish between "full-scale" ethnography and other forms of "ethnographic" studies. For her, this knowledge is essential if researchers are to claim that they are doing ethnography, not merely adopting ethnographic techniques. In this way, she draws a set of distinctions similar to those we described at the beginning of the section.

Her concern reflects the early stages of the relationship between ethnography and education that characterize the period from the the mid-1970s to the early 1980s. For an earlier argument on misappellation in education, see Ray Rist (1980). In this period of educational research, qualitative research and ethnographic research were emerging as a viable approach in Education. This period contrasts with the current state-of-affairs in which a significant body of research across different qualitative traditions and disciplinary perspectives has been accepted and published as evidenced by recent handbooks (Denzin, & Lincoln, 1994a; LeCompte, Milroy, & Preissle, 1994) and discussions of qualitative research (e.g., Guba, 1990; Jacob, 1987) . As we will illustrate in the next section, the current ethnographic studies in education build on historical roots, while adapting ethnography to the questions, purposes, and theories of Education as an academic field of study.

The issues identified in this section show ethnography to be a theoretically driven approach that is situated within a particular site, a discipline within a field. These sites, and their related questions, purposes, and theories shape the practice of ethnography. Viewed in this way, ethnography is a situated approach to the study of everyday life, and ethnographic practices reflect the inquirer's disciplinary grounding and his or her logic-in-use. Thus, theory, purpose, and practice within the academic site help distinguish different views on ethnography, implicate particular relationships between researcher and member of the social group being studied, and distinguish it from other forms of qualitative research.

ETHNOGRAPHY AND ETHNOGRAPHIC STUDIES OF AND IN EDUCATION

In this section, we examine what counts as ethnography in relationship to Education, and how this relationship reflects the academic field of the researcher—Anthropology, Sociology and Education. As part of this discussion, we will illustrate how ethnographic studies have contributed to the development of an academic field of Education that has its own theories, purposes, questions, practices, and literature.

Heuristically, there are two ways of distinguishing among ethnographic studies focusing on education as a site for inquiry: (1) ethnography and ethnographic studies *of* education; and (2) ethnography and ethnographic studies *in* education. The first, prototypically involves anthropologists and sociologists using education as a place of study to which they bring theoretical frames, tools of inquiry, and a history from their field and discipline within the field to construct an understanding of what counts as education to a local group. From this perspective, educational sites, such as schools, are primarily physical sites that become locations for the pursuit of social science research through ethnography and ethnographic research. Theories, questions and goals of this research are framed by the home disciplines and academic fields of the researcher, and not necessarily by educator's needs, issues or concerns (Gilmore, & Glatthorn, 1982; Green, & Wallat, 1981; Heath, & Peters, 1984; Spindler, 1982).

The second set, studies *in* education, can be heuristically defined as studies grounded in knowledge derived from the field of Education and the historical background of ethnography in anthropology and sociology. These studies, however, are guided by educational questions, purposes, needs, and concerns, which, as argued previously, shape the specific character of *ethnography in education*. From this perspective, education is both a physical site and an intellectual one with its own knowledge base, questions, and purposes. Ethnography *in education* is conducted by those inside this academic field, for example, teachers, students, teacher educators, administrators, using ethnographic perspectives and ethnographic tools for Education's purposes.

While this distinction is useful heuristically in framing the difference, in actual practice, the boundaries are often blurred (Geertz, 1983). Social scientists *of education* often collaborate with researchers and practitioners in education and employ the many kinds of knowledge generated within the disciplines *of education*; and those *in education* often employ frames, modes of inquiry and findings from the disciplines within the fields of anthropology and sociology. Thus, rarely is any ethnography or ethnographic study only *of education* or only *in education*. Nonetheless, the distinction is useful in examining the intellectual sites within which ethnography and ethnographic studies on education have been located.

This section begins with a brief discussion of ethnography of education to set the frame for the general discussion of this relationship and to provide a basis for readers to distinguish between this view and the ways that ethnography is currently in use in education. The discussion of ethnography in education provides a general argument about this conceptualization and then moves to specific examples of ethnographic research across multiple sites within education and the purposes each serves. The first part of this argument describes studies and directions that have been undertaken

by university-based researchers to illustrate how this perspective has contributed to a knowledge base for the field of Education. This discussion is followed by two newer areas of use that are currently contributing to this knowledge base: Teachers as ethnographers and students as ethnographers.

Ethnography *of* Education

The need for theory–method considerations in ethnography and ethnographic research of education is clear in the arguments presented by Heath (1982). To help shape the importance of this issue, we discuss briefly the educational ethnographer's task as framed within cultural anthropology. While specific areas of focus may differ within and across disciplines and theories guiding collection, analysis and interpretation may vary from one discipline to another, the general theory–method task remaining constant. What follows, then, is a sketch of the task; it is not a description of how to accomplish this task since that requires knowledge of questions, theories, and purpose of the research.

The ethnographer of education's task is to describe the culture of the social group being studied and to identify specific cultural patterns and structural regularities within the process of continuity and change that are ongoing dimensions of everyday life (Heath, 1982). One of the definitions of culture used frequently in ethnographic studies of education is one posed by Ward Goodenough (1981) for cognitive anthropology. Briefly, within this tradition, culture is defined as the norms that are constructed for ways of perceiving, believing, evaluating, and acting within a social group.

Another way of viewing the ethnographer's task is to see it as one of constructing a cultural grammar or abstract theory that describes the rules or norms that individuals within a society, community, or group have to know, produce, predict, interpret, and evaluate in a given setting or a social group in order to participate in socially and culturally appropriate ways (Heath, 1982; Zaharlick, & Green, 1991). To develop a theoretically driven working model of life within a social group, the ethnographer selects particular theoretical frameworks to guide analysis of the patterns and practices of members and how these bits of everyday life frame a particular view of the social organization. Through this lens, the ethnographer identifies key events or incidents (e.g., recurrent events and events that have sustaining influence); describes these events or incidents in functional and relational terms; explores links to other incidents, events, phenomena, or theoretical constructs; places the events in relation to other events or wider social contexts; and then constructs a description so that others may see what members of a social group need to know, produce, understand, interpret, and produce to participate in appropriate ways.

Viewed in this way, the task of the ethnographer of education is to understand what counts as education to members of the group and to describe how this cultural practice is constructed within and across the events and patterns of activity that constitute everyday life. To accomplish this, ethnographers must set aside their own definitions of actors, places, time(s), actions, events, and other aspects of everyday life (cf. Spradley, 1980), and identify and describe the emic (insider) terms for these dimensions of everyday life. In other words, the ethnographer seeks understanding of the ways in which members of the group name, organize, and interact both in local events and across events over time. In this way, the ethnographer can identify what counts as education, who has access to education, who the actors are that are involved in education within and across events, what relationships exist between and among actors and events, and what factors support and constrain participation among other issues. Through analysis, the ethnographer also identifies the norms and expectations, roles and relationships, and rights and obligations of membership in a society, a community, a group or a classroom. In this way, the ethnographer makes extraordinary the ordinary, and makes visible the invisible patterns of ordinary life within a group.

This brief description of the ethnographer's task indicates the complexity of the task facing an ethnographer *of education* located in the social sciences and suggests further reasons for understanding the theoretical framework guiding individual ethnographies as well as studies stemming from particular sites. Spindler (1982) provides an example of why such knowledge is necessary and illustrates how he frames differences among perspectives. In discussing the "ethnography of schooling," he illustrates one way of defining disciplinary sites and institutional sites. As discussed earlier, Spindler's approach is grounded in anthroethnography, specifically a psychological anthropology focus. In defining an institutional site, Spindler makes a distinction between the "ethnography of schooling" and "educational ethnography."

The terms "ethnography of schooling" and "educational ethnography" mean nearly the same thing but are not exactly synonymous. At least in my usage, "educational ethnography" refers to the study of any or all educational processes whether related to a "school" or not. "Ethnography of schooling" is therefore a little narrower in that it refers to educational and enculturative processes that are related to schools and intentional schooling, though this concept leaves room for studies of playgrounds, play groups, peer groups, patterns of violence in schools and other aspects of school related life. (p. 2)

Thus, Spindler defines and frames different foci and inquiry related to ethnography and education. At the same time, he also indicates that some sites, questions, and foci are not part of or available to those within each perspective. In framing this distinction, he is creating a parallel argument to Harrington's (1982) presented previously, about the variation within an academic site. In drawing this distinction, he illustrates how intellectual sites influence the definition of the institutional site itself (e.g., education, schooling). The ethnography of education, then, can be viewed as consisting of a series of disciplinary sites and institutional sites that frame and are framed by theory–method relationships and research practices, for example, cognitive anthropology, psychological anthropology, and cultural ecology. As argued previously, these variations shape questions and reflect different logics-in-use (Pelto, & Pelto, 1978).

These differences are only problematic if we assume that we can ignore them and try to aggregate unproblematically data across studies, as if they all belonged to a single perspec-

tive. However, if we understand that the differences reflect the situated nature of ethnography and ethnographic research, then we can understand how such research varies according to questions, goals, techniques, practices and purposes of members of a social group (the ethnographers) located in a particular site (disciplinary, institutional, and physical). In constructing such understandings, we can productively engage in dialogues across perspectives and seek approaches to bringing together studies from different perspectives in ways that honor the differences, yet provide insights into the nature of educational practices of a group or institutional site. Green, (1983a) used this argument in constructing a synthesis of the 10 NIE research studies funded under the title "Teaching as a Linguistic Process in a Cultural Setting."

Viewed in this way, ethnography of education, like other forms of ethnography discussed previously, can be understood as the work of people living in a particular time and place, undertaking the study of social and cultural practices of everyday life from particular points of view for particular purposes. From this perspective, then, no single definition of ethnography of education exists, only situated definitions. What is common, however, across these different perspectives is the goal of generating knowledge about the social and cultural practices related to phenomena that researchers have named as "educative." Just what will count as the practice of educating, what slice of society will be examined (e.g., ethnic communities, classrooms and schools as communities, speech communities, etc.), and what tools the ethnographer will use depend on the theoretical framework and intellectual position selected.

Ethnography *in* Education: Framing Education as a Site of Ethnography

In the previous section, we discussed how social science researchers using ethnography and ethnographic research have viewed education as a physical and institutional site for applying disciplinary perspectives and research agenda. Traditionally, education has not been considered a field in the same ways that Anthropology and Sociology have been considered. Some have argued that it is not a field in the sense of having disciplinary frames, knowledge, and modes of inquiry; rather, it is a place to which researchers bring other theories and methods.

Given the scope and depth of the research that has been undertaken over the past three decades, we argue that Education is a field in the sense of having its own (a) history of inquiry, and (b) knowledge base that needs to be accounted for in conducting inquiry and interpreting and reporting of data. To illustrate the basis for this claim, we provide a brief history of research within one area of Education, research on teaching. In 1963, Donald Medley and Harold Mitzel (1963), in the first *Handbook of Research on Teaching* (Gage, 1963), argued that there was little direct observational research in classrooms. In 1973, Travers published the second *Handbook of Research on Teaching,* in which Barak Rosenshine and Norma Furst (1973) found that researchers had created more than 125 systems for observing but these had little or no reliability or validity data. Building on a conceptual argument by Nathan Gage, they called for and framed a research tradition that is known as process-product research. At the same point of time, Michael Dunkin and Bruce Biddle (1974) published a review of systematic observational studies on teaching. They found that most studies were framed by personal, philosophical, experience- or commitment-based beliefs about teaching. There were few empirical or theoretically based studies. In addition, they concluded that there had been little research on teaching (and by implication, little research in education in general). They further argued that the primary focus of educational research at that time focused on issues of learning. In making this claim, they separated the two processes for heuristic purposes. They concluded their synthesis with a call for examining the language of the classroom in order to explore further research on teaching, a call that echoed an earlier one by Smith and Ennis (1961).

Ethnographic research was not represented in either of the first two handbooks or in the synthesis by Dunkin and Biddle (1974), since what little ethnographic research existed at that time was conducted in anthropology and sociology. That research did not examine classrooms as cultural sites but focused on education in other cultures or education at the societal level. Additionally, this work was not readily available since the key journal for this work, *The Anthropology & Education Quarterly,* had not published its first volume until 1975.

In the two decades since that period, there has been a substantial growth of research studies and systematic theory building from a broad range of perspectives including ethnography in and of education. This growth and the shift in recognition of ethnographic research is visible in the third *Handbook of Research on Teaching* (Wittrock, 1986). When this volume was published, three chapters foregrounded ethnographic research and ethnography as a method for educational research (Cazden, 1986; Erickson, 1986; Evertson, & Green, 1986). This handbook, therefore, reflected a shift in frameworks, in research practice, and in the knowledge base. The decade following the 1986 *Handbook of Research on Teaching* is characterized by a plethora of new handbooks across different areas or disciplines within education including Curriculum, Early Childhood Education, English Language Arts, Teacher Education, and Reading among others and an increase in the number of journals publishing research on teaching, including ethnographic studies of life in classrooms. These handbooks and journals reflect the growth of educational research and the development of a knowledge base for the field of Education to which ethnographic studies have made a major contribution.

In just over three decades, then, Education has developed a comprehensive knowledge base that includes work grounded in a variety of disciplines. This body of work includes studies of education and educational processes and practices from other fields, as well as studies in education that often draw on knowledge from these other disciplines and fields. These different traditions and foci within education can be conceived of as branches in the sense that Anthropology and Sociology have branches. In other words, they are intellectual sites for research in education, each focusing on

particular theories, processes, practices, questions and research agenda.

Ethnographic research in and of education has contributed to the growing knowledge base of Education in different ways. Given the scope of work from this tradition, it may be thought of as an area of study and not just a method of research. However, as we have described in this section, these two ways of generating knowledge about education are not the same. Metaphorically, while these two sites of ethnography may be overlapping locations, they are not the same locations. Each is guided by different theories, goals, values, and purposes that shape the use of a common set of tools. In the next section, we will illustrate the range of work and the variation in what counts as ethnography and ethnographic research in education.

ETHNOGRAPHY-IN-USE AMONG TEACHERS AND RESEARCHERS LOCATED IN CLASSROOMS

One way to describe the variation in the intellectual sites associated with ethnography and ethnographic research *in* education is to examine the knowledge bases employed in the studies, who counts as an ethnographer, and the research agenda each addresses. Our discussion below is not intended to be comprehensive, but to illustrate one way in which variation of ethnography and ethnographic studies in education might be described. Given space limitations we only discuss two areas, and even within these two areas we discuss a few topics, issues, and questions. The two areas were selected to highlight research directions and issues of interest to those concerned with the communicative arts and to illustrate how ethnographic research is contributing to the construction of the knowledge base of Education. The areas selected include: studies that have focused on classroom language (including multiple languages in classrooms), and studies of learning and knowledge in education. These categories are presented for heuristic purposes and reflect the primary focus of the different studies or focus on different places of education. These areas, therefore, provide a means of examining a limited, yet focused, view of research on *ethnography in education.*

Ethnographic Studies of Classroom Language, Social Organization and Linguistic Diversity in Classrooms

One of the primary areas of ethnographic research in education has been research that focuses on language or communication in classrooms. This area of ethnographic studies is interdisciplinary in that the studies in this area draw on frameworks from ethnography of communication, interactional sociolinguistics, social semiotics, functional linguistics, and studies of language learning in classroom. The earliest collection of published ethnographic work in this area is entitled, *Functions of Language in the Classroom,* edited by Courtney Cazden, Vera John and Del Hymes (1972). These studies were the stimulus for other ethnographic research and contributed to the convening of a panel of international scholars in 1974 by the National Institute of Education (NIE) that conceptually framed a program of research on "Teaching as a linguistic process in a cultural setting." This panel consisted of researchers from linguistics, anthropology, education, and child development. These interdisciplinary scholars framed a research call that led to the funding of 10 research studies in 1978 from a range of theoretical frameworks but with a common goal—to understand how language use shaped access to schooling, how students learned language in school, and how the language use influenced the teacher's assessment of academic competence. The findings of this work were synthesized by Judith Green and colleagues (see Green, 1983a, 1983b; Green, & Smith, 1983).

During the same period, a number of edited collections and volumes reporting studies within this growing area were also published (e.g., Bloome, 1985; Cook-Gumperz, 1986; Gilmore, & Glatthorn, 1982; Green, & Wallat, 1981; Mehan, 1979; Wilkinson, 1982). As indicated previously, in 1986, this area of research was also represented in three chapters in the third *Handbook of Research on Teaching* (Wittrock, 1986): Cazden's chapter, "Classroom Discourse," Erickson's chapter, "Qualitative Methods on Research on Teaching," and Evertson and Green's chapter, "Observation as Theory and Method." Additionally, in 1988, Cazden published a book, *Classroom Discourse,* a term that captures a subset of the work in this area. This book brought together ethnographic and other research on classroom language concerned with questions of access, cultural variation, effective instruction, and learning. These books, therefore, represent ethnographic research on classroom language conducted in the United States and primarily, but not exclusively, in monolingual classrooms.

These publications along with other studies on classroom language, in the United States, the UK and elsewhere, can be viewed as constituting the beginning of a recognized knowledge base on classroom language in the United States on which subsequent studies of classroom language in education have been built. Note that none claimed to be a comprehensive review. Green's mandate was to synthesize and summarize the NIE funded studies, Wilkinson's book by its very nature was not intended to be comprehensive, and Cazden made clear that she is not attempting a comprehensive view but rather her own view. The point is not that they were comprehensive (either alone or collectively) but rather that their presence marked the emergence of a recognized knowledge base in education in the United States on classroom language. One further indication of the establishment of a knowledge base in education on classroom language is the establishment of research and theoretically oriented journals devoted to the topic: for example, *Linguistics and Education* edited and published in the United States and *Language and Education* edited in the UK and Australia and published in the UK.

Analysis of the focus of studies within this area of concentration shows that, regardless of the particular topic, the research examining classroom language has a common set of concerns—the social and cultural dynamics of the classroom. To show the range of issues addressed and different purposes for research from this perspective, we highlight a series of studies. These studies make visible areas of common concern, the interdisciplinary nature of research in this area, issues of variation, and contributions of this work to the knowledge base in education.

A series of studies have examined how the structure of language use defines classroom culture, pointing out who gets to use what language (or languages), when, for what purposes, and with what social, cultural, and educational consequences (e.g., Au, 1980; Michaels, 1981; Philips, 1983). Of major concern has been the lack of access to appropriate and effective instruction and the misevaluation of student performance and competence. Thus, one of the sites in which ethnographic studies of classroom language have located themselves has been in the dialectic between access to academic language and achievement and students' home and community language and culture. While some researchers have constructed this dialectic to be one of congruence or incongruence (e.g., Au, 1980; Michaels, 1981), others have viewed the dialectic as defining dimensions of teacher-student talk (e.g., Floriani, 1993; Foster, 1995; Gilmore, 1987; Gutierrez, 1993; Kantor, Green, Bradley, & Lin, 1992; Lin, 1993; Mehan, 1979; Santa Barbara Classroom Discourse Group, 1992). Another set of studies has examined how language use shapes situated definitions of what counts as content area knowledge including literacy (e.g., Bloome, & Egan-Robertson, 1993; Cochran-Smith, 1984; Kantor, Miller, & Fernie, 1992; Myers, 1992), science (e.g., Bleicher, 1995; Lemke, 1990), mathematics (e.g., Brilliant-Mills, 1993; Campbell, 1986), and mathematics-science relationships in classrooms (Weade, 1992). (See also Emihovich, 1989.)

Social organization issues have also framed ethnographic studies of language in the classroom. Two examples illustrate how ethnographic research from differing perspectives has provided new understandings about the relationship between social organization and language. These studies show how ethnographic research often provides new ways of understanding old issues within education (e.g., grouping). They also illustrate further the interdisciplinary nature of ethnographic research.

Hilda Borko and Margaret Eisenhart's (1989) study of the language of different reading groups within the same classroom found that students learned how to talk and use written language appropriate to their reading group. When students did not use spoken or written language indicative of their reading group, it raised questions for the teacher about their reading group placement. Moving from one reading group to a higher group was not just a matter of reading achievement per se but required display of the spoken and written language appropriate to the higher reading group. However, once a student learned the spoken and written language of a particular reading group, it was difficult to display the language of a different reading group that might indicate a higher group placement. Additionally, if the student was placed in a higher reading group, but displayed the language from the lower reading group—which is what the student might expect to display,—this display would raise questions about whether the higher placement had been justified. Similarly, a series of ethnographic studies by James Collins (1987) shows that grouping placements had less to do with academic competence than with students' social and linguistic behavior and what the teacher "took up." This research on classroom discourse and the social organization of the classroom, including grouping and other patterns of organizing students, makes visible ways in which classroom patterns and practices create differentiated language and learning environments, even within the same classroom and with the same teacher.

The research agendas of Borko and Eisenhart, and Collins concern issues of equity and evaluation. At the same time, their studies provide theoretical constructs in education about education. Further, the juxtaposition of these studies illustrates how two ethnographic studies can provide data on a common issue and how the findings of one can extend or contribute to those of another. For collections of ethnographic studies concerned with issues of equity that do not focus on language use in classrooms see, for example, Trueba, Guthrie, & Au, 1982; Arvizu, & Saravia-Shore (1990). Geertz (1983) provides an argument about theorizing in ethnography that provides an understanding of how such juxtapositions contribute to the development of a field. This argument, while not specifically focusing on ethnography in education, has implications for future construction of knowledge from such local studies in education:

> The major theoretical contributions not only lie in specific studies—that is true in almost any field—but they are very difficult to abstract from such studies and integrate into anything one might call "culture theory" as such. Theoretical formulations hover so low over the interpretations they govern that they don't make much sense or hold much interest apart from them. That is so, not because they are not general (if they are not general, they are not theoretical), but because, stated independently of their applications, they seem either commonplace or vacant. One can, and this in fact is how the field progresses conceptually, take a line of theoretical attack developed in connection with one exercise in ethnographic interpretation and employ it in another, pushing it forward to greater precision and broader relevance, but one cannot write a "General Theory of Cultural Interpretation." Or, rather, one can but there appears to be little profit in it, because the essential task of theory building here is not to codify abstract regularities but to make thick description possible, not to generalize across cases but to generalize within them. (pp. 25, 26)

These studies show that the construction of knowledge about learning in groups in classrooms is not merely a process of aggregation. Additionally, with regard to intellectual sites, the ethnographic studies by Borko and Eisenhart, and Collins illustrate the interdisciplinary character of such research. These studies are located in the knowledge base that has been developed in education about classroom language and in the knowledge base developed about the social organization of classrooms and schools, and in knowledge from anthropology and sociolinguistics. It is the comingling of these multiple knowledge bases that creates an intellectual context for theory–method connections and for the interpretation of data.

Another area that ethnographic studies of classroom language have addressed is multiple languages in classrooms. Studies in education have examined how shifts of language are employed in teacher–student interaction (e.g., Ernst, 1994; Guthrie, 1985; Guthrie, & Guthrie, 1987; Heras, 1993;

Oreallana, 1995; Tuyay, Jennings, & Dixon, 1995), student–student interactions (Duran, & Szymanski, 1995; Floriani, 1993; Gumperz, & Field, 1995) and in establishing or erasing borders between the classroom community and the home and neighborhood community (e.g., Willett, & Bloome, 1992). In these studies, and in ethnographic studies of classroom language in general, issues of language are not separated from social and cultural issues. For example, in Larry Guthrie and Grace Pung Guthrie's (1987) study of two bilingual classrooms, they found that the teachers' orchestration of the language used was both influenced by and created social dynamics in the classroom; and these social dynamics either facilitated or hindered the students engagement in academic learning (see also Gutierrez, 1995).

This study also illustrates the ways in which knowledge from particular studies informs the construction of knowledge within a field. To construct their conceptual framework they (Guthrie, & Guthrie, 1987) grounded their study in a variety of fields: "anthropology, education, linguistics, psychology, and sociology" (p. 206). Citing Susan Ervin-Tripp and Claudia Mitchell-Kernan (1977), they note five themes that situate their theory–method relationships and that are found in other studies in education of classroom language:

1. First, the data source for studies of conversation or children's language should be natural language in context. (p. 207)
2. …the study of discourse includes elements beyond the sentence level … it has become apparent that multiple constraints beyond the sentence level operate on the production of speech. (p. 208)
3. [T]he social and situational context affect[s] linguistic rules and output. … In the mutual construction of their discourse, actors make selections about what they want to say next (semantic options), about how to say it (social options), and about the form it will take (linguistic options). At the basis of all these choices, and impinging upon them, is a series of factors which can act as constraints. At the most general level, these include social and cultural facts such as social status and cultural norms. At the most narrow level are facts within the interaction itself, such as particular prosodic or phonological variations. (p. 209)
4. The fourth theme is that linguistic rules are variable. … For example, … phonological rules vary according to the situation. It should not, however, be assumed that there is any regular one-to-one correspondence between particular constraints and rules and particular discourse features. Constraints may operate singly or in combination and across the various discourse and linguistic levels. Factors of social status, for example, can just as well influence code choice as phonological variation; a contextualization cue as subtle as rise in intonation can result in a change of code, definition of the situation, or phonological choice. (p. 209)
5. [C]onversational utterances can serve multiple functions in context. (p. 210)

But their study was also grounded in experience with and concern for teaching and teacher education. They write,

> Prospective and practicing teachers should be provided with examples of the various functions that L1 may serve in [bilingual education] instruction. Mere use of L1 is not the issue; it is *how* the bilingual teacher uses the students' language that is important. (p. 227)

The implications of their above research are not specific classroom applications but theoretical constructs in education, at the level noted earlier by Geertz (1973).

Also of prominent concern in the study of multiple languages in the classroom has been questions of how choice of language—by the school, teacher, and students—structures social relationships between the student and the school, and provides or denies access to academic knowledge and achievement. For example, Henry Trueba (1989) has shown how immigrant students to the United States, who are nonnative speakers of English, are not only at risk of experiencing cultural trauma but also at risk of being constructed as learning disabled or otherwise incompetent. Part of what Trueba shows is that success and failure in school and classrooms are socially constructed (see also Bloome, 1989; Gumperz, 1986). Trueba's research agenda (see also Trueba, Jacobs, & Kirton, 1990), which is part of the intellectual site in which his study is located, is twofold: (1) to describe the experiences of some nonnative English speaking immigrant students in U.S. schools with a concern for social justice; and (2) to raise theoretical issues about how success and failure are constructed.

Similarly, a practice-based study by Nan Elsasser and Patricia Irvine (1985) shows how students' language can be taken from them, constructing them as incompetent. The students, enrolled in a writing program at the College of the Virgin Islands, were expected to write in English and to revile writing in their native Creole.

> Experience has shown us that the writing problems of West Indian students are not due to "interference" in the structural linguistic sense of the term; rather, we find their reluctance to write directly attributable to the denigration of their native language and to their conviction that they do not, in fact, possess a true language but speak a bastardized version of English. It is difficult if not impossible to write without a language, and it is emotionally draining to attempt to develop voice and fluency in an educational system which has historically denigrated one's own language. (p. 406)

Their study was located in the effort to transform that course in the writing program; specifically, to "integrate the study of Creole and English" (p. 406). That is, no dichotomy was created between the study of social and educational life and social action. Indeed, it is through social action in the classroom that social, cultural, and linguistic phenomena become clear. Their research agenda is mutually concerned with social and cultural change and with effectiveness (in this case, the effectiveness of writing instruction).

Part of what Elsasser and Irvine (1985) show, as do studies by many other teacher researchers, some of which will be highlighted in the next section, is that one site of ethnographic studies in education is local knowledge and experience of curricular and instructional practice and its transformation. Further, they illustrate that who is an ethnographer in education is not confined to university-based "outsiders" studying the other, but includes teachers (and as described later, students) as well as other "insiders." While part of the knowledge base defining theory–method relationships in such studies involved classroom language, and local knowledge and experience, it also involves knowledge of the efforts of educators to transform the language and languages of the classroom.

Ethnographic Studies of Learning and Knowledge in Education

Unlike psychological studies of learning and knowledge that begin with a priori definitions of knowledge and learning, the key question that ethnographers in education ask is: what counts as knowledge and learning in classrooms to teachers and students? That is, both knowledge and learning are treated as folk terms used by members of the community, in this case the classroom community, to designate particular social and cultural phenomena and relationships among these phenomena. From this perspective, knowledge and learning do not exist separate from the cultural and social constructions of members of the classroom.

In the general field of education, during the 1970s, a beginning knowledge base on classroom learning was developed by educational researchers who sought to identify in a systematic manner those factors that lead to greater academic achievement as well as ways in which children think. One area of this research is known as process-product studies, which correlated classroom factors with outcome measures. This approach led to the development of concepts, such as 'time-on-task' and 'academic engaged time', as major correlates of "learning" (e.g., Denham, & Lieberman, 1980). Another set of studies that examined what so-called effective teachers did in their classrooms led to the identification of a set of teacher behaviors associated with effective instruction (see Brophy, & Good, 1986; Rosenshine, & Stevens, 1984). Both sets of studies located classroom learning in academic lessons. Unasked were the kinds of questions that ethnographers in education might ask: for example, what counts as learning in and across "lessons" and time in this classroom; who has access to this learning; how do students perceive, understand, and participate in learning?

Ethnographic studies have begun to provide new insights into the ways in which learning is socially constructed in classrooms. For example, in a series of ethnographic studies of middle school classrooms, David Bloome (e.g., Bloome, & Argumedo, 1983; Bloome, Puro, & Theodorou, 1989) described how teachers and students coconstructed lessons and how they equated accomplishment of the lessons with academic learning. That is, 'doing lessons' was equated by members of the classroom with academic learning. Bloome described this phenomenon as cultural and social, and labeled it procedural display.

> [Procedural display is] (a) the display by teacher and students, to each other, of a set of academic and interactional procedures that themselves count as the accomplishment of a lesson, and (b) the enactment of a lesson is not necessarily related to the acquisition of intended academic or nonacademic content or skills but is related to the set of cultural meanings and values held by the local education community for classroom education. (Bloome et al., p. 272)

Although the metaphor is not perfect, procedural display can be compared to a group of actors who know how to perform their parts in a play, know their lines and how and when to say them, but who may have little or no understanding of the substantive meaning or significance of the play.

The construct, procedural display, challenged previous work that focused on observable behavior at the surface level. This construct shows that it is no longer possible to correlate surface level features of classroom life (e.g., academic engaged time) with outcome measures as a definition of learning. Learning in classrooms is a problematic construct because, among other reasons, teachers and students, in situ, hold definitions of what counts as learning and what does not count as learning and may orient their behavior to those definitions. These definitions are artifacts of both the broader classroom culture and the particular cultural dynamics of any specific classroom. (see also Fernie, Davies, Kantor, & McMurray, 1994; Myers, 1992; Prentiss, 1995; Rex, 1994; Santa Barbara Classroom Discourse Group, 1992).

Bloome's ethnographic studies of procedural display are located in knowledge bases associated with classroom language studies, educational studies of learning, achievement, and effectiveness, discussions by ethnographers in education about definitions of learning in classrooms (e.g., Erickson, 1982; Green, Kantor, & Rogers, 1991; Spindler, & Spindler, 1987), as well as the ethnography of communication. This multidisciplinary perspective not only frames theory–method relationships but provides a means for problematizing basic concepts in education such as learning, achievement, lesson, accomplishment, teaching, and so forth (see also Weinstein, 1991) Furthermore, the problematizing of such basic concepts in education provides an intellectual site for ethnographic studies in education.

In a series of studies, Luis Moll and his colleagues have raised questions about the location of knowledge in classrooms (e.g., Gonzales et. al., 1993; Moll, & R. Diaz, 1987; Moll, & S. Diaz, 1987; Moll, & Greenberg, 1990). Typically, knowledge in classrooms is viewed as located in the teacher or textbook with each individual student viewed as a potential receptacle for that knowledge. Moll and his colleagues have suggested that knowledge be viewed as a series of funds, distributed among people within a social group (such as a household or community). Access to knowledge needs to be viewed within the context of the social network and social dynamics that connect the funds of knowledge within the social group. As the design of their research projects makes clear, such a conception of knowledge is not only applicable to students but also to teachers, in that it extends the boundaries of classroom learning beyond the classroom walls.

> Our research project, still in progress, consists of three main, interrelated activities conducted simultaneously as part of a research / teaching system: (1) an ethnographic analysis of the transmission of knowledge and skills among households in a Hispanic community of Tucson; (2) creation of an after-school laboratory where researchers and teachers use community information to experiment with literacy instruction; and (3) classroom observations in which we examine existing methods of instruction and explore how to change instruction by applying what is learned in the after-school site. … We build on the idea that every household is, in a very real sense, an educational setting in which the major function is to transmit knowledge that enhances the survival of its dependents. The content and manner of this transmission, the households' zones of proximal development if you will, are the central features of the ethnographic study. In order to examine the instructional potential of these household activities, we have created an after-school "lab" within which researchers, teachers, and students meet to experiment with the teaching of literacy. We think of the lab setting, following Vygotsky, as a "mediating" structure that facilitates strategic connection, multiple paths, between classrooms and households. The goal of the lab is to support new teaching practices that make ample use of both the school's and community's resources. (p. 320)

As part of the ethnographic endeavor, Moll and his colleagues have collaborated with teachers and helped them conduct ethnographic studies of the households and communities of their students, gaining knowledge that can be used in their teaching. They have also collaborated with teachers in bringing parents into the classroom to share funds of knowledge from their households and communities. Like other ethnographers in education, the theoretical constructs about knowledge developed by Moll and his colleagues hover close to educational settings, both the classroom and other settings; and, like others, involve change, both as a consequence of the research and as part of the research.

The ethnographic studies highlighted in this section show the ways in which ethnographic studies in education have created the beginnings of a knowledge base on learning and knowledge. This knowledge base, in contrast to previous approaches, is framed more by questions and dialectics than by accumulated bits of abstracted knowledge. Such studies ask questions about what counts as knowledge and learning, where is it located, who gets to define it, how, and for what purposes. This research shows that such definitions are part of the situated tensions that teachers, students, parents, researchers, and others must address, especially as related to equity and effectiveness agendas.

SUMMARY OF ETHNOGRAPHY-IN-USE AMONG TEACHERS AND RESEARCHERS LOCATED IN CLASSROOMS

The research agenda of ethnographic studies in education can be viewed as framing a series of dialectics related to equity and effectiveness in education. Within the area of equity, the studies frame questions about access and cultural and social change in and through educational institutions: Does a focus on access obfuscate the need for cultural and social change in educational institutions? Does a focus on cultural and social change ignore the current needs of people from non-dominant communities to survive and succeed in the dominant culture? How, when, and where can questions of access and social and cultural change be brought together? Within the area of effectiveness, the studies frame questions about teacher practice, evaluation, decision making, and academic achievement: Who gets to define academic achievement? when? where? and how? How do such definitions themselves situationally define knowledge, learning, teaching, decision making? These questions are not static, but change and evolve. From the perspective of the novice ethnographer in education, the task is to locate one's study within appropriate knowledge bases (both within education and from disciplinary and multidisciplinary perspectives) and research agendas in education, with associated theory–method relationships, as well as to locate one's study in an ongoing, evolving set of dialectics.

Ethnography-in-Use Among Students Located in Classrooms

In a small number of elementary, middle school, and secondary classrooms, students have taken up ethnography and ethnographic inquiry. Although conceptions of ethnography and ethnographic research are imported from the social sciences, how student ethnography and ethnographic inquiry gets defined depends on which students and teachers are using it, and how they frame the academic agenda of the classroom. In other words, student ethnography and ethnographic inquiry is situated in the particular social and cultural dynamics of a particular classroom, in its academic curriculum, and in the disciplinary and multidisciplinary perspectives associated with ethnographic research in the social sciences that the teacher elects to use as a frame. Theory—method relationships in student ethnographic inquiry, therefore, are framed by efforts to transform the classroom and the relationship of students to academic and community knowledge.

In this section, we discuss a small number of published descriptions of students as ethnographers to illustrate how the ethnographic inquiry gets defined by three academic agenda, which often overlap. The three academic agenda are: (1) the exploration of students' own communities, (2) the promotion of the learning of academic, disciplinary, based knowledge, and (3) social and political change in students' communities. In addition, each of the three academic agenda provides a different response to the questions: Who is an ethnographer? where and when was the ethnography undertaken? for what purpose? in what ways? with what outcome? These questions parallel those asked of any social group by an ethnographer and make visible ways in which ethnography has become a resource for everyday practice and academic study in educational settings.

Students' Ethnographic Study of Their Own Communities

One agenda of students' ethnographic study of their own communities has been to make their community's heritage, knowledge, and way of life, visible and respected. A similar agenda has been pursued by educators who have involved students in collecting and publishing oral histories and folk knowledge from their own communities (e.g., Montero-Sieburth, in press; Wiggington, 1986). Also similar educational efforts have involved students as sociolinguists of their own communities (e.g., Cheshire, & Edwards, in press; Thomas, & Maybin, in press; Wolfram, in press). One such project is reported in complementary chapters by Carmen Mercado (in press), and Marceline Torres (in press), a university professor and middle school teacher, respectively, who collaborated on a students-as-ethnographers project. Mercado writes:

> I did not set out to improve the reading scores of the sixth graders in Torres' class, even though that is what occurred. When I asked to be adopted by the class of my former graduate student, my purpose was to demonstrate to students and others that "under-achieving" students are capable of "college work."... What began by posing a simple, but unexpected, question: "What do you want to learn about?" led to introducing students, first by me and then by Torres, to the ways of thinking and using language of ethnographic researchers. ... Ethnographic research contrasts sharply to the type of library research typically emphasized in schools. That "knowledge is all round us," and that it is "in people," is significant for students who do not see their world, their experiences, their forms of expression, in the texts they are required to read.

For Mercado and Torres, student ethnography and ethnographic inquiry was located in the dismantling of deficit models of urban students and in redefining knowledge and relocating it "in people." As Mercado explains, such relocations of knowledge involve shifts in social relationships.

> Because constructing knowledge in this manner involves a relentless search to understand that which compels, through the eyes of different people, students engage in observations of and conversations with others whom *they* regard as authorities. Engaging in the practices of ethnographic researchers enables students to relate to their peers, their families, and members of their immediate community, as sources of academic knowledge.

Torres describes two types of events that defined social relationships for the students-as-ethnographers: "letters home" and "celebrations."

> After deciding on a research topic and question, I had the students write letters to their parents, telling them about the research topic and why they were interested in it. ... They provoked conversations and letters back from parents as well as parent involvement. The "celebrations" were monthly meetings I arranged that were attended by students and parents. At the celebrations, students presented their research or gave a progress report... letters home and the celebrations help redefine the possibilities of middle school classrooms.

These social relationships and social identities are part of the intellectual site of the ethnographic inquiry; that is, part of the theory–method connection. Unlike traditionally conceived ethnographic research in the social sciences, in which there is a distinction between the researcher and the researched, in the context of students studying their own communities, similar to what Jones (1988) has called native anthropology, students with the help of their teachers, are adapting ethnographic perspectives and techniques to study the community from within the community, as an insider.

Torres and Mercado engaged the students in a great deal of writing—what they call scribing, planning, reflecting, and sharing, and as such closely aligned ethnographic inquiry with writing. Thus, theory–method relationships were framed by the educational agenda of the students-as-ethnographers project: recreating definitions and locations of knowledge, how to write and who is a writer, and educationally support-ive social relationships. But the educational agenda and the research agenda come together and overlap with a political agenda. Mercado writes,

> Especially those of us who come from marginalized communities, *we* need to *tell* our *own* stories, *we* need to *inform* others of *our* cultural and linguistic heritages, and *we* need to *preserve* these treasures (original emphases)

It is within these multiple agenda, then, that Torres and Mercado have situated and defined ethnography and ethno-graphic inquiry.

Students as Ethnographers and Disciplinary-Based Knowledge

A second way that students have taken up ethnography and ethnographic inquiry has been to engage students in ethnog-raphy as a resource for the acquisition of academic, disciplin-ary-based knowledge. In a collaborative ethnographic study (Yeager, Floriani, & Green, in press), Beth Yeager, a 5th- and 6th-grade teacher argues that disciplinary-based knowledge is not just knowledge of history or science. Rather, as she framed for students and parents, disciplinary knowledge is knowl-edge of how members of a discipline construct knowledge. Thus, Yeager told her students that they were to become mathematicians, social scientists, artists, writers among other positions to learn how to construct knowledge consistent with that used by members of each discipline.

Viewed from the perspective of "knowledge how," Yeager et al. (in press) argue that a discipline can be viewed as a community, a social and cultural group, with its own ways of acting, believing, thinking, feeling, valuing, and using lan-guage (cf. Goodenough's, 1981, definition of culture). Thus, as a social and cultural group, a disciplinary community can be studied in the same manner that other social and cultural groups can be studied, employing ethnography and ethno-graphic inquiry. Additionally, within education, such knowl-edge can be used as a focus for the curriculum rather than, or in addition to, the bits and pieces of information constructed through such disciplinary actions. In this way, Yeager et al. (in press) argue, knowledge can be viewed as an outcome of the actions of members of a discipline or group.

> I have become concerned with helping my students acquire disci-pline-based knowledge. I want my students to understand how discipline knowledge is the product of actions of people and how they "take up" the actions associated with particular disciplines. I want them to be able to "envision" themselves as anthropologists, writers, scientists, and mathematicians.
>
> To put my goals into practice, I create opportunities to explore how people in each discipline go about their work ... What the ethnographic study has contributed to this process is a language to describe what it is I do and how we, the students and I, construct a common language for looking at learning and for exploring how others engage in similar processes in all aspects of everyday life.

For Yeager and her students, ethnography and ethnographic perspectives became resources for such an inquiry. Yeager is a member of the Santa Barbara Classroom Discourse Group, which is a group of university researchers and teacher re-searchers involved in the collaborative study of classroom life. Collaborative ethnographic research has been ongoing in her classroom since 1991. She has involved both 5th and 6th grade students in ethnographic research. The study reported here was begun in the 1991 school year, but draws on re-search across all years.

As in the case of Mercado and Torres, the original purpose of the ethnographic research was not to use ethnography with students. For Floriani and Green, the goal was to document how the teacher constructed a community of learning with students. However, as is the case in ethnography, the re-searchers become responsive to the members' goals and needs. Thus, the traditional role of ethnographer became reshaped by Beth Yeager:

> I set the conditions for Ana and Judith's entry to afford students an opportunity to become co-researchers in the ethnography and to establish a particular relationship between Ana and Judith as researchers and those of us in the classroom—"I would like you to be members of the community and to participate in and contrib-ute to the life of this group."...
>
> Additionally, I asked Ana and Judith to share their fieldnotes and purposes for doing ethnography with the students. I used this sharing to help shape and define what anthropologists do and to set the stage for students to take up the roles and language of anthropologists as we began the study of history as a social science.

Thus, ethnography and ethnographic perspectives were used not only by the university researchers and teacher researchers but also by students-as-researchers as a frame—or, in Yeager's words, a language—for exploring disciplinary knowledge and classroom life (including how they, as students, learn).

In this section, we are focusing primarily on the students' take up of ethnographic perspectives for the study of disci-plinary knowledge and of their classroom. Unlike the students in the previous section, the students in Beth Yeager's class did not take up ethnography to explore their home communities or cultural heritage. In other words, their use of ethnography was situated in a different agenda and thus defined differ-ently. Ethnography, for them, was a way of studying everyday life in their classroom as well as accessing disciplinary knowl-edge, not only in social science but in all areas of the curricu-lum.

Although Yeager provided the students with demonstra-tions and models of how members of academic disciplines construct knowledge (e.g., through videotapes of scientists in different fields doing their work; through examining the research processes of Ana and Judith), the primary means for engaging students in the ethnographic study of academic disciplines was to ask them to engage simultaneously in the role of a member in the discipline while reflecting on their thinking and what they were doing. This dialectical process was used throughout the year across discipline areas. High-lighted throughout the cycles of activity (units) through which the year was organized were seven principles or themes about inquiry (Yeager et al., in press):

1. Questions are formulated and reformulated throughout the inquiry process;
2. Data are constructed not found;

3. Observation is a selective process guided by personal as well as formal frames of reference;

4. Observation and data construction require a descriptive language;

5. Interpretation is based on evidence and point of view, not merely personal opinion;

6. Within a group, multiple interpretations of a text (visual, oral, aural, written) are possible and probable; and

7. Multiple ways of presenting information exist.

Regardless of the cycle of activity, whether mathematics, history, literature, natural sciences, academic writing, and so forth, the seven principles guided student inquiry and over time became a framework for students to understand themselves (as individuals and as a social group) as well as disciplinary communities. The seven principles also became a way for students to challenge each other's construction of knowledge within a particular unit of study, which broadened the definition of disciplinary inquiry to include the interaction that members of an academic community have with each other, through presentation, discussion, and writing. Students were expected to provide evidence for their claims about both content area learning and themselves as learners. (Brilliant-Mills, 1993; Floriani, 1993; Heras, 1993; Tuyay, Floriani, Yeager, Dixon, & Green, 1995).

The taking up of ethnographic inquiry by students in Yeager's class was a means of redefining academic knowledge in the classroom, and of making the processes of disciplinary-based academic communities open and accessible to students. This educational agenda became the context for defining what counted as ethnographic inquiry. That is, although building upon ethnographic perspectives and practices from outside the classroom, Yeager and her students redefined ethnographic inquiry in terms of their educational agenda. It became both a set of principles and a set of related activities that were recycled across various units of study representing multiple disciplinary communities.

Students as Ethnographers and Social and Political Change

In a sense, each of the studies of student-as-ethnographers involves social and political change. Torres and Mercado used students-as-ethnographers to counter deficit models of urban students, to validate community and family members as sources of knowledge, and to make visible the students' cultural and linguistic heritage. Yeager used students-as-ethnographers to open up academic disciplines and make them accessible as well as to make their own learning processes and practices available to them. In this section, we will discuss a students-as-ethnographers study which had an explicit agenda of social and political change to illustrate how such an agenda defines ethnography and ethnographic inquiry.

With the support of a cooperating teacher and the school administration, Ann Egan-Robertson (a university researcher) created a writing club in an urban school. Egan-Robertson describes her purpose as follows:

I had the opportunity to work with a small, multiracial group of young women in a students-as-ethnographers project during the winter and spring of 1993. This project was a community writing club that I formed out of their eighthgrade English language arts class. Like other educators who work with teenagers, I am committed to finding ways of empowering students as active participants in our democracy and as readers, writers, and life-long learners. I am especially concerned about those students, all too numerous, who act as though their living does not matter. (Egan-Robertson, in press).

Egan-Robertson began the writing club by describing previous students-as-ethnographers projects in the Bronx (Mercado, in press; Torres, in press); Detroit (Curry, & Bloome, in press; Schaafsma, in press); the Piedmont Carolinas (Heath, & Branscombe, 1986); Saginaw (Robinson, & Stock, 1990); and Santa Barbara (Yeager et al., in press).

As I told them about each of these projects, I gave a couple of examples of questions and topics that the other student ethnographers had pursued and related those questions and topics to potential avenues for them. For example, tying to the Saginaw project [Robinson, & Stock, 1990], I said "You might want to ask, 'What's it like growing up as a female teenager in Riverside? What's it like growing up as an African-American young woman in Riverside? As a Latina? Or as a white young woman?" This particular wording I used made an intertextual link between the extant students-as-ethnographers projects and their own project that proved to be very important. Another important framing I made in this initial meeting was the particularity of my offered questions. Rather than leaving the topic at "What's it like being a young woman growing up in Riverside?", I brought to that gender category the added categories of race and ethnicity.

Thus, although not determining the questions and topics that would guide the students' ethnographic inquiry, Egan-Robertson grounded their studies in previous student-as-ethnographers projects, both as intellectual sites (e.g., what questions and frames had been employed) and as a set of activities (e.g., use of ethnographic techniques, interviewing people in the community, etc.). About the questions that guided the students' ethnographic inquiry, Egan-Robertson writes:

From the start, students raised and discussed such serious questions as: "Why do men rape women?" and "Why do kids call me a 'wannabe' when I say I'm Puerto Rican?" Students began field notebooks at their first meeting, recording questions and writing on topics. While they generated many questions, each student eventually settled on one to pursue:

DeLayne: How can you avoid becoming an alcoholic if your parents are alcoholic?

Denise: Is racism a problem in Riverside?

Felicita: How do you deal with teenage pregnancy?

Sandra: Does music affect the way we think and feel about people?

Shanae: What's it like being or having two nationalities?

Marielis: What can help teenagers stay off the streets?

The questions and issues raised by the students are political ones, that derive from their own experiences as teenagers in their city. The questions are also related to the construct of personhood.

Personhood refers to how a culture or subculture, such as a school, defines "person" and what attributes it associates with "person" (Besnier, 1993; Kondo, 1990). Personhood includes the ways that people construct identities in relation to one another. Personhood is not given or predetermined but is established through everyday interactions, which in turn, are influenced by historical and institutionalized contexts and narratives (Dubois, 1969; Galwatney, 1981; Street, 1993a; West, 1993). More simply put, to ask about personhood is to ask, "What does it mean to be a person in a particular cultural group, at a particular time, in a particular event?" (Egan-Robertson, in press)

The construct of personhood is an explicitly political question in the context of racism both in the students' city, in the United States in general, and in many other places in the world. Thus, Egan-Robertson viewed the students-as-ethnographers project as a way for the students to reconstruct personhood for themselves.

Egan-Robertson provided an opportunity for the students to examine how members of their own communities constructed and communicated knowledge about people's lives. Among other activities, she had the students interview two community activists, one an actress and director, the other a poet and playwright. The interviews with these activists connected the students with community-based ways of identifying, gaining, and representing knowledge. They learned about the importance of stories told at kitchen tables, the narratives that ordinary people told, and community theater. They began to view family and community members as oral historians and theorists.

In a sense, what Egan-Robertson did parallels Yeager's invitation to students to be ethnographers of academic disciplines, learning how members of a discipline construct and represent knowledge. But instead of focusing on academic communities and academic scholars, Egan-Robertson connected the students with their own communities and with community activists.

At the end of the project the students wrote up what they had learned, using a variety of formats that they had learned through their inquiry.

> The way students wrote up their ethnographic reports was profoundly influenced by the literacy practices they encountered through their inquiry: seeing the Health Peer Educators' play, and hearing about Ashton's and Cruz's work in the political theater. The students also had the opportunity to work with Ashton as they wrote up their research. All of these activities led the students to write monologues, skits, and poetry. The students' writing reflects recent changes in ethnography, moving toward interdisciplinary perspectives and paying more attention to writing style (e.g., Holloway, 1991). Their writing is based on what they learned about themselves and their various communities as they did the ethnography. As they wrote, they used the community practices they accessed during their inquiry (Egan-Robertson, in press).

Thus, there was not a single, fixed definition of ethnographic research. Rather, it was defined by the educational agenda, both academic (e.g., improve student writing) and affective (e.g., improve student self-esteem), and by political agendas (e.g., counter racism, reconstruct personhood, contribute to the community). Further, as the students learned more about community-based practices for constructing and representing knowledge, those practices influenced the ongoing ethnographic inquiry;—how and where the students defined, gathered, interpreted, and represented data.

SUMMARY OF ETHNOGRAPHY IN EDUCATION: TOWARD THE CONSTRUCTION OF A DISCIPLINARY FOCUS WITHIN EDUCATION

In previous section on ethnography in education, we illustrated how ethnography and ethnographic perspectives have become a language of education, a productive resource for students for academic study, a way of taking action while learning content, and a way of bridging the proverbial gap between theory, research, and practice that has characterized much education research. In each example, students became ethnographers for particular purposes and engaged in ethnography in particular ways. In each, however, they shared a common concern for the study of culture and everyday life as constructed by members of a group. In this way, they were consistent with the purposes and goals of ethnography as framed within the social sciences, but were using ethnography for educational purposes. These studies, and those in the previous sections on ethnography in education, show how ethnography in education has contributed to a knowledge base for education.

These studies also show how ethnography frames a language of educational practice and everyday life. The scope of work presented suggests that ethnographic research, with its theories of culture and its concern for how members construct patterns of everyday life, is becoming an area of concentration within education and not merely a method for qualitative research. However, as illustrated across the examples in this section on ethnography in education, variation exists in this area just as in disciplines in anthropology or sociology. These variations, however, do not fracture the discipline; rather, they provide a rich source of information across levels of study, foci and purpose. This information provides a rich view of how local knowledge is constructed in particular schools, classrooms or groups, and how this knowledge is consequential for students as they build their repertoires for learning across intellectual and physical sites of schooling.

ORDINARY PEOPLE, ETHNOGRAPHY, AND ETHNOGRAPHIC WRITING

In this last section we discuss ordinary people as ethnographers. This section is based on and borrows from Bloome, Sheridan, & Street (1993). We focus on one example, the Mass-Observation Project. We begin with a brief description of the Mass Observation Project and then discuss issues involved in writing for the Archive and in reading materials in the Archive. Throughout we list questions about ethnography and ethnographic writing that are raised by the Mass-Observation Project. As with previous sections, our purpose is to illustrate how ethnography and ethnographic inquiry are located in particular intellectual sites. In this case, the intellectual site is located in the relationship of the ordinary people who write for the Mass-Observation Project and the scholars and others who read what is written.

The Mass-Observation Project and Archive

Mass-Observation (MO) started in 1937 as a 'people's anthropology' of life in Britain. Ordinary people were asked to write about their daily lives and events in their community. Other methods were also used to collect information about the lives of ordinary people: surveys, observations, interviews. The first phase of MO occurred in 1937 until 1950 with a good deal of attention devoted to the recording of civilian life during the World War II. The papers from that research were brought to The University of Sussex and the Mass-Observation Archive opened in 1975.

The second phase began in 1981. David Pocock and Dorothy Sheridan recruited people from all parts of the UK to write about their lives, either in the form of a diary or more often in the form of detailed replies to questions on specific themes. Since 1981 an enormous bank of written information about life in the UK has been accumulating, including over 400,000 pages of typed and handwritten material representing the combined contributions of over 2,500 volunteer writers.

Since its beginning, the basic process has remained the same. The Archive asks volunteers throughout the UK to write about specific events and issues. The people—known as Mass-Observation correspondents—send their writings to the Mass-Observation Archive Project at The University of Sussex Library which stores them. The MO correspondents have no official training as anthropologists, sociologists, and so forth, although a few may have taken higher education courses in those or related fields. University researchers, undergraduate and graduate students, and others, come to the Archive, and read what has been written. For a fuller account of how the project was launched and how it relates to the work of earlier MO, see Sheridan (1993).

Reading Mass-Observation Writing

There are many ways of reading the materials in the Mass-Observation Archive, we describe four here. Each way of reading involves assumptions about the nature of ethnographic writing and the nature of knowledge.

Reading Mass-Observation Writing as Knowledge Transmission. One way of reading is to assume that the writer is sending information he or she has gathered about the world to the Archive. Ordinary people are transmitting knowledge about their daily lives and communities to scholars, students and others. The MO correspondents can make available to people using the Archive knowledge about daily life in the UK that is otherwise unavailable, or at least, very difficult to get. Further, they make available knowledge from one period of time that may be useful to people decades later. One implication of reading the Archive materials as knowledge transmission is that the MO correspondents are defined as reporters or as field workers, gathering information and passing it on.

There is variation in the styles of writing used by the MO correspondents: some respond with exposition, others with narrative, some write as if writing a letter to a friend, and occasionally, a few may write a poem as part of their response to a directive. One way to view the variety of ways of responding is that they are transmitting different types of knowledge and different contexts of knowledge (e.g., personal context, community context, historical context).

There are limitations to reading the Archive materials as "knowledge transmission." First, everyone has his or her biases and perspectives. What gets reported often reflects that. Many MO correspondents are aware that they have biases and they will often note in their writing that they are only describing things from their own perspective. The MO correspondents often make special efforts to gather information from other people so that what they report is not limited to their own point of view.

A second limitation in reading MO writing as knowledge transmission is that sometimes MO correspondents have other purposes than just knowledge transmission. They may be commenting on an event or giving a political opinion. Some MO correspondents enjoy the intellectual stimulation and writing practice involved in responding to a directive, and so they are not just reporting. Writers may also be constructing personalities / identities as writers that are different from how they represent themselves in other contexts. For instance, they may present themselves as "researchers," as "social commentators," as "ordinary people" (see below), all of which affect the "knowledge" they are "transmitting."

A series of questions can be posed about reading the Archive materials as "knowledge transmission":

• What is being reported?
• Who is doing the reporting?
• What kind of report is it?
• What is the nature of the knowledge that is in the report?
• What kinds of knowledge are being transmitted?
• What contexts of knowledge are being implied?
• What kind of reader is being imagined?
• In what way is the knowledge from different reports cumulative?
• What limitations are there about the knowledge being transmitted?

Reading Mass Observation Writing as Knowledge Construction. Readers are affected by what they already know about the topic and by the experiences they have had. Thus, reading is not just a matter of getting knowledge from the written text but is a process of knowledge construction. Similarly, when people write, both what they write and how they write are influenced by their knowledge and experiences in general, by their knowledge and experience as writers and readers, and by their purposes for writing and reading.

One important implication derived from viewing reading as knowledge construction is that the responses of the MO correspondents might be considered reports of their perceptions, memories, and interpretations of events rather than just unmediated descriptions of events. From the viewpoint of reading as knowledge construction, the MO Project is like a survey or a large-scale experimental task. The directive is like a survey questionnaire or an experimental prompt, and what the MO correspondents write is like an answer to a survey question or a response to an experimental condition, respectively.

To the extent that researchers, students, or others using the Archive are interested in people other than the MO correspondents,—that is, they are using the MO Project as a representative sample,—the following questions should be asked:

- How well do the MO correspondents represent the broader population?

- What segments of the population do they represent?

- To what degree and how can inferences be made from their responses to the perceptions, views, and interpretations of others?

There is at least one more important implication of reading the MO Archive as knowledge construction. Researchers and others using the Archive are themselves readers. Their background knowledge, experiences, and purposes affect their understanding and interpretations of what they read and write no less than what occurs for the MO correspondents. The disciplinary background researchers and students bring to their reading also affects their understanding and interpretation. Given reading as knowledge construction, researchers' reports—like the writings of the MO correspondents—are also constructions of knowledge and not just factual reports.

Reading Mass Observation Writing as Social and Cultural Practices. Through their writing, the MO correspondents are establishing various social relationships with both the Archive and with the scholars and others reading the Archive materials. By how and what they write, the MO correspondents are promoting a particular social identity for themselves. This social identity may be working class, writer, ordinary person, artist, teacher, parent, son / daughter, elder, observer, responder, or more subtle and complex social identities that are difficult to describe within a few words. The social identities they present are part of the message and information communicated to the reader.

The writer's establishment of a social identity has implications for the reader's social identity and may promote a particular kind of reading. For example, the MO correspondent who presents an identity as an observer, promotes a reading of reports from field workers. The MO correspondent who writes as a son about his family, promotes perhaps a voyeuristic reading. The MO correspondent, who presents herself as an 'ordinary' person, may be inviting the reader to be a coconspirator in writing a history of 'ordinary' people. As the writers establish and maintain a social relationship with the MO Archive and Project they involve themselves in a set of social and cultural activities they might not otherwise be involved in (e.g., the cultural practice of making history by recording it). Writers may also be trying to influence opinion of future generations or they may be promoting an explicit or implicit political agenda.

It is not just the writing of the MO correspondents that needs to be viewed as social and cultural practice, but also the writing and reading of scholars using the MO Archive. One implication for scholars is to be aware of the assumptions and limitations of various social and cultural practices with regard to knowledge, description, interpretation, and narrative. Part of this awareness involves questioning the match, complementary nature, mismatch, or incompatibility of the writing and reading practices of researchers with those of the MO correspondents they are reading.

Reading Mass Observation Writing as Contested Social Practice. It was suggested in the previous section, that mismatches and incompatibility may occur between the writing and reading practices of MO correspondents and the scholars and others who come to the Archive to read the materials there. One set of conflicts may occur over how the MO correspondent and the researcher are defining each other (as discussed earlier). Conflicts may also occur in assumptions about the nature of knowledge. For example, a directive may be organized to elicit expository responses (following a "scientific" model of knowledge) while MO correspondents may choose to write narratives instead, redefine the question, or ignore the directive completely and write about something *they* believe that people using the Archive should know about and be interested in.

There may also be a conflict in how researchers using the Archive present their findings. Some researchers may package their findings from the Archive as scientific reports and coherent histories although the MO Project and Archive collection itself is not a single coherent history.

Incorporating issues from the previous sections and recognizing that writing and reading practices associated with the MO Project and Archive may involve contested social practices, there are questions about reading MO writing that should be asked:

How are MO correspondents defined?—as recorders, as subjects, as readers, as mediators, as interpreters, as authors, as actors.

How is the relationship of the MO correspondents to others defined?—as representative of a group, as a representative from a group, as marginal, as atypical.

How is the writing of MO correspondents defined?—as report, as correspondence, as field notes, as diary, as data, as letters.

How is the directive defined?—as prompt, as task, as experimental condition.

How are the researchers defined?—as interpreters, writers, field workers, surveyors, readers, as well as by disciplinary identities (as anthropologist, as historian, as sociologist, etc.).

How is knowledge defined?—as events, as a collection of facts, as perceptions, views, and interpretations, as social practices, as background and experience, as representative of ideas.

How is knowledge produced?—extracted, discovered, transmitted, created, constructed, collected, organized.

How is knowledge presented—as description, as personhood, as hierarchies of concepts, as social practice, as narrative, as carnival.

Do particular uses of the Archive usurp the role of the MO correspondents as researchers themselves, and as researchers, their 'right' to provide interpretation of events?

Conflicts among MO correspondents and those who use the Archive will not be resolved by merely acknowledging all sides as valuable and ignoring what the conflicts reveal about the various enterprises that come under the rubric of ethnographic writing and reading. Rather than viewing conflicts as problems requiring resolution, the conflicts can be viewed as points of inquiry revealing even more insight about ethnographic writing and reading.

Conclusions of Ordinary People as Ethnographers

The questions that we have raised about reading MO writing apply broadly to the writing and reading of ethnography and ethnographic inquiry (there are, of course, other similar questions that need to be asked but were omitted for lack of space). These questions constitute an intellectual site, not only for the writing and reading of ethnography and ethnographic inquiry, but also for how ethnographic writing is employed to build knowledge and how such knowledge is integrated with other sources of knowledge. In brief, the theory–method domain of ethnography and ethnographic inquiry includes the writing and reading involved, as well as how relationships with other sources of knowledge are built.

FINAL COMMENTS

It is no longer possible to view ethnography and ethnographic research as monolithic. In our discussion of ethnography and ethnographic research as situated inquiry, we identified a series of intellectual sites which has contextualized how ethnography and ethnographic research has been taken up by social scientists, educational researchers, teachers, students, and ordinary people. The sites we have identified are not intended to be comprehensive; rather, they are illustrative of how various intellectual sites influence the relationship between theory and method.

We have treated ethnography and ethnographic research as a set of social and cultural practices employed by members of various 'communities': disciplinary-based communities, educational research communities, and classroom communities. As such, ethnographic practices—like any set of social and cultural practices—are ways that people in a site act and react to each other in pursuit of an agenda; including research agenda, educational agenda, and social, cultural and institutional change agenda. Like any set of social and cultural practices, although based on past practices that provide people with 'folk' models of what the practices 'look like,' how they are to be enacted, and what meaning and significance they have, no set of practices, including ethnographic practices, are fully predetermined. As such, ethnography and ethnographic research continues to evolve and change as a consequence of the new sites (intellectual, topical, institutional, educational, physical, geographical, social, and cultural sites) in which it is situated, and as a consequence of the people who take it up and the agenda they pursue.

References

Agar, M. (1980). *The professional stranger*. New York: Academic Press.

Arvizu, S., & Saravia-Shore, M. (1990). Cross-cultural literacy: An anthropological approach to dealing with diversity. *Education and Urban Society, 22*(4), 364–376.

Atkinson, P. (1990). *The ethnographic imagination*. London: Routledge.

Atkinson, P., Delamont, S., & Hammersley, M. (1988). Qualitative research traditions: A British response to Jacob. *Review of Educational Research, 58*(2), 231–250.

Au, K. (1980). Participation structures in a reading lesson with Hawaian children. *Anthropology and Education Quarterly, 11*, 91–115.

Besnier, N. (1993). Literacy and feelings: The encoding of affect in Nukulaelae letters. In B. Street (Ed.), *Cross-cultural approaches to literacy* (pp. 62–86). Cambridge: Cambridge University Press.

Birdwhistell, R. (1977). Some discussion of ethnography, theory, and method. In John Brockman (Ed.), *About Bateson: Essays on Gregory Bateson* (pp. 103–144). New York: E.P. Dutton.

Bleicher, R. (1995). High school students presenting science: An interactional sociolinguistic analysis. *Journal of Research in Science Teaching, 31*(7), 697–719.

Bloome, D. (Ed.). (1985). Literacy and schooling. Norwood, NJ: Ablex.

Bloome, D. (1989). Beyond access: A sociolinguistic and ethnographic study of reading and writing in a culturally diverse middle school classroom. In D. Bloome (Ed.), *Classrooms and literacy*. Norwood, NJ: Ablex.

Bloome, D., & Argumedo, B. (1983). Procedural display and classroom interaction at the middle school level: Another look at academic engaged time. *Middle school research: Selected studies 1983.*

Bloome, D., & Egan-Robertson, A., (1993). The social construction of intertextuality in classroom reading and writing lessons. *Reading Research Quarterly, 28*(4), 304–333.

Bloome, D., Puro, P., & Theodorou, E. (1989). Procedural display and classroom lessons. *Curriculum Inquiry, 19*(3), 265–291.

Bloome, D., Sheridan, D., & Street, B. (1993). *Reading mass observation writing* (Occasional Paper #1). Brighton, England: University of Sussex Library.

Borko, H., & Eisenhart, M. (1989). Reading ability groups as literacy communities. In D. Bloome (Ed.), *Literacy and classrooms* (pp. 107–134). Norwood, NJ: Ablex.

Brilliant-Mills, H. (1993). Becoming a mathematician: Building a situated definition of mathematics. *Linguistics and Education, 5*(3&4), 301–334.

Brophy, J., & Good, T. (1986). Teacher behavior and student achievement. In M. Wittrock (Ed.), *Handbook of research on teaching* (3rd ed., pp. 328–375). New York: Macmillan.

Campbell, D. (1986). In J. Cook-Gumperz (Ed.), *The social construction of literacy.* New York: Cambridge University Press.

Cazden, C. (1986). Classroom discourse. In M. Wittrock (Ed.), *Handbook of research on teaching* (3rd ed., pp. 432–463). New York: Macmillan.

Cazden, C. (1988). *Classroom discourse.* Portsmouth, NH: Heinemann.

Cazden, C., John, V., & Hymes, D. (Eds.). (1972). *Functions of language in the classroom.* New York: Teachers College Press.

Cheshire, J., & Edwards, V. (in press). Knowledge about language in British classrooms: Children as researchers. In A. Egan-Robertson, & D. Bloome (Eds.), *Students as researchers of culture and language in their own communities.* Cresskill, NJ: Hampton Press.

Clifford, J. (1988). *The predicament of culture.* Cambridge, MA: Harvard University Press.

Clifford, J., & Marcus, G. (Eds.). (1986). *Writing culture: The poetics and politics of ethnography.* Berkeley, CA: University of California Press.

Cochran-Smith, M. (1984) *The making of a reader.* Norwood, NJ: Ablex.

Collins, J. (1987). Using cohesion analysis to understand access to knowledge. In D. Bloome (Ed.), *Literacy and schooling* (pp. 67–97). Norwood, NJ: Ablex.

Cook-Gumperz, J. (Ed.). (1986). *The social construction of literacy.* New York: Cambridge University Press.

Corenstein, M. (1992). Panorama de la investigación etnográfica en la educación en México: un primer acercamiento. In M. Beltran & M. Campos (Eds.), *Investigación etnográfica en educación* (pp. 359–376). Mexico City: Universidad Nacional Autónoma De Mexico.

Curry, T., & Bloome, D. (in press). Learning to write by writing ethnography. In A. Egan-Robertson & D. Bloome (Eds.) *Students as researchers of culture and language in their own communities.* Cresskill, NJ: Hampton Press.

Denham, C., & Lieberman, A. (Eds.). (1980). *Time to learn.* Washington, DC: National Institute of Education.

Denzin, N. (1989). *The research act: A theoretical introduction to sociological methods* (3rd ed.). Englewood Cliffs, NJ: Prentice-Hall.

Denzin, N., & Lincoln, Y. (Eds.). (1994a). *Handbook of qualitative research.* Thousand Oaks, CA: Sage.

Denzin, N., & Lincoln, Y. (Eds.). (1994b). Introduction: Entering the field of qualitative research. In N. Denzin & Y. Lincoln (Eds.), *Handbook of qualitative research.* Thousand Oaks, CA: Sage.

Dubois, W.E.B. (1969 [1973 reprint]). *The Philadelphia Negro.* Philadelphia: University of Pennsylvania Press.

Dunkin, M., & Biddle, B. (1974). *The study of teaching.* New York: Holt, Rinehart, & Winston.

Duran, R., & Szymanski, M., (1995) Cooperative learning interaction and construciton of activity. *Discourse Processes, 19*(1), 149–164.

Duranti, A., & Goodwin, C. (Eds.). (1992). *Rethinking context: Language as an interactive phenomenon.* Cambridge: Cambridge University Press.

Egan-Robertson, A. (in press). We must ask our questions and tell our stories: Writing ethnography and constructing personhood. In A. Egan-Robertson & D. Bloome (Eds.), *Students as researchers of culture and language in their own communities.* Cresskill, NJ: Hampton Press.

Egan-Robertson, A., & Willett, J. (in press). Students as ethnographers, thinking and doing ethnography: A bibliographic essay. In A. Egan-Robertson & D. Bloome (Eds.), *Students as researchers of culture and language in their own communities.* Cresskill, NJ:

Hampton Press.

Ellen, R.F. (Ed.). (1984). *Ethnographic research: A guide to general conduct.* New York: Academic Press.

Elsasser, N., & Irvine, P. (1985). English and creole: The dialectics of choice in a college writing program. *Harvard Educational Review, 55*(5), 399–415.

Emihovich, C., (1989). *Locating learning: Ethnographic perspectives on classroom research.* Norwood, NJ: Ablex.

Erickson, F. (1982). Taught cognitive learning in its immediate environment: A neglected topic in the anthropology of education. *Anthropology and Education Quarterly, 13*(2), 149–179.

Erickson, F. (1986). Qualitative methods on research on teaching. In M. Wittrock (Ed.), *Handbook of research on teaching* (3rd ed.), (pp. 119–161). New York: Macmillan.

Ernst, G. (1994). *Anthropology and Education Quarterly, 25* ( ),

Ervin-Tripp, S., & Mitchell-Kernan, C. (1977). Introduction. In S. Ervin-Tripp & C. Mitchell-Kernan (Eds.), *Child discourse.* New York: Academic Press.

Evertson, C., & Green, J., (1986). Observation as theory and method. In M. Wittrock (Ed.), *Handbook of research on teaching* (3rd ed., pp. 162–214). New York: Macmillan.

Fernie, D., Davies, B., Kantor, R., & McMurray, P. (1993). Becoming a person in the preschool: Creating integrated gender, school culture, and peer culture positionings. *Qualitative Studies in Education., 6,* 95–110.

Floriani, A. (1993). Negotiating what counts: Roles and relationships, texts and contexts, content and meaning. *Linguistics and Education, 5*(3&4), 241–274.

Foster, M. (1995). Talking that talk: The language of control, curriculum and critique. *Linguistics and Education, 7*(2), 129–150.

Gage, N. L. (1963). Paradigms for research on teaching. In N. L. Gage (Ed.), *Handbook of research on teaching.* Chicago: Rand.

Galwatney, J. (1981). *Drylongso: A self-portrait of black America.* New York: Random House.

Geertz, C. (1973). *The interpretion of culture.* New York: Basic Books.

Geertz, C. (1983). *Local knowledge.* New York: Basic Books.

Gilmore, P. (1987). Sulking, stepping and tracking: The effects of attitude assessment on access to literacy. In D. Bloome (Ed.) *Literacy and schooling* (pp. 98–120). Norwood, NJ: Ablex.

Gilmore, P., & Glatthorn, A. (Eds.). (1982). *Children in and out of school.* Washington, DC: Center for Applied Linguistics.

Gilmore, P., & Smith, D. (1982). A retrospective discussion of the state of the art in ethnography and education. In P. Gilmore & A. Glatthorn (Eds.), *Children in and out of school* (pp. 2–18). Washington, DC: Center for Applied Linguistics.

González, N., Moll, L., Floyd-Tenery, M., Rivera, A., Rendón, P., Gonzales, R., & Amati, C. (1993). *Teacher research on funds of knowledge: Learning from households* (Research Report). Tucson, AZ: University of Arizona, National Center for Research on Cultural Diversity and Second Language Learning.

Goodenough, W. (1981). *Culutre, language, and society.* Menlo Park, CA: Cummings.

Graddol, D., Maybin, J., & Stierer, B. (Eds.). (1994). *Researching language and literacy in social context.* Clevedon, UK: Multilingual Matters.

Green, J. (1983a). Exploring classroom discourse: Linguistic perspectives on teaching-learning processes. *Educational Psychologist, 18*(3), 180–199.

Green, J. (1983b). Research on teaching as a linguistic process: A state of the art. *Review of Research in Education, 10,* 151–252.

Green, J., & Bloome, D. (1983). Ethnography and reading: Issues, approaches, criteria and findings. *Thirty-second yearbook of the National Reading Conference.* Rochester, NY: National Reading Conference.

Green, J., Kantor, R., & Rogers, T. (1991). Exploring the complexity of language and learning in the classroom. In B. Jones & L. Idol (Eds.), *Educational values and cognitive instruction: Implications for reform* (Vol. 2, pp. 333–364). Hillsdale, NJ: Erlbaum.

Green, J., & Smith, D., (1983). Teaching and learning: A linguistic perspective. *Elementary School Journal, 83*(4), 353–391.

Green, J., & Wallat, C. (Eds.). (1981). *Ethnography and language in educational settings.* Norwood, NJ: Ablex.

Guba, E. (Ed.). (1990). *The paradigm dialog.* Thousand Oaks, CA: Sage.

Gumperz, J. (1986). Interactional sociolinguistics. In J. Cook-Gumperz (Ed.), *The social construction of literacy* (pp. 45–68). New York: Cambridge University Press.

Gumperz, J., & Field, M. (1995). Children's discourse and inferential practices in cooperative learning. *Discourse Processes, 19*(1), 133–148.

Gumperz, J., & Hymes, D. (Eds.). (1972). *Directions in sociolinguistics: The ethnography of communication.* New York: Holt, Rinehart & Winston.

Guthrie, G. P. (1985). *A school divided: An ethnography of bilingual education in a Chinese community.* Hillsdale, NJ: Erlbaum.

Guthrie, L., & Guthrie, G. P. (1987). Teacher language use in a Chinese bilingual classroom. In S. Goldman, & H. Trueba (Eds.), *Becoming literate in English as a second language* (pp. 205–234). Norwood, NJ: Ablex.

Guthrie, L., & Hall, W. (1984). Ethnographic approaches to reading research. In P.D. Pearson, R. Barr, M. Kamil, & P. Mosenthal (Eds.), *Handbook of reading research* (pp. 91–110). New York: Longman.

Gutierrez, K., (1993). How talk, context, and script shape contexts for learning: A cross-case comparison of journal sharing. *Linguistics and Education, 5*(3&4), 335–366.

Gutierrez, K. (1995). Unpacking academic discourse. *Discourse Processes, 19*(1), 21–38.

Hammersley, M. (1990). *Classroom ethnography.* Milton Keynes, UK: Open University Press.

Hammersley, M. (1992). *What's wrong with ethnography?* London: Routledge.

Hammersley, M., & Atkinson, P. (1983). *Ethnography: Principles and practices.* London: Tavistock.

Harrington, C. (1982). Anthropology and education: Issues from the issues. *Anthropology and Education Quarterly, 8*(4), 323–335.

Heath, S. (1982). Ethnography in education: Defining the essential. In P. Gilmore & A. Glatthorn (Eds.), *Children in and out of school* (pp. 33–58). Washington, DC: Center for Applied Linguistics.

Heath, S., & Branscombe, A. (1986). Intelligent writing in an audience community: Teacher, student, and researcher. In S. Freedman (Ed.), *The acquisition of written language: Response and revision.* Norwood, NJ: Ablex.

Heath, S. B., & Peters, S. (1984). Ethnography and education: An uneasy union? *Reviews in Anthropology,* 52–57.

Heras, A. (1993). The construction of understanding in a sixth-grade bilingual classroom. *Linguistics and Education, 5*(3&4), 275–300.

Holloway, (1991).

Howe, K., & Eisenhart, M. (1990). Standards for qualitative (and quantitative) research: A prolegomenon. *Educational Researcher 19*(4), 2–9.

Hymes, D. (1982). What is ethnography? In P. Gilmore & A. Glatthorn (Eds.), *Children in and out of school* (pp. 21–32). Washington, DC: Center for Applied Linguistics.

Jacob, E. (1987). Qualitative research traditions: A review. *Review of Educational Research, 57*(1), 1–50.

Jones, D. (1988). Toward a native anthropology. In J. Cole (Ed.), *Anthropology for the nineties: Introductory readings.* New York: Free Press.

Kantor, R., Green, J., Bradley, M., & Lin, L. (1992). The construction of schooled discourse repertoires: An interactional sociolinguistic perspective on learning to talk in preschool. *Linguistics and Education., 4*(2),131–172.

Kantor, R., Miller, S., & Fernie, D. (1992). Diverse paths to literacy in a preschool classroom: A sociocultural perspective. *Reading Research Quarterly, 27*(3), 184–201.

Kondo, D. (1990). *Crafting selves: Power, gender, and discourses of identity in a Japanese Workplace.* Chicago: University of Chicago Press.

LeCompte, M., Milroy, & Preissle, J. (1994). *The handbook of qualitative research in education.* New York: Academic Press.

Lemke, J. (1990). *Talking science.* Norwood, NJ: Ablex.

Lin, L. (1993). Language of and in the classroom: Constructing the patterns of social life. *Linguistics and Education, 5*(3&4), 2367–2410.

Medley, D., & Mitzel, H., (1963). Measuring classroom behavior by systematic observation. In N.L. Gage (Ed.), *Handbook of research on teaching.* Chicago: Rand.

Mehan, H. (1979). *Learning lessons.* Cambridge, MA: Harvard University Press.

Mercado, C. (in press). When young people from marginalized communities enter the world of ethnographic research: Scribing, planning, reflecting, and sharing. In A. Egan-Robertson & D. Bloome (Eds.), *Students as researchers of culture and language in their own communities.* Cresskill, NJ: Hampton Press.

Michaels, S. (1981). "Sharing time": Children's narrative styles and differential access to literacy. *Language in Society, 10*(3), 423–442.

Moll, L., & Diaz, R. (1987). Teaching writing as communication: The use of ethnographic findings in classroom practice. In D. Bloome (Ed.), *Literacy and schooling.* Norwood, NJ: Ablex.

Moll, L., & Diaz, S. (1987). Change as the goal of educational research. *Anthropology and Education Quarterly, 18*(4), 300–311.

Moll, L., & Greenberg, J. (1990). Creating zones of possibilities: Combining social contexts for instruction. In L. Moll (Ed.), *Vygotsky and education: Instructional implications and applications of sociohistorical psychology* (pp. 319–348). New York: Cambridge University Press.

Montero-Sieburth, M. (in press). Reclaiming indigenous cultures: Student-developed oral histories of Talamanca, Costa Rica. In A. Egan-Robertson & D. Bloome (Eds.), *Students as researchers of culture and language in their own communities.* Cresskill, NJ: Hampton Press.

Myers, J. (1992). The social contexts of school and personal literacy. *Reading Research Quarterly, 27*(4), 296–333.

Oreallana, M. (1995). Literacy as a gendered social practice: Tasks, texts, talk, and take-up. *Reading Research Quarterly, 30*(4), 674–708.

Pelto, P., & Pelto, G. (1978). *Anthropological research: The structure of inquiry* (2nd ed.). Cambridge: Cambridge University Press.

Philips, S. (1983). *The invisible culture: Communication in classroom and community on the Warm Springs Indian Reservation.* New York: Longman.

Prentiss, T. M. (1995). Constructing literacy practices: An analysis of student lived and perceived experiences in high school English. *Journal of Classroom Interaction, 30*(2), 27–39.

Rex, L. A. (1994). A social view of composing from insiders' perspectives: The roles and relationships of teachers and students. *Forty-third yearbook of the National Reading Conference.* Chicago: The National Reading Conference.

Rist, R. (1980, February). Blitzkreig ethnography: On the transformation of a method into a movement. *Educational Researcher,* pp. 8–10.

Robinson, J., & Stock, P. (1990). The politics of literacy. In

J. Robinson, *Conversations on the written word: Essays on language and literacy.* Portsmouth, NH: Boynton/Cook.

Rosenshine, B., & Furst, N. (1973). The use of direct observation to study teaching. In R. M. W. Travers (Ed.), *Second handbook of research on teaching* (pp. 122–183). Chicago: Rand.

Rosenshine, B., & Stevens, R. (1984). Classroom reading instruction. In P. D. Pearson, R. Barr, M. Kamil, & P. Mosenthal (Eds.), *Handbook of reading research* (pp.745–798). New York: Longman.

Sanday, P. (1976). Emerging methodological developments for research design, data collection, and data analysis in anthropology and education. In C. J. Calhoun & F. A. J. Ianni (Eds.), *The anthropological study of education* (pp. 173–188). The Hague: Mouton.

Santa Barbara Classroom Discourse Group (Green, J., Dixon, C., Lin, L., Floriani, A., Bradley M., Paxton, S., Mattern, C., & Bergamo, H.). (1992). Constructing literacy in the classroom: Literate action as social accomplishment. In H. Marshall (Ed.), *Redefining learning: Roots of educational change* (pp. 119–151). Norwood, NJ: Ablex.

Schaafsma, D. (in press). Plants for peace: Telling stories with Mrs. Rose Bell in the Dewey Center Community writing project, Detroit. In A. Egan-Robertson & D. Bloome (Eds.), *Students as researchers of culture and language in their own communities.* Cresskill, NJ: Hampton Press.

Sheridan, D. (1993). Ordinary hardworking folk: Volunteer writers in mass-observation, 1937–50 and 1981–91. *Feminist Praxis, 37/38 .*

Smith, B. O., & Ennis, R. (1961). *Language & concepts in education.*

Smith, L. (1990). Critical introduction: Whither classroom ethnography? In M. Hammersley, *Classroom ethnography* (pp. 1–12). Milton Keynes, UK: Open University Press.

Spindler, G. (Ed.). (1982). *Doing the ethnography of schooling: Educational anthropology in action.* New York: Holt, Rinehart & Winston.

Spindler, G., & Spindler, L. (1983). Anthroethnography. *Anthropology and Education Quarterly, 14*(3), 191–194.

Spindler, G., & Spindler, L. (Eds.). (1987). *Interpretive ethnography of education at home and abroad* (pp. 1–10). Hillsdale, NJ: Erlbaum.

Spradley, J., (1980). *Participant observation.* New York: Holt, Rinehart & Winston.

Street, B. (Ed.). (1993a). *Cross-cultural approaches to literacy.* Cambridge: Cambridge University Press.

Street, B. (1993b). Review article. *Journal of Research in Reading, 16*(2), 165–174.

Thomas, K., & Maybin, J. (in press). Investigating language practices in a multilingual London community. In A. Egan-Robertson & D. Bloome (Eds.), *Students as researchers of culture and language in their own communities.* Cresskill, NJ: Hampton Press.

Torres, M. (in press). Celebrations and letters home: Research as an ongoing conversation of students, parents, and teacher. In A. Egan-Robertson & D. Bloome (Eds.), *Students as researchers of culture and language in their own communities.* Cresskill, NJ: Hampton Press.

Travers, R.(1973). *Handbook of Research on Teaching* (2nd ed.). Chicago: Rand.

Trueba, H. (1989). English literacy acquisition: From cultural trauma to learning disabilities in minority students. *Linguistics and Education, 1*(2), 125–152.

Trueba, H., Guthrie, G., & Au, K., (1982). *Culture and the bilingual classroom: Studies in classroom ethnography.* Rowley, MA: Newbury House.

Trueba, H., Jacobs, L., & Kirton, E. (1990). *Cultural conflict and adaptation: The case of Hmong children in American society.* New York: Falmer Press.

Tuyay, S., Floriani, A., Yeager, B., Dixon, C., & Green, J. (1995). Constructing an integrated, inquiry-oriented approach in classrooms: A cross-case analysis of social, literate, and academic practice. *Journal of Classroom Interaction, 30*(2), 1–15.

Tuyay, S., Jennings, L., & Dixon, C. (1995). Classroom discourse and opportunities to learn: An ethnographic study of knowledge construction in a bilingual third-grade classroom. *Discourse Processes, 19*(1), 75–110.

van Maanen, J. (1988). *Tales of the field: On writing ethnography.* Chicago: University of Chicago Press.

Vidich, A., & Lyman, S. (1994). Qualitative methods: Their history in sociology and anthropology. In N. Denzin & Y. Lincoln (Eds.), *Handbook of qualitative research* (pp. 23–59). Thousand Oaks, CA: Sage.

Weade, R. (1992). Locating learning in the times and spaces of teaching. In H. H. Marshall (Ed.), *Redefining student learning: Roots of educational change* (pp. 87–118). Norwood, NJ: Ablex.

Weinstein, C. (1991). The classroom as a social context for learning. *Annual Review of Psychology, 42,* 493–525.

West, C. (1993). *Race matters.* Boston: Beacon.

Wigginton, E. (1986). *Sometimes a shining moment: The foxfire experience.* New York: Anchor Books.

Wilkinson, L. (Ed.). (1982). *Communicating in the classroom.* New York: Academic Press.

Willett, J., & Bloome, D. (1992). Literacy, language, school and community: A community-centered perspective. In C. Hedley & A. Carrasquillo (Eds.), *Whole language and the bilingual learner* (pp. 35–57). Norwood, NJ: Ablex.

Wittrock, M. (Ed.). (1986). *Handbook of research on teaching* (3rd ed.). New York: Macmillan.

Wolcott, H. (1975). Criteria for an ethnographic approach to research in schools. *Human Organization, 34*(2), 111–127.

Wolcott, H. (1982). The anthropology of learning. *Anthropology and Education Quarterly, 13*(2), 83–108.

Wolcott, H. (1987). On ethnographic intent. In G. Spindler & L. Spindler (Eds.), *Interpretive ethnography of education at home and abroad* (pp. 37–60). Hillsdale, NJ: Erlbaum.

Wolfram, W. (in press). Dialect awareness and the study of language. In A. Egan-Robertson & D. Bloome (Eds.), *Students as researchers of culture and language in their own communities.* Cresskill, NJ: Hampton Press.

Yeager, B., Floriani, A., & Green, J. (in press). Learning to see learning in the classroom: Developing an ethnographic perspective In A. Egan-Robertson & D. Bloome (Eds.), *Students as researchers of culture and language in their own communities.* Cresskill, NJ: Hampton Press.

Zaharlick, A., & Green, J. (1991). Ethnographic research. In J. Flood, J. Jensen, D. Lapp, & J. Squire (Eds.), *Handbook of research on teaching the English language arts* (pp. 205–225). New York: Macmillan.

17

REMAKING SENSE, RESHAPING INQUIRY: FEMINIST METAPHORS AND A LITERACY OF THE POSSIBLE

Lorri Neilsen

MOUNT SAINT VINCENT UNIVERSITY

The invisible woman in the asylum corridor sees others quite clearly, including the doctor who patiently tells her she isn't invisible.... The invisible woman has great compassion. So, after a while, she pulls on her body like a rumpled glove, and switches on her voice to comfort the elated doctor with words (Morgan, 1970).

Unable to see her, I speak in a kind of blindness, not knowing what dance is being made of me, what puns of the thumb, tough similes of the fingers, how I translate into bone (Atwood, 1995).

Our responsibility as literacy educators, we claim, is to bring literacy to life. We are midwives, we think, who watch reading and writing of the word become the Freirean reading and writing the world, who see inquiry into literacy as a process of changing the abstract noun into the transformative verb. Becoming literate is a form of intellectual inquiry, in teaching and in life. So we stand behind or beside, offer skills, arrange perspectives, invite dialogue, nudge, nurture, critique. And wait.

Over the years, as a feminist teaching literacy and the inquiry process, I have come to realize that only when we come to an understanding of the cultures of the home, the school, and the academy as sites of struggle and hope, encoded and inscribed with politically-charged values, expectations, and assumptions, do we begin to see inquiry and research in literacy as partial, limited, shifting, and actively constructed. We also see literacy as not merely an intellectual activity, but as a way we are in the world (Neilsen, 1989). Teachers who come to this understanding begin to see their own literacy as they see and know themselves: instrument, aspiration, connection, limitation. They begin to see themselves as integral, and hence responsible, to these cultures into which they inquire.

This process requires more than changing a noun to a verb. It is more than the cognitive transformations we often hope for, and it is much deeper. For the literacy we have been fostering in schools and in inquiry these many years has been a literacy devoid of our response-ability: of our ability, as passionate and breathing creatures, to respond to our world. To live in it, here: now, with all the ecological implications and baggage of a past and future together. Literacy, more than the head, is also of the heart, and of the body. Of many bodies, breathing together. To be attuned to the world in ways that make us clear-eyed conspirators in life we must pull literacy off the page and out of the individual intellect into our sense-making, body-resonant and earthly-connected selves. It is this aim that shapes the work I do as a literacy researcher and teacher educator.

Claiming feminist as a descriptor for my work and my life (and I cannot separate these) poses challenges not only as an academic but as a researcher. I know I want, like Marge Piercy, to see the earth split open, to see notions of science / inquiry and literacy turned in our collective hands, held against the heat of the sun until their essences have evaporated, their core images bleached, their edges blurred and rendered invisible. Our modernist notions have reified science and literacy, so that definitions meant in their day to clarify have, instead, closed off possibilities. But an exploration of a postmodern stance, a stance which makes essences and foundations problematic, does not mean that nothing exists, that no positions are taken. It only means that we must be comfortable marking a path on shifting ground, easy with the notion of seeing meaning between the cracks, locating signifiers in spaces that were not there yesterday and may not be there tomorrow.

It is this project of creating a path by walking which I describe here. Revisioning research into literacy required me to revise the work that I do with teachers. My teaching in feminist inquiry and literacy research have changed dramatically over the last 10 years as my senses of what counts as research and what counts as literacy continue to change. At this writing, I believe feminist inquiry to be a stance to the world which knows interpretation to be an ecological process, a project of integrating and furthering sustainable growth. We are connected, and we are response-able. And bringing history into our present, we are always just beginning.

IMPOSSIBLE METAPHORS

Traditional notions of literacy and literacy research have been guided by impossible metaphors which constrain our notion of literacy. Like carefully-dressed, clipboard-carrying assistants trailing theory down its many well-defined hallways only to discover darkness, dead ends, or a painted movie set, these metaphors have succeeded in shaping methods of inquiry. But they have not achieved what we hoped they would achieve: robust and generative understandings of what literacy is and does and can be; ways of supporting and sustaining growth in literacy for children of all cultures, between and within our national and global communities; educational reform, including schooling practices which invite students and teachers into, rather than alienate them from, themselves, their communities, and a sense of all that is possible.

Even our pluralizing the concept of literacy—computer, media, visual, among others—has not mitigated the stifling effects of how we think about those literacies; how we tend to define, and hence confine; to describe, only to prescribe; and to teach, which, too quickly, turns to test. The results are more than disastrous. They are dehumanizing.

The guiding metaphors which have taken us away from ourselves, turning us away from the possible, are multiple. Three I have found to be pervasive—the industrial model, the medical model, and the training model—have roots in educational research, but the growth still creeps among the public and policymakers, covering more ground than we have any hope of reclaiming. Each of these models is informed by a verbocentric ideology; each separates reading and writing from other ways of knowing. Each is more limiting than enabling.

The industrial, or mechanistic model (A. Neilsen, 1989) characterizes literacy in terms of parts and components within a well-functioning machine. Learning literacy involves learning perfectible subskills; teaching literacy involves sequencing the instruction of these skills in such a manner as to result in a well-functioning machine. In society, this industrial metaphor plays itself out in functional notions of literacy as a competence which is definable and measurable. It is also autonomous, largely pan-contextual, and inert.

The medical metaphor characterizes our literacy in terms of wellness or pathology. Terms such as deficiency, diagnosis, and treatment mark this approach to teaching and learning how to read and write. This view of literacy is similar to the industrial metaphor in that diseased parts and aberrant behavior can, with the correct treatment, be replaced or eradicated. "Healthy" literate behavior is normal, standardized behavior: school reading and writing become the primary indicators of literacy and the sites for evaluation and assessment. Compliance becomes a marker for health. Like the industrial, functional view, the medical metaphor has definable boundaries for literate and nonliterate, and abnormal and normal.

The most popular metaphor for literacy education is the training center, a place where children, like caged animals, learn to press the right buttons to receive their reward. The rewards range from stickers to smiley faces to gold stars to scholarships. Those who do not perform as required receive frowns, F's, the threat of being held back, or continual reminders of their status in the academic basement. The legacy of behaviorism lingers: during his first year of school my youngest son's teacher devised a sticker system to encourage his sitting still to do his worksheets. My refusal to allow this both shocked and puzzled her: she sincerely believed that he would work for stickers. In the same way, our classroom practices assume a stimulus / response path into literacy which have the effect of disembodying text, textual practices, and knowing itself. And like the medical and industrial models which are its companions, the training model assumes cause and effect, and a dangerous linearity, instrumental utility, and predictability.

Each of these metaphors externalizes the learning and teaching of literacy, perpetuating the myth that literacy is something we think about and do, rather than something we live (Lytle, 1991; L. Neilsen, 1989). Each of these metaphors spawns research activity that serves to encode further the power of the metaphor in practice. How many years, for example, will we continue to isolate strategies for reading comprehension, teach them to an isolated sample in an anywhere-but-here classroom, and turn the results into textbook activities and teacher materials for widespread application? How much longer will we entertain the naive notion, whether it is wrapped in the garb of skill kits, whole language or process writing pedagogy, that there is *One Right Way?*

But, more germane to this discussion is that these metaphors for literacy learning and research are verbocentric and patriarchal: they reinforce the text's power to create us in its image, an image whose values include preservation of the hierarchy, of competition, and of accountability, and whose means of naming the world have limited imaginings of text and textuality. Outside the discursive and textual practices we call literacy and literacy research there remain silent presences awaiting ears to hear, hands to touch. By looking to the spaces, the presences between, and their many shifting forms, we can seek revisionist and feminist metaphors of the possible. Like Shakespeare's sister, these presences may have been there all along, if we would only imagine them.

Countless feminist researchers and educators have written about the tendency for institutions to appropriate text into their discursive practices in ways that alienate, silence, and violate the majority of the world's population striving for a literacy of the possible (Rockhill, 1987; Smith, 1990). As Magda Gere Lewis tells it:

if we are not men, if we are not economically advantaged, if we survive by the labour of our hands, if we are not heterosexual, and if we do not embody and display the valued assets of the privilege of Euro-American culture, schools are not the sites of possibility which the rhetoric of educational discourse wishes to portray (1993, p. 193)

As a researcher and teacher educator, I must work on my own practice. I must seek an integrity between my pedagogy and my inquiry so that these practices continually find each other out. The questions, then, are not about course syllabi but about daily work in the relations among people and ideas. What do I do in my own classroom to perpetuate silence and disembodied knowing about literacy? And, by promoting principles of feminist inquiry that have evolved in my practices as a researcher, how do I avoid creating another regime which silences and alienates teachers from themselves and their inquiry? How do I engage in my own inquiry to nudge myself toward a more response-able way of living?

LIVING INQUIRY

The nights are cooler now that summer is passing; they seem darker, full of unplayed drama. An early morning walk reveals the goldenrods, now as tall as my child, and the velvet white stalks of pearly everlasting along the path. The air is heavy, even sweet, and the woods are so silent that, when I step on the spongy moss, I cannot hear my steps. It is only the tensing, and then breaking, of filament against my skin, a spider web spun across trees in the night, which reminds me that I am both myself and Other here. Here? Where is here? In these woods, in this part of the country, this season of my life, of my mind, of my body; this world of worlds.

Now what kind of blissed out academic prose is this, you may wonder? Bear with me. August is a rich month for me and it demands my experience of it by mediation of all my senses and means of understanding: somatic and kinaesthetic, visual, verbal. And so I walk, smell, swim, watch the stars, draw, write poetry, eat the summer harvest from the garden, sleep near an open window. I come to embody August.

Similarly, I come to embody inquiry and writing. Words have shaped, guided, informed, constrained, and told my life across many texts and many years. I sometimes see my writing in that cinematic trick-cum-cliche of the 1940s, the black and white pages of a calendar flipping, scrolling into another time and place, another dimension. Trinh T. Minh-Ha, describing Helene Cixous' writing as a process of inscribing, notes that the forms of Cixous' texts "cancel themselves out as they appear, (and) challenge the work's status as object (temporal, finite). Infinitely dividing and multiplying, they are engaged in a movement of otherness which never comes back to the same (1991, p. 141).

My love affair with words, like any love affair, is fraught with tension and passion. To begin writing, I do a dance I have since found is common: I read, I tidy the house, I ponder, flirt with an approach and then, with a shrug, abandon it, pore over books and papers and leave them open on the floor, the desk, the bed. I embrace the rhythm of certain ideas (right now I am waltzing with both Franck's notion of the reflex arc

and Haraway's revisionist take on objectivity). I will move across many floors of understanding, shadow dancing with many theories, until the gestures, the nuances of these ideas become part of me, part of how my mind moves into words and the life they carry. (Here, I am also tempted to play with an eating metaphor, describe how I chew on certain ideas, letting their juices drain down the back of my throat into some river of theoretical waters. The comparisons are many).

I will create a working environment, for a week or a month, that looks to others as though the room has been tossed by the mafia. My mind will buzz with words, with continuities and discontinuities, and I will argue with myself until I reach clarity, insouciance, arrogance, humility, or boredom; any of these states will be fine. It is the processing, the induction, after all; the reaching for a state "in medias res," hearing the hum in the center of silence. To write, I must wade into a textual ocean and disappear in order to appear. I come to embody words.

This state, I assure you, has nothing to do with finding the Muse, or being a prose prima donna. I believe insight (or perception, or creativity, whatever one wants to call the state) has more to do with how attuned we are to the world around us, how passionately we want to apprentice ourselves to its offerings, to cultivate awareness, than with divine intervention or cosmic chicanery.

Similarly, when I draw, an avocation of my youth which tapped me forcibly on the shoulder when I began teaching courses in feminist inquiry, I must become so saturated with my seeing that my fusion with the so-called object transcends conventional physical borders. Franck (1993) calls this a state of seeing / drawing, meditative activity that requires not that I "look at" (for that is what separates us from objects, creating other), but see: fully perceiving, the body, the eye, the hand becoming acutely sensitive antennae. Words fail here: I can only describe the state as a high thin wire of concentration, immensely relaxing, a state, paradoxical as this sounds, so "inside" the activity and myself that I am open to the universe.

And that is where writing and inquiry begin, I believe. At a place, or is it space? as individuals where we are so attuned to the process that we are connected to the world. This space is where literacy lives and breathes, where struggles and connection shift and strain. It is not an easy place to be in, but it is alive.

Name a human experience that calls on us as fully human and multidimensional and we all can list examples of that state of being. Settling into the fourth mile in a long run, kneading bread in the quiet of the morning, sitting in the audience in the last act of Les Miz, breast-feeding a child, weeding a garden, holding the hand of a dying friend in the dank and acrid smell of a hospital room, playing a video game, tinkering at the piano late on a winter's night. Each of these experiences opens up our perceptual pores, awakens in us a dimension, a responsiveness to the world in all its pain and beauty which may have lain dormant for some time. Typically, though, we let the stirring giant go back to sleep again, promising ourselves to allow life in more often.

What I want for myself and hope for children is to be fully alive, to be a sensuous, sensual, somatically-aware being, one who feels and knows anguish and joy, sees the particulars of the world as well as its wholeness, celebrates and challenges what we mean by human in a diverse world.

Berman (1989) agrees. He is not, I think, hyperbolic in his assertion that when we lose awareness of our bodies, our sense of ourselves as a tiny cell in a larger living planet, we look for isms, and "from there it is a short step to seeing other isms as life-threatening, and to seeing the Other as an enemy" (p. 343). The despair of mothers of sons across enemy lines is silent testimony to our failure as a species to cherish life more than the contest of ideologies. The alarming rate of extinction of species on this planet reminds us, on that rare occasion when we stop to think about it, how we have made an Other of the organism which feeds us. Creating an Other allows us to avoid response, and hence, response-ability. Our romance with Cartesian simplicities has been a costly one, and we must draw it to a close. (But we must be careful, too, not to recast our talk of our humanity in neo-romantic terms: we fool ourselves if we think that a spine-tingling chorus of "We are the World" can make us feel sufficiently at one with the universe to drown out cries of terror or fill the tomb-like silence of famine).

WHEN WE DEAD AWAKEN

My aim, as a researcher and an educator, is to hone my own response-ability, and to foster that ability in others. In part, this response-ability must start with a "coming to our senses" that affirms our humanity:

> There is, here, a stretching out to a Gaia-politik, the conviction that the flesh of my body is also the flesh of the earth, the flesh of experience. To know your own flesh, to know both the pain and joy it contains, is to come to know something much larger... (Berman, 1989, p. 344).

Once that awareness is reawakened, once we begin to hear, see, know, feel, and touch again, our alienation from others—from colleagues, from ideas, from the many Others we create to simplify our thinking and to dull our feeling—seems to diminish. We come back to ourselves, back to who we are and where we live. As researchers, we are better equipped to communicate our experience when we see the inquiry process as a relationship, not only among people or participants, but with our unarticulated selves and the earth which bears us.

One of the great disjunctures of education is the fact that, as adults, we are alienated from the thinking and feeling of our body selves (John-Steiner, 1985); but children, the putative beneficiaries of the school structures and curricula we create on their behalf, are not: they passionately and with joy use all their senses and abilities to create knowledge and to embrace the world (Gardner, 1982; John-Steiner, 1985).

Greene (1988) claims that the passivity and disinterest prevalent in classrooms, particularly in the areas of reading and writing, is a result of our failure to educate for freedom in schools. To do this, we must focus on "the range of human intelligences, the multiple languages and symbol systems available for ordering experience and making sense of the lived world" (p. 125). Literacy educators are only now recognizing the powerful effect on learning and development of what Suhor has called transmediation (Suhor, 1984), moving across sign systems in a way that Siegel (1994) claims "offers learners rich potentials for gaining new insights and perspectives on the texts and concepts being explored—understandings that might remain untapped if language were the sole sign system used" (p. 3)

But how can we focus on the range of human possibility in children, when we fail to nurture those same possibilities, the uses of myriad symbol systems and ways of knowing, in ourselves? Where do we demonstrate or nurture our transmediative potential as adults? We can descry education's neglect of the arts and know that it is a long-standing neglect, borne of a utilitarian, functional, and materialist approach to education. We know that our attempts to weave the arts into curricula are an uphill struggle. We know that there remains a hierarchy of symbol systems and intelligences which define schooling and literacy: verbal and mathematical literacy continue to claim most of the nation's attention and the taxpayer's dollar. We watch, too, as the association of early literacy learning with nurturing and motherhood (Grumet, 1988; L. Neilsen, 1993b) becomes a double-edged sword: the body and the role of the mother in early education is at once idealized and trivialized. The embodied knowing associated with early learning, fully human sense-making, is tolerated until later school years, when induction into the Word of the father becomes necessary. Reading and writing become objects of study and control, separate from the learner, and employed to meet the ends of various contests of merit and manipulability, including assessment.

Nevertheless, in spite of these overwhelming obstacles, we have not adequately addressed our own complicity: what are we, as educators, doing to awaken in ourselves the responsiveness necessary to hone, promote, and celebrate our own multiple ways of knowing the world, of making sense? What are we doing to resist institutional practices which stifle our growth as professionals?

The metaphors we have used for literacy shape the educators as well as the learners. If we seek other metaphors, we may find that our perspective on literacy and learning changes, and so do we. In seminars on qualitative and feminist inquiry, I have attempted to promote new perspectives on our many human literacies in the hope that educators will take these perspectives into their lives and their classrooms and, as a result, teach with more confidence, autonomy, humility, and joy. Some may prefer to call these approaches methods of inquiry; perhaps they are simply (and complexly) the ways in which we are in many ways human. And perhaps, as researchers and educators, we can argue for their cultivation not as curricula, but as habits of mind (L. Neilsen, 1993).

CREATING A PATH BY WALKING

It will be hot in the city today but, here, on the rocks of Peggy's Cove, the early morning air is cold. The sun will burn off the fog by ten, but for now, we have sweaters and jackets as we walk among the whale-sized rocks whose lines dip toward the

Atlantic. Teachers all, we are careful to wear our sensible shoes; the notice posted near the lighthouse reminds all visitors that the sea here is merciless, that waves can, and do, reach up over the rocks and pull us in. I choose to walk among the rocks and around the cove itself, stopping to admire the brightly-colored homes of the residents. What must these people think when visitors arrive, as we have, at 7:00 a.m.? What must it be like having your community be the most well-known tourist attraction on the East coast of Canada?

Agnes is on the wharf, talking to the fishermen who are loading their lobster traps. John is behind the lighthouse, at the edge of the water, using a tape recorder to capture the sound of the waves crashing against the boulders. Linda is perched next to a pool, a microcosm of aqualife nestled in the boulders, observing the movements of insects and suckers. Patricia is sketching, using an HB pencil to show the play of shadow and line in the rocks as the sun begins to break through the fog. At the peak of the largest boulder, I can see Allison, prone on the grey expanse, a notebook in her hand. Near the shore, Carole aims her camera at a gull poised like a weathervane against the sky.

We are here before the busloads of tourists, and for a reason. The stunning beauty of Peggy's Cove is guaranteed to pull us out of words and texts and ideas into the physical power of the so-called natural world. It is guaranteed to bring us to our senses, and it does. This day-long event for graduate students, one which I often include when I am teaching a summer course, serves to remind us, as teachers, how bound we are to rooms and desks and constructions of words in various formats and guises. Invariably, we renew our long-forgotten commitment to worlds beyond the page when we are free to roam, to explore using all our senses, to record and reflect. And when we return to text, it is with revised, sense-charged notions. Typically, a day such as this produces poetry, which always surprises the writer: she or he will return to class the next day, poem in hand, full of wonder and renewed inspiration. I felt alive again on those rocks, and I wrote this: Is this real research, she will ask?

And it is here, then, that we can begin. What is research? Who does it? What counts as knowing, and whose knowing is valued? From the outset, I make my agenda explicit. As a researcher and as a teacher educator, my aims include the following:

(1) To demystify and to reclaim research and the inquiry process.

(2) To encourage the use of multiple sign systems, particularly as they reawaken body understanding and aesthetic sensibilities, in order to open up the inquiry process, and in so doing, to revitalize professional commitment.

(3) To promote an understanding of our multiple selves in relation to the cultures of the home, the school, and the academy and in so doing, promote our response-ability in those cultures.

(4) To encourage resistance of practices in the educational and institutional hierarchy which de-value situated inquiry and multiple ways of knowing; and to be open to understand how I am co-opted by those practices, and how I perpetuate them.

To Demystify and to Reclaim Research and the Inquiry Process

> As people mature, they cease to believe in sides or Headmasters or highly ornamental pots. At any rate … it is notoriously difficult to fix labels of merit in such a way that they do not come off (Woolf, 1929, p. 101)

Coming to the point of being able to articulate these aims for teaching and research has been a long and difficult process. Woven in the story of who I am and what I do as a researcher are, of course, the stories that form my history as a student, a teacher, a graduate student, and an academic (L. Neilsen, 1993). My struggle, which was much less painful than most, has served to remind me of my responsibility to other students, particularly women, who have felt outside themselves, silenced, and trivialized in education as a whole, and in the research process in particular. After all, research has created "a place where none of us lives and works—an 'objective' place wherein we are contrasted, compared, designed, and interpreted" (Chandler, 1992, p. 130). The study of research perspectives is often characterized by curricula which present research as "hygienic" (Stanley and Wise, 1993, p. 114) and "out there." This disjuncture between our intellectual work and our lives is crazy-making, creating invisible women (and men) walking the corridors of academe in search of something familiar to their lived worlds. Desperate for connection, we relent, and like Morgan's invisible woman, don a body and voice not our own, but which render us, for the time being, visible and heard.

The language of theory creates a valuing of propositional knowledge (Eisner, 1988), which generalizes more than it particularizes, and whose coin is the testable assertion. But, as Eisner states, our reliance on propositional knowledge diverts our attention from what he calls direct experience because we "know more than we can tell" linguistically (p. 16). Propositional knowledge is not only often contradictory to experience, particularly the experience of women and underrepresented groups in education, but its lifeless disembodied nature can, in fact, distort experience, and close possibility: "Our awareness is always limited by the tools we use. When those tools do not invite further sensory exploration, our consciousness is diminished" (p. 16). In effect, Stanley and Wise claim (1993), "there is a power relationship between theory and experience, and one consequence is that women are not only alienated from theory but also experience itself" (p. 162). We cannot see ourselves in the research reports and theoretical treatises that shape the research enterprise, and in trying to see ourselves in those terms, we blunt and diminish our exploration. Coming to research, we are required to wear the body of knowledge like a glove, and speak words only to make others happy.

We learn posturing so well that we risk mistaking it for the "real thing." Teachers who are also students of educational inquiry, are doubly obligated to be in drag; not only must they wear the dress of academic theory and jargon, but in their own work in classrooms, they have been expected for years to be "professionals": to silence or mask their preferences, their cultural biases, their ethnicity and their politics to uphold a discourse of neutrality and objectivity. They must play their role so well that they are capable of inspiring shock in the student who sees them in blue jeans at the market, buying oranges and wine with their partner.

The task of demystifying and reclaiming research and the inquiry process begs the question, "What counts as research?" Discussions around the seminar table with teachers invariably reveal how deeply encoded conventional notions of research have become. Men and women alike, even those who have conducted their own classroom research, continue to believe that "real" research searches for an objective truth, is synonymous with "science," is conducted in institutions elsewhere by funded academics, and has little practical relevance to their home or their working lives. Research is logical, value-free, tidy, and replicable. Academic practices, which so often go unchallenged or deconstructed (and which I realize I perpetuate even in this article), reify text as the sole purveyor of research knowledge, elevate "scientists" and "science," and perpetuate verbocentric practices in inquiry at all levels. The practices of quoting research to settle issues of "proof" and of lifting arguments with a highly developed set of bibliographic muscles prevent everyone around the table—faculty and student alike—from recognizing the validity and authenticity of their own experience and from learning to open that experience to scrutiny.

As the seminar facilitator, my task becomes showing the many ways we can take apart existing research "products," to look behind them to see how they are constructed within political and personal exigencies and constraints, and to recognize their fleeting and mutable nature. Teachers who want to explore, for example, classroom talk, and who see that other researchers have published studies in that area, must be first convinced that classroom talk is not closed as a topic, "been done," or "covered already." They must then work to understand that their perspective on the subject will be unique. (Much of the work I do, I realize, is enmeshed in the problems created by our lack of professional esteem, how we are schooled to defer). I remind people that everybody comes from somewhere, including a researcher. Using my own studies works well: I can explain how the historical influences and relations of ruling within the field of literacy research and within my particular institution shape the way in which I do inquiry and write about it. The text they read, then, is connected to a face, a voice, and a history, none of which are "objective" or unflawed. The words I wrote, the published text, can then be seen as partial, provisional, exploratory, tentative.

What works best to dismantle notions of "research" and "researcher," however, has been to invite teachers to engage in their own inquiry; in particular, inquiry that arises from their own experience, not as individuals, but as situated, relational beings. This "kitchen table" inquiry, as I call it, aims to "create a space in the academy to make our inquiring selves the center of our own inquiry: the daily micropolitical acts, the many issues, circumstances, and challenges of the ordinary which reveal the politics of our behavior in our conflicting identities and relations" (L. Neilsen, 1993, pp 6–7). Such inquiry both reveals experience and makes it problematic, and because it is dialectical, it serves necessarily to change the circumstances in which we live and work by forcing new

syntheses, different identity relations. Like tai chi, the movements are not static; the body moves fluidly from one position to another, poised momentarily, each movement leading to the next in order to maintain balance. At each position, our perspective changes. To do inquiry, as we do tai chi, we learn to recognize that we have been making those movements all along, albeit with less purposefulness and discipline. Stylized moving with awareness, in tune with the world, makes inquiry come alive.

To Encourage the use of Multiple Sign Systems, Particularly as They Reawaken Body Understanding and Aesthetic Sensibilities, in Order to Open up the Inquiry Process, and in so Doing, to Revitalize Professional Commitment.

> The governing of our kind of society is done in concepts and symbols. (Smith, 1987, p. 87)

The work of C.S. Peirce provides a basis for an understanding of sense-making, or meaning-making as a semiotic activity. A sign, he claims, is "something that stands to somebody for something in some respect or capacity." We make sense through a process of semiosis, in which our responding to a sign creates a "thirdness," our meaning or apprehension of / for the sign. What we have ignored in literacy education research, with only a few notable exceptions (Harste, 1989; Siegel, 1994), is the potential for semiotics in extending our understanding of reading and writing and the transmediative power of alternative sign systems in learning. Even those attempts to see literacy as a semiotic activity have tended to focus more on alternative modes of cognition, rather than full-bodied perspectives on learning. Not only has our classroom practice in supporting literacy learning been affected; so too has our inquiry. What counts as research and inquiry continues to be what can be documented and written in conventional text.

In Siegel's (1994) discussion of transmediation, the process of boundary crossing / mixing among sign systems in order to explore one way of knowing in terms of another, she draws on children's work in schools. But the potential for such transmediation holds for the research process in academic institutions as well:

> "Transmediation thus stands as a critique of the status quo in schools, where the emphasis on rote learning and the display of ready-made knowledge has dulled the minds and senses of a generation of students and led them to believe that there is no ambiguity in learning, no risks to be taken, no new knowledge to be made". (p. 4)

So too are teachers dulled in their means of recognizing and creating the conditions for meaningful inquiry. Research is often presented as a product, a current truth, a template for teaching. Why watch this reading group, they may wonder, when the list of readings from my graduate course tells me that children will do X, Y, and Z, anyway? Why not simply read what others have studied rather than watch, hear, draw, record, smell, or interact in the busyness of classroom life in front of me? Here again, the dominant metaphors for literacy learning, mediated through the printed word, shape teachers' practice. A simple shift in metaphorical thinking, from "if it's broke, fix it" to "if it's alive, feed it," might make all the difference, not only in the way she or he teaches, but in the means they use to begin their own inquiry.

The courses I have taught in inquiry (whether a general course in qualitative inquiry, or more specifically, feminist inquiry), have invited teachers to go beyond conventional texts and ways of knowing to exploring—or renewing—their multiple ways of making sense of the world. The courses require them to engage in learning using many sign systems (from music to the visual arts to performance art, among others), to communicate their learning using those systems, and to consider their classroom teaching in light of these multiple sense-making literacies. What are they doing about stretching themselves as fully sense-making humans, and what kind of environment are they creating for their students to do the same?

With the permission (or perhaps, requirement) to explore sign systems other than conventional written text, teachers exchange insights using video, pencil and charcoal drawings, watercolor and oil paintings, dramatic performances, scripted plays, musical compositions, photographic essays, computer graphics, children's books, fabric arts, dance, and comic routines. Typically, they relish the freedom that such expression affords, but they are also somewhat reticent to declare their enthusiasm to their colleagues. As exciting and renewing as these media are, they are nevertheless held in the same regard among professionals as they are in the school system: making a video for a university course, for example, is not considered as "rigorous" as reading three books and writing a term paper. Teachers begin to see that, regardless of the work in discourse these many years, only one definition of "text" prevails.

Like emerging limbs of a sapling, our many ways of knowing the world can be cut off early in our lives. School becomes a site for learning compliance, and robust and fecund creativity—the sort we see in artists and highly productive people—is seldom nurtured. The stories often told about highly creative people, such as those studied by Ghiselin (1952) or John-Steiner (1985), indicate that they often endure or ignore schooling to keep their creativity alive. But, unfortunately, so do we all. As adults, we squirrel away our instinctive needs to work in differing sign systems by slotting them into home or extracurricular activities such as organized art and music lessons; we trivialize these needs as childish or as play (and hence disruptive of our work ethic); or we meet the needs in socially approved and sanctioned ways, allowing glimpses of the possible only through the doodlings on the cover of a notebook, the dramatic hallway impersonations of a teacher or colleague, or the performative art of lying our way out of trouble or obligation.

But mature trees can often, given the proper conditions, support diverse growth, and I have found consistently in my inquiry courses that teachers who conduct their own inquiry into making meaning in diverse ways will renew their professional enthusiasm. Bridging various sign systems, playing with their intereducative potential, reminds teacher researchers that they are "whole" beings, aesthetically and somatically "real" and alive. Their confidence in having risked and

thrived, the inter-relationality of the learning that ensues, and the liberation from the word as the only signifier, all combine to shift ground, to propel them forward to a fertile awareness of themselves and their own students.

Piaget's student, Howard Gruber describes the "whole thinking" person as working with a number of interacting subsystems. Gardner's description of Gruber's perspective touches closely on the notion of transmediation, albeit in terms sounding more structural than semiotic: "A creative individual typically spawns a network of enterprises—a complex of searches that engages his [sic] curiosity over long periods of time. These activities usually sustain one another and give rise to an incredibly active creative life" (Gardner, 1982, p. 354.). Not surprisingly, the creative individual, Gardner claims, also experiences a "strong, almost primordial tie to the subjects of his [sic] curiosity ... a special intimacy with the natural world" (p. 355), a pleasurable tie with the work he compares to sexual involvement with a loved one. It may well be that opening our senses opens awareness, and such awakenings kindle or rekindle desire in all its forms.

Sign systems, however well we explore them, and however well we integrate or encourage transmediation among them, are not neutral, nor sapped of ideology. They are politically charged, encoded in our social practices in ways that can build empires and assign value. At a pragmatic level, disciplines and activities in schools are marked, encoded with political, economic and social importance or irrelevance. When teachers realize their response-ability in these cultures for assigning and assuming value to certain sign systems, it can open understanding about the everyday, and create opportunities to challenge the given, the values which form an unproblematized backdrop to everything they do. Suddenly, they will see schools in a different light, their work both as belonging to a culture of its own creation and responsible for its critique and renewal. They begin to question the verbo-centric bias in the public education system which marks survivors and champions as those who learn to negotiate and perpetuate the relations of ruling (Smith, 1987).

To Promote an Understanding of Our Multiple Selves in Relation to the Cultures of the Home, the School, and the Academy and in so Doing, Promote Our Response-Ability in Those Cultures

So, I think ... "our" problem, is how to have simultaneously an account of radical historical contingency for all knowledge claims and knowing subjects, a critical practice for which recognizing our own "semiotic technologies" for making meanings, and a no-nonsense commitment to faithful accounts of a "real" world, one that can be partially shared and that is friendly to earthwide projects of finite freedom, adequate material abundance, modest meaning in suffering, and limited happiness. (Haraway, 1991, p. 187)

While we engage in ongoing debates about the nature and existence of truth, looking askance at those claims that "no truth" exists as being equally problematic and equally modernist (if that matters), we still have to live and work, teach children, feed the dog, and pay for groceries. Some of us, like Stanley and Wise (1993), answer the phone to hear threats and abusive comments about lesbians and gays; others hide from a man who hits when he drinks; and still others watch as the administrative position available in the school, and toward which they have directed all energies, goes to a youthful member of the "old boys' club."

This is not mere information; these are experiences that matter, that bring us to our senses. These are the "stones in our shoe" (L. Neilsen, 1994). We are eldest in a large family from rural Canada, or we are the child of an alcoholic, a new citizen of the country, or the sister of a man who has just died of AIDS. Each of us comes from somewhere, but that "somewhere" casts a different shadow in each of our encounters with others. The recognition that each of us is a constellation of differing positions according to the culture or context in which we find ourselves—and that these "multiple selves" negotiate and monitor ever-changing positions in a complex web of relations in the world—need not be an awareness which strikes fear of chaos. It can, instead, be a liberating recognition that the "self" is provisional, growing, elusive, but nevertheless, for the time being, here. Such awareness also brings with it the obvious: that the self is as the self does. We are what we do.

This kaleidoscope of shifting selves that we carry into the world each changing day, creates a similarly complex set of relations for the teacher encountering a roomful of children, each of whom brings equally complex kaleidoscopes and webs of relations. The study of teachers' lives, whether described from narrative, postmodern, or critical perspectives, is beginning to inform our understanding about actual people doing messy work in classrooms. Researchers who make it a point to "come clean," about their own experiences will, as Stanley and Wise (1993) put it, "present analytic accounts of how and why we think we know what we do about research situations and the people in them" (p. 166). We drop masks: by divulging who we are and where we come from, we are less likely to dismiss others' understandings as deficient, wrong, or lost in false consciousness.

When I work with teachers in inquiry seminars, they work with the situations or issues in their own home, work, or community which trouble, chafe, or intrigue them in some way. Research closer to home is less likely to be turned into an object, an Other, and the participants in the inquiry are more likely to have a face and a voice. These are situations from which the researcher cannot stand outside, but in which she participates, and often, through the process, inspires or affects change. Thus, this "kitchen table" inquiry has a particularly striking effect on peoples' assumptions about researcher stance. Questions about research ethics rise to the forefront.

In a recent discussion, an art teacher described her colleague's recent practice of using a repetitive, cut and paste task with paper in her first grade classroom. Although the teacher had observed the class only one day, she judged her colleague as having "taught art badly," of having stifled the children's creativity. But, someone in the seminar group asked, could there be other explanations? What are the assumptions here about inquiry and about teaching art? Another offered an alternative perspective on the activity: was this teacher, perhaps, aiming to provide young children with an opportunity to practice motor skills and task completion, and not seeing this activity as related at all to art? How do we frame what we do? How do we frame what we see? Ought we to judge? How does the observed see herself and her intentions? How does the researcher see the teacher? Whose perspective is closer to "true"? Are our observations different when we see ourselves as colleagues, not researchers? What is a research stance? Who benefits from it? Who decides?

It becomes more difficult, as we engage in inquiry closer to the communities in which we live, to put on the body of a researcher like the rumpled glove, and to speak words outside of ourselves. It becomes more difficult, as we sit in a circle around the kitchen table, the seminar table, or the staff room table, to point a finger at others in the circle who do not meet our standards, or see from our perspective. For this reason, I believe it is important that our inquiry be situated in places we know, and in which we participate. It is only then that we face our response-ability, are less cavalier with our notions of what counts as ethical, and what constitute integrity and community. Flying into data plantations, in the colonialist version of "objective" research, has always allowed for the kind of symbolic violence that, around home or the kitchen table, would be resisted, might be considered intrusive, assumptive, arrogant, and exploitative.

To Encourage Resistance of Practices in the Educational and Institutional Hierarchy Which Devalue Situated Inquiry and Multiple Ways of Knowing; and to be Open to Understand How I am Co-opted by Those Practices, and How I Perpetuate Them.

> ...(academic scholarship) is in the mind, in logic, in a form of discourse which totally erases the body, the emotional, the symbolic, the multiplicities and confusions—and in all ways orders the chaos of our lived experiences so that we no longer feel their power, their immobilizing conflicts, as we live them. (Rockhill, 1987, 7)

My doctoral studies were filled with what might be called transmediative experiences. I particularly recall one "writing seminar" held by Donald Murray in which we engaged in another creative process, such as playing the piano or drawing, and wrote about how the processes informed one another. In other seminars writing as an art form was valued, encouraged, and expected; discursive, highly bibliographic academic writing played a part, but not the major part, in my studies. The education department in which I now teach has long held a reputation for holistic teaching practices, albeit varying interpretations of those, and for response-able, flexible, constructivist pedagogy. Students in our graduate program typically must spend the first part of their studies unlearning the institutional expectations and assumptions about university teaching and academic work they brought with them. It takes several months of waiting before I or my colleagues hear the incoming question "Is this what you want?" shift to "Let's talk about what I / we need to do, and how I / we can make that happen."

Still, as fortunate as I have been as a graduate student studying inquiry and a faculty member both teaching and engaging in it, tensions remain. The symbolic order of educational research marks doctoral institutions such as the one I attended, as being from a "soft" research perspective, not "rigorous" or a place where "real" research is funded or pursued. The narrative and reflexive research practices associated with institutions such as these are often labeled unscientific, merely anecdotal. Regardless of the educational site, from an elementary to a university classroom, ways of pursuing our knowing have become gender coded, inscribing a public / private separation, where stories and the "personal" are considered of the private sphere, usually associated with women, and which run counter to the goals of the school which intends to prepare people, especially males, for induction into public life (Nicholson, 1994, p. 79).

Outside the places where I am able to live and work I realize, as Helene Cixous so accurately names it, I must salute and show my identity papers, or in Virgina Woolf's terms, to identify my Headmaster. While students in our program speak in passionate tones of the dramatic changes in their perspectives—indeed in their lives and their relationships with colleagues, family, and friends—as a result of studies in which they can explore alternative notions of literacy and inquiry, the universities which maintain the status quo, the patriarchal symbolic order, are nevertheless considered to be legitimate universities, the "scholarly" institutions. They are places where, the student query "what do you want?" is answered by the prevailing master narrative or the accompanying bibliography.

In the meantime, I continue to celebrate and support, theoretically and empirically, work which, by redefining literacy and inquiry, seems to be want to redefine scholarship as we know it. In a time of decaying institutions and irrelevant structures it is necessary that we engage in inquiry which calls on an understanding of our whole signifying beings and in so doing rewrites our institutional practices. We are at a critical point; we must realign signifiers in new fusions of possibilities. How many years and how many millions of dollars will we continue to spend on dead and dangerous metaphors, grasping for new ways to revive them? How many years do we expect a love of literacy to survive with the heart cut out of it, when we allow it to walk among us, disembodied, a head on a stick?

The inquiry I explore and which I propose here is not, nor should it be, the only form of inquiry offered or explored in feminist courses, or in any research program, for that matter. After all, theory as regime creates its own problems of oppression. What should these efforts be called? Feminist standpoint inquiry? situated, reflexive research? feminist ethnomethodology? interpretive inquiry? response-able research? perhaps this work is a step toward the joining of partial views and voices into a collective subject position. Or perhaps the work is more interesting for the new spaces it creates, the positions it disrupts.

And so the circle turns, and this time the view is different. I consider it a step toward achieving Haraway's "earthwide projects" and Berman's "gaia politik" to resist institutional practices which continue to define, and hence constrain research that grows out of a particular context by attempting to name it, and to compare it to others' in different classrooms, and other inquiry collectives. Whose ends does it serve for us to agree on a definition of qualitative, or feminist, or science—to put fences around our isms and marshall our forces—if children and adults continue to wander the earth deadened to its promise and its pain? Virginia Woolf reminds me that we cease believing in sides as we mature, and the labels we use will come off anyway. Experience tells me, also, that even when I refuse a label, others will affix it on the work to quiet their own uncertainty. I cannot help that; but I can help myself and others teach and learn in more responsive ways.

Over the last 5 years my work with teachers has changed. Variously, I have encouraged a focus on observation, reflection, reflexivity, and resistance, sometimes, or usually, all at once. The ways of inquiring and "telling" have included most aesthetic and technological media available. The "sites" for inquiry have ranged from a girls' soccer season to an immigrants' social club to the local newspaper, an individual's experience of racism in school, the experience of motherhood, to the conversational dynamic of our graduate seminar. In all cases, the researcher—with her perspectives, dilemmas, insights, and activity—is the sphere from which the inquiry begins, the axis on which the related and relational worlds spin.

Throughout these explorations, I have encouraged the body awareness and attunement that brings alive teacher researchers too long buried under dry and bloodless words. I have argued for the validity of inquiry that arises out of uncertainty, and indeed, invites more troubling of experience. And I have worked to support as many strategies for seeing, hearing, documenting, and codifying—a triangulation of methods, if you will, especially of methods that invite many forms of representing how we know.

A classroom, however, is still a classroom, and my own practices with people are open to question and to critique. For some, I realize, the kind of situated inquiry I promote creates its own form of tyranny, opening issues a person would rather not address. My pedagogy can be a breath of fresh air for some, a terrifying open space with no guide posts for others. I must learn to adapt practices that recognize such differences. I must also recognize my own complicity in maintaining the symbolic order that excludes underrepresented and silenced groups, and places students at the bottom of a hierarchy (L. Neilsen, 1993). Grades and other such markers are still there, in spite of our work to take evaluation out of institutional practice. We can support growth through critique and conversation, create all the communities of inquiry we wish, but the grade sheets continue to appear on our desks.

It is instructive to continue to ask the impossible: how can educational institutions, and the practices of pedagogy themselves (however "empowering") avoid becoming sites of oppression, silencing in their own way? We cannot aspire to other, more ideal classrooms, for I do not believe they exist. Classrooms are still situated within academic institutions which promote competition, and which, through policies and discourse, find ways of excluding many combinations of identities, and the lived realities they hold, all in the name of standards and rigor.

FEMINIST METAPHORS

Robin Morgan's Invisible Woman "sees others quite clearly, including the doctor who patiently tells her she isn't invisible." She "pulls on her body" and "switches on her voice" and, in so doing, calls attention to herself. Better to suffer this, she thinks, than for the young doctor to learn that "he himself is insane. Only the strong can know that" (p. 326).

Historically, voice—and its companion notions of ventriloquism, silence, and muteness—has been a productive metaphor for women's experience of teaching and learning in the world (Belenky, Clinchy, Goldberger, & Tarule, 1986; Fine, 1992; Gere Lewis, 1993). But, is voice the foundational sound of our "true" selves, or do we produce many tones in many ways over many years? And from where do voices emanate? Equally compelling and useful has been the metaphor of the body, the corporeal being, whether we articulate it in terms of invisibility, embodied knowing / disembodied knowing, skin as a cover, role-playing or masks (Belenky et al., 1986; Grumet, 1988; Minh-Ha, 1991). Too often, however, we use the metaphor of body as an entity distinct from the mind. Cartesian perspectives on our work in the world have helped to form a basis for the metaphors for literacy which we now find wanting. What might happen if, we opened the gates separating mind, body, the world?

Shakespeare's sister, the 16th century fictional young woman born with a gift of poetry, is the ghost in our collective consciousness, reminding us all of the blunted possibilities of women's imaginings. Virginia Woolf, describing how the downward spiral to the young woman's death might have occurred, imagines her facing the impossible: "all the conditions of her life, all her own instincts, were hostile" to the development of her talent. Between her and the incandescence of mind needed to write poetry, were attitudes, social practices, and assumptions which were insurmountable, even in her own mind. "Her mind must have been strained by the need of opposing this, of disproving that" (p. 53), writes Woolf. In fact, Shakespeare's sister, shut in by the gates created in her world, would never have sought the horizon of her talents at all; from where she stood, it was impossible to even be aware of a horizon, let alone seek its possibilities.

Little has changed where issues of knowledge and inquiry for women and underrepresented groups are concerned. I continue to hear challenges about the "validity" or "reliability" of my argument for a living inquiry: how then can we compare, prove, sort, categorize, or place value such inquiry in the academy? A kitchen table metaphor for inquiry has a decidedly homespun, anti-intellectual flavor, challenging received notions of formal academic propriety. And yet I will continue to invite my colleagues to the conversation there. Such a conversation causes us all to examine again the split between the public and the private spheres: one, the political and social external world, and the other, the realm of privacy and subjectivity.

This, then, has been education. As Nicholson (1994) writes: "As one moves from the elementary to graduate and particularly professional schools, one finds an institution less and less "homelike" and increasingly dominated by characteristics associated with the public world and masculinity" (p. 80). A living inquiry, as comfortable in the kitchen as the seminar room, attempts to bring research home (L. Neilsen, 1994), to be named and recognized in the same way that we continue to lobby for recognition of unpaid labor, for the value of story beside statistic. It is work of the heart, the hands, our sense-making bodies.

The issues are ones on which the world can tilt: learning about the world as through the body is inseparable from the mind; creating the discursive world from the axis of experiences of the silenced, the unnamed, and the disregarded; exposing and composing our lives as researchers by including and examining who we are and what we do in the name of inquiry. Such issues are issues of legitimacy, if we choose to use a morally-laden term, or perhaps, issues of value. What and who and how do we value, what means and why, when we set out on the inquiry path?

But like the histories of midwifery or herbal medicine—from necessary practice to a position outside the realm of "acceptable medical practice" to a growing, if qualified return to "legitimacy"—the history of inquiry, at least its history within the last 20 years, has been a battle of "regimes of truth" (Gore, 1993). But who is right is not nearly as interesting or productive as questions such as "Who benefits?" "What is the legacy of our work?" "Who and what are we not hearing, seeing, knowing?" Women who assisted at the birth of children are neither right or wrong; they are variously witches, shamans, friends, lovers, pariahs, health care providers, and licensed midwives. The work is necessary, and will be done. The times assign place, and the politics ascribe value.

In fact, it is not my intention to force the adoption of my research and teaching practices on anyone, only to invite teachers to embrace them, take them in, like Shakespeare's sister, for a time, to reawaken aspects of themselves and their professional lives, to live the inquiry, and to be confident in its own particular truth. These practices of feminist inquiry, while they are satisfying and challenging, are part of the diversity and richness that marks the inquiry process as a whole, part of a mix of perspectives and methods we need to spark learning and force change. Such diversity, to the extent that the practices are not oppressive or irresponsible, is to be embraced in the same way our multimodal literacies ought to be embraced. My argument is that feminist inquiry of the sort I practice and support, ought not, like the talents of Shakespeare's sister, be blunted by the thick resistance of the status quo. Nor ought it to be skewered on a standard to which it does not aspire: to be the whole answer. Such feminist praxis ought to claim a space in the house we are constructing, not perceived as a faint shadow in an asylum hallway. After all, as Haraway notes, "we could use some enforcible, reliable accounts of things not reducible to power moves and agonistic, high status games of rhetoric" (1991, p. 188).

Metaphors become our lenses, our seat on the ferris wheel, our foot on the rocky bottom of the ocean. They shape how we respond, and even who we are. Our metaphors for teaching and learning literacy with and for ourselves and our students have diminished our possibilities, closed us from the constellations of codes and living responses that life opens up to us. Thirsty children are given recipes for water; soul-diminished teachers are given keys to the textbook storeroom. Both ought to be out looking for the horizon unravelling it, creating surprise.

No single metaphor can be selected here to speak for a feminist method of inquiry. But I am aware that metaphors that make sense—shape sense—for me in my teaching and inquiry practices are metaphors that call on the "body resonant." Living inquiry means that a relational being, living in overlapping worlds, touches and responds to those around her as she pursues the work she deems important. As she moves within / out of these worlds, she and they are changed. More than speaking a single voice, her presence re / sounds, re / verberates; her senses take in all that surrounds her, and she in turn, gives back. Her many-toned voice is part of her presence; sometimes a song, sometimes a cry, or a whisper. Her body lives in the world—mind, emotion, and sentience as a breathing whole—like a cell lives within a larger being, exchanging life-giving synapses of the heart, the mind, and all that she is. Our body resonant is less like a corporeal entity, and more like a permeable membrane balancing forces of air and water, fire and earth. Literacies of the body resonant are living literacies. They are the joy and pain of engaging ourselves in the many ways that our sensory systems offer, knowing all the while that we are not aiming to reach an ideal holism, but rather to be awakened to the knowledge that links meanings with bodies, here and elsewhere. I am urging abandonment of metaphors for literacy that do not fit our world,

that cut off our circulation, parch our possibilities and clutter our lives with miseducative and unsustainable activity. We need complex, situated metaphors, opening a "view from a body, always a complex, contradictory, structuring and structured body, versus the view from above, from nowhere, from simplicity" (Haraway, 1991, p. 195).

No god's (or goddess') eye view is enough, and we have had too many in the inquiry business in education who aspire to that seat. Meanwhile, as academic arguments rage in the etherworld, the discursive system where "system / atic" inquiry is enforced, a Kurdish child new to Canada enters a school in Nova Scotia speaking no English. She feels the cold in the outside air and in the classroom climate. She aches with knowledge she cannot tell, and she sits near the window, her pencil poised on a paper with words to copy. Disembodied words, that do not touch any experience she knows. Elsewhere, the mother of two children enters a literacy program after 30 years of illiteracy and confesses that she no longer feels like a nobody. Literacy will make her somebody, she believes.

No body. Some / body. Dis / embodied. Our metaphors for literacy have created a world of schooled people outside their bodies, outside themselves, unable to connect their life to their words. New ways of imagining our literacies and our possibilities might help us all read, write, sing, touch, hear, and in richer ways resonate with the lives and the struggles of travelers we have missed on the paths. We are passionate, resonant bodies seeking connection and survival; it is a compassionate literacy to which we must aspire.

References

Abbs, P. (Ed.). (1987). *Living powers: The arts in education.* London: The Falmer Press.

Atwood, M. (1995). *Morning in the Burned House.* Toronto: McClelland and Stewart, pp. 14–15.

Babbitt, S. (1993). Feminism and objective interests: The role of transformation experiences in rational deliberation. In L. Alcoff & E. Potter (Eds.). *Feminist epistemologies.* London: Routledge.

Belenky, M., Clinchy, B., Goldberger, N., & Tarule, J. (1986). *Women's ways of knowing: The development of self, voice, and mind.* New York: Basic Books.

Berman, M. (1989). *Coming to our senses.* New York: Bantam Books.

Burt, S., Code, L., & Dorney, L. (Eds.). (1993). *Changing patterns: Women in Canada.* Toronto: McClelland and Stewart.

Chandler, S. (1992). Displaying our lives: An argument against displaying our theories. *Theory into practice, 31,* 126–131.

Code, L. (1993). Taking subjectivity into account. In L. Alcoff & E. Potter (Eds.). *Feminist epistemologies.* London: Routledge.

Cook, J., & Fonow, M. (1990). Knowledge and women's interests: Issues of epistemology and methodology in feminist sociological research. In J. M. Nielsen (Ed.). *Feminist research methods: Exemplary readings in the social sciences.* Boulder: Westview Press.

Eisner, E. (1988). The primacy of experience and the politics of method. *Educational Researcher.* June / July, 15–20.

Flax, J. (1990). *Thinking fragments: Psychoanalysis, feminism, and postmodernism in the contemporary west.* Berkeley: University of California Press.

Franck, F. (1993). *Zen seeing, Zen drawing.* New York: Bantam Books.

Gardner, H. (1982). *Art, mind, and brain.* New York: Basic Books.

Gergen, K. J. (1991). *The saturated self: Dilemmas of identity in contemporary life.* New York: Basic Books.

Gheselin, B. (1952). *The creative process.* New York: New American Library.

Gore, J. (1993). *The struggle for pedagogies: Critical and feminist discourses as regimes of truth.* New York: Routledge.

Greene, M. (1988). *The dialectic of freedom.* New York: Teachers College Press.

Grumet, M. (1988). *Bitter milk: Women and teaching.* Amherst, MA: University of Massachusetts Press.

Haraway, D. (1991). *Simians, cyborgs, and women: The reinvention of nature.* New York: Routledge.

Harste, J. C., Woodward, V. A., & Burke, C. L. (1984). *Language stories and literacy lessons.* Portsmouth, NH: Heinemann.

Hekman, S. J. (1990). *Gender and knowledge: Elements of a postmodern feminism.* Boston: Northeastern University Press.

John-Steiner, V. (1985). *Notebooks of the mind: Explorations of thinking.* Albuqerque, NM: Unviersity of New Mexico Press.

Lave, J., & Wenger, E. (1991). *Situated learning: Legitimate peripheral participation.* New York: Cambridge University Press.

Lewis, M. G. (1993). *Without a word: Teaching beyond women's silence.* New York: Routledge.

Lytle, S. (1991). Living Literacy: Rethinking development in adulthood. *Linguistics in Education, 3,* 109–138.

Minh-Ha, T. (1991). *When the moon waxes red: Representation, gender, and cultural politics.* New York: Routledge.

Minh-Ha, T. (1993, October 14). Public lecture. Halifax, N. S. James Dunn Theatre, Dalhousie Univeristy.

Morgan, R. (1970). The Invisible Woman. In F. Howe (Ed.). (1993). *No more masks: An anthology of twentieth century American poets.* New York: Harper Collins., p. 326.

Morrison, T. (1992). *Playing in the dark: Whiteness and the literary imagination.* New York: Vintage Books.

Neilsen, A. (1989). *Critical thinking and reading: Empowering learners to think and act.* Urbana, IL: National Council of Teachers of English and ERIC.

Neilsen, L. (1989). *Literacy and living: The literate lives of three adults.* Portsmouth: Heinemann Educational Books.

Neilsen, L. (1993a). Exploring reading: Mapping the personal text. In S. Straw & D. Bogdan (Eds.). *Teaching beyond communication.* Portsmouth: Boynton-Cook / Heinemann.

Neilsen, L. (1993b). Women, literacy, and agency: Beyond the master narratives. *Atlantis, 18*(1 & 2), pp. 177–189.

Neilsen, L. (1993c). Authoring the questions: Research as an ethical enterprise (A response to Ridgeway, Dunston, and Quian. *Reading Research Quarterly),* 28(4), 350–353.

Neilsen, L. (1994a). *A stone in my shoe: Teaching literacy in times of change.* Winnipeg: Peguis Publishers.

Neilsen, L. (1994b). *The academy of the kitchen table.* Unpublished manuscript.

Nicholson, L. J. (1994). Women and schooling. In L. Stone (Ed.). *The education feminism reader.* New York: Routledge.

Okely, J. (1992). Anthropology and autobiography: Participatory experience and embodied knowledge. In J. Okely & H. Callaway, (Eds.). *Anthropology and autobiography.* London: Routledge.

Rockhill, K. (1987, Winter). The chaos of subjectivity in the ordered halls of academe. *Canadian Woman Studies, 8*(4), 1987.

Rogers, A. G. (1993). Voice, play and a practice of courage in girls' and women's lives. *Harvard Educational Review, 63*(3), 265–295.

Schniedewind, N. (1987). Teaching feminist process. *Women's Studies Quarterly,* XV: 3 and 4 (Fall / Winter), pp. 15–31.

Siegel, M. (1994, April). Metaphor and the curricular possibilities of transmediation. Paper presented at the annual meeting of the American Educational Research Association. New Orleans, LA.

Smith, D. (1990). *The conceptual practices of power.* Toronto: University of Toronto Press.

Stanley, L. (Ed.). (1990). *Feminist praxis: Research, theory and epistemology in feminist sociology.* London: Routledge.

Stanley, L., & Wise, S. (1993). *Breaking out again: Feminist ontology and epistemology.* London: Routledge.

Suhor, C. (1984). Towards a semiotics-based curriculum. *Journal of Curriculum Studies, 16*(3), 247–257.

Suleiman, S. R. (1992). Feminism and postmodernism: A question of politics. In C. Jencks (Ed.). *The postmodern reader.* London: St. Martin's Press.

Woolf, V. (1929). *A room of one's own.* London: The Hogarth Press.

·18·

MAKING 'COLLABORATION' PROBLEMATIC IN COLLABORATIVE SCHOOL–UNIVERSITY RESEARCH: STUDYING WITH URBAN TEACHER RESEARCHERS TO TRANSFORM LITERACY CURRICULUM GENRES

Christine C. Pappas
UNIVERSITY OF ILLINOIS AT CHICAGO

Those who have been involved in school–university collaborations have frequently remarked that "collaboration is not always an easy process" (Oja & Smulyan, 1989, p. x), or have characterized it as a very "messy," "uncertain," and time-consuming enterprise (e.g., Bickel & Hattrup, 1995; Miller, 1990; Oakes, Hare, & Sirotnik, 1986; Prawat, 1991; Sirotnik, 1988). However, despite these difficulties, for several decades now many have taken on the challenge to create communities that educate both those of the university and the schools by expanding relationships and social networks with each other (Lieberman, 1986, 1992; Nespor & Barylske, 1991; Sirotnik & Goodlad, 1988; Tikunoff, Ward, & Griffin, 1979).

I will argue that this messiness in these collaborations is largely due to new conceptualizations about power/participant structures and the nature of knowledge, which, in turn, have required changes in educational research methodologies. The major aim of this chapter is to insist that because of these changes about power/knowledge, *collaboration* itself in collaborative arrangements has to be made constantly problematic—that is, it has to be an ongoing, integral facet of methodological concern.

This chapter has been organized into three major sections. The first section sketches the changing power/knowledge perspectives that underlie collaborative school–university research projects. It starts by offering a framework for 'voice' from the work of Bakhtin (1981, 1986) to clarify whose voices have been privileged and whose voices have been silenced in traditional educational research. Then, because I believe that school–university collaborations are part of the larger challenge to traditional educational research, four areas of critique are briefly covered. At the end of this first section, characteristics of *collaborative action research*—which is the term frequently used to refer to many current school–university partnerships—are outlined to show how this research has been influenced by these four types of criticisms.

The second section describes a particular collaborative research action project in which I am involved that centers on

The research reported in this chapter has been supported by grants from Spencer Foundation and the Center for Urban Educational Research and Development, University of Illinois at Chicago. The views expressed are solely the responsibility of the author.

I wish to acknowledge the helpful advice and feedback I received on an earlier draft of this work from Vicki Chou, Micky Donahue, Fran Falk-Ross, Annette Henry, Celia Oyler, Bill Schubert, Tim Shanahan, and Steve Tozer. Of course, I am responsible for any leftover errors. I am also indebted to my other university research collaborators on our project—Diane Escobar, Shannon Hart, Jane Liao, Linda Montes, Caitlyn Nichols, Dian Ruben, Hank Tabak, and Liliana Barro Zecker.

215

urban elementary teacher researchers' attempts to change their literacy curriculum so that it realizes the aims of what Willinsky (1990) has called the "New Literacy." More specifically, these efforts consist of teachers redefining literacy by studying their roles and instructional interactions to make reading and writing more connected and meaningful to the real lives of their students. After covering the theoretical background of the project, various methodological techniques that we have employed—mostly in collecting data—are described so as to illustrate more generally the range of approaches being used in many collaborative projects. Then, there is a special focus on how videotaping has been used as a methodological instrument in our study to examine together the classroom interactions in our collaborative action research.

The third section identifies important ongoing issues and challenges for school–university collaborations. Since one cannot write a "methods" chapter without addressing the traditional research conventions of validity and reliability, changes in these two concepts are discussed first, and then two issues of representation are considered.

SECTION 1: CHANGING PERSPECTIVES REGARDING POWER AND KNOWLEDGE: THE DEVELOPMENT OF COLLABORATIVE ACTION RESEARCH

Changing Voices in Educational Research

Changes in power and knowledge exemplified in school–university collaborations are frequently expressed as finding, gaining, hearing, or creating *voices* (e.g., Gitlin & Russell, 1994; Miller, 1990; Richardson, 1994a; Schratz, 1993). Bakhtin's (1986) conception of 'voice' provides a useful initial frame to examine the kinds of relationships that are developed in these collaborative arrangements.

'Voice' is Bakhtin's notion for the "speaking personality, the speaking consciousness" (Holquist & Emerson, 1981, p. 434). Indeed, for Bakhtin, utterance (his term for text or the *real unit* of speech communication [oral or written]) exists only by being produced by a voice. Voice, here, is a point of view that always enacts particular social values by addressing—or being in dialogue with—other voices (Cazden, 1992; Wertsch, 1991). And, because language is fundamentally dialogic in that we use and create language by speaking with others, any new instance of use is entwined with other previous uses and voices. There is, then, *conflict* in this process—in Bakhtin's (1981) words, "[Language] is populated—overpopulated—with the intentions of others. Expropriating it, forcing it to submit to one's own intentions and accents, is a difficult and complicated process" (p. 294).

In such a view, because our language is already used and reflects previous *and* present speakers, the finding of our voice also involves hearing the echoes of others (Burbules, 1993). This may explain why the challenge of *altering* the traditional relation regarding power/knowledge between educators in universities and schools has been so distinctive

and also so difficult in collaborative ventures. These enterprises represent new ways to conduct educational research that are marked by attempts to develop a climate of open participation by partners so that the dialogue between them is one of discovery and exploratory, but frequently marked with uncertainty. Thus, there is a commitment to "see things through," and, despite the conflict the effort entails, a struggle to ensure that *all* voices are heard and valued.

Challenges to Traditional Educational Research

Most of traditional educational research—with its dichotomized stance on 'theory and practice'—has emphasized the view that researchers from the university produce the theoretical background for all and any educational innovation (Altrichter, Posch, & Somekh, 1993; Burbules, 1993; Carr & Kemmis, 1986; Cochran-Smith & Lytle, 1990, 1993; Gitlin & Russell, 1994; Lytle & Cochran-Smith, 1992). In such a hierarchical process, changes occur according to what has been termed a *technical rational view,* which has three major assumptions: that there are general solutions to practical problems; that such solutions can be developed outside of particular, practical classroom situations (that is, in university or other research or administrative centers); and that these solutions can then be translated into the teachers' actions in the classroom through training, publications, or administrative directives (Altrichter et al., 1993; Schon, 1983, 1987, 1991; Wells, 1994b). Clearly, in this "outside-in" assumption that sees knowledge for teaching being generated at the university and then used in schools (Cochran-Smith & Lytle, 1993), the *voices of teachers*—their speaking personalities or consciousnesses, their points of view, in Bakhtin's sense—have been missing. According to Gitlin (Gitlin, 1990; Gitlin et al., 1992), traditional educational research rarely involves a level of question-posing from teachers. As a result, this research silences teachers-as-subjects and "strengthens the assumptions that practitioners do not produce knowledge, that their personal knowledge is not useful" (Gitlin, 1990, p. 444). Little opportunities are available for teachers-as-subjects to play any role in the research process (Agar, 1980).

In the past couple of decades or so, different questions have been posed in educational research (Apple, 1993; Gitlin, et al., 1992; Ladwig, 1991; Noffke & Stevenson, 1995; Richardson, 1994a, 1994b): Who owns knowledge in education? Who benefits from research? To answer these questions, criticism of traditional educational research has been great, and embodied in this challenge are many influences that have contributed to the development and nature of school–university collaborations. I very briefly cover four of these influences: (1) the movement from quantitative to more qualitative studies and methodology; (2) critique from humanistic psychology and feminist theories on research; (3) the strong movement of teacher research; and (4) the increased emphasis of socioconstructivist or sociocultural views of learning.

Emphasis on Qualitative Research. Consideration about who owns knowledge in education and benefits from research has led to the view that alternative approaches in educational inquiries have to emphasize the importance of meaning *in context* (Mishler, 1979). According to Schratz (1993), many researchers have been disturbed that educational research, based on positivist models and quantitative measures, has led to too much 'noise reduction.' In his words:

> [V]ariables, experimentation and operationalization usually [transfer] the original 'voices' of its research subjects into statistical data, mathematical relations or other abstract parameters. Therefore, very little is left of the social context in which educational practices occur. What is left over represents the 'noise' in the transmission of data and is reduced to its minimal disturbance in the research process. Thus the original voices from the field become the disembodied voices in the discourse of quantitative research presented through reports, articles and books. (p. l)

The applicability of quantitative, experimental methodologies to educational settings has been questioned because too often they restrict the researcher's attention to short-lived events, isolated variables, and a very narrow range of meanings. Such a research product, therefore, provides an extremely simplified picture of a complicated classroom reality (Oja & Smulyan, 1989). Moreover, because it necessitates that conditions of the experiment be kept constant, which conflicts with a teacher's needs to modify and improve the so-called 'treatment' throughout the research process, the usefulness of the research for teachers to inform their future practice is also limited (McCutcheon, 1981) or even antieducational (Torbert, 1981). In short, traditional educational research uses instruments of doubtful ecological validity (Walker, 1993).

Thus, new qualitative approaches in educational research—ranging from ethnographic studies, naturalistic inquiry, or case studies to more recent enterprises such as action research, biographical analyses, and profile studies—have been developed to study the context of classrooms and schools, which are the settings that constitute teachers' realities. Using techniques to minimize interference or disturbance, researchers attempt to study and understand the actual lived experiences of education. Even within these qualitative paradigms, reconceptualizations have emerged because the theory and methods in these fields—from which educational researchers have typically drawn on—have been reconsidered. For example, in anthropology, the traditional picture of the ethnographer as an objective, authoritative, politically neutral observer who is above and outside of the phenomenon being studied has been replaced with one where the ethnographer is seen as always being historically and culturally situated (Bruner, 1993). This means that because subjectivity is an integral component of all aspects of the research process, it has to be identified and acknowledged throughout (Peshkin, 1988; Reason, 1994b; van Maanen, 1995).

Ideas from Humanistic Psychology and Feminist Theories. The purpose of newer qualitative approaches is to change the nature of educational knowledge by admitting the emotive and frequently the more vexing qualities of individuals into the research process. This focus on *persons* has its roots in humanistic psychology (Reason, 1994a). For example, Heron and others (Heron, 1981a, 1981b, 1992; Reason, 1988; Reason & Heron, 1986) have argued that traditional research methods in the social sciences are just not adequate, appropriate, or relevant for the study of persons, who are self-determining. That is, because such an approach excludes human subjects from the various facets of the inquiry process, including the knowledge of its outcomes, it cannot make any valid claim as a science of persons. For example, Heron (1981a) has argued:

> [P]ersons, as autonomous beings, have a moral right to participate in decisions that claim to generate knowledge about them. Such a right ... protects them ... from being managed and manipulated. ... [T]he moral principle of respect for all persons is most fully honored when power is shared not only in the application... but also in the generation of knowledge. (p. 155)

Thus, such a view argues that since participants in educational research are authors of their own intentions, choices, and actions, methods must be used to respect such agency in the generation of knowledge.

A similar stance is offered by feminist theories, many of which take seriously Foucault's (1980) notion of power-knowledge and how discourse is organized by sets of understandings that legitimate particular social attitudes and practices (Fairclough, 1992; Gore, 1993). As Luke and Gore (1992) argue, "A poststructuralist feminist epistemology accepts that knowledge is always provisional, open-ended and relational" (p. 7). This is because knowing is always a contextual matter—it is located in a historical and cultural context, and for that reason, there can be no finite or unitary truths. Moreover, there is an acknowledgement that this social inquiry is value laden (Lather, 1992; Neilsen, 1989).

Cameron, Frazer, Harvey, Rampton, and Richardson (1992) offer three major characteristics—which are similar to those of Heron's above—of what they term as 'empowering research.' The first argues that persons should not be treated as objects. That is, empowering research is research *with* subjects by seeking their active cooperation; it is always attempting to make research methods be more open, interactive, and dialogic. The second point argues that subjects have their own agenda, and therefore research should try to address them. Finally, the third argues that in the research process there should be efforts to give feedback to, and share knowledge with, subjects.

Teacher Research. Although the concept of teachers reflecting on their practices to construct their own theories of teaching and learning can be found as early as Dewey (1904) and Lewin (1948), the more current notion of teacher as researcher is most frequently traced to the idea of "action research" characterized in the work of Stenhouse (1985) and others (Elliot, 1985, 1991; Nixon, 1981).

Cochran-Smith and Lytle (1990, 1993) define teacher research as systematic, intentional inquiry by teachers. It is *systematic* in that there are ordered ways of gathering and documenting information or experiences in a written form, as well as ordered ways of recollecting, rethinking, and analyzing classroom events (for which there may be only partial or even unwritten records). Although insights can always be gained through more spontaneous teaching-learning activities, teacher research is an *intentional,* planned endeavor. Finally, it is *inquiry* because it emanates from, or generates questions about, classroom events, and involves reflection by teachers to make sense of their experiences. There is a "Researching" (Berthoff, 1987)—looking and looking again at what happens in the classroom; it is taking on a learning stance toward classroom or school life.

Cochran-Smith and Lytle (1993) claim that knowledge for teaching promoted by teacher research is "inside/outside" and is intended "to call attention to teachers as knowers and to the complex and distinctly nonlinear relationships of knowledge and teaching as they are embedded in the contexts and the relations of power that structure the daily work of teachers and learners in both the school and the university" (p. xi). Thus, teacher research promotes a new, distinctive way of knowing of teaching, one that privileges teachers as those who have the authority to know—"to construct Knowledge (with a capital K) about teaching, learning, and schooling" (p. 43). Here, then, there is no need to "translate" findings in the traditional educational research sense, for teacher research is steeped in praxis (Lather, 1986a); it is critical reflection *on* practice (Noffke & Stevenson, 1995).

Some argue that there are alternative paradigms available for the teacher researcher (McCutcheon & Jung, 1990), and that there is a typology of forms possible in teacher research (Cochran-Smith & Lytle, 1993). Nevertheless, advocates of teacher research argue that not only does teacher research provide useful knowledge for teachers themselves or their own schools, it also generates knowledge for the larger educational community by contributing greatly to the general knowledge base for teaching (Cochran-Smith & Lytle, 1993; Duckworth, 1987; Hollingsworth & Sockett, 1994; Watt & Watt, 1993; Wells, 1994b).

Socioconstructivist and Sociocultural Views of Learning. Through their own research, teachers often inquire with their students, thereby enabling these students to be also empowered as knowers. Indeed, the notion of learners as active meaning makers, and learning as a fundamentally social and constructive activity, are concepts that have challenged traditional curriculum, teaching, and learning, as well as traditional educational research.

These ideas argue against the traditional curriculum, a model that Freire (1972) has criticized as the "banking concept of education," where knowledge is seen as deposits into the heads of learners who are thought of as empty vessels. The kind of teaching–learning relationship being promoted here, then, is not one of transmission and reception, but instead is realized through collaborative interaction. As such, it also questions an individualistic conception of learning by emphasizing that learning activities take place not *within* individuals but in transactions *between* them (Wells & Chang-Wells, 1992). Thus, it reflects a sociocultural theory based on Vygotsky's (1962, 1978) view of learning that has been extended by others (Gutierrez, 1994; Moll, 1990; Newman, Griffin, & Cole, 1989; Wells, 1994a; Wertsch, 1985, 1989, 1991). From such a perspective, the teaching–learning relationship represents the coconstruction of meaning and knowledge in which the teacher shares his or her expertise to

guide and assist learners to construct their own. As Kreisberg (1992) has articulated it, there is an emphasis here of power relationships as being *power with,* not *power over.*

School–University Collaborations as Collaborative Action Research

Challenges to traditional educational research have originated from many fronts. The four I have briefly sketched have contested and interrupted common views of power/knowledge and theory/practice, and these changes have provided a foundation on which many school–university research collaborations have been, and can be, built. Emphasis on keeping true to the personal, original voices in educational contexts has led to more qualitative approaches. Such interpretive orientations aim to be "empirical without being positivist; to be rigorous and systematic in investigating the slippery phenomenon of everyday [classroom and school] interaction and its connections, through the medium of subjective meaning, with the wider social world" (Erickson, 1986, p. 120). Humanistic psychological views and feminist theories have argued that participants in such endeavors need be more involved and considered throughout the whole process of research. Socioconstructivist/sociocultural views offer new conceptualizations about how teachers and students might work together so that knowledge can be seen as their joint construction of meaning (Miller, 1992; Oyler, 1993; Wells, 1994a; Wells & Chang-Wells, 1992). This classroom collaboration between teachers and students represents a constant struggle after our long-lasting transmission-oriented tradition in schooling. And, although the teacher–student collaboration in the classroom has not always been very explicit in the writings of collaborative studies, there is a *parallel* effort being enacted between participants in most school–university partnerships (Oyler & Pappas, 1992, also in preparation). To understand how teachers make sense of teaching and learning—to acknowledge and value their ways of knowing—fundamentally changes the discourse about theory and practice. Indeed, as van Manen (1990) argues, "We need to invent a concept of pedagogical reflection and action that effectively blurs and blocks the idea of the theory--practice relation" (p. 154). Such an enterprise rests on new assumptions about power/knowledge relations between school- and university-based researchers, and attempts to develop methodologies to empower these voices in research projects.

Currently many of these more recent partnerships are considered—either by name and/or by nature—to be collaborative action research. A general aim of collaborative action research (CAR) is the modification and elaboration of theories of teaching and learning. This research can take different forms, depending on the purpose of particular projects and the ways in which teachers or other school personnel are involved. However, according to Oja and Smulyan (1989), there are four major characteristics that CAR projects have in common. (Only a brief description is possible here—see Adelman, 1993; Kyle & Hovda, 1978; Oja and Smulyan, 1989, for more detailed and historical discussions.)

First, of course, CAR is *collaborative in nature*. That is, it permits mutual understanding among the participants through democratic decision making for some common action. There is an emphasis for both teachers and university researchers to work together to set common goals, plan the research, analyze data, and report results.

Responsibilities and roles are determined together, which may shift during the course of a project, but teacher- and university-researchers contribute their own knowledge and insights to the process. There is an assumption that participants communicate frequently and openly to prevent any possible conflicting perceptions stemming from their different social networks, values, expectations, and so forth, and to encourage and support teachers' ongoing practice and responsibilities.

Second, and obviously, CAR projects *focus on practice*. Most of the time CAR addresses the immediate problems defined by participating teachers. Sometimes, university researchers may have a particular issue or topic of interest for consideration and invite teachers to participate with them in investigating it. Or, teachers or a school may identify the problem and ask for university researchers' collaboration to help examining and studying it. Nevertheless, within each framework, there is a teacher-as-researcher emphasis of some kind.

Third, CAR enhances teachers' *professional development* by supporting or providing the impetus to improve and change their classroom practice. Through CAR they construct new knowledge to deal with their immediate difficulties, expand their professional knowledge, and acquire research skills for future teacher inquiry.

The last characteristic of successful CAR stresses the need for a *project structure* that enables the above three elements to occur. This structure requires: regular and open communication among participants; democratic project leadership; recurring cycles of planning, acting, observing, and reflecting; and positive relationships with the school or schools in which the project is conducted.

In the next section more specific methodologies are addressed by describing a particular collaborative action research project that focuses on changes in literacy teaching and learning in urban schools.

SECTION 2: AN EXAMPLE: STRUGGLES TO TRANSFORM LITERACY CURRICULUM GENRES TO PROMOTE NEW LITERACY GOALS

Theoretical Background of the Project

Our school–university research project involves collaboration with a small group of elementary teachers in two Chicago schools (8 in one school; 6 in the other) who have been attempting to develop literacy practices that are more "holistic" and student-centered. Thus, their approaches have involved moving away from transmission-oriented curriculum by adopting more socioconstructivist and sociocultural views of teaching/learning, as noted in Section 1. A major focus of

these teachers' struggles to be agents of change in their classrooms has centered around their questions of when and how to share authority and power with their students, most of whom are poor and who come from various ethnolinguistic backgrounds. That is, as these teacher researchers have begun to utilize a more collaborative style of teaching, they have grappled with new ways to fashion instructional interactions so they can share their expertise, but at the same time foster and facilitate children's active construction of their own knowledge and expertise (Kreisberg, 1992; Martin, 1993; Wells & Chang-Wells, 1992). Thus, as indicated in the introduction of the chapter, their inquiries involve efforts to implement "New Literacy" curriculum (Willinsky, 1990)—to make reading and writing more personally meaningful and powerful by connecting these processes to the real lives of students. In Willinsky's words:

> The New Literacy speaks directly to teachers reasserting control over the work that goes on in the class, even as it attempts to hand a greater part of the locus of meaning over to the student. It represents a taking hold of the curriculum by the teacher at a fundamental level by challenging the meaning of literacy in the classroom as well as the nature of a teacher's work with the students. (p. 18)

In our project the study of these changes has centered around the analysis of classroom discourse. Classroom discourse is the medium by which most teaching takes place and in which students demonstrate to teachers much of what they have learned (Barnes & Todd, 1995; Cazden, 1986, 1988; Christie, 1987, 1989; Edwards & Westgate, 1994). As Lemke (1985a) has stated it, "Classroom education, to a very large degree, *is* talk: it is the social use of language to enact regular activity structures and to share systems of meaning among teachers and students" (p. 1).

Thus, this is a social-semiotic perspective (Halliday, 1978, 1993; Halliday & Hasan, 1985; Lemke, 1990; Young, 1992) that focuses on how these various educational routines are structured and shift during a school day. That is, these shifts in activities or routines are encoded in behavioral patterns, as well as through changing, corresponding linguistic patterns to express these different classroom meanings (Bloome & Bailey, 1992; Erickson & Shultz, 1977; Green, Kantor, & Rogers, 1991; Santa Barbara Classroom 1992). Using a term suggested by Christie (1987, 1989, 1993), I have called these demarcated event/participant structures or routines "curriculum genres" (Pappas, 1990, 1991, in press). That is, particular curriculum genres are particular activity structures, that is, each curriculum genre represents a socially recognizable sequence of actions that realizes particular meanings or purposes for teachers and students in the overall classroom curriculum. Thus, a curriculum genre, as an "action genre," is analogous to Bakhtin's (1986) idea of "speech genre."

Classroom discourse studies have indicated that most of the typical classroom talk in curriculum genres has properties that make it quite different from talk in most other settings. First, this talk is dominated by teacher questions, typically a certain kind of questions termed "pseudo" questions—ones for which the teacher already *knows* the answers (Dillon, 1994; Edwards & Mercer, 1987; Ramirez, 1988; Shuy, 1988;

Young, 1992). Second, these questions are frequently embedded in a characteristic initiate-respond-evaluate (IRE) talk structure that is controlled by the teacher (Cazden, 1988; Edwards & Mercer, 1987; Lemke, 1990; Sinclair & Coulthard, 1975; Young, 1992). In this IRE pattern, the teacher *initiates* a sequence or interaction by calling a child to respond, then the nominated child *responds* to the initiation or question posed by the teacher, and finally the teacher *evaluates* what the child has said before calling on the next child, and on and on. This IRE structure is the essence of traditional transmission-oriented education.

Children have unique personal characteristics, and in urban schools they come from a variety of cultural and linguistic backgrounds, which means that they also bring their own complex "ways with words" to classroom interactions (Heath, 1982, 1983; Lindfors, 1987; Michaels, 1981; Philips, 1972, 1983). The traditional IRE talk structure, with its strict teacher-dominated, turn-taking format, has been shown to affect minority students' learning adversely because it does not provide many opportunities for negotiation or consideration of these children's styles of interaction (Au & Jordan, 1981; Delpit, 1988, 1992; Foster, 1992; Heath, 1983; McCollum, 1991; Michaels, 1981; Philips, 1972, 1983; Reyes, 1991, 1992).

What is central in the present project, then, is how these urban teachers are trying *alternatives* to these IRE patterns to realize New Literacy ideas. By giving their students more control of their own literacy learning, they are attempting to transform literacy curriculum genres so that both teacher and student "voices" are privileged in collaborative transactions. Thus, struggles to develop curriculum genres that accommodate for diversity in this complex way are at the root of these teacher researchers' change.

Methodologies for Collaboration

Methodologies in our school–university collaboration have evolved over our almost 6-year partnership. My relationship with the teachers at the two schools began in 1989, the year when I began teaching at the University of Illinois at Chicago. This was also the year when Chicago Reform was initiated where school personnel at each Chicago public school worked together with its Local School Council to develop a Fifth-Year Plan. Teachers in the two schools sought me out for collaboration as they began to implement their respective plans, which called for their reexamining their language and literacy curriculum to make it more "holistic."

Throughout the years a small group of teachers from each school and I would meet regularly to discuss their inquiries about their struggles to enact collaborative styles of teaching literacy. As I had time, I would also observe in their classrooms, audiotape interactions in various curriculum genres, and write up fieldnotes that I would share with the teachers to promote ongoing investigation and discussion. Finally, external research support enabled us to extend this collaborative action research in a more systematic way. By using videotaping and other ethnographic techniques, we have been attempting to document the *process* by which urban elementary teachers develop culturally and linguistically responsive literacy pedagogy. However, I will concentrate mostly on what has been employed during the past school year (1994–95), which has been mostly a "data collection" year, to be followed by a year of our transforming, and writing up these data together. The purpose here is not to set forth some kind of methodological "ideal," but instead to be illustrative of some of the typical techniques that are being used in collaborative ventures. Moreover, my aim is not to be exhaustive in citing, or referring to, other projects, so those that are mentioned reflect the ones that have most informed our work.

Journals. In our study, teachers determine and choose the area—the curriculum genre—in which they do their literacy inquiries. In the fall I gave them a form that asked them what they would be studying during the year—the major questions they would be attempting to address in their inquiries, when they would be "doing" the inquiries, and in what initial ways we could help or support their inquiries. I also encouraged them to use their own private research journal, which is quite a common tool for reflection and documentation in collaborative work with teacher researchers (Clandinin & Connelly, 1991; Connelly & Clandinin, 1988; Miller, 1990; Stevenson, Noffke, Flores, & Granger, 1995). Because only some of the teachers had previously kept a journal, I shared with them the chapter of Altrichter et al. (1993) on "The Research Diary," which provides a rationale and useful suggestions for using one.

Many collaborative projects also use dialogue journals (Clandinin, 1993; Miller, 1990; Robinson, 1994; Stevenson et al., 1995), sometimes in addition to the private journals kept by teachers, where university- and teacher-researchers correspond back and forth to (and among) each other. This is particularly frequent when there is also a professor–student relationship present in the collaboration (e.g, see Gitlin's [Gitlin et al., 1992] Educative Research project that is part of a Cooperative Masters of Education Program, and Wells' [1994b] graduate courses on "Action Research in Language and Learning").

In our project teachers sometimes spontaneously refer to entries they have noted down in their journals during our weekly school meetings, and at our individual end-of-the-year interviews with them, they more purposefully consulted them (as well as their fieldnotes—see below) to talk to us about what stood out for them during the past year regarding their inquiries. Next year, as we begin to write up the past year's research, I expect that teachers will rely on these journals more in their further analysis, interpretation, and reflection of our collaborative research. Thus, journals—either private or dialogue— represent an important resource in collaborative research, as well as valuing of teachers' knowledge and voice in the process of research.

Fieldnotes. Another feature of many collaborative projects involves observations in particular teachers' classrooms by others—other teachers or outside university personnel—that are recorded through fieldnotes (Clandinin & Connelly, 1991; Connelly & Clandinin, 1988; Hollingsworth, 1994). In our project, three 2-member teams of university researchers—one at each of the two schools and one who worked in the four bilingual classrooms at both schools—completed the fieldnotes, which usually complemented videotaping records. Because I was in *all* of the 14 teachers' classrooms regularly to observe their inquiries (and several of the teachers had two inquiries), and could not manage in any practical way regularly to write up in-depth fieldnotes, I developed shortened versions of fieldnotes that I called "Summary/Queries." Instead of providing rich description and comments of what I saw or heard, which is what the other university researchers did, I provided a brief summary with perhaps a pertinent example or two of interaction and then posed questions or provided other comments for the teachers to consider relative to their inquiries. As I observed, I might have also thought of an article or book that could be helpful in a particular teacher's thinking about the problem or issue he or she is presently tackling, and I might have added a note that I would soon be bringing in that resource for his or her consideration. The teachers have reported that both of these versions of fieldnotes have been extremely invaluable in their inquiries.

Of course, writing fieldnotes has been a mainstay of ethnographic and qualitative research, but what is different in collaborative studies is that these fieldnotes are shared with teachers in an ongoing way. That is, unlike noncollaborative ethnographies where the researcher "keeps" the fieldnotes and rarely ever discloses them with the "subject(s)" of research, the purpose of observation here is to give feedback and support on what the teachers are attempting to accomplish in their inquiries.

In our case, then, one of our major university-researcher roles in our collaborative project was to observe (and videotape—see the next subsection) classroom activities and interactions in the various curriculum genres that constituted the teachers' inquiries. Therefore it was important that the teachers received our (my and other university researchers') fieldnotes of these observations as quickly as possible.

The university personnel were prepared for this task by reading and examining various perspectives on fieldnotes in qualitative research (Bogdan & Biklen, 1982; Delamont, 1992; Patton, 1990). We worked on devising a general framework that we could all follow but that still allowed for openness for our different styles. That is, we recognized that there is no such thing as "pure" description since "doing" fieldnotes is "the very act of constructing *data* out of *experience*" (Wolcott, 1994, p. 13).

Although I had anticipated that the past year of the project would mostly consist of "gathering data," the documentation of classroom life and talk could not be seen as *merely* description because some aspects of ongoing analysis and interpretation by all of us—university- and teacher-researchers—would be required to understand and support the course of the teachers' investigations. Thus, we also relied on Wolcott's (1994) recent suggestions on description, analysis, and interpretation of qualitative data to keep our use of fieldnotes (and other kinds of data) in a larger perspective during the past year.

This practice of sharing of fieldnotes (and other data gathered by different techniques) in an ongoing fashion is

distinctive in collaborative projects. It is also similar to methods employed in school profile studies in England (Rudduck, 1993) where outside researchers do fieldwork and rapid reporting on a topic or "area of significance" (Walker, 1980) that is identified ahead of time by a particular school. This approach also shifts the notion of the outside researcher as the prime interpreter of the data to the school audience—who was also the sponsor and subject of the research. Sometimes some version of this approach (but usually done by outside researchers *with* school personnel) is used as the initial phase in a longer project to identify the topic(s) to be studied in the latter phases by the collaborative school–university team (e.g., Oja & Smulyan, 1989).

Regular Meetings. We had weekly meetings of the university- and teacher-researchers at each school (as well as several meetings with all of the teachers), which were also videotaped. At these meetings, edited classroom videotapes of one or sometimes two teachers were examined— see below for a more detailed account of these meetings.

Having regular meetings between university- and teacher-researchers where all talk about and examine issues relevant to the project is a very common feature in collaborative studies, and for some, transcriptions of these conversations consist of one of the major sources of data (e.g., Hollingsworth, 1994; Miller, 1990). Rereading of these transcripts enables the collaborative group to identify themes and consider new interpretations.

Individual Interviews/Conversations. We had many incidental and informal conversations throughout the year, some of which were audiotaped, some of which were captured as "additions" to fieldnotes if they had been recently related to something that had happened in the classroom regarding a particular teacher's inquiry. We (the respective university research team and myself) also had individual end-of-the-year interviews with the teachers about what stood out for them—both ups and downs—regarding their inquiries. They prepared in advance for these conversations by going through their journals and fieldnotes.

The use of individual interviews or conversations that serve as data resources is frequent in collaborative projects. Members of the collaboration team may interview other teachers or school personnel, parents, or students on a particular topic or issue (Bickel & Hattrup, 1995; Connelly & Clandinin, 1988; Oja & Smulyan, 1989; Rudduck, 1993; Watt & Watt, 1993), and then analyze and interpret these together. In our case, the interviews provided a means to get the teachers' perspectives on what they believed were the critical points of their inquiries.

Summary. I have tried to describe some of the methodological tools that we have employed in our project to illustrate the typical approaches of collecting data in various collaborative projects. These are not the only ones we used in our project (for example, teachers also had their own audiotape recorders and taped certain classroom interactions when we were not present), nor do I suggest by the above list that these are the only ones available in collaborative action research projects (for example, see Walker 1993 in the use of photographs). However, it is important to note that most collaborations use several techniques in the research process to provide triangulation, and that these methods are sensitive to *being* collaborative.

In some projects—like ours—university researchers have major responsibilities collecting data in teachers' classrooms; in others, university personnel—especially if they also have roles as professors in courses, or if they are leaders of professional development school projects—serve mostly as facilitators of teachers' action research, where teachers collect most of the data in their own classrooms. The arrangements in collaborative ventures are quite varied.

Using Videotape as an Instrument in Collaborative Action Research

As already noted, videotaping was a major tool of data collection in teachers' classrooms and documentation of our collaborative work. Two-member teams, who worked with the same teachers the whole year, did the classroom videotaping. One person in the team operated the camera, and the other took the fieldnotes. The duration of these videotaping sessions varied according to the length of the curriculum genres in which teachers had their inquiries—as short as 20 minutes or as long as over an hour long. If we had shown the entire classroom videotape recording, we would have had no time for examination or discussion at our weekly meetings. Thus, an edited version (usually 10–15 minutes long) of one or two teachers' classroom footage was shared at these meetings. Since we did not want university researchers to make all of the decisions on what should and should not be included in an edited videotape, we developed a form that asked for teachers' input. After each videotaping session in a teachers' classroom, they noted on this form the "good" parts and "vulnerable" parts that they thought would be important to include in the editing. Using that as a guide, and the fieldnotes that were taken to complement the videotaping (which, as I have already noted, were given to the teacher within a day or so after our visit), we selected several portions that we believed captured the focus of the teacher's inquiry to date. The teacher then shared the video in an "author's chair" fashion a week or so later. Also, we found it useful to provide a brief note, on which we listed short descriptors of the edited segments, for everyone at the meeting so that we could all better follow what would be shown.

Below we focus on Dorothy's sharing of her inquiry of her Teacher-Led Reading-Aloud Curriculum Genre. Excerpts are provided both of her edited tape of the classroom discourse for a particular day, and the meeting discourse between her, other teachers in the group at her school, and university researchers (the research team who had been working with her in collecting the data, and myself).

Several teachers at this school and the other had been doing inquiries in the Teacher-Led Reading-Aloud Curriculum Genre, but each teacher had a different focus and specific questions that he or she was investigating. In her previous teaching experience, Dorothy had always felt more comfortable in dominating the discussions about books. However, in the past year she had wanted to understand her 3rd-grade, mostly Mexican-American students' responses to the multicultural literature she had collected during the summer to share for the year. Thus, she had an important reason to examine and change the typical ways she conducted the reading-aloud routine so as to encourage more student initiation and response to these books.

In a recent article, Mehan (1993) tells why he has used videotape as an instrument in educational research. He states, "[C]ognitive skills don't reside in the heads of people, including children in schools, they reside in social situations which are composed of people..." (p. 94). This is a 'situated cognition' perspective (Lave, 1988; Rogoff & Wertsch, 1984) that emphasizes that student performance varies as a function of the situation in which they find themselves. Thus, videotape enables the researcher, Mehan argues, to listen and look at this social life in classrooms more closely than is otherwise possible.

What I want to stress, here, is how listening to discourse afforded by videotape permits *teacher researchers,* like Dorothy, to "see" critical dimensions of their inquiries. It helps them—in collaboration with others—interrupt and examine carefully the everyday routines of teaching–learning they have chosen to investigate.

Throughout the year, Dorothy had drastically changed her style of interaction by providing "spaces" for student initiation. Here, we will be focusing on the classroom discussion that was initiated by a student question as she read *Darkness and the Butterfly* by Grifalconi (1987), and then our subsequent examination of that episode in our weekly meeting conversation that occurred a few weeks later when Dorothy shared the edited version that included that classroom footage. Thus, two types of discourse are provided here: first, discourse from the meeting is provided, then classroom discourse from the videotape, followed by more on our discussion in our meeting.

In our meeting that day we had already seen other segments of the videotape. Now we were noting on our editing sheet that the next part had to do with a boy's interruption of Dorothy's reading by asking, "Is that a poem?" I had been in the classroom that day, too, and I was recalling—before we had as yet viewed this particular videotape segment—my impression of it. (Present at the meeting that day were teacher researchers Dorothy, Hawa, Sonia, and Sue, and university researchers Chris, Diane, and Shannon.) Table 1 presents the explanation of transcription conventions.

Chris: This was really great in lots of ways. Again there's the notion of intertextuality cause they were talking about things they did on poetry. But it doesn't get to--you didn't ask the kid "well why did you think..."

Dorothy: I see, I did ask [pointing to the video screen]--somebody said it was a story though, so I moved it which kind of didn't make sense, but...

Chris: Which is okay, too. We should listen to it.

{Weekly Meeting, March 29, 1995}

Initially I brought up the idea of intertextuality as it occurred in the classroom discourse as I remembered it. "Intertextuality," as we have been using it in our project,

TABLE 18–1. Conventions of Transcription

Unit:	Usually corresponds to an independent clause with all dependent clauses related to it (complex clause or T-unit). Sometimes includes another independent clause, if there is no drop of tone and was added without any pausing. Units here are punctuated as sentences.
Turn:	Includes all of a speaker's utterances/units.
Key for Speakers:	First name is listed for university- or teacher-researcher. C, C1, C2, etc., are noted for individual children (with "m" or "f" to refer to the gender of a child): C is used if a child's voice cannot be identified; Cs represents many children speaking simultaneously.
– –	False starts or abandoned language replaced by new language structures.
. .	Small/short pause within unit.
. . . .	Longer pause within unit.
. . .	Breaking off of a speaker's turn due to the next speaker's turn.
< >	Uncertain words
(***)	One word that is inaudible or impossible to transcribe.
(*** ***)	Longer stretches of language that are inaudible and impossible to transcribe.
Underscore:	Emphasis.
# #	Overlapping language spoken by two or more speakers at a time.
CAPS	Actual reading of a book.
{ }	Teacher's miscue or modification of a text read.
[ ]	Identifies what is being referred to or gestured and other nonverbal contextual information.
. . . .	Part of a transcript has been omitted.

follows Bloome's (Bloome & Bailey, 1992; Bloome & Egan-Robertson, 1993) and Lemke's (1985b) ideas on the topic. When teachers leave "spaces" for student initiation, children frequently make intertextual links in the classroom discourse; that is, they connect other books, songs, movies, prior curricular information they have studied, personal stories from their home and community, and so forth, with the topic being discussed. According to Bloome, for these student offerings to be considered as instances of intertextuality, they must be proposed, recognized, acknowledged, and have social significance for the participants. Thus, intertextual links that begin from student initiation are characteristic of collaborative talk, which is something that Dorothy and the other teachers in the project are attempting to promote.

As you will see in the following excerpt, when the student asked about whether the book was a poem, the students, who had some earlier curricular experience regarding poems, had brought in their own ideas about the characteristics of them, mostly to argue that the present book was not a poem, but a story.

[Dorothy is reading about the part of the book where Osa, who is a girl who afraid of the dark, is talking to the Wise Woman, who is trying to help Osa overcome her fear. A boy in the back of the room raises his hand. Dorothy acknowledges him and he asks a question.]

Dorothy: . . . . "BUT LOOK AT THAT LITTLE BUTTERFLY, OSA; SHE MUST THINK SHE IS THE SMALLEST OF THE SMALL. DARKNESS PURSUES HER TOO––YET *SHE* FLIES ON!" SLEEPILY, OSA THOUGHT ABOUT THAT. "MAYBE SHE HAS A SECRET?" {AND} THEN SHE SHOOK HER HEAD. "BUT I HAVE NO WINGS TO FLY." OSA HEARD THE WISE {WOMAN CALL FORTH}: "YOU WILL FIND YOUR OWN WAY. YOU WILL SEE." OSA NODDED, AND BEFORE SHE KNEW IT, SHE FELL INTO A DEEP SLEEP. . . .

Cm1: That's a poem?

Dorothy: Pardon me?

Cm1: That's a poem. Or is that a poem or is it a story?

Dorothy: Is this a poem or is it a story? What do you think?

Cm1: # A story. #

Cs: # Story. #

Dorothy: Why do you think it's a––excuse me, why do you think it's a story? Who else thinks it's a story?

Cs: [About 9 kids raise their hands.]

Dorothy: Cm2, why do you think it's a story?

Cm2: It doesn't have things(?) that rhyme.

Dorothy: It doesn't have very many rhyming words.

Cm2: It doesn't have stanzas.

Dorothy: It doesn't––it's not written in stanzas, good.

Cm3: It doesn't have four lines. . .

Dorothy: Okay, do some stanzas have four lines? Do all stanzas have four lines in a poem?

Cs: No.

Dorothy: No, do all stanzas have rhyming words?

Cs: No.

Dorothy: Is it too long?

Some Cs: # Yes. #

Some Cs: # No. #

Dorothy: Well, we haven't read very long poems, I agree. But poems can be very, very long. They can be longer than a story. (***) Do you think this story could be made into a poem?

Cs: Yes.

Dorothy: Probably so, probably so.

{Edited videotape shared March 29, 1995 from classroom videotape, March 1, 1995}

Actually, although the author/illustrator of the book, Grifalconi has written this book as a story, she has also included poem-like qualities in it, both in its format and in its lyrical phrasing. So, Cm1's question was probably a very reasonable one. And, the idea that there were not any stanzas in the book is not really accurate because the text was written in a stanza-like fashion—with each line beginning with a capital letter, for example. However, this was probably not very noticeable to the students since usually there was only one "stanza" per page and they would not have been able to see the punctuation from their seats.

Dorothy has subsequently looked at this book and the student's question about it quite differently since we have examined it in our meeting, but here in the upcoming excerpt of the meeting discussion her attention is on other facets of the interaction.

Diane: I thought that was a really good wrap up question, "Can this be made into a poem?" And all the kids answered, "Yeah, sure."

Dorothy: Well they did––they did kind of do a little bit of that when we kind of went in and out of poetry. I couldn't get them to come up with a poem. We had a theme to send to the..dental week or something and they just...

Chris: [facing Dorothy] See, it's just that the kind of conversation would have been quite different if you had said, "Tell me why did you– –what makes you say that, what makes you think that this might be a poem?"

Dorothy: Mmm, I'm getting too direct here [pointing to the video screen]. The question is becoming looking for an answer instead of just a comment and let them go in what direction they– –And I can hear that now, where I could never hear that, I mean, I wouldn't– –I thought that was good! [As Dorothy talks, she waves her hand in front of her face as if to wave off her own lack of hearing herself before now.]

Chris: Yeah, yeah.

Dorothy: I mean I'm beginning to see that because you cut them off you're looking for yes or no, or the whole class responds...

Chris: Usually, yeah, usually there is a whole– – yeah, there's a real clue when the whole class is going "yeaaah" or "noooo" [lowers her voice and makes it long, like a mechanical answer, and the whole group laughs]. You know that "whoops, I'm definitely asking a pseudo question here!" But you know there's some points where that might be appropriate because you're trying to make connections to other kinds of instruction, you know.

Hawa: Or sometimes you get them when they say "yeah" and you ask them "why?" and they say, "uh, well, uh..."

Sonia: That's because they expect this, they expect...

Chris: Well, you know people call this procedural display and mock participation. In other words, kids know the routine but sometimes there's no– –and lots of teachers accept that they've understood and it's really just surface procedures so people call it procedural display and mock participation. It's that IRE where the teacher does this, the kids say that, and teacher evaluates. It's the kind of thing that you guys are trying to challenge.

Sonia: It's hard...

Dorothy: It's hard, but it's neat though [pointing to the video screen]. It's hard too because– –I think this is the first time that I've seen value in looking at my video. I can relate to things now and actually I heard that and it sounded awful. I mean just the kids says, "yesss" and before perhaps I would have thought, "Gee, isn't that good, they're all responding [sort of with an exaggerated smile as if to show how silly that was].

Shannon: And they all got the right answer.

Dorothy: And not even the right and wrong answer but just that they were...

Chris: Engaged.

Dorothy: [pointing to Chris] Yes, engaged. And somebody wasn't. Which isn't as good as...

Chris: Yeah, a kid could be looking over there [Chris turns in her seat to look away from the group] and said "yeah."

Dorothy: Right.

Chris: Well, maybe you can hear it because you have gone beyond in your inquiry in some way.
....[The discussion then changed topic to see and consider the last segment of the video.]
{Weekly Meeting, March 29, 1995}

There are two important, interrelated points I want to emphasize about this discussion. The first is that Dorothy had come to a critical understanding about her interactions with students in her inquiry. That is, she decided that what had been "comforting" to her or evidence of engagement in the responses of "yes" or "no" from students in certain classroom interactions is now problematic and indicative of mostly mock participation and procedural display (which I put a label to, drawing again from some ideas in Bloome' s [1994] work) instead of more substantive meanings being developed. Thus, besides teachers making the effort to provide opportunities for students' initiations around books in classroom discourse, their learning best how to contingently respond to students' initiations to sustain and extend them is an issue in developing collaborative talk.

The second point is Dorothy' s belief that there was great value in viewing the videotape of her classroom interactions because it enabled her to "hear" what she had not been able to hear before. Thus, she might have missed an important opportunity to respond to her student's question on this particular day in a way that might have contributed to her understanding of her students' understanding of this book, which was at the core of her inquiry. However, with the help of the videotape, she was given a chance to become more explicitly aware of what she has to do in the future to accomplish that goal in her inquiry.

Now, it might seem to readers of this chapter that I was extremely fortunate to have Dorothy's overt testimony on the value of videotaping as an important tool in her teacher inquiry, but many of the teachers have commented on its utility. In fact, it was teachers who had suggested its use in the first place, since they are unable to observe each other in their classrooms.

Moreover, although we had not expressly asked for it, several of the teachers discussed the advantages of the use of videotape in their inquiries in our individual end-of-the-year interviews. For example, in the beginning of her conversation with us, Hawa, who teaches second grade at the same school as Dorothy, listed what she saw as the "pluses" in her inquiry for the year, which also focused on the Teacher-Led Reading-Aloud Curriculum Genre. She stated that it had helped her better prepare for teaching—that is, she is now more aware how important it is to choose good literature and for what purpose. Moreover, it helped her think of sharing power with kids, since before then she had just wanted kids to listen to a book and afterwards to answer yes or no to the questions she had for them. Then she more specifically addressed how the videotape particularly contributed: "Another one was seeing yourself after you had– –did a read-aloud ... seeing yourself on tape, saying 'ooh I did that,' or 'didn't do that,' or 'that was good,' or 'I liked that.' That's one of the positive things I liked about it, too."

Sarah, a colleague at the same school who taught a 2nd-grade bilingual class, also remarked on positive benefits of videotape. She felt that the sharing of videotapes promoted collaboration. She thought that it got the teachers in the group talking to each other at the meetings, of course, but also that it spilled over in that it fostered conversations about what they were doing among their group when they saw each other in the halls, at lunch, or other times in school. Videotape, she also said, gave her "... 'a third eye' ... it gave me not only a resource but also an outlet ... to what was going on and what carried on. ... It makes everything self-conscious..."

In attempting to establish trustworthiness, qualitative researchers have frequently relied on videotape. For example, Lincoln and Guba (1985) comment on how videotape recordings (and cinematography) can provide the means to "capture and hold" episodes in the classroom that can later be examined and compared with other data, thereby furnishing referential adequacy for interpretations in studies. Certainly, videotape will serve this function for all of us in the research process in our collaborative project. But importantly, as I have tried to emphasize here, its utility from the teacher researchers' perspective is that videotape also directly informs their inquiries by enabling them to relive "being there," making it possible for them—actually, all of us who are attempting to document the changes—to interrupt, carefully examine, and transform their everyday routines in the classroom.

SECTION 3: ONGOING ISSUES AND CHALLENGES FOR COLLABORATIVE ACTION RESEARCH

There are many ongoing issues and challenges in present and future collaborative action research. However, here, I have concentrated on three, interrelated ones that have been especially relevant in our project, and are also likely to be pertinent in other collaborative school–university arrangements.

Issues of Validity and Reliability

Because collaborative action research involves an expanding notion of legitimate knowledge, teachers who have historically been silenced, now have opportunities to develop their voice. And, in telling their educational stories, they have the *right* to debate and challenge the authority of others—university researchers certainly, as well as business people and parents, and district and state policy makers. Thus, when the central purpose of the educational research process is to empower voice, concepts of validity and reliability have to be reconceptualized. For example, as Gitlin et al. (1992) argue, old views of validity have to be altered.

> The validity or 'truthfulness' of the data can be understood no longer as something extracted by [a university researcher] armed with a set of research procedures, but rather as a mutual process pursued by [university- and teacher-researchers] ... that recognizes the value of practical knowledge, theoretical inquiry, and systematic examinations. The [university] researchers' knowledge is not assumed to be more legitimate than the [teacher researchers'], nor is their role one of helping the needy other. Rather, the researcher and [teacher researcher] attempt to come to a mutual understanding based on their own strongly articulated positions. (p. 27)

Thus, validity cannot be ignored, as Lather (1994) has recently argued, because "[it] is a 'limit question' of research,

one that repeatedly resurfaces, one that can neither be avoided nor resolved, a fertile obsession given its intractability..." (p. 37), but it has to be viewed differently from established renditions of it. In collaborative inquiry, all those involved are both *coresearchers*—everyone is involved in the thinking and decisions that generate ideas, manage the project, and come to conclusions about the whole research experience—and *cosubjects*—everyone participates in the inquiry enterprise that has been researched (Reason, 1994a). In such a reciprocity, validity has more to do with validating and developing insights among university- and teacher-researchers; it involves a dialogue on how to interpret data by considering alternative perspectives (Altrichter, 1993), or as Lather (1986b) suggests, it is 'catalytic validity,' which is the capacity of the research process to foster participants' knowing of their reality and urge them towards self-determined action. Thus, accomplishing a new rigor to promote a "validity of knowledge in process" (Reason & Rowan, 1981) is an ongoing challenge in collaborative action research.

Reliability has been seen in a new light as well. Naturally occurring situations, such as those found in classrooms, are very changeable. Moreover, the aim of collaborative action research is to disrupt the status quo by developing and putting into practice certain action strategies in the hope to change and improve it. Consequently, the traditional idea of reliability as a kind of "repeating the research," that is, the ability of different independent researchers being able to come up with the same conclusions by using the same procedures, is clearly problematic in collaborative research (Altrichter et al., 1993; Gitlin et al., 1992). When voice is the goal of research, it is not expected (indeed, nor even desirable) that team members of university- and teacher-researchers would initially come up with the same conclusions. Procedures have to be evolved in particular projects. As Gitlin, et al. (1992) argue: "Reliability ... cannot be based on duplicating procedures, but rather must center on attempts to satisfy the underlying principle of voice and its relation to a particular type of school change" (p. 28). Thus, because particular procedures cannot be applied unchanged from context to context, each collaborative project has its own challenge in developing its specific "reliability of voice."

Issues of the Representation of Teacher Researchers

It has been a practice to use pseudonyms for the names of participants (and their schools, communities, etc.) in educational research, and strong arguments have been lodged for the need to protect their identity (e.g., see Delamont, 1984, 1992). However, many teacher researchers, seeking recognition for their contributions in the collaborative work they do with university researchers, no longer want anonymity (although there are still others, who, due to the various circumstances teachers find themselves, do not wish to be so visible). In 1990, Shulman offered a useful discussion on the difficulties and ethical dilemmas that occur around this issue, especially on the vulnerability of teachers who forego anonymity and end up receiving disapproval and recrimination from their colleagues and administrators. Much more has to be examined on this topic, but here I want to focus on tensions that arise around the issue of representation in writing up the work of collaborative school–university projects. Concerns are certainly present when the teachers are anonymous, but I will concentrate mostly when they are not.

Since 1990, it has become even more common to identify teachers in collaborative work, although it is done several ways. The cases where teacher researchers are authors of their own chapters within a book in which university researchers in the same project also have their own chapters and/or coedit the volumes are more straightforward. However, in other authoring situations, issues regarding the representation of teachers who wish to be identified are more difficult to sort out.

Any time a university researcher, who has a commitment to study and understand the perspective of an interacting individual, authors a text describing that individual, the sticky area of representation is evoked (Lincoln & Denzin, 1994). As Nespor and Barylske (1991) argue, representation is "not just a matter of epistemology or method, but a matter of power" (p. 806). When we (university researchers) represent others, there is always the potential to reduce them; that is, the relations of power in this discourse favor the representers (the university researchers) over the represented (the teachers we write about).

For example, many collaborative studies use narrative approaches in which interviews are gathered over time. Usually, the university researchers suggest an overall frame for the discussions, frequently identifying various topics, but for the most part teachers have considerable control over what they talk about and how they talk (see Cortazzi '1993' for a good review and critique of this approach and various schemes of narrative analysis). Once the interviews are transcribed, teachers are usually given these transcriptions for their review, elaboration, and clarification. Is this enough of a safeguard for the collaborating teachers when university researchers then write an article selecting quotes from these transcriptions— even when these quotes are long enough to give readers a good sense of these teachers' voices—to make theoretical points? (See Rudduck, 1993, for a discussion on issues regarding direct quotation.)

Or, how about me as the author of this chapter, writing about our project? I have checked with Dorothy and the other teachers about how I have written about them, but is this enough? (Dorothy O'Malley and the other teachers, Sarah Cohen, Hawa Jones, and Sonia Torres Pasewark, whose discourse is included in the excerpts have reviewed and have given me an okay on what I have written herein.) And, what about cases where university- and teacher-researchers are coauthors of a text, and presumably where the teachers have had ample opportunities to write segments of the text and to review other parts written by the university researchers? In these texts, there are genuine occasions to refer to the larger collaborative enterprise as a "we" experience. But, because such texts frequently focus on the teachers' experiences in their schools and classrooms, these teachers are usually written up in the third person. Is this just a more subtle way for the university researcher to inflate his or her control in the power relation with the teacher?

Thus, as Lincoln and Denzin (1994) state, "Writing the present is always dangerous, a biased project conditioned by distorted readings of the past and utopian hopes for the future" (p. 575). It is likely that there will be many instances where university- and teacher-researchers in collaborative action research will have constructed a common social network, and will have come to some consensus in the interpretations of the data of their projects—even if they have agreed to disagree or have included different perspectives. Nevertheless, it is also clear that much more work will be required on the problem of power and method in the production of academic discourse (Ladwig & Gore, 1994). *New* genres of discourse will need to be developed so that all participants' voices are realized in a democratic way, and undoubtedly this will be no easy task if we are reminded how hard it has been to include genres stemming from qualitative paradigms into educational research books and journals.

The Issue of Claiming Expertise Without an Authoritarian Voice and Its Implications in the Representation of University Researchers

There is another issue that is closely related to the issue of representation of teacher researchers. In many ways, it is the other side of the same coin for it considers university researchers' struggles to shed their authoritarian voices in collaborative arrangements, but at the same time their resistance to express the details of their part of the dialogue that they have with teacher researchers.

In the efforts to develop and leave "spaces" for the voices of teachers who have been historically silenced, there has been a tendency on the part of university researchers to draw back so as not to impose these outsiders' views too much. Yet, a "true" collaboration has to have both university- and teacher-researchers claiming their respective expertise in the research process (Oyler & Pappas, 1992, also in preparation). This is because in such a partnership there is an assumption that neither is more needy of the other, or that neither contributes knowledge to the collaborative process that is more legitimate (Gitlin et al., 1992; Treleaven, 1994). Too frequently, teachers sharing authority with their students have been conceived of as merely teachers moving away from the "hard place" of authoritarianism to the other side of the dichotomy, namely the "soft place" of abdicated authority (Oyler, 1996; Oyler & Becker, in press). Such a view does not regard this sharing of authority as the coconstruction of knowledge by *both* teachers and students. Thus, so as not to make the same mistake, university participants have to overcome their reluctance not to share their ideas or interpretations in collaborative inquiry.

That does not mean that in so doing , there would not be times when university researchers might go beyond their "claiming expertise" in their interactions with teacher researchers. For example, in the weekly meeting discourse provided in the previous section there were places where I shared my expertise, first by my asking her to reexamine her responses to the boy's question, since I thought it was so relevant to her inquiry, and then later when I brought up the terms "mock participation" and "procedural display" to put a name on the phenomenon that Dorothy and the other teachers were recognizing *and* questioning in their practice. However, as I have reflected on my responses in this discourse with Dorothy, I felt that I might have cut her off a couple of times, and although I believe that my role is to ask questions for the teacher researchers to consider, I have also wondered if I might have been too pushy—that is, gone over some collaborative boundary, so to speak. What I am leading up to is that I am now publicly vulnerable in this exchange in terms of collaboration. However, as I have read and reviewed the many writings on collaborative action research, I have noticed that it is rare to find quotes of the discourse used by university researchers in this work. Thus, besides making problematic of the representation of teacher researchers, we have to think long and hard about why university researchers have been unable to represent themselves—warts and all—in academic discourse. Consequently, this is another ongoing challenge in developing new genres to report on collaborative action research.

Summary and Making 'Collaboration' Problematic to "Keep Voices Alive and Well"

Throughout this chapter I have stressed the importance and difficulty of making 'collaboration' ever present in the methodologies in collaborative action research. Because of the dominant perspectives in educational research, only by being vigilant in the entire collaborative research process will there be any chance to "keep authentic voices alive and well" (Schratz, 1993). To return to the Bakhtinian framework offered in the first section of the chapter, as attempts are made to include the point of view and "speaking consciousness" of both university- and teacher-researchers in the dialogue of collaboration, there will be an ongoing conflict in this process because of this history.

Thus, methods of collaborative inquiry for social change cannot be conceived of in "mechanistic," superficial terms (Schensul & Schensul, 1992). Indeed, as Walker (1993) argues,

> [Q]uestions about objectivity and subjectivity, representativeness, reliability, validity … are often described as though they were simply technical problems, capable of reasonable resolution, but in practice they appear as moral dilemmas, concerned with selection, framing, judgment, risk and making one interpretation rather than another. (p. 90)

Moreover, as it challenges the traditional hierarchical differences between university researchers and teacher researchers within the educational community, collaborative action research represents a new activism to become practically critical as to promote democratic schooling (Gitlin, A., 1994; Noffke & Stevenson, 1995). That is, there is also a struggle to incorporate here a "political view of validity" (Gitlin, et al., 1992). Thus, as in jazz, new improvisations will need to be woven into the methods of this research (Oldfather & West, 1994) to achieve these good intentions of inclusion and emancipation.

References

Adelman, C. (1993). Kurt Lewin and the origins of action research. *Educational Action Research, 1,* 7–24.

Agar, M. (1980). *The professional stranger: An informal introduction to ethnography.* New York: Academic Press.

Altrichter, H. (1993). The concept of quality in action research: Giving practitioners a voice in educational research. In M. Schratz (Ed.), *Qualitative voices in educational research* (pp. 40–55). London: Falmer Press.

Altrichter, H., Posch, O., & Somekh, B. (1993). *Teachers investigate their work: An introduction to the methods of action research.* London: Routledge.

Apple, M. (1993). *Official knowledge: Democratic education in a conservative age.* New York: Routledge.

Au, K. H., & Jordon, C. (1981). Teaching reading to Hawaiian children: Analysis of a culturally appropriate instructional event. *Anthropology and Education Quarterly, 11,* 91–115.

Bakhtin, M. M. (1981). *The dialogic imagination: Four essays by M. M. Bakhtin.* In M. Holquist (Ed.) (M. Holquist & C. Emerson, Trans.) Austin TX: University of Texas Press.

Bakhtin, M. M. (1986). *Speech genres and other late essays.* In C. Emerson & M. Holquist (Eds.) (V. W. McGee, Trans.). Austin, TX: University of Texas Press.

Barnes, D., & Todd, F. (1995). *Communication and learning revisited: Making meaning through talk.* Portsmouth, NH: Boynton/Cook.

Berthoff, A. E. (1987). The teacher as REsearcher. In D. Goswami & P.

R. Stillman (Eds.), *Reclaiming the classroom: Teacher research as an agency for change* (pp. 28–39). Portsmouth, NH: Boynton/Cook.

Bickel, W. E., & Hattrup, R. A. (1995). Teachers and researchers in collaboration: Reflections on the process. *American Educational Research Journal, 32,* 35–62.

Bloome, D. (1994). Reading as a social process in a middle school classroom. In D. Graddol, J. Maybin & B. Stierer (Eds.), *Researching language and literacy in social context* (pp. 100–129). Bristol, PA: Multilingual Matters.

Bloome, D., & Bailey, F. (1992). Studying language and literacy through events, particularity, and intertextuality. In R. Beach, J. L. Green, M. L. Kamil, & T. Shanahan (Eds.), *Multidisciplinary perspectives on literacy research* (pp. 181–210). Urbana, IL: National Conference on Research in English.

Bloome, D., & Egan-Robertson, A. (1993). The social construction of intertextuality in classroom reading and writing lessons. *Reading Research Quarterly, 28,* 305–333.

Bogdan, R. C., & Biklen, S. K. (1982). *Qualitative research for education: An introduction to theory and methods.* Boston: Allyn & Bacon.

Bruner, E. M. (1993). Introduction: The ethnographic self and the personal self. In P. Benson (Ed.), *Anthropology and literature* (pp. 1–26). Urbana, IL: University of Illinois Press.

Burbules, N. C. (1993). *Dialogue in teaching: Theory and practice.* New York: Teachers College Press.

Cameron, D., Frazer, E., Harvey, P., Rampton, M. B. H., & Richardson, R. (1992). *Researching language: Issues of power and method.* London: Routledge.

Carr, W., & Kemmis, S. (1986). *Becoming critical: Education, knowledge and action research.* London: Falmer Press.

Cazden, C. B. (1986). Classroom discourse. In M. C. Wittrock (Ed.), *Handbook of research on teaching* (3rd ed., pp. 432–463). New York: Macmillan.

Cazden, C. B. (1988). *Classroom discourse: The language of teaching and learning.* Portsmouth, NH: Heinemann.

Cazden, C. B. (1992). Whole *language plus: Essays on literacy in the United States and New Zealand.* New York: Teachers College Press.

Christie, F. (1987). The morning news genre: Using a functional grammar to illuminate educational issues. *Australian Review of Applied Linguistics, 10,* 182–198.

Christie, F. (1989). Language development in education. In R. Hasan, & J. R. Martin (Eds.), *Language development: Learning language, learning culture* (pp. 152–198). Norwood, NJ: Ablex.

Christie, F. (1993). Curriculum genres: Planning of effective teaching. In B. Cope & M. Kalantzis (Eds.), *The powers of literacy: A genre approach to teaching writing* (pp. 154–178). Pittsburgh, PA: University of Pittsburgh Press.

Clandinin, D. J. (1993). Teacher education as narrative inquiry. In D. J. Clandinin, A. Davies, P. Hogan, & B. Kennard (Eds.), *Learning to teach, teaching to learn: Stories of collaboration in teacher education* (pp. 115). New York: Teachers College Press.

Clandinin, D. J., & Connelly, M. (1991). Narrative and story in practice and research. In D. A. Schon (Ed.), *The reflective turn: Case studies in and on educational practice* (pp. 258–281). New York: Teachers College Press.

Cochran-Smith, M., & Lytle, S. L. (1990). Research on teaching and teacher research: The issues that divide. *Educational Researcher, 19,* 2–11.

Cochran-Smith, M., & Lytle, S. L. (1993). *Inside/outside: Teacher research and knowledge.* New York: Teachers College Press.

Connelly, M., & Clandinin, D. J. (1988). *Teachers as curriculum planners: Narrative of experience.* New York: Teachers College Press.

Cortazzi, M. (1993). *Narrative analysis.* London: Falmer Press.

Delamont, S. (1984). The old girl network: Recollections on the fieldwork at St. Luke's. In R. G. Burgess (Ed.), *The research process in educational settings: Ten case studies* (pp. 15–38). London: Falmer Press.

Delamont, S. (1992). *Fieldwork in educational settings: Methods, pitfalls and perspectives.* London: Falmer Press.

Delpit, L. D. (1988). The silenced dialogue: Power and pedagogy in educating other people's children. *Harvard Educational Review, 58,* 379–385.

Delpit, L. D. (1992). Acquisition of literate discourse: Bowing before the master? *Theory into Practice, 31,* 296–302.

Dewey, J. (1904). *The relation of theory to practice in education: The third NSSE yearbook* (Pt. 1). Chicago: University of Chicago Press.

Dillon, J. T. (1994). *Using discussion in classrooms.* Buckingham, England: Open University Press.

Duckworth, E. (1987). *"The having of wonderful ideas" and other essays on teaching and learning.* New York: Teacher College Press.

Edwards, A. D., & Westgate, D. P. G. (1994). *Investigating classroom talk.* London: Falmer Press.

Edwards, D., & Mercer, N. (1987). *Common knowledge: The development of understanding in the classroom.* London: Routledge.

Elliot, J. (1985). Facilitating action research on teaching: Some dilemmas. In R. Burgess (Ed.), *Field methods in the study of education*

(pp. 235–262). London: Falmer Press.

Elliot, J. (1991). *Action research for educational change.* Milton Keynes: Open University Press.

Erickson, F. (1986). Qualitative methods in research on teaching. In M. C. Wittrock (Ed.), *Handbook of research on teaching* (3rd. ed., pp. 119–161). New York: Macmillan.

Erickson, F., & Schultz, J. (1977). When is a context? Some issues and methods in the analysis of social competence. *The Quarterly Newsletter of the Institute for Comparative Human Development, 1,* 5–12.

Fairclough, N. (1992). *Discourse and social change.* Cambridge: Polity Press.

Foster, M. (1992). Sociolinguistics and the African-American community: Implications for literacy. *Theory into Practice, 32,* 303–311.

Foucault, M. (1980). Truth and power. In C. Gordon (Ed.), *Power/knowledge: Selected interviews and other writings 1972–1977* (pp. 109–133). New York: Pantheon.

Freire, P. (1972). *Cultural action for freedom.* Harmondsworth: Penguin.

Gitlin, A. (1994). The shifting terrain of methodological debates. In A. Gitlin (Ed.), *Power and method: Political activism and educational research* (pp. 1–7). New York: Routledge.

Gitlin, A., Bringhurst, K., Burns, M., Cooley, V., Myers, B., Price, K., Russell, R., & Tiess, P. (1992). *Teachers' voices for school change: An introduction to educative research.* New York: Teachers College Press.

Gitlin, A., & Russell, R. (1994). Alternative methodologies and the research context. In A. Gitlin (Ed.), *Power and method: Political activism and educational research* (pp. 181–202). New York: Routledge.

Gitlin, A. D. (1990). Educative research, voice and school change. *Harvard Educational Review, 60,* 443–466.

Gore, J. M. (1993). *The struggle for pedagogies: Critical and feminist discourses as regimes of truth.* New York: Routledge.

Green, J. L., Kantor, R. M., & Rodgers, T. (1991). Exploring the complexity of language and learning in classroom contexts. In L. Idol & B. F. Jones (Eds.), *Educational values and cognitive instruction: Implications for reform* (pp. 333–364). Hillsdale, NJ: Erlbaum.

Grifalconi, A. (1987). *Darkness and the butterfly.* Boston: Little Brown.

Gutierrez, K. D. (1994). How talk, context, and script shape contexts for learning: A cross-case comparison of journal sharing. *Linguistics and Education, 5,* 335–365.

Halliday, M. A. K. (1978). *Language as social semiotic: The social interpretation of language and meaning.* London: Edward Arnold.

Halliday, M. A. K. (1993). Towards a language-based theory of learning. *Linguistics and Education, 5,* 93–126.

Halliday, M. A. K., & Hasan, R. (1985). *Language, context, and text: Aspects of language in a social-semiotic perspective.* Victoria, Australia: Deakin University Press.

Heath, B. (1982). What no bedtime story means: Narrative skills at home and school. *Language in Society, 11,* 49–76.

Heath, S. B. (1983). *Ways with words.* Cambridge: Cambridge University Press.

Heron, J. (1981a). Philosophical basis for a new paradigm. In P. Reason & J. Rowan (Eds.), *Human inquiry: A sourcebook of new paradigm research* (pp. 19–35). New York: John Wiley & Sons.

Heron, J. (1981b). Experiential research methodology. In P. Reason & J. Rowan (Eds.), *Human inquiry: A sourcebook of new paradigm research* (pp. 153–166). New York: John Wiley & Sons.

Heron, J. (1992). *Feeling and personhood: Psychology in another key.* London: Sage.

Hollingsworth, S. (1994). *Teacher research and urban literacy edu-*

cation: Lessons and conversations in a feminist key. New York: Teachers College Press.

Hollingsworth, S., & Sockett, H. (Eds.). (1994). *Teacher research and educational reform. Ninety-third yearbook of the NSSE* (Pt. 1). Chicago: University of Chicago Press.

Holquist, M., & Emerson, C. (1981). Glossary. In (M. Holquist (Ed.), M. Holquist & C. Emerson, Trans.). *The dialogic imagination: Four essays by M. M. Bakhtin* (pp. 423–434). Austin, TX: University of Texas Press.

Kreisberg, S. (1992). *Transforming power: Domination, empowerment, and education.* Albany, NY: State University of New York Press.

Kyle, D., & Hovda, R. (Eds.). (1978). The potential and practice of action research: Parts I and II. *Peabody Journal of Education, 64.*

Ladwig, J. C. (1991). Is collaborative research exploitative? *Educational Theory, 41,* 111–120.

Ladwig, J. C., & Gore, J. M. (1994). Extending power and specifying method within the discourse of activist research. In A. Gitlin (Ed.), *Power and method: Political activism and educational research* (pp. 227–238). New York: Rutledge.

Lather, P. (1986a). Research as praxis. *Harvard Educational Review, 56,* 257–277.

Lather, P. (1986b). Issues of validity in openly ideological research: Between a rock and a soft place. *Interchange, 17,* 63–84.

Lather, P. (1992). Critical frames in educational research: Feminist and post-structural perspectives. *Theory into Practice, 31,* 87–99.

Lather, P. (1994). Fertile obsession: Validity after post-structuralism. In A. Gitlin (Ed.), *Power and method: Political activism and educational research* (pp. 36–60). New York: Routledge.

Lave, J. (1988). *Cognition in practice.* New York: Cambridge University Press.

Lemke, J. L. (1985a). *Using language in the classroom.* Victoria, Australia: Deakin University Press.

Lemke, J. L. (1985b). Ideology, intertextuality, and the notion of register. In J. D. Benson & W. S. Greaves (Eds.), *Systemic perspectives on discourse: Selected theoretical papers from the 9th international systemic workshop, Vol. 1* (pp. 275–294). Norwood, NJ: Ablex.

Lemke, J. L. (1990). *Talking science: Language, learning, and values.* Norwood, NJ: Ablex.

Lewin, K. (1948). *Resolving social conflicts.* New York: Harper & Row.

Lieberman, A. (1986). Collaborative research: Working with, not working on. *Educational Leadership, 43,* 28–33.

Lieberman, A. (1992). The meaning of scholarly activity and the building of community. *Educational Researcher, 21,* 5–12.

Lincoln, Y., & Guba, E. (1985). *Naturalistic inquiry.* Beverly Hills, CA: Sage.

Lincoln, Y. S., & Denzin, N. K. (1994). The fifth moment. In N. K. Denzin & Y. S. Lincoln (Eds.), *The handbook of qualitative research* (pp. 575–586). Thousand Oaks, CA: Sage.

Lindfors, J. W. (1987). *Children's language and learning.* Englewood Cliffs, NJ: Prentice Hall.

Luke, C., & Gore, J. (1992). Introduction. In C. Luke & J. Gore (Eds.), *Feminisms and critical pedagogy* (pp. 1–14). New York: Routledge.

Lytle, S. L., & Cochran-Smith, M. (1992). Teacher research as a way of knowing. *Harvard Educational Review, 62,* 447–474.

Martin, L. (1993). Understanding teacher change from a Vygotskian perspective. In P. Kahaney, L. A. M. Perry, & J. Janangelo (Eds.), *Theoretical and critical perspectives on teacher change* (pp. 71–86). Norwood, NJ: Ablex.

McCollum, P. (1991). Cross-cultural perspectives on classroom discourse and literacy. In E. H. Heibert (Ed.), *Literacy for a diverse society: Perspectives, practices and policies* (pp. 108–121). New York: Teachers College Press.

McCutcheon, G. (1981). The impact of the insider. In J. Nixon (Ed.), *A teacher's guide to action research* (pp. 186–193). London: Grant McIntyre.

McCutcheon, G., & Jung, B. (1990). Alternative perspectives on action research. *Theory into Practice, 29,* 144–151.

Mehan, H. (1993). Why I like to look: On the use of videotape as an instrument in educational research. In M. Schratz (Ed.), *Qualitative voices in educational research* (pp. 93-105). London: Falmer Press.

Michaels , S. (1981). "Sharing time": Children's narrative styles and differential access to literacy. *Language in Society, 10,* 423–442.

Miller, J. L. (1990). *Creating spaces and finding voices: Teachers collaborating for empowerment.* Albany, NY: State University of New York Press.

Miller, J. L. (1992). Exploring power and authority issues in a collaborative research project. *Theory into Practice, 31,* 165–172.

Mishler, E. G. (1979). Meaning in context: Is there any other kind? *Harvard Educational Review, 49,* 1–19.

Moll, L. C. (Ed.). (1990). *Vygotsky and education: Instructional implications and applications of sociohistorical psychology.* Cambridge: Cambridge University Press.

Neilsen, J. M. (1989). Introduction. In J. M. Neilsen (Ed.), *Feminist research methods: Exemplary readings in the social sciences* (pp. 1–37). Boulder, CO: Westview Press.

Nespor, J., & Barylske, J. (1991). Narrative discourse and teacher knowledge. *American Educational Research Journal, 28,* 805–823.

Newman, D. P., Griffin, P., & Cole, M. (1989). *The construction zone: Working for cognitive change in school.* Cambridge: Cambridge University Press.

Nixon, J. (Ed.). (1981). *A teacher's guide to action research.* London: Grant McIntyre.

Noffke, S. E., & Stevenson, R. B. (Ed.). (1995). *Educational action research: Becoming practically critical.* New York: Teachers College Press.

Oakes, J., Hare, S. E., & Sirotnik, K. A. (1986). Collaborative inquiry: A congenial paradigm in a cantankerous world. *Teachers College Record, 87,* 545–561.

Oja, S. N., & Smulyan, L. (1989). *Collaborative action research: A developmental approach.* London: Falmer Press.

Oldfather, P., & West, J. (1994). Qualitative research as jazz. *Educational Researcher, 23,* 22–26.

Oyler, C. J. (1993). *Sharing authority in an urban first grade: Becoming literate, becoming bold.* Unpublished dissertation, University of Illinois, Chicago.

Oyler, C. J. (1996). *Making room for students: Sharing authority in Room 104.* New York: Teachers College Press.

Oyler, C. J., & Becker, J. (in press). Teaching beyond the progressive-traditional dichotomy: Sharing authority and sharing vulnerability. *Curriculum Inquiry.*

Oyler, C. J., & Pappas, C. C. (1992, October). *Claiming and sharing our authority in collaboration.* Paper presented at the Bergamo Conference, Dayton, OH.

Oyler, C. J., & Pappas, C. C. (in preparation). *School–University collaborations: Acknowledging the parallel of power and knowledge.*

Pappas, C. C. (1990, July). *The reading-aloud curriculum genre: Exploring text and teacher variation.* Paper presented at the Seventeenth International Systemic Congress, Stirling, Scotland.

Pappas, C. C. (1991, April). *The reading-aloud curriculum genre: Book genre and teacher variation.* Paper presented at the annual meeting of the American Educational Research Association, Chicago.

Pappas, C. C. (in press). Reading instruction in an integrated perspective: Collaborative interaction in classroom curriculum genres. In S. Stahl & D. A. Hayes (Eds.), *Instructional models in reading.* Mahwah, NJ: Erlbaum.

Patton, M. Q. (1990). *Qualitative evaluation and research methods.* Newbury Park, CA: Sage.

Peshkin, A. (1988). In search of subjectivity—one's own. *Educational Researcher, 17,* 17–22.

Philips, S. U. (1972). Participant structures and communicative competence: Warm Springs children in community and classroom. In C. B. Cazden, V. P. John, & D. Hymes (Eds.), *Functions of language in the classroom* (pp. 370–394). New York: Teachers College Press.

Philips, S. U. (1983). *The invisible culture: Communication in the classroom and community on the Warm Springs Indian Reservation.* New York: Longman.

Prawat, R. S. (1991). Conversations with self and settings: A framework for thinking about teacher empowerment. *American Educational Research Journal, 28,* 737–757.

Ramirez, A. (1988). Analyzing speech acts. In J. L. Green & J. O. Harker (Eds.), *Multiple perspective analyses of classroom discourse* (pp. 135–163). Norwood, NJ: Ablex.

Reason, P. (Ed.). (1988). *Human inquiry in action.* London: Sage.

Reason, P. (1994a). Three approaches to participative inquiry. In N. K. Denzin & Y. S. Lincoln (Eds.), *The handbook of qualitative research* (pp. 324–339). Thousand Oaks, CA: Sage.

Reason, P. (1994b). Human inquiry as discipline and practice. In P. Reason (Ed.), *Participation in human inquiry* (pp. 40–56). London: Sage.

Reason, P., & Heron, J. (1986). Research with people: The paradigm of co-operative experiential inquiry. *Person Centered Review, 1,* 456–475.

Reason, P., & Rowan, J. (1981). Issues of validity in new paradigm research. In P. Reason & J. Rowan (Eds.), *Human inquiry: A sourcebook of new paradigm research* (pp. 239–262). New York: John Wiley & Sons.

Reyes, M. de la Luz. (1991). A process approach to literacy instruction for Spanish-speaking students: In search of a best fit. In E. F. Heibert (Ed.), *Literacy for a diverse society: Perspectives, practices, and policies* (pp. 157–171). New York: Teachers College Press.

Reyes, M. de la Luz. (1992). Challenging venerable assumptions: Literacy instruction for linguistically different students. *Harvard Educational Review, 62,* 427–446.

Richardson, V. (1994a). Conducting research on practice. *Educational Researcher, 23,* 5–10.

Richardson, V. (Ed.). (1994b). *Teacher change and the staff development process: A cage in reading instruction.* New York: Teachers College Press.

Robinson, H. A. (1994). *The ethnography of empowerment: The transformative power of classroom interaction.* Washington, DC: Falmer Press.

Rogoff, B., & Wertsch, J. V. (1984). *Children's learning in the zone of proximal development.* San Francisco: Jossey-Bass.

Rudduck, J. (1993). The theatre of daylight: Qualitative research and the school profile studies. In M. Schratz (Ed.), *Qualitative voices in educational research* (pp. 8–22). London: Falmer Press.

Santa Barbara Classroom Discourse Group. (Dixon, C., de la Cruz, E., Green, J., Lin, L., & Brandts, L.). (1992). Do you see what we see? The referential and intertextual nature of classroom life. *Journal of Classroom Interaction, 27,* 29–36.

Schensul, J. L., & Schensul, S. L. (1992). Collaborative research: Methods of inquiry for social change. In M. D. LeCompte, W. L. Milloy, & J. Preissle (Eds.), *The handbook of qualitative research in education* (pp. 162–200). San Diego, CA: Academic Press.

Schon, D. A. (1983). *The reflective practitioner: How professionals think in action.* New York: Basic Books.

Schon, D. A. (1987). *Educating the reflective practitioner: Toward a new design for teaching and learning in the professions.* San Francisco: Josssey-Bass.

Schon, D. A. (Ed.). (1991). *The reflective turn: Case studies in and on educational practice.* New York: Teachers College Press.

Schratz, M. (1993). Voices in educational research: An introduction. In M. Schratz (Ed.), *Qualitative voices in educational research* (pp. 1–6). London: Falmer Press.

Shulman, J. H. (1990). Now you see them, now you don't: Anonymity versus visibility in case studies of teachers. *Educational Researcher, 19,* 11–15.

Shuy, R. (1988). Identifying dimensions of classroom language. In J. L. Green & J. O. Harker (Eds.), *Multiple perspective analyses of classroom discourse* (pp. 115–134). Norwood, NJ: Ablex.

Sinclair, J. M., & Coulthard, R. M. (1975). *Toward an analysis of discourse.* London: Oxford University Press.

Sirotnik, K. A. (1988). The meaning and the conduct of inquiry in school-university partnerships. In K. A. Sirotnik & J. I. Goodlad (Eds.), *School–university partnerships in action* (pp. 169–190). New York: Teachers College Press.

Sirotnik, K. A., & Goodlad, J. I. (Eds.). (1988). *School–university partnerships in action.* New York: Teachers College Press.

Stenhouse, L. (1985). *Research as a basis for teaching.* London: Heinemann.

Stevenson, R. B., Noffke, S. E., Flores, E., & Granger, S. (1995). Teaching action research: A case study. In S. E. Noffke & R. B. Stevenson (Eds.), *Educational action research: Becoming practically critical* (pp. 60–73). New York: Teachers College Press.

Tikunoff, W., Ward, B., & Griffin, G. (1979). *Interactive research and development on teaching: Final report.* San Francisco: Far West Laboratory for Educational Research and Development.

Torbert, W. R. (1981). Why educational research has been so uneducational: The case for a new model of social science based on collaborative inquiry. In P. Reason & J. Rowan (Eds.), *Human inquiry: A sourcebook of new paradigm research* (pp. 141–151). New York: John Wiley & Sons.

Treleaven, L. (1994). Making a space: A collaborative inquiry with women as staff development. In P. Reason (Ed.), *Participation in human inquiry.* London: Sage.

van Maanen, J. (1995). An end to innocence: The ethnography of ethnography. In J. van Maanen (Ed.), *Representation in ethnography* (pp. 1–35). Thousand Oaks, CA: Sage.

van Manen, M. (1990). Beyond assumptions: Shifting the limits of action research. *Theory into Practice, 29,* 152–157.

Vygotsky, L. S. (1962). *Thought and language.* Cambridge, MA: MIT Press.

Vygotsky, L. S. (1978). *Mind in society: The development of higher psychological processes.* Cambridge: Cambridge University Press.

Walker, R. (1980). The conduct of educational case studies: Ethics, theory and procedures. In W. B. Dockrell & D. Hamilton (Eds.), *Rethinking educational research* (pp. 30–62). London: Hodder and Stoughton.

Walker, R. (1993). Finding a silent voice for the researcher: Using photographs in evaluation and research. In M. Schratz (Ed.), *Qualitative voices in educational research* (pp. 72–92). London: Falmer Press.

Watt, M. L., & Watt, D. L. (1993). Teacher research, action research: The logo action research collaborative. *Educational Action Research, 1,* 35–63.

Wells, G. (1994a). The complimentary contributions of Halliday and Vygotsky to a "language-based theory of learning." *Linguistics and Education, 6,* 41–90.

Wells, G. (1994b). *Changing schools from within: Creating communities of inquiry.* Portsmouth, NH: Heinemann.

Wells, G., & Chang-Wells, G. L. (1992). *Constructing knowledge together: Classrooms as centers of inquiry and literacy.* Portsmouth, NH: Heinemann.

Wertsch, J. V. (1985). *Vygotsky and the social formation of mind.* Cambridge: Cambridge University Press.

Wertsch, J. V. (1989). A sociocultural approach to mind. In W. Damon (Ed.), *Child development today and tomorrow* (pp. 14–33). San Francisco: Jossey-Bass.

Wertsch, J. V. (1991). *Voices of the mind: A sociocultural approach to mediated action.* Cambridge, MA: Harvard University Press.

Willinsky, J. (1990). *The new literacy: Redefining reading and writing in the schools.* New York: Routledge.

Wolcott, H. F. (1994). *Transforming qualitative data: Description, analysis,, and interpretation.* Thousand Oaks, CA: Sage.

Young, R. (1992). *Critical theory and classroom talk.* Clevedon, England: Multilingual Matters.

·19·

POETIC REPRESENTATION

Laurel Richardson

OHIO STATE UNIVERSITY

How we write has consequences for ourselves, our disciplines and those publics we serve. *How* we are expected to write affects *what* we can write about. The *form* in which we write shapes its *content*. Prose is the form in which social scientists are expected to report their findings. Yet, virtually absent is any analysis or critique of this literary form as the sole legitimate carrier of knowledge.

For nearly a decade I have been exploring alternative forms of staging sociological texts (cf. Richardson 1990, 1992a, 1992b, 1993, 1995, 1996, forthcoming; Richardson & Lockridge 1991). My purposes have been several: to examine how knowledge claims are constituted in social scientific writing; to write more interesting sociology; and to reach diverse audiences. In this paper, after briefly discussing some postmodernist writing issues, I discuss one alternative way of staging findings, "poetic representation." I consider two kinds of poetic representation, the longer narrative poem and lyric poetry. My intent is not to argue that poetic representation is the only or even best way to represent all social scientific knowledge; but I do claim that poetic representation is a method for seeing the conventions and discursive practices we take for granted, and, that for some kinds of social scientific knowledge, poetic representation may be preferable to prose representation.

My theoretical positioning is that of a feminist-postmodernist-interpretivist. The core of that position is the *doubt* that any discourse has a privileged place, any method or theory a universal and general claim to authoritative knowledge. Truth claims are suspected of masking and serving particular interests in local, cultural and political struggles. Wherever truth is claimed so is power: the claim to truth is a claim to power. Once the veil of privileged truth is lifted, the opportunities for rethinking how we think and who can think and what we can think are legion; also comes the possibility of alternative criteria for evaluating social scientific production. Moral implications, practical applications, aesthetic pleasure, performativity, credibility, become other possible criteria for choosing one discourse over another. Social scientists can, with philosophical impunity, interrupt their own discursive spaces, reflect on their modes of production, their power interests, and explore writing / performing / teaching / sharing their knowledge *both* as a "science" *and* as a public or aesthetic or practical or morally charged discourse.

Language is a constitutive force, creating a particular view of reality. This is as true of writing as it is of speaking, and as true of science as it is of poetry. Producing "things" always involves value—what to produce, what to name the products, and what the relationship between the producers and the products will be. Writing "things" is no exception. Writing always involves what Roland Barthes calls "the ownership of the means of enunciation." (Shapiro, 1985-86, p. 195). A disclosure of writing practices is thus always a disclosure of forms of power (Derrida, 1982). No textual staging is ever innocent (including this one).

Social scientific writing, like all other forms of writing, is a sociohistorical construction that depends upon literary devices (e.g., narrative, metaphor, imagery, invocations to authority, and appeals to audiences) not just for adornment, but for *cognitive* meaning. The truth value of social scientific writing depends upon a deep epistemic code regarding how knowledge *in general* is figured. Imminent in the prefiguring are metaphors so entrenched and familiar that they do their partisan work in the guise of neutrality, passing as literal (Derrida, 1982). For example, the grammatical split between subject and object goes wholly unnoticed as a metaphor for the separation of "real" subjects and objects, for "objectivity," and a static world, fixed in time and space. The temporal and human practices that reified the objects are rendered invisible, irrelevant. The technical mechanisms of explanation are quarantined from the human processes of interpretation. The actual linguistic practices in which the researcher / writer is engaged are hidden; but they are not eradicated.

A deep and totally unnoticed trope used by social scientists is reporting their findings in *prose*. In this chapter, I have myself used the prose-trope and will use it for the next several pages. Its conventions allow me to stage my arguments in a way that are familiar to the reader, which is my goal in this chapter. The reader is not distracted by a different genre, and I am aided in my argument by the invisible power inherent in the adoption of conventional writing (essayic prose). Those conventions are particularly helpful in making abstract arguments, which I am rhetorically interested in doing before I demonstrate violations of those conventions.

In conventional social scientific writing, not only are the arguments written in prose, but the findings are, too. I however, wish to challenge, this ossification—prose reified as the only way to write "findings." In what follows, I discuss two kinds of research findings staged as poetic representations: first, the writing-up of an in-depth interview as a narrative poem; and, second, the transformation of ethnographic materials into lyric poetry.

FROM IN-DEPTH INTERVIEW TO NARRATIVE POEM

In the routine work of the sociological interviewer, the interview is tape-recorded, transcribed as prose, and then cut, pasted, edited, trimmed, smoothed, and snipped, just as if it were a literary text, which it is, albeit usually without explicit acknowledgment or recognition of such by its sociological constructor. Normatively, underlying this process is the belief that the purpose of the text is to convey information, as though information consists of facts or themes or notions which exist independently of the context in which they were told, as if the story we have recorded, transcribed, edited and rewritten as snippets is the true one: a "science" story. Using standard writing conventions, including the use of prose, conceals the handprint of the sociologist who produced the written text.

Ironically, prose might not be the most "accurate" (i.e. "valid" and "scientific") way to "report" speech. According to the oral historian, Dennis Tedlock (1983), when people talk, whether as conversants, storytellers, informants, or interviewees, their speech is closer to poetry than it is to sociological prose (p. 109). Nobody talks in "prose." Everybody—so-called literate and nonliterate, adult and child, male and female—speaks using a poetical device, the pause. Indeed, in American speech, estimates are that about half of the time we are speaking, we are not; we are pausing (p. 198). And some 25% of pauses cannot be explained by physiological needs for breath or grammatical demands for closure, such as at the ends of sentences or clauses (p. 198). Unlike prose, poetry acknowledges pauses through the conventions of line breaks, spaces between lines and between stanzas and sections; a poem, therefore, more closely mimics actual speech by building its text upon both sounds and silence.

Most important, poetry and its related genres are both written and oral traditions. They can be read or performed. Drama (e.g., Ellis & Bochner, 1991; McCall & Becker, 1990; Richardson & Lockridge, 1991; Richardson, 1993, 1996), "ethnographic fiction" (e.g., Ellis, 1995; Krieger, 1983; Stewart, 1989), responsive reading (e.g., Richardson, 1992a), and poetry bring social theoretic understandings "live" to different audiences: poetry bars, theaters, policy-making settings, literary conventions, street scenes, and mass media.

I have used poetic representation to "report" the "findings" of an interview I had with "Louisa May." One evening, as part of a larger project on "unwed mothers," I completed an in-depth interview with Louisa May. I transcribed the tape into 36 pages of prose, and then shaped the transcript into a 5-page poem. In so doing, I drew upon both scientific and literary criteria. In fashioning her poem, I used only her words, tone, and diction, but relied upon poetic devices such as repetition, off-rhyme, meter, and pauses to convey her narrative. The speech style is Louisa May's, the words are hers, but the poetic representation is my own construction.

The way in which I have constructed the poem inscribes the interactional nature of the interview, the "talk" is one which has been produced in a particular kind of speech context—the sociological interview. I am the implied listener throughout the poem; when Louisa May speaks to me about the interview process itself, her words are italicized. The poem "shows" the sociological "buttress" to the "conversation," reminding the reader that this is a rendering of a particular kind of speech performance. Louisa May's story arises in the context of an interview; the context is written into the poem. Since an interview is a jointly constructed text arising from the intersection of two subjectivities in a particular social context (see especially Mischler, 1986), framing the "findings" as though they are independent of the method in which they were produced is falsifying, although a standard claims-making procedure.

Since "Louisa May's Story of Her Life," has been constructed as a poem, listeners / readers are not deluded into thinking that they are reading the one and only true story about her; rather, the facticity of its constructedness is ever present. As the poetic form plays with connotative structures and literary devices to convey meaning, poetic representations of "findings" have a greater likelihood of engaging readers in reflexive analyses of their own interpretive labors of the researcher's interpretive labors of the speaker's interpretive labors. The construction of "text" is thus positioned as joint, prismatic, open, and partial.

I have presented "Louisa May" to diverse audiences. The responses have been uniformly strong, sometimes heated. The "genre-breaking" writing displayed unexamined but foundational assumptions regarding the nature of "theory," "data," "findings," "authority," and "authorship." Poets theorize about the social construction of "normality," genre boundaries, and authorship. Women's studies audiences theorize the poem as a method of revealing "findings" as masculinist—with poetry "feminizing" the product and its production. General audiences have used "Louisa May" as a springboard for discussing societal issues. Oral historians have seen poetic representation as a method of capturing an "essence," that is lacking in their own conventions. Social workers and policy makers claim the poem has altered their stereotypical thinking. Some social scientists, and even some with constructionist and postmodernist leanings, though, have challenged the "validity" of the poem, demanding to see the transcript, although not to hear the tape, see a videotape, or talk directly to Louisa May—all possible grounds for establishing validity that do not privilege a written document. I have been variously accused of exploiting Louisa May, of fabricating her, and of being her. I doubt if these accusations would have been made by poets or sociologists or feminists had I written conventionally.

For sociological readers, in addition, the poem may seem to lack certain sociological data. But this poem is based on Louisa May's sense of what is relevant, not the sociologist's; it is her narrative. For example, Louisa May does not talk about her education or occupation. Uneasiness that readers might have over their apparent lack of knowledge about Louisa May, I submit, reflects on the readers' unexamined assumptions. If they wonder, for example, how Louisa May supports herself and her daughter, are they tapping into their stereotypes about *unwed* mothers? Would they wonder about "support" if Louisa May were married or were Louis M.? If they feel they cannot understand her unless they know about her educational level, are they telling us about the place of education in their own lives? More generally, have the categories of sociology been so reified that even interpretivists feel they have to refract a person's life through a sociologically prescribed lens?

Here is "Louisa May's story," a poetic representation, a transcript masquerading as a poem / a poem masquerading as a transcript.

LOUISA MAY'S STORY

The most important thing
to say is that
I grew up in the South.
Being Southern shapes
aspirations   shapes
what you think you are
and what you think you're going to be.

> *(When I bear myself, my Ladybird
> kind of accent on tape, I think, OH Lord,
> You're from Tennessee.)*

No one ever suggested to me
that anything
might happen *with* my life.
I grew up poor in a rented house
in a very normal sort of way
on a very normal sort of street
with some very nice middle class friends

> *(Some still to this day)*

and so I thought I'd have a lot of children.

I lived outside.

Unhappy home. Stable family, till it fell apart.
The first divorce in Milfrount County.

So, that's how that was worked out.

ii

Well, one thing that happens
growing up in the South

is that you leave. I
always knew I would

> I would leave.
> *(I don't know what to say…
> I don't know what's germane.)*

My high school sweetheart and I married,
went north to college.
I got pregnant and miscarried,
and I lost the child.

> *(As I see it now it was a marriage
> situation which got increasingly borrendous
> where I was under the most stress
> and strain without any sense
> of how to extricate myself.)*

It was purely chance
that I got a job here,
and Robert didn't.
I was mildly happy.

After 14 years of marriage,

That was the break.
We divorced.
A normal sort of life.

iii

So, the Doctor said, "You're pregnant."
I was 41. John and I
had had a happy kind of relationship,
not a serious one.
But beside himself with fear and anger,
awful, rageful, vengeful, horrid,
Jody May's father said,
"Get an Abortion."

I told him,
"I would never marry you.
I would never marry you.
I would never.

"I am going to have this child.
I am going to.
I am. I am.

"Just Go Away!"

But he wouldn't. He painted the nursery.
He slept on the floor. He went to therapy.
We went to LaMaze.

> *(We ceased having a sexual relationship directly
> after I had gotten pregnant and that has never
> again entered the situation.)*

He lives 100 miles away now.
He visits every weekend.
He sleeps on the floor.
We all vacation together.
We go camping.

I am not interested in a split-family,
her father taking her on Sundays.
I'm not interested in doing so.

So, little Jody May always has had a situation which is
normal.

Mother—bless her—the word "married" never crossed
her lips.
(I do resent mother's stroke. Other mothers
have their mother.)
So, it never occurs to me really that we are unusual in
any way.

No, our life really is very normal. I own my house.
I live on a perfectly ordinary middle-class street.

So, that's the way that was worked out.

iv

She has his name. If she wasn't going to have a father,
I thought she should have a father, so to speak.

We both adore her.
John says Jody May saved his life.

OH, I do fear that something will change—

v

(Is this helpful?)

This is the happiest time in my life.

I am an entirely different person.

With no husband in the home there is less tension.
And I'm not talking about abnormal families here.
Just normal circumstances. Everyone comes
home tired.

I left the South a long time ago.
I had no idea how I would do it.

So, that's the way that worked out.
(I've talked so much my throat hurts.)

FROM ETHNOGRAPHIC MATERIALS TO LYRIC POETRY

I presented "Louisa May" to an ethnography conference, along with a drama based on responses to the poem at a sociology conference. Considerable discussion followed; some conferees feared for ethnography's future. But a conference organizer and coeditor of *The Journal of Contemporary Ethnography (JCE),* stood up in the front row of the overfull auditorium and said with cheeky good humor: We are the ethnographers. We decide what constitutes ethnography. She then invited me to send poems, with or without an introduction, to *JCE.* I sent the following, "Nine Poems: Marriage and the Family," without justification or explication.

MARRIAGE AND THE FAMILY

Legacy

To comfort the mother
of the third born daughter
her father names her
after his own mother.

The third born becomes a mother.

She learns her namesake died
of pleurisy or suicide.
Her father doesn't remember.
Says it doesn't matter

Marriage

I used
to think it was
cute to have a lit-
tle shadow go in and out
with me.

The Good Doctor Said

Your son has inoperable
brain tumors. At puberty
he'll get progressively
weaker on his left side
until he takes to bed
catches cold and dies.

Treat him as normal.

Lullaby

Time
goes
slowly
thinking
about
dying
giving
me
more
time
to
think
about
dying

When he was a baby,
I wondered if he
would die in his sleep,
In my sleep.

Bill said it didn't matter.
Death, he said, is best
after a good night's sleep.

Taking Him to the Vet

He's shameless, Doctor.
Walks around with no clothes.
Growls at pussies,
sniffs.
Pees in public with others
of his sex and species,
impervious to breed.

I do believe he would bite
the hand that feeds him.

At night
He pants and moans and salivates.
He's shameless.

Will his Blue Cross cover?
How soon can you fix him?

Custody

See how the orange is segmented:
naturally. How apples resist
paring. How ocean water fills
a glass. My glass. Full tide
hovering at the rim. My hand
holding the ocean still,
still the undertow. See my hand
through the glass.

Being Single Is

drying a wishbone
by the kitchen window
'til the bone is chipped

to bits by trinkets
placed beside it,
or it rots, because

there is no one
to take one end
you the other

pulling, wishing
each against each
until the bone

breaks.

Surrounded By Men

Short ones, lover and friend,
beer drinking on the back porch,
comparing the lengths of their
manuscripts, their tenures.
Wisps of Tennyson and Chaucer.

Tall ones, sons, territorizing
the front yard. Shooting rockets,
burning fingers, spilling rock salt.

Commanding the living room, Father,
dead already eight years, today,
swollen with waiting-

Even The Knives Sleep

If I were a fork, I would know my place,
to the left of the plate, tines beckoning
a hand to cradle me,
me holding meat for the knife.
The blade slips between my tines
scraping edges.
There is no pain, and after

I am bathed in water
and returned to the space
I share with others of my kind.
We nestle together, edges cradling edges.
I am safe in the drawer.
Even the knives sleep.

Some reviewers wanted to know: How are these poems ethnography? Although initially I resisted writing about the poems, I decided that to do so afforded me an opportunity to think more about how knowledge-claims are constituted and supported. I am particularly interested in how my own branch of knowledge—that based on ethnographic qualitative research—is constituted as authoritative. I focus here primarily on issues of narrative and validity.

Poststructuralism proposes that systems of knowledge are narratively constructed. Traditionally, ethnographies, oral histories, social histories, biographies, and other qualitatively based research are constructed with fairly straightforward, obvious, and visible plot lines. The author intends that the reader "gets *the* story." "The story" is understood as taking place within or reflecting a particular social order or culture. Writing in-depth interviews as a long narrative poem, then, although transgressing representational practices, coheres with the narrative traditions of qualitative research. These transgressive writings reinscribe the possibility of "the plot line," the story, even as they challenge the *format* through which the story is told.

In "Nine Poems," however, the narrative is only implied. Nine Poems are short, *lyric poems,* each a "mini-narrative," an episode, representing an emotionally and morally charged experience. The order of the poems implies a plot, but the "spaces" between the poems invite greater readerly responses and interpretive work than would a long narrative poem. The nine poems could also be reordered, implying yet different plots. Subsuming "Nine Poems" under the rubric, "Marriage and the Family," moreover, implies a *metanarrative,* the sociocultural construction of those two concepts "marriage" and "family," and a seeming relationship between them, "marriage *and* the family." The implied narrative would change, if "Nine Poems" were subtitled, "Gender" or "Maturing," or "Socialization" or "Treason" or "Paper Airplanes."

If a goal of social science is to retell "lived experience," to make another world accessible to the reader, then, I submit that the lyric poem, and particularly a sequence of lyric poems with an implied narrative, may come closer to achieving that goal than other forms of ethnographic writing.

Lyric poetry may come closer to presenting "lived experience" for literary, sociological, and cultural reasons. "Poems exist in the realm of making (*mimesis*) rather than of knowing or doing; they are representations of human experience ... not speech uttered by, or speech acts performed by individuals who happen to be poets" (Borroff, 1993, p. 1032). That is, lyric poems are consciously constructed through literary devices such as sound patterns, rhythms, imagery, and page layout to evoke emotion. Like the lived experiences they represent, poems are emotionally and morally charged. Lyric poems concretize emotions, feelings, and moods—the most private kind of feelings—in order to recreate an experience in another person. A lyric poem "shows" another person how it is to feel something. Even if the mind resists, the body responds to poetry. It is *felt*. To paraphrase Robert Frost, poetry is the shortest emotional path between two people.

Sociologically, each lyric poem represents a "candid photo" or an "episode" or an epiphany. People organize their sense of Self around and through such epiphanous moments (Denzin, 1989). Everyday life experiences are not organized around the long biographical account, the epic poem, the life history. Rather, people tell stories about events in their lives; the meaning of the event changes through the invocation of different implied narratives. Further, not all events are stuffed into the same narrative. A life may have a "plot line," but not everything lived—nor everything of import to the person—fits neatly into "a" plot. We are not characters. Our lives are not morals. They are not even ethnographic narratives.

Cultures provide prefabricated narratives for hooking up the events of our lives. As cultural studies and discourse analyses demonstrate, those narratives are multiple, contradictory, changing, and differentially available. As agents in our own construction, we choose among available "cultural stories," apply them to our experiences, sometimes get stuck in a particularly strong "meta-narrative," often operate with contradictory implied narratives, and sometimes seek stories which transgress the culturally condoned ones. Any or all of these processes through which the self is constructed and reconstructed may be going on simultaneously. Lyric representation mimics the complexity and openness of this human process—"shifting subjectivities"—by which we come to know, and not know, ourselves, and know ourselves, again, differently.

In addition to these narrative issues, "Nine Poems" raises another question: validity. In the long narrative poem, "Louisa May's Story" the reader is told that all the words, rhythms, and sound patterns come from an in-depth interview with Louisa May. Although I crafted the poem, my voice is distinguished from Louisa May's. That is, although the format is transgressive, in the production and sharing of "Louisa May" I adhered to a scientific protocol.

In "Nine Poems," however, the reader is not told the source of the poems. No "subversive repetition" of science practices is proffered. The poet and the poems are conflated. Are the poems from the life of a particular person, and if so, is that person one and the same as the poet? Or, did the poet compile the poems from interviews with different people or from a variety of texts?

But, does it matter—ethnographically—whose life is represented, or whether the poems represent a particular life? These questions are not asked in standard ethnographic codifications, where an "ideal-typic" portrait may be presented or a series of quotes from different interviews are collated under a theme, sometimes (I am told) quotes from the researcher, herself, secreted in amongst the others. If you care about whether the "I" of the poems is the "I" writing this essay, I ask you to ask yourself, "Why?" Do you have validity questions? Reliability questions? Truth questions? Emotional identification / disidentification con-cerns? "Nine Poems" brings these ethnographic issues—always present, usually suppressed—into critical awareness.

If we suppose that the poems are a representation of a particular life, they simply fit within the tradition of making an individual (e.g., the jackroller, the children of Sanchez, Don Juan, etc.) the center of ethnographic writing. But if the poems are thought of as a representation of my own life, then the writing belongs to the newly developing sociology of subjectivity (Ellis & Flaherty, 1992; Ellis, 1995; Richardson, 1995). In literary writing and ethnographies of the self, the boundary line is personal; the boundary is between the foreign territory of one person's psyche and that of another. The Other that is the foreign territory, the "terra exotic," is the *inner experience,* the inner life of the writer. Writing about the Self as both subject and object distances the Self from the usual codifications of ethnography, even while the writing points out how the Self depends upon social and cultural discourses to "know" itself, to position itself. Lyric poems have the capability of reducing the "distance" between the "I" and the "Other" and between the "writing-I" and "experiencing-I" of the writer, and thus move us to rethink the boundaries between ourselves and our "work," help us feel how ethnography might be situated within the "Self" (Krieger, 1991).

I would submit that "good" ethnography, like "good" literary works, invites the reader to *experience* a culture or an event. If one wants to *feel* what the plague was like, one can read DeFoe's *Journal of the Plague Year,* which purports to be factual but is in fact a work of imagination. If one wants to *feel* what it was like to survive the Buffalo Creek disaster, one can read Kai Erikson's *Everything in Its Path,* which is categorized as ethnography, and reads like good fiction. If one wants to *feel* what it is like to experience emotional depression, one can read William Styron's *Darkness Visible,* which is a personal account by a novelist that exposes institutionalized medical ignorance, as might a good ethnography. In all of these instances—and many others—the reader is not simply "told," s/he *feels* the experience. In this deepest sense, ethnographic writing, then, is allied to the rhetorical and emotional center of literary writing.

How does the lyric poem fit in, then? The lyric poem's task is to represent actual experiences—episodes, epiphanies, misfortunes, pleasures—to capture those experiences in such a way that others can experience and *feel* them. Lyric poems, therefore, have the possibility of doing for ethnographic understanding what normative ethnographic writing cannot.

The question—"How is lyric poetry ethnography?"—must be, I submit, inverted. The question should rather be, "When is lyric poetry *not* ethnographic?" As an opening move to answer that question, I would suggest that had Keats' "Ode to a Nightingale" first appeared in a journal of ornithology, this fact would have forever influenced how the ode was read and understood by the literary critic. Knowledge is always contextual, legitimated by gatekeepers, and always exists inside a "meta-narrative." For now, "Nine Poems" appearing in *JCE* and in this book as ethnographic representation "is" ethnographic writing.

CONCLUSION

How we write has consequences for what we can know. Poetic representation is one possible way of knowing. By examining the foundations of our claims to authoritative knowing and by exploring alternative representations, we may all be more knowledgeable.

References

Borroff, M. (1993). Cluster on the poetic: from Euripides to Rich. *Publications of the Modern Language Association of America PMLA, 108*, 1032–1035.

Denzin, N. K. (1989). *Interpretive interactionism.* Newbury Park, CA: Sage.

Derrida, J. (1982). *Margins of philosophy* (A. Bass, Trans.). Chicago: University of Chicago, Press.

Ellis, C. (1995). *Final negotiations: A story of love, loss, and chronic illness.* Philadelphia: Temple University Press.

Ellis, C., & Bochner A. (1992). Telling and performing personal stories: The constraint of choice in abortion. In C. Ellis & M. G. Flaherty (Eds.), *Investigating subjectivity: Research on lived experience* (pp. 79–101). Newbury Park, CA: Sage.

Ellis, C., & Flaherty M.G. (Eds.). (1992). *Investigating subjectivity: Research on lived experience.* Newbury Park: Sage.

Krieger, S. (1983). *The mirror dance: Identity in a woman's community.* Philadelphia: Temple University Press.

Krieger, S. (1991). *Social science and the self: Personal essays on an art form.* New Brunswick, NJ: Rutgers University Press.

McCall, M. M., & Becker, H. S. (1990). Performance science. *Social Problems, 32*, 117–132.

Mischler, E. G. (1986). *Research interviewing.* Cambridge, MA: Harvard University Press.

Richardson, L. (1990). *Writing strategies: Reaching diverse audiences.* Newbury Park, CA: Sage.

Richardson, L. (1992a). Resisting resistance narratives: A representation for communication. *Studies in Symbolic Interaction, 13*, 77–82.

Richardson, L. (1992b). The consequences of poetic representation: Writing the other, rewriting the "self." In C. Ellis & M. G. Flaherty (Eds.), *Investigating subjectivity: Research on lived experience* (pp. 124–141). Newbury Park, CA: Sage.

Richardson, L. (1993). Poetics, dramatics, and transgressive validity. *The Sociological Quarterly, 35*, 695–710.

Richardson, L. (1995). *Vespers. Chicago Review, 41*(2 & 3), 129–146.

Richardson, L. (1996). Educational birds. *Journal of Contemporary Ethnography, 25*, 6–15.

Richardson, L. (forthcoming). *Fields of play: Constructing an academic life.* New Brunswick, NJ: Rutgers University Press.

Richardson, L., & Lockridge E. (1991). The sea monster: An ethnographic drama. *Symbolic Interaction, 14*, 335–341.

Shapiro, M. (1985-86). Metaphor in the philosophy of the social sciences. *Cultural Critique, 2*, 191–214.

Stewart, J. O. (1989). *Drinkers, drummers and decent folk: Ethnographic narratives of Village Trinidad.* Albany, NY: State University of New York Press.

Tedlock, D. (1983). *The spoken word and the work of interpretations.* Philadelphia: University of Pennsylvania Press.

20

ALTERNATIVE METHODOLOGY FOR DIAGNOSTIC ASSESSMENT OF WRITTEN AND VERBAL RESPONSES TO WORKS OF ART

Carol Susann Stavropoulos

UNIVERSITY OF GEORGIA

Instruments currently available to assess written statements about works of art do not adequately account for cognitive conceptions of learning. That is, they do not discriminate between the learner's knowledge-base and knowledge-seeking strategies, higher-order and lower-order understandings, and misunderstandings. The development of an assessment instrument, referred to as a Diagnostic Profile of art understandings, begins to lessen this gap in art education research on student assessment (Stavropoulos, 1992).

A study by Koroscik, Short, Stavropoulos, and Fortin (1992) found that components of a student's knowledge-base and knowledge-seeking strategies can be reflected in written statements about works of art. The purpose of this chapter is to focus on the interaction between the knowledge-base and knowledge-seeking strategies employed in the process of transfer. Building upon this theoretical framework and related research, the chapter will present categories for an alternative assessment instrument referred to as a Diagnostic Profile of art understandings.

The steps taken to develop and test the quality of this alternative assessment instrument will be summarized as follows: (a) the theoretical foundation directing the inquiry, (b) methodologies used in the development of assessment categories, (c) description of the Diagnostic Profile, (d) validity and reliability studies conducted to establish instrument quality, (e) the educational importance of future applications of an alternative methodology for assessing understandings of art, and (f) implications for the field of art education.

An oil painting entitled, *The Birthday,* painted between 1915 and 1923 by artist Marc Chagall was the primary focus of the research of Koroscik et al. (1992). Numerous criteria directed the selection of *The Birthday* in that study, for example, it is highly representative of the artist's style, there is a sizable body of literature available on the work, it represents a moderate level of abstraction, and it has a theme to which many can relate (p. 156). *The Birthday* (see Plate 20–I) will be used throughout this chapter as a convenient way of providing illustrations of knowledge-base and knowledge-seeking strategies.

THE LEARNER'S KNOWLEDGE-BASE

The sum total of what an individual already knows is referred to as *prior knowledge* in the learning literature (Alexander, Schallert, & Hare, 1991). The importance of prior knowledge has been examined in such fields as computer programming (Linn, 1985), mathematics (Schoenfeld, 1985), medicine (Lesgold, et al., 1988), art education (Koroscik, 1982), and reading comprehension (Alvermann, Smith, & Readence, 1985; Wilson, & Anderson, 1986).

Prior knowledge has at least two facets: knowledge-base and knowledge-seeking strategies. In accounting for learning outcomes through transfer, Koroscik has proposed a theoretical framework highlighting the learner's knowledge-base and choice of knowledge-seeking strategies. Both facets must be engaged to some degree in order for transfer to occur (Koroscik, 1992–93, p. 7).

Koroscik (1992–93) defines the *knowledge-base* as "all the accumulated knowledge, skill, and experience a student currently possesses, including what the learner already knows about the material being studied" (p. 7). Emphasizing the learner's active role in this construction of knowledge, Koroscik's model of art learning differentiates knowledge-base from strategies that students use to acquire new

PLATE 20–I Marc Chagall. *The Birthday*, 1915–1923, oil on cardboard, 31 3/4 × 39 1/4 in/80.5 × 99.5 cm.
The Museum of Modern Art, New York; acquired through the Lille P. Bliss Bequest.

knowledge and make use of existing knowledge. The learner can access relevant prior knowledge or irrelevant prior knowledge from the knowledge-base. Additionally, the strategies students employ in accessing knowledge in their possession range in effectiveness. Based on the interplay between knowledge-base and knowledge-seeking strategies, at least four conceivable learning outcomes can be isolated. These outcomes exist along a continuum (1992–93, 1993):

1. The learner does not possess adequate prior knowledge nor are effective knowledge-seeking strategies employed.
2. The learner possesses relevant prior knowledge but employs ineffective knowledge-seeking strategies.
3. The learner uses effective knowledge-seeking strategies but does not possess adequate prior knowledge.
4. The learner possesses relevant prior knowledge and uses effective knowledge-seeking strategies.

The interaction between the knowledge-base and knowledge-seeking strategies explains why learning outcomes can differ, and provides a foundation for developing a more comprehensive approach for assessing student understandings of artworks. An evaluative account and / or characterization of the outcomes that occur along these learning continua can distinguish less successful learners from more successful ones (Koroscik, 1982, 1990a, 1990b).

The Function of Prior Knowledge

Vosniadou and Brewer (1987) state, "the acquisition of new knowledge from experience makes little sense without assuming some prior knowledge within which the new experience is interpreted; otherwise the new experience will be unintelligible" (pp. 51, 52). Therefore, for meaningful learning to occur, information to be learned must be connected to prior knowledge (Prawat, 1989; Vosniadou, & Brewer, 1987). Often students have difficulty in accessing, or fail to transfer their existing knowledge to new information (Alvermann, et al., 1985; Bransford, Sherwood, Vye, & Rieser, 1986). The extent to which learners can activate and transfer prior knowledge influences the degree to which new information and ideas are comprehended (Bransford, & Johnson, 1972; Dooling, & Lachman, 1971).

Encounters with visual art are interpreted through a student's existing knowledge of art. For example, students would need to know something about Marc Chagall before they could understand Chagall's influences on the French poet Paul Eluard (Crespelle, 1970), the Russian printmaker El Lissitzky (Alexander, 1978; Bolliger, 1957; Compton, 1985; Jager, 1970), and / or the Canadian choreographer Ginette Laurin (Pontbriand, 1990).

Formal and Informal Knowledge

Confrontations with a work of art such as Chagall's painting *The Birthday,* have the potential to trigger a wide spectrum of prior knowledge within the learner's / student's / art viewer's knowledge-base. The degree to which general or art-specific prior knowledge is activated determines understanding (Koroscik, 1982).

A student can accumulate general knowledge that is related to art from everyday experience, that is, *informal knowledge* (Prawat, 1989). It is possible to rely on informal knowledge to identify the subject matter in *The Birthday*. For example, a student might cite the table in a home where enjoyable meals are served each day.

Prior knowledge specific to art might encompass viewing and art-making experiences that can be gained as a result of formal education. Knowledge gained in this manner can be referred to as *instructed* or *formal knowledge* (Prawat, 1989). For instance, the art teacher could instruct students that the interior space of *The Birthday* includes a bed. While students possess informal descriptive knowledge regarding beds, a bed cannot easily be identified in *The Birthday*. In the painting, the bed is actually cut off at the right-hand side of the composition, slightly tilted in perspective, and covered with scarves and what may be a pillow. As such, identification of the bed is difficult. Without instructed knowledge of the subject matter, the student might miss noting details that suggest that the interior space is actually Chagall's living quarters.

Informal and instructed knowledge can coexist in the student's knowledge-base. For example, a student might draw upon informal knowledge of birthday cake after the teacher has provided instructed knowledge of the birthday cake.

A question explored in this chapter is "What aspects of the knowledge-base should be the focus of an assessment instrument?" In terms of evaluation, this is an important question because there are direct relationships between the content taught in the classroom, learning outcomes or understandings that result, and existing assessment tools (Hamblen, 1988). If an assessment instrument is to measure outcomes that are reflective of student understandings, its dimensions should be representative of content that can bring about those understandings. However, there remains still much debate over the content of art education curricula, and what learning outcomes are considered desirable.

Dimensions of Art Understanding

While terminology may vary somewhat in analyzing works of art, art educators often use language that can be characterized as follows:

- *formal*—elements or principles of design, media, technique
- *descriptive*—objects, subject matter
- *interpretive*—meaning, emotion, feeling, expression
- *historical*—names, dates, information regarding the artist, and the artist's background

Recent college textbooks for the teaching of methods to prospective art teachers align curricular objectives in responding to works of art along formal, descriptive, interpretive, and historical dimensions of art understanding (Herberholz, & Hanson, 1990; Herberholz, & Herberholz, 1990; Hurwitz, & Day, 1991; Linderman, 1990; Wachowiak, & Clements, 1993). Art education textbook series, teacher guides, and curricula at the primary, elementary, and high

school levels incorporate formal, descriptive, interpretive, and historical dimensions of art understanding in suggested classroom lessons and topics of study (Briere, 1988; Brommer, 1982; Chapman, 1987, 1992; Fichner-Rathus, 1986; Hobbs, & Salome, 1991; Hubbard, 1987; Hubbard, & Rouse, 1981; Mittler, 1994; Mittler, & Ragans, 1992a, 1992b; Ragans, 1995). Even the National Teacher Examination (NTE) speciality area in art education and NTE core battery tests on general knowledge contain standardized assessment of formal, descriptive, interpretive, and historical dimensions of the prospective teacher's knowledge-base (DeMauro, 1989; NTE, 1987).

Current theories in art education incorporate perspectives based on formal, descriptive, interpretive, and historical foundations (Clark, Day, & Greer, 1987; Efland, 1990; Hurwitz, & Day, 1991; Smith, 1989). Cognitive theorists and researchers in the field of art education use similar distinctions to describe responses to works of art (Efland, 1990; Koroscik, 1990a, 1990b; Koroscik, Osmond, & DeSouza, 1988; Koroscik, et al., 1992; Parsons, 1987), as do art criticism specialists (Barrett, 1990, 1994a; Carney, 1994; Feldman, 1994). The underlying assumption is that each dimension of art facilitates art understanding in particular but overlapping ways. Therefore, an assessment instrument for art education might reflect the degree to which formal, descriptive, interpretive, and historical concepts and strategies incorporating their use are contained within the student's knowledge-base.

KNOWLEDGE-SEEKING STRATEGIES

Strategy refers to a spectrum of methods that assist knowledge acquisition and utilization (Prawat, 1989, p. 2) . According to Alexander, et al. (1991) "the learner builds a meaningful framework from existing knowledge that will facilitate the interchange between what is already known and what is to be understood" (p. 331). Koroscik (1992–93) defines *knowledge-seeking strategies* employed in art learning situations as "the cognitive steps a student takes to construct new understandings, to seek new knowledge, and to apply previously acquired knowledge, skill, and experience (p. 7)." Efland (1990) contends that assessment of art understandings should focus on strategies used to organize knowledge. Therefore, an instrument that assesses art understandings should represent the student's employment of knowledge-seeking strategies.

As students construct new understandings, it is important that knowledge-seeking strategies are adopted to make efficient use of the knowledge-base. However, relevant knowledge that could prove useful in learning situations often remains inactive (Bransford, et al., 1986; Schoenfeld, 1985). Failure to access relevant knowledge might be due to gaps in the learner's knowledge of certain routines, processes, and strategies. According to Koroscik et al. (1992), "if a student chooses a search strategy that is inappropriate, there is little chance relevant knowledge will be transferred even if the student possesses it. And if effective search strategies are employed but the student's knowledge-base is lacking, understanding will be impaired or misguided" (p. 164).

Efland (1990) states, "the naive learner may have knowledge but not know how to apply it to new situations" (p. 52). More experienced art viewers "need to acquire procedures for using what they already know in order to identify what they don't know, thus organizing the search for new information" (Koroscik, 1988, p. 11).

Therefore, the concerns identified by Koroscik (1988) and Efland (1990) indicate a need for assessment tools including an inventory of learning strategies and outcomes. A model of learning and assessment should also differentiate between the types of prior knowledge that are brought to bear on understanding a work of art. This approach is superior to classical models that tend only to focus on the student's knowledge-base (Efland, 1990).

TRANSFER

Transfer is the result of employing knowledge-seeking strategies to make connections between the characteristics of the artworks and the student's accumulated knowledge or knowledge-base (Koroscik, 1992–93, 1993; Koroscik, et al., 1992). The connections a student may make might be referred to as "building bridges" (Nickerson, 1985). The "bridges" students build when viewing works of art can determine whether they arrive at lower-order understandings, higher-order understandings, and/or misunderstandings. According to Parsons (1990), a student may make connections

> between the various aspects of the work itself (internal connections), and of any of those with the artist, with the history and culture within which the work was created, and/or the present art world and social setting in which it is viewed, including the emotional and intellectual state of the viewer. (p. 42)

Both instructed knowledge of formal, descriptive, interpretive, and/or historical dimensions of art and/or informal knowledge can be involved in transfer. Just as prior knowledge (both formal and informal) are unique to individuals, so too are the connections one brings to a work of art.

According to Prawat (1989), "the breadth and depth of a concept's connectedness—that is, how many other ideas it is connected to—is a good measure not only of its meaningfulness but also of its potential contribution to the coherence of a cognitive structure" (p. 8). Therefore, the organization of connections between the learner's knowledge-base and the characteristics of the work of art can range from simple to more complex in structure.

Efland (1990) suggests that deeper understandings are evidenced when concepts are integrated, (e.g., concepts acquired in the studio surface in critical and/or historical discussions about works of art). The literature on the phenomenon of transfer supports the view that deeper understandings happen when previously synthesized material from one learning situation aids in the successful understanding of another.

Low-Road Transfer and Lower-Order Understandings

Perkins and Salomon (1987) characterize the most common form of transfer as *low-road transfer*. The process of low-road transfer can involve lower-order knowledge-seeking strategies such as application of familiar vocabulary, recall of facts, correct description of instances, and/or memorization. These knowledge-seeking strategies tend to occur as the automatic consequence of varied practice and are familiar operations performed intuitively and automatically (Perkins, & Salomon, 1987; Salomon, & Perkins, 1989).

For example, *The Birthday* depicts an interior space. This deduction might be based on the identification of furnishings such as a table, floor, and walls. Since the idea of these items within an interior space is not new, the need to think deeply about this aspect of the work is lessened. Understanding the concept of interior space represented in *The Birthday,* through low-road transfer, requires almost automatic recall-oriented associations rather than reflective thinking.

High-Road Transfer and Higher-Order Understanding

High-road transfer is defined by Perkins and Salomon (1987) as "deliberate mindful efforts to represent principles at a high level of generality, so that they subsume a wide range of cases" (p. 288). High-road transfer is a controlled and nonautomated process which demands greater mental effort (Perkins, & Salomon, 1987; Salomon, 1983; Salomon, & Perkins, 1989). According to Salomon and Perkins, when mindful processes are evoked, an obvious response might be withheld in favor of a closer examination of the underlying meaning. Looking closer at the problem facilitates alternative strategies, choices, and connections, which lead to the construction of new structures of understanding. Perkins and Salomon claim that high-road transfer is brought about by an ability to abstract and apply principles under appropriate conditions (pp. 290, 291).

For example, the relationship of levitation to the notion of love is cited frequently in the historical literature on *The Birthday.* The sensation brought about by love does not literally cause lovers to defy the laws of gravity and hover above the ground. It is an abstraction to reference the principle of gravity from the context of science and apply it to the context of *The Birthday.* For high-road transfer to occur, a richer set of connections must be made as in the following example:

> The lighthearted, weightless sensation of love is symbolized by the two floating figures.

As illustrated, the process of high-road transfer involves the construction of meaning through a meshing of concepts. Meshing of concepts requires more than simply identifying that the couple in *The Birthday* are kissing. Constructing meaning in high-road transfer is a higher-order skill which promises deeper understandings and greater retention (Efland, 1990; O'Neal, 1992; Perkins, & Salomon, 1987; Salomon, & Perkins, 1989).

Understandings may therefore be said to vary in degrees of cognitive complexity (Efland, 1990; Nickerson, 1985; Parsons, 1987, 1990). According to Nickerson, "the richer the conceptual context in which one can imbed a new fact, the more one can be said to understand the fact" (pp. 235, 236).

Misunderstandings

Misunderstandings about works of art can impede meaningful learning (Efland, 1990; Efland, Koroscik, & Parsons, 1991; Koroscik 1990b; Parsons, 1990). According to Feltovich, Spiro, and Coulson (1988), some misunderstandings are more entrenched than others. An assessment instrument should be able to distinguish the misunderstandings a student brings to potential learning situations in art. To assess misunderstandings, a knowledge of the kinds of mistakes students make and their causes is required (Perkins, & Simmons, 1988).

One reason students do not fully understand works of art is because prior knowledge and / or the employment of a particular knowledge-seeking strategy prevents learning. When one learning encounter impairs another, negative transfer has occurred (Perkins, & Salomon, 1987, p. 287). Some misunderstandings are equivalent to negative transfer. For example, prior knowledge in reference to Marc and Bella Chagall's married life could inhibit an understanding of *The Birthday*. In this instance, a student might mistake the flowers Bella holds in her hand for a bridal bouquet. Based on this finding, the student might interpret the painting as a commemoration of Marc and Bella's wedding day. Actually, Bella brought the flowers to decorate Marc's apartment for his birthday celebration before the couple was married.

Other reasons students do not fully understand works of art is because they do not have an adequate knowledge-base and / or their knowledge-seeking strategies are limited. In these cases, terms like misunderstandings can be misleading because there is the implication that an error has been made "when the only error might be a limited frame of reference beyond which the student has no experience" (Confrey, 1987, p. 97). Supporting this stance, Parsons (1990) states "a child's present conceptions represent not a false, but a partial and incomplete understanding" (p. 41). Many young children would understand the birthday celebration depicted in *The Birthday*. However, a young child would not be expected to understand the metaphysical connotations attached to the imagery of Marc Chagall. While a young child may relate to the imagery, he / she may actually have an incomplete understanding of Chagall's paintings.

Multiple Interpretations

People generate many different interpretations of a work of art. If we are to assess a person's understanding of a work of an artist, we must first determine, at least to some extent, what understandings are desirable. According to Parsons (1990), desirable understandings are more easily identified in math and science because "a mis-conception contrasts naturally with a correct conception. It is much clearer in math and science which are the correct conceptions" (p. 40). Calling for a middle ground, experts agree that multiple interpretations of works of art are certainly possible, however, some interpretations are more convincing than others (Barrett, 1994b; Koroscik, 1992–93; Parsons, 1990, 1992). The field of medicine can lend a clue to this dilemma.

In medicine, assessment of a patient's symptoms and treatment plans are sequential diagnostic processes. Once a patient's symptoms have been assessed, the doctor arrives at a diagnosis, and the treatment plan is elected (Miller, & Keane, 1972). For instance, multiple treatment plans exist for sufferers of migraine headache. The treatment of choice may have as much to do with the particular doctor, his or her training, experience, and philosophies, as it does with the patient. For instance, after ruling out the presence of a brain tumor or other such brain disorders, one general practitioner might prescribe narcotic pain medication to ease a migraine, while another might prescribe a high dose of aspirin. A university physician, because of campus drug problems, might be cautious about prescribing narcotic drugs for headaches. As an alternative, exercise and over-the-counter medications such as Tylenol®, may be recommended. One neurologist might suggest biofeedback while another may suggest a change in diet. A doctor of holistic medicine might suggest a stress management program, while still another might prescribe allergy tests or an optometry examination.

Hypothetically all of these treatment plans would seem to be legitimate and logical courses of action, even though they differ drastically. In the same vein, interpretations of art may vary, but still be legitimate and logical. For example, one critic may view a photograph by Mapplethorpe through the lens of technique and conclude that Mapplethorpe possesses notable skill in the mastery of photography. Another critic may view the same work through a descriptive lens and determine that the artist uses subject matter that some would consider offensive. Viewing the work of Mapplethorpe through an interpretative perspective, one might infer that he is communicating problems of society.

Parsons (1990) states a key question in this debate: "by whose standards are some interpretations to be judged less acceptable?" (p. 40). The answer to Parsons' question is suggested through the previous medical example. Like doctors, students come to art learning situations equipped with differing backgrounds, experiences, and understandings. Therefore, students may understand works of art differently. To gauge the nature and extensiveness of students' prior knowledge, learning outcomes in relation to art must be looked at with some flexibility.

LEARNING OUTCOMES

Efland (1990) points out that classical approaches to assessment in art education tend to focus on recall of vocabulary, definitions, and / or facts. Knowing to recall, define, and use specific vocabulary are examples of knowledge-seeking strategies that can result in lower-order learning outcomes. Recalled information, including definitions, often appears in a student's recitation of historical information and / or facts about an artwork. Lower-order outcomes can also be aligned with the learner's knowledge of formal qualities, subject matter (description), and expressive (interpretive) content of an artwork.

When students explore works of art for deeper understanding they engage a different set of knowledge-seeking strategies. For instance, when students apply search strategies involving analysis, comparisons, questions, judgments, interpretations, explanations, extensions and / or challenges of the ideas of authorities, higher-order learning outcomes can occur (Stavropoulos, 1992–93a, 1992–93b). Higher-order outcomes can also be associated with formal, descriptive, interpretive, and historical dimensions of the learner's knowledge-base.

The range of lower-order and higher-order outcomes within the formal, descriptive, interpretive, and historical dimensions of the learner's knowledge-base will be illustrated in the sections that follow.

Formal Dimension of the Learner's Knowledge-Base

Formal qualities of artworks can be identified and discussed in reference to all periods and movements in the history of art. Barrett (1990) describes *form* as an artwork's structure, arrangement, and organization of the composition, construction, and elements and principles of design (p. 24). Barrett's description of medium, the material from which the art object is made (p. 26), is also related to the formal dimension.

Susan Compton, an art historian specializing in 20th-century Russian art, writes extensively on Russian artist, Marc Chagall. In a text documenting the work and life of Marc Chagall, Compton (1985) provides an account of information within the formal dimension for each of the artworks he produced. In reference to *The Birthday,* the medium employed by Chagall, oil paint on cardboard, is identified by Compton. It is important for any art historian to identify media for the reader. However, if a student simply names the medium as oil painting or identifies *The Birthday* as a painting, based on recall of a teacher's lecture, such an outcome could be considered evidence of shallow knowledge-seeking strategies and low-road transfer. There are numerous other formal qualities a student could also note in *The Birthday,* as follows:

- compressed space
- strong diagonals
- multiple points of view
- defiance of normal proportion
- asymmetrical balance
- saturated hues

Knowledge that *The Birthday* is a painting is obvious, and it is based on the practice of looking at other paintings. When knowledge is the consequence of varied practice, (e.g., a great deal of experience looking at paintings), low-road transfer has occurred (Salomon, & Perkins, 1989).

Comparing *The Birthday* to a preparatory sketch, Compton (1985) provides further discussion of formal qualities:

> Whereas the drawing establishes the magical relationship of the hovering figures and indicates the detailed elements of the still-life on the table, the role of the table itself has become less important in the oil. For instead of being based purely on a triangle, the final composition depends on the balancing of the diagonals on the left by additions on the right, where the bed and shawl above it have been added. Likewise, the area above the table has been enlivened by a window. (p. 191)

Pointing to compositional devices employed by Chagall, Compton analyzes qualities within the formal dimension. This analysis of the underlying structure of *The Birthday* is mastered by looking closely at balanced diagonals defined by different images in the work. A student might arrive at a higher-order understanding of *The Birthday* by looking closely at its formal qualities. For example, a student might respond as follows:

> Red / orange draws attention to the floor area, while the color black is important in shading and defining images in the work.

In this example, the student has employed knowledge-seeking strategies to access relevant prior knowledge of the effects and functions of color. The student has then applied this knowledge to *The Birthday*. The student is able to describe the impact of color in *The Birthday* and its tendency to draw the viewer's attention. The student has also determined that the use of black functions in modeling images in the work. This is high-road transfer because the student expended "greater mental effort" in performing an analysis of the formal qualities in *The Birthday* based on the effects and function of color. This analysis was facilitated by a "closer examination" of the underlying effects of the elements of design (Perkins, & Salomon, 1987; Salomon, 1983; Salomon, & Perkins, 1989).

A close examination of the work does not guarantee a high-road transfer, however, as evidenced in the misunderstanding revealed in this student's statement about *The Birthday:*

> The colors Chagall selected to paint *The Birthday* represent the primary color scheme.

While there may be subtle traces of shades, tints or tones of primary colors, the overall color scheme of *The Birthday* is not based on this triadic group of colors. No particular color scheme can be discerned in *The Birthday,* only a brilliant vermilion dominates within a polychromatic family of colors. In this example, meaningful learning is impeded because the student has inaccurate knowledge of what constitutes a primary color scheme.

To assess levels of art understanding, instruments need to focus on the formal dimension of the learner's knowledge-base. The learner's formal knowledge-base might be verified in statements regarding the elements of art, organizational principles of design, surface characteristics, compositional devices, abstract, real and nonobjective qualities, technique, and materials.

Descriptive Dimension of the Learner's Knowledge-Base

In Compton's (1985) formal analysis of the composition of *The Birthday,* she also identifies figures, a still-life, table, bed, shawl, and window within the interior space. According to Barrett (1990), "descriptive statements are verifiable by observation and an appeal to factual evidence" (p. 12). Barrett explains that critics can obtain descriptive evidence by looking directly at what is seen in the work, that is, *internal description.* Barrett goes on to explain that "describing is a logical place to start when viewing an exhibition or a particular photograph because it is a means of gathering basic information upon which understanding is built" (pp. 12, 13). Compton's use of description is generally confined to the subject matter. However, Barrett states, "descriptive statements about subject matter identify and typify persons, objects, places, or events in a photograph. When describing subject matter, critics name what they see and also characterize it" (p. 17). The following is another historian's descriptive characterization:

> Chagall rented a room from a policeman, and that is what we see, faithfully reproduced: Bella's scarves hung up on the wall, the Ilitch church through the window (it also figured in *Over Vitebsk*), the *fortochka*, a small opening in the top of the window that is a typical feature of Russian houses, even the birthday cake on the table. (Makarius, 1988, p. 74)

A student may also describe subject matter of *The Birthday* as follows:

> This is a picture of a man and a woman in a room kissing.

In this description, the student identifies the subject matter in the painting, including a man, woman, and the room. The student also mentions the action of kissing. Describing familiar images and actions requires a shallow, recall-oriented knowledge-seeking strategy. This is an example of low-road transfer because the knowledge-seeking strategy employed by the student does not lead to the construction of new structures of understanding.

In the statement that follows, the student has also identified the subject matter and the act of kissing:

> There is a woman kissing a man who is suspended above her. She is also hovering above the ground. Perhaps it was the kiss that caused the couple to float.

Yet in this statement the student has searched for additional descriptive information. The search has prompted the student to provide a reason why the figures are shown floating. This statement is an example of high-road transfer because the student has made a controlled mental effort to explain the floating figures. The resulting higher-order understanding is supported by the scholarly literature on *The Birthday* which describes the painting in much the same way (Compton, 1985; Kamensky, 1989; Makarius, 1988; Sweeney, 1946; West, 1990).

Sometimes students make statements that are clearly contradictory to scholarly interpretations such as:

> It appears the woman is kissing a ghost since he is floating in the air.

The student uses descriptive language in identifying the male figure in *The Birthday* as a ghost. Actually, Marc Chagall is portrayed as a man, not a ghost. The student's statement reveals a misunderstanding based on the subject matter. In this case, informal knowledge that ghosts float has impaired potential learning. Perkins and Salomon (1987) might say this as an instance of negative transfer. The student employed knowledge-seeking strategies that caused irrelevant information to be applied from his or her knowledge-base.

Interpretive Dimension of the Learner's Knowledge-Base

According to Barrett (1990), "interpretation occurs whenever attention and discussion move beyond offering information to matters of meaning" (p. 34). There is fairly consistent agreement across the art history literature as to meanings of *The Birthday*. Note the interpretive similarities in the following statements spanning 39 years:

> In 1915 he [Chagall] had painted the first of what was to become a long series of paintings of lovers, each celebrating an anniversary of his marriage with Bella, her birthday, or his or their daughter, Ida's. (Sweeney, 1946, pp. 36, 37)
>
> Love as romantic transcendence is most popularly expressed in the work of Marc Chagall (born 1887), as in *The Birthday*, which is so much in the spirit of our notions of perpetual courtship: the exchange of gifts on anniversaries; the perpetuation of courtesies and gallantries practiced before marriage. The charm and popularity of Chagall are in good measure traceable to our belief that the substance of love consists of just such rituals as the one celebrated in *The Birthday*. (Feldman, 1967, p. 24)
>
> … this celebration by the lovers is equally fantastic, for their joy has levitated them from the ground. (Compton, 1985, p. 15)
>
> *The Birthday* celebrates Chagall's reunion with Bella, whom he married in Vitebsk on 25 July 1915. It is the first of the famous motif of lovers floating in the air—to which Chagall would return again and again. This highly improbable stance adopted by the figures illustrates, both literally and metaphorically, the transports of love, but the interior is teeming with realistic detail. (Makarius, 1988, p. 74)

Each statement suggests *The Birthday* is about the ritual of a birthday. Each statement interprets the subjects as lovers. Since the theme of couples is easy for young people to relate to, it would not be unusual for a student to arrive at an accurate interpretation of *The Birthday* as follows:

> The couple shown kissing in the picture are truly head over heels in love … floating on air.

The student has closely examined the physical positioning of the figures in *The Birthday*. This knowledge-seeking strategy has facilitated access to relevant prior knowledge. First, the man and the woman are kissing and the student knows to classify them as a couple. Second, the student determines that the couple must be in love because they are represented as floating in air. Finally, the student associates the couple's incredible stance as reflecting two people that are "head over heels in love." High-road transfer is reflected in this statement because the student has constructed several new structures of understanding about the painting.

Sometimes ideas are not interrelated and result in lower-order understanding of *The Birthday* as follows:

> The painting transmits a joyous, happy mood.

In this case, the student uses obvious adjectives to refer to the work of art. While the painting does transmit a joyous and happy mood, the student has not given any reasons to support that interpretation. This statement is an example of low-road transfer because a quick summation about mood is usually arrived at "intuitively and automatically" (Perkins, & Salomon, 1987).

When a student attempts to interpret meanings of *The Birthday*, it is possible to form a misunderstanding of the work as follows:

> The work has a violent theme, a young couple in troubled times do not know how to release their aggression, so they take it out on each other.

The student has employed appropriate and useful knowledge-seeking strategies; however, the interpretation of a "violent theme" is diametrically opposed to the prevalent interpretation of the painting. The student has misinterpreted the painting by drawing upon incongruent information from his or her knowledge-base. Perkins and Salomon (1987) might also call this a negative transfer.

Historical Dimension of the Learner's Knowledge-Base

Historical knowledge might include factual information such as the name of the artist; personal data, such as age, sex, race; title and / or date of the work; historical period / movement; and information regarding where the artist lived and worked. Many sources on Chagall verify factual information of that nature (Arnason, 1976; Compton, 1985; de la Croix, & Tansey, 1980). It is necessary for historians to provide dates, titles, and information about artists, and these facts can also be useful in the classroom. However, when a student merely recites historical facts about a work of art, a lower-order understanding is the result. In responding to *The Birthday*, a student may recall factual information as follows:

> The painting is called *The Birthday*. It was painted by the artist Marc Chagall in 1915–1923.

The student has given the title of the work of art, the artist name, and the date the work was created. Yet the student has not used this factual information to learn anything new—even though the title gives a strong clue as to the meanings of the work. Ineffective knowledge-seeking strategies used to access memorized information from the knowledge-base prevent the construction of new structures of understanding in this example.

However, facts in the learner's knowledge-base can be useful in the construction of new understandings, as shown in the following example:

> The woman in *The Birthday* looks a lot like the woman depicted in a portrait called *Bella with a White Collar,* also by Marc Chagall. Chagall used the same woman as a model for other paintings. Bella is probably his wife.

In this example, the student has employed knowledge-seeking strategies to access relevant factual knowledge about another work by Chagall. Art historians explain that Chagall is well known for the series of paintings depicting his love for his wife, Bella. The student has expended "greater mental effort" to recall another one of these works by name. This is an example of high-road transfer because the "closer examination" resulted in construction of new structures of understanding. The comparison of the two works stimulated the student to correctly hypothesize an underlying theme present in many of Chagall's artworks.

Using knowledge-seeking strategies to access information regarding other works of art does not guarantee a higher-order understanding of *The Birthday* as shown in the following example:

> Salvador Dali, the surrealist, has done many paintings that show human figures and other objects suspended in space: *The Madonna of Port Lligat, The Disintegration of the Persistence of Memory,* and *The Sacrament of the Last Supper,* to name a few. Since figures are suspended above the ground in *The Birthday*, this work by Chagall must be an example of Surrealism.

While mental energy is expended in making an interesting association between Dali and Chagall, the conclusion reached in this example is a reflection of misunderstanding. This misunderstanding might be due to a limited frame of reference (Confrey, 1987, p. 97). The Surrealists' concern with the "omnipotence of the unconscious mind" (Preble, & Preble, 1985, p. 378) was not considered in the statement. While aspects of Chagall's work are irrational, the unconscious is not a characteristic associated with *The Birthday*. Thus, the original misunderstanding has been compounded because of the attempt to compartmentalize the work of Chagall into one particular movement or style (Feltovich, et al., 1988; Perkins, & Simmons, 1988). When students learn about the history of art, they commonly associate artists with a particular period, movement, or style. There is not always consistent agreement in the art history literature on the stylistic categorization of Chagall's paintings. For example, in specifying stylistic influences on Chagall's work, Arnason (1976) discusses Chagall as follows:

> From his background he acquired a wonderful repertoire of Russian-Jewish folk tales and a deep and sentimental attachment to the Jewish religion and traditions. There was also inbred in him a fairytale sense of fantasy. Out of these elements emerged his personal and poetic painting.... In Paris, Chagall entered the orbit of Apollinaire and the leaders of the new Cubism, as well as that of Modigliani, Soutine, and Jules Pascin. Chagall's Russian paintings had largely been intimate genre scenes, often brightened by elements of Russian or Jewish folklore. Bakst's school caused him to make bold efforts using fauve colors and constricted space. His intoxication with Paris opened a floodgate of experiments in fauve color and cubist space, and above all of subjects filled with lyric fantasy. Within two years of his arrival, Chagall was producing mature and weirdly poetic paintings. (p. 282)

The literature offers several viewpoints as to the historical period in which Chagall's work best fits. According to de la Croix and Tansey (1980), Chagall "accepted many aspects of the most sophisticated theories and practices of the times— Expressionism, Cubism, Fauvist color" (p. 832).

Assessing Learning Outcomes

Verbal responses to works of art can provide evidence of learning outcomes within the formal, descriptive, interpretive, and historical dimensions of the learner's knowledge-base. These learning outcomes reflect a variety of knowledge-seeking strategies that can account for degrees of lower-order and higher-order understandings. Therefore, the development of alternative methods for assessing student understanding might focus on profiling the range of these learning outcomes.

AN ALTERNATIVE ASSESSMENT METHODOLOGY

The quality of assessment instruments used in education is critical because teachers, researchers, and evaluators come to conclusions and base important decisions on the results produced by such instruments (Fraenkel, & Wallen, 1990, p. 126). Current conceptions of learning discussed in this chapter form a theoretical framework upon which an assessment instrument for art education can be grounded. The theoretical framework of learning suggests that categories within an alternative assessment instrument might: (a) represent students' knowledge-base and knowledge-seeking strategies, and the process of transfer; (b) encompass terminology reflective of the field of art education; (c) be responsive to the educator with a background in the arts; and (d) be diagnostic in discriminating among lower-order and higher-order understandings, and misunderstandings.

Development of Categories

The research by Koroscik et al. (1992) motivated the development of an alternative assessment methodology that profiles lower-order and higher-order understandings, and misunderstandings of artworks. Results of study indicate that student understanding can be facilitated by presenting artworks within comparative contexts. Understanding is further facilitated when verbal cues are provided. Through an analysis of qualitative data, the research team found evidence to support the independent functioning of a student's knowledge-base and knowledge-seeking strategies. These findings indicate that a diagnostic assessment of art learning must encompass both facets of learning.

Further analysis of written statements from the Koroscik et al. (1992) study (also known as the Chagall Study) reveals a continuum of learning outcomes. These learning outcomes occur within the formal, descriptive, interpretive, and historical dimensions of art understanding. By adopting Guba's (1978) naturalistic inquiry methodology (also in Patton, 1990), written statements can be reduced and organized into diagnostic categories within the formal, descriptive, interpretive, and historical dimensions of art understanding.

According to Guba (1978), developing category systems first requires overcoming the problems of convergence and divergence. The first problem, *convergence,* arises "because the naturalistic inquirer must derive a set of units or categories within which he will classify and interpret observed outputs" (p. 50). Initially, when sorting data into categories, the researcher might ask: "do the same kinds of observations or comments recur at different times, from different informants or documents, in somewhat different contexts?" (p. 53).

In developing the diagnostic categories, convergence is addressed by seeking out these "recurring regularities." The rules of internal homogeneity and external heterogeneity are applied as recurring regularities were identified. *Internal*

homogeneity refers to the extent to which the data hold together in a meaningful way (Guba, 1978, p. 53). *External homogeneity* refers to the extent to which the categories differ from one another, that is, the difference should be "bold and clear" (p. 53).

The problem of *divergence,* as identified by Guba (1978), involves "the 'fleshing out' of categories with whatever additional information is required for completeness and thoroughness" (p. 49). A three-step process assisted the development of categories: extension, bridging, and surfacing. First, *extension* was employed by building on items of information already known. In the case of the Chagall Study (Koroscik, et al., 1992), student responses had already been identified as formal, descriptive, or interpretive in nature. These dimensions served as bases for more detailed categories. According to Guba, the evaluator "uses these items as bases for other questions or as guides in his examination of documents. Amoeba-like, he inches his way from the known to the unknown" (p. 70).

The second step in devising categories involved *bridging,* that is, making connections among different items. According to Guba (1978):

the inquirer begins with several known, but apparently disconnected, items of information. The term "disconnected" simply means that their relationships are not understood. That there are relationships is a premise of high probability because the items have been placed into the same category. The evaluator now uses these two points of reference for further inquiry in an effort to identify the connections and understand them. (p. 59)

Categories derived from the Koroscik et al. (1992) qualitative data, and sample statements representing each category facilitate the bridging process. First, the relationship of categories within the formal, descriptive, interpretive, and historical dimensions is studied for its connectedness. Also, the relationship of written statements representing individual categories is studied for its connectedness. Once the connections are identified, the third step of surfacing is carried out. According to Guba (1978) *surfacing* involves proposing and verifying new categories or information that should fit into the evaluation system (p. 59). The procedure of surfacing validates the appropriateness of examining supplemental data for "information that ought to be found in the field and then verifying its existence" (p. 59). A broad range of data is gathered from student populations representing a range of ages and abilities. These diverse and varied data sources aid in the expansion, refinement, and applicability of the diagnostic categories.

Koroscik's (1992–93) art learning model also qualifies as a surfacing directive. Grounded in cognitive learning theory, Koroscik's model represents facets that can be assessed in art education, including knowledge-base and knowledge-seeking strategies. Learning outcomes reflective of this model are easily identified in the Koroscik et al. (1992) data, and they mesh with categories previously established through extension and bridging. Therefore, the overall structural format for the Diagnostic Profile of art understandings is tied directly to Koroscik's art learning model.

Through extension, bridging, and surfacing, each learning outcome conveyed by students within the formal, descriptive, interpretive, and historical dimensions has been translated into a diagnostic category. Further, diagnostic categories within the formal, descriptive, interpretive, and historical dimensions have been characterized as lower-order and higher-order understandings, and misunderstandings (Stavropoulos, 1992, 1992–93a).

THE DIAGNOSTIC PROFILE

Grounded in current conceptions of learning, an alternative assessment methodology, referred to as the *Diagnostic Profile,* was developed from the categories. The Diagnostic Profile encompasses terminology reflective of the field of art education, and is responsive to the educator with a background in the arts. Categories within the Diagnostic Profile represent the application of the student's knowledge-base and knowledge-seeking strategies through the process of transfer. Further, this assessment instrument is diagnostic in its ability to discriminate between lower-order and higher-order understandings, and misunderstandings.

The Diagnostic Profile assesses student understandings from written and / or transcribed verbal statements about works of art. Written statements can be stimulated by a range of art reproductions, slides of artworks, actual works of art in museums or galleries, and the students' own artwork.

The Four Dimensions of the Diagnostic Profile

The Diagnostic Profile comprises four dimensions: formal, descriptive, interpretive, and historical. Each dimension contains a series of categories describing student learning outcomes (see Appendix A). All the dimensions within the Diagnostic Profile can be used for a complete analysis. However, a teacher may wish to employ selected dimensions in the analysis of written statements.

Formal dimension. Categories within the formal dimension represent a range of learning outcomes related to the formal qualities of artworks: elements of design (e.g., line, shape, color, texture); organizational principles of design (e.g., repetition, variation, transition, balance, unity); technical processes or media (e.g., impasto, printmaking, drawing, ink); and art styles (e.g., abstract, nonobjective, realistic).

Descriptive dimension. Descriptive dimension categories include learning outcomes related to the subject matter of artworks: objects or figures (e.g., images, symbols); artforms (e.g., landscape, still-life); and activities or actions.

Interpretive dimension. The categories within the interpretive dimension provide a broad spectrum of learning outcomes related to: expressive qualities of artworks; personal meaning and interpretations; and interpretive perspectives.

Historical dimension. The learning outcomes within the historical dimension categories focus on: personal data about the artist (e.g., name, race, birthplace); historical data about the work (e.g., title, date); classifications (e.g., Impressionism, Surrealism); stories, inspirations, mythology regarding the artwork; purpose, function, use of the artwork; and significance.

Identifying Scoring Units

Single words, clauses, sentences, phrases, and / or paragraphs can be used as units of analysis within students' written statements about works of art. As individual scoring units are identified, they are characterized as lower-order understandings, higher-order understandings, and / or misunderstandings.

A scoring unit can be a word, or a group of words in a clause or phrase, that may or may not comprise a whole sentence. A scoring unit can have one or more of the following in various combinations: subject noun, object noun, verb, adjective. Each of the following phrases equal a single scoring units:

- *a dog and a cat* (subject noun + subject noun)
- *a dog was running* (subject noun + verb)
- *the dog was running after a cat* (subject noun + verb + object noun)
- *the black dog was running after a white cat* (adjective + subject noun + verb + adjective + object noun)

Sometimes there are multiple scoring units in one sentence. Usually, these compound sentences are separated by coordinating conjunctions (e.g., then, and, but, or, however) or by punctuation (e.g., a dash, comma). Examples of compound sentences equal to two scoring units are shown below:

- *a dog is running after a cat* while the *pet owner watches* (subject noun + verb + object noun) [conjunction] (subject noun + verb)
- *a dog and a cat are in the background,* and *a hamster is in the forearound* (subject noun + subject noun + object noun) [conjunction] (subject noun + object noun)
- *a dog and a cat are playing with a ball while the children watch* (subject noun + subject noun + verb + object noun) [conjunction] (subject noun + verb)

Scoring units: Lower-order understandings. Each single word, clause, or sentence can be used as a unit of analysis for lower-order outcomes. For instance, a student can arrive at a lower-order understanding of *The Birthday* by simply identifying and / or describing an image as follows:

- man in the air

This statement is the equivalent of one scoring unit. The student recognizes a "man," and his placement, as "in the air." Simply recognizing an image, and it's location in the picture plane constitutes a lower-order understanding.

Scoring units: Higher-order understandings. Clauses, phrases, sentences, and / or paragraphs can be used as units of analysis for higher-order outcomes. Often, parts of higher-order units have been previously scored according to their lower-order content. For this reason, scoring for higher-order understanding is essentially a second screening or double-coding of a statement. For example, in the following statement, the student performs a higher-order formal analysis of *The Birthday* based on the elements of design:

• red / orange draws attention, black is important as a shading / defining color

In this example, the student has employed knowledge-seeking strategies to access relevant prior knowledge of the effects and functions of color. It is important to note that this analysis cannot be performed without the lower-order outcome of identification of color. Therefore, lower-order outcomes are analyzed separately from higher-order-outcomes.

Scoring units: Misunderstandings. Sometimes students misunderstand a work of art. Instances of misunderstandings are reflected in responses that contain incorrect information and / or conclusions. Students can arrive at misunderstandings with or without providing a supportive explanation for their response. For example, in the following statement the student has misunderstood *The Birthday*:

• the people are unhappy

The people in *The Birthday* are happily in love; therefore, this statement is contrary to the scholarly interpretations of the work. To arrive at this misunderstanding, the student renders the lower-order description of "people," and then applies lower-order interpretive language to characterize the people as "unhappy." If the student can provide reasons, explanation, and / or arguments to support the "unhappy people" point of view, such strategies applied in misunderstanding *The Birthday* would be considered higher-order.

Color Codings

Units within the written statement are first distinguished according to formal, descriptive, interpretive, or historical dimensions. It is also helpful to note the misunderstandings in this initial screening. This step is expedited by consistently color coding each unit with a transparent marker as:

• formal dimension—yellow
• descriptive dimension—orange
• interpretive dimension—pink
• historical dimension—green
• misunderstanding—double code with dimension color and blue

The process of color coding student responses is accomplished by studying one scoring unit at a time. For instance, the scoring unit, "there is contrast between black and white,"

is coded with a yellow marker because the student is referring to formal qualities. The scoring unit, "a dog is running," is coded with the orange marker because the student is describing subject manner. The scoring unit, "this gives me a happy feeling," is coded with a pink marker because the student is using interpretive language. The scoring unit, "Marc Chagall," is coded with a green marker because the student is giving historical information in reference to the artist's name.

The same color coding system is used to screen higher-order outcomes. When scoring lengthy statements, drawing a circle, or using a bracket to indicate the location of the higher-order outcome is clearer.

If a student incorrectly states that the artist is "Vincent Van Gogh," the statement would be double-coded green for the historical information and blue for the misunderstanding. If a student states, "the people in *The Birthday* are unhappy," the word "people" is coded orange, "unhappy" is coded pink, and " *The Birthday*" is coded green. In addition, since the student misunderstood the interpretive dimension of the work, the statement would also be double-coded with blue.

Assigning Category Codes with the Diagnostic Profile

After each unit has been color coded, the rater analyzes one dimension of the written statement at a time. The units of one particular color are analyzed according to the categories within the dimensions of the Diagnostic Profile.

The rater writes the category code next to each unit in the written statement. Lower-order outcomes can be revealed by the use of a single word, sentence, or phrase. Higher-order outcomes can be revealed by a phrase, sentence, and / or paragraph. The supportive responses (see Appendix B) are useful as standard examples that meet the criteria of particular categories.

Within each dimension (e.g., formal, descriptive, interpretive, historical) categories are coded with a letter. The letters stand for the particular dimension in the Diagnostic Profile:

"F" = Formal Dimension
"D" = Descriptive Dimension
"I" = Interpretive Dimension
"H" = Historical Dimension

Besides the letter code indicating the particular dimension in the Diagnostic Profile, a numerical code also appears next to each category. Categories that have numerical codes 0" through "4" are representative of lower-order outcomes. Categories with numerical codes "5" and higher are considered higher-order outcomes. Categories identified with negative numbers "–1" through "–3" delineate misunderstandings.

Both the letter and the corresponding number are combined to represent each of 60 categories within the Diagnostic Profile. For example, the category code "F2" illustrates a lower-order outcome in the formal dimension; the category code "D5" is considered a higher-order outcome within the descriptive dimension; and the category code "I10" is representative of a higher-order outcome within the interpretive dimension.

Tally of Scores

A matrix can be constructed to tally the outcomes, as shown in Figure 20–1 below:

	F	D	I	H
Lower-order				
Higher-order				
Misunder-standing				
Total				

FIGURE 20–1 Diagnostic profile assessment tally sheet.

To record outcomes of a single student or an entire class, list each outcome on the appropriate line (lower-order understanding, higher-order understanding, or misunderstanding). As outcomes are recorded they should be placed under the appropriate dimension column.

Diagnosis: A Sample Scored Statement

The sample scored statement shown in Figure 20–2 has been stimulated by a series of related artworks. A key artwork, *The Birthday,* is placed within a context of other works of art inspired by the artist Marc Chagall, as follows:

- *Chagall,* a dance choreography by Ginette Laurin, 1988
- *To Marc Chagall,* a poem by Paul Eluard, 1911–1915
- *And Came the Dog and Ate the Cat,* a lithograph by El Lissitzky, 1919

In the scholarly literature on *The Birthday,* experts agree that certain characteristics are significant. These characteristics can be organized according to the dimensions of the Diagnostic Profile, as follows:

- Formal   = juxtaposition, abnormal anatomical proportion
- Descriptive = floating, suspended figures
- Interpretive = lovers, relationship, romance
- Historical = Fauvist, Surrealist, Expressionist influence

Such a literature review on the key artwork, *The Birthday,* provides a baseline to judge students' statements about the artwork. If a student arrives at one or more of these understandings of *The Birthday,* they would receive a score that represents an agreement with the literature review in each dimension (category codes "F8," "D6," "I9" and / or "H9") as constructed in Figure 20–2:

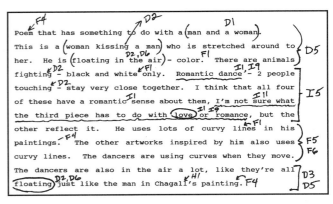

FIGURE 20–2 Sample scored statement.

Each of 27 items scored in the previous statement have been tallied as shown in Figure 20–3:

	F	D	I	H	Total
Lower-order	1,1,1,4,4,4	1,2,2,2,2,2,3	1,1,1	1	17
Higher-order	5,6	5,5,6,6	5,9,9,11		10
Misunder-standing					
Total	8	11	7	1	27

FIGURE 20–3 Tally of diagnostic profile scores.

Graphic Displays of Data

With simple computations based on the 27 items scored with the Diagnostic Profile (shown in Figure 20–3 above), the teacher can reach both qualitative and quantitative assessments of the student's knowledge-base and employment of knowledge-seeking strategies, discussed in the following sections.

Column graph. By constructing a simple column graph, the number of outcomes scored in the various dimensions can be quantified. Frequency of these responses with the formal, descriptive, interpretive, and historical dimensions of the Diagnostic Profile are organized into a column graph (Figure 20–4). The column graph can display visual evidence

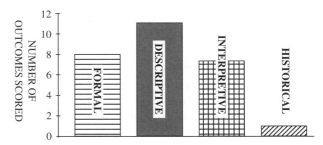

FIGURE 20–4 Knowledge-seeking assessment column graph: Frequency of responses within the formal, descriptive, interpretive, and historical dimensions of the diagnostic profile.

of the student's concentration of search strategies in one dimension over another.

Pie chart. The pie chart shown in Figure 20–5 is similar in purpose to the column graph above. Like the column graph, the pie chart provides visual evidence of the student's concentration of search strategies in one dimension over another. However, the actual percentage of responses within the various dimensions of the Diagnostic Profile has been added to the pie chart. In the graphic depiction, the learner's knowledge-seeking strategies within the formal descriptive, interpretive, and historical dimensions of understanding are displayed.

Analysis of the pie chart provides specific quantitative information about the learner's response. Figure 20–5 illustrates that 29.63% of the student's knowledge-seeking strategies occur in the formal dimension, 40.74% are located within the descriptive dimension, 25.93% are found in the interpretive dimension, and only 3.70% are concentrated in the historical dimension.

Histogram. The extent of formal, descriptive, interpretive, and historical understanding can also be plotted from the tally sheet of diagnostic scores. A frequency distribution of individual scores can be depicted graphically to illustrate the degree of cognitive complexity reflected in the written statement. Based on the frequency of response (vertical axis), and the scores received in individual diagnostic categories within each dimension (horizontal axis), a histogram can be constructed, as shown in Figure 20–6.

The histogram in Figure 20–6 provides a more detailed visual account of the learning outcomes in the various dimensions. A diagnostic account of these learning outcomes can be extracted directly from the language used in the categories of the Diagnostic Profile. In the case of the sample statement, the student has concentrated knowledge-seeking strategies in the descriptive dimension, explaining the activities and actions taking place in the artworks. However, the histogram reveals that the student has also employed knowledge-seeking strategies involving the construction of a question pertaining to the meaning of the artworks (category

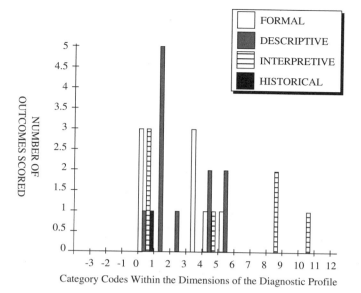

FIGURE 20–6 Degree of cognitive complexity histogram: Extent of formal, descriptive, interpretive, and historical understandings.

code "I11"). As a result of this knowledge-seeking strategy, the student has arrived at an interpretive understanding of the artworks reflective of the scholarly literature on the works of art (category code "I9").

Bar graph. Based on the tally of scores (Figure 20–3), the presence of lower-order and higher-order understandings also can be displayed in a bar graph. As shown in Figure 20–7, the bar graph makes diagnostic discriminations between learning outcomes reflective of lower-order and higher-order understandings. In addition, these learning outcomes have been isolated within each dimension of the student's knowledge-base (i.e., formal, descriptive, interpretive, and historical).

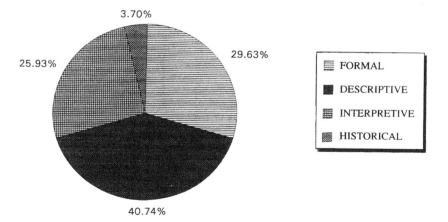

FIGURE 20–5 Knowledge-seeking assessment pie chart: Percentage of responses within the formal, descriptive, interpretive, and historical dimensions of the diagnostic profile.

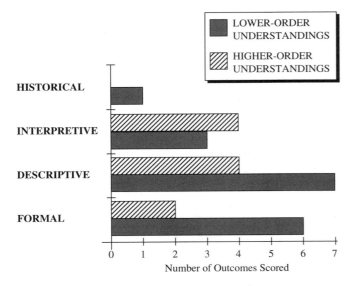

FIGURE 20–7 Diagnostic assessment bar graph: Lower-order and higher-order understandings within the formal, descriptive, interpretive, and historical dimensions of the diagnostic profile.

ESTABLISHING THE QUALITY OF THE DIAGNOSTIC PROFILE

The quality of the Diagnostic Profile assessment was ascertained through traditional test and measurement procedures. These procedures are of two basic types: studies of validity, and studies of reliability. Generally, validity refers to the extent to which the instrument provides an accurate picture of the phenomena examined; and reliability refers to the extent to which the measurement procedure yields the same answer and whenever it is used (Kirk, & Miller, 1990). Validity and reliability studies enhance the likelihood that appropriate inferences will be drawn from data the instrument provide (American Psychological Association, 1985; Fraenkel, & Wallen, 1990; Krathwohl, 1988; Leedy, 1989; Messick, 1989). Overall, these validity and reliability procedures apply equally well to qualitative and quantitative data (Kirk, & Miller, 1990, p. 19). However, in selected instances the procedures have been redefined "to fit the realities of qualitative research, and the complexities of social phenomena" (Strauss, & Corbin, 1990, p. 249, 250).

Validity of the Diagnostic Profile has been estimated by two content validity studies, two criterion-related studies, and a construct validity study. Reliability of the Diagnostic Profile has been estimated by inter-rater and intra-rater reliability studies. Results of these studies are summarized in the following sections.

Content Validity

Two experts served as independent judges for content validity studies. One of the independent judges is an art educator who specializes in evaluation in art education. The expertise of the second independent judge is in the application of non-Western art history to art education. Each of these two independent judges assessed the content of the Diagnostic Profile. A summary of the results of the analyses performed by the independent judges follows.

Importance and appropriateness of content. Judgments were rendered on the importance and appropriateness of categories in assessing art understandings. With a few minor exceptions, the diagnostic categories were considered important and appropriate.

Practicality. The complexity of the analysis performed by the Diagnostic Profile justifies its length, according to an independent judge. In addition, this judge responded positively to the procedural and administrative aspects of the Diagnostic Profile. She found the training procedures to be reasonable, and the methods of coding and reporting data were judged to be clear and concise.

Applicability to artforms. The independent judge with the art history specialization was asked to rate the diagnostic categories in terms of their applicability to a variety of artforms. Since the categories were originally derived from Western art, the results provided by the independent judge are encouraging. She verified that 98% of the categories could apply to Western art and fine art, and that 90% be used for non-Western art. In addition, the Diagnostic Profile is highly rated for its applicability to popular arts, folk art, crafts, antiques and heirlooms, and cultural artifacts.

Applicability to data. Both judges indicate that a diagnostic assessment can be applied to a variety of data. These might include written statements about a single work of art or multiple works of art, written statements that have been verbally cued, and oral statements that have been transcribed.

Diagnostic capabilities. The independent judges agree that the Diagnostic Profile could be used to determine formal, descriptive, interpretive, and historical understandings of art. The experts also indicate that the Diagnostic Profile could be used to assess understandings of students in kindergarten through grade 12. Furthermore, the Diagnostic Profile can be used to assess the understandings of undergraduate and graduate students.

Future implications. The Diagnostic Profile is judged to be clear "conceptually and in its application." An independent judge states the instrument and the theoretical model are "well-conceived." There is also support for using the Diagnostic Profile in art education research, program assessment, teacher assessment, student assessment, student self-assessment, and curriculum development. In conclusion, one independent judge states, "I find the implications for teacher training and on-going self evaluation (by the teacher) to be extremely intriguing."

Criterion-Related Validity

Two criterion-related studies were conducted with a 3rd / 4th-grade art class and an 8th-grade art class (Stavropoulos,

1992–93b). The focus of these studies was on the relationship between an external criterion and the Diagnostic Profile findings. The principal investigator observed 3rd / 4thgrade and 8th-grade students and the instruction they received over a period of several weeks. A summary of these observations serves as an external criterion.

Data in the form of written statements were gathered from students at the end of the observational periods. The written statements were then scored with the Diagnostic Profile. The degree of criterion-related evidence of validity was reflected in how well the external criterion predicted student performance as assessed with the Diagnostic Profile.

3rd / 4th-grade class. Student writing samples were expected to be heavily influenced by the art teacher's instruction. During the 6-week observational and instructional period, students participated in the following activities:

- *lecture format*—students viewed slides in a dark room as the teacher read a script
- *questioning*—students were asked to recite historical facts about an artist and his artwork
- *reinforced vocabulary terms*—students repeatedly identified various art terms

Results of this study demonstrate an extremely strong relationship between the external criterion and the assessment of the 3rd / 4th-grade students' written statements. This criterion-related evidence of validity offers verification regarding the Diagnostic Profile's ability to discriminate lower-order understandings (see Stavropoulos, 1992–93b).

8th-grade class. Observations of the 8th-grade class revealed that students received instruction that encouraged higher-order thinking skills such as:

- *research*—students searched through classroom resources to learn about works of art
- *"put it in writing"*—students found the words to express their ideas in a cohesive written format
- *constructing arguments*—students were required to defend their stance with reasons
- *criticism*—students described, analyzed, interpreted, and judged works of art
- *aesthetic inquiry*—students considered social and cultural issues in the selection of artworks for a museum

The teacher's implementation of these instructional strategies encouraged students to become active participants in their own learning. As predicted, higher-order thinking skills were exhibited by the vast majority of students in the 8th-grade class.

Results of this study demonstrate a strong relationship between the external criterion and the assessment of the 8th-grade students' written statements with the Diagnostic Profile. This criterion-related evidence of validity provides convincing evidence of the Diagnostic Profile's effectiveness in discriminating higher-order understandings (see Stavropoulos. 1992–1993b).

Construct Validity Study

The objective of the construct validity study was to determine whether constructs in the Diagnostic Profile could be supported with a comprehensive data base. Results indicate that all categories within the Diagnostic Profile could be supported by responses from the data base (see Appendix B). A strong relationship was found between the data and the constructs in the Diagnostic Profile. Consequently, the Diagnostic Profile discriminated lower-order understandings from higher-order understandings, and identified misunderstandings.

According to Fraenkel and Wallen (1990) construct validity involves a variety of procedures that include evidence of content validity and criterion-related validity (p. 133). Therefore, construct validity of the Diagnostic Profile was further amplified by the favorable results of the content validity and the criterion-related validity studies previously discussed.

Rater Reliability

Reliability tests of the Diagnostic Profile focus on inter-rater and intra-rater consistency.

Participants. The principal investigator, an expert at using the Diagnostic Profile, served as the criterion rater. Since written statements about works of art are generated in art classrooms, it made sense for art teachers to serve as raters. Since the teachers in the study were to provide information to assist in the refinement of the Diagnostic Profile, they were selected on the basis of their commitment to assessment in art education. Both teachers had embarked on graduate work, and they were compensated $300 for participating in the rater-reliability studies. Therefore, the teachers had a stake in the results.

Data base. The Diagnostic Profile can be used to assess written or transcribed verbal statements about works of art. Since people respond in many different ways to works of art, a comprehensive data base of written and transcribed verbal statements was gathered for the studies. The data base reflects variance in several areas: size of class, age, sex, ethnicity, grade level, economic standard, cultural background, and academic abilities.

Inter-Rater Consistency

The focus of the inter-rater reliability study was on how consistently three different raters assign scores to written statements using the Diagnostic Profile. The teachers learned how to use the Diagnostic Profile during several practice sessions.

Findings. Calculation of average reliability between pairs of raters was based on 109 checks. In the three comparisons, average reliabilities verified a "very strong association" in the assignment of scores as follows:

- 0.97—teacher A and teacher B
- 0.96—teacher A and the criterion rater

• 0.98—teacher B and the criterion rater

Several factors should be considered when interpreting the strong association between the raters' scores: (a) the teachers had an unusually high commitment level, (b) the teachers were financially compensated, and (c) the teachers received intensive practice sessions. Under normal circumstances, reliability would be expected to be somewhat lower. However, this study presents convincing evidence that with a reasonable amount of training art teachers can be taught to reliably score written responses with the Diagnostic Profile.

Intra-Rater Consistency

The intra-rater consistency study involved the comparison of scores assigned to identical written statements at different points in time. Four weeks elapsed between the two scoring periods, and no practice sessions were held for the intra-rater study.

Findings. The average reliability between time one and time two (i.e., four weeks later) was based on 42 checks. A "very strong association" was indicated between the scores as follows:

• 0.86—teacher A
• 0.88—teacher B
• 0.98—criterion rater (e.g., principal investigator)

Although there was a noted decline in the abilities of the teachers to apply the Diagnostic Profile, the retention rate held strong even after a 4-week interval.

The data suggest that the intervening time (4-weeks), does not adversely affect an art teacher's ability to reliably score written responses to art using the Diagnostic Profile. As the inter-rater and intra-rater studies involved the same participants and some of the same data, the limitations discussed in the inter-rater study apply to the findings of this study.

EDUCATIONAL IMPORTANCE OF FUTURE APPLICATIONS OF THE DIAGNOSTIC PROFILE

The Diagnostic Profile has the potential to assess understandings of students in kindergarten through grade 12. In addition, the Diagnostic Profile is also judged to be useful in assessing the understandings of college undergraduates and graduate students (Stavropoulos, 1992). Through both small and large scale research studies, assessment provided with the use of the Diagnostic Profile can demonstrate the effectiveness of teaching and learning. Therefore, the importance of the research contained in this chapter lies in future applications of the Diagnostic Profile assessment methodology.

Research on Art Education Programs

The Diagnostic Profile provides a means of assessing alternative art education programs, such as discipline-based art education (DBAE). In a recent report submitted to the Getty Center for Education in the Arts, the Diagnostic Profile was reviewed:

> The project team is very excited about the analytic scoring system [Diagnostic Profile] because it allows the team to assess constructs such as problem solving, higher-order thinking, and other sophisticated constructs that cannot be assessed using holistic scoring. It provides a mechanism to probe the viability of the theoretical framework.... The potential of this system to document the impact of DBAE based instruction far exceeds anything that is currently available (Getty Center for Education in the Arts, 1991, pp. 21–22)

DBAE programs have been assessed with the Diagnostic Profile. For example, one quasi-experimental study focuses on the effects of a DBAE program on elementary students' written statements about artworks (French, 1992; Stavropoulos, 1994). Three intact 4th-grade classrooms received either a writing intensive approach to DBAE, a nonwriting approach to DBAE, or a traditional studio-based approach to art education throughout the school year. Long-term effects of these art curricula on 4th-grade students' ability to engage in higher-order thinking skills was determined by a qualitative analysis of pretest and posttest data with the Diagnostic Profile. According to the Diagnostic Profile analysis, both the nonwriting DBAE approach and the DBAE writing intensive approach had a notable impact on student ability to write about the art stimuli. However, the writing intensive approach to DBAE influenced students' ability to effectively discuss and understand a work of art most significantly. Further, the Diagnostic Profile was found to be extremely applicable and instrumental in making such discriminations.

Curriculum

Potential learning outcomes are reflected in categories of the Diagnostic Profile. These learning outcomes correspond to a novice-to-expert continuum and provide a hierarchical framework of art learning. The Diagnostic Profile can therefore serve as a curriculum scheme from which to design and guide instruction.

Research on Teachers

The Diagnostic Profile might also be used in research on teachers. For example, an independent judge suggests exploring teachers' attitudes toward using the Diagnostic Profile by asking:

> How does the ability to generate supportive evidence of student learning outcomes with the Diagnostic Profile heighten teacher confidence and morale, sense of accomplishment, and self esteem? Will using the Diagnostic Profile prompt ownership of the instrument?

Another study might be conducted to examine differences in how teachers interpret curricula. This research direction builds upon the two criterion-related validity studies performed on the Diagnostic Profile. Both the 3rd/4th-grade teacher and the 8th-grade art teachers teach concepts of discipline-based art education; however, the art teachers sharply contrast in how they operationalize discipline-based art education (Stavropoulos, 1992, 1992–93b). While it is clear that the two art teachers are dissimilar in their background qualifications and in the educational levels they teach, fluctuation in meeting discipline-based curricular objectives may be attributed to other variables. The Diagnostic Profile might be useful in isolating these variables.

Self-Assessment

The Diagnostic Profile might also be used to assess student understandings of artworks. It seems most appropriate to develop a form of the instrument for students to use in self-assessments. This feedback might help students grasp more fully aspects of their own educational progress.

Large-Scale Studies

The Diagnostic Profile enables random sampling from large populations. Results provided by large-scale studies can assist in designing more effective curricula, demonstrate to parents that art programs make a difference, and assist in advocacy efforts by providing comparative data. Such efforts might help secure funding for future research in art education and assist policy makers in arriving at more equitable decisions about the allocation of educational resources.

IMPLICATIONS FOR ART EDUCATION

The Diagnostic Profile contributes to the advancement of the field of art education by providing a means to assess student understandings of visual art. Standardized tests are not useful for assessing understanding because they are recall-oriented. They do not provide students with the opportunity to use their prior knowledge to demonstrate organizational skills, give explanations and reasons for choices, and present arguments.

The instrument discussed in this chapter is diagnostic in its ability to discriminate among lower-order and higher-order understandings, and misunderstandings reflected in written statements. Learning outcomes in relation to the student's knowledge-base and choice of knowledge-seeking strategies can also be verified in written statements. When students write about works of art, their thinking processes can unfold, and their understandings are revealed (Efland, et al., 1991). Therefore, writing activities allow students to apply their prior knowledge to organizing information and to explaining answers or solutions related to works of art.

The Diagnostic Profile encompasses terminology reflective of the field of art education. Therefore, the Diagnostic Profile is responsive to educators who have backgrounds in the visual arts. Studies reported in this chapter indicate that the Diagnostic Profile is consistent and effective in: assessing formal, descriptive, interpretive, and historical understandings of artworks; and providing a reliable and valid assessment of student understandings of artworks. The Diagnostic Profile is unique in that it reflects current conceptions of art learning, and provides an analysis of student's thinking and understanding of visual art. The Diagnostic Profile goes beyond description based upon memorization and recall by: (a) delineating the student's construction of knowledge from a writing sample, (b) characterizing the interplay between students' knowledge-base and choice of knowledge-seeking strategies, (c) assessing a range of understandings and misunderstandings, and (d) diagnosing attributes and constraints in learning. With the capability to assess student understandings and misunderstandings of art, the Diagnostic Profile offers opportunities to reconfigure instructional materials to improve teaching and learning of the visual arts.

References

Alexander, S. 1978). *Marc Chagall: A biography.* New York: G. P. Putnam's Sons.

Alexander, P. A., Schallert, D. L., & Hare, V. C. (1991). Coming to terms: How researchers in learning and literacy talk about knowledge. *Review of Educational Research, 61*(3), 315–344.

Alvermann, D. E., Smith, L. C., & Readence, J. E. (1985). Prior knowledge activation and the comprehension of compatible and incompatible text. *Reading Research Quarterly, 29*(4), 420–436.

American Psychological Association. (1985). *Standards for educational and psychological testing.* Washington, DC: American Psychological Association.

Arnason, H. H. (1976). *History of modern art: Painting, sculpture, architecture.* New York: Harry N. Abrams.

Barrett, T. (1990). *Criticizing photographs: An introduction to understanding images.* Mountain View, CA: Mayfield.

Barrett, T. (1994a). *Criticizing art: Understanding the contemporary.* Mountain View, CA: Mayfield.

Barrett, T. (1994b). Principles for interpreting art. *Art Education, 47*(5), 8–13.

Bolliger, H. (1957). *Marc Chagall: The graphic works.* London: Thames & Hudson.

Bransford, J. D., & Johnson, M. K. (1972). Contextual prerequisites for understanding: Some investigations of comprehension and recall. *Journal of Verbal Learning and Verbal Behavior, 11,* 717–726.

Bransford, J., Sherwood, R., Vye, N., & Rieser, J. (1986). Teaching thinking and problem solving: Research foundations. *American Psychologist, 41*(10), 1078-1089.

Briere, M. (1988). *Art image* (Vols. 1–6). Champlain, NY: Art Image.

Brommer, G. F. (1982). *Discovering art history.* Worcester, MA: Davis.

Carney, J. D. (1994). A historical theory of art criticism. *Journal of Aesthetic Education, 28*(1), 13–29.

Chagall, B. (1973). *First encounter.* New York: Schocken Books.

Chapman, L. H. (1987). *Discover art* (Vols. 1–6). Worcester, MA: Davis.

Chapman, L. H. (1992). *A world of images.* Worcester, MA: Davis.

Clark, G. A., Day, M. D., & Greer, W. D. (1987) . Discipline-based art education: Becoming students of art. *Journal of Aesthetic Education, 21*(2), 129–196.

Compton, S. (1985). *Chagall.* New York: Harry N. Abrams.

Confrey, J. (1987). Misconceptions across subject matters: Science, mathematics and programming. In J. D. Novak (Ed.), *Second International Seminar on Misconceptions and Educational Strategies in Science and Mathematics Education* (Vol. 1, pp. 81–106). Ithaca, NY: Cornell University Press.

Crespelle, J. P. (1970). *Chagall.* New York: Coward-McCann, Inc.

de la Croix, H., & Tansey, R. G. (1980). *Gardener's art through the ages.* New York: Harcourt, Brace and Jovanovich.

DeMauro, G. E. (1989). The least and most difficult content areas on the NTE speciality area test in art education. *Visual Arts Research, 15*(1), 48–54.

Dooling, D. J., & Lachman, R. (1971). Effects of comprehension on retention of prose. *Journal of Experimental Psychology, 88,* 216–222.

Efland, A. (1990). An approach to the assessment of art learnings. *Arts and Learning Research, 8*(1), 50–65.

Efland, A., Koroscik, J., & Parsons, M. (1991). *Assessing art learning based on the novice-expert paradigms: A progress report.* Paper presented at the annual meeting of the National Art Education Association, Atlanta.

Feldman, E. B. (1967). *Varieties of visual experience.* New York: Harry N. Abrams.

Feldman, E. B. (1994). *Practical art criticism.* Englewood Cliffs, NJ: Prentice-Hall.

Feltovich, P. J., Spiro. R. J., & Coulson, R. L. (1988). *The nature of conceptual understanding in biomedicine: The deep structure of complex ideas and the development of misconceptions,* (Technical Report No. 440). Center for the Study of Reading. Urban-Champaign, IL: University of Illinois Press.

Fichner-Rathus, L. (1986). *Understanding art.* Englewood Cliffs, NJ: Prentice-Hall.

Fraenkel, J. R., & Wallen, N. E. (1990) . *How to design and evaluate research in education.* New York: McGraw-Hill.

French, M. (1992). *Effectiveness of a DBAE program: Pre- and posttest SDP analysis of written statements from three elementary classrooms.* Unpublished master's thesis, The Ohio State University.

Getty Center for Education in the Arts (1991, March). *Progress report on regional institute project on student assessment.* Unpublished report, The Ohio Partnership for the Visual Arts, The Ohio State University.

Guba, E. G. (1978). *Toward a methodology of naturalistic inquiry in educational evaluation* (CSE Monograph series in evaluation, No. 8). Los Angeles: University of California.

Hamblen, K. A. (1988). If it is to be tested, it will be taught: A rationale worthy of examination. *Art Education, 41*(5), 59–62.

Herberholz, B., & Hanson, L. (1990). *Early childhood art.* Dubuque, IA: Wm. C. Brown.

Herberholz, D., & Herberholz, B. (1990). *Artworks for elementary teachers: Developing artistic and perceptual awareness.* Dubuque, IA: Wm. C. Brown.

Hobbs, J., & Salome, R. (1991). *The visual experience.* Worcester, MA: Davis.

Hubbard, G. (1987). *Art in action* (Vols. 1–8). San Diego, CA: Coronado.

Hubbard, G., & Rouse, M. J. (1981). *Art: Meaning, method and media* (Vols. 1–5). Chicago: Benefic Press.

Hurwitz, A., & Day, M. (1991). *Children and their art.* New York: Harcourt, Brace and Jovanovich.

Jager, N. (Ed.). (1970). *Russian art of the revolution.* Brooklyn, NY: Brooklyn Museum of Art.

Kamensky, A. (1989). *Chagall: The Russian years 1907–1922.* New York: Rizzoli.

Kirk, J., & Miller, M. L. (1990). *Reliability and validity in qualitative research.* Newbury Park, CA: Sage.

Koroscik, J. S. (1982). The effects of prior knowledge, presentation time, and task demands on visual arts processing. *Studies in Art Education, 23*(3), 13–22.

Koroscik, J. S. (1988). *The acquisition of art knowledge: A theoretical framework for curriculum development in art education* (Grant No. 8720287). Washington, DC: U. S. Department of Education.

Koroscik, J. S. (1990a). The function of domain-specific knowledge in understanding works of art. *Inheriting the Theory: New Voices and Multiple Perspectives on DBAE.* Proceeding of a national invitational seminar sponsored by the Getty Center for Education in the Arts. Los Angeles: J. Paul Getty Trust.

Koroscik, J. S. (1990b). Novice-expert differences in understanding and misunderstanding art and their implications for student assessment in art education. *Arts and Learning Research, 8*(1), 639.

Koroscik, J. S. (1992–93). Assessing student learning in the visual arts: Application of a theoretical model. *Arts and Learning Research, 10*(1), 5–15.

Koroscik, J. S. (1993). Learning in the visual arts: Implications for preparing art teachers. *Arts Education Policy Review, 94*(5), 9, 10, 20–25.

Koroscik, J. S., Osmond, A. H., & DeSouza, I. (1988) . The function of verbal mediation in comprehending works of art: A comparison of three cultures. *Studies in Art Education, 29*(2), 91–102.

Koroscik, J. S., Short, G., Stavropoulos, C., & Fortin, S. (1992). Frameworks for understanding art: The function of comparative art contexts and verbal cues. *Studies in Art Education, 33*(3), 154–164.

Krathwohl, D. R. (1988). *How to prepare a research proposal: Guidelines for funding and dissertations in the social and behavioral sciences.* New York: Syracuse University Press.

Leedy, P. D. (1989). *Practical research: Planning and design.* New York: Macmillan.

Lesgold, A., Rubinson, H., Feltovich, P., Glaser, R., Klopfer, D., & Wang, Y. (1988). Expertise in a complex skill: Diagnosing x-ray pictures. In M. T. H. Chi, R. Glaser & M. J. Farr (Eds.), *The nature of expertise* (pp. 311–342). Hillsdale, NJ: Erlbaum.

Linderman, M. G. (1990). *Art in the elementary school: Drawing, painting and creating for the classroom.* Dubuque, IA: Wm. C. Brown.

Linn, M. C. (1985). The cognitive consequences of programming instruction in classrooms. *Educational Researcher, 14*(5), 14–29.

Makarius, M. (1988). *Chagall.* New York: Portland House.

Messick, S. (1989). Validity. In R. L. Linn (Ed.), *Educational measurement* (3rd ed., pp. 13–104). New York: Macmillan.

Miller, B. F., & Keane, C. B. (1972). *Encyclopedia and dictionary of medicine and nursing.* Philadelphia: W. B. Saunders.

Mittler, G. (1994). *Art in focus* (3rd ed.). New York: Macmillan.

Mittler, G., & Ragans, R. (1992a). *Exploring art.* Lake Forest, IL: Macmillan.

Mittler, G., & Ragans, R. (1992b). *Understanding art.* Lake Forest, IL: Macmillan.

National Teacher Examination (1987). *Programs bulletin of information, 1987–88.* Princeton, NJ: Educational Testing Service.

Nickerson, R. S. (1985). Understanding understanding. *American Journal of Education, 93,* 201–239.

O'Neal, J. (1992). Wanted: Deep understandings. *Update, 34*(3), 1–6.

Parsons, M. J. (1987). *How we understand art: A cognitive develop-*

mental account of aesthetic experience. New York: Cambridge University Press.

Parsons, M. J. (1990). A comparison of novice-expert and developmental paradigms in terms of their use in work on the assessment of student learning in art education. *Arts and Learning Research, 8*(1), 30–49.

Parsons, M. J. (1992). Cognition as interpretation in art education. In B. Reimer & R. Smith (Eds.), *91st Yearbook of the national society for the study of education: Arts and aesthetic knowing* (chap. IV). Chicago: National Society for the Study of Education and University of Chicago Press.

Patton, M. Q. (1990). *Qualitative evaluation and research methods.* Newbury Park, CA: Sage.

Perkins, D. N., & Salomon, G. (1987). Transfer and teaching thinking. In D. N. Perkins, J. Lochhead & J. Bishop (Eds.), *Thinking: The second conference.* Hillsdale, NJ: Erlbaum.

Perkins, D. N., & Simmons, R. (1988). Patterns of misunderstanding: An integrative model for science, math, and programming. *Review of Educational Research, 58*(3), 303–326.

Pontbriand, C. (Ed.). (c. 1990). *Festival internationale de novelle dance.* Canada: Editions Parachute.

Prawat, R. S. (1989). Promoting access to knowledge, strategy, and disposition in students: A research synthesis. *Review of Educational Research, 59*(1), 1–41.

Preble D., & Preble, S. (1985). *Artforms.* New York: Harper & Row.

Ragans, R. (1995). *Arttalk* (2nd ed.). New York: Macmillan.

Salomon, G. (1983). The differential investment of mental effort in learning from different sources. *Educational Psychologist, 18*(1), 42–50.

Salomon, G., & Perkins, D. N. (1989). Rocky roads to transfer: Rethinking mechanisms of a neglected phenomenon. *Educational Psychologist, 24*(2), 113–142.

Schoenfeld, A. H. (1985). *Mathematical problem solving.* New York: Academic Press.

Smith, R. A. (Ed.). (1989). *Discipline-based art education: Origins. meaning, and development.* Urbana-Champaign IL.: University of Illinois Press.

Stavropoulos, C. S. (1992). *A diagnostic profile of art understandings based on verbal responses to works of art.* Unpublished doctoral dissertation, The Ohio State University.

Stavropoulos, C. S. (1992–93a). Alternative methodology for assessing student learning in visual arts: The diagnostic profile of art understandings. *Arts and Learning Research, 10*(1), 16–32.

Stavropoulos, C. S. (1992–93b). Characterizing the cognitive complexity of students' written statements about works of art: An alternative assessment strategy. *Arts and Learning Research, 10*(1), 33–47.

Stavropoulos, C. S. (1994). Distinguishing the effectiveness of a writing intensive DBAE curriculum: A quasi-experimental study comparing three elementary classrooms' written responses to a work of art. *Arts and Learning Research, 11*(1), 25–40.

Strauss, A., & Corbin, J. (1990). *Basics of qualitative research: Grounded theory procedures and techniques.* Newbury Park, CA: Sage.

Sweeney, J. (1946). *Marc Chagall.* New York: Simon & Schuster.

Vosniadou, S., & Brewer, W. F. (1987). Theories of knowledge restructuring in development. *Review of Educational Research, 57*(1), 51–67.

Wachowiak, F., & Clements, R. D. (1993). *Emphasis art: A quality art program for elementary and middle schools* (5th ed.). New York: Harper Collins.

West, S. (1990). *Chagall.* New York: Gallery Books.

Wilson, P. T., & Anderson, R. C. (1986). What they don't know will hurt them: The role of prior knowledge in comprehension. In J. Orasanu (Ed.), *Reading comprehension: From research to practice* (pp. 31–48). Hillsdale, NJ: Erlbaum.

APPENDIX A :
DIAGNOSTIC PROFILE OF ART
UNDERSTANDINGS

FORMAL DIMENSION

Elements of Design and Principles of Organization,
Media and Technique

Lower-Order Understandings

F0   Immature judgment, nebulous or unclear formal statement.

F1   General recognition / identification / definition of elements, principles, marks, graphic details, grounds and / or perspective.

F2   Identifies abstract, real, or nonobjective qualities.

F3   Points out style or personal method used by the artist or ethnic group.

F4   Correctly classifies work in terms of technique processes, media and / or materials used .

Higher-Order Understandings

F5   Student actively searches work for formal understanding (e.g., compound sentences, complex thought structures, connection-making, comparisons, speculation, hypotheses, and / or conclusions).

F6   Analyzes work in terms of the elements of design (e.g., line, shape, color, texture).

F7   Analyzes work in terms of the principles of design (e.g., repetition, variation, action / movement, balance, unity, dominance, contrast).

F8   Formal agreement with literature review.

F9   Supported judgment and / or aesthetic reasoning (formal).

F10   Formal questioning.

F11   Extends and / or challenges technicians' appraisal regarding the technical process / medium utilized to make the work, through convincing argument which includes supportive examples or evidence. Extends and / or challenges historians' or critics' analysis of the work in reference to the elements and principles of design, through convincing argument which includes supportive examples or evidence.

Misunderstandings

–F1   Incorrect formal appraisal (Supported)

–F2   Incorrect formal appraisal (Unsupported)

–F3   Illogical formal findings

DESCRIPTIVE DIMENSION

Objects, Images and Scenes

Lower-Order Understandings

D0   Immature judgment, nebulous or unclear descriptive statement.

D1   Identifies lists, and demonstrates a general recognition of images, scenes, and / or symbols .

D2   Student lists and / or explains activities (verb / and at least one noun).

D3   Identification of artforms (e.g., landscape, portraiture, caricature, still-life, street scene) .

D4   Examines and describes surface details of images.

Higher-Order Understandings

D5   Student actively searches work for descriptive understanding (e.g., compound sentences, complex thought structures, connection-making, comparisons, speculation, hypotheses, and / or conclusions).

D6   Descriptive agreement with literature review.

D7   Supported judgment and / or aesthetic reasoning (descriptive).

D8   Descriptive questioning.

D9   Extends and / or challenges historians' and / or critics' description of the work through convincing argument which includes supportive examples or evidence.

Misunderstandings

–D1   Incorrect descriptive appraisal (Supported)

–D2   Incorrect descriptive appraisal (Unsupported)

–D3   Illogical descriptive findings v

INTERPRETIVE DIMENSION

Meaning, Emotion, Feelings, and Expression

Lower-Order Understandings

I0   Immature judgement, nebulous or unclear interpretive statement.

I1   General interpretive language.

I2   Uncustomary / unexpected impression (viz., personal).

I3   Relates work to "popular culturer (e.g., names pop culture).

I4   Correctly relates work to a culture or religious belief system.

Higher-Order Understandings

I5   Student actively searches work for interpretive understanding (e.g., compound sentences, complex thought structures, connection-making, comparisons, speculation, hypotheses, and / or conclusions).

I6   Personal interpretation based on description of images, scene, and / or symbols.

I7   Personal interpretation based on analysis of elements of design (e.g., line, shape, color, texture).

I8   Personal interpretation based on analysis of principles of design (e.g., repetition, variation, dominance, balance, transition, unity, contrast, movement, action).

I9   Interpretation agreement with literature review (e.g., cites conventional, feminist, psychoanalytic, Marxist interpretive perspectives).

I10 Supported judgment and / or aesthetic reasoning (interpretive).

I11 Interpretive questioning.

I12 Extends and / or challenges historians' and / or critics' interpretation of the work through convincing argument which includes supportive examples or evidence.

Misunderstandings

−I1 Incorrect interpretive appraisal (Supported)

−I2 Incorrect interpretive appraisal (Unsupported)

−I3 Illogical interpretive findings

HISTORICAL DIMENSION

Historical Background Classifications and
Shared Understandings

Lower-Order Understandings

H0 Immature judgment, nebulous or unclear historical statement.

H1 Artist's name(s), or ethnic group.

H2 Personal data or background about artist (e.g., age, sex, race, culture, where artist was born, lived, worked and / or "stories" about artist's life) or ethnic group.

H3 Title or date of work(s), the place or person(s) the work might depict.

H4 Identifies, sorts, or classifies work(s) according to culture, period, movement, societies and associations; and / or form(s).

Higher-Order Understandings

H5 Student actively searches work for historical understanding (e.g., compound sentences, complex thought structures, connection-making, comparisons. speculation, hypotheses, and / or conclusions).

H6 Discusses the artist's inspiration or mythology about the origin of the form in a supportive explanation of the work.

H7 Provides a supportive explanation of the work in reference to its purpose, function, or use.

H8 Makes comparison(s) of other works by same artist or ethnic group(s) or different artist(s) and / or ethnic group(s).

H9 Historical agreement with literature review (e.g., cites cultural significance of work in reference to artist, context, movement, ethnic group and / or society).

H10 Supported judgment and / or aesthetic reasoning (historical) .

H11 Historical questioning.

H12 Extends and / or challenges historians' and / or critics' appraisal, analysis, and / or theories applied to the work of art or artist through convincing argument which includes supportive examples and evidence.

Misunderstandings

−H1 Incorrect historical appraisal (Supported)

−H2 Incorrect historical appraisal (Unsupported)

−H3 Illogical historical findings

APPENDIX B : SUPPORTIVE RESPONSES FOR DIAGNOSTIC CATEGORIES

Sample student responses are given to support each category within the Diagnostic Profile. Following each sample is a code number that corresponds to the artwork, group of artworks, or artist that stimulated the response as shown below:

(0) The artist, Marc Chagall.

(1) *The Birthday,* a painting by Marc Chagall, 1915–1923.

(2) *Chagall,* a dance choreography by Ginette Laurin, 1988.
To Marc Chagall, a poem by Paul Eluard, 1911–1915.
And Came the Dog and Ate the Cat, a lithograph by El Lissitzky, 1919.
The Birthday, a painting by Marc Chagall, 1915–1923.

(3) *The Holy Coachman,* a painting by Marc Chagall, 1911–1912.
I and the Village, a painting by Marc Chagall, 1911–1912.
The Fiddler, a painting by Marc Chagall, 1912–1913.
The Birthday, a painting by Marc Chagall, 1915–1923.

(4) *Jawlensky and Werefkin in a Meadow,* a painting by Gabriele Munter, 1908–1909.
Untitled #2, a painting by Richard Lindner, 1962.
The Dance of Life, a painting by Edvard Munch, 1899–1900.
The Birthday, a painting by Marc Chagall, 1915–1923.

(5) *Los Mismos,* aquatint print from the Disasters of War series, by Francisco Goya, 1919.

(6) The artist, Vincent Van Gogh.

Expert statements about works of art were also part of the sample selection. These statements were appropriated from two sources. Some expert statements came directly from books on art history and art techniques. Other statements were solicited from persons with advanced knowledge in visual art, art education, or art history. These statements are coded with the word "expert."

SUPPORTIVE RESPONSES: FORMAL DIMENSION

Lower-Order Understandings

F0 Immature judgment, nebulous or unclear formal statement.

I like it because it has orangish-red in it (1).

the work is very good and detailed (5).

F1 General recognition / identification / definition of elements, principles, marks, graphic details, grounds and / or perspective.

red, blue, green (3).

perspective used (2).

F2 Identifies abstract, real, or nonobjective qualities.

a little abstract especially in distorting the features of the body (3).

none are realistic, again abstract (3).

but they are not realistic portrayals, the last one looks almost real with very little abstraction if any at all (3).

F3 Points out style or personal method used by the artist or ethnic group.

Van Gogh has an unusual brush stroke—very wild with energy (6).

F4 Correctly classifies work in terms of technique processes, media and / or materials used.

the way the paint is applied it seems to have been thinned and soaked into the canvas (3).

a 'collage' type picture, meaning that several pictures are painted on top of each other (3).

they used a shading technique (5).

one color will fade into the next (3).

Higher-Order Understandings

F5 Student actively searches work for formal understanding (e.g., compound sentences, complex thought structures, connection-making, comparisons, speculation, hypotheses, and / or conclusions).

he uses lots of curved lines in his paintings. The other painting inspired by him also uses curved lines. The dancers are using curves, when they move (2).

abstract work—a man and a woman . . . the pieces all fit to make up the images, yet they are all different shapes and colors (4).

F6 Analyzes work in terms of the elements of design (e.g., line, shape, color, texture).

red / orange draws attention, black is important as a shading / defining color (3).

some [colors] are soft and timid while others harsh and bright (3).

the shapes of the faces are very similar (3).

F7 Analyzes work in terms of the principles of design (e.g., repetition, variation, action / movement, balance, unity, dominance, contrast).

dominant figures that the eye is attracted to (3).

detail around the sides draws the eye outward (3).

each has a main focal point (3).

black and white suggest opposition and contrast (2)

F8 Formal agreement with literature review.

Goya used an aquatint method of printing (expert).

F9 Supported judgment and / or aesthetic reasoning (formal).

doesn't give my eye a focal point, it isn't pleasant to look at (3).

cluttered . . . too many contrasting views (3).

the color white is used effectively as a receding color (3).

F10 Formal questioning.

We have studied many painting by Chagall in class. Has

Chagall ever worked in any other media, such as wood, clay, or printmaking? (0).

F11 **Extends and / or challenges technicians' appraisal regarding the technical process / medium utilized to make the work, through convincing argument which includes supportive examples or evidence. Extends and / or challenges a historian's or critic's analysis of the work in reference to the elements and principles of design, through convincing argument which includes supportive examples or evidence.**

Tamarind Book of Lithography states the stone should be lavigated before resensitization with acetic acid, in preparation for the second printing. However, when lavigating the stone there is the risk of scratching its surface, making additional lavigating necessary. With too much lavigating there is a good chance the ghost image would be lost on the stone, making further detailing of the image and future registration impossible. I have found the use of bleach cleanser to be a suitable alternative to the lavigation method. The mild abrasive in the cleanser removes the old ink, and the bleach eliminates the oil deposits. Resensitization with acetic acid is not affected (expert).

Misunderstandings

–F1 **Incorrect formal appraisal (Supported)** .

Marc Chagall does not proportion feet & hands correctly—they are stretched out (2).

you can tell it's a black and white etching because of the deep lines and dark color (2).

–F2 **Incorrect formal appraisal (Unsupported).**

its done in ball-point pen (5).

each painting uses the same color scheme of primary colors (3).

–F3 **Illogical formal findings.**

painting looks almost one-dimensional (4).

SUPPORTIVE RESPONSES: DESCRIPTIVE DIMENSION

Lower-Order Understandings

D0 **Immature judgment, nebulous or unclear descriptive statement.**

I like it because of the people (1).

D1 **Identifies, lists, and demonstrates a general recognition of images, scenes, and / or symbols (nouns).**

man and woman (4).

body, face, village, church, cabins (3).

image of an animal, a cow, and two people (3).

D2 **Student lists and / or explains activities (verbs).**

2 people starting to kiss (3).

man in air—backwards (2).

men fighting with each other (5).

this is an image of a person that appears to be flowing or flying near a church (3).

D3 **Identification of artforms (e.g., landscape, portraiture, caricature, still-life, street scene)**

land types (5).

portrait of a couple (1).

D4 **Examines and describes surface details of images.**

the faces look like skeletons (5).

goat face and a human face (3).

scarves on the wall have a detailed paisley pattern (1).

Higher-Order Understandings

D5 **Student actively searches work for descriptive understanding (e.g., compound sentences, complex thought structures, connection-making, comparisons, speculation, hypotheses, and / or conclusions).**

humans in inhuman states, and nonhumans in human states (3).

there is a woman kissing a man who is stretched around her, he is floating in the air . . . there are animals fighting . . . 2 people touching very close together . . . the dancers are also in the air a lot, like they're all floating just like the man in Chagall's painting (2).

D6 **Descriptive agreement with literature review.**

man playing the fiddle - standing on top of the world (3).

portrayed in a floating, distorted manner (3).

killing, rape (5).

D7 **Supported judgment and / or aesthetic reasoning (descriptive).**

I don't like this piece because of the man's body and how its disfigured (4).

I don't like this painting because the man's neck in the picture makes me feel strange and uncomfortable (4).

D8 **Descriptive questioning.**

why are the walls of the apartment pictured in *The Birthday* decorated with colorful scarves? Was there a special reason for the scarves to be hung in this way? (1).

a robot's knee is showing—why? (4).

why is the lady so big? (4).

D9 **Extends and / or challenges historians' and / or critics' description of the work through convincing argument which includes supportive examples or evidence.**

because the "bed image" is cut off at the right of the composition, slightly tilted in perspective, and covered with scarves, it could be very well be a pillow rather than a bed (1).

Misunderstandings

–D1 **Incorrect descriptive appraisal (Supported).**

it appears the woman is kissing a ghost since he is floating in the air (4).

the look on the man and woman's face appears to be angry and they look as though they are arguing (1).

–D2 Incorrect descriptive appraisal (Unsupported).

black and white monsters (2).

–D3 Illogical descriptive findings.

there are martians invading a planet (1).

SUPPORTIVE RESPONSES: INTERPRETIVE DIMENSION

Lower-Order Understandings

I0   Immature judgment, nebulous or unclear interpretive statement.

I like it because it makes me happy (1).

I1   General interpretive language.

this work is very violent (5).

vulgar, disgusting (5).

I2   Uncustomary / unexpected impression (viz., personal).

murder, hate, killing—things I like (5).

I3   Relates work to popular culture (e.g., names pop culture).

Fiddler on the Roof (3).

Bart Simpson (5).

I4   Correctly relates work to a culture or religious belief system.

Reference to Christianity in all of them—the symbol of the cross (3).

A couple of them have a Christian theme (3).

Higher-Order Understandings

I5   Student actively searches work for interpretive understanding (e.g., compound sentences, complex thought structures, connection-making, comparisons, speculation, hypotheses, and / or conclusions).

they all involve two people or two major subjects; deal with love; romance in a bazaar way; eerie kind of love; not ordinary (4).

I6   Personal interpretation based on description of images, scene, and / or symbols.

man bending over woman—To me this signifies that a man bends over backward to make a woman happy (4).

a couple sitting on a hillside and they seem content with each other (4).

I7   Personal interpretation based on analysis of elements of design (e.g., line, shape, color, texture).

almost wicked because of the dark colors (3).

it looks like a happy wedding reception, but the bride is in red and the guests are in white (4).

I8   Personal interpretation based on analysis of principles of design (e.g., repetition, variation, dominance, balance, transition, unity, contrast, movement, action).

a light and joyous feeling caused by the delicate motion of the dancers—graceful movement (2).

create a sense of anxiety because there appears to be haphazard movement within each scene (2).

I9   Interpretation agreement with literature review.

someone being head over heels in love ... floating on air (3).

dreamy—reminds me of a dream. I think of floating—I like it—different (4).

it is about the horrors of war (5).

I10   Supported judgment and / or aesthetic reasoning (interpretive).

My favorite piece is the last one because its simple and peaceful (4).

Looks romantic—I like it—it reminds me of happy moments (4).

I11   Interpretive questioning.

were any other contemporaries of Chagall working with the theme of love during this time? (0).

did the euphoria of their love cause them to have an outer body experience? (1).

I12   Extends and / or challenges historians' and / or critics' interpretation of the work through convincing argument which includes supportive examples or evidence.

the title of the painting suggests the work should be interpreted as the celebration of a birthday. However, the two lovers pictured may have just been married. The woman holds the traditional bridal bouquet, they are so in love they have defied gravity (1).

Misunderstandings

–I1   Incorrect interpretive appraisal (Supported).

all of these figures have very blank frozen looks on their faces ... I see it as being sick of the everyday monotony of life or as being bored with each other (4).

all of the people seem sad, with their heads hung, or facial expressions (4).

–I2   Incorrect interpretive appraisal (Unsupported).

these artworks are about a man and woman interacting, generally sexually (4).

I'd say it looks like jealousy (4).

–I3   Illogical interpretive findings

to me seems satanist. Like there is a heaven and hell (2).

all of them have a violent theme, a young couple in troubled times does not know how to release their aggressions, so they take it out on each other (2).

SUPPORTIVE RESPONSES: HISTORICAL DIMENSION

Lower-Order Understandings

H0   Immature judgment, nebulous or unclear historical statement.

I like it because it is Surrealistic (1).

H1   Artist's name(s), or ethnic group.

the work is painted by Marc Chagall (1).

H2   Personal data or background about artist (e.g., age, sex, race, culture, where artist was born, lived,

worked and / or "stories" about artist's life) or ethnic group (e.g., culture, county, sex of artist).

he was born in Russia (0).

he had a studio in Paris (0).

H3   Title or date of work(s), the place or person(s) the work might depict.

the work is entitled *The Birthday* and was painted in 1915 (1).

outside the window is a view of Vitebsk (1).

H4   Identifies, sorts, or classifies work(s) according to culture, period, movement, societies and associations; and / or form(s).

Like the Impressionists, Van Gogh painted the light with his favorite color yellow (expert).

Chagall accepted the sophisticated theories and practices of the times: Expressionism, Cubism, and Fauvist color (expert).

Higher-Order Understandings

H5   Student actively searches work for historical understanding (e.g., compound sentences, complex thought structures, connection-making, comparisons, speculation, hypotheses, and / or conclusions).

this painting [*The Birthday*] incorporates the pure saturated color of the Fauvist, and the floating figures are reminiscent of Surrealism. In examining the tilted perspective of the table, and the multiple points of view, Cubist qualities become apparent (expert).

H6   Discusses the artist's inspiration or mythology about the origin of the form in a supportive explanation of the work.

Chagall's imagery is representative of his early life in a Russian village (0).

the Bwami society is compared to a tree with far reaching roots (expert).

H7   Provides a supportive explanation of the work in reference to its purpose, function, or use.

warriors' tunics were occasionally worn by kings (expert).

H8   Makes comparison(s) of other works by same artist or ethnic group(s) or different artist(s) and / or ethnic group(s).

a comparison of Chagall's interpretation of war with Picasso's in the Guernica illuminates the broad scale of expressive emotion upon which art can play (expert).

H9   Historical agreement with literature review (e.g., cites cultural significance of work in reference to artist, context, movement, ethnic group and / or

society).

Chagall portrays the trials and persecutions of the Jewish people (0).

H10   Supported judgment and / or aesthetic reasoning (historical).

this is a successful work of art because it can touch people of different ages. Children can relate to the child-like quality of the execution—exact representation is not important, figures float about the picture plane. The work can remind the adult of happy childhood dreams and memories (1).

H10   Historical questioning.

the work of Chagall seems to have elements of several different styles and movements (Expressionism, Fauvist color, Fantasy, Surrealism, etc.). In what period of art history is Chagall's work most associated? (0).

H12   Extends and / or challenges historians' and/or critics' appraisal, analysis and / or theories of the work with supportive examples, explanation, and / or evidence.

West (1990) reminds us that "indeed all such stories by Bella and Chagall himself must be read with the knowledge that they were writing retrospectively, and could thus construct their interpretations to suit themselves" (p. 80). I question West's (1990) remarks, that in essence tend to reduce the credibility of the remembrances of Bella Chagall. It may be possible that Bella Chagall's 1939 dedication to Marc Chagall, *First Encounter* (Chagall, 1973), provides the context for a deeper understanding of the painting *Above the Town?* This 1917 painting depicts Bella and Marc floating in the sky over Vitebsk . It is interesting to note that the view from the window of *The Birthday* has also been identified as Vitebsk. And further, Bella has on the same dress as she wears in *The Birthday;* Marc wears a similar green shirt and black pants. Could *Above the Town*, painted two years later than *The Birthday*, record the imaginary flight over Vitebsk that summer evening? (expert).

Misunderstandings

–H1   Incorrect historical appraisal (Supported).

the stories reflected in the works are from the past, maybe in the 19th century (3).

–H2   Incorrect historical appraisal (Unsupported).

its abstract expressionism (3).

–H3   Illogical historical findings.

the painting looks like it was done back in the era of Napoleon (2).

21

A NATIONAL POLICY PERSPECTIVE ON RESEARCH INTERSECTIONS BETWEEN LITERACY AND THE VISUAL / COMMUNICATIVE ARTS[1]

Anne P. Sweet

OERI, U.S. DEPARTMENT OF EDUCATION

The focus of this chapter is on national education research programs in literacy and the visual/communicative arts from a federal policy perspective. A discussion on general trends and issues that are on the horizon within the national education sphere is undertaken. An examination of the Office of Educational Research and Improvement's (OERI) Research and Development Centers Program is presented within the context of a restructured OERI—the result of new legislation reauthorizing the existence of OERI as a federal research agency. Justification for an expanded view of the definition of literacy is offered. The intersections between literacy, the visual, and communicative arts are explored and the likelihood of carving out a niche for cross-cutting research in these areas is evaluated. Finally, directions are suggested for future K–12 literacy research that may be supported by OERI.

THE NATIONAL LEGISLATIVE ARENA: LAYING THE GROUND WORK FOR A NEW VISION OF SYSTEMIC EDUCATION REFORM

The last decade of this century is proving, legislatively, to be a unique time during the history of American education. Congress has set into motion a series of bold education reform initiatives that will substantially affect literacy, the communicative, and visual arts. These initiatives include the Goals 2000: Educate America Act, the School-to-Work Opportunities Act, expansion of the Head Start program, and the restructuring of the Elementary and Secondary Education Act.

The Goals 2000: Educate America Act establishes a framework to identify world-class academic and occupational standards. Among other actions, this legislation:

- Codifies into law six National Education Goals established in 1990 by the President and the nation's Governors at the National Education Summit held in Charlottesville, Virginia. These goals deal with school readiness, school completion, student academic achievement, leadership in mathematics and science, adult literacy and safe and drug-free schools. Two added goals relate to parental participation and professional development of teachers. Goal 6 captures the literacy landscape: "Every adult American will be literate and possess the skills necessary to compete in a global economy…";

- Supports the development and adoption of challenging national performance standards (currently viewed as model content standards) that define what all students should know and be able to do in core subject areas including language and the arts, and supports local reform efforts to make these standards operational in every school and classroom throughout the nation;

- Strengthens and improves teacher training, textbooks, instructional materials, technologies and overall school services so that students will have the tools to achieve higher standards;

[1] The opinions expressed in this chapter are those of the author. No official endorsement by the U.S. Department of Education is intended nor should be implied.

- Encourages the development of innovative student performance assessments to gauge students' progress;
- Establishes a National Skills Standards Board to promote the development of occupational skill standards that will define what workers will need to know and to ensure that American workers are better trained and internationally competitive;
- Increases flexibility for states, school districts and schools by waiving rules and regulations that might impede local reform and improvement; and,
- Establishes a National Education Standards and Improvement Council (NESIC) to certify voluntary national state content, student performance, and opportunity-to-learn standards, and assessment systems.

Although the new National Partnership for Educational Excellence encourages a bottom-up approach, the federal government has played a key role in setting high standards. Title II of the Goals 2000 Act, created NESIC, in part, to work with a host of organizations to determine criteria for certifying that the national content standards that are or have been developed by national organizations of subject-matter experts in each subject area, including English and the arts, are (1) internationally competitive; (2) reflective of the best knowledge about teaching and learning; and (3) developed through a broad-based, open adoption process. However, there was little support for NESIC as reflected in amendments introduced to Congress to eliminate its formation. The thinking behind these amendments stemmed from a pervasive view that national standards should be put forth as models that are available for state and local school districts to use as exemplars in establishing their own sets of standards. Opportunity-to-learn standards faced similar opposition. Most recently, the 1996 federal budget bill that was signed into law on April 26, 1996, includes amendments that eliminate the authorization of NESIC and eliminates opportunity-to-learn standards from Goals 2000 and the Elementary and Secondary Education Act.

OERI's Mission and the Research and Development Centers Program

Public Law 103-227 went into effect on March 31, 1994, having been signed into law by President Clinton. The Goals 2000: Educate America Act and the Educational Research, Development, Dissemination, and Improvement Act of 1994 (Title IX) are included under this new law. Title IX authorizes a new OERI, giving it a broad mandate to conduct an array of research development, dissemination, and improvement activities to bolster education for all students. Under the new authorization, OERI has been granted legislative provisions to reinvent itself. Central to OERI's new mission is its charge to provide national leadership in expanding fundamental knowledge and understanding of education; promoting excellence and equity in education and the achievement of the National Educational Goals by spurring reform in the school systems of the United States; promoting the use and application of research and development to improve practice in the classroom; and, monitoring the state of education. A key facet of Public Law 103–227 is that the OERI mission be accomplished in collaboration with researchers, teachers, school administrators, parents, students, employers, and policy makers.

Inherent is the federal government's responsibility to provide leadership in the conduct and support of scientific inquiry into the educational process. This includes the call for basic and applied research as pathways to improved practice. In so doing, OERI is propelled by the need for a stable, coherent, and long-term agenda in which the commitment to build knowledge, the identification of promising approaches, and the provision of technical assistance to those responsible for educating our nation's youth are included.

Among the set of principles that OERI must adhere to in order to realize its mission is one that speaks of preserving and enhancing the infrastructure of educational research and development. This means that OERI must continue to support work that is vital to the sustenance of education-related inquiry and ensure that the researcher talent pool flourishes. This principle comes with the recognition that all members of the education community must be supported in their professional development, including the efforts of researcher practitioners who are seeking to create the future in terms of their own vision. In so doing, OERI should confirm the belief that theory is grounded in practice. Moreover, it should actively support the notion that researchers and practitioners may assume alternating roles—that is, researchers and practitioners are teacher and learner, leader and follower. Collaborations among teacher-researcher colleagues should increase the likelihood that the fruits of OERI-sponsored research will be readily assimilated into everyday practice in classrooms. Finally, OERI should sustain its commitment to nurturing a program of research that is multidimensional and interdisciplinary.

The OERI is assuming a different structure as prescribed by the authorization legislation. New policies are to be guided by a research priorities plan developed by the agency's Assistant Secretary, in collaboration with a National Educational Research and Policy Priorities Board. OERI assumes an administrative structure that includes: National Research Institutes, a National Education Dissemination System, the National Center for Education Statistics, the National Library of Education, and the establishment of any other units deemed appropriate by the agency head (Assistant Secretary). The OERI research and development activities fall under the National Research Institutes, of which there are five: (1) The National Institute on Student Achievement, Curriculum, and Assessment; (2) The National Institute on the Education of At-Risk Students; (3) The National Institute on Early Childhood Development and Education; (4) The National Institute on Educational Governance, Finance, Policy–Making and Management; and (5) The National Institute on Postsecondary Education, Libraries, and Lifelong Learning. Each Institute will coordinate research and development centers, field-initiated research programs, special studies, and form lineages with the Office of Reform Assistance and Dissemination, which is a part of the National Education Dissemination System.

Within this structure, each of the National Research Institutes will carry out a research and development (R&D) program for improving federal, state, Indian tribal, and local education policies and practices that is tailored to suit each Institute's particular mission. Within each Institute, a variety of strategies will be available to meet the research, development, and dissemination objectives although these strategies are likely to be confined by budgetary constraints. Each R&D program may conduct a portion of its activities internally but will achieve its objectives largely through awarding grants (including cooperative agreements) and contracts; providing technical assistance; conducting research syntheses; awarding graduate fellowships to individuals from groups traditionally underrepresented in the field of education; and selecting fellows to work within the agency. In addition, each Institute will coordinate its efforts with fellow Institutes, the regional laboratories, and other education agencies.

National programs for supporting research and achieving the Institutes' missions include Field Initiated Studies (FIS) and the National Research and Development Centers Program. Field initiated research is defined by the legislation as research in which topics and methods of study are generated by investigators, including teachers and other practitioners. The FIS competitions will reflect the missions of the Institutes.

By and large, however, the national R&D Centers will be the principal vehicles through which the Institutes' missions will be fulfilled. The legislation stipulates that no less than one third of the funds made available to the each Institute will be allocated to R&D Centers. In the language of the legislation, it is acknowledged that Centers are best designed to provide for and maintain a stable foundation of long-term research and development on core issues and concerns. The law calls for applicants for Center grant awards to demonstrate that they have assembled a group of high quality researchers sufficient to achieve the Center's mission, that the proposed organizational structure will facilitate achievement of the mission; and that the Center Director and support staff will devote a majority of their time to the Center's work. With the new authorization comes an Education Department thrust toward funding fewer R&D Centers at significantly higher dollar amounts—the law declares that no Centers may be competed for less than $1.5 million annually.

Until recently, OERI supported 20 national research Centers that engaged in long-term programmatic research. Three of these Centers, in particular, were devoted predominantly to the study of K–12 literacy issues—the National Reading Research Center, the National Research Center on Literature Teaching and Learning, and the National Center for the Study of Writing and Literacy. Sweet and Anderson (1993) provided an informative discussion on the process that unfolded in setting a federal agenda for research on reading and holding a national R&D Centers Program competition in this area. The process resulted in the awarding of a National Reading Research Center to the University of Georgia and the University of Maryland, College Park collaboration, a 5-year grant that commenced in March 1992. The majority of these Center awards, excluding the National Reading Research Center, expired in late 1995. The lines of predominantly kindergarten through grade 12 literacy research that have been supported by the Office of Research in OERI are seated within the National Institute on Student Achievement, Curriculum, and Assessment.

In the most recent Educational Research and Development Centers Program competition, the Secretary of Education gave absolute preference to those R&D Center applications that met the following general priority: Each national research and development center must

(a) Conduct a coherent, sustained program of research and development to address problems and issues of national significance in its individual priority area, using a well-conceptualized and theoretically sound framework;

(b) Contribute to the development and advancement of theory in the area of its individual priority (i.e., a priority specific to the mission of a particular R&D Center);

(c) Conduct scientifically rigorous studies capable of generating findings that contribute substantially to understanding in the field;

(d) Conduct work of sufficient size, scope, and duration to produce definitive guidance for improvement efforts and future research;

(e) Address issues of both equity and excellence in education for all students in its individual priority area; and

(f) Document, report, and disseminate information about its research findings and other accomplishments in ways that will facilitate effective use of that information in professional development for teachers, families, and community members, as appropriate.

There are seven absolute priorities, each of which points toward the problems that an R&D Center should address under a particular priority. These are:

1. Enhancing young children's development and learning;
2. Improving student learning and achievement;
3. Improving student assessment and educational accountability;
4. Meeting the educational needs of a diverse student population;
5. Increasing the effectiveness of state and local education reform efforts;
6. Improving postsecondary education; and
7. Improving adult learning and literacy.

Although K–12 literacy-related research may have been proposed under the majority of those absolute priorities enumerated above, absolute priority (2): Improving student learning and achievement, is the absolute priority under which most K–12 literacy research is apparent. Under this absolute priority, a national research and development center must

(a) Conduct research and development on improving student achievement, which must comprise research and development on improving learning, teaching, and assessment within a content area; and

(b) Include in its work, research or development related to the following topics:

(1) How students acquire knowledge and skills;

(2) Curriculum and effective instruction, including the use of technology, which reflects current un-

derstanding of cognitive development, the social context of learning, and student motivation;

(3) Effective professional development for teachers and other school professionals; and

(4) Assessment for improving teaching and learning, including the technical quality of such assessments.

The language in the general priority and priority (2) is excerpted from the *Federal Register Notice of Final Priority* which was published on September 14, 1995. It is in this notice of final priorities that the baseline for a 1996 competition for the Educational Research and Development Centers Program is made explicit. As a matter of course, OERI, through a series of meetings, regional hearings, and *Federal Register Notices,* solicited advice from parents, teachers, administrators, policy makers, business people, researchers, and others to identify the most needed research and development activities. After reviewing this advice, the Secretary published a notice in the *Federal Register* on April 10, 1995, inviting written public comments on proposed priorities for seven national research and development centers that would carry out sustained research and development to address nationally significant problems and issues in education. After reviewing these written public comments, OERI's National Educational Research Policy and Priorities Board made recommended changes to the Assistant Secretary. The Department incorporated these recommendations into the notice of final priorities. On September 14, 1995, the Secretary also published a notice in the *Federal Register* inviting applications under this competition.

The 1996 Educational Research and Development Centers Program competition was completed early in the year. It resulted in the awarding of seven national research and development Center grants. Although none of these 5-year grants is devoted exclusively to K–12 literacy research, the National Research Center on Student Learning and Achievement in English, awarded to the University at Albany, State University of New York, in collaboration with the University of Wisconsin at Madison, has a mission that is devoted to improving the teaching and learning of English, including students' skills with oral and written language and literature. This Center's scope also includes other academic subjects (e.g., math, science) where, increasingly, English skills are needed. There is the possibility that OERI will commence an R&D Center competition for research in reading after the current Reading Center grant award expires in early 1997. If substantial strides in students' achievement are to be realized, then research in reading must remain as a national priority. At the time of this writing, the fate of an OERI sponsored R&D Center for research in reading-literacy remains unsealed.

LAYING THE GROUNDWORK FOR A NATIONAL AGENDA ON LITERACY RELATED RESEARCH

A decade ago, schooling in the United States was literally turned upside down as national attention became critically focused on the quality of education that children were receiving and on the ability of educators to provide students with the tools that they needed to compete successfully in American society and in a global economy. The release of the landmark report, *A Nation at Risk,* marked the beginning of a series of national studies and reports that deluged the national scene with analyses, criticisms, and recommendations for American education. These publications set into motion an education reform movement that has since maintained momentum. In *Integrated Language Arts: Controversy to Consensus* (Morrow, Smith, & Wilkinson, 1994), Louise Cherry Wilkinson described the need for a general and national educational forum in which the problems of education can be examined in light of research from a range of relevant disciplines. In so doing, she made a timely observation about research and the national debate on educational reform:

> Too often, analyses of very complex issues and problems occur within a single discipline. Aspects of a problem that are unfamiliar to members of the discipline are ignored, and the resulting analysis is limited in scope and thus unsatisfactory. Furthermore, when educational issues are investigated by members of one discipline only, there is seldom an attempt to examine related issues from other fields or to apply methods developed in their fields that might prove illuminating. The national debate on educational reform has suffered from this myopia, as problems and issues are identified and analyses and solutions often are proposed within confines of a single disciplinary boundary. In the past, national discussions have been ill informed or uninformed by current research partly because there are far too few mechanisms for interdisciplinary analyses of significant issues. (p. xvii)

It is in the spirit of this observation that the following discussion proceeds strategically to make explicit the intersections that occur naturally across those disciplinary boundaries related to literacy. In this vein it becomes apparent that expanding traditional conceptions about literacy and the boundaries between learning disciplines is not only justifiable, but critical if we are to transform much more fully into a nation of learned, literate Americans. In the following section(s), what we know via research about the connections across the English language arts, the communicative arts, and the visual arts is discussed.

English Language Arts: Research Intersections

Through the years researchers have tended to study isolated pieces of the learning puzzle within restricted domains (e.g., beginning reading). It is not until very recently that researchers have begun to focus on learning as a process within the dynamics of various contents and contexts. New directions in research represent a shift in the way that researchers and practitioners have come to view learning, particularly language learning. Formerly, it was widely held that listening, speaking, reading, writing, and response to literature were discrete operations, learned largely through behavioral mechanisms, in hierarchical progression. As new theories of learning replaced this notion, a paradigm shift occurred in the view of language learning. The concern with form and structure gave way to the study of language function. In turn, this shift signaled a new generation of research investigation focusing on larger units of language in the context in which language is used and developed (Shuy, 1984).

There is a concrete connection between language and thought. Attention to this connection has its roots in philosophy (Schlesinger, 1971) and has been firmly established through research from many disciplines—ranging from research in hemisphericity (e.g., Gazzaniga, 1985), to research in cognitive science that is linguistically-based (e.g., Graesser, Millis, & Long, 1986). The primacy of language in cognition has been established by a large body of research which demonstrates that language is a form of thought; it is a mediator of thought, and it is a tool for enhancing thought (Marzano, 1991).

Clearly, there are common threads that weave a tapestry across the language arts. These threads are woven together through language and thought. The complex interplay between language and thought and the acquisition of reading, writing, listening, speaking, and content knowledge forms the basis for integration among the language arts. The discussion below will highlight these cross-cutting relationships based on what is known from research. The reader should note, however, that research knowledge about any one set of these relationships is not mutually exclusive. That is, the research findings often times cut across several dimensions (e.g., writing, literature, social interactions). The intricate nature of these relationships does not allow the research findings to fit neatly into discrete categories. In addition, linkages across literacy (including all the language arts) and the visual / communicative arts will be explored in the following discussion. In so doing, connections among these modes of discourse will be made explicit.

Reading, Writing, and Thinking Connections

Recent research supports the premise of modern theorists (Squire, 1984; Tierney & Pearson, 1983; Wittrock, 1984; and others) that reading and writing can be viewed in terms of the same general cognitive process—that is, gathering ideas, questioning, and hypothesizing. Reading and writing appear to differ, however, in the extent to which students call upon these cognitive strategies. These similarities and differences have been illustrated in studies by Langer (1986), Ryan (1985), and others. It is here that the cross path between the reading and writing processes adds power to student learning. McGinley and Tierney (1989) suggested that these similarities and differences may account for the advantages afforded when reading and writing work together. These advantages become apparent through the findings of recent studies.

A strand of experimental studies has focused on sharing from reading to writing. Bereiter and Scardamalia (1984) found that writing in conjunction with reading proved to be a powerful vehicle for learning, even more powerful than direct instruction. Conversely, some researchers have studied the influence of writing on reading. For instance, Clark's (1988) research showed that, not only did first graders write better when they were permitted to spell in free form, their reading achievement and word recognition ability improved as a result of the activity. These studies, among others, have shown that writing led to improved reading achievement, reading led to better writing performance, and combined instruction led to improvement in both reading and writing (Tierney & Shanahan, 1991). A clear understanding of the shared knowledge development that might accrue from comprehensive, integrated reading and writing instruction is not apparent, hence there is a need for more experimental studies of reading and writing relations. Although studies have shown that instruction can have joint benefits for reading and writing achievement, they generally lack the detailed descriptions necessary to allow such findings to be applied broadly to instructional practice.

Another fruitful avenue of research is looking at how reading and writing can be used in combination to influence learning and thinking. The findings from several studies suggest that combined reading and writing fosters a more inquisitive attitude to learning, and that it facilitates the expansion and refinement of knowledge. The integrating effects that writing has upon long-term learning, especially of key issues related to a topic, have been affirmed in studies by Copeland (1987), Hayes (1987), and others. The effects that writing has upon thinking, however, may be even more important. One research finding that has been consistent thus far is that writing prompts readers to engage in the thoughtful exploration of issues, whether it be in the context of studying science, social studies, or literature. The effects that writing about literature have upon thinking and learning are explored in the works of Marshall (1987) and Salvatori (1985). Salvatori, for example, demonstrated that writing prompted readers to be less passive and more reflective, evaluative, and enthusiastic.

Similar findings have been forthcoming in studying the effects of writing upon reading in science and social studies (Newell, 1984; Penrose, 1988). Writing's association with greater student engagement with a content topic—for example, examining evidence, or marshaling ideas and reconstructing them—is indicated by findings from both of these studies. In a study by Tierney, Soter, O'Flahavan, and McGinley (1989), the question of whether thoughtful engagement would be attributed to writing alone, reading alone, or the effects of reading and writing together, was addressed. In their findings, it was suggested that if cognitive engagement in a task is reflected in more comments about thinking, more evaluative thinking, or a greater willingness to revise one's position, then reading and writing in combination is more likely to induce learners to be more engaged (Tierney & Shanahan, 1991).

Taken together, based on the research findings discussed above, it can be inferred that writing in conjunction with reading prompts learners to be more thoughtfully engaged in learning. Langer and Applebee (1986; 1987) extended this work by conducting a 3-year study that investigated the effects of different kinds of writing assignments upon thinking in high school science and social studies. They found that writing activities contributed to better learning, especially of less familiar material, than when reading was done alone; they also found that different kinds of writing tasks prompt different kinds of cognitive engagement. McGinley and Tierney (1988) extended this work and found that reading and writing served complementary as well as unique ways of thinking about topics.

Despite the substantial body of evidence accumulating to support a holistic view of language use as the way to promote academic achievement in any discipline, language for learning activities remain unavailable to most students (Healy & Barr, 1991). In Applebee's (1980) yearlong study of writing across the curriculum in secondary school, he found that pupils had few opportunities for doing expressive writing to aid their learning in content area classrooms. The findings of this study were confirmed by later studies (Applebee, Langer, & Mullis 1987). In sum, consistent support for viewing writing as a powerful tool for the enhancement of thinking and learning is provided by these research studies. Hence, writing is not only a medium of thought, but also a vehicle for developing it (Nickerson, 1984). Moreover, writing and reading together engage learners in a variety of reasoning operations—more so than when writing or reading are apart or when students are given a variety of other tasks to do along with their reading. Support for McGinley and Tierney's (1988) argument that "literacy should be understood as the ability to enlist a repertoire of discourse forms to explore and extend thinking and learning" (p. 13) is also provided by the work discussed above.

According to results from the 1992 NAEP reading assessment (Mullis, Campbell, & Farstrup, 1993) and the 1992 NAEP writing assessment (Applebee, Langer, Mullis, Latham, & Gentile, 1994), recent reforms in reading and writing instruction are taking root, although most teachers rely on eclectic approaches that draw from varied instructional traditions. Teachers of 4th-grade students who participated in NAEP's reading assessment reported that almost all (98%) were receiving at least moderate emphasis in integrated reading and writing instruction, while this approach was central for teachers of 54% of students. Interestingly, teachers of 8th-grade students who participated in NAEP's 1992 writing assessment also reported that integration of reading and writing was being given heavy emphasis for 54% of students in grade 8. These findings are consistent with research wherein the effectiveness of integrating reading and writing instruction has been demonstrated (Harste, Short, & Burke, 1988).

Finally, it must be recognized that research of this sort is in its infancy. Research in reading and writing remains largely unintegrated. Many more studies need to be conducted, especially those that consider the possibility that students can be taught to use reading and writing together in a strategic way, based on learners' goals and the thinking operations that these goals trigger.

Reading, Literature, and Discussion Connections

Readers both transform and are transformed by literary works. This phenomenon has become apparent through research findings on response to literature. This means that the reading experience is influenced by the stances that readers take toward texts (Britton, 1984; Rosenblatt, 1985; and others) as well as the cognitive and psychological processes they bring to the reading process (Applebee, 1978; Holland, 1985; and others). Although interpretations may differ from reader to reader, common meanings within communities of readers come forth where readers share common backgrounds, psychological predispositions, and interpretive strategies (Beach & Brown, 1987; and others).

The relationship between level of reading proficiency, frequency of reading, and knowledge about literature is supported by substantial evidence. In an analysis of National Assessment of Educational Progress (NAEP) data, Ravitch and Finn (1987) reported that 11th-grade students averaged 48% incorrect responses in answering questions about authors, texts, and literary periods. Successful performance on the test, however, was directly related to the degree of leisure reading as well as the amount of instruction and homework students received. Based on this finding, it seems plausible that students acquire more knowledge about literature from additional reading. In addition, results of NAEP's 1990 reading assessment were presented in the report, *Reading In and Out of School* (Foertsch, 1992), where students who reported reading novels, poems, or stories on a daily basis for school assignments had higher average reading proficiency than students who reported doing so less frequently.

Moreover, there is evidence that discussions about what is read are related to reading proficiency. Studies of group discussion in literature indicate that high school students perceived little opportunity to express or reflect on private responses in larger group discussions (Gross, 1984). Discussion in classrooms is rare according to recent reviews of research (see Dillon, 1984). It has been observed that older students have fewer opportunities to engage in oral language experiences, such as small group discussions, theater and drama, and public speaking events in the classroom where, too often, teacher talk overwhelms student talk (Cazden, 1988; Wagner, 1991). As students advance through the grades, opportunities for them to use oral language in the classroom appear to decrease. Research shows that patterns of discourse that favor teacher talk in lieu of student talk severely restrict students' learning potential via their own spoken language. Not a great deal has happened to alter a phenomenon so common that, in her study of secondary English classrooms, Alvermann (1986) described discussion as the "forgotten language art." This is unfortunate because, as studies by Graup (1985) and others have found, students in discussion groups evidenced better comprehension than did individuals who did not participate in discussion groups (Beach & Hynds, 1991). These findings are supported by data presented in *Reading In and Out of School* (Foertsch, 1992)—1990 NAEP reading assessment results indicated that students who said that their teachers never asked them to talk about what they had read, to explain their understanding of what they had read, or discuss their interpretations, had a lower average reading proficiency than those students who reported engaging in these activities. This finding is similar for students who engage in discussion outside of school—according to the *Reading Report Card for the Nation and the States* (1993), 1992 NAEP reading assessment results indicated that students who reported at least weekly discussion about their reading with friends or family had higher average reading proficiency than students who reported little or no such discussion.

Many research studies (e.g., Berrill, 1988; Martin, 1983) have shown that students, given opportunities to talk and listen, can and do converse in productive ways to learn in all areas of the curriculum. In the case of literature, for example, encouraging students' personal responses improve their ability to construct meaning (Eeds & Wells, 1989; Galda, 1983). Over time, students develop more and more complex responses to literature that help them become better at constructing meaning. Questions, rethinking, and refined understandings result when students discuss their understandings of themes or concepts that appear in text (Langer, 1991; 1992). Moreover, Almasi and Gambrell (1994) found that students in peer-led discussions were able to recognize and resolve sociocognitive conflicts better than students in teacher-led discussions. Overall, their findings indicated that peer-led discussions produced richer and more complex interactions than did teacher-led discussions.

Thus, students' discussion in classrooms is important to their learning. Through research, Paley (1981) has shown that discourse among all ages serves as a catalyst for the development of logical reasoning skills in which students hear different points of view and collaborate to solve problems. The assumption that student-to-student verbal interactions about content improve learning and increase the level of thinking (Marzano, 1991) is supported through much of the research on small group interactions within the cooperative learning literature. Nystrand and Gamoran (1991) conducted a large scale study on instructional discourse, student engagement, and literature achievement. Using data on literature instruction from 58 8th-grade English classes, they found significant relationships with achievement: (a) students' disengagement adversely affected achievement; (b) procedural engagement (focus on classroom rules and regulations) had an attenuated relationship to achievement; and (c) substantive engagement (sustained commitment to the content and issues of academic study) had a strong, positive effect on achievement. All features of substantive engagement in this study involved reciprocal interaction and negotiation between students and teachers. Thus, the great importance of connecting literature and other texts with a variety of experiences and the prior knowledge of the reader has begun to become apparent. The notion that simply acquiring information—for example, facts and dates—amounts to significant learning, has been put to rest by the research findings cited above and related studies. More research is needed, particularly research that examines how certain instructional techniques—for example, discussions, journal writing, and formal papers—foster students' interpretations of literature and elaborations of response.

Speaking, Listening, and Learning Connections

Speaking and listening (oral language) are interrelated processes that occur within the context of social interaction. Oral language development is inextricably related to the development of literacy and learning in the content areas. The effective use of oral language is a powerful tool for communicating and learning. Current language research confirms the importance of oral communication in children's social and cognitive development and provides the impetus to integrate speaking and listening activities. Moreover, it points to the importance of taking into account the interactive nature of communication and the context variables which may influence this process. The research of King (1984) and others confirms the human potential to construct meaning through language and to use language to learn. The research of Cazden, John, and Hymes (1972) brings attention to the functions of language and to communicative competence within the social context of the classroom. The social nature of learning implies that, because each context is different, participants must always evaluate what to say, consider options, and make choices. One choice is when and how to initiate an interaction with someone. Learning rests on taking these risks (Cook-Gumperz, 1986; Hansen & Graves, 1991). The importance of social interaction in the advancement of learning, as postulated by Vygotsky (1978) in what he referred to as a child's *zone of proximal development*, is now supported by a growing corpus of research literature. For example, Wilkinson's (1984) research points to the value of small group, peer-peer interaction for promoting academic and social learning. Children who rely on each other for help learn more than those who work alone (Cazden, 1988).

Theorists of situated cognition posit that there is no cognitive core that is independent of context and intention (Brown, Collins, & Duguid, 1989; Greeno, 1988; Resnick, 1990). The study of shared reasoning within the structure of discussions in school settings is proving to be a particularly promising area of research (Resnick, Salmon, Zeitz, Wathen, & Holowchak, 1993; and others). Social interaction provides a social support system, particularly for the acquisition of procedural knowledge (Brown & Palinscar, 1989; Pontecorvo, 1993). Devescovi and Baumgartner (1993), having analyzed joint book-reading with pairs of young children, concluded that peer interaction provided the context within which children transferred skills acquired through interacting with adults; moreover, this acquired knowledge was further developed and new knowledge was formed. Pontecorvo and Girardet (1993) found that students' engagement in small group discussions about content created extremely rich situations in terms of the production of high-level reasoning even in young children, similar to *cognitive apprenticeship* (Collins, Brown, & Newman, 1989) wherein reasoning is both a situated and a distributed action occurring in a social context of negotiation with others and with the task. This generation of work reflects a new perspective on learning and instruction in educational settings in which language is not only essential to the social construction of knowledge, but is an essential means of cultural transmission. Within this perspective, cognitive functioning is part of a larger social functioning that is situated in a cultural environment. Thus, cognition and learning, regarded as sociocognitive development, become elements of a deep socialization process in which they cannot be separated (Light & Butterworth, 1992; Perret-Clermont, 1993).

Children's stories, both oral and written, have been the subject of important research on the development of children's ability to construct coherent text (e.g., King & McKenzie, 1988). Many recent studies have shown that children learn the structure as well as the linguistic features of narrative discourse, as they hear stories told and read (e.g., Cox & Sulzby, 1984). Children often display their knowledge by *talking like a book* when they pretend to read their favorite stories (e.g., Pappas & Brown, 1987). These studies suggest that reading aloud to children facilitates the development of narrative competence, particularly literate narrative. Moreover, the research suggests that communicative competence in the classroom cannot be broken down into fragments out of context, without destroying the essence of the process (Pinnell & Jaggar, 1991; Wilkinson & Spinelli, 1982).

Morrow (1988), in studying young children's literacy development, found that participation in one-to-one read-aloud events increased the quality and complexity of the children's responses. Also, repeated experiences with stories fostered a wider variety of responses and more complex, interpretive comments than did single readings of stories. Readers construct meaning as they interact with peers and adults in discussing stories (Jett-Simpson, 1989). This research, along with related studies (e.g., Teale & Sulzby, 1987; and others) has demonstrated that storybook reading involves far more than reading aloud the words of an author. The discussion among readers and listeners that occurs in response to the shared text is integral to the story-time experience. Eeds and Wells (1989) presented evidence that children support one another in their efforts to understand and reflect on stories. Dyson's (1983) research led her to conclude that children's interactions contribute substantially to intellectual development in general and literacy growth in particular, given tasks worth talking about and permission to talk. Moreover, Dyson (1987) and other researchers surmised that children engage in their most intellectually demanding work when they share ideas and opinions about stories, and share experiences related to stories read or told to them.

Broadly, research supports the integration of speaking and listening and the development of language curricula that provide students with opportunities to use language for a wide variety of purposes, in different situations, and with different audiences. For young children, Paley (1990) concluded that stories should be written down for retelling and dramatization. Related research (Goodall, 1988; Prater, 1987; and many others) has shown that wordless picture books can encourage a variety of stories based on the same illustrations (Bromley, 1992). Recent research has indicated that it is important to provide children with positive experiences involving stories and other literature on a daily basis (Morrow, O'Connor, & Smith, 1990). Opportunities for such experiences have included reading and retelling stories, discussing stories critically, role-playing, responding to stories both orally and in writing or through expressive art (e.g., drawing), and sharing books with peers. Pinnell and Jaggar (1991) pointed to studies of classroom processes (e.g., Delamont, 1983) to show that oral language functions in subtle, yet immensely important ways to give students access to learning.

Literacy, Communicative and Visual Arts Connections

Elkind (1988) observed that, in the study of literacy, it is important to look back to the images and feelings that pre-

cede the words and to explore the relationships between the way children see the world and the way it is interpreted in print. Although there is growing sentiment among educators for the integration of literacy and the visual/communicative arts, a comprehensive search of the literature produced very few empirical studies conducted on this topic during the past decade. The majority of studies that were conducted involved the use of drama in literacy learning. There is evidence that informal drama enhances children's oral language fluency, critical thinking, literacy learning, self-confidence, and feeling (Booth, 1987; Paley, 1981; Stewig, 1983; Wagner, 1988, 1991). As Christie (1990) observed, a growing body of research indicates that when children are given opportunities to engage in dramatization in *literate* play settings supplied with reading and writing material, they incorporate literacy into their play episodes readily. Research in play has pointed to young children's ability to shift into alternative roles and take on the perspective of others (Rubin, Fein, & Vandenberg, 1983; Wolf & Heath, 1992) in coming to understand the bounded and negotiated nature of theatrical interpretation (Wolf, 1994). In studying how children moved from a perception of drama as uninhibited expression to one that is bounded and negotiated as influenced by careful text interpretation, Wolf concluded that more opportunities need to be provided for children to "enter into an extended relationship with written text where they can discuss, dispute, challenge, and confirm each others' suggestions for text interpretation" (p. 42, 43). Tierney (1992) surmised that activities involving dramatic presentations will become more prevalent as the use of multimedia in classrooms increases.

Research conducted on classroom drama and the reading–writing process has shown that there is a significant, positive relationship among them. Students' participation in dramatic activities following reading improved their comprehension of text (Gray, 1987). Wagner (1986) found that role-playing helped writers identify the viewpoint of their intended audience when they were composing persuasive letters and develop their arguments accordingly. The results of Kardash and Wright's (1987) meta-analysis of 16 studies involving the use of drama with students in kindergarten through grade 7 indicated that drama had a moderately positive effect on their achievement in reading and on their oral language and written communication.

Researchers have found that children's narrative competence is dependent on encounters with many stories (Galda, 1984; Pellegrini & Galda, 1982; and others) in activities such as listening to someone tell a story, participating in storybook readings with adults, engaging in sociodramatic play, and taking part in dramatic reenactments of storybooks. Silvern, Taylor, Williamson, Surbeck & Kelly (1986) studied dramatic story reenactments (DSRs) with early elementary students and found that participants in DSRs, with or without adult guidance, recalled stories that they had reenacted better than children who participated in story discussion only. Martinez (1993) studied the use of DSRs in conjunction with early literacy development, as fostered by various forms of play. Having explored the question of why kindergarten children in a particular classroom were so intent on dramatizing stories from literature, she concluded that the literature-rich environment encouraged children to initiate these dramatizations, which in turn, likely nurtured the development of children's sense of story.

Studies (Dyson, 1982; Gundlach, 1982; and others) conducted on young writers have shown that children rely on varied media, especially drawing, as they learn about the critical features (structures and strategies) of each. Also, children's understanding of the drawing symbol system likely serves as a transition to the writing symbol system (Dyson, 1982; Ferreiro & Teberosky, 1982). Moreover, young children's texts are commonly composed of varied media, including drawing, writing, and talking. Dyson (1986) described how young children use drawing and talking as transitions to writing and concluded that "to understand the beginnings of literacy, researchers cannot be interested only in text... we have to look for its beginnings in all the kinds of making that children do. In this way, we will begin to understand, appreciate, and allow time for the often messy, noisy, and colorful process of becoming literate" (p. 408,409). Other researchers (Sulzby & Teale, 1991; Teale & Sulzby, 1987) who have studied emergent literacy have corroborated this observation.

In addition to the studies cited above, a review of the literature also yielded numerous, mostly descriptive accounts reported in magazines for teachers which largely described a range of promising practices. An initial account (Catchings, 1984) reported that integrating art lessons with reading activities raised children's reading test scores. A host of accounts described the use of drama and related strategies that helped children digest expository text (Putnam, 1991), decide how to make their writings better (Knipping, 1993), and described ways in which drama could be a frequent component of a teacher's lesson plans (Flynn & Carr, 1994). Other descriptions focused on visual and verbal / writing systems that mutually reinforced each other in an integrated approach to teaching art (Ernst, 1994); that led to students' in-depth written and oral responses to pictures (Stewig, 1986); that honored students' use of color, texture and dimension to communicate significant details in their writing (Hubbard, 1990); and, that led students to consider multiple interpretations with stories (Whitin, 1994).

Even fewer than the number of research studies and reports of promising practices relating to literacy and the arts are the actual number of integrated literacy / arts programs that have been implemented in the United States. As Sautter (1994) noted, compared to research in other areas of education, research into the effect of arts education on reading (and other subjects) is rather sparse and more research is clearly needed. Nonetheless, he argued that from the standpoint of education reform, there is not enough time to wait for more research to be done before creating more arts-integrated schools. One such program is the SPECTRA+ Program, which is a 4-year arts education model that was initiated in 1992. The empirical evaluation report (Luftig, in press) described the program's effects on 615 students at grades 2, 4, and 5 in two school districts. The 1993–94 data indicated that SPECTRA+ students benefited significantly in terms of their academic achievement and affective well-being. An-

other program of note is titled *Different Ways of Knowing* (DWoK). The DWoK, sponsored by the Galef Institute of Los Angeles, was designed to offer a thematic, interdisciplinary elementary social studies / literature curriculum that specifically encourages diverse forms of expression in the academic curriculum, including the visual and performing arts. In the third of a series of annual reports describing this national longitudinal study (Catterall, in press), significant effects of the program on student learning outcomes and on student achievement motivation and engagement were described, including indices of increased achievement in language arts, social studies content, and mathematics.

Yet another promising program is now in the planning stages by the College Board and Getty Center for Education in the Arts. This 4-year project is being designed to show how the arts can unify and strengthen the high school curriculum. The program will examine how different approaches to teaching that include the arts as a core element enhance student achievement. By late fall 1995, up to seven schools will be selected for the study. The high schools will develop and test model curricula integrating the teaching of the arts with more traditional core subjects such as history, literature, and science. A crucial element of the project will be the involvement of school districts, state agencies, and local universities in exploring the implications of unified high school curricula in such areas as student assessment, teacher preparation, and college admission. A nationwide survey conducted by the College Board in conjunction with this project revealed that there are very few well-established interdisciplinary programs of study including the arts in our nation's schools today.

In sum, research on the development of literacy through the arts is in its infancy. Programs such as those referenced above are creating a foundation of sound research upon which integrated curricula including literacy and the arts can be built. There is much to be learned about the efficacy of this approach to learning channeled through an expanded view of literacy.

We know that the construction of meaning involves multiple levels and forms of communication. Literacy is a complex system of interrelated processes and the development of literacy draws upon social and emotional experiences as well as cognitive ability. As such, the arts may provide one way for students to gain new insights into what they read and write. Hoyt (1992), a program specialist for Chapter 1 services, provided the following advice:

> As we strive to help children make connections between their world and the world of print, we need to keep in mind that it isn't enough to have a reader's time and attention. We need to help learners activate their senses, their imaginations, their emotions and all their life experiences while interacting with text. With the support of multiple communication systems, even learners with special needs can bring life into the words on the page. (p. 584)

This ardent recommendation, coupled with the absence of a direct, broad-based core of research in this arena, points to the need for an expanded research agenda.

AN EXPANDED VIEW OF LITERACY LEARNING: A NICHE FOR THE VISUAL AND COMMUNICATIVE ARTS

The ways in which we conceive of learning and alternative ways of knowing are expanding our notions about what it means to be literate in today's society. A heightened awareness of multiple paths to learning and knowledge construction has begun to emerge. Reading and writing are at the core of traditional notions of literacy. It is generally accepted that reading is comprehending, that is, the construction of meaning. Readers construct meaning by interacting with text (Pearson, 1986) on the basis of their existing or prior knowledge about the world (Rumelhart, 1985). Writing is commonly viewed as a process through which writers make meaning and communicate it through composing (Flower & Hayes, 1984; Langer, 1986).

There are many pathways to learning and knowledge acquisition. When viewed as a cohesive whole, these pathways expand the boundaries of literacy in the traditional sense. The visual and communicative arts combine richly to provide abundant avenues that lead to what Eisner (1994) terms, multiple forms of literacy. Multiple forms of literacy constitute pathways that hold the potential to enable students not only to construct meaning but to diversify and thereby deepen the meaning they construct. Hence, education is viewed as a process that involves fostering students' ability to construct, diversify, and deepen meaning. In order to do so it is necessary for students to become skilled in the construction of such meanings within a variety of the forms that are available, including words, pictures, drama, music, mathematics, dance, and the like.

Related to this notion is Gardner's (1983) theory of multiple intelligences, which encompasses seven distinct intelligences: linguistic, musical, logical-mathematical, spatial, bodily-kinesthetic, interpersonal, and intrapersonal. According to this theory, different cultures value different intelligences. For example, spacial intelligence is valued in Eskimo cultures because physical survival depends upon discerning subtle differences in snow and ice surfaces. Linguistic and logical-mathematical intelligences have been traditionally valued in American culture. Eisner (1994) pointed out that limiting forms of representation to number and word has a handicapping effect on children whose aptitudes are in other areas. Moreover, students whose aptitudes are congruent with these predominantly valued forms of intelligence receive unfair status advantages in gaining access to systems throughout society at large, whether it be entry into highly esteemed colleges and universities or highly specialized jobs and professional careers. The broadening of our definition of intelligence, when combined with an expanded view of literacy that encompasses the visual and communicative arts, has the potential to make schooling relevant to the lives of all children across the diverse spectrum of backgrounds and subcultures. The education provided by our schools under this model includes a plethora of opportunities for children to develop their capacities and deepen their constructions of meaning through a variety of forms and experiences.

Eisner (1994) presented a cogent argument concerning matters of meaning and the different kinds of meaning that different forms of representation make possible. In *Cognition and Curriculum Reconsidered*, he addressed himself to the ways in which different kinds of meaning can be secured and the conditions within curriculum and teaching that foster what might be regarded as multiple forms of literacy:

> What does it mean to secure poetic meaning, and what does poetic meaning help one understand? What kinds of meaning are accessible through the visual world? And how does one learn to read those meanings, not only within what we call works of art but within the environment at large? The curriculum that is made available to students in school is, in an essential sense, a means through which students can learn to encode and decode the meanings made possible through different forms of representation. Through this process, different kinds of intelligences are cultivated or, more broadly, cognition itself is expanded. (p. 23)

In effect, broadening the definition of literacy to include multiple forms of representation holds the potential to expand ways of knowing and the extent to which new knowledge is internalized by the learner.

The concept of multiple forms of representation is bolstered by the dual coding theory (Paivio, 1986), which posits that information that is encoded mentally in two ways is better comprehended and recalled than information encoded in only one way. This theory holds that cognition consists of two separate but interconnected systems. One is a verbal system that specializes in processing language, and the other is a nonverbal system (e.g., as images) for processing world knowledge of objects and events. Research (Mayer & Anderson, 1991; Sadoski, Goetz, & Fritz, 1993; Sadoski, Paivio, & Goetz, 1991) has shown support for this theory's assertion that when information is encoded both ways, it is elaborated, thus providing increased comprehension and strengthened memory trace. According to the dual coding theory, concrete language has a natural advantage over abstract language because it easily evokes integrated mental images. For example, the phrase *blue horizon* readily conjures up a mental image whereas the phrase *critical juncture* is more tentative. By and large, verbal and nonverbal codes are considered to be cumulative in effect. Moreover, dual coded information (concrete language) is likely to be recalled twice as fast as single coded information (abstract language). Broadly conceived, the dual coding theory provides a further basis for expanding the boundaries of traditional literacy to include the visual and communicative arts, replete with multiple codes and images that deepen students' comprehension.

Instructional Implications

There are a variety of ways to symbolize thoughts, experiences, and perceptions. Cecil and Lauritzen (1994) have added their voice to the growing notion that the arts can enhance literacy and tap linguistic, musical, logical-mathematical, spatial, body-kinesthetic, interpersonal and intrapersonal intelligence and that through these modes students can demonstrate their understanding of ideas. Moreover, they and others (e.g., Gallas, 1994) contend that if children experience an expression through the arts and relate that expression to literacy (e.g., read a story and depict a main theme visually), both symbol systems are improved. Research findings in recent explorations of emergent literacy (e.g., Morrow, 1993; Teale, 1986; Teale & Sulzby, 1987) have bolstered primary teachers' knowledge that it is sound educational practice to allow children to draw a picture and then dictate a story to accompany it, or write it themselves using invented spellings. It is through this synergy across communication systems that children generate new meanings and expand existing ones as they labor to express themselves through a variety of forms or media. Lessons learned from research on emergent literacy have demonstrated the potential of this blend and flow across multiple ways of knowing to bolster literacy development. Emergent literacy research may be viewed as providing an impetus toward an expanded view of literacy that is still in its infancy.

Central to this expanded view of literacy is the recognition that different meanings are embedded within different forms (Eisner, 1994). These meanings can be distinguished from one another through distinctive features which allow individuals to both construct and experience particular kinds of meanings. The meanings related to each form are unique. One form or pathway cannot substitute for another, and each complements another. For example, the unique qualities of a text can combine with the unique qualities of an image to yield meaning that is expanded beyond that which could be created from either one solely. Research has demonstrated that concepts can be made clearer through the visual image. For example, in addition to reading conventional text, important lessons in ecology and the environment can be underscored and brought to life by showing children photographs of the erosion of the architectural monuments in Italy and Greece (Godfrey, 1992). With regard to visualization activities in a program that integrates literacy and the arts, it has been shown that encouraging children to actively visualize words and concepts may not only help them to enjoy reading more, but it can also improve their understanding of what they read (Long, Winograd, & Bridge, 1989; and others).

We have only to look back to the personal journals of Einstein, Darwin, and McClintock to further substantiate and exemplify the different meanings that emanate from different forms and that constitute alternate pathways to knowing. These eminent scientists described experiencing a mental process in which intuition, imagination, metaphor, and visualization combined to form creative thinking that enabled them to gain new and important insights (Fox-Keller, 1983; Rothenberg, 1979). Einstein related that "words or the language, as they are written or spoken, do not seem to play any role in my mechanism of thought... the... elements are, in my case, of visual and some of muscular type" (Hadamard, 1949, p. 142). Often lost in descriptions of individuals who exhibited a genius of one sort or the other is the widely agreed upon judgment among researchers that preparation is one of the most important conditions of creativity. Based on studies in this arena, it appears that a long period of time is essential for creative productivity even, for example, the most talented of our composers, painters, and poets (Hayes, 1990). It may be safe to conclude that schooling should not only provide our

children with the essential foundations of learning, but with abundant opportunities to use a broadened realm of expressive modes to study about and communicate their understanding of the world. This includes encouraging children to think divergently rather than convergently and pushing the boundaries of their thinking and communication through primacy of expression.

In a discussion on expanding the definition of narrative to include broader realms of communication and expression, Gallas (1994) presented a conceptual framework which suggests that for children in schools, deep transformative learning takes place when language is defined expansively. In *The Languages of Learning: How Children Talk, Write, Dance, Draw, and Sing Their Understanding of the World*, Gallas, a teacher researcher, wrote:

> Children's narratives are not naturally confined to the spoken or written word. From early childhood on they tell stories in dramatic play, in their drawings and paintings, in movement and spontaneous song. As they move further into the adult world of signifying, spoken language does begin to take precedence, but in essence children do not *naturally* limit the forms that their expressions take. Because adult communication relies so heavily on spoken and written language, however, schools necessarily reflect that orientation and channel children's narratives into a very narrow realm of expressions, in effect limiting rather than broadening the child's expressive capabilities. (p. xv)

It is commonly the case that society at large relegates the adaptive use of song, movement, painting, sculpting, drama, and poetry to a small segment of our population. It does not necessarily follow that those areas of expression are available to only a few people who comprise an elite subculture of our society. Rather, it is more likely that these individuals have made a conscious choice to express meaning via these alternate pathways. Alternate forms of expression and meaning can be made available to all children in our schools. Gallas continued:

> When children are continuously offered opportunities to express their stories about the world through many avenues, they show that the power and range of their intellectual and creative pursuits are unbounded; they create new kinds of learning communities that offer membership to every child; they teach us that the process of education transcends methodology and curriculum and is situated in the realm of possibility. They change our conceptions of who teaches whom in the classroom. Once we begin to understand the many paths that narrative can take through the modalities of talk, song, art, and movement into the written word, the practice of teaching and the process of learning are mutually transformed. (p xvii)

Thus the arts hold the potential for offering students a way of pushing the boundaries of their learning. Dramas, poems, paintings, and the like provide forms of expression through which children can tell their stories and teachers can piece together a more complete picture of who their students are, what they understand, and what they can do. The essence of the message is that there are different ways of knowing and understanding the world, and there is a variety of forms that expression can take.

Drama, for example, is a highly effective mode of self-expression through which children can develop their communication abilities while fostering their creative imaginations. Cecil and Lauritzen (1994) maintained that children who are learning English as a second language (ESL) can more clearly begin to grasp concepts and have access to a variety of ideas through this unique and compelling art form. In a creative climate, literacy and the arts can blend and flow with synergy, and the uniqueness of each individual can emerge. Moreover, for ESL students or others with special needs (e.g., language delays), songs with their rhyme, rhythm, and repetition are particularly potent paths to language competence and literacy (Jalongo & Bromley, 1984).

Rudolf Arnheim (1969) argued in *Visual Literacy* that our visual perception of the world undergirds our cognitive processes, and that visual literacy and the enlightened eye are substantial life-long contributions to both intelligence and an aesthetic enjoyment of the universe. If this is indeed the case, photography, as a distinct art form, holds the potential to engage children in meaningful interactions with their world and facilitate the growth of visual-spatial intelligence and literacy. Gardner's (1990) ARTS PROPEL project uses photography as a means of offering many opportunities for students to engage in a host of authentic literacy experiences and intrinsically motivated learning. The photographic project is filled with occasions for dialogues, the use of a student-maintained portfolio of photographs, and a written journal. These components encourage literacy and effectively facilitate habits of working, self-initiated assessment, and self-sustained learning (Zessoules & Gardner, 1991). Moreover, Schwartz (1988) asserted that through photographic projects children become involved in their own self-motivated education and learn to read, to write, and to communicate with others, as well as to learn the art and techniques of photography.

This multiliterate approach to learning not only allows children to express themselves freely but also allows teachers to assess what students know in a variety of ways. A prime example of this assessment strategy is implanted within the Concept-Oriented Reading Instruction (CORI) model under development at the National Reading Research Center (NRRC), which is funded through a cooperative agreement with the U.S. Department of Education. The CORI model, designed to foster students' amount and breadth of reading, intrinsic motivations for reading, and strategies of search and comprehension, contains a framework which has five phases of reading instruction in a content domain: observing and personalizing, searching and retrieving, comprehending and integrating, communicating with others, and interacting with peers to construct meaning (Guthrie, McGough, & Bennett, 1994). Measures of learning include an assessment that traces students' performance as they use their knowledge and strategies to learn a new concept in a content domain like science. Within this performance assessment instructional unit, the broadest possible range of reading competencies is covered, including integrating illustrations with text—that is, students' expressing what they learn through drawing. Preliminary examination of individual student cases, gleaned from the federal monitor's (Sweet's) examination of case data collected in an ongoing study at the NRRC, showed that some students reveal content knowledge in their drawings that is not communicated in their writings about the same topic.

Instructional Implications for Content Disciplines

In the expanded view of literacy discussed in this chapter, I have focused on the visual and communicative arts within the social contexts of learning. This expanded view of literacy bears direct implications for instruction in subject disciplines that include science, mathematics, geography, and history, particularly since many schools are moving toward merging these disciplines with literacy learning. It seems desirable to provide students with instruction that promotes the interrelatedness of learning in lieu of parceling knowledge into conceptually discrete bundles. This means providing integrated experiences across curriculum areas and disciplines instead of segregating knowing into separate isolated packages. Research has begun to accrue most predominantly in literacy learning and science as a discipline. For example, Alvermann and Hinchman (1991) concluded that instruction can be designed to help students learn science content at the same time that they are learning science and reading process skills. Glynn (1994) found a model for teaching science concepts with analogy to be effective in connecting these concepts to new knowledge that students acquire from reading textbooks. Guthrie et al. (1994), in the concept-oriented reading instruction model described earlier in the chapter, found that helping students search for, comprehend, and integrate relevant scientific information enhances learning. Hynd, McNish, Qian, Keith, & Lay, (1994), in investigating the role of text and other factors in learning counterintuitive physics concepts, found a perceived lack of textbooks' effectiveness at inducing conceptual change. Finally, Morrow, Cunningham, and Murray-Olsen (1994), in examining current strategies for literacy development in early childhood science texts, found that textbook publishers used limited strategies to teach science that included integrated language arts elements. More research on the connections between literacy and science learning is indicated. Additionally, research is needed on literacy learning and learning in the adjunct disciplines of history, geography, and mathematics. For instance, as yet we know little about children's misconceptions of history and how these may be fostered inadvertently in some forms of text such as historical fiction.

The intersections between literacy learning and learning in content disciplines give rise to a host of important questions and considerations for research and practice, a full discussion of which is beyond the scope of this chapter. One such consideration that bears mentioning, however, is learning that occurs in out-of-school settings such as in the home and community (e.g., museums). We know that isolating the teaching of content is not productive. As Greeno (1989) observed, if the transfer of learning is to occur for students, then they need to see the connection between what they learn in school to what they experience outside of school. The school knowledge they acquire and the relationships they learn need to be situated in tasks that are somewhat parallel to life beyond the classroom. Content learning that is seated solely in the discrete structure of a discipline may have the effect of limiting students' ability to transfer and apply this knowledge in nonschool settings. Csikszentmahlyi and Hermanson (in press), in a discussion of museums and motivation to learn, pointed out that learning transcends knowledge acquisition to involve an open process of interaction with the environment. Although cognitive processes are commonly regarded as more important than affective processes for learning, Schiefele (1991) and others have concluded that affective processes are at least as important for evoking broader conceptual understanding.

In conjunction with this supposition, another consideration that bears mentioning is the relationship between school learning and motivation. Motivational constructs have been found to predict school achievement (Wigfield & Eccles, 1992; and others). They have also been found to predict the use and self-regulation of cognitive strategies for learning from text (Nolen, 1988; Pintrich & DeGroot, 1990) and gaining conceptual knowledge (Deci, Hodges, Pierson, & Tomassone, 1992; and others). Although student self-reports have been used most frequently in motivation-related research, teacher perceptions also appear to be important. Researchers have reported that teacher perceptions of student engagement were found to have reciprocal effects with students' self-report of perceived control and academic performance (Skinner, Wellborn, & Connell, 1990) and reciprocal effects with teachers' own behavior as well as with students' self-reports of engagement (Skinner & Belmont, 1993). Moreover, Sweet and Guthrie (1994), in an exploratory study to investigate teachers' perceptions of students' motivation to read in school-based settings, found that students perceived by teachers to be highly motivated to read also had high report card grades in all school subjects and vice versa. Although we do not have fully developed theories of motivation that are specific to literacy acquisition, researchers have made substantial strides in examining more fully motivations as they relate specifically to literacy events. Gambrell and Morrow (in press) report on several other of these new studies. Thus, affective as well as cognitive and social aspects of learning are important factors that must be considered in planning for instruction within the broader context of literacy learning, discipline-based learning, and knowledge construction.

In sum, the various symbolic forms used in our society to create and convey meaning—literary text, mathematics, science, art, music, dance, poetry, and the like—possess their own parameters of possibility for the construction and recovery of meaning. Moreover, individuals actively maneuver within their environment through those forms offered by the culture at large via the languages, concepts, theories, and technologies that permit them to develop higher levels of cognitive functioning in different fields of competence and knowledge. In the school context, available forms of discourse are explicit and are organized as sets of concepts and procedures. Languages, sciences, arts, technologies, and cultural artifacts (e.g., books and instructional materials) are the means through which students' thinking and learning are expanded and modified (Pontecorvo, 1993). Given this knowledge, a host of issues and resultant questions that may comprise a research agenda for teaching and learning a broader range of literacy skills comes into play. For example: What kinds of meaning are available through the various symbolic forms? When symbolic forms are combined, how is students' learning affected? How do students learn to *read* or construct meaning from various symbolic forms, and how can teachers best teach them to do so? Finally, how might students work with different symbolic forms and how might teachers evaluate what students learn? Research that brings us closer to providing answers to these and related questions is necessary under an expanded view of literacy. Answers to these types of questions are of crucial importance to the formation of curriculum policy. In turn, curriculum policy that is informed by a global view of literacy has the potential to deepen our children's thinking and learning substantially and thereby enable American students to become more competitive, internationally.

NATIONAL CONTENT STANDARDS FOR ARTS EDUCATION: HOW THEY RELATE TO LITERACY LEARNING

The U. S. Department of Education, other federal agencies, and foundations have made grants to major professional and scholarly organizations to develop voluntary national standards in different subjects that are designed to be internationally competitive. These standards are meant to serve as national benchmarks that states may use as guidance in developing their own standards. Standards being developed are of two kinds—content and performance. On the one hand, content standards are meant to define what all students should know and be able to do, to live and work in the 21st century. They describe the knowledge, skill, and understanding that students should have in order to attain high levels of competency in challenging subject matter. On the other hand, performance standards are meant to identify the levels of achievement in the subject matter that are set forth in the content standards. They state how well students demonstrate their competency in a subject.

A great deal of activity has already taken place in the movement to develop model content standards. The National Council of Teachers of Mathematics has prepared mathematics standards, and two key professional associations in literacy, the International Reading Association and the National Council for Teachers of English, coalesced to develop English Language Arts standards. The U.S. Department of Education has funded the creation of model content standards in areas including English, the arts, civics and government, foreign languages, geography, history, and science.

The national standards for arts education were completed in March 1994. The national standards for arts education are comprehensive in scope. Essentially, the standards delineate what students should know and be able to do by the time they graduate from high school: communicate at a basic level in the four arts disciplines—the visual arts, theatre, music, and dance; communicate proficiently in at least one art form; develop and present basic analyses of works of art; possess an informed acquaintance with exemplary works of art from a variety of cultures and historical periods; and, relate various types of arts knowledge and skills within and across the arts disciplines.

In the arts standards document, it was acknowledged that the arts are important to life and learning. In particular, it was recognized that there are a host of connections between and among the visual arts and literacy/communicative arts. Certain affirmations best captured these connections:

- The arts are a way of knowing. Students grow in their ability to apprehend their world when they learn the arts. As they create dances, music, theatrical productions, and visual artworks, they learn how to express themselves and how to communicate with others;
- The arts are indispensable to freedom of inquiry and expression;
- The modes of thinking and methods of the arts disciplines can be used to illuminate situations in other disciplines that require creative solutions; and
- The arts provide forms of nonverbal communication that can strengthen the presentation of ideas and emotions (*National Standards for Arts Education,* pp. 8, 9).

Although this discussion is limited to the visual arts section of the standards document, similar affirmations were stated for other arts areas in their respective sections.

A basic premise of these standards was that students in all grades will be actively involved in comprehensive, sequential programs that include creating, performing, and producing on the one hand, and study, analysis, and reflection on the other. Essentially, these standards provided a framework for helping students learn the characteristics of the visual arts by using a wide range of subject matter, symbols, meaningful images, and visual expressions, to reflect their ideas, feelings, and emotions; and to evaluate the merits of their efforts. The standards addressed these objectives in ways that promote acquisition of and fluency in new ways of thinking, working, communicating, reasoning, and investigating. They emphasized student acquisition of the most important and enduring ideas, concepts, issues, dilemmas, and knowledge offered by the visual arts. These included developing new techniques, approaches, and habits for applying knowledge and skills within the visual arts and to the world beyond.

It is evident that the national standards for arts education clearly relate to literacy and literacy instruction. Arts instruction and literacy instruction hinge upon expression as a primary mode of communication. The same tenet holds for art instruction as for literacy instruction—expression is a process of conveying ideas, feelings, and meanings through the selective use of the communicative possibilities of the visual arts, reading, writing, and oral language. To meet the standards, students must learn vocabularies and concepts associated with various types of work in the visual arts. Moreover, students must demonstrate their developing artistic competence through their literacy abilities and communicative art skills: "As they develop increasing fluency in visual, oral, and written communication, they must exhibit their greater artistic competence through all of these avenues." (*National Standards for Arts Education,* p. 49)

In the arts standards document, it was asserted that the problem-solving activities inherent in art making help students develop cognitive, affective, and psychomotor skills.

Moreover, it was maintained that students get to select and transform ideas, discriminate, synthesize and appraise, and apply these skills to their expanding knowledge of the visual arts and to their own creative work. Children come to understand that making and responding to works of visual art are inextricably interwoven and that perception, analysis, and critical judgement are inherent to both. According to the standards document, arts education cultivates the whole child, gradually building many kinds of literacy while developing intuition, reasoning, imagination, and dexterity into unique forms of expression and communication.

ARTS EDUCATION RESEARCH AGENDA FOR THE FUTURE: HIGHLIGHTS AND INTERFACE WITH LITERACY RELATED ISSUES

In response to the continuing need and recognition of the importance of research on arts education, the Office of Educational Research and Improvement (OERI) and the National Endowment for the Arts (NEA) formed an alliance to facilitate the development of a research agenda in this domain. The result was a publication titled *Arts Education Research Agenda for the Future* (1994), which contains a national agenda for arts education research developed primarily through collaboration among and with arts educational professional organizations. The purpose of this document was to stimulate discussion among researchers and the broader community about the best directions for future research in the arts disciplines. A major goal was to engender research, in part, that sheds light on the fundamental question: Does arts education enhance the development of cognitive capacities, motivation to learn, self-esteem, appreciation of multiple cultures, performance and creative capacities, and appreciation of the arts? This question was posed with an eye toward improving our understanding of important aspects of arts education, as well as our understanding of other subject areas. It is anticipated that the arts research agenda will serve as a springboard for fostering similar efforts within other agencies, foundations, associations, and organizations concerned about the future of arts education as well as continued dialogue about research among representatives of the various arts disciplines.

This research agenda was by no means exhaustive. It contained sets of research questions organized into three areas: (1) curriculum and instruction; (2) assessment and evaluation; and (3) teacher education and preparation. There were several research questions posed under curriculum and instruction that addressed integrated curricula in the arts and across other subject areas. The three questions posed in this section of the agenda were: (a) What characteristics of artistic practice and arts education contribute to the development and implementation of cohesive and integrated curricula in the arts and across other disciplines? (b) How can the allocation and scheduling of instructional time and space contribute to more cohesive curricula within the arts and across all subject areas? and (c) How does an integrated curriculum that cuts across subject areas affect the individual arts disciplines? Although these types of research questions represented a starting point, clearly they were quite general in nature, did not seat the arts within any particular subject matter, and did not seek to explore the intricacies of the relationships between the teaching and learning processes that unfold within the arts and other school subject domains. The agenda can and should likely be expanded to provide focus to research on the intersections between the arts and related subjects such as literacy and the communicative arts.

NATIONAL ARTS EDUCATION SURVEY: HOW IT CAN STIMULATE CROSS-CUTTING RESEARCH INQUIRY

The National Endowment for the Arts (NEA), through OERI, is supporting the development, administration, and analysis of a survey on the status of arts education in American schools in 1994. Public school principals were surveyed recently in order to document the current status of arts education as well as the growth or decline of the arts in schools over a 5-year period. The survey is meant to serve as a tool to inform policy developments and program planning for the NEA, OERI, and the Department of Education at large, as well as other public and private agencies by providing national-level data to provide answers to such questions as who is currently teaching the arts in grades K–12, what types of courses and instruction are students receiving, and to what extent are community arts resources being utilized in education programs? An earlier nationwide survey on the status of arts education was conducted by the National Arts Education Center at the University of Illinois (Leonard, 1991). Since that time, there has been no follow-up information available to identify changes in schools' approaches to arts education. Data from the new survey will not only render a more current picture of the status of arts education, but will allow for comparative analyses with a previous data source. It is anticipated that the *Arts Education Research Agenda for the Future,* coupled with the results of a *National Arts Education Survey,* will lead to the identification of numerous avenues for research inquiry.

Overriding issues to be addressed at the national level include answers to the following questions: Will federal dollars be forthcoming to support new avenues of research that are identified through these and related endeavors? If so, when and how much? Will research dollars be funneled through OERI? If so, how will monies be channeled to the research community—through R&D Center or other grant programs? And, which research issues are apt to receive priority attention?

NATIONAL ASSESSMENT OF EDUCATIONAL PROGRESS IN READING, WRITING, AND THE ARTS

The National Assessment of Educational Progress (NAEP) is a survey of the educational achievement of our nation's students in which changes in achievement are traced over time.

NAEP, the nation's primary indicator of what school children know and can do, emerged in 1969 as an educational indicator designed to provide useful information to educators and policy makers. The NAEP, a Congressionally mandated activity conducted through the U.S. Department of Education's National Center for Educational Statistics, was specifically designed to:

- Collect data from nationally representative samples of fourth, eighth and twelfth graders, reporting trends over time;
- Assess student achievement in reading and mathematics every 2 years, science and writing every 4 years, and history\geography at least once every 6 years;
- Detail performance by a cross section of students in each subject assessed, highlighting home and school factors related to achievement; and
- Report teachers' descriptions of their backgrounds, teaching experience, and instructional approaches.

A key characteristic of NAEP has been its objective to change and keep pace with current interests in education. The NAEP continually attempts to reflect changes in curriculum and educational objectives and respond to changes in assessment technology, such as adopting innovations in performance testing, including oral reading, and portfolios of reading and writing samples.

The NAEP's 1992 reading assessment was based on a newly developed framework that emerged though the consensus process. This framework portrays reading as a dynamic, interactive, and constructive process that is purposeful and meaning-oriented and that involves a complex interaction between the reader, the text, and the context. In this view of reading, the definition of literacy has been expanded beyond text comprehension and has advanced toward an interdisciplinary perspective. The 1992 NAEP reading assessment includes a consideration of reading for literacy experience, reading to be informed, and reading to perform a task. Constructing, extending, and examining meaning are critical aspects of the framework. The NAEP assessment asks students to build, extend, and examine text meaning from four critical stances: initial understanding, developing an interpretation, personal reflection and response, and demonstrating a critical stance. These stances provided a frame for generating questions and considering student performance at all grade levels.

Guided by the tenets of the reading framework, the NAEP reading assessment now includes longer passages of text that are more representative of the types of materials students typically encounter, including a range of literary, informational, and document materials. The questions that accompany the passages ask students to interpret, reflect on, and evaluate what they have read. At least half of the student response time at grade 4 and approximately three-quarters at grades 8 and 12 are devoted to questions requiring students to construct their responses, including at least one question per passage of text that calls for an extended response equaling a paragraph or more. There are some instances where students are required to integrate information from two passages in order to answer certain questions. The reader is referred to *Reading Assessment Redesigned* (Langer et al., 1995) for a more in-depth discussion of these points.

At grade 4, paper-and-pencil assessment questions have been supplemented with the *Integrated Reading Performance Record,* a special study which consists of interviews with individual students about their independent and school-based reading experiences, and analyses of their oral reading behavior. Interview results are linked to students' performance on the written assessment. At grades 8 and 12, a portion of students are given a compendium of short stories, titled *The NAEP Reader,* from which to select and read one story, and then to answer open-ended questions about what they have read. These stories are drawn from a wide variety of sources, including short story collections, literature anthologies, and literary magazines.

For the area of writing, a new assessment was developed to assess fourth, eight, and twelfth graders. This assessment includes 25- and 50-minute prompts and also provides space for students to plan and revise their writing. The *Nation's Writing Portfolio* includes three samples of 4th- and 8th-grade students' best writing, along with a teacher questionnaire and letters from students explaining their selections. Teachers assist students in selecting their best writing for the portfolio. The questionnaire that teachers respond to focuses on student assignments and instruction provided to students. Clearly, when one contrasts the most recent NAEP assessments with those used in prior years, it is evident that substantial progress has been made in redesigning the NAEP to more closely reflect current knowledge about students' learning and how best to gauge that learning.

What about arts education assessment? In the 1970s, NAEP conducted visual arts and music assessments. Since that time, however, this practice ceased. Most recently, the National Assessment Governing Board (NAGB), with funding from the National Endowment for the Arts, and in collaboration with the Getty Center for Education in the Arts, commissioned the development of a consensus framework for a planned national assessment of student performance in the arts in 1997, although field testing is ensuing in 1995 and 1996. As of this writing, limited funding will restrict the 1997 arts assessment to grade 8. The challenges encountered when building consensus for the reading framework and designing NAEP assessments in reading and writing were formidable. The challenges presented by engaging in an analogous process for the arts are equally imposing and strikingly unique. The task of designing an arts assessment is confounded by the fact that, at present, the arts are often a marginal experience for students at the elementary and middle school levels, while they are an elective subject(s) in secondary school. Moreover, arts education in many schools has been scaled down considerably, seldom including dance and theatre. The 1997 NAEP Arts Education Assessment is being designed in such a way as to acquire information that "will indicate where arts education needs to be strengthened and extended so that future citizens may fully realize their human heritage." (NAGB, 1994, p. 10)

The model of arts learning that will underlie the NAEP Arts Education Assessment has emerged through the NAEP Framework consensus process and been influenced by the National Content Standards for Arts Education. This model projects a vision of arts education that integrates the aesthetic, social, cultural, and historical contexts of the arts with the knowledge and skills necessary to participate in the arts. NAEP is attempting to portray arts education as closely as possible to a vision of the arts as basic, unified, and pervasive. Given this objective, skills will not be considered as separable, and the achievement of students will be reported as a whole according to the various artistic processes. The assessment will consist largely of multiple related exercises organized around an arts activity—for example, theatre or dance. Portfolios will be explored extensively in a special study.

A topic for debate has been how to capture the interdisciplinary nature of much artistic work—the writing, design, and illustration of books; musical theatre; architecture. The NAEP Assessment includes all four strands—dance, music, theatre, and the visual arts—in the assessment, although the strands are separate. Design and media arts will be included within these strands as integral components. There are plans to conduct a special study to examine the interdisciplinary nature of the arts and explore the technical challenges associated with attempting to assess interdisciplinary action in this realm.

One of the biggest challenges faced in designing the NAEP arts assessment is how to gauge students' prior knowledge and experience with the arts. For example, without musical training, most students would not be able to perform successfully in items that require them to read music. Therefore, in order to obtain a valid assessment of students' performance in questions of this kind, their prior experience and training with the four different art forms should be determined. Another challenge is the difficulty inherent in reliably producing individual scores derived from a group assessment activity. An activity, such as a drama reenactment, is multidimensional whereas an individual item or set of items is constructed to measure a unidimensional quality. For this reason, it may become necessary for group assessment activities to be reported separately from students' performance in individual items. Also, group assessment activities are very costly to conduct, particularly when one considers that scorers must be employed to set up the activities as prompts for student action and interaction, provide the materials needed for each activity (e.g., musical instruments, art supplies), shoot videos of students engaging in each activity, and rate students' performance. Technical issues aside, NAEP assessment in the arts will take its place alongside of other arts assessments that have been or are being developed. However, NAEP can accomplish certain goals that no other assessment can when it comes to understanding what K–12 students know and can do because it is a large-scale, national assessment. Much can also be learned from other assessments, such as The Advanced Placement Studio Art Portfolio, an exemplary visual arts assessment from the College Board, and the portfolio assessments being developed by ARTS PROPEL in Pittsburgh and by the Florida Institute for Art Education in Florida.

CONCLUSIONS AND DIRECTIONS FOR FUTURE RESEARCH

The OERI, under its reauthorization, will function through an institute structure, as described earlier in this chapter. An important association through which the Institutes will achieve their missions is the Research and Development Centers Program. The OERI's national institutes, and the R&D Centers that are supported through these institutes will be driven by problem-centered research, which is a departure from years past wherein discipline-centered research shaped the nature of the research questions that were pursued. Problem-centered research is a practice-oriented approach to producing new knowledge. Research of this genre beckons the convergence of multiple disciplines and thereby accommodates an evolving, expanded view of literacy. Research of this kind invites knowledge integration activities. It is imperative that OERI supports domain knowledge integration activities in order to inform the ongoing national debate on educational reform. Domain knowledge integration may be viewed both as an end and as a means to an end. The objective of integrating knowledge across domain boundaries must be made explicit at the front end of the research enterprise. In so doing, research perspectives on a singular problem or issue multiply many fold and a wider lens is created to accommodate interdisciplinary inspections of the same problem or issue. Therefore, systematic views from different but complementary angles are sought here. Knowledge integration activities should facilitate analyses of complex issues and problems that transcend a single discipline. This approach holds promise for serving as a profitable vehicle through which interdisciplinary analyses of significant issues can occur.

In addition, it must be considered that this type of activity holds the potential to change substantially the nature of the research questions posed for exploration as well as the choice of methods used to explore these questions. Moreover, this approach can capitalize on research methods developed across a variety of disciplines that might add clarity to defining problems as well as seeking solutions. It is highly probable that questions of the variety posed on the same topic will lend themselves to a variety of research methodologies, thereby ensuring the collection of both quantitative and qualitative data, in tandem, that ultimately interface to tell a *bigger* story. Thus, genuine knowledge integration becomes a generative process which results in the creation of new knowledge that is inherently interdisciplinary. Designing research activities and creating funding mechanisms that enable this type of research inquiry to flourish would represent a sharp turn away from the all-too-prevalent myopic vision that advances simplistic solutions to a complex web of problems.

With specific regard to literacy, complex interactions between language and thought and the acquisition of reading, writing, listening, speaking, and literature/content knowledge have been shown to exist, although this line of research inquiry is still in its infancy. These cross-cutting relationships came to light as a result of recent changes in research focus on literacy, which include the development of interest in the early years of language acquisition and the emergence of studies on multiple aspects of the language arts and their relation to one another. It was not until very recently that researchers began to focus on the cross-dynamics among the English language arts, taking into account the content and context of learning. Many more studies must be conducted in order to clarify our understandings about the nature of these intersections and their implications for instructional practice. In addition, it is the case that systematic research inquiry on the interactions between literacy, the communicative, and visual arts is scant. This arena is a fertile ground where future research focus is warranted. The dynamics between the English language arts and the visual arts need to be examined with an eye toward the development of prototypical models for instruction.

Moreover, careful research that examines integrative instructional trends that are evident in classrooms across the country needs to be undertaken. As Dorothy Strickland pointed out in *Integrated Language Arts: Controversy to Consensus* (Morrow et al., 1994),

> ...Drawing upon the best research from the past and merging it with more contemporary research findings, today's educators are making significant changes in the way literacy is taught. Terms such as literature-based curriculum, language across the curriculum, whole language, emergent literacy, and integrated language arts are used to describe the particular thrust of those changes. Regardless of the heading under which they appear, however, these curricular changes are very similar in that they emphasize process rather than product and view language as a complex whole rather than as a series of fragmented parts. (p. xix)

The curricular changes that Strickland had characterized share the common feature of intersecting the language arts and to a certain extent, the communicative/visual arts. They share an additional trait in that all of them lack substantial research investigation. That is, although these curricular changes (e.g., whole language, literature-based reading programs, and integrated language arts instruction) can trace their roots back to Dewey (1943), Smith (1971) and others, proponents rely on the vast bodies of research on how students learn, how students learn to read and write, and what constitutes effective instructional strategies in literacy. The paradigms themselves, as recently transformed into practice, are just becoming the subject of vigorous research inquiry. Proponents of these movements refer to the substantial bodies of research on learning, language, reading, writing, literature, instructional strategies, and social interactions to inform the knowledge base from which they operate. Doing so, however, can only be considered a starting point. It is clear that research utilizing a variety of methodologies is needed on all of these language oriented, process-type paradigms in order to explore and determine the instructional efficacy of each.

Significant changes in the methodologies used to study the language arts in particular have begun to emerge. Recently, a variety of perspectives from which to study the English language arts has become popular, including views based on anthropology, psychology, and ethnography. Future directions for research, in order to be fruitful, must expand efforts to study the integrative effects and interactions among and across the English language arts and the visual arts as well as other forms of knowing. There is a pressing need to broaden the study of teaching, learning, and skill development in context over extended periods of time. This type of inquiry requires the conduct of longitudinal studies. Moreover, there is a need to inform these lines of inquiry by conducting research that is based on different kinds of research paradigms including qualitative, quantitative, experimental, and ethnographic methodologies. National research programs such as those supported by OERI and other federal agencies are challenged to take these considerations into account and to provide supportive leadership that would broaden as well as integrate the study of literacy and literacy development.

At the policy level, what can we hope to gain from an R&D Center(s) that focuses on teaching and learning and that incorporates issues pertaining to literacy? We can anticipate that the educational research which will be conducted over the 5-year grant award period will make some contributions to policy and practice that will influence immediate and specific applications in the field. This expectation may not always materialize to the extent that many policy makers, practitioners, and others may wish. Although an R&D Center holds the promise of generating research findings over a 5-year grant period that can be useful in the relative near-term, many factors impinge upon this supposition, including the maturity of research lines of inquiry, research-problem orientation, and level of Center funding— to name but a few. More profitably, in order to increase the frequency and effectiveness of useful findings, we may look toward the Center's constructing, challenging, or changing the way policy makers and practitioners think about problems. Taken a step further, as Shavelson (1988) observed, we can look toward bringing science to bear on the mind frames of practitioners and policy makers in order to better understand how educational research might shape the policy debate or reconceptualize the nature of problems confronting practitioners. In so doing, we may become better able to formulate research questions, design studies, and translate our findings in ways that influence not only specific literacy practices but the construction of knowledge on the part of policy makers and practitioners. This end result is likely to alter the very nature of the research enterprise and positively impact the ways in which education research generally and literacy research specifically is viewed from both within and outside of the education arena.

References

Almasi, J. F., & Gambrell, L. B. (1994). *Sociocognitive conflict in peer-led and teacher-led discussions of literature* (Reading Research Report No. 12). National Reading Research Center: Universities of Georgia and Maryland at College Park.

Alvermann, D. E. (1986). *Discussion: The forgotten art: Becoming literate in the secondary school.* Paper presented at the annual meeting of the American Educational Association, San Francisco. (ERIC Document Reproduction Service No. 269 717).

Alvermann, D. E., & Hinchman, K. A. (1991). Science teachers' use of texts: Three case studies. In C. M. Santa & D. E. Alvermann (Eds.), *Science learning: Processes and applications.* Newark, DE: International Reading Association.

Applebee, A. (1978). *The child's concept of story.* Chicago: University of Chicago Press.

Applebee, A. (1980). *A study of writing in the secondary school* (Final Report NIE-G-79-0174). Urbana, IL: National Council of Teachers of English.

Applebee, A., Langer, J. A., & Mullis, I. V. S. (1987). *The nation's report card: Learning to be literate in America.* Princeton, NJ: National Assessment of Educational Progress.

Applebee, A. N., Langer, J. A., Mullis, I. V. S., Latham, A. S., & Gentile, C. A. (1994). *Writing report card.* Washington, DC: National Center for Education Statistics, U.S. Government Printing Office.

Arnheim, R. (1969). *Visual thinking.* Berkeley, CA: University of California Press.

Beach, R., & Brown, R. (1987). Discourse conventions and literary inferences. In R. Tierney, P. Anders, & J. Mitchell (Eds.), *Understanding readers' understanding* (pp. 147–174). Hillsdale, NJ: Erlbaum.

Beach, R., & Hynds, S. (1991). Research on response to literature. In R., Barr, M., Kamil, P., Mosenthal, & P. D. Pearson, (Eds.), *Handbook of reading research* (Vol. 2, pp. 453–489). White Plains, NY: Longman.

Bereiter, C., & Scardamalia, M. (1984). Learning about writing from reading. *Written Communication.* 1(2). 163–188.

Berrill, D. P. (1988). Anecdote and the development of oral argument in sixteen-year-olds. In M. MacLure, T. Phillips, & A. Wilkinson (Eds.), *Oracy matters* (pp. 57–68). Milton Keynes, UK; Philadelphia: Open University Press.

Booth, D. (1987). *Drama words.* Toronto, Ontario: Language Study Centre, University of Toronto.

Britton, J. (1984). Viewpoints: The distinction between participant and spectator role language in research and practice. *Research in the Teaching of English, 18,* 320–331.

Bromley, K. (1992). *Language arts: Exploring connections.* Boston: Allyn & Bacon.

Brown, A. L., & Palinscar, A. S. (1989). Guided, cooperative learning and individual knowledge acquisition. In L. B. Resnick (Ed.), *Knowing, learning, and instruction: Essays in honor of Robert Glaser* (pp. 393–451). Hillsdale, NJ: Erlbaum.

Brown, J. S., Collins, A., & Duguid P. (1989). Situated cognition and the culture of learning. *Educational Researcher.* 18(1), 32–42.

Catchings, Y. P. (1984). Art joins the reading circle. *Instructor, 94,* 150, 151.

Catterall, J. S. (in press). *Different ways of knowing: 1991–94 National Longitudinal Study Final Report.* Los Angeles: The Galef Institute.

Cazden, C. B. (1988). *Classroom discourse: The language of teaching and learning.* Portsmouth, NH: Heinemann.

Cazden, C., John, V. P., & Hymes, D. (1972). *The functions of language in the classroom.* New York: Teachers College Press.

Cecil, N., & Lauritzen, P. (1994). *Literacy and the arts for the integrated classroom.* New York. Longman.

Christie, J. (1990). Dramatic play: A context for meaningful engagements. *The Reading Teacher, 43*(8), 542–545.

Clark, L. K. (1988). Invented versus traditional spelling in first graders' writings: Effects on learning to spell and read. *Research in the Teaching of English, 22,* 281–309.

Collins, A., Brown, J. S., & Newman, S. E. (1989). Cognitive apprenticeship: Teaching the crafts of reading, writing, and mathematics. In L. B. Resnick (Ed.), *Knowing, Learning, and instruction: Essays in honor of Robert Glaser* (pp. 453–494). Hillsdale, NJ: Erlbaum.

Consortium of National Arts Education Associations (1994). *National standards for arts education: What every young American should know and be able to do in the arts.* Reston, VA: Music Educators National Conference.

Cook-Gumperz, J. C. (1986). *The social construction of literacy.* Cambridge: Cambridge University Press.

Copeland, K. A. (1987). *Writing as a means to learn from prose.* Doctoral dissertation, University of Texas at Austin.

Cox, B., & Sulzby, E. (1984). Children's use of reference in told, dictated, and handwritten stories. *Research in the teaching of English, 18,* 345–365.

Csikszentmahlyi, M. & Hermanson, K. (in press). Intrinsic motivation in museums: Why does one want to learn? In J. H. Falk & L. D. Dierking (Eds.), *Public Institutions for personal learning: Establishing a research agenda.* Washington, DC: American Association of Museums.

Deci, E. L., Hodges, R., Pierson, L. H., & Tomassone, J. (1992). Autonomy and competence as motivational factors in students with learning disabilities and emotional handicaps. *Journal of Learning Disabilities, 25*(7), 457–471.

Delamont, S. (1983). *Interaction in the classroom: Contemporary sociology of the school* (2nd ed.). London: Methuen.

Devescovi, A., & Baumgartner, E. (1993). Joint-reading a picture book: Verbal interaction and narrative skills. *Cognition and Instruction. 11*(3&4), 299–323.

Dewey, J. (1943). *The child and the curriculum: The school and society.* Chicago: University of Chicago Press. (Originally published 1900)

Dillon, J. T. (1984). Research on questioning and discussion. *Educational Leadership, 42,* 50–56.

Dyson, A. H. (1982). The emergence of visible language: Interrelationships between drawing and early writing. *Visible Language, 6,* 360–381 .

Dyson, A. H. (1983). The role of oral language in early writing. *Research in the Teaching of English, 17,* 1–30.

Dyson, A. H. (1986). Transitions and tensions: Interrelationships between the drawing, talking, and dictating of young children. *Research in the Teaching of English, 20*(4), 379–409.

Dyson, A. H. (1987). The value of "time off task" Young children's spontaneous talk and deliberate text. *Harvard Educational Review, 57,* 396–420.

Eeds, M., & Wells, D. (1989). Grand conversations. An exploration of meaning construction in literature study groups. *Research in the Teaching of English, 23,* 4–29.

Eisner, E. W. (1994). *Cognition and curriculum reconsidered* (2nd ed.). New York: Teachers College Press.

Elkind, D. (1988). *The hurried child.* Reading, MA: Addison-Wesley.

Ernst, K. (1994). Writing pictures, painting words: Writing in an artists' workshop. *Language Arts, 71*(1), 44–52.

Ferreiro, E., & Teberosky, A. (1982). *Literacy before schooling.* Exeter, NH: Hienemann.

Flower, L., & Hayes, J. (1984). Images, plans, and prose: The representation of meaning in writing. *Written Communication. 1,* 120–160

Flynn, R., & Carr, G. (1994). Exploring classroom literature through drama: A specialist and a teacher collaborate. *Language Arts, 71*(1), 38–43.

Foertsch, M. A. (1992). *Reading in and out of school.* Washington, DC: U.S. Department of Education.

Fox-Keller, E. (1983). *A feeling for the organism.* New York: Freeman.

Galda, L. (1983). Research in response to literature. *Journal of Research and Development in Education, 16,* 1–20.

Galda, L (1984). Narrative competence: Play, storytelling and story comprehension. In A. D. Pellegrini & T. D. Yawkey (Eds.), *The development of oral and written language in social contexts* (pp. 105–117). Norwood, NJ: Ablex.

Gallas, K. (1994). *The languages of learning: How children talk, write, dance, draw, and sing their understanding of the world.* New York: Teachers College Press.

Gambrell, L. B., & Morrow, L. M. (in press). Creating motivating contexts for literacy learning. In L. Baker, P. Afflerbach, & D. Reinking (Eds.), *Developing engaged readers in home and school communities.* Hillsdale, NJ: Erlbaum.

Gardner, H. (1983). *Frames of mind.* New York: Basic Books.

Gardner, H. (1990). Multiple intelligences: Implications for art and creativity. In W. J. Moody (Ed.), *Artistic intelligences: Implications for education.* (pp. 11–27). New York: Teachers College Press.

Gazzaniga, M. S. (1985). *The social brain.* New York: Basic Books.

Glynn, S. M. (1994). *Teaching science with analogies: A strategy for teachers and textbook authors.* (Reading Research Report No. 15). National Reading Research Center: Universities of Georgia and Maryland at College Park.

Godfrey, R. (1992). Civilization, education, and the visual arts: A personal manifesto. *Phi Delta Kappan, 73,* 596–600.

Goodall, J. (1988). *Little red riding hood.* New York: McElderry.

Graesser, A. C., Millis, K. K., & Long, D. L. (1986). The construction of knowledge structures and inferences during text comprehension. In N. E. Sharkey (Ed.), *Advances in cognitive science* (pp. 125–157). New York: Ellis Horwood.

Graup, L., (1985). Response to literature: Student-generated questions and collaborative learning as related to comprehension (Doctoral dissertation, Hofstra University). *Dissertation Abstracts International, 47,* 482A.

Gray, M.A. (1987). A frill that works: Creative dramatics in the basal reading lesson. *Reading Horizons, 28,* 5–11.

Greeno, J. G. (1988). *Situations, mental models, and generative knowledge.* Report No. IRL88–0005. Palo Alto, CA: Institute for Research on Learning.

Greeno, J. G. (1989). Perspectives on thinking. *American Psychologist. 44*(2), 134–141.

Gross, B. (1984). Private response and public discussion: Dimensions of individual and classroom responses to literature (Doctoral dissertation, Rutgers University, 1984). *Dissertation Abstracts International, 45,* 03A.

Gundlach, R. A. (1982). Children as writers: The beginnings of learning to write. In M. Nystrand (Ed.), *What writers know* (pp. 129–147). New York: Academic Press.

Guthrie, J. T., McGough, & Bennett, L. (1994). Concept-oriented reading instruction: An integrated curriculum to develop motivations and strategies for reading (Report No. 10). Athens, GA & College Park, MD: National Reading Research Center at University of Georgia and University of Maryland, College Park.

Hadamard, J. (1949). *An essay on the psychology of invention in the mathematical field.* Princeton, NJ: Princeton University Press.

Hansen, J., & Graves, D. H. (1991). The language arts interact. In J. Flood, J. Jensen & J. Squire, (Eds.), *Handbook of research in the English language arts* (pp. 805–819). New York: Macmillan.

Harste, J. C., Short, K. G., & Burke. C. (1988). *Creating classrooms for authors: The reading and writing connection.* Porthsmouth, NH: Heinemann.

Hayes, D. A. (1987). The potential for directing study in combined reading and writing activity. *Journal of Reading Behavior, 19*(4), 333–352.

Hayes, J. R. (1990). Cognitive processes in creativity (Report No. 18). Berkeley, CA & Pittsburgh, PA: National Center for the Study of Writing at University of California at Berkeley and Carnegie Mellon.

Healy, M. K. & Barr, M.A. (1991). Language across the curriculum. In J. Flood, J. Jensen & J. Squire, (Eds.), *Handbook of research in the English language arts* (pp. 820–826). New York: Macmillan.

Holland, N. (1985). Reading readers reading. In C. Cooper (Ed.), *Researching response to literature and the teaching of literature* (pp.3–21). Norwood, NJ: Ablex.

Hoyt, L. (1992). Many ways of knowing: Using drama, oral interactions, and the visual arts to enhance reading comprehension. *The Reading Teacher, 45*(8), 580–584.

Hubbard, R. (1990). There's more than black and white in literacy's palette: Children's use of color. *Language Arts, 67*(5), 492–500.

Hynd, C. R., McNish, M. M., Qian, G., Keith, M., & Lay, K. (1994). *Learning counterintuitive physics concepts: The effects of text and educational environment.* (Reading Research Report No. 16). National Reading Research Center: Universities of Georgia and Maryland at College Park.

Jalongo, M. R., & Bromley, K. D. (1984). Developing linguistic competence through song picture books. *The Reading Teacher, 37,* 840–845.

Jett-Simpson, M. (1989). Creative drama and story comprehension. In J. W. Stewig & S. L. Sebasta (Eds.), *Using literature in the elementary classroom* (pp. 91–109). Urbana, IL: National Council of Teachers of English.

Kardash, C., & Wright, L. (1987). Does creative drama benefit elementary school students: A metaanalysis. *Youth Theater Journal, 1*(3),11–18.

King, M. L. (1984). Language and school success: Access to meaning. *Theory into Practice, 23,* 175–182.

King, M. L., & McKenzie, M. G. (1988). Research currents: Literary discourse from the child's perspective. *Language Arts, 65,* 304–314.

Knipping, N. (1993). Let drama help young authors "re-see" their stories. *Language Arts, 70*(1), 45–50.

Langer, J. A. (1986). Reading, writing and understanding: An analysis of the construction of meaning. *Written Communication. 3*(2), 219–267.

Langer, J. A. (1991). Discussion as exploration: Literature and the horizon of possibilities. In G. Newell & R. Durst (Eds.), *The role of discussion and writing in the teaching and learning of literature.* Norwood, MA: Christopher-Gordon.

Langer, J. A. (1992). Academic learning and critical reasoning: A study of knowing in academic subjects (Final Report, Grant No. RED). Washington, DC: U.S. Department of Education

Langer, J. A., & Applebee, A. N. (1986). *Writing and learning in the secondary school* (National Institute of Education Grant No. NIE-G-82-0027). School of Education, Stanford University.

Langer, J. A., & Applebee, A. N. (1987). *How writing shapes thinking.* Urbana, IL: National Council of Teachers of English.

Langer, J. A., Campbell, J. R., Neuman, S. B., Mullis, I. V., Persky, H. R., & Donahue, P. L. (1995). *Reading assessment redesigned: Authentic texts and innovative instruments in NAEP's 1992 survey.* Washington, DC: National Center for Education Statistics, U.S. Government Printing Office.

Leonard, C. (1991). *Status of arts education in American public schools.* Urbana, IL: Council for Research in Music Education, University of Illinois at Urbana-Champaign.

Light, P., & Butterworth, G. (1992). *Context and cognition: Ways of learning and knowing.* New York: Harvester Wheatsheaf.

Long, S., Winograd, P., & Bridge, C. (1989). The effects of reader and text characteristics on imagery reported during and after reading *Reading Research Quarterly, 24,* 359–371.

Luftig, R. L. (in press). *The schooled mind: Do the arts make a difference? An empirical evaluation of the Hamilton Fairfield SPECTRA+ Program. Part 2.* Hamilton, OH: Fitton Center for the Creative Arts.

Marshall, J. D. (1987). The effects of writing on students' understanding of literary text. *Research in the Teaching of English, 21,* 31–63.

Martin, N. (1983). Language across the curriculum: A paradox and its potential for change. In *Mostly about writing: Selected essays* (pp. 100–111). Upper Montclair, NJ: Boynton/Cook.

Martinez, M. (1993). Motivating dramatic story reenactments. *Reading Teacher. 46*(8), 682–688.

Marzano, R. J., (1991). Language, the language arts, and thinking. In J. Flood, J. Jensen, J. Squire, (Eds.), *Handbook of research in the English language arts* (pp. 559–586). New York: Macmillan.

Mayer, R. E., & Anderson, R. B. (1991). Animations need narrations: An experimental test of a dual coding hypothesis. *Journal of Educational Psychology, 83*(4), 484–490.

McGinley, W., & Tierney, R. J. (1988). Reading and writing as ways of knowing and learning (Tech. Rep. No. 423). Champaign, IL: Center for the Study of Reading, University of Illinois.

McGinley, W., & Tierney, R. J. (1989). Traversing the topical landscape: Reading and writing as ways of knowing. *Written Communication, 6,* 243–269.

Morrow, L. M. (1988). Young children's responses to one-to-one story readings in school settings. *Reading Research Quarterly, 23,* 89–107.

Morrow, L. M. (1993). *Literacy development in the early years: Helping children read and write* (2nd ed.). Needham Heights, MA: Allyn & Bacon.

Morrow, L. M., Cunningham, K., & Murray-Olsen, M. (1994). *Current strategies for literacy development in early childhood science texts.* (Reading Research Report No. 11). National Reading Research Center: Universities of Georgia and Maryland at College Park.

Morrow, L. M., O'Connor, E. M., & Smith, J. (1990). Effects of a storytelling program on the literacy development of at-risk kindergarten children. *Journal of Reading Behavior, 20*(2), 104–141.

Morrow, L. M., Smith, J. K., & Wilkinson, L. C. (Eds.). (1994). *Integrated language arts: Controversy to consensus.* Boston: Allyn & Bacon.

Mullis, I. V. S., Campbell, J. R., & Farstrup, A. E. (1993). *Reading report card for the nation and for the states.* Washington, DC: National Center for Education Statistics, U.S. Government Printing Office.

National Assessment Governing Board (1994). NAEP Arts Education Consensus Project: Arts Education Assessment Framework. Washington, DC: National Assessment Governing Board.

National Endowment for the Arts & U.S. Department of Education, OERI (1994). *Arts education research agenda for the future.* Washington, DC: U.S. Government Printing Office.

Newell, G. (1984). Learning from writing in two content areas: A case study/protocol analysis. *Research in the Teaching of English, 18,* 205–287.

Nickerson, R. S. (1984). Kinds of thinking taught in current programs, *Educational Leadership, 42,* 26–37.

Nolen, S. B. (1988). Reasons for studying: Motivational orientations and study strategies. *Cognition and Instruction, 5*(4), 269–287.

Nystrand, M., & Gamoran, A. (1991). Instructional discourse, student engagement, and student achievement. *Research in the Teaching of English. 25*(3), 261–290.

Paivio, A. (1986). *Mental representations: A dual coding approach.* New York: Oxford University Press.

Paley, V. G. (1981). *Wally's stories.* Cambridge, MA: Harvard University Press.

Paley, V. G. (1990). *The boy who could be a helicopter: The uses of storytelling in the classroom.* Cambridge, MA: Harvard University Press.

Pappas, C. C., & Brown, E. (1987). Learning to read by reading: Learning how to extend the functional potential of language. *Research in the Teaching of English, 21,* 160–184.

Pearson, P. D. (1986). Twenty years of research in reading comprehension. In T. E. Raphael (Ed.), *The contexts of school-based literacy* (pp. 43–62), New York: Random House.

Pellegrini, A., & Galda, L. (1982). The effects of thematic-fantasy play training on the development of children's story comprehension. *American Educational Research Journal, 19,* 443–452.

Penrose, A. M. (1988 April). *Examining the role of writing in learning factual versus abstract material.* Paper presented at the American Educational Research Association, New Orleans, LA.

Perret-Clermont, A. N. (1993). What is it that develops? *Cognition and Instruction, 11*(3&4), 197–205.

Pinnell, G. S., & Jaggar, A. M. (1991). Oral language: Speaking and listening in the classroom. In J. Flood, J. Jensen & J. Squire (Eds.), *Handbook of research in the English language arts.* New York: Macmillan.

Pintrich, P. R., & DeGroot, E. V. (1990). Motivational and self-regulated learning components of classroom academic performance. Special section: Motivation and efficacy in education: Research and new directions. *Journal of Educational Psychology, 82*(1), 33–40.

Pontecorvo, C. (1993). Social interaction and knowledge acquisition. *Educational Psychology Review, 5,* 293–310.

Pontecorvo, C., & Girardet, H. (1993). Arguing and reasoning in understanding historical topics. *Cognition and Instruction,* (3&4), 365-395.

Prater, J. (1887). *The gift.* New York: Viking/Penguin/Puffin.

Putnam, L. (1991). Dramatizing nonfiction with emerging readers. *Language Arts, 68*(6), 463–469.

Ravitch, D., & Finn, C. E. (1987). *What do our 17-year olds know?* New York: Harper & Row.

Resnick, L. B. (1990). Literacy in school and out. *Daedalus, 119,* 169–185.

Resnick, L. B., Salmon, M., Zeitz, C. M., Wathen, S. H., & Holowchak, M. (1993). Reasoning in conversation. *Cognition and Instruction. 11*(3&4), 347–364.

Rosenblatt, L. (1985). Viewpoints: Transaction versus interaction—A terminological rescue operation. *Research in the Teaching of English, 19,* 96–107.

Rothenberg, A. (1979). *The emerging goddess: The creative process in art, science and other fields.* Chicago: University of Chicago Press.

Rubin, K. H., Fein, G. G., & Vandenberg, B. (1983). Play. In P. H. Mussen (Ed.), *Handbook of child psychology* (4th ed., pp. 693–774). New York: Wiley.

Rumelhart, D. E. (1985). Toward an interactive model of reading. In H. Singer & R. B. Ruddell (Eds.), *Theoretical models and processes of reading* (3rd ed., pp. 722–750). Newark, DE: International Reading Association.

Ryan, S. M. (1985). An examination of reading and writing strategies of selected fifth grade students. In J. Niles & R. Lalik (Eds.), *Issues in literacy: A research perspective* (pp. 386–390). Thirty-fourth Yearbook of the National Reading Conference, Rochester, NY: National Reading Conference.

Sadoski, M., Goetz, E. T., & Fritz, J. B. (1993). Impact of concreteness on comprehensibility, interest, and memory for text. *Journal of Educational Psychology 84*(4), 444–452.

Sadoski, M., Paivio, A., & Goetz, E. T. (1991). Commentary: A critique of schema theory in reading and a dual coding alternative. *Reading Research Quarterly 26*(4), 463–484.

Salvatori, M. (1985). The dialogical nature of basic reading and writing. In D. Bartholomae, & A. Petrosky (Eds.), *Facts, artifacts, and counterfacts* (pp. 137–166). Upper Montclair NJ: Boynton/Cook.

Sautter, R. C. (1994). An arts education school reform strategy. *Phi Delta Kappan, 75*(6), 432–437.

Schiefele, U. (1990). Interest, learning, and motivation. *Educational Psychologist, 26*(3&4), 299–323.

Schlesinger, M. (1971). Production of utterances in language acquisition. In D. I. Slobin (Ed.), *The ontogenesis of grammar* (pp. 63–101). New York: Academic Press.

Schwartz, B. (1988). Photography and self-image. *Arts and Activities, 44,* 24–25.

Shavelson, R. J. (1988). The 1988 Presidential address: Contributions of educational research to policy and practice: Constructing, challenging, changing cognition. *Educational Researcher, 17*(7), 41, 22.

Shuy, R. (1984). Language as a foundation for education: The school context. *Theory into Practice, 23,* 167–174.

Silvern, S., Taylor, J., Williamson, P., Surbeck, E., & Kelly, M. (1986). Young children's story recall as a product of play, story familiarity, and adult intervention. *Merrill-Palmer Quarterly, 32,* 73–86.

Skinner, E. A., & Belmont, M. J. (1993). Motivation in the classroom: Reciprocal effects of teacher behavior and student engagement across the school year. *Journal of Educational Psychology, 85*(4), 571–581.

Skinner, E. A., Wellborn, J. G., & Connell, J. P. (1990). What it takes to do well in school and whether I've got it: A process model of perceived control and children's engagement and achievement in school. *Journal of Educational Psychology, 82*(1), 22–32.

Smith, F. (1971). *Understanding Reading.* New York: Holt, Rinehart & Winston.

Squire, R. J. (1984). Composing and comprehending: Two sides of the same basic processes. In J. M. Jensen (Ed.), *Composing and comprehending* (pp. 23-31). Urbana, IL: National Council of Teachers of English.

Stewig, J. W. (1983). *Informal drama in the elementary language arts program.* New York: Teachers College Press.

Stewig, J. W. (1986). *Visual and verbal literacy.* Paper presented at the 76th NCTE Conference, San Antonio, Texas (November 21–26) ED278028.

Sulzby, E., & Teale, W. (1991). Emergent literacy. In R. Barr, M. L. Kamil, P. B., Mosenthal & P. D. Pearson (Eds.), *Handbook of reading research* (Vol. 2, pp. 727–757). New York: Longman.

Sweet, A. P., & Anderson, J. A. (1993). Making it happen: Setting the federal research agenda. In A. P. Sweet & J. A. Anderson (Eds.), *Reading research into the year 2000* (pp. 37–64). Hillsdale, NJ: Erlbaum.

Sweet, A. P., & Guthrie, J. T. (1994). Teacher perceptions of students' motivation to read (Reading Research Report No. 29). National Reading Research Center: Universities of Georgia and Maryland at College Park.

Teale, W. H. (1986). Home background and your children's literacy development. In W. H. Teale and E. Sulzby (Eds.), *Emergent literacy: Writing and reading* (pp. 173–206). Norwood, NJ: Ablex.

Teale, W. H., & Sulzby, E (1987). Literacy acquisition in early childhood: The roles of access and mediation in storybook reading. In D. A. Wagner (Ed.), *The future of literacy in a changing world* (pp. 111–130). New York: Pergamon Press.

Tierney, R. J. (1992). Ongoing research and new directions. In J. W. Irwin & M. A. Doyle (Eds.), *Reading and writing connections: Learning from research* (pp. 246-259). Newark, DE: International Reading Association.

Tierney, R. J., & Pearson, P. D. (1983). Toward a composing model of reading. *Language Arts, 60,* 568–580.

Tierney, R. J., & Shanahan (1991). Research on the reading-writing relationship: Interactions, transactions, and outcomes. In R. Barr, M. Kamil, P. Mosenthal & P. D. Pearson (Eds.), *Handbook of reading research* (Vol. 2, pp. 246–309). White Plains, NY: Longman.

Tierney, R. J., Soter, A., O'Flahavan, J. F., & McGinley, W. T. (1989).

The effects of reading and writing upon thinking critically. *Reading Research Quarterly, 24*(2). 134–173.

Vygotsky, L. (1978). *Mind in society.* Cambridge, hA: Harvard University Press.

Wagner, B. J. (1986). The effects of role-playing on written persuasion: An age and channel comparison of fourth and eighth graders. *Dissertation Abstracts International, 47,* 11–A. (University Microfilms No. 87–05196)

Wagner, B. J. (1988). Research currents: Does classroom drama affect the arts of language? *Language Arts, 65,* 46–55.

Wagner, B. J. (1991). Imaginative expression. In J. Flood, J. M. Jensen, D. Lapp, & J. R. Squire (Eds.), *Handbook of research on teaching the English language arts* (pp. 787–804). New York: Macmillan.

Whitin, P. (1994). Opening potential: Visual response to literature. *Language Arts, 71*(2), 101–107.

Wigfield, A., & Eccles, J. S. (1992). The development of academic task values: A theoretical analysis. *Developmental Review, 12,* 265–310.

Wilkinson, L. C. (1984). Research currents: Peer group talk in elementary school. *Language Arts, 61,* 164–169.

Wilkinson, L. C., & Spinelli, F. (1982). Conclusion: Application for education. In L. C. Wilkinson (Ed.), *Communicating in the classroom* (pp. 323–327). New York: Academic Press.

Wittrock, M. C. (1984). Writing and the teaching of reading. In J. M. Jensen (Ed.), *Composing and comprehending* (pp. 77–83). Urbana, IL: National Council of Teachers of English.

Wolf, S. A. (1994). Learning to act/acting to learn: children as actors, critics, and characters in classroom theater. *Research in the Teaching of English, 28*(1), 6–9.

Wolf, S. A., & Heath, S. B. (1992). *The braid of literature: Children's worlds of reading.* Cambridge, MA: Harvard University Press.

Zessoules, R., & Gardner, H. (1991). Authentic assessment: Beyond the buzzword and into the classroom. In V. Perrone (Ed.), *Expanding student assessment* (pp. 47–71). Alexandria, VA: Association for Supervision and Curriculum Development.

22

LEARNING WITH MULTIPLE SYMBOL SYSTEMS: POSSIBILITIES, REALITIES, PARADIGM SHIFTS AND DEVELOPMENTAL CONSIDERATIONS

Robert J. Tierney

OHIO STATE UNIVERSITY

...Paintings continue to help Kunwinjku to understand the fundamental connection between individuals, and the social and ancestral order. Kunwinjku experience the worth of the knowledge revealed in paintings because it helps to structure so many aspects of their experience of the world in a way that makes such experience intelligible ... the experience of understanding the artistic system takes the revelations of the truth of knowledge relating to the Ancestral Beings. Paintings help to create the meaningful texture of their religious understanding.

—Taylor, 1987, pp. 336–338

...I'm a discourse surfer.... Of all of the things I have done, discourse surfing makes me the happiest. And, not incidentally, for me in deep ways it is the most powerful tool of all the tools I've learned to use....
Discourse surfers can surf any discourse if they are good enough. I'm not that good: I have a favorite spot, at which I'm most content, but there are plenty of great coves and public places where great things happen.

—Stone, (1995), p. 165

...the electronic future was not there in an envelope that we could either open or ignore, we have made it inevitable through countless acts of acquiescence.

—Bickert, (1994), p. 220

In contrast to Bickert, my thesis is that, under certain conditions, multimedia environments (involving the use of more than one medium, and regardless of whether it be the electronic environment or involving everyday media such as paper, string, glue, tape) can serve as the basis for the social construction of self and others, making multiple probes about issues or concepts and problem solving, and empowering students in a host of ways. The presence of multiple symbol systems allows for constructing oneself and for achieving different "takes" on an issue or problem with one "take" supporting (complementing, extending, or challenging) another—that is, different ways of knowing and being known.

While I have not focused on theory so much as described practices, the descriptions lend themselves to sociosemiotic (e.g., Taylor, 1987), marxist (e.g., Habermas, 1983) and cognitive (e.g., Bruner, 1990) perspectives on learning. When such perspectives are applied, media can be seen as embedded within cultural practices and serving to signal and shape values as well as transform, challenge and shape self and others—both socially and culturally.[1]

There are several key words that help capture the view that I am espousing. They are: learner-centered, multisymbolic, perspectival, communal, generative, developmental, systemic, representational, indeterminate, ongoing, and empowering. *Learner-centered* is intended to highlight the preeminent position of the student. I envision that our goal is not to have the media or an activity displace the student, but have the students achieve ownership of the media whereby they can use the media in various ways including developing representations of their own meaning making. *Multisymbolic* (as contrasted with unisymbolic or a reliance upon a limited range of media) is intended to highlight the

---

[1] Gee (1990) has described Discourse as "...a socially accepted association among ways of using language, of thinking, believing, valuing and acting that can be used to identify oneself as a member of a socially meaningful group or "social network" or to signal (that one is playing) a socially meaningful "role" (p. 143).

pursuit of media in various combinations. Media used together or in concert serve as ways of crisscrossing explorations en route to achieving multiple perspectives or being *perspectival*. Sometimes these perspectives are achieved by individuals working in collaboration with oneself; at other times they are achieved in collaborations with others. *Communal* is meant to suggest the various senses of community that media afford including the multiple roles in the context of ongoing conversations / collaborations with oneself and others. I have chosen the word *generative* as a way of pursuing a view of multimedia which involves new and open-ended uses rather than canned and receptive uses of knowledge. The word *developmental* reflects a concern with how media use shifts over time. As educators we need to develop an environment whereby we are sensitive to the students' emerging uses of media, developing expertise, growing understandings with media and expanding possibilities for media. *Systemic* reflects concerns with how media are woven into the social fabrics of the individual and group's experiences and relationships within different institutions such as schools.[2] *Representational* is used to suggest that these media afford new ways to represent ideas especially in combination with other ideas.[3] *Indeterminate and ongoing* refer to the constant shifts that are incurred with meanings associated with such representation such that meaning should never be viewed as fixed.[4] Finally, *empowering* is meant to suggest that the study of multimedia also has to do with empowering individuals within different institutions. In other words, as individuals do or do not gain access and expertise, they may gain or lose access to certain opportunities which may carry with them an increase or decrease in power or the opportunity to participate in certain decision making.[5]

To illustrate the integration of media in teaching and learning and the conditions necessary for media to act as a meaning making tool, let me begin by offering three examples. The first describes my son's recent involvement with boogie boarding. The second is taken from one of the many projects pursued at one of the preschools within the Reggio Emilia project in Italy. The third is derived from my involvement with the Apple Classroom of Tomorrow; specifically, from my observations of students at West High School in Columbus, Ohio (Tierney, Kieffer, Stowell, & Desai, 1992).

Boogie Boarding

My son (Shaun), when he was nine years old, became rather engaged with boogie boarding on a recent extended trip to Australia. While his introduction to the sport had begun on

FIGURE 22–1 Shaun and his cousins outfit themselves.

[2] Green, Weede and Graham (1988) discuss schooling as "learning to student" rather than learning as may otherwise be defined. Street (1984) discusses the differences that may exist between literacy practices as defined within the institution of schools versus other cultural settings. The former tending to treat text as autonomous and the acquiring of pyschological competence of a series of skills versus acquiring literacy practices.

[3] The Cognition and Technology Group at Vanderbilt University have used the term representational literacy to refer to the flexible use of multimedia for communications and learning.

[4] Bloome (1993) provides a detailed discussion of the indeterminate nature of meaning in reading and writing that can be extended to other forms of representation and argues for the "refractive" versus "reflective" nature of ongoing meaning making.

[5] Critical theorists, sociolinguists, and various systemic linguists have underlined the extent to which various forms of literacy can serve to exclude or empower individuals or groups. (see Fairclough, 1992; Lemke, 1990; Luke, 1988; Wignell, Martin and Eggins, 1982). There have been a number of discussions to the extent to which technology may exclude certain groups from being afforded access. For example, with the advent of e-mail certain groups have the potential to shift all communications to e-mail thus excluding those who do not have or choose not to use this technology.

FIGURE 22–2 The group make their way through the waves in hopes of being optimally placed to catch certain waves .

the East Coast of the United States, his sustained and in-depth engagement occurred in Australia where his cousins loaned him a boogie board and engaged him in conversations about boogie boarding, including cutting, doing spinners and going for the better waves. With a little encouragement and without much of the paraphernalia (flippers, wet suits, gloves, helmet etc.), my son set out on his first trip to the beach with his cousins—a kind of an initiation for which my son needed little prodding. At the beach he watched other boogie boarders and, alongside his cousins, made his way through the breakers close to the shore where he caught (OOPS, almost caught) his first wave. In the ocean, he watched his cousins who were quite good and full of expert advice and whom he hoped would watch his successes. Once on shore again, the conversations represented a mixture of expletives about the great waves that were caught, some of the stunning wipeouts and analyses of how to better "read" the waves. Away from the shore, the conversations as well as the discussion of the

equipment continued—the advantages of wet suits, flippers, the kind of boogie board needed to maximize possibilities. Then there were the videos of surfing, magazines and posters being reviewed and analyzed. Then the return trips to the beach to try boogie boarding again and again—each time under somewhat different wave conditions. Before too long, boogie board posters surrounded bedroom walls and my son was negotiating with us how to apply his savings toward the purchase of his own "manta" board, flippers, and so forth. He began reading the newspaper for information about tides and weather forecasts as well as anything that might pertain to surfing conditions. Conversations addressed the sand bars, the uniqueness of each wave, each wave set, the dangers of rips, kinds of conditions, as well as issues of balance, weight distribution and the relationship of body position to direction and speed. And, sharks, stingers and seaweed were discussed.

It was not until I wrote this piece on boogie boarding that I truly realized what boogie boarding entailed. Consider, if you will, what my son learned: First, he learned a very sophisticated skill in becoming "a boogie board rider." Such expertise, while seemingly frivolous, should not be slighted; it entails a knowledge of the ocean, especially waves, currents, tides, the dangers of rips, different kinds of breaks, and sealife. It also entails an understanding of flotation, momentum, water temperature, body temperature, sunlight—especially ultraviolet light, the effects of salt water, pollution, and the characteristics of various materials (rubber, foam, salt water, fiberglass) and their effects on one another.

Consider also the media that were used. My son enlisted conversations, photos, magazines, videos, first hand experience, observations, self and peer analysis and advice across a range of situations. At the same time he sent letters and e-mail messages back to the United States to friends about surfing and used his expertise to have conversations with grandparents, uncles, and his little brother. The media were rarely separate and discrete from these interactions; indeed, the media were embedded within and a part of the social situations. The media were a vehicle for learning (prompting questions, arousing interests, affording comparisons and connections, analysis, evaluation and goal setting). And, to be a boogie board rider entailed walking, talking, watching, and analyzing boogie boarding.

There is a great deal more that could be said. But suffice it to say, my son's learning experience represents a kind of real world learning experience that involves various media in a complex and dynamic fashion that is inseparable from the learning experience itself. The media were used in combination with one another as boogie boarding was explored, problems were solved, new perspectives achieved, expertise developed and knowledge advanced.

Learning experiences such as this parallel some of the descriptions of learning in classrooms that afford similar possibilities with media. The projects that are pursued in conjunction with the Reggio Emilia preschools represent such situations. The Long Jump project is one such project.[6]

---

[6] Unfortunately, a detailed description of the Reggio Emilia's educational approach is beyond the scope of this paper since it would require an extensive discussion of a range of features: the involvement with parents and the community, the integrative nature of projects, the practical

FIGURE 22–3 Shaun experiences the thrill of riding the wave just below its shoulder and cuts across the surface.

FIGURE 22–4 Shaun cuts then turns trying to maximize his ride prior to deciding to exit the wave.

nature of these projects, the discussions among teachers regarding the development of projects, the use of children's ideas and multiple representation. I will focus on the use of media as a symbol system to represent, explore and engage with new ideas, and so forth.

Reggio Emilia "The Long Jump Project"

The Long Jump Project involved the development of an athletic event by four children who volunteered to plan and design it with occasional input from the whole class and the community. While some activities emerged, others were planned or facilitated by the teachers. The teachers identified the long jump events as an activity in which the students could become engaged and in so doing would learn about measurement, jumping, events, tools, and a host of other things. The project began with conversations surrounding the possibility of the class holding a long jump event. Those children who volunteered to organize the event began their extended exploration and preparation by studying how experts (i.e. Olympic athletes) do the long jump. They did so by discussing videos of athletes jumping and then pursuing the long jump themselves. There was a kind of spontaneous sharing of knowledge of jumping in conversations that related to what they were seeing and what they themselves could do or might do. Their conversations included a mix of observations, some firsthand experiences experimenting with the long jump and illustrations generated by the children. They needed not only to understand the long jump, but to be aware of how to actually organize an event which involved classmates being long jumpers and comparing the distances that they jumped. Discussions, observations and planning involved developing suggestions / plans for the physical space needed to run an event requiring a pit, a place to run to the pit, a spot to launch the jump and an area for spectators and judges. To these ends, an array of media was used, including drawing plans of the field, using replicas of people as a way of simulating jumping, enlisting strings and other media to assess distances jumped, and so forth. These experiences led to questions and further analyses and other problems to be solved (e.g., how to compare the length of the jumps with strings) and all of these rolled over to an expanding understanding which then informed plans. Sometimes in conversations peers advised one another, compared their observations, discussed replays of the simulations with replicas, examined one another's drawings and made decisions regarding what media tool would best serve certain purposes. Sometimes the discussions led to disagreements. For example, a lengthy discussion surrounding issues such as measuring distances never reached resolution (i.e. the comparative worth of strings and rulers). Also, the children became engaged in lengthy discussions of rules and etiquette as the students practiced the context of long jumping and used replicas or figures of jumpers jumping to simulate the event. Forman (1993) provides a chronological listing of activities involved in the project:

Looking at and acting out photographs of Olympic long jumpers
Verbal outpouring of initial knowledge of long jump making an initial sketch of track, jumpers and how to score
Drawing the track layout
Experimenting with running speed x jumping distance
Laying out the track in the courtyard with white chalk
Debating about handicap for girls using small replica objects
Designing six posters for rules to the long jump
    Place to start
    Three false starts allowed

    Speed and place of run-up
    The touch of the foot
    Measurement of the footprint
Presenting the rules to the whole class
Designing training, clothes, diet
Making posters calling for registration of each participant
Making posters for designating ability flights
Making posters for calendar of competition by ability flights
Writing a letter of invitation to all children of the school
Designing posters of citywide advertising
Writing the rules for prizes
Writing the closing speech for the competition
Making a poster of rules for measuring three jumps per person
Learning to measure distance—six phases
    Using string to record the distance jumped
    Trying to use the tape measure
    Correcting the tape measure
    Transcribing tape measure symbols to paper
    Comparing the tape measure to carpenter's rule.
    Reinventing convention place value notation
Preparing insignia for each jumper to wear at meet
Writing rules for the referee and assistants
Implementing the plans: the day and the final competition
    The run and the long jump measuring each jump with string
    Posting the strings on the wall
    Using the tape to measure the longest strings
    Awarding the trophies
    The kisses from the misses and misters (Forman, 1993, pp. 173–174)

During their experimentation and exploration, teachers supported the students and prompted comparisons, speculations, evaluations and further planning by them. Oftentimes the teachers encouraged the children to use props or illustrations to externalize their thoughts or to show them to others, and discussed ways in which they might share what they were doing with less informed others. To these ends, various symbol systems were used including different symbols for the same object (e.g., P for person or the use of small figurines) as they explored the long jump through diagrams and photographs and used a tape measure and carpenter's rule to explore ways to measure distance. Sometimes the discussion focused on the worth of different symbolizations and created what Forman described as "the type of constructive conflict we deem to be the power of this multisymbolic approach to education" (p. 187). As Forman stated, the essence of the project involved the following:

As these children sought to gain a more coherent understanding of time, distance, and rules of equity, they externalized their nascent theories as icons, gestures, speech, text, pictograms, diagrams and notations. These symbols were embedded in the coherence of a real-world event which in turn helped convert a random list of symbols into a symbol system. This holism assures that the symbol system will ultimately converge to deepen knowledge rather than increase facts. (p. 188)

In a host of ways the Reggio Emilia approach resembles the kind of learning with media engaged by my son as he developed expertise in boogie boarding. Just as my son enlisted a range of overlapping media, these preschoolers enlisted a variety of media throughout the project—even for the same activity. The extended projects involved a host of planned and unplanned learning about sports, materials, the world around us, working with others, problem solving and the use of media. Also, the use of media and the projects themselves were socially constituted—that is, it is impossible to separate long jumping or boogie boarding from the other social negotiations and events that were occurring / developing. Just as these explorations are inseparable from the social fabric of the learning situation, the media serve as vehicles for learning and become part of what is being learned. In other words, the conversations, observations, and use of other tools have a symbiotic relationship with the events themselves.

Apple Classroom of Tomorrow[sm.]

The third situation involving media is drawn from one of the many projects that were observed in conjunction with a 6-year study of computer appropriation in a learning environment (an Apple Classroom of Tomorrow[sm.] site) that provides students as much access to computers as students in regular classrooms have to books, pen and paper. The Apple Classroom of Tomorrow[sm.] represents an attempt to provide students with state-of-the-art technology in a constructive learning environment wherein they enlist media to explore topics, solve problems and pursue their own projects. Students are able to interact with a community of learners in various subject areas within a context that allows them to explore and learn with a range of multimedia software, data bases, and word processing software. For example, in their science or history class, they might pull together projects using PageMaker, HyperCard and SuperCard, using a mix of scanned images, video, and multilevel stacks of ideas. They also have access to computers at home where they can pursue classwork or projects that they might decide to initiate themselves. Some may say that the site is too rare to be generalizable; I would disagree and argue that, as Clark and Salomon (1986) state, such a level of investment may be necessary to study the impact of computer media upon learning and to develop the culture of the classroom technology to the point at which computer use is universally appropriated. The site involved similar careful planning as that carried out by the teachers at the Reggio Emilia school. Projects and units were selected, planned and implemented with student problem solving and issues in mind. Throughout the projects the ACOT teachers considered ways to facilitate student engagement with issues, concepts and problems as they used media as adjuncts to their learning and simultaneously studied the value of the media for so doing. The students themselves provided one another help in various forms including expertise, if needed, as well as ongoing critical feedback.

The projects with which the students were engaged represented a wide range of problems, topics and issues. Students might be given the tasks such as developing and launching their own rockets; developing video portfolios about themselves; constructing a scaled-down version of the city of Columbus; helping develop leaflets for community agencies using desktop publishing and pursuing projects tied to different topics and themes. Often projects involved an extended exploration of a topic. Take, if you will, their exploration of

one such topic—the China project. This project was one of many projects in which students were encouraged to explore topics using a range of media as vehicles for such explorations and to culminate their explorations in the presentation of an exhibit or demonstrations for others (classmates, teachers, students in other classes, and interested public). The China project coincided with a rare exhibition of Chinese artifacts dating back to the earliest emperors in China. The students were encouraged to explore various facets of life in China during early imperial dynasties and, to these ends, were given access to the exhibit and other resources including experts of that period, video and laser disks. The students grouped themselves in terms of their interests and in the context of conversations with the collaborators, began gathering resources in the form of books, pamphlets, photographs, videos or other forms of resources. With the computer-based technologies and other media, each project became a composite of media involving the development and capturing of conversations, observations, scanned images, video clips, or experiencing firsthand food of the times, different ways of dressing, sporting activities, and so forth. The explorations of their specific topic involved a mix of conversations that were tied to readings, viewing films, examining actual artifacts at the exhibit, these aforementioned firsthand experiences and interviews with experts. Each student's explorations took a variety of different turns as they explored their topic with these media.

The media served as vehicles for developing understandings as well as a kind of portfolio from which they could either keep track of their explorations and palate from which they could pursue their own expressions or customized presentations. The students could be seen discussing what they wanted to do as they directed one another's attention to material that they had located in books and other reference material stacked on the floor, portions of video that they had discovered as well as scanned images and text that they had generated. As the stacks of material were examined the explorations of the topic and their projects moved forward. Sometimes the discussions centered upon the scope of the topic (what was relevant, what was irrelevant, how ideas were related); at other times the discussion focused on how the different media could complement one another or which medium was more effective. As they explored different topics they generated video screens which combined text, images and sound and these screens connected with one another sequentially and hierarchically. With the electronic media that they were using, they could insert graphics buttons, which, if clicked upon, accessed other layers of information (perhaps a map depicting the Great Wall, additional information on related events, a graphic display of the sequence of events, a video clip, etc.). The technology appeared to increase the likelihood of being able to pursue multiple lines of thought, as well as entertain different perspectives. Ideas were no longer treated as unidimensional and sequential; the technology allowed students to embed ideas within other ideas, as well as other forms of multilayering and interconnecting between ideas. The students spent a great deal of time considering how ideas were laid out—that is, how the issues that they were exploring might be explored across an array of still pictures, video segments, text segments and sound clips. It was apparent that the students in the high access classroom had begun exploring images, sound tracks, and text interconnected in very complex ways (i.e., multifaceted, multilayered ways) using a smorgasbord of image, sound, and print. The presentations themselves included the computer-based presentation of a mix of multilayered visual information together with text on various facets of a topic. Supplementing the technology-based presentations were food tasting, posters, verbal presentations and demonstrations of sports.

The multisymbolic or multimedia texts that they created were, as the students stated, "more inviting, dynamic and open than regular text." Students realized the possibility of developing texts that were more pictorial and concrete at the same time as they allowed for making connections between concepts that were more complex, multilayered and immediately accessible. In conjunction with being able to explore the integrated use of various graphics (animation, video segments, scanned images or various ways to graphically depict data), they began to utilize various media as a way of achieving different perspectives on issues they were exploring in physics, history, and other subjects. Just as an author might look for the right word or twist in their text, these students were exploring ways to integrate images with written text to achieve different takes and twists. They found themselves free to develop texts that were nonlinear and multilayered.

If outsiders come to these learning situations with traditional views of media and learning, they may not realize what is occurring. Some might view these learning situations as different forms of project learning; others might see them as ways to make learning more concrete. However, educators attuned to the role of the media in transforming ways of knowing are likely to recognize that these situations represent environments where students are exploring their world with media that afford the enlistment of multiple symbol systems. Moreover, they are apt to see some confirmation of Olson's (1974) contention that the symbol systems create new possibilities for ways of knowing, including deepening and shifting understanding as well as transacting with others. These situations represent learning conditions that reflect an orientation to learners, learning and the role of media which is less traditional—especially in terms of the nature of knowledge, the pursuit of knowledge and the role multiple media assumes.

MAKING THE SHIFT

Obviously, media or various symbol systems can serve several masters. Indeed, some media may be enlisted solely as ways to enhance textbook-like approaches to teaching and learning. For example, images and sound may be embedded with an approach to teaching and learning which is rote and survey-like. Alternatively, media can be enlisted as vehicles for crisscrossing the exploration of topics and cases (or instantiations), affording different *takes* on a topic and facilitating the development of understandings that are transfer-

able to other situations. Accordingly, media may be used as a meaning-making tool that affords not only access to ideas but also ways to achieve *different* constructions and different takes on one's own multimedia compositions or those of others. The uses of these resources are not seen as ends unto themselves or as affording a comprehensive or definitive understanding but as a vehicle for achieving perspectives and making meanings.

Drawing upon work and studies of early literacy development (Harste, Woodward, & Burke, 1984), Seigel (1984) suggests that children have the potential to use symbol systems in concert with one another. By so doing, these symbol systems afford alternative perspectives that inform one another and invite reflection and invention. In other words, she argues that meaning and signification, not language, should be at the center of teaching and argues for a higher status for media. She and others emphasize, however, that to achieve these ends, displacement of the preeminent role granted print or the reverence for print's authority over other media is required (e.g., Bolter, 1991; Lanham, 1993; Lemke, 1994). 'Logophobia,' a term coined by Jacques Derrida, aptly captures the preoccupation with written language to the exclusion of other symbol systems.

In many classrooms as students move through the grades there may exist a tendency to stress the written text over and apart from other media. The stress is placed upon learning of the written language rather than learning with language. Many have argued that there exists a kind of verbocentricity that separates written language from other ways of knowing and that gives written language a status not only apart from but superior to other sign systems or media. Their argument is that the preeminence of language reflects the tendency for the language of schooling to be the object of learning rather than a resource for exploration. As an object, language constrains learning by emphasizing convention as being more important than invention and revering recitation, memorization and preset outcomes.

Moving toward the use of other symbol systems is not straightforward and appreciating what might be entailed in the shift is to see that it demands more than simply ridding ourselves of logophobia. The enlistment of a range of symbol systems does not ensure a shift away from how knowledge is viewed in schools and especially the orientation to the transmission and display of knowledge rather than to exploration and debate, problem solving or ongoing dialogue. Resnick (1989), Seely-Brown, Collins, and Duguid (1989) and Spiro, Coulson, Feltrovich, and Anderson (1988) suggest that schools often treat knowledge and the learning of knowledge in a fashion that is inconsistent with how we understand that knowledge is actually acquired and structured. For instance, schools may approach knowledge as more generalizable and absolute than it actually is. Accordingly, rote learning and recall of factual information from lecture or textbook rendering are stressed, giving preeminence to the scope rather than the depth of knowledge. In the "real world", knowledge and the pursuit of knowledge appear to be quite different. Explorations of topics or engagement with problems are usually firsthand rather than summarized by others. In turn, a premium is placed upon one's ability to apply knowledge of situations rather than to recall facts. Experiences with case-like leanings from a variety (but not exhaustive set) is viewed as developing expertise.

Similarly, schools may mirror an approach to learning that is antithetical to our current views of scholarly inquiry. While some schools have tended to approach inquiry positivistically and reductionistically, science has shifted to relativism or constructivism and sociolinguistics. For example, schools may approach knowledge as absolute, rather than relative. Some schools may emphasize preset objectives and measurable outcomes rather than emerging orientations and open-endedness. Of direct relevance to media, schools may highlight knowledge as generalizable and decontextualized rather than context-specific and derivative of the methods employed for different takes or perspectives. Media can serve such ends and perpetuate decontextualized learning *or* media can serve to contextualize learning including the heightening of context and virtual as well as firsthand encounters.

These days, the frameworks informing views of learning include ethnographies of communication, social semiotics, linguistic anthropology, sociolinguistics and sociohistories. Accordingly, while schools may view literacy as a set or series of fixed skills, researchers have shifted to the appreciation of the nature of literacy as indeterminate and ongoing. While schools have tended to treat education as dealing with cognitive outcomes which are apoliticial, researchers have become increasingly concerned with the social dynamics and the political nature of what and how we teach.

Whether the media are software or involve "hands on" activities, educators need to consider the extent to which the software or activity lends itself to meaning making by the students, alternative ways of knowing including ways that are less obsessed with the written or spoken word as the sole vehicle and the power of the media to democratize, engage, empower and enhance the voices of students. Software that allows the possibility of using multimedia in generative, open-ended, flexible and empowering ways is to be preferred to software or activities that are prepackaged, preset, canned and constraining. Sometimes media detract from sustained engagement with ideas and perpetuate secondary almost summary-like renditions and engagements with ideas. Sometimes they do not. If these assumptions are accepted, then our goal would seem to be to engage students with the media whereby they can extend, alter (refract vs. reflect), create, speculate and use rather than recant or cut and paste the ideas of others. This entails preference being given for media that students will find inviting and useful for explorations of topics, problem solving and developing their own constructions or virtual words. It also entails affording students access to media that will afford them clout, opportunities and access to possibilities. Of course, media may result in the opposite—for example, if students are constrained and given access to media in a very limited fashion (preset and controlled by others) or are given such restricted access to media resources that they remain dependent upon others or are unable to realize the possibilities with the media.

Often when schools consider a shift toward multimedia they focus on the supplies and materials they need or what they can afford in terms of technology. These are important considerations, but they should not be seen as more important than a consideration of how students and teachers view the role of the software or media's contribution. Sometimes the possibilities with software are limited by the orientation of the teacher or the predisposition of the students and how the media are integrated. For example, an emphasis upon the quality of a finished product may discourage students from taking risks and pursuing their own explorations of ideas and contribute to students' superficial use of the media and, in turn, limited exploration of topics. Sometimes the possibilities with media are constrained simply by resources and tend to perpetuate inequities that may preexist in school funding. Sometimes the possibilities are constrained by the nature of schooling, especially the extent to which schooling maintains control over the media, student learning with media and possible uses.

How we appropriate technology can have a profound effect on its eventual integration into our lives. Let me offer an autobiographical account to illustrate this point. The 1950s in Australia were a period of very rapid change in terms of technology. Two major shifts occurred relative to everyday media—families began to install phones in their homes (or I should say the post office did) and television was introduced to Australia. The shifts in views and uses of these media represented shifts in how individuals viewed technology as well as shifts in the technologies themselves. For example, initially the technologies appeared to have been used somewhat ceremoniously rather than spontaneously or incidentally. Expectations shifted from an initial reverence for the equipment to expectations that equipment should meet the users' needs (whether it be remote control, ear phones or speakers, etc., a wide array of choices in the physical and electronic features as well as programming capabilities). There was also a shift in the accessibility and control as the technology was improved to create more flexibility such as interfaces with other technologies including answering machines, faxes, VCRs, computers, and so forth. Eventually the technology itself became more integrated with our everyday lives. Let me illustrate:

I was 9 years old when the telephone was finally connected in my house. When the telephone was introduced, it was placed upon a special telephone table in the hallway along with its own little seat. Calls were a formality in lots of ways. They were often scheduled rather than enlisted incidentally. It was not initially a vehicle for lengthy conversations or spontaneous extended chats, but usually something that was an event of some proportion. Sometimes letters were written to apprise someone that you would call. Likewise phones were not used to deal so much with folks in your neighborhood, but places to which you could not walk or to which you might not carry a note. Oftentimes I would be asked to "run a message" from home to a neighbor's house. Also, for many years the telephone was not a substitute for the telegram. Indeed, I had a part-time job on weekends delivering telegrams on my bicycle. A person would not call to check on when you were leaving or coming. With the introduction of the telephone came telephone numbers not unlike addresses. To look at the telephone use nowadays we see a technology that is everyday, incidental, accessible and that affords new ways of exploring ideas and relationships. Telephones are no longer viewed as a luxury but a necessity and the uses of the telephone are still expanding. Its use is woven into the fabric of everyday life for a range of purposes; communication, accessing information of certain kinds instantly, a means of negotiation, ways to achieve immediate feedback and to leave and send messages. For those of us who are e-mail users it integrates our written mail to a telephone via a computer such that we can exchange notes back and forth without the constraints of distance and time interfering with the ongoing communication and exchange of information that we need.[7] The telephone now serves as a bulletin board for us or others as well as means of having food or other goods delivered to our door.

Television came to Australia with the Melbourne Olympic games in 1956. Prior to that time and for several years thereafter, radio was the primary vehicle for entertainment and broadcast news. Several of my friends had TV sets prior to my own family. Geoff Brown's family had one of the first sets and I still recall arriving at Geoff's house on a Friday night to watch my first TV show. I still have a vivid recollection of the living room darkened as if we were at a movie theater and our group glued to the set as we watched an old Edward G. Robinson movie. Watching TV became a regular Tuesday night event as my friends and I met at the Foxes' house to watch the Mickey Mouse club prior to going to Boy Scouts. A year or so later we bought our set. I already knew lots about televisions from being at my friends' houses. While turning the TV set off and changing channels was something that was similar to the radio and something that we all could do (but carefully), other fine tunings etc. were under the control of my father or older brother. Nowadays televisions afford us access to a wide range of viewing experiences that we might otherwise not have had. These range from seeing sports and other ways of life or world events as they unfold. Nowadays, my 5-year old controls a remote (sometimes channel surfing), manipulates the video player and witnesses people, places events as if he were there. The TV is also used for videogames, to make and play back video. Nowadays video screens have become commonplace as well as interactive but as yet only beginning to be enlisted to make and edit videos. With the advent of user friendly video production capabilities, it has also the potential to be a palate from which they can create their own video and text images as they engage simultaneously with others engaged from afar in also doing so. ...

While my autobiographical account or similar accounts may bring to the fore the shifts that occur with the integration of technology in one's lifetime over time, it should be noted that developmental studies of the appropriation of multiple symbol systems, especially tied to technological possibilities, are sorely lacking. We have studies that describe the extent to which technology is being used, but no studies (of which I am aware) that address these issues across time. There is also a dearth of longitudinal studies describing the engagement of individuals or societies with media. While we have detailed descriptions of the nature of students' development tied to written language, similar studies of students' development of other symbol systems, such as video, separately or in combination with other media do not exist. While we have several different views of the integration of technology in the curriculum, we have few sustained studies.[8]

In my own work, I have tended to adopt the close-up lens within an institution constrained by curriculum, resources and teachers' changing views. With this close-up lens, what I have found in media use in classrooms is that individuals approach the introduction of media differently. In my observations of students in the ACOT classroom, I encountered a wide range of individual differences including varied dispositions with respect to appropriation and use of media. Interestingly, Seigel also suggests, but does not account for, the existence of individual differences with which students engage in the use of symbol systems. We live in a world that introduces us to new media possibilities and many of us approach these situations differently. Let me offer a final aside as an illustration of this point:

> My two sons are rather shy and reserved when you place them in new situations. Recently they temporarily relocated in Australia where they encountered a whole range of new people and situations. Like many children, they are initially hesitant and perhaps withdrawn. However, once they learn the ropes or warm up to new people they become very interactive and explorative. Fortunately, they have cousins who have helped them with the transition. It is as if their confidence grows with the verbal and nonverbal conversations that are pursued. They begin to make the most of the situation in ways that you can never fully predict. Sometimes they embark upon experiences with others that open whole new worlds of possibilities to them, including long-standing relationships. Sometimes, they want out. As a parent I spend a great deal of my time being concerned about their engagement in these foreign situations and anxious that they will take advantage of the opportunity. I try to help them participate or simply become less wary. At the same time, I need to be very cautious that my goals for my children do not override a consideration for them, who they are etc.. Fortunately, my children will not shy away from letting me know what they are ready for and interested in pursuing and what they are not.

I would think that most of you are aware of situations similar to what I have described. But what has this got to do with the issues being addressed in this handbook? I would hypothesize that an introduction to and subsequent participation with media is not unlike my description of my sons in a new country. As mentioned earlier, often when schools consider a shift toward multimedia, they focus on the supplies and materials they need or what they can afford in terms of technology. These are important considerations, but they should not be seen as more important than a consideration of how the media might be integrated to meet individual

---

[7] Various discussions and some research have focused on the nature and effects of e-mail. Reinking (1994) discusses e-mail and selected research on the effects of this medium on communication (e.g., Neilson, in press). A recent article by Mann (1995) describes e-mail use with comparisons to the use of pneumatic tubes in the late 1800s in Europe and discussed Verdi's rather prolific use of this medium rivaling some e-mail users of today.

[8] As such studies are considered, one should recognize the differences that may exist across institutions. Schools, for example, may operate with media as they have done with other literacy in ways that limit access and restrict possibilities. Bloome (1994) suggests that curriculum and administrative constraints may predispose a view and use of media which delimits the possible integration of multimedia either by groups or individuals within these institutions.

needs. In planning for any kind of integration, we need to adopt a developmental orientation relative to media's fit in the classroom with regard for the students individually and collectively. If we are to enhance learning with multimedia we need a fuller understanding of issues of development lest we fail to appreciate and therefore dismiss the developments that are occurring and the factors that contribute to such developments.

Learning to do research on multimedia: some lessons

For a period of 6 years I was engaged in a series of studies directed at many of these same issues as I pursued my work in a site (the Apple Classrooms of Tomorrow[sm.] [ACOT[sm.]]) that afforded students access to state-of-the-art technologies with dynamic multimedia capabilities (see previous discussion). These studies included:

- attempts to define in broad and specific terms the nature of individual student learning that occurs as students appropriate the use of computers—in particular, longitudinal studies of students' computer acquisition appropriation over extended periods of time;
- attempts to define the specific impact of certain facets of video and HyperCard applications;
- attempts to define the specific assessment practices that are or might be enlisted by teachers, students or others—in particular, studies focusing upon the use of portfolios and the nature of teacher and student ongoing decision-making.

If you recall, the Apple Classroom of Tomorrow[sm] (ACOT[sm]) site afforded students as much access to computers as students in regular classrooms have to books, pen and paper. Students were able to interact with a community of learners in various subject areas within a contact that allows them to explore and learn with a range of multimedia software, data bases, and word processing software. For example, in their science class or history class, they might pull together projects using Page Maker, HyperCard and SuperCard, using a mix of scanned images, video, and multilevel stacks of ideas. They also had access to computers at home where they can pursue classwork or projects that they might decide to initiate themselves.

In discussing computer acquisition, it is important to distinguish site from setting. I would define the site as a location, whereas setting is much more relative. Site does not serve the same function as setting for inhabitants. As I studied the engagement of different ACOT students, it was apparent that they have had different experiences, especially over time. There may be one site, but within that site there are multiple settings. The variations that occurred across individuals might be viewed as a kind of aptitude treatment interaction. However, I would suggest that the type of variation that I encountered was more complex than a simple two-factor interaction. There seemed to be a myriad of factors interacting with one another within the site. Moreover, as new applications emerged over time, new possibilities were grafted onto others. It is as if to study the impact of technology is to study change on top of change (see Reinking, & Bridwell-Bowles, 1991). Some specific technologies (e.g., HyperCard) had a major impact on students' uses of technology. But in ACOT the students had a certain history that predisposed them to consider the possibilities with certain technologies in terms of how they linked with other technologies, classwork and so on. In other words, in ACOT technology did not exist in isolation but interacted with other technologies, as well as an array of variables, for example, the nature of the units of study; the nature of the student's goals, collaborations, view of expectations, expertise and approach; the nature and style of teacher and technological support; and so on. In other words, to study the impact of technology, involved the following: (1) recognizing that to study technology is akin to studying a moving target; (2) appreciating how technology is woven into the fabric of classroom; and (3) affording different perspectives on learning within the site—including takes across individuals, units of study and time.

In my own work, the lesson that I found hardest to learn was tied to my own verbocentric orientations and the past lens with which I wanted to study technology. As Olson suggested the function of media is not so much to convey old knowledge in new forms but rather to cultivate new ways of exploring and representing these ideas. The ramifications of this notion for studying computer appropriation seem immense. Put simply, I needed to see students appropriating technology on its own terms. It was not until by looking and listening closely to what the students were saying and doing that I began to realize that the lens that I had adopted was restricting our view of what was occurring. Indeed, I had unwittingly adopted the view of technology as merely an adjunct to learning—an adjunct that made learning more effective. Most past examinations have been restricted to the use of traditional indices that may not reflect the true nature of computer literacy (Baker, Herman, & Gearhart, 1988; Ross, Morrison, & Smith, 1989). As Baker, Gearhart, and Herman (1990) suggested, traditional indices do not appear to address the types of skills students acquire in high computer access classrooms. Or, as Ross et. al., commented, learning to use computers may expand the ability to use particular skills with the computer but not other abilities apart from them.

There was a need to characterize data in nonverbocentric fashion—that is, ideas that may not be unidimensional and sequential; ideas within other ideas, as well as multilayering and the complex ways in which ideas may be interconnected. There was a need to capture what was entailed as students began spending a great deal of time considering how ideas layout—that is, how the issues that they were exploring might be represented dynamically and complexly across an array of still pictures, video segments, text segments and sound clips interconnected in very complex ways (i.e., multifaceted, multilayered ways). With the introduction of desktop publishing, scanning capabilities and hypermedia, some major shifts occurred in how students represented ideas and approached the integration of ideas from various sources. Students realized the possibility of developing texts that, to use their words, were "dynamic rather than static," their approach to ideas became less logophobic or verbocentric, less linear and unidimensional. In conjunction with being able to explore the integrated use of various graphics (animation, video segments, scanned images or various ways to graphically depict data), they began to utilize various media as a way of achieving different perspectives on issues that they were exploring in physics, history and other subjects. Just as an author might look for the right word or twist in their text, these students were exploring ideas in new ways that very few past examinations had attempted to detail.

In addition, the types of involvements with technology also involved issues of power and relationships. These relationships involved teacher with student, student with student, student with other high schools students, students with the outside world, students with parents, and so forth. With the introduction of these multimedia came new possibilities for individuals and groups—an opportunity to achieve new relationships with oneself, new levels of decision making and different aspirations.

Attempts to portray computer appropriation and use such portrayals require a form of dynamic and interactive evaluation in which the students and teachers collaborate in the form of dynamic and reciprocal data analysis, collection and interpretation. In an attempt to involve myself in this dialectic, I extended our interaction with students and teachers beyond standard classroom observation followed by a set of predefined debriefing questions. I attempted to engage in a conversation with both students and teachers as the students progressed through these learning situations. The teachers shared with us their goals, plans and expectations for the projects, as we observed the students involved in lectures, class activities, and interactions with their peers outside of class. Through these observations and conversations we attempted to draw sketches of the students in the process of learning and thinking. These sketches attempted to visually represent the connections that the students were making in their thinking, their developing understandings, as well as their reactions to the interactive learning process. The students were asked to comment upon the sketches in terms of the adequacy of the representations. Had we indeed captured the nature of their thinking? What had been left out? Were the connections that we were making about their learning correct? Had we identified all aspects of the social setting as it impacted the development of their thinking? The sketches were also shared with teachers as our emerging understandings were compared with their perceptions of the learners. What emerged from these sketches and the conversations that occurred around them was a richer understanding of the students and the dynamic nature of their learning. As we talked with the teachers and students it quickly became apparent that students make numerous connections as they attempt to understand complex ideas, all of which are not apparent in any single observation, nor are they accessible from any one measure of student performance. As noted earlier, to accurately portray or to effectively assess learning, we need to develop collaborative and interactive methods for data collection, analysis and interpretation. I would suggest that if we are to capture the dynamic nature of learning which occurs in multiple settings we must find ways to capture the multiple voices, and in so doing renegotiate assessment in the classroom.

Summary and Remarks

Kozma (1991) has stated:

> ...that capabilities of a particular medium, in conjunction with methods that take advantage of these capabilities, interact with and influence the ways learners represent and process information and may result in more and different learning (p. 179).

Through the ages peoples have appropriated symbol systems as metaphorical vehicles with generative syntax and these symbol systems have afforded new possibilities for engagement with self, others and this world. Our various means of representation serve to open us to new possibilities, including achieving new insights and ways of transacting with others, ourselves, and ideas and problems. Recent descriptions of preschools in Italy and the United States describe similar phenomena when very young children are given the opportunity to use different media or symbol systems to explore their world or problem-solve. Their cutting and pasting, drawings, talk, play, and use of other media are used to achieve different perspectives on their world, to solve problems, make plans, and communicate with others. With advances in technology, the same is apparent with electronic media. Projects are apt to involve a mix of transactions including talk, faxes, word processing, scanning; video as different media are accessed separately and together for purposes of composing communications, pursuing problem solving, and as a means of exploring ideas, perspective taking and deepening or acquiring new understandings. I would suggest that the projects occurring in conjunction with the Apple Classroom of Tomorrow, the Reggio Emilia schools and my son's boogie boarding, share many things—especially the power of the symbol systems to engage students in deep and complex explorations of issues as well as constructive discussion and debate. At the same time these sites may be more an exception than a rule. Historically, classrooms have tended to access a limited range of media and the orientation to these media has been limited. Despite the recent developments with electronic media and the simultaneous access to video, graphics, other images, sound and text, the question remains: will multimedia be meaningfully integrated into the classroom? Will we simply acquiesce or will we recognize and embrace the potential to use multimedia as a tool to transform our lives?

Finally, I close with the following sketch that tries to capture some facets that I have addressed: the emphasis upon people rather than media, different individuals or the same person assuming multiple roles and achieving multiple perspectives, people engaged in a range of media reflecting varying technologies, people also engaged in conversation and reflection and an environment that is integral to the explorations occurring.

FIGURE 22–5

References

Baker, E. L., Gearhart, M., & Herman, J. L., (1990). *The apple classroom of tomorrow: 1989 evaluation study.* Los Angeles; UCLA Center for the Study of Evaluation.

Baker, E. L., Herman, J. L., & Gearhart, M. (1988). *The apple classroom of tomorrow: 1988 evaluation study.* Los Angeles UCLA Center for the Study of Evaluation.

Bickert, S. (1994). *The Gutenberg elegies: The fate of reading in an electronic age.* Boston: Faber & Faber.

Bloome, D. (1993). Necessary indeterminacy and the microethnographic study of reading as a social process. *Journal of in Research Reading, 16*(2), 98–111.

Bloome, D. (1994). Response to McCarthey: On the nature of language in classroom literacy research. *Reading Research Quarterly, 29* (3), 232–241.

Bolter, J. D. (1991). *Writing space: The computer, hypertext, and the history of writing.* Hillsdale; NJ: Erlbaum.

Brown, J., Collins, A., & Duguid, L., (1989). Situated cognition and the culture of learning. *Educational Researcher, 18*(1), 32–41.

Bruner, J. (1990). *Acts of meaning.* Cambridge, MA; Harvard University Press.

Clark, R., & Salomon, G. (1986). Media in teaching. In M. Wittrock (Ed.), *Handbook of research on teaching* (pp. 464–478). New York: Macmillan.

Fairclough, N. (Ed.), (1992). *Critical language awareness.* London, Longman.

Forman, G. (1993). Multiple symbolization in the long jump project. In C. Edward, L. Gandini & G. Forman (Eds.), *The hundred languages of children* (pp. 171–188). Norwood, NJ: Ablex.

Gee, J. (1990). *Social linguistics and literacy: Ideologies in discourses.* New York: Falmer Press.

Green, J. L., Weade, R., & Graham, K. (1988) Lesson construction and student participation: A sociolinguistic analysis. In J. Green & J. Harker (Eds.), *Multiple perspective analyses of classroom discourse* (pp. 11–48). Norwood, NJ: Ablex.

Habermas, J. (1983). *The theory of communicative action* (2 Vols.). Boston: Beacon.

Harste, J., Woodward, V., & Burke, C. (1984). *Language stories and literacy lessons.* Portsmouth, NH: Heinemann.

Kozma, R. B. (1991). Learning with media. *Review of Educational Research, 61*(2), 179–212.

Lanham, R. A. (1993). *Hypertext: The convergence of contemporary critical theory and technology.* Baltimore: Johns Hopkins University Press.

Lemke, J. (1990) *Talking science: Language, learning & values.* Norwood, NJ: Ablex.

Lemke, J. L. (1994). *Multiplying meaning: Composing multimedia text.* Paper presented at the meeting of the American Educational Research Association, New Orleans, LA.

Luke, A. (1988). The political economy of reading instruction. In C. Baker & A. Luke (Eds.), *Toward a sociology of reading instruction* (pp. 3–26). Philadelphia: John Benjamin.

Mann, C. C. (1995). Email by any other name. *Technology, 17*(4), 54–56.

Neilson, L. (in press). Coding the light. In L. Neilson & J. Willinsky (Eds.), *Coding the light: Gender, generation, and technologies of metamorphoses.* New York: Teachers College Press.

Olson, D. (1974). Introduction. In D. Olson (Ed.), *Media and symbols: The forms of expression, communication and education.* Chicago: National Society for Study of Education.

Reinking, D. (1994). *Reading and writing with computers: Literacy research in the post-typographical world.* Paper presented at the National Reading Conference, San Diego.

Reinking, D., & Bridwell-Bowles, L. (1991). Computers in reading and writing. In R. Barr, M. L, Kamil, P. Mosenthal & P. D. Pearson (Eds.), *Handbook of reading research, Vol. 2,* (pp. 310–340). New York: Longman.

Resnick, L. (1989). Learning in and out of school. *Educational Researcher, 18*(1).

Ross, S. M., Morrison, G., R., Smith, L. J. (1989). *What happens after ACOT? Outcomes for program graduates one year later.* Final report to Apple Computer, Inc. Memphis, TN: Memphis State University.

Siegel, M. (1984). *Reading as signification.* Unpublished doctoral dissertation, Indiana University, Bloomington; IN.

Spiro, R. J, Coulson, R. L., Feltovich, P. J., & Anderson, D. K. (1988). *Cognitive flexibility theory: Advanced knowledge acquisition in ill-structured domains* (Tech. Rep. No. 441). Urbana-Champaign, IL: University of Illinois, Center for the Study of Reading.

Stone, A. R. (1995). *The war of desire and technology at the close of the mechanical age.* Cambridge, MA: MIT Press.

Street, B. (1984). *Literacy in theory and practice.* Cambridge: Cambridge University Press.

Taylor, L. (1987). *'The same but different': social reproduction in innovation in the art of the Kunwinjka of western Arnhem land.* Doctoral dissertation, The Australian National University.

Tierney, R. J., Kieffer, R., Stowell, L., & Desai, L. (1992). Computer, acquisition: a longitudinal study of the influence of high computer access on students' thinking, learning and interactions. (Apple Classrooms of Tomorrow Report #16). Cupertino CA: Apple Computer.

Wignell, P., Martin, J., & Eggins, S. (1982). The discourse of geography: Ordering and explaining the experiential world. *Linguistics and Education, 1*(4), 359–392.

Part
·III·

RESEARCH ON LANGUAGE LEARNERS IN FAMILIES, COMMUNITIES, AND CLASSROOMS

INTRODUCTION

Victoria Chou

UNIVERSITY OF ILLINOIS AT CHICAGO

The nine chapters in part III use divergent research methods to portray language learners in dramatically different settings. Using innovative assessment approaches, discourse analysis, videotape and photography, and qualitative and ethnographic methods, these researchers focus on language learners shaped differently by race and ethnicity, gender, class and income, place, and age and generation. The authors remind us of learners older than those traditionally studied in K–12 settings. They study learners from the same family or the same community, variously defined, and learners who meet as strangers to one another. They portray language learners in, but mostly out of, formal school settings—from classrooms to homes to streets and other public spaces. They examine learners individually and learners in communication with one another. They reveal a variety of learners' literacies in terms of print, talk, and sign. The authors, themselves representative of a wide spectrum of literacy educators, come to know language learners in very different ways, and, together, they enlarge our view of who language learners are.

In the opening chapter, "Telling Their Stories, Singing Their Songs," Mara Krechevsky and Ulla C. Malkus focus on understandings of the preschool learner that stretch us beyond the linguistic and logico-mathematical. They describe how Project Spectrum, a research initiative based at Harvard Project Zero and Tufts University, deploys innovative assessments that provide opportunities for young children to express their strengths in different content areas. These alternative assessments are mapped onto the seven different intelligences identified by Howard Gardner in his well-known theory of multiple intelligences. Because the assessments enable teachers to recognize and appreciate multiple dimensions of what learners know, teachers are better able to structure classrooms and teach to accommodate individual abilities. Krechevsky and Malkus show readers how original assessments in the areas of language, visual arts, movement, and music can provide great depth and insight to profiles of individual preschoolers' abilities.

Claire Ramsey in "Deaf Children as Literacy Learners: Tom, Robbie, and Paul," draws attention to younger learners who are bilingual and bicultural. She writes of primary-grade deaf learners who use American Sign Language (ASL) as their preferred and primary mode of communication. She argues persuasively for a view of deaf education pedagogy that originates in a cultural view of deaf people. Such a view suggests that deaf children are members of an ethnolinguistic group using ASL, a genuine language maintained by a community of deaf signing people. Children growing up in a deaf community in an English speaking context are, effectively, bilingual or potentially bilingual. Ramsey studied how three deaf 2nd-grade boys proficient in face-to-face ASL approached literacy in settings where both signing and print coexist. In their mainstreamed classroom, where the boys were viewed as disabled, proficiency in ASL did not (could not) foster interaction with hearing classmates who did not know how to sign. In contrast, in their deaf classroom, where ASL communication was accepted as a matter of course, early literacy efforts were supported by ASL. Ramsey's observations lead her to conclude that literacy development is as systematic and rule-governed, as inclined toward sense-making, for ASL-signing children as it is for English-speaking children.

In "Youth Genre in the Classroom: Can Children's and Teachers' Cultures Meet?" Colette Daiute shifts to middle childhood and early adolescent learners. She explains aspects of *youth genre*, featuring discourse rooted in and influenced by youth peer culture. She finds that learners adopt youth genre to relate to one another, seeking to make sense of their world, without having to adopt the dominant adult school language—teachers' talk—completely. Across several transcripts of conversations of older children, Daiute shows us how youth genre is repeatedly characterized by features of reciprocity, experimentation, sense making, playfulness, and affectively charged language. We observe children solving a variety of challenging academic problems in intense give-and-take interactions, in contrast to adults' more characteristic internalized working out of problems. Daiute speculates that youth genre works to scaffold learners' understanding of difficult problems, where less familiar adult or school genre may inhibit learners' understanding. She makes a series of specific recommendations to teachers for inviting children to use youth genre as a tool for learning in intellectually challenging and collaborative contexts.

The next three chapters portray adolescent and young adult learners. In "Bridging Home and School Literacies: Models for Culturally Responsive Teaching, A Case for African-American English," Carol D. Lee recalls the earlier theme of bilingualism, in this case, studying adolescent learners whose home literacies vary from their school literacies. In particular, she reviews discourse and rhetorical forms identified as part of the African-American verbal tradition. Then, drawing from the literature on effective teaching and learning, she shows how adolescents who are proficient in the nuances of this tradition can learn to extend their knowledge to other verbal traditions and acquire important literary concepts and strategies. In an intervention study, she illustrates that the metaphoric reasoning and ironic reasoning demanded by African-American adolescents' signifying dialogue can productively be tapped to interpret the predominantly white, male, and western literature in the school curriculum. Lee makes a convincing case for using this kind of cultural modeling as a scaffolding vehicle for all students to illuminate the "rites of passage" required in secondary English classrooms. She argues that capitalizing on home languages that differ from Edited American English advances literacy development and supports a model of culturally responsive pedagogy.

In contrast to Lee, in "Student Conversations: Provocative Echoes," Eleanor Binstock examines the nature of youth genre across cultures. Videotaping conversations over a year's time, Binstock engaged a group of Latino students attending an alternative high school on Chicago's south side in correspondence with a group of African-American students attending an alternative high school on the city's west side. The strategy enables us to learn what students who would not normally encounter one another reveal in dialogue together. The peer video conversations provided students with opportunities to name their experiences, to disclose life texts to one another, and to create new meanings within and between groups. The extended video conversations additionally allowed misunderstandings to be resolved and meanings clarified. Binstock's analyses of conversational excerpts reveal the sophisticated ways in which students employ rhetorical echoes to influence and shape mutual interaction: to underscore a point or a theme, to challenge and react, to ease border crossings among strangers. Educators, in turn, are afforded privileged opportunities to experience the diverse perspectives of cultural others.

In "Street Literacy," Dwight Conquergood takes readers further yet outside the adolescent mainstream and explores the outlawed literacy of street youth, encoded in graffiti writing. He reveals the oppositional, yet intricately coded language of signs in the context of the public subjection of street youth to search warrants, strip searches, and fingerprinting. He heightens our awareness of the tensions elicited by this form of visual communication: its hypervisibility and its secrecy. When he decodes graffiti writing's alphabetic, iconographic, and corporeal dimensions in a photographic journey, he also comments on the playful, creative character of the writing. Conquergood captures the familiarizing, communal aspects of street literacy that draw its members into tightly knit groups. He shares three levels of performance featured in gang graffiti writing: collaborative writing constituting a well-orchestrated ensemble performance (e.g., of "making a wall"), using body surfaces to mirror and extend graffiti on buildings, and reading "play."

Adults in intergenerational familial relationships are the learners in Vivian Gadsden's chapter. In "Intergenerational Discourses: Life Texts of African-American Mothers and Daughters," Gadsden examines the convergences of issues of gender, race, and culture within the intergenerational oral and written discourses (life texts) of African-American women. In reviewing current understandings and unresolved issues in the field of intergenerational literacy learning, she addresses the researcher's role in disclosing—and therefore making vulnerable—what is typically not disclosed to outsiders. She frames her subsequent discussion by presenting both current and historical contexts for African-American women's literacy. Gadsden then examines the oral and written life texts of two and three generations of African-American mothers and daughters, predominantly from rural South Carolina. The discourses, in effect, create possible meeting places for women and girls to learn from one another, to come to respect persistence in the face of travails, and to share aspirations and concerns about achieving life goals, including the goal of literacy. The author closes the chapter by considering implications of these convergences for practice and research.

The last two chapters in the section predominantly address the literacy experiences of adult learners. In "Community Literacy: From Home to Work and Back," Gary Pharness and Lee Weinstein call upon their own histories as learners to help them understand the adult learners with whom they work. They argue that, additionally, an appreciation of adult learners' many contexts—family, community, and workplace—is essential in promoting their literacy, and doing so with integrity. They claim that these contexts can be understood through learners' own narratives, which can be the literature in a curriculum that connects isolated learners of diverse ethnicities and breaks down barriers. These narratives inform educators about what is and is not important to the adult learner and where educators might intervene, principles that have been realized at Invergarry Learning Centre in Surrey, B.C., Canada and in the journal *Voices*. Pharness and Weinstein raise thought-provoking questions about the relationships between concern for individual workers' literacy and stories, workers' performance in the workplace, and the collective building of community. They end the chapter by describing two community-building literacy projects in which they are presently involved: one, an intergenerational literacy project called Rainmaker; the other, a literacy project with a First Nations' aboriginal community.

Finally, Hal Adams' chapter, "A Grass Roots Think Tank: Linking Writing and Community-Building," amplifies the experience of linking literacy to community action. He documents how African-American parents in a west side Chicago elementary school so deepened their understandings of their own and others' experiences through processes of writing and discussion that they became motivated to take action to improve the quality of life in their community. Adams describes how the idea of a writing group founded on the notion that "every person is a philosopher" gave rise over time to parents' increased confidence in the worthwhileness of their experiences. Parents who initially joined the group to find out how to help their children with schoolwork returned to make sense of their experiences and to affirm each other's role in their common struggles against the stresses of poverty. Adams chronicles how the parents published their work in *The Journal of Ordinary Thought,* gave readings to audiences that included their children's classes, encouraged the founding of a neighborhood men's writing group and, eventually, initiated the Austin grass roots think tank that took concrete action to remedy community problems identified in the writing of community citizens.

Across the chapters in this section, all the authors conceive of language learners as distinctively influenced by their particular social and cultural contexts. Some learners' environments are nurturing, supportive, or at least relatively benign; others dwell in exceptionally hostile and oppressive, even menacing, surroundings. Across the chapters, we receive privileged glimpses of learners' lives, revealing the undeniably powerful influences of family and community, gender and race and ethnicity, age, and language(s).

The authors do not speak as a group, but a recurrent theme in their work is how the multiple influences imprinted in the learners can be called forth to serve as positive resources. The authors review a variety of ways to assess what learners know. In particular, the value of intensely personal oral and written narratives dominates the chapters. These narratives or life texts, as some authors have termed them, create extraordinary potential for self-knowledge and existential understandings; for community building and for educating others; and for community action, when used in learning environments where trust and respect prevail. The authors show how literacy learning as a social, contextualized process, can become entwined with the inscription of learners' lives in personal narratives. Collectively, these pieces yield important insights into how learners' social and cultural histories can contribute to our understanding of how, why, and when individuals learn and use literacy.

Finally, it comes as no surprise that we repeatedly come across the terms *sense making, risk taking,* and *playfulness* in this section. Over and over, the authors document language learners' affectively charged, intentional pursuit of meaning in the world around them. Interestingly, a number of authors profile learners bridging two languages by using the more familiar, more known language to make sense of the less familiar language. These specific efforts among bilingual and bidialectal learners are yet another instance of learners' proactive efforts to negotiate meaning-meaning across boundaries of culture and difference.

23

TELLING THEIR STORIES, SINGING THEIR SONGS

Mara Krechevsky

HARVARD UNIVERSITY

Ulla C. Malkus

WHEELOCK COLLEGE

Walk into a typical preschool classroom and what are you likely to find? A variety of learning centers and materials, such as an art table, a nature area, a dramatic play area, blocks, puzzles, a math area, a reading corner, and a writing table, among others. Despite the diversity suggested by this array, much of the assessment of children's cognitive development has focused on two symbolic domains: language and mathematics. This conception of development is based on traditional notions of intelligence that take a unitary view of the human mind (Sattler, 1988). This model has had enormous impact not just on the way children are viewed in school but on Western thinking about intelligence in general. Children who do not exhibit competence in language and logic are often identified as at-risk for school failure. Some of these children may eventually fall through the cracks of the educational system if their strengths in other areas go unrecognized.

The aim of this chapter is to examine an approach to assessment that encourages teachers to look at young children's cognitive development in a more pluralistic way. Project Spectrum, a research initiative based at Harvard Project Zero and Tufts University, was developed as a way to uncover the many dimensions of the preschool learner's mind. Spectrum is an attempt to give children the opportunity to speak, sing, dance, draw—to express themselves in activities that are meaningful to them. We chose to focus on early childhood because of the relative plasticity of the young mind and the diversity of the preschool environment. We also saw assessment as a useful point of leverage for effecting educational change. The Spectrum assessments give teachers a framework for observing children and shaping their teaching and classrooms accordingly.

The Spectrum assessment framework is based on Howard Gardner's theory of multiple intelligences (Gardner, 1983) and David Feldman's theory of nonuniversal development (1980, 1994; see also Ceci, 1990; Fodor, 1983; Keil, 1986). Instead of limiting our assessments to linguistic and logical-mathematical competencies, as many standardized tests do, the Spectrum approach addresses a broader range of abilities, including musical, spatial, bodily-kinesthetic, and social skills. In this chapter, we discuss the principles behind our assessment approach that enabled us to identify the full spectrum of abilities exhibited by preschool children. After a brief theoretical overview, we summarize the Spectrum approach to assessment and describe its underlying principles, providing examples from the domains of language, art, music, and creative movement.

BRIEF THEORETICAL OVERVIEW

The unitary view of intelligence was first proposed by Charles Spearman (1904, 1927). Spearman used statistical analyses of individuals' performances on a battery of tests to assert that a single general capacity underlies all intellectual activities. This point of view was furthered by Alfred Binet's (Binet & Simon, 1916) development of a measure that would predict which children would benefit from remedial help in school (Fancher, 1985). Although Binet did not suggest that his measures identified a single entity that could be considered a "general intelligence," his mental tests yielded a single numerical score. This "mental age" and later the "intelligence quotient" (IQ) were often regarded as a measure of general intelligence.

In contrast to the factor-analytic procedures used by researchers like Spearman to identify intellectual capacity, Gardner surveyed a wide range of evidence to support a more

The research reported in this chapter has been supported by generous grants from the William T. Grant Foundation, the Rockefeller Brothers Fund, and the Spencer Foundation. We are grateful to Howard Gardner, Thomas Hatch, Mindy Kornhaber, and Julie Viens for many helpful comments on earlier drafts.

pluralistic view of intelligence. For example, he looked at the development of abilities in a variety of domains of knowledge. He also examined the neurobiological literature to determine whether there was evidence for the separation of different mental functions in the brain. Other sources of evidence included literature on the existence of special populations like prodigies, idiot-savants, and autistic individuals; cross-cultural data; and a plausible evolutionary history. Based on this review, Gardner identified at least seven different intelligences: linguistic, logical-mathematical, musical, spatial, bodily-kinesthetic, interpersonal, and intrapersonal. Almost all human beings possess all of these intelligences; however, we differ in the relative strengths and weaknesses of individual cognitive profiles. Also, one never finds an intelligence in isolation; all meaningful tasks, roles, and products involve a combination of intelligences.

The research of David Feldman focused on the development of ability within particular domains of knowledge. According to Feldman, development within domains—areas of knowledge and practice ranging from language and music to map-making and chess—can traverse a continuum from universal to unique. For example, language is considered a universal arena of development, with virtually all individuals developing relatively high levels of performance, while the contributions of a writer like Toni Morrison would be considered unique. Other types of nonuniversal development include cultural (e.g., oral storytelling in nonliterate societies), discipline-based (e.g., poetry), and idiosyncratic (e.g., free verse). Project Spectrum's assessments are intended to address the nonuniversal end of Feldman's continuum of development. This chapter describes a set of measures designed to identify abilities that many teachers may currently overlook or consider "fringe" domains of cognitive growth.

The Spectrum Approach to Assessment

The Spectrum classroom encompasses learning activities in seven different content areas. Using multiple intelligences theory as a starting point, we conducted observations in preschool classrooms and consulted with teachers to determine which areas we would address. Through this process, we hoped to create developmentally appropriate assessments that were both grounded in theory and reflected the preschool environment. We also met with subject matter experts and reviewed the literature in different domains to ensure that the assessments tapped key abilities in each area. The list of 15 assessment activities is given below.

AREAS OF COGNITIVE ABILITY EXAMINED IN PROJECT SPECTRUM

Movement

Creative Movement Curriculum

Assesses children's abilities in five areas of dance and creative movement: sensitivity to rhythm, expressiveness, body control, generation of movement ideas, and responsiveness to music.

Obstacle Course

Assesses skills found in a variety of athletic activities such as coordination, timing, balance, and power.

Language

Storyboard Activity

Assesses a range of language skills including use of temporal markers, complexity of vocabulary and sentence structure, use of dialogue and narrative voice, and thematic coherence.

Reporter Activities

Assess children's abilities to describe experiences or events with regard to such criteria as level of detail, accuracy of content, relationships among events, and sentence structure.

Mathematics

Dinosaur Game

Assesses children's understanding of number concepts, counting skills, abilities to adhere to rules, and use of strategy.

Bus Game

Assesses children's abilities to create a useful notation system, perform mental calculations, and organize number information for one or more variables.

Science

Assembly Activity

Assesses children's mechanical abilities. Successful completion of the activity depends on fine motor, visual-spatial, observational, and problem-solving abilities.

Treasure Hunt Game

Assesses children's abilities to make logical inferences. Children are asked to organize information to discover the rule governing the placement of various treasures.

Sink and Float Activity

Assesses children's abilities to generate hypotheses based on their observations and to conduct simple experiments.

Discovery Area

Assesses children's observational skills and appreciation and understanding of natural phenomena through yearlong natural science activities.

Social

Classroom Model

Assesses children's abilities to observe and analyze social events and experiences in their classroom.

Peer Interaction Checklist

Assesses the behaviors in which children engage when interacting with peers. Different patterns of behavior yield distinctive social roles such as facilitator and leader.

Visual Arts

Art Portfolios

Contents of children's art portfolios are reviewed twice a year and assessed on criteria that include use of lines and shapes, color, space, detail, and representation. Children also complete four structured activities to supplement their portfolios.

Music

Singing Activity

Assesses children's abilities to maintain accurate pitch and rhythm while singing as well as their abilities to recall a song's musical properties.

Music Perception Activity

Assesses children's abilities to discriminate pitch. Activity consists of song recognition, error recognition, and pitch discrimination.

The assessments include both structured (e.g., music perception) and unstructured (e.g., creative movement) measures. Record keeping takes the form of scoresheets, observational checklists, and anecdotal descriptions. Although many of the assessments yield quantitative as well as qualitative results, the numerical data were used primarily for research purposes. At the end of the year, the information collected on children is described in a "Spectrum Profile," a narrative summary of children's areas of strength, either relative to their peers or to themselves. In addition to the profiles, parents receive a Parent Activities Manual with suggestions for out-of-school activities, grouped according to content area. As many schools and homes may not be equipped to address the full range of intelligences, a list of community resources is also included to provide additional services and programs.

Spectrum's approach to assessment is founded on four educational principles: emphasizing children's strengths, integrating curriculum and assessment, embedding the assessments in real-world activities and using materials that are authentic to the domains being assessed (see also, Krechevsky, 1991). Many of these principles are becoming accepted practice in the field (see, e.g., Bredekamp & Rosegrant, 1993; Meisels. Dorfman, & Steele in press). In the rest of this chapter, we describe how these four principles have been applied in the areas of language, art, music, and creative movement. Where relevant, we also place the Spectrum assessments in the context of past and current research on child development.

The preliminary results reported here are drawn from three preschool classrooms at the Eliot-Pearson Children's School at Tufts University in Medford, MA. These data were collected from 1985–88 on a sample of primarily European American, middle-income children, with an average class size of 20 children. Clearly, the way in which different abilities are expressed varies across cultural contexts, and many of the Spectrum assessments and scoring rubrics may need to be modified for other settings. (For a more complete description of the Spectrum assessment program and the preliminary results reported in this chapter, see *Project Spectrum: Preschool Assessment Handbook* (Krechevsky, 1994).

Emphasizing Children's Strengths: A Look at Language

Perhaps the most important feature of the Spectrum assessment approach is its emphasis on identifying children's strengths. Rather than focusing on areas of weakness and trying to remediate them, the Spectrum measures explicitly target areas of strength. For instance, Spectrum's assessments in language provide a fine-grained analysis of children's skills in that domain, focusing on exceptional linguistic abilities. Teachers can then use this information to build on those competencies, perhaps using them to shore up areas where children are not as strong.

Many current researchers in the area of language development recommend that measures of young children's development focus on emergent literacy skills (e.g., Hiebert & Calfee, 1992; Snow, Tabors, Nicholson, & Kurland, in press; Sulzby, 1985; Teale, 1988). Sulzby (1985), for example, has devised a classification scheme for young children's emergent reading of storybooks. This scheme addresses children's shift from attending primarily to pictures to focusing more on print, and their shift from "reading" that relies on the conventions of oral language to "reading" that reflects the conventions of written language.

The above measures focus on the developmental sequences of emergent literacy through which virtually all children pass. In contrast, the Spectrum measures target nonuniversal development (toward the unique end of Feldman's continuum of development). The Spectrum language assessments examine both invented and descriptive narrative. The Storyboard Activity, Spectrum's invented narrative measure, is designed to tap such components of linguistic ability as thematic coherence, nature of narrative structure, and sentence structure. Children are asked to generate their own tales using a three-dimensional storyboard, including evocative props, creatures, people, and an ambiguous-looking landscape. Table 23–1 lists the component skills targeted by the Storyboard Activity.

After identifying children's primary language functions (e.g., use of descriptive, investigative, conversational, or storytelling language), teachers can assess their performance on each subskill. The scoring rubrics allow teachers to identify and document a range of linguistic competencies. For example, the category of expressiveness refers to sound effects used in support of a child's story. Level 1 is defined as "child uses little or no emphasis in her story; story is presented in a monotone voice;" Level 2 refers to children who use occasional sound effects (character voices, emphasis, singing); and Level 3 describes children who consistently use sound effects, lively character voices, and vivid narration.

While some children demonstrate unusual imaginative language skills, others may reveal strong descriptive narrative competence. Spectrum's Reporter Activities elicit children's abilities to report content accurately, to report detail selectively, and to identify sequential or causal relations. The assessment consists of a "Movie Report" and "Weekend

TABLE 23–1. Skills Targeted by the Storyboard Activity

STORYBOARD OBSERVATION SHEET

Child   Date

Age   Observer

Please comment as much as possible on the following:

physical manipulation of props   –   for example, child seems overwhelmed by props or seems more interested in setting up scene than in telling story

transformation of materials/activity   –   for example, child uses clay arch as rainbow or uses extra props box as a ship

skills from different domains   –   for example, child sings her story or counts the objects on the storyboard

Be specific and detailed in your account of these and any other visual cues so that the scorer has a more complete sense of the physical dynamics of the child's storytelling.

Primary Language Function:	Language Skills:		Comments:
_____ storytelling	Nature of Narrative Structure	☐	
_____ interacting with adult	Thematic Coherence	☐	
_____ investigating	Use of Narrative Voice	☐	
_____ describing	Use of Dialogue	☐	
_____ labeling or categorizing	Use of Temporal Markers	☐	
	Expressiveness	☐	
	Level of Vocabulary	☐	
	Sentence Structure	☐	
	TOTAL	☐	

Scorer _____

Date _____

News." In the Movie Report children watch a short movie or video and then recount what happened. The Weekend News Activity offers children regular opportunities to describe their weekend experiences. In addition to some of the language skills addressed in the Storyboard Activity, the Reporter Activities yield information pertaining to accuracy of content, expansion of main events, and relationships between events.

In the Storyboard Activity, most children in a Spectrum class of 3- and 4-year-olds were able to use both dialogue and narration. Several children also created a storyline that combined characters, props, and action in a common narrative problem. In the Reporter Activities, individual differences emerged in children's abilities to use language relevant to the experiences that they were describing (e.g., using phrases like "I goed there" as opposed to "My father bringed me to the museum with knights with different kinds of helmets".) (We recognize the experientially dependent nature of the measures reported here and the need for further field-testing.) One boy's strength showed up in the imaginative detail of his movie report. He reported with great zeal that he saw a dog chase a cat, a kitty cat climb a tree, a bald eagle, a runaway bull, an ostrich, a dog that barked, and pigs that were killed for bacon. None of these features were in the film. While the detail in his report was rich and abundant, it was low on accuracy.

Not only do the measures just described provide a framework for assessing children's language abilities, the activities also enrich a teacher's curriculum by eliciting children's invented and descriptive narrative. Teachers can use their knowledge of children's competences to provide additional experiences in their areas of strength as well as to help them in areas in which they are struggling. For instance, if children exhibit a strength in language but not in creative movement, teachers can suggest that they act out a story or create movements to represent evocative words or expressions. The Spectrum approach offers one possible means for nurturing children's self-esteem as a direct result of meaningful work.

Integrating Curriculum and Assessment: The Case of the Visual Arts

A second educational principle that underlies the development of the Spectrum measures is blurring the line that traditionally divides curriculum and assessment (see also, Teale, 1988; Teale, Hiebert, & Chittenden, 1987). The Spectrum materials are designed to resemble other classroom activities and, ideally, are conducted by the teacher over time in the children's classroom. The Spectrum visual arts assessment is a particularly good illustration of this principle in that it builds on the teacher's regular art curriculum, supplementing it with four targeted exercises.

While many preschool environments are rich with artistic experiences, most teachers devote little attention to assessment in this area. Even when teachers do assess artistic ability, their assessments focus primarily on such exercises as collecting self-portraits in portfolios (see also Harris, 1963). Traditional spatial measures include asking children to copy block designs and geometric patterns (Wechsler, 1967). The assessment guidelines developed by the National Association for the Education of Young Children suggest that artwork be collected to document "children's progress in the division and use of space, awareness of shapes, fine-motor control and eye–hand coordination, and sensitivity to materials" (Cherry, 1990, p. 60). While these categories address some of the same elements covered by the Spectrum assessments, they overlook such capabilities as expressiveness, imagination, and generativeness.

The Spectrum art assessment is embedded in a curriculum with a variety of activities entailing both two-dimensional (paint, markers, crayons, chalk) and three-dimensional (clay, wood-working, sculpture, collage) work. Much of this work is collected in portfolios and assessed at the end of each semester. Four targeted exercises give teachers the opportunity to compare children's work when presented with the same task and materials. The scoring categories used to monitor children's work in the portfolios include use of lines and shapes, color, composition, use of detail, expressiveness, and representation. Four additional categories—consistency, imagination, variety, and sense of completeness—help teachers record their overall impressions of children's work.

The four targeted exercises ensure that children complete a range of art projects they might not otherwise attempt. To establish a baseline for children's representational abilities, two of the Spectrum drawing activities entail drawing a farm animal and a picture of the child with his or her family. To make them meaningful to children, drawings are incorporated into group and individual books. The third drawing exercise is designed to tap children's abilities to use their imagination. For this activity, children are read a story about a strange creature visiting the planet and then asked to depict the creature. The fourth exercise is an open-ended, three-dimensional project incorporating such materials as clay, plasticine, wood scraps, popsicle sticks, and paste.

Most of the scoring categories used by Spectrum address whether children's abilities are characteristic or distinctive for their age group. For example, with regard to composition, preschool children often depict objects and figures in a scattered fashion around the page. Objects may be related to one another, but not to the page as a whole. Objects are also typically depicted in space as children understand them in relation to themselves. However, children with a strength in composition are most likely to portray objects in relation both to one another and the page. Some may use a baseline with a sky in their representational work. Their drawings may also demonstrate a sense of perspective, including such features as occlusion (partial view), three-dimensionality, and profile.

Most preschool children in the Spectrum classrooms produced art characteristic for their age. They often drew stick figures and "tadpole" people and used the materials in exploratory ways. As in language, some children exhibited distinctive ability in certain categories only. For example, one girl whose work was mainly exploratory demonstrated an unusual use of color. In each of her drawings and paintings she drew the color spectrum, varying it slightly with each piece. She also frequently experimented with color-mixing in her paintings. Another boy concentrated on representational drawings with markers. He demonstrated an unusual command of detail, perspective, and composition. Some of his drawings showed figures in profile or partially obstructed objects. His use of lines also conveyed a sense of motion.

The Spectrum art portfolio integrates assessment with curriculum by situating the measures in the context of regular classroom activities. Again, as we saw with the language assessments, one contribution of Spectrum's visual arts assessment is that it gives teachers a frame of reference and a vocabulary for documenting their impressions of children's work. Teachers can come to understand the learner more completely. Instead of just saying, "I like your painting," or "This drawing is really good," teachers can differentiate and describe children's products according to a range of artistic features.

Contextualizing Assessment: The Movement Curriculum

Much of the way we think about and analyze children's development in early childhood programs is influenced by the division of human development into four domains: cognitive, physical, social, and emotional (e.g., Bredekamp & Rosegrant, 1993). Early childhood researchers and educators often refer to this four-part scheme both implicitly and explicitly in studying and tracking children's progress in different areas. For example, progress reports for young children focus primarily on the cognitive sphere of development, often addressing early symbol acquisition. If domains other than language and math are addressed at all, they are often lumped together in such phrases as "expresses ideas and emotions through drama, music, dance, and art," or they reflect mainly basic skills, for example, "can grip a pencil, uses glue to make collage, participates in finger plays."

The Spectrum approach, on the other hand, considers problem solving in areas like movement, visual arts, and music to reflect cognitive abilities analogous to those identified in language and math. We drew upon the concept of adult "end-states"—or significant roles in our society—to define the types of abilities we wanted to elicit. For instance, we looked at such vocations as storyteller, reporter, singer, naturalist, and mechanic in developing our assessment activities. By embedding the Spectrum assessments in meaningful, role-related activities, we were hoping to look beyond skills useful in the school context to include the range of abilities called upon in real-world situations.

Reflecting the abilities of athletes and dancers, Spectrum's assessments in the movement domain address both athletic and creative movement. Although movement is an important part of many early childhood programs, experiences in this area often revolve around such gross motor activities as running, jumping, balancing, and climbing. As children get older, a greater emphasis is placed on fine-motor development through activities like using scissors, holding markers, and playing with small manipulatives. As suggested earlier, assessments in this area typically focus on broad stages of development, with little opportunity for child input or choice (see, e.g., Folio & Fewell, 1974; Haines, Ames, & Gillespie, 1980; McCarthy, 1972). While the movement theorist Laban (1960), among others, has created a notational and interpretive scheme for tracking children's growth in creative movement, teachers often find such procedures too complex for classroom use.

Since many preschool programs already include an athletic or outdoor activity time, we focus here on the more expressive dimensions of physical development. The Spectrum creative movement assessment is embedded in an ongoing classroom curriculum. Activities elicit five key abilities in creative movement and dance: sensitivity to rhythm, expressiveness, body control, ability to generate movement ideas, and responsiveness to music (see below for scoring criteria).

CREATIVE MOVEMENT SCORING CRITERIA

Sensitivity to Rhythm

Ability to synchronize movements to stable and changing rhythms (generated by an instrument or recorded music) or to set one's own rhythm.

Child attempts to move with the rhythm as opposed to being unaware of or disregarding rhythmic changes. Child can set a rhythm of her own through movement and regulate it for desired effects. Take note whether she uses one part of the body, for example, swinging her arm, or whether she moves her whole body in synchrony.

Expressiveness

Ability to evoke moods or images through movement. Stimulus can be verbal image, prop, or music.

Child is comfortable using gestures and body postures to express herself. She responds vividly to different verbal images and/or moods and tonal qualities of different instruments, for example, drum and bell. She also varies her response to music selections, interpreting the quality of music in her movements, for example, light and fluid movements for lyrical music versus strong and staccato movements for a march.

Body Control

Ability to place body, and to isolate and use body parts effectively, to achieve desired effects, for example, to freeze, balance, melt, and the like.

Child can play, sequence, and execute movements efficiently. Her movements do not seem random or disjointed. She accurately executes movement ideas proposed by adults or other children. Look for whether child can freeze her body when asked. Also notice *body awareness* (ability to identify and use different body parts like hips and shoulders, and to understand their functions) and *movement memory* (ability to replicate her own movements and those of others).

Generation of Movement Ideas

Ability to invent novel movement ideas or to offer extensions of ideas, for example, suggesting that classmates make their raised arms float like clouds in the sky. Execution of movement is not necessary to excel in this category.

Child responds immediately to ideas and images with original interpretation.

Responsiveness to music

Ability to respond in different ways to different kinds of music (combines sensitivity to rhythm and expressiveness).

Notice whether child responds primarily to rhythm or to mood of music, or to both. Also notice *use of space,* that is, ability to explore available space comfortably using different levels (high, middle, low) and to move easily and fluidly around the room. Look for whether child anticipates others in shared space or experiments with body in space, for example, turning and spinning.

For instance, in addition to asking children to execute specific movement sequences like balancing and skipping, we give children the opportunity to invent their own ideas for movement—important skills for choreographers. As a foundation for movement expressiveness, children explore different levels of space, for example, walking in "high" and "low" space. Later in the year, teachers can determine children's understanding of the use of space by providing them with a variety of images (melting snowpeople, popcorn popping) and observing their responses. Rhythmic sensitivity is another important skill for dancers. To develop children's rhythmic sensitivities, teachers present them with objects with a regular beat like clocks and metronomes. Children also dance to different tempos of music. Teachers document their observations by completing an observational checklist immediately following each movement session.

As stated earlier, one of the distinguishing features among children's responses to the Spectrum movement activities is their ability to generate their own movement ideas, rather than watching and imitating what other children do. While many children simply repeat the teacher's ideas, some expand upon or generate their own novel movements, for example, suggesting that children pretend to be "clocks." One girl revealed unusual movements that reflected both the tempo and mood of the accompanying music. At the conclusion of one piece, she deliberately tried to end her dance in a pose that matched the quality of the music. Some children exhibited good body control and were confident and agile in their movements but were hesitant to experiment with more expressive types of movement. The strengths of these children might have been elicited more fully through athletic challenges rather than the creative movement sessions.

The Spectrum creative movement curriculum contextualizes assessment by enabling teachers to look at children's abilities as they participate in activities authentic to the domain of dance. By designing our assessments with end-states like "dancer" in mind, we hope to ensure that the abilities being tapped are worthy of recognition and support.

Creating "Intelligence–Fair" Assessments: The Music Domain

Finally, the Spectrum assessments are based as much as possible on measures that are what we call "intelligence-fair." Instead of looking at abilities through the windows of language and logic, like many standardized tests, the Spec-

trum measures use materials that reflect the characteristics of the domain being examined. For instance, the athletic movement component involves children completing an obstacle course while the mechanical science assessment entails presenting children with simple machines to take apart and reassemble. In music, in particular, the Spectrum approach departs from traditional paper-and-pencil measures. Instead of focusing on verbal or written responses, the music assessments rely on children singing songs and playing simple instruments.

Assessment of young children's musical competencies has traditionally centered on the ability to distinguish differences in rhythm and pitch (Deutsch, 1983; Dowling & Harwood, 1986; Miller Walker, 1992). Many of the assessments of young children's musical abilities rely on paper-and-pencil measures that were originally designed for older children (Miller Walker, 1992). For example, some of these assessments involve asking children to draw circles around pictures representing "same" and "different" sounds. One music educator argues that there are no appropriate standardized tests for preschool children (Flowers, 1993). Although some researchers in early childhood assessment are beginning to recognize the need to include music, among other art forms, as an important area of child development, these assessments mainly address children's levels of engagement and participation, rather than differentiate the quality of musical competence (Meisels, 1993; Schweinhart & McNair, 1991).

The Spectrum music assessments tap children's abilities in production and perception. The production measure, the Singing Activity, looks at the ability of children to sing new and familiar songs. Core components include grouping of notes, clarity of rhythm, contour of phrases, and singing in tune. For example, contour refers to the up-and-down motion of the melody. Children receive credit for adhering to the general direction of a phrase, even if individual notes are not accurate. Clarity refers to children's ability to project an accurate sense of rhythm. Credit is given if they sing notes on the appropriate beats; if children are vague about the rhythm or invent their own rhythm during the song, they receive no credit.

On the birthday song exercise, part of the production measure, most of the children in the Spectrum classroom sang all the lyrics accurately and exhibited a strong sense of rhythm. A smaller group showed awareness of pitch distinctions, but few were able to maintain the correct key throughout the song. Several children who exhibited outstanding musical ability were also taught a more challenging tune. Although their singing did not reflect the mood or feeling of the melody, they were able to reproduce difficult pitches and intervals and to recreate the song's beginning octave jump.

Complementing the production measure, a Music Perception Activity taps children's abilities to perceive differences in musical qualities like pitch and rhythm. We designed the assessment to be "intelligence-fair" by using a performance-based mode of response for eliciting children's perception abilities. Children are asked to play Montessori bells, which all look alike but yield different tones. Thus, the bells eliminate the visual cues of instruments like xylophones and keyboards. The perception activity consists of five parts: song recognition, error recognition (identifying incorrect versions of well-known tunes), two pitch-matching exercises, and free play.

Most of the children participating in the Spectrum assessment were able to match pitches when asked to identify two bells that sounded the "same" from a series of three-bell sets. Two children who demonstrated unusual sensitivity to the manner in which the bells were played also commented on the different tones created by the wooden and plastic mallets. In the error recognition exercise, one boy articulated subtle distinctions among incorrect versions of the tune, characterizing the differences as "a little the same," "a lot different," and "a very lot different." During free play, some children were reluctant to touch the bells or played entire songs using only one bell, while others explored different arrangements and experimented with volume and rhythm on a number of bells.

As with any assessment, teachers should never rely on just one type of measure for determining perception and production abilities. The Spectrum activities are a vehicle for identifying children's strengths or testing emerging hypotheses about where children's strengths may lie. An important, supplementary source of information—which can also be considered "intelligence-fair"—is observing children's other musical activities in and outside of the classroom. Such observations are essential for additional documentation of children's growth in the domain.

CONCLUDING NOTE

Clearly, much of the work reported here is still in a preliminary stage. For example, the Spectrum activities need to be field-tested with larger and more diverse samples of children. Further, it would be a mistake to interpret this chapter as recommending that all children need to be assessed on all Spectrum measures. Given the daily challenges faced by teachers of young children in terms of class size, limited staff support, lack of time, and scarce resources, we believe it is most important to focus on those children who are not being adequately served by the traditional curriculum.

In this chapter, we have tried to suggest an alternative way of conceptualizing children's abilities in the communicative and visual arts. Rather than restricting our notion of cognitive activity to language and math, we consider problem solving in the visual arts, movement, and music to represent "intelligences" as well. The Spectrum framework offers a tool for differentiating and documenting aspects of children's development, which too often go unnoticed. If we begin to recognize and support children's strengths in a wider range of areas, we are likely to increase the chances for all children to experience success in domains valued in school. Ultimately, the promise of this approach will be realized when children's distinctive cognitive profiles can be discerned and nurtured in their educational, home, and community contexts.

References

Binet, A., & Simon, T. (1916). *The development of intelligence in children* (E.S. Kite, Trans.). Baltimore: Williams & Wilkins. Reprinted in 1973, New York: Arno Press.

Bredekamp, S., & Rosegrant, T. (1993). *Researching potentials: Appropriate curriculum and assessment for young children, Vol. I.* Washington, DC: National Association for the Education of Young Children.

Ceci, S. (1990). *On intelligence … more or less: A bioecological treatise on intellectual development.* Englewood Cliffs, NJ: Prentice-Hall.

Cherry, C. (1990). *Creative art for the developing child* (2nd Ed.). Carthage, IL: Fearon. Cited in S. Bredekamp, & T. Rosegrant, (1993). *Reaching potentials: Appropriate curriculum and assessment for young children, Vol. I,* (p. 60). Washington, DC: National Association for the Education of Young Children.

Deutsch, D. (1983). *Psychology of music.* New York: Academic Press.

Dowling, W., & Harwood, D. (1986). *Music cognition.* New York: Academic Press.

Fancher, R. (1985). *The intelligence men, makers of the IQ controversy.* New York: Norton.

Feldman, D. H. (1980, 1994). *Beyond universals in cognitive development* (2nd ed.). Norwood, NJ: Ablex.

Flowers, P. (1993). Evaluation in early childhood music. In M. Palmer & W. L. Sims (Eds.), *Music in prekindergarten* (pp. 37–43). Reston, VA: Music Educators National Conference.

Fodor, J. (1983). *The modularity of mind.* Cambridge, MA: MIT Press.

Folio, M., & Fewell, R. (1974). *Peabody developmental motor scales and activity cards.* Allen, TX: DLM Teaching Resources.

Gardner, H. (1983). *Frames of mind: The theory of multiple intelligences.* New York: Basic Books.

Haines, J., Ames, L. B., & Gillespie, C. (1980). *Gesell preschool test.* Flemington, NJ: Programs for Education.

Harris, D. B. (1963). *Children's drawings as measures of intellectual maturity: A revision and extension of the Goodenough Draw-a-Man Test.* New York: Harcourt, Brace & World.

Hiebert, E. A., & Calfee, R. (1992). Assessing literacy: From standardized tests to portfolios and performances. In S. J. Samuels & A. E. Farstrup (Eds.), *What research has to say about reading instruction* (pp. 70–100). Newark, DE: International Reading Association.

Keil, F. C. (1986). On the structure-dependent nature of stages in cognitive development. In I. Levin (Ed.), *Stage and structure* (pp. 144–163). Norwood, NJ: Ablex.

Krechevsky, M. (1991). Project Spectrum: An innovative assessment alternative. *Educational Leadership. 50*(2), pp. 43–48.

Krechevsky, M. (1994). Project Spectrum: Preschool assessment handbook. Cambridge, MA: Harvard Project Zero.

Laban, R. (1960). *The mastery of movement* (2nd ed.). London: McDonald & Evans.

McCarthy, D. A. (1972). *McCarthy's scales of children's abilities.* New York: The Psychological Corporation.

Meisels, S. J. (1993). Remaking classroom assessment with the work sampling system. *Young Children, 48*(5), 34–40.

Meisels, S. J., Dorfman, A., & Steele, D. M. (in press). *Contrasting approaches to assessing young children's school readiness and achievement.* Paper commissioned by the National Center for

Education Statistics, Office of Educational Research and Improvement, and the U.S. Department of Education.

Miller Walker L. (1992). Assessment in early childhood music. In B. L. Andress & L. Miller Walker (Eds.), *Readings in early childhood music education* (pp. 100–106). Reston, VA: Music Educators National Conference.

Sattler, J. M. (1988). *Assessment of children* (3rd ed.). San Diego: Sattler.

Schweinhart, L. J., & McNair, S. (1991). *The new child observation record*. Ypsilanti, MI: High/Scope Educational Research Foundation.

Snow, C., Tabors, P., Nicholson, P., & Kurland, B. (in press). SHELL: A method for assessing oral language and early literacy skills in kindergarten and first grade children. Paper submitted to *Journal of Research in Childhood Education*.

Spearman, C. (1904). The proof and measurement of association between two things. *The American Journal of Psychology, 15,* 201–292. Excerpted in J. J. Jenkins, & D. G. Patterson (Eds.), (1961), *Studies in individual differences: The search for intelligence* (pp. 59–73). New York: Appleton-Century-Crofts.

Spearman, C. (1927). *The nature of intelligence and the principles of cognition.* London: Macmillan.

Sulzby, E. (1985). Kindergartners as writers and readers. In M. Farr (Ed.), *Advances in writing research, Vol. I: Children's early writing development.* (pp. 127–199). Norwood, NJ: Ablex.

Teale, W. H. (1988). Developmentally appropriate assessment of reading and writing in the early childhood classroom. *The Elementary School Journal, 89*(2), 173–183.

Teale, W. H., Hiebert, E., & Chittenden, E. (1987). Assessing young children's literacy development. *The Reading Researcher, 40,* 772–777.

Wechsler, D. (1967). *Wechsler preschool and primary scale of intelligence.* New York: Psychological Corporation.

24

DEAF CHILDREN AS LITERACY LEARNERS:
TOM, ROBBIE, AND PAUL

Claire L. Ramsey

UNIVERSITY OF CALIFORNIA, SAN DIEGO

INTRODUCTION

In this chapter I describe three young literacy learners in a public elementary school program for hearing impaired children. As in most deaf education settings, literacy in English is the dominant instructional goal. In contrast to most deaf education settings, however, in this classroom, discourse was structured by American Sign Language (ASL). Indeed, ASL was the primary medium of instruction for all school subjects, including English, as well as for social life among the deaf children and their teachers. In this setting, the presence of one deaf adult who is a native signer of ASL generated a context where deaf children could both engage in learning and express themselves as learners through their incipient ASL/English bilingualism. Although they found the learning tasks focused on reading and writing English to be difficult, the children's interest in language, writing, and other people, coupled with their ability to express their ideas through ASL, provides many insights into the nature of the literacy learning task for deaf children.

BACKGROUND

Currently most deaf children are enrolled in regular public elementary schools (Schildroth, 1988) in education programs where their time is distributed among special classes for deaf students and classes and activities where they are "mainstreamed" or integrated with hearing children. Signing interpreters are often provided in integrated settings. In special classes, a pedagogy called "total communication" (TC) is followed. Total communication teachers are generally hearing speakers of English who use spoken English accompanied by signs as the medium of instruction. Deaf adult staff members are rarely found in elementary TC settings (Woodward, Allen, & Schildroth, 1988). The twin objectives of public school hearing impaired programs are to allow for instruction with normally hearing agemates as much as possible and to facilitate the acquisition of English among the deaf children. Despite the existence of such programs, and the highly intensive and technical methods for educating deaf children which have been developed over the years, deaf students in the United States generally fail to achieve competence in English and assimilation with hearing people that their education is expected to provide (Allen, 1986; Commission on Education of the Deaf, 1988; Quigley & Paul, 1984). As their school careers proceed, deaf students fall more and more behind their hearing agemates.

Although a great deal is known about the disappointing outcomes of schooling for many deaf students (e.g., Allen, 1986), many questions remain about the everyday enactment of deaf education. Trends in communication and instruction come and go in a virtually data-free vacuum. In addition, mainstreaming, although widespread, is also poorly understood, especially its potential effects on deaf students' learning (Commission, 1988; Ramsey, 1994). These gaps in knowledge have generated provocative theoretical and practical questions about deaf children's early school lives, especially their learning of basic literacy (Commission, 1988; Erting, 1981; Johnson, & Erting, 1989; Johnson, Liddell, & Erting, 1989; National Institute on Deafness and Other Communication Disorders, 1989; Padden & Ramsey, 1993; Quigley & Paul, 1984; Ramsey, Sterne, & Padden, 1994).

How do deaf children tackle basic literacy skills? What do they do with language in contexts where print and signing coexist? To shed light on this question, I spent a school year with three deaf second graders, Tom, Robbie, Paul, and their teachers, and classmates. I observed and participated in instructional and noninstructional school activities, using two video cameras to videotape instruction, booksharing, writing, reading, classes with hearing children, and visits from local deaf community members. I made 68 visits and recorded 250 hours of videotape. I studied the school context from "top to bottom," in order to isolate the school's many influences on the deaf children's opportunities to participate in learning. At the institutional level, I noted practices that reflected national legislative goals for educating children with disabilities and traced ways in which the school's organizational response to these ideals negatively affected the deaf children, especially in integrated settings (Ramsey, 1994). In contrast, the special self-contained classroom for deaf children was organized by the teachers of the deaf, according to their educational goals for the children. Notably, deaf community norms, especially norms for use of signed communication, also shaped life in the special classroom (Ramsey, in press). In the local context of the deaf students' activities during literacy instruction, I noted the powerful influence of the social life of the classroom, where both ASL and English were used and valued. This paper focuses on Tom, Robbie, and Paul as learners, and on their notions about language and literacy, revealed in their activities and in their comments on reading, writing, signing, and talking.

The Boys, Their Teachers, and Their School

Tom, Paul, and Robbie were the only deaf children in second grade during the study year, although they were part of a larger special class that included deaf third graders who signed, and a group of hard-of-hearing second and third graders who spoke English and did not sign. The three boys (who all turned 9 during the study) were good friends who used signing as their primary and preferred mode of communication.

Tom has a profound, bilateral sensorineural hearing loss caused by meningitis, contracted when he was 12 months old. (The names of the school and all participants have been changed to protect their privacy). The only child of hearing, English-speaking parents, Tom entered the preschool hearing impaired program at Aspen School when he was 3 years old. His mother signed and his father signed "some." Both parents expected that Tom would be an ASL-signing deaf community member when he grew up.

Paul has a profound sensorineural hearing loss in his left ear, with no response to testing in his right ear. His deafness was also caused by meningitis when he was around 12 months old. Paul entered the Aspen School hearing impaired program when he was 5 years old, having had no previous schooling. He was an only child who lived in an extended family household with his parents, and his mother's sister and her sons, whom he referred to as his "brothers." His parents spoke English, although only his father was a native speaker. Paul's father, a beginning signer, was the only member of the household who signed.

Robbie has a profound sensorineural hearing loss in his left ear and a severe sensorineural hearing loss in his right ear. Robbie was born deaf, of unknown causes. Robbie and his parents participated in a university-based "parent-infant program" when he was a baby. When he was three, he joined the

Aspen School preschool program. (He and Tom entered the same year.) He was the middle child in a hearing English-speaking family, with an elder brother and a baby brother. According to the teachers, his mother signed and his father was a beginning signer.

Aspen Elementary School, the site of the study, is a public elementary school in an unincorporated urban area in the western United States. About 350 students attend the school. Nearly half of them qualify for the free or reduced price lunch program. Deaf and hard-of-hearing students comprise about 10% of the school population.

Robbie, Paul, and Tom spent half days in a self-contained special classroom for the deaf and half days in integrated settings, primarily a regular 2nd-grade classroom. As spoken English was the medium of instruction and the hearing teachers and students did not sign, an interpreter accompanied deaf children during mainstreaming periods. The boys joined the hearing children's class for math, social studies, art, science, and "specialist" classes (PE, music and library).

Three adults worked with the boys and their deaf and hard-of-hearing classmates. Ms. Roberts and Ms. Adams are teachers of the deaf and both are hearing, native speakers of English, who each learned ASL as an adult, after leaving graduate school. Mrs. Hart is the instructional assistant in the classroom. In contrast to Ms. Roberts and Ms. Adams, Mrs. Hart is a deaf native signer of ASL, and has deaf parents, children, and grandchildren. She began acquiring English speaking ability during her early school years. She had good second language competence in written English, but little confidence in her writing ability. Although she could detect speech and use spoken English intelligibly, she would not speak on the telephone. She identified herself as a culturally deaf person.

Bilingualism in Deaf Education

Since the early 19th century, American deaf education pedagogy has cycled through several major ideological changes. (See Lou, 1988, for a detailed review of this history.) Early 19th century deaf education was conducted through signing. By the late 19th century "oral" methods (where students learned to "lipread" and to speak) were dominant. Oralism, in turn, was displaced by total communication in the 1960s. Total communication returned signing to the classroom, although not the sign language of deaf people, ASL, nor their communication practices. Rather, several groups of educators fashioned systems of signing that they hoped would provide not only media for communication and instruction but models of English that would be clearly visible to deaf students. These systems are often referred to as "manually coded English" or by trademark names such as "SEE." In practice, total communication methods depend upon the medium of speech combined with one of these systems of signs, a method of communication that is not comfortable for most deaf adults. Neither oral methods nor the TC pedagogy have significantly altered the depressed schooling outcomes of deaf students. (See, Ramsey, 1989 and Supalla, 1986 for discussions of the formal linguistic and sociolinguistic weaknesses of the manually-coded English systems, and of communication practices in TC classes.)

As educational methods in classrooms for deaf children fluctuated, communities of deaf adults remained linguistically stable, using, maintaining, and elaborating their language as any speech community would over time. They transmitted ASL to their children (hearing and deaf) via precisely the same interactional paths that all communities use to pass on linguistic heritage to younger generations. Deaf people who did not grow up in deaf communities (e.g., those from hearing families) gained access to the deaf community and to ASL at various points in their lives (at school from deaf adults in nonclassroom settings, or from native-born deaf peers), and entered the world of deaf signers of ASL. Although ASL is signed language embedded in an English speaking context, it is unrelated to English, maintained by a cohesive speech community of deaf signing people and their deaf and hearing children.

In recent years deaf Americans, especially those who are teachers of the deaf, have spearheaded a reevaluation (at both the grass roots and professional levels) of the education that is offered to deaf children. The recurring problem, long noted by both deaf people and by teachers, is the difficulty of communication (and hence of teaching and learning) in classrooms for deaf students organized according to oral or TC pedagogies. As deaf adults began participating in and directing the discourse about the education of deaf children, images of deaf students began to change. Descriptions of deaf children as disabled persons needing auditory and speech rehabilitation began to fade. In their place, descriptions of deaf people as an ethnolinguistic group arose, where the young need "bilingual education" using ASL as the medium of instruction, not "special education" using invented or artificial languages or mechanistic methods. This cultural view of deaf people, existing alongside recent realizations of the multicultural nature of contemporary American life, has given rise to a new deaf education pedagogy, termed bilingual–bicultural (or bi–bi) education.

The analogy between the bilingual educational needs of deaf children and those of hearing ethnic minority children is not perfect. Critically, approximately 90% of deaf children are born into families of hearing people who have never met a deaf person and have little access to the deaf community, to its language and its practices. Unlike most Hispanic children, for example, most deaf children do not go home from school to deaf communities or to homes where all family members sign. Nonetheless, the powerful arguments in favor of using a natural human language, with an established "speech" community of signers and a historically-transmitted set of communication practices, have convinced some teachers and parents that ASL should be the medium of instruction for deaf children. Although only a few schools for deaf students have formally adopted a bi-bi stance toward education, many teachers and parents of deaf students see deaf children's educational needs from a nonmedical perspective, and make efforts to arrange for their children to have access to deaf native signers, and ASL and ASL-based communication practices at school.

Aspen School is such a case. While it is not formally a "bi-bi" school, ASL and deaf community ways with language are present in the classroom for deaf children. During her 12-year tenure in elementary deaf education classrooms, Ms. Roberts had begun taking ASL courses at night, believing that she could communicate and teach more successfully if she could use the language of deaf adults. In addition, when a position for an instructional assistant opened in her classroom, she encouraged the hiring of a deaf native signer, and Mrs. Hart joined the staff. Ms. Adams had recently received an M.A. in deaf education, after which she undertook a 2-year course in sign language interpreting to build her ASL skills. All three women believed that ASL was the best teaching tool they could bring to their classroom to help their deaf students learn and develop. With very little outside guidance, they attempted to make their classroom a culturally and linguistically friendly place for the deaf students.

Two Classrooms

Each school day Robbie, Tom, and Paul moved between the "deaf classroom" and the "mainstreaming classroom." In these two settings, they found a range of opportunities for using language face-to-face. It is important to understand the stark contrast between the deaf classroom, where teachers viewed the deaf children as bilingual (or potentially so), and mainstreaming settings, where teachers viewed the deaf children as disabled and in need of access to hearing children as language models.

Instruction in the mainstreaming classroom was teacher-centered, with an interpreter signing the teacher's speech for the deaf children. Since the teacher held the floor much of the time, most face-to-face communication in this room was among children, either "underground" and unofficial, or during recess or transitions between activities. I closely examined interactions among deaf and hearing children in this classroom to see how they managed to make contact with each other and to look for any hints that the deaf students were being assimilated into the mainstream hearing classroom culture. This is a positive outcome that administrators, policy makers, and parents have come to expect from integrated classrooms, although it is not clear how assimilation takes place when hearing children do not sign, and deaf children cannot speak.

Ideals about fostering opportunities for deaf children to mix with hearing children were not easily converted into practice. In fact, they were often incompatible with deaf children's specific educational needs. Since there was very little provision for teaching the hearing children to sign, and hearing and deaf peers could not communicate easily with each other, contexts of mainstreaming created constraints for the deaf children's communication. Although a sign language interpreter was always available to mediate their interactions, she did not have a niche in the hearing children's social life at school, and they avoided using her to communicate with the deaf children unless a dispute needed to be resolved.

For their part, the deaf children saved their interactional energy for communicating with other signing deaf children. They engaged with hearing children rarely, and only for instrumental purposes, for example, to manage classroom business. Interaction initiated by hearing children with deaf children consisted of evaluations, directives, and unintelligible signing. This limited range of caretaker-like functions contributed to the status of "exotic mascots" that was often assigned to the deaf children in mainstream settings, where they were observed, commanded, praised or chided, but rarely included as peers in the group life of their hearing classmates.

In contrast, life in the deaf classroom was organized to promote a great deal of interaction and communication. This was facilitated by the teacher-student ratio, with three teaching adults working with only five or six students. Instruction took place through small group conversations, and children and adults were engaged with each other much of the time. Social life in the self-contained classroom was intelligible and engaging, structured as it was by ASL. Neither the three boys nor the adults used manually coded English for face-to-face communication. All participants, including the two hearing teachers of the deaf, signed ASL with varying degrees of skill. This was confirmed by a panel of native signer judges, none of whom knew the children or their teachers.

Yet, even in this intelligible classroom setting, patterned choices of interactional partners were based upon signing ability and gender. Tom, Robbie, and Paul preferred to interact with signers and with other boys. They did not favor their hard-of-hearing classmates in the deaf classroom who did not sign. Mrs. Hart was the preferred adult conversant. At the ages of eight and nine, the three boys were developing knowledge about the complicated linguistic world that all deaf people inhabit, where signing people and speaking people coexist. As the school year unfolded, I interviewed the boys about their lives at school. Each offered his observations about people at school and about communication, and made claims about his own writing, reading, and language. Additionally, the boys expressed some unconventional beliefs about hearing children's language and literacy.

Who Is Deaf?

All three focal boys asserted that they were deaf. Both Robbie and Paul assured me that they would be deaf when they grew up. Tom told me that Jesus would make him a hearing person, although when asked exactly how this would happen, he explained that the Jesus account was "just pretend." It is possible, however, that the second graders' definitions of "deaf" would undergo some change as they grew older. The deaf third grade students in the classroom expressed less certainty about their future status. One third grader told me that he would be both deaf and hearing when he grew up.

Robbie, Paul, and Tom made clear their knowledge that deaf people signed and hearing people did not. Hearing people could be diagnosed by their practice of talking to communicate. People who appeared to be able to both speak and sign had no clear status. Accordingly, the adults in the deaf classroom presented a problem. When confronted with the facts that we could all talk as well as sign, the children proposed various solutions. Paul declined to explain how Mrs. Hart could both talk and sign. He stated that she could

talk and that she was deaf, then summed up with a shrug, "I don't know." He was certain, however, that Ms. Roberts was deaf, and claimed that he did not know about Ms. Adams. Robbie resolved the problem by claiming that we were all both deaf and hearing. Tom claimed that I was hearing, that Mrs. Hart was "a little bit deaf" and that Ms. Roberts was a deaf person who could, for an unexplainable reason, talk. (Recall that Mrs. Hart was deaf, and Ms. Adams, Ms. Roberts, and I were all hearing signers.)

Tom also identified as "hearing" the hard-of-hearing children in his classroom who used hearing aids but did not sign. He laid out his reasoning on this topic by describing his hard of-hearing classmate Drew's flaws as a signer, explaining, "She can't use her fingers right. It's awful." Tom reported that his parents were hearing people who could sign a little bit, then emphatically changed his mind, "NO, my mom and dad are hard-of-hearing." (See Padden & Humphries, 1988, for a discussion of the phenomenon of deaf children's definitions of "deaf" in the fuller context of American deaf culture.)

The boys' friendships and choices of interactional partners during instruction, and during lunchtime and recess (which were integrated activities) as well as their explicit expressions of friendship, complemented their claims about who fit into which category. The deaf children preferred to interact, eat, and play with other deaf children and stated this preference when asked. Paul explained to me that his friends were Robbie, Tom, and the deaf boys in the 3rd-grade group, and then very sweetly announced his affiliation with Tom, "Tom is my deaf."

Dealing with Hearing Children

The hearing 2nd-grade children in the mainstreaming classroom presented a less confusing diagnostic problem. According to Robbie, Paul, and Tom, these children were all hearing, and hearing children differed from deaf children in their communication abilities. For example, Robbie claimed that he himself never used his voice or tried to speak, and stated, "I sign, I'm deaf." In contrast, he maintained that hearing people (both his neighbors at home and his hearing classmates) simply did not sign, "They are hearing. Hearing people don't sign." Tom explained that the people in the mainstreaming classroom talked, and "I can't understand talking." Paul conceded that the children in the mainstreaming classroom were "different," and that they could do "a little bit of signing." In contrast, he reminded me that in the deaf classroom, "people know how to sign."

Although the boys willingly constructed categories for the various people in their worlds and acted on their preferences to play with children they could sign with, they obviously had interactions with hearing people. Robbie revealed that there were activities where hearing and deaf people could adjust to each other. (This is notable since, of the three boys, Robbie was the most uncooperative with any nonsigning substitute teachers who were temporarily assigned to the classroom.) For example, he claimed that math was hard, but it did not require "talking," so math lessons could take place among the hearing children. In his out-of-school life, he reported that playing Nintendo with nonsigning hearing neighbor children was "easy, easy, easy" because it only involved "hitting the buttons" and "being careful." For his part, Tom maintained the less charitable stance that people who could only sign a little bit were "stupid."

It is clear that these deaf children lived in the so-called "hearing world." Over the course of their young lives, they had observed hearing people and deaf people, as well as the activities that took place in their lives. Not surprisingly, they had formed preferences and certain (reasonable) beliefs about their own communication, especially about whom they could successfully communicate with and which activities might allow specific kinds of nonsigning interaction. The point here is that, in the context of their current school life, the focal boys were not only unconfused about their identities as deaf boys, they had begun to form a set of related beliefs about what "deaf" and "hearing" meant.

Relating Communication and Literacy: "Hearing Children Can't Sign and Can't Read"

The boys each outlined definitions of "reading and writing" suggesting that they expected that a connection between language used face-to-face and written language could be discovered or created. Their claims about deafness and the reading and writing abilities of hearing children with no access to signing and finger spelling indicated the symbolic order they were attempting to place on their social school world. In their world, both print and hearing people played prominent roles, and both needed to be accounted for.

For children conventionally regarded as suffering a "communication disorder," the deaf boys had made surprisingly careful observations of communication practices in their social world at school. Specifically, they related their notions about categories of people, ways of communicating, and reading and writing in unconventional, but reasonable ways.

Robbie conceded that reading was hard, yet he claimed that hearing children would find reading even harder than deaf children, since hearing children could not fingerspell. He claimed that signing and fingerspelling helped with reading, while talking did not. Further, he claimed that "deaf people can write fast, and hearing people can't. Hearing people can't sign and deaf people write fast." Despite Robbie's child-like logic, he was approaching language use face-to-face and in print as metalinguistic objects about which speculations and statements could be made. Although he had not discovered the exact nature of the relation, he clearly assumed that one existed, and that it could be stated at a metalevel.

Tom was also casting around for an account of relations among symbol systems, social identities, and general language abilities. Initially he reported that the hearing children were "stupid." He told me that they did not even have reading or spelling lessons, a sensible comment since he was never present in the mainstreaming classroom for these lessons and hence had never observed the hearing children engaging in spelling and learning-to-read rituals. (He actually regarded the perceived absence of reading books in the mainstreaming classroom as a positive feature. At one point during the school year, he reported that he preferred the mainstreaming class-

room for exactly that reason, since he disliked reading.) Despite this, he reported that learning to read was easy if you were smart (as he was), and that "girls" (specifically, his mom) loved to read. He preferred skateboarding over any school-like activity, such as reading.

Tom claimed that writing was hard and that the adults in the deaf classroom had various reasons for making their students write. He claimed that Mrs. Hart made him write because she was a mean and strict person, but that the other teachers made him write "because I make mistakes, and it's hard." Tom explained that the hearing children knew how to write and that it was easy for them. He concluded, however, that writing was not important.

Paul, who was a relatively new signer and was the last of the three boys to put reading and writing to use, had strong opinions about his own literacy skills. Simply put, he was thrilled that he could read and write, and took our interview as an opportunity to demonstrate his abilities by reading a familiar text, *The Little Red Hen,* to me. He told me that reading was both easy and important, "because it's my favorite" and claimed that anyone could write. In Paul's view, writing was important "because you need to write to work." He was less clear about the hearing children's literacy skills and practices, having no opinion on hearing children's reading and guessing that writing was "the same" for deaf and for hearing children.

From their comments during interviews and conversations over the course of the study year, it was clear that the deaf children were alert to some of the ways that social life interacted with symbolic life. For example, they recognized that there were categories of people who conducted their social lives via distinct symbolic means—hearing people talk and deaf people sign. At the same time, in their own writing activities, it appeared that they were trying to forge for themselves relations among the symbolic means that were available to them in their school social world, especially during activities that centered on literacy.

Doing Writing

As I got to know the boys, I asked them many times in many different ways what they did when they wrote. Not surprisingly, I was unsuccessful in getting Robbie, Tom, and Paul to put their mental processes into explicit language. They had not yet developed the ability to reflect on or communicate about their own intellectual activities. Yet, even though they could not report their own mental processes, the boys' communication with others and their signing to themselves during writing can be analyzed as externalized traces of the internal relations they were forging between their own face-to-face language and print.

Although each boy engaged in the same school activity, "writing," each had his own way of approaching the task, and each depended on the social setting of the deaf classroom, as well as his ability to use ASL, as resources when confronting the task of writing.

Writing time took place daily in the deaf classroom, generally right before or directly after lunch. This event always took place at the "horseshoe table," a U-shaped table located at the side of the classroom. The children sat around the outside of the U, and one adult sat inside the U, all on low, child-sized chairs. If other adults were there, they sat with the children on the outside of the U.

There were no specific lessons about "English" or writing planned for these periods. The goal, according to Ms. Roberts, was to provide a time when the deaf students could practice getting their ideas out of their heads and onto paper via whatever means they wished to use. One adult was always available to help the children (often all three of them were present), the children were free to converse with each other, and a variety of resources was available (e.g., word lists, calendars, maps, books, and scratch paper). Instruction about English, and about such matters as the format of arranging written text on the page occurred in context, in response to the children's questions or problems with the immediate task. (During "language lessons," another daily instructional event, a more explicit version of English instruction was provided.) Within this social and symbolic setting, the focal boys took somewhat different paths to accomplishing the task of "writing."

"To write you have to be smart ... and ask.": The case of Robbie. Robbie's expressed attitude toward writing was that individuals and social settings both contributed to the accomplishment of writing. He clearly felt that his own contribution was being "smart." The contribution of the social setting was to answer or to provide resources when he asked questions and to provide partners and raw material for conversation. Like the other two boys, he assumed that support would be available whenever he needed it. He did not regard communication with peers and adults in the deaf classroom as troublesome or difficult, but as a routine feature of life. Unlike many deaf school children, he did not struggle to communicate with anyone in his classroom.

Robbie regarded himself as an expert on spelling and writing. He often offered unsolicited corrections to his friends' texts, reminding Paul, for example, that writing "two sister" was wrong—if there were two, then Paul had to add an "s" to sister to make it right. Even in cases where writing was not the task, Robbie stood his ground on his current suppositions about representing English. The three focal boys argued at length one day about creating a sign name for "Little Red Riding Hood." Although Tom and Paul proposed calling her RED, using a traditional ASL lexical item, Robbie argued long and hard that the sign should reflect features of the print letter R. His suggestion was to include an R handshape borrowed from fingerspelling to adequately represent her name, as a manually coded English system would. Although the boys' interactional world was structured by signing and ASL, and not by English, their access to English provided an avenue for making English, and representations of English words in spelling and writing, a topic of conversation.

Although Robbie himself volunteered information and instruction about writing to his peers (such that his bossiness was sometimes resented), when he required assistance himself he never asked peers for help, but always turned to an adult. He often used his voice (although it was generally unintelligible) in his attempts to solicit information about

English. Robbie's selective use of his voice is intriguing, especially since he identified himself as a deaf person who signed. In fact, as noted, he had denied speaking, told me that he never used his voice, and pouted and moped when the speech teacher came to pull him out for speech lessons. His use of his voice when he solicited help from signing people during literacy activities suggested that he had included spoken pronunciation of words as one feature of literacy tasks that he could exploit under very specific circumstances. That is, this strategy was useful only when his interlocutor could both talk and sign and was otherwise known to him as a helpful, supportive adult. At this stage of his life, he refused to exploit this sound resource when the interlocutor did not sign.

When Robbie sat down to write, he focused on his text. In addition to asking adults for assistance with vocabulary, he also turned inward, signing and fingerspelling to himself. He worked on ideas and planned texts with self-directed signing, which was sometimes translated from ASL to written English. He often monitored his sentences by reading and signing the text to himself after he had written it. During writing, he interacted with peers for various alternative purposes, to make personal comments about drawings or to gossip in ASL with Paul about Tom's dreamy, inattentive behavior.

"Mrs. Hart makes me write because she's mean, and I make mistakes.": The case of Tom. In second grade, Tom disliked school and viewed writing as well as reading as difficult potentially error-ridden tasks that included an element of punishment. Where Robbie and Paul treated print as a puzzle to be solved, Tom regarded it as dangerous territory.

Yet Tom's dislike of school tasks did not mean that he inhabited a symbolic wasteland. Although he was known to the other children and adults in the deaf classroom as both a good storyteller (a positive characterization) and a daydreamer (a negative characterization), he regarded himself as a creative person who "adores making things up." The truth is, however, that Tom often disengaged from ongoing school life to daydream and fantasize about Michael Jackson's dance moves, or about one of his other heroes from movies or television. He made varying accounts of his tendency to avoid schoolwork, including the outlandish explanation to Mrs. Hart (which he only attempted to use once) that he could not watch her signing or read that day because his eyes were slanted, since his grandfather on his mother's side was Japanese American.

Despite his resistance to engaging in the school activity of writing, his writing time activities suggested that he was actively involved in the enterprise of using symbols. At the very least, his idiosyncratic version of writing activities (which sometimes resulted in no writing) promoted the task of finding equivalents between signs and print words. It also gave him access to a unique social world which was structured by his preferred language, ASL, where the content and topic of conversation was writing, English, signing and the relations among them. Tom spent a great deal of writing time making elaborate drawings, from which he signed exciting stories. When encouraged to write his stories, he relied on the adults or the other children to help him with words or with spelling. Like Robbie, he signed to himself to plan and monitor texts, although for Tom the process of putting his signed plans into print was very difficult.

"I love to write because it's my favorite.": The case of Paul. Of the three boys, Paul most recently acquired language and used print. He turned nine early in the study year and had only begun to learn to sign 3 years before. The teachers reported that during first grade he did not communicate fluently or often. According to Ms. Roberts, "something clicked" during second grade, and she was very pleased with his growing willingness to communicate and his interest in language.

Paul himself seemed to be aware of his growth. He was wildly proud when he memorized a spelling list, for example, and often tried to engage adults in spelling games. He began a conversation one day by announcing an inventory of signs, the English glosses for which he could spell by himself, and he sometimes stood at the chalkboard and produced long written inventories of words he knew. However, his hold on English was tenuous and he often lost confidence in his knowledge about words. Almost by reflex, one day he asked Lawrence (a hard-of-hearing classmate who was a beginning signer) to help him spell "school." Despite his pride in his growing sign and English print vocabularies, Paul was accustomed to not knowing how to spell all the words he wanted to write. However, he remembered part way through Lawrence's help that he could spell and write "school" by himself, so he blocked out Lawrence's fingerspelling by covering his own face with a book.

Paul maneuvered through the social life of writing time with functional ease, although he was not a skilled signer yet, and he could not always express himself in signing. He spent time carefully drawing pictures in his journal, and often sat quietly, thinking about his stories. His writing often began as an inventory of single words or very short sentences, like "Snow fun. Sled with brother." He asked for assistance with words from both peers and adults. However, he resisted teachers' attempts to model composing processes (e.g., What did the boy do next? What is in that box? How did the girl feel when she saw the Christmas tree?).

Paul's most serious social obstacle during writing time was getting the attention of potential interlocutors. He often tried to initiate conversations, got no response, then sat quietly and waited for someone to respond to him, as other people signed. (Ramsey et al., 1994 note a similar circumstance involving a "new signer" in an ASL-structured deaf education setting.) Whatever he lacked in communicative competence, Paul, like the other boys, operated as if he assumed that the social world of writing time was ultimately supportive and intelligible. He trusted that there were people who assumed that his signing, gesturing, and movement were meaningful and that they would attend to the meaning he was trying to express.

When he was writing, Paul worked with great concentration and disliked being bothered or interrupted. He had learned to use sternly explicit language with his peers during literacy activities. For example, when Tom interrupted his school work and was seeking a playmate or someone to tell stories or giggle with, Paul routinely looked him in the eye and signed, "Stop it. I'm going to ignore you." When Tom was acting especially irritating, Paul and Robbie openly gossiped about him and shared their disapproval of his dreamy, silly ways.

Language and Literacy in ASL-Signing Deaf Children.

The interaction between face-to-face language and written language during Tom's, Robbie's, and Paul's literacy activities suggested that intelligible access to other people in the classroom setting fostered their engagement with the people around them, with themselves, and with the symbolic tasks of writing. First, the boys' certainty about who was deaf and who was hearing interacted with their observations about the ways different kinds of people communicated and extended to speculations about the ease with which different kinds of people could approach literacy. The boys appeared to expect that a relationship between ASL used face-to-face and English print could be either discovered or imposed upon their symbolic life during writing. The three boys approached writing in different ways, but all used ASL consistently, representationally, and heuristically with others to discuss topics, recount narratives, and to seek and offer help. They used ASL directively, signing to themselves to plan and monitor their own writing.

Despite their avoidance of English-based systems of signing, the data suggest that the boys knew something about English and about demonstrating school competence. When the adults asked them to "sign that in a sentence," the boys sometimes used English-like signs as embellishments to their performance although these performance sentences were almost never committed to print.

Relations Between Face-to-Face Language and Written Language

Among these three deaf children, face-to-face language and written language interacted in complex, theoretically intriguing ways. Robbie, Tom, and Paul are active social beings who observed and were able to comment on the "real" world around them at school. In addition, they engaged in strategic activities during writing in an effort to discover and create relations between their social lives, their internal mental lives, and their writing. I believe that both their capacities for expressing themselves and their strategies for writing were made possible by their ability to use ASL as their primary language and by their developing ASL/English bilingualism. Although they might appear to outsiders as "special education" students with a communication disability, they were unconfused about their own identities as deaf children who signed, and they were alert to and interested in the people around them. What is of most interest here is their forceful attempts to understand the relations between a person's way of communicating and his or her ways of learning and using print, and their own struggles to discover or impose this kind of relation between ASL and English. Their activities suggest that the social resources of the classroom, built around ASL, contributed to their early literacy.

Dyson (1991) outlines a view of writing development among hearing, speaking children that can also shed light on the deaf children's strategies for literacy learning and on the supportive role of ASL in these processes. In Dyson's view, written language is a symbol system with its own integrity, which children explore as their symbolic development unfolds. Written language itself is one of several culturally provided symbolic options. Children's explorations of this system are systematic and principled and follow predictable patterns whether they are English speaking children exploring written English or ASL-signing children exploring the written variety of another language such as English. Following Dyson's conception of early literacy development, I found that Robbie, Tom, and Paul:

- searched for equivalents between ASL and print English through translation processes;

- experimented with the forms of signs and of words in attempts to create relations between them as when the boys discussed whether or not Little Red Riding Hood's sign must include an "R";

- depended upon their stronger system, ASL, to help them in their attempts to solve the puzzles of English, as when they held metalevel discussions in ASL about English spelling and grammar;

- took conscious and reflective control of their own processes of thinking and writing, as when they planned and monitored their uses of English through ASL;

- actively participated in a social and cultural world that included English, print, sound, and hearing people from their vantage points as signers of ASL.

This study was informed by a theoretical frame that combined an emphasis on the role of social and cultural life in learning with a focus on children as users of symbols who forge relations among the symbol systems to which they have access. This is not a framework designed to account for the problems of deaf children's development. Rather, it is a set of statements about human development, especially about the unfolding of our heritage as symbol users during childhood. Particularly since deaf children are expected to become as "normal" as possible, accounts of development under normal circumstances serve as excellent guides to understanding their development. I argue that deaf children's deepest needs, as well as their developmental accomplishments, are not critically different from those of any young children.

In their early school lives, deaf children need access to symbol systems and to other people, especially to natural human language and members of the speech community that use it. They need intelligible social settings, where they can not only understand and be understood by adults and peers but also comprehend the structure of activities and fully participate in them. Finally, deaf children need paths for engaging with the complex social settings where they are expected to learn. The findings of this study suggest that classroom settings structured by deaf ways and by ASL can provide these features and, in the process, promote acquisition of English and the development of literacy.

References

Allen, T. (1986). Patterns of academic achievement among hearing impaired students: 1974 and 1983. In A. Schildroth & M. Karchmer (Eds.), *Deaf children in America* (pp. 161–206). San Diego: College-Hill Press.

Commission on Education of the Deaf. (1988). *Toward equality: Education of the deaf.* Washington DC: U.S. Government Printing Office.

Dyson, A. (1991). The word and the world: Reconceptualizing written language development or, Do rainbows mean a lot to little girls? *Research in the Teaching of English, 25,* 97–123.

Erting, C. (1981). An anthropological approach to the study of the communicative competence of deaf children. *Sign Language Studies, 32,* 221–238.

Johnson, R., & Erting, C. (1989). Ethnicity and socialization in a classroom for deaf children. In C. Lucas, (Ed.). *The sociolinguistics of the deaf community* (pp. 41–83). New York: Academic Press.

Johnson, R., Liddell, S., & Erting, C. (1989). *Unlocking the curriculum.* Washington, DC: Gallaudet University Research Institute.

Lou, M. (1988). The history of language use in the education of the deaf in the United States. In M. Strong (Ed.), *Language learning and deafness (pp. 75–98).* Cambridge: Cambridge University Press.

National Institute on Deafness and Other Communication Disorders (1989). *A report of the task force on the national strategic research plan.* Bethesda, MD: National Institutes of Health.

Quigley, S., & Paul, P. (1984). ASL and ESL? In R. Fewell, (Ed.), *Young sensory impaired children: Topics in early childhood special education, Vol. 3.* (pp. 17–26). Austin, TX: Pro-Ed.

Padden, C. & Humphries, T. (1988). Deaf in America. Cambridge, MA: Harvard University Press.

Padden, C., & Ramsey, C. (1993). Deaf culture and literacy. *American Annals of the Deaf, 138*(2), 96–99.

Ramsey, C. (1989). Language planning in deaf education. In C. Lucas, (Ed.), *The sociolinguistics of the deaf community* (pp. 123–146). San Diego, CA: Academic Press.

Ramsey, C. (1994). The price of dreams. *Implications and complications for deaf students of the full inclusion movement.* In O. P. Cohen, & R. C. Johnson (Eds.), Gallaudet Research Institute Occasional Paper, 94-2. Washington, DC: Gallaudet University.

Ramsey, C. (in press). A deaf person in the classroom: Using ASL to support deaf children's English literacy. In P. Higgins & J. Nash, (Eds.), *Understanding deafness socially* (2nd. ed.). Springfield, IL: Charles C. Thomas.

Ramsey, C., Sterne, S., & Padden, C. (1994). Deafness, ethnicity, and learning to write. Working paper, Research Program in Language and Literacy. La Jolla, CA: University of California, San Diego.

Schildroth, A. (1988). Recent changes in the educational placement of deaf students. *American Annals of the Deaf, 133,* 61–67.

Supalla, S. (1986). *Manually coded English: The modality question in signed language development.* Unpublished master's thesis, University of Illinois, Urbana-Champaign, IL.

Woodward, J., Allen, T., & Schildroth, A. (1988). Linguistic and cultural role models for hearing impaired children in elementary school programs. In M. Strong (Ed.), *Language learning and deafness* (pp. 184–191). Cambridge: Cambridge University Press.

GLOSSARY

American Sign Language (ASL)
A signed language used among deaf people in North America, unrelated to English.

Bilateral hearing loss
Hearing loss in both ears.

Deaf (profound, severe)
Audiological condition of having impaired hearing. Profound losses are those measured at 91 dB or more. Severe losses are those measured between 71 and 90 dB.

Face-to-face language
Term used where "talk" or "oral language" might be used in descriptions of discourse among hearing people. These terms have specific connotations in the context of deafness and are avoided in this report.

Fingerspelling
Strings of handshapes that function as signed letter names for the alphabet.

Hearing
People who are not deaf. To the children in the study, "people who cannot sign."

Hearing impaired
The preferred term in educational contexts to refer to the condition of deafness.

Mainstreaming
The practice of integrating able-bodied and disabled students in classrooms and other school settings.

Sensorineural
Hearing loss originating in the inner ear or auditory nerve. Contrasts with conductive hearing loss, caused by problems in the transfer of sound energy through the outer or middle ear.

25

YOUTH GENRE IN THE CLASSROOM: CAN CHILDREN'S AND TEACHERS' CULTURES MEET?

Colette Daiute

CITY UNIVERSITY OF NEW YORK, GRADUATE SCHOOL

Teaching can be characterized as the art of communicating across cultures. In every classroom, there exists a need for communication across the cultures of childhood and adulthood as well as across ethnic cultures. Nevertheless, children's discourse tends to be ignored or seen as something to be corrected. This chapter discusses *youth genre*—a form of discourse characteristic of children—and explains how it is a tool for learning.

Culture typically refers to ethnic and national groups, but childhood is also a culture. Children share symbols, practices, and values. They create rituals. They interpret the world around them in some similar ways. And they share a common language—a language that is different in several important ways from that of adults in their community (Daiute, 1993a). Childhood culture is embedded within traditional, ethnic cultures as it builds on the local adult world and sometimes forms in reaction to that world (Fiske, 1989; Willis, 1990). Childhood culture is dynamic, changing as children mature, and changing more quickly than traditional cultures. Childhood culture, like traditional cultures, is created in context and collaboration as children engage in activities that challenge them and that have meaning in their lives. The essence of childhood culture occurs in language, activities, and objects that children create to impose meaning on the world around them. Thus, sayings, games, clothing styles, musical tastes, and other shared obsessions are evidence of children's cultures. Overshadowed by traditionally noted ethnic and gender cultures, youth culture has not been recognized as an important force in children's lives, especially in their lives in school.

To some extent, children's culture is created by adults who cast their young in a role—like apprentices preparing for the real thing. Adults also construct institutions based on their notions of what appeals to children, as they have in television and advertising aimed at young audiences. Children are influenced by these products; yet they also construct their own culture as they interpret and *re*construct the legacies offered by adults. Although many of us live with and teach children, few adults listen intently enough to children to become privy to the meanings and symbols of childhood culture. Teachers and parents who are sensitive to children's culture recognize the signs and symbols, perhaps noting "what third graders are like" or "interaction patterns typical of middle schoolers." Nevertheless, neither educators nor researchers have devoted much attention to understanding youth culture as a positive resource for children's cognitive development and learning.

Unfortunately, when youth culture is recognized it tends to be characterized in negative terms. Habits of dress, interest in electronic media, slang, and behaviors of youth culture are typically seen as undesirable. Demonstrations of youth culture are often seen as antithetical to learning. Some children fall collectively into antisocial behavior, but many participate in language and behavior that establish solidarity with a peer group. Children bring to the world unique perspectives with which they create meaning out of the world around them. Within some of the forms that are not so desirable to adults, children are making sense of the crises and stresses they observe. Language, dress, behavior, music, and visual creations by children not only set them apart as a group but also embody their interpretations of the adult world, not always reflecting an ideal world. Peer group identity has taken hold, moreover, in younger children, so children's culture begins to exert itself from 8 or 9 years.

A feature of childhood culture is its discourse—the language and underlying orientations that shape children's language. Discourse is one aspect of childhood culture that relates to literacy and learning in profound ways. Certain characteristics make up what I have called *youth genre,* after Bakhtin's notion of regularized speech genres (Bakhtin, 1986; Daiute, 1993a). Youth genre is a speech genre, influenced by children's status as children. Children spontaneously construct their speech genres based on their own developmentally evolving perspectives, using patterns of thought that influence their theory building about other phenomena. Like the mature speech genres discussed by Bakhtin, youth genre reflects the structures and meaning-making practices of one culture that children participate in and that becomes increasingly important in middle childhood and adolescence—the culture of their peers. Since orientations and understandings as well as specific linguistic sequences constitute youth genre, it occurs across national culture and gender groups, even though children incorporate aspects of the dominant discourse in their talk.

The following conversation between two 4th-grade boys in a Midwestern city classroom is characteristically childlike. The boys were writing a report about the rain forest, which they had been studying in science and social studies.

Richard:	We saw what?
Nicholas:	We heard bees, insects.
Richard:	Yeah.
Nicholas:	The tree was humongous.
Richard:	The.
Nicholas:	Trees were.
Richard:	Did I spell humongous right?
Nicholas:	No.
Richard:	Oops. …
Nicholas:	Let's just put giant.
Later:	
Nicholas:	No. Let's say, it was the biggest rain forest in the world, the Amazon.
Richard:	No, no it was biggest rain forest we saw in our life.
Nicholas:	Let's say it was the Amazon rain forest, the biggest one in the world.
Richard:	Okay, world. That ain't how to spell world.
Nicholas:	Unclear comment
Richard:	That's word. That ain't world.

This conversation includes several characteristics of youth genre. Richard and Nicholas worked interdependently; they experimented; their affect seems to be entwined with their thinking, and they worked in the details rather than through plans.

The boys built their conversation and thinking in a reciprocal way. They assumed a mutual orientation to the task at hand—writing a story situated in the rain forest. They asked each other questions, listened to, and built upon answers to those questions. Richard and Nicholas engaged in joint problem solving, identifying problems like which word to use and proposing solutions like using *giant* because they could spell that. Although they did not always agree on the solution to all the issues they raised, they maintained a mutual stance as evidenced by "let's" and by clarifying their own positions "Did I spell *humongous* right?"

Another aspect of youth genre that Richard and Nicholas' conversation illustrates is the experimental and creative quality of children's intellectual discourse. They tested ideas when they said "It was the biggest rain forest in the world," "… in the Amazon," "… that we saw in our life." Through this progression of alternatives, they explored understandings about the rain forest and how to talk about it. This type of experimenta-

tion is rarely audible in adult problem solving, which tends to occur via planning (Flower & Hayes, 1981). Similarly, exaggeration is a characteristic of youth genre, serving as a tool for hypothesis testing. The boys' suggestions of *humongous* and *biggest rain forest in the world* reflect a typical way that children make descriptions, especially around subjects with which they are not familiar (Daiute, 1990, 1993b). Finally, Richard and Nicholas' conversation shows how children use affectively charged language, disagreeing in a forthright way, "That ain't world."

A conversation by two 3rd-grade girls in an Eastern city writing a report about their class trip to the Gardener Museum reflects these aspects of youth genre in somewhat different ways.

Lisa:	Okay, does this sound good ? "When we went to the th-third floor, we wanted to know if we could go up to the fourth floor."
Kay:	They said we couldn't because that's where Elisabel, Isabella, was … like, that's where Isabella lived.
Lisa:	Okay, that's great. And then we would say, then we could say, "We couldn't cuz that's where. "
Kay:	Isabella lay-lived.
Lisa:	Lived.
Kay:	That's her bedroom.
Lisa & Kay:	And that's where she lay, she lays.
Kay:	She did ?
Lisa:	No.
Kay:	They buried her there ?
Lisa:	I think so.
Kay:	No, I think—
Lisa:	NO, they didn't!!!!
Kay:	No I think, I think—
Lisa:	they didn't bury her, cuz who would want her to be in a
Kay:	museum
Lisa:	a museum, cuz then her body would like…
Kay:	rot?
Lisa:	yeh… okay.
Kay:	So, yeh.
Lisa:	I know, she would turn to aaa (cough)
Kay:	(unclear) … so they said.
Lisa:	she would sorta like form into the way she would like be, turned into ashes or something.
Kay:	(anxious giggle)
Lisa:	I know… Did you know that when we went there, when I was on the third floor, it gave me the creeps, cuz of those stairways, and it was dark sometimes and then light?

Lisa and Kay's conversation was animated. Lisa seems to have been pulled into an inquiry about Mrs. Gardner based on her affective reaction to Kay's proposal that the patron of the museum had been buried on the fourth floor of the museum, where the children were not permitted to go when they visited the museum. Lisa's comment "NO, she didn't!!!!" was marked by intensity and argumentative stance. Kay obviously understood this stance as directed toward the inquiry rather than toward her, so the intellectual discussion proceeded with Kay building on Lisa's discovery that a human body could not be buried in a museum because it "would rot." Thus, Lisa and Kay's affective reactions to material served as catalysts to their cognitive work. Strong affective reactions like, "NO, they didn't !!!!" seem to have organized the girls' understanding because such remarks involved the children in exploring some aspect of the subject matter, as they took a stand on a particularly salient aspect of it. Many children draw on affective resources, especially when working with peers who do not constantly encourage them to be more "logical," as adults do (Daiute, 1993a; Daiute, Campbell, Griffin, Reddy, & Tivnan, 1993). In this way, children's affective orientations to an intellectual task organize intellectual interactions, such as when they become intrigued with figuring out some aspect of a task. This emotional stance on the task involves intensity, excitement, and other types of affective engagement.

A third excerpt by two 3rd-grade boys indicates a predominantly playful orientation to task, with the reciprocity, experimentation, and sense making done in the context of child-like verbal and social play.

Russ:	Put Mr. Columbus.
Andy:	Mr. Columbus.
Russ:	Columulumbus.
Andy:	Colum, Columbumps (laughter).
Russ:	Lumberjack (laughter).
Andy:	Colombos, Columbus, Columbus.
Russ:	Colummmmmbababababababbbb. Ohhew. B U S. I think that's how you spell it.
Andy:	Col-um-bus. Ya, you're right.
Russ:	Christopher Columbus. Collumm.
Andy:	Ya, where Columbus, Columbus. The Spaniard Christopher Columbus discovered America. Now do you know how to spell the last three letters of Christopher Columbus? Oh, I already asked you. Forget it.
Russ:	Actually he rediscovered American.
Andy:	No. U.S.
Russ:	And he even made friends with some Indians.
Andy:	Discovered!
Russ:	Ya, Discovered Japan (laughs) !
Andy:	Well, no. Discotti, discovered it. No, we're fine *Redis*-covered then.
Russ:	Okay, rediscovered America. No! It should be New England.
Andy:	Ya, 'cause he did.
Russ:	No, that was in revolutionary times.
Andy:	Rediscovered.
Russ:	I wonder if it should be New Spain or New England ?
Andy:	Forget it, I mean. Rediscovered America!
Russ:	No, rediscovered the West Indies, thinking it was Japan.
Andy:	Ya! Ya! Nice. All right. We got a smart person here, like moi! (giggle) No, rediscovered R E whoah! R E S C, S C O. Oh, I've got to find the V. I forgot where the V is.

As in this writing session excerpt of Andy and Russ' report about an important event in the European Renaissance, a common characteristic across children's talk is its playfulness (Daiute, 1990). Children who work with peers on challenging academic activities play with ideas and concepts as Andy and Russ did around places and characters' perceptions and Lisa and Kay did around physical concepts (what would happen to a dead body in the museum?). Some children role-play, put themselves into stories, and tease each other, expressing feelings about their relationship to each other and to the task,

as did Andy when he expressed his satisfaction with Russ' sentence and his own fact recall, *a smart person like moi.*

In summary, these excerpts reveal several orientations that characterize youth genres: reciprocity, experimentation, playfulness, affect, and sense making. Children tend to talk as one, interrupting each other, finishing each other's sentences and, even when disagreeing, orienting to their tasks mutually. They play with ideas, sounds, and each other, and draw on their affective resources in ways that might seem illogical. Children's works seem to evolve as an interplay of mind in context, while adults' works seem to evolve more fully in their minds where the contexts have been internalized. The close scrutiny we have devoted to such interactions in previous research indicates these youth genre features serve as strategies children use in their intense pursuit to make sense of the world around them. These attempts are sometimes hidden from adults because the process of children's sense making tends to be different from our own process of understanding. Underlying what might appear to be impolite, chaotic discourse is a probing experimentation, in which children select and explore problems that extend beyond their comfortable understanding. Our research has shown that such intense interaction tends to form a coherent discourse that is richer and more productive than conversations some of the same children have with their teacher (Daiute, Campbell, et al., 1993).

In spite of the common orientations underlying youth genre, there is also diversity in how individual children combine youth genre features. For example, the excerpt from one of Lisa and Kay's collaborations was responsive, exploratory, affective, and meaning-based but not as playful as that of Andy and Russ. All the children progressed in their thinking by posing alternatives, but Lisa and Kay tended to explore an alternative in depth while the Richard–Nicholas and Andy–Russ pairs went for breadth.

The six children whose conversations are presented above come from four different ethnic/racial groups, including African-American, European American, Asian American, and Latino. Since the youth genre features I have outlined are orientations rather than specific sequences, these apply to different dialects and, I believe, different languages. The experimentation that Andy and Russ do through verbal play, Lisa and Kay do through a more affectively charged series of responses. Youth genre may, in fact, function as a unifying language for children—a language that they can use to relate as a group without adopting a mainstream, adult, school language completely.

Youth culture and discourse are not, however, monolithic. Longer excerpts illustrate how children weave their youth genre with their ethnic and gender genres. Like adults, children are influenced by all the cultures in which they participate, so youth culture is not isolated from these other influences. Youth culture and youth genres overlap the ethnic, gender, and other cultures with which they are entwined. What educators typically ask children to do when they enter school is to function almost exclusively in the culture of the school—which in many cases matches none of the multiple cultures children live in outside of school, neither their ethnic nor youth culture. This issue is, of course, especially acute for children from minority groups. The children in our studies were attending desegregated schools, which means that they were working in a mainstream cultural model (Nelson-LeGall, 1994). Children in such situations may engage in a different discourse than they do in their neighborhoods, and a common peer culture discourse may be preferable to or more familiar than a mainstream adult discourse.

Children sometimes adopt specific youth genre features from the discourse of an ethnic group, as with "Yo!" which occurs in some African-American argot via popular media. Although children may adopt features of mainstream discourse into their youth genre (white middle-class boys calling each other by their last names as in sporting events), popular culture theory would predict this to occur less frequently than adoption from a minority culture, because youth culture is formed in part to distinguish itself from mainstream culture (Willis, 1990).

Television, popular music, and other electronic media serve a unifying function for youth culture. Certain symbols, discourse features, themes, and styles that appear in the visual, aural, and print media appeal to many children, so these media serve as a kind of meeting place. A cycle of influences has been established in the media by the fact that marketing research of children's preferences guides program development, and children are, in turn, influenced by the specific creations they experience in the media. Musical styles, modes of dress and discourse contribute to unify children across races, classes, genders, and continents. Children's interpretations and actions in relation to such media may differ across traditional cultures, but as a group that has some developmental as well as social perspectives in common, children in the middle years appear to make many similar interpretations in media worlds.

These descriptions of youth genre have evolved from research on children's conversations rather than being imposed from a priori categories; yet these qualities are also consistent in several ways with recent cognitive-developmental descriptions of thought by 8- to 11-year-olds (Daiute, 1993a). Youth genre features are consistent with thinking that has an "in-the-moment" quality (Case, 1991). Perception tends to dominate reflection at first, which is illustrated by Andy and Russ' play originating with letter sounds and progressing to aspects of meaning related to the topic. When mutually orienting themselves to the collaborative writing task, children also share their ideas and the labors of writing, including generating content, noting spelling mistakes, and typing. The mutually oriented, playful alternative-posing strategy reflects children's skill at using support to handle multiple variables of a complex task. Although the developmental stage theory proposed by Jean Piaget (1926) has been shown to require more sensitivity to cross-cultural factors and flexibility, general characteristics of thought seem to apply. For example, at younger ages children tend to focus on single aspects of a problem, gradually becoming facile at coordinating multiple variables in a complex problem. Similarly, at younger ages children tend to focus on salient features like visual images or sounds only later to begin explicitly manipulating abstract principles. These youth genres are also defined by how they differ from adults' approaches as identified in

research. The concept of youth genre, however, incorporates a sociocultural understanding of child development—an understanding that children are socialized to the values and practices of people around them.

Involvement in youth culture and the use of youth genre changes over time for children. Throughout childhood, the peer group becomes an increasingly salient reference point, with a general interest in others in the primary years, to a same-sex group focus in third and fourth grades, and increasingly differentiated social identities in adolescence (Erikson, 1956). Similarly, as children progress through these intricate peer orientations, their focus on their own ethnicity ebbs and flows as the multiple frames of reference have an impact on identity (Daiute & Shaw, 1993; Deaux, 1993; Heath & McLaughlin, 1993).

HOW DOES YOUTH GENRE SUPPORT CHILDREN'S LEARNING?

Educators need to pay attention to youth genre because it serves children as a tool for thinking and learning. In several studies, my colleagues and I have found that the more children tended to use youth genre around academic tasks, the more they made advances in challenging academic writing projects. For example, children who balanced their conceptual and linguistic play with more metacognitive talk, like labeling, explicit planning, and evaluation, tended to gain higher scores on their reports than did children who took a predominantly metacognitive approach (Daiute, 1990). In another study we found that children who engaged with partners in ways that were reciprocal, affectively charged, playful, and experimental tended to improve more on their academic writing than children who took fewer of these orientations (Daiute & Dalton, 1993; Daiute, Campbell, et al., 1993). These findings are consistent with the fact that metacognitive training tends to help only older children approaching adolescence (Bereiter & Scardamalia, 1987; Daiute, 1990; Palincsar & Brown, 1984). I interpret these findings to mean that as a familiar strategy, youth genre helps children focus on and master unfamiliar material. If each utterance serves the dual functions of imparting information and reflecting on information (Lotman, 1990), then a child's using his/her familiar language may better serve both functions than using a foreign language—like adult discourse. When children use developmentally inappropriate or unfamiliar discourse, such as discourse imitated from adults, while working with new material, the demands may be so great or so confusing that engaging in both a reporting function and an interpretive function may be impossible. Moreover, the very nature of youth genre, with its experimental, meaning-making and affective resources, is quite adapted to reflection and discovery, which may be most helpful when children encounter new material. More metacognitive orientations like analysis and planning are apt for refinement in later phases of acquaintance with a subject matter.

In addition to the form of youth genres, the content of children's conversations with peers appears to be around issues that interest and challenge them. For example, in spite of the teacher's insistence that spelling was not important, third graders tended to focus on spelling as well as rhetorical features and critical content when they worked with their peers (Reddy & Daiute, 1993). Similarly, children explored a range of issues indicating that they were making sense of the values and meanings in relation to subject matter (Daiute & Shaw, 1993; Daiute, Campbell, et al., 1993). In analyses of conversations in one group of third graders, we found that they talked about issues of life and death, intergroup relationships, the best way to begin news stories, and many other important topics that were not explicitly part of the curriculum but that came into play in writing critically about the experiences they had in their classrooms (Daiute & Griffin, 1993).

Teachers have to work hard to keep youth genre out of the classroom—requiring quiet classrooms, separating children from their friends, using their own logic as a standard, and inculcating metacognitive strategies. Since youth genre somehow operates in spite of such organizations, some teachers create classroom communities that include children's voices and make youth genre not only a strategy for learning but also an object of study in comparison to school discourse.

In classrooms where children have the opportunity to engage in extended dialogue with peers as well as teachers, children rely on youth genre, like the dialects of their family backgrounds, to make sense of the material and skills they are trying to master. Teachers who are sensitive to children's need to draw on youth genre have ways of inviting it into the classroom to serve children as they work with challenging material, including the mastery of school-based adult genre.

Inviting Youth Genres into the Classroom

Teachers can structure the classroom so that children's discourse is a resource for intellectual development rather than a problem. Teachers need not use youth genre themselves, nor mention it explicitly, but by creating certain types of meaningful, challenging, collaborative contexts, they can invite children to use youth genre in the classroom. In this section, I suggest several ways of inviting children to use youth genre as a tool for learning.

Restructure the classroom so that children can use youth genre around important content. Adults often conflate the forms and contents of children's talk. It is very easy to assume that children are not talking about anything important when their talk is silly, imprecise, or emotional. On the contrary, children often rely on their spontaneous childlike language when they are engaged in profound inquiry. Just as Andy and Russ explored the important historical issue of what counts as a discovery in the midst of play with language and interpersonal relations, children have explored scientific, literary, and mathematical concepts in playful, affective, socially oriented language. For this reason, teachers should construct some challenging academic activities for children to do in dyads or small groups. Several consistent features of the tasks in our

research over 12 years seem to be optimum for engaging inquiry within youth genre.

The following task conforms to several principles that engage children's intellectual inquiry.

> You have been asked to write a science textbook for next year's fourth grade. This text will be in story form to help children gain deeper knowledge of the way in which our planet depends on the rain forests. As part of creating this textbook, write some of the following stories:
> Imagine you and your friend have been transported to the rain forest. You are walking along and you see a group of people burning down trees. Tell a story about what happens and why it is important.

This task was developed with several classroom teachers around material that children were having difficulty in mastering—understandings about the local and global interdependencies among flora, fauna, and people in the Amazonian rain forest (Daiute, Hartup, Sholl, & Zajak, 1993). Thus, at the center of the task was a difficult problem. Moreover, the children had the opportunity to work with several aspects of the subject matter in a series of similarly structured tasks. For example, while one story starter centered around competing needs of people who wanted to use the rain forest for local development and those who needed it for a more distant global balance, other tasks involved aspects of the rain forest habitat, including dangerous animals, the prevalence and paucity of certain types of food, and the outsiders' difficulty in finding their way in the rain forest. Before doing this writing, the children had a range of types of exposure to information and issues about the rain forest, including teacher-led discussions, readings, talks with environmental groups, educational videos, picture books, and so forth, so the children had information to draw upon. This information may, however, have been inert, and the collaborative narrative task engaged them in incorporating that tacit knowledge into their active meaning making.

Unfortunately, when teachers design collaborative learning activities, they often do so around "manageable" tasks that tend not to be intellectually challenging. Several common peer-mediated activities include applying editing checklists to peers' papers, brainstorming lists of topics, and practicing spelling. In contrast, our research suggests that teachers should invite children to put their heads together around the challenging new material of the day, as in this project, to write narrative texts about the rain forest for the next year's class. We found in our research, moreover, that working with concepts just after they had been introduced by the teacher proved to be a successful application of peer interaction (Daiute, Campbell, et al., 1993). Although it may seem counter intuitive to involve children in working together on material that they do not yet know much about, children tend to use the peer collaboration context to bring up related background knowledge, to identify relevant problems, and to develop their own inquiry goals in relation to the material. Similarly, many teachers engage large groups of children in making "maps" of words and concepts that children already know in relation to a new unit of study. Working on a concrete task with a peer creates an extended and critical context in which to develop this knowledge in depth.

Collaborative projects should also play an explicit role in the classroom or school culture, so embedding tasks as part of a school newspaper, textbook, or extended letter provide a meaningful social context. Purposeful projects provide contexts, explicit goals, and audiences that invite children to frame their knowledge and work in ways that enhance the development of knowledge.

In our studies, children were required to create a written product as the focal point of their collaboration and problem solving. This written product not only provided an anchor for the children's talking and thinking, but it was also the type of intellectual object that children are required to use for subsequent learning in school. Thus, written language became an object of focus and inquiry as well as a tool for learning. As a matter of fact, we have found that even when children work with their best friends, they focus intensely on the text form and content and thus on written language and subject matter (Daiute, Hartup et al., 1993).

While collaboration is important for involving children in intellectual conversations with peers as well as teachers, it is important to balance collaborative tasks with similar individual tasks. Working individually on a similar piece about the rain forest allows children to transfer into their own personal repertoire some of the knowledge and strategies they explored when they were stretched in peer interaction.

Since youth genre tends to involve extended, sometimes tangential exploration, it is essential that children have ample time in each session for these collaborative projects. The richness of youth genre is in the posing of alternatives, focusing on some intriguing topic within an apparent tangent, and the gradual development of issues that children fix on affectively as they react to something in the task or to a partner's comments. Rather than being a waste of time, such forays into meaning that occur in youth genre around challenging topics are unique to peer interaction. Some of the same children who raised and explored probing questions with peers were intellectually cautious and taciturn when working with the teacher. Of course, teachers should work so that children feel safe with them, but their role is most profitably one of being the informant about the school culture and creator of engaging classroom contexts rather than trying to talk children's language. Children need to have the teacher's structure, support, and follow-up to peer talk. In other words, teachers can allow children to integrate their explicit teaching—content and skills—in the context of what the children know and how they know it.

Finally, youth genre is sometimes enriched by the use of multiple media. Just as oral language provides a rich, culturally salient context for written academic tasks, visual media can engage children with ideas and knowledge from various points of view. In research where children had access to images and sounds as they wrote their reports, we found that low-achieving students were able to think and write with much more skill than when they did not have access to visual media (Daiute, 1992; Daiute & Shaw, 1993).

Involve children in some explicit work on multiple cultures and discourses. For many of the same reasons why children need to use youth genres, they need to use their native languages and dialects to support classroom learning. Teacher can involve children in language research. Children can observe, videotape, and take notes on other children playing in the playground, on teachers talking to one another, and on their parents' behavior. (Heath & Mangiola, 1991). Children can also increase their awareness about language, culture, and power relations by writing plays and creating imaginary cultures. Invite children to create rituals and names for classroom contents and strategies.

Teachers can also do research on the themes and practices of the classroom, as do anthropologists. Teacher research is a good way to explore any questions about teaching and learning in the classroom, and it can be targeted at understanding how children's ways of talking reveal underlying orientations to school, subject matters, and knowledge. Such teacher research can reveal the topics and issues that children find intriguing and challenging. You can engage in research focusing on how children use language, paying attention to the imprecise phrasing, silly episodes, or tangents. If you pay attention to how they ask questions, describe, and explain, you can gain insights into the ways of thinking behind childlike language. A teacher-led research project on the youth genres in the classroom can be an entry point for understanding students' perspectives (Cochran-Smith & Lytle, 1992).

Children can act as experts, offering teachers information about their language and thinking, prompted by the teachers, questions about what they are thinking when they are engaged in challenging problems.

Teachers can help the children understand school-based knowledge or practice as a culture. Cultural mores underlie every aspect of the curriculum including topics, tasks, and assessments. Although education is in large part enculturation, the subject matter and methods are typically presented as objective and universally valued. Teachers can recognize and encourage youth culture at the same time as they make clear that they also represent diverse cultures.

Cultural differences in discourse become more marked in adults; thus in some cultures adults tend to give messages via stories that carry internal messages rather than spout explicit rules, but an interesting topic of study would be to explore differences between adults' and children's discourse within a culture.

Recognize the youth genres in your classroom. An important basis for teachers' work is understanding youth genre in the classroom and on the playground. Teachers can make an effort to understand how children interpret the world, in particular, the world in school. They can recognize the orientations (attitudes, outlooks) that underlie youth genre by noticing the symbols and orientations children have toward tasks, relationships, and physical phenomena. If teachers listen to the topics of children's spontaneous conversations during relatively unstructured time—walking to and from your room, during art, around journal writing, on the playground, they can learn more about children's concerns, needs, and spontaneous strategies. The curriculum goals may not change, but ways of allowing children to participate in those goals may be quite different when children can draw on their strengths.

In the first section of this chapter, I explained the characteristic orientations of youth genre. When trying to recognize youth genre, you can learn about the specific brand of youth genre in your classroom by paying attention to the following outward signs. The topics that interest children hold keys to their culture. Nine- and ten-year old boys' interest in physical play and girls' interest in relationships are central themes. Topics that fascinate children can be related to subject matter to provide a base for new knowledge.

One problem for some teachers is that topics that fascinate children may seem taboo. Children are drawn to issues of life and death, identity, and injustice. For example, Lisa and Kay, like many other children, explored the issue of where Mrs. Gardner's body went after she died, and many children in that group were concerned over why they were not permitted to visit the fourth floor of the museum, which these and other children explored as an issue of justice as well as intrigue. Similarly, Andy and Russ became involved in exploring the issue of how Native Americans are slighted when people say that Christopher Columbus discovered America. In another dyad of third graders, a black girl and a white girl explored issues of identity by playing with the idea that they were sisters in a story where they had similar interests and personalities. Children tend to explore such issues through the details of specific events rather than to state explicitly that they are interested in "justice," "life and death," or "identity," so we need to be astute listeners to the underlying themes of children's talk. When such topics emerge as recurrent themes underlying children's conversations, it is the optimal time to explore such issues in relation to subject matter in your curriculum.

Another factor worthy of attention when basing new material on children's interests is that there may be gender differences in youth genre preferences. For example, while most children are fascinated by the issues mentioned above, girls and boys tend to differ in their focus on the ways in which they explore these issues, with girls tending to focus on issues of life/death, justice, and identity in relationships, and boys around events (Gilligan, 1982). It is important to be aware, however, that such gender distinctions do not apply in all contexts or for all children. Children's values reflect those of their parents, but there are kid values too. For example, friendship is in many cases more important to children than individual achievement.

When children depict violent scenes, they may be revealing stresses and trying to gain some control over phenomena that are difficult to understand (Bettelheim, 1975). The issues and values reflected in children's conversations reflect their family mores, too, so the themes are complex. To respect children's family values and to avoid reading complex themes too simplistically, some teachers may stay away from big issues in the classroom. One problem with such avoidance is that the issues form the basis of children's concerns and questions. Linking these concerns to academic knowledge can help children understand the value in what they are presented in school and can help with the develop-ment of knowledge, which builds on prior knowledge and questions.

One way of finding out about current concerns and symbols is to ask children each year to create a book about their culture—what is important in their lives. When we did such a project, we were struck with the nature of symbols that children expressed and explored—the sophistication and diversity of their interpretations (Daiute & Shaw, 1993). For example, all the children selected an image of a Hershey bar, which one child had digitized into the computer in this multimedia project (Daiute, 1992). While this image seemed commercial and trivial compared to the possible images children could have gathered considering that they had photographic equipment, film, free processing, and access to lots of print and physical materials, the ways in which children wrote about this image were wide-ranging and profound. For example, one child used the image of a Hershey bar wrapper as a springboard to offer a sketch of her family relationships, all centered around their interest in candy, but going well beyond sweets. Another child who was an immigrant, discussed the image as an example of American culture, offering several ways in which the wrapper represented a culture where he evidently still felt very much like an outsider.

Children's interaction styles are important marks of youth genre, and as discussed above, important tools for learning. Their banter, laborious explanations, exaggeration, and teasing are all part of the problem-solving process.

Recognizing youth genre may be easier when contrasting it with adult genre—in particular school-based discourse. What teachers can do is to make explicit the orientations that underlie their own school discourse and relate these to the specific forms of their speech.

Many parents and teachers have had the experience of feeling like they were speaking a different language when speaking to children from 8 years up to early adolescence. Children seem to veer from the point, but we have to remember that our point may not be theirs. Children seem to be imprecise, but an important difference is that children explain with examples, details, sensations, while we tend to label our messages more explicitly, especially as they regard children. Interestingly, as most parents know, explicitness alone does not ensure that adults can communicate with children.

Teacher talk was noted as a form of discourse by Heath (1978), and others have noted major patterns of teachers' classroom talk including the Initiation-Response-Evaluation pattern noted by Mehan (1979). Guitierrez (1993) has described three patterns of teacher interaction in process writing classrooms. Cognitive science researchers examining interaction patterns across reading, writing, and math contexts noticed a variety of metacognitive strategies including planning and revising (Collins, Brown, & Newman, 1989; Flower & Hayes, 1981; Palincsar & Brown, 1984) with goal statements and explicit reflection as prominent features of experts' talk. Of course, not all adults are experts, nor all children novices (Daiute & Dalton, 1993), but teachers typically function as experts in classrooms. Interestingly, some children can assume certain features of teacher talk during their interactions, but these are usually minimal compared to their use of youth genre. Thus, as shown in research on adults, teacher talk is not a monolithic genre, but there are some consistencies across previous descriptions of literate adults' approaches to reading and writing tasks, and these contrast to youth genre talk.

To explore adult/child differences as they are played out in the classroom, my colleagues and I did a study comparing children's peer interactions around literacy to teacher–student collaborations and found contrasts for each of the major youth genre characteristics. These contrasts are not absolute, and they vary across different adults. Teacher and youth genres contrast in several ways. The teacher's comments tended to maintain individual control, in contrast to the children's reciprocal orientation to each other and to their tasks. The teacher consistently referred more to her student partners than to herself, but organized those references in specific ways, such as when asking children "Do you want to type now?" or "Do you remember when (something specific happened)?" While the children tended to approach their literacy tasks playfully, experimenting and approximating, the teacher's movement through steps of a task and her reflections about it suggested recursive phases of planning and other strategic approaches. While the children eventually found effective writing strategies and demonstrated increasing control over written language through their effortful, probing, and playful work with ideas and text sequences, the teacher's talk suggested that she came to the task with definite ideas about how to make a good text—the elements that were required and the desired effects of different strategies. Another contrast is that the teacher's talk was more explicitly cognitive, including labeling, verbs of cognition, strategies, and content. Finally, the teacher used her talk to structure ideas and the composing process, while children seemed to use their talk and their interactions with peers to figure out what they were thinking. This sense-making quality of the children's peer talk sometimes became theory building, as when 8-year-old Brant explored his belief that news stories do not have to be true and, in fact, they were more interesting if not true.

In spite of the striking nature of these contrasts, I must reiterate that the teacher's interactions, like the speech genres they characterize, are not absolute. For example, the teacher was sometimes playful, yet her entry into youth genres tended to occur only with certain children.

Recognize subjectivity in the classroom. Just as no one curriculum is the right curriculum, there is no one way to orient one's self to the classroom. As we recognize how affect figures into learning and development, we can begin to recognize the diverse orientations that children have toward subject matter, situations, and people in school. A child's affective orientation toward school is influenced by experiences, cultural values, emotional factors, and emerging interpretations of the environment. It is crucial to understand this kind of subjective stance on school because it can block or facilitate learning. It is the rare child (or even adult) who can separate his or her subjective formulations from cognitive aspects of school tasks. Multicultural understandings have paved the way for diversity in the classroom, but not enough has been said about the affective stances that organize interactions in school.

In education we have tended to think about affective issues in rather limited ways. The tradition of positive reinforcement is entrenched. While positive responses to children cannot be criticized, the role of positive reinforcement is problematic. There is such an emphasis on positive response that negative responses tend to be offered implicitly as in the statement— *Do you really want to be doing that now?* When discussions of affect in the classroom do occur they tend to focus on positive reinforcement and self-esteem. In the many attempts to build a positive basis for children's work, the tasks children are asked to do are often simplified and segmented to ensure their success. But, limiting tasks to make them manageable does not necessarily engage children affectively in ways that support development of discourse and thinking. Children need meaningful contexts of challenging activities that can draw on important affective aspects of their lives, such as interpersonal orientations, personal experiences, interpretations and evaluations of the world around them. Since such affective states are to some extent culturally determined, having extended projects rather than worksheets allows children a fuller range of responses, even though these present challenges and a full range of affects.

In our comparison of teacher–child and child–peer interactions, a striking difference between children's and teacher's talk was that children used a range of explicit negative as well as positive evaluations while the teachers' explicit evaluations were only positive. Children tended to take each other's evaluations at face value, sometimes asking the partner to say more about what he or she meant by a negative evaluation, sometimes disagreeing with the negative evaluation, and less often simply reposting with an unrelated negative evaluation. What is more important is that children used a range of affectively charged interactions that were not characteristic of the teacher's talk. For example, children alternately expressed joy, conflict, surprise, anxiety and other emotions. This range of affect occurred mostly in the peer interactions, perhaps appropriately kept in check when the children worked with the teacher who guided a logical approach to the task (Daiute, Campbell, et al., 1993). Thus, the nature of children's peer interactions suggests that children can profitably draw on affect for intellectual work.

One of the great challenges for classroom teachers is that children's needs and understandings do not exist in compartments, that is, cognitive, social, or emotional. Classroom teachers are trained to deal with the cognitive child—a child who does not exist. Children whose social and emotional needs are met elsewhere may be able to work in a compartmentalized fashion, but even those children are not best served by an exclusively cognitive reference point. The classroom teacher works on the cognitive child, and some permit social interaction in the classroom. A prevalent idea is that the counselor and family work on the affective child, peers work on the social child, especially on the playground and other nonschool settings. But children's needs are not so easily separated. The many different professionals who work with children can collaborate to serve their needs; thus, home–school, counselor–teacher collaborations would be helpful.

We need to organize classroom experience in a more integrated way.

It appears that many classroom teachers are aware of children's affective orientations in the classroom, often referring to children's "personalities." An exciting current area for research and practice is to increase awareness of the nature and importance of affective strategies in the classroom, to recognize how integral affect is to learning, and to learn how to support affective strategies while guiding children in developmentally appropriate ways toward metacognitive approaches. This, in turn, may diminish the separatist and limited view that affect comes before and after learning rather than as fuel for learning in an ongoing way.

Children's social interactions in the classroom reveal how they integrate, social, cultural, and affective resources to organize cognitive work. Adults are crucial to establishing the types of environments where children can turn these needs into intellectual functions rather than purely to survival or pleasure. Teachers need to think about how they respond to children working in youth genre and how they support childhood discourse when it seems to flounder or go awry.

When structuring the classroom and interacting with children, teachers should try not to abstract away from what appear to be children's affective stances. Sarah Freedman has observed a major distinction between the organization of education in Great Britain as structured around child development and in the United States around curriculum (Freedman, 1994). In research comparing classrooms in Britain and the United States, Freedman found that British teachers tended to negotiate a curriculum with each child based partly on values in the school culture but determined mostly by the child's interests, needs, and modes of operating at the time. Based partly on being able to work with children over several years, these British teachers directly addressed each child's affective orientation—what the child was interested in at the time, how the child wanted to work, what "mood" the child was in, what exigencies were occurring that might have an impact on the particular writing assignment in question. In contrast, the teachers in the United States organized their classrooms and their work with children around the curriculum, so children's specific cultural, cognitive, and affective factors had little or no impact on what was expected of them. In the United States an assignment was rigid while in England it was by definition tailored to the child. One aspect of this comparison by Freedman that is particularly relevant to the discussion in this chapter is that the brand of child-centered approach in England was not only focused on the child's skills and needs as assessed by the teacher but by the ongoing influence of the child herself. When children's interpretations and intentions are incorporated in this way, the categories in the classroom go beyond culture and cognition.

Try to interpret the child's world from his or her perspective.
A 3rd-grade boy was having difficulty in writing. While most of his classmates produced page after page of stories and journals, he had difficulty with the fiction genre. We know from previous research that children tend to have a penchant for certain genres, therefore this child may have been one for whom nonfiction was basic. During a collaborative writing activity, this boy, who worked jocularly with his friend, proposed a sentence that his partner found particularly funny. The partner laughed and laughed, falling off his chair, true to his dramatic orientation, saying "write another one, write another one." The formerly blocked writer, who was quite facile at punning, added several more sentences, complicating the predicament of the main character. When the teacher saw the resulting piece she was disappointed because the text appeared in comic book-like bubbles, but she refrained from instructing the child to use more extended prose form until after speaking with him. The teacher asked the child to talk about the story. She asked about Morris falling off his chair, and the child beamed because his friend had found his idea so funny. The teacher then realized that this child had found his genre—at least a genre that could form the basis of some fluency in writing and finding a voice. Realizing the meaning of this story—talk bubbles and all—for this boy, the teacher asked him to read it aloud so that the entire class could appreciate it. This teacher recognized many aspects of youth genre, including the need for genuine peer support and affect, especially this particular child who thrived on peer support. The teacher disliked comic books and wanted to privilege the prose genre, which she believed children needed for success in school, but in this case she subsumed her values to the value of this experience for the child. As the child became comfortable writing in the comic book genre, the teacher began to make connections with prose, providing translations herself and eventually creating activities that would involve the child's shuttling between familiar and unfamiliar modes of expression.

Emphasize function and sense as well as form and structure. Recognizing children's culture implies new roles for teachers and parents. They need to create contexts where the child's culture can flourish around academic as well as social issues. Supporting this youth culture also requires that the teacher take a stand in relation to it. While some teachers want to become part of youth culture, others stand respectfully back from it. Projects like writing a handbook for children in a lower grade or building a clubhouse engage children in meaningful, purposeful problem solving. The requirements of time for children to develop ideas in such contexts with peers suggest the need to move beyond the notion of the skills in sequence curriculum, which may allow teachers mere minutes to "cover" a topic. The structure provided by such projects to produce culturally meaningful artifacts differs markedly from lessons, tests, and worksheets that reify pieces of curriculum. Such isolated activities may be useful for rote learning but do not require the kind of intellectual engagement that leads children to seek out their peers for collaborative problem solving.

Invite conflict. One striking difference between teachers' and children's conversations and their contributions in conversations was that the teacher exerted all her control in positive terms. Very little conflict or disagreement was stated explicitly. Children across sociocultural groups in these studies tended to express disagreements and conflicts openly, apparently as part of the problem-solving process. Girls and boys tended to do so differently, and African-American children tended to do so to a greater extent than European American children, but all children tended to do so more than the teacher. Although argument and counterargument are so important in intellectual work, children are engaged in such discourse only as they move toward high school. When children do engage in argumentative discourse, it is typically in an abstract form of exploring points of view on topics in essays or taking stands in debates. These activities would also be valuable for younger children.

The process of conflict could also be encouraged in classroom discourse. One way to allow children to explore ideas through disagreeing is to let them work with peers. We have found that children tend to disagree around issues that they want to understand but realize they do not. We have also noticed that children have a range of ways to resolve disagreements, many of which expand intellectual inquiry. Other researchers have also found that disagreeing is an essential aspect of cognitive development (Bearison, Magzamen, & Filardo, 1986), but productive disagreements do not overwhelm discussion. Children could be encouraged to discuss the topics about which they disagree, which would allow the teacher to monitor the process, and, more important, such discussions would reveal the topics that children find interesting and challenging.

Issues Around Inviting Youth Genre Into the Classroom

Some valid concerns can be raised about integrating youth genres into the classroom.

The need to learn school discourse. Some educators believe that the implicit job of American education is to engage children in mainstream school language, behaviors, and points of view. Debate about this goal is currently in progress around the meanings and methods of multicultural education, and an issue related to this phenomenon of youth genre is one that has been raised on behalf of minority children (Delpit, 1986). While some educators and theorists argue for challenging goals of social reproduction, others argue that, at least until the goals change, teachers should offer explicit instruction in all forms and subject matters required for a successful career in school.

One aspect of the argument for explicit instruction has been to raise questions about the value of "child-centered" practices common throughout the 1970s and 1980s, including open education and process of writing. According to one version of the argument for explicit instruction, these and other methods are successful only for children who are already privvy to mainstream practices (Delpit, 1986). Child-centered practices have also been criticized for having the goal of fluency and creativity, which minority children already possess, when what they need is to learn the rules of school. There has been little discussion in the context of this critique of how to evolve a form of explicit instruction that takes into account developmental factors. Various forms of explicit instruction have failed the same children that it is supposed to

help, and much of the discussion proposes the modeling of adult, metacognitive language and behaviors on children who are really too young to benefit from the methods described. The concept of scaffolding within the sociocultural approach takes the child into consideration by positing the gradual transfer of responsibility from the adult who has created a learning scaffold to the child, but the processes for such a transfer are extended over so much time that we need deeper understandings about how the scaffold and the emerging form underneath it relate to each other. Dyson (1993) has proposed the permeable curriculum, where the teachers' and children's worlds can meet. I am proposing that youth culture and youth genre be seen as strategies and objects of study so that children can use them in school to make sense of the multiple demands upon them.

This paper has discussed youth genre as a tool for children rather than the endpoint of education. Inviting youth genre into the classroom does not mean that children are left to flounder or to figure out on their own what they are supposed to do and to know. Rather, children use youth genre as a familiar tool so that they can work with new material.

The argument has also been made that learning a new domain is learning a new language, therefore, emphasis has been made on learning "science talk," for example (Lemke, 1990). While language is the socially mediated focus on knowledge, it is not the same as having the knowledge. Children, like great scientists, may use unscientific language (and thought) to explore and achieve scientific understanding. Moreover, they may use their most spontaneous everyday language to mediate difficult scientific understanding; thus, youth genre is an appropriate tool.

As all teachers know, children do not develop merely through exposure and repetition. One reason why learning takes time is that children need to consider and to reconstruct knowledge in their own terms. Youth genre provides a framework for thinking in a way that allows children to have mastery over unfamiliar material as they draw on the social and subjective skills at sense making they use in spontaneous learning. Allowing youth genre in the classroom can mean making the most out of the time spent on explicit instruction. The planned invitation of youth genre is akin to providing books, paper, and activities. The class can be prepared so that children use their spontaneous, meaning-oriented discourse after the teacher has imparted new material.

Youth genre as a haven. Another issue around merging youth genre into the classroom is that children may need to keep their culture separate to feel safe—safe to use their own language, to take intellectual risks, and to work from their own values. In fact, some scholars believe that youth culture is an ongoing deliberate reaction to adult culture as part of identity formation, especially in adolescents (Willis, 1990). Thus, attempts to pull youth culture into the mainstream may threaten it. A teacher's blurring the distinctions between adult and youth culture may be threatening to some children, but at the same time not providing contexts where children can draw on their meaning-making strategies, may leave these children out of the classroom circle. The multiple cultures in the classroom can all have a voice toward common ends.

Some Necessary Changes Beyond the Classroom

In many places, teachers have the power to create classroom cultures. Nevertheless, the culture beyond the classroom also plays a role in determining the extent to which children are allowed access to their familiar discourses as tools for learning in school. That most people participate in multiple discourse communities should be acknowledged beyond the classroom as well. If children are going to understand and participate in multiple discourses, school activities should include more collaboration between teachers and children, administrators, teacher and children, and parents and schools. Such collaborations, like meaningful collaborations among children, challenge existing boundaries in education. Activities that enable people with different formal roles in education to work together toward shared goals can be contexts for authentic communication. If these activities are important, then people can use their authentic discourses to common ends and common developments. Thus, acknowledging and working with youth genre—like the other genres at play in school—is a significant step toward multicultural understanding.

References

Bakhtin, M. M. *Speech genres and other late essays* (V. W. McGee., Trans). (1986). Austin, TX: University of Texas Press.

Bearison, D. J., Magzamen, S., & Filardo, E. K. (1986). Socio-cognitive conflict and cognitive growth in young children. *Merrill-Palmer Quarterly. 32,* 51–72.

Bereiter, C., & Scardamalia, M. (1987). *The psychology of written composition.* Hillsdale, NJ: Erlbaum.

Bettelheim, B. (1975). *The uses of enchantment.* New York: Knopf.

Case, R. (1991). *The mind's staircase: Exploring the conceptual underpinnings of children's thought and knowledge.* Hillsdale, NJ: Erlbaum.

Cochran-Smith, M., & Lytle, S. (1992). *Inside/outside.* New York: Teachers College Press.

Collins, A., Brown, J., & Newman, S. (1989). Cognitive apprenticeship: Teaching the crafts of reading, writing, and mathematics. In L. Resnick (Ed.), *Knowing, learning, and instruction: Essays in honor of Robert Glaser.* Hillsdale, NJ: Earlbaum.

Daiute, C. (1990). The role of play in writing development. *Research in the Teaching of English. 24,* 4–47.

Daiute, C. (1992). Multimedia composing: Extending the resources of kindergarten to writers across the grades. *Language Arts, 69,* 250–260.

Daiute, C. (1993a). Youth genres and literacy: Links between socio-cultural and developmental theories. *Language Arts, 70,* 402–416.

Daiute, C. (Ed.). (1993b). *The development of literacy through social interaction.* San Francisco: Jossey-Bass.

Daiute, C., Campbell, C. H., Griffin, T. M., Reddy, M., & Tivnan, T. (1993). In C. Daiute (Ed.), *The development of literacy through social interaction.* San Francisco: Jossey-Bass.

Daiute, C., & Dalton, B. (1993). Collaboration between children learning to write: Can novices be masters? *Cognition and Instruction. 10,* 1–43.

Daiute, C., & Griffin, T. (1993). The social construction of written narratives. In C. Daiute (Ed.), *The development of literacy through social interaction.* San Francisco: Jossey-Bass.

Daiute, C., Hartup, W. W., Sholl, W., & Zajak, R. (1993). *Peer collaboration and written language development: A study of friends and acquaintances.* Paper presented at the Society for Research in Child Development Meeting in New Orleans, LA.

Daiute, C., & Shaw, T. (1993). *The lived diversity of children's identities as revealed through their writing.* Paper presented at the American Educational Research Association Convention, Atlanta, GA.

Deaux, K. (1993). Reconstructing social identity. *Personality and Social Psychology Bulletin, 19,* 4–12.

Delpit, L. (1986). Skills and other dilemmas of a progressive Black educator. *Harvard Educational Review, 56,* 379–385.

Dyson, A. H. (1993). *Social worlds of children learning to write in an urban primary school.* New York: Teachers College Press.

Erikson, E. H. (1956). Identity in the life cycle. In G. S. Klein (Ed.), *Psychological issues.* New York: International Universities Press.

Fiske, J. (1989). *Understanding popular culture.* Boston: Unwin Hyman.

Flower, L., & Hayes, J. R. (1981). The pregnant pause: An inquiry into the nature of planning. *Research in the Teaching of English, 15,* 229–244.

Freedman, S. (1994). *Exchanging writing/exchanging cultures.* Cambridge, MA: Harvard University Press.

Gilligan, C. (1982). *In a different voice.* Cambridge, MA: Harvard University Press.

Guitierrez, K. (1993, April). *Scripts, metascripts, and counterscripts.* Paper presented at the American Educational Research Association, Atlanta, GA.

Heath, S. B. (1978). *Teacher talk: Language in the classroom.* Arlington, VA: Center of Applied Linguistics.

Heath, S. B., & Mangiola, L. (1991). *Children of promise: Literate activity in linguistically and culturally diverse classrooms.* Washington, DC: National Educational Association.

Heath, S. B., & McLaughlin, M. W. (Eds.). (1993). *Identity and inner-city youth: Beyond ethnicity and gender.* New York: Teachers College Press.

Lemke, J. L. (1990). *Talking science: Language, learning, and values.* Norwood, NJ: Ablex.

Lotman, U. (1990). *The universe of discourse.* Bloomington, IN: Indiana University Press.

Mehan, H. (1979). *Learning lessons: Social organization in the classroom.* Cambridge, MA: Harvard University Press.

Nelson-LeGall, S. (1994, October). Self-regulation in African-American children. Invited address at The Graduate School and University Center of the City University of New York.

Palincsar, A. S., & Brown, A. (1984). Reciprocal teaching of comprehension-fostering and comprehension-monitoring activities. *Cognition and Instruction, 1,* 117–175.

Piaget, J. (1926). *The language and thought of the child.* New York: Harcourt, Brace and Jovanovich.

Reddy, M., & Daiute, C. (1993). The social construction of spelling. In C. Daiute (Ed.), *The development of literacy through social interaction. New directions in child development sourcebook.* San Francisco: Jossey-Bass.

Willis, P. (1990). *Common culture: Symbolic work at play in the everyday cultures of the young.* Boulder, CO & San Francisco: Westview Press.

26

BRIDGING HOME AND SCHOOL LITERACIES: MODELS FOR CULTURALLY RESPONSIVE TEACHING, A CASE FOR AFRICAN-AMERICAN ENGLISH

Carol D. Lee

NORTHWESTERN UNIVERSITY

Zora Neale Hurston's Janie Starks of *Their Eyes Were Watching God* philosophically proclaims,

Ah know all dem sitters-and-talkers gointuh worry they guts into fiddle strings till dey find out whut we been talkin' 'bout. Dat's all right, Phoeby, tell 'em. Dey gointuh make 'miration 'cause mah love didn't work lak they love, if dey ever had any. Then you must tell 'em dat love ain't somethin' lak uh grindstone dat's de same thing everywhere and do de same thing tuh everfything it touch. Love is lake de sea. It's uh movin' thing, but still and all, it takes its shape from de shore it meets, and its different with every shore (1990, p. 182).

The narrator's voice opens Toni Morrison's *The Bluest Eye* with

Here is the house. It is green and white. It has a red door. It is very pretty. Here is the family. Mother, Father, Dick, and Jane live in the green-and-white house. They are very happy. See Jane. She has a red dress. She wants to play. . .

Here is the house it is green and white it has a red door it is very pretty here is the family father dick and jane live in the green-and-white house they are very happy see jane she has a red dress she wants to play . . .

Hereisthehouseitisgreenandwhiteithasareddooritisveryprettyhereisthefa milymotherfatherdickandjaneliveinthegreenandwhitehousetheyareveryh appyseejaneshehasareddressshewantstoplaywhowillplaywithjane...

Quiet as it's kept, there were no marigolds in the fall of 1941. We thought, at the time, that it was because Pecola was having her father's baby that the marigolds did not grow. A little examina-

tion and much less melancholy would have proved to us that our seeds were not the only ones that did not sprout; nobody's did. Not even the gardens fronting the lake showed marigolds that year. But so deeply concerned were we with the health and safe delivery of Pecola's baby we could think of nothing but our own magic; if we planted the seeds, and said the right words over them, they would blossom, and everything would be all right.... (1970, pp. 1–3)

These two slices lifted from two classic African-American novels share several provocative characteristics. Each speaks in the voices of African-American English, the first in the vernacular and the second in a standard variety. The blackness swirling beneath the standard syntax represents a deep structural level of African-American culture. Morrison (1984) acclaims that African-American fiction often embodies attributes that reflect a black cultural tradition:

There are things that I try to incorporate into my fiction that are directly and deliberately related to what I regard as the major characteristics of Black art, wherever it is. One of which is the ability to be both print and oral literature.... It should try deliberately to make you stand up and make you feel something profoundly in the same way that a Black preacher requires his congregation to speak, to join him in the sermon, to behave in a certain way, to stand up and to weep and to cry and to accede or to change and to modify—to expand on the sermon that is being delivered. (p. 341)

The attributes Morrison identifies include "an affective and participatory relationship between the artist ... and the audience," the influence of superstition and magic as ways of knowing, and the presence of ancestors as characters, narrators, elders, a pervasive and timeless presence who act as a kind of chorus. In the first three paragraphs of the opening of *The Bluest Eye,* Morrison "signifies" on or critiques a set of cultural assumptions that lie beneath the 1950s Dick and Jane basal readers. Signifying is a form of discourse within the African-American English speech community. It involves critique and often sarcastic or ironic commentary couched in language that is highly figurative and makes use of creative plays on the sounds and rhythms of words. Her opening "Quiet as it's Kept," with its vernacular expression, invites an intimate listener. Her invocation of magic, saying "the right words over them" recalls the role of superstition and magic in the folk beliefs of traditional southern African-American culture.

The vernacular and the standard syntax both exemplify and extend the talk of ordinary black folk on street corners, in barber shops, churches and at home. Hurston and Morrison's use of language that is both public and singular is reflected in Toni Morrison's (1984) commentary about African-American autobiography:

> The autobiographical form is classic in Black-American or Afro-American literature because it provided an instance in which a writer could be representative, could say, 'My single solitary and individual life is like the lives of the tribe; it differs in these specific ways, but it is a balanced life because it is both solitary and representative.' (p. 339)

While the vernacular variety of African-American English is devalued in formal schooling, its structure and spirit are celebrated in diverse ways by some of the most startling authors in the canon of African-American fiction, poetry and drama. What is the dark pathway that leads these writers—Richard Wright, Ralph Ellison, Toni Morrison, Alice Walker, Zora Neale Hurston, Ishmael Reed, Sterling Brown, Gwendolyln Brooks, Sonia Sanchez, Amiri Baraka, Haki Madhubuti—to explore the magical underworld of this speech community through literary tropes and forms?

What engenders their love of language and literature, so that they are personally steeped in the great dances with language and divine like insights into the human experience reflected in the literatures of writers from around the world and across human history? I believe it may be their conscious immersion in the nuances of the African-American verbal tradition that leads them to push that tradition to its ever changing limits, while at the same time learning to appreciate the variations on language play that are evident in the traditions of meaning making in literature of all parts of the world. What role can schools play in drawing students to the edge of this language whirlpool and inspiring them to taste the waters? I will argue in this chapter that a model of cultural responsive pedagogy (Ladson-Billings, 1990,1991) does offer one possible answer.

Another attribute these two selections of fiction by Hurston and Morrison share is that they are difficult for novices to penetrate, yet offer multiple nuances of meaning to the initiated. Their semantic and structural difficulties are worth the effort they require. In terms of their accessibility to the uninitiated, they share bonds with W.B. Yeats, John Donne, Fyodor Doestoevsky, James Joyce, and others elected to the school canon of white western European and white, often male, U.S. writers who dominate the literature anthologies and reading lists of U.S. high schools (Applebee, 1993). It is possible that if we can illuminate the rites of passage required of our novice initiates in schools serving poor African-American, Native American, Latino and Latina, Hmong, Innuit, and Native Hawaiian students, among others, we can build bridges for all our students to become highly literate lovers of books. Building such bridges from the communities of ethnically and linguistically diverse students to the libraries in our schools is the subject of this chapter. The lens through which I view this construction is that of speakers of African-American English.

PROBLEMS IN THE FIELD

Current research findings document that reading comprehension can be explicitly taught (Pearson & Dole, 1987). There is also a body of research that suggests that while reading comprehension can be taught, teachers and basal reading programs often take students through activities requiring very literal levels of comprehension without teaching students how to construct inferences and read between the lines (Durkin, 1978–79). Much reading research has focused on processes involved in comprehending expository texts at the elementary school level or the college level. Within the research literature on teaching students how to read literature at the secondary school level, very little attention has been paid to teaching ethnically diverse literatures or teaching ethnically diverse students who are underachieving. In reviewing submissions to *Research in the Teaching of English,* Sandra Stotsky (1992) notes, "we have received too few ethnographic studies of effective literacy teaching of children at risk and low-achieving children. We need detailed descriptions of the contexts and conditions for successful classroom instruction, descriptions that provide some evidence of these children's growth as readers and writers" (p. 247).

The research which I describe in this chapter works on the assumption that reading literature is a strategy-directed activity (not strategy governed) requiring complex problem solving. According to Dole Duffy, Roehler, and Pearson (1991), "Strategies are thought of as conscious, instantiated, and flexible plans readers apply and adapt to a variety of texts and tasks.... Skills, by contrast, are viewed as highly routinized, almost automatic behaviors" (p. 242). Problem solving in an effort to construct interpretations of rich literature is complex because efforts do not necessarily lead to single right and wrong answers, while at the same time, solutions are constrained by authorial intent as conveyed in the language and rhetorical structure of the text in question. The knowledge required to play this game of interpretation includes knowledge of literary genres, literary techniques, other writings by the author, and knowledge of the social world reflected historically and culturally in the work in question .

The research I cite also assumes certain tenets about learning and teaching.

These tenets include the following:

(1) Reading is an active process of constructing meaning, which implies that readers must
    (a) know what to pay attention to in the text,
    (b) monitor their ongoing understanding as they read,
    (c) be flexible enough to test their understandings by evidence in both the text and the social world as they know it,
    (d) be willing to hold conclusions in abeyance while waiting for confirmation,
    (e) alter those understandings when the evidence warrants revision,
    (f) transform their understandings into some form that is different from the literal text—perhaps through writing, drawing or dramatizing, and
    (g) find ways to apply their understandings to contexts outside the text that are meaningful to them. (Anderson & Pearson, 1984; Dole et al., 1991; Garner, 1987; Spiro, 1980)

(2) Learning new concepts is most efficient when students are able to draw upon knowledge of concepts, procedures and strategies that they know well in order to construct for themselves a mental representation of the new concept, procedure or strategy. This process is one of construction because students figure out how the new and old knowledge are linked, how they are the same, how they differ, sometimes resulting in qualitative or quantitative changes in the original understandings (Spiro, 1980).

(3) Developing what Gardner (1991) calls genuine understanding or disciplinary expertise requires many opportunities to practice new procedures and strategies or to apply new concepts in problems that increase over time in complexity and to apply this evolving knowledge in multiple contexts that are socially meaningful.

(4) While learning to apply this evolving knowledge, the student must receive strategic support or coaching while in the act of practice (Collins, Brown, & Holum, 1991).

(5) Finally, the student must have opportunities to apply this new knowledge independently in settings and contexts that differ in small but meaningful ways from the contexts and settings in which the knowledge was learned, as evidence of some level of independent mastery.

While these tenets of learning, teaching and reading literature are not unique to any special ethnic or language community, their application, I believe, demands attention to the language, the social norms, and the cultural histories of the students one is teaching. Admittedly, this challenge becomes more difficult and complex when the student population is heterogeneous in terms of language, ethnicity and/or class.

However, while the data on achievement in integrated school settings are hopeful (Orfield & Ashkinaze, 1991), there still remains a significant difference in levels of achievement as measured by standardized test score data between white, middle-class students and students from poor, ethnically and linguistically diverse communities (Mullis, et al., 1991). While there are certainly reasons to question the validity of total reliance on standardized achievement measures of reading (Wolf, Bixby, Glenn, & Gardner, 1991), there are insufficient data on other more authentic forms of assessment to gauge achievement nationally and across large-scale school systems. In addition, demographic data indicate that by the middle of the 21st century, the majority population of the United States will be of people of color, and significant numbers of large, urban school districts contain many schools whose majority student population is "minority" and homogeneous (i.e., Chicago, Atlanta, New York, Detroit, Milwaukee). Thus, the need to address ethnic and language diversity is demanded both by current theories of learning, theories of reading comprehension, and by current and projected demographics.

In the sections that follow, I will describe research in which competencies in a devalued language variety, specifically African-American English, were used to teach important literacy concepts and strategies. I will also describe research that has uncovered the impact of such competencies on the acquisition of literacy both in and out of school. I conclude by arguing that the lessons learned from these research efforts looking at the relationship between competencies in African-American English and the acquisition of literacy offer important insights about supporting the literacy development of other students whose home language differs from the Edited American English (see Smitherman, 1994) that serves as the primary medium of instruction and the idealized standard of traditional U.S. schooling.

RESEARCH IN LANGUAGE AND LITERACY

African-American English

Black English or African-American English is one variety of English spoken by most African Americans. Research in linguistics from the 1970s used the label Black English Vernacular or BEV. Recently, African-American linguists have begun to use the label African-American-English and African-American English Vernacular. In this essay, I will alternate in using both labels, sometimes for historical accuracy and at other times for stylistic diversity. Labov (1972) reported that 80% of the black population in the United States spoke Black English at the time of his research. Lucas (1987) estimates that 60 to 70% of African-Americans speak Black English. These high percentages are reinforced considering that there are both standard and vernacular varieties of Black English and by the fact that code switching is an accepted linguistic phenomenon within many speech communities. According to Orlando Taylor (1992) there are both standard and vernacular varieties of African-American English. While most research has focused on the vernacular, insufficient attention has been paid to its standard variations. Both standard and vernacular varieties have been described in terms of phonology, intonation, modes of discourse, and lexicon (Dillard, 1972; Mitchell, 1969; Smitherman, 1977). Smitherman documents the following categories of black discourse forms: call and response, signification, tonal semantics, and narrative sequencing. Other research analyzes the historical roots of African-American English and argues that there are Africanisms evident in the phonology, syntax and lexicon of African-American English (Mufwene, 1993; Smitherman, 1977; Turner, 1949; Vass, 1979). Smitherman (1977) has called African-American English as "Africanized English" (p. 103).

As with other vernacular varieties of English, Black English Vernacular has been stigmatized in the larger society and specifically in schools. Since BEV was viewed as having low status and speakers of BEV were seen as being "culturally deprived," curricula aimed at fixing this "cultural deprivation" were organized explicitly during the 1960s and 1970s, and attention to language use as a prelude to effective reading was a central premise of these curricula (Bereiter, 1965; Bereiter & Engleman, 1966). Under the assumption that African-American English interfered with the development of early reading abilities, basal readers in the primary grades were developed using African-American English Vernacular as the medium of communication and spelling reflected the so-called "dialect." In addition, highly prescriptive reading and language arts curricula such as the popular DISTAR program specifically had as one its goals the eradication of speech patterns of BEV. Research in the effectiveness of the "dialect" readers showed mixed results, with no clear advantage of using such readers to improve the early reading abilities of low-income African-American students. In fact, there is evidence that these "dialect" readers may have interfered with students' abilities to read (see Hall & Guthrie, 1980 for a full review).

By contrast, Labov (1972) shattered the myth that African-American English Vernacular was inferior and incapable of expressing complex thinking. On the basis of extensive ethnographic research in several urban centers, Labov demonstrated what he called "the logic of nonstandard Black English." Labov's work was followed by a number of studies that documented the rich and artistic qualities of BEV along with historical studies of its evolution (Abrahams, 1970; Kochman, 1972; Smitherman, 1977).

African-American English, Signifying and the Teaching of Literary Interpretation

Signifying is a form of discourse practiced widely among speakers of African-American English across generations. "Your house is so poor, they tore it down to put up a slum" (p. 111) and "Your house is so small, I walked through the front door and tripped over the back fence" (p. 113) are typical examples of signifying (Percelay, Ivey & Dweck, 1994). Signifying has been defined both in terms of its functions within a speech act (Abrahams, 1970; Kochman, 1972) as well as a rhetorical stance, an attitude toward language and a means of cultural self-definition (Cooke, 1984; Gates, 1984, 1988; Mitchell-Kernan, 1981; Smitherman, 1977). Signifying can be used for the following functions within a speech act:

(1) challenge and maintain a friendly, but intense verbal duel,
(2) persuade—to direct through indirection . . .,
(3) criticize or insult either through carp or innuendo,
(4) praise...,
(5) reverse a relationship,
(6) to show off... (Lee, 1993).

As an attitude toward language, signifying involves speaking with innuendo and double meanings, playing rhetorically upon the meaning and sounds of words, and being quick and witty in one's response. Mitchell-Kernan (1981) describes signifying as a "way of encoding messages or meanings which involves, in most cases, an element of indirection" (p. 311). Smitherman (1977) summarizes the formal properties of signifying in the following way:

> indirection, circumlocution; metaphorical-imagistic (but images rooted in the everyday, real world); humorous, ironic; rhythmic fluency and sound; teachy but not preachy; directed at persons or persons usually present in the situational context (siggers do not talk behind yo back); punning, play on words; introduction of the semantically or logically unexpected. (p. 121)

Popular categories of signifying include playing the dozens (i.e., talking about yo' mama), and cappin' or sounding (outperforming in a verbal duel of friendly insults), as in the following examples:

> Dozens—Yo mamma so skinny, she do the hula hoop in a Applejack!
> Cappin' or sounding—Someone says, "I went to your house and wanted to sit down. A roach jumped up and said 'Sorry, this seat is taken. '"You respond, "I went in yo house and stepped on a match and yo mama said, 'Who turned off the heat?'" (See Mitchell-Kernan, 1981; Percelay, et al., 1994; Smitherman, 1977; Taylor, 1982 for additional examples.)

It should be noted that the descriptive lexicon for categories of signifying and the term *signifying* itself change from one generation to another. Youngsters today do not use the terms signifying, dozens or sounding. However, the rhetorical characteristics and communicative functions of signifying and its various categories have remained consistent across many generations. When I first began this line of research, my teenage children became active researchers, bringing in current examples of signifying on television, the radio, and in rap music, while my mother and her friends shared examples and reminisced about their experiences signifying across their life-span.

Signifying is not limited to insult, but may also be both *metaphoric and informative* as in the following example, taken from Mitchell-Kernan (1981):

> (Grace has four kids. She had sworn she was not going to have any more babies. When she discovered she was pregnant again, she wouldn't tell anybody. Grace's sister came over and they had the following conversation.)
> Rochelle: Girl, you sure do need to join the Metrecal for lunch bunch.

Grace: (noncommitally) Yea, I guess I am putting on a little weight.

Rochelle: Now look here girl, we both standing here soaking wet and you still trying to tell me it ain't raining (p. 323)

In addition, signifying can serve *ironic functions* as in this next example, also taken from Mitchell-Kernan (1981). Mitchell-Kernan was conducting doctoral research on language patterns in the black community, including signifying. A young man in the park approaches her and she explains her interest in signifying. In the midst of their conversation, the young man flirts with the researcher through rapping and at the same time engages in a verbal duel through signifying. Rapping in this instance is not to be confused with the current genre of rap music, but rather is in this example a category of signifying talk in which young men, in particular, flirt and demonstrate braggadocio by playing with the sounds and innuendo of words. In the midst of their signifying dialogue, the young man responds:

> Baby, you a real scholar. I can tell you want to learn. Now if you'll just cooperate a li'l bit, I'll show you what a good teacher I am. But first we got to get into my area of expertise. (p. 323)

A full analysis of the ironic nature of the full dialogues from Mitchell-Kernan (1981) quoted above are described in Lee (1994c).

African-American adolescents, in particular, regularly produce and interpret such figurative and ironic talk. I have argued that to process such figurative and ironic talk demands both metaphoric reasoning and ironic reasoning (Lee, 1993, 1994c). To reason or infer metaphorically involves establishing an unstated relationship between the topic and the vehicle of the metaphor, and then building levels of parallel associations that extend to the topic of the metaphor (Booth, 1974; Winner, 1988). Ironic reasoning differs from metaphoric reasoning in that the reader or listener must reject the surface meaning of the passage and then construct levels of meaning that are in contrast or even contradiction to the literal interpretation of the oral or written text. If underachieving African-American adolescents are able to carry out metaphoric and ironic reasoning in the contexts of signifying dialogues in their homes and communities, then they should be able to apply those reasoning strategies to texts of literature in the school curriculum where full interpretation demands a similar use of strategies.

Cultural Scaffolding: Bridging Home and School Knowledge

A classic problem in learning is where someone has schemata or organized bodies of knowledge of content, strategies or procedures that are applicable to a problem she is trying to solve, but cannot seem to make the connection between her existing knowledge base and the new problem (Rumelhart, 1980; Spiro, 1980). When a person is trying to solve a novel problem—whether one of literary interpretation or mathematical problem solving—she may not make the connection between her prior knowledge and the problem posed. This lack of connecting may be because the prior knowledge is

tacit, having evolved in everyday learning and socialization. Since that knowledge is known tacitly and not consciously, the realms in which the knowledge is applicable are often limited to the contexts in which it evolved. Such is the case with African-American adolescents' use of signifying. They can participate in signifying dialogue with little conscious reflection and can interpret signifying turns of talk with little conscious reflection. However, when asked what they did to arrive at the interpretations they construct, my research suggests that they are usually at a loss for words (Lee, 1993).

Where there is an overlap between what Moll and Greenberg (1990) refer to as "funds of knowledge in community contexts and funds of knowledge required to solve school based problems in an academic discipline," a potential model for what I call cultural scaffolding (Lee, 1993, 1995) exists. Cultural modeling as a scaffolding device is what I have attempted to illustrate in the research on signifying and literary interpretation that I describe in this chapter.

Signifying serves as an effective source for modeling powerful strategies for interpreting fiction because it overlaps both community-based and school-based funds of knowledge in ways that are complex. In texts of African-American fiction which are referred to by some as "speakerly" texts or "talking books" (Gates, 1988; Hurston, 1935; Reed, 1974), characters speak in language that reflects the many voices of the African-American speech community. Alice Walker (1988) comments about the source for the character Celie in *The Color Purple:*

> Celie speaks in the voice and uses the language of my stepgrandmother, Rachel, an old black woman I loved. Did she not exist; or in my memories of her, must I give her the proper English of, say, Nancy Reagan?
>
> And I say, yes, she did exist, and I can prove it to you, using the only thing that she, a poor woman, left me to remember her by—the sound of her voice.
>
> Her unique pattern of speech. Celie is created out of language. In *The Color Purple,* you see Celie because you 'see' her voice. To suppress her voice is to complete the murder of her. And this, to my mind, is an attack upon the ancestors, which is, in fact, war against ourselves.
>
> For Celie's speech pattern and Celie's words reveal not only an intelligence that transforms illiterate speech into something that is, at times, very beautiful, as well as effective in conveying her sense of her world, but also what has been done to her by a racist and sexist system, and her intelligent blossoming as a human being despite her oppression demonstrate why her oppressors persist even today in trying to keep her down.... (pp. 63–64)

In such "speakerly" texts, authors use tropes, images, proverbial statements, allusions, discourse patterns, and narrative structures that are deeply entrenched in the language and lived experience of many in the African-American community. Through such rhetorical techniques, these authors couch multiple layers of nuanced meanings that wait to be unearthed by active readers. In some "speakerly" texts, such as *Their Eyes Were Watching God* (Hurston, 1990), *The Color Purple* (Walker, 1982), "My Man Bovanne," (Bambara, 1972), and *Mumbo Jumbo* (Reed, 1972), signifying, in particular, acts as both a rhetorical tool and a theme. Detailed analyses of the uses of signifying as both rhetorical tool and theme are available in Lee (1993), Gates (1988), and Smitherman (1977). Jones (1991) provides a comprehensive analysis of the role of African-American oral patterns in African-American fiction.

To interpret complex literature requires knowledge of literary techniques, the structure of genres and the implications of those structures for interpretations of the work, and knowledge of what may be the archetypal themes explored in other works by an author. Efforts to construct interpretations of complex problems posed in fiction also require the reader to have knowledge of social norms, the social world in which the fiction is cast. Knowledge about contemporary and historical life in the African-American community is another form of prior knowledge which African-American adolescents potentially bring to the reading of African-American literary texts. However, it is crucial to point out that these links of linguistic and social knowledge are only potential levers for these students as readers. When either source of prior knowledge is either tacit or incomplete, appropriate activation of such prior knowledge during reading needs explicit support before, during, and after the act of reading. At the same time, the problem of interpretation is fundamentally of a different order when a novice reader brings neither the linguistic knowledge nor the social knowledge to a literary work in question. The conditions under which cultural scaffolding can occur, then, are not simple, yet the right mix can provide powerful learning experiences for students who traditionally underachieve.

I will describe below an instructional intervention based on the cultural scaffolding I have described (Lee, 1991, 1993, 1994b, 1995) . The intervention took place in two urban high schools in a large midwest school district. The participants were high school seniors. Among the four classes participating in the quasi-experimental treatment, only 8.25% scored above the 50th percentile in reading comprehension on the standardized achievement test used by the district. At the time of the study, the graduate rates in the two schools were 39.8 % and 50.9% respectively.

Earlier in this chapter, I referred to a set of basic tenets of learning and teaching. In the school intervention in which signifying was used as a cultural scaffold, these tenets were incorporated as part of the daily routine of instruction. It was necessary to model the strategies good readers use to know when to slow down their reading and pay close attention to details that the author uses to flag down the reader with a sign in invisible ink that says "Pay Attention To Me For Gold Lies Beneath the Surface." To accomplish this cultural modeling, the students were given a series of extended dialogues replete with signifying. They were asked to tell what each turn of talk in a signifying dialogue meant, since in such talk the words are never meant to be interpreted literally. The students had no trouble summarizing what each speaker meant. The challenge came when they were asked: (1) what strategies they used to know that the interpretation they made was appropriate, and (2) how they knew when to interpret figuratively and when to interpret literally. The purpose of these last two questions was to help the students construct strategies from their own storehouse of tacit knowledge that they would make explicit and public. From this process, the students

came to articulate a set of conditions requiring inferencing, often of either metaphor or irony. These conditions are listed in Table 26–1. This process required the students actively to construct their knowledge of strategies by linking old and new knowledge.

Once this milestone of coming to understand what Rabinowitz (1987) calls "rules of notice" had been addressed, consistent with the tenets of learning and teaching referred to earlier, the students needed opportunities to apply these "rules of notice" to literary texts, in this instance texts for which they had meaningful prior social knowledge. Applying these "rules of notice" to the literary texts demanded that they extend their knowledge again to include monitoring their on-going understanding as they read, testing their evolving understandings against the text and their knowledge of the world, and being flexible in their on-going interpretations. Use of small group work provided the environment for both application and strategic coaching by the teacher.

In the use of small group work, another kind of cultural scaffolding occurred. While Slavin and associates have documented that cooperative work groups have proved successful with African-American students (Slavin & Oickle, 1981), Boykin and associates have extended analyses of the effectiveness of small group work with African-American students to include cultural foundations as explanations for their success (Boykin, 1994). Boykin (1994) has outlined nine characteristics of what he calls Afro-cultural ethos:

(1) spirituality—an acceptance of a nonmaterial higher force that pervades all of life's affairs;
(2) harmony—This implies that functioning is inextricably linked to nature's order and one should be synchronized with this order;
(3) movement—a premium placed on the interwoven amalgamation of movement, (poly)rhythm, dance, and percussion embodied in the musical beat;
(4) verve—receptiveness to relatively high levels of sensate (i.e., intensity and variability) of stimulation;
(5) affect—the centrality of affective information and emotional expressiveness and the equal and integrated importance of thoughts and feelings;
(6) expressive individualism—a uniqueness of personal expression, personal style, and genuiness of self-expression;
(7) communalism—a commitment to the fundamental interdependence of people and to the importance of social bonds, relationships, and the transcendence of the group;
(8) orality—the centrality of oral/aural modes of communication for conveying full meaning and the cultivation of speaking as a performance;
(9) social time perspective—commitment to a social construction of time as personified by an event orientation (p. 184).

According to Boykin's research, the inclusion of these attributes in the environment of classes where African-American youngsters are taught is associated with academic achievement. In a series of studies conducted by Boykin and his associates, when groups of African-American elementary students were given different conditions in which to carry out academic tasks, the students preferred conditions of cooperation rather than competition and the students learned more when working in small cooperative groups. Boykin (1994) provides a full overview of these studies.

In the intervention based on signifying, the teacher first modeled how she marked the opening of *Their Eyes Were Watching God* and asked students what stood out for them from the opening page and why. As an essential part of the protocol of the teaching, the teacher always demanded that students prove any assertions they made, either about why a passage stood out for them, or about what that passage meant. From the group modeling, students were then divided into small cooperative work groups each day. They received a set of challenging questions demanding that they read between the lines, that they make inferences based on divergent sources within the text, and that they extend their interpretation of the work to what the text said about the world (Hillocks & Ludlow, 1984). The teacher served as coach by sitting in each group in order to determine if the group was on the right track, if the group was confused, or if the group was avoiding complexity and opting for simplistic responses. The teacher would then give advice or ask a devil's advocate question where appropriate. This use of small cooperative groups focusing on challenging questions and teacher coaching continued across two novels for a total of six weeks. A detailed description of classroom talk and the evolution of students' understanding are given in Lee (1993, 1994b) . The daily routines included teacher modeling, small cooperative group work with teacher coaching and finally writing a response to at least one of the challenging questions.

By the time the classes reached the second novel, *The Color Purple,* the lines of authority had changed. Analysis of transcripts of classroom talk from the end of the intervention shows that students were now initiating the questions, rather than the teacher, and the students were dominating the talk. The percentages of teacher talk to student talk dramatically shifted by the end of the instructional unit (Lee, 1994b). I have argued (Lee, 1994b) that this dramatic shift occurred because students were explicitly taught the rules they needed to know and were strategically coached in their application. Delpit (1988) has argued strongly that minority students often feel lost in classes where they are asked to apply rules about writing and reading that they do not know. Many wonderful pictures of classrooms in which students are actively engaged in discussing and critiquing literature abound. However there is little evidence that these students are African-American, Latino or Native American, for example, and insufficient description about how the students reached this level of expertise.

In order to determine whether the students had internalized the reading strategies and whether they had developed habits of mind that allowed them to attack really difficult literary problems with patience, steadfastness, and sophistication, they were given pre- and posttests. For both the pre- and posttests, the students were given a short story that had not been read before in class and a series of questions ranging from literal to inferential, to questions asking them to apply themes from the stories to real-life contexts. A full description of the tests—including pre- and posttests as well as tests of knowledge of signifying and prior social knowledge relevant to the texts in the instructional unit—is given in Lee (1993). Each of the four classes in the quasi-experimental treatment achieved a statistically significant gain from pre- to posttest over the classes in the control treatment. The instructional intervention has been repeated with similar results.

The lessons from this example of cultural scaffolding are important. First, it demonstrates the practical power of building on the language patterns that students from speech communities whose language varieties are devalued in traditional school settings. Second, it links philosophical and ethnographic arguments for what Ladson-Billings calls culturally responsive pedagogy (Au & Kawakami, 1994; King, 1991; Ladson-Billings, 1990; Villegas, 1991) to other mainstream research in reading comprehension (Barr, Kamil, Mosenthal & Pearson, 1991), literary schemata (Beaugrande, 1987), and cognition in everyday contexts (Lave, 1988; Rogoff & Lave, 1984). I point out these connections because there has been a tendency to see calls for cultural responsivity in language arts teaching as ghettoized arguments that apply only to disenfranchised minorities or linked to self-esteem efforts, but not intellectually stimulating teaching. I have addressed the implications of this line of thought for teacher training in Lee (1993) .

In addition, there is a growing body of research documenting community-based funds of knowledge as sources for cultural scaffolding. Some of this work has occurred in schools, some in other community settings, but all hold strong implications for teaching and learning to read and write well.

Related Research

Several studies investigate the impact of oral narrative styles on the support for literacy learning in classrooms. Taylor and Lee (1987), Michaels (1981, 1986), and Cazden, Michaels, and Tabors (1985) looked at a common speech event in primary level classes called *sharing time,* where children may bring objects from home and tell stories about these objects or stories about personally meaningful experiences. One goal of such lessons is for the teacher to act as coach and to support children in being articulate, including details about their experiences, and sequencing their narratives in such a way as to approximate either traditional story grammar structure or the logical linear expository style of writing and speaking that is valued by schools. These researchers found that the African-American children in their studies often related stories in what Michaels labeled a "topic associative" style. In this topic associative style, the stories told by African-American children contained segments of the narrative that on the surface appear to bear no explicitly stated relationship to one another. The teachers listening to these stories did not provide the kind of scaffolding support to the African-American children because they could not make sense of the stories. Michaels argued that segments of the stories were often linked by the narrator's internal point of view that was not articulated and must be inferred by the listener. This narrative structure is in direct contrast to the sequential series of events and the explicit thematic cohesion of the topic-centered style expected by the school. Since the teachers in the study were able to perceive some rudimentary aspects of the topic-centered storytelling style in the narratives of the white children, these teachers were able to intercede at appropriate moments to make suggestions to the students about adding details, enriching language, and making explicit the point of the narrative. Cazden (1988) extended the findings of this line of research by asking groups of white adults and black adults to read and evaluate samples of topic-centered and topic-associative narratives. The white adults found the episodic stories of the African-American children hard to follow and made the assumption that the child who wrote the story was likely a low-achieving student. Black adults, on the other hand, were more likely to evaluate positively both the topic-centered and topic-associative stories. The black adults recognized the differences in the stories, but also appreciated the artistic qualities of both.

Using both a sociolinguistic and literary analysis of a topic-associative story taken from the corpus of narratives collected in the Michaels studies, Gee (1989a) argued that the topic-associative story structure was characterized by high literary elements and was more complex than the topic-centered style advocated by schools. From a practical standpoint, however, what it means to help African-American children who demonstrate this topic-associative narrative style to develop further that narrative style is still an open question. I have advocated cultural modeling in which, in this example, the topic-associative narratives would be used as objects of study, as case studies or data from which the children could infer formal properties of stories (Lee, 1994a). The students would then be supported in incorporating these formal properties both in their oral and written narratives. Research efforts are underway in this regard. (Carol Lee of Northwestern University and Wade Boykin of Howard University are initiating such a study under the auspices of the Center for Research on the Education of Students Placed at Risk (CRESPAR). I have also discussed the concept of language expertise within minority speech communities (Lee, 1994a). In the African-American speech community, such experts would include preachers, rappers, politicians and writers, all who have historically served as orators or wordsmiths through both oral and written media. In other words, it is possible that much can be gained by supporting the extension and refinement of the topic-associative narrative style, especially when one considers the detrimental effects of efforts to eradicate its use in school.

Hyon and Sulzby (1994), in a recent study, collected oral narratives from 48 African-American kindergarten children. These stories were produced in a context other than the sharing time activity reported in Michaels (1981, 1986). In contrast to Michaels, Hyon and Sulzby found that 33.3% of the narratives were in the topic associative style, while 58.3% were in the topic-centered style. These findings are significant; yet, they do not negate the arguments that have been made regarding the usefulness of building on indigenous narrative

styles in order to support school-based literacies. It is important to recognize the diversity of oral genres, including a diversity of oral narratives, within various speech communities. Sufficient research has not been conducted on the emergence of oral narrative styles among African-American children in different contexts, at home, among peers, in school settings, in community institutions such as social clubs and churches. The attention paid to Michaels' characterization of the topic-associative style has in part been a result of lack of information on other manifestations of narratives within this population. For teachers, the range of language competencies that African-American and other linguistically diverse youth bring to the school setting, for example, should be viewed as a pool of potential resources from which to draw, rather than a simplistic label that fits every African-American child one meets. As relates to the Hyon and Sulzby (1994) study, I would argue that one third of the total corpus is not insignificant and that additional criteria for the presence of elements of the African-American verbal tradition may reveal new insights. Ball (1992) and Smitherman (1994) offer potential examples of criteria by which to evaluate oral and print texts produced by speakers of African-American English.

In addition to looking at narrative styles, research has also focused on issues of expository style. Ball (1992) studied expository writing samples from African-American high school students. In both their personal writing and writing done at school, the students exhibited three expository structures that Ball indicates are rooted in African-American verbal traditions. Although the students were not conscious of their overt use nor why they used these structures, the students showed a preference for these African-American expository styles.

The expository structures included what Ball calls circumlocution, narrative interspersion, and recursion. Significantly, Ball's description of the expository pattern of circumlocution among African-American adolescents is very similar to the pattern described by Michaels as topic-associative narrative style among African-American primary school students. In both patterns of organization, "thematic development was typically accomplished through anecdotal association" (Ball, 1992, p. 509). In the narrative interspersion pattern, "the speaker or writer intersperses a narrative within expository text" (p. 511). In this pattern, often the narrative is expected to communicate the main point of the essay.

In the third pattern, recursion, "the speaker dicusses a topic and then restates it using different words or images" (Ball, p. 511). Ball illustrates this pattern by references to the organizational pattern of Martin Luther King's speech "How Long? Not Long." One of the more important implications of Ball's research, consistent with that of Lee (1994a), is that these organizational patterns were observed in vernacular speech patterns and were, perhaps unconsciously, adopted by students into their school-based writings. Further, there are expert uses to which these patterns are applied by ministers, orators who are often political leaders, and by creative writers. As Gee (1989a) and Lee (1994a) observed, it may be possible to build on these tacit vernacular patterns in order to develop expertise in school-based writing. There may be differences between the traditional academic essay and oral argumentative and narrative genres in terms of what characterizes optimal writing. However, it may well be the case that (1) transfer to the more conservative academic prose may be easier with cultural scaffolding, and (2) that such efforts to scaffold may expand the range of acceptable patterns of organization in academic prose. Certainly, Smitherman (1977; p. 19) has challenged those boundaries by publishing academic prose that incorporates uses of Black English Vernacular.

Smitherman (1994) studied samples of narrative, expository, and persuasive writing from the National Assessment of Educational Progress (NAEP) from 1969, 1979, 1984 to 1988–89. Extending earlier research by Chaplin (1987) and Scott (1981), Smitherman analyzed the writing samples for examples of Black English Vernacular syntax and black discourse styles. Scott (1981) and Chaplin (1987) had documented that black discourse patterns highly influenced the evaluation of African-American student writing. Smitherman extrapolated the following features as characteristic of an African-American discourse style:

(1) Rhythmic, dramatic, evocative language. Example: "Darkness is like a cage in black around me, shutting me off from the rest of the world."

(2) Reference to color–race–ethnicity (that is, when topic does not call for it).
Example: "I don't get in trouble at school or have any problems with people picking on me I am nice to every one no matter what color or sex. "

(3) Use of proverbs, aphorisms, Biblical verses: Example: "People might have shut me off from the world cause of a mistake, crime, or a sin.... Judge not others, for you to will have your day to be judge"

(4) Sermonic tone reminiscent of traditional Black Church rhetoric, especially in vocabulary, imagery, metaphor. Example: "I feel like I'm suffering from being wwith world. There no lights, food, water, bed and clothes for me to put on. Im fighten, scared of what might happened if no one finds me. But I pray and pray until they do find me."

(5) Direct address-conversational tone. Example: "I think you should use the money for the railroad track... it could fall off the tracks and kill someone on the train And that is very dangerius. Don't you think so. Please change your mind and pick the railroad tracks. For the People safelty O.K." [From letter-writing, persuasive task]

(6) Cultural references. Example: "How about slipping me some chitterlings in tonite"

(7) Ethnolinguistic idioms. Example: "... a fight has broke loose"; "It would run me crazy ...."

(8) Verbal inventiveness, unique nomenclature. Example: [The settlers] were pioneerific"; "[The box] has an eye look-out"

(9) Cultural values-community consciousness. Expressions of concern for development of African Americans; concern for welfare of entire community, not just individuals, as for example several essays in which students expressed the view that recreational facilities would have to be for everybody, "young and old, and homeless among Blacks"

(10) Field dependency. Involvement with and immersion in the events and situations; personalizing phenomena; lack of distance from topics and subjects. (pp. 86, 87)

Smitherman found a decline in BEV syntax in narrative writing between 1969 and 1979 (Smitherman & Wright, 1983). Smitherman predictably found that BEV syntax was the most significant predictor of the rater's score. In contrast, however, from an analysis of NAEP essays of 1984 and 1988-89, Smitherman notes "the more discernibly African American the discourse, the higher the primary trait and holistic scores; the less discernibly African-American the discourse, the lower the primary trait and holistic scores" (p. 93). This finding is significant because of the sample size and the strength of the correlations. Smitherman posits that the shift in the unstated criteria of NAEP raters may have been influenced by the efforts of organizations such as the Center for Applied Linguistics, the National Council of Teachers of English, and the Conference on College Composition and Communication to "sensitize teachers to the linguistic-cultural norms of the African-American speech community" (p. 95).

Language and Literacy in Community Contexts

The discourse and rhetorical forms that have been identified as part of the African-American verbal tradition are developed and honed in community contexts, including the family and community institutions. Two classic studies of how reading and writing were used in one poor rural (Heath, 1983) and one poor urban (Taylor & Gaines, 1988) African-American community, document the myriad ways that reading and writing were used and how children were socialized into certain attitudes about language, what makes for a good story, and what quality of questions are worth asking (Heath, 1983). Both Heath, and Taylor and Gaines argue that the rich experiences with language that African-American children have in their family and community lives present a bountiful repertoire for teaching in school contexts. The challenge, however, has been how to translate these language experiences to uses in specific pedagogy and content. The uses of reading and writing within these two African-American communities are similar, including both functional and aesthetic uses. These studies contradict popular assumptions that because students from this population living in poverty tend to score lower on standardized tests of academic achievement and attend school districts with inordinately high drop-out rates (Kaufman, 1991; Mullis, et al., 1991), that their families and communities are either illiterate or have low levels of literacy. Heath (1983) and Taylor and Gaines (1988), among others, present a very different picture of poor African-American urban and rural communities. It is important to note, however, that in a follow-up study by Heath (1989) of families from Trackton who moved into an urban community, the language interaction between parents and children had lessened and peers were a primary source of socialization.

Williams (1991) studied how a group of middle-class African-American families socializes their young children through stories and joint construction of stories of personal experience. Stories reflecting African-American narrative conventions and rhetorical tools were used to reinforce the children's identities as African-Americans, and included learning how to deal with conflicts arising from racism. Potts (1989) analyzed stories of personal experience from young children living in public housing projects in Chicago. He found the stories to be structurally complex. Potts concludes, "These children were especially adept at 'evaluating' or communicating the personal meaning of past experiences. In this corpus of narratives can be seen the incipient skills for becoming participants in an important tradition in Afro-American communities" (p. 25).

Moss (1994) carried out an ethnographic study of literacy acts within some African-American churches. She analyzed rhetorical structures of sermons in black churches and documented how print and oral media are jointly used in literacy acts. Moss' analyses of the argumentative structure of sermons delivered in the African-American church are of interest to those considering the possible uses of rhetorical models from the African-American verbal tradition for teaching in school contexts. Mahiri (1991) looked at language uses among African-American adolescent and preadolescent males and their coaches in a Youth Basketball League. Mahiri found that the young men developed skills in argumentation and routinely employed rhetorical techniques like signifying to dramatize their points of view. Like Moss, Mahiri documented many uses of literacy that were supported through this community institution. Delain, Pearson and Anderson (1985) found that proficiency in African-American English served as a predictor of general language ability.

CONCLUDING THOUGHTS

The acquisition of a language or a particular language variety involves more than learning a lexicon and syntax. Language competency involves knowing not only what to say, how to say it, where to say it, but also requires the invocation of certain worldviews and social norms (Gee, 1989b; Saville-Troike, 1989). Identity is tied to language acquisition and use. The acquisition of language competency also demands the assumption of cultural competencies. Due to this connection, Farr (1991) recommends that schools attend to bidialectism, bilingualism and biculturalism. DiPardo (1993) conducted case studies of language minority students in a writing program for basic writers in a major U.S. university. She found that both African-American tutors and students in the program showed great ambivalence about adopting

Edited American English and an academic expository essay style into their writing and personal communication. DiPardo concludes that those who design basic writing programs within universities must consider more carefully the goals of such programs and their possible impact on students.

Language is a complex symbol system through which we learn, think and are socialized. Bruner (1990) argues that "culture . . . shapes human life and the human mind, . . . [and] gives meaning to action by situating its underlying intentional states in an interpretive system. It does this by imposing the patterns inherent in the culture's symbolic systems—its language and discourse modes, the forms of logical and narrative explication" (p. 34). Wertsch (1991) uses the analogy of a psychological tool kit with which humans are endowed. This tool kit includes a variety of symbol systems and is shaped by culture and history. Language use is one big ticket item in such a tool kit.

Heath (1989) admonishes educational institutions to acknowledge and make productive use of the language competencies of language minority students:

> The school has seemed unable to recognize and take up the potentially positive interactive and adaptive verbal and interpretive habits learned by Black American children (as well as other nonmainstream groups), rural and urban, within their families and on the streets. These uses of language—spoken and written—are wide ranging, and many represent skills that would benefit all youngsters: keen listening and observational skills, quick recognition and nuanced roles, rapid-fire dialogue, hard-driving argumentation, succinct recapitulating of an event, striking metaphors, and comparative analyses based on unexpected analogies. (p. 370)

Practitioners and researchers in literacy education would do well to pick up the gauntlet.

For schools to either ignore or depreciate the significance of indigenous language competencies is to lose a potentially powerful cognitive tool in the psychological tool kit of both youngsters and adults. The admonition that Heath makes about African-American youngsters rings true for students from all corners of the tapestry of languages and language varieties that constitute language use in the United States.

References

Abrahams, R. (1970). *Deep down in the jungle: Negro narrative folklore from the streets of Philadelphia.* Chicago: Aldine.

Anderson, R. C., & Pearson, P. D. (1984). A schema-theoretic view of basic processes in reading comprehension. In P. D. Pearson, R. Barr, M. L. Kamil & P. D. Mosenthal (Eds.), *Handbook of reading research,* (Vol. 1, pp 255–291). White Plains, NY: Longman.

Applebee, A. (1993). *Literature in the secondary school: Studies of curriculum and instruction in the United States.* Urbana, IL: National Council of Teachers of English.

Au, K., & Kawakami, A. J. (1994). Cultural congruence in instruction. In E. Hollins, J. King & W. Hayman (Eds.), *Teaching diverse populations.* Albany, NY: State University of New York Press.

Ball, A. F. (1992, October). Cultural preference and the expository writing of African-American adolescents. *Written Communication, 9*(4), 501–532.

Bambara, T. C. (1972). My man Bovanne. In *Gorilla, my love* (pp. 1–10). New York: Random House.

Barr, R., Kamil, M. L., Mosenthal, P. D., & Pearson, P. D. (Eds.). (1991). *Handbook of reading research (Vol. 2).* White Plains, NY: Longman.

Beaugrande de, R. (1987). Schemas for literary communication. In L. Halasz (Ed.), *Literary discourse: Aspects of cognitive and social psychological approaches* (pp. 49–99). New York: Walter de Gruyter.

Bereiter, C. (1965). Language problems for culturally deprived children. *Language programs for the disadvantaged: Report to the NCTE Task Force on teaching English to the disadvantaged.* Urbana, IL: National Council of Teachers of English.

Bereiter, C., & Engleman, S. (1966). *Teaching disadvantaged children in the pre-school.* Englewood Cliffs, NJ: Prentice-Hall.

Booth, W. (1974). *A rhetoric of irony.* Chicago: University of Chicago Press.

Boykin W. (1994). Harvesting culture and talent: African American children and educational reform. In R. Rossi (Ed.), *Educational reform and at risk students.* New York: Teachers College Press.

Bruner, J. (1990). *Acts of meaning.* Cambridge, MA: Harvard University Press.

Cazden, C. (1988). *Classroom discourse: The language of teaching and learning.* Portsmouth, NH: Heinemann.

Cazden, C., Michaels, S ., & Tabors, P. (1985). Spontaneous repairs in sharing time narratives: The intersection of metalinguistic awareness, speech event and narrative style. In S. Freedman (Ed.), *The acquisition of written language: Revision and response.* Norwood, NJ: Ablex.

Chaplin, M. (1987). An analysis of writing features found in the essays of students in the National Assessment of Educational Progress and the New Jersey high school proficiency test. Unpublished manuscript, Rutgers University, Department of English, Camden, NJ.

Collins, A., Brown, J., & Holum, A. (1991, Winter). Cognitive apprenticeship: Making thinking visible. *American Educator, 15*(3), 6–11, 38–46.

Cooke, M.(1984). *Afro-American literature in the twentieth century: The achievement of intimacy.* New Haven, CT: Yale University Press.

Delain, M., Pearson, P., & Anderson, R. (1985). Reading comprehension and creativity in Black language use: You stand to gain by laying the sounding game. *American Educational Research Journal, 22*(2), 155–173.

Delpit, L. (1988). The silenced dialogue: Power and pedagogy in educating other people's children. *Harvard Educational Review, 58*(3), 280–298.

Dillard, J. (1972). *Black English.* New York: Random House.

DiPardo, A. (1993). *A kind of passport: A basic writing adjunct program and the challenge of student diversity.* Urbana, IL: National Council of Teachers of English.

Dole, J. A., Duffy, G. G., Roehler, L. R., & Pearson, P. D. (1991, Summer). Moving from the old to the new: Research on reading comprehension instruction. *Review of Educational Research, 61*(2), pp. 239–264.

Durkin, D. (1978–79). What classroom observations reveal about reading comprehension instruction. *Reading Research Quarterly, 15,* 481–533.

Farr, M. (1991). Dialects, culture and teaching the English language arts. In J. Flood, J. M. Jensen, D. Lapp & J. R. Squire (Eds.), *Handbook on research on teaching the English language arts* (pp. 365–371). New York: Macmillan.

Gardner, H. (1991). *The unschooled mind: How children think and how schools should teach.* New York: Basic Books.

Garner, R. (1987). *Metacognition and reading comprehension.* Norwood, NJ: Ablex.

Gates, H. L. (1984). *Black literature and literacy theory.* New York: Methuen.

Gates, H. L. (1988). *The signifying monkey: A theory of Afro-American literary criticism.* New York: Oxford University Press.

Gee, J. P. (1989a). The narrativization of experience in the oral style. *Journal of Education, 171*(1), 75–96.

Gee, J. P. (1989b). Literacy, discourse, and linguistics. *Journal of Education* [special issue].

Hall, W. S., & Guthrie, L. F. (1980). On the dialect question and reading. In R. Spiro, B. Bruce & W. Brewer (Eds.), *Theoretical issues in reading comprehension: Perspectives from cognitive psychology, linguistics artificial intelligence and education* (pp. 439–452). Hillsdale, NJ:Erlbaum.

Heath, S. B. (1983). *Ways with words: Language, life and work in communities and classrooms.* New York: Cambridge University Press.

Heath, S. (1989). Oral and literate traditions among Black Americans living in poverty. *American Psychologist, 44*(2), 367–373.

Hillocks, G., & Ludlow, L. (1984). A taxonomy of skills in reading and interpreting fiction. *American Educational Research Journal, 21,* 7–24.

Hurston, Z. N. (1935). *Mules and men.* New York: Harper & Row.

Hurston, Z. N. (1990). *Their eyes were watching god* (1937). New York: Harper & Row.

Hyon, S., & Sulzby, E. (1994). African American kindergarteners' spoken narratives: Topic associating and topic centered styles. *Linguistics and Education, 6*(2), 121–152.

Jones, G. (1991). *Liberating voices: Oral tradition in African American literature.* New York: Penguin Books.

Kaufman, P. (1991). *Dropout rates in the United States: 1990.* Washington, DC: National Center for Education Statistics.

King, J. (1991). Black student alienation and Black teachers' emancipatory pedagogy. In M. Foster (Ed.), *Readings on equal education. Vol. 11: Qualitative investigations into schools and schooling.* New York: AMS Press.

Kochman, T. (1972). *Rappin' and stylin' out: Communication in urban Black America.* Urbana, IL: University of Illinois Press.

Labov, W. (1972). *Language in the inner city: Studies in the Black English vernacular.* Philadelphia: University of Pennsylvania Press.

Ladson-Billings, G. (1990). Like lightning in a bottle: Attempting to capture the pedagogical excellence of successful teachers of Black students. *International Journal of Qualitative Studies in Education, 3*(4), 335–344.

Ladson-Billings, G. (1991). Returning to the source: Implications for educating teachers of Black students. In M. Foster (Ed.), *Readings on equal education Vol. 11: Qualitative investigations into schools and schooling.* New York: AMS Press.

Lave, J. (1988). *Cognition in practice: Mind, mathematics and culture in everyday life.* New York: Cambridge University Press.

Lee, C. D. (1991). Big picture talkers/words walking without masters: The instructional implications of ethnic voices for an expanded literacy. *The Journal of Negro Education, 60*(3), 291–304.

Lee, C. D. (1993). *Signifying as a scaffold for literary interpretation: The pedagogical implications of an African American discourse genre.* Urbana, IL: National Council of Teachers of English.

Lee, C. D. (1994a). Slipping into the breaks and looking around: Towards a theory of African American literary expertise and its implications for school based literacies. Paper presented at the Annual Conference of the NCTE Assembly for Research: The Multiple Discourses of Writing and Literacy, Chicago.

Lee, C. D. (1994b). The interplay of cultural modeling and the organization of instruction effective for culturally diverse students: Knowing when fat meat is greasy. Paper presented at the Annual Meeting of the American Educational Research Association, New Orleans, LA.

Lee, C. D. (1994c). *Signifying in the zone of proximal development.* Manuscript submitted for publication.

Lee, C. D. (1995). A culturally based cognitive apprenticeship: Teaching African American high school students skills in literary interpretation. *Reading Research Quarterly, 30*(4) 608–630.

Mahiri, J. (1991, Summer). Discourse in sports: Language and literacy features of preadolescent African American males in a youth basketball Program. *Journal of Negro Education, 60*(3), 305–313.

Michaels, S. (1981). "Sharing time" Children's narrative styles and differential access to literacy. *Language in Society, 10,* 423–442.

Michaels, S. (1986). Narrative presentations: An oral preparation for literacy with first graders. In J. Cook-Gumperz (Ed.), *The social construction of literacy* (pp. 94–115). New York: Cambridge University Press.

Mitchell, C. (1969). Language behavior in a Black Urban Community (unpublished doctoral dissertation). Berkeley, CA: University of California, Press.

Mitchell-Kernan, C. (1981). Signifying, loud-talking and marking. In A. Dundes (Ed.), *Mother wit from the laughing barrel* (pp. 310–328). Englewood Cliffs, NJ: Prentice-Hall.

Moll, L., & Greenberg, J. (1990). Creating zones of possibilities: Combining social contexts for instruction. In L. Moll (Ed.), *Vygotsky and education: Instructional implications and applications of sociohistorical psychology,* (pp. 319–348). New York: Cambridge University Press.

Morrison, T. (1970). *The bluest eye.* New York: Holt, Rinehart & Winston.

Morrison, T. (1984). Rootedness: The ancestor as foundation. In M. Evans (Ed.), *Black women writers (1950–1980): A critical evaluation* (pp. 339–345). New York: Doubleday.

Moss, B. J. (1994). Creating a community: Literacy events in African-American churches. In B. J. Moss (Ed.), *Literacy across communities* (pp. 147–178). Cresskill, NJ: Hampton Press.

Mufwene, S. (1993). *Africanisms in Afro-American language varieties.* Athens, GA: University of Georgia Press.

Mullis, I. V., Dossey, J. A., Foertsch, M. A., Jones, L. R., & Gentile, C. A. (1991). *Trends in academic progress: Achievement of U.S. students in Science. 1969–70 to 1990; Mathematics, 1973 to 1990; Reading, 1971 to 1990, Writing, 1984 to 1990* [Prepared by Educational Testing Service]. Washington, DC: Office of Educational Research and Improvement, U.S. Department of Education.

Orfield, G., & Ashkinaze, C. (1991). *The closing door: Conservative policy and Black opportunity.* Chicago: University of Chicago Press.

Pearson, P. D., & Dole, J.A. (1987). Explicit comprehension instruction: A review of research and a new conceptualization of instruction. *Elementary School Journal, 88*(2), 151–165.

Percelay, J., Ivey, M., & Dweck, S. (1994). *Snaps.* New York: William Morrow.

Potts, R. (1989, April). West side stories: Children's conversational narratives in a Black community. Paper presented at the biennial meeting of the Society for Research in Child Development.

Rabinowitz, P. (1987). *Before reading: Narrative conventions and the politics of interpretation.* Ithaca, NY: Cornell University Press.

Reed, I. (1972). *Mumbo jumbo.* Garden City, NY: Doubleday.

Reed, I. (1974, June). Ishmael Reed: A self interview. *Black World,* 20–34.

Rogoff, B., & Lave, J. (Eds.) (1984). *Everyday cognition: Its development in social context.* Cambridge, MA: Harvard University Press.

Rumelhart, D.E. (1980). Schemata: The building blocks of cognition. In R. J. Spiro, B.CCC. Bruce, and W.F. Brewer (Eds.), *Theoretical issues in reading comprehension* (pp. 34–58). Hillsdale, NJ: Erlbaum.

Saville-Troike, M. (1989). *The ethnography of communication.* New York: Basil Blackwell.

Scott, J. (1981). Mixed dialects in the composition classroom. In M. Montgomery (Ed.), *Language variety in the south: Perspectives in black and white.* Tuscaloosa, AL: University of Alabama Press.

Slavin, R. E., & Oickle, E. (1981). Effects of cooperative learning teams on student achievement and race relations: Treatment by race interactions. *Sociology of Education, 54,* 174–180.

Smitherman, G. (1977). *Talkin and testifyin.* Boston: Houghton Mifflin.

Smitherman, G. (1994). The blacker the berry, the sweeter the juice: African American student writers. In A.H. Dyson & C. Genishi (Eds.), *The need for story: Cultural diversity in classroom and community.* Urbana, IL: National Council of Teachers of English.

Smitherman, G., & Wright, S. (1983, March). Black student writers, storks and familiar places: What can we learn from the National Assessment of Educational Progress? Paper presented at the annual convention of the Conference on College Composition and Communication, Detroit. [Also, (1983, December). *Interim Research Report.* Urbana, IL: National Council of Teachers of English.]

Spiro, R. (1980). Constructive processes in prose comprehension and recall. In R. Spiro, B. Bruce & Brewer W. (Eds.), *Theoretical issues in reading comprehension* (pp. 245–278). Hillsdale, NJ: Lawrence Erlbaum and Associates.

Stotsky, S. (1992). From the editor. *Research in the Teaching of English, 26*(3), 245–248.

Taylor, D., & Dorsey-Gaines, C. (1988). *Growing up literate: Learning from inner-city families.* Portsmouth, NH: Heinemann.

Taylor, M. (1982). The use of figurative devices in aiding comprehension for speakers of Black English. Unpublished doctoral dissertation, University of Illinois, Urbana, IL.

Taylor, O. (1992, June). Toward a redefinition of standard Black English. Paper presented at the African American English in Schools and Society Conference, Stanford University, Stanford, CA.

Taylor, O., & Lee, D. (1987). Standardized tests and African-American children: Communication and language issues. *Negro Educational Review, 38*(2/3), 67–80.

Turner, L. (1949). *Africanisms in the Gullah dialect.* Chicago: University of Chicago Press.

Vass, W. K. (1979). *The Bantu speaking heritage of the United States.* Los Angeles: Center for Afro-American Studies, University of California.

Villegas, A. M. (1991). *Culturally responsive pedagoy for the 1990's and beyond.* Washington, DC: ERIC Clearinghouse on Teacher Education.

Walker, A. (1982). *The color purple.* New York: Simon and Schuster.

Walker, A. (1988). Coming in from the cold. In *Living by the word* (pp. 54–68). New York: Harcourt, Brace and Jovanovich.

Wertsch, J. (1991). *Voices of the mind: A sociocultural approach to mediated action.* Cambridge, MA: Harvard University Press.

Williams, K. (1991). Storytelling as a bridge to literacy: An examination of personal storytelling among Black middle-class mothers and children. *The Journal of Negro Education, 60*(3), 399–410.

Winner, E. (1988). *The point of words: Children's understanding of metaphor and irony.* Cambridge, MA: Harvard University Press.

Wolf, D., Bixby, J., Glenn, J., & Gardner, H. (1991). To use their minds well: Investigating new forms of student assessment. In G. Grant (Ed.), *Review of Research in Education, 17,* 31–74. Washington, DC: American Educational Research Association.

27

STUDENT CONVERSATIONS:
PROVOCATIVE ECHOES

Eleanor Binstock
NATIONAL-LOUIS UNIVERSITY

Prologue: Many Literacies, Many Cultural Styles

I can't look up to my brother. He is locked up,
so [pause], how could I look up to him?
Before, I admired him; he had like a lot of girls and stuff.
I thought he was slick and badass', playing around.
Now he ain't got no girls.
You don't see any of his ladies out here visiting him,
or any of his boys visiting him.
Nobody cares. You get locked up, so what—"Oh, well, that's it."
Now that I look at him, I see him as another one that
didn't get away, just like that.
He ain't bad no more, he just ended like that.

—Maria, student at "West" High

As the high school students in my research group swap stories on videotape, their adolescence extends across streets of culture and consciousness. For them, the research is a forum in which to talk about their lives, and the videotape their passageway to voices and images not otherwise accessible. The technical process seems simple: conversation at one school is videotaped and played back at the second school where students watch, then respond on videotape for playback at the first school. The recording of the conversations on videotape inscribes them, fixing them in time; it captures and transports discourse, normally a "fleeting event" (Ricoeur, 1991). This enables Latino and African-American students on Chicago's west and south sides respectively to correspond with one another for a year, within and between their two alternative high schools. The lively combination of text and image brings students together, sustaining their interest and challenging them to "read" and respond to each others' stories of lived experience.

For example, Maria, a student at "West," one of the two alternative high schools, relates a story about her brother. Her narrative conveys a poignant scenario of gang lifestyle, disintegration of family, divergent messages of success, and images of lost hope and lost respect. It assembles a reality and brings it to life for audiences from diverse backgrounds. Maria describes her brother's situation in a world they share with many of their Mexican and Puerto Rican friends. She laments his fall from social stature and the disintegration of their relationship. She depicts the texture of their lives together, intertwined with those around them.

In this chapter, videotaped student conversations lead us to consider the readability of students' oral texts and the literate qualities associated with constructing and interpreting these oral texts. We also examine how their conversation illuminates connections between them and the circumstances of their world, as we listen to the echo-structure of their conversations, the familiar ring of their voices.

CONVERSATION AS TEXT

As they talk about their lives, the students from the two schools exercise their capacity "to constitute their worlds as they begin to name them" (Greene, 1986, p. 782). This potential to create meaning through conversation is what initially inspired the research, what was to become a transnarrative journey into language, culture, and lifetexts. Constructing and interpreting lifetexts (the word I use for the oral text we create in representing our lived experience) are literate acts, like the composing and reading of written texts, even though literacy is usually related to written texts only, a facility with "letters." Although not in use today, "oracy" is a word that was used by Andrew Wilkinson to indicate literacy of the spoken, specifically the relating of people to people. It was intended to correspond both to literacy, traditionally connoting the relating of people to books, and to numeracy, the relating of people to things (Watson, 1993). It is in the spirit of oracy that I argue for the literacy of the spoken word.

To speak of the readability of oral text identifies it with written text. According to Geertz (1983), the textual analogy is used by social scientists to accommodate a blurring of boundaries between systems and ideas and is the broadest and least well developed of the recent "refigurations" of social thought which see social institutions, customs, and changes as "readable." Both Bakhtin and Ricoeur corroborate this correspondence of forms. For Bakhtin, each of us has a dialogue with existence which takes on the textual form of a novel; the text we write is called life (Holquist, 1990). Ricoeur (1981) considers experience and consciousness structured like language and, therefore, all human experience and interactions interpretable as some kind of text.

Just as with our reading of the written text, we bring to the reading of lifetexts what we already know—our longings, trusts, biases, and (mis)understandings. We approach truth only in "transaction" (Rosenblatt, 1978) with the text, rather than in search of a priori meaning.

Language, Culture, and Oral Texts

For Wittgenstein (1973), "to imagine a language means to imagine a form of life" (p. 8e). It is in our imaginations where we first acknowledge pluralities of language and forms of life. Once in this knowledge, we are less apt to experience or engender cultural dissonance and more apt to recognize many lives, many languages. And to recognize the language of cultural "others" is to begin to grasp something about their forms of life.

Within "arche-writing," Derrida's term for language, he names

> all that gives rise to an inscription in general, whether it is literal or not and even if what it distributes in space is alien to the order of the voice: cinematography, choreography, of course, but also pictorial, musical, sculptural "writing." (1976, p. 9)

In Derrida's image of the ark, all forms of "writing," all manners of inscription are contained (as were all forms of being in the biblical ark). His image evokes Eisner's view of literacy, with its many voices:

> …one of the major aims of education is the development of multiple forms of literacy. What we ought to develop, in my view, is the student's ability to access meaning within the variety of forms of representation that humans use to represent the contents of their consciousness. (Eisner, 1994, p. x)

If we recognized the variety of literacies, we would "contribute to greater educational equity for students, especially those whose aptitudes reside in the use of forms of representation now marginalized by our current educational priorities" (p. x). This applies to the high school students taking part in video conversations, casualties of a public school system which, unwilling (or unaware of how) to accommodate their learning styles and language, drops them from the rolls. But many of these students are capable of producing exceptionally wise, poetic oral prose. If teachers would accept and nurture the variety of expressive forms, while at the same time consider with their students the ethical guidelines for these forms, students could become more discerning and independent learners and communicators, trusting they will be accepted more wholly, cultural style and all.

Culture is shared learned behavior and language habits are part of it. In what Heath (1983) terms the "language socialization process," children learn to use language based on their culture's values, social legacies, styles of face-to-face interactions, and patterns of adjusting to the external environment. They become acculturated to the interactions between themselves and their parents; the ways in which reading and writing are used; and the content, enactment, and uses of storytelling—practices which lead to distinct learning styles. When the school fails to accept children's unique learning styles or communication styles, it contributes to sustaining cultural inequities still deeper than those identified by Eisner above:

> …unless the boundaries between classrooms and communities can be broken, and the flow of cultural patterns between them encouraged, the schools will continue to legitimate and reproduce communities… who control and limit the potential progress of other communities and who themselves remain untouched by other values and ways of life. (Heath, 1983, p. 369)

What is considered in one milieu to be communicative competence may not be considered so in another, unaccepting milieu. The teachers in Heath's study learned how to incorporate their students' ways of "talking, knowing, and expressing knowledge" into the classroom ethos, enabling children from different communities to learn how to make choices among uses of languages and to understand that these choices are connected to life chances, instead of "growing restless in the uncertainties" of a system intolerant of their cultural style (1983, p. 343).

It is clear in the student conversations that communicative competence is in part related to one's command of the nuances and subtexts of language in context and that it emanates from and generates personal courage and conviction. The peer conversations I witness are filled with language and forms of life native to the communities in which the students are growing up. Although I have built friendships and collegiality in these communities over the years, listening to the peer conversations is often like being privy to the stories of travelers from unimagined lands (Jefferson, 1995). Yet these are the everyday lands of our urban terrain, so their unfamiliarity may underscore the distance between that terrain and a more privileged academic community.

Conversation as Correspondence

The video conversations engage students in expressing and interpreting lived experience. Their lifetexts are constituted and reconstituted in iterations of their own experiences and those of others; they become at once readers and authors as their stories converge and intersect with others. Often this is literally so, as in:

> an overlapping-turn structure similar to the overlapping speech that is common in ordinary Polynesian conversations, and

especially in the stylized speech event called "talk-story." Here, a story is co-narrated by more than one person, and the speech of the narrators is also overlapped by audience response. (Cazden, 1988, p. 71)

There are talk-stories in the student conversations. They arise when speakers share common backgrounds or are tuned in to the same story, as in the following example from South, where not only is the story remarkable, but it could be the expression of a single voice (a slash indicates interrupted speech):

Kevin: You can write a story, you ain't even got to gangbang. You can wear out the ordinary—wear all yellow, go into somebody neighborhood, you walkin' [pause], people be looking, "Who is that mark, who is that punk motherfuck–." I know, I know, I'm not– I can't say everybody bad out here 'cause I know I do devious things myself. We be outside, somebody strange be walking down the street, we be like, "Man, who the hell is that stud, who that punk is?" You know. We do it ourselves, that's why I can't trip on nobody else. I'm just saying it happens everyday.

Darryl: Like, "Who is that, that nigger?" you know.

K: "Look at that phone man, let get that, let get that."

D: "Let's get this coat, he just like a nerd, let's bang"/

K: /"Yea, let's bang that mug."

D: Especially when niggers get under the influence of drugs they be, like, ah, they snap then. Get under influence of drugs, they go crazy. They take care of you.

K: Man, they'll smack the fuck out you man.

D: They he ready to fight they homeys.

K: Don't get in no crap game, no dice game. It will be on then/

D: /Be smoking mud or something, man.

K: Beat me out in front of her house man, all this, all that, then it be on all over again/

D: /homeys killing each other up.

K: That's why you got to watch yourself, you know, you ain't got no friends or nothin' you know. I don't care what nobody say, you ain't got no friends, you got a lot of associates.

D: That all there is.

K: You could have a friend, now, 'cause it some people out here/

D: /it some friends that'll stick by you like this, you know.

K: And then it's some people out here [pause], ain't your friends.

D: Like we here right now, I'm talking to you, this for an example you know, we here right now, I'm to you, and when you leave I can be like– all man, you know, people out here.

K: Or like say, for instance, you know, alright, say Sam your friend, you know, I'm your friend, we shaking hands, you say "I love you"—he love me—you know-ing inside you really ain't got no love for me and I ain't got no love for you. Or, you know, I get locked up or he get locked up and I suppose' to be his homey and I try to call him and tell, send his money or something, you know, I be jumpin, "All– all man, I got to break, you know."

D: It's people out here that's a fool. ... They get a little money in they pockets, they go up you know. They use' to be your homeys from way back in the days, they get some loot in they pockets, they be like, "What's up man, all yea man, what's up man," you know.

K: They be trying to tell you to break North, you know what I'm saying, "I'm big now, I don't want to be around you." Then, you understand, when they go to jail you understand, all that, when they call, soon as they fall off, they see you outside, "All man, what's up man, let's get a St. Ides or something." You be looking at them like, "All yea nigger, the other day you was drinking cases of fifth of Hennessy, now you want to get a .40 St. Ides with me, man. Break North, man." There's a lot of perpetrator studs out here, that's all, trying to high cap.

D: They think they get the money, they think they got the power and everything, you know. You can make money just like they too.

Kevin and Darryl are partners in narrative; together they shape the story—its content, flow, and tempo. Their storytelling resonates with their environment and serves to corroborate their individual perceptions of what is going on in a world they share. Their talk-story confirms the correspondence between them, as well as between the story and the sociocultural texture of their worlds. It may even be seen to confirm the accuracy of how they read the goings-on of their environment. Later in this conversation, it becomes obvious how the structure and rhythms of Kevin's stories are in tune with those of his life experience:

Kevin: I–
you know,
they sell drugs out there.
It dope fiends out there, it crack houses out there.
It no change, it's everywhere.
It ain't gon' change, you know.
Long as the stuff keep comin' over here
and people keep gettin' it and baggin' it up,
it always gon' be.
Long as people see six-point star and five-point star,
the gangbanger gon' be here.
Long as people see a liquor store
the drinks gon' be here.
Long as people know where to get a gun,
the gun shop gon' be here.
So where's it gon go? Where it been before.
It ain't gon' change.

The repetition in his speech mimics the ineluctability of his environment—"it always gon' be.... It ain't gon' change." The gangbanger, the abuse of liquor, the gun shops, will continue in perpetuity until the conditions in which they incubate change: as long as such-and-such persists, then such-and-such "gon be here ... gon' be here ... gon' be here." The sound and form of his speech, as in a fugue, reiterate the enduring patterns of his environment. "So where's it gon' go? Where it been before. It ain't gon' change," he recapitulates in his closing, as in a musical coda, transforming consciousness into poetic language.

Not only are his speech and narrative creative renditions of his environment, but Kevin himself is in sync with it. He allows as much in his opening words, in his "I-they" switch, that he is not apart from it but a part of it, in tandem with it. Bakhtin says nothing is in itself: "existence is an event of co-being, a web of interconnections so extensive that it cannot be known by only one of us. Its form is fluid, manifest in an ongoing and endless creation and exchange of meaning" (Holquist, 1990). The web of dialogue, too, pervades more than is knowable at one time, always at once more mysterious and more telling than any single one of its strands or motifs. Kevin's ability to connect the otherwise unordered pieces of his environment into a logical order—"Long as the stuff keep comin' over here … long as people see six-point star and five-point star… long as people see a liquor store … long as people know where to get a gun…"—is an indication of his communicative agility in transliterating a grammar of daily life in one milieu (his neighborhood) to a grammar of language in another (the logic of argument in discourse).

In another conversation, between Sonja and William at "South" School, we experience a *pas de deux* in which the participants know the steps because they have danced the dance. As Tannen (1989, p. 18) says, "Finding a way into a conversation is like joining a line of dancers. It is not enough to know where other dancers have been; one must also know where they are headed."

The considerable conversational two-stepping at South (much more than at West), suggests it is a style well known and practiced by African-American students there, surely by the more skilled orators. It is a style also well remembered by this Jewish writer from her childhood—uncles and aunts gathered around a wood-burning stove, seemingly all speaking at the same time in what begins as serious, but inevitably lapses into comedic exaggerations of truth. The difference here is that Sonja does not allow William to lapse into comedy, and remains herself dead serious.

(A slash indicates interrupted and interrupting speech. Indented dialogue indicates continuation of prior interrupted speech):

Sonja:	Do you know what sellin' drugs gets you into,/
William:	/Yeah. I know what drugs get/
Sonja:	/huh?
William:	I know what it do, but/
Sonja:	/I used to sell drugs./
William:	/it's like this, see/
Sonja:	/Do you wanna be six feet under for somebody else's fault?
William:	I don't know,/
Sonja:	/Do you wanna end up in jail/
William:	/see (…)/
Sonja:	/for the rest of your life?

She asks why he does not get a legal job and he laughs, "'Cause me and a legal job ain't gonna work out right now." He has a police record, he explains.

"That's the purpose in why you supposed to tell 'em you goin' to school," Sonja argues, "they don't ask you all that on no application."

William retorts, a smile on his face, "I'm not made to flip hamburgers." Laughing, he gets a rise from another boy in the group. William repeats: "I'm not made to flip hamburgers."

Sonja shifts perspective:

Sonja	I know– I know quite a few people that's thirty years old, thirty-five years old and sellin' drugs. But when

they kids ask them where they get the money from, they always say, "UNHH," and have a stupid look on they face/

William:	/Whatchya gonna/
Sonja:	/you know. They have a stupid look on they face yet here they got all the money to buy all the gym shoes and take care they kids and stuff but as soon as they kids ask 'em, "Hey, Daddy, where you get all the money from"/
William:	/It's like this,/
Sonja:	/Then what you gonna tell 'em, you out there doin' wrong but you want them to do better than what you doin'?
William:	Okay, but say you can't get no job. You ain't got nowhere else to turn to but to sell drugs."
Sonja:	Well see, you still don't see what I'm gettin' at: you gonna be sellin' drugs for the rest o' your life.

William and Sonja engage each other in what Rosen (1984, pp. 12–14) calls "the story grammars of [their] society, [their] culture," grammars in which they are comfortable and competent because they share the forms of life in which those grammars are grounded. Neither is threatened by the other as they step in and out of each other's words and back into their own. They would have had difficulty sustaining such conversation had they not shared a full body of assumptions about the world and one another. When, for example, blacks and whites are interacting and such assumptions cannot readily be shared, there is a lack of ease or comprehension. Some of this lack "must be caused, or at least exaggerated, by cultural differences—by the different contexts in the mind, the expectations about form and topic, that black and white listeners bring to the listening task" (Cazden, 1988, p. 25). It is an apparent difference in social grammar or expectation that will cause dissonance between West and South in an example cited later.

Conversation as Echo

The most extraordinary, and certainly most enchanting aspect of the peer conversations is its echo-like quality, within the group conversation and between groups in video conversation. Within and across space and time, the echo signals the contextual and historical underliers of the students' lives. These underliers reflect and give rise to certain languages, certain forms of life. They are forceful antecedents of custom and attitude, and they resound in the conversations. Echoes of culture and history are fundamentally reincarnations of the past in the present, like recapitulative cycles of being—the archetype in the fetus, the child in the adult, for example. These echoes prompt feelings of familiarity, of having been here before, of having heard or seen this before:

> Utterances are not indifferent to one another, and are not self-sufficient; they are aware of and mutually reflect one another. These mutual reflections determine their character. Each utterance is filled with echoes and reverberations of other utterances to which it is related by the communality of the sphere of speech communication. (Bakhtin, 1986, p. 91)

The stories told by Maria and by Kevin and Darryl contain this communality, a continuity characterized by repetition and reflection. One common application of the echo is in verse, where one line repeats the end of the preceding line to supply an answer to the question contained within it, or to give a holistic sense. In the peer conversations, the echo gives this continuous sense between the ethos and the oral text, as we have already seen. And, as we will soon see, through reverberation and response, the echo also suggests congruity, or at least continuity between the Latino and African-American students.

The echo also facilitates or reinforces learning and communicative agility, because responding to the echo—reading and interpreting it—requires one to recognize connections between then and now, this and that, oneself and another. The most dynamic narrative element to emerge from the conversations between the Latino students at "West" School and the African-American students at "South" School, the echo appeared as corroboration, challenge, and collaboration, each with rules, mood, and consequence:

> …not only formally distinct speech events but all kinds of casual talk are rule-governed, and … the mechanisms which underlie speaker coordination can be studied empirically by examining recurrent strategies, responses they elicit, and ways in which they are modified as a result of those responses. (Gumperz, 1977, p. 196)

The video conversations are like call and response to expressions of lived experience. They stir up the interlocutors and myself as well, as I gain understanding of the forces and boundaries of the mother tongue—not only that of my hosts, but of my own. The echo harkens back in time and forward to the future; it mirrors meaning and summons a literacy of sound and voice. It is evident in the following three sequences (excluding intervening utterances of classmates) from a conversation in which Maria expresses her frustration with the system and the school curriculum, and her impatience with racism. Her ideas and feelings emanate from several places: her personal sense of schooling, family, and life; the mosaic of talk in her daily conversations with friends, family, and teachers; the music she listens and responds to; the television programs she watches; and the news she hears from the streets and the media. She reconstitutes her experience in a soliloquy on fairness, dignity, history, racism, voice, and change. Her words echo the circumstances of her life now and of a time before:

Maria: …the system isn't perfect. The system, it's– it's not fair. It was probably fair for the people that made it at that time but it's not fair now for other people like minorities. It's not– it's obvious that– that you know, the government wasn't made, like, for minorities because minorities probably wasn't out there at the time. They didn't have a voice, so now that we do have a voice we– you know, want to change because the system is not perfect, you know. They make a lot of mistakes, a lot of big mistakes, okay.

Maria has an historical awareness: what may have been fair representation at one time is not now so. The system is not quite "of [all] the people," or "for [all] the people." Moreover:

Maria: Like the history, like George Washington and all that. I mean how are you goin' to compare to Martha Washington, or George Washington? You can't compare to that people. I mean that you can't– your parents can't even compare to that people, so you kind of feel left out when you read that history, because you know damn well that they're not—not talking about your people and, it's not to be racist [pause], that we're racist again' all White people, but that's not fair. How would the White people feel if we came out teaching them the Mexican culture, or the Puerto Rican culture, the African culture [pause]? They wouldn't like it. They'll probably be mad just as well as we did. That's right, we're teaching them something they're not, you know. You can't make 'em– you can't– we can't, you know, erase the color of our skin, can't erase our heritage. I mean we could probably lie about who we are and all that, but deep down inside we know we can't lie to ourselves.

In the excerpt above, Maria develops the historical theme begun earlier, crowning it with a switch of subject and object—a hypothetical turning of the tables ("How would the White people feel if we came out teaching them the Mexican culture, or the Puerto Rican culture, the African culture…?"), making sure a multicultural audience will identify with the incongruity she is explaining.

In the next excerpt, she challenges her sister's teacher, whose attitude resonates with, even corroborates Maria's prior argument about unfairness:

Maria: My little sister asked her to help her for her math. The teacher says, "Why don't you ask your parents?" And then she said, "Oh, let me take that back, I wouldn't expect your parents to know this." What the fuck does she mean by that, just because my parents are Mexican or something like that? That is why I know right away they don't expect—the teachers in there don't expect— there are a lot of teachers that are ignorant and racist. They have got to learn, too. They don't know everything and they expect us to fail. They do.

Maria's oral text is antecedent for Darryl and will be echoed by him at the next session at South. Her ideas will be reincarnated by his words in a perpetual cycle of disclosure and reknowing. Oral texts, like the written, come from and go to many places, assembled and rechanneled through the listener/speaker back into the world in a new configuration, welcoming and facilitating new generations of thought and knowing.

The peer video conversations are mirrors of the self and others: they reflect and generate images of selves in definition. They give rise to collaborative knowledge-building, and provide an arena for those less knowledgeable or less articulate to learn from peers who are more so, central to Vygotsky's concept of social learning and the contributions of "more capable peers" (1978, p. 86). Vygotsky's model is like that of apprenticeship, learning by witnessing and emulating competent practice. Bruner (1986) describes this emulative learning as the "method of the well-conceived tutorial or small discussion group" in a world where "we cease thinking of the growth of the mind as a lonely voyage of each on his own" (p. 142).

In the session following Maria's exposition on fairness and racism, Darryl echoes many of her themes. Although he does not seem here as practiced or skilled a speaker as she, he speaks with equal passion. The example shows how the echo operates corroboratively and collaboratively among less and more capable peers:

> Darryl: Because sometimes, you know, they do tell us that we can't accomplish, that we can't do this and we can't do that. They don't respect us [pause]—the past and stuff. They always put us down and tell us that we are gonna be dumb forever, you know. But we gotta come up and show 'em that we ain't gonna be dumb. . . .

He expresses solidarity with Maria by echoing her concerns, if not her words. He holds them up as a mirror to his own lifetext and, strengthened by this new alliance, takes her argument a step further: "…we gotta come up and show 'em. …" The echo is capable of conflating boundaries between cultures and languages, experience and lifetext, and often, even author and reader.

Echoes in Groupspeak. Bourdieu (1993) says there is an "objective relationship between corresponding languages, that is to say, the relationship between the groups speaking those languages" that transcends the conversational situation and determines linguistic interaction. He calls this phenomenon "linguistic power relations" (p. 82). This is evident in the next examples where West is challenging a prior videotape in which South called them stupid, and South subsequently answers. Within groups, the echo contributes to the construction of the argument. Between groups, it provides the scaffolding on which the challenge is mounted. The challenge is a version of the echo, derived from a source and directed back at it. It is not as much imitative as defiant.

West will challenge South's foul language and their use of inverted gang signs to show extreme disrespect. They are reacting mostly to South's accusations that West is stupid (for discussing family problems). Everyone fails to realize that whereas it is okay at West to talk about one's dysfunctional family life, it is apparently forbidden to do so at South. So South, thinking West is obviously violating rules that apply in all cultures, calls West "stupid." Kochman (1981) says this is due to a clash of cultural styles in which, for example, in the case of blacks and whites interacting, each may behave according to their own cultural norms, yet in the eyes of the other be perceived to be in violation.

> Maria: Okay, why are you calling us stupid, alright? If you think we are stupid, then back up your attitude, why are we stupid? Okay, just don't be saying we are stupid and then you don't got nothin' to say about it. You know, if I am going to say you're stupid, then I am going to tell you why I think you are stupid, right?
> Ines: They think it is fun and games.
> Eddie: They were probably thinking we weren't serious but we were serious. We were trying to talk about something important.

West's request for South to "back up your attitude" confirms that West does not know what they did "wrong" to incur South's censure. While the Latino students at West consider it within the rules to discuss their families' dysfunctions, the African-American students at South, not sharing this rule, feel justified mocking and challenging West for doing so. Were they to get to know each other better, as I did in my two years with them (in person and in the transcripts) they would likely learn to be sensitive to "linguistic power relations" and to be more tolerant, to see friction and misunderstanding as a result of cultural variance rather than the inadequacy of any individual.

Later at South, where the videotape of West has just been viewed, William and Kevin respond in the form of a challenge also. Although brief, they offer a vivid picture of the dangers and frustrations of life in their environment. They use repetition and irony. This repetition, or echo, serves to emphasize and corroborate what each of them knows:

> William: Let them come in our 'hood.
> Kevin: Let 'em come in our 'hood.
> William: Let them come to our motherfucking castle.

With 19 words they reveal a world of information. Instead of replying directly to West's requests for South to back up their accusations, South tells West they need to understand that what must be conveyed about the lives of students at South is so complicated and deeply embedded in the ways of the neighborhoods in which they live, that words are not enough. If West wants to understand South, they will have to come over there in person to see for themselves what is going on. And if West thinks that life for South is so great, they have another "think" coming. Further, the invitation to come to "our motherfucking castle" seems to be an escalation of the combative tone of West's earlier response. A dare to West to "cross the line" into South turf, this invitation holds an unmistakable threat of violence. All this is said using eight basic words, a core phrase of five words repeated three times with variations (in parentheses): "Let them ('em) come in (to) our. …" The word "'hood" is repeated once and then again in sarcastic aggrandizing, expressed in two words. So it basically takes eight words to encapsulate a world. To some extent, that world is unspeakable, calling to mind Rosenblatt's (1978) caution that language may be:

> not simply the inked marks on the page or even the uttered vibrations in the air. The visual or auditory signs become verbal symbols, become words, by virtue of their being potentially recognizable as pointing to something beyond themselves. (p. 12)

Peer conversation is a conduit to students' (children's) ways of knowing and communicating. Greene (1986) says that if we understood how children reach for meaning and coherence we could make it possible for them to "join the conversation" of cultural ways of knowing so that they might overcome their powerlessness and passivity:

> …paying a new kind of attention to children's lived lives has to do with our current recognition that much of what passes for learning represents a mastery of terminology, not a becoming different, not an entering the conceptual order, or the great "conversation." We cannot know this if we do not listen to children, talk with children, play with children, even dance with children. (p. 782)

Listening to Students

Peer video conversations offer rich opportunities for listening to the language of students' lives—their passions, disappointments, and their issues with the schools that renounce them. Only when we appreciate the particularities of their stories and ethos can we join them in conversation, be privy to their passages:

> I research the spoken and written words of the students to learn what they know, what they want, and how they live. Their speeches and writings are privileged access to their consciousness. I examine the words and themes most important to them so I will have reality-materials for the class studies. (Shor & Freire, p. 9).

Through listening, we can come to know students. The "social texts" that emerge from their conversations with each other and with us present "patterns, motifs, themes, characters, imagery, as clues to meaning" (Shor & Freire, 1987, p. 24). These are the clues that lead us to them so that we may engage with them in the studies of the curriculum.

Travelers to Unimagined Lands

To share community in spite of the roads that separate us, we need to join together in search of a common language:

> This is not an external matter of simply adjusting our tools, nor is it even right to say that the partners adapt themselves to one another but rather, in the successful conversation they both come under the influence of the truth of the object and are thus bound to one another in a new community. To reach an understanding with one's partner in a dialogue is not merely a matter of total self-expression and the successful assertion of one's own point of view, but a transformation into a communion, in which we do not remain what we were. (Gadamer, 1975, p. 341)

Learning together in dialogue transforms knowers and the known. We come into knowing and being in the world, says Grumet (1992), out of the dialogue we have with the world of our experience. Peer conversation is a supportive venue for students to grapple with personal and generational concerns. Together they can seek the conversation that will guide them through the mystery that they themselves are, or, in Husserlian fashion, inspect the conversation that each of them is, to approach the mystery of language (Gadamer, 1975). Shared stories spill over into one other, reinforcing, refuting, changing each other. They mingle together transformingly, an ideal way for (young) children to begin learning that there are many stories that can be theirs, and many lands that they can call their own.

We have looked at some striking properties of high school student conversation: its "literacy;" its textuality; its attachment to temporal and situational context; its poetry. We have seen video as a means of generating conversation where distance would forbid, of confronting and penetrating borders normally hostile to interpersonal interaction. We have looked at the echo carrying meaning across place and time; reflective and resonant and indicating meaning beyond itself. Careful listening can yield for students and their teachers a renewed sensitivity to the diversity of life experience and cultural consciousness.

As teachers and researchers we can become facilitators in what bell hooks (1994) calls a "coming to voice," which she explains as "not just the act of telling one's experience [but] using that telling strategically—to come to voice so that you can also speak freely about other subjects" (p. 148). Putting words to experience is tantamount to reflective action, the criterion for self-determination. Teachers who aspire to guide students toward these ends will find their work easier once they allow for student voice as classroom text. Only then can forms of life and language be shared.

_____ *References* _____

Bakhtin, M. M. (1986). *Speech genres and other late essays.* Austin, TX: University of Texas Press.

Bourdieu, P. (1993). *Sociology in question.* London: Sage.

Bruner, J. (1986). *Actual minds, possible worlds.* Cambridge, MA: Harvard University Press.

Cazden, C. B. (1988). *Classroom discourse: The language of teaching and learning.* Portsmouth, NH: Heinemann.

Derrida, J. (1976). *Of grammatology* (G. C. Spivak, Trans.) Baltimore: Johns Hopkins University Press.

Eisner, E. (1994). *Cognition and curriculum reconsidered.* New York: Teachers College Press.

Gadamer, H-G. (1975). *Truth and method.* New York: Continuum.

Geertz, C. (1983). Blurred genres: The refiguration of social thought. In *Local knowledge: Further essays in interpretive anthropology.* New York: Basic Books.

Greene, M. (1986). Landscapes and meaning. *Language Arts, 63*(8), 776–781.

Grumet, M. R. (1992). Existential and phenomenological foundations of autobiographical methods. In W. F. Pinar & W. M. Reynolds

(Eds.), *Understanding curriculum as phenomenological and deconstructed text* (pp. 28–43). New York: Teachers College Press. (Original work published in the 1970s)

Gumperz, J. J. (1977). Sociocultural knowledge in conversational inference. In M. Saville-Troike (Ed.), *Linguistics and anthropology* (pp. 191–212). (Georgetown University Round Table on Languages and Linguistics.) Washington, DC: Georgetown University Press.

Heath, S. B. (1983). *Ways with words: Language, life, and work in communities and classroms.* New York: Cambridge University Press.

Holquist, M. (1990). *Dialogism: Bakhtin and his world.* London: Routledge.

hooks, b. (1994). *Teaching to transgress: Education as the practice of freedom.* New York: Routledge.

Jefferson, M. (1995, March 26). A journey to a mysterious country: The mind. In *Arts and Leisure. The New York Times,* p. 7.

Kochman, T. (1981). *Black and White: Styles in conflict.* Chicago: University of Chicago Press.

Ricoeur, P. (1981). *Hermeneutics and the human sciences.* New York: New Directions.

Ricoeur, P. (1991). *From text to action.* Evanston, IL: Northwestern University Press.

Rosen, H. (1984). *Stories and meanings.* Sheffield, England: National Association for the Teaching of English.

Rosenblatt, L. (1978). *The reader, the text, the poem: The transactional theory of the literary work.* Carbondale, IL: Southern Illinois University Press.

Shor, I., & Freire, P. (1987). *A pedagogy for liberation: Dialogues on transforming education.* South Hadley, MA: Bergin & Garvey.

Tannen, D. (1989). *Talking voices: Repetition, dialogue, and imagery in conversational discourse.* Cambridge: Cambridge University Press.

Vygotsky, L. S. (1978). *Mind in society. The development of higher psychological processes.* In M. Cole et al. (Eds.), Cambridge, MA: Harvard University Press.

Watson, D. J. (1993). Community meaning: Personal knowing within a social place. In K. M. Pierce & C. J. Gilles (Eds.), *Cycles of meaning: Exploring the potential of talk in learning communities* (pp. 3–15). Portsmouth, NH: Heinemann.

Wittgenstein, L. (1973). *Philosophical investigations.* (G.E.M. Anscombe, Trans.). New York: Macmillan.

28

STREET LITERACY

Dwight Conquergood

NORTHWESTERN UNIVERSITY

What I'm writing here
Is the heart
Broken in half

> Ghetto Boy explaining to Dwight Conquergood a
> graffito symbol he has just drawn on a Chicago
> rooftop wall during videotaping of the documentary
> *The Heart Broken in Half*

(Conquergood, & Siegel, 1990; see Plate 28–1).

Gang graffiti is vilified by outsiders as a spectacle of filth, scene of vandalism, both symptom and source of social disorder and decay. In the middle-class imaginary, it is a metonym for incivility and barbarism: "wild, graffito-like scratchings" (Freedberg, 1989, p. 425). Ghetto Boy, however, subversively reframed graffiti as "writing." With this assertion, he contested official control over the meanings and interpretations of literacy by disrupting its associations with refinement and the educated person. Ghetto Boy's metacommunicative statement unsettled the literate–illiterate hierarchy that naturalizes class privilege and supports the uneven distribution of

PLATE 28–1

cultural capital (see Marvin, 1994; Bourdieu, 1984). According to official definitions of literacy, "graffit writing" is an oxymoron, and the hooligan who "commits graffiti" is the anathema of a literate person.

Recent ethnographic studies of literacy open a space for Ghetto Boy's expansion of what counts as writing (Street, 1994; Boyarin, 1993). Invigorated by ethnographic theories and field methods, this new literacy research has four distinguishing features: (1) it foregrounds the politics of literacy, focusing on how it is implicated in the distribution of power and authority; (2) it shifts emphasis from abstract standards to concrete practices of literacy, a shift from normative to performative literacy; (3) it dismantles the orality–literacy dichotomy that dominated previous literacy research (Goody, 1986; Olson, 1994; Ong, 1982) and emphasizes the overlap, exchange, and interaction between oral and literate channels of communication within specific contexts; (4) it abandons the conformist ideal of a singular literacy, opening the door to multiple and nonstandard literacy practices, variously called "local literacies," "vernacular literacies," and "grassroots literacies" (see Street, 1994; Fabian, 1993). In recognition of the conceptual replenishment that a political perspective brought to literacy research, this new approach was named the "ideological model" of literacy (Street, 1994). Rockhill (1994, p. 171) sets forth the tenets of the ideological model: "The construction of literacy is embedded in the discursive practices and power relationships of everyday life: it is socially constructed, materially produced, morally regulated, and carries with it a symbolic significance which cannot be captured by its reduction to any one of these."

My ethnography of Chicago gang graffiti writing builds upon the ideological model of literacy but pushes it into even more radical territory. "Local" and "vernacular" are not strong enough adjectives to capture the moral outrage and repression that this literacy practice provokes. Graffiti writing is a counterliteracy that challenges, mimics, and carnivalizes the "textual power" (Scholes, 1985) that underwrites private ownership of property and the regulation, control, and policing of public space. This outlawed literacy grotesquely mirrors and mocks the literate bureaucracy that administers licenses, receipts, badges, diplomas, ordinances, arrest warrants, green cards, and other deeds of power and possession. What distinguishes graffiti writing from other subaltern literacies is its criminalization: more than an illegitimate literacy, it is illegal. To understand the complicated meanings of this counterliteracy, it must be situated within the discursive and visual practices of power and control that it struggles against.

THE VISUAL PREDICAMENT OF GANG CULTURE

Gang graffiti writing is a very ambivalent form of visual communication that pivots on a dialectic between display and disguise, visibility and veiling, spectacle and secrecy; it is communication that is simultaneously conspicuous and camouflaged. Street youth go to great lengths and risk to make spectacles out of their writing on the wall even as they take care to mask their messages. This ocular paradox is rooted in and a response to the visual politics of the dominant culture. Donna Haraway reminds us that "vision is *always* a question of the power to see—and ... the violence implicit in our visualizing practices" (1991, p. 192). Like most subordinate groups, street youths suffer from both too little visibility, and too much visibility. Either they are willed to disappear or they are rendered hypervisible within the scopic regimes of power. They are shuttled back and forth between erasure and exposure, being ignored and being exhibited by the ruling classes. Postcolonial critic Homi K. Bhabha (1994, p. 236) speaks of "the marginalized, the displaced, the diasporic" whose "very presence is both 'overlooked'—in the double sense of social surveillance and psychic disavowal— and, at the same time, overdetermined—psychically projected, made stereotypical and symptomatic."

Street youth are articulate about mainstream visual practices that refuse to see and recognize them. Chiquito, an "illegal alien" [sic] from Guatemala who also happens to be a member of the Almighty Latin King Nation of Chicago, protested:

We want to be recognized.
We want to be seen—not shoved to the side.
In the eyes of people,
We are the criminals, the drug dealers.

His words resonate with those of the protagonist of Ralph Ellison's novel *Invisible Man* who expressed the existential strain of living with relentless effacement, "you often doubt if you really exist" (1952, p. 4), and explained it as a socially constructed and political act of exclusion: "I am invisible, understand, simply because people refuse to see me. ... When they approach me, they see only my surroundings, themselves, or figments of their imagination—indeed, everything and anything except me" (p. 3). Adrienne Rich (1986, p. 199) affirms that "invisibility is a dangerous and painful condition. ... When those who have power to name and to socially construct reality choose not to see or hear you ... there is a moment of psychic disequilibrium, as if you looked into a mirror and saw nothing."

The politics of who is visible and who is invisible are embedded in the politics of literacy and textual bureaucracy, what Michel de Certeau (1984, p. 140) named "intextuation." In addition to the fact that Chiquito is poor, young, orphaned, and a person of color, another reason that he must struggle just for simple recognition of his humanity—the everyday acknowledgements that a white, middle-class person can take for granted—is that he is "undocumented," he has neither green card nor social security number, he is one of the phantom people *sin papeles* (without papers). His elder sister, Maria, who at the age of 20 became the head of the family of four siblings after her mother's death, also complained:

Dwight, I can't be going around telling people I don't have papers.
You don't know how much that hurts us,
Not having papers. I had that good job in the factory—processing chickens—
And I was making $350 a week,
And I lost that job
Because I don't have papers.

It is no wonder that *Shadow* is one of the most common tags, nicknames, that Chicago street youth take for themselves.

Although these so-called "undocumented aliens" are denied papers that would enable them to secure nonexploitative employment, they, with cruel irony, are heavily "documented" by the police and legal system. On May 1, 1992, I testified in court to forestall deportation proceedings against Chiquito. The prosecutor presented a bulging file of papers that documented the 26 times Chiquito had been arrested for misdemeanors, most of them Disorderly Conduct, which Chiquito explained to me, "That means walking down the street if you're a person who looks like me—I just be walking down the street," or Mob Action, which he translated, "That means standing on a street corner with your friends." As the prosecutor displayed the fat file of Chiquito's documented transgressions, Maria astutely observed: "They just look at his file, not his face." When the identity of street youth and that of their families and neighborhoods is continuously erased or exiled to shadowy margins, then writing in illegal letters on the wall, "Here the Sun Shines," is Chiquito's brave gesture of refusal to a regime of power that banishes all of his kind from view, and, quite *literally,* has initiated deportation proceedings against him (see Plate 28–2).

The insult of effacement is compounded by surveillance. In the ocular politics of the ruling classes, subordinate groups are expunged from spaces of respectability, and then rendered hypervisible in the surreal zone of panoptic power (Foucault, 1977). Susan Buck-Morse (1989, p. 347) observed: "For the oppressed ... existence in public space is more likely to be synonymous with state surveillance, public censure, and political powerlessness." They are specularized and spectacularized in myriad and demeaning ways. The intimate spaces of their homes and bodies are overexposed. Once, a tactical squad of police officers kicked in the door of Chiquito and Maria's apartment, confusing it with that of one big-time drug dealer. While officers held guns to their heads, including 4-year-old Juanita's, police ransacked their humble

PLATE 28–2

furnishings: they pulled out and dumped dresser drawers, rifled through closets, emptied cabinets, stripped beds, overturned furniture, opened cushions, ripped off the backs of the television set and the stereo, pulled apart toys, fingered through family photograph albums, broke framed pictures. Having satisfied themselves that these Guatemalan youngsters were not major criminals, the law enforcement officers left without cleaning up the mess, leaving behind a baseball bat (one of their break-in tools) to add to the clutter. I arrived on the scene soon after Maria, still stunned by the assault, called me. Almost every inch of their homespace had been physically searched right down to Maria's carefully nursed plants, which had been uprooted and the flower pots spilled.

Even the personal space of the body is not safe from mandatory exposure. Body frisks and pat-downs often are preludes to strip searches. Since marijuana dealers sometimes conceal contraband in their underwear, Chicago police use this information as an excuse to pull down the pants of youth they stop on the street or in the park. This unauthorized police practice is more about public humiliation than the control of marijuana trafficking. Several of my neighbors and friends in the Big Red tenement—(where I lived during the early months of fieldwork, see Conquergood 1992a)—complained to me that police officers had deliberately pulled down their shorts in front of their girlfriends, sisters, and mothers, in order to embarrass them. Like the grotesquely invasive body searches that are part of the induction into jail and prison, these street strips function as degradation rituals in which the most private parts of street youth are subjected to the "compulsory visibility" of the state (Feldman 1991, p. 173). When I would return in the evening to my apartment in the Big Red tenement, I never became accustomed to the frequently encountered and eerie spectacle of half a dozen youths, most of whom I knew and tutored, spreadeagled against the wall while the hands of the state searched their bodies.

State surveillance is mimed and proliferated by the visual vigilance of private citizens. Chicago community councils, homeowners' associations, and block clubs form pervasive "Neighborhood Watch" groups with telephone trees and hotlines to police stations (see plates 28–3, 28–4). These grassroots scopic campaigns are set up to see some people and complexions in sharper focus than others, a class and color-coded way of seeing that is not lost on the youth themselves:

> How do you think that makes us feel, Dwight,
> When we see all those signs with eyes up in the windows of those fine houses?
> 'Warning
> Neighborhood Watch
> WE CALL POLICE'
> That means
> NO BLACK TEENAGERS ALLOWED IN THIS NEIGHBORHOOD.
> That's what those signs be saying.

These glaring signs of surveillance stand in stark contrast to the optics of intimacy that are captured in a phrase of leave-taking common in latino neighborhoods: "nos vemos," "we will see each other." *Nos vemos* expresses a supportive way of seeing that is connected to the security of togetherness and mutual affirmation, not the security of property and the state.

The hypervisibility and objectification of street youth are extended by new surveillance and computer mapping technologies that consolidate massive data bases on street gangs. Hidden cameras monitor public spaces and entrap graffiti writers. Chicago police use night-sensor goggles recycled from the Persian Gulf War to search and seize gang members after dark. These arrest records, along with an array of other information—addresses of those arrested, addresses of those recently released from prison, telephoned complaints of private citizens, as well as information compiled by

PLATE 28–3

neighborhood watch and community groups—are stored in geo-coded databases, "geo-archives." The technology-driven scrutiny, documentation, and mapping of the movements of street youth and other stigmatized groups are accelerating. The Illinois Criminal Justice Information Authority has developed Spatial and Temporal Analysis of Crime (STAC) computer mapping software, which it promotes through workshops, conferences, and a widely circulated newsletter, *STAC News*. According to Rebecca Block (1991, p. 15) of the

PLATE 28–4

Authority's Statistical Analysis Center, "Computer mapping technology, coupled with the technology necessary to store and organize vast amounts of geo-coded data, has expanded extremely rapidly in the last year or two, and there is no end to the expansion in sight."

When street youth are subjected to search warrants, strip searches, fingerprinting, and an array of invasive visual technologies, when the human face of their experience is displaced by a mug shot, then densely coded, creatively masked communication and secrecy provide a refuge from the gaze of gang squads and tactical units, a shield against the surveillance of panoptic powers. Dick Hebdige captures the creative response to these optical dilemmas with the conundrum that aptly titles his book on youth subcultures, *Hiding in the Light* (1988, p. 35): "Subculture forms up in the space between surveillance and the evasion of surveillance, it translates the fact of being under scrutiny into the pleasure of being watched. It is a hiding in the light."

The fingerprint is in many ways emblematic of the optics of domination. It is an ocularcentric documentation of the presence, the touch, of transgressive bodies for penal purposes of discipline and control. Most of the time, subaltern groups are unable to register their presence in mainstream spaces. However, within the space of law enforcement and prosecution, their silent, tactile traces are pressed into harsh visibility and rendered severely legible. It is within this context of ocular politics and the criminalization of the subordinate classes that graffiti writing needs to be understood as 'fingerprints in your face.'

When the technology of fingerprinting transcodes the embodied touch of a living person into a legible text for visual perusal and inspection, it mimes the "intersemiotic translation" (Fine, 1984) of dominant literacy that transposes embodied oral performance, the spoken word, into a visual text, what Johannes Fabian (1993, p. 87) called "disembodied literacy." Carolyn Marvin (1994, p. 129) affirmed: "A mark of literate competence is skill in disguising or erasing the contributions of one's own body to the process of textual production and practice." New computer technology further disembodies the fingerprinting process as digital biometric scanners replace the press of flesh from inkpad onto paper. Graffiti writing as counterliteracy disrupts "the disembodied bourgeois text" (Marvin, 1994, p. 141), reconnects letters with bodies, and reincarnates writing. Although graffiti texts communicate complex and coded messages to other gang members (Conquergood, 1994a), most outsiders are not versed in the code and cannot read them for content in the same way that they read conventional texts. Their disturbing impact on middle-class citizens is derived from their indexical force, not their referential meaning. Property owners react to graffiti writing with revulsion because they viscerally experience it as a flagrantly sensuous sign of gang *presence,* as the contaminating touch of grotesque bodies out of place. They describe it in body-charged imagery: a wound, scar, defacement, violation, rape, excrement, human sewage, the territorial markings of a wild animal. While most mainstream texts dispassionately foreground referential meaning and hide the historical-material and embodied operations of text-production, graffiti writing seethes with and is haunted by the performing presence of its producers. It is reviled and feared precisely for being the polluting point of corporeal contact in the "metonymic chain of contagion" that leads back to the dangerous classes (Stallybrass, & White 1986, p. 138). In *Crimes of Writing*, Stewart (1991, p. 226) observed that graffiti, unlike pornography, was not "a crime of content" but "a crime in mode of production."

Graffiti gives new meaning to Mary Louise Pratt's (1992) study of the "contact zone" as an intercultural space of friction, struggle, and resistance that stimulates new genres of writing that mimic and subvert dominant rhetorics of power. She speaks of

> the possibilities and perils of writing in ... 'contact zones,' social spaces where disparate cultures meet, clash, and grapple with each other, often in highly asymmetrical relations of domination and subordination—like colonialism, slavery, and their aftermaths as they are lived out across the globe today. (p. 4; see also Mignolo, 1995)

Gang graffiti writing performatively constitutes middle-class and public spaces into contested zones of contact, site-specific theaters of defiance where excluded others re-present themselves. It is interesting to note that in Chicago the street term for writing graffiti and other displays of gang identity is "reppin'," short for *representing* (Conquergood, 1992b). Graffiti writing articulates cross-class antagonisms by bodily *contact* with, touching, public space and private property. In doing so, it upends the hierarchy of the senses: sight, the highest sense, is collapsed into touch, the lowest sense (Gilman, 1991, p. 32), a reversal of the fingerprinting process. While official literacy is associated with detachment, distance, disclosure, and a scene of solo production and reception— (writing and reading are typically figured as private, contemplative activities)—graffiti writing is characterized by contact, coding, collaboration, and collusion.

GANGSTER GRAMMATOLOGY

In addition to its intense body-consciousness and performative aspects, graffiti writing has a number of other features that uncannily resemble Derrida's grammatology project. Ulmer (1985) explicates Derrida's "grammatology" project—his later creative experiments with writing and stylistic innovations—and sets it against his earlier and enormously influential program of philosophical studies known as "deconstruction." A distinguishing hallmark of grammatology is its trickster disruption of boundaries and transmodal jostlings, particularly the way it plays with and across the border between words and pictures, its grafting of visual items onto verbal texts. Ulmer (pp. 98, 99) identified this "intermedia" coarticulation of both verbal and nonverbal materials as "double-valued Writing, ideographic and phonetic at once." Influenced by studies of Mayan hieroglyphics and other non-Western writing systems, Derrida (1976, p. 90) described grammatology as "picto-ideo-phonographic" writing.

Graffiti writing likewise irreverently mixes and mingles visual and verbal modes of communication, transposing,

to create hybrid scripts. These playful, intricate, and elaborate transfusions between semiotic systems are, of course, key strategies for encrypting and hiding messages from the uninitiated. But the sheer creativity and boundless signifying energy of graffiti exceed the need to simply mask and conceal. There is a strong pleasure dynamic to graffiti writing. Street youth revel in the pleasures of underground semiosis, they take intense delight—as both performers and audience—in the kinetic energies of "breaking and remaking" the codes of master discourse (Conquergood, 1992c, p. 84; see also Gates, 1988; Gilroy, 1995). Gang graffiti writing is oppositional and transgressive, to be sure, but it is not formless or disorganized. Like other guerrilla formations, it has its own internal structure and highly efficient strategies for mobilizing meaning. Whatever else one wants to say about gang youth, one cannot say that they are unstructured or disorganized.

Structuralism in the Streets

Street literacy embraces three signifying modes: the alphabetic, iconographic, and corporeal. Plates 28–5 and 28–6 spell out complete words, "King Love" and "Queen Love." This straightforward graffiti proclaims the ethos of solidarity, camaraderie, and bonding that are key to gang *esprit de corps*. They are examples of the poeticizing and eroticizing of space, what I have discussed elsewhere as the transformation of bleak, benighted inner city terrain into a "hood," an intimate space of warmth, familiarity, and intense fellowship (Conquergood, 1994a). They also are metadiscursive statements: all forms of gang *representing* ("reppin'"), including graffiti writing, are interpreted by participants as expressions of love, "throwing up our love": in the words of Latino Boy, "we write our love on the wall."

Straightforward spelling of complete words is actually the exception, rather than the norm, of gang graffiti writing. A more common alphabetic form is the construction of gang logos, by using the initial letters of a gang name, that function as acronyms. An example is the "ALKQN" on the left side of Plate 28–6, which stands for Almighty Latin Kings and Queens Nation. Plate 28–7 demonstrates the coarticulated display of these three aspects of graffiti writing. The LK

PLATE 28–6

PLATE 28–7

letters constitute the logo for the Latin Kings. The figure of the crown between the letters "L" and "K" is the icon that stands for the Latin Kings. The figure inside the shield underneath the crown is the pictorial representation of the embodied hand-sign of the crown. The two images of the crown, one iconographic, the other a pictograph of the corporeal hand-sign of the crown, are, in effect, mirror images of each other, albeit on different registers (Plate 28–8). Plate 28–9 is a photograph of the corporeal performance of making the crown handsign, in street argot called, "throwing up the crown." Note that Chiquito is wearing a tee shirt that advertises Corona beer. The Corona beer advertising campaign is of course, means "crown" in Spanish, and the colors, gold and black, are the emblematic colors of the Latin Kings. (The street term for signifying gang allegiance by wearing, for example, black and gold, is "flying the colors.") John Fiske (1989, p. 15) coined the term "excorporation" to describe how subordinate cultures raid, refashion, and redeploy mainstream symbols for subversive ends. By strategically wearing the "Corona" tee shirt while performing the embodied handsign, Chiquito achieves the same doubling effect seen in Plate 28–8, although this time the modes are corporeal and alphabetic. He is also "signifying" on a commercial product associated with yuppies and upscale culture (see

PLATE 28–8

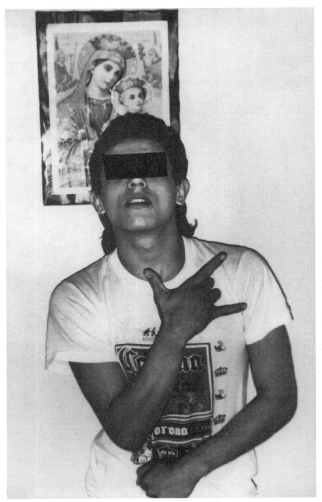

PLATE 28–9

In addition to delight in doubling, elaboration, and embellishment, gangster grammatology is characterized by turnings, flips, indirection, intricacy, and affirmation by negation. This complex and multichannelled play of symbols is structured along an agonistic division between two hostile factions. Most gangs in Chicago are aligned with one of the two supergang confederations: the People Nation, or the Folks Nation (for more detailed discussion of gang organizations, see Conquergood, 1994a). This binary opposition underpins all gang communication and provides a basic grid for particular graffiti. Since the Gangster Disciples is the largest gang in Illinois, its icon, the pitchfork, stands in for all Folks Nation gangs. Likewise, the initial "D", for Disciples, stands as a logo for the entire Folks Nation. All People Nation gangs represented by the number 5, such as a five-point star, and Folks Nation gangs by the number 6, such as a six-point star. A common feature of gangster grammatology is the agonistic manipulation of the signifying letters, icons, numbers, and handsigns of the other, hostile nation, in street slang called, "throwing down" the rival nation. These semiotic manipulations fall into three patterns: inversions (turning symbols upside down), reversals (spelling letters backwards), fractures (breaking symbols).

The complexity and sophistication of this signifying system are best illustrated with concrete examples. Plate 28–10 is a graffito written entirely in the alphabetic mode, but eight

of the 13 letters have been either inverted or reversed. It displays the name of a gang member with his gang affiliation and local branch. The first word is GARFIELD, his street tag or nickname, taken from Garfield the cool cat. The most important thing for a street youth to decipher when encountering any graffiti writing in Chicago is, which nation claims this turf? People or Folks? The first letter in "Garfield" would signal immediately to a streetwise youth that this site was People territory. The "G" is reversed because it stands for the Gangsters, aligned with the Folks Nation (Imperial Gangsters and Gangster Disciples are both Folks Nation gangs). The streetwise youth would read the reversed "G" as an indirect way of proclaiming People Nation turf by "throwing down" the emblematic letter of a Folks Nation gang, a common strategy of affirmation by negation. This reading would be corroborated by proceeding through the other letters of GARFIELD. "A" is inverted because, as every streetsmart Chicago youth knows, it stands for Ambrose, another Folks Nation gang. "R" is reversed because it stands for Royals, short for Simon City Royals, one of the largest gangs of the Folks Nation. "F" is reversed, of course, because it stands for Folks. "E" is reversed because it stands for the Latin Eagles, another Folks Nation gang. The inverted "L" and reversed "D" need to be taken together, standing for Latin Disciples, sometimes called Maniac Latin Disciples, a Folks Nation gang. From reading Garfield, a youth would know beyond the shadow of a doubt that he or she was on People Nation turf. From the next unit, a street-literate youth could read the precise identity of the particular People Nation gang, including further detail of the specific branch of the gang. Garfield is a member of the Clark Street and Winnemac Street branch of the Latin Kings gang (the subsection branches of a gang are named after the intersecting streets, the streetcorner, where the homeboys hang out; for more detail about gang organizational structure see Conquergood 1994a). The "C" is reversed to throw down the Insane Spanish Cobras, aligned with the Folks Nation. Note that the "L," previously inverted, escapes defacement because in this unit it stands for the Latin Kings.

While Plate 28–10 was written entirely in the alphabetic mode, Plate 28–11 extends the resources of street literacy into the iconographic mode, and also includes an example of the "fracture" pattern of semiotic defacement. The left panel displays a six-point star fractured by the number 5. From that "graffeme" alone, a streetwise youth would read this section of the park as belonging to the People Nation (I coin the term "graffeme" in order to discuss basic microunits within a complex graffiti text—obviously, I am punning on "grapheme" and other structuralist terms). From the right panel he or she could read the identity of the specific gang, in this case the Latin Kings. The right panel also demonstrates a combination of alphabetic and iconographic modes locked into an affirmation by negation. The unadulterated letters "LK," standing for Latin Kings, are placed strategically on top of the inverted pitchfork, icon of the Disciples, the largest Folks Nation gang.

Plate 28–12 displays another proclamation of Latin Kings' space. This graffiti text draws on top or bottom, up or down

PLATE 28–10

PLATE 28–11

PLATE 28–12

PLATE 28–13

spatial symbolism: the alphabetic "LK" astride an inverted pitchfork and an inverted cross with three dots. A cross with three dots is an icon for Folks Nation gangs, and a cross with two dots is an icon for People Nation gangs. The Old English "LK" is followed by a smaller "ST" for "Street," to punctuate the fact that this specific section of the Latin Kings is the Lawrence and Kedzie streetcorner branch (I lived inside this section for 4½ years; see Conquergood 1992a). The Lawrence and Kedzie homeboys delight in the fact that the letters of their branch duplicate the LK of Latin Kings. Note, also, that the "T" in upper right corner is written as an inverted pitchfork, thus mirroring the inverted icon in the lower left corner.

Plate 28–13 displays an elaborated variation of the same Latin Kings proclamations that we have seen in Plates 28–5 to 28–12 (with the exception of Plate 28–10, all these photographs were taken within two blocks of the Big Red tenement). At the top of the left panel is the word "AMOR," which, of course, is Spanish for "love" that we saw spelled out in plates 28–5 and 28–6. In addition to that explicit meaning, there is a hidden meaning. Latin Kings gang members confided to me that "AMOR" also stands for Almighty Masters of Revolution, thus making it a true acronym, and adding another level of meaning to the politics of language. The O in AMOR is actually an inverted O or A fusion, which is the logo of Orchestra Albany, a Folks Nation gang. The reversed R we have seen already in Plate 28–10, and would read this as "throwing down" the Simon City Royals gang. Note that in this graffeme the "A" is not inverted, but it could have been, as we saw in Plate 28–10. There is always room for choice, variation, and innovation within this signifying system.

The centerpiece of this panel depicts the drama of two rival crowns locked in conflict, and counterbalanced by four opposing icons. The dominant crown on top is the icon of the Latin Kings that we would recognize from Plate 28–7. It

stands astride another crown, but the bottom crown is of a different style, and it is inverted. The bottom crown is the icon of the Imperial Gangsters, a Folks Nation gang that has excorporated the crown of the Imperial Margarine brand logo (see Plate 28–14). Note the same reversed G that we saw in Plate 28–10 inserted into the middle of the inverted crown, a grafting of the alphabetic onto the iconographic mode. The two icons on top of the crowns are the five-point star, an icon for all People Nation gangs for which the number 5 is sacred, and a dandy's cane, one of the icons for the Vice Lords. The Latin Kings and the Vice Lords are the two largest gangs of the People Nation. By inserting the cane in a spatially privileged section of this text, that is, the top half, the Latin Kings who wrote this text are signaling solidarity with their Vice Lords brothers. The two counterbalancing icons in the bottom, polluted space of this text, are, on the left, an inverted cross with three dots, which, we remember from Plate 28–12, is an icon for all Folks Nation gangs, and an inverted diamond transected by a horizontal S, the icon of the Insane Spanish Cobras, a Folks Nation gang.

PLATE 28–14

The middle panel displays a more complex five-pointed crown, which is actually the more commonly used icon of the Latin Kings. The choice of crown styles, either three-point or five-point, is another example of variation even within a highly structured system. The choice not available for a graffiti writer aligned with the People Nation would be a six-point crown because that would signify allegiance with the Folks Nation. One of the reasons a five-point crown is slightly preferred to the three-point style is that its points enumerate the five cardinal virtues of the Almighty Latin King Nation: Love, Honor, Obedience, Sacrifice, and Righteousness. To punctuate the fact that this icon also functions as a mnemonic device for the five sacred values, note the dots drawn above each of the five points of the crown. Also note the number 5 emblazoned on the crown. The word KINGS is spelled out underneath the crown, an example of the alphabetic mode underlining the iconographic mode, and there is

a numerological significance to the fact that KINGS is a five-letter word.

The right panel features a large polluted icon, inverted pitchfork of the Folks Nation, counterbalanced by alphabetic inscriptions. The ALKN on top stands for Almighty Latin Kings Nation. The reversed D at the bottom stands, of course, for the Disciples, largest gang of the Folks Nation. On the other side, separated by the middle tine of the pitchfork, is a K. It has not been reversed; it mirrors the K on top, and the Ks we have seen in previous plates, which stood for Kings. However, that reading is not possible because of the spatial position within the text of this particular K. As it is in the polluted bottom space, alongside the reversed D and inverted pitchfork, this K cannot stand for Kings. It stands for Killers. The reversed D and the K actually comprise a single graffeme; they must be read together as Disciple Killers, a grim example of affirmation by negation.

Four alphabetic graffemes on a boarded-up window of the Big Red tenement display this same stark strategy of affirmation by negation (see Plate 28–15). By now it would be clear to the reader that Big Red is located in the heart of Latin King turf, particularly the Lawrence and Kedzie branch of the Latin Kings gang. Plate 28–15 demonstrates how the Latin Kings at this site affirm their identity against enemies. Each graffeme combines a reversed letter that stands for a rival Folks Nation gang, followed by K which stands for Killers (note that the K is grafted onto the reversed letters in the top two graffemes). Reading from left to right and top to bottom, this graffiti panel proclaims Big Red as located in the territory of [Gangster] Disciple Killers, [Latin] Eagles Killers, [Simon City] Royals Killers and [Insane] Popes Killers. There is also a local history behind the choice to desecrate these particular four gangs, out of all the dozens of possible Folks Nation gangs that could have been targeted at this proclamation. As a resident of Big Red I was aware that the selection of

PLATE 28–15

PLATE 28–16

PLATE 28–17

PLATE 28–19

PLATE 28–18

killed allegedly by a member of the Latin Eagles and whose memory is inscribed in the top right graffeme.

Just four blocks west of the Big Red tenement is Kimball Street, the dividing line between People Nation and Folks Nation territory in this section of northwest Chicago. The photographs in Plates 28–16 to 28–18 were taken on the west side of Kimball Street, on the Folks Nation side. Plate 28–16 shows the icon of the pitchfork standing right side up, alongside the letters MLD, which stand for the Maniac Latin Disciples. Plate 28–17 proclaims the territory of the Insane Spanish Cobras Nation in both alphabetic and iconographic modes, with the icon of the diamond transected by the horizontal S grafted on to the letter N. Plate 28–18 proclaims the turf of the Simon City Royals Nation with the Folks icon of the cross with three dots astride inverted icons and letters of the Vice Lords. It is interesting that in the bottom polluted half of this graffiti text the letters V and L for Vice Lords have been both inverted and reversed, a double defacement. The top hat and cane, Vice Lord icons, likewise have been inverted, and, to clinch the desecration, an inverted 5 has been emblazoned on the inverted top hat.

Plates 28–19 to 28–21 all are graffiti writings of the word FOLKS, but written on different turfs. Any streetwise youth

PLATE 28–20

these four rival gangs was not random. Each graffeme represented the name of an enemy gang allegedly responsible for the killing of a local Latin King homeboy. "Local knowledge" (Geertz, 1983) enables one to read particular stories and commemorations out of this panel. I knew and went to the funerals of most of the youths whose murders were marked by these graffemes; I tutored the young Latin King who was

PLATE 28–21

PLATE 28–22

would know that the rendition of FOLKS in Plate 28–19 was written on Folks Nation turf because the second letter, O, doubles as a six-point star. This interpretation is reinforced immediately by the third letter, a reversed L, which signals that the third and fourth letters, LK, are to be read as a graffeme that throws down the Latin Kings. Plate 28–20 is the same word FOLKS, but written on People Nation territory, specifically Latin Kings gang turf. The F is inverted to pollute the Folks Nation, the O is written as an inverted O or A fusion, the logo of the Orchestra Albany Folks Nation gang. While the L was reversed in Plate 28–19, it is unadulterated in this text and separated by a hyphen from the following letter K to highlight the fact that these two letters are to be read as a separate graffeme affirming the Latin Kings. The alphabetic rendering of Folks towers over two polluted icons of the Folks Nation. On the left, there is the inverted icon of the Insane Spanish Cobras that we have seen before. The inverted icon on the right is quite interesting because it represents an innovation that we have not seen in previous plates. It is an inverted pitchfork, but if you look closely, each one of the three tines is punctuated by a dot, thus transforming the pitchfork into a cross with three dots, another popular icon of the Folks Nation. The pitchfork and the cross with three dots have been conflated in this double inversion. The name

Chiquito spelled out at the right identifies the writer or creator of this text. Note that the T in Chiquito doubles as an inverted pitchfork.

Plate 28–21 represents another innovation on how a Latin Kings gang member writes the word Folks. This vertical writing in the alphabetic mode quite creatively draws on spatial symbolism to intensify affirmation by negation strategy. The F for Folks suffers a triple negation: it is inverted, reversed, and placed at the bottom of this column of letters. The LK, for Latin Kings, almost jumps off the column as this graffeme surges toward the top. This style of vertical writing was developed as a creative response to the limitations and possibilities of utility poles as surfaces for inscription (see Plate 28–22).

These inventive, playful, and intensifying innovations within the basic signifying system are deeply meaningful to street youth. Gang graffiti writers love to talk about their rhetorical art and to comment on the level of skill and creativity of other writers. Several times during the course of my fieldwork I have been taken on walking tours down back alleys and underneath bridges where articulate gang members take pride and pleasure in delivering detailed and insightful commentary on various graffiti walls in a presentational style that resembles that of docents at art galleries and museums. Although these "gallery" tours are typically organized for my benefit, they always attract an appreciative audience of other gang members who, although cognoscenti of the streets, never tire of hearing graffiti texts explained, discussed, and contextualized. Audience members monitor the performance of the "docent" and interject comments that enrich, or sometimes contest, the "docent's" commentary. If the "docent" does not have the requisite cultural authority, he or she will be quickly replaced by a more knowledgeable member of the audience who steps forward and takes over the role.

Scripting in the Streets

Although I have tracked through several graffiti texts in order to illustrate the structural conventions and complexity of this writing system, gangster grammatology exceeds the "model of the text" (Ricoeur, 1972) and pushes toward performance. According to Ulmer (1985, pp. xii, xiii):

> Grammatology as composition (Writing) is not confined to books and articles, but is addressed more comprehensively to the needs of multichanneled performance.... Writing as Derrida practices it could be called Scripting.... It is to the program of grammatology what a screenplay is to a film—a set of descriptions and directions which for its full effect must be 'enacted.'

Gang graffiti constitutes embodied, performative writing at every level of production and reception. Even as literal inscriptions on material surfaces we have seen how they are

read by mainstream authorities as dangerous scripts haunted with the performing presence of transgressive bodies and portents of more to come. Gang graffiti points to the scene of enactment and connects with performance on three levels: collaborative writing as ensemble staging; reciprocal doublings between bodies and buildings; interpretive collusions and the play of reading.

Collaborative writing as ensemble staging. While official literacy education enjoins linear activities of solo writing and silent reading, graffiti writing is a dynamic group performance characterized by complex interactions among the participants where oral and literate modes of communication are in constant exchange (see Plate 28–23; see also Camitta 1993; Shuman 1993). The borders between writing and reading, production and reception, actors and audience, collapse as questions, commentary, criticism, and suggestions circulate simultaneously and continuously throughout the collaborative event of "making a wall," "putting up a wall,"—(also called "piece," "set," "envelope," the street terms for graffiti writing). The coperformers are mutually supportive of one another's efforts, but are not shy about counterbalancing praise and criticism. The evaluative terms alternate between "fresh" and "phony": the former bespeaks highly skilled execution with a distinctive flair, and the latter refers to work that is amateurish, unimaginative, and careless.

The performance event of "making a wall" is a preeminently social process that requires planning, preparation, cooperation, and carefully coordinated interactions within the team. The paint and tools must be procured; no easy task because the sale of spraypaint and broad-tipped magic markers to minors was banned in Chicago (in 1995, the sale of these items was banned outright). Sites are selected strategically to maximize the impact display of but also with an eye for cover and ease of execution during the actual staging event. Since it is illegal to write graffiti on walls, scouts must be posted to warn of the approach of police or vigilant citizens. Alleys, rooftops, and the undersides of bridges offer sheltered staging grounds, which, when coupled with darkness, enable prolonged group performances that yield some of the most elaborate graffiti displays. But one thing that makes a "piece"

PLATE 28–23

PLATE 28–24

really "fresh" is the daring and challenge posed by the location, the scripting that takes place on the face of public facades, 'in the face' of heavy surveillance. The complementary "set" in Plate 28–24 is appreciated for its panache within the performance community of the local homeboys because the graffiti panels jump out from the well lighted facade of a busy shopping mall. The Latin Kings letters and icons on this building compete with other signs of proprietorship. The spacing of the panels creates a dramatic tension and magnitude of scale but can also be explained in terms of constraints of execution within such a busy, public place. The writer of the fractured six-point star on the left selected a panel that was near the alley, thus offering a quick exit. The writer of the LK astride an inverted pitchfork on the right likewise selected a panel near an intersection with multiple escape routes.

The danger of getting caught heightens the need for secrecy and contributes to the drama, excitement, and esprit de corps of these ensemble performances. It also encourages the development of considerable technical skill and improvisational savvy. The deft strokes, efficient movements, and well orchestrated interactions are based on endless rehearsals of solidarity, called "hanging out together" or "hanging together," in which the art of "doing things together" gets finely tuned (see Becker, 1986). The art of scripting in the streets pivots on the ability to adapt to local environment, work with found materials, perform under pressure, and collaboratively improvise solutions to technical problems (see Plate 28–25; see also Harrison-Pepper, 1990; Schechner, 1993). It is an example of what de Certeau (1984, pp. xiv, 29) called "makeshift creativity," a mobile art of "making do."

Reciprocal doublings between bodies and buildings. We have already seen in Plate 28–7 how graffiti writing copied the corporeal performance of "throwing up the crown." Like the facades of buildings, the surfaces of the body are transformed into a mise-en-scene for performing gang identity, "reppin'." The body becomes a mirror and mobile extension of graffiti writing on buildings. The same People Nation-Folks Nation agon is transcoded onto the body in terms of left side of the body associated with People Nation and right side of the body aligned with Folks Nation. The left-right distinction is from the point of view of the actor; it is stage left, and stage right. For example, the bill of a baseball cap is raked to the left to 'rep' affiliation with People Nation gangs, and to the right for Folks Nation gangs. In addition to tattoos (Plates 28–26, 28–27), there are myriad ways of using the body to 'rep' gang nation affiliation: a belt buckle left of center for People Nation, and right of center for Folks Nation, an earring in left or right ear, a jacket tossed over the left shoulder or the right shoulder, jeans torn on the left or right leg, a pants pocket pulled out on the left or right side, wearing bib overalls with one strap up and the other unbuckled and dangling, wearing a colorcoded bandana handkerchief in the left or right rear pocket, hair braided down on one side and left unbraided on the other side, a tattoo on the left or right shoulder or thigh, standing "in position" with either the left or right foot turned out, leaning against a wall in low-rider pose with either the left or right knee bent, and so forth. Street youth transform themselves into "the body of the signifier" and thus participate in what Michel de Certeau (1986, pp. 39, 44) called "the intimacy of Exteriority."

Plate 28–27 demonstrates the reciprocal reppin' ("representing") between buildings and bodies, the mirror extension and reinforcement between alphabetic or iconographic and corporeal modes of street literacy. In addition to the tattoos all over his body, the Latin King standing stage-left to the graffiti written on the wall is reppin' with his body in a

PLATE 28–25

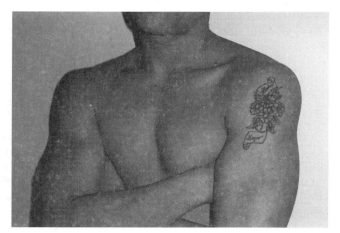

PLATE 28–26

PLATE 28–27

PLATE 28–28

precisely coded way called "crossing up." True to his Latin Kings (People Nation) allegiance, he is "crossing up" to the left by placing his right hand over his *left* wrist, which remains pressed close to his body. Street youth aligned with the Folks Nation would "cross up" to the right by placing the left hand over the *right* wrist. The hand held closest to the body is the one that counts within this corporeal grid of left or right distinctions. A variation of this gestural practice involves crossing the arms so that the right hand grips the left *upper* arm, signifying People Nation alliance, and vice versa for Folks Nation (review Plate 28–2).

The legs and feet also are choreographed to rep' gang identity. The Latin King in Plate 28–28 has turned out his *left*

foot to signify People Nation alignment, which simultaneously displays the Converse tennis shoe logo, a five-point star. Folks Nation gangs also rep' by wearing Converse tennis shoes, but they fold down the flaps, thus breaking the five-point star. Note also that he has laced up five eyelets (Folks Nation gang members lace up six eyelets). Leaving the laces untied is part of street style. When gang members need laces tightened for traction when running from police or rival gangs they will tie the laces behind the heel or underneath the arch of the foot inside the shoe.

Plate 28–29 demonstrates a two-handed way of throwing up the crown. At this point the reader should review Plate 28–9 for a single-handed version of throwing up the crown, but note that the handsign is positioned over the *left* shoulder, a highly meaningful detail. Just as graffiti writing on buildings is a collaborative enterprise, so is the scripting on and with the body often a joint performance. Plates 28–30 and 28–31 enact variants of throwing up the crown: plate 28–30 is the collaborative version of the two-handed crown handsign in Plate 28–29, and Plate 28–31 is the collaborative version of the handsign in Plate 28–9. While throwing up the crown note that both sets of performers are simultaneously throwing down digital inverted pitchforks.

The stylized handshake enacts the interlocking relationships, camaraderie, and solidarity that define the gang ethos. Each street gang performs an elaborate and intricately choreographed rite of handshaking that incorporates a joint performance of the digital handsign of the respective totemic symbol (crown, pitchfork, eagle, etc.) extended into a series of bonding gestures that celebrate corporeal contact (these may include tapping the heart, multiple variations of inter-

PLATE 28–29

twining fingers and "giving skin," and kisses). Plates 28–32 to 28–34 document key movements within the sequence of this kinetic performance. The underground "books," "manifestos" that each gang develops (see Conquergood 1994a, p. 28, n. 6) contain exegetical commentary that deepens the meaningfulness of these embodied performances. I quote from the King Manifesto: "A fist upon our heart... It means, 'I DIE FOR YOU' for you are flesh of my flesh, blood of my blood,

son of my mother who is the Universal Nature and follower of Yahve." Many working-class latinos refer to one another as camales, which means closer than a brother, literally "flesh" (Limon, 1994).

PLATE 28–31

PLATE 28–30

PLATE 28–32

PLATE 28–33

PLATE 28–35

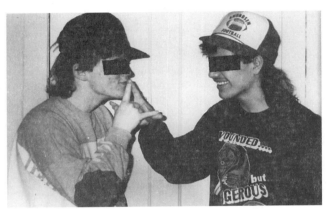

PLATE 28–34

Scripting in the streets gives a new dimension to what Michail Bakhtin (1986, p. 6) called "bodies of meaning." It is a powerful pedagogy that deeply engages the body as a way of knowing. Peter McLaren (1995, p. 46) compared and contrasted the visceral power and intimacy of streetcorner knowledge with the disembodied and distant nature of classroom knowledge:

> Streetcorner knowledge is epistemologically different from traditional conceptions of school knowledge. It is a type of mimesis or visceral/erotic identification.... In the streets, what mattered most was always somehow 'felt,' whereas classroom knowledge was often sullied by an inflated rationalism and logocentrism. In the streets, students made use of more affective engagement with symbols marked by the emotive rather than the rational.

Children learn street literacy, particularly the corporeal mode, through imitation and gestural play (see Plate 28–35). The little Khmer refugee boy on the right is miming the "crossing up" display he has seen the big boys perform on the streets. He is not yet in control of the technique because he is "crossing up" to the right, which, particularly if he were a few years older, would be a dangerous mistake to make within Latin Kings territory (see also Plate 28–36).

The walls of buildings are eroticized as the sensuous surfaces of the "hood," the intimate spaces of the homeboys and homegirls, the collective body of the gang. Likewise,

bodies are scripted as metonymic extensions of the hood, walking condensation symbols of gang geography, able to animate or antagonize the urban spaces they pass through. Perhaps the most poignant and compelling example of the meaning-making convergence between bodies and buildings is the RIP (Rest In Peace) death murals inscribed near the site where a street youth "went down" (died) for the hood (see Plate 28–37).

Interpretive collusions and the play of reading. Interpretation of a graffiti text is contingent upon performance. Instead of a disembodied, compliant consumer of communication, the reader is engaged as a dynamic player who *enacts* textual meanings. Since graffiti texts are intricately coded, cryptic, collusive, and context specific they demand a knowledgeable and energetic "interpretive community" that is able to supply the subtext, furnish supplementary readings, activate and play with conventions, generate interpretations, and cocreate or contest meanings (see Fish, 1980; Radway, 1984). Graffiti writing is an excellent example of what Roland Barthes (1974) called "writerly" texts wherein readers or audiences are scripted as active agents and coproducers of meaning, in contrast to "readerly" texts that position the reader as a passive depository of messages. In place of a disembodied

PLATE 28–36

PLATE 28–37

aesthetics of distance and detachment, street "protocols of reading" (Scholes, 1989) constitute a call to participate and connect, an aesthetics (and ethics) of contact, interaction, and collective life.

All manners of punning and visual-verbal play continuously exercise imaginations and keep the performance community interpretively alert and alive to witty flips and new twists and surprises of meaning. Fiske (1989, p. 107) argued that the pleasure of punning is its rough-house creativity, the way it tricks and startles the reader or audience into participatory play with meanings: "puns invite producerly readings, there is a pleasure in spotting and solving the pun. ..." Through visual alterations the Latin King writer of the graffiti text in Plate 28–38 teases out a pun from the name of a rival gang, "disciples." Although this is a classic pun, a play between written and oral forms of language, many graffiti texts create visual puns through optical illusions and tricks of the eye.

Mexico, the signed author of the text in Plate 28–39 has disrespected his rivals, the Latin Eagles, by turning their icon, an eagle, on its head, and bracketing it with a reversed letter "E" and the letter "K", which stand for "Eagles Killers." What makes this inversion witty as well as grim is that the upside down eagle's head is "crowned" by the icon of the Latin Kings, a five-point crown. Further, the neck of the upended eagle's head with elongated beak can be read as forming the letter "L" for "Latin" followed immediately by 'K,' which can now be read as Kings. The letter "K" thus doubles and signifies simultaneously two different meanings: when part of the graffeme reversed-E K, it means Eagles Killers; when part of the graffeme LK (with the L formed from neck and beak of upended eagle's head), it means Latin Kings. The meaning is in the movement, the unfixing and remobilizing of the signifiers, and their dancing, doubling, shape-shifting play across modes of representation (see Sanchez-Tranquilino, & Tagg, 1992).

Plate 28–40 represents an even more subtle and complex optical transformation. In this graffiti text the Lawrence and Kedzie branch of the Latin Kings gang has conflated the icons of two enemy gangs: the heart with devil's horns and tail is the icon of the Latin Disciples, and the heart with wings is the icon of the Latin Lovers, both Folks Nation gangs. This hybrid heart with devil's horns and tail as well as wings has been turned upside down and fractured, a double disfigurement. But there is one detail inconsistent with the overall strategy of "throwing down" the coupled icons: the wings remain right side up, even though the heart to which they are affixed has been inverted. This disruption of the pattern opens up another way of looking at the image: if you look at it long enough, it transforms into a chicken, specifically a chicken in distress with its hanging head, flustered wings, and the inverted curved horns as legs create a pigeon-toed effect. My Latin Kings neighbors relished this visual pun, delighted in

PLATE 28–38

PLATE 28–39

PLATE 28–40

the way the upside down icons of their rivals perceptually dissolved into a chicken in distress, with all the ridiculing power of that image. The dishonorable connotations of the chicken are played out in embodied performance as well. I have seen Latin Kings mimic the Latin Eagles handsign, which is interlocking thumbs with the fingers spread like eagles' wings, but then start nervously fluttering their fingers while vocally imitating the clucks and squawks of a chicken.

Puns and verbal–visual play excite and encourage active engagement with texts, close reading gives way to a participatory theater of proliferating interpretations. Street literacy gives new meaning to Barthes' (1974) theory of "writerly" texts—which makes the activity of reading coextensive with that of writing—because on the streets, reading, quite literally, often incites a performative rewriting of graffiti texts. Plate 28–41 documents the common practice of rewriting, or writing over, the graffiti texts of rival gangs. The Simon City Royals, a major Folks Nation gang, had dared to enter and appropriate Latin Kings' territory by marking it as their "camp." No self-respecting Latin King could countenance this flagrant violation of territorial boundaries, the gang equivalent of a nation-state planting its flag inside another country's borders (see Conquergood, 1994b). The Latin Kings reclaimed and reterritorialized their space by writing their letters over those of the insurgents. Significantly the Latin Kings

reestablished their dominion by deliberately writing on top of the offending letters instead of cleaning the slate and then putting up their own insignia. By not erasing but leaving the Simon City Royals graffiti in view but now reframed as a conquered relic, the Latin Kings dramatized their prowess, their "juice," in the ongoing struggle for territory and respect. Their status is enhanced by the palimpsest effect of writing

PLATE 28–41

over the text of a rival gang, which now serves as an aggrandizing foil to the lustrous insignia of the triumphant gang.

Plate 28–42 demonstrates an improvisatory variant on the practice of rewriting graffiti texts. The graffito inscribed on my personalized Northwestern University stationery is an ironic mirror image and subversive doubling of my name, "Dwight," from the letterhead. The writer, Hitman, is a Latin King who seized the opportunity to "signify" (Gates, 1984) on my name when he found my memo tablet that I had brought to a tutoring session with him. He mimicked and carnivalized the conventions of official literacy and the insignia of institutional authority by rewriting my name within the conventions of street literacy and textual power displays. His translation and critical reframing of my name, my identity, is an important reminder that all writing is a creative act of interpretation and relocation. Hitman's appropriation of my name unsettles the hierarchy of textual authority that underpins academic ethnographic writing (Clifford, & Marcus, 1986). Typically it is the more powerful participant in the ethnographic encounter who writes and makes texts, and the subordinate other who is written about, textualized. In this chapter, I have been taking examples of street literacy and analyzed and recontextualized them within the discourse of ethnographic analysis. Disrupting this process, Hitman took my printed name from a Northwestern University memo tablet and translated it into

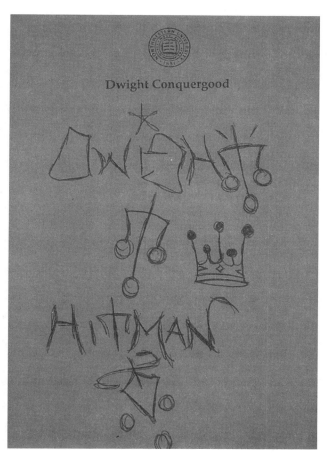

Dwight Conquergood

PLATE 28–42

the discourse of gang graffiti. This is instructive, critical, and fair play.

CONCLUSION

It is the truism of critical pedagogy and emancipatory literacy that schools should teach by engaging the creativities, competencies, and capacities of students: "[Emancipatory] literacy . . . is grounded in a critical reflection on the cultural capital of the oppressed" (Freire, & Macedo, 1987, p. 157). Gang youth are one of the most stigmatized groups of students, seen exclusively in terms of their difference, deficits, deviance, and danger. Going against the grain of popular perception and public policy, this chapter excavates the complex, intricate, subjugated knowledges and interpretive skills that gang youth learn and perform on the streets with great authority. "Critical reflection", however, is the key term because just as it is counterproductive to vilify and further marginalize street youth, it is unhelpful to romanticize gang culture. As several examples make clear, street literacy is connected to violent action, although I hasten to point out that mainstream literacy is not innocent of battle metaphors, militaristic rhetoric, and actual declarations of war. It would be hypocritical to suggest that street youth were violence-prone, and mainstream culture was violence-pure. Violence at all levels must be resisted. The implicit and overarching argument of this chapter is that there are insights and capacities embedded in street literacy that can be recuperated by progressive educators for positive pedagogical ends.

Street literacy develops an impressive, albeit underground, body of knowledge and skills that are based on cooperative and interdependent learning that is embodied, coexperienced, refreshed and kept exciting through improvisation and play. It is difficult for most citizens, progressive educators included, to see anything of value in street culture because our perceptions are skewed by prevailing media metaphors that depict gangs as malignant microbes ("plague," "cancer," "blight," "disease," "scourge," "virus," "infestation," "epidemic of violence"), or vicious animals ("wilding packs," "superpredators," "roving," "prowling" beasts of prey from the "urban jungle" seized with "pack frenzy"), or violent terrorists (youths who "menace" and "terrorize neighborhoods," creating "explosions of violence" and "little Beiruts" in the inner city). It is difficult to think of groups other than gang youth that are publicly characterized as germs, animals, and monsters. Nonetheless, some educators have penetrated this sensationalist demonology and called for intervention programs that build on the capacities, communal strengths, and hopeful yearnings of street youth (Johnson, & Johnson, 1993; Rodriguez, 1994). In Chicago, the deeply committed and long-term work of Marvin Garcia at the Pedro Albizu Campos High School, Luis Rodriguez and Patricia Zamorra with Youth Struggling for Survival, Maria Dalida Benfield and Christopher Bratten with Video Machete, Lisa Kenner at the Juvenile Temporary Detention Center (Audy Home), and Meade Palidofsky with Music Theatre Workshop, all offer positive, hopeful, and inspiring examples of critical pedagogical strategies that tap into the intelligence, talent, and, yes, humanity of street youth.

At the turn of the last century, Jane Addams (1972 [1907], p. 66) wrote a book about street youth and gangs and how she and her Hull House workers were able "to utilize the gang spirit and to turn its collective force towards" successful drug rehabilitation programs. Instead of seeing street youth as problems, "delinquents," she focused on their potential, capacities, and energies, their "quest for adventure" (p. 57) and "spirit of revolt" (p. 117). She pointed out the political-economic conditions of oppression instead of blaming the poor for the circumstances within which they were forced to live. Above all, she called for new, insightful, and more compassionate ways of seeing urban youth and responding to their needs: "We fail to understand what he wants or even to see his doings, although his acts are pregnant with mean-ing, and we may either translate them into a sordid chronicle of petty vice or turn them into a solemn school" for civic responsibility and social justice (p. 161). She concluded *The Spirit of Youth and the City Streets* with this haunting image:

> We may either smother the divine fire of youth or we may feed it. We may either stand stupidly staring as it sinks into a murky fire of crime and flares into the intermittent blaze of folly or we may tend it into a lambent flame with power to make clean and bright our dingy city streets" (pp. 161, 162)

In the wake of the 1992 Los Angeles uprising, this passage stands as unheeded warning and critique of contemporary public policy that sees urban youth in terms of problems and pathologies instead of their potentials, possibilities, hopes, and struggles.

References

Addams, J. (1972 [1909]). *The spirit of youth and the city streets.* Urbana, IL: University of Illinois Press.

Bakhtin, M. M. (1986). *Speech genres and other late essays,* (V. McGee, Trans.; C. Emerson, & M. Holquist, Eds.). Austin, TX: University of Texas Press.

Barthes, R. (1974). *S/Z* (R. Miller, Trans.). New York: Hill & Wang.

Becker, H. S. (1986). *Doing things together.* Evanston, IL: Northwestern University Press.

Bhabha, H. K. (1994). *The location of culture.* New York: Routledge & Kegan Paul.

Block, R. (1991). *Early warning system for street gang violence crisis areas: Automated hot spot Identifiction in law enforcement.* Chicago: Illinois Criminal Justice Information Authority, Statistical Analysis Center.

Bourdieu, P. (1984). *Distinction: Social critique of the judgement of taste.* (R. Nice, Trans.). Cambridge, MA: Harvard University Press.

Boyarin, J. (Ed.), (1993). *The ethnography of reading.* Berkeley, CA: University of California Press.

Buck-Morse, S. (1989). *The dialectics of seeing: Walter Benjamin and the arcades project.* Cambridge, MA: MIT Press.

Camitta, M. (1993). Vernacular writing: varieties of literacy among Philadelphia high school students. In B. Street (Ed.), *Cross-cultural approaches to literacy* (pp. 228–246). Cambridge: Cambridge University Press.

Clifford, J., & Marcus G. (Eds.), (1986). *Writing culture: The poetics and politics of ethnoraphy.* Berkeley, CA: Universityof California Press.

Conquergood, D. (1992a). Life in big red: Struggles and accommodations in a Chicago polyethnic tenement. In L. Lamphere (Ed.), *Structuring diversity: Ethnographic perspectives on the new immigration* (pp. 95–144). Chicago: University of Chicago Press.

Conquergood, D. (1992b). *On reppin' and rhetoric: Gang representations* (CUAPR working papers no. 92–19). Evanston, IL: Northwestern University, Center for Urban Affairs and Policy Research.

Conquergood, D. (1992c). Ethnography, rhetoric, and performance. *Quarterly Journal of Speech, 78,* 80–97.

Conquergood, D. (1994a). Homeboys and hoods: Gang communica-tion and cultural space. In L. Frey (Ed.), *Group communication in context: Studies of natural groups* (pp. 23–55). Hillsdale, NJ: Lawrence Erlbaum.

Conquergood, D. (1994b). For the nation! How street gangs problematize patriotism. In H. Simons & M. Billig (Eds.), *After postmodernism: Reconstructing ideology critique* (pp. 200–221). London: Sage.

Conquergood, D [Producer & Director], & Siegel, T. [Producer & Director]. (1990). *The heart broken in half* [Videotape]. New York: Filmmakers Library.

de Certeau, M. (1984). *The practice of everyday life,* (S. Randall, Trans.). Berkeley, CA: University of California Press.

de Certeau, M. (1986). *Heterologies: Discourse on the other* (B. Massumi, Trans.). Minneapolis, MN: University of Minnesota Press.

Derrida, J. (1976). *Of grammatology* (G. Spivak, Trans.). Baltimore: Johns Hopkins University Press.

Ellison, R. (1952). *Invisible man.* New York: Vintage.

Fabian, J. (1993). Keep listening: Ethnography and reading. In J. Boyarin (Ed.), *The ethnography of reading* (pp. 80–97). Berkeley, CA: University of California Press.

Feldman, A. (1991). *Formations of violence: The narrative of the body and political terror in Northern Ireland.* Chicago: University of Chicago Press.

Fine, E. (1984). *The folklore text: From performance to print.* Bloomington, IN: Indiana University Press.

Fish, S. (1980). *Is there a text in this class?: The authority of interpretive communities.* Cambridge: Harvard University Press.

Fisk, J. (1989). *Understanding popular culture.* Boston: Unwin Hyman.

Foucault, M. (1977). *Discipline and punish: The birth of the prison,* (A. Sheridan, Trans.). New York: Pantheon.

Freedberg, D. (1989). *The power of images: Studies in the history and theory of response.* Chicago: University of Chicago Press.

Freire, P., & Macedo D. (1987). *Literacy: Readin the word and the world.* South Hadley, MA: Bergin & Garvey.

Gates, H. L. (1988). *The signifying monkey: A theory of Afro-American literary criticism.* New York: Oxford University Press.

Geertz, C. (1983). *Local knowlede: Further essays in interpretive anthropology.* New York: Basic, Books.

Gilman, S (1991). *Inscribing the other.* Lincoln, NE: University of Nebraska Press.

Gilroy, P. (1995). '… to be real': The dissident forms of black expressive culture. In C. Ugwu (Ed.), *Let's get it on: The politics of black performance,* Seattle, WA: Bay Press.

Goody, J. (1986). *The logic of writin and the organization of sociey.* Cambridge: Cambridge University Press & Kegan Paul.

Haraway, D. (1991).*Simians, cybors, and women: The reinvention of nature.* New York: Routledge.

Harrison-Pepper, S. (1990). *Drawing a circle in the square.* Jackson, MS: University Press of Mississippi.

Hebdige, D. (1988). *Hiding in the light: On images and things.* New York: Routledge & Kegan Paul.

Johnson, D. W., & Johnson R. T. (1993). Put gang dynamics on your side. *Education Digest, 59,* 35–38.

Limon, J. (1989). Carne, carnales, and the carnivalesque: Bakhtinian batos, disorder and narrative discourse. *American Ethnologist, 16,* 471–486.

Marvin, C. (1994). The body of the text: Literacy's corporeal constant. *Quarterly Journal of Speech, 80,* 129–149.

McLaren, P. (1995). *Critical pedagoy and predatory culture.* New York: Routledge & Kegan Paul.

Mignolo, W. (1995). *The darker side of the Renaissance: Literacy, territoriality, and colonization.* Ann Arbor, MI: University of Michigan Press.

Olson, D. (1994). *The world on paper: The conceptual and cognitive implications of writing and reading.* New York: Cambridge University Press.

Ong, Walter (1982). *Orality and literacy: The technologizing of the word.* New York: Methuen.

Pratt, M. L. (1992). *Imperial eyes: Travel writing and transculturation.* New York: Routledge & Kegan Paul.

Radway, J. (1984). *Reading the romances: Women. patriarchy. and popular literature.* Chapel Hill, NC: University of North Carolina Press.

Rich, A. (1986). *Blood. bread. and poetry.* New York: Norton.

Ricoeur, P. (1971). The model of the text: Meaningful action considered as a text. *Social Research, 38,* 529–562.

Rockhill, K. (1993). Gender, language, and the politics of literacy. In B. Street (Ed.), *Cross-cultural approaches to literacy* (pp. 156–175). Cambridge: Cambridge University Press.

Rodriguez, L. J. (1994, November 21). Turning youth gangs around. In *The Nation,* 605–609.

Sanchez-Tranquilino, M., & Tagg, G (1992). The Pachuco's flayed hide: Mobility, identity, and buenas garras. In L. Grossberg, C. Nelson & P. Treichler (Eds.),*Cultural Studies* (pp. 556–570). New York: Routledge & Kegan Paul.

Schechner, R. (1993). *The future of ritual: Writings on performance and culture.* New York: Routledge.

Scholes, R. (1985). *Textual power.* New Haven & Kegan Paul: Yale University Press.

Scholes, R. (1989). *Protocols of reading.* New Haven, CT: Yale University Press.

Shuman, A. (1993). Collaborative writing: Appropriating power or reproducing authority? In B. Street (Ed.), *Cross-cultural approaches to literacy* (pp. 247–271). Cambridge: Cambridge University Press.

Stallybrass, P., & A. White (1986). *The politics and poetics of transgression.* Ithaca, NY: Cornell University Press.

Stewart, S. (1991).*Crimes of writing: Problems in the containment of representation.* New York: Oxford University Press.

Street, B. (Ed.), (1993).*Cross-cultural approaches to literacy.* Cambridge: Cambridge University Press.

Ulmer, G. (1985). *Applied grammatology: Poste(e)-pedagogy from Jacques Derrida to Joseph Beuys.* Baltimore: Johns Hopkins University Press.

·29·

INTERGENERATIONAL DISCOURSES: LIFE TEXTS OF AFRICAN-AMERICAN MOTHERS AND DAUGHTERS

Vivian L. Gadsden

UNIVERSITY OF PENNSYLVANIA

Intergenerational literacy and the broader issues of family and intergenerational learning have been the center of discussions in educational research and practice for more than three decades. Compelling historical accounts of African-American education during slavery and reconstruction (Anderson, 1988, 1995) highlight the importance that ex-slaves and freed men and women assigned to literacy as an intergenerational legacy to ensure citizenship and the enrichment of the black family. In a work focused on family literacy in the 19th century home of Cotton Mather, Monaghan (1991) provides a critical analysis of literacy interactions between Mather and his children, attending specifically to issues of race, class, and gender within the household and the community. Durkin (1966, 1976), at the height of the antipoverty movement and early years of Head Start, studied low-income African-American children and parents in Chicago, focusing on how parents assisted their children in developing literate ability.

More recently, longitudinal ethnographic research demonstrates how issues of class, race, and social and political history are intergenerationally represented, understood, and enacted within different communities (e.g., Heath, 1983; Taylor, 1983; Taylor & Dorsey-Gaines, 1988; Taylor & Strickland, 1989). For instance, Purcell-Gates (1995) leads readers through a series of life and literacy events of a low-literate Appalachian family and describes the efforts of a mother and her son to improve their literacy. This and other research situate the problems and successes of literacy within a larger discourse of life circumstances and pose a range of questions about literacy learning; cultural rules, norms, and roles within families and communities; and the constraints imposed by societal constructs such as gender bias and racial discrimination.

These and other studies connote newly-expanded conceptualizations and approaches to studying and supporting literacy development. They also enhance our understanding of the intergenerational, social, and cultural contexts that create opportunities for that development. Rather than assuming a unilinear focus on children in K–12 schools, these literacy analyses integrate into a more comprehensive framework issues from different domains, age ranges, and areas typically absent in traditional discourses in the field. Such analyses increasingly suggest that while many of the issues have been excluded historically from the primary discourses of literacy research, they are neither outside the domains of literacy nor oppositional to the purposes of literacy practice as it has emerged over the past decade. Instead, the issues are strongly connected to the premises that literacy is a social process reliant for meaning on contexts and that this meaning is embedded deeply in the lives of learners. By focusing on the social processes of reading and writing, literacy research and practice have begun to provoke discussions about how life events, cultural traditions, family beliefs, gender roles, and

This work was supported by funding from the Spencer Foundation/National Academy of Education and the National Center on Adult Literacy at the University of Pennsylvania, which is part of the Educational Research Development Center Program (Grant No. R1 17Q00003) as administered by the Office of Educational Research and Improvement, U.S. Department of Education, in cooperation with the Departments of Labor and Health and Human Services. The opinions expressed here do not necessarily reflect the position or policies of any of these organizations.

individual behaviors intersect and contribute to our understanding of how, why, and when individuals learn and use literacy; why some approaches to instruction engage learners more effectively than others; and what supports are necessary to help learners affect change in their lives.

This chapter examines the intersection of critical issues in the life-course and self-perception of two and three generations of African-American mothers and daughters, connected through biological ties, cultural history, social experiences, and educational aspirations. Specifically, I examine how issues of gender, race, and culture are raised and personal responses shared within the oral and written discourses. The content of these discourses forms here what I call "intergenerational life texts," that is, the accumulation of events and circumstances that affect the daily lives of learners and the ways they think about literacy, use it, and convey messages about its meaning across multiple generations and contexts.

In examining life texts as oral and written discourses, this chapter focuses on the development, uses, and sharing of reading and writing within two communities of African-American women and girls, and the meanings attached to the relationships that evolve from sharing these literacies. The issues of temporality, age, and agelessness are critical to this discussion which attempts to understand better *when and where* these women and girls meet around and about literacy, and create opportunities to engage in difficult conversations about family expectations, race, education, and persistence. The conjunctive adverb "when," rather than denoting a specific time, connotes activities and discourses that occur between girls and women—language, postures, and symbolic acts that inform us about who the women and girls are, what the literacies are that they value most, where they meet and for what purpose(s), how they come to meet, how they sustain literate relationships, and why these relationships are sustained.

This chapter is divided into four sections. The first section presents some of the current conceptualizations and issues in intergenerational literacy learning. The second describes the current and historical context for African-American women's literacy. The third presents the oral and written narratives from case studies with African-American women across two and three generations. The fourth summarizes the ways in which literacy converges for these different generations of women and the implications of these convergences for practice and research.

DEFINITIONS AND DISCOURSES IN INTERGENERATIONAL LITERACY

Definitions of intergenerational literacy learning typically have included a focus on the nature of literacy within each generation and the mechanisms (e.g., local programming and recruitment) and approaches (e.g., literature-based instruction) used to convey reading and writing abilities (Gadsden, 1993b). Intergenerational literacy has come to be associated almost solely with families and often is used interchangeably with family literacy. However, intergenerational literacy includes more than the family, although families create obvious intergenerational connections. Indeed, intergenerational literacy may be conceptualized more broadly as a wide array of participants—parents, grandparents, teachers, and children— learning and teaching one another about literacy.

Much practice and research on intergenerational literacy are developed out of an assumption that in settings where children and adults have opportunities to interact over periods of time, adults transmit knowledge, beliefs, and practices to children either through direct teaching or informal activities (e.g., Pellegrini, Brody, & Sigel, 1985). Such transmission and learning may take place in formal settings such as schools where adult teachers share with children the strategies for reading and writing and facilitate the development of these abilities using a set of accepted approaches. It may take place within homes—between parent and child, grandparent and grandchild, or other adult–child configurations. The relationship may include an adult relative modeling a variety of literacy behaviors, talking about literacy, or demonstrating the value and importance of literacy by engaging children in activities requiring increasingly sophisticated literate ability. Intergenerational literacy learning may be a part of relationships established in community settings such as churches in which an adult helps a child understand the written ritual of the church or participate in literacy activities integrated into the church program, such as singing in a choir. It is tied as well to family literacy programs in which parents are assisted in supporting their children's literacy development or where parents and children learn together.

While several forms and formats are evident in family and intergenerational literacy programs, there is some agreement that such programs are designed largely to improve literacy for adults (typically parents) and children in a family and to increase the likelihood that children in the family will experience fewer literacy problems than their parents (Gadsden, 1993b). Many intergenerational literacy programs are located in schools, churches, community centers, libraries, and private agencies; others may be linked to existing efforts described in Chapter 1, compensatory education, adult education, Head Start, and welfare initiatives. The programs may be defined broadly as intergenerational or multigenerational but include only a limited literacy strand, or they may involve adults and children in one family. Some programs simply pair one child in a family with an adult outside the family who volunteers to assist the child by tutoring, book reading, or mentoring. Rarely, even now, do programs expand to include more than two members within a single family (typically a parent and a young child) around a set of teaching and learning approaches (see Gadsden, 1994). Programs sometimes are developed around a mix of approaches, but are as likely to be built around a single philosophy or strategy.

Although the populations of programs may include a variety of cultural and ethnic groups, a few programs are designed specifically to support literacy development among certain language and cultural groups (e.g., African-Americans, Mexican Americans, and Asian and Eastern European immigrants). Others may be ecumenical in their programmatic appeal. Many programs attempt to respond to the goals of a small community network; some are appended to existing adult literacy programs.

Despite growing scholarly interest in intergenerational literacy, striking examples of uncharted possibilities in the field exist. One such example is the exchange of responsibility between parents (particularly limited English-speaking, immigrant parents) and children when parents' low literacy makes them dependent on literate children to complete daily tasks requiring reading and writing (see Weinstein-Shr, 1991). Likewise, little work examines the relationships between parent and child learning when the child assumes a dominant role in supporting the parent's reading (i.e., teaching the parent to read) or what the multiple configurations of parent–child learning are within a home or other social context. That is, how are the different kinds of literacies—oral, writing, reading, and other visual forms—shared, understood, accessed, and used by adult and child learners working together? What are the trade-offs in power, skills, knowledge, practical applications, and the representations of people learning literacy and the processes of learning and teaching themselves?

These questions are related to larger issues about the nature and meaning of intergenerational learning and transfer—primarily whether, how, and under what circumstances behaviors, beliefs, and attitudes are conveyed from one generation to another. Researchers here might examine the degree to which parents and families, in fact, influence children's literacy. They might address how parents convey to children beliefs about their ability to succeed, the value attached to the family itself, the importance of education, and ways of thinking about issues and solving problems; they might explore how to model appropriate behaviors that children use and apply to different situations in their lives. Whatever their origins, these behaviors, beliefs, and attitudes appear to be influenced by a range of life experiences and result in intergenerational family practices and shared expectations (Baydar, Brooks-Gunn & Furstenberg 1993; Kreppner & Lerner, 1989).

Another relatively unexplored area of study centers on a tacit assumption that intergenerational literacy and learning is "women's work." Research studies in K–12 settings and intergenerational and family literacy program efforts focus disproportionately on women and mothers, in part, because women have been the most active participants in adult literacy programs. In addition, women's roles as mothers have positioned them historically as children's first socializers and teachers. Several intergenerational literacy studies examine mother–child reading (Pellegrini, 1991; Pellegrini, Perlmutter, Galda, & Brody, 1989), while mother's education is used typically as the primary predictor of children's academic achievement.

Despite the gender-specific nature of much of intergenerational literacy research, current discourses do not focus on specific issues about gender—either women or men, mothers or fathers, girls or boys. Rather, the discourses on intergenerational literacy have been developed around some basic assumptions about who would learn (children) and who would convey that learning (mothers), with few studies examining questions about father-child literacy or the effect of women's changing role in society on intergenerational learning. In recent years, however, interest in women's roles, debates about family values, and conversation about fathers' involvement in children's development have begun to transform the substance and form of conceptualizations of intergenerational literacy, and new approaches for studying and working with parents, children, and families.

CURRENT AND HISTORICAL CONTEXT FOR AFRICAN-AMERICAN WOMEN'S LITERACY

Although recent international foci on women and literacy, particularly within home contexts and parent–child relationships, increasingly are being reported (e.g., Mwiria, 1993; Stromquist, 1992; Young & Padilla, 1990), the literature on women learning literacy is impoverished. Like women in many other cultural groups, African-American women as mothers are implicated throughout conversations about literacy and children's achievement; yet their history, literacy contributions, and literacy experiences are rarely a part of the discourses in literacy studies, family literacy efforts, or intergenerational learning. African-American women's literacy and their role in educational movements represent an almost invisible subset of the existing work on women and historical accounts of African-American culture (Morris, 1986). In the accounts that do exist, African-American women's roles have ranged from mothers and teachers in the emancipation of the 4,500,000 African-Americans (almost half of whom were women) from slavery to leadership in the citizenship campaigns of the 1950s and 1960s (see also Harris, 1995).

Morris (1986) and Holt (1990) chronicle the difficult, if not precarious, position in which African-American women found themselves shortly after slavery, having earned their freedom in a society in which women—black and white—were assigned low status and in which blackness was equated with intellectual inferiority. As Anderson (1988) suggests, African-American women in the South who had been teachers in secret learning places during slavery and in classrooms subsequent to slavery existed, acted, and held personal definitions of themselves and their abilities that contrasted with prevailing popular opinion about African-Americans in general and about African-American women in particular.

The absence of a literacy history that provides a comprehensive analysis of the campaigns and movements that occurred within the African-American community explains the still unexplored areas of African-American women's roles in citizenship campaigns. What we know about this history acknowledges the role of women such as Ella Baker whose ideas about galvanizing the black vote by teaching literacy to a potential black electorate sparked efforts leading to the Southern Christian Leadership Conference's citizenship campaign. Critical to the quieted discourses of Baker and other African-American women was a sense of literacy as a tool for citizenship, self-defense, and protection of the group.

The work of Ida B. Wells-Barnett, a journalist and eventually a publisher, is one example of the value assigned to the written word and the ability to execute the word in self-defense. In the early 1900s, determined to address the postbellum crimes against blacks throughout the country, Wells-Barnett provided a prescriptive, intellectual account of the "social and economic captivity" which was perpetrated against blacks through racism and lynching. In a harsh response to a series of investigations which Wells-Barnett had conducted about lynchings, a white male Southerner wrote: "The Negroes in this country are wholly devoid of morality, the women are prostitutes and all [a]re natural thieves and liars" (see Lerner, 1972, p. 436).

The retort of African-American women was to take the pen and, in a statement published by the National Association of Colored Women (NACW), leaders of the colored women's club movement declared the intergenerational purpose of their work for literacy and education:

> Now for the sake of thousands of self-sacrificing young women teaching and preaching in lonely southern backwoods, for the noble army of mothers who have given birth to these girls, mothers whose intelligence is only limited by their opportunity to get at books, for the sake of the fine cultured women who have carried off the honors in school here and often abroad, for the sake of our own dignity, the dignity of the race, and the future good name of our children, it is 'mete, right and our bounden duty' to stand forth and declare ourselves and principles, to teach an ignorant and suspicious world that our aims and interests are identical with those of all good aspiring women. Too long have we been silent. ... (quoted in Lerner, 1972, p. 442).

The legacy represented by this declaration—the culture of African-American women and the intergenerational transmission of beliefs and attitudes about learning that are nurtured within many African-American communities—has been steeped historically in images, perceptions, and illusions about the nature of the black woman. Similar to women from other cultural and ethnic groups, African-American women are often challenged and challenge themselves around questions of who they are or are not, how they have changed or have not changed, and what successes they are capable or not capable of achieving. Unlike the culture of women generally, however, the culture of black women is characterized by a distinctively race-centered perspective in which the social processes of sexism and racism stand not in tandem but in relation to each other. Thus, in many ways the development of views about literacy—together with the contexts in which these views are developed and in which literacy events occur, are created, and are enacted—is not embedded in a natural life discourse but is initiated as a response to or preparation for life (not simply as a woman, but as a black woman) in American society.

The prices that are tagged to this identification, the path less traveled by women outside the African-American community, and the difficult road to accepted and acceptable private and shared discourses are the literacy legacies of many African-American women—what Hill-Collins (1996) has called "visionary pragmatism" or what I refer to as limitless possibilities against guarded hopes. In the next section, I present literacy narratives from case studies with African-American women and girls across two and three generations, focusing on: (1) the complexities of intergenerational communication around literacy, race, and gender, and (2) the ways in which views of literacy are transmitted and literate activities such as journal and letter writing serve as mediators for difficult topics and familial problems implicated in limitless possibilities and guarded hopes.

INTERGENERATIONAL DISCOURSE: MEETING PLACES FOR WOMEN AND GIRLS

I used to sit and wonder, "What will my children become?" I guess I wasn't like many girls of my time. As a child, I had dreams that seemed so big; they were bigger than anything I had ever known or seen. I wanted to go places and do things that I was made to feel were impossible for a Black girl. I wasn't even sure that the places existed but I thought if I could think of such places, they had to exist. As I grew older, I came to know that such places did exist, that the choices we make sometimes limit whether and when we go to these places and learn new things. I knew that even if I made the choice to do otherwise, the Jim Crow laws would not allow me to enter some places. For the past 60 years, I have argued my case for equity and I have used my teaching of literacy as a way to come to grips with the barriers before me, making sure they would not be obstacles for my children and the other little treasures of this community. I have been happy in this struggle and have wanted my daughters to be happy like me. But I wanted them to have a different kind of happiness. I wanted them to be in a position to ask for what they wanted—to demand it—and be sure that they could be in a position to get it. I wanted them to be wives and mothers, but I wanted them to somehow be the voice of my discontent and the voice of my pleasure and pride as a Black woman... to speak with eloquence and confidence, to be fighters and nurturers, leaders and pursuers of dreams. I guess I still don't understand impossible. I have often spoken of these things and thought it was time to write them for you to remember.

—Ms. Cenia, an 81-year-old mother, grandmother, and teacher

The text has been translated from Gullah to standard English at the request of many of the informants. The realm of possibility mapped against the perception of limitations in intergenerational literacy perhaps is captured most eloquently in this quotation from a self-described perpetual learner and teacher and oft-described ageless entity. The intergenerational nature of learning, as it occurs in families and other contexts, is both inviting and problematic for teachers, learners, and users of literacy. It thrusts into an academic sphere issues that were once the natural preserve of informal discussions and private traditions within families and cultural and ethnic groups. To study intergenerational literacy is to make public, formal, and vulnerable both the processes by which literacy is constructed and conveyed (through oral and recorded messages) and the actual activities associated with learning, understanding, using, and valuing knowledge. Intergenerational literacy research and practice hinge on assumptions that literacy is a critical part of learners' social and cultural evolution, and that whether and how learners choose to use this knowledge connotes or demonstrates the degree to which they have accepted, modified, sustained, or transformed the intergenerational messages about literacy—in short, the degree to which they have "bought into the system."

What genres have been created by women and life texts shared between women and girls, mothers and daughters, sisters and sisters, grandmothers and granddaughters, or teachers and students? Who are the people involved in intergenerational learning? Where do they come to share knowledge and experiences, and with what effects? What are the bounties of knowledge and intricacies of learning in the relationships between learners across generations, and how do they negotiate these relationships? What does it mean to be literate, and what selfhood is disclosed and personal opportunities provided to African-American women who are literate (Gadsden, 1993a)?

The term, "meeting," is used here to label these sharings of discourses. However, the term has a range of meanings and uses. Consider the following common uses:

> I can meet you at the corner, to indicate place for gathering.
> I will see you at the meeting, that is, a business or social event for a stated cause.
> I have always wanted to meet him, for example, a long-awaited introduction.
> Then, our eyes met, indicating the preface to romantic possibilities.
> It is where the two roads meet—to indicate a convergence of formerly discrete points.

In the text that follows I have conceptualized "meeting" of women and girls in two ways. In the first, the girl in each woman and the woman in each girl attempt to reconcile their common histories and destinies. They grapple with insecurities, aspirations, and expectations—unresolved issues that are sometimes unsuccessfully submerged in the daily acts and demands of being assigned roles by virtue of their race, income or poverty, age, or gender itself. Second, they talk about common and unique strengths.

The narratives are divided into three text groups. Text Group 1 includes a grandmother, mother and daughter who, through written and oral discourse, attempt to unpack the long unspoken questions of gender and race and of intergenerational tensions that overwhelm their caring. Text Group 2 focuses on written conversations about the meaning of persistence. Text Group 3 describes the uses of written literacies as a way to uncover experiences of hardship and fear of failure between mother and daughter.

The narratives are part of two intergenerational literacy studies. Those in Groups 1 and 2 are gleaned from my work with three of four generations of African-American families from rural South Carolina. The informants in this work include 25 families across the four generations: (1) adults who at the beginning of the study were in their 70s and 80s, and (2) their children, grandchildren, and great-grandchildren. Beginning in the second generation, I interviewed the children who had stayed in the small community and those who had moved north. I have attempted to interview a cross-section of informants in each location. Interviews were conducted with the members of the first cohort and with selected children in the second and third cohorts. Over 700 hours of interviewing were conducted in both the rural communities and the northern cities where many of the children now live. In-depth,

follow-up interviews were conducted with a representative group of families for the third and fourth generations. I observed the informants in multiple contexts and examined their written family histories, letters, and stories; listened to their oral histories; and reviewed existing reading texts and materials in the homes. Either as a result or in spite of this work, many of the informants have begun to exchange their written texts with each other and with me.

The narratives in the third text group are lifted from work with African-American and Latino Head Start families in Philadelphia. Supported by a grant to the National Center on Adult Literacy, this study focused on parent literacy and parent learning, particularly examining the family as a system of learning and the role of literacy in that learning. With more than 40 participants over 2 years, the study provided a perspective on how families living in poverty perceive literacy and gain access to literacy and the need to provide literacy. The relationship between the parents' desire to improve their literacy, their intent to ensure their children's success, and their representations of the harshness of poverty in their daily lives threaded the conversations and our work with the Head Start program and the parents.

The commentaries in this paper are from interviews I conducted with eight women. The commentaries centered on three themes (1) the role of literacy and the relationship of literacy to life goals and expectations, (2) purposes and uses of literacy, and (3) incentives and obstacles to literacy. Each commentary and theme connect a variety of life events around issues of womanhood and race.

MEETINGS AROUND GENDER AND RACE: WHERE PRACTICAL REALITIES MEET LIMITLESS POSSIBILITIES

Two kinds of literacy discourses are provided within three generations of Ms. Lannie's family: the oral and written discourses of Ms. Lannie, an 82-year-old mother with eight years of schooling; her daughter, Pat, a 50-year-old teacher with a master's degree; and Melanie, Pat's 16-year-old daughter. Their journal accounts in an intergenerational women's group meet around unspoken love and a common bond in the experiences of race and gender. Ms. Lannie commented:

> My dear, reading and writing is the one thing that everybody should want to learn. I always wanted to be a good reader; people give you so much respect when you are learned. There is no substitute, though, for having good old mother sense. But back to this thing about being a woman. You know, Black women always must be ladies. People don't expect that we can be; slavery taught us that. Well, the truth is that I have never known a woman in this community who did not do her best for her children. Women take care of the children. They're the only ones who always know how children are doing in school; they are the protectors of their children. It has always seemed wrong that with all the responsibility that women have, we don't all know how to read.
>
> My most difficult experience was trying to prepare my girls for the challenges. I was caught between wanting them to conquer the world and finding a husband. I bought them books, I read to them

and mostly told them stories. I told them stories often about the great women in the Bible. When I learned about great women who were Black, I didn't tell them much about these women at first—maybe I didn't think I measured up. I wasn't sure that the stories were always true, how the women I had read about made the choices that they did. I didn't know what to tell my daughters about what to expect, but I could tell them that if these women could make it, so could they.

This is a quiet community. Women in this community are strong. I know that if Harriet Tubman could take slaves to freedom, I could make sure my children were prepared to fight the system. Black women are strong women; we survived over 200 years of slavery, not once giving up on our children. No matter how much life challenges us and how much we are denied, we force our way in and make people listen.

Ms. Lannie's daughter, Pat, spoke of the stated valuing of literacy and the images of a woman—her mother—for whom literacy was important but for whom education had not been accessible. We begin to see the respect that defines the relationship, the issues that potentially complicate that relationship, and the shared views and behaviors that have sustained it. In a written journal account, Pat wrote:

My mother is an interesting woman. We had a relationship based on respect ... and trust. She reinforced the issue of self-pride as a woman and as a Black person. When I was a little girl and I saw her reading, I wanted to read. We rarely left notes to each other; we relied almost always on telling someone else. We practiced the oral tradition in our house. What I remember most fondly is the way she would listen to me read. I would tell her about my plans for being an important, educated person. She used to give me mixed messages. For example, she made a point of telling me that I should get married after college, but seemed relieved when I said I was going on to graduate school. The culture of women, as you call it, was that literacy gave women options, that those options created more problems than they eliminated, that the options had to be used, and that no difference existed between literate and illiterate women. On any given day, you could be assigned the stereotypical images. Learned people were expected to know how to respond to the system in ways that showed off how literate they were, their intellect, to speak for the least of your sisters and brothers.

The greatest impact of my mother's literacy for me and the legacy she gave me is my desire to read things written about and by Black women. By telling me about my responsibility to the community, I understood that learning was more than what I got for myself. It was for generations of women to come. What is shocking to me is to compare my mother's stories of racism with my daughter's stories of racism and sexism and to know that discrimination is here for a long time. I think my mother prepared me for womanhood by making sure I was literate. I think that's what she felt she had to give me and my sisters. I try to give that to my daughter, perhaps less successfully than my mother. The enemies and barriers were more obvious when I was growing up; your place as a woman, as a Black person, and as a literate person was clear. Your decision was whether and how you would rise above the barriers, accept them, or try to remove them. You knew that while you might have the support of women in word, the struggle may have to be yours [alone]. I don't think she [mother] has ever believed that I understand that!

She has always felt that I take the education for granted and that I don't understand how many sacrifices were made. It might be that I have not paid enough dues. But you never know how

much is enough. My mother took a little education and made it count for her children.

After reading her daughter's entry, Ms. Lannie commented not about the personal statements of her daughter but about her own role as a mother, seemingly not as a form of self-centeredness or resistance but as a way to delay a response to Pat or me. She subsequently spoke about how touched she was by her daughter's admissions but did not want to respond to them publicly. In short, she was choosing who the audience would be for her response. Instead, she talks about her valuing of literacy, introducing the commentary with an approving tribute to her daughter:

Pat, smart girl!! But no patience with people sometimes. She was always a good reader and always wanted to read. ...

I may not be the best reader, but my role as a mother and wife made me want to use the reading that I could do to make sure that opportunities were available for my family and myself. Thank God, I never had to work in a White woman's kitchen. Sometimes, I look at my children, and I can't believe how learned they are. You see what Pat can do. ... Ah, I need to tell her that.

I wonder what it would have meant for my literacy not to have been Black or a woman, you know, at the time I was. You know, in our little women groups [in the community], we used to get together and talk about what we wanted for our children. Our Sunday School was the Bible reading class. Men always taught the classes, teach the women. You could say that they couldn't trust women with the Word. No telling what we might do. Defrock them!

Probably the thing that makes me downright mad is how strong the prejudice was here. If I had had more grades, what a joy it would have been to read different books to my children, expose them to the fine readings early. My children are wonderful. I tried to teach them not to hate. You know racism is a terrible thing, and Black girls are the victims of so much. How do you say, be strong, fight for your rights, study hard, don't let racism get in your way, and don't let what others think they know about you, whatever the source—research or whatever—make you believe that you are not the best. Pat is a fighter; she is her mother and father's child now. ... Now we have to work with that Melanie. I just want Melanie to understand the important things in her young life.

Ms. Lannie and Pat shared beliefs and views, but their experiences differed. Although well educated, Pat had never attempted to use the written word as a way to engage or come to seek greater understanding and communication between her mother and herself. Whatever their differences, however, they also shared a common interest—Melanie—the granddaughter and daughter who represented the possibilities for the future. Ms. Lannie sought a shared discourse with Melanie whose experiences were similar to, yet vastly different from, her own. Ms. Lannie and Melanie were able to cohere around many common beliefs and experiences that the absence of an intervening generation allows, a cohering that would not have been possible for Ms. Lannie and Pat. Despite the opportunities that a missing generation of discourse offers, however, Ms. Lannie and Melanie were daunted equally often by the distance created by the missing generation. They suffered from an inability of the first generation to understand the third and of the third to understand the first, reflected in Melanie's journal:

Sometimes Grandma gets on my last nerve! But sometimes what she says makes me feel so much better. She treats me as though I don't think. I guess she has seen so much, she wants the best for me. It's a funny thing. Even though she gets on my nerves sometimes, there is nothing I can't ask her or tell her. She just nods and makes the hardest question seem like an easy thing to answer. I feel so confused sometimes. I tell Grandma. "Girl," she says, "it's the times you're living in. You can't help but be confused. But keep your feet to the ground, believe in yourself, and trust in God. You have a family that loves you, and a strong mama and grandmama."

Like other children, Melanie was more likely to speak about her grandmother in loving rather than negative terms. What was striking was her stated desire to unpack the negative responses that did not allow her to demonstrate caring. After many conversations, Melanie decided to begin writing notes to Ms. Lannie. The first, short note was the beginning of ongoing sharing of literacies and experiences, many of which center around parsing the changing expectations of girls and women within and outside of African-American communities and the implications of racism in the daily life experiences of both:

Dear Grandma,

Although we do not always agree, you are my best friend. There is no problem that I can't share with you. Thank you for being there for me.

Love,

Mel

Ms. Lannie responds:

Dear Melanie,

I wish I could write this better, but I hope you understand what I am trying to say. Your words are beautiful. When I see you, I see all of the things I wanted for myself and never had a chance to do, all the things that I wanted for your mother and she just didn't or couldn't do them. You are so much like me—when you're feisty. You have the weight of all of our hopes and failures. It's a hard road to travel. But I believe in you and love you.

Love,

Grandma Lannie

Both Ms. Lannie and Pat indicated that they had attempted to shelter Melanie from confusion and self-doubt that result from, as Pat suggests, "the insidious nature of racism." Each identified difficulties in helping Melanie both prepare for and balance the problems that each felt Melanie had already begun (and will continue) to confront through harsh experiences in "unlikely places." What each has decided is that at the center of her talk to and with Melanie is the communication of love and caring. Melanie's first short note, thus, became the point of entry for this talk.

Meetings of Respect and Persistence

I have identified two dominant themes in the interviews with the informants. One focuses on the concept of individual and family persistence as a survivalist quality, enabling the individual to continue in the midst of human conflict and strife. As a motivational/metacognitive variant, persistence encourages the learner to (1) assess, plan, monitor, and continually weigh the potential difficulties of learning and schooling against the opportunities they provide, and (2) develop and use strategies and resources to rise above obstacles.

Relatively little work on African-American families speaks to the issue of persistence outside of motivation within school contexts. In this research, persistence refers to the emotional and human stamina of the individuals studied—stamina to demand education for their children, to insist on learning to read, to cling to a belief in schools and the people in them, and to seek alternatives to human and educational plight. Persistence also refers to the immutability of aspirations associated with literacy beliefs, practices, and strategies despite their transformation within families over time, as a result of migration and a variety of life events. In this work, the need for persistence appears to be inherent in the African-American experience. Ms. Addy, an octogenarian with "high school grades," describes this in a statement of her sense of family life and learning:

Family life isn't just about having children; no, it's about planning for them and them planning for themselves, *too*. Well … and being Black, a mother, and having children. When I was a child, well, things were a lot harder [than today]. But, despite the hard times, my parents talked about the future as though things were really going to be different for me! They had absolutely no idea as to how it would happen or what it would take exactly, but they knew it would take *hard work!* School was one place where I was going to be prepared, not only to help myself but to help the family.

Here's the thing. You knew you were Black and poor—a given during my young days [and early adulthood]. You knew that the White people in the community were not going to give you a break, and in fact, we made our breaks. So, you had to figure out what you wanted to achieve, how to get there, and what to do when you got there. There was no confusion about the fact that when you learned to read and write and if you became highly educated, you were supposed to share the knowledge and the struggle so that kids and families understood not only that you got to where you were but what it took—that you needed to continue the struggle as a Black person, primarily for your family, and to make sure you were learning what you needed to improve the community. Parents prepared you to think about the struggle in the long-term, prepare for the [hurtles], and for what you needed to do if you didn't jump them. I don't know if you understand what I am talking about! In some ways, what children and parents are experiencing today is not that different from my childhood and my early years as a parent.

Life for Black people has changed as my daughter says in the "quantity" of opportunities or what seems to be quantity, not in the quality of the opportunities. My grandchildren are victims of racism, a different kind, just as I was. But, you know, they don't know how to plan for hard times *and* good times, like we were taught to do. They only plan for the good times.

Sometimes it seems like even the ones who did well in school don't always understand, or may be they just aren't willing [to understand] the next step in the struggle. Not just our children—all of them (Black and White!). Instead of trials and errors, they seem to have a wagonful of errors for every trial! So they are always starting over or picking up where they left off in school or whatever, rather than continuing on their planned course.

Ms. Addy's daughter, Ina, writes:

If there was one thing that my parents taught me, it was to think about what and who I wanted to be: how do you make it; how to hang in the picture long enough to make it. Well, you begin by reading. What made a difference in our little country community was that we knew everybody—you know the principal could just as soon come to your house as your kin. The other thing was that our parents expected us to demonstrate that we were learning something and what we were learning. Educated or not, many parents wanted to hear children read and made them read; they trusted schools in a way that their children find it hard to do. The encouragement they gave us said that we had to persist in the face of difficulty and that persistence was tied to the struggle of … not Black people in general but to the values of our small community.

Don't get me wrong, not everything was happy or pleasant, not everyone cared about other to do people. But, I think people who were not successful saw their failures as individual, not family, and kind of kept hope for their sisters and brothers and their own children.

So, educated or not, successful or not, as one informant said, "you had this plan"—sometimes an intuitive sense of the journey of learning and living. Learning was equated with literacy, and living demonstrated the functions and uses of literacy. In learning and living, the individual was expected to persist; the family was the context for crafting and strengthening that persistence.

Meeting of Past and Present: Literacy of Hope and Fear

Increasingly, reports from practitioners indicate that the intensity of problems facing many learners may exceed the ability of programs to support families learning literacy. The intergenerational meeting of children and parents often results in parents attempting to reconcile past hopes and present fears. Letter writing and the act of journal writing often provided safe places for the mothers in a small literacy program to reflect on this push-pull of past and present and its implications for their future. In the renderings that follow, neither speaker is over the age of 30. Both have worked intermittently, both want to improve their literacy, both have children and aspirations for their children, and both live in low-income homes. Although both seek to "make a difference" in their homes and community, neither understands fully what the scope of her rights and responsibilities is or might be in the future. Little in either one's education or experience has exposed her to more than the limits of possibility. Karen, a mother of two wrote:

If I had been a better student, I wouldn't be poor, at least not as poor, I don't think. But you know, my husband finished school, and he has been laid off, laid off more than once, and he is poor. I do think that if you have reading and writing you have a better chance, but if you are poor, no one seems to take you seriously. In school, the way teachers teach make you not want to learn, make reading seem hard. Then [the stories] weren't even interesting. It would have been nice to read that a girl like me made it out of the ghetto and be able to understand what I had read. I am going to go and take some classes to improve my reading—as soon as my baby goes to Head Start. Maybe if they [her children] see me reading, they will want to read, too, and make it out of this neighborhood. But education gives you one way out, and some people do it.

Alisha, a mother of three, faces the fear for her children's future and her inability to mediate the problems they will confront:

What I would like my children to understand is that they don't have to be poor—that literacy is theirs for the tryin'. The problem isn't that I don't know what to say to them; it's that I don't know how to back up what I'm saying. Old people use to tell us to work hard in school, but [in truth], some of us weren't taught much reading in school. People who are literate and well educated, they run the world, but how many of them started off poor. I don't mean their White grandparents, I mean them. What I am going to tell my children is that they have to do good work in school, and I need to be able to help them. If you are [literate], I think you just know better where to find the things you need. You don't have to be as embarrassed as if you are poor and illiterate.

Desperate to enter into a conversation with her adolescent daughter, Alisha shares in a letter with Lisa her personal disappointment at having gotten pregnant as a teenager and her hopes for Lisa:

I want you to know I love you. I want you be a good student. I want you to make it. I don't want you to become pregnant like me. You do have opportunities. I want you to go to college. I want you to be happy.

Lisa, unwilling to be engaged or to engage her mother about the difficult topic of sexual activity, responds in a letter with an answer to the unasked question about her sexual activity:

Dear Mom,

I love you, but sometimes… I get so tired of you not trusting me. I plan to be somebody and I will not get pregnant. You think I am having sex, but I am not. I want to get out of this neighborhood and get you out of here too. I need you to believe in me.

Your daughter,

Lisa

The tradition of letter writing in the families I have studied allowed women to talk about a variety of issues. I have read letters kept by family members—family texts that included letters written between children and parents; siblings and siblings; and among parents, children, and other family members. A few of these letters were written in the early 1900s and typically conveyed the state of the individual's life, rarely mundane details. In volumes such as Gutman's (1976) and Blassingame's (1977) historical works, this purposeful picture of letter writing is presented, for example, letters of slaves both to family members and to white sponsors. These letters provided the context for understanding the travails of the African-American in search of a place to succeed and a time in which to be successful. The women who wrote spoke of both successes and problems, often seeking assistance for their hardship and support for their advancements.

A primary communicative device prior to the advent of telephones, letters for African Americans (as is true of other Americans) were the vehicle to exchange ideas and experiences. Unlike the letters of other Americans, however, many of the letters of African Americans from slavery through recent times have been laced with messages of life in a society where race is still the most prominent and divisive issue. African-American women such as Alisha and Lisa continue to bear a significant burden in this discourse and have begun their own written discourse to unravel the complexities of their lives and to lift the tension between hope and despair.

CONCLUSION:
THE EVOLVING INTERGENERATIONAL CONTEXT AND THE CONVERGENCES OF LITERACIES

What does it mean to be a woman and then to be an African-American woman wanting to provide a legacy of hope for the next generation? Responses to this question are riddled with issues about self-definitions, personal analyses, and choices, particularly for mothers who, in aiming to convey to their daughters the possibilities for their future, feel compelled to remind them of a real or perceived limit to their acceptance (Hill-Collins, 1996). The definitions and development of literacy within the lives of these three groups of women and of African-American women historically are centered around the notion of community, including the need to rise above societal obstacles, to chart a course often unlike that of the women's nonblack peers, to be responsive to the collective mission of the group, and to commit to the nurturance of children for an apparent race-unfriendly world. So embedded in the definition of woman is the concept of cultural uplift that the women find it difficult, if not impossible, to separate their identities from the struggle. This message of struggle is a part of the message within each of the legacies of the women described in this chapter—women in search of the freedom to be themselves. The ease with which the message about literacy and access is conveyed is increased when a generation of responsibility is removed (e.g., in the case of Ms. Lannie, Pat, and Melanie) and when each succeeding generation becomes a part of the evolving historical context.

In this chapter, through oral and written literacies the mothers and daughters negotiate limitless possibilities against guarded hopes or Hill-Collins' "notion of visionary pragmatism." The intergenerational context for interpreting, valuing, and assigning purposes to literacy evolves as the possibilities for literacy become apparent for these mothers and daughters who have varying levels of literacy. The narrative texts presented suggest issues that have implications for research and practice.

First, families serve as the most obvious intergenerational context. Although they sometimes impose boundaries, that is, on the ways that individual family members come to define and articulate life needs and goals, they provide in other cases spaces for expansive ways of thinking and exploring possibilities despite obstacles. How literacy can assist families to remove boundaries and realize opportunity is perhaps the most important question and challenge facing family and intergenerational literacy programs. What are the messages that parents want to convey to their children about literacy, what messages do children hear, and how can programs assist parents and children most effectively in learning literacy? What are the strengths of families? Who are the mothers and fathers in these families, and how do programs build on parents', children's, and families' strengths? How do programs make useful, rather than problematic, the issues of race, class, and gender? Because these issues are common to the experiences of families, intergenerational learning efforts will be affected by them and by learners' perceptions about their importance to the culture of the family itself (Gadsden, 1994).

Second, the life texts of the women and girls suggest that literacy activities also create points of entry for beginning and sustaining discourses that continue throughout the life-span of children and adults. For the mothers and daughters here, the topics that emerge are both complex and difficult to discuss. Yet, the literate activities of reading and writing contribute to their intergenerational learning by offering both a means to create and to continue conversation—that is, written and readable discourses—and a place for the conversations to be inscribed—that is, the family.

Third, literacy activities such as interactive journal writing and letter writing hold much of the same promise as a communicative medium as they do in school-based relationships between teachers and students. Parents and children who have varying levels of literacy have opportunities to reflect on issues critical to them, to share ideas with each other, and to practice their writing and reading. In the work that my research team has done with Head Start parents in Philadelphia, parents comment consistently on the value of the journals and letter writing as activities to "make them write."

For practice, these life texts imply that intergenerational and family literacy efforts have a variety of stimuli upon which to build relationships within families. Journal and letter writing, autobiographical analyses, and biographical writings provide learners with a way to improve their literacy, share life stories, and explore difficult questions with each other. I do not suggest here that parents and children no longer engage in talk but that a richer follow-up to these oral discourses is to be found in the written discourses within families. Activities developed around intergenerational life texts encourage the learner to investigate cultural myths and family legends and to compare these across contexts and storytellers. The mix and match of oral and written tradition within the cultural community of the learner assumes a larger image.

In considering interactive journal and letter writing as approaches to increasing intergenerational literacy, researchers and practitioners might be mindful also that these activities presuppose a level of competence or appreciation of the letter as a familiar document and that the value of this medium may not apply to all families. For example, Purcell-Gates (1995) found letters to be outside the experiences of the mother and son with whom she worked over time. After informing the young mother that her son was unfamiliar with postcards or letters, to Purcell-Gates' surprise, the mother responded, "No one writes us 'cause they all know we can't read."

By using African-American women's life texts as a context for the discussion of intergenerational literacy, I have attempted to position the issues of gender, culture, and race as powerful influences and sources of shared meaning and literacy—as sources of information which can be used planfully by programs and researchers to understand better the nature of intergenerational learning, the lives of learners, and appropriate approaches and materials to be used with different populations. Equally important, however, is the need for attention to women's issues in literacy discussions and inquiry into the multiple ways in which mothers and fathers, as women and men, come to influence the literacy development of children as they reconcile their own life options with their literacy and educational goals.

References

Anderson, J. D. (1988). *The education of Blacks in the South. 1860–1935.* Chapel Hill, NC: University of North Carolina.

Anderson, J. D. (1995). Literacy and education in the African-American experience. In V. L. Gadsden & D. A. Wagner (Eds.), *Literacy among African-American youth* (pp. 19–38). Cresskill, NJ: Hampton Press.

Baydar, N., Brooks-Gunn, J., & Furstenberg, F. F. (1993). Early warning signs of functional illiteracy: Predictors in childhood and adolescence. *Child Development, 64*(3), 815–829.

Blassingame, J. W. (Ed.). (1977). *Slave testimony: Two centuries of letters, speeches, interviews, and autobiographies.* Baton Rouge, LA: Louisiana State University Press.

Durkin, D. (1966). *Children who read early.* New York: Teachers College Press.

Durkin, D. (1976). *Teaching young children to read.* Boston: Allyn & Bacon.

Gadsden, V. L. (1993a). Literacy, education, and identity among African-Americans: The communal nature of learning. *Urban Education, 27*(4), 352–369.

Gadsden, V. L. (1993b, October). *Persistence, literacy, and schooling: The intergenerational transfer of meaning in African-American families.* Paper presented at the meeting of the National Academy of Education and the Spencer Foundation. University of Michigan, Ann Arbor, MI.

Gadsden, V. L. (1994). Understanding family literacy: Conceptual issues facing the field. *Teachers College Record, 96*(1), 58–86.

Gadsden, V. L. (1994). Representations of literacy: Parents' images in two cultural communities. In L. M. Morrow (Ed.), *Family literacy: Multiple perspectives to enhance literacy development* (pp. 287–303). Newark, DE: International Reading Association.

Gadsden, V. L. (1995).

Gutman, H. G. (1976). *The Black family in slavery and freedom. 1750–1925.* New York: Pantheon Books.

Harris, V. J. (1995). Using African-American literature in the classroom. In V. L. Gadsden & D. A. Wagner (Eds.), *Literacy among African-American youth: Issues in learning, teaching, and schooling,* (pp. 229–260). Cresskill, NJ: Hampton Press.

Heath, S. B. (1983). *Ways with words.* Cambridge: Cambridge University Press.

Hill-Collins, P. (1996). Searching for sojourner truth: The visionary pragmatism of Black women's social theory. In *Fighting words: Knowledge, power, and the challenges of Black feminist thought.* Minneapolis, MN: University of Minnesota Press.

Holt, T. (1990). "Knowledge is power": The Black struggle for literacy. In A. A. Lunsford, H. Moglan & J. Slevin (Eds.), *The right to literacy,* (pp. 91–102). New York: Modern Language Association.

Kreppner, K., & Lerner, R. M. (1989). Family systems and life-span development: Issues and perspectives. In K. Kreppner & R. M. Lerner (Eds.), *Family systems and life-span development* (pp. 1–13). Hillsdale, NJ: Erlbaum.

Lerner, G. (1972). *Black women in White America: A documentary history.* New York: Vintage.

Monaghan, E. J. (1991). Family literacy in early 18th century Boston: Cotton Mather and his children. *Reading Research Quarterly, 26,* 342–370.

Morris, A. D. (1986). *The origins of the civil rights movement: Black communities organizing for change.* New York: Free Press.

Mwiria, K. (1993). Kenyan women adult literacy learners: Why their motivation is difficult to sustain. *International Review of Education, 3*(May), 183–192.

Pellegrini, A. (1991). A critique of the concept of at risk as applied to emergent literacy. *Language Arts, 68,* 380–385.

Pellegrini, A., Brody, G. H., & Sigel, I. (1985). Parents' book-reading habits with their children. *Journal of Educational Psychology, 77,* 332–340.

Pellegrini, A., Perlmutter, J. C., Galda, L., & Brody, G. H. (1989). *Joint book reading between Black Head Start children and their mothers.* Unpublished manuscript. University of Georgia, Institute for Behavioral Research, Athens, GA.

Purcell-Gates, V. (1995). *Other people's words: The cycle of low literacy.* Cambridge, MA: Harvard University Press.

Stromquist, N. P. (Ed.). (1992). *Women and education in Latin America: Knowledge, power and change.* Boulder, CO: Lynne Rienner.

Taylor, D. (1983). *Family literacy: Young children learning to read and write.* Exeter, NH: Heinemann Educational Books.

Taylor. D., & Dorsey-Gaines, C. (1988). *Growing up literate: Learning from inner-city families.* Portsmouth, NH: Heinemann Educational Books.

Taylor, D., & Strickland, D. (1989). Learning from families: Implications for educators and policy. In J. Allen & J. Mason (Eds.), *Risk makers, risk takers, risk breakers: Reducing the risks for young literacy learners* (pp. 251–276). Portsmouth, NH: Heinemann Educational Books

Weinstein-Shr, G. (1991, April). *Literacy and second language learners: A family agenda.* Paper presented at the annual meeting of the American Educational Research Association, Chicago, IL.

Young E., & Padilla, M. (1990). Mujeres Unidas en Accion: A popular education process. Special Issue: Community-based education: II. *Harvard Educational Review, 60*(1), 1–18.

30

COMMUNITY LITERACY:

FROM HOME TO WORK AND BACK

Gary Pharness
HASTINGS INSTITUTE, VANCOUVER, B. C. CANADA

Lee Weinstein
ADULT EDUCATIONAL CONSULTANT

The constant presence of family and community is found in all literacy work that attempts to build, redefine, and nurture learners in settings that draw their strengths from the needs and interactions of their participants. Community literacy is that literacy which reaches out to a defined neighborhood and to those who live and work within its boundaries. Community literacy exists at its best when all interested residents can shape and define the learning opportunities.

In this chapter, we argue not only that an understanding of adult learners' family, community, and workplace contexts is most powerful in literacy learning but that these contexts are best understood through learners' own narratives. It is the singular context that directs each of us as educators to learn afresh what is and is not important to the learner, and it is this story that tells us where we might best step into the learner's life.

Although the authors work in different arenas—community, workplace, and neighborhood-based—our view of literacy shares a common perspective. We believe that all of us have many personal literacies and each literacy has its own texts. These texts are the histories of our families, communities, and workplaces. In creating these texts, we are creating a literature. The use of that literature as curriculum reduces the separations of teacher from learner, curriculum from learner, and both from community. We believe that to teach literacy with this analysis requires the teacher to engage in the same process that he/she asks the learners. In understanding what we do, it is important for us to look at where we as workers come from. As an example, our own stories follow.

GP: Shortly before I turned three my grandfather came to live with us. With the arrival of my grandfather, I was intro-duced to reading. My grandfather was bald except for a short fringe of hair which seemed to wrap around the sides of his head like a narrow collar. And, although he was bald, he was more than vain about this collar. He dyed it red, using a toothbrush to apply watered-down oxblood shoe polish. Soon after his arrival he taught me the method of applying the polish to his hair. And during the procedure, which usually lasted an hour, he would read to me from either the *Bible* or from Dale Carnegie's *How to Win Friends and Influence People*.

Understandably, these two books are beyond the comprehension of a small child; however, they were exciting to me. My grandfather was a very attentive man. He realized my need for language; and, not only did he read, but he sang. He paused often to repeat a sentence or explain a word. More often than not, he would draw my attention to the sounds of a word and then help me struggle through to what to him was a satisfactory pronunciation. Another habit of his, which was annoying at the time, was the way he enjoyed the cadence of prose by emphasizing sound within a line. I soon learned to associate my grandfather's voice changes with certain meaning within the line. This was my introduction to books, and to reading. My grandfather also introduced me to carpentry. He allowed me to hammer alongside him high on a roof; and, while I missed nails, bent nails, and watched nails roll down the roof and over the eaves, my grandfather shouted, laughed, sang, and talked. My grandfather brought more than books and reading to our house, he brought language.

LW: My Dad, whose first language was Yiddish, was the model for my reading. He taught himself to read at the public library. He was an eclectic and passionate reader. His most used possession was the library card. My earliest and fondest memory, outside of playing baseball with him, was going to the main branch of the library in New Rochelle, New York.

When I was 8 or 9 years old my mother and father introduced me to independent reading. Now that I look back, it seemed odd that they had certain books that they told me I had to try. It was okay if I didn't like them and I didn't have to finish them, but I had to read twenty or thirty pages. Perhaps the reason it seemed tolerable was that my reading time extended my bedtime by 45 minutes. Another advantage was that my parents didn't check up on me to see if I followed instructions. There were no reports and no time limit to complete the readings. They only asked me to tell them what I thought about the books.

There weren't a lot of books on the "required list," but I knew they were important to my parents and they hoped would be important to me. The overflow books in the house were kept in the bookcase next to my bed. One night, with nothing to read, I found on the shelf a book of Twain's short stories. The first story was "The Jumping Frog;" because the stories were not longer than 25 pages, I could read two mini books a night. In each story I walked through a new town filled with characters that I couldn't wait to get to know. What was most important about the books I found in my room was that in a house where no secrets were allowed I had something of my own.

By junior high school I had an interesting outlook on the world. I was conservative in my tastes and politics. My brother had enlisted in the Marines and as he went south, Paris Island became the benchmark of what made a man, that is, until it became clear he didn't quite fit into the Corps. My vocabulary expanded to include the terms: brig, AWOL, M.P., St. Alban's Hospital, and Section 8 discharge. Into that fractured consciousness my radio dial hit WBAI in 1967. With no parental filter, I heard for the first time Phil Ochs, Tom Paxton, Lenny Bruce, and others. The words, songs, and attitude on WBAI were exciting, bordering on the illegal, to me.

While I was on vacation during my junior year in college, my father came downstairs and gave me one of the library books he had checked out that week, E. L. Doctorow's *The Book of Daniel.* It was a fictional account of the Rosenberg children and how they coped with and survived in the world after their parents were executed.

My Dad and I talked about what it was like during the McCarthy era and the earlier memories of his dad, who was an organizer for the Garment Workers' Union. As he talked about his early Post Office union activities and his flirtation with the Abraham Lincoln Brigade, I found myself embarrassed at my arrogance and how little credit I had given him. More important, I realized how much I enjoyed my new found connection with him.

My new respect for him gave my father the permission he needed to tell me stories of his life. Instead of having the dialogue between us based upon my bizarre behavior, politics, and dress, we had a positive reason to be in the same room. As I read *The Book of Daniel,* we talked about the Rosenbergs, the Peekskill riots, and what it was like to hear Paul Robeson live. I told him how happy I was for the book he gave me and I thought Doctorow did me a favor by writing it.

"Call him up," he said, "he just lives in New Rochelle." I laughed and told him that it would be crazy, and he'd hang up. "You're the one who is crazy. He would love to know you liked his book. Every author is happy to know if a reader liked his work." I did call Doctorow, and told him his book helped me connect with my father. He was very gracious and appreciative that I called.

GP: After starting school, I was placed in an adjustment room which had been created for children who demonstrated difficulty in settling down to kindergarten routines. All in all, this was a positive experience for me. It allowed me to look at and to try to read the many books in the room. Of more importance, our teacher, Miss Runberg, read to us for about 2 of the 3 hours we were in school. She read Mother Goose, fairy tales, folktales, and a continuing story of Uncle Wriggly, a story about an old rabbit; and, when reading about this rabbit, she always put long whiskers around her mouth and long fluffy ears on her head and then she would twitch her lips and shake her ears. It was wonderful and it was the last year I ever liked school.

During grade 1, I went to an old Carnegie library after school and on weekends. It had a fireplace which was used during the winter, and a large stage. The story lady read twice a week from a comfortable, overstuffed chair which always was to the side of the fireplace. The story lady read beautifully. In winter, the library staged children's theatre on Saturdays. The entertainers performed with breathtaking grace. By grade 3, the librarians allowed me the run of the place. From that time on, I especially enjoyed the stories of Grimm and Andersen, Harris and Aesop. I also read Sleeping Beauty, The Wizard of Oz, and Alice's Adventures in Wonderland. And, I continued to read about explorers, pirates, gunfighters, Indians, the Civil War, and New York gangsters. Along with these stories I read *Tobacco Road* and *Studs Lonigan.*

Inevitably, at an early age, I was drawn into the human spirit of my family and neighborhood through stories full of sin and hope, violence and joy, sorrow and redemption, hatred and promise and loss and love. It was in the telling of stories that my neighbors and family took on life, and fixed their place as detailed portraits in my memory. Uncle Harold is one such story.

who:	Uncle Harold,
what:	death,
how:	killed on motorcycle,
when:	1939, and
why:	he turned around to kiss his girlfriend.

These were stories about family that seemed to mean a lot to everyone, whether living or dead. And, as much as any living thing, I remember the darkening light and lifeless air of the foundry where my father worked; a loveless misery generated from its heat and noise and strength, then passed on from father to son. However, I was unable to carry for all my working days the burden of being a foundryman, or to hand it down to my own son.

LW: After college I started teaching social studies in an alternative school at Washington Irving High in New York City. The program was on the twelfth floor of a 6,000-student all-girls public school. I taught western civilization for one period in the regular school and any kind of social studies course that would keep five other classes interested.

Everyday for the first month I wanted to quit. The girls thought I had nothing to offer them and I ended up unsuccessfully pandering to them just to keep their interest. The low point was at 1:00 p.m. everyday when I'd get in the TV and we'd watch a game show. Whatever the mandate of the New York State Department of Education was, it wasn't happening in my room.

Then it struck me to bring in some black American literature that I found exciting. So I ran off some Julius Lester's stories from *Black Folktales* and *Long Journey Home* on an old Gestetner and formed a reading circle in my classes. As the stories spoke to my students and I valued the writings, the classwork assumed an importance it hadn't had before. Friends of my students started cutting out of their school and showing up for class. Students would frantically practice the text to be read during their turn. Discussions were as exciting as the stories they were reading.

What we can learn from our own literacy acquisition and practices allows us to work with others with more integrity. Implicitly or explicitly, our histories as laborers and skilled workers inform us about most facets of working with learners and employees.

SHARING WRITING, SHARING LIVES AT INVERGARRY LEARNING CENTRE

At Invergarry Learning Centre, we experience learners' sharing of their lives through writing. The Centre is unique in that it is a wholly adult learning environment housed in its own building, under the auspices of the Surrey School District. The Centre is staffed by people who favor a writing-process approach to literacy, and the staff and administrator develop funding proposals which access resources to put beliefs into concrete actions. More than anything else, we want to build a sense of community with learners.

The literacy program at Invergarry was founded on the principle that language learning best occurs when learners create their own text from the experiences, competencies, struggles, and triumphs in their lives. Learners are encouraged to write and critique each other's work in small groups. Many of us write side by side with the learners, whose writing is published in our journal, *Voices*. These writings support our literacy philosophy: everyone is a writer and has a story to tell, and through this telling we can better understand our place in the world. Toby, a young man from Mississippi in a class at DeBerry Prison recounts:

> So the next day Davie got me into a reading class and the teacher did not mind that I could not read too good. He handed me a book (Harry Crew's *A Childhood: Biography of a Place*) one day and told me to read just a couple of lines out loud to him. So I started to read and something in the book told me that it was a good book and the teacher knew that I liked it. If I like the book I could read it if I would not let no one have it or lose it. So, I left and went back to my unit and started reading it and a week later I was finished with the book and give it back.

> The teacher asked me if I like it and to tell him about it. So I began telling about the book. And how it somehow changed me just a little. The teacher then told me that there was a good story inside of me and he wanted me to write a short story for him, so I wrote a story about prison and what I thought about it. And that story came right out of me. It was at the first time I've ever wrote anything like that. So the next day I gave it to my teacher and he liked it and said it was good and that. He said that he thought there was a book in me. And if I keep writing I might get to it. (*Voices*, Fall 1990, pp. 78, 79)

Student writing and other dialogues help make the Invergarry literacy program a place where a sense of community grows and is nurtured.

The consequences of turning memories into text must be recognized and validated in any literacy program. This validation can best occur by printing these texts as elegantly as monies allow and using them as curriculum between like-minded programs. *Voices* grew out of an intent to create a beautiful product which would feature the writing of not just our students, but students around the world. These stories would be accompanied by photographs whose art and composition would add to the text.

We set about writing proposals to the government to get a literacy magazine funded. What we knew, beyond all else, was that this magazine, *Voices,* would treat writing as people read writing in their everyday lives. We wanted a magazine of stories without comprehension questions, spelling lists or myriad exercises subtracting from the joyful experience of recreational reading. We also, in our enthusiasm, wrote teacher/practice articles in the first six issues. While the teacher practice pieces ended by the seventh issue, *Voices* eventually grew to a 3000-subscriber base in 12 countries. We ran stories and photos from Capetown, South Africa; New York City; Chicago; Toronto; and other cities and countries—all without a comprehension question, cloze exercise, or single paid advertisement. As we learned about what issues were present in learners' lives, we subsequently recognized the need to include access to services within the centre's mandate: free legal services, refugee settlement, health care, counseling, day-care services, and work opportunities and training, to name a few, all of which work *against* isolation and *toward* building connections in ways that make sense to learners and practitioners. Acknowledging and addressing these kinds of issues has traditionally been seen as being outside the purview of the classroom teacher and administrator. However, we believe that the separation of learners' issues from prescribed curriculum has only served to perpetuate a larger system which, wanting to appear to address people's needs and concerns, in fact neither allows for real change nor reduces the isolation already experienced by many adult literacy learners and practitioners.

THE VALUE OF WORKERS' STORIES: OVERCOMING THE PREVAILING DISCONNECTEDNESS

Workers' stories take us back to places and people we have known before, remind us of our common roots, and give us back some of the community we thought we had left behind. Also, employee stories nurture any of us who, after reading the first line or paragraph, want to know, for the sake of shared humanness, what happened to the people in the stories. Through these writings we learned of people's jobs, families, histories, joys, and demons. And, in a more specifically penetrating way, the stories we read today give meaning to many of the kinds of work we had performed but at the time had missed the meaning of, having taken with us only the experiences. It is from our range of work experience and from those who worked alongside that we have come to understand how their language and story have shaped our literacy. Thinking about language in this way instructs us as to how language work can build learning communities from fragmented work environments. Writing groups and peer expectations are important to colearners. Group discussion about reading and writing not only generates mental stimulation between work peers, but it also confirms the importance of peer nurturing. This accords with Deutsch (1982), who suggested that cognitive growth may be the best therapy and the best means of self-realization. Writing about language development, Deutsch and others indicated that it must be continuous, sustained, connected, and relevant. Practiced in the workplace, these ideas significantly change attitudes and relationships, breaking down barriers among employees and slowly transforming fragmented worksites into learning communities.

The following piece by Deborah Lee, formerly a learner and now a consultant in the Vancouver Municipal Workplace Language Program, gives expression to this:

Learning English in the Workplace

Many times I have feelings deep in my mind. I don't know how to tell others, but when I write them down it's easier. From the writing I can find out my mistakes which I couldn't in the past. If I wanted to express something, in this program, but I didn't know how to write in English, I could use my own language and the teachers and I would then translate the words back into English. In this way I learned lots of new words, and I am no longer afraid to express myself. Since beginning, I continue to write and build up my interest and extend my thinking. (*Voices*, Spring 1991, p. 61)

What Deborah experienced in the above passage is experienced by many learners and therefore is not unique to those members of the community having English as an additional language. Crucial to building communities of learners and helping people such as Deborah is the understanding by teachers that literacy issues exist in real life contexts. The lack of literacy skills or confidence in acquiring those skills, often reinforced by the various institutions that propose to develop these skills, can adversely affect adults' self-esteem.

Our approach differs drastically from the following, more typical, scenario:

A corporation acknowledges that a given number of employees are experiencing difficulties with language. Most of this difficulty is in the area of basic literacy skills. Many of the employees are at work at the lower levels of the organization. To mediate this language problem, it is necessary to bring in an educator or "rent a teacher" to do a needs assessment and a task analysis. Many employees are seen to have English as an additional language or are identified as representing a specific race. Finally, the program is designed, then implemented. Attention is given to the method of program evaluation but seldom to how evaluation fits into company philosophy or how it addresses assessment outside language-related issues.

This approach, in a practical way, views the employee as an individual with language deficits. As such, the work of the program concentrates on filling in the gaps or deficits in employee's language ability. For the most part, classes consist of a number of learners having the same general ability and representative of a particular department or work function within the corporation. In short, employees are brought together for the purpose of remediation. This structure of literacy around what essentially is a class, race, and deficit model serves to further fragment the workplace and to separate employees from one another.

Fundamental to prescribed and dictated workplace programs is subservience to the dictates of the corporation. And, all too often, because they too work in large bureaucracies, educators model this behavior of deference. How many times do we see teachers thrilled to find themselves talking with managers, condescending towards employees, and advocating continuation of the status quo? The kinds of questions we ask determine the responses we get back. If the questions are employer-focused, we exclude employee's participation. This prescriptive focus asks: What specific language skills do our employees need to have? How does our organization use language and what do we need to do to help our employees construct language in the same way as we do? These questions outline the employer's goals but fail to help employees accomplish their full measure of literacy.

The kinds of questions we ask may need to be directed more specifically at employees or to answer questions about how employees interact. For example, what role does literature created by coworkers play in transforming the workplace into a more thoughtful and rewarding experience? Does a more thoughtful and rewarding workplace encourage employees to think about performance in terms of production, and so forth? How does our limited knowledge of how others work and live influence our personal and societal expectations of worker/learners? If we truly understand the dynamics which promote literacy, it is crucial that educators and people who implement literacy programs for any community of learners honestly express the value they place on individual members' literacy. When we fail to extend our own literacies to others, we have missed the opportunity to invite our learners and our employees to participate in and strengthen a literate society.

In the workplace context, writing memos, preparing documents, and filling in forms, along with being able to read and comprehend such materials, are pragmatic needs as well as aids to workplace function. However, these activities sometimes evoke a negative response to the question "Why should I learn to read and write better?" or "Why do I want to become literate?" Many employees, at all levels of the organization, interpret language activity of this kind as forms of employer and union control, worker compensation control, or something over which the boss has ultimate authority. Employees identify those who have power in the organization as being the same people who control print, revising what is fact and restructuring what is true.

To counteract and change this belief, learners need to have the opportunity to engage themselves with their work peers in the collaborative writing process to begin to practice collaboration in their respective worksites. This writing collaboration, in the form of "Would you take a look at this?" gives back to the presenter not only comment on the writing from the peer but a possible invitation to coffee or lunch, or maybe the discovery that both parties have some common interest. On a day-to-day basis, we see employees sharing life experiences, discussing books and film, getting together for recreational activities and exploring together ways in which work problems can be solved.

Literature is often seen as not having a place in workplace literacy programs. However, it is important for workplace programs to value literature of all kinds for the purpose of promoting literate behaviors. All too often employees are forced to work with safety and health manuals, business and technical writing texts, workplace policy booklets, and everyday workplace documents of memos, reports, and correspondence.

In contrast, at a lumber manufacturing site, MacMillan-Bloedel, Ltd., a growing library is well used. Employees contribute books, magazines, and other print text to the library, and suggest other possible inclusions. This employee interest in books has given rise to many discussions around style, diction, structure, and organization of text. One employee, a shop steward, wrote a piece for the regional International Woodworkers of America paper. After publication, he discovered that an editor had changed some of his vocabulary and slanted some of his meaning to take a harsher union position. At first, the employee questioned his writing, but then set about writing a piece, again for the paper, on how language has the capacity to create positive or negative responses to all union issues.

A program at the City of Vancouver's Manitoba Works Yards illustrates the value of an on-site library and the importance of literature. Here, a class of nine Italian and nine Portuguese males, and one each of male and female natural-born Canadians, made use of literature extensively to enhance and to explore their own personal stories. All males in this group worked in traditional male jobs: laborer, jack hammer and tool operator, heavy equipment operator, engineering, and surveying. The lone female worked as the crew dispatcher within the central engineering complex. Much of their work, although seemingly physical in nature, also required various kinds of thinking. Within the class setting, literacy tasks ranged from letter-sound association work to pronunciation, the writing of simple sentences, preparation of memos and more detailed reports, communicating ideas at a union meeting, and taking minutes in class for the purpose of accessing job postings, listing and minutes taking as a required skill for advanced job status.

A quick look at class ethnicity suggests the importance for instructors to have some general knowledge of world literature. Both English speakers were originally from the Canadian Prairies. W. O. Mitchell's story, "The Painted Door," set in the

Canadian Prairies of the 1930s, spoke of a life and place both learners knew intimately, although they were of different genders.

For the Italians, Silone's *Bread and Wine* proved more than useful when we were looking at City street names. Even after many years on the City's street crews, most of the men still had trouble remembering names of streets. Pronunciation also proved difficult. We took a break from the tedious work of reading the street names on the City map to read the beginning of *Bread and Wine.* Since most of the Italians had been to Rome, they knew the names of the roads leading to Rome. The excitement around this recognition encouraged these learners to continue trying to learn: their visible success and ability to correctly pronounce street names in Italian and the general feeling of knowing a past landscape contributed to their successful outlook. Indeed, the reading of *Bread and Wine* prompted a discussion about how our earliest remembered landscapes are always our points of reference. And, for a brief while, the natural English speakers saw the Italians talking and gesturing animatedly, carried beyond the usual struggle with English by the fluency of their first language.

The literature need not be from the student's homeland. Three of the Portuguese started their lives as fishermen and the sons of fishermen. They loved *The Old Man and the Sea,* parts of *Big Two Hearted River* and passages from *Jaws.* Always, the important consideration is that the story speaks strongly the life of the reader. Literature not only helps employees connect the external world to their personal internal world, but it also serves to reinforce for the learner the whole notion that writing about one's personal life differs little from commercially published literature in either content or significant meaning.

In yet another context, a group of 12 employees are gathered around a large boardroom-like table. All are attending the workplace language program in an on-site classroom provided by their employer. The employer and the six unions support the program which is open to all employees who want to attend the program, based on self-identified need. There are a couple of Vietnamese, three Chinese, four Canadians, a Serbian, a Croatian, and a Greek. Of these learners, other than the Canadians, five are naturalized citizens, and the remainder are immigrants.

The range of formal and informal learning experience found within this group is broad. While two come from rural areas of Asia and one comes from rural Europe, the rest come from large cities. Two of the workers who have rural backgrounds never attended school; however, their thinking is as sharp as any other person in the class. One city-born-and-raised student dropped out of school at age 9 because of family sickness. All in all, these 12 hold nine grade 12 diplomas, six B.A.s, five master's, and four doctorates among them.

A sampling of titles taken from this group's writings reinforces the sense of a range of schooling and, more important, personal interest: "Professions," "Christmas Gifts," "Dreams," "Masks," "Love is Blue," "Overdue It," "Parent/Teacher Meeting", "Rice Cooker," "A Text for my Drawings," "Meeting the Challenge," "My Uncle," "The Despair I Have Fought," "Samos," "The Meaning of Marriage," "Use of Words," "Computer Aided Learning," "Wood Products," and "Canadian

Democracy," to name a few. Learners see how the writing of a story brings about discovery, then gives meaning to one's experience in ways that go beyond routine writing exercises. In the following piece, Guadalupe Aguilar confirms his experience of having educated himself:

Self-Educated Man

I reside in Lockhart, approximately 30 miles south of Austin, the capital of Texas. My hometown is famous for its barbecue and sausage. People come from all over Texas and out of the state to eat at Kruz Market.

As a child and as a young man growing up in this town some of the things I remember most are working in the fields, picking cotton, hoeing, and picking corn. Very vividly, I remember those hot summer months. As we went about doing our work, hoeing cotton, a rain cloud would form on the horizon. Always I'd say to myself, "Come on this way rain cloud, I need a rest from this hot sun." Most of the time the rain cloud would just go the other way.

But as hot as those summer months were, and it gets hot in Texas, I was glad to be working in the hot sun rather than attending school. School was a very bad experience for me. I couldn't speak a word of English when I first started the First Grade. I remember standing with my dad, outside the Third grade class, crying, not wanting to go inside the classroom. You would think that by the Third grade a child would be used to attending school, but I wasn't.

I didn't learn English until maybe the Third or Fourth grade. By the time I left school I was 17 years old and I was in the Eighth grade. I had learned practically nothing.

Fortunately I developed a liking for reading. I started by reading newspaper comics. Then I progressed to the front page and the sports page.

Ironically, I think I learned more after I left school, because then I got interested in books. Books fascinated me. They opened a new world to me. I have never been too far away from home, that's why I especially like to read about faraway places. I also like to read about history, religion, and UFO information.

It wasn't easy learning to read. Many times I'd come across a word that I couldn't understand. By taking my time and concentrating on the sentence and the whole paragraph, I could figure out what the word meant. Sometimes I'd use a dictionary or ask somebody what that particular word meant.

I learned to read because I enjoy reading. It was precisely that enjoyment of reading that kept me from being illiterate.

As the years went on, I read more books. Consequently I improved my vocabulary. But I know I still have much to learn. That's why today I attend a reading class at my place of employment, Southwest Texas University, Grounds Department, in San Marcos, Texas.

Even though I can read efficiently enough, I have difficulty writing. That's why I attend this class to learn to write with more proficiency.

My goal is to some day attend college classes at my place of employment. I dare to dream that some day I could obtain a college degree. (*Voices*, Fall 1992, p. 50)

After reading Guadalupe's work, how many of us can say we have given such eloquent clarification to our life experience? Thinking back on work and school, Guadalupe concluded that attending school was a less preferable choice to working in the hot Texas sun. Throughout this short piece the writer's joy of reading and wonder of books balances and minimizes his failure at school. And, speaking of tone, the line, "Come on this way rain cloud, I need a rest from this hot

sun," certainly possesses all the strength of a good blues line and is followed by the timeless resignation of "Most of the time the rain cloud would just go the other way."

In seeing themselves as writers, we have found it important that learners use writing to redefine themselves in the world. Subsequently, programs and learners must value that writing by finding ways to make the writing available to others through publishing, then using it as curriculum. The ability to do these things with print is part of a process which offers learners opportunities to make their own choices and to be more in control of their lives. It is through such a connection with print and dialogue that learners can identify and address educational and social barriers. Moreover, equally as important as the methodology and the materials teachers and learners use for reading and writing are the relationships, trust, and value established between teachers and learners. When we make this part of our collective understanding of literacy, we collaboratively build a community. It seems perverse to claim a desire to make learners feel valued in a program, to encourage them to open up, and to develop personal relationships with colearners and instructors, but not to have the institution and its agents extend to learners their personal educational commitment beyond the language program.

When program providers help employees understand that many work cultures make up their organization and that these work cultures share certain histories, goals, and practices which connect the organization's various operational sections, a more desirable workplace literacy scenario can be imagined. It becomes easier for the employer to see the importance of building the language program so that it reflects the appropriate indigenous curriculum needs of the employees, not the prescribed curriculum which the provider most often brings. Such a program makes itself open to all employees within the corporation who want to attend. Employees then identify their own reasons for attending. The management and the union executive recognize that the program is inclusive and not subject to management and union agenda. Similarly, singular ethnicity, job type, and specific worksite become less than desirable foci upon which to build a program or class. Further, in the interest of achieving more than rhetorical change, the program extends opportunity to employees to make the daily conditions of work congruent with corporate philosophy about literacy, that is, the idea of flattening the workplace now actively translates into the practice of consulting with all or nearly all employees to better understand how to make decisions in the corporate culture.

Where do we draw the line as literacy workers ... in the classroom, home, neighborhood, city hall or workplace? The only reason to stop our analysis in the classroom or with the family is that it saves the trouble of connecting what we do to who we do it to and what happens to them when it is done or because mandates have never been broadened to allow these connections to be made. For the learners with whom we work, the time set aside for class competes with needs such as child care, health care, nutrition, cultural change and heritage language, adequate housing, and networks of support.

How can we say to learners that we want to be their partner, but do not carry this too far and remember that this is only school? If we are going to have integrity in our educational approach, we need to value learning by connecting experiences in the classroom back to the family, work, and community. If a program is going to espouse value and respect for learners, and view their experiences as central to the learning process, then all aspects of that program, from intake to evaluation to curriculum, need to reflect those beliefs. That same pedagogy requires literacy educators to consider issues in learners' lives which extend beyond the classroom to their families and communities.

We are really talking about intergenerational literacy and about using available resources to create authentic connections between different and otherwise isolated groups in our society. Literacy practice can speak to neighborhoods and communities where there is a need for quality child care to be readily available and affordable. It can presume that parents want to help and teach their children, and that parents and other adults have skills and experience that are worthwhile to impart to children (even if as adults they are not confident in their skills with print). Community literacy can allow professionals such as literacy teachers and early childhood educators to facilitate learning in an atmosphere which can encourage the sharing of knowledge and the acquiring of new knowledge. It can mean recognition that all cultures have rich traditions which must and can be affirmed in the literacy process. We envision community literacy as a vehicle through which people can begin to imagine the conditions that would help make and keep a society whole and healthy.

Community literacy models can build upon existing community strengths. Program designers need to explore relationships among individuals in otherwise unrelated groups: the work lies in finding what these relationships may be. The ways in which federal and provincial or state dollars are made available for new initiatives are not always well thought of. Many program administrators wrongfully spend time and limited resources simply getting projects started, whereas those resources can be used to enhance relationships which already exist. Community literacy models could have the potential to be effective because of their emphasis on community strengths. In less tightly connected areas, the dissolution of community, the transient nature of populations, the fear of crime and violence, the suspicion that comes from not knowing one's neighbors and their histories, and increased demographic changes, can all be seen as opportunities to establish community literacy practice. At the same time, there is a need to bring together different generations of different groups in positive, sharing, community-building activities. Community literacy can offer some of the glue to cement these connections.

For the last 2 years, Lee Weinstein and five others have been working in an intergenerational literacy project called Rainmaker in East Vancouver. With federal and provincial funding and an Apple Foundation donation of computers, we established a public space literacy project in a welcoming "inner city" elementary school of about 255 children, of whom 50% are First Nations (native Indian), 40% Asian

(Chinese and Vietnamese), 5% each of Spanish-speaking, and Canadian-born of Northern European origin. The Rainmaker room offers schoolchildren, parents, and community residents the opportunity to identify what they would like to learn with assistance from the Rainmaker staff. Guiding the project is the idea of reducing feelings of isolation and increasing feelings of connection. A parallel goal is to develop a center for learning and educational processes which could be adapted and eventually owned by community stakeholders.

In addition to workplace literacy, Gary Pharness has recently been involved in a community literacy project with a First Nations aboriginal community. People in the community wanted to become literate about who they were and they wanted to reinforce the positive aspects of their cultural heritage and present-day culture. However, the "mission" existed in a fragmented and factionalized state and, like much in public education, did not collectively hold a world view sufficiently strong enough to refashion its membership into a community or to restructure the existing system into a useful and purposeful institution. Fragmentation had resulted because 39 children had been removed from the community and many more members had moved away because living there was so bleak. The Indian leaders looked to bring back their children and encourage the return of their members, to establish independence and self-reliance from the government, to create safe day care and group home environments for the children, to build social structure and create economic development, and to provide schooling and training within the community.

On a day-to-day basis, the development of literacy and the building of community seldom elicited the excited response people need to develop and extend beyond their current position. However, the promise for literacy and the hope for community directed the struggle to emerge from the status quo. The First Nations people began to look at the power of language to describe community and to communicate a shift in power. Questions such as, "Who owns the housing?" and "Who is responsible for housing?" translated easily into illuminating descriptive contrasts: community housing committee versus the Department of Indian Affairs; social services' apprehension of children versus day care, group home and the training of community members for foster parenting; external policing, for example, the Royal Canadian Mounted Police, sheriffs, and Federal Bureau of Investigation versus internal local policing. The descriptive power of language to penetrate the experience of the individual and the community helped to understand the past and marked the beginning of a vision capable of illuminating the future.

This is the stuff of community literacy. It has the ability to develop educational plans which access funding to connect individuals and groups to one another. For some, this awareness may also include challenging the very systems under which we are funded, and working to create more honest and equitable means of supporting community literacy work. Taking a holistic approach which validates participants' strengths, literacy practitioners can assist in introducing groups to one another around those strengths to engage in community building, viewing language and literacy as paths for exploration and expression. Perhaps then we could, to use Freire's words, begin reading the world in such a way as to rewrite the human story in ways more humanly satisfying to us all. (Virginia Sauvé, quote written for a focus paper by Lee Weinstein, National Family Literacy Conference, Ottawa, Canada, September 1994).

Reference

Deutsch, W. (Ed.), (1982). *The child's construction of language behavioral development.* San Diego, CA: Academic Press.

31

A GRASS ROOTS THINK TANK: LINKING WRITING AND COMMUNITY BUILDING

Hal Adams

UNIVERSITY OF ILLINOIS AT CHICAGO

In a small wooden structure across the blacktop playground from their children's elementary school, a handful of adults smoke cigarettes, eat doughnuts, drink coffee and talk about their lives. The focus of the discussion is a short piece one of them wrote last weekend.

The author is 23 years old, pregnant with her third child. Her oldest is seven. She has no husband, no job, little formal education and uncertain housing. Because of her situation she thinks she is a failure. Her writing is self-critical. She fears she has violated God's plan for her life. She is weeping as she responds to others' comments, though the comments are gentle. They say it is not God's plan that she has violated, but her own. They say she is following God's plan by preparing for her baby's arrival and providing for her other children as best she can. The conversation alternately focuses on her writing, offering her emotional support, and debating religion. She begins to reconsider her writing and her views.

Sometimes these meetings unfold as literary criticism sessions, other times as church revivals, coffee klatches, therapy groups, or political caucuses. But mostly they are writing workshops, which turn out to be a kaleidoscope of possibilities and enactments. The participants are preparing their work for publication in a magazine that will be distributed in their school and community. The magazine is called the *Journal of Ordinary Thought*.

For 3 years I have been offering a parent writing program in local elementary schools in Chicago. The purpose of the program is to increase community involvement in the schools and demonstrate the link between education and community life. This is the story of that effort in one school. It began as a writing class for parents and grew into a community-building program that called itself a grass roots think tank.

EVERY PERSON IS A PHILOSOPHER

The school is in Austin, a poor black neighborhood on the west side of Chicago. Everybody in the group lives in the neighborhood, most of them all their lives. Two mornings a week we gather, usually 10 or 12 of us, to write and talk about life. It was not always relaxed, especially not the first day. People were anxious then. They had come because they wanted to help their children with their school work. Only a couple viewed themselves as writers, and here I was, the outsider from the university, under scrutiny, asking everyone to write freely about their experiences. I insisted that each of them had stories worth writing. Even strangers would be interested, I told them. They were doubtful, but polite. I persisted.

Every person is a philosopher, I said, thinking of the Italian Marxist, Antonio Gramsci, who thought people with power maintain dominion over ordinary people through the control of ideas as much as through the exertion or threat of force (Gramsci, 1971). If ordinary people develop confidence in their own ideas, Gramsci reasoned, they can challenge the control others hold over them. I was thinking also of the Brazilian educator, Paulo Freire, who thought ordinary people limit themselves by rejecting ideas that grow from personal experience and instead adopt ideas from the class that rules them (Freire, 1964). These ideas tend to justify class and race privilege. If ordinary people learn to recognize the alien ideas they have adopted, they are able to discard them and act in their own interest. Last, I was thinking of the Caribbean revolutionary, C. L. R. James, who thought the artistic expressions of ordinary people contain truths essential for social change (Buhle, 1988; Grimshaw, 1992). If ordinary people recognize the truths within their art, James concluded, they are more likely to trust their capacity to make a better world.

The ideas of these three thinkers can be summarized like this: Ordinary people hold the key to a better world; experience is the best guide to thinking and action; to achieve social progress people must think for themselves and reach their goals through self-activity rather than rely on outside authority to think or act for them; it is the responsibility of everyone to strive for a better world; those who are not political in this broad sense are illiterate, no matter how well they read and write.

I was in a poor neighborhood on Chicago's west side, facing 10 mothers and grandmothers who had vast experience in raising their families while keeping life and limb together under harsh conditions. Gramsci's, Freire's, and James' emphasis on the experience and thinking of ordinary people was compelling. The parents were intrigued by the idea that it is people leading ordinary lives who understand the world most clearly and create the truest meaning of their situation. Heads began to nod.

Near the end of the first session, having discussed lofty ideas about the importance of experience and the role of the ordinary person in creating a better world, the parents wrote what was on their minds. "Use your own language," I urged, "don't worry about spelling and grammar. If you don't know a word, leave a blank space; we'll figure it out later." Everyone gave me something.

The papers were so brief and cautious I was tempted to dismiss them as shy attempts to "get over" on the first day, to avoid drawing attention to themselves. Perhaps the good stuff would come later. But more was there than immediately apparent. Several papers, for instance, made reference to religious practices and beliefs. Looked at as a whole, they formed a religious theme that could not be denied. I typed all the submissions and distributed them at the next meeting. The group focused its attention on one, which read, in its entirety: *I went to church Sunday. I had a good time.*

If the author were to write more about this topic, I asked, what would you as a reader like to know? They gently began to ask questions aimed partly at the author, partly at the group. Why do you go to church? How did you choose this church? Do your children like it? What happened in church Sunday that made it a "good time?" Each question sparked discussion. People offered opinions on the differences between churches, the role of pastors, how churches have changed, their importance in African-American communities, disputes and disagreements within churches, and so on. They talked about how church communities and religious beliefs had helped them in everyday living and during crises.

From a simple two-sentence piece of writing I had nearly dismissed as "getting over" grew a discussion about how people create institutions to deal with the difficulties they face and how articles of belief influence everyday life. The discussion had its effect. The author had new directions to pursue, and others who were stimulated by the piece began writing ideas of their own.

The lessons were not lost on the group:

1. Even apparently simple writing contains meaning for the group.
2. The group helps develop the meaning in a piece of writing.
3. Writers develop their work by discussing it with others.
4. Writing by one person stimulates writing by another.

PRIMACY OF EXPERIENCE

The writing group was a place to identify questions from the gritty reality of life experience and to address them in discussion and writing. Nothing in these meetings took precedence over the experiences of the members. The parents took to this idea quickly. It was as if it affirmed an approach to learning that they already intuitively had accepted, namely, that life is the best teacher. Within a few months, armed with the confidence that its perspectives on the community were valid, the group would begin to take action on issues raised in the writing.

The meetings were conducted as writing workshops. I collected the writing, commented on it, and photocopied some for the class to read and discuss in future sessions. All discussion started with a member's writing. Discussion often went off in disparate directions, but inevitably it returned to the writing.

Mary was a leader but she was not a confident reader or writer. At each meeting the group would encourage her to write, but to no avail. A tape recorder and individual attention helped, but she still refused to write. One day, months later, she appeared with a piece of writing and proudly distributed it to the group. She had written it over the weekend with help of her teenage daughter and two of her daughter's friends. The four of them were lounging about in Mary's bedroom one night discussing their relationships with men. Mary asked them if they would help her write something summarizing their discussion. Mary spoke while her daughter wrote and the others made suggestions. This grim piece, the result of that cross-generation writing session, clicked immediately with the writing group and brought expressions of understanding that came from places formerly kept secret. An old bond was deepened between Mary and her daughter in the writing of the piece, and a new bond was forged in the group with the reading and the discussion of it:

> Males obsession over females. It starts with friendship, then they fall in love. The relationship begins wonderful; the nice secrets they share, gifts, romantic dinners, and the first time they make love. That's when the changes begin. The female is not allowed to have other male companions, no going out with her friends. All she can do is sit at home and wait for him. Then they have children and it really gets bad. The crying and fighting starts. All of a sudden the female loses interest and breaks the relationship off. Some get away, others can't. They are chased, harassed, and some even get killed in the process. Then all the male can say is, "If I can't have her, no one else can." Don't ever think you have made the right choice because you never know.

This story, based upon the experiences of Mary and her young friends, prompted others to tell similar stories about sexual relationships. A furious discussion followed about the oppressive conditions under which black men and women live in the United States and the stress these conditions place on intimacy between black men and women.

The group members brought new writing every session. They wrote about commonplace and extraordinary experiences: bus rides, kids getting ready for school, funny episodes, scary times, childhood memories, illness, death. The group discussions that followed the reading of these pieces always demonstrated the complexity of experience, including experiences that appeared trivial at first. It became second nature for the group to explore each story for its broader implications.

One mother wrote about taking a summer trip as a teenager with her mother and aunt to the southern United States. She was surprised that life in the rural South was so different from the northern city life she had always known. She disliked being in the South because there was nothing for her to do. After the others read her story they identified words they considered to be essential to it, even words the author did not use: surprised, different, peaceful, safe, friendly, boring, caring, violence, drugs. Using these key words as a point of departure, the parents discussed the difference between northern urban and southern rural life. How did values differ in the two regions? Was life safer in the South than in the North? Were families closer in the South? Was the educational system better? Did it cost less money to live in the South?

The parents' attention was rapt during the reading of these experience-based stories, and the ensuing discussions were intense. The stories rolled on, about family life, raising children, relations between the sexes, living amid violence, finding affordable housing, dealing with the public aid system, and surviving as women. The mothers came first to the writing group because they wanted to learn how to help their children with school work. They returned for the chance to explore the meaning they had gleaned from lives lived under stress of poverty, and because it was comforting to make explicit to each other the common struggle they shared.

PUBLISHING

Inside the front cover of the *Journal of Ordinary Thought* (*JOT*) is its statement of purpose: "The *Journal of Ordinary Thought* publishes reflections people make on their personal histories and everyday experiences. It is founded on the propositions that every person is a philosopher, expressing one's thoughts fosters creativity and change, and taking control of life requires people to think about the world and communicate the thoughts to others. *JOT* strives to be a vehicle for reflection, communication, and change."

It was time to publish writing from the parent group. I previously had published *JOT* in other settings: a public assistance office and a single residency hotel for formerly homeless people. The writing group's response to these earlier issues was positive. They liked the plainly-written style and the stories by people who lived lives similar to their own. They were fascinated by the prospect of seeing their names in print. The decision to publish was unanimous.

A few weeks later the group published an issue of *JOT* featuring writing by its members. The magazine's appearance in the dead of winter must have taken some bite from the Chicago wind because group members were dashing without coats between the school and the little back building where we met, waving copies. It was high drama. They were celebrating having published a magazine that would cast them in a new light in the community, as writers and thinkers to be taken seriously.

The magazine contained several stories about family life and, as a portent of what was to come later, a few about violence in the community. The family, troubled as it may be, was viewed in the writing group as a buffer against the harsh outside world. Charlene's piece reflected both of these themes and, by implication, suggested a relationship between them. She foreshadowed the strong fear of violence that other group members would pursue later in their writing. The security of her home, described in the opening, three-sentence paragraph, allowed her the psychological protection one evening to reflect on this disturbing experience:

I have put my kids to bed, finally. My house is peaceful, quiet. I will do some writing.
Two weeks ago I was standing at the bus stop. I noticed a guy walking up wearing house shoes. There were three other ladies standing there too. He was standing there looking at everyone's purses. He was moving a little closer every second, so I moved up a little closer to the pole at the bus stop. My heart was really pumping hard. I turned to the left to see if the bus was coming. It was, thank God. The bus pulled up and I rushed to the door as it opened. I did not want to be the last person to enter, but the lady behind jumped in front of me. I entered the bus gripping my purse real hard. As I sat at my seat I asked the lady why she jumped in front of me. She told me she too was frightened that she was going to have her purse taken. I finally felt at ease for a while.

The story, interesting in its own right, opened the door for others to write later of experiences more frightening than Charlene's. The group began to explore the violence that, while it surrounded them, did not overwhelm them.

Alberta, like Charlene, introduced a topic that would become a theme for the group as time passed. In only a few lines, she explored tension within the family, between men and women, in particular.

My brother called. He wants some money. I want to give it to him, but he don't work like he could. I wish he could get the right job and clean himself up. He only had one real job, and then didn't do so well. I don't want to give him money to waste up on something else. The world is such a mess, not like it used to be. I know it has to change.

The explicit recognition by the group of the tension between men and women, introduced here by Alberta, was a primary factor in establishing a separate writing group for men within a few months. Starting the men's group and openly discussing the tensions eventually increased the potential for men and women from the neighborhood to collaborate as the group evolved toward community action.

Publishing the magazine changed the group. Commitment to the writing sessions soared and almost nothing took precedence over the writing class. Membership grew. The group was asked to speak at several university classes. The children's teachers began to take notice of the parents' writing.

Influencing the Classroom

The stories the group published were not primarily about children, nor were they written primarily for children. From the beginning the authors wrote for themselves and each other, which is good because honest self-expression is the best way for adults to win children's respect and attention. Children learned from seeing adults tell stories about lives fully lived. The parents' history was the children's history, and committing it to writing demonstrated the truth in the adage that people are accumulated history. It was good to convey to children that experience counts, and that we are all philosophers interpreting the experience that forms our lives. There was wisdom in the stories for anyone in the community who read them, including children. Children grasped the meaning of some of the stories while the meaning of others eluded them. Even stories beyond their reach, however, made a point with the children: there were stories from the neighborhood worthy of publication and there were adults close to the school who cared enough to write them.

The parents began visiting primary-grade classes as guest authors. The purpose was to show the children that adults familiar to them were writing and publishing, reinforcing the idea that literacy was an everyday, important part of their community. The children enjoyed seeing familiar faces in the magazine, and gave close attention when the mothers read their work. Karen read her piece to her daughter's 1st-grade class.

> Let me tell you what a bad day I had. First I woke up late. The kids were hungry. I had to iron. I had washed only one of every sock. Finally we got out the door and wouldn't you know it, we missed the bus. So, I walked to get my check, but the lady said it was not there. My caseworker said I missed my appointment, which I didn't know about, and I had only one day to get my medical card. I got to the doctor, but he was gone for the day. Then I got some money to go to the store only to find that what I wanted was not on sale anymore. So I went home and cooked what I had. There was not enough for me, so I went to bed hungry. Now that's a bad day, but everybody has them.

The first graders gave it a positive review. The children's comments showed an understanding of the subtle message of Karen's story: Bad days are hard, but they can be handled. It was tiring and difficult to run around town with your kids, the children agreed, and scary to go bed hungry, but at the same time it was pretty funny that only one sock from each pair had been washed. The children emerged from Karen's reading with an understanding that one can survive a bad day with dignity and humor. Equally important, they developed new respect for Karen for having written about her bad day.

A Men's Group

The inclusion of men in the writing group on a regular basis was problematic for several reasons. The school had become the almost exclusive place for the women to meet socially;

men in live-in relationships with women receiving public aid often remained in the background for fear that their known presence would reduce the women's already-meager public aid checks; most important, living in poverty strained the relations between the sexes because men were unable to find decent jobs to support their families, often leaving women with the sole responsibility for raising children.

It was gratifying then, when two young men from the neighborhood asked to start a men's writing group. They had seen *JOT* and thought they could recruit several men to a group to work toward publishing a men's magazine. The women and the school administration enthusiastically agreed to have the men meet at the school once a week. Four men attended the first meeting, but the group quickly grew to 12. All were in their late teens and twenties; some were former or current gang members; most were not employed; and only one had a secure, well-paying job. The group met for a year and published two issues of a magazine called *Through the Eyes of a Villain.*

I objected to the title at first, arguing that it made them sound evil. "That's the point," they explained. "That's the irony. We are seen as evil. Our music strikes people as evil; our appearance strikes people as evil. They have to listen carefully to rap music to discover it is far more complex than 'bitches' and 'hoes' and violence. They will have to read the magazine to see beyond their fears, to realize we are men thinking about the world and how to remake it."

One piece in *Through the Eyes of a Villain* described the author as waking up one morning "unemployed, but not without work to do." It was an important phrase because this author and his writing group were taking a new look at their community. The men approached this task by offering highly personal critiques of two cultures—mainstream U.S. culture and the street culture of their neighborhood. Their critique of the mainstream was angry. Their critique of the street was poignant. Both cultures, the mainstream and the street, have ravaged the young lives of these men. The men expressed surprise that they had survived the racist violence of the mainstream and the street violence of the neighborhood. Here we are, they said with some surprise, in our twenties, still alive and out of jail. Who would have thought? As Derrick put it:

> Growing upon the Westside is a task all people can't do. There is a fear of death that haunts the neighborhood. Many people are scared because of drive-by shootings and drug sales on the corner, to come outside or even let their children play in front of their own houses. I can see where they're coming from. Sometimes I feel like that, because I'm a Black man on the Westside of Chicago who has seen about everything from group beat downs, to getting shot, to getting cut, to shooting first, to seeing murder, to kicking it with murderers. I ain't saying that I'm a bad guy or a nice guy, but I came a long way. All the things I did in my life, I'm surprised I didn't go to jail or die, but I know I came a long way. I got a long way to go. Looking back through all the madness, I believe I was possessed, but now I feel peace and blessed and the demons have left and I can start with my self evolution, evolving to a peaceful state.

The men wrote about what most men think about—what does it take to be a man? Existing on the outside of the only two cultures they knew, they faced a void they sought to fill with their manhood. They recognized the tremendous potential in the world and in their own lives for creativity on the one hand and for barbarism on the other. At this point in their lives, like C. L. R. James, they were seeking an artistic solution to the crisis. Most of them made rap music and they all wrote. It was no escapist art in which they were involved. It was art that told the truth, for them the only path to being human and to manhood. Kevin wrote:

> Life, it's a hard subject to talk about because I'm having a hard time dealing with it. A buddy of mine was smoked about a month and a half ago on the South Side. It was gang related. Another one of my homies had his picture taken with a 12 gauge. The last thing he saw was the flash. It was drug related. When I lived in California one of my boys got beat down by some Bloods over his truck... I could go on and on with these types of stories, but it's hard, especially when it's one of your boys. Each time I heard the bad news I wanted to strap up and take care of business. But who gives me the right to kill another muthafucker just cause he killed my boy? Like I said in the beginning, life, it's hard to talk about. We're becoming extinct, being hunted by our own kind. ...

A GRASS ROOTS THINK TANK

Before the men's group was formed, the women had become more active in the school. Writing and group discussion seemed to make them more free to offer public opinions about school policy. Several ran for the local school council, which in Chicago has considerable power in neighborhood schools. As their confidence grew, some parents who previously had viewed their classroom volunteer role as primarily disciplinary began to take a different initiative with students. Linda contributed to the discussion of this process with "Parent Volunteer":

> There is a child in the classroom where I volunteer. His name is Marvin. He is so cute. He has a problem reading, but he is trying hard. He also has a problem with adding and subtraction, but he is learning. When the teacher passes out the homework he gets his and puts it in his bag. The next day she asks the kids to bring up their homework, and she asks Marvin for his. He says, "My mom wouldn't help me." So, I suggest, "Marvin, do the best you can. Try by yourself, and if you can't get some part, leave it blank." For a while he wasn't bringing in any homework, but boy, now he's doing it and turning it in....

The discussion of Linda's piece, where members reassessed their roles as parents in the classrooms, was part of a larger discussion about the relationship of neighborhood culture to the educational process. The physical environment, family traditions, educational expectations, child rearing practices, family structure, and community institutions were described in writing from a personal perspective.

Toward the beginning of its second year of existence the writing group began to discuss taking action on issues that had arisen in the writing. As members continued to write about the experience of living in the community, the group expressed an awareness that the community environment was related closely to the quality of education their children received in school. They convened a meeting to discuss the

matter with about 30 neighbors. To get the ball rolling, members of the writing group read selections from writing in progress. Three authors who subsequently published their works in *JOT* caught the attention of the meeting. Paulette went first with a piece she called, "Abandoned Buildings":

> I imagine people staying around abandoned buildings. Sometimes you have to pass these buildings. You're actually scared to walk by them because you never know who might be inside. Sometimes you know they are inside watching you come by, but you don't know who is there. It might be a drug addict or someone to kill you. So when you pass these buildings, you have to watch carefully.

Joyce followed with "Dangerous World":

> It is a dangerous world today. Something I wonder about a lot is how my children will live in this world. I know it's coming to an end one day. I hope and pray I will live to see my children grow up and make something out of themselves.
>
> So much is happening out there every day of their lives. I see things and hear things—people and deaths, and so many young people killing one another over nothing. That's why I worry about a lot of things. I pray to God every day that nothing will happen to my kids. I tell him, don't forget us down here. Just keep watching over us and everybody in the world.

Theresa read last with an untitled piece:

> Most everywhere you go in the 29th ward there is a vacant building. Some are torn halfway down or boarded up. Some were boarded up but the drug dealers have taken the boards down and made the buildings into spots to sell drugs, or they take someone in there to rape or kill.
>
> One night I was going to work. After taking the kids to the babysitter, I was on my way back to Central and Washington to catch the bus when I happened to walk by a vacant building and heard a lady screaming. I did not stop because I was the only one walking on the street that night. I was frightened. I ran fast and prayed—just get me to the bus stop and then, please bus, hurry up!

Each author's story was greeted with nods and murmurs of approval. As it happens, there was a large abandoned apartment building next to the school playground. At the time of the community meeting it was well known as a center for drug activity, and a few years earlier a woman had been raped in the building. It is no wonder the three essays struck a responsive chord.

It was agreed that the group would do something to stop drug activity near the school, but there were no illusions about the limited effect a victory would achieve. Everyone knew if the dealers were removed from the school area they simply would set up shop in another place, but at least parents would not have to worry about their children passing by drug deals on their way to school. People understood the complex nature of the problem. The deeper social and economic problems would not be solved by removing drug activity from the school area or, for that matter, even by eliminating drugs from the entire neighborhood. Many expressed sympathy for the young people selling drugs. There was strong sentiment in the discussion for the group not to take an unalterable position against the desperate people, some of whom were acquaintances, who had turned to selling drugs as a last resort. What appeared on the surface to be a simplistic solution (get drug sales away from the school) was in fact a solution that took into account complex social factors beyond the comprehension of many people not from the community. The lesson here is that long-term solutions to the complex problems of poor communities cannot be found without the broad, realistic perspectives that can be developed only by community residents.

At least once a month for the next year the writing group met not as a writing group, but as the Austin Grass Roots Think Tank. The Think Tank was an organization committed to planning community action based on ideas that grew from the writing of ordinary citizens who lived in the area. During the Think Tank meetings the group discussed what to do about the abandoned building next door. They took pictures of the many vacant buildings in the area and wrote stories about their experiences with them. They called in the police to discuss increased security (to little avail) and invited the city housing department staff to explain procedures for addressing the matter. They discovered how to do a title search to identify the owners of abandoned buildings. They learned about housing court. They sent representatives to testify in court several times during the year, and on two occasions rented buses to carry groups of people to the downtown courtroom. They invited building owners to meetings to discuss the threat their buildings posed to the children. With pressure from the court and the Think Tank, the owners of the building next to the school agreed to secure their building, post a guard during school hours, clean the area, and report to the school office each day.

The Men's and Women's Groups Unite (Sometimes)

As time passed, the men's writing group joined the Think Tank sessions. The effect was significant as both sexes offered their often differing perspectives on common problems. At one meeting, for instance, Detrich read a piece in which she asserted that black women coped better than men with drugs, poverty and violence. She concluded that it was difficult to find "a good Black man." Joe uncurled his long limbs, reached for a paper of his and said, "Yeah, women go through a lot we don't understand, but we go through things women don't understand. Check this out." He began to read about hanging out with his buddies after a writing group session:

> ...An hour later I smoked a blunt and drank a couple of brews with my buddies in the alley behind my house. I turned to walk away and there was an unmarked police car flying towards me. In my neighborhood cops like to hit you, so I was hoping they would drive right by. All four doors flew open and the car screeched to a stop. I took a step back and threw my hands up. I was snatched and thrown roughly against the gate alongside my buddies. ... One cop (started yelling), "Hit him, hit him, hit him, hit him! One of you fuckers is going to jail." ... one (of the cops) reached into my underwear looking for dope. My cousin came out of the house to see what was going on. "What the fuck do you want," one of the officers asked... "you're going to jail too, motherfucker, put that bag of dope on him. ..."
>
> I got angry at myself. I felt like a sellout. I was afraid. It was five of them with guns, but that was no consolation. I kept quiet

because I was afraid they'd make good on their threats. They left as suddenly as they came. "Get out of the alley," they warned, leaving us spread eagle against the fence.

> ...I think I've been searched by the police at least a hundred times, but I've never gotten used to it. Each time it's like being raped. Sometimes they even do it with a gun to my head or ribs. I told my mom what happened and she said I shouldn't hang with my friends. My aunt called and told me to stay out of the alley. My alley!...

A heated discussion followed the reading of Detrich's and Joe's papers with all the men and some of the women initially siding with Joe, and most of the women taking the position of Joe's mother and aunt that Joe should not be hanging out in the alley. Eventually the group decided there was an overriding matter that concerned everyone in the room: the tension in the community regarding its diverse expectations of the police. At the time of this writing, the Think Tank is debating a program to address this issue.

By becoming more active in the school as volunteers and policy makers, by addressing community issues that have an impact on education, and by basing these actions on experiential writing, the Grass Roots Think Tank has taken beginning steps toward realizing the visions of Gramsci, Freire, and James who imagined a primary role for ordinary people in changing society. The steps are encouraging when one considers the pressure in contemporary society against such political initiative. (Gramsci would call it self-activity.) Democracy has been reduced in popular consciousness to the occasional casting of a ballot. True community action based upon collective deliberation is rare, and those who engage in it are often viewed cynically as being naive. The Think Tank and the *Journal of Ordinary Thought* are instances of participatory democracy in practice.

Looking Ahead

The Grass Roots Think Tank would like to expand the concept of a writing-based community organization beyond its current location in one school. It would like to establish writing groups around the neighborhood in different settings: housing complexes, churches, libraries, public aid offices, and so on. Each group will be responsible for publishing its writing. Periodically the expanded organization will convene forums where the writing groups will make their work available to each other. Ad hoc action committees with participation from several writing centers will form around shared community concerns. In this way people from several community bases will be working on issues of common interest.

The early success of the Think Tank was largely a function of its nonhierarchical, informal, organizational character. Individual, experiential writing and group discussion drive the Think Tank. Thus, it relies simultaneously on both highly independent and highly collective activity. Any expanded version of the program must preserve this mode of operation to preserve the intimate atmosphere. Otherwise, new, honest writing about personal experience will not be forthcoming.

Moving from writing groups to action groups is both the most promising and problematic aspect of an expanded Grass Roots Think Tank. It is promising because the movement from writing to action will be based on perceptions of the community by people at its roots, a condition implicit in the ideas of Gramsci, Freire, and James. It is problematic because there will be no central staff to assume responsibility for organizing action programs and moving them forward. But one simultaneously cannot have self-activity by community residents and central control of them. Central control often discourages ordinary citizens and otherwise weakens their initiative. It is the philosophy behind the Think Tank's organizational approach that people will be more likely to take control of their community if they are not expected to hand over their initiatives to a central administrative body.

We propose to set in motion a process where residents of the community can examine with each other the weighty matters of family, community, and economic development. The process will rely heavily on writing and publishing by community residents. We do this to demonstrate the critical role literacy plays in community development, and because community writing is an effective way to reveal the profound wisdom and understandings residents can develop by examining their community experiences.

The time is ripe for such initiatives in poor communities where people often are discouraged by their chronically limited economic prospects. It is clear that help from the outside is not immediately forthcoming. Self-activity is now the only real alternative. A writing-based community project offers a practical way for citizens to be involved at the center of a process that will address their own futures. The precise direction the community will take in the process is not certain. But that is the nature of self-direction, and it is part of the reason it appeals to people who have long since become skeptical of solutions imposed from the outside.

References

Buhlé, P. (1988). *C. L. R. James: The artist as revolutionary.* New York: Verso.

Freire, P. (1964). *Pedagogy of the oppressed.*

Gramsci, A. (1971). *Selections from the prison notebooks.* New York: International Publishers.

Grimshaw, A. (Ed.), (1992). *The C. L. R. James reader.* Oxford: Blackwell.

RESEARCH ON LANGUAGE TEACHERS: CONDITIONS AND CONTEXTS

INTRODUCTION

Dorothy S. Strickland

RUTGERS UNIVERSITY

The scene is a 10-year college reunion. Three friends, all teachers, are renewing their friendships. After comparing vital statistics about marital status and offspring, they begin to talk about their work. They discover that they all work in districts characterized as "difficult." Two complain about being totally burned out. One comments that today's students do not want to learn, lack respect for authority, and are out of control most of the time. Another says that she has little complaint about her students, "After all, many of them come from tough circumstances." Instead, she is fed up with the administrative bureaucracy. She contends that they go out of their way to stifle teacher creativity and effectiveness with onerous paperwork requirements and endless restrictions on what teachers may or may not do in the classroom.

The third concurs that reaching many of her students is difficult and agrees that dealing with the central office bureaucracy is a headache producer. Quite unexpectedly, however, she eagerly begins to share a new innovation that she is trying out in her classroom. She is experimenting with the use of drama in her language arts and social studies programs. With great enthusiasm, she reports, "There seem to be endless ways to link creative drama, literature, history, and writing. The students love to role-play scenes from their reading and to 'perform' poetry. Some have used the computer to collaborate on writing plays. Performances have been videotaped and shared with other classes and at home." Most important, she adds, "Creative dramatics seems to build on the natural expressiveness and creative energy that her students possess." To her amazement, she explains, "Student interest is up and discipline problems down." She wonders if the other two have tried any of these ideas, and seeks their advice and opinion.

One can conjecture about the many reasons these teachers vary so widely in their response to somewhat similar circumstances. The most obvious explanation is that, although similar, their situations are not identical. And certainly, each of these teachers is an individual personality with certain predisposed ways of handling difficult situations. Still, the question of why some teachers and administrators remain resourceful and optimistic despite difficult conditions is a highly important one. Disgruntled, ineffective educators only exacerbate situations that are difficult to begin with. Their very presence has an adverse effect upon the lives of students and contributes to the public's misimpression of educators as less well trained and effective than other professionals. On the other hand, educators whose professional stance includes a sense of optimism and inquiry are likely to have a positive effect on students and demonstrate a personal commitment to ongoing professional development. These are the types of individuals we want to attract to schools of education. Once there, we need to prepare them well and nurture them as practitioners.

Preservice and inservice educators, associated with a variety of disciplines and working in a variety of contexts, comprise the *WHO* of research on teaching the communicative and visual arts. An examination of issues related to these individuals is key to broadening our professional understanding and interpretation of the ways in which print and visual arts, as well as oral language performance and interpretation, play continuing and changing roles in language education. In this part of the handbook, we examine research on language teachers and the conditions and contexts in which they teach. We discuss the increasing assortment of programs offered at the preservice level and the kinds of inservice support offered to practicing professionals. Special issues are addressed that confront teachers in the current wave of reform. These include the current emphasis on multicultural education and the challenges posed by the ever-increasing diversity of the school population. The need to bring teachers together from various disciplines within the communicative and visual arts to create and implement curriculum is also addressed. The voices of teachers and administrators are heard, including those who teach in traditional as well as nontraditional settings.

Improvement in the conditions and quality of teachers and teaching has been a continuing source of concern to educators from the earliest history of schooling in the United States:

It is undeniably true that for many years the teaching profession has been held in less high regard in the United States than its due; the teachers have been ranked and rated more by their salaries than by their service to public. Teachers' salaries are inadequate, and the professional requirements are correspondingly low. The profession has suffered because almost any kind of amateur can get permission to instruct school children. If it were not that the average public school teacher has given the public much more than he has received, it would have gone hard with the schools and education in our country. (Department of Interior Bureau of Education, 1918, p. 208)

Concern for the status of the teaching profession continues to undergo constant public criticism and the scrutiny of educational researchers. Current reforms in teacher education and at the district and school levels are addressed by several authors in this section. Significant changes in traditional university-based programs as well as alternative certification, programs connected with professional development schools, and the Teach For American initiative. Nearly all of these programs are relatively new and require continued scrutiny. Nevertheless, they are viewed as attempts to be more responsive to needs within schools and classrooms and for that reason they are hailed as innovative and hopeful alternatives to existing programs that are badly in need of reform.

In an attempt to re-create schools as places where students and teachers work together, some school districts are attempting to redefine the roles of teachers. Curricula are being revised and instructional methods altered to reflect more interdisciplinary approaches. The integration of the communicative and visual arts would appear to be natural points of linkage. In general, however, several authors in this section concur that linking the domains of visual and verbal expression continues to be a need both in teacher education programs and in the classroom. Olson laments the lack of communication between art and English language arts teachers, stating that the actual setting of the school frequently works against the formation of a close partnership between the two areas of communication and expression. Mesa argues not only for the integration of the communicative and visual arts, but decries the fact that the arts are often thought of as less intellectual or important as other areas of the curriculum. He reminds us that good art instruction calls for rigorous intellectual skills, imagination, and the ability to conceptualize.

Grossman, Valencia, and Hamel raise a key point of tension as we move toward a more interdisciplinary view of the communicative and visual arts. They remind us that current reforms within literacy education require greater teacher expertise in all aspects of the English language arts. Yet, reforms across and beyond subject matter areas would appear to ask teachers to act as generalists. Providing teachers, especially new teachers, with the fundamental background they need to design and implement integrated curricula will be a growing challenge for teacher education in the future.

Redefining of the role of the teacher is also the thrust of the chapter by Vacca, Vacca, and Bruneau. They encourage the concept of *teaching as a reflective practice* as it is increasingly used to describe both teacher development and the practice of teaching as a thoughtful, highly professional activ-

ity. They call for a high level of problem solving and intellectual inquiry among teachers and state the need for professionals to develop the ability to identify and understand problems of practice as well as to develop the ability to hypothesize alternatives, place new actions into practice, and evaluate the results of their teaching action. They cite examples of individual and collaborative work in which classroom teachers and university teachers and researchers problem-solve together. Grossman, Valencia, and Hamel also call for greater collaboration between faculties in education and in arts and sciences within colleges and universities, and between university-based teacher education programs and schools.

Concern for preparing and supporting teachers who work with students from diverse linguistic and cultural backgrounds is expressed by several authors. As teachers and principals struggle to redesign their schools to meet the challenges of the 21st century, they are faced with the reality that the public schools must educate more children from diverse bacgrounds than ever before and that they must do it better than ever before. As an administrator, who is neither an artist nor an art educator, Mesa speaks passionately about art as central to our need to express human experience and thought. He has a special concern for the decreasing role given to art in the education of ethnically and linguistically diverse students. Viewed as far away from the basics, art departments are most likely to suffer from budget cuts. Although Mesa deplores these cuts for all students, he views them as doubly harmful for students in areas of high academic risk where large numbers of ethnically and linguistically diverse students are concentrated. Unlike more advantaged children, these students are not likely to have rich experiences with art outside the classroom.

Teacher education programs that prepare teachers to work with the increasingly diverse populations found in our nation's schools are discussed in the chapter by Tinajero and that of Grossman, Valencia, and Hamel. They are also the focal point of the Willis and Harris chapter. Willis and Harris cite numerous researchers, who stress the belief that improved understandings of the role of culture in literature instruction during preservice education will improve literature instruction for all students. They share some of the instructional techniques they use with preservice students to build community, model instructional strategies, and offer opportunities for students to experience strategies they might eventually use as teachers.

No doubt the diversity among learners and the teaching environments in which they are taught will only increase in the coming years. So too, the modes of communication will continue to expand and change in our society. The concept of what it means to be literate and what teachers must do to support learners in their attempts to acquire knowledge and develop as literate members of our society will also change. Thus, the challenge to attract and nurture teachers, such as the one enthusiastically experimenting with drama described at the beginning of this introduction, will only become greater.

Throughout Part IV, the contributors offer an agenda for research on teachers and teaching that goes well beyond the collection of evidence regarding best methods, time on task, or stating instructional objectives. Simply modifying the framework within which teachers operate will neither improve teachers nor the teaching of the English language arts. Moreover, it will do little to bring the communicative and visual arts closer together as a unified whole. Teaching is an uncertain and vulnerable activity. The fact that this is unlikely to change, is not all bad. Though the uncertainties make teachers vulnerable, they also invite opportunities to construct effective, dynamic learning environments for everyone involved. We can help counterbalance the uncertainties that teachers face by connecting them to other teachers to lessen the loneliness and lack of support they experience; by allowing them the rewards that come from recognition, accomplishment, and professional control; by enabling them to acquire and generate new knowledge; and by encouraging them to take charge of their own professional development". (Goodwin, 1987, p. 35)

References

Department of the Interior Bureau of Education. (1918). The educational system of South Dakota. Bulletin, No. 31. Washington, DC: U.S. Government Printing Office.

Goodwin, L. (1987). The realities of teaching. In F. Bolin & J. Falk (Eds.), *Teacher renewal: Professional issues, personal choices*. New York: Teacher College Press.

32

PREPARING LANGUAGE ARTS TEACHERS IN A TIME OF REFORM

Pamela L. Grossman, Sheila W. Valencia, Frederick L. Hamel

UNIVERSITY OF WASHINGTON

INTRODUCTION

Myriad in number and diverse in intent, reform efforts are currently challenging the educational status quo. Some of the reforms are aimed at increasing access to quality education for all students. These reforms include the movements to eliminate tracking in schools and to educate special education students in regular classrooms. Other reforms hope to create greater national consensus on standards for students and teachers alike. Goals 2000 legislation requires that we define what students should learn and make explicit the criteria for acceptable performance. At the same time, the National Board for Professional Teaching Standards has begun to create standards for expertise in teaching. Other reforms are aimed at giving teachers a more active role in determining school policies through site-based management and in assessing student learning through classroom-based and performance assessments. Not surprisingly, language arts has occupied a central role in many of these reform efforts, as the literacy abilities of students continue to concern both educators and the public.

At the same time, the field of language arts itself has undergone a number of reforms. Over the past two decades, basic and applied research in literacy has changed what we teach, how we teach, and how we assess student learning in the language arts (cf. Hillocks, 1986; Pearson & Fielding, 1991; Resnick & Resnick, 1992). For example, reading is now understood as the process of constructing meaning rather than the translation of icons; writing is viewed as a complex series of processes for a variety of purposes and audiences, rather than as a product; and new approaches to literary criticism have challenged the purely text-based models of close reading that defined New Criticism. Literature-based reading instruction, reader response theories, and writing

process have all found their way into classrooms. In addition, the curriculum of language arts has expanded beyond the traditional areas of reading, writing, listening, and speaking to include visual literacy and an emphasis on thematic or interdisciplinary curriculum. Finally, assessment within the language arts has shifted away from sole reliance on standardized tests to include more authentic, performance-based assessments, as well as classroom-based evidence of student growth (Valencia, Hiebert, & Afflerbach, 1994). Taken together, these multiple reform efforts represent a dramatic departure from the language arts curriculum and instruction of the past.

Given the breadth and multifaceted nature of the subject matter, preparing capable and knowledgeable language arts teachers can be a complicated task at any time. The complexity of the task increases during periods of reform. In this chapter, we explore the challenges of preparing language arts teachers both within the specific context of the subject matter, which presents its own unique dilemmas, and within the context of these larger reform efforts.

BREADTH OF SUBJECT MATTER

Any discussion of preparing language arts teachers must confront the breadth of the subject matter and its implications for teacher education. Whether depicted as the traditional tripod of language, literature, and composition, or the four areas of reading, writing, listening, and speaking, the subject matter is extremely broad and ill-defined (Applebee, 1974; Elbow, 1990). This breadth invariably creates dilemmas in preparing teachers to teach language arts.

One dilemma concerns the subject matter preparation for prospective language arts teachers. Because the field is composed of many distinct disciplines, there may be an inevitable trade-off between breadth and depth of preparation in the content areas of language arts. For example, should we require that prospective elementary school teachers take at least one course in all of the areas that might reasonably be considered part of the language arts curriculum as part of their undergraduate programs? If so, they might be required to take courses in literature, writing, rhetoric, speech communications, drama, and language acquisition. Such a requirement threatens to sacrifice depth of understanding in any one particular area for overall breadth. Similarly, what majors should be recommended for prospective secondary language arts teachers? The traditional English major is likely to focus almost exclusively on literature (Graff, 1987) and give shorter shrift to other components of the language arts. At the same time, prospective teachers who major in communications or journalism may find themselves relatively less well prepared to address the literature component of most secondary language arts classes.

These issues are accentuated, in part, because there is no direct higher education equivalent for "language arts." Instead, a number of university departments overlap the territory encompassed by this school subject, including English, Communications, Speech Communication, Drama, and Comparative Literature. Learning language arts for teaching can thus occur in a wide variety of academic departments, no single one of which captures the entire school subject.

The breadth of the school subject also creates dilemmas for research efforts in English education. For example, researchers have concentrated particularly on elementary teachers' understandings and beliefs about reading, while all but ignoring their knowledge of literature. In contrast, a number of studies have investigated secondary English teachers' knowledge and understanding of literature, but researchers have seldom looked at their knowledge of the reading process. Few studies have attempted to study teachers' understandings of the full spectrum of language arts. As Nancie Atwell's (1987) portrayal of her own development as a teacher suggests, teachers' beliefs about the teaching of writing and the teaching of reading may develop in isolation; changes in teachers' beliefs and practice in teaching writing are not necessarily accompanied by changes in the teaching of reading. These issues of breadth affect not only teacher education and research but language arts classrooms, as teachers must make decisions about what aspects of this many-faceted subject to include in their curriculum. The lack of definition of language arts may create greater autonomy for teachers, which in turn, places greater demands on teachers' individual knowledge and skill (Grossman & Shulman. 1994).

ELEMENTARY AND SECONDARY LANGUAGE ARTS: SEPARATE WORLDS?

Language arts is susceptible to fragmentation not only by the breadth of its content but by grade level as well. Researchers and teacher educators alike have often tended to treat elementary and secondary language arts as separate worlds. Traditionally, elementary teacher educators have focused more on teachers' knowledge of the processes of language acquisition, reading, and writing. Because elementary teachers have relied in the past upon basal readers, the selection and instruction surrounding particular literature has not been seen, until recently, as the primary responsibility of the individual teacher; the textbooks provided both reading selections and suggestions for instructional strategies. In contrast, secondary teacher educators have focused more on the content of the curriculum. However, with the recent popularity of literature-based instruction at the elementary school, the subject matter preparation of prospective elementary teachers in literature will become increasingly important. Similarly, the numbers of secondary students experiencing difficulty in reading and writing, and the increased emphasis in secondary language arts on the processes of writing and interacting with texts suggest that secondary teachers' understandings of the processes involved in reading and writing will attract more attention as well.

These differences in perspective dependent upon grade level are also reflected in the membership and concerns of national organizations concerned with the teaching and learning of language arts. The National Council of Teachers of English (NCTE) and the International Reading Association (IRA) are the two largest professional organizations associated with language arts education. While the sizes of their memberships are similar, the distribution of members representing elementary and secondary education is reversed. Based on data on journal subscriptions, approximately 70% of IRA members have an elementary focus and 30% a secondary focus, while 30% of NCTE membership represent an elementary emphasis and 70% a secondary emphasis. This suggests that elementary and secondary language arts teachers may be reading different journals, attending different conferences, and generally remaining isolated from one another, making it all the more difficult to ensure an articulated curriculum and shared understandings across the grades. The sequestering of teachers by grade level also closes off opportunities for teachers to learn from one another. Teacher educators may also reflect this division by grade level, as they may belong to different professional organizations and work in different arenas in teacher education programs.

MULTIPLE VERSIONS OF ENGLISH/ LANGUAGE ARTS

Both accounts of actual classroom practice and theoretical analyses suggest that there are multiple, and often conflicting, "versions" of language arts operating within schools (see Applebee, 1974; Barnes, Barnes & Clarke, 1984; Dixon, 1969; Gere, 1992; Grossman, 1993; McEwan, 1992; for discussions of various traditions and versions of language arts and their implications for teaching). Five distinct versions of language arts might include: personal growth version; disciplinary knowledge version; basic skills version; transformative/critical literacy version; and cultural heritage version.

Each of these versions poses somewhat different goals for the teaching of language arts and implies different sets of assumptions about the nature of the subject matter. For example, a basic skills version may emphasize the acquisition and command of reading and writing skills. Skills may be depicted as discrete and detachable into isolated subskills. In contrast, a personal growth version of the subject matter emphasizes the centrality of the learners' growth as an individual; the purpose of language arts instruction, in this version, is "to enable pupils through reading and writing to change their experience of the world" (Barnes et al., 1984, p. 247). A cultural heritage version of English highlights the importance of literature in conveying common cultural knowledge and values, while a version that focuses on critical literacy might focus on teaching students to use language to critique and transform social inequities. Finally, a disciplinary knowledge version might focus attention instead on helping students acquire the ways of knowing that characterize the disciplines of literature and language arts (Applebee, 1994).

Teachers also possess different theoretical orientations to instruction. Much of the research in elementary literacy teaching and teacher education describes a range of teacher's orientations to instruction (e.g., top-down, bottom-up, interactive), each of which may carry various approaches to curriculum and instruction (e.g., whole language, literature-based, explicit instruction, direct instruction). Adding further to the complexity, the multiple interpretations of approaches such as whole language and literature-based curricula make shared understanding and discussion among teachers difficult at best (e.g., Hiebert & Colt, 1989; Scharer, Freeman, Lehman, & Allen, 1993; Zarrillo, 1989).

The fact that multiple versions of the language arts curriculum exist within actual classrooms creates additional challenges for the preparation of language arts teachers. First, because approaches to language arts instruction have changed dramatically over past two or three decades, prospective teachers have had experiences in learning to read and write during their own educations that differ from what is being advocated in their teacher education programs. Second, because there are always likely to be different versions of language arts instruction operating within different classrooms, prospective teachers are likely to encounter dissonance between the recommendations of their language arts methods courses and the classroom practices they encounter during field experiences and student teaching. Understanding how new teachers position themselves among these competing versions of language arts instruction has become a central focus of research in this area.

As suggested earlier, these specific characteristics of the subject matter of language arts raise dilemmas for the preparation of teachers. Given the breadth of the subject matter and the tendency for the individual components of the larger subject to be treated separately, teacher educators face the challenge of creating coherent programs for prospective language arts teachers. The fragmentation by grade level suggests that programs to prepare language arts teachers may differ rather dramatically, depending upon the level for which teachers are being prepared. Finally, the multiplicity of theoretical orientations to language arts instruction almost guarantees that prospective teachers will encounter conflicts in instructional philosophy among their own experiences as students, their coursework in teacher education, and their experiences in actual classrooms.

RECENT RESEARCH ON PREPARATION OF LANGUAGE ARTS TEACHERS

While language arts educators may disagree on the definition of the content, there is general agreement that learning language arts for teaching requires understanding of both the content of the subject matter and approaches to teaching the subject matter to make it accessible to diverse learners. However, the preparation of language arts teachers has been a relatively unexplored area of research until relatively recently (Alvermann, 1990; Guthrie, Seifert, & Mosberg, 1983; O'Donnell, 1979; Quisenberry, 1981). In the past decade, a number of studies have focused on the development of prospective language arts teachers, focusing particularly on the knowledge and beliefs prospective teachers hold about teaching the language arts and how these beliefs are influenced by their professional preparation. Studies on the preparation of language arts teachers have focused on at least three areas; (1) teachers' subject matter knowledge and understandings in various aspects of language arts (most often, literature, reading, and writing) and how these understandings are acquired during both liberal arts and professional education; (2) teachers' pedagogical content knowledge, or understandings of approaches to teaching language arts and how these understandings are acquired during preservice education; and (3) how teachers' experiences as students and student teachers mediate their efforts to translate their understandings of how to teach language arts into classroom practice.

The Question of Subject Matter Knowledge

Research on teachers' knowledge of the subject matter has tended to concentrate more on the school subjects of math and science than on language arts. In part, this may reflect the difficulty of disentangling knowledge of the content, per se, (e.g., knowledge of rhetoric and writing) from knowledge of teaching the content (e.g., knowledge of teaching writing) in the language arts. Another explanation may be the epistemological diversity within the discipline itself . (See Shanahan, 1994, for a discussion of the variety of perspectives on teachers' knowledge in language arts.) Recent changes in approaches to teaching language arts, however, may put even greater demands on teachers' knowledge of literature and of writing. For example, literature-based reading programs in elementary schools presume that teachers have broad knowledge of both high quality literature for children and the pedagogical knowledge of how to use literary texts to promote both basic literacy and literary understanding. Similarly, proposals for classroom-based assessments assume that teachers possess appropriate knowledge of the content and the processes involved in student learning. In order to meet the challenge of these proposed reforms, those concerned with teacher preparation may need to reconsider issues related to prospective teachers' subject-matter backgrounds.

The research on teachers' content knowledge within the language arts has focused particularly on secondary school teachers, although a number of studies have investigated preservice elementary teachers' beliefs and understandings.

As part of a larger study on knowledge growth among beginning secondary teachers, Grossman (1991) explored the knowledge and beliefs two preservice teachers held about literature and how these beliefs affected their classroom practices. Grossman identified distinctive orientations toward literature held by the two teachers—an orientation to the text and an orientation to the reader, which are loosely related to different schools of literary theory. These predominant orientations shaped the teachers' goals, the kinds of activities they planned for students, and the nature of questions they asked during classroom discussions. Other work seems to confirm that preservice secondary teachers enter teaching with specific orientations toward literature that influence their beliefs about teaching (Clift, 1987; Holt-Reynolds & McDiarmid, 1993). Researchers at the National Center for Research on Teacher Learning are currently studying how prospective teachers develop these beliefs and knowledge about literature during their undergraduate courses in English and how these beliefs are affected, in turn, by teacher education.

Clift's (1991) study describes the first 2 years of one young teacher's experiences in learning to teach in a secondary literature class. The study identifies the large gaps that exist in the teacher's knowledge, gaps that make teaching problematic. Clift suggests that knowledge of the subject matter of literature, particularly knowledge of literary analysis plays a significant role as it interacts with knowledge of pedagogy, assessment, management, student diversity, and self-image.

In general, the studies of teacher knowledge at the elementary level have defined subject-matter knowledge as knowledge of the reading process and reading skills—that is, decoding, comprehension, vocabulary, study skills and the like (cf. Alvermann, 1990; Bednar, 1991, Evans & Johnson, 1991). This emphasis on the teaching of reading is understandable at the elementary level, given national reports about students' limited abilities to read and comprehend complicated material (Williams, Reese, Campbell, Mazzeo, & Phillips, 1994), concerns about the quality of reading instruction (Durkin, 1978), and recent metacognitive and cognitive research about the reading process (e.g., Cross & Paris, 1988; Duffy et al., 1987; Palinscar & Brown, 1984). More recently, however, with an emphasis on process writing and literature-based instruction, a few studies have examined teachers' knowledge of literature and writing.

Relatively few studies have looked at elementary teachers' knowledge of literature and its relationship to classroom instruction. A recent study conducted by the National Center for the Learning and Teaching of Literature (Walmsley & Walp, 1989) concluded that although teachers strongly believed that literature should be a major part of the elementary curriculum, their main reason for using literature was to encourage a love of reading and books, and to teach reading skills rather than to "explore literary responses or develop literary knowledge." They had no coherent, articulated philosophy of literature's role in the language arts program, the connections between reading and literature, or the role of writing in literary understanding (Walmsley, 1992). Similarly, other studies (e.g., Scharer et al., 1993) have found that literature-based instruction is used primarily as a vehicle for teaching reading rather than for literary understanding. Furthermore, in the few instances in which teachers' knowledge of literature has been investigated, it is often assessed by having teachers identify the titles and/or the content of children's literature rather than literary understandings (e.g., Cunningham & Stanovich, 1990; Johnston, et al., 1990). Walmsley and Walp conclude that many elementary teachers have limited formal training in literature. Taken together, the limited scope of this line of research on experienced teachers' understanding of literature suggests that we have much to learn about preservice elementary teachers' knowledge and beliefs in this area.

Research on elementary teachers' knowledge of writing is also limited. An early study (Walmsley, 1980) found that elementary preservice teachers knew almost nothing about teaching writing. More recently, Gambell (1991) found that most of the preservice teachers in their study were frustrated and unsure of themselves as writers, knowing little about various approaches to writing or modes of writing. Three studies conducted by researchers at the National Center for Research on Teacher Education add to the concerns. Schmidt and Kennedy (1990) found that preservice, beginning, and experienced elementary teachers held a wide diversity of beliefs about teaching writing, including a process approach, skills approach, and a form/function approach. Teachers did not have a uniform perspective nor did they discriminate among them. They adopted an all inclusive perspective toward writing, believing that being good at writing requires "everything from factual knowledge about the parts of speech to the use of an iterative writing process." The preservice teachers in this study represented this all encompassing view almost twice as often as the more experienced teachers.

Florio-Ruane and Lensmire (1990) looked closely at what prospective elementary teachers learned about writing in a preservice class. Initially, these teachers knew little about how students learned to write and about the forms and functions of writing. They envisioned teaching writing as direct explanation. The course was designed to transform their prior experiences and beliefs about teaching writing by having the prospective teachers redefine and learn about writing and work directly with students. Although the prospective teachers experienced difficulty when the course challenged their visions of teaching or threatened their control, working directly with children and using their acquired subject-matter knowledge helped them to understand students' writing in a new way. The researchers suggest that by focusing on children's writing, relying on subject matter and developmental knowledge, rather than on teaching strategies, these preservice teachers were able to see children and teaching in a new way.

Ball and Mosenthal (1990) examined the impact of the Teacher's College Writing Project on preservice and inservice teachers. Although the teacher educators themselves had strong subject-matter knowledge of the writing process, text characteristics, and types of genres, analysis of the program and interviews with the participants revealed that the primary goal of the program was not to develop teachers' subject-matter knowledge. Instead, the goal was to help teachers engage students in writing and to support the concept of students and teachers as colearners. The researchers question how teachers can facilitate students' learning in writing, without a deeper knowledge of writing.

Process-oriented approaches to teaching writing assume some knowledge about the nature of writing and composing, and the ways in which the demands of writing may vary depending upon the nature of the writing task, the specified audience, and the genre, among other factors. Lack of this knowledge among teachers may help explain why process-oriented writing instruction all too often reduces the complexity of the writing process to a linear, lock-step series of discrete stages (Applebee, 1986). Acquiring beliefs about the appropriateness of process-oriented instruction without also acquiring a deeper understanding of writing may contribute to this pattern among both elementary and secondary language arts teachers.

While research on language arts teachers' understandings of subject matter is still relatively new, initial findings suggest that what teachers both know and believe about the processes of literary interpretation and written composition affect the ways in which they implement curriculum and orchestrate classroom instruction. Given the increasing emphasis on literature-based curriculum at the elementary level, teacher education programs may need to reconsider the kinds of knowledge and experiences prospective elementary teachers may require in order to help students construct their own interpretations of literature. Both elementary and secondary teachers may require greater knowledge of writing in order to provide appropriate instruction for students that honors the complexity of writing for different purposes and audiences. In concentrating primarily on literature and composition, this area of research has neglected to investigate what teachers need to know about oral communication in order to incorporate more opportunities for students to develop their skills and understanding of spoken language. Any consideration of prospective teachers' preparation in these areas would seem to require the collaborative efforts of faculties in both education and the arts and sciences, a point we return to later in this chapter.

The Transition to Pedagogical Reasoning

Research on the preparation of prospective language arts teachers has also examined the development of pedagogical content knowledge among beginning teachers. Shulman (1987) calls such pedagogical reasoning "the capacity of a teacher to transform the content knowledge he or she possesses into forms that are pedagogically powerful and yet adaptive to the variations in ability and background presented by the students ... to think one's way from the subject matter as understood by the teacher into the minds and motivations of learners" (p. 15, 16). In looking at this shift from knowledge of the subject, per se, to knowledge of how to represent the subject matter for diverse learners, most research has focused on identifying the importance of subject-specific methods courses in the formation of pedagogical content knowledge for language arts and on the difficulties facing prospective and beginning teachers as they make this shift to a more pedagogical consideration of subject matter.

Recent studies have explicitly resisted the popular notion that subject-matter knowledge, a few generalized pedagogical principles, and classroom experience can suffice as teacher preparation in the language arts. Several studies have demonstrated that understanding of the subject matter alone does not necessarily enable prospective teachers to rethink the content from a pedagogical perspective. Clift (1987) studied six university seniors, three of whom were English majors with no intention to teach and no coursework in education, and three were English majors who were becoming certified in secondary school teaching. Her analysis suggested that the English majors located expertise for textual interpretation with the teacher/professor, while the education students favored the construction of personal understanding. The prospective teachers emphasized the learner's experiences with literature, seeing themselves as educators first and subject-matter specialists second; the English majors cast learners in a more passive role, as consumers of the details of literature brought to them by knowledgeable teachers. As Clift concluded, "English majors ... may develop a schema for teaching and learning English that has a strong orientation to the text ... but virtually no orientation to the reader. Prospective teachers, by contrast, may be guided to develop schema that take the learner into account..." (p. 234). The study suggests that preservice English education programs serve to modify and expand novice's initial orientations to literature and to help them develop pedagogical reasoning.

Another study (Grossman, 1990) looked at first year secondary English teachers, three of whom had completed a teacher education program and three of whom entered teaching without professional preparation. The case studies of these six teachers show important differences between these two groups of beginning teachers with respect to their purposes for teaching English, their understanding of students, and their approaches to selecting and organizing content. The author comments that while "all prospective secondary teachers face the task of rethinking their subject matter from a more pedagogical perspective" (p. 143), teacher education can help beginning teachers establish a framework within which to accomplish this task.

Part of the task of developing pedagogical content knowledge involves confronting one's implicit assumptions about the teaching and learning of language arts. A number of studies have looked at strategies for uncovering preservice teachers' prior assumptions and helping teachers to reflect on them. Many authors point to the power of asking students to engage in autobiographical writing as part of this process. Sperling (1994), for example, asked preservice English teachers to write about their own classroom experiences and to identify the personal metaphors they held for teaching English. Her analysis of student writing suggests that allowing prospective teachers to reflect critically in a social context on their metaphors encourages their ability to imagine alternative choices in teaching and the potential impact of these choices on students' opportunities to learn. In a related study, White and Smith (1994) suggest that English education students' construction of personal teaching metaphors provides an occasion for dialogue as competing ideas, assumptions, and beliefs are revealed. In a series of qualitative case studies, Fox (1995) provides further evidence supporting the importance of self-reflective examination of preexisting beliefs through the uses of narrative and autobiography in English methods courses. Others have also used literacy histories or reflective journals in preservice reading education classes to help students develop insights into literacy, literacy learning and teaching (Bednar, 1991; Hermann & Sarracino, 1993; Meyer, 1993; Pultorak, 1993; Stansell, 1994). Although all these studies conclude that such reflective experiences are important vehicles for preservice teachers to confront their past experiences, not all have been equally successful at promoting renewed visions. Resistance to change may be a result of confronting negative past experiences or it may be related to the way the journals or autobiographies are supported and used in preservice courses.

From a slightly different perspective, Florio-Ruane (1994) explored how reading and writing autobiographies helped prospective elementary teachers address issues related to teaching culturally and economically diverse students. She found that having prospective teachers read autobiographies of culturally diverse authors elicited personal narratives from preservice teachers which focused on issues of ethnic identity and difference, language and schooling. Such explorations of both their own and others' autobiographies may help preservice teachers acknowledge and investigate the resources that culturally diverse students bring to school.

Other studies have addressed elementary preservice teachers' theoretical orientations, beliefs about, and strategies for teaching reading (cf. DeFord, 1985). For the most part, these studies focus on the changes of teaching beliefs and practices as part of coursework or practicum experiences. Several studies suggest that it is difficult to change preservice teachers' beliefs about teaching reading, even when students are engaged in coursework and a related practicum (Davies, 1990; Evans & Johnson, 1991; Herrmann & Sarracino, 1993; Moore & Harris, 1986; Wallhausen, 1990; Wham, 1993). For example, Wallhausen (1990) used qualitative and quantitative methods to examine preservice elementary teachers' knowledge of reading theory and instructional methods as well as their beliefs. The teachers learned the content knowledge taught in their methods class more rapidly than they were able to change their beliefs or translate knowledge into actual practice. She concludes that teachers' past experiences and the stress of a practicum experience interfere with their ability to mediate theory and practice.

Other researchers suggest that specific strategies used in methods classes may actually promote change in knowledge and in understanding of teaching practices. Some recent studies have documented students' learning in restructured constructivist elementary literacy courses (Hermann & Sarracino, 1993; Hollingsworth, 1989). For example, Hermann and Sarracino restructured their course to engage prospective teachers in reflective inquiry. The content of the course changed from topics about literacy to theories influencing the development of literacy. The structure of the course was altered to include a mentoring program, individual tutoring of children, and professional collaboration partnerships among the preservice teachers and the

instructors. The changes were difficult for both students and instructors but some changes were noted for all students in how they thought about literacy instruction, and the social and emotional aspects of becoming a teacher. At the secondary level, Fox (1995) found that preservice teachers engaged in constructivist coursework, especially recursive inquiry and reflection, made adaptations in their approaches to the teaching and learning of English.

These studies indicate that understanding one's own implicit assumptions and beliefs about the teaching and learning of language arts represents a critical stage in the development of pedagogical content knowledge. Literacy autobiographies, reflective journals, and critical reflection can all help surface these implicit assumptions. Prospective teachers may also need to confront differences between their own experiences as learners in language arts classrooms and the kinds of teaching and learning that are currently being advocated. This disjunction is particularly apparent in the field of writing, in which dramatic shifts in classroom practice have occurred over the past two decades. Experiences in working directly with children can also support the development of pedagogical thinking and the reexamination of theoretical assumptions.

Learning to Teach in Context

A number of studies illustrate the importance of field experiences in shaping prospective teachers' beliefs about the teaching and learning of language arts. As many studies of teacher education have demonstrated (Feiman-Nemser & Buchmann, 1985; Lanier & Little, 1986), student teachers must traverse two worlds—the world of the university and the world of the schools. Student teachers may find it difficult to reconcile the perspectives on teaching the language arts they encounter in teacher education courses with the kinds of activities they observe in classrooms.

Clift (Clift, Merg, & Eggerding, 1994) explored the tensions two student teachers experienced between the goals of their English education program and the pressures of the student teaching context. The student teachers reported that the expectations of their cooperating teachers conflicted with their emerging pedagogical beliefs about English and with their images of teaching. Moreover, Clift found that the teacher education program did little to ease this tension. In following 25 preservice English teachers through their professional preparation, Ritchie and Wilson (1993) found that although students began to revise their views about the teaching and learning of language arts during teacher education, their experiences both as students and as student teachers within more traditional classrooms proved more powerful. The preservice teachers did not totally transform their beliefs about the teaching of writing and literature. Instead, as the researchers conclude, "students were merely adding new, alternative notions to their existing traditional views, and they did so with little apparent sense of tension or conflict" (p. 76). When student teachers entered the classroom, their fragile understandings of new approaches to teaching writing and literature faltered and they often reverted to more traditional practices.

Other research supports the difficulties student teachers and beginning teachers face in implementing new visions of teaching writing in classroom settings (Gomez, 1990; Gomez & Comeaux, 1990). In a study of eight secondary English education students from different universities, Gomez and Comeaux found that these preservice teachers had been taught process-oriented methods of teaching composition and entered their student teaching situations idealistically regarding their ability to carry out these ideas in the classroom. By the end of student teaching with ethnically diverse populations, however, their concerns had shifted away from the subject matter to classroom management and they became disillusioned with their students' ability to succeed in the language arts classroom. The authors conclude that student teachers need more time to reflect on the failure of instructional strategies with particular students. In a related study that followed three graduates into their first year of teaching, Gomez found a similar pattern of idealism followed by disillusionment. This work suggests that as preservice teachers develop new ideas about teaching language arts, they may need help in adapting their ideas and strategies specifically for diverse learners.

Other researchers agree that field experiences play an important role in fostering preservice teachers' learning (Blanton & Moorman, 1985; Evans & Johnson, 1991; Hollingsworth, 1989; Michelson, Duffy, & Lasovage, 1984). Hollingsworth followed preservice teachers before, during, and after a 5th-year teacher education program. Through interviews and observations of 14 elementary and secondary preservice teachers, she found that students' incoming beliefs about reading served as filters for understanding the content they learned and how classrooms functioned. Furthermore, these preservice teachers had to have managerial routines in place before they could focus on learning about reading or teaching reading and they had to have both subject-matter knowledge and managerial routines in place before they could focus on their students' learning. Given the power of field experiences, researchers in this area suggest various models such as early multiple field experiences to foster mediation of beliefs and practices, and greater coordination between field and coursework to insure opportunities to apply new concepts.

As these researchers suggest, prospective teachers may find it difficult to resolve conflicts that arise between visions of language arts instruction encountered in language arts education classes and the realities that confront them in actual classrooms. In order to support prospective teachers' transformed visions of teaching and learning the language arts, teacher educators must work with classroom teachers who share common visions and find settings for student teaching in which new teachers are able to explore what it means to put these ideas into practice.

However, even in supportive settings, prospective teachers are still likely to hold seemingly inconsistent beliefs about the teaching and learning of language arts, particularly if their own experiences as students differ dramatically from the new ideas they are encountering. As studies of student learning have vividly demonstrated, the process of conceptual change is rarely simple or linear, and new understandings are initially layered upon older and perhaps inconsistent prior beliefs (Smith, diSessa, & Roschelle, 1993/1994). Recent theoretical study suggests that prospective teachers will need opportunities to work out these new ideas in the context of classroom practice and with the support of knowledgeable mentors who can help them identify and explore inconsistencies in their beliefs and practice.

CHALLENGES FOR THE FUTURE

The existing research suggests that much work needs to be done if teacher education is to support current reform efforts. New reforms within the teaching of language arts suggest that more emphasis may need to be given to the subject-matter preparation of prospective language arts teachers. Curriculum frameworks that ask teachers to engage students in active and thoughtful interpretation of literary works place new demands on teachers' own grounding in interpretive frameworks and strategies. The adoption of literature-based instruction at the elementary level puts greater demands on teachers' knowledge of literature. The increasing diversity of students in regular classrooms suggests that secondary school teachers will need to develop a deeper understanding of the teaching of reading to help struggling readers. Similarly, process-oriented writing instruction may assume greater knowledge of writing and composing than did more traditional instruction. In order to create and scaffold appropriate writing assignments (Langer & Applebee, 1986) and to provide instruction that supports students' writing, elementary and secondary teachers may need a deeper understanding of rhetoric and composition processes. Finally, the movement towards classroom-based and performance assessments requires greater subject-matter understandings on the part of teachers.

Teacher education cannot solve the problem of subject-matter knowledge for prospective teachers without the full participation of arts and sciences faculty. Efforts to rethink the subject-matter preparation of elementary teachers in literature or writing must include faculties from both education and English (Tyson, 1994). A number of pilot projects, have tried to develop stronger linkages between education, and arts and sciences faculty (Tyson, 1994).

The movement toward more inclusive schools and classrooms may also place greater demands on teachers' pedagogical content knowledge. As teachers become responsible for meeting the needs of a wider range of students, including special education students and students who speak English as a second language, they will need to increase their instructional repertoire and to develop a better understanding of reading and language acquisition among different populations of students.

At the same time that prospective teachers may need deeper understanding of the individual language arts, they also need help seeing the connections among the various threads that constitute the subject matter. Language arts is an inherently interdisciplinary subject matter. In order to orchestrate a coherent language arts curriculum in the classroom, prospective teachers may need more help in reflecting on what constitutes the warp and weft of this admittedly diffuse subject.

A curious dilemma arises if we juxtapose the need for prospective teachers to be more deeply prepared in various aspects of the language arts with the current calls for more cross-disciplinary and interdisciplinary curriculum at both the elementary and secondary levels. While reforms within the subject matter would seem to require even greater subject-matter expertise in order to succeed, reforms beyond the subject matter might be interpreted as calling for the preparation of teachers as generalists. Some have even questioned if we should be preparing language arts teachers, per se, if our goal is a truly integrated curriculum. This emphasis on the importance of interdisciplinary work and integrated curriculum may undermine the efforts of teacher educators to focus on subject-specific pedagogy within the teacher education curriculum.

However, we know very little about what kinds of understandings are necessary for teachers to design and implement integrated curricula. Some might argue that prospective teachers first need a thorough understanding of a specific discipline before they are able to engage in interdisciplinary work, while others might argue that the emphasis on separate disciplines undermines the focus on integration. Future research will need to look more carefully at the kinds of subject-matter and curricular understandings required for responsible interdisciplinary curriculum (Gardner & Boix-Mansilla, 1994). In short, this tension between the push toward a greater emphasis on subject-specific pedagogy in teacher education and the growing demand for interdisciplinary programs will need to be addressed by teacher educators at both the elementary and secondary levels.

Even if teacher educators succeed in engaging students in new ways of thinking about language arts instruction, they will still need to deal with the difficulties new teachers face in implementing these new visions in more traditional classrooms. The gulf between university exhortations and classroom practices, a perennial problem of teacher education, is unlikely to disappear in the near future. Most public school teachers have been in the classroom on an average of 15 years, and 75% of them plan to remain in teaching as long as they are able (Choy et al., 1994). This suggests that a majority of practicing teachers, the pool of cooperating teachers, was prepared prior to many of the current reforms. The reform of classroom teaching cannot rely on newcomers alone. Much recent work on the reform of teacher education has been devoted to ways of bridging this gulf through professional development schools (Darling-Hammond, 1994; Goodlad, 1990; Holmes, 1990) or various other forms of collaborations between schools and colleges of education. Such collaborations try to connect ongoing professional development with preservice education. However, we have relatively little evidence of how effective professional development schools can be on a large scale.

New research on cognition highlights the importance of context in problem solving and casts new light on apprentice-ship models of learning (Brown, Collins, & Duguid, 1989; Lave, 1988). Student teaching represents one form of an apprenticeship model. While the apprenticeship form of learning during student teaching in the past has focused primarily on the acquisition of practical knowledge, recasting student teaching as a *cognitive* apprenticeship (Brown, Collins, & Duguid, 1989) could help students wrestle more actively with the theoretical implications of classroom routines and practices and to puzzle over the tensions between what they have been taught at the university and what seems to work, or not work, in the classroom. In order to create this kind of apprenticeship model in student teaching, there will need to be greater mutual understanding on the sides of both university-based and field-based teacher educators. This vision of cognitive apprenticeship seems to underlie the hopes of the professional development school movement (Holmes, 1990).

Even if these collaborations could be created and sustained, however, teacher educators would still face challenges within the apprenticeship model. Apprenticeship models of any kind may be most appropriate when the goal is stability of practice (Dewey, 1904/1965; Grossman, 1992). At a time of dramatic reform, the apprenticeship model can only work if there are enough master teachers who are successfully implementing these reforms with whom to place prospective teachers. Even in these ideal situations, apprenticeship models still provide only a single "case of teaching" for prospective teachers to learn from. Work on knowledge acquisition in complex, uncertain domains illustrates the importance of multiple cases for learning (Spiro, Carlsen, Feltovich, & Anderson, 1988). This need for prospective teachers to encounter variations in practice, to consider how the same theories or ideas can unfold differently in different contexts, argues for any form of field experience to include multiple placements and to be supplemented by some form of case-based teaching in the university curriculum (Grossman & Shulman, 1994).

Current reform efforts cannot succeed without careful attention to the content and processes of both teacher education and continuing professional development. Teacher educators will need to reconsider the subject-matter knowledge and pedagogical content knowledge required in order for language arts teachers to teach for understanding in increasingly diverse classrooms, even as they rethink the structures and experiences through which prospective teachers acquire this knowledge. Such changes will require greater collaboration between faculties in education, and in arts and sciences within colleges and universities, and between university-based teacher education programs and schools. While the obstacles to such collaboration are well known (Sirotnik & Goodlad, 1988), the number of efforts currently underway in the reform of teacher education and professional development provide opportunities to study natural variations among these efforts and to make recommendations about the best ways to sustain collaborative efforts to rethink the preparation of language arts teachers.

References

Alvermann, D. E. (1990). Reading teacher education. In W. R. Houston (Ed.), *Handbook of research on teacher education*. New York: Macmillan.

Applebee, A. N. (1974). *Tradition and reform in the teaching of English: A history*. Urbana, IL: National Council of Teachers of English.

Applebee, A. (1986). Problems in process approaches: Toward a reconceptualization of process instruction. In A. Petrosky & D. Bartholomae (Eds.) The teaching of writing. 85th Yearbook of the National Society for the Study of Education. (pp. 95–113). Chicago, IL: University of Chicago Press.

Applebee, A. N. (1994). Toward thoughtful curriculum: Fostering discipline-based conversation. *English Journal, 83*(3), 45–52.

Atwell, N. (1987). *In the middle: Writing, reading, and learning with adolescents*. Portsmouth, NH: Heinemann.

Ball, D. L., & Mosenthal, J. H. (1990). *The construction of new forms of teaching: Subject matter knowledge in in-service teacher education* (Report No. 90–8). East Lansing, MI: National Center for Research on Teacher Education.

Barnes, S., Barnes, D., & Clarke, S. (1984). *Versions of English*. London: Heinemann Educational Books.

Bednar, M. R. (1991, December). *Teacher cognition: Preservice knowledge and reflections about the reading process*. Paper presented at the 41st Annual Meeting of the National Reading Conference, Palm Springs, CA.

Blanton, W. E., & Moorman, G. B. (1985). The devil's advocate: Field experiences: Aids or impediments to classroom reading instruction. *Reading Research and Instruction, 25*(1), 56–59.

Brown, J. S., Collins, A., & Duguid, P. (1989). Situated cognition and the culture of learning. *Educational Researcher, 18*(1), 32–42.

Choy, S. P., Bobbitt, S. A.., Henke, R. R., Medrich, E. A., Horn, L. J., & Lieberman, J. (1994). *American's teachers: Profile of a profession*. Washington, DC: U.S. Department of Education.

Clift, R. T. (1987). English teacher or English major: Epistemological differences in the teaching of English. *English Education, 19*(4), 229–236.

Clift, R. T. (1991). Learning to teach English—maybe: A study of knowledge development. *Journal of Teacher Education, 42*(5), 357–372.

Clift, R. T., Merg, L., & Eggerding, S. (1994). Mixed messages in learning to teach English. *Teaching and Teaching Education, 10*(3), 265–279.

Cross, D., & Paris. S. (1988). Developmental and instructional analysis of children's metacognition and reading comprehension. *Journal of Educational Psychology, 80*(2), 131–142.

Cunningham, A., & Stanovich, K. (1990). Assessing print exposure and orthographic processing skill in children: A quick measure of reading experience. *Journal of Educational Psychology, 82*(4), 733–740.

Darling-Hammond, L. (1994). *Professional development schools: Schools for developing a profession*. New York: Teachers College Press.

Davies, K. S. (1990). Novice teachers: Do they use what we teach them? *Reading Horizons, 30*(2), 24–34.

DeFord, D. (1985). Validating the construct of theoretical orientation in reading instruction. *Reading Research Quarterly, 20*(3), 351–367.

Dewey, J. (1904/1965). The relation of theory and practice in education. In M. Borrowman (Ed.), *Teacher education in America: A documentary history* (pp. 140–171). New York: Teachers College Press.

Dixon, J. (1969). *Growth through English*. Oxford: Oxford University Press.

Duffy, G. G., Roehler, L. R., Sivan, E., Rackliffe, G., Book, C., Meloth, M. S., Vavrus, L. G., Wesselman, R., Putnam, J., & Bassiri, D. (1987). Effects of explaining the reasoning associated with using reading strategies. *Reading Research Quarterly, 22*(3), 347–368.

Durkin, D. (1978). What classroom observations reveal about reading comprehension instruction. *Reading Research Quarterly, 14*(4). 481–533.

Elbow, P. (1990). *What is English?* Urbana, IL: National Council of Teachers of English.

Evans, A. D., & Johnson, C. S. (1991, March). *Theoretical orientations and content knowledge of pre-service reading teachers: A preliminary investigation into cognitive apprenticeships*. Paper presented at the 19th Annual Pacific Northwest Research and Evaluation Conference, Vancouver, WA.

Feiman-Nemser, S., & Buchmann, M. (1985). Pitfalls of experience in teacher preparation. *Teachers College Record, 87*(1), 53–65.

Florio-Ruane, S., & Lensmire, T. (1990). Transforming future teachers' ideas about writing instruction. *Journal of Curriculum Studies, 22*(3), 277–289.

Florio-Ruane, S. (1994). The future teachers' autobiography club. Preparing educators to support literacy learning in culturally diverse classrooms. *English Education, 26*(1), 52–66.

Fox, D. L. (1995). From English major to English teacher: Two case studies. *English Journal, 84*(2), 17–25.

Gambell, T. J. (1991). University education students' self-perceptions of writing. *Canadian Journal of Education, 16*(4), 420–433.

Gardner, N., & Boix-Mansilla, V. (1994). Teaching for understanding—within and across the disciplines. *Educational Leadership, 51*(2), 14–18.

Gere, A. R. (Ed.). (1992). *Language and reflection: An integrated approach to teaching English*. New York: Macmillan.

Gomez, M. L. (1990). *Learning to teach writing: Untangling the tensions between theory and practice*. (ERIC Document No. ED322 101).

Gomez, M. L., & Comeaux, M. A. (1990). *Start with the stone—not the hole: Matching novices needs with an appropriate program of induction*. (ERIC Document No. Ed 327 541).

Goodlad, J. (1990). *Teachers for our nation's schools*. San Francisco: Jossey-Bass.

Graff, G. (1987). *Professing literature: An institutional history*. Chicago: University of Chicago Press.

Grossman, P. L. (1990). *The making of a teacher: Teacher knowledge and teacher education*. New York: Teachers College Press.

Grossman, P. L. (1991). What are we talking about anyhow? Subject matter knowledge of secondary English teachers. In J. Brophy (Ed.), *Advances in research on teaching* (Vol. 2) *Subject matter knowledge*. Greenwich, CT: JAI Press.

Grossman, P. L. (1992). Why models matter: An alternate view on professional growth in teaching. *Review of Educational Research, 62*(2), 171–179.

Grossman, P. L. (1993). *English as context: English in context*. (Tech. Rep. #593-2). Center for Research on the Context of Secondary School Teaching, Stanford University. Stanford, CA.

Grossman, P. L., & Shulman. L. (1994). Knowing, believing, and the teaching of English. In T. Shanahan (Ed.), *Teachers thinking, teachers knowing: Reflections on literacy and language education* (pp. 3–22). Urbana, IL: National Council of Teachers of English.

Guthrie, J., Seifert, M., & Mosberg, L. (1983). Research synthesis in reading: Topics, audiences, and citation rates. *Reading Research Quarterly, 19*(1), 16–27.

Hermann, B. A., & Sarracino, J. (1993). Restructuring a preservice literacy method course: Dilemmas and lessons learned. *Journal of Teacher Education, 44*(2), 96–106.

Hiebert, E. H., & Colt, J. (1989). Patterns of literature-based reading instruction. *Reading Teacher, 43*(1), 14–20.

Hillocks, G. Jr. (1986). *Research on written composition.* Urbana, IL: National Conference on Research in English.

Hollingsworth, S. (1989). Prior beliefs and cognitive change in learning to teach. *American Educational Research Journal, 26*(2), 160–189.

Holmes Group. (1990). *Tomorrow's schools: Principles for the design of professional development schools.* East Lansing, MI: The Holmes Group Inc.

Holt-Reynolds, D., & McDiarmid, G. W. (1993, April). *How do prospective teachers think about literature and the teaching of literature* (Tech. Rep.). National Center for Research on Teacher Learnings, East Lansing, MI: Michigan State University.

Johnston, P. H., et al. (1990). *Teachers' evaluations of teaching and learning in literacy and literature* (Report Series 3.4). Albany, NY: Center for the Learning and Teaching of Literature.

Langer, J. A., & Applebee, A. N. (1986). Reading and writing instruction: Toward a theory of teaching and learning. In E. Z. Rothkopf (Ed.), *Review of research in education. Vol. 13* (pp. 171–194). Washington, DC: American Educational Research Association.

Lanier, J. E., & Little, J. W. (1986). Research on teacher education. In M. C. Wittrock (Ed.), *Handbook of research on teaching,* (3rd ed., pp. 527–569). New York: Macmillan.

Lave, J. (1988). *Cognition in practice.* Cambridge: Cambridge University Press.

McEwan, H. (1992). Five metaphors for English. *English Education, 24,* 101–128.

Meyer, R. J. (1993, December). *Preservice teachers' literacy autobiographies and teacher development.* Paper presented at the annual meeting of the National Reading Conference, Charleston, SC.

Michelson, S., Duffy, G. G., & Lasovage, J. (1984). An exploration of preservice teachers' conceptual change during reading methods instruction. In G. H. McNinch (Ed.), *Reading teacher education. Fourth yearbook of the American reading forum,* (pp. 13–16). Athens, GA: American reading forum. (ERIC Document Reproduction Services No. ED290134).

Moore, B., & Harris, B. (1986). *An assessment of preservice teachers' knowledge of instructional strategies for teaching phonics.* (ERIC Document No. ED298 445).

O'Donnell, R. C. (1979). Research in the teaching of English: Some observations and questions. *English Education, 10*(3), 181–183.

Palinscar, A. S., & Brown, A. L. (1984). Reciprocal teaching of comprehension-fostering and comprehension-monitoring activities. *Cognition and Instruction, 1*(2), 117–175.

Pearson, P. D., & Fielding, L. (1991). Comprehension instruction. In R. Barr, M. Kamil, P. Mosenthal, & P. Pearson (Eds.), *Handbook of reading research, Vol 2* (pp. 815–860). New York: Longman.

Pultorak, E. G. (1993). Facilitating reflective thought in novice teachers. *Journal of Teacher Education, 44*(4), 288–295.

Quisenberry, J. B. (1981). English teacher preparation: What's happening? *English Education, 13*(2), 70–77.

Resnick, L. B., & Resnick, D. L. (1992). Assessing the thinking curriculum: New tools for educational reform. In B. Gifford & M. O'Connor (Eds.), *Future assessments: Changing views of aptitude, achievement, and instruction* (pp. 37–75). Boston: Kluwer.

Ritchie. J., & Wilson, D. (1993). Dual apprenticeships: Subverting and supporting critical teaching. *English Education, 25*(2), 67–83.

Scharer, P. L., Freeman, E. B., Lehman, B. A., & Allen, V. G. (1993). Literacy and literature in elementary classrooms: Teachers' beliefs and practices. In D. J. Leu & C. K. Kinzer (Eds.), *Examining central issues in literacy research, theory, and practice* (pp. 359–366). Chicago: National Reading Conference.

Schmidt, W., & Kennedy, M. (1990). *Teachers' and teacher candidates' beliefs about subject matter and about teaching responsibilities* (Research Report). Office of Educational Research on Teacher Education.

Shanahan, T. (1994). *Teachers thinking, teachers knowing.* Urbana, IL: National Council of Teachers of English; National Conference on Research in English.

Shulman, L. S. (1987). Knowledge and teaching: Foundations of the new reform. *Harvard Educational Review, 57*(1), 1–20.

Sirotnik, K. A., & Goodlad, J. I. (1988). *School-university partnerships in action: Concepts, cases, and concerns.* New York: Teachers College Press.

Smith, J. diSessa, A., & Roschelle, J. (1993/1994). Misconceptions reconceived: A constructivist analysis of knowledge in transition. *Journal of the Learning Sciences, 3*(2), 115–163.

Sperling, M. (1994). Moments remembered, moments displayed: Narratization, metaphor and the experience of teaching. *English Education, 26*(3), 142–156.

Spiro, R. J., Carlson, R. L., Feltovich, P. J., & Anderson, D. K. (1988). *Cognitive flexibility theory: Advanced knowledge acquisition in ill-structured domains* (Tech. Rep. No. 441) Urbana, IL: Center for the Study of Reading.

Stansell, J. C. (1994). Reflection, resistance, and research among preservice teachers studying their literacy histories: Lessons for literacy teacher education. In C. K. Kinzer & D. J. Leu (Eds.). *Multidimensional aspects of literacy research, theory, and practice, Forty-third yearbook of the national reading conference.* Chicago: National Reading Conference.

Tyson, H. (1994). *Who will teach the children? Progress and resistance in teacher education.* San Francisco: Jossey-Bass.

Valencia, S.W., Hiebert, E. H., & Afflerbach, P.P. (1994). Authentic reading assessment: Practices and possibilities. Newark, NJ: International Reading Association.

Wallhausen, H. A. (1990). *The effect of first teacher education courses on students' perception of the reading process.* (ERIC Document No. ED 322 490).

Walmsley, S. A. (1980). What elementary teachers know about writing. *Language Arts, 57*(7), 732–734.

Walmsley, S. A. (1992). Reflections on the state of elementary literature instruction. *Language Arts, 69*(7), 508–514.

Walmsley, S. A., & Walp, T. P. (1989). *Teaching literature in elementary school: A report of a project on the elementary school antecedents of secondary school literature instruction* (Report Series 1.3). Albany, NY: Center for the Learning and Teaching of Literature.

Wham, M. A. (1993). The relationship between undergraduate course work and beliefs about reading instruction. *Journal of Research and Development of Education, 27*(1), 9–17.

White, B., & Smith, M. W. (1994). Metaphors in English education: Putting things in perspective. *English Education, 26*(3) 158–176..

Williams, P. L., Reese, C. M., Campbell, J. R., Mazzeo, J., & Phillips, G. W. (1994) . *1994 NAEP Reading: A first look—Findings from the national assessment of educational progress.* Washington DC: National Center for Educational Statistics, U.S. Government Printing Office.

Zarrillo, J. (1989). Teachers' interpretations of literature-based reading. *The Reading Teacher, 41*(1), 22–28.

33

BECOMING A MEMBER OF A PROFESSIONAL LANGUAGE LEARNING COMMUNITY

Janet L. Olson

BOSTON UNIVERSITY SCHOOL FOR THE ARTS, CHAIR, ART EDUCATION

INTRODUCTION

It is not easy for a teacher from one discipline to enter the domain of another, especially when one is entering an area viewed as essential to good education from one often viewed as a frill. Such is frequently the case when the value of language and visual arts is assessed, even by experts. When this happens, that is, when one feels judged as an educator by the ability to express oneself with words, art teachers often feel intimidated by both English and language arts teachers. Word people, of course, frequently feel intimidated in the area of studio arts and are often quick to declare that they cannot draw.

Nevertheless, the priority given to each of these subject areas is quite different, both within and without the school setting. For example, the student unable to draw to an acceptable level of accomplishment is rarely viewed as having a learning disability. But the student with artistic skills who has great difficulty with the language arts is frequently labeled as having learning disabilities. Drawing well is viewed as a special gift that requires very little work or practice to improve upon, whereas improvement in language arts is almost always considered essential. Needless to say, such attitudes, when prevalent, can inhibit the building of bridges between the visual and language arts.

Similarities

In spite of these obstacles, art teachers with deep concern for students with good visual skills but who perform poorly in academic subjects, should put their personal insecurities aside in order to make a concerted effort to build connections between these two areas for the sake of learning. By so doing, they will be surprised to discover the natural liaison between these two domains. Thus, when art teachers find themselves entering the professional language learning community, they should focus first on the many similarities shared by the two areas. Focusing on the similarities is far more productive than dismissing the possibility of a close educational partnership based on differences. Unfortunately, very few art teachers and both English and language arts teachers are aware of how much they have in common.

GOALS

Both the language and visual arts claim to be forms of communication concerned with thinking. Each discipline professes to be a primary means of knowing, experiencing, and understanding the world around them; and each discipline claims to facilitate creativity and self-expression while transmitting a historical and cultural record of human achievement (Greene, & Petty, 1975; National Council of Teachers of English, 1976; Qualley, 1986). Finally, each discipline believes that children have a natural desire to draw (Wilson, & Wilson, 1982) and to write (Calkins, 1986), respectively. It is reasonable to assume, therefore, that if educational goals and beliefs for teaching visual and verbal expression are viewed as being complementary rather than different, mutually supportive rather than both competitive and different, the learner might benefit a great deal.

Verbal and Visual Development

There are many more specific characteristics that the two areas have in common. For example, it is interesting to observe that children develop visual and verbal language in a highly similar sequence. The first babbling sounds that babies make are similar to their very first marks on any surface (paper, wall, high chair tray) with any marking tool (crayon, fingers, stick). In each case children are experimenting with a range of possibilities. By repeating sounds and marks they discover the ability to control and to be intentional with their actions (see Figure 33–1). When children begin to use a single word referential designator such as "mommy", "daddy" or "chair," it is developmentally similar to what happens when children begin to assign meaning to their marks, such as the 3-year-old who says "snow" after making the white marks around the periphery of her painting (see Figure 33–2). Combining two words to make an early sentence form, such as "me up" or "me go," is similar to visual combines, such as the first "tadpole" people (see Figures 33–3 and 33–4) that children make as they gradually develop their visual language (de Villiers, & de Villiers, 1979; Fein, 1993; Gardner, 1981; Glazer, 1989; Kellogg, 1970).

Active language processing develops gradually, including evidence of more complex talking, vocabulary expansion, increased sensitivity to syntax, sounds, and meaning. This stage of development is similar to what happens when children expand their visual vocabulary to include a range of visual symbols including people, animals, houses, trees, and so on throughout the preschematic stage of visual development. During the preschematic stage, images seem to float in space over the entire picture plane without a sense of gravity (see Figure 33–5). When children progress to the schematic

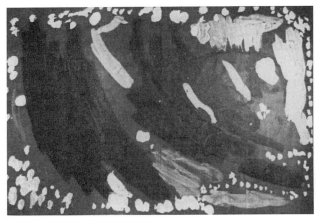

FIGURE 33–2 Child names white marks "snow" around the periphery.

FIGURE 33–3 First visual combine, a "tadpole" person.

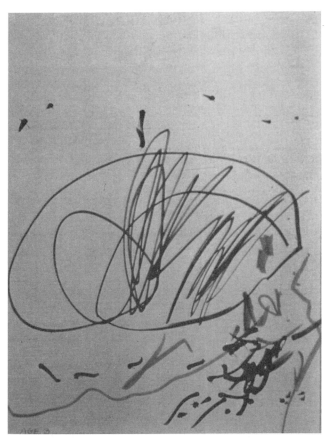

FIGURE 33–1 Markmaking stage of development.

stage of visual development, they show evidence of understanding their place in relationship to the world. Images no longer float, but are placed firmly on a groundline, with the sky at the top of the page (see Figure 33–6). At this stage of development children are able to articulate both visual and

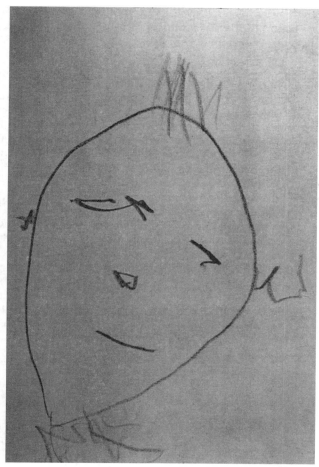

FIGURE 33–4 More developed combine,
a "tadpole" person.

FIGURE 33–5 Preschematic stage of visual development,
floating images.

verbal stories with confidence. From this point on, students will develop more advanced visual and verbal skills, and realism of expression gradually becomes a critical factor (Goodnow, 1977; Hurwitz, & Day, 1991; Lowenfeld, 1957; Pinker, 1994).

When this happens, self-confidence is challenged and teacher attitudes play an important role if self-confidence is to be enhanced. However, if visual ability is not valued or understood as a vehicle of communication by teachers or parents, students naturally conclude that verbal communication is more important than visual communication and that their so-called "gift" is not really important after all. With this devaluation, the visual and verbal partnerships can breakdown and, as a consequence, the two forms of communication will no longer benefit from their initial, and in my view, quite natural, interactive complementarity. Such a breakdown puts students with stronger visual than verbal skills at a marked disadvantage. No longer are their strengths valued or used as a tool for learning in their area of weakness. Hence a close working relationship between art teachers and language arts teachers is essential to prevent, and cer-

FIGURE 33–6 Schematic stage of visual development,
groundline and sky.

tainly to alleviate, such problems if and when they arise (Olson, 1992).

Parts of Speech and Elements of Design

When one probes more deeply into the similarities between visual and verbal expression, one quickly sees obvious connections. For example, both forms of communication have their own basic parts or elements. The eight parts of speech, of course, are the noun, verb, pronoun, adjective, adverb, preposition, conjunction, and interjection. Similarly, depending on how one counts, there are also eight visual elements, including the dot, line, shape, value, texture, color, space, and movement. Artists can feature each of the visual elements individually, even when the subject of an image is the same, such as a shoe, as demonstrated in Figure 33–7.

Authors and artists use these basic parts of speech and visual elements to *compose* or to *construct* either a literary or a visual image. The unique manner in which the author and the artist both compose their work is referred to as *style* (voice or vision). Occasionally terminology separates us, even when the meaning or the intention is very much the same. For example, artists speak of portraits and figure studies, and authors speak of character development. Artists speak of landscapes, interiors and still lifes and authors speak of set-

tings and props. Artists speak of tryptichs, a sequence and/or a body of work, and authors speak of a plot or a sequence of events. And both speak of their own point of view or perspective.

Both the artist and the author communicate their stories or concerns by employing their own chosen art form, and yet the creative process for each is very similar. Both the artist and the author go through a period of rehearsal, preparing their work space and getting ready for the process. Donald Murray (1984) describes the writing process as a sequence of collecting, focusing, ordering, drafting and clarifying, and then returning to any step in the sequence again and again until the author decides that the writing is finished. The visual artist works in a similar manner.

What would happen if a choice between the two forms of communication was never required and students of all ages were encouraged to move naturally between both forms of expression? This natural process would allow insight to be translated from one form to the other as necessity dictates, such as when this 5-year-old practiced writing G's (for girl) and drawing girls in the same image (see Figure 33–8). Is it possible that a higher level of literacy could be achieved if both forms of communication were encouraged, especially for

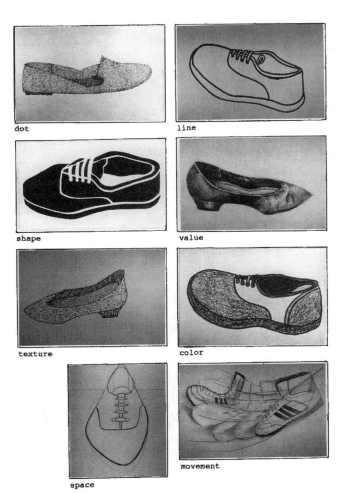

FIGURE 33–7 Eight visual elements.

FIGURE 33–8 Child moves naturally between visual and verbal forms of expression.

those students who have difficulty in expressing themselves with words?

In order to research this possibility, an art teacher decided to explore the potential of such a partnership. Could the writing process be used to draw upon her area of strength (painting) and translate her visual expressions and insights into her area of weakness (writing)? Could one of her paintings (see Figure 33–9) inspire a piece of creative writing? Following Donald Murray's (1984) model of collecting, focusing, ordering, drafting and clarifying, she proceeded to put the visual—verbal partnership to the test. Figures 33–10 through 33–22 describe the entire translation process that was employed and the final piece of writing that was the result of the process (see Figure 33–23). This art teacher concluded that the writing process was definitely effective and served to translate and to inspire a level of creative writing she had never before achieved. She also concluded that without the original visual image, her level of verbal expression would have been inferior by comparison.

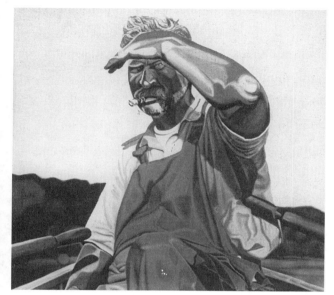

FIGURE 33–9 Painting chosen to inspire the writing process.

As one continues to research the similarities between the two forms of expression and communication, it becomes increasingly obvious that visual and verbal forms of expression have much in common. It is entirely natural for both children and adults to move comfortably between the two forms of communication if impediments are not created that lead to their separation.

AUTHORS AND ARTISTS

Many adults continue the natural inclination to move freely between the visual and verbal forms of expression, as evidenced by viewing the personal letters written by both artists

Process Log

This paper was an enormous challenge to me for three very specific reasons:

1. I have never tried to write fiction before.
2. Even though I have done a lot of work helping children learn how to translate their images into words, I have never tried it myself. That may seem strange, but I think teachers are often guilty of this.
3. Since writing does not come naturally to me, it is an enormous struggle. My skills are still very weak and probably not equal to the goal I set for myself.

My first task was to choose a painting from my portfolio to write about. I wanted both the painting and the writing to be fictional, eliminating other influences as much as possible. I wanted the image and the word to be intimately related, both filtering throught the artist/writer. Even at that, fiction is never completely so, it's always influenced greatly by the personal experiences of the creator. I chose Ole Randall, a fictional character to write about.

FIGURE 33–10 Page 1 of the writing process, translating from the visual image to the verbal form of expression.

I started by brainstorming for 10 minutes. By studying the painting, I listed any word that popped into my head:

Ole
strong
old
piercing
looking
rugged
weathered
farmer
fisherman
sensitive
caring
silent
reflective
lake
Minnesota
immigrant
Norway
Viking
fjord
seeking
searching
new land

calm lake
still water
not moving
weathered
tanned
squinting into sun
looking back
at peace
strong arms
manual work
field work
work clothes
simple
earthy

new life
masculine
simple
limited palette
blue
orange
white
burnt umber
steel grey hair
cigar
half burnt

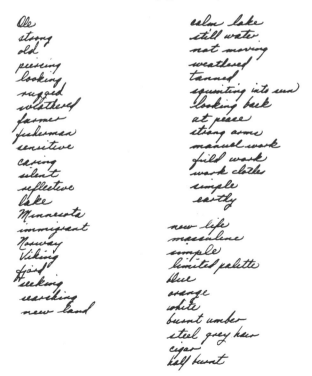

FIGURE 33–11 Page 2 of the writing process, translating from the visual image to the verbal form of expression.

and writers such as Pablo Picasso, Vincent Van Gogh, Edouard Manet, Mark Twain, Virginia Woolf, Victor Hugo and others (Hamilton, 1987). Numerous authors and writers also recognize the close relationship between writing and the making of art. Unfortunately, art teachers rarely make reference to the artist as writer. William Blake, Edvard Munch, Alexander Calder, Kathe Kollwitz, Piet Mondrian, Paul Klee, Wassily Kandinsky, Egon Schiele are just a few examples of the many artists who have used verbal expression to inform and augment their art (Hayes, 1987; Kandinsky, 1981; Schiele, 1985; Torjusen, 1986), and contemporary artists, such as Jenny Holzer, Jennifer Bartlett or Faith Ringgold, continue to do so (Wallis, 1991; Witzling, 1991). Conversely, language arts teachers are rarely interested in the drawings, paintings or sculptures executed by writers such as Edgar Allen Poe, e. e. cummings, Dylan Thomas, Federico Garcia Lorca, T. S. Eliot, Henry Miller, Gunter Grass and John Updike, just to name a few (Hjerter, 1986; Oppenheimer, 1987; Young, 1973). Such individuals are sensitive to the admonition of Goethe who once said:

> We ought to talk less and draw more. I personally should like to remove speech altogether and communicate everything I have to say in sketches. My poor little bit of sketching is priceless to me; it helped my conception of material things; one's mind rises more quickly to general ideas, if one looks at objects more precisely and keenly. (Hjerter, 1986, p. 16)

CURRICULUM CONTENT

It is interesting to note, during these times of educational self-study and evaluation, that the visual and language arts seem to be following an inverse pattern of emphasis regarding instructional methodologies and goals. Historically it has been the case that the visual arts have placed emphasis upon the creative process by focusing on the subject, namely, the child as artist. The language arts, by contrast, have been subject-matter oriented to the extent that students have been encouraged to model their writing on certain classical paradigms of writing. In other words, self-expression has been encouraged in the former case, whereas, in the latter case, the subordination of self-expression to content and correct grammar tended to be the rule.

Now, these priorities in pedagogy are in the process of being reversed. The language arts is placing greater emphasis upon creative writing by attending to whole language approaches to the process of writing with attention to the child as writer. Conversely, art education, in many quarters, is taking a more academic approach to methodology by stressing the elements of design, criticism, art history, and familiarity with classical art objects as prerequisite to the actual making of art objects.

There is great danger, given this exchange of instructional strategies, that the language and visual arts will simply pass

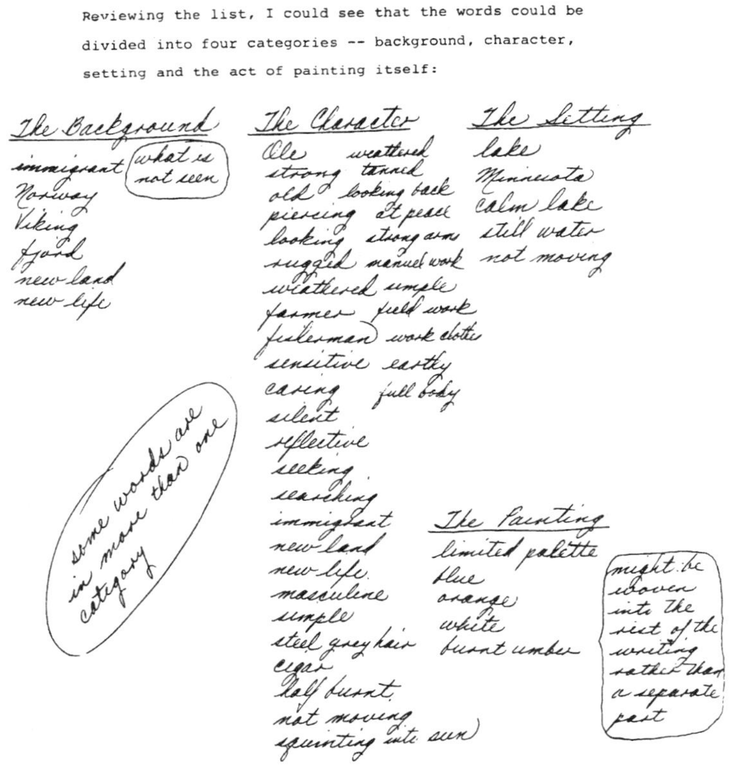

Reviewing the list, I could see that the words could be divided into four categories -- background, character, setting and the act of painting itself:

FIGURE 33–12 Page 3 of the writing process, translating from the visual image to the verbal form of expression.

A third list was devoted only to the character -- his appearance, personality, work and history:

The Character (Ole Randall)

Appearance	Personality	Work
strong	strong	farmer
old	sensitive	fisherman
piercing	easing	manual work
looking	silent	field work
rugged	reflective	
weathered	seeking	
masculine	searching	
steel grey hair	masculine	
cigar	simple	
half burnt	at peace	
not moving	earthy	
squinting into sun		
weathered		**History (background)**
tanned		immigrant
looking back		new land
strong arms		new life
work clothes		

FIGURE 33–13 Page 4 of the writing process, translating from the visual image to the verbal form of expression.

At this point, I thought I was ready to begin the writing. I wrote in a linear form, beginning with the discovery of a small, forgotten photo. No one knew who the man was, but it became the inspiration for the painting.

I remember when I first layed eyes on him. I was looking through some very old photographs in my in-law's living room. A very small black and white photo fell to my feet from between the pages of the album. It had been bent, creased and stuffed between the pages long ago. I picked it up and felt a strong rapport with this man peering out at me. Who was he? a family member? a friend? Nobody knew. Nobody could remember. I simply put the photo back in the book and returned the album to the shelf. I didn't give the picture much more thought.

But that image came back to me every once in a while. I found myself thinking about it and I began to wonder if I could do something with it. Could I give it life? Could I give it a past and a future? As an artist I wanted to try.

It was several months before I was able to look at the photo again. I slipped it into my purse and took it home with me. I spent much time looking at

FIGURE 33–14 Page 5 of the writing process, translating from the visual image to the verbal form of expression.

this little worn photo wondering who this man was. He gradually became a symbol of my past. I could see him sailing the Norwegian fjords and struggling for his very existence in a poor country with few opportunities

I finally got to the fictional part, describing the person in my painting. My voice sounded very matter-of-fact and wooden. I was simply reporting.

Ole [Randall was his name] is a strong man. He came to this country many years ago seeking a new life, a better life. He would not forget the past, but he would look forward to the future. Settling in the lake country of Minnesota he would have daily reminders of the fjords he left behind. Ole was a hard worker.

Ole is one with the land. His weathered body was at peace with the earth. He raises his tanned, muscular arm to squint at the setting sun. He is old now and he can look back and reflect on a life of honest work and personal fulfillment. Ole is not

FIGURE 33–15 Page 6 of the writing process, translating from the visual image to the verbal form of expression.

I stopped writing after the character description. I wanted to weave in material about the act of painting, but I needed to return to the image and draw out more information. I made another list specifically focussed on the act of painting. Notice the notation I made to myself.*

The Act of Painting

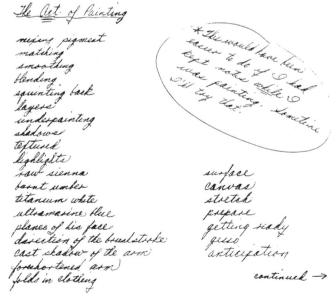

mixing pigment
matching
smoothing
blending
squinting back
layers
underpainting
shadows
textured
highlights
raw sienna
burnt umber
titanium white
ultramarine blue
planes of his face
direction of the brushstroke
cast shadow of the arm
foreshortened arm
folds in clothing

surface
canvas
stretch
prepare
getting ready
gesso
anticipation

This would have been easier to do if I had kept notes while I was painting. I'll try that. Sometime

continued →

FIGURE 33–16 Page 7 of the writing process, translating from the visual image to the verbal form of expression.

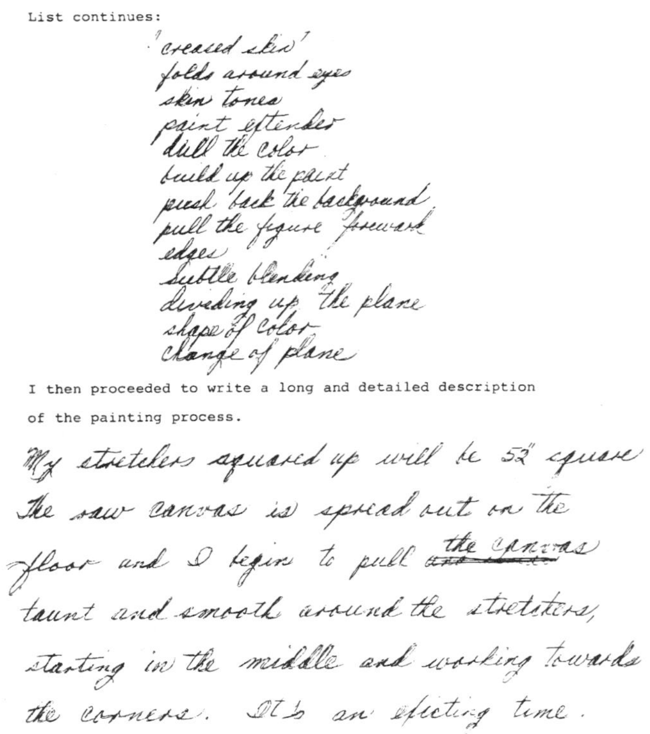

List continues:

'created skin'
folds around eyes
skin tones
paint extender
dull the color
build up the paint
push back the background
pull the figure forward
edges
subtle blending
dividing up the plane
shape of color
change of plane

I then proceeded to write a long and detailed description of the painting process.

My stretchers squared up will be 52" square. The raw canvas is spread out on the floor and I begin to pull the canvas taunt and smooth around the stretchers, starting in the middle and working towards the corners. It's an exciting time.

FIGURE 33–17 Page 8 of the writing process, translating from the visual image to the verbal form of expression.

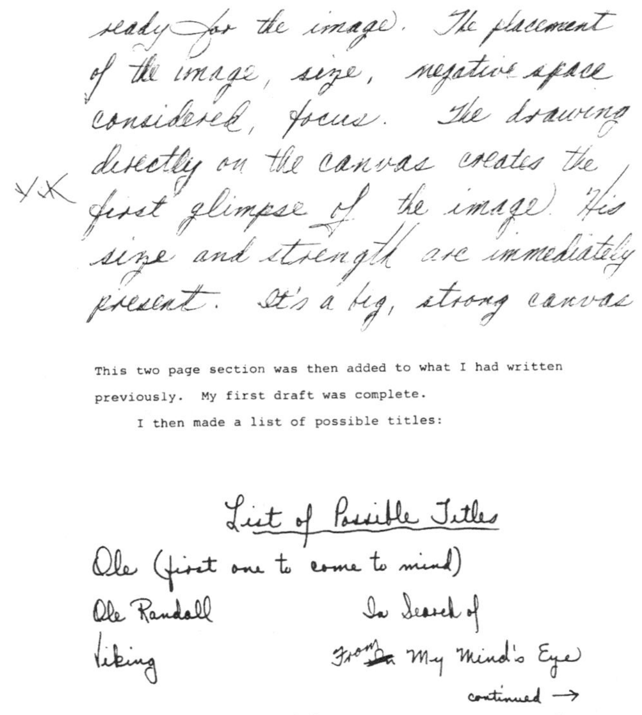

ready for the image. The placement of the image, size, negative space considered, focus. The drawing directly on the canvas creates the first glimpse of the image. Its size and strength are immediately present. It's a big, strong canvas

This two page section was then added to what I had written previously. My first draft was complete.

I then made a list of possible titles:

List of Possible Titles
Ole (first one to come to mind)
Ole Randall   In Search of
Viking   From My Mind's Eye
continued →

FIGURE 33–18 Page 9 of the writing process, tanslating from the visual image to the verbal form of expression.

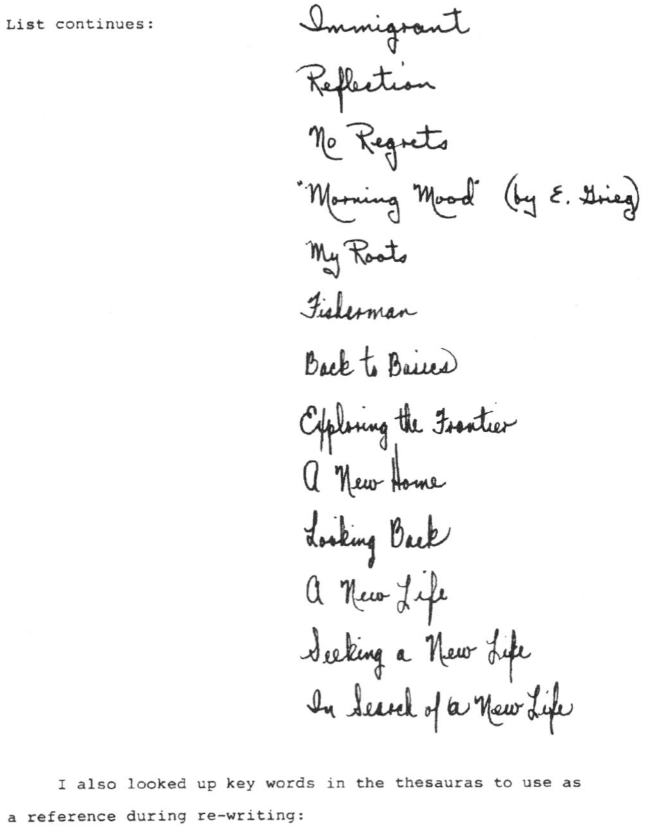

List continues:

Immigrant
Reflection
No Regrets
"Morning Mood" (by E. Grieg)
My Roots
Fisherman
Back to Basics
Exploring the Frontier
A New Home
Looking Back
A New Life
Seeking a New Life
In Search of a New Life

I also looked up key words in the thesauras to use as a reference during re-writing:

FIGURE 33–19 Page 10 of the writing process, translating from the visual image to the verbal form of expression.

each other by, without ever learning anything from the other. This is extremely unfortunate since, as this chapter has tried to demonstrate, these two fields have so much in common and have much to learn from each other. A greater level of communication between the language and visual arts through a spirit of mutual support will finally benefit the student most of all (Olson, 1992).

It is fair to assume, then, that becoming more fully aware of artists who write and writers who make art can provide profound insights for educators — not just theoretically but in the practice of the classroom. Each art form can benefit enormously when art and language arts form a partnership for the sake of learning. The integration of visual and verbal expression provides a more complete picture of communication and allows each art form to benefit from the special insights of the other. This connection also encourages a higher level of literacy for all students, especially for those students more inclined toward artistic expression — what is called the visual or the spatial learner (Dixon, 1983; Olson, 1992).

For this to happen, art teachers ought to become more involved with the larger educational community, making connections with other subject areas, for the sake of learning. In general, art educators, it seems to me, have been too much concerned with the child-artist and too little concerned with the child-learner. On the other hand, English and language

FIGURE 33–20 Page 11 of the writing process, translating from the visual image to the verbal form of expression.

I worked on possible outlines:

1. Finding the photo
2. Getting ready (stretching the canvas, etc.)
3. The Character
4. Painting
5. Conclusion

1. The Character

2. The Character + painting terminology

3. Rehearsal (anticipation + stretching the canvas)

4. the small photo (replacing it)

1. the character
2. the process
3. the rehearsal
4. the source of the inspiration
close with Murray's quote

FIGURE 33–21 Page 12 of the writing process, translating from the visual image to the verbal form of expression.

It seems necessary for me to write my first draft in a very linear, sequential form before I can play around with the parts. I guess I have to "see" it. Insight may then come at the strangest times. While brushing my teeth one morning, I suddenly realized that I was including much more than what was necessary. I didn't need to go into great detail about finding the photo and stretching the canvas. Writing it all out served a good purpose, however. It refreshed my memory concerning the entire creation of the painting, but it was clear that the finished piece of writing would be much more effective if I simply focused on the strength of the character. Then I could gradually weave in the painting descriptions.

The re-writes went through many messy changes:

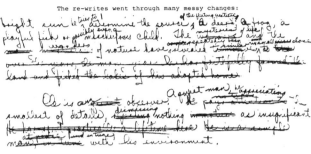

And finally, I closed with Murray's words simply because I thought they were very appropriate.

FIGURE 33–22 Page 13 of the writing process, translating from the visual image to the verbal form of expression.

arts teachers ought to investigate what a difference an image can make in order to understand the entire picture of a child's expression. Only when educators systematically assume the comprehensive responsibility for educating the whole child will it be possible to view both the visual and the language arts as offering necessary and essential dimensions for every child's education. When this happens, the formative partnership between the language and the visual arts will make it much more difficult to simply cut or reduce an area of instruction due to budgetary constraints.

THE EDUCATION OF TEACHERS OF VISUAL AND LANGUAGE ARTS

Chapters 34 and 36 focus on the preparation and certification requirements for English and language arts teachers. Unfortunately, these programs of study do not often require a visual arts course. If such a course is required, it is generally satisfied with taking an art history course or a studio course, rather than an art education course that would emphasize the artistic development of children. Even when an art education course is required, it is often taught as an art appreciation course rather than an opportunity to build bridges between the two areas of specialization that might ultimately make a significant difference in the classroom.

Art teachers are prepared for state certification in a variety of ways. They are expected to have a broad background in studio art, as well as experience in the history of art, criticism and aesthetics. In addition, art teachers are expected to have background in the artistic growth and development of

FROM MY MIND'S EYE

The air is still. It causes not a single ripple on the clear Minnesota lake. Ole Randall sits quietly. He's a vision of solitude, sensitive to the slightest movement near the opposite shore. Peering into the bright sun, he tries to determine the source of the fleeting gesture. A deer? A frog? A leaping bass? Or maybe a playful child. The mysteries of life and the wonders of nature have oft been revealed to him in such small pieces. Ole is an observer. A quiet, contemplative man, he appreciates the slightest clue to lifes' many treasures.

Ole is getting on in years. The lake is a soothing reflection of his old Viking past. In his youth he sailed the Nordic fjords imagining a more prosperous land, one of opportunity. He left and never returned, and yet he never forgets. The lake is a daily reminder of the beautiful Norwegian fjords he left years ago.

As a young immigrant farmer, he worked hard, having the advantage of both a strong mind and a strong body. He worked the fields in the scorching summer sun and drilled holes through the frozen lake for fish during the long, intensely cold Minnesota winter. His weathered body adapted to the rigorous demands of each season.

A rare man is he. In tune with his environment, as are the trees and the animals he lovingly observes. He looks straight into the future, not with regret or apprehension, but anticipating the day his beloved earth embraces and protects his tired body in never ending rest.

Ole's strong arm is raised to his forehead, shielding his eyes from the blinding sun. The burnt umber tones are brushed across the strongly defined muscular structure of the arm. The upper arm is foreshortened to create a strong illusion and depth of vision. He squints. Squeezing white pigment into the raw skin tones reveals the brilliant light and the contrasting shadows cast across his weathered face, challenging the artist. His face, the varied textures, the changing planes, minute shapes and lines fitting together like life's puzzle. Nothing can escape the painters' eye. The image is released from the deep crevices of my soul. I am one with my painting. There is no separation, no dividing line. My own history, my own past, my very roots are revealed in its' form. The painting is finished. The struggle is over, the artist has spoken. I stand back to see what hath been wrought -- a new life. A "thing" has been created from mere earthy pigments.

It was only a few short weeks ago that this large, tightly stretched canvas was lovingly prepared in uncertain anticipation. As the writer's blank page, it waited for the first mark, the first stroke of the brush.

Artists make me see what I can write. Reflected light, stillness captured, one simple curved line that leaves out and keeps in. When the writing doesn't come, I look at paintings, and especially drawings. If I could draw I wouldn't have to write. (Murray, 1984, 227)

FIGURE 33–23 Final writing example, inspired by the visual image.

children, classroom management and be able to design developmentally appropriate curriculum. A student attending a liberal arts college either majors in art education or majors in art studio and minors in art education. A student who attends an art school, usually majors in art education after completing an intense studio core program during the first 2 years. Many students choose to fulfill certification requirements at the masters level after devoting their entire undergraduate experience to the study of art. In most cases, freshman English, in order to demonstrate verbal competency, is the only English course required for graduation and certification.

Students in each area proceed on a narrow path of specialization, with little consideration given to how their respective subject relates to the other. If teachers were educated to *recognize* and to *analyze* the close relationship between artistic and verbal development, and communication and expression, children would be the beneficiary of a higher level of respect and understanding. A close partnership between the two areas of *communication* and *expression* could potentially elevate the level of student learning. With so many similarities between the visual and the language arts, I believe each teacher would benefit enormously from taking courses in each area of specialization, in order to solidify the partnership.

The Public School Setting

Communication between art and language arts and English teachers is made difficult by the usual educational setting in the public school. At the elementary level, language arts teachers are generally considered classroom teachers and are responsible for a small group of children for an entire academic year. They usually teach in their own classroom setting and are fully responsible for that environment. Very often, the special areas of instruction, including visual art, provide time in the daily schedule for the classroom teacher to have planning time. Consequently, classroom teachers are rarely involved with the curriculum content in these areas.

Art teachers, on the other hand, either welcome individual classes to their own art rooms, or they move from classroom to classroom, known widely as "art on a cart!" It is not unusual for art teachers to meet as many as 300 to 800 students in a single week. Some hardworking art teachers are able to integrate an individual art lesson with a classroom unit of study, but in many cases the requests are more than one art teacher can accomplish.

At the middle and high school levels, the isolation of one subject from another grows more profound. Some high schools are even designed in such a way that the arts (visual arts, music, theater and dance) are dedicated to their own wing, as though they have no connection whatsoever with the academic subjects. I know of at least two high schools where the arts are even located in their own separate building.

On the surface, this may not seem to be reason for dismay, but it sends a very subtle message that art is separate and different from more serious learning. The physical design of these schools also makes it almost impossible for visual art teachers and language arts teachers to converse about particular students, curriculum design and any kind of possible partnership between the two areas.

No wonder teachers, students, administrators and parents have come to the conclusion that art is a frill, rather than an integral part of the school curriculum. Unfortunately, the students who could benefit most from a close partnership between the visual and language arts are not being well served and consequently, are not reaching their full educational potential.

CONCLUSIONS

In this chapter, a strong case for collaboration between the visual and language arts has been made. Before the beginning of this research project, the visual and language arts areas were viewed as being worlds apart; but after entering the language arts community, enormous similarities and valid educational reasons for ongoing collaboration were found. The fears that were often expressed by both visual and language arts teachers were often based on very early school experiences, and these impressions were frequently reinforced at the college level where specialization is considered both natural and essential. As educators, however, we have a responsibility to serve students by attending to all aspects of aptitude and potential. Certainly, this is an invitation to build whatever bridges are necessary for the sake of more complete learning.

The American poet e. e. cummings seemed to understand very well the unique and even necessary partnership between the visual and the verbal modes of expression in the following lines:

> Tell me, doesn't your painting interfere with your writing? Quite the contrary: they love each other dearly. (Hjerter, 1986, p. 109)

References

Calkins, L. M. (1986). *The art of teaching writing.* Portsmouth, NH: Heinemann.

de Villiers, P. A., & de Villiers, J. G. (1979). *Early language.* Cambridge, MA: Harvard University Press.

Dixon, J. P. (1983). *The spatial child.* Springfield, IL: Charles C. Thomas.

Fein, S. (1993) *First drawings: Genesis of visual thinking.* Pleasant Hill, CA: Exelrod Press.

Gardner, H. (1981). *Artful scribbles.* New York: Basic Books.

Glazer, S. M. (1989). Oral language and literacy development. In D. S. Strickland & L. M. Morrow (Eds.), *Emerging literacy: young children learn to read and write* (pp. 16–26). Newark, DE: International Reading Association.

Goodnow, J. (1977). *Children drawing.* Cambridge, MA: Harvard University Press.

Greene, H., & Petty, W. (1975). *Developing language skills in the elementary schools.* (5th ed.). Boston: Allyn & Bacon.

Hamilton, C. (1987). *The illustrated letter.* New York: Universe Books.

Hayes, M. C. (1987). *Three Alexander Calders: A family memoir.* New York: Universe Books.

Hjerter, K. G. (1986). *Doubly gifted: The author as visual artist.* New York: Harry N. Abrams.

Hurwitz, A., & Day, M. (1991). *Children and their art* (5th ed.). New York: Harcourt, Brace and Jovanovich.

Kandinsky, W. (1981). *Sounds.* (E. R. Napier, Trans.). New Haven, CT: Yale University Press. (Original work published 1912).

Kellogg, R. (1970). *Analyzing children's art.* Palo Alto, CA: Mayfield.

Lowenfeld, V. (1957). *Creative and mental growth.* New York: Macmillan.

Murray, D. (1984). *Write to learn.* New York: Holt, Rinehart & Winston.

National Council of Teachers of English. (1976). *A statement on the preparation of teachers of English and the language arts.* Urbana, IL: National Council of Teachers of English.

Olson, J. L. (1992). *Envisioning writing: Toward an integration of drawing and writing.* Portsmouth, NH: Heinemann.

Oppenheimer, H. (1987). *Lorca the drawings: Their relation to the poet's life and work.* New York: Franklin Watts.

Pinker, S. (1994). *The language instinct: how the mind creates language.* New York: William Morrow.

Qualley, C. A. (1986). *Quality art education.* Reston, VA: National Art Education Association.

Schiele, E. (1985). *I, eternal child* (A. Hollo, Trans.). New York: Grove Press.

Torjusen, B. (1985). *Words and images of Edvard Munch.* Chelsea, VT: Chelsea Green.

Wallis, B. (Ed.), (1991). *Blasted allegories.* Cambridge, MA: MIT Press.

Wilson, B., & Wilson, M. (1982). *Teaching children to draw.* Englewood Cliffs, NJ: Prentice Hall.

Witzling, M. R. (Ed.). (1991). *Voicing our visions: Writings by women artists.* New York: Universe Books.

Young, N. (Ed.), (1973). *The paintings of Henry Miller: Paint as you like and die happy.* San Francisco: Chronicle Books.

·34·

TEACHER PREPARATION IN THE LANGUAGE ARTS: A SYNTHESIS

Josefina Villamil Tinajero

UNIVERSITY OF TEXAS AT EL PASO

Ana Huerta-Macias

NEW MEXICO STATE UNIVERSITY

INTRODUCTION

Teacher education programs have undergone significant changes in the last few decades as they become more responsive to needs within the schools and classrooms. These changes have impacted teacher preparation programs in all areas of the curriculum including the language arts. This article describes recent developments in the area of teacher preparation with a focus on the language arts. We first present a historical perspective of teacher education programs and then focus on educational reform and renewal.

BRIEF HISTORICAL PERSPECTIVES ON TEACHER EDUCATION

Research indicates that some universities had established their own schools of education in the early 1900s, long before normal schools became teachers colleges and more than half a century before they evolved into universities. These schools of education were supported mainly by male high school teachers who had viewed university training "…as a way to protect themselves from the rising feminization and falling prestige of their calling" (Labaree, 1992, p. 138). However, this move to protect the male orientation of the high school teaching profession failed, and the schools then adapted by preparing the same male high school teachers as educational administrators. The result was that these early, university-based schools of education focused on the

preparation of school administrators as opposed to classroom teachers (Labaree, 1992). Thus, it was the normal schools that carried the major responsibility of formalizing programs for the training of teachers in the United States. It was also predominantly women who were being trained in these schools, as women public school teachers far outnumbered the male teachers. Kline and Dye (1992), for instance, indicated that at the end of the 1870 school year there were 5 male teachers in the Cleveland public schools versus 164 female teachers—a trend that continued into the 20th century. The first normal schools in Cleveland were private and were established in the post civil war period. Public normal schools were then established in response to the growing need to train urban as opposed to rural public school teachers. The urban teachers were dealing with problems in late 19th century Cleveland not encountered by rural teachers such as an "…increasing immigrant population, the dilemma of dual income homes leaving children in many instances to their own devices, the problem of health, sanitation…" (p. 4). Thus, there was a growth of public normal schools that continued into the early 20th century not only in Ohio but in other states as well. Bennie (cited in Warner, 1990) describes the establishment of the first normal schools in Texas:

Barely 30 years after becoming a state, Texas established its first teacher education institution, the Sam Houston Normal Institute at Huntsville in 1879. The importance Texans placed on quality elementary and secondary education is shown by the fact that the Institute was established four years before the opening of the state university. As the population began to expand over the state, other

428

teacher education facilities were opened. Normal schools were established in Denton 1901; San Marcos in 1903; Canyon in 1910; Commerce in 1917; Nacadoches (sic) in 1918; and Alpine in 1919. (p. 27)

The concept for those schools was borrowed by American reformers from the Prussians, who had a seminary-type school specifically for training teachers. However, as these normal schools were established in the states in the late 19th and early 20th centuries, the plans for them grew increasingly different from the original visions for such schools. Horace Mann, an American educator, had envisioned the ideal for these schools as a center specifically for teacher training. Yet, over time and with a demand for accessibility to higher education, these schools were generally treated as additional centers for advanced education rather than for teacher training (Eisenmann, 1991).

Squire (1991) additionally notes that while most elementary school teachers in the early 20th century had been trained in these 2-year normal schools, they were not trained in the teaching of English as subject matter. This lack of course work in English as subject matter was still apparent, even in universities, in the early decades of this century. A professor at Boston University noted, for instance, that in 1930 when he began teaching "not a single course on teaching reading was offered in the nation's colleges" (p. 6).

During the 1930s and early 1940s, teaching training centers and laboratory schools were established by universities throughout the country as they experimented with progressive education. These centers, which had a strong following, are said to have been responsible for training of an entire generation of teachers. Some of these university centers grew into centers for research and for training teacher educators as well as educational administrators. Teachers College at Columbia University, for example, became a major center for teacher education and research at this time.

It was not until after World War II, however, that with pressure from organizations such as the National Council Teachers of English (NCTE) and International Reading Association (IRA), stronger certification standards were recommended for teachers and that emphasis was laid on preparation for teaching the language arts. In the 1950s and 1960s there was a school reform movement to strengthen academic achievement. This led not only to funding for projects on curriculum development and teaching in English but also to the establishment of summer training institutes for teachers which focused on language, literature, and composition (Squire, 1991).

The centers which were created in the 1930s and 1940s were closed by the 1960s and 1970s as teacher educators moved away from these demonstration centers and laboratory schools to the real world of the classroom. Currently, however, there is a resurgence of centers which are gaining attention in language arts preparation, such as the Center for Study of Writing at Berkeley and the Centers of Excellence Program by NCTE which recognizes exemplary classrooms and schools.

Teacher preparation programs have continued to move toward a "field-based" approach by integrating more actual classroom experience into teacher training. This is evident in the alternative programs which will be discussed later in this paper. However, before discussing alternative programs it is appropriate here to take a look at those skills and knowledge bases within the area of language arts that are the focus of teacher education programs. Space limitations, however, preclude an explanation of the many areas in which language arts teachers are expected to develop expertise. A listing of some of the general areas of teacher preparation is provided. This list is based on recent trends and issues in the language arts as identified by NCTE.

Teacher Preparation in the Language Arts

Discussions from the Commissions of the NCTE (Suhor, 1993) indicated increased attention to (1) the social and critical aspects of language; (2) multicultural issues within the curriculum (such as gender awareness and sexual orientation in literature selection); (3) a broader understanding of visual language (for example, film, television, graphs and photographs); (4) the teaching of writing as a process with the inclusion of spelling, grammar and vocabulary within the context of the student's writing; (5) the inclusion of reading and writing practices within literature studies; and (6) the combination of books and technology to form a new kind of instruction text. Two areas merit some elaboration: visual arts and technology in teacher preparation.

Teacher Preparation in the Visual Arts. There is a dearth of literature in the area of teacher preparation in the visual arts—to include art, music, drama, film, and dance—as compared to the language arts. Nonetheless, research in this area suggests trends toward postmodernism in art education (MacGregor, 1992); preparation for the teaching of arts within a multinational context (Zimmermann, 1990); and training in the development of a variety to skills such as critical thinking, cooperative work, organization and problem solving, and communication through dance and other comparable visual art forms (Overby, 1992).

The impact of postmodernism on the arts is one where less attention is paid to differences between what is known as high art and popular art, and where the emphasis is on the construction of art forms, each with its own unique interpretation, through social interactions. Thus, as MacGregor (1992) says, educators are now forced "to take note of voices often ignored in the establishment of educational priorities" so that curriculum development is now more "accommodative" and "elastic" (p. 4).

Following along the lines of a postmodern attitude, teacher education in the visual arts is increasingly focused on teaching the arts within a multinational-multicultural context. There is a thrust to internationalize the art curricula, and thus teacher art education, that it is now more global in perspective. Multicultural art programs have been sparse. Nonetheless, there have been a few projects in the past 10 years that have addressed this change to pluralism in the arts. These range, for instance, from a teacher preparation program to prepare in-service and preservice teachers to teach students from three cultural backgrounds to a large school district curriculum project where art was one of a number of curricular areas incorporated into a multicultural approach to education (Zimmermann, 1990, p. 2). Community-based art education is another aspect of the change in the teaching of the arts within a multicultural context. This involves the presentation of art in such a way that the audience can gain insight into local and global issues and thus relate it to their own lives. These community and global extensions of the visual arts have created an issue in the area of teacher preparation. The issue is that art teachers cannot be expected to have the knowledge that is required about the many different cultures and communities within the United States and internationally to teach the visual arts from a global perspective. Thus, there is a call for the development of practical materials in this area, along with a request for support from school administrators, government policy makers, private foundations and university teacher educators.

The changes which have occurred in dance education typify what is happening within the area of the visual arts, and by extension, within teacher education programs for the visual arts. The more recent guidelines in the area of dance education curriculum include attention to not only specific dance technique and vocabulary but to (1) historical and cultural information, (2) the production of unique, creative, and expressive dance studies, (3) analyses and critical examination of professional and peer performance, and (4) the recognition of the relationship of dance to the arts. Dance elements are also integrated into other subject areas, including for example, physics. In the physics class principles of momentum, force, velocity, and energy are applied to dance to improve dance performance (Overby, 1992, p. 2). Thus, there is a move in dance, as in other forms of visual art, toward greater depth, broader national and international perspectives, and an integration with other subject areas.

Technology in Teacher Preparation. Technology is becoming the focus of much discussion not only within the language arts but in all literacy development across the curriculum. Training in the use of technology for the language arts is increasingly impacting teacher education. In his discussion about the role of computers in teaching the language arts, Bruce (1991) indicates that they can be:

1. A tutor to individualize instruction and record student progress,
2. A tool that can aid in reading, revision of texts and spelling,
3. A way to explore language as they manipulate and interact with it in various ways,
4. A medium which makes possible new forms of communication and "hypertext" which use tables, charts, graphs, pictures, sounds, video and text, and
5. An environment for communication including electronic networks that permit new forms of meaningful interaction.

Griest (1993) further elaborates on how technology is revolutionizing the language arts such that "whole language practices that do not evolve into whole media practices stop way short of a whole classroom" (p. 10). An example of how technology is impacting the language arts in critical and constructive ways is in the areas of reading and literature.

Earlier literary texts were considered static, and the student's role was to appreciate the printed words on the page and giftedness of the author. Now, with technology, texts have become fluid and students analyze texts not in passive but in active ways. Students can deconstruct texts as they move from a single linear channel to one of hypertext. Hypertext, or hypermedia, engages them in the process of text production with all forms of visual art, so that students are no longer just consumers whose role is to admire someone else's print (Griest, 1993). Technology has also made its way into assessment in the language arts as new software allows teachers to use text, images, and sound to document their student's processes and products as they go about using written and oral language (Barrett, 1994).

Teacher preparation programs have begun to integrate technology into their programs of study. Reading courses at New Mexico State University, for instance, include a review and evaluation of a variety of computer software. Preservice teachers are given the opportunity to (1) learn how to use these programs in the classroom; (2) talk about how they might be applied in reading and language arts classrooms in the schools; and (3) evaluate them in terms of usefulness, cost, multicultural perspectives, ease of integration into the curriculum, and so forth (V. D. Thompson, personal communication, May 1995).

The role of technology in teacher preparation, then, is a central one in that it will impact the teaching of all of the traditional language arts—reading, writing, literature—as well as create new areas of teaching—hypertext, telecommunications, visual arts—that we must integrate into our teacher education programs.

As teacher education programs adapt to these evolving areas of instruction, there is yet another change which is affecting preparation in all areas of the curriculum, the language arts, in particular—the increasing diversity in our nation's classrooms.

Preparation for Student Diversity

The major challenge for the future of teacher education programs in the language arts is preparing teachers to work with the increasingly diverse populations found in our nation's schools. Projections are that by the year 2000, almost 50% of the children in our classrooms will be culturally and linguistically different; that is, "minority" (Sosa, 1993). This means that every classroom teacher will be working with SAEs (students acquiring English). The English as a second language (ESL) teacher will no longer be able to take sole responsibility to assist those students who are developing English literacy, for these students will be present in all classes regardless of whether they are designed as ESL, language arts, science, social studies, or math classes. Thus, language arts teachers need some background in second language acquisition, the use of sheltered English, and ESL. How can teacher education programs in the language arts integrate all of the above? That is, how can we best prepare teachers in the language arts who have the skills and knowledge bases required to successfully teach students in the 21st century? The following sections explore the traditional university-based teacher education programs and take a look at the educational reform movement, including alternative certification programs, Teach for America, and professional development schools.

Traditional University-Based Programs. Although traditional preservice teacher preparation programs differ remarkably from one another in their structure and orientation, they are also remarkably similar in many respects. Until a few years ago, teacher preparation programs were, almost exclusively, university based, with their teacher preparation unit at each institution responsible for program design, for curriculum design, development and implementation and for delivery of instruction with little or no input from practitioners.

With few exceptions, traditional teacher preparation programs in every state established broad academic requirements for the initial teaching certificate which included a college BA or BS degree, general education coursework, studies of subject matter, pedagogical studies and coursework in special education. The majority of teacher preparation units also established assessment requirements such as basic skills, subject matter and general knowledge exams. As recently as 1994, less than one third of the states, however, required assessment of teaching performance for the initial teaching certificate (Andrew, 1994). While most states had requirements for the initial elementary and secondary teaching certificate in the study of teaching and schooling (development of a basic repertoire of teaching strategies, methods of teaching elementary school subjects), only about one third of the states required the study of self (teacher as learner) and knowledge of alternative ways of organizing schools (Andrew, 1994).

In addition, as recently as 1994, almost one third of the states required no field experiences prior to student teaching. For those states which did have a field experience requirement, the requirement ranged from only 40 clock hours to 300 hours of field and clinical experiences, with the majority of states falling in the lower range of the continuum (Andrew, 1994). Among those states requiring field experiences prior to students teaching, only 11 required students to spend some time in multicultural settings, and only one state required videotaped feedback.

While almost all of the states required student teaching experience (which ranged from 8 full-time weeks to 18 full-time weeks), the majority required only 8 to 12 full-time weeks. In addition, seven states required no visit by a supervisor and only 14 states required master teacher training (Andrew, 1994).

In spite of a variety of similarities, traditional preservice teacher education programs do differ from one another in their structure and orientation (Kennedy, 1991). According to Kennedy, some preservice teacher education programs are 4 year programs, with teacher education integrated throughout the 5 years. Fifth-year programs allow undergraduates to major in a liberal arts discipline and then switch to specialized education courses at the graduate level. Five-year teaching programs are becoming the norm, and about 25% of newly hired teachers hold master's degrees (Teaching Teachers, 1995, p. 70).

Teacher education programs also differ in the number and mix of professional courses they require as well as in the assessment requirements. They also differ in the noneducational requirements for the initial teaching certificate and field experiences. Some programs emphasize liberal arts education, while others emphasize research on teaching. Still others emphasize the craft of teaching. Some programs require basic skills exams in reading, math, and writing, while others include spelling and still others require an assessment of teaching performance (Andrew, 1994; Kennedy, 1991). Programs also differ in the noneducational and special requirements for teaching certificates. Some programs require U.S. citizenship, an oath of allegiance and screening for moral character (Andrew, 1994). They also differ in the kind of teachers they hope to produce and in their tacit theories of how novices can learn to teach (Kennedy, 1991).

Teacher Education Reform. A number of organizations, foundations, and individuals have sought ways in which to change the manner in which teachers are prepared and certified. They have been particularly concerned about teachers' continuing professional development. Although the great majority of the new teaching enthusiasts are graduates of schools of education, more and more are entering the teaching profession through alternate routes, including alternative certification routes, the Teach for America programs, which enlist liberal arts graduates from elite schools. Other programs are attracting military retirees and recently unemployed defense workers to teaching (Teaching Teachers, 1995, p. 69). A small percentage is enrolled in programs at newly restructured, reformed schools of education, which teacher educators, policy makers, and the public hope will produce what past reforms have failed to accomplish: better schools and better teachers through better teacher education (Winitzky, Stoddart & O'Keefe, 1992, p. 3).

Alternative Certification Programs. Certification programs which provide an alternative to the traditional teacher preparation programs in the United States have increased dramatically over the last two decades. In the 1980s only a handful of states provided programs that led to certification without the traditional course of study through a university or college. Yet, this number quadrupled in the late 1980s and by 1990 there were 33 (and possibly as many as 48) states implementing alternative certification programs (Hawley, 1990).

While the first alternative certification (AC) programs were spurred by the long-term teacher shortages, particularly in math, science and specialties such as bilingual education, AC programs which are being implemented currently are not limited to the sole purpose of increasing the supply of available teachers. Among the objectives of some AC programs are minimizing the costs and time for teacher education, encouraging well-qualified professionals to come into the field of education, and providing a model for teacher education reform. In this section, the concept of AC will be discussed and sample programs will be described. Since the literature does not single out language arts as a specific topic within the area of AC, the authors will here provide a general description of AC programs and concerns. It is safe to assume, we believe, that the information presented applies to preparation for teaching the language arts as well as math, science, and other areas.

At this point, a working definition of AC program is appropriate. While definitions of AC programs vary according to different groups, institutions, and researchers, the American Association of Colleges for Teacher Education (AACTE) generally characterizes these programs as "any significant departure from the traditional undergraduate route through teacher education programs in universities and colleges" (cited in Hutton, Lutz, and Williamson, 1990). Alternative certification programs are to be distinguished from other types of programs which allow teachers to practice without certification, such as teacher certificate or emergency waiver programs. Additionally, AC programs are defined by states and typically include selective admission standards, a supervised internship-mentor supervision program, a streamlined curriculum of formal coursework which may or may not involve a university or college, and an examination to assure competency in the subject to be taught (Baird, 1990; Cornett, 1990; Hawley, 1990).

It was mentioned above that while increasing the supply of teachers is still one of the primary purposes of AC programs, additional objectives include facilitating the entry of professionals into teaching and providing a model for teacher education reform. State models in Texas and Connecticut, which fulfill each of these purposes will be described in the following sections. Another AC program, Teach for America, which is not state based, will also be described.

Alternative Certification Programs in Texas. Texas passed a law in 1985 for licensure of college graduates who had not completed a Teacher Education Program by passing a competency test, serving an internship, taking training in teaching methods and also taking courses from a university program. Three different programs have resulted from this: higher education, educational service center, and school district models. The higher education model includes coursework and supervised in-school training during the intern's first year of teaching. The educational service center programs rely on field-based experiences with mentor supervision. School districts participate in models which they have designed using staff development as the primary basis for preparation (Cornett, 1990).

Since 1989 all AC programs in Texas brought before the State Boards must undergo a developmental process which calls for the participatory involvement of classroom teachers, district administrators, education specialists from education service centers and representatives from higher education faculty and administration. The purpose of this is to strengthen the quality of the program and foster broad-based participation as programs are developed and refined. As an additional effort to maintain quality, interns in AC programs are provided with multiple levels of support. Support is provided by the principal of the school where the intern is placed, by trained observers, by a program supervisor who serves as a liaison between the program director and the interns, and by mentors who receive training in monitoring, clinical supervision, peer coaching, communication and conferencing skills (Texas Education Agency, 1991–92).

These programs have brought a dramatic increase in the number of AC students. The number of interns jumped from 276 in 1985–86 to 1,965 in 1991–92; likewise, the number of programs went from one (in Houston) in 1985–86 to 21 in 1991–92. Moreover, the Texas program shares-characteristics with other programs with respect to the higher numbers of minorities and males being recruited for these programs. In 1991–1992, for example, 34% of the total number of interns in Texas-based AC programs were males and 50% were minorities (Texas Education Agency, 1991–92).

Some highly successful models have introduced AC programs at the post baccalaureate level. Such is the case at the University of Texas at El Paso where students who already have college degrees and work experiences in other fields are recruited. This program requires university coursework over summer, fall and spring semesters. During the fall and spring a student simultaneously works as an entry-level teacher in one of the 10 participating school districts in the area. Interns take the required state certification exams during their second summer in the program. Upon successful completion, students are recommended by the university for a Texas Teacher Certificate (UTEP/ACP, 1995).

Alternative Certification Programs in Connecticut The AC program in Connecticut was instituted in 1987. Its primary objectives were "…To bring exceptionally qualified individuals with diverse backgrounds into the profession … a secondary agenda … was to create an external catalyst for change in Connecticut's fourteen standard teacher education programs" (Bliss, 1990, p. 36). Competitive entry for this program is based on minimum criteria which include:

- a Bachelor's degree with a major in the intended teaching field
- GPA of at least B
- an essay describing the desire to become a teacher
- a passing score on the Connecticut's content area exam
- proof of registration for Connecticut's content area exam
- experience in working with children or adolescents

Alternative certification is available in the areas of elementary education (grades 4–8); secondary education (English, foreign language, mathematics, science, history and social studies), and art and music (K–12).

The initial part of the program consists of the successful completion of an 8-week, full-time, noncredit summer program. The curriculum consists of a coherent integrated group of courses which are organized in thematic blocks. These blocks, for instance, include student as learner, teaching the learner and problems of learners. The sessions utilize lecture, small group discussion, case teaching and forums with experienced teachers.

After completing the summer program and after accepting a regular teaching position in a public school, a temporary

90-day teaching certificate is issued to the AC teacher. Once the 90-day period is over, and upon recommendation of the superintendent, an Initial Educator Certificate is issued by the State Department of Education which is enough for 1½ years. At the end of this period, and after the teacher has passed an assessment on the Connecticut teaching competencies, a Provisional Educator Certificate is issued. The teacher must then complete, within 3 to 8 years, 30 credit hours in a planned program beyond the bachelor's degree after which a Professional Educator Certificate is issued. In order to keep this certificate, 90 contact hours of professional development must be taken every 5 years (Bliss, 1990).

The program has resulted in a dramatic increase in the number of teachers (60% of whom entered teaching from another field) and their salaries in the state. In a few years Connecticut moved from seventh place in teacher salaries to second place behind Alaska with an average teacher's salary of $40,346 in 1990.

The reaction by supervisors to the AC teachers has been highly positive with respect to their personal qualities as well as their teaching. These results have been attributed to the high standards of the program as well as the demanding schedule and heavy workload—all of which have also brought about an esprit de corps among the participants. The strong mentor program—2 years with a state trained mentor and district appointed supervisor—has also been recognized as highly important to the program's success.

The program has also achieved its objective of serving as a catalyst for teacher education reform in Connecticut. Faculty members in some universities have reexamined the curriculum and organizational structure of the courses. In at least one university, the core courses were organized thematically in a highly integrated sequence. Thus, the program is reported as meeting its goals of (1) attracting highly qualified individuals into teaching who demonstrate a heightened sense of professionalism; and (2) serving as a catalyst for change in Connecticut's standard teacher education programs (Bliss, 1990).

Teach for America. Teach for America (TFA) is another popular program which deserves mention here. This program seems to be sweeping the country as a modified Peace Corps program where teachers work toward certification through placement in school districts which already have existing mechanisms for AC. The program which is in part supported by private industry, requires a 2-year commitment on the part of cities and rural areas. The program trains teachers in an 8-week preservice institute held at the University of Southern California in Los Angeles during the summer, prior to their placement. This institute includes a 6-week national component which revolves around student-teaching in Los Angeles' year around schools and 2-week on-site induction into the schools and communities in which corps members will be teaching. The institute is mostly staffed by active teachers from the placement sites who aim to provide corps members with the practical skills as well as a theoretical background which they feel is essential before they go into the classrooms. These novices then enter the schools as 1st-year teachers and are paid entry level salaries. Ongoing professional develop-

ment is provided through support groups, workshops, and university programs. Additionally, TFA has a local office which provides its members with transitional help and ongoing direct support. The program is evaluated internally through its Director of Research and Evaluation who identifies strengths and weakness of the program.

Teach for America program appears to be highly controversial. While some praise the program others feel that this "emergency" type credentialing of teachers leaves them without crucial preparation in the general areas of child growth and development—knowledge essential to effective teaching (Lawton, 1991). The classes at the preservice institute have been criticized as being mostly irrelevant to the daily work of the members in the classroom. The lack of strong mentor teachers who could truly provide guidance by working closely with the corps members has also been cited as a major weaknesses of the program. The frustration from the lack of an adequate mentorship system was expressed by a corps member graduate as he reflected on his training experiences, "many TFA student teachers were consigned to the back of the room, observing the 'master' teacher at work and occasionally making cameo appearances before the class. Other so-called mentors dropped the full load of planning, teaching, and grading on the TFA neophyte, sometimes even leaving the student teacher alone in the room" (Schorr, 1993, p. 316).

Other critics claim that ghetto children are being shortchanged by TFA's brief 8-week training (Parker, 1992). Defenders of the program point out that their rigorous screening process (which includes a written essay, two interviews, a sample teaching session, and demonstration of a high-level commitment, academic excellence, leadership, maturity, flexibility and a sensitivity to diversity) allows them to recruit only the most bright and able arts and science graduates, including minorities, who would not otherwise serve the school. Thus, the controversy continues which will provide more insights on its relative strengths and weaknesses.

In brief, the existing research (Baird, 1990; Hawley, 1990; Hutton, et al., 1990; Littleton, Beach, Larmer, & Calahan, 1991) on the effectiveness of alternative certification programs has concluded that these programs have:

- attracted higher numbers of individuals into teaching
- helped to decrease teacher shortages
- increased the available pool of teachers
- prepared individuals who are at least as likely as traditionally prepared teachers to stay in the profession
- attracted higher numbers of minorities, males and matured (ages 25–40) persons into teaching
- prepared teachers who appear to be at least effective as the traditionally prepared teacher (a factor that is difficult to measure due to the weaknesses and inconsistencies of evaluation systems reported in the literature)
- fostered more collaborative relationships between universities and school districts as innovative teacher preparation programs are explored
- served as a catalyst for teacher education reform, par-

ticularly with respect to the importance of field-based experiences which are supervised and mentored

- increased in number due to state mandates to explore alternative ways of preparing teachers. (Baird, 1990; Bliss, 1990; Cornett, 1990; Dial, 1992; Dill, 1990; Hawk & Schmidt, 1989; Hawley, 1990; Hutton et al., 1990; Littleton et al., 1991.)

Fenstermacher (1990) has succinctly identified three issues which continue to be at the core of the discussion around the preparation of teachers and which are best represented not as extremes but as continua: (1) Training which occurs close to practice versus training which occurs far from practice; (2) Training emphasizing pedagogical methods versus training emphasizing academic content; and (3) Training conforming to practice versus training revising practice. However the discussions over the merits of one form of teacher preparation over another will continue until the profession can address the purpose of teacher preparation programs. What does that body of knowledge that is crucial to effective teaching consist of? What are the specific criteria or standards by which we can judge teacher education? What skills can we expect from a novice teacher? What about those skills that we can expect teachers to develop only through the course of the first 5 or 6 years of experience in the classroom such as reflective thinking and change regarding one's practice? Some educators such as Goodlad (1990) have provided a point of departure for these discussions. Fenstermacher (1990) has concluded through his research on teacher education that when done well,

> …Initial teacher preparation is a process of preparing teachers who are critically reflective in their practice, teachers who do not simply know and apply operation skills, but who can think through the adjustment of these skills based upon increasing familiarity with context … to equip the novice teachers to be discerning when considering the purposes, procedures and consequences of teaching. (p. 70)

It is this ability to be discerning and reflective which is central to the discussion of alternative certification versus traditional teacher education programs, and which many feel gives the traditional programs the superiority of reformed programs. There is also debate which surrounds other forms of professional preparation for teachers—including professional development schools to which we now turn to.

EDUCATION REFORM AND RENEWAL

In the last two decades, reformers have been working to change the teaching profession, particularly in the training of new teachers (Goodlad, 1994a, Holmes 1990). Goodlad's Center for Educational Renewal and the Institute for Educational Inquiry have created and sustained one of the most effective movements for the simultaneous renewal of teacher education and public schools in the United States. Currently, 16 settings in 14 sates are involved in advancing the Goodlad agenda. In keeping with the basic agenda of simultaneous renewal, each setting consists of one or more institutions of higher education working in close collaboration with one or more school districts and one or more partner schools within each district (Goodlad, 1994b).

Goodlad and other reformers contend that teacher education must undergo serious renewal in tandem with the reform of public schools and refer to their reform as simultaneous renewal. Goodlad (1994b) has suggested that "teacher candidates intern and practice their skills in exemplary sites and that stronger links be established between universities and schools." The Holmes Group Report (1986) also has suggested that "universities and colleges expand their teacher education programs to include cooperation with school districts to provide demonstration sites for practicum experiences, as well as bring exemplary teachers from the schools to the universities and colleges." (Welch and Kukic, 1988).

Professional Development Schools

According to Winitzky, et al. (1992), of the many reform efforts, "the professional development school (PDS) is particularly promising because its aim is to link the university and the public school and by so doing link theory with practice" (p. 3).

In response to the Goodlad agenda, throughout the country, schools and universities are cooperating in the creation of partner schools in order to enhance the clinical experiences provided for preservice teachers, to improve professional development, and to create settings that can contribute in various ways to improved learning for young people. Sometimes these schools are called professional development schools, sometimes they are referred to as clinical settings. The Center for Educational Renewal headed by Goodlad has chosen to refer to them as "partner schools" in order to emphasize the importance of the roles of both school and university educators as they join in the simultaneous renewal of schooling and the education of educators (Porter, 1994).

These new structures in teacher preparation have been referred to in a number of ways: "Key Schools" (Wise, 1991), "Professional Development Schools" (Holmes Group, 1986, 1990) or "Partner Schools" (Goodlad, 1990). The Wyoming School-University Partnership has chosen its own unique name for partner schools—Center for Teaching and Learning. The University of Texas at El Paso refers to them as Centers for Professional Development. All, however, seem to share a common vision. According to Harris and Harris (1992–93), "all reconceptualize teacher education around a model of professional-school partnerships which link colleges of education and schools or school districts" (p. 1). They are considered the counterpart in education of teaching hospitals in medicine. According to *U.S. News,* "about 200 institutions have established such programs, which provide real-world settings in which prospective teachers and experienced teachers can hone their professional skills, especially classroom techniques. The extended immersion in professional development is a far cry from the traditional training of most of the nation's 2.8 million teachers and most teachers-to-be" (Teaching Teachers, 1995, p. 70).

Harris and Harris (1992–93) define partner schools as places where university and school educators collaborate on a renewal agenda structured by Partner School functions, such as: (1) preservice education for new teachers; (2) in-service education (staff development) for practicing teachers in the school; (3) curriculum development to improve the learning experiences of pupils; and (4) research and evaluation to foster university and school inquiry.

Goodlad (1990) "believes a wide variety of laboratory settings and exemplary schools must be available to teacher education students for observation, hands-on experiences, internships, and residencies. Clinical arrangements demand close collaboration between the schools and the university, and clearly delineated connections between classwork and fieldwork. For a school to qualify as a clinical site, its teachers and administrators must demonstrate their willingness to engage in constant, critical review and renewal of the school's structure and performance" (Clark, 1990, p. 5).

Research by Harris and Harris (1992–93) has shown that effective collaboration in Partner Schools is distinguished by four attributes:

1. Common goal— The simultaneous renewal of schools and the education of educators are supported by both university and school educators.
2. Participants and participation—Both university and school educators are represented and actively share expertise in all organizational facets.
3. Equity and trust—University and school educators engage in dialogue by which they build on each other's expertise, focus on insights from research and experience, acknowledge legitimacy of different perceptions, and avoid paternalistic or reductionist attitudes.
4. Self-interest and selflessness—Partners seek to improve in their own stewardship roles for the mutual benefit of all without becoming overly concerned with investments.

According to Harris and Harris (1992–1993), "a number of such schools have been established across the country. Typically, they are jointly operated by a university and a school district. Teachers and professors work side by side to induct new teachers into the profession and to engage in ongoing research about teaching. The professional development school not only elevates and enhances the education of future teachers but also offers professional renewal for the teachers employed in the schools" (p. 38).

The professional development schools movement has been supported by various organizations and associations. Among the most well-developed networks are the American Federation of Teachers' Professional Practice Schools, the Ford Foundation's Clinical Schools Project, and John Goodlad's Center for Educational Renewal (Goodlad, 1990; Goodlad, 1994a; Goodlad, 1994b).

Goodlad has also created a coalition to reform teacher education. Through the Center for Educational Renewal, he has established school-university partnerships throughout the United States. His main argument is that we must require teachers to receive their clinical preparation in professional development schools that include teachers and university faculty working together.

Professional development schools have impacted teacher preparation in several important ways. First, it has intensified fieldwork. According to Lawton (1991) "one substantial reform advocated by an increasing number of educators is the creation of new structures in teacher preparation that extends and intensifies student fieldwork. In the mid-1980s two major critical reports, *A Nation Prepared* by the Carnegie Forum on Education and the Economy (1986) and *Tomorrow's Teachers* called for the invention of a new model for teacher education: Professional development or professional practice schools, clinical schools similar to teaching hospitals in the field of medicine." (p. 38).

According to Welch and Kukic (1988), "The value of clinical practicum experience as part of classroom teacher preparation is unquestionable. However, it has been suggested that the extension of practicum teaching experiences be carefully considered" (Holmes Group, 1986). Pugach (1987), while supporting the need for practicum experience, has raised concerns regarding quality control as to the selection of sites, cooperating teachers, and the evaluation process. Consideration also must be given to how school districts select mentor teachers, the frequency of supervision by university supervisors, the number and variety of sites, how to minimize the mere imitation of mentor teacher behaviors rather than the development of individual skills, and how to maximize opportunities for investigation and problem solving (Holmes Group, 1986).

CONCLUSION

In sum, "a new view of teacher education is emerging as university and school educators combine their insights and expertise. This view is that excellent teacher education is more likely to occur when the university and schools form a seamless web of theory and practice. This will be accomplished when university theorists and researchers understand the problems of practice and identify with the demands of real-world teaching and when their university-based courses become relevant and applicable. When practitioners join in supervising, mentoring, evaluating, and recommending new teachers their living laboratories become exemplary sites of excellence in learning and teaching" (Harris & Harris, 1992–93, pp. 7, 8).

References

Andrew, T. E. (1994) *The NASDTEC manual 1994–95*. Manual on certification and preparation of educational personnel in the United States. National Association of State Directors of Teacher Education & Certification. Dubuque, IA: Kendall/Hunt.

Baird, A. W. (1990). Alternative certification of teachers. *School Business Affairs, 58*(8), 18–21.

Barrett, H. C. (1994). Technology-supported assessment portfolios. *The Computing Teacher, 21*(6), 9–12.

Bliss, T. (1990, published 1992). Alternate certification in Connecticut: Reshaping the profession. *Peabody Journal of Education, 67*(3), 35–83.

Bruce, B. (1991). Roles for computers in teacher in the English language arts. *Handbook of research on teaching the English language arts.* New York: Macmillan.

Carnegie Forum on Education and the Economy. (1986). *A nation prepared: Teachers for the 21 century.* Report of the Task Force on Teaching as a Profession. New York: Carnegie Forum.

Clark, R. W. (1990). *What school leaders can do to help change teacher education.* Washington, DC: American Association of Colleges for Teacher Education. (ERIC Document No. 335 302)

Cornett, L. M. (1990, published 1992). Alternative certification: State Policies in the SREB states. *Peabody Journal of Education, 67*(3), 55–83.

Dial, M. (1992). A comparison of retention rates of alternatively certified and traditionally certified teachers. [EJ 448493]. *ERS-Spectrum, 10*(3), 10–14.

Dill, V. (1990). Support of the unsupportable. *Phi Delta Kappan, 72*(3), 198–99.

Eisenmann, L. (1991). Teacher professionalism: A new analytical tool for the history of teachers. *Harvard Educational Review, 61*(2), 215–224.

Fenstermacher, G. D. (1990, published 1992). The place of alternative certification in the education of teachers. *Peabody Journal of Education, 67*(3), 155–185.

Goodlad, J. (1990). *Teachers for our nation's schools.* San Francisco: Jossey-Bass.

Goodlad, J. (1994a). *Educational renewal: Better teachers, better schools.* San Francisco: Jossey-Bass.

Goodlad, J. (1994b). The national network for educational renewal. *Phi Delta Kappan, 75*(8), 632–638.

Griest, G. (1993). You say you want a revolution: Constructivism, technology, and language arts. *The Computing Teacher, 20*(7), 8–11.

Harris, R. C., & Harris, M. F. (1992–93). Partner schools: Places to solve teacher education problems. *Action in Teacher Education, 14*(4), 1–8.

Hawk, P. P., & Schmidt, M. W. (1989, September–October). Teacher preparation: A Comparison of traditional and alternative programs. *Journal of Teacher Education, 53*, 58.

Hawley, W. D. (1990, published 1992). The theory and practice of alternative certification: Implications for the improvement of teaching. *Peabody Journal of Education, 67*(3), 3–34.

Holmes Group. (1986). *Tomorrow's teachers.* A report of the Holmes Group. East Lansing, MI: Holmes Group.

Holmes Group. (1990). *Tomorrow's schools: Principles for the design of professional development schools.* A report of the Holmes Group. East Lansing, MI: Holmes Group.

Hutton, J. B., Lutz F. W., & Williamson, J. L. (1990). Characteristics, attitudes, and performance of alternative certification interns. *Educational Research Quarterly, 14*(1), 38–48.

Kennedy, M. M. (1991). Some surprising findings on how teachers learn to teach. *Educational Leadership, 49*(3), 14–17.

Kline, M., & Dye, C. M. (1992). *The Cleveland city normal school, 1874–1936.* Paper presented at Mid-Western Educational Research Association. Chicago. (ED 358 011)

Labaree, D. F. (1992). Power, knowledge, and the rationalization of teaching: A genealogy of the movement to professionalize teaching. *Harvard Education Review, 62*(2), 123–154.

Lawton, M. (1991). The new recruits: Teach for America readies its second batch of teachers, *Teachers Magazine, 3*(1), 16, 17.

Littleton, M., Beach, D., Larmer, B., & Calahan, A. (1991). An effective university-based alternative certification program: The essential components. *Teacher Education and Practice, 7*(1), 37–43.

MacGregor, R. N. (1992). Post-modernism, art educators, and art education. Bloomington, IN: Adjunct ERIC Clearinghouse for Art Education. (ED 348 328)

Overby, L. Y. (1992). Status of dance in education. Washington, DC: ERIC Clearinghouse on Teacher Education. (ED 348 368)

Parker, F. (1992). *U.S. teacher education trends, 1990–92.* School of Education and Psychology, Western Carolina University. (ED 340 711). Unpublished manuscript.

Porter, W. (1994). *The Wyoming school-university partnership.* Brochure. University of Wyoming: School of Education.

Pugach, M. (1987). The national education reports and special education: Implications for teacher preparation. *Exceptional Children, 53*, 308–414.

Schorr, J. (1993). Class action: What Clinton's national service program could learn from Teach for America. *Phi Delta Kappan, 75*(4), 315–318.

Sosa, A. (1993). *Thorough and fair: Certain routes to success for Mexican-American students.* Charleston, WV: ERIC Clearinghouse on Rural Education and Small Schools.

Squire, J. (1991). The history of the profession. In J. Flood, J. M. Jensen, D. Lapp, & J. Squire (Eds.), *Handbook of research on teaching the English language arts.* New York: Macmillan.

Suhor, C. (1993). *Trends and issues in English instruction, 1993*—Six summaries of informal discussion of the Commissions of the National Council of Teachers of English. (ED 369 083)

Teaching teachers: Graduate schools of education face intense scrutiny. (1995, April 3). *U.S. News and World Report.*

Texas Education Agency. (1991–92). *Alternative teacher certification in Texas.* Austin, TX: Texas Education Agency.

Warner, A. R. (1990). Legislated limits on certification requirements: Lessons from the Texas experience. *Journal of Teacher Education, 41*(4), 26–33.

Welch, M., & Kukic, S. (1988). Utah's response to critical issues and needs: An experimental field-based preparation program for teachers of mild to moderately handicapped students. *Teacher Education and Special Education, 11*(4), 172–179.

Winitzky, N., Stoddart, T., & O'Keefe, P. (1992). Great expectations: Emergent professional development schools. *Journal of Teacher Education, 43*(1), 3–18.

Wise, A. E. (1991). We need more than a redesign. *Educational Leadership, 49*(3), 7.

Zimmerman, E. (1990). Teaching from a global perspective. Bloomington, IN: ERIC Clearinghouse for Social Studies/Social Science Education. (ED 329 490).

35

EXPLORING VOICES OF THE LANGUAGE ARTS UNIVERSE: FROM TIN CAN TELEPHONES TO SATELLITE MISSIONS

Debra Bayles

SAN DIEGO STATE UNIVERSITY

Nancy Roser

UNIVERSITY OF TEXAS AT AUSTIN

The voices that inform and influence the language arts professional are many and diverse. Melissa, a white female from a middle-class home, attended a large state university, graduating recently as an elementary teacher at the age of 24. When asked how she prepared for the first few days of her first teaching assignment in an inner-city school, she explained:

> I felt very unprepared to do first grade … I didn't know what the big picture was supposed to look like. Fortunately, my aunts that were living in Houston both had taught first grade before. So, while I was there, I spoke with them a whole lot and that helped me get a better picture of what it was going to be like. And I also called Angie and I asked her if I could look at her journal [from our college methods course]. And I talked to Cindy and Jess. And I started going back over notes from our class, because I felt like my professor had really focused a lot on emergent readers and I felt like, at the time, I was kind of like, "Come on, come on! Get to the third grade and the older stuff!" 'cause that's where I was at in my student teaching. But, now I'm thankful (laughs) I took good notes. I also went through *The Art of Teaching Writing* and *Invitations*. I read *Transitions* 'cause I knew that would be really helpful because she seems to focus more on first grade in that one. I was just getting a feel for it, because I didn't know, you know? We had the new teacher inservice at the school, and there was this new teacher, and I met her. This was her first year too, but she had done her student teaching in first grade. And, she and I have become extremely close, you know, because we're both going through the exact same thing and I felt very comfortable talking to her because she's my age and um, we just kind of hit it off right away—

Linda, also a white, middle-class woman, was certified as a teacher through an alternative certification program after completing a Bachelor's degree in another field and working for a year. As she began her fourth teaching year, she talked about the "voices" of influence:

> I majored in Interior Design. Worked for a year—that's it—and was not happy. And somehow, I've always liked kids and somehow—I can't remember—I found out about this Alternative Certification Program. I thought about going back to school, [but] it was an extra 60 or 70 hours. So four years ago I trained for a month, and then started teaching. So I have NO background. And I'm just—experimenting. It's just like, I go to a workshop: "Okay, I'll try THAT!" My first year, I taught first grade and that's my FIRST YEAR! I mean, you know, no background, so I can't, I tell you, I can't remember that first year. It was just like every day, hey, it's just a new experience! And then, after that first year, I thought, "Okay, I sort of understand this, maybe, a little." Then they switched me to second. So, the second year I was in the second. And my third year I was in second. And then, this year, my fourth year, they switched me back to first. I'm experimenting. I don't know what's going on in those kids' heads. But I try, you know, I just try to read things and go to workshops, and just try everything I can, and try to just hit the different needs. I mean, I hear that some kids can't read phonetically, that they just have to have the whole word. So I just try to hit it, all aspects, and hope I reach them. And the ones that I don't reach, it's difficult, because you don't know what's wrong with them! You really have to be an expert, and I mean, good grief! You all are studying it still!

Tom is also white and of middle-class background. He completed an anthropology degree at a state university and began work in Mexico. Realizing that his home culture was vastly removed from that where he was working, he returned to the university, planning to obtain an education degree and teach students from his own culture. Beginning his first year of teaching in an inner-city school, he noted the irony of his placement, and emphasized his lack of knowledge about how to create lessons to which his African-American students could relate:

> I make it up. I mean, I've always been that way, and I'm pretty good at just making things up as I go, but, like lesson plans? I mean, I write them absolutely just so that when the principal comes in there, she can look at something and I have something written down. And I don't do it, any of it. I mean, I'm lost. I'm floundering. I don't know what to do. I want to do so many things that I just can't do. I don't know how to do them. We do, response charts, we do response journals; we did that morning journal [as in student teaching].

Melissa, Linda, and Tom all teach 1st- and 2nd-grade students. All three sincerely hope that their students will become lifetime readers and writers, and they try to reflect this goal in their language arts teaching. Yet although the general school populations and grade assignments are similar for these teachers, their conversations about what it means to teach communicative arts suggest interesting differences. For example, when asked where she turned for knowledge in her early days of teaching, Melissa readily listed colleagues, books, and university courses. Linda mentions in passing that she reads for ideas, but offered workshops as her primary information source. And Tom admits he either makes things up or relies upon ideas from his student teaching experience.

In talking with Melissa, Linda, and Tom, (as well as many other teachers) about the ways they select and approach their teaching goals, we have come to believe that regardless of the diversity of the settings or responsibilities, all teachers' experiences influence and are influenced by highly personal views of what it means to teach and "to know." This personal view is akin to a mental environment for teaching—a teacher's mental "place" or personal world view which colors his / her perception of all other environments and experiences. In this chapter, we suggest that inquiry into teaching the visual and communicative arts should explore the mental "environments" from which teachers perceive, select, interpret, and respond to the voices in their worlds.

The question of how we might learn about and from the mental environment of an individual is certainly challenging. However, some researchers and theorists (e.g., Bakhtin, 1993; Connelly & Clandinin, 1985; Elbaz, 1983, 1990; Leont'ev, 1978; Munby, 1987, Vygotsky, 1962, 1978) suggest that patterns in an individual teacher's comments or ways of talking about teaching may offer important insights as to the "voices" teachers rely upon and respond to. Although we use the terms "voice" and "dialogue" throughout this chapter, we do not mean to claim that the "voices" with which teachers interact are predominantly verbal, nor do we wish to suggest that there is a limited number of voices which can be classified and categorized. Rather, we posit that thinking of education as a process of learning to converse with the world may allow us to explore the environments in which

teachers live and work as dialogic interactions with various knowledge sources. From the cacophony of competing "voices" (diverse knowledge sources in numerous representations) teachers are in a constant process of selecting those with which to interact. Interaction with such voices (dialogue) yields knowledge, which then colors all future actions and interpretations.

LEARNING TO TEACH AS LEARNING TO CONVERSE

Melissa, Linda, and Tom's comments demonstrate that the number of voices with which teachers may converse about teaching ideas and practices appears, if not limitless, at least potentially overwhelming. That number grows even larger if other voices such as those of parents, administrators, and students are included. How does a teacher choose which voices to converse with? What consequences do these choices carry? To address these questions, we adopt a simple communications metaphor (spanning from tin can telephones to satellites) to represent an ever-widening and increasingly sophisticated sphere of reach, range, and access to the voices that inform and influence the professional. For us, this metaphor captures a portion of the complexity involved in teaching and learning the visual and communicative arts. It also suggests important considerations (from both research and practical perspectives) for helping teachers and researchers address the responsibilities and challenges involved in the "New Literacy" (Monson & Monson, 1994; Willinsky, 1990) and its evolving postmodern curricula (Doll, 1993).

Beginning to Call and Respond: Talking on a Tin Can Telephone

We live in a universe of discourse (Moffett, 1968). Voices of people and of ideas (e.g., spoken, written, or captured in some other medium) continually compete for our attention—inviting us to engage in dialogue with them toward various ends (Bakhtin, 1981, 1993). However, when a child enters the world, it is likely that his / her early interactions or "conversations" arise primarily from a desire to satisfy physical needs (Leont'ev, 1978). Thus, infants enter the grand conversation of the world by "calling" for help in addressing their personal needs. These calls are met with various responses—from which, over time, the language learner achieves a range of communication strategies. For many young children, the number of voices recognized as available for "dialogue" (Bakhtin, 1981, 1993) may be limited to parents, well-known friends, close relatives, or caregivers. Communication at this stage is relatively simple, concrete, focused, and proximal—much like conversation along the single string of a tin can telephone.

Over time, children participate in a number of routine or similar interactions/dialogues (such as storybook reading, mealtime talk, and religious rituals) in which they learn how more elaborate language events unfold. For example, as a parent reads aloud to a child, the adult's pauses may signal a space for questions and responses; adult comments model how readers think and talk in a particular circumstance. In these ways, children learn how to enter the conversation, and which responses are valued by other participant(s) (Bruner, 1981; Grice, 1975; Magolda, 1992; Tannen, 1986).

Through opportunity, experimentation, and practice, the tin can user (the young communicator) continues to develop greater communicative competence, becoming aware of an increasing number of voices with which to interact—albeit on a one-to-one or one-at-a-time basis. Similarly, teachers functioning at a "tin can level" of communication may approach the world through a series of simple, two-way conversations. In tin can talk, the teacher as speaker may assume an informing, authority role (with students); at other times, the teacher as listener may assume the receiver's role (with principals, policies, curriculum, or "expert" opinions). As long as the roles, messages, and turns are predictable and clear, tin can communicators are generally comfortable (Belenky, Clinchy, Goldberger, & Tarule, 1986). However, in the interview segments above, Tom expresses the frustration of a tin can telephone stage (and with its limited range and number of informing voices) as he strains toward the "life-line" of his student teaching experience.

Upgrading Communication Equipment to "Direct Dial" and Creating a Personal "Telephone" Directory. Although simple, two-way communication is important, it is limited by both space and time. As children interact with an increasingly broad array of individuals and ideas (through preschool and elementary experiences, community activities, family gatherings), they encounter views and communication patterns which differ from those of their home and immediate surroundings. Suddenly, the world seems filled with voices (friends, books, television, other media), all competing for attention. Of necessity, language users begin to replace the string and tin cans of simple interaction patterns with the wires and receivers of more advanced technology and communication. Now they hear the dial tone of possibilities—recognizing that numerous calls can be made across space and time: books can be read, authorities can be contacted, and conversations can be initiated and terminated over longer distances.

In addition to its enhancement of communicative reach, the "advanced technology" of broadened communicative experience increases the need for decision making on the caller's part. From among an ever-widening range of dialogue possibilities, language learners must decide *whom* to call upon (or respond to) *and for what purposes* (e.g., calls can be made for information, affirmation, or entertainment). Because some "numbers" are called more frequently, they can soon be dialed automatically. These "numbers" may represent developing areas of interest, relationship, and knowledge (e.g., the voice of a favorite book, the advice of an athletic coach, the intrigue of particular hobby pursuits, etc.). Over time, learners of language develop a set of "telephone manners"—characteristic ways of calling upon and responding to others in dialogue (Bakhtin, 1993). Familiar interaction patterns make dialogic roles predictable and support further learning (Bruner, 1981; Kelly, 1955; Vygotsky, 1978). Conversely, "numbers" called infrequently are less well-known, and thus require the development of some organization system (i.e., a directory, a storage system, or computer menu) to enable the caller to readily retrieve them.

Like all language learners/users, as teachers come to recognize the need to communicate with a more complex array of voices (dealing with groups of students rather than individuals, or interacting with special needs students), they also may desire a "directory" to assist them in contacting and engaging in dialogue with particular voices. Generally speaking, teachers at this "direct-dial level" approach the world from a "look-up-the-number-and-punch-it-in" perspective, viewing one of their roles, for example, as "looking up" diagnoses and "punching in" appropriate prescriptions. Teaching strategies may be committed to memory (or catalogued in one's directory) and then called up in particular settings to address specific situations.

Teachers seem to begin to develop their directories of "numbers" (their teaching strategies, expectations, approaches, and information sources) during their experiences as students (Holt–Reynolds, 1991; Lortie, 1975). They extend their "directories" during their teacher education programs, as instructors emphasize particular perspectives. Across teaching experiences and staff development, still other voices inform and demand inclusion; for example, the voices of administrative authority and of public opinion are rarely, if ever, silent. Further, throughout teacher education and ongoing inservice efforts, the voices of research and good practice are continually extolled. If we think of each voice as a potential source of teacher knowledge—a directory entry—then the task of identifying and organizing the access "numbers" is overwhelming. Given the number of teaching decisions to be made on an almost moment-to-moment basis (Clark & Peterson, 1986), having a complete and organized directory is surely a great boon for a teacher. Fortunately, the task can be simplified by adopting or adapting an existing categorization system. For example, Doyle's (1990) concept of codifiable knowledge provides one helpful way to categorize a directory. Using Doyle's work as a frame, we describe some "directory entries" a teacher might consider building.

Building a Personal Teaching Directory With Doyle's Categories

Doyle (1990) uses the term "codifiable" to describe findings of research studies with relatively clear results. He claims that many specific teaching practices are growing more sophisticated and can be referenced as an array of useful alternatives from which a teacher might choose to achieve specific goals in a given context. Teachers turning to such practices might be considered to be conversing with the "voice" of a particular researcher, or perhaps with the "voice" of a reasoned philosophy. Doyle offers three categories for organizing codifiable research findings: (a) Descriptions of teaching practices, (b) Pedagogical content knowledge, and (c) How classrooms work.

Descriptions of Teaching Practices. Teachers who believe that learning unfolds in logical, predictable ways might organize their directories with codifiable voices that inform their teaching practices. Descriptions of reciprocal teaching / learning, as well as derivatives of the older process-product studies (e.g., allocating time for specific tasks) offer relatively clear-cut, codifiable findings. Such work might be indexed under the name of a particular strategy (K–W–L), under its general focus (levels of questioning), or under the "voice" of the particular researcher with whom it is associated [i.e., Palinscar & Brown (1984) for reciprocal teaching].

Pedagogical Content Knowledge. Doyle (1990) describes pedagogical content knowledge as the knowledge teachers need about a subject in order to represent and convey it to their students. Shulman (1987) suggests that each field of study includes principles of conceptual organization and inquiry—content which influences the methods of presentation teachers should use. Although there is more to learning to teach than acquiring specific content and congruent presentation knowledge, notions of a subject/method match are still reflected in methods courses and textbooks. These "voices" may suggest, for example, specific strategies for teaching within a particular discipline (the scientific method for science experiments or genre studies in English). Teachers who believe that teaching involves matching content and method would probably list "voices" of pedagogical content knowledge prominently in their directories. Prospective teachers in particular often hold the view that a "right way" exists for teaching a given topic in a specific subject area.

How Classrooms Work. Doyle (1990) lists a third area of codifiable knowledge as inquiry into how classrooms work—understanding patterns and rhythms in classrooms and how teacher actions influence student learning. Researchers working in this area act on the notion that the classroom tasks and learning activities a teacher chooses reflect intentional, larger learning goals. Such tasks may enhance or constrain student interaction and achievement—depending upon several factors. Studies in this area include investigation of teacher planning (Clark & Peterson, 1986), teacher use of questioning taxonomies (Bloom, Englehart, Furst, Hill & Krathwohl, 1956), and student–teacher verbal interactions in the classroom (e.g., Cazden, 1988; Mehan, 1985). Teachers may catalog these studies in their personal directories so as to interact more efficiently with "voices" of careful and informed observers.

Direct Dial: Limited Service Area

Although building a directory should be an ongoing process involving a teacher's personal reflections and views of the field, some teachers limit their directory entries by including only those numbers consistent with a particular program bias—or they may fail to update their directories on a regular basis. As a result, they may find themselves with too limited a list—one in which numbers which might have proved helpful in specific settings are missing or inaccessible. The

breadth and accessibility of any teacher's directory of knowledge sources affects students. For example, teachers who habitually call only certain numbers and "speak in inflexible ways" may be approaching their students and their teaching decisions honoring only certain values and knowledge sources. They may expect their students to call and respond to designated numbers in the same manner as they do. If so, the "directory" of teacher knowledge and dialogue may constrain the potential for students' dialogue. Identifying and responding to voices in the language arts universe may mean opportunity to profit from dialing a range of numbers, engaging in conference calls (multiple sources), or completing other "telephone" maneuvers (Au & Kawakami, 1985; Cazden, 1988).

Even with a fairly complete directory, the direct-dial approach still limits the reach, range, and access of communication because it fails to encompass a myriad of connections—particularly those demanded by social context. Further, "direct-dial" teachers, like their tin can telephone counterparts, may tend to complete only one call at a time. As though working a switchboard, they may repeatedly plug in a prerecorded approach to achieve a particular teaching goal, often leaving some student calls waiting. Thus, while clearly an improvement over the single tin can telephone, the direct-dial communicative approach is not without important shortcomings as well.

LAUNCHING SATELLITE MISSIONS: EXPLORING THE UNIVERSE OF DISCOURSE

The concept of codifiable knowledge sources and teaching "directories" suggests several voices with which professional teachers interact. The seemingly clear information delineated by ordered voices can make learning to teach seem like a deceptively simple, direct dialogue, wherein a teacher (as alluded to earlier) memorizes routine steps or relationships as a "number" in a directory and then matches a given routine with an appropriate situation or teaching goal. However, few studies yielding codifiable findings (like those noted in the previous section) address the question of how a teacher comes to know *which* routine or task to use in a given setting or the reasons for altering a routine or task.

Indeed, the whole question of how a teacher interprets classroom scenes and invents solutions to teaching problems has spawned a new area of inquiry in teacher knowledge research, the results of which Doyle (1990) labels as "less codifiable." "Less codifiable" findings include reports of teachers' personal knowledge, such as the individual meaning teachers attribute to particular events, as well as personal insights and inventions in teaching. This research often includes teachers' views as represented by a researcher, but even more recently, is reported by the teachers themselves (see, for example, Cochran-Smith & Little, 1993; Hudelson & Lindfors, 1993; Patterson, 1993). In spite of its potential contribution to understanding learning to teach, research into less codifiable areas is often labor intensive, relying heavily on case study methods and attempts to make explicit implicitly held knowledge. Results are often difficult to summarize and directly apply to teacher knowledge bases—as well as difficult to list in teaching "directories."

The reality of teaching, then, is far more complex than controlled two-party conversations or even ready direct-dial access to extensive, well-organized "directories" of knowledge. The metaphor must be extended; it requires still more reach and range. Even at its best, direct dialing allows communication access only within the earth's boundaries (or the confines of a particular teacher's directory). For those who would explore and address the complex influences of individual experience and background learning upon, the communicative arts—something much more sophisticated is required to traverse the "universe of discourse" (Moffett, 1968). It is at this point in considering the development of teacher knowledge and communicative skill that we find it helpful to liken the dialogic process to the detaching of a satellite from a fixed orbit, allowing its communication equipment to send and receive messages from an infinite number of points, as determined by its location (goals and setting) at any particular juncture (time). The perspective broadens, the vantage is unique, new knowledge is constructed.

In this way, each teacher can be viewed as a unique satellite, moving freely to explore the universe of discourse. (Students, too, are individual satellites—able to direct their own communication and exploration, able to interact with others in multiple ways across contexts.) To undertake a mission, however, communication equipment must be developed and installed. The less codifiable research findings reviewed below may be considered as attempts to illuminate the "program" from which a teacher functions as a communication satellite.

Less Codifiable Voices: Interacting With Images

Writing in 1983, Elbaz suggested that teachers' practical knowledge develops in three areas. The first, termed "rules of practice," are brief, clearly formulated statements prescribing how to behave in frequently encountered teaching situations. These very explicit rules portend Doyle's (1990) codifiable category, although it is not clear whether teachers determine these rules by listening to their personal voices of experience, or by turning to other voices to determine the "right" and "wrong" of various behaviors (Belenky, et al., 1986). However, the next two levels identified by Elbaz are clearly representative of less codifiable knowledge. The second level, "practical principles," includes broader, more inclusive statements of knowledge that embody a rationale, derived from personal values as well as outside influences. Elbaz drew upon the notion of "images" to capture a teacher's knowledge and purposes at the third or most general level. According to Elbaz, images (values, feelings, needs, beliefs) orient a teacher's general conduct and may be similar to the notion of "environments" discussed at the beginning of this chapter.

In extending Elbaz's (1983) work, Clandinin (1985) suggests that *images* refer to a special kind of knowledge teachers develop and use which is "neither theoretical, in the sense of theories of learning, teaching, and curriculum, nor merely practical, in the sense of knowing children" (p. 361). For Clandinin, "a teacher's special knowledge is composed of both kinds of knowledge, blended by the personal background and characteristics of the teacher and expressed by her in particular situations" (p. 361). Clandinin posits that images grow out of teachers' private and personal experience, and sometimes include a detailed visual component. While Clandinin acknowledges that a teacher's verbal use of an image might indicate its centrality in his or her mental representation of the world, she is careful to note that verbal mention alone is insufficient evidence of an image's function. Rather, Clandinin holds that a key feature of an image is its *expression in action.* She cautions researchers to go beyond simple interview data in determining teachers' images, stressing detailed, in-depth discussion, participant observation, and other triangulation techniques as essential for determining actual, influential images teachers hold.

A Linguistic Connection: Expressing World Views in Metaphors. Munby (1986,1987) also drew heavily from Elbaz's (1983) concept of images in researching teacher knowledge, but in contrast with Clandinin (1985), Munby stresses attention to a teacher's *verbal* use of metaphor. Munby (1986) claims that a teacher's persistent use of a metaphor may serve as an important indicator from which to examine his or her world view. While Munby's work (1986,1987) might appear to contradict Clandinin's cautions about the importance of metaphor *in action,* he notes that the *persistence* of the metaphor is important. Munby also acknowledges that even in the case of persistent metaphor reference, the actual relationship of an expressed metaphor to a teacher's world view may not always be clear to the teacher or to the researcher.

Additionally, while Munby (1987) holds that teachers choose particular metaphors for important reasons, he also recognizes that teachers may use a metaphor merely as an aspect of a "folk tradition of ways to speak about the events of school" (p. 397). Thus, it seems that while Munby does not explicitly state the same cautions as Clandinin (1985), he too implies the need for researcher care in interpreting teachers' metaphors. The exercise of caution in interpreting metaphor/practice links seems particularly germane in light of conflicting results in research aimed at detecting links between teachers' classroom actions and their articulated beliefs [e.g., as measured on the TORP survey (DeFord, 1981)]. DeFord reported a strong relationship between teachers' beliefs and their instructional approaches. However, Duffy (1981) and Hoffman and Kugle (1982) failed to confirm a strong link between teachers' instructional practices and their beliefs as expressed on DeFord's instrument. Richards, Anders, Tidwell, and Lloyd (1991) found that while the majority of their informants taught reading comprehension in a manner consistent with their beliefs (as determined from a beliefs interview), a change in teacher beliefs tended to precede a change in practice—underlining the need for long-term inquiry in teacher belief research. Thus, although these studies focus on beliefs as expressed through researcher-generated sentences and interview questions as opposed to gathering teachers' personal metaphors, the underlying concern of accurately relating beliefs and practices continues in teacher knowledge research.

If, however, teacher metaphors can be reliably linked to actual teaching practice (e.g., Richards, Gipe, & Duffy, 1992), the linguistic focus of Munby's work may provide a link between Bakhtin's dialogic philosophy and actual teaching behavior. If one's knowledge is acquired and altered in part by one's dialogic interactions (Bakhtin, 1993; Vygotsky, 1978), then perhaps a person's dialogic patterns or choices may offer an important foundation from which to explore his or her world view. Nevertheless, we also believe that it is important to exercise caution in limiting exploration of teachers' possible mental environments or world views to strictly verbal indicators. Since the notion of metaphor includes visual as well as verbal connotations, it seems to include possibilities for referencing visual or other tacit influences which should not be overlooked in exploring teacher knowledge. This may be especially important, for as Grossman and Shulman (1994) note, "That we implicitly adopt a theoretical stance when we teach does not necessarily mean that we are explicit about our assumptions or about the limitations inherent in any single critical theory" (p. 7).

It is interesting to note that as researchers attempt to characterize the knowledge teachers develop, the teacher knowledge literature refers to both verbal and visual representations. Researchers and thinkers such as Bruner (1986), Connelly and Clandinin (1990),Gardner (1987), Sternberg (1981), and others suggest that individuals may develop particular ways of knowing which are less verbocentric (Leland & Harste, 1994), or which draw on particular aspects of a given linguistic genre, such as the use of narrative story "to know." This interplay suggests something of the complexity of dealing with the concept of knowledge acquisition and representation, as well as in dealing with questions about how such knowledge might be stored or accessed. At this juncture, we wish to reiterate our view that one's "dialogue" with the world is not limited only to verbal interaction. As mentioned earlier, our use of the terms "dialogue" and "voice" throughout the chapter is meant to extend verbocentric notions to include any interaction between a person and a potential knowledge source, whether predominantly visual or verbal. However, since humans generally do not communicate in visual formats alone, we believe exploration of teachers' mental environments through linguistic patterns may fruitfully begin with verbal information but include attention whenever possible to visual (and other) notions held by particular individuals.

Another important consideration in dealing with teacher knowledge research revolves around the question of defining teacher knowledge as opposed to teacher beliefs. According to Buchmann (1984) something is accepted as knowledge when it can be publicly supported with evidence. "Codifiable" information and research results (Doyle, 1990) would likely fall within this definition of knowledge. It follows then, that ideas not publicly supported would be characterized as beliefs. Yet, the thorny issue of whether a particular belief might function as knowledge within a teacher's thought processes (independent of its public acceptance) remains a matter of debate. Researchers like Nespor (1987) have written extensive pieces proposing differences between the two concepts. Others, like Kitchener and King (cited in Magolda, 1992) note similarities, suggesting that beliefs may function as knowledge depending upon the certainty a person feels about their truth and usefulness. At this point in teacher knowledge research, the more compelling questions may center on identifying (through exploring dialogic patterns) what ideas particular teachers hold and how those ideas and patterns relate to teaching practice, rather than whether an idea is categorized as a belief or as knowledge.

TEACHER DEVELOPMENT AS SATELLITE MISSIONS: MULTIPLE AND CONSTANT SIGNAL EMISSION AND RECEPTION

If the development of all human activity is goal directed such that a person's motives transform and create anew (Leont'ev, 1978), then it is likely that each teacher/learner is in a continual state of choosing which voices to respond to (as well as which calls to make) from ever-evolving contexts. This constancy of change implies the need for a more distal, flexible, and multifaceted communication scheme—more a moving satellite than the earthbound or more fixed transmission points of the direct-dial telephone system. At any given time, a moving satellite's sensory system may scan incoming data and revise its course to fix on signals which best match immediate motives and goals.

Just as the communication equipment of a satellite must be developed and programmed, so too, might we consider the development and "programming" of teacher communications. Because voices are educative, and education is conversation (Arnett, 1992), the more "conversational" experiences teachers have, the more options they develop for taking part in a still wider set of calls and responses—within a much broader community. Through their conversations, and through their dialogues with knowledge sources, teachers develop more beliefs, build more familiarity with varying conversational conventions, and become increasingly selective in directing attention to voices that inform. Just as person and role are defined through interaction, so is the person/role defined more broadly through increased interaction (Bakhtin, 1993; Leont'ev, 1978; Vygotsky, 1978). And, although language is (and has been) the dominant way of making meaning, it is not necessary that dialogue include only verbal interactions; the "arts" are also ways of "mediating experiences" (Leland & Harste, 1994) and of conversing with the voices of the world.

Satellite System Malfunctions: A Caution

Although the notion of individuals functioning as satellites freed from the earth's gravitational pull, able to communicate from unlimited positions for a myriad of purposes is appealing, the metaphor also presents inherent concerns and challenges. We deliberately chose to couple the term "mission" with the satellite metaphor to suggest the need for researchers and practitioners alike to view the exploration of teachers' mental environments as new and somewhat tentative. Mission directors surely take great care in interpreting their investigations and discoveries, in making recommendations, and in deriving applications from their explorations. So, too, must researchers of teacher knowledge.

In reviewing teacher knowledge research up to 1990, Kagan (1990) suggests the "Goldilocks principle" to summarize the strengths and weaknesses of the work thus far. She notes that some studies conceptualize teacher knowledge and/or cognition in ways "too small" for reasonable application in teacher education or education in general. In the future, researchers undertaking small-scale studies must clearly articulate their research goals and views to help readers aptly connect study results to related information. Conversely, Kagan also suggests that many teacher knowledge studies are "too big"—too vague, general, or ambiguous to be translated into concrete terms. Again, studies contributing to the "big picture" of teacher knowledge surely have a place in exploring and explicating teachers' mental environments, but it is incumbent upon researchers to communicate how they view their study as contributing to a particular educational conversation.

Kagan (1990) also lists some problems in past research on teacher cognition which future researchers may want to consider. First, research in this area often suffers in clarity since the same term is used, at times, for different concepts or products. If we are to engage in dialogue about knowledge, such a dialogue can surely be enhanced by careful use and definition of particular terms as we view them (Alexander, Schallert, & Hare, 1991). Second, since it is difficult to assess teacher knowledge or beliefs directly, researchers should exercise caution and be extremely clear about the kinds of inferences they make within a given study. This can be difficult, given the time-consuming nature of many methods used to elicit and assess teacher thinking. As a result, advances in this area may depend upon insights derived from case study work and grow in a way that differs from traditional "scientific" theory building. Recognizing this possibility may help researchers and research consumers develop a useful set of expectations from which to interpret and discuss such work. Finally, Kagan notes the difficulty of making comparative judgments among teachers with respect to teacher knowledge and beliefs. Questions such as "What's good?" or "What's bad?" or "Are all self-reflective thoughts helpful and of equal value?" will, of necessity, be raised and require response in future inquiry and dialogue.

EXPLORING THE MENTAL ENVIRONMENT FRONTIER: MISSION POSSIBLE

To explore the mental environments of others, we might first explore our own voices—both the ones to which we attend and the ones in which we speak. As we contemplate the myriad voices in which we speak, for example, we may become more sensitive to characteristics of others' voices. Further sensitized, we become better able to help others investigate their own voices and dialogues. We come to recognize the importance of understanding the goal or motivation of persons with whom we interact. As Nespor (1987) wrote:

> If we are interested in why teachers organize and run classrooms as they do we must pay much more attention to the goals they pursue (which may be multiple, conflicting, and not at all related to optimizing student learning) and to their subjective interpretations of classroom processes. (p. 325)

This is particularly important since:

> We do not know very much about how beliefs come into being, how they are supported or weakened, how people are converted to them, and so on. Socialization, the social context of the school and other processes and constraints have been suggested as likely sources of beliefs, but just how they operate on beliefs is far from clear. (p. 326)

As teachers come to know their own voices and discover the multitude of voices with which they can interact, they will need, in turn, to learn to call upon and respond to the voices of their students, discovering the discourse patterns from which specific students function and experimenting with options for helping students expand their discourse skills and knowledge. Such exploration has been well established in the work of Mehan (1985), Cazden (1988), Heath (1983), Au and Kawakami (1985), and others. The voices of the teachers at the beginning of this chapter—Melissa's, Linda's, and Tom's—will change and refocus as their points of reference change and they are influenced by a broader knowledge base.

Finally, as we explore the grand conversation of education and all its glorious potentials for dialogic interaction, Arnett (1992) astutely reminds us of the essential qualities of agency and respect within all interaction: "Dialogue is an invitation, not a demand, nourished not so much by the guarantee that it will happen as by patience" (p. 4).

References

Alexander, P. A., Schallert, D. L., & Hare, V. C. (1991). Coming to terms: How researchers in learning and literacy talk about knowledge. *Review of Educational Research, 61*(3), 315–343.

Arnett, R. C. (1992). *Dialogic education: Conversation about ideas and between persons.* Carbondale, IL: Southern Illinois University Press.

Au, K., & Kawakami, A. J. (1985). Research currents: Talk story and learning to read. *Language Arts, 62*(4), 406–11.

Bakhtin, M. M. (1981). *The dialogic imagination.* (C. Emerson, & M. Holquist, Trans., M. Holquist, Ed.) Austin, TX: University of Texas Press.

Bakhtin, M. M. (1993). *Toward a philosophy of the act.*

(V. Liapunov, Trans., M. Holquist, Ed.) Austin, TX: University of Texas Press.

Belenky, M. F., Clinchy, B. M., Goldberger, N. R., & Tarule, J. M. (1986). *Women's ways of knowing. The development of self, voice, and mind.* New York: Basic Books.

Bloom, B. S., Englehart, M. D., Furst, E. J., Hill, W. H., & Krathwohl, D. R. (Eds.), (1956). *Taxonomy of educational objectives: The classification of educational goals. Handbook 1: Cognitive domain.* New York: David McKay.

Bruner, J. (1981). The pragmatics of acquisition. In W. Deutsch (Ed.), *The child's construction of language.* New York: Academic Press.

Bruner, J. (1986). *Actual minds, possible worlds.* Cambridge, MA: Harvard University Press.

Buchmann, M. (1984). The use of research knowledge in teacher education and teaching. *American Journal of Education, 592*(4), 421–439.

Cazden, C. B. (1988). *Classroom discourse.* Portsmouth, NH: Heinemann.

Clandinin, D. J. (1985). Personal practical knowledge: A study of teachers' classroom images. *Curriculum Inquiry, 15*(4), 361–385.

Clark, M. C., & Peterson, P. L. (1986). Teachers' thought processes. In M. C. Wittrock (Ed.), *Handbook of research on teaching* (3rd ed., pp. 291–310). New York: Macmillan.

Cochran-Smith, M., & Lytle, S. L. (1993). *Inside/outside: Teacher research and knowledge.* New York: Teachers College Press.

Connelly, F. M., & Clandinin, D. J. (1985). Personal practical knowledge and the modes of knowing: Relevance for teaching and learning. In E. Eisner (Ed.), *Learning and teaching the ways of knowing* (pp. 174–198). Chicago: University of Chicago Press.

Connelly, F. M., & Clandinin, D. J. (1990). Stories of experience and narrative inquiry. *Educational Researcher, 19*, 2–14.

DeFord, D. (1981). Validating the construct of theoretical orientation in reading instruction. *Reading Research Quarterly, 20*(3), 351–367.

Doll, W. E. (1993). *A post-modern perspective on curriculum.* New York: Teachers College Press.

Doyle, W. (1990). Themes in teacher education research. In W. R. Houston, M. Haberman, & J. Sikula (Eds.), *Handbook of research on teacher education.* New York: Macmillan.

Duffy, G. (1981, April). *Theory to practice: How does it work in real classrooms?* Paper presented at the annual meeting of the International Reading Association, New Orleans, LA.

Elbaz, F. (1983). *Teacher thinking: A study of practical knowledge.* London: Croom Helm.

Elbaz, F. (1990). Knowledge and discourse: The evolution of research on teacher thinking. In C. Day, M. Pope, & P. Denicolo (Eds.), *Insight into teachers' thinking and practice* (pp. 15–42). London: Falmer Press.

Gardner, H. (1987). The theory of multiple intelligence. *Annals of Dyslexia, 37*, 19–35.

Grice, H. P. (1975). Logic and conversation. In P. Cole, & J. Morgan (Eds.), *Syntax and semantics: Speech acts, Vol. 3.* New York: Academic Press.

Grossman, P. L., & Shulman, L. S. (1994). Knowing, believing, and the teaching of English. In T. Shanahan (Ed.), *Teachers thinking, teachers knowing: Reflections of literacy and language education* (pp. 3–22). Urbana, IL: National Council of Teachers of English.

Heath, S. B. (1983). *Ways with words: Language, life, and work in communities and classrooms.* New York: Cambridge University Press.

Hoffman, J. V., & Kugle, C. L. (1982). A study of theoretical orientation to reading and its relationship to teacher verbal feedback during reading instruction. *Journal of Classroom Interaction, 18*(1), 2–7.

Holt-Reynolds, D. (1991). *Practicing what we teach* (Research Report 91–5). National Center for Research on Teacher Learning. East Lansing, MI: Michigan State University.

Hudelson, S. J., & Lindfors, J. W. (1993). *Delicate balances: Collaborative research in language education.* Urbana, IL: National Council of Teachers of English.

Kagan, D. M. (1990). Ways of evaluating teacher cognition: Inferences concerning the Goldilocks principle. *Review of Educational Research, 60*, 419–469.

Kelly, G. A. (1955). *The psychology of personal constructs.* New York: W. W. Norton.

Leland, C. H., & Harste, J. C. (1994). Multiple ways of knowing: Curriculum in a new key. *Language Arts, 71*, 337–345.

Leont'ev, A. N. (1978). *Activity, consciousness, and personality* (M. J. Hall, Trans.) Englewood Cliffs, NJ: Prentice-Hall.

Lortie, D. C. (1975). *Schoolteacher.* Chicago: University of Chicago Press.

Magolda, M. B. B. (1992). *Knowing and reasoning in college: Gender-related patterns in students' intellectual development.* San Francisco: Jossey-Bass.

Mehan, H. (1985). The structure of classroom discourse. In T. van Dijk (Ed.), *Handbook of discourse analysis, Vol. 3.* London: Academic Press.

Moffett, J. (1968). *Teaching the universe of discourse.* Boston: Houghton Mifflin.

Monson, R. J., & Monson, M. P. (1994). Literacy as inquiry: An interview with Jerome C. Harste. *The Reading Teacher, 47*, 518–521.

Munby, H. (1986). Metaphor in the thinking of teachers: An exploratory study. *Journal of Curriculum Studies, 18*(2), 197–209.

Munby, H. (1987). Metaphors and teachers' knowledge. *Research in the Teaching of English, 21*, 377–397.

Nespor, J. (1987). The role of beliefs in the practice of teaching. *Journal of Curriculum Studies, 19*(4), 317–328.

Palincsar, A. S., & Brown, A. L. (1984). Reciprocal teaching of comprehension-fostering and comprehension-monitoring activities. *Cognition and Instruction, 1*, 117–175.

Patterson, L. (1993). (Ed.). *Teachers are researchers: Reflection and action.* Newark, DE: International Reading Association.

Richards, J., Gipe, J. P., & Duffy, C. A. (1992, April). *Beginning professionals' metaphors in an early field placement.* Paper presented at the annual meeting of the American Educational Research Association, San Francisco.

Richards, V., Anders, P., Tidwell, D., & Lloyd, C. (1991). The relationship between teachers' beliefs and practices in reading comprehension instruction. *American Educational Research Journal, 28*(3), 559–586.

Shulman, L. S. (1987). Knowledge and teaching. Foundations of the new reform. *Harvard Educational Review, 57*(1), 1–22.

Sternberg, R. (1981). *Beyond IQ: A triarchic theory of human intelligence.* New York: Cambridge University Press.

Tannen, D. (1986). *That's not what I mean! How conversational style makes or breaks relationships.* New York: Ballantine.

Vygotsky, L. S. (1962). *Thought and language.* Cambridge, MA: M.I.T. Press.

Vygotsky, L. S. (1978). *Mind in society.* Cambridge, MA: Harvard University Press.

Willinsky, J. (1990). *The new literacy: Redefining reading and writing in the schools.* New York: Routledge.

36

TEACHERS REFLECTING ON PRACTICE

Richard T. Vacca, JoAnne L. Vacca, and Beverly Bruneau

KENT STATE UNIVERSITY

In the foreword to *Teachers Are Researchers,* Nancie Atwell (1993) notes that when she started teaching she was more the "technician" than the reflective teacher that she is today. As a technician, Atwell relied on "outside" expertise—for example, the authors of reading and writing programs—to inform her teaching. She viewed her role as managing the students, the paper work, and the programs that she used. The more she taught, however, the more she became dissatisfied with classroom practice. Gradually, she began to observe and reflect on what literacy learners actually do when they use language to construct meaning; she inquired into the problems and uncertainties of learning and teaching literacy in a classroom context. Reflective teaching allowed her to respond to what students needed to know and do to become effective readers and writers. Rather than relying on outside experts, reflective inquiry allowed Atwell to construct knowledge of literacy learning and teaching inside her head to better inform her practice.

Nancie Atwell's transformation as a teacher is not unlike others who engage in reflective teaching. The phrase *reflective teaching* is used increasingly to describe both teacher development and the practice of teaching. This chapter begins with an exploration of the meaning of reflective teaching, demonstrates the connection between reflective teaching and best literacy practice, and provides examples of teachers and teacher educators reflecting on their practice.

REFLECTIVE TEACHING

Reflective teaching, the ability of teachers to function as professional problem solvers, has emerged in response to the technical view of teaching developed through the process product research prevalent during the 1970s (Richardson, 1990). Driven by an increasing political emphasis on teacher accountability, researchers focused on identifying teacher competencies that were essential to facilitating the learning of basic skills (Rupley, Wise, & Logan, 1986). During the same period, elementary reading instruction was dominated by basal readers and their accompanying teacher manuals that prescribed and sequenced instructional activities (Shannon, 1983). Apple (1987) describes the reliance of classroom teachers on experts to prescribe plans as the "deskilling" of teaching. Effective teachers were considered to be good managers of lessons planned by experts.

Important changes occurred during the 1980s which currently challenge the technical view of teaching. Qualitative researchers began to explore the complexities of classroom life (Richardson, 1990) and to validate the importance of classroom teachers' practical knowledge of interactions with students (Cochran-Smith & Lytle, 1993). The emerging holistic approach toward literacy instruction requires teachers who can create learning opportunities based on observation of student abilities and interests (Goodman, 1990) and encourages teachers to become "active agents" developing their own literacy curriculum (Maguire, 1989). Effective literacy education requires teachers who are empowered, careful thinkers about their day-to-day interactions with students— teachers who are able to reflect on their practice.

Reflective thinking in teaching can be traced to John Dewey who advocated that teachers must be thoughtful students of their own practice rather than followers of prescriptions or routines (LaBoskey, 1994). An important component of reflective teaching is consideration of beliefs, goals, and practice which Dewey (1993) described as "the active, persistent, and careful consideration of any belief or supposed form of knowledge in light of the grounds that support it and the consequence to which it leads" (1933, p. 9)." Zeichner and Liston (1987) conclude that the purpose of reflection on practice is to help teachers better understand and control their own teaching and learning.

More recently, Schon (1983, 1987) has described reflection as central to growth and development within all the professions. According to Schon, professional problems are complex, often dilemma ridden in which there is no easy answer, and unique to each particular situation. Professionals need to develop the ability to identify and understand problems of practice as well as to develop the ability to hypothesize alternatives, place new actions into practice, and evaluate the results of their teaching action.

Critical to this problem-solving process in education is the teacher's own knowledge. In contrast to the belief that experts hold the knowledge necessary to improve teaching, the reflective perspective values the situational knowledge, "Knowledge in action" held by classroom teachers (Richardson, 1990; Schon, 1991). Through the process of reflecting on their own practice, teachers can become aware of their intuitive knowledge as well as engage in problem solving which strengthens teaching ability. Reflection promotes "knowledge on practice," which is the heart of professional growth.

Oberg and Field (1986) have suggested that as teachers begin to describe problems, they have opportunities to articulate why they have engaged in particular actions. This exploration enables teachers to examine their intuitively held beliefs, an understanding which becomes the base for new knowledge and individual control for classroom decision making. Classroom decision making from a reflective viewpoint requires concrete problem solving. The reflective problem-solving process includes: problem identification, problem framing—considering which features to attend to; generating tentative solutions; gathering additional evidence; reframing in light of new evidence; implementing new procedures; and evaluating the implementation (Moore, 1992).

Researchers have described the content of teacher reflections. Van Manen (1977) has identified three levels of reflection: technical, practical, and critical. Technical reflection enables teachers to consider what works within their classrooms as they attempt to solve day-to-day problems. Practical reflection includes the consideration of educational goals and alternative ways of teaching. Critical reflection examines the ethical and political issues of teaching. What are our assumptions and aims? How do these aims affect our students? Most recently, Zeichner (1993) has suggested that we reconsider Van Manen's levels of categories of thinking. Zeichner argues that if we view technical reflection as a lower level than critical reflection, we are in essence "devaluing" teachers' day-to-day thinking. Rather, Zeichner suggests that we view Van Manen's categories as domains of reflection; valuing that all three are important and that, in reality, teachers move among the levels in a reflexive manner.

Along with a problem-solving approach, reflection requires a particular attitude toward teaching as a problem-solving activity. Dewey identified necessary dispositions which Ross (1987) has summarized as: open-mindedness, the ability to suspend judgment to consider alternatives; responsibility, the ownership of consequences for actions; and, whole-heartedness, which includes both feelings of self-efficacy and a commitment to continuous professional development.

Critical to the process of reflecting on practice is the disposition that teaching is "problematic" (Ross, 1987). Teachers need to view their practice as one that involves problem solving and that this problem solving will contain some degree of ambiguity. Teaching is also complex and solving one particular problem often results in the emergence of related problems (Lambert, 1985). Reflection requires a professional stance which is comfortable with ambiguity, is patient with complex problem solving, and which is open toward multiple sources of information (Kitchener & King, 1981).

More recently, researchers have further emphasized that reflective teaching includes cognitive consideration of classroom problems and also promotes an advocacy for student development. Drawing on the work of Noddings, Valli (1990) describes an ethic of caring as necessary for reflectivity. Noddings' (1984) descriptions of a "caring teacher" in which teachers model the process of concern for others, engage in facilitative dialogue, provide opportunities for students to practice care, concern, and connection, as well as confirm students' abilities fit well with a problem-solving, facilitative approach toward teaching. Reflective teaching from a caring perspective requires teachers to be concerned with students' cognitive and affective development.

Additionally, Valli (1990) describes a critical component of reflection which maintains that knowledge, society, and schools are socially constructed representing the bias of the dominant culture (Giroux & McLaren, 1987). Reflection on teaching from a critical perspective involves an examination of individual, institutional, and societal assumptions which maintain unjust structures and includes an active role of teachers as change agents (Valli, 1990).

Through the process of reflecting on practice teachers are able to better understand their professional thinking and, thereby, better control decisions made within their classrooms. Reflection on practice places a high value on teachers' individual development and knowledge. Reform efforts have emphasized the need for teacher reflection, the consideration of teachers' voices in educational decision and policy making, and the collaborative development of practice in which teachers and researchers together explore how best to educate today's students (The Holmes Group, 1990). Central to this reform are teachers who are able to think carefully about their practice.

THE CONSTRUCTIVIST CONNECTION

Best literacy practice and reflective teaching are grounded in a constructivist view of learning. Constructivism provides a compelling explanatory framework for understanding the way human beings acquire knowledge. Constructivist thinking has powerful links to many fields of inquiry, including psychology (Bruner, 1974; Piaget, 1967; Vygotsky, 1962), linguistics (Halliday, 1977), sociology (Berger & Luckmann, 1966), and philosophy (Polanyi, 1958). From a literacy perspective, children construct knowledge about reading and writing as they interact with people, processes, ideas, and things within a social context that both shapes and constrains that knowledge.

When constructivist principles are applied to the acquisition of knowledge about teaching, teachers are viewed as engaging in a process of seeking and making meaning from personal, practical, and professional experiences (Vacca, Vacca, & Gove, 1995). Best literacy practice and reflective teaching support the role that inquiry plays in meaning making. Literacy learners and teachers are active participants who engage in literacy events and self-examination to make sense of problematic situations that they encounter on an everyday basis.

In the literacy field, constructivist principles have had a major impact on classroom practice, teachers' beliefs about practice, and their self-perceptions. Research related to children's oral language and literacy development in early childhood, comprehension processes, and reader response represent three areas of theoretical and practical inquiry firmly grounded in a constructivist framework.

Oral Language and Literacy Development

Piaget (1967) theorized that children do not internalize knowledge directly from the outside but construct it from inside their heads as they interact with their environment (Kamii, 1991). From a constructivist perspective, children are not passive learners who wait to be taught, but rather they are producers of knowledge who try to make sense of everything that they encounter in the environment.

Studies of children's language and literacy development have been rooted in Piagetian and Vygotskian cognitive, social constructivist perspectives (Goodman, 1990; Ruddell, Ruddell, & Singer, 1994). Researchers from different cultural contexts have explored, among other things, how children decide what is readable, how children compose and comprehend written language, what knowledge children have about written language, and how their perceptions of knowledge change over time. Ruddell and Ruddell (1994, p. 96) acknowledge that much is still unknown about children's oral language and literacy development, but at least five conclusions can be drawn: (1) children are active participants in their own language and literacy development. Driven by a need to construct meaning and make sense of their worlds, children build theories and test hypotheses about language and literacy as they interact with people, processes, and things in their environment; (2) children exhibit rule-governed behavior that reflects their current understanding of how language works; (3) because they are active constructors of meaning, children develop and use literate activity well before school entry; (4) children's language and literacy development are influenced by their world knowledge, social and cultural interactions, and language environments, and (5) home and community language learning environments are often rich in ways not fully explored or understood.

Comprehension Processes

As children grow as language users, the learning that is essential to their social and cognitive development, Wells and Chang-Wells (1992) argue, is that which is likely to engage children actively in solving problems of increasing levels of difficulty. Flood and Lapp (1991) suggest that contemporary literacy practice, particularly as it manifests itself in comprehension instruction, should be based on constructivist principles. Children who engage in learning literacy and in using literacy to learn, build on their own experiences, knowledge,

and values. That is to say, they use what they already know to give meaning to new events and experiences.

Schema is a term used by constructivists to describe how human beings organize and construct meaning in their heads. Schemata represent elaborate networks of concepts, skills, and procedures that are used to make sense of new stimuli, events, and situations (Neisser, 1976). Schemata, based overwhelmingly on research evidence, play an important role in language comprehension (Anderson, 1994). As a result of a schema-theoretic view of language comprehension, there has been a significant shift in comprehension practice over the past two decades. The shift has been away from an emphasis on skills instruction to process-centered approaches that emphasize inquiry and problem solving among students as teachers scaffold instruction.

Langer and Applebee (1986), for example, suggest that instructional scaffolding is an appropriate metaphor for process-oriented literacy learning supported by constructivist principles. Scaffolding provides learners with the instructional support and guidance that they need to do new things with language. Applebee (1991) notes that the concept of instructional scaffolding can be applied to several dimensions of the environment of teaching and learning language—from classroom dialogue, to texts, to instructional activities. The criteria for effective scaffolding include student *ownership* for learning, *appropriateness* of instructional tasks to build upon the skills that students already have, *support* that guides students' learning and develops strategy awareness and use, *collaboration* in which teachers create environments for exploration that are nonevaluative, and students' *internalization* of strategies for effective problem solving.

Reader Response

Rosenblatt (1938) theorized that human beings bring to the reading act distinctive personality traits, world views, and preoccupations of the moment which influence their understanding of literary texts. Literature study involves an exploration of meaning that underscores a reader's personal interpretations of the text. Literary interpretation, therefore, involves a transaction between reader and text in which the meaning of the literary work does not reside in the text, but is constructed by the reader. As a result, each reader comprehends a literary text differently because every reader will bring unique contributions to the reading act. Several literary theorists, such as Bleich (1975, 1978) and Holland (1975, 1985) assert the total authority of the reader in text interpretation. Bleich (1975) contends that literary response begins in complete subjectivity and is then transformed into judgments that appear to be objective.

From a classroom perspective, reader response practice focuses on eliciting and nurturing students' interactions and transactions with texts. Teachers create classroom environments in which students feel free enough to respond openly to a text and then to explore their responses as they seek to clarify and extend their initial thoughts and feelings. In response-based classrooms, teachers demonstrate that meaning is constructed socially as well as within each individual reader as students share interpretations with one another and engage in further analysis of the text.

Literacy practice—as exemplified by literacy development in early childhood, comprehension, and reader response practices— and reflective teaching are rooted in constructivist principles. Advances in literacy practice have required teachers to reconceptualize their own professional roles by engaging in a process of reflection and self-examination. How teachers engage in reflective teaching, and the tools that they use for self-examination and problem solving vary from context to context.

HOW TEACHERS ENGAGE IN REFLECTION

Over the last decade, teacher educators and researchers in the College of Education at Kent State University have explored a number of ways in which teachers inquire into their own practice; how teachers become aware of their intuitive knowledge as they problem-solve. They have examined two major means used by classroom teachers to experience meaningful professional development: writing and dialogue.

Writing

Holly, in her 1989 book, *Writing to Grow: Keeping a Personal-Professional Journal,* discusses the use of logs, diaries, and journals by educators "to explore and grow from experience and reflection on practice" (p. 5). She cites the benefits of journal writing that accumulated from analysis of her long-term research with seven classroom teachers who "learned to wonder on paper about themselves, their students, and their profession…" (p. 5). Holly explains how teachers explore links between teaching and professional development, how teachers identify and think about their own circumstances and experiences, and how these influence and shape their teaching and professional development. Holly's study of seven teachers delved into teachers' joys and frustrations expressed through their writing in diaries, journaling, and meetings in seminar groups. Manna and Misheff (1987) and Vacca et al. (1995) explore the use of reading autobiographies. According to Smyth (1989), encouraging teachers to develop (in writing) a personal biography and professional history allows them to overcome unwillingness to question where certain teaching practices came from. "Simply asking teachers to reflect on the stories they already tell can provide a natural bridge to a serious inquiry about the very deep layers of value and belief…"(Mattingly, 1991, p. 255). Vacca et al. describe and suggest the development of an autobiographical narrative as a powerful tool to help teachers link their personal histories as readers to their instructional beliefs and practices. Autobiographical narrative helps teachers inquire into the past so as to better understand what they do in the present and what they would like to do in future classroom situations. They suggest asking questions such as, "How did you learn to read?", "What home reading experiences do you recall?", "What kinds of instructional activities were you involved in as an elementary school child?", "Which ones do you recall fondly?" The sharing of narratives with others is accomplished by asking, "what beliefs, values, and attitudes are an integral part of the various stories?" "How do teachers' personal histories of reading and learning to read influence where they are philosophically and where they would like to be?"

Group Meetings and Dialogue Sessions

Clemente (1992) studied how teachers developed as meaning makers in an educational change environment over a 2-year period of time. She was a participant in a collaborative university–school district change project, functioning as a participant observer, interacting with teachers during group meetings, both informal and formal. Clemente's field notes about these meetings revealed data about the impact that teachers' experience in an educational change project had on them. Among her findings she reports that, as teachers acted and reacted in their working environment to make sense of their experiences, their role perceptions changed. They expanded their own roles and began to take curricular risks. The teachers were supportive of one another in this urban school system as they gained a new perspective on their roles. Furthermore, as the teachers interacted in meetings over time, their personality and people-to-people skills influenced their participation and perception of their roles. Several of the teachers showed movement to the level of introspective questioning. As one teacher said, "Am I doing what I am supposed to be doing? Now I question everything I do." During the informal meetings where participants gathered to talk about their classroom practice, frustrations were vented. These were sessions where teachers chose to work with others who had similar philosophies as a means of improving their teaching practices. These "situational aspects" were "supportive oases of confidence, trust, rapport, and friendship."

Where teachers were philosophically similar to one another, there was less confrontation and better communication. "In these situations… communication… went smoothly because there was a basis of trust and confidence in one another" (Clemente, 1992, p. 191). Clemente's findings corroborate the previous findings of Holly (1989) that the increased opportunity to interact with teachers, regardless of the setting, would be perceived as beneficial by teachers … who viewed their colleagues as valuable resources. Likewise, Lieberman (1988) also found that when teachers meet together their success is enhanced by the colleagueship they feel with other teachers and with principals.

In a recent study, Ruttan (1994) observed and interviewed two student teachers over an 8-week period of time, placed in the supportive setting of Professional Development Schools. She concludes that the "supportive stance of the cooperating teachers contributed a secure educational context." This context enabled the student teachers to problem-solve and to experiment. They were able to demonstrate mature levels of reflection. They both indicated that their journal writing and participation in the study itself, and conversations and interviews with the researcher helped them focus on literacy teaching, learning, and to reflect about their teaching practices. Opportunities to relate their new knowledge to past experiences are important. Again, having similar philosophies and the opportunity to share perspectives about literacy teaching and learning were important and should be considered when placing a student teacher with a cooperating teacher. Affective issues should be taken into consideration; attempts to make complementary matches between the student teachers and the cooperating teachers are important.

Ambrose, Vacca, and Vacca (1992) describe a long-term university–school district collaboration in teacher education built around an inquiry orientation. Experienced teacher leaders who worked with university preservice interns met once every 2 weeks in a cohort seminar with the project codirectors. These faculty associates reported their role as "professionally rewarding and personally satisfying because of the sustained, intense involvement with interns and their colleagues." Furthermore, the cohesiveness and identification with a select group of peers seemed to "enable the teachers, as it does the interns, to engage in public discourse about existing practice. It provides a much needed sounding board for reflection." This process has also been credited by teachers who are faculty associates for their willingness to assume more responsibility for present and future direction in program development and to replace traditional university supervisors.

In a recent study, Waldron (1994) explores reflective practice in art education using an inquiry model for staff development. She combined journal writing with dialogue sessions to engage five visual art teachers in systematic reflection over a 12-week period of time. Her intent was to describe the processes of reflective teaching and collegial dialogue of inservice art teachers. She described teachers, thinking about their episodes of practice—how they make sense of them and how they learn from them. Teachers were provided with journals, notebooks and supplies to be used for individual reflection and preparation for five seminar sessions, each lasting 90 minutes. Their written entries addressed two major areas: personal concerns about individual practice and reactions to aspects of the collegial dialogue in seminar sharing sessions. According to one experienced teacher, "it has been good for me to journal about my art teaching and daily ups and downs ... for the conscious awareness it brings. I've found I'm reflecting more carefully and slowing down my high-speed chase through the days." Another reported that she enjoyed the gatherings but, "I still find it hard to find the time to write it all down." Time was a major theme. Waldron found that the journaling process and time were somewhat problematic. Keeping a professional journal is a technique which requires time to cultivate in order for the journaling teacher to be comfortable with the process, to make it a natural habit, and to find a personal style so that the journal can become a meaningful, useful, and professional growth tool. The dialogue sessions were useful in exploring concerns and frustrations and personal or professional issues identified by both early career and veteran art teachers. Frustrations expressed by early career art teachers dealt more often with "constraints they felt to be directed at them personally which infringed upon their time, while veteran art teachers were more often frustrated by outward directed concerns, those that interacted with the school, community, and field" (p. 129). Waldron concludes that changes were evident in teachers' growth in the process of engaging in reflection.

CONCLUSION

This chapter examined reflection on the part of teachers. How teachers engage in reflective teaching was followed by a section in which the constructivist roots of literacy theory and practice were explored. The final section presented examples of individual and collaborative work in which classroom teachers and university teachers and researchers problem-solve together. As LaBoskey concludes, "The charge of the teaching profession is precious—the minds and lives of our children. We cannot afford to have teachers who are unwilling or unable to analyze the sources, meanings, and implications of their beliefs about their students and the learning process..." (1994, p. 122).

References

Ambrose, R., Vacca, J., & Vacca, R. (1992). A university collaboration of an inquiry orientation. In A. Frager & J. Miller (Eds.), *Using inquiry in reading education,* (pp. 49–55). Oxford, OH: College Reading Association.

Anderson, R. C. (1994). Role of the reader's schema in comprehension, learning, and memory. In R. B. Ruddell, M. R. Ruddell & H. Singer (Eds.), *Theoretical models and processes of reading* (4th ed.). Newark, DE: International Reading Association.

Apple, M. W. (1987). The de-skilling of teaching. In F. S. Bolin & J. M. Falk (Eds.), *Teacher renewal: Professional issues, personal choices* (pp. 59–75). New York: Columbia Teachers College Press.

Applebee, A. N. (1991). Environments for language teaching and learning: Contemporary issues and future directions. In J. Flood, J. M. Jensen, D. Lapp & J. R. Squire (Eds.), *Handbook of research on teaching the English language arts.* Newark, DE: International Reading Association and National Council of Teachers of English.

Atwell, N. (1993). Foreward to *Teacher as Readers.* In L. Patterson, C. Santa, & K. Smith, (Eds.), *Teachers as researchers.* Newark, DE: International Reading Association.

Berger, P. L., & Luckmann, T. (1966). *The social constitution of reality.* New York: Anchor Books.

Bleich, d. (1975). *Readings and feelings: An introduction to subjective criticism.* Urbana, IL: National Council of Teachers of English.

Bleich, D. (1978). *Subjective criticism.* Baltimore: Johns Hopkins University Press.

Bruner, J. (1974). *Beyond the information given: Studies in the psychology of knowing.* London: George Allen & Unwin.

Clemente, R. (1992). *Teachers as meaning-makers in an educational change initiative.* Doctoral dissertation, Kent State University.

Cochran-Smith, M., & Lytle, S. (1993). *Inside outside: Teacher research and knowledge.* New York: Teachers College Press.

Dewey, J. (1933). *How we think: A restatement of reflective thinking to the educative process.* Boston: D. C. Heath.

Flood, J., & Lapp, D. (1991). Reading comprehension instruction. In J. Flood, J. M. Jensan, D. Lapp, & J. R. Squire (Eds.), *Handbook of research on teaching the English language arts.* Newark, DE: International Reading Association and National Council of Teachers of English.

Giroux, J. A., & McLaren, P. (1987). Teacher education and the politics of engagement: The case for democratic schooling. *Harvard Education Review, 90,* 113–127.

Goodman, Y. M. (Ed.). (1990). *How children construct literacy: Piagetian perspectives.* Newark, DE: International Reading Association.

Halliday, M. (1977). *Learning how to mean.* New York: Elsevier.

Holland, N. (1975). *5 readers reading.* New Haven, CT: Yale University Press.

Holland, N. (1985). Reading readers reading. In C. Cooper (Eds.), *Researching response to literature and the teaching of literature, points of departure.* Norwood, NJ: Ablex.

Holly, M. (1989). *Writing to grow: Keeping a personal–professional journal.* Portsmouth, NH: Heinemann Educational Books.

Holmes Group Report. (1990). *Tomorrow's schools: Principles for the design of professional development schools.* East Lansing, MI: The Holmes Group.

Kamii, C. (1991). What is constructivism? In C. Kamii, M. Manning, & C. Manning (Eds.), *Early literacy: A constructivist foundation for whole language.* Washington, DC: National Education Association.

Kitchener, K., & King. P. (1981). Reflective judgment concepts of justification and their relationship to age and education. *Journal of Applied Developmental Psychology, 2,* 80–116 .

LaBoskey, V. (1994). *Development of reflective practice: A study for preservice teachers.* New York: Columbia Teachers College Press.

Lambert, M. (1985). How do teachers manage to teach? Perspectives on problems in practice. *Harvard Educational Review, 55,* 178–194 .

Langer, J. A., & Applebee, A. N. (1986). Reading and writing instruction: Toward a theory of teaching and learning. *Review of Research in Education, 13,* 171–194 .

Lieberman, A. (1988). Teachers and principals: Turf, tension, and new tasks. *Phi Delta Kappan, 69,* 648–653.

Maguire, M. (1989). Understanding and implementing a whole language program in Quebec. *The Elementary School Journal, 90,* 143–160 .

Manna, A., & Misheff, S. (1987) . What teachers say about their own reading development. *Journal of Reading, 31,* 160–169.

Mattingly, S. (1991). Narrative reflections on practical actions: Two learning experiments in reflective story telling. In D. Schon (Ed.), *The reflective turn,* (pp. 235–257). New York: Columbia Teachers College Press.

Moore, S. T. (1992). *A context for growth: The lived experience of an emergent teacher educator.* Unpublished doctoral dissertation, Virginia Tech, Blacksburg, VA.

Neisser, U. (1976). *Cognition and reality: Principles and implications of cognitive psychology.* San Francisco: Fleerman.

Noddings, N. (1984). *Caring: A feminine approach to ethics and moral education.* Berkeley, CA: University of California Press.

Oberg, A., & Field, R. (1986, April). *Teacher development through reflection.* A paper presented at the annual meeting of the American Educational Research Association, San Francisco.

Piaget, J. (1967). *The development of thought: Equilibrium of cognitive structures.* New York: Viking.

Polanyi, M. (1958). *Personal knowledge.* London: Routledge.

Richardson, V. (1990). The evolution of reflective teaching and teacher education. In R. T. Clift, W. R. Houston, & M. C. Pugach (Eds.), *Encouraging reflective practice in education: An analysis of issues and programs* (pp. 3–19). New York: Teachers College Press.

Rosenblatt, L. M. (1938). *Literature as exploration.* New York: Nobel & Noble.

Ross, D. (1987, October). *Reflective teaching: Meaning and implications for preservice teacher educators.* Paper presented at the Reflective Inquiry Conference, Houston, TX.

Ruddell, R. B., & Ruddell, M. R. (1994). Language acquisition and literacy processes. In R. B., Ruddell, M. R., Ruddell & H. Singer, (Eds.), *Theoretical models and processes of reading* (4th ed.). Newark, DE: International Reading Association.

Ruddell, R. B., Ruddell, M. R., & Singer, H. (Eds.). (1994). *Theoretical models and processes of reading* (4th ed.), Newark, DE: International Reading Association.

Rupley W., Wise, B., & Logan, J. (1986). Process product research on effective teaching: A primer for a paradigm. In J. Hoffman (Ed.), *Effective teaching of reading: Research and practice* (pp. 39–52). Newark, DE: International Reading Association.

Ruttan, D. (1994). *A qualitative case study of the influence of the student teaching experience on the perspectives of two student teachers in regard to literacy teaching and learning in kindergarten.* Doctoral dissertation, Kent State University.

Schon, D. A. (1983). *The reflective practitioner: How professionals think in action.* New York: Basic Books.

Schon, D. A. (1987). *Educating the reflective practitioner: Toward a new design for teaching and learning in the professionals.* San Francisco: Jossey-Bass.

Schon, D. A. (1991). *The reflective turn: Case studies in and on educational practice.* New York: Teachers College Press.

Shannon, P. (1983). The use of commercial reading materials in American elementary schools. *Reading Research Quarterly, 19,* 65–84.

Smyth, J. (1989). Developing and sustaining critical reflection in teacher education. *Journal of Teacher Education, 40*(2), 2–9.

Vacca, J., Vacca, R., & Gove, M. (1995). *Reading and learning to read* (3rd ed.). New York: Harper Collins.

Valli, L. (1990). Moral approaches to reflective practice. In R. T. Clift, W. R. Houston & M. C. Pugach (Eds.), *Encouraging reflective practice in education: An analysis of issues and programs* (pp. 39–56). New York: Teachers College Press.

Van Manen, M. (1977). Linking ways of knowing with ways of being practical. *Curriculum Inquiry, 6,* 205–228.

Vygotsky, M. (1978). *Mind in Society.* (M. Cole, V. Johnsteiner, S. Scribner, & E. Souberman, Eds. and Trans.), Cambridge, MA: Harvard University Press.

Waldron, D. (1994). *Reflective practice in art education: An inquiry model for staff development.* Doctoral dissertation, Kent State University.

Wells, G., & Chang–Wells, G. L. (1992). *Constructing knowledge together: Classrooms as centers of inquiry and literacy.* Portsmouth, NH: Heinemann.

Zeichner, K. (1993, August). *Research on teacher thinking and different view of reflective practice in teaching and teacher education.* A keynote address presented at the Sixth International Conference of the International Study Association on Teaching Thinking, Goteborg, Sweden.

Zeichner, K., & Liston, D. (1987). Teaching student teachers to reflect. *Harvard Educational Review, 57,* 23–48.

37

PUTTING IT IN PERSPECTIVE:
ADMINISTRATING ART EDUCATION
FOR LITERACY

Richard P. Mesa

MILLS COLLEGE

I try to tell students, 'You have the eye. You issue your own artistic license.' And then you see them start to make choices in the class. And then you have to back that up by giving them more choices and leeway and materials and by saying, 'Here is the assignment. The assignment is perspective. Or the assignment is symmetry. Meet those two expectations and then you may do it whatever way you want.' And if they didn't meet the expectation of perspective, they did this with a free will. And the consequences are there. It doesn't mean the piece is not beautiful.

—Alice LaTouche, Teacher, Lockwood Elementary School

INTRODUCTION

Several years ago the San Francisco Art Institute hosted a symposium whose theme, *Towards A Culturally Inclusive Art Education,* provided its participants with an excellent opportunity to articulate why art is an essential component of a child's education. This chapter offers my key note address to that symposium as the theoretical rationale for art education, placed in the perspective of furthering literacy in our schools. This rationale is followed by a discussion of three central challenges facing administrators of art education, and suggestions for meeting these challenges from the point of view of a superintendent of schools.

Art: Linking Culture and Literacy

As an educator, as a teacher, particularly one who sees the arts play a very central role in the education of the young, I thought I would comment in a way that may be different from what you are accustomed. What I would like to talk about is the transmission of culture to the young and the increasing

problem that is emerging in our society. I also want to talk about the cultural exclusion we see all around us, including the development of racial ambivalence and of the cultural discontinuity that affects the motivation of young people. I will try to relate this as best as I can to art education and why it is so important in the schools.

To begin with, I know very little about art, at least visual art; I was an English teacher, so I knew the arts from the perspective of literature. But I know that human beings have had a compulsion since the very beginning to commemorate what they feel, experience and see—to record what they have seen and to transmit it to someone who was not at a particular place to see the hunt or the birth of a child or whatever. We know that there are cave drawings and other early recordings of humanity's need to commemorate what it has felt and experienced. We know that art is not a frivolous experience, it is not something one does in one's spare time, but is central to our need to express our experiences and thoughts. Through language, through drawing, through music, that need to commemorate, express and record human experience is very important to human development. Clearly, people in societies and civilizations in different parts of the world have taken different routes, and have fulfilled this need in a variety of ways. Nevertheless, in whatever media human beings have used to express, record and commemorate their feelings, there are clearly universal aspects, as well as differences. I am a little puzzled by the topic of this symposium, which implies a need to be culturally inclusive of the arts. I wonder if true art is not already universally appealing. The first thing a conqueror does is loot to the art treasures of the conquered and take them back home and display them, not only as a symbol of conquest but also of

451

what is most desirable in victory. I've experienced this personally.

In 1975, I was lucky enough to be asked to teach at the University of Santiago de Compostella in Spain for a summer. My wife and I and two of our children toured Spain, of course, and we found ourselves at a remote little seaport museum. Someone had told me that I should go there because one of Montezuma's headdresses is there. I expected that the museum would be grand, that it would take pride in and somehow feature the headdress of Montezuma, one of the great figures in Mexicaul history. Well, here it was, under a dusty glass covering in this isolated little museum. The headdress obviously had not been featured for a long time. It would have been priceless in Mexico, but it was almost lost in Spain. I asked myself why art invaluable to the heritage and history of conquered people, is taken for casual display by the conquerors. Nevertheless, here it was, surge kept after more than 400 years.

Perhaps "cultural inclusion" is a natural consequence of war trade and coexistence, and what I saw as art was an example of the historical tendency of powerful conquerors to steal the art treasures of the weak. But the distribution, the theft of these treasures is rather selective; selective in the sense that what is stolen is then exhibited to show indirectly that the conquerors in fact conquered, that they had the capacity to take these treasures and exhibit them back in their homelands. Napoleon exemplified this when he brought the ancient Egyptian obelisk back for display on the Paris square as a symbol of his power to conquer. This kind of theft is selective because it tends to feature that which manifests the power of those who have conquered, but perhaps it misses the nuances that can sustain, educate, and enable a people to feel pride in what they have developed and created. These treasures may be literature or art that protests, art that defies, art that expresses dangerous ideas. That kind of art is taken and hidden away, allowed to gather dust and grow shabby; it is not exhibited, not manifest. Through time, for the people who are colonized or conquered, these symbols are lost. This art, this expression of ideas that could revive a spirit, that could cause rebellion, that could cause reaction to oppression, is removed and not allowed to be shown until the conquerors have recast history so that it proves to their own advantage.

I think that this experience of not sharing complete access to the art of a people has a crippling, stunting effect. I do not know about this as an arts educator, because I am not an artist or an art educator, but I do know as an educator that one of the most serious problems we deal with in young people today is the cultural ambivalence they feel. Everyone in this audience has experienced some ambivalence of identity, but an ambivalence of identity as it relates to one's culture or race is deep and serious. We have experienced it if we are Mexican American and do not know whether we should allow ourselves to be more American or stay loyal to being Mexicans. As a consequence of not knowing where we fit, of not knowing where we belong, we go back and forth between being derisive toward the native culture and angry toward the dominant. This anger blinds students to the benefits of society, such as school.

Three years ago, I was asked to help write a curriculum for a Mexican art museum in San José. As part of the process of developing this curriculum, we took some students through to get their reactions, to get some sense of the questions they would ask, to better understand what we might need to teach these young people about art. They walked through in a matter-of-fact way and looked at the art exhibits, not with what we expected to be curiosity and respect for the art, but almost as if they were walking by the food displayed in the latest fast food store on the corner. Then the man who was developing this museum started to ask the young people questions about who they thought had made certain objects. Silence, they did not know. He said, "People from the New World, your ancestors, made these. They were Aztecs, they were Mayans, they were many different Nations, but they were your ancestors." The students kidded around with each other, and their interest grew a little bit.

Then he asked if they had ever heard their parents talk about some of the people he had mentioned. One kid raised his hand and said, "Yes, my mother told us about the Indians who were traveling down through what is now called Mexico, looking for a place to live. She said when the Aztecs saw an eagle perched on a cactus, devouring a snake, that would be the place." That drew a little bit more interest from the students. Then the museum director asked how they thought a certain stone carving was made. "They had tools, chisels and stuff." "Chisels," the director repeated, "Is that what it takes to cut stone?" One kid said, "Well, obviously a steel chisel." When the director explained that there were no metal chisels then, that the people did not know about metals hard enough to cut stone but still carved so exquisitely, delicately, the kids became really interested. One asked how these people did that without tools harder than the stone. The kids started to guess; they said it must have been a stone harder than this stone. They decided the Aztecs must have been very wise and really wanted to create this carving if they were going to take the trouble to find a stone that could cut a stone.

These students' respect for the Aztecs and Mayans, for ancient art, and teacher lead them to discover answers to their own questions. What was happening, I could see, was a connection between children and art and their heritage though a description of history and a modeling of respect for artistic creation. The connection that was made there led to more curiosity, more interest on the part of these young people, and many of them became active in the establishment of this small art museum.

I use this small example to elaborate several points that I began to make earlier. One is that the deliberate transmission of culture to the young almost never happens, even in the dominant culture. It rarely happens in relationship to a child's home culture. The connection between the culture and these young people began with derision of what they saw; it began with a matter-of-fact disregard until someone began the process of making the connections, of talking about how important these things were to them. It is my opinion that one of the most critical things young people suffer from today is that adults spend so little time with the young; the interaction between adults and young people is decreasing rapidly and it is cutting down enormously on the opportunity for transmission of culture to take place.

Anyone who teaches the primary grades will tell you that children, in kindergarten especially, behave very differently now than they used to. Many reasons are given; some people blame it on the fact that the parents have been on drugs, and the children are exposed to drugs at a prenatal stage. But I think the one thing we can say about most young people is that, for a variety of reasons, adults spend much less time with them. Prior to World War II, and before television, according to some studies, the typical parent spent upwards of 2½ hours with their children, at dinner, talking, prior to putting them to bed and so on. Since the onset of tract housing and freeways and of homes removed from places of work, where parents often have to commute an hour or more to work; since both parents need to work to survive economically; since television has come along and taken up much of the time that was spent talking, the amount of time that parents or supportive adults spend with children has been incredibly reduced. This was different when I was growing up in a large, migrant family. I first learned about art from my brother.

I think an artistic streak runs in my family. My brother, Louis, was a folk artist who drew beautifully. He made a gallery on a twelve-inch by tenfoot-long plank he found. He brought it into the house, and on it he drew a caricature of each member of the family; it was hilarious. He nailed it up on the wall and it became our family gallery. His son Bob makes money by painting designs on these low rider cars; he also paints beautifully. My son Tom is attending the art school in Oakland. His daughter Justine and my grandson Conor have shown great interest and aptitude in drawing and creating. I do not know where it comes from, but somehow the talent and the need to create, to draw is passed on. But I can remember spending hours with Louis. He would take my younger brother and me (we were the babies of the family and Louis was among the oldest, so 15 years separated us) to the dump before Christmas. We would find things to make toys with, since we could not buy them. The time we spent talking about how to make things both useful and beautiful transmitted values, hopes and ideas to us. He taught us to see beauty and reality in the unlikeliest materials. We also learned who we were; that we were connected to him and our family.

When there is no transmission of culture to the young, the cultural disconnection results in a cultural ambivalence, a loss of identity, a discontinuity that is devastating to the young because they lack confidence in who they are. Worst of all, they do not believe they are as good as someone else who seems secure in a sense of belonging and identity. That loss of confidence, that loss of a sense of who they are is distracting. It creates a dynamic in young people that often has terrible consequences. They can internalize that lack of confidence as the belief that trying is futile, or they can become angry about it and take an opposition stance to a society to which they know they do not belong. Of course, there are those few who do transcend this feeling and go on to do very well. But most do not.

I am convinced that loss of culture also robs young people of the capacity to express themselves, and therefore it erodes their capacity for language. It is commonly known that one of the reasons we press the arts as being so basic in school—I am trying to do this in the Oakland School District, and I have tried to do it in every district I have led—is that through the arts comes the concrete experience of language. In literature classes, I remember when the teacher talked about the mood of a story. I did not know what she really meant until I heard mood related to music. Of course, I could tell immediately if music was solemn, if it was bright, if it was happy; and then I could relate that concrete experience in music to the more abstract conception of mood in literature. If I am shown what symmetry or texture is in art, then I can take that concrete experience and use it in a metaphorical way to express observations elsewhere, quite apart from that context of art. If I use the term texture to describe an abstract conception, such as the texture of my life, I can communicate what I mean exactly, because we all know textures physically, concretely. Perspective I know visually, from art; when I hear that abstract term perspective applied elsewhere I apply the visual images to the abstraction and understand it. I did not just understand it, I grasped it.

Now let me relate the association between artistic experience and abstract concept to an expression or experience that is close to my own background. If someone says to me that something feels like *un grito de ganas,* how many of you know what this means? When one hears un grito, there is no equivalent to it. When the *mariachi* sings so passionately that those listening cannot help but let out this *grito;* those who have experienced it know exactly what I mean. The *grito* expresses a feeling to anyone who has had that experience— *se siente como un grito,* it feels like that cry—it is part anguish, part passion, complete yearning. That is how this cultural experience, artistic because it comes from music, causes you to relate the cry to your own often unarticulated feelings. And because you feel it and there is a word connected to that feeling, you can now use it metaphorically; you can now use the word to convey the emotion metaphorically, like a poet. The definition of a poet is someone who can describe concrete experience in language that evokes memories, thoughts, feelings or ideas. It is art which links the abstract and the concrete, that opens intelligence and thought, that keeps people powerful. If this were not true, why would the conquerors steal it?

PUTTING THEORY INTO PRACTICE: IMPROVING OUR SCHOOLS

As the participants of the San Francisco Art Institute Symposium have discovered, it can be reenergizing to remind ourselves why art education is so important to the young people we serve: it motivates students with its dual offerings of cultural inclusion and the shared human experience; it provides a vehicle for literacy by asking students to express and commemorate feelings and abstract ideas; it possesses the power to revive a spirit.

Even when we are armed with a renewed energy for art education, however, formidable challenges face those of us who wish to administrate art education in today's schools. For the last 5 years I faced these challenges as the Superintendent of Oakland Unified School District, an urban school district in northern California. As the sixth largest district in the state, it serves over 50,000 students from diverse ethnic, linguistic, and economic backgrounds (OUSD, 1994). The young people who succeed as students and citizens in Oakland schools often do so by successfully navigating very challenging life circumstances. At the same time, however, too many of our students are not able to overcome all of the obstacles facing them to achieve the benefits of an education. While the inner-city crises of violence, poverty, addiction, and racism intensify the challenges to administrating art education discussed in this chapter, three central challenges: (l) Justifying Art Education; (2) Financing Art at Time of Budget Crisis; and (3) Updating Classroom Pedagogy confront school administrators across the country. Though none of these challenges operates independently of the others within the reality of a school district, each does present identifiable elements which justify their perhaps artificial separation in this text.

Challenge: Justifying Art Education

A primary challenge that faces us is ourselves. Public school administrators are lacking in art education. This gap in knowledge is not necessarily the fault of the administrators themselves; art education is rarely included in an administrative job description. From the beginning, Americans have viewed and structured their schools as something Puritanical, no-nonsense, basic skills oriented. In the first published curriculum for the Oakland Public Schools, adopted in 1868, art was included in the elementary curriculum only as it conformed to the rote requirements of the three Rs, only as it could be organized into discreet, verifiable uniform units:

First Grade Course of Study

Printing and Drawing — Printing letters on the blackboard, at least 15 minutes by each division, daily. Printing on the slate, daily, at least 15 minutes. One division shall be sent to the blackboard, while the other is at work on the slates. [See page 26, Wilson's Manual. Drawing, both on the slate and blackboard, as directed in Wilson's Manual, pp. 51–55; Calkin's Manual, 94 to 98(p. 33)].

In schools taking this approach, an education in art hardly seems required of the teacher, let alone the administrator. Instead, the official job descriptions of the Superintendent and principals in 1868 focused exclusively on the administrator's responsibility to maintain strict order and adherence to carefully prescribed norms:

> (The Superintendent) shall advise with those through whom, either directly or indirectly, the school appropriations are expended, that there may result greater uniformity in their plans and more economy in their expenditures.
> The Principals of the schools shall examine all the class books of the other teachers as often as once a month, and give such direction and assistance as may be necessary to secure accuracy and uniformity (p. 11)

In more recent years, public school administrators have been selected and trained to run their schools and districts according to the principles of corporate management. In their history of public school administration, *Managers of Virtue*, authors Tyack and Hasnot (1982) examine how the turn of the century in America brought with it "a conception of leadership designed to consolidate power in large and centralized organizations, whether steel mills, large department stores, or city school systems". Today a candidate for a superintendency can expect to field substantial questions about budget development, human resource management, mediation of contending political factions, labor relations, statistics, litigation, and so on; in over a dozen interviews for administrative positions, I have never once been asked a question which implied that I should possess or would be valued for possessing knowledge of the arts.

Whether actively discouraging art education by precluding it from administrative job descriptions or discouraging it more passively through the process of elimination, schools sometimes bring together those students and teachers who are enthusiastic about and carefully educated in art with administrators who are not equipped to fully appreciate what they are doing. A teacher of Cantonese bilingual classes in Oakland designed a lesson in which she used 16-fold origami boxes to teach principles of fractions to her first graders. As she was guiding her students through the folding process, an administrator came into the room to observe. The teacher was excited to show off the innovative and challenging work; her students were doing. The observer's response: "Where's the work that goes with this?" A central function of the school administrator is advocacy, and one is not likely to advocate what one does not see or understand.

Beyond advocating, administrators are responsible for justifying educational programs to their many constituents: school board members, teachers, parents, the business community, state and local governments; to ensure the place of art in the curriculum. Without tools to justify arts education as essential to the academic learning of children, they are then also unable to develop plans and policies of operationalization, or the measures by which to evaluate the effects of art education. Without substantive evaluation data, the cycle closes back in on itself as the administrator is left without the proof of educational success.

SOLUTION: LEARN FROM THE TEACHERS AND STUDENTS

Administrators need to see and make clear the connection between art and the academic outcomes for which they are held most strictly accountable: improvements in language, mathematics, science and the social sciences. In urban districts these clear connections are especially hard to come by in the light of the serious and almost insoluble problem of raising the achievement of a disproportionate number of poor and minority students who are now failing in school. District and school administrators would gladly justify and institutionalize art education if they could see the conceptual and practical connections between art education and the so-called "basics" for which they are held accountable. Fortunately, these connections can be made through art; teachers can teach maths, reading, verbal expression, and writing through and as a part of art lessons.

Beyond the most obvious solution of altering the administrative credentialing requirements and job descriptions to include art education, administrators can draw on the resources already contained within their districts. Administrators who seek, talk with, and observe teachers educated in the arts will be provided with an impressive collection of strong justifications for art education. The information gathered and art lessons learned from teachers and community members of the Oakland Public Schools while writing this article are offered throughout this chapter as proof, in part, of the vast resources available to administrators of art education. While many of the justifications gathered from the classrooms and art studios are included in the Pedagogy Section of this chapter, one justification which received unanimous mention is offered here.

The educators with whom we spoke were careful to emphasize that they see the arts as a natural, if not instinctual means of communication and learning for children. And because art is a natural way of knowing for children, the authority of creation is invested in them, and they become responsible for identifying and sharing their knowledge with others. This field note description of an elementary teacher's plan for teaching writing through art justifies art education as a means of using knowledge that is native to a child to facilitate the acquisition of a new knowledge—literacy:

> From the beginning of the year Theresa AuYoung asks first graders to keep a journal. At first they mostly draw what is on their minds and then scribble "pretend writing" or random-looking lettering underneath. The only requirement is that they can share with Mrs. AuYoung and other students in the class what they have recorded in their journals. If they can do this, then they have succeeded in understanding a central purpose of writing - to reveal and make permanent our thoughts. As the year progresses the writing becomes more legible, coherent, and often takes over from the importance of the illustration (although Mrs. AuYoung would prefer that it did not).
> Mrs. AuYoung shows parents how the students' writing is improving, and they are impressed. But she tells her students to savor their very first journal entries - to remind themselves of how smart they were before they knew how to write, how rapidly their writing skills developed when their minds were allowed to flow freely, and so that they can share their artistic talent with their children while remembering themselves their first writing experiences and how they developed.

Before children can read and write or add and subtract, they can draw, sing, pretend, act out and tell stories. Before the human race invented reading, writing and arithmetic, they engaged in those endeavors we now call artisitic expression. As this teacher shows, using art to precede and set the stage for the "basic" skills is not only natural, but fundamentally important. As this method works as a means of education between teacher and student, so it can work as a means of education between teacher and administrator.

CHALLENGE: FINANCING ART AT A TIME OF BUDGET CRISIS

The budget crisis being suffered by inner city school districts is a magnification of the budget problems facing schools nationwide. A great deal has been written documenting the decline of the public's willingness and ability to fund public schools in the 1990s; in Oakland a most telling statistic is that 460 million have been cut in the last 4 years equaling 20% of our budget and aborting, among many other things, our elementary music program. Quality art education is dependent upon projects, which require primary sources, materials and supplies. While extravagance is not a perquisite of art education, a certain degree of expendability is. A teacher from a year-round inner-city elementary school describes the budgetary Catch-22 which binds her as she tries include art in her class:

> The materials are expensive and many of them aren't the usual materials that are ordered for elementary schools and you find it difficult to get the materials. And they're consumables so sometimes they can't even be bought out of the little budget that we try to have to let each teacher go shopping. [Administration] really doesn't want you to buy consumables with it. So while I can buy brushes, I'm discouraged from buying paint. And while I can by clip boards, I'm discouraged from buying the art paper to go on the clip board.

Damage done by budgetary limitations and questionable priorities increases exponentially in combination with other challenges. For example, because many administrators are unversed in art education, established curriculum in this area is limited or even nonexistent. The burden is then transferred to the teacher to create a curriculum, lesson units and materials. Paradoxically this extra work places art officially outside of the standard curriculum, so that money spent on it is seen as an extra expense, to be paid when there is money left over. If only one or a few teachers within a school community are trained in art pedagogy, the special supplies are being purchased for a select group and liable to be viewed as favoritism.

Comparisons between corporate management and school management suggest that the departments which maintain the greatest financial stability and are most clearly linked with profit-proven (or, in the language of schools, basic skills) output are the most important. Viewed as far away from the academic "basics," art departments in schools are routinely appropriated less funding—whether it be through dollars in a budget to spend or through faculty appointments, materials, and time in the master schedule. Even while such a utilitarian means of evaluation relegates art departments to stepchild status, schools are highly aware of how important student art work is to their image. Back-to-school nights, assemblies, bulletin boards, newsletters, classroom parties and school-wide celebrations—none of these aspects of school life would be complete without the artwork of students and teachers. However, money and time are rarely budgeted to pay for these projects and displays in the formal way that it is made available to pay a coach, fund a field trip or finance a department. One elementary teacher with extensive formal training in art confessed that she purposely avoids revealing to her colleagues the extent of her experience in art: "Cheap labor," she commented matter-of-factly.

SOLUTION: TAP INTO COMMUNITY RESOURCES

The problems facing schools today, financial and otherwise, require the cooperation of local and extended communities for valid and lasting solutions. The California High School Task Force acknowledged this need for new kinds of symbiotic community–school relationships when it proposed that the high school become "the center of a network of community services that might include government, health and youth organizations" (California Department of Education, 1993, p. 1). This cogent advice sheds some light on the task of funding art education as well—turn to the community. Many schools have already discovered and implemented artists-in-residence programs which bring professional poets, dancers, theater technicians, and artists of all kinds into classrooms to supplement the teachers' knowledge with their expertise. In addition, many of the country's urban public school districts have established magnet schools organized around a theme of the arts (Fliegel, 1993) in partnership with artists' unions, professional performance organizations and nonprofit art agencies.

Community collaboration toward art education can take place on a smaller scale as well. A pair of local business owners brought a straightforward and mutually beneficial idea to the Oakland's public schools in 1993 when they offered to display and sell student artwork from the walls of their jewelry gallery (White, 1993, p. x). Each class displaying its work is then responsible for deciding how their profits will be spent. Jan Christiansen-Heller remembers the development of the project's fiscal philosophy from the initial thought was that students could be empowered to direct funds into things they themselves wanted, perhaps field trips more art supplies. But without, she is cautions to add, "Getting hooked into the entrepreneurship of it. That is, we didn't want the money to benefit them only. It had to benefit a larger group." Several of the classes which have displayed their work have opted to donate the proceeds from their work to various community charities, and the project now includes a more organized means of sharing with students the wide range of charities available to receive their donations.

This business–community–school collaboration is reaping a number of benefits. It promotes appreciation of art within the community. It demands that students take themselves and their art seriously, by working hard to create a finished product that is worthy of display, by discussing their work with opening night gallery audience, and by making decisions about how their profits will be spent. Christiansen-Heller likes the way the project brings parents in closer touch with their children, and with their children as artists:

> The kids come in and their folks have made them dress up a little nicer than normal. And they're pleased to see their artwork up. I'll never forget one woman came in with her son, who was in junior

high, and said, "Oh my God, I didn't realize he was an artist."

While extolling the social benefits of the program, Christiansen-Heller is careful to point out that the project continues because, and only as long as it benefits her business. "We all need to make a living. Obviously people come into the shop because their children are having an art show. And hopefully they'll make a connection, and want to support this kind of business." Rather than discrediting business owners as anti-school or anti-charity, Christiansen-Heller's words prove that there is a beneficial and lasting future in community-based support for art education.

SOLUTION: USING ART AS A PREVENTATIVE MEASURE

The cost of dealing with those students who are not able to succeed in school is a problem which extends beyond campus boundaries to society-at-large. Angry and alienated because of racial prejudice, unemployable because they lack the literacy and technical skills increasingly required by the modern job market, they often turn to crime. In Oakland today, school age children are currently incarcerated in juvenile detention facilities, where it costs a great deal a year to house each inmate. The problems of financing school failures can also be viewed as a justification for art education. Studies of the problems of incarcerated youth show that the great majority did poorly in school, often because of their inability find a place where they could feel accepted and establish an identity. Students who fail classes, fight with peers, act out in class and drop out of school, can also be characterized as students who have not been made to feel welcome in school. In addition to fostering a sense of community, the arts, as much as any other academic or athletic activity, integrate students. Students' interests in the arts cross racial or ethnic foundations. In Oakland, the ethnic and racial composition of bands, orchestras, art projects and performing groups is as varied as are our student bodies. Working together in friendship and with common interests, students drawn to art projects are offered a way to participate in and contribute to their school community.

CHALLENGE: UPDATING CLASSROOM PEDAGOGY

The epidemic of failure in inner city schools, with dropout rates as high as 70% between the seventh and twelfth grades in urban schools and test scores in the lowest quartile, begs us to take a frank and self-critical look at what we are doing in the classroom. Our charge to educate children from a variety of ethnic, linguistic, and economic backgrounds is forcing us to acknowledge where standard classroom practices are failing. We are in real need of classroom practices which do not depend on authority models that feed off of, or worse yet, create feelings of being devalued, and which do not present didactic teacher-centered instruction as the only way to learn. If there is an insidious effect on students' self-conception when they are cast as passive learners who must receive knowledge as presented and interpreted by higher authority, then conversely, there must be a sense of liberation and empowerment when students come to realize that they do not have to depend on higher authority for their own discoveries in making sense of the world.

A study conducted by the Oakland School District designed to evaluate the kind of instruction that students receive, found that while equal amounts of classroom time were devoted to instruction across the educational and socioeconomic levels, this instruction was too often teacher directed. As a result, less than 2% of classroom time was spent on such important matters as open-ended problem solving, debate of moral and ethical issues, and interactive collaboration (Institute for Effective Leadership, 1990). These findings reached across all schools and student ability levels, reminding us that all children require improved pedagogy which casts them as active learners, learners who want to take responsibility for creating and using knowledge.

In Oakland we know first hand that working with ethnically diverse students also means working with linguistically diverse students and this fact has led to the realization of how language-dependent instruction in our classrooms is. While interviewing art teachers for this article it was not uncommon to hear classroom situations such as the following described: a bilingual primary class with 30 students, 28 of whom spoke Cantonese as their primary language, one who spoke Russian and one who spoke a West African language; or, a class of 27 5th/6th grade Limited English Proficient students combined at a year-round school, with one student arriving two thirds of the way through the year speaking no English whatsoever. The students in these classes will and do fail if their only avenue for instruction is through the English language. They rightfully become frustrated when instruction is lowered in its intellectual content because of their limitations in English— they need to continue to take on learning challenges as they learn a second language, rather than having to wait until after they learn the second language. We cannot rely solely on bilingual teachers and ESL departments to handle this demand in our classrooms; this year the State of California alone is thousands of teachers short of the projected number of credentialed bilingual teachers needed by the public schools.

A direct extension of inadequate pedagogy is the standardized testing we have relied upon to evaluate our students' learning. Art educators have long felt the inadequacies of standardized testing. With its reliance on items which can be met with discreet, quantifiable answers, standardized testing has left them and their discipline completely out of the evaluation picture. The fact that art has not been testable is often extended to mean that it cannot be evaluated nor can it be put on the same level of importance as other subjects which can be tested in this standardized way. The truth is that good art instruction calls for equally if not more rigorous intellectual skills than standardized tests. Art calls for the ability to conceptualize. It requires the student to visualize a creation before creating it. It calls for imagination; the imagination of places, times, scenes perhaps never before experienced. We all know what a fine job science fiction has done of predicting most of today's technology. Artists

compose, communicate, express and evoke feelings far beyond the quality of expression test items can possibly reflect. What collection of multiple choice questions could prove a student's knowledge of perspective as well as the drawings illustrating this article?

Solution: Design a curriculum around concepts and values

The purpose and design of curriculum plays an important part in determining the status of the arts. If the curriculum is intended to drill students in basic skills and to teach by rote the rules and facts related to a subject matter, there will be no place for the arts in the classroom. If, on the other hand, the purpose of the curriculum is to give students access to powerful ideas, the arts have a central place. Powerful ideas consist of important concepts, insightful theories, values, and issues in a discipline. They embrace the ethical and moral questions with which all of us struggle. In rewriting our curriculum in Oakland, we formed representative committees for each academic subject, and asked the teachers within each to identify the powerful ideas of their disciplines. These ideas became both the foundation and framework for Core Curriculum, which advocates learning powerful ideas from an early age and transferring them across the disciplines.

"Learning," art educator Elliot Eisner tells us, "Takes place when the abstract idea can be connected to an image in our experience" (1990). Eisner's words remind us that the arts not only contribute their own powerful ideas to the curriculum, they also provide concrete experiences by which students can understand the abstract ideas of other academic subject matters. The perspective art assignment which illustrates this chapter was designed by a teacher looking for learning objectives which could link the two grade levels combined within her elementary classroom. The assignment's requirement that the students visualize and draw perspective in railroad tracks disappearing into the horizon offers students the opportunity, through the concrete experience of drawing, to experiment with new knowledge. The children know that their drawings need to look like what they see in the real world. They know that things look smaller as distance increases, and they know they have to learn certain techniques to create the illusion of nearness and distance. In creating perspective, they have learned that how reality looks depends on where you stand, and that what you see is partly what your mind creates, that perspective is subjective. While the children may not yet have words to express these sophisticated ideas, they will know them experientially.

The following excerpt from an interview with the teacher of the perspective exercise illustrates how important ideas and experience come together in the rigorous work of learning through art. When asked what she felt were the most difficult concepts for students to learn in this assignment, Ms. LaTouche identified the creation of an illusion of reality - both in perspective and color:

> I'm very particular about insisting that they understand that the further the ties get away not only the more narrow they are (*she points to the width of the individual railroad ties*) but they're

more narrow this way (*she points to the distance in between the individual ties*)... Because they would make every line the same thickness all the way up. So, I did a lot of nagging. I know they can do it. Before I give them this lesson I've known my kids a long time and I've given them a lot of opportunities to use rulers. I put a big piece of paper up on the wall and I say the directions are not to draw your first horizontal line in the middle, but to draw it closer to a third of the way from the top. And so they have to have some experience with a ruler before you even get here ... I also tell them that when they're looking at a field you never see one color. And we spread all our crayons out and we look at all the colors that could possibly be used. And of course I have some students that refuse to listen to me. But there are some students that say, "OK. I could use green but I could use more than one green and I could make some darker and some lighter and I could put some yellow in there." And what you're doing, you're just expanding their minds to accept another idea.

As the children respond to the assignment, they calculate the placements of objects, the ratio of size to location of the object to create the illusion of distance, the point from which the audience or observer of the drawing viewing the scene, the composition of color, so that in one project they work with several powerful ideas: illusion, ratio and audience, to name just three. The opportunities for discussion and explication of these ideas is where art is a powerful vehicle for "expanding minds" to accept new ideas.

Art is well suited to furthering a curriculum designed around powerful ideas and values even when it is not being taught as the focal academic subject. In a bilingual primary grade classroom, a teacher uses art as one of many tools in planning a class party. The teacher has deftly designed party planning into a lesson which asks the young students to read, write, discuss and debate, and calculate. But it is when the students are asked to illustrate their party lists that important issues surface for discussion and decision. The following is an excerpt from field note observations of the party planning lesson:

> When students are asked what they would like to eat at their party they call out suggestions which the teacher records on the board. Students are asked to illustrate the list to prove that they understand the translations between English and Cantonese. The students' pictures spark a conversation about the difference between Chinese, American, and African party food. Once the list is complete, a survey is conducted: How many people would like each item listed? Cookies—only 3 people raise their hands. Three out of 30 students want cookies - is the percentage high enough to justify bringing in cookies? If one person brings in a batch or box of cookies that will be at least 20 cookies, how many cookies would each of the 3 cookie people need to eat in order to finish all the cookies? How does the class feel wasting food?

SOLUTION: USE ART TO OVERCOME THE LIMITATIONS OF LANGUAGE

In addition to raising and illustrating powerful ideas, art is an excellent means of sheltering instruction of any academic subject for English language learners. The following excerpt from an interview with a middle school teacher demonstrates how the use of an art project can allow teachers to maintain the depth of their subject area when working with students of varying levels of proficiency in the English language .

> You'll get that occasional child that just comes right here, right from another country and can't say "Hello" even. That's the student that I had. And he was totally coached by his Vietnamese-speaking peers in the class. I didn't know how much he could take and transfer. And use. And that was the real assessment. His assessment was the construction of the module. He was able to demonstrate through that module his understanding of a self-supporting structure up in space that would be run solely on the solar light it would capture. This told me a lot. Where the children in my class have a lot of social language, I wasn't quite sure where their academic level of fluency in Vietnamese was until I could see it expressed ... To the child that's different art may be the only means of assessing- in math and science and social studies and in reading. That may be it.

This teacher's approach to teaching science through art sheltered, and enriched, her students' learning on several levels: it enabled the brand new English learner to express his sophisticated knowledge of science and space; it honored the talents of her bilingual students; it encouraged her more advanced English learners to use their knowledge of English and school to enrich their native language; it provided both herself and her students with a genuine, multileveled assessment of all the powerful ideas and sills learned in this lesson.

CONCLUSION

Art transmits culture to the young, to the generations that follow. Many children today are cut off from the many avenues by which it comes to children. Conquest, colonization and its deliberate efforts to disconnect conquered people from language, art and culture, erosion of the extended family and radical changes in family composition, and the economic necessity of the salaries of two working parents, as well as other factors have greatly reduced the amount of time adults and children have together, and with that the opportunities for children to feel connected to their heritage.

The arts play an essential and powerful role in passing on the culture, values and hopes they embody. Whether the arts be the masterworks of a people or the humble folk tales and family craftings, they embody and ideas, images in concrete ways upon which children build language, concepts and understandings, and other abstractions. Art is a way to provide the image to which learners later connect the idea to be grasped.

It is imperative that superintendents and other educational leaders be aware of the powerful role the arts can play in helping them achieve the goals for which they are held accountable: academic learning and basic skills. We who have these responsibilities can learn from teachers who teach the arts not only for their intrinsic worth. but also for their powerful promise they carry for other valuable learning.

References

California Department of Education. (1993). *Second to none: A vision of the new California high school.* Sacramento, CA: Author.

Eisner, E. (1992). *Phi Delta KapDan, 73.*

Fliegel, S. (1993). *Miracle in East Harlem: The fight for choice in public education.* New York: Time Books.

Institute for Effective Leadership. (1990). *Evaluation of teaching and learning behaviors in Oakland unified school district.* Oakland, CA: Author.

Oakland Unified School District. (1994). *Education plan.* Oakland, CA: Author.

Public Schools of the City of Oakland. (1868). *Department of public schools by laws of the board of education, and the rules and regulations of the Public schools of the city of Oakland.* San Francisco: Edward Bosqui.

Tyack, D., & Hasnot, E. (1982). *Managers of virture: Public school leadership in America 1820–1980.* New York: Basic Books.

White, E. C. (1993, May 18). Children's art has a purpose. *San Francisco Chronicle.*

38

PREPARING PRESERVICE TEACHERS TO TEACH MULTICULTURAL LITERATURE

Arlette Ingram Willis and Violet J. Harris

UNIVERSITY OF ILLINOIS AT URBANA-CHAMPAIGN

Several years ago during a final field experience a prospective teacher wrote:

> Both Willie and Elisha are the stereotypical "scary" African-American male(s). They are very tall, muscular, and dark. However, it has been wonderful for me, as a person with very little contact with African-Americans, to have these two young men in class.

This statement was made by one of our "top" students. A student who had excelled during her academic undergraduate education and one who received an uncontested "high rating" as a prospective teacher educator from her supervisors and cooperating teachers. The student is not a "bad" person. However, her journal entry reacquaints us with the notion that understandings of race, culture, and ethnicity are ever present in our consciousness. Until recently, it has been considered "polite not to notice" incidents of racism in education (hooks & West, 1991). As bell hooks (1992) has observed in similar instances, "For my colleagues, racism expressed in everyday encounters … is only an unpleasantness to be avoided, not something to be confronted or challenged. It is just something negative disrupting the good time, better not to notice and pretend it's not there" (p. 61). However, racism is here as an ugly unfortunate part of life in American society. Racist acts, unintentionally committed by well-intended folk, are a part of the lived reality, in and out of school, for culturally and linguistically diverse children. How can we better educate preservice teachers to understand the relationship among language, culture, and literacy as they prepare to teach all of our children?

The student's entry served as a wake-up call for us. First, the student has described the men, all the important ones, in our lives – fathers, friends, husband, brothers, and sons. She has also revealed that she suffers greatly from stereotypical notions – notions perpetuated in media about African-American males. What other stereotypical notions might she harbor: African Americans are poor students? Or worse, African-American parents are not interested in the education of their children? Do we want someone whose limited and biased understanding of African-Americans teaching our children? No. Second, we were prompted to consider whether or not other students in our classes also held similar viewpoints and stereotypical notions about culturally and linguistically diverse groups. Finally, we were encouraged to examine the stereotypical notions of race that all of us carry.

As unpleasant as the student's journal entry was, it has challenged us to confront the necessity of preparing teacher educators for the rapidly changing public school population. Current estimates of school populations reveal a rising number of children from African, Asian, and Latino backgrounds and speculate that by the year 2000 (only 4 years from now) one out of every three Americans will be a person of color (*The Nation Prepared*, 1986). By way of comparison, recent statistics of preservice educators suggest that they are: European American (92%), female (75%), and middle class (80%) (Fuller, 1992; Ross & Smith, 1992). What should students learn in their undergraduate training that will predispose them to have a more democratic approach and less racialized attitude toward all their future students?

Our university, like many throughout the country (Bulter & Schmitz, 1992) requires that all undergraduate students take at least one non Western course. The intent of the legislation was to help diversify the students experiences and to help them acknowledge and respect differing perspectives. In addition, there was the tacit assumption that students would also want to investigate more closely the domestic minority groups in this country. However, conversations with undergraduates reveal that they have taken anything from Chinese painting to Chilean basket weaving. While not the intent of the requirement, students are often able to skirt the requirement by taking such courses. The intent of the requirement is to prepare students for diversity within their future careers; currently, the requirement is unenforceable. It is clear that such feeble attempts to broaden student knowledge bases are not what students need as they move from collegiate life to the work force. They need more than a surface acquaintance with issues of diversity. They need a series of courses that would help them understand the domestic minority and new immigrant populations that are appearing in growing numbers in America's public schools (Ross & Smith, 1992).

In teacher education we cannot trust the responsibility to anyone else or any other course; the responsibility is ours. We are obligated to make changes in our courses that will better prepare all students to meet the changing demographics of America's classrooms with high expectations for all students, literature that would validate the life experiences of all students, and instructional methods that are culturally sensitive and responsive. We believe that the most effective way to reform and improve literacy education begins in our colleges and universities by better informing and preparing prospective teacher educators to address their own ethnicity, learn the historical and social experiences of domestic minority groups, construct new understandings of the role of culture in language, literacy, literature, and empowerment in schooling (Barrera, 1992). Therefore, it becomes imperative that multicultural teacher education courses, and multicultural literature courses, not merely *teach* about multicultural education, but that they *become* multicultural environments.

THEORETICAL PERSPECTIVE

In this chapter we will review three distinct but interrelated areas of research: multicultural teacher education, social constructivist theories of school based literacy, and multicultural literature. Each area has received considerable attention in the professional literature and may serve as frameworks for developing courses to better educate preservice teachers for the changing student populations. Recent census projections of a growing culturally and linguistically diverse school population by the year 2000 have sounded an alarm to teacher educators to begin to better prepare prospective teachers for a changing student body. Educators have noticed that while the school population is growing increasingly diverse (linguistically and culturally), the teacher education population continues to be dominated by European American females. The university and college faculties instructing them are also predominantly (94%) European American and middle class (Fuller, 1992). Second, the concerns of educators are framed in discussions of teacher/student understandings and interactions (Au, 1993; Delpit, 1988), the cultural gap between the school and communities (Au, 1980; Cook-Gumprez, Gumprez, & Simons, 1981; Heath, 1983), and effective instructional strategies for children in multicultural settings (Au, 1993; Barrera, 1992). Popular and professional literature on the need for improved multicultural education programs, in its varying forms – cultural awareness, cultural sensitivity, human understanding,

and ethnic studies – as part of teacher education programs is filled with discussions of knowledge bases and understandings necessary to improve the education of culturally and linguistically diverse students. Yet, the professional literature lacks a framework for preservice course design, instruction, and evaluation. This chapter will provide readers with a glance into the complexity of conjoining the work of several theorists from various domains into a workable course that trains teachers to use and teach multicultural literature as one response to meeting the challenge of teacher preparation. As a way of organizing the many theoretical positions that supply the underlying structure of multicultural literature we will offer a brief review of three broad domains: multicultural education, school-based literacy, and the changing role of the canon.

Theoretical Notions About What Constitutes Multicultural Teacher Education

It is important to understand that multicultural literature is a subset of a broader domain of knowledge: multicultural education. Three particularly influential theorists have offered insight into different ways of thinking about multicultural education and how it is conceived and taught. First, Sleeter and Grant (1988/1993) have suggested five different ways educators can think about multicultural education. They suggest (a) teaching the exceptional and culturally different, (b) human relations, (c) single-group studies, (d) multicultural education, and (e) education that is multicultural and social reconstructionist.

Second, the work of McCarthy (1993) has also described different ways of thinking about multicultural education. He argues that there are three general approaches: "*cultural understanding* suggests that all cultural groups have parity and cultural differences are recognized, *cultural competence* suggests that cultural pluralism should have a central place in the school curriculum, and *cultural emancipation* suggests that a reformist multicultural curriculum can boost school success and economic futures of minority youth" (pp. 291–293). McCarthy maintains that to deny the importance of race, as central to the debate of multicultural education, is to hinder real progress toward change.

Third, James Banks (1994), a noted authority on multicultural education, reacquaints his readers with his 1988 outline of approaches to multicultural curriculum reform. The approaches are: "*the contributions approach*—that focuses on heroes, holidays, and discrete cultural elements; *the additive approach*—that adds content, concepts, themes, and perspectives to the curriculum without changing its structure; *the transformation approach*—where the structure of the curriculum is changed to enable students to view concepts, issues, events, and themes from the perspective of diverse ethnic and cultural groups; and *the social action approach*—where students make decisions on important social issues and take actions to help solve them" (p. 25).

Importantly, in his 1994 text, Banks identifies two opposing groups that have debated over the content of school literacy instruction. The groups are known as the traditionalist and the multiculturalist. Simply stated, the traditionalist refers to those individuals who wish to retain the literary canon. The multiculturalist refers to those individuals who wish to broaden the canon to include the works of women and people of color. We, too, will use these terms for ease of reference throughout this chapter.

The body of literature that addresses the teaching of multicultural education courses to preservice teachers is also an important consideration to include in this review. It is to this body of research that we will now turn.

Theoretical Notions About Teaching Multicultural Education Courses to Preservice Teachers

As noted by Willis and Meachem (in press) the majority of the empirical research on multicultural teacher preparation has emphasized the description and evaluation of curricular innovations designed to improve the multicultural preparedness of predominantly white preservice teachers (Burstein & Cabello, 1989; Cooper, Beare, & Thorman, 1990; Ladson-Billings, 1991; Larke, Wiseman, & Bradely, 1990). The research focuses on either expanding the multicultural knowledge base of preservice teachers or increasing the receptivity of white preservice teachers to the task of teaching children of color. Of interest to researchers has also been the assessment of attitudes of preservice teachers related to issues of race, culture, and inequality (Ginsburg & Newman, 1985; King, 1991; Watson & Roberts, 1988). Several noted researchers and cultural theorists (hooks, 1992; Ladson-Billings, 1994; Sleeter, 1994) have commented that the issue of race must not be ignored, dismissed, or subsumed under the multicultural label. Race, when discussed has usually focused on people of color. This discursive slant has the effect of concealing the concept of white identity or "whiteness" from critical indention into the discourse of multicultural education (Willis & Meacham, in press). Consequently, white preservice teachers are not provided with the opportunity to examine their own racial and cultural identities and to investigate the influences of such identities on their efforts to teach children from different racial, class, cultural and linguistic backgrounds. McIntosh (1990) asserts that, the absence of a racial discourse on whiteness reinforces the widely accepted myth that whiteness is "morally neutral, normal, and average, and also ideal" (p. 32). Nieto (1992) argues the same point in a somewhat different manner. She states "white people, as the majority of U.S. society, do not often think of themselves as ethnic which is a term they reserve for other, more easily identifiable groups. ... Whiteness is an important factor, but it is not an exclusively determining one in defining a group. The term European American also implies culture, something that many European Americans lament they do not have" (p. 16).

The ethnographic research of Christine Sleeter (1993), among others, with in-service teachers suggests the need for more extensive training at the preservice level. Sleeter's 2-year study documents the voluntary involvement of in-service teachers in multicultural education workshops. During the 2-year study she observed the following: teachers' exposure to multicultural education workshops and activities, teachers in their classrooms, and individual interviews (p. 159). Her data reveal that there is little apparent transfer of multicultural knowledge gained or activities to classroom practice by in-service teachers (p. 160). Therefore, Sleeter argues that preservice teacher education programs may offer the optimal conditions for effecting change in teacher understanding and knowledge of multicultural education (p. 160).

A second domain of knowledge that is helpful to review when considering the teaching of multicultural literature courses is the research on literacy, more specifically school-based literacy.

Theoretical Notions of School-Based Literacy

Several contemporary positions on literacy serve to enlighten our understanding of how literacy is defined in the field and how it is defined in practice. In this section we will offer a brief look at several definitions. First, Cook-Gumprez (1986) describes two competing definitions of school literacy that are useful in our discussion of the role of literacy training during preservice education. She states, "inherent in our contemporary attitude to literacy and schooling is a confusion between a prescriptive view of literacy, as a statement about the values and uses of knowledge, and a descriptive view of literacy, as cognitive abilities which are promoted and assessed through schooling" (p. 14). Second, a more expansive definition of how literacy is conceptualized is offered by Freire and Macedo (1987). They suggest that, "literacy becomes a meaningful construct to the degree that it is viewed as a set of practices that functions to either empower or disempower people. In the larger sense, literacy is analyzed according to whether it serves a set of cultural practices that promotes democratic and emancipatory change" (p. 141). Further, they clarify their position on literacy by noting that, "for the notion of literacy to become meaningful it has to be situated within a theory of cultural production and viewed as an integral part of the way in which people produce, transform, and reproduce meaning (p. 142). Third, more general discussions of literacy define literacy as *functional, cultural,* or *critical*. Each of these concepts also refers to very different ways of thinking about literacy. *Functional literacy* refers to mastery of the skills needed to read and write as measured by standardized forms of assessment. This view of literacy is similar to Cook-Gumprez's notion of a descriptive view of literacy. The functional view promotes literacy as a cognitive set of skills that is universal, culturally neutral, and equally accessible through schooling and based on a positivistic ideology of learning. Further, this view is heavily dependent on the use of standardized testing measures as a proving ground for literacy acquisition. Most basal reading series and programmed reading approaches embrace the functional/descriptive view of literacy.

Cultural literacy is a term that is most often associated with E. D. Hirsch's 1987 book, *Cultural Literacy: What every American needs to know.* Hirsch defines cultural literacy as "the network of information that all competent readers possess. It is the background information, stored in their minds, that enables them to take the point, grasping the implications, relating what they read to the unstated context which alone gives meaning to what they read" (p. 2). Cook-Gumprez (1986) labeled this form of literacy "prescriptive." In effect, this form of cultural literacy validates language forms, experiences, literature, and histories of some and marginalizes or ignores the language forms, experiences, literature, and histories of others. In the United States, the prescriptive view can be seen in the use of standard English, Eurocentric ways of knowing and learning, a Eurocentric literary canon, and a conventional unproblematic rendering of U.S. history. This form of the cultural/prescriptivist view marginalizes the pluralistic composition of American society by devaluing the language, contributions, and histories of some groups. Traditional or conventional approaches to school-based literacy take this form. McLaren (1988) argues that there is a second form of cultural literacy. He writes that this form of cultural literacy "advocates using the language standards and cultural information students bring into the classroom as legitimate and important constituents of learning" (p. 214). Cultural literacy, thus described, suggests that the language and experiences of each student who enters the classroom should be respected and nurtured. This form of cultural literacy recognizes that there are differences in language forms, experiences, literature, and histories of students that will affect literacy learning. Social constructivist theories fall into this prescriptive/cultural literacy category. These approaches to literacy emphasize the active engagement of learners in making meaning from print, the social context of literacy learning, and the importance in recognizing individual and cultural differences.

Critical literacy refers to the ideologies that underlie the relationship between power and knowledge in society. The work of Brazilian educator Paulo Freire has been influential to U.S. efforts to adopt a critical literacy position. Freire, among others, suggest that literacy is more than constructing meaning from print. Literacy also must include the ability to understand oneself and one's relationship in the world. Giroux's (1987a) discussion is worth quoting here at length:

> As Paulo Freire and others have pointed out, schools are not merely instructional sites designed to transmit knowledge; they are also cultural sites. As sites, they generate and embody support for particular forms of culture as is evident in the school's support for specific ways of speaking, the legitimating of distinct forms of knowledge, the privileging of certain histories and patterns of authority, and the confirmation of particular ways of experiencing and seeing the world. Schools often give the appearance of transmitting a common culture, but they, in fact, more often than not, legitimate what can be called a dominant culture (p. 176).

Giroux goes on to state that:

> At issue here is understanding that student experience has to be understood as part of an interlocking web of power relations in which some groups of students are often privileged over others. But if we are to view this insight in an important way, we must understand that it is imperative for teachers to critically examine the cultural backgrounds and social formations out of which their students produce the categories they use to give meaning to the world. For teachers are not merely dealing with students who have individual interests, they are dealing primarily with individuals

whose stories, memories, narratives, and readings of the world are inextricably related to wider social and cultural formations and categories. This issue here is not merely one of relevance but one of power (1987a, p. 177).

Similarly, Apple (1992) has argued for nearly a decade that, "…it is naive to think of the school curriculum as neutral knowledge. … Rather, what counts as legitimate knowledge is the result of complex power relations and struggles among identifiable class, race, gender, and religious groups" (p. 4). Critical literacy draws attention to the historical, political, cultural, and social dimensions of literacy. Most important, this form of literacy focuses on power relations in society and how knowledge and power are interrelated. Educationalists, practitioners in particular, have not yet fully grasped this position of literacy. The other forms of literacy, functional/descriptive and cultural/prescriptive do not include, among other things, the notion of power relations in literacy instruction.

Philosophically, social constructivist notions (a form of prescriptive/cultural literacy) may be seen as comparable to those espoused by critical literacy. From the schema theorists of the early 1980s to the social constructivist theories of the 1990s, literacy development is understood to be a "meaning making process" — that is, socially mediated (Meek, 1982). Drawing primarily on the work of Goodman (1989; Halliday 1975; Vygotsky, 1978), a number of literacy researchers have stressed the universality of language learning. For example, Goodman's discussion of the philosophical stance of whole language is that:

> At the same time that whole language sees common strengths and universals in human learning, it expects and recognizes differences among learners in culture, value systems, experience, needs, interests and language. Some of these differences are personal, reflecting the ethnic, cultural, and belief systems of the social groups pupils represent. Thus teachers of whole language programs value differences among learners as they come to school and differences in objectives and outcome as students progress through school (p. 209).

However, we would argue that the role of culture in social constructivist theories is not as well defined as it needs to be in a pluralistic or multicultural society. While it is fair to say that unidimensional views of culture would not be supported by social constructivist, it is also fair to say that the multilayered complexity of culture, especially the cultures of historically oppressed groups, is not explicitly addressed by them either. By way of example, we will examine the prescriptive/cultural literacy foundation of whole language.

Goodman (1986) argues that "language begins as means of communication between members of the group. Through it, however, each developing child acquires the life view, the cultural perspective, the ways of meaning particular to its own culture" (p.11). But this definition fails to acknowledge that in addition to acquiring culturally "neutral" knowledge, some children must also acquire a Eurocentric cultural perspective to be successful in school. It is not sufficient to suggest that the language and culture of every student is welcomed, supported, and nurtured in school without explicitly addressing the power relations in institutions, social practice, and literature that advantage some and hinder others (Delpit, 1988; Reyes, 1992). School-based literacy, in its varying forms, fails to acknowledge explicitly the richness of the cultural ways of knowing, forms of language other than standard English, and the interwoven relationship among power, language, and literacy that silences many children of color (Fine, 1987). To fail to attend to the plurality of diversity within the United States—and to fail to take seriously the historic past and the social and political contexts that have sustained it—is to dismiss the cultural ways of knowing, language, experiences and voices of children from diverse linguistic and cultural backgrounds. This is not to imply that programs not based on such theories need to be scrapped. It does mean that social constructivist theories need to be reworked to include the complexities of culture that are currently absent. It will also mean that teacher education will need to: (1) make explicit the relationship among culture, language, literacy, and power; and (2) train teachers to use cultural information to support and nurture the literacy development of all the students who enter their classrooms.

It is important to note that both multiculturalist and those who endorse holistic notions of literacy point to the social construction of knowledge and the importance of the role of culture in school-based literacy. There is an important difference, however, in how each group of theorists defines culture. Research by Delpit (1988), among others, suggest that culturally and linguistically diverse children must adopt a knowledge and proficiency in "school-literacy" which differs from their knowledge of the home and community understandings of language. Multiculturalists argue, that is not sufficient for holistic programs to merely acknowledge that children bring to school with them cultural and linguistic differences. Nor is it sufficient to suggest that the language and culture of every student is welcomed, supported, and nurtured in school without also explicitly addressing the power relations in institutions, social practice, and literature that advantage some and hinder others (Delpit, 1988; Reyes, 1992). Recent ethnographic literacy research studies of the role of culture in elementary school and community environments of linguistically and culturally diverse groups have suggested that traditional and new approaches to literacy instruction have not prepared teachers for linguistic and cultural difference (Barrera, 1992, Gutierrez, 1992; Reyes, 1992; Willis, 1995).

Preservice literacy teachers need more than knowledge of cultural and linguistic differences of U.S. populations. It is important that teachers understand the cultural and linguistic differences in ways that are affirming and supportive. Moreover, it is crucial that teachers know how to support cultural and linguistic differences toward literacy development. They also need experiences and skills to take with them into their classes (Banks, 1994).

Multiculturalists have adopted more inclusive notions of culture that explicitly include the cultures of the dominant as well as domestic minority groups. They consider gender, language, social class, age and sexual preference in definitions of each cultural group. Moreover, multiculturalists acknowledge the diversity within all domestic minority groups and within European American culture.

ADOPTING A MULTICULTURAL PERSPECTIVE

Jackson and Solis' (1995) have observed that "in the discourse on multiculturalism that has emerged since the mid-1970s, the primary focus of the literature and research has been on the curriculum and the canon" (p. 6). So too, research efforts toward a better understanding of multicultural education have focused on the canon and the curriculum and instructional strategies. We will briefly explore each area as it relates to the teaching of multicultural literature.

The Canon and the Curriculum

The content of the high school English curriculum has been the subject of many heated debates, conferences and journals in the last few years. The battle is being waged by two opposing groups. The first group consists of supporters of the canon (Bloom, 1987; D' Sousa, 1991; Hirsch, 1987). The second group consists of those who wish to see the canon reconceptualized (Gates, 1992; McCarthy, 1993; Morrison, 1992).

At issue is the retention of the traditional canon or the expansion of the canon to include works by women and authors of color. Retention of the canon means the continued use of the same "classic" literature that has been the staple for nearly a century. Reconceptualization of the canon means, among other things, the inclusion of what is commonly defined as multicultural literature. Harris (1992) defines multicultural literature as "...literature that focuses on people of color (such as African-Americans, Asian Americans, Hispanic Americans and Native Americans), on religious minorities (such as the Amish or Jewish), on regional cultures (such as Appalachian and Cajun), or the disabled, and on the aged" (p. 175). One can read most discussions of the debate, however, as centering on the inclusion of literature written by women and authors from diverse backgrounds as part of the set of works that are important for study.

Karen Peterson (1994) reports on a recent survey by The College Board citing the following top 20 books as those most frequently recommended for high school seniors and college freshmen: *The Scarlet Letter, Huckelberry Finn, The Great Gatsby, Lord of the Flies, Great Expectations, Hamlet, To Kill a Mockingbird, The Grapes of Wrath, The Odyssey, Wuthering Heights, The Catcher in the Rye, The Crucible, Gulliver's Travels, Julius Caesar, Of Mice and Men, The Old Man and the Sea, Pride and Prejudice, The Read Badge of Courage, Romeo and Juliet,* and *Death of a Salesman* (*USA Today*, 1994, December 27). According to spokesman Fred Moreno, The College Board examined curriculum guides, private school reading lists, research surveys, federal reports and other sources in conducting the survey. A review of the titles notes that the list favors the literature of European or European American males and includes only three titles by women authors. The list does not include any works by authors from historically underrepresented groups. The marginalization of the works by women and people of color prompted traditionalist E. D. Hirsch to observe that "This is a very traditional list that doesn't reflect new thinking. ... It is clearly defective in not including books such as *Black Boy* (Richard Wright), *Song of Solomon* (Toni Morrison) and *I Know Why the Caged Bird Sings* (Maya Angleou)." He later predicted that it may take another decade before the list is more representative.

The most comprehensive look at secondary literature curricula is offered by Arthur Applebee (1993) in his paper "Literature in the secondary school: Studies of curriculum and instruction in the United States." In this paper he examines literature and literature instruction in public and private schools. Applebee notes that literature instruction includes a variety of facets, but none so important as the book-length works used to convey a sense of who and what literature is important to study.

Applebee's (1989, 1992) nationwide survey reports the consistent use of canonical literature in our nation's high schools. He cites the continual use of works by Shakespeare, Steinbeck, Dickens and Twain, yet few works by women and minority authors. [Applebee sites, similar traditional approaches to high school literature had been observed by Tanner (1903) and Anderson (1963)]. Further analysis by Applebee reveals only one European American female author and two African-American authors (one female, one male) among the top 50 listed authors. Applebee (1992) draws some important conclusions from his study:

(1) a comparison of the studies reveals little change in the nature of the selections in the 25-year period,
(2) marginal increases in titles by women and diverse authors, and
(3) few book-length works by women and diverse authors have entered the canon.

If Applebee's conclusion about the importance of book-length works is correct, students are receiving a very narrow view of what literature, values, and people are important. As Applebee (1991) puts it, "Whether intentional or not, schools have chosen to ignore diversity and assimilate everyone to the "classical" culture that found its way into schools before the turn of the century" (p. 235). He goes on to state that "we are failing in a fundamental way to open the gates of literacy to the majority of the students we teach." (p. 235). His suggestions for change include the challenge of expanding the canon to be more reflective of the history, life experiences, culture, and literature of all Americans. Applebee argues that the expansion of canon begins with preservice programs that require students to read and discuss book-length works written by authors of underrepresented groups. Moreover, Applebee suggests that preservice English courses may help students develop a repertoire of effective teaching strategies to use when teaching the literature.

Applebee's suggestion for canon expansion does not acknowledge the need for increased understandings of the role of culture and language in multicultural literature instruction. It is important to expand the canon, but expansion without sufficient understandings of the role of culture and language in the literature of diverse groups, will give preservice teachers inadequate knowledge by which to instruct students. Preservice teachers need more than a list of multicultural books to read and discuss, they need to understand the histories and cultures that support the writing of the literature. In addition, they need instructional strategies to help students understand, appreciate, and enjoy each work.

Graff's (1992) findings of the undergraduate English curricula offered nationwide suggest that there has been little substantive change in the literature offered to English majors. Generally, the literature that dominates college and high school English curriculum offers a very narrow view of the world; one that is not part of the cultural schema of every student. In addition, research by Au (1993) notes that most preservice teacher education courses are dominated by traditional transmission models of literacy instruction that support a mainstream middle-class perspective of literacy and inadequately address the needs of culturally or linguistically diverse students. Preservice teachers need to be taught strategies to make the implicit knowledge about the culture described in literature explicit to learners of different cultures. Giovanni (1994) declares that, "In the universities we have seen white men declare time and time again that they cannot teach women, they cannot teach Blacks, they cannot teach Native Americans, because they do not have any 'experience' in this area. Yet we who are Black and women and not white males are expected to teach literature written by them because it is 'universal'? I think not. It is called education because it is learned. You do not have to have had an experience in order to sympathize or empathize with the subject" (p. 109). Research on cultural schema has documented improved understanding, enjoyment and memory of literature that acknowledges and supports the cultural knowledge of readers (LeSound, 1988).

An important caveat is worth mentioning. Simply adding materials to the curriculum, without reforming the curriculum or training teachers, legitimates the continued use of the dominant cultural perspectives and paradigms in schools. Apple (1992) notes that "controversies over 'official knowledge' that usually center around what is included and excluded in textbooks really signify more profound political, economic, and cultural relations and histories. Conflicts over texts are often proxies for wider questions of power relations" (p. 5).

Instructional Strategies

Recent research on school literacy either ignores or minimizes the need to broaden teacher knowledge and understanding of cultural variables inherent in literacy programs (Garcia, Pearson, & Jimenez, 1994). Researchers and practitioners of school literacy approaches tend to discuss literacy with vague, muddled notions of the role and importance of cultural knowledge.

Au (1993) offers a theoretical framework for preservice elementary teachers founded on social constructivist notions of literacy instruction. The theoretical framework is based on field-based research conducted by several researchers in linguistically and culturally diverse settings including Au's (1980) work with Hawaiian children; Heath's (1983) research with working class African-American and European

American communities, schools, parents, children and teachers; and the Spindler and Spindler (1990) research among Menominee (Native American) people. An analysis of the findings of these researchers and others has led Au to conclude that what is needed is a redefinition of school literacy. Specifically she suggests that school literacy be redefined through types of texts; instruction centered on meaning; writing based on students experiences; culturally responsive instruction; and critical literacy (p. 30). Au argues that perhaps the most effective time to train teachers to think differently about the culture, language, and literacy development of culturally and linguistically diverse children and to learn how to create culturally responsive strategies and culturally sensitive interactional responses is during their preservice training.

Barrera's (1992) observation of elementary (K–6) classroom teachers' literacy instruction in culturally and linguistically diverse communities finds that in-service teachers exhibit "cultural gaps" in knowledge necessary for successful literacy development. She defines a "cultural gap" as a "void in teachers' knowledge bases about culture as it relates to literacy and literature" (p. 227). Her discovery of the "cultural gaps" exhibited by teachers in content selection and communication patterns and interactions has sounded an alarm in literacy theory and praxis. For example, Barrera reports content and communication "gaps in cultural knowledge" exhibited by the teachers. In content, she notes, the language and literature used in the classroom do not reflect the culture, language, histories and lives of the children but are dominated by literature written by European Americans that reflected themes, characters and experiences from the mainstream culture (p. 230). In the area of communication she has observed teachers' failure to understand the interactional patterns and shared meanings of the language of the children. Failure in this area has resulted in literacy activities that are more reflective of mainstream or "school" culture and literature than the culture, language and literature of the children in the classroom. Barrera explains that "The school culture can be seen to reflect the dominant class and, so too, the cultures of literacy and literature embedded within the school culture. For this reason, the teaching of literacy and literature are considered to be neither acultural nor neutral, but cultural and political" (p. 236).

Barrera's research reveals that in-service teachers are often unaware of the need to address cultural and linguistic difference in their selection of instructional strategies, interaction patterns and materials. She offers a theoretical framework for teaching about culture arguing for improved understandings in three knowledge dimensions (cultural, cross-cultural, and multicultural). Barrera defines each of the knowledge dimensions as: *cultural knowledge*—meaning making is culturally mediated and human meaning is cultural meaning; *cross-cultural knowledge*—literacy and literature are cultural phenomena and practices in literacy and literature differ across cultures; *multicultural knowledge*—cultures involve relations power and literacy teaching is culturally mediated" (p. 232). Finally, she points out that theories that guide teacher education programs need to make explicit the role of culture in literacy and to

train teachers to be culturally sensitive and responsive and seldom has the impact of the cultural knowledge of the teacher in decision making been considered. We suggest that an ideal place to begin is in preservice teacher education courses.

Some very interesting work is being conducted by Richard Beach (1994), Spears-Bunton (1992), Jordan and Purves (1993), and Willis (1995), among others, as researchers seek to understand how the use of multicultural literature affects teacher educators and students. Some research studies suggest that: (a) white high school and college students may be unaware of their biases toward multicultural literature, and (b) there may be a tacit resistance on the part of white high school, college and university students to multicultural literature. While others suggest that:(a) reading multicultural literature can improve understanding of self and others, and (b) discussion of multicultural literature can lead to behavioral and attitudinal change.

What appears clear to us from our work in the area is that new knowledge bases are needed by students in which they can begin to understand a more inclusive sociohistorical view of education, the role of literacy attainment in the United States, the role of culture in language and literacy acquisition and use, and the role of multicultural understandings of power relations within school settings and how these are practiced, intentionally or unintentionally by classroom teachers. Then, students can take their newly acquired knowledge into the classroom in terms of praxis, from the creation of an atmosphere of tolerance, high expectations for all students, the sensitive and careful selection of materials, informed choices of instruction and student-teacher interactions that welcome, respect, and acknowledge all learners. It is simply unacceptable to claim "I didn't know," there is an obligation to learn if you do not know.

In summary, researchers in each area of literacy above have suggested specific improvements in teacher education programs to better prepare prospective teachers for a culturally and linguistically diverse student body of the future. Moreover, a common notion expressed in each area is the belief that improved understanding(s) of the role of culture in literature instruction, during preservice education will improve the literature instruction for all students. As Reyes has pointed out, "one size does not fit all." Reyes (1992) argues that teachers use theories and strategies based upon research with mainstream populations, hoping that "…the high rate of success with process instruction reported for mainstream students will magically happen for culturally and linguistically diverse learners" (pp. 436–437). How can we build upon the theories of multicultural education and school-based literacy so that they enhance the literacy development of all children? We believe that teacher training in multicultural literature is one response.

We believe that courses in multicultural literature are an excellent starting point to develop the understandings preservice teachers need in multicultural education and literature. In such courses prospective teachers can learn to examine their own cultural and linguistic assumptions, confront their biases, and learn skills and practices that will enable them to respond to the literacy needs of all children in culturally sensitive and responsive ways. Banks (1994) describes the exposure of a multicultural perspective during preservice training as a way "to examine and clarify their recall and ethnic attitudes, and to develop the pedagogical knowledge and skills needed to work effectively with students from diverse cultural and ethnic groups" (p. vi).

EDUCATIONAL IMPLICATIONS

Several theoretical positions have proven influential in helping us design courses that address multicultural education, the social construction of knowledge (especially its role in literacy development), and multicultural literature. Philosophically, we have grounded our work on notions found in the critical literacy paradigm. In keeping with the critical literacy theory, we are not suggesting any set "how-to" rules. Later, in this section we will suggest several activities that have proven helpful to encouraging our students to adopt a more critical understanding of literacy. However, at this point it is important that we offer some contextualizing of critical literacy as it is being applied in U.S. contexts.

A starting point for a corresponding critical literacy pedagogy in U.S. schools is offered by Giroux (1987b):

> The type of critical pedagogy being proposed here is fundamentally concerned with student experience; it takes the problems and needs of the students themselves as its starting point. This suggests both confirming and legitimating the knowledge and experiences through which students give meaning to their lives. Most obviously, this means replacing the authoritative discourse of imposition and recitation with a voice capable of listening, retelling, and challenging the very grounds of knowledge and power.... It is important to stress that a critical pedagogy of literacy and voice must be attentive to the contradictory nature of student experience and voice and therefore established the grounds whereby such experience can be interrogated and analyzed with respect to both strengths and weaknesses. (p. 43)

Critical literacy, so defined, strongly supports current socioconstructivist theories espoused in new holistic approaches to school-based literacy programs. Most important, however, critical literacy theory goes beyond generic references to culture, and specifically acknowledges the historical and social contexts that have given rise to domestic minority cultures' language, literature, and experiences in the United States. Many have experimented with adopting Freire's pedagogical style to U.S. contexts (Shor, 1987).

In what follows we will describe how we have melded multicultural notions of knowledge about the role of history, language, and literacy, social constructivist notions of literacy and Freireian techniques in preservice English/Language Arts courses. At the onset let us state that we use literature, particularly the literature written by members of underrepresented domestic minority groups which has historically been minimized in schools and universities, as an avenue to discuss deeper issues of the affects of historical contexts on relationships of power, language, and literature. As Banks (1994) suggests:

> The most meaningful and effective way to prepare teachers to involve students in multicultural experiences that will enable them to know, care, and to participate in democratic action is to involve teachers in multicultural experiences that focus on these goals. When teachers have gained knowledge about cultural and ethnic diversity themselves, looked at that knowledge from different ethnic and cultural perspectives, and taken action to make their own lives and communities more culturally sensitive and diverse, they will have the knowledge and skills needed to help transform the curriculum canon as well as the hearts and minds of their students. (p. 28)

Several course experiences/activities illustrate how we have approached the task of teaching and using multicultural literature.

(1) We begin by creating atmospheres where it is safe to share who and what you believe without fear of punishment or reprisal. Next, there is a sense of colearnership within the classrooms. Our roles as teacher, colearner, and listener are best described as one of facilitation. Although we do relinquish a total nonauthoritative stance, in reality we do not completely relinquish our roles as teacher/educator because we constantly serve as sources of information in and outside of class. However, throughout our courses we do gradually transfer much of the responsibility for class content and discussions to the students. Thus, students become active critical constructors of our multicultural community. Our success has been enhanced by the enrollment of students who represent linguistic and cultural groups outside of the mainstream. In addition, we have called upon our colleagues, former students, staff, and community people to speak to our classes. It is important that our students hear many different voices speak about their life experiences, educational roadblocks, and engagement with literature. The firsthand experiences help our students better understand the complexity of multiculturalism and the importance of offering a balanced literary diet to their future students.

Students must, however, begin by participating in the course. Beginning the first moment they step into the classroom they are called upon to participate in some fashion, from learning the names of their classmates to moving furniture. Each student is required to participate in all activities. Great effort is made to create a safe, comfortable atmosphere during the first few weeks so that students can share with one another in an environment in which all listen and can respond in supportive manners.

(2) With Hansen-Krening's (1992) permission students respond to the following question on the first day of class, "How do your cultural perspectives affect the students you teach?" Following Hansen-Krening's technique, students are asked to respond to the same question on the final day of class. The responses are compared to graph changes in perspective as a result of participation in the course.

(3) Students are asked to explore their own ethnicity through the writing of an autobiographic essay which becomes part of classroom discussions over the next few weeks. Research by Britzman (1986) and Hansen-Krening (1992), among others, has shown that many preservice teachers are unaware of the cultural values, beliefs, and perspectives they bring to teaching. Several researchers have noted the importance of beginning by helping students acknowledge their

own cultural heritage and perspectives (Barrera, 1992; Britzman, 1986; Hansen-Krening, 1992).

(4) Students are asked to individually define commonly used, yet often misunderstood terms regarding multicultural education. This activity is followed by small group and large group discussions of the terms. Students are required to canvass the campus seeking the "person on the street" response to the same words. Finally, all responses are read, compared and contrasted to those offered by experts in the field.

(5) Students select a 'popular' text on issues of race, culture, or multicultural education. Students are asked to write a response to the reading that will be shared in the class. It is during the small group discussions that most students encounter perspectives that vary from their own. Small group discussions are followed by large group discussions where students share their perspectives with one another. Students may rethink their initial response after hearing the viewpoints of others.

(6) After writing, reading, talking, and viewing issues of diversity we move into theoretical discussions of teaching literature. The work of Rosenblatt (1933/1995) and Atwell (1987) forms the core of our discussions. However, we also read Au to balance our understanding of how to implement social constructivist theories in multicultural settings.

(7) We begin our wide reading of the multicultural literature section of the course with the selection of novels for grades 6–12. The novels are selected by small groups of students and represent each domestic minority group and European Americans. In an effort to share multicultural literature it is important not to dismiss the diversity within the European American community. Students select novels from a predetermined list created by the instructor.

(8) Each small group reads and responses to their novel. The members of the group are responsible for creating a packet of information on the novel that consists of a summary, a biography of the author, a list of pertinent historical facts and events which occurred when the novel was written and that cover the time period discussed in the novel, a lesson about the novel and supporting materials, and at least two reviews of the article. The novel packets will become a quick resource of activities and information for the students in the future.

In our courses we attempt to nurture the ability to think critically and reflectively about the integrated nature of knowledge, language, and literature. Our roles (teacher, colearner, and facilitator), the gradual release of power, and the voices and experiences of others help empower our students to make culturally sensitive and responsible instructional decisions, as well as to feel a deeper sense of commitment to the course and the subject matter.

Multicultural literature becomes a bridge we transverse to better understandings of ourselves, our history, and our society. Learning about multicultural literature requires that students read widely the literature of each domestic minority group. In addition, it is equally important that students are given opportunities to discuss their responses to the readings with others who have read the same novel. The discussions allow students to share their growing understandings, misunderstandings, and knowledge of different cultures. The in-class discussions allow students to hear one another's perspectives and revisit their own. The class, in effect, is socially constructing knowledge about culture and literature.

References

Apple, M. (1992). The text and cultural politics. *Educational Researcher, 21*(7) 4–11,19.

Applebee, A. (1989). *A study of book-length works taught in high school English courses.* Albany, NY: Center for the Learning and Teaching of Literature.

Applebee, A. (1991). Literature: Whose heritage? In E. H. Hiebert (Ed.), *Literacy for a diverse society: Perspectives, practices, and politics* (pp. 228–236). New York: Teachers College Press.

Applebee, A. (1992). Stability and change in the high school canon. *English Journal, 81*(5), 27–32.

Applebee, A. (1993). *Literature in the secondary school: Studies of curriculum and instruction in the United States.* Urbana, IL: National Council of Teachers of English.

Atwell, N. (1987). *In the middle: Writing, reading, and learning with adolescents.* Portsmouth, NH: Boynton/Cook.

Au, K. (1980). Participation structures in a reading lesson with Hawaiian children: An analysis of a culturally appropriate instructional event. *Anthropology and Education Quarterly, 11*(2), (91–115).

Au, K. (1993). *Literacy instruction in multicultural settings.* New York: Holt, Rinehart & Winston.

Banks, J. (1994). *An introduction to multicultural education.* Boston: Allyn & Bacon.

Barrera, R. (1992). The cultural gap in literature-based literacy instruction. *Education and Urban Society, 24*(2), 227–243.

Beach, R. (1994). *Research on readers' response to multicultural literature.* Paper presented at the annual meeting of the American Educational Research Association, New Orleans.

Bloom, A. (1987). *The closing of the American mind: How higher education has failed the democracy and impoverished the souls of today's students.* New York: Simon & Schuster.

Britzman, D. (1986). Cultural myths in the making of a teacher: Biography and social structure in teacher education. *Harvard Educational Review, 56*(4), 442–456.

Bulter, J., & Schmitz, B. (1992). Ethnic studies, women studies, and multiculturalism. *Change, 24*(1), 34–41.

Burstein, N. D., & Cabello, B. (1989). Preparing teachers to work with culturally diverse students: A teacher education model. *Journal of Teacher Education, 18,* 9–16.

Cook-Gumprez, J. (1986). *The social construction of literacy.* Cambridge: Cambridge Universtiy Press.

Cook-Gumprez, J., Gumprez, J., & Simons, H. (1981). *School home ethnography project* (Final Report). Washington, DC: National Institute of Education.

Cooper, A., Beare, P., & Thorman, J. (1990). Preparing teachers for diversity: A comparison of student teaching experiences in Minnesota and South Texas. *Action in Teacher Education, 12*(3), 1–5.

Delpit, L. (1988). The silenced dialogue: Power and pedagogy in educating other people's children. *Harvard Educational Review, 58,* 280–298.

D' Sousa, D., (1991). *Illiberal education: The politics of race and sex on campus.* New York:Free Press.

Fine, M. (1987). Silencing in public schools. *Language Arts,62*(2), 157–174.

Freire, P., & Macedo. (1987). *Literacy: Reading the word and the world.* South Hadley, MA: Bergin & Garvey.

Fuller, M. (1992). Monocultural teachers and multicultural students: A demographic clash. *Teaching Education, 4*(2), 87–93.

Garcia, G., Pearson, P., & Jimenez, R. (1994). *The at-risk situation: A synthesis of reading research* (Special Report). Champaign, IL: Center for the Study of Reading.

Gates, H. L. , Jr. (1992). *Loose canons: Notes on the culture wars.* New York: Oxford University Press.

Ginsburg, M., & Newman, K. (1985). Social inequalities: Schooling and teacher education. *Journal of Teacher Education, 36,* 49–54.

Giovanni, N. (1994). *Racism 101.* New York: William Morrow.

Giroux, H. (1987a). Critical literacy and student experience: Donald Graves' approach to literacy. *Language Arts, 64*(2), 175–181.

Giroux, H. (1987b). Introduction. In P. Freire & D. Macedo, *Literacy: Reading the word and the world.* Westport, CT:Bergin & Garvey.

Goodman, K. (1986). *What's whole language?* Portsmouth, NH: Heinemann.

Goodman, K. (1989). Whole-language research: Foundations and development. *Elementary School Journal, 90,* 207–221.

Graff, G.(1992). *Beyond the culture wars: How teaching the conflicts can revitalize American education.* New York: W. W. Norton.

Gutierrez, K. (1992). A comparison of instructional contexts in writing process classrooms with Latino children. *Education and Urban Society, 24,* 244–262.

Halliday, M. (1975). *Learn how to mean.* London: Edward Arnold.

Hansen-Krening, N. (1992). Authors of color: A multicultural perspective. *Journal of Reading, 36*(2) 124–129.

Harris, V. (1992). *Teaching multicultural literature in grades K–8.* Norwood, MA: Christopher.

Heath, S. (1983). *Ways with words: Language, life, and work in communities and classrooms.* Cambridge: Cambridge University Press.

Hirsch, E. D., Jr. (1987). *Cultural literacy: What every American needs to know.* New York: Houghton Mifflin.

hooks, b. (1992). *Black looks: Race and representation.* Boston:South End Press.

hooks, b. & West, C. (1991). Breaking bread: Insurgent black intellectual life. Boston: South End Press.

Jackson, S., & Solis', J. (1995). *Beyond the comfort zones: Multiculturalism and teacher education.* West Port, CT: Bergin & Garvey.

Jordan, S., & Purves, A. (1993). *Issues in the response of students to culturally diverse texts: A preliminary study.* Albany, NY: National Research Center on Literature Teaching and Learning.

King, J. E. (1991). Dysconscious racism: Ideology, identity, and the miseducation of teachers. *Journal of Negro Education, 60,* 133–146.

Ladson-Billings, G. (1991). Beyond multicultural illiteracy. *Journal of Negro Education, 60,* 147–156.

Ladson-Billings, G. (1994). *Your blues ain't like mine: Keeping issues of race and racism in the multicultural agenda.* Paper presented at the annual meeting of the American Educational Research Association, New Orleans.

Larke, P. J., Wiseman, D., & Bradley, C. (1990). The minority mentorship project: Changing attitudes of preservice teachers for diverse classrooms. *Action in Teacher Education, 12*(3), 5–11.

LeSound, S. (1988). Using an advance organizer to set the schema for a multicultural lesson. *Journal of Reading, 25,* 12–18.

McCarthy, C. (1993). After the canon: Knowledge and ideological representation in the multicultural discourse on curriculum reform. In C. McCarthy, & W. Crichlow, (Eds.). *Race identity and representation in education.* New York: Routledge.

McIntosh, P. (1989). White privilege: Unpacking the invisible knapsack. *Peace and Freedom,* 10–12.

McLaren, P. (1988). Culture or canon? Critical pedagogy and the politics of literacy. Book Review. *Harvard Education Review, 58*(2), 213–234.

Meek, M. (1982). *Learning to read.* Portsmouth, NH: Heinemann.

Morrison, T. (1992). *Playing in the dark.* Cambridge, MA: Harvard University Press.

The Nation prepared: Teachers for the twenty-first century: The report of the task force on teaching as a profession(1986). New York: Carnegie Forum on Education and the Economy, 79.

Nieto, S. (1994). Lessons from students on creating a chance to dream. *Harvard Educational Review, 64*(4), 392–425.

Peterson, K. (1994, December 27). 'Scarlet' has 'A' position on reading lists. *USA Today,* p. D1.

Reyes, M. de la Luz. (1992). Challenging venerable assumptions: Literacy instruction for linguistically different students. *Harvard Educational Review, 62,* 427–446.

Rosenblatt, L. (1995). *Literature as exploration* (4th ed.). New York: Modern Language Association. (Originally published 1938)

Ross, D., & Smith, W. (1992). Understanding preservice teachers' perspectives on diversity. *Journal of Teacher Education 43*(2), 94–103.

Shor, I. (Ed.).(1987). *Freire for the classroom: A sourcebook for liberatory teaching.* Portsmouth, NH: Boynton/Cook.

Sleeter, C. (1993). How white teachers construct race. In C. McCarthy, & W. Crichlow, (Eds.), *Race identity and representation in education.* New York: Routledge.

Sleeter, C. (1994). White racism. *Multicultural Education, 1,* 5–39.

Sleeter, C., & Grant, C. (1988/1993). *Making choices for multicultural education: Five approaches to race, class, and gender.* New York: Macmillan.

Spears-Bunton, L. (1992). Literature, literacy, and resistance to cultural domination. In C. Kinzer & D. Leu (Eds.). *The forty-first Yearbook of the National Reading Conference, Literacy research, theory and practice: Views from many perspectives* (pp. 393–401). Chicago: National Reading Conference.

Spindler, G., & Spindler, L. (1990). *The American dialogue and its transmission.* London: Falmer Press.

Vygotsky, L. (1978). *Mind in society: The development of higher psychological processes.* In M. Cole, V. John-Steiner, S. Scribner, & E. Souberman (Eds.), Cambridge, MA: Harvard University Press.

Watson, K., & Roberts, R. (1988). Multicultural education and teacher training: The picture after Swann. *Journal of Multilingual and Multicultural Development, 9,* 339–352.

Willis, A. (1995). Reading the world: Contextualizing the school literacy experiences of a young African-American male. *Harvard Educational Review, 65*(1), 30–49.

Willis, A., & Meacham, S. (in press). Unveiling the complexities and emotional challenges of teaching preservice multicultural education courses. *Journal for the Assembly on Expanded Perspectives on Learning.*

EXPANDING INSTRUCTIONAL ENVIRONMENTS: TEACHING, LEARNING, AND ASSESSING THE COMMUNICATIVE AND VISUAL ARTS

INTRODUCTION

Nancy Roser
UNIVERSITY OF TEXAS AT AUSTIN

Not so very long ago, establishing an "instructional environment" meant ensuring a comfortable classroom temperature or arranging desks so that natural light traveled over the students' left shoulders and perhaps even placing a green plant or a poetry anthology on each teacher's desk. Things have changed. As Tway (1991) indicated in her chapter in the *Handbook on Research in Teaching the English Language Arts* (Flood, Jensen, Lapp, & Squire), the classroom environment is an instructional tool, and "…can be set up in such a way that it issues … invitation[s] to learning" (p. 427). Although the physical environment of the classrooms has lost none of its importance, teachers and researchers have broadened their notions of instructional environments and now consider the social, psychological, technical, spatial, aesthetic, management (and still other) aspects of teaching and learning both inside and outside of traditional schooling.

The authors in this part of the handbook also paint the instructional environment with broader strokes, as they describe both the teaching and learning opportunities that occur within redefined classrooms as well as those that exist in the "real world" of work, technology, and the arts.

First, Morrow and Tracey build a theoretical and research base for creating classroom environments that support elementary children's literacy learning. Pellegrini describes ways in which different instructional contexts are accompanied by specific sorts of dramatic play and oral language. Wolf, Edmiston, and Enciso describe the place of drama in classrooms as a vehicle for exploring meanings beyond print, and for making classrooms places for the integration and expression of ideas. In addition to addressing storytelling and the importance of narrative in the environment, Scala and Schroder, in their chapter describe a specific aesthetic educational program at The Lincoln Center for the Performing Arts. Wells and Chang-Wells address how problem-solving discussion (within an inquiry-based science curriculum) can be viewed as part of group processing—movement toward building shared, coconstructed understanding of individual meanings.

Venezky recounts and critiques innovations that extend and change students' experiences with text and predicts even greater changes for the text itself. The changes he describes are of text as a multimedia, participatory experience—including custom publishing, hypertext, and interactive fiction. Sticht's chapter focuses on the language and literacy learning of diverse adult learners—including the immigrant, the job-seeker, and the incarcerated.

Chapters by Baines and by Butler also stretch the contexts for literacy learning to show (respectively) the history and uses of film as a component of media literacy, and the potential of electronic discourse communities as instructional environments. Shiring reviews the effects of students' television viewing habits, and offers classroom innovations with television as well. Wood and Nicholson consider newspapers, magazines, and on-line text as new essentials of the classroom literacy environment. The last chapter by Farr and Jongsma, includes research on metacognition as a means of understanding the learner's self-assessment within the instructional context, as well as a preview of multimedia assessments.

Altogether, the chapters contribute to an increasingly complex display of teachers' and researchers' roles as creators, inhabitants, participants, and observers of newly defined instructional environments. From library corners to virtual classrooms, the challenge grows.

39

INSTRUCTIONAL ENVIRONMENTS FOR LANGUAGE AND LEARNING: CONSIDERATIONS FOR YOUNG CHILDREN

Lesley Mandel Morrow

RUTGERS UNIVERSITY

Diane H. Tracey

KEAN COLLEGE OF NEW JERSEY

Given a choice of topics to study—animals, plants, or space—the students in Mrs. Martinez's first grade selected animals. They decided to design a veterinarian's office in the dramatic play area of their classroom. The class visited a veterinarian to gain some background knowledge to help with their plan. They agreed that there should be a waiting room with chairs and a table filled with magazines and books. Mrs. Martinez suggested hanging some posters and pamphlets about good health practices for pets, which she had obtained from the veterinarian. The children placed reading materials in the waiting room and made posters that listed the doctors' hours, a "No Smoking" sign, and a sign that read, "Check In With The Nurse When You Arrive." The nurse's table contained forms for patients to fill out, as well as a telephone, telephone books, appointment cards, and a calendar. The veterinarian's office was supplied with patient folders, prescription pads, white coats, masks, gloves, cotton swabs, a toy doctor's kit, and stuffed animals. Blank paper, a stapler, pencils, markers, colored pencils, and crayons were placed in the area as well. The classroom computer was relocated to the dramatic play area for the purpose of keeping patient records and other files in the veterinarian's office. The center design was a collaborative effort on the part of the teacher and children.

After preparing the environment with the children, Mrs. Martinez discussed and modeled the use of the various materials. She said: "You can read to pets in the waiting area and there are materials to write with. The nurse can ask you to fill out forms while waiting for your turn to see the doctor. The doctor can fill out forms about the condition of a patient or prescriptions for medicine. The nurse can fill out appointment cards. She might like to talk to patients on the phone about problems their pets are having, and schedule appointments. She can write bills for visits, accept payments, and give receipts."

The following is an observation of a thematic dramatic play episode that occurred in this center and included literacy activity.

Tiffany sat in the waiting room reading the story, "Are You My Mother," to her pet monkey. Tyshell joined her with her cat and listened. She asked if she could have her turn in reading. Before they finished, the nurse called Tiffany to answer some questions about her monkey's problems. Tiffany asked Tyshell if she would watch her monkey while she talked to the nurse. Tyshell agreed, and read to her cat and the monkey. When Tiffany finished filling out forms for the nurse, she watched the two pets for Tyshell while she spoke with the nurse. To occupy the stuffed animal pets, Tiffany decided to draw a picture for them. She described her illustration as she composed it.

This anecdote from a study by Morrow (1990) describes a classroom environment that provides an atmosphere that motivates the desire to read and write. The teacher along with the children prepared the physical environment. The teacher described and modeled the use of materials in the literacy-enriched play area. After this initial guidance she acted as a facilitator with students in need of direction. Shortly thereafter she allowed the play to take place on its own, and she took the role of a participator. The children were given time to work in a social collaborative setting, and engage in dramatic role-playing that was integrated with a content area theme. In the dramatic play children participated in real-life behaviors concerning the care of pets, visiting a veterinarian's office, and were involved in meaningful and functional literacy activities. The environment contained challenges for children, opportunity for choice, activities at which they could succeed, and a setting in which social collaborative literacy activities could take place. The teacher in this classroom is aware that the visual presentation of her room will have a dramatic effect upon motivating children to participate in communication of varied kinds.

OVERVIEW

The purpose of the present chapter is to describe instructional environments, and factors within instructional environments, which promote language and literacy learning in young children. As the topic of environment is so broad, it is often recommended that one should focus on specific dimensions of the concept (Tway, 1991). Therefore, for the purpose of this discussion, the term environment will be viewed as the physical environment (the visual presentation of materials and the arrangement of classroom space) and the social behaviors within the classroom.

The chapter begins with a broad discussion of philosophical and theoretical beliefs related to the relationship between young children's literacy learning and their environment. These include the emergent literacy philosophy, the integrated language arts perspective, the National Reading Research Center's engagement perspective and a discussion of motivation theory. Following the theoretical and philosophical foundations, the chapter focuses more specifically on research findings and practical information related to creating physical and social environments which facilitate literacy learning in young children.

PHILOSOPHICAL AND THEORETICAL INFLUENCES FOR THE DESIGN OF EARLY LITERACY INSTRUCTIONAL ENVIRONMENTS

Early Literacy Constructs

A conceptual change regarding children's early reading and writing development has taken place over the past two decades. The term *emergent literacy* is now used to describe the development of literacy as a continuous experience, "emerging" from birth onward (Clay, 1966). In this philosophy, children at all ages possess certain literacy skills, though the skills are not fully developed nor conventional as we recognize mature reading and writing (Teale, 1986). Emergent literacy acknowledges children's scribble marks on a page as rudimentary writing, even if characters are not discernible. Similarly, a child is involved in legitimate literacy behavior when he or she narrates a familiar storybook while looking at the pictures and occasionally at the print. Although the reading is not conventional, the child gives the impression of reading through tone of voice, attention to print, illustrations, and following left-to-right progression (Sulzby, 1985). The emergent literacy perspective allows us to recognize that children come to school with a background of experiences which they use to understand the functions of oral and written language (International Reading Association, 1989). For example, many children can read environmental print, such as familiar signs and labels, and can differentiate between drawing and writing. Similarly, many children associate books with reading and expect that written text communicates a sensible message. Children's background experiences, including their cultural and language environments, become the stepping-stones for further literacy development.

Emergent literacy is not tantamount to the concepts of pre-reading or reading readiness, which are both traditional conceptions of children's literacy development prior to their ability to read conventionally. The reading readiness model implies that children know little about literacy before coming to school. In this model prescribed reading readiness skills are taught systematically with the assumption that all children are at fairly similar levels of development when they come to preschool or kindergarten. The activities that have taken place under this rubric are typically not authentic reading or writing. Rather, reading readiness skills focus on relatively abstract and isolated activities, and mastering these skills has been seen as necessary before formal reading can begin. Many of these activities have little meaning or function for the child (Teale & Sulzby, 1986).

In contrast to the reading readiness model, research in the area of emergent literacy has studied young children's literacy development in the home, prior to children's entry into school. For example, in her seminal work, Durkin (1966) studied the home and family background variables of early readers, children reading prior to their entrance into first grade. Her results indicated that early readers had been read to since a very young age, they had their questions regarding reading and writing answered, they had come from homes in which parents themselves were avid readers and in which reading was a frequent source of pleasure and relaxation. These children expressed fascination with early writing, and subsequently, were given access to writing materials and encouraged to explore with these materials. Other studies have found strong relationships between the home environment and levels of emergent literacy development as well (Anbar, 1986; Clark, 1976; Schickedanz, 1986, 1993). Studies of emergent literacy behaviors related to invented spelling, writing, and print conventions have also been completed (Clay, 1987; Sulzby, 1986).

The social aspect of the home environment, as well as the physical environment as described above, has been documented as being significant in children's emergent literacy development. Teale (1982) views the development of early literacy as the result of children's involvement in reading and writing activities mediated by more literate others. According to this view, it is the social interaction in these activities that makes them so significant to the child's development. Not only do interactive events teach children the societal function and convention of reading and writing; they also link reading with enjoyment and satisfaction and thus increase children's desire to engage in literacy activities. Teale's emphasis on the social aspects of reading development reflects Vygotsky's (1978) more general theory of intellectual development, that higher mental functions really are internalized social relationships. It also reflects Piaget's (Piaget & Inhelder, 1969) theory that literacy learning happens best in an atmosphere that encourages social, collaborative interactions in which youngsters interact with their environment and peers through exploration, experimentation, and social negotiation.

Language Arts Perspective

The language arts perspective, like the emergent literacy perspective, contributes to the foundation of our knowledge regarding the relationship between the classroom environment and children's early literacy development. The language arts perspective suggests that reading and writing will result from a concerted series of authentic, meaningful, and functional experiences that use varied genres of children's literature as their main source for actively involving children in reading and writing. Those experiences take place within rich literacy environments created specifically to encourage social collaboration during periods set aside for independent reading and writing where children practice skills that they have been taught. Instruction includes a conscious effort to integrate literacy learning throughout the school day within different content areas, and it emphasizes learning that is self-regulated with self-selection and student choice. Teachers and children become responsible for deciding instructional strategies, organizations, activities, and materials. The overall goal of the language arts perspective is to develop not only competent strategic readers, but readers who are motivated to read for pleasure and for information. Learning theories undergirding the approach have been described by Dewey (1966), Piaget and Inhelder (1969), and Vygotsky (1978), as well as in philosophies and viewpoints identified more generally as integrated language arts, literature-based instruction, whole language, language experience, and the writing process approach (Bergeron, 1990; Goodman, 1989; Graves, 1975; Stauffer, 1970).

The Engagement Perspective on Reading

The concept of engagement, as defined by the National Reading Research Center (1991), also contributes to the foundation of knowledge on which the relationship between children's environment and their literacy development is understood. Engaged readers are *strategic* readers who possess multiple skills which enable them to read independently and comprehend what they read. Engaged readers become *knowledgeable* from information they learn through reading. These readers are able to transfer and apply their knowledge into new contexts. Engaged readers are *motivated* to read

voluntarily for pleasure and for information, and are *social* in their approach to learning and using literacy.

The engagement perspective on reading suggests that children need to be actively involved with the reading materials in their environment to achieve optimal literacy success. Recently, educators and researchers have begun to use concepts such as children's theater, music, art, film, and creative movement to increase and enhance children's engagement with literacy materials (Moore & Caldwell, 1993). Other modes of increasing children's engagement with literature, such as storytellings and retellings, use of flannel boards, roll movie stories, audiocassettes, chalk talks, prop stories, puppets, slides, photographs, computers, and videos have been well documented by Morrow (1993). Clearly, the engagement perspective holds strong implications for designing educational environments for young children's literacy development.

Motivation Theory

In a survey of classroom teachers concerning priorities for research in the 1990s, motivating children to read and write was ranked high on the list of suggestions (O'Flahavan, Gambrell, Guthrie, Stahl, & Alverman, 1992). Teachers recognize the importance of motivation in the development of children's literacy skills, and are most interested in learning new ways to motivate their students. Motivation theory, the engagement perspective, emergent literacy constructs, and the language arts perspective, all contribute to the knowledge base on which our understanding of the relationship between children's early literacy learning and their environment is based.

Motivation is defined as initiating and sustaining a particular activity. It is considered the tendency to return to and continue working on a task with sustained engagement (Maehr, 1976; Wittrock, 1986). A motivated reader chooses to read on a regular basis, and for many different reasons. Researchers have found that experiences which afford students the opportunity for (1) success, (2) challenge, (3) choice, and (4) collaboration, are likely to promote motivation.

When providing an environment that will foster *success,* a student must perceive that there is some *challenge* to the activity at hand, but it is one that he/she can accomplish. When the task is complete the student must perceive success (Ford, 1992; McCombs, 1989; Spaulding, 1992; Turner, 1992). Tasks are only appropriate if perceived to be challenging, that is, not too hard, and not too easy. When tasks are viewed as too easy, children become disinterested, if they are too difficult they become frustrated. Intrinsic motivation is enhanced when one perceives oneself to be competent or successful in challenging situations (Rodin, Rennert, & Solomon, 1980; Spaulding, 1992).

Providing children with the opportunity to make *choices* about the literacy tasks to participate in, offers students responsibility, and empowers them with control over the situation. Choice needs to involve multiple modalities for learning such as more traditional avenues with pencil and paper experiences as well as developing literacy skills through the use of technology, drama, or the visual arts. Choices like challenge and success instill intrinsic motivation (Lepper, 1988; Morrow, 1992; & Turner, 1992). Finally, motivation is increased through activities which offer opportunities for social *collaboration.* It has been found that when children have the opportunity to engage in learning through social situations involving collaboration with the teacher or peers, they are likely to get more done together than they could do alone, and are more intrinsically motivated to participate than when they work alone (Brandt, 1990; Oldfather, 1993). Recent investigations by Gambrell, Palmer, and Coding (1993) and Gambrell, Almasi, Xie, and Heland (1995) support the findings of the research reported here that success, challenge, choice, and collaboration are indeed elements that promote motivation for reading and writing in children.

CREATING ENVIRONMENTS THAT SUPPORT LITERACY LEARNING AMONG YOUNG CHILDREN

The emergent literacy perspective, the language arts perspective, engagement theory and motivation theory all suggest compatible factors which contribute to creating high quality environments for children's literacy learning. Emergent literacy constructs and the language arts perspective both describe strategies that encourage *Literacy Rich Physical Environments* in classrooms. The perspectives of emergent literacy, language arts, and engagement all suggest the importance of *Social Cooperative Learning,* whether they are experiences in which teachers scaffold and model behavior for children, engage in interactive mediation with children, or when children work with peers. Finally, the engagement perspective speaks of *motivation* as a construct to be nurtured within the literacy environment. The remaining sections of the chapter apply the philosophical and theoretical information presented thus far, to the actual creation of environments that promote reading and writing for young children.

Research Concerning Literacy Rich Physical Environments that Motivate Reading and Writing

As mentioned earlier, observations of homes where children learned to read without direct instruction before coming to school have taught us much about literacy rich environments. Parents in these homes read to their children, often read themselves, were supportive of their children's literacy activities, and had reading and writing materials in their homes (Durkin, 1966; Morrow, 1983; Taylor, 1983; Teale, 1984).

Historically, theorists and philosophers who studied early childhood development emphasized the importance of the physical environment in learning and literacy development. Pestalozzi (Rusk & Scotland, 1979) and Froebel (1889) described real-life environments in which young children's learning could flourish. Both described the preparation of manipulative materials that would foster literacy development. Montessori (1965) described a carefully prepared classroom environment intended to promote independent learning and recommended that every material in the environment has its specific learning objective. The objectives and materials she recommended were more highly structured than those of Pestalozzi and Froebel, who allowed for more natural learning situations in which children explored and experimented with materials in their environment.

Piaget (Piaget & Inhelder, 1969) found that children acquire knowledge by interacting with the world or the environment. Those who interpret his theories into educational practice involve children in problem-solving situations where they can assimilate new experiences into what they already know. Learning takes place as the child interacts with peers and adults in social settings, and conducive environments (Vygotsky, 1978). Ideal settings are oriented to real-life situations, and materials are chosen to provide opportunities for children to explore and experiment. Dewey (1966) probably would have agreed with the educational settings described by Piagetians. In addition, Dewey believed in an interdisciplinary approach. In other words, learning takes place through the integration of content areas. He believed that storing materials in subject area centers encouraged interest and learning.

Based on these discussions, any classroom designed to provide a literacy rich environment and optimum literacy development will offer an abundant supply of materials for reading, writing, and oral language. These materials will be housed in a literacy center. Literacy development will be integrated with content area teaching reflected in materials provided in content area learning centers. Materials and settings throughout the classroom will be designed to emulate real-life experiences and make literacy meaningful to children. They will be based on information children already possess, and will be functional so that children can see a need and purpose for using literacy. Careful attention to a classroom's visual and physical design contributes to the success of an instructional program. Preparing a classroom's physical environment is often overlooked in planning instruction. Teachers and curriculum developers tend to concentrate on pedagogical and interpersonal factors, but give little consideration to the visual and spatial context in which teaching and learning occur. They direct their energies toward varying teaching strategies while the classroom setting remains relatively unchanged. When program and environment are not coordinated, "Setting Deprivation" often results, a situation in which the physical environment fails to support the activities and needs of students (Spivak, 1973).

While the learning environment is often viewed as background or scenery for teaching and learning, there is another way to view the physical environment and the teacher's role in creating it. This view recognizes that by purposefully arranging the environment, teachers acknowledge the physical setting as an active and pervasive influence on their own activities and attitudes, as well as those of the children in their classrooms. Appropriate physical arrangement of furniture, material selection, and the visual aesthetic quality of a room provide a setting that contributes to teaching and learning (Loughlin & Martin, 1987; Morrow, 1990; Phyfe-Perkins, 1979; Rivlin & Weinstein, 1984; Sutfin, 1980). For example, design of spatial arrangements alone affects children's behavior in the classroom. Field (1980) observed that rooms partitioned into smaller spaces facilitated such behaviors as peer and verbal interaction, fantasy, associative, and cooperative play more than did rooms with large open spaces. Nash (1981) and Moore (1986) found that children in carefully arranged rooms showed more creative productivity and greater use of language-related activities than did children in randomly arranged rooms. Children in these carefully arranged rooms also demonstrated more engaged and exploratory behavior and more social interaction and cooperation than did children in moderately or poorly defined settings.

In another example of the effects of the physical environment on children's behavior, combining the block and housekeeping areas of a classroom increased mixed-sex grouping among 3- and 4-year-olds, as well as relevant, constructive use of the block area by girls (Kinsman & Berk, 1979). Montes and Risley (1975) found that storing toys on open shelves rather than in boxes led to easier selection, more time spent playing, and more immediate involvement. The introduction of thematic play materials into the dramatic play area of a laboratory playroom and of a preschool classroom, led children to more elaborate and longer dramatic play sequences (Dodge & Frost, 1986; Woodward, 1984). Studies that investigated the role of literacy-enriched dramatic play areas based on themes being used in the classroom stimulated increased use of literacy activity and the enhancement of literacy skills (Morrow, 1990; Neuman & Roskos, 1990, 1992). Other researchers have found that dramatic play with story props has improved story production and comprehension, including recall of details and ability to sequence and interpret (Mandler & Johnson, 1977; Saltz & Johnson, 1974).

Preparing Literacy Rich Physical Environments that Motivate Reading and Writing

The research that investigates the physical design of classrooms strongly suggests that by purposefully arranging the space and materials, teachers can use physical environments as an active, positive and pervasive influence on instruction. Educators must think of their classrooms as places to project a visual atmosphere that communicates a definitive message. The following describes the visual presentation of a literacy rich physical environment to motivate reading and writing based on the research discussed in the previous section.

Literacy rich classrooms are filled with visually prominent functional print—labels on classroom items and areas; signs communicating functional information and directions, such as *Quiet Please,* and *Please Put Materials Away After Using Them;* and charts labeled *Helpers, Daily Routines, Attendances,* and *Calendar* to name a few (Morrow, 1993; Schickedanz, 1986). A notice board in a prominent place in the room can be used to communicate with the children in writing. Experience charts are used to display new words generated from themes, recipes used in the classroom, and science experiments conducted.

Each classroom has a literacy center which includes space and materials for writing, reading, oral language, and listening. The center is positioned in a portion of the classroom that is visible. It should be visually attractive and physically accessible. The effort of creating an inviting atmosphere for a classroom literacy center is rewarded by an increased interest of children in participating in activities offered. This center is essential for children to enjoy immediate access to literature. Researchers have found that children in classrooms with literacy centers read and write more often than do children whose classrooms do not have such materials (Morrow & Weinstein, 1982, 1986).

Although the literacy center needs to be visible and inviting, it should also have some privacy and physical definition for its users with partitions. Five or six children should be able to work in the center at a time. All children should be able to take materials from the center to use in other parts of the room.

Literacy centers should have pillows, rugs, and a rocking chair for comfort and softness. Books are stored in open-faced bookshelves for displaying titles about themes being studied. Regular bookshelves are also available to house five to eight books per child at three to four grade levels. Books are color coded by categories, and represent different genres of children's literature such as picture storybooks, poetry, informational books, magazines, biographies, fairy tales, novels, realistic literature, cookbooks, joke books, craft books, and so forth. Books are rotated on and off the shelves regularly.

There is a system for children to check books out of the classroom literacy center to take home and read. Logs are provided to record books read and tasks completed during periods of independent reading and writing. There is a writing area or "Author's Spot," with a computer, various types of writing paper, blank booklets, and writing utensils such as markers and pencils for creating original stories and books. There are posters displayed to point out the joys and importance of reading and writing and a bulletin board that provides a place for children to display their work. Literacy manipulatives such as felt boards with story characters from pieces of children's literature are included. These manipulatives have been found to motivate children to engage in storytelling, storybook reading, and writing, providing a means for active involvement (Morrow & Weinstein, 1982, 1986). These materials include puppets, taped stories with headsets, chalk-talks, roll stories, prop stories, and so forth. These materials encourage the use of communicative and visual arts.

Programs that motivate early literacy development require literacy rich environments that recognize the need for an integrated approach to literacy learning and recognition of individual differences and levels of development. Classrooms that use the philosophies and theories outlined earlier in this chapter are arranged in centers with sections dedicated to content areas, such as social studies, science, art, music, math, literacy, dramatic play and block play. Centers contain materials pertinent to the content area and materials that are added are specific to the themes being studied such as nutrition or animals. Each subject-specific center is equipped with materials devoted to that content, but includes literacy materials as well. They contain things to read, materials with which to write, things to listen to and talk about. These materials create interest, new vocabulary and concepts, and a reason for participating in literacy activities. With each new theme studied, additional books, posters, artifacts, music, art projects, dramatic-play materials, and scientific objects can be added to create new interest. The materials are often activity oriented, and designed so that children can use them independently or in small groups. The classroom floorplan in Figure 2, provides an illustration of this type of learning environment.

When preparing the centers for a Nutrition unit, for example, a teacher may add to existing center materials in the following way:

Art Center. Include play dough for making play food, and a recipe poster for making the dough; include cooking and health magazines, dry foods to make collages (macaroni, peas, seeds), fruit and vegetables for printing with paint.

Music Center. Various songs on nutritional topics can be added to this center, such as "Chicken Soup with Rice." All tapes should be accompanied by lyrics.

Dramatic Play Center. Turn this area into different ethnic restaurants and include menus, receipts, order-taking slips, recipes, and 3 × 5 cards for new recipes, cookbooks, baking utensils, empty food boxes, signs commonly seen in restaurants, a cash register, play money, food posters, cooking magazines, and waiter and waitress clothing.

Block Center. In order to create places that food comes from, such as farms and supermarkets, the following items can be added: farm props (animals and plants), supermarket props (empty food boxes, receipts, play money, and bags), environmental print signs and posters displaying food information.

Outdoor Play. When providing for role-playing at a lemonade stand the following items can be added: tables, signs with prices, play money, a cash register, receipts, recipe charts with directions for making lemonade, paper and pencils.

Math Center. Various foods can be used as counters, such as macaroni or wrapped hard candies. Include counting books that contain foods and blank books for children to create their own number book of different foods.

Science Center. Materials for nutrition projects may be added: planting equipment, recipes and the ingredients needed, foods to be classified into food groups, seed packages, and foods to be tasted. There should be charts and journals to record progress of growing plants. There should be informational books about food and good nutrition.

Social Studies Center. Pictures of food from the different food groups can be placed on maps to show where they are produced. Recipe books and recipes from home representing different cultures should be added.

Literacy Center. Books and magazines about good nutrition need to be added and pamphlets about good nutrition. The Author's Spot can add an index card box for sharing recipes.

Centers are separated by furniture that holds their materials and serves as partitions. Center materials can be stored on tables, in shelves, or in boxes that are labeled and the area often includes a bulletin board for displays. The equipment in the centers is accessible for children and has a designated spot for storage, so that children can find them easily and return

them easily. The number of items in each center increases as the year progresses and is introduced by the teacher according to its purpose and use (Montessori, 1965).

In addition to generating a literacy rich environment, and an interdisciplinary approach, the room is designed to cater to different teaching methods, organizational strategies, and grouping procedures so that the individual differences in instructional needs of all children can be accommodated. The centers provide space for independent or social collaborative learning, exploration, choice, and self-direction. There is place for whole-class instruction, small-group meetings, and individualized learning. The materials in this center provide for choice, challenge, success, and for use alone or collaboratively. They involve the children in communicative and visual arts.

Research Concerning Social Contexts as Environments that Motivate Reading and Writing

Emergent literacy constructs, the language arts perspective, the engagement perspective, and research on motivation theory, all discuss the importance of social collaboration and interaction with adults and peers as an important factor for literacy learning. Therefore it is necessary to translate this theoretical construct into practice and include it as an environmental context to promote literacy in classrooms.

When children work in small groups in which social interactions are cooperative, their achievement and productivity increase (Johnson & Johnson, 1987; Slavin, 1983). Yager, Johnson and Johnson (1985) posit two important elements in the dynamics of cooperative learning: (a) oral interaction among students, and (b) heterogeneity among group members. According to their findings, cooperative learning succeeds because it allows children to explain material to each other, to listen to each others's explanations, and to arrive at joint understandings of what they have shared. The cooperative learning setting enables "more capable peers" to offer support to others. Cazden (1986) points out that peer interaction allows students to attempt a range of roles they would be denied by traditional student–teacher participant structures. Forman and Cazden (1985) also indicate that Vygotsky's theory (1978) led them to conclude that an interactional transformation can occur among peers when one student is observing, guiding, and correcting as another performs a task. The students accomplish more together than either could accomplish alone. Working in peer dyads allows for similar learning opportunities as tutoring. Forman and Cazden's discussion reflects both Dewey's (1966) argument that children engaged in task-oriented dialogue with peers can reach higher levels of understanding than they do when teachers present information didactically, and Piaget's (Piaget & Inhelder 1969) suggestion that childhood peers serve as resources for one another in cognitive development.

With less dependence on the teacher for instance, learning appears to be more intrinsically motivated (Wood, 1990). Children who ordinarily work alone choose to collaborate in cooperative settings—even forming friendships— and there is greater acceptance of differences among students (Slavin,

1990). High and low achievers work together in cooperative learning settings, and positive relations increase among children from varied racial and ethnic backgrounds (Kagan, Zahn, Widaman, Schwarzwald, & Tyrell, 1985; Morrow, 1992). Finally children with special problems such as physical disabilities, emotional handicaps, and learning difficulties are more likely to be accepted by other children in cooperative learning settings than in traditional classrooms (Johnson & Johnson, 1981; Lew, Mesch, Johnson, & Johnson, 1986; Morrow, 1992).

Research has confirmed the importance of providing children with daily opportunities for storybook reading. Many of these studies have illustrated that with a strong emphasis on storybook reading children learn concepts about books and print, they become more sophisticated in the form and structure of written language, they develop vocabulary, comprehension, and a sense of story structure (Feitleson, Kita, & Goldstein, 1986; Snow & Pearlman, 1985; Wells, 1985). It has been found however, it is not simply the reading aloud that provides beneficial outcomes, but the verbal interaction that occurs between adult and child during this experience (Morrow, O'Connor, & Smith, 1990). A read-aloud event involves social relationships among people: teachers and students, parents and children, authors and readers. Because reading stories to children is a social activity, children almost never encounter simply an oral rendering of text. Rather, the author's words are augmented and shaped by the interpretation and social interaction of the adult reader and the child as they cooperatively negotiate and reconstruct meaning from text (Morrow, 1988). Researchers agree that what the adult and child talk about in the interaction holds the key to the effect of storybook reading. Vygotsky (1978) describes cognitive development as growing out of social interactions. From that perspective, the importance of read-aloud events is their social interactiveness, with the adult serving initially as mediator between text and child and providing the opportunity for both adult and child to make or take meaning from the text.

Experiences with children's literature, however, need to go beyond storybook reading. Studies have confirmed the importance of providing children with frequent literature experiences in active and pleasurable ways by reading and telling stories to children, dealing with stories through literal, interpretive, and critical discussions, integrating literature into themes being studied throughout the curriculum, having children share books they have read, responding to literature through written and oral language, and participating in independent reading and writing periods (Heath, 1980; Hoffman, Roser, & Farest, 1988; Roser & Martinez, 1985). Additional experiences that provide challenge, choice, success, and collaboration are participating in literature experiences using manipulatives described in the physical environment section for story retellings, and rewritings (Gambrell, Kapinus, & Koskinen, 1991; Sulzby, 1985).

The importance of the social context as an environmental factor that positively affects the literacy learning of children from diverse backgrounds and ability, has been positively documented for those identified as at-risk, average achievers, and the gifted, as well as children from diverse races and cultures. For example, in studies with at-risk kindergartners

and children from diverse backgrounds in first, second, and third grade, several interactive social strategies were used, including daily storybook reading, story retelling, use of literature manipulatives, and periods of independent reading and writing (Morrow, 1992; Morrow et al., 1990). The investigators found that the experimental groups scored better than the control group on measures of comprehension, retelling, and extent of voluntary participation in literacy activities during independent reading and writing. In these investigations, as well as in others, the social interaction that occurred between adult and child and among the children themselves seems to be a major factor responsible for the positive outcomes.

Preparing the Environment for Social Interaction During Literacy Events

The nature of social interaction between adults and children during storybook reading, and between children during work in independent small groups, has been studied to determine what actually occurs. Several studies have suggested that a child's literacy development is influenced by the type and amount of verbal interaction that takes place between an adult and a child during story reading. By imitating the model provided by an adult reader and reenacting a story-reading event, a child can vicariously experience independent reading (Flood, 1977; Pellegrini & Galda, 1982). Studies in school settings indicate that eliciting children's active responses to literature enables them to integrate information and relate various parts of a story. A teacher's reading style can also have an effect on how well children comprehend stories (Dunning & Mason, 1984; Peterman, Dunning, & Mason, 1985). Story-reading interactions should be flexible and develop over time; adults tend to change their interactive styles as children change the nature of their responses. Several investigators have identified adult initiated verbal interactions during storybook reading that appear to be beneficial in enhancing literacy development. These social interactive behaviors include adults acting initially as *managers,* introducing the story by providing background information about the book. Adults act as *prompters,* inviting children to ask questions or comment about the story. They also *scaffold* responses for children when they are not responding. As *supporters and informers,* adults invite children to respond, they share reactions, they explain, answer questions, provide information, relate comments to real-life experiences, and offer positive reinforcement for children's participation. The number of words used and questions asked or answered by children, the number of pre- and poststory evaluative questions asked by the adult, the number of instances of positive reinforcement by adults, and the number of references to the child's own experiences, are predictors of success in early literacy development (Flood, 1977; Martinez & Teale, 1993; Morrow & Smith, 1990; Roser & Martinez, 1985).

When investigating the size of group and the type of interaction that takes place, it appears as if whole group, small group, and one-to-one storybook-reading settings all have their pros and cons. However, reading to children in small groups was found to be more socially active than the other two settings. The children responded quickly to adult prompts. The small-group atmosphere was lively. The children interacted with the teacher and among themselves. They offered comments, repeated what others had said, or elaborated on the responses of their peers. Children acted as a team, often responding in unison. The children took over the discussion of the story, and each child participated equally in the conversation (Morrow & Smith, 1990).

Under what circumstances do young children socially interact in the most productive way when participating in periods of independent reading and writing? What is the nature of the literacy and social activity that occurs? Most research on cooperative group learning has been done with elementary school children (Johnson & Johnson, 1987; Slavin, 1983). Not as much attention has been paid to environmental contexts that promote cooperative endeavors with young children. The research that has been completed suggests that the ultimate goal for periods set aside for independent reading and writing is for students to learn to direct their own behavior, make decisions, work together, stay on task, and be accountable for completing tasks. After many years of investigating with informal, moderate, and formal structures, it has been found that initially children need more formal guidelines to begin cooperative activities, and after practicing can participate with less formal structures. Students need guidelines for participating in periods of independent reading and writing such as: (l) Decide who you will work with; (2) Choose a reading or writing activity from the literacy center; (3) Do only one or two activities in a given period; (4) Use materials in or outside of the literacy center; (5) All activities must include reading and writing; (6) Handle materials carefully; (7) Speak in soft voices; (8) Put materials back in their place before taking more; (9) Try new activities you have not done before; (10) Work with people you have not worked with before; (11) Stay with a group to complete tasks; (12) Record completed tasks in your log; (13) Be ready to share completed tasks with the class.

In addition to general guidelines, rules for cooperating may include:

When Working in Groups

Select a leader to help the group get started
Give everyone a job
Share materials
Take turns in talking
Listen to your friends when they talk
Respect what others have to say
Stay with your group.

Helpful Things to Say to Group Member

Can I help you?
I like your work.
You did a good job.

Check How Well You Cooperated and Check Your Work

Did you say helpful things?
Did you help each other?

Did you share materials?
Did you take turns?
Did you all have jobs?
How well did your jobs get done?
What can we do better next time?

When first initiating periods of independent reading and writing, some teachers assign children to groups, decide which activity they will participate in, and select leaders to organize the activity. Other teachers have children sign up for activities and groups before the period begins. After participating in assigned groups with assigned activities, children can eventually make these decisions themselves, that is, choose people with whom to work, pick leaders, and select tasks. To help children select activities, a list of things to do during periods of independent reading and writing can be posted such as: (l) Read a book, a magazine, or a newspaper; (2) Read to a friend; (3) Listen to someone read to you; (4) Listen to a taped story and follow the words in the book; (5) Use the felt board with storybook and felt characters; (6) Use the roll movie with its storybook; (7) Write a story; (8) Draw a picture about a story you read; (9) Make a story you wrote into a book; (10) Make a felt story for a book you read or story you wrote; (11) Write a puppet show and perform it; (12) Make a taped story for a book you read or story you wrote; (13) Check out books to take home and read; (14) Use Activity Cards for projects you select to do.

Activity cards containing steps for carrying out the activities help children organize their work. The role of the teacher during this time is to model behavior and act as a facilitator in the classroom.

During periods of independent reading and writing children engage in a variety of literacy activities that are both social and collaborative in nature. For example, children may write their own stories, and then prepare felt characters, or a roll movie for presenting them. Children demonstrate comprehension of stories read by retelling them onto a tape for others to listen to, retelling it with puppets, or through dramatic presentations. The manipulative literacy materials in the literacy center allow the children to read and write through many different modalities. Children also engage in specific social behaviors that help the literacy activity to occur. They collaborate on tasks which helps to get them completed more quickly. There is peer tutoring when youngsters help each other with reading words, coming up with ideas, or spelling. Social conflicts also occur when students have difficulty deciding about taking turns, and sharing materials, as well as cognitive conflicts, when youngsters disagree about spelling a word, or what should happen next in a story they are writing. According to Piaget and Inhelder (1969) conflict enables children to study the options and negotiate a compromise or problem solve until a joint decision can be reached (Morrow, Sharkey, & Firestone, 1993).

The following episodes describe children participating in literacy activities in an environment that provides physical and social contexts that promote motivation to read and write. Children are involved in social cooperative literacy activities using materials from a literacy rich environment which includes books, writing utensils, and multimedia activities that foster the use of communicative and visual arts.

Rodney and Kirtus were sitting comfortably on the carpet, leaning against pillows, and sharing a book about snakes. Rodney said to Kirtus, "Yo! Look at this!" as he held out the page for Kirtus to see. Rodney and Kirtus were fascinated as they continued to read and look at the pictures. They discussed as they went along.

Sholanda and Kendra, squeezed tightly into one rocking chair, were also sharing and reading the same book. Marcel, Kimba, and Terrence snuggled under a shelf—a private spot filled with stuffed animals—taking turns reading together.

In the Author's Spot, Ramon and Kira were writing a Rebus story on the computer. They found just the right graphics on the computer for specific words they chose to illustrate.

Elvira, Emily, and Howard had just finished cooperatively writing their own original episode for the "Reading Rainbow" television program. They featured the book *Petunia,* for the farm unit they had been learning about. They wanted to produce a video of the episode and sought help from the teacher on how they might proceed.

Tashiba and Angela decided to read the story *The Mitten.* Occasionally Angela helped Tashiba with a word when she had difficulty. After Tashiba read it, the two girls acted it out with stick puppets and a large mitten prop. They hoped to perform it for the class during sharing time.

Terrence was writing a story with Charlene about the "Old West" and how buffaloes were a source of clothing and food. Terrence spelled buffalo with one *f* and Charlene argued that there were two. Terrence said he was sure there was only one. They talked back and forth for a while, getting a bit angry with each other and then decided to look it up in the book where they had read about the animals. They found that Charlene was correct that there were two *f*'s not one. After settling their conflict, they continued writing their story. After it was edited, they made their story into an illustrated book.

At the end of this period of independent reading and writing some of the children were given the opportunity to perform for the class. Some simply described the project they were working on. Others acted out a puppet show, while reading a story from a book read, or telling a story that was read. Another group presented a play about a story they had written.

CONCLUDING REMARKS

Environments to motivate reading and writing in early childhood classrooms have been discussed. Ideas have been drawn from emergent literacy constructs, the language arts perspective, the engagement perspective on reading, and motivation theory to demonstrate how these philosophies and theories can be transformed into practice. The environments that were described included physical and social contexts. Holdaway's theory (1979) of developmental learning has been utilized in this discussion. (1) Children would be able to *observe* literacy behavior, such as being read to or seeing peers and teachers engaged in reading and writing, (2) Children would be engaged in collaboration and cooperation through sharing materials with peers, and working on joint projects, as well as interacting with adults who provide models for literacy activity, encouragement, motivation, and help, (3) Children would be involved in *practicing* skills they had been learning during periods of independent reading and writing, and (4) Children would be involved in *performance* by sharing completed reading and writing activities with others. In addition, through the physical environments described and the social contexts for shared storybook experiences and independent reading and writing, they are provided with a motivating atmosphere that encourages the use of communicative and visual arts. There are *challenging* materials, and activities that involve children in *social collaboration,* with *choices* of what they would like to do and with whom, and the opportunity for *success* in the literacy activities undertaken.

References

Anbar, A. (1986). Reading acquisition of preschool children without systematic instruction. *Early Childhood Research Quarterly, 1,* 69–84.

Bergeron, B. (1990). What does the term whole language mean? A definition from the literature. *Journal of Reading Behavior, 23,* 301–329.

Brandt, D. (1990). *Literacy as involvement: The acts of writers, readers, and texts.* Carbondale, IL: Southern Illinois University Press.

Cazden, C. (1986). Classroom discourse. In M. C. Wittrock (Ed.), *The handbook of research in teaching* (3rd ed., pp. 432–463). New York: Macmillan.

Clark, M. M. (1976). *Young fluent readers.* Portsmouth, NH: Heinemann.

Clay, M. M. (1966). *Emergent reading behavior.* Doctoral dissertation, University of Auckland.

Clay, M. M. (1987). Implementing reading recovery: Systematic adaptations to an educational innovation. *New Zealand Journal of Educational Studies, 22,* 35–58.

Dewey, J. (1966). *Democracy and education.* New York: Free Press. (Original work published in 1916)

Dodge, M., & Frost, J. (1986). Children's dramatic play: Influence of thematic and nonthematic settings. *Childhood Education, 62,* 166–170.

Dunning, D., & Mason, J. (1984, November). *An investigation of kindergarten children's expressions of story character intentions.* Paper presented at the annual meeting of the National Reading Conference, St. Petersburg, FL.

Durkin, D. (1966). *Children who read early.* New York: Teachers College Press.

Feitleson, D., Kita, B., & Goldstein, Z. (1986). Effects of listening to series stories on first graders' comprehension and use of language. *Research in the Teaching of English, 20,* 339–356.

Field, T. (1980). Preschool play: Effects of teacher/child ratios and organization of classroom space. *Child Study Journal, 10,* 191–205.

Flood, J. (1977). Parental styles in reading episodes with young children. *Reading Teacher, 30,* 864–867.

Ford, M. E. (1992). *Motivating humans.* Newbury Park, CA: Sage.

Forman, E., & Cazden, C. (1985). Exploring Vygotskian perspectives in education: The cognitive value of peer interaction. In J. Wertsch (Ed.), *Culture, communication, and cognition. Vygotskian perspectives.* Cambridge: Cambridge University Press.

Froebel, F. (1889). *The education of man.* Clifton, NJ: Augustus M. Kelly. (Original work published in 1926.)

Gambrell. L. B., Almasi, J. F., Xie, Q., & Heland, V. (1995). Helping first-graders get off to a running start in reading: A home-school-community program that enhances family literacy. In L. M. Morrow (Ed.), *Family literacy: Multiple perspectives to enhance literacy development.* Newark, DE: International Reading Association.

Gambrell, L. B., Kapinus, B. A., & Koskinen, P. S. (1991). Retelling and the reading comprehension of proficient and less proficient readers. *Journal of Reading Behavior, 84,* 356–362.

Gambrell, L. B., Palmer, B. M., & Coding, R. M. (1993). *Motivation to read.* Washington, DC: Office of Educational Research and Improvement.

Goodman, K S. (1989). Whole language research: Foundations of development. *Elementary School Journal, 90,* 207–220.

Graves, D. H. (1975). An examination of the writing process of seven-year-old-children. *Research in the Teaching of English, 9,* 227–241.

Heath, S. B. (1980). The function and uses of literacy. *Journal of Communication, 30,* 123–133.

Hoffman, J. V., Roser, N. L., & Farest, C. (1988). Literature strategies in classrooms serving students from economically disadvantaged and language different environments. In J. E. Readence, & R. S. Baldwin (Eds.), *Dialogues in literacy research: Thirty-seventh yearbook of the National Reading Conference* (pp. 331–338). Chicago: National Reading Conference.

Holdaway, D. (1979). *The foundations of literacy.* Sydney: Ashton Scholastic.

International Reading Association. (1989). *Literacy development in early childhood (Pre-school through third grade).* Newark, DE: International Reading Association.

Johnson, D. W., & Johnson, R. T. (1981). Effects of cooperative and individualistic learning experiences on interethnic interaction. *Journal of Educational Psychology, 73,* 444–449.

Johnson, D. W., & Johnson, R. T. (1987). *Learning together and alone* (2nd ed.) Englewood Cliffs, NJ: Prentice-Hall.

Kagan, S., Zahn, G., Widaman, K. F., Schwarzwald, J., & Tyrell, G. (1985). Classroom structural bias: Impact of cooperative and competitive classroom structures on cooperative and competitive individuals and groups. In R. Slavin, S. Sharan, S. Kagan, R. H. Lazarowitz, C. Webb, & R. Schmuck (Eds.), *Learning to cooperate, cooperating to learn* (pp. 277–312). New York: Plenum Press.

Kinsman, C., & Berk, L. (1979). Joining the block and housekeeping areas: Changes in play and social behavior, *Young Children, 35,* 66–75.

Lepper, M. R. (1988). *Motivational considerations in the study of instruction. Cognition and Instruction, 5,* 289–309.

Lew, M., Mesch, D., Johnson, D. W., & Johnson, R. T. (1986). Positive interdependence, academic and collaborative skills group contingencies and isolated students. *American Educational Research Journal, 23,* 476–488.

Loughlin, C. E., & Martin, M. D. (1987). *Supporting literacy: Develop-*

ing effective learning environments. New York: Teachers College Press.

Maehr, M. L. (1976). Continuing motivation: An analysis of a seldom considered educational outcome. *Review of Educational Research, 46,* 443–462.

Mandler, J., & Johnson, N. (1977). Remembrance of things parsed: Story structure and recall. *Cognitive Psychology, 9,* 111–151.

Martinez, M. G., & Teale, W. H. (1993). Teachers' storybook reading style: A comparison of six teachers. *Research in the Teaching of English, 27,* 175–199.

McCombs, B. L. (1989). Self-regulated learning and academic achievement: A phenomenological view. In B. J. Zimmerman & D. H. Schunk (Eds.), *Self-regulated learning and academic achievement: Theory, research, and practice* (pp. 51–82). New York: Springer.

Montes, F., & Risley, T. (1975). Evaluating traditional day care practices: An empirical approach. *Child Care Quarterly, 4,* 208–215.

Montessori, M. (1965). *Spontaneous activity in education.* New York: Schocken Books.

Moore, B. H., & Caldwell, H. (1993). Drama and drawing for narrative writing in primary grades. *Journal of Educational Research, 87*(2), 100–109.

Moore, G. (1986). Effects of the spatial definition of behavior settings on children's behavior: A quasi-experimental field study. *Journal of Environmental Psychology, 6*(3), 205–231.

Morrow, L. M. (1983). Home and school correlates of early interest in literature. *Journal of Educational Research, 76,* 221–230.

Morrow, L. M. (1988). Young children's responses to one-to-one story readings in school settings. *Reading Research Quarterly, 23*(1), 89–107.

Morrow, L. M. (1990). Preparing the classroom environment to promote literacy during play. *Early Childhood Research Quarterly, 5,* 537–554.

Morrow, L. M. (1992). The impact of a literature-based program on literacy achievement, use of literature, and attitudes of children from minority backgrounds. *Reading Research Quarterly, 27,* 250–275.

Morrow, L. M. (1993). *Literacy development in the early years* (2nd ed.). Boston: Allyn & Bacon.

Morrow, L. M., O'Connor, E., & Smith, J. K. (1990). Effects of a story reading program on the literacy development of at risk kindergarten children. *Journal of Reading Behavior, 22,* 225–275.

Morrow, L. M., Sharkey, E., & Firestone, W. A. (1993). Promoting independent reading and writing through self-directed literacy activities in a collaborative setting. *National Reading Research Center, Research Report No. 2,* (pp. 1–26). Georgia & Maryland: University of Georgia and Maryland.

Morrow, L. M., & Smith, J. K. (1990). The effect of group setting on interactive storybook reading. *Reading Research Quarterly, 25,* 213–231.

Morrow, L. M., & Weinstein, C. S. (1982). Increasing children's use of literature through program and physical design changes. *Elementary School Journal, 83,* 131–137.

Morrow, L. M., & Weinstein, C. S. (1986). Encouraging voluntary reading: The impact of a literature program on children's use of library centers. *Reading Research Quarterly, 21,* 330–346.

Nash, B. (1981). The effects of classroom spatial organization on four- and five-year-old children's learning. *British Journal of Educational Psychology, 51,* 144–155.

National Reading Research Center. (1991). Conceptual framework: The engagement perspective. *In National Reading Research Center: A proposal from the University of Maryland and the University of Georgia* (pp. 8–10). Athens, GA and College Park, MD.

Neuman, S., & Roskos, K. (1990). The influence of literacy-enriched play settings on pre-schoolers' engagement with written language. In J. Zutell & S. McCormick (Eds.), *Literacy theory and research: Analyses from multiple paradigms. Thirty-ninth yearbook of the National Reading Conference* (pp. 179–187). Chicago: National Reading Conference.

Neuman, S., & Roskos, K. (1992). Literacy objects as cultural tools: Effects on children's literacy behaviors in play. *Reading Research Quarterly, 27*(3), 202–225.

O'Flahavan, J. Gambrell, L. B., Guthrie, J., Stahl, S., & Alverman, D. (1992, April). Poll results guide activities of research center. *Reading Today* (p. 12). Newark, DE: International Reading Association.

Oldfather, P. (1993). What students say about motivating experiences in a whole language classroom. *The Reading Teacher, 46,* 672–681.

Pellegrini, A., & Galda, L. (1982). The effects of thematic fantasy play training on the development of children's story comprehension. *American Educational Research Journal, 19,* 443–452.

Peterman, C. L., Dunning, D., & Mason, J. (1985, December). *A storybook reading event: How a teacher's presentation affects kindergarten children's subsequent attempts to read from the text.* Paper presented at the annual meeting of the National Reading Conference, San Diego.

Phyfe-Perkins, E. (1979). *Application of the behavior-person-environment paradigm to the analysis and evaluation of early childhood education programs.* Doctoral dissertation, University of Massachusetts.

Piaget, J., & Inhelder, B. (1969). *The psychology of the child.* New York: Basic Books.

Rivlin, L, & Weinstein, C. (1984). Educational issues, school settings, and environmental psychology. *Journal of Environmental Psychology, 4,* 347–364.

Rodin, J., Rennert, K., & Solomon, S. (1980). Intrinsic motivation for control: Fact or fiction. In A. Baum, J. E. Singer, & S. Valios (Eds.), *Advances in environmental psychology.* Hillsdale, NJ: Erlbaum.

Roser, N., & Martinez, M. (1985). Roles adults play in preschool responses to literature. *Language Arts, 62,* 485–490.

Rusk R, & Scotland, J. (1979). *Doctrines of the great educators.* New York: St. Martin's Press.

Saltz, E., & Johnson, J. (1974). Training for thematic-fantasy play in culturally disadvantaged children: Preliminary results. *Journal of Educational Psychology, 66*(4), 623–630.

Schickedanz, J. A. (1986). *More than the ABC's.* Washington, DC: National Association for the Education of Young Children.

Schickedanz, J. A. (1993). Designing the early childhood classroom environment to facilitate literacy development. In B. Spodek & O. N. Saracho (Eds.), *Language and literacy in early childhood education: Yearbook in early childhood education* (Vol.4). New York: Teachers College Press.

Slavin, R. E. (1983). Non-cognitive outcomes. In J. M. Levine & M. C. Wang (Eds.), *Teacher and student perceptions: Implications for learning* (pp. 341–366). Hillsdale, NJ: Erlbaum.

Slavin, R. E. (1990). *Cooperative learning: Theory, research and practice,* Englewood Cliffs, NJ: Prentice-Hall.

Snow, C., & Pearlman, R. (1985). Assessing children's knowledge about book reading. In L. Galda & A. Pellegrini (Eds.), *Play, language, and stories.* Norwood, NJ: Ablex.

Spaulding, C. I. (1992). The motivation to read and write. In J. W. Irwin & M. A. Doyle (Eds.), *Reading/writing connections: Learning from research* (pp. 177–201).

Spivak, M. (1973). Archetypal place. *Architectural Forum, 140,* 44–49.

Stauffer, R. G. (1970). A reading teacher's dream come true. *Wilson Library Bulletin, 45,* 282–292.

Sulzby, E. (1985). Children's emergent reading of favorite story books. *Reading Research Quarterly, 20,* 458–481.

Sulzby, E. (1986). Kindergarteners as writers and readers. In M. Farr (Ed.) *Advances in writing research: Vol. 1. Children's early writing.* Norwood, NJ: Ablex.

Sutfin, H. (1980). *The effects on children's behavior of a change in the physical design of a kindergarten classroom.* Doctoral dissertation, Boston University.

Taylor, D. (1983). *Family literacy.* Exeter, NH: Heinemann Educational Books.

Teale, W. (1982). Toward a theory of how children learn to read and write naturally. *Language Arts, 59,* 555–570.

Teale, W. (1984). Reading to young children: Its significance for literacy development. In H. Goelman, A. Oberg, & F. Smith (Eds.), *Awakening to literacy.* Exeter, NH: Heinemann Educational Books.

Teale, W. (1986). The beginning of reading and writing: Written language development during the preschool and kindergarten years. In M. Sampson (Ed.), *The pursuit of literacy: Early reading and writing.* Dubuque, IA: Kendal/Hunt.

Teale, W., & Sulzby, E. (Eds.), (1986). *Emergent literacy: Writing and reading.* Norwood, NJ: Ablex.

Turner, J. C. (1992, April). *Identifying motivation for literacy in first grade: An observational study.* Paper presented at the annual meeting of the American Educational Research Association, San Francisco.

Tway, E. (1991). The elementary school classroom. In J. Flood, J. M. Jensen, D. Lapp, & J. R. Squire (Eds.). *Handbook of research on teaching the English language arts.* New York: Macmillan.

Vygotsky, L. S. (1978). *Mind in society: The development of psychological processes.* Cambridge, MA: Harvard University Press.

Wells, G. (1985). *Language development in the pre-school years.* Cambridge: Cambridge University Press.

Wittrock, M. C. (1986). Students' thought processes. In M. C. Wittrock (Ed.), *Handbook of research on teaching* (pp. 297–314). New York: Macmillan.

Wood, K. (1990). Collaborative learning. *Reading Teacher, 43*(4), 346–347.

Woodward, C. (1984). Guidelines for facilitating sociodramatic play. *Childhood Education, 60,* 172–177.

Yager, S., Johnson, D. W., & Johnson, R. T. (1985). Oral discussion, group to individual transfer, and achievement in cooperative learning groups. *Journal of Educational Psychology, 77,* 60–66.

40

DRAMATIC PLAY, CONTEXT, AND CHILDREN'S COMMUNICATIVE BEHAVIOR

A. D. *Pellegrini*
UNIVERSITY OF GEORGIA

Over the past decade or so researchers have renewed their interest in the role of dramatic play in the lives of children, particularly as it relates to children's performance in school. Dramatic play is defined as fantasy, or pretense, play where children enact, either socially or alone, some make-believe theme. The commonality among these different labels is that children suspend reality in their interactions with peers, adults, and props. While recognized as a hallmark of the preschool period, dramatic play can be observed from the toddler period, throughout childhood, and into adulthood (see Fagen, 1996). Researchers, however, have been most interested in the ways in which aspects of young children's dramatic play, such as the oral language that accompanies dramatic play, relate to various educational and developmental outcomes, such as literacy. To this end, a number of integrative reviews have been written on the role of dramatic play in children's social and cognitive development (e.g., Christie & Johnsen, 1983; Rubin, Fein, & Vandenberg, 1983; Smith, 1982) and in oral language and literacy development (Fein, 1980; Garvey, 1984; Pellegrini, 1985a; Pellegrini & Galda, 1993; Wagner, 1992). The reader interested in general reviews of the role of dramatic play on aspects of children's development is referred to these excellent pieces.

In addition to the current interest in dramatic play, researchers are also currently interested in the various "contexts" of development and education. Much effort has been expended on exploring the influence of aspects of social context on children's development and learning. Students of children's play, too, have examined the role of social context, as well as physical context, in children's pretend play, language, and literacy (Haight & Miller, 1992; Morrow & Rand,

1991, this handbook; Neuman & Roskos, 1991; Vukelich, 1991) and social behavior (Howes, 1992).

In this chapter, I will attempt to extend the current research traditions in dramatic play and contextual influences on development and education. Specifically, I will first, and briefly, define what I mean by dramatic, or pretend, play. Second, I will outline my conceptualization of context. In this section, I will stress the transactional nature of context, or the ways in which children and the social and physical environments affect each other. Third, I will review the ways in which different contextual arrangements are accompanied by specific sorts of dramatic play and oral language.

DRAMATIC PLAY

For the purpose of this chapter, dramatic play will not be differentiated from fantasy, pretense, or symbolic play. Dramatic play is defined as the nonliteral (or symbolic) behavior that children use to transform (or change) the identities of objects, actions, and people (Fein, 1981; Garvey & Kramer, 1989). Children engage in dramatic play in many different social configurations: alone, with a parent, or with a peer, and with a variety of physical props, ranging from no props to explicitly defined theme, or replica, toys, such as Barbie dolls. Further, dramatic play, like other forms of play (see Fagen, 1981; Pellegrini & Boyd, 1993; Rubin, Fein, & Vandenberg, 1983), follows an inverted developmental U-function, first appearing around 1½ years of age, peaking during the late preschool/early primary school period, and then declining (Fein, 1981).

Work on this chapter was partially supported by a grant from the National Reading Research Center and the Institute of Behavioral Research, both at UGA.

For the purposes of this chapter, dramatic play is interesting because of the types of oral language that children use when playing. Specific design features of social dramatic play relate to the forms of language which children use in a variety of important situations, such as school literacy events. In this section I will outline some of these design features of dramatic play and note the accompanying forms of oral language.

Fein (1981) analyzed pretense play in terms of the following design features: decontextualization, object substitution, and role-playing. Decontextualization involves framing realistic events in fantasy; for example, pretending to eat dinner. Object substitution involves having one thing (e.g., a prop, gesture, or utterance) to represent something else; for example, a child verbally defines a stick as "my sword." Role-playing has players enacting real and pretend roles.

In one of those earlier reviews referenced above, I showed the ways in which these features of play related to children's language and literacy (Pellegrini, 1985). Suffice it to say that social dramatic play is characterized by a very specific sort of oral language. As Halliday (1969–70) noted 25 years ago, the "Imaginative Function" of language, or that form of language used when children engaged in social pretense, is elaborated, or decontextualized. In this register linguistic meaning is verbally encoded through cohesive ties (Halliday & Hasan, 1976), such as endophora and conjunctions. Others (e.g., Bernstein, 1960; Cook-Gumperz, 1977; Olson, 1977; Snow 1983) have also pointed out that the features of this register are similar to the register of school, and more specifically to the language of literacy (Olson, 1977).

As they engage in social dramatic play, children are learning to use this register while they are simultaneously learning other pragmatic and discourse level skills; thus, pretense may be a practice or learning venue for these important language skills (Garvey & Kramer, 1989).

I will briefly review those linguistic forms which correspond to the design features of pretend play. Of course these designs features co-occur; consequently, linguistic forms will also co-occur. So, for example, decontextualization, role-play, and object substitution often co-occur as, for example, when children pretend to build a "fort," each child dramatizes a different role, using pretend tools. Decontextualization is often realized linguistically with temporal (e.g., *and then*) and causal (e.g., *'cause*) conjunctions; thus, decontextualized drama often has a narrative structure (Wolf & Grollman, 1982).

Role-play is typically realized through the use of explicit linguistic reference, such as *I'll be the boss.* In this case the pronoun *I* is linguistically defined by its tie to *boss,* thus minimizing ambiguity. Similarly, such explicit reference is used with object substitutions. Indeed, such explicit definitions as, *Here's my hammer,* to transform a real stick into a pretend hammer, are not only used referentially in fantasy, but they are also used to signal other children that the event they are participating in is fantasy. Each of these language forms, in turn, has important implications for children's early school-based literacy and the interested reader is referred to numerous reviews on the topic (Christie, 1991; Pellegrini, 1985a,b; Pellegrini & Galda, 1993).

Recently, Catherine Garvey (Garvey & Kramer, 1989) analyzed the forms of language that young children (i.e., preschoolers) used to announce to their partners that "*This is play.*" Announcing "*This is play*" was labelled metacommunication, by Bateson (1956), and has been thoroughly studied (e.g., Auwarter, 1986; Giffin, 1984) since that time. Metacommunication is observed in dramatic play because of the communicative problems inherent in social pretending: enacting a decontextualized event; coordinating, negotiating, and clarifying the multiple meaning inherent in pretend scenes; and entering and terminating the pretend frame (Garvey & Kramer, 1989). Children use a specific register, marked by specific verb tenses, modal auxiliaries, and sentence/discourse complexity to metacommunicate in pretend play.

Past tense is used to "set the stage", or provide the background for the upcoming play episode, while present tense is used to enact the episode (Garvey & Kramer, 1989); for example, "*Once there was a little boy and he lost in the woods.*" Future tense is often used to plan the upcoming episode (Pellegrini, 1985b); for example, "*Let's pretend that you're gonna fall in the hole.*" Children more frequently use past and future tense verbs when they engage in fantasy play compared to nonpretend peer discourse (Pellegrini, 1986). This is commonsensical to the extent that in fantasy children are talking about things that are not there; past and future tense verbs also mark nonpresence. Further, the planning, assignment, and negotiation of pretend episodes necessitates using past tense.

Modal auxiliaries are used to mark mood, such as obligation (e.g., *You have'ta*), often at the onset of an episode (Garvey & Kramer, 1989). Regarding linguistic complexity, it is well documented that children use complex language during social pretense. As noted above, verbal explication is necessary in pretend because of its inherent ambiguity. At the utterance level, we know that in children's fantasy, compared with nonfantasy, language is functionally more diverse (Pellegrini, 1982). Similarly, children's choice of verbs is more diverse in fantasy than in nonfantasy (Wolf, Goldfield, Beeghly, & Cardona, 1985, cited in Garvey & Kramer, 1989). The actual verbs used in fantasy are often those that encode verbal and mental processes (Pellegrini & Galda, 1993).

By extension, complexity at the discourse level is another characteristic of pretend discourse. Just as sentence level complexity is the realization of explicit meaning, so too, at the discourse level. In fantasy, as noted above, children define potentially ambiguous terms, such as pronouns, with cross-sentential ties and use a variety of conjunctions to organize ideas across the play discourse (Pellegrini, 1982, 1986).

Garvey and Kramer (1989) raise an obvious, but often overlooked, point. The development of these language features, which we assume develop in the context of fantasy, is also developing in children's nonpretend discourse. Indeed, for some features, such as the use of adjectives to elaborate meaning (Pellegrini, 1986), there is no difference between fantasy and nonfantasy; children's use of these terms increases across the preschool period. Rather than minimizing the role of pretend play in learning and developing these forms, I would argue that pretend play is a vital part of children's everyday life which they delve in and out to learn and practice all sorts of new behaviors. I will also argue that pretend, or dramatic, play is one of the most important contexts for learning and development during the early childhood period. As part of this argument, I must first define context.

What is Context?

Context is a term very frequently used in educational, psychological, and anthropological research. Context is often defined in terms of social dimensions and physical dimensions (e.g., Caldwell & Bradley, 1984; Wachs, 1990). Social dimensions of context can be further refined by considering the number of participants, as in social network theory (e.g., Cochran & Riley, 1988), the status of the participants, as in peer versus adult interaction (e.g., Tudge & Rogoff, 1989), or the specific relationships between participants, such as friends versus nonfriends (Hartup, 1996). Physical dimensions of context can be proximal, such as the props in the dramatic play center of a classroom, or distal, the number of books read to a child across the school year.

Many conceptualizations of context, as noted by Bronfenbrenner (1979) and Hinde (1980), share two unfortunate, and interrelated, features. First, many dichotomize social and physical contexts by looking at the ways in which variables in each, independent of the other, relate to children's behavior. Second, context is often conceptualized in unidirectional terms; that is, the environments are sometimes seen as "coercing" (Barker, 1968) behaviors in children. Examples of this sort of work include looking at "effects" of classroom structure on children's behavior (see Minuchin & Shapiro, 1983, for a review) and the role of activity centers on children's pretend play and literate behavior. The assumption behind these conceptions, not unlike those of S-R psychologists, is that social and physical aspects of context shape children's behavior; the organism is a passive recipient of environmental stimuli.

Again evoking Bronfenbrenner (1979) and Hinde (1980), we know that contexts and persons are transactional; that is, they affect each other. Specifically, children often self-select themselves into desirable contexts and then interact with the contexts in such a way as to make it most suitable for them. For example, certain children may choose to engage in dramatic play on the playground, enacting Power Rangers; these children choose other like-minded individuals; individuals' behavior, in turn, influences others' behavior (e.g., cooperative acts are reciprocated). Additionally, individuals influence aspects of the physical context of the playground (e.g., a slide becomes a launching pad). In this latter case, it is important to recognize that individuals also change physical aspects of their environment to suit their needs.

Even in cases where children are not free to choose the location or their playmates for activities, as is the case in many academic settings, children can choose how they define that context; they can read, clandestinely, daydream, or act out. To

ethologists, such as Hinde (1980), and ethnographers, such as Erickson and Shultz (1977), it is assumed that people choose their "niche" and "furnish" it in their own ways: People affect context and contexts affect people.

In this section I review research on a more specific level of context—social participation in dramatic play. I argue that social participants, who may be superficially similar (such as peers), often play differential roles in children's play, depending on their relationships. By relationships I mean, the interactional history between two people (Hinde, 1980). Interactional history, as noted above, is affected in a dialectical way, by individual and situational variables. This history, in turn, influences future interactions. For example, children in a classroom may be assigned by their teacher to "play" at the same center. Because of similar interests and repeated interactions, these children become friends; their friendship, in turn, affects their play. The specific relationships that I will be concerned include, from the peer world, sibling and friendship relationships and, from the adult–child world, attachment relationships.

The importance of examining context in terms of relationships, I think, is that it specifies more exactly the social arrangements that relate to learning and development. For example, conceptualizing context in terms of peer interaction or adult–child interaction is often too global because there are different sorts of relationships within each of these configurations, each of which relates differentially to children's dramatic play and language.

My examination of social contexts and the specific types of relationships that comprise social context, begins with descriptions of naturalistic studies of children playing with a parent, or more exactly, mother, and siblings. The value of examining naturally occurring dramatic play, especially if it is embedded in a longitudinal research design, is straightforward enough, at least for me: It provides insight into the ways in which pretense play and language *actually* develop across childhood. By contrast, laboratory studies of these sorts of interactions, while useful at later stages of theory testing, inform us as to what *can* develop (McCall, 1977).

The paucity of naturalistic, longitudinal research on children's play is quite surprising, especially in light of the popularity of dramatic play and language in the child development and educational literatures. There are two noteworthy exceptions, Wendy Haight and Judy Dunn. Both researchers have spent substantial amounts of time in homes observing and recording the play and language between children and their parents, siblings, and peers. Haight's (Haight & Miller, 1992) longitudinal study of the pretend play of middle-class children from 12–48 months of age found that children's primary playmate was mother until 36 months, after which children played with siblings and peers, thus supporting the notion that pretend develops in an interpersonal context (Vygotsky, 1978). Also in support of Vygotskyan theory, children appropriated responsibility from mother (e.g., more frequently initiating play) with age. By the time children were 48 months, their play with peers and siblings was more involved (i.e., longer episodes) than their play with mothers. Thus, mothers seem to introduce children to social fantasy by initiating play themes and modeling fantasy language; by their third birthday children were able to use these strategies with other children.

Dunn's (Dunn, 1988; Dunn & Dale, 1984) observations of young children in their homes point to clear differences in the ways in which mothers and older children play with the younger sibling. While mothers' play with children is very supportive it is often not as active as the play with an older sibling. For example, mothers are frequently observers of their children's pretend while older siblings often take a complementary pretend role (Dunn, 1988). Further, mothers' play with 2-year-olds often involves replica toys or objects whereas play with older siblings was less object-oriented and more frequently involved young children using language to sustain the pretend (Dunn & Dale, 1984). It may be that youngsters enjoy playing with an older sibling more than with mother; thus, they are more willing to comply with the demands of the older child (Dunn, 1988) and engage in a form of social pretend that is rather cognitively demanding.

MOTHER–CHILD PRETEND PLAY AND ATTACHMENT RELATIONSHIPS

In these two instances I have sketched differences in the pretend play of young children when they play with an adult (in the form of mother) and other children, including siblings. Taking a relationship, perspective, I would expect there to be different sorts of play exhibited between mothers and children as a function of their relationships history. Most research in this area utilizes attachment theory as a measure of the mother–child relationship. Generally, attachment is a measure of the degree to which children and their mothers have a secure or insecure relationship. Attachment relationships are thought to provide the basis for children's interactions with parents, other adults, and peers. Secure, compared to insecure, attachment relationships are characterized by more synchronous and flexible interactions between mothers and children (see Bretherton & Waters, 1985, for a summary).

The pretend play of securely attached children is more frequent and more synchronous (e.g., positive and responsive) with their mothers and with their peers, compared to their insecurely attached counterparts (Howes, 1992). Correspondingly, securely attached children, compared to insecurely attached, are more successful at initiating play with their mothers (Roggman & Langlois, 1987) and engaging in longer and more complex forms of fantasy (Slade, 1987a, 1987b).

This brief foray into attachment relationships was meant to be an illustrative, rather than exhaustive, discussion of the ways in which one aspect of social context, mother–child interaction, can be more clearly specified in terms of their relationships history. If this variable were to be disregarded, and only mother–child interaction were to be studied, an interesting and important aspect of social context would be missed. In the next section I will illustrate the ways in which different sorts of peer relationships relate to children's pretend play and language.

PEER PLAY, SIBLINGS, AND FRIENDSHIPS

Peer play has received much attention in the educational and developmental literature. Attachment theorists, for example, have discussed children's peer relations, friendship, and play patterns as an outgrowth of the attachment relationships (Howes, 1992). Other theorists have contrasted peer interaction with adult–child interaction as a venue for stimulating children's social cognitive development. Providing the foundation for the facilitative role of peers on development, Piaget's (1983) theory stressed the role of conceptual conflict and resulting reequilibration that typifies the reciprocal roles that peers take with each other. This is contrasted with the more subordinate, and complementary roles that children take when interacting with adults. While the contrastive role of peers and adults in children's cognitive development has yielded some very interesting findings and brought us closer to explicating the role of social context in development (e.g., Tudge & Rogoff, 1989), not all peer interactions are alike. Just as attachment history influences the quality of mother–child play, so too with peer interactions.

At a very basic level, it is illustrative to note that children's pretend play differs as a function of their playmates. For example, Kramer, Bukowski, and Garvey (1989) found that the language of preschoolers varied significantly across different triadic partners. By way of explanation for the seemingly unreliable behavior of play behavior, researchers have explored a number of avenues. Doyle (1982), for example, has suggested that preschool children's familiarity with each other has an important impact on their pretend play. When comparing the social and cognitive dimensions of the preschoolers play, Doyle found that children's interactions were more cooperative, active (i.e., involved), and dramatic in familiar dyads, compared to interactions with unfamiliar peers. Familiar children were also more willing to imitate their peers' play than the play of unfamiliar peers.

Familiarity is necessary, but not sufficient, for another important dimension of peer interaction: friendship. By friendship I mean dyadic groupings that make reciprocal choices of each other. So friends would nominate each other as friends and would also be observed interacting with each other. Obviously, children must be familiar with each other before they can be friends. Indeed, the degree to which children are familiar with each other, in terms of spending time in proximity to each other and sharing similar play preferences, is a very good predictor of their becoming friends (Hartup, 1983). Thus, friends, like other familiar peers, know, (usually) trust, and reinforce each other.

The level of trust between preschoolers who are friends, compared to nonfriends, is indicated by the high levels of self disclosure during social pretend play (Howes, 1992). Not surprisingly, the play between preschoolers who are friends, compared to nonfriends, is longer and more harmonious (Gottman, 1983). When conflicts do arise, friends are more likely to resolve the conflicts and resolve them equitably (Hartup, 1996). Play for friends, because of these features, tends to reinforce the strength of the friendship. Children enjoy playing with their friends and consequently they exert many cognitive resources to maintain it, the end result being complex and sustained interaction.

Another close relationship, like attachment and friendship, is the sibling relationship. Siblings are, generally, very familiar and trusting of each other (Dunn, 1988). Younger siblings, specifically, tend to follow the lead of older siblings in pretend play. Indeed, Dunn suggests that older siblings are more able than mothers to elicit sophisticated levels of pretend from their younger siblings; for example, fantasy of siblings is more symbolic than the mother–child play. Further, siblings maintain fantasy more frequently through linguistic interaction, while mothers and children's play is more directly tied to physically present objects.

CONCLUSION

To sum up, I have illustrated the ways in which particular aspects of context affect the pretend play and accompanying oral language of young children. I focused on one dimension of the social groupings of pretend—the nature of children's relationships with their playmates. Examining specific relationships between children and the age-mates and adults enables us to more clearly understand the actual processes of social interaction responsible for learning and develop-ment. The brief review presented here suggests that trust, modeling, and mutual reinforcement are important aspects of close relationships which are important for children's development. The trust and enjoyment typical of play between children and others with whom they have a close relationship allows them to express themselves, imitate and disagree with others, as well as compromise, all in the service of maintaining enjoyable social interaction.

That these sophisticated language forms and social behaviors occur in pretend play probably has something to do with the fact that children, and adults, enjoy this activity. This is not to say, of course, that there are other equally enjoyable events which may have enriching effects on children's language and representational capacity. Another likely candidate, of course, is joint book reading. Parents and children enjoy this activity and children may learn similar linguistic forms here as they do in pretend. (For contrasting data see Goelman, 1996; Snow et al., 1976). It would be interesting to compare the ways in which children listen to books read by siblings and friends.

The goal of research in pretend play, from my perspective, is to identify the places where and participants with whom children play. This should be done in a variety of situations, including home, playground, and school; of course, the situations must be studied across time.

References

Auwarter, M. (1986). Development of communicative skills. In J. Cook-Gumperz, W. Corsaro, & J. Streeck (Eds.), *Children's worlds and children's language* (pp. 205–230). Berlin: De Gruyter

Barker, R. (1968). *Ecological psychology.* Stanford, CA: Stanford University Press.

Bateson, G. (1956). The message is " This is play." In *Group processes: Transactions of the second conference* (pp. 145–242). New York: Josiah Macy Foundation.

Bernstein, B. (1960). Language and social class. *British Journal of Sociology, 2,* 217–276.

Bretherton, I., & Waters, E. (1985). Growing points in attachment theory and research. *Monographs of the Society for Research in Child Development, 50,* (1–2, Serial No. 209).

Bronfenbrenner, U. (1979). *The ecology of human development.* Cambridge, MA: Harvard University Press.

Caldwell, B., & Bradley, R. (1984). *The HOME Inventory.* Little Rock, AR: University of Arkansas.

Christie, J. (Ed.), (1991). *Play and early literacy development.* Albany, NY: State University of New York Press.

Christie, J., & Johnsen, P. (1983). The role of play in social-intellectual development. *Review of Educational Research, 53,* 93–115.

Cochran, M., & Riley, D. (1988). Mother reports of children's personal networks. In S. Salzinger, J. Antrobus, & M. Hammer (Eds.), *Social networks of children* (pp. 13–147). Hillsdale, NJ: Erlbaum.

Cook-Gumperz, J. (1977). Situated instructions. In S, Ervin-Tripp & C. Mitchell-Kernan (Eds.), *Child discourse* (pp. 103–124). New York: Academic Press.

Doyle, A. (1982). Friends, acquaintances, and strangers: The influence of familiarity and ethnolinguistic background on social interaction. In K. Rubin, & H. Ross (Eds.). *Peer relationships and social skills in children* (pp. 229–252). New York: Springer.

Dunn, J. (1988). *The beginnings of social understanding.* Cambridge, MA: Harvard University Press.

Dunn, J., & Dale, (1984). I a Daddy: 2-year-olds' collaboration in joint pretend with sibling and with mother. In I. Bretherton (Ed.), *Symbolic play* (pp. 131–158). New York: Academic Press.

Erickson, F., & Shultz, J. (1977). When is a context? *Newsletter of the Institute for Comparative Human Cognition, 1,* 5–10.

Fagen, R. (1981). *Animal play behavior.* New York: Oxford University Press.

Fagen, R. (1996) Animal play, games of angels, biology, and Brian. In A. D. Pellegrini (Ed.), *The future of play theory: Essays in honor of Brian Sutton-Smith.* Albany, NY: State University of New York Press.

Fein, G. (1980). Echoes from the nursery: Piaget, Vygotsky, and the relationships between language and play. In E. Winner & H. Gardner (Eds.), *Fact, fiction, and fantasy* (pp. 1–14). San Francisco: Jossey-Bass.

Fein, G. (1981). Pretend play in childhood: An integrative review. *Child Development, 52,* 1095–1118.

Garvey, C. (1984). *Children's talk.* Cambridge, MA: Harvard University Press.

Garvey, C., & Kramer, T. (1989). The language of social pretend play. *Developmental Review, 9,* 364–382.

Giffin, H. (1984). The coordination of meaning in the creation of shared make-believe reality. In I. Bretherton (Ed.), *Symbolic play* (pp. 73–101). New York: Academic Press.

Goelman, H. (1996). Literate apprenticeships and oral discourse. In K. Reeder, J. Shapiro, R. Watson, & H. Goelman, (Eds.), *Literate apprenticeships: The emergence of language and literacy in the preschool years.* (pp. 101–118). Norwood, NJ: Ablex.

Gottman, J. (1983). How children become friends. *Monographs of the Society for Research in Child Development, 48,* (Serial No. 201).

Haight, W., & Miller, P. (1992). *The ecology of everyday pretending.* Albany, NY: State University of New York Press.

Halliday, M. A. K. (1969–70). Relevant models of language. *Educational Review, 22,* 26–37.

Halliday, M. A. K., & Hasan, R. (1976). *Cohesion in English.* London: Longman.

Hartup, W. (1983). Peer relations. In E.M. Hetherington (Ed.). *Manual of child psychology* (Vol. 4, pp. 103–196). New York: Wiley.

Hartup W. (1996). The company they keep. *Child Development, 67,* 1–13.

Hinde, R. (1980). *Ethology.* London: Fontana.

Howes, C. (1992). *The collaborative construction of play.* Albany, NY: State University of New York Press.

Kramer, T., Bukowski, W., & Garvey, C. (1989). The influence of the dyadic context on the conversational and linguistic behavior of its members. *Merrill Palmer Quarterly, 35,* 327–341.

McCall, R. (1977). Challenges to a science of developmental psychology. *Child Development, 48,* 333–344.

Minuchin, P., & Shapiro, E. (1983). The school as a context for social development. In E.M. Hetherington (Ed.), *Manual of child psychology* (Vol. 4, pp. 197–274). New York: Wiley.

Morrow, L., & Rand, M. (1991). Preparing the classroom environment to promote literacy during play. In J. Christie (Ed.), *Play and early literacy development* (pp. 141–166). Albany, NY: State University of New York Press.

Neuman, S., & Roskos, K. (1991). The influence of literacy enriched play centers on preschoolers conceptions of the function of print. In J. Christie (Ed.), *Play and early literacy development* (pp. 167–188). Albany, NY: State University of New York Press.

Olson, D. (1977). From utterance to text. *Harvard Educational Review, 47,* 257–281.

Pellegrini, A. D. (1982). The construction of cohesive text by preschoolers in two play contexts. *Discourse Processes, 5,* 101–108.

Pellegrini, A. D. (1985a). The relations between symbolic play and literate behavior. *Review of Educational Research, 55,* 107–121.

Pellegrini, A. D. (1985b). Relations between preschool children's symbolic play and literate behavior. In L. Galda, & A. D. Pellegrini (Eds.), *Play, language, and stories* (pp. 79–98). Norwood, NJ: Ablex.

Pellegrini, A. D. (1986). Play centers and the production of imagina-

tive language. *Discourse Processes, 9,* 115–125.

Pellegrini, A. D., & Boyd, B. (1993). The role of play in early childhood development and education: Issues of definition an function. In B. Spodek (Ed.), *Handbook of research on the education of young children* (pp. 105–121). New York: Macmillan.

Pellegrini, A. D., & Galda, L. (1993). Ten years after: A reexamination of symbolic play and literacy research. *Reading Research Quarterly, 28,* 163–175.

Piaget, J. (1983). Piaget's theory. In W. Kessen (Ed.), *Manual of child psychology* (Vol. 1, pp. 103–128). New York: Wiley.

Roggman, L., & Langlois, J. (1987). Mothers, infants, and toys: Social play correlates of attachment. *Infant Behavior and Development, 10,* 233–237.

Rubin, K., Fein, G., & Vandenberg, B. (1983). Children's play. In E. M. Hetherington (Ed.), *Manual of child psychology* (Vol. 4, pp. 693–774). New York: Wiley.

Slade, A. (1987a). A longitudinal study of maternal involvement and symbolic play during the toddler period. *Child Development, 58*(A), 367–375.

Slade, A. (1987b). Quality of attachment and early symbolic play. *Developmental Psychology, 23,* 78–85.

Smith, P. K. (1982). Does play matter? Functional and evolutionary aspects of animal and human play. *The Behavioral and Brain Sciences, 5,* 517–523.

Snow, C. (1983). Literacy and language: Relationships during the preschool years. *Harvard Educational Review, 83,* 165–189.

Snow, C., Arlman-Rupp, Hassing, Y., Jobse, J., Joosten, J., & Vorster, J. (1976). Mothers' speech in three social classes. *Journal of Psycholinguistic Research, 5,* 1–20.

Tudge, J., & Rogoff, B. (1989). Peer influences on cognitive development. In M. Bornstein, & J. Bruner (Eds.), *Interaction in human development* (pp. 17–40). Hillsdale, NJ: Erlbaum.

Vukelvich, C. (1991). Materials and modeling: Promoting literacy during play. In J. Christie (Ed.), *Play and early literacy development* (pp. 215–231). Albany, NY: State University of New York Press.

Vygotsky, L. (1978). *Mind in society.* Cambridge, MA: Harvard University Press.

Wachs, T. (1990). Must the physical environment be mediated by the social environment in order to influence development? *Journal of Applied Developmental Psychology, 11,* 163–178.

Wagner, B. (1992). Imaginative expression. In J. Jensen (Ed.), *Handbook of research on teaching the English language arts* (pp. 787–804). New York: Macmillan.

Wolf, D., & Grollman, S. (1982). Ways of playing. In D. Pepler, & K. Rubin (Eds.), *The play of children.* Basel, Switzerland: Karger.

41

DRAMA WORLDS:
PLACES OF THE HEART,
HEAD, VOICE, AND HAND
IN DRAMATIC INTERPRETATION

Shelby Wolf
UNIVERSITY OF COLORADO AT BOULDER

Brian Edmiston & Patricia Enciso
OHIO STATE UNIVERSITY

We accept the fact that the actor infuses his [sic] own voice, his own body, his own gestures—in short his own interpretation—into the words of the text. Is he not simply carrying to its ultimate manifestation what each of us as readers of the text must do? (Rosenblatt, 1978, p. 13)

The combination of reading with dramatic interpretation—infusing text with the lively play of voice, body, and gesture—is a notion that seems to hover in America's literacy education and goes in and out of focus depending on the historical period (Robinson, Faraone, Hittleman, & Unruh, 1990). As Martin (1992) suggests, "perhaps at one time in American history our country could afford schools that severed heads from hands and hearts," but this is no longer the case. Instead, she reminds us that schools should be places where "mind and body, thought and action, reason and emotion are all being educated" (pp. 86, 87). Yet, how do we build a place in school where integration rather than separation is the norm? Rosenblatt's (1978) metaphor for the connections between drama and reading can be a powerful reminder of possibilities, for it invites us to establish new connections among students' textual experiences and the social and imaginative worlds students create together.

In advocating classroom drama, we support literacy which shifts meaning and control from teachers and texts to students and teachers who create meaning together as they interpret, dramatize, and dialogue with texts. We regard literacy as much more than reading, writing and speaking, and listening. Literacy is "reading the world" (Freire, 1972) and "working the world" (Willinsky, 1990) as much as it is reading or working a text. The classroom that uses drama for alternative modes of meaning making is a place where "students and teachers can also be empowered to rethink the world-in-progress and their place in it" (Apple, 1990, p. xii). It is a place that deliberately constructs and reconstructs spaces for learning that can include students' multiple social, cultural, and expressive knowledge. Thus, drama educates for a freedom of the imagination in which students of diverse cultural backgrounds can connect with and transform texts in dramatic interpretations and thereby "surpass the given and look at things as if they could be otherwise" (Greene, 1988, p. 3).

This chapter is designed to serve as a map to places where the integration of drama with literacy exists—places of the heart, head, voice, and hand—all of which lie in the realm of what Stanislavski (My Life in Art, cited in Cole & Chinoy, 1970) terms "the magic if":

I came to understand that creativeness begins from that moment when in the soul and imagination of the actor there appears the magical, creative *if* … that is, the imagined truth which the actor can believe as sincerely and with greater enthusiasm than he believes practical truth, just as the child believes in the existence of its doll and of all life in it and around it. From the moment of the appearance of *if* the actor passes from the plane of actual reality into the plane of another life, created and imagined by himself. Believing in this life, the actor can begin to create. (pp. 494, 495)

It is the notion of shifting planes and altering perspectives by entering a conditional world that is important for players reading, writing, or enacting a piece of literature or exposition. To be able to cast themselves in the space and time of others, to walk between the pages of a book and imagine "what would happen if …," not simply to mouth the lines and mimic the motions, but to understand, create, and convey meaning—this echoes Rosenblatt's (1978) description of the "ultimate manifestation" that readers as well as actors must do.

As children read and enact their interpretations, they express not only the possible worlds of other characters in time and space but the actual minds and imaginative possibilities of their own reality. Writers, too, must be able to see their work as more than "dummy runs" (Britton, 1972); as they create stories, letters, documents, scientific or historical reports they also engage in "social work" (Dyson, 1993). Writers in schools use situations to complete both the official work of the classroom and the unofficial work of negotiating their social positions with teachers and peers. Drama experiences, like children's play, can enable students to construct purposes and audiences for their writing. Thus, they simultaneously accomplish the official work of the classroom curriculum, while they move across perspectives and positions to "place" themselves in multiple social roles both within and outside the world of the classroom.

We begin this chapter by discussing two kinds of classroom drama—each of which encompasses a variety of specific dramatic forms—for commonalties and contrasts. We then look at these two kinds across the body of dramatic enactment. We first explore the heart and the head of drama, combining them to emphasize their integration. We then carry these concepts into the voice and ultimately the hand to show how drama fuses emotion and intellect through communicative channels and action. Throughout these sections, we emphasize Heathcote's (1984) notion of "framing." We suggest that children in drama not only try on particular roles, but experience feelings of commitment and responsibility to dramatic encounters as they interact with new perspectives.

KINDS OF DRAMA

Although drama appears in multiple forms, here we explore two perspectives on drama— one which pays close attention to the text on the page and one that emphasizes text as a starting point for exploring meanings beyond the page. The first entails dramatizing at the *center of text* and the second involves dramatizing at the *edges of text*. Yet, rather than dichotomize these two dramatic forms, we emphasize that

both are art forms and both are learning processes. Hughes (1991) has clarified that there is actually "a complex dialectic" between "drama as an art form" and "drama as a learning process." The first focuses on "actor/audience relationship and the semiotics of performance" while the second "accentuates the paradoxical nature of play in which the child can be engaged in a fictional world while simultaneously reflecting upon its symbolic significance" (p. 1). He goes on to say:

The debate, between those supporting Drama as a learning medium and those proclaiming the primacy of the art form, has led to a wide variation in teaching practice. There are some who say *I teach for art;* others see the extension of human empathy as essential. In Australia, the majority of educational Drama teachers seem to view both concerns as important. (p. 1)

In this chapter, we take the relationship of drama with written literary text—particularly the proximal distance between the two—to be a productive focus for understanding drama and literacy education and research. Yet, like literary genres which Fowler (1982) suggests are "not permanent classes but … families subject to change" (p. v), the lines between different dramatic forms often blur. More important, the distance between literary text and dramatic enactment often works in accordion-like fashion—shrinking and stretching to meet the needs of the moment. Our point here is not to set up definitive categories, but rather to look at two large families of drama as they exist in classrooms today.

Dramatizing at the Center of Text

Dramatizing at the center of the text places the written piece of literature or exposition at center stage. Children read, interpret, and negotiate the enactment of text adhering (more or less) to the characters, dialogue, and plot written on the page. Even when written texts are adapted for various forms of production, McCaslin (1990) suggests that playwrights "must make every effort to retain the essential elements of the source material so as not to disappoint or offend the audience" (p. 161). Many teachers rely on professional playwrights and published suggestions (Wills, 1989), while others prefer to transform tradebook texts with their children, enacting particular scenes or transforming entire pieces for the classroom stage. No matter who serves as playwright—teachers, children, or professional playwrights—there is a sense of remaining "true" to the text on the page.

There are multiple forms that emphasize dramatizing at the center. Table 41–1 lists and defines three current forms:

Although Siks (1983) suggests that in story theatre "players are guided to *tell the story,* to be true to its intent, rather than to aim to elaborate, digress, or change its theme" (p. 48), her description could apply to all three of the forms above. As McCaslin (1990) explains, in all of these forms "the primary virtue is the text" (p. 280).

Dramatizing at the Edges of Text

When dramatizing at the edges of text, the players do not have a script, though a story may become a "narrative prop"

TABLE 41–1. Dramatizing at the Center of Text

Story Theatre

In story theatre, a narrator (usually the classroom teacher) tells or reads a story with children seated in a semicircle. Siks (1983) tells us that there are three basic rules to follow: (a) *the rule of the theatre*—in which children take on character or scenic roles and move on stage to enact a part and off to be an audience for other roles, (b) *the rule of instant action*—the children must move the instant a role is called for and then quickly exit, and (c) *the rule of instant cooperation*—since roles are not assigned, children must cooperate to allow individuals to take on specific parts, though at times, parts can be taken by more than one player. This last rule also emphasizes the equal distribution of roles so the play is not dominated by a few eager volunteers (p. 48).

Readers Theatre

Readers theatre is "a form of group storytelling in which two or more readers present a piece of literature by reading aloud from hand-held scripts" (Robertson, 1990, p. 2). Children (a) read a story, (b) make selective and analytical choices in transforming the story into a script through social negotiation, (c) formulate, practice, and refine their interpretations, (d) perform for an audience, and (e) evaluate their performance (Shanklin & Rhodes, 1989). Readers theatre is often defined by its emphasis on language; performances involve no use of costumes or props; actors face the audience rather than each other; characters are brought to life through choices in voice and minimal gestures (Busching, 1981; Landy, 1982; Robertson, 1990; Sloyer, 1982).

Classroom Theatre

Classroom theatre is a blend of creative drama and readers theatre that ultimately has much in common with regular theatre. Classroom theatre takes and reshapes the best from both worlds—offering children opportunities to (a) participate in theatre games to exercise their voices and bodies as well as build concentration, and (b) collaboratively produce theatrical interpretations of selected scenes in published texts (Wolf, 1994, 1995). Children are encouraged to think like actors, using the technical vocabulary of the theatre and the strategies of those on the stage—marking their scripts to note body movement and intonation, arranging for a prompter if needed, and running their lines repeatedly, though they can enact the final performance with hand-held scripts.

(Heath & Branscombe, 1986) around which students and teacher raise questions and enact possible situations. Rather than providing students with words to interpret and enact, the whole or parts of the narrative become a prop or "pretext" for creating a play world which intersects and interacts with both the world of the story and the actual world of the students. The pretext, as defined by Rogers and O'Neill (1993), is the shared beginning point for wide-ranging explorations of human relations and interpretations. Students' interpretive actions and discussions around the pretext will be informed by their personal and social experiences, their ideas of cultural norms and expectations, and the imaginative power they bring to experiencing, rethinking and transforming human dilemmas. Students' interpretations and creations of texts arise through improvised encounters which enable them to explore the ambiguities and possibilities of the text. Though at various points in the work some students may watch as others show or demonstrate, no

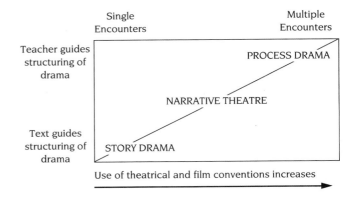

FIGURE 41–1 Features of Dramatizing at the Edges of Text

final performance is being prepared: the process is the product. In a sense, by dramatizing at the edges of the text, children's interpretive processes and perspectives, as well as the teacher's role in structuring those processes and perspectives are drawn into the center. As Heathcote (1984) stresses, "When it comes to the interpretation of ideas it is the child's viewpoint which is important ... he [sic] is offering a viewpoint and in return the teacher may offer another one" (p. 85).

Dramatizing at the edges of the text may take many forms and be referred to by various names. The terms drama in education and educational drama (Bolton, 1979; Heathcote, 1984) are used more generically. Story drama (Booth, 1985, 1994, 1995), narrative theatre (Edmiston, Enciso, & King, 1987), and process drama (O'Neill, 1991; O'Toole, 1992) are three other descriptive terms. These forms of drama are not distinctive and in practice overlap. However, all of these forms of drama are distinguished by their attention to process and the teacher's selection of and participation in encounters that may be actually evident in a text or only implied.

As seen in Figure 41–1, the teacher may focus on one encounter with children that is fairly close to the actual text. The teacher may make dramatizing at the edges of the text more complex in two ways: (1) increase the number of encounters, and (2) rely less on encounters in the actual text and more on his or her own aesthetic structuring of the drama.

There are many forms that emphasize dramatizing at the edge of text. Table 41–2 lists and defines three current forms, although it is important to remember that the lines between these kinds of dramatizing are often blurred. These approaches to drama, particularly process drama, may seem to require considerable skills and knowledge related to theatre and playwriting. Although "doing drama" in these ways may seem daunting, very rich, accessible drama experiences can be created with reference to some widely known conventions and principles of sociodramatic play. The following touchstones may be useful to a beginning drama and literacy educator:

(1) The source for creating dramatic images and encounters is as limitless as the whole array of theatrical and film

TABLE 41–2. Dramatizing at the Edges of Text

Story Drama

Story dramas (Booth, 1995) are generally very focused on a single encounter or several brief encounters that are elaborated on and interpreted over time. As teachers work in this way, they use the text as a basis for determining which characters will be encountered, what problems inherent in the story are of concern, and what decisions and actions need to be taken. The players, in turn, interpret the story in ways which are meaningful to them—an interpretation which may ignore subtle details of the story or alter the story in substantive ways (e.g., changing the ending). Although their personal interpretations are elicited, players are also working within a shared social context. Thus, the story becomes a pretext to involve the children in ways of negotiating and dealing with imagining alternative possibilities beyond those in the text as well as those which they encounter in their actual lives.

Narrative Theatre

In narrative theatre (Edmiston et al., 1987), the teacher also relies on the text, and may actually read from it. He or she does so initially to guide students' actions and interpretations of the words of the characters or narrator in a story. However, in narrative theatre, students may be involved in numerous encounters covering the full chronology of the story while the teacher or students read excerpts from the text to set the scene or, as in readers theatre, devise possible interpretations of a character's meaning. Narrative theatre could be located at the midpoint of the continua in Figure 41–1. Dramatic encounters will be shaped by both the text and the teacher. The characters and the author's words can be used, as well as the students' own writings and interpretations. The teacher will both structure encounters and participate in imaginary interactions with the students. The students could be engaged in encounters implied by the circumstances of the story but also in encounters imagined by the students and teacher.

Process Drama

Process drama relies more on the teacher's knowledge of aesthetic structuring through improvisation and the use of theatrical and film processes and conventions in order to create multiple and carefully sequenced ways of creating dramatic art with students (O'Neill, 1991, 1994). As with story drama and narrative theatre the teacher can enter into the fictional world of a text. The text can provide them with an initial dilemma or situation. However, the original text will soon be supplemented by the texts which arise among students and teacher as they interact (Enciso & Edmiston, in press). It is not that a text is absent from this approach to dramatizing, instead it is "under construction."

conventions (e.g., tableaux, dreams, multiple 'selves' speaking across time and space, etc.). Nearly every film uses time shifts, overheard conversations, or setting changes. Teachers who begin to pay attention to the ways in which filmmakers and theatre directors create situations or encounters among characters may try these out with students as they read, interpret, and write texts. A number of excellent publications are also available that fully describe a series of drama encounters and/or describe theatrical and film conventions that can be used in drama (Bolton, 1992; Morgan & Saxton, 1987; Neelands, 1990; O'Neill & Lambert, 1983; O'Neill, Lambert, Linnell, & Warr-Wood, 1976; O'Toole & Haseman, 1988; Swartz, 1988; Tarlington & Verriour, 1991).

(2) Following the reading of a story or some part of a story, drama can begin with the simple invitation, "Let's imagine that. ...." Just as children often initiate play by entering into an imaginary situation from a book and assign themselves and their friends various roles (Wolf & Heath, 1992), so also students in supportive classrooms will adopt imaginary perspectives. Students' involvement in these encounters is often generated and guided by the features of play that have always attracted children: They are invited to "be a head taller" (Vygotsky, 1978), to imagine themselves as participants in a world where they have power to make choices, to take action, and to interpret circumstances. In drama, adults and students speak and interact together with the understanding that the students have an urgent responsibility to find out, make decisions, or interpret data. As in play, students are thinking through situations while they are in the midst of them, as participants who have the authority to act. They are not talking about what they would do if they were a certain character—they are doing it and finding out what it means to *be* in a situation and experience the consequences of actions.

(3) Students may adopt and shift perspectives as a group rather than as individual actors. For example, children can imagine they are the parents of children who live near Red Riding Hood's family and are concerned about Little Red Riding Hood's late return from her grandmother's house. They can also shift perspectives to test out possible meanings or thematic directions implied by the story. For example, if they shift to the perspective of wolves' parents, they entertain a completely different view of 'wolfish' behavior than that portrayed in the folktale. Having taken both parental views (and other possible perspectives related to the story), students are in a position to advise community members on safety or animal–human coexistence.

(4) Teachers enter the drama world and adopt positions alongside or in opposition to the students. Evaluative statements and questions are raised as possibilities that can be considered rather than regarded as authoritative judgments that must be accepted. In the scenario described above, for example, the teacher could adopt the position of a forest ranger who raises questions about the students' proposed standards for safety or planned education of young animals and humans. The teacher could shift to another perspective, such as an editor of the local newspaper who sends the students/reporters to conduct interviews about safety practices.

(5) In a drama world the teacher can always place herself in a position of relative (and often fictional) incompetence. She needs their help or she needs to know something from them. She can become very inept; for example, she could represent Red Riding Hood's parent who has no idea how to track wolves. In addition, the students can often be cast as "experts" so that they interact from positions of strength and competence. Students could be expert planners who create a wildlife refuge. They could be journalists who are expert at writing for a newspaper or creating a newspaper layout. The teacher can still "teach" but now she can do so indirectly and in response to students' needs. Extended uses of this strategy, called "mantle of the expert" by Dorothy Heathcote, are

described in Bolton (1992), Heathcote and Bolton (1995), Heathcote and Herbert (1985), and Wagner (1985).

DRAMA WORLDS

Blurred and at times extinguished by standardized expectations for response, Rosenblatt's (1978) image of reader as active interpreter through multiple channels of communication is more often a metaphor for reading than a reality. Yet, dramatizing at the center and at the edges of the text creates places that bring the vision to actuality. These places exist in the hearts, heads, voices, and hands of children and their teachers as they interpret and integrate the texts on the page and the texts of their lives.

Places of the Heart and Head

Rather than separate intellect from affect, drama, like life, weaves the two together—integrating mind and emotion within the experience and action of specific situations. As Dewey (1934) noted, the arts are experienced intellectually, emotionally, and consciously in a "union of sense, need, impulse and action" (p. 25). Vygotsky (1986) also emphasized this union by suggesting that thought is not individual and detached, but socially and emotionally constructed:

> Thought is not begotten by thought; it is engendered by motivation, i.e., by our desires and needs, our interests and emotions. Behind every thought there is an affective-volitional tendency, which holds the answer to the last "why" in the analysis of thinking. A true and full understanding of another's thought is possible only when we understand its affective-volitional basis (p. 252).

Many of Vygotsky's examples of the emotional motivation behind thought come from his discussions of the dramatic interpretation of literature. Vygotsky's interest in theatre was one that began in childhood and extended throughout his life. As Vygotsky's sister explained, "I don't think there was any period in his life when he did not think or write about the theatre" (Levitin, 1982, cited in Wertsch, 1985, p. 4). Leaning on the work of Constantin Stanislavski, actor and artistic director of the Moscow Art Theatre, Vygotsky suggests that underneath the written or spoken text lies the subtext of thought and emotion. An understanding of the subtext or the "inner life" of the text is critical to actors in the theatre (Stanislavski, 1961). They need not only deliver lines on stage, but also create hypothetical affective worlds of their characters off stage by negotiating among actors, for the "full person" has to interact with other characters/players. The collaborative and often conditional nature of the construction of meaning brings actors away from the isolated roles of fixed characters. Instead, they must play off each other's roles, listen to the sounds of other's emotional subtexts, and respond to meet or question interpretations.

For Dorothy Heathcote (1980), the dramatic intersection of heart and head occurs when children in classrooms learn to "read implications"—to discover the meanings which lie behind words, meanings which affect the lives of human beings. She dramatizes predominantly at the edges of texts, as children create characters, scenes, and interactions which *will* be structured by the teacher and *may* be structured by a text. Heathcote pioneered the strategy of "teacher-in-role" — the practice of teacher structuring from within the drama by participating in fictional encounters alongside the students. Johnson and O'Neill (1984) explain Heathcote's position: "...the teacher, as the most mature member of the group, has not merely a right but a responsibility to intervene, since learning is the product of intervention" (p. 12).

In order to help children and their teachers learn to listen to and talk with implication, Heathcote and Horda (1980) led teachers and upper elementary school students in a variety of interpretations surrounding Percy Bysshe Shelley's famous sonnet *Ozymandias*—a tale of a tyrant's power and his lost civilization. In one activity, the children constructed a museum with waxworks that captured events they believed would "show the slow fall of the dynasty of Ozymandias to the strangers who finally conquered" (p. 13). The children then explained their exhibits to museum visitors:

Ch. 1 (As Ozymandias) I see the ships on the horizon and I know deep within my heart that the end has come.

Ch. 2 (The attacker) With pride I hold this dagger in my hand to kill the King of Kings, Ozymandias King of Kings.

Ch. 3 (servant of the King) Oh the agony that I could not save my king. (p. 22)

The words the children used reveal mental states which are much dependent on emotional interpretation. As Ozymandias, the child uses the words "deep within my heart" to suggest that although the mental leap from ships on the horizon to certain doom is a feat of cognitive problem solving, it is sparked by a highly intuitive emotional reaction. The attacker holds his dagger "with pride" transforming a violent act into a moment of intense patriotism for his own country. And the servant does not distantly discuss the events that occurred after the King's death, but the "agony" that he felt. As Heathcote suggests,

> Attitudes shape happenings, and events are their result. Each event, which is the result of attitudes, creates another shift in attitude (either by change or by refusal to change) and so creates another event. So the story is what we find we have made, as a result of the seesawing between attitude producing action, and action changing attitude (p. 5).

Thus, the stories of Ozymandias that these children *made* highlight both the emotional motivation of thought and their effect on other people. People in their events stress what Vygotsky (1986) calls "the personal needs and interests, the inclinations and impulses, of the thinker" (p. 10).

Yet, the intersection of head and heart is more intriguing when we consider not only individual motivations, but what happens when the motivations of one meet those of another. One can easily imagine the scene between Ozymandias, his attacker, and his protective servant. Lovers are not the only characters on the stage or in life who are "star crossed," for intentions conflict and/or merge through events, solidifying or transforming subsequent attitudes. Still, the issue here is not whether Ozymandias and his attacker could ever agree, but whether the children in these encounters can see another's point of view. Through the revelation of their highly emotional motivations, can players hear the *implications* of the others' lines? Heathcote believes that they can for "the point of view we have in life often cannot be changed, but in play and art we can adapt different ways of involving ourselves in the occasion" (pp. 4, 5).

A more recent study of drama and reading was developed by Jeffrey Wilhelm (1994, in press) for his 6th grade 'resistant' readers, who tended to read only for explicitly stated or plot information. In an effort to enable his students to recognize their authorial power relative to literature, he involved them in improvisations of brief episodes from *The Incredible Journey* (Burnford, 1961). Students spoke as if they were characters, creating responses that were replete with implications, innuendo, and possible motivations. They explored meanings implied by the text and, at the same time, began to reinvent the meaning of reading. As one boy stated, "If you're not there, in the story, you're not even reading."

Whether working at the edges or at the center of text, children learn to read and enact implications. In a study of text-centered classroom theatre (Wolf, 1993, 1994), one group of children prepared a production of *Tikki Tikki Tembo* (Mosel, 1968)—the story of two brothers who unwittingly take turns falling into the local well. Because of the brevity of his name, Chang is quickly rescued, though he is long-suffering for the accident of birth order which relegates him to secondary status. However, "Tikki tikki tembo–no sa rembo–chari bari ruchi–pip peri pembo" lies long at the bottom of the well while Chang rushes about in an effort to save him and simultaneously speak his brother's great long name with reverence. A key *implication* of this text is the relationship between Chang and his mother—for she gives Chang little credit and much grief as she dotes on her oldest son.

Two of the children who worked on this production explored the emotions behind the actions in their journals. Henry, who played Chang, wrote, "I am an unwanted boy. I act smart." This brief but telling description captures the cyclical nature of attitudes shaping action and action constructing attitudes. Chang is unloved and "unwanted" so he attempts to capture his mother's attention by "act[ing] smart." From the many discussions that surrounded this production, Henry let it be known that he well understood how children could be ignored and perhaps abused. In one interpretation of the scene, the mother was supposed to yell loudly at Chang, *"Tiresome child, what are you trying to say?"* After shrinking away from the intense eye gaze and loud shouts of his "mother," Henry stopped the scene explaining, "Cause I have enough of that at home." Perhaps because all the players could appreciate Henry's position, they offered a substitute for menacing violence with a world-weary voice of a mother burdened with daily duties as well as an incessantly tiresome boy jabbering at her side.

In his own journal entry, Bobby (who played the "mother") reflected on the nature of unwanted boys, but he wrote from the parental point of view expressing the overall disappointment that became the essence of his character:

> Have you rea[d] Tiki tiki tebo? No then I will tell you all abawt it. it is abawt a mother and two boys in cinu [China] the two boys wer stopied [stupid] din't lisin to thary [their] Mother thay [they] are lucke thay are alive.

He supplemented his words with an illustration of himself as parent looming over his two sons floating in the well. The words that appear in the bubble extending from his mouth are "I told yoo so." Never a part of the original script, these four words capture the tiredly bitter denunciation of two disobedient sons, and are reflective of the analytical conversation of the mind and heart. To get inside another character, speak her speech and think her thoughts, Bobby attempted to explain action through intention. The mother had a hard life, taking care of two relatively disobedient sons. Bobby did not see her anger directed at Chang as much as at her "favorite son" Tikki Tikki Tembo who proved to be just as disobedient when he too tumbled into the well.

As the production progressed, the boys decided to change the "mother" into a "father" and Bobby was able to understand the parental perspective even more by thinking about his own father:

Bobby: Well, … just because like if you're a father and your favorite son is like on a baseball team … and you expect him to do very, very good … and you tell him like [deep voice] "Okay, now go and strike out this guy and make a big home run" [normal voice] and— you don't and it gets him really upset and he's like [deep voice] "you coulda done better than that." [Returning to the story] He's my most honored son and he does almost whatever I tell him to do and [then] he disobeys me and he goes in and he nearly DROWNS himself. So you know.

Shelby: So you're /irritated./

Bobby: /That. Ya./ Ya. Just like my father sometimes.

Bobby's choices reveal the disappointment of a father whose instructions were ignored. As Bobby explained his reasoning, he moved in and out of the role of the character through pronoun shifts, speaking as both character ("He's *my* most honored son and he does almost whatever *I* tell him to do") and as self ("Just like *my* father sometimes"). Shifting from the textual scene to a hypothetical and metaphorical situation ("like if you're a father and your favorite son is like on a baseball team") allowed Bobby to enter into the thoughts and emotions of his character—to analyze and to feel the irritation of a father whose son had let him down.

When shifting into the character's world, children's analyses often fall into the hypothetical realm as they justify their decisions based on details they notice in illustration or word, on understandings they have about similar characters in real life, and on their own motivations and intentions. In the world of drama, children may or may not *identify* with the character, but they come to *believe* in the possibility of their character. They construct a narrative world for their characters, imbuing them with intentions, motivations, and reasoning that is often not explicit on the page. The performance is only the surface level; through their decisions the children build a narrative foundation for what occurs on the surface. However, new understandings of alternative perspectives are not simply confined to the moment of performance or even postperformance reflection. Often, there are hints that the understandings children have gained in drama will become a part of what they know about the world. As they learn to read the subtext of particular situations, they come to see the implications for their own lives.

Fifth-grade students working with Brian Edmiston (1993a) engaged their hearts and heads as they dramatized at the edges of *The Journey: Japanese Americans, racism and renewal* (Hamanaka, 1990), a picture book about the experience of Japanese Americans who had been interned during World War II. The children's teacher read and discussed the text and then Edmiston worked in process drama to set up a series of dramatic encounters at the edges of the text. His goal was to bring the children to a decisive point in U.S. history when Japanese-American citizens had to decide whether or not to sign a Loyalty Questionnaire. Those who signed renounced their allegiance to the Japanese emperor and effectively to Japanese culture but were faced with conscription into the U.S. Army. Those who refused faced being branded as traitors and being sentenced to prison. Drawing on details of the book, the students first created "photographs from family albums" which illustrated both their Japanese and American heritage. Then Edmiston briefed some students playing the role of FBI agents about the Presidential decree which required them to arrest the Japanese Americans. Finally, in pairs, with one as an FBI agent and the other as a Japanese American the arrests took place.

In the so-called "relocation centers," the internees recalled what happened to them and shared their inner thoughts. One said, "There must be some mistake, we are Americans." Another replied, "I don't want to be American if they treat us like this." The FBI agents advised the soldiers at the camp that, for example, "They need to accept the facts ... this is not their country." Then the students shifted perspective to their future and spoke their thoughts as they looked back on their memory of those events. An FBI agent said, "I didn't realize it would be like this; I'm so sorry."

Edmiston next asked them to return to the internment camps and also adopted the position of an internee. He told them that he had heard that they would be let out of the camp if they all signed a piece of paper and renounced allegiance to Japan. There followed a heated and insightful discussion among the students which was intensified when Edmiston repositioned himself as the camp commander demanding a response. Their comments ranged from the boy who said, "I am proud to be Japanese. I will not say I am not Japanese just to get out of this place" to the girl who lamented, "I have to sign, my poor little baby and when she was born in the concentration camp she would die and if I sign I can never speak of my homeland again but my baby will live to tell the truth about the foolish Americans so it won't happen again."

Finally, the students concluded their work by depicting a sculpture which would show what the Japanese Americans wanted all Americans to know. The students became statues with inscriptions which they spoke aloud. One girl stated,

I've been in concentration camps, my sister's died and my daughter's gone away, but I know one thing after living through all I've gone through, you've got to be good to yourself and when doing that you can't be bad to anyone else. You try to be the best person you can be and in doing that you don't hurt anyone else.

Another said simply, "We're all different and we should be proud of all of our cultures."

The 5th-grade students were not only thinking about the experiences of Japanese Americans, they were affectively engaged as they imagined they were involved and implicated in the events of the 1940s. While dramatizing at the edges of the text, the students thought and felt deeply about the themes of the book. Their interpretations of the situations described, illustrated and implied in the original text were placed at the center of the classroom interactions as the teacher structured a sequence of encounters.

The students described above, who were dramatizing at the center and at the edges of texts, all readily adopted and switched perspectives several times. They experienced and explored attitudes as much as they adopted points of view. They also made connections between the people described in the texts and their own experiences—webs of feeling and thought which were inextricably bound together. These students' interpretations endorse the position of Ellen Langer (1989) who categorically rejected any artificial separation of feeling from thought: "Neither separating these two functions, nor trying to reduce one to the other, seems to me to make sense. Nor is it enough to see them as simply related. [We should view] them instead as part of one total simultaneous reaction" (p. 174).

Places of the Voice

In this section we discuss three definitions of voice: (a) one of vocal interpretation, marked by stress, tone, accent, and characterization; (b) one of perspective and the facility with which children and teachers shift perspectives to explore their perceptions and attitudes within situations; and (c) one of voice in terms of whose voices are heard in the classroom.

In dramatizing at the center of the text, voice is most often seen as vocal interpretation. Anger, affection, threat, tristeza, excitement, and ennui all emerge in the voice. As Bakhtin (1986) suggests, an utterance is a complex integration of word choice, emphasis, and attitude which the voice can either hide or reveal. The voice puts life to words, reflecting or obscuring the context, the manner, and the intent of the speaker. The phrase, "It's all right," for example, can be the soothing voice of a mother to a crying child, the art critic's sarcastic dismissal of a less than stunning painting, the suppressed frustration of a host to a guest who has just broken a favored momento, or the injured athlete's anxious assurance to a coach in the hopes of returning to the field. In each interpretation of the phrase, decisions in vocal attitude and emphasis highlight or shadow the inner thoughts or subtext of the speaker's meaning. A similar multifaceted construction of a phrase is described by Roman Jakobson (1960):

A former actor of Stanislavski's Moscow Theater told me how at his audition he was asked by the famous director to make forty different messages from the phrase *Segodnja vecerom* 'This evening,' by diversifying its expressive tint. He made a list of some forty emotional situations, then emitted the given phrase in accordance with each of these situations, which his audience had to recognize only from the changes in the sound shape of the same two words. For our research work in the description and analysis of contemporary Standard Russian ... this actor was asked to repeat Stanislavski's test. He wrote down some fifty situations framing the same elliptic sentence and made of it fifty corresponding messages for a tape record. Most of the messages were correctly and circumstantially decoded by Muscovite listeners (pp. 354, 355).

A dictionary definition of the phrase 'This evening' does little to enlighten the listener; it is the vocal shaping of the context which provides the sense, not simply the meaning (Vygotsky, 1986).

Similarly, in text-centered drama, changes in tone mark the students' adoption of the external features of their characters as well as the internal features as they voice inner speech to demonstrate the thinking of their characters in their analyses, stage whispers, and asides. In exploring voice in classroom theatre, Wolf (1995) followed the vocal interpretation of three children—Bart, Stella, and Tomás—as they enacted William Steig's (1982) *Dr. De Soto*—the story of a mouse dentist with a problem. While Dr. De Soto ordinarily refuses to treat animals dangerous to mice, he and his wife decide to treat a fox in a moment of weakness. Under the influence of gas, the dapper but devious fox reveals his plan for the ultimate demise of his helpers. In the face of such a threat, the De Sotos spend a worrisome night wondering how they will be able to insert a new gold tooth without self-sacrifice. They devise a marvelous plan, affixing the tooth and resolving their problems by offering the fox a secret formula which will rid the patient of further toothaches. The fox quickly agrees and his teeth are painted with the secret formula. However, after he is told to hold his teeth together tightly for a full minute, he discovers that he cannot open his jaws. His teeth are glued together! The De Sotos smile victoriously as the fox stumbles away.

In the final performance of their play, Bart (as the fox) swaggered onto the classroom stage, his top hat tipped recklessly to the side. Tomás (as Dr. De Soto) wore a white coat and was in the midst of organizing his "instruments" (a child's toy doctor kit) when Bart entered. Tomás immediately began to pace back and forth, shooting nervous glances in Bart's direction. He then hid under the desks to create the effect of having disappeared into the fox's mouth. Bart pretended to snap his jaws shut and then chortled loudly at his own humor. But Tomás emerged from the desk and said *"Be serious"* in an authoritative "get down to business" tone. After the operation, Bart ran his tongue over his teeth and exclaimed *"My it feels good, honey!"* Then he tucked his head down and lowered his voice to a stage whisper, *"I really shouldn't eat them. On the other hand, how can I resist? Ya!"* Later while applying the "secret formula," Tomás painted Bart's fake fox teeth carefully with a paintbrush, while Bart leaned in to accommodate the process. Yet, when he realized that his teeth were stuck together, Bart leapt off the stool and turned in amazement to face the clever doctor and his wife. As Stella,

who played both wife and narrator read the lines: *"The fox was stunned. He stared at Doctor De Soto, then at his wife. They smiled, and waited,"* she looked up from her script and joined Tomás in a heartfelt grin, their eyes, all the while, on Bart. The eye gaze, touch, tone, and intonation all combined to join the characters in the time, space, and relationships of the play. While Bart's eyes registered stunned disbelief, his actions and those of the successful De Sotos, created a believable scene.

Each of the children leaned on the language in the play to communicate their character and scene. Very early in rehearsals, Bart began to add "cocky" additions such as "honey" and "baby" to the end of his lines. He only added one or at most two words to the entire script and the additions appeared at different points in different rehearsals. In discussions with fellow players, he did not appear to have a fixed plan of where these additions should fall, only that they should be inserted at some point. In the final performance, however, he added the word "honey" to his first line, and this addition, combined with his "jive" tone, set the entire audience into giggles. Their reaction seemed to trigger an alternative decision in Bart, for he then abandoned his more conservative plan of only one or two additions and instead added *six* new endings which included one "baby," two uses of "honey," and three supplementary expressions of either "Ya!" or "Ah!" The audience went wild. Through cocky endearments slurred carelessly over the tongue, Bart copped an attitude with his character—a fox who was sly and sinister but humorous as well.

The character of the dentist was less dramatic, and Tomás played it accordingly. He adopted a professional air—though he did appear to be extremely nervous at first sight of the fox. His face was set in a serious expression, and his vocal interpretation was a careful match—deep-voiced and dignified. Stella, too, was more serious. She played the part of Mrs. De Soto but had no character lines. Instead, she read all the narrator's lines, emphasizing the words with a slight increase in volume. After Tomás, her husband, succeeded in gluing the fox's teeth together, Stella read, *"The fox was stu::nned"* elongating the vowels with a musical lilt. Her choice emphasized a key word to show that the De Sotos' trick had worked, and her musical tone highlighted the pleasure of her character's success. Had she been able to express her character's inner thoughts, they would no doubt be striking a triumphant chord.

In dramatizing at the edges of text, students adopt multiple perspectives and speak in many voices. In their interactions, their discourse becomes what Bakhtin (1981) calls "multivoiced", if they talk about different concerns from varied points of view. Their voices are not only vocal interpretations of imaginary people's expressions, but a montage of multiple positions and perspectives on the world. As Carroll (1980) has shown, in such dramatizing students use different genres and also shift among different registers and modes as they use language for multiple purposes and varied audiences.

Working at the edge of the *Dr. De Soto* (Steig, 1982) text, Edmiston (1988) led 1st-grade students to imagine they were all mice dentists wondering what to do about foxes and other dangerous animals in need of dental care. The De Sotos had come to them for advice asking whether they should help the suspicious fox who needed a new tooth. As the children wondered about dangerous animals, they made signs for their offices (some consulted the text for their words while others wrote their own), they made a television commercial advertising their offices for all "nice animals," and they practiced what to do if a fox came to their offices. They gave varied vocal interpretations and used language in multiple ways.

If with Vygotsky (1986) we connect language with thought and feeling, we realize that as students talk they do more than use words, they explore alternative ways of thinking and feeling about the world. The possible worlds created in dramatizing at the edge of the text open up limitless opportunities for social interactions and explorations in multiple dramatic encounters. In every encounter, students adopt positions or points of view from which they can voice their reactions and thereby create new meanings and understandings. As they find new voices, they also see the world in new ways. The mice dentists in Edmiston's study (1988) were not only talking as animals, they were thinking and feeling about multiple ways of reacting to dangerous situations where they could keep enemies out, warn them to stay away, attack them, ignore the danger, be clever and outwit them, talk nicely to them, and so forth.

As students engage in dialogue, their voices intermingle and their meanings and understandings continue to develop and change. For Bakhtin (1981), genuine dialogue is much more than a conversation; in dialogue we listen to each other, exploring social and cultural references and experiences, and change the way we think in doing so. A script contains repeated encounters where students can see how characters do (or do not) listen to each other and react to what others say and do. Plays are concerned with how characters change or resist change in the situations they find themselves. The De Sotos in the text considered but did not agree with those who refused to help foxes—they changed their ideas and came up with a novel way of protecting themselves and the fox from his desires to eat mice. In dramatizing at the edge of the text, each encounter between teacher and students or among the students is an opportunity for dialogue and change in understanding. Although students in improvised dramatic encounters may talk but not listen, the 1st-grade mice dentists dialogued with each other and considered multiple ways of dealing with danger—some agreed, some disagreed, and many changed from their original positions.

The teacher, who functions as playwright, stage manager, director, and actor (Edmiston, 1993b) is critical in promoting dialogue through both external and internal facilitations. Structuring externally is what good teachers do all day long as they help students create limits for their work together. This is essential in dramatizing at the edges of texts to ensure that encounters or tasks do not end before they have begun. It is also critical that students explore possibilities with others as well as express themselves. The teacher can be clear about choices and about a task's purpose or outcome. For example, at one point, the 1st-grade students chose what to work on—the dentist office notices, the letters, or the commercial. All knew who their audiences were, the purpose of their task,

and what to do when they had finished. The teacher can also set up encounters with dramatic constraints (Bolton, 1992) or other obstacles which increase dramatic conflict but create spaces where students can interact with each other. Students may, for example, interact in pairs, make a tableau in small groups, or collectively demonstrate an event. For a few minutes in the text-edged *Dr. De Soto* work, half the students were foxes and the others were mice hiding to watch them. They were all constrained by their physical separation; the foxes could not eat the mice even if they wanted to and the mice had to watch and listen if they wanted to try to figure out if all foxes were dangerous. Since some foxes behaved like dogs and others were planning to eat chickens or Little Red Riding Hood some children were still unsure whether or not to trust the one who had come to Dr. De Soto.

Structuring internally the teacher enters the drama world and encounters the students. The 1st-grade students talked with their teacher—she was a fox with a toothache and they decided that they were mice pretending to be wolves. Some children were unsure whether or not to trust the fox. They asked her about what she liked to eat and whether she liked to eat mice. She drew on the original text and said that she would not want to eat a mouse dentist, but she did love mice and licked her lips. In reflection, the children all agreed that they had to be cautious. Recognizing that the power relations among teacher and students can become malleable in fictional encounters, the teacher may construct various positions of power relative to the students—higher, equal to, or lower (Morgan & Saxton, 1987). She does so in order to present students with other voices with which they can dialogue and discover new perspectives, create new understandings and find new voices in reaction. When the teacher was a mouse dentist she and the children had an equitable power relationship so the children could more easily agree or disagree with her. When the teacher was the fox being interviewed, in one sense she was more physically powerful since she could have attacked them. Still, in another sense the children could exercise more power since they were outwitting the fox. The children were, however, listening intently to what the fox was saying and to one another's ideas—they wondered together about trusting foxes and about the nature and meaning of trust. The multiple encounters possible in dramatizing at the edges of the text allow students to adopt and shift perspectives many times. In doing so, students' interpretations and understandings can become more complex. Some 1st-grade students who were very trusting became more cautious by the end of the drama, others who had been ready to kill all foxes came up with a plan similar to the De Sotos—they decided to give him more gas and then lead him outside when he was half asleep.

In these dramas, students' ideas are given a platform or stage that enables them to test their voices through perspectives and situations that are quite unlike the ones they encounter in typical classroom contexts. As Delpit (1988) and others have argued, power differentials are inherent in classroom interactions; and these differentials can be used to silence children who are uncertain about the purposes of the teacher's instructions, who do not accept the premises of the approach to teaching and learning in the classroom, or who recognize that their voice, because of their race, ethnicity, class, or gender is not going to be heard. Dramatizing encourages teachers to use and shift their power in a way that may make our beliefs and practices relative to our students more explicit and open to change. As described above, in dramatizing at the edge or at the center of texts, teachers must create openings for dialogue, and then they must listen. It is the kind of listening Delpit describes that requires:

> ...not only open eyes and ears, but open hearts and minds. We do not really see through our eyes or hear through our ears, but through our beliefs. To put our beliefs on hold is to cease to exist as ourselves for a moment—and that is not easy.... it means turning yourself inside out, giving up your own sense of who you are ... but it is the only way to learn what it might feel like to be someone else and the only way to start the dialogue" eliminated quick work (p. 297).

Places of the Hand

In this section, the "hand" serves as a metaphor for the integration of all that players do to take a text into action and create their own interpretive stances. Though we do not wish to dichotomize, we find it useful to distinguish between two kinds of stance—physical movement and mental action. The first stance is the physical attitude demonstrated by the player through body movement and orientation, gesture, eye gaze, facial expression, and the use of props. The second stance is the mental attitude and action that is aroused by physically shifting into the possibilities of a play world, and by allowing interactions in that world to affect and change the players' understandings and attitudes. Wertsch (1991) explains:

> When action is given analytic priority, human beings are viewed as coming into contact with, and creating, their surroundings as well as themselves through the actions in which they engage. ... This contrasts ... with approaches that treat the individual primarily as a passive recipient of information from the environment (p. 8).

In stressing action, we move from the transmission of meaning to the generation of meaning, for mental action is "often socially distributed and it is connected to the notion of mediation" (p. 14). In stressing dramatic action, we note that students not only discover new possibilities, they also transform *themselves* in the process of transforming the words or situations of a text. Maxine Greene (1988) states it succinctly: "It is, actually, in the process of effecting transformations that the human self is created and recreated" (p. 21).

As Kenneth Burke (1969) noted, dramatic action can be contrasted with movement—action is consciously willed and the result of a choice, whereas movement can be reactive and instinctual. Vygotsky (1978) argued that paradoxically in play we are more in conscious control than we are in non-play situations because in play every action becomes significant. Thus in drama, students tend to be more deliberate and conscious of their actions especially as symbolic meanings are generated during a sequence of encounters.

In text-centered drama, the focus is often on the body or the first stance. Physicalization calls for the player to embody the emotion of the words in the text into the motion of the character. Stanislavski argues that the gesture can often contain the key to meaning: "If the intellect can inhibit, and the emotions are fickle where can an actor begin in his exploration of a role? The answer is with what is most immediately available to him [sic], what responds most easily to his wishes—his body" (Benedetti, 1982, p. 67). Langer (1953) explains that each utterance must spring from thought and feeling which begins inside the speaker's body, "so the actor has to create the illusion of an inward activity issuing in spontaneous speech, if his [sic] words are to make a dramatic and not a rhetorical effect" (pp. 315, 316).

Wolf (1994) followed three children—Jewel, Catalina, and Maia—as they enacted *Mirandy and Brother Wind* (McKissack, 1988)—a story about an African-American girl who persuades the wind to instill his spirit into her friend Ezel, and together the two children high step their way to first prize at their community cakewalk. The physical movements the children chose were carefully planned. Maia, in her role as Mirandy, for example, incorporated a number of movements which she designed in rehearsal and repeated in the final performance. When she warned Orlinda not to tease about Ezel, Maia approached Jewel with her hands on her hips, flung back her head, and walked away. When she was in the barn, supposedly regretting a foolish mistake, she paced back and forth with her finger to her cheek, as though in studied concentration. When she danced across the floor, she kicked her thin legs high at the fan that Jewel held out to her. And when she was presented with the cake, she turned proudly toward the audience, holding the cake up like a well-earned prize.

Weeks after the final performance, the girls were able to hold on to the physical patterns they established for their characters. When Wolf asked them to pose in character for a photograph, they immediately chose the scene of the confrontation between Mirandy and Orlinda when Mirandy boldly announces that she and Ezel will win the cakewalk, while Orlinda and her friend look skeptically on. As Jewel, Catalina, and Maia took up their own positions, Jewel who played Orlinda adopted the hands-on-hips stance of Mirandy, leaning toward Maia with a smirk on her face. Maia did not take the stance offered by the text but instead folded her arms in stubborn defiance. Still, the thrust of Maia's chin was a mirror image of Mirandy's and revealed the determination that was strong in the character as well as in the child. Just as the character of Mirandy in the story captured Brother Wind, Maia captured the character in the thrust of her chin. The girls' body positions demonstrated an understanding and internalization of the story's central mood and the primary attitude of the characters that helped establish this mood. Such perceptions did not receive specific labeling in their talk before the photo. These understandings emerged from extended discussion as well as physical exploration of the story. Through their positionings, the girls expressed their textual understandings of character both in posture and in facial expression.

Enciso (1990, 1991, 1996) shows that as readers, we may go "inside" a book as we adopt the perspectives of characters, empathize with them, spy on them, argue with them, and even try to lend them our help and advice. However, when we *talk* about literature, we are always outside the world of the story and are no longer experiencing it except in retrospect (Edmiston, 1993a). In drama, however, we can enter the world of the story with others. Our private world of literature can become a drama world, a public shared world of the text in which we can walk around and interact with other people in role. Heathcote (1984) uses the phrase "now and imminent time" to describe the feeling that an experience is happening now rather than in the past. In drama, we feel we are in the middle of events that concern us or are happening to us because in our imaginations we are in the same world as in the story. What we say and do within the drama is not just a detached comment about the world of the story. On the contrary, every action and inaction affects that world directly and affects the person we imagine ourselves to be in the drama world.

Working at the center of text often spreads out to the edges. In other words, *physical stance* within an interpretive text action can sometimes motivate a *mental stance* that leads to a highly personal reaction. This is exemplified in the work of Nancy King (1981) who often uses drama to move from literature to life. Working with the text of *The Big Wave* (Buck, 1948), she asked students to enact scenes in the book that affected them most deeply. One group formed a huge wave and swept everything up in its path. King (1981) explains:

> The villagers tried to flee, to protect themselves as best they could, but the power of the wave was too much. Soon everything was swept away and nothing remained but an empty, silent space.
>
> As the lone child returned to the quieted waters she looked around in horror at the emptiness. Slowly the full meaning of what had happened penetrated her being, and she sank to her knees and rocked with despair. Clutching her small toy to her chest, she crooned a chant that was half sound, half sob. Then there was only silence.
>
> …The group was preparing to discuss their feelings about the book when one member of the class who had been watching, an eight-year-old boy, suddenly got up from his seat. Without paying any attention to anyone else, he ran to the girl, knelt down in front of her, took her face in his hands, and said, "Come with me. You can live with me and my family. We will help you." The girl looked at the boy as if not fully understanding his words. "Come," he repeated. "Come with me to my family in the mountains. There you will be safe." The girl followed the boy, still holding on to his hand. She left the space in the middle of the room and sat down in a seat next to his (p. 165).

The physical stance of one child—sinking to her knees, rocking in anguish, grasping a toy as if it could save her—led to a mental stance in another child—a boy who thought he *could* save her by offering her a place to stay, taking her hand, and leading her away from the scene of her pain. Later, in a discussion of times when he himself had felt terribly alone, he explained his actions, "When I saw [her] all alone, it reminded me of how I feel, and I just wanted her to know that she still had a friend" (p. 165).

In dramatizing at the edges of the text, players also consciously use and link their "hands": their bodies demonstrate physical attitudes which others interpret and they take actions in dramatic encounters which transform texts, situations and themselves. Gavin Bolton (1981) describes a particularly vivid example. At the resolution of process drama work which took place in South Africa several years ago with black school students, Bolton positioned them as old people looking back on the changes which had taken place during the imaginary time of their lives. They imagined that apartheid had ended. One student extended his hand to Bolton—a white teacher. Bolton read his gesture and shook hands as the student said with confidence and dignity, "Now we are equal."

Throughout the Japanese American work (Edmiston 1991, 1993a), players demonstrated their mental and emotional attitudes through physical action. For example, some of those who were arrested initially resisted—their bodies struggling against the arresting agents. Others were stoically still as they packed their belongings with dignity. In the internment camp as they deliberated over whether or not to sign the loyalty statement some sat hunched over in despair, while others sat upright as they refused to reject their cultural heritage. Players repeatedly took action to express their reactions. They had many choices—how to react to racist remarks, how to act when arrested, whether or not to sign. Their actions and reactions also affected each other and led to further reactions. When some were resisting arrest, others argued that they should not behave in such an undignified way. When one wanted to join the army, others tried to talk her out of this decision. When one jumped up and cried out that they were being denied justice, others leapt to their feet as well.

The "hand" or the active mental and physical stances represented in the body cannot be separated from the heart, head, or voice. Instead, they intersect and influence each other within the individual and among individuals. Eisner (1985) is highly critical of the discourse of separate "domains" of knowing—cognitive, affective and psychomotor—for it tends to reify distinctions and privilege discursive and logical thinking, rather than emphasize that processes of meaning making involve all modes of being and interacting. In drama, we understand through shaping and reading movements and actions as much as through our words and emotions. In other words, we cannot extend our hand without putting heart, mind, and voice behind it.

CONCLUSION: DRAMA WORLDS IN SEARCH OF A CLASSROOM

In the 1920s, Pirandello wrote a play in which six characters unexpectedly appeared in a theatre rehearsal to tell their stories. They described themselves as unused creations of the author's imagination and performed key scenes which, though never written, contained the content of their lives. Their search for an author stemmed from their desire to play their parts not for eternity, but "only for a moment." As the lead character explains, "The drama is in us, and we are the drama. We are impatient to play it" (1922, p. 219).

In much the same way, dramatizing at the center and at the edges of text are rarely used creations searching for classrooms that will make room for the integration and expression of the head, heart, voice, and hand. The "places" that we have described in this chapter have no borders. Instead, thought and emotion, articulation and gesture all merge in environments where children and teachers act together to negotiate the dramatic interpretation of texts through multiple voices, perspectives, and symbolic systems. While the voice of written texts is stronger in text-centered forms, children's individual and negotiated needs and narratives are heard throughout.

In literacy instruction we often focus on children's identification of discrete elements, but we ignore the possibilities of discrete elements in other symbolic systems and their potential for use of metaphor, emphasis, and parallelism. Moreover, we ignore uses of pause, nonverbal gestures, and facial expressions or eye gaze as symbolic elements to underscore, complement, or negate verbal meanings. The enactments described here combine the verbal with the nonverbal to create a theatre in the round of children's interpretations of texts and their needs to express these interpretations. The texts they ultimately enact are rich orchestrations of multiple symbolic systems which simultaneously analyze the action of the story with a call for action in the real world.

Much of the current work in restructuring and rethinking education, particularly in literacy education, is on putting theory into practice—taking into account the multiplicity of voices and perspectives in text interpretation, reminding teachers of the power of negotiated action through group work and peer discussion, as well as reflecting on the possibilities for mental action through alternative symbolic systems; but we continue to measure new theories with old practices. We test students, but we do not carefully examine the breadth or depth of their knowledge. We do not acknowledge authentic deeds accomplished by verbal displays of knowledge as well as by other symbolic systems.

As teacher education programs introduce these issues to beginning teachers, there is a tendency to ignore the students in the cycle (Wolf, Carey, & Mieras, 1996). Much of the discussion in education is about teachers as reflective practitioners and stresses theories into practice in terms of interpretation of text, movement into action, with action by teachers to create a context for learning given analytic priority. Yet it is critical to remember that students are reflective practitioners as well (Edmiston & Wilhelm, in press). The students described here immersed themselves in written story in order to tell a number of stories about who they were and what they knew. These children were not passive recipients of knowledge, but active participants who were able to generate, negotiate, and enact their own understandings. Moreover, the children were given opportunities to reflect on their learning and their creation of a learning environment in their actions, their writing, and their talk. They played and worked not only in "now and imminent time" (Heathcote, 1984), but beyond the vivid immediacy of the moment to make decisions for how they would live their lives.

The negotiation and interpretation of text is a living, protean, and richly varied creation in a classroom of children. Children of different linguistic, cultural, social backgrounds bring diverse gifts, symbols, and methods of accomplishing tasks in language, art, music, and drama. While some children leap to the director's role seeing the scene as a unified whole, others add the much needed creative details, while still others provide stability, decoding expertise, humor, artistic advice, or practical experience about the way things work in the real world. In traditional classrooms, children's individual thoughts and talents are often separated from their peers as children work in isolation and through uniform symbolic systems for expression. But in the collaborative work of dramatic interpretation, individuals come together to create new understandings. In the enactments of seemingly simple scenes, multiple sources of knowledge meet together; individual stories, voices, dialects, accents, resources, and reflections flow into a rich representation of a community of learners. The multiplicity and diversity of contributions represented here offer just a glimpse into the resources available when children have opportunities to call on personal experiences, narratives, and ways of working in the world. In such an atmosphere, cultural preferences as well as individual learning styles, find room for expression.

Nearly 60 years ago, Rosenblatt (1978) reminded us of the links between literacy and drama. Yet, drama still hovers outside of classrooms and rarely appears in the research literature (Wagner, in preparation; Wolf & Enciso, 1994). Although there is much anecdotal information on the "benefits" of drama, teachers and researchers need to more formally substantiate and carefully describe the transformations that occur when children meet drama. The research studies we have presented here will hopefully serve as a spark to fire the imaginations of teachers and researchers willing to offer children more room for expression and eager to think in new ways about how meaning is created in the world. As teachers and researchers of drama, we find ourselves in much the same position as Pirandello's (1922) lead character, for we are impatient to see drama play its role in more and more classrooms. The drama worlds that we have described here offer children and their teachers much needed room for interpretation and expression. Is this not simply carrying to its ultimate manifestation what each of us as teachers and researchers of literacy must do?

References

Apple, M. (1990). Introduction to J. Willinsky. *The New Literacy.* New York: Routledge.

Bakhtin, M. (1981). *The dialogic imagination.* (M. Holquist, Ed. & Trans.). Austin, TX: University of Texas Press.

Bakhtin, M. (1986). *Speech genres and other late essays* [C. Emerson & M. Holquist (Eds.) & V. W. McGee (Trans.)]. Austin, TX: University of Texas Press.

Benedetti, J. (1982). *Stanislavski: An introduction.* New York: Theatre Arts Books.

Bolton, G. (1979). *Towards a theory of drama in education.* London: Longman.

Bolton, G. (1981). Drama in the curriculum. *2D: Drama & Dance, 1,* 9–16.

Bolton, G. (1992). *New perspectives on classroom drama.* London: Simon & Schuster.

Booth, D. (1985). Imaginary gardens with real toads: Reading and drama in education. *Theory into Practice, 24,* 193–198.

Booth, D. (1994). Entering the story cave. *NADIE Journal, 18*(2), 67–77.

Booth, D. (1995). *Story drama.* Markham, Ontario: Pembroke.

Britton, J. (1972). *Language and learning.* New York: Penguin.

Buck, P. (1948). *The big wave.* New York: John Day.

Burnford, S. (1961). *The incredible journey.* Boston: Little Brown.

Burke, K. (1969). *A grammar of motives.* Berkeley, CA: University of California Press.

Busching, B. A. (1981). Readers theatre: An education for language and life. *Language Arts, 58,* 330–338.

Carroll, J. (1980). *The treatment of Dr. Lister: A language functions approach to drama in education.* Bathurst, Australia: Mitchell University.

Cole, T., & Chinoy, H. K. (1970). *Actors on acting: The theories, techniques, and practices of the world's great actors, told in their own words.* New York: Crown.

Delpit, L. (1988). The silenced dialogue: Power and pedagogy in educating other people's children. *Harvard Educational Review, 58,* 280–298.

Dewey, J. (1934, 1958). *Art as experience.* New York: Capricorn Books.

Dyson, A. H. (1993). *Social worlds of children learning to write.* New York: Teachers College Press.

Edmiston, B. (1988). *Unfoxing language with Dr. De Soto.* Unpublished manuscript.

Edmiston, B. (1991). Planning for flexibility: The phases of a drama structure. *Drama/Theatre Teacher, 4*(1), 6–12.

Edmiston, B. (1993a). Going up the beanstalk: Discovering giant possibilities for responding to literature through drama. In K. Holland, R. Hungerford & S. Ernst (Eds.), *Journeying: Children responding to literature.* Exeter, NH: Heinemann.

Edmiston, B. (1993b). Structuring drama for reflection and learning: A teacher-researcher study. *Youth Theatre Journal. 7*(3), 4–12.

Edmiston, B., Enciso, P., & King, M. L. (1987). Empowering readers and writers through drama: Narrative theater. *Language Arts, 64,* 219–228.

Edmiston, B., & Wilhelm, J. (1996). Playing in different keys: Research notes for action researchers and reflective drama practitioners. In P. Taylor (Ed.), *Researching drama and arts education: Paradigms and possibilities 85–86.* New York: Falmer Press.

Eisner, E. (1985). *The art of educational evaluation.* Philadelphia, PA: Falmer Press.

Enciso [Edmiston], P. (1990). *The nature of engagement in reading: Profiles of three fifth-graders' engagement strategies and stances.*

Enciso, P. (1991). Creating the story world: A case study of a young reader's engagement strategies and stances. In C. Cox & J. Many (Eds.), *Reader stance and literary understanding: Exploring the theories, research and practice* (pp. 75–102). Norwood, NJ: Ablex.

Enciso, P. (1996). Why engagement in reading matters to Molly. *Reading and Writing Quarterly: Overcoming Learning Difficulties, 12*(2), 171–194.

Enciso, P., & Edmiston, B. (in press). Drama and response to literature: Reading the story, rereading "the truth." In N. Karolides (Ed.), *Reader response in elementary classrooms: Quest and discovery.* New York: Erlbaum.

Fowler, A. (1982). *Kinds of literature: An introduction to the theory of genres and modes.* Cambridge, MA: Harvard University Press.

Freire, P. (1972). *Pedagogy of the oppressed.* Harmondsworth: Penguin.

Greene, M. (1988). *The dialectic of freedom.* New York: Teachers College Press.

Hamanaka, S. (1990). *The journey: Japanese Americans, racism and renewal.* New York: Orchard Books.

Heath, S. B., & Branscombe, A. (with Thomas, C.). (1986). The book as narrative prop. In B. B. Schieffelin & P. Gilmore (Eds.), *The acquisition of literacy: Ethnographic perspective* (pp. 16–34). Norwood, NJ: Ablex.

Heathcote, D. (1980). *Drama as context.* Great Britain: The National Association for the Teaching of English, Aberdeen University Press.

Heathcote, D. (1984). Drama as challenge. In L. Johnson & C. O'Neill (Eds.), *Dorothy Heathcote: Collected writings on education and drama* (pp. 80–89). Evanston, IL: Northwestern University Press.

Heathcote, D., & Bolton, G. (1995). *Drama for learning: Dorothy Heathcote's mantle of the expert approach to education.* Portsmouth, NH: Heinemann.

Heathcote, D., & Herbert, P. (1985). A drama of learning: Mantle of the expert. *Theory into Practice, 24*(3), 173–180.

Heathcote, D., & Hovda, R. (1980). Drama as context for talking and writing: 'The Ozymandias Saga' at Broadwood Junior School, Newcastle upon Tyne. In D. Heathcote, *Drama as context.* Great Britain: National Association of Teachers of English.

Hughes, J. (1991). Drama in education: The state of the art, an Australian perspective. In J. Hughes (Ed.), *Drama in education* (pp. 1–12). Rozelle, Australia: Educational Drama Association.

Jakobson, R. (1960). Closing statement: Linguistics and poetics. In T. Sebeok (Ed.), *Style and language* (pp. 350–377). Cambridge, MA: MIT Press.

Johnson, L., & O'Neill, C. (1984). Introduction. In L. Johnson and C. O'Neill (Eds.), *Dorothy Heathcote: Collected writings on education and drama* (pp. 9–13). Evanston, IL: Northwestern University Press.

King, N. (1981). From literature to drama to life. In N. McCaslin (Ed.), *Children and drama* (pp. 164–177). New York: Longman.

Landy, R. J. (1982). *Handbook of educational drama and theatre.* Westport, CT: Greenwood Press.

Langer, E. J. (1989). *Mindfulness.* Reading, MA: Addison-Wesley.

Langer, S. K. (1953). *Feeling and form.* New York: Charles Scribner's Sons.

Martin, J. R. (1992). *The schoolhome: Rethinking schools for changing families.* Cambridge, MA: Harvard University Press.

McCaslin, N. (1990). *Creative drama in the classroom.* New York: Longman.

Mckissack, P. C. (1988). *Mirandy and Brother Wind,* illustrated by J. Pinkney. New York: Alfred A. Knopf.

Morgan, N., & Saxton, J. (1987). *Teaching drama: A mind of many wonders.* Portsmouth, NH: Heinemann.

Mosel, A. (1968). *Tikki Tikki Tembo,* illustrated by B. Lent. New York: Scholastic.

Neelands, J. (1990). *Structuring drama work.* Cambridge: Cambridge University Press.

O'Neill, C. (1991). *Structure and spontaneity: Improvisation in theatre and education.* Unpublished doctoral dissertation, University of Exeter.

O'Neill, C. (1994). Here comes everybody: Aspects of role in process drama. *NADIE Journal, 18*(2), 37–44.

O'Neill, C., & Lambert, A. (1983). *Drama structures.* London: Hutchinson.

O'Neill,, C., Lambert, A., Linnell, R., & Warr-Wood, J. (1976). *Drama guidelines.* London: Heinemann.

O'Toole, J. (1992). *The process of drama: Negotiating art and meaning.* New York: Routledge.

O'Toole, J., & Haseman, B. (1988). *Dramawise.* Portsmouth, NH: Heinemann.

Pirandello, L. (1922). Six characters in search of an author. In E. Bentley (Ed.), *Naked masks: Five plays by Luigi Pirandello.* New York: E.P. Dutton.

Robertson, M. E. (1990). *True wizardry: Readers theatre in the classroom.* Rozelle, Australia: Primary English Teaching Association.

Robinson, H. A., Faraone, V., Hittleman, D. R., & Unruh, E. (1990). *Reading comprehension instruction 1783–1987: A review of trends and research.* Newark, DE: International Reading Association.

Rogers, T., & O'Neill, C. (1993). Creating multiple worlds: Drama, language, and literary response. In G. E. Newell & E. K. Durst (Eds.), *Exploring texts* (pp. 69–89). Norwood, MA: Christopher-Gordon.

Rosenblatt, L. (1978). *The reader, the text, the poem: The transactional theory of the literary work.* Carbondale, IL: Southern Illinois University Press.

Shanklin, N. L., & Rhodes, L. K. (1989). Comprehension instruction as sharing and extending. *The Reading Teacher, 42,* 496–500.

Siks, G. B. (1983). *Drama with children.* New York: Harper & Row.

Sloyer, S. (1982). *Readers theatre: Story dramatization in the classroom.* Urbana, IL: National Council of Teachers of English.

Stanislavski, C. (1961). *Creating a role.* New York: Theatre Arts Books.

Steig, W. (1982). *Dr. De Soto.* New York: Scholastic.

Swartz, L. (1988). *Dramathemes.* Markham, Ontario: Pembroke.

Tarlington, C., & Verriour, P. (1991). *Role drama.* Portsmouth, NH: Heinemann.

Vygotsky, L. S. (1978). *Mind in society.* Cambridge, MA: Harvard University Press.

Vygotsky, L. S. (1986). *Thought and language.* Cambridge, MA: MIT Press.

Wagner, B. J. (1985). Elevating the written word through the spoken: Dorothy Heathcote and a group of 9- to 13-year-olds as monks. *Theory into Practice, 24*(3), 166–172.

Wagner, B. J. (in preparation). *What is learned through classroom drama.*

Wertsch, J. V. (1985). *Vygotsky and the social formation of mind.* Cambridge, MA: Harvard University Press.

Wertsch, J. V. (1991). *Voices of the mind: A sociocultural approach to mediated action.* Cambridge, MA: Harvard University Press.

Wilhelm, J. (1994). *Developing readers: Teaching engaged and reflective reading in the middle school.* Unpublished doctoral dissertation, University of Wisconsin, Madison.

Wilhelm, J. (in press). *Developing readers: Teaching engaged and reflective reading with middleschoolers.* New York: Teachers College Press.

Willinsky, J. (1990). *The new literacy.* New York: Routledge.

Wills, B. S. (1989). Theatre education: Approaching a new decade. *Designs for Arts in Education, 90,* 24–29.

Wolf, S. A. (1993). What's in a name? Labels and literacy in readers theatre. *The Reading Teacher, 46*(7), 540–545.

Wolf, S. A. (1994). Learning to act/Acting to learn: Children as actors, characters, and critics in classroom theatre. *Research in the Teaching of English, 28*(1), 7–44.

Wolf, S. A. (1995). Language in and around the dramatic curriculum. *The Journal of Curriculum Studies, 27*(2), 117–137.

Wolf, S. A., Carey, A., & Mieras, E. (in press). What is this literachurch stuff anyway? Preservice teachers' growth in understanding children's literary response. *Reading Research Quarterly, 31*(2), 130–157.

Wolf, S. A., & Enciso, P. (1994). Multiple selves in literary interpretation: Engagement and the language of drama. In D. J. Leu, & C. K. Kinzer (Eds.), *Multidimensional aspects of literacy research, theory, and practice: Forty-third Yearbook—National Reading Conference* (pp. 351–360). Chicago: National Reading Conference.

Wolf, S. A., & Heath, S. B. (1992). *The braid of literature: Children's worlds of reading.* Cambridge, MA: Harvard University Press.

42

FROM STORYTELLING TO GOING ON-LINE: LANGUAGE AND LITERACY OPPORTUNITIES IN THE ELEMENTARY SCHOOL

Marilyn C. Scala and Virginia C. Schroder

MUNSEY PARK ELEMENTARY SCHOOL, MANHASSET, NY

Literacy thrives in environments rich in conversation, so that educators constantly seek innovative methods to foster meaningful conversations within curricula boundaries, without increasing the burden of content to be taught.

Two tools for encouraging literate conversations are storytelling and technology—the old and the new. Storytelling encompasses personal narratives, myths and fables, and the performing arts, while technology assumes a broad definition that embraces television, video, and computer use. Both can be woven into the fabric of existing subject matter, offering new venues from which to see and explore content, and new opportunities for language growth and exchange.

The intellectual, social, and aesthetic values of literacy are learned individually, in small groups, and in whole class settings. However, storytelling and technology are best used in interactive settings where students are exposed to multiple perspectives and global understandings.

In this chapter storytelling and technology are examined in light of their effectiveness as aids to literacy and language development.

STORYTELLING: RATIONALE FOR USE

The telling of stories is part of our daily lives and provides a natural environment for teaching language and literacy. Storytelling is a universal experience, encompassing that which is oral and written. Originally, storytelling was an oral tradition and the means for elders to pass down a culture's values to their young. Families for generations have told stories to entertain, express hopes and fears, instill values,

and pass on family traditions. Now storytelling is valued not only for its family traditions but for its benefits to children's literacy. It is a natural link between home and school. It is listening to a parent, teacher, or librarian read a wonderful book. It is family and personal stories told in unique narratives. As Heather Forest, a professional storyteller for over 20 years, says, "Storytelling is a root of language" (Shedden, 1990, p. 11).

Learning history through journals and letters is history by storytelling. The telling of stories includes myths, folktales, legends, fairy tales, tall tales, and fables of all cultures so that:

> students begin to know the stories that people everywhere, throughout time, use to teach their young the rules for human conduct, through metaphors for bravery, greed, faithfulness, envy, change, pride.... Children can look deeply into myths, see themselves, and make connections between themselves and all the people who live and have lived (Reinehr, 1987, p. 7).

Storytelling enriches existing curriculum with aesthetic principles. Aesthetic knowing is a synthesis of cognitive, affective, intellectual, and emotive skills (Sienkiewicz, 1986). While listening to and telling stories in an endless variety of ways, students develop language skills, gain confidence, and learn how to think inventively and take appropriate risks. When students and teachers create stories about their experiences, they include their interpretation of that experience. By listening to the perspectives of others, students expand their ability to make sense of the world through more generalized knowledge and understanding. Developing skills of perception affects their lives as citizens in a global community. Aesthetic education is not an enrichment of academic programs but an integral part. Storytelling is not a separate entity but a part of the curriculum in reading, writing, show and tell, and much that teachers already do.

Storytelling embraces all that is communicative and visual. It is appropriate for all grade levels. It fosters cognitive, language, and social development in students, and connects reading, writing, listening, and speaking with performing arts skills.

Research shows that storytelling improves retention. "Stories are more easily remembered and recalled than a series of unrelated 'facts'. For example information is more readily retained when reading a journal of a Civil War soldier or watching parts of the Civil War film series by Ken Burns. Rudyard Kipling said that if history were taught in the form of stories it would never be forgotten (Hamilton, & Weiss, 1990, p.132). All students benefit from storytelling, and it is especially an important resource for students with reading difficulties. Hamilton and Weiss (1990) found that listening skills, comprehension, and confidence improve with these activities.

WAYS TO USE STORYTELLING

Several types of storytelling for classroom use are discussed in this chapter. Teachers encourage family stories; they retell myths and fables; and they incorporate literature into readers' theater and story theater. Partnerships with cultural institutions offer another resource for communication and literacy.

Family Stories

Shelley Harwayne, in a class in New York City's P.S. 149, gathered students in a comfortable circle to share stories, memories, and moments. She told her class:

> In every family there are stories we tell over and over. These are stories that hold us together as a family; stories of coming to America, of how one child got his name, of the day we found a turtle on the highway, or named our dog, or got stuck in a rainstorm(Calkins, 1991, p.28).

Then she told a story of her own. This warm-up and the intimacy of the group experience released a flow of stories from the students. Classrooms are turned into communities by shared stories (Calkins, 1991).

When listeners are actively involved, there is more intense focus between teller and audience, whether between teacher and students or student and student. Teachers find students very supportive of each other as they coach one another in their storytelling skills.

Family stories give teachers insight into how families interpret their experiences. They are also good beginnings for research skills. Gathering family stories requires interviewing, note-taking, oral storytelling, and writing. Children become involved in this type of research because they are writing about events close to them and about which they have knowledge (Harste, Short, & Burke, 1988).

Ralph Fletcher (1993), in conducting reading and writing workshops for teachers, intersperses his classes with personal stories and poems as well as trade books. These stories trigger

ideas, helping teachers connect with their own stories. Teachers who on Monday felt they were not writers and had no stories to tell, by Friday had formed an intimate community as they shared their narratives. They left the group experience trusting their personal voices and respecting the stories of the others. Teachers also gained insight from their experiences confronting the empty page in this workshop as "students." Nancie Atwell, in her book *In the Middle,* (1987), shares valuable techniques on how to confer with students so that they can discover what is significant in their everyday lives.

Readiness to write often comes from storytelling, shared responses to literature, and journals and writers' notebooks. After sharing thoughts and stories, it is natural to record the memories and moments in writing (Calkins, 1991, p. 31).

Professional Storytelling as a Resource

Marni Schwartz, a storyteller, also believes that telling personal narratives is the way to introduce children to storytelling. Her students find their stories by searching for story memories from books read, movies, TV, and family experiences, and sharing them in what she terms "a fabulous 'jam session' of tellers" (Schwartz, 1987, p. 605). When children choose myths and fables to learn, they need to prepare and work on them as they would a piece of writing to make it their own. Schwartz stresses that students need a variety of models and time to bring them to life. Her students research versions of a story or film to find the way they want to present it. They draft a telling much as they would a piece of writing, experimenting with introductions and endings.

In storytelling, as opposed to plays, students are encouraged to visualize the story in scenes rather than memorize a script. Heather Forest says she creates a story by putting the motion picture image in her mind into words (Shedden, 1990, p.12). It is important to retain key phrases, though, because the impact lies in the language such as, "Then I'll huff and I'll puff and I'll blow your house down" (Cullinan, 1989, p. 63). Drawing story sequences and story mapping are effective ways to visualize the story while learning it. By not memorizing, students are encouraged to make the story their own and are released from the constraints of a right or wrong way. Since children are exposed to powerful visual sources:—television, movies, picture books—it is important to let them rely on their own visual imaginations in storytelling so that they can trust in their own ability to form images.

When children are read to, they learn about story structures. When they tell stories, they learn to manipulate and control them. As they internalize these structures, comprehension improves considerably. Listening skills improve. When a story is told rather than read, the bond between teller and audience facilitates a more focused listening. In storytelling children are more involved and more likely to use imagination to create alternative solutions to problems. The classroom, as a storytelling community, becomes a safe environment in which to take risks, elaborate, invent, explore and grow (Trousdale, 1990, p. 173).

Just as a piece of writing enables teachers to know a child better, storytelling helps the teacher to see a child in a different way. Children bring to storytelling the authority of personal information and knowledge, imagination, and problem-solving strategies. The process provides ways to construct meaning and to verbalize experiences. Much of the power is in the sharing, the relationship and interaction established between teller and the audience through body language and eye contact. When teachers assess students' growth after storytelling activities, they find that the experiences improve self-esteem as well as language and aesthetic perceptions. Children of all abilities are enthusiastic in their comments after storytelling experiences. Many especially express pride in overcoming their anxiety of speaking in front of a group (Hamilton, & Weiss, 1990, p.15). Becoming a confident and competent speaker is a lifelong skill.

When children tell stories of their own experiences, as well as historical and fictional ones, they become more socially aware and responsible (Dyson, 1990, p. 194). Learning is the process of connecting current experiences to past stories. Through discourse and reflection across ethnic and religious lines students and teachers reach new understandings. Storytelling takes students from their personal environment to more global understandings.

Maxine Greene, Professor of Education and Philosophy at Teachers College, Columbia University, states that stories encourage reflection on the diversity of human experience and help us recognize that there are always multiple perspectives (Dyson, 1990, p.194). Reinehr believes in the power of a story to fill children with hope. She states that we need stories of every genre, "told and retold by every culture throughout time, because we all need redefinitions of what it means to arrive safely after difficult journeys" (Reinehr, 1987, p. 1). She uses *The Lion, the Witch and the Wardrobe* by C. S. Lewis (1950), *Harriet the Spy* by Louise Fitzhugh (1964), *The Hobbit* by J. R. R. Tolkien (1937), fairy tales, myths, and legends of Native Americans as examples of literacy journeys. Although vocabularies are enriched, of equal importance is the fact that these stories provide a medium in which diverse people can stay in tune with each other. Through stories—oral, written, sung, performed— teachers can promote an increased understanding of the past and present.

Readers' and Story Theater

Readers' theater is a kind of oral storytelling in which literature is the focus. Students read orally from scripts adapted from selections of literature. Voice and some facial expressions and gestures make the characters and narration come alive. Stories with dialogue and a strong plot work best. Students and teachers can adapt scenes from a book to discover the various points of view of the characters. When groups give different readings of the same story, children realize that reading is an open process of constructing meaning and that there are many interpretations of texts. (Harste et al., 1988) Like storytelling, there is an audience. Unlike plays, there are no costumes, sets, or memorized lines.

Story theater is another way to extend meaning through storytelling. In story theater, a narrator reads while players perform the action described. Simple poems, folktales, and stories with plenty of action and less dialogue work best.

Teacher Training in Aesthetic Education

School districts across the country are working collaboratively with performing arts institutions to enhance their curriculum with the philosophy of aesthetic education. The Lincoln Center Institute was created in 1975 by Lincoln Center for the Performing Arts in New York City. Its goal was to further a commitment to education by providing aesthetic education programs to teachers and students. The Institute is associated with Teachers College of Columbia University and Dr. Maxine Greene, and also with the education department of The Museum of Modern Art. Dr. Greene describes aesthetic education and authentic learning as a matter of going beyond. "Is it not exploration generated by wonder, curiosity, open questions?... And is there not a special pleasure, a delight found in the discovery, in the sometimes startling realization that what is being learned affects the manner in which we make sense of our world?" (Greene, 1980, p. 9, 10.) She goes on to say that the more informed we are, the more sensitive we are to the complexity of the world.

Lincoln Center teaching-artists work directly with teachers during summer sessions and with teachers and students during the school year with the work of art as the text. Mark Schubart, President of the Institute, states that its purpose is to enhance children's perceptions and their ability to express themselves and communicate creatively, not to train a generation of professional artists. It is an interdisciplinary process with the goal of teaching aesthetic perception and how these understandings relate to other aspects of life, not the acquistion of knowledge about a specific body of literature or specific performance skill (Schubart, 1972). It is in this philosophy that aesthetic education and literacy as well as aesthetic education and curricula become natural partners in our schools.

Teachers and students explore aesthetic issues in dance, music, theater, and visual arts. The workshops include hands-on activities such as movement exercises and improvisation with professional artists as well as attendance at performances in the various art forms. Within this structure, teachers find ways to relate dance, music, drama, and visual arts to areas of the curriculum. For example, in their classrooms teachers and children collaborate in small groups creating movements to discover how choreographers use dance as an expression of the social issues of a time. Baroque style dance is examined for the political/social/musical climate in which it was developed. Poetry and drama combine in a workshop with the theme, youth and democracy, as explored by Paul Lawrence Dunbar, Langston Hughes, Alice Walker and others. Jazz is studied to learn how this conversational music reflects the America in which it developed. The Greek myth of Orpheus and the Andean mountain tale of Delgadina are examined through language, movement, dance, and improvisation. Educators and artists adapt fairy tales, fables, and legends into contemporary lessons evoking insight and identificaton. Teachers "learn how artists make aesthetic choices; how to develop skills of perception, communication, and understanding applicable to other curriculum subjects and to other aspects of life" (Summer Session Bulletin, 1994). In workshops, the use of observation, questioning, and studio projects fosters awareness of diverse cultures. Literature as an art form is explored through active engagements in the same way teachers explore literature in their classrooms through reader responses.

Key elements in the Lincoln Center philosophy of aesthetic education are collaborative and interactive teaching and learning. Teaching is seen as a lifetime journey of personal and professional growth. Teachers are asked to integrate new information into their teaching, to approach their jobs in new ways, and to recognize that everyone is a learner, adults and children alike (Sienkiewicz, 1986, pp.146, 147).

Exploration is done within small groups in a nonjudgmental environment. Sensorimotor skills are unified with cognitive skills. In 1993–94, 1,500 teachers from 260 schools participated in the Lincoln Center Institute partnership. Teachers and teaching artists made aesthetic education part of the classroom experience for 100,000 students. The Institute's model is being developed in other cities across the country. Partnerships of school districts, colleges, cultural institutions, and artists are fostering aesthetic education as a significant component of education today.

There are many ways and reasons to tell a story. The pleasures of stories are obvious. But the importance lies in their educational value. Using storytelling as a tool across curriculum areas teaches not only the components of reading, writing, listening, and speaking but also aesthetic understanding and collaboration which will provide today's students with the balance they need for the 21st century. When asked how they implement various aspects of storytelling in their classrooms, teachers report that networking with colleagues and sharing expertise are the most valuable and time-efficient ways to branch out into new delivery methods.

TELEVISION AND VIDEO: RATIONALE FOR USE

About 30 years ago, educational television joined the ranks of filmstrips and movies as one of the technological tools available for classroom use. When videos were developed the scope of television use in education became even broader. Teachers could purchase preprogrammed videos to augment the curriculum, or tape programs from commercial TV to use in the classroom (Wilson, & Tally, 1991, p. 9). Many educators believe that the promise of these innovative tools has never been fulfilled. Indeed, it is estimated that as of 1992, only about half of the nation's teachers had experienced using television and technology in their teaching (Texaco / Thirteen: National Teacher Training Institute 1991–92).

Television as an entertainment medium has sometimes been blamed for a decline in literacy, language use, and curiosity about the real world. Studies have shown that a steady diet of solitary TV viewing results in a reduced ability to form oral sentences or solve verbal problems (Cheney, 1983, pp. 54–58). Other studies, however, conclude that although television viewing does not augment vocabulary development in young children, it does not adversely affect it either. The impact of television viewing on children seems to depend on what is viewed, who is doing the viewing, and what preceeds or follows the viewing. For every study made, other studies show reverse findings. It is agreed, however, that television could exert a more powerful influence on social and language growth than it has (Comstock, 1991).

While there is still much to learn about the most effective ways to integrate TV, film, and video into existing classroom programs, progress has been made in understanding their potential. Knowledgeable teachers recognize that today's technology can bring the real world into the learning environment, and take students where they could not otherwise go—beyond classroom walls. As a result, TV and videos expand students' horizons while they close the gap between those students who are well traveled and experienced, and those whose experiences are limited. Language skills and vocabulary develop as children discuss programs, analyze issues, compare information, and construct their own understandings through further inquiry and exploration (Peterson, 1992, pp. 75, 76).

WAYS OF USING TELEVISION AND VIDEO

Using what they have learned about the media, students can prepare their own televised or taped presentations for their classmates to critique. For example, in an upper elementary classroom, students analyze commercials taped from television. They look for examples of various types of advertising, comparing them and discussing their effectiveness. These students then create their own commercials, defending choice of media and style, and evaluating the effectiveness of their presentations. Here, TV and video are being used as interactive tools that enhance literacy. They support the teacher's goals of language development as students become aware of the power of their words. Working with television in this way also creates sensitive viewers who are aware of the "programming" that commercial television imposes on its public. These students are learning to question both the value and the integrity of the televised message. The commercials can be rerun, segments can be reviewed, and viewing can be stopped so that students can ask and answer questions or discuss what they have seen.

When a classroom of students is operating from within a framework of language and experience, cooperation in problem solving is facilitated and increased. As students begin to make connections between the immediate worlds of home, classroom, and community, and the world that television portrays, they move in their thinking from the particular to the general, from a "self" view to a global view. With guidance and experimentation, they learn to interpret what they see and hear—to analyze, synthesize, and evaluate. The group mix is enriched by the variety of approaches, interests, and abilities that each member brings (Peterson, 1992, p. 80).

The creative use of television and video as technological tools also recognizes the individual learning styles of students. As teachers move away from lecture-based instruction toward multimedia classrooms, they are reaching those students who need more than written or auditory signals to become engaged. Moreover, when students work within a learning community as members of a team, the learning is increased and retained (Peterson, 1992). The teacher, as guide, allows time for each student to work at a comfortable pace. The teacher also arranges a schedule that encourages cooperative group work as well as individual investigation and research.

Television programs are linear; they have beginnings, middles, and endings. But taped programs can be manipulated to suit classroom needs. They can be stopped and started at will. They can be edited so that only certain information or sequences are viewed and reviewed. Different programs can be spliced together to highlight particular content. Programs can be viewed alone, in small groups, or as a whole class.

Videos and television programs motivate students. They can be used as the primary content deliverer, or to review and assess information. Through television, teachers can bring into the classroom specialists and experts in a given field of study. Television used in this way expands the classroom experience beyond the printed page. The content is more likely to be relevant, current, and interdisciplinary. A program about math can also involve the world of art. A program about the art world can include content about history. Video equipment can be paused or stopped to allow the teacher to check for comprehension, discuss new vocabulary, or to introduce some hands-on activities. Since television and videos used interactively work well for many learning styles, all students experience success.

TEACHER TRAINING FOR TELEVISION AND VIDEO USE

The National Teacher Training Institute (NTTI) is one organization working to educate teachers regarding the best use of television and video. Founded in 1990, the Institute recognizes the power and duty of the media to bring teachers beyond the use of TV as a passive activity. Through the facilities of public television networks nationwide, NTTI trains teachers to work with their colleagues creating video-enhanced lessons through a series of seminars and workshops. The authors of the training videos are teachers working hand-in-hand with instructional designers and media specialists. Together, they create and tape effective lessons plans that are accompanied by written teachers' guides (Texaco / Thirteen NTTI, 1991–92).

Four basic steps for opting to use television and videos as part of a lesson are taught:

- Think about the topics to be taught, then investigate the kinds of videos that are available. Survey what is available. The curriculum is the basis for choice, not the other way around.
- Develop lead-in activities.
- Determine when to use the video, or segments of it.
- Decide how much to use, but do not overuse it.

Utilization strategies are also taught, including:

- Selecting segment(s) to be targeted.

- Providing a focus or task for viewing.
- Using pausing techniques for predicting or analyzing.
- Checking for vocabulary and comprehension.
- Fostering interaction by using an acetate sheet over the screen so that students can write on it.
- Using only the video portion when the sound tract is either too sophisticated or too elementary, or to encourage students to predict the content.
- Providing hands-on activities to reinforce the content and insure students' understanding. (Texaco / Thirteen NTTI. 1991–92.)

In the New York metropolitan area, once NTTI training is completed, teachers can count on support from Learning Links, an electronic communication and information service sponsored by the New York Tri State Public Broadcasting System. Learning Links provides teachers and students with a multitude of services, including program listings, database resources, discussion forums, and classroom activities for all aspects of the curriculum. This service is especially valuable, since the response to problems and questions is rapid, and the information is current. There are replicas of the NTTI and Learning Links networks throughout the United States, and a national consortium located in Chicago which provides technical and content support to all local networks. (Texaco / Thirteen NTTI. 1991–92.)

RATIONALE FOR COMPUTER USE

In a Long Island, New York 5th-grade science classroom, groups of students are busily working. One group is gathered around the computer drafting a letter to fellow students in Seattle, Washington. They are using notes from interviews and readings about their Long Island community, its history, population, habits of energy use, and power sources. Another group is formulating questions that they will use in a telephone interview with the local power plants public relations office. They refer to an outline that they have received from a team of researchers and scientists investigating patterns of acid rain throughout the Americas. The teacher is helping other students add to a map of the community, locating small factories, bus routes, and points of interest that the students want to include. The completed map will be sent to a classroom in southern California, which will, in turn, send their community map to Long Island. Still another group of students is discussing the designs of several sample rain collectors that they have built. They are concerned with stability, ease of use, and freedom from contamination. They glance at questions about these issues on the chalkboard near them, to keep their focus clear.

This class is involved with National Geographic's Kids Network Acid Rain Program, designed to help students explore an environmental issue through authentic research and a series of hands-on experiments. Once the students have constructed their rain collectors, they will learn to read the pH scale and use pH paper to measure the acidity of local rainwater. Students investigate the possible causes of acid rain locally by noting commuter habits as well as access to and use of mass transit. They also investigate the presence of such potential polluters as factories and fossil-fuel burning power plants. They share their findings with like groups in other parts of the continent through a central command location. Then they analyze the geographic patterns they have observed, and make predictions and recommendations based on their findings (National Geographic Society, 1989).

When computers first entered the educational scene, they were used primarily as managerial tools by teachers, or to provide skills practice and drill. Increasingly, computer systems are supporting the instructional process in ways that are interactive and collaborative.

There are vast differences between "electronic classrooms," depending upon how teacher and students interact with the computer and its components, and upon the function of the technology within the curriculum. In some instances, interaction is limited because the teacher retains total control of the equipment and the scope for its use is narrow. In these situations, CD-ROM resources and laser discs are used predominantly to provide yet another view of material that has traditionally been retrieved from books. Although there is movement and sound as well as printed material, the students are passive viewers and receptors of information. Here, the advantages of technology use lie in its motivational aspects and the immediacy of the data received. What is missing is the opportunity for building language and communication skills.

In other electronic classrooms, however, the curriculum is designed to move away from lecture-based instruction toward discovery learning that fosters creative and critical thinking and personal involvement with the content. Telecommunication networks such as America On-line's National Geographic services and the many student forums and bulletin boards offered by AOL, CompuServe and the Internet are used to promote deeper investigations and inspire cooperative learning and teaching. Communication among students is encouraged as small groups work together at computers. Since students both learn and help others learn, skills and information are retained.

Today's teaching involves using technology to inspire students to investigate within the classroom and beyond it as well. For example, after viewing a program about a threatened species, students might set up an investigation of a species within their own surroundings. The computer can assist them in locating research about the subject, organizing data within a database or on a spreadsheet, and collating the findings into a report. Through a computer networking program, students might contact other students similarly engaged, sharing information, examining theories, and generating new questions to be explored. The flexibility of interaction between user and computer allows it to be manipulated in ways that go beyond the limitations of books and lectures (Thornburg, 1989). This implies that hands-on science and textbook science are not enough for today's classrooms. But neither can technological tools stand alone; each must be integrated.

When the goal is language growth, the ideal computer programs will include problem solving, collaboration, and networking with others. The gathering, sorting, analyzing, synthesizing, evaluating, and reporting that is done will be for real reasons that validate writing, reading, and communicating. Part of the learning must include an opportunity for critical analysis of the information itself. Authentic engagement means that students need to question their sources as they research, rather than accept all computer or television-generated data as accurate. Becoming a critical consumer is part of technology's challenge (Dipinto, & Turner, 1994; Kinnaman, 1994).

It is the teacher who must select this software with curricula objectives and the needs of the students in mind. As with the traditional components of any unit of study, the teacher will consider the purpose for using the technology, who will be using it, and whether it will effectively satisfy the users' needs (Hirschbuhl, 1994). With the proliferation of computer software programs, this is not an easy task. To complicate the issue further, it is likely that the teacher has never been educated to consider the best qualities of interactive media.

TEACHER TRAINING FOR COMPUTER USE

In-service teacher training for computer literacy should be a feature in every school district budget. As teachers are trained to use visual and interactive media with planning and thoughtfulness, students will also be instructed to see more than just the content that programs offer. They will learn to see the background, the people involved, the larger view. As much as possible, the teachers capitalize on the ability of computers to capture the students' attention, to make them curious and keep them curious. In other words, teachers go beyond the program as simply another source of information. By monitoring and tailoring programs for specific purposes, teachers encourage students to construct their own knowledge, and to validate what they hypothesize, so that content is truly learned and remembered. They can delete non-essentials, and add components that necessitate group work and conversation. They can use technology to bridge curriculum areas, encouraging thematic work and connections between traditional disciplines so that relationships are emphasized and content is seen as relevant to the real world (Kari, & Nojd, 1991).

The involvement and interest of students provide the impetus for growth in the use of technology in the classroom. But teachers must provide the structure within which the initial exploration takes place, and the scheduling that allows it to continue. This means a change in the roles of the teachers. There is no longer a need for the "sage on the stage" approach. What is needed is the "guide on the side," a partner in the learning process (Wilson, & Tally, 1991). Having studied and selected beforehand those components best suited for the students and the learning objectives, the teachers develop a way to use technology as part of the curriculum (Thornburg, 1989). Technology does not take the place of hands-on activities, or reading and writing, but supports them and gives richer meaning to them.

The inescapable necessity of technological tools offers a real challenge to teacher preparatory institutions. By the year

2000, an estimated 75% of today's teachers will no longer be teaching. Unfortunately, the recruits that are being educated to replace this retiring group will be no better equipped to deal with the tools of technology than their predecessors of 30 years ago (Dipinto, & Turner, 1994). In most preparatory schools, technological training consists of word processing skills, with some database and spreadsheet instruction included. When television, films, and videos are used in teacher training courses, they are not perceived as interactive tools.

Teachers can learn through workshops, but they also profit from an opportunity to build supportive networks with other teachers. The teachers with whom we spoke credited their expertise with technological tools to conferences, peer networking, professional journals and magazines, as well as inservice course work. Each believed that without this support, they would have grown more slowly. As with young students, learning is best done when it is collegial. Teachers, as students, need to talk with others who are exploring new ideas. Together, they can trouble shoot, imagine, create, publish, and spread the wealth. It is easier for a teacher to be a guide through new terrain in the classroom when there are others available to give ongoing support.

Funding for teacher in-service training and purchasing the technological tools needed to keep abreast of today's fast-paced information explosion places an onerous burden on school districts. Some districts are involving their surrounding business communities as partners in educational endeavors. In addition to providing potential financial assistance, such a partnership establishes a vehicle for communication about the education of tomorrow's employees and a network for mutual growth. Just as schools need to take their cues about what is needed for the business world of the future, businesses need to be informed about what today's students have to offer them. Public relations are improved as barriers between home, schools, and businesses are breached. Other school districts are seeking funding through grants to foundations supporting educational advances. The NTTI manual and periodicals such as *Technology and Learning* offer suggestions for funding and grant proposals.

CONCLUSION

In trying to meet the expanding needs of today's classrooms, teachers must find unifying tools to facilitate learning. From storytelling to technology, teachers and students explore and expand literacy and communicative skills.

Major implications for classrooms of the future are:

1. Storytelling, used throughout the curriculum, promotes historical and personal understanding.
2. Students of the future must be proficient in interactive technology.
3. Aesthetic education, with its emphasis on respecting multiple perspectives, is a critical component in classrooms that are global in outlook.
4. Students must be able to work collaboratively in a team environment.
5. Learning tasks must be relevant and authentic, connecting students to problems, situations, and issues that affect them and their world.
6. The teacher is less an information transmitter and more a partner/facilitator in the learning process.
7. To build and maintain links to new expertise, teachers must network through conferences, collegial workshops and seminars, and telecommunications.

References

Atwell, N. (1987). *In the middle: Writing, reading and learning with adolescents.* Portsmouth, NH: Boynton/Cook Publishers.

Calkins, L. M. (1991). *Living between the lines.* Portsmouth, NH: Heinemann Inc.

Cheney, G. A. (1983). *Television in American society.* New York: Franklin Watts.

Comstock, G. (1991). *Television and the American child.* New York: Academic Press.

Cullinan, B. E. (1989). *Literature and the child.* (2nd ed.). Fort Worth, TX: Harcourt, Brace and Jovanovich.

Dipinto, V., & Turner, S. (1994). Teachers and students as co-conspirators in learning. (Summary). *Proceedings of the 1994 national educational computing conference: Recreating the revolution.* pp. 68, 69.

Dyson, A. H. (1990). Diversity, social responsibility, and the story of litteracy development. *Language Arts, 67,* 192–205.

Fitzhugh, L. (1964). *Harriet the Spy.* New York: Dell Publishing.

Fletcher, R. (1993). *What a writer needs.* Portsmouth, NH: Heinemann.

Greene, M., (1980). *Themes, a teacher talks to teachers: Perspectives on the Lincoln Center Institute.* New York: Lincoln Center Institute, No. 1, pp. 5, 9,10.

Hamilton, M., & Weiss, M. (1990). *Children tell stories: A teaching guide.* Katonah, NY: Richard C. Owen.

Harste, J. C., Short, K.G., & Burke, C. (1988). *Creating classrooms for authors.* Portsmouth, NH: Heinemann.

Hirschbuhl, J. (Ed.). (1994). *Computers in education,* (6th ed.). Guilford, CT: Dushkin Publishing Group.

Kari, J., & Nojd, O. (1991). Interactive video in teaching. *Institute for educational research: Theory into practice,* (pp. 2–5, 13, 26).

Kinnaman, D. (1994). The problem with information in the information age. *Technology & Learning.* 94.

Lewis, C.S. (1950). *The lion, the witch, and the wardrobe.* New York: Macmillan.

National Geographic Society. (1989). *National geographic kids network: Introduction.* (video). Washington, DC.

Peterson, R. (1992). *Life in a crowded place.* Portsmouth, NH: Heinemann.

Reinehr, F. (1987). Storyteaching. *Teachers & Writers, 18,* 1–7.

Schubart, M. (1972). *Performing arts institutions and young people: Lincoln Center's study, The hunting of the squiggle.* New York: Praeger.

Schwartz, M. (1987). Connecting to language through story. *Language Arts, 64,* 603–660 .

Shedden, M. (1990, July 18). Telling stories in the TV age. *Newsday,* p. 11 .

Sienkiewicz, C. L. (1986). *From theory to practice: The development of the Lincoln Institute's model of aesthetic education.* Ann Arbor, Ml: University Microfilms International.

Summer Session Bulletin (1994). New York: Lincoln Center Institute for the Arts in Education.

Thirteen / Texaco. *National teacher training institute: Science, television & technology. 1991–1992.* New York.

Thornburg, D. (1989). *Education, technology, and paradigms of change for the 21 st century.* Starsong Publications.

Tolkien, J. R. R. (1937). *The Hobbit.* New York: Ballantine Books.

Trelease, J. (1982). *The read-aloud handbook.* New York: Penguin.

Trousdale, A. M. (1990). Interactive storytelling: Scaffolding children's early narratives. *Language Arts, 67,* 164–173.

Wilson, K., & Tally, W. (1991). Designs for discovery: Interactive multimedia learning environments at Bank Street College. *Center for Technology in Education.* pp. 6–17.

· 43 ·

"WHAT HAVE YOU LEARNED?":
CO-CONSTRUCTING THE MEANING OF TIME

Gordon Wells

ONTARIO INSTITUTE FOR STUDIES IN EDUCATION

Gen Ling Chang-Wells

TORONTO BOARD OF EDUCATION

Have you ever tried making a water clock from pieces of wood left over from renovation, a plastic spoon, a yogurt carton and bits and pieces of string? At the suggestion of their teacher, the first author constructed such a device—with the help of the directions in a junior science guide—and took it to the combined grade three and four class in which the two authors were collaborating in a study of the grade three students as they worked on the theme of time. When it was finally set up, the teacher asked some of the children who had been watching to demonstrate how it worked to the rest of the class. Unfortunately, it failed to work as expected. However, suggestions for fixing it were not slow in coming and soon an animated discussion was in full swing, as competing proposals were put forward, justified and evaluated. By the end of the day, some of the most enthusiastic engineers had succeeded in making it work.

We want to hold on to this event for a moment, and say a little more about its significance, as we perceive it. For it has come to function as an icon for us as we have thought about the actuality of classroom activity from the perspective of its role in bringing the resources of the past to bear in equipping each new generation of students to meet the challenges of their future. As we shall try to show, this unplanned situation epitomized many of the characteristics of the social constructivist model of learning-and-teaching which we wish to explore through a more detailed examination of some of the episodes that occurred during the course of these students' study of time.

During the preceding weeks, the children we had been observing had engaged in a variety of activities designed to help them understand the need for a standard method of measuring time. They had also learned about some of the earliest timing devices by constructing simple versions for themselves and then using them to measure how long it took them to perform an activity such as walking round the room. The model water clock, complete with its striking mechanism, was intended to add a further dimension to their study, by showing how the problem of marking the passage of time in a

The observations and analysis which form the major part of this paper, arose from an ongoing collaborative project between Gen Ling Chang-Wells, a teacher with the Toronto Board of Education, and Gordon Wells, a researcher at the Ontario Institute for Studies in Education. Earlier versions were presented at the Annual Conference of the Canadian Council of Teachers of English, Calgary, April 29, 1992, under the conference theme "Remembering the Past; Remembering the future," and at the First Conference for Sociocultural Research, held in Madrid, September 1992. The preparation of the paper was made possible, in part, by a grant from the Spencer Foundation to the Ontario Institute for Studies in Education.

We should like to express our gratitude to Miriam DiGiuseppe, the former Principal of Orde St. Public School in Toronto, for allowing us to conduct the research, and the grade three children for their enthusiastic participation. Without their collaboration and their reflections on what they had been doing, the writing of this paper would not have been possible. We should also like to acknowledge the helpful comments we received in the preparation of the paper from Patrick Allen and Myriam Shechter.

regular manner could be solved by the use of a number of simple mechanical principles in combination. It was, one might say, a way of reconstructing the past with the intention that the children should grasp the principles involved in order to be able to use them in solving problems in the future.

However, as it transpired, the imperfect workmanship succeeded in teaching another lesson. Instead of serving merely as a demonstration of how the problem might have been solved in the past, the water clock became a problem in its own right. To it the children brought their own original and creative solutions, testing them in debate and subsequently in action, until they had created a functioning device that was better than the one the adult had originally constructed. What they demonstrated in the process was that the most effective way to foster children's thinking and problem-solving ability is to present them with a challenge that engages their interest and invites them to create their own solutions. They certainly benefited from the experience, but probably the person who learned most from this incident was the one who had designed the model as no more than a demonstration.

Before going on to look at further episodes from these children's study of time, therefore, we should like to develop these ideas a little further by presenting a brief account of recent work in sociocultural theory, as it applies to learning and teaching in schools. We believe that the insights that this theory offers can help us understand, and perhaps reinterpret, some of the most enduring characteristics of classroom practice.

BRINGING THE PAST INTO THE FUTURE

Let us start with a quotation from Leont'ev, who, with Vygotsky, is one of the founders of sociocultural psychology. Describing the cultural continuity which makes human society uniquely different from that of all other species, he writes: "a special form of transmitting the achievement of preceding generations to the next takes place in human society; that is, the achievements are embodied in the material and spiritual products of human activities and specific human psychological abilities can be developed through the mastery of these products by each person" (quoted in Amano, 1991). More recently, Michael Cole has made a similar point: "Human beings live in an environment transformed by the artifacts of prior generations ... the basic function [of which] is to coordinate [them] with the physical world and each other" (1991, p. 6).

Central to the thinking of this school, then, is the idea that the artifacts that were invented in the past to solve the problems that were encountered then can serve as a sort of external cultural memory, encoding the interactions of which they were previously a part and carrying their potential for solving similar problems into the present and future. In order to benefit from this legacy, however, each new generation has to be inducted into the cultural practices in which they are used and be able to recognize when and how they are relevant.

But it is not simply to physical tools that these writers refer, nor to such social practices as marriage customs or legal procedures. More important is the recognition that language, both spoken and written, and the uses we make of it for remembering, reasoning, evaluating, as well as communicating, are also cultural artifacts and practices, and that these, too, have to be learned and mastered through social interaction in the context of joint activity. Thus all the higher mental functions, as Vygotsky (1978, 1981) called them, first exist and are encountered *inter-mentally,* in interactions between people; only when they are appropriated and internalized do they function *intra-mentally,* as a resource for individual thinking and problem solving.

Inspired by this theory, a considerable amount of research has taken place in recent years into the forms of adult–child interaction that facilitate children's cognitive and linguistic development (e.g., Newman, Griffin, & Cole, 1989; Rogoff, 1990, 1992; Wells, 1986; Wells & Chang-Wells, 1992; Wertsch, Minick, & Arns, 1984). Vygotsky described this contingently responsive tutorial behavior as "working in the learner's zone of proximal development;" more recently it has been variously described as "scaffolding" (Wood, Bruner, & Ross, 1976) or "prolepsis" (Wertsch & Stone, 1985). Whatever the term used, what is emphasized in all these accounts is the way in which the tutor (whether parent or teacher) takes the learner's attempt to perform some part of the task and appropriates it into her or his more mature version, thereby giving it a significance which it does not yet have for the learner. In so doing, the tutor both enables the learner to contribute as much as he or she is able to the performance of the task and, at the same time, to become aware of the functional relationship between the constituent actions and the goal of the task as a whole. From participation in such shared task performances, the learner in turn appropriates the tutor's version and, having internalized it, is eventually able to perform it on his or her own. In this way, knowledge, both substantive and procedural, that is first encountered and mastered in social interaction, becomes an intellectual "tool-kit" for thinking and problem solving carried out by the individual alone.

Thus far, we have concentrated on learning as the remembering of the past through the taking over of the achievements of previous generations. But, as the metaphors of "scaffolding" and "prolepsis" make clear, this theory also involves a kind of remembering of the future, as the teacher, based on his or her own past experiences, projects a more complete version of a task than the learner is currently able to achieve and assists and guides the learner's performance in such a way as to bring that future about (Cole, 1991). Indeed, on a larger time-scale, education can be seen as a form of apprenticeship, as more mature members of a culture—parents, teachers and educational policy makers—drawing on their interpretations of their own remembered past experiences, project expectations about the future lives of the children in their care, and create opportunities for them to appropriate the cultural resources of knowledge and skills that they themselves have found important.

However, to place the emphasis almost exclusively on reconstructing the past for an imagined future has serious limitations. First, there is increasing likelihood that the future today's students actually encounter will be very different from that which we imagine; by equipping them only with the resources of the past, therefore, we will render them less able to solve the problems, unforeseen by us, with which they will actually have to cope. Equally important, if we emphasize tradition and authority at the expense of originality and creativity, we shall fail to do justice to the transformative nature of learning and to the possibility that this implies for change and improvement, both for the individual and for society as a whole.

Two further points must therefore be added to provide a more balanced account. First, it must be emphasized that internalization does not imply a simple copying from the outside in. In all cases, in taking over, or appropriating, a cultural artifact or practice, the learner necessarily constructs a new internal version, which builds upon and is shaped by what he or she can already do and understand. At the same time, in the process of internalization, the learner also "grows into" the organizing cognitive structures associated with the artifact or practice; this results in a modification of the individual's own cognitive organization and thus changes the way in which he or she perceives, interprets and organizes the world (Nicolopoulou, 1991; Rogoff, 1992). In other words, the outcome of the process of internalization is a transformation of the way in which an individual participates in a social practice, such that he or she is able to engage more effectively in the relevant activities.

Secondly, it is important to recognize that all action is creative, in the sense that each occasion of interaction with the social and material world is different from all previous occasions and demands a response which is unique to the particularities of the present moment. It may also be creative in the further sense that the solutions constructed for the problems encountered often go beyond previous achievements to create new artifacts which, in turn, have the potential to enhance the cultural resources to be used in solving future problems. Thus, just as the learner is transformed by appropriating the problem-solving resources inherited from the past, so can present problems be transformed by the new insights that learners are able to bring to bear on them.

Therefore, if we are to make good use of the insights to be derived from sociocultural theory to enhance our understanding of the goals and means of education, a concern with cultural reproduction and continuity needs to be complemented by an equal concern with cultural renewal and an encouragement of the creativity that makes this possible.

The remainder of this chapter explores what these ideas might look like in practice, through a collaborative investigation undertaken by both authors into the learning and teaching that took place in one unit of work in science—the study of time which was referred to in the introduction. However, because of the limits of space, we shall focus mainly on a single event—the discussion which occurred at the end of the unit, in which the teacher and children reviewed the work they had done in the preceding weeks. As we have argued elsewhere (Wells, 1995), of all the components of an inquiry-based curriculum approach, the final retrospective review is probably the most important—for both students and teacher-in the opportunities it provides for them jointly to construct a common understanding of what has been achieved, and how,

and to identify topics and issues that are recognized as needing further investigation. But before turning to the discussion, we must first provide some context by saying a little about the participants in the discussion and about their classroom environment.

The School and Classroom Context of the Investigation

The school in which this investigation took place is situated in an inner-city area in Toronto. Due to its location, close to Chinatown and also to a number of large corporate office buildings and hospitals, the students come from a wide variety of backgrounds. Some are children of relatively recent immigrants, who work in service jobs nearby; others are children of doctors, lawyers, and other professionals, who have chosen the school because of its reputation and because of the day-care facilities that it provides. It should also be noted that this school is one of the few that offers heritage language instruction, in Chinese and in Spanish, as part of its regular program; in the last few years, it has also included a black studies program as part of its curriculum. The makeup of the combined grade three and grade four class is fairly typical of the school as a whole. Children of Caucasian descent, for whom English is the first language, are in a minority, although most of those who are bilingual in English and another language have been resident in Canada since birth, or at least since they began to attend school. There are, however, several children who have arrived in the last year or two, and they are still receiving special help in learning English as a second language. The class also has several children who are withdrawn for additional help in literacy or with other special needs.

Although the class includes children from two grades, whose current levels of attainment span a very wide range, the teacher tries to create a single community in which each child is challenged to address the topic being studied at a level appropriate to her or his ability. For much of the time children work in groups, sometimes self-selected and sometimes chosen by the teacher. In all cases, the groups are encouraged to develop their own ways of working cooperatively, but with the requirement that each child play a part in achieving the goal that is jointly negotiated. On the present occasion, as an experiment, the teacher has decided to divide the class, with one half engaging in a unit on forensic science and the other half making a study of time.

Since this study took place in January and February, the children already had some experience of engaging in sustained inquiry. In the previous term, they had done work in science on sound and on light and color, and in social studies they had carried out library-based research on a Canadian province or a foreign country. Concurrently with the work on time, they were also studying endangered spaces and species. Evidence of the resources they had used and of the meanings they had made with them was to be seen on shelves and tables in all parts of the classroom and displayed on bulletin boards around the walls and in the adjoining corridor. From these same sources it was evident that, wherever possible, connections were also made between these topics of inquiry and the children's work in math, literature, art and drama. The study of time should be seen, therefore, against the background of a curriculum that was both integrated and challenging.

Co-constructing the Meaning of Time

The discussion which is the focus of this chapter occurred at the end of the unit of study on time and served as an occasion for the children and their teacher to make connections among the various activities in which they had engaged and the artifacts of various kinds that had mediated both their practical activity and the sense that they had made of what they were doing. It started with the teacher gathering the children on the rug and inviting them to think about what they had learned during the preceding 5 weeks. Almost all the topics that were considered in the following 40 minutes were generated from this initial invitation. They are summarized in Table 43–1. The duration of each topic, in number of exchanges, is shown in parentheses in the final column.

Set out like this, the discussion can be seen to have had an impressive agenda, one that very few teachers would consider possible to treat in any depth with 8- and 9-year-olds. What was it, then, that enabled this group of children to remain interested and involved from beginning to end of this long and challenging discussion?

The first part of the explanation, we believe, is to be found in the rich variety of practical work that the children had engaged in, from which they had acquired first hand knowledge about several of the topics that were raised. Through the activities of attempting to invent a method of measuring time, experimenting with pendulums, and constructing either a

TABLE 43–1. An Overview of the Review Discussion

Episode	Topic	Initiator	No. of Exchanges
1	Introduction: personal responses	Teacher	(3)
2	Accuracy: need for standard measurement—comparing various methods used by groups	Auritro	(10)
3	"Processes of science": fair test, variables—reviewing experiments on pendulums	Bianca	(20)
4	Checking knowledge of units of time	Tema	(16)
5	Previous work with pendulums—personal recollection	Tema	(4)
6	Sources of power for clocks and timers—students' personal experiences	Bianea	(4)
7	Basis for units of time in earth's movement—demonstration using various artifacts	Teacher	(13)
8	Time differences between time zones—exploring personal anecdotes, using globe	Bianca	(40)

"water-clock" or a "rolling-ball-clock," they had experienced, in practice, what it is to "do science." They had also found themselves faced with problems they had attempted to solve in a (relatively) principled and systematic manner. Personal experiences from outside the classroom provided a further source of information on which they could draw.

However, that is to tell only part of the story. As Driver (1983) argues, on the basis of observation of many classrooms in which children engage in practical activities in science, "hands-on" activities do not lead to the development of an understanding of scientific principles unless they are accompanied by "minds-on" activities as well. In this unit, numerous instances of such sense making occurred in the conferences that took place while the activities were being planned and in progress, and in class discussions that occurred after each one to underline the significance of what had been done. Limitations of space make it difficult to do more here than hint at the richness of these continuing discussions. Mention must also be made of the various books the teacher had assembled, which the children had been encouraged to consult for specific purposes and to browse through more generally. Equally important were the science logs that the children kept, for these were another tool for sense making. Rather than simply using them to report what they had done, the children were encouraged to write in their logs about what they had learned and about their reflections on the experience; they were also encouraged to note questions to which they wished to obtain answers. Finally, mention must be made of the connections that were noted in passing between their science investigations and the work they were doing in mathematics.

This review discussion was not an isolated event, therefore, but a part of this teacher's overall approach to the learning and teaching of science in her classroom and, indeed, to learning and teaching in all areas of the curriculum. As she explained, there are three aspects of doing science that she wishes the children to gain from the work that they do in each unit: the concepts appropriate to the topic, the processes of observation and experimentation and of making sense of the results, and the language for talking, reading and writing about the topics that they study. One of the overall purposes of this discussion, then, was to continue to weave connections among all the three.

However, an equally important aim was to bring together the meanings that individual children had been making, both alone and in their separate groups, and to construct a shared understanding of what had been done and found. By bringing her own more systematic knowledge of the various topics associated with the theme of time to this co-constructive process, the teacher also wanted the children to have an opportunity to take over some of the ways of talking and thinking about these matters that are practiced in the wider culture.

What we wish to explore, then, is the way in which these various aims were achieved in the moment-by-moment unfolding of this particular discussion. In the process, we hope to show how collaborative talk of this kind makes possible the co-constructive and transformative knowledge building that was described in the introductory section of this chapter. Furthermore, since discourse is itself a cultural artifact, which learners have to appropriate through participation in actual occasions of use, a close examination of selected episodes from this particular classroom discussion should enable us to gain a better understanding of how this process of appropriation takes place.

The Need for a Standard Method of Measuring Time

The teacher opens the discussion with a very general question: "What have you learned about time?" Tema, Emily, and Jamilla obviously hear the question as a request to tell about what they have personally learned, and each contributes an interesting idea.

(Note: In this and the following transcripts, . = 1 second of pause; * = a word that was inaudible; < > enclose segments where the transcription is uncertain; <u>underlining</u> indicates segments that were spoken simultaneously; CAPS = a segment spoken with emphasis.)

1	Tema:	It's not just everything is the same thing . some people might want to set their clocks faster or slower or right on time
2	Teacher:	Emily
3	Emily:	Time does not have to be telled by clocks and watches we can–we also * it can also have different sort of timers
4	Teacher:	OK, we learned about different . types . of timers (writing on board) . clocks or even watches, right? And I think what Tema said I would rephrase it as time is a form of measurement, right? (writing) a . form . of . measurement, right? just as distance is a form of measurement . What else did you learn about time? . anything else? Jamilla?
5	Jamilla:	We learned that it um– you don't necessarily have the um– the coo– the watches like um the, minute hand, the hour hand, the second hand, you can also– you can also use water and <things like that> construct watches and um . construct clocks and it doesn't have to be um um someone– someone special makes them to be *
6	Teacher:	Uh-hmm, right (accepting) So a timing device like a clock or watch may not have the minute or hour hand, you can use the water . to represent the– the minute hand for example . or use something else to represent it . Yes, what else did we study in the whole unit of time?
7	Auritro:	Counting isn't always accurate
8	Teacher:	Counting is not accurate, so there are certain ways of . timing that some are more accurate and some are less accurate, for example like counting . What is more accurate than counting?
9	Bianca:	Using the stop-watch
10	Teacher:	Using stop-watches . What about the things you made? .. of the various things you've made what are some of the timing devices you all made?

In their idiosyncratic detail, these answers are not untypical of children, or even of adults, who lack experience of engaging in metacognitive talk. In these circumstances, they tend to provide answers which are at the "local and specific level." As is apparent here, an invitation to reflect does not in itself enable reflection. More has to be done. In fact, as is suggested by the research on adult–child interaction (Bruner, 1983; Cross, 1977; Wells, 1986), it is the follow-up to a child's contribution that is crucial for the development of a conversation; it is also this move, in particular, that makes a qualitative difference to what the child learns from the interaction as a whole (Wells, 1996). Here, in the teacher's follow-up moves in turns 4 and 6, it is evident that, as she echoes back what the children have said, she is doing three things. First, she is providing an opportunity for the children to discover how their contributions have been understood and giving them a chance to make a repair if needed. Second, whilst accepting the child's idea, she introduces an alternative way of articulating the response, thereby bringing it closer to the register conventionally used in the wider culture for "talking science" (Lemke, 1990). Third, and perhaps most important from the metacognitive perspective, she "steps up" the children's responses to a level of talking about their personal experiences in a way that reflects a principled understanding of the topic rather than a simple telling of what they have personally learned. In other words, she is encouraging talk which requires transformation of their personal knowledge rather than merely knowledge-telling (Bereiter & Scardamalia, 1985).

In such sequences, the teacher uses her follow-up moves to model this complex but powerful thinking skill; that is, she takes the child's contribution and, in her response to it, demonstrates how one can extrapolate from a range of specific experiences a principle which applies to those past experiences and possibly to similar future ones as well. An obvious example of this occurs in turn 4, where Tema's observation is utilized to form the basis for the introduction of the scientific "thematic formation" (Lemke, 1990) "x is a form of y."

In the next sequence, Auritro, the fourth child to offer a personal response to the original question, not only picks up on the teacher's intervening amplification of time as a form of measurement, but extends it by tacitly juxtaposing standard and nonstandard methods of measurement. Counting belongs to the latter class, which "isn't always accurate" (7). Comparing Auritro's contribution to those of the preceding three children, it is clear that he is expressing an idea that has wider application and one which evidences an ability to extrapolate and articulate a principled understanding from particular physical experiences. To provide a bedrock of such experiences is, in fact, one of the teacher's priorities, as she believes that it is a necessary basis for engaging the children in talk which has the potential for knowledge transformation. In Auritro's case, he and a few other children had chosen to investigate the use of nonstandard methods of measuring time, such as counting, clapping, and pouring an agreed amount of water out of a pop bottle, in order to measure the duration of activities such as walking from one end of the hallway to the other. In so doing, they had confronted the issue of these methods' reliability.

In her follow-up to Auritro's introduction of the topic of accuracy of measurement, the teacher makes explicit Auritro's tacit comparison by reposing it in the form of a question: "what is more accurate than counting?" (8). This question enables those children who have investigated time by using standard measurements, or those who constructed devices such as a salt timer, to bring in their expertise. Thus, the topic is extended both in "depth and breadth," as the teacher put it, and the children are provoked to think beyond the local level or the single case as they draw upon their collective experiences to arrive at understandings which will have wider and future applications.

Following the request for specific examples (10), the next 20 turns are spent in recalling the various devices that different children had experimented with. Then, in turn 31, the teacher poses a question which is in some ways the obverse of the one asked earlier: "Of all that you have done ... which are the ones that are the <u>least</u> accurate as a kind of . timing device?" Her intention here is to invite the children to go beyond the devices themselves to a consideration of their relative accuracy. Then, in the following sequence, as she follows up their suggestions with a request for a justification (33), a new issue is brought into the discussion.

33 Teacher: Counting or stamping your feet and using your heart-beat or walking round the room . that is the least accurate
Why? Why is it least accurate?
34 Bianca: If you < use > your heart-beat sometimes your heart-beat gets faster, like fai– um– like you've– like you've been– you've got um so many–like a lot of energy and then <you're trained> to get your heart-beat and then because you've got a lot of energy you feel like running around, and then you start running around– your heart-beat's going to get faster < so it changes>
35 Teacher: And I think er Bianca is bringing things to another part of this science unit <that you have learned about> . "the processes of science" (writing on board) .

Once again, it is a child's contribution which provides an entry to the new topic. For although, in itself, Bianca's answer is largely anecdotal in intention, the teacher recognizes in it an opportunity to bring into the discussion a fundamental principle to be observed in carrying out experiments, and one that the children have encountered in several of the earlier activities. In her follow-up move, the teacher makes this connection (attributing it to Bianca) and announces this new topic, writing it on the board to underline its importance, "The Processes of Science." Then, following the lead provided by Bianca's reference to the variability of the heart-beat as a measure, she reminds the children of how they have talked about the need to control the variables in an experiment and, in turn 40, she poses the question: "Why must we control our variables?"

The first answer she receives shows that Tema has at least a partial understanding of what is at issue and so, to signal this, the teacher repeats the key word "accurate" in the follow-up move. However, since this is not a fully adequate answer, she asks a probe question to elicit an alternative within the frame that Tema and she have jointly provided: "if we don't control our variables, x is not accurate." This is obviously a

difficult question for 8-year-olds to answer in that form. However, Bianca finds an alternative, but appropriate, solution by repeating a phrase that has been used on a number of previous occasions: "It's not a fair test" (43).

40 Teacher: OK . why must we control our variables?
41 Tema: Because if we don't, the time won't be accurate and so you won't get the correct timing
42 Teacher: Not so much the time is not accurate, what is not accurate?
43 Bianca: It's not a fair test

THE PRINCIPLE OF "A FAIR TEST"

The problem of how to make sure that their experiments were "fair tests" had been introduced in the very first activity of the unit. Some had chosen to try to construct a salt timer that would measure exactly 30 seconds. Emily, Veronica and Lily had chosen to invent a way of measuring how long it took to empty a bottle of water. In a conference with their teacher when they had gathered their materials, the teacher had presented them with two problems to solve: the first was to invent a method of measuring how long the emptying took, and the second was "to make sure your test is fair." To help them understand what was meant by a fair test, she had discussed a number of possible variables with them:

Teacher: The meaning of "fair test" is if you empty a bottle–say if you fill the bottle half . and Veronica fills her bottle full . would it be a fair test?
Veronica: No
Emily: No . you have to– if I filled my bottle half and to make that a fair test she would fill her bottle half
Teacher: That's right . and what about Lily's bottle?
Emily: She would fill her bottle <u>half</u>
Teacher: <u>half</u>
So all your three bottles must have the same amount of water
Now how do you ensure the same amount of water?
Emily: Well.
Teacher: Do you just estimate?
E and V: No

A few minutes later, after they had considered possible solutions to these problems, the children returned to their corner of the classroom and carried out the first trial, clapping plastic cups together to mark the beat and counting the number of claps that were made before the bottle was completely emptied. In the first trial, Lily's bottle was only half full, so the trial was aborted and they returned to the bucket to fill all their identical FiveAlive bottles "to the brim." Then they took it in turns to empty their bottles, with one child clapping and the third counting the number of claps. Lily, who went first, took four claps. Emily and Veronica each emptied theirs in a count of three. Emily, who has assumed the role of group leader, pauses for a moment's reflection:

Emily: I know, me and Veronica are tied
Do you know why you were slow? (to Lily)

When Lily does not answer, she puts the question again in a different form:

Emily:	What we did– . what we did was we . did a method by timing Now, d'you guys think it was a fair match?
Veronica:	Yeh Emily: Do you? (doubtfully)
Veronica:	Cos we each used the same . <thing>

At this point, Emily goes to fetch their science logs so that they can record their results. But the problem of the discrepant results is obviously still bothering her for, when they have finished writing, she returns to it again.

Emily:	I want to ask you some questions before we do something Why do you think it was a fair match?
Veronica:	Cos the bottles were filled to the exact same amount . because exactly the same *
Emily:	Yeah, like we counted EXACTLY . *
Veronica:	<u>Yeh</u> like I **** –
Emily:	Now . why d'you think . she lost? (referring to Lily) Why?
Veronica:	Cos she was –
Emily:	Probably she poured it- probably she poured it slow
Veronica:	Like she goes like this (demonstrating) and then she –

While Veronica is speaking, the teacher joins the group to find out how they are getting on. Emily and Veronica describe what they have been doing, ending with a summary of their recent conversation. The teacher's follow-up question prompts Emily into a statement that recognizes that, for the test to be fair, the angle of pouring must also be controlled.

| Teacher: | OK, so you– so that is a good observation– you observed . that Lily's count . was more . than both of you . and you figure that it's because of the way she poured it . Now, how can you make sure . that it's a fair test between all three of you? |
| Emily: | Well . a fair test– well I don't really think it's fair now because . it was fair we put it the same size of the cup by the measuring cup, but I don't think it was fair because we poured it– we turned it right over . and Lily just poured it like this, kind of so I don't think it was fair . (T:Uh-huh) I that– I think that's why she um– . was slow |

Writing in her log book later, Emily included the following observation:

Test 1

It wasn't a fair match because Lily tilted her bottle sideways.
Our method was claping.
and for the activity as a whole:

What I learn

I learned that if the bottle has a small mouth the water will come out slower than a wide mouth bottle.

From the episode that we have just summarized, it seems clear that Emily, at least, has developed some understanding of the principle of a fair test and, as leader of the group, she has also drawn the other two girls into using this principle in the consideration of their results. However, it is worth noting that, in her original posing of the question to her friends, she uses the expression "a fair match." In taking over the teacher's concept, it seems, she has assimilated it to her own concept of a competition and, as a result, she has recast the results of their first trial in terms of Lily having "lost."

There are various ways in which this might be viewed: as an indication of a discrepancy between Emily's understanding of the principle and the more conventional interpretation; as evidence of the connections she has made between a new idea and a domain which is both familiar and significant to her; or as a novel application of the principle of a fair test. All of these would, we think, be valid interpretations. But what seems most important to us about this episode is the clear evidence it provides for the way in which the children are actively making sense of what they observed in the trial, using the concept of "a fair test" as a tool to help them do so, and gaining a greater understanding in the process.

In fact, in the next activity, in which the children had experimented to discover which variables affected a pendulum's period of swing, there was further opportunity to appreciate the importance of changing only one variable at a time in order to ensure that the test was fair. It is to a collaborative reconstruction of the different groups' experiences with pendulums that the teacher now turns in the review discussion.

| 44 Teacher: | Remember when you did the pendulum, when one group did the bob . changing the weight of the bob, one group changing the type of bob, one group changing the release height . and all of us did changing the length . that– what– when you want to change the release height what was constant? What was the variable we held constant? |

Emily's group, which on this occasion also included Bianca and Jamilla, had tested the effect of changing the weight of the bob. Over a period of some 30 minutes, they had systematically added one washer at a time to their string pendulum and timed the number of complete swings in 30 seconds. The following extract captures something of the quality of their engagement in the task.

Lily has just added the fourth washer and Emily, who is responsible for timing each trial with the stopwatch, prepares to start.

Emily:	OK, ready?
Bianca:	No .. we've got to measure it to forty-four [B takes the tape-measure and, while V holds the pendulum horizontally, she measures its length]
Veronica:	Forty-four?
Bianca:	Yes
Emily:	On your marks .. get set, go!
ALL:	One, two, three .... (continue counting) [Veronica sways from side to side with the pendulum, making as if to push it on each swing] .. nineteen, twenty, twenty-<u>one</u>
Emily:	<u>Stop!</u>
B and V:	Twenty-one (laughing)
Bianca:	Look, twenty-two, twenty-two, twenty-one, twenty-one (reading the results from the chart on which Jamilla is entering them after each trial)

Emily: Five (instructing them to make the bob up to 5
                washers)

While Lily is adding the next washer, Emily has nothing to do and she idly swings the stopwatch by its carrying strap. As she is watching it swing, she suddenly sees the significance of what she is doing and announces: "I've got a pendulum." Jamilla immediately picks this up and starts to swing the kiss-curl on her forehead, announcing that she too has a pendulum. She is followed by Bianca, who swings her pony-tail as a pendulum, and finally by Veronica who, not to be outdone, shakes her whole head to make her loose hair swing as a pendulum. They all laugh with pleasure at the discovery of this extension of their understanding of what may function as a pendulum.

By now, the extra washer has been added and Emily is keen to proceed. But there is a problem. The knot is not secure.

Veronica: No wait
Lily: Uh-oh . that not way to tie it on
Veronica: I started to hold them and they ***
Bianca: I'm wonderful at tying knots, I love them
            I mean I like tying them

While Bianca is retying the knot, the teacher approaches to check on how they are progressing.

Teacher: What did you get, guys?
Bianca: We got a pattern of twenty-two, twenty-two. twenty-one. twenty-one
Jamilla: two. twenty-one. twenty-one
Bianca: We want to see what it's going to be this time
Emily: I predict the more washers there, the less * swing
Bianca: I think this time maybe we'll get something like nineteen, eighteen or twenty . something like that
Jamilla: Maybe
Bianca: Maybe
Emily: I predict twenty dead . bet you have twenty

As the teacher walks away, they prepare to start the next trial. But first Bianca insists that they must measure the string to make sure that it is still the right length. As she does so, she notices that, with all the tying and untying, the string is fraying.

Bianca: Cos it's actually .. it's actually the string that's breaking . see
Veronica: Yeah, it's the string
Bianca: So what we have to do is– the string's probably getting shorter by the minute
Emily: I don't get it
Bianca: Because it's breaking, you know these things are getting heavy on the string and if they're all unpleating . next thing you know it'll be tearing off

Finally, however, the knot is firmly tied, the length of the pendulum checked, and the trial completed. The result is as before: twenty-one swings. After considerable further discussion, they decide that changing the weight of the bob does not systematically affect the period of swing. This is captured in the following extracts from Emily's journal. The first entry was written before she carried out this activity:

My Observation
I found out that the longer the string is, the less swings.

The shorter the string is, the more swings.
I think I know why! Because if you have a long string you can make it sway more. If you sway it more it will take longer to sway so it will have less swings. But if you have a short string it will go fast because it cannot sway so much. Probably it is also the wight.

This second entry was written when the group had finished the trials involving changing the weight:

My Observation
I learned that adding more washers make no difference.
Not even the count of swings.
I thought it would put more wight on the string so it
will go slower each time. Our score was all 21.

When it is their turn to report, then, there is a wealth of shared experience within the group on which to draw. However, for Veronica, who is chosen to speak for the group, it is still a difficult task to express what she knows in a form that is explicit enough for others to understand. Nevertheless, with prompting questions from the teacher and contributions from other members of the group, a satisfactory account is constructed. Finally, after the last group has reported in similar vein, the teacher invites the whole class to join with her in drawing a conclusion about the principle's more general applicability:

72 Teacher: So that is an example of what we mean by "a fair test"
              . . . it's very important in science
              Those are some of the science processes
              you have to think about . OK?

"What Time is it in Scotland?"

At this point, we want to move on more rapidly to an episode that occurred some 10 minutes later. In the interim, the group had reviewed the designing and making of water timers and rolling ball timers as further instances of the "science processes you have to think about" (72). Then the teacher had reopened the more general discussion of what they had learned about time and, on the basis of Tema's contribution—

91 Tema: I learned that time may not only be in seconds, you may, see it as a minute, a second–and a second is made up of . quite a few fast counts

she had spent a few minutes in checking that the children knew the constituency relations among seconds, minutes, hours, days, weeks, months and years (92–129).

Next followed another opportunity for students to talk about what they had learned (130–159), which the teacher followed with an episode of more direct teaching about the basis for the different units of time in the movement of the earth on its axis, and in its orbit around the sun. This latter topic was also developed dialogically, but interspersed with longer turns by the teacher, in which she accompanied her explanation with demonstration, using two of the balls from the rolling ball timer to represent the earth and the sun.

The episode to be examined next followed directly from the one just described, and was originated by Bianca. In a pause that occurred while two children were going to fetch the globe, she raised her hand to indicate that she had a contribution to make.

204 Teacher: Yes . while . somebody's doing it (= fetching the globe), Bianca you have a question?

205 Bianca: Well, um, you know last night I was going to bed something like quarter to ten– I can't exactly remember but um my sister said that um– I asked her um "guess how lo– guess what time it is in Scotland" (Bianca has recently arrived in Toronto from Scotland) and she goes "I think it's um about ten o'clock" and I go "But it's only ten o'clock here it can't be ten o'clock over there" (T: Mm) . so I counted back five for the time difference and I said "It's actually four thirty um in the afternoon and they're just about to have their cookies"

206 Teacher: Very good . Now Bianca's bringing up another point

Given the point at which she makes this contribution, it is likely that Bianca has already made the connection between the time differences between different countries and the rotation of the earth in relation to the sun. However, because other children may not have followed this implicit connection, the teacher makes it explicit by relating the anecdote to her previous explanation and by once again demonstrating the two movements of the earth, this time using the globe to represent the earth and Angeline, who is sitting at one end of the semicircle of children, to represent the sun. Then, against this general background, she goes on to consider Bianca's example in detail, correcting, in passing, the error that Bianca had made in carrying out the rather difficult operations involved in calculating the time difference between the two countries.

Although the teacher had not embarked on the discussion with a preplanned agenda of her own, the topic of time zones would obviously have been a candidate item for inclusion on such a list. Therefore, when Bianca presents an opportunity to bring it into the discussion, the teacher is pleased to take it up. Once again, what the teacher later described as "a teachable moment," has arisen. This is made particularly clear in her focusing move, "Now, Bianca's bringing up another point" (206), in which she deftly accomplishes two purposes, first, that of authorizing the relevance of Bianca's anecdote and, second, that of signaling that the topic is one of general importance, that merits further discussion.

In fact, this topic is pursued for the remainder of the lesson, as it is one that is of personal significance to many of the children. Drawing on anecdotes similar to Bianca's, contributed by children with relatives in Hong Kong, the Philippines and other countries, the teacher is able to help the children to attach real-life significance to the concept of time zones, and the differences in time between them, which might otherwise have been too abstract for them to grasp. One of these anecdotes, in particular, is worth quoting in full.

The class contains quite a number of Chinese Canadian children, and Emily, whose family comes from Hong Kong, has just been recounting a conversation with her father about the time difference between Hong Kong and Toronto:

258 Emily: …say it was nine o'clock and I asked Dad "What's it like in Hong Kong now?" and he said "It's– it's the same time but it's the morning, nine o'clock in the morning"

As the teacher recaps and makes the connection with Bianca's example, Lily, another Chinese Canadian girl, raises her hand. As the teacher immediately recognizes, this is an important moment. Lily has only been living in Canada for just over a year, and is usually very reticent about speaking in front of the whole class. On this occasion, however, she clearly feels her story is sufficiently important for her to request an opportunity to tell it.

266 Teacher: …that's why your Dad says Hong Kong to here is a twelve hour difference, that's exactly . half way round for time whereas . Scotland to here is five hours difference
Yes, Lily

267 Lily: When I was in China . my Mum always called me at the night and er– and I– I don't like– I don't er I don't want to wake up and my– my Grandmother say You have to wake up, your mother on– in the phone."
So I have to listen to him

268 Teacher: That's right . she says– Lily says that when she was in China . where's China? you show me (to Lily) [Lily points to the position of China on the globe]

269 Auritro: Er you just –

270 Teacher: There, China's over here . (pointing) and her Mum was in .
Canada

271 Lily: Canada

272 Teacher: –her Mum called at say two o'clock in the afternoon, say now, cos the sun is there two o'clock I would say it's roughly here . is she still asleep?

273 Children: Yeh

274 Bianca: Two in the morning, **

275 Teacher: Now, it's really not as much as Hong Kong, * slightly less, but she's still asleep . so that's why she was telling us her grandmother said "Your mum is on the phone, get up! Your Mum is calling you"– which means phoning for you– and she says "Why does she phone me at night?" But is it night for your Mum?

276 Lily: No

277 Children: No

278 Teacher: No, it's daytime . and say if Lily comes over– the earth moves here and it's daytime (i.e. in China) and Lily calls her Mum . Lily phones her Mum, would her Mum be awake or asleep?

279 Children: (laugh) Asleep

280 Teacher: See now why? do you see it now with the globe and the sun

281 Children: Yes

As in learning their first language, what prompts children to take risks in using the linguistic resources they are learning in a second language is so often the combination of having something they feel it is important to say and an audience who will be interested to hear it. This is what happens here. As with other children's contributions, the teacher picks up Lily's anecdote and retells it to give it added effect, using it at the same time as a particular case of the more general principle that is under discussion. Whilst illustrating the rich resource for developing understanding that is to be found in multicultural classrooms such as this, this episode also exemplifies very clearly just what is meant by the co-construction of meaning.

LEARNING FROM THE PAST: LEARNING FOR THE FUTURE

In the introductory section of this chapter, we outlined a way of thinking about education in which teaching was characterized as the provision of opportunities for learners to appropriate the achievements of past generations—as these are embodied in cultural tools and their associated practices—and to transform them into a personal resource for individual thinking and problem solving now and in the future. This discussion, we want to suggest, is an excellent exemplification of this process in action. In order to justify this claim, we should like to revisit the section of the discussion concerned with "the processes of science," in order to consider it from this point of view.

The principle of "a fair test" is just such an intellectual artifact—or tool—and one which is of central importance for the way in which scientific understanding is advanced in our culture. Indeed, it is so central that it is easy to ignore its artifactual nature. Yet this principle, which is taken for granted as necessary in any experimental attempt to understand relationships of cause and effect in the material world, was developed in the course of practical activity by our forebears over many generations in the past. That it is a tool that has to be learned in action was made very clear in the course of the activities in which the children engaged and in the accompanying discourse.

We have already seen how Emily and her friends grappled with the problem, as they reflected on the probable reason for Lily "losing the match." Now we want to consider the experience of Auritro and his group as they tested the effect of changing the type of bob on their pendulum and in the subsequent discussions.

In the class discussion which was held at the end of the experimental work on pendulums, it was finally agreed that it was only changing the length of the pendulum that changed its rate of swing, and a rhyming slogan was coined to make this finding memorable: "The longer the string, the slower the swing." However, earlier in this session, when the groups described what they had done and reported their results, Auritro's group had reported results that were anything but conclusive. The problem, it transpired, was that, in changing the type of bob, they had been unsuccessful in keeping the length of the string constant. Now, compared with the results obtained by the other groups, who had been more successful in changing only one variable, theirs were impossible to interpret. Asked to comment on them, he described them as "pretty wacky," and when they were displayed using another artifact—that of graphing—it was clear that, as he put it, they

were "all over the board." This evaluation is confirmed by the entry he had already written in his log:

Topic: Swing time
Question: Will the type of bob change the swings?
> Well it was confewsing for us wich is Me, Kelvin, Benjamin and Tsz-yeung. We made another pendeleum and testing lots of things. First we checked the lengths. The first and second time the lengths where different. The last time it was same but counts were different. Heres the chart:
> We used Nails, washers, screws and a cup

Nail	=	24 going back and fourth
Washer	=	23 "
Screw	=	21 "
Cup	=	23 "

> going back and fourth counts as one swing.

> I think what we had observed was right but was wrong. We had done something wrong with Nail and screw. I dont how that happend but it did. I think our counting was wrong.

However, in the second section of the present review discussion, in which the experiment with pendulums was reviewed from the perspective of "the processes of science," these difficulties were no longer alluded to. Instead, it was the principle of a fair test that was emphasized, with its operationalization in the controlling of variables. Through the successive sequences of discourse, the experiences of the separate groups were jointly reconstructed as instances of carrying out a fair test. As the teacher explained afterwards, since the children now knew that only length affected the rate, what in her view was important to emphasize in the discussion was not whether they had succeeded in holding all but the experimental variable constant, but the fact *that* they had attempted to do so and understood why this was important.

Another way of looking at this episode is as a particularly clear example of the general principle of cultural learning, discussed earlier, in which the learner is enabled to take over the culturally accepted practice by being taught to use an artifact or tool in which the outcome of past achievement is encoded. Here it is the meaning of a fair test that the teacher wishes the students to take from their practical work and the accompanying discussions. Therefore, by appropriating what actually happened in Auritro's group and reinterpreting it in terms of what would have happened if they had followed the cultural practice associated with the use of this principle, the teacher is helping the children to take over the practice, together with the understanding that it embodies, as a tool that they can use in all future scientific experiments.

Overall, then, one of the teacher's intentions for this discussion is that the children should draw on their various group experiences of practical work and on other relevant information to construct a *shared* understanding, but one that is also informed by the publicly accepted account of the phenomena that they have been investigating. The children are certainly willing and able to play their part: following the initial "macro" question asking what they had learned, they eagerly offer a wide range of important topics for discussion (cf. Table 43–1). However, as might be expected of children of this age, these are largely in the form of observations and anecdotes drawn from personal experience; therefore, in order to create what Edwards and Mercer (1987) refer to as culturally appropriate "common knowledge," a considerable amount of "follow-up" work is required on the part of the teacher. On each topic, this is achieved, first, by eliciting similar observations and recollections from other members of the group so that, together, their contributions are built into a shared account, and then by extending and reinterpreting their contributions, drawing on the linguistic register that is more generally used to talk about the related activity in the culture. In this way, while encouraging and valuing the ideas and experiences that the children are keen to contribute, the teacher, as "an authoritative representative of the educated culture" (Edwards & Mercer, 1989, p. 97), provides an opportunity for the children to take over and internalize her organizing cognitive structures and associated language so that, in the future, they will be able to deploy these resources when engaging in further activities for which they are relevant.

Learning About Time: Through the Children's Eyes

The emphasis in the chapter so far has been on an exploration of what the children had learned from their study of time, as seen through the lens of the collaborative meaning making that occurred in the final discussion. However, as will be clear by now, this discussion was itself an occasion of learning, as important as any of the activities that were reviewed during its course. For, as well as clarifying and extending the science concepts associated with those activities, the discourse that the teacher and children co-constructed itself provided a model, on the intermental plane of public discourse, for the intramental dialogue of inner speech in which individual thinking and problem solving is conducted.

In *Thinking and Speech*, Vygotsky (1987) hypothesized a developmental progression in the learning of any aspect of cultural knowledge, from adult-assisted interpersonal interaction, through interaction with peers, to a stage when the individual is able to function autonomously under the control of the discourse structures internalized from social interaction. In this section, we shall look again at what the children were learning, focusing here on how they were appropriating the concepts and processes of science as evidenced in their talk and writing.

One very clear example of this developmental process in action was seen in the episode quoted earlier, in which Emily initiated a review of the results of the bottle-emptying task. Attempting to explain to herself and her friends why Lily had taken longer than Veronica and herself to empty her bottle, she drew upon her interpretation of the language that she had just recently encountered in the conference with the teacher and couched her questions in terms of "a fair match," in which Lily "lost." Interestingly, Emily's conflation of "a fair test" with a fairly conducted competition came into play again in the final practical activity, when she and her group designed and made their own water clock. However, they were not content to make just one; at Emily's suggestion, they decided to make two identical water clocks so that, in addition to making sure that their experiment constituted "a fair test," they could also have races between them.

Two years later, however, her understanding had changed. In an interview at the end of her grade five year, she was asked about things she had learned it was important to do when "doing science." Without hesitation she replied:

> I think you have to be . um . consistent and do fair tests for everything.

And when asked what she understood by "a fair test," she replied:

> You have to keep everything the same and if you
> change a thing you have to change it all

In the intervening years, Emily had continued in the same class with the same teacher and many of the same children. During that time many other science topics had been investigated, always with opportunity for practical work and often involving experiments. Certainly the issue of fair tests had been discussed on more than one occasion and, from taking part in these activities and discussions, Emily's understanding had gradually been transformed until it approximated more closely the conventional version.

Here, the value of collecting longitudinal data is particularly clear, for it allows us to see that, as Vygotsky (1987) pointed out, concepts are not learned instantaneously in their mature form, but are appropriated and modified over numerous occasions of use in settings in which they are relevant to the task in hand.

A second feature of Emily's discussion with her peers that is worth commenting on is its reflective nature. This stance was almost certainly taken over from the review discussions with which the teacher ended most activities, and from her repeated injunctions to the children to use the writing of entries in their science logs to reflect on what they had learned.

We have already quoted Auritro's log entry, in which he tried to explain to himself why his group's testing of different types of bob had been unsuccessful. Here is another reflective entry that attempts to draw conclusions from a series of experiments involving pendulums. It was written by Jamilla, who had been the record keeper for the group that tested changing the weight of the bob. After each child had made a pendulum with a washer and a randomly cut length of string and counted the number of swings it completed in 30 seconds, the pendulums were arranged on a chart in the order of the number of swings completed. From the resulting display, it was clearly apparent that "the longer the string, the slower the swing."

> I noticed that when we made a chart, the person who had
> the longest string had the smallest amount of counts.
> Why? I think it was the length of which the string was.
> Why? The release height does not matter, and the
> weight of the bob does not matter.
> Why? Bianca, Veronica, Emily, and I did a test on
> weight of the bob. Other groups did tests and it did not matter.
> Only the length matters because it takes a longer or shorter
> time.

In all these entries, it is a personal observation or discovery that provides the point of departure and the writing serves not only to communicate that information but also acts as a "tool" with which to make sense of its significance.

Not all the children were able to make such sophisticated use of their writing, of course, and some relied more on pictures and diagrams than on written text. The teacher deliberately encouraged such "picture writing" by those children for whom the writing of text was a painful struggle. She was more concerned that every child should experience the value of recording and reflecting than that they should produce conventional text. For example, Lily, the newly-arrived Chinese girl, put considerable effort into drawing and labeling the materials that her group had used in constructing a timer that would measure 30 seconds, based on the design of an hour-glass, but using salt instead of sand. Nevertheless, despite her limited command of English, she also wrote the following account of what, for her, was either the most memorable aspect of the experiment or the aspect that she felt most able to write about. In any event, she succeeds in giving a graphic account of how the teacher helped them to solve the "parbom" (problem) they encountered in trying to make the right-sized aperture in the paper diaphragm between the two pop bottles that, taped together, formed the two parts of the "hour-glass."

> Emily Veronica and I try to maked good but every time we do tat we has a little parbom, first time the hole is very bag only 7 secon and tn we try to do it slowly so Emily pat in sum salt and this time we taked 25 sicon and the last time we do that Emily pat in sum salt and only 27 and Mrs X. was come in and she tell us how to do it she take a bag funnel a madm funnel and a little funnel and she sad the bag one is father the madm one is mom and the little one is baby. So Mrs X take the baby and count to 30 and she take the mom the mom is 20 agn Mrs X take the father the father is 14 now Mrs X and us know the baby is the roret (correct) one so we copy the hole forkm baby funnel wnet we finisht we trn (try) this time we got 30.

Even at the age of eight or nine, then, many of the children in this class were capable of reflecting, in speech and writing, on what they were doing, and were able to understand the relationship between the "hands-on" practical work, which they enjoyed so much, and the "minds-on" spoken and written discourse in which they planned and reflected on what they were doing and learning. Through these interrelated activities, carried out jointly with their peers and with their teacher, they were taking over the knowledge and artifacts of previous generations and using them to make and communicate their own sense of the puzzles and problems they encountered in the present.

At the end of the year—some months after the end of the unit on time—we interviewed two groups, one of boys and the other of girls, to ask, once more, "what have you learned?" The answers they gave confirmed our expectations. Although none of those interviewed recalled the episode with the malfunctioning water clock, with which we introduced this chapter, they did remember many of the activities they had carried out, and they referred to their logbooks to make sure they got the details right.

Asked which they considered most important—practical activities, reading, writing or talking—the girls responded as follows:

Veronica:	I think the writing–
Bianca:	All of them
Emily:	Yeh all of them, but I think one thing um very important is that we all discussed about it, like talked
Veronica:	What I think is because um you need to write for er– and you need to read to get the idea and then you need to talk to get the– er talk to the other person to get the idea of what you're going to do and who's going to do what so that you don't get into a big fight when you're doing it
Bianca:	Yeh and I think the fun activities are important cos you can also have some fun doing your science and the writing's good because it builds up your * and your language your brain and also discussing about it it builds up your confidence to talk about things and also your– er your language skills and things like that and I also think the reading's very good because in most jobs you do have to know how to read and to write
Jamilla:	You also learn about math sort of because you're doing um– . science is a lot of patterns and things like that and math is also patterns and things like that so you get a lot of everything just by doing science
Emily:	And you learn a LOT

Asked the same questions, the boys gave very similar answers. They, too, had enjoyed the practical activities and could recall many of them in considerable detail. Auritro and Benjamin, for example, explained very clearly why their salt timer had taken longer to run through in one direction than in the other. The problem, they were convinced, was that, in piercing the hole in the paper diaphragm, they had created the equivalent of a valve: the pierced paper opened up to let the salt pass through easily in one direction but, when the timer was inverted, the weight of the salt tended to push the paper back into its original, unpierced position, thereby slowing down the rate at which the salt passed through. However, because this reasoning took place only after the pop bottles had been securely taped together, they had not had the opportunity to empirically verify their hypothesized explanation.

The boys also recognized the value of the reading and writing. In fact, they tended to place more emphasis on reading than the girls had done. But reading, writing, and talking were all seen as complementary activities which, when carried out in a collaborative group, enabled real progress to be made in the construction of group and individual knowledge. This is how Auritro put it:

> If you know something that– you know something that somebody else doesn't know, somebody else knows something that you don't know, then you can add those ideas together

And, on the role of reading and writing, the group had this to say:

Auritro:	You read the– once you do the science experiment, you experiment about it, then if there's a book about that animal– that creature, you could read about it and then you could write about it and you could make a whole new thing of it .

Benjamin: And you can er- like if there is a book on flower– on a flower–certain kind of flower and you're um you're experimenting with it you can mix the breeds and then like and then write er write down what you've experimented with .

Steven: After you've finished an experiment you should always write it up in the science log. Because if you want to do that experiment again you might forget how to do it

Teacher: So that's one good reason for writing, so that you have a record of what you've done. Are there any other reasons you can think of for writing?

Steven: Writing books to help others to understand

Auritro: Yeh, understand the **

Teacher: You mean you write to help other people understand or you write to help yourself understand?

A and S: Both

Auritro: You help yourself by reading and then you write it down so other people can understand

Steven: Well wouldn't that be copying the book?

Auritro: No .. you have to read from a book because once . you read the book and you know– and you know a little bit and you read the book and you get a little bit more. You can write your own book, some more, and then you could like publish it and then give it to a science fair and then people could read it. If you know something little, and that book doesn't have it in there, you could add it up together and then you get another book.

Auritro, it appears, already has a well-developed, if intuitive, understanding of the intertextual nature of reading and writing and of the way in which knowledge is collaboratively and progressively constructed through reading, writing, and talking.

CONCLUSION

In presenting an analysis of the review discussion with which the unit culminated and of some of the activities on which it was based, we have tried to show how learning in science—or in any other curricular area—can be seen as part of a continuing cultural process of appropriating the achievements of the past and transforming them into a resource for creative and innovative problem solving in the present and future. In the episodes selected from the discussion, we have seen how the experiences of the immediately preceding few weeks were collaboratively reviewed and their meaning reinterpreted in terms of principles and practices that previous generations had invented to make sense of the phenomena in question. Similar discussions had also occurred in relation to the various activities in which the children had engaged throughout the unit; however, this one had particular importance in that it was used as an occasion for making connections among these individual topics in order to achieve a more integrated understanding of the theme of time.

Such opportunities to synthesize and reflect on what has been learned occur all too rarely under the pressure that many teachers feel to hurry on in order to cover the recommended curriculum. Yet they constitute an essential element of any curricular unit, if school learning is to be more than the accumulation and memorization of isolated bits of information (Wells, 1995).

But it has also been one of our aims to show how, in appropriating the knowledge and artifacts from the past, children use them for their own purposes and put their own stamp upon them. The episode in the review discussion in which the basis for the different time zones is explored provides a clear example of the former. For Lily, who has rarely spoken in the whole class group, the new understanding she has achieved of the personal experience of being phoned by her mother in the middle of the night is significant enough for her to break her silence with a brief story that enables her to become a fully participating member of the classroom community. In a different vein, Emily's personal interpretation of a fair test as involving competition ("a fair match") is an example of the latter. But perhaps more significant than either of these rather specific examples is the tenor of the discussion as a whole, with its numerous examples of the children's ability to infuse general concepts with their own personal and particular meanings and at the same time to reframe those personal meanings in more public terms that make them relevant and, therefore, worthy of sharing.

A second theme of the chapter has been the dual role of discourse in the learning and teaching of science. On the one hand, "doing science" is to a considerable degree a matter of participating in the various discourses by means of which the scientific community addresses the problems of current concern and creates and debates novel solutions that have the possibility of transforming and extending previous knowledge; therefore, one of the major goals of the science curriculum must be to enable students to gain sufficient control of these specialist discourses to be able to use them in constructing their own knowledge. On the other hand, as we have seen, it is also in the ongoing discourse of the classroom that the teacher and students create the forum for co-constructing the meanings in terms of which they make their own sense of these specialist discourses and of the situations to which they apply.

The same arguments could be made for the other subjects in the school curriculum. In all areas, one of the major goals of education is for students to appropriate the modes of discourse that are specific to the different discipline-based ways of doing and knowing so that they are able to take part in those practices and, in so doing, to make them part of their own resources which they can use for their own purposes. At the same time, it is in the more familiar patterns of classroom discourse with their peers and teachers that students are enabled to build bridges between these specialist discourses and those with which they are familiar from their experiences at home and in the larger community. It is, therefore, in providing them with opportunities for apprenticeship into the discourses of the disciplines, we believe, that teachers will most fully achieve the aims that are captured in the phrase "language across the curriculum" (Wells, 1994).

Despite the theme of the volume in which this chapter occurs, as may have been noticed, we have not singled out literacy for special attention. This is because, like the children, we see it as an integral component of any unit of study. To do science—or history, or mathematics—is necessarily to engage in reading and writing, along with doing and talking—in order to formulate and address the problems and issues that seem worthy of sustained attention with respect to the topic under investigation. As we argued earlier, language and literacy are cultural tools for thinking, feeling, and communicating with. Like other tools, they are best mastered, not through decontextualized exercises, but through appropriate use in situations of significance to the user.

This chapter started with an account of just such a situation, in which the real problem posed by the malfunctioning water clock led to a creative solution which required the integration and application of a variety of cultural tools, including logical reasoning, reading of the junior science guide, and talk for coordinating joint activity. In this situation, perhaps more than in any other we have described, the children really showed what they had learned.

We should, therefore, like to end this chapter by quoting Emily's insightful conclusions about the year's work. In the end-of-year discussion referred to above, the children were asked how they, if they were responsible, would plan the work for the next year's students. This is Emily's reply:

> We should give the children—the grade threes that came—to go through the "Innovations" [the resource book they had used][4] and then I would ask them questions, like what we did or what we remember, like "What is science?" "What did I think of it?" and I would– I think I would start them by um– giving-start with projects– not projects but making things, and then I think I would um– few days later I would gather them on the carpet and they all share what they observed and then see they'll become like us, just writing them in our books...

—Innovations in Science. (1991). Toronto, Ont: Holt, Rinehart & Winston.

References

Amano, K. (1991, January 2). E-mail communication, XLCHC.

Bereiter, C., & Scardamalia, M. (1985). Children's difficulties in learning to compose. In G. Wells & J. Nicholls (Eds.), *Language and learning: An interactional perspective* (pp. 95–105). London: Falmer Press.

Bruner, J. S. (1983). *Child's talk: Learning to use language.* New York: W. W. Norton.

Cole, M. (1991). *Remembering the future.* University of California, San Diego, CA: Laboratory of Comparative Human Cognition.

Cross, T. (1977). Mothers' speech adjustments: The contribution of selected child listener variables. In C. E. Snow & C. Ferguson (Eds.), *Talking to children: Language input and acquisition* (pp. 151–188). Cambridge: Cambridge University Press.

Driver, R. (1983). *The pupil as scientist?* Milton Keynes, UK: Open University Press.

Edwards, D., & Mercer, N. (1987). *Common knowledge: The development of understanding in the classroom.* London: Routledge.

Edwards, D., & Mercer, N. (1989). Reconstructing context: The conventionalization of classroom knowledge. *Discourse Processes, 12,* 91–104.

Lemke, J. L. (1990). *Talking science: Language, learning and values.* Norwood, NJ: Ablex.

Newman, D., Griffin, P., & Cole, M. (1989). *The construction zone: Working for cognitive change in school.* Cambridge: Cambridge University Press.

Nicolopoulou, A. (1991, January 1). E-mail communication, XLCHC.

Rogoff, B. (1990). *Apprenticeship in thinking.* New York: Oxford University Press.

Rogoff, B. (1992, September) *Observing sociocultural activity on three planes: Participatory appropriation, guided participation, apprenticeship.* Paper presented at the First Conference on Sociocultural Research, Madrid.

Vygotsky, L. S. (1978). *Mind in society.* Cambridge, MA: Harvard University Press.

Vygotsky, L. S. (1981). The genesis of higher mental functions. In J. V. Wertsch (Ed.), *The concept of activity in Soviet psychology* (pp. 144–188). Armonk, NY: Sharpe.

Vygotsky, L. S. (1987). *Thinking and speech.* (N. Minick, Trans.) In R. W. Rieber & A. S. Carlton (Eds.), *The collected works of L. S. Vygotsky. Vol. 1,* (39–285). New York: Plenum Press.

Wells, G. (1986) *The meaning makers: Children learning language and using language to learn.* Portsmouth, NH: Heinemann.

Wells, G. (1994). Text, talk and inquiry: Schooling as semiotic apprenticeship. In N. Bird et al. (Eds.), *Language and learning* (pp. 18–51). Hong Kong: Department of Language in Education and the University of Hong Kong.

Wells, G. (1995). Language and the inquiry-oriented curriculum. *Curriculum Inquiry, 25,* 233–269.

Wells, G. (1996). Using the tool-kit of discourse in the activity of learning and teaching. *Mind, Culture and Activity, 3,* 74–101.

Wells, G., & Chang-Wells, G. L. (1992). *Constructing knowledge together: Classrooms as centers of inquiry and literacy.* Portsmouth, NH: Heinemann.

Wertsch, J. V., & Stone, A. (1985). The concept of internalization in Vygotsky's account of the genesis of higher mental functions. In J. V. Wertsch (Ed.), *Culture, communication and cognition: Vygotskian perspectives* (pp. 162–179). Cambridge: Cambridge University Press.

Wertsch, J. W., Minick, N., & Arns, F. J. (1984). The creation of context in joint problem-solving. In B. Rogoff & J. Lave (Eds.), *Everyday cognition: Its development in social context* (pp. 151–171). Cambridge, MA: Harvard University Press.

Wood, D., Bruner, J. S., & Ross, G. (1976). The role of tutoring in problem-solving. *Journal of Child Psychology and Psychiatry, 17,* 89–100.

44

THE LITERARY TEXT: ITS FUTURE

IN THE CLASSROOM

Richard L. Venezky

UNIVERSITY OF DELAWARE

The literary text is under siege on several fronts. First, as a subclassification of *books* it is viewed by some as a dying remnant of the age of paper, a time period that, like the stone age and the bronze age, will be viewed primarily as a transition to a higher and more satisfying form of life. Enthusiasts of the electronic age have forecast the doom of books (and other forms of print) since at least the late 1970s (e.g., Lancaster, 1978). One member of the publishing trade predicted about 10 years ago that the how-to-book would be the first printed genre to reach extinction, driven "the way of the buffalo" by the videodisk (Goodrum & Dalrymple, 1987, p. 160). That both buffalo and how-to-books are plentiful today is a testament to more than the difficulties of prediction.

Just 9 years ago, in a paper entitled "The paperless society revisited," F.W. Lancaster found the decline of paper accelerating. Of books in particular, he claimed, "...the printed book will be replaced by something quite different from anything we have yet seen, and this will occur because the medium replacing it will be widely perceived to be better" (Lancaster, 1987, p. 217). At the same time, various gatherings of scholars, educators, librarians, computer scientists, lexicographers, and the like have pondered the future of the book, generally finding cause for concern over the future of printed materials. The U.S. Congress in 1983, concerned over the impact of new technologies on books, authorized the Library of Congress to do a study of the "changing role of the book in the future" (Senate Concurrent Resolution 59, approved November 18, 1983). Although the publications that resulted from this study (The Book in the Future Project) revealed no consensus on the impact of technology on book production, a sense of inevitable change permeated the various contributions (Cole, 1987; Joint Committee on the Library, 1984). More recently, the 10th Annual Conference of the University of Waterloo Centre for the New Oxford English Dictionary and Text Research selected as its title "Reflections on the Future of Text,"

with papers scheduled on a variety of topics, including speculations on the nature of the electronic text.

Ironically, the electronic publishing explosion, with a laser printer and a page composition program on every desk, has led not to a decline in the sale of paper but to a noticeable increase. According to the latest edition of the *Statistical Abstract of the United States,* the total quantity of books sold in the United States has continued to increase roughly at the same rate as the population has increased. Elementary, high school, and college textbook sales did decline slightly from 1990 to 1991, but trade books (both juvenile and adult) made larger gains. Thus, while more and more material is being issued on CD-ROM and more and more archives are popping up on the Internet and the World Wide Web, total book production continues at a steady pace.

The potential replacement of the paper-based literary text by glowing images on a screen does not within itself alter the text itself. *The Name of the Rose* is *The Name of the Rose,* appearing as Mr. Ecco planned and published it, whether on paper, CD-ROM, diskette, or any other delivery medium. However, an even larger threat to the survival of printed fiction is envisioned through the deployment of hypertext. Robert Coover, who directs the Brown University Hypertext Fiction Workshop, calls hypertext fiction "a potentially revolutionary space, capable, exactly as advertised, of transforming the very art of fiction" (Coover, 1992, p. 24). George Landow, author and editor of a number of (printed) texts on hypermedia, hypertext, and literary studies, posits (with no apologies to Vico) three ages in the history of literacy, corresponding to (1) the invention of writing, (2) the invention of movable type printing, and (3) the invention of hypertext (Landow, 1992).

Hypertext derives from ideas first advanced in the 1940s but not developed until the 1960s (Conklin, 1987). In its most general form, hypertext is a scheme for creating a web or net composed of nodes and links between nodes. The nodes might be patches of text, as in a novel, or discrete facts, pictures, charts, or any other two-dimensional form. Links can be given any labels desired: definition, pronunciation, comment, history, biography, and so forth. They function to connect one node to another so that the label given signals to the reader / navigator what might be expected if a particular link is followed. Hypermedia extends hypertext to another dimension, allowing video, sound, and potentially any other media to occur at the nodes. Otherwise, however, the basic plan of nodes and links is the same as for hypertext.

Hypertext could be used to supplement a text through the addition of links from words, sentences, sections, and so forth to explanations, definitions, alternate wordings, and other supporting comments, or to alter the linear transversal of the text through links that allow alternate paths for the reader. For example, the lines for a character in a play might be linked so that the reader could progress through a single role without encountering scenes in which the character was absent.

Confronted with these two challenges—a movement toward electronic delivery of texts and the potential of hypertext and hypermedia, what future does the literary text have in the classroom? What follows is one view of this future, derived from working in both the literary and the technological sides of the house.

THE EVOLUTION OF TEXTBOOKS

Modern American textbooks are a creation of the second half of the 19th century when the common school movement created a large market for textbooks, and new canals and roads allowed national distribution of materials at low costs. Large speciality printing houses like Truman & Smith in Cincinnati, Ohio could do a multimillion dollar business in textbooks by marketing across the entire country. Ray's *Practical Arithmetic* and the *McGuffey Readers* were successful not just because of their intrinsic merits as pedagogical materials but also because of the distribution and marketing skills of their publishers (Sutton, 1961). The evolution of the textbook, however, has extended over several thousand years.

Within Western education, most historians trace textbook usage to the Greek schools prior to the Golden Age of Greece. "Homer was the first and the great reading book of the Greeks... Then followed Hesiod, Theognis, the Greek poets, and the fables of Aesop" (Cubberley, 1920). In the Golden Age, which followed the defeat of the Persian army at Plataea in 479 B.C.E., the arts curriculum first emerged, combining the contrasting views of Plato and the orator Isocrates. For Plato, subjects such as grammar, arithmetic, geometry, and music were preparatory for philosophy. For Isocrates, rhetoric not philosophy was the peak of intellectual and moral development. The resulting curriculum (*enkyklios paideia*), which the Romans eventually inherited, consisted of seven "liberal arts": grammar, rhetoric, dialectic, arithmetic, geometry, astronomy, and music. The texts that supported this curriculum were the original works in these areas by Plato, Aristotle, Isocrates, Ptolemy and others.

By the end of the Roman Empire, various writers, including Capella, Cassiodorus, Isidore of Seville, Augustine, and Boethius had synthesized and summarized the knowledge of the ancient world, usually in a single text. The seven liberal arts, as presented in these works, constituted the standard curriculum, and therefore the required preparation for theology until the 13th century (Chall & Mirsky, 1978). The three verbal arts (grammar, dialectic, rhetoric) were the introductory curriculum, known as the *trivium,* while the four mathematical arts (arithmetic, geometry, astronomy, music) defined the advanced curriculum and were collectively known as the *quadrivium.*

After Rome was sacked in 410 C.E., European learning continued in the monasteries, which also took on the work of preserving and copying manuscripts. Many secular writers like Caesar, Cicero, and Virgil were retained originally as models for Latin prose, but by the later Middle Ages were read for their own content. The authors of the church and ancient classics (*auctores*) were treated in the classrooms as authorities and were revered by students. "Students read *auctores* under a master who dictated explanatory notes of his own, themselves usually derived from earlier authorities" (Thomson & Perraud, 1990).

Textbooks were circulated as manuscripts, generally equivalent in to a modern text of 70–137 pages, and were sometimes in catechetical (question–answer) form (Cubberley, 1920). The catechism, whether for religious or secular subjects, was the primary instructional device evidenced in early textbooks. Through the Dark Ages, instruction was based mostly upon religious texts, including the Bible and the writings of the church fathers, but with the awakening of intellectual life in Europe in the 13th century, classical works were rediscovered, primarily through contact with Moslem learning in Spain. Within a century Aristotle, Euclid, Ptolemy, Cicero, Galen, Hippocrates, and other classical writers were standard fare in the European universities, where they remained until the mid-18th century. Although most textbooks up to the 16th century were written in Latin, the Protestant Reformation initiated a flood of vernacular materials. By 1529 Martin Luther published in German his translation of the New Testament, the *Greater* and *Smaller Catechisms,* and his own version of a primer. By the end of the 16th century, primers in vernacular languages contained the alphabet, syllable tables, and even occasional secular material, all oriented toward teaching children to read and to know the primary church rituals (Davies, 1974) .

Although the primer began as a religious text, it evolved over several hundred years into a secular introduction to reading. It was for most of this time, however, a dour repository of the prayers and other basic church materials that children were expected to know by rote. The first illustrated schoolbook was Comenius's *Orbis Pictus,* issued in 1654. This became the model for primers like the *New England Primer,* and eventually the ABC books and secular primers. However, well into the 18th century in England, schooling for young children was based upon the primary religious texts. John Locke, born in 1632, described his first school books as "The Horn Book, Primer, Psalter, Testament, and Bible" (cited in Cubberley, 1920, p. 439).

The colonial settlers in North America brought with them English textbooks and continued to import textbooks from England until well into the 19th century. But textbooks were also published in the Colonies, beginning with the first press established in Cambridge, Massachusetts in the mid-17th century. Primers and ABC books were among the staples of the Colonial and early National Period press. Textbooks were also among the first books to receive copyright protection in the United States when the first copyright law was adopted in 1790. John Barry's *Philadelphia Spelling Book,* Jedidiah Morse's *American Geography,* and Samuel Freeman's *Columbian Primer* were among the first materials to be protected. For several centuries elementary textbooks were undifferentiated by age or grade level and gave little, if any, pedagogical advice to the teacher. Complex prose and an adult vocabulary were common until the 1820s and 1830s when the ideas of Rosseau and Pestalozzi began to influence American educational thought and practice.

Textbook Sales

With the common school movement came a rapid expansion in school attendance, encouraged by tax supported schools and compulsory attendance laws. In parallel with this enrollment increase came an equally rapid increase in textbook publication. The total value of book production in the United States increased through the second quarter of the 19th century at nearly twice the rate of increase in the total U.S. population, growing from $2.5 million in 1820 to $5.5 million in 1840 and $12.5 million in 1850, with textbook sales accounting for almost a third of these totals (Trübner, 1859). School materials were purchased not only by parents and individual schools but more and more by school districts. With the introduction of age-graded schools, textbooks for the elementary grades began to be issued in graded series, with a separate book designated for each grade level. Earlier graded series had been published, particularly for reading, but the widespread development of graded series for reading and mathematics did not occur until the second quarter of the 19th century (Venezky, 1990).

Elementary and secondary textbook sales in the United States totaled $1.974 billion in 1991, up just slightly over sales in 1990 (U.S. Bureau of the Census, 1993). However, increases over the past decade in total dollar volume have been created by price increases and not by expanded sales. From 1982 until 1991, textbook expenditures increased by 85% while the quantity of books sold declined by 11.6%.

Authorship

Sullivan (1927, p. 9) noted that "When people could not read, who wrote the ballads of a nation may have been more important than who made the laws. After literacy and schools became general, the authorship of school text-books became important." Authorship of elementary textbooks has shifted since the 17th century from the single writer who truly wrote and edited the work to committees of authors, selected as much for their name, gender, or race appeal as for their abilities to write instructional materials. Modern elementary textbooks are most often not written by the people listed as authors, but by writing houses that specialize in the development of textbook series, or by in-house editors / writers.

Textbooks today, however, are assembled more than they are written, leading to what Jacques Barzun described as the impersonal voice. "The truth drones on with the muffled sound of one who is indeed speaking from a well" (Barzun, 1945). With some texts, especially those created through the electronic contributions of large numbers of people, the notion of authorship may not apply. The National Library of Medicine, for example, has created a hepatitis data base through consensus of experts. Perhaps we have finally arrived at virtual authorship.

THE LITERARY TEXT

The modern literary text used in the classroom generally takes one of three forms: either a published work of fiction as presented by the author, or a published work accompanied by a critical apparatus or pedagogical notes, or an anthology with pedagogical accompaniments. Although anthologies and excerpted works have been declared "ineffable trash" by at least one college president, they remain popular in both elementary and secondary classrooms, mainly because of their instructional value. A typical high school anthology presents a wide range of literary genres—short stories, poems, speeches, biographies, essays, plays, and so forth, usually organized around major themes; for example, the American dream, transitions, the individual. Also included are pedagogical materials: explanations of metaphors, historical references, discussion questions, vocabulary notes, and so on. Elementary readers are reduced versions of the high school texts, generally with tighter lesson plans and more student activities.

As more and more school districts move away from basal reading series, teachers will more and more be required to create their own anthologies and to develop or borrow the instructional materials to accompany the readings they select. But no matter where the lessons originate, they will no doubt continue to be composed of both literary works and instructional aids. That is, the content of the literary text in the elementary and secondary classroom is not a function of the medium through which the text is realized, but the developmental levels of the students, the goals of literature instruction, the context of classroom instruction, and the interests and abilities of teachers. Limitations of cost and of bulk force the setting of priorities in what to include in an anthology or in the number of paperback novels to buy for a class, but these do not shape the balance of different contents so much as limit the total quantity of material made available for instruction.

FORMS OF TEXT DELIVERY

Strengthening of Printed Texts

Given the nature of the literary text, how might it change as a result of electronic technologies? First, it is worthwhile to consider technological advancements that would further entrench printed works. Although most speculation about the future of the book is done within the context of electronic delivery of text, two sets of advancements have begun to alter the cost and convenience of book production. One set has simplified the printing process by allowing printing directly from computer files without the need for film negatives and metal plates (Anonymous, 1994). Besides reducing the complexity of the printing process, this technique enables printing on demand, thus reducing the publisher's need to carry costly inventories of books, and increasing the ability to issue revised editions at a low cost.

A second set of advancements, consisting of both technological and production changes, facilitates custom publishing of texts and textbooks. A system introduced in 1989 combined editing, formatting, pagination, indexing, printing, and binding in a single device (McDowell, 1989). With such a system, an instructor could add or subtract readings in a literary anthology, incorporate different explanatory notes, questions, suggestions for projects, and references to local events, places, and people. The desired number of texts would then be printed and bound, with the instructor's name and class imprinted on the cover and the title page.

Of course, copyright restrictions place serious limitations on the extent of customizing possible. Some customized book services are restricting changes to materials on which they own the copyrights. Other services are developing large data bases for particular areas, with public domain materials, materials for which they own the copyright, and materials for which they have gained permission for use (Cairns & Feinstein, 1982). Costs are still relatively high for custom textbooks and some publishers require instructors to guarantee sales of 150 or more copies, thus limiting the process primarily to high enrollment college courses. Nevertheless, a number of major publishers, including McGraw-Hill, Addison-Wesley, Harcourt Brace, and Prentice-Hall, have entered this rapidly expanding market and others are expected to offer the same services soon.

As custom publishing costs decrease, school districts will find advantages in producing their own reading and literature materials. For publishers of basal readers, one opportunity for retaining market share may be to develop data banks of different reading materials along with supporting instructional components, and to offer custom design of anthologies. Customization could extend not just to the selection of readings, but also to the format and content of the lesson plans for the readings. Whether new vocabulary is presented before or after a reading selection, the extent of background information included, the type of extension activities, and other instructional decisions could be left as options for the purchaser.

The Electronic Supplement to the Text

The digital press and custom publishing may increase the viability of printed literary texts. Nevertheless, technological advances in data storage and transmission, along with the continued decline in prices for multimedia systems, will make certain types of electronic delivery attractive. Most of this advantage, however, is for the materials that supplement literary selections and not for the selections themselves. It is instructive, nevertheless, to consider different levels of electronic texts, progressing from supplementary materials to total on-line delivery of readings and everything that might accompany them.

To begin, consider a printed anthology of readings with a companion CD-ROM that contained background information on the selections and their authors, vocabulary lessons, suggestions for projects, and self-evaluation questions along with answers and explanations. Students might begin a lesson with a whole class discussion on the selection to be read. Then, working in small groups, students would access specific directions from assigned sections of the CD-ROM, including questions or issues to guide their reading. After reading all or part of the selection, the groups would return to the computer system to assess their understanding, obtain further information on the selection, or receive further assignments. Also contained on the CD-ROM could be excerpts from other works by the authors in the anthology, oral presentations of some of the selections, and discussions with the authors.

Teachers could use the electronic resource imagined here in several ways. As a teacher resource the CD-ROM could guide the development of lessons around each reading selection, provide models for teaching particular concepts, perhaps through short film clips of expert teachers doing lessons, and present specific student materials that could be selected and edited for printing. Alternatively, the teacher could select portions (film clips, readings, etc.) for presentation to the whole class through a projection system.

The Electronic Textbook

At the opposite end of the spectrum is the fully electronic textbook. This is clearly a possibility now, but not a particularly desirable one yet. Portable (i.e., laptop) computers of the power required for sustained reading by students are still too expensive, too heavy, and too limited in screen quality to be considered as replacements for printed books. But what if these barriers were removed? What if, over the next decade or two, a device were developed with the same or better resolution as modern books (including color illustrations), weighing no more than a hardback novel, and costing no more than a dinner for two at a four-star New York City restaurant? We should assume that by the time such a device were available, it would also have the ability through wireless communication to access large data banks anywhere in the world, send and receive voice and mail messages, and link directly to similar machines of classmates and teachers. Would we welcome such a device as a replacement for printed books or would nostalgia lead us, like the scent of flowers, back to printed texts?

For many books, particularly those of limited permanence such as school textbooks, such a device might be welcomed. But would we forsake our shelves of treasured volumes, our hardback editions of Shakespeare, Milton, and Chaucer, and our original editions of Nabakov, Cather, Rhys, and Firbank? For many, books are not just for reading; they are also a physical statement of who we are and what we value. An electronic book could reflect images of words and lines onto the retina as well as a printed book but may not substitute so well for its physical presence. Perhaps the printed textbook and the electronic textbook will coexist, the former restricted to elegantly bound volumes that mark the cultural qualifications of their owners, and the latter to everything else. But the resolution of this issue does not depend upon hardware alone, as the next section suggests.

THE TEXTBOOK AS NETWORK

Whatever the delivery mechanism, printed page or electronically activated surface, the textbook might still be a linear sequence of pages. Hypertext, which is dependent upon software and not any particular hardware, offers a possibility for altering this linear arrangement. As noted above, hypertext represents for some a revolution comparable to that created by the invention of writing itself. It is further claimed that by incorporating the reader into the creative process of writing, humanity will be released from the confining grasp of single authored works and passive reading (Bolton, 1991). Interactive fiction is not only a revolution in our time, it also "restores a theoretical innocence to the making of literary texts" and will require "a simpler, more positive literary theory" (p. 147).

Removing the "hype" from hypertext is not an easy job, given such exaggerated claims swaddled in the mushy lexicon of politicized literary theory, but hypertext has been used in enough applications to have its virtues and drawbacks made evident. To understand what hypertext (or hypermedia) is and what it might do to change the literary textbook, I will present four levels or types of hypertext structures as they might be applied to literary textbooks and comment on the advantages and disadvantages of each.

The Annotated Text

Simplest of all hypertext structures both to understand and to create is the annotated text. Imagine an anthology of readings for a classroom, any anthology, with table of contents, index, introductory remarks, reading selections, footnotes, glossary, and all the other appendages of a classroom text. Now transform the textbook into electronic form with all the nonlinear elements—table of contents, index, footnotes, etc.—accessible directly from where they apply. For visual convenience, assume that the existence of such supporting material is signaled by particular graphic devices: background color of a word in context, labeled button or other icon in a margin, and so forth. Navigation through the text is by "point and click," that is, by moving a cursor or other pointing image to a specific location on the computer screen and clicking a specified button, as on a computer mouse.

Within the text certain words are highlighted, indicating that information about these words is available. In a row below the text window are located various icons or buttons. Some, like the left and right arrows, allow linear sequencing forward or backwards in the main body of the text. Other buttons access specific sections of the text (e.g., table of contents, index, glossary) or resources (e.g., pronunciation, note pad). To open the text, the student selects the text title from a list or points and clicks on the representation of the book on a bookshelf. However selected, the initiating process brings to the screen a title page, followed by a table of contents. A student might point and click on a specific title to bring that selection to the screen, or select some other part of the text or one of the on-line resources.

As the text is read, various branches can be taken by a student. A definition for an unfamiliar word might be requested from a general dictionary which is available for any word in the text, or, if a word is highlighted, specific information on that word might be obtained. In these and in most other cases where specific assistance is requested, a text window appears on the screen, overlaying the main text window. Once the new information is read, the student closes the extra window by pointing to and clicking on a *close* button, or moves the window to where it does not interfere with the main text being displayed. When this is done, attention is returned to the point from which the last branch was taken.

From the index, pointing and clicking on an entry brings to the screen the text in which the selected term or phrase occurs. That is, instead of page numbers, the index entries have (invisible) links to not only the appropriate pages, but the places on the page where they occur. Other resources might be added that do not typically occur in a printed text, such as a speech system that will pronounce index or dictionary words or even read the text aloud, but otherwise this option makes an annotated textbook more accessible without changing its basic form. It has many advantages over a printed text, especially in navigation and in modification.

A student can move back and forth easily from literary text to author and editor notes, definitions, and the like. An on-line note pad can allow copying of small portions of text and the recording of student notes, all of which could be printed. The addition of teacher or student notes to the main system, either as a supplement to the notes provided by the editor or as a replacement, is also a possibility. If the appropriate software is provided, such changes would be easy to make and would allow adaptation or customization of a textbook by an individual teacher or by a school district.

The primary drawback of such a plan is the cost of providing a sufficient number of computers so that an entire class could be reading a textbook at the same time. Furthermore, if no printed editions are available, then students will need portable computers so that they can read away from class. Nevertheless, if the present exercise is a reverie about what might be, then cost should not be allowed to interrupt it. First we need to determine what benefits might accrue from new technologies; then the costs can be considered against these outcomes.

Hopscotching Through the Linear Text

A second level of hypertext is created by threading alternate pathways through a linear text such as a story or play. Events described nonchronologically in a story might be linked so that a reader could encounter them in either chronological order or reverse chronological order, that is from the most recent back to the most distant in time, or in the order selected by the author. Descriptions of characters, their thoughts and activities, could be linked so that a reader could follow a single character at a time, returning to pick up another after completing the text portions for one. For plays the linkages could create pathways based on characters, locales, or any other property of the plot, characters, or action.

This is a rather weak and limited use of hypertext but one which might serve didactic purposes. Pathways in this context could be viewed as study aids, much like a keyword in context index. They do not create a new text so much as they provide convenient access for study purposes of an existing text. Therefore, the best pathways will be those that allow discovery of the writer's mechanisms for character and plot development, description, and other elements of style. There is, furthermore, no limitation on where such pathways might extend so that different works by the same author might be linked as might works by different authors. Portrayals of Shakespeare's women—Desdemona, Cordelia, Gertrude, Lady Macbeth, and others—might be linked as might Shakespeare's Shylock and Christopher Marlowe's equivalent character, Barabas.

Extending this idea to its current limits creates Mosaic, World Wide Web, and other Internet resources that link through key words to archived documents all over the world. Imagine electronic demons that wander day and night throughout the Internet, seeking on-line documents and indexing important words within them. From a master index the equivalent of pathways is created so that, for example, a patient navigator of the network could flit from one occurrence of "lexicography" to another, encountering the Oxford Text Archives in Oxford, England, the Hebrew Dictionary Project in Jerusalem, the Dictionary of Old English Archives in Toronto, and dozens more document collections and sites. At this point the literary textbook becomes a small stitch in a larger, multicolored fabric.

Interconnectivity of the type described here, whether within a single text or across texts, does not ipso facto yield an interesting or useful resource. For example, random connections within a text would have no particular value, nor would those generated by someone with limited insight into the significance of the story, its method of construction, and its stylistic merits. Although a few such pathways might lead to the discovery of interesting relationships, most would be dead ends, and in time the reader would learn that following the nonlinear links was a waste of time. Only pathways created by an experienced critic or instructor would, in general, be useful for students, and these could be used either to supplement and automate (in some sense) what a critic or instructor typically writes about a literary text, or they could be structured to lead a reader to discover particular relationships.

What is critical here is the understanding that the value of the linkages is dependent upon the insights of the critic / instructor and not on some magical properties of the hypertext system. Dull, unimaginative analyses of a work, rendered into hypertext, remain dull and unimaginative. If anything changes with the hypertext version, it is that the lack of imagination becomes evident more rapidly. This means that so long as literary works are to be taught in the classroom, the need for human insight into these works will remain. Furthermore, although hypertext systems like those described here may be valuable for classroom instruction, students will still need access to the literary works themselves, and this requires either high quality, inexpensive portable computers or printed texts.

Interactive Fiction

The first step toward a form of fiction that is not based on a traditional, linear text is what is now called "interactive fiction." In this genre, brief episodes are written and linked so that the readers can thread their own pathways through the episodes. Navigation is either through overt choices that are offered at the end of an episode or through branching that links particular words, clauses, and so forth across episodes. In a novel by Michael Joyce, one of the first examples of interactive fiction, episodes correspond roughly to the amount of text that can appear in a single screen window. The reader can follow a default path through the episodes, or select alternate paths by responding to queries at the ends of episodes. Alternatively, some words within episodes are linked to other episodes and can be selected, thus bringing the linked episode into the main reading window.

It is possible in an interactive fiction work to return to the same episode many times or to follow a constrained path, if the author provided one, such that the story becomes linear. Two readers of the same interactive work may have little overlap in what they encountered. There is, therefore, no fixed work that can be analyzed, criticized, or in other ways treated as a linear work might be treated. Yet, contrary to the sense of infinite paths, an interactive fiction work with a finite number of episodes will have a finite number of realizations, if loops are not allowed. A clever author could develop alternate interpretations of characters, alternate plots, and alternate outcomes, expanding dramatically what has been realized in the past with interactive movies where the audience decides at a few specified junctures which of a small number of options will occur next.

The question of importance here is whether or not this form of hypertext will render obsolete the literary textbook as it exists today or even as it might exist as annotated or hopscotched hypertext. As interesting as interactive fiction might appear to be, it faces a highly uncertain future as a literary form. The most charitable statement that could be made is that the literary world would welcome a new approach to the construction of fiction if its best products possessed the richness and depth that the best of linear fiction possesses. Whether we subscribe to Bloom's (1973) "Anxiety of Influence" or to some other criterion of quality for fiction, we continue to judge each work on some set of merits. Even though what we include in classroom anthologies is not based strictly upon merit, as the temperament of the times demands something else, we still resist inclusion of works that are without aesthetic merit, regardless of their authorship. So far the interactive fiction oeuvre has been competition for video games but not for serious fiction.

One particular problem with interactive fiction is the complexity of maintaining coherence. To write an interesting story that is original in the sense of the unexpected is a nontrivial task that few writers succeed at. To expect success at this task with multiple pathways is perhaps to expect the impossible unless the pathways are severely constrained. A well crafted story requires an extraordinary effort on the part of the writer, as the *Paris Review* interviews with famous writers have often demonstrated. To expect that each of a series of alternative pathways through a story will exhibit high aesthetic quality is to expect too much. Perhaps the initial challenge for interactive fiction writers should be simplified: to produce a work with only a few paths, but with each possible traversal yielding a work of merit by some generally acceptable set of standards.

A second concern with interactive fiction is with the role of the reader. Beyond the hype of liberating the reader from the viewpoint and perspective of a single author lies a question of what the reader seeks in serious fiction. Is it an opportunity to superimpose one's own will on the work or is it to discover the will of the author, to be engaged by her or his craft, and to discover something new and unexpected? Does a serious reader, on learning of the father's perfidy in *A Thousand Acres,* want to dictate what the daughters should do next or even choose among alternative actions, or does the reader want to see where the author goes next? I do not read Jane Smiley or any other serious writer with the intent of altering their presentation; I read to be absorbed in what they choose to present and in the order they present it. An author might suggest skipping a particular chapter, as Maugham does in *The Razor's Edge,* but even this is more a device to engage the reader than it is a serious invitation to alter the order of the text or to take an active role in the creation of the story. Transforming reading into a quasi-literary form of Dungeons and Dragons may, in the end, be neither a threat to serious linear fiction nor to video games.

Beyond Interactive Fiction

If the future for interactive fiction may not be so certain, are there alternative forms of electronic texts that might be more successful? One possibility is the mixing of print, voice, music, and video. Texts on tape exist now, as do musical works with narrative voice (e.g., Schünberg's *A Survivor of Warsaw*), and many movies have used text to convey information to the viewer, although usually as an introduction or coda, but no work that I am familiar with has intermixed major stretches of printed text with voice, music, and video. What I imagine is still linear: a text dissolves into music, voice, or video, and then returns to text. Segments or pages of text are displayed at a rate controlled by the reader. At some point, rather than the next page appearing, a voice begins to speak. Perhaps it is the author, explaining in a bygone "gentle reader" style something about the text. Perhaps it is one or more of the characters talking. Or a video might begin. Imagine, for example, *Rashamon,* where each character's tale is presented as a video clip. This is multimedia of a special type and it presents many of the compositional problems of interactive fiction, but perhaps teams of writers, composers, and film directors will collaborate on such works.

CONCLUSIONS

More speculations might be offered on combining electronic media to create new types of fiction. But none imagined so far invalidates or replaces the basic function of fiction, that of a private conversation between author and reader. Electronic technologies hold great promise for expediting the study of literary texts through the linking of multimedia resources to the text itself. Having the author's voice and the voices of insightful critics readily available, to have immediate access to definitions, alternate readings, earlier editions, and all the other components of a critical apparatus will open opportunities to both the instructor and the reader that are not available now. But the literary textbook is a long way from being replaced by electronic text delivery. When computers are so inexpensive, so portable, and possess such high quality display devices that they do everything that a printed textbook now does, we probably will welcome them as replacements for some texts and as alternate means for reading, particularly in traveling about when we do not wish to transport a briefcase full of books. This replacement of the printed textbook by electronic devices will occur gradually over time as the quality of computer systems improves and their costs decline. By the time that textbooks are fully replaced, whether this be in 10 years or 500 years, we will have already accepted the electronic substitute as an obvious improvement.

We have no memory today of the time when textbooks were made of clay tablets or quires of papyrus, nor do we lament their passing, even though they lasted nearly a thousand years. There will probably be a time in the future when memory of books printed on paper sheets gathered between covers will disappear. Audiences in theaters, should there still be such assembly places, will express mild surprise and benign amusement when viewing videos of reading in the 20th century, and librarians (or their equivalents) will puzzle over the tactical problems in our time of providing space for so many millions of printed volumes. Yet we have no reason to believe that the cognitive processes involved in writing or reading of good fiction will change dramatically in the near or distant future, nor the need to teach plot, character, author intent, or any other component of the fictive process. In other words, there is no imminent threat to the content of the literary textbook from technology. Its future continues to lie within the hands of educators who select the canon and the methods for its presentation. Whether the aesthetics of literature will continue to be appreciated, even by a few, depends more on the backbone of the language arts educators than it does on how many pixels can be packed onto a delimited surface or how cheaply solid state devices can be manufactured.

But however safe the literary textbook may be for the immediate future, the technologies described here offer opportunities for advancing literary instruction that should not be ignored. All of them place more resources in the hands of teachers and students than ever before, and require, for full utilization, more independent exploration and testing by students than is common now in language arts classrooms. Students will need encouragement and instruction in how to use on-line information, such as author comments, instructor interpretations, definitions, and so on, to improve their understanding and appreciation of works of fiction. Perhaps even interactive fiction will prove useful as a writing tool, allowing testing of alternative plots, characterizations, and so forth, much as computer simulations of new car designs are used today. We are far beyond the era of computer-as-threat; each new technology can be evaluated for its potential in enhancing literary instruction, as well as for its potential drawbacks. In a world in which only a small proportion of even the college-educated adults read serious fiction, we can use all the help we can get in making reading enjoyable, rewarding, and enhancing.

References

Anonymous (1994, September 14). Digital press to be tested. *The New York Times*, p. D7.

Barzun, J. (1945). *Teacher in America*. Boston: Little, Brown.

Bloom, H. (1973). *The anxiety of influence: A theory of poetry*. New York: Oxford University Press.

Bolton, J. D. (1991). *Writing space: The computer, hypertext, and the history of writing*. Hillsdale, NJ: Erlbaum.

Cairns, C. E., & Feinstein, M. H. (1982). Markedness and the theory of syllabic structure. *Linguistic Inquiry, 13*(2),193–225.

Chall, J. S., & Mirsky, A. F. (Eds.). (1978). *Education and the brain (Yearbook of the National Society for the Study of Education. 77th. Pt. 2)*. Chicago: National Society for the Study of Education.

Cole, J. Y. (Ed.). (1987). *Books in our future: Perspectives and proposals*. Washington, DC: Library of Congress.

Conklin, J. (1987). Hypertext: An introduction and survey. *Computer, 20*(9),17–41

Coover, R. (1992, June 21). The end of books. *The New York Times Book Review*, pp. 1, 23–25.

Cubberley, E. P. (1920). *The history of education*. Boston: Houghton Mifflin.

Davies, W. J. F. (1974). *Teaching reading in early England*. New York: Harper & Row.

Goodrum, C. A., & Dalrymple, H. (1987). The computer and the book. In J. Y. Cole (Ed.), *Books in our future: Perspectives and proposals* (pp. 150–178). Washington, DC: Library of Congress.

Joint Committee on the Library, Congress of the U. S. (1984). *Books in our future: A report from the librarian of Congress to the Congress*. Washington, DC: Author.

Lancaster, F. W. (1978). *Toward paperless information systems*. New York: Academic Press.

Lancaster, F. W. (1987). The paperless society revisited. In J. Y. Cole (Ed.), *Books in our future: Perspectives and proposals* (pp. 212–218). Washington, DC: Library of Congress.

Landow, G. P. (1992). *Hypertext*. Baltimore: Johns Hopkins University Press.

McDowell, E. (1989, October 23). Facts to fit every fancy: Custom textbooks are here. *The New York Times*, pp. D1, D11.

Sullivan, M. (1927). *Our times: The United States 1900–1925: Vol. II. America finding herself*. New York: Charles Scribner's Sons.

Sutton, W. (1961). *The western book trade: Cincinnati as a nineteenth-century publishing and book trade center*. Columbus, OH: Ohio State University Press.

Thomson, I., & Perraud, L. (1990). *Ten Latin schooltexts of the later Middle Ages*. Lewiston, NY: Edwin Mellen Press.

Trübner, N. (Ed.) (1859). *Trübner's bibliographical guide to American literature*. London: Trübner.

U. S. Bureau of the Census (1993). *Statistical abstract of the United States* (113th ed.). Washington, DC: Author.

Venezky, R. L. (1990). The American reading script and its nineteenth-century origins. *Book Research Quarterly, 6*(2), 16–28.

45

INSTRUCTIONAL ENVIRONMENTS FOR LANGUAGE AND LITERACY: CONSIDERATIONS FOR THE ADULT LEARNER

Thomas G. Sticht

PRESIDENT, APPLIED BEHAVIORAL AND COGNITIVE SCIENCES, INC.

The design of instructional environments for language and literacy learning by adults is made difficult by the great diversity of adults as individuals and by the situational and organizational contexts in which adults are found. Because of this diversity, adult educators need to possess an extensive body of knowledge and professional expertise that goes well beyond what is typically the case today. These three topics, the diversity of adult learners, the diversity of learning contexts, and the professional education of adult educators, are discussed in this chapter.

THE DIVERSITY OF ADULT LEARNERS

Adult language and literacy learners form a breathtakingly diverse group. Among others, it includes college students taking English courses at the university; new immigrants who need to learn the English language as a second language, out of school; native born adults who are seeking to develop basic and intermediate language and literacy skills, and mature adult employees who need to upgrade their language and literacy skills in the wake of changes in their work environments.

Immigrants / Foreign Born

In this chapter, attention will focus on the language and literacy development of adults who are not enrolled in higher education at the postsecondary level. This narrows the field somewhat but still includes a great diversity of adults, including immigrants.

Immigrants arriving in the United States frequently enroll in English as a second language (ESL) programs. The diversity of educational backgrounds among these new arrivals is extensive; some have higher education degrees; others are without formal education and are totally illiterate in any language, and thousands of others fall in between these extremes. They are all grouped together by their need and desire to learn to speak, read and write the English language of their newly adopted homeland.

A U.S. Department of Education (1993, pp. 15–22) study reports that during 1991–92, federally funded adult education programs enrolled about 756,000 adults in ESL. Almost all of these adults were foreign-born, and about half had arrived in the United States after 1990. Sixty-seven percent of the ESL enrollees were Hispanic, 22% Asian/Pacific Islander, 8% White, non-Hispanic, 2% black, non-Hispanic, and slightly less than 1% were American Indian/Alaskan Native.

Over half (53%) of ESL enrollees had attained at least a high school education, another 23% had completed a postsecondary (4-year college) degree, and 47% had no high school diploma. About 92% said they read "well" or "very well" in their native language, while 8% said they read "not at all" or "not well" in their native language. The ability to read in their native language was directly and positively related to their ability to speak English.

Sixty-two percent were under age 30, and only 11% were over age 40. Most (51%) had never married and 63% had no children living in the household. About one third of the ESL students with young children in the household reported that they provided some intergenerational transfer of literacy by reading with their children nearly everyday.

Committed as they must be to meeting the demands of daily living while still spending precious hours in learning the English language, these new citizens-to-be pursue this study openly, with the admiration and encouragement of their families, friends, and, for those lucky enough to find work, their employers.

Native Born Adult Learners

The undereducated, native born citizens of the United States include those for whom life has been rough, for whom learning in school may have been very difficult, leading to a decision to drop out of school without having achieved higher levels of language or literacy, those for whom decisions made in the passions of youth brought early parenthood and an existence on welfare, or those engaged in jobs where new ways of work have upgraded the demands for language and literacy skills. These are the adult learners who are stigmatized in the mass media as the "functionally illiterate."

For these learners there is frequently little joy in "going back to school." Unlike those studying ESL, the native-born who seek basic literacy education often feel that there is nothing to be proud of in going for "remedial" education. Too often for these adults, language and literacy learning is an embarrassment—an activity to be concealed. In these cases, the design of the instructional environment may include changing loss-of-face names like "adult literacy program" to face-saving names like "job skills enhancement program." Participation in these adult education programs is often clandestine, and not to be divulged to one's families, friends, or employers.

The U.S. Department of Education (1993, pp. 22–29) reported that, in federally funded adult education programs, about 414,000 adults enrolled in Adult Basic Education (ABE) and 612,000 in Adult Secondary Education (ASE) during fiscal year 1991–92. Over 90% of these enrollees were U.S. citizens by birth, most (61%) were white, non-Hispanic; black, non-Hispanic (22%), Hispanic (12%), American Indian/Alaskan Native (3%) and Asian / Pacific Islander (2%) made up the remainder of the ethnic distribution of the enrollees.

For 82% of the ABE / ASE adult students, English was the language spoken at home, with Spanish the next most frequent language spoken at home. Over two thirds (68%) of the ABE/ASE students were under age 30, and only 8% were over age 45. Most (61%) were women, most (52%) had never been married, and most (63%) had no children in the house under the age of 6. Those with young children (about 37%) said that they read with their children about once a week on average.

The typical ABE / ASE adult student dropped out of school after completing 10 years of schooling. Eighty-nine percent had no high school diploma, 8% had a diploma, and 3% had a postsecondary degree.

A local perspective. In San Diego, research is under way to better understand the education of adults in an inner-city, economically depressed area served by four continuing education centers that are part of the San Diego Community College District, Continuing Education Division (McDonald, Huie, Sticht, & Grimes, 1994). District data indicate that of

28,822 adult students served from 1992–93, 90% were ESL students and only 10% were ABE students. This may reflect the negative feelings that frequently accompany "going back to school" that many native-born adult students report (McDonald, et al., 1994, pp. 35, 36).

The diversity of ESL clients in the San Diego study sites is much greater than that suggested by the U.S. Department of Education report. At just one of the four adult continuing education centers where research is underway, enrollment data show that there are learners from 108 different nations, speaking over 70 languages. At the centers involved in the study, there are large enrollments in beginning ESL, and then enrollments plummet and very few adults are found in advanced ESL, possibly because they are able to gain employment with lower levels of language skills (McDonald et al., 1994, pp. 25–34). Whatever be the case, these new immigrants are an inspiration to adult educators. Many are here in the United States studying to become citizens, "American-style" parents, workers, and friends with their new neighbors. Many have survived the horrifying experiences of famine, floods, war, genocide, infanticide, wife-burning, and extreme poverty in their native lands.

In San Diego, as in the rest of the nation, the awesome task of the adult educator is to design instructional environments that will serve well this diverse population of language and literacy learners.

THE DIVERSITY OF INSTRUCTIONAL CONTEXTS

The adult educator's task is made even more difficult because diversity is also constituted by the contexts in which adults learn. Unlike children, who face compulsory education demands by attending more or less homogeneous public schools for 12 to 13 years, adult language and literacy learners are not typically faced with compulsory education, nor are they neatly housed in schools. The various situational and institutional contexts in which adult learners may be found constrain the types of instructional environments that adult educators can provide.

Self-instructional Programs

Adults may choose to learn in a variety of contexts. They may study alone at home, using language tapes, computer software, books, or even products such as Hooked on Phonics™ with SRA™ kits ("used by over 62 million people around the world") that rely on the mass media of television and radio to bombard the airwaves with advertising aimed at the adult learner/consumer.

Adult learners may be attracted to such products because they offer flexibility in terms of time of use, number of repetitions of a lesson, and, perhaps most important, anonymity. Adult educators may be engaged in developing these types of products for self-study. With such materials, it is important to keep the operating instructions as simple as possible, so that non-English speaking or less literate adults are able to use the

products. In language learning, there must be special attention given to providing information feedback to the learners
so that they can know how well they are doing and whether
they are proceeding correctly in areas such as pronunciation
and appropriateness of syntax and vocabulary.

Military Contexts

Educators working in military contexts are strictly bound by
the amount of time that is provided for instruction. Such
time pressures may be even greater under a major mobiliza-
tion like the Vietnam war. Military management may provide
as little as 45 hours or as much as 3 months for an instructional program in reading or mathematics, depending upon
the circumstances. Socialist, Marxist or "critical literacy"
aimed at overthrowing the hegemony of the governing
classes through revolution are notions that are not typically
valued as goals of military literacy programs. Instead, it is
generally expected by military management that the program
will produce measurable improvements in job tasks requiring
reading or mathematics.

In such cases, the adult educator may have to work with
adult learners whose participation in the program is mandatory, who are excused from their daily job and whose full time
is dedicated to learning in the program. They may often be
exhausted from overnight training activities. The educator
may have to develop or use existing job-related materials to
accomplish a significant amount of literacy development in a
fairly narrow domain in a short amount of time. Nationally
normed and job-related tests may have to be administered to
document learning gains in the programs.

In 1980–81, when the military was enlisting only volunteers and spending billions of dollars to recruit higher ability
personnel, they were still providing basic skills instruction to
over 220,000 service personnel, which was equivalent to all
the basic skills enrollments in 25 states (Sticht, 1982, Table 16,
p. 47). With the end of the cold war and the downsizing of the
military services, there were fewer enrollments in basic skills
courses, but as recently as 1990 the military provided literacy
instruction for over 75,000 adults (Villanueva, Lamb, & Chin,
1991, appendix). Adult educators need preparation for work
in military contexts that serve the needs of both the service
members and their organizations.

Jails and Prisons

As sad as it is to say, one of the "growth" areas for adult
language and literacy providers are the thousands of city jails
and state and federal prisons, so-called "correctional" institutions, that have and continue to proliferate throughout the
United States. With over a million prisoners behind bars,
perhaps most of whom are undereducated, adult educators
must understand the cultural contexts of institutions that
many view as existing to punish, not rehabilitate (Newman,
Lewis, & Beverstock, 1993, p. vii).

In jails, the prisoners may be highly transient, shuffled
among different facilities, and released and readmitted repeatedly. They may be able to grab only a few hours of

instruction at one facility before being moved elsewhere.
Guards and other personnel may resent the educational
opportunities to prisoners, taunt them and discourage learning. The prevalence of violent gangs may limit the work of
the adult educator because gang leaders may discourage
participation in education (Newman et al., 1993).

Unlike the military, where specific organizational outcomes in the form of improved job-related reading and math
skills are expected, many correctional institutions have no
particular institutional goals for education, but rather a less
direct outcome in mind—lowered recidivism. Toward this
end, institutions are likely to look more favorably on those
programs that help prisoners make successful transitions into
civilian life than those oriented toward "improving one's
potential" in some more abstract sense.

Adult educators must be prepared to work in correctional
institutions under conditions of what is often heavy-handed
security, including censorship of materials, that limit what
they teach and how they teach. In jails, brief, self-contained
lessons, perhaps computer-based, focused on a particular
topic may be useful in working among the highly transient
inmates. In prisons, where long-term programs may be possible, programs aimed at improving self-image, such as high
school completion, or integrated basic skills, life skills, and
vocational skills may be desired and developed by the adult
educator to help improve each prisoner's personal potential,
contributing to a more successful transition to civilian life
and lowered recidivism (Newman et al., 1993, p. 37). In
accomplishing the latter, it is essential that adult educators
coordinate "inside" educational programs with "outside" programs that aid in prisoner re-entry into civilian life.

The Job Corps

The War on Poverty of the 1960s produced many intervention
programs for youth and adults. Vocational training was the
major focus of many youth programs, with some attention to
remedial academic education, and attainment of a high school
equivalency degree. The most prominent and enduring of
these programs was the Job Corps, which is still in operation.

Adult educators who wish to work in Job Corps centers
teaching literacy skills must be prepared to follow a highly
systematized, competency-based, computer-managed instructional (CMI) program developed, in part, to meet the
demands of the "open entry / open exit" policy of the Job
Corps that permits students to start or leave the program
whenever they want. The CMI system tests students and
analyzes their needs for basic skills instruction. Teachers
assign instructional materials according to this computer test
analysis. For instance, based on a student's reading level,
appropriate math instructional materials can be assigned.
Progress tests are scored and recorded automatically by the
CMI system so that students can progress rapidly through the
program. With the CMI system, it is expected that teachers
can spend less time on record keeping and more on working
with students individually or in small groups.

In 1991–92, participants in the Job Corps were economically disadvantaged, mostly male ($\frac{2}{3}$), high school dropouts

(80%), minorities ($\frac{2}{3}$) who had never been employed. Reading skills on entry were around the 7th-grade level. Students improved on average length of stay of 7.6 months to around the 8.4 grade level (U.S. Department of Labor, 1992). By contemporary standards of having literacy skills at or above Level 3 of the National Adult Literacy Survey, this would leave the majority of Job Corps "graduates" functionally illiterate (National Education Goals Panel, 1995, p. 8).

Workplace Learning Contexts

The U.S. Department of Education funds partnerships of educational providers and various businesses to develop and conduct basic skills (English as a second language, reading, writing, mathematics) programs for employees. As in the military, socialist-Marxist ideas that are sometimes part of "critical literacy" are not usually valued in workplace programs. Rather, literacy instruction in workplace programs generally conforms to traditional values of "the American work ethic" and is consistent with the concepts of capitalism, competitiveness and private enterprise. The programs may be expected to produce changes not only in employees' basic skills, but also in one or more aspects of productivity on their job. Indeed, the federal regulations that govern program development generally require that the language and literacy programs be developed using materials relevant to the jobs done in the workplace, though this does not apply to programs for completing the General Educational Development (GED), high school equivalency certificate.

In workplace-based programs, if the education is on duty time, the adult educator will frequently have to develop brief (20–50 hour) programs because employers cannot afford to spare employees off a production line or from another position for long periods of time. Classes may be run on or off duty from midnight to eight in the morning or at other odd hours to match the shifts that employees are working. Classes may be held in well-furnished and quiet offices, noisy, makeshift space in the company cafeteria, or specially designed learning centers fully equipped with text, video and audio materials, computers, and audiovisual equipment.

Recent research on workplace literacy programs suggests that such programs may indeed contribute, not only to improving adults' literacy and numeracy skills, but also to improving productivity on the job . In one recent study, six manufacturing companies in Chicago, making products ranging from hydraulic valves to bubble gum, provided basic English language, reading, and mathematics education for over 700 employees (Sticht, 1994a). In evaluation studies conducted in the companies, supervisors reported that the programs had a variety of positive effects on organizational effectiveness, including improvements in job training, on the job performance, promotability of participants, and productivity, such as scrap reduction, reduced paperwork, less waste, and other efficiencies. In turn, employees reported that the language and literacy programs had helped them on their job, at home, and in their communities. Some were stimulated to continue their education at local community colleges.

Community Colleges and Adult High Schools (Local Education Agencies)

Approximately 1.8 million adults enrolled in 1991–92 in federally-funded ESL, ABE, or ASE programs. Ninety-four percent of ESL and 85% of ABE/ASE adult learners enroll in public school systems (local education agencies) or community colleges (U.S. Department of Education, 1993, pp. i, 21, 28).

Community colleges and adult high schools are typically state-funded bureaucracies which scramble to get Full Time Equivalents—FTEs. The FTEs are the number of student contact hours that would be obtained with a full time student. The FTEs are typically based on average daily attendance, and because adults are not usually full-time students it may take quite a few adults to accumulate enough hours to make up one FTE.

In a "teacher as researcher" study conducted in the San Diego continuing education centers mentioned above, over 80 adult students in one classroom came and went during a semester to make up an average daily attendance of 22 students (Bundy, 1995). The latter was the number required to conduct the class and if there were not 22 students enrolled at the outset of class, the class would be canceled and the teacher would have been out of a job for the semester.

This uncertainty of enrollments and availability of funds for classes has led many institutions to hire part-time teachers who work without health or retirement benefits. In the San Diego continuing education centers where research is underway, in 1993 there were 63 full-time and 523 part-time teachers. The uncertainty inherent in this system leads to staff morale problems and frequent hardships for teachers who may have to work at two or three jobs to support their families. This may detract from the quality of education that can be delivered, and it makes it difficult to get many of these adjunct teachers to attend staff development activities on a voluntary basis.

Because of the transient nature of many adult students, due to work schedules, problems with transportation and child care, and other personal problems, many community colleges and adult schools run what are known as "open entry/open exit" classrooms in which adults may enroll at any time and drop out at any time (as in the Job Corps). Needless to say, this demands a great deal of flexibility on the part of the teacher and the students to constantly accommodate newcomers. It may limit the propensity to engage in cooperative group or team projects. It has also led to the development of "learning centers" in which teachers may act more as facilitators of self-study activities by directing students to appropriate workbooks, audiotapes, videos, or computer programs.

Community-Based Organizations (CBOs)

There are a large number of community-based groups that are typically nonprofit, charitable organizations that provide a variety of services to community residents, often including ESL, ABE, and ASE programs. About 4% of ESL and 5% of ABE/ASE adult students funded by the Adult Education program of the U.S. Department of Education enrolled in CBOs in 1991–92 (U.S. Department of Education, 1993, pp. 21, 28).

Many of these organizations have sprung up to serve the educational needs of particular segments of the adult population for whom special laws, policies and funding have been provided by various government agencies. For instance, the Association of Farmworker Opportunity Programs includes 37 CBOs in 48 states and Puerto Rico which provide disadvantaged migrant and seasonal farmworkers with education, training, and employment opportunities. These organizations are funded through the Department of Labor's Job Training Partnership Act (JTPA), Title IV §402 (Association of Farmworker Opportunity Programs, 1991, p. iv). In program year 1991, some 50,000 farmworkers were served in the program. About 45% of these workers received classroom training (Strong et al., 1993, p. 1–6).

While CBOs that receive federal and state funds are typically constrained in various ways by the rules and regulations governing their funding sources, many CBOs exist that are completely independent of any government agencies and operate with the extensive use of volunteers and funding by public donations. Organizations such as Laubach Literacy Action and Literacy Volunteers of America (LVA) may sometimes work with government grants, but in principle they are independent, charitable organizations funded through memberships and the benevolence of individuals, businesses, and private foundations. In 1992, Laubach served some 147,000 students with 98,000 tutors, while LVA served 65,000 adults with 55,000 tutors and administrators (Business Council for Effective Literacy, 1993, No. 34, pp. 6, 7).

While organizations like Laubach and LVA have their established teaching methods and materials that each new tutor must learn to use, other CBOs may follow their own lead and permit greater or lesser initiative on the part of individual teachers for conducting their classrooms the way they want. Still others are constrained by the federal, state, and local regulations that their funding sources impose with regard to amount of time for education, the focus of the education (e.g., high school completion; employability), the contents of education (e.g., programs funded by the JTPA are being directed to incorporate the competencies developed by the Secretary of Labor's Commission on Achieving Necessary Skills, (SCANS) 1991, p. vii), and methods of program evaluation (e.g, use of nationally normed, standardized tests of English, reading, or mathematics).

Many CBOs are involved in the new family literacy initiatives of the federal government's Even Start legislation or the work of the National Center for Family Literacy (Sticht, 1994b). Such programs bring a new dimension to adult education because adult educators must work with and learn about early childhood education to promote the intergenerational transfer of new language and literacy skills from parents to their children (Sticht, Beeler, & McDonald, 1992a, b).

NEW DIRECTIONS FOR THE PROFESSIONAL EDUCATION OF ADULT EDUCATORS

Designing instructional environments that are conducive to

sustained and effective learning is not a simple matter, considering the diversity of adult learners. Across contexts, mostly part-time adult educators are asked to promote learning among some of the most difficult-to-teach learners in the nation under substandard and generally underfunded circumstances. Still, in 1991, in a national survey of schools of education, no higher education programs were found that were designed to produce professional adult educators who could serve the broad diversity of adult learners in the different organizational and intergenerational contexts reviewed above (Sticht, McDonald, & Huie, 1992).

There are many indicators that the programs offered for adult ESL and literacy education in many institutional settings are not working very well. It is instructive to review a few items that illustrate certain beliefs and practices that are widespread which seriously reduce the effectiveness of educational programs for youth and adult learners. This is necessary to counter the claims of those who would argue that there is no need for professional development of adult educators or research on adult instruction and learning because, "We already know what to do; what we need is more money with which to do it."

The items below do not form an exhaustive listing of educational problems plaguing adult education, but rather a sampling of beliefs, practices, and outcomes which indicate that, indeed, many times people, even experienced professionals, do *not* know what to do, and in fact many may harbor beliefs that actually detract from the development of excellent programs for youth and adults. These are beliefs and practices that an adult educator must learn about and be prepared to overcome.

Cultural Beliefs That Hinder Adult Education

Item 1: On Sunday, October 13, 1991 The San Diego Union newspaper reprinted an article by Joan Beck, columnist for the *Chicago Tribune* that argued for early childhood education because, "Half of adult intellectual capacity is already present by age 4 and 80 percent by age 8. The great education researcher Dr. Benjamin Bloom reported in scholarly studies in the 1960s that helped establish the importance of early learning. No matter how good schools are, how capable and caring the teachers, they will not have as much effect on a child's permanent level of intelligence as has the environment in which he has lived before he started to first grade. A school may teach him a zillion facts and inspire him to use the mental capacity he has, but the opportunity to influence his basic intelligence—considered to be a stable characteristic by age 17—is greatest in early life."

The influence of such beliefs was illustrated a year earlier in the same newpaper on October 14, 1990, in an article in which a staff member of the California state library system was interviewed. The staff member, in charge of the library's family literacy programs, was quoted as justifying the importance of family literacy (in which parents' literacy skills increase and are transfered to their children) in this way "Between the ages of zero to 4 we have learned half of everything we'll ever learn in our lives. Most of that has to do with language, imagination, and inquisitiveness." What hope, then, does that leave for improving the parent's language or literacy skills?

Item 2: A December, 1989, report summarized a study of how recruits designated as "low aptitude" on the basis of their scores on basic skills (reading and mathematics) tests fared some 20 years after military service. Researchers funded by the Department of Defense stated in the report that, "Military training for marginal youth may be too little, too late. To compensate for the deficits which the underprivileged bring with them would require more than a little extra training, and maybe a complete restructuring of current pedagogical practices." On February 24, 1990, the Director of Accession Policy of the Department of Defense commented on the report in the *Washington Post*. "The lesson is that low-aptitude people, whether in the military or not, are always going to be at a disadvantage. That's a sad conclusion." Then on April 8, 1990, Jack Anderson's column in the *Washington Post*, quoted one of the researchers as saying, "…by the age of 18 or 19, it's too late. The school system in early childhood is the only place to really help, and that involves heavy participation by the parents."

Neither the articles about intellectual development in early childhood nor the Department of Defense study elicited responses from the adult (or any other) education field challenging these conclusions and beliefs about human cognitive development. Yet, if true, these beliefs about intellectual, linguistic, and literacy development would have dire implications for the achievement of Goal 6 of the National Education Goals, which states that by the year 2000 all adults will be literate. Further, these beliefs denigrate as nearly futile the work of those involved in the language and literacy education of youth and adults in any setting, including the military, job training, corrections, adult basic education, workplace literacy, and even family literacy.

Educational "Malpractice"

Item 3: In the late 1980s and early 1990s, a major international corporation acted to improve its competitiveness by improving the quality of its products. As one part of its strategy for quality improvement, it moved to improve its employees' basic skills. It made a commitment of $25 million to this effort. In a decentralized manner, various plants implemented their own basic skills programs. One purchased computers worth thousands of dollars and subscribed to a telecommunications network that claimed to make 1 year's improvement in basic skills for every 10 hours of instruction. Another plant contracted with a major learning center company that stated that it would increase basic skills by 1 year for every 60 hours of instruction. Other plants contracted with community colleges that simply offered to teach basic skills, with no guarantees of gains.

No one wondered how people who had not learned basic skills well in their school days, could now be expected to learn in 10 or 60 hours what the normal child takes a full year to learn in and outside school. No one knew what the basic skills that were used on the job actually were and how the training in the basic skills programs was supposed to be transferred to

the worksite. No one understood standardized testing and how test artifacts such as regression to the mean could produce a year of gain with no basic skills training at all. No one evaluated the effects of basic skills training on work quality and productivity. Following critiques of their programs, the corporation initiated activities to develop "functional context" workplace literacy programs that taught basic skills contextualized within work tasks requiring those skills.

Item 4: An adult basic skills program in the Appalachian region applied to the U.S. Department of Education for recognition as an "exemplary" program. In its application, the program operators noted that they administered the Tests of Adult Basic Education as pre- and posttest measures. To give the adult learners the opportunity to really show what they could do, the tests were administered ignoring the time limits. Additionally, because so much improvement was typically made, the easy form of the test was generally given as the pretest and a more difficult form as the posttest.

No one noted that by ignoring the time limits, the test was no longer "standardized," and therefore the raw scores had no meaning when converted to "grade levels." Hence adult learners were misinformed about their literacy skills. No one paid attention to the fact that random marking of the easy version of the test could produce nothing less than a grade 1.0 score, while random marking of the more difficult test, frequently given as the posttest could produce nothing less than a grade 3.0 score. Hence, random marking of the different forms as pre- and posttests could produce a gain of 2 years. The U.S. Department of Education designated the program as "exemplary."

The items above indicate that many educational program providers are so untutored and inept with respect to the use of instruments such as standardized tests that, if in the practice of medicine professionals misused medical test instruments the way adult educator misuse cognitive test instruments, they would be sued for malpractice.

Limited Outcomes

Item 5: Although 1.8 million new adult learners enrolled in federally funded adult ESL and ABE / ASE programs in 1991–92, 17% (300,000) dropped out before receiving any instruction, about 36% left their programs before completing 12 hours of instruction, and 50% of all new starters were no longer active after 16 weeks. The median hours of instruction completed were 43 (U.S. Department of Education, 1993, pp. i, ii). This is not enough time to become proficient in English as a second language or to overcome years of educational problems.

Item 6: In the mid 1960s, when the Adult Education Act was first passed, "functional literacy" was designated as having reading and mathematics skills equivalent to those of a typical grade school student who had completed the eighth grade (i.e., who had reading skills at the 8.9 grade level). In the national survey of young adult literacy in 1985 it was found that one out of five (20%) young adults read with skills below that of typical eighth graders (Kirsch & Jungeblut, 1986, p. 40). Further studies have shown that (1) for 1991–92,

56,000 Job Corps learners entered reading on the average with 7th grade skills and left reading at the mid 8th-grade level (Sticht & Armstrong, 1994, p. 150); (2) averaged over 7 years from 1985 to 1992, adults in California's adult basic education programs who are assessed by the Comprehensive Adult Student Assessment System entered adult basic education reading at the mid 6th-grade level and left reading at the mid 7th-grade level (p. 144); (3) in New York city, data for 5 years from 1985 to 1990 showed that adults who entered programs at around the 2nd grade level left reading at about the 3rd grade level, those entering at the 4th-, 6th or 8th-grade levels also made about 1 year of gain on the Tests of Adult Basic Education. Data available for some 788 learners who had been enrolled in these New York city adult basic education programs for 3 years showed that 93% entered reading below the 6.9 grade level and two thirds of these learners read below the 4.9 grade level at entry. On average, these 3-year learners made a gain of around 16 months to about the mid 6th-grade level. (pp. 147, 152).

In general, studies of adult basic education indicate that most students enter reading at levels that would define them as functionally illiterate and leave at levels that would still define them as functionally illiterate by most contemporary standards. Given the dearth of research on adult literacy learning, it is difficult to estimate how much gain adult students retain after leaving their programs.

THE WELL SPECIALIST

The items reviewed above indicate the beliefs and practices that hinder the development and implementation of programs of excellence for underserved youth and adults. They illustrate widely held beliefs about human intelligence and cognitive abilities, and their development that are, most simply put, wrong. They reveal widespread ignorance about the nature and use of instructional tools such as standardized tests. They indicate that many programs are not, in fact, attractive enough to retain adults for long periods of time and they do not make adults broadly literate in the relatively brief periods of time that adults remain in the programs.

In 1991, a project was initiated to address the need for a new breed of adult educators which could meet the challenges of adult education across the life-span and from one generation to the next (Sticht et al., 1992). Called the Workforce Education and Lifelong Learning Specialist (WELLS), the degree program was established at the San Diego State University, College of Education, Department of Educational Technology, to produce adult educators specializing in the education and training of underserved youth and adults to prepare them for productive, well-paying work, responsible parenting, participatory citizenship, and community development.

The WELLS' Domains of Competence

The items cited above clearly indicate the need for adult education specialists who are professionally educated and trained to engage in their educational practice. A summary description of the contents of the WELLS curriculum to educate such specialists is presented in Table 45–1.

By studying the cognitive science foundations of education, the educational arts and sciences, and culture and human resources policies and practices, the WELLS is prepared with the broad knowledge base needed to work in an adaptive mode in any institutional context and with the diversity of adult learners discussed above.

While the WELLS' preparation includes considerable classroom instruction, much of it is laboratory work in developing instructional materials, and field work to learn about adult cognition, language, and literacy in home, work, and community settings, and adult education in real instructional settings (although many of the first generation of WELLS students are already working in adult education settings and want to develop a greater degree of professional competence).

To provide a field setting for research and internships by WELLS students, the San Diego State University, Department of Educational Technology joined forces with a local non-

TABLE 45–1. Domains of knowledge and skill for the Workforce Education and Lifelong Learning Specialist (WELLS).

Cognitive Science Foundations of Education Develops an understanding of human growth and cognitive development within a framework based on research from studies in anthropology, sociology, psychology, linguistics, philosophy, and computer sciences. Integrates biological, cultural & social foundations of cognition and the intergenerational transfer of cognitive abilities (knowledge; thinking skills); oral and written language; graphic tools of thought; academic bodies of knowledge (math; science; history; geography; etc.) workforce bodies of knowledge; and the applications of knowledge in the everyday world. Develops an integrated understanding of learning in childhood and adulthood as influenced by culture and other context factors.

Educational Arts and Technology Develops competence in using a variety of problem solving methods (including qualitative and quantitative research methods); technologies for instructional development, delivery & evaluation; methods for teaching basic academic skills, workforce skills, personal management skills in various contexts; multicultural education for ethnic, gender, age and organizational diversity; learner-centered, participatory education methods for empowering youth and adults in the education process; aiding the teacher as inquirer in action research to improve the delivery of education programs; functional context education.

Culture and Human Resources Policies and Practices Develops an understanding of cultural beliefs about cognitive development and how these beliefs are translated into policies and practices; federal, state, and local policies and laws regarding various funding "streams" such as the Job Training Partnership Act (JTPA) the Family Support Act and JOBS; the Adult Education Act, etc. and how to obtain funding for programs from these sources. Methods of work analysis to establish cognitive, social, and technical skills for work for counseling youth and adults for employment and for curriculum development. The cultures of various work organizations and organizational development. Methods for community development.

TABLE 45–2. An article about teacher-research project in the *Community Exchange* newspaper

SDCCD Teachers Become Researchers

To Improve Adult Basic Education

Teachers in the San Diego Community College District (SDCCD) are also becoming researchers. They are studying in adult basic education.

Begun in March 1993, ten Teacher as Researcher projects are underway. These projects are sponsored by the CWELL Action Research Center.

In one project, "Families Learning English Together," Marjorie Howe, SDCCD Home Economics Resource Instructor and Esther Garcia, SDCCD ESL / Child Development Instructor have joined forces.

They are developing new course curriculum and instructional materials to help Limited English Proficient (LEP) parents, especially mothers, and their preschool children integrate better into the community by: 1) developing their skills in accessing community resources, locating and using medical services, using the library, shopping for family necessities, and communicating at a basic level with school personnel at their child's school; and 2) expanding their basic survival English in the context of family situations.

In another project, "Intergenerational Transfer in the GAIN / ABE Classroom," Instructor Judy Quinton is documenting the intergenerational transfer of cognitive skills from parent to child in her classroom.

Judy is documenting this phenomenon through a literature review of the topic; various surveys, journal writing by students directed towards how their own attendance at school affects their children, and encouraging parents to participate with their children in various activities.

More innovative and exciting Teacher as Researcher projects will be featured in future editions of *The Community Exchange*!

profit educational R&D organization, the Applied Behavioral & Cognitive Sciences, Inc. and the San Diego Community College District, Continuing Education Division (SDCCD / CE) to create the San Diego Consortium for Workforce Education and Lifelong Learning (CWELL). The CWELL established an Action Research Center (ARC) which, among other things, has stimulated over a dozen teachers in four continuing education centers to engage in what is called the "teacher as researcher" project. In this project, teachers participate in Friday or Saturday seminars, conferences and one-on-one meetings with staff researchers in the ARC. They develop, carry out, and report research projects. In some cases they engage adult learners as researchers to help adult learners develop critical thinking skills along with language and literacy skills.

To encourage and recognize the work of the teacher researchers, stories are printed in the *Community Exchange*, a newspaper published three times a year by the CWELL Action Research Center. Four thousand copies of the newspaper are distributed locally and nationally. Table 45–2 shows an article from the first issue of the *Community Exchange* that recognized the work of three of the teacher researchers.

The specialists are expected to participate in the activities of the research center and learn how to participate in action research. They also learn how to help other adult education teachers engage in action research projects as a form of staff development aimed at improving instructional environments for language and literacy learning by adults across the lifespan, from one generation to the next, and in any of the diverse contexts in which adults engage in learning.

References

Association of Farmworker Opportunity Programs (1991). *National directory of farmworker services*. Washington, DC.

Bundy, L. F. (1995). Empowerment skills for ESL students. In B. A. McDonald, C. J. Huie & T. G. Sticht (Eds.), *Teachers as researchers in adult English as a second language and literacy learning classrooms*. San Diego, CA: San Diego Community College District, Continuing Education Division, Action Research Center.

Business Council for Effective Literacy. (1993). *LVA & Laubach revisited*. New York.

Kirsch, I. S., & Jungeblut, A. (1986). *Literacy: Profiles of America's young adults* (Report No. 16-PL-02). Princeton, NJ: National Assessment of Educational Progress, Educational Testing Service.

McDonald, B. A., Huie, C. J., Sticht, T. G., & Grimes, W. B. (1994). *Learning in the action research center (ARC) community: Inquiry, reflection and change in the delivery system for continuing education services for adults in the San Diego Community College District*. San Diego, CA: San Diego Community College District, Continuing Education Division, Action Research Center.

National Education Goals Panel (1995).

Newman, A. P., Lewis, W., & Beverstock, C. (1993). *Prison literacy: Implications for program and assessment policy*. Pennsylvania, PA: University of Pennsylvania, National Center on Adult Literacy.

Secretary of Labor's Commission on Achieving Necessary Skills. (1991). *What work requires of schools: A SCANS report for AMERICA 2000*. Washington, DC: U.S. Department of Labor.

Sticht, T. G. (1982). *Basic skills in defense. Professional Paper 3–82, HumRRO-PP-3-82*. Alexandria, VA: Human Resources Research Organization.

Sticht, T. G. (1994a). *Workplace literacy programs for ten manufacturing companies in the Chicago, Illinois area: A report of process and outcomes*. Des Plaines, IL: THE CENTER: Workplace Education Division.

Sticht, T. G. (1994b). *Family literacy: A world movement*. El Cajon, CA: Applied Behavioral & Cognitive Sciences.

Sticht, T. G., & Armstrong, W. B. (1994). *Adult literacy in the United States: A compendium of quantitative data and interpretive comments.* Washington, DC: National Institute for Literacy.

Sticht, T. G., Beeler, M. J., & McDonald, B. A. (1992a). *The intergenerational transfer of cognitive skills: Vol. I: Programs, policy, and research issues.* Norwood, NJ: Ablex.

Sticht, T. G., Beeler, M. J., & McDonald, B. A. (1992b). *The intergenerational transfer of cognitive skills: Vol. II: Theory and research in cognitive science.* Norwood, NJ: Ablex.

Sticht, T. G., McDonald, B. A., & Huie, C. J. (1992). *Getting WELL: Workforce education and lifelong learning: Designs for professional education and action research to improve the education and training of underserved youth and adults.* El Cajon, CA: Applied Behavioral & Cognitive Sciences.

Strong, M., D'Amico, R., Clüver, A. F., Sloan, E., Uratsu, C., Weinstock, P., & Rogers, K. (1993). *Evaluation of the JTPA Title IV migrant and seasonal farmworker program. Final report.* Washington, DC: U.S. Department of Labor.

U.S. Department of Education. (1993). *National evaluation of adult education programs. Second interim report. Profiles of client characteristics.* Washington, DC: Division of Adult Education and Literacy.

U.S. Department of Labor. (1992). *Job corps in brief: Program year 1991.* Washington, DC: Employment and Training Administration, Job Corps.

Villanueva, T., Lamb, T. A., & Chin, K. B. O., (1991, October). *Fundamental skills training/education programs in the military.* San Antonio, TX: Paper presented at the annual meeting of the Military Testing Association.

·46·

FILM, VIDEO, AND BOOKS:
SOME CONSIDERATIONS FOR LEARNING
AND TEACHING

Lawrence Baines

FLORIDA STATE UNIVERSITY

I remember, when I was a boy, Douglas Fairbanks was the model for me. Adolphe Menjou was the model for my brother. Of course those men were playing the roles of mythic figures. They were educators toward life. (Campbell; in Campbell & Moyers, 1988, p. 15)

It has been a 100 years since the Lumiere brothers charged admission in the basement of the Grand Cafe in Paris, France to show features such as *La Sortie des Usines Lumiere* (*Workers Leaving the Lumiere Factory*). It has been almost as long that film has been under consideration for use in public schools. Film has never managed to gain a permanent foothold in the American secondary school curriculum but has somehow managed to stay alive through the years on the fringe of respectability as a subject worthy of academic study. Once upon a time (before World War II), using film in the classroom was considered the cutting edge of technology in American education. With the introduction into schools of the computer (and the mass of technological apparatus that has come with it) film's central position as the medium of choice for the technologically-minded teacher has been lost.

Yet, the value of film has never resided in its technological novelty, arresting as it must have seemed to the first spectators who witnessed those life-like images flicker across the bedsheet screen in the basement of the Grand Cafe. As books transport us through a "lived-through" experience with words (Rosenblatt, 1978), so films offer an aesthetic "lived-through" experience with pictures (Amelio, 1972; Durgnat, 1967; Eidsvik, 1978; Lacey, 1972; Miller, H., 1979; Smith, 1969). But, there is something more in films—something that invites us to lose ourselves to its vicarious world of image and sound. Perhaps because "a picture is irrefutable" (Postman, 1985),

film has the feel of authenticity and truth. Film's convincing veracity is one reason some educators have been clamoring for the inclusion of film studies in the curriculum for the past 100 years.

FILM AS A HYBRID ART

With the spread of newer electronic media such as CD-ROM, laser discs, cable television, and interactive computers, the boundaries of media have become quite blurred. Accurate conclusions cannot be drawn about the content of moving pictures based upon the devices used in conveying them. One could see *Citizen Kane* on a cable television station during "Orson Welles Week"; rent the tape at a local video rental store, take it home and play it on a home VCR; or attend a screening of the film at a local art-house movie theater (if one still exists in your neighborhood). Indeed, the makers of interactive video computer systems are beginning to use clips from the movies as basic components of their programs.

Since the parameters of what constitutes film are ever-expanding, a more encompassing definition of film study is being developed. Nichols (1992) writes that contemporary film studies programs "very often include an examination of television or other media, and many television or mass media programs include courses in aspects of film" (p. xi). However, for purposes of this chapter, film will refer to all productions shot with a movie camera (camcorders included) that were *not* shot specifically for, and limited to, television.

In reality, the convergence of media makes it difficult to define where film ends and television begins. Some of the top-grossing commercial films of 1993, are based upon old television series—*The Addams Family Values* ($44.4 million), *The Beverly Hillbillies* ($41.6 million), and *The Fugitive* ($179 million) (Klady, 1994). The 1976 commercial network showing of the film *Gone with the Wind* (in two parts) garnered a viewership of almost 34 million Americans, making it the seventh and eighth most watched television programs of all time. Videos of television series (such as the complete *Star Trek* and *Star Trek Next Generation*) sell on the shelves of video stores alongside *Apocalypse Now.*

Representative of the confusion over content and medium is the case of The Teenage Mutant Ninja Turtles. Initially a Saturday morning show for children, the Turtles quickly became the subjects of some of the best-selling books and most lucrative films of the decade. The number one children's best seller in 1990 was the initial offering in a long series to come, *Teenage Mutant Ninja Turtles,* by B. B. Hiller, which sold about 1.8 million copies. In fact, eight of the ten best-selling children's books of 1990 were books about Michaelangelo and the gang. The Turtles' third, and least financially rewarding big screen adaptation (the first film grossed over $133 million), *The Teenage Mutant Ninja Turtles 3,* grossed $42.3 million in 1993 (the thirty-first highest grossing film of the year). By comparison, the award-winning film *The Piano* grossed about $15.5 million (Klady, 1994, p. 14).

The money that Americans spend on recreation and entertainment has been steadily increasing over time, with expenditures on electronic media constituting the lion's share (Kaestle, Damon-Moore, Stedman, Teisley, & Trolluiger, 1991, pp. 153–166). Using data from the Bureau of Labor Statistics, employment experts at *Business Week* calculated that 12% of all new jobs in 1993 were generated by firms in the fields of entertainment and recreation, eclipsing the number of employees hired by the health-care industry (Mandel et al., 1994).

In 1993, Americans spent more on entertainment than ever before, including $58 billion on VCRs, TVs and prerecorded music and videotapes; $19 billion on cable television; and $13 billion on movie admissions and video rentals. In total, Americans spent $341 billion on ways to have fun. By comparison, $270 billion was spent on all the secondary and elementary schools in the country, public and private combined (Landler, 1994, p. 66).

THE INTRODUCTION OF VIDEO

In 1978, R.C.A. introduced the first programmable VCR into the American market and the first video rental store franchises sprang up around the country. By 1987, Americans were spending more on renting videos than on going to see films in theaters (Barry, Butterworth, Clark, Korman, & Pinkwas, 1993). Videocassette rentals boomed from 200 million units in 1982 to 3.6 billion rentals in 1992 (Bennett, 1994, p. 109). Network television, video, and cable have negatively affected the absolute number of ticket sales, in America and abroad, for some time. In fact, for the past 40 years, the number of theater patrons has been steadily declining in the United States, Great Britain, Japan, Italy, West Germany, and France (Doherty, Morrison, & Tracey, 1987; Ganley & Ganley, 1987.

The college campus used to be the progressive show place for the cinema, and film societies often sponsored festivals and offered subscriptions to screenings on campus. Byrne writes that "at the height of the film-society expansion in the late 1960s there were more than 4,000 individual societies functioning actively" (1971, p. 2). But, video has moved film events from the theater near campus to the dorm room of the student who has television with the 45-inch screen, 4-head VCR, Dolby stereophonic sound, and a refrigerator full of beer. At Yale University, the number of film clubs on campus dropped from seven to one between 1986 and 1990 (Hickenlooper, 1991, p. 364).

Surprisingly, despite video's penetration into the American market, revenue from films has managed to rise. In 1993, films generated over $5 billion in sales and, for the first time in 5 years, the number of ticket sales climbed to 1.1 billion tickets (from 924 million in 1992), (Klady, 1994, p. 3).

Ninety-seven percent of American have at least one television, 23% own personal computers, 73% own VCRs (Brower, 1994, p. 17), and 62% of American households subscribe to cable television (*World Almanac,* 1993, p. 295). To be sure, of the 18–27 hours a week that students watch television (Bennett, 1994, p. 103; Csikszentmihalyi & Larson, 1984, p. 8), many hours involve watching films. In a recent study of talented teens, it was found that watching television occupied 9.2% of a gifted teenager's waking hours, attending media events or concerts about 1%, and reading accounted for 3% (Csikszentmihalyi, Rathunde, & Whalen, 1993, p. 220).

FILM AND HUMAN RESPONSE

A short video, taken by nonprofessional camera operator George Holliday on his Sony camcorder, is a contemporary example that helps illustrate the power of film. On March 3, 1991, Holliday happened to record a scene in which Los Angeles police officers repeatedly beat a motorist, Rodney King, whose automobile they had stopped. Holliday's video was the focal point of an ensuing trial, which resulted in the acquittal of the four police officers, and precipitated a reign of violence and brutality in areas in Los Angeles and around the country. King and his attorneys eventually sued the city of Los Angeles and collected over $38 million.

Undoubtedly, film has the capability to foster intense emotional responses (Cantor, 1991, Zillmann & Bryant, 1986). Film and the visual media have been integral in electing government officials, determining the success or failure of a business, helping shape world opinion. Leni Reifenstahl, the head of film propaganda for Nazi Germany, was vital in elevating Hitler to the level of popularity and power that gave him reign to create the Germany of the 1930s. Expert speculate that the Berlin Wall may never have fallen if it were not for the impact of film, video, and television (Murray-Brown, 1991).

Since film has the capacity to provide a pictorial representation of lived experience (Langdorf, 1991), the moving image will almost always be more convincing than words. Consider the effects of films such as *Jaws* (1975), *Easy Rider,* (1969), *Boyz 'n the Hood,* (1992), and *Schindler's List,* (1993) on American attitudes toward sharks, hippies, urban neighborhoods, and the treatment of Jews in Nazi Germany. In the same year that *Schindler's List* (1993) was released, the legislature of the state of Florida mandated that the Holocaust be covered in every school in the state.

The poet Richard Wilbur (1970) writes, "Even the worst movie has much of the authority of the actual, and quite without knowing it one comes out of the theater brainwashed into scanning the world through the norms of the camera" (p. 167). Kraft, Cantor, & Gottdiener (1991) hypothesize that one reason that the film seems so much like actual experience is that film's structure mimics human interaction with the natural world. Viewers understand that when a scene cuts to a high angle camera shot, the characters being filmed will appear small and insignificant because they have previously looked down upon people from an elevated position (such as a tall building) and seen the same kind of image.

The trend in research on media effects has been away from the concept of viewer as passive agent to the reformulation of the viewer as active communicator (Anderson & Anderson, 1993; Rubin, 1993; Scholle, 1991). The uses and gratifications model, which assumes that certain human behaviors are motivated by the satisfaction of perceived needs, has quite a bit of empirical evidence in its favor (Blumler & Katz, 1974; Rosengren, Wenner, & Palmgreen, 1985). According to the uses and gratifications model, a young man who has become disconcerted when he notices that he is gradually losing hair, will be receptive to products that he perceives as reme-dies for his baldness.

The uses and gratifications model has been recently supplemented by examination of the complex web of processes that transpire within viewers which serve to motivate them to think and behave in certain ways, sometimes called audience activity research (Kellerman, 1985; Levy & Windahl, 1984; Lin, 1993; Wenner, 1986). For example, say the balding young man mentioned earlier happened to see a product advertised on television that promised to relieve his hair loss, and he immediately went to the drug store to purchase it. Audience activity research would examine the mental processes of the young man during different phases of the process—from the factors that contributed to his receptiveness to the advertisement to his selection of the product at the drugstore.

Through the analyses of uses and gratifications and audience activity research, one begins to understand the complexities involved in characterizing how an individual responds to film.

The Payne Fund studies, a series of 12 experiments carried out between 1929 and 1932, represent one of the first important investigations into the effects of watching movies on the behavior and attitudes of children. Some film scholars have justly criticized the Payne Studies for the lack of rigor in some experiments, for using a strong moralistic tone in reporting the results of the experiments, and for the conception of

children as passive receivers of information. Yet, few media educators today would quarrel with the three major conclusions from the studies: (a) Motion pictures serve as a potent medium of education; (b) The subject matter of many motion pictures may not be appropriate for children; and (c) The motion picture is only one influence in the complicated, ever-changing worlds of children (Charters, 1933; Holaday & Stoddard, 1933).

In the 1960s, Bandura studied how children responded to watching certain violent images on television and found that prolonged exposure to images of violence "tends to reduce the child's inhibitions against acting in a violent, aggressive manner" (Bandura, 1968, p. 126). Greeson and Williams (1986) found that junior and senior high school students were less inhibited about violence after viewing selected videos from M.T.V. A host of studies (Bandura, 1986; Hansen & Hansen, 1990a, 1990b, 1991; Sherman & Dominick, 1986) have found exposure to videos with extreme amounts of sex or violence may affect the social judgments and the personal value systems of viewers.

Eisenman, Girdner, Burroughs, and Routman (1993) found that even showing a single, short film can alter human perceptions and behavior. In their experiment, 211 college students in Mississippi were shown a film *Who is David Duke?* which provided evidence that Duke was anti-black, anti-Semitic, and pro-Nazi. Before the film was shown, 35 of the 211 students perceived Duke as anti-Semitic. After the film, 129 students perceived Duke as anti-Semitic. Before the film, 47 students said they would vote for Duke and after the film, only 33 students kept their pro-Duke position.

The viewing of specific films has also been linked experimentally with childhood phobias, traumas, and nightmares (Cantor, 1991; Cantor & Reilly, 1982; Sarafino, 1986), sensual arousal (Hansen & Krygowski, 1994), empathy (Davis, Hull, Young, & Warren, 1987; Tamborini, Salomonson, & Bahk, 1993), the use of preventive measures to combat AIDS (Maibach & Flora, 1993), the desensitization to portrayals of sexualized violence and rape (Linz, 1989; Linz, Donnerstein, & Penrod, 1988; Oliver, M., 1993) and other effects.

In a recent study of the role of the cinema in urban poor areas of Southern India, Dickey (1993) found that films served as powerful factors in the shaping of moral codes of viewers and that much of the structure of social interaction in the Indian urban community under study revolved around attending and discussing movies. In the city of Madurai (Tamil Nadu, India), where "cinema is everywhere" (p. 3), 85% of adults went to the movies at least three times a month and the state's last five Chief Ministers have been either film actors or directors.

Schneller (1988) found that small town youth in Israel spent large amounts of time watching video as compared with their central city peers. Schneller suggests that video watching in this particular rural community had become so prevalent among small town youth that it greatly reduced the time spent in person-to-person socializing activities.

Boorstin (1962), Kernan (1990), Ong (1967, 1982), and McLuhan (1962, 1964, 1967) have alerted us to the truth that politics has been forever changed by film, videotape, and television. Most candidates for major political offices today have multiple media advisors on staff to keep them apprised of modulations in public opinion. Attors for Ivan Boesky (charged with insider trading) and William Kennedy-Smith (charged with rape) both hired public relations agents to help represent their client's case to the media. In the confirmation hearings of Supreme Court Justice Clarence Thomas in 1991, both Thomas and the woman who accused him of sexual harassment, Anita Hill, were represented by public relations specialists (Schlesinger & Tumber, 1994).

Media researchers and public relations professionals have come to realize that the moving picture has an impact on audiences not only at the moment of exposure, but also potentially in any subsequent communicative transaction. (Alexander, 1993; Fry, Alexander, & Fry, 1990).

FILM STUDY IN SCHOOL—VERY BRIEF HISTORY

Robert Neal (1913) was perhaps the first to suggest that the study of film be integrated into the language arts curriculum, though he did so with much ambivalence. Neal wrote, "The moving picture is not an invention of the devil. There is a great deal in it, at the present stage of its development, that we have to think of with all the optimistic faith summonable, in order not to regard it as excessively satanic" (p. 68).

Once film was established as a mass medium, a small contingent of educators has seemingly always been around to lobby on its behalf. But, these groups have never been large enough or organized enough to affect permanent alterations in the school curriculum. The film study movement enjoyed the peak of its popularity during two periods — the 1930s and the late 1960s. In 1930, movie houses sold almost 5 billion tickets in the United Sates (compared to 1.1 billion in 1993) (Golenpaul, 1994). In the 1930s, the sheer popularity of cinema helped propel the film study movement into prominence for a period of time before it was abruptly cut off by the beginning of World War II. In the 1970s, it was the "Back to Basics" movement that eventually drove most of the film study movement's contributions to the curriculum (which were put in place in the middle to late 1960s) into quiet oblivion.

The passages below will give a brief idea of the dialogue that has ensued over the years regarding the study and use of film in school.

1915
Moving pictures everywhere will become a valuable adjunct in the mastery of skill in English composition. (Gerrish, 1915. p. 230)

1923
It is useless to condemn moving pictures; we may as well condemn all novels. ... Why not bring the movies into the schoolroom? (Cunningham, 1923, p. 490).

1936
I submit now that motion-picture appreciation is here to stay. The momentum it has created will insure its adoption, gradually but surely, not only into the high schools, but also into teacher-training institutions. (Dale, 1936, p. 113).

1948
The next ten years should show a great increase in the intelligent use of films and in the establishing of motion picture appreciation units by English teachers. (Finch, 1948, p. 170)

1952
It may properly be said that virtually every state supports to some degree a film program because every state has one or more libraries which provide films on a rental basis to the schools. (Meierhenry, 1952, p. 188)

In motion pictures the spurt of interest that occurred about fifteen years ago has died down. (Boutwell, 1952, p. 131)

1964
One believes that with the continually growing enthusiasm for film among young intellectuals, good film teachers will be easier to find in the future. ... One concludes that the future is bright for the study of film. (Selby, 1968, 226, 227).

1970
Movies are moving into the high school. The proliferation of film societies on the college level is now commonplace. (Carrico, 1970, p. 97)

1978
(In retrospect regarding his 1964 study) Looking backward, I would say that my optimism for the importance of the film as an art form in secondary school was unfounded. (Selby, 1978, p. viii)

1981
No one doubts that language, reading, and writing are central to school programs or that they are the proper business of English language arts teachers; but most people, teachers included, have strong reservations about media studies. (Karl, 1981, p. 139)

1992
With research that suggests how effective film can be, why does the medium continue to be regarded critically by school administrators, school board members, and the general public? (Lankford, 1992, p. 3)

The ebb and flow of film studies have always been tied to the social and economic climate of the nation as a whole. When times get tough, "frills" such as film study are the first courses to get cut. In this, the American educational system is not alone. Media studies, once mandated as a core subject in the English language curriculum in England, has been recently removed (Coughlan, 1993).

CURRENT AVAILABILITY / USAGE OF VIDEO AND FILM IN SCHOOLS

As early as 1982, 40% of all public school districts had VCRs. By 1985, 95% of all districts of over 1,000 students had VCRs (Quality Education Data, 1986). Today virtually every public elementary and secondary school in America, regardless of size or relative wealth, has access to VCRs (Digest of Education Statistics, 1993; Ely & Minor, 1993).

Although it is known that VCRs, computers, and audiovisual equipment are available in almost all schools, the degree to which teachers use video and film in instruction remains a mystery and must be inferred from surveys revealing the types and amounts of equipment available or from usage data from schools' regional service center (Boone, Marak, & Wilkins, 1989; Digest of Education Statistics, 1993; Main & Roberts, 1990; Quality Education Data, 1993). In one of the few studies of film use in schools, Lynch (1986) found that 60% of English teachers at the secondary level classify themselves a low or nonusers of film and that few teachers "teach film as film" (p. 250). Due to the dearth of data on film use in schools, little can be said with certainty about the ways in which teachers routinely use films or their overall effectiveness in using them.

FILM AND VIDEO COPYRIGHT LAWS AND THE CLASSROOM TEACHER

The Copyright Revision Act of 1976 was enacted to enforce long-standing copyright laws that previously had no enforcement provisions. Section 110 of the law authorizes the use of copyrighted work, such as videotapes, for use in educational settings (Miller, J., 1988). A teacher may use prerecorded videotapes and films provided certain criteria are met: (a) The film is shown in a face-to-face teaching situation; (b) a teacher, student, or guest speaker shows the film in an educational setting (such as a classroom or an auditorium) as part of an instructional plan; (c) the film is shown only to students, the teacher, and the guest speaker; (d) the copy of the film or videotape is a legal one.

Actually, very few lawsuits have ever been brought against teachers or educational institutions for copyright violations of videotapes or films. When lawsuits have been instigated, the guilty parties have exhibited blatant copyright abuses, such as the mass distribution of pirated videotapes. One of the landmark cases in copyright legislation has to do with an educational services company (called BOCES) operating out of Buffalo, New York. BOCES regularly taped programs from cable television programs without permission, made copies of them, then circulated them throughout the school district. The judge ruled against BOCES and fined them $63,500 in statutory damages (Resch & Schicker, 1992, p. 134)

Technically, the Copyright Revision Law of 1976 makes it illegal to show movies that serve as pure entertainment to students. According to the law, the film needs to be part of the instructional plan of the teacher.

FUNCTIONS OF FILM AND VIDEO IN THE CONTEMPORARY CLASSROOM

Suhor (1986) analyzed the number of articles concerning nonprint media appearing in the journals *College English, College Composition and Communication, English Journal,* and *Elementary English* (later, *Language Arts*) during the period 1961–78. Suhor found that of the 1799 articles about nonprint media, all but 55 could be classified as falling into one of six groups: theoretical, practical, referential, analytical, mechanical, and qualitative.

I have chosen to sort film into five categories based upon how a teacher might use it in the classroom. The categories are as follows: (a) film as a teaching tool, (b) film as a component of media literacy, (c) film as art and artifact, (d) film as student project, and (e) film as a supplement to the study of literature.

Film as a Teaching Tool

Perhaps the least controversial use of film in the secondary classroom has been its use as an instructional tool to bolster student achievement. Many studies since the 1940s, including a good deal of research performed by the offices of the U.S. armed forces, have tested the effectiveness of film in helping to educate students, workers, and soldiers. The results of such tests often yielded bold praise for the medium of film as a tool for instruction. However, as Clark (1983, 1985, 1991, 1992) has repeatedly pointed out, media comparison studies that find greater learning gains in the newer media often fail to consider "novelty effects." In addition, the failure of researchers to maintain adequate control over aspects of the instructional design sometimes translates into unequal presentation of content to participants. Thus, when Clark writes, "During the early days of the motion picture, studies tended to favor movies over teachers" (1992, p. 806), he means that the superiority shown by films was due to differences in content in the studies, not due to some mystical, enriching power of the medium of film.

Conversely, Ullmer (1994) and Kay (1991) contend that the differential content in studies that find superior achievement in newer media might instead be the result of a natural propensity of the newer medium. That is, each medium possesses its own strengths, some of which make it more appropriate than other media for particular kinds of learning. In the medium-driven configuration, results are thought to be traceable to the inherent advantages and appeals of the delivery systems themselves. Such a philosophical stance would seem to substantiate one of McLuhan's infamous convictions, that "the medium is the message."

Researchers in the field of educational technology (Cennamo, 1993a, 1993b; Krendl, 1986; Saloman, 1983, 1984, 1992; Saloman & Leigh, 1984) have found that humans perceive learning to be easier from the moving image (using media such as film, video, interactive video, and television) than from books. Perhaps its reputation as an "easy" medium and its consistent record of educational gains are two reasons for the endurance of film as a teaching tool in a variety of fields. This is not to say that the use of film has become ubiquitous across subject areas, but that a small group of educators in a variety of subject areas regularly use film.

A glance at recent publications reveals that film is being used to teach about madness (Fleming, Piedmont, & Hiam, 1990), mathematics, (Kelly, Wiebe, & Hynes, 1993), critical thinking skills (Guista, 1992; Remender, 1992), the German language and culture (Flippo, 1993), children's social development (Boyatzis, 1994), law (Anderson, 1992), race relations (Loewen, 1991), popular culture (Groce, 1992), sociology (Berg, 1992; Tipton, 1993), propaganda (Rhiel, 1993), attitude toward the elderly (Cross, 1989), race relations (Manley, 1994), biology (Faulkner, 1993) and, of course literature.

Film as a Component of Media Literacy

One could reasonably argue that the birth of the media literacy movement in America began shortly after the invention of the motion picture. Today, media literacy (also known as "visual literacy" or "critical viewing skills") occupies a space inclusive of cultural and anthropological studies, pop culture, television, advertising, radio, music, newspapers, news reporting, computers, interactive video, virtual reality, photography, and film. According to the National Telemedia Council, media literacy is "the ability to access, analyze, evaluate and create information in a variety of media formats including print and non-print" (Telemedium, 1994. p. 28).

Deconstruction, once a literary term for literary analysis, serves as a major theme throughout the literature on media literacy. According to Considine and Haley (1992), "Media literacy means evaluating and analyzing the form, content, origin, and impact of media messages" (p. 19). The techniques of the French literary postmodernists (such as Baudrillard, 1983, Derrida, 1992; Lyotard, 1984) are invoked in the deconstruction of media messages in advertising (Glasgow, 1994), feature films (Palmer, 1989), and other media, though they are not often mentioned by name.

There is some evidence that the media literacy movement is gaining some momentum. Portions of *The Goals 2000: Educate America Act,* signed by President Clinton in April 1994, contain provisions for the establishment of standards for media literacy at the elementary and secondary levels. Interestingly, the standards are recommended within the standards for arts, not English. The states of North Carolina, Florida, and New Mexico already have provisions promoting the teaching of media literacy in school, while Hawaii and California were considering its addition in 1994. Brown (1991) and Bazalgette, Sevoty, & Savino (1993) have chronicled the rise of media education worldwide. Some evidence exists that film education may even be on the ascent in the new Russia (Drobashenko & Sadchikov, 1992).

In 1934, William Lewin wrote, "The contemporary movie, like the contemporary novel, the contemporary drama, the newspaper, the magazine, the radio... is something to enjoy, to discuss, to analyze, to think about, something to use as a starting point from which to move toward an appreciation of the best things that life and literature have to offer" (p. 38). Such a critical stance would seem as apt for media literacy today as it was for the film study movement of 1934.

Film as Art and Artifact

One of the strengths of film is its ability to capture and preserve moments in time. Most of us remember certain events, places, and persons with more clarity if we have photographs or movies to help jar our recollections. With film, as with literature, newer words do not replace older works, but are annexed into the domain's cumulative archives. Zefferelli's *Hamlet* (1990, starring Mel Gibson) does not supplant Kline's *Hamlet* (1990, starring Kevin Kline), which does not supplant Richardson's *Hamlet* (1969, starring an elderly Nicol Williamson), which does not supplant Kozintsev's *Hamlet* (1964, a Russian film starring Innokenti Smoktunovsky), which does not supplant Gielgud's *Hamlet* (1964, starring Richard Burton), which does not supplant Kurosawa's *The Bad Sleep Well* (an adaptation of Hamlet set in modern Japan, 1960, starring Tohiro Mifune) which does not supplant Olivier's *Hamlet* (1948, starring Laurence Olivier), or any of the 10 other versions of *Hamlet* made since 1915 (Esner, 1985; McMurtry, 1994).

The body of work that is "film" is continually expanding. Kaes (1992) writes that, "Film constitutes a collective memory that, however much it splinters into innumerable individually remembered images, forgets nothing." (p. 317).

Since film is generally accepted as an authentic record of events, some anthropologists have argued against the use of film in describing customs or cultures. The fear is that documenting events by using film may actually inhibit objective discussion and analysis (Raymond, 1991). Certainly, there is a grain of truth in the statement that film is an unwitting part "of and ideological conspiracy in which we are invited to look back at our past through the distortions of our present culture" (Giddings, Selby, & Wensley, 1990, p. xi).

Semiotics, or the science of signs, allows scholars to examine the ways in which media images represent reality and ideology (Gibson, 1979; McArthur, 1992; McGinty, 1987; Rank, 1991; Scholes, 1982). In studying the semiotics of the mass media, critics such as George Gerbner (1988, 1992), assert that the film presented by personalities of the mass media often reinforces stereotypes and reduces the complexities of real life. Truly, the mass media are often blamed for creating conflict, fabricating (or prefabricating) history, and manipulating interpretation of world events in such a manner as to bolster its audience share. It is not uncommon for contemporary analysis of media to hold film responsible for oppressing or suppressing a particular segment of society. One recent study (Everett, 1994) blamed the American mass media for damaging the self-esteem of all ethnic minority children through the uniform portrayal of a unicultural world.

Works such as *Teaching the Sixties* (Workman, 1992), *Projections of War* (Doherty, 1993), *Hollywood as Historian* (Rollins, 1983), and *American History / American Film* (O'Connor & Jackson, 1980) advocate analysis of film as a document of social history as well as its value as an artistic creation. Knight (1972) claims that "the most interesting use of film in English teaching is its use to increase an understanding of the formal qualities of art" (p. 36). In an earlier study of film at the secondary level, Selby (1968) found that schools rarely, if ever, considered the aesthetic properties of film.

Cocteau called film "a petrified fountain of thought" (in Plimpton, 1989, p. 248). In terms of diversity and ubiquity, film offers semioticians and aesthetes a resource for analysis unrivaled in the world of art.

Film as Student Project

The portability and affordability of the camcorder has democraticized film and video and allowed teachers and students the luxury of considering its use for the classroom. Steinman (1993) has described how a video camera might be used in a science class to monitor experiments. Beasley (1994), Berwick (1994), Brown (1993), Catron (1991), Faulkner (1993), Hannafin (1991), Lang (1986), Turner (1989), and others have discussed the advantages of using video camcorders to enhance the student's learning experience in a variety of fields. Baines (1995) and Lasky (1990) have contended that use of the camcorder helps students attain a deeper sense of media literacy than that attained through simply studying media messages.

Using the camcorder as a format for creative endeavors by students would seem to be an obvious match with some educational reform efforts aimed at "empowering students" and getting the teacher "off the stage as a sage." Higgins (1991) views the camcorder as an opportunity to implement the philosophies of Freire in the classroom. Higgins writes, "If one does not work actively against the canons of visual representation, or at a minimum question them, one is working to support the existing methods of shaping reality. ... The education of students in video production is a political activity" (p. 26).

Burns (1991) has even suggested that using the camcorder to shoot videos should be the equivalent of publishing works in print for faculty under consideration for tenure at the postsecondary level. The camcorder opens the possibility for a permanent record of individual progress and activity. Some states, such as Vermont, already advocate the inclusion of videotape in the state-mandated portfolio for each student in public school.

Film as a Supplement to the Study of Literature

A teacher of English is most likely to use a film when it relates directly to a literary work covered in class (Lynch, 1983). The most popular techniques of teachers who use film with literature involve either asking students to compare a film with a recently completed novel or showing the film as a sort of reward for getting through the book. Although students tend to enjoy watching films without having to think about them or discuss them much, allowing the student to remain passive viewers has probably drawn the strongest criticism in the literature (Considine & Haley, 1992; Gardner, P., 1992; Watson, 1990).

A growing sect of educators has shown interest in the use of filmed adaptations as a device for improving the comprehension skills of low-achieving students. Goldman (1990), McKenzie (1993), Shiring (1990), and Squires (1990) have found filmed adaptations effective in filling in gaps for reluctant readers or special populations, such as students designated as "at-risk." McDonald (1983) suggests using film to improve the language skills of students. Bottge and Hasselbring (1993) argue that videos may help low-achieving students to construct mental models that are richer than those derived solely from text (in Skolnik & Smith, 1993, p. 23).

The differences and similarities between film and the novel have been debated at length (Admussen, 1978; Aycock & Schoenecke, 1988; Beja, 1979; Biro, 1982; Bluestone, 1957; Boyum, 1985; Cohen, 1979; Costanzo, 1985, 1992; Cox & Many, 1989; Esner, 1985; Fadiman, 1978; Gardner, P., 1991; Giddings et al., 1990; Harrington, 1977; Hulesberg, 1978; Jinks, 1974; Kawin, 1977; Kittridge & Krauzer, 1979; Klein & Parker, 1981; Knight, 1972; Magill, 1976; Magney, 1972; Manchel, 1990; Marcus, 1971, 1977; Maynard, 1971; McConnell, 1979; McDougal, 1985; Miller, G. 1980; Miller, J., 1986; Millichap, 1983; Murray, 1972; Oliver, 1989; Peary & Shatzkin, 1977, 1978; Richardson, 1969; Ross, 1991; Self, 1987; Sheridan, Owen, Macrorie, & Marcus, 1965; Sinyard, 1986; Sohn, 1970; Speigel, 1976; Street, 1983; Wagner, 1975; Weinberg, 1973; and others).

When discussing the similarities in the two media (film and the novel), scholars usually conclude that both film and literature are narrative arts—both exist to tell a story. Miller (1986) asserts that the two media share the capability to create an invisible structure to which the viewer or reader responds. Like a reader who must ignore the construction of the text in order to continually derive meaning from it (Iser, 1989), the viewer is rarely conscious of every cut or change in camera angle. Yet, it is the cut and the angle of the camera that give much of film its meaning (Kraft, 1986, 1987).

A third similarity is that much of the jargon of literary criticism is equally applicable to film. Plot, symbolism, theme, tone, characterization, foreshadowing, and setting are terms as applicable to film as text.

Despite the similarities, most writers agree with Bluestone (1957), that "the film and the novel remain separate institutions, each achieving its best results by exploring unique and specific properties" (p. 218). The differences between the film and the novel noted most often in the literature are these: (a) Film is dominated by the image, while literature is bound by the word. (b) Time constraints limit what films can and cannot do. (c) Novels are usually produced by an individual working alone for a limited audience, while films are made by group of individuals for a larger audience. (d) With film, star power almost always wins out over storyline if the two should ever collide (Baines, 1993).

An intriguing area of exploration is the degree to which writers of novels have been influenced by films and other mass media. Hamilton (1990) chronicled the efforts of Faulkner, Fitzgerald, Chandler, and others who dabbled in screenwriting for Hollywood. Hamilton found that the lure of money and steady work was irresistible to writers, famous or not, who usually had to eke out a living on the paltry royalties from books.

Others who have examined the effects of film and nonprint media on the literary achievements of writers have found a certain symbiosis between writers and filmmaking. For example, Millichap (1983) asserts that Steinbeck drew his documentary style "from the photography and films of the period" (p. 176). Early filmmaker D.W. Griffith is said to have often consulted the work of Charles Dickens in the making of his films. It was also through Dickens' novels that Russian director Eisenstein uncovered the ideas of montage, dissolve, and close-up (Eisenstein, 1949).

It is probable that popular novelists such as Grisham, Crichton, and Walker consider the possibility of screen adaptations before they even pick up their pens or turn on their computers. Certainly, a writer would find it difficult to ignore that a filmed adaptation earned $350 million or so at the box office in a year (as Crichton's *Jurassic Park* did in 1993).

FILM AS FILLER

The view of film as "trash culture" persists as the dominant image that many educators hold today toward motion pictures. Even though teachers cannot legally show students rented films as entertainment (because it is a violation of copyright laws), administrators still view the use of films as somehow taking time away from other areas of "more serious study" (Perry & Gluckman, 1990). It is not uncommon for a teacher who uses film often to be viewed as lazy or incompetent by fellow teachers and administrators, regardless of the benefit students may reap in their interactions with film. When the Education Secretary for England, John Patten, was asked why he was considering the elimination of media studies in English schools, Patten replied that media studies were a "cultural Disneyland for the weaker-minded" (*Clipboard*, 1994, p. 15).

One of the biggest obstacles to the use of film in school has always been its identification with "light entertainment." Gutenberg created movable type so that mankind could read and understand the Word of God (the *Bible*). On the other hand, the Lumiere brothers created film to astound and entertain a paying audience. Perhaps the different circumstances involved in the inceptions of print and film help account for some of our lingering sentiments about them.

FILM, VIDEO, AND LINGUISTICS

In a study of the language of novels and the films adapted from them, Baines (1993) found a dramatic difference in how language is employed in novels and in film. In brief, a novel exhibited a greater variety of words, more polysyllabic words, and significantly longer, more complex sentences than did its film adaptation. Language in film tended toward repetition, simplicity, and the use of short, direct sentences.

Obviously, in its current manifestation, film does not come close to the richness of the linguistic environment available through books. Critics of nonprint media are correct when they note that entrance into undergraduate or graduate study at the postsecondary level still requires satisfactory scores on standard tests such as the Scholastic Aptitude Test (SAT) and Graduate Record Exam (GRE), which lean heavily on linguistic and logical assessments of intelligence. However, film's strong points are not words, but accessibility, immediacy, and the ability to communicate visually and aurally at the same time. Only the most bookish of us would rather read a five-page description of a sunset than view its Technicolor glory on the big screen while listening to Samuel Barber's *Adagio for Strings*.

Many educational reformers (Gardner, H., 1983, 1991, 1993 among the most prominent) have recommended that schools broaden their concept of literacy. Whether or not schools will undertake such a transformative view of literacy

remains to be seen. Two things are indisputable—film cannot do what books can; books cannot do what film can.

THE FUTURE OF FILM AND VIDEO

The field of data compression has the potential to change film and video as they currently exist. Technologies utilizing data compression procedures are currently being used in relation to the development of High Density Television (HDTV), the transference of motion pictures to compact disc, and the further advancements of interactive technologies. Media will continue to converge, as telephone companies experiment with video communications, and video companies play with the possibilities of digital technology. Tele-Communications Inc., the largest cable operator in the United States will have lain $2 billion worth of fiber-optic cable by 1996 (Beachum, 1993). Meanwhile, the world's largest entertainment company, Time Warner, is building a fully interactive experimental cable television system in Orlando, Florida, and scientists promise that virtual reality will alter the human conception of "visualization" and "experience" (Auld & Pantelidis, 1994; Helsel, 1992).

In the current milieu of exploding technologies, those who advocate film study in school find themselves in the awkward position of advocating the use of a medium that is no longer considered technologically advanced. The film study movement of the 1930s was the result of the public perception of film as a high-tech medium, as well as the movie house's central position in the social lives of students. Research over the past 30 years has shown overwhelmingly that it is television that occupies the central position in the social lives of students today. Also, as we venture into the next millennium, the obsession of forward-thinking educators is with computers and telecommunications, not with film.

While trends in technology and education would seem to warrant a bleak forecast for film study in the classroom, two factors militate against such negativism. First, many newer electronic technologies are based upon the moving image. The motion picture, now with a history of more than 100 years, is in the unique position of being the most established electronic communications medium of the day still in widespread use. As Culkin (1972) has noted, "A lot of things have happened since 1900 and most of them plug into the wall" (p. 88). Knowledge of how and why we create meaning through viewing a film is the kind of literacy that is transferrable to the real world, a world inundated with visual and aural stimuli.

Second, because film study has become subsumed under the mantle of mass media (which includes the computer, CD-ROM, interactive video, and other electronic devices), its fortunes have become inextricable with those of other, newer media. Thus, as the push for the infusion of technology in schools grows, the acceptability of mass media including film also grows.

Unlike most elementary and secondary schools, other factions of American society have shown a genuine willingness to work with film. Today, police officers use videotape to record evidence at the scene of a crime, doctors probe with tiny cameras to observe and record the workings of a patient's internal organs, mom and dad use video to record the development of their child, beginning with the baby's first movements inutero.

Over 50 years ago, Hoban wrote, "Motion pictures have all the vital ability to influence and improve education that the printing press had five hundred years ago" (1942, p. 4). While film has never reached the pinnacle of influence predicted by Hoban, no other medium has better represented life in the 20th century.

References

Admussen, R. (1978). Novel into film: An experimental course. *Literature/Film Quarterly, 6*(1), 66–72.

Alexander, A. (1993, March). Exploring media in everyday life. *Communication Monographs,* 55–61.

Amelio, R. (1972). *Film in the classroom.* Cincinnati, OH: Standard Publishing.

Anderson, D. (1992). Using feature films as tools for analysis in a psychology and law course. *Teaching of Psychology, 19*(3), 155–158.

Anderson, J., & Anderson, B. (1993). The myth of persistence of vision revisited. *Journal of Film and Video, 45*(1), 3–12.

Auld, L., & Pantelidis. V. (1994, January/February). Exploring virtual reality for classroom use. *Tech Trends,* 29–31.

Aycock, W., & Schoenecke, M. (Eds.). (1988). *Film and literature: A comparative approach to adaptation.* Lubbock, TX: Texas Tech.

Baines, L. (1993). Aspects of language in literature and film (Doctoral dissertation, The University of Texas, 1993). *Dissertation Abstracts International, 54*(4), 1268.

Baines, L. (1995, February). Scripting screenplays. An idea for integrating reading, writing, and media literacy. *English Journal,* 86–91.

Bandura, A. (1968). What TV violence can do to your child. In O. Larsen (Ed.), *Violence and the mass media.* New York: Harper & Row.

Bandura, A. (1986). *Social foundations of thought and action.* Englewood Cliffs, NJ: Prentice-Hall.

Barry, J., Butterworth, B., Clark, B., Korman, K., & Pinkwas, S. (1993, September). Nonstop revolution. *Video,* 58–61.

Baudrillard, J. (1983). *Simulations.* New York Semiotext.

Bazalgette, C., Sevoty, E., & Savino, J. (1993). *New directions: Media education worldwide.* London: British Film Institute.

Beachum, F. (1993, September). Fifteen years. *Video,* 77–81.

Beasley, A. (1994). The camcorder revolution. *School Library Media Activities Monthly, 10*(5), 38–39.

Beja, M. (1979). *Film and literature: An introduction.* New York: Longman.

Bennett, W. (1994). *The index of leading cultural indicators.* New York: Touchstone.

Berg, E. (1992, October). An introduction to sociology using short stories and films. *Teaching Sociology,* 265–269.

Berwick, B. (1994, April). Kids behind the camera: Education for the video age. *Educational Leadership,* 52–54.

Biro, Y. (1982). *Profane mythology.* Bloomington, IN: Indiana University Press.

Bluestone, G. (1957). *Novels into film.* Los Angeles: University of California Press.

Blumler, J., & Katz, E. (Eds.). (1974). *The uses of mass communications: Current perspectives on gratifications research.* Beverly Hills, CA: Sage.

Boone, B., Marak, D., & Wilkins, C. (1989, January). The impact of high technology. *Educational Technology,* 38–42.

Boorstin, D. (1962). *The image.* New York: Harper & Row.

Bottge, B., & Hasselbring, T. (1993, April). Taking work problems off the page. *Educational Leadership,* 31–38.

Boutwell, W. (1952, March). What can we do about movies, radio, television? *English Journal,* 131–136.

Boyatzis, C. (1994, April). Using feature films to teach social development. *Teaching of Psychology,* 99–101.

Boyum, J. (1985). *Double exposure: Fiction into film.* New York: Universe Books.

Brower, A. (1994, June 6). Home technology key to the future. *Brandweek,* 17.

Brown, J. (1991). *Television "critical viewing skills" education.* Hillsdale, NJ: Erlbaum.

Brown, K. (1993). Video production in the classroom. *Tech. Trends, 38*(3), 32–35.

Burns, G. (1991, Fall). Production theory as administrative research. *Journal of Film and Video,* 30–40.

Byrne, R. (1971). Study of film. In L. Deighton (Ed.). *The encyclopedia of education, Vol. 4*(pp. 1–9). New York: Macmillan.

Campbell, J., & Moyers, B. (1988). *The power of myth.* New York: Doubleday.

Cantor, J. (1991). Fright responses to mass media productions. In J. Bryant & D. Zillmann (Eds.), *Responding to the screen: Reception and reaction processes* (pp. 169–197). Hillsdale, NJ: Erlbaum.

Cantor, J., & Reilly, S. (1982). Adolescents' fright reactions to television and films. *Journal of Communication, 32*(1), 87–99.

Carrico, J. (1970). Film and the teaching of English. In A. Schillari & J. Culkin (Eds.), *Films deliver* (pp. 97–115). New York: Citation.

Catron, L. (1991). Camcorder 101: Buying and using video cameras. *Teaching Theatre, 2*(2), 5–8.

Cennamo, K. (1993a). Students' perceptions of the ease of learning from computers and interactive video: An exploratory study. *Journal of Educational Technology Systems, 21*(3), 251–263.

Cennamo, K. (1993b). Learning from video. Factors influencing learners' preconceptions and invested mental effort. *Educational Technology Research and Development, 41*(3), 33–45.

Charters, W. (1933). *Motion pictures and youth. A summary.* New York: Macmillan.

Clark, R. (1983). Reconsidering research on learning from media. *Review of Educational Research, 53,* 445–459.

Clark, R. (1985). Confounding in educational computing research. *Journal of Educational Computing Research, 1*(2), 28–42.

Clark, R. (1991, February). When researchers swim upstream. Reflections on an unpopular argument about learning from media. *Educational Technology,* 34–38.

Clark, R. (1992). Media use in education. In M. Alkin (Ed.), *Encyclopedia of educational research, Vol. 3* (pp. 805–814). New York: Macmillan.

Clipboard (1994, Summer). International clippings, p. 15.

Cocteau, J. (1989). In G. Plimpton, (Ed.), *The writer's chapbook.* (p. 248). New York: Viking.

Cohen, K. (1979). *Film and fiction. The dynamics of exchange.* New Haven, CT: Yale University.

Considine, D., & Haley, G. (1992). *Visual images.* Englewood, CO: Teacher Ideas Press.

Costanzo, W. (1985). *Double exposure. Composing through writing and film.* Upper Montclair, NJ: Boynton/Cook.

Costanzo, W. (1992). *Reading the movies.* Urbana, IL: National Council of Teachers of English Press.

Coughlan, S. (1993, April 23). Battle of the books. Media's removal as a required component of English. *Times Educational Supplement,* N4008, p. I.

Cox, C., & Many, J. (1989). World of possibilities in response to literature, film, and life. *Language Arts, 66*(3), 287–294.

Cross, C. (1989). The influence of a positive portrayal of specific elderly individuals in a film series on the cognitive, affective, and behavioral components of children's attitudes toward the elderly. (Doctoral disseratation, The University of Maryland at College Park, 1989). *Disserfation Abstracts International, 50,* 3799A.

Csikszzentmihalgi, M., Rathunde, K, & Whalen, S. (1993). *Talented teenagers.* New York: Cambridge University Press.

Csikszentmihalyi, M., & Larson, R. (1984). *Being adolescent.* New York: Basic Books.

Culkin, J. (1972). A schoolman's guide to Marshall McLuhan. In T. Giblin (Ed.), *Popular media & the teaching of English* (pp. 82–90). Pacific Palisades, CA: Goodyear.

Cunningham, A. (1923, September). Teaching English with the movies. *English Journal,* 488–490.

Dale, E. (1936, February). Teaching motion picture appreciation. *English Journal,* 113–120.

Davis, M., Hull, J., Young, R., & Warren, G. (1987). Emotional reactions to dramatic film stimuli. *Journal of Personality and Social Psychology, 17,* 616–640.

Derrida, J. (1992). *Acts of literature.* New York: Routledge.

Dickey, S. (1993). *Cinema and the urban poor in South India.* New York: Cambridge University Press.

Digest of Educational Statistics (1993). Washington, DC: National Center for Education Statistics.

Doherty, T. (1993). *Projections of war.* New York: Columbia University Press.

Doherty, D., Morrison, D., & Tracey, M. (1987). *The last picture show?* London: British Film Institute.

Drobashenko, S., & Sadchikov, I. (1992, Spring/Summer). The main tendencies of the film education system in Perestroika. *Journal of Film and Video,* 91–96.

Durgnat, R. (1967). *Films and feelings.* Cambridge, MA: MIT Press.

Eder, B. (1993, September). 15 titles that shook the world. *Video,* 68–84.

Eidsvik, C. (1978). *Cineliteracy.* New York: Horizon.

Eisenman, R., Girdner, E., Burroughs, R., & Routman, M. (1993, Fall). *Adolescence,* 527–532.

Eisenstein, S. (1949). *Film form: Essays in film theory.* New York: Harcourt, Brace and Jovanovich.

Ely. D., & Minor, B., (Eds.). (1993). *Educational Media and Technology Yearbook,* 1993.

Esner, A. (1985). *Filmed books and plays.* Lexington, MA: Lexington Books.

Everett, S. (1994). The endangered post-modern childhood. *Intermedia, 22*(2), 30–33.

Fadiman, R. (1978). *Faulkner's intruder in the dust. Novel into film.* Knoxville, TN:University of Tennessee Press.

Faulkner, S. (1993). Videomicroscopy using a home camcorder. *American Biology Teacher, 55*(5), 304–306.

Finch, H. (1948). In G. Elliot, *Film and education.* New York: Philosophical Library.

Fleming, M., Piedmont, R., & Hiam, C. (1990). Images of madness: Feature films in teaching psychology. *Teaching of Psychology, 17*(3), 185–187.

Flippo, H. (1993, Fall). Marlene Dietrich in the German classroom. *Die Unterrichtspraxis,* 132–139.

Fry, V., Alexander, A., & Fry, D. (1990). Textual status, the stigmatized self, and media consumption. In J. Anderson (Ed.), *Communication yearbook 13* (pp. 519–544). Newbury Park, CA: Sage.

Ganley, G., & Ganley, O. (1987). *Global political fallout. The first decade of the VCR.* Norwood, NJ: Ablex.

Gardner, H. (1983). *Frames of mind.* New York: Basic Books.

Gardner, H. (1991). *The unschooled mind.* New York: Basic Books.

Gardner, H. (1993). *Multiple intelligences. The theory in practice.* New York: Basic Books.

Gardner, P. (1991, October). Narrative crossings: Film adaptations in the literature class. *Teaching English in the Two-Year College,* 217–224.

Gardner, P. (1992). Makers and users of knowledge. Literary recreation in the classroom. *Journal of Teaching Writing, 11*(1), 19–33.

Gerbner, G. (1988). *Violence and terror in the mass media.* Paris: Unesco.

Gerbner, G. (1992). Persian Gulf War, the movie. In H. Mowlana, G. Gerbner & H. Schiller (Eds.), *Triumph of the image* (pp. 243–265). Boulder, CO: Westview Press.

Gerrish, C. (1915, April). The relation of moving pictures to English composition. *English Journal,* 226–230.

Gibson, J. (1979). *The ecological approach to visual perception.* Boston: Houghton Mifflin.

Giddings, R., Selby, K., & Wensley, C. (1990). *Screening the novel.* London: Macmillan.

Glasgow, J. (1994). Teaching visual literacy for the 21st century *Journal of Reading, 37*(6), 494–500.

Goldman, M. (1990, November). American fiction for reluctant readers. *English Journal, 78,* 79.

Golenpaul, D. (Ed.). (1994). *Information please almanac.* New York: McGraw-Hill.

Greeson, L., & Williams, R. (1986). Social implications of music videos for youth. *Youth & Society, 18,* 177–189.

Groce, S. (1992, January). Teaching the sociology of popular music with the help of feature films. *Teaching Sociology,* 80–84.

Guista, M. (1992, October). Siskel and Ebert, move over. *Teaching English in the Two Year College,* 206–209.

Hamilton, I. (1990). *Writers in Hollywood.* New York: Harper & Row.

Hannafin, K. (1991). Technology and the support of at-risk students. *Journal of General Education, 40,* 163–179.

Hansen, C., & Hansen, R. (1990a). Rock music videos and antisocial behavior. *Basic and Applied Social Psychology, 11,* 357–370.

Hansen, C., & Hansen, R. (1990b). The influence of sex and violence on the appeal of rock music videos. *Communication Research, 17,* 212–234.

Hansen, C., & Hansen, R. (1991). Schematic information processing of heavy metal lyrics. *Communication Research, 18,* 373–411.

Hansen, C., & Krygowski, W. (1994, February). Arousal-augmented priming effects: Rock music videos and sex object schemas. *Communication Research,* 24–47.

Harrington, J. (1977). *Film and/as literature.* Englewood Cliffs, NJ: Prentice-Hall.

Helsel, S. (1992, May). Virtual reality and education. *Educational Technology,* 38–42.

Hickenlooper, G. (1991). *Reel conversations.* New York: Citadel Press.

Higgins, J. (1991, Fall). Video pedagogy as political activity. *Journal of Film and Video,* 18–29.

Hoban, C. (1942). *Focus on learning. Motion pictures in the school.*

Washington DC: American Council on Education.

Holaday, P., & Stoddard, G. (1933). *Getting ideas from the movies.* New York: Macmillan.

Hulesberg, R. (1978, Winter). Novels and films. A limited inquiry. *Literature/Film Quarterly,* 57–65.

Iser, W. (1989). *Prospecting: From reader response to literary anthropology.* Baltimore: Johns Hopkins University Press.

Jinks, W. (1974). *The celluloid literature.* Beverly Hills, CA: Glencoe.

Kaes, A. (1992). History and film. In B. Murray & C. Wickham (Eds.), *Framing the Past* (pp. 298–324). Carbondale, IL: Southern Illinois University Press.

Kaestle, C., Damon-Moore, H., Stedman, L., Tinsley, K., & Trollinger, W. (1991). *Literacy in the United States.* New Haven, CT: Yale University Press.

Karl, H. (1981). What it means to be media competent. In C. Cooper (Ed.), *The nature and measurement of competency in English* (pp. 139–163). Urbana, IL: National Council of Teachers of English.

Kawin, B. (1977). *Faulkner and film.* New York: Ungar.

Kay, A. (1991, September). Computers, networks, and education. *Scientific American,* pp. 138–148.

Kellerman, K. (1985). Memory processes in media effects. *Communication Research, 12,* 83–121.

Kelly, M., Wiebe, J., & Hynes, M. (1993, September). Teaching mathematics with technology. *Arithmetic Teacher, 41–43.*

Kernan, A. (1990). *The death of literature.* New Haven, CT: Yale University Press.

Kittridge, W., & Krauzer, S. (Eds.). (1979). *Stories into film.* New York: Harper & Row.

Klady, L. (1994, January 24). WB grabs top share of 1993. *Variety,* 14–21.

Klein, M., & Parker, G. (Eds.). (1981). *The English novel and the movies.* New York: Ungar.

Knight, R. (1972). *Film in English teaching.* London: Hutchinson Educational.

Kraft, R. (1986). The role of cutting in the evaluation and retention of film. *Journal of Experimental Psychology, 12*(1), 155–163.

Kraft, R. (1987). The influence of camera angle on comprehension and retention of pictorial events. *Memory & Cognition, 15,* 291–307.

Kraft, R., Cantor, P., & Gottdiener, C. (1991, October). *Communication Research,* 601–616.

Krendl, K. (1986). Media influence on learning. *Educational Communications Technology Journal, 34,* 223–234.

Lacey, R. (1972). *Seeing with feeling. Film in the classroom.* Philadelphia, PA: W.B. Saunders.

Landler, M. (1994, March 14). Are we having fun yet? May be too much. *Business Week,* p. 66.

Lang, F. (1986). Shooting essays. *Teaching English in the Two-Year College, 13*(4), 281–289.

Langsdorf, L. (1991). The emperor has only clothes: Toward a hermeneutic of the video text. In A. Olson, C. Parr & D. Parr (Eds.), *Video: Icons and values* (pp. 45–62). Albany, NY: State University of New York Press.

Lankford, M. (1992). *Films for learning, thinking, and doing.* Englewood, CO: Libraries Unlimited.

Lasky, K. (1990). Perceptions of television programming among college students with varying degrees of video production experience. *Educational Research Quarterly, 14*(2), 48–52.

Levy, M., & Windahl, S. (1984). Audience activity and gratifications: A conceptual clarification and exploration. *Communication Research, 11,* 51–77.

Lewin, W. (1934, January). The business of running a high school movie club. *English Journal,* 38.

Lin, C. (1993, December). Modeling the gratification-seeking process

of television watching. *Human Communication Research,* 224–244.

Linz, D. (1989). Exposure to sexually explicit materials and attitudes toward rape: A comparison of study results. *Journal of Sex Research, 26*(1), 50–84.

Linz, D., Donnerstein, E., & Penrod, S. (1988). Effects of long-term exposure to violent and sexually degrading depictions of women. *Journal of Personality and Social Psychology, 55,* 758–768.

Loewen, J. (1991, January). Teaching race relations from feature films. *Teaching Sociology,* 82–86.

Lynch, J. (1983). *Film education in secondary schools.* New York: Garland.

Lynch, J. (1986). Film education research: An overview. *Teaching English in the Two-Year College, 13*(4), 245–253.

Lyotard, J.(1984). *The postmodern condition.* Minneapolis, MN: University of Minnesota Press.

Magill, F.(Ed.). (1976). *Cinema: The novel into film.* Pasadena, CA: Salem Softbacks.

Magney, C. (1972). *The age of the American novel: The film aesthetic of fiction between the two wars.* New York: Ungar.

Maibach, E., & Flora, J. (1993, August). Symbolic modeling and cognitive rehearsal. *Communication Research,* 517–545.

Main, R., & Roberts, L. (1990, December). Educational technology in California public schools. *Educational Technology,* 7–19.

Manchel, F. (1990). *Film study: An analytical bibliography, Vols. 1–4.* Cranbury, NJ: Associated University Press.

Mandel, M., Landler, M., Grover, R., DeGeorge, G., Weber, J., & Rebello, K. (1994, March 14). Entertainment, *Business Week,* pp. 58–64.

Manley, T. (1994). Teaching race and ethnic relations. *Ethnic and Racial Studies, 17*(1), 135.

Marcus, F.(Ed.). (1971). *Film and literature: Contrast in media.* London: Chandler.

Marcus F. (Ed.). (1977). *Short story, short film.* Englewood Cliffs, NJ: Prentice-Hall.

Maynard, R. (1971). *The celluloid curriculum: How to use movies in the classroom.* Rochelle Park, NJ: Hayden.

McArthur, D. (1992). Sign function and potential of the printed word. *Visible Language, 26*(3), 282–297.

McConnell, F. (1979). *Storytelling and mythmaking: Images for film and literature.* New York: Oxford University Press.

McDonald, B. (1983). *Basic language skills through films.* Littleton: Libraries Unlimited.

McDougal, S. (1985).*Made into movies: From literature to film.* New York: Holt, Rinehart, & Winston.

McGinty, S. (1987, January). Deconstructing "Citizen Kane." *English Journal,* 46–50.

McLuhan, M. (1962). *The Gutenberg galaxy.* Toronto: The University of Toronto Press.

McLuhan, M. (1964). *Understanding media: The extensions of man.* New York: Signet.

McLuhan, M. (1967). *The medium is the message.* New York: Bantam Books.

McKenzie, B. (1993). Ten innovative uses of video with at-risk students. *Clearinghouse, 66*(1), 238–240.

McMurtry, J.(1994). *Shakespeare films in the classroom.* Hamden,CT: Archon.

Meierhenry, W. (1952). *Enriching the curriculum through motion pictures.* Lincoln, NE: University of Nebraska Press.

Miller,G.(1980). *Screening the novel: Rediscovered American fiction in film.* NewYork: Ungar.

Miller, H. (1979). *Films in the classroom: A practical guide.* Metuchen, NJ: Scarecrow.

Miller, J. (1986). *Subsequent performances.* London: Faber.

Miller, J. (1988). *Using copyrighted videocassettes.* Friday Harbor, WA: Copyright Information Services.

Millichap. J. (1983). *Steinbeck and film.* New York: Ungar.

Murray, E. (1972). *The cinematic imagination: Writers and the motion pictures.* New York: Ungar.

Murray-Brown, J. (1991). Video ergo sum. In A. Olson, C. Parr, D. Parr (Eds.), *Video: Icons and values* (pp.17–32). Albany, NY: State University of New York Press.

Neal, R. (1913, December). Making the devil useful. *English Journal,* 658–660.

Nichols, B.(1992).Film studies. In E. Laskin (Ed.), *The American Film Institute guide to setting started in film,* (pp. xi–xiii). New York Prentice-Hall.

O'Connor, J., & Jackson, M. (Eds.). (1980). *American history, American film.* New York: Ungar.

Oliver, C. (Ed.). (1989). *A moving picture feast: The filmgoer's Hemingway.* New York: Praeger.

Oliver, M. (1993, February). Adolescents' enjoyment of graphic horror. *Communication Research,* 30–50.

Ong. W. (1967). *The presence of the word.* New Haven, CT: Yale University Press.

Ong. W.(1982). *Orality and literacy.* New Haven, CT: Yale University Press.

Palmer, R. (Ed.). (1989). *The cinematic text.* New York: AMS Press.

Peary, G., & Shatzkin, R. (Eds.). (1977). *The classic American novel and the movies,* New York; Ungar.

Peary, G., & Shatzkin, R. (Eds.). (1978). *The modern American novel and the movies.* New York: Ungar.

Perry, A., & Gluckman, I. (1990). Using (and misusing) movies. *Principal, 70,* 59–61 .

Postman, N. (1985). *Amusing ourselves to death.* New York: Penguin.

Quality Education Data (1986). *Microcomputer and VCR usage in schools. Denver: Quality Education Data.*

Quality Education Data (1993). State school guide. Denver: Quality Education Data.

Rank, H. (1991). *The pitch.* Park Forest, IL: Counter-propaganda Press.

Raymond, C. (1991). Increasing use of film by visually oriented anthropologists stirs debate over ways scholars describe oher cultures. *Chronicle of Higher Education, 37*(28), A5.

Remender. P. (1992). Using feature films to encourage critical thinking. *Southern Social Studies Journal, 17*(2), 33–44.

Resch, K., & Schicker, V. (1992). *Using film in the high school curriculum.* Jefferson, NC: McFarland.

Rhiel, M. (1993, Spring). Teaching Arturo Ui: Triumph of whose will? *Die Unterrichtspraxis,* 67–69.

Richardson, R.(1969). *Literature and film.* Bloomington, IL: Indiana University Press.

Rollins, P. (Ed.). (1983). *Hollywood as historian.* Lexington, KY: University Press of Kentucky.

Rosenblatt, L. (1978). *The reader, the text, the poem.* Carbondale, IL: Southern Illinois University Press.

Rosengren, K., Wenner, L., & Palmgreen, P. (1985). *Media gratifications research: Current perspectives.* Beverly Hills, CA: Sage.

Ross, N. (1991). Literature and film. *ELT Journal, 45*(2), 147–155.

Rubin, A. (1993, March). Audience activity and media use. *Communication Monographs,* 98–105.

Saloman, G. (1983). The differential investment of mental effort in learning from different sources. *Educational Psychologist, 18,* 42–50.

Saloman, G. (1984). Television is "easy" and print is "tough." *Journal of Educational Psychology, 76,* 647–658.

Saloman, G. (1992). New information technologies in education. In M. Alkin (Ed.), *Encyclopedia of educational research, Vol. 3* (pp. 892–903). New York: Macmillan.

Saloman, G., & Leigh, T. (1984). Predispositions about learning from print and television. *Journal of Communication, 34,* 119–135.

Sarafino, E. (1986). *The fears of childhood.* New York: Human Sciences Press.

Schlesinger, P., & Tumber, H. (1994, June/July). The politics of crime reporting. *Intermedia,* 16–19.

Schneller, R. (1988, June). Video watching and its societal functions for small-town adolescents in Israel. *Youth and Society,* 441–459.

Scholes, R. (1982). *Semiotics and interpretation.* New Haven, CT: Yale University Press.

Scholle, D. (1991, Spring/Summer). Reading the audience, reading resistance. *Journal of Film and Video,* 80–90.

Selby, S. (1968). The study of film as an art form in American secondary schools (Doctoral dissertation, Columbia University, 1968). *Dissertation Abstracts International, 24*(12), 5098.

Selby, S. (1978). *The study of film as an art form in American secondary schools.* New York: Arno Press.

Self, R. (1987). Film and literature: Parameters of a discipline. *Literature/Film Quarterly, 15*(1), 15–21.

Sheridan, M., Owen, H., Macrorie, K., & Marcus, F. (1995). *The motion picture and the teaching of English.* New York: Appleton-Century-Crofts.

Sherman B., & Dominick, J. (1986). Violence and sex in music videos: TV and rock 'n' roll. *Journal of Communication, 36,* 70–93

Shiring, J. (1990, October). Free reading and film. *English Journal,* 37–40.

Sinyard, N.(1986). *Filming literature: The art of screen adaptation.* London: Croon Helm.

Skolnik, R., & Smith, C. (1993). Utilizing video technology to serve the needs of at risk students. *The Journal for Vocational and Special Needs Education, 16*(1), 23–31.

Smith, R. (1969). Film, new media and aesthetic education. *The Journal of Aesthetic Education, 3*(3).

Sohn, D.(1970). *Film: The creative eye.* Dayton, OH: Pflaum.

Speigel, A. (1976). *Fiction and the camera eye.* Charlottesville VA: University Press of Virginia.

Squires. N. (1990). A Freireian-inspired video curriculum for at-risk high school students. *English Journal, 79*(2), 49–56.

Steinman, R. (1993, April). Cameras in the classroom. *Science Teacher,* 16–19.

Street, D. (Ed.). (1983). *Children's novels and the movies.* New York: Ungar.

Suhor, C. (1986). Media and English: What happened? *Teaching English in the Two-Year College, 3*(4), 254–260.

Tamborini, R., Salomonson, K., Bahk, C. (1993, October). The relationship of empathy to comforting behavior following film exposure. *Communication Research,* 723–738.

Telemedium (1994, Summer). What is media literacy? p. 28.

Tipton, D. (1993, April). Using the feature film to facilitate sociological thinking. *Teaching Sociology,* 187–191.

Turner, D. (1989). The art teachers' new tool: The video camcorder. *School Arts, 89*(4), 27–28.

Ullmer, E. (1994). Media and learning: Are there two kinds of truth? *Educational Technology Research and Development, 42*(1), 21–32.

Wagner, G. (1975). *The novel and the cinema.* Cranbury, NJ: Associated University Presses.

Watson, R. (1990). *Film and television in education: An aesthetic approach to the moving image.* London: Falmer Press.

Weinberg, H. (1973, Spring). Novel into film. *Literature/Film Quarterly.* 98–102.

Wenner, L. (1986). Model specification and theoretical development in gratifications sought and obtained research. *Communication Monographs, 53,* 160–179.

Wilbur, R. (1970). A poet at the movies. In T. Ross (Ed.), *Film and the liberal arts* (pp. 167–170). New York: Holt, Rinehart, & Winston.

Workman, B. (1992). *Teaching the sixties.* Urbana, IL: National Council of Teachers of English Press.

World Almanac (1993). New York: Newspaper Enterprise Association.

Zillmann, D., & Bryant, J. (1986). Exploring the entertainment experience. In D. Zillmann & J. Bryant (Eds.), *Perspectives on media effects* (pp. 303–324). Hillsdale, NJ: Erlbaum.

47

ELECTRONIC DISCOURSE COMMUNITIES: THEORY, PRACTICE, AND RESEARCH

Wayne M. Butler

UNIVERSITY OF MICHIGAN

Some contemporary literacy educators might be startled if they were to walk into one of the hundreds of university, college, and high school classrooms where students learn literacy on-line. They would see a score of students sitting in front of personal computer monitors, their hands alternately perched over keyboards and reaching reflexively for mouses, their fingers flailing away at keyboards in a flourish, pausing intermittently to read off their monitors not only the words they are writing but those of their peers as well. The relative lack of human voices would be underscored by the clackity clack of keys. Although these students might, during certain class meetings anyway, seem mute and silent, they are anything but isolated and alone; they are linked, through their networked computers, into a literate learning community in which more of them will participate in the class's meaning-making discourse than they typically would in traditional classrooms, they will contribute to a textual conversation made up of more diversity in voices and perspectives than would be possible in other settings, and they will be more engaged and active learners than they might be in more traditional literacy environments.

Major shifts in the ways in which we conceive of literacy—the acts of reading, writing, and meaning making through text—parallel the advances in technology. More important, perhaps, than the changes in the physical conditions under which texts are produced, and perhaps even more important than the way in which literacy is taught, is the effect of literacy technologies on language itself and what it means to be literate. The confluence of language and literacy theories, pedagogical practice, and technology have resulted in what might be called electronic discourse communities; ones founded on contemporary social views of language, literacy and education; ones bulwarked by the new network technologies that become both simpler to use and offer greater access within and across networks; and ones that already are

reaching out beyond classrooms and school buildings and into a site where virtual communities exist in cyberspace.

Before embarking on a physical description of pedagogy in and research concerning electronic discourse communities, it is important to define what might be meant by "literacy" for the purpose of this chapter. We have long abandoned a narrow vision of literacy as the ability to decode and encode texts. Most theorists and researchers agree on a broader view of literacy, one that, of course, requires encoding and decoding, skills but goes beyond to what James Boyd White describes as more than

> the capacity to understand the conceptual content of writings and utterances but the ability to participate fully in a set of social and intellectual practices. [Literacy] is not passive but active, not imitative but creative, for participation in the speaking and writing of language includes participation in the activities it makes possible. (Robinson, 1990, p. 17)

And, just as the definition of literacy has moved from the ability to read and write to the ability to participate in and contribute to the social and intellectual practices of a literate culture, the notion of computer literacy, one that began with the idea that it was enough to know how to operate a computer, has taken on broader ramifications as technology has ushered in the information age. This chapter does not address how computers might be used to help readers and writers learn the decontextualized skills that are thought to contribute to literacy but rather how computer technology creates a means of literate communication wherein students learn to read and to write by reading and writing within a community, albeit a virtual one, of other readers and writers.

Computer technology is an encompassing term that includes hardware, such as mainframes, PC compatibles, Macintoshes and CD-ROM players, and sundry software applications, such as drill and practice, word processing, and hypertext programs, each of which might deserve separate discussions on their effects on literacy. Furthermore, the various developmental stages at which readers and writers might use technology each suggests different possible effects. What follows, however, is a description, analysis, and discussion of one way in which technology, in the form of local (LAN) and wide (WAN) networks, is affecting how more and more students at a growing number of institutions are learning how to write. Since such electronic writing is being done within a community of writers, members of the community are readers, too.

WHAT IS AN ELECTRONIC DISCOURSE COMMUNITY?

On one level, an electronic discourse community can be housed in a physical place, a classroom, perhaps one designed exclusively for the English department, with a dozen to thirty personal computers. Another setting might be a library with a bank of personal computers or a general purpose computer lab of a dozen or so computers in which teachers reserve times for classroom meetings or individual students drop in during study halls, lunch hours, between classes, or after school. In such places, the desks, tables, and carrels on which the machines sit may be arranged in rows as in a traditional classroom. In other places the tables might be arranged around the perimeter of the room, the monitors facing inward, with a large conference table in the middle. While yet in other settings the furniture may be clustered in pods, with four or five computers per pod and four to five pods per room. On another level, the electronic discourse community is not a physical space at all. Instead, members of the community may be sitting at home, in a classroom, or in a public library at a personal computer, one with a modem connecting the computer to the telephone line that links them with a virtual community, one that exists in cyberspace.

The physical relationship among the computers, though each configuration can create different dynamics (Boiarsky, 1990), is less important than the technological relationship among the machines. The computers in an electronic discourse community are not stand-alone machines running software based on behavioristic notions of programmed learning and electronic workbooks or word-processing programs with spell and style checkers. Such stand-alone configurations, after all, suggest individualistic models of learning, ones in which writers and readers interact with the machine and interface with software in attempts to master literacy skills, often in the absence of authentic communication. The electronic discourse community comes to being in one of two ways. In one scenario, the computers are linked together by cables and network software into a local area network (LAN) that allows applications, such as word processors, and files, ones consisting of both student and professionally produced texts, to be shared among those on the network. While the LAN links anywhere from several to a hundred microcomputers through a local server, other networks can be created through mainframes or powerful personal computers linked together over vast geographical

areas into wide area networks (WAN), such as the Internet, that expands the infrastructure of electronic discourse communities from the classroom to the truly global level.

In addition to electronic literacy tools such as word processing, desktop publishing and, in the truly cutting edge environments, hypermedia and hypertext programs, the network will include computer-mediated conferencing programs such as e-mail and synchronous or "real-time" conferencing. E-mail can support one-to-one messaging and can offer discussion lists where participants broadcast their messages to all those subscribed to the discussion group or list. Whereas e-mail operates asynchronously, that is, allowing participants to send and receive messages at their leisure, synchronous conferencing programs, ones that operate in real time, require participants to be logged onto the network at the same time so they can participate in text-based discussions with other members of the discourse community. In such programs, participants have access to both a text editor with which they compose their contributions and a communal transcript to which their contributions are appended, thus allowing all members of the community to engage in a discussion. At the local level, community members include both classmates and teachers; at the WAN level, community members include millions of potential participants.

Merely buying computers and linking them together into a local area network is not enough, however, to build an electronic discourse community. As Gail Hawisher and Cynthia Selfe (1991) have pointed out, network technology can and has been used to promote top-down, teacher-centered pedagogies and behavioristic models of skills acquisition. Underlying the technological infrastructure of electronic discourse communities are social theories of language, literacy, and pedagogy.

Theoretical Basis for Electronic Discourse Communities

During the last several decades a number of strands running through the fabric of what we call literacy education have recognized that language—its acquisition and its use—though comprised, perhaps, of discrete skills and used by individuals, is essentially a social act. For Lev Vygotsky, "Development in thinking is not from the individual to the socialized, but from the social to the individual" (Gere, 1987, p. 81). Dialogue models of language acquisition theorize that the construction of meaning through language is an interactive process between language producers and language perceivers. When discussing the prelingual stage of a child's language acquisition, Jerome Bruner (1981) explains that "formats," cognitive schemata that language learners must develop in order to manipulate the conventions of conversation, are developed through the interaction of the child with its environment and caretakers (p. 44). A number of contemporary rhetorical theorists have focused on the social aspects of language and communities. Lester Faigley's (1986) "social view," Kenneth Bruffee's (1986) "social constructionism," and James Berlin's (1988) "social-epistemic," are related, as Berlin notes, "because they share a notion of rhetoric as a political act involving a dialectical interaction engaging the material, the social, and the individual writer, with language as the agency of mediation" (p. 488). Contemporary literary critics also recognize the role "community" plays in the meaning making process. Stanley Fish (1980) and David Bleich (1975) both contribute to the notion that "it is interpretive communities, rather than the text or the reader, that produce meaning and are responsible for the emergence of formal features" (p. 14). Bleich, when discussing his conception of the interpretive community, writes.

> Interpretation is always a group activity, since the individual interpreter is creating his statement in large part with an eye towards who is going to hear it. That is his community, whether it is of students, teachers, reviewers, or critics. ... For this reason interpretation is a communal act. (pp. 94, 95)

PEDAGOGY IN NETWORKED LITERACY CLASSROOMS

What teachers and students actually do in networked classrooms grows out of the collaborative learning pedagogies that model social views of language. At the outset of her book, *Writing Groups: History, Theory, and Implications,* Anne Ruggles Gere (1987) lists the various names and phrases from "writing groups" to "intensive peer review" that have been applied to pedagogical practices modeling social views of cognition, language, and literacy. To these could be added James Moffet's (1968) "naturalistic curriculum," Robert Slavin's (1983) "cooperative learning," and George Hillocks (1986) "environmental mode" pedagogy. What all these techniques have in common, of course, is the recognition of social dynamics in any learning situation which asks students to work together to solve problems. "Collaborative learning," a specific version of group work, "assumes a socially derived view of knowledge and opposes a fixed and hierarchical one" (Gere, p. 75). In practice, the role of the teacher is to create "conditions in which students engage in conversation, both face-to-face conversation and conversation displaced into writing" and "social structures in which students can learn to take over the authority of learning as they gain the ability and confidence to do so" (Bruffee, 1985, pp. 8, 13).

The types of pedagogical practices often employed in the networked classroom, those based on collaborative learning, have been explained by Thomas Barker and Fred Kemp (1990) in an essay entitled, "Network Theory: A Postmodern Pedagogy for the Writing Classroom." They argue that the computer-based collaborative-learning classroom places social constructivist learning theory at the very center of pedagogy, thereby undermining the proscenium style of teaching that places the teacher on the stage and the students in the audience. The proscenium classroom, according to Barker and Kemp, enforces notions of the teacher as sole authority and arbiter of knowledge, a model in direct opposition to contemporary learning, pedagogical, and critical theories that view knowledge as a social construct. Writing in the computer-networked setting becomes a tool for communication, not simply a product for an evaluator. Furthermore, students' texts rather than instructors' evaluations become the focus of class activity. Barker and Kemp write, "Network

theory ... empowers the student writer ... [and] rejects elitist epistemologies which support an 'information transfusion' or teacher-centered model of instruction in favor of social constructivist models which privilege a communal process of knowledge making" (1990, p. 26).

Attempts to separate the acts of reading and writing in the networked classroom create a false dichotomy because members of the electronic discourse community are bound to one another through text. What they write is always to be read by others in the community; what they read has been written, for the most part, by others in the community. What follows is a survey of how literacy educators have used network pedagogy to help students gain what Robert Scholes (1985) calls "textual power," by helping them

> to see that every poem, play, and story is a text related to others, both verbal pre-texts and social sub-texts, and all manner of post-texts including their own responses, whether in speech, writing, or action ... (to understand) the web (of interaction and intertextuality), to make it real and visible..., to cast their own strands of thought and text into this network so that they will feel its power and understand both how to use it. ... (pp. 20, 21)

Teaching Critical Reading and Literary Interpretation

In those courses in which, critical reading & texts represents the content, a typical instructional sequence begins with students reading the text. The "discussion" of the text can then be conducted in one of several ways. For example, students might compose on a word processor a response-statement to the poem or short story under study. If the focus text is nonfiction, students write on their word processor a critical analysis of the piece, focusing on the main ideas, the mode of development, the line of argument or other salient features. These response statements are then copied to an e-mail conference or a real-time electronic conference, a procedure which allows students to publish their readings for the entire community.

Once these initial reactions are posted, on-line discussions about both the focus text and the community's responses to the text ensue. Students are offered time (class time if using a LAN with limited nonclass time access; nonclass time if students have access to the LAN after hours or if working on a WAN) to read the responses written by others in the community (students may read all classmates' reactions or just those of some predefined subgroup, depending on the class size) and engage in on-line discussions that focus on the range of possible readings inspired by the focus text as evidenced by the range of readings offered by community members. Students describe and analyze the differences among the various readings and their interactions with one another to negotiate for "best" or "strong" readings (Butler, 1992).

During such negotiations, those whose readings are challenged are placed in the rhetorical situation of having to argue for their reading by further explicating the focus text and supporting their argument with details from the reading selection. Those mounting the challenges then need to offer, in response to the writer's argument for her reading, counter arguments. Such interaction forces the critic to offer more detail about the stimulus text and the writer's response to it. Students often are asked to postulate how and why a single text can lead to the multiple interpretations that inevitably arise during such activities. Throughout these on-line discussions of readings, students are using language in a social setting to communicate, express, analyze, and argue about language. And, each member of the community is not only writing with a purpose, but reading in an intensive literacy environment in which their communication with peers is all through text. In such settings, participants learn literacy "from the class of discourses, ... through engaging in discourse" (Cooper & Selfe, 1990, p. 867).

The on-line instructional sequence described above can be applied to various learning situations by changing the stimulus for the discussion. In the rhetoric classroom, the stimulus might be an important text which tackles a controversial issue, such as George Wald's treatment of the creationism versus evolutionism debate in "The Origin of Life" (Butler & Kinneavy, 1991). In other composition classrooms focusing on cultural criticism through ethnographic writing, ethnographies become the sites of electronic interaction (Faigley, 1992). Socially constructing knowledge through networks, furthermore, need not be confined to the English classroom. In history classrooms, for instance, where on-line writing-to-learn is used as a vehicle to study history, the stimulus might be an historical text or issue such as "Should the U.S. participate in WWI?," an activity in which students, who have researched various positions from the points of view of historical figures from the period, argue the issue by taking on the personas of these historical figures (Wax & Butler, 1993).

Teaching Writing On-Line

In the writing classroom, the stimuli for text-based social interaction can be student drafts. The traditional activities of peer editing and critiquing take on a new dynamic when students submit their drafts electronically to the community and the community members offer on-line critiques through real-time electronic conferencing or e-mail. Because using e-mail or electronic conferencing does not support the writing of marginalia or intratextual commentary, peer critics are encouraged to comment on the communicative rather than surface features of drafts. And, since the on-line peer critique process is interactive, writers are engaged with their readers in the discussions of their texts.

Stimuli for on-line discussions need not be only published or student-drafted formal texts. Since, for example, many electronic conferencing programs allow participants to compile and print transcripts, these records of the discussions can be used as stimuli for follow-up discussions or sources for writers. In the composition classroom in which argumentation is the focus, transcripts capturing on-line debates about a controversial issue can provide writers evidence of the various points of view surrounding the issue. In the history classroom in which students have argued an issue on-line from the various perspectives of historical personas, students use the transcripts as sources for research papers. Such uses of electronic conference transcripts serve

the purpose of validating and privileging the language and socially constructed knowledge of the electronic discourse community and thus permitting students to use their language to study their language.

RESEARCH ON ELECTRONIC DISCOURSE COMMUNITIES

Electronic discourse communities are relatively new literacy sites and those who have taught in, researched, and written about them have articulated a diverse, if not always unified, set of observations and questions. Using various research methods including linguistic analysis, discourse analysis, ethnography, and experimental studies, researchers have described the characteristics of language used in electronic conferences, analyzed how electronic conferencing fosters environments considered crucial in the learning and teaching of reading and writing, and studied the effects of writers' participation in electronic discourse communities on writing achievement. Despite what Hawisher and Selfe (1991) have called the "rhetoric of technology," that is, discourse about technology and literacy characterized "uncritical enthusiasm" (p. 56), caveats, critiques, and contradictory findings abound.

Characteristics of Language On-Line

Investigators of electronic conferencing have argued that interactive writing serves to bridge some of the gaps between speaking and of writing, bringing reading, writing, and speaking closer together than previously believed possible. Faigley (1992), for example, notes, "The result is a truly hybrid form of discourse, something between oral and written, where the conventions of turn-taking and topical coherence are altered. Another difference from oral discussion is that students can move back and forth in the emerging transcript to check what was 'said' earlier" (p. 168). Murray (1985), who analyzed discourse features of two computer scientists using electronic conferencing, concludes that the language of electronic conferencing is semipermanent, can be partly planned, is subject to time delays, and lacks visual paralinguistic and nonlinguistic cues. To avoid ambiguity, users articulate topic shifts and gloss reference items. The electronic discourse reveals less fragmentation than oral discourse, change of voice is handled through pronoun use and choice of diction, and the interaction of these characteristics results in complex turn-taking, with conventional turn-taking principles of oral discourse being violated.

Perceived Benefits

Perhaps more important than the effect of electronic conferencing on language itself are the cultural aspects of electronic discourse communities, that is, how participating in such environments affects how literacy is learned and taught and how it affects members of the communities. A number of researchers have commented on how electronic conferencing can create conditions believed to be conducive to the learning of writing. When discussing the possible advantages of synchronous communication with basic writers, Thompson (1988) notes that electronic conferencing is "promising for basic writers because it offers them a link between their generally adequate oral language skills and their weak, reluctant writing" (p. 17). Joy Kreeft Peyton and Trent Batson (1986) claim that "the network provides the conditions now considered crucial for writing development: a close relationship between reading and writing activities; writing with a strong sense of context with a known and present audience" (p. 6). According to Schriner and Rice (1989), electronic conferencing "promotes a new sense of community, rather than isolated study" (p. 478).

Electronic discourse communities provide not only environments considered crucial for writing development, but they also tend to undermine the authority structures of traditional academic discourse, ones in which teachers dominate, a minority of students control what little student talk there is (Karp & Yoels, 1983), and women and minorities are marginalized. Such shifts in who contributes when and how are crucial in electronic communities built on social constructivist assumptions that such learning sites must encourage and privilege student to student interaction in meaningful ways to negotiate problems concerning the creation, comprehension, and interpretation of texts. Various studies have confirmed, that within electronic communities not only does student discourse take an equal or more dominant place as compared to teachers' discourse (Butler, 1992; Butler & Kinneavy, 1991; Faigley, 1992), but females (Bump, 1989; Selfe, 1990) and minorities (Butler, 1992; Faigley, 1992) have better opportunity to participate in meaning-making discourse. In an ethnographic study of a college writing-intensive literature classroom, for example, Butler found that over the course of four real-time electronic conferences throughout a 15-week semester, 100% of the students participated in each session and student turns accounted for 89% of the classroom discourse, with the teacher and participant observer accounting for the rest of the turns. During those four, 1-hour sessions the average student took 4.4 turns per session. The most active student (a Caucasian female) took 6.25 turns per session while the least active (an Asian-American male) took 1.5 turns per session. The males, who comprised 60% of the class population, accounted for 59% of the turns with the females accounting for 41% of the turns.

A number of reasons exist as to why the traditionally marginalized find more space in electronic discourse than they do in the oral discourse of traditional classrooms. Hiltz and Turoff (1978) and Faigley (1992) note that because within electronic conferences all participants can contribute simultaneously, it becomes more difficult for one person to dominate (including the teacher), and no one can be interrupted. Also, because only participants' words are transmitted, computer conferencing is less intimate and self-exposing than face-to-face verbal interaction and therefore nonverbal cues such as personal mannerisms and handicaps do not influence the message. Thus, write Hiltz and Turoff, participants "can feel more free to express disagreements or suggest potentially unpopular ideas. In addition, statements may be considered on their merit rather than by the status of their proponents" (p. 27). Kiesler, Siegal, and McGuire have speculated that "charismatic and high status people may have less influence, and group members may participate more equally in computer communication" (Hawisher, 1992, p. 88). As a result of more participants contributing to community discourse than might otherwise be possible in traditional educational settings, members are exposed to a greater diversity of ideas (Langston & Batson, 1990; Schwartz, 1990).

Participants in electronic discourse communities have demonstrated and reported positive attitudes and behaviors toward membership and participation in networked environments. Faigley (1990) describes the phenomena of his students arriving early to and leaving late from his networked computer classroom. Schriner and Rice (1989) report that most of their students who used electronic conferencing as a supplement to their normal class activities, often logged on everyday while some logged on more than once a day, and Hiltz (1990) writes of electronic conference participants perceiving electronic conferencing as "fun."

Butler (1992) reports that college students who had just completed a writing-intensive literature course in a networked classroom using electronic conferencing attested to differences between their learning styles and attitudes as compared with other courses taken across the university, including previous English courses. When asked to compare their learning styles in the electronic discourse community with those of other courses in the university, 84% claimed they were more active learners. When asked to compare their learning styles in the networked course with those of previous English courses, 92% felt they were more active. And, when compared to previous English classes in traditional academic settings, 100% claimed that they enjoyed the computer-based course more. When asked how much they learned about language, literature, and writing in the electronic discourse community as compared with in previous English courses, 69% felt that they had learned more. A similar anonymous survey completed by at-risk high school students studying American History in a networked writing classroom revealed that 71% felt working with the networked computers improved their classroom behavior, 81% claimed they were more engaged in learning, and 90% felt they learned more about history than they had in other history classes completed during high school (Wax & Butler, 1993).

Gail Hawisher (1992) draws upon Erving Goffman's terms "absorption" and "engrossment" to label the increased levels of participant involvement reported by those studying electronic conferencing. Citing Andrew Feenberg's analogy between conferencing and game playing, that "we are drawn in by interest in the next step in the process of interaction more than by any other motive," Hawisher surmises:

> Such gaming intrigues participants and probably in part accounts -for why students remain after class to continue both asynchronous and synchronous on-line discussions: They want to see what happens next. Since the entire game consists of reading and writing, we might say that participants are involved in a game of literacy. ... (p. 88)

Caveats, Criticism, and Contradictions

Electronic discourse communities, however, are not utopian literacy sites. What some researchers have considered the benefits of electronic conferencing, that is, the increased amounts of electronic text students produce (Butler & Kinneavy, 1991; Schriner & Rice, 1989), can also lead to communication anxiety (Hawisher, 1992) and sensory overload (Butler, 1992; Hawisher, 1992) as a result of technostress (Bump, 1990) and the seemingly incoherent and disunified discourse. Neuwirth et al. (1993) add to the list of disadvantages, including "concurrent network interaction," lower communication efficiency, less effective discourse production, emotionality and uninhibited remarks (flaming) because of the written medium and "less reflective responses because of the pressures of interactive communication" (p. 207). A number of studies suggest that despite the more egalitarian access to meaning-making discourse provided by electronic conferencing, true equality may not always be achievable. And, the several studies that have looked for significant gains in writing achievement of those students working within electronic discourse communities as compared to those working in traditional classrooms have found little.

Much of the criticism of networked interaction comes from those who have experienced the downside of the kinds of conversations that mask writers' identities. Within these electronic discourse communities in which more candid contributions by participants whose identities can be masked by pseudonyms or by the lack of paralinguistic cues and social markers, candor can turn into rancor. Susan Romano (1993), in a critique of what she calls the "egalitarianism narrative," studied the content of Mexican-American students' electronic conference messages looking for evidence of not merely more turn-taking but if their words concerning a play, *Los Vendido,* had any impact on influencing the stereotypes of Mexican-Americans held by their Anglo classmates. What she found, however, was despite the fact that the nine Hispanic students (out of a class of 19 students) contributed nearly half the text within a real-time electronic conference, "university-educated Mexican-Americans are mentioned only five times" (p. 24). What Romano observed made clear to her "that because opportunity exists for the marginalized to either center themselves or validate the margins does not mean they will welcome that opportunity" (p. 10). Alison Regan (1993), in her study of networked discourse in a class debating current gay rights issues, writes

> the voices of gay and lesbian students and instructors are at least as silenced in the networked classroom as in the traditional classroom, and may in fact be more silenced, for the electronic medium provides homophobic students with the space to express themselves in ways that serve to further suppress gay and lesbian voices. (p. 13)

In the study cited earlier in which Butler (1992) found certain egalitarianism in quantitative terms, a content analysis of students' electronic messages and an interaction analysis of whose messages were actually read, considered, and integrated into the communal knowledge of the discourse community revealed much to support Romano's critique of the egalitarianism narrative. More access and participation in the written conversations did not necessarily lead to more power for females, nonnative speakers of English, and those whose literacy skills, in terms of reading ability and writing fluency, lagged behind those of their more influential classmates. By the end of a 15-week semester, once students' identities were both constructed by themselves and by their classmates, those who most influenced topic strands, communally negotiated interpretations of literary texts, and were most often identified by their peers as intellectual leaders demonstrated characteristics of traditional academic discourse. The leaders wrote well, were assertive rather than qualifying, and "spoke" in teacherly, authoritative tones. English as a second language students whose impromptu online contributions were often ungrammatical and difficult to comprehend, those with poor typing skills who felt handicapped by the velocity of the real-time conferencing, and those with most problems comprehending, reflecting upon, and writing about the literary selections and their peers' online texts were read less often and were taken less seriously by others. Based on his observations Butler concludes, "when given the opportunity to restructure the discourse of education, the community relied on the old blueprints to build new walls" (p. 391).

Several researchers have measured growth in the writing achievement of students participating in electronic.' discourse communities. Although many proponents of on-line literacy surmise that students become better writers because they write more text more often, entertain a more diverse range of perspectives and ideas, develop a better sense of audience, and write for real purposes, several studies that have looked systematically at writing achievement cannot demonstrate that students writing on networks outperform those who do not. Gail Hawisher (1992) reports on studies by Hiltz (1990) and Neuwirth et al. (1993) that found no improvement in student writing, but Hawisher notes that Hiltz attributed her lack of positive findings to possible shortcomings in the holistic scoring system.

More extensive and thorough studies, however, have also failed to demonstrate that students writing on networks, in comparison with students learning to write in traditional settings, produce significantly better formal, academic texts. David Bartholomae (1993), in his role as outside evaluator for the Electronic Networks for Interaction (ENFI) Consortium, collected essays from the beginning, middle, and end of both ENFI and non ENFI basic writing classes at three postsecondary institutions. His analysis of almost 3,000 pages of text from both groups led Bartholomae to conclude, "I do not believe that the ENFI writers write any better than the non-ENFI writers" (p. 259). He did not notice, moreover, significant interdraft revisions in either group. His descriptions of ENFI produced texts as compared to non-ENFI produced texts revealed that "ENFI essays were less formal, more colloquial, less predictable, more individualized, less likely to present themselves as texts, and more likely to imagine a direct form of address" (p. 240). He tempered his findings, however, by noting that even though the ENFI essays were less formal and less predictable, "to my mind this is an advantage" (p. 261). He recommends:

For teachers who are eager for students to see the effects of a conversational style, for teachers who are eager for students to talk back to experts or break the format of the book report of the term paper, the networks could be seen as beneficial. (p. 261)

In another type of analysis of ENFI writing, Mary Fowles (1993) administered to 228 ENFI and 230 non-ENFI students from five ENFI Consortium sites writing prompts derived from the Educational Testing Service's Pre-Professional Skills Test. Students wrote pretests at the beginning of the semester and posttests at the end. A team of nine trained readers evaluated the essays following the ETS's Guidelines for Free-Response Scoring. Interreader discrepancy rate was 3.45%, which Fowles characterizes as "respectable" (p. 271). The results revealed that both groups improved slightly from pre- to posttest, but "since gains were nearly the same for both groups, the use of the ENFI network did not appear to contribute significantly to student writing ability" (p. 271).

CONCLUSION

What emerges, then, from the research on writing and reading in electronic discourse communities are theoretical perspectives from which to view these new sites and contradictory findings concerning the efficacy of learning to write well with the aid of networked computers. This latter fact, however, must not deter literacy educators from pursuing, indeed embracing, these new technologies for a number of reasons.

First and foremost is the fact that for better or for worse, electronic conferencing has gone beyond a novel way to teach students how to write. Local area networks now serve as hamlets connecting to wide area networks, which have expanded from military to university communication networks, growing presently into the Internet, that vast web of interconnected networks on which the Information Superhighway will be based. In many educational settings today, students sitting at their personal computers on local area networks have instant and transparent access to the millions of people worldwide who have become part of what Howard Rheingold (1993) has called the virtual community. Conservative estimates consider 5,000 the number of "attached regional, state, federal, campus, and corporate networks" (Fraase, 1993, p. 10) consisting of 750,000 computers. Others estimate 25 million people have access to the Internet alone (Elmer-Dewitt, 1994), excluding those who interact textually on local area networks and the commercial networks like America On-Line and Prodigy. Estimated Internet growth is as much as 10% a month (Fraase, 1993). Whereas in the early days of networked communication relatively few government and educational scientists and researchers populated virtual space, the educational, political, commercial, and recreational worlds are now on-line. The Internet includes on-line publications, retail services, access to local and national politicians, and recreational newsgroups. The Internet is a vast textual space, one in which the ability to read and write for civic, corporate, and personal reasons becomes increasingly crucial.

If we return for a moment to James Boyd White's definition of literacy as "the ability to participate fully in a set of social and intellectual practices" and understand that those practices are, or at least will become, inseparable from computer-mediated communication, we as literacy educators would be remiss not to usher our students into the age of on-line literacy.

References

Barker, T. T., & Kemp, F. O. (1990). Network theory: A postmodern pedagogy for the writing classroom. In C. Handa (Ed.), *Computers in society: Teaching composition in the twenty-first century* (pp. 1–27). Portsmouth, NH: Boynton/Cook.

Bartholomae, D. (1993). "I'm talking about allen bloom": Writing on the network. In B. Bruce, J. K. Peyton & T. Batson (Eds.), *Network-based classrooms: Promises and realities* (pp. 237–262). Cambridge: Cambridge University Press.

Berlin, J. A. (1988). Rhetoric and ideology in the writing class. *College English, 50,* 477–494.

Bleich, D. (1975). *Readings and feelings: An introduction to subjective criticism.* Urbana, IL: National Council of Teachers of English.

Boiarsky, C. (1990). Computers in the classroom: The instruction, the mess, the noise, the writing. In C. Handa (Ed.), *Computers and community: Teaching composition in the twenty-first century* (pp. 47–67). Portsmouth, NH: Boynton/Cook.

Bruffee, K. A. (1985). A *short course in writing* (3rd ed.). Boston: Little Brown.

Bruffee, K. A. (1986). Social construction, language, and the authority of knowledge: A bibliographical essay. *College English, 48,* 773–790.

Bruner, J. (1981). The pragmatics of acquisition. In W. Deutsch (Ed.), *The child's construction of language* (pp. 39–55). New York: Academic Press.

Bump, J. (1990). Radical changes in class discussion using networked computers. *Computers and the Humanities, 49,* 49–65.

Butler, W. M. (1992). *The social construction of knowledge in an electronic discourse community.* Unpublished doctoral dissertation, The University of Texas, Austin.

Butler, W. M., & Kinneavy, J. L. (1991). The electronic discourse community: God, meet donald duck. *Focuses, 4*(2), 91–108.

Cooper, M., & Selfe, C. (1990). Computer conferences and learning: Authority, resistance, and internally persuasive discourse. *College English, 52,* 847–869.

Elmer-Dewitt, P. (1994, July 25). Battle for the soul of the internet. *Time,* pp. 50–56.

Faigley, L. (1986). Competing theories of process: A critique and a proposal. *College English, 48,* 527–543.

Faigley, L. (1990). Subverting the electronic workbook: Teaching writing using networked computers. In D. Daiker & M. Morenberg (Eds.), *The writing teacher as researcher: Essays in the theory of class-based research* (pp. 290–311). Portsmouth, NH: Boynton/Cook.

Faigley, L. (1992). *Fragments of rationality: Postmodernity and the subject of composition.* Pittsburgh, PA: University of Pittsburgh Press.

Fish, S. (1980). *Is there a text in this class: The authority of interpretive communities.* Cambridge, MA: Harvard University Press.

Fowles, M. (1993). Designing a writing assessment to support the goals of the project. In B. Bruce, J. K. Peyton & T. Batson (Eds.), *Network-based classrooms: Promises and realities* (pp. 263–285). Cambridge: Cambridge University Press.

Fraase, M. (1993). *The mac internet tour guide: Cruising the internet the easy way.* Chapel Hill, NC: Ventana Press.

Gere, A. R. (1987). *Writing groups: History, theory, and implications.* Carbondale, IL: Southern Illinois University Press.

Hawisher, G. E. (1992). Electronic meetings of the minds: Research, electronic conferences, and composition studies. In G. E. Hawisher & P. LeBlanc (Eds.), *Re-imagining computers and composition: Teaching and research in the virtual age* (pp. 81–101). Portsmouth, NH: Boynton/Cook.

Hawisher, G., & Selfe, C. (1991). The rhetoric of technology and the electronic writing class. *College Composition and Communication, 42,* 55–66.

Hillocks, G. Jr., (1986). *Research on written composition: Directions for teaching.* Urbana, IL: National Council of Teachers of English.

Hiltz, S. R. (1990, June). Collaborative learning: The virtual classroom approach. *T.H.E. Journal,* pp. 59–65.

Hiltz, S. R., & Turoff, M. (1978). *The network nation: Human communication via computer.* Reading, MA: Addison-Wesley.

Karp, D. A., & Yoels, W. C. (1983). The college classroom: Some observations on the meanings of student participation. In H. Robboy & C. Clark (Eds.), *Social interaction: Readings in sociology* (2nd ed., pp. 195–210). New York: St. Martin Press.

Langston, M. D., & Batson, T. (1990). The social shifts invited by working collaboratively on computer networks: The ENFI project. In C. Handa (Ed.), *Computers and community: Teaching composition in the twenty-first century* (pp. 140–159). Portsmouth, NH: Boyntonl-Cook.

Moffett, J. (1968). *A student-centered language arts curriculum, grade k-13: A handbook for teachers.* Boston: Houghton Mifflin.

Murray, D. E. (1985). Composition as conversation: The computer terminal as medium of communication. In L. Odell & D. Goswami (Eds.), *Writing in nonacademic settings* (pp. 203–228). New York: Guilford Press.

Neuwirth, C. M., Palmquist, M., Cochran, C., Gillespie, T., Hartman, K., & Hajduk, T. (1993). Why write-together-concurrently on a computer network? In B. Bruce, J. K. Peyton & T. Batson (Eds.), *Network-based classrooms: Promises and realities* (pp. 181–209). Cambridge: Cambridge University Press.

Peyton, J. K., & Batson, T. (1986). Computer networking: Making connections between speech and writing. *ERIC/CLL News Bulletin, 10*(1), 1–7.

Regan, A. (1993). "Type normal like the rest of us": Writing, power, and homophobia in the networked composition classroom. *Computers and Composition, 10*(4), 11–23.

Rheingold, H. (1993). *The virtual community: Homesteading on the electronic frontier.* Reading, MA: Addison-Wesley.

Robinson, J. L. (1990). *Conversations on the written word: Essays on language and literacy.* Portsmouth, NH: Boynton/Cook.

Romano, S. (1993). The egalitarianism narrative: Whose story? which yardstick. *Computers and Composition, 10*(3), 5–28.

Scholes, R. (1985). *Textual power: Literary theory and the teaching of English.* New Haven, CT: Yale University Press.

Schriner, D. K., & Rice, W. C. (1989). Computer conferencing and collaborative learning: A discourse community at work. *College Composition and Communication, 40,* 472–478.

Schwartz, J. (1990). Using an electronic network to play the scales of discourse. *English Journal, 79,* 16–24.

Selfe, C. (1990). Technology in the English classroom: Computers through the lens of feminist theory. In C. Handa (Ed.), *Computers and community: Teaching composition in the twenty-first century* (pp. 118–139). Portsmouth, NH: Boynton/Cook.

Slavin, R. (1983). *Cooperative learning.* New York: Longman.

Thompson, D. (1988). Interactive networking: Creating bridges between speech, writing, and composition. *Computers and Composition, 5*(3), 2–27.

Wax, R., & Butler, W. M. (1993). *The Pioneer High School—University of Michigan connection: Writing to learn history on-line.* Unpublished manuscript, The University of Michigan, The English Composition Board, Ann Arbor.

48

THE FUTURE OF TELEVISION IN THE HOME AND IN THE CLASSROOM: EVIDENCE FOR IMPACT

Joan M. Shiring
UNIVERSITY OF TEXAS AT AUSTIN

For good or for ill, television has become an integral part of Americans' lives. This ubiquitous medium can be a treasure chest offering viewers *Sesame Street*, Ken Burns' *The Civil War*, and Alex Haley's *Roots*, or a Pandora's box unleashing *Let's Make a Deal*, *Beavis and Butt-Head*, and "professional" wrestling. At its best, television informs, entertains, enhances global communications, provides companionship, and offers time-saving services (e.g., college courses, exercise classes, home shopping). At its worst, it bores, perpetuates stereotypes, wastes valuable time, isolates family members, and prevents people from engaging in more meaningful activities.

So where does this situation leave viewers now, on the brink of the 21st century? Chances are great that in the years to come television will remain a double-edged sword to society. Before speculating on possible future roles of television in the home and classroom, though, it would be wise to examine some general trends associated with the medium today. As Igor Stravinsky astutely noted in his autobiography, "I cannot know what tomorrow will bring forth. I can know only what the truth is for me today" (1936, p. 10). Consequently, this chapter presents a brief, introductory overview of research in four areas related to television viewing: (a) typical habits of children and teenagers; (b) possible effects on family dynamics; (c) general effects on vocabulary growth and reading achievement; and (d) interesting uses of television in classroom settings.

One caveat: this chapter's length obviously precludes an in-depth analysis of any of these complex issues. Rather, information presented here offers readers a broad, general picture of television as it affects many young people today. For more detailed, thorough treatments of topics and research related to television and its effects on children and teenagers see Berry and Asamen (1993), Bryant (1990), Comstock and Paik (1991), and Zillman, Bryant, and Huston (1994).

TYPICAL VIEWING HABITS OF CHILDREN AND TEENAGERS

During the Watergate and Iran-Contra hearings, the American public heard two questions repeatedly: "What did the President know?" and "When did he know it?" Similarly, where television viewing is concerned, parents, educators, advertisers, and A. C. Nielsen pollsters want to know the answers to two key questions: "What are young people watching?" and "When are they watching it?" The answers are neither easy nor readily accessible. At the most basic level, the term "television viewing" lacks a precise definition among researchers. With 98% of American households in the 1990s owning television sets, and two thirds having two or more sets, the television tends to be on much of the time in millions of households (Comstock & Paik, 1991). People wander in and out of the room while the set is on, chat, eat, do homework, play with games and toys, read the newspaper, talk on the phone, cook, work on hobbies, and attend to myriad chores. Consequently, some family members may be truly concentrating on programs, other members may be virtually ignoring the TV set, or (most likely) the viewers will experience a range of engagement levels over the course of several hours.

Given that key limitation, researchers have nevertheless gathered data at different times and in different studies that suggest some significant patterns and habits. For example, kids and cartoons go together like peanut butter and jelly. The Saturday morning audience at its peak includes more than half of all children aged 2–11 years. Even so, 95% of the average child's viewing during the week is of programs not specifically produced for youngsters (Comstock & Paik, 1991). Clearly, children are watching adult-oriented programs on the "boob tube" in record numbers—morning, noon, and night. In fact, one of the most quoted statistics on young people's is habits asserts that by high-school graduation, the average student will have spent more hours viewing television than in the classroom: 16,000–20,000 versus 14,000 (Fosarelli, 1986).

Other researchers similarly attest to the fact that television is one of the major components in children's and teenagers' lives. Several studies tracking young people's television viewing (Comstock, Chaffee, Katzman, McCombs, & Roberts, 1978; Robinson, 1990; Tangney & Feshbach, 1988; Timmer, Eccles, & O'Brien, 1985) conclude:

- Television occupies more time than any other out-of-school activity;
- Television accounts for half or more of all leisure time;
- Television occupies proportionately more free or leisure time among children than adults; and
- The amount of television viewed by teenagers, while less than consumed by children, ensures that the medium occupies a similar position of prominence in their lives.

Although millions of American children and teenagers are obviously enamored of television, some differences in viewing habits do emerge which depend on the young person's socioeconomic status, race, and intellectual ability. Not too surprisingly, several major studies reveal that generally, as a family's socioeconomic level increases, the members' television viewing decreases (Anderson, Mead, & Sullivan, 1986; California Assessment Program, 1988; Keith, Reimers, Fehrmann, Pottebaum, & Aubrey, 1986; Neuman, 1988). Additionally, these researchers note that often, as family income increases, the parents' assessment of television as a worthy educational tool decreases. Educators should not leap to the conclusion, though, that greater viewing in impoverished families is necessarily a bad thing. As researchers point out, young people not fluent in English or coming from homes with few printed educational materials (e.g., books, newspapers, encyclopedias, magazines) can benefit greatly from television's rich resources.

One exception to the inverse relationship between income level and amount of television viewed occurs within African-American families. Several studies conducted during the past two decades suggest that at every social stratum, African Americans tend to watch more television and to have more positive attitudes toward the medium than do their Anglo counterparts (Anderson et al., 1986; Anderson & Williams, 1983; Bogart, 1972; Greenberg & Dervin, 1973; Medrich Roizen, Rubin, & Buckley, 1982; Tangney & Feshbach, 1988).

Along with the factors of socioeconomic status and ethnicity, a young person's intellectual abilities will often affect both the amount of television watched and the nature of the programs selected. Robert Abelman, in his article "Television and Gifted Children: What the Research Says" (1992), summarizes some important findings on bright children's interactions with the medium. He notes that intellectually gifted 4- and 5-year-olds actually spend more hours in front of the television set than other children of their age. Television, however, does not displace reading. As Schramm, Lyle and Parker (1961) similarly observed, "[These gifted youngsters] have an almost inexhaustible fund of energy for mental activities. They did *more* of everything—more television, more movies, more reading, more discussing, more investigating on their own" (p. 79). Abelman also notes that very young gifted children today are more inclined to seek out educational programs (e.g., *Sesame Street*, *Reading Rainbow*, *Carmen San Diego*) than cartoons, and to watch them with greater devotion than other children. In turn, these children rapidly outgrow the programs, moving on to adult-oriented comedies and action–adventure shows. During adolescence, intellectually gifted teens tend to be drawn toward more sophisticated fare (e.g., the evening news, adult educational programs, reality-based shows).

This pattern is markedly different from that of children and teens at the other end of the intellectual spectrum. In general, the lower the youngsters' mental abilities, the more likely they are to be heavy viewers (6 or more hours a day) who prefer shows emphasizing fantasy, comedy, cartoons, and violence. These contrasting viewing patterns for the gifted and those of lower mental ability have held true across four decades of research on British and American viewers, with the preferences continuing throughout adulthood (Beentjes & van der Voort, 1988; Himmelweit & Swift, 1976; Maccoby, 1954; Schramm et al., 1961; Sprafkin & Gadow, 1986; Williams, 1986). One exception to these patterns occurs when gifted young people and those financially well off experience a great deal of conflict in their social relationships (e.g., with parents, siblings, peers). In such cases, television viewing can become quite heavy, serving as an escape from unpleasant reality (Abelman, 1992; Maccoby, 1954; Schramm et al., 1961).

Related Video Media: Videocassettes, Video Games, and Music Videos

By the late 1980s videocassette recorders (VCRs) were in more than half of all American homes; experts predict that at the end of this century VCRs will be in nine out of ten households (Klopfenstein, 1989). That is the good news—and the bad news. Today's youngsters clearly feel at ease with VCRs, seeing the machine not as something separate or added onto their TV, but rather an essential part of it. Jokes abound concerning adults' inability to program their VCRs to tape a show, but American youngsters do not appear to be similarly "VCR-impaired." A study by Sims (1989) examining the viewing habits of more than 2,500 persons aged 2 years and above resulted in three major findings: (a) children and teenagers use VCRs much more than adults—approximately 3 to 5 hours per week, (b) young people use VCRs primarily for prerecorded tapes (e.g., rented movies), and (c) young viewers rarely look at taped TV shows more than once. Cohen and Cohen (1989) arrived at a similar conclusion concerning adolescents' familiarity with VCRs (e.g., 90% of the teenagers knew the functions of all the buttons vs. 40% of the adults).

Other researchers reiterate the finding that young people in households with VCRs typically see more movies per week, and more rented movies with restrictive ratings (PG–13 and R). One might expect that parents in households with access to VCRs, basic cable, and premium services (e.g., HBO, Cinemax, pay-per-view) would actively exert restrictions on their child's or teen's viewing, but this does not appear to be the case (Atkin, Heeter, & Baldwin, 1989; Greenberg & Heeter, 1987; Kim, Baran, & Massey, 1988; Lin & Atkin, 1989). Occasionally parents express a slight concern over their sons' viewing choices (apparently fearing that adolescent males will seek out more violent or sexually explicit materials) than will females. In general, though, households with the most diverse media access seem to opt for a laissez-faire attitude toward youngsters' television and movie selections.

Acknowledging children's and teenagers' fondness for VCRs and rented movies, television viewing of both commercial and cable channels still accounts for more time than all other media combined. Video games, for instance, do not appear to consume a significant chunk of most youngsters' free time. Although little formal research has been done on this topic, Kubey and Larson (1990) conclude that young people (especially boys) enjoy using the television on occasion for video games, but find the sophisticated arcade games more arousing and emotionally gratifying. Studies by Dominick (1984) and Selnow (1984) concur with these general findings.

As children move into adolescence, though, music begins to compete with television for teenagers' attention. Adolescents typically spend less media time supervised by their parents, preferring instead to watch television and listen to music either alone or with peers. With the advent of Music Television Video (MTV) in 1981, teenagers could watch the tube and listen to their favorite songs at the same time. Today, MTV appears to be a significant part of adolescent culture, influencing teenagers' speech, fashions, attitudes, and dances (Seidman, 1985).

Teenagers with access to MTV typically watch 30 minutes a day, with males apparently enjoying the station more than females. Several studies provide explanations for this male preference for rock videos (Brown, Campbell, & Fisher, 1986; Greenfield et al., 1987; Kubey & Larson, 1990; Zillman & Mundorf, 1987). Female viewers complain that music videos tend to be pitched more to males' desires than their own, frequently presenting women as sex objects, often in various states of undress. In turn, this male-oriented sexual imagery can be threatening to young girls trying to come to terms with their own sexuality. Finally, female viewers are more likely to enjoy just listening to songs, preferring to create their own imaginative scenarios rather than view the visuals on MTV. Having said that, the young women concede that rock videos are here to stay. (It is rather ironic than MTV should end up being the first serious effort by the television industry to provide regular programming for adolescents.) Ultimately, teenagers in the l990s—like young people in previous generations— find music in all its forms to be a significant part of their lives.

TV VIEWING AND EFFECTS ON FAMILY DYNAMICS

As mentioned earlier, television is America's most ubiquitous medium, reaching 98% of the nation's households. With two thirds of these homes enjoying the luxury of two or more television sets, some changes in family behavior patterns are bound to occur (Comstock & Paik, 1991). During the first half of this century and the early days of television, mothers usually stayed home and families often sat down to an evening meal together. Obviously, many societal factors besides television's proliferation have influenced today's changing family patterns (e.g., rising divorce rates, two-career families, expanded extracurricular activities for kids, more after-school jobs for teens). For all these reasons, many parents find themselves caught up daily in an exhausting whirlwind of career demands—carpooling, household chores, shopping, cooking, and child care. With schedules so hectic and varied, individual family members often resort to popping something in the microwave for dinner, then heading to the nearest TV set to eat, view, and relax—each at his or her own convenience. When parents do fix dinner for everyone or attend to household chores, television often serves a custodial function, keeping the kids out of the parents' way so that the adults can work more efficiently. For example, in one survey of mothers by Gantz and Masland (1986), the subjects interviewed estimated that most mothers of children aged 2 to 12 used television as a babysitter for about 3.5 hours a day.

Studies in recent years on families' viewing habits have noted several important trends. In the 1950s and early 1960s families tended to gather around one television set to watch their favorite programs, often chatting and exchanging comments and opinions about the shows and advertisements. For today's families who own only one set, such joint viewing and conversation continue to be typical behaviors (Bower, 1985). With the nation's tremendous increase in households with multiple sets, cable systems, and VCRs, however, this viewing tradition has become the exception rather than the norm. For example, Bower points out that for about 50% of all viewing time, children and adults watch television separately. Other researchers concur with these general findings and offer some additional conclusions (Baron, 1985; Kubey & Czikszentmihalyi, 1990; Lawrence & Wozniak, 1989; McDonald, 1986):

- As multiple sets increase, whole-family viewing decreases; this effect is especially strong in low socioeconomic households;

- Most coviewing occurs among persons within the same general age range, whether children, teenagers, or adults; and

- When parents and children watch programs together, both groups perceive the experience as a positive one, although not as rewarding as other shared family time (e.g., playing games, doing arts and crafts projects, cooking, eating outside, going to social and cultural events).

Clearly, television viewing as an activity is becoming more individualized and intragenerational, rather than intergenerational, not only in America but worldwide. For example, in 1992 Jude Collins investigated 300 adolescents in a working class district of Belfast, Ireland. Surprisingly, more than two thirds of the teenagers had TV sets in their bedrooms, with 70% of these young people stating that they preferred to watch alone versus viewing programs in the company of others. Similarly, a study in Beijing, China (Ekblad, 1986) noted that even young children often preferred to be alone when watching television, especially when the home was rife with conflict.

Given the norm in American culture of quasi-harried adults, hectic schedules, youngsters with strong viewing preferences, and multiple-media homes, educators should not be surprised that parents are not as effective as they could or should be in controlling their kids' television habits. Reviews of studies on parental control, mediation, and program selection conclude the following (Alexander, 1994; Comstock & Paik, 1991; Dorr, Kovaric, & Doubleday, 1989; McLeod, Fitzpatrick, Glynn, & Fallis, 1982; Winn, 1985):

- Television habits are very difficult to break;
- Parents acknowledge the need to restrict their children's viewing and to discuss programs, yet parent–child coviewing occurs least often with younger children who need it the most;
- Multiple TV sets make it more difficult for parents to limit hours watched and shows seen;
- Parents' involvement with children's and teenagers' television viewing ranges from at best moderate to all too often nonexistent.

Clearly, television plays a key role in family life today. On the positive side, family viewing can be a quick, easy, inexpensive way for parents and children to share time with each other. The medium can provide topics for discussion, offer common experiences, suggest valuable moral lessons, and encourage physical intimacy (e.g., snuggling, touching, hugging, stroking). On the negative side, television can become an "in loco parentis" black box, exposing children daily to a steady stream of inane, violent, and inappropriate material. At its most damaging, the "boob tube" can serve to fragment families, driving children, teenagers, and parents into different rooms for hours, days, and weeks of isolated viewing and noncommunication. (Note: The subject of television violence and its possible effects on children is an exceedingly complex one, far beyond the limited scope of this chapter. For further reading on research related to television violence and aggression, see Zillmann et al., 1994, Chap. 3.)

EFFECTS ON VOCABULARY GROWTH AND READING ACHIEVEMENT

For over 30 years researchers have examined youngsters' television viewing in order to determine possible effects on vocabulary development and reading scores. This section highlights some recent reviews of research and summarizes major findings.

Vocabulary Growth

A good place to start might be with *Sesame Street*, first aired in 1970 and now America's most extensively researched children's educational program. The show is viewed regularly (i.e., four or more times weekly) by an estimated 50–60% of all children between the ages of 2 and 5 (Comstock & Paik, 1991). Some critics worry that the program's rapid pace and visually complex graphics may gain children's attention but could interfere with real learning. The research, though, suggests that such concerns are unfounded (e.g., Anderson & Collins, 1988; Davies, 1989). In 1989, Children's Television Workshop compiled an exhaustive *'Sesame Street' Research Bibliography*, concluding that the show's format was good not only for attracting and holding a child audience, but for transmitting information as well.

A sampling of some of the bibliography's studies illustrates this point. Ball and Bogatz (1970), for example, noted that young children's viewing of the show led to improvements in letter recognition, word recall, number skills, and cognitive reasoning. A 2-year longitudinal study conducted in the 1980s also demonstrated that the more time children spent watching *Sesame Street* between the ages of 3 and 5, the more their vocabulary scores improved over time (Rice, Huston, Truglio, & Wright, 1990). Even when factors such as parent's education, preschool experience, and birth order were controlled, *Sesame Street* viewing made an independent contribution to vocabulary development. Two other studies revealed additional vocabulary growth when mothers in the United States and Israel actively watched and discussed *Sesame Street* with their preschool children (Lemish & Rice, 1986; Salomon, 1977).

Several researchers have noted that whereas regular viewing of *Sesame Street* typically leads to increased vocabulary growth in preschoolers, the viewing of animated cartoons results in no such positive effect (Harrison & Williams, 1986; Rice et al., 1990). Thus, many shows designed merely for young children's entertainment do not apparently yield the same positive effects as quality educational programming does.

Reading Achievement

Once children enter school and begin to read and write, the youngsters' language and learning processes become increasingly difficult to isolate and analyze in controlled settings. Similarly, the relationship between television viewing and reading achievement is an exceedingly complex one for researchers to evaluate. Many interpenetrating factors contribute to children's and adolescents' viewing and reading patterns: time devoted to television and reading, type and quality of programs watched and materials read, age, socioeconomic and educational levels of family members, attitudes and behaviors modeled by adults, accessibility to television and print materials, and youngsters' innate interests and ability levels, to name a few. For more detailed information on this topic, see, Comstock and Paik (1991) and Reinking and Wu (1990).

In general, reviewers of research conducted prior to 1980 did not find television wielding a pervasive negative effect on reading achievement (Hornik, 1981; Morgan, 1980). Some of the earlier studies that had suggested a negative correlation (e.g., Childers & Ross, 1973) tended to be dismissed in later years because sample sizes were small and the investigators had not controlled for such critical variables as intelligence, socioeconomic status, and availability of educational resources. Consequently, many researchers in the decades between 1950 and 1980 concluded that either a negative effect did not exist, or that their methodologies were not sophisticate enough to discern more subtle patterns.

With advanced statistical analyses and major national studies such as the National Assessment of Educational Progress (NAEP), some of these research liabilities have begun to be addressed. Given larger data bases and additional opportunities for in-depth secondary analyses of interrelated factors, researchers have noted some significant trends emerging. Perhaps the most important finding is that the relationship between television viewing and reading achievement appears to be curvilinear (Fetler, 1983; Mullins, 1992; Neuman, 1988; Roberts, Bachen, Hornby, & Hernandez-Ramos, 1984; Searls, Mead, & Ward, 1985; Williams, Haertel, Haertel, & Walberg, 1982). Specifically, moderate television viewing (i.e., 2 to 3 hours a day) is linked with an increase in reading achievement. In turn, children and teenagers who are heavy viewers (4 or more hours a day) tend to have appreciably lower reading scores.

This general pattern appears consistent regardless of the sex or age of the young person. Some researchers conjecture that watching television a few hours a day may enhance students' reading abilities by providing helpful background knowledge, piquing interest in various subjects for further reading, encouraging imaginative role-playing, and stimulating discussions with peers and adults about issues raised. For students in homes where English is not the first language, television can also help develop a more extensive vocabulary. To explain the decline in reading scores for heavy viewers, Williams (1986) posits his "displacement" theory. That is, for youngsters in first and second grade who experience difficulties when learning to read (e.g., those with lower mental abilities or learning disabilities), television can become an easy, pleasurable escape from their daily, anxious school environment. Thus the vicious cycle begins. The children can not read, so they do not enjoy the activity. Since they do not enjoy it, they often refuse to do out-of-class reading, choosing instead to relieve their stress by watching television. The more they watch, the less they practice—and the farther they fall behind in their reading proficiency with each successive year.

Out-of-class reading is a type of homework, and it might be worthwhile to cite a few salient studies exploring television's general impact on young people's homework. Somewhat surprisingly, when Fetler (1984) looked at his sample of almost 10,600 eighth graders tested through the California Assessment Program, he discovered only a minute negative association between homework done while watching television and scholastic achievement. Keith et al. (1986) echoed these findings when they looked at 28,000 seniors and the time these teens spent watching television and doing homework. According to these researchers, no strong relationship exists between television viewing and homework because they do not apparently compete for the same blocks of time. The investigators note that these two activities do not seriously conflict with each another to affect students' grades because the amount of homework demanded of the teenagers is so modest. Mullins' (1992) more recent analysis of NAEP data from 1982 to 1990 offers a similar conclusion. In 1990, most 9-year-olds reported doing less than 1 hour of homework each night; at ages 13 and 17, only about one third spent as much as 1 hour per night on homework. Clearly, long hours spent struggling over homework assignments seems to be rare.

TELEVISION IN CLASSROOM SETTINGS

In the 1980s, the great proliferation of satellite systems, cable networks, VCRs, and videocassettes resulted in television's real birth as a convenient, effective tool in many classrooms around the world. Although the medium's educational potential has only begun to be tapped, television can serve many functions in today's schools. For example, teachers use television, videodiscs, and VCRs to introduce classroom topics and extend the traditional curriculum, concretize difficult concepts with engaging visuals, tape students' performances for feedback and evaluation, connect reading materials with related films, link students in remote sites to faculty and educational resources, and provide teachers with helpful in-service training (e.g., demonstrations of innovative teaching practices conducted in real classroom settings). With so many options to explore, therefore, this section focuses on research in three areas related to educational television: (a) postsecondary television courses in the United States, (b) the "Channel One" controversy, and (c) some innovative uses of television in elementary and secondary schools.

Postsecondary Television Courses in the United States

Given America's obvious love affair with television, educators might assume that the United States would lead the world in the educational use of this medium. But they would be wrong. In 1991, Titti Forsslund, head of the Research Division of the Swedish Educational Broadcasting Company, compiled a bibliography of international studies on educational-television use. Based on this research (conducted mainly in the 1980s), she concluded that elementary and secondary teachers in the United States use educational television (e.g., educational videos, educational series shown on commercial and cable channels) far less than their colleagues in many industrialized nations. Japan and Great Britain lead the list, followed by the Netherlands, Israel, Australia, Sweden, Canada, and Belgium. According to her data, only 54% of the teachers in America incorporate educational videos / programs in any consistent manner into their classrooms. Obviously, the use of educational television by teachers is dependent on many factors, a critical one being the number of quality series broadcast for students. In Japan and Britain, for example, where almost every elementary school relies regularly on educational television, 30-40 educational series are produced. By contrast, only 10 series are typically available to Sweden's teachers, with many shows being repeats.

In terms of educational television, the United States does lead the way in one area, though: televised courses for postsecondary students. Many colleges and universities are relying increasingly on multichannel cable systems as an inexpensive, convenient way to disseminating information to students. Although no reliable, national agency tabulates data on enrollments and drop-out statistics for televised college courses, Zigerell, O'Rourke, and Pohrte (1980) reviewed research on instructional television in postsecondary institutions. According to their findings, more than 1,800 of the nation's 3,000 colleges and universities offered about 2,300 televised courses. Half a million students were enrolled in these courses—300,000 in closed-circuit courses on campuses and 200,000 in courses designed for home viewing.

What exactly constitutes an instructional-television course or "telecourse"? Although no precise definition exists, the term often describes a sequenced learning system comprising 30–60 minute video programs (borrowed; rented; or viewed on closed-circuit campus, commercial, or cable channels), textbooks, and additional resources (e.g., study guides, maps, suggestions for further reading). Evaluation materials—tests, papers, projects—can be mailed to the institution or handled on campus. Typically, people use these televised programs as a convenient way to (a) earn credits for college courses; (b) update their professional skills in such areas as law, real estate, the health sciences, and teaching; and (c) enjoy "general interest," informal courses. Thus, anyone with access to a television might, on any given Saturday morning, be able to delve into the mysteries of Chemistry 101, grapple with the intricacies of the latest tax laws, or appreciate the subtleties of Japanese flower-arranging.

Some universities, however, have envisioned even greater opportunities for students taking telecourses. Wayne State, Ohio, for example, acknowledging the many barriers employed adults contend with when trying to earn degrees (e.g., limited time, jobs far from classroom sites, excessive costs for student fees) developed a consortium entitled "To Educate the People." This special program allows adults employed full time to earn a bachelor's degree by combining telecourses with weekly conferences and periodic on-campus weekends (Feinstein & Angelo, 1977). In turn, several other universities, colleges, and community colleges have adapted Wayne State's videos and curricula to fit their own local needs (Lynch, 1980). In 1980, the Walter Annenberg Foundation, in conjunction with the Corporation for Public Broadcasting, committed over $150 million for a 15-year project focusing on the development of college telecommunication materials (Zigerell et al., 1980).

Telecourses, however, are not for everyone. As Zigerell et al. (1980) note in their summary of research, up to 50% of university students enrolled in telecourses drop out, with rates even higher in community colleges and open-admission schools. Clearly, telecourses require high levels of maturity, discipline, and self-motivation—qualities often dormant in postsecondary students who have just left high school. These researchers also lament the distressingly low numbers of African Americans and Hispanics enrolled in American telecourses. They comment too, that in the United Kingdom, very few blue-collar students participate in telecourses; most people taking the courses are middle-class teachers and technicians seeking additional qualifications.

For students who do complete university telecourses, though, their level of satisfaction with the course is often equal to that of students in parallel "live" sections (i.e., with professors teaching directly to students in the room). Researchers at Michigan State University—a pioneering school in telecommunications—have tracked student satisfaction with telecourses since the 1950s. In the 1980s, Michigan State offered over 400 such courses to 62,000 students across campus (Creswell, 1986). Typically, these courses consist of videotapes showing professors lecturing and conducting demonstrations in front of a live student audience. The tapes are then fed to a multichannel, closed-circuit cable system, which in turn runs the tapes at different times throughout the week in dormitories, classrooms, and campus centers. In order to survey students' opinions over the years, each semester researchers conduct phone interviews with random samples of students from both the live and taped class sections. Topics of inquiry include opinions on course quality, organization, methods of evaluation, and impact of audiovisual aids, in conjunction with information on student demographics (e.g., age, major, grade point average, grade expected in the course). In his overview of Michigan State's research on instructional television, Creswell concludes that the professor's personality and knowledge are the keystones to student satisfaction. The actual method of information delivery—taped or live—is not really a crucial factor. In fact, many students prefer the flexibility that comes with taped lectures and the opportunity for repeated viewings of tapes.

According to Creswell, students who have completed telecourses are typically quite positive when asked if they would take another telecourse. Not too surprisingly, the medium's biggest drawback focuses on the students' inability to ask questions and discuss issues with professors. This key disadvantage, of course, gets to the core of a basic, unspoken assumption about undergraduate teaching at many major institutions—that somehow the timeworn format of large-hall, lecture / demonstration classes with little student interaction (whether taped or not) is the best way to cover material in core courses. For administrators, telecourses are certainly cost effective, since hundreds of students can be enrolled in one course with few concerns about room-capacity limits. Admittedly, some courses do offer weekly "discussion" sections, typically led by graduate students. However, these graduate students who serve as teaching assistants often have no formal training in pedagogy, and the weekly meetings still offer fewer opportunities for discussion than if students met in smaller groups with a professor for each class.

In order to overcome the problem of student passivity in traditional telecourses, some high schools and postsecondary institutions have turned to two-way interactive telecourses to encourage student participation. Since this mode of instruction is still in its infancy for many school districts and universities, relatively little in-depth, formal research has been conducted on two-way telecourses. One investigator who has assessed the effectiveness of several two-way telecourses is Jerry McClelland (1987) at the University of Minnesota, St. Paul. In the mid-1980s the university used two-way television to connect multiple sites for four interactive telecourses. Two of the four courses linked a primary-site high school with several smaller high schools in order to give students in the sparsely populated areas access to a foreign language class and a vocational education class. The other two telecourses linked university professors teaching a professional education course and a food preservation course on the main campus with adults in classrooms at distant sites. Video cameras and monitors were set up so that all the teachers could send views of themselves, students, or visual aids to students at remote sites by pressing buttons on a panel beside them. The technology was simple enough that no technician was needed to manage the equipment.

After analyzing videotapes of class sessions and interviewing teachers and learners, McClelland arrived at two major conclusions. The good news is that the instructional–television technology did not appear to be a significant intrusion on the flow of lessons in any of the telecourses. That is, the teachers—with practice—demonstrated a good deal of skill in coordinating the technology and class activities so that students at distant sites could see and hear content to be learned. On the downside, though, all the teachers tended to focus on the class before them and to ignore pupils at the remote sites. Rarely did teachers call the distanced students by name or direct questions or comments to them. In McClelland's words, the remote sites became "invisible classrooms." Additionally, at the secondary level, a social hierarchy developed. For example, a student at one primary site joked to a new exchange student that their class was linked up with another class "in the boon-docks." Later, students at the remote site referred to themselves as "boonies" (p. 2). These and other comments over a period of time created a contrast between the "in" school at the primary site and the "out" school at the remote site. In sum, telecourses in the future could provide top quality, specialized instruction to students across the nation, regardless of their school's location or size. Still, teachers conducting these courses must make a concerted effort to create a truly balanced, supportive community of learners among all the students linked electronically.

The Channel One Controversy

Virtually all teachers and principals in the 1990s would like their students to be educated consumers and thoughtful media critics as the world barrels into the "Telecommunication Age." Unfortunately, the cost of setting up a good school video system for hands-on student experiences (e.g., with adequate television monitors, videocassette recorders, a closed-circuit cable system, satellite dish, installation and technical assistance) frequently daunts administrators, especially when their schools may still lack basic textbooks, desks, and classrooms. In the late 1980s, Chris Whittle of Whittle Communications, recognizing both schools' need for technical equipment and advertisers' desire for access to a large teenage audience, developed his controversial "Channel One" project (Wulfemeyer & Mueller, 1990). Beginning in

1990, Whittle Communications agreed to donate video hardware and software worth $50,000 to a secondary school to use as the faculty saw fit, if one condition were met. Each day, at a designated time, all teachers would show their students the 12-minute "Channel One" program. Students would watch a 10-minute summary of current events featuring attractive young news readers, state-of-the-art graphics, and attention-getting "fast facts" and pop quizzes. However, students would also be exposed to a mandatory 2 minutes of commercials pitching products specifically targeted to teens (e.g., Clearasil, Levi's jeans, Nike tennis shoes). At the end of a 3-year period, schools could either continue the program or they could cancel the contract and return the equipment.

And therein lies the heart of the controversy. Critics argue that commercials have no place in the daily curriculum, that advertisers are taking advantage of a captive audience, and that administrators are being seduced by the lure of needed video equipment (N.Y. rejects, 1989; Rudinow, 1989 / 90). In truth, the Channel One program—now in over 8,000 schools with more than seven million student viewers—does give Madison Avenue executives their largest captive teenage audience ever (Reilly, 1989). Corporate giants apparently have no qualms about paying $150,000 for a 30-second commercial and, as of 1994, Chris Whittle claims a 99% renewal rate for schools and advertisers (Elson, 1994). Additionally, reviews of research on adults' and students' reactions to "Channel One" reveal basically positive attitudes (Carlin, Quinones, & Yonker, 1992; Knupfer, 1993; Wulfemeyer & Mueller, 1990). In general, researchers conclude the following:

- Channel One appears to be accomplishing its primary instructional goal. Most students' knowledge of current events increases after watching the program.
- Most secondary students and their teachers feel that their schools should continue showing Channel One.
- Students seem to enjoy the program's fast-paced format. In turn, the teenagers tend to watch more television news than they did before Channel One came to their schools. However, the show does not seem to create an increased interest in newspaper reading.
- In most cases, Channel One information is not consciously integrated into the daily lesson. Little discussion typically occurs before or after the program. Whittle Communications does offer instructional materials to teachers, but these resources receive little use in the classroom.
- Students viewing Channel One do not pay too much attention to the commercials, commenting that the ads are really no different from the ones they see at home. Approximately 80% of the characters in commercials are Caucasian; African-American, Hispanic, and Asian characters are not well represented.
- Public-service ads constitute 15% of Channel One's 2-minute commercial segment, a significantly higher percentage than that on most commercial television stations in the United States.
- Many schools are using the video equipment for more than Channel One viewing. For example, some schools use the system for video school announcements; other schools

extend that idea to include support for community events.

Innovative Uses of Television in Elementary and Secondary Schools

Nancy Signorelli, in an article for the *Journal of Early Adolescence*, reflects on the critical role commercial television plays in today's society: "For the first time in human history a centralized commercial institution rather than parents, church, or school tells most of the stories most of the time" (1987, p. 255). As mentioned earlier, research suggests that many parents are not actively mediating their children's television viewing. Consequently, young people can grow up with the misbegotten notion that all life's problems are easily solvable (usually within a 30-minute time frame) by wise-cracking kids or fallible adults who may squabble with each other, but ultimately do the right thing and love each other unconditionally. For many of today's youngsters, especially those who grapple with poverty, stressful life events, and unstable parents, television can serve as a poorly woven safety net, temporarily distracting them from their daily pain with fantasy-world settings, facile stereotypes, glib advice, and quick solutions to complex problems. And what happens when the television is turned off and reality hits? Children and adolescents are often left feeling confused, frustrated, and somehow betrayed.

All is not lost, however. When the right medium—in this case, television—is wed to the right message, good things can happen in the classroom. Several researchers, for example, have observed that quality programming geared toward adolescents (e.g., the *Freestyle* series, after-school specials), when accompanied by teachers' guides and discussion, can produce positive changes in students' attitudes (Johnston & Ettema, 1982; Singer, 1979; Williams, LaRose, & Frost, 1981). For years, teachers and students have benefited from PBS' broadcasts and instructional materials for productions such as *A Tale of Two Cities*, *Henry V*, *Middlemarch*, *The Power of the Word*, and *Voices and Visions*. Unfortunately, the dearth of quality programming on a regular basis leaves students in the lurch much of the time.

One recent study that reveals the positive effects quality programming can have on teenagers is the "Degrassi Junior High" research intervention conducted by Yale professors Dorothy Singer and Jerome Singer (1994). In the late 1980s a joint United States–Canadian television series was developed for PBS entitled *Degrassi Junior High*. First aired in 1988, the program ran for four seasons, two as *Degrassi Junior High* and two as *Degrassi High*. Targeted at an 11- to 15-year-old audience, the series attempted to portray realistically the complex problems contemporary adolescents face. Topics for episodes included sexual awareness, pregnancy, shoplifting, alcoholism, drugs, illness, and death, along with the more common teen issues of popularity, friendships, grades, and parent–child relationships. According to the series' producer, Kate Taylor, the writers made a point not to offer easy solutions; instead, myriad options for problem solving were presented.

In the Singer study, 284 students in grades 5 through 8 in two Connecticut communities were selected to participate. The students came from ethnically diverse, blue- and white-collar family backgrounds. For the study, videotapes of five episodes were shown in class to the students; topics for these particular episodes included lying, dating, jealousy, peer pressure, self-image, alcoholism, and latch-key kids. Some viewings were accompanied by class discussion, others were not. At the conclusion of the study, Singer and Singer noted that students' and teachers' overall responses to the episodes were extremely positive. Teachers reported that after viewing the shows, youngsters were significantly more open about discussing general issues, personal problems, and effective coping strategies than they had been before the study started. The participants found the class discussions very helpful and asked for additional tapes to watch. In fact, home viewing of the "Degrassi" series by students in the study was seven to eight times greater than that done by students not in the study. It is a sad side note, therefore, that the series was cancelled after the 1991 spring season, due to low ratings and funding problems. Perhaps if more teachers had information about and access to well-written programs such as this, more series could be produced for use in the classroom.

Several other researchers have also studied the effects of using videotapes to depict both realistic problems young people encounter and possible coping strategies for handling these situations. As Yale psychologists Robin Harwood and Roger Weissberg explain, "Unlike live modeling, [videomodeling] has the capacity to focus the observer's attention on relevant aspects of an interaction, replaying and analyzing important details, and depicting them again as a whole. This capacity may be particularly important for children with social skills deficits" (1987, p. 354). Some studies, for example, have focused on the use of videomodeling in and out of school to help juvenile delinquents acquire needed behavioral and social skills. In general, the investigators conclude that the combination of videomodeling, role-playing, and discussion is a very helpful technique for producing behavioral changes (Goodwin & Mahoney, 1975; Kennedy, 1984). Other researchers and educators have used videomodeling and feedback to help teenagers deal with contraceptives (Gilchrist & Schinke, 1983), alcohol (Baker Udin, & Vogler, 1975), and cigarettes (Botvin, Renick, & Baker, 1983). Finally, this strategy of videomodeling and coaching appears to work equally well with younger children who are extremely shy, fearful, and withdrawn at school (Kendall & Morison, 1984).

Another exciting, innovative way for teachers to use videotapes in the classroom focuses on the teaching of reading via taped, closed-captioned television programs. In 1983, the National Captioning Institute funded a collaborative effort among researchers at their institute, education professors at the University of Maryland, and reading specialists in Washington, DC's public schools to help hearing students improve their reading skills (Jensema, Koskinen, & Wilson, 1984). After a pilot study and subsequent program modifications, the researchers selected 10 capable, experienced teachers (all master's and doctoral students) and 35 students in grades 2 through 6 for the project's second study. Seventy-five percent of the students were remedial readers who read below the

3rd-grade level. Teachers were given videotapes of closed-captioned, high-interest programs (e.g., cartoons, situation comedies), along with scripts of the telecasts' subtitles and a packet of instructional materials (e.g., ideas for reading activities, sample lesson plans, possible topics for discussion). Teachers were asked to teach two lessons per week for a 3-week period.

Although these two studies were brief and exploratory in nature, the results were nevertheless extremely encouraging. All the teachers indicated that they would like to use captioned TV in their regular classrooms at least once a week. Additionally, every teacher rated the quality of students' learning as "good" or above. In turn, students obviously found the taped shows and scripts highly motivating. For example, 90% of the children stated that they would like to learn with closed-captioned TV in school; several students reported that reading with these tapes was their favorite time of the day. This finding is especially significant, since almost all students in the study were considered reluctant learners. Clearly, the use of closed-captioned videotapes to promote vocabulary growth and reading fluency in poor readers and nonfluent, English-language speakers remains a potentially rich area for future research.

As educators increasingly experiment with video technology in all subjects and grade levels, the future will also assuredly bring new periodicals and magazines for sharing classroom ideas and instructional strategies. One current resource highly recommended by Susan Mernit, a senior editor of *Instructor*, is *Cable in the Classroom Magazine*, a guide to listings and teaching materials that accompany public broadcast and cable television shows. [For more information on this monthly, call 1-800-216-2225 or write to *Cable in the Classroom Magazine*, 86 Elm St., Peterborough, NH 03458.] Mernit endorses this particular magazine in an article she wrote for *Instructor* entitled "Get with the Program: Teach with TV" (1991). The author kindles her readers' imaginations by sharing eight creative teachers' innovative ideas for giving students hands-on learning experiences with video technology. Across the nation children and teenagers are bustling around with television monitors, VCRs, and video-cameras to integrate reading, writing, listening, and speaking. For example, some of the ideas described in the article include the following: scripting and preforming video book reviews for the local cable station; writing weather forecasts; researching and debating current events seen on *CNN Newsroom;* making storyboards and videotapes of major curriculum projects; and producing an hour-long cable show called *Homework Helpline*, a fast-paced teen show filled with music, interviews, study tips, and craft activities. As one teacher explains, "The visual immediacy of television can really help students make connections between what they know and what they watch. It's a mighty big world out there, and television brings it right into my classroom" (p. 44).

CONCLUSION

So, what lies ahead for Americans on the brink of the Tele-communication Age? Whether consumers are ready or not,

construction on the infamous "information superhighway" has begun, and pondering its effects on daily life can be a fruitful—if somewhat frightening—endeavor. The recent confluence on technologies (e.g., the digitalizing and compressed storage of audio and video communication, combined cable / fiber-optic wiring, computer-controlled selecting and patching mechanisms for meshing relayed information) virtually assures video's expanded influence in homes of the 21st century.

Telephone, computer, and cable systems—once separate entities—now are merging to form unified "mega-information" networks. For example, Tele-Communications, Inc., is now marketing a cable decoder capable of providing access to 540 channels (Elmer-Dewitt, 1993). To date, the content of most of these channels remains undetermined. However, given corporations' penchant for profit, odds are long that educational programming for children and teens will be a scheduling priority. Fortunately for kids, Michael Eisner, chairman of Walt Disney Company, recently teamed up with Ameritech, BellSouth, and Southwestern Bell to distribute movies, interactive games, and other programs via two-way video systems (Greenwald, 1994). Not to be outdone, Bell Atlantic recently spent $11 billion for cable systems and equipment to bring two-way television to eight million homes by the year 2000 (Greenwald, 1994).

Nicknamed "smart TVs," these new two-way television sets combining audio, video, and computer information will offer virtually limitless services to American homes and businesses. People will be able to bank, pay bills, make travel reservations, play interactive games, shop in video malls, work at home, select movies (and change the endings, if desired), access libraries, order business materials, receive health care, communicate with government officials, and possibly even vote (Hight, 1994). Young people will be able to study any subject at any level of difficulty, given the right teacher and the right technology.

So far, so good. But is there a downside to this surfeit of channels, information, and services? Will America become a wired nation of people "cocooning" in homes—paradoxically linked electronically yet isolated physically, unified technologically yet fragmented communally? Will television in the future really make people smart, or will it become, in Marie Winn's words, the "plug-in drug," used much like alcohol and drugs to fend off depression, loneliness, anxiety, and conflict? Since no one knows what the future holds, Neil Postman (1992) suggests that the final word should go to Stephen Vincent Benet. In *John Brown's Body* the author, musing upon the effects of new technologies in the 20th century, ends his poem thus:

> If you at last must have a word to say,
> Say neither, in their way,
> "It is a deadly magic and accursed,"
> Nor "It is blest," but only "It is here."

(1927, p. 377)

References

Abelman, R. (1992). Television and gifted children: What the research says. *Roeper Review, 15*(2), 80–84.

Alexander, A. (1994). The effect of media on family interaction. In D. Zillman, J. Bryant & A. Huston (Eds.), *Media, children, and the family: Social scientific, psychodynamic, and clinical perspectives* (pp. 51–59). Hillsdale, NJ: Erlbaum.

Anderson, B., Mead, N., & Sullivan, S. (1986). *Television: What do national assessment results tell us?* Princeton, NJ: Educational Testing Service.

Anderson, D., & Collins, P. A. (1988). *Television's influence on cognitive development*. Washington, DC: U.S. Department of Education, Office of Educational Research and Improvement.

Anderson, W. H., Jr., & Williams, B. M. (1983). TV and the black child: What black children say about the shows they watch. *The Journal of Black Psychology, 9*(1). 27–42.

Atkin, D., Heeter, C., & Baldwin, T. (1989). How presence of cable affects parental mediation of television viewing. *Journalism Quarterly, 66*(3), 557–578.

Baker, T., Udin, H., & Vogler, R. E. (1975). The effects of videotaped modeling and self-confrontation on the drinking behavior of alcoholics. *The International Journal of the Addictions, 10*(5), 779–793.

Ball, S., & Bogatz, G. A. (1970). *The first year of "Sesame Street": An evaluation*. Princeton, NJ: Educational Testing Service.

Baron, L. J. (1985). Television literacy curriculum in action: A long-term study. *Journal of Educational Television, 11*(1), 49–55.

Beentjes, J. M., & van der Voort, T. J. (1988). Television's impact on children's reading skills: A review of research. *Reading Research Quarterly, 23*(4), 389–413.

Benet, S. V. (1927). *John Brown's body*. New York: Doubleday.

Berry, G., & Asamen, J. (Eds.). (1993). *Children and television: Images in a changing sociocultural world*. Newbury Park, CA: Sage.

Bogart, L. (1972). Negro and white media exposure: New evidence. *Journalism Quarterly, 49*(1), 15–21.

Botvin, G., Renick, N., & Baker, E. (1983). The effects of scheduling format and booster sessions on a broad-spectrum psychosocial approach to smoking prevention. *Journal of Behavioral Medicine, 6*(4). 359–379

Bower, R. T. (1985). *The changing television audience in America*. New York: Columbia University Press.

Brown, J., Campbell, K., & Fisher, L. (1986). American adolescents and music videos: Why do they watch? *Gazette, 37*(1–2), 19–32.

Bryant, J. (Ed.). (1990). *Television and the American family*. Hillsdale, NJ: Erlbaum.

California Assessment Program. (1988). *Annual report, 1985–1986*. Sacramento, CA: California State Department of Education.

Carlin, T., Quinones, Z., & Yonker, R. (1992). *The perception of the educational value of Channel One among secondary level teacher and students*. (ERIC Document Reproduction Services No. ED 347 980)

Childers, P. R., & Ross, J. (1973). The relationship between viewing television and student achievement. *The Journal of Educational Research, 66*(7), 317–319.

Children's Television Workshop. (1989). *"Sesame Street" research bibliography*. New York: Children's Television Workshop.

Cohen, A., & Cohen, S. (1989). Big eyes but clumsy fingers: Knowing about and using technological features of home VCRs. In M. Levy (Ed.), *The VCR age: Home video and mass communication* (pp. 135–147). Newbury Park, CA: Sage.

Collins, J. (1992). Secondary school children and their television. *Educational Media International, 29*(4), 221–228.

Comstock, G., & Paik, H. P. (1991). *Television and the American child*. San Diego: Academic Press.

Comstock, G., Chaffee, S., Katzman, N., McCombs, M., & Roberts, D. (1978). *Television and human behavior*. New York: Columbia University Press.

Creswell, K.W. (1986). Does instructional TV make the grade? *Journal of Educational Television, 12*(1), 19–27.

Davies, M. M. (1989). *Television is good for your kids*. London: Hillary Shipman.

Dominick, J. (1984). Videogames, television violence, and aggression in teenagers. *Journal of Communication, 34*(2), 136–147.

Dorr, A., Kovaric, P., & Doubleday, C. (1989). Parent–child coviewing of television. *Journal of Broadcasting & Electronic Media, 33*(1), 35–51.

Ekblad, S. (1986). Social determinants of aggression in a sample of Chinese primary school children. *Acta Psychiatrica Scandinavica, 73*, 515–523.

Elmer-Dewitt, P. (1993). Take a trip into the future on the electronic superhighway. *Time, 141*(15), 50–55.

Elson, J. (1994). Whittling down. *Time, 144*(7), 31.

Feinstein, O., & Angelo, F. (1977). *To educate the people: An experimental model for urban higher education for the working adult*. (ERIC Document Reproduction Services No. ED 146 880)

Fetler, M. (1983). *Television and reading achievement: A secondary analysis of data from the 1979–80 National Assessment of Educational Progress*. (ERIC Document Reproduction Services No. ED 229 748)

Fetler, M. (1984). Television viewing and school achievement. *Journal of Communication, 34*(2), 104–118.

Forsslund, T. (1991). Factors that influence the use and impact of educational television in school. *Journal of Educational Television, 17*(1), 15–30.

Fosarelli, P. (1986). In my opinion: Advocacy for children's appropriate viewing of television—what can we do? *Children's Health Care, 15*(2), 79–80.

Gantz, W., & Masland, J. (1986). Television as a babysitter. *Journalism Quarterly, 63*(3), 530–536.

Gilchrist, L. D., & Schinke, S. P. (1983). Coping with contraception: Cognitive and behavioral methods with adolescents. *Cognitive Therapy and Research, 7*(5), 379–388.

Goodwin, S., & Mahoney, M. (1975). Modification of aggression through modeling: An experimental probe. *Journal of Behavior Therapy and Experimental Psychiatry, 6*(3), 200–202.

Greenberg, B., & Dervin, B. (1973). Mass communication among the urban poor. In C. D. Mortensen & K. K. Sereno (Eds.), *Advances in communication research* (pp. 388–397). New York: Harper & Row.

Greenberg, B. S., & Heeter, C. (1987). VCRs and young people. *American Behavioral Scientist, 30*(5), 509–521.

Greenfield, P., Burzone, L., Koyamatsu, K., Satuloff, W., Nixon, K., Brodie, M., & Kingsdale, D. (1987). What is rock music doing to our youth? A first experimental look at the effects of rock music and music videos. *Journal of Early Adolescence, 7*(3), 345–364.

Greenwald, J. (1994). Lights! Camera! Dial tone! *Time, 144*(10), 56, 57.

Harrison, L., & Williams, T. M. (1986). Television and cognitive development. In T. M. Williams (Ed.), *The impact of television: A natural experiment in three communities* (pp. 87–142). New York: Academic Press.

Harwood, R., & Weissberg, R. (1987). The potential of video in the promotion of social competence in children and adolescents. *Journal of Early Adolescence, 7*(3), 345–358.

Hight, B. (1994, October 26). Report offers city guidance on fiber optics. *Austin American-Statesman*, pp. B1, 3.

Himmelweit, H., & Swift, B. (1976). Continuities and discontinuities in media usage and taste: A longitudinal study. *Journal of Social Issues, 32*(4), 133–156.

Hornik, R. (1981). Out-of-school television and schooling: Hypotheses and methods. *Review of Educational Research, 51*(2), 193–214.

Jensema, C., Koskinen, P., & Wilson, R. (1984). Teaching reading to hearing children via captioned television. *Computers, Reading, and Language Arts, 2*(1), 20–23.

Johnston, J., & Ettema, J. (1982). *Positive images: Breaking stereotypes with children's television*. Beverly Hills, CA: Sage.

Keith, T., Reimers, T., Fehrmann, P., Pottebaum, S., & Aubrey, L. (1986). Parental involvement, homework, and TV time: Direct and indirect effects on high school achievement. *Journal of Educational Psychology, 78*(5), 373–380.

Kendall, P. C., & Morison, P. (1984). Integrating cognitive and behavioral procedures for the treatment of socially isolated children. In A. W. Meyers & W. E. Craighead (Eds.), *Cognitive behavior therapy with children* (pp. 261–288). New York: Plenum Press.

Kennedy, R. L. (1984). Cognitive behavioral interventions with delinquents. In A.W. Meyers & W.E. Craighead (Eds.), *Cognitive behavior therapy with children* (pp. 351–376). New York: Plenum Press.

Kim, W., Baran, S., & Massey, K. (1988). Impact of the VCR on control of television viewing. *Journal of Broadcasting & Electronic Media, 32*(3), 351–357.

Klopfenstein, B. (1989). The diffusion of the VCR in the United States. In M. Levy (Ed.), *The VCR age: Home video and mass communication* (pp. 21–39). Newbury Park, CA: Sage.

Knupfer, N. (1993). *Channel One: Reactions of students, teachers, and parents*. (ERIC Document Reproduction Services No. ED 362 176).

Kubey, R., & Czikszentmihalyi, M. (1990). *Television and the quality of life: How viewing shapes everyday experience*. Hillsdale, NJ: Erlbaum.

Kubey, R., & Larson, R. (1990). The use and experience of the new video media among children and adolescents. *Communication Research, 17*(1), 107–130.

Lawrence, F., & Wozniak, P. (1989). Children's television viewing with family members. *Psychological Reports, 65*(2), 396–400.

Lemish, D., & Rice, M. L. (1986). Television as a talking picture book: A prop for language acquisition. *Journal of Child Language, 13*(2), 251–274.

Lin, C., & Atkin, D. (1989). Parental mediation and rulemaking for adolescent use of television and VCRs. *Journal of Broadcasting & Electronic Media, 33*(1), 53–67.

Lynch, E. (1980). A description and analysis of the consortium process and development of the American government telecourses for national distribution (Doctoral dissertation, North Texas State University, 1981). *Dissertation Abstracts International, 41*(8), 3447, 3448A. (University Microfilms No. 8100096)

Maccoby, E. (1954). Why do children watch television? *Public Opinion Quarterly, 18*(3), 239–244.

McClelland, J. (1987). *Use of two-way interactive television in education*. (ERIC Document Reproduction Services No. ED 288 503)

McDonald, D. G. (1986). Generational aspects of television coviewing. *Journal of Broadcasting & Electronic Media, 30*(1), 75–85.

McLeod, J., Fitzpatrick, M., Glynn, C., & Fallis, S. (1982). Television and social relations: Family influences and consequences for interpersonal behavior. In D. Pearl, L. Bouthilet, & J. Lazar (Eds.), *Television and behavior: Ten years of scientific progress and implications for the eighties* (Vol. 2, pp. 272–286). Washington, DC: U.S. Government Printing Office.

Medrich, E., Roizen, J., Rubin, V., & Buckley, S. (1982). *The serious business of growing up: A study of children's lives outside school*. Los Angeles: University of California Press.

Mernit, S. (1991). Get with the program: Teach with TV. *Instructor, 100*(8), 42–44.

Morgan, M. (1980). Television viewing and reading: Does more equal better? *Journal of Communication, 30*(2), 159–165.

Mullins, I. (1992). *Trends in school and home contexts for learning*. (ERIC Document Reproduction Services No. ED 353 330)

N. Y. rejects commercial classroom news program (1989, June 17). *San Diego Union*, p. A10.

Neuman, S. B. (1988). The displacement effect: Assessing the relation between television viewing and reading performance. *Reading Research Quarterly, 23*(4), 414–440.

Postman, N. (1992). *Technopoly: The surrender of culture to technology*. New York: Knopf.

Reilly, P. (1989). Whittle sticks by Channel One rollout. *Advertising Age, 60*(11), 3.

Reinking, D., & Wu, J. (1990). Reexamining the research on television and reading. *Reading Research and Instruction, 29*(2), 30–43.

Rice, M. L., Huston, A. C., Truglio, R., & Wright, J. C. (1990). Words from "Sesame Street": Learning vocabulary while viewing. *Developmental Psychology, 26*(3), 421–428.

Roberts, D. F., Bachen, C. M., Hornby, M. C., & Hernandez-Ramos, P. (1984). Reading and television predictors of reading achievement at different age levels. *Communication Research, 11*(1), 9–49.

Robinson, J. (1990). Television's effects on families' use of time. In J. Bryant (Ed.), *Television and the American family* (pp. 195–210). Hillsdale, NJ: Erlbaum.

Rudinow, J. (1989/90). Channel One whittles away at education. *Educational Leadership, 47*(4) 70–73.

Salomon, G. (1977). Effects of encouraging Israeli mothers to co-observe "Sesame Street" with their five-year-olds. *Child Development, 48*(3), 1146–1151.

Schramm, W., Lyle, J., & Parker, E. (1961). *Television in the lives of our children*. Stanford, CA: Stanford University Press.

Searls, D. T., Mead, N. A., & Ward, B. (1985). The relationship of students' reading skills to TV watching, leisure time reading, and homework. *Journal of Reading, 29*(2), 158–162.

Seidman, S. (1985). Music videos: Why they're effective and what we can learn from them. *International Journal of Instructional Media, 12*(1), 61–64.

Selnow, G. (1984). Playing videogames: The electronic friend. *Journal of Communication, 34*(2), 148–156.

Signorelli, N. (1987). Children and adolescents on television: A consistent pattern of devaluation. *Journal of Early Adolescence, 7*(3), 255–268.

Sims, J. B. (1989). VCR viewing patterns: An electronic and passive investigation. *Journal of Advertising Research, 29*(2), 11–17.

Singer, D. G. (1979). The constructive uses of television in the classroom. In S. L. Lustman (Ed.), *Proceedings. International year of the child: Child advocacy* (pp. 255–266). New Haven, CT: Child Study Center, Yale University.

Singer, D., & Singer, J. (1994). Evaluating the classroom viewing of a television series: "Degrassi Junior High." In D. Zillman, J. Bryant, & A. Huston (Eds.), *Media, children, and the family: Social scientific, psychodynamic, and clinical perspectives* (pp. 97–114). Hillsdale, NJ: Erlbaum.

Sprafkin, J., & Gadow, K. (1986). Television viewing habits of emotionally disturbed, learning disabled, and mentally retarded children. *Journal of Applied Developmental Psychology, 7*(l), 45–59.

Stravinsky, I. (1936). *An autobiography*. New York: Simon & Schuster.

Tangney, J., & Feshbach, S. (1988). Children's television-viewing frequency: Individual differences and demographic correlates. *Personality and Social Psychology Bulletin, 14*(1), 145–158.

Timmer, S., Eccles, J., & O' Brien, K. (1985). How children use time. In F. T. Juster & F. P. Stafford (Eds.), *Time, goods, and well-being* (pp. 353–382). Ann Arbor: Institute for Social Research, University of Michigan.

Williams, P., Haertel, E., Haertel, G., & Walberg, H. J. (1982). The impact of leisure-time television on school learning: A research synthesis. *American Educational Research Journal, 19*(1), 19–50.

Williams, T. M. (Ed.). (1986). *The impact of television: A natural experiment in three communities*. New York: Academic Press.

Williams, T. M., LaRose, R., & Frost, F. (1981). *Children, television, and sex role typing*. New York: Praeger.

Winn, M. (1985). *The plug-in drug: Television, children, and the family* (2nd ed.). New York: Viking.

Wulfemeyer, K. T., & Mueller, B. (1990). *Commercials in the classroom: A content analysis of "Channel One" advertisements*. (ERIC Document Reproduction Services No. ED 323 575)

Zigerell, J., O'Rourke, J., & Pohrte, T. (1980). *Television in community and junior colleges: An overview and guidelines*. (ERIC Document Reproduction Services No. ED 206 329)

Zillman, D., & Mundorf, N. (1987). Image effects in the appreciation of video rock. *Communication Research, 14*(3), 316–334.

Zillman, D., Bryant, J., & Huston, A. (Eds.). (1994). *Media, children, and the family: Social scientific, psychodynamic, and clinical perspectives*. Hillsdale, NJ: Erlbaum.

49

NEWSPAPERS AND ON-LINE TEXT:
ESSENTIALS OF THE LITERACY ENVIRONMENT

Karen D. *Wood*

UNIVERSITY OF NORTH CAROLINA AT CHARLOTTE

Jim Nicholson

PHILADELPHIA DAILY NEWS

According to Sullivan (1993), it was the French historian de Tocqueville who, upon visiting the United States, observed that newspapers are not just a means to preserve freedom, they are a means to preserve civilization. Apparently, more than a century ago, the press was recognized as an educative institution, and as this chapter reveals, the emphasis on the role newspapers can play in educating society has steadily increased.

Newspapers constitute the material most read by adults. Data from the Newspapers Publishers Association reveal that more than 113 million adults read the newspaper on a daily basis. The average reader spends 62 minutes reading the Sunday newspaper and 45 minutes reading one or more daily newspapers (Cheyney, 1992). Since newspaper reading is viewed as largely an adult activity, it is an extremely motivating instructional medium for students of all age levels. The purpose of this chapter is to review existing research on the benefits of using newspapers in the classroom, to trace the history of the Newspapers in Education Program and, to look at present and future uses of the newspaper as advances in technology continue to make dramatic changes in our lifestyles.

HISTORY OF THE NEWSPAPER IN EDUCATION PROGRAM

It was in the 1930s that the *New York Times* began the first newspaper in education program (Wilson, 1994), but it was not until 1952 that a communications milestone became

marketable and radically altered the environment. This new environment provided a fertile seedbed for a formal, nationwide program.

Television, an experimental medium from the late 1930s through the 1940s, suddenly showered the American landscape with hundreds of thousands of incandescent specks that landed in the living rooms. The infant medium quickly demonstrated its awesome power to tether and transfix entire families, irrespective of generational lines.

In 1952 the circulation manager at the *Des Moines Register* became concerned about the impact television was having on reducing newspaper reading nationwide. C. Ken Jefferson, with the help of the International Circulation Managers Association, initiated a program designed to encourage future readership by providing schools with newspapers to distribute to their students. Thus, the Newspaper in Education (NIE) program was born. It officially assumed the name "NIE" in 1976. Since 1958 it has functioned under the auspices of the American Newspaper Publishers Association Foundation (ANPA) (Wanta and Brierton, 1992).

By the early 1990s, NIE had encompassed more than 62,000 teachers and two million students in almost 26,000 schools (Wanta and Brierton, 1992). Editors and publishers agreed that, as circulation of newspapers continued to plummet through the 1960s, part of their agenda included capturing a future market while there was still time. The newspaper industry became "alarmed by long-term declines in readership" and realized that they had to do more to "woo the audience critical to their future, children and teenagers" (Walsh, 1991). *USA Today*, for example, began offering a

20-page catalogue of educational products designed to help teachers use the splashy national newspaper in the classroom. Among its products was a guide titled "How to Teach Math with USA Today" (Walsh, 1991).

Currently, NIE programs offer a wealth and a variety of resources for teachers, students, and the community in general. The results of surveys by the ANPA Foundation and the International Newspaper Promotion Association, as reported by DeRoche (1991), along with the most recent findings of Media General Research (1993), revealed the following:

1. Eighty-nine percent of respondents reported offering an NIE program through the year in 1992 versus 81 percent in 1989.
2. The number of teachers and students served by NIE programs has increased significantly since 1989.
3. Elementary schools are the most frequent participants in NIE programs.
4. More newspapers are evaluating the effectiveness of their NIE programs usually via surveys and feedback.
5. More than half of the respondents publish features geared specifically to youth.
6. The major purposes of NIE programs were to increase readership, serve the community and promote awareness of freedom of the press.
7. Most of the NIE programs offered curriculum materials such as filmstrips, video and other instructional aids in addition to newspaper tours and outside speakers and promotional presentations.
8. The majority of the newspapers' publishers offer the paper at a reduced rate to schools.
9. More than one-third of the newspapers reported offering an adult literacy program.
10. Majority of the programs conducted workshops for teachers and / or parents with many offering college or in-service credit.

In major studies conducted by the Newspaper Advertising Bureau (NAB 1977; 1980), it was concluded that the Newspaper in Education program can provide many of the prerequisites for later adult newspaper reading (Wanta & Brierton, 1992).

However, a 1992 study (Stone & Grusin) submitted to the American Newspaper Publishers Association Foundation, found that NIE exposure by itself is a lesser influence on later newspaper use than is the quality of the NIE experience. How many times per week or minutes per day is not as significant as the extent to which the students found the experience enjoyable. It was also found that receiving the newspaper in the classroom can compensate in some respects for not having one in the home.

The search for a quick, easy fix to declining newspaper readership is what Jack D. Lail, (1995) metro editor of the *Knoxville News-Sentinel*, terms "protecting the franchise, instead of developing the franchise" by supporting mediums beyond newprint and thus enhancing the newspaper's name and credibility as an information source.

But the failure to confirm any latent benefits of NIE programs in no way deterred the enthusiasm of NIE advocates or impeded the program's growth, which would indicate a widespread and popular response to the more immediate benefits (DeRoche, 1991; DeRoche & Skover, 1983).

The NIE programs, which can vary from locale to locale, have received high marks from educators, journalists, students and parents alike (NAB, 1980). NIE-type programs have since spread to countries which include England, New Zealand, and South Africa.

Gwen Kirk, who manages the national program for the Newspaper Foundation of America, commented that, "Our goal is to enhance a cooperative relationship between the press and the schools to provide educational opportunities for students" (Wilson 1994).

The *Commercial Appeal* in Memphis, Tennessee, which has one of the oldest NIE programs in the country, has distributed newspapers to classrooms for the past 27 years and has encouraged teachers to use the newspapers as a "teaching tool by providing creative curriculum, teacher workshops and credit courses at Mid-South Universities" (Flanagan, 1995).

Tennessee was tied with four other states (Mississippi, New York, Louisiana and Texas) and the District of Columbia, for the highest illiteracy rate (16% of the population) in the United States (U.S. Office of Education Research and Improvement, 1993). This newspaper provides a snapshot of how an aggressive NIE program can reach out to the inhabitants of its circulation area.

In the 1994–95 school year, 550 schools in the Mid-South participated in the *Commercial Appeal*'s NIE program. More than 20,000 newspapers were provided each week to the schools at a discount, involving more than 16,500 students in NIE program topics such as reading, math, economics, and geography (Flanagan, 1995).

More than a decade ago (1983), DeRoche and Skover observed that "research and evaluation experts should study the impact of this instructional tool on reading achievement, habits and attitudes over the long term. Teachers, administrators, reading specialists, parents, and others should examine existing research, talk to teachers and students who have used newspapers in their classroom and decide for themselves whether this medium will help students learn to read and, equally important, read to learn" (p. 19).

Unfortunately, research since 1983 has remained sparse. But now the technological revolution threatens to overtake events and make any academic research on the current use of newspapers as a learning tool, well, academic.

The computer age has pushed this classroom learning tool, the newspaper, to the precipice of change and uncertainty. The "newspaper" of the 21st century, say some media futurists, may not even vaguely resemble what the teacher is passing out to the class today.

The following sections will examine the research on the benefits of using the newspaper in more detail, including its value for elementary, middle / secondary, and special needs students. The last section of this chapter speculates about the role of the newspaper in education in the 21st century.

THE VALUE OF NEWSPAPERS IN THE CLASSROOM: WHAT RESEARCH REVEALS

According to DeRoche (1991), newspaper in education research has been termed interesting to read about, in need of more comprehensive study with greater control of variables, and sparse and irrelevant. While ideas abound for using the newspaper in the classroom, it is evident that the research supporting its use is indeed sparse, though not necessarily irrelevant. One of the reasons offered for the paucity of current research is that in the late 1970s, leaders from the American Newspaper Publishers Association Foundation and school administrators called for evidence that newspapers in classrooms will pay off in terms of increased reading achievement, reading habits and attitudes toward reading. As newspapers in education programs throughout the nation have steadily grown, along with teacher testimony supporting their value, the research interest dissipated in the 1980s (DeRoche, 1991). This section will report on some of the studies and major findings.

Research has shown that the more students are exposed to the newspaper, the more their attitudes about its value to them as involved, concerned citizens increases. Whitaker (1969) used newspapers to teach a unit on laws affecting our youth with sixth graders and found that such a unit can improve students' attitude toward the law. Verner and Murphy (1977) found that using the newspaper as an instructional resource increased students' attitudes toward their city, community, school, and nation.

In a study conducted by West (1979), students exposed to newspapers for instruction versus those students exposed to textbooks only reported more belief in the newspaper as an exciting, responsible, and valuable means of learning about events around them. The researcher reported that using newspapers in the classroom may establish a daily newspaper reading habit and that students learned the benefits of all media.

Research has also shown that students who use newspapers in their classes tend to be more socially and politically aware of current events, have more positive attitudes toward newspapers, read newspapers outside of school, and interact with parents and other adults about the content of newspapers (Dubuque Telegraph Herald, 1984; Newspaper Advertising Bureau, 1980; Rhoades, 1982; Stone, 1988).

A survey conducted by the Oklahoma Newspaper Advertising Bureau shows that those who read the newspaper regularly tend to be more active voters. The survey revealed that voters read more national, state, and local news and were more inclined to read the editorial page than nonvoters. This research suggests that getting students to stay more informed on social issues via the newspaper will incline them to want to have a voice in political issues.

NIE coordinators from the *Dubuque Telegraph Herald* (1984) surveyed fourth and fifth graders to determine their awareness, usage, and attitudes toward the local newspaper. They compared one school in which the newspaper was used weekly throughout the year to another school (the control group) which did not use the newspaper. Their findings showed that the experimental group read more local and national news and demonstrated a greater interest in local government, neighborhood events, current issues, and foreign affairs. Both the experimental and control groups reported difficulty on the pretest administered prior to the study but twice as many control group students reported having problems on the posttest.

Windhauser and Stone (1981) examined the reading habits of 738 college students to determine if exposure to newspapers in elementary or high school resulted in increased newspaper use in college. Their findings showed that students exposed to newspapeer programs in school reported more daily reading and that parental interaction with children about the newspaper had a positive effect on readership.

A similar study of college students by Rhoades (1982) used newspaper in education students (NIE) and nonnewspaper in education students (non-NIE). The study found that the NIE group spent more time reading the newspaper and acquiring news from all major news media, expressed a greater interest in the news and were more informed about current events.

An examination of the later reading habits of students exposed to the Newspaper in Education program was undertaken by Wanta and Brierton (1992). A total of 235 respondents was included in the survey. The results showed that students involved in the NIE program were more likely to cultivate the newspaper reading habit than others. Statistically significant results were found for most, but not all, of the variables examined in the study. For example, the researchers concluded that activities with high student involvement and teacher–student interaction were more highly correlated to later reading frequency. Specifically, those activities associated with newspaper use involved taking current events quizzes, clipping and saving articles, discussing articles in class, and analyzing newspaper contents. Those activities not associated with higher newspaper reading use involved merely delivering newspapers to a classroom and allowing class time to read them.

Research synthesized from a number of studies offers the following conclusions regarding the value of using newspapers in the classroom (DeRoche, 1991; DeRoche and Skover, 1983; Newspaper Advertisers Bureau, 1977; 1980; Ringler & Rhodes, 1990; Stone & Grusin, 1992; Wanta & Brierton, 1992):

1. Daily newspapers are a valuable and useful instructional tool.
2. Daily newspapers are a useful aid in helping young and adult learners master the skills of reading and writing.
3. Using newspapers on a regular basis in classrooms improves the reading interests and the newspaper reading habits of learners.
4. Instruction in using the newspaper helps students have less trouble reading the newspaper.
5. Newspaper use seems to influence classroom verbal interactions, student motivation, school attendance, and student behavior.
6. The use of the newspaper has been demonstrated to increase students' interest and knowledge of world affairs and current events.

7. Newspaper use helps students to become more involved in political issues in the community and the world at large.

8. Exposure to a newspaper in education program is associated with higher levels of newspaper use by young adults.

9. The long-term effects of the exposure are strongest for minorities.

10. Parents, teachers and students, alike, tend to respond positively to the use of the newspaper.

The next three sections will examine the research more thoroughly by citing studies done on newspaper use in the elementary grades, middle and secondary grades and with special needs students.

NEWSPAPER USE IN THE ELEMENTARY GRADES

Measuring the impact of newspaper use in education is difficult because of the inability to control the many variables involved. Many studies reported were action research conducted by teachers in their own classrooms. These and other studies varied in terms of duration of the treatment period, type of instruction, variables examined, and use of a control group, to name a few. As mentioned previously, the bulk of such research that is available took place nearly two decades ago.

Update NIE (1977) conducted a study on 442 low-income first graders who participated in an experimental reading and writing project employing newspapers and other reading materials. The results showed that the project group outperformed the control group on the posttest.

The *Commercial Appeal* (1980) reported a school-wide study which revealed gains in reading comprehension and vocabulary on a standardized reading test for classes using the newspaper.

One of the most comprehensive studies on the use of the newspaper to teach reading was conducted over a 3-year period in Stockholm , Sweden (Edfelt, 1990). Called Project NewRead, the study involved nine experimental classrooms in grades one through nine, and 7,515 students in the same grades comprised the control group. The newspaper was used as the sole reading text by the experimental group for two years.

The researcher reported "stunning" results with the experimental groups surpassing the control group one-half to a full year in reading development. Specific findings included an increased respect for the opinions of others, highly developed metalinguistic ability, increased capacity for listening, and an increased motivation to read and learn independently.

The Newspaper Advertising Bureau (1982) examined the effects of newspaper use in the school on newspaper readership when the students become adults. Based upon interviews of over 3,000 adults, the results showed that the influence of school use of newspapers was greatest among minorities who did not have a newspaper at home. Apparently, childhood exposure to newspapers fosters adult newspaper reading.

Stone and Grusin (1992) conducted focus groups with individuals who had attended one of 50 schools with extensive NIE programs. Their 2-year study involved interviews with 644 young adults. Similar to the previous study (NAB, 1982), they reported that the impact of the newspaper in education program on cultivating black young adult readers was "formidable." They also concluded that merely having the newspaper available in the classroom is not sufficient. The experience must be enjoyable, positive, interactive, and involve effective instructional methods.

Recognizing the paucity and limitations of existing research, Ringler and Rhodes (1990) investigated the relationship between classroom newspaper reading and students' reading habits, comprehension, and ability to write a newspaper article. A total of twenty classes in grades 4–6 participated in the study with 239 students assigned to the experimental group and 188 students in the control group. A curriculum based upon the whole language philosophy integrated with the newspaper was employed for the school year. In addition to the positive reactions of both teachers and students, participants outperformed nonparticipants in terms of writing ability and reading performance. Not only did students show higher scores in newspaper writing but their scores in general writing improved as well. The researchers concluded that "reading newspapers should become a regular part of the classroom instructional program" (p. 38).

NEWSPAPER USE IN THE MIDDLE AND SECONDARY LEVEL

Studies with upper-level students have examined the effects of newspaper instruction on students' reading achievement, comprehension, vocabulary, writing performance, verbal interaction, political participation, knowledge of government, and on newspaper reading skills in general.

In order to more accurately assess the effectiveness of the newspaper in education program, the American Newspaper Publishers Association (ANPA) commissioned the Educational Testing Service to develop the Newspaper Reading Test. The first research study which used that test was conducted by Diederich in 1971. The participants included 13,000 students in grades seven through twelve who were divided into groups: one in which the newspaper in education program was used and one in which newspapers were not used. The data revealed that 13% more students in the newspaper group scored above the national norm on the test than in the control group. Diederich reported that gains this large are rarely observed in typical reading improvement programs.

Wardell's (1973) study of 300 ninth graders showed improvements in various reading-related skills such as differentiating main ideas from details, distinguishing fact from opinion, locating information and ability to read the newspaper using specially prepared newspaper exercises.

Adams and Cook's (1977) study used seventh graders enrolled in a 26-lesson program designed to increase their reading skills. Each student was given a newspaper each day, along with a study guide to assist their reading. The researchers reported that the reading ability of the students did improve over the 12-week period.

A study by Norman (1978) and one sponsored by the *Milwaukee Journal / Milwaukee Sentinel* (1980) both found increased verbal interaction by students involved in using the newspaper instructionally. The latter study reported that eighth graders who used newspapers were superior to the nonnewspaper group in verbal skills, newspaper knowledge, and current events.

The Flanders Interaction Analysis Scale was used in the Norman study which revealed significant changes in the amount and quality of student talk in the experimental classes (newspaper use) versus the control group classes.

The NIE Information Service (1987) examined the effects of newspaper use on the writing performance of students in grades eight through twelve over a 6-month period. The results showed that all of the experimental groups that used the newspaper with related instruction made gains in writing skills, whereas the group not using the newspaper showed no improvement.

A 1989 investigation by Palmer examined the effects of using the newspapers in combination with normal class instruction. The study involved 627 at-risk students in middle and secondary schools. An analysis of the pre- and posttest scores revealed increased improvement in reading vocabulary and comprehension, and in writing performance.

Although empirical research is scant, practical publications abound illustrating the many ways in which the newspaper can be applied to the study of any discipline. One of the most popular of these publications is Cheyney's (1992) third edition of *Teaching Reading Skills through the Newspaper*. In addition to suggestions for how to read the newspaper with skill and comprehension, each of the chapters focuses on integrating the newspaper with the teaching of social studies, science, language arts, and mathematics.

THE USE OF THE NEWSPAPER WITH SPECIAL NEEDS STUDENTS

The limited number of studies on the effectiveness of newspaper use with special needs students involved mostly upper-level students. In one 9-week study (Stetson, 1970) including 107 special needs students, a standardized test was used to measure pre- and posttest gains. Results revealed that students in a teacher-directed newspaper use group experienced greater gains in reading skills than those students who used the newspaper on their own. The central group showed no gains in reading scores. Similarly Vernor and Siedow (1978) wanted to determine if the newspaper can be used as the sole instructional material for improving the reading achievement of high school-level special education students. One group used the newspaper as a resource while another received instruction in the parts and organization of a newspaper. Both groups showed gains in reading achievement in addition to more positive attitudes toward politics and newspapers in general.

Curtis and Shaver (1980) used as sample of 22 special needs students drawn from eight secondary schools to determine what effect exploration of contemporary social problems would have on students' attitudes toward funda-

mental freedoms, critical thinking abilities, self-esteem, reading comprehension, and school attendance. The program spanned a 5-month period and incorporated a wide variety of print materials such as newspapers, magazines, government reports, and books. The reseachers used an inquiry–problem identification model of instruction requiring students to collect and analyze information, take a position on certain issues and develop a plan of action. Based on their findings, the researchers concluded that appropriate and interesting social studies content for special needs students can increase interest in contemporary problems. No significant differences were found for the other variables under study.

Clearly, empirical data on newspaper use with special needs students are sparse and limited largely to the 1970s and 1980s. However, numerous practitioner-oriented publications have addressed its many benefits for special populations. Vail, Monda and Koorland (1989) advocate the use of the newspaper with Behaviorally Disordered (BD) students who they say are often unmotivated by traditional classroom materials. Since the newspaper is living history, it can be used to help students deal with problems in their own lives. For example, students can develop graphs of various job opportunities in the classfield ads, make checklists of job requirements and design charts comparing projected earnings with monthly expenditures.

In a previous article, Monda, Vail and Koorland (1988) recommend using the newspaper with Learning Disabled (LD) students who often experience failure with traditional content area methods and materials. Such students may be characterized as passive participants who need direct involvement in motivating activities. They suggest that the newspaper be used as a supplement for LD students, focusing on specific skills in reading / language arts, and mathematics.

Since the newspaper is largely an adult medium, LD and BD students do not feel embarrassed by its use as when they are assigned lower-level materials different from their peers. Everyone in a heterogeneous classroom may be working on the newspaper, while the activities assigned to the special needs students can be adapted to meet varying ability levels.

The newspaper is a recognized instructional tool for teaching English as a second language (ESL) learners. The recently published book, *Using the Newspaper to Teach ESL Learners* (Olivares, 1993) builds on a foundation of sound pedagogical theory and includes numerous suggestions for practitioners. Olivares advocates including ESL learners in cooperative groups while using the newspaper to foster interpersonal communication skills. With the help of peers, students identify, label and categorize information in a meaningful language and print context.

NEWSPAPER IN THE 21ST CENTURY

It does not take a futurist or visionary to see that the electronic superhighway will be a dominant force in the lives of Americans in the next century. The blueprints are already off the drawing board and the surveyor stakes have been driven for the route that this information mega-transitway will take into the year 2000; right through the center of the average citizen's life.

And as a significant portion of the older generation tentatively steps out into the computer net traffic, the younger generation is already crowding the lanes that have been paved by present technology and are running wide open.

This younger generation are also school children whose reading and other learning skills have been enhanced considerably by using the newspaper as a classroom teaching tool. So how does the Newspaper in Education program, whose success has steadily escalated in the past four decades, not only keep up, but keep from getting run over especially if newspapers are in the twilight of their history as some critics contend? "Newspapers, more and more, are coming on-line with computers. The idea of using newspapers as a teaching tool in schools won't change that rapidly. They'll still be using printed material. A lot of teachers are print oriented" (DeRoche, 1995).

Jack Lail, metro editor of the *Knoxville News-Sentinel* noted that "In the 21st Century, newspapers will still be using NIE programs. A strong NIE program is a big plus." But he is clear in his view that newspapers, like any other life form, must adapt or perish.

"Newspapers have to get into the game. They have to do more than put day-old copy on the street. They have to get connected. We have to look at educational resources. Newspapers generally react for the wrong reasons," said Lail (1995). "They are trying to protect their franchise instead of developing it." Lail went on to explain that "protecting" the franchise is simply the short-sighted view of trying to corner readers and corral new ones by beating them over the head with a rolled up newspaper. He said the long-term goal should be to employ advanced technology with the newspaper which will enhance the overall credibility of the newspaper and support programs which will associate newspapers in the public mind with being a knowledge center.

Some newspapers such as *Raleigh, North Carolina* are giving an 800 telephone number out and have a bulletin board with special areas for kids where resources are attainable. He cited the CIA Worldbook, which features in-depth area studies of countries. Lail's own paper has an aggressive NIE program.

Even the publisher of *Tomorrow's Morning*, a nationally distributed children's newspaper, has a strong sense that the massive daily information flow's future cannot be bound inside six or eight columns of newsprint. Publisher Adam Linter said that he wants to make his business more of a literary company, not just a newspaper. He said a lot of companies do not understand that the "digital highway" is here and that kids are more comfortable with the computer. In fact, they would rather send a message over a computer than a telephone (Boneberg, 1994).

A year ago his company started working on a book, a television show, and a CD-Rom game. They also have news spots on local radio and had planned to join the America On-Line computer network with forums and uploading / downloading capabilities. The potential for on-line networking with schools is overwhelming.

There are more than 1.2 million users of the Prodigy network and its feature, Homework Helper. Reviewers are calling this database an "impressive industrial-strength research tool that parents will want as much as their kids" (Healy, USA Today, 1995). There is no need to look for news articles in the library archives. The built-in intelligence allows students to pose a question in plain English. The features allow students to narrow or extend their searches, retrieve information appropriate to their reading levels, copy maps, charts, photos and click on a definition for unknown words (Healy, 1995). Similarly, Knight Ridder, Inc. has developed "media-line," an on-line computer service that provides teachers with lesson plans, current events texts, and graphics to aid their instruction. Students, too, can log-on to the system to access information for research papers.

Jan Vincens Steen (1992), NIE project supervisor in Norway, conducted a survey to determine: (a) Will NIE have any value in the 21st century and, (b) What effect will the use of NIE have in the next century?

He asked these two questions of three groups: the Newspapers circulation leaders at a circulation conference in Bergen, Norway on May 9, 1992; NIE specialists from all over Norway at the National NIE Conference in Nesyben held May 11 to 13, 1992; and an international conference of NIE specialists which convened in San Fransico on May 19, 1992. He found that everyone believed NIE would have a value in the next century "with only one noting that this is actually dependent on the credibility maintained by newspapers in the future." It was mentioned that newspapers have the "advantage that you can bring them with you again and again" and that children learn better through the use of printed words than through the use of computers and television.

Regarding the effect NIE will have in the 21st century, the respondents made comments such as the following:

- Because of rapid changes in the world (new governemnts, independent states) newspapers will be the textbook that tells pupils about these changes.
- It will be good for democracy (this is if all newspapers are not controlled by too few words).
- We need to develop critical readers of the media.
- The "return to reading" will produce individuals who have far greater depth concerning knowledge and its appreciation.

Steen further offered that in the 21st century, instead of newspapers in print, there could well be computer versions where the readers only print out what they want to read, and only pay for these pages. Family members, and schools alike, might choose pages appropriate to their objectives.

One prototype of this 21st century newspaper is here and is being developed by Roger Fidler, director, Knight Ridder Inc., Information Design Laboratory in Boulder, Colorado.

This "newspaper" is a portable, battery-operated flat-panel screen some nine inches wide, a foot high and an half-inch thick similar to the size of a typical magazine. The device would weigh a little over a pound, far less than the Sunday edition of the local newspaper. Fidler calls it a "personal information appliance" or it could be termed a newspanel. It could contain a trove of news, graphics , audio and even video, representing more than a year of Sunday papers. Through fiber-optic lines and radio links, it might connect to databases of news and entertainment from around the world (Gilder, 1993).

On the face of this tablet is something that looks a lot like the page of a newspaper. It contains headlines for featured stories followed by their first few paragraphs and a jump to an inner page. The jump, unlike the usual newspaper, is electronic and immediate with the click of an arrow or a mouse. Discreetly placed ads are at the bottom of the page (Gilder, 1993). The electronic tablet, as conceived by Fidler, has no keyboard, but instead enables the user to touch an icon with a pen or a finger to page through it. Eventually, a voice command will be used in this capacity.

Fidler has said that the first generation tablets could begin appearing by 1996 for $1500 to $2500 and drop in price to $500 by the year 2000 (Aumente, 1994).

Fidler has been active since 1981 in developments which would be the transformation of print media from pigmented ink on paper to digital ink displayed on portable information appliances (Fidler, in press).

According to Gilder (1993), computers will soon "blow away the broadcast television industry, but they pose no such threat to newspapers. Indeed, the computer is a perfect complement to the newspaper. It enables the existing news industry to deliver its product in real time. It hugely increases the quantity of information that can be made available, including archives, maps, charts and other supporting material. ...It empowers the reader to use the 'paper' in the same way they do today." (p. 142)

Computer newspapers, traditional newspapers, on-line services, are the medium, but it may be the message—and credibility of that message—which determines the 21st century role of Newspapers in Education.

Fidler (1995) commented, "I think newspapers are in a strong position to go into the 21st Century. The future is not so much will they publish, but who will publish. There will be a shaking out in the industry of newspapers too disconnected from their communities. Credibility will be an important factor."

SUMMARY

Even though the Newspapers in Education program has not been encompassed by academic scrutiny and evolution and, despite the less than certain latent benefits the newspaper industry may garner in terms of lifelong readership, NIE has stood the populist test of time. It is a program which has shown immediate and obvious benefits to hundreds of thousands of children and provided teachers with an instructional device which can transcend the tedium of blackboards and books. The overwhelming consensus is that "News" In Education, even if the medium is not columns of newsprint, will be with us through the next century. The reportage of current events shaping and re-shaping the world appears to be just as important to the youngsters who also inhabit that world; and they have responded well to the stimuli.

References

Adams, A., & Cook, S. (1977). Seventh graders in Raleigh use newspapers for a 12-week course. *Southern Newspaper Publishers Association Bulletin*, (August), 22.

Aumente, J. (1994, October). Panel Vision. *American Journalism Review*, 34–39.

Boneberg, K. (1994). *Dallas Morning News*, (January, 18) p. 5c.

Cheyney, A. B. (1992). *Teaching Rading Skills Through the New spaper*. (3rd edn.). Newark, DE: International Reading Association.

The Commercial Appeal (1980). Achievement soars with newspapers. *The Teacher's Notebook*, Memphis.

Curtis, J., & Shaver, J. (1980, April). Slow learners and the study of contemporary problems. *Social Education*, 302–309.

DeRoche, E. F. (1991). *The Newspaper: A Reference Book for Teachers and Librarians*. Santa Barbara, CA: ABC-CLIO, Inc.

DeRoche, E. F. (1995). Personal communication.

DeRoche, E. F., & Skover, L. (1983). The American Newspaper Publishers Association Foundation, *Newspaper Research Journal*, 4(2) 23–30.

Diederich, P. (1971). *Test results of using newspapers to teach reading*. Paper presented at the International Reading Association Convention, May, 1974.

Dubuque Telegraph Herald (1984). *NIE Newsletter*, Newspapers in Education Survey.

Edfelt, A. (1990). Teaching analytical reading with newspapers as sole reading test. *Research Bulletins, 14, 4*. University of Stockholm.

Fidler, R. (1995). Personal communication.

Fidler, R. (in press). *Mediamorphosis, Understanding New Media*, Los Angeles: CA: Pine Forge Press.

Flanagan, I. C. (1995). All about Kidzine. *The Commercial Appeal*, March 8, p. 2E.

Gilder, G. (1993). *Forbes ASAP*, (October, 25).

Lail, J. D. (1995). Personal communication.

Media General Research (1993). *Survey of Newspaper in Education Programs and Literacy Programs*, 1992. Reston, VA: American Publishers Association Newspaper Foundation.

Milwaukee Journal / Sentinel (1980). *Reading Papers Can Help Students*. (September), 11.

Monda, L. E., Vail, C. O., & Koorland, M. A. (1988). Newspapers and LD Students. *Journal of Reading, 31*(7) 678–9.

Newspaper Advertising Bureau (1977). *The Infleuence of Childhood Experience with Newspapers on Adult Newspaper Habits*. New York: Newspaper Advertising Bureau, Inc.

Newspaper Advertising Bureau (1980). *Daily Newspapers in American Classrooms*. New York: NAB.

Newspaper Advertising Bureau (1982). *Assessing the Impact of Newspaper in Education Programs: Changes in Student Attitudes, Newspaper Reading and Political Awareness*. New York: NAB.

NIE Information Service (1987). Florida Research Study Finds a Write Connection. (November).

Norman, B. (1978). *Changes in classroom verbal interaction as a result of the newspaper's instruction use.* Unpublished report.

Olivares, R. A. (1993). *Using the Newspaper to Teach ESL Learners.* Newark, DE: International Reading Association.

Rhoades, G. (1982). *Newspaper in Education (NIE) and News Media Use.* A Review from the Southwest Education Council for Journalism / Mass Communications Annual Conference. (October).

Ringler, L. H., & Rhodes, C. S. (1990). *The Relationship between Students' Newspaper Reading and Students' Habits, Attitudes, Writing Ability and Reading Comprehension.* School of Education, New York University.

Steen, J. V. (1992). The effect and value of newspapers in education in the twenty-first century. *Educational Media International, 29*(3) 193–95.

Stetson, E. (1970). The effectiveness of newspaper use on reading achievement of secondary special education students. *Journal of Reading, 13*, 26–28.

Stone, G. C. (1988). Measuring adult readership potential of the newspaper in education program. *Newspaper Research Journal,* (Winter) 77–86.

Stone, G. C., & Grusin, E. K. (1992). *NIE's Cultivation of Young Adult Newspaper Readers.* Reston, VA: American Newspaper Publishers Association Foundation.

Sullivan, B. L. (1993). Foreward to *Using the Newspaper to Teach ESL Learners* by R. A. Olivares. Newark, DE: International Reading Association.

Update NIE. (1977). Right to read succeeds in Durham. Also reported in the *Southern Newspaper Publishers Association Bulletin.* (September) 1.

Vail, C.O., Monda, L.E., & Koorland, M.A. (1989). Behavior disordered students use the news. *Journal of Reading, 32*(4) 364–5.

Verner, Z., & Murphy, L. (1977). Does the use of newspapers in the classroom affect attitudes of students? *The Clearing House, 50*(8) 350–351.

Verner, Z., & Siedow, M. (1978). In Verner, Z. *Newsbook of Reading Comprehension Activities.* Houston, TX: Clayton Publishing Co.

Walsh, M. (1991). The paper chase. *Teacher Magazine, 3*(3) 26–7.

Wanta, W., & Brierton, P. (1992). *The Newspaper in Education program: Types of activities and later reading habits.* Paper presented at the Annual Meeting of the Association for Education in Journalism and Mass Communication. Montreal, Canada.

Wardell, P. (1973). *The development and evaluation of a reading program designed to improve specific skills in reading a newspaper.* Unpublished dissertation, Boston MA, Boston University .

West, J. (1979). *A study of using the newspaper in teaching language arts in middle school.* Unpublished master's thesis. Columbia SC, University of South Carolina. Also reported in *Southern Newspaper Publishers Association Bulletin.* (February), 26.

Whitaker, V. (1969). *A study of the newspaper in teaching a greater respect for the law.* Unpublished master's thesis. San Diego CA, San Diego State University.

Wilson, L. (1994). Newspaper–school programs seek to teach kids, encourage readership. *Dallas Morning News*, May 10.

Windhauser, J., & Stone, G. (1981, October). Effects of NIE on adult newspaper use. *Newspaper Research Journal.* 22–31.

50

READING COMICS, THE INVISIBLE ART

Shirley Brice Heath and Vikram Bhagat

STANFORD UNIVERSITY

Ask any youngster about reading comic books or newspaper comic strips, and you are sure to meet with mixed reactions, ranging from vigorous justification to outright denial. Kids seem to know instinctively that comic books are "forbidden fruit" or "light reading"—a highly marginalized art form that suggests frivolous interests and low abilities (Dorrell & Carroll, 1981; Krashen, 1989). Everywhere, print-only books hold the highest position for literacy achievement; art forms that mix words with stylized pictures in bold colors receive attention primarily as commercial trivia.

Yet around the world, concerned educators use comics to invite new readers into literacy habits, to teach English, to explore science and literature, and to carry out political education. Some countries, such as Mexico, have a well-established tradition of comic books, and city street vendors count them among their best-selling wares. Indian families whose children can read English give them comics in English that feature Hindu mythology and tales of historical figures, political and social. Since the 1940s, comic strip artists in Australia have used their medium to characterize foreigners and to represent language varieties as well as to poke fun occasionally at habits seen as peculiarly Australian (Foster, 1991). Within the United States, cartoonists receive hundreds of letters weekly from young readers, asking questions, protesting changes in characters, and offering ideas. Many adults develop a love of comics as children and later collect old comics, check garage sales for caches of particular favorites, and readily offer their opinions about new comic figures that come not only in comic books but also in an array of commercial products. Children's clothing, as well as toys, board games, and television programs, expand print versions of cartoon characters' lives within the United States.

What then are comics, and what do they share with art and literature? What challenges to cognitive processing do they offer, and how do these differ from those of literature that are filled only with words? What do we know about comics and their use in different settings and for various purposes in different parts of the world? Answers to these questions suggest that by exploring comics, we can understand more deeply the combination of the visual and the communicative that underlies this entire volume, for within comics, the verbal and pictorial communicate in tight combination through word and picture. This combination seems to be one that comes naturally in early stages of children's art. Numerous studies of children's early interpretations of picture books, as well as illustrated texts with words, and their own drawings, indicate the extent to which picture and word work together as children develop their initial concepts of literacy (Winner, 1982, especially chap. 5; Wolf & Heath, 1992).

Yet academics who study reading habits and literacy development have given relatively little attention to children's interest in combinations of pictures and words in the stylized forms of comics. However, scholars interested in popular culture and cognitive processing of visual images with written words have devoted considerable attention to the ebb and flow of the popularity of comics since World War II. Regarded as popular literature in a "hybrid form of narrative art," comic books and comic strips interact extensively with other forms of literature. For example, Dick Tracy was inspired by Sherlock Holmes (Inge, 1989, p. 196). Superheroes in American comics have much in common with folk tales of frontiersmen such as Davy Crockett and Paul Bunyan (Inge, 1989), Many of the trappings around comics resemble those of literature: secondary texts document the history of cartoon creators' lives as well as offer deconstructions of their pictorial and verbal representations (Schmitt, 1992); deluxe editions of favorites are available, and collectors prize early originals in good condition (see, for example, Cahn, 1986 and other texts listed in Inge, 1988, 1989).

Vikram Bhagat is a junior at Stanford University with an undeclared major. In 1990, he was named a "Promising Young Writer" by the National Council of Teachers of English. He hopes to study economics and enjoys reading comics of all sorts, especially "Garfield" by Jim Davis.

In the 1990s major figures in the art world of comics, such as Will Eisner and Scott McCloud, began to encourage serious consideration of cognitive issues as well as recognition of the long history of "juxtaposed pictorial and other images in deliberate sequence, intended to convey information and / or produce an aesthetic response in the viewer" (McCloud, 1993, p. 9). Messages conveyed in ancient hieroglyphics in several parts of the world depended on stylized pictorial representations. Illuminated manuscripts incorporated the pictorial with written text. Comics produced as early as the 1400s separated stylized pictures from words, the former conveying resemblance and the other meaning. This division became increasingly strict for the next 500 years, until artists' disillusionment following World War I led them to Dadaism and caricatures emphasizing unpredictability and the symbolic in both pictorial and verbal representations. Ambiguity and confusion, often masked as naivete, marked pre-World War II comic book characters, such as Krazy Kat, and Mutt and Jeff in the United States. These characters became known to Americans first in comic strips and only later were these strips collated and reprinted into hardcover bound "comic books." The first glossy full-color softback ancestor of the comic book so familiar today was issued in 1933 as *Funnies on Parade*, and in 1934 *Famous Funnies* became the first monthly comic magazine and continued publication for over 20 years (Berger, 1973; Inge, 1988, 1989; Kunzle, 1973).

By World War II, popular culture unabashedly combined words and pictures as authors flaunted a disregard for the status quo and advocacy of alternative "superhero" approaches.

Comic art took off, drawing from and interpreting current societal issues as well as celebrating particular types of characters and action. During and following World War II, Action Comics brought several superheroes into circulation—heroes who would still be known at the end of the century. *Superman* (1938) was followed by *Batman* (1939) and *Wonder Woman* (1941), characters who used their superhuman powers to bring about good and order in the world around them. Numerous imitators and kinsmen developed over the next two decades with Captain America and the short-lived competition of Captain Marvel from Fawcett Comics.

During the 1950s and 1960s, satire surfaced in characters such as Beetle Bailey and Pogo. Teen romance in characters such as Archie and his friends spoke directly to adolescent interests, as did the continuation of old favorites such as Donald Duck and Mickey Mouse for the very youngest readers and those who had come to know these characters in movie cartoons of Looney Tunes. Marvel Comics created an overnight sensation in the United States with Spider Man, a hero, but one with numerous human characteristics and foibles. Additional genres that emerged during these decades were crime comics, inspired by gangster movies, and bearing some resemblance to the horror tales of Edgar Allen Poe. Titles such as *Tales from the Crypt* vied with *Crime Suspense Stories* (Inge, 1988, 1989).

Comics of political satire as well as promotion of new themes, such as feminism, children's dominance over their parents, and the bizarre and yet human characteristics of animals, came to be increasingly popular in the late 1970s.

New titles, such as *Amazing Spider Man,* were now possible, because a code of censorship established in 1954 banning any treatment of crime, violence, drugs, or sexual innuendo in comics was considerably softened in 1971. The absolute divide between good and bad, right and wrong, that had clearly defined superheroes as supergood came down, and comic heroes were portrayed as facing ambiguities and succumbing to temptation from societal forces.

COMICS AS EDUCATIONAL INFLUENCE AND SOCIAL COMMENTARY

Librarians and other educators interested centrally in motivating the habit of reading, as well as linguists eager to promote development of vocabulary not easily acquired through vocabulary workbooks, agree that comics develop both literacy and language competency. Repeatedly, studies have shown that "nonreaders" are attracted to comic books and that many adults with firm habits of reading attribute their continuing enthusiasm for reading to their early devotion to forms of light reading that often included comic books. During the 1970s, literacy advocates from libraries and language classrooms flooded journals such as *The Reading Teacher, School Library Journal,* and the *Journal of Reading* with articles offering both research and programmatic statements about the merits of comic books. In the 1980s, several scholars in second language acquisition and literacy research reminded educators of the proved potential of comics for advancing educational goals (Dorrell, 1987; Krashen, 1989).

But comics in the 1990s seem to do more than these educators advocated and to address in numerous ways some fundamentals of reader response theory and literary interpretation. Marvel Comics leads the way in both its comic books and collected comics in making clear the links between literature and life, as well as the ties between themes addressed in the late 1990s and those taken up as far back as the Classics. Moreover, the view that their editors express is that their literature can appeal to all ages. A recent survey of comic book stores in a West coast university town revealed that anywhere from 25% to 50% of comic book buyers are under the age of 18, but all clients purchased comic books for their own reading and not primarily for collecting. Most stores cited *X-men* as being by far the most popular among younger customers, although the list of high-sales image comics for those in the age range 18–28 included such titles as *Cyberforce, Sandman, Spawn, Wildcats, X-force* and *X-man.* Japanese animation comics were in high demand as well, particularly ones such as *Sanctuary.* Youth and adults explained that for them, comics convey "real-life" adventures and issues. Many other readers across the nation must agree, for Marvel sells 3 million comic books a year to those between the ages of 6 and 11, another 3 million to those aged 11 to 17, and about a million to readers over 17, with over 90% of these male readers. In 1991, retail sales reached $400 million in the 5,000 specialty comics shops in the United States. Data on national sales and buying trends came from *American Demographics* (1991, May, p. 16).

X-men, a publication of comic-book giant Marvel Comics under the editorship of Bob Harras, enjoys extremely high readership in the 15–18 range. A Saturday morning cartoon show features the same characters, as do numerous video games. Animated adventure games of the same name have been developed for both the Sega and Nintendo home entertainment systems as well as entertainment systems found in many video arcades. Introductions to the comic books link readers with complex political issues and speak of their texts as "modern fables" that address such matters as the "evils of unreasonable prejudice and insensitive government policy." Such comments directly address the combined helplessness and urge for political resistance in their comic characters, linking their feelings with those of people who feel a sense of powerlessness to overcome what some have called "mindless bureaucratic constraints on their lives."

An analysis of the September 1995 issue of *The Uncanny X-men*, titled "Deadly Messengers," reveals two features rarely addressed in the literature on comic books. Words and not pictures dominate its pages. Graphic and colorful illustrations abound, but often only a single visual image appears on a page. Often pages contain multiple drawings placed at random and multiply layered. The clues that readers must use to understand the mass of visual images are the words. Instead of being incidental to understanding the storyline, as some critics of comics allege, words give the dominant portions of the storyline. With the text deleted, this comic book would be incomprehensible, but if the dialogue were retained and the illustrations omitted, the story would make sense. Illustrations appear to link the dialogue to its appropriate speaker, much as "he said" and "she said" phrases do in literature.

A second observation regarding this issue of *X-men* relates to the advanced level of the language used. Not only do readers need to understand the words of the dialogues, but many of these vocabulary items compare favorably with the most advanced vocabulary-building lists prepared for the Scholastic Assessment Tests. Within only the first three pages of the comic book, words such as the following appear: *justifiably, traipsing, foreboding, telepathically, subterfuge*, and *estrangement*. This level of vocabulary continues throughout the work. The bulk of the readership for *X-men* consists of 15–18-year-olds who count this as "light reading," while groaning over vocabulary drills and SAT-preparation classes. The language of *X-men* characters also features "sound" words, such as *klik, blam, wham, kreash, bam*, and *whoosh*. These interjections appear mixed with dialogue that makes use of both high-level vocabulary and high-tech or sci-fi jargon. For example, one character states: "My Mutant ability allows me to siphon psionic and even physical residue from the recently deceased." This statement is followed by *bam* when he strikes a rival character. The speaker proceeds "Remnant energy that I can transmute into raw physical power!"

The *X-men* comic books, therefore, defy traditional assumptions regarding the nature of comic books and the "low-level" skills necessary to read them. Yet certain features also echo trends in language use in comic books, such as the reflection of social dialects. For example, this particular issue features a female who says "Ah reckon this is the place t'be if'n ah need a bite." Colloquialisms such as "y'll" appear throughout the issue, perhaps reminding older readers of the rendering of southern dialect in *Li'l Abner* comics. Bold type and numerous punctuation marks break the text in each speech bubble, and rectangular boxes often provide background narrative information.

THE ART OF CREATING AND READING COMICS

To create comics, artists have a wide range of choices: linear sequence of blocks of pictures and words, whole-page or large-block single cartoons, or whole-page mixed layouts of blocks, circles, and other pictorial presentations (Eisner, 1992). Within comic books produced in the United States, the linear sequence of blocks has been dominant, with covers generally displaying the superhero or primary characters in a whole-page portrayal of action. Within the line-up of blocks, artists select not only their ways of portraying characters' actions and emotions, but also patterns of key word choices. "Bam!" came to be associated early with the first superheroes of Buck Rogers, Dick Tracy, and Wonder Woman, many of whom became television and motion picture characters as well. Later comics, such as those of the Marvel Comics Group, expanded vocabulary level and created more complex plots, many of which were linked to social issues.

To understand this sequential art of comics, readers must process the meanings of the staccato rhythm of unconnected moments that come between the panels of comics—the empty space that comic arts call "the gutter." The imagination of the reader fills the visual gaps, just as it does the verbal gaps in literary language. Abstract representations, as well as pictorial renderings of parts for the whole, enable readers to follow the sequence of actions, emotions, and development of complication, because they tap into the reader's stored experiences and competence with imagination. To understand *Archie* takes some experience with the culture dominant among young people during its years of creation from the 1940s onward. Today, to grasp *X-Men* requires considerable knowledge of the vocabulary linked to the science of space and computer and artillery technology. Vocabulary recognition and inferencing come through contextual clues hidden in pictorial details and linked to experiential knowledge of readers who are often also viewers of these same types of episodes on television or in video games.

Some artists create their cartoons or strips in response to gaps that young readers themselves report in their knowledge or experience, particularly in science. Here the artist's success depends on responding appropriately and not didactically to the curiosity and creativity of readers. For example, Jok Church, creator of the comic, *You can with Beakman & Jax*, a syndicated feature that responds to science questions from middle childhood readers (between the ages of 6 and 12), uses his comics to answer questions such as what fingernails are made of or what snot is. Each segment frames a question and takes readers through the answer, giving a story that involves Beakman and Jax, the comic's characters. Humor, information, eye-catching graphics, and a related experiment draw readers to the comic, as well as to its weekly television counterpart *Beakman's World.* In 1995, the comic characters went on the World Wide Web to answer young readers' science questions, supplementing the letters received from more than 100 youngsters each week who follow the antics of Beakman and Jax. [Data for this discussion came from Heath's interviews with Jok Church and joint participation with him in a 1994 conference sponsored by the Poynter Media Institute of Reading in America.]

Several countries similarly depend on young readers' attraction to comics to teach science. For example, in South Africa in 1990, the Storyteller Group began publishing *99 Sharp St.,* a series of comics that depended on young readers in workshop sessions to let artists know their interests. Taking great care to launch this medium, relatively unknown in South Africa, the Storyteller Group workshopped with numerous groups to create characters and language that would reach the bulk of middle and secondary school students. The multilingual population of South Africa, as well as regional variation in cultural values and habits, and general unfamiliarity with reading as a habit made such workshops necessary. Throughout these interactive sessions, editors and artists worked directly with young people and watched and listened as they acted out what they would do in particular segments of action plots. Teachers helped the artists create images of sufficient detail and general familiarity to meet the experiences and comprehension level of most South African students. The resulting uses of colloquial language, detailed artwork, and adventuresome characters won praise, not only from young readers but also from educators and adult literacy instructors as well as English as a second language program personnel. By the end of its first 2 years, the comic series reached a circulation of more than 750,000. Educators began thinking seriously about visual literacy and the ways in which readers interpreted diagrams, sketches, and abstract and fragmented pictures to create their sense of story. Within the next 5 years, several additional series, stressing not only science but also public health concerns and literature by black South African writers, reached learners across the age span. In preparation for the national elections in the spring of 1994, the Storyteller Group prepared posters and polling booth displays to help South Africans understand details of the voting process.

The results of research on the impact of comics for a variety of uses, from schools to savings programs, indicated that readers saw the pictorial and verbal representations of their own experiences as strong motivation not only to read but to extend what were for many narrow ways of using textbooks— often the only written text in their previous experience. Moreover, many students talked of the personal value that the comic books had for them, echoing a point made by a young township South African writer in the mid-1980s who had access to American comic books through his grandmother's employer. In his autobiography he wrote that comic books went with him everywhere until his English reached a level where he could read extensive literary writings (Mathabane, 1986). Today comic books, puppets, drama, and discussion of the variety of meanings that texts and pictures hold, have

entered numerous classrooms for the first time. Practice teachers and experienced teacher trainers use comics in their demonstration projects for rural teachers and other educators unfamiliar with reader response theories and active classroom discussion. A series for television on science concepts began to supplement the comic books in 1994, reinforcing and expanding the idea of finding and testing scientific and mathematical ideas in everyday practice. [Information given here on The Storyteller Group is drawn from interviews Heath held with staff members and educators in late 1994 and early 1995, as well as publications of the Group (see especially Bahr & Rifkin, 1992). Special thanks go to Peter Esterhuysen, editor, and Patricia Watson, researcher and staff member of The Storyteller Group, for their discussions of visual literacy and their experiences in numerous workshops throughout South Africa.]

In numerous countries, comic books appear when all else seems to fail to motivate reading or to alter attitudes and behaviors—for either the good or ill of society. In the late 1970s, German educators tried to use the comic medium to educate school children about the Third Reich. Censors not yet ready to expose some of the darkest chapters of the period shut down the effort. However, in the early 1990s, in the face of growing right-wing extremism among young Germans, the government's Centre for Political Education and the Reading Foundation combined to prepare a 200-page comic book biography of Adolph Hitler for 15- to 17-year-olds that teachers in several subject areas used to combat the Hitler-inspired racism, and anti-foreigner attitudes some youth in this age group found increasingly attractive. Ironically, in the 1930s and 1940s cartoon broadsides as well as posters and pamphlets, had spread Nazi propaganda and exploited mythic superhero figures to generate acceptance of Hitler as a dictator.

Fifty years later, the same medium embedded within political education efforts once again tried to offer a realistic portrayal of the events of World War II and the activities of the Third Reich. Research carried out in pilot studies in the early 1990s to compare the amount of information retained from comic books and standard history books indicated greater retention of information from the comic book as well as more vigorous discussion and debate that expanded concepts of the comic book presentation. Development of the comic book depended in large part on documentary sources, so that the speech balloons contained original statements by actual characters. Artists, historians, and youth policy experts teamed up to spread use of the comic book and its accompanying media package in schools and youth organizations. These comic book materials (like many in the United States) are complemented by a computer game entitled *Der Diktator* in which players receive points for successfully resisting various stages of a political leader's ascension to dictatorship (Bendelow, 1993).

ENVISIONING AND ENCODING INFORMATION

Interpretation of both the words and pictures of comic books depends on gaps and fill-in, on absences and presences.

Readers understand them by bringing to bear both their real-world information and creativity in image building and meaning making. By the 1970s, European scholars began to describe a theory of aesthetic response (Ingarden, 1973; Iser, 1978) that gave readers new kinds of credit as interpreters and as sense makers whose views of the meanings of literary art need not match those of literary critics. Any notion of a single meaning of artistic works or literary texts now met with strong resistance as theorists celebrated the power of readers to interpret texts and fill in their indeterminacies by image building and intersubjective communication of meaning.

Scholars interested in the relationship between visual images and real-world appearances debated similar issues. With particular attention to interpretation of films and photographs, some argued that viewers had to develop special conceptual categories and processing strategies to understand pictures (Snyder, 1980). Others gave more credence to the dominance of real-world informational cues in understanding visual images in the media and art (Messaris, 1994, especially chap. 1).

From time to time since the 1950s, when educators launched an intense struggle to discredit comic books (Wertham, 1954), scholars have debated the relevance of reading comics to "actual" reading skills and cognitive processing. For example, a common sense approach by proponents of comic books asserts that the linear dimensions of comic reading gives practice in left-to-right eye movements necessary for reading printed text. But close study of eye movements in reading comics indicates that the eye moves between words and pictures rapidly, so that neither the word nor the picture text remains linear in a left-to-right pattern (Barker, 1989). Instead, readers often, at the very least, do a double reading—following the multiple readings of pictures and sometimes their "sound words" (such as "Wham!"). This following of several narratives at a time parallels the mental activities of youngsters channel surfing and following several television programs while also doing homework or playing a card or board game with a friend. While adults tend to ask learners to have a single focus of attention, comics—especially comic books—promote multiple layers of attention and habituate readers to relating such layers to one another.

In addition, comics employ archetypal symbols as a kind of vocabulary of "design language" to support verbal messages. Dark colors, places of height and of hiding, and contrasts of small and large sizes convey patterns of repetition and sequence that parallel in many ways the patterning of folktales revealed by Propp (1975; Brent, 1991). Spatial patternings also indicate concepts such as the divergence between what a character is saying and what he or she is thinking. Marvel Comics often achieves this effect either by layering the same character in such a dual state or by including the overt action in the regular sequence and separating the covert thoughts of the character in another location on the page. Youngsters who report on their reading of comics often reveal how well they know just what is going on in the complexities of human emotion in the characters they read (see, for example, such testimonies in Krashen, 1989).

It is clear that neither presentation nor plot line in comics is straight; it is often by no means obvious. Adult readers often turn to youngsters to explain the humor in Garfield or the message of *Doonesbury* or *Calvin and Hobbes*. Increasingly, comic strips and books leave open endings, relate to current events, and call for a breadth of types of experiential knowledge that adult readers will not have. The "flash of meaning" approach found in MTV and animated films also appears in comics, where only a hint of something that has passed or of something to come appears. This approach may, for example, allow some readers to employ a one-character-after-another reading of speech balloons. In the Marvel Comics, these balloons appear in small parts, cutting the image; hence, some readers follow a single character's words through a full page and then return to another's, and so on, for the full page.

The conventions of reading *visual* images in comics as elsewhere in art, rather than being a separate arbitrary set, depend on readers making use of not only their experiences with similar techniques of other media, but also their understanding of conflicts of power, matching of wits, and access to special technologies that characters (and readers) may have or imagine to be possible. At its most basic level, the encoding of visual images follows unmediated experience for many young readers, making it unnecessary for them to acquire a particular set of conceptual categories or analytical strategies to understand what is going on (Messaris, 1994). But it is important to remember that visual displays encourage a diversity of individual viewing styles as well as rates of reasoning, understanding, and personalizing what is being seen: to borrow an analogy from broadcasting, "visual displays are simultaneously a wideband and a perceiver-controllable channel" (Tufte, 1990, p. 31). Sighted individuals have the capacities to edit, structure, feature, ignore, classify, scan, or integrate visual information; they can either take in, reject, or reshape visual information through experiential, attitudinal, and situational stimuli. "Seeing is believing," not because everyone sees the same image, but because seeing is strongly influenced by human capacities to integrate visual information with other kinds of knowledge and context-shifting abilities. It is difficult, if not impossible, for neurologically normal human beings not to layer information from a variety of sense sources (eyes, smell, touch), as well as cognitive and affective dimensions. All of these combinations, plus their context sensitivity to the moment of reading, contribute to the multiple meanings that words and pictures give in the visual displays of comics. Anecdotal evidence of this phenomenon often appears when adults who were devoted to comics as children recall their small intricate drawings, the gloss of covers, and the warm cozy hiding places in which they used to steal away to read them. Little of their plots or conventions is remembered, but certain visuals in the books and sensual responses to reading them flood back from memory.

At the end of the 20th century, the term *comic* for comic books is probably more inappropriate than at any time in their history. Most of those preferred by today's young readers have little that is directly comic. They speak to readers about loss of control, struggles with parents and bullies, and the contradictions of women as nurturers and as superheroes. In Marvel's *The Fantastic Four*, for example, Susan Richards as Invisible Woman faces a son who wonders why his parents are not at home more often. She suffers a miscarriage as a result of her superheroine-like activities. Vietnam veterans write about their war in *Nam,* done for Marvel Comics, and teenage titans move about the world facing famine, political intrigue, and floods. Family obligations, education, drugs, crime, and political and philosophical debates enter their texts. Editors defend the trend away from adventuristic humorous stories by pointing to the maturing experiences many young people face early in life today. In addition, they argue that these are issues and concepts that other reading materials for young people often ignore or treat in didactic ways. Comics give voice to parts of young readers' experience and imagination;

they play a key role in cross-media theme development, and they illustrate multiple ways of presenting information— verbal, visual, and graphic. In the words of Stan Lee, publisher of Marvel Comics, "the illustrated format of comic books favorably competes with *any* and *every* form of literature." In an era when literary texts and age-old literary themes enter new forms every year—from films to adventure games in arcades to hypertext—the visual and verbal powers of comics may be one of the most powerful and productive forms of preparation and motivation available to invite new readers into literacy habits.

References

Bahr, M., & Rifkin, C. (1992). *Interim research report—storynet.* Melville, SA: The Storyteller Group.

Barker, M. (1989). *Comics, ideology, power and the critics.* New York: Manchester University Press.

Bendelow, P. (1993, October 1). Comics bid to stem the Nazi tide. *Times Educational Supplement,* p. 33.

Berger, A. A. (1973). *The comic stripped American.* New York: Walker.

Brent, R. S. (1991, Spring). Nonverbal design language in comics. *Journal of American Culture.*

Cahn, J. M. (1986). *The teenie weenies book: The life and art of William Donahey.* La Jolla, CA: Green Tiger Press.

Dorrell, L. D. (1987). Why comic books? *School Library Journal, 34*(3), 30–32.

Dorrell, L. D., & Carroll, C. E. (1981). Spider-man at the library. *School Library Journal, 27*(10), 17–19.

Eisner, W. (1992). *Comics and sequential art.* Princeton, WI: Kitchen Sink Press.

Foster, J. (1991). From "ulla dulla mogo" to "serene azure vault of heaven": Literary style in Australian children's comic books. *Journal of Popular Culture, 25*(3), 63–77.

Ingarden, R. (1973). *The literary work of art.* (G. Grabowicz, Trans.). Evanston, IL: Northwestern University Press.

Inge, M. T. (1988). Comic books. *Handbook of American popular literature* (pp. 74–99). New York: Greenwood Press.

Inge, M.T. (1989). Comic strips. *Handbook of American popular culture* (2nd ed., pp. 196–219). New York: Greenwood Press.

Iser, W. (1978). *The act of reading: A theory of aesthetic response.* Baltimore: Johns Hopkins University Press.

Krashen, S. (1989). Language teaching technology: A low-tech view. In *Georgetown University round table on languages and linguistics, 1989* (pp. 392–340). Washington, DC: Georgetown University Press.

Kunzle, D. (1973). *The early comic strip.* Berkeley, CA: University of California Press.

Mathabane, M. (1986). *Kaffir boy.* New York: Plume.

McCloud, S. (1993). *Understanding comics: The invisible art.* New York: Harper Perennial.

Messaris, P. (1994). *Visual literacy: Image, mind, & reality.* Boulder, CO: Westview Press.

Propp, V. (1975). *Morphology of the folktale.* (2nd. ed.). Austin, TX: University of Texas Press.

Schmitt, R. (1992). Deconstructive comics. *Journal of Popular Culture, 25*(4), 153–161.

Snyder, J. (1980). Picturing vision. *Critical Inquiry, 6*(3), 499–526.

Tufte, E. (1990). *Envisioning information.* Chesire, CN: Graphics Press.

Wertham, F. (1954). *Seduction of the innocent.* New York: Rinehart.

Winner, E. (1982). *Invented worlds: The psychology of the arts.* Cambridge, MA: Harvard University Press.

Wolf, S. A., & Heath, S. B. (1992). *The braid of literature: Children's worlds of reading.* Cambridge, MA: Harvard University Press.

51

ACCOUNTABILITY THROUGH ASSESSMENT AND INSTRUCTION

Roger Farr

INDIANA UNIVERSITY

Eugene Jongsma

DIRECTOR OF EDUCATIONAL ASSESSMENT, HARCOURT BRACE SCHOOL PUBLISHERS

LANGUAGE-RELATED ASSESSMENT ON THE THRESHOLD OF A NEW CENTURY

The widespread demand for educational accountability has been reviewed and analyzed many times (e.g., Farr, & Olshavsky, 1980). At the same time that this demand to endorse and promote the use of traditional forms of assessment appeared, the development of theory about how people think, learn, and express themselves has called for the development of assessments that reflect the processes those theories describe (Anderson, & Pearson, 1984; Johnston, 1986).

Emerging theory has been highly convincing and persuasive as it defines language use as a *thinking process* (Williamson, 1983), and acceptance of this description has led to the questioning of assessment that attempts to break meaning-making down into a list of skills that can be measured with a host of tests. This attention to theory–practice mismatch has become a major criticism of assessment (Farr, Carey, & Tone, 1986; Froese, 1987; Valencia, & Pearson, 1987).

Most tests that have been mandated in a majority of the states in recent decades are of this type (Afflerbach, 1990), and concern about being accountable to them has tended to recommend teaching strategies that present learning and thinking with language as isolated skills that can be drilled in very short and inauthentic meaning bites. Across schools and teachers, this has curtailed instructional emphases that meet individual student needs for comprehending and expressing oneself. Thus standardized tests have not mod-eled or measured the emerging definitions of the meaning-making process in any convincing way.

Current models of literacy begin with the user's reasons for making meaning, with an examination of how those reasons combine with the user's understanding of author purpose or any audience involved, with the user's application of personal background, and with adjustments and revisions made as the user self-evaluates how well the process is meeting his or her needs. All this is meshed in a process within the so far impenetrable "black box" of language and thinking (Hambrick, 1991), a highly complex behavior that seems to defy stratification and any attempt to describe it with ordered sets of prioritized skills (Farr, & Tone, 1982).

We now understand that processes like reading operate in ways that extend far beyond a single language mode. People make meaning using a rich mixture of signs and expressions. These include complex semiotic input and communication (Suhor, 1982), including dance and body language (Beyond words..., 1988; Leung, 1986) and extensive use of drama (Fiala, 1979). They can involve appreciation and response to music as well as its expression; and they tap a host of visual environments and expressions (Siegel, & Carey, 1989). Golson and Kirscht (1983) discuss Langer's explanation of how *presentational* and *discursive symbolism* fuse art and knowledge and recommend an increasingly attractive instructional approach (Harp, 1987).

This goes beyond the intention of teaching language development across the curriculum to a genuine integration of disciplines (Duke, 1987; Kaltsounis, 1990; Rabson, & Warshaw, 1980). It stresses the interactive nature of the arts with special attention given to broad-based learning and language development (Hoyt, 1992; Spillane, 1987).

Criticism of standardized testing has rightly focused on its attention to isolated behaviors measured in unrealistic (invalid and inauthentic) ways (primarily with responses to multiple-choice items). This does not necessarily condemn the norm-referenced, multiple-choice testing of reading, for example, as valueless; but it certainly challenges the use of its data as the sole or even primary basis of broad-based educational decision making. Such tests produce but one type of information that helps underline the need for assessment that can indicate how well students make meaning of topics that cross many disciplines (as comprehenders and expressers) from the access they have to an incredibly rich mix of various media.

That is what life is like, especially in a world served by newly developed technologies; and that is what we are supposedly eager to prepare students for, so that development of these meaning-making processes is presumably what we would like to assess. It is a challenge, but the technologies that provide an ever-richer environment for learners have also begun to provide the means to attempt to do this.

The long time span over which this realization about educational assessment needs gained force would suggest that test makers have not been highly responsive to criticism or theory development; yet given the traditionally cautious and conservative tendency of assessment designers and publishers, criticism of reading assessment in particular and of assessment of language development in general has indeed served as analysis that has had some impact on assessment over the years (Farr, & Tone, 1994a):

- Standardized testing of reading, which has continued to draw the most prevailing criticism, has responded by attempting to provide and promote diagnostic applications of its results, by increasing the length of passages, and by using title-like questions that attempt to establish a purpose for reading. The criticisms of such issues and responses were discussed by Farr and Beck (1994).

- The new understanding of how thinking processes appear to work developed during decades of theory making that has emerged at the same time that public concern—even panic—about the quality of education has grown dramatically (Afflerbach, 1990). Ironically, the latter has reinforced a dependency on and demand for the kinds of assessment that the new theories question. While the ever-increasing cost of our schools is an enduring motivation for public demand for educational accountability, the widely reported decline of scores on tests such as *The Scholastic Achievement Tests,* an instrument used to screen college applicants, was the primary factor for many years. That the college-bound students taking such tests had grown and changed dramatically—in number, background, and attitudes—did not assuage the public clamor for more effective, and usually rigid, instructional objectives. To the general public this would be evident in improved test scores. Thus criterion testing matched more directly to instructional objectives has gained considerable popularity among educators and other citizens who are interested in

customizing assessments to show if particular students have mastered particular objectives they believe are important. While this coverage of numerous subskills may have customized the faith that many have in a skill-drill approach to instruction, it has flown in the face of 30 years of developing theory about how people construct meaning by using language and other means of expression.

- Schools have been as conservative as test makers in implementing alternative assessment (Cawelti, 1994), but in recent years, new *performance assessments* have been developed in response to emerging theory about language use and development (Farr, & Greene, 1993; Farr, & Tone, 1994b; Smith, 1991). In response to this broader concept of literacy, these instruments examine student products as well as the processes, which created them; and integrate different language behaviors. As the description of recently developed performance reading and writing tests will show, once one depends on student expression to demonstrate comprehension, the integration of similar language processes can occur naturally. Such assessments also facilitate cross-curricular integration, for the subject matter selected can come from science, social studies, or other disciplines.

- The brief description of *portfolio assessment* later in this chapter suggests how other forms of expression can be integrated with the assessment of reading and writing (Farr, 1990). In such collections, artwork is frequently as important as written expressions, which may be lyrics set to music or critical and appreciative descriptions of art, music, dance, and other forms of expression.

- Finally, the extended description near the end of this chapter of an assessment instrument under development demonstrates how *multimedia technologies* now available in some schools can link the comprehension of various types of text, audio, and video sources of information. The new instrument suggests much potential for assessing responses to different expressions, such as the written word, music, the graphic and other arts, and the dramatic arts with interactive activities that respond to a meaningful task.

Such trends in assessment development are responses to our growing understanding of how people learn, think, and express themselves.

Portfolio Assessment is a Promising Response to Concerns About Validity

If a major concern about language testing is that it invalidly reflects the behavior or behaviors it measures—that it does not provide or consider genuine purposes for reading, writing, speaking, listening, or drawing that relate realistically to student backgrounds and interests—the growing popularity of *portfolio assessment* is an encouraging response (Tierney, Carter, & Desai, 1991; Valencia, 1990; Valencia, Pearson, Peters, & Wixson, 1989). Simply described, portfolio assessment is the practice of keeping lots of specimens of student writing, drawing, and thinking together so that they can be analyzed by both the student and teacher over time to improve learning and instruction.

Portfolios can also be used quite effectively to demonstrate student performance to parents, administrators, and others. Since the contents are usually so uniquely personal, each portfolio requires special attention that places considerable demands on such viewers; but the effort frequently rewards the assessor with a perspective on the student as a thinker and language user that cannot easily be acquired in other ways. The literature of language education includes a growing number of testimonies to this effect (Johns, & Leirsburg, 1992; McRobbie, 1992; Miller, 1992; Wiggins, 1989; Wolf, 1992). This approach to accountability assessment, however, is still evolving. A report by Gentile (1992) of the analysis of 4,000 student portfolios showed that they had promise for informing audiences interested in accountability. Similarly, the NAEP 1992 Writing Portfolio Study (Gentile, Martin-Rehrman, & Kennedy, 1995) showed that writing portfolios can be valuable supplements to other forms of assessment.

Portfolios do not facilitate the kind of quantifiable comparisons that those demanding school and student accountability have come to expect, and they challenge the objective evaluator to define the educational outcomes that are the basis of his or her criticism and/or concerns (Tierney et al., 1991; Russavage, 1992).

There are, however, numerous considerations that help insure the success of portfolio assessment for both instruction and accountability, (Farr, & Tone, 1994b):

- It is vital in such a system, that the collection center as much as possible on reaction to, and uses of, texts that the student has read; but the portfolio should contain a mix of multiple kinds of expression and interests. It can include different kinds of journal entries, notes, clippings, favorite pictures, audio- and videotapes of student thoughts and projects, records and other information on computer discs, and reactions of the journal keeper, his or her peers, parents, the teacher, and others.

- The collection should include numerous specimens of student thinking and notes and drafts reflective of language and thinking processes. It needs to be more than just the student's best work.

- The student should have primary control of the collection, have ready and regular access to it, and be guided and even be required to evaluate, analyze, and reorganize it frequently and regularly. A good portfolio system usually provides some printed aids to guide the student in that direction. At the same time, the student is aware that his or her teacher, parents, school administrators, and even fellow students may be looking at it and evaluating it informally from time to time.

- Regular and relatively frequent teacher–student conferences are essential to assure that the portfolio supports and promotes self-assessment strategies that can guide future reading, writing, and other expression (Farr, & Tone, 1994b, chap. 5).

Basically, portfolio assessment appears to restore faith in trained teacher judgment; but many critics question its dependability as an accountability measure, arguing that with ongoing teacher and student control of the collection, it could be manipulated to suggest better performance than that which exists. Teachers who cull student collections to leave just the best pieces for outside inspection may have little faith in the outside observer to use a fuller collection to consider student's thinking, expressions, and interests as a process. Teachers who limit the collection to just final drafts of student writing (and even particular types of writing) are denying its potential to reflect the multimedia that surely influences the student's thoughts.

Due to of its potential to reflect student thinking more validly, the portfolio is being considered in some places as assessment that reports on school and teacher accountability; but this practice works only when the audience understands the importance of assessing student meaning-making as a process. Educating those who would examine portfolios for accountability, as well as those who guide their development, and developing the mutual trust among all who examine them is an apparent problem yet to be adequately solved (Kemp, Cooper, & Davies, 1991).

In an attempt to conduct broad assessment using portfolios one approach pulls random samples from the universe in a classroom to show a supervisor, in a school to show to the press, or in a school system or state for accountability purposes. A principal or supervisor, for example, may be invited to select six or ten student portfolios at random to examine. It is important in such a practice, to make sure that the persons inspecting the random collection know what to look for (as those in studies of the potential of portfolios are trained to do); and teachers can make sure that the viewers know how the collections were gathered and are maintained and can make some suggestions for things to look for. The importance of tapes, drawings, pictures, and even student-made models of settings, situations, and other creative ideas needs to be understood. It is especially important that viewers know when they are looking at portfolios whose owners have been encouraged to be "inclusive," keeping notes, drafts, and ideas for future expressions and reading.

Generally, however, use of portfolios in broad accountability programs, such as those that have been used in some states (Kapinus et al., 1994; Koretz et al., 1992; New Mexico, 1991-92; Snider et al., 1994) tends to structure portfolio content in a fashion that may limit the inclusion of multimedia materials. Yet the value of miscellaneous contents to support a student's language development is too important to let limitations that may appear necessary for accountability uses influence portfolio assessment in the classroom.

Other approaches attempting to make portfolios more usable for accountability purposes have supported comparison among students and have specified the kinds of reading and writing students should be able to do. They have dictated particular contents—a practice which can limit use of the portfolio by the student for self-assessment. This is problematic: If the ultimate purpose of educational assessment—in language use, for example—is to develop more effective language users, then its primary purpose ought to be to contribute to developing the students as self-assessors. Teachers, school systems, and critics cannot be following people around all their lives to see if they are using language effectively and advising them on how to improve their language processes. The only sure source of that ongoing, personal guidance is the student himself or herself!

Self-Assessment is Promoted by a Growing Emphasis on Metacognition

Whether metacognition is by definition and necessity a conscious effort as theorists such as Brown (1975), Paris Wasik and Van der Westhuizen (1988) and Wagoner (1983) contend; an active control of a hidden process, as suggested by Block (1992), or a broader, more generic kind of knowledge about comprehension that can for example, have an automatic impact on one's processing of text, (Flavell, 1979)—it is, nonetheless, the essence of the development of a reader. It is certainly an indication that a language user has some idea of how he or she comprehends and of what to do when comprehension is not taking place. Both researchers and educators have begun to take more notice of it.

As researchers have focused on metacognition (Paris, & Oka, 1986); (Paris et al., 1988), (Wagoner, 1983); strategies for collecting data on the mental processes it employs have been developed as questioning either during or after a text is read (Olshavsky, 1976–77; Powell, 1989). Related techniques have been devised for instruction. "Think-alongs" are running verbal or written stream-of-conscious reports that can be used to gather data on student processing of texts while they read (Farr, & Greene, 1992). Researchers get students to report aloud about their ongoing reactions to texts by modeling the process for the subjects. This modeling is used not only for research, but primarily as a teaching device in which the teacher reveals what she or he is thinking as a text is read. It invariably demonstrates how background is called up by texts and contributes to the comprehension of it. It reveals problems with diction and language structures. At the same time, the process becomes a model for students to follow. As they think aloud about their reactions and the various thoughts that a text provokes, the experience promotes and develops student metacognition.

Standardized tests have added items that purport to measure metacognition, and basal series offer activities to build it and explanations of how it can be developed to teachers (Farr, 1989). There are many classifications of reading strategies that suggest metacognitive questions a reader can ask himself or herself, but generally they can be grouped with eight icons that help a reader remember them:

1. Do I have a specific purpose as I read this story/book/text? What do I want to know after reading this? What is my specific purpose for writing this? What do I want my audience I am writing to know?

2. Have I thought about what I already know about this topic before I begin to read or write (or as I am reading or writing)?

3. Have I thought about the ideas I will probably find in reading this or that I intend to write? Have I done this before I began to read and write? What do the title, the pictures, and other clues tell me to expect?

4. As I am reading or writing, do I think about what is coming next? What predictions can I make?

5. Do I picture in my mind what I am reading or writing? Am I able to visualize this?

6. Do I ask myself as I read and write, "Is this making good sense?" How do the ideas fit together?

7. Do I change my mind and revise the meaning I am making if necessary? Do I make changes if things don't make sense? Do I need to change direction in my thinking?

8. Do I need to reach out for help from other things I have read or written? from my classmates? from my parents? from my teachers? from classroom resources?

FIGURES 51–1

This metacognitive checklist is not all-inclusive, and individual teachers and readers may easily think of other questions they want to ask themselves each time they read and write. But the strategic self-questioning prompted by these icons does demonstrate the simplicity and common sense of useful metacognitive behavior. They can be adapted easily for meaning-making using any kind of communication, including music, motion, and drawing. If young learners were to remember and ask just these, they would be in the practice mode to develop metacognitive strategies that could strengthen their ability to communicate and to comprehend by processing ideas, descriptions, and other information more effectively.

Much of the work by researchers on metacognition appears to be on efforts to test theoretical definitions of it, to analyze it in terms of types and types of strategies that it involves to help define it, and to come to grips with it by reviewing the theory and research that have helped create a broader understanding of literacy.

While all this is a useful and potentially valuable emphasis, the technical distinction between a definition of *cognition* and *metacognition* becomes somewhat academic; although it seems possible that a part of the complex interactions involved in meaning-making might include self-questioning habits and approaches to dealing with difficult text, that operate without deliberate commitment or attention but which can be developed and incorporated by classroom and self-instruction.

Portfolio assessment, conducted effectively, is the ideal tool to promote student self-assessment (Herter, 1991; Sunstein, 1992). It structures the comparison of current to past efforts while providing the incentive to plan for future reading, writing, and other expression. It can incorporate the reactions of teachers, fellow students, and parents to its contents and be a concrete and wholly valid demonstration of strengths and areas that need attention. Indications of reactions to larger portfolio projects, however, indicate that while critics and the public may find portfolios fascinating and enlightening about student thinking and processes, they still seek assessments that show how a student's performance compares to that of other students, or how it compares to accepted benchmarks or standards.

Performance Tests and Portfolio Assessment Appear to be Valid Assessment

One response in recent years to the criticism of the validity of tests that assess language use has been the development of *performance assessments* by several publishers, states, consortia, districts, and individual schools (Beaverton... District, 1984; Coley, 1990; Farr et at., 1989; Ferrett, 1991; O'Neil, 1992). They are also in use in England (Lutrario, 1991). They aim at capturing genuine reasons for reading and writing. Like the portfolio, performance assessments can provide a more valid assessment of language behaviors, and they can easily incorporate other kinds of input and expression. At the same time, they can best be prepared through an implementation of field tryout results that are actually used in structuring them. This procedure can provide a framework and extensive samples for comparison of results to the performance of students deemed typical of the age tested.

These tests vary in format and scoring. Some, for example, ask students to complete open-ended questions after reading a selection, while others require students to produce longer, extended responses. Extended performance assessments generally include the following characteristics:

- *A passage (or a group of texts) related to a particular topic or problem as a "prompt" to promote student writing.* Across a basal reader, for example, or a test publisher's system, these problems will encompass numerous genres, subject content areas, graphic format, and styles. Some may be charts, maps, lists, photos, or other graphic materials. Many such prompts are as generously illustrated as typical reading materials that the students might frequently encounter.

- *An assigned task for responding to the textual prompt, usually in writing.* These tasks establish a purpose for writing that would seem appropriate for the grade level, and they identify the audience for whom the student is writing. The types or styles of writing required of the student vary across different assessment prompts, from personal letters or journal entries to reports to employers or school administrators. They can be as simple—in a basal unit assessment, for example—as writing a conclusion for an unfinished story, or as complex as analyzing and synthesizing opposing arguments, charts, letters, speeches, and technical articles related to a societal problem (a college competency measure). They can be designed for kindergartners or beginning first graders as the request for an original captioned picture, or for elementary children as letters of advice to characters with problems- or directions-based descriptions provided.

- *A brief, but relatively complete explanation to the student about how the response will be evaluated.* This scheme is often presented to the student in outline or bulleted form.

- *A prewriting guide that the student can use in preparing to write the response.* These are designed to logically serve the assigned task and are often relatively simple. They may suggest a chart (for comparisons, for example) or a form of an outline. These are usually optional and the student is advised that he or she can organize and prepare to write using any other system that seems effective and comfortable.

- *A self-evaluation guide to direct revision and other polishing and checking.* This component may be as simple as a short set of questions that the student can ask himself or herself about the first draft. While these questions focus on content and always encourage the student to review the task and audience and to self-evaluate from that perspective, they frequently also remind the writer to look for clarity and mechanical errors. Almost all performance assessment instruments encourage the student to revise as a final draft and give the student the time to allow for that. Depending on the use that will be made of the student response, the planning notes and early drafts may or may not be kept with the final draft. An example of how the full response can be useful is its inclusion in a student's portfolio. These sets of notes, draft, and final draft provide the student with an excellent record of her or his processing of information using language.

- *A scoring system expanded as a rubric that the rater of responses can follow.* These systems are often quite simple: the response may be rated on as few as two, and often just three, general categories, such as *Reading* (understanding / comprehension of the text), *Writing* (organization, mechanics), and *Accomplishment of Task* (consideration of audience in terms of the assigned task and content). Seldom does such a scheme include more than four general categories, and although the categories may be defined or expanded as subfactors, these are not rated separately. A general category called Reading, for example, may be described in terms of accuracy of details reported, completeness of details in terms of those needed to complete the task effectively, understanding of relationships, or other subfactors. These are explained in a very simple chart.

- *A simple rating scheme that seldom ranges more than 1–5 (with 1 usually low) and are frequently rated 1, 2, or 3.* A description of each rating usually appears in a table with each number described or defined for each general category. An expanded rubric may explain each general rating in terms of each subfactor. The authors are not aware of any such system which encourages raters to average or subsume the ratings for the categories into a single score for a particular student's response as an overall, and overriding rating.

- *A full set of "model" or "anchor" papers as examples of ones that would get a particular score in each particular major category.* Since this component of the performance assessment package can be the most important scoring aid in it, it should include at least two samples or anchors for each score within each category. These should be drawn from responses acquired through a sizable tryout of the assessment, should be selected by a group of scorers who are in agreement about them, and should be significantly different in some aspect that was suggested by the complete set of responses in the tryout.

A vital part of this collection should be a very carefully written annotation that accompanies each sample paper, explaining what the scorers who rated it with the number it represents saw in it. Some authors and publishers of such tests strongly advise that rating be done primarily by matching student responses to these anchor papers and that if this were done with genuine care, the rubric could often be laid aside.

A published series of performance assessment instruments that contains all of these components is described by Werner (1992). As the description of the multimedia assessment project below indicates, components including sound, moving videos, and other media can be added to various types of print in creating performance assessment prompts of the future.

That administrators, parents, and other members of the community, such as journalists with an educational beat, appear to readily accept performance assessment should not come as a great surprise. Why shouldn't a chance to look at a paper based on a seemingly valid experience and rated in several key ways be more meaningful to such an audience than the statistical data provided by nationally administered norm-referenced tests? Meyer, Schuman, and Angello, (1990) explain how aggregated analyses of portfolios can meet the needs of audiences that have depended on standardized test results, and Simmons (1990) reports research indicating that they can be adapted to serve accountability needs. Moss, et al. (1992) suggests how the assessment information should be reported.

What a school relying on performance testing to account should do is to explain how their scoring system has been developed, so that a 4 in Writing does indeed represent an excellent performance—compared to the broad sample of like-aged students used to develop the test (if it is from a major publisher) or a large sample of local students (if developed locally). In the latter case, it can be explained that the score also reflects the judgment of a panel of teachers who cooperated to develop the test. At the same time, a truly interested reporter, administrator, or critic can be introduced to the anchor samples and rubric and be invited to assess a sample of papers.

Why Should we Feel the Need to Rely on a Single Type of Assessment?

Why should our educational system and society be obligated to rely on any single approach to assessment? In truth, and in current practice, we do not. Standardized testing can afford the kind of comparison to the norming sample that many citizens seeking educational accountability seem to appreciate and demand. But while relying on and reporting it, educators (and journalists, too) would do well to explain that the multiple-choice format of standardized testing is criticized by many educators and theorists as a far cry from the actual reading process. Multiple-choice items on standardized writing tests may call for editorial recognition of correct mechanical form but are only that—an indication that a student can recognize correct usage (spelling, punctuation, diction, number agreement, etc.) when presented with an isolated focus. *Such tests are hardly a valid representation of whether students can write with a genuine purpose for a particular audience!*

If you want a comparison of how your students do as copy editors of canned, limited, and isolated text (an admittedly a typical language behavior) when their performance is compared to a national sample used to norm that test, the results of a standardized instrument can be useful. If you can get scores on the same test of students from other locales, you are provided some more comparisons—on those multiple-choice responses to very isolated skills and fragmented focus on meaning-making. Many of the critics who demand such scores may not understand them well, but they should be encouraged to press publishers for clear descriptions of the norming populations they are comparing their students to. Teachers inclined to rely on the diagnostic aspects of those tests, should be reminded that a limited number of items on a particular skill can serve only as an initial indication; the standardization of the instrument does not make them any more useful than that. *If you want to know if your students can write, you had better look to other assessments!*

Teachers have always created criterion-referenced tests for their individual classrooms and have based grades and instructional emphasis on the results. Students can identify prescribed, if limited, objectives that they have not yet mastered. The primary advantage of criterion-referenced tests is that they can be tailored for particular students in a specific classroom in any one year. Their highly prevalent use in wider educational arenas, as state competency exams, for example, is a phenomenon that began over 20 years ago and then virtually swept the nation (Farr, & Olshavsky, 1980). Results from these tests are of use to teachers who support or are obligated to support the criteria (particular performance objectives) used to prepare them. In that regard, they can be diagnostic, as well as dictatorial.

If such tests and the administration of them do not change

significantly over time, scores on them can be used to compare student performance to that of students who have taken them previously. Any critics who have helped articulate the objectives will surely use the scores on them to judge the schools' accountability, but everyone should be aware that these instruments are rarely normed before use and that whatever percentages are purported as "acceptable," "excellent," or whatever are arbitrarily established. Furthermore, people who rely on reports of scores on criterion-referenced tests should examine the test's content and the objectives that dictate it.

Most significantly, like the nationally standardized test, they are almost certainly made up of multiple-choice items that can be challenged as an invalid representation of the way that students are expected to use—and actually do use—language. While they are used, and misused, by other assessment audiences, they are of most value to the teacher who teaches to a rather specific and lengthy set of objectives.

In the 1990s, some schools are using performance assessment-often in addition to standardized and criterion-referenced tests (Hansen, 1992). While portfolios and other approaches are generally and correctly classified as assessment of performance (Feuer, & Fulton, 1993), the discussion here centers on a more particular approach that uses textual prompts to generate student writing (Farr, 1993; Farr, & Farr, 1990; *Indiana Performance Assessment '92*).

The results of such assessments are highly useful to both teachers and students! and representatives of these schools can add: "If you would like to see how our students performed while actually reading and writing for what we hope you will believe is a meaningful purpose, we have something else to show you. Our students read and used a particular text to complete a particular task. Their responses were scored in several key ways, and those scores can be related to carefully articulated criteria and sample papers that were written by real students of equivalent ages and that got similar scores from a panel of teachers and educators who read them and agreed about their merit. We invite you to react to how useful or meaningful you think the tasks assigned are for our students and how appropriate the texts are for the students and the tasks."

If those interested in educational accountability can get score percentages for other locales, they can make that comparison as well. Interestingly, such users are apt to become so interested in the task, the text, and the individual student responses that they may forget about the need for numbers to tell them how the students are reading and writing. If that happens, the performance assessment test has lived up to its very valuable potential to link the various assessment audiences in order to demonstrate student performance in a far more valid manner than standardized tests have or can.

It would be misleading to ignore the concerns of some test experts about the use of tests such as performance assessments and portfolios (Beck, 1991). The features of developing performance assessments that can be argued to be a form of standardization rely on the subjective judgment of the raters involved in the procedure. Even if that judgment is unanimous, that degree of subjectivity, such experts' advice, does

not recommend making wide-sweeping educational decisions on the basis of score reports that they produce. Even the most enthusiastic supporters of portfolio assessment note problematic issues that need to be considered and addressed (Valencia, & Calfee, 1991).

Others look on developments like portfolio assessment as opportunities but express concerns about how effectively the collections will be used (Calfee, & Perfumo, 1993). Grant Wiggins expects much of such assessment reforms but expresses concerns that they may fail if the high stakes attached to them force too heavy a reliance on them before problems such as task validity, score reliability, methods of portfolio sampling, and those related to the generalizability of results are solved (Brandt, 1992)

Such concerns reflect the emphasis on formal assessment that has come about in the past several decades and on its use in holding schools more accountable. This has developed as a response to criticism of the schools, which in turn has intensified as scores dropped on tests like those used to predict how well students will do in college. Few standardized tests were administered evenly and widely enough over the years to make comparison of widespread student performance across time periods very dependable, but the general interpretation of the media, public, and educational decision makers was to confirm the criticism and to demand more accountability reported in test scores (Farr, & Fay, 1982).

The increase in reliance on standardized tests led, in turn, to reasonable concerns about how well tests can measure educational accomplishments without narrowly beginning to dictate the curricula they purported to measure. So, more and more tests were constructed by states and local school districts to match their particular educational goals and curricula and to measure minimally acceptable results (Farr, & Olshavsky, 1980). These criterion-referenced measures are now in place in a majority of states and schools systems and have tended to be administered in addition to, not in place of, standardized testing. Many educators became alarmed about the narrowing influence of the testing phenomenon on what is taught, noting that teachers will tend to emphasize what is on tests holding them accountable at the expense whatever the tests do not cover.

All this occurred as slowly emerging theory began to explain language development, as one example, as meaning-making that responds to individual student needs, interests, and backgrounds. This perspective invariable integrates different language behaviors, thinking, and learning in complex ways that defy skill stratification and sequencing. So, it was that newer forms of assessment have attempted to examine student efforts in performing real tasks that integrate these abilities (Farr, & Tone, 1982; Pikulski, 1989).

At the same time that performance assessment has developed, both standardized and criterion-referenced testings have continued. The interlocking purposes of the different forms of assessment serve a variety of audiences. (See Farr, & Tone, 1994b, chap. 6).

So we are left with the seemingly sensible conclusion that most information is useful and that different types of assessment produce different kinds of information that may be useful to different assessment audiences but that are, depending on the type, more useful to some audiences than to others (Farr, 1992). To clarify this issue adequately, we need first to rethink and to carefully articulate what it is that we expect to achieve with instruction and what we want to learn from assessment. Such an effort could reasonably be tied to a study of how assessment results are and have been used and misused.

Any contention that most assessment should be useful to someone must yet face the long-held and sensible objection that testing uses up two valuable educational commodities: time and money. An increased emphasis on assessment means that more time is being spent on test taking and less on learning. If we are to endorse all types of assessment as of value and each type as the best suited for a particular audience or two, aren't we contributing to the overuse of testing?

This argument seemed particularly acceptable as states and schools added rather massive testing programs that theory could not endorse as very valid. But alternative performance assessments in use today, and most certainly portfolio assessment, are practice of the very processes they assess. Analysis of student efforts from both types serve instruction in potentially highly effective ways. Above all, they promote self-evaluation and develop metacognition. In short, this type of assessment has to reflect instruction so directly that it is rather meaningless to try to tell them apart or to fret about how much time is used (Paulson, Paulson, and Meyer, 1991). Both the class time and the portion of the instructional budget dedicated to them are serving double duty.

The Time has Arrived to Assess Student Ability to use Multimedia

Concerns about how literate our students are constitute a vital issue that can certainly be informed by assessment. We are at the doorstep of the 21st century, and it is time to acknowledge that the best way to assess students' ability to think is to see if they can apply the meaning they make. In doing that, we recognize that the various language behaviors are complexly linked as thinking processes. And we know that people make meaning in more ways than just reading, listening, speaking, and listening. They observe or view things, and they visualize. They communicate with body movements, and structure that into dance. They listen to more than words. They respond to and make nonlanguage sounds using all kinds of instruments.

None of this input and output is isolated, the way that tests try to do. Varied responses come from a synthesis of all kinds of perceptions. Midway into the 1990s we can demonstrate all of this on our home computers, which give us the printed word, moving videos, graphic stills, a host of sounds including the human voice, animated games and stories, and almost unlimited access to information. We store an encyclopedia on a tiny silver disc, and we can go on-line to great libraries near and far and to a host of specialized information sources.

Are we interested in knowing how well our students can function in such an almost unbelievably rich multimedia environment? If the development of assessment moves with the tortoise-like caution and deliberation of the past, all the stimuli our students must process everywhere else may make school itself seem obsolete. *If assessment has seemed a peculiarly unrealistic experience before, it could seem humorously esoteric to them in the near future!*

Does it seem unreasonable then that some assessment specialists are developing instruments that exploit the *multimedia* stimuli that many school computers will soon be capable of providing.

Technology is Suggesting new Formats

Multimedia is a difficult term to define because it means so many things to so many people. Generally, "multimedia means that more than one medium of communication is employed to deliver a message" (Kanning, 1994, p. 40). Advances in computer technology have enabled developers to integrate the presentation of text, still images, animation, video, and audio into a single program or product. CD-ROM has become the primary source of delivering multimedia, but videodiscs, slide shows, digitized sound sources, illustrative libraries, scanners, and the developing information highway are examples of other means of delivery.

Multimedia is clearly the technology trend of the 1990s (Owens, 1992). Two million CD-ROM discs were sold in 1993. That number is expected to climb to 64 million by 1997 (Betts, 1994). The number of CD-ROM drives (the devices that play CD-ROM discs) is expected to increase by 260% between 1991 and 1996 (The New Multimedia, 1994). By the end of 1992, there were about 900,000 CD-ROM drives in use. In one year, that number had surged to 10.5 million (Shields, 1994). With prices of computer hardware dropping relatively dramatically, many school districts are acting quickly to acquire multimedia, raising their technology standards to require a CD-ROM drive in any new computer that is purchased.

What has captured the imagination of educators and developers is the interactive capability of multimedia. Interactive multimedia requires the user to be an active participant, not a passive bystander as in so many early skill-and-drill software programs. Interactivity is made possible through the use of *hypermedia* software systems. These allow users to create, annotate, and link information from a variety of media sources.

These systems possess three characteristics that differentiate them from past "linking" systems. First, information does not have to be linked sequentially. Associations can be created across a variety of dimensions. Second, the systems are not limited to text. Links can be established between multiple types of media (text, video, and still images, for example). Third, navigational systems can be created to guide users, or users are free to create their own navigational systems.

Interactive Multimedia Software can Present Powerful Assessment

In the past few years, hypermedia, or multimedia authoring systems have become more sophisticated, more powerful, and yet easier to use. This surely accounts for the surge of interest in, and creation of, multimedia products (Pryor, 1992). Interactive multimedia software has several promising characteristics that make it a powerful tool for both learning and assessment. The presence of these characteristics and the degree to which they are operative varies from application to application. Nonetheless, proponents usually cite the following as characteristics of the genre:

- Because multimedia presentations can link various types of media, they can create *rich learning environments*. For example, in addition to just reading about a tropical rain forest, a student may be able to view a video of cutter ants at work, hear an audio clip of the nocturnal sounds heard there, and watch an animation sequence that shows how rain forest plants decay and provide a source of nutrients for the next generation. This mix of information can be presented as a real-world context, and it quickly engages the genuine interest of most students.

- Interactive multimedia presentations emphasize self-direction and thus provide *learner control*. That is, they allow the learner to determine the path of his/her study. This "inquiry-driven" approach encourages, and even requires in many instances, students to ask questions, seek out information, and solve problems. Learning takes place on the student's terms, not the terms of the teacher or the product developer. Inherent in this learner control is self-pacing and multiple routes to the same information.

- By providing information in a variety of formats (such as text, video, and images), and by allowing multiple paths through that information, interactive multimedia is accessible to *multiple modalities*. It accommodates different learning styles and makes itself more available to children with special needs. For example, a second-language track has become fairly standard on many multimedia programs, so the learner has a choice as to which language to use.

The technology that presents and supports multimedia is still in its infancy, but the amount of literature describing it is increasing (Cannings, & Finkel, 1993). Much of the research that has been conducted has focused on conceptualizing the design features of multimedia presentations and investigating their effectiveness:

Ferretti (1993) conducted a Delphi study to identify research questions that could guide the study of interactive multimedia with special education populations. He found the most frequently cited topics to be (1) design issues affecting the efficacy of interactive multimedia; (2) the multimedia environments, (3) navigational tools; and (4) strategies for promoting the transfer of learning.

In a comprehensive review of the literature, Litchfield (1993) focused on four areas: (1) instructional strategies (including cooperative learning); (2) branching (navigation and learner control); (3) affective features (learning styles and motivation); and (4) types of media (interactive videodiscs, hypermedia and hypertext).

Some investigators (Park, & Hannafin, 1993) have tried to shape a conceptual framework for organizing research and learning theory as they relate to interactive multimedia.

Schwier (1993) has created a classification scheme for multimedia interaction based on the degree of control and type of cognitive engagement experienced by learners. Allred and Locatis (1988) compared the effectiveness of three methods of designing interactive multimedia.

One of the few studies that investigated assessment issues related to multimedia was conducted by Baird and Silvern (1992). They investigated the interaction between instructional mode (computer vs. paper/pencil) and testing mode.

Cates (1992) predicted that the new interactive hyper- and multimedia technologies will have promising potential to evaluate metacognition.

An Exploratory Project Suggests the Potential of Multimedia Assessment

The authors have been exploring the potential of multimedia for assessing important language arts outcomes. They have created a prototype software program called "Lost in a Storm" for use with upper elementary students.

The program presents a simulation activity in which students play the role of a newspaper reporter for a small local paper. They are told that two children participating in a cross-country skiing event have disappeared due to a bad snow-storm. The local sheriff and rescue teams have been searching for them. The task for the students using this program is to gather background information and write a newspaper story about the incident for the morning edition.

To help them accomplish their task, students are provided with tools commonly used by newspaper reporters—a telephone, a tape recorder for recording interviews, and a reporter's notebook for recording information that is collected. These tools are presented as icons which the student can activate with the computer mouse when needed.

While working through the simulation activity, students engage in a variety of activities designed to tap their reading, writing, listening, and organizational skills. They read background information about the incident, generate interview questions, conduct a phone interview with the sheriff and an interview with one of the rescued boys at the local hospital, and generate planning questions for their news report. During these activities, they can record information they gather in their reporter's notebook, use their tape recorder to check the accuracy of their notes, and read verbatim transcripts of their interviews as an additional check on their notetaking.

When students feel they have collected enough information, they may begin drafting their newspaper account. A window interface is provided for entering text. Students have the option of opening their reporter's notebook, which appears in a window adjacent to the writing/drafting window. They may also retrieve their tape recorder and replay any of the interviews to verify their notes. Two other tools they may access while they are drafting their article are a dictionary and a book of instructional tips on writing newspaper stories. Students may print their notes and drafts for use off-line as well as save their work for access through the program later.

This activity yields different types of assessment information. Several different kinds of information are tracked and saved as separate files to be used for evaluative purposes after the student has completed the activity. The program is structured to provide teachers with the opportunity to assess student process as meaning is made from the program. Teachers can ask the following revealing questions:

- *What kinds of interview questions did the student generate?*

  The quality of the interview questions gives insights into the student's comprehension of the incident. They reveal, for example, what the student recognizes as important and what he or she feels needs to be reported (as a response to the assigned task).

- *Did the student take notes of the interviews?*

  The student's notetaking reveals his or her engagement with the program and grasp of individual study skills.

- *If the student did take notes, how accurate and complete were they?*

  The quality of the student's notes reflects both listening skills and notetaking ability.

- *Did the student check the accuracy of the notes?*

  This observation enables teachers to evaluate the student's self-assessment and self-monitoring ability.

- *What type of planning questions did the student generate?*

  The quality of the planning questions provides additional clues to the student's comprehension and his or her ability to differentiate important details from trivial information.

- *Did the student make revisions to his/her initial draft of the news report? If so, what types of revisions were made?*

  Each draft of the news report is saved as a separate file so that the teacher is able to trace the student's thinking and revision strategies over multiple drafts. These insights provide valuable information for guiding future instruction.

- *What does the final news report reveal about the student's reading comprehension? writing ability? and ability to accomplish the task?*

  A 4-point rubric is used to score the final report for the three-dimensions listed above. Benchmark responses help teachers apply the rubric.

Using instruments that have interactive multimedia, such as the sample described above, to assess the language arts offers several promising features. First, it allows the assessment to occur in a more naturalistic context. Assessing listening skills by having students take notes of a phone interview, for example, is much more realistic than traditional paper / pencil tests of listening ability.

Second, the assessment focuses more on process than product. Because interactive multimedia authoring systems enable educators to compare a wide array of behaviors and performances, emphasis can be placed on examining the processes the student is using rather than on judging only the final product of his or her work.

Third, the results of the assessment are not effected because the assessing process is transparent to the student; for he or she becomes involved in it as an inquiry-driven activity that has been designed in an attempt to make it enjoyable. By

opting for particular media, the student moves behind the scenes of the incident to gather important information. These options built into the multimedia instrument also provide the student with a chance to customize the assessment to match his or her meaning-making strengths. For example, it permits students to listen to an audio version of texts that can also be read or to complete the program in a language other than English.

All of the discussion thus far has centered on the student as a "receiver" or "participant" in a multimedia program created by others. But there is another side of multimedia assessment that may make it even more powerful. It is now possible for students themselves to create and produce interactive multimedia presentations of their responses. Language arts teachers have traditionally relied on the representation of knowledge through the written and spoken word. But multimedia authoring tools will allow students to represent knowledge in vastly different ways—through films, through art, through music and a host of combinations of text and media. This will come as a blessing to manly students who feel ill-equipped or disinclined to use the traditional ways of expressing what they have learned. Student-created multimedia presentations will offer teachers a completely new vehicle for evaluating student performance. We are only beginning to explore this possibility.

Multimedia Should Lead the way to Future Assessments

In recent years, the concept of literacy has been broadened beyond reading and writing. Many people now talk of "visual literacy," "computational literacy," "computer literacy," "scientific literacy," and more. Each of these types of literacy has traditionally been viewed by most educators in isolation with its own vocabulary and conventions. Interactive multimedia holds the promise of bringing many of these "literacies" under a single umbrella. As they are combined—or allowed to interact as they do in reality—they will promote assessment of the combined uses.

Some have called this comprehensive concept "information literacy" (Hancock, 1993). Information literacy is defined by an individual's ability to:

- recognize a need for information;
- identify and locate appropriate information sources;
- know how to gain access to the information contained in those sources;
- evaluate the quality of information obtained; organize the information; and
- use the information effectively.

Proponents of this *information literacy* perspective envision a literate-rich environment in which students engage in active, self-directed learning activities; pose questions about the content being learned; reflect on and assess their own learning; and take responsibility for their own learning. In such an environment, the role of the teacher changes from teller and dispenser of knowledge to facilitator, mentor, and coach.

In a very real sense, this is already happening with the development of performance assessment and the increasing reliance on portfolios, which virtually rely on the student's involvement as a self-assessor. As interactive multimedia contributes to our valuing of information literacy, our view of literacy assessment will continue to change and expand. Technology will change what we assess and how we assess it just as an increasing understanding of language and thinking processes has already done that to a significant degree.

References

Afflerbach, P. (Ed.). (1990). *Issues in statewide reading assessment.* Washington, DC: ERIC Clearinghouse on Tests, Measurement, and Evaluation. (Document ED 360 315).

Allred, K. F., & Locatis, C. (1988). Research, instructional design, and new technology. *Journal of Instructional Development, 11*(1), 2–5.

Anderson, R. C., & Pearson, P. D. (1984). A schema-theoretic view of basic processes in reading. *Handbook of reading research* P. D. Pearson (Ed.), (pp. 255–292). New York: Longman.

Baird, W. E., & Silvern, S. B. (1992). Computer learning and appropriate testing: A first step in validity assessment. *Journal of Research on Computing in Education, 25*(1), 18–27.

Beaverton (Oregon) School District #48. (1984). *Analytical scoring guide, Handout #4.*

Beck, M. D. (1991, April). *Authentic assessment for large-scale accountability purposes. Balancing the rhetoric.* Paper presented at the annual meeting of the American Educational Association, Chicago.

Betts, F. (1994). Making decisions about CD-ROMs. *Educational Leadership, 51*(7), 42.

Beyond words: A program for movement observation and analysis. (1988). Final Report. New York: Laban/Bartenieff Institute of Movement Studies. (ERIC Document ED 299 243).

Block, E. L. (1992). See how they read: Comprehension monitoring of L1 and L2 readers, *TESOL Quarterly, 26*(2), 319–343.

Brandt, R. (1992). On performance assessment: A conversation with Grant Wiggins. *Educational Leadership, 49*(8), 35–37.

Brown, A. L. (1975). The development of memory: Knowing, knowing about knowing and knowing how to know. *Advances in Child Development and Behavior, 10,* 103–151.

Calfee, R. C., & Perfumo, R. C. (1993). Student portfolios: Opportunities for a revolution in assessment. *Journal of Reading, 36*(7), 532–537.

Cannings, T. R., & Finkel, LeRoy (Eds.). (1993). *The technology age classroom.* Wilsonville, OR: Franklin, Beedle and Associates.

Cates, W. M. (1992, April 20–24). *Considerations in evaluating metacognition in interactive hypermedia/multimedia instruction.* Paper presented at the annual conference of the American Educational Research Association, San Francisco. ERIC Document ED 349 966.

Cawelti, G. (1994). *High school restructuring: A national study.* Arlington, VA: Educational Research Service.

Coley, R. J. (Ed.). (1990). Testing. *ETS Policy Notes, 2*(3), 1–13.

Duke, C. R. (1987) *Integrating reading, writing, and thinking skills into the music class. Journal of Reading, 31*(2), 152–157.

Farr, R. (1989). *Gathering information to plan instruction: Informal assessment strategies.* In B. E. Cullinan, et at. (Eds.), Teacher's Strategies Book, (pp. 65–82). Orlando, FL: Harcourt, Brace and Jovanovich.

Farr, R. (1990). Setting directions for language arts portfolios. *Educational Leadership* 48(3), 103.

Farr, R. (1992). Putting it all together: Solving the reading assessment puzzle. *The Reading Teacher.* 46(1), 26–37.

Farr, R. (1989). Writing as a means of reading assessment. *Educational Leadership, 46*(6), 86–87.

Farr, R. C. (1993). *Unit integrated performance assessment: HBJ treasury of literature.* Orlando, FL: Harcourt, Brace and Jovanovich.

Farr, R., & Beck, M. (1994). Evaluating language development: Formal methods. In J. Flood, J. M. Jensen, D. Lapp & J. R. Squire (Eds.), *Handbook of research on teaching the English language arts.* (pp. 489–501). New York: Macmillan.

Farr, R., Carey, R., & Tone, B. (1986). Recent theory and research into the reading process: Implications for reading assessment. In J. Orasanu, (Ed.), *Reading comprehension: From research to practice.* Hillsdale, NJ: Erlbaum.

Farr, R., & Farr, B. (1990). *Integrated assessment system/language arts performance assessment.* San Antonio: The Psychological Corporation.

Farr, R., & Fay, L. (1982). Reading trend data in the United States: A mandate for caveats and caution. In G. Austin & H. Garber (Eds.), *The rise and fall of national test scores.* (pp. 83–141). New York: Academic Press.

Farr, R., & Greene, B. G. (1992, March 5–7). *Using verbal and written think-alongs to assess metacognition in reading.* Paper presented at the 15th annual meeting of the Eastern Educational Research Association. (ERIC Document ED 364 576).

Farr, R., & Greene, B. (1993). *Indiana performance assessments '92: Final report.* Bloomington, IN: Center for Reading and Language Studies and Indiana State Commission for Higher Education.

Farr, R., & Olshavsky, J. Edwards. (1980). Is minimum competency testing the appropriate solution to the SAT decline? *Phi Delta Kappan, 61,* 528–530.

Farr, R., & Tone, B. (1982). *Text analysis and validated modeling of the reading process (1973–1981): Implications for reading assessment.* Washington, DC: National Institute of Education.

Farr, R., & Tone, B. (1994a). Choices and opportunities. In *Education Catalog 1994.* Fort Worth: Harcourt Brace College Publishers.

Farr, R., & Tone, B. (1994b). *Portfolio and performance assessment Helping students evaluate their progress as readers and writers.* Fort Worth: Harcourt Brace College Publishers.

Ferrett, R. T. (1991). Reading & writing. *Thrust for Educational Leadership, 21*(2), 38–41.

Ferretti, R. P. (1993). Interactive multimedia research questions: Results from the Delphi study. *Journal of Special Education Technology, 12*(2), 107–117.

Feuer, M. J., & Fulton, K. (1993). The many faces of performance assessment. *Phi Delta Kappan, 74*(6), 478.

Fiala, B. (1979). Spotlighting Classroom drama. *P.E.N.* (Primary English Notes) Rozelle, Australia: Primary English Teaching Association. (ERIC Document ED 276 044).

Flavell, J. H. (1979). Metacognition and cognitive monitoring: A new area of cognitive-developmental inquiry. *American Psychologist, 34*(10), 906–911.

Froese, V. (1987, May 2). *Language assessment: What we do and what we should do!* Paper presented at the Northwest regional conference of the National Council of Teachers of English. Vancouver, Canada. ERIC Document ED 291 104.

Gentile, C. (1992, April). *Exploring new methods for collecting students' school-based writing.* NAEP's 1990 Portfolio Study. Washington, DC: Prepared by Educational Testing Service for the National Assessment of Educational Progress 1990, Writing Assessment for National Center of Education Statistics, Office of Educational Research and Improvement, U.S. Department of Education.

Gentile, C., Martin-Rehrman, J., & Kennedy, J. H. (1995, January). *Windows into the Classroom: NAEP's Writing Portfolio Study* (Report 23-FR 06). Washington, DC: Office of Educational Research and Improvement, U.S. Department of Education.

Golson, E. B., & Kirscht, J. (1983, March, 17–19). *On making the I universal: From Langer to Britton to Kinneavy.* Paper presented at the 34th annual meeting of the Conference on College Composition and Communication. (ERIC Document ED 237 992). Bloomington, IN: ERIC Clearing House on Reading, English, and Communication.

Hambrick, K. (Ed.). (1991). *Making connections II: Four educational perspectives.* 2nd Symposium proceedings. Occasional Paper No. 33. Charleston, West Virginia: Appalachia Educational Lab.

Hancock, V. E. (1993). *Information literacy for lifelong learning.* Washington, DC: ERIC clearing house on information resources. ERIC Digest. ERIC Document ED 358 870.

Hansen, J. B. (1992). *A purpose driven assessment program.* Paper presented at the annual meeting of the American Educational Research Association. (ERIC Document ED 344 928).

Harp, B. (1987). When the principal asks: "Why are your kids doing art during reading time?" *The Reading Teacher, 41*(3), 346–347.

Herter, R. J. (1991). Writing portfolios: Alternatives to testing. *English Journal, 80*(1), 90–91.

Hoyt, L. (1992). Many ways of knowing: Using drama, oral interactions, and the visual arts to enhance reading comprehension. *The Reading Teacher, 45*(8), 580–584.

Indiana Performance Assessment '92. (1992). Bloomington, IN: Center for Reading and Language Studies, Indiana University.

Johns, J. L., & Leirsburg, P. V. (1992). How professionals view portfolio assessment. *Reading Research and Instruction, 32*(1), 1–10.

Johnston, P. (1986). Assessing the process and the process of assessing in the language arts. In J. Squire (Ed.), *The dynamics of language learning: Research in the language arts.* Urbana, IL: National Council of Teachers of English.

Kaltsounis, T. (1990). Interrelation between social studies and other curriculum areas: A review. *Social Studies, 81*(6), 283–286.

Kanning, R. G. (1994). What multimedia can do in our classrooms. *Educational leadership, 51*(7), 40–44.

Kapinus, B. A. et al. (1994). The Maryland School Performance Assessment Program: A new view of assessment. In S. W. Valencia et al., (Eds.), *Authentic reading assessment: Practices and Possibilities.* Newark, DE: International Reading Association.

Kemp, D. Cooper, W., & Davies, J. (1991). The role of administration in portfolio assessment. *California Curriculum News Report, 16*(3), 3, 4.

Koretz, D. et al. (1992). *Can portfolios assess student performance and influence instruction? The 1991–92 Vermont Experience.* Los Angeles: Rand.

Leung, K. (1986, March 31-April 4). *Facilitating speech, language and auditory training through tap dancing and creative movement.* Paper presented at the 64th annual convention of the Council for Exceptional Children. Reston, VA: ERIC clearing house on handicapped and Gifted Children. (ERIC Document ED 269 908).

Litchfield, B. C. (1993, April 12–16). *Design factors in multimedia environments: Research findings and implications for instructional design.* Paper presented at the annual meeting of the

American Educational Research Association. Atlanta Washington, DC: ERIC clearinghouse on Information resources. (ERIC Document ED 363 268).

Lutrario, C. (1991). *English INCA (Integrated National Curriculum Assessment) Teacher's Guide.* London: Harcourt, Brace and Jovanovich.

McRobbie, J. (1992). Using portfolios to assess student performance. *Knowledge Brief,* No. 9, Far West Laboratory for Educational Research and Development.

Meyer, C., Schuman, S., & Angello, N. (1990). *Aggregating portfolio data,* (Rev. ed.). Lake Oswego, OR: Northwest Evaluation Association.

Miller, M. A. (1992). The ins and outs of portfolios. *Communique, 20*(6), 3, 4.

Moss, P. A. et al. (1992). Portfolios, accountability, and an interpretive approach to validity. *Educational Measurement: Issues and Practice, 11*(3), 12–21.

New Mexico portfolio writing assessment 1991–92: Administration Manual. (1992). Sante Fe: New Mexico State Department of Education.

The new multimedia. Electronic Learning, 13(8), 56–57.

O'Neil, J. (1992). Putting performance assessment to the test. *Educational Leadership, 49*(8), 14–19.

Olshavsky, J. E. (1976–77). Reading as problem solving: An investigation of strategies *Reading Research Quarterly, 12*(4), 654–675.

Owens, P. (1992). Multimedia Educational Software: A radical new era for software design and authorship. *Journal of Computing in Higher Education, 3*(2), 3–20.

Paris, S. G., & Oka, E. R. (1986). Children's reading strategies, metacognition, and motivation. *Developmental Review 6,* 25–56.

Paris, S. G., Wasik, B. A., & Van der Westhuizen, G. (1988). Meta-metacognition: A review of research on metacognition and reading. In John E. Readence et al., (Eds.), *Dialogues in literacy research.* Thirty-seventh Yearbook of the National Reading Conference.

Park, I., & Hannafin, M. J. (1993). Empirically based guidelines for the design of interactive multimedia. *Educational Technology, Research and Development, 41*(3), 63–85.

Paulson, F. L., Paulson, P. R., & Meyer, C. A. (1991). What makes a portfolio a portfolio? *Educational Leadership, 48*(5), 60–63.

Pikulski, J. J. (1989). The assessment of reading: A time for change? *The Reading Teacher, 43*(1), 80–81.

Powell, J. L. (1989, June). *How well do tests measure real reading?* Bloomington, IN: ERIC Clearinghouse on Reading and Communication Skills.

Pryor, B. W. (1992, August 4–7). *Streams of knowledge, streams of action: The river of research and development at technology based learning and research,* Arizona State University. Paper presented at the meeting of the Association of Management. Las Vegas. (ERIC Document ED 352 949).

Rabson, B. B., & Warshaw, R. K. (Eds.). (1980). *PALS Project: Art as a learning strategy: A guide for teachers and students.* New York: Learning to Read Through the Arts Programs.

Russavage, P. M. (1992). Building credibility for portfolio assessment. In *Literacy: Issues and practices.* 1992 Yearbook of the State of Maryland International Reading Association Council, Vol. 9.

Schwier, R. A. (1993, January 13–17). Classifying interaction for emerging technologies and implications for learner control. In *Proceedings of selected research and development presentations* at the Convention of the Association for Educational Communications and Technology, New Orleans.

Shields, J. (1994). CD-ROM hits its stride. *Technology and Learning, 15*(1), 33, 34.

Siegel, M., & Carey, R. F. (1989). *Critical thinking: A semiotic perspective*. Bloomington, IN: ERIC Clearinghouse on Reading and Communication Skills and National Council of Teachers of English.

Simmons, J. (March 1990). Adapting portfolios for large-scale use. *Educational Leadership, 47* (6), 28.

Smith, C. B. (Ed.). (1991). *Alternative assessment of performance in the language arts: What are we doing now? Where are we going?* Proceedings of a national symposium. Bloomington, IN: ERIC Clearinghouse on Reading and Communication Skills.

Snider, M. A., et al. (1994). Rhode Island's literacy portfolio assessment project. In *Authentic reading assessment: Practices and Possibilities.* S. W. Valencia et al.(Eds.). With comments by Robert C. Calfee. Newark, DE: International Reading Association.

Spillane, R. R. (1987). *Arts education is not a frill!* Alexandria, VA: National School Boards Association.

Suhor, C. (1982, April 27–30). *Reading in a semiotics-based curriculum.* Paper presented at the 27th annual meeting of the International Reading Association. (ERIC Document ED 215 299).

Sunstein, B. S. (1992). The personal portfolio: Redefining literacy, re-thinking assessment, re-examining evaluation. *Writing Notebook: Creative Word Processing in the Classroom, 9* (4), 36–39.

Tierney, R. J., Carter, M. A., & Desai, L. E. (1991). *Portfolio assessment in the reading-writing classroom.* Norwood, MA: Christopher-Gordon.

Valencia, S. (1990). A portfolio approach to classroom reading assessment: The whys, whats, and hows. *The Reading Teacher, 43* (4), 38–40.

Valencia, S., Peason, P. D., Peters, C. W., & Wixson, K. K. (1989). Theory and practice in statewide reading assessment: Closing the gap. *Educational Leadership, 46* (7), 57–63.

Valencia, S. W., & Calfee, R. (1991). The development and use of literacy portfolios for students, classes, and teachers. *Applied Measurement in Education, 4* (4), 333–345.

Valencia, S., & Pearson, P. D. (1987). Reading assessment: Time for a change. *The Reading Teacher, 40* (8), 726–732.

Wagoner, S. A. (1983). Comprehension monitoring: What it is and what we know about it? *Reading Research Quarterly, 18* (3), 328–346.

Werner, P. H. (1992). Integrated assessment system. *Journal of Reading, 35* (5), 416–418.

Wiggins, G. (1989). Teaching to the (authentic) test. *Educational Leadership, 46* (7), 41–47.

Williamson, L. E. (1983, May 2–6). *NAEP literacy data: Students deficient in using language.* Why? Paper presented at the 28th annual meeting of the International Reading Association. (See conclusions). (ERIC Document ED 241 904).

Wolf, D. P., et al. (1992). Good measure: Assessment as a tool for educational reform. *Educational Leadership, 49* (8), 8–13.

RESEARCH PERSPECTIVES ON CURRICULAR, EXTRACURRICULAR, AND POLICY PERSPECTIVES

INTRODUCTION

James R. Squire

HARVARD GRADUATE SCHOOL OF EDUCATION

Research findings alone do not determine policy decisions. As the discussions in this part indicate, policy decisions are influenced by political, economic, and professional considerations as the leading edge of the profession seems to move continuously from one major thrust to another.

Too often, in American schools at least, the partisans of one approach or the other become so emotionally committed that they seem not to admit compromise. Thus, during recent years, the advocates of whole language and the leading "phonickers" seem more intent on scoring points on one another than on seeking a reasonable balance between skill and instruction in reading, writing, and literature experience. Yet some of the experimental programs discussed in this part have achieved their own balance over the course of their development. The Benchmark School model, for example, as discussed in this part by Irene Gaskins, demonstrates the success of a widely varied, eclectic approach in the instruction of delayed readers. The Reading Recovery program also targets the delayed reader with a wide spectrum of strategies; Marie Clay and Gay Su Pinnell's chapters describe the program's attempts to balance those strategies in a manner that is consistent with the specific needs of each learner. Kathryn Au and Claire Asam contribute a description of the integration of a process approach to literacy into the mastery-driven Kamehameha Elementary Education Program. California underwent a similar transformation in creating its Literature-Based curriculum. The state's attempts to infuse literature into a skill-based curriculum are chronicled by Phillip Gonzales and Mel Grubb.

This is an active, energetic time for curriculum reformers in every state. Strong reform efforts began particularly after the publication of the federal report on *A Nation at Risk* in 1984 and presently show no sign of abating. These efforts are typically realized in the creation of curricular standards. The purpose and parameters of the modern vehicle of reform are explored in the chapter by P. David Pearson, C. Jane Hydrick contributes a paractical view of this approach to reform, acknowledging pragmatic obstacles in her chapter "Setting Opportunity-to-Learn Standards." The paramount role of assessment in the movement to reform literacy education is explored by Louise Wilkinson and Elaine Silliman's chapter "Alternative Assessment, Literacy Education, and School Reform."

The current dynamic climate necessitates discussions of where the accountability for change will ultimately rest. Robert Shafer's chapter discusses the various social and political institutions vying for the right to determine policy and set standards while Richard Allington and Sherry Guice examine the issues which define each contender. Sharon O'Neal and Susan Streeker investigate the potential effects of their efforts on textbook and instructional materials.

Presently, educators at many levels are attempting to standardize curriculum. The case study conducted by Karen Wixson, Charles Peters, and Sheila Potter, provides a keen portrait of this process at the state level in describing Michigan's development of its curricular standards. By contrast, John Richmond's chapter, which describes the United Kingdom's implementation of its curriculum, portrays a national approach to standardization. Should national standardization become a reality, cross-national studies of literacy achievement, such as the one presented here by Warwick Elley, may serve as our most indispensable design resources.

Despite the likelihood of such a movement, some of the major statements interpreting research emerging from the national curriculum study centers could have even greater long range impact. For example, the National Reading Research Center (NRRC) has investigated approaches to creating self-determined, motivated readers. Relying on the NRRC's extensive research, John T. Guthrie, Ann McCann, Cyndie Hynd and Steve Stahl describe classroom contexts which will promote life long literacy engagement. Similarly, 10 years of research support Sarah Warshauer Freedman, Linda Flower, Glynda Hull, and J. R. Hayes' report on the classroom implications of studies at the National Center for the Study of Writing. The pioneering collaboration of university and classroom described by Jeanne Paratore and Roselmina Indrisano in their chapter on the Boston University-Chelsea Project also promises to influence profoundly future instructional practices.

52

WHO DETERMINES POLICY, POWER AND POLITICS AND WHAT ARE THEIR ATTITUDES?

Robert E. Shafer

ARIZONA STATE UNIVERSITY

The answer to the above question is a complex one. If one looks at case studies of changes in policies affecting literacy education in a comparative way, the answer becomes complicated to the point that any unified answer may not be possible. The question may be answered only in a particularized way. The social and political forces that determine power and therefore influence policy in the United States in 1995, are different from those that determined power and influenced policy in 1965, or in 1945. Similarly, in the UK, New Zealand or South Africa differing social, political or ideological forces determine varying clusters of power that effect or determine policy on educational matters. The particular decision makers involved also carry attitudes that shape their decisions. It seems a simple proposition, although complex in the process of analyzing any individual policy change or determination. But is it a simple matter at all? Policy changes or determinations are made by human beings, individually or collectively and human beings are knowledgeable about matters of language and literacy in varying degrees, but all have attitudes about language—attitudes that may strongly affect their decisions. Politicians are no different from anyone when it comes to attitudes toward language. Their attitudes toward language influence their policy decisions relating to standards in the English Language Arts.

THE STUDY OF LANGUAGE ATTITUDES

The study of language attitudes became important in the sociolinguistic research of the 1960s. In Labov's (1966) well-known study of the social stratification of English in New York City, varieties of language attitudes of New Yorkers and "outsiders" were revealed toward New York City speech. These attitudes were pervasive throughout the social structure. Labov reasoned that certain phonological variables could be cues to a person's social status; that is, when one heard these cues, attitudes emerged in the listener concerning the type of person who was speaking. In testing this hypothesis, Labov presented various samples of speech, each of which contained one of the variables found for a certain social class, to listeners who were then asked to make an estimate of the probable occupation of the speaker. The occupations ranged on a social scale from "television personality," which was presumed to have the highest social status speech, to "factory worker," which was presumed to have the lowest social status speech. Labov (1966) also found that in general, these judgments made were good predictors of the speaker's social class. Social stratification then, he concluded, exists not only with respect to the various elements of language, it also exists in the attitudes people have concerning these elements. There is further evidence that such attitudes toward dialects on the part of a given individual may not only reflect his attitudes toward the social class of a person speaking a particular dialect, but that his reactions may also include a whole set of other attitudes relating to the qualities of the dialect itself or more broadly, also concerned with those persons who speak that dialect. Apparently, language attitudes group themselves across and among various ethnic groups and social strata as well as sex, age and other factors. As Shuy and Williams (1973) have pointed out:

> In the broadest sense, such attitudes, if they be defined, may begin to reveal the affective dimensions of dialect stereo-typing. (p. 18)

Considerable research has already been done on the effect language attitudes have on stereotyping teachers' attitudes and behavior regarding the speech of their pupils. Little research has been done on the attitudes of politicians and other policy makers and decision makers—outside the teaching profession—whose attitudes and behavior affect educational policy. Such language attitudes seem to have affected policy decisions in the past to the extent that they have swayed national policy and have resulted in significant policy changes in the English speaking world. Often these attitudes are masked as "philosophical differences" and are therefore present in the realm of values and ideology. One of the possibilities explored in this chapter is the extent to which language attitudes may be used to pursue a social agenda. Actually, they extend not only to language but to the learning and teaching of language and seem to be particularly concerned with the learning and teaching of the mother tongue at least in the English speaking world.

The IRA/NCTE Standards Matter

When Janice Anderson, Interim Director of the Office of Educational Research and Improvements' Fund for the Improvement and Reform of Schools and Teaching (FIRST), quoted in *The Council Chronicle* (NCTE / IRA, 1994), notified the National Council of Teachers of English (NCTE) and the International Reading Association (IRA) that the funds for their Standards Project were being cut off after the first 6 months, one of her objections was that the proposed standards "focused too much on process" rather than "content" and did not address "issues" of a particular canon for children's literature and "standard spelling" versus "invented spelling." Although other reasons were also given, these, in particular, reveal attitudes which, although they may be characterized as stemming from "philosophical differences", are more rightly to be seen as language attitudes, These attitudes reveal a lack of professional knowledge which today is part of the preparation to teach and is therefore specialized knowledge which is not held by legislators, bureaucrats, school board members, many school administrators, and other citizens unless they have had recent training which involves this particular knowledge. A "particular canon" for children's literature, for example, means specified books which would be required for children to read and study in every school district in the country. Most teachers do not want such a "canon" because they know that most of the literature-based reading programs used in today's schools draw upon the plethora of high quality children's books of a wide diversity which they can tailor to individual children, classes, schools and communities. They already know that this literature exists and they are using it. Of what use would an unchangeable list of books prepared by someone in a far off place be to them?

The objection to "too much process" and not enough "content" reveals an attitude stemming from a lack of professional knowledge that educators have developed through their own experience as teachers and writers and through research. Many years ago, teachers concentrated almost exclusively on the written product, believing that the processes by which students achieve that product were largely unknown. As the decades passed and studies of creative processes and cognitive processes multiplied and ethno-methodological ways of studying writing were applied to students' writing in schools and colleges, many teachers began to become aware of this research and certainly by the beginning of this decade, many teachers had not only heard of the writing process and

"process writing" but had incorporated it into their teaching. A term like "writing process" or process writing carries with it to those who have been made aware of the implications of hundreds of studies conducted over the last several decades. To those who have not yet been made aware of this exploration of the processes involved in writing, the term may sound like jargon.

"Standard spelling" versus "invented spelling" to the uninitiated, sounds as though it cannot really be an issue at all. Obviously, the logic probably goes—there is only one correct way to spell—the standard way. Why would any group of teachers want to invent another?

Although teachers have noticed the invented spelling of their young pupils for decades, a recent scientific investigation of inventive spelling was done by Charles Read (1975). His book, *Children's Categorization of Speech Sounds in English,* was published as Research Monograph #17 in 1975. Read studied the ways in which children categorize distinct speech in which sounds based on phonetic similarities and differences. He found that children recognize specific and sometimes subtle phonetic relationships and proposed that these judgments may influence children's initial encounters with spelling and reading. For one aspect of his research, he studied the invented spellings created by children in preschool and early elementary school grades and inferred from their spellings, aspects of their categorization of speech sounds. The invented spellings indicated how children group sounds together for spelling purposes in certain specific situations:

> …These can be regarded as 'forced choice' situations in that the children sought to spell messages at will, using a limited set of known spellings. That is when the children wished a phone whose spelling is not suggested by the letter-names, they typically chose a known spelling for what seemed to them to be a similar sound. Ordinarily, they knew spellings for several phones, each related to the target phone in different ways, so that the direction in which the children typically made their choice suggests which similarities are most prominent. (p. 15)

Read (1975) found that many of his nonstandard spellings occurred regularly, when the same general principle seems to have been applied in the spelling of different sounds. It usually turned out that there was a plausible explanation in terms of the phonetic similarity, and rarely any other. Read noted further:

> …Many parents may quite unknowingly pass along to their children, even at the scribbling stage, the belief that English spelling is governed by a standard of correctness, and that it is hazardous to predict the spelling of words. This attitude is probably a prevailing one in our society. (p. 19)

Here, Read (1975) points out a significant language attitude about spelling which clearly affects not only parents but certainly legislators, bureaucrats, school board members and school administrators as they act in their various professional roles. Read went on to show that "children in kindergarten and first grade often share some of the categorical judgments seen in the invented spellings." This results in the "spontaneous linguistic performance" of invented spelling, "the phonetic basis of which is quite clear in certain cases" (p. 20).

Perhaps the most significant implication of Read's research is that children's grouping of speech sounds into phonemes allows them to make up an orthography which may initially ignore phonetic or even phonemic distinctions, but that they will make up a system of invented spelling which will not at once be standard spelling, is inevitable. But such a system will reflect their own organization of speech sounds and by continued exposure to standard orthography through reading and writing in a continuously encouraging and accepting atmosphere, standard spelling will appear. That this is *not* done through memorizing lists of "spelling demons" or reading red-penciled incorrectly spelled words over and over again has become obvious to many teachers in the past decades. Teachers expect "invented spelling" on the part of their elementary school pupils and know, as a result of Read's research, and other similar scholarly work in this area, that the first invented spellings will contain consonants alone. The vowels appear later. Read's research also indicates:

> ...It appeared that none of these children had any special difficulty in adopting standard spelling.... It seems more adequate to regard their spelling as based on tacit hypotheses based on phonetic relationships and sound spelling correspondences, which the child modifies readily as he or she encounters new information about standard spelling. (p. 30)

Many teachers have come in the past decade since Read's research to expect the phenomenon of invented spelling on the part of their first, second and even their 3rd-grade students and many parents are familiar with it in their children's writing during preschool years. There are still some principals who refuse to allow teachers to post children's writing which involves invented spelling on bulletin boards for fear that parents will see it. But many teachers have used children's writing with invented spellings as an opportunity to explain the phenomenon to parents so that they will not censor children at home for doing invented spellings, but regard their appearance as a natural step toward learning standard spelling and the conventions of writing.

But we cannot expect legislators, school board members and other citizens, all of whom influence educational policy and may, indeed, write and review standards, curriculum documents and new policies in the English Language Arts, to know of Read's (1975) research or its implications. We can expect them to listen carefully to teachers, researchers and curriculum workers on matters of curriculum and educational policy—or can we?

A NATIONAL CURRICULUM IN ENGLAND AND WALES

In his book, *English Teaching Since 1965: How Much Growth?*, David Allen (1980) describes his mood as an English teacher in the England of the early 1960s:

> It was an exhilarating, buoyant time of high hopes, of great ferment. Each new book seemed to stretch the boundaries of my subject. There was a confidence that we English teachers were doing a vital job. To subscribe to the *Use Of English* was to draw on a source of energy. This vigorous enthusiasm was sometimes

lifted to the level of crusade, to the humor of teachers of more workaday subjects.... One of the critical centres was the belief that children should be more involved, that lessons should have more give and take, that what children brought to their learning was important. For that reason alone, conversation and discussion were important; many remembered their own passive learning and encouraged children to talk round experience, exchange views. Above all, English should be enjoyable, for joy was seen as a great mover and an admirable stirring of mind and heart together. Drama made a deep contribution and literature, an indispensable part of our work, was the main source of enjoyment. (pp. 1, 2)

This model of teaching and learning described elsewhere as a "personal experience model" (Shafer, 1983) had been developing in England (and other countries as well) since the 1930s. The model had been refined over several decades and except for a small conservative group, had achieved acceptance by most teachers and by most segments of the British public. During the 1940s and 1950s, the British primary school had become widely recognized as a model of excellence in education. The Education Act of 1944 extended the movement of "informal education" into the postwar period. The focus continued on the use of personal experience and activity as the basis for classroom organization, teaching and learning, giving shape to an integrated primary curriculum, in which reading and writing were used as a means of learning and were not taught as ends in themselves. Visitors came from a variety of countries to see these schools in action, and in the 1960s, many Americans visited them. British teachers came to the United States to give workshops in "open education" and many schools were built on the open model.

In August 1963, the Minister of Education, Edward Boyle, asked the Central Advisory Council for Education in England to review primary education in England in all its aspects and also to consider the transition to secondary education. The report of this review, *Children and Their Primary Schools* (more widely known as the Plowden Report), was released on October 28, 1966. The recommendations of this report for children's writing were entirely consistent with the personal experience model and proposed that the primary schools continue in that tradition:

> What is most remarkable now in many infant schools is the variety of writing: writing rising out of dramatic play, writing associated with and explaining the models that are made, writing which reflects the sharpening of senses.... Much of the writing derives from the experience of individual children. (p. 218)

It seems clear that the Plowden Report cemented many of the practices of primary education which had developed during the child-centered decade from 1930 onward, and which had become known as "open education" or "informal education" or the "unified curriculum." Such educational practices also came to be called the "integrated day" or simply the "informal approach" to education. Using personal experience in writing and reading was a substantial part of education theory and practice arising from this position, placing value on using children's interests and experiences in all areas of schooling.

The concepts of personal experience and informal education were tested again in the 1970s, when the then Secretary of State for Education, Margaret Thatcher, set up a committee under the chairmanship of the noted Oxford University historian, Sir Alan Bullock, to inquire into the teaching of reading and other uses of English. The Committee report (1975), *A Language for Life,* proved to be another endorsement of the personal experience model. In the recommendations devoted to writing, the Bullock Report came out strongly in favor of writing as an activity integrated with other language experiences and not as a separate subject. The report commented on the fact that writing in the secondary schools had traditionally been used to assess the students' knowledge of the subject matter, but noted that there had been an increase in the amount of personal writing in recent years. In acknowledging the necessity to encourage personal, spontaneous writing, and also noting the teacher's desire to foster growth of technique in writing, the report recommended attention to "the fact that the writer's intention is prior to his need for technique.... The teacher who aims to extend the pupil's power as a writer must therefore work first upon his intentions and *then* upon the techniques appropriate to them" (p. 164). Such statements served not only as a confirmation of the personal experience model of reading and writing within the British educational tradition, but also as validation of the efficacy of the model in education practice in primary and secondary schools.

The 1960s saw a growing debate between teachers and others within the education professions and a small group of conservatives, who in 1969 began "the Black Papers," a series of attacks on educational practices of the day—including calls for a "return" to using only standard English in schools and increasing the teaching of formal grammar. In their recent history of the teaching of English in England, Burgess and Martin (1996) put it this way:

> We think the story goes like this. Through to the beginnings of the 1960's, a new progressive framework was being constructed in which the central elements were comprehensive schooling, an altered examination system, the emergence of new subject teaching associations and the steady accumulation of agreed lines of a common English teaching practice. How deeply this was founded it is hard to tell. It is possible to overestimate the depth and degree of agreement but also to underestimate the durability. The 1960's and early 1970's look like years of consolidation of this framework as well as of development and innovation. A central element in this was the emergence of the School's Council with something like general acceptance of a role for professional, teacher responsibility in curriculum and examinations reform. (p. 9)

As criticisms mounted, and teachers spent more time on the defensive, an attack came from one whom teachers considered their friend—a Labour prime minister. In 1976, at Ruskin College of Oxford University, James Callaghan called for a new demand for efficiency and value for money and a "relevant" curriculum. He agreed, surprisingly, with the conservative right that "lowered school standards" were supposedly somehow responsible for the country's dire economic plight.

Margaret Thatcher became Prime Minister in 1979, with the advent of a new conservative government. During her first two terms poverty and unemployment both increased and affected the atmosphere of most schools as the stresses pressed hard on the teachers. There were increased legislative attacks on unions which served to increase the tensions between the government and the main teachers' organizations, leading to a growing politicization of previously politically neutral teachers' associations. Ignoring the improvement and achievement as measured by examination results, Thatcher declared that education was "a disaster area" and for this, she blamed teachers, teacher educators, and the local education authorities.

In the 1980s there had been any number of government reports dealing with curriculum matters. There was also a plethora of inspectorate reports on individualized schools and colleges. By the mid-1980s, government interest and concern for matters of curriculum were firmly established in the public mind. It now became quite normal for ministers and inspectors to make detailed comments on questions of curriculum; for example, matters of teaching grammar and the place of various works of literature in the school program.

Kenneth Baker succeeded Sir Keith Joseph as Minister of Education in 1985, and began immediately to make pronouncements concerning a national curriculum. These were made to appear as though they were natural extensions of previous policies and development. They were all made to fit neatly together—the importance of education for the economy, the need to ensure basic educational standards, the desirability of putting curbs on the power of the teaching profession over curriculum matters.

Prime Minister James Callaghan's call for the making of a "strong case for the so-called core curriculum of basic knowledge" was answered in the Education Reform Act of 1988. A 10-subject curriculum was approved and a National Curriculum Council based in York was appointed with the staff to develop the attainment targets within the "key stages." A separate Examinations and Assessment Council was created for evaluation purposes. Pupils were to be tested at ages 7, 11, 14, and 16.

The working group on school subject English took as its starting point the report of the Kingman Committee (1988) which was still sitting when the national curriculum was introduced so that the English working group got a late start because Baker did not wish to appoint it until the Committee had made its report. The Kingman Committee (chaired by Sir John Kingman, Vice-Chancellor of Bristol University) was supposed to recommend a model of the English language, whether spoken or written, which would serve as the basis of how teachers are trained to understand how the English language works and which would also inform professional discussion of all aspects of English teaching; recommend and guide teachers on how far and in what ways the model should be explicit to pupils, to make them conscious of how language is used in a range of contexts; and to recommend what, in general terms, pupils need to know about how the English language works and consequently, what they should know and be able to do involving the workings of the language. But this charge masked the government's real intention and their language attitudes. Duncan Graham, First Director of the

National Curriculum Council notes the government's "feelings" and those of the right-wing conservatives about the state of English teaching (Graham & Tyler, 1993):

> A more fundamental problem was the growing feeling that teachers should no longer correct mistakes in spelling or punctuation such as the use of full stops and capital letters, because it obstructed children in their creative writing. Formal grammar teaching had largely disappeared as a part of the philosophy that had been seen in mathematics: children could only learn through enjoyment and should not be inhibited by the use of such words as noun, pronoun, and verb. They would learn the structure of language through use. The same arguments dictated that children should never be asked to learn a list of spellings (sic) because it was mechanistic, with the words being used out of context. Children should learn spelling by putting their own thoughts on paper and then being gently reminded when a word was misspelt (sic) in context. Too many teachers did not even do that. (p. 45)

The "feeling" that Graham cites, which was extensively referred to in the press and on TV, indicated the language attitudes of journalists and of the "mandarins" as the top government ministers in the Conservative Party were referred to—confusing invented spelling with "mistakes," referring to identifying parts of speech in the peer editing of student's papers as unwillingness to teach formal grammar and describing using peer editing by pupils as "teacher unwillingness" to "correct mistakes." These attitudes, undoubtedly, came from the Minister's own memories of schooling and a lack of knowledge of current research and practice.

Certainly the same attitudes were widely held by many members of the public and by many top government officials. The Kingman Committee (1988) recommended a model which involved:

1. The forms of the English language, e.g., sounds, letters, words, and how these relate to meaning,
2. Communication and comprehension—how speakers and writers communicate and how listeners and readers understand them,
3. Acquisition and development—how the child acquires and develops language, and
4. Historical and geographical variation—how language changes over time, and how languages which are spread over territories differentiate into dialects or, indeed, into separate languages. (p. 17)

The Committee rejected the teaching of formal grammar but took a position for the teaching of Standard English. The Kingman Report (1988) was something of an embarrassment to the government because it was expected that the Committee would strongly recommend the teaching of formal grammar, which they did not. The Committee had both English teachers and linguists as members. They took both oral and written testimony from a number of specialists in language teaching and referred to many recent studies of the teaching of grammar. Their position on grammar was stated as follows:

> Widely divergent views are now held on the value of the formal elements of knowledge about language. Many people believe that standards in our use of English would rise dramatically if we return to the formal teaching of grammar which was normal practice in most classrooms before 1960. Others believe that explicit teaching or learning of language structure is unnecessary. We believe that both these extreme viewpoints are misguided. Research evidence suggests that old-fashioned formal teaching of grammar had a negligible, or because it replaced some instruction and practice in composition, even, a harmful effect on the development of original writing. We do not recommend a return to that kind of grammar teaching. It was based on a model of language derived from Latin rather than from English. However, we believe that for children not to be taught anything about language is seriously to their disadvantage. (p. 12)

Professor Brian Cox of Manchester University had been an author of one of the Black Papers. He had also been a member of the Kingman Committee. Undoubtedly, when the Minister of Education at the time, Kenneth Baker, appointed him Head of the Working Group to prepare proposals for English in the National Curriculum, he considered him a "safe" appointment, leaning to the conservative position on the teaching of English.

In the primary and secondary proposals which the Working Group developed, specific knowledge about language, for example, grammatical knowledge, was considered an integral part of work in English, and not a separate body of knowledge to be added on to the traditional English curriculum. The notion was that as pupils extend their skills, abilities, and understandings in speaking, listening, reading and writing, the teacher's role is to highlight those aspects that will lead to a greater awareness of the nature and functions of language. This awareness should in turn, contribute to the pupils' own sensitivity as language users. For this reason the Working Group did not propose that knowledge of language should have its own profile component. To treat it separately, they thought, would be to risk giving rise to the misconception that it should be separately taught, and evaluated, rather than integrated within the speaking, listening, reading and writing activities of the English curriculum. Accordingly, the content they saw as essential to knowledge of language was incorporated in the three profile components, speaking and listening, reading, and writing, both in the statements of attainment and in the programs of study. Although the Working Group report showed a number of ways in which grammar could be taught inductively, including a long illustrative account of such a practice in a classroom dialogue, the reception of the final report by the press and the ministers was to the effect that grammar had been neglected completely. In his book, *Cox on Cox,* Brian Cox describes the reception of his Committee's proposals by the Minister and the press:

> When our first report on the primary stages was submitted to Mr. Baker at the end of September 1988, he felt that we had given insufficient emphasis to the teaching of grammar. In his proposals, printed at the front of the report, he asked that "the programs of study for writing should be strengthened to give greater emphasis to the place of grammatical structure and terminology within the matters, skills and processes otherwise covered. This was seized upon by the press, which in headlines proclaimed that the Report was weak on grammar.... The *Mail On Sunday's* headlines (13 November, 1988) were: 'Thatcher Furious With Trendy Experts' and 'English Report Fails The Test.' The article began: 'A report telling schools to ignore English teaching in favor

of trendy methods has infuriated Mrs. Thatcher,' and continued by saying that the lengthy report "dismisses grammar in a few paragraphs." (p. 7)

In his books, *Cox on Cox: An English Curriculum for the 1990s* (1991) and *The Great Betrayal* (1992), Brian Cox details the various pressures on the Working Group as they struggled to prepare the "statements of attainment" and "programs of study" for subject English in the National Curriculum. Unfortunately, the greatest travail for English teachers dealing with the National Curriculum was yet to come.

The years 1991 and 1992 saw the Working Group's proposals tried out in many schools. In July 1992, the government, through a report of the National Curriculum Council (*National Curriculum English: The Case for Revising the Order*) indicated its intention to rewrite the Orders that the Cox Committee had so carefully developed. As the government pushed on with its plans to revise the "attainment targets" in English through late 1992 and early 1993, the various government proposals began to leak out to the press. In the February 3, 1993 *Independent,* a number of these changes to the original recommendations of the Cox Committee was described as follows:

> …Teachers will have to correct six and seven year olds who speak dialect and persuade them to speak "standard" or grammatically correct English. They must wait until the pupils are about sixteen before explaining that the use of split infinitives in speech is sometimes socially acceptable. Critics say the proposals, which are expected to be approved by the National Curriculum Council tomorrow, are a triumph for traditionalists. They will anger English teachers, who are already threatening a boycott of national testing at fourteen. The document shows that the English curriculum for all state school pupils, age five to sixteen, will be laid down in unprecedented detail and that the way teachers teach is to be prescribed in the National Curriculum for the first time. At about age thirteen, pupils will be taught to use apostrophes and speech marks accurately. Sixteen year olds will be required to learn how to use a semicolon and a colon. Eleven year olds should be taught to use commas. Seven year olds will have to use capital letters and full stops (periods) in most sentences and sound out letters in an unfamiliar word to show they have been taught to read partly by the phonics method favored by the traditionalists. (p. 1)

Other similar strictures dealt with the use of Standard English, defined as "grammatically correct English spoken in any accent." The document also proposed that according to the account of the February 3, 1993 *Independent,* 7-year-olds should be "sensitively" introduced to Standard English, to use sentences in which the subject and verb agree, the syntax is logical and verb tenses are correctly used. Most 9-year-olds should say "isn't" and "haven't" rather than "ain't" and most 11-year-olds should use negatives, comparatives and superlatives correctly, as in "we haven't seen anybody" and "the smaller of the two but the smallest of the three" (p. 3).

These and similar proposals were continuously leaked out to the press during the Spring of 1993, and there was much discussion among teachers and school administrators. It became clear that civil servants, acting at the behest of John Patten, then Minister of Education, had rewritten the English "attainment targets" and tests without the approval of Professor Cox or any of his Committee members, or consultation with any teachers' groups. On June 1, 1993 over 93% of the teachers and school administrators in England and Wales successfully refused to give the tests and only "a handful" of schools actually gave them.

An analysis of the revised proposals which ultimately became the actual Orders was carried out by the National Association of Teachers of English (NATE) and reported on by its past chairperson, Henrietta Dombey (1993), at the organization's conference at the University of Brighton. Though it is not possible to cite her complete report, certain aspects of her presentation are quoted in their entirety since they clearly reveal the language attitudes of those who did the revisions:

> The linguistic trip wires, the concern with the niceties of Standard English, and with form at the expense of function, are there in Writing too, and make an even heavier presence now that spelling and handwriting have been brought back into the Writing fold. The very first statement requires the average five year old to "identify where full stops (periods) should go in their own writing." At age seven, "children should write sentences in which," as in their spoken language, "subject and verb agree." The theme continues. At age nine, they must "use correctly and understand the function of nouns, pronouns, adjectives and adverbs." At age eleven, "they must write in complex sentences, controlling syntax and connectives and spell correctly polysyllabic words (such as accommodate and irrelevant) that do not conform to regular patterns." As we go up the levels, these formal niceties are increasingly accompanied by more substantial requirements to do with conveying ideas and themes, writing with conviction and clarity, until at sixteen, the pupil is required to "write confidently in a personal style." But an impersonal style is required much earlier, at age eleven. Pupils must now achieve the impersonal before the personal, running counter to all we know of writing development. And again, we need to be aware of what has been lost. All reference to audience and purpose have disappeared, as has the word "appropriate." So much for our substantial body of research into writing development, started by James Britton's research team at the London Institute over twenty years ago. Story structure has gone too, apart from the sequencing of events. So much for the work on narrative over the last fifteen years. Gone too are revising and redrafting, never mind all the work on this, largely inspired by Donald Graves, carried out on both sides of the Atlantic in the last two decades, an awareness of the differences between spoken and written English has, of course, completely disappeared. Learning to write has been reduced to little more than a matter of learning correct forms and to use these on demand. (p. 10)

After the boycott, which attracted international attention, the School Evaluation and Assessment Authority was merged with the National Curriculum Council to form the School Curriculum and Assessment Authority and a reevaluation of English in the National Curriculum was undertaken. A new English Order was produced in 1995 and sent out for consultations. At present, the Conservative government's attempts to influence the content of the English curriculum to suit the language attitudes of a few of those in the highest circles of government, do not seem to be evident in the new proposals. A further study by Professor Ronald Carter (1993) of the University of Nottingham indicates how far the government proposals went, how deeply embedded their procedures were to change the tests and what their ultimate political goals may have been.

> During the past few years, a number of linguists and English language specialists, myself included, have found ourselves at the centre of cultural debates about the English language, its teaching, and its formation as a subject in the new National Curriculum. It has been a fascinating, if somewhat enervating exercise. ... The fascination comes from interrogating and attempting to understand better the ways in which the very terms of debate are rooted in ideologies, in the relationship between language and power, and in particular, in the different understandings of what is the *proper* in Proper English.... This will provide the main focus. This article is not about the rights and wrongs of split infinitives or subject verb agreements, but rather about the attitudes to such matters which the discourses about them reveal. (p. 4)

Carter begins his article with a much quoted statement by the British heir to the throne, Prince Charles, which he deems a useful starting point: The statement was made in 1989, one week after the publication of the Cox Report:

> We've got to produce people who can write proper English. It's a fundamental problem. All the people I have in my office, they can't speak English properly, they can't write English properly. All the letters sent from my office, I have to correct myself, and that is because English is taught so bloody badly. They want people who write good English in right place for the future, it cannot be done with the present system and all the nonsense academics come up with. It is a fundamental problem. We must educate for character. This matters a great deal. The whole way schools are operating is not right. I do not believe English is being taught properly. You cannot educate people properly unless you do it on a basic framework and drilling system. (Prince Charles, 28 June, 1989)

Prince Charles also made pleas for the centrality of Shakespeare in the curriculum and in a subsequent speech on the degeneracy of the modern English language, particularly in relation to the *Book of Common Prayer*. He also argued with great conviction that God speaks English (Carter, 1993, p. 5). The keyword "proper" used by Prince Charles is also revealing of an attitude—an attitude concerning the views of English and English teaching encoded in terms of social propriety. Also the word "drill" reveals an attitude toward teaching which is that teachers instruct pupils in the correct forms of the language—using techniques which allow pupils regular practice in these forms. The word "drill" is especially revealing in that it derives from a militaristic context, in fact from the army parade ground. It seems to reveal an attitude toward the relationship of the individual pupil or student who is required to be in step with a series of instructions issued by someone invested with authority. Language drills provide the all-important framework within which differences are, albeit superficially, eradicated and order established.

Carter also points out that the word "standards" must be noted as revealing of an attitude. He points out that "especially in the discourses of many politicians and their media allies, there is a constant slippage from the word 'standard' to educational, behavioral and social *standards.*" To illustrate this, he cites an example provided by the former Chairman of the British Conservative Party, now a television personality and a past member of the Kingman Committee:

> ...We've allowed so many standards to slip.... Teachers weren't bothering to teach kids to spell and to punctuate properly.... If you allow standards to slip to the stage where good English is no better than bad English, where people turn up filthy—all those things cause people to have no standards at all, and once you lose standards then there's no imperative to stay out of crime. (Norman Tebbit, Radio Four, 1985)

Here we have standards for language use magically transformed into standards for behavior. The language attitudes become attitudes toward persons exhibiting antisocial behavior. Antisocial or criminal behavior is associated with speakers of incorrect language and English teachers are at fault because they allow this to happen. The whole process illustrates the unambiguous connection between standard language and social and political power and helps explain the much quoted statement that any standard language is no more than a dialect with an army and a navy. In the history of the English language, such a process accelerated during the 18th century, in particular, coinciding with the economic growth of a centralized nation state linguistically based on the East Midlands' dialect of the southeast of the country. Ann Shreeve (1993) comments on Carter's (1993) article in her editorial in *English in Education*:

> He comments on what we know about language—that it is subject to change; that it reflects and encodes social and cultural patterns; and that it is rooted in texts and context. He juxtaposes this with a government whose aim is to control a culturally diverse society by imposing national unity through a monocultural national curriculum. Imposing "proper language" is one way in which the government has sought to do this—a sort of "ethnic cleansing through language" which could silence many groups in society by undermining their confidence to speak out.

Decision making about school matters—particularly curriculum matters in England and Wales—had largely been done in the years before the establishment of the national curriculum by the appointment of national committees or commissions which were given a specific charge. These committees made a thorough study of the issue using the testimony of experts, professional associations, and scholarly leaders. The committees' recommendations are then formalized in a report to the key government official who may or may not accept it in part or on the whole. It is then translated into official policy. Until the advent of the National Curriculum, specific matters of curriculum content such as the teaching of grammar had rarely been dealt with by the government and were left to the local education authorities and individual schools. The advent of the National Curriculum in 1988 represented a complete change in national policy. In contrast, in the American system where the power for educational policy decision making is centered in the 50 states, the federal government historically has had only the power to initiate, recommend, and fund (usually a key incentive) programs. The recent move by the federal government to fund national content standards in the various subject fields, perhaps in the hope of establishing a national testing program, may signal an attempt to change national policy on curriculum development by shifting power to the federal government through a national testing program.

As we see from a recent bill introduced to Congress to make English our national language, we need to recognize that every time the question of language surfaces, as it has in this bill, we must consider Gramsci's words:

> ...It means that a series of other problems are coming to the fore: the formation and enlargement of the governing class, the need to establish more intimate and secure relationships between the governing groups and the national "popular mass," in other words, to reorganize the cultural hegemony. (Gramsci, 1985)

The cutting off of funds to the NCTE / IRA Standards Project may be viewed as a signal that the issue of language may well be coming to the fore again in our country and it may well be, in Gramsci's words revealing of a change in our own social and political relationships. We would do well to examine the language attitudes of our own educational policy makers and decision makers whether on local district school boards, in state legislatures, or the Congress of the United States. When the critical question came before British teachers and educators, they acted with a unified, professional perspective. Will we do likewise?

References

Allen, D. (1980). *English teaching since 1965: How much growth?* London: Heinemann.

Burgers, T., & Martin, N. (1990). The teaching of English in England, 1945–1986. in J. Britton, R. Shafer, & K. Watson (Eds.), *Teaching and Learning English Worldwide.* Clevedon, Avon: Multilingual Matters.

Carter, R. (1993). Proper English: Language, culture and curriculum. *English in Education, 27*(3), 3–14.

Cox, B. (1991). *Cox on Cox: An English curriculum for the 1990's.* London: Hodder and Stoughton.

Cox, B. (1992). *The great betrayal.* London: Chapman.

Dombey, H. (1993, Summer). Building site or battleground. *National Association for the Teaching of English News,* pp. 7–12.

Graham, D., & Tyler D. (1993). *A lesson for us all: The making of the national curriculum.* London: Routledge.

Gramsci, A. (1985). In J. Forgacs & R. Smith, (Eds.), *Selections from cultural writings.* London: Lawrence and Wishart.

Labov, W. (1966). *The social stratification of English in New York City.* Washington, DC: Center for Applied Linguistics.

NCTE/IRA. (1994, June 3, 5). Say standards effort will continue. *The Council Chronicle,* Urbana, IL: National Council of Teachers of English.

Plowden, L. B. (1967). *Children and their primary schools.* London: Her Majesty's Stationery Office.

Read, C. (1975). *Children's categorization of speech sounds in English.* Urbana, IL: National Council of Teachers of English.

Shafer, R. E. (1983). A child's power to share: The development of a personal experience model of the writing process. In B. Kroll & G. Wells, (Eds.), *Explorations in the Development of Writing.* London: John Wiley.

Shreeve, A. (1993). Editorial. *English in Education, 27*(3), p. 2.

Shuy, R., & Williams F. (1973). Stereotyped attitudes of selected English dialect communities. In R. Shuy & R. Fasold (Eds.), *Language attitudes: Current trends and prospects.* Washington, DC: Georgetown University Press.

U.K.: Department of Education and Science. (1975). *A Language for life* (Bullock Report). London: Her Majesty's Stationery Office.

U.K.: Department of Education and Science. (1988). *Report of the Committee of Inquiry into the Teaching of English language* (Kingman Report). London: Her Majesty's Stationery Office.

53

ALTERNATIVE ASSESSMENT, LITERACY EDUCATION, AND SCHOOL REFORM

Louise C. Wilkinson
RUTGERS UNIVERSITY

Elaine R. Silliman
UNIVERSITY OF SOUTH FLORIDA

LITERACY AND THE ROLE OF LITERACY EDUCATION

Literacy is more than learning to read and write. Listening, speaking, reading, writing, and spelling are interrelated, since all are communicative processes. Literacy includes both oral and written communications. At one level, being literate is a confirmation of the social identity as a full participant in a community. In addition, since language transcends immediate temporal and spatial constraints, it is a potentially powerful metacognitive tool for creating, understanding, and revising ideas about the world. This chapter presents an analysis of literacy and its assessment in the context of American education reform, particularly with regard to the systemic school reform movement.

Integrated perspectives about the relationships between language and learning share the view that integrating communicative processes—listening, reading, speaking, and writing—is the route to literacy. This view undergirds the *emergent literacy* and *whole language* educational approaches, have been applied in regular education settings (Weaver, 1991) and in special education settings with students described as learning disabled (Rhodes & Dudley-Marling, 1988). This perspective is consistent with recent research on the *writing-process* or *authoring* approaches (e.g., Sulzby, 1990), including integration into *whole literacy* programs involving cultural minority children (Au, Scheu, Kawakami, & Herman, 1990; Bloome, Harris, & Ludlum, 1991; Kawakami-Arakaki, Oshiro, & Farran, 1988; Shuy, 1988; Staton, 1988; Teale & Martinez, 1989). The *communication-process* perspective in language learning disabilities is similar, with its emphasis on the integration of language intervention into regular and special education classrooms (Silliman & Wilkinson, 1991).

Being literate can be seen as a continuum that transcends the oral and written media of communication, with different discourse styles overlapping both media (Wallach, 1990).

Consider the following example. Across the oral and written media, one can select more literate styles—styles that are more linguistically explicit, content-focused, and impersonal; alternatively, one can use a more personal, communication-focused, and less explicit oral style. The selection of a style is dependent on several factors including:

- the purposes for communicating,
- the role relationships between discourse partners,
- the temporal and spatial aspects of the discourse, and
- the medium of communication.

Because communication is purposeful, the selection of a style is heavily influenced by the first factor—the goal or purpose.

The Purposes of Communication

It is interesting to note that the functional nature of classroom communication has not been a major focus in past research on literacy learning.

Understanding the purpose of communication is relevant regardless of whether the task is one of comprehending or producing narrative and expository discourse in either the oral or written domain (Brown & Palincsar, 1987; Palincsar & Brown, 1984, 1987).

In the next section, other important aspects of verbal communication are considered, including: (a) the relationships between speakers, (b) constraints imposed by temporal and spatial elements, and (c) the choice of the medium (oral versus written). Adequate understanding of these aspects of communication is a necessary background for connecting literacy to learning.

Speakers' Roles

During conversations, speakers and listeners constantly monitor and negotiate the use of language as interaction unfolds (Biber, 1988; Horowitz & Samuels, 1987). Social and cultural experiences influence the selection of discourse style and particular choices of words. Consider the following example of an individual presenting a lecture. In this situation, the speaker cannot assume that the audience is familiar with basic definitions and applications; thus, the speaker must organize discourse in a more linguistically explicit, or literate, manner. But, the speaker can still monitor whether listeners seem to understand and be interested in the topic and how it is being presented. As a result, the speaker has opportunities to clarify what is being said or revise how it is being said as these active feedback signals are processed and interpreted. The audience must also select more literate comprehension strategies because selective attention to essential information is crucial, as is continuous monitoring by each participant of his or her state of comprehension (Horowitz & Samuels, 1987; Sternberg, 1987).

Alternatively, when the relationship is one of reader–author, direct feedback is not possible, but variation does exist. Harste, Short, and Burke (1988) and Meyer (1987) note that writing, during its production, involves speaking to a real or imagined audience. The actions of reading and listening, in turn, are dependent on inferring the speaker–author's plans, or underlying purposes, for communicating the message. Thus, identical to the speaker–listener role relationship, the author–reader relationship is foremost of all social interactions (Anders & Pearson, 1987; Meyer, 1987). It involves the construction of dialogue between the author and reader in which the reader acts as an interpreter of the author's purposes and meanings. The reader, in turn, becomes an interpreter of his or her own intentions and meanings when these are written down for others to interpret (Tierney, Lazansky, Raphael, & Cohen, 1987).

Temporal and Spatial Aspects of Communication

Temporal and spatial factors affect communication to a great extent. For example, in the case of one family member writing to another, the presumption is that a high degree of shared knowledge exists about family members. This familiarity forces the choice of a more oral and personal style of communication. Also, when communication takes place in a shared physical setting within the same temporal framework, the need for linguistic explicitness is reduced. In contrast, when

the speaker is giving a lecture and visual aids (transparencies and videotapes) are used as referents, the style becomes more literate. When communication is displaced in time and space, as is the case when the speaker is an author and the listener is a reader who is unfamiliar with the topic, then the entire communicative context of interaction must be reconstructed using verbal means alone. This reconstructive process is the recreation of what an audience needs to know in order to meet the purposes of communication (Cazden, 1988).

The Medium of Communication

Differences between the oral and written media influence comprehension and production. When discourse is written down, it has permanency. The reader can work with an understanding at his / her own rate and use different metacomprehension strategies (Anders & Pearson, 1987; Baker & Brown, 1984a, 1984b; Biber, 1988; Gavelek & Raphael, 1985). Metacomprehension strategies are concerned with how cognitive activity is modified in order to facilitate and monitor one's state of comprehension (Gavelek & Raphael, 1985; Palincsar & Brown, 1984; Paris, 1991). For example, the selection of metacomprehension strategies depends on how the purposes of reading are understood and the type and complexity of discourse structure, such as narrative versus expository structures. Comprehension breakdowns may be intentionally repaired by rereading, looking up unfamiliar words, self-questioning, or, even, asking another for assistance. Essential information may be identified by skimming content, underlining, outlining, or note-taking for subsequent summarization.

Similar to the more skillful reader, the skillful author also can engage in a more controlled way in planning, organizing, editing, and revising the content to be communicated, as well as the linguistic forms of communication, over a period of time (Raphael, Englert, & Kirschner, 1989). As a literate mode of communication, writing is more integrative than the oral mode. Large amounts of information can be condensed into the discourse through such linguistic devices as subordination, nominalization, adverbing (Biber, 1988; Scott, 1988, 1989), and other cohesive devices that tie meaning together semantically within-and-across sentence boundaries (Hasan, 1984a). Hasan (1984b) has refined the notion of cohesion into one of cohesive harmony, the process by which chains of reference thematically unite semantic and syntactic information. A working knowledge of "cohesive harmony" influences knowledge of literacy, including children's developing metastrategies for becoming more effective speaker-authors or listener–readers of narrative and expository discourse (Cox, Shanahan, & Sulzby, 1990; DeStefano & Kantor, 1988; Eller, 1989).

Finally, regardless of the style of communication, the oral medium places a premium on "speed of production and comprehension" (Biber, 1988, p. 42). Speaking is bounded in time and is often fragmented in character because of transient breakdowns in planning or executing what to say. False starts, silent and filled pauses, revisions, and word and phrase repetitions are common. As a consequence, listeners must also work under the pressure of time in order to understand what is being said, as anyone knows who has ever sat in a classroom trying to make sense of the vast array of information being communicated.

In sum, this brief discussion has provided an expanded perspective on literacy, to include both oral and written domains. At the broadest level, being literate is a confirmation of the social identity as a full participant in a community. In addition, since written language can transcend immediate temporal and spatial constraints, it is a potentially powerful metacognitive tool for creating, understanding, and revising ideas about the world. We will now discuss some recent changes in education policy in the United States that may powerfully affect classrooms and the roles of literacy educators.

CURRENT TRENDS AND NEW DIRECTIONS IN AMERICAN EDUCATION: SCHOOL REFORM

Recently, the concept of systemic school reform (SSR) has been introduced into the public debate about education in the United States, as a way to improve schooling throughout the country (Consortium for Policy Research in Education, 1991). Its introduction will change American classrooms and have profound consequences for the ways in which language and literacy are taught, learned, and assessed.

The importance of the *systemic school reform* is exemplified by recent legislation introduced by the Clinton administration's major school reform bill, *Improving America's Schools Act of 1993* (Goals 2000). The SSR is the foundation for the legislation.

The SSR refers to the process of making and implementing educational policy; the notion is to make it more like effective teaching and learning in classrooms and less like a top-down "teaching is telling" mandate from high level administrators and legislators (Elmore, 1993). The SSR emphasizes the need to find ways of communicating more effectively, so that making educational policy is a good process for all involved.

The concept incorporates a design for a systemic state structure that supports school-site efforts to improve classroom learning and instruction. The idea is that the structure be based on clear and challenging standards for students' learning; policy components would be tied directly to standards that support each other and guide classroom teachers and building administrators about how to optimize instruction. Thus, the states are seen as the critical providers of two fundamental aspects for universal educational excellence: (a) a unifying vision and set of goals, and (b) a coherent system of instructional guidance.

Common Vision of SSR

Regarding the first aspect, each state must provide coherent direction for educational reform throughout the state and each state must have a common vision of what schools should be like. The value of providing an intellectually stimulating and engaging education for all students is at the heart of the matter. Equity and equality reign here. Both coherence and a point of view must be accommodated.

Elements

Regarding the second aspect, the elements of SSR address how to provide a coherent system of instructional guidance. These elements include the following:

1. *Curriculum frameworks and materials:* Curriculum frameworks set out the best consensus in thinking in a field about the knowledge, processes, and skills that students need to know in each core curriculum area. The emphasis is on in-depth understanding, higher-order thinking, problem solving, hands-on experiences, and the integration of content and pedagogy. One often cited successful example of a curricular framework is the *National Council of Teachers of Mathematics* (NCTM, 1989) mathematics standards. Schools will select specific curriculum materials that support the instruction guided by the frameworks.

2. *Teacher education and professional development:* States should ensure that both new and continuing teachers have both the knowledge of subject matter, pedagogy, and instructional skills so that they can teach the content specified by the frameworks. States must support excellent programs to prepare teachers and exhibit a commitment to the continuing professional development of teachers.

3. *Accountability assessment:* States must develop a system to measure and report what students know, which is tied to what the curriculum frameworks specify. Assessment instruments require attention and support commensurate with the significant role they play in the system. Instruments must be developed that reveal the knowledge assumed to have been learned; exclusively relying on paper-and-pencil multiple choice tests will not address this need.

4. *Governance:* For SSR to work, the responsibilities and accountability must be clearly specified. The literature suggests that three critical ingredients are necessary for instructional success: a staff of well-trained professionals who use their knowledge with their students to meet goals; an internal governance structure that allows teachers to be decision makers; a well-supported and flexible infrastructure that supports teachers in this work.

5. *Finance:* States must ensure that schools have sufficient resources to implement the other elements in a high quality way.

The SSR dictates a focus on outcomes, where students' performance on learning tasks is the product to be measured (not processes, thinking, talking). The focus is on teaching and learning subject matter, not affective development, emotional well-being, social adjustment.

Blueprint for Action

What does this imply in terms of an immediate blueprint for action? Elmore (1993) has argued that for SSR to succeed, the action focus should be on deploying resources against students' performance, that is, to achieve the greatest percentage of children performing at the highest possible levels. To do this, educational administrators need to act as managers of performance, and not the role of power brokers whose main aim is to protect their turf and their budget. In terms of policy, the philosophy of "less is more" reigns; that is, less bureaucratization and rigid rules allow more flexible and creative problem solving by teachers and administrators to attain the goal of maximizing students' learning. Teachers must be seen by themselves and by others as the individuals mainly responsible for problem solving and should be given maximum autonomy to achieve their goals. Schools, in turn, are seen as performance centers, where the most important task is to achieve increased student learning and performance. The notion of the school as a cog in the wheel or unit in a big bureaucracy must be abandoned. Finally, there must be an emphasis on the professionalization of teachers, as exemplified in the NCTM frameworks, where the concept is of the teacher at the leading edge of problem solving. The focus is on developing the knowledge of the child and consistent improvement in the child's demonstration of that growing knowledge by his / her performance on assessment instruments.

Unanswered Questions

The SSR emphasizes a focus on teaching and learning content matter as demonstrated in performance assessments, which are often synonymous with the notorious "high stakes" exams. The focus is on outcomes, not processes. The SSR takes the point of view that all American children are to be included in this new plan; little is said about individual differences and diversity among children. The emphasis is on empowering teachers, which is typically heard as "regular education" teachers. There is no mention of other educational professionals.

These issues raise certain questions about the utility of the SSR approach. The first question is what does the curriculum framework really mean? How can it be adapted to address diverse populations of children? How are teachers equipped to do this well and be fair to each child? Second, the assumption that educators can just focus on learning of content, and ignore all the distractions—such as affective, emotional, and social factors—is naive. If learning were that simple, then we would have approached it without needless interference from these other psychological factors. Children do differ in their readiness to learn, their motivation to learn, their ability to focus and sustain learning in classrooms—and in countless other ways. Do we just assume that the same presentation of materials stage-managed by one regular education teacher will be sufficient for all children in her classroom? What about class size? Further, is school just for learning content matter—or should it include learning about how to get along with each other, citizenship, sharing, and other values that undergird our democracy.

The inclusion of the professional development of teachers is laudable and essential; the implication from the SSR discussions is that this constitutes professional development only for regular education teachers. Where do special educators, school psychologists, speech and language pathologists, school counselors, among other specialists, fit in? How will their expertise with special populations of children best be used—if at all? How can regular education teachers optimally deal with the increased diversity of the student body in their classes without assistance of these experts? Doesn't professional development include ways for all educational professionals who can assist students in finding ways to work together for the benefit of children?

Finally, about assessment, the critiques of "high stakes" standard examinations have permeated recent debates on American education. It is important that the SSR supports implications of alternative assessment.

THE ROLE OF ALTERNATIVE ASSESSMENT FOR LITERACY EDUCATION IN SCHOOL REFORM

The combined effects of the SSR movement, with its emphasis on standards and assessments and the implementation of the full inclusion mandates (increasing with class variation among students) will change American classrooms substantially, and therefore significantly affect teachers' work with children. Several competencies will be essential for teachers to develop and expand, including alternative assessment, instructional technique, and strategies for interdisciplinary collaboration among education professionals.

In this chapter, we focus on one of these key new competencies for literacy educators—alternative assessment, particularly the use of observational methods to reveal children's literacy competencies and the critical importance of interdisciplinary collaboration in assessment, so that a full picture of the child's strengths and weaknesses may emerge.

Classroom teachers are faced with the challenge of variability among students in their language and literacy skills and how best to assess and promote the development of these skills. The variability among students within the same grade has increased in many cases due to two reasons. One concerns changes in the cultural diversity of American schools. The other source of variability arises from recent efforts to include more students with learning disabilities in regular classrooms. As a result, teachers, clinicians, and others are looking for alternatives to standardized tests, which are limited in the information provided, particularly about the progress of individual children. Thus, teachers need to be aware of specific ways to support students' development of competence in language and literacy. Additionally, teachers have to have adequate means for assessing children's progress.

In a previous work, we presented an approach for adequately assessing growth in the language and literacy skills of school-age children, with focus on: print-awareness, word recognition, vocabulary acquisition, sound–symbol connections, and comprehension (Wilkinson & Silliman, 1994). Our approach, using the *Observational Lens Model*, is a qualitative one, in which the actual language and literacy behaviors of students are described over time and students' progress is documented. Our perspective emphasizes the need for careful and frequent monitoring of students' development of these and other key language and literacy behaviors. This perspective is also compatible with the integrated language arts view. We believe that adequate assessment must include the collection of actual performance samples, observations of classroom interaction, and interviews with children and teachers.

Previous work by the authors illustrates the critical importance of teachers' developing and applying knowledge of alternative assessment techniques. To develop this point of view, we provide some background on one student, Jamie, who had attended a regular education classroom, but was subsequently referred to a combination inclusion and regular education program. The goal of the program for Jamie was to support her development of the essential literacy skills needed so that she could return to a regular classroom.

Jamie

The focus of this discussion is Jamie, a child with a language learning disability (LLD). She has been selected because her language learning and literacy problems are typical of many children with an LLD.

Jamie was born following a normal pregnancy and delivery on November 6, 1984. She is the second of two daughters in a working-class family. All developmental milestones, with the exception of speech and language development were reported to be within normal limits. She did not begin to combine two words together until age 4 and had a significant phonological process disorder. In April 1991, Jamie was 6½ years old and enrolled in a half-day kindergarten program. She was receiving pull-out speech and language services. Her school system referred her to the Communication Development Program, a cooperative public school program, for a full case study evaluation. The speech-language pathologist providing her services in kindergarten found significant language comprehension and production problems in combination with the phonological disorder. Jamie's mother viewed her difficulties as primarily involving articulation. She also wanted Jamie to be able to recite the alphabet and to be able to read and write simple sentences. Despite her communication problems, Jamie showed persistence in trying to make herself understood. She fully used what she had available to be an active participant in conversation, a quality she still displays.

Because of her developmental and educational difficulties, Jamie was eligible for placement in the Communication Development Program, publicly funded special education program in the Chicago area. She has attended this program since September 1991 when she was 6 years 10 months old. This program is specifically designed for students with LLD from kindergarten through high school. Its philosophy is grounded to the integration of communication and students' communication goals across all areas of the curriculum. The approach is transdisciplinary and theme-based. Speech-language pathologists are also classroom teachers and collaborate with special education teachers, social workers, occupational therapists, and career educators, among others. Instructional principles are translated into practices in which speaking, listening, reading, writing, and spelling are integrated across the curriculum for two purposes: (a) to support the development of literacy and (2) to support the development of metacognitive and metalinguistic strategies for becoming active, reflective, and successful learners. Jamie remained in the program for 3 years and has been a participant in a longitudinal study on the assessment of her progress. One focus in the assessment of her progress has been her increasing ability to attend in more intentional and analytical ways to the phonological structure of oral language, what we all refer to as changing levels of phonological awareness. Jamie has been supported in learning strategies for word recognition in both reading and spelling. At the same time, through immersion in multipurpose literacy activities, Jamie has been supported in understanding that print, whether read or written, has communicative functions and meaning. She now reads, writes, and spells with some proficiency. Standardized tests failed to reveal the nature of her progress or describe her strategies and her difficulties as a "non-comprehending" reader and writer.

Observation for Assessment

We used the observational approach to document and assess the changes that Jamie underwent during the past 3 years in the Communication Development program; this approach is incorporated within our *Observational Lens Model* (Wilkinson & Silliman, 1994).

The plan for the assessment of progress was developed collaboratively in order to incorporate multiple perspectives — those of the teacher / clinician, the program supervisors, the researchers, and Jamie. A combination of observational techniques was used to implement the plan. For example, using video as a narrative tool, the teacher / clinician videotaped at least three times during a unit, including an end-of-unit assessment activity ("What Was Learned"). She also used a variety of other narrative tools to document ongoing progress. These included: (a) systematic, daily, on-line observations of significant behaviors that Jamie demonstrated (summarized weekly); (b) the development of a language / literacy portfolio collection (with Jamie's assistance); and (c) written evaluations of changes observed in Jamie and in herself as a teacher. To illustrate the use of observation for assessment, we have selected a 2-month period, when Jamie was placed in the special program described above. This analysis shows the utility of the approach that we suggest teachers take when attempting to understand a child's strengths and weaknesses.

Analysis of the videotapes proceeded in three phases. First, running records were prepared of the videotaped activities (approximately 2 hours). Running records represent an example of a narrative tool. Their purpose is to obtain a chronological record of the activities that occurred. These records were then verified for accuracy by the teacher / clinician and the program supervisors. During analysis, a question arose regarding the nature and scope of Jamie's phonological awareness in the oral domain and its relationship to her awareness that print serves a variety of communicative functions. This question stimulated the second phase of assessment and led to the application of another narrative tool, the critical incident. Five critical incidents were identified, with two each in November and December and one from January. The designation of critical incidents was a joint decision of both the teacher/clinician and the program supervisors. Finally, using observational tools, the critical incidents were transcribed so that the dynamics of actual verbal interaction could be closely examined. These tools include: Running records, critical incidents, and transcribed critical incidents.

Steps for Observational Assessment

As teachers plan literacy activities and curricula, they may want to consider using observational methods as a way to document and better understand the progress made by individual children in their acquisition of key language and literacy skills. Observation as one method of assessment is becoming more popular in both regular and special education classrooms for two reasons. First, the limitations of formal standardized assessment procedures have been recognized. Second, systematic observation links together assessment and instruction (Wilkinson & Silliman, 1990). We offer four suggestions as general guidelines for teachers and speech-language clinicians. Readers need to draw on their own experiences and apply any of these ideas to their own particular classroom situations.

Formulate the question and select the appropriate kinds of observation. The first step in using observational assessment successfully is often the most difficult. This step requires one to define the focus of observation; that is, teachers and other educational staff need to consider the purpose of assessment and formulate the question to be asked clearly and specifically. An important point to remember in question formulation is that not all levels of communicative behaviors can be observed simultaneously. Also, defining in advance the behaviors to be observed is essential. Unless workable definitions are agreed on, observers will be less reliable in identifying particular instances of these behaviors.

In the case of Jamie, a specific purpose of observations was to assess the nature of progress that she made in developing strategies for word recognition. This focus involved relationships among phonological awareness, print awareness, and spelling as these were implemented within a classroom approach that emphasized literacy functions and learning-how-to-learn. Another purpose concerned how the teacher used discourse scaffolding to support Jamie's efforts to progress from being a novice with these key language and literacy skills to becoming more of an expert. It is clear from the kind of strategies being cultivated for phonological awareness, print awareness, and spelling that a fairly fine degree of detail would have to be captured by the observations; thus, the application of regular, close-up, and even microclose-up lenses seemed appropriate. The choice of running records, critical incidents, and transcriptions followed from the decisions made about the level of detail

needed to see progress in strategy use for cultivating these essential skills.

Recognize key language and literacy skills in real-time usage. A second step for teachers is to look for specific examples of language and literacy skills as they *actually occur in classroom activities,* such as the reading activities observed with Jamie. Campione and Brown (1987) suggest that, in documenting progress, the teacher should not be concerned with how much overall improvement can be demonstrated in a child's performance. Rather, the focus should be maintained on how much discourse support a child needs from the teacher to attain a specific level of learning and, as a next step, be able to apply that learning to new situations that increasingly diverge from the original situation. Another way of stating this concept is to think of helping the child move along a continuum where the child starts as a novice and becomes more of an expert within a specific domain.

Over the 2-month period of observation, Jamie continued to need relatively high levels of discourse assistance from the teacher/clinician to be able to participate in classroom activity. For example, at the end of the 2-month period, Jamie still required external guidance for the more complex word recognition activities, such as reading of the "What We Want to Know" questions in the dinosaur activity. Although high levels of discourse support from her teacher were still necessary, Jamie increasingly took on more responsibility for her own learning with less assistance. For example, in different activities, she began to use some self-monitoring strategies more effectively and to retrieve some spelling forms on her own or with minimal guidance. However, Nelson (1989) reminds us that simply noticing an increased frequency of occurrence of a particular behavior is insufficient evidence that the child has actually learned (internalized) that behavior. Documentation of authentic progress must provide ample and convincing evidence that the key language or literacy skill is firmly under the control of the child, who can now use it functionally and appropriately.

Document progress clearly and with ongoing observations. Documenting progress for a particular child needs to be ongoing, a kind of formative assessment, and includes quantitative and qualitative data. Some of the specific methods that can be used were outlined in the discussion on Jamie.

There are, however, literally thousands of specific observational methods available. Howell and Morehead (1987) discuss a wide variety of charting procedures for assessing changes on a daily, weekly, or monthly basis. However tempting it may be to reduce the assessment of progress to a set of neat charts, lines, or tables with frequency counts, teachers should not succumb! These kinds of "categorical" data have some limited utility, but cannot be sufficient for documenting progress of key language and literacy skills (see Silliman & Wilkinson, 1991, for a more complete discussion on advantages and disadvantages of categorical systems). In developing a broad framework for the assessment of progress, teachers will need to rethink assessment data "...as any recordable data from which inferences about learning and teaching can be drawn" (Weaver, 1991, p. 212).

A broad framework must include other methods, such as narrative ones, if adequate understanding is to result. Portfolios (a narrative method) can be maintained for each child. Dialogue journals (also a narrative method) help children make transitions from more oral styles of communication to more literate styles of communication. They also provide a written record over time that can be evaluated for evidence of real change in communicative strategies for the expression of purpose and meaning. Categorical methods, such as rating scales, can add to the richness of assessment if constructed with appropriate items. Watson and Crowley (in Weaver, 1988) offer several suggestions that can be included in rating scales: (a) the types of assistance sought for problem solving (e.g., child seeks assistance only from teacher, seeks assistance from others, etc.); (b) the extent of risk taking (e.g., the child contributes his or her own topics, tries to paraphrase what has been read, attempts to invent best-fit predictions for an unfamiliar word, etc.); and (c) the attitude toward reading and writing (child prefers books with predictable structure, enjoys shared writing, etc.).

The guiding concept is for teachers to use whatever kinds of specific observational methods that seem most appropriate in order to capture what the child knows about language-literacy connections at that time. This information will assist the teacher in designing the most appropriate curriculum and learning activity, one that builds on existing knowledge and challenges the child to reach for the next level. For example, the broad assessment framework used with Jamie allowed her teacher / clinician to revise teaching strategies. These revisions included building in more systematic and developmentally appropriate phonological awareness activities, providing Jamie with more encouragement to take risks in applying invented spellings, and altering the nature of discourse scaffolding to give Jamie (and the other students) increased responsibility for collaborating in decision making. *Use the observational data as a way to share insights.* Finally, teachers and speech-language clinicians can consider using the metaphor of the *Observational Lens Model* as a way to talk about what they see and how they interpret the significance of those observations. A shared frame of reference made possible through systematic observation facilitates teachers being able to talk with each other and other educational professionals.

It is no small matter how classroom teachers, speech-language clinicians, special educators, and other specialists learn to communicate with one another in order to attain proficiency in the use of observational assessment. Teachers and clinicians can move to new professional competencies as they collaborate more effectively in ongoing assessment and intervention. In a real sense, new professional communicative competencies are required for this kind of collaboration to happen. The focus of collaboration would be the child, the classroom, and how to design the most effective instruction to maximize children's acquisition and applications of key language and literacy skills. Examples of successful collaboration in both the regular and special education settings are found in Silliman and Wilkinson (1991).

TABLE 53–1. Jamie's case evaluation in November 1993

Jamie's Evaluation

Jamie was referred for a case study evaluation by her educational team in November 1993. The reason for the case study was to update information on her levels of functioning in order to assist her educational programming. Assessments consisted of: (1) Speech and language assessment; (2) educational assessment; (3) psychological assessment; and (4) a social developmental study. An integrated set of programming and educational objectives was then prepared. The actual assessments were conducted by members of Jamie's educational team for the 1993–94 school year. These team members included her classroom teachers (a speech-language pathologist and educator), the school psychologist, and a school social worker.

Team Recommendations

The educational team concluded that Jamie relied on her strengths in socialization, including her emerging discourse skills. For example, she now initiated conversation with adults and peers and attempted to assist her classmates. She had also begun developing metacognitive skills as demonstrated through an emerging ability to identify activities that were easy or hard for her and attempting to apply strategies to assist herself with difficult tasks. In mathematics Jamie independently used strategies and showed an interest in the further development of skills. Her overall profile indicated continued need for the support of her communication, including all aspects of literacy learning. High levels of scaffolding support remained necessary for Jamie to engage in more complex cognitive, communicative, and linguistic activities and to attempt applications to novel situations. Moreover, the team believed that her decoding difficulties seemed to hamper her text comprehension. Integrated educational and communication goals included: (1) continued use of verbal and nonverbal cues and comprehension facilitating strategies, such as clarification requests and revisions, to support language comprehension; (2) use of editing strategies, dictionaries, word charts, and sound patterns to support more conventional spelling and the composition of written expression; (3) use of phonemic segmentation and blending strategies to aid in recognizing unfamiliar words and to increase sight vocabulary; and (4) enhancement of problem-solving abilities by supporting increased responsibility for practical decision making.

CONCLUSION

The analysis of Jamie's literary skills presented above is an illustration of how careful observation of a child's behavior in the classroom can reveal literary competencies and areas that need to be targeted for growth. After 3 years in the special Communication Development program, Jamie made substantial progress in developing the requisite literacy skills in the academic and social domains. Table 53–1 shows the summary recommendation by the interdisciplinary team which has overseen her case in her third year.

The integration of the information gathered from alternative assessments, specifically observational methods, is clear and significant. Such careful documentation of Jamie's actual literacy usage is essential for successfully implementing the team's recommendations.

In sum, using observation as one component for assessing progress in children's language and literacy development is becoming more popular in American elementary schools. The model and specific techniques presented here illustrate the utility of such an approach. Documenting progress through observational methods can be a vehicle for teachers to optimize their understanding of children's knowledge and how that knowledge changes over time, sometimes in subtle ways. Observational methods can thus provide crucial information on the relative success of choices made about curriculum, learning activities, and teaching strategies.

References

Anders, P. H., & Pearson, P. D. (1987). Instructional research on literacy and reading: Parameters, perspectives, and predictors. In R. J. Tierney, P. L. Anders, & J. N. Mitchell (Eds.), *Understanding readers' understanding: Theory and practice* (pp. 307–319). Hillsdale, NJ: Erlbaum.

Au, K. H., Scheu, J. A., Kawakami, A. J., & Herman, P. A. (1990). Assessment and accountability in a whole literacy curriculum. *Reading Teacher, 43*, 574–578.

Baker, L., & Brown, A. L. (1984a). Metacognitive skills and reading. In P. D. Pearson (Ed.), *Handbook of reading research* (pp. 353–394). New York: Longman.

Baker, L., & Brown, A. L. (1984b). Cognitive monitoring in reading. In J. Flood (Ed.), *Understanding reading comprehension*. Newark, DE: International Reading Association.

Biber, D. (1988). *Variation across speech and writing.* New York: Cambridge University Press.

Bloome, D., Harris, O. L. H., & Ludlum, D. E. (1991). Reading and writing as sociocultural activities: Politics and pedagogy in the classroom. *Topics in Language Disorders, 11*(3), 14–27.

Brown, A. L., & Palincsar, A. S. (1987). Reciprocal teaching of comprehension strategies. In J. O. Day & J. G. Borkowski (Eds.), *Intelligence and exceptionality: New directions for theory, assessment, and instructional practice* (pp. 81–132). Norwood, NJ: Ablex.

Campione, J. C., & Brown, A. L. (1987). Linking dynamic assessment with school achievement. In C. S. Lidz (Ed.), *Dynamic assessment: An interactional approach to evaluating learning potential* (pp. 82–115). New York: Guilford Press.

Cazden, C. B. (1988). *Classroom discourse: The language of teaching and learning.* Portsmouth, NH: Heinemann.

Consortium for Policy Research in Education (1991). *Policy Briefs, Putting the pieces together: Systemic school reform.* RB-06-4/91, Rutgers, The State University of New Jersey.

Cox, B. E., Shanahan, T., & Sulzby, E. (1990). Good and poor elementary readers' use of cohesion in writing. *Reading Research Quarterly, 25*, 47–65.

Curriculum and Evaluation Standards for School Mathematics (1989). National Council of Teachers of Mathematics, Reston: VA.

DeStefano, J. S., & Kantor, R. (1988). Cohesion in spoken and written dialogue: An investigation of cultural and textual constraint. *Linguistics and Education, 1*, 105–124.

Eller, R. G. (1989). Ways of meaning: Exploring cultural differences in students' written compositions. *Linguistics and Education, 1*, 341–358.

Elmore, R. (1993, November). An overview of systemic reform: Benefits and potential pitfalls. *CEPA-NJ Newsletter,* Rutgers, The State University of New Jersey

Gavelek, J. R., & Raphael, T. E. (1985). Metacognition, instruction, and the role of questioning activities. In D. L. Forrest-Pressley, G. E. MacKinnon, & T. G. Waller (Eds.), *Metacognition, cognition, and human performance,* (Vol. 2, pp. 103–136). New York: Academic Press.

Harste, J. C., Short, K. G., & Burke, C. (1988). *Creating classrooms for authors.* Portsmouth, NH: Heinemann.

Hasan, R. (1984a). Ways of saying; ways of meaning. In R. P. Fawcett,

M. A. K. Halliday, S. Lamb & A. Makka (Eds.), *The semiotics of culture and language* (pp. 105–162). Dover, NH: Frances Pinter.

Hasan, R. (1984b). Coherence and cohesive harmony. In J. Flood (Ed.), *Understanding reading comprehension* (pp. 181–219). Newark, DE: International Reading Association.

Howell, K., & Morehead, M. (1987). *Curriculum-based evaluation for special and remedial education.* Columbus, OH: Charles E. Merrill.

Horowitz, R., & Samuels, S. J. (1987). Comprehending oral and written language: Critical contrasts for literacy and schooling. In R. Horowitz & S. J. Samuels (Eds.), *Comprehending oral and written language* (pp. 1–52). New York: Academic Press.

Kawakami-Arakaki, A. J., Oshiro, M. E., & Farran, D. C. (1988). Integrating reading and writing in a kindergarten curriculum. In J. M. Mason (Ed.), *Reading and writing connections* (pp. 199–218). Boston: Allyn & Bacon.

Meyer, B. J. F. (1987). Following the author's top-level organization: An important skill for reading comprehension. In R. J. Tierney, P. L. Anders, & J. N. Mitchell (Eds.), *Understanding readers' understanding: Theory and practice* (pp. 59–76). Hillsdale, NJ: Erlbaum.

Nelson, K. E. (1989). Strategies for first language teaching. In M. L. Rice & R. L. Schiefelbusch (Eds.), *The teachability of language* (pp. 263–310). Baltimore: Paul H. Brookes.

Palincsar, A. S., & Brown, A. L. (1984). Reciprocal teaching of comprehension fostering and comprehension monitoring activities. *Cognition and Instruction, 1,* 117–175.

Palincsar, A. S., & Brown, D. A. (1987). Enhancing instructional time through attention to metacognition. *Journal of Learning Disabilities, 20*, 66–75.

Paris, S. G. (1991). Assessment and remediation of metacognitive aspects of children's reading comprehension. *Topics in Language Disorders, 12*(1), 32–50.

Raphael, T. E., Englert, C. S., & Kirschner, B. W. (1989). Acquisition of expository writing skills. In J. M. Mason (Ed.), *Reading and writing connection* (pp. 261–290). Boston: Allyn & Bacon.

Rhodes L. K., & Dudley-Marling, K. (1988). *Readers and writers with a difference: A holotic approach to teaching learning disabled and remedial students.* Portsmouth, NH: Heinemann.

Scott, C. M. (1988). Spoken and written syntax. In M. A. Nippold (Ed.), *Later language development* (pp. 49–95).

Scott, C. M. (1989). Learning to write: Context, form and process. In A. G. Kamhi & H. W. Catts (Eds.), *Reading disabilities: A developmental language perspective* (pp. 261–302). Boston: College-Hill Press.

Shuy, R. (1988). Identifying dimensions of classroom language. In J. L. Green & J. O. Harker (Eds.), *Multiple perspective analysis of classroom discourse,* (Vol. 28, pp. 115–134). Norwood, NJ: Ablex.

Silliman, E. R., & Wilkinson, L. C. (1991). *Communicating for learning: Classroom collaboration and observation.* Gaithersburg, MD: Aspen.

Staton, J. (1988). An introduction to dialogue journal communication. In J. Staton, R. W. Shuy, J. K. Peyton & L. Reed (Eds.), *Dialogue journal communication: Classroom, linguistic, social and cognitive views* (pp. 1–32). Norwood, NJ: Ablex.

Sternberg, R. J. (1987). A unified theory of intelligence and exceptionality. In J. D. Day & J. G. Barkowski (Eds.), *Intelligence and exceptionality* (pp. 135–172). Norwood, NJ: Ablex.

Sulzby, E. (1990). Assessment of emergent writing and children's language while writing. In L. M. Morrow & J. K. Smith (Eds.), *Assessment for instruction in early literacy* (pp. 83–109). Englewood Cliffs, NJ: Prentice-Hall.

Teale, W. H., & Martinez, M. G. (1989). Connecting writing: Fostering emergent literacy in kindergarten children. In J. M. Mason (Ed.), *Reading and writing connections* (pp. 177–198). Boston: Allyn & Bacon.

Tierney, R. J., Lazansky, J., Raphael, T., & Cohen, P. (1987). Author's intentions and readers' interpretations. In R. J. Tierney, P. L. Anders & J. N. Mitchell (Eds.), *Understanding readers' understanding: Theory and practice* (pp. 205–226). Hillsdale, NJ: Erlbaum.

Wallach, G. P. (1990). Magic buries Celtics: Looking for broader interpretations of language learning and literacy. *Topics in Language Disorders, 10*(2). 63–80.

Watson, D., & Crowley, P. (1988). How can we implement a whole language approach? In C. Weaver (Ed.), *Reading process and practice* (pp. 232–279). Portsmouth, NH: Heinemann.

Weaver, C. (1988). *Reading process and practice.* Portsmouth, NH: Heinemann.

Weaver, C. (1991). *Understanding whole language: From principles to practice.* Portsmouth, NH: Heinemann.

Wilkinson, L. C., & Silliman, E. R. (1990). Sociolinguistic analysis: Nonformal assessment of children's language and literacy skills. *Linguistics and Education, 2,* 109–125.

Wilkinson, L. C. & Silliman, E. R. (1994). Assessing student's progress in language and literacy: A classroom approach. In L. Morrow, L. C. Wilkinson & J. Smith (Eds.), *Integrated language arts: Controversy to consensus* (pp. 241–270). Needham, MA: Allyn & Bacon.

·54·

SETTING OPPORTUNITY-TO-LEARN STANDARDS

C. Jane Hydrick

CLASSROOM TEACHER

There are too many variables in the human experience that cannot be leveled with money alone. Yet consider the challenge to a level playing field by this range in expenditure per pupil: in one metropolitan area, one school with a per pupil expenditure of $1732 is 15 miles away from a school where the per pupil expenditure is over $15,000. You can imagine the disparity in opportunities to teach and opportunities to learn. Even within a single district, every school may be operated under the same per pupil expenditure, but the schools' physical plants, environments, resources and climates of support are very different. The standards on the property manifests may be exact in terms of expenditure and number, but the realities for the teachers and students vary greatly.

Each day, schools, teachers and students deal in greatly varying degrees with hurdles such as class size, quality and appropriateness of teacher preparation and ongoing teacher in service, inequitable access to resources, lack of vigorous involvement of all learners in decision making, little parental and community support, and funding formulas and voucher systems that exacerbate the inequities. Kozol's 1991 book, *Savage Inequalities*, presented the classroom realities of teachers and students whose daily classroom experiences characterize the disheartening, angering, shameful extreme of inequity of opportunities; and provided a focus for advocates of equitable funding and opportunities for teachers and students.

Gonzalez (1993) reports that in 1991 the National Coalition of Advocates for Students offered a set of 10 basic rights that it felt comprised equal opportunities for all students:

1. Children are entitled to have parents, advocates, and concerned educators included in all decisions affecting their education.
2. Children are entitled to learn in an integrated, heterogeneous setting responsive to different learning styles and abilities.
3. Children are entitled to comprehensible, culturally supportive, and developmentally appropriate curriculum and teaching strategies.
4. Children are entitled access to a common body of knowledge and the opportunity to acquire higher-order skills.
5. Children are entitled to a broadly-based assessment of their academic progress and grading structures that enhance individual strengths and potential.
6. Children are entitled to a broad range of support services that address individual needs.
7. Children are entitled to attend schools that are safe, attractive and free of prejudice.
8. Children are entitled to attend school unless they pose a danger to other children and school staff.
9. Children are entitled to instruction by teachers who hold high expectations for all students and who are fully prepared to meet the challenge of diverse classrooms.
10. Children are entitled to equal educational opportunity supported by the provision of greater resources to schools serving students most vulnerable to school failure: low income, minority, or immigrant students. (p. 24)

The notion of delivery standards catapulted into public debate with the January 24, 1992 report from the National Council on Education Standards and Testing, which separated delivery standards from content and performance standards. "School delivery standards should provide a metric for determining whether a school 'delivers' to students the 'opportunity to learn' well the material in the content standards" (p. E-5). Content standards developed by the National Council of Teachers of Mathematics (NCTM) became the prototype for content standards developed in other subject-matter areas, and spawned projects and programs that had as their focus student and teacher performance and assessment in terms of the content standards.

As a result of the ensuing political debate on delivery standards, the notion of delivery standards became law as opportunities to learn in Section 213 of the March, 1994, Goals 2000: Educate America Act. Opportunity-to-Learn standards, formerly delivery standards, were defined as ones "that will establish a basis for providing all students a fair opportunity to achieve the knowledge and skills set out in the voluntary national content standards." Specific elements designated in Section 213 as opportunities to learn were:

(A) the quality and availability to all students of curricula, instructional materials, and technologies, including distance learning; (B) the capability of teachers to provide high-quality instruction to meet diverse learning needs in each content area to all students; (C) the extent to which teachers, principals, and administrators have ready and continuing access to professional development, including the best knowledge about teaching, learning, and school improvement; (D) the extent to which curriculum, instructional practices, and assessments are aligned to voluntary national content standards; (E) the extent to which school facilities provide a safe and secure environment for learning and instruction and have the requisite libraries, laboratories, and other resources necessary to provide an opportunity to learn; (F) the extent to which schools utilize policies, curricula, and instructional practices which ensure nondiscrimination on the basis of gender; and (G) other factors that the Council deems appropriate to ensure that all students receive a fair opportunity to achieve the knowledge and skills described in the voluntary national content standards and the voluntary national student performance standards certified by the Council.

The voluntary national content standards which are referenced in Goals 2000 are currently being written for many subject-matter areas and some, such as those completed by the NCTM and the Music Educators National Conference (MENC), are published and available now. In the preface to the music standards, it states that students cannot be expected to meet the standards unless they are "given reasonable opportunities to learn the skills and knowledge specified" (p. vi). To that end, the music opportunity-to-learn standards include standards for every aspect affecting the classroom from staffing, curriculum and scheduling, to facilities, materials and equipment. The MENC document (1994) concludes from practice and history that there exists a "high correlation between effective student learning in music and the existence of the favorable conditions specified in the opportunity-to-learn standards" (p. vii).

The belief that opportunities for achievement must precede fair assessment is articulated further in the New Standards Project statement of principles. The New Standards Project, originally a joint program of two organizations (The National Center on Education and the Economy, Rochester, New York, and the Learning Research and Development Center at the University of Pittsburgh), and continuing as a partnership with states and local school districts to design and administer a new system of standards and assessments, has termed its tenth project principle "The Social Compact." It is essentially an acknowledgment of the high stakes involved with assessment of student performance, and a pledge, in view of those high stakes, by the New Standards Project to

do everything in [their] power to ensure all students a fair shot at reaching the new performance standards, and to prevent

students' performance on the new assessments from being used as the basis for awarding a diploma or any other form of credential unless all students in the jurisdiction awarding the credential have had an opportunity to prepare themselves well. This means that they will be taught a curriculum that will prepare them for the assessments, their teachers will have the preparation to enable them to teach it well, and there will be an equitable distribution of the resources the students and their teachers need to succeed. (p. 11)

The Social Compact states that, although educators ought to be held accountable for bringing each child up to world-class standards, educators cannot accomplish the tasks on their own. The Social Compact lists several elements as necessary support for educators: "the support of families, high quality early childhood programs, health care and other resources to make it possible for all our children to succeed in school" (p. 11).

It was a presidential agenda priority of National Council of Teachers of English (NCTE) President Hydrick that NCTE assume a national leadership position in delivery standards, and lead other associations in ensuring that the debates, efforts and works in standards projects serve at least as catalysts for declaring as untenable the de facto standards in opportunities to teach and learn which have dominated too many of our schools and classrooms: de facto delivery standards that, if not recognized, addressed and corrected, would, Hydrick believed, effectively countermand any possibilities or hope that may have resided in the content standards efforts.

To reconfirm NCTE's national leadership in learner advocacy and delivery standards, Hydrick held an Invitational Conference on Opportunities-to-Learn / Delivery Standards, July 29–31, 1994 in Washington, DC. Representatives from subject-matter organizations, educational policy and advocacy groups attended. Although it was the first time that many of the groups had collaborated, particularly on the issue of opportunity-to-learn standards, at the conclusion of almost three days participants agreed that opportunity-to-learn standards have relevance to the missions of all represented organizations, and that the organizations shared a common vision of teaching and learning environments which provide equal opportunities to learn.

Representative organizations included the NCTE, Teachers of English to Speakers of Other Languages, Speech Communication Association, Brooks Associates, National Middle School Association, National Board for Professional Teaching Standards, National Parent Teachers Association, College Language Association, National Association for Bilingual Education, National Science Teachers Association, National Council of Teachers of Mathematics, National Council for the Social Studies, Music Educators National Conference, Alliance for Curriculum Reform, National Council for Geographic Education, International Reading Association, and the American Association of Colleges for Teacher Education.

Conference participants drafted four documents, three of which pertain specifically to collaborative efforts in opportunities to learn. The first document, a summary report of the conference, has been endorsed by the conference participants.

SUMMARY REPORT

An invitational conference on Opportunities-to-Learn / Delivery Standards sponsored by the National Council of Teachers of English was convened in Washington, DC. July 29–31, 1994. Participants in the conference included representatives (listed above) of subject-matter organizations, educational policy, and advocacy groups.

Participants agreed that Opportunities-to-Learn / Delivery Standards (OTL standards) have relevance to the missions of all represented organizations, and that we share a common vision of teaching and learning environments which provide quality opportunities to learn.

Recognizing the strength of a collective voice and a shared plan of actions, the participants proposed the following actions to guide our efforts to impact the OTL standards debate and to influence the implementation of OTL standards at local, state and national levels—

- develop a statement of principles for OTL standards and invite endorsement from a wide range of subject-matter organizations, educational policy, and advocacy groups

- prepare a proposal for participation by subject-matter organizations in consortia which apply for an OTL Standards Development Grant as provided for in Section 219, Goals 2000 legislation; to invite other subject-matter organizations to join in this proposal to submit the unique expertises of the subject-matter organizations as a vital component of any consortium developing OTL standards

- participate individually and collectively in public hearings, state panels, and other such forums which address OTL standards

- present collective views regarding OTL standards to the National Education Standards and Improvement Council (NESIC), which is authorized to certify voluntary, national OTL standards (Section 213 c1, Goals 2000 legislation)

- contribute individually and collaboratively to the development of state models for OTL standards

- promote public awareness of OTL standards legislation and its implications for national education standards; engage in an education process to make the public aware of the value of OTL standards (increase public awareness of the effects of opportunities to learn on each member and facet of our local, state and national communities)

- maintain open communications within and among all participating organizations regarding OTL standards.

The participants of this conference proposed the above actions which each participant's organization(s) could adopt and implement either individually or collaboratively in a variety of ways and in varying degrees.

The second document, a statement of principles regarding opportunity-to-learn standards, has passed a first-stage endorsement by the subject-matter organizations, educational policy, and advocacy groups who participated as well as some that were unable to attend.

Opportunity-To-Learn Standards Statement of Principles

At a 1994 conference on Opportunity-to-Learn Standards, sponsored by the National Council of Teachers of English, participants agreed that opportunity-to-learn standards provide a framework that makes it possible for all students to have equitable access to high quality education.

Why are opportunity-to-learn standards necessary ?

The opportunity to learn is the inherent right of every student in America. Educators, parents and other members of a student's many communities share a common interest in the educational success of each student and in the role of education in our democratic society. Full, positive participation in democracy is contingent upon every student's access to quality education. Such access to high quality education should not be dependent upon the specific community in which a student lives. By focusing and building upon the strengths of learners, opportunity-to-learn standards can help insure equitable access to high quality education for all students in America.

What should opportunity-to-learn standards do?

Opportunity-to-Learn standards should

- enable all students to achieve high content standards and to learn to their full potential

- be directly tied to students' learning and performance in content standards

- consider the diverse, multiple ways students learn

- enable all teachers to teach all students

- be supported by the best classroom practice and research

- include on-going professional development of educators

- be based on research on how effectively schools use resources

- address necessary conditions and resources for successful learning in our schools, as well as effective use of resources including safe, secure environments free of prejudice and violence; attractive, comfortable environments that invite learning, risk taking and problem solving; updated library, media centers and technologies

- consider opportunities for preschool and beyond school learning

Opportunity-to-learn standards at their best should reflect America's commitment to equitable access to high quality education for all students. States and schools that meet opportunity-to-learn standards will enable students to become lifelong learners and lead productive, rewarding lives.

SUMMARY

Opportunity-to-learn standards should provide:

- time for students to learn and reflect
- time for teachers to plan, learn, teach and reflect
- appropriate learning resources
- resources from the community

The third document is a proposal for participation by subject-matter organizations in consortia which apply for an opportunity-to-learn standards development grant as provided for in Section 219, Goals 2000 legislation. The consortia are defined as groups which include the participation of

(a) state-level policy makers, such as Governors, State legislators, chief state school officers, and State school board members;

(b) local policy makers and administrators, such as local school board members, superintendents, and principals;

(c) teachers (especially teachers involved in the development of content standards) and related services personnel;

(d) parents and individuals with experience in promoting parental involvement in education;

(e) representatives of business;

(f) experts in vocational-technical education;

(g) representatives of regional accrediting associations;

(h) individuals with expertise in school finance and equity, the education of at-risk students, and the preparation and training of teachers and school administrators;

(i) curriculum and school reform experts;

(j) representatives of advocacy groups, including student and civil rights advocacy groups;

(k) representatives of higher education; and

(l) secondary school students.

Section 219 also includes a statement of the purposes and uses for the opportunity-to-learn standards.

(a) provide all students with an opportunity to learn;

(b) assess the capacity and performance of individual schools; and

(c) develop appropriate actions to be taken in the event that the schools fail to achieve such standards.

Additionally, all consortia are directed to

(a) draw upon current research about student achievement and the necessary conditions for effective teaching and learning; and

(b) provide for the development of more than one draft of standards which incorporates the comments and recommendations of educators and other knowledgeable individuals across the nation.

Although he cautioned that opportunity-to-learn (OTL) standards were still at the "emerging idea stage," Andrew Porter (1994), a leading writer on opportunities to learn, shared an optimism about the potential helpfulness of Goals 2000 and NESIC:

From my perspective, the concept of OTL standards seems headed in about the right direction. Clearly, OTL standards are not going to become a major new form of school-by-school accountability. If they are to have any influence on school improvement, it will be through persuasion provided by visions of good education practice and information from OTL indicators on progress toward school improvement. (p. 31)

The keynote speaker at the OTL conference was Judge Eugene Reese, Circuit Judge in Montgomery (Alabama)

county. The April 6, 1993 *Wall Street Journal* printed the surprising news that Judge Reese, in a March 1993 ruling, had declared the Alabama state's entire public school system unconstitutional because it did not give students an adequate education. Prior to Reese's ruling, courts in other states had based their decisions on school financing procedures, ruling that there existed discrimination against poor students, that children had a right to an equitable education. In the *Wall Street Journal*, Helen Hershkoff, "a lawyer for the American Civil Liberties Union, termed Reese's decision "a landmark because it recognizes that children have a right not only to an equitable education but also to an adequate education" (p. B1). The article credited lawyers and education specialists with agreeing that the most controversial part of the decision was that it "specifies criteria necessary for schools to meet constitutional muster." Although Alabama's state constitution was quoted in the judge's ruling, other states have similar constitutions and would, therefore, be subject to similar rulings.

Reese began his keynote address with a quote from another landmark decision almost 40 years earlier, *Brown vs. Board of Education*:

Today, education is perhaps the most important function of state and local governments. Compulsory school attendance laws and great expenditures for education both demonstrate our recognition of the importance of education to our democratic society. It is required in the performance of our most basic public responsibilities, even service with the armed services. It is the very foundation of good citizenship. Today, it is a principal instrument in awakening the child to cultural values, in preparing him for later professional training and in helping him to adjust normally to his environment. In these days, it is doubtful that any child may reasonably be expected to succeed in life if he is denied the opportunity of an education. Such an opportunity where the state has undertaken to provide it, is a right which must be made available to all on equal terms. (p. 3)

In the conclusion of the court case document, Reese acknowledged Alabama Governor Hunt's admission that "deficiencies exist in Alabama's public school system and that additional funds are needed to remedy some of the unsatisfactory conditions" (p. 122). Reese stated further, however, that "The real issue here is whether these deficiencies and conditions rise to the level of deprivations of constitutional and statutory rights. In the opinion of the court, they do" (p. 122). Reese invoked the Alabama state constitution to substantiate that Alabama's school-age children should be provided with "substantially equitable and adequate educational opportunities."

In a 1993 National Governors' Association publication, *The Debate on Opportunity-To-Learn Standards*, author Traiman suggested that the debates surrounding opportunities to learn focus on several general areas: defining opportunities to learn; the purposes and uses of opportunity-to-learn standards; when, how, and by whom should opportunity-to-learn standards be developed; and the appropriate federal role in opportunity-to-learn standards. Since that publication, the language of Goals 2000: Educate America Act has provided the guidelines for all those once-debated general areas.

What remain to be hotly debated, of course, are the implementation and effects, both short-term and long-term, of the Goals 2000 legislation. Common sense and perhaps a single trip to a classroom would tell us that every item in the Goals 2000 laundry list of opportunity-to-learn standards comes with a price tag. We know that a large part of every school district's budget is designated to support curriculum, instructional materials and resources, capable teachers, professional development, and safe and secure facilities. Common sense and perhaps a single trip to a classroom would also tell us that not every child in any one school district, much less in all American districts, has equitable access to opportunity-to-learn standards.

Research studies will continue to deliver conflicting analyses on the effectiveness of class size, per-pupil spending, and all the other necessary conditions for effective teaching and learning. Research data are helpful, yet in Alabama alone, Judge Reese reported a $55,000 disparity between the highest and the lowest classroom annual expenditures; schools with no playground equipment; textbooks not available or several decades old; and unsafe buses. Kozol's report of the disparity in America's schools is equally depressing and portrays schools and districts across the country. It takes money to fix toilets so that they flush, to buy books, to make buses safe, to provide professional development for teachers, to patch holes in floors and ceilings, and to repair furnaces. Alabama's and America's schools have problems that need money, not data, to solve. Money alone is not the solution, but without money, opportunities to learn cannot improve.

There is Goals 2000 funding to develop opportunity-to-learn standards, but there are no funds to support opportunities to learn. Our National Education Goals are for school readiness; school completion; student achievement and citizenship; teacher education and professional development; world leadership in mathematics and science; adult literacy and lifelong learning; safe, disciplined, and alcohol- and drug-free schools; and parental participation. Consortia will be funded to deliberate how we might achieve these goals. We will have our destinations and our road maps, but no cars!

United States Representative Major R. Owens of New York, Chairperson of the House Education and Labor Subcommittee on Select Education and Civil Rights, held great promise for opportunities to learn and made this statement for the March 23, 1994 *Education Week*:

> If it does not cost a penny or require elected officials to do anything differently than they did the day before, we have embraced it. And, as a result, urgently needed education reform has begun and ended with a stream of photo opportunities and press releases. Opportunity-to-learn standards are an antidote to this consuming, vacant chatter, a font of truth that promises to set out for parents, teachers, and communities a more practical projection of what must be done to achieve educational excellence. To end the cynical swindling of the children of America, opportunity standards must be a component of any education-reform package. (p. 35)

The participants of the July 1994 Conference on Opportunities-to-Learn / Delivery Standards in Washington, DC, also held great promise for opportunities to learn. Opportunities to learn are now, through Goals 2000, a component of our currently legislated education-reform package. We cannot know yet if opportunity-to-learn standards will be the harbinger of realized opportunities for students who have had limited or no access to those opportunities, or if opportunity-to-learn standards will be the harbinger of more vacant chatter. We can know, however, that unless equitable opportunities to learn are realized for all students, our National Education Goals will never be realized.

References

Civil Action No. CV-90-883-R. (1993). Alabama Coalition for Equity, Inc. vs Guy Hunt. Circuit Court for Montgomery County, Alabama.

Gonzalez, R. D. (1993). Language, race, and the politics of educational failure: A case for advocacy. *NCTE Concept Paper Series 10*.

Kozol, J. (1991). *Savage inequalities*. New York: Crown.

Music Educators National Conference. (1994). *Opportunity-to-learn standards for music instruction*. Reston, VA: P. R. Lehman, Project Director.

National Council on Education Standards and Testing. (1992). *Raising standards for American education: A report to Congress, the Secretary of Education, the National Education Goals Panel, and the American people*. Washington, DC: U. S. Government Printing Office.

New Standards Project. *New Standards Project*. Pittsburgh, PA: Author.

Porter, A. (1994). *The uses and misuses of opportunity-to-learn standards*. Unpublished manuscript.

Public Law 103–227. (1994, March 31). 103rd Congress: Washington, DC.

Reese, E. (1994). *Opportunity-to-learn standards*. Washington, DC. National Council of Teachers of English.

Staff. (1993, April 6). *Wall Street Journal*, p. B1.

Staff. (1994, March 23). Opportunity to achieve: The debate over standards and equity. *Education Week*, pp. 33–36.

Traiman, S. L. (1993). *The debate on opportunity-to-learn standards*. Washington, DC: National Governors' Association.

STATE CURRICULAR FRAMEWORKS AND STANDARDS IN THE COMMUNICATIVE ARTS

Sharon O'Neal

TEXAS EDUCATION AGENCY

Susan Strecker

UNIVERSITY OF TEXAS AT AUSTIN

The ideal school is an earnest, cheerful, hard-working community without any internal strife or discord. To bring about and maintain such a condition the community, the school board, the teacher and the pupils must all work in harmony, to the end that the school may accomplish its proper work of developing character training, intelligence, and giving skill in using knowledge that is of most value in every-day life. (*Course of Study for Elementary Grades: Public Schools of Texas*, 1927).

To examine this excerpt in light of today's cry to establish standards in public education is to be struck with the similarity of the goals in 1927 and today. The focus on a common set of content standards has been the centerpiece of the 1990s national educational reform movement. This 1927 report to public schools asked the community, the school board, the teacher and the pupils to work in "harmony" toward a common set of goals. These goals were to provide students with useful strategies and information for use in their everyday life. Educators and communities are still struggling with these same issues. Today reformers ask teachers, administrators, and communities to work together toward a common set of content and performance standards so that students might be successful in the world outside of school. For teachers of the communicative arts, the goal seems simple enough: establish what all students should know and be able to do as they read, write, listen, and speak and describe what quality performance in each of those areas would look like. But language arts educators, like those in the other content areas, have faced serious questions as they proceed in this effort. For example, who decides what is contained in these content and performance standards? If the standards are rigorous, will resources be made available so that teachers might teach those standards and students might learn them? Should the standards be global or specific?

An examination of standard setting efforts indicates that the path to accomplishing such harmonious goals as the development of content and performance standards is riddled with complex and difficult issues for all involved. The purpose of this chapter is to examine the complexity of standard setting in the communicative arts and draw conclusions and implications for schools and states engaged in similar efforts.

WHAT COUNTED YESTERDAY

In the spring of 1937 the president of the Vidrine, Louisiana school board made his annual recruiting trip to the colleges and universities in the area. He succeeded in recruiting several young women, one of whom, Miss Curl, became a third grade teacher the following fall. At the time of her hiring she was told she had been selected because she was single, did not speak French, and did not have a Cajun surname.

Most of the children in Vidrine came from monolingual French-speaking homes and the president of the school board, even though he was of Cajun heritage, was interested in immersing the students in English as quickly as possible. Miss Curl's students loved talking to one another during class and passing notes. They often preferred recess to spelling practice. These students also enjoyed hearing a good story read aloud, and were willing to work hard for their teacher when they were reasonably sure of success and were interested in the topic at hand. Miss Curl's students came from various home backgrounds, some better able to provide for their children's well-being than others. She never knew the parents of her students well. The parents were uncomfortable coming to school because they spoke little or no English and in many cases, had never experienced school themselves.

Obviously the president of the school board in that small town in south Louisiana in 1937 had very explicit content and delivery standards. Clearly he felt that the children should leave his district speaking English, and toward that end, instruction should be delivered in English only.

Sixty years later Ms. Curl's class sounds familiar. Today's teachers of the language arts find themselves in classes with students whose first language is not English. Whether the students come from well-heeled suburbs or public housing projects, some of their parents and guardians are better able to provide nurturing home environments than others. Today's third grade classrooms still have students who love to talk and pass notes. Students are still begging their teacher to read just one more page of classics such as *To Kill a Mockingbird* (Lee, 1988) or such lighthearted texts as *The Twinkie Squad* (Korman, 1992).

But were those district "standards" in harmony with Miss Curl's goals? Were her goals in harmony with the broader community of Vidrine? Were her goals shaped in any way by state laws or rules and regulations? Did they influence student assessment, instruction and textbook selection? More important, did her goals promote life long readers and writers?

WHAT COUNTS TODAY

The Current Standards Movement

National attention has illuminated both the perils and merits of standards. In 1989, at an education summit in Charlottesville, Virginia, then president George Bush met with the nation's governors. Together they set national education goals that emphasized an increase in school readiness, high school graduation rates, and school safety, as well as calling for rigorous academic standards across the subject areas. (U.S. Department of Education, 1990). In January 1990, President Bush presented these goals in his State of the Union Address, and in February that year the National Governor's Association endorsed the goals. By April 1991, the Bush Administration proposed the "America 2000" legislation. Two key components of that legislative effort were implementation of national voluntary academic standards and development of a national achievement test.

President Clinton's new administration also embraced America 2000, and with minor changes the initiative was renamed "Goals 2000." In *Goals 2000* the national achievement test has been de-emphasized, but the debate over the development of rigorous national standards in each of the disciplines continues. At the same time the Education Department, in an effort to move the standard discussion to a more local level, has awarded more than $3 million for six states to develop content standards in the English language arts. Other states have received funding to examine English language arts

in a multidisciplinary context (McNeeley, 1995). Thus, the impetus for state and local standards development has come in response to national dialogue and resulting legislation.

The Role of National and State Standards

Based on the United States Constitution, traditionally states have had responsibility for public school education—what public school students are taught and what subject matter is tested, which books and materials are used, and how teachers are trained. But the American public has of late been disappointed with the work of the states in the public schools. Both the America 2000 and Goals 2000 reports reprimanded public education for the mediocre and undemanding work required of students (U.S. Department of Education, 1990, 1994). Establishing national content standards was an effort to make public schools more challenging and to make students more academically and economically competitive.

Language arts educators have not yet had the opportunity to examine national standards, because thus far, none exist. In 1992, the Standards Project for English Language Arts (SPELA) was federally funded for a brief time by the Education Department, but funding was withdrawn after the first year of activity. SPELA was criticized for including too much attention to settings in which language arts education was successful and not providing enough specificity about skills and knowledge in the English language arts. The SPELA language played well among those serving disenfranchised children who felt discussions of resources needed to achieve standards might entice more money into poor schools. Conservatives, however, found language about resources to be an attempt to micromanage English language arts education at a national level (Diegmueller, 1994). Currently, both the National Council of Teachers of English and the International Reading Association have continued national standards work.

The intent was for national content standards to establish a consistent framework to guide public education in the states. The framework would then initiate sweeping systemic changes. For example, once states embraced rigorous goals in each content area, changes in student and teacher assessment programs, professional development efforts, and instructional materials would be aligned with the content standards. (See Figure 55–1)

Even without national standards, states have always articulated goals implicitly in the curriculum documents they publish, the tests they require, or the textbooks they adopt. In states with no mandates, textbooks have been the de facto required curriculum. With the first wave of reform in the early 1980s many states employed sanctions regarding promotion, retention, high school graduation tied to statewide testing programs. In these states, test results also became the basis of teachers' evaluations and thus, became performance standards for both teachers and students. Teachers began to teach toward the test, regardless of its integrity, because the results were part of their own evaluation. Therefore, both in states where reform has been a top-down effort and in states where the effort has been more respectful of the individual teacher in the classroom, standards have existed.

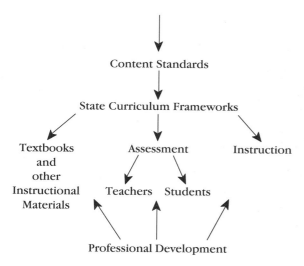

FIGURE 55–1 Relationship between and among content standards, state curriculum frameworks, and state level decisions

States often explicitly lay out the what, when, and how of the delivery of content in documents known as frameworks. These frameworks, however, serve differing purposes. In Texas, frameworks serve as guides for local districts while in California they also serve as directives to publishers wishing to participate in state textbook adoptions. Still other states use frameworks as a rationale for certain types of instruction. Perusal of these frameworks provides an overview of what is perceived by state departments to be the critical elements in the language arts.

Common Threads in State Frameworks

In 1991 state supervisors of reading and English language arts met to determine the role of content standards and their impact on such state work as curriculum development, textbook and materials adoption, student and teacher assessment, and professional development guidelines. The supervisors chose to collect all state frameworks in reading and literacy and determine their points of agreement. Four common threads were identified (Kapinus, 1995).

First, all state documents agreed on the definition of reading as a strategic process during which meaning is constructed through dynamic interaction among the reader's background knowledge, the ideas suggested by the written language of the text, and the context of the reading situation. Documents also agreed that practiced readers draw from a number of resources as they read in order to comprehend text. These resources include semantic, syntactic, structural, and phonemic cues of written language, as well as the reader's experiences and beliefs.

Second, all the documents reviewed predicted that the literacy demands of the world beyond the classroom will become increasingly complex. The global economy will require students to work with diverse groups of individuals. Since future workers must be able to contribute to and draw from group efforts within organizations and across conti-

nents, the document stressed the need for students to practice working with others toward a common goal. In addition, technologies were noted in all documents as becoming more an everyday part of a worker's life. Students engaged in the language arts must learn to access and produce information via technology. State documents clearly emphasized that future employers will seek individuals with the ability to gather, process, synthesize, analyze, apply, and represent information in varied formats and for various purposes. Such analysis will be required of workers at all levels. Thus, students of the language arts must be asked to generate their own understandings and develop unique approaches for completing tasks and solving problems. Such changing conditions were reported by every state.

States also reported increased student achievement in reading, writing, and oral communication. At the same time, however, states noted a widening gap between the knowledge and skills that students needed for classroom success and the knowledge and skills necessary for success in the world outside of school. This disparity influenced all state efforts in the development of critical content standards.

Third, all documents agreed that literate individuals must not only possess an array of strategies and knowledge, but also use them in flexible ways. Good readers were defined as those who could monitor their use of strategies and check their effectiveness by interrogating both themselves (Am I understanding this?) and the author (Is this making sense? Can she say that?) as they read. Therefore, state frameworks recommended that instruction include strategies to assist readers in becoming flexible thinkers who could generate hypotheses and sound theories. All documents concluded that students must not only be able to read well, but must also be able to use language in all its forms to communicate and solve problems.

Finally, the state documents expressed the belief that all children need to reach their full potential as readers, writers and communicators. Since that potential was noted as highly influenced by the context in which instruction occurs, teachers were asked to vary the nature of instruction and the amount of instruction according to the needs of individual students. All states stressed the importance of building on each student's unique cultural background.

Current State Standards Projects

Currently many states are pursuing the development of content and performance standards in addition to their work in the area of curriculum frameworks. Like the frameworks, the standards contain points of agreement. For example, states agree that reading, writing, listening and speaking (and sometimes viewing) should be practiced in various contexts and for a variety of purposes. However, the formats of the state standards documents and the level of detail vary significantly. Some documents provide prescriptive "standards" at various grade levels, while others offer general content standards that span the grades.

For example, Virginia provides the following standard at grade six:

> The student will ... employ standard written English: subject–verb and pronoun antecedent agreement, consistent tense inflections, adverb inflections and comparison inflections. (Virginia Department of Education, 1995, p. 20)

The document from Delaware is less directive, providing standards for grade-level clusters. For example, in Delaware in grades 6 through 8, the standard addressing conventions of language read as follows:

> Students will use written and oral English appropriate for various purposes and audiences. (Delaware Department of Public Instruction, 1995, p. 10)

Unlike the Virginia document, the standard articulated in Delaware describes "appropriate" conventions in its section on performance indicators rather than in the standard itself.

Vermont approaches standards differently from both Virginia and Delaware. While Vermont does not yet have a final standards document, current drafts include language arts standards in an interdisciplinary document. Vermont curriculum standards are categorized as "Transdisciplinary Content Standards" or "Field of Knowledge Content Standards." Standards attending to listening, speaking, reading, writing, and viewing are seen embedded across both categories. These standards are intended for all students of grades K–12. Such skills as "communication" are part of the Transdisciplinary Content Standards. The content standard addressing conventions of language reads as follows:

> Each student with a common core of knowledge and skills writes effectively for a variety of purposes and skills.... Evaluates both process and product with regard to conventions (spelling, usage, and punctuation), forms of expression (style and voice), process (drafting, revising, and editing), and tools (technology and media). (The State of Vermont Department of Education, 1995, pp. 6–7)

Struggling with how to format these language arts standards is only one of the challenges before the states. Additionally, states wrestle with how to provide clear and common terminology, as well as with conflicting purposes.

Language Arts Standards: Common Definitions or Multiple Meanings?

A clear understanding of the terms used to describe standards is critical to the success of reform. Multiple definitions of terms such as content standards, performance standards, opportunity to learn standards, delivery standards, and assessment standards add to the confusion. If those terms are not clearly defined, the task of reform can become unmanageable. As Pearson (1993) noted in his analysis, the standards movement originally involved two concepts: content standards and performance standards. A Standards Glossary provided by *Education Week* (Wolk, Edwards, & Olson, 1995) stated that *content standards* spell out the subject-specific knowledge and skills that schools are expected to teach and students are expected to learn. The term *performance standard*, on the other hand, is most often defined as the parameters that determine the quality of student performance (Pearson, 1993). The *Education Week* Glossary noted that

performance standards gauge the degree to which students have met the content standards. Such standards specify how students will demonstrate their skill. In other words, how good is good enough on any given content standard? *Education Week's* Glossary also defined opportunity to learn standards as those standards which specify the materials, environments and resources students need to meet the performance standard. Other standards terms exist, including delivery standards, evaluation standards, instructional standards; but content and performance, seem to be at the heart of the major efforts taking place at both the state and the national level. While the opportunity to learn standards are addressed in many state documents in the form of vignettes or examples, most decisions regarding students' opportunities to learn are being made at local levels where funds for resources are appropriated.

The Purpose of Standards in Elevating Instruction

Even more problematic than the debate over terminology are differences in perception about what constitutes the elevation of standards or content rigor. While most have agreed that content standards define what students should know and be able to do in a given subject area, the "standard" descriptor can vary from meaning "basic" or "adequate" to "superior" (Eisner, 1995). Each definition significantly alters the substance of content standards.

The American public seems to view content standards as the basic skills and strategies that students need for adequate performance in and out of school. As reported in *First Things First: What Americans Expect From Public Schools* (1994), a "report card" from the public on the educational reform movement, respondents perceived standards as a way to raise the level of basic skills. Surveys indicated that 88% of the American people felt that raising "standards" should include requiring students to speak correct English in order to receive a high school diploma; 82% felt that all children at the end of first grade should have knowledge of punctuation and spelling. Tougher standards for promotion and retention were also overwhelmingly endorsed. Such findings were also supported by recent Gallup polls which tapped public opinion regarding school reform. These polls found the public highly interested in insuring that all students received a firm knowledge of "the basics" (Elam, Rose, & Gallup, 1994). Furthermore, those responding felt strongly that promotion and high school graduation should be tied to "basic subject matter" tests. At the June 1995 meeting of the Texas State Board of Education, board members called for specific attention to spelling, grammar, and phonics in their long-range plan for education in the state (Texas Education Agency, 1995). The popular press is filled with examples of the public equating a return to basics as a means of raising the standards in American education (Henry, 1994; Will, 1995).

The view held by the general public is significantly different from that of professional educators. The Council of Chief State School Officers surveyed educators and found that written composition and higher level comprehension and thinking skills were their top priorities for language arts standards

(Kapinus, & Verrico, 1995) . These different perceptions of standards have resulted in conflicts at the state level (Flanagan, 1995). For example, in the spring of 1995, the Michigan State Board of Education reported dissatisfaction with the Michigan English Language Arts Framework. This framework was criticized for lack of attention to basic skills and a denial of Western culture. When Idaho produced a draft framework in that same year (Flanagan, 1995, pp. 1, 8) which focused on holistic, student-centered language arts classrooms, their new commissioner of education initially banned its distribution. The California Department of Education has revamped its 1986 framework for teaching the language arts through child-centered and literature-based instruction. California is now developing a document which includes more structured phonics and a basic skills approach (Diegmueller, 1995).

ONGOING ISSUES

Is the public demanding one thing and the academic community providing another in standards documents? In other words, are educators' goals in harmony with the broader community? Public pressure has led state legislatures to demand more rigorous academic standards for all students in public schools. However, the task, of defining those standards is the responsibility of the state departments of education. Traditionally the states have turned to their colleagues in the field, that is, groups of highly qualified teachers, representative of a variety of school districts, who debate and ultimately prescribe the nature of those standards. Even though the teachers' views are diverse, they may not represent the public views as to what should count in classrooms. Conflicts then arise between the public and the academic community regarding the quality of the specified outcomes or standards. For standards to work, the public at large, as well as educators, must have a say in setting standards. Otherwise, educators may produce standards for which there is no market (Manno, 1995).

Perhaps, as recommended in the 1927 course of study, successful teachers have always worked in harmony with others in their educational community, just as Miss Curl was working in harmony with her school board president. Moreover, successful teachers have always expected the most from their students. Rigorous standards can move more teachers toward higher expectations of all students.

Today in Vidrine, Louisiana, another third grade teacher, Mrs. Monier, has taken Miss Curl's place. Her children no longer come from monolingual French-speaking homes. The parents of her children are comfortable at school and are actively involved in school functions. While Miss Curl was expected to teach all children English, Mrs. Monier is expected to provide instruction such that all her third graders pass the criterion-referenced test that accompanies the basal reader.

When asked what she considered the most essential language arts goal for her third graders, Mrs. Monier stated without hesitation, "To love reading!" Mrs. Monier surrounds her third graders with language that appeals to them, such as humorous poetry and award-winning trade books. She noted that, although standardized test scores are important, she evaluates her professional worth using other criteria. "It means more to me when the librarian tells me my students ask for authors by name, or when I see them carrying a book to read on the bus, or when they ask me for recommendations about what to read over a school holiday." Like many master teachers of the language arts, Mrs. Monier views reading and writing skills as critical tools that all children must have. Equally important, however, is her clear expectation that her students will read interesting and challenging texts and become expert users and lovers of the language arts. If language arts standards are adopted at state and national levels, will Mrs. Monier be limited or liberated in her work with third graders?

YESTERDAY AND TODAY: SIMILAR CHALLENGES

Effective communication may be the most critical skill a teacher can impart to her students. An individual skilled in the language arts can bring diverse groups together to achieve loftier goals than either side could have accomplished alone. The general public and educators are united in their desire to raise both content and performance standards in this area. Yet, the path to harmonious goals and standards is filled with complex and difficult issues. Clear and common terminology, understandable formats, and unity of purpose are just some of the challenges in the development of standards at both national and state levels. Nonetheless, standards development holds promise for systemic educational reform in the language arts.

The challenges of the past and the issues facing language arts educators today are similar. In 1934, a report from the Division of Supervision (Texas State Department of Education, 1934) offered these words:

> Standardization has its perils as well as its distinctive merits, but at present we know of no better way to meet the general problems of unification and orderly procedure in the interrelated units of a public school system than through the development and promulgation of definite and rather arbitrary standards. It is to be hoped, however, that no standard fixed by the State Department of Education will interfere with any real freedom belonging to a local school system in connection with its own school problems.

Many questions remain as language arts educators not only decide how to participate in the development of standards, but whether to participate. Some scholars and educators have advised against participation, fearing that the "perils" would outweigh the "merits" of the efforts. Yet educators are increasingly accountable to the public. Content and performance standards will be at the heart of the assessment instruments and systems used for that accountability. Rigorous, well-conceived standards, tied to robust and valid accountability measures, may raise expectations in a positive way for both teachers and students. Such standards could, in fact, serve to liberate rather than limit the teacher of the language arts.

References

Cohen, D. (1995). What standards for national standards? *Phi Delta Kappan, 76,* 751–757.

Delaware Department of Public Instruction. (1995). *New directions Delaware first in education: State of Delaware English language arts curriculum framework.* (Document Control Number 95-01/95/05/05). Dover, DE.

Diegmueller, K. (1994, March 30). English group loses funding for standards . *Education Week,* 1, 9, 16 .

Diegmueller, K. (1995, June 14). California plotting new tack on language arts: State to wed phonics and whole language. *Education Week,* 1, 12.

Eisner, E. W. (1995) . Standards for American schools: Help or hindrance? *Phi Delta Kappan, 76,* 758–764 .

Elam, S. M., Rose, L. C., & Gallup, A. M. (1994) . The twenty-sixth annual Phi Delta Kappa Gallup poll of the public's attitudes toward the public schools . *Phi Delta Kappan, 76,* 41–64 .

Flanagan, A. (1995, June) . Idaho' s content-area frameworks back in circulation. *The Council Chronicle,* 1, 8, 9.

Henry, T. (1994, December 12). College level literacy less than impressive. *USA Today,* p. 1.

Kapinus, B. (1995). *Points of agreement: A consensus map of state and national reading literacy frameworks.* Washington, DC: Council of Chief State School Officers.

Kapinus, B., & Verrico, B. (1995). *State's status on standards: Findings from the conference on standards-focused collaboration to improve teaching and learning.* Washington, DC: Council of Chief State School Officers.

Korman, G. (1992). *The twinkie squad.* New York: Scholastic.

Lee, H. (1988). *To kill a mockingbird.* (4 ed.). Warner Books.

Lewis, A. C. (1995). An overview of the standards movement. *Phi Delta Kappan, 76,* 744–750.

Manno, B. V. (1995). The new school wars: Battles over outcome-based education. *Phi Delta Kappan, 76,* 720–726.

McNeeley, M. (1995). *Looking across standards: Status of state efforts.* Paper presented at the Council for Chief State School Officers National Conference on Large Scale Assessment, Phoenix, AZ.

Olson, L. (1995, April 12). The view from the classroom. *Education Week,* 47–48.

Pearson, P. D. (1993). Standards for the English language arts: A policy perspective. *Journal of Reading Behavior, 25,* 457–475.

Public Agenda. (1994). *First things first what Americans expect from the public schools* (A report from Public Agenda). New York, NY: Johnson, J. & Immerwahr, J.

Texas State Department of Education. (1927, September). *Course of Study for Elementary Grades,* (No. 226, p. 18). Austin, TX.

Texas State Department of Education. (1934). *Standards and Activities of the Division of Supervision,* (No. 334, p. 107). Austin, TX.

U.S. Department of Education. (1990). *America 2000: An Education Strategy.* Washington, DC.

U.S. Department of Education. (1994). *Goals 2000: Educate America Act.* (document control number 103–446). Washington, DC.

Vermont Department of Education. (1994). *Content standards for Vermont common core framework for curriculum and assessment.* (draft). Montpelier, VT.

Virginia Department of Education. (1995). *Language arts standards of learning for Virginia public schools.* (draft). Richmond, VA.

Will. G. W. (1995, July 2). Schools fail on reading, writing [editorial section]. *The Austin American Statesman.*

Wolk, R. A., Edwards, V. B., & Olson, L. (Eds.) (1995, April 12). On assignment special pull out report: Struggling for standards [Special issue]. *Education Week.*

·56·

STATE CURRICULAR FRAMEWORKS AND THE REAL LIFE OF THE CLASSROOM

·56A·

READING RECOVERY: A SUMMARY OF RESEARCH

Gay Su Pinnell

OHIO STATE UNIVERSITY

Reading Recovery demonstrates what is possible when we put into action current knowledge about how young children learn literacy; in doing so, it challenges present systems and prompts both visionary thinking and problem solving. Briefly defined, Reading Recovery (RR) is a tutorial for children who are having difficulty in learning to read and write after approximately one year of school. It is usually described as an early intervention program; however, RR defies a simple definition. This systematically designed program involves layers of intersecting variables and integrated components, many of which are not obvious even to those who teach children in RR or who have studied it intensively. Teaching procedures, adjustment of instruction to learners, instructional decision-making, training and self-reflection on the part of teachers, ongoing evaluation and research, as well as a colleguial network of support and expectations—all contribute to RR's success.

Unique features and results of RR have captured public attention in a way unprecedented for a "program." In this chapter I summarize what we know about RR and what we have learned through research connected with the program. First, RR is briefly described. Then, research on program success, on teaching and learning, and on teacher development is reviewed. Finally, research related to implementation is presented. Where they are available, sound critical reviews are noted.

READING RECOVERY AS AN EARLY INTERVENTION PROGRAM

Since RR has been described in numerous publications, no attempt will be made here to describe the program in detail (for further information see Clay, 1993a, 1993b; Clay, in press; DeFord, Lyons, & Pinnell, 1991; Lyons, Pinnell, & DeFord, 1993; Pinnell, 1989 and Pinnell, Fried, & Estice, 1991). The program is designed to help lowest achieving 1st-grade children develop effective strategies for reading and writing. In RR, these initially struggling children make accelerated progress, reaching average levels of their particular class or group. The goal is to assist children in constructing the inner control that will enable them to continue to learn independently as they read more difficult and varied texts (Clay, 1991a). The ability to learn more about reading through reading is characteristic of good readers.

The program in the United States involves first graders only, although when full coverage (defined as approximately 20% of the age cohort or all children who need one-to-one help) is achieved and more resources become available, continuing instruction at the beginning of second grade is recommended for those children who enter RR late in their 1st-grade year. Children are selected for RR through a combination of teacher judgment and independently administered assessments (Clay, 1993a, 1993b); they receive individual tutoring until they show evidence of independent, strategic reading of texts and can demonstrate ability to participate in classroom reading instruction at average levels for their class or school. Then, the program is "discontinued" for that student and another enters the program.

Materials

Books are considered the key material for RR. Little existing research focuses on the texts themselves. Peterson's (1991) analysis of the texts used in the program indicates that the twenty levels of difficulty into which the books are organized serve several purposes for teachers, including tracking progress of children and book selection for individual children. The levels, however, serve only as a rough guide for selection; there is no prescribed sequence. Peterson states that in selecting the easiest books for children at the beginning of their programs, teachers look at both text characteristics (the layout of text, predictability, knowledge required to understand concepts, and so on) and student characteristics. She also cautions teachers that books in RR are selected for individual children's needs in learning to read; classroom literacy programs require a much broader range of difficulty and type of text.

Reading Recovery Teacher Training

Reading Recovery operates within an educational system through four key programs: (1) intensive, daily, one-to-one, 30-minute instruction for children; (2) an in-service program through which educators are instructed in teaching; (3) a network of professional support for teachers and administrators involved in the program; and (4) a research program to continuously monitor program results and provide support for participating teachers and institutions (see Clay & Watson, 1982; Gaffney & Anderson, 1991).

The in-service program for teachers is a yearlong experience during which teachers meet in weekly classes taught by a trainer (called "teacher leader" in the United States, "tutor" in New Zealand, Australia, and England, with both terms used in Canada). Extensive use is made of a one-way glass screen to view live lessons. Teachers in the class take turns teaching behind the screen while their peers observe, and, guided by the leader, talk aloud about the lesson. This process of articulating observations is a hallmark of initial training. Trained teachers participate continuously in professional development as long as they are involved in RR. The program also provides continued training at conferences for teachers and an annual institute for teacher leaders.

Implementation and Quality Control

A structured process guides the dissemination and expansion of RR. School districts enter a long-term planning process beginning with preparation of a leader who is specially prepared to train teachers and oversee the program. Pursuing a full year course of study, teacher leaders are prepared at university training sites. At the same time, a "site coordinator" undertakes administrative leadership for the program in a given school district or consortium of districts. As part of the agreement with the regional training center, the sponsoring agency (school district or consortium), agrees to follow the *Guidelines and Standards for the North American Reading Recovery Council* (1993). The guidelines contain standards that are essential for assuring quality services to children.

The name "Reading Recovery" was designated a trademark and/or service mark of The Ohio State University in December 18, 1990, an action taken to identify sites that meet the essential criteria as defined in the guidelines for an RR program. On an annual basis, programs are granted a *royalty free* license to use the name. Every district that has an RR program is reviewed annually to determine which district has met the standards and guidelines. Reading Recovery is a nonprofit program; training is a university function, not a business venture.

Current Status in North America

Reading Recovery was piloted in the United States in 1984–85 and has been adapted and tested across sites that vary by region, economic group, culture, and linguistic background. In 1994, 22 regional training centers existed to prepare the key personnel in the United States, teacher leaders. Reading Recovery programs are supported by a network of 388 RR sites, representing 7,784 schools that span North America. Personnel at sites within this network provide training and continuing education, coordinate the collection of research data on RR children, disseminate awareness information and develop program guidelines. Over 11 years, from 1984 through 1995, 519 RR teacher leaders and 12,084 RR teachers have served a total of 229,254 "at-risk" 1st-grade students in 2,543 United States school districts. In 1994–95, 46,637, or 81% of all 1st graders who completed the program, met the stringent discontinuing criteria after an average of 17 weeks of daily lessons. It is estimated that the program will serve more than 100,000 children during the 1995–96 academic year.

Evidence of Program Effectiveness

A body of research and program evaluation illuminates both the achievements of RR and the interacting factors contributing to success. This section presents the research that provides evidence of success. Critics of the program (Hiebert, 1995; Shanahan & Barr, 1995) suggest that research does not go far enough; indeed, traditionally designed empirical studies are few in number and scope because of the limitations involved in large scale field research. Longitudinal studies have been limited by loss of subjects and lack of resources to conduct exhaustive testing programs, and almost all have been conducted on new implementations during their first year. Most system implementers want to study the program from its onset even though we know that it takes about three years to pick up pace and deliver quality intervention. Nevertheless, the body of evidence is considerable, particularly if one considers the range and variety of settings within which the program has been tested. For example, extensive information on individuals has been collected in New Zealand (Kerslake, 1992), the United States (The Ohio State University, 1994), and England (Hobsbaum, 1994). At this point in time, RR has gone farther than any other early intervention program to collect data on every subject involved.

Early Research and Continuing Data Collection in New Zealand

Clay's initial research in New Zealand was conducted in several phases, from a development project (1976–77), to field trial research (1978), to one-year follow-up research and replication studies (1979), and a three-year follow-up, completed in 1981 (reported in Clay, 1993b). Now, the Ministry of Education undertakes national monitoring annually (Kerslake, 1992). To answer the question, "How do these children compare with all their classmates?" Clay compared RR children with a nonequivalent control group consisting of all the children who had not been selected for RR. She found that children who were tutored in RR and successfully discontinued made accelerated progress and scored, even several years after tutoring, within the average band. In addition to confirming RR's positive impact on children, Clay's first research indicated that children with incomplete programs (not enough time) did not spontaneously shift into the average group. She recommended that time be provided the following school year for children to complete their programs and that is now the practice in New Zealand.

Clay replicated her original study in 48 schools and found similar results; it was also clear from this research that lower entry scores implied more individual tutoring time for students. Her research documented the successful delivery of the program at locations distant from the original university development area. It confirmed the success of RR with varying populations and led to the adoption and maintenance of RR as a national program. Monitoring of the program by the New Zealand Ministry of Education indicates that with more than 20% of the age group receiving RR, fewer than 1% of the age cohort is referred for further services (see Clay, 1993b; Kerslake, 1992). Two British school inspectors (Frater & Staniland, 1994) who visited New Zealand to make a careful evaluation before recommending RR for adoption, suggested that the low and generally stable figures for the proportions of pupils referred on for longer term help prompt further thought. Most prominently perhaps, they suggest that the scheme may have told us something fundamental about the remedial nature of much of the incidence of early reading difficulty encountered not only in New Zealand but in similarly long-established education systems in other advanced industrial societies (HMSO, 1993, p. 12).

Recent research from New Zealand focused on children for whom English is a second language (Smith, 1987, 1988, 1994). The study addressed the question of the suitability and long term benefit of the program for this population. From 1986 to 1991, ESOL and non-ESOL children were compared on entry and exit data and postprogram progress. A measure of average book level indicated that statistically significant progress was made (p <.001) by both groups in their RR programs. At the third year follow-up more than 50% of children in both categories (ESOL=21, 57%; non-ESOL=26, 70%) were reading material at a difficulty level 13+ months beyond their chronological age. The study confirmed previous longitudinal studies indicating immediate and long-term success for children who receive RR programs; it also indicated that these findings are applicable to ESOL children in New Zealand.

Empirical Studies in the United States

Although the New Zealand research was impressive, it was necessary to test the program's potential for success in the United States. Two empirical studies were undertaken during the first years of the project in Ohio.

The purposes of the Ohio longitudinal study (Pinnell, 1989), initiated during the first full year of RR in the United States, were to explore: (1) whether the program could succeed with low-achieving children; and, (2) whether those children maintained their gains. The study used standard empirical design to demonstrate RR's impact when compared to existing (and typical) programs. The results of the study were positive for RR. Effect sizes were substantial in the first

year's comparison but diminished by the fourth year after the treatment period, a phenomenon that may be explained by dwindling sample size and increasing variability. Nevertheless, the study confirmed RR's immediate and long-term positive effects.

Zutell and DeFord (1994) used the same sample of subjects (n=54) to take a focused look at abilities and strategies. They compared the remaining RR students, 23 control students, and a randomly selected group (n=53) of fourth grade students on responses to the *Qualitative Inventory of Word Knowledge* (Schlagal, 1989). They found that while statistical analyses indicated no significant differences among groups, clear trends did emerge from the data. Reading Recovery students, on an average, performed noticeably closer to children in the general population than did students who had received the other form of instructional support. Over 20% of the control group performed at frustration level. Comparisons of percentages of misspellings indicated that a lower proportion of the control group students produced misspellings that followed "logical" patterns. They concluded that in spelling ability, the profile of the RR group was similar to that of the random sample group while the control group data indicated a higher percentage of students performing at lower levels.

The second study (see Pinnell, Lyons, DeFord, Bryk, & Seltzer, 1993) was designed in response to challenges about the delivery system of RR. This study was designed to address specific questions by comparing RR with:

(1) other one-on-one interventions;
(2) traditional RR teacher training with a condensed program that did not utilize key teacher training procedures; and
(3) group instruction based on RR principles.

The study again confirmed the program's successful instruction with effect sizes of 1.5 in the first year and 0.75 in the second year when groups were compared on text reading level. The analysis provided evidence that success was related to several interacting factors. One-on-one setting, a lesson framework with intensive experiences in reading and writing, and long-term teacher training were all necessary but not sufficient to explain RR's success. The nature of training provided by teachers emerged as a factor of critical importance. This research prompted more detailed examinations of the subtle differences in the instructional program provided by the teachers.

Replications of the Process

Over the last 10 years RR has accomplished what it is designed to do. A total of 88,187 individuals made accelerated progress, caught up with their grade-level peers and became independent readers and writers. In each single case we can be sure of this because what happens to each individual provides the data on which the success of the program is judged. Reading Recovery records the proportion of individuals who meet the tough exit criteria. The large majority of children provided at least 60 days of RR tutoring become independent readers at grade level (as measured by an outside examiner).

In addition to the extensive data collected to document children's 1st-grade year and their success in the program, follow-up studies are conducted at many RR sites. Three examples are presented here. Researchers at Texas Woman's University (1994) examined the literacy performance of previously discontinued RR children two and three years beyond the 1st-grade intervention. They compared discontinued RR children with a random sample of classroom peers. The data included performance on a test of oral reading as well as information about the perceptions of classroom teachers of literacy. Former RR children performed well above grade-level placement on oral reading and compared well with their classroom peers. Classroom teachers perceived these former RR children to be within average range in terms of literacy and classroom behaviors.

The University of Arkansas (1994) reports a comparison of formerly discontinued RR children with a random sample of children. Second-grade follow-up studies indicate that children continued to make gains with no need for remedial reading instruction and, on average, exceeded the achievement of a random sample of 2nd-grade children on measures of spelling, dictation, and oral reading. A third-grade follow-up study of 53 formerly discontinued children indicated that their average exceeded the achievement of a random sample of 3rd-grade children on measures of spelling, dictation, and text reading. At the East Baton Rouge Parish Reading Recovery site, researchers (Elliott, 1995) administered spelling, dictation, and oral reading measures individually to discontinued RR students (N=43) and a random sample of 3rd-grade students. They also administered the Louisiana Educational Assessment Program (LEAP). In third grade, former RR students scored slightly higher than those of the random sample group on spelling, dictation and oral reading. Results of an analysis of the language arts component of LEAP indicated that 85% of formerly discontinued RR students achieved the performance standard. These students, by the selection criteria, had been in the lowest achieving group in first grade.

Long-term Benefits

Any analysis of long-term benefits must acknowledge that intervening variables make it difficult to accurately determine the value of an approach. Over a period of years, systemic factors such as subsequent instruction, promotion and disciplinary policies, special education, and individual life circumstances, act as intervening variables affecting a student's progress, despite a successful early intervention. Studies in New Zealand and the United States indicated long-term benefit from early tutoring in RR. An Australian study, not designed to look for a continuing effect on the progress of individuals involved in RR, discovered such an effect as a serendipitous outcome (Rowe, 1988).

Preventative efforts make sense but are difficult to measure. For example, it is hard to convince the public of the value of preventative health care because when we look at healthy individuals we cannot know with certainty that they would have required expensive services without the intervention. We cannot calculate the true cash value of RR by figuring the cost per test point gained or even by reducing numbers in remediation. In some areas of high need, so many children qualify for Title 1 that without full coverage and an orchestrated range of interventions, including enhanced opportunities and dynamic teaching in classrooms, the effect will not be noticeable.

One benefit may be reduction of the need for some kinds of special education services. One district in Massachusetts (Moriarty, 1995) reports reduction in retention and a drop from approximately 18% to 3% in referrals to special education in the primary grades. Much has been written about the misclassification of children as handicapped (see Allington & McGill-Franzen, 1990). Classification, according to researchers like Allington and McGill-Franzen, may result in a "blame-the-victim" mentality that ultimately deprives the student of the instruction needed to achieve. It is time, they say, to stop "focusing on the unnecessary labeling of children as a prerequisite to their receiving instructional support." Clay (1990) advocates using RR as a period of diagnostic teaching before labeling children in any way as requiring longer-term individual help. She writes,

> If we accepted an open definition of learning difficulties, we would diminish the need to debate what constitutes learning disabilities. This would encourage researchers, educators, and policy makers to provide early intervention for all low-achieving children, based on specialized teaching responsive to individual behaviors. (p. 16)

Intervention prior to labeling is taken seriously in Canada. A recent Royal Commission Report on Learning from Canada (1995) recommends:

> …that no child who shows difficulty or who lags behind peers in learning to read be labeled "learning disabled" unless and until he or she has received intensive individual assistance in learning to read which has not resulted in improved academic performance. (Vol. G, Recommendation 33)

Reading Recovery, which is designed to adjust to the individual, is an example of an early intervention approach that has potential for reducing the numbers of children ultimately diagnosed as learning disabled. At this time, "learning disabled" can refer to a variety of problems, and behavioral characteristics may be dependent on the diagnostic measures used to identify children. In a study comparing children classified as learning disabled with RR children not so identified, Lyons (1989) found that at the beginning of their programs, classified children had a greater tendency to rely on visual information, neglecting meaning and language cues. By the end of their programs, the two groups became more alike, using a balanced set of strategies to read. Both groups were highly successful readers. Differences in children's behavior patterns required teachers to conclude that the study provided evidence that RR was an effective approach whether or not children had been previously classified as learning disabled. Different studies might find other kinds of imbalance, but individually constructed programs can help children use their strengths in different ways to become flexible, fluent readers.

The Ohio State University (Pinnell, Lyons & Jones, 1995) reports that of 40,493 RR program children (selected as the lowest achieving children) in 1993–1994, 457 (1.1%) were later referred for Learning Disability (LD) screening. Of 5,466 program children in Ohio that same year, only 0.9% were referred for LD screening. There is no way to know how many would have been referred without RR; but experts suggest much higher proportions. This is at such a time when the United States Department of Education (1990) reports that the LD population has doubled. Coopers and Lybrand (1994) recently found that in New York City the cost is $23,598 for full time special education students. Providing extra services to students who remain in classrooms creates an add-on cost of $5,059 per student in addition to the base of $5,149 each year. As a "first net," RR has the potential to reduce special education referrals, retention, and the need for remedial services with consequent savings (see Lyons, 1994; Lyons & Beaver, 1995).

Success in Diverse Settings

Reading Recovery has been shown to be successful in a wide range of urban, rural, and suburban school settings. Hiebert (1994), in a critique of the program, has suggested that RR is effective in suburban districts, but questions whether it is worthwhile to provide it for poor children in urban districts where it is harder to achieve full coverage for children who need extra help. Children who enter the program with less knowledge will have longer programs in RR, but they do succeed. Areas of high need usually require more problem solving and greater efforts on the part of administrators. More time is required to move the greater distance to full implementation (serving approximately 20%) in such districts. But, success has been demonstrated, establishing a reason for making this extra effort.

In a study of children who were served by RR in the New York area in 1990–91, Jaggar and Smith-Burke (1994) compared RR children with a group of children drawn from the "waiting list." These children had scored low but were not the lowest scorers in their schools. The schools in the study, however, for economic and other reasons, had high numbers of children who qualified for RR and low resources to provide the program. Thus, the "waiting list" children were considered by teachers in the school to need extra help. Of RR children who received at least 60 lessons and / or were discontinued (n=328), 78% were successful in the program, meaning that they achieved at least grade level status (defined by average band) for their class or school and showed evidence of a self-extending system for reading (see discontinuing criteria in Clay, 1993). Of the comparison group, 71% were reading below grade level even though many received some type of supplementary instruction. Higher coverage in RR could have benefited the "waiting list" children.

District #2, New York City, (see Jaggar & Smith-Burke, 1994) an area of economic disadvantage that has a highly diverse population, reports a steady increase in the percentage of children who successfully discontinued the program (from 57% in 1990 to 95% in 1994). This progress can be attributed to increased coverage and analysis of the system over time. A June 1994 follow-up study of 198 second graders showed that at the end of second grade, 86% of the RR children who successfully discontinued from the program in first grade scored within or above the grade-level average band in text reading (20.33–30.27; equivalent to a range between end of second grade to grade 6) compared to 75% of a random sample of children not selected for RR. As a group, the RR children had a mean text reading score of 27.06 (equivalent to grade 4) while the random sample mean score was 25.3 (equivalent to grade 3). A small number (n=27) of formerly discontinued third graders followed. At the end of third grade, 82% of the RR children, compared to 87% of the random sample children scored within or above the average band (29.88–34.34; grades 5–8). As a group, these RR third graders had a mean text reading score of 31.56 (grade 6) which is similar to the random sample (32.11; grade 7). There appear to be variations from year to year, however these results indicate a remarkable achievement for these initially struggling children. The District #2 project demonstrates what can be achieved with continuous effort in an urban setting.

In Boston and surrounding areas, Lesley College reported that 93.3% of second graders who were RR children in first grade were reading materials identified by classroom teachers as at grade level or above. Of second graders who participated in RR (N=146), 94.9% read materials at or above grade level, with 92.3% reading at above average grade level (Fountas, 1994). As the British inspectors stated, "The essential conditions for the success of RR, as a system, lie in the coherence, the resourcing, and the reach of the support and quality assurance structures which are put in place for its implementation" (HMSO Report, p. 23).

Some educators have combined RR with other approaches to meet the demands in high-need areas. Dorn (1994), with a colleague, Allen, reports the simultaneous implementation of RR with a specially designed small group model in the state of Arkansas. The small group program was similar to that described by Pinnell and McCarrier (1994), although adapted at the local level. Extensive staff development was provided for RR teachers; they taught small groups of low achieving children during half of the day, devoting the rest of their time to tutoring four RR students daily in individual lessons. Each small group lesson was approximately 45 minutes in length.

The program was based on an organizational structure suggested for areas that serve large numbers of at-risk children. Based on a combination of teacher ranking (by kindergarten teachers and first grade teachers in collaboration), classroom observation, standardized test, and observation survey (Clay, 1993a), the lowest ranking children were selected. Of those students the lowest achieving were selected to receive RR and the remaining children were placed in a small group program, five students per group. When a child exited the RR program (through moving or discontinuing), the lowest achieving student in the group was placed in RR. It is important to note that prior small group membership was not a criterion for selection if, at the point of vacancy, another child were more in need. A priority was placed on reserving the individual tutoring for the children who needed it most.

Intervention services for a total of 231 children were analyzed. Of this number, 95 (41%) received RR tutoring only; 93

(40%) received group services only; and 43 (19%) received a combination of group service and RR, although not simultaneously. Of the 95 children who received RR services with no prior experiences in a group program, 72 (76%) were discontinued in an average of 65 lessons. Of the 93 children who received only small group instruction, 28 (30%) reached successful levels of reading achievement at an average of 48.5 lessons. Of the 43 children who were served by the group prior to entering RR, 24 (55%) were successfully discontinued from RR in an average of 25 lessons. This group had received an average of 40 group lessons prior to entry. A higher percentage of children probably would have reached average reading levels with more time in the school year. The 11 teachers involved in this study each served an average of 21 low achieving children in some type of intervention during the first grade year and an average of 11.3 children per teacher reached average reading levels for their schools. Dorn raised several cautions in interpreting these data. First, she recognized that the confusions of the lowest achieving children are diverse and that multiple assessment must be used in assigning children to the appropriate level of intervention. Second, she affirmed RR as the most effective program for the lowest children, who must have individually tailored lessons. The group provided support but could not reach the high discontinuing rates yielded by RR. It was, however, an added benefit that 30% reached average levels without requiring RR. Third, 19 (6% of the at-risk population) children were served first in the group and then entered into RR but were not discontinued. These children, however, made notable gains in all areas when compared with a state random sample of first grade students. Dorn concluded that this model has efficacy for serving larger numbers of children *during the first grade year.*

Contextual Factors in the Implementation of Reading Recovery

It is not enough to design effective procedures for tutoring children. Any successful program must have a way of delivering the program. In the guidebook for teachers, Clay stated that "the plan of operation must allow for teachers to differ" (Clay, 1993b, p. 62). At the same time, processes must be in place to assure quality service. Program implementers give particular attention to contextual factors that may influence the delivery system. For example, in the United States, RR is seen as a school and district commitment rather than one of a single teacher. An important contextual factor is the partnership that exists between classroom teachers and RR teachers.

In a study of RR in 12 schools situated in Auckland, Otago, and Southland, New Zealand during 1986 and 1987, special attention was given to context (Glynn & McNaughton, 1992). The sample represented a range of schools but was neither a random sample nor a systematical representation of possible schools. The subjects were 42 individual children who were entered in RR and 41 children of similar age who did not experience RR. Data were gathered over a 2-year period. In each school when an RR child (called "target") entered the program, a comparison child of approximately the same age

was also selected. Neither the research team nor the schools wanted to prevent children who might need RR from being selected; therefore, comparison children were chosen who were of similar age and scored toward the lower end of the distribution but for whom a place in RR was not available. Thus, comparisons were among initially unequal groups in schools where coverage provided for service to all children who needed intervention.

Glynn and his team found that while participating in RR, target children made substantially more progress than comparison children, gaining over four levels more than those who began at the same reading levels. After release from RR, the rate of gain decreased (a typical circumstance since children are no longer expected to make accelerated progress without one-to-one teaching), and the control subjects were allowed to catch up. The explanation that researchers gave for the slower progress after release from RR was that students were generally placed in classrooms reading in book levels lower than what they could read; therefore "it appears that in effect many target children made little progress until their reading groups caught up with the level they had attained some months earlier at discontinuation" (p. 124). They hypothesized that this practice was to allow children to consolidate skills, but that children might not be challenged enough by this practice. They also noted extreme variations in the attitudes of classroom teachers towards target children. The researchers found greatest benefit for the children entering RR with the lowest text reading levels. Caution must be observed in the interpretation of this study. Two unequal groups were compared and membership of the sample groups varied markedly from one testing time to another. This factor is compounded because the sample was small and not randomly selected.

Glynn recommended a conservative cut-off point, considering text reading only, for entry into RR with the idea that fixed criteria would prevent children from receiving tutoring when they do not need it. There are two arguments against this recommendation. First, in beginning reading it is critical to use multiple measures. Children are acquiring knowledge along several dimenations and have not yet been integrated; therefore, using one task will not give us a true picture of who the children in difficulty are. Literacy involves a complex interrelationship of abilities; to measure only one aspect of reading may provide a false picture. Writing skill is as important for literacy learning as reading skill.

Second, any prevention program inherently runs the risk of serving some children who might succeed without it; but at the entry point we cannot predict in any satisfactory way which individuals will make good progress. Provision of the program to approximately 20% of the first graders will be the best compromise between risk and cost. In low economic areas with high need, children's programs may be longer; therefore, more resources will be needed and coverage may need to be extended into second grade.

What we can derive from Glynn's study is a recognition of classroom factors as important in the continued progress of RR children. A United States study by White (1992) indicates the complexity and impact of the school context and confirms the importance of partnership between the RR and classroom teachers in helping children transfer their skills from individual lessons to classroom work. White found that even so seemingly insignificant a factor as proximity of the classroom and the instructional space for RR can have facilitative or negative effects. The study revealed contextual factors that can affect the delivery of the program as well as the different perspectives and decision-making styles of local educators. In another New Zealand study, Smith (1984, 1988) also found that factors involving subsequent instruction were the single strongest influence on children's post RR progress.

Schnug (1991) studied RR from the point of view of the student. In a 2½ month case study of two male students, Schnug examined the patterns of instructional activities that occurred over time in RR lessons and in the classroom setting. A unique aspect of his study is the descriptions of students' self-reports. Schnug was interested in students' perceptions of their performance and abilities as they learned to read. The researcher found that both students were highly influenced by the context. While opportunities were available in both settings, RR provided more routines that required a sustained and open-ended reading or writing response. Routines in classroom reading generally produced more close-ended responses as imposed by instructional materials such as worksheets. One subject's more active participation appeared to work to the other one's advantage; the more hesitant child was allowed to turn down invitations to participate in the classroom. Schnug's study reveals how an active teacher in RR can create opportunities for children who might be reluctant to participate in classroom settings. Both students became more active in the classroom over time, and both saw themselves as good readers.

Askew and Frasier (1994) have suggested that teachers' perceptions of children's abilities figure heavily in their continued progress and opportunities to learn beyond the 1st-grade year. Their study of the program's sustained effects on the cognitive behaviors of 2nd-grade children suggested that former RR children, when compared to a randomly selected average group that did not receive the intervention, were more overtly signaling their problem-solving strategies while reading text. This factor did not appear to affect reading ability in general, and may have been an artifact of the researchers' observational skills and sensitivity to subtle aspects of behavior. Former RR children also compared well with their peers in oral retelling tasks designed to measure comprehension of text. The researchers noted problems with retelling as a measure since both groups, random sample and former RR students, appeared to see the task as socially inappropriate without a logical audience.

Additionally, Askew and Frasier found that former RR children compared well with their 2nd-grade peers on fluency indicators. They noted, however, that in many instances for both groups, teachers' perceptions did not match actual student performance, suggesting that either teachers were making their judgments on a broad range of classroom behaviors rather than on specific reading behaviors or that they were using a comparative scale, ranking some students as "low" even if most were well within average range.

Reading Recovery has been implemented with remarkable fidelity in all five countries of implementation; yet, different problems and dilemmas continue to arise. For example, in New Zealand children enter school on their fifth birthday and encounter a print-rich environment in classrooms. By their sixth birthday they have had a year of literacy experience. In the United States and Canada, children enter kindergarten anywhere between ages 4 and 7, and kindergartens vary widely. This circumstance prompts continuous problem solving, which is assisted by the program's guidelines and standards. This document also acknowledges, however, that "no set of guidelines will ever address the range of issues that will arise" (Reading Recovery Council of North America, 1993, p. iii). The guidelines are intended to be used as a guide by educators who have been trained in the rationales behind their use rather than as an arbitrary set of rules.

Research on Reading Recovery and Home Relations

In a unique descriptive study of RR children's home experiences, Holland (1991) discovered that the achievements children made in school tutoring carried over to the home environment. Through interviews and observation, Holland studied the family literacy experiences of 13 children for a period of 1 year. Families were, in general, in economically depressed circumstances. She found that parents, siblings, and other caregivers supported and appreciated children's efforts in a variety of ways, for example, by listening to them read and talking with them. These families tended to depend on the school for writing materials. Early in children's programs, the cut up sentence was highly valued, but, increasingly, both parents and children depended on the little books that came home everyday. Holland reports that "during the year, more than seven hundred RR books were taken home by these thirteen first-grade children, but only one child lost a book" (p. 157).

Children tended to initiate reading sessions at home; usually they captured more than one family member. Holland described the book as a "literacy tool that drew the whole family together to support the young reader's need to share reading … when no one was available, children read the books to themselves or to dolls, stuffed animals, and family pets" (1991, p. 157). The study demonstrated that parents, formerly concerned about their children's progress, were able to observe their children successfully reading and writing. By the third interview most parents believed that their children were good readers. Holland's research indicates the power of sending into homes literacy materials that children can control themselves.

English researchers (Moore & Wade, 1994) interviewed a group of parents (N=47) from diverse socioeconomic and ethnic backgrounds. They report that parents had been invited to observe reading sessions and that this experience influenced the kind of help they gave their children at home; for example, they were more aware of the importance of praise. These parents were impressed with their children's enthusiasm for the stories they encountered in RR and stated that progress had extended into other areas of the school curriculum and that their children read more on their own time. Twelve of the 47 children whose parents were interviewed were second-language learners; and these parents were as positive about the program as were the single-language parents.

Descubriendo la Lectura: Reading Recovery in Spanish

One of the most interesting and exciting new developments in RR is the reconstruction of the program in Spanish (Escamilla, 1994). In consultation and with the permission of Clay, teachers and administrators in Tucson, Arizona, made the commitment to develop and study the application of RR in Spanish. This reconstruction of the program is designed to serve native speakers of Spanish who are having difficulty in learning to read in their first language. From a theoretical standpoint, this study is significant for three reasons. First, it utilizes the knowledge base and theoretical framework from two important fields (bilingual education and RR) for the purpose of addressing a large and growing need in our country. This need is how to assist Spanish-speaking children who are having difficulty in learning to read without prematurely submerging them in English and without permanently placing them in classes for slow learners (p. 59). Second, the study provides a model for constructing RR programs in other languages. Third, it demonstrates learning and teaching processes across languages.

Descubriendo la Lectura (DLL), as the reconstructed program was called, is equivalent in all major aspects to the program designed by Clay. Escamilla (1994) studied 180 1st-grade, Spanish language dominant students from six elementary schools. She compared three groups: (1) the lowest achieving children, identified by teacher ranking and the six observational measures (Clay, 1993a), who were entered in DLL (n=23); (2) control group students (n=23) who were selected on the same basis and could have benefited from DLL but were from two schools that had no DLL program; and (3) a comparison group (n=134) composed of all 1st-grade students who were from the six schools in the study and were not identified as needing DLL (that is, not in the lower 20% of the class).

Subjects were tested at the beginning of 1991 and again at the end of the year. In addition to Clay's measures, Escamilla used the *Aprenda* Spanish Achievement Test (1991). Although several tests favored the control group in the fall, Escamilla found the DLL group and control group to be similar at the year end. There were statistically significant differences between those two groups and the comparison group (p < .01) in the fall. Spring measures indicated that the DLL group significantly outperformed the control group (p < .05) on all measures. Mean scores of the comparison group (Fall and Spring) provided a picture of what average progress meant in first-grade. By the spring testing, DLL students had reached average levels for the class on all measurement task. This was not true of the control group, which remained far behind the comparison group. "In fact, on all measurement criteria used in the study, DLL students not only caught up with their average peers, but surpassed them at statistically significant levels" (p. 86). Escamilla concluded that "the data

reported establish that the DLL program achieved acceleration with Spanish-speaking students who were struggling while learning to read in Spanish" (p. 86). This research provides evidence of the promise of *Descubriendo la Lectura*; however, as Escamilla notes, the numbers of children were small. It is also the case that DLL is still under careful development and scrutiny by its implementers. More research is needed to determine effectiveness and also to provide information about the ways in which teachers and children work together, and the differences in emphasis that will be related to the differences between English and Spanish. The DLL continues to be an integral part of the North American RR effort.

Research on Teaching and Learning

The statewide experimental study referred to above (Pinnell, et al., 1993) showed superior results for one-to-one instruction using RR procedures by trained teachers. Researchers were interested to note that the alternatively trained teachers (two initial weeks and some follow-up) provided lessons that on the surface were almost identical to RR lessons in that approximately the same amount of time was spent on each element of the framework. Materials were the same for RR and the alternative program. Clearly there was a need to look beyond the surface elements uncovered by the statewide study.

The Nature of Teaching in Reading Recovery

Reading Recovery is an individual program in that the teacher works from the child's responses and knowledge base. The theory on which RR is based (see Clay, 1991a) suggests that support for individuals' learning is provided from moment to moment teacher–child interactions. The power of the program lies in the teacher's ability, in the context of continuous text, to direct the child's attention to "the clearest, easiest, most memorable examples with which to establish a new response, skill, principle or procedure" (Clay, 1993b, p. 8). This powerful teaching occurs throughout the 30-minute lesson, which is structured around six general components that must be present everyday:

(1) reading many known stories;
(2) independently reading a story that was read once the previous day while the teacher observes and assesses progress;
(3) writing a message or story, with support by the teacher for the construction of words;
(4) working with letter and "making and breaking" words to learn how they work (using magnetic letters);
(5) putting together a cut-up sentence (from the story above); and
(6) reading a new book introduced by the teacher.

In the RR lesson, children have the opportunity to connect reading and writing and to engage in problem solving while reading. Children work out problems by searching for and using information from a variety of sources such as experience, knowledge of language, and visual information from print. Although challenge is inherent in the activity, the RR teacher is also concerned with ease and fluency. Text selection and instructional support make it possible for children to see themselves as doing what good readers do (DeFord, 1991). DeFord suggests that RR children's rereading of texts helps them to orchestrate strategies more effectively and focus on meaning while becoming more fluent.

The RR lesson has been described as "a highly organized, intensive, and, it must be stressed, enjoyable occasion. Moreover, it is not confined to reading alone—writing and good deal of speaking and listening also features strongly" (HMSO, 1993, p. 5). The activities of the lesson put the child in control of his / her learning. The teacher's goal is to help children to become independent, strategic users of literacy. Only by engaging in the use of strategies, with the support of another with greater expertise, will the child be able to take over the learning. Although not developed using Vygotsky's theory, RR has been interpreted as an example of an apprenticeship model, in which the child works alongside a more expert writer and reader who demonstrates and supports the novice's efforts. The teacher identifies the child's areas of strength and existing knowledge and assists in the use and extension of that knowledge (Clay & Cazden, 1990; Gaffney & Anderson, 1991). "Acceleration is achieved as the child takes over the learning process and works independently, discovering new things for himself inside and outside the lessons. He comes to push the boundaries of his own knowledge, and not only during his lessons" (Clay, 1993b, p. 9)

Studies of Teacher Behavior and Student Outcomes

Studies of RR have documented teacher–child interactions that appear to be related to successful student outcomes. These studies involved the detailed analysis and categorization of the types of interactions that were observed in taped lessons. Several studies of instruction (see Lyons, 1991; Lyons, 1993; Lyons & White, 1990) provided a pattern of evidence suggesting that successful teachers help children become flexible problem solvers who focus on meaning. Teachers' comments during lessons supported children's use of the full range of information needed for reading (e.g. meaning, picture clues, syntax, and visual detail). Lower student outcomes were associated with an overemphasis on one source of such information. Videotaped lessons, taken at two points in time, were analyzed to determine the prompting and reinforcing statements made by teachers. The analysis indicated that higher student progress was associated with consistent balance between attention to text-level strategies and letter-, or word-level strategies. Successful teachers appeared to be helping students analyze words using larger chunks of information and they were more specific and more responsive to specific child behaviors that indicated problem solving (Pinnell, 1993). These studies were conducted on quite small samples of teachers. Further investigations are needed involving larger numbers of RR teachers.

Frasier (1991) observed two RR students with differing profiles of progress for a period of 6 months. Based on behavioral evidence, Frasier compared the use of strategies by the two readers and also examined the teacher's prompting for strategy use. One child made accelerated progress in RR and the other was not successful. This research indicated that while both readers made progress in learning and evidenced the development of strategies, the two readers differed in several ways: for example, oral language behaviors, print awareness behaviors, linking behaviors and risk-taking behaviors as well as the way in which they interacted with the teacher. The high progress student had more initial control of oral language and more readily noticed and used visual information in print. The slow progress child required more prompting from the teacher to take on every new behavior. Consistent with Glynn's recommendations (Glynn, et al., 1989), Frasier concluded that the slow progress child required more time in the program. These results, however, should not be generalized to indicate that children who come into the program with low scores will make slow progress; many children who initially have a low knowledge base make accelerated progress. More research is needed, such as that undertaken by Clay and Tuck (1991), that looks closely at children who do not make accelerated progress in RR.

As an alternative to defining success in terms of student outcome measures, Handerhan (1990) conducted a qualitative investigation using multiple ways of viewing success. She contended that success can also be defined through perceptions of students and teachers and through observed actions. In her study of successful teachers, using this multifaceted definition, Handerhan found that while the four teachers she studied structured their lessons in similar ways, there were variations across teachers in use of time, choices of materials and instructional actions. Interactions between the student–teacher pair who consistently fell at the higher end of the success continuum were varied and represented a wide repertoire of strategies. Children were invited to "play" with language in many different ways and for different purposes. Handerhan described a narrower range of interactions for the dyad at the lower end of the continuum. Iversen and Tunmer (1993) report results of a quasi-experimental study in which two nonstandard versions of RR were compared. Three matched groups of RR children were compared:

(1) one group received an RR program designed by the researchers to include explicit code instruction involving phonograms;
(2) the second group received "traditional" RR instruction that did not include recent refinements; and
(3) the third group received a "standard intervention," defined as either Chapter 1 or a state-supported program called Literacy.

Both RR groups were superior in performance to the third group and achieved equal levels of reading performance; however, the group receiving the modified program made quicker progress, resulting in somewhat shorter programs. While the researchers concluded that the more rapid progress in the program was strongly related to the development of phonological skills, two things must be noted. First, what was described as the "traditional group" (group 2) was equal to or better than the special program group on the phonological test assessments at the end of the RR program; and second, the special program group (group 1) had a full RR program within which to learn their phonological skills.

Several factors make it important to exercise caution in interpreting the study. The RR groups were selected for convenience (two teacher classes) rather than using random assignment or other techniques for matching; therefore, we cannot assume that they were equivalent. One of the researchers, a New Zealand tutor, conducted both RR classes making experimenter bias a possibility. Since the same teacher educator had not participated in RR for several years, the experiment was conducted without access to refinements in the program that had taken place in the preceding 3 to 4 years. So, RR in this experiment did not have the benefit of the in-depth work on words, called "making and breaking," which now features more prominently in RR lessons. Revisions in the program are related to recent research on phonological awareness, onset and rhyme, and analogy (see Clay, 1993b, p. 44). The major focus of the program, however, is still on meaning and on reading and writing extended text. In any study of variations on a program, it is a dangerous assumption to conclude that the variant produces good outcomes. It may be that the program is sustaining the progress despite the variant. Nevertheless, the work of these researchers confirms the power of the lesson framework and raises important issues related to the role of phonological awareness in reading progress.

DeFord (1994) examined differences among high and low progress students. In a comparative descriptive study she selected students (n=12) and teachers (n=8) half of whom represented higher and lower outcomes in the program. Her analysis of videotapes of lessons, student writing books, pre- and post-test measures, and lesson records indicated marked patterns of interactions across the beginning, middle, and end of program designations. This analysis focused on the writing section of the RR lesson. In this section of the lesson, teachers and children collaborate to write a message on one page of a writing book while using a "practice" page for word construction and other kinds of practice and analysis. Teachers watch for appropriate opportunities to use scaffolding tools such as "hearing sounds in words," in which the teacher draws squares for each phoneme (and for each letter, as the child becomes more advanced) and invites the child to say the word slowly to identify sounds and construct the word. Teachers also find opportunities to help children construct unfamiliar words from words they know and see patterns and relationships in word clusters. The whole process, with the goal of producing a message composed by the child, offers chances for children to examine the links between oral language and written symbols.

DeFord suggested that higher outcomes were related to teachers' supporting efforts at independent problem solving and making decisions about how to use tools such as hearing and recording sounds in words and analogies across the child's program. Copying had little value; independent phonological analysis (using hearing sounds in words techniques), generating new words from known examples, and fluent word writing facilitated rapid progress. This analysis confirms the importance of writing in the lesson framework.

DeFord found that the most effective teachers allocated more time to writing and concluded that writing is especially helpful early in the child's program. By taking advantage of and fostering the reciprocity between reading and writing, teachers helped children build networks of understanding "until the systems of knowledge held in reading and writing converge" (DeFord, 1994, p. 53). These networks, she hypothesized, would be powerful sources of personal knowledge for children's continued learning in classrooms.

Studies of Teacher-Student Interactions

Studies of teaching, while helpful to program developers in refining teacher training, fall short of explaining the dynamic and interacting processes that lead to student learning in RR. With the consistent lesson framework and emphasis on conversation as a support for learning (Kelly, Klein, & Pinnell, 1994), RR has been viewed by some researchers as an ideal setting for examining teacher-child interactions and their relationship to learning.

A number of studies have used RR as the setting to study interactions between children and teachers. Askew (1993) analyzed taped interactions between children and their teachers across four readings of the same text. This study of repeated readings revealed that children's behaviors indicating monitoring, error detection, and self-correction increased as texts became more familiar. These familiar texts do not represent "memorized" renditions but strong linguistic resources which the reader can access when cued by print. Fluent reading also increased and teacher intervention decreased. Askew's analyses support the inclusion of multiple readings of the same text because they provide a chance to engage in fluent reading and independent problem solving.

Using a sociocultural framework, a group of researchers (Wong, Groth, & O'Flahavan, 1994), analyzed five RR teachers' interactions with children in two contexts, familiar reading of known stories and reading new stories. They characterized teacher–student interactions using five categories for teacher behavior:

(1) telling—to provide the word or an explanation;
(2) modeling—to explicitly demonstrate an act;
(3) prompting—to focus attention on visual, structural, or meaning cues available in the text;
(4) coaching—to take the reader outside the reading act to focus on how the student performs or responds; and
(5) discussing—to talk about the text in a way that focuses attention on the meaning of the story.

The researchers found that teachers were less directive when students reread familiar texts and tended to behave as "coaches" to support students' attempts. In new texts, however, there was an increase in teacher behaviors such as modeling, prompting, and discussing comments that fostered efficient processing of continuous texts. The researchers stated that "teachers trained in RR seem to know from moment to moment what text to focus on, when and how to prompt, when to tell, when to coach, and when to allow readers to direct their own reading" (p. 23). These comments capture the goal of RR teaching, toward which both initial training and continuing teacher development are directed.

Case studies of teachers have further illuminated the decision-making process. Elliott (1994) employed a qualitative case study approach to examine decision making by one effective RR teacher. Her study reveals that the teacher's knowledge was built upon multiple sources of information—knowledge of the child, pedagogical content knowledge, and knowledge of content. Pedagogical content referred to the teacher's understanding of her role in assisting children to read and write. Knowledge of content referred to understandings specific to the ideas, facts and concepts associated with emergent literacy; that is, the teachers's personal theory. These knowledge sources intricately linked to the kind of reasoning the teacher used to make decisions for individual children. Elliott described what she observed as "responsive teaching," a process of observing and interpreting information about one child's reading / writing behaviors forming a transaction with the teacher's knowledge base and the process of making decisions. That is, the process is not one of applying a particular teaching move to a particular response but of constantly synthesizing and analyzing relative to the individual.

Dorn (1994) examined the types of conversations that occurred between the teacher and child during the period of a child's program called "Roaming around the Known." Teachers are directed by the RR guidebook as follows:

> For the first two weeks of the tutoring programme stay with what the child already knows. Do not introduce any new items of learning...
>
> Go over what he knows in different ways until your ingenuity runs out, and until he is moving fluently around this personal corpus of responses, the letters, words and messages that he knows how to read and write. [MR1]... the most important reason for roaming around the known is that it requires the teacher to stop teaching from her preconceived ideas. This will be her focus throughout the programme. (Clay, 1993b, pp. 12, 13).

Dorn suggests that this context is comparable to the mother-child dyad. She conducted case studies of one teacher and two African-American male students in a small rural shcool; all "roaming" sessions were audiotaped and video recorded; sessions were observed and written productions were collected.

To analyze the data, Dorn identified a series of nested contexts: literacy events, literacy episodes, literacy conversations, and literacy statements. She found that three types of talk worked together to support the child's development of inner control:

(1) child talk;
(2) teacher feedback talk, in which the teacher responded to the child's demonstrations of literacy use; and
(3) teacher feed-forward talk, in which the teacher tried to activate the child's preexisting knowledge for use in a new situation.

Her analysis of the language in sessions suggested that both kinds of teacher talk facilitated children's literacy growth. Teachers took the opportunity to talk aloud, describing the child's accomplishments with regard to reading and writing. Children also began to articulate specific knowledge about literacy, providing the teacher with further overt evidence of understanding; however, Dorn concluded that the teacher's responses to the child's demonstrations of literacy were of greater importance than the child's ability to articulate. The teacher skillfully used language in a mediating way to help the child access prior knowledge. As children gained experience, they tended to exercise greater control in the reading activity and the teacher's role of assistance varied in response to the behaviors signaling children's knowledge; for example, Dorn observed transitions from teacher-regulation to child-regulation in literacy events. Dorn's study confirms the central role of observation in RR teaching. After entry to the program, some children find it hard to make accelerated progress a circumstance that provides additional challenges for RR teachers. If a child is making slow progress, teachers must assume that they have not adequately adapted the program to meet the student's needs. A reexamination of teaching is required (Clay, 1993b). To meet these idiosyncratic needs, teachers must reexamine their teaching behavior and their analyses of the child's difficulties. The goal is to gain new or additional insights into what may be interfering with progress. Lyons' (1994) case study is of an effective RR teacher working with a hard-to-teach child who was successfully discontinued. The study revealed that this excellent teacher could:

(1) describe specific behaviors that suggested where, when, and under what conditions the student's processing was breaking down;
(2) use the student's behaviors to infer the cognitive and perceptual processing going on "inside the head" to build a theoretical rationale for *why* the breakdown might be occurring; and, then
(3) determine a course of action and specific teaching procedures to help the student learn how to help him / herself acquire and use effective reading and writing strategies.

The RR lesson provides an intimate setting within which teacher and child are collaboratively immersed in reading and writing. Wong et al's (1994) analysis reveals that teachers' scaffolding comments occurred not in isolation but "dynamically as the teachers attempted to find the appropriate support for the student at the right time" (1994, p. 21). It is the spontaneous nature of the interaction that is so difficult for research to capture and press into a formula that may be directly taught to teachers and transferred to other situations or programs. As they interact, the teacher structures behaviors to meet the student where he or she is in learning. In times past, this kind of powerful teaching might have been described as an "art" or something that a "born teacher" might do. We know from RR that teachers can learn to interact with students to promote learning and that this skill can be refined and extended over time, given a high quality professional development program.

Research on Teacher Learning

Reading Recovery training has been described (Alverman, 1990; Pinnell, 1994) as an inquiry-oriented model for teacher education, an appropriate description because all components of the staff development model involve teachers in searching and reflection. Each young student represents an individual investigation through which teachers learn as they "follow" the child's progress and make hypotheses about the nature of his or her learning . The teacher uses opportunities that arise from several sources:

- the texts children encounter
- their responses to those texts
- the conversations in which they engage
- the messages composed and written.

From those sources, teachers learn to craft teachable moments; their learning is supported by the leader's guidance and their talk with others. According to Clay and Watson (1988), "the key word in the development and implementation of this inservice program was ... observation, and the unique feature was the potential for multilevel observation and learning that was embedded in the situation" (p. 192). Two components—talking while observing and the reflective discussion—make up the major part of the teacher education program. Each case, example, or demonstration presented gives every teacher a chance to reflect on his / her own teaching. This reflective / analytic experience helps teachers construct and refine their theoretical explanations and go beyond procedures. Through shared experiences, a culture is created that supports teachers' learning.

Impact of Reading Recovery on Teachers

Every study of teachers involved in RR has revealed a powerful impact on individuals. In the United States, researchers followed one group's shifts through recording informal discussions held every two weeks (see Lyons et al., 1993). Teachers moved from a focus on mechanics and logistics to a willingness to examine theory. However, the study revealed that learning, even with weekly classes and support, took time. An Australian study (Geeke, 1988) provided evidence that the RR training course had a strong impact on teachers' views. Teachers valued the learning that occurred. In both United States and Australian studies, teachers commented on the intensity of the training and the anxiety connected with teaching "behind the screen." A more recent Australian study from a different state was entitled *Changing Lives* (Power & Sawkins, 1991). The results confirmed the potential of the program for teacher change and yielded comments that the in-service sessions were "intense," "exhausting," and "stressful." As in the initial United States study, teachers were concerned about teaching loads and scheduling. In all three studies there was an initial desire on the part of teachers to be told "the answers" and frustration that points were turned back to the group for decision making.

Shannon (1990) undertook an year-long study of a 12-member RR teacher class. Her objective was to study the role of verbal challenge and teacher response during live demonstrations. Shannon identified 19 categories of verbal challenge and 21 categories of response. She particularly noted the role of exploratory questions, for which the leader had no specific response in mind. She found generally stable patterns of questioning and response across the 8 months of the study; however, changes in focus and changes in teacher acquisition of knowledge were evident in their ability to evaluate, describe and explain behavior. The researcher hypothesized that the opportunity to observe authentic lessons is a key factor in teachers' ability to interpret and transfer learning to their own teaching.

Two other studies focused on the nature of interactions during in-service sessions. In an year-long study of one teacher group, Wilson (1988) recorded and analyzed behind-the-screen and discussion sessions. She found that over the course of the year teachers increased in their interactions, grew in their ability to describe specific behavior, and were more likely to challenge each other's statements. Rentel and Pinnell's (1987) study of teachers' language focused on growth in ability to provide evidence or "grounds" for statements. They found that teachers grew in their ability to make statements that were supported by specific evidence from student behavior.

Teacher Learning Over Time

Research is needed that goes beyond the training year to discover whether teachers can sustain ongoing development without continuous support. Woolsey's (1991) case study of one teacher indicated the difficulty she experienced in coping with the internal and external forces that impinged on her learning and on the changes she wanted to make in her classroom teaching. (This teacher taught RR for one half the day and a 1st-grade classroom the rest of the day.) School district requirements, other teachers' expectations and opinions, and her own built-in fears were all barriers to continued growth for this teacher. It was only during the second year after training that she was able to change her classroom practice to be more consistent with the theoretical shifts she had made during RR training. Another interpretation of Woolsey's research is that theoretical concepts deepen and become more generalizable in the years after initial RR training.

Teacher Learning Over Time

Using an interpretive case study approach, Lyons (1991) examined the development of one RR teacher's understanding and questioning practices over time. Videotapes of teaching were first analyzed by experts and then discussed with the case study teacher while viewing the videotape. Lyons recorded the teacher's comments. Over a 3-year period the teacher continued to grow in her understanding of how to prompt and / or ask questions that enabled a student to construct learning. Her approach to instruction became more skillful and complex throughout the investigation period. Lyons identified Phase 1 as "trying out" the prompts and questions suggested by RR training, Phase 2 as using prompts and questions to test her hypotheses about the child's behavior and then to support the student's problem solving, and Phase 3 as prompting and questioning in response to students' behaviors. The teacher moved from the first phase, in which, by her own account, she was "parroting questions according to the book," to the third phase when she demonstrated her ability to respond to unexpected answers, to reframe the situation, to step out of her original perspective to take into account the student's perspective. The study also indicated the value of this teacher's opportunity to talk about her own work with others. With system support and an inquiry approach learning is continuous. Lyons (1991) replicated this study with six RR teachers leaders in training. The teachers collected and analyzed observational notes of student behavior, running records of oral reading and writing samples to determine shifts in student learning. Subjects also used journals to record personal reflections about the effects of their teaching decisions on student learning, and they tape-recorded, analyzed, and evaluated their interactions (verbal and nonverbal) with students throughout the in-service course. The teachers and the researcher met weekly to analyze and evaluate the consequences of their instruction. Lyons' analysis of the audiotaped lessons and of teachers' personal reactions as documented in journals and conversations with colleagues, indicated that as teachers became more sensitive to emerging behaviors signaling student change, they began to tailor their own behaviors to meet the students' developing abilities. The study suggested five general principles of learning and teaching:

(1) assisted performance by another more expert helps individuals—both students and teachers—expand and reorganize their understandings;
(2) the language that surrounds events within an RR lesson mediates performance and creates systems of change;
(3) conversation has an important role in teachers' learning; ongoing discussions provide a scaffold for the growth of understandings and a way to mediate performance by providing bridges between what the teacher already knows and what he / she needs to know to teach effectively;
(4) collaboration enables teachers to develop theoretical and practical knowledge; and,
(5) the major shifts in teacher theory development are given impetus by learning the RR teaching procedures and are greatly influenced by the in-service course.

Lyons (1993) concluded that this model enables teachers to internalize and transform psychological processes. This incorporated a way of "learning how to learn" into their own instructional repertoires. Lifelong learning is a result of the process. It appears that the idea of social construction of knowledge applies not only to children but to teachers as well. The teacher's construction of his / her own knowledge is a critical factor in RR teaching.

Another study (Lyons, 1994b) focused on thirteen RR teachers in training at three and again at six months. In training sessions these teachers assisted one another to engage in thinking about their instructional decision-making, called "pedagogical reasoning" in this study. Support took the form of "chains of reasoning" cooperatively built by the group. Teachers reported that this process increased their decision-making power in individual teaching. Lyons (1994) claims that an important factor in RR teaching is how "teachers consult with each other to develop a theoretical base that is grounded in action. They are encouraged to approximate, to generate hypotheses about what the student has learned and controls, to challenge one another, and to provide alternative explanations for the student's behavior with supporting evidence for their hypotheses" (p. 285). Peer consultation is a requirement from the beginning of training and throughout a teacher's particpation in the program. This study also showed the powerful role of the RR teacher leader in guiding the process.

Studies of teacher learning represent a relatively unexplored yet significant dimension of RR. More research, with larger numbers, is needed; yet, an open-ended survey of 205 RR teacher leaders supports the findings of case studies. In a lengthy questionnaire, teacher leaders revealed their perspectives on their own training and their role as teacher leaders (Pinnell, Lyons, Constable & Jennings, 1994). The value of talk with colleagues emerged as a major factor in their learning. During the first year of training, and in subsequent years, respondents reported that reflection, dialogue, and the opportunity to articulate new understanding increased learning. The support of colleagues was valued by teacher leaders, especially after the training year. For these leaders, learning to teach is facilitated through talk with others who share their mission and vision.

Research on Implementation

Most innovations are confined to small demonstrations that are described in the literature but not taken to a large scale because dissemination processes are not in place. RR has reached a large scale by replicating the innovation in new settings (Wilson & Daviss, 1994). Hiebert (1994) says that "once a program is in place, there appears to be considerable fidelity in the results. Even when the number of tutees jumps 100% as it did at OSU from 1986–87 to 1987–88, similar levels of oral reading were maintained with the same percentage of the cohort" (p. 21). Clay (1994) has recognized systemic factors in the design and implementation system for RR.

> ...my personal orientation in developing RR was to take account of the complex interdependence among parts of the system.... In an effective intervention the interdependence of variables demands a systemic plan, for an innovation cannot move into an education system merely on the merits of what it can do for children (p. 128).

Innovators must see change "as a problem of instructional linkage in which there is likely to be conflict about issues which will affect the survival of new programs" (p. 128).

Education experts not directly associated with the program (for example, Adams, 1990; Allington & Walmsley, 1995; Slavin & Madden, 1987) have recognized the potential of RR and encouraged dissemination. Consistent success rates across hundreds of school districts, in urban, rural, and suburban settings, serving "at risk" students in multiethnic and multilinguistic classrooms, indicate that the current method of implementing, disseminating, evaluating and ensuring program quality has been maintained over the decade that RR has been in existence in North America.

Adapting and Changing Reading Recovery

In each new adoption systemic variables require changes in RR in order to deliver the program to the new system. Delivery systems must be devised to ease the transition without eliminating essential components of the program. For example, assessment procedures were tailored to the United States system; books had to vary to reflect local groups and cultures; incentives such as university credit were devised to reward teachers and maintain quality; and new administrative and financial structures were created. Reading Recovery now has a range of alternative structures that are responding to local conditions. Survival requires that the program must continue to be cohesive. Adaptations must preserve integrity (Dunkeld, 1991).

In the 12 years since its introduction in the United States, RR itself has changed in response to the growing body of knowledge about how children learn to read and write. Based on Clay's 1963–66 research (reported in Clay, 1982), hearing sounds in words and visual analysis were included in the RR program from the beginning, well in advance of the field's recognition of the importance of these factors. Changes occurred in the training over a period of years in response to new published research. More attention was given to children's learning of how to work at the subword level of analysis. Minor changes were gradually incorporated into the RR training. Differences between the second and third editions of *The Early Detection of Reading Difficulties* (Clay, 1979, 1985) reveal refinements in the procedures that had just been made when the program was first tested in the United States. A stronger theoretical statement informed teaching as *Becoming Literate: The Construction of Inner Control* (Clay, 1991) was published; experienced teachers and teacher leaders studied this volume intensively during the following year. A comprehensive review of research and publication about onset and rhyme and analogy contributed to revision of a new edition of RR teaching procedures, *Reading Recovery: A Guidebook for Teachers in Training* (Clay, 1993b). This volume separated the *Observation Survey* (Clay, 1993a) from the RR program; teachers in training use both documents. Space here does not permit a detailed analysis of the changes in RR; however, procedures for working with words are presented with more elaboration than in previous editions. The focus of the program remained on whole text, with meaning as the center; but teachers learned to help children learn how "words work" to assist their problem solving while reading and writing. Changes in practice are in the process of gradual assimilation.

A dynamically changing theory is valued in RR. The system of implementation and teaching practice are constantly examined in search of the most effective procedures. Individuals have tried applying the principles of the program for other purposes, for example, Bradley's (1991) work with adult emergent readers. Investigation regarding children who do not succeed in the program is continuous (see Clay & Tuck, 1991). Research projects are underway at many of the regional training centers; in addition, adjustments in implementation are investigated whenever necessary.

Moreover, systems are in place to assure that both teachers and teacher leaders receive up-to-date knowledge of new developments in the program. Continued training for teachers takes place on a regular basis; there are also professional development opportunities for teacher leaders. Reading Recovery has developed a self-renewing system, one that accommodates changes, which result from sound research and from carefully monitored developments. Otherwise it would become outdated as society and theory changed around it.

Intangibles in the Implementation of Reading Recovery

Weaving these elements together are the intangibles revealed in the survey of teacher leaders (Lyons, et al., 1994). The 205 responding teacher leaders, trained at 16 different regional sites and representing differing years of experience, were articulate in their descriptions of how much they had learned in RR training and how they had grown in their professional roles. These teacher leaders responded in terms of their roles both as teachers of children and as teacher educators, since this duality is a feature of their position.

Becoming Part of a Community. They supported the "sense of community" that they felt through interactions with their colleagues. Indeed, discussion with colleagues was seen as a principle element in learning during the training year, but experienced teachers were even more enthusiastic about the role of colleagues in their continued learning. As part of the initial training, teacher leaders (as well as teachers) learn a common language that they can use to talk with one other about their teaching; this conversation continues across sites, regions, and continents, as evidenced by the communication among teachers at international institutes.

Working Closely with Children. Teacher leaders valued their continued work with children. Reading Recovery teacher leadership is different from other staff development roles in that the teacher educator also practices daily through work with children. Leaders reported that they continue to learn from their own experience of teaching children.

Continuing to Learn. Everyone involved in RR sees him / herself as a learner. Teachers do not have to be defensive about "less than perfect" lessons. Everyone knows that individuals are developing their skills and learn from one another. Reading Recovery contributes to the creation of learning so that improvement is a constant goal.

Holding a Common Vision. Everyone involved in RR shares a vision that is built through case after case of success on the part of students who were the lowest achievers in reading. It is a vision of what is possible. British inspectors suggested that the results of RR "show what can be achieved by the combination of decisive policy and professional will" (Frater & Staniland, 1994, p. 149).

Among others, intangible characterisitcs such as sense of community, closeness to children, continued learning, and common vision form the foundation that makes RR a cohesive system. In the implementation of the program, varied patterns emerge, but the whole is disciplined piece of work that is focused on student success (Clay, 1994).

References

Adams, M. (1990). *Beginning to read: Thinking and learning about print.* Cambridge, MA: MIT Press.

Allington, R. L., & McGill-Franzen, A. (1989). Different programs, indifferent instruction. In D. Lipsky & A. Garther (Eds.), *Beyond special eduction* (pp. 3–32). New York: Brookes.

Allington, R. L., & Walmsley, S. R. (1995). *No quick fix: Rethinking literacy programs in America's elementary schools.* New York: Teachers College Press.

Alverman, D. E. (1990). Reading teacher education. In W.R., Houston, M., Haberman & J., Sikula, (Eds.), *Handbook of research on teacher education: A project of the Association of Teacher Educators.* New York: MacMillan. (pp. 687–704).

Aprenda–Technical Data Report. (1991). The Psychological Corporation. San Antonio: Harcourt, Brace and Jovanovich.

Askew, B. J. (1993) The effect of multiple readings on the behaviors of children and teachers in an early intervention program. *Reading & Writing Quarterly: Overcoming Learning Difficulties, 9,* 307–316.

Askew, B. J., & Frasier, D. F. (1994). Sustained effects of reading recovery intervention on the cognitive behaviors of second grade children and the perceptions of their teachers. *Literacy, Teaching and Learning: An International Journal of Early Literacy, 1,* 7–28.

Bradley, D. H. (1991). *Reconceptualizing literacy learning for adult new literates in one-to-one teacher/student interaction.* Unpublished doctoral dissertation, The Ohio State University, Columbus, OH.

Clay, M. M. (1979). *The early detection of reading difficulties.* Auckland, New Zealand: Heinemann.

Clay, M. M. (1982). Observing young readers; Selected papers. Exeter, NH: Heinemann.

Clay, M. M. (1985). *The early detection of reading difficulties.* (2nd ed.). Auckland, New Zealand: Heinemann.

Clay, M. M. (1990). The reading recovery programme, 1984–88: Coverage, outcomes and education board district figures. *New Zealand Journal of Educational Studies, 25,* 61–70.

Clay, M. M. (1991). *Becoming literate: The construction of inner control.* Auckland, Heinemann.

Clay, M. M. (1993a). *An observation survey of early literacy achievement.* Portsmouth, NH: Heinemann.

Clay, M. M. (1993b). *Reading recovery: A guidebook for teachers in training.* Portsmouth, NH: Heinemann.

Clay, M. M. (1994). *A guidebook for reading recovery teachers.* Portsmouth, NH: Heinemann.

Clay, M. M., & Cazden, C. B. (1990). A Vygotskian interpretation of reading recovery. In L. Moll (Ed.), *Vygotsky and education: Instructional implications and applications of sociohistorical psychology* (pp. 206–222). New York: Cambridge University Press.

Clay, M. M., & Tuck, V. (1991). *A study of reading recovery subgroups: Including outcomes for children who did not satisfy discontinuing criteria* (Tech. Rep.). Auckland, New Zealand: Ministry of Education.

Clay, M. M., & Watson, B. (1982). An inservice program for reading recovery teachers. In M. M. Clay (Ed.), *Observing young readers.* (pp. 192–200). Portsmouth, NH: Heinemann.

Coopers & Lybrand (1994). *Resource allocations in the New York City Public Schools.* L.L.P., 1251 Avenue of the Americas, NY, New York, 10024.

DeFord, D.E. (1994). Early writing: Teachers and children in reading recovery. *Literacy, Teaching and Learning: An International Journal of Early Literacy, 1,* 31–57.

DeFord, D. E., Lyons, C. A., & Pinnell, G. S. (1991). *Bridges to literacy: Learning from reading recovery.* Portsmouth, NH: Heinemann.

Dorn, L. (1994). *A Vygotskian perspective on literacy acquisition: Talk and action in the child's construction of literate awareness.* Unpublished doctoral dissertation, Texas Woman's University, Denton, TX.

Dunkeld, C. (1991). Maintaining the integrity of a promising program: The case of reading recovery. In D. DeFord, C. Lyons & G. S. Pinnell (Eds.), *Bridges to literacy.* Portsmouth, NH: Heinemann.

Elliott, C. B. (1994). *Pedagogical reasoning: Understanding teacher decision making in a cognitive apprenticeship setting.* Unpublished doctoral dissertation, Texas Woman's University, Denton, TX.

Elliott, C. B. (1995). *The East Baton Rouge Parish Reading Recovery Project: Third grade follow-up study of literacy proficiency.* Unpublished report.

Escamilla, K. (1994). Descubriendo la Lectura: An early intervention literacy program in Spanish. *Literacy, Teaching and Learning: An International Journal of Early Literacy, 1,* 77–90.

Fountas, I. (1994). *Reading recovery in Massachusetts.* Lesley College Boston, MA.

Frasier, D. F. (1991). *A study of strategy use by two emergent readers in a one-to-one tutorial setting.* Unpublished doctoral dissertation, Columbus, OH.

Frater, & Staniland (1994). Reading recovery from New Zealand: A report from the Office of Her Majesty's Chief Inspector of Schools, *Literacy, Teaching and Learning, 1,* 141–159.

Gaffney, J. S., & Anderson, R. C. (1991). Two-tiered scaffolding: Congruent processes of teaching and learning. In E. H. Hiebert (Ed.), *Literacy for a diverse society.* New York: Teachers College Press.

Geeke, P. (1988). *Evaluation report on the reading recovery field trial in Central Victoria, 1984.* Australia: Centre for Studies in Literacy, University of Wollongong.

Glynn, T., & McNaughton, S. (1992). Early literacy learning: A tribute to Marie Clay. *Educational Psychology, 12*(3, 4), 171–176.

Her Majesty's Office for Standards in Education (HMSO). (1993). Reading recovery in New Zealand: A report from the office of Her Majesty's Chief Inspector of Schools. London: HMSO.

Hiebert, E. H. (1994). Reading recovery–Some new caveats and cautions. *Educational Researcher.*

Holland, K. E. (1991). Bringing home and school literacy together through the Reading Recovery program. In D. E. DeFord, C. A. Lyons & G. S. Pinnell, (Eds.), *Bridges to literacy: Learning from reading recovery.* (pp. 149–170). Portsmouth, NH: Heinemann.

Iversen, S. J., & Tunmer, W. E. (1993). Phonological processing skills and the Reading recovery program. *Journal of Educational Psychology, 85,* 112–126.

Jaggar, A. M., & Smith-Burke, M. T. (1994). *Follow-up study of reading recovery children in community school district #2, New York City.* New York: Reading Recovery Project, School of Education, New York University.

Kelly, P., Klein, A., & Pinnell, G. S. (1994). Reading Recovery: Teaching through conversation. In D. Lancy (Ed.), *Children's emergent literacy: Social and cognitive processes.* Westport, CT: Praeger.

Kerslake, J. (1992). *A summary of the 1991 data on reading recovery.* Research and Statistics Division Bulletin, No. 5. Wellington, New Zealand: Ministry of Education.

Lyons, C. A. (1989). Reading recovery: A prevention for mislabeling young at-risk learners. *Urban Education, 24,* 125–139.

Lyons, C. A. (1991). A comparative study of the teaching effectiveness of teachers participating in a year-long and two-week inservice program. In J. Zutell & S. McCormick (Eds.), *Learning factors/teacher factors: Issues in literacy research and instruction* (pp. 367–675). Fortieth Yearbook of the National Reading Conference. Chicago: National Reading Conference.

Lyons, C. A. (1993). The use of questions in the teaching of high-risk beginning readers: A profile of a developing reading recovery teacher. *Reading & Writing Quarterly: Overcoming Learning Difficulties, 9,* 317–328.

Lyons, C. A. (1994a). Reading recovery and learning disability: Issues, challenges and implications. *Literacy, Teaching and Learning: An International Journal of Literacy Learning, 1,* 109–120.

Lyons, C. A. (1994b). Constructing chains of reasoning in reading recovery demonstration lessons. In C. K. Kinzer & D. J. El (Eds.), *Multidimensional aspects of literacy research, theory and practice.* (pp. 276–286). Forty-third Yearbook of the National Reading Conference. Chicago: National Reading Conference.

Lyons, C. A., & Beaver, J. (1995). Reducing retention and learning disability placement through reading recovery: An educationally sound cost-effective choice. In R. Allington & S. Wamsley (Eds.), *No quick fix: Redesigning literacy programs in America's elementary schools.* (pp. 116–136). New York: Teachers College Press and the International Reading Association.

Lyons, C. A., Pinnell, G. S., & DeFord, D. E. (1993). *Partners in learning: Teachers and children in reading recovery.* New York: Teachers College Press.

Lyons, C. A., & White, N. (1990). *Belief systems and instructional decision: Comparisons between more and less effective teachers.* (Tech. Rep.): The Ohio State University.

Moore, M., & Wade, B. (1994). Reading recovery: Parents' views, *English in Education, 27,* 11–17.

Moriarty, D. J. (1995, January 25). Our reading recovery results: "Conclusive." *Education Week.*

Peterson, B. (1991). Selecting books for beginning readers: Children's literature suitable for young readers: A Bibliography. In D. E. DeFord, C. A. Lyons & G. S. Pinnell (Eds.), *Bridges to literacy: Learning from reading recovery.* (pp. 119–148). Portsmouth, NH: Heinemann.

Pinnell, G. S. (1989). Reading recovery: Helping at-risk children learn to read. *The Elementary School Journal, 90*(2), 159–181.

Pinnell, G. S. (1993). Teaching for problem solving in reading. *Reading & Writing Quarterly: Overcoming Learning Difficulties, 9,* 289–306.

Pinnell, G. S. (1994). An inquiry-based model for educating teachers of literacy. *Literacy, Teaching and Learning: An International Journal of Early Literacy, 1,* 29–42.

Pinnell, G. S., Fried, M. D., & Estice, R. M. (1991). Reading recovery: Learning how to make a difference. In D. E. DeFord, C. A. Lyons & G. S. Pinnell. (Eds.), *Bridges to literacy: Learning from reading recovery.* (pp. 11–36). Portsmouth, NH: Heinemann.

Pinnell, G. S., Lyons, C. A., Constable, S., & Jennings, J. (1994, December). *The voices of teacher educators: Reading Recovery teacher leaders' reflections on their learning and teaching.* Paper presented at the National Reading Conference, San Diego, CA.

Pinnell, G. S., Lyons, C. A., DeFord, D. E., Bryk, A., & Seltzer, M. (1993). Comparing instructional models for the literacy education of high risk first graders. *Reading Research Quarterly, 29,* 8–39.

Pinnell, G. S., Lyons, C. A., & Jones, N. (1995). What difference does reading recovery make? Response to Hiebert. *The Network News, 7,* 18–22.

Power, J., & Sawkins, S. (1991). Changing lives: Report of the implementation of the reading recovery program on the North Coast. Northern Rivers: University of New England.

Reading Recovery Council of North America. (1988). *Guidelines and Standards for the North American Reading Recovery Council.* (2nd ed.), 1993, July. Columbus, OH: The North American Reading Recovery Council.

Rentel, V. M., & Pinnell, G. S. (1987, December). *A study of practical reasoning in Reading Recovery instruction.* Paper presented at the meeting of the National Reading Conference, St. Petersburg Beach, FL.

Royal Commission Report on Learning, (1995). *For the love of leanring,* (Vols. 5 and 6). Canada.

Rowe, K. (1988). *Literacy programs study: Reading recovery.* Melbourne, Australia: Ministry of Education.

Schnug, J. R. (1991). *Learning to read in an intervention program and the classroom reading group.* Unpublished doctoral dissertation, The Ohio State University.

Shanahan, T., & Barr, R. (1995). *Reading Recovery: An independent evaluation of the effects of an early instructional intervention for atrisk learners.* Reading Research Quarterly, *30*(4).

Shannon, D. (1990). *A descriptive study of verbal challenge and teacher response to verbal challenge in reading recovery teacher training.* Unpublished doctoral dissertation, Texas Woman's University, Denton, TX.

Slavin, R. E., & Madden, N. A. (1989). Effective classroom programs for students at risk. In R. E. Slavin, N. L. Karweit, & N. A. Madden (Eds.), *Effective programs for students at risk* (pp. 23–51). Boston: Allyn & Bacon.

Smith, P. E. (1987). Mana reading recovery follow-up report. *Unpublished end of year report, 1987.*

Smith, P. E. (1988). Mana reading recovery follow-up report. *Unpublished end of year report, 1988.*

Smith, P. E. (1994). Reading recovery and children with English as a second language. *New Zealand Journal of Educational Studies, 29,* 141–155.

Texas Woman's University: College of Education and Human Ecology (1994, Fall). *Reading recovery report 1988–94,* (Report No. 5). Denton, TX: Texas Woman's University.

U.S. Department of Education. (1990). *Twelfth annual report to Congress on the Implementation of the Education of the Handicapped Act 9.* Washington, DC: U.S. Office of Special Education and Rehabilitative Services.

University of Arkansas at Little Rock. (1994). UALR highlights of reading recovery research. *Reading Recovery, 1,* 4.

White, N. (1992). *Social constructions of literacy learning: At risk first graders making sense of instruction in the classroom and an early intervention program.* Unpublished doctoral dissertation, The Ohio State University, Columbus, OH.

Wilson, V. (1988). *A study of teacher development in an interactive inservice setting.* Unpublished doctoral dissertation, The Ohio State University, Columbus, OH.

Wilson, K., & Daviss, B. (1994). *Redesigning education.* New York: Henry Holt.

Wong, S. D., Groth, L. A., & O'Flahavan, J. F. (1994). *Characterizing teacher-student interaction in reading recovery lessons.* (Rep. No. 17). National Reading Research Center: Universities of Georgia and Maryland.

Woolsey, D. P. (1991). Changing contexts for literacy learning: The impact of reading recovery on one first-grade teacher. In D. E. DeFord, C. A. Lyons, and G. S. Pinnell (Eds.), *Bridges to literacy: Learning from reading recovery* (pp. 189–204). Portsmouth, NH: Heinemann.

·56B·

INTERNATIONAL PERSPECTIVES ON THE READING RECOVERY PROGRAM *

Marie M. Clay

UNIVERSITY OF AUCKLAND

THE OPPORTUNITY

I used to just throw my book down because it was too hard to read but now I can read any book in the world.

—A Reading Recovery student

That is what Reading Recovery (RR) does. It puts a limited number of children who might have been confused by early literacy instruction back in touch with the communicative arts. It is an early literacy intervention program designed for children who clearly show that they have already become at-risk in literacy learning in their classroom program. Two of Her Majesty's Inspectors in Britain studied RR in operation across New Zealand and reported that, "It is much more than a set of procedures to be used with a child. It is a way of establishing an early intervention program in an education system in order to reduce reading and writing difficulties in the primary school" (Frater & Staniland, 1994). Any child entering the program is taken from where he is to somewhere else, working up from what he already knows, using his strengths and what he does well. The lessons are individually designed, differ from day to day, and emphases change according to individual need across the series of lessons.

Analogies can be misleading but let me try one. The instruction is not a packaged recipe for all learners and it cannot work for a whole class of children. It is more like a dose of antibiotics, taken only when essential, after professional appraisal, given as a full course of treatment, and varied to suit the precise condition of each individual.

We aim to minimize a seemingly chronic problem found in every country with universal education—reading difficulties. To cope with this problem in the past, education systems have expanded legitimate labels like learning disability and dyslexia to cover children who do not need those labels, and administrators have tried remedial approaches one after another with extremely limited results. Societies have come to accept literacy difficulties as always being with us but have settled for much greater numbers than are necessary.

Reading Recovery research presents a challenge to this state of affairs, suggesting only 1–2% of an age cohort in school will require assistance with literacy learning which starts early and continues for several years. Other lowest achievers between 6 and 7 years can become readers and writers. The special situations that allow the lowest achievers to learn quickly and catch up with their classmates involve teaching them one at a time, and not in a prescribed sequence such as occurs in class or group instruction. If we problem-solve each individual case we are able to hand over literate 7-year-olds to the education systems with an inner control over literacy learning which enables them, in a good classroom program, to continue to learn within the average band.

Across the world RR is a target for copyists who want to help more children. These innovators modify, simplify, and design cheaper versions that make the very compromises that have led to weak solutions to this problem in the past. They advocate, but they do not observe, develop, try out, research, check, and provide data. They live by assurances or single demonstration with a case or small group. It seems that few people are prepared to consider "a different program for

* The Auckland College of Education has hosted the Reading Recovery National Centre in New Zealand for many years now, and the National Trainer-Co-ordinators have trained Australian, British, Canadian, and some United States trainers and tutors to lead programs back home. Many New Zealand tutors and trainers have by now served a period overseas to our benefit as well as to the benefit of their host country and such exchanges will be of value as new theories and future circumstances bring continuing adjustments.

655

every child" in this hard-to-teach group, even though most people would expect their doctors to treat them as individuals, and most teachers of writing, art and drama would plan for individual creativity to thrive. Such respect for individual learning also applies to seemingly low achievers when the foundation of later learning is being laid down.

Literacy, defined here as performance in reading and writing, could be likened to an individual sport like golf or swimming; a personal coach can teach to the strengths of an individual, go around his weaknesses, and gradually lift the challenge. Reading Recovery designs individual solutions, from its theory and research to its delivery and daily instruction, and results appear in a relatively short period of time! A mother, having just consented to her child joining the program, said, "I doubt that they can do it in such a short time but I'll keep an open mind. It ought to take longer," than about 12–20 weeks to get to average levels of the class.

One-to-one teaching is not merely a convenient or privileged delivery tactic; it is the only delivery system that could arise from a theory which says that the causes of the difficulties are multiple, they differ from child to child, and each child has a different profile of strengths. This is heretical in an academic world that spends much energy searching for one explanation for reading difficulties; therefore RR's approach stands somewhat in isolation. Many who admit it works still do not accept our explanations of why it works, and the practice will not survive unless its supporting theories are understood. Our challenge is simple: we have to enable children who are hard-to-teach able to read and write in ways that make it possible for them to learn in class without any further special help.

Reading Recovery can have three positive outcomes, which create a win-win-win situation:

(1) We aim to get about 90% (of those who enter) to work independently in the average group of their classrooms without further extra help.
(2) Some children need to complete this treatment in the next school year because they entered too late in the year to have a full program.
(3) We provide diagnostic teaching which identifies about 1% of the age group (or up to about 10% of the intake group) for referral for a specialist report and appropriate longer-term help, after their time in Reading Recovery.

These outcomes are replicated by individual cases daily, in New Zealand probably 40–50 children complete their program each school day and in the United States RR may be completing programs at the rate of 500 children per school day.

The lowest achieving children in the 6-year-old group are selected not excluding any child for any reason in an ordinary classroom, a challenging position adopted to ensure reliability of teacher judgement. It also takes care of other values like children's rights, fairness and equality, and social, cultural and linguistic inequities (Sylva & Hurry 1995).

Most children are flexible learners and can learn in classrooms with very different reading programs. Reading Recovery switches from group instruction to the child's own competencies and provides a second chance to learn literacy

for those who make a struggling beginning. However, at the end of an individual program a child must have regained the flexibility required to work with any classroom program.

In time, RR gets "good press" for surprisingly good results in different countries and finds its way into important documents at country level. In England press comment moved from 3-inch high headlines in the *Sunday Times* claiming, "This Program Fails" in February 1992 to part of a main editorial in the *Independent* in February 1995 which read:

> ...To most people outside educational politics it (Reading Recovery) sounds like a simple idea. Six year olds who are lagging behind in their reading are given half-an hour of individual tuition every school day for 16 weeks by a highly trained teacher... Expensive? Of course. But the cost for each child is less than the cost of administration alone for a child who requires 'a statement' for special needs...

By 1995 an independent academic research appraisal funded by politicians had reported the success of children in some tough urban settings in England (Sylva & Hurry, 1995).

The idea is simple but the program is complex; it calls for shifts in the thinking of those who train to be RR teachers; and it is hard for researchers and evaluators to understand a program which breaks with so many established parameters. This program aims to get rid of literacy difficulties, to accept an hypothesis of multiple causation, and has a theory to explain why it succeeds even when it flies in the face of much experience and established practice.

Reading Recovery professionals have to solve problems about children's learning, about teachers' learning and about making the program work in education systems, which I graph as three concentric circles. Trainers and tutors train to become specialists in these three areas of problem solving.

A PERSONAL VIEW OF HISTORY

My contacts with reading difficulties date from the 1940s when I entered teachers college and university and set out to complete a case study of one child. I was on teaching practice in a class of 11-year-olds and selected a child having difficulty with reading. I was given no framework for my study, no books to read, and no prescription of what to do and how to do it. I was required to give instructional help which I did but as I have no memory of the outcome I wonder what either of us learned. My university courses about atypical children were heavily influenced by child psychologists in Britain like Burt and Schonell, and by Professor Ralph Winterbourn who developed the psychological service for the New Zealand Department of Education and the counseling service for New Zealand secondary schools. I was appointed to teach a special class for mildly mentally retarded children, which was Winterbourn's special area at that time. I taught most of them to read with some success, was surprised at their progress, and wrote a paper about it. The literature review discussed the work of Monroe, Fernald, Gates, Burt, Schonell, and Helen M. Robinson, most of whom referred in some limited way to spelling and writing as well as reading. Winterbourn trained two reading specialists, Ruth Trevor who established reading clinics in New Zealand over the next 20 years, and Yvonne Malcolm, known especially for bringing the International Reading Association to New Zealand.

My plans in 1949 to study with Schonell in Britain were thwarted by his move to the University of Queensland, Australia and I went instead to the University of Minnesota and studied with Guy Bond (a student of Arthur Gates, whose "Improvement of Reading" is still on my bookshelf). Under Bond's supervision, I taught children with reading difficulties in my minor courses, completing my major in developmental child psychology. The courses I had planned to take in special education no longer existed, so I talked my way into the Institute of Child Welfare, and studied research on children and clinical child psychology. For personal interest I took "Theater for Children" in 1951 and still have my production script for a Chinese play with full stage design and costumes for three dragons, an interest never allowed to flourish.

The concepts of brain damage, brain dysfunction and learning disability were on the rise; Strauss and Lehtinen had published two challenging books, and Sam Kirk was in Chicago beginning his work in this area. Clinics were seen as the answer to severe reading difficulties from 1950–70 and psychological tests for assessment included the Illinois Test of Psycholinguistic Abilities and the Frostig Test of Visual Perception, new instruments designed to produce definitive diagnoses leading to prescriptions for instruction. With them came countermovements, weak by comparison, but destined to oust the clinical, diagnostic test approach in due course (Wiederholt, 1977).

While at home with my own preschool children in the 1950s I taught remedial reading at my kitchen table overlooking the Rangitoto channel and particularly remember two interesting 11-year-old boys. After a slow start each made alarming progress, alarming because it was unexplainable by existing theories about learning to read. It is food for thought when one's theories do not explain one's successes!

Schonell's research from Australia was widely read in the British Commonwealth. Canada had a strong group of academics leading clinical and classroom programs, and the research of people like Daniels and Diack (1956) was influencing approaches to reading problems in the United Kingdom. Led by medical advocates the concept of dyslexia and the teaching programs it spawned spread across the globe in this period.

At this time in New Zealand the Chief Inspector of Primary Schools, Brian Pinder, concluded that the existence of reading clinics diminished the responsibility of classroom teachers for literacy instruction and defined every teacher as a teacher of reading, which was, perhaps the origin of the sound and pervasive literacy teaching of classroom teachers in the New Zealand Primary School today.

By the mid-1970s the critique of the special psychological tests gained ground, followed in the 1980s by the sociologists' strident attack on the concept of learning disability and how it was being overgeneralized to populations to whom it probably did not apply. Psychological publications stressed that the numbers of people being labeled as having difficulties increased but programs did not demonstrate a reduction in the size of the problem (Gittleman, 1985).

I published my first critique of the learning disability concept in Clay, 1972 and I was ready to put the brake hard down on the overgeneralization of legitimate conditions to children who did not need the labels. I began what I describe as my long and lonely swim against the accepted tide of theory and practice. In Clay, 1987 I published a stronger statement called "Learning to be learning disabled" presenting arguments about the definition problem, the diagnostic tools and the failure of this path of research to provide programs which reduced the size of the problem. Reports appeared showing that increasing numbers of people were being labeled in this way. Bluntly, I wanted to remove as many of these potentially learning disabled children from that category as I could. Today RR's challenge to teachers in the first year of school is "Take as many of the potential Reading Recovery children away from Reading Recovery as you can by teaching them well" and the appeal to psychologists and administrators is, "Give as many children as need it a second chance at literacy learning before you categorize or label them as special kinds of learners."

A growing disenchantment with learning disability gave way to a new popular diagnosis of attention deficit disorder (ADD) with questioning articles now appearing in major psychological journals.

Country by country. Briefly, what was happening in the countries where RR is now being tried out? (See Pinnell, this volume, pp. 638–654 for the situation in the United States.) New Zealand had high expectations from classroom teachers, and a diminishing number of reading clinics. The education system never adopted learning disability or dyslexia concepts but instead appointed Reading Resource Teachers to provide itinerant assistance to children with reading difficulties. These teachers supported and supplemented the classroom teachers' work. A voice for learning disability was maintained by the Specific Learning Disability (SPELD) organization of parents and interested public, who brought authorities from dyslexia or learning disability programs in the United States, Britain and Australia to annual conferences in New Zealand.

In Australia the position was similar with greater diversity from state to state, a stronger learning disability movement, and exploration of new teaching strategies at different sites by people like Kemp, Elkins and members of the staff of Macquarie University. A strong countermovement toward improving classroom teaching grew up with an emphasis on books, language, messages and writing, an example of a defiant call encountered in several countries that quality classroom teaching was the way to reduce and eliminate reading difficulties. In part they were right.

In Canada the movement to improve classroom teaching was supported by authorities in the reading field like Robertson, Jenkinson, Downing, and innovative academics at the Ontario Institute for Educational Studies like Smith, Wallach, Wells, and Olson, with support from visiting British authorities on literature and writing like Meek, Britton, and Wilkinson. In each province there was strong clinical leadership from many people like Grace Walby in Manitoba.

In England opposing theories flourished side by side. Dyslexia still has a strong hold today in the treatment of reading difficulties drawing new energy from research in neurological science. Research from Oxford and Cambridge by Bryant, Bradley, and Goswami led many to design programs on a most-important-single-variable assumption that reading difficulties would be overcome by increasing phonemic awareness. This nudged a long-overdue revision of unsound practices in the teaching of "phonics" as if English had a regular orthography. On the other hand the ideas of those with a literary theory of learning to read encouraged a faith in children's ability to learn if they were read to, from good trade storybooks, a move which became linked with a goal of working with each child individually until she or he became a reader and writer. This confused the essential need for "individual teaching for some" with the difficulty of delivering it effectively to all. Most children do not need it; some do. For some people psychological theories and psychologists were seen as the problem, perhaps the cause, behind reading difficulties. Therefore an admirable advocacy for reading stories which was needed in classroom programs became confused with the need of some learners to get extra and special help. Good classroom teaching will never suit every learner and something extra should be available for some.

The combined effects of teaching practices, theories, academic endeavour, and public and political awareness lead countries to travel along different paths in evolving improved literacy programs. Some cross-fertilization of ideas is accompanied by serious doubts that what works in one place could work in another but there have been strong movements driven by the assumptions of teachers and teacher educators, each emphasizing their own "significant variables" for primary school literacy learning. Notable is the doggedness with which Australia, New Zealand, and Canada, while strongly influenced by British and American practices and publications, have striven for the local integrity of what they do, evolving programs which do not mimic the perplexing diversity of practices in England, or the polarity and pendulum swings of change that occur in the United States.

Reading Recovery's History

In New Zealand. It was 25 years after my time in Minnesota before I began on RR. I taught Developmental Psychology and clinical child psychology for 30 years to educators and educational psycholosists, and carried out a variety of research projects, some directed toward early literacy. I became involved with the International Reading Association in Auckland, and was elected President of this Association 30 years later in 1992–93. My connections with the United States were rewarding because I learned a lot about my own country during my stay there, and about cultural differences, and how to switch from culture to culture. This prepared me in small ways for my recent challenges.

Reading Recovery started in 1976 at the University of Auckland in a lean-to behind an old house in Wynyard Street with one teacher teaching hard-to-teach children behind a one-way screen and myself observing and recording. We

discarded what did not work, related what worked to existing theoretical writing, enlarged the team in 1977 to seven, continued the sifting process, wrote a teachers' manual and felt that we had "something that worked." We got permission to carry out field trials in schools with five teachers paid by the National Department of Education. We selected schools in average to poor areas, varying in size and in organization, avoiding the advantaged districts. Principals released their best teachers for the job and we began the development of our several levels of training for RR professionals.

By the end of 1977, we had a well-documented miracle full of surprises. The research design had been carefully selected not in ignorance of traditional research designs but to answer the relevant questions at that point in time. Five issues were considered.

(1) The questions were: "What was possible for the lowest achievers? What percentage could learn to read? Could any children reach average levels for class? and if so what percentage could reach such levels?" The theoretical question was "Could we take children who were falling further and further behind their age / class peers and teach them to do what competent children were learning to do" as described by Clay (1966, 1972)?

(2) No competing programs existed. Therefore, research designs comparing programs (such as a quasi-experimental design with randomized groups) would only answer the question, "Was it better than an alternative program?" We needed to ask, "How do the outcomes compare (a) with the individual's past record of progress?" and (b) "Where were individuals in relation to the class group?" Such questions continue to be critical in evaluations of RR.

(3) At that time the experimental designs were not recommended as appropriate for an extreme tail-end segment of the total population.

(4) Success could not be judged by standardized tests in New Zealand at the time of the initial research (a) because none were available for the age group and (b) because RR is directed toward schools managing their own programs in the interests of their local population and not necessarily matching national norms. All the other children in the same classes, that is, all the better performers, create the school-based relative standard for entry and outcome against which the program's effectiveness in practice was judged.

(5) Statistical analyses of changes across groups would be mere approximations of success which could not guide the clinical treatments of individuals, so real-world differences recorded as data for individual cases were essential.

In this first study we were also investigating the way the program might work in schools and we deliberately placed as few organizational constraints as possible on the RR teachers' decisions; we asked them to tell us how to make the program work in schools of different sizes and populations.

The results of every child who entered the program, not excluding anyone, were published in the manual for teachers (Clay, 1979, pp. 74–79) contrary to misreporting in many reviews. Three group results were reported—Discontinued from the program, Not Discontinued, and the Comparison group for age/class peers in the same school. The Not Discontinued group included the seven children who were referred to psychologists (reported in Clay, 1979, p. 80), the children who had short, incomplete programs which were continued in the next year, and four children who left the schools before their programs were completed. Thus the tables account for all children in the study. In a later study Clay and Tuck (1993b), showed that "carried over" children took the same time and had the same discontinuing rates as children who completed their programs within the school year.

The first research design apparently addressed administrators' questions about children's progress and demonstrated that they could have discontinued children in high numbers, with low numbers of referrable children, and that children who entered late in the school year would need to complete their programs in the subsequent year. Within a month the Director-General of Education called for a seminar to discuss the report's implications for the development and expansion of the program across the country. Where was this surprising solution which defied traditional parameters supposed to go? The notes I prepared for that seminar were pretty much on target for the next 10 years. I missed some of the problems but I had a pretty good view of what could happen in our small country, and anything beyond these shores was not to be dreamed of.

The snowball began to roll. One hundred teachers were trained in Auckland in 1979–80, the program began a slow expansion throughout New Zealand with national implementation across the country during 1983–88 (Clay, 1990) and the analysis set the model for an economical, national monitoring system based, not on a sample, but on the total population served and discontinuing rates (Kerslake, 1993). From a birth cohort of 50,000 6-year-olds in 1994 a prevention program was provided for 14,500 each year, about 9,000 of them became independent readers and writers, 3,400 were identified for completion of their lessons in the following school year and 1043 were referred for specialist reports (Kerslake, 1994). The efficiency of this implementation has had a good press (Frater & Staniland, 1994).

The emigration of Reading Recovery. In 1983 came the challenge to transfer RR first to Victoria, Australia and 18 months later to Columbus, Ohio. Could what worked in New Zealand be replicated in another country? Education is usually not considered to be exportable as education systems are organized and managed differently with different political agendas and a superior result from a program on home ground did not justify the optimism about replication in another education system. Thirty years after my experiences in Minnesota I was still deeply impressed with how different education is in different countries.

My talk on RR at the Darwin Reading Conference of the Australian Reading Association triggered developments in Victoria and Canberra. A Bendigo administrator, Peter Hunt, thought RR worth trialling. Joan Smith trained in Auckland, returning to Bendigo in 1984 with Jeanette Methven, a New Zealand tutor. Hints that this program would only work under

the close guidance of Marie Clay had to be laid to rest and I did not visit Victoria until the end of the year, leaving guidance of the development to the Director of Reading Recovery in New Zealand, Barbara Watson. Peter Geekie (1992) with Brian Cambourne studied the initial year of the program in Bendigo from the point of view of how teachers, school staff, parents and the community saw the program.

In sequence three trial training programs for tutors were initiated, in Victoria at the Bendigo College of Advanced Education, at La Trobe University, and at Melbourne University. Victoria did not train a RR trainer until 1994 but in some years tutors were sent to the Auckland College of Education for training. Parallel developments occurred in the Catholic schools, and in other Australian states—sometimes the lead has been taken by Catholic education and sometimes by the state system.

The Canberra system sent two tutors to New Zealand for training in 1986 and has run a system-wide implementation for 8 years in almost all its schools but only serving about 13% of its hard-to-teach children. This is called partial implementation when a school does not deliver the program to all who need it and this leads to a questioning of the program if the problems are not cleared by expansion of the coverage. Another early stronghold was establisred in Wagga Wagga. The New South Wales program began to expand in the late 1980s with help from the New Zealand National Trainer, and tutors on leave from New Zealand served both the State and Catholic education systems. Queensland now has an expanding program and Australia now has three RR trainers.

Australia made a unique contribution to RR by having a member speaking in the Federal Parliament sufficiently well-briefed by an alert tutor to have a description of the program entered into Hansard, the parliamentary record. Representations were also made to a Federal Parliamertary Commission which recommended two literacy programs, Reading Recovery and First Steps, and suggested that states might select one or the other! This was strange since if First Steps were to be directed to classrooms RR would still be useful as a backup supplementary program for those with literacy learning difficulties.

Note that early initiatives by educators came to the notice of State and national administrators by first making the program work in schools rather than by academic argument or espousal. This was probably the only possibility since the program turns its back on so much past thinking and practice.

From the early Australian experience we learned to adjust to some education system differences: different policies for entry to school, use of the first year of school as a preparatory program in contrast to the expectation that 5-year-olds would learn to read and write, variation of curriculum and materials with nothing like the many little story books in New Zealand classrooms, and concern that the program's assessment tasks for selection and progress checks might perform differently on "new soil."

In the United States and Australia we faced the challenge of getting teachers to teach differently, to use a theory predicated on the constructive child, and to hold complex variables in mind when making teaching decisions at all times.

The insistence that the teacher should be very observant of the learner's behavior made some Australian teachers uncomfortable, as if this were an intrusion on privacy to peer into and discuss the detail of a child's response but being observant has become accepted as essential in a program that helps children proceed along idiosyncratic paths.

By May 1984 colleagues in the United States were asking how to prepare for a September start when we had only just begun in Victoria. (The extensive research from the United States is reviewed in this volume by Pinnell, pp. 638–654.) In the United States the program faced a new variable, the existence of established provisions for children with reading difficulties at this age level. There were "reading teachers," and federally-funded programs for socially disadvantaged children, and programs for the "learning disabled," and a common practice of schools to employ paraprofessionals to work with children needing "extra help." Reading Recovery had to compete for the same pool of resources, and for the children to be served. The conflict emerged early in Ohio in one district with a strong skills-based program for children with literacy difficulties. Reading Recovery was criticized for not delivering success to every child, and the existing program claimed superior results.

In 1995 in the United States, "Over the last 10 years in 1,905 school districts and 5,523 schools Reading Recovery has accomplished what it was designed to do. A total of 88,323 individuals have … caught up to their grade-level peers…" (Pinnell, Lyons, & Jones, 1995). The program continues to expand and has a place in current discussions in the United States about special services in least restrictive environments for special needs children (Lyons, 1994, 1995).

Canada, benefiting from the proximity of Ohio State University, had tutors trained for British Columbia, Manitoba, Newfoundland, Nova Scotia, and Scarborough, Ontario which led to the creation of a Canadian National Training Institute in 1993, backed by sterling efforts from administrators. Canada had three trainers by 1996. The Canadian Royal Commission on Learning recently reported to the Minister of Education and Training, with recommendation 33 being:

> That no child who shows difficulty or who lags behind peers in learning to read be labelled 'learning disabled' unless and until he or she has received intensive individual assistance in learning to read, which had not resulted in improved academic performance (1994).

This is what we would like to see in all countries; give children a second chance for literacy learning in an individual program before they are labeled.

England's interest began later in 1989, starting in Surrey after several talks given in England between 1981 and 1989. Surrey found funds to train a tutor in New Zealand, who returned to set up a successful local implementation model backed by strong administrators in tough economic times (Wright, 1992). A training for tutors began in the UK in 1991, and over 2 years nine New Zealand Reading Recovery personnel helped the Institute of Education, University of London to mount training programs for teachers and tutors for geographically-spread sites in boroughs and counties. The Institute trained further tutors in 1993–94, and completed 3 pilot years with temporary support from the central government. The HMI report on the New Zealand program was an independent document of importance to developments in England and the program found its place in the National Commission on Education report "Learning to Succeed." Northern Ireland and Jersey have new programs and the first class of teachers for Wales have trained for English-medium schools. The Government also commissioned an independent research study (Sylva & Hurry, 1995).

On my computer I have copies of most of the United Kingdom press reports which have on the whole made our task difficult, but with the publication of the research commissioned by the government, RR's press in England has become positive. It took 3 years.

Politics in the United Kingdom induced a twist into the implementation of this program. It was delivered mostly to inner city schools recording the lowest scores, where many children had free lunches. Together politicians, economic issues and the predominant message of the press over 4 years pushed out of sight the fact that as almost every school has its children who have difficulties, almost every school requires a make-up program. *Resourcing should not be linked to poverty*; it should be based on learning need and all schools should have access according to demonstrated best learning needs, not socioeconomic need. The English counties like Surrey and Cheshire which have introduced Reading Recovery without government assistance will be free to demonstrate what the program can do for young children's literacy difficulties. The lowest achievers in any school, in any sector of society, need access to this supplementary program.

Reading Recovery operates in a window of opportunity through which an individual child passes only once, and that window has nothing to do with needing a free lunch. When RR is new, it is fragile and does not demonstrate clearly what it can achieve. It needs administrative leadership, and planful political support for best results in an education system.

The cutting edge of the research for RR is delivery in Spanish for Hispanic children in various parts of the United States and interest has been shown for other language adaptations, such as French for Canada. It is not possible to deliver this program immediately in another language as redevelopment is required to suit the characteristics of that language, and this involves much more than mere translation and takes about 3 years of trials. The Spanish experience has demonstrated that redevelopment takes time and must be done with care. But it is interesting because we can expect to get another level of understanding about the reading process across languages. Full translations into Spanish of the teachers' manuals are a current development and would open the doors to trials in Mexico, Central and South America led by bilingual tutors from the United States. Rather belatedly I have come to understand what we are struggling with in trying to make this program work in different countries. I think of each country, or state or province as a young river, on a course of development that is undergoing changes of a complex kind, and our early intervention is like a standard boat tossed into several different turbulent rivers and struggling to master the rapids and stay afloat in each of them. The central tenets of teaching on this program, "tentativeness, flexibility and problem-solving," are necessary.

THREE CONCENTRIC CIRCLES: IMPLEMENTING, TEACHING AND LEARNING

Evaluation studies of new educational developments do not necessarily arise from a theoretical hypothesis. Discovering what was workable in RR led to the construction of a theory to explain this, the reverse of most academic inquiry. On the one hand teachers had children they could not teach, and on the other, educational psychologists had too many referrals and few effective treatments for the hard-to-teach literacy problems. I worked with a team to find a research-based solution to these problems. The program was constructed by a problem-solving approach to an unstructured problem (although Robinson's (1993) authoritative work in this area is critical of the path we took). Theory did not drive practice; rather there was a circle of influence from practice to theory, and back to practice, informed and altered by data from day-by-day documentation of changes in children and an imperative that it must be workable in schools. No particular school of thought on literacy learning drove the exploration, but new work at the time included Bruner (1957, 1973), Cazden (1972), Chomsky (1972), Donaldson (1978), Graves (1978), Miller (1967), Read (1975), Smith (1971), the Russian school of developmental psychologists, and information processing psychologists like Rumelhart (1994).

A typical research review assumes that theory comes first, and is subsequently applied to practice, and we gamble on whether teachers and education systems can work from the theoretical account. I recommend that a critique of RR should reverse the cycle, start with the outer circle and ask:
(1) Can this education system put the program in place? and
(2) Can teachers be trained to teach children and achieve change? before asking the question from the inner circle,
(3) What theoretical assumptions do the data on children's learning support or challenge? Critiques usually try to answer question (3) but this is only relevant if the first two questions can be answered affirmatively. Readers of reviews should first be assured that the conditions in questions (1) and (2) have been met. Therefore, I will comment with this approach in mind.

The Outer Circle: Working in Schools Systems

At what age should RR be available? The general statement would be that selection should occur as soon after entry to school as we can reliably identify children falling behind their same age peers in the new classroom, and the timing has to be problem-solved in each education system. In New Zealand it is after 1 year of school (i.e., around the sixth birthday), after a fair chance to settle in the school, to adjust to demands, and to begin to learn. Two reasons for this timing are that (1) reviews of research reiterate that we cannot predict literacy problems well enough before instruction begins, and (2) a "multiple causation" theory includes lack of learning opportunities in life or school contexts as well as

problematic learning histories, and does not relate only to a child's potential for learning. Reliable prediction of which individuals will fail or succeed is not achieved before the onset of instruction.

Across the world further questions are raised. Should entry be earlier in places in the United Kingdom where the school entrant could enter school at just over 4 years of age? or do we wait until after 7 years for the child who begins schooling at 6 years?. What could be recommended for countries which begin school at 7 years? In the United States does the kindergarten count as school and what about half-day kindergarten?

Age of entry is an example of how implementation of the program must be problem-solved in every country because of differences in societies, in populations and in education systems, as well as politics, economic theories, social problems and religions. On the other hand a country's theories of child development and learning, of literacy learning, and of early intervention must also be taken into account. Surprisingly, about 6 years is a practical compromise and we have enough experience on the ground to show that this works. The factors to be weighed are age, time at school, general preparedness and some things about child development. We had to have learners with two qualities: first, what they knew had to be woven into a fabric of interacting response systems which they controlled (for islands of knowledge about specific aspects of literacy processing would not make an effective reader or writer) and second, the learners had to become relatively independent of teachers so that they could work well in classrooms.

The negative consequence of starting too early is giving individual teaching that would not have been needed if we had waited longer, and the negative results of waiting too long are that the time it takes to deliver an effective program lengthens the longer the children have been in formal instruction, and therefore fewer children can be served for the same teaching resource.

Absence of Teacher or Learner from Daily Lessons. This threatens the accelerative learning needed for children to catch up with their classmates. The difficulty of getting children to school every day requires attention but getting parental permission for the child to join the program offers an opportunity to negotiate for special help from the family to have the child at school. After several research studies the variable "teacher not available to teach" emerged as a bigger problem than child absence. Despite excellent reasons why the trained teacher should perform other duties in school or in society it is absolutely necessary for the RR children to receive a lesson a day. This frequent contact allows yesterday's responding to be still clear in the minds of both teacher and child. For schools this means release of an effective teacher for 2 hours a day (varied according to training status and the school's need) and without pulling that person off their allotted task. The potential for accelerated learning is reduced if the teacher is not available to teach daily. The lessons must occur in an intensive series and the same number of lessons spaced out over time is a poor substitute resulting in poorer learning.

The Length of the School Year. This determines how many days the teacher has to teach. Different models for three or four terms, and all-year-round schools can create difficulties with the "a lesson every day" demand.

The learning needs of individual children do not align with the school year of teaching. In New Zealand schools it was easy to continue to teach the children who were not yet ready to leave RR in the next school year, until they reached one of two outcomes, discontinued or referred. (Teacher leaders in the United States and Canada are called Tutors of Teachers in New Zealand, Australia, and the United Kingdom.) An incomplete series of lessons occurs only when a child leaves the school and attends a new school which does not provide RR assistance, a very rare occurrence in New Zealand. In some other countries like the United States with a shorter school year and different promotion practices it is often unworkable to continue RR help in the next school year, but solutions to this problem are being formulated.

How Long Does This Supplementary Program Take? The time in the program is surprisingly brief. With consistency across the world the time in an efficient program averages from 12 to 20 weeks thus providing a guideline within which to shape our expectancies and policies. The fact that individuals spend different lengths of time in the program is irritating for researchers and administrators; they would like a fixed number of treatments for all, a prescribed turnover point, "all change here," but the discontinuing criteria require a teacher to ensure, as best as she can, that a child is now sufficiently independent to survive in the classroom without further help. Reviewers also find it difficult to understand the flexibility with which this program adapts to individual learners so that time in the program was reported as 15 weeks for research convenience in one study (Center, Wheldall, Freeman, Outhred, McNaught, 1995) and 20–26 weeks in another (Sylva & Hurry, 1995). Unfortunately figures in reviews can become the reference for new research or implementations. The capacity of the program to adapt in length to the learning needs of individuals is critical to (a) learning and (b) effective implementation.

Discontinuing Rates Across Different Countries. Comparisons of the rate at which children leave this program at average levels of performance can be made within an education system but must be handled cautiously across countries. It is now clear that they depend on program delivery factors such as the average number of children passing through a half-hour teaching slot in the year, the length of the school year, and whether daily lessons are delivered. If the question is, "What percentage of the intake group will be discontinued?" then in the real world the following statistics apply.

No. of children a teacher serves in a year in a 30 min. teaching slot	No. of children with a full programme	Possible Discontinuing Rate
1	1	100%
2	1	50%
2	2	100%
3	2	67%

In each 30 minute teaching 'slot' New Zealand teachers tend to get two children out of the program and take a third child in, to be continued in the next school year. This is considered "best practice" and results in about 67% discontinued per calendar year! The Ministry of Education Research Division's annual figures published and available on request show, that in New Zealand 0.2–1.5% of the age cohort is referred for longer-term assistance in a calendar year (Clay, 1993b, p. 84).

This sampling of some of the implementation issues illustrates why a sound approach to evaluating the children's learning would be to start an evaluation by satisfying oneself and one's readers that the implementation of the RR program to be studied was an effective one.

The Second Circle: Training Teachers For Problem Solving

The training course for RR teachers is a year-long period of change. Change during that year is a unit of learning in itself. Geekie (1992) reported a shift over a year from widespread scepticism to obvious commitment among RR teachers and among schools. Teaching improves after training and more children are discontinued in less time. Research reports need to record how long a program has been in place together with details of teaching experience beyond training.

In all countries teachers bring to their teaching, assumptions which are sometimes country-specific and sometimes more general. Such assumptions call for small adjustments in training courses in each country, but because RR must not limit the progress of any child by its practices and policies all teachers are required to open up their local clusters of assumptions to new alternatives.

(1) Some assumptions are about *curriculum sequences* that should occur, including inflexible beliefs that a child must know (A) before she or he can try to do (B)! Assumptions like this underpin programs which teach a letter a day for a whole year in some kindergartens, or require children to know all letter-sound relationships before they try to read, or insist that children read before they try to write.

(2) Some assumptions are about *task difficulty* and the *assumed limitations for learning that children have.* There are assumptions about "*hard things*" that must be left until later (such as comprehension), or "*things that must come first*," or "*things that will require many repetitions.*" Teachers think, "It will be hard and I will have to help you," or "I will have to simplify it for you," or "I will have to instruct you until you can learn for yourself." A RR teacher must invite learners to deal with *complex texts,* to l*earn at a faster rate than average,* and to become independent learners who initiate, process, monitor, and self-correct, expanding their own literacy processing system while reading and writing independently.

These assumptions of curriculum sequence or teaching sequence are inappropriate in RR; they are assumptions devised for group instruction, and are not suited to individual learning, looking for a fast track to success and taking different paths to common outcomes. To accelerate the progress of a child with a low repertoire a teacher must find any route to the desired outcome and allow for the entire range of idiosyncratic competencies to support the struggling learner. A teacher must monitor her own assumptions about learning and about an individual child to take advantage of every incipient opportunity to "leap forward."

(3) On the other hand there are sets of assumptions which limit progress because they take for granted that all competencies needed for literacy behaviors will emerge in some natural way when the learner is ready, causing a teacher to wait for these emerging competencies to reveal themselves. Some teachers do not want to govern the amount of challenge in a reading text, nor consider a gradient of difficulty, nor think about how a new competency can be helped to emerge from what is already known. This is not the place to debate this matter in relation to classroom learning but these things are not true for those learners who, by definition and selection, are finding learning extremely difficult.

The challenges in training teachers lie in uncovering hidden assumptions made by teachers in each country that are antagonistic to the progress of hard-to-teach children. We need them to become more flexible and tentative, to observe constantly and alter their assumptions in line with what they record as the children work. They need to challenge their own thinking continually. Such change begins during their training year but teachers discontinue more children in the next 2 years as they become familiar with the program and how it can work. They learn to use the rationales for decision making which make the teaching and the organization of the program run more effectively. Due to the complexity of what is being learned, the individual learning trajectories of the children and the incomplete theory out of which teachers work, there will always be problems to solve. Teachers need to recognize that they start with diverse assumptions about learning to read and write and these differences are a strength within their collegial network.

In different countries there have been differing degrees of willingness to consult peers, and for tutors or trainers to form networks, to seek a second opinion, and to overcome the unreliability of one person's decision by pooling knowledge in network decision-making. Such consultation is self-correction behavior aimed at catching the errors in individual judgements; it is essential.

Sometimes the emphasis during training in sessions behind the one-way-screen is on putting what you see into words, but equally important is the articulation of how what you see conflicts with what you had assumed. Bringing the implicit, whether observed or assumed, into a verbal form which allows discussion and revision is an essential part of training in each country. As a College of Education Dean said to his peers,

> Reading Recovery has managed to operationalize that vague notion that teachers ought to reflect on their own practice. That behind the glass play by play analysis and the collegial debriefing with the teacher after her teaching session represent some of the

best teacher education I have witnessed in my 28 year history in the field (Pearson, 1994).

The Inner Circle: The Learning of the Children

Children's learning has not shown clear differences across countries, except for those created by different classroom programs (i.e., different learning opportunities) or associated with age. Culture and language have created interesting questions but no big problems.

Independent reviewers from the United States and the United Kingdom who are not inolved in devising or delivering RR, provide the following characterizations of the program's background theory. Both reviews say that Clay (1979) describes reading as "a message-gaining, problem-solving activity which increases in power and flexibility the more that it is practised." Wasik and Slavin (1993) list the components of the reading model as perceptual analysis, knowledge of print conventions, decoding, oral language proficiency, prior knowledge, inference making, reading strategies, metacognition, and error detection and correction strategies. They omit "visual" from perceptual analysis, translate phonemic awareness into decoding and create an unexplained metacognition component, all of which are imprecise and could mislead. They select three major theoretical principles for mention: (1) that reading is considered a strategic process that requires the integrating of letter–sound relationships, features of print, and language which is derived from the interaction of the reader's unique background and the print; (2) reading and writing are interconnected and the child must make the connections; and (3) children learn to read by reading and only by reading frequently can the child come to detect regularities and redundancies present in written language. I would not quarrel with the words used above or with the following. "There is no systematic presentation of phonics yet during the reading and writing activities letter–sound relationships are taught as one of the basic strategies for solving problems" (p. 183).

Sylva and Hurry (1995) reiterate the message-getting, problem-solving activity quoted above and add that children make use of a variety of strategies to help them in this problem-solving activity, the most central of which are: (1) their understanding of the concepts of print, (2) their phonological awareness of sounds in words and letters and letter strings on the page, (3) their understanding of the meaning of the text; and (4) their knowledge of syntax. "Meaning is not derived from the print alone but also from the knowledge of the world that readers bring to the task, for example, their knowledge of the language of books and language in general, their prior knowledge of the subject matter of the text, their ability to make inferences." The goal of RR is to help children to use all the skills and strategies that they have at their disposal (and to) "encourage children to monitor their own reading, detecting and correcting errors by checking responses against all possible strategies." This improves children's reading and writing "over a wide range of skills," described as a broad spectrum approach.

Against that reporting one can set less accurate accounts of RR's theory given by Center et al. (1995), Hiebert (1994),

Iversen and Tunmer (1993), Razinski (1995), Shanahan & Barr (1995). Center et al., for example report the theory in this way: "reading is viewed as a psycho-linguistic process in which the reader constructs meaning from print," and most readers would then place it in the wrong theoretical camp with psycho-linguistics rather than information processing.

Variants Within the Learning Theory. To be an effective program RR must be responsive to the discourse of new research and theory and not be locked into the theory of the late 1970s when it was developed (Pearson, 1994). In the early 1970's its practices may have appeared ahead of research in some areas but as more information and new theory becomes available, areas of uncertainty should be informed and practices should change. Three examples illustrate past or potential changes:

(1) Recent research on phonemic awareness called for little change in actual procedures because in 1976–77 we observed that children who had extreme difficulty with "hearing sounds in words" needed effective teaching which was built into the program from the beginning, an example of practice ahead of theory. New information confirmed that practice; it changed what teachers read during training, and it led to an increase in emphasis on the reciprocity of reading and writing (see Wasik & Slavin, 1993).

(2) In one area of uncertainty we still search for a stronger theoretical basis for how the child weaves visual perception learning into his early construction of inner control over literacy and recent eye movement research inches us closer to this possibility (Rayner & Pollatsek, 1989). The reader cannot use his phonemic awareness in the service of reading or writing without some new visual perception operations!

(3) A thorough review of the arguments about onset and rime, and analogy clarified how children can develop effective procedures for handling three different categories of spelling clusters in English that are phonologically regular, orthographically regular, or irregular, with the same cognitive strategy. This allowed for better teaching in the "making and breaking" segment of the lesson (which existed in the first edition of the procedures manual) and without either a prescriptive teaching sequence or an undue stress upon regularity and word families that would be inappropriate for the English language.

The dynamically changing theory is concerned with how we understand the sequence of changes in ways in which children process complex arrays of information as they learn to read and write. A multivariate theory of such changes (rather than a single causal theory) forces an openness to new knowledge. If "Reading Recovery helps children to integrate a wide range of skills involved in reading and writing" (Sylva & Hurry, 1995) then there are a myriad of unknowns hidden in the verb "to integrate" when it is combined with a developmentalist's interest in "change over time." Much of it has to do with how and what the constructive learner learns from his own decision processes when problem-solving continuous text. What is challenging for theory construction is that during the time of reading and writing acquisition each one of the multivariate processes is in a formative stage.

New editions of teachers' text covering theory (Clay, 1991), assessments (Clay, 1993a), and teaching procedures (Clay, 1993b) are essential for a program that is evaluating, and responding to shifts in available knowledge.

Variants from Outside the Program. When variants which are theoretically incompatible with the program are introduced into the program as research variables and good results reported, it is not acceptable merely to claim that the variant produced the good outcomes for it is plausible to suppose that the broad program may have sustained progress despite the variant. Hatcher (1994) for example, introduced a systematic, detailed and prescriptive phonological training into his recommended program and, unless we are shown otherwise, one might hypothesize that the wrap-around RR program carried the variant to its success.

Children with English as a Second Language. It has been reported that these children are, or should be excluded from selection (Hiebert, 1994). This does not happen in the five countries where their progress has been watched. They are probably the group of children who derive most benefit in subsequent years from having had this supplement early because language was the major block to their learning and they had 30 minutes every day with a teacher who increased their time for talking and personalized their instruction. Hobsbaum's study (1995) from England reported satisfactory progress for children who spoke more than one language.

Reading Recovery in Another Language. If special care is taken to redevelop the observation (assessment) tasks and the instructional procedures then the "window of opportunity" for an early intervention in literacy learning appears able to cross language barriers and remain effective. For children learning to read and write English no important differences appear in what it is the children need to learn to do in different countries. However, since teaching began in Spanish (Escamilla, 1994) we have had to consider that there is more involved than theoretical concepts and assessment tasks. The timing in acquisition and the emphases during instruction for effective processing in another language might change. After an early discovery in studies of early writing that English-speaking children hear the consonants of the language easily and have problems with hearing the vowels and by contrast, Spanish-speaking children hear the vowels and miss out the consonants at first (Ferreiro & Teberosky, 1982) our current questions are about (a) the role of the syllable in Spanish literacy acquisition, (b) whether the linguistic discovery of onset and rime applies to Spanish? (c) how to help beginning readers cope with many long words in their first books? and (d) for languages with much more regular letter–sound relationships than English (Spanish, Maori, and German, for example) how might RR teachers tell whether the learner who has become a rapid decoder of regular phoneme–letter relationships is taking full account of meaning and language structure? These aspects of processing may be more readily observed in the oral reading of English than in more regular languages.

A Possible Neglect of Writing. Progress in RR is measured in terms of both reading and writing progress and the child is expected to survive back in the classroom in both curriculum areas. A large body of research shows that readers and writers have to develop phonemic awareness, and build the use of the sound system of their spoken dialect and language into their developing network of strategies for two similar but different processing systems, reading and writing. Researchers who continue to separate reading and writing and their respective theories, do not model the actual or potential links between these two activities, and reviewers tend to skip over the writing in RR and its contributions. If children can use their knowledge about reading and writing to support each other then these two activities have reciprocal effects on each other. Teachers with very different assumptions can retard the progress of children in reading when they skip the writing or give it minimal attention, assuming that they should and can give priority to reading and attend to writing as a later learning task.

CONCLUSIONS

A good review will be referred to when the original studies are forgotten; it summarizes the position to date and acts as a bulwark saving readers from the need to return to original sources. Reviewers therefore have a responsibility to understand and report previous research accurately before biasing the subsequent course of practice, research, and theory with their conclusions. Whether we like it or not Herber (1994) has shown that we do not usually review back more than 21 years and it is 19 years since RR began its development and 16 years since the first reports were available. Already the decade of the 1970s is outside the reviewer's ken; therefore, while this is not the place for a meta-analysis of reviews it is important to stress that, internationally, accurate reviewing is very important and seldom achieved.

To take just one example, several reviews echo the claim that RR only used in-program tests and had no standardized test as a beyond-program measure (Center et al., 1995) but that problem was recognized from the beginning. Training sites have used local standardized instruments; the Burt test from NZCER in New Zealand; in the United States the most successful being the Woodcock Reading test; and in England the British Intelligence Scale (Reading), although this test is not available for use by teachers. Outside the United States some favor the Neale Reading Test but as it has four unconnected and not comparable standardizations at this time, a reader needs to be told clearly which editions and which norms are being reported.

In research studies across the world measurement instruments are added to the RR measures for several reasons: (1) to test alternative theories; (2) to measure outcomes on standardized measures which were designed usually with different theories in mind; (3) because new instruments become available; and (4) to allow for comparisons across populations and even countries. What the researcher, administrator, and teacher understand by the test labels will depend on the theory they are committed to, the implementation question they have in mind, or the practices they have experience with. One can "read" the phrase "a test of explicit phonics" in nine or ten different ways depending on one's professional role (theorist, teacher or administrator) and if there is no explicit specification of what is taught, how it is taught, and how it is embedded and used in the acts of reading and writing one is left to one's own constructed interpretation. Is the achievement the memorizing of words (Sylva & Hurry, 1995), or a metacognitive awareness that makes sense of phenomena like down / blown or light / bite in English, or a set for diversity, or elaborate teaching sequences (Hatcher, 1994)? Could this be abstracted to the principle of knowing how to use analogy with the flexibility to say, "If it is not like this word I know then it might be like that one," a simple tactic to achieve many complicated solutions (Clay, 1993b)?

One-to-one tutoring as reviewed by Allington (1994), Pikulski (1994), and Wasik and Slavin (1993), is a potentially effective means of preventing student reading failure. It deserves an important place in discussons of reform in preventive, compensatory, remedial, and special education strategies. "If we know how to ensure that students will learn to read in the early grades, we have an ethical and perhaps legal responsibility to see that they do so. Preventive tutoring can be an alternative for providing a reliable means of abolishing illiteracy among young children who are at risk for school failure" (Wasik & Slavin, 1993, p.158).

High rates of success for RR have encouraged a frequent error in education, the error of over-extension of its potential and consequential misapplications. It would be unfortunate to lose the specialist solution because of this. No one claimed that RR would be an effective solution to anything but the learning problems of the lowest achievers in the second year of school; no one claimed it would improve the *mean scores* of the age cohort; no one claimed that it would provide the answers to all literacy difficulties; no one claimed its theory to hold for all literacy learning.

Complex issues require specialist solutions. An educational treatment finely tuned to a particular challenge should not be expected to solve all literacy problems. Its success is captured in the Sylva and Hurry synopsis "...a powerful intervention over a broad spectrum in the short term, and for the most disadvantaged and the lowest achieving children.... Reading Recovery was more powerful even one year after the end of the intervention for the disadvantaged children and it is highly effective (also) in changing the behaviours of those who fail to discontinue." This demonstrates something more like "a change of status theory" of literacy acquisition, the child going through the door into the world of written language rather than a theory which emphasizes a slow accumulation of knowledge, and that change of status might be considered a citizen's right. We want to know much more about how tutoring works and how to maximize its effectiveness (and minimize its cost).

The explorations of teacher training and support, the delivery of teaching, the management at the school, district and state / country level of the program demonstrate that any further research on RR should, for economy's sake, study the outcomes in learning only in places where it can be established that: (1) the teachers are in or beyond their second year of teaching after training and are part of the recommended support system offered by tutors / teacher leaders, and (2) the program is implemented according to state or national guidelines. The schools should follow the local guidelines for program delivery and the implementation should be in its fourth year. I am still inclined to the opinion that a follow-up study should follow the childen over time together with the age / class group in their school for that is the valid comparison group against whom their entry and exit criteria are judged. Under the above conditions it would be good judgment to carry out a cost effectiveness study.

With that approach in place and with any other qualifications appropriate for real-world research, academic researchers might be justified in using the changes in learning to shape and evaluate theoretical constructs about literacy learning.

Such choice conditions are unlikely for, as the then Dean of the College of Education, University of Illinois, David Pearson (1994) reported, he searched with others for 2 years for financial and / or political support to conduct a substantive and effective cost-benefit analysis of RR to "alleviate the lingering doubts of sympathetic supporters and to disarm opponents," but without success. An alternative model used

in the Rowe (1995) study from Victoria, Australia provides an example of a well designed follow-up study.

In this early intervention program 6-year-olds become competent 7-year-old readers and writers. It will not help older children become anything but 7-year-old readers. Therefore sound school reading programs for 8–18-year-olds are still necessary to take full advantage of the foundation skills that RR establishes.

Reading Recovery must have what Wilson and Daviss (1994) call "the power of the redesign process in industry":

- capitalizing on success
- improving quality
- expanding usefulness and
- keeping the selling price of each unit as affordable as possible for as many consumers as possible.

They warn that the redesign process does not develop without normal growing pains.

One thing we have learned internationally. Children do not have to be slow learners. We have created and categorized slow learning children by the ways in which we package and deliver our age-bound cohort structure for instruction. Reading Recovery set out to deliver learning opportunities differently. And that perhaps is the general message which this paper can contribute to the topic of this volume.

References

Allington, R. L. (1994). The schools we have. The schools we need. *The Reading Teacher, 48*(1), 14–29.

Bruner, J. S. (1957). On perceptual readiness. *Psychological Review, 64*, 123–152.

Bruner, J. S. (1973). Organization of early skilled action. *Child Development, 44*, 1–11.

Canadian Royal Commission on Learning, (1994). *For the love of learning*. Ontario: Ministry of Education and Training.

Cazden, C. (1972). *Child Language and Education*. Cambridge: Harvard University Press.

Center, Y., Wheldall, K., Freeman, L., Outhred, L., & McNaught, M. (1995). An evaluation of reading recovery. *Reading Research Quarterly, 30*(2), 240–263.

Chomsky, C. (1972). Stages in language development and reading exposure. *Harvard Educational Review, 22*, 1–33.

Clay, M. M. (1966). *Emergent reading behaviour*. Doctoral dissertation: University of Auckland Library, Auckland.

Clay, M. M. (1972). Learning disorders. In S. J. Havill & D. R. Mitchell (Eds.). *Issues in New Zealand Special Education*. (pp. 230–243) Auckland: Hodder and Stoughton.

Clay, M. M. (1972). *Reading: The patterning of complex behaviour*. Auckland: Heinemann Education.

Clay, M. M. (1979). *The early detection of reading difficulties: A diagnostic survey with Reading Recovery procedures*. Auckland: Heinemann Education.

Clay, M. M. (1987). Learning to be learning disabled. *New Zealand Journal of Educational Studies, 22*(2), 155–174.

Clay, M. M. (1990). The Reading Recovery programme, 1984–88;

Coverage, outcomes, and Education Board district figures. *New Zealand Journal of Educational Studies, 25*(1), 61–70.

Clay, M. M. (1991). *Becoming literate: The construction of inner control*. Auckland: Heinemann Education.

Clay, M. M. (1993a). *An observation survey of early literacy development*. Auckland: Heinemann Education.

Clay, M. M. (1993b). *Reading Recovery: A guidebook for teachers in training*. Auckland: Heinemann Education.

Clay, M. M., & Tuck, B. (1990). *A study of Reading Recovery subgroups*. Report to the Ministry of Education Research Division, Wellington. Republished in abbreviated form in Clay, (1993b) above.

Daniels, J. C., & Diack, H. (1956). *Progress in reading*. Nottingham: University of Nottingham, Institute of Education.

Donaldson, M. (1978). *Children's Minds*. Glasgow: Fontana.

Escamilla, K. (1994). Descubriendo la lectura: An early intervention literacy program in Spanish. *Literacy, Teaching and Learning: An International Journal of Early Literacy, 1*(2), 77–90.

Ferreiro, E., & Teberosky, A. (1982). *Literacy Before Schooling*. Portsmouth, NH: Heinemann Educational Books.

Frater, G., & Staniland, B. (1994). *Reading Recovery in New Zealand: A report from the office of Her Majesty's Chief Inspector of Schools (Ofsted reports)* London: Her Majesty's Stationery Office. Reprinted in *Literacy, Teaching and Learning: An International Journal of Early Literacy*, (1994), *1*(1), 143–162.

Geekie, P. (1992). Reading Recovery: It's not what you do, its the way that you do it. In M. Jones & E. Baglin Jones, (Eds.), *Learning to behave: Curriculum and whole school management approaches to discipline*, (pp. 170–188). London: Kegan Paul.

Gittleman, R. (1985). Controlled trials of remedial approaches to reading disability. *Journal of Child Psychology and Child Psychiatry, 26*, 167–192.

Graves, D. (1978). *Balance the basics: Let them write*. New York: Ford Foundation.

Hatcher, P. J. (1994). *Sound linkage: An integrated programme for overcoming reading difficulties*. London: Whurr.

Herber, H. (1994). Professional connections: Pioneers and contemporaries in reading. In R. B. Ruddell, M. R. Ruddell & H. Singer, (Eds.), *Theoretical models and processes of reading*. Newark, DE: International Reading Association.

Hiebert, E. (1994). Reading Recovery in the United States: What difference does it make to an age cohort? *Education Researcher, 23*(9), 15–25.

Hobsbaum, A. (1995). Reading Recovery in England. *Literacy, Teaching and Learning: An International Journal of Early Literacy, 1*(2), 21–40.

Iversen, S. J., & Tunmer, W. E. (1993). Phonological processing skills and the Reading Recovery program. *Journal of Educational Psychology, 85*, 112–126.

Kerslake, J. (1993). A summary of the 1992 data on Reading Recovery. *The Research Bulletin* (May). Wellington: Ministry of Education. (Also annual summaries for 1994, 1995, and 1996).

Lyons, C. (1994). Reading Recovery and learning disability issues, challenges, and implications. *Literacy, teaching and learning: An international journal of early literacy, 1*(1) 81–93.

Lyons, C. (1995). Reducing retention and learning disability placement through Reading Recovery: An educationally sound, cost-effective choice. In R. L. Allington & S. A. Walmsley (Eds.) *No quick fix: Redesigning literacy programs in America's elementary schools*. New York: Teachers College Press.

Miller, G. A. (1967). *The psychology of communication*. New York: Basic Books.

Pearson, D. (1994). Notes on Reading Recovery Opportunities and Obligations. Speech to Deans of Colleges of Education with Reading Recovery training Programmes. Personal communication.

Pikulski, J. J. (1994). Preventing reading failure: A review of five effective programs. *The Reading Teacher, 48*(1), 30–39.

Pinnell, G. S., Lyons, C., & Jones, N. (1995). Response to Hiebert: What difference does it make? *Network News (Winter)*. Columbus, OH: Reading Recovery Council of North America.

Rayner, K., & Polletsek, A. (1989). *The Psychology of reading*. Englewood Cliffs, NJ: Prentice-Hall.

Razinski, T. (1995). Commentary: On the effects of Reading Recovery: A response to Pinnell, Lyons, DeFord, Bryk and Seltzer. *Reading Research Quarterly, 30*(2) 264–270 / 276–7.

Read, C. (1975). *Children's categorization of speech sounds in English*. Urbana, Illinois: National Council of Teachers of English.

Robinson, V. (1993). *Problem-based methodology*. Oxford: Pergamon Press.

Rowe, K. J. (1995). Factors affecting students' progress in reading: Key findings from a longitudinal study. *Literacy, teaching and learning: An international journal of early literacy, 1*(2) 21–40.

Rumelhart, D. (1994). Toward an interactive model of reading. In R. B. Ruddell, M. R. Ruddell & H. Singer (Eds.). *Theoretical models and processes of reading*. (pp. 864–894) Newark, DE: International Reading Association.

Shanahan, T., & Barr R. (1995). Reading Recovery: An independent evaluation of the effects of an instructional intervention for at-risk learners. *Reading Research Quarterly, 30*(4) 958–997.

Smith, F. (1971). *Understanding Reading*. New York: Holt, Rinehart & Winston.

Sylva, K., & Hurry, J. (1995). *Early intervention in children with reading difficulties: An evaluation of reading recovery and a phonological training*. (Short and Long Reports). London: Thomas Coram Research Unit, University of London.

Wasik, B. A., & Salvin, R. E. (1993). Preventing early reading failure with one-to-one tutoring: A review of five programs. *Reading Research Quarterly, 28*, 179–200.

Wiederholt, J. L. (1977). Interaction between special and regular educators: Serving the mildly handicapped. *Journal of Special Education, 11*(2), 151–200.

Wilson, K. G., & Daviss, B. (1994). *Redesigning education*. New York: Henry Holt.

Wright, A. (1992). Evaluation of the first British Reading Recovery programme. *British Educational Research Journal, 18*(4) 351–368.

CHANGE THROUGH COLLABORATION: THE BOSTON UNIVERSITY–CHELSEA PUBLIC SCHOOLS PARTNERSHIP IN LITERACY

Jeanne R. Paratore and Roselmina Indrisano

BOSTON UNIVERSITY

In 1989, Boston University entered into a historic contract with the Chelsea Public Schools, agreeing to manage all aspects of its educational system for the next 10 years. Under the agreement, elected officials delegated the authority granted to them by the city charter to a university appointed management team through June 1998. The school committee retained the right to review all actions of the management team, and by a two-thirds vote, to override any action of the management team. Also, by a simple majority, the agreement established the school committee's right to terminate the partnership. Further, the governor established an oversight panel for monitoring the university's compliance with laws governing the management of the public school systems.

As described in a report to the legislature (Sears, 1994), 17 long-term goals, listed in Table 56C–1, were identified for the partnership. Initiatives and activities designed to achieve these goals are many and varied. Several articles and reports describing specific programs have been published (see, for example, Indrisano, & Paratore, 1994). This chapter will address activities of the partnership only as they relate to teaching and learning in literacy.

WHAT DID WE KNOW AS THE PARTNERSHIP BEGAN?

In 1987 one year before the signed agreement between the Chelsea Public Schools and Boston University, an evaluation team from Boston University conducted a comprehensive review of educational opportunities in the city of Chelsea. As part of this process, a team of literacy professionals, including Boston University faculty, graduate students and in-service teachers from area urban and suburban schools, visited 55 elementary classrooms and interviewed 21 teachers, gathering information about instructional practices in reading and writing. In its final report, the literacy study team concluded that the children of Chelsea were members of a caring and concerned educational community; most classrooms were organized and serious, and children were clearly aware of instructional routines; transitions from one activity to another were generally orderly and efficient. At the same time, however, it was clear that instructional practices in literacy had not kept pace with current research and theory. Among the many observations, three major concerns emerged. First, in almost every classroom, children were tracked in three reading groups, each instructed with a different level of the basal reading program, with substantially more than half of the children placed in below-grade-level texts. Overwhelming research evidence suggested that this practice was harmful for many children (Allington, 1984; Good, & Marshall, 1984; Slavin, 1986). The negative findings reported so frequently in professional literature were on display in most of the classrooms: when compared to their higher performing peers, children in low-ability groups spent far more time reading words in isolation, spent more time reading workbook pages and less time reading connected text, and spent more time answering low-level questions.

Second, reading instruction was centered on assignment of selections from the reading anthology, followed by oral

A version of this chapter has been published in the *Journal of Education,* Vol. 176, a themed issued on the Boston University–Chelsea Public Schools Partnership.

TABLE 56C–1. Boston University-Chelsea partnership goals

1. Revitalize the curriculum of the city's school system.
2. Establish programs for the professional development of school personnel and for the expansion of learning opportunities for parents.
3. Improve test scores of students in the school system.
4. Decrease the dropout rate for students in the school system.
5. Increase the average daily student attendance rate for the school system.
6. Increase the number of high school graduates from the school system.
7. Increase the number of high school graduates from the school system that go on to attend four-year colleges.
8. Increase the number of job placements for graduates of the school system.
9. Develop a community school program through which before-school, afterschool, and summer programs are offered to students in the school system and through which adult education classes for inhabitants of the city are offered.
10. Identify and encourage the utilization of community resources.
11. Establish programs that link the home to the school system.
12. Decrease teacher absenteeism in the school system.
13. Improve the financial management of the school system and expand the range of operating funds available to the school system.
14. Increase salaries and benefits for all staff, including raising the teacher salary average to make it competitive with the statewide average.
15. Construct effective recruiting, hiring, and retention procedures for all staff members.
16. Establish student assessment designs and procedures that are of assistance in monitoring programs and that act as incentives for staff members in each school.
17. Seek to expand and modernize physical facilities in the school system.

short-answer responses and the completion of workbook pages. Opportunities for students to work independently consisted primarily of workbook pages and worksheets; children rarely had opportunities to talk, and were seldom encouraged to build on their knowledge as a way to prepare for reading or as a bridge to written composition; they had few opportunities to write and virtually no instruction in the writing process. These practices were inconsistent with evidence that children learn best in classrooms where they are provided with regular and sustained instruction in the processes that will lead them toward independence in reading and writing (e.g., Graves, 1983; Tierney, & Cunningham, 1984).

Third, classrooms were generally not "print-rich" environments. The primary, and often the only, text the children read was a basal reader. With very few exceptions, when classroom bookshelves were available at all, they held instructional textbooks, usually outdated. There were few books for recreational reading, and those that were available were typically very old and usually not appropriate with regard to either students' reading or interest levels. In many classrooms, books were stacked on top of each other, suggesting that students were not invited or encouraged to select from even the few available titles. Outside of the classroom, the school

libraries held limited resources with few high-quality, multicultural children's books. It was clear that children lacked environments that would demonstrate how books and print could entertain and sustain them and how reading and writing could be used to help meet social needs in and out of school.

While these observations were clearly discouraging, interviews with teachers were encouraging. In interview after interview, teachers cited lack of opportunity for professional development as a major concern. These were not teachers who were resistant to change. Rather, these were teachers whose professional setting had offered them few opportunities and resources to explore new educational practices. They were eager to examine instructional issues and to explore ways to improve their students' achievement.

To begin the work, teachers and university faculty identified and planned frequent, systematic, school-based opportunities in collegial settings to explore effective instructional practices in literacy. Then, within these settings, the instructional issues that caused the greatest immediate concern were explored.

HOW DID WE WORK TOGETHER?

...no innovation has a realistic chance of succeeding unless teachers are thoroughly involved in the process, unless teachers are able to express, define, and address problems as they see them, unless teachers come to see the innovation or the change as theirs. The ultimate outcome of the innovation (or of a replication, we could add) depends on when and how teachers become part of the decision to initiate change. (Moll, 1992, p. 229)

From the beginning it was understood that the success of the partnership would depend upon a true collaboration between classroom teachers and university faculty. It must be said that the unprecedented nature of the partnership and the resulting confusion over roles and responsibilities made it difficult, at first, for teachers to trust that collaboration was the goal. However, 5 years later, teachers and faculty involved in classroom change in literacy agreed that the work is best described as coteaching.

Guiding Principles

Steps toward change in literacy instruction were built on a set of principles that guided initial efforts and that continued to be important to the partnership. First, the goals for professional development were set collaboratively. The concerns of teachers and university faculty were discussed openly; priorities were agreed upon and a plan of action was negotiated. Second, it was understood that the collaboration between Chelsea teachers and university faculty would be long-term; the 10-year term of the university–school partnership established by the contractual agreement ensured an ongoing commitment of resources and time. Third, as described by Goldenberg and Gallimore (1991), effective change is based on an "interplay between research knowledge and local knowledge," (p. 2), the latter defined as the understanding that comes from direct experience in the classroom and community. The instructional models that became the basis for classroom literacy instruction emerged from examination and discussion of current research and theory, and the reality of the classrooms in which they would be implemented.

Professional Development Opportunities

Few of the early efforts toward professional development were comprehensive, system-wide efforts. In an attempt to diminish the widespread belief that Boston University was involved in a "takeover" of the schools, initial meetings grew out of specific invitations from either individuals or small groups of teachers or from an administrator. As a result, in the beginning years of the partnership, the professional development initiatives in literacy were sometimes unevenly distributed throughout the city, since teachers and administrators in some buildings simply initiated more requests for assistance than those in others did . This is not to suggest that the beginnings were unproductive . In fact, concerted efforts in a smaller number of grades and classrooms led to the development and refinement of instructional models and to the emergence of teachers who quickly became viewed as "resident-experts" by their colleagues. By the beginning of the fifth year, administrators, teachers, and university faculty codeveloped a systematic, sustained, district-wide plan for introducing effective instructional practices in literacy.

The progress from individual or small group to system-wide efforts was marked by a series of professional development opportunities. They included: summer institutes; classroom demonstrations; city-wide in-service sessions; courses offered on-site and at the university, the latter often supported by scholarships; school-based seminars; curriculum committees; internships in the university's assessment center; institutes for administrators; participation and presentations at local, regional and international conferences; and city-wide grade-level bimonthly seminars. It is not possible to provide a detailed description of all these activities, therefore only those that have been most productive will be described.

The first professional development opportunity offered to the teachers was a summer institute in literacy, one of four planned for the core curriculum areas. This opportunity was offered on a voluntary basis. A major goal of the literacy institute was to discuss current research and its application to the classroom. To implement these understandings, teachers prepared a series of model lessons at kindergarten, primary and intermediate grade levels for teaching fiction and exposition. At the end of the institute, the teachers wrote to their colleagues to introduce the lessons that would be distributed to the entire staff.

Following this introductory session, a group of 1st- and 2nd-grade teachers from one building asked if they could continue to meet with university faculty during the school year to explore issues and concerns in literacy instruction. Of particular interest was developing an integrated model for regular and Chapter 1 instruction and connecting instruction and assessment. Careful planning and scheduling by the building principal permitted all 1st- and 2nd-grade classroom and Chapter 1 teachers to be released at the same time to attend weekly seminars on topics of concern. This series continued for 2 full years.

During the same time period, in all elementary schools and in the middle school, university faculty and doctoral students responded to teachers' and administrators' requests for demonstration teaching. Teachers and university faculty agreed that a demonstration teacher would be assigned to two classrooms in each of the buildings for the academic year. Demonstration lessons occurred once each week and were coplanned and cotaught by the university and local teachers. Teachers throughout the buildings were released to observe the demonstrations, and to participate in a discussion group that met immediately following the lesson.

These two professional development activities represented the most comprehensive and successful efforts during the initial years. The insights that were gained guided the planning for the most recent and most ambitious activity, city-wide, grade-level, biweekly seminars, initiated in the fifth year of the partnership. At the end of the 2-year implementation period, every teacher in grades 1 through 8 completed a minimum of at least six sessions on literacy instruction.

The format of the sessions varied with the topic and included: presentations and demonstrations by university faculty and Chelsea teachers; discussion groups and workshops. Each seminar ended with a plan for classroom implementation, and began the next week with a critical analysis of the implementation. The discussion often resulted in suggestions for revising the instructional plan based on the teachers' experiences.

Focus of Professional Development Opportunities

Since the start of the partnership, the focus of professional development initiatives has been threefold: (1) classroom contexts (2) instructional strategies and (3) classroom assessment.

Classroom Contexts. Seminars, courses and meetings related to this topic address the ways in which classroom organization influences students' access to and opportunities for reading and writing. Teachers explore ways in which to organize classrooms so that children are explicitly invited to read and write during both instructional and independent learning periods of the day. Emphasis is placed on the selection of high-quality children's literature that is diverse in subject matter, literary genres, and cultural and ethnic representation. Also, discussion addresses ways in which to organize classroom reading centers where books and magazines are displayed so that children are invited to read, and ways in which to organize writing centers where tools to support the writing process are readily available.

Teachers also investigate flexible-grouping practices. The full range of grouping options is presented and discussed, including whole-class, teacher-led and student-led small groups; small, cooperative groups; peer dyads; and individual learning. Emphasis is placed on keeping the grade-level curriculum constant for all students, while using various grouping options to provide some students with additional challenge and others with additional help. Two particular grouping models are emphasized, one for use when students are reading a common text (Paratore, 1991) and one when students are reading multiple texts (Reutzel, & Cooter, 1991).

Finally, in order to support implementation of an in-class Chapter 1 instructional model in which Chapter 1 teachers and regular education teachers team-teach for 60–90 minutes per day, strategies for coteaching were explored.

Instructional Strategies. Demonstration lessons, seminars, courses, and discussion focus on understanding and applying current research and theory in literacy instruction to classroom practice.

First- and second-grade teachers explore research-based strategies for teaching phonics and other decoding strategies within meaningful contexts. Building on the work of several researchers, most particularly Adams (1990), they develop and implement daily classroom routines for engaging students in word-building activities and the compilation of personal dictionaries. Also, they engage students in writing from the start, emphasizing invented spellings and drawings as a way to respond to reading. Teachers use choral readings and rereadings as a way to give every child access to books on the first day and every subsequent day of the school year.

In every grade, emphasis is placed on creating authentic situations for reading and writing in which the reading and writing tasks assigned to students represent activities that students encounter both inside and outside of school. As teachers plan literacy activities, they consider and incorporate into the lesson plan practices that mature readers routinely use. This principle affects long-held beliefs about how children learn to read. For example, instead of admonishing students "not to look ahead" prior to reading a story, teachers encourage students to preview the text and talk with a student near them, making predictions and formulating questions. After reading, student-centered book talks and discussions replace the question-and-answer periods that for many years characterized teachers' interactions with students after they had read a selection. Also, the practice of using workbook pages and worksheets for practice in reading and writing has been abandoned in favor of having children keep reading journals. Students' written responses are guided by a reader response model that emphasizes three types of response: aesthetic—how does the selection make the reader feel, think, act? strategic—what particular reading strategy will help the reader comprehend more fully, and generative—how can the reader relate the text to other texts and experiences in order to formulate new hypotheses, plans or ideas (Indrisano, & Paratore, 1992).

Finally, while skill instruction remains an integral part of the teaching of reading, teachers have abandoned the practice of following a rigid "scope and sequence" for one in which skills and strategies are selected to be relevant to the type of text the students are reading. Teachers examine the selected text and choose the comprehension skill or strategy that would most likely support comprehension and critical thinking. For example, understanding cause and effect is introduced and practiced when children are reading myths, since so many episodes and event sequences in mythology are dependent on understanding causal relationships. Understanding time order is introduced when students read historical fiction, since the sequence of events over time has particular significance in understanding prose of this type.

When planning skill instruction, teachers consider and explicitly teach three levels of knowledge (Paris, 1984) and implement an instructional model which emphasizes gradual release of responsibility from teacher to student (Pearson, & Gallagher, 1983).

Classroom Assessment. This topic has been the least comprehensively addressed and implemented. At the end of the fifth year, no district-wide, in-service sessions or meetings had yet focused on literacy assessment. On the other hand, there had been numerous opportunities for teachers to join on-site courses and seminars on assessment, and approximately 30 elementary school teachers chose to participate in these over the course of several semesters.

Assessment courses have focused on classroom assessment for the purposes of informing instructional decision making. Building on research and theory in literacy assessment (e.g., Johnston, 1992), the following principles have been emphasized: (1) Routine instructional settings provide the most authentic, and therefore the most valid, opportunities for assessment; (2) Multiple sources of data should be used to judge students' literacy knowledge, including samples from different types of literacy tasks and different curricular areas; (3) Literacy assessment should include systematic and routine opportunities for students to reflect on their own work and assess their performances; (4) Assessment tasks should provide varying levels and types of teacher interventions (i.e., demonstration, guided practice and independent practice), enabling teachers to make judgments about the instructional conditions under which students are most successful.

WHAT HAVE WE LEARNED?

Teaching and learning in Chelsea have changed. It is, however, important to acknowledge at the beginning of this discussion that only now are "hard data" being collected to validate this claim. When an unprecedented partnership between a large, private university and a small, impoverished, urban school district is widely described as a takeover, professors of good will have a serious choice. They can come to the partnership as researchers, with all the attending requirements of science, or as colleagues, constrained only by a commitment to the teachers and to the children. The latter course was chosen. Now, in the sixth year of the project, many local teachers and university faculty have joined together as coresearcher teams, and more scientific evidence will be gathered. Until those data are available, observations and samples of the children's work are offered as evidence of the changes in literacy instruction and learning.

The Teachers and the Classrooms

A walk through the nearly century-old school buildings in Chelsea in 1994 makes visible the changes in the classroom environment. From the physical arrangements that encourage collaboration as well as independence; to classroom libraries where books are exhibited on shelves or in brightly colored crates, arranged by topic and theme; to writing centers where books authored by the children themselves are widely displayed beside child-created dictionaries and thesaurus, the classroom invites the children to join a community of learners.

The most important educational outcome of the physical changes in the classrooms is the resulting change in the ways literacy is taught. Visits to classrooms reveal scenes such as the following: children reading grade-appropriate books of high literary quality or award-winning selections from literature anthologies; children reading a story with a partner, helping each other as they come to difficult words or challenging ideas; children working in pairs and small groups, collaborating, explaining, clarifying and defending their ideas about the stories and books they read and write; children keeping reading journals in which they record their individual responses to the books and selections they read; children meeting in small, student-led groups to discuss the books they are reading and the stories they are writing; teachers actively engaged with children, sometimes leading an introductory lesson in front of the whole class, other times meeting with a small group of students to provide additional instruction or practice on a specific skill or strategy, sometimes listening to individual children read or having a conference to discuss a child's recent piece of writing.

In connection with various professional development activities, teachers have offered written reflections of how the recommended changes have influenced their teaching actions and children's opportunities to learn. Samples from a few teachers provide some indication of teachers' response to the instructional changes. One teacher commented on the practice of keeping writing folders and reviewing children's work over time:

> I was able to expect more writing from my students and was able to be on top of their strengths and weaknesses. Often, I did not demand as much writing from my second language students. In the past, my students kept a writing folder in which their work went home daily. I had no way to compare their September writing with their June writing. In keeping a portfolio, I know exactly what the children need help in. With my Chapter 1 coteacher, we can make extra help groups and be successful with them.

Another teacher considered the gradual release model of instruction and the emphasis placed on demonstration, guided practice and application as an instructional model:

> I am less afraid to stop and seize the moment of a student faltering and turn it into a strategy session, modeling for everyone so we appreciate each other's attempts to "figure it out" and learn more.

Another teacher commented on the ways the recommended literacy practices had influenced the opportunities she provides the students:

> I have been attempting to build in more opportunity for the students to reflect on their own writing and to help them become aware of their own personal literate growth. Daily, the children are engaged in peer conferencing and editing with frequent teacher modeling to keep them on track … we have been exposing the children to a variety of authors, tapes and interviews to familiarize them with a model to show the importance of experiences and ideas that spark writing … the children are writing more and even asking for writing time. Using a response journal has definitely given them the knowledge that their literate opinions are valued and important.

Another teacher commented on the coteaching model and on its influence on her own teaching:

> I had a wonderful experience in working with [a colleague]. I learned many things from her. Her idea of having the children do their story map and then highlighting with a yellow crayon the points that they wanted to include in their summary was very beneficial to me. The children found that this method helped them organize their thoughts and the summary was written with less difficulty. The extra help groups were able to take their group map and then write individual stories. A feeling of accomplishment was [evident] throughout the room.

In these examples and in the many other written comments, there are a few common themes: teachers emphasize purposeful and meaningful reading and writing tasks and consistently provide students more time to read and write; teachers provide students more scaffolding and support, and engage in daily activities that give some students extra help and others additional challenge; teachers routinely involve students in the process of assessment and emphasize the development of self-motivated, self-directed learners.

Importantly, the isolation that is too often the accepted condition for elementary teachers has given way to consultation during the challenging task of implementing innovations. These conversations often result in invitations to visit colleagues' classrooms and ultimately, to additional discussion, enriched by shared experience. The professional development seminars that follow these activities are enhanced by the pragmatic insights and probing questions that result from the teachers' experiences in collaboration.

Among the most personally satisfying milestones has been the teachers' interest in and commitment to join Boston University faculty as coresearchers and copresenters. Teachers are eager to share their experiences in this effort toward school reform and have joined in preparing and delivering papers at local, regional and international conferences.

Children's Classroom Performance in Reading and Writing

At this point, data from students are only anecdotal, emerging from portfolio samples and classroom observations that teachers have chosen to share. As limited as these are, they do provide some preliminary information about how children are performing in literacy.

Are Children Learning to Read and Write Words? When the work in Chelsea classrooms began, more than half the students simply did not have the opportunity to read grade-appropriate text. Judged to be low-performing readers, they were tracked in below-grade-level text and rarely moved beyond it. One of our major goals was to change this practice. To do so, teachers were asked to assume that, given enough teacher intervention and practice, all children would be able to successfully read grade-appropriate text. How has this worked? Interviews with regular classroom teachers, demonstration teachers and lead teachers suggest that with very few exceptions, children are successfully reading grade-appropriate text. One lead teacher reported that during her visits to elementary and secondary classrooms, she consistently observed that one-half to three-quarters of the students could read, without any help, grade-appropriate tradebooks on the very first reading; the remaining students could read the text successfully following teacher and student support activities such as read-alouds, choral-readings and partner-readings.

Evidence of children's developing fluency at the word level can also be derived from students' writing samples. Are students able to use their knowledge of sound / symbol relationships to spell words? Samples displayed in Figures 56C–1–56C–3 are typical of the growth children demonstrated in one 1st-grade classroom.

This child, who is bilingual, was reluctant to write more than two sentences at the beginning of the year. In September, she represented words using their initial sound only and she was able to copy the word "duck" from the chalkboard (Figure 56C–1). In January, she was writing substantially more, but still struggling with word–sound associations, as her invented spellings reveal: "He pat [put] on his cos

[clothes]" (Figure 56C–2). In June, although her writing still contained spelling errors, her errors were either consistent with the sounds in the English language (e.g. "mayd" for "made") or indicative of an emerging awareness of irregularly spelled words ("seid" for "said", Figure 56C–3) Further, her June sample was well-organized, accurate and complete in detail, suggesting strong story comprehension.

Are Children Able to Comprehend and Talk About Books? Perhaps the best measure of students' ability to build meaning and understanding as they read, and to relate and connect the texts they are reading to their own lives comes from students' book talks. In the sample presented in Table 56C–2, a heterogeneous group of 3rd-grade children discussed the book, *Knots on a Counting Rope*. Although the teacher was present in this group, she played a minor role; the children, directed the discussion themselves. The students' awareness of classroom routines in reading was evident when one student asked: "Should I do a quick summary?" Further, the value of understanding the process for getting an answer, not just the answer itself, was evident when another student asked: "…about the summary … did you just get that summary up in your mind or something?" The first child responded by describing the steps he followed: "Ya, I like this story a lot so I just paid a lot of attention to the story. And then I got a lot of pictures in my mind and so I made up words and put it in the summary." The other student is still not satisfied, so she says: "Can I ask one more question?"…. "How do you get these good stories up in your mind?" And the first child responds, "I just—when I read those sentences I get a lot of pictures in my mind so I put it in words." As the discussion continues, other children offer their ideas for summarizing as they read. Of importance is not just the children's interest in and

FIGURE 56C–1

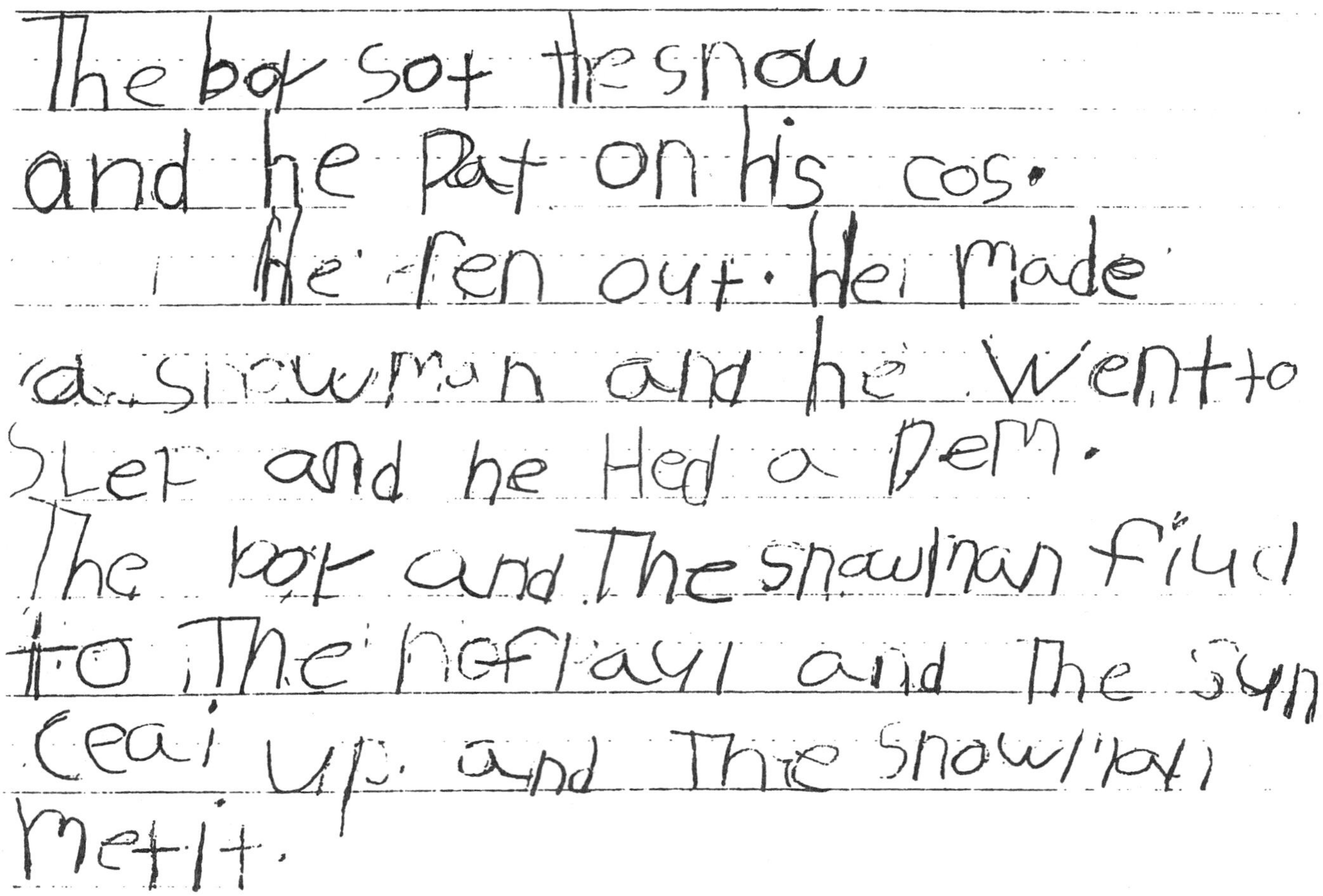

The boy sot the snow
and he pat on his cos.
He fen out. He made
a snowman and he went to
slet and he hed a dem.
The boy and the snowman fiud
to the noflayl and the sun
ceai up and the snowman
metit.

FIGURE 56C–2

TABLE 56C–2. Knots on a Counting Rope Discussion

M. He learned how to ride horses. He didn't know what the color blue was and now he knows what the color blue is.
T. How did he learn about the color blue?
M. Because he could picture it in his heart.
T. Anyone have any questions they want to ask?
S. How did he picture it? He didn't know blue so how did he picture it?
M. He could see by his heart.
S. What does that mean, by his heart?
M. He could see by his heart.
T. Can you see in your heart or can you...
M. Feel, you feel in your heart.
S. Should I do a quick summary?
T. If you'd like.
S. In the beginning the wind was going boyeee. Then they said, "A boy was going to be born and he had a dark curtain over his eyes" and the grandfather took him out to see morning. And two great blue horses rode up and looked at him and he reached his arms out to the blue horses. And they said that gave him the strength to live. And that's why they called him Boy-Strength-of-Blue-Horses.
T. Can you tell us something he learned?
S. He learned to ride a horse. I learned he could do the same thing people who aren't blind could do. He learned to ride a horse in a race like people who can see.
T. Do you want to ask anyone anything? Does any one want to ask Stephen anything?
M. I have something. About the summary... did you just get that summary up in your mind or something?
S. Ya, I like this story a lot so I just paid a lot of attention to the story. And then I got a lot of pictures in my mind and so I made up words and put it in the summary.
M. Can I say one more question?
S. O.K.
M. How do you get these good stories up in your mind?
S. I just—when I read those sentences I get a lot of pictures in my mind so I put it in words.

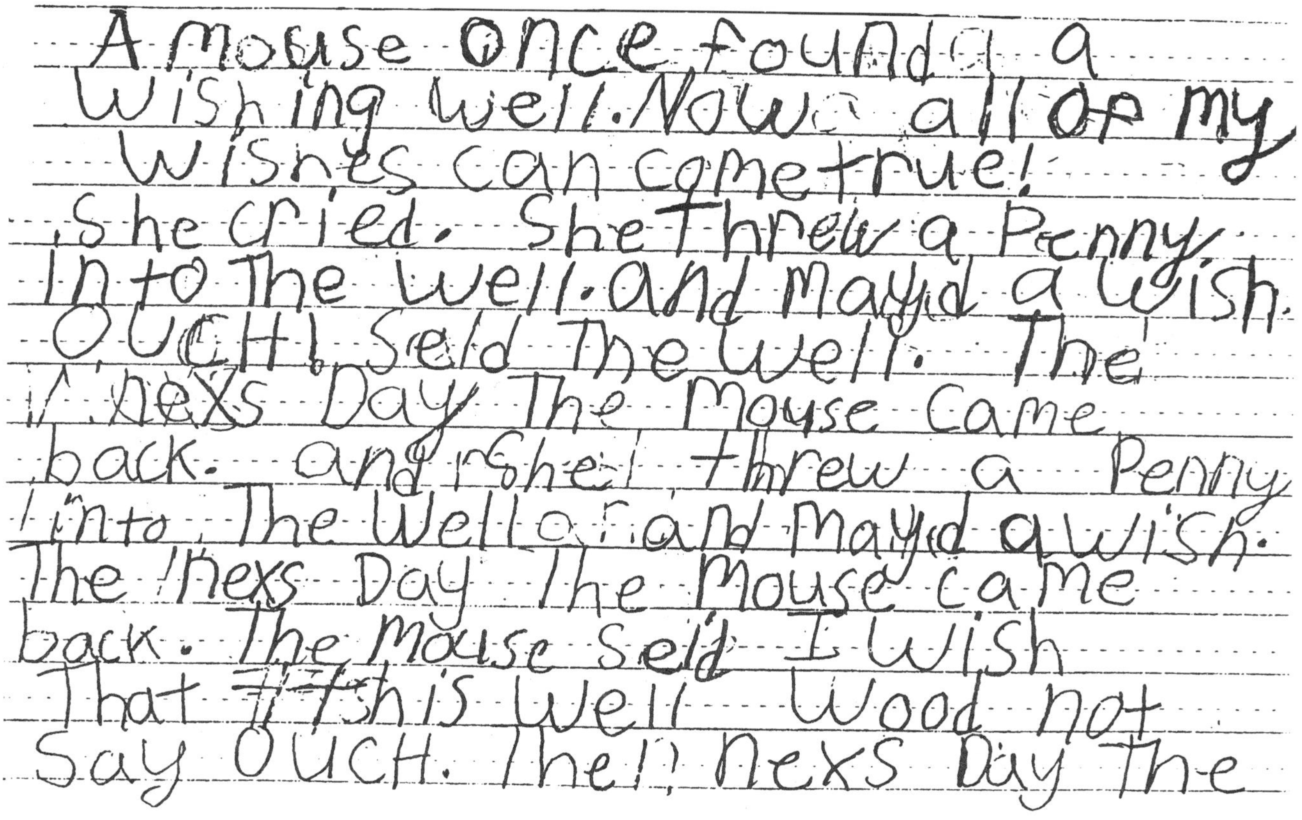

A mouse once found a wishing well. Now all of my wishes can come true! she cried. She threw a penny into the well and mayd a wish. OUCH! seld the well. The nexs Day the mouse came back. and she threw a penny into the well. and mayd a wish. The nexs Day the mouse came back. The mouse seld I wish that this well wood not say OUCH. The nexs Day the

FIGURE 56C–3

understanding of the details of the story, but their awareness and discussion of the strategies that are helpful to them in constructing meaning as they read and their ability to share their understanding with their peers. Such explicit discussion also provides teachers with a "window" on the children's thinking processes, in this case leading the teacher to reteach and review strategies for summarization, as it became apparent that children had insufficient understanding.

CONCLUSION

Achieving reform through a university–school collaboration has been a significant challenge. The unprecedented nature of the partnership, the scope of responsibility, the sometimes ineffective lines of communication, have caused local teachers and university faculty alike to, at times, question the

likelihood that the agreement could have positive outcomes. Yet, on reflection, most conclude that efforts that are being made will make a difference in the lives of the children who are the primary concern. As the partnership continues, the words of one teacher are instructive in defining its purpose:

> I think when you want to change something, you really don't want to change it, but you want to make it grow. And, instead of change, we should talk more about growth, and start from what really exists and make that better… A good leader, I think, empowers the people, and then guides the growth… It's not just a professor or a superintendent, but a good teacher who's a leader of the classroom who empowers the children and guides their growth. I was thinking that Boston University faculty have brought me information, inspiration and support. I've started to think that is really what we want to bring to our children: information, inspiration, and support. So it really is much more basic than people think. It's more empowering to guide growth, than to enforce change.

References

Adams, M. J. (1990). *Beginning to read: Thinking and learning about print*. Cambridge, MA: MIT Press.

Allington, R. L. (1984). Content coverage and contextual reading in reading groups. *Journal of Reading Behavior, 16*, 85–96.

Goldenberg, C., & Gallimore, R. (1991). Local knowledge, research knowledge, and educational change: A case study of early Spanish reading improvement. *Educational Researcher, 20*, 2–14.

Good, T., & Marshall, S. (1984). Do students learn more in heterogeneous or homogeneous groups? In P. L. Peterson, L. C. Wilkinson, & M. Hallinan (Eds.), *The social context of instruction* (pp. 15–38). New York: Academic Press.

Graves, D. (1983). *Writing: Teachers and children at work.* Portsmouth, NH: Heinemann.

Indrisano, R., & Paratore, J. R. (1992). Using literature with readers at risk. In B. E. Cullinan (Ed.), *Invitation to read: More children's literature in the reading program* (pp. 138–149) . Newark, DE: International Reading Association.

Indrisano, R., & Paratore, J. R. (1994). The Boston University/Chelsea public schools partnership. *Journal of Education, 176.*

Johnston, P. H. (1992). *Constructive evaluation of literate activity.* New York: Longman.

Moll, L. C. (1992). Literacy research in community and classrooms: A sociocultural approach. In R. Beach, J. Green, M. L. Kamil, & T. Shanahan (Eds.), *Multidisciplinary perspectives on literacy research* (pp. 211–244). Urbana, IL: National Conference on Research in English and National Council of Teachers of English.

Paratore, J. R. (1991). *Flexible grouping; Why and how.* Needham, MA: Silver Burdett Ginn.

Paris, S. (1984). Teaching children to guide their reading & writing. In T. Raphael (Ed.), *The school contexts of literacy* (pp. 115–130). New York: Random House.

Pearson, P. D., & Gallagher, M. C. (1983). The instruction of reading comprehension. *Contemporary Educational Psychology, 8,* 317–344.

Reutzel, D. R., & Cooter, R. B. (1991). Organizing for effective instruction: The reading workshop. *The Reading Teacher, 44,* 548–554.

Sears, D. (1994). *The Boston University / Chelsea partnership: Third report to the legislature.* Boston: Boston University, Office of the President.

Slavin, R. E. (1986). *Ability grouping and student achievement in elementary school: A best evidence synthesis.* Baltimore: Johns Hopkins University Press.

Tierney, R. J., & Cunningham, J. W. (1984). Research on teaching reading comprehension. In P. D. Pearson, R. Barr, M. L. Kamil & P. Mosenthal (Eds.), *Handbook of reading research* (Vol. 1, pp. 609–656). New York: Longman.

·56D·

TEACHING THE DELAYED READER:
THE BENCHMARK SCHOOL MODEL

Irene W. Gaskins

BENCHMARK SCHOOL, MEDIA, PA

There are various ways in which children learn the processes needed to be readers. We know this because most children learn to read and they learn in very different programs. For many it does not seem to matter where the program starts, nor what order it follows. These students apparently are able to add for themselves what teachers leave unsaid. All students, however, are not able to learn despite the program or to fill in the gaps when procedures are not explicitly explained. Some children must have a program that starts where they are, proceeds according to the competencies they develop, and teaches explicitly what they do not figure out on their own.

For these children, learning to read was placed in jeopardy by theoretical assumptions about how reading is acquired and the specific curriculum built around those assumptions (Clay, 1991). Even if a program has a strong record of achievement with most children, it may still be a bad match for the way in which some children learn. In such cases, the children who are not flexible enough to adapt their way of learning to the school's curriculum develop reading competencies at a slower rate than their classmates and slip further and further behind. These children need the opportunity to begin again in a rich literacy environment conducive to the way in which they learn and where a high percentage of student time is spent on task, engaged in meaningful reading and writing activities (R. W. Gaskins, 1988). Benchmark School was founded to provide that opportunity.

Benchmark School is a day school with a full elementary curriculum for 6- to 14-year-old children in grades 1–8. The children who attend Benchmark have experienced difficulty in learning to read, despite average or above intelligence, and their difficulties are not attributable to primary emotional or neurological difficulties. Most of the 175 students who attend the school each year enter the school as 7- to 9-year-old beginning readers, although some enter when they are as old as 11, reading several years below their grade placement, and have a history of reading difficulties dating back to first grade. At the root of these children's difficulties in learning to read seems to be a mismatch between the way they learn and the way they were taught.

For some, pacing seems to have been an issue, thus they fell behind others for whom the pace of instruction was more appropriate. These delayed readers may have needed instruction characterized by more frequent teacher mediation, smaller units of instruction, and much repetition. For other delayed readers, initial instruction assumed prerequisite skills that the students did not yet possess, such as the ability to segment words into individual sounds or to notice visual patterns in words. These students might have experienced more success had the program capitalized on the considerable background of knowledge and love of a good story that they brought to literacy learning. For still others, the major difficulty at the time they entered Benchmark did not lie in acquiring a beginning-level sight vocabulary. They could

---

The final draft of this chapter is the result of weekly small-group discussions of earlier drafts with the extraordinary teachers and supervisors of Benchmark School who over the past years have implemented the principles and practices elaborated in this chapter. The helpful suggestions and editing of Benchmark Board of Directors' Deputy President Robert Gaskins and the following members of the staff are gratefully acknowledged: Susan Audley, Anita Bair, Cheryl Cress, Betsy Cunicelli, Joan Davidson, Katie Donnelly, Marjorie Downer, Thorne Elliot, Renee Erickson, Eleanor Gensemer, Tom Hurster, Lisa Kascavage, Sally Laird, Helen Lawrence, Eric MacDonald, Dorothy O'Donnell, Colleen O'Hara, Mika Okawa, Joyce Ostertag, Nancy Powell, Melissa Radico, Pam Rappolt, Sharon Rauch, Theresa Scott, Jackie Sheridan, Linda Six, Marianne Smith, Jean Stakias, and Beth Wahl.

memorize or sound out words. However, these children seemed not to attend to the text for the purpose of constructing meaning. Some were stranded at the word level of processing text, others relied too heavily on background knowledge, seeming to arbitrarily disregard text. Most demonstrated cognitive styles and temperaments such as impulsivity, rigidity, and passivity that interfered with their ability to figure out strategies for effectively dealing with print and constructing understanding. Instruction was needed to help these students develop the notion that reading is a process of making meaning that is based on the constraints of contiguous text. They also needed to develop an awareness of their styles and the value of reflection, flexibility, and active mental processing, and learn how to take control of style, temperament, and tasks.

These examples of mismatches between learner characteristics and learning environments illustrate just a few of the learning differences exhibited by Benchmark students. The characteristic these students share is that, despite being bright, they were among the few in their pre-Benchmark classes who did not respond successfully to the reading programs that seemed to work for their classmates. (Those who repeated kindergarten or first grade also did not respond to a second chance to learn to read in the program.) In addition to delayed reading achievement and learning style differences, Benchmark students often exhibit an overlay of emotional responses to their reading difficulties as well as maladaptive strategies for coping with the confusions they encounter in reading.

Teaching Benchmark's delayed readers to read at a level commensurate with their age and potential is a slow process, perhaps because there is more to achieving success in reading than learning how to read (I. W. Gaskins, 1984). Students also need to learn how to orchestrate and apply strategies for the completion of real-life tasks and those assigned across the curriculum (Gaskins, Guthrie, et al., 1994; Gaskins, Satlow, Hyson, Ostertag, & Six, 1994), as well as how to take charge of the styles and temperaments that got in the way of their learning in the first place (Gaskins & Baron, 1985).

Benchmark teachers strive to help these delayed readers become proficient, self-regulated, and life-long readers by creating a learning environment in which students can capitalize on their strengths and develop inner control over knowledge, strategies, and motivation across the curriculum (Gaskins & Gaskins, in press). The challenge is to plan and deliver instruction that matches the many combinations of pace, developmental level, style, temperament, and feelings that exist in a class, as well as to guide students to substitute more functional strategies for those that have not proved productive. Success for Benchmark students depends on teachers who understand the factors that make reading difficult, know their students well, and meet students where they are with respect to pace, developmental level, cognitive style, temperament, and feelings.

In order to provide appropriate instruction for Benchmark's delayed readers both professional development and program development are ongoing. (See I. W. Gaskins, 1994a, for a discussion of professional development at Benchmark, and Pressley, Gaskins, et al., 1991, for an inter-view study about staff reactions to program development for strategy instruction.) As a result of staff collaboration, reflection on practice, and research, a few basic principles of instruction have evolved during the school's 25-year history. These principles, however, as well as the total program, are continually fine-tuned, adapted, and changed as the staff learns more about teaching delayed readers. (I. W. Gaskins, 1988; I. W. Gaskins, Cunicelli, & Satlow, 1992). Six of these guiding principles are: (1) understand students as individuals and let their strengths and needs dictate what methods might work and how instruction will proceed; (2) determine the desired outcomes of instruction and explicitly teach students how to accomplish these outcomes, then scaffold instruction and gradually release responsibility to the students; (3) create a safe environment for risk taking where learning from errors and problem solving are celebrated; (4) plan, yet be dynamic and flexible, being conscious of creating a high degree of student time on task; (5) teach reading skills and strategies actively and responsively across the curriculum; and (6) encourage extensive reading and sharing (I. W. Gaskins, 1980; Gaskins & Elliot, 1983; Gaskins & Gaskins, in press).

The remainder of the chapter outlines some of the approaches Benchmark teachers use to help students understand not only what they read but also the reading processes, and how to take control of styles, temperaments, emotions, and tasks. The program is based on the belief that delayed readers need a variety of reading and writing experiences, as well as explicit instruction in strategies for both identifying words and constructing meaning. Waiting for development to occur or immersing students in literacy activities without appropriate mediation does not foster development (Cunningham & Allington, 1994).

The Benchmark program has been described as a whole language program by some experts (I. W. Gaskins, 1994b) because of the richness of literacy experiences and the responsiveness of teachers to individual students. Yet, contrary to many whole language programs, explicit instruction in decoding, comprehension, and writing is a hallmark of Benchmark instruction because Benchmark's delayed readers, as well as many other students, demonstrate time and again that they need instruction that explains what they are learning, why it is important, when they can use it, and how to do it (Chall & Squire, 1991; Hiebert, 1991; McCaslin, 1989; Pearson & Fielding, 1991). Explanations and teacher responsiveness are the distinguishing characteristics of teacher--student interactions at Benchmark (Gaskins, Anderson, Pressley, Cunicelli, & Satlow, 1993).

Similar to Pearson (1993), the Benchmark staff believes that instruction should emphasize: (a) the structure and patterns in words, text, and knowledge, (b) inferences based on the text and the reader's background knowledge, and (c) monitoring for meaning making. In addition, Benchmark students profit from explicit guidance in analyzing the components of a task and matching those components with appropriate strategies to control task, text, situation, and person variables (I. W. Gaskins, 1994a). The key to achieving these goals is meaningful interactions between teachers and students.

UNDERSTANDING READING AND WRITING PROCESSES AND TEXT

In this section instructional procedures that Benchmark teachers use to guide students in their understanding of reading and writing processes and text are described. These include repeated readings, reading group instruction, word identification lessons, writing lessons, independent reading, and literature lessons. Benchmark teachers have found that, regardless of age or reading level, new-to-Benchmark students need guidance to make sense of the reading and writing processes. As part of frequent teacher–student interactions, teachers mediate students' learning experiences so that they become aware that the construction of meaning should guide what they do as they read and write. Teachers discuss with students why making sense of what they read and write is important, emphasizing that reading and writing are done for a purpose. They are meant to serve a function, such as to entertain or to help complete a task. If students are not able to create meaning, they will not achieve their purpose.

Strategies are explicitly taught that place students in control of problem solving and meaning making. These include monitoring (such as stating what they have read in their own words to check understanding) and fix up strategies for detecting and correcting errors and for clarifying fuzzy comprehension (such as rereading or discussing their confusion with a peer). Teachers model aloud their own thinking processes for error detection and meaning making, then guide students as they practice these strategies in their own text. Catching students in the act of applying appropriate meaning-making strategies, and expressing the connection between the processes they used and the results they achieved, reinforces for students the fact that improvement in reading and writing is linked to recognizing, correcting, and learning from errors, as well as to asking questions when attempts at problem solving do not result in the construction of meaning.

Repeated Readings

Echo reading and choral reading of predictable books are frequently used methods for introducing reading as a meaning-making process to Benchmark's beginning readers. In implementing this technique, the teacher first reads a section to students, engaging them, as he reads, in eliciting background knowledge and making predictions. The teacher next reads the selection a second time as students point and follow in their books. Next, the teacher reads the selection one line at a time with students echo reading after each line. This is followed by choral reading. The teacher may also read only parts of the text, allowing students to supply what would make sense in the predictable sections. In addition, he may allow a few students to read the text together, but he will chime in when needed to ask how they might solve a meaning-making problem. Finally, he may ask volunteers to read portions, again chiming in to support when necessary, often asking a student how he or she could solve the dilemma of meaning making. Throughout this process the pace is lively and a spirit of fun prevails. Young children love reading the stories they have memorized from repeated readings to anyone who will listen and as often as they will listen.

Students may also listen repeatedly to taped books. Older delayed readers find this particularly helpful because it provides an opportunity to experience books written at a level that matches more closely their conceptual, rather than their reading, level. They read a portion of the text repeatedly until they reach a criterion of 99–100% accuracy when reading the text without the tape. Not only are books for independent reading taped, but content-area books used in middle school may also be taped. These repeated-reading procedures (echo reading, choral reading, and taped books), can occur many times a day for as many days, months, or years as is deemed necessary to develop a confident, independent reader.

In addition to supporting students in the reading of text, repeated-reading procedures benefit students affectively. Students experience what it feels like to read like a good reader, feel good about experiencing success, and begin to believe again that they can become successful readers.

Reading Group Instruction

Instruction about meaning making takes place daily in reading groups of generally two to four students. The materials vary for these groups, for just as there is no one right reading method for all children, there is also no one best text. Basal readers with controlled vocabularies allow some students to feel most successful, while for other students trade books seem more motivating and appropriate. Teachers are free to use whatever texts seem to work for individual children. Students are grouped for instruction based on the instructional needs they share and the text the teacher determines is the best match for them.

During the 40-minute reading-group lessons, students are explicitly taught strategies for detecting and processing print information to construct meaning. The outcome teachers seek is that students will demonstrate active involvement in reading by using such strategies as surveying, accessing background knowledge, predicting, reading for a purpose, self-monitoring, changing a prediction based on information in the text, integrating new information with prior knowledge, and implementing decoding strategies to unlock unknown words. Beginning with the youngest students and for several years thereafter, each process is explicitly taught one at a time, with the teacher providing instruction, guided practice, and gradual release of responsibility to the students for one strategy over a period of at least 6–8 weeks before a new strategy is introduced. As each new strategy is introduced, instruction includes daily guidance, practice, feedback, and cuing in orchestrating all the strategies that students have learned to date. The goal is that over time, with this kind of daily scaffolding, students will gradually assume executive control and the disposition to apply these strategies on their own. The experience of the Benchmark staff is that it takes from 4–7 years for most of Benchmark's delayed readers to learn to orchestrate and apply appropriate strategies to match a learning situation.

Problem Solving for Words. Prior to reading a new selection, students are introduced to three to five words from the selection that they may not have encountered previously in the text which provide opportunities for working on print by applying a variety of problem-solving strategies. Before the lesson begins, the teacher of beginning readers places on sentence strips sentences from the text containing the target words for the day. Teachers of more advanced readers may place the target words on word cards. On one side of the word card is written in large type and below that the word is written in context. In the right-hand corner the word is written again and has beneath it known words that will help decode the spelling patterns in the word. On the other side of the card the word may be written in isolation to allow practice toward developing automaticity. When the procedure for introducing new words is first introduced, the teacher initiates a discussion about the value of applying problem-solving strategies to unknown words and why problem solving to figure out new words will be part of each lesson. He explains that it is important that the reader determine the sense the author is trying to convey; thus when a reader encounters an unknown word that interferes with making meaning she must use problem-solving strategies to figure out its pronunciation. The teacher brainstorms with students how they might solve the problem of an unknown word, then adds and teaches a few problem-solving strategies of his own, such as decoding unknown words by using known words with the same spelling pattern as the unknown word or using the initial consonant and context. Next, the teacher models the process of problem solving when an unknown word is encountered.

Explicit explanations of decoding processes are followed by guided practice during which the teacher provides feedback to students about their application of decoding strategies. With beginning readers the teacher or a student reads a sentence on a sentence strip saying "blank" for the target word. Students are asked what clues they can use to pronounce the word. At this point students would not pronounce the word even if it is in their sight vocabulary, rather they would share with their classmates the strategies they could use to decode the word and make sense of the text. One student may suggest that she would read on and see if the text provided additional clues, while another might suggest that he would guess what the unknown word is based on the initial consonant and what makes sense. A third student might say that the word has the same group of letters at the end that are found in a word he already knows, thus he would use the word he knows to decode the unknown word (e.g., being able to decode "mouse" because "house" is a known word). Still another student might point out that the identity of the word is obvious because of the predictable rhyming pattern in the text. All these suggestions are regarded as equally acceptable and high praise is given by the teacher as each student exhibits these good problem-solving strategies. Of course, when the students' decoding suggestions are not as functional as they might be, the teacher asks for more information and gently guides the student to an appropriate problem-solving strategy. The goal is to help students acquire a network of effective strategies for operating on the text, with the ultimate goal being automatic use of analogous word patterns as found among good readers (Stanovitch, 1984). For beginning readers, teachers often introduce new words a few days before they will be encountered in the reading group selection and place the words on word-ring cards similar to the word cards described above. These are reviewed nightly as part of homework. When word-ring words are recognized instantly as sight words, they are removed from a student's word ring.

Strategies for Meaning Making. Next, the teacher discusses the need to be active processors and constructive learners beyond the word level. The group is taught explicitly how to implement an active-reader strategy and why using strategies to be actively involved in processing text is important. During reading-group lessons for the first month of school the focus strategy for beginning readers may be making predictions by surveying the title and pictures of a selection and relating this text information to their background knowledge. As students become somewhat independent in applying one strategy, additional active-reader strategies are introduced. The gradual introduction of meaning-making strategies continues through the grades and includes setting purposes; making inferences about relationships in the story based on background knowledge, such as the relationship between character traits and the resolution of the story problem; and analyzing the structure of the text for story elements, theme, evidence of genre, and organizational characteristics of exposition. (See Gaskins & Elliot, 1991, for additional details about strategy instruction at Benchmark.)

Each day the teacher leads a discussion of the what, why, when, and how of the strategy, then models, by thinking out loud, the process for implementing the strategy. In later lessons, once a strategy is introduced, students are encouraged to share their ideas about the why, when, and how of implementing the strategy, with modeling alternating between the students and the teacher as circumstances dictate.

Talk about words and text processing is the focus for the first 10–15 minutes of the 40-minute reading group. The remainder of the time is devoted to silent reading and discussion, although talk about words and text processing goes on continually as teachers cue students to orchestrate specific active-reader strategies to construct understanding.

Monitoring Silent Reading. In classes where students are in the early stages of learning to read, students remain at the reading table with the teacher for silent reading so that the teacher can support students in their reading, as well as gather information about how each student learns. Observing the silent reading of two to four beginning readers who are reading the same selection is usually quite easy because most of these students whisper read; however, observing true silent readers is also possible by watching students as they proceed down a page and by initiating mini-conferences with them as they read. As students read silently, Benchmark teachers act as facilitators and consultants who quietly interact with individual students to discuss strategies and information and to observe students' attention to print and how they process information.

An important part of the teacher's job is to assess and record the operations each student attempts to implement and the kinds of operations that are not yet employed (Clay, 1991). These observations determine the next steps in instruction. The teacher is also interested in whether or not students are aware of their own reading behaviors and can assess accurately their progress toward meaning making. In addition, the teacher wants to discourage students from practicing inefficient or ineffective habits that remain from their early struggles in learning to read.

As the teacher listens and observes, he may follow students' eyes and note how their markers move down the page. In doing so, he may discover a student who is skimming, apparently more intent on looking like a speedy reader than reading for meaning. He engages the student in a brief conversation about the text, perhaps initiated by, "I was surprised by the things that happened on this page; was there anything that surprised you when you read it?" If, after a follow-up comment or two, it is clear that the child is confused about the information on the page, the teacher tries to lighten the moment by saying something like, "No problem, I often catch myself daydreaming when I'm reading. What do you think I do when I discover that I don't know what I've read?" On another occasion, the teacher may see a twinkle in a child's eye or hear a muffled giggle. He might comment to the child, "I can tell you are really actively involved in what you are reading; 1 laughed when I read that part, too." Another child may have come to a dead stop in her reading with her finger under a word. Noticing this, the teacher may ask, "What are you thinking?" If the child confirms that she is stuck on a word, the teacher praises her for monitoring her reading and asks what problem-solving strategies she has already tried, then he guides her in applying a strategy for decoding the word.

As a general rule, students are encouraged first to attempt to problem solve on their own when meaning making breaks down, then ask for assistance if confusions persist. A frequent teacher response to requests for assistance is, "What have you already tried?" Students enjoy these brief mini-conferences with the teacher and quickly learn that admissions of confusions and tales of successful problem solving earn praise and respect from both teacher and classmates. Even more important to students, is the realization that they are on the road to establishing inner control over important reading processes.

Students tend to complete the silent reading of a selection at different times. In some classes, as they finish, they take a card and pencil from the middle of the table and jot down notes (sometimes using invented spelling) to use during discussion. These notes are usually related to their purpose for reading. Some hold the card and pencil for a few seconds, then realizing that confusions exist they turn back to the text and reread. During this process, the teacher may discuss notes individually with a student or praise someone for being a good detector of fuzzy comprehension. In other classes, teachers may give those who finish first cards on which questions have been written that necessitate students returning to the text to gather information. Students generally enjoy the opportunity to become an expert on one of the interpretative or critical-thinking questions that the teacher plans to ask during discussion.

Collaborative Construction of Meaning. Discussions of the selection that the group read silently often begin by a teacher asking if anyone needs clarification or with students sharing what they have written on cards, most often something that relates to their purposes for reading or the objective of the lesson. Personal, affective responses are also shared, as well as the strategies students used to construct understanding. During an explanation in response to a student's request for clarification, students may refer to a chart in the classroom where Benchmark's framework for learning and understanding is displayed as a reminder for students to analyze the task, monitor for sense, look for patterns, and make inferences. Emphasis is often placed on practicing the strategy that was the objective of the lesson and sharing how the strategy was used.

In contrast to the traditional Initiate Respond Evaluate (IRE) pattern of teacher initiating a question, having a student respond, and evaluating the student's response, Benchmark teachers encourage group members to initiate the topics for discussion and to respond to one another's requests for clarification and to what others share. A common response made by a Benchmark teacher when students do not comment spontaneously after a student shares is, "Susan seems to be saying..., what do the rest of you think?" Responsiveness, rather than passing judgment, facilitates a collaborative effort toward constructing meaning (Gaskins, Anderson, et al., 1993). In such discussions, meaning is jointly negotiated with each participant constructing a meaning a little different from what would have been constructed individually (Pressley, El-Dinary, et al., 1992).

Word Identification Lessons

Most students who attend Benchmark (including students who have acquired a sight vocabulary that enables them to read books at early-reader levels) have failed to construct a dependable means of decoding unknown words. Thus, a word identification program was developed to meet this need (Gaskins, Downer, et al., 1988; Gaskins, Gaskins, & Gaskins, 1991, 1992) . In fast-paced, game-like, 20-minute group lessons students are guided to see patterns in words and to develop an awareness of concepts about print that is essential to independent and automatic decoding. Students are taught easily visualized concrete key words (e.g., tent, rain, ship, frog, skunk) that contain high-frequency phonograms (spelling patterns) and, in the early grades, they use these words to construct structured language experience stories collaboratively. As students explore the key words visually and play games with them that reinforce relationships between sounds and symbols, they become increasingly sensitive to the discriminating features of words and the predictability of letter sequences. Key words are prominently displayed on the classroom word wall and throughout the day students use those words to pronounce unknown words that have similar spelling patterns to words on the wall. For example, when a student encounters "bent" as an unknown word, she might use the known word "tent" from the word wall to decode it. She might also use "can" and "her" to decode "banter." This practice of using known words to decode unknown words is further enhanced by extensive reading of simple predictable books that provide additional words to be used in identifying unknown words by analogy (Adams, 1990; Cunningham & Allington, 1994).

Writing

For many of Benchmark's beginning readers, writing is the breakthrough to reading. At least this has often been the case when students use invented spelling and write on topics about which they are very familiar (I. W. Gaskins, 1982; 1991). Benchmark's writing program is a process approach that guides students through the recursive steps from rehearsal to publication. Students engage in daily sustained writing wherein they choose their own topics and are taught to plan, organize, and elaborate ideas. By writing about what they know and receiving explicit instruction about how to improve their writing, students tend to become enthusiastic writers who learn to view writing as communicating ideas.

Writing at Benchmark begins with planning. For some Benchmark students, planning for writing is begun at home as homework. Students brainstorm about a topic of their choice and about which they know a lot, then jot a few notes in preparation for the next day's writing. As they brainstorm ideas, they may discover that they do not know enough, thus part of the planning process becomes reading to gather information. For beginning readers the planning process is slightly different. They often draw a picture to illustrate their ideas, then with the assistance of parents label their pictures with some of the words they will need to write their piece in class the next day. Throughout the school during the daily 40-minute writing period, students in collaboration with teachers and/or peers discuss what they plan to write before they write.

The daily writing period often begins with the teacher explicitly teaching some aspect of the writing process (it might even be planning) that the previous day's writing suggested needs emphasis. Teachers may also model their thought processes as they write part of a piece on the chalkboard to illustrate a particular point. In the primary classes, students may be explicitly taught how to construct a paragraph and how to write letters, especially a thank-you note and a friendly letter. Intermediate-level classes may learn how to put paragraphs together with transition sentences, as well as how to write introductory and concluding paragraphs. As students progress through the school, many genres of writing are taught. For example, both mini-lessons and large-group instruction are provided to explicitly teach the skills and strategies needed for writing responses to what has been read, such as summaries, character sketches, and research reports. Students are also taught how to write pieces patterned after various forms of literature and expository text and how to use writing to learn concepts, especially those taught in social studies and science.

Once a piece is planned, the focus during writing is, first, on getting one's ideas on paper, then on making sure that the ideas are organized and clearly presented. The mechanics of writing are a major concern only when the piece is in the last stages of development and headed for publication. Almost all entering-Benchmark students are overly concerned about correct spelling. To discourage a preoccupation with spelling at the early stages of the composing process, teachers give a consistent response to requests for how to spell a word, "Write down the sounds that you hear; right now we are interested in getting your good ideas on paper." Students are also encouraged to use their word-wall words to encode words with spelling patterns that are being learned in word identification lessons. For example, to spell "that", a student would be encouraged to use the key word "cat".

Throughout the school first to eighth graders can be seen collaborating with others as they write. At Benchmark students are encouraged to use other students as resources, thus they frequently write in groups of three or four where they share plans for their pieces, as well as seek feedback on drafts and collaborate about revisions. The process of sharing and giving feedback has been modeled by teachers, thus students know how to make good use of their time collaborating with peers. If they become "stuck" for something to write, students read what they have written to one or more of those in the group and request suggestions either for ways to elaborate on ideas in the composition or for additional information (or clarification) that might interest a reader. In addition, checklists are often posted in classrooms that provide criteria for components of a well-written selection. The processes of sharing and collaborating seem to help students develop a sense of audience and reinforce the fact that meaning is at the core of writing, as it is in reading.

After spending the majority of the writing period engaged in putting ideas on paper, the class or writing group may reconvene to share. Several students usually volunteer to read their compositions aloud and request feedback. Feedback begins with a comment telling the author what the listener liked about the piece and often is followed by a question about additional information that the listener would like to learn about the topic. The following day students may choose to revise their compositions based on feedback and thus begin to take the composition through the editing-revision process to publication, or they may choose to write a new piece.

Writing instruction for beginning readers at Benchmark is adapted to accommodate their limited encoding ability. Each day after the teacher's brief instruction, students spend a few minutes discussing their notes, drawing, and discussing ideas with those in their group, then each writes a composition on every other line in a journal. As these beginners complete a line or sentence, the teacher asks them to share quietly what they have written. As the child shares, the teacher writes in standard spelling above the invented spelling what the child shared (initially students' writing may be only a series of consonants, plus lines that designate that the rest of the word's spelling was unknown). After a few days of journal writing, it is common to see the beginning readers turning back in their journals to copy the teacher's correct spelling of a word that was used on a previous occasion. In doing so, they learn not only to discriminate carefully the individual features of the word, but also to group sequences of letters together to expedite the painstaking copying of words into their new composition. Drawing a picture and having a teacher write on the lines above the invented spellings are phased out as soon as students demonstrate that these supports are no longer needed.

In the process of writing and sharing, Benchmark's delayed readers have multiple occasions to think about relationships between sounds and symbols and to read and reread their compositions. Writing, as a result, becomes another opportunity for students to articulate their awareness of phonology and print, to construct meaning, and for the teacher to hold back and let students use what they know. Writing becomes an opportunity to read!

Independent Reading and Literature Lessons

Few would dispute that children learn to read by reading and being read to, yet in catch-up programs these are often missing ingredients (Allington & McGill-Franzen, 1989). However, even when the intent is to include independent reading and teacher read-aloud opportunities, convincing delayed readers to read or listen for pleasure is not always as straightforward as putting books in their hands or reading to them. Other factors must be considered; for example, the fact that reading cannot be separated from a reader's purposes, prior knowledge, and feelings (Smith, 1994). Without the intent to either enjoy or learn from what is read and the expectation that enjoyment or learning is possible, looking at a page of words may be little more than a mindless passing of the reader's eyes over text. Engagement based on intent and positive expectations is crucial to meaning making. And meaning making is what reading is all about.

Clearly, the more students read, the more they will learn about the processes they can use to become better readers. Thus, it is crucial that teachers provide an approach to reading that addresses or counteracts the negative feelings and attitudes that may have become a habitual response to the delayed reader's difficulties in learning to read. These responses may include expectations for failure, the belief that reading is too effortful in view of the return, and the preferred self-image of a nonreader. Dealing with these issues includes providing a safe environment where teachers mediate understanding and enjoyment as students read texts that interest them and about which teachers desire only honest personal responses.

Independent Reading During School. There are many occasions during the day when students practice reading. As discussed above, they practice reading as part of reading-group lessons, writing instruction, and repeated reading. In addition, Benchmark students are allotted time to practice reading while the teacher is with their classmates for reading-group instruction. During this silent-reading time students read stories in basal readers and trade books that are written at their independent level (the level at which they can accurately read 99–100% of the words). When they complete reading a book or selection, they respond to what they have read by choosing from a menu of possible responses that have

been introduced one at a time and taught explicitly. Some students choose to write a review, others a summary, while still others prefer to write answers to questions related to the teacher's instructional objective or to discuss what they read with peers or the teacher. Active engagement with lots of easy-reading text is the goal of independent reading time. Benchmark teachers have discovered that the number of words read correlates with progress in reading, a conclusion supported by research (Guthrie & Greaney, 1991; Taylor, Frye, & Maruyama, 1990); thus, they strive to have students engaged in reading for 80% of their seatwork time.

Independent Reading at Home. Benchmark students also read at home. As part of their homework, they are required to read independently for a minimum of 30 minutes each day. For beginning readers this often means reading aloud the predictable books they have practiced at school. Teachers of beginners also send home teacher-composed stories that feature words from stories read in reading group. As readers establish competency as beginning readers, they begin to select books from the school library for their 30 minutes of home reading. Books in the library are color coded to roughly approximate traditional basal reader levels. For example, all books that could be read easily by a child reading at preprimer level are coded red, primer level is coded yellow, and so forth. Students have the opportunity to visit the library daily to select books for home reading at their independent level, although in some classes, students in one reading group may elect to read the same trade book in order to support one another and enjoy discussion of the same book. Students may also choose books that interest them that are above their independent level, but these are to be read after 30 minutes of independent reading is completed. Books that students read independently are not intended to be challenging. Instead, independent books are to be books that students can read effortlessly, so that reading will be a successful experience, motivating students to accomplish the volumes of reading that lead to progress in reading. With the exception of beginning readers, most independent home reading is silent reading. An alternative to reading at one's independent level is to select a taped book and to follow along as the book is read on tape for as many times as necessary to be able to read a section fluently to a teacher the following day.

Students often write book notes or summaries about their home reading. Often these notes or summaries are used as a way to foster practice of the strategy being taught in reading group. Books (or chapters in books) read at home each evening are discussed at school the next day. Sometimes these discussions take place in a conference with the teacher, sometimes with a peer, and on other occasions books read at home are discussed in small groups. One of the students' favorite activities for responding to books is to present 2-minute book commercials. Students, especially those who read taped books, are often asked to choose a section of the book to read aloud to a teacher or peer as a means of monitoring fluency.

Parent Read Aloud. While students are in the library, they also select a book for a parent to read aloud. Each evening parents are asked to read to their Benchmark student for a minimum of 15 minutes. In the primary grades the parent-read-aloud book is almost always good literature at the child's conceptual level. However, as Benchmark students reach the higher grades and are engrossed in Benchmark's grade-level-appropriate social studies and science programs, parents often spend the 15-minute parent-read-aloud time reading nonfiction selections related to the concepts being taught in social studies or science.

Benchmark Literature Program. Benchmark also has designed a read-aloud literature program, originally based on *A Curriculum for English* (1966), but which has been modified, reorganized, and updated by the staff. The program is implemented daily by classroom teachers and language specialists (Gaskins & Elliot, 1983) for the purpose of both enjoyment and helping students become aware of the characteristics of various genres. As part of this 20-minute-a-day program, approximately 10 genres are presented, one during each month of the school year (e.g., realistic fiction, folktales, historical fiction, myths, etc.). Examples of each genre of literature are read to students and patterns found in each are discussed and become part of the background knowledge students use to predict and understand other texts. Discussions of these literature patterns are also part of the discussion of the trade books and stories read in reading group and at home.

In their many mediated encounters with text throughout the school day, Benchmark students become aware of structure and patterns in texts, make inferences between the text and their background knowledge, and monitor their reading for sense making. However, the job of helping delayed readers does not stop with mediating these processes. Students also must be taught to orchestrate these strategies to complete real-world and school tasks and to overcome the maladaptive nonreading factors that often coexist with delayed reading, such as disorganization, inattention, passivity, rigidity, impulsivity, and nonpersistence (I. W. Gaskins, 1984). These issues are discussed in the next section.

TAKING CONTROL OF STYLES, TEMPERAMENTS, EMOTIONS, AND TASKS

Follow up of Benchmark students over 25 years suggests that teaching students to read well is not enough. Unless teachers address the styles, temperaments, beliefs, and behaviors that initially contributed to students' difficulties in learning to read, delayed readers may return to the mainstream only to experience difficulty again, despite being able to read at or near grade level. The significant results of Benchmark's year-long cognitive training project (Gaskins & Baron, 1985) highlighted the benefits of making students aware of personal characteristics that can impede learning and flexible problem-solving and teaching them *how* to manage them. To accomplish the goal of helping Benchmark students control styles, temperaments, emotions, and tasks both stand-alone and embedded programs are provided.

Stand-Alone Programs

Programs both to support students in achieving awareness and control over issues that may interfere with their achieving well in academic or social situations and to support teachers in endeavoring to guide students to take charge of styles, temperaments, emotions, and tasks are part of Benchmark's across-the-curriculum program for delayed readers. These programs include a Support Services department staffed by psychologists, counselors, and social workers who serve as classroom consultants to teachers, conduct weekly class meetings, see students individually or in small groups for problem-solving sessions, address emotional overlay and resulting emotional issues, and lead parent groups. In addition, a team of placement counselors work with parents and graduating students to place students in schools that are an appropriate academic match for their abilities and the way they learn. This team also follows and supports former Benchmark students throughout their school years. Additional special programs for dealing with styles, temperaments, emotions, and tasks include a mentor program (R. W. Gaskins, 1992), courses in how the brain works (Psych 101 and LAT; Gaskins & Elliot, 1991), after-school guided study, and an Outward Bound-type program, to mention only a few. In addition to the programs outlined above, teachers address issues of control over style, temperament, emotion, and task as part of their daily teaching.

Embedded Programs

Goal Setting. Regular weekly goal-setting conferences are a key factor in helping students deal with style issues and are one of the cornerstones of the Benchmark program. Students from the youngest to the oldest take part in conferences with their teachers to set goals and review progress. The first goal-setting conference of the year often includes not only the teacher and student, but also the student's parents. During these weekly conferences a style, temperament, feeling, or task issue that needs to be changed or adapted is identified, then those attending the conference clarify and refine a contract stating in measurable, observable terms what the student will accomplish during a specified period of time and how the student, teacher, and parents will collaborate to achieve these goals.

For example, a teacher may open a conference by inviting the student (and parents, if present) to share the student's strengths. Next, an issue that seems to be interfering with the student's academic progress may be addressed. After some discussion, those present may agree that attention and active involvement in learning are major concerns. The teacher might ask the student and others to describe how they would expect the student's behavior to look when she is attending and actively involved. What behavior would they be able to observe? Next, those present might brainstorm to determine the observable behaviors that would count as attentiveness and active involvement and conclude that these behaviors are: having eyes on the speaker for discussion or instruction and eyes on the text when that is the expectation, as well as contributing ideas to group discussion, summarizing what has been learned, and / or critiquing what was in the text or contributed by others. Some or all of these behaviors would become the agreed upon goals. The teacher would next ask the student what the expectancy for meeting the goals should be and over what time period, as well as what support she would like in meeting her goals. A contract is then drawn up that includes the terms discussed. Sometimes parents promise a reward, such as lunch at McDonalds, if the student achieves five consecutive days with pluses on the goal card.

Initially teachers attempt to make the goals easily attainable, and increase expectations over time. Thus, the goal for the first week might be for the teacher to catch the student with eyes on the speaker more times than not during reading-group prereading activities, with the expectation several weeks later that eyes must be on the speaker 9 out of 10 times that the teacher observes the student and that the student participates three times during reading group discussion. For monitoring attentive behavior, the teacher may use a card or bookmark on which the goal is written. As the lesson proceeds he tells the student to make check marks on the card whenever he observed the student with eyes on the speaker. At the end of reading group the student would receive a plus on her goal card if there were a certain amount of marks on the card. Eyes on the text may be monitored similarly with the teacher marking the card as the student reads. As part of the collaborative agreement, the student may ask the teacher to help her focus by cuing her on the first occasion of inattentiveness.

Teachers regularly cue students to remember their goals and suggest strategies that students might implement in a particular situation to achieve their goals. Student progress is monitored daily, usually using a goal card taped to the student's desk or, for older students, a goal sheet placed in front of a student's notebook. At the weekly goal conference the student and teacher discuss progress and determine if any changes need to be made in goals or the collaborative roles of those involved. The goal card or goal sheet is often sent home as a means of communicating with parents about the student's progress. Parents sign the goal card or goal sheet, often adding comments, and return it to the teacher.

Task Analysis. Analyzing a task is important, whether the task is reading to gain ideas or reading for pleasure. However, as students move out of the beginning stages of reading, they discover that the tasks of reading to participate in a discussion or for pleasure are relatively uncomplicated when compared to most life or school tasks. For one thing, they often receive considerably more adult mediation as they accomplish these short-term, daily school tasks. On the other hand, delayed readers often experience a different situation when they encounter tasks that require planning for events over time, such as the need to write a report for a Scout meeting or complete a written list of directives left by a parent that need to be completed prior to his arrival from work. Even when they can read the text involved, Benchmark's delayed readers often find such tasks frustrating and to be avoided, usually because they are unaware of how to analyze the task into

component parts or make and execute a plan of action to complete each part systematically.

Tasks involving reading are complicated because they necessitate individuals being aware of, and taking control over, at least four variables: task, text, situation, and person (Gaskins & Elliot, 1991). The complexity of a task is further compounded by the parts into which each of these variables can be broken. Tasks that teachers assign are often much more complicated than most teachers realize and are usually not accompanied by the explicit explanations and the scaffolding delayed readers need to meet with success. Having experienced the fact that delayed readers usually do not fill in the gaps for the procedures that a teacher leaves unstated, the Benchmark staff has designed a number of procedures to teach delayed readers how to navigate the complexities of task completion.

Analyzing the task is often introduced to students as a problem-solving task, followed by an explicit explanation of the what, why, when, and how of task analysis. For example, a teacher might posit, "What would you do if you had the task of taking care of your neighbor's house while she was on vacation?" Through brainstorming, the teacher would take students through the process of breaking the job into parts and making a plan for the completion of each part in light of situation and person variables, such as the situation of having soccer practice and homework responsibilities most evenings and the personal characteristic of procrastination. The teacher might continue the strategy discussion something like this:

During the next 4 or 5 years at Benchmark you will be hearing a great deal about analyzing the task. The reason this goal is important is that many school and life tasks seem overwhelming, not because they are too difficult to achieve, rather because we do not break them into manageable parts and work on them a little at a time. It is sort of like eating an elephant; you have to eat it one bite at a time. Just as you wouldn't eat an elephant in one sitting without getting pretty sick, you also cannot complete a science project the night before it is due and expect not to experience some problems. The good thing about task analysis strategies is that you can use them for tasks in and out of school. They are a means of problem solving, a way to accomplish any job you have to tackle.

The teacher working with older students might continue the explicit explanation of task analysis as explained below, writing the steps for task analysis on a chart or the chalkboard, underlining the first letter of the action word, and grouping the steps into categories of task, plan, and do.

Here are some general steps you might use in analyzing a task. First, put the task in your own words to be sure that you really understand what the task is. If you have any doubts about your interpretation of the task, it is a good idea to check your interpretation with someone you know who has a good track record for interpreting tasks correctly. Once you get straight what it is you need to accomplish, break the task into small manageable parts and make a plan for how you will accomplish each part. Next you need to analyze text, situation, and personal characteristics that could cause difficulties in completing the task and add to your plan strategies for dealing with these factors. Once you have completed the planning stage by making a list of all the parts of the task, as well as how and when you will accomplish each part, you are ready to implement your plan.

The chart the teacher constructed to explain the process would include: *P*ut task in own words; *C*heck understanding with someone; *B*reak task into parts; *M*ake a plan for each part; *A*nalyze text, situation, and person; *A*dd to the plan; *D*o it. These steps remain visible in the classroom throughout the year, with students often devising a mnemonic to aid in remembering the steps. (PCB the task and MAA a plan, then do it.)

Students are explicitly taught how to employ each part of the process before they tackle applying the entire process on their own. For example, a class may have the task of preparing for an essay test in social studies that will be given when the class completes a unit in 4 or 5 weeks. The part of the task on which the teacher may choose to focus for this unit of instruction is how to answer an essay question. The teacher would walk students through the process of analyzing the task (being prepared to take an essay test in 4 or 5 weeks) and scaffold instruction so that as a class the plan would be accomplished, with perhaps the difference from most school situations being that the students would know from the beginning what the one or two essay questions would be. In addition to teaching the social studies concepts for the unit, the teacher would explicitly teach students how to gather the information they will need to answer the essay questions. Near the completion of the unit, the teacher would provide explicit instructions and guided practice in how to answer an essay question. The strategy is one that during the past few years Benchmark students have dubbed A-NOW. The letters of the acronym stand for: *A*nalyze the question and write it in your own words; brainstorm *N*otes listing everything you can

think of that is related to the question; *O*rganize your notes; and *W*rite your essay. For an excellent description of how a teacher guides students through the process of completing a task, see a case study of Sharon Rauch's reading group instruction in Gaskins and Elliot (1991).

CONCLUDING REMARKS

Benchmark's program is designed for children who must have a program that starts where they are, proceeds according to the competencies they develop, and teaches explicitly what they do not figure out on their own. To provide this, the staff must understand the factors that make reading difficult, know their students well, and meet students where they are. The program is based on the belief that delayed readers need a variety of reading and writing experiences, instruction using a variety of methods and materials that are eclectic and flexible, and a lot of reading in easy material. Benchmark students also need explicit instruction in strategies for identifying words, constructing meaning, and dealing with styles, temperaments, emotions, and tasks. During instruction, Benchmark teachers emphasize: the structure and patterns in words, text, and knowledge; inferences between the text and the reader's background knowledge, and monitoring for meaning making. In addition, the staff provides stand-alone and embedded programs to help students deal with styles, temperaments, emotions, and tasks. The emphasis is on goal setting and task analysis as the staff guides students in analyzing the components of a task or situation and how to match those components with appropriate strategies to control task, text, situation, and person variables. The program works because of caring, knowledgeable staff members who know how to initiate and sustain meaningful interactions with students and their families.

References

Adams, M. J. (1990). *Beginning to read: Thinking and learning about print*. Cambridge, MA: MIT Press.

Allington, R. L., & McGill-Franzen, A. (1989). School response to reading failure: Chapter 1 and special education students in grades 2, 4, and 8. *Elementary School Journal, 89,* 529–542.

Chall, J. S., & Squire, J. S. (1991). The publishing industry and textbooks. In R. Barr, J. L. Kamil, P. Mosenthal, & P. D. Pearson (Eds.), *Handbook of reading research* (Vol. 2, pp. 120–167). New York: Longman.

Clay, M. M. (1991). *Becoming literate: The construction of inner control*. Portsmouth, NH: Heinemann

Cunningham, P. M., & Allington, R. L. (1994). *Classrooms that work: They can all read and write*. New York: Harper Collins.

A Curriculum For English. (1966). Lincoln, NB: University of Nebraska Press.

Gaskins, I. W. (1980). *The Benchmark story*. Media, PA: Benchmark Press.

Gaskins, I. W., (1982). A writing program for poor readers and the rest of the class, too. *Language Arts, 59,* 854–861 .

Gaskins, I. W. (1984). There's more to a reading problem than poor

reading. *Journal of Learning Disabilities, 17,* 467–471.

Gaskins, I. W. (1988). Helping teachers adapt to the needs of students with learning problems. In S. J. Samuels & P. D. Pearson (Eds.), *Changing school reading programs* (pp. 143–159). Newark, DE: International Reading Association.

Gaskins, I. W. (1991). And it works for them, too! In J. T. Feeley, D. C. Strickland, & S. B. Wepner (Eds.), *From writing process to reading process: K–8 teachers share their literacy programs*. New York: Teachers College Press.

Gaskins, I. W., (1994a). Knowing how to learn. In K. McGilly (Ed.), *Classroom lessons: Integrating cognitive theory and classroom practice*. Cambridge, MA: MIT Press.

Gaskins, I. W. (1994b). Creating optimum learning environments: Is membership in the whole language community necessary? In F. Lehr & J. Osborn (Eds.), *Reading, language, and literacy: Instruction for the twenty-first century* (pp. 115–130). Hillsdale, NJ: Erlbaum.

Gaskins, I. W., Anderson, R. C., Pressley, M., Cunicelli, E. A., & Satlow, E. (1993). The moves and cycles of cognitive process instruction. *Elementary School Journal, 93,* 277–304.

Gaskins, I. W., & Baron, J. (1985). Teaching poor readers to cope with maladaptive cognitive styles: A training program. *Journal of Learning Disabilities, 18,* 390–394.

Gaskins, I. W., Cunicelli, E. A., & Satlow, E. (1992). Implementing an across-the-curriculum strategies program: Reactions to change. In J. Pressley, K. Harris, & J. Guthrie (Eds.), *Promoting academic competence and literacy in school* (pp. 411–426). Boston: Academic Press.

Gaskins, I. W., Downer, M., Anderson, R. C., Cunningham, P. M., Gaskins, R. W., Schommer, M., & the Teachers of Benchmark School (1988). A metacognitive approach to phonics: Using what you know to decode what you don't know. *Remedial and Special Education, 9,* 36–41, 66.

Gaskins, I. W., & Elliot, T. T. (1983). *Teaching for success: Administrative and classroom practices at Benchmark School.* Media, PA: Benchmark Press.

Gaskins, I. W., & Elliot, T. T. (1991). *Implementing cognitive strategy instruction across the school: The Benchmark manual for teachers.* Cambridge, MA: Brookline Books.

Gaskins, I. W., Guthrie, J. T., Satlow, E., Ostertag, J., Six, L., Byrne, J., & Connor, B. (1994). Integrating instruction of science, reading, and writing: Goals, teacher development, and assessment. *Journal of Research in Science Teaching, 31,* 558–565.

Gaskins, I. W., Satlow, E., Hyson, D., Ostertag, J., & Six, L. (1994). Classroom talk about text: Learning in science class. *Journal of Reading, 37,* 2–9.

Gaskins, R. W., (1988). The missing ingredients: Time on task, direct instruction, and writing. *The Reading Teacher, 41,* 750–755.

Gaskins, R. W., (1992). When good instruction is not enough: A mentor program. *The Reading Teacher, 45,* 568–572.

Gaskins, R. W., & Gaskins, I. W. (In press). Creating readers who read for meaning and love to read. The Benchmark School reading program. In S. A. Stahl & D. A. Hayes (Eds.), *Instructional models in reading.* Hillsdale, NJ: Erlbaum.

Gaskins, R. W., Gaskins, J. C., & Gaskins, I. W. (1991). A decoding program for poor readers—and the rest of the class, too! *Language Arts, 68,* 213–225.

Gaskins, R. W., Gaskins, J. C., & Gaskins, I. W. (1992). Using what you know to figure out what you don't know: An analogy approach to decoding. *Reading and Writing Quarterly: Overcoming Learning Difficulties, 8,* 197–221.

Guthrie, J. T. & Greaney, V. (1991). Literacy acts. In R. Barr, J. L. Kamil, P. Mosenthal, & P. D. Pearson (Eds.), *Handbook of reading research* (Vol. 2, pp. 680–696). New York: Longman.

Hiebert, E. H. (1991). Research directions: Literacy contexts and literacy processes. *Language Arts, 68,* 134–139.

McCaslin, M. M. (1989). Commentary: Whole language: Theory, instruction, and future implementation. *The Elementary School Journal, 90,* 223–229.

Pearson, P. D. (1993). Teaching and learning reading: A research perspective. *Language Arts, 70,* 502–511.

Pearson, P. D., & Fielding, L. (1991). Comprehension instruction. In R. Barr, J. L. Kamil, P. Mosenthal, & P. D. Pearson (Eds.), *Handbook of reading research* (Vol. 2, pp. 815–860).

Pressley, M., El-Dinary, P. B., Gaskins, I. W., Schuder, T., Bergman, J. L., Almasi, J., & Brown, R. (1992). Direct explanation done well: Transactional instruction of reading comprehension strategies. *Elementary School Journal, 92,* 513–555.

Pressley M., Gaskins, I. W., Cunicelli, E. A., Burdick, N.J., Schaub-Matt, M., Lee, D. S., & Powell, N. (1991). Strategy instruction at Benchmark School: A faculty interview study. *Learning Disability Quarterly, 14,* 19–48.

Smith, F. (1994). *Understanding reading: A psycholinguistic analysis of reading and learning to read* (5th ed.). Hillsdale, NJ: Erlbaum.

Stanovich, K. E., (1984). The interactive-compensatory model of reading: A confluence of developmental, experimental, and educational psychology. *Remedial and Special Education, 5,* 11–19.

Taylor, B. M., Frye, B. J., & Maruyama, G. (1990). Time spent reading and reading growth. New York: Longman. *American Educational Research Journal, 27,* 351–362.

EFFECTIVE LITERACY INSTRUCTION:
FINDINGS OF THE KAMEHAMEHA ELEMENTARY
EDUCATION PROGRAM

Kathryn H. Au and Claire L. Asam
UNIVERSITY OF HAWAII

For 23 years, members of the staff at the Kamehameha Elementary Education Program (KEEP) carried out research and development efforts aimed at improving the school literacy achievement of students of Native Hawaiian ancestry. In this chapter we discuss lessons learned during the last 5 years of KEEP's work, which focused on the development and implementation of a whole literacy curriculum, including a system of portfolio assessment tied to standards. Detailed accounts of KEEP's earlier work are available elsewhere (Au, Crowell, et al., 1986; Tharp & Gallimore, 1988).

BACKGROUND OF KEEP

In general, Hawaiian students tend to have low scores on standardized achievement tests, especially in reading (Kamehameha Schools, 1993). KEEP was established in 1971 with the goal of bringing Hawaiian students in the elementary grades to parity with national norms in the language arts.

KEEP's initial program development work took place in a laboratory school, where both of us served as teachers. Under the influence of behaviorism, the curriculum that evolved in KEEP's early years, the Kamehameha Reading Objectives System (KROS; Crowell, 1981), took a mastery learning approach to skills. This curriculum, however, differed from others of the time in emphasizing comprehension, even at kindergarten and 1st-grade levels.

In 1978, after the comprehension-oriented curriculum showed promising results, KEEP began disseminating to public school classrooms. The strategy was to improve students' reading achievement by developing the instructional expertise of classroom teachers. The members of the staff of

KEEP, known as consultants, were based in public schools to provide in-service support to teachers.

Over a 16-year period, KEEP expanded steadily to schools on three islands. In 1994, the last year of its operation, KEEP's curriculum was being used by 176 teachers, affecting 3,476 students in 9 elementary schools. Most of KEEP's students were Native Hawaiians; from low-income families, including many families on welfare; and speakers of Hawaii Creole English, a nonmainstream variety of English.

CURRICULUM AND ASSESSMENT

From 1978 to 1989 we continued to use the comprehension-oriented curriculum. Students also received systematic instruction in skills such as word identification and sight vocabulary, and their progress was charted using criterion-referenced tests. Beginning in 1984, teachers were introduced to the process approach to writing, although students' progress in writing was not systematically evaluated.

In the spring of 1989, due to internal and external evaluations that showed low levels of reading achievement in KEEP classrooms, we came under pressure to overhaul the program. We decided to develop a whole literacy curriculum, drawing upon the social constructivist perspective (Au & Asam, 1994).

Six Aspects of Literacy

The curriculum we designed addressed six aspects of literacy (Au, Scheu, Kawakami, & Herman, 1990):

(1) ownership,
(2) reading comprehension,
(3) the writing process,
(4) language and vocabulary knowledge,
(5) word reading strategies and spelling, and
(6) voluntary reading.

The first aspect of literacy, ownership, also served as the overall goal of the curriculum. Ownership has to do with students valuing their own ability to read and write (Au, Scheu, & Kawakami, 1990). Students who have ownership of literacy have a positive attitude toward reading and writing and make literacy a part of their everyday lives.

The second aspect of literacy was reading comprehension. In the whole literacy curriculum, comprehension was seen to involve a dynamic interaction among the reader, the text, and the situation or social context in which reading took place (Wixson, Peters, Weber, & Roeber, 1987). Drawing on reader response theory, the curriculum gave equal attention to the aesthetic and efferent stances (Rosenblatt, 1978).

Use of the term *writing process* for the third aspect of literacy conveyed a view of writing as dynamic and nonlinear, including such activities as planning, drafting, revising, editing, and publishing (Graves, 1983).

Language and vocabulary knowledge, the fourth aspect of literacy, involves the ability to understand and use appropriate terms and structures in both spoken and printed English. It includes the ability to learn the meanings of new words encountered during reading (Herman & Weaver, 1988).

In the fifth aspect of literacy, word reading strategies and spelling, the curriculum drew on Clay's (1985) notion that effective word identification requires the simultaneous use of information from different cue systems: meaning (i.e., passage and sentence context), structural, and visual.

In voluntary reading, the final aspect of literacy, students select the materials they wish to read, either for information or pleasure. Ideally, students also choose the times when they will read (Spiegel, 1981). In short, the whole literacy curriculum brought writing to the same level of importance as reading and gave equal attention to the affective and cognitive dimensions of literacy, in keeping with a social constructivist perspective.

Cultural Responsiveness

The commitment of KEEP to cultural responsiveness in instruction remained unchanged in the shift to the whole literacy curriculum. Culturally responsive instruction allows students to achieve academic goals through means consistent with the values and standards of behavior of the home culture (Au, 1993). For example, many Hawaiian families attach great value to the well-being of the extended family or 'ohana (Gallimore, Boggs, & Jordan, 1974). The ability to work with others for the good of the family is judged more important than a person's individual achievements. In contrast, schools typically place greater value on individual achievement. Three specific aspects of culturally responsive instruction played a prominent part in both KEEP's old and new curricula: peer teaching–learning interactions (Jordan, 1985), a style of

classroom management described as "a smile with teeth" (D'Amato, 1988), and the talk story style of discussion (Au & Mason, 1983). All three build on students' preferences for cooperative, group activities as opposed to competitive, individualistic ones.

Writers' and Readers' Workshops

Instruction in the whole literacy curriculum occurred in two blocks of time called the writers' workshop and the readers' workshop. The writers' workshop typically began with a mini-lesson and teacher and student sharing, followed by a period when students did their own writing (Calkins, 1991; Graves, 1983). Teacher and peer conferences occurred during this time. Near the end of the workshop, the teacher generally gathered the students together for the author's chair (Graves & Hansen, 1983), a time when one or two students read their drafts or published books aloud to the class and received feedback about their piece.

The organization of the readers' workshop varied more than that of the writers' workshop, due primarily to the teacher's decision about when to schedule sustained silent reading and teacher read-alouds. The workshop often began with the teacher reading aloud or conducting a mini-lesson. Then the teacher met with students in small groups to discuss works of literature. Teachers used different approaches to grouping. In the primary grades, students were grouped by ability about half the time, and by interest (for example, in reading a particular book, or in doing research on a particular topic) the rest of the time. In the upper grades, students were usually grouped by interest. Small-group discussions generally began with students sharing their writing in response to literature. When not with the teacher, students read independently or with a partner, wrote in their literature response logs, and worked on individual and small-group projects.

Benchmarks and Portfolio Assessment

The portfolio assessment system designed as part of the whole literacy curriculum was anchored to standards, which we termed grade-level benchmarks. The benchmarks described the desired achievements of the hypothetical average student at the end of each grade. The sources for the benchmarks were (1) the state department of education's language arts curriculum guide, (2) the reading objectives of the National Assessment of Educational Progress (1989), (3) a well-known standardized test series used in the state's evaluation program, and (4) recently published basal reading, language arts, and literature programs. In areas not traditionally evaluated, such as ownership and voluntary reading, we developed benchmarks based on available research and our observations in classrooms.

In keeping with the spirit of the whole literacy curriculum, the benchmarks were stated holistically yet with wording specific enough to guide the efforts of teachers and students. Examples of benchmarks for ownership of writing at the 3rd-grade level included the following:

- Shows interest in others' writing
- Writes outside of school
- Third-grade benchmarks for the writing process included:
- Selects own topics for writing
- Tries to make writing interesting for the reader

Among the reading comprehension benchmarks at third grade were the following:

- Shares written responses to literature in a small group
- Comprehends and writes about theme / author's message

Many of the benchmarks reflected our concern with process, but we were concerned with product as well (cf. Delpit, 1988). For example, we included a benchmark indicating that the holistic quality of students' writing samples had to be judged at grade level with respect to an anchor piece.

Students' performance in the six aspects of literacy could be measured against the benchmarks and their performance rated as above, at, or below grade level. This made it possible to report program results in terms of the number or percentage of students above, at, or below grade level for each aspect of literacy (for a full discussion of the portfolio assessment system, refer to Au, 1994; Carroll, 1993).

Although its primary purpose was program evaluation, KEEP's portfolio assessment system also provided teachers with detailed information about students' progress. Teachers could use this information to guide and improve instruction in the six aspects of literacy. In addition, the system allowed students to become aware of the expectations for their grade level, to set their own goals, and to monitor their own progress.

Approach to Teacher Development

Once a school elected to become involved with KEEP, teachers volunteered to participate in the program. Each volunteer was assigned to a KEEP consultant, who usually worked with 8 to 10 teachers. The consultants were experienced teachers who had completed a one-year course of study to become proficient both in the KEEP curriculum and in approaches to supporting teacher development.

The consultants' work centered on classroom observations, followed by individual meetings for the purpose of feedback and discussion with the teacher. Consultants also conducted demonstration lessons and held workshops. As in most traditional teacher education approaches, the consultants usually spent more time informing and less time working with teachers on collaborative problem solving. Although the teacher–consultant relationship was generally a positive and supportive one, it did not tend to foster feelings of equality or to promote teachers' sense of responsibility for their own professional development (Giuli, 1985).

Consultants tended to devote the greatest amount of time to teachers with the lowest levels of expertise. Most of the KEEP schools experienced high levels of teacher turnover. The rate could be as high as 33% in a given school and averaged 20% per year across all KEEP schools. Many new teachers were recent college graduates who wanted help with the basics of classroom organization and management. Consultants seemed to work effectively with new teachers, who accepted a rather directive form of assistance. However, most consultants seemed uncertain about how to work effectively with highly experienced teachers. As discussed below, consultants had to overcome a reluctance to work intensively with experienced teachers.

Implementation of the Whole Literacy Curriculum

Year 1. We developed the whole literacy curriculum rapidly, under pressure to make changes in KEEP and to show better student achievement results. As a result, when the curriculum was introduced in the fall of 1989, teachers and consultants had not had a chance to contribute to its development. The KEEP consultants and public school teachers alike spent Year 1 struggling with the change in philosophy, from a behavioral, mastery learning curriculum to a constructivist, holistic one. Many consultants and teachers liked the new philosophy but felt unsure about how to translate the ideas into practice. Few changes took place in classroom organization and instruction, and no attempt was made to implement portfolio assessment.

Years 2 and 3. During Years 2 and 3, we intensified staff development efforts for both consultants and teachers. With the philosophical changes well underway, we felt we could focus on the details of the readers' and the writers' workshop. In the readers' workshop, most teachers began to use children's literature in place of basal readers. In kindergarten and first grade, big books and shared reading became common. In the writers' workshop, students wrote and published pieces on topics of their own choice. Observers noted a high level of student engagement in authentic literacy activities, and teachers expressed enthusiasm about students' positive attitudes toward reading and writing. Most teachers did not yet feel comfortable with portfolio assessment, so consultants took the responsibility for managing the portfolios and collecting the benchmark data in classrooms.

Despite signs of change, the achievement results during Years 2 and 3 proved disappointing (Au, 1994). Results for ownership, voluntary reading, and word reading strategies looked promising, but results were poor for the aspects of literacy demanding higher level cognitive processing: reading comprehension, the writing process, and language and vocabulary knowledge. In these aspects, about two thirds of the students scored below grade level.

At this point, we had to address the question of why the whole literacy curriculum had not proved effective with Hawaiian children. One possibility was that the design of the curriculum could not meet the needs of Hawaiian students in learning to read and write. Another possibility was that the curriculum had not shown a positive effect because it had not been adequately implemented. We thought the second possibility was more likely.

Years 4 and 5. At the beginning of Year 4, to test the possibility that inadequate implementation was the problem, we undertook the Demonstration Classroom Project (DCP). The purpose of the project was to show that the whole literacy curriculum, when fully implemented, could make a measurable difference in the students' literacy achievement. In order to assess implementation, we devised classroom checklists, one for the readers' workshop and one for the writers' workshop, listing items central to our vision of classrooms.

The KEEP staff worked with a small group of demonstration teachers, those judged most willing and able to achieve full implementation of the whole literacy curriculum in their classrooms. The project involved 13 teachers and 281 students during Year 4, increasing to 29 teachers and 608 students in Year 5. The demonstration teachers were asked to select a focus, either the readers' workshop or the writers' workshop. Both years, the vast majority of teachers chose to focus on writing (11 in Year 4 and 26 in Year 5).

Demonstration teachers entered into a rigorous process of staff development. Once a month, the consultant and an outside observer took detailed notes on events in the classroom during the writers' or the readers' workshop. On the basis of their observations, they noted the classroom checklist items present and absent and met with the teacher to discuss the results. The teacher then set goals for the coming month. During both Years 4 and 5, the demonstration teachers enjoyed extraordinary success in fully implementing their chosen workshop. While they started with about 50% of the items in place, they had implemented about 90% by the end of the school year.

The DCP led to a dramatic turnabout in student achievement. In the writing process in particular, student achievement reversed the pattern shown in the previous 2 years. Now, two thirds of the students showed achievement at or above grade level. This pattern of achievement held across the board, in upper grade as well as primary classrooms. Results for reading comprehension showed improvement as well. However, with only two classes focusing on the readers' workshop in Year 4, and only three in Year 5, these results were not considered robust. Portfolio results for Years 2 and 3 were available for a subset of teachers, and comparisons showed that these teachers achieved better results with their students in Years 4 and 5 (for full reports of implementation and achievement results, refer to Asam, Au, et al., 1994; Asam, Blake, et al., 1993).

Go with the Goers

Prior to the DCP, KEEP consultants had tried to achieve across-the-board implementation of the whole literacy curriculum by working with all teachers, including those with little or no experience in the profession. Consultants appeared to believe that teachers experiencing the greatest difficulty implementing the curriculum should receive the most help. Consequently, consultants did not spend much time with the teachers most capable of implementing the curriculum at a high level.

We knew consultants would need to organize their time differently to ensure that some teachers would achieve full implementation of the whole literacy curriculum. We adopted a strategy described by Peters and Waterman (1982) as that of small wins, building from a small group of people most likely to be successful. During a visit to KEEP, Jan

Turbill and Brian Cambourne, educators experienced in assisting teachers in the transition to whole language, described the process to us succinctly: Go with the goers. That became our motto.

At the start of Year 4, we asked each consultant to think about her pool of teachers and to commit herself to working intensively with just one teacher who had the potential of achieving full implementation of either the writers' or the readers' workshop by the end of the school year. We used the term *demonstration teachers* to describe these candidates for full implementation. The demonstration teachers were generally implementing about half to three fourths of the items in the writers' or the readers' workshop (as indicated by the classroom checklist) and ready to work toward implementing all or nearly all the items.

We referred to the other teachers receiving KEEP's services as either *emergent* or *recruitment* teachers. Emergent teachers could be expected to become demonstration teachers in 1–2 years, with the consultant's support. An emergent teacher was implementing about one fourth to one half of the features of the curriculum and was ready to work toward implementing about three fourths of the features. Recruitment teachers could be expected to become demonstration teachers in 3–4 years and were implementing relatively few features of the curriculum.

In collaboration with their consultant, teachers analyzed their teaching and identified their current level of program implementation, according to the classroom checklist. Teachers determined their level of involvement with KEEP, whether they wished to become demonstration, emergent, or recruitment teachers. Most of the demonstration and emergent teachers had been associated with KEEP for several years and had similar levels of knowledge of the curriculum. Demonstration teachers often differed from emergent teachers, not just at the level of program implementation but in the time and effort they were willing to commit to their professional development at that particular juncture. Recruitment teachers generally had not previously been associated with KEEP and / or were new to the teaching profession.

Most consultants found it difficult to accept the logic of going with the goers, of working intensively with just the demonstration teachers. Some consultants had become comfortable serving in the role of answer-givers with new teachers, and they were uncomfortable with their new role, which required that they work collaboratively with expert teachers who knew as much (and sometimes more) about instruction in the whole literacy curriculum. Some consultants believed that giving a great deal of support to a small group of teachers would contribute to a perception of favoritism at their schools, since teachers had the expectation that everyone would receive the same services.

We replied to these concerns by advising the consultants that KEEP's resources needed to be distributed on the basis of potential benefit to students. We reminded consultants that the practice of working with all teachers had not resulted in gains in student achievement. We argued that resources should go to the teachers who had the best chance, at that point, of fully implementing the curriculum and improving students' achievement.

The small-wins strategy differs from the usual approach to curriculum change. Often, a district mandates the change, with the expectation that all teachers will move forward at the same time. Resources to support the change effort are scattered rather than focused, and the effort fails. The small-wins strategy is based on the expectation that change will be initiated by a small group of highly committed goers. Resources are directed toward the goers to ensure their success. In the case of KEEP we found that the first wave of goers (demonstration teachers who began in Year 4) managed to succeed at a level exceeding our expectations. Year 5 went more smoothly than Year 4, in part because the first group of goers served as examples and advisors to the second group.

Give Teachers Different Kinds of Support

Published reports suggest that many teachers require 5 years or more to complete the paradigm shift from a behavioral, skills orientation to a holistic, constructivist orientation (e.g., Routman, 1991). Our work at KEEP supports this estimate. It took 4–5 years for most of the KEEP consultants, as well as the teachers, to make the shift. In the model of professional development we followed in the DCP, we looked at the development of teachers, expertise in the whole literacy curriculum as a process taking 4–5 years. Services to teachers' differed depending on their decision to assume the role of recruitment, emergent, or demonstration teacher.

Services to recruitment teachers centered on workshops, both large- and small-group events. Consultants held meetings with small groups of recruitment teachers and made arrangements for them to visit demonstration teachers. However, consultants seldom observed recruitment teachers or provided them with individual feedback. Consultants referred to these efforts as "planting the seeds" to develop the teacher's knowledge of the whole literacy curriculum and to establish a working relationship with KEEP. Recruitment teachers tried to implement what they learned in workshops, using their more experienced colleagues as resources.

With emergent teachers, consultants increased their focus on the classroom checklist. They worked with emergent teachers to assess their current level of implementation and identify goals for improving implementation. Consultants engaged in activities such as conducting demonstration lessons, observing in classrooms, and holding individual meetings with these teachers. Teachers and consultants planned lessons together and began to engage in collaborative problem solving.

With demonstration teachers, consultants worked on the same activities but in a more fast-paced and exacting manner. A monthly cycle of teacher goal setting, consultant support for meeting goals, and feedback to the teacher was established and maintained throughout the school year. Consultants also took steps to involve 2nd-year demonstration teachers in staff development activities for 1st-year demonstration teachers and others.

In staff development programs in some districts, the approach is to give all teachers the same information and types of support. Our experience suggests that such an undifferentiated approach does not work. We found it more effective to rely on teachers' judgments of their own level of expertise and desire to engage in professional development activities. We tailored professional development activities to the teachers' needs and interests in becoming expert at holistic, constructivist forms of instruction.

Outsiders, such as the KEEP consultants, can act as catalysts for change. Over the long term, however, change is best sustained through a steadily expanding network of demonstration teachers within each school. With both instructional expertise and knowledge of the school context, these teachers are in the best position to prepare other teachers to become skilled in an innovative curriculum so as to sustain change.

Bolster a Holistic Curriculum with Systematic Instruction and Benchmarks

The results of the DCP showed us that the whole literacy curriculum could make a difference in students' achievement. However, we learned that positive results were obtained with only full, not partial, implementation of the curriculum. There were striking differences between students' achievement in Years 2 and 3 versus Years 4 and 5.

During Years 2 and 3, we saw promising results in ownership, voluntary reading, and word reading strategies. These results seemed to be related to changes in classrooms as teachers began to adopt portions of the whole literacy curriculum, becoming more student-centered in their teaching and giving students more choice during literacy activities. Students developed positive attitudes toward literacy, they did more reading on their own, and by doing more reading they improved their word reading strategies.

Yet during Years 2 and 3, achievement in reading comprehension, the writing process, and language and vocabulary knowledge lagged. With the KEEP students, we found that building a positive attitude toward literacy was not sufficient. Improvements in these aspects of literacy apparently depended upon teachers providing students not just with choice but with systematic instruction.

During Years 4 and 5, teachers learned about the aspects of literacy that needed improvement, and the demonstration teachers in particular received considerable support for improving their instruction. For example, they learned to provide mini-lessons to meet specific needs and to demonstrate writing techniques by sharing their own writing with students.

We asked teachers and consultants to concentrate on implementing portfolio assessment, paying special attention to the grade level benchmarks. Interestingly, the benchmarks themselves provoked little discussion. Teachers agreed from the start that the benchmarks reflected important and appropriate outcomes for students at those grade levels. However, they questioned whether it was realistic to expect their students to reach the benchmarks.

During Years 4 and 5, in order to implement portfolio assessment, the demonstration teachers had to become thoroughly familiar with the grade-level benchmarks. They learned to provide instruction to enable students to meet the benchmarks. They became aware of the benefits of introducing students to the benchmarks as well. To the teachers' surprise, the majority of students showed that they could meet the grade-level benchmarks. Several teachers even asked us to change the grade-level benchmarks to make them more difficult. For example, we were asked to move a benchmark for research report writing from third to second grade.

Our experience with the use of grade-level benchmarks suggests that standards can be useful in raising teachers' expectations of student achievement. However, we know that the process of instituting standards will not make a difference in the absence of a high level of support for teacher development. Our studies of the implementation of the KEEP whole literacy curriculum suggest that teachers must first become comfortable with the new philosophy and the instructional practices associated with it. Once changes in instruction are underway, teachers can turn their attention to changes in assessment. Assessment may drive instruction in the sense that assessment associated with benchmarks or standards gives teachers a sense of direction. But as our work at KEEP demonstrates, changes in assessment, including the introduction of benchmarks, do not automatically lead to changes in instruction.

We learned during Years 2 and 3 that it was easy to be distracted by rather superficial changes in classrooms that did not lead to meaningful changes in students' literacy achievement. Therefore, during Years 4 and 5, we paid close attention to cognitive dimensions of performance. We looked not just at whether students were writing, but at how well they were writing; not just at whether students were reading, but at how well they were reading.

During Years 4 and 5 we emphasized accountability for students' achievement. For one thing, we conducted an audit of the portfolio assessment results for each classroom. Knowing that the results would be audited, consultants and teachers took extra care to document students' progress on each of the benchmarks. Many teachers taught their students to identify evidence of their own achievement, and this process heightened students' awareness of the benchmarks and their own progress as literacy learners.

We asked the consultants to prepare brief presentations on each of their demonstration classrooms, for discussion at retreats held in the middle and at the end of the school year. We had the consultants focus on the changes teachers had made to improve implementation in their classrooms and student achievement results. The presentations had the effect of making consultants and teachers closely monitor both classroom implementation and student achievement, because they knew that others were following their work with interest.

Summary

Work during KEEP's last 5 years demonstrated that a whole literacy curriculum could have a positive effect on the achievement of students of diverse cultural and linguistic backgrounds. However, we learned that holistic, constructivist curricula will only have positive effects under certain conditions. First, full implementation of holistic curricula may depend on the use of a strategy of going with the goers. Change did not come about until we focused on the goers and had them focus either on the writers' workshop or the readers' workshop. Second, holistic curricula probably need to be supported by professional development efforts tailored to teachers' needs and interests. To bring about change, resources should be committed to demonstration teachers who can eventually serve as mentors for other teachers at their schools. Third, holistic curricula are more likely to be effective if they include benchmarks or standards to raise teachers' expectations and guide instruction. Finally, systematic instruction tied to benchmarks appears to be needed to improve achievement in the writing process and reading comprehension, the most cognitively demanding aspects of literacy.

References

Asam, C., Au, K., Blake, K., Carroll, J., Jacobson, H., Kunitake, M., & Scheu, J. (1993). *The demonstration classroom project: Report of year 1*. J. Carroll (Ed.), Honolulu, HI: Kamehameha Elementary Education Program, Kamehameha Schools.

Asam, C., Blake, K., Carroll, J., Jacobson, H., Kunitake, M., Oshiro, G., & Scheu, J. (1994). *The demonstration classroom project: Report of year 2*. J. Carroll (Ed.). Honolulu, HI: Kamehameha Elementary Education Program, Kamehameha Schools.

Au, K. H. (1993). *Literacy instruction in multicultural settings*. Fort Worth, TX: Harcourt, Brace and Jovanovich.

Au, K. H. (1994). Portfolio assessment: Experiences at the Kamehameha Elementary Education Program. In S. W. Valencia, E. H. Hiebert, & P. P. Afflerbach (Eds.), *Authentic reading assessment: Practices and possibilities* (pp. 103–126). Newark, DE: International Reading Association.

Au, K. H., & Asam, C. L. (1994, October). *Improving the achievement of students of diverse backgrounds: Changes in curriculum, assessment, and teacher development*. Paper presented at the inaugural Guy Bond Commemorative Reading Conference, University of Minnesota, Minneapolis.

Au, K. H., Crowell, D. C., Jordan, C., Sloat, K. C. M., Speidel, G. E., Klein, T. W., & Tharp, R. G. (1986). Development and implementation of the KEEP reading program. In J. Orasanu (Ed.), *Reading comprehension: From research to practice* (pp. 235–252), Hillsdale, NJ: Erlbaum.

Au, K. H., & Mason, J. M. (1983). Cultural congruence in classroom participation structures: Achieving a balance of rights. *Discourse Processes, 6*(2), 145–167.

Au, K. H., Scheu, J. A., & Kawakami, A. J. (1990). Assessment of students' ownership of literacy. *The Reading Teacher, 44*(2), 154–156.

Au, K. H., Scheu, J. A., Kawakami, A. J., & Herman, P.A. (1990). Assessment and accountability in a whole literacy curriculum. *The Reading Teacher, 43*(8), 574–578.

Calkins, L. M. with Harwayne, S. (1991). *Living between the lines*. Portsmouth, NH: Heinemann.

Carroll, J. (Ed.) (1993). *Literacy curriculum guide.* Honolulu, HI: Kamehameha Elementary Education Program, Kamehameha Schools.

Clay, M. M. (1985). *The early detection of reading difficulties* (3rd ed.). Auckland: Heinemann.

Crowell, D. C. (1981). *Kamehameha reading objective system.* Honolulu, HI: Kamehameha Schools, Center for Development of Early Education.

D'Amato, J. (1988). Acting: Hawaiian children's resistance to teachers. *Elementary School Journal, 88*(5), 529–544.

Delpit, L. D. (1988). The silenced dialogue: Power and pedagogy in educating other people's children. *Harvard Educational Review, 58,* 280–298.

Gallimore, R., Boggs, J. W., & Jordan, C. (1974). *Culture, behavior and education: A study of Hawaiian-Americans.* Beverly Hills, CA: Sage.

Giuli, C. (1985). *Responsive consulting: Test of a model* (Tech. Rep. No. 131). Honolulu, HI: Kamehameha Schools, Center for Development of Early Education.

Graves, D. (1983). *Writing: Teachers and children at work.* Exeter, NH: Heinemann.

Graves, D., & Hansen, J. (1983). The author's chair. *Language Arts, 60*(2), 176–183.

Herman, P. A., & Weaver, C. R. (1988). *Contextual strategies for learning word meanings: Middle grade students look in and look around.* Paper presented at the annual meeting of the National Reading Conference, Tucson, AR.

Jordan, C. (1985). Translating culture: From ethnographic information to educational program. *Anthropology and Education Quarterly, 16,* 105–123.

Kamehameha Schools (1993). *Native Hawaiian educational assessment, 1993.* Honolulu, HI: Office of Program Planning and Evaluation, Kamehameha Schools Bernice Pauahi Bishop Estate.

National Assessment of Educational Progress (1989). *Reading objectives, 1990 assessment* (No. 21-R-10). Princeton, NJ: Educational Testing Service.

Peters, T. J., & Waterman, R. H., Jr. (1982). *In search of excellence: Lessons from America's best-run companies.* New York: Warner Books.

Rosenblatt, L. (1978). *The reader, the text, the poem: The transactional theory of the literary work.* Carbondale, IL: Southern Illinois University Press.

Routman, R. (1991). *Invitations: Changing as teachers and learners K–12.* Portsmouth, NH: Heinemann.

Spiegel, D. L. (1981). *Reading for pleasure: Guidelines.* Newark, DE: International Reading Association.

Tharp, R. G., & Gallimore, R. (1988). *Rousing minds to life: Teaching, learning and schooling in social context.* Cambridge: Cambridge University Press.

Wixson, K. K., Peters, C. W., Weber, E. M., & Roeber, E. D. (1987). New directions in statewide reading assessment, *The Reading Teacher, 40*(8), 749–754.

·56F·

CALIFORNIA'S LITERATURE-BASED CURRICULUM AND THE CALIFORNIA LITERATURE PROJECT

Phillip C. Gonzales
CALIFORNIA STATE UNIVERSITY, DOMINGUEZ HILLS

Mel Grubb
LOS ANGELES COUNTY OFFICE OF EDUCATION

INTRODUCTION

With the publication of the *English-Language Arts Framework* in 1987, California began a reform effort that is revolutionizing both its schools as well as many throughout the United States. The *Framework* brought together research on effective schooling practices and newer notions regarding literacy. Major changes resulted in the language arts school programs both in content and the way in which instruction is delivered. This reform effort took place at several levels. It affected the State curriculum review process, textbook adoption criteria, local school district staff development, assessment procedures, and university teacher training. Most instrumental in this reform effort has been the California Literature Project.

Educational reform is never easy. It calls upon teachers, administrators, parents, business and the entire educational community to reexamine and revamp current educational ideals and practices and to replace them with rethought curriculum and educational strategies and activities. While sometimes change for change's sake can revitalize our profession, reasoned change based on the current thinking in a profession is difficult to affect, much less to sustain. In California, educational reform was seen as a change that was to take place over time and to include multiple facets and principles for it to be effective. This chapter will discuss the California literature / language arts program that is part of this reform effort and the California Literature Project, its principal change agent.

CHARACTERISTICS OF THE CALIFORNIA LITERATURE-BASED PROGRAM

Before the 1987 *Framework*, California's language arts curriculum had students experiencing instruction that was teacher centered and textbook dependent. It used literature only to support direct instruction and practice of those discrete and isolated skills presumed to result in better readers and writers. Reading and writing processes were taught in isolation, not in the service of constructing meaning, and with little relation to what was understood about learning and teaching. Tests involved multiple-choice questions focusing often on low-level facts from a short reading selection. Writing in response to literature was virtually a nonexistent practice. Writing assessment was a multiple-choice test measuring student understanding of standard American edited English.

Moving a state as large as California away from such a skills-based language arts curriculum was a major undertaking. The earliest agreement among *Framework* developers was the establishment of literature as the core of the language arts curriculum. Major changes called for by the California *English-Language Arts Framework* included:

A move to	and away from
• literature-based instruction	• isolated skills instruction
• integrated language arts	• fragmented reading and writing

- meaning-centered / thinking curriculum
- strategic constructivist experiences
- skills taught in the service of meaning
- phonics in context, concluded by grade 3
- student-centered curriculum
- collaborative learning
- quality programs for ALL students
- authentic/performance assessment

- mastery learning
- information banking
- scope and sequence of skills
- phonics taught in isolation
- teacher-centered curriculum
- competitive ranking
- tracking with differentiated programs
- multiple-choice testing

Language arts became a discipline concerned with major universal themes, the human condition, exploring life experiences, and social agendas introduced through quality literature. Whole works of quality literature, unabridged or unaltered in any manner that varied from the original, replaced shortened, language-changed versions of well-known selections. The teacher continued to introduce and facilitate lessons, but students now became the workers, collaborating in their meaning-seeking and sense-making generation of new insights and interpretations. Instruction became student-centered. It honored student voices and encouraged critical and thoughtful exploration of literature in the supportive environment of the classroom.

A TYPICAL LESSON

The traditional passive language arts lesson in which teachers assigned readings, students answered textbook questions and then completed dittoed worksheets was replaced by a lesson in which students collaborated in making sense and seeking personal meaning in response to literature.

In a typical literature-based lesson, the teacher begins by focusing student attention on the important issue central to literature to be read. Students draw on prior knowledge and experiences, often share related anecdotes, express opinions through anticipation response activities, and begin to speculate on what the literature may be presenting as an additional experience or interpretation.

The new selection is introduced and the reading begins. The teacher guides students as they experiment with ideas, think divergently by sharing personal experiences related to the text, and question character motivation. Students learn to take risks in expressing opinions and challenging the text. They visualize characters or scenes and express these interpretations through active performances. Alternative scenarios are explored and questions are raised regarding how the story and its characters evolved. Students in groups and individually are challenged to generate and honor different and possible multiple meanings in interpretations. The teacher creates situations where the impact of cultural and / or psy-

chological nuances displayed in the literature can be discussed. Ideas, interpretations, and opinions are encouraged but are not allowed to be shared without challenge or support. Students are taught to use clues and evidence both from the passage to draw conclusions as well as from their personal experience. Students are encouraged to consider how the author led them to believe as they do about the literature's issues and social situations.

Frequently, the lesson culminates in some project, demonstration, performance, or exhibition developed by students working collaboratively and assuming primary responsibility for its planning and delivery. Typical activities may involve a change in genre, a revision of the story to tell it from another's point of view, a change of time frame or culture, or comparison with current events or related literature.

Although the specifics of lessons may vary considerably, there are common elements found in most:

- Focus is on the story
- Students are encouraged to explore the issues within the selection of literature
- Creative, reasoned ideas are tested
- Students create their own understandings
- The literature is revisited several times each for a different reason
- All students have a common experience but their interpretations may vary
- Skills are introduced in context and serve the meaning-focus of the lesson

Although literature study often continues over an extended period of time, it is dynamic, students are excited when involved in it, and motivation is high. In all cases, this construction of meaning has been built upon the student's prior experiences and results with the student leaving experiences with the text knowing more about himself, his peers and his world.

While individual lessons may vary considerably, the following are offered as examples of the type of development that results in a literature-based program:

Example I

In kindergarten through second grade, children are learning to read and write as they read and respond to entertaining works of literature. Students reading and rereading literature become so familiar with the meaning and language of stories and poetry that they begin to associate sound–symbol associations with print and to anticipate and recognize the language of texts. Their attention is focused on the story or poem and its meaning. They are led to see personal connections between the literature and their own lives. They begin to practice the behaviors of literate readers and writers under the guidance of the teacher.

In a primary classroom, children begin a lesson by relating personal experiences regarding their own 'horrible, terrible, no good, bad day' to others prior to engaging with *Alexander's Terrible, Horrible, No Good, Bad Day*. The story is read. Students act out parts of the story using realia and reader's theater speaking parts. Lines from the story are reread in a pair-share format and students talk about how they would have felt if they had experienced what Alexander suffered in the story. Students continue their meaning search by speculating about the characteristics of the very bad days that their teacher, parents, friends, and so forth, may experience. Relating this issue to their own lives, students visually depict what their own bad day might include. Finally, the story is rewritten to tell about Alexander's wonderful terrific, very good day.

Example II

In grades 3–6, students refine literate behaviors and are encouraged to increase their reading and writing fluency through practice and selective feedback. Students explore multiple possibilities of meaning and experiment with their personal interpretations as they write responses to the literature or plan enactments of the story.

In an intermediate language arts lesson, students may interview neighbors, friends or family members who may have been victims of a robbery regarding that experience. Selected life experiences are enacted by groups of students who plan out the drama, create the dialogue, and present the performance after rehearsal. Students may poll communities regarding the incidence of crime in their area, if community members believe adolescent law breakers may be punished or rehabilitated, and potential preventive measures. All these activities precede the reading of Langston Hughes' *Thank You, M'am.* In the reading of this short story, students interview both the boy and Mrs. Washington regarding their role in the story. Students learn to dialogue with the text by entering sentences or phrases from the story in one column of a dialectic journal and their own response in the second column. They speculate on what a meeting 20 years later might be like between the two main characters in the story. Then, the whole class may decide to put the boy on trial with class members serving as jurors, prosecutors, witnesses, judge, and defense attorneys. Finally, students record through newspaper formats and news broadcasts, a retelling of events of the story.

Example III

In grades 6–9, students are led to formulate and express opinions based on evidence and support from the text or their personal experiences. They consider how the story might have been different if presented from the perspective of a different culture or time period. Ambiguities in the text are examined and students are taught how to 'read against the cultural grain' by taking issue with the author's message. Clarity in student discussion or response in writing is sought.

Middle school students reading Gary Soto's *Pacific Crossings* come to understand how culture helps determine why we behave the way we do. This literary selection is used as a study of the differences between Japanese and American cultural groups. They begin by dramatizing culture capsules (aspects of culture such as behavior, language, values, use of language, etc., different in two or more cultural groups) depicting some difference among groups for the purpose of discussion and analysis. They explore differences among class members in dress, use of language, preferences, behavior, and so forth, to see how perceptions are formed. In a 'quickwrite,' students write about a time they visited a new area where the people acted and talked in ways that were different from their own. As final preparation for the story, students explore stereotypes they hold about Japanese behavior, gender roles, their work ethic, and so forth. In the first reading of the story *Pacific Crossings*, students compare table manners of the Japanese with their own, gender and age roles and status, dress and statements of values. Their own homes and those of the Japanese family in the story are similarly compared regarding possessions, construction, and so forth. Rituals such as greetings, sitting down to eat, coming of age, and ceremonies of the Japanese family are analyzed and dramatized as well. This cultural comparison culminates by having groups of students perform aspects of culture that were in the story but were different from their own. Finally, students write a short story about someone from a foreign country coming to visit them in their city.

Example IV

High school students begin to analyze the structure of the text and its language to understand how the author produced his / her effect. The social complexities of a story are unraveled and differing cultural options are explored. Additionally, aesthetic appreciation of stories and poems are developed.

In a secondary language arts classroom, students read Zora Neal Hurston's *Their Eyes Were Watching God* to explore the struggles people face in trying to find happiness. Students begin the lesson by speculating on the differences between the lives of the poor and the more affluent, the rural and the urban, and the people in the 1920s and today. Students explore what life would have been like, what the concerns would have been, how vital their lives would have been. In reading the novel, students would be guided to challenge and reflect critically on the text by agreeing or disagreeing, arguing, endorsing, questioning, and/or wondering about the relationship of this story to today's world and whether rural America was similar to or different from urban America in the 1990s, to conjecture whether that life exists today as it did in the 1920s in rural America, and whether the values that motivate the characters are like the values of people in the students' experiences. This exploration of story set in time and place and its relationship to the universality of humanity and its concerns would be highlighted using mini dramatizations of story parts, creating poetry to express emotions felt in various parts of the story, character interpretation papers, use of talk show formats, recording in dialectical journals, biographical writing, and chronicling the changes and growth of character in the story as she moved from a young lady to an older woman. In students looking for the life's lessons in the text, its essential story line would be re-presented but in a different time period and using a different culture. They explore it metaphorically and in terms of a rich tapestry of life. Students would explore how writers from the Harlem Renaissance have much to say to the reader today. By analyzing the language of the dialogue, we would want students to come to understand and perhaps appreciate the speech patterns that added a rich texture to the reading. Parallels between the story and the experiences of students are explored through writing of a reflection paper in which students consider the lessons from the literature and its relationship to their own lives.

ASSESSMENT

Realizing that a new language arts curricular program obviously required a newer understanding of reading, the California Learning Assessment System (CLAS) (Early Reading Instruction, 1993) defined reading for California schools as follows:

> Reading is the process of constructing meaning through transactions with the text. In this view of reading, the individual reader assumes the responsibility for interpreting the text, guided not only by the language of the text but also by the personal experiences, cultural experiences, and prior knowledge that the reader brings to the task. Rather than believing that the meaning resides solely within the words on the page, this view of reading emphasizes the role of the individual reader in making meaning through a process that brings together textual and contextual evidence and the distinctive experience and perspective of the reader as meaning-maker.

The CLAS was designed to authentically evaluate the success of the new language arts curriculum. The CLAS had the following characteristics:

(a) It resembled what good language arts teachers did in their classroom. Good assessment was believed to be indistinguishable from good teaching. The assessment was to involve a multiday format including sections for reading, discussion, and writing.

(b) It was constructivist, allowing students to have common experiences but to respond to them idiosyncratically. While understandings and interpretations were based on the literature read, individual connections were encouraged.

(c) Opportunities for collaboration abounded in the middle section of the test that was not scored. Collaboration involved layering of ideas, some developed in earlier exercises of the assessment, added to by continued thought later, refined through discussion with peers, and finally, was used as prewriting for the third section of the assessment, an extended writing in response to or related to the literature selection,

(d) Multiple opportunities were present for students to demonstrate what they were thinking and coming to know. The assessment offered visualization possibilities, use of symbolization, expression of metaphorical thinking, writing to generate, further develop and clarify thoughts,

collaborative talk to encourage students to develop insights and layer interpretations together, to find connections between the work of literature and their personal lives and experiences.

(e) Assessment scales examine not whether the students arrive at the 'correct answer' but rather the quality of thinking their responses show in response to the text. Teacher / assessors allow for divergence of response and multiple reasoning routes that support the students' conclusions.

(f) Assessment allows districts and schools to understand the success of their language arts program as well as how well students are internalizing the strategies of the constructivist approach that encourage them to construct understandings beyond the school setting. As noted in CLAS training materials (1993) for scorers, these strategies include:

1. Demonstrate intellectual engagement with the text:
   —experiment with ideas, think divergently—share personal experiences related to the text, question a character's motivation, take risks, express opinions, speculate, hypothesize, visualize characters or scenes, explore alternative scenarios, raise questions, make predictions, and think metaphorically.
2. Explore multiple possibilities of meaning:
   —consider cultural and / or psychological nuances and complexities in the text.
3. Fill-in gaps:
   —use clues and evidence in the passage to draw conclusions, make warranted and plausible interpretations of ideas, facts, concepts, and / or arguments.
4. Recognize and deal with ambiguities in the text:
   —Give specific examples from the story that do not make sense to you, look at polar opposites, report conclusions to the class.
5. Revise, reshape, and / or deepen early interpretations.
6. Evaluate, examine the degree of fit between the author's ideas or information and the reader's prior knowledge or experience.
7. Challenge and reflect critically on the text by agreeing or disagreeing, arguing, endorsing, questioning, and / or wondering.
8. Demonstrate an understanding of the work as a whole.
9. Attend to the structure of the text:
   show how the parts work together; how characters and / or other elements of the work are related and change— freeze frame; sequence the events of the text through graphics, visual demonstrations, role-playing, charts, graphs, posters, murals, storyboards.
10. Show aesthetic appreciation of the text; consider linguistic and structural complexities.
11. Allude to and / or retell specific passage(s) to validate and / or expand ideas.

CLAS as a statewide evaluation system helped focus educator attention on the importance of the reform effort. Translating the intents of the *English Language Arts Framework* continued through additional California Department of Education documents published since 1987.

SPECIAL PUBLICATIONS

The California Department of Education has also published additional papers supporting the intents of the *English-Language Arts Framework*. Among these publications are:

California Department of Education, Bilingual Education Office. 1990. *Bilingual Education Handbook: Designing Instruction for LEP Students.* Sacramento, CA: California State Department of education.

California Department of Education, Bilingual Education Office. (1990). *Caught in the Middle.* Sacramento, CA: California Department of education.

California Department of Education, Bilingual Education Office. (1991). *It's Elementary.* Sacramento, CA: California Department of education.

California Department of Education, Bilingual Education Office. (1991). *Second to None.* Sacramento, CA: California Department of education.

Gonzales, P. C. (1988). *Equity and Access in a Language Arts Program for ALL Students.* Sierra Madre, CA: The Kaw Company and the California State Department of Education.

Gonzales, P. C., & Melvin H. G. (1993). *Grouping Students for Effective Language Arts Instruction.* Sacramento, CA: California State Department of Education.

California Department of Education, Bilingual Education Office. (1993). *The Framework in Focus,* Sacramento, CA: California Department of education.

TEACHER CREDENTIALING

To promote conformity in preservice teacher training, California's Commission on Teacher Credentialing has established standards for the regular evaluation of teacher education programs. To be approved to offer a credential program, school of education programs must help its preservice teachers learn how to deliver *Framework* consistent instruction. At California State University, Dominguez Hills, for example, all teachers in training learn how to provide whole language instruction, writing as a process, emergent literacy planning for elementary through high school levels—all in a language arts teacher training program that focuses on literature study. Methods classes in English language arts teach a constructivist pedagogy. English as a second language, and Sheltered and Specially Designed Academic Instruction (SDAI) are also embedded into all courses. Multicultural concerns such as cultural matching, socialized and culturally dependent learning orientations, and culturally determined content-embedded cognitive development are regularly addressed in the Teacher Education Department credential courses.

Thus, the California literature-based language arts reform effort trumpeted changes in the manner in which instruction

was to be provided in the State. However, announcements of change will never by themselves result in wholesome differences in curriculum nor instruction. A vehicle for helping teachers both understand and implement the new language arts program was needed.

THE CALIFORNIA LITERATURE PROJECTS ROLE IN THE FORMULATION OF THE CALIFORNIA LITERATURE-BASED CURRICULUM

In California, the reform effort established a philosophical *Framework* calling for changes in language arts instruction, program quality review criteria employed by State officials as they approved curriculum programs throughout California, textbook adoption review criteria and procedures, and initiated a new Statewide assessment system. The Department of Education through legislated funding established the California Literature Project (CLP) to provide training for teachers expected to guide and effect these changes. The CLP was designed to focus directly on classroom instruction, the rejuvenation of teachers, and the establishment of a rigorous language arts program for every student.

The CLP was established in 1985 as a staff development effort to help train English / language arts teachers to teach a literature-based, meaning-centered curriculum. In 10 years, it has evolved into a major instrument for change in language arts instruction. The CLP began with an institute held on one university campus for approximately 100 teachers from throughout California. After two additional years of similar statewide institutes, the project moved to five State University campuses throughout California. Today, there are nine regions housing the CLP. Some of these regions support institutes at more than one satellite site. In the summer of 1993 a statewide residential California Spanish Literature Project was offered with all literature and pedagogy read and discussed in Spanish. In 1994, Spanish CLP institutes were offered at two locations in California. At present, a Japanese CLP institute is under development.

The primary mechanisms for the staff development effort of the CLP are its summer institutes offered through the CLP. These institutes are designed to model some of the best current thinking on the teaching of language arts. Articles written by such well-known academicians as Rosenblatt, Langer, Vygotsky, Squire, Wells, Greene, Pearson, Scholes, Wittrock, Freire, and many others provide much of the basis for the CLP pedagogy. The goal of the institutes is to help English / language arts teachers understand constructivist pedagogy and learn curricular and instructional strategies for implementing a literature-based, student-centered program for all students.

CLP SUMMER Institutes

In the CLP Summer Institute, each of the 4 weeks has an instructional theme tied to planned outcomes. Week one is titled *Literature as Experience* and looks at the "Teacher as Reader." During this week teachers explore literature as active constructors of meaning. The four objectives for the week are that teachers will

1. discover, interpret, and apply insights into meaning of selected literature,
2. experience the impact of visualization, writing, and enactment on comprehension,
3. read and respond orally and in writing to adult works of prose and poetry, and
4. define a problem in implementing a literature-based curriculum and pedagogy of tolerance and inclusion for their own students.

For week two, *Using Language to Learn,* focuses on the "Teacher as Learner." During this week teachers reflect on their personal learning processes. The four objectives for this week are:

1. collaborate with other teacher-learners to strengthen the understanding that differences in background experience are not learning deficits but do contribute to the achievement of all students,
2. participate in core, extended (nonfiction) and recreational reading program of instruction to focus on organizational and inventional strategies for encouraging wide, sustained reading and writing,
3. use written and oral language to deepen engagement in learning, and
4. refine insights into individual teaching / learning problems.

Week three, *Affirming What is Known,* looks at the "Teacher as Professional." During this week teachers come to understand more about the teacher as decision maker. The four objectives for this week are:

1. assess your classroom needs for learning in language arts,
2. examine a variety of materials and strategies appropriate to the needs of particular students,
3. use technology in ways that may help provide access to the core curriculum for particular students, and
4. review relevant California Department of Education documents.

Week four, *Exploring Solutions,* is concerned with the 'Teacher as Practitioner." This week focuses on establishing the role of instructional architect. The two objectives for this week are:

1. reflect on the ways in which the experience of literature can increase multicultural tolerance and inclusion, and
2. develop an instructional plan to field test in the first two months after the teachers return to their classrooms.

In this approach to teacher education, the learner is not told how to teach, he / she experiences the model eventually to be put into place in the classroom. This new teacher-learner has an 'honored voice' actively creating ideas testing hypotheses, and generating insights about teaching and learning. The learners construct personal understandings and individual realities. Participants engage in directive experience, collaborative invention, personal insight, individual reflection, and academic application. The partici-

pating teachers assume responsibility for their learning. They learn to approach discussions with an attitude of trust. They assume others have something to say. Teachers engage in open-ended investigation of life's issues in selections of literature. Teachers come to realize that their purpose is not to judge but to understand. Teachers become a community of learners. New and experienced teachers are immersed in environments where they actively question, hypothesize, investigate, imagine, and debate substantive topics in a manner that could be replicated in their classrooms.

Teachers leave the 4-week institute with a tentative "Curriculum Action Plan" that they use with their students when they return to their classroom. On six different occasions during each of the following two years, the teacher-participants return to a CLP follow-up day. They bring student work that reflects what is occurring in their classroom. During the follow-up, they interact with their CLP Institute peers exploring what is working and where they need help and guidance in implementing their Action Plans. They reflect upon their successes noting student performances and growth. During the second year of follow-up, CLP teachers develop staff development workshops based on their classroom experiences using literature-based lessons.

ONE SITE

In 1994, approximately 1,000 teachers attended a 4-week CLP Institute at 12 sites throughout the State and read, discussed, and learned more about the teaching in a literature-based classroom. In one region, California State University, Dominguez Hills (CSUDH) and its satellite sites at CSU Northridge and Cal-Poly Pomona, over 200 teachers participated.

Using "Crossing Borders" as the theme, and inclusion and tolerance as organizing concepts, teacher participants experienced a "constructivist" approach to language arts education. Although the term *constructivist pedagogy* was relatively new, its influence and philosophy had always underwritten the California *English-Language Arts Framework*. The CLP teacher-leaders coached the CLP participants as they assumed responsibility for their learning. One teacher participant wrote: 'We approached our discussions with an attitude of trust. We assumed others had something to say. We didn't measure the contributions of our fellow teachers by some impersonal standard. We engaged in open-ended investigation of life's issues in selections of literature. Our purpose was not to judge but to understand. We became a community of learners."

The 4-week CLP Institutes in 1994 used *Palace Walk, Tracks,* and *M Butterfly* as the core texts read by the teacher participants. In addition, grade-alike books and picture books were read. Pedagogical articles emphasizing themes of inclusion and access written by Banks, Greene, and others along with California State Documents were also examined. One journal entry at the CSUDH CLP Summer Institute read: "I expected a traditional 'tell me / show me' summer program where CLP teacher-leader-experts led us to 'truths' and 'facts' through lectures and step-by-step cookie-cutter instruction."

Instead, what occurred was participants were asked to examine and understand themselves as learners and how they come to make meaning. Participants learned what it was like to feel confused when they encountered situations where a peer's ideas contradicted their own. They explored how they were similar to and different from other individuals in the teaching community. In the end, they came to comprehend firsthand the 'constructivist pedagogy' they experienced for 4 weeks.

Speakers are limited to only those who could add to the experience of the text. Two provocative speakers, Dr. Terry Tafoya, a native American psychologist, and Dr. Amir El-Araf, Vice President at CSU Dominguez Hills, shared cultural background that provided insight into *Tracks* and *Palace Walk*, respectively. One teacher reported that he better understood the notion that literature was written in a cultural context with its societal norms and that considerations of behavioral expectations are time bound and not necessarily reflecting today's reality in the same area with today's populations.

How successful was the 4-week CLP Institute? One elementary bilingual teacher said, "What a treat. I love this summer.... I was able to read books and discuss them with other adults. It's so intellectual. And I can see how to do this in my classroom...."

To provide a working CLP classroom model, 43 middle school students and three teachers who would be their English teachers the following fall attended a 4-week CLP Student Academy held on the CSUDH campus. Led by CLP teacher-leaders, these students read literature, they composed poetry, discussed issues related to multiculturalism, tolerance and inclusion, and learned firsthand what it was like to construct and test their own meaning in response to literature. In the Student Academy, an anthology of multicultural literature served as the core text. The mother of one of the participants said, "I can't thank you enough for the experience my son had this summer. He never wanted to miss class, he read at night instead of watching television, and his experience going to the Simon Wisenthall Museum of Tolerance will never be forgotten." Another parent reported, "At first, my daughter fought the idea of attending the CLP. I had to bribe her to attend the first day. By the end of the 4 weeks, she was thanking me for having sent her and she cried because it was over." A CLP teacher who worked with many of the previous year's Student Academy participants during the past school year reported that she could not believe how much more confident her students were in school. They wrote better and wanted to read. Their discussions were more thoughtful. She went on, "In my case, I can't tell how much my experience working the Student Academy meant to me. I am a changed teacher. I expect and get more from my students. Their work was much improved. My teaching is also better. I thank you."

CLP PROVIDES LEADERSHIP

Teachers from the CLP have for 10 years been expected to assume leadership roles in the reform of language arts curriculum and instruction in the State. Their involvement is varied:

(1) The CLP teachers provide *staff development* services for schools and districts throughout the State. Typically, each workshop guides teachers through an exploration of literature where new understandings are constructed in a manner resembling how a similar process can be enacted with teachers' students back in their classrooms. Some of these topics include: the role of phonics in a literature-based program, performance assessment in a literature-based program, teaching skills in context, writing to learn and writing in response to text, interdisciplinary teaching and the role of literature in other disciplines, using technology in a literature-based classroom, literature in an ESL classroom, among others.

(2) The CLP teachers were among the developers of the California statewide performance assessments for language arts called California Learning Assessment System (CLAS). They worked directly with testing companies and assessment consultants in the development of a literature-based assessment reflective of a meaning-centered approach. Staff-development sessions for teachers and administrators related to the instructional practices resembling the new assessment system were also conducted by CLP teachers.

(3) The State has a *recommended literature list* for K–8 and for 9–12 as well as for K–8 for books in Spanish developed in part by CLP teachers. These recommended lists were offered in districts and schools as guides to be used in the construction of their own list. The CLP teachers also serve as a resource to districts and schools as they update their literature selections.

(4) Schools and districts have come to rely on CLP teachers who teach in *bilingual* settings to assist their teachers to provide literature-based programs in the primary language of their students. This is not only because they believe that literature-based programs are good but because they have come to see that the strategies used for assisting students in constructing meaning from the text provide for better users of language and more skilled readers and writers than when taught in tracked linguistic programs.

(5) A core group of CLP teachers from throughout California has taken the philosophy and practices of the *Primary Language Record* (developed by the London Education Authority) and adapted them for local classroom use as the *California Learning Record*. This student observation system has become more and more in use as teachers put into place a literature-based program along with performance assessment. CLP teachers have developed a 7th- through 12th-grade version of the record that is being used more frequently as student portfolios are being used throughout California schools. Parents' support for the *California Learning Record* results from their involvement in gathering initial information and the value of the data collected to show growth that is used in parent conferences.

(6) The CLP teachers are also involved in a satellite transmitted staff development program received throughout California. This service called the Educational Telecommunications Network (ETN) is transmitted out of the Los Angeles

County Office of Education CLP and shows CLP teachers presenting lessons consistent with the *English Language Arts Framework*. Viewing teachers throughout California interact with teachers in the studio regarding the classroom scenes shown. To date, over 100 hours of language arts programming have been broadcast. Beginning in 1995, actual language arts classroom instruction in 4th- to 6th-grade CLP classrooms will be broadcast to schools throughout the United States as part of a Federally funded Star Schools project.

(7) Additional *special projects* involving CLP teachers include programs such as Reading Recovery, the Language Arts Middle School Demonstration Project, California Restructuring and other State initiatives. Additionally, CLP teachers are responsible for curriculum workshops, conference presentations, and site-based new teacher mentoring. Many CLP teachers teach education methods courses offered in teacher credential programs in State universities. A significant number of CLP teachers are now in doctoral programs throughout the United States.

(8) Special *study groups* have been sponsored to investigate topics of concern to smaller groups of CLP teachers. At CSUDH, for example, groups of teachers have established "Teacher as Researcher" groups, Multimedia Media Institutes, Literature for Gangs, ESL / Bilingual Literature Approaches, Emergent Literacy in Middle School, Parent Education, CLP for Administrators, CLP for College Professors, Portfolio Assessment, Interdisciplinary Instruction, Multicultural Literature, Beginning Literacy, and others. Each group meets for one or more weeks during the summer and during two to three follow-up dates during the academic year.

(9) Realizing that nothing drives educational reform better than an *assessment* system, in 1986 California Department of Education began designing its authentic language arts assessment program in writing. This was followed by the California Learning Assessment System (CLAS) in language arts in 1992. The CLP teachers were among those selected to develop, field test, revise, and score these tests.

The legislation to refund the CLAS was vetoed by Governor Wilson in 1994 after yielding to pressure from conservative fundamentalist Christian groups. Yet, the impact of the training and widespread use of the assessment prototypes are still felt throughout the State.

(10) The final piece of the reform puzzle was that of teacher training conducted by universities in California. California Literature Projects are located at *teacher-training* institutions throughout California. Usually, an English or Education professor involved in teacher training or some well-known and respected teacher from the region serves as the site director. The summer institutes, follow-up meetings, and much of the training of the CLP occur at university sites. At several university sites, CLP teachers teach methods courses for students in preliminary teaching credential programs. Often, CLP teachers are master teachers helping new student teachers. At CSUDH, for example, 25 CLP teachers have taught part-time in the Teacher Credential Program—primarily in the area of English language arts methodology. Faculty members frequently work with CLP Institutes as featured speakers, with CLP staff development providers functioning as coaches, and as participants in varied CLP activities.

HOW STUDENTS AND TEACHERS FARE

Much of the evaluative information regarding the results of the reform effort in California is anecdotal since the defunding of the CLAS in a recent legislative session. Nevertheless, educators have found changes in English language arts instruction to be remarkable. Typical of California teachers employing a student-centered, literature-based, meaning-seeking, constructivist approach to language arts instruction are classroom environments alive with student work in progress and products that reflect new learning. Interactions within lessons bring students together as pairs or small groups coming to better understand the works of literature they are reading. These students share insights, they test ideas, explore issues and opinions with their peers, and transmediate metacognitively in planning and enacting performances, demonstrations, or exhibitions in which the results of their literature study are displayed.

The inclusion of ALL students (ESL, gifted, average, remedial, and Title I) was found by many teachers to result in richer discussions, introduction of different perspectives, and a sharing of a multitude of prior experiences that contributed to a more dynamic construction of meaning. Detracking was one of the more complex efforts in the language arts reform. Districts and schools were successful when they involved students, teachers, and most important, the parents. Today, school districts are beginning to see an overall improvement of students who often would have dropped out of school and at the same time no decrease in student achievement for the students who would have been placed in advanced classes.

Informal surveys tell us that students are more willing to take risks with new ideas, they tend to be more creative in generating ways of demonstrating their understanding, they are more motivated to respond to writing prompts assigned to elicit a response to text, they become more independent, sometimes impatient with teachers who spend too much time explaining how to do assignments, and they develop closer relationships with their peers. One student reported, "I feel stronger. I hear myself think and want to share my ideas with others. I enjoy hearing what others believe and challenge them to find support for these opinions in the literature or from their own lives."

Some teachers have difficulty letting go of 'control' in the classroom. Coming from an education approach in which the teacher was central to all that occurred in the room, some teachers are reluctant and slow to turn over responsibility for learning to the students. These same teachers hold on to the format of questioning for correct answers, linguistic study, and testing protocols even as they begin to experiment with constructivist literature-based instruction. At times, teachers dislike the up-front planning for their lessons—but realize its payoff and power when students begin to operate more independently. Finally, teachers accustomed to 'grading' the work of students struggle with how to evaluate the more collaborative, generative, and organic learning that occurs in constructivist literature-based lessons.

CONCLUSIONS

The publication of the California English-Language Arts Framework heralded the beginning of education reform in California. Today's language arts education in the State incorporates effective schooling practices and new notions of literacy. It replaced a skill's curriculum with a literature-based, meaning-centered program. It resulted in improvement of the literature selections available to students. The *Framework* helped alter what was a teacher-centered program to one that has become more student-centered. And, it spurred the development of an assessment instrument that more closely reflected how well language arts teachers taught. Assisting this effort are the new assessment system and the new teacher training credential programs. The California Literature Project as a State initiated staff development program has been central to the change in the teaching and learning in language arts introduced by the *Framework*. By engaging a teacher-centered change agent and by enlisting successful teachers from throughout the State in a consistent effort, California is now leading the language arts curricular reform in the United States.

References

CLAS Training Materials for Language Arts. (1993). Sacramento, CA: California Department of Education.

Early Reading Instruction: A Balanced Approach. (1993, October 21). Teleconference by Educational Telecommunications Network, Los Angeles Count Office of Education, Downey, CA.

THE INTRODUCTION OF THE NATIONAL CURRICULUM FOR ENGLISH

John Richmond

UNIVERSITY OF NOTTINGHAM

THE HISTORY OF THE LEGISLATION

In 1988 the government of the United Kingdom passed the Education Reform Act. Among other measures, the Act announced the introduction of a national curriculum, with an assessment and testing system, for children between the ages of 5 and 16 in state schools in England and Wales. (Private schools are not obliged to follow the national curriculum.) Parallel arrangements introduced a statutory curriculum in Northern Ireland. In Scotland, the authorities decided to pursue the goal of a national consensus on the curriculum without legislation, and this has been achieved. The national curriculum in England and Wales includes nine subjects. Three of these subjects, English, mathematics and science, are described as core subjects.

This chapter intends to explain something of the experience of the design and implementation of the national curriculum for English. The curriculum orders for English are substantially the work of a committee established by the government in 1988 and chaired by Professor Brian Cox. The Cox Committee's Report (Department of Education and Science, 1989a) drew on the work of another committee established by the government in 1987 and chaired by Sir John Kingman, which had published a report the previous year (Department of Education and Science, 1988) offering a model of the English language for teachers and attempting to answer the question, "What do teachers need to know about language?" The national curriculum for English (Department of Education and Science, 1989b) and its assessment arrangements took effect in schools from September 1989. In 1992, the government ordered a revision of the curriculum orders for English. In 1993 it ordered a further revision of the orders for all national curriculum subjects. The further revised orders will, when published in January 1995, apply in schools from September of that year. The government currently promises that there will be no further revision to the national curriculum for 5 years from 1995.

WHERE WE HAVE BEEN AS LANGUAGE EDUCATORS

In order to set these bald facts in the context of language teaching and learning, I am going to offer a summary, using headlines only, of the main lines of progress in language education, as I see them, in the UK over 25 years. The ideas in the summary will, I guess, be familiar to most readers; 25 years ago, they were new to all but a few pioneering language educators in the English-speaking world. In the intervening time, there has been a constant dual effort among inquiring English teachers: both to generate new insights and, as important and in recent years more important, to defend those insights and their practical outworkings against ignorant and destructive attacks.

The energies we have brought to language education have moved us beyond:

the exercise of language as a set of drills and routines, divorced from real acts of communication and comprehension;

the idea that language is in itself neutral, value-free;

a curriculum of short tasks, each apparently unconnected with what had preceded or would follow;

the setting of tasks within which the student had little or no control;

a tendency to value the written language over the spoken;

classrooms of isolated individuals performing competitively against each other and only for the teacher;

the assumption that the teacher's role is simply to issue

instructions to students to do things with language, and then make judgements on what they have done;

an overriding preoccupation with correctness;

a narrow range of formats and purposes for language use; and

monocultural, monolingual assumptions.

By the same token, our energies have taken us toward:

the use of language as an expression of the desire to mean, and achieve in real acts of communication and comprehension;

an awareness of what social purposes people use language for, and what representations of the world are constructed for them through language;

a curriculum with a shape and sequence to it, understood by teachers and learners;

the setting of tasks within which students have the opportunity to make decisions about what to say, read, and write, and how best to plan their work;

a recognition that speech, as language in its primary mode, is inherently valuable and must be the basis on which competence in reading and writing is built;

classrooms where students can collaborate with one another, and criticize and admire each other's work;

the assumption that the teacher is involved in the work of the classroom as a user of language, albeit with special expertise, and is prepared to write, read, listen and talk along with the students;

a primary concern with the substance of what students say, read and write, and how they apprehend the meaning of what others say, read and write, with a concern for control of conventions following from that;

a broad variety of formats and purposes for language use; and

multicultural and multilingual expectations.

It is easy to abuse the past. The past is not here to answer back. Since language education began, there have been teachers who have helped their students to a confident control of their language and to a sense of how to use it to interpret and affect the world, whether or not those teachers would have described what they did in terms quite like those of my second list. However, I do think that the understandings in the second list have been achieved much more widely now than a generation ago.

ENGLISH AS A POLITICAL INSTRUMENT

Despite this progress, there are still numerous classrooms and schools that have not moved far away from the kinds of practices on my first list. The reason is not that there has been no recent activity in curriculum development in English on the part of government, teachers, and other professionals in language education; there has been much. Part of the reason

is that language education has been, in the last decade, the subject of conflict between government and professionals, between those with power but without much knowledge and those with knowledge but without much power. I am sorry to say that the government in the UK has used the teaching of English—and in particular its ability through the media to manipulate public perceptions of how effectively English is taught in the schools—as a political instrument.

I am a supporter of the principle of a national curriculum, which I think should apply both to state and to private schools. Government and professionals should be able to agree upon the broad framework of knowledge, understanding, and skill within which teaching and learning should take place. For one thing, we teachers know more than we did about language learning, and if those fundamental insights are evident in the broad framework, they have a powerful capacity to encourage better teaching and discourage worse. For another thing, I believe that all our students have a common right to the kinds of activities and experiences which a curriculum based on those fundamental insights can provide, though to put something into a piece of law does not in itself guarantee that common right.

In the mid-1980s, however, when the government first had the idea of a national curriculum, it had no intention of promoting what I will call "a meaning-making approach" to language learning. It wanted a back-to-basics curriculum, with an admixture of great literature for the older students, which it hoped would sweep aside what it regarded as a dubious progressivism which had infected all areas of the curriculum, but most particularly English. It had neither respect for, nor understanding of, the fundamental insights about language learning. (As an aside, it is fascinating to see how the words "fundamental" and "basic" have acquired such different connotations in education.) The government usually preferred to listen to a tiny group of unofficial voices given considerable influence on educational policy making, through an overlapping network of think tanks and policy units whose musings went into pamphlets which had privileged access to ministers' desks and to the front pages of newspapers.

Let me give examples. All the English teachers I have met believe, as does the government, that students should be introduced to magnificent literature. The phrase "magnificent literature" is a category which will sometimes overlap with a conventional definition of the literary canon, while also including material which governments are unlikely to have heard of. Like the government, English teachers believe that students should be helped to a confident control of the conventions of written language. But in the UK, English teachers have come to the realization that all the topics of genuine debate within English—for example, the question of what counts as literature, or of how to foster students' developing control of the writing system, or of what constitutes effective initial teaching of reading, or of the variety of accents, dialects, and languages spoken by students and the special role of standard English amid that variety, or of the extent to which English teaching should consider media texts, including some of the products of popular culture, or of the use of grammatical terminology in teaching—are regularly parodied and sloganized with a constant eye to the political advantage of striking a particular public posture, regardless of its truth value.

THE NATIONAL CURRICULUM FOR ENGLISH IN BRIEF

Despite this, the requirements of the national curriculum for English currently in force do, on the whole, promote a meaning-making approach to language learning—something not dissimilar in principle to the points on my second list—although there are numerous detailed criticisms to be made of omissions, contradictions and inconsistencies. Here is a summary (necessarily very selective) of the requirements of the national curriculum for English in England.

KEY STAGE 1 (5–7-YEAR-OLDS)

Speaking and Listening

Offer a variety of planned situations and activities which:

encourage the development of pupils' ability to describe experiences, state information, express opinions, articulate feelings;

encourage the development of pupils' powers of concentration and sense of appropriate response—their grasp of how speakers and listeners behave toward each other.

Use a full range of groupings and audiences, from pairs to large groups, involving adults as well as pupils.

Reading

Show children how to make sense of texts using the whole range of psycholinguistic cues. Emphasize meaning.

Make available the widest possible range of engaging and appropriate reading material.

Develop the partnership between home and school.

Show children how reading and writing develop interdependently. Use reading to enrich oral work and drama.

Encourage the beginnings of explicit understanding of structure and conventions in written texts.

Writing

Make connections between children's spoken language and their developing sense of the nature of writing.

Give children an understanding of the composition process: planning, drafting, changing, polishing.

Give children models of, and invite them to try for themselves, a wide variety of kinds of writing. See that writing reaches a varied readership.

Pay attention to spelling, punctuation and layout in the context of children's own writing.

Foster a comfortable and legible handwriting style.

Encourage an awareness of some of the functions of writing. Encourage play with written language. Teach some grammatical terms in the context of discussion of children's writing.

KEY STAGE 2 (8–11-YEAR-OLDS)

Speaking and Listening

Provide opportunities for children to increase the complexity, clarity, and precision of their spoken language in situations and activities across the whole curriculum.

Develop children's spoken responses to fiction, nonfiction, poetry, and plays.

Give children a more developed understanding of the possibilities for and demands on spoken language brought about by working in groups.

Give children opportunities to reflect on their own effectiveness in the use of spoken language.

Discuss variations of accent and dialect in English. Teach about the forms and functions of standard English.

Reading

Show children how to read different kinds of texts (e.g. fiction, poetry, databases, information books) in different ways. Encourage active research reading of information texts.

Continue to provide a widening repertoire of reading material.

Provide guidance for children in reflecting, in speech, and in writing, on their reading.

Encourage different kinds of performance reading.

Discuss texts with children which make playful or imaginative use of language (e.g., advertisements, word games, graffiti).

Writing

Help children to develop a firmer control of structure and organization in the different kinds of writing they attempt.

Provide contexts for the use of writing as a tool of learning across the whole curriculum.

See that children's writing reaches a varied readership.

Teach about the special role of standard English in writing, and about occasions on which writers will deliberately use nonstandard forms. Teach something about the history of writing.

Help children to develop a more advanced understanding and control of spelling, punctuation and layout in the context of their own writing.

Foster a comfortable, legible, and fluent handwriting style.

KEY STAGES 3 AND 4 (12–16-YEAR-OLDS)

Speaking and Listening

Give students opportunities to develop sophistication and skill in using, interpreting and responding to spoken language in a wide range of social and cognitive situations.

Give students increasing opportunities to develop proficiency in spoken standard English.

Give students opportunities to reflect on their own effectiveness in the use of the spoken word. Encourage them to respect their own language(s) and dialect(s) and those of others.

Teach about some of the range of styles and registers of spoken language.

Reading

Help students to develop as critical readers who form judgements about authors, characters, viewpoints, textual structures.

Help students to develop as skillful researchers who know how to use texts to advance their learning and who understand something of the range of information texts employed in the modern world.

Introduce students to the richness of contemporary writing and to some pre-20th century literature including Shakespeare.

Introduce students to a range of media texts and to a discussion of their purposes, effects, and intended audiences.

Teach about some of the main characteristics of literary language.

Teach about some aspects of historical change in English.

Writing

Help students take control of the process of composition (drafting, redrafting, revising, proof-reading) to an advanced stage.

Foster in students a more conscious sense of the choices and techniques available to a writer in aiming at particular effects and in appealing to particular audiences.

Foster in students an understanding of a wide range of the purposes and formats for writing in the adult world.

Help students take control of all aspects of the writing system (spelling, punctuation, layout) to an advanced stage.

Encourage students to reflect on and talk about the activity of writing.

Teach about some of the main differences between speech and writing.

MAKING ECCENTRIC PROPOSITIONS INTO COMMON SENSE

We have various individuals and organizations to thank for the fact that so much has been salvaged from the intellectual struggle which preceded the publication of the national curriculum for English. The most important group is the Cox Committee itself. Its members argued for a description of English which most English teachers share, and turned those arguments into firm proposals despite considerable pressure to abandon them. They then, with persistent determination and some cunning, saw to it that the proposals became law with the minimum compromise necessary. They were helped in this by some members of Her Majesty's Inspectorate—an independent body which advises the government on the content of the curriculum and the quality of schools and which, as a result of the independence of much of its advice in recent years, has had its numbers and its power drastically reduced. Numerous teachers' organizations, including the National Association for the Teaching of English, submitted evidence, suggested draft sections, offered ideas and advice.

But there is a wider acknowledgment than that to be made, and one whose lessons are longer lasting. It has to do with creating common sense. If enough people consistently and open-mindedly develop, promote, and practice a certain understanding of language education; if enough people have a shared view about the kinds of societies which classrooms should be, and the kind of influence on society which they want its future citizens to exert; and if they manage to articulate that, then they feed a process whereby the daring insight, the eccentric proposition, becomes, over time, the major body of common sense. Thus when a destructive and retrogressive power attempts to impose itself, it discovers, for one thing, that it is hard to assemble and vet committees which can be required to do its exact bidding. Further, it discovers that out there among professional educators, by far the largest body of articulated thought (whatever differences of emphasis on specifics there may be within that body) represents a vision of the subject, the teacher, and the learner which is too dynamic and too confident to be quashed easily.

In all the topics of debate within English mentioned earlier, there are stories to be told in detail about the progress of the argument. I will tell stories belonging to two of the areas. The first belongs to the area of grammar and the second, knowledge about language.

The Kingman Report

The question which the government gave the Kingman Committee when it was established in 1987, 'What do teachers need to know about language?', is a legitimate and important one. The difficulty lay in the fact that it wished the Committee to arrive at one simple answer to the question: an answer which it had in its mind before the Committee began its work. It wished the Committee to decide that teachers need to know, above all, about the grammar of sentences. The decline in old-fashioned grammar teaching was, the government believed, both a cause of and a metaphor for a decline in educational standards generally. In the more extreme versions of this position, informality of dress, lack of respect for authority, and even the occasionally disappointing performance of our national cricket team were attributed by politicians, journalists and other social commentators to the collapse of parsing and clause analysis.

The Kingman Report profoundly disappointed those who had commissioned it. It was against old-fashioned grammar teaching and learning by rote, and proposed that teachers should develop a wide range of perspectives on language, including attention to some formal aspects of written and spoken language (one of which, it acknowledged, is sentence grammar) but also introduce the social context of language use: how speakers and listeners, readers and writers behave toward each other and change that behavior according to situation and purpose, both interpersonally and in mass uses of language. The Report offered some thoughts on early language acquisition and on historical and geographical variation in English.

The model of the English language by which the Kingman Report represented these ideas is deeply imperfect. Some of its details are simply wrong. There is no reference to social variation in accents and dialects of English; there is no attention to language learning beyond the early acquisition of speech. However, the Report was sufficiently unsatisfactory from the government's point of view for the Secretary of State at the time to describe it, on the day of its publication, as an "interesting" report; code for "not what we wanted to hear".

The Language in the National Curriculum Project

Despite its disappointment, the government decided to spend £21 million on a 3-year project, the Language in the National Curriculum (LINC) project, to disseminate the Kingman model to all primary teachers and all secondary English teachers in England and Wales. Having so publicly got itself on to a hook, it needed to be equally public about getting itself off. It was determined, at least, to exercise tight control over the project, and directed that there would be a scheduled training program using an approved training package. The package would be produced by an eminent linguist in a few weeks of his spare time. A giant piece of educational pyramid selling would ensue, with close supervision being maintained for 3 years to see that the package went down the line without being damaged or dropped.

Eighteen months later, the sadder and wiser senior civil servant in charge of the project told me: "We lost control of LINC after three weeks." I will say some more about this piece of carelessness in a moment. By this time (late 1988), however, the Cox Committee was well into its work and the government instructed it to ignore the complexities of Kingman's model, and to concentrate, so far as knowledge about language was concerned, simply on sentence grammar. There was to be a separate section of the English orders, called knowledge about language, which would mean sentence grammar. Teachers would teach grammar using pieces of

great literature as models; students would learn how the English stylists handled subordination, modifiers, pronouns and complements; naturally, as a result, they would once again (as had happened in the past) be able to handle these things properly themselves.

I have already said that the English orders were hammered out over a period of months of tense negotiation and compromise between members of the Cox Committee, civil servants and ministers, amid threats of resignation and rumors of dismissal. The orders had no separate section on grammar. It was agreed, rightly, that metalanguage—including the metalanguage of sentence structure, appropriately treated—is one of the tools of the English teacher's trade. The requirements for knowledge about language are divided among the three sections on speaking and listening, reading, and writing. Six aspects of language are required to be studied: accent, dialect and standard English; the functions, registers, and styles of speech; historical change in English; the nature of literary language; the functions, registers, and styles of writing; and some of the characteristic differences between speech and writing. That these aspects of language study, however partial and uneven they may seem, gained admittance to the curriculum orders, represents a significant political achievement in the circumstances. Much of this territory was unfamiliar, in a teaching sense, to teachers. The nature of literary language is obviously, at first glance, the most familiar topic; in a timely way this requirement invited discussion of newer literary theories and their application to reading texts in classrooms.

Once the national curriculum for English became law, the government asked the LINC project, as an additional and complementary responsibility to that which it already had, to help teachers approach the knowledge about language elements in the orders. A group of 25 people, of whom I was one, under the direction of Professor Ronald Carter of the University of Nottingham, wrote a collection of professional development materials between September 1989 and July 1990, when they were delivered to the Department of Education and Science (Professor Carter having persuaded the Department that more than a few weeks of his spare time were needed to do the job properly). The materials fulfilled the promise of the outline plan which had been approved in autumn 1989 by the project's steering committee. In the interim, suggestions and criticisms made by the committee had been accepted by writers of the materials, parts of which had been revised accordingly. It was therefore a surprise to be told a few days after delivery that the materials would not be acceptable to the government without substantial further revision (dissenting voices on the steering committee having been overruled). The materials were further revised over the next 7 months, but in May 1991 were finally rejected.

LANGUAGE STUDY OR GRAMMAR EXERCISES

What was the problem? The LINC project's interpretation of the model of the English language in the Kingman Report generated a set of linked perspectives on language study which I will summarize under five headings. We recommended that, whether in the course of other activities within the English curriculum or as specific investigations, teachers might look explicitly at language as follows:

(1) Language Variety: between speech and writing; of accents and dialects; of functions, registers, and genres in speech and writing, including those of literature; as evident in differences and similarities between languages, including comparisons of words and scripts;

(2) Language as Social Construct and Constructor: as evident in speaker–listener, reader–writer relationships, for both interpersonal and mass uses of language, and including a particular concern for the ways in which social power is constructed and challenged through language;

(3) Language Acquisition and Development: as evident in babies learning to talk; in children learning to read and write; in the potentially lifelong expansion of all our language repertoires;

(4) History of Languages: as evident in historical change in English, and in some of the world's other languages, ancient and contemporary—ephemeral as well as long-term change;

(5) Language as System: as evident in vocabulary—connotations, definitions and origins of words; in grammar—the functions and forms of words in groups; in phonology—the sound systems of spoken language; in graphology—the systems of marks that give us written language (including spelling, punctuation, layout, and handwriting); in the structure of longer pieces of text (e.g., conversations, stories, arguments, descriptions, reports).

The problem was that genuine attempts, such as this one, to interpret the Kingman model in ways which would help teachers address with their pupils the knowledge about language elements of the national curriculum, was not what the government really wanted, even though that was what it had officially asked for. What it really wanted was that which the Kingman and Cox Committees had been expected to deliver, but had not: a primer of grammar exercises. The fact that the LINC materials contained more attention to grammar, in the course of trying to fulfill the brief their writers had actually been given, than any materials produced by a major curriculum development project in the UK so far, was not the point.

There is a happy ending to this story. The government's letter of final rejection of the materials did contain the minor consolation that the government was:

content for the latest versions of the LINC units to continue to be used for the purpose of in-service training of teachers.

Whether or not it was truly content we cannot say; but the government could not help the fact that thousands of photocopies of the draft materials, in whole or in part, were circulating in the country. The leaders of the LINC project decided to produce a visually more attractive version of them, looking in fact remarkably like a published book (or rather the insides of a ring-binder folder) except for the lack of a publisher's name and an ISBN. A designer and printer worked speedily on this version of the materials for us, and two copies were delivered

to each of the local education authorities in England and Wales in October and November 1991. It is impossible to say how many further copies of *Language in the National Curriculum—Professional Development Materials* (University of Nottingham, 1991) have since been made; 30,000 would be a minimum. About 1,000 copies have so far been sold outside of the UK, and copies are still available from Professor Carter at the University of Nottingham.

The LINC project generated two official publications. *Knowledge about Language and the Curriculum: The LINC Reader* (Carter, 1990) has sold very well, largely because local education authorities, enraged by the censorship of the professional development materials, spent some of the money allocated to them for the LINC project in 1991 and 1992 on bulk orders. Equally successful has been *Looking into Language: Classroom Approaches to Knowledge about Language* (Bain, Fitzgerald, & Taylor, 1992), a collection of case studies of knowledge about language drawn from the huge harvest of records of work done within the project.

As a result of the work of the LINC project, there is now a much more developed understanding of the ways of studying language than there was in 1989. With that understanding, many teachers have designed sequences of work which address the requirements for knowledge about language in the national curriculum, and have seen how opportunities can be taken to reveal and extend children's knowledge about language throughout the English curriculum and beyond. There is every reason to suppose that this learning will continue.

READING STANDARDS: HARD TO MEASURE, EASY TO EXPLOIT

The second of my stories belongs in the area of the teaching of reading, and to get a proper sense of the political significance of this debate in the UK, we need to go back to a time long before a national curriculum was thought of: to the early 1970s. It was a time of widespread national concern about reading standards. They had fallen sharply in recent years, according to press reports of a study of some 11- and 15-year-old readers by two educational psychologists (Start & Wells, 1972). The government decided to act. It set up a committee, chaired by Sir Alan Bullock, to investigate the problem. The Bullock Committee examined the findings of the study, and in its Report, *A Language for Life* (Department of Education and Science, 1975), urged great caution in interpreting them. One reason for this advice was that the Committee was critical of the testing methods that had been used:

We do not regard these tests as adequate measures of reading ability. What they measure is a narrow aspect of silent reading comprehension .

A second reason for caution was that the test results actually underestimated what many 15-year-olds could do as readers. They were too easy for them, so there was a "ceiling effect," with more successful 15-year-old readers bunched together at the top of the available scale. Third, the Committee pointed out that the sample of children which the researchers had intended to test was not large enough to have national significance:

> If national standards are under discussion, then one needs either a national sample or a collection of a large number of local surveys which taken together represent accurately the national population. Such a collection does not exist....

Fourth, some of the language used in the tests had aged since they were originally devised. The researchers themselves pointed out the limitations of phrases like "mannequin parade" and "pacific settlement of disputes" as items on the basis of which to measure present-day children's meaningful recognition of written language.

There were other drawbacks as well. Nonetheless, the Committee squared up to the findings of the survey as they stood. Contrary to the unequivocal reports whose urgency had been the spur to the setting up of the committee in the first place, it summarized:

> There is no evidence of a decline in attainment over the years in the lowest achievers among 15-year-olds. Since national surveys were instituted in 1948 the standards of the poorest readers have risen, and the gap between the most able and least able has narrowed. This reflects upon the capacity of existing tests to measure the achievement of the most able readers; [Conclusion 14]

and

> There was no significant change in the reading standards of 11-year-olds over the decade 1960–1970, but such movement as took place after 1964 was in all probability slightly downwards. [Conclusion 15]

What the Bullock Report Recommended

The Report then went far beyond the narrow definition of its brief, to make a comprehensive statement about language and learning, including the teaching of reading. The Report's conclusions and recommendations about the teaching of reading include the following:

7. The level of reading skill required for participation in the affairs of modern society is far above that implied in earlier definitions of literacy.

56. There is no one method, medium, approach, device or philosophy that holds the key to the process of learning to read.

58. A detailed understanding of the reading process should inform decisions about the organization of teaching, the initial and in-service education of teachers, and the use of resources.

62. The learning of sound–symbol correspondences should take place in the context of whole word recognition and reading for meaning. It is important ... that children should ...have had a full range of pre-reading experiences.

66. The most effective teaching of reading is that which gives the pupil the various skills he or she needs to make the fullest possible use of context cues in search for meaning.

73. It should be established from the beginning in the mind of the child that reading is primarily a thinking process, not simply an exercise in identifying shapes and sounds.

79. Reading schemes which use contrived and unnatural language prevent children from developing the ability to detect sequential probability in linguistic structure.

83. The difference in [teachers'] effectiveness lies not in their allegiance to any one method but in (a) the quality of their relationships with children, (b) their degree of expert knowledge, and (c) their sensitivity in matching their teaching with each child's current learning needs.

The Report's great achievement was to place on official record the complexity of the job that teachers of language do; in the area of reading, it ought not to have been possible for any responsible person to suggest again that one-dimensional quick fixes using some kind of transmissional rote would be the salvation of any teacher or learner; it ought not to have been possible ever again to escape the Report's emphasis on the multiskilled, meaning-making nature of all language learning. The Report shifted official support away from the set of practices summarized in my first list above, and toward that in my second. When the members of the Cox Committee came to formulate their proposals on the teaching of reading for the national curriculum, they drew on the professional consensus which the Bullock Report had done so much to establish, as can be seen by comparing the conclusions and recommendations just quoted with the reading sections of the national curriculum summarized earlier.

Short Memory and Malicious Intent

Nonetheless, in 1991, 16 years after the publication of the Report, with the national curriculum already passed into law and being taught in the schools, a violent argument about reading standards, complete with corrupt news management and vitriolic reporting of that news, broke out in the UK. A pamphlet entitled *Sponsored Reading Failure* (Turner, 1991), was seized on by the government and most of the popular newspapers as clear proof of a disastrous fall in reading standards. "Trendy" teachers using "progressive" methods of teaching reading were to blame. The teaching of reading was presented as offering a simple choice of two (and only two) methods. Either teachers used phonics, or they used "real books." Those who chose to use real books, so the pamphlet said and, much more important, so the press reportage ran, had abrogated their responsibility to teach. Children stumbled from one confused encounter with a book, unaided by the teacher, to the next. Hence the national decline.

Those who obtained a copy of the pamphlet discovered that its findings had been reported on the basis of a tiny, statistically utterly insignificant sample of children, using a discredited test administered in highly artificial circumstances. That did not matter. The pamphlet's destructive political purpose had been achieved so far as its authors were concerned. The attempt to offer phonics as an idea in opposition to real books; to suggest that if the St George of the former could slay the dragon of the latter, all would be well in the fair land of Albion; such banality plumbed great depths. Every government document on the subject of reading, from the Bullock Report up to and including the sections on reading in the national curriculum for English, had agreed that phonics, the apprehension of symbol-to-sound correspondences, is one but only one of the range of cues by which readers apprehend meaning in texts. The material which children read has to be apprehended using the whole range of cues which generate meaning in the reader's brain, including the vitally important semantic and syntactic cues. There was equally strong agreement in all the documents that the reading material which children are offered should encompass a wide range of appropriate and engaging literature and information texts.

The government commissioned an investigation by Her Majesty's Inspectorate into the scandal which the pamphlet had uncovered. Predictably, the Inspectorate rejected the pamphlet's findings. No single method of teaching reading had taken the country by storm, it said. Almost 95% of the schools in its sample made at least some use of reading schemes, and did not rely entirely on real books. It was critical in equal measure of fundamentalist phonics teaching which pays no attention to meaning, and of a misunderstanding of the "real books method" which imagines that their use equals giving no guidance to young readers at all.

It is sobering to go back to the Bullock Report's list of conclusions and recommendations, and see it carefully picking its way through the discussion after, no doubt, listening to the same dissonant collection of voices. English teachers have made so much actual progress, in so many directions, since 1975. But in spite of that progress, so far as a widespread lay opinion has it, they are still blundering around in a large field of factionalism and ignorance. Those who help maliciously to form that lay opinion carry a heavy weight of responsibility for the time and effort wasted, the damage done.

THE FIRST REVISION OF THE ENGLISH CURRICULUM ORDERS

In 1992, the government decided on a major revision of the national curriculum for English, despite the fact that the curriculum orders had only recently been agreed upon after intensive debate and negotiation. (Indeed, there were still at that time some years within the 5 to 16 range which the national curriculum had not yet formally touched, since it was introduced as a rolling program intended to take 5 years to complete.) It used controversies such as the two which I have recounted to justify a public position that there was an intellectual and pedagogical need to change the orders significantly. The decision went against the wishes of the great majority of teachers, who had been getting accustomed to the orders, and who thought that, on the whole, they offered a framework for promoting effective teaching, allowing the right amount of professional autonomy and choice, and based on a thoughtful consensus on how children best learn to use English and to study its use. There was widespread agreement on the desirability of a number of detailed changes, but a strong feeling that the essential spirit of the orders should be preserved. Unfortunately, it was precisely the spirit of the orders which the government did not like. It found it galling that its own legislation had produced a document so distant from what it had intended 7 years previously. The areas in which it insisted on change were those which we had identified earlier: it wanted more insistence on standard English

from the earliest age, and less tolerance of nonstandard forms, even in the speech of very young children; it wished to exclude any reference to the needs and abilities of bilingual children learning English (except in Wales); it wanted more mechanistic approaches to the teaching of reading, and especially an emphasis on phonics; it wanted sentence grammar to be the only element of knowledge about language to which students were introduced; it wanted to remove media education from the statutory curriculum; it wanted less drama; it wanted children principally to read the works of authors in a literary canon which it established.

The publication of the government's new proposals in April 1993 was greeted with deep resentment by most teachers, though the reaction was tempered by a recognition that, in some aspects of presentation and layout, the proposals were clearer. At this point, however, something unexpected happened.

Dispute Over Assessment

A dispute, parallel with that over the curriculum, broke out between the government and language educators over the assessment and testing system for the national curriculum. In order to understand this dispute properly, we need to know something about the history of the national examination system in the UK.

Students have for many years taken a national examination at 16. Before the national curriculum, examination syllabuses exercised a decisive effect on the curriculum in secondary schools, particularly in the upper years. From 1963 to 1987, a dual system operated, in which higher-attaining students took the General Certificate of Education at Ordinary Level and lower-attaining students took the Certificate of Secondary Education. In 1988, this was replaced by a common system known as the General Certificate of Secondary Education (GCSE), which aimed to test students at 16 across virtually the whole attainment range. The GCSE was widely welcomed by teachers, parents, and students. Under the dual system in the 1970s and 1980s, English teachers had conducted a long campaign in support of coursework methods of assessment. This action had the effect of establishing the GCSE in English as an examination which could be taken partly or wholly by coursework methods. More than 70% of schools chose 100% coursework examination syllabuses in 1991. National standards of attainment in English at 16 have risen significantly since 1988, although there have been some who have liked to suggest, despite the evidence from the annual research carried out by examination boards and the government's advisory agency on assessment, that it has been easier to get good grades through coursework than in an end-of-course examination.

When it introduced the national curriculum, the government had decided to establish a 10-level scale, which would encompass the range of attainment likely to be reached in each national curriculum subject by the great majority of students from age 5 to age 16. It took the end of the school years in which students turned 7, 11, 14 and 16 as the moments in their career when they would be tested and given a level. Teachers and students were familiar with examinations at age 16. However, national testing at 7, 11 and 14 was a complete innovation. The 10-level scale in English produced numerous theoretical and pedagogical absurdities and inexactitudes, as the scale's linear set of discrete criteria came face to face with the essentially recursive nature of language development. To quote one example from among many, in order to gain level 6 for writing, a student must, among other things, be able to:

> recognize when redrafting and revising are appropriate and act accordingly, either on paper or on a computer screen.

In order to gain level 7, students must be able to:

> demonstrate an increased awareness that a first draft may be changed, amended and reordered in a variety of ways.

It is unclear how the second set of criteria is describing an essentially more advanced group of attainments than the first. Nonetheless, English teachers scratched their heads and made the best of it. The pilot tests for children at age 7 and 14 could broadly be defined as good pieces of language education. They provided opportunities for a broad range of speaking and listening, reading and writing activities, appropriate to the attainment range for the age in question, to be assessed over a period of 3 or 4 weeks. (The first 11-year-olds were not due to be tested until 1994, and so no one had then thought in detail about the nature of their tests.)

The dispute, when it came, was not over the need, in principle, to have an assessment system: an organized way of making judgments on which teachers and learners can act, and a reliable record of achievement. There was general agreement, whatever teachers' views about the shortcomings of levels, that every student should have some sort of accumulating record of progress. The dispute was over the government's decision in 1992 to exclude from its testing system at 7, 11 and 14 all elements other than short, timed, externally set tests, and to severely limit the proportion of the GCSE examination which could be assessed by coursework. This decision seemed likely to cause particular difficulties for English, where achievement can only properly be assessed by using whole examples of reading, writing, and speech produced in a range of purposeful communicative contexts, and where English teachers, as we have seen, greatly valued coursework methods of assessment at 16, and were glad when it seemed that they were to be adopted at the lower ages.

To make matters worse, the decision then influenced the curriculum revision, with the government arguing that the curriculum must be simplified so as to justify simpler tests. If the national curriculum had made it a requirement that students should be tested on a wider range of knowledge, understanding, and skill than any short, timed test could measure, the government reasoned that the curriculum must change. It would not recognize that old-style tests were not up to the new job.

Revision of the Revision

The moment of publication of the revised proposals for English coincided with a unanimous boycott by teachers of the new tests for 14-year-olds. This was a shocking humiliation for a government which had assumed, a few years previously, that it could always drive through its reforms, however unpopular. Up to this point, the government had had two advisory agencies, one for the curriculum and one for assessment. It combined these into one, and appointed Sir Ronald Dearing, an open-minded civil servant with some sympathy for the teachers' case, as chairman of the new School Curriculum and Assessment Authority. Sir Ronald rapidly announced a further full-scale review of the national curriculum and its assessment system, whose aim was to achieve a degree of professional consensus and industrial peace. Strange to recount, the revised proposals for English were themselves revised only months after their publication. Once again, there has been impassioned debate, tense negotiation and cunning maneuver, with clear evidence of the government intervening to reverse specific recommendations made by the writing group it appointed through its own advisory agency. These reversals were, of course, in the familiar ideological battlegrounds mentioned throughout this chapter. The departure from the (renamed) Department for Education in July 1994 of two government ministers most intransigently opposed to the view of the majority of English teachers means, I understand, that the final form of the re-revised curriculum orders, to be published in January 1995, will represent more closely a meaning-making definition of language education than would otherwise have been the case. A compromise over testing, with teacher assessment and short external tests both playing a part in the system, looks likely to be accepted though not welcomed by teachers.

CONCLUSION

This has been an account of a few highlights only of an extraordinary political battle over curriculum reform in language education. The destructiveness of the battle has, mostly, been unnecessary. It would have been perfectly possible, had the government wished to, for it to introduce a rational set of curriculum orders and assessment arrangements for English which were properly demanding, were likely to promote the best teaching and discourage the worst, were informative to parents, employers, the interested general public, and to itself, without the bitterness, the mess, the exhaustion on all sides. Actually, language educators want what the government officially also wants: confidently literate, articulate children and young people, broadly cultured, excited by knowledge, proud of their own achievements as users and students of language and appreciative of the achievements of others. History seems to show that it is difficult for major change to occur without some degree of struggle, and no doubt that would have been true in the present case, even with a more cooperative and trusting relationship between government and professionals. The sadness is that very often the government chose to adopt a discourse of derision, slandering and parodying English teachers' work, both in its private discussions and in its public statements. The price paid for this decision has been the confusion and low morale which English teachers have suffered as they have seen themselves traduced in the media as "a national problem" which heroic government intends to solve; as they have seen one "definitive" set of instructions superseded before they have barely had a chance to interpret them in the classroom; and as their intellectual energy has been distracted from long-term learning for the benefit of their students to the rearguard defense of fundamental understandings which they thought, wrongly, had been established beyond doubt.

Despite all this, a true report on the national curriculum and its testing system must record that the great majority of language educators accept that they have come to stay. Few want to go back to a time when responsibility for the content, methodology, and assessment of language education lay with the individual school and teacher, heavily influenced in the upper years of secondary education by examination syllabuses. Most English teachers agree that, whatever contests the future holds, curriculum reform in language education should be conducted within a framework of the entitlement of all students to a common language curriculum which government and professionals construct for them, however painfully.

References

Bain, R., Fitzgerald, B., & Taylor, M. (Eds.). (1992). *Looking into language: Classroom aproaches to knowledge about language.* London: Hodder and Stoughton.

Carter, R., (Ed.). (1990). *Knowledge about language and the curriculum: The LINC reader.* London: Hodder and Stoughton.

Department of Education and Science. (1975). *A language for life.* (the Bullock Report), London: Her Majesty's Stationery Office.

Department of Education and Science. (1988). *Report of the Committee of Enquiry into the teaching of the English language* (the Kingman Report), London: Her Majesty's Stationery Office.

Department of Education and Science. (1989a). *English for ages 5 to 16* (the Cox Report) London: Her Majesty's Stationery Office.

Department of Education and Science. (1989b). *English in the national curriculum.* London: Her Majesty's Stationery Office.

Language in the National Curriculum Project. (1991). *Language in the national curriculum—professional development materials,* Nottingham: University of Nottingham.

Start, K. B., & Wells, B. K. (1972). *The trend of reading standards,* National Foundation for Educational Research.

Turner, M. et al. (1991). *Sponsored reading failure,* Campaign for Real Education.

CROSS-NATIONAL STUDIES OF LITERACY

Warwick Elley

UNIVERSITY OF CANTERBURY, NEW ZEALAND

There are many reasons why comparative studies of student achievement in literacy, across educational systems, might prove fruitful for policy makers. Educators around the world vary in their policies and theories concerning the optimum strategies for teaching children to read and write. What is traditional in one country is regarded as eccentric in another. If there are differences in the effectiveness of their instructional strategies, resources, and policies, then cross-national empirical studies have the potential to identify the most and least successful, and to explore the correlates of various approaches. Curriculum specialists and teachers in each country also appreciate having hard data on the relative strengths and weaknesses of their reading and writing programs, when viewed in an international perspective. The achievement levels of comparable samples of students in similar countries provide a useful framework within which their school systems can be evaluated.

A study involving many countries also has the opportunity to separate the effects of factors that are similar across systems, and those that are different. For instance, if the age at which instruction is begun varies from one country to the next, but is uniform within countries, then it takes a cross-national study to determine whether it is a key factor or not. In this sense, the world represents a huge "educational laboratory."

Among the variables that do vary markedly across countries are the level of per student funding; the amount of teacher education; the age at which children are introduced to literacy; the length of the school year; the amount and type of homework; the extent to which phonics is stressed in reading programs; the emphasis placed on real literature versus graded texts; the extent of grouping and reading around the class; the typical size of the class; the amount of reading done in school; the involvement of parents; the availability of books; and the complexity of the orthography of the language. If such factors are really important, international studies should confirm it for us. Literacy educators in all countries have much to learn from one another.

CHALLENGES IN CROSS-NATIONAL STUDIES

It takes but little reflection, however, to reveal a host of obstacles that the would-be international researcher faces. Literacy, more so than numeracy or scientific abilities, is firmly embedded in the culture and language in which it is encountered (Levine, 1986; Purves, 1992). For instance, the prestige accorded to imaginative literature, as opposed to oral eloquence or clarity of exposition, varies across cultures; the value of taking a critical perspective is cherished in some countries, while the need to respect and honor the written word is more important in others. Furthermore, many reading and writing tasks surely differ in their significance and their difficulty level across languages, and translation from one to the next may well distort differences in achievement levels, and in the impact of instructional variables. How then, can tests be developed that are equally unbiased for all? How can such tests reflect differences in curricular emphases across countries? How can the researchers accommodate differences in traditions of test format?

Comparison of student samples across countries is also fraught with problems, especially when educators follow different policies of school entry ages, promotion and retention policies, curriculum sequencing, drop-out rates, and mainstreaming of handicapped students and immigrants from other cultures. Under such circumstances the selection of truly representative samples, comparable across many countries, is no easy task. It is no wonder that many are sceptical about the viability and validity of international comparisons (Jaeger, 1994; Moses, 1991; Westbury, 1992).

THE INTERNATIONAL ASSOCIATION FOR THE EVALUATION OF EDUCATIONAL ACHIEVEMENT

One organization that has attempted to meet these linguistic and technical challenges is the International Association for the Evaluation of Educational Achievement (IEA). Since the early 1960s this association of educational researchers has been conducting surveys of student achievement in its member countries, with increasing levels of sophistication in procedures.

Founded in a small way in 1959, IEA has developed into a federation of committed researchers from some 50 countries, and now has a full-time Secretariat located in The Hague, the Netherlands. The IEA Assembly, or governing body, meets annually in order to plan and discuss its projects. Surveys of large representative samples of students have now been conducted, at two or three age levels, in subjects as diverse as reading, mathematics, science, foreign language, civics, writing, computers, literature, and preprimary education. Also, student attitudes, teaching practices, and local policies are put under the researchers' microscope.

The main purpose of this chapter is to review the methodologies and interpret some of the salient findings of the cross-national studies of reading, writing, and literature. How helpful have these enormous surveys been in clarifying policy issues in IEA member countries? The recent work of American researcher Harold Stevenson and his colleagues comparing U.S. and Asian students and policies will also be included. There are other organizations that plan and conduct international surveys of student achievement (e.g., The International Assessment of Educational Progress [IAEP] associated with Educational Testing Service in the United States) but they have not focused on the measurement of literacy. There are also a number of cross-national collaborative surveys under way in adult literacy, but they are not yet far enough advanced to warrant inclusion in this article. Small studies that compare local samples in only two countries have also been excluded.

Pioneering Studies

The first reported attempt to conduct an international survey of literacy across several countries and languages was the pilot study of reading comprehension which was incorporated in a series of surveys conducted by IEA in the early 1960s (Foshay, 1962). Twelve countries, all European except Israel, participated in this exploratory study. Achievement tests of reading, along with tests of mathematics, science, and geography were administered to cross-sectional samples of 13-year-olds in each country. Resources for the study were slim, no precedents were available, no clear hypotheses were set, and it is not surprising that serious problems arose in the comparability of the samples and the suitability of the tests. Many of the challenges outlined above became painfully obvious to the researchers.

The desired samples of 600–1000 pupils were intended to be chosen by community rather than by school, and were to be based on the researchers' judgment of representativeness, guided by results of previous local surveys. In the event, some countries produced socioeconomically biased and/or numerically inadequate samples making comparisons of mean scores questionable. Furthermore, in spite of some pilot testing of the tests, the translation procedures adopted for the

reading tests were too haphazard to escape the criticism that the tests were not equivalent across countries (Downing, 1973).

The final form of the reading test consisted of five passages and 33 multiple-choice questions, but no time limit was imposed, so that the conditions of testing were not well standardized. To overcome differences in students' test sophistication across countries, a practice test was devised and administered before the main testing and opportunities were provided for pupils to discuss the nature of the task.

Despite the looseness of translation (undertaken by one researcher, and without back translation), it is important to note that the items appeared to "behave" in similar fashion in each country, as indicated by a median correlation of 0.87 between the difficulty indices of the reading test across the 12 nations. Surprisingly, this was a higher figure than was found in the other subjects. Thorndike's optimistic conclusion, in the final report, is worthy of note. A difficult item is a difficult item "regardless of the school system in which the pupil has been educated, or the language in which his schooling has been couched" (Thorndike, in Foshay, 1962, p. 33).

Numerous analyses were attempted to explore the patterns of results. Boys' scores were superior to girls', on all tests except reading, where the girls performed consistently better; the distribution of scores was wider in the UK than in other countries; and the differences in mean scores in reading, relative to nonverbal ability, provided some evidence of the relative success of the school systems in reading instruction. However, such findings should have been regarded as tentative, in view of the inadequate samples. Perhaps the firmest conclusion that could be drawn was an encouraging one, that a cross-national study of this sort was considered feasible in reading. The researchers believed that the cultural and technical challenges could be met, and overcome.

The IEA Survey of Reading Comprehension in 15 Countries

The next international survey of reading comprehension was the 15-nation survey at three age levels, conducted by IEA under the direction of Robert Thorndike (1973). This study, which was one of the IEA six-subject survey of 1970–71, capitalized on the experience gained in the earlier study, (Foshay, 1962), and was itself the source of a number of lessons for future studies.

In order to ensure maximum collaboration and minimal bias in the project, an international steering committee was established, which collaborated with national advisory committees in each of the 15 participating countries. Plans were developed to test representative samples of pupils at ages 10, 14, and the final year of school in each country. This proved to be a mammoth enterprise, which finally led to the testing of over 103,000 students. After discussion of various options, the committees prepared tests of reading comprehension of the traditional kind—self-contained paragraphs of continuous prose, followed by multiple-choice questions which could be answered by referring back to the passage as required. All countries were invited to contribute items and passages, so that cultural bias would be kept to a minimum. The tests were developed and trialled in several countries, and only those items were selected which were felt to be appropriate by the advisory committees of each country. At each population level the final reading tests contained about 50 items, which were administered to students in two testing sessions of between 25 minutes (age 10) and 50 minutes (age 17–18).

Short tests of word knowledge and reading speed were also administered, but these were given less weight in the international analyses as they did not show satisfactory equivalence across languages. (Thorndike, 1973, pp. 29–36; 131–132; Walker, 1976, p. 114). Neither skill proved to be easy to translate without affecting difficulty levels substantially. It was learned that whenever the translation depends considerably on a single key word, the potential for change in difficulty level as a result of the translation was too large. Languages differ too much in their potential for providing synonyms of similar levels of familiarity, and usage.

Background questionnaires designed to elicit information on the circumstances of the students' home and school were also completed by the students and their teachers, with a view to testing hypotheses about the influence on achievement of home environment, book resources, instructional policies, teacher variables and the like.

Despite meticulous planning for obtaining good representative samples of students at each level, several countries were unable to meet the requirements, and their results therefore had to be regarded with some caution. As the target population at the 10- and 14-year levels was an age group rather than a grade group, many pupils were omitted in some countries because they fell outside the typical grade for their age. In five countries these omissions represented more than 10% for at least one age level (Thorndike, 1973, pp. 47, 48).

Reliability checks on the reading comprehension tests showed respectable coefficients (0.75 to 0.85) in most cases, although they were generally low in the developing countries. From 20% to 40% of items in two such countries showed correct answers no higher than chance levels, which makes identification of significant patterns of correlations problematic. Attempts to identify reading subskills were unsuccessful, as the correlations between the hypothesized subscores were generally as high as their respective reliability coefficients, so that most analysis was carried out on total comprehension score. A comparison of difficulty indices across countries showed very similar patterns in English-speaking countries, and a median correlation of 0.75 across different languages. This is a respectable figure, but considerably lower than that found in the Foshay (1962) study. Thorndike attributed the discrepancies to translation problems, and cultural differences, but concluded that the figures were high enough to indicate "a substantial core of similarity in the reading comprehension task as one goes from country to country" (Thorndike, 1973, p. 164).

Numerous statistical analyses were conducted on the results, including comparisons of country means and standard deviations, and multiple regression analyses with background variables. The former comparisons showed predictably large differences in mean scores between developed and lesser-developed countries, but less predictable small differences within those groups. At the highest age level, a correlation of –0.60 between mean score and percentage of students still in school complicated the interpretation, and this retentivity factor also affected the spread of scores. At the two lower age levels, however, retentivity was much less of a problem in this respect. Table 57–1 shows the mean scores for each country for each population.

The correlations with home background variables showed consistently significant relationships with two composite variables—socioeconomic status, and level of reading resources—but only modest relationships with parental help, and level of parental interest. When combined in multiple regression analyses, the "home factors block" produced correlations of 0.38 and 0.40 for 10- and 14-year-olds respectively. However, once this amount of variance was removed, school type and instructional variables produced disappointingly small improvements in the prediction of students' scores, at the individual level, and not much more at the school level. Where correlations were strong in one country, they were weak in the next. Thorndike was forced to conclude that "little emerges that helps to understand what a school can do to foster better achievement in its students" (Thorndike, 1973, p. 117).

When national mean scores in reading were lined up alongside national means on other variables, highest correlations were found with availability of reading materials, hours of instruction in the mother tongue, parental education and hours reading for pleasure. These findings were in line with prediction.

The major benefits of this mammoth exercise were the confirmation of the belief that it could be done, and the consequent lessons for those who would try again. The so-called "Olympic Games" aspect of the mean scores also generated considerable interest, exchange of ideas, and revisions of policy in some countries. The potential for drawing conclusions about effective instruction, however, was largely unrealized.

TABLE 57–1. Mean Scores in Reading Comprehension for 15 Education Systems (from Thorndike, 1973)

Country	Pop I (10 Yrs)	Pop II (14 Yrs)	Pop IV (17–18 Yrs)
Belgium (Fl)	17.5	24.6	25.0
Belgium (Fr)	17.9	27.2	27.6
Chile	9.1	14.1	16.0
England	18.5	25.3	33.6
Finland	19.4	27.1	30.0
Hungary	14.0	25.5	23.8
India	8.5	5.2	3.5
Iran	3.7	7.8	4.4
Israel	13.8	22.6	25.2
Italy	19.9	27.9	23.9
The Netherlands	17.7	25.2	31.2
New Zealand	–	29.3	35.4
Scotland	18.4	27.0	34.4
Sweden	21.5	25.6	26.8
United States	16.8	27.3	21.8
Median	17.6	25.5	25.2

Amongst the chief reasons for this disappointment were those acknowledged by Thorndike himself. Without a survey below age 10, it was difficult to throw light on the major influences on reading acquisition, as the critical stage in this enterprise is probably between 6 and 9 years in most countries. However, the group administration of tests and questionnaires to whole classes in many schools was widely felt to be problematic at these tender ages. Questionnaires to teachers also have distinct limitations in capturing key differences in classroom processes, especially when they put questions which can be answered only by Yes or No answers.

Another problem concerned the unit of analysis. Since the sampling was done by schools, students' scores and teachers' responses were averaged for schools, not self-contained classes, so that any variation in teacher effectiveness within a school was neutralized. The link between student and teacher was lost in this enterprise, making the identification of important teacher influences less likely. Furthermore, the effects of teaching are subtle and elusive. The kinds of questions that can be asked in questionnaires to students are bound to miss many of them, and the fact that reading is a cumulative skill, depending much on early training and experience, makes the identification of significant influences in the current school year of 10- and 14-year-olds rather improbable. Only a good pretest could avoid this weakness, but none was used in the study.

Added to this is the fact that schools vary much less than homes in their quality (Thorndike, 1973, p. 99). Teachers require certificates of competence, and governments usually attempt to standardize much of the learning which occurs in schools. Parents are not subjected to these constraints, and family backgrounds vary much more in consequence. It should not be surprising, then, that little variance in student performance was attributable to schools. This is not to say that they do not contribute much to student learning. They clearly do. But the model of analysis in the IEA studies focused on contributions made by different agencies to student variance, not to changes in student means. The fact that all variance associated with the home was removed first in the analyses, without calculation of joint and unique variance for home and school, only served to reduce further the apparent contribution of the school.

Another possible weakness of the study was revealed by an analysis of the test questions themselves. At all three levels, 75% to 80% of the items measured inferential reading skills. It is possible that the emphasis placed on such basic reasoning ability, as opposed to literal reading skills, made it difficult to measure the impact of different teaching methods. The survival of inferential items, after item analyses, may of course be a result of the translation requirement. Other items may be more affected by a change of language.

Other commentators on this IEA survey of reading comprehension identified different problems. Downing and Dalrymple-Alford (1974–75) pointed to the weaknesses in sampling and the lack of clear-cut hypotheses to test, while Theisen, Achola and Boakari (1986) were concerned with the neglect of "within-country factors" in the measurement. Many education systems are far from uniform in their cultural and curricular emphases.

Nevertheless, the exercise was a distinct step forward in bringing an empirical dimension to the study of comparative reading, and provided the world with a clear example of what might be achieved with some modifications in design and procedure. Furthermore, many participating countries found specific benefits in the results. National reports of the findings, when viewed in relation to those of other countries, gave rise to more informed debates about methods and policies. In Hungary, for instance, the relatively low scores were "like a bolt from the blue" (Bathory & Kadar-Fulop, 1974). Professional educators and the general public reacted strongly, methods of teaching were reexamined, silent reading was given greater emphasis, and a diverse range of innovations were developed and evaluated.

By contrast, New Zealand educators gained much in confidence from the knowledge that their students achieved at relatively high levels. Closer analyses of the reasons for these findings were stimulated (Guthrie, 1981; Purves, 1979) and many educators and researchers visited New Zealand to study their reading programs.

Swedish authorities also gained strong reassurance from the IEA studies that their educational reforms had been successful in reducing inequalities between schools and districts. The between-school variance in Sweden was very low, relative to that of other countries.

Researchers also made good use of the IEA data base to test new models (Bulcock, Clifton, & Beebe, 1978; Munck, 1979) and many participants reported improvements in their national research and test development skills.

The IEA Survey of Literature in 10 Education Systems

An IEA study of achievement in literature provided even greater challenges than the one of reading. However, preliminary studies of literature response of 13- and 17-year-olds were conducted during the mid- 1960s (Purves & Rippere, 1968), and the results were promising. While some elements of literature proved too diverse across cultures to make for common assessment, other elements were clearly possible candidates for assessment. So IEA resolved to conduct a larger study with special focus on literary responses to specific texts and on attitudes toward, and interest in, literature. This survey was conducted at secondary school level only, on populations of 14-year-olds and students in their preuniversity year (Purves, 1973). Poetry works proved to be unsuitable across cultures, as was knowledge of works and literary terms, so attention focused on self-contained short stories. In a preliminary study of item format in literature testing, Choppin and Purves (1969) had shown that multiple-choice tests measured essentially the same literary abilities as were measured by open-ended items on the same literature passages. They therefore recommended the use of multiple-choice items in the final study.

In line with IEA procedures, an international steering committee was established and countries were asked to submit test materials. Four countries provided passages for pretesting and six countries undertook pilot testing on their students. Four long passages were eventually selected as suitable in all 10 countries that participated: "The Sea," "I See You Never," "The Use of Force," and the "Man by the Fountain." Each passage gave rise to about 18 questions. Measures of response preference were also devised, pretested, and revised. Eventually, a format was agreed to, where students were asked to rank the five most important questions (out of 20) that one should ask about each passage. Attitude and interest scales were also prepared, along with questionnaires for students, teachers and schools. Not all of these proved successful, or as reliable as had been hoped, and some of the findings were accordingly regarded with uncertainty. Nevertheless, the achievement tests proved sufficiently reliable (around 0.7 to 0.8), to identify large group differences.

The results of the literature tests for each country are given in Table 57–2 broken down into Interpretation and Comprehension categories. It should be noted that the student samples were substantially the same as those participating in the reading comprehension survey, and were subject to the same limitations.

As in the Reading Comprehension Survey, New Zealand students showed the highest achievement levels at both 14 and 18 years, but the results for the older group must be interpreted in the light of the low retention rates for students in New Zealand (13%), as well as those of England (20%) and Italy (16%). By contrast, 75% of U.S. students stayed at school until grade 12. In order to compensate for these differences in retention rates at age 17, the researchers attempted a further analysis, in which they compared the mean scores of the top 9% of Population IV students in each country. The result was that the rank order changed to produce the highest mean for England, followed closely by the United States, Sweden, and New Zealand, but with little change in the others. However, the adjustment probably overcorrects, as the assumption underlying it, that only less able students (in Literature) drop out of school, is a debatable one. For the older age groups, national differences in retention rates will continue to complicate interpretation of relative performance levels.

Student achievement in literature is partly a function of the traditional curricular emphasis given to different aspects of literary study by teachers—historical, linguistic, moralistic, critical, or psychological. Students in all countries did tend to read texts and then to discuss them in class, followed by some form of writing. However, the nature of the talk differed across countries, and these differences were believed to be reflected in the students' ranking of response preferences. Students in most countries rated highly such questions as "What happened in this story?" and "Has anything in this story a hidden meaning?" However, they differed in their rating of the remaining questions. Students in Belgium and Italy emphasized the formal and impersonal; students in Chile, England, and Iran the personal and content-oriented responses. Again, others stressed historical or moral interpretations. Interestingly, there was a substantial correlation between teachers' ranking of the response questions and those of their students. The researchers concluded that teachers do "succeed in imparting to their students a preferred way of approaching literary works" (Purves, 1973). One cannot, of course, rule out the general influence of community or parental expectations.

Reading interests were found to differ more between genders and age groups than they did across countries. In all countries, books of humor tended to be most popular at age 14, followed by adventure, sports, romance, and mystery, while poetry, art, science, and politics attracted very few. The older age group added current events, history, and biography to the popular category—again consistently across countries. The youth culture for teenagers is virtually universal—apparently more biological than cultural.

There were some clear-cut gender differences, of course—boys opting for sports and mystery, and girls for romance and sometimes poetry—but these too were remarkably consistent across cultures.

As in the case of reading, the chief conclusions drawn were that the enterprise of assessing groups of students in many diverse countries on a common test is possible, but only in a limited set of literary outcomes: comprehension and interpretation of literary texts, and stated responses to such texts. As before, the major sources of variance were found at home and in the community rather than in the school, "...the differences between high-achieving and low-achieving schools are explained by the culture that they serve." (Purves, 1973, p. 312). However, as in the reading study, a great deal of variance was unexplained.

In another analysis, the degree of gain which occurred in student mean scores from Population II to IV shows that 17-year-old students achieve at much higher levels than 14-year-olds on the same literary exercises. Girls also achieved at higher levels than boys in literature (Walker, 1976). The patterns in student response to literature were interesting, as they appeared to reflect differences in instruction but were also sufficiently consistent across countries to show differences according to the text read. "Response to literature is a learned behavior" (Purves, 1973, p. 315). It is modified by what the student reads and is affected by the students' culture and school. Curriculum developers and teachers have to make choices, and their choices appear to make a real difference in students' literary responses, if not in their abilities.

TABLE 57–2. Mean Scores in Literature for 10 Education Systems (from Purves, 1973)

Country	INTERPRETATION		COMPREHENSION	
	Pop II (14 Yrs)	Pop IV (17–18 Yrs)	Pop II (14 Yrs)	Pop IV (17–18 Yrs)
New Zealand	10.0	14.9	8.7	11.9
Finland	9.0	13.3	8.2	10.5
USA	8.8	12.1	7.7	9.8
Belgium (Fr)	8.3	11.6	7.6	9.8
England	8.3	14.7	7.8	11.7
Sweden	8.3	12.7	7.6	10.7
Italy	7.8	10.7	8.6	10.3
Belgium (Fl)	6.8	10.9	7.1	9.3
Chile	4.1	8.8	5.3	9.4
Iran	2.1	3.1	3.9	5.0

The IEA Written Composition Survey

While the challenge of assessing reading and literature across languages and cultures was found to be daunting, the cooperative methods used to develop and screen the tests produced results which appeared to largely meet the challenge. The test questions tended to operate in similar fashion in all countries. However, the challenge presented by a cross-national study of writing was even greater. Writing educators recognize that most acts of writing are culturally determined, and that even when teachers claim to be stressing clarity and organization, for instance, their interpretation of these actions may well vary across countries (Purves, 1993, p. 17).

Nevertheless, IEA set out to explore such complexities in a survey of performance in written composition in 14 countries (Gorman, Purves, & Degenhart 1988; Purves, 1992). Three populations A, B and C participated at ages 12–13, 15–16, and 17–18 respectively, but the main focus of attention was given to Population B (15–16 years).

After useful cross-national discussions of an appropriate model of school writing the researchers settled on a diverse range of writing tasks to use in their surveys. Students in each country were selected by stratified random probability procedures, and those selected wrote on three tasks rotated from a set of nine. Each wrote a functional task, a descriptive-expository letter and one of either an argument, a narrative or a reflective essay. The finished products were graded on a 5-point scale by internationally trained marking panels, but major differences in teachers' values emerged during this task, differences which effectively prevented any meaningful cross-national comparisons of relative achievement levels. Some marking juries emphasised product in their judgment of quality, while others focused more on aspects of form, with the result that discrepancies in means and variance amongst markers were unusually large, and correlations amongst grades across individual tasks were too low to justify combining of tasks into reliable total scores (Lehmann, 1992). This was a disappointment to the researchers, but a finding which may not have surprised those who stress the role of culture in students' composing processes.

Nevertheless, Purves (1992) reports a number of findings of interest which can only be interpreted within a cross-cultural context. Although the tasks did vary in difficulty, the order of difficulty was not the same across countries. Narrative tasks tend to be easier at age 15, but the functional task was better done in New Zealand and the Netherlands, and the expository task in Hungary. Reflective compositions were not well done in most countries, especially New Zealand, but Hungarian students had most difficulty with argument, Dutch students with narrative, and Finnish and German students with exposition. Such variations mirrored well the curricular emphases placed on such tasks in the school. Student performance in writing is related to instruction and "the ease or difficulty appears to depend on practice or exposure" (p. 152).

Another clear cut finding is that girls achieve at higher levels than boys at all ages and in all writing tasks (in 113 out of 114 comparisons), especially in Finland, Sweden, and New Zealand, but much less so in the United States, Germany and several developing countries. At the younger ages the girls' superiority showed up more in narrative, at the older ages in expository and reflective writing.

As predicted, there was clear evidence of growth in writing performance with age, and the influence of the home was consistently evident in the various multiple-regressional analyses that were undertaken. However, little more emerged from the international study of predictor variables in home, school, and community, as the reliability of the measures used did not favor such analysis (Lehmann, 1992).

More interesting was an analysis of the content of one of the writing tasks in nine countries—that which asked students to write a letter of advice to a younger pupil who was soon to enrol at the school. How could such students improve their marks in writing when they attended this school? (Taukala & Degenhart, 1992, p. 126).

In all countries (at Population B level) students' priority advice referred to matters of presentation, especially to handwriting, format, spelling and punctuation. Either these are the features that their teachers are most likely to mark, or those that most readily come to mind—perhaps because of parental expressed expectations, as well as those of their teachers. Such a finding is inconsistent with the priorities of many teachers, especially those who value process writing. The researchers did note, however, that these presentation factors tended to be stressed more by less able writers.

Presentation factors accounted for 37% of the variance in student advice, and was especially strong in Chile, the Netherlands, England, and Germany. Next in order of importance was advice relating to content, especially about relevance, amount, and fact (Finland and Germany), or interest, imagination, originality (New Zealand). Process factors—planning, revision, topic choice—figured prominently in Chile, Sweden, and New Zealand, and organizational factors in Thailand, Finland, the Netherlands, and England. Style and general classroom tactics received little attention in any country.

Across countries, there were clearly strong common threads running through the students' perceptions of good writing, but there were enough differences in emphasis to give educators in each country pause for thought.

IEA Study of Reading-Literacy in 32 Countries

The most recent cross-national study of literacy undertaken by IEA was the Reading–Literacy survey of 32 countries (Elley, 1992, 1994) which took place in 1990–91. Building on the lessons learned from earlier surveys, the International Steering Committee for the project consulted widely, invited many national centers to participate, and worked cooperatively to ensure that all countries contributed to the study's design and to the measuring instruments.

The essential differences in design between the Thorndike survey of reading comprehension in 1970–71, and that of 1990–91 were:

1. The younger age levels were changed from 10 years to 9 years to improve the chances of identifying key factors in the reading acquisition phases.

2. A wider range of test materials was trialled and used, including narrative, expository, and documents (charts, maps, and graphs). Some were brief, others were over 1,000 words.

3. A greater variety of test items was used, including multiple-choice, completion and some sentence answers.

4. Students were tested in intact classes, with a view to clarifying teacher effects on student achievement.

5. Greater efforts were made to assess the volume and character of students' voluntary reading activities.

6. A systematic attempt was made to relate a country's test scores to community expectations, and to the level of economic and social development of each country.

7. Technical advances included the use of Rasch analyses for item selection and scaling, and Lisrel path analyses and other multivariate analyses of the completed data.

Other improvements were proposed, such as the use of pre- and posttests, the testing at adjacent class levels, and the use of more performance type tests, but logistical and financial constraints made them impracticable in many countries. Some countries made use of "national options" to augment the international core of literacy tasks and questions set.

After consensus had been reached by national representatives on the overall design and variables to include in the study, 20 countries contributed test materials for screening. These were sifted and revised by the Steering Committee, and duly studied and rated for suitability by national committees in each country. The surviving materials were pilot tested in over 30 school systems, on judgment samples of 9- and 14-year-olds. After scoring, coding, and analysis by Rasch procedures, the final items were selected and approved in joint consultation sessions. Only those items which were acceptable in all countries, were of appropriate difficulty level, and conformed to the Rasch criteria of "good fit" in and across all countries, were selected. Many items were dropped because they could not be translated fairly, or were culturally unsuitable in one or more countries. Participating countries also contributed to the formulating of hypotheses to test, and worked collaboratively on the tasks of developing the questionnaires for principals, teachers, and students and on the measures of voluntary reading activities. (For further details, see Elley, 1993.)

Representative samples of students for the final testing (in the eighth month of the school year) were selected in a two-stage or three-stage randomly stratified sampling strategy, supervised by an independent sampling judge, and strict rules were laid down for ensuring that the samples were as comparable as possible. Nevertheless, a few countries tested samples of students who turned out to be somewhat older or younger than those of other countries, largely because of differences in retention and promotion policies. These discrepancies were identified, and their effects estimated for fairer interpretation of differences among national means. For instance, the results for the Netherlands and Canada (BC) were underestimated for Population A (9 years); and those of Canada (BC), Italy, Hungary, Spain, and Belgium (Fr) for Population B (14 years). For future studies it was felt important that adjacent age groups be assessed to make better provision for such discrepancies.

Guidelines for translation of test materials built on those of earlier IEA studies, requiring parallel translation by two experts, and some back translation. The Rasch analyses and correlational studies were also undertaken to identify any distortions, and to check on the effects of any translation problems. As in the earlier studies of reading, these proved to be manageable, and the differences in rank order of difficulty between items were very similar for countries which tested in English and those which translated the measuring instruments. Correlations clustering around 0.93 were found. This was an encouraging sign, indicating that, once again, the items behaved in similar fashion across countries and languages. However, many items measuring vocabulary, beginning reading skills, and comprehension had already been dropped in the development phases.

More problematic was the case of several countries whose 9-year-olds had difficulty in handling the formal timed test situation (e.g., Denmark, the Netherlands, and Germany) and whose scores are probably underestimated at the younger age. There also was some concern that the response rates for schools were below 85% of the planned samples in the United States, Zimbabwe, Nigeria, and Thailand—which may have somewhat inflated their scores.

MAIN FINDINGS OF THE IEA READING–LITERACY SURVEY

In the light of such cautions, what can be concluded from the 1990–91 IEA Survey of Reading-Literacy? First, as Table 57–3 shows, the mean achievement scores highlighted the superiority of Finnish students in all aspects of reading, clearly ahead of the other high achievers, Sweden, France, and New Zealand—at both age levels. Students in the United States and Italy showed high levels of achievement at the 9-year level, but their 14-year-olds did not match these levels. The consistently high achievement shown by Finnish students, across all domains, again raised the question of the importance of their transparent orthography (Kyostio, 1980; Linnakyla, 1993). The Finnish language is, more than any other language, phonetically very regular. However, the benefits of any such regularity were not obvious in the case of other countries, as the correlation between the rated phonetic regularity of the language and a country's achievement levels was near zero. This issue was raised again, and also dismissed, by Lee, Stigler and Stevenson (1982) (see below). Other explanatory factors, such as the strength of Finland's literacy traditions, its linguistic homogeneity, its well endowed school system, and the high status of teachers were probably all supporting factors (Elley, 1992; Linnakyla, 1993).

Another clear-cut finding which emerged from the comparison of mean scores was the size of the gulf between developed and developing countries. Without exception, countries with low economic indicators have large literacy problems, and no country had students who achieved at high levels which did not also fund its school system generously. Quality education does not come cheaply anywhere.

TABLE 57–3. Mean Scores in Total Reading Literacy Achievement for 32 Education Systems (from Elley, 1994)

Country	Pop A (9 Yrs)	Pop B (14 Yrs)
Belgium (Fr)	507	481
Botswana	–	330
Canada (BC)	500[a]	522[a]
Cyprus	481	497
Denmark	475	525
Finland	569	560
France	531	549
Germany (E)	499	526[a]
Germany (W)	503	522
Greece	504	509
Hong Kong	517	535
Hungary	499	536[a]
Iceland	518	536
Indonesia	394	–
Ireland	509	511
Italy	529	515[a]
The Netherlands	485[a]	514
New Zealand	528	545
Nigeria	–	401
Norway	524	516
Philippines	–	430
Portugal	478	523
Singapore	515	534
Slovenia	498	532
Spain	504	490[a]
Sweden	539	546
Switzerland	511	536
Thailand	–	477
Trinidad/Tobago	451	479
United States	547	535
Venezuela	383	417
Zimbabwe	–	372
Mean	500	500

[a] Underestimated due to differences in age of sample.

Third, the gender differences favoring girls at age 9, although not unexpected, were impressive in their consistency. Girls excelled in virtually every country in narrative and expository reading, and in most cases in document reading. However, by age 14 the gender gap had narrowed substantially in most countries, except in narrative reading (Wagemaker, 1996). The explanations for consistent female superiority at the younger age are not yet final, but probably reflect the influence of predominantly female teaching forces, and the slower rate at which young boys are attracted to book-related activities. Boys report reading fewer books at this age in most countries (Guthrie & Greaney, 1991). Interestingly, countries which started reading instruction earlier tended to have longer and persisting gender gaps. An early start for later maturing boys may well be counterproductive (Elley, 1992).

Other consistent findings across countries were seen in the reading difficulties experienced by students whose mother tongue was different from that of the school, except for the interesting case of Singapore. Here, the fact that three-quarters of their students learned to read first in English, which was not the language of the home, did not prevent them from achieving at high levels, at both age levels.

As expected, urban children generally outshone rural pupils in reading, although the differences were negligible in Scandinavia, New Zealand, and several wealthy OECD countries. One unexpected finding was the discovery that age of beginning instruction does not show a clear relationship with reading performance, even at age 9. Indeed, four of the highest achieving 10 countries in Population A (age 9) delayed formal instruction until age 7, and only one began at age 5. This counterintuitive phenomenon deserves closer scrutiny.

Another surprise emerged from the effects of TV viewing. Predictably, at age 9, heavy TV viewers scored lower in most countries, but in Scandinavian countries as well as Portugal and Italy, the best readers were found to be heavy viewers, at 3 to 4 hours each day (Elley 1992, p. 72). Closer examination revealed an interesting lesson for reading researchers. Children in these countries observe many imported TV films with subtitles in their own language. The regular experience these children had of reading captions at high speed, with genuine motivation and plentiful cues, is apparently an important ingredient in promoting fluent reading skill. No other interpretation is readily available, and there is both anecdotal and experimental evidence to support it (Neuman & Koskinen, 1992).

As in earlier surveys, the pervasive influence of the home was demonstrated in national and international analyses, whether indicated by parents' education, reading materials at home, or material possessions. Access to books was a salient factor in the international analyses—whether at home, school or community. While causal interpretations are always uncertain, the data are certainly consistent with the conclusion that an abundance of classroom book corners, school libraries, and community libraries are key ingredients in making for a healthy national literacy level.

As for instructional factors, the findings were not as clear as the researchers had hoped. Once again, the limitations of questionnaire data in surveys describing teaching processes were all too apparent (Lundberg & Linnakyla, 1992; Postlethwaite & Ross, 1992). Nevertheless, a few outcomes deserve special mention. In most countries, students of female teachers showed higher achievement levels than those of male teachers; better educated teachers also tended to produce students with higher scores. Viewed internationally, countries with smaller classes produced better results, but this variable is not easily entangled from other positive factors associated with greater wealth. Countries which allocated more time to silent reading in class, more reading aloud by the teacher, and more assigned homework tended to produce better results, other things being equal (Elley, 1992). However, there was no support for the view that countries with longer school years, or more formal testing of students will achieve at higher levels.

A question to pupils about "the best way to become a good reader" in each country produced some interesting contrasts, especially amongst those students who actually qualified as good readers (the highest 20%). While most such pupils supported the view that it is important to like reading, and to have ample time to read, good readers in the higher scoring nations more often stressed such factors as having many good books around, having a lively imagination, and developing an extensive vocabulary. By contrast, good readers in low-scoring nations more often stressed the value of learning to sound out the words and having lots of drill at the hard things. The causal links in these contrasting perceptions of good students clearly deserve more study.

Within countries, many other findings emerged which were valued by policy makers. For many nations, it was the first time a national assessment had been undertaken, and it was thus a valuable indication of their relative status and a useful experience for their researchers.

Finnish educators were encouraged by the clear-cut indications of the success of their reading programs, and the evidence that their standards had clearly improved since the first IEA reading study, on those tasks common to the tests used both in 1971 and in 1991 (Linnakyla, 1993). By contrast, Venezuelan and Belgian authorities, amongst others, planned wholesale investigations and revisions of their reading programs, as their achievement levels were less impressive. The Danish Ministry of Education allocated an extra U.S. $1.8 million to improve the teaching of reading following their disappointing results. Policy makers in Singapore have gained in confidence about the effectiveness of their recent liberal reforms in reading instruction. Hungarian educators have also received some comfort about their improved achievement levels between the two IEA surveys. New Zealand educators gained some support for particular practices (building up classroom libraries, devoting more time to silent reading, teacher reading aloud, gaining parental support), and a reassurance about the performance levels of Maori students, relative to other indigenous peoples in other countries. However, the findings about the relatively low performance of many 9-year-old boys and Pacific Islanders, and the comparatively high TV viewing hours, for instance, have caused concern and policy investigations. Further follow-up studies of high-achieving schools, relative to socioeconomic background, promise to produce richer interpretations—and more issues to investigate.

Internationally, the IEA results have been incorporated in the OECD international data base, and reported as a key indicator of educational performance (OECD, 1993).

HAROLD STEVENSON'S CROSS-NATIONAL STUDIES OF ACHIEVEMENT

Traditionally the IEA surveys have focused on the achievement levels of nationally representative samples of students, in a wide range of education systems. By contrast, Harold Stevenson and James Stigler, psychologists at the University of Michigan have undertaken, with their colleagues, a series of cross-cultural studies of American and Asian students in selected cities, assumed to be representative of each country. With smaller samples, and fewer countries, Stevenson has been able to study the students' learning contexts in greater depth, using interviews and observational techniques, in addition to teacher questionnaires.

In their first study, Stevenson, Stigler, Lucker, and Lee (1982) investigated the relative frequency of reading disability in grade 1 and grade 5 pupils in Minneapolis (USA),

Taipei (Taiwan) and Sendai (Japan). The researchers began by making an intensive analysis of the reading curricula of each country, and devised tests which were believed to be equivalent in language demands and conceptual load in English, Chinese and Japanese. The tests covered the letters of the alphabet, vocabulary, reading aloud and reading comprehension of phrases, sentences and paragraphs—assessed by multiple-choice and true–false items.

The investigators deliberately avoided direct translation, choosing instead to select items which were deemed to be functionally equivalent in each country. A passage about the Statue of Liberty for American children was equated with a similar passage about the Great Wall for Chinese pupils. This approach enabled the researchers to use items which depended for their difficulty on single letters, words or phrases, as well as on longer texts.

Children from two classes in each of 10 judiciously selected schools in each city were tested, individually, on each of the reading tests. In addition, a number of other cognitive tasks (memory, spatial ability, coding) and tests of general knowledge and mathematics were given. The tests were designed and administered at progressively more advanced grade levels, so that students stopped when they reached their upper limit. Four years later, the grade 1 sample was retested on the same tests.

The predicted differences in rates of reading disability among the three countries did not occur. Indeed, the incidence figures for severe disability (2 grades below classmates) were very similar across all three national groups. For grade 5 children they were 3%, 2% and 8% for American, Taipei and Japanese children respectively. When judged by the criterion of one standard deviation below estimated IQ, the figures were 6.3%, 7.5% and 5.4% respectively. There was no support here for the widespread belief that the orthographic systems of Chinese and Japanese prevented the development of reading disabilities. The differences which did occur in the patterns of reading scores were better explained by differences in learning contexts than in orthography.

Nevertheless, when judged by the number of grade 5 students who failed to reach a standard one grade below their own in reading, the Taiwanese students achieved best (only 12% below), followed by Japanese (21%) and American (31%). Paradoxically, the American students also had more students scoring *above* grade level (40% vs. 33% and 29% respectively). The greater variability in U.S. classes was attributed in part to such classroom effects as grouping and teacher beliefs in native ability, as well as one orthographic advantage, that which enabled high-achieving American children to sound out unfamiliar words. The researchers found clear-cut differences favoring the Taipei children at both grade levels, yet there were no such differences in the cognitive tests. Closer analysis showed that the achievement differences could best be explained in terms of both the quantity and the quality of time spent on reading. For instance, Taiwanese grade 1 students were in school for 240 days; American students for only 178 days. Moreover, Taiwanese students spent an average of 77 minutes each weekday on their homework, while American students devoted only 14 minutes . At grade 5 level, the mean times spent on homework were 13 hours per week in Taipei, compared with 6 hours in Sendai and 4 hours in Minneapolis.

Observational studies of the students at work furthermore showed that while American children spent much more time "off-task," wandering about, talking, asking irrelevant questions and the like, Chinese students tended to stay on task, most of the time. Other factors which were ruled out as explanatory factors were the educational level of the children's parents and their teachers (which favored Americans), or the relative amounts of time devoted to reading and language in the daily timetable. As for the orthographic factors, the researchers concluded that learning to read in Chinese requires more cognitive demands than English—some 3,000 individual characters and many thousands of words that are formed by combining them (Stevenson, & Stigler, 1992). Japanese also requires the mastering of four different scripts. By contrast English is relatively straightforward.

Despite the overall superiority of the Chinese reading scores (see Table 57–4), American parents expressed much higher levels of satisfaction with their children's schooling than Chinese parents. Adult expectations of student achievement appears to be much higher in Asia. Lapointe, Mead and Phillips (1989) found similar trends in their surveys of mathematics and science.

Finally, interviews with parents revealed that American grade 5 children spent much more time at play per week (20 hours vs. 8 hours) and watching TV (14 hours vs. 11 hours) and fewer children regularly read the newspaper (24% vs. 56%). Education is clearly taken more seriously in Taiwanese homes.

CONCLUSIONS

At the outset, the question was posed whether the enterprise of conducting cross-national studies of literacy was profitable—or even possible.

On balance, this reviewer believes that the outcomes of these studies to date are themselves strong evidence that the enterprise is worth the cost and effort. Indeed, international organizations such as OECD and World Bank have made extensive use of IEA results, and national governments are quoting IEA findings increasingly, to inform local debates on academic standards. Many other findings, of greater or lesser certainty have emerged, findings which could not have been arrived at any other way, findings which could only be inter-

preted against the backdrop of an international study. Moreover there are benefits for the participants when undertaking cross-national collaborative research studies, in mounting first-time surveys in many countries, and in gaining access to useful measuring instruments for local and cross-cultural studies. Traditions have been questioned and new policies considered as researchers talk through the many issues that arise in conducting a joint project. More policy makers are learning the valuable lesson that it is possible to gain empirical data to inform decisions which have previously been settled by tradition, or by the force of personalities. Findings about relative achievement levels, about age of entry, gender differences, influence of TV, or orthography, minority languages, access to books, and the value of distinctive methods have all been elaborated above.

As for the question of feasibility across all the literacy domains, the evidence to date is mixed. There is little doubt amongst those who participated in the recent IEA Reading–Literacy Survey, that one can assess reading competence across cultures. The iterative processes involved in meeting together to plan projects, and discuss criteria, in item writing, in collaborative reviewing, in rating for suitability, in trialling, analyzing, and checking for unsuitability, ensures that cultural biases are reduced to an absolute minimum. The fact that the resultant items behaved in such a similar way statistically across cultures and languages, regardless of topic, skill, and format in the final tests, confirms Thorndike's dictum (1973) that a typical reading item does measure comprehension. After all these precautionary measures are taken, a difficult item in one country turns out to be a difficult item in all countries, and the rank order of difficulty is virtually the same—in reading comprehension. Such an outcome is reassuring. It is possible, then, to assess reading across countries, well enough to draw useful conclusions.

The evidence in measuring achievement in literature, in the home language, is less secure, but some aspects of interpretation and response to specific literary texts did produce enough promise to warrant the effort. Educators in individual countries did learn something about their programs. For cross-cultural writing, however, the findings were not as comparable across countries, as the researchers had hoped. Consensus was persistently lacking in the qualities that make up a good piece of writing. While there were numerous perceived benefits on the part of the participants, the implications for policy or practice were less obvious than in the case of reading.

One of the virtues of cross-national studies often proclaimed by IEA supporters is that multivariate analyses can help identify factors which contribute to better instruction. While there have been numerous hints and hypotheses emerging from the IEA data bases, it must be conceded that this aspect of the cross-national surveys of literacy has been disappointing to date. As long as information about instruction is collected by questionnaires—with their acknowledged weaknesses of exaggeration, distortion, and social desirability effects, many crucial variables will go untapped. The more intensive data-gathering strategies employed by Stevenson, Stigler and colleagues, as outlined above, have clearly been more productive in teasing out critical variables.

TABLE 57–4. Mean Performance of Children on Reading and Mathematics Tests (adapted from Stevenson et al.; 1985, p.731)

		JAPAN	TAIWAN	USA
GRADE 1	Vocabulary	7.2	10.8	10.0
	Comprehension	22.8	25.7	21.3
	Mathematics	20.1	21.2	17.1
GRADE 5	Vocabulary	47.0	49.8	48.4
	Comprehension	82.5	84.6	82.7
	Mathematics	53.3	50.8	44.4

Few who have tried it think that cross-national studies are easy. Apart from the challenges posed by different languages, and different traditions in educational policies and testing procedures, there are frequently problems of funding, communication, variations in sampling, and limited control over test administration—not to mention frustrations caused by social desirability responses. However, when a determined steering committee has the support of talented organizers and computer processors, widespread cooperation and plausible outcomes can be generated. Not all objectives may have been achieved, but enough has been learned to inform future studies, and to help build up a more comprehensive knowledge base in literacy education.

References

Bathory, Z., & Kadar-Fulop, J. (1974). Some conclusions for curriculum development based on Hungarian IEA data. *Comparative Education Review, 18*(2), 228–236.

Bulcock, J. W., Clifton, R. A., & Beebe, M. J. (1978). Reading competency as a predictor of scholastic performance: Comparisons between industrialized and third world nations. In D. Feitelson (Ed.), *Cross-cultural perspectives on reading and reading research.* Newark, DE: International Reading Association.

Choppin, B. H., & Purves, A. C. (1969). A comparison of open-ended and multiple-choice items dealing with literary understanding. *Research in the Teaching of English, 3*(1),15–24.

Downing, J. (1973). *Comparative reading.* New York: Macmillan.

Downing, J., & Dalrymple-Alford, E. (1974–75). A methodological critique of the 1973 IEA survey of reading comprehension in fifteen countries. *Reading Research Quarterly, 10,* 212–29.

Elley, W. B. (1992). *How in the world do students read?* The Hague: International Association for the Evaluation of Educational Achievement.

Elley, W. B. (1993). Developing the IEA reading literacy tests. *Scandinavian Journal of Educational Research, 37*(1), 27–42.

Elley, W. B. (Ed.). (1994). *The IEA study of reading-literacy: Achievement and instruction in 32 school systems.* Oxford: Pergamon Press.

Foshay, A. W. (Ed.). (1962). *Educational achievements of 13 year olds in twelve countries.* Hamburg: UNESCO Institute of Education.

Gorman, T. P., Purves, A. C., & Degenhart, R. E. (Eds.). (1988). *The international writing tasks and scoring scales: The international study of achievement in writing.* Oxford: Pergamon Press.

Guthrie, J. T. (1981). Reading in New Zealand: Achievement and volume. *Reading Research Quarterly, 17*(1), 6–27.

Guthrie, J. T., & Greaney, V. (1991). Literacy acts. In R. Barr, M. L. Kamil, P. Mosenthal & P. D. Pearson (Eds.), *Handbook of reading research,* Vol. 2. New York: Longman.

Jaegar, R. M. (1994). Evaluating policy inferences drawn from international comparisons of students' achievement test performance. *Studies in Educational Evaluation, 20,* 23–39.

Kyostio, O. K. (1980). Is learning to read easy in a language in which the grapheme-phoneme correspondences are regular? In J. F. Kavanagh & R. L. Venezky (Eds.), *Orthography reading and dyslexia.* Baltimore: Baltimore University Press.

Lapointe, A. E., Mead, N. A., & Phillips, G. W. (1989). *A world of differences: An international assessment of mathematics and science.* Princeton: IAEP, Educational Testing Service.

Lee, S. Y., Stigler, J. W., & Stevenson, H. W. (1982). Beginning reading in Chinese and English. In B. R. Foorman & A. W. Sieger (Eds.), *Acquisition of reading skills: Cultural constraints and cognitive universals.* Hillsdale, NJ: Erlbaum.

Lehmann, R. H. (1992). The achieved quality of essay ratings. In A. C. Purves (Ed.), *The IEA study of written composition II: Education & performance in fourteen countries* (Appendix B). Oxford: Pergamon Press.

Levine, K. (1986). *The social context of literacy.* London: Routledge.

Linnakyla, P. (1993). Exploring the secret of Finnish reading literacy achievement. *Scandinavian Journal of Educational Research, 37*(1), 63–74.

Lundberg, I., & Linnakyla, P. (1992). *Teaching reading around the world.* The Hague: International Association for the Evaluation of Educational Achievement.

Moses, S. (1991, September). International comparison no easy feat. *APA Monitor* (pp. 26, 27). American Psychological Association.

Munck, I.M.E. (1979). *Model building in comparative education: Applications of LISREL method to cross-national survey data.* Ph.D. dissertation, University of Stockholm.

Neuman, S. B., & Koskinen, P. (1992). Captioned television as comprehensible input. *Reading Research Quarterly, 27*(1), 94–106.

OECD (1993). *Education at a Glance.* Paris: Organisation for Economic Cooperation and Development.

Postlethwaite, T. N., & Ross, K. (1992). *Effective schools in reading: Implications for educational planners.* The Hague: International Association for the Evaluation of Educational Achievement.

Purves, A. C. (1973). *Literature education in ten countries.* Stockholm: Almqvist & Wiksell.

Purves, A. C. (1979). *Achievement in reading & literature in the secondary schools: New Zealand in an international perspective.* Wellington: New Zealand Council for Educational Research.

Purves, A. C. (Ed.). (1992). *The IEA study of written composition II: Education & performance in fourteen countries.* Oxford: Pergamon Press.

Purves, A. C. (1993). The IEA reading literacy study: A brief history. *Scandinavian Journal of Educational Research, 37*(1),15–26.

Purves, A. C., & Rippere, V. (1968). *Elements of writing about a literary work: A study of response to literature.* Champaign, IL: National Council of Teachers of English.

Stevenson, H. W., & Stigler, J. W. (1992). *The learning gap.* New York: Summit Books.

Stevenson, H. W., Stigler, J. W., Lucker, G. W., & Lee, S. Y. (1982). Reading disabilities: The case of Chinese, Japanese and English. *Child Development, 53,* 1164–1182.

Taukala, S., & Degenhart, E. (1992). Pupil perception of writing instruction in schools. In A. C. Purves (Ed.), *The IEA study of written composition II: Education and performance in fourteen countries* (pp. 103–128). Oxford: Pergamon Press.

Thiesen, G. L., Achola, P. W., & Boakari, F. M. (1986). The underachievement of cross-national studies of achievement. *Comparative Education Review, 27*(1).

Thorndike, R. L. (1973). *Reading comprehension achievement in fifteen countries.* Stockholm: Almqvist & Wiksell.

Wagemaker, H. (Ed.). (1996). *Are girls better readers?* The Hague:

International Association for the Evaluation of Educational Achievement.

Walker, D. A. (1976). *The IEA six subject survey: An empirical study of education in twenty-one countries.* Stockholm: Almqvist & Wiksell.

Westbury (1992). Comparing American & Japanese achievement. Is the United States really a low achiever? *Educational Researcher, 21,* 18–24.

·58·

NATIONAL CENTERS :
DO THEY MATTER TO SCHOOLS?

LITERATURE CURRICULUM:
ISSUES OF DEFINITION AND CONTROL

Richard L. Allington and Sherry Guice

STATE UNIVERSITY OF NEW YORK AT ALBANY

The National Research Center for Literature Teaching and Learning opened its doors in 1987 (as the Center for Literature Teaching and Learning), funded primarily "to stimulate reform in the teaching of literature" (Langer, 1992). The original mission focused largely on literature curriculum and instruction in American high schools. With reauthorization, as the National Research Center for Literature Teaching and Learning (NRCLTL) in 1990, the scope of inquiry was broadened to include the literature curriculum pre-Kindergarten through grade 12. This broader scope was needed because literature was earning an increasingly important role in the elementary school curriculum as schools engaged in a fairly rapid curricular shift—away from a mastery-focused, skills-based, and hierarchical curriculum plan for reading and language arts lessons and toward a more literature-based, integrated, and process-oriented curriculum (Pearson, 1993).

The NRCLTL has supported a variety of studies of the elementary, middle, and secondary literature curriculum (although the elementary literature curriculum is usually firmly imbedded in the reading and language arts curriculum). In this report, we discuss one theme that has routinely emerged across a significant number of the NRCLTL investigations: How is a literature curriculum defined? We also explore a second theme that has emerged, primarily, from our own NRCLTL research: Who controls the curriculum? While the discussion of these two themes does not adequately represent either the scope or the nature of the work completed at the NRCLTL, we believe these themes represent important and recurring questions that have been too little discussed in the literacy teaching and research communities.

HOW IS A LITERATURE CURRICULUM DEFINED?

As a first step in studying curriculum, we must decide which sort of curriculum will become the focus. Following a tradition in curriculum studies we can talk of the planned (or formal) curriculum, the delivered (or enacted) curriculum, and the experienced (or received) curriculum. At the NRCLTL studies have been carried out that locate the primary research questions in each of the three curricula (and most studies do focus primarily on a single curriculum type). Thus we will briefly review major findings of relevant studies following the three-type scheme.

The Planned Curriculum

Applebee reported on the texts most frequently named for use in high school English courses. The analysis suggested "a curriculum dominated by familiar selections drawn primarily from a white, male, Anglo-Saxon tradition" (Applebee, 1992, p. 7). Most schools relied on literature anthologies as well as lists of individual books as instructional materials. Applebee (1993b) also studied a collection (n=42) of high school literature anthologies. He reported that anthologies seemed to be narrowing their collections with the number of unique works declining substantially over the past 30 years. At the same time, the representation of alternative literary traditions has improved with the inclusion of works by women and ethnic minority authors. In fact, for many students, it seemed that the anthologies used might offer the best hope for

Prepartation of this report was supported under the Educational Research and Development Center program (Grant # R117G10015) as administered by the Office of Educational Research and Improvement, U.S. Department of Education. The findings and opinions expressed here do not necessarily reflect the position or policies of the sponsoring agency.

exposure to nontraditional literatures since the book-length literary works most commonly assigned in American high schools were authored, overwhelmingly, by males of an Anglo-Saxon heritage (48 of the 50 most frequently used texts).

More recently, Applebee (1993a, 1996) has noted that there seem to be only few basic schemes for structuring a curriculum. The simplest, and surprisingly common, device is a *catalog* of items within a domain but without any cumulative structure. He notes that a catalog approach to spelling or vocabulary might entail simply listing words by orthographic pattern or simple frequency of use. Likewise, a K–12 literature curriculum that simply listed age-appropriate core books to be read would also fit the catalog classification. A key facet of catalog structure is the lack of any strong conceptual links among the various elements.

A second structuring device is the *collection*. In this case, the elements form a "set" identified from some center or focus. Applebee identifies the Great Books plan as a collection curriculum as well as other curriculum formed around reasonably well-defined topics (e.g., modes of discourse). A third device is a *sequential* plan; perhaps organizing literature by date of publication or a social studies curriculum that follows historical eras. A fourth device, the *episodic* structure, relates elements to each other and to a central focus or idea. Chronologically organized sets of texts, for instance, might have as a focus literature as representative of the historical era. The final device, *integrated* curricular structure, might be illustrated by a curriculum that had students read "a cross-cultural collection of stories illuminating culturally different assumptions about the relationships among old age, wisdom, and respect" (Applebee, 1993a, p. 17).

While Applebee originally presented these organizing structures in a reconsideration of curriculum as conversational domains, he also reports on a study of how such devices mediate the conversations that occur in the classroom (Applebee, Burroughs, & Stevens, 1994). In that study of high school English instruction, it was noted that the most common organizing devices were catalog and sequential curriculum plans with few collection, episodic, or integrated curriculum plans evident. The curriculum plans varied from a simple listing of a collection of novels deemed age-appropriate for different grade levels to carefully integrated English and World Cultures courses where the literature read focused on developing an understanding of a variety of specific cultural groups.

Thus, the studies of the planned literature curriculum in American high schools provide us with reasonably good evidence that few school systems have developed complex curriculum schemes and few have developed curriculum that fosters much linkage between the literature studied in the various courses or between literature and other curriculum areas. Literature anthologies still form the backbone of the literature curriculum at many high schools and the instructional plans that accompany these materials offer little integration or linkage among selections included, much less other texts teachers might use alongside the anthology or in other English courses.

Several NRCLTL studies have reported on the planned literature curriculum in elementary schools, although here literature is usually firmly embedded in the reading and language arts curriculum. Allington, Guice, Michelson, Baker and Li (1996) report that few elementary teachers articulated a clear role for literature beyond developing an enjoyment of reading or teaching and practicing reading skills. In addition, literature was only rarely and loosely linked to writing activities and rarely integrated with other subject areas.

The planned curriculum of several school districts was characterized (Allington, 1994a) as falling generally into one of four broad classification schemes focusing on the curriculum materials selected and the roles the materials played. The *basal* curriculum plan was organized around commercial anthologies that provided an array of literary selections along with more traditional reading and writing skills lessons. In this scheme, full-length literature was rarely declared part of the curriculum although such works might be read aloud to students by the teacher or be read independently by children (e.g., requiring book reports). The *basal and books* scheme placed literature anthologies at the center of the curriculum with full-length books at the periphery, but still included. This curriculum plan might offer a list of core books for each grade level or simply designate books to a separate independent, but daily, reading experience. The *books and basal* plan placed full-length children's literature at the center of the curriculum with literature anthologies available but not a requisite. In some books and basal plans a core reading list had been developed for each grade, in others particular themes had been identified for different grade levels, and in others individual teachers simply selected books for classroom collections that students might draw from. In this plan the anthologies were most often to be used to provide greater variety of literature as well as a selection of skills lessons that teachers might draw from. In the *books* scheme, full-length children's literature was the curriculum focus. Again, as with the books and basal scheme, there was a variety of patterns for organizing the selected children's literature. In some schools, students seemed to have much greater choice in the selection of the books to be read, while in others the choice of books was either determined by a district-wide committee of teachers or by individual teachers themselves. In the six districts studied, there were variations from teacher to teacher on how the same curriculum framework was interpreted and enacted. The curriculum plans of only a few teachers in any district were classified as books plans.

Strickland, Walmsley, Bronk, and Weiss (1994) reported on a much larger and geographically diverse sample of elementary school teachers but with similar results. In this case the curriculum schemes were broken down into finer, but comparable, segments. Only 2% of the teachers reported using a basal anthology solely, while 39% reported using an anthology supplemented by trade books, 24% reported a balanced use of an anthology and trade books, 18% reported using trade books supplemented by basal anthologies, and 18% reported using trade books exclusively. These two studies suggest that the elementary literature curriculum is largely undefined although it seems as though catalog and collection schemes dominate in those schools that have attempted to define a literature curriculum.

While Applebee's classifications of curriculum structures provide one way of thinking about the literature curriculum, we might also use the three-part classification scheme adapted by Farrell (1991) to attempt to categorize the curriculum located in schools. The descriptors—mastery models, heritage models, and process models—offer a sort of shorthand for describing broad emphases that differentiate one curriculum from another. He suggests that *mastery* models are typified by lists of component skills, thought to be ordered by complexity, to be mastered sequentially. Such lists are at the root of diagnostic-prescriptive teaching, the dominant model in reading and language arts instruction over the past 30 years (1965–95) and, to a lesser extent, a traditional model for English instruction at the secondary level. The *heritage* models reflect a cultural transmission emphasis and often, in the case of literacy education, include lists of important literary works that students will read. Proponents include E. D. Hirsch, Diane Ravitch, and Allan Bloom, just to name a few authors of recent works evangelizing heritage models of literature curriculum. The *process* models are characterized by a student-centeredness with an emphasis on the interests, curiosity, and motivations of learners and a rejection, largely, of reliance on adult-constructed curriculum frameworks. Process models fill academic journals and recent teacher training textbooks and are promoted especially by whole language theorists and advocates such as Ken Goodman, Yetta Goodman, Lucy Calkins, Nancie Atwell, and Jane Hansen.

No matter how we examine the reports, the preponderance of evidence suggests that both the high school and the elementary school literature curricula are typically organized around lists of skills to be mastered or books to be read—either mastery or heritage models of curriculum—usually organized around a catalog structure. While process approaches to curriculum and instruction have wide popularity in the professional journals and books, there is but a smattering of evidence that process approaches have yet substantially altered the planned curriculum in most American schools or classrooms.

Schools do seem to be struggling with redefining curriculum, especially the role of literature in the literacy curriculum (Walmsley, 1991). But the historical emphasis on skills-based scope and sequence charts and the prevailing influence of assessment programs based on those models have created a difficult transition period. Walmsley and Walp (1989) argued that elementary schools "seem to have made more progress in articulating specific teaching routines and book lists than they have in resolving such issues as the relationship between reading skills and literary strategies, between reading achievement and literary knowledge, and between reading experiences and literary experiences" (p. 37). Freeman (1994) contrasts the elementary literature curriculum with the elementary literature-based curriculum noting that few schools have a literature curriculum though many have implemented literature-based instruction. As Applebee (1993a) notes, "None of these [popular] approaches sits in comfortable relationships to a constructivist framework, primarily because each ultimately turns the curriculum into a body of knowl-

edge and skills that must be imparted. Such a vision trivializes the role of the learner as an active participant in a socially constructed world, and distorts the ways that skills develop in the process of mastering complex tasks" (p. 5).

One primary finding of the various NRCLTL studies is the difficulty schools have in articulating any coherent literature curriculum for K–12 much less a comprehensive curriculum that fosters thoughtful, integrated teaching and learning. But the difficulty is not simply one faced by schools since there is rather little evidence, as Applebee points out, that the profession has resolved this issue in any satisfactory way. In addition, as Farrell (1991) suggests, we know little about the effects of different curricula on learners and learning, especially the effects of a particular curriculum across a school career (K–12). However, given the scant evidence that school districts typically adopt a single literature curriculum framework, K–12, coupled with the impatience of those supporting a school reform agenda, it seems unlikely that such studies will ever be conducted. That is perhaps the sort of goal that now seems to be such a perfect choice for a large-scale, longitudinally-funded research effort. But it is also the sort of study that probably could not be carried out naturalistically, since schools with a coherent K–12 literature curriculum even now exist only in the visions of a very few folks.

The Delivered Curriculum

Perhaps predictably, the NRCLTL studies of instruction indicate that rather few of the classroom environments studied are well captured by the phrase "thoughtful literacy." Whether reading Applebee et al. (1994), Allington et al. (1996), Walmsley and Walp (1989), Walmsley, Fielding, and Walp (1991), McGill-Franzen and Lanford (1994), Purves (1992), or Afflerbach and Johnston (1993), one comes away with a pervasive feeling that most students are told what to read and given a series of questions to answer, either orally or in writing, with few opportunities to discuss, explore, or expand meanings. While there are exceptions to this generalization in these reports, such classrooms still seem rare.

Langer (1992, 1995a, 1995b) and Miller (1993) perhaps best describe alternative pedagogies and the difficulty of developing those pedagogies within the existing curriculum frameworks and classroom contexts, although Stayter and Close (1991) provide a moving and detailed accounting of one teacher's journey in that direction. If nothing else, the various NRCLTL research reports suggest both how much remains to be done to foster classrooms where thoughtful literacy is the goal and how large that task will be in terms of time and effort.

Received Curriculum

Fewer NRCLTL reports present analyses of the received curriculum, although studies such as those reported by Langer (1991), Applebee et al. (1994), McGill-Franzen and Lanford (1994), and Walmsley et al. (1991) offer some evidence on student literary experience. But we know less than we could about how different literature curriculum schemes effect the learners who might experience them. This is, in part, because we found a slim variety of literature curriculum emphases and structures in both elementary and secondary schools and found much common in the way students experienced the literature curriculum. Still, the NRCLTL reports noted above do offer us glimpses of what sort of classrooms might be created from the descriptions of those rare classrooms where the literature curriculum provided rich, thoughtful, and integrated experiences for children and adolescents.

WHO CONTROLS THE LITERATURE CURRICULUM?

Given the findings of the various NRCLTL studies concerning the nature of the literature curriculum, many will see a need for some sort of immediate action; some immediate reform. In fact, as noted earlier, a central mission of the NRCLTL was to stimulate reform in the teaching of literature. But the hard question is: How best can we stimulate what kind of reform? While there seems to be general agreement among the various researchers at the NRCLTL that a more thoughtful approach to literature teaching is needed, there would likely be substantially less agreement on what sort of reforms are most needed and on how best such reforms might be stimulated. In this section, we explore some issues related to initiating reforms in literature curriculum and instruction with a particular emphasis on issues of authority, power, and influence in educational policy making.

Recently, there has been much debate about the effects of the various reform initiatives that were implemented, often with much fanfare, during the past decade or so. Much opinion and some evidence has been amassed that suggests that the increasing centralization of educational decision making has failed to achieve the sorts of effects on classroom practice that optimistic policy makers had hoped for. In other words, increased mandates have not resulted in substantial improvements in American education. As a result, there has been much discussion about giving teachers more authority in curriculum decisions often under the broadly construed term "empowerment." This approach would undo much of the centralization of educational decision making and would, advocates argue, give teachers more authority, power, and influence in educational processes. However, there is yet little evidence that such moves would foster the development of more thoughtful curriculum, especially curriculum that presented a coherent plan for the use of literature across a school career, K–12.

Rowan (1990) contrasts these two current, but often conflicting, approaches to educational reform activities. *Control* strategies, he argues, attempt to shape reform through mandated practices. The mandates may come from federal, state, district, or building levels, usually issued by an education agency official or a school district or building administrator. Examples of mandates might include educational arenas as diverse as student attendance, assessment of achievement, salary structure, teacher professional development, as well as curriculum mandates and textbook mandates. While federal education agencies are largely barred from the latter two areas, state-, district-, and building-level mandates concerning curriculum and textbooks have been widely practiced. Activities such as state textbook adoption, state curriculum mandates, district textbook mandates, district or school textbook coverage schedules and monitoring schemes, all seem examples of control strategies found fairly commonly in American elementary schools today.

Commitment strategies, according to Rowan, work to foster educational reform by enhancing the commitment and expertise of educators for improving practice. One aspect of commitment strategies has been to attempt to increase teacher participation in the educational decision-making process. Most proposals for "shared decision-making" or "site-based management", focus on decentralizing the decisions about curriculum, budget, and staffing. In addition, many advocates also emphasize enhancing teacher collegiality and reducing the professional isolation of teachers from their colleagues.

However, studies of implementations of "shared decision-making" and "site-based management" do not consistently report that participating teachers realize enhanced autonomy (Smylie, 1994). Instead, participation may lead to increased pressure for compliance to local norms and increased administrative monitoring of such compliance. Similarly, efforts to enhance teacher collaboration in planning instruction may actually work to restrict perceived autonomy as teachers feel more compelled to adopt group norms.

Within the literacy education community, there has been widespread criticism of the use of control strategies and a chorus of voices calling for increased use of commitment strategies. A particular focus has been on decentralizing curriculum decisions (e.g., Freeman, 1988; Shannon, 1991)—returning to teachers the authority to make many decisions, including those about the texts used in the classroom. But the issue seems not quite so straightforward given the power structure currently found in most K–12 educational settings.

Ruth (1991) distinguishes *power* from *influence* in educational policy making. Power involves having the legal authority to make demands and set constraints upon people. Influence, while related to power, involves a different sort of relationship between those participating in decision-making events. But both power and influence play important roles in constraining curriculum determinations.

Currently, teachers report that they have little influence on curriculum decisions, at least as far as text selection is concerned. In a recent large-scale federal study, only about one third of elementary school teachers reported that they thought they had a great deal of influence in the process of establishing curriculum for goals. Teachers in "central city" schools were the least likely to report influence on curriculum. Only about a quarter of central city elementary teachers felt curriculum was an area in which they exerted a great deal of influence. Teachers in rural and small town schools were most likely to report feeling influential (38.5%) but even here the majority of elementary teachers felt establishing curriculum goals was an area in which they exerted little influence. More teachers working in schools with few minority students reported that they had a "great deal of influence" on curriculum matters compared to teachers working in elementary schools with more minority students (greater than 20% of enrollment). In addition, more teachers working in small elementary schools, regardless of community, reported the feeling that they had a great deal of influence compared to teachers in the largest schools. Thus, teachers working in large (enrolling over 750 students), central city schools with a significant minority enrollment (over 20%), were the teachers least likely to report exerting a great deal of influence on curriculum matters (National Center for Educational Statistics, 1993).

These findings suggest that curriculum decisions are largely made by someone other than teachers, usually someone distant from the classroom. The situation varies by size of the school district and by region, with some states exercising greater authority over curriculum decisions than others. Many of the NRCLTL studies have been conducted in New York state, where there is a state curriculum plan for English / Language Arts which must be reflected in district curriculum but no mandate to adopt the state plan. There is no state textbook adoption and no state textbook committee (save one for referrals of materials charged as containing "seditious" or "disloyal" content). The authority for the selection of textbooks lies with local school boards (Rockmuller, 1993), as do most curriculum decisions, save the distribution of courses required to earn a Regent's diploma (New York State School Boards Association, 1992). While some other states do feature state textbook selection committees and state mandated curriculum, it is still most often the case that considerable latitude is allowed to schools in both selection and implementation of curriculum, more so at the elementary school levels.

Generally the authority of state legislatures to establish curriculum standards has been upheld by the federal courts as have the implied powers of local school boards in these areas. In fact, local boards have considerable discretion in the curriculum decisions. "Probably in no area of school operation have the courts been more liberal in interpreting implied powers of local boards than in curriculum matters" (Reutter & Hamilton, 1976, p. 128). This includes the power to make textbook decisions.

This power would be revoked or restricted by many reformers. As Freeman (1988) argues, concerning the California English/ Language Arts Framework, "The potential for change is enormous but only if teachers and students are empowered by the reforms ... when teachers are allowed to develop curricula based on their understanding of the research and on the needs of students, then the revolution called for in the Framework can become a reality" (pp. 241, 242). Comments such as these have become increasingly common in some of the educational reform literature, especially those addressing reform of literacy and literature instruction in American schools (K. S. Goodman, 1989; Y. Goodman, 1989; Jones, 1990; Shannon, 1991). However, the authority, or control, over curriculum is currently set, by law and regulation, outside classroom walls and the recent movement toward establishing national standards seems to suggest a shifting influence and power away from local and state education agency offices, even further removed from classrooms and teachers and their students.

In our own work at the NRCLTL we have found that an important influence on curriculum decisions is what we have dubbed "a press for standardization" of the curriculum (Allington et al., 1996). This press is exerted from a number of sources both within a school and from outside. Regardless of the source, however, a common feature of this pressure is the constraints teachers feel over control of the curriculum.

Within the School Press

The press for standardization from within can stem from the negotiations that accompany the selection of literature to be used in a classroom. For instance, it has been common in the schools we have studied for groups of teachers to work to define a curriculum around a set of core books to be read in a particular course (World Literature) or at a particular grade level (3rd-grade core books). During one focus group meeting a new 4th-grade teacher told us of having several books unknowingly displayed in her room that were included on the 5th-grade core books list. Another teacher noticed these books, and then proceeded to remove them from her display, noting that fourth graders were not allowed to read those books.

In another school we studied, the discussion of children's books in a Teachers as Readers group led to reconsideration of the use of a tradebook in some classrooms. The particular book in this case was Cynthia Rylant's (1989) autobiography, But I'll be Back Again. The discussion was initiated around commonalties in her autobiography and Rylant's (1992) novel Missing May. However, the conversation drifted toward the appropriateness of the autobiography for elementary school children since she included references to an emerging sexuality, menstruation, undergarments, and her first elementary school kiss. The strong feelings of inappropriateness of these topics held by some teachers were vigorously debated by others. In the end, however, those arguing for using the autobiography seemed to give in to the opponents as a general agreement about recommending its use in the middle school or high school emerged. Proponents of the book were uncomfortable with the end result, but seemed less comfortable using the book over the objections of colleagues.

Finally, we have reported on the experiences of one of our teacher collaborators who felt enormous pressure from colleagues (and union officials) to conform to tradition and resist the implementation of a literature-based curriculum (Michelson, 1994). Krissa (a pseudonym at her request) did ultimately end her resistance and incorporated more traditional aspects of reading and language curriculum into her lessons. As Barksdale-Ladd (1994) notes, such social influences are powerful in schools and teachers regularly reported succumbing to compliant agreement just to get along with other teachers. One of her participating teachers noted, "I want everybody to be happy."

In each of the four school districts we studied, there existed similar sorts of press for standardizing the literature curriculum. Even when no formal core book list had been developed, teachers talked to us about "fourth grade books," for instance, and noted that individual teachers protected certain titles they used in their classrooms and restricted the use of other titles deemed inappropriate by colleagues for other reasons.

Press From Outside the School

In another school district, a school board member wondered aloud what was so difficult about delineating which books children would be reading on which days at any grade level. In his view, an adequate curriculum plan would provide a detailed framework for literature selections including a common pacing schedule for completing those books. He evidenced little concern about the specific books to be included but argued for a standard plan across all schools.

In another report (Allington, 1994b) we discuss a communication from a state education agency that noted, "the nature of the educational support services program ... requires that there be some consistency of implementation on a district-wide basis." The communication goes on to recommend that programs "be supervised and coordinated from the central office to ensure a consistent philosophy of instruction, congruence and articulation across the program, and uniform record keeping" (p.12). This occurred in a context of state education agency mandate for shared decision making in local education agencies!

We heard several rationales for standardization from administrators in the schools we studied. One argument concerned intradistrict student mobility, a common situation, especially in school districts that enroll many children from low-income families. The more standardized curriculum, it was argued, allows for an easier transition for students moving from School A to School B within the district. While no one seems to have gathered any sort of data to support this hypothesis, it was a most common rationale for a common curriculum district-wide.

A second argument we heard stemmed more from concerns about monitoring teacher performance. In this case, the more standard curriculum was viewed as ensuring a more equitable instructional environment for students. The common curriculum would work to provide all students with similar high-quality experiences. Without a common curriculum plan, administrators feared increased variation in the nature and quality of instruction offered across classrooms. Again, we know of little research to support this contention.

A third argument for standardization was related to the one just above, but it was argued more from a parent / citizen perspective. In this case, the standard curriculum was seen as one way of reducing parental / citizen concerns about variations in instructional quality across classrooms in the district. One administrator noted that standardization reduced the number of questions parents had about, "Why Johnny isn't reading *Charlotte's Web* in his third grade classroom, while their neighbor's child, Katie, is reading it in her third grade classroom." It was felt that when curriculum plans were more standardized across a district, both administrators and teachers were less open to criticism of differential quality and had to less often explain variation in curriculum opportunities.

Albert Shanker (1994), head of the American Federation of Teachers, echoes many of these arguments as he argues for national curriculum content standards:

> We generally agree, for example, that students in high school should study English ... but we have not tried to come to any agreement about what those courses should include or what students who take them should know or be able to do. State curriculum guidelines are usually broad recommendations rather than specific curricula. In principle, this leaves decisions about exactly what our students will be taught to our 15,000 school districts. In practice, this decision is often left to individual teachers, who are encouraged to select on the basis of their own interests or the interests of their students. We are accustomed to this relaxed, take-your-pick attitude towards curriculum and standards, but we pay heavily for it. It means we have no way of making sure that all our students have the advantage of a first-rate curriculum. ... Successful learning to some extent depends on continuity, and our ad hoc standards and curriculum mean that there can be enormous variations, even within a school. Teachers can never be sure of what students entering their class in September have already covered. (p. 7)

Shanker's arguments for national standards, like those of others, would reduce the influence of teachers and administrators, local and state boards of education, superintendents and chief state school officers, and set curriculum content standards nationally.

Though a long-held tradition, local control of curriculum seems almost surely to be on the decline. Chester Finn (1991), only one of the policy makers that initiated the national standards movement, argues that the "antiquated devotion to 'local control' of schools" must be rejected. "We must," he says, "recognize that local control today is indistinguishable from maintenance of the status quo..." (p. 234). He goes on to suggest that if local control (here meaning nonfederal control) were the solution, then our schools would already have adapted to the societal shifts that demand a more demanding curriculum. He notes that the almost 100,000 local school board members are simply not up to the task of reforming American education.

While one can view all of this rhetoric about national curriculum content standards with substantial skepticism (as we do), support for standardization of curriculum experiences seems to come from many quarters—administrators, parents, legislators, and the head of a major teacher union. While advocates for personalized, child-centered and teacher-developed curriculum abound in the education profession (and especially in colleges and universities), both inside and outside of the profession there is more talk about curriculum standards and standardization than talk of teacher empowerment and child-centered educational practice.

SUMMARY

Our intent in this chapter has not been to specify the nature of an ideal literature curriculum nor to suggest who should control that curriculum. Rather, we have sought to raise what seem to us to be especially pertinent, current issues about the teaching of literature in American schools. While advocates often argue around issues of curriculum, too often the arguments seem, to us at least, to miss the critical marks. Hardly anyone that we are aware of argues that infusing the school curriculum with literature is a bad idea. So we can leave those arguments behind.

But how should a literature curriculum be defined and who should control the definition and delineation of the curriculum? While many literacy educators would place children and teachers more directly in control of which literature is read in our schools, such plans seem to garner little support among school administrators, state education agency personnel, legislators, parents, citizens, and federal policy makers. As we near the turn of the century, it may be time for a broader-based discussion of just what roles literature can play in the education of children and youth (Langer, 1995b) and just how we will decide who determines those roles and which texts are used to fulfill them.

References

Afflerbach, P., & Johnston, P. (1993). Writing language arts report cards: Eleven teachers' conflicts of knowing and communicating. *Elementary School Journal, 94,* 73–86.

Allington, R. L. (1994a). Reducing the risk: Integrated language arts in restructured elementary schools. In L. M. Morrow, L. C. Wilkinson, & J. Smith (Eds.), *The integrated language arts: From controversy to consensus* (pp. 193–214). Boston: Allyn & Bacon.

Allington, R. L. (1994b). What's special about special programs for children who find learning to read difficult? *Journal of Reading Behavior, 26,* 1–21.

Allington, R. L., Guice, S., Michelson, N., Baker, K., & Li, S. (1996). Literature-based instruction in schools serving large numbers of children from low-income families. In M. Graves & B. Taylor (Eds.), *The First r: The children's right.* New York: Teachers College Press.

Applebee, A. N. (1992). The background for reform. In J. A. Langer (Ed.), *Literature instruction: A focus on student response* (pp. 1–18). Urbana, IL: National Council of Teachers of English.

Applebee, A. N. (1993a). *Beyond the lesson: Reconstructing curriculum as a domain for culturally significant conversations* (Report No. 1.7). Albany, NY: National Research Center for Literature Teaching and Learning, State University of New York.

Applebee, A. N. (1993b). *Literature in the secondary school: Studies of curriculum and instruction in the United States.* Urbana, IL: National Council of Teachers of English.

Applebee, A. N. (1996). *Transforming traditions: Toward a curriculum of knowledge in action.* Chicago: University of Chicago Press.

Applebee, A. N., Burroughs, R., & Stevens, A. (1994). *Shaping conversations: A study of continuity and coherence in high school literature curricula* (Report No. 1.11). Albany, NY: National Research Center for Literature Teaching and Learning, State University of New York.

Barksdale-Ladd, M. A. (1994). Teacher empowerment and literacy instruction in three professional development schools. *Journal of Teacher Education, 45,* 104–111.

Farrell, E. (1991). Instructional models for English language arts, K–12. In J. Flood, J. Jensen, D. Lapp, J. Squire (Eds.), *Handbook of research on teaching the English language arts* (pp. 63–84). New York: Macmillan.

Finn, C. E. (1991). *We must take charge: Our schools and the future.* New York: Free Press.

Freeman, Y.S. (1988). The California reading initiative: Revolution or merely revision? *New Advocate, 1,* 241–249.

Freeman, Y. S. (1994). Celebremos la literatura: Is it possible with a Spanish reading program? In P. Shannon & K. Goodman (Eds.), *Basal readers: A second look.* Katonah, NY: Richard C. Owen.

Goodman, K. S. (1989). Whole language research: Foundations and development. *The Elementary School Journal, 90,* 207–221.

Goodman, Y. (1989). Roots of the whole language movement. *The Elementary School Journal, 90,* 113–127.

Jones, N. K. (1990). Getting started: Creating a literate classroom environment. In D. Stephens (Ed.), *What matters? A primer for teaching reading* (pp. 49–61). Portsmouth, NH: Heinemann.

Langer, J. A. (1991). *Literary understanding and literature instruction* (Report No. 2.11). Albany, NY: National Research Center for Literature Teaching and Learning, State University of New York.

Langer, J. A. (1992). Rethinking literature instruction. In J. A. Langer (Ed.) *Literature instruction: A focus on student response* (pp. 35–53) Urbana, IL: National Council of Teachers of English.

Langer, J. A. (l995a). *Envisioning literature: Literary understanding and literature instruction.* New York: Teachers College Press.

Langer, J. A. (1995b). Literature and learning to think. *Journal of Curriculum and Supervision, 10,* 207–226.

McGill-Franzen, A., & Lanford, C. (1994). Exposing the edge of the preschool curriculum: Teachers' talk about text and children's literary understandings. *Language Arts, 71,* 264–274.

Michelson, N. (1994, December). *A teacher learning to learn in the context of a mandated language arts change.* Paper presented at the National Reading Conference, San Diego.

Miller, S. M. (1993). Why a dialogic pedagogy? Making space for possible worlds. In S. M. Miller & B. McCaskill (Eds.), *Multicultural literature and literacies: Making space for difference* (pp. 247–266). Albany, NY: State University of New York Press.

National Center for Educational Statistics (1993). *Schools and staffing in the United States: A statistical profile, 1990–91* (Report NCES 93–146). Washington, DC: U.S. Department of Education, Office of Educational Research and Improvement.

New York State School Boards Association (1992). *School Law 1992.* Albany, NY: Author.

Pearson, P. D. (1993). Teaching and learning reading: A research perspective. *Language Arts, 70,* 502–511.

Purves, A. C. (1992). Testing literature. In J. A. Langer (Ed.), *Literature instruction: A focus on student response* (pp. 19–34). Urbana, IL: National Council of Teachers of English.

Reutter, E. E., & Hamilton, R R. (1976). *The law of public education.* Mineola, NY: Foundation Press.

Rockmuller, S. (1993). *School law in New York State: A manual for parents.* East Chatham: Longview.

Rowan, B. (1990). Commitment and control: Alternative strategies for the organizational design of schools. In C. B. Cazden (Ed.), *Review of research in education, Vol. 16.* Washington, DC: American Educational Research Association.

Ruth, L. P. (1991). Who determines policy? Power and politics in English language arts education. In J. Flood, J. Jensen, D. Lapp & J. Squire (Eds.), *Handbook of research on teaching the English language arts*. New York: Macmillan.

Rylant, C. (1989). *But I'll be back again.* New York: Orchard Books.

Rylant, C. (1992). *Missing May.* New York: Doubleday.

Shanker, A. (1994). National standards. In C. E. Finn & H. J. Walberg (Eds.), *Radical education reforms*. Berkeley, CA: McCutchan.

Shannon, P. (1991). Basal readers and the illusion of illegitimacy. In P. G. Altbach et al., (Eds.), *Textbooks in American society* (pp. 217–233). Albany, NY: State University of New York Press.

Smylie, M. A. (1994). Redesigning teachers' work: Connections to the classroom. In L. D. Hammond (Ed.), *Review of research in education, Vol. 20* (pp.129–177). Washington, DC: American Educational Research Association.

Stayter, F., & Close, E. (1991). *Journeying toward collaboration* (Report No. 6.6). Albany, NY: National Research Center for Litera- ture Teaching and Learning, State University of New York.

Strickland, D. S., Walmsley, S. A.; Bronk, G. T., & Weiss, K. (1994). *School book clubs and literacy development: A descriptive study* (Report No. 2.22). Albany, NY: National Research Center for Literature Teaching and Learning, State University of New York.

Walmsley, S. A. (1991). Literacy in the elementary classroom. In A. C. Purves & E. M. Jennings (Ed.), *Literate systems and individual lives: Perspectives on literacy and schooling* (pp. 139–164). Albany, NY: State University of New York Press.

Walmsley, S. A., Fielding, L., & Walp, T. (1991). *A study of second graders' home and school literary experiences* (Report No. 1.6). Albany, NY: National Research Center for Literature Teaching and Learning, State University of New York.

Walmsley, S. A., & Walp, T. (1989). *Teaching literature in the elementary school* (Report No.1.3). Albany, NY: National Research Center for Literature Teaching and Learning, State University of New York.

TEN YEARS OF RESEARCH: ACHIEVEMENTS OF THE NATIONAL CENTER FOR THE STUDY OF WRITING AND LITERACY

Sarah Warshauer Freedman
UNIVERSITY OF CALIFORNIA AT BERKELEY

Linda Flower
CARNEGIE MELLON UNIVERSITY

Glynda Hull
UNIVERSITY OF CALIFORNIA AT BERKELEY

J. R. Hayes
CARNEGIE MELLON UNIVERSITY

Writing matters—for what people learn, for how they grow and develop and for how they function in society. It also matters for society as a whole—for our position in the global marketplace and for the transmission and transformation of our culture. Writing is the active side of literacy, the side that allows us to contribute to change, to protect our rights, to take control of our lives. Clearly, what we know about writing development in our schools, our communities and our workplaces is essential to our individual and cultural well-being. Over the past 10 years the National Center for the Study of Writing and Literacy has focused its attention on how literacy, and in particular, writing, functions in our society and how it is taught, used, and learned in schools, communities, and workplaces. Our goal has been to contribute to higher levels of writing achievement for an increasing proportion of our population.

It is important to state from the outset that within the area of literacy, writing is a young area of study and indeed has been the forgotten one of the three Rs. Writing research only began to develop in the 1970s, and there was no significant federal investment in writing research until the Center was first funded in 1985. Reading and literacy are often

Although this report is authored by the four Center co-directors, all the Center project directors have made substantial contributions. Summaries of projects are drawn from reports and other documents authored by the researchers themselves. Much gratitude also goes to all project assistants as well as to Andrew Bouman. The authors thank Julie Kalnin for providing a first draft of the section on the M-CLASS research.

The publication of this report was supported under the Educational Research and Development Center Program (Grant No. R117G10036 for the National Center for the Study of Writing) as administered by the Office of Educational Research and Improvement, U.S. Department of Education. The findings and opinions expressed in this report do not reflect the position or policies of the Office of Educational Research and Improvement or the U.S. Department of Education. In addition to the U.S. Dept. of Education, research was supported by the Bingham Trust, the British National Foundation for Research in Education (NFER), Carnegie Mellon University, The Howard Heinz Endowment, National Center for Research in Vocational Education, Oakland Unified School District, Rockefeller Foundation, Spencer Foundation, University of California, and University of London Institute of Education.

considered synonymous terms, with writing left out of the equation. Given the newness of writing as a field of research, much remains to be done; we know much less about learning to write than we know about learning to read or learning to do mathematics.

Having said that, given 10 years of sustained research, the Center has been able to reach large numbers of practicing teachers because from its start, the Center joined forces with the National Writing Project, an already well-established network which has trained 1,318,174 teachers of writing to date, with 163 sites representing every state in the nation and many foreign countries. Since both the Writing Project and the Center have been based at the University of California at Berkeley, collaboration has been natural, intense, and ongoing. Writing Project teachers now depend on the work of the Center as a significant part of their professional development. The Center's research agenda was shaped from the start by what teachers wanted to know, by the knowledge that they felt would help them do their jobs better. To be certain that Center research projects remained focused on teachers' needs, the projects have involved important collaborations with teachers. In addition, the Center has reached beyond the National Writing Project network, to administrators, policy makers, and others interested in literacy education in general and writing in particular—from the Chief State School Officers to the national PTA, from the American Society for Curriculum Development to the National Association of Elementary School Principals, from the Council of Great City Schools to teachers' organizations such as the National Education Association, the National Council of Teachers of English, the National Council of Teachers of Social Studies, the International Reading Association, and Teachers of English to Speakers of Other Languages. Above all, the Center has aimed to fund "practice-sensitive research" while at the same time to promote "research-sensitive practice."

Center research projects and activities have been tied together to address three interlocking sets of questions:

1. ABOUT WRITING: What writing demands are made upon students in key educational, family, community, and workplace settings?
   - What relationships exist between the writing practices of schools as compared to families, communities, and workplaces?
   - How do these writing practices both support and require higher-order thinking and learning across the curriculum and across the grades?
2. ABOUT LEARNING: How do students meet these demands?
   - What variation exists in students' ways of writing? How is this variation related to familial and community experiences? to language background?
   - How do students' ways of writing—their strategies—change over time? How do students adapt what they know and negotiate new literacy practices?
   - How does students' writing figure into the language life of these settings, that is, what is its interrelationship

with students' ways of speaking? with their ways of reading? How do these interrelationships change over time?

3. ABOUT INSTRUCTION: How do teachers help students meet these demands? How can student progress be measured?
   - What challenges do teachers in varied settings face as they work amidst a diversity of literacy practices, of learners, and of technological tools? What is the nature of helpful teacher behavior in writing instruction across settings? What institutional structures are needed to support important instructional changes?
   - What instructional strategies promote both writing and learning across the curriculum and across the grades?
   - What purposes does writing assessment serve—at the level of the classroom, school, district, state, and nation? What is involved in creating assessments designed to fulfill varied purposes?
   - How does assessment influence instruction, both in terms of how and what students are taught and in terms of how the results affect the school site?
   - How does writing assessment relate to the assessment of reading and oral language development? (Dyson & Freedman 1991, pp. 2, 3)

Answers to these questions are designed to help teachers and public officials deal with the most pressing literacy issues we face as we strive to reach national goals and set high standards for the next generation and as we strive to advance the position of the United States in the global economy.

To address these questions Center research projects have been broadly conceived to cover many areas and represent varied constituents and points of view. Projects have first of all focused on a range of settings—the schools from kindergarten through twelfth grade, community colleges, universities, community centers, home and family settings, workplaces. Center projects have also focused on the learning of varied types of writing—from academic arguments to writing pamphlets for community distribution; from stories, poems, and plays to historical narratives to learn about history and logs to learn about science; from personal autobiographies and college admissions essays to instructions in a manufacturing plant. Projects have further examined how computer technology affects writing and also how writing growth is related to growth in reading and oral language. Center researchers have studied the work of prize-winning college students, students labeled "remedial" at the high school and college levels, young children just learning to put pencil to paper, and second language learners—from child immigrants to immigrant workers. Center researchers also have looked comparatively at how writing is learned in Britain, where there is a long history of writing in the schools. In addition, Center projects have focused on how to assess writing, determining how to get reliable scores for something as inherently subjective as judgments of writing quality, and at the same time projects have explored the movement toward portfolio assessment, from both practical and policy angles. To conduct our research, we have relied on the expertise not only of teachers in the schools but also of an interdisciplinary team of scholars—from education, linguistics, English, history, anthropology, and psychology. We have designed many types of studies—large-scale projects that look nationally and internationally at how writing is taught and learned, longitudinal studies of individual development across time, and case studies to understand how writing functions in the workplace. Our methods have included ethnographies and other forms of descriptive research to develop theories, traditional experiments to test theories, and large-scale surveys to provide information about the status of the field.

Results from 10 years of research on writing, learning, and instruction have led us to conclude that written language, which is fundamentally active in nature (compared to the usually more reactive quality of reading), has the potential to have significant effects on performance in most areas of the curriculum, in many community-based endeavors, and in the high-performance workplace. Through conducting our research, we have located five areas in which writing and knowledge about writing are essential: (a) in communities of teacher researchers, where writing and reflection can help build a professional teaching force; (b) in multicultural and multiracial learning communities where writing can provide the base for motivating student achievement; (c) in the increasing range of settings populated by large numbers of nonnative speakers of English; (d) in the high-performance workplace, if employees are to become maximally productive; and (e) in the variety of settings where evaluating written language is essential. In the following sections, we provide examples of the impact of our work in these five critical areas.

TEACHER RESEARCH, TEACHER REFLECTION: BUILDING A BASE FOR THE ACHIEVEMENT OF LEARNERS

In the Center's projects that involve teacher research, we find a striking role for writing in the professional development of teachers, based on reflection and inquiry that grows out of various forms of teacher research. This includes Freedman and Simon's M-CLASS (Multicultural Collaborative for Literacy and Secondary Schools) project, Dyson's project with elementary teachers, Schecter's project with Writing Project teacher researchers, Flower's MTV (Making Thinking Visible) Project, and also efforts of the National Writing Project (NWP) through the Urban Sites Network and other teacher research activities. The national teacher-research agenda has mobilized a teacher movement, creating a new cadre of professional teachers who better understand their students and their students' learning needs and who are well positioned to serve as leaders in the educational reform movement. Writing offers these teachers the necessary tools for inquiry and reflection and makes this proactive form of teacher development and educational reform possible. Reform projects such as the Coalition of Essential Schools, as well as other major reform efforts that rely on

teacher leadership, report that the teacher leaders are usually those who have developed their skills of reflection and inquiry through writing; many have been involved in teacher professionalization programs that stress writing and teacher research.

The central purpose of the Center's M-CLASS teacher-research project was to explore what is involved in literacy learning and using literacy to learn in 8th-, 9th-, and 10th-grade, urban, multicultural classrooms (Freedman, 1994b; Freedman, 1996; Freedman, Simons, & Kalnin, in preparation). The 24 participating English and social studies teachers, six from each of four sites (Boston, Chicago, New Orleans, and San Francisco), worked for 2 years to think through and articulate the underlying tensions in their schools, classrooms, and communities; to explore their theories of teaching and learning; and to understand the opportunities before them. In the course of their work, the teacher researchers discovered the importance of writing in helping them reflect on and better understand their students. By writing about and reflecting on their students and their teaching, this multicultural group of teacher researchers delved into the issues that make life in their classrooms both challenging and interesting.

For example, in Boston, Roberta Logan, an experienced teacher researcher with the NWP Urban Sites Network and leader of the Boston M-CLASS site, encouraged her colleagues to write in order to reflect on their practice. Recognizing that the teachers were not used to writing about their work, she pushed them to write regularly early on in their process:

> I guess the one thing I should say is, the piece of advice I can share is, try to begin to write. Just write about your classroom in some way or another even if it is not focused on your particular [research] question... Try and write about it with some amount of regularity, even if it's just a little bit just to get started, because I'm sure there are highlights or things that you want to begin to record now.

She continued by emphasizing the importance of journals and stream of consciousness writing to help ideas flow:

> Once you get in the habit of writing, it will flow easier. Not everybody keeps a journal, but it's a good way to start. I'm a journal druggie. I've kept journals for a really long time just personally, but in reality, journals are really unfocused. They are real stream-of-consciousness writing.

Tom and Kathy Daniels, teacher researchers from the Chicago group, illustrate the benefits of advice like Roberta's as they explain how regular journal writing for their research projects led them to new understandings about their students:

> For both of us, the act of writing a daily journal, focusing on our Introduction to H. S. English classes, was especially important. Each day we looked back at each student in the class, noted what he or she did, and looked back at interactions between students and teachers. Occasionally we re-read entries from the previous week or month. Both of us took more time for reflection than ever before. We began to see patterns.... Our students began to emerge as separate and distinct persons in a way that helped us better understand their outlook on life, their method of operating in school, their view of themselves, and how they thought others saw them. (Daniels, & Daniels, 1994, p. 10)

Tom then explains that his growing understanding led him to improve his teaching:

> Based on that information, I began treating each one in a way I thought would help them. I always did that before, but now I had much better information.

Kathy adds:

> I don't think I have ever been so aware of individual students as I was last year. I came to know them all, not just the "stars" or the problems. Through their writing, I shared all the ups and downs of that rather chaotic freshman year, and I became acutely aware of the need to provide a kind of safe haven.

Tom next tells how the act of writing helped him clarify his thinking, leading him to a new level of awareness about his role in the classroom:

> I'm the kind of person who really doesn't become conscious of his thinking until he writes it down. This year I did much more writing about what I thought. As a result, I understood my strengths and weaknesses much better. I could observe myself when I was slipping back into the old ways of teaching or thinking. (p. 10)

Like Tom and Kathy, other M-CLASS teachers had similar experiences: writing consistently helped them reflect on and then improve their classroom practice.

Using another approach to teacher reflection, Dyson collaborated with skilled primary teachers in urban schools to examine the language resources for literacy learning that young children bring to school, particularly as members of various ethnic and cultural communities. (Dyson, in press). She worked with the teachers to examine the ways in which those resources influence the teaching and learning of written language in classrooms. The teachers in her project met with her to present case studies of children from their classroom, which included general introductions to each child and specific information about the children's participation in writing activities. The teachers reflected on such issues as (a) with whom children interacted during writing; (b) the themes, structures, and styles that figured in children's writing; (c) the responses that the children benefited from—or offered—others about texts; (d) any links between children's texts and their in-school relationships and their out-of-school lives. The teachers also talked about (e) their relationship with the child's family and, at times, with other teachers who worked with (or had worked with) the child. These reports led to ongoing analytic discussion of the students across classrooms and to joint writing with Dyson. In this way the teachers brought together their constructions of children's actions and their own responses to those actions. The descriptions reveal the teachers' understandings of literacy learning as articulated in their day-to-day experiences with children. This joint analysis of commonalties and differences in the teachers' constructions or narratives of everyday teaching led the teachers to formulate understandings of what difference sociocultural difference makes in the daily work of teaching.

Flower's MTV (Making Thinking Visible) classroom research project involved teachers and students in using collaborative planning, a technique in which a writer works with a planning partner to generate ideas for writing. Collaborative planning provides a window through which to view the processes of thinking and writing. In Flower's MTV, project, a team of 14 teacher researchers worked together for 4-years to implement collaborative planning strategies in their classrooms, to examine how students collaborated, and to write about what they observed. A full report of this project is contained in Flower, Wallace, Norris, and Burnett (1994).

The purposes of the MTV project were threefold: (a) to help students develop a repertoire of strategies for planning and writing; (b) to encourage students to reflect on their own problem-solving strategies and become more aware of themselves as thinkers; and (c) to discover ways in which classroom inquiry conducted by teachers and students can enhance teaching and help make the processes of thinking, planning, and writing more visible.

As the MTV teachers worked to understand their students' thinking processes and to help their students develop and become aware of their strategies for writing, they depended on their own writing and discussions of their writing to help them understand their students. They wrote a series of brief discovery memos that were shared with other members of the project. These memos recorded and commented on classroom observations, giving everyone an ongoing story of the students. Later, these memos were combined into extended papers that documented the kinds of thinking and reflection that were happening in many different contexts—for example, in developmental writing classes at a community college, in teacher education courses, in remedial and gifted high school programs, in community literacy projects, and in programs for technical and professional writers in the workplace.

Unlike the Center's other teacher-research projects, Schecter's study did not form a new teacher-research group but rather studied how a well-established group functioned She focused on a teacher-led group sponsored by a National. Writing Project site and was especially concerned with the kinds of support teachers need if they are to conduct classroom research; the effects of becoming researchers on teachers' views of classroom practice and their self-images as professionals; the kinds of knowledge that research by teachers can contribute to the field of composition study; and the forms used to present this knowledge in written texts.

In the course of doing research, the teachers routinely shared their writing with their colleagues. Schecter found that the amount and kinds of writing the teachers did depended on their purposes for engaging in teacher research: some were interested in using teacher research to empower other teachers, others hoped to stimulate social change, while others hoped mainly for personal professional development. For all of them, however, writing was a central part of the teacher research enterprise and was valued as a prime method of reflection. Marilyn, who hoped her teacher research would empower others, says, "Writing is essential ... It's not just thinking about teaching and thinking about some changes or even the process of research. Looking at your kids and the data through writing forces you to consider other hypotheses." Moreover, according to Marilyn, writing is also a sign that a teacher believes that what she is doing is important, that "this matters to me and I want it to be good" (Schecter & Parkhurst, 1993, p. 780). Kate, who cared most about social change, hoped to use writing to reach people in positions of power who could affect life in schools. Paula, who was involved in the group for her own professional development, had the most ambivalent attitude toward writing, but even she used journal writing to help her reflect on her teaching.

Across all of the Center's teacher-research efforts, regardless of the goal of the project or the structure of the teacher research group, writing played a powerful role. Creating a cadre of highly reflective teachers is essential to improving instruction, and teacher writing drives the reflective process. As school reform efforts are demonstrating, we must depend on reflective teachers as essential contributors to any national effort aimed at improving student achievement. Further, if schools are to become professional workplaces, writing will have to become integral to teachers' work and to their identities as professionals.

INTERCULTURAL COLLABORATION THROUGH GROWTH IN WRITING

One of the biggest challenges facing the United States today is finding ways for varied cultural groups to come together in multicultural classrooms and communities. Research at the Center has not only shown several ways in which writing and instruction in writing can be organized to promote writing growth in the multicultural classroom but has also helped students and teachers move beyond multicultural awareness to new forms of intercultural collaboration. First, research at the Center is helping teachers understand and teach to the logic of learners, especially those at risk. Second, writing makes the tacit expectations of different discourses and literate practices in our society more explicit, as students are expected to move from acts of personal reflection, to problem analysis, to reasoned argument. In teaching strategies for writing, we are also teaching students the strategies for intercultural collaboration, for reading and communicating across differences. Finally, writing and writing instruction can unlock the door to personal and social empowerment for students by first letting people bring their voice to the table in a way that informs, reasons, moves, and persuades. Writing also supports the larger goals of social civility, bringing people into collaboration and community building, by giving them the tools to cross the boundaries of race, class, culture, or discourse and the power to be full participants in a range of settings in our literate world.

The Logic of Learners

Teachers become more effective when they understand the logic of learners: when they know why some students seem to be walking to a different drummer, appear to misunderstand instructions, or even choose to resist learning that conflicts with other values or habits of mind at home or in their community of peers. Motivating at-risk children to learn is one of the keys to success, and understanding students' assumptions and their approaches to school or their interpretation of writing tasks lets teachers give students the help they really need.

Ogbu and Simons lay some valuable groundwork for understanding students' worlds through a 2-year study of the ways in which knowledge about minority communities can inform the teaching of writing. Data for the study are a subset of the data collected for John Ogbu's Community Forces and Minority Education Strategies Project. The Community Forces Project looks at the cultural models and educational strategies of what Ogbu has described as "voluntary" minority groups (Chinese American) and "involuntary" minority groups (African-American, Mexican American) to identify those models and strategies which contribute to success in school and those which are less useful.

The Ogbu and Simons study shows that the cultural models (assumptions and values) and the educational strategies that minority groups bring to school can help explain educational differences. In a survey of 2,285 African-American, Asian American, and Mexican American students, Ogbu saw that while the adult community strongly supported success in school and did not see it as a threat to ethnic identity, African-American and Mexican American students stigmatized their peers who got good grades for "acting white." Although all three communities see education as necessary to "making it" in life, the African-American community and its students see that road littered with barriers of prejudice and discrimination. Moreover, they believe that experience and common sense, as opposed to book learning, play a relatively larger role in making it than the other groups report.

However, when one looks at students' oppositional behavior in school, there seems to be a discrepancy between what African-American and to a lesser degree Mexican American students say and what they do. Ogbu and Simons reveal an opportunity for learning that writing instruction is ideally suited to exploit: in both the quantitative and ethnographic dimensions of this study these students revealed their ambivalence about crossing cultural boundaries and adopting mainstream values and strategies for success in life—ambivalence they may not even be consciously aware of. Our attempts to teach writing (including the conventions of mainstream English) will be more effective if we address the reasons that students that have to resist such learning as well as the reasons they have to perform. On top of that, writing is the tool which lets students themselves address their own ambivalence and examine the cultural models and assumptions that they hold.

Anne Haas Dyson's (1993) study of elementary school writers (kindergarten–grade 3) shows how children's sociocultural experience—of growing up as a person of a particular race, class, and gender—shapes their growth in literacy. The project focused on young school children from low-income, minority homes and examined how children's diverse cultural resources—their experiences with literary, popular, and folk traditions—figure into their learning to write; the various ways they use those resources in composing activities; and how they use writing to negotiate their complex social identities in their interactions with teachers, peers, and community members. Dyson's project confronts the difficulties of teaching the social act of writing to children from different social backgrounds and it also deepens our understandings of good writing instruction. One of the recent signal improvements in instruction has been the growing use of research-based teaching techniques focusing on the writing process and on writing as a social and cognitive event. As elementary school teachers follow the suggestions of this recent writing research, they begin to direct children to write to real audiences, with a genuine reason to share ideas, and to rely on audiences, such as classmates and teachers, for feedback and evaluation regarding successive drafts.

Not surprisingly, these curricula lead children to practice an unfamiliar set of social skills for relating to a general reading audience. But as Dyson shows us, individual children respond quite differently to this set of goals for writing and communication. For example, children are taught that these reading audiences have new expectations for clarity, interest, and informativeness, and teachers try to embody these expectations for their students. These are important goals, but they are not the only goals that people bring to writing, and in practice Dyson finds that these challenge the assumptions that individual children already have about how to relate to an audience through language.

In a 1-year-long case study, a part of the larger project, Dyson observed a verbally gifted, African-American 1st-grader struggle to understand why audiences for his writing should be "allowed" to make demands for clarity and the like. He often wrote compositions that had a musical quality and relied on plays-on-words, verbal imagery, and rhyming to delight his peers. While he felt that a written piece should be performed and appreciated like artwork, some of his classmates insisted instead that a written piece needed to communicate information.

This case study, like the project as a whole, shows that children's cultural knowledge may often be at odds with the best educational practices. In teaching young children to write, teachers must integrate their instruction with children's individual expectations for how a written piece should be evaluated, what it should achieve, and how real audiences play a role in its successive drafts. When writing teachers successfully mediate these forums, they win the enthusiasm and participation of their students. Dyson showed how the gifted teacher of these students was able to lead them to appreciate and practice both the performative and communicative aspects of their writing.

This research helps elementary school teachers foster their students' abilities to express themselves and cooperate socially in a multicultural classroom. It shows how writing can develop children's audience-sensitivities—to help them accept different points of view and share ideas. In the innovative writing classrooms that Dyson studied, teachers arranged their lesson plans so that children relied on their peers for feedback about their compositions and ideas for new compositions. Not only did children share ideas about writing, they also shared opposing ideas on important topics. But this atmosphere of learning is only possible when teachers also recognize the different kinds of language experience and practices (especially those valued in the child's home and community) that individual children bring with them. When teachers see all these styles as resources, learning flourishes.

Dyson's study also shows how writing teachers have a unique opportunity to motivate children to follow their directions. Writing teachers can win children's trust and cooperation by encouraging children's own ideas of how readers and audiences relate to one another. Writing teachers also have a unique opportunity to learn about their students' differing ways of sharing and communicating ideas. In an innovative writing classroom, children can find an audience in the skilled writing teacher for self-expression and for guidance in addressing other important audiences.

Understanding the logic of learners is equally important when older students are attempting a difficult task. In the Writing of Arguments across Diverse Contexts Flower and her a colleagues (Flower, 1994; Flower et al., 1990; Flower, & Petraglia, 1992; Higgins, 1992); studied the construction of arguments in school and out by inner city teenagers, precollege minority freshmen, returning women in community college, college student mentors, and a multicultural neighborhood group. Flower and her team found that when college students are asked to take on demanding writing tasks and to juggle a number of competing goals, they may make choices and set priorities that differ from what the teachers expect. And teachers, blind to that logic, miss the opportunity to teach the students real questions, difficulties, and needs.

One part of Flower's study takes us into a college dorm room where freshmen minority students work together to plan their essays on issues of minority students and education. Their course in argument writing asked them to plan collaboratively, defining an open question and taking a rival hypothesis stance to their question—that is, a stance that considered genuine alternative hypotheses or different perspectives on the problem and the evidence for each hypothesis before coming to a resolution. The essays that these students wrote suggested that they had difficulty with generating genuine rival hypotheses (as opposed to simply asserting a claim or thesis), and also with presenting adequate evidence to evaluate any of their claims.

However, an analysis of each student's planning sessions also suggests that a significant part of their problem solving was devoted to other problems that the teacher did not anticipate, did not see, and did not address in her teaching or comments. In particular, the analysis of the conflict episodes in students' planning processes pointed to three concerns. First was the problem of creating and using evidence. The second involved students' desires to address real readers with their arguments. The final area of concern for these minority students involved questions of their own identity and their place in this new, largely white institution. These concerns led to conflicting goals for writing.

For instance, one student produced a well-written paper that failed to meet the goals of the assignment. Instead of recognizing some of the valid arguments various writers in their source material were making, she took a single position. What happened? Why did she fail to take a rival hypothesis stance? The tapes of her collaboration revealed two important things: her own experiences as an African-American led her to question what she viewed as faulty generalizations about African-Americans in what she had read for the assignment. For this student, the most important goal in writing this paper was to speak loudly and clearly to the research community which she believed perpetuated such generalizations. The second point to note about this student's apparent "failure" to carry out the assignment was that she was in fact doing what many teachers long to promote—imagining herself as a person with a purpose writing to a real audience—and in this case to the intimidating world of the research community. The logic of her performance was the logic of a mature and committed writer. But all that the teacher saw was a paper that failed to use the assigned argument structure.

The ways in which students negotiated their conflicting goals often led them to make choices dictated by problems the teacher never saw. Their negotiations led to a logic and a text that apparently "failed" to meet some assignment demands, when in fact students were choosing to negotiate a different, and to them, more compelling problem. Both sets of goals are necessary, but when teachers uncover the logic of these negotiations, they become more effective at diagnosing the students' writing problems and teaching to students' real needs. Understanding a student's logic does not mean replacing the instructional goals of a class with those of each student. However, it does mean teaching to the genuine conflicts that students face and to the process of negotiating multiple voices, expectations, and demands that all writers must juggle (Flower, 1994).

Making Literate Practices and Strategies Explicit

The responsibility for intercultural understanding is not only the job of teachers but of students as well. Yet how can students be expected to negotiate the maze of American culture and its multiple discourse communities, each with their conventions, roles, and appropriate languages? Such negotiation can become even more complex when it involves understanding multiple perspectives from the past, which normally occurs in history instruction. One answer is provided by writing, which helps students take part in intercultural collaboration by making different ways of talking, thinking, and being explicit. It prepares students for productive work across differences in disciplines and discourses.

Downey's project (1996) takes us to 3rd-, 4th-, and 5th-grade social studies classes where writing is the key to helping students think like historians. Data were collected in urban classrooms in the San Francisco Bay Area with a diversity of students, including recent immigrants from Central America and Asia. Students in the study used a wide-ranging collection of historical materials and participated in a curriculum that included different kinds of writing (such as personal narratives, biography, historical fiction, and expository writing).

Instead of memorizing names and dates, these children learned about the context of life in other times and places through engaging in historical perspective taking, which involved them in understanding the values, assumptions, and everyday habits of people who lived in the past. In particular, they engaged in historical imagination about people's lives and actions in ways that replaced historical stereotypes with a more accurate understanding of historical people and events. In the process, students learned to make causal connections

between events over time. Writing played a central part of learning to think like historians.

For example, the third graders in this project had trouble sorting out whether Columbus, the Indians or the Pilgrims came first—of seeing a logical order to past events. An even harder task for the fifth graders was to imagine the life of American Indians, their food gathering and life style, in a way that distinguished it from going out to play or shoot deer, with a handy berry drink. Narrative writing was the place where students worked on such historical thinking, by writing about events such as a story of what was happening and trying to make their events make sense given what they had learned about the past. It was also the place where they learned how to discern and build causal connections between historical "facts" and the artifacts and context of life—that is, what it could mean in terms of survival if you did not find berries or missed your deer. Although students wrote from the perspectives of historical characters and cultural groups, they did not adopt their values but rather worked to understand how differences in cultures and traditions can shape identity and action—a sophisticated thinking skill. Thus, when the fifth graders took the role of Spanish colonists writing a letter to a cousin in Spain about their perception of the Indians and the struggle for land, they had to make the radical transition from an Indian point of view, to attitudes that made "Spanish sense."

It is important to note that the historical thinking that Downey is studying does not come easily—many students had difficulty with perspective taking and then with taking the more sophisticated step of building causal links and making "historical" sense. Teaching history through writing is powerful because it goes directly to the heart of historical thinking, and it lets teachers not only give explicit instruction but gain a new insight into the historical worlds students are constructing. Through this research Downey discovered ways by which to make the writing assignments and instruction more acutely attuned to the difficulties that children have, especially those who are not native speakers of English. In particular, Downey found that student conferences, a key feature of process-based writing instruction, were also important in history instruction. These conferences became the place where teachers not only noted writing problems, and checked for historical understanding, but helped students make these historical thinking–writing connections. Downey's work shows the advantages and challenges of integrating history with the language arts in the intermediate grades.

Sometimes making strategies explicit has a large impact because students already know a great deal—and need to figure out how the new literate practices of school are different. Higgins (1992) worked with nontraditional students—low-income returning women students who came to community college with significant life experience in making arguments for themselves and their children to institutions and social agencies.

The nontraditional students in this study do indeed use written argument in their nonacademic lives. However, such arguments typically depend on external factual evidence or "proofs"; hence, this experience did not prepare the women to produce the warrants and extended reasoning that academic argument requires, nor did it prepare them for the different patterns of reasoning expected in their required course. Their academic writing forced them to deal with the (often conflicting) expectations of their teacher, a departmental review board at the community college, and the other members of the class.

For instance, all three groups shared a number of criteria (such as the appropriate use of organizational conventions); however, a close look at the goals and strategies of each group showed that students and teacher gave high priority to additional goals, such as influencing certain readers or using writing to explore charged issues in their own lives. Juggling all these goals—and the strategies to carry them out in the same text—is a significant problem for many inexperienced (and experienced) writers. Although the teacher offered students standard patterns for organizing an argument, what they needed more were strategies for making their own path of personal reasoning explicit.

Where could instruction make a difference? Higgins, study suggests that, first, teachers need to address these conflicts directly in their teaching—learning to negotiate competing goals is a necessary part of learning to write. Second, the standard practice of teaching argument often assumes that students will "find" evidence and support from outside authorities and organize it into a paper. But, in fact, college writing typically asks students not to find but to create a line of reasoning that supports claims with evidence, inferences, and good arguments. This study revealed that students are indeed doing this kind of reasoning in their planning—but not in their papers. The instruction that these students need is how to lay out their reasoning in text, how to make their own path of personal case building explicit in the text.

Community Building and Collaboration

As the traditional promises of education and advancement begin to ring hollow, educators are seeking ways by which to make learning count both in school and in the workplace and community. Writing—especially strategic training in writing—unlocks the door to rhetorical empowerment, to participation in community building, to bringing a stronger voice to the table. Center projects have shown how to make this process a reality. One did it by creating an international exchange of writing that motivated students to write to be understood and that allowed for comparisons of learning to write in different countries. Another project has made writing and collaboration a tool for making changes in inner-city neighborhoods by adapting the Center's research-based strategies to support collaboration among mixed groups of residents. In doing so, it has shown how school / community / university partnerships can be linked to community building in urban centers.

In Freedman's project (Freedman, 1994a, 1995) writing exchanges between paired classes of British and American students in grades six through nine not only motivated students to make their writing work; it revealed some important differences in how teachers in both countries looked at motivation. The writing exchanges showed the kinds of

classrooms that led students to higher levels of achievement. In particular, students who achieved the most were in classes where the teacher expected them to produce lengthy academic pieces and where they were given several months to craft each one. In order to get young adolescents excited about producing such extended work, these teachers worked together with their students to form a classroom community where writing activities kept the students' interest while at the same time pushed them to meet demanding academic challenges. This new kind of research-sensitive practice, which we call a negotiated curriculum, moves beyond fixed programs aimed at an idealized whole class. It also moves beyond the individualized "learner-centered" curriculum of the 1960s which is inadequate since it carries the implication that teachers concern themselves only with individuals and not with the community as a whole. A negotiated curriculum incorporates ways of leading discussions, and building activities, and frequently writing which emerge from the interests of the community of students in the classroom.

In Peter Ross' class students at the equivalent of 8th-grade level worked for 2 months on short stories, which they put together as a class anthology to send to students in the United States. Peter's students wanted more time to do a better job. As one of his female students explained, "He [the teacher] gave us about two months or more," but "he said it had to go on a particular Tuesday and I said I needed some more time." In the end one of the young men, who wanted more time, wrote a spy story of over 5,000 words, packed with action and compelling detail.

As another example of an extended activity, Peter's class worked collaboratively for several months to put together a 119-page book about the school. The book contained photographs of the students in Peter's class, of the school secretaries, the cooks, and the library. It also included a copy of the school rules, a written piece on form tutors and the "head of year," and a weekly schedule of classes. In addition, there was an entry on the physical structure of the school, what classes there were, who taught what, and uniforms. Following these general items was a series of chapters on each subject taught at the school and final chapters on such topics as community activities, trips, and a recounting of a bomb scare at the school. After completing this project, the class produced a 183-page book about the community surrounding the school.

In classrooms like Peter's teachers worked with their students to decide on writing activities, routinely bringing in issues close to the students' home communities and social and political issues that affected their lives. These teachers saw their job as setting motivating contexts for a particular group of students that would generate enthusiasm for writing in a variety of ways, for a variety of audiences. They understood that not all their students will be motivated by the same activity. When certain students were not motivated, the teachers helped them find something more motivating but equally academically challenging. Students experienced no stigma if they chose a different activity than the majority of the group. In the end, however, the teachers expected their students to master a variety of types of writing and to stretch beyond immediate and concrete concerns to consider more abstract issues and ideas. If students did not practice and master certain types of writing, the teacher considered it his or her failure in setting motivating contexts. This approach, which was more common in Britain than in the United States, provided an extremely powerful frame which allows students flexibility while giving both teachers and students important responsibilities.

In fact, this same finding was supported in Freedman and Simon's M-CLASS teacher research project. In the M-CLASS schools, mostly located in poverty-stricken, violence-ridden areas where drop-out rates and low-test scores are daily news, most Americans seem to doubt the possibility for academic achievement. However, Freedman and Simons are finding that community building through negotiation over important and substantive issues is a key to the M-CLASS teachers' successes. Still, their road is often a rocky one as Brenda Landau's story illustrates.

An African-American herself, Brenda teaches high school social studies in one of the toughest areas of Chicago. When she first attempted to open up the curriculum of her African-American history course to student negotiation, her students, many of whom were also African-American, were reluctant to accept her invitation. On the second day of class, Brenda asked the students to write a journal entry telling her what they wanted the class to cover. Only a few students responded. As Brenda reports, "Most of the students did not do the assignment. I asked them why and several said that they did not know what I wanted them to say. We discussed the fact that the class was not going to be what I wanted them to say, but that we were going to try to identify and express things they were concerned about, their conflicts about multicultural issues and conflicts about their own identities."

After this discussion Brenda tried a second time, asking students to describe where the study of African-American history should begin. Again students failed to respond. Brenda then laid out a general structure for the class, including time for student input through journals and discussions and launched into a 3-week lesson on Ancient African kingdoms. The students were not particularly responsive in class until a well-publicized shooting of a 7-year-old child who was walking from his Cabrini-Green (a Chicago public housing project) apartment to his school nearby. One student responded angrily in his journal:

> As I got off the bus at Kimball and Lawrence, I saw these two ladies reading the front page of the Sun Times. I glanced at what it said, and to see what was in there. There was a picture of Cabrini Green with the headline that read The Killing Ground. I thought to myself, why is it now that the media makes a big deal about a killing of a boy. Little kids get killed everyday and there aren't any big headlines! I thought why now, why not earlier?

From this journal entry and the discussion which followed the shooting, Brenda saw that when the class linked African-American history to current events, the students had a lot to say. Soon afterward, one student commented in her journal: "This class is not long enough. I need more time to express myself and for the rest of the students to express themselves. We have some pretty important stuff to say." This comment

struck Brenda as a significant clue to how she might redesign her course curriculum. She decided to allow students to bring the world outside into the classroom, where they could safely discuss and write about how current events related to African-American history and to their own lives.

As a result, Brenda writes, the class altered its rules of operation. The students decided that the group needed at least one class period, per week, to discuss whatever they wanted. They made three basic rules: that students respect one another's rights and opinions, that students could only speak when recognized, and that the teacher would only answer questions directed at her. The group also decided to watch the evening news daily and to take 15-minutes of each class period to discuss current events.

While the students had not responded to Brenda's earlier invitations for their participation, she found that when she was more open about the ways by which they could participate, a negotiated curriculum began to emerge. Asking students to outline the course curriculum in journal entries did not spark collaboration, but students' desire to discuss and write about contemporary African-American issues led them to reshape the curriculum. Brenda was flexible enough to turn over one day a week, and 15-minutes each day to issues which the students wanted to raise, despite her own full agenda of African-American history. She relinquished that position of power, but in order to do so, ironically, she had to draw on her reputation for "toughness" to manage the intense discussions which ensued in her multicultural classroom:

> I told them that there are rules in here to guide you. And I am an authoritarian. Otherwise, there would be no way I could hold those two classes together. They are predominantly male, predominantly gang (with emphasis). If I didn't have a very strong personality and if my reputation was not throughout the school that you know, "She's tough. I don't fool around, but she's fair. Okay?", they would be really at each other's throats.

Brenda's experiences reveal a true balance between a classroom in which the teacher is in total control and one in which there is a complete partnership with students. She used her authority quite deliberately to allow students space in the curriculum, not free rein. The careful balance of power yielded impressive changes in Brenda's classroom. When she opened up the discussion to students, not only was Brenda able to teach more effectively, but she learned a great deal also. She discovered, for instance, through their journal entries and classroom talk that some of her students were ardent racial separatists. In her opinion, their interpretations of current events were distorted by a lack of information about African-American history:

> I listened to all of this and then when they got into the separatist bit I asked them, "Well how many of you are old enough to vote?" Well only maybe one or two.
> And I said, "If you were old enough to vote, would you participate?"
> And they said, "No."
> And I said, "You wouldn't?"
> And they said, "No."
> And I said, "Why?"
> "Because it's not going to change anything in the Black community. It's not going to change the poverty. It's not going to change

the crime. It's not going to change the drugs. It's not going to change the gangs."

I was active in the Civil Rights Movement and I've spent may be ten years in Social Services working with gangs. Let me tell ya, I had to sit and listen, and I mean I learned a lot in that one session.

Brenda felt compelled to propose an alternative position to students and did so in response to the students' strong opinions. She states her goal:

My goal is to get them to the point where they realize that the only way they can make a difference is that they have to participate to a certain point. They have to. And one of the ways that you have to, is that you have to exercise that voting right. If I don't teach them anything more than that, then I will have accomplished something.

Brenda knew she needed to work to counteract the ignorance of African-American history which she believed led to her students' tendency to live in "the here and now." Students no longer could ask Brenda what she wanted them to write, but they had identified and now began to express their concerns and their conflicts about multicultural issues and about their identities. If Brenda had retained tight control of the curriculum, she may never have learned that many of her students held beliefs which she felt needed to be argued openly in an African-American history course; she might never have been able to help students confront and examine the rationale for and the consequences of a separatist ideology.

Later in the year, when she was reflecting on the changes that took place in her classroom, Brenda commented that until students began to take part in the curriculum, it was as if they were not physically present. She spoke clearly of the importance of creating an atmosphere in which students bring their interests and concerns to the teaching–learning process:

These kids have taught me something. When I walked in, the first thing I learned—these were kids who had self-esteem which was on the floor and we were walking with it. And when we began to interact, and I began to earn their trust—that was the main thing, they had been so done in for so long that when I finally began to earn their trust, behind this defensive mechanism of rebellion were the wonderful minds. They had some knowledge which had been picked up in the street which was totally crazy in relationship to African-American History and multiculturalism and in addition to that that they weren't succeeding because nobody was tuning in to what they wanted to discuss. It was back to the 1950s where they weren't in the classrooms, basically. They weren't there. And all of a sudden you're given this opportunity to be there and to participate. For me, it was when I saw that light behind their eyes—that this was a beginning.

By encouraging students to share their "street knowledge" and by offering her own experiences and those of other African-Americans, as well as her "book" knowledge, Brenda allowed her students to enter into the African-American history curriculum in meaningful ways. The students had something important to think about and something important to read and write about.

In Flower's study of argument writing in diverse contexts, writing crosses the boundaries between schools and communities, and it takes the results of educational research with it into inner-city neighborhoods. Collaborative planning is a problem-solving strategy for writing that developed out of the Center's initial research into an educational practice that high schools and college teachers adapted to a wide range of students (Flower, et al., 1994). This study takes us to an inner-city neighborhood where adults on different sides of a controversial issue learned collaborative planning and used writing to deal with multiple viewpoints. The members of the multicultural Landlords and Tenants project at Pittsburgh's Community Literacy Center met to construct a memorandum of understanding that would define the problem from both perspectives and at the same time it offered guidance to both groups in resolving conflicts.

The success of this initial project led to collaboration with Pittsburgh's major community development organization and another partnership with a neighborhood-based planning group. It showed, first of all, that the Center's research-based educational strategies for collaborative planning are translating well to community settings where people are using writing to draft better understandings and plans of action. An educational approach to community issues and research-based literacy instruction is proving its power in these nontraditional settings.

The study also revealed why attempts to build consensual arguments and texts in such contexts can falter. In tracing the points of conflict and negotiation in these planning and writing sessions, Flower observed how a group comes to premature agreement over a concept, even though the analysis showed that each member held a very different set of meanings and goals associated with that concept—differences which later surfaced as conflict. Although many theories of argument assume that persuasion must lead to consensus and agreement, this study showed how community members designed a written document, based on problem scenarios and "what if" alternatives and solutions, that let them maintain different, often conflicting, values and perspectives, and still come to consensus through shared action. In this case the action they took was a written guidebook that honored differences while it resolved conflict.

In another study within the multi-context project, Flower looked at what a growing number of community service projects have recognized: literacy is a powerful link between our colleges and communities. Mentoring younger students is a way to address urgent social needs, benefiting marginalized teenagers who need intellectual strategies for negotiating their worlds more constructively as well as college students who often feel alienated from public life. However, Flower's study of community literacy—based on collaborative planning, problem solving and writing—offers a model that goes well beyond traditional tutoring. College students worked as collaborative planning partners with inner-city teenagers at the Community Literacy Center, helped the younger writers address issues that affect their lives, from risk and respect, to violence and school reform. Each semester, high school age writers not only published a written document but planned and held a public community conversation to present their arguments.

In this context we see the teenage writers move from a rhetoric of complaint and blame to collaborative problem solving as they learn strategies for defining and analyzing problems, for taking rival points of view, and for articulating issues. Community literacy motivates students on the margins of school to seize writing as a tool for making themselves valued and heard. At the same time, the college students embark on a vigorous course of mutual learning as they understand and respond to an intercultural discourse. Tracking the conflicts and negotiations behind students' reading and writing showed them how to work hard to integrate their "academic" knowledge of literacy and intercultural communication with their experiential knowledge as a writing mentor. One such conflict, for instance, stems from students' commitment to respecting and supporting the perspectives of their teenage writer (rather than dictating what they might say), while at the same time wanting to exercise the authority of their own expertise as a writer / mentor and help teens produce an effective public document.

This study documented a process of mutual learning in which both groups of students not only developed their own skills as writers, but used writing to cross barriers of race, culture, socioeconomic status, and discourse. This is not a trivial crossing: multicultural education can build awareness of difference, but raise the question of how to respond to it in productive ways. Writing and planning together—as a collaborative process focused on community issues—creates a productive relationship in which students can move beyond the awareness of cultural difference to the practice of intercultural collaboration.

LEARNING TO WRITE IN ENGLISH: A STUDY OF NEW IMMIGRANT ADOLESCENTS

Elisa is 13 years old, small and dark-complexioned, her high cheekbones and very straight black hair reflecting her Indian heritage. A newly arrived immigrant from Honduras and a village girl, she and her sister lived with their grandmother for 8 years until their mother, who had immigrated earlier to the United States, was able to send for them. Upon arriving in the United States, Elisa was literate in Spanish, having completed the 6th grade, although her writing was not as developed as her reading. She knew very little English, although she could respond to questions like "what is your name?" She knew, however, that English was very important to her mother, who was an energetic and ambitious single woman who worked two jobs, and who insisted that her daughters watch only English language television.

Lilian at 12 is big for her age, blond and blue-eyed, and a new immigrant from a small village in Mexico. Before coming to the United States, Lilian had yet to travel even to the country seat a few miles away from her village. Here she lives in an urban area in a three-bedroom apartment that is shared by two families and other relatives; her family was struggling to keep food on the table and pay the rent. Her English abilities were close to zero when she arrived; she knew a few words like dog, cat, and ice cream, but she could read and write in Spanish. She confides that she had not been a very good student in Mexico.

Martin was born in Shanghai in the People's Republic of China. His father was a technician, and his mother, a primary school teacher of English. After coming to the United States as tourists and then staying on illegally, they both took jobs in a Chinese grocery store, and his mother also worked cleaning houses. Martin began studying English in the 4th grade in China; he was 13 when he arrived in the United States. He scored quite low for oral English skills and "0" for reading and writing when he was tested, but he knew some basic English. Lively, outgoing, confident, and aggressive, Martin says one of his priorities in school is studying English. When asked about his future, he said he wanted to *churen toudi,* or "rise head and shoulders above other people."

Audrey's father is a pastor who moved to the United States when he was offered a position in a Chinese community church. Born in Taipei, Audrey is 12 and had completed elementary school in Taipei and had gone to "night school" for training in English. She reported having plenty of opportunities to speak English at home and with kids in the neighborhood, but she also spoke Taiwanese and Mandarin. Audrey is not very motivated to learn English or to do well in school, and a year after moving to the United States her written Chinese was beginning to deteriorate. But Audrey is an accomplished musician, playing the cello, the piano, and singing in the choir, and she says she would like to be a music teacher.

These young people have something in common with many children in many countries all over the world: they are just in the process of learning, often from scratch, the language in which they are to receive the bulk of their schooling. For these students learning to write in a language other than their first presents big hurdles, partly because we know relatively little about how writing ability in a second language develops. Educators often assume that non-English-background students must acquire a certain level of English before they can profit from the instructional approaches used with native English-speaking students (though this level remains undefined). It is also often assumed that when such students exit from ESL (English as a second language) tracks, they should write like native-speaking students, and conversely, when they do not, then they are not ready for "mainstream" classes.

Guadalupe Valdés (Valdés, 1993; Valdés & Sanders, in press) and Sau-ling Wong (Wong & Zou, 1993; McKay & Wong, 1996) complicate and challenge these assumptions in their Center project, The Writing of Non-English Background Students. Conducting detailed case studies of Latino-background and Chinese-background students, including those introduced above, they describe the acquisition of writing abilities by eight young people over a 2-year period. They also create fine-grained portraits of writing instruction within ESL or "sheltered English" classes, illustrating writing assignments and describing instructional practices. They finally take us into students' communities and homes, reminding us how performance in school often takes its cue from social, economic, and cultural circumstances that originate beyond the schoolhouse door.

One important contribution of the part of the study led by Valdés, focusing on the Latino-background students, is a detailed description of students' language development across 2 years. To trace students' growth, a total of four English language assessments and one Spanish language assessment were carried out. At the outset all students were literate in Spanish, being able to read aloud confidently from a 6th-grade level book and to answer comprehension questions. All students were also able to write a bit about themselves in Spanish, although their abilities varied widely. Students' listening comprehension abilities in English were shown to be developing more rapidly than their speaking abilities, though they were generally unsuccessful at the outset in taking part in the assessment activities. Finally, in general, students' writing abilities in English were nonexistent.

From this modest beginning, Valdés traces students' growth; for some students the progress was remarkable indeed.

Here is a sample of what Elisa, 13, was able to write about her family on the first assessment:

thes tha paper
door
window
mesuring spoon
spatula o turner
postre
measurins cup
teacher
sister
brother
granmother
name
period

And here is the writing sample that she produced for her last assessment 2-years later:

I woke up on Saturday morning, it was cold and dark. I had breakfast with my sister, mom and dad. I knew that that day I was going to have fun. My mom and dad were getting read to go to work and my sister to go out with her friends.

When everybody had already left it was about six-thirty a.m. I started getting read. I went in the shower and spent 30 minutes. When I got out of the shower it was about 7:00 AM. I put lotion all over my body and put on my favorite underwear, pair of jeans, T.shirt, jacket and pair of shoes, I was feeling fresh and clean, I guess I was ready

I phoned my friend Rolando to tell him that I was ready. I wait for him for ten minutes. When I saw him coming, I saw a big limousine too. He asked me; "do you want to come in"? I said yes.

We went to San Francisco, we stay there for almost two hours. There we ate another funer breakfast.

I asked him if he wanted to go shopping with me. He answer yes. We went to almost all the malls in San Francisco. We spent almost all morning and part of the afternoon shopping then we went for a big dinner at Sizzzler.

At this point Elisa was able to meet practical writing needs, to take notes on familiar topics and to respond in writing to personal questions. She could write simple letters, brief synopses and paraphrases, and accounts of work and school experience. She demonstrated an ability to describe and to narrate in paragraphs. Though she had not yet learned to use cohesive devices and some of her verb inflections were inaccurate, her writing was generally comprehensible. She had a way to go before she would write on a par with her native English counterparts, but her growth was nonetheless impressive.

Valdés points out that not all Latino-background students fared so well; indeed, after 2 years of schooling, the four Latino focal students demonstrated different levels of English language development and different rates of growth in the four language modalities. All four students started at almost zero English, but two became fluent speakers, while two others acquired little spoken English during the 2-year period. The two fluent speakers, including Elisa, learned to write well enough to participate in selected mainstream classes, while the other two students developed very little ability to write in English. The different levels of development were influenced by a complex web of factors: the students' different responses to instruction, teachers' perceptions of their abilities, students' family backgrounds, their psycho-social development as adolescents, the circumstances which surrounded their immigration, and their hopes about what they could accomplish in the United States.

Valdés's studies of the Latino students suggest a strong relationship between the development of oral productive skills and the development of writing abilities. This, however, was not always the case for the Chinese-background students that Wong studied. For example, Martin, who is described earlier, started out with the highest proficiency (among those students who were studied) in English writing, and throughout the 2 year period he did better at writing English than speaking or comprehending it. Similarly, another student in the cohort made terrific strides in writing, but had difficulty even with everyday listening comprehension after 2 years. This finding contradicts the widely held notion that development in English always proceeds from listening to speaking to reading to writing, and that students who do not speak English well are not ready to tackle writing. It is also important to note here that for both Latino- and Chinese-background students, the development of writing ability may depend on the development of productive—oral or written—skills as opposed to receptive skills. Again, the importance of writing as the proactive branch of literacy comes to the fore.

Perhaps the most important contribution of Valdés and Wong's work is that they began the big and significant task of illustrating and analyzing levels and stages of writing development among Latino- and Chinese-background students. Such research is rare and time consuming, but it is necessary if we are to give teachers a much-needed sense of what is possible for non-English-background students, for how quickly some such students can be expected to develop, and what their writing can be expected to look like and when. Valdes and Wong's work can also help mainstream teachers to be more comfortable with the writing that non-English-background students produce, being assured that non native-like syntax does not mean that students cannot benefit from instruction in mainstream classes, and that such students who still make mechanical errors in their writing can nonetheless exhibit and acquire sophistication in other areas of writing. In short, Valdés and Wong's work goes some distance in helping teachers to be more hopeful in their dealings with ESL students and more helpful in assisting those students with the considerable challenge of getting an education in English.

CHANGING WORK, CHANGING LITERACY? HIGH PERFORMANCE WORKPLACES AND SKILL REQUIREMENTS

Most of the Center's projects have naturally taken place within the context of schools (and other educational institutions or organizations). But recent global economic developments and widespread national concerns about the future of work and the transition from school to work made it critical to study literacy and writing requirements and practices outside school as well. Flower's work with community organizations is an important step in this direction, as is Schriver's research on assessing drug-education literature. Hull, however, has focused squarely on the workplace.

During the past 10 years the way we think about work has changed and changed radically. Gone are the days, it is said, when North Americans (as well as citizens in virtually all industrialized countries) were expected to check their heads at the factory door and settle in for 8 hours of repetitive, routine, perhaps physically demanding or even debilitating but certainly mind-numbing labor. The claim is that, in order to be nationally and globally competitive, North American industries must adopt new technologies and new forms of work organization often labeled "high performance." Although definitions of what constitutes a "high performance" workplace do vary, these freshly organized workplaces are usually said to push responsibility and authority to lower levels of the organization, to reduce or even eliminate middle management in order to increase the flow of information, and to create cross-functional teams that can respond more rapidly to customers and that can suggest ways to improve work processes continuously. A recent article titled, "The New World of Work" in *Business Week* captures something of the public perception of the extent and severity of the change: "Mobility. Empowerment. Teams. Cross-training. Virtual offices. Telecommuting. Reeingineering. Restructuring. Delayering. Outsourcing. Contingency. If the buzzwords do not sound familiar, they should: They are changing your life. The last decade, perhaps more than any other time since the advent of mass production, has witnessed a profound redefinition of the way we work" (Hammonds, Kelly, & Thurston, p. 76).

The question becomes, what do people need to know and to be able to do in order to function well in the new world of work—both those adult workers who now hold entry-level industrial and service sector jobs, and the young people who will hopefully move into these jobs in the future? More particularly, what is the role of written literacy in these factories of tomorrow? Hull's project is showing specifically how writing and reading are used in changing workplaces and how the

knowledge and skill of workers, especially immigrants and minorities, might be drawn upon more effectively to help workplaces reach constantly sought, higher levels of productivity. But this project is also shedding light on the nature of high performance work organizations, illustrating the difficulties that companies experience as they attempt cultural and structural change and the ways in which old practices and modes of organization die hard. Most significantly, Hull and her colleagues (Hull, Jury, Ziv, & Katz, 1996; Hull, in press; Gee, Hull & Lankshear, in press) suggest that literacy practices might be a good measure of high performance work systems. That is, an audit of writing and reading requirements, responsibilities, and rights and their distribution across a workforce can provide an important indication of the extent to which a company offers workers the chance to participate in decision-making and the authority to do so.

To illustrate these themes from Hull is project, let us turn to an evening during the second shift at an electronics factory in the Silicon Valley of Northern California. This circuit board assembly plant is a Fortune 500 company with annual revenues in excess of $1 billion. It represents "high end" manufacturing, focusing on high quality and the full range of services—design, assembly, quality checks, testing, and packaging of circuit boards for diverse products, from helicopters to elevators to computers. The plant has also adopted practices associated with "high performance," such as self-directed work teams and decentralized decision making and continuous improvement and the use of flexible technologies. According to the plant manager, in order to become a high performance workplace, "First you have to create a culture, where people believe that they can make decisions without being put in a penalty box." As will become apparent, however, this factory is closer to traditional rather than high performance work organizations, despite the fact that it has tried to adopt certain high performance practices.

Ernie, a lead assembler in the hardware and wave solder department, is an immigrant from the Philippines with an interest in new management ideas such as quality circles and self-directed work teams. On this evening Ernie is facing a problem that is not uncommon among contract manufacturers in the circuit board industry. His department has received some old circuit boards from a customer, and the workers are supposed to update those boards by soldering some components onto them. Ernie's job is to figure out, by reading all the documents and examining the sample board and checking the kit, exactly what is to be done to the old boards, with what parts, in what order. Significantly, he is the only frontline worker in his group who is required to read the MPI (manufacturing process instructions), which makes him a literacy broker of sorts. After he has deciphered the problem, he will, as the lead worker, explain it to the rest.

To carry out this task, Ernie has, as he soon realizes, some inadequate written instructions, an outdated drawing (the numbers on the drawing have changed, and so have the shapes), and a bill of materials. As is his usual procedure, Ernie compares the written texts with the components in the kit, poring over a variety of forms of representation for a while, and it is then that he realizes that they do not match:

that is, the components do not look like what the drawing says they should look like, and in fact, attaching them to the board presents some technical problems. At this point Ernie tries to flag down the engineer, who is on his way out of the door, to ask him about the discrepancy. But the engineer gives Ernie short shrift, simply telling him to "lap solder" a wire, a solution that Ernie believes would not provide the most reliable connection. Next Ernie goes to another part of the factory where parts for old boards are stored to see if the customer had provided a sample board to go by. And sure enough, there is a sample board, but it is plugged into a system, and Ernie is told that he will need to get permission from the person who oversees that area to take the board. That person is unavailable. Thus, Ernie looks at the sample board without taking it out of the system that it is connected to, and he constructs his own drawing of it, and he writes his own parts list as best as he can.

He then goes to his supervisor's office, a woman named Margie, spreads out all the drawings and components, kneels down beside her, and they both hold the board that needs to be modified and talk their way through the problem. They were very concerned with how to get that component soldered on properly, and they go back and forth about whether it would be all right to tilt it so as not to have to attach such a long lead line; they both disagree with the engineer's solution of a lap solder. The supervisor keeps pressing Ernie toward a particular solution to the problem, but he persistently doubts that it will work—partly because he is unsure of the drawing he had made so quickly, and partly because he feels that he does not have the written authority through MPI to proceed. Finally, after manipulating the component, situating it this way and that on the board for about six pages of transcript, the supervisor asks to see the official documentation, realizes how inadequate it is, and joins Ernie in complaining about the engineer who should have updated the drawing and provided sufficient instructions and thereby given them the authority to do their work, but did not.

Margie finally decides that Ernie should go ahead and put the components on; they will curve the lead to get more length out of it, but as Ernie argued, they will not tilt the component. But just to be sure, because they do not have written authorization—a deviation approval to alter the board in this way—they will contact the program administrator, Ron, whose name the supervisor notices on one of the documents. This administrator is assumed not to know anything about production, but to have the authority needed to deviate from the MPI. "I hope my eyes serves me right when I look at this part," Ernie says a little nervously as they wait for the program administrator to appear.

The program administrator arrives with an enormous red three-ring binder in his arms; it contains every single document about this project, its history, all the communications with the customer, the MPIs, the material transfers, the deviations, and so forth. With Margie's permission Ernie explains the problem, and then Ron flips through his big notebook to see, in his words, "If I have anything in writing on this." Ron cannot find permission from the customer to change the board in the ways Ernie has outlined, but he says he may have seen such a letter on someone's desk, and that therefore they

should go ahead with the work. Ernie asks if he can look one more time at the sample board that is now in a locked department, and Ron agrees. Everyone walks to the department where old parts are stored, the security guard opens the door, and Ernie looks at the board and says immediately, "I did the right drawings." He makes a new sample board, using the new parts and based on the earlier discussion, his drawings, and the customer's sample board. He then proceeds to instruct the other workers as to how they should alter the board. Almost an hour has elapsed since Ernie first identified the problem.

This "work event" and millions similar to it—where the smooth flow of production is interrupted and an employee joins collaboratively with others to use texts and talk and problem solving to set it in motion again—are played out in factories across the United States everyday. Literacy plays a big role in the event narrated above, as it does in the work life of most high performance companies. A great deal of this literacy comes about as a result of international certification standards, which require that every single procedure for every action in an entire factory, as well as every deviation from those instructions, and deviations from the deviations of the instructions, and so on, be documented—be written down, distributed, and referred to as necessary. Other literacy requirements arise because of the nature of the work in new industries. In contract manufacturing, for example, a company survives by making products for its customers quickly, accurately, and cheaply, and by doing so again and again, over time, as was the case with the old boards that Ernie had to alter. These relationships require a thick paper trail—witness the three-ring binder in the previous example—and adherence to a literacy-driven notion of "traceability." In many factories the ante for literacy is also raised when workers are required to take in-house courses on how to participate in self-directed work teams or are asked to enroll in specialized study to upgrade their skills, as in "pay-for-knowledge" systems.

The texts that saturate new workplaces are accompanied by rules of use, rules that are often complex, that grow out of social relations in particular companies and the history of industries, and that participants must decipher and master if they are to be considered fully literate at work. Much previous research on workplace literacy has consisted of readability analyses of work-related texts done in an effort to determine the grade level needed to comprehend them. Hull's research has begun to suggest how much more we need to understand about how texts are used in factories and other workplaces and about the rules and strategies that govern who constructs, reads, and uses these texts and how and for what purpose. In the above example, Ernie was quite aware of how tightly authority was wedded to MPI where his own work activities were concerned, and both he and his supervisor knew better than to ignore these instructions, even when they recognized them to be incomplete and inaccurate. Rules of use for literate activity will differ from workplace to workplace and from industry to industry, but the existence of the rules will not, especially as literacy demands grow in frequency and complexity and as workplaces change. This project suggests that one challenge for teachers of writing and English is to find ways to teach prospective workers how to size up a given work environment's literacy practices.

An analysis of the literate practices and the rules that govern the use of texts in a given workplace also provides a window on the extent to which a factory has achieved the "high performance" ideal of shared decision making and worker empowerment. It is clear from Hull's project and other research that the majority of workers want a voice in their companies' operations, and it is also clear that most workers experience a big gap between their desire to participate and the reality of opportunities to do so. Ernie, for example, talked again and again to the researchers about his interest in participating in team meetings, a high performance practice that his company reserved for managers, engineers, and supervisors. Ironically, many of these upper-end employees also complained about not being heard, albeit in a different way. One engineer said, "The five white guys [in top management] want to 'empower' us, but they don't want to give us full control." Significantly, not being heard in team meetings was paralleled by constraints on literacy. As a lead in his work area, Ernie was expected to read manufacturing process instructions and explain them verbally to the others in his group, who were not expected to read (because they were assumed, on the basis of their immigrant and ethnic status, not to be able to). His reading served certain functions, most often identification, verification, and receiving instructions. But he was not authorized to alter existing texts, even if outdated or otherwise erroneous, or to create texts which instruct others, even when he had the knowledge to do so and his superiors had dropped the ball. The texts that Ernie did create were unofficial ones, texts that he wrote on scraps of paper pulled from his pocket nervously, texts that were not sanctioned by the company and that had no authority.

Hull's research suggests that as more and more companies recognize the good sense of moving toward "high performance" work organizations, it would also make good sense for these companies to examine and reconceive the literate practices that weave throughout the work that gets done. Is literacy set up to control? Are writing and reading practices strictly meted out, with certain workers having the authority to produce texts of particular sorts, and others having the responsibility to read them, and still others denied the right and responsibility of either? Then you probably have a traditionally organized workplace. Are writing and reading responsibilities—but especially writing—distributed across the workforce, with line workers able to participate in the writing and revision as well as the reading of manufacturing process instructions? Do they have access to the big red binders which hold the history of products? Do they have access to whatever training they need to make participation a right and reality? Then you are probably moving more in the direction of the high performance ideal.

WRITING ASSESSMENT

Where do students stand in relation to their individual growth, to their peers in the United States, and to children in other countries? This is a question that is increasingly on the minds of parents, teachers, policy makers, and the public at large; writing assessment plays an essential role in answering it. Writing assessment also helps give us clues about whether our instructional practices are working. As a field, writing assessment is necessarily diverse as it aims to set national educational policy or to help a single child in one classroom, as it is used for placement, diagnosis, or grading. It may involve objective tests, holistically evaluated essays, personal journals, or all of these. It may be limited to a single 20-minute writing sample or it may encompass a whole year's work. Because of the diversity of the field and the urgency of the questions, the Center has taken a strategic approach to the study of assessment by concentrating on just three central topics. The first is the highly visible but poorly defined topic of portfolio assessment, which is being widely promoted in schools across the country. The second topic concerns the validity of holistically scored writing samples; such samples are widely used for assessment, but their validity is rarely questioned. The third topic concerns the impact of often hidden cultural differences between readers and writers that influence how we routinely assess the writing we read.

Portfolio Assessment

Although portfolio assessment enjoys great popularity among educators nationwide, there is little agreement about its goals or the methods by which it should be carried out. To find out what people mean when they say that they are "doing portfolios," Center researcher Robert Calfee surveyed 150 sources, including states, school districts, schools, and individual teachers. The survey focused on four questions: How did you get into portfolios? What does the concept mean in practice? How do you do it? and What do you see as the effect of portfolios for your students and for you? In addition, Calfee and his team conducted a 2-day working conference with 24 respondents to obtain information in more depth (Calfee & Perfumo, in press).

Calfee learned first that teachers involved in the portfolio movement feel a strong sense of commitment and personal renewal. Teachers feel ownership of this "bottom-up" movement and report that the movement has provided them with the opportunity to rethink the meaning of their work and their relation with their students. This kind of rethinking enables them to act in ways that affirm their status as professionals.

Although Calfee's respondents claimed that an important purpose of portfolios was to assess students' progress, they did not provide a clear account of how progress was to be measured. In fact, across the varied classrooms the portfolio concept amounts to a virtual anarchy in which "anything goes" in deciding what to include in a portfolio and how to evaluate it. At the classroom level, then, the reliability of the assessment was simply not discussed.

Teachers also showed a definite aversion to evaluation and to the assigning of grades. Teachers were willing to judge individual compositions but were uncomfortable about assessing an entire portfolio. The following comment was typical: "I wish grades would just go away."

Calfee's research demonstrates how important the portfolio assessment movement has been for the personal and professional development of many teachers. It has stimulated a great deal of reflection on fundamental issues of teaching and has afforded teachers a satisfying way to express their professionalism. Calfee further shows that for some teachers portfolios may be most important as a teaching tool—a focus for student–teacher discussions of writing. But it is not as yet clear what role the portfolio movement will play in assessment. The teachers in Calfee's study who "do portfolios" do not seem inclined to use them for grading nor is their attention focused on measurement issues.

Holistic Scoring of Writing Samples

Holistically scored writing samples are widely used to assess students' writing skills and to predict later writing performance. For example, a single holistically scored essay may be used to decide whether a student should be placed in one writing course or another, the underlying assumption being that a student's performance on one holistically graded essay is a useful predictor of how that student will do on later essays such as those that the student writes in school. Further, in some forms of portfolio assessment, it has been proposed that holistically graded essays be used to track students' development over the course of a semester or a school year. The underlying assumption here is that students' performance on such tasks is stable enough that developmental changes would be evident. Given the importance of these applications, it is surprising that the reliability of holistically graded essays for serving these purposes has not been clearly established. Although considerable attention has been paid to rater reliability, that is, the extent to which two raters can agree in evaluating the same essay, very little has been devoted to validity, or the extent to which the student's performance on one essay is related to that student's performance on another. If the validity of holistically scored essays is low, then great caution should be exercised in using them for placement or the assessment of student writing development.

To explore this important issue, the Center sponsored a study designed by J. R. Hayes (Hayes, Hatch, & Silk, 1996) to obtain estimates of the validity of holistically scored writing samples. The data for this study are derived from about 1000 essays, written by 250 students in 13 writing classes at two universities. The essays were selected by the classroom teacher as representing the most important assignments in the course.

In this study, the objective was to answer the question, "To what extent is student writing performance consistent across successive essays?" The basic measure in this study was the correlation between a judge's rating of students' performance on one essay and that same judge's rating of the same students' performance on another essay. If the students who performed well on one essay also performed well on the second, then these correlations, which are measures of validity, would tend to be high.

Averaged over all classes and all judges, the correlation between students' performance on one essay and their performance on another was 16, which is extremely low. Such low correlations suggest that placement tests based on single holistically scored essays are hazardous. Further, they suggest that holistically scored essays are not likely to be effective if used to track students' development over the course of a semester or a year. These results call into question the widespread reliance that the writing community has placed on holistically scored essays and suggests that we need to look for measures of writing skill that have greater validity.

In response to these findings, Hayes and his colleagues are now assessing the validity of a variety of measures of writing skill which could provide teachers with reliable information that they could use to shape instruction for individual student's needs.

Cultural Differences between Readers and Writers

Understanding the nature of cultural differences is an important first step in developing methods for helping writers—both in school and in the workplace—to avoid communications that misfire from the audience's perspective. Research at the Center is helping writers respond to readers' needs in positive ways that reflect their understanding of their audience's culture and values.

In one project Schriver (in press) explored how 11- to 21-year-old students, drawn both from inner-city and suburban schools, responded to drug education literature. This literature was representative of over 100 brochures, hand-outs, and fact sheets that the researchers collected from national and local drug prevention agencies. The writers who design the literature, employed both by government and private agencies, differ from their audiences in age and point of view and, often, in race and social class as well. These differences were frequently evident in the students' responses to the brochures.

Although the students who evaluated the brochure represented the age range for which this literature was designed, many students felt "talked down to." Both the language and graphics suggested to the students that the materials were meant for a much younger audience. One junior high school student felt that the pictures made the brochure seem "...too kiddy [meaning childish] ... it is something you would give to sixth graders." A 9th-grade student complained, "If I saw this on a rack, I wouldn't read it. If I looked at the picture I'd think it was for 8 year olds and I wouldn't read it." Another felt that "the author thinks the reader is naive and isn't smart enough to make her own decisions."

Some students found the brochures racially offensive. For example, one student questioned the significance of a line drawing of a black youth in one of the brochures, "Why is a black man on the inside? Why are black people in all these brochures? I resent this crap!"

Many comments reflected the social distance that the students perceived between themselves and the authors of the brochures. One student remarked, "Well, it seems it's just the facts, and it's goody-goody. You know, 'Don't do this, don't do that'." Another said she thought the author was "The establishment. You know, the system." Others described the author of the brochures as "a person who is definitely NOT street smart." In fact, one person said, "Oh he's so-o-o-o street smart" to which another student shouted "NOT!" Still another characterized the author as "Someone who would never come to my neighborhood." Schriver's study shows that even when writers have the best intentions, cultural differences can still have an important impact on readers when communication crosses cultural lines.

A second Center project focused on another instance in which readers misinterpreted writers' intentions, but in this case the salient difference was age. Schriver and her colleagues found significant differences in the way college applicants and faculty and admissions counselors judged the applicants' essays. In particular, essays that the students judged to be creative, intelligent, and mature were often perceived by university staff as pretentious, pedestrian, or naive. Such negative judgments significantly reduced the probability that counselors would recommend that the student be admitted.

Presumably, cultural differences of the sort that influence the assessment of college applications as well as drug education literature can also influence the assessment of applications for employment or for bank loans as well as the evaluation of student writing in school. Such research can do more than describe the negative effects of cultural difference; it can also point to ways of enhancing communication across varied types of cultural boundaries.

CONCLUSION

Center research has shown, not that writing per se is the solution to all our educational difficulties—there is no magic—but rather that writing education and writing-centered activities—from teacher research to partnerships in the schools, the workplace, and the community—can deliver something unique. Writing-based literacy develops social and intellectual capacities in learners and promotes powerful literate practices and skills that can unlock the door to higher levels of performance and success. Ultimately, writing-based literacy is a major factor in solving some of the most pressing problems in education and in our society at large.

We know that research priorities often change as public interests shift. But if there is anything we have learned from our intense and long-term studies at the Center over the past 10 years, it is the centrality of writing and literacy for an individual's success in school and the workplace and its importance to the effective functioning of the larger community. In the future we will need to identify and continue to learn more about the key sites in schools, workplaces, and communities where writing matters most.

References

Calfee, R. C., & Perfumo, P. (Eds.). (in press). *Writing portfolios: Promise and peril.* Mahwah, NJ: Erlbaum.

Daniels, T., & Daniels, K. (1994). The value of teacher research: Lerning about ourselves and our students. *Best Practice 6.* Evanston, IL: National Louis University and North Central Regional Educational Laboratory.

Downey, M. T. (1996 January). *Writing to learn history in the intermediate grades* (Final Report). Berkeley, CA: University of California, National Center for the Study of Writing and Literacy.

Dyson, A. H. (1993). *Social worlds of children learning to write in an urban primary school.* New York: Teachers College Press.

Dyson, A. H., & Freedman, S. W. (1991). Critical challenges for research in writing: 1990–1995 (Tech. Rep. 1B). Berkeley, CA: Center for the Study of Writing.

Dyson, A. H. (with A. Bennet et al.). (in press). *What difference does difference make? Teacher reflections on literacy, diversity, and the urban primary school.* Urbana, IL: National Council of Teachers of English.

Flower, L. (1994). *The construction of negotiated meaning: A social cognitive theory of writing.* Carbondale, IL: Southern Illinois Univerity Press.

Flower, L., Stein, V., Ackerman, J. Kantz, M. J., McCormick, K., & Peck, W. C. (1990). *Reading-to-write: Exploring a cognitive and social process.* New York: Oxford University Press.

Flower, L., Wallace, D., Norris, L., & Burnett, R. (1994). *Making thinking visible: Writing, collaborative planning and calssroom inquiry.* Urbana, IL: National Council of Teachers of English.

Freedman, S. W. (1994a). *Exchanging writing, exchanging cultures: Leassons in school reform from the United States and Great Britain.* Cambridge, MA and Urbana, IL: Harvard University Press and National Council of Teachers of English.

Freedman, S. W. (with Simons, E. R. & Roy, C., and with New Orleans teachers Alford, K., Galley, R., Herring, S., Smith, D. W., Valenti, E. & Ward, P.). (1994b). Teacher researchers together: Delving into the teacher research process. *The Quarterly, 16*(4), 8–17.

Freedman, S. W. (1996). Moving writing research into the 21st century. In L. Bloom, D. Daiker, & E. White, (Eds.). *Composition in the 21st Century: Crisis and Change* (pp. 183–193). Carbondale, IL: Southern Illinois University Press.

Freedman, S. W., Simons, E. R., & Kalnin, J. (in preparation). *Multiculturalism is the mainstream: Teacher researchers build multiethnic literacy communities in urban classrooms.*

Freedman, S. W. (1996). Crossing the bridge to practice: Rethinking the theories of Vygotsky and Bakhtin. *Written Communication, 12*(1), 74–92.

Gee, J., Hull, G., & Lankshear, C. (in press). *The new work order: Education and literacy in the new capitalism.* Sydney, Australia: Allen & Unwin.

Hammonds, K., Kelly, K., & Thurston, K. (1994, October 17). The New World of Work, *Business Week,* pp. 76–87.

Hayes, J. R., Hatch, J. A., & Silk, C. M. (1996 May). *Experimental approaches to evaluating writing (Final Report). Study 1. In search of writing ability: Exploring consistency of student performance on holistically scored writing tasks.* Berkeley, CA: University of California, National Center for the Study of Writing and Literacy.

Higgins, L. (1992, May). *Argument as construction: A framework and method.* Unpublished doctoral dissertation, Carnegie Mellon University, Pittsburgh, PA.

Higgins, L., Flower, L., & Petraglia, J. (1992). Planning text together: The role of critical reflection in student collaboration. *Written Communication, 9*(1), 48–84.

Hull, G. (Ed.). (in press). *Changing work, changing workers: Critical perspectives on language, literacy, and skill.* Albany, NY: State University of New York Press.

Hull, G., Jury, M., Ziv, O., & Katz, M. (1996, February). *Changing work, changing literacy? A study of skill requirements and development in a traditional and restructured workplace* (Final Report). Berkeley, CA: University of California, National Center for the Study of Writing and Literacy.

McKay, S., & Wong, S. (1996). Multiple discourses, multiplie identities: Investment and agency in second language learning among Chinese adolescent immigrant students. *Harvard Educational Review,* 66(3), 577–608.

Schecter, S., & Parkhurst, S. (1993). Ideological divergences in a teacher research group. *American Educational Research Journal, 30*(4), 771–798.

Schriver, K. A. (in press). *Dynamics in document design: Creating texts for readers.* New York: John Wiley & Sons.

Valdés, G. (1993, December). *The writing of non-English background students (Final Report). Introduction and Part 1: The study of the Latino-background students.* Berkeley, CA: University of California, National Center for the Study of Writing and Literacy.

Valdés, G., & Sanders, P. (in press). Latino ESL students and the development of writing abilities: A guide for teachers of composition. In C. Cooper & L. Odell (Eds.), *Eliminating error.* Urbana, IL: National Council of Teachers of English.

Wong, S., & Zou, J. (1993, December). *The writing of non-English background students (Final Report). Part 2: The study of the Chinese-background students.* Berkeley, CA: University of California, National Center for the Study of Writing and Literacy.

·58C·

CLASSROOM CONTEXTS PROMOTING LITERACY ENGAGEMENT

John T. Guthrie
UNIVERSITY OF MARYLAND

Ann McCann
ELEMENTARY SCHOOL TEACHER

Cyndie Hynd and Steve Stahl
UNIVERSITY OF GEORGIA

BACKGROUND

This chapter is based on investigations at the National Reading Research Center (NRRC) that are related to the growth of literacy engagement in elementary school children. At the NRRC, our overarching goal is to study how to cultivate self-determining readers who are the architects of their own learning. Our research is unified by an *engagement perspective* which suggests that productive learners are: motivated, strategic, knowledgeable, and collaborative. Engaged students participate in literacy activities to gain knowledge, perform tasks, and enjoy literary experiences. Motivated by a variety of purposes, they use higher-order strategies such as searching, summarizing, and connecting ideas across genres. Engaged readers are knowledgeable, using what they already know to gain new understandings through text, and they collaborate by socially constructing meanings with peers. Within the NRRC, there are five divisions of research, one of which is related to literacy in conceptual areas such as science and social studies. Within this division we are examining the question: What classroom contexts are associated with growth of literacy engagement in integrated learning situations? To address this question, we are designing and implementing classroom contexts that are intended to promote literacy engagement.

LITERACY ENGAGEMENT IS AN AIM OF INSTRUCTION

Helping students become lifelong readers is a goal shared by most literacy educators. When students learn to enjoy a variety of genres, teachers feel a genuine sense of accomplishment. However, too few students develop into interested, involved readers. Diary studies, surveys, and the 1992 National Assessment of Educational Progress, document that a shocking number of students are alliterate, choosing not to read despite their cognitive ability. For example, 25% of grade 4 and 50% of grade 8 students report reading once a month or less for their own interest. This lack of voluntary reading is problematic, considering that wide reading is associated with recreational enjoyment, reading achievement and general knowledge (Stanovich & Cunningham, 1993), as well as community participation and workplace productivity (Guthrie, Schafer, & Hutchinson, 1991). People extend their minds, their sense of self and their social experience through reading widely and frequently.

Although comprehension has been the primary goal of elementary reading instruction in the past (Pearson & Fielding, 1991), this goal is insufficient. We should not assume that students who can comprehend texts will choose to do so. Developing students' basic skills does not assure that they will

The work reported is a National Reading Research Center project of the University of Maryland and the University of Georgia. It was supported under the Educational Research and Development Centers Program (PR/AWARD No. 117A20007) as administered by the Office of Educational Research and Improvement, U.S. Department of Education. The findings and opinions expressed in this report do not reflect the position or policies of the National Reading Research Center, The Office of Education Research and Improvement, or the U.S. Department of Education.

753

be inclined select books, read at appropriate times, persist through difficult material, and gain satisfaction from reading. Comprehension must be supplemented by motivation for reading as an objective of instruction. The construct of engagement enables us to join the motivational with the strategic and conceptual aspects of literacy.

To address the development of reading, we emphasize the importance of *literacy engagement*. An engaged reader chooses to read frequently for a variety of reasons, and comprehends the texts appropriately within their context. Comprehending a book entails the deliberate use of prior knowledge and meaning-making strategies (Dole, Duffy, Roehler, & Pearson, 1991), but intrinsic motivation is needed to develop these higher-order strategies and extend them to critical evaluation and the synthesis of diverse sources of information. Intrinsic motivation empowers students to become self-regulating readers who direct their own knowledge acquisition and personal development (Deci, Vallerand, Pelletier, & Ryan, 1991). In brief, engaged readers and writers are strategic, motivated and knowledgeable about the content of their literacy activities.

Strategies for Reading

We believe that a few, broad strategies are useful in higher-order literacy. First, the ability to search for books, resources, and information within texts, is increasingly important to students (Armbruster & Armstrong, 1993) as well as adults (Dreher, 1993). Second, strategies for comprehending texts, including inferring, summarizing, and self-monitoring are indispensable (Dole et al., 1991). Third, students need to be able to synthesize ideas from multiple texts that contain illustrations and documents (Mayer, 1993). Fourth, higher-order problem-solving processes such as clarifying ideas, using analogies, shifting frames of reference, establishing criteria for judging ideas in text, analyzing text structure, and identifying themes in literature are valuable (Collins-Block, 1992). Fifth, strategies for composing should be targeted in instruction, particularly when students are "reading to write" (Flower et al., 1990). Planning, note-taking, organizing, illustrating, integrating, composing and evaluating woven into a network surround student self-expression related to learning from text.

Motivations for Strategic Reading

In our perspective, motivations are internalized goals that lead to reading behavior and strategies (Pintrich & Schrauben, 1992). In this goal-oriented view, motivations are "reasons for reading." One basic distinction drawn in the literature on motivation is between the intrinsic and the extrinsic motivation. Intrinsic motivation refers to the performance of activities for their own sake. Pleasure is inherent in the activity itself (Gottfried, 1985). Extrinsic motivation refers to reasons that originate from outside the learner, such as rewards and recognition.

The richness of motivation for reading is being explored by Wigfield (1994) with a combination of methods including open-ended interviews with students, and factor analysis of self-report data on student questionnaires. He reported clear distinctions among several intrinsic motivations including: (1) curiosity, (2) aesthetic involvement, (3) social interaction, (4) challenge, and (5) self-efficacy, and several more extrinsic motivations such as: (6) recognition, (7) grades, (8) competition, (9) compliance, and (10) work avoidance (Wigfield, 1994). Studies show that intrinsic motivations generally tend to decrease during elementary school (Harter, Whitesell, & Kowalski, 1992), although intrinsic motivations increase strategy learning (Corno & Kanfer, 1993), and accelerate students' amount and breadth of reading (Guthrie, Van Meter, Dacey, & Wigfield, 1994).

Conceptual Learning from Text

Although the motivational literature has established a link between intrinsic motivations and the use of higher-order cognitive strategies, the use of a strategy is not usually the endpoint of a literacy activity. Most frequently, school-based literacy is a vehicle for gaining knowledge, which consists of a richly interconnected set of concepts and relations among concepts. Consistent with previous research, we view concepts as rule-based mental representations (Holland, Holyoak, Nisbett, & Thagard, 1986). For young children and adults (Neisser, 1987), concepts expand through the acquisition and differentiation of particular features and the elaboration of relations among the features. Concepts are not usually formed from a single exposure to information, nor are they memorized, like facts. Concepts need to be constructed; that is, people need to create a personal understanding of a concept. Spiro, Coulson, Feltovic, and Anderson (1994) suggest that people form concepts by viewing the same topic from different angles to get a full understanding. Learners construct more elaborate concepts by assimilating or accommodating new information into already existing knowledge structures. When new information fits well with existing knowledge, learners add the new piece of information to the schema. When new information contradicts existing schema, then some sort of reorganization takes place. Therefore, the construction of richly elaborated concepts requires active thinking about new information and how it fits with what one already knows.

To foster higher-order thinking during reading, use of multiple texts may be critical. Wineburg (1991a, 1991b) and Perfetti, Britt, Rouet, Mason, and Georgi (1993) assert that the use of multiple sources offering different perspectives on the same topic can foster the development of more elaborate concepts in all students. Stahl, Hynd, McNish, and Bosquet (in progress), note that high school students who read multiple documents about an incident in history go through a process of integration that is not possible for students who read one text. Because intrinsic motivation is necessary for the formation of richly elaborated, coherent concepts (Pintrich, Marx, & Boyle, 1993), education should support conceptual learning from multiple texts by undergirding students' intrinsic motivations for reading (Head, & Sutton, 1985).

RATIONALE FOR INTEGRATED INSTRUCTION

Many teachers embrace the integration of reading instruction. According to 1992 NAEP data, 97% of a national sample of grade 4 teachers reported that they placed at least a moderate emphasis on integrating reading and writing (Mullis, Campbell, & Farstrup, 1993). In states with standards-oriented reform programs, such as California, Connecticut, Kentucky, and Maryland, instructional integrations were especially prominent. An NRRC study of the systemic reform program of Maryland, which highlights higher-order reading, showed that district-level policies emphasized new goals for incorporating "real-world" reading (trade books rather than text books) and integrations into the curriculum. The largest single policy impact of the Maryland School Performance Assessment program has been to integrate the curriculum (Guthrie, Schafer, Afflerbach, & Almasi, 1994).

Integrations of reading instruction, however, are not always successful. The 1992 NAEP data showed that integrating reading and writing did not show positive effects on achievement (Mullis et al., 1993). Furthermore, researchers rarely investigate other types of integration, such as the integration of language arts and content subjects, although depictions of instructional practices are beginning to be available (Calfee, 1994; Lapp & Flood, 1994; Stevenson & Carr, 1993). Although Meece, Blumenfeld, and Hoyle (1988) are optimistic that project-based teaching in science can help students "think like a scientist," and Brown (1992) found that conceptual knowledge of science was accelerated in integrated instruction, these findings have not addressed reading and language arts.

A few integrated instructional approaches in reading and language arts are designed to foster selected cognitive or social processes besides basic reading comprehension. For example, some programs emphasize the metacognitive strategies involved in problem solving, integrating, and decision making (Collins-Block, 1992). Other programs focus on the social collaboration in peer-led literature discussion groups (Almasi & Gambrell, 1994). Self-expression through the arts and drama and also writing is underscored in many literature-based programs (Lapp & Flood, 1994); critical thinking is highlighted in inquiry-oriented approaches (Brown, 1992; Calfee, 1994); whereas conceptual knowledge learning is foregrounded in secondary school content area literacy (Hynd, McNish, Qian, Keith, & Lay, 1994). Although these approaches are innovative, they are not as fully comprehensive as we believe they could be. We need to find frameworks that include these themes in order to support the development of all of the diverse aspects of literacy engagement.

The instructional framework that we are evolving is consistent with reviews of the motivational literature (Ames, 1992; Ford, 1992; Maehr & Fyans, 1989). Our framework portrays engaging classroom contexts as: (1) *observational,* encouraging students to initiate learning with "real-world" problems and observations (Lepper, 1988; Newby, 1991); (2) *conceptual,* with a focus on substantive topics rather than rewards or skills (Maehr & Fyans, 1989); (3) *self-directed,* supporting student autonomy and choice of topics, books and peers (Skinner & Belmont, 1993); (4) *metacognitive,* with explicit teaching of reading strategies, problem solving and composing (Collins-Block, 1992); (5) *collaborative,* emphasizing social construction of meaning in communities of readers and learners (Almasi & Gambrell, 1994); (6) *expressive,* creating opportunities for self-expression thorough writing, debating and group work (Oldfather & Dahl, 1994); and (7) *coherent,* containing connections between classroom activities and tasks across the day, week and month (Gamoran & Nystrand, 1992). Our theoretical expectation is that the salience of each of the following classroom qualities will influence the development of literacy engagement.

Inquiries into Integrated Instruction—Elementary

A collaborative team of teachers, reading specialists and University-based researchers at the National Reading Research Center is studying a comprehensive form of instruction that we describe as Concept-Oriented Reading Instruction. At present, three schools near College Park, Maryland, are setting up this instructional approach in year-long programs, and we are charting remarkable growth in children's literacy engagement. To capture the aspects of the classroom context that nurture this enhanced literacy engagement, we videotaped one grade 3 and one grade 5 classroom during the Fall of 1993, obtaining multiple samples of the classroom interactions that were representative of the instructional program. Teachers identified lessons or days that they expected to be characteristic of the program. Thirty-minute portions of classroom interaction were videotaped on eight different occasions for grade 3; 30 minutes of classroom interaction on eight different occasions were taped for both grades 3 and 5 separately. These tapes were analyzed holistically by the first author to identify recurring themes using an analytic inductive method (LeCompte, & Priessle, 1993), revealing seven dimensions. These results were triangulated with the participating teachers. At the end of the academic year, the teachers wrote retrospective accounts of their instruction excerpted here to illustrate each dimension. The findings will be described in concert with findings from inquires at the secondary level.

Inquiries into Integrated Instruction—Secondary

What does integrated education look like at the high school level? By the time students get to high school, curriculum has been departmentalized. Although integrations are more difficult to accomplish in these conditions, we observed integrations occurring naturally in our studies at the high school level. Our observations of integrations were made as part of a study of the effect of text in helping students learn counterintuitive ideas in science. In this study, students and teachers were videotaped and interviewed during instruction. Field note transcriptions and analysis of videotapes and interviews provided us with not only a view of student learning, but also a view of integrated curriculum.

At our target school, integrations occurred in two ways. In one, content teachers included instruction in areas like reading, writing, discussion, math, science, and history as part of their course curriculum. A physics teacher, for example, taught students to take advantage of the organized structure of the textbook in order to search for information in a research project. Students learned the value of peer discussion, because they are given time to discuss scientific ideas among themselves before they shared their ideas with the teacher and a wider range of students. Finally, they learned the history of science (e.g., the evolution of thinking from Aristotle, Galileo, Newton, and Einstein). Later, we describe portions of a unit where students integrate several subject areas into the learning of a physics topic.

In another type of integration, teachers followed what has become known as the "middle-school model." The particular application of the model we observed, teachers in English, science and social science shared the same students. Throughout the school year, teachers planned thematic units that integrated the three subjects. In English, students learned to engage in scientific writing such as is needed in lab reports and learned to report historical research, as well. They read literature that was tied to the theme and discussed the relation between their reading and the topics they were investigating in the other classes. They took field trips with all three teachers attending, so that they could help students observe phenomena from several perspectives. In order for this type of integration to be successful, a team of teachers must work well together and be committed to the extra planning and preparation time. The principal must also be committed to the concept of integration, as was the case in the school we studied. He was interested in developing many options for schooling in the same building—schools-within-schools—and increasing the number of integrations that occur.

Both kinds of integrations embody the characteristics of integrated instruction observed at the elementary school level. That is, the classroom contexts were: observational, conceptual, self-directive, metacognitive, collaborative, self-expressive, and coherent. We will organize our descriptions around these themes.

QUALITIES OF CLASSROOM CONTEXTS

Observational

Elementary School Level. Students receiving Concept-Oriented Reading Instruction began their literacy experience with observations of the "real world" around them. Observing the natural environment, such as trees, grass, and plants, or the social environment, including friends, politicians, or homeless people, was intrinsically motivating, and thought provoking. Students personalized their observations by noticing features that were intriguing and important to them. These personal interests formed the basis for questions and a point of departure for instructional units. Teachers returned to observational activities to enable students to integrate the knowledge gained through literacy and to rekindle their curiosities. One grade 5 teacher summarized the observational dimension of instruction by saying:

Instruction in reading/language arts and science began with first-hand experiences that raised awareness levels in students. From examining the components of a habitat firsthand, to observing crickets up close, to dissecting owl pellets, students developed a springboard that led to further questioning and interest. As interest developed through these experiences books available to the students became the tools necessary to complete the process.

In the Concept-Oriented Reading Instruction we studied, students explored objects and events in their world. After experiencing an initial fascination with tangible objects, students began to wonder and ask conceptual questions. Students brainstormed and explicitly stated the questions they wanted to explore with additional observations, data collecting, reading, writing and discussion. Observing the "real world" was a point of departure for extended literacy, and it provided a frame of reference that enabled students to select reading and writing activities and to self-monitor their pursuits.

Grade 3 classrooms studied the adaptation of animals to their environments beginning with a unit on birds. By observing bird nests, attempting to build their own bird nest, drawing feathers, recording behavior at feeding stations, simulating the gizzard in a classroom experiment, and visiting a display of stuffed birds, students gained knowledge and long-lived curiosity. Students kept journals of their observations and one student reported that:

We built our nest with leaves, grass sticks and twigs. Mud too. But first we looked for each of these things at the playground. Clay was to stick our nest together because if we didn't have clay our nest would break. We called the clay mud. I learned that it's hard to make a nest unless you really try to. I learned that birds have a hard time making nests but we read a book that helped us learn and I found out that if you try with a group it might be easy. And you might make a lot of friends.

Grade 5 teachers initiated the year with a unit on adaptation of plants and animals to the environment. One classroom explored insects beginning with crickets and another explored plants beginning with flowers. To observe insects and life cycles, students collected crickets from the back-yard of the school and collected data on the location in the school wildlife habitat area in which they were found, leading to classroom aggregations of individual data. Students brainstormed different ways to learn more about crickets including classroom observations and experiments, additional field observations, reading, and discussing. Students selected an area of interest to them about crickets: habitat or food preference, habits of movement, and interest groups chose a method of study and pursued the approach for approximately two weeks. Grade 5 science goals consisted of habitat, food webs, life cycles and breeding, feeding and shelter as aspects of adaptations.

Secondary School Level. Instruction in high school physics classes was grounded in students' observations of "real-world" tangible objects and events. Students used their observations to give their learning a personal direction. In a gravity unit, the students began with a laboratory investigation. Students brought eggs they had placed in "safe" cartons and dropped them out of the window to observe and time how they fell. Before they engaged in the drop, students were asked to speculate what weight and different shapes of containers would do to the fall and to write about that. One student, M. B., bragged that he was making his heavier "to make sure it will drop fast and break". (He had the nonscientific conception that gravity pulls objects of greater weight to the ground at greater speed) and put nails in the bottom of his carton, making it the heaviest in the class. When he actually dropped the egg, he was astounded that his carton did not fall any faster than others that were much lighter. "How did you make yours go so fast?!" he asked another student. Later on this observation gave him motivation to read about and discuss the problem with other students.

In the three-subject integration, students studied the Greeks in history and Aristotelian classification systems in science class. In English, they studied Greek literature. Because the city in which the school was located, near Athens, Georgia, had many examples of Greek architecture, students took a walk to observe examples of Greek culture. Each teacher accompanied these students and helped them pay attention to aspects of Greek architecture and other Greek influences (in education and art, for example). Students took notes on their observations and wrote a journal on the experience.

Conceptual

Elementary School Level. The leading edge of the typical integrated instructional unit in Concept-Oriented Reading Instruction was conceptual. As ways of representing and understanding the world, concepts can be learned through a variety of observations, literacy activities, discussions, and contemplation. Teachers continually reintroduced higher-order conceptual orientations such as the adaptation of plants to the environment, or the relationships of structure, form, and function in the life of a bird or animal. Growth of conceptual understanding was the recurring purpose for many classroom activities, serving as the basis for explaining the observations about an object, and providing a motivation for the students to exercise critical judgment during reading, writing, and discussion. One grade 3 teacher noted that:

> "The lines between each 'subject' became so blurred that it would have sometimes been difficult to discern what to call it." "We might be reading content books about birds and writing to extend thoughts and concepts. Our daily schedule was far less tied to the clock than before. Reading time blended into science, and language occurred at all times. Planning became less concerned with preparation of specific lessons and discreet skills and more concerned with the ideas we were seeking today, this week, and this month."

For example, grade 3 students in Concept-Oriented Reading Instruction focused on learning about birds and their environments. Student questions were placed on the classroom walls, forming the cornerstone of a coherent sequence of learning activities that connected science with language/ arts activities. Students were excited and gratified by having their questions legitimated and publicly displayed. Grade 3 conceptual goals included understanding structural charac-

teristics of birds such as beaks and feathers, and functional characteristics such as flying, feeding, and breeding that aid survival.

Secondary School Level. Teachers in both types of integration focused on conceptual development. The goal of each unit was developing understanding of concepts related to that unit, and students were persistent in finding answers to their personal questions about each topic. In the physics integration, W. J. rolled two balls down a ramp and timed them. One was made of wood and the other steel, and he was confused when the time was the same. "I know that all objects are supposed to fall at the same rate. I learned that a long time ago. But no one ever told me why. I need to know why." Several other students in the class told him that they had read an explanation of gravity earlier. The teacher showed him a copy of the text and he read the explanation. This vignette shows the need for students to understand the phenomena they observe. Because they were focused on learning, these students could use the resources of the classroom, including other students, the teacher, and texts, to help them.

In the three-subject integration, the same emphasis held. One teacher explained,

> In everything we did, the goal was conceptual development. While students learned about early times in history, for instance, they learned about archeology and the tools archaeologists used to uncover evidence of early times in science. We tried to focus on that level of integration of learning in every unit.

Self-directive

Elementary School Level. Teachers encouraged students to assume responsibility for their own learning by providing them with a series of bounded choices. Teachers created options from which students could select, and students were encouraged to generate their own plans and preferences wherever possible. Group sets of different folktales were made available to students. Folktales were from different cultures around the world, including Native America. Topics were related to earth–man, or animal–man relationships. Students chose a folktale of interest and worked in pairs, or groups to read. Story elements were discussed, written in journals, and shared on posters in the room. Students directed their learning by choosing subtopics within the conceptual domain, identifying books and resources useful for pursuing those subtopics, working with peers who shared the same subtopics, and developing their internal standards for judging their own literacy. One grade 5 teacher noted that:

> Students were most enthusiastic when they had ownership of learning tasks. Tremendous interest and selection of books from the classroom library occurred when students were working on self-selected topics. Many times students read books they were using in their project during free time reading and recorded them on their book logs.

Secondary School Level. Teachers encouraged students to be independent learners and to direct their own learning. One way in which this was done in the physics class was to have students create their own science experiment. After coming up with a topic for the study, students gathered resources, planned, implemented, and wrote about their research, with the teachers' direction in strategies for conducting the research. In the three-subject integration, students were also taught strategies for writing and studying that would make them more independent learners. Students were given several ways to control their own learning. One teacher commented:

> A big part of our curriculum project is that the students choose topics for writing and research that relate to what we're studying. Students work together on projects of their choosing, and they decide what the final product will look like.

Metacognitive

Elementary School Level. Teachers emphasized strategy development. For example, summarizing and note-taking were taught explicitly through modeling, scaffolding, and coaching. Whole class discussions and peer-led conversational groups were conducted to enhance verbal awareness and shared consciousness of strategies for reading and writing. Explicit strategy teaching was one of the basic distinctions between concept-oriented reading instruction and most forms of whole language instruction. As one grade 3 teacher noted:

> I spent a lot of time in situated reading strategy instruction. Together we would compare fiction and non-fiction books and how to enjoy them. We discussed parts of a book, how to read the information, note taking strategies, and compiling information. With narrative selections we often talked about common literary elements—character analysis, figurative language, setting and authors' style or purpose. We compared these to the facts, ideas, and explanations that might be included in a good summary of an information book.

In Concept-Oriented Reading Instruction, teaching students how to search was fundamental to enabling them to pursue their interests and answer the questions generated from their observational activities. Students were encouraged to choose subtopics for learning, and to search for books, resources, references, pictures, and explanations of the topics they chose. Initial searches began with a question formulated by each student after firsthand observations keyed-off new ideas. Students began to wonder about new concepts they had not considered before. They found their answers in the classroom books. Students were taught how to search for books in the school library, locate books in the classroom, collect, and use the table of contents, index, headings, and pictures as guides to discovering answers to their questions. Strategies for searching were taught explicitly through teacher modeling, peer modeling, teacher scaffolding, guided practice, and team work. Typically, teachers presented a directed lesson using a class set of one book for all students, emphasizing book organization, relevance of information, appropriateness of detail, extensiveness of the search, and distinguishing among facts, explanations, and opinions.

Grades 3 and 5 students were taught four fundamental processes of search that have been identified by previous investigators (Armbruster, & Armstrong, 1993), including:

(1) Goal formation, which refers to knowing what you want to find or having an objective for the search activity; (2) Categorizing, which refers to understanding how things are organized; (3) Extracting, which refers to finding critical details, note-taking, paraphrasing, and summarizing, within a book or resource; and (4) Abstracting, which refers to putting ideas together and forming a general understanding. Teachers modeled each of these stages, students discussed them in groups and recorded progress toward each of them in their journals.

To help students in fully comprehending and integrating the texts they found during their search activities, teachers emphasized: determining the topic of a text selection, detecting critical details, summarizing the text, making comparisons between texts, relating illustrations to text, developing criteria for evaluating a book, and critically reflecting on the organization of information and the author's point of view. In thematic units, students become aware of how different narrative and informational texts help us understand a theme in different ways.

Teachers used multiple trade books for all aspects of instruction. Grade 3 students began the year by reading *Owl Moon* by Yolen. At later points in the unit they read *White Bird* by Bulla and *Wingman* by Pinkwater, as well as poetry on birds. Within these books teachers' emphasized imagery, aesthetics of language, and characterization, as well as the traditional constituents of setting, plot, conflict, and resolution. Third graders were taught to use information books to pursue the interests they formulated during the observing and personalizing phase of instruction. "Practice Searches" were conducted, first using teacher-generated questions and later students formulated their own questions and found appropriate informational texts. To help students comprehend books such as *Birds: How to Watch and Understand the Fascinating World of Birds,* teachers provided explicit instruction in identifying topic, details, and writing summaries. Through teacher modeling, peer modeling, and small group discussion students were provided instruction in "fix-up" strategies, enabling students to: (a) use pictures, illustrations, diagrams, and graphs; (b) refer back to their own questions; (c) look up vocabulary in an index glossary or dictionary; (d) break text into parts and put it back together; (e) ask peers and teams; (f) form images about what they know; (g) reread the text in a new way; (h) slow down or speed up; and (i) consult their own background knowledge. In addition to comprehension strategies, students' were taught note-taking and critical reflection on information from expository books. Students learned to critique books using their own questions, interests, and topical knowledge as criteria for judgement.

Grade 5 students who were studying adaptation of plants and animals to the environment read narratives of *Song of the Trees* by Taylor, *Tuck Everlasting* by Babbitt, *Top Secret* and *The Gift of the Tree* by Tresselt. Informational books were interwoven with these narrative books about the theme. For example, *Animal Adaptations* by Penny, was used extensively in one grade 5 classroom to convey the concept of adaptation and to provide a context for instruction in reading strategies. With these materials, teachers emphasized metacognitive strategies of identifying topics, determining important details, and summarizing sections of texts. They helped students to interpret illustrations, relate text to illustrations, and integrate information across texts. In grade 5 "fix-up" strategies were also taught including referring text against their questions, looking up vocabulary and index glossary and dictionary, subdividing and reuniting portions of texts, consulting peers, forming images, and adjusting speed of reading. Instruction in these cognitive strategies began with an appraisal of strategies students currently possessed, through class discussion and student written statements of strategies they favored. While avoiding strategies that most students already possessed, teachers provided modeling, scaffolding, and guided practice in learning new strategies within the conceptual domain of instruction. When strategies were situated within concepts, their usefulness became apparent to students.

Secondary School Level. As in the integrated instruction at younger levels, teachers in the high school also emphasized strategies. For example, searching for resources and writing reports were explicitly taught. In the very first unit of the three-subject integration, the English teacher started teaching the kids research skills. She taught them about library usage, how to use the computer to search for resources, use the word processor and hypercard, and the conventions for writing in history as opposed to writing in science. They used these skills to complete projects such as the Greek cultural project.

In the physics classroom, the teacher taught students to use journals and logs to keep track of their thinking processes as they completed research projects. She met with students individually as well as with the whole class to explicitly teach students the writing skills necessary for reporting science projects.

Collaborative

Elementary School Level. Teachers created opportunities for students to participate in five different types of social structures, including whole class, collaborative teams, pairs, idea circles, and individual work. Whole-class discussions were held to give directions, organize teams, model strategies, read aloud and entertain or group reports. Time for individual work was provided daily for reading, writing, and reflection. Pairs of students and collaborative teams worked on all phases of instruction. At the outset of the instructional unit the teacher assigned students to teams, but during the middle of a unit students formed interest groups for particular aspects of projects. Within teams students combined their observations, collected data, discussed strategies, and prepared their displays of writing for other student teams. A fourth form of social interaction was idea circles. This structure was designed to enable students to articulate their ideas with a new group of students. In idea circles, students synthesized what they had been learning recently in their project. It was a challenge for students to share conceptual understandings, and perceptions of their own literacy strategies with classmates who are not on their team. Participating in varied social structures was motivating, and it fostered interest in the books and writing activities that were the subject of collaborative activities. One grade 5 teacher noted that:

> Students have learned a lot more about analyzing their reading through idea circles and have enjoyed reading more because of it. The group dynamics of the reading group are different this year and help students to be better readers than usual. In idea circles students who usually do nothing are persuaded by others to do the reading and thinking necessary for a grid group discussion— much better than me bugging them. Most of the students are learning to look for different things in stories and books especially motives of characters and authors' techniques for organizing information to keep you interested.

Secondary School Level. Teachers in both the physics course and the three-subject integration provided a number of opportunities for students to work collaboratively. Students in science classes worked with partners or in groups of three to complete laboratory explorations. Later, they joined with other lab groups to share data. In these collaborations, students helped one another with both procedural and conceptual parts of their tasks. The following vignette shows how this collaboration helped one student learn a concept.

M. B. (the student who made his egg carton heavier so that it would fall faster) recorded other students' data on a data table. As he looked at the data he said to the person sitting next to him, "That means that mass doesn't make a difference. That can't be. Mass has to make a difference!" Another student who was listening said that it didn't. M. replied, "I believe it does. I don't care what anyone else thinks." Still another student then said, "M, there was this guy named Galileo. He proved that things fell at the same rate." Others joined in to explain the concept to him. At that point, M. made another comment about how he was not going to change his mind and fell silent. Later he read a text about gravity. When another student expressed disbelief, M. was the first one to point out the fact that objects of differing masses fall at the same rate.

Students in this class also relied on peer tutors to help them with problem solving. Students were often the ones who spoke up during whole group discussion to explain concepts to other students who were having difficulty. When the teacher posed a question, she had students discuss it together before they answered. In these ways, students learned the value of teamwork and sharing ideas. In the three-subject integration, students also collaborated in a variety of ways. For instance, they worked together on projects about Greek culture in groups and formed study groups in English as a way of helping them prepare for tests in English, history and science.

Self-expressive

Elementary School Level. A prominent dimension of the classroom context was student self-expression. From the outset of the instructional units when students posed and published their own questions, to the end of the units when students presented their books to other students, self-expression was honored. Not only were students delighted when their thoughts were accepted in class discussion or posted on classroom displays, they also aspired to be good at explaining their poems, experiments or written descriptions of invented animals. Particularly as they gained in-depth knowledge of concepts students felt compelled to express their expertise to others. As one grade 3 teacher noted:

> They made posters, wrote stories, and yes, reports they presented to other classes. But the important point here is that the motivation to communicate was started by the observation and was an outgrowth of that engagement. Observation led to reading motivation, but we also got motivation for writing that surprised us.

In Concept-Oriented Reading Instruction, students became experts on the topic they had chosen to learn about. As they gained knowledge, and the self-efficacy that accompanies it, students wanted to express their understandings to others. To foster this self-expression, teachers provided instruction that enabled students to present their understanding in many forms, including a written report, a class-authored book, dioramas, charts, and informational stories. Teachers coached students in identifying their audience, organizing their message to the audience, identifying critical details, and elaborating their writing. Students were encouraged to express their understandings about the topics of personal interest in a variety of coherent, persuasive and accurate communications to classmates or other audiences of their choosing.

Grade 3 teachers invited students to make charts about their observations of birds. One class created wall displays of the materials found in bird nests. Another class created charts of adaptive features such as beaks and feet. Students wrote journals which were shared with other students, and small classroom teams composed books on their favorite bird which were illustrated, covered, and shared with other teams. In a book about humming birds, the "chapter" on beaks was entitled *Beaks about Humming Birds:*

> The humming bird beaks are very sharp. Their beaks are big as a glue top and long as a glue stick. Their beaks are sharp like a needle and shaped like a "v". A humming bird's beak is small. The parents' beaks are four inches long. Humming birds poke thin beaks into a flower to find out whether it is sweet. They pick hay, grass, and strings with their beaks. Their beaks are good because they can protect themselves by their beaks and they know how to make nests using their beaks.

Grade 5 students communicated their understanding of adaptation of plants and animals to the environment through writing journals, reporting experiments, exhibiting their interpretations of class data, and engaging in two synthesis projects. The first synthesis consisted of inventing an animal, in which each student team selected a habitat, such as the desert. Each student invented an animal and wrote an essay describing the animal and what adaptations enabled this creature to survive in its environment. A second synthesis project consisted of writing informational stories in which each student selected an animal that she was interested in learning more about. They read and discussed their ideas with other students, and composed a narrative about their animal in a form of informational fiction. One story was entitled "Through the Pearl Colored Eyes of the Snow Leopard." It began:

> As the sun rose high above the mountain-filled land of Asia, there in the cliff side two bright eyes appeared. Beautifully and half awake an Asian snow leopard walked out tiredly. Its broad paws, like snow pads, supported the mother snow leopard as she walked down the mountain side.
>
> The warm climate took over all coldness from last night's rainstorm. Her mate lay restlessly in their cave home on the mountainside resting with babies. The male snow leopard, as all do, weight around 100 to 160 pounds. The mother snow leopard set out to find food. Snow leopards eat monkeys, antelope, muntjacs, jackals, peacocks, snakes, sheep, goats, and dogs. 'What should we eat today?' thought mama snow leopard." [Eight pages and six illustrations later this story ends, as follows:]. "At the beginning of November they were ready for the long winter. The mother and father checked to make sure they had all of their food. Then they put their young ones to bed. She had already eaten. They sat to watch the last leaves falling off the trees. Her mate stared into her eyes and saw the reflection on the pearl colored eyes of the snow leopard!"

Students composed imaginative, knowledge-rich tales about a day gecko, praying mantis, wild horse, squirrel, and other creatures. To support their writing, students read descriptive and figurative language in books such as *Tuck Everlasting, Moon of the Chickapee.* They were encouraged to apply these writing styles in their books. Informational stories were a popular form of art for expressing interests and exchanging expertise.

Secondary School Level. Students expressed themselves in varied forms. In the three-subject integration, for example, they learned debate techniques in English, studied the origins of debating in history as a topic related to learning about Roman culture, and engaged in debates about medical issues in their science class. This formal method of expression was counterbalanced by more subjective and personal forms such as journal writing, discussion, and informal presentations of their project work to other members in class. In the history class, too, they made portfolios that represented their personal development as a form of self-expression. In the physics integration, students expressed themselves through laboratory explorations, discussion of their interpretations, and a variety of writing activities.

Coherence

Elementary School Level. The instructional framework for enhancing literacy engagement contained interconnected student activities across the day, week and month. As students observed phenomena, read about the topic, wrote about their related experiences, and learned literacy strategies within the theme, students integrated their school life. *Coherence* refers to connections across activities on many levels, including substantive topical linkages, and parallels between the processes of reading and writing. For example, as students learned to support broad principles with details in describing their experience narratively, they began to write up simple science experiments using the same processes. One grade 3 teacher reported that:

Interested students went beyond the classroom to the library and to newspapers, anyplace, for more information on the subjects they were studying in class. My children learned that you don't have to have the same book to explore, investigate, enjoy personal experiences, and gather information. Tradebooks enable students to learn to read, establish strategies, and continue to gain knowledge about their own goal.

In one grade 5, Concept-Oriented Reading Instruction classroom, students experienced coherence through the concept of adaptation. In their initial observational activities, students considered the adaptive characteristics of a hillside behind the school. Gathering plants and insects provided opportunities for exciting, hands-on observations. Questions that children inevitably posed became the basis for concept learning. Self-directed learning began with permitting students to ask their own questions and keep their own journals. Metacognitive strategies for literacy, including finding books, searching for information, comprehending text and enjoying folktales were linked to the theme of adaptation of animals to the environment. When the texts were fused with the observational activities, and reading/writing merged with learning about the hillside behind the school, students unified their school experience. Collaborative teams that shared books about the common theme of adaptation, learned about the useful portions of the books; and they also learned about the processes of constructive social interaction. Finally, when students gained command of the concepts they were exploring, and they gained a sense of competence with the tools of literacy, they became expressive. Ideas about mutual adaptation of plant and animal worlds that emerge from observations, questions, reading, and discussion were synthesized through a variety of communicative arts. Coherence culminates in the integration of literacy as an avenue of engagement between self, the social and the natural worlds.

Secondary School Level. We observed highly interconnected learning activities in both types of integrations. The fabric of reading, writing, discussion, and content learning appeared to be seamless. Literacy was situated in specific tasks related to students' learning of content, making them relevant and purposeful. In the physics class students read texts to help them explain their lab observations. They wrote journal entries about their thinking process, and discussed their thoughts with peers. In the three-subject integration, students read literature learning about theme, figurative language, and political conflict at the same time. Connections between the literature they were reading and the time period they were studying in history were abundant. These interconnections afforded students with ways of looking at the world that encouraged critical thinking.

CONCLUSION

The notion of engagement moves teachers and researchers beyond models of literacy as a language process or a set of cognitive competencies. An engaged reader, of any age, possesses a desire for literacy. Her intrinsic motivation powers her conceptual understanding and aesthetic enjoyment, which foster a lifelong disposition for reading. However, literacy engagement does not spontaneously arise for all students, and engagement is not sustained for long periods unless teachers nurture it. Our collaborative inquiries reveal that the tapestry of literacy engagement is best supported in classroom contexts that contain integrated instruction. Because engagement unites motivations with strategies and conceptual learning, it is sensible that classroom integrations of conceptual, strategic and motivational themes should be particularly promising. Many questions arise from our view of engaging classrooms: Does integrated instruction work well for multicultural populations? Can it be instituted school-wide? What are the professional development experiences needed to support teachers in these classrooms? What are the costs? Although not all these questions are addressed yet, we are optimistic that answers will be forthcoming as an increasing number of literacy professionals build integrations into the classrooms for which they are responsible.

References

Almasi, J. F., & Gambrell, L. B. (1994). *Sociocognitive conflict in peer-led and teacher-led discussions of literature* (Research Report No. 12). Athens, GA: National Reading Research Center.

Ames, C. (1992). Achievement goals and the classroom motivational climate. In D. Schunk, & J. Meece (Eds.), *Student perceptions in the classroom.* Hillsdale, NJ: Erlbaum.

Armbruster, B. B., & Armstrong, J. O. (1993). Locating information in text: A focus on children in the elementary grades. *Contemporary Educational Psychology, 18*(2), 139–162.

Brown, A. (1992). Design experiments: Theoretical and methodological challenges in creating complex interventions in classroom settings. *The Journal of the Learning Sciences, 2,* 141–178.

Calfee, R. (1994). Critical literacy: Reading and writing for a new millennium. In N. J. Ellsworth, C. N. Hedley, & A. N. Baratta

(Eds.), *Literacy: A redefinition* (pp. 19–39). Hillsdale, NJ: Erlbaum.

Collins-Block, C. (1992). Strategy instruction in a literature-based reading program. *The Elementary School Journal, 94*(2), 139–151.

Corno, L., & Kanfer, R. (1993). The role of volition in learning and performance. In L. Darling-Hammond (Ed.), *Review of research in education* (pp. 301–341). Washington, DC: American Educational Research Association.

Deci, E. L., Vallerand, R. J., Pelletier, L. G., & Ryan, R. M. (1991). Motivation and education: The self-determination perspective. *Educational Psychologist, 26*(2 & 4), 325–346.

Dole, J. A., Duffy, G. G., Roehler, L. R., & Pearson, P. D. (1991). Moving from the old to the new: Research on reading comprehension instruction. *Review of Educational Research, 61*(2), 239–264

Dreher, M. J. (1993). Reading to locate information: Societal and educational perspectives. *Contemporary Educational Psychology, 18*(2), 129–139.

Flower, L., Stein, V., Ackerman, J., Kantz, M., McCormick, K., & Peck, W. (1990). *Reading to write: Exploring a cognitive and social process.* New York: Oxford University Press.

Ford, M. E. (1992). *Motivating humans: Goals. emotions, and personal agency beliefs.* Newbury Park, CA: Sage.

Gamoran, A., & Nystrand, M. (1992). Taking students seriously. In F. M. Newman (Ed.), *Student engagement and achievement in American secondary schools.* New York: Teachers College Press.

Gottfried, A. E. (1985). Academic intrinsic motivation in elementary and junior high school students. *Journal of Educational Psychology, 77*(6), 631–645.

Guthrie, J. T., Schafer, W. D., Afflerbach, P., & Almasi, J. (1994). *Policies for integrated reading instruction related to a state-wide improvement plan.* Paper presented at the annual meeting of the American Educational Research Association, New Orleans, LA.

Guthrie, J. T., Schafer, W. D., & Hutchinson, S. R. (1991). Relations of document literacy and prose literacy to occupational and societal characteristics of young black and white adults. *Reading Research Quarterly, 26*(1), 30–48.

Guthrie, J. T., Van Meter, P., Dacey, A., & Wigfield, A. (1994). *Literacy engagement: Changes in motivations, strategies and amounts of reading during a year of concept-oriented reading instruction* (Research Report in preparation). College Park: University of Maryland, National Reading Research Center.

Harter, S., Whitesell, N. R., & Kowalski, P. (1992). Individual differences in the effects of educational transitions on young adolescents' perceptions of competence and motivational orientation. *American Educational Research Journal, 29*(4), 777–808.

Head, J. O., & Sutton, C. R. (1985). Language, understanding, and commitment. In L. H. T. West, & A. L. Pines (Eds.), *Cognitive structure and conceptual change* (pp. 91–100). Orlando, FL: Academic Press.

Holland, J. H., Holyoak, K. J., Nisbett, R. E., & Thagard, P. R. (1986). *Induction: Processes of inference, learning, and discovery.* Cambridge, MA: MIT Press.

Hynd, C. R., McNish, M., Qian, G., Keith, M., & Lay, K. (1994). *Learning counterintuitive physics concepts: The effects of text and educational environment.* (Research Report). Athens, GA: National Reading Research Center.

Lapp, D., & Flood, J. (1994). Integrating the curriculum: First steps. *The Reading Teacher, 47*(5), 416–419.

LeCompte, M. D., & Priessle, J. (1993). *Ethnography and qualitative design in educational research* (2nd ed.). San Diego, CA: Academic Press.

Lepper, M. R. (1988). Motivational considerations in the study of instruction. *Cognition & Instruction, 5*(4), 289–309.

Maehr, M. L., & Fyans, L. J. (1989). School culture, motivation and achievement. In M. L. Maehr, & C. Ames (Eds.), *Advances in motivation and achievements: Motivation enhancing environments,* (Vol. 6, pp. 215–247). Greenwich, CN: JAI Press.

Mayer, R. E. (1993). Illustrations that instruct. In R. Glaser (Ed.), *Advances in instructional psychology* (pp. 253–285). Hillsdale, NJ: Erlbaum.

Meese, J. L., Blumenfeld, P. C., & Hoyle, R. H. (1988). Students' goal orientations and cognitive engagement in classroom activities. *Journal of Educational Psychology, 80,* 514–523.

Mullis, I. V., Campbell, J. R., & Farstrup, A. E. (1993). *NAEP 1992 reading report card for the nation and the states.* Washington, DC: Office of Educational Research and Improvement.

Neisser, U. (1987). *Concepts and conceptual development: Ecological and intellectual factors in categorization.* Melbourne: Cambridge University Press.

Newby, T. J. (1991). Classroom motivation: Strategies of first-year teachers. *Journal of Educational Psychology, 83*(2), 187–194.

Oldfather, P., & Dahl, K. (1994). Toward a social constructivist reconceptualization of intrinsic motivation for literacy learning. *Journal of Reading Behavior, 26*(2), 139–158.

Pearson, P. D., & Fielding, L. (1991). Comprehension instruction. In R. Barr, M. L. Kamil, P. Mosenthal, & P. D. Pearson (Eds.), *Handbook of reading research.* New York: Longman.

Perfetti, C. A., Britt, M. A., Rouet, J. F., Mason, R. A., & Georgi, M. C. (1993). *How students use texts to learn and reason about historical uncertainty.* Paper presented at the annual meeting of the American Educational Research Association, Atlanta, GA.

Pintrich, P. R., Marx, R. W., & Boyle, R. A. (1993). Beyond cold conceptual change: The role of motivational beliefs and classroom contextual factors in the process of conceptual change. *Review of Educational Research, 63*(2), 167–199.

Pintrich, P. R., & Schrauben, B. (1992). Students' motivational beliefs and their cognitive engagement in classroom academic tasks. In D. H. Schunk, & J. L. Meese (Eds.), *Student perceptions in the classroom* (pp. 149–184). Hillsdale, NJ: Erlbaum.

Skinner, E. A., & Belmont, M. J. (1993). Motivation in the classroom: Reciprocal effects of teacher behavior and student engagement across the school year. *Journal of Educational Psychology, 85*(4), 571–581.

Spiro, R. J., Coulson, R. L., Feltovich, P. J., & Anderson, D. K. (1994). Cognitive flexibility theory. Advanced knowledge acquisition in ill-structured domains. In R. B. Ruddell, M. R. Ruddell, & H. Singer (Eds.), *Theoretical models and processes of reading* (pp. 602–615). Newark, DE: International Reading Association.

Stahl, S., Hynd, C. R., McNish, M., & Bosquet, D. (in progress). *Multiple documents in history.* Athens, GA: National Reading Research Center.

Stanovich, K., & Cunningham, A. (1993). Where does knowledge come from? Specific associations between print exposure and information acquisition. *Journal of Educational Psychology, 85*(2), 211–230.

Stevenson, C., & Carr, J. F. (1993). *Integrated studies in the middle grades: Dancing through walls.* New York: Teachers College Press.

Wigfield, A. (1994). *Dimensions of children's motivations for reading: An initial study.* Paper presented at the annual meeting of the American Educational Research Association, New Orleans, IA.

Wineburg, S. S. (1991a). Historical problem solving: A study of the cognitive processes used in the evaluation of documentary and pictorial evidence. *Journal of Educational Psychology, 83,* 73–77.

Wineburg, S. S. (1991b). On the reading of historical texts: Notes on the breach between school and academy. *American Educational Research Journal, 28,* 495–519.

·58D·

STANDARDS IN THE LANGUAGE ARTS

P. David Pearson

MICHIGAN STATE UNIVERSITY

Beginning in 1989 when the governors blessed the concept of standards as a major tool of educational reform in our nation, the public rhetoric about high and rigorous standards has gathered momentum steadily throughout the early 1990s. Encouraged by the success of the curriculum standards in mathematics (NCTM, 1989) federal and state policy makers supported the development of standards in other curriculum areas. The early 1990s saw federally sponsored curriculum standards projects funded in the arts, civics, English, geography, history, science, and foreign language (even if not all met with uniformly high success, including the Standards Project in English Language Arts). In an even earlier effort, the National Board for Professional Teaching Standards (NBPTS, 1990) began the process of developing standards to guide the creation of assessments for the advanced certification of teachers. States got into the standards business very early, some even before the watershed governor's conference of 1989 (e.g., California,, 1989), and the momentum for state and local standards development was enhanced by federal legislation promoting their development and mandating their use.

The purpose of this chapter is to acquaint the reader with the state of standards in the English language arts as the profession readies itself to enter a new century of curriculum development, debate, and reform. In accomplishing this purpose, I hope to provide insight on several issues:

(1) What are standards?
(2) What does (did) the standards terrain in English language arts look like in the middle of the last decade of the 20th century?
(3) What sorts of standards are possible? likely to be set?
(4) What are the dangers in this whole process?
(5) What, if anything, do we as a professional community have to gain by participating in a standards setting effort?

DEFINING STANDARDS

The dictionary definition

The dictionary is an informative starting point in our quest to understand standards (Merriam-Webster, 1983). These four definitions are instructive for our efforts because they capture the variety of meanings that people in our field extend to the term:

> *standard* (stan' derd): (1) something that is established by authority, custom, or general consent as a model or example to be followed; (2) a definite level or degree of quality that is proper or adequate for a specific purpose; (3) a carefully thought-out method of performing a task; (4) any measure by which one judges a thing good, authentic, or adequate. Synonyms: criterion, gauge, yardstick, touchstone, test.

The first definition captures the idea of standards as a vision of what we are about, what we stand for, and what we want to encourage in curriculum reform. Definitions 2 and 4 are more likely to become operationalized as tests or assessments; taken together, they could specify *what counts as evidence of meeting a standard* as well as *"how much"* of that evidence is required for meeting it. Definition 3 is a little different since it deals more with process than outcome. The clearest example is the "standard" routine one has to follow to receive high marks in a ice-skating or gymnastics competition; the closest example in teaching and learning might be meeting a standard for working one's way out of a math problem or a writing difficulty by employing a problem-solving heuristic.

Metaphors from the field

Dictionaries are not our only source of insight about the meaning of standards. Based upon an inspiration by Elizabeth

---

An earlier version of this paper was published as a policy piece in *JRB: A Journal of Literacy*.

Stage (1992), my colleague Lizanne DeStefano and I (DeStefano, & Pearson, 1994) have been collecting metaphors from different speakers and writers—metaphors they have used to explain what they mean by standards. Our search for metaphors has been fascinating and instructive, especially when we attempt to attach them to the four dictionary definitions we have found.

Group 1. Identity, priorities, and *core values*—this is the essence of these metaphors. Consistent with dictionary definition #1, they deal with issues such as what we stand for, who we are, and what constitutes our essence. We have found:

- a banner on a pole (carried by a standard bearer, the leader of the parade)
- a foundation or platform (on which we stand)
- a vision (a dream of the possible)
- a framework or a blueprint (from which we will fashion our entire effort)

These "identity" metaphors tend to show up in broad goal and missions statements. The 1989 Mathematics standards (NCTM, 1989), for example, intentionally incorporated the standard bearer metaphor to characterize what the whole movement was about. Romberg (1993), writing about the math standards, reiterated this metaphor in the title of his article, "NCTM Standards: A Rallying Flag for Mathematics Teachers." Sizer and Rogers (1993) talk about standards as "images of excellence." It is largely this metaphor that stands behind the standards effort of the NBPTS, most notable when they talk about standards as a way of enhancing the professional stature of teachers (NBPTS, 1990).

Group 2. This set connotes *direction* or *momentum*. Consistent with the first definition, they address the question, Where are we headed? Our search through the standards literature revealed many:

- an engine (of reform)
- a mountain to be climbed (with many routes to the top)
- target
- milestone
- guidance system

Stage (1992; 1993), in discussing the standards work in science, has demonstrated just how richly one can extend these metaphors. The mountain, for example, permits many extensions: We all want to get to the top, but there are many routes. Some go straight up the slope while others meander along a less acute angle of ascent. Some stop to take stock or appreciate the journey itself while others wear blinders that limit vision to nothing but the goal. Some do it on their own while others assemble considerable assistance in the form of maps, machinery and guides.

The engine metaphor has been used by leaders of the New Standards Project (Simmons, & Resnick, 1993) to emphasize the critical role that standards and, even more important, the assessments that accompany them will play in stimulating real reform in our nation's schools. As far as a dictionary match goes, the metaphors in Group 2 are most consistent with

definitions 1 (identity) and 3 (processes); while they do address, at least implicitly, issues of identity, they can also specify procedures and methods of accomplishing goals.

Group 3. The metaphors in Group 3 connote either the *type* or *the level of performance* involved in gathering evidence about meeting standards. They provide answers to one of two questions: (1) What counts as evidence (definition 4) that a person has achieved a standard? or (2) How high a score or level (definition 2) do you have to achieve on a particular measure to demonstrate that you have mastered the standard? These metaphors include...

- high jump bar
- hurdle
- thermometer
- boundaries
- test itself
- litmus test
- rubric

These performance-oriented metaphors, which identify either the measure of a standard or the degree of achievement on that measure needed to meet a standard, are probably the most common meaning of standard in everyday discourse. When people talk about meeting a standard, this is the meaning that underlies their use of the term. It is certainly the meaning that underlies the use of standards, for example, in athletics; each spring, our sports pages report the list of college athletes who have *qualified* for the National Collegiate Athletic Association finals because they have reached the standard. The qualification dimension is critical in the standards conversation. It emerges in the form of certification for teachers (NBPTS, 1990 or INTASC, 1993), initial mastery (as in the New Standards Project) for students, and a host of other gatekeeping functions.

Test, litmus test, and rubric foreshadow one of the stickiest of all issues in the standards conversation—the relationship between standards and assessment. In the minds of many, there is no substantial difference between standards and assessment because assessments are means that the field will use to evaluate whether students, teachers, or schools have met the standards. It is a small step from this observation to the conclusion that standards will become just one more tool to alienate those groups of students who are not currently well served by our schools and therefore do not perform well on those indices typically used to evaluate performance. The rubric metaphor, because it comes from recent developments in performance and portfolio assessment, raises the possibility of greater equity. Whether these new traditions prove any more empowering and useful to those populations traditionally marginalized by our schools is an open question, one that can be answered only by observing their impact.

Group 4. The metaphors in Group 4 connote transactions among individuals and / or politics about meeting particular responsibilities. They include

- responsibilities (of students, teachers, and schools)
- rights (that students or parents or teachers possess)

- opportunities (that schools and teachers are obligated to provide to students and parents)

These metaphors are related to none of the definitions found in the dictionary. This is not surprising because these metaphors are relatively new in the national standards dialogue. These metaphors have arisen because some groups have come to regard standards as a way of ensuring that the clients they represent get a fair shake from the educational system.

Within this set of metaphors, standards become a compact: "We will hold our kids accountable to achieving particular performance standards if you will guarantee resources (plant facilities, materials, and teacher expertise) and curriculum that will gain them access to the higher literacies." New labels such as delivery standards and opportunity to learn standards have arisen to accommodate these transactional relationships. They represent a twist on the use of concept of standards that even our lexicographers have not yet discerned. But, they are likely to dominate the standards discussion in the future. The fact that between 1993 and 1995 an increasing number of sessions on the annual program of American Educational Research Association addressed these transactional standards, suggests that they have captured the attention of the educational research and policy community.

In a very broad sense, professions, including teacher education, have always recognized this transaction between accountability and resources. While one may argue about the appropriateness or rigor behind accreditation standards, such as those of the NCATE (National Council of Accreditation in Teacher Education, 1994), colleges that hold themselves accountable to these standards are promising to provide a level of resources and curricular opportunity sufficient to allow their students to meet licensure or certification requirements. High schools that submit themselves to accreditation by regional bodies make a similar implicit contract with their students. Those who currently favor delivery and opportunity to learn standards as the quid pro quo for content and performance standards would probably agree with the goal of accreditation efforts but criticize them for their predisposition toward compliance rather than vision and their privileging minimal over high and rigorous standards.

As a political phenomenon, opportunity to learn standards have proved the most controversial to implement. While logic of the argument seems self-evident—that individual entities, be they persons, teachers, schools, or states, ought not to be held accountable to performance standards unless the authorities holding them to account provide resources and opportunity, the politics are anything but self-evident. In fact, many politicians fought hard to either eradicate or dilute the opportunity to learn language when standards bills went through the Congress in 1994.

Types of Standards

As the standards movement has gathered momentum through the early 1990s, the typology of standards expanded correspondingly (NCEST, 1992). We began with basically two concepts, content standards (what students should know

and be able to do) and performance standards (how much is enough on any given content standard), and now we have expanded the category to include delivery standards, opportunity to learn standards, assessment standards, instructional standards, and standards for the process by which standards are created, discussed, adopted, and adapted (National Educational Goals Panel, 1993).

Content Standards. In the national lingo, content standards (what some call curriculum standards) answer the question, What should students know and be able to do? Not surprisingly, they also answer the question, What should teachers teach? They can be very broad:

> Students will construct meaning from written text,

moderately broad:

> Students in grades K–4 will respond effectively and cognitively to significant aspects of narrative, such as character, mood, tone, plot, and authorial craft,

or very specific:

> Students in grade 9 will demonstrate mastery over the essay form of writing by composing a tightly organized, grammatically acceptable, compelling essay of 500–600 words detailing the costs and benefits of environmental legislation.

Depending on the language used and the curricular grain size used, they can resemble the well-worn (worn out?) behavioral objectives of the mastery learning movement of the 1960s and 1970s or broad statements of goals or curricular intent. While some have focused on statements implying student accountability, others (e.g., Marshall, 1993) have focused on curricular opportunity in redefining content standards as the curricular experiences in which every student has a right to participate. For example,

> Students should experience multiple opportunities to read complete, authentic texts in a variety of genres.

The early versions of the federally defunded Standards Project for English Language Arts (SPELA) had settled, at least tentatively, on standards for teaching and learning, standards that implied both opportunity and student knowledge. For example,

> Students make active use of what they already know, what they learn through inquiry, and their reflections on learning to become more sophisticated at making meaning, solving problems, and constructing new knowledge.

The principle of the SPELA was to create standards that implied accountability for both students (growth in constructing meaning and solutions) and teaching (providing a classroom ecology in which students are encouraged to integrate rather than compartmentalize knowledge). Hence, the SPELA dual commitment to standards for *teaching and learning.*

Performance Standards. In the national lingo performance standards answer the question, How much is good enough? They describe and prescribe the specific levels of performance on specific tasks that students need to achieve in order for schools and society to conclude that they have met a standard. The achievement levels sponsored by National Assessment

Governing Board for the 1992 National Assessment of Educational Progress state-by-state trial are prototype performance standards; they define the precise cut score that a student must achieve in order to be classified in the basic, proficient, and advanced levels of achievement. If one had access to a rubric for scoring a writing prompt accompanied by anchor papers illustrating each score point in the rubric, one would have a clear picture of the performance standards for at least that particular task.

The Arts Standards project (Consortium of National Arts Education Associations, 1994) took an interesting approach on performance standards. At least for the higher grades, their current plan is to present a fairly broad content standard, such as:

Standard: Understanding how music relates to the other arts, followed by "achievement" standards, at both proficient and advanced levels.

Proficient: Students describe both common and unique features of two or more arts within a particular historical period, style, or culture (e.g., Baroque, African-American, Japanese).

Advanced: Students describe the similarities and differences in the use of elements, processes, and organizational principles among the arts in the 18th, 19th, and 20th centuries.

It is at the interface between content standards and performance standards that we would expect both the professional and the public debates to become heated. In the language arts, for example, it is one thing to hold a national conversation about the literacy curriculum—debating the type of tasks, contexts, and collaboration that students ought to experience, but it is quite another to pinpoint a specific score on a specific exam that students must achieve or a specific set of criteria that students must meet before we can declare them literate. Experience bears out this expectation. During the development of tools for the New Standards Project, it was always the specification of "how much is enough" that kindled the most vehement debates. For example, we had no trouble agreeing that students should "read widely", but the process of agreeing on a performance standard which specified a certain number of books per year (see New Standards, 1995) proved to be quite contentious within our ranks.

Delivery Standards. Delivery standards are included as a historical footnote only. They entered the standards dialogue fairly early on in the conversation. As groups such as the National Governor's Conference, the National Council on Standards and Testing, and the National Goals Panel debated the question of how to invest schools in content and performance standards, those who worried about the plight of teachers, especially teachers who had to cope in underfunded urban and rural schools, began to argue that schools, teachers, and students could and should not be held accountable to higher standards unless they could be assured that they would receive the resources needed to achieve them. Delivery standards soon became the "quid pro quo" in the standards dialogue; the bargain seems to be transparent: Give us more and better schools, materials, and professional staff, and we will give you students who achieve higher scores on tougher standards. Now that the term opportunity standards is being extended to embrace resources, the term delivery standards has fallen into disfavor.

Opportunity to Learn Standards. This has been the very latest entry into the standards dialogue. While related to delivery standards in the sense that they both represent the allocation of resources to teaching and learning, opportunity to learn standards emphasize curricular opportunity more than material resources. They provide an answer to the question, What evidence is there that students have had an opportunity to participate in a curriculum that would help develop the skills, understandings, and dispositions that would enable them meet the standards to which they are being held accountable? Opportunity standards can be viewed as the obligations that schools have to their clients, the students and parents of our country. The logic of opportunity standards can be extended upward in the political hierarchy: schools are obliged to provide opportunities to students and parents; districts are obliged to provide opportunities (or at least the resources that make it possible to create opportunities) to schools; states to districts; and the federal government to the states. The concept is, in principle, quite useful, especially in contrast to the notion of delivery standards. It allows us to point out, for example, that even though two groups of students may have equal material resources, they may be receiving vastly different, and hence inequitable, curricula. Starting in 1994, the terms delivery standards and opportunity to learn standards came to be used interchangeably, thus denying us the capacity to distinguish among notions such as material resources (buildings, teaching materials), teaching capacity (better student to teacher ratios) and curricular opportunity. By 1995, the term delivery standards had been subsumed under opportunity to learn.

Assessment Standards. These are the standards that we use to evaluate the quality and validity of our assessment tools. Assessment standards are not new. For about the last 3 decades, the American Educational Research Association (AERA), the American Psychological Association (APA), and the National Council on Measurement in Education (NCME) have collaborated to define, elaborate, and disseminate standards for the productive use of a variety of measurements of human behavior (1985). These standards, intended to guide test constructors and test users in the application of assessment, deal with a wide range of technical, epistemological, and ethical issues in the construction and use of data from a wide range of types of tests, assessments, and evaluation procedures, including many informal and clinical procedures. More typical of recent entries into this effort are the assessment standards developed jointly by the National Council of Teachers of English (NCTE) and the International Reading Association (IRA) or the assessment standards evolving from the effort to develop national standards in science. The NCTE / IRA joint statement on *Standards for the assessment of reading and writing* (1994 cf., p. 2452) is a prototype for these sorts of standards. The standards are provided, according to the task force that drafted them, "to guide decisions about assessing the teaching and learning of reading and writing." Unlike the AERA / APA / NCME statement, the NCTE / IRA standards de-emphasize technical aspects of assessment in deference to their epistemological bases, ethical characteristics, and political uses. The literacy assessment standards are much more likely to discuss under whose aegis the assessment was created and the consequences of their use. More on this document is given later in this chapter.

Also interesting are the assessment standards for the science standards movement. As of early 1995, they were working on five standards, which taken as a unit, examine most of the types of decisions for which assessment data are used in our culture:

- Assessment in the service of teaching and learning (teacher perspective—what teachers have to know in order to deliver instruction).
- Assessment in the service of learning (student perspective—what students have to know to evaluate their own learning).
- Assessment for decisions about individuals (the importance of fairness and equity for high stakes assessment).
- Assessment in the service of policy (how to help policy makers make good decisions).
- Assessment to monitor the system (how to balance the assessment of attainment [student achievement] and opportunity to learn [holding the system to account]).

Standards for Standards. As redundant as it may sound, we do have standards by which to judge the validity and efficacy of standards that are created by various groups. In 1993, the National Educational Goals Panel commissioned a committee of distinguished Americans to develop standards that could be used to evaluate standards that are currently being developed by the various national standards movements as well as standards developed by the states. In summary form, these are the standards they developed. "For subject-specific standards to be judged worthy of certification (p. iv)," they must be

1. world class
2. important and focused
3. useful
4. reflective of broad consensus-building
5. balanced between competing requirements for depth versus breadth, specific versus flexible, theory versus fact-driven, knowledge versus application, forward-looking versus traditional
6. accurate and sound, clear and usable
7. assessable
8. adaptable
9. developmentally appropriate

NAVIGATING THE CURRENT STANDARDS TERRAIN

It is no mean feat to keep straight the various standards movements currently active in the field of the English language arts, let alone the field of education more broadly construed. Not only do their names contain many overlapping terms and phrases, but their purposes and conceptual structures are often intertwined. In the ensuing section, I attempt to describe these various standards setting efforts in the hope that all of us, including myself, can ferret out commonalties and uniquenesses among the projects.

National Standards Projects within the English Language Arts Field

The English Standards Project. The English Standards Project experienced a rocky beginning. It started as a federally funded collaborative project of the Center for the Study of Reading, the IRA and the NCTE to set standards for the teaching and learning of the English language arts, K–12. The SPELA agreed to set content standards for the teaching and learning of the English language arts. The project tried to describe what students "should know and be able to do" at various stages of their school careers.

The project began in October 1992 and was slated for federal funding until October 1995. It was obligated to deliver a set of curriculum standards to the Office of Educational Research and Improvement by the October 1995 ending date. The primary governing body was a National Board which bore the responsibility for setting broad policy directions for the project and receiving, reviewing, critiquing and endorsing the standards developed by the project. The actual writing of the standards was to have been completed by three task forces, one each for Early School, Middle School, and Secondary School. These three task forces were to have met approximately twice yearly in weeklong retreats to draft and revise standards in response to review by the profession. Each of these task forces was supported by a staff member and an Executive Secretary, whose responsibility was to translate the work of the Task Force at these retreats into language that could be shared broadly for review, critique, and consensus.

Between Task Force meetings, IRA and NCTE were to engage in broad-based critique and consensus processes within their organizations. Additionally by working through state departments, other professional organizations, and other interested groups, the project was to have extended this critique and consensus process as far and wide as possible. There was even a process by which *any* group of interested individuals could bid to become a task force charged with "official" review responsibilities.

That I talk about this project in the past tense should not be dismissed as a grammatical error; the project no longer exists, at least under federal sponsorship. On March 18, 1994, the University of Illinois received a letter from officials within the Department of Education terminating the project as of March 20, 1994. Specifically, the Department of Education officials criticized the project on two counts: (1) introducing process criteria and opportunity to learn standards into what they (the Department) said should be exclusively content standards, and (2) failing to address key issues in the field, such as invented spelling (it was not clear which side they wished us to take) and the "canon" in children's literature.

Diane Ravitch, in her recent book on Standards (Ravitch, 1995) commented that the project could not even agree on whether English should be taught, referring no doubt to the fact that in its guiding principles, SPELA came out foresquare for supporting and honoring students' primary languages and cultures while they were in the process of developing competence in all aspects of English.

Shortly after the demise of the federally sponsored project, IRA and NCTE each committed $500,000 of organizational resources to completing the project with federal support, and, of course, without federal oversight. At one point, the Department of Education considered funding a second English standards project; however, they received so many letters from schools, local organizations, and individual teachers of reading, language arts, and English, that they decided to "leave it to the profession." During the period from Fall, 1994 until March, 1996, at which point the Standards were released, committees comprised of IRA and NCTE members worked feverishly to complete the document and to negotiate the political support within the organizations and the broader profession of language arts educators to guarantee their acceptance upon release. Initial public reaction to the standards was decidedly mixed. Many commentators from the news media (e.g., the *New York Times* and the *Washington Post*) responded quite negatively, calling the standards vague and useless and accusing the project of a variety of sins, ranging from the overuse of educational jargon to a disregard for the importance of learning standard English to abandoning traditional values in English in favor of promoting cultural relativism. Others, however, praised the standards for avoiding the very temptation (cited as a weakness by the press) to provide standards that were so specific as to marginalize the role of states, districts, schools, communities, and individual teachers in crafting local standards and curriculum frameworks and for creating an inclusive net that recognizes and celebrates the cultural and linguistic contributions of the myriad ethnic groups that comprise our national heritage. Their ultimate impact, I believe, will only be known a decade from now.

There are many lessons to be learned from SPELA, most of which are inappropriate for an encyclopedia entry. Two, however, are fundamental, and should never be forgotten by the profession. First, professional groups may be better off without federal entanglements. What we gain in dollars to get the work done may not be worth the potential loss of our professional efficacy and independence. Second, history, I believe, will demonstrate that we were right to link teaching and learning as seamless and complementary constructs. Even though in the process of linking them, we were accused of infusing opportunity to learn into content standards, that is, and most of us believe this to be true, the only defensible ethical position to take. It is unethical to create standards for student performance or teacher performance without providing for delivery standards (resources) and opportunity to learn (access to the curriculum).

The New Standards Project. This assessment-driven reform effort, headed by Lauren Resnick of the Learning Research and Development Center at the University of Pittsburgh and Mark Tucker of the National Center for Education and the Economy, is a consortium of 17 states and 7 major cities which has taken on the task of developing a system of alternative examination procedures (portfolios and instructionally embedded performance exams) as the cornerstone of curriculum reform in schools. A basic assumption is that our current crop of norm-referenced standardized tests and criterion-referenced curriculum tests are responsible for much of the narrow, irrelevant, and uninteresting curriculum that our teachers and students have to endure. Therefore, the argument goes, if we could only create an examination system that was thoughtful, challenging, relevant, and interesting, we would spawn a whole new generation of curricula. These new curricula would at once satisfy students' needs for relevance, teachers' needs for efficacy, parents' needs for assurance, and the needs of business and industry for a workforce of literate, collaborative, internationally competitive problem solvers. In short, since bad assessments got us into our current curricular troubles, good assessments can jolly well get us out!

About 5,000 K–12 teachers across the country, at one time or another, have been involved in the work of the New Standards Project, attending national or local workshops and/or experimenting with NSP materials and processes in the classroom. The NSP Literacy Unit, housed at the NCTE from 1991–1996, has had a three-stage history. In the first stage (1992), teachers from NSP partners were brought together to score integrated English language arts tasks for writing and response to a reading. This initial work introduced performance assessment, including scoring rubrics, anchor papers, and performance standards, to thousands of teachers who had not previously been involved in performance scoring and established the NSP goal and message as a serious endeavor.

Thousands of teachers across the country were brought together to develop a second batch of (hopefully) more sophisticated language arts performance tasks—tasks which would provide students with the opportunity to read and respond to entire pieces of worthwhile literature and write to thematic related prompts which would respect the basic principles of process writing as it has evolved over the last quarter century. Task development required that teachers find reading selections which would elicit engagement from 4th, 8th, and 10th graders; develop and pilot questions on these selections, questions which would challenge the reader to think about the reading selection at several different levels of cognitive and aesthetic engagement; develop rubrics and scoring procedures for piloted tasks, including experiments with both holistic and analytic scoring procedures; and prepare interpretative commentaries on scored tasks, complete with examples of student responses at each score level. During the development of tasks, there were experiments with various types of scoring and with a process for certifying various kinds of scores. The goal in stage 2 task development was to develop a large pool of tasks sampling all parts of English and the English language arts curriculum. These tasks were accompanied by scoring guide consisting of rubrics, benchmark papers representing various score points in the rubric, and interpretive summaries describing how the rubric was applied to each benchmark paper. The basic idea was to make available to teachers in New Standards partners a large set of assessment tools from which they could select those most relevant and appropriate to their situation. What would set these tasks apart from others is the broad-based consensus underlying their development (thousands of teachers from all around the country would have agreed upon their efficacy and validity) and the availability of nationally constituted benchmarks for calibrating the performance of students, schools, or even districts.

Stage 2, the portfolio stage, began in 1993 and has continued to progress ever since. Based upon the advice of experienced portfolio users, New Standards developed agreements with 21 teams of teachers around the country to craft a New Standards portfolio system during the 1993–94 school year. The long-range goal was to develop the materials, procedures, and staff development resources needed to implement a real portfolio assessment system, one that would have consequences for individual students and schools, by the 1998–99 school year. The short range goal was to build the materials and expertise within New Standards partners to implement a portfolio tryout in the 1994–95 school year. Working closely with our 21 portfolio consultant teams (3 teams at each of the elementary, middle and high school levels), they developed–through a process of successive iterations—outlines, menus, rubrics, handbooks (for students and teachers) and standards for our portfolio system. After a year of experimentation, they settled on a standards-based approach for a 1994–95 tryout. In the standard based system, teachers and students are provided with a menu of standards, along with examples of the range of entries that might be used to demonstrate mastery of each standard, as targets to guide the development of New Standards portfolios for each student. The key information is provided in the form of a student portfolio handbook in which the standards and the guidelines for portfolio preparation are presented in language that is (hopefully) accessible to the target student audience. The challenge here is that if the student is the client for the assessment system (and the audience for the materials developed), communication with other key stakeholders (teachers, parents, and policy makers) will be transparent. During 1994–95 school year, about 2,000 teachers in the NSP Project piloted this process and participated in partner scoring conferences in the spring and the first national bench marking of portfolios during the summer of 1995.

Performance tasks developed in stage 2 were added to the portfolio as a "common tool" (Valencia & Place, 1994) and an audit mechanism. Teachers at each NSP site included a commonly scored integrated language arts performance task. The inclusion of this task, along with the appropriate scoring materials, permitted NSP to evaluate scoring consistency across sites. The utility of this common tool in calibrating between site scoring is critical. Clearly, a system in which individuals from different sites come together for direct moderation of scoring practices is preferable but also more expensive. If it can be demonstrated that one or two commonly scored tasks can be used to compare scoring tendencies across sites, then the profession may have a cost-effective way of establishing statewide, national, or even international benchmarks.

Stage 3 of New Standards will come after this portfolio pilot / tryout phase, when the assessment system (some combination of portfolios, on-demand performance tasks, and / or projects) is used to make decisions of consequence about individual students (for example, does the evidence presented support a decision to award a diploma or a certificate on initial mastery?) or schools or districts (does the program provide evidence of promoting accomplishment among its students *OR* does the program offer students the opportunity to learn the knowledge and skills they will need to demonstrate mastery?). The assumption that New Standards is making, of course, is that when schools have in place assessment systems that are challenging, engaging, and based upon completely open and transparent standards, all the stakeholders (students, teachers, parents, and policy makers) will—perhaps even collaboratively–build, support, and participate in high quality curricular programs.

NAEP Achievement Level Standards. The National Assessment Governing Board (NAGB), for the 1992 trial state-by-state assessment in reading, writing, and mathematics (and for the 1994 trial assessment in reading), decided to develop a new, more publicly accessible system of reporting NAEP results. In the previous system, the proportion of students who perform at or above key 50 point intervals (e.g., 250, 300, 350, etc.) on the NAEP scale is reported; these 50 point intervals are anchored by items judged by experts to be prototypical of those intervals. In the system proposed by NAGB, these 50 point intervals and the items representing them would be replaced by categories based upon standards defining broad performance levels (below basic, proficient, and advanced) accompanied by items that typify those levels. In order to anchor these levels within the set of items and tasks within the NAEP framework, NAGB proposed a process of using the judgments of representatives from the professional and lay communities to set cut scores for basic, proficient, and advanced levels of performance. As of the summer of 1993, American College Testing Company, the contractor for NAGB had completed the process, using the modified Angoff procedure, in which professional and lay judges predict the proportion of students at each performance level who will answer each item correctly or who will perform each task (e.g., a writing prompt or an open-ended response to literature probe) at a given level of sophistication. From these judgments, cut scores are established for the borderlines among below basic, basic, proficient, and advanced levels of performance. The net result of all this effort is the capacity to report the percentage of students who perform at each of these performance levels.

Without question, this is the most wide-scale attempt in the United States to use performance standards to report student achievement data. The attempt has been met with considerable criticism, both from the English Language Arts community and the broader assessment community. The nature of the criticisms range from the basic invalidity involved in trying to reduce something as complex as reading or writing to a cut score on a test, to problems with the Angoff procedure as a means of setting cut scores (DeStefano, &

Pearson, 1994), to the construct validity of the entire NAEP operation (Bruce, Osbom, Commeyras, 1993)

The Joint NCTE / IRA Task Force on Standards for the Assessment of Reading and Writing. In 1994, the governing boards of NCTE and IRA approved a set of standards for evaluating literacy assessments; they were developed by a joint task force that had worked on the project since 1991. These are *not* performance standards that, once applied to assessments, could be used to evaluate whether students had met a standard. Instead they are standards that can be used to evaluate *tools* that we use to assess language and literacy. In essence, they hold assessments to account:

1. The interests of the student are paramount.
2. The primary purpose of assessment is to improve teaching and learning.
3. Assessment must reflect and allow for critical inquiry into curriculum and instruction.
4. Assessments must recognize and reflect the intellectually and socially complex nature of reading and writing and the important roles of school, home, and society in literacy development.
5. Assessment must be fair and equitable.
6. The consequences of an assessment procedure are the first, and most important, consideration in establishing the validity of the assessment.
7. The teacher is the most important agent of assessment.
8. Assessment process should involve multiple perspectives and sources of data.
9. Assessment must be based in the school community.
10. All members of the educational community–students, parents, teachers, administrators, policy makers, and the public–must have a voice in the development, interpretation, and reporting of the assessment.
11. Parents must be involved as active, essential participants in the assessment process.

These are radical assessment standards. If taken seriously, they would lead to a complete overturn of our current assessment systems, at least in the United States. The requirements for involving teachers, students, parents, and the community in the assessment process would lead to a major alteration of the very process of developing assessment procedures, not to mention a significant change in the way data are reported to various constituencies.

The Pacesetter Initiative of the College Board. With strong representation from the English language arts profession, the College Board has embarked upon a new curriculum development initiative that has major implications for the teaching and learning of the English language arts at the secondary level. Building on the success and popularity of its advanced placement syllabi and assessments, the College Board is trying to build a rigorous, thoughtful, and inviting curriculum for all students, not just those who are bound for college (see Payzant, & Wolf, 1993; Wolf, 1988). The controlling metaphor is, "entering the cultural conversation," and the basic idea is to challenge all students with the best and most interesting of classic and contemporary texts; relevant,

lively, collaborative discussions; and thoughtful writing opportunities. While this effort is not a standards setting effort per se, it will unquestionably influence other standards setting efforts by providing compelling models of the kind of curricular outcomes and performance assessments we could expect as students near the close of their formal school experience.

The National Board for Professional Teaching Standards. The NBPTS is a national, broad-based movement to create a system for the *voluntary advanced certification* of teachers at all levels and in all fields. It often gets confused with English standards efforts because the very first project out of the chute was to create a set of standards and accompanying assessments to evaluate teachers of the English language arts at the early adolescent level. The NBPTS selected a committee of teachers and English language arts professionals from around the country to create these standards. At the very same time, they created an Assessment Development Laboratory at the University of Pittsburgh to create an assessment system capable of evaluating the "certifiability" of English language arts teachers; in other words, the system was designed to evaluate whether teachers met the standards developed by the national advisory committee. When one examines the standards that the committee developed for evaluating whether teachers meet "high and rigorous" standards, it is easy to see how they might get confused with standards for curricula that students receive. Many of the standards used to describe what teachers should know and be able to do could, with minor rewording, be used to describe what students should know and be able to do. For example, Standard VI, for Reading, reads,

> Accomplished Early Adolescent / English Language Arts teachers engage their students in reading and responding to literature, and in interpreting, and thinking deeply about literature and other texts.

It is not too difficult to move from this standard about teaching to a standard about learning; it might read something like,

> Accomplished adolescent readers engage texts thoroughly, respond openly to literature, interpret what they read, and think deeply about literature and other texts.

Granted that each needs considerable unpacking (which, by the way, is accomplished in a section entitled, *Elaboration* in the NBPTS document), but the commitment to high and rigorous standards and literature-based approaches to the teaching of reading is clear.

Over the past several years, the initiatives to build a teacher assessment based upon these standards have been provocative and controversial. In 1993, the Assessment Development Laboratory at the University of Pittsburgh implemented a substantial field trial of its exercises for the Early Adolescence / English Language Arts effort. The reaction of the teachers who volunteered to be a part of the trial was overwhelmingly enthusiastic; even though they viewed the process as time-consuming, intrusive, and difficult, they found it to be a professionally challenging and rewarding experience. Nonetheless, grave concerns about the reliability, equity, and cost of the process prompted NBPTS to issue a second contract to the Educational Testing Service (ETS) to develop an assessment process that met these concerns. At the time this chapter was written, the NBPTS was in the process of evaluating the process developed by ETS. This set of events underscores another deeper debate in the field of assessment. At issue is whether assessment is conducted within a measurement or an interpretive (Delandshre, & Petrosky, 1994; Moss, 1994) framework. Within a measurement framework, privilege is accorded to concepts such as reliability, generalizability, and utility. Within an interpretive framework, the privileged constructs are difference, multiple perspectives, and the public presentation of rationales underlying decisions and judgments (much in the spirit of legal judicial opinions). Another factor which will ultimately determine the success of the NBPTS is cost, both monetary cost and energy costs. As indicated, the individual investment of candidate time and energy is enormous, well beyond anything currently at work in the teaching profession. Equally as expensive is the assessment process. Conducted by peers who have successfully stood for certification themselves and who have received many days of training for the complex scoring procedures, the assessment and scoring will conspire with other factors to drive the examination costs to a very high, perhaps prohibitive level. In the early years, NBPTS has underwritten the training and examination costs; it remains to be seen whether the system can stand on its own in a marketplace economy.

The NBPTS effort shares much in common with the curriculum standards movements in the various subject matter areas. What all these efforts seem to have in common is the development of fairly broad and theoretically grounded guiding principles that are rendered increasingly more specific until they provide some guidance to answer the question. What would count as evidence that the student (or teacher) had met the standard? Equally clear, even though it is not always explicitly stated, is a commitment to a broad notion of assessment that goes beyond multiple-choice tests to include long-term, environmentally situated, client-centered assessments.

DANGERS

The arguments against standards are grave, familiar, and convincing, and they should be taken seriously by all members of the profession, including those who are strong advocates for standards. The common theme uniting the criticisms is the concern for the loss or erosion of local and individual autonomy and voice in the name of global consensus (or intrusion, as is often implied).

Standards will Create a National Curriculum. No discussion of standards omits the obligatory critique that standards will lead to a national curriculum. And no amount of repetition of the "Why can't national standards accommodate a wide range of local curricula?" seems to quell this criticism. In truth, we should not be surprised at the ubiquity of this concern; in a nation so committed to local control of educa-

tion, what is more surprising is that a national discussion is tolerated at all. Two factors, I believe, account for our tolerance of a national discussion. First, the educational community has been so badly battered by the accusation that our workforce has lost its competitive edge that we are more willing than ever to consider national solutions (NCEST, 1992). Second, and more positive in tone, many educators believe that a national framework with lots of room for local variation and adaptation is not a bad idea. I suspect that many of us yearn for some shared national values; this yearning is captured in the appeal of phrases such as "entering the cultural conversation," the current theme of the Pacesetter effort sponsored by the College Board. Many of us appear to want to be a part of a "variations on a theme" enterprise in which there is room for both common and unique curricular elements.

They will Spawn a National Test. They could easily do this, and many policy observers in Washington have suspected that the movement toward state-by-state NAEP was the first step toward a national test. Those who advocate assessment as the engine of school reform (e.g., Simmons, & Resnick, 1993) are likely to prefer a national system of assessments to a national test. Such a system, they argue, would permit states, districts, and schools to develop and maintain their own assessment tools; through a system of benchmarking across schools, states, and even nations, the various tools would be benchmarked to a common set of standards. The portfolio, defined as a cumulative record of individual accomplishment, is the most commonly mentioned framework for such a system.

Whether such a system is viewed as a contentious instance of top-down intrusion or as an opportunity for schools, teachers, and students to show their mettle in a national forum is as much a matter of perception as reality. To one educator, national standards will constrict the range of assessment tasks to a myopic view of student achievement and, in the process, narrow the range of instructional possibilities in classrooms. To another they paint an exemplary portrait of what a literate person can do and invite students to paint their own personal portraits of achievement. The central question is whether a national system of assessment, benchmarked to permit substantial variation in assessment tools, is any less intrusive than a national test. That question is at present only answerable in the abstract.

They will became minimal standards. This criticism of standards appears to have little merit in the current debate. To the contrary, the rhetoric focuses on creating high and rigorous standards, albeit standards that are within the reach of all students.

They Represent Federal Intrusion. Until the death of the National Education Standards and Improvement Council (NESIC) in the 1995 Congress, federal control of standards remained a genuine concern. Among other functions, NESIC was to have reviewed national and state standards and assessments to ensure their compliance with nationally developed criteria. The professions and the public have to be vigilant to make sure that even when the federal government supports standards development financially, it refrains from exerting any direct or indirect control over the direction that standards take. If standards are to achieve any sort of credibility among teachers, they must be viewed as a professional activity, one in which classroom teachers are fully vested and invested. The negative experience of the English standards underscores the need for this sort of vigilance. Perhaps the positive side of the losing of federal support for the English standards will be the independence the profession gains by funding the project with its own resources.

They Will Become Just Another Tool of Exclusion and Marginalization. Any savvy member of a minority group should be suspicious about the current standards movement. Based upon previous incarnations of standards, be they labeled standards, objectives, competencies, goals, or outcomes, they have every right to assume that the current standards effort will continue to exclude and marginalize minority students. When standards are instantiated as test scores, the negative consequences for minority group members can be quite severe and are well-documented (see Chachkin, 1989; Durán, 1983; Garcia, & Pearson, 1994).

However, the metaphors of transaction (cf. Group 4 on p. 2–3) should they be realized as a part of our current reform movement, may give minority group-members reason to anticipate change. These transactional standards are causing us, as a profession, to rethink our notion of equity. With Brown versus The Board of Education, we adopted equal access as the basic criterion of equity; separate schools were viewed as inherently unequal, and the path to equality consisted of providing access to all. With the affirmative action movement of the 1970s, the equity criterion shifted to opportunity; every individual deserves an equal opportunity to compete for the good life, the good job, or the good educational experience. With the current standards movement, we have moved to an equity at the outcomes level; equality is not achieved until all students are able to achieve high standards. This implicit equity is captured in Simmons' statement, as quoted in an interview by O'Neil (1993):

> We have to shift the discussion away from whether we should hold students to high standards and toward what resources we need to get everybody to meet these high standards. This is where the delivery standards come in. They focus attention on whether or not students have had the opportunity to meet high standards. In the past, I think we mistakenly decided to wait until we got the resources to hold the students to high standards. The students are paying a price for that delay. (p. 20)

Irrespective of types of standards we are referring to, they must be inclusionary rather than exclusionary. They must invite people into the conversation rather than keeping them out. I know of no sure fire way to guarantee inclusion; but the most important safeguard is to keep the process open so that we can all see what is being valued and privileged in the standards that we set.

They Will Hurt Students. The "standards are bad for kids" position is most often an extension of either the "narrowing the curriculum" or the "standards exclude" argument. It is hard to argue with this position. Standards, especially as they are instantiated in tests, have been responsible for narrowing curriculum. While this restriction function is especially true for minimal competencies and the tests that accompany them, it is also true for tests designed for students at the high end of the performance scale. For example, each year, thousands of students spend millions of hours and dollars practicing for the SAT or ACT entrance examinations; while their scores surely improve, it is not certain that they have actually acquired any worthwhile knowledge.

Standards, under the guise of entrance or qualifying exams, have served to exclude students from particular schools, universities, or programs. The consequences of low scores on high stakes tests are familiar to all of us, and their impact is exacerbated by the fact that all too often, a single test is the sole criterion used to make the decision.

I know of no way to eliminate completely the potential harm of standards. If standards exist and if meeting them or failing to meet them bears consequences for individuals, then some students will experience the "joy of victory" and others, the "agony of defeat." Perhaps the best we can hope for is to make the standards completely transparent so that everyone will be able to see what we mean by them. By opening our values to public scrutiny, we permit evaluation of their potential for harm; standards and assessments that are left unseen and unstated are more likely to be arbitrary and harmful.

They Will Become Fixed and Static. Of all the concerns raised about standards, their potential for orthodoxy concerns me most. Eisner (1993) in a recent essay raising concerns about the standards movement, expressed this concern eloquently:

> …I cannot help but wonder whether this emphasis on standards is likely to move schools in the direction that I value. I do not value schools that regard children as an army marching toward fixed and uniform goals. Standardization is already too pervasive in our culture. We need to celebrate diversity and to cultivate the idiosyncratic aptitudes our students possess. (p. 23)

The danger of orthodoxy will be all the greater if and when many in the profession have worked very hard to develop an initial consensus. Those who come late to the party will be reluctant to undo or overturn the work of their colleagues. I hope that we can overcome this conservative disposition. Nothing has greater potential to destroy the professional and instructional value of standards than reverence for their quality and elegance or respect for the process that spawned them. We must demand generativity and dynamism for the standards and the process by which they are created. Review and revision should be continuous. Only partly in jest, some in the English standards project have suggested that they always bear a DRAFT stamp emblazoned boldly across each page; others have suggested that only disc copies (perhaps with an embedded time-released virus) be distributed for fear that the printed page will elicit too much respect.

The Impact of Standards as an Approach to Reform

The beguilingly simple logic of standards-based reform and assessment (set clear and transparent outcomes, establish equally clear assessment tools and criteria for meeting standards, and develop instructional programs that lead to mastery of the standards) is not new. In adopting standards-based reform for the teaching profession we would be returning to something like the logic of the competency based movement of the 1970s. Standards, competencies, and criteria bear a strong family resemblance to one another, the common thread being the early establishment of expected outcomes as the basis for evaluating both individual progress and institutional capacity to deliver quality instruction. The most notable difference is that standards, in contrast to the earlier competency-based movement of the early 1970s, are likely to bite off pretty big "competency chunks." In contrast to earlier movements, current efforts may truly represent "high and rigorous" standards of performance. So we may avoid the proliferation of minute behavioral precision so prevalent in the objectives of the competency-based movement.

The logic of standards, as well as other outcomes-based efforts, is that if you hold folks accountable for standards at the end of the process, you can eliminate the compliance mentality of our current certification systems and give both individuals and institutions lots of latitude in deciding how to "get there." This sort of logic places a high premium on performance standards and the assessments that accompany them. One wonders if our current crop of certification assessments are up to the challenge. To raise this point as a concern is to suggest the possibility, which is proving accurate in content standards efforts and teaching standards movements, that the biggest impact may be in the area of assessment. In privileging portfolios and exhibitions at the expense of test scores as evidence of competence, licensibility, and certifiability, we may leave an indelible mark on teacher education. If assessment becomes something future teachers do to and for themselves (rather than something we do to them), we, as teacher educators, may find ourselves in a whole different power relationship with our students.

WHY SUPPORT STANDARDS?

The concerns and the dangers notwithstanding, I believe there are several compelling reasons for us as a field of professional educators to engage in this process.

We could create a forum for a national conversation about what we value in teaching and learning. While local conversations about what we value are more likely to impact instruction, a grand national conversation is also needed. First, equity concerns demand that local groups become aware of the array of curricular possibilities that they might consult in building their own curriculum. Second, a national conversation is needed to celebrate the best practices of our nation's teachers. As Hoffman and Stage (1993) point out in discussion the movement in science standards,

> We need national standards to highlight and promote the best practices of these heroes. We must make their curriculums the exemplars—the core of teacher preparation programs, the models for instructional materials and assessments, and the basis on which science programs are judged. (p. 29)

Third, a national conversation will allow all of us in the profession to embrace a larger notion of community and encounter a larger pool of professional colleagues.

We could create an expectation that all of those of us who call ourselves teachers are willing to expose our real standards to public scrutiny. It is my strong conviction that our educational worlds are full of standards. We give grades, we set cut points for entry into special programs and institutions, and we track students. And for each of these decisions, we have implicit (occasionally explicit) standards of performance. The problem in most of these situations is that no one knows what the standards really are. As a result, they end up as the special property of those students (and parents) who manage to figure out what the real rules of the game are; the remainder of the students (and parents), in order to maintain their self-esteem, develop a sense of cynicism about the nature and futility of schooling. The current standards movement, with its emphasis on public discussions of values and student work, could put an end to this unequal distribution of privilege. Standards which are publicly displayed and discussed are much less likely to remain the special property of the privileged few who get told or figure out what the rules are.

We might influence both public and professional investment of time and resources. We need greater investment in education at all levels—national, state, and local—in our attempts to improve education and to promote challenging expectations of all students. Our public bodies—school boards, trustees, legislatures, and Congress—must *invest* in and be *invested* in the educational enterprise. Increased public awareness and increased public support may be the most important lesson to be learned from our colleagues in mathematics.

We can create a healthy tension between commonality and diversity within the field. We could provide a clear statement of our common values and an equally clear commitment to diversity and variation within that common frame. We want to be in a position to honor both local knowledge and national values. And we do not want the tension to disappear because, if and when it does, we may find ourselves on the verge of either a national orthodoxy or a large set of local orthodoxies. If standards can perform this function, they can be a catalyst for local curriculum reform. Sizer and Rogers express the sentiment that I am searching for quite concisely in discussing ways to achieve a balance between "civic virtue and individual liberty":

> Achieving a balance depends upon our ability to honor the individual school as the proper locus of accountability while also acknowledging that the school cannot manage this responsibility in isolation. (p. 25)

We could ensure a challenging, supportive, and thoughtful curriculum for all students. One of the greatest challenges to the standards movement is inclusivity. Earlier incarnations of standards movements have often excluded "special" students from mandates to meet a particular standard. The notion of *special* is usually extended to students who fit one of the categories of special education, students who speak English as a second language, and students who qualify for compensatory programs or assistance, such as Title 1. In fact, many current mandatory assessment programs allow schools to excuse particular categories of students from the assessment. If we truly believe in the transactional ideas expressed earlier in this chapter (cf, p. 2–3, see also Simmons, & Resnick, 1993), then we will extend high and rigorous standards to all students as we seek the resources needed for each and every student to achieve them. If we do this right, and if we can find the resources we need, we might reduce the likelihood that the quality of the education a student received could be an accident of residence, curriculum, or teacher expertise.

We could create a process for using standards. The balance between national vision and local knowledge will be difficult to maintain. If we fail to create expectations about how local conversations on standards and curriculum might proceed, we may fail to realize the variations on a theme metaphor. In some instances the national standards may be adopted rather than adapted, in which case local ownership is not likely to occur. The short history of the impact of the mathematics standards suggests that in some districts, the school board members examine a one-page summary of the standards, vote to adopt them, and go on to the next item of business, fully expecting teachers to regard them with the same cynicism they accord to other curricular documents. To prevent this, we might, for example, suggest that local groups engage in the same sort of public discourse that created the standards document in the first place. We might make recommendations such as, a diverse representation of stakeholders at the table, teams to craft their own local vision, widespread distribution and public discussion of any document.

We could establish a symbiotic relationship between standards and scholarship. I see two possible relationships between standards and scholarship: (1) the influence of research on the development of standards, and (2) the research opportunities that might be provided by the standards movement.

Our standards for the teaching and learning of any subject matter or process, including teacher education, ought to be as well grounded in theory and research as they are in best practice. Whether they are or not depend primarily upon three factors. First, if those involved in writing, reviewing, and approving are positively disposed toward research, then the standards are likely to reflect what research has taught us about the teaching and learning of various subjects. Perhaps we ought to examine the roster of task force members and board members in all standards projects to evaluate commitment to evidence rather than tradition, ideology, or political position. Second, if we rely equally on best practice and research for our ideas about standards, then they will reflect research to the degree that best practice also reflects research. Those of us who have been active in research about school curriculum are likely to be vain enough to conclude that *best* practice reflects research more than does practice per se. But there could be significant discontinuities. Whether best prac-

tice and research map onto each other well is open to question, and I think we will have to see what emerges from the consensus process that will guide the development of the standards. Third, to the degree that members of the various research communities demand a strong voice in the standards setting effort, the standards will reflect our best and most current research. We tried, in the Standards Project for the English Language Arts, to provide multiple paths and opportunities for involvement, response, and critique. And members of our research community did avail themselves of those paths and opportunities until, that is, the project was scrapped.

As members of the research community, we have an incredible opportunity to conduct research about standards. There are several levels and types of research that ought to be conducted as this process plays itself out in various venues. Here is just a sampling of research studies that someone ought to conduct

1. Ethnographies of the process by which standards are set within the various standards efforts, including analyses of the political role played by various individuals and constituencies.
2. Sociological analyses of the source and impact of ideas on the standards that are set as well as the impact of standards on practice.
3. The role and influence of the feedback (critique and consensus) process on standards development and revision.
4. Literary analyses of the form and content of the standards, including critical studies of the power relations implicit in the language of the standards and the symbolic role of the metaphors that undergird them.
5. Studies focused on the impact of standards on groups that have been marginalized by previous standards efforts.
6. Analyses of the relationship between standards and assessment. It will be especially interesting to see if the rhetoric of alternative assessment that pervades the movement will persist after content standards have been developed and schools try to establish performance standards to determine whether students have met them. What will happen once we become aware of the high cost of portfolios and performance assessments and are reminded of the efficiency and cost-effectiveness of standardized tests?

Regardless of the label we get saddled with—researcher, teacher educator, practitioner, client of the educational system—there is much work to be done in the standards arena. In fact, it is a unique venue in the sense that all of us can lay claim to a significant stake in the outcomes. I would like to think that we all hope they turn out to be a positive force for improving life for students and teachers in our schools and universities. I would also like to think that we all know that hoping will not make it so. If we want standards to have a positive impact, then we—collectively and individually—will have to shape their destiny.

References

Bruce, B., Osborn, J., & Commeyras, M. (1993). *The content and curricular validity of the 1992 National Assessment of Educational Progress in Reading:* A report to the National Academy of Education.

California State Department of Education. (1989). *English-language arts framework.* Sacramento, CA: Author.

Chachkin, N. J. (1989). Testing in elementary and secondary schools: Can miscue be avoided? In B. Gifford (Ed.), *Test policy and the politics of opportunity allocation: The workplace and the law* (pp. 163–187). Boston: National Commission on Testing and Public Policy, Kluwer.

Consortium of National Arts Education Associations. (1994). *National standards for education in the arts: What every young American should know and be able to do in the arts.* Washington, DC: Consortium of National Arts Education Associations.

Delandshere, G., & Petrosky, A. R. (1994). Capturing teachers' knowledge: Performance assessment (a) and post-structruralist epistemology (b) from a post-structuralist perspective (c) and post-structuralism d) none of the above.*Educational Researcher, 23*(5), 11–18.

DeStefano, L., & Pearson, P. D. (1994).*Content validation of the 1992. NAEP in Reading: Calssifying items according to the Reading Framework.* Unpublished manuscript.

DeStefano, L., & Pearson, P. D. (September, 1994). *The current standards terrain.* Paper presented at the 75th Anniversay conference of the College of Education at the University of Illinois at Urbana-Champaign, Champaign, IL.

Durán, R. P. (1983). *Hispanics education and background: Predictors of college achievement.* New York: College Entrance Examination Board.

Eisner, E. (1993). Why standards may not improve schools. *Educational Leadership, 50*(5), 22–23.

García, G. E., & Pearson, P. D. (1994). Assessment and diversity. In L. Darling-Hammond (Ed.), *Review of Research in Education* (337–391), Vol. 10. Washington, DC: American Educational Research Association.

Hoffman, K. M., & Stage, E. K. (1993). Science for all: Getting it right for the 21st century. *Educational Leadership, 50*(5), 27–31.

International Reading Association, & National Council of Teachers of English. (1996). *Standards for the English language arts.* Urbana, IL: National Council of Teachers of English.

Interstate New Teacher Assessment and Support Consortium. (1993). *Model standards for beginning teacher licensing and development: A resource for state dialogue.* Washington, DC: Council of the Chief State School Officers.

Marshal, J. (1993). *A vision of standards for American high school* (Tech. Rep.). Urbana, IL: The Standards Project for English Language Arts.

Merriam-Webster. (1983). *The Merriam-Webster dictionary.* Springfield, MA: G&C Merriam.

Moss, P. (1994). Can there be validity without reliability? *Educational Researcher, 23*(2), 5–12.

National Board for Professional Teaching Standards (NBPTS). (1990). *Initial policies and perspectives of The National Board for Professional Teaching Standards.* Detroit, MI: NBPTS.

National Council for Accreditation of Teacher Education. (1995). *Standards, procedures and policies for the accreditation of professional educational units.* Washington, DC: National Council for the Accreditation of Teacher Education.

National Council on Education Standards and Testing. (1992). *Raising standards for American education.* Washington, DC: U. S. Government Printing Office.

National Council of Teachers of Mathematics. (1989). *Curriculum and evaluation standards for school mathematics.* Reston, VA: NCTM.

National Educational Goals Panel. (1993). *Promises to keep: Creaitng high standards for American students* (report on the review of education standards from the Goals 3 and 4 Technical Planning Group. Washington, DC: National Educational Goals Panel.

O'Neil, J. (1993). On the New Standards Project: A conversation with Lauren Resnick and Warren Simmons. *Educational Leadership, 50*(5), 17–21.

Payzant, T. W., & Wolf, D. P. Piloting Pacesetter: Helping at-risk students meet high standards. *Educational Leadership, 50*(5), 42–45.

Ravitch, D. (1995). National standards in American education: A citizen's guide. Washington, DC: Brookings Institute.

Romberg, T. (1993). NCTM's standards: A rallying flag for mathematics teachers. *Educational Leadership, 50*(5), 36–41.

Sizer, T. R., & Rogers, B. (1993). Designing standards: Achieving the delicate balance. *Educational Leadership, 50*(5), 24–26.

Simmons, W., & Resnick, L. (1993). Assessment as the catalyst of school reform. *Educational Leadership, 50*(5), 11–16.

Smith. M. (June, 1993). *The Clinton agenda for educational reform.* Paper presented at the Large Scale Assessment Conference, Albuquerque, NM.

Stage, E. (September, 1992). Status report on the standards movement in science. Paper presented at the joint IRA / NCTE meeting on standards, Chicago, IL.

Standards for educational and psychological testing. (1985). Washington, DC: American Psychological Association. Introduction and Validity, pp. 1–18.

Stage, E. (January, 1993). *Standards for science in the 21st century.* Paper presented at the meeting of the Standards Board for English Language Arts, Chicago.

Valencia, S. W., & Place, N. (1994). Literacy portfolios for teaching, learning, and accountability: The Bellevue Literacy Assessment Project. In E. Hiebert, P. Afflerbach, & S. Valencia (Eds.), *Authentic reading assessment: Practices and possibilities* (pp. xx). Newark, DE: International Reading Association.

Wofl, D. P. (1988). *Reading reconsidered: Literature and literacy in the high school.* The College Entrance Examination Board, New York.

DEVELOPING STATE STANDARDS IN ENGLISH LANGUAGE ARTS: A CASE STUDY

Karen K. Wixson
UNIVERSITY OF MICHIGAN

Charles W. Peters
OAKLAND SCHOOLS

Sheila A. Potter
MICHIGAN DEPARTMENT OF EDUCATION

State standards setting initiatives are the result of factors such as the role of state standards and assessments in the 1994 Elementary and Secondary Education Act (ESEA) reauthorization, the availability of federal support for state standards projects, and the passage of Goals 2000 legislation which calls for competency in areas such as English language arts and establishes the National Education Standards Improvement Council (NESIC) to certify voluntary national standards in these subject areas. Curriculum development activities similar to these state standard setting initiatives are not new, but the level of scrutiny and direction from the national level is much higher than ever before.

The process of developing standards in English language arts is complicated by the fact that this area is an amalgam of the fields of reading, writing, listening and speaking, and literature which have a long tradition of operating fairly independently of one another. The separation of the fields comprising the English language arts is evident in everything from professional organizations and publications, to teacher preparation programs, to national and state level objectives and assessments. The history of separation made the process of developing integrated, K–12 English language arts standards extremely difficult. This situation was made even more complex by the lack of national standards in English language arts to serve as a model for state standards development projects until 1996.

This chapter describes the process, emerging content, and some of the problems encountered within the Michigan English Language Arts Framework project, a state standards development effort funded by the U.S. Department of Education in 1993. This information is provided in an effort to help others embarking on similar efforts at the local, state, or national level.

AN OVERVIEW OF MELAF

The Michigan English Language Arts Framework (MELAF) project was a 3-year grant to the Michigan Department of Education in collaboration with the University of Michigan. The major purposes of this project were to bring state goals and objectives in the areas of listening and speaking, reading, writing, and literature together into a unified framework that integrated curriculum, instruction, and assessment through specific content, opportunity-to-learn, and performance standards, and benchmarks for early elementary, later elementary, middle, and high school levels.

The organizational structure of the MELAF project included project Codirectors Karen Wixson (University of Michigan) and Sheila Potter (Michigan Department of Education), Demonstration Project Manager Charles Peters (Oakland Schools), a Steering Committee comprised of representatives from business, labor, government, and education, an Equity Advisory Panel, Grade Level Task Forces, a Teacher Education Task Force, an Evaluation Advisory Panel, and Demonstration Districts to assist the project in piloting standards and developing sample instructional units and classroom assessment procedures.

The first year of the MELAF project, 1993–94, was devoted to developing drafts of a vision statement, content standards and grade level benchmarks. These drafts were approved by the Michigan State Board of Education in August 1994 for public hearings and field review. Following an 18-month review period, the revised content standards in English language arts and the other areas of the academic core curriculum were to be written into law—a first in Michigan.

The activities for the second year of the MELAF project (1994–95) focused on reviewing and revising the vision statement, content standards, and benchmarks, developing of drafts of opportunity-to-learn standards, and designing guidelines for in-service and preservice teacher education. In addition, Demonstration Districts worked to implement the draft content standards and benchmarks, develop district level guidelines for curriculum and instruction, and create sample units of instruction.

The final phase of the MELAF project (1995–96) focused on developing and piloting informal classroom assessment procedures and performance standards, reviewing and revising opportunity-to-learn standards, and piloting, reviewing, and revising teacher education guidelines and recommendations. The standards were finalized as part of the larger framework, and both the content and the process used for development were disseminated to other states. The completed content standards were then used as the basis for revisions in statewide assessments of student progress and high school proficiency examinations.

The National Context

To understand state standards projects, it is important to be aware of the larger national and state contexts in which they have been operating. The larger context for current curricular reform efforts in Michigan and in many other states can be linked to the Governors' Education Summit convened by President Bush in Charlottesville in 1989. Stimulated by a series of reports in the early to mid-1980s such as *Nation at Risk: The Imperative for Education Reform* (1983), summit participants resolved to set National Education Goals and to invest energy toward their realization by the year 2000. Six goals were announced in early 1990 by a bipartisan task force led by then Governor Clinton, and a National Education Goals Panel was established to measure progress toward the goals in 1991.

Although two of the goals focused on improving student achievement in challenging subject matter, there was little consensus on the knowledge, skills, and abilities worthy of being taught and assessed. In 1991, Congress and the National Education Goals Panel created the National Council on Education Standards and Testing (NCEST) to consider establishing, for the first time, national academic standards

in the United States. The report of the *Council, Raising Standards for American Education* (1992), revealed that such standards were desirable and feasible and recommended the creation of voluntary nationwide education standards that would clearly identify what "all students should know and be able to do to live and work in the 21st century."

In 1994, President Clinton signed into law the *Goals 2000: Educate America Act,* which modified the six national goals and expanded them to include two new goals for teacher development and parent involvement. Goal Three is most pertinent to the MELAF project because it calls for "competency in English, mathematics, science, foreign languages, civics and government, economics, arts, history and geography." Goals 2000 also established the National Education Standards Improvement Council (NESIC) which was intended to monitor progress toward goals and work with appropriate organizations to determine the criteria for certifying voluntary national standards.

The first voluntary national standards were developed by the National Council of Teachers of Mathematics in 1988 and the U.S. Department of Education has since funded professional groups for the development of national standards in the other areas identified in Goal Three. Grants such as the one awarded to the MELAF project have also been made available for states to develop their own versions of voluntary national standards. Although funding was discontinued for the national standards project in English language arts in 1994, the International Reading Association and the National Council of Teachers of English continued to work on this project with their own resources. Although the federal government had announced an upcoming competition for a national standards project in English language arts, no request for proposals was ever issued. The result of this situation was that MELAF and other state standards projects had no national standards in English language arts with which to work until the NCTE / IRA standards were issued in 1996.

The State Context

Educational reform was mandated in Michigan with the passage of Public Act 25 of 1990 by the state legislature. Known as the Quality Issues Package, this law was aimed at raising standards for public schools by providing financial incentives for schools to develop a school improvement plan, to engage in an accreditation process, to produce an annual report for the community, and to provide a core curriculum for all students. In 1991, the State Board of Education published the *Model Core Curriculum Outcomes* document designed to guide local districts in establishing a core curriculum as required by Public Act 25. This document was based on the *Michigan K–12 Program Standards of Quality* (1984) and the *Essential Goals and Objectives* in each subject area developed between 1984 and 1991. The language arts section contained a total of 144 outcomes listed separately for reading, writing, listening and speaking, and literature.

The legislation passed in 1991 directed the Michigan Department of Education to develop graduation proficiency exams in communication arts, mathematics, and science based on the Model Core Curriculum Outcomes. Students in the high school graduating class of 1997 and beyond are required to pass these assessments to qualify for a state endorsement on their diploma. The high school proficiency test in the area of communication arts was defined as separate reading and writing assessments because the Model Core Curriculum Outcomes had been developed separately in reading and writing. Frameworks for the high school proficiency tests in reading and writing were developed independently by the Michigan Reading Association and the Michigan Council of Teachers of English respectively. As the frameworks were being developed for the high school proficiency tests in reading and writing, work began on the MELAF proposal to integrate state curriculum and assessment in reading, writing, listening and speaking, and literature.

Prior to MELAF, the Michigan Department of Education (MDE) had been unsuccessful in its attempts to get the state professional organizations in the separate areas of English language arts to work toward an integrated set of objectives in communication arts. The availability of federal funds to develop English language arts standards provided an opportunity for MDE to achieve this goal. As a result of the MELAF project, the reading and writing components of the communication arts high school proficiency test are administered at the same time and students must pass both assessments to receive the communication arts endorsement. There are also plans to develop and implement new, integrated English language arts assessments to replace the current, unintegrated Michigan Education Assessment Program (MEAP) tests and high school proficiency tests by 1999.

The MELAF project grant was awarded to the MDE along with two other curriculum frameworks projects in mathematics/science and geography in 1993, and a fourth grant was awarded in the area of social studies in 1994. Subsequent to the start of MELAF and the other curriculum frameworks projects, Public Acts 335, 336, and 339 were signed into law in December 1993. Public Act 336 altered the entire funding structure of public education in Michigan, while Public Acts 335 and 339 expanded Public Act 25 to include additional quality measures, the most notable of which was a required State Board of Education Core *Academic* Curriculum. For schools to be accredited, they were required to provide Core Academic Curriculum to the State Board of Education in the areas of mathematics, science, reading, history, geography, economics, American government, and writing.

The State Board of Education used the five curriculum frameworks projects to develop Michigan's new Core Academic Curriculum content standards in the areas designated in Public Act 335, and to assist with the creation of pupil performance standards and opportunity-to-learn standards. The initial work of these projects was approved by the State Board of Education in August, 1994 as the draft *Core Academic Curriculum Standards* document. Following an 18-month period of review and public hearings and approval of the revised document by the State Board of Education, the revised Core Academic Curriculum Standards were to be forwarded to the Joint Committee on Administrative Rules of the Michigan legislature. With the approval of the Joint Legislative Committee, the content standards in the areas of the Core Academic Curriculum were to be written into law.

Several of the factors just described made the MELAF project significantly more complex than originally planned. Specifically, the work of the project was complicated by the need to work together with the other curriculum framework grant projects and legislative action to mandate an academic core curriculum. Although these factors made the project more difficult, they also increased its potential impact—for good or for ill.

THE MELAF PROJECT

The ultimate goal of the MELAF project was substantive change in English language arts instruction that enabled *all* students to become responsible, productive, literate citizens in the 21st century. Our experience in Michigan with reform in the area of literacy education (cf. Peters, Wixson, Valencia, & Pearson, 1993) had taught us that nothing less than an inclusive process leading to systemic change at district, school, and classroom levels would be sufficient to achieve this goal. Keeping this in mind, the primary objective of the MELAF project was to develop a statewide framework that integrated the English language arts through:

(a) a vision statement for English language arts;
(b) K–12 content, opportunity-to-learn, and performance standards;
(c) grade-level benchmarks for K–3, 3–6, 6–9, and 9–12;
(d) guidelines for curriculum, instruction, assessment, and professional development; and
(e) sample units of instruction.

In addition, the MELAF project was designed to: develop an inclusive process that worked from both the top-down and the bottom-up to develop a framework that aligned curriculum, instruction, and assessment; support and develop demonstration projects for implementing the framework at the local level; incorporate the framework into teacher preparation programs and certification standards; and, finally, to inform the development of statewide assessments and proficiency tests.

How MELAF Works

Perhaps it is easier to understand the process that was used to accomplish the MELAF objectives through a description of the key groups within the project (see Figure 58E–1).

Michigan Department of Education Codirector's Group. The opportunity to coordinate standards development in several major areas of the curriculum was created when MDE received more than one curriculum framework grant. To facilitate this coordination, the codirectors of the various curriculum standards projects met regularly. Although this added another layer of meetings and administration to each of the projects, all have benefited from the opportunity to share with others engaged in similar efforts.

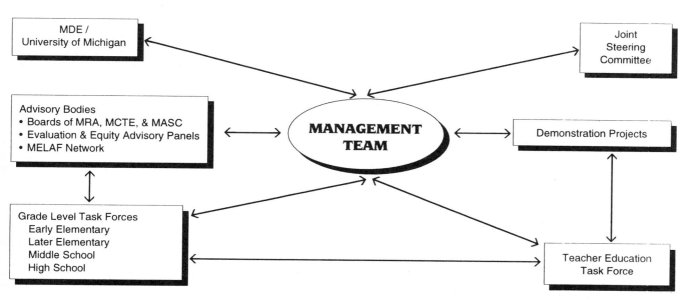

Figure 58E–1. Organizational chart of Michigan English Language Arts Framework project

The codirectors' group became even more important with the passage of legislation mandating the academic core curriculum in the areas of the curriculum standards projects. Through the efforts of the codirectors, we have been able to present a consistent portrait of the constructivist perspective on teaching and learning promoted by the standards in each of the core curriculum areas. This was the first time, at least in recent history, that there had been a coordinated effort to develop and represent state standards or goals in the major areas of the curriculum, and it has made a significant difference in how these standards were promoted through professional development and translated into local curriculum.

Joint Steering Committee. Each of the curriculum framework grant projects was required to establish a Steering Committee comprised of educators, business leaders, and representatives of government and labor to oversee the state standards projects. When Michigan was awarded more than one curriculum framework grant, MDE established a Joint Steering Committee to oversee the work of these frameworks grants in the areas of English language arts, social studies, geography, mathematics, and science. This Joint Steering Committee was in the unique position of being able to respond to the activities of these projects in a manner that ensured consistency and coherence in the resulting curriculum frameworks across subject areas. Ultimately, the Joint Steering Committee reviewed the curriculum framework documents for each subject area before they were submitted to the State Board of Education for final approval.

Broad-based steering committees are intended to involve representatives of those segments of society with an abiding interest in quality education in the standards development process. The support and input of the Joint Steering Committee was invaluable to the work of the curriculum standards projects. They raised key questions that were likely to be raised by other noneducators and offered helpful advice about both the content and process of the standards development effort.

Management Team. The MELAF Management Team was the central cog in the wheel of this project. Because MELAF was so large and complex, this was the one mechanism where representatives of all the components of the project came together to coordinate their efforts. The Management Team consisted of the Codirectors, Demonstration Project Manager, and Task Force Cochairs. The Management Team also created an Equity Advisory Panel to join them in their work and ensure that equity issues were dealt with substantively at every step of the development and dissemination process.

As the primary decision-making body of MELAF, the Management Team was responsible for activities such as selecting the members of the Task Forces, deciding about the direction of the project, preparing draft documents, and planning for meeting agendas. This group was ultimately responsible for the final revisions of all documents submitted by the MELAF project to the State Board of Education for approval.

Equity Advisory Panel. The Equity Advisory Panel was formed to ensure attention to issues of diversity in all project discussions and in the development of all written documents. Members of this group were experienced with a wide range of equity issues in education including gender, racial, and ethnic bias, and the needs of bilingual / LEP, special education, and Title 1 populations.

The charge to the Equity Advisory Panel was twofold. First, they were expected to participate directly with the Management Team and Grade Level Task Forces in the development of the various types of standards at the heart of the final framework document. Their second charge was to review thoroughly all documents as they were prepared for distribution to the field with an eye toward equity concerns. Panel members also provided other project members with relevant reading materials and made presentations on specific equity issues when appropriate.

Grade Level Task Forces. The Grade Level Task Forces were focused on four developmental levels, early elementary, later elementary, middle, and high school. As the primary document writing groups within MELAF, it was important that they represent as broad a group of educators from as many regions in the state as possible. The Grade Level Task Force members were selected by the Management Team through a process involving the solicitation of nominations through the newsletters of the Michigan Council of Teachers of English, Michigan Reading Association, and Michigan Association of Speech Communication.

The eight members of each Grade Level Task Force were selected according to the following guidelines: Each task force was comprised of a majority of classroom teachers, at least one administrator, at least one individual who worked with special populations, a balance between individuals whose primary perspective was reading and those who focused more on writing, at least one person who worked in the area of listening and speaking, individuals from districts who represented a balance of geographic and demographic characteristics, and individuals who represented a variety of racial and ethnic backgrounds. In addition, where possible, we were interested in selecting individuals with expertise in working with bilingual and limited English proficient students and people with experience using technology in English language arts. A state grant also allowed us to include an additional member on each task force from the Upper Peninsula.

The four Grade Level Task Forces met on the same day and in the same location approximately six times during the first two years allowing for both within level and across level discussions. During the first year of the project, the Grade Level Task Forces developed the draft content standards and grade-level benchmarks that were presented to the Joint Steering Committee and approved by the State Board of Education for field review and public hearings.

During the period of review and public hearings, the Grade Level Task Force members served as facilitators in statewide field reviews of the content standards and benchmarks. At each meeting educators, community members, parents, and others were invited to respond to the standards and benchmarks. Unlike previous statewide field review activities in Michigan, the current effort viewed the involvement of larger segments of the community from the earliest stages of the process as critical to the overall success of curricular reform.

The Grade Level Task Force members were also responsible for analyzing the results of field reviews and public hearings, revising the content standards and benchmarks, and drafting performance and opportunity-to-learn standards. In addition, they worked with the Demonstration District personnel, the Management Team, and the Teacher Education Task Force to develop a Framework Guidebook that included guidelines for and examples of local curriculum, instruction, and assessment and professional development activities.

In the final phase of the project, the Grade Level Task Forces were reorganized into a series of work groups focused on specific tasks related to completing the larger set of framework documents and activities. These groups focused on a variety of development activities such as creating performance standards, conducting workshops and preparing materials related to public education, describing a curriculum planning process for use by local districts, developing parent support materials, and coordinating publications of writings by project members.

Teacher Education Task Force. A Teacher Education Task Force was an essential piece of the curricular reform effort, because standards can never be realized fully without appropriate in-service and preservice education. The primary work of the Teacher Education Task Force focused on developing guidelines for teacher education and state certification consistent with the content standards and benchmarks and assisting local districts in planning for appropriate staff development. The Teacher Education Task Force also worked together with the Grade Level Task Forces and Demonstration Districts to develop a network of teacher researchers engaged in reflective practices that included implementing content standards and benchmarks. This type of network was essential for validating the work of the writing groups and provided models for implementing the standards at the local level.

The development of guidelines for teacher preparation included an examination of existing guidelines such as those published by the National Council of Teachers of English, the International Reading Association, the Entry-Level Standards for Michigan Teachers, and the National Board of Professional Teaching Standards and considering them in light of the MELAF content standards and benchmarks. The Teacher Education Task Force then developed models appropriate for preparing Michigan English language arts teachers and conducted discussions of these guidelines with representatives of teacher education programs throughout the state.

Demonstration Districts. A unique feature of the MELAF project was the role played by the local districts that served as Demonstration Districts (Fleischer, Koch, Lewis, & Roop, 1996). The work of these districts provided a critical perspective that has long been absent from curricular reform efforts in Michigan—the classroom perspective. Although MDE has a long history of collaborating with professional organizations in the development of goals and objectives for each of the language arts areas, the goals and objectives were never tried out in the classroom prior to statewide dissemination and adoption. It was essential that teachers have an opportunity to try out the proposed content standards and benchmarks so that their experiences could inform the review process and provide new models for developing local K–12 English language arts curricula (Casteel, Roop, & Schiller, 1996).

The local districts that were part of the MELAF project represented different demographic regions of the state including small rural districts and large urban and suburban districts, districts with above average socioeconomic indicators and districts with below average socioeconomic status, districts with homogenous populations and districts with racially and ethnically mixed populations. These districts were selected because they had already started to develop their own K–12, integrated English language arts curricula prior to their involvement with MELAF. As a result, these sites provide other local districts and teachers with a place to observe best practices in operation.

Work with Demonstration Districts provided models for the professional development activities that are essential for the successful implementation of the new standards. As part of the professional development activities in these districts, teachers and administrators from all of the sites attended one or two, week-long summer workshops for three consecutive summers that provided opportunities for in-depth exploration of topics and issues related to integrated English language arts. Participants studied the content standards, worked on instructional units that incorporated the content standards and benchmarks, and investigated topics for teacher-research projects related to the standards. During the second and third summers, teachers articulated the implications of the standards for their district curriculum and explored the creation of classroom assessment procedures consistent with district curricula and state content standards as a means of developing performance standards.

Participants in each of the Demonstration Districts also kept journals that served as the basis for a case study for each of their districts. The case studies were designed to help other districts in the process of translating the new standards, benchmarks, and performance standards into local curricula. Throughout the project, Demonstration District participants continued to meet regularly both within and across their districts to bring the standards and benchmarks to life in real classrooms and to provide much needed models for how to accomplish this type of curricular reform.

Evaluation Advisory Panel / Case Study Evaluator. The Evaluation Advisory Panel was formed in recognition of the importance of ongoing evaluation in curriculum reform projects such as MELAF. This group consisted of five members, two from Michigan and three from outside the state, with combined expertise in policy, literacy, and multiple forms of evaluation.

The Evaluation Advisory Panel was convened by phone or in person at least two or three times each year to advise the Codirectors and Management Team on opportunities and methods for continuous evaluation. This group also assisted in the hiring of a case study evaluator and in advising this individual as he constructed an in-depth case study analysis of the project. In addition to the first year report of the case study evaluator, evaluative information included data from minutes, transcripts of meetings, reflective writings, focus group reflections, and questionnaires.

Resource Groups. Several different types of organizations served as resource groups for MELAF. First, the Boards of Directors of the Michigan Reading Association, the Michigan Association of Speech Communication and the Michigan Council of Teachers of English provided feedback and input to the project. In addition, these professional organizations joined together to reactivate a Literacy Consortium which was formed in 1983, but was inactive for many years. The Literacy Consortium is working together with the MDE to plan and develop professional development activities related to the new reading and writing high school proficiency tests and the emerging integrated English language arts curriculum.

The MELAF Network was another resource group formed from the nominees who were not selected as members of the Task Forces and other local educators who expressed an interest in the work of the project. This group assisted the Management Team in reviewing draft documents and was called on periodically to provide information about related activities in their area of the state and to disseminate information at the local level.

Vision and Content Standards

The vision statement and content standards for English language arts accepted by the State Board of Education on April 18, 1995 are presented in Tables 58E–1 and 58E–2. Generally, the response to the draft content standards presented at public hearings and review sessions in the fall of 1994 was quite favorable. Of the 2,439 comments received regarding the proposed English language arts standards, 58%

TABLE 58E–1. English Language Arts

Vision Statement and Goals

The English language arts are the vehicle of communication by which we live, work, share, and build ideas and understandings, for the past, present and future. Through the English language arts skills, we learn to appreciate, integrate, and apply what is learned for real purposes in our homes, schools, communities, and workplaces.

The English language arts encompass how people communicate as well as *what* they communicate. The *process* includes skill and strategies used in listening, speaking, reading, writing, and viewing. The *content* includes the ideas, themes, issues, problems, and conflicts found in classical and contemporary literature and other texts, such as technical manuals, periodicals, speeches, and videos. Ideas, experiences, and cultural perspectives we discover in texts help us shape our vision of the world. The insights we gain help us understand our cultural, linguistic and literary heritages.

The ultimate goal for all English language arts learners is personal, social, occupational, and civic literacy. A literate individual:

- communicates skillfully and effectively through printed, visual, auditory, and technological media in the home, school, and workplace;
- thinks analytically and creatively about important themes, concepts, and ideas;
- uses the English language arts to identify and solve problems;
- uses the English language arts to understand and appreciate the commonalities and differences within social, cultural, and linguistic communities;
- understands and appreciates the aesthetic elements of oral, visual, and written texts;
- uses the English language arts to develop insights about human experiences;
- uses the English language arts to develop the characteristics of lifelong learners and workers, such as curiosity, persistence, flexibility and reflection;
- connects knowledge from all curriculum areas to increase understanding.

favored acceptance as written, 31% supported acceptance with revision, and 11% were opposed.

The specific comments received were very helpful to MELAF in revising the standards. In several instances, comments revealed misunderstanding of the intent of specific standards suggesting that the language of the standards was not clear enough. For example, the proposed content standard 2, entitled Language, read: *All students will understand and make thoughtful use of the forms and features of the English language that vary within and across different linguistic communities and contexts.* This standard was interpreted to mean that students who did not speak a dialect would be taught to do so. Feedback regarding this misunderstanding enabled MELAF to revise this standard to make clear its intent (see Table 58E–2).

Some critics argued that the proposed standards did not attend to classic literature or basic skills and that the intention was to disregard all things traditional. Although this was not the intent, the failure to mention these items specifically in the proposed standards allowed for this misinterpretation. This feedback allowed MELAF to understand better the concerns of others and to clarify the intent of the proposed standards. Of course there were and are some who did not and will not support the more holistic, social-constructivist bent of these standards and would prefer a more traditional, basic skills curriculum. As one State Board member put it, "I don't doubt the quality of the work. It's just that you've built a colonial, and I want a ranch." At present, however, there is widespread support of the revised content standards in Michigan and beyond.

WHAT WE HAVE LEARNED

As the field moves toward developing integrated, K–12 English language arts standards, there are numerous conceptual, procedural, and political issues that must be addressed. These include ideological and philosophical differences that exist within and across the various areas of English language arts, issues of turf and tradition that work against collaboration among professional organizations, and issues of community involvement, project management, and politics. These critical components in the reform process must be attended to if integrated English language arts standards are to serve as a positive influence on curriculum, instruction, and assessment.

Conceptual Issues

While those involved in the development of the MELAF standards share a social-contructivist perspective on English language arts, philosophical and ideological differences about the best practices associated with this perspective still exist. These differences manifest themselves in critical, and sometimes acrimonious, discussions about who controls the curriculum, how and when skills are taught, and what are desirable assessment practices.

In MELAF, philosophical differences have been apparent in a number of conversations about topics such as how

TABLE 58E–2. Michigan Core Curriculum Content Standards for English Language Arts

Revised April 18, 1995

Content Standard 1: Meaning and Communication
Focus on meaning and communication as they listen, speak, view, read, and write in personal, social, occupational, and civic contexts.

Content Standard 2: Language
Use the English language effectively in formal situations within schools, communities, and workplaces by building upon an understanding of their own and other language patterns.

Content Standard 3: Literature
Interact with a wide variety of classic and contemporary literature and other texts for information, ideas, enjoyment, and understanding of their individuality, our common humanity, and the rich diversity in our society.

Content Standard 4: Voice
View themselves as effective speakers and writers and demonstrate their expressive abilities by creating oral, written, and visual texts that engage their audiences.

Content Standard 5: Skills and Processes
Demonstrate, monitor, and reflect upon the skills and processes used to communicate through listening, speaking, viewing, reading, and writing.

Content Standard 6: Genre and Craft of Language
Explore and use the characteristics of different types of texts, aesthetic elements, and mechanics—including text structure, figurative and descriptive language, spelling, punctuation, and grammar—to construct and convey meaning.

Content Standard 7: Depth of Understanding
Demonstrate understanding of the complexity of enduring issues and recurring problems by making connections and generating themes within and across texts.

Content Standard 8: Ideas in Action
Apply ideas and issues drawn from texts to their lives and the lives of others.

Content Standard 9: Inquiry and Research
Define and investigate important issues and problems using a variety of resources, including technology, to explore and create texts.

Content Standard 10: Critical Standards
Develop and apply personal, shared, and academic criteria for the enjoyment, appreciation, and evaluation of their own and others' oral, written, and visual texts.

specific the grade-level benchmarks should be; whether there is a content in English language arts or it is primarily a process; what terms best communicate the intent of the content standards, for example, metacognition versus reflection, meaning making or meaning; whether literature or text should be the focus of English language arts; and how decisions are made about the canon. Discussions that focus on such issues are at the heart of what constitutes an integrated English language arts curriculum and should lead to clarification and understanding of the different perspectives that exist in the field. However, overly dogmatic positions can lead to paralysis and paradigm zealots can frustrate the process.

If we believe in respect for diverse perspectives, then we must accommodate a range of viewpoints in our collaborations to produce an integrated English language arts curriculum. Compromise in these situations does not mean violating beliefs and principles; it means learning where the commonality exists. In the end, compromise must prevail if the development and implementation of the framework is to go forward.

Professional Collaboration

Successful integration requires working closely with all the key professional organizations that are directly affected by the new integrated English language arts framework. In Michigan these professional organizations include the Michigan Council of Teachers of English (MCTE), the Michigan Reading Association (MRA), and the Michigan Association of Speech Communication Association (MASC). Although a Literacy Consortium was formed among these groups in 1983, these groups do not have a history of working together closely on important curricular issues.

For example, when the existing Michigan Educational Assessment Program (MEAP) reading test was substantially changed in the mid- to late 1980s, only MRA was involved in the process (Peters et al., 1993). Or, when new literature objectives were developed recently, MCTE took full responsibility for developing them. While these efforts had major implications for the English language arts curriculum, collaboration among the relevant professional organizations did not occur. Even at the national level where the International Reading Association (IRA) and the National Council of Teachers of English (NCTE) worked on national English language arts standards, integration was difficult to accomplish and the national speech and communication organization was not even involved.

In statewide projects such as MELAF where territorial boundaries of professional organizations are blurred to achieve integration of the English language arts, there are some who perceive this blurring as a loss of control that threatens the existence of a particular organization or professional identity. Consequently, tensions develop and become more important than the lofty goals of the framework. For example, not all professional organizations were involved in selecting the members of the MELAF Management Team. Although there was no intention to exclude leaders from any professional organization in selecting the Management Team, the perception was that one organization was trying to control the Management Team membership and, as a result, the decisions that would be made about integration. Projects such as MELAF need to think carefully about the implications of any decision on all groups. Past approaches to reform did not require this type of collaboration; current ones do.

A sometimes overlooked contributor to issues of collaboration among professional organizations in English language arts is the current state of preservice teacher preparation programs and certification requirements. It is not uncommon to have entirely separate groups of faculty, sometimes in different departments, oversee the preparation of elementary teachers focusing on language arts and secondary English teachers. There is rarely any overlap in either course content or practica experiences, which virtually eliminates any possibility of providing prospective teachers with an integrated, K–12 perspective on English language arts. Certification requirements usually reflect this separation, rather than lead the field in another direction. This is another example of why reform efforts such as MELAF need to address a whole array of concerns simultaneously. If the entire system is not brought into alignment, standards projects designed to promote systemic reform are not likely to succeed.

Community Involvement

Community members, parents, and business leaders are seeking a more prominent role in curricular reform initiatives than in the past. As important stakeholders in the educational system, policy makers expect individuals and groups representing these constituencies to be involved in curricular reform efforts. The Joint Steering Committee (see above) addressed this need directly. Business leaders, government officials, and community members were given active decision-making responsibilities as the standards were being developed instead of perfunctory roles of reviewing finished products with little chance for input. Another constituent group that was not included in the Joint Steering Committee, but must not be overlooked, is parents. Partially as a result of feedback from public hearings and review sessions, MELAF now has parents directly involved in the development of dissemination materials. The lesson here is that the support of the community at large is necessary for curricular reform and that this requires direct input from all relevant constituencies into the process itself.

The concept of community support should also be extended to include members of the educational community not directly involved in the particular curricular reform effort. It is very easy for the educators involved in a project such as MELAF to be viewed by their colleagues as an "elite" group that has special opportunities that do not apply to everyone. MELAF worked very hard to address these concerns through activities such as the MELAF Network (see above), updates in organization newsletters, special teacher-to-teacher publications, and interactive sessions at regional and state conferences.

Project Management

No matter how well intended or conceived, curriculum development projects are not likely to succeed without management procedures that promote the collaboration, communication, and consensus necessary to produce acceptance and support. Among the lessons we have learned in this area is the importance of coordination and communication at multiple levels of organization. For example, the Codirectors' Group and the Joint Steering Committee (see above) coordinated the activities of the curriculum frameworks projects in all the areas of the academic core curriculum. Within MELAF, the Management Team coordinated the activities of the different Task Forces and the Demonstration Districts and a group of facilitators both internal and external to the Demonstration Districts coordinated activities across districts. Other examples of coordinated activities within MELAF include the Equity and Evaluation Advisory Panels (see above).

We have also learned some things about the planning of various large group meetings and work sessions. For example, an advantage of having the different Grade Level Task Forces meet in the same location and on the same day was that it promoted a K–12 perspective on curriculum development. However, we also found that "writing by committee" with groups of 10–12 or more was not the best use of the expertise provided by the Task Forces. Rather, the experiences of the members of these groups provided an excellent base for a small writing team to develop draft materials to which Task Force members could then respond. In addition, it worked well to subdivide the larger group into small, cross-grade, working groups focused on preparing materials on specific topics to be presented to the entire group for feedback and revision.

Political Considerations

There is a new political context in which educators must operate. If we do not get involved, we are likely to have new English language arts standards imposed on us. This means we must deal with a process that can be both unpredictable and inflexible. We have learned that, although we cannot control the process, we can anticipate problems and develop appropriate responses. Two examples in Michigan will help illustrate how we need to be prepared to respond to this new political context.

Timelines always seem to be an issue in curricular reform projects, but the problems were compounded in Michigan with the state legislature's mandated changes in the state curriculum. The completion date for the content standards and benchmarks had to be accelerated because public hearings and legislative dates had to be accommodated. Legislators share educators concern for improving the quality of education, but have different timelines and approaches for solving the problems. What we learned was to be flexible in responding to these mandates, and to "let go" of our work before we are completely satisfied with it so that it can be examined critically by all the stakeholders in the process.

Another important political consideration is the changing role of community groups and their desire to monitor closely proposed changes to the curriculum. Groups from both ends of the political spectrum want control over the content of the curriculum. Each has developed a certain litmus test for the appropriateness of proposed curricula, and one of them is the language used in documents such as the content standards. Certain terms act as lightening rods (e.g., multiculturalism, values, respect for diversity, attitudes) and produce immediate response because they suggest a "political" agenda to certain individuals and groups. Such groups will sometimes mount an assault on the entire process that puts the entire framework in jeopardy. Many of these groups are well orga-

nized and very sophisticated when it comes to finessing the political system. What we have learned is to avoid certain types of language, study well the concerns of the opposition, and be prepared to respond to specific issues in public forums.

For example, in Michigan the content standards were required to go before a series of public hearings where all people were invited to respond. We knew that if we did not actively work to get parents and other community members who supported the direction the framework was taking out to these hearings, the only voices policy makers would have heard were those in opposition. Policy makers look more to the public than ever before and if conscious efforts are not made to provide them with a more representative view, they may infer that the public speaks with one voice.

SUMMARY AND CONCLUSIONS

The hallmark of the MELAF project is the process used to develop the components of the framework. The process is inclusive; it involves multiple levels and cycles of review and revision, working from both the "bottom-up" and the "top-down" to impact districts, classrooms, and individual students. Both the substance of the resulting framework and the processes used for development provide direction to districts within Michigan as well as to other states in creating systemic change and improving teaching and learning in the English language arts.

State standards development activities should not be undertaken lightly. Because they must transcend special interests for the broader purposes of the effort, they are extremely difficult to create and sustain. Even when the many levels of organization and aspects of curriculum development are negotiated successfully, there are no assurances that these projects will result in the expected changes. Although these projects are well intended, it is best to be prepared for unanticipated consequences (cf. Linn, Baker, & Dunbar, 1991).

EPILOGUE

Several significant events have occurred since we wrote this chapter. Most notably, the election of more conservative policy makers in the fall of 1994 resulted in less support for systemic reform initiatives such as standards development at both the state and national levels. In Michigan, this trend was evident in the change from a *mandated* academic core curriculum to *voluntary* standards and benchmarks. The move from mandated to voluntary standards encouraged the State Board of Education to make changes in the English language arts content standards appearing in Table 58E–2 before approving them in July 1995, despite the fact that these were the standards that had resulted from the public hearing process described previously.

The State Board of Education also required the MELAF project to pursue alternative instructional approaches to implementing the content standards—with an emphasis on the role of phonics in beginning reading instruction. As a result of this charge, we identified a group of K–2 teachers who use a variety of instructional practices from elementary schools that have demonstrated success by achieving state accreditation. These teachers wrote a series of mini case studies describing their instructional practices for inclusion in and dissemination with the final set of project materials.

A noteworthy conclusion to the MELAF project was the dissemination conference being held in July 1996. Forty district teams were selected from applications from around the state to participate in a 3-day conference intended to initiate professional development activities around Michigan similar to those developed in collaboration with the Demonstration Districts. A MELAF participant was assigned to each district team as a facilitator in developing district plans for professional development. In addition, district teams were grouped into regions and worked together with a coordinator from their region to plan cross-district professional development activities. Regional proposals received small seed grants to initiate these professional development activities in 1996–97.

The final framework documents were to be presented to the State Board of Education in the fall of 1996 for their approval and subsequent dissemination to local districts. Despite the decreased support for systemic reform initiatives such as this one in Michigan, these efforts are continuing and promise to have a significant impact on the way we go about the business of teaching and learning in this country.

References

Casteel, J., Roop, L., & Schiller, L. (1996). "No such thing as an expert": Learning to live with standards in the classroom. *Language Arts, 73,* 30–35.

Fleischer, C., Koch, R., Lewis, J., & Roop, L. (1996). Learning to walk it, not just talk it: Standards and Michigan's demonstration sites. *Language Arts, 73,* 36–43.

Linn, R. L., Baker, E. L., & Dunbar, S. B. (1991). Complex, performance based assessment: Expectations and validation criteria. *Educational Researcher, 20,* 15–23.

National Commission on Excellence in Education. (1983). *A nation at risk: The imperative for educational reform.* Washington, DC: U.S. Department of Education.

The National Council on Education Standards and Testing. (1992). *Raising standards for American education.* Washington DC: U.S. Government Printing Office.

Peters, C. W., Wixson, K. K., Valencia, S. W., & Pearson, P. D. (1993). Changing statewide reading assessment: A case study of Michigan and Illinois. In B. R. Gifford (Ed.), *Policy perspectives on educational testing* (pp. 295–385). Norwell, MA: Kluwer.

·VII·

VOICES FROM THE FIELD

INTRODUCTION

Lee Galda

UNIVERSITY OF GEORGIA

Bernice E. Cullinan

NEW YORK UNIVERSITY

Literacy is no longer just knowing how to read and write—it encompasses much more: critical viewing and listening, using technology, and recognizing persuasive techniques in political campaigns or advertising, for example. When a game changes, the players on the field must change. Therefore, to obtain a broad perspective on the contemporary literacy game, we invited contributions from long-standing literacy developers, such as teachers, and also from writers of children's books, and people who work in publishing, television, technology, art, and music. The chorus of voices from the literacy field grows large.

Our chorus of voices from the field includes writers, artists, illustrators, publishers, filmmakers, television producers, art critics, art educators, computer programmers, and children. Children, the primary focus of our work, have ideas about reading, writing, listening to music, watching films, or looking at book illustrations and art. Six-year-old Arianna Rubin responded with this note:

> Dear Lee: I would realy like to be in this. I tink it is vary cool. I'm talking about your book. from Arianna Rubin. P.S. Thanks

Arianna's gracious words and thumbs up signal demonstrate the range of her communicative repertoire; she includes both visual and verbal systems to express delight. Her message, illustrative of young children, combines art and words to convey meaning. Later, she sent this explanation:

> Sometimes I don't look at the pictures in the book. I try to make my own up. For example, when they talk about mermaids in the sea I think about The Little Mermaid and try to get pictures from movies.
>
> When I write I also draw pictures. The pictures show my readers what things look like. For example, I wrote a story called Jim and Jan and I drew pictures of where they were, not just what they were doing.

For Arianna, as for many children, writing and drawing are parts of a communication system that works together to convey meaning and emotion. Her older sister, Aviva, says she sees pictures in her head when she reads and she prefers her visions of characters to the ones artists draw.

Five-year-old Adam, a child frequently towed along through art galleries by his parents, began to look actively at paintings when he saw several Van Gogh self-portraits hung side by side and discovered they were quite different. An astonished and bemused cluster of adults nearby listened as he blurted: "Look, Mommy! This one looks smooth up close and kinda like skin and this one has speckles and this one has lots of color dots unless you get far away." Although he did not have a sophisticated vocabulary to describe the evolution of Van Gogh's technique, he was making meaning from paintings and beginning to read the language of art. His understanding of the language of music causes him to beg, with tears in his eyes, that anything played in a minor key be turned "Off! Off!"

Today's children are media alert. They learn early how to "read" the genre of children's magazines; they figure out a magazine's consistent format and turn to their favorite part rapidly. They develop a preference for art and artists in their picture books and gradually recognize the writing style of the authors they read. Some children outdistance adults around them in using the language of computers, especially for computer games. Many manage to channel surf across several television stations to keep track of five different programs at the same time. Some notice how cameramen use light and angle to frighten or startle them in the films they see. Some notice that advertisers try to manipulate them to buy their products. Children learn to play the communication game quickly.

Those of us involved in education, writing, illustrating, filmmaking, television, publishing, technology, music, and art recognize the virtual explosion in communicative possibilities available to us. We recognize, however, that among the possibilities there also lie perils.

VOICES FROM THE WORLD OF THE CLASSROOM

Children come to school today with far more information than those who came 10 years earlier. Today's children grow up with Sesame Street, Barney, magnetic ABCs on the refrigerator, interactive computer games, newspapers, magazines, and cassette players at their fingertips. They hear about social problems in their world through television newscasts and, although some part of their knowledge is only surface level, they sound glib in their pronouncements about a variety of social issues.

Students often have an overload of superficial information and questionable news from the street: this creates new challenges for teachers who want them to make sense of what they know and to think critically about real-world issues. In this regard, Ann Alejandro describes how visual arts play a crucial role in her Hispanic students' language learning in southwest Texas. Sometimes their real world is overwhelmingly ever present and numbing. Alejandro makes a powerful case for bringing beauty into all children's lives so that they can create worlds like happy dreams.

Teachers help students become aware of the ways in which symbols influence our thinking and create belief systems. Michelle Carey, for example, shows how her 3rd-grade students move from exploring visual symbols to examining literary symbols in imaginative literature. Richard Kerper questions the kinds of meaning making he sees valued in schools and looks carefully at the types of information students can gain from illustrations in nonfiction texts. A poet, Michael Strickland, guides students to explore poetry, music, and words as they create their own symbols. He includes performance as a natural part of every session so that students learn how to express themselves verbally. Teachers work along with their students to probe new definitions of literacy—they learn to master new aspects of technology without being controlled or misled by it.

VOICES FROM THE WORLD OF CHILDREN'S BOOKS

Current definitions of literacy incorporate visual as well as verbal formats; educational issues surround both formats and are similar. Mental processes that underlie all forms of literacy involve thinking, expressing ideas, evaluating ideas, and making connections. Fortunately, learning in one medium contributes to understanding in others. Voices to speak from this domain include writers, illustrators, a teacher of aesthetics, and art critics.

Master storyteller and poet Jane Yolen addresses differences between a tale apprehended by ear and one taken in by the eye. Acknowledging that although print may intimidate some, Yolen believes that the eye and the ear are different listeners. Good storytellers hold listeners through a magical combination of art and word weaving. Jan Greenberg, aesthetics teacher, concentrates on perception in the arts and believes art should be integrated into classrooms. In *The Painter's Eye* and *The Sculptor's Eye*, Greenberg introduces basic principles of art along with the language to talk about them. She argues convincingly that we appreciate more fully what we know best and understand well.

Two-time Newbery Award winner Katherine Paterson discusses her role as a storyteller who writes novels; she says novels are 'stories in the flesh.' Paterson tries to involve basic human senses (sight, hearing, taste, touch, and smell) in her words because readers must use them to create their own images; that is how readers make Paterson's stories come to life. W. Nikola-Lisa writes picture books, which is quite a different process from writing novels. Instead of describing every sensual detail, he must allow illustrators to tell the rest of his story. He continues to be pleasantly surprised as artists extend his texts and enrich his stories. Barbara Kiefer uses picture books to help children and adults learn about art. She encourages learners to consider artists as meaning makers who make visual choices; she asks students to make connections between art in picture books and art in their wider world. Steve Tozer and Victoria Chou examine a book, *The Stinky Cheese Man*, that plays against literary and artistic conventions for the sake of humor. Wildly popular with students and teachers, this book is both subtle and blatant in story, art, and design.

It is clear to teachers that students accept art as a way to make meaning. Beginning writers often draw first and write later. One day when asked what he was going to write about, Billy answered, "How do I know? I haven't drawed it yet!" Students use their notebooks as a place to think, plan, draw, discover, reflect, develop ideas, and sketch plans for drawings they will make and poems they will write. Teachers also see students use writing to express meaning in artists' workshop (Ernst, 1994). Ernst shows that students in kindergarten to grade 4 use writing in artists' workshop to express their thinking, to show meanings in their pictures, to assess and revise their work, to describe their process, to plan ahead, and to reflect on their learning and thinking (p. 45). She compares art exhibits to publishing in that both help students celebrate their work, find an audience, and receive encouragement to become better writers and artists.

Visual literacy and print literacy may be reciprocal: we use pictures to make meaning about text and we use text to make meaning about pictures. Certainly, parallels exist in the interplay between words and pictures. One teacher said, "My kids don't know where writing ends and art begins." The truth may be that writing and art are on a continuum as part of the same thing—a way to express meaning about our world. The issue remains unresolved: Will school curricula include instruction in critical viewing as well as in critical reading and listening?

VOICES FROM THE WORLD OF FILM AND TELEVISION

The ability to create images, to see things in our mind's eye, and to visualize objects and events not physically present is a major function of the human mind. We could never have our great cathedrals, skyscrapers, or the Golden Gate Bridge if someone had not imagined them first. Television and films spell out images on screens. They make images explicit; viewers do not need to work hard to create their own mental images. Healy (1990) believes that good learning and good problem solving require active involvement, persistence, and imagination. She fears that a great deal of television watching creates passive learners who give up easily (p. 201).

Studies show that the amount of information presented on television news is minimal compared to the amount presented in a newspaper such as the *New York Times, The Wall Street Journal,* or *The Washington Post.* The entire transcript of a 1 hour telecast fills less than half a page in a newspaper. The telecast includes pictures—which some say are worth a thousand words—but the depth of coverage is minimal.

Television reports the news and moves on—it does not hold still for reexamination, questioning, or looking at alternate explanations. A critical reader goes back to examine statements, the level of documentation, the sources of information. Critical readers assess the credibility of information, and the qualifications of a writer. This kind of checking is extremely difficult with a telecast. Readers determine the length of time print remains visible for its reanalysis, or evaluation. But television directors and cameramen control what we see and how long we see it. Can we teach students to be critical viewers of the media? Is our imagination stunted in its growth from watching a lot of television, computer screens and films?

Educators work in the field of film and television to make it responsive to learners. At the same time people who create media programs consider their audience and adapt their work to function effectively in a democratic society. Voices from this section of the field include artistic creators and producers of film and visual media. Marc Brown, creator of picture books, tells how he adapted his book character Arthur to the screen and interactive CDs. The childlike Arthur in aardvark form faces the same kind of emotional and social problems that any human child faces. Vulnerable and lovable, Arthur serves as a model for viewers who see possible ways to face their own life problems. Kathy Waugh, senior editor of children's programming, explains why she features the Arthur stories on a television series. Viewing the films leads to reading the books and she sees books as the key

to understanding one's own life, one's history, and one's place in the larger world. Twila Liggett, one of the first to present high quality literature on television, describes the research and development of the notable series *Reading Rainbow.* She also reports the dramatic effects that the series has on children as readers. Lauren Wohl, from Disney Press and Hyperion Books, transcribes comments from a session in which children under age 9 view the film *Bambi.* She observes that indeed children *do* read images on a screen that become new dimensions to explore in books. Victoria Chou and Steve Tozer, professors of education, interview Steven James, a filmmaker, who created *Hoop Dreams.* The filmmaker talks about how the film evolved, who he considers its audience, and what he hopes the film will accomplish.

VOICES FROM THE WORLD OF ART AND MUSIC

Children's development of aesthetic taste hinges on their experience with art and music. In this section, we let two people speak for themselves—one through his writing and the other through a personal interview. Philip Yenawine, art educator, describes his work with children at the Metropolitan Museum of Art and the Museum of Modern Art in New York City. Yenawine believes that children develop visual literacy when they have an informed guide to help them explore art. The guide also models a vocabulary to talk about art. Josephine Peyton Young interviews (her cousin) songwriter Caroline Peyton who discusses how she selects topics and creates images to convey her message. The popular songwriter tries to capture experiences that are gone and turn them into something tangible through her song lyrics.

VOICES FROM THE WORLD OF PUBLISHING AND TECHNOLOGY

Publishers have reason to be concerned that readers are an endangered species. The number of daily newspapers has declined steadily during the past decade. Book sales in the United States rank only twenty-fourth worldwide. Although publishers are necessarily concerned about making return to stay in business, they are also concerned about the intellectual level required to maintain an informed citizenry. A democracy cannot survive without active, engaged, and knowledgeable participating citizens.

Reading provides more than information; it has a cumulative effect on all language related skills. More reading results in better reading comprehension, writing style, vocabulary, spelling, and grammatical development. People who read know more about their world than those who do not. They are more curious, have greater understanding, and make more informed choices. Active citizens need to read to stay informed.

Students who use computers have advantages over those who do not. McDermott (1989) found that daily use of computer software programs helped kindergarten children learn to write and read better than children taught through traditional methods. Children who have access to computers excel because they can manipulate a mouse better than a pencil, and it is easier for them to recognize a letter rather than having to draw it from scratch again and again. Older students who use computers write more willingly, research more extensively and read voraciously, than students who do not have access to computers. Computer access seems to be necessary to remain an informed citizen.

In the final section, publishers speak about magazines, textbooks, trade books, and computer graphics. Tamara Hanneman Rubin is editor of *Storyworks,* a classroom magazine for students in grades 4, 5, and 6. Hanneman Rubin explains the considerations she has in choosing the content and illustrations for each issue. Joy Chu, a talented book designer, reviews her thoughts as she works with a manuscript and an illustrator to create a design for a picture book that flows, urges a reader to turn the pages, and holds together as a unified experience. You can always spot a book that Joy Chu designs; it is elegant, breathtaking, and a work of art. Roger Rogalin, formerly with the American Association of Publishers and currently with Macmillan Publishers, discusses political implications of publishing in regard to developments in literacy and technology. Anthony Lucki, Harcourt Brace Publishers, describes the effect of technology on publishing. He recognizes the impact of technology on

the way we now define literacy to indicate its fluidity or flexible nature: we negotiate meaning, we write as a recursive process. Suzanne Singleton, curriculum consultant, describes the process of creating a basal reading program, a collaborative process involving hundreds of people over a 3-year time span. Program authors, selected on a variety of criteria—area of expertise, gender, geographical location, and cultural background—shape the philosophy and much of the content of a program. Finally, Barbara Baskin, computer program writer and professor of education, explains the role of computer graphics in literacy attainment. She recognizes that some students are more comfortable and literate in microworlds than their teachers and addresses the issue of whether the intrinsic quality of the medium or the information obtained draws students to its use.

As literacy educators, we dare not be too enamored with the possibilities of technology: easy access to information, attractive media displays, and appealing interactive elements—that we ignore its potential dangers. Possibly students will think less critically, some may be less imaginative, and some may be influenced by advertising and its attendant materialism. Who controls the news we hear and the information we receive determines the direction our lives take. The overwhelming appeal of progress forces us directly into accepting these challenges. Schools must give students access to books, newspapers, magazines, computers, and all other available sources of information. We must also educate students in the processes of critical evaluation; only then can we guarantee a viable democracy.

References

Ernst, K. (1994). Writing pictures, painting words: Writing in an artists' workshop. *Language Arts, 71,* 44–52.

Healy, J. M. (1990). *Endangered minds: Why children don't think and what we can do about it.* New York: Simon & Schuster.

McDermott, V. (1989). *The effect of access to computers on children's writing.* Ph.D. dissertation, New York University.

.59.

VOICES FROM THE WORLD OF
THE CLASSROOM

LIKE HAPPY DREAMS: INTEGRATING VISUAL ARTS, WRITING, AND READING

Ann Alejandro

RIO GRANDE RIVER VALLEY SCHOOL DISTRICT

I have taught in southwest Texas for 15 or 16 years. In 1991–92 and 1992–93 I built two reading–writing communities with primary students in two districts. I have been their teacher, and they have been mine as we have worked together to create worlds "like happy dreams." This is our story.

TWENTY MILES SOUTH: THIRD GRADE, 1992–93

This year, we are 33 third graders in two language arts blocs, 12 of whom began the current school year reading at the readiness or 1st-grade levels. We are all Hispanic: 26 are classified as "at risk"; 19, limited English speakers; 17, the children of migrant farm workers; 2, learning disabled; 1, emotionally disturbed; and 31 are receiving public assistance. According to the 1990 census, 60% of the community respondents said that they did not speak English "very well," 76% of those 25 or older did not graduate from high school, nearly 65% of school-aged children lived below the poverty line, and 16.4% of the adult population are unemployed.

Once a week for the last 3 weeks, someone in our community has been killed. We have a population of 1,500, three gas stations, one cafe, no public library, and a postage-stamp-sized post office that opens from 9:00 a.m. until 10:30 a.m. and 11:30 a.m. until 4:00 p.m. All you can see from anywhere you stand in our town are farmed fields, tumbledown shacks and implement sheds, a cotton gin, a chemical supply, and an airstrip for the crop dusters. Our families have worked on these farms and ranches, sometimes for generations, and now the jobs are fewer and farther between.

We work together in this state that has threatened to close its public schools unless compromises can be reached about how to distribute education funding fairly and, for the last few years, has demanded that public schools address and fix the crises of high drop-out rates, gang violence, and terrible standardized test scores, particularly among minorities. When our local administrators responded to the threats of the governing state education agency (both of which demanded that we get "back to basics"), we were nearly denied the privilege of out-of-town field trips (for which we ourselves had already raised the money at school fairs and carnivals) because such a reward, our administration felt, should be earned by performing well on the TAAS tests.

"Art" has been relegated to a nonbudgeted craft activity involving paper plates and Popsicle sticks. For music, the children sing to records once a week for 25 minutes. Since we do not have sinks in our classrooms, painting is trouble and cleanup impossible, especially on the days we have no running water. Since our district lives under the gun of what the Education Agency will do to us unless we get our scores up in reading, writing, and math and "cover" all the test objectives, art and beauty are frivolities in which we just cannot indulge our students.

When I began working with primary-age children in our area, I doubted whether any of them had really seen, heard, or read anything truly beautiful in their lives. They had missed it, even when it was around them, because nobody had shown them how to see it. Sometimes a crop flowering or ready to harvest is beautiful, and a scraggly rose bush in a grand-mother's yard or even the chickens bred for cock-fighting can be beautiful. But the students did not recognize the beauty. The school library has many beautiful art books, but most of them stay on the shelves. At the beginning of the school year, none of my students has ever seen a real painting or sculpture or stained-glass window, and most have never seen a real Christmas tree.

TWENTY MILES EAST: SECOND GRADE, 1991–92

I had begun to use art extensively in my language arts instruction the previous year with second graders in a different district, 20 miles from the district where I work now, but with parallel populations and situations of difficulty. Because I believe that most writing is visually dependent, I am convinced of the parallels between teaching children how to draw and teaching them how to read and write. In all cases, students need to learn *how* to *see*, to interpret data from the world, the canvas, and the page. We see whole texts in paintings, in the scenes of life around us, and in the books we read. I believe children can understand thematic wholes as they look back on the events of books, the composition of paintings, and the unfolding autobiographies of their own lives. Conversely, I recognize that when we analyze the small components of paintings—dots, circles, curved lines, straight lines, texture, angles, genre or media, use of color, mood, atmosphere, and even conflict of character or plot—we use thought processes similar to those involved in creating or analyzing components of the texts we read and write. Sounds, words, sentences, punctuation, spelling conventions, genre, paragraphs, poetic language, metaphor, character development, and style provide an interplay of parts that contribute to a harmonic, full-blown whole. I believe that immersion in art can parallel and enhance immersion in text: When we read and write, we use the same critical thinking and decision-making brain power that we use when we paint or respond to paintings. Probably the same comparisons among musical, sculptural, and printed compositions can be made; it is a theory I have not had time to test yet.

Ironically, my art-centered classroom began as a direct response to the state-mandated reading, writing, and math test that these second graders would be taking in October of their 3rd-grade year, a test which would measure their 2nd-grade "skills mastery." Every teacher in the state was given enough worksheet preparation materials for this test to reforest the Amazon River Basin. The idea of the writing test was simple: Students would be given a "prompt" and would then generate a draft of a process analysis, a description, or a narrative from that prompt. Their papers would then be scored holistically by two or more state-trained readers. Based on these writing samples, combined with scores on the objective (bubble-dot) components of the writing portion of the test—capitalization, punctuation, spelling—students would have either "mastered" or "failed to master" the test objectives, and their teachers and districts would be held accountable for the results. A student could compose a decent writing sample and still fail the writing test; likewise, it was very possible to master the objective component but freeze up or compose "off the prompt" on the writing sample and fail. My students would be all of 8 years old when they took it, after months of summer vacation and then 7 weeks of cramming for it, in another grade, with another teacher.

The Lure of Paintings

These writing "prompts" consisted of cartoon line drawings, the quality of which was disgusting to the imagination of any child who had ever held a crayon. As I thought about inviting the children to write descriptively, I threw away the prompts and invested in a set of slides and transparencies of famous paintings and a set of slim, inexpensive paperbacks in the *Art*

for Children series (Raboff, 1988a, 1988b, 1988c, 1988d). I also stole all my mother's art books, set them in stacks on the tables in our classroom, and watched my students change. During small-group reading sessions, I shared little bits of two lovely books by Gladys S. Blizzard: *Come Look With Me—Enjoying Art With Children* (1990), a volume of portraits accompanied by engaging, thought-provoking questions like, "What do you think the little girl is staring at so intently?" and *Come Look With Me—Exploring Landscape Art with Children* (1992), with similar questions and situations inviting children to imagine, pretend, and immerse themselves in the landscapes. As all these treasure books were out on the tables all the time, my students came to the classroom early and stayed late, gathering around the books, laughing, talking, showing, and exclaiming, or sneaking off to corners to look at books all by themselves. They could not wait to finish assignments to explore the books in the free time I gave them, and for several days, I mostly watched, listened, and offered a few comments when students brought me pictures to look at.

When it was time to become art critics, we began looking at slides in whole-group settings, observing colors, background, foreground, different media, and mood. The children began to observe character and plot, and we talked about how "every picture tells a story." Brainstorming, we imagined names, feelings, and relationships among the subjects painted. They noticed that each painting had its own time of day, source of light, and weather, and they soon made comparisons between paintings and artistic styles. Quickly, they observed contrasts between cool and warm colors; and they made comments like, "It's very hot in this scene, and the men are very tired" (in response to a Frederic Remington desert scene) and, "Renoir likes to paint in the springtime."

They had no interest in relying on the text descriptions even when they could read them; nobody needed to explain these pictures to any of these little people. On the day I decided it was time to let them choose their favorite painting to describe, no child could be dissuaded from the painting he had chosen, the one that elicited the strongest emotional response. Although some of my cowboys would have no truck with anything but Remingtons, and most girls grabbed for the books of Renoir, Cassatt, and Monet, I was very pleased that many boys were drawn to Da Vinci portraits of women and Millais's drowning "Ophelia," and several girls loved Van Gogh's portraits of peasant men and the "Bedroom at Arles."

The 7-year-olds drafted their descriptions, and, that night, when I read them to my mother, she was able to identify each artist whose work the children had described. They had enabled an adult to "see" what they had described in words.

Children as Art Critics

In the following days, we revised our drafts for correctness only because the students had already found plenty to say. We prepared our descriptions for publication. Responding to Michelangelo's stylized, early "Doni Tondo," Cynthia, whose only pair of shoes were so tight that they make her cry, wrote in her final draft:

This is a round picture. Joseph is holding God. And God is puling Mary's hair and she is reaching to get God. Mary and Joseph are very proud of baby Jesus. Baby Jesus has curly hair and he is looking at Mary and Mary is looking at baby God. Mary has an ovl chin and a ovl face. and Mary has on pink and blue and green. Joseph has orinoge and gray and a mustache. And there are some men fighting in the background. There are some mountains in the background.

It was the most she ever wrote in the entire year and one of two discourses she ever completed.

Lorraine, an award-winning artist who turned all she read, wrote, or painted into love stories, was especially drawn to the rich colors and fairy-tale qualities of the paintings of Marc Chagall. She combined two rough drafts as she completed her interpretation of Chagall's "The Three Candles":

A Description of the Tree Candles

In this painting there is a woman and a man getting married. It seems like thay like each other. In the Backgrownd thar are green leaves and three candles and a goat and two people are out of the house that is red. This is a picture of angels flying in the sky. Thar is six houses and one car and flowers are by the angels. White rings are floting arownd. There is a clown standing on the fints. The people at the botum of the bride have a magic wone and thar pontin it to the air. And the air is red. And thar is earth all over. The magic angel is floting in the sky making drems come true for the womarl and a groom. And thay lived happile ever affter.

The End

Responding to the same painting, "The Cowboy," by Remington, Rigo and Daniel took different angles. Remembering to describe in detail, Rigo wrote:

I see a wonderful picture by Frederic Remington. I see one man riding on a strong horse and I see 46 rocks on the ground. The hores is slipeen off a mountain and I can see 4 horses, and the man has a hat on his head and he has a gun and bullets and he is wereng broun. He has a brown hat and brown short pants. The Shadow is broun and the background is blue, brown, and gray and I see that it is in the evnen. . . .

Daniel really was a cowboy who worked on a ranch with horses and cattle everyday after school, and he had had a few spills and close calls that became part of his description-turned-narrative: "This is a picture of a man riding as fast as he can on his horse on a very hot day. He's very tired. He is hitting his horse with all his fears. He doesn't care if he Fall's down...." Daniel was a talented clay sculptor of horses and cowboys. Later in the year, he also won an award for one of his paintings in the annual area-wide creative arts contest sponsored by our junior college. All dressed up in a western suit, he showed up at the awards ceremony at the college with his parents, who spoke very little English, beaming for him, shaking my hand, and asking, "Es good boy? He give you no trouble?" Yes, I said, he was a very good boy and never any trouble. A few days after school let out for the summer, Daniel's parents got into an argument, and his father killed himself in front of the children. I have no idea what became of Daniel. There was speculation that his mother may have moved the family back to her people in Mexico. I am holding on to the arts magazine in which his painting was printed, in case I ever see him again.

Dana had a twin sister in the other 2nd-grade classroom, and they were always dressed exactly alike—like princesses. Dana also had a younger sister, and her narratives were always characterized by beautiful girls or young women who had, specifically, no brothers, sisters, husbands, or children. Although she had not read any of the written description of the painting, her final copy appeared on my desk like this:

A Description of Diego Rodriguez De Silva y Velasquez's "The Infanta Margarita" by Dana Tristan.

This is a painting of a beautiful little girl. She is wearing a beautiful blue dress. She looks like a princess. She has a white face and a silver necklace on her neck. She has an olive green bow on her hair. The background is mostly black. She has a blue bow in front of her dress. She has gold on her dress, too. She feels so wonderful that she is a princess. It looks like she lives in a beautiful red orange castle. She is rich. She has black beautiful eyes. She has long light blond hair. She made that beautiful leathered dress that she worked on it for several days. She is in a dark room that there's no light in. She is not married. She does not have any kids or brothers or sisters.

She has a lot of jewels. She is sweet and thoughtful. She wears a lot of gold on her dress every day. She wears a little bit of makeup and lipstick. She cares for everybody. She is always happy. She looks like she lives in France.

I copied all the pictures, typed all the text, made book covers, and bound our volume of art criticism to present as Mothers' Day gifts. All year long, the children were more excited on "Authors' Day," when their bound books come to the room hot off my presses, than they were at Christmas parties or Easter egg hunts. They were just as delighted to read their classmates' words in print as they were their own, a consistent response each time I brought completed copies of one of the seven class sets of chapbooks we published that year. After the children pored over their anthologies for a long time, we had Author's Chair in the reading circle, and each author read his own contributions. Then they autographed copies for one another, the school library, the principal, and the superintendent.

Combining Paintings to Tell Stories

A few days later, I cut out quality artwork from calendars, magazines, old date books, catalogues, and journals; and I laminated them for the next series of "prompts," the narratives. Before school, I covered all the desks and much of the floor with these prints of paintings and sculptures. The students already knew that narrative structure required characters, a setting, a problem to solve, and the solution to the characters' problem; but before we began using paintings and sculpture as the stimulus for writing, all these elements had to come out of their own heads, and some of the stories had an uninspired sameness as the young writers borrowed ideas from each other. When they walked into the room filled with art, I asked them to pretend to be in an art gallery, looking quietly and carefully at each print, taking plenty of time, and then choosing four prints to incorporate into a story. I instructed the students to pick one or two character pictures; a setting picture; an event picture (if they had only picked one character picture); and one picture they absolutely did not like because it bothered them, scared them, or made them feel uneasy.

They chose their four pictures with great care, frequently changing their minds. The room stayed very quiet as they frowned, walked, picked, rejected, and finally chose. For prewriting, they began to take notes and wanted me to come to their assistance: "What do you think his name could be, Miss?" "Where do you think this picture is?" "Why don't this person's eyes match?" "Is this a lady or a man?" I answered all of them, "You decide." The resulting narratives were rich and complex, and I am convinced that the element of tension created by the one "disturbing" picture lifted these stories out of the trite, bland, and predictable. The students truly had wrangled with the resultant conflicts, and not one "formula" story came out of this assignment. We were all convinced that we were wizards.

Test Results

My principal resigned under pressure due to the campus' previous years' low state-test scores, and over the summer, the administration hired a new principal who would whip us all into shape and make those scores come up. After spending 20 minutes with him and hearing his plans to push me back into basal readers and "preparing for the tests," I resigned. The second graders from that school came back as third graders and, 7 weeks into the new school year, took the all-important state test, the results of which were published in December. Third grade writing had moved from 38 mastery the previous year to 88 mastery. Reading scores went up from 28 student mastery in 1991 to 80 in 1992. The school received a $30,000 bonus from the state for significant improvement, and the superintendent attributed the gains to the strong new campus leadership. Nobody knew that, in second grade, my students had hardly ever heard a mention of that test. I had never told them that we were preparing to "master test objectives." We had been too busy loving what we read and what we wrote.

COMING HOME

I applied to teach elementary school in my own home district, where I had always attended school and previously had taught at the high school before moving to our junior college to work in the writing lab. My criteria for teaching assignments were exclusive: My students could not consider themselves too big to sit in my lap or hold my hand, and they had to believe in Santa Claus. When no calls came, I prepared to home-school my own children and those of my relatives and a few friends who, like me, felt our kids were being robbed by the district's emphasis on mastery of basic skills and test-taking practice. But 2 days before in-service for the academic year began, the principal from the school where I now work called. (The campus was 20 miles from me in the other direction, 4 miles from the farm and ranch which had more or less supported my father's family all through my childhood, and less than 300 yards from some of my brother's cotton fields. I was, in

many ways, back home.) This tiny community is part of our local school district and has one school serving grades Pre-K through 8. The principal offered me kindergarten but asked me to take third grade, which I did, taking all my art books, posters, slides, videos, prints, paintbrushes, and clay with me to the new classroom where I would be obliged to prepare the incoming third graders for their early October testing.

Boot Camp Art and Writing

Astonished and overwhelmed by my students' "deficiencies," their lack of experience in reading, writing, and especially *seeing* (connecting language to visual stimuli and sensory experience), I began the same processes of using the art slides and prints, having 7 weeks to give the children the tools with which to compose narratives, descriptions, or process analyses. This did not include reading "skills" measured by the test, so we dived deeply and hardly came up for air as we struggled for words, descriptors, sense, rudimentary organizations, and structures for ordering language. I only remember four things about those 7 boot camp weeks: I brought huge buckets for watering horses to use as sinks, and we filled them with water from the hose outside, passing it through the window whenever we needed water for painting, making, or cleanup, and for our process analysis. Instead of describing "How I Clean Up My Room" or "How I Get Ready for School in the Mornings," we cooked clay dough on hot plates and colored it with dry tempera powder. As their hands turned wonderfully red and green and purple while they squeezed and kneaded the magic goo, the students did not know they were prewriting. The next day, our hall bulletin board was covered with baggies of brightly colored play clay and sentence strips completed by small groups describing the process stages for "How to Make Your Own Clay Dough and Enjoy it With Your Frends." My principal said, "I see," and asked some of my students to write down the recipe so that he could make the clay with his preschool daughter.

Pope Julius and the Texas Education Agency Have Their Standards

I showed the students pencil-sketch studies (prepainting?) and the resulting Sistine Chapel frescoes, asking the children to make the connection between vision—the beginning work, the germinating idea from the artist's eye—and revision—literally, seeing again, making the final product ready for the eyes of an audience. We talked about the kinds of changes we must make as we move from writer to reader of what is written. Using transparencies of their own writing, I taught them how to score writing holistically, using the same measures which their test evaluators would use. Within hours, they could evaluate accurately the strengths and weaknesses of their discourses. "See it in your head," I kept telling them. "When you read, don't depend on looking at somebody else's pictures of what you're reading. There won't be any pictures on the reading test. When you write, see it in your head like it was a movie or a painting. Let your readers know exactly how you see what you see. Don't leave any white spaces on your canvas."

It's Not Cute. It's Messy. It Has Misspelled Words.

When I look back, I think the most important part of those first weeks stemmed, once again, from my aversion to "canned" methodology. It seems to be a necessity that an elementary school bulletin board, usually teacher-made, must be "cute," the product of some pre-prepared activity from a cute teacher magazine, with little precise worksheets to duplicate, color, cut out, and write in response to seasonal or thematic carica-tures about "spring" or "puppy love." Grown-ups walk down the halls and say, "Oh, isn't that a cute idea?" Most cute ideas make for lousy reading and writing experiences, completely lacking in authenticity of students' voices and passions. I think groups of students should design, make, and caption their own messy, error-plagued, crooked bulletin boards. Because I honestly felt that about a third of my students stood a chance of mastering their reading and writing test objectives, I took that third to the library during our enrichment period at the end of the day, as my miracle-working, full-time aide kept the others for reading or completing final copies of their writing; pulled out the grown-up art books and set them beside my own collection; invited small groups of students to research their favorite artists and compile examples of their work from magazines (again, stolen from my mother, who parted with them for the good cause); and directed the groups to com-pose teaching bulletin boards for the rest of the students in the classroom and the school. When the bulletin boards were complete, each member of the different groups would explain different aspects of the artists' lives and work to the rest of the class.

The groups chose Michelangelo and Da Vinci (spin-offs of which resulted in brief studies of scientific invention, Biblical history, architecture, and the Renaissance), Georgia O'Keeffe, and Marc Chagall. The resulting scratched-out, messy bulletin boards that they made were the project's crowning glory, and little Debbie Gauna, who is almost too shy to speak above a whisper and who has shingles activated by the stress of major state-mandated tests, concluded her part of her group's bulle-tin board caption with the statement, "Marc Chagall's paint-ings look like happy dreams."

Deliverance

All Texas students took the same standardized tests on the same days. I felt riding on me the hopes of my last year's students, now third graders, and my new group, with whom I had worked these 7 weeks. Our school's third graders' read-ing scores rose from 48% of the students passing the previous year to 66% passing. Writing rose from 20 to 55%. The district thought the achievement was significant. Having read the results of what my last year's 7-year-olds in the other district had accomplished, I did not. We had merely done the best we could, limited by our ill-prepared circumstances, in 7 weeks that left me bone-weary. I was furious at a state that measured my 8-year-olds' skills and my own teaching ability by the

standard of one yardstick which had little or nothing to do with the real, always emerging literacy experiences that my students and I needed, wanted, and loved.

The Consequences of a Day

The pressure of that test off, the real fun and authentic learning could begin. Preparing for our upcoming field trip to the San Antonio Museum of Art where our students could view one of the best Hispanic folk-art collections in the nation, we spent a few weeks looking at and talking about the differ-ence between the artistic expressions and media of everyday people from cultures all over the world and those of the trained artists, Michelangelo and Da Vinci. We talked about flatness versus real, three-dimensional perspective; about the differences between painted wood and polished marble; and about children's toys compared to hammered gilt altar pieces. Our generous librarian supplied us with carts of Post-It tagged books showing the masks, weavings, furniture, and religious idols from cultures all over the world. When we went to the museum, we had a context that ranged from Hispanic folk art to masterful, prized examples of Phoenician glass and pottery; Greek and Roman statuary; Native American ceremonial robes; stone-carved Mayan and Aztec cooking utensils ("My grandma has a *molca jete* just like that for grinding her chiles"); and pioneer American quilts and crocheted bed-spreads. The Lure of The Mummies hit them hardest (and me, too). The children kept gravitating back to the second coffin of some minor Pharaoh's third cousin, wanting to touch it, to open it, to understand the hieroglyphs, and to see the mummy, which was not there.

For lunch, we went to the Japanese Sunken Gardens, where the children, in the rain, raced, screaming among the secret paths, pagodas, bridges, waterfalls, and ponds in which giant goldfish went into bread-crumb feeding frenzies. A lady asked me if I was a sponsor of a Christian school because the children, even in the ecstasy of exploration, had remembered to say, "Excuse me, ma'am." She had even overheard one of them chanting to herself, "Oh, thank you, Jesus, for letting us come here"—somewhere beautiful, away from the sheds, the windblown grit, the tin sheds, the Quonset hut cotton gin, the flat fields, and the thorny mesquite trees.

The day never left us as we continued to read and write all year long; the students continually made connections be-tween what they saw that day and the material we explored and made back in the classroom. For Halloween, their three-dimensional papier-mache masks harkened back to the cer-emonial masks they had seen either in books supplied by the library or on the field trip to the art museum; and it was clear that their own sculptures drew from those they had seen as examples of the masks of China, India, Africa, Native America, South America, and Mexico. These creations were of such high quality that they drew crowds to the lobby of one of our biggest area banks, where they were displayed for several weeks. As we spent weeks in January and February reading the myths and creation stories of various worldwide cultures and religions, the students reminded me of the Buddhas, urns, *retablos*, totems, and carvings of gods and goddesses they had seen during their 2-hour tour of the art museum. When we read "Pygmalion and Galatea," several reminded me of the memorable marble sculptures from the classical age. Our observation of the quiet textures and description of the small hospital courtyard, so valuable because of its comfort to the protagonist of *Sadako and the Thousand Paper Cranes* (Coerr, 1977), led the students to make comparisons with the serene composition of the Japanese Sunken Gardens they had visited. And, finally, when we read *The Day of Ahmed's Secret* (Heide & Gilliland, 1990), the children were able to identify the setting (country and city—illustrated in water colors with teeming, emotive detail) when they recognized the pyramids of Giza in the background of one of the pages.

Phrases like, "It looks like …" and, "It reminds me of …" consistently appeared in their oral language and descriptions of their own story settings, which became more descriptive and visual. Their handmade Big Books became rich volumes of detailed print and vividly painted illustrations. Without my teaching them the literary definitions of schemes and tropes, many students began using poetic language in their journal responses to the questions I had posed, as well as in their own descriptions and stories. Natural-born metaphor makers, the children now had fairly rich artistic backgrounds to draw from as they painted with words—and with color.

Painting and Writing Who We Are

Throughout the year, I have periodically used lessons from *Drawing With Children* by Mona Brookes (1986) to give my students formal, sequenced instruction in the use of line, color, perspective, and drawing what they really see. I am hard to please. I never saw blue clouds shaped like wads of cotton candy, I know that trees are not rectangles topped off by loopy ovals, birds are not upside down letter m's, people's bodies are not shaped like sticks, and houses do not float on spaces of white air. To teach my children to draw what they see instead of careless, dim representations of what they vaguely remember having seen, I have had temper tantrums: "You go outside, and you look at those cars, and you break them up into lines and ovals and circles and dots, and you make me a car that looks like a car!" "Look out there at that playground and that sky! Do you see any white spaces? Does the sky start 7 inches above the ground? Is all the grass one flat color, like a carpet? Give me a background!"

Challenged by people who have wondered if I interfere with my students' personal creativity by giving them formal art instruction with high critical standards, I have answered that creativity, like any natural potential, is a capacity that either levels off and becomes ordinary or is challenged to achieve higher and higher planes of expression. Some creativity survives in some rare children in spite of the ways in which schools attempt to kill it; but most creativity in most children has to be elicited and then channeled toward a set of culturally accepted standards. (Why else do we teach?) Otherwise, our language would not have any conventions of spelling, punctuation, semantics, or pronunciation, and nobody would understand anything anyone else ever said or wrote.

In other words, I know my students are geniuses, but I will not tell them that until they show me that they are. Our whole academic year works toward their recognition of

genius in themselves and their ability to go out independently like the people in the Nike commercials, and "Just do it." Approaching the end of this school year, most of them have taken on the attitude of, "Sure. I can do that. What do you want next?"

To make memories of who we are right now, we read an English–Spanish book written and illustrated by a young woman raised not 200 miles from us, who experienced almost exactly the same childhood traditions as ours—county fairs, eating *nopalitos*, cakewalks at parish festivals, religious pilgrimages to the Rio Grande Valley, *posadas* at Christmas, *pinatas* for *cumpleanos*, *sandia* on summer evenings, and *tamaladas* for New Year's Eve. Using Carmen Lomas Garza's *Family Pictures Cuadros de Familia* (1990) as their springboard, my students painted and then wrote vignettes describing their favorite family and cultural traditions. We displayed them all over the room and out in the hall. "This lady's from Kingsville, Miss? I been to Kingsville. We went to the beach, too. Just like that author."

We will wrap up this 3rd-grade year with one more reading–writing–art book that we will make ourselves after reading and thinking about Leila Ward's (1978) lyrical portrait of the inherent wonders in the life a Kenyan child who opens her eyes upon every day: *I Am Eyes / Ni Macho*. With simple, subdued illustrations by Nonny Hogrogian, a two-time Caldecott medalist, *I Am Eyes* teaches *seeing* as well as classifying beginning, ending, or rhyming sounds of words with pages that read, "I see sunflowers and skies, … stars and starlings, … donkeys and monkeys, … kites and Kilimanjaro, … And everywhere / where I am eyes, I see butterflies."

This past summer, my "at-risk" exiting third graders responded to *I Am Eyes* by describing either the world they inhabited or the one they want to inhabit someday, covering their pages with tempera-paint illustrations and leaving just enough unpainted space to print their final copies of "I see." From the perspective of being in the starry purple space and looking down on the blue-and-brown planet earth, partly covered with swirls of white clouds, Efrain wrote:

I See a Lot of Things

I see my family at the river.
I see my brother and me playing in the backyard.
I see my brothers and sisters swimming.
I see the earth from out space.
I see the Milky Way.
I see my whole family at the beach.
I see the sky torning into blue berries.
I see the trees at my house so beautiful.
I see my mom baking a cake for my teachers.
I see New York City turnin into popsides.
I see my teachers famous.
I see my whole friends and teachers singing at school in the library.

POSTSCRIPT: DWELLING IN POSSIBILITY

Reform continues. The future of public education in our state is out there and looking pretty ragged. Our district, with a capital base of per-pupil wealth at $65,523 compared to the state average of $178,277, has just lost more than a million dollars in state funding and fired 43 of its support personnel— many of whom worked everyday in the classrooms with us, with our students. They were vital. Eight people on our campus lost their jobs, and probably more will have to go next year. The legislature removed the possibility of merit pay raises for all teachers who had not already achieved "career-ladder" status. On the last day of work on our campus, everybody cried as we waited and watched our coworkers get axed. Our principal, red-eyed, said that it was the worst day of his life. We left the campus for summer vacation feeling kicked in the teeth.

In response to these worst-case events and data like the classroom profile that I received at the beginning of this year (the statistics compiled by the census bureau, the lice, the impetigo, the handicaps, the single parents and poverty levels, the simultaneous mandates for change and back-to-basics, the insanity and threats over district- and statewide scores, the programs piled on programs, the goal of minimal skills proficiencies), I take comfort from the knowledge that my students and I can always fall back on Botticelli and Picasso, on tribal masks and Homer.

We can always keep the quest for understanding beauty and making beauty at the heart of our curriculum, as long as we do not tell anybody that is what we are doing, and we can always strive for meaning that matters to us. I can keep throwing away most of those practice test worksheets, or using them for rough sketches or drafts; and at least for the time being, we can still take one field trip that transports us from where we are, where we live. We can imagine anything for ourselves. I can keep screaming at my district, "*Never* remediate. *Always* enrich. Treat students as if they were all gifted and talented, and they will show you that in some way, or in many ways, they are." Maybe someday, somebody will believe me. Meanwhile, like Debbie Gauna, we can think about reading and writing and painting a world that we can make "like happy dreams."

References

Blizzard, G. S. (1990). *Come look with me—Enjoying art with children*. Charlottesville, VA: Thomasson-Grant.

Blizzard, G. S. (1992). *Come look with me—Exploring landscape art with children*. Charlottesville, VA: Thomasson-Grant.

Brookes, M. (1986). *Drawing with children*. New York: St. Martin's.

Coerr, E. (1977). *Sadako and the thousand paper cranes*. Illustrated by R. Himler. New York: Putnam.

Garza, C. L. (1990). *Family pictures cuadros de familia*. San Francisco: Children's Book Press.

Heide, F. P., & Gilliland, J. H. (1990). *The day of Ahmed's secret*. Illustrated by T. Lewin. New York: Morrow.

Raboff, E. (1988a). *Diego Rodriguez De Sila Y Velasquez*. New York: Harper & Row.

Raboff, E. (1988b). *Frederic Remington*. New York: Harper & Row.

Raboff, E. (1988C). *Marc Chagall*. New York: Harper & Row.

Raboff, E. (1988d). *Vincent Van Gogh*. New York: Harper & Row.

Ward, L. (1978). *I am eyes / ni macho*. Illustrated by N. Hogrogian. New York: Greenwillow.

SYMBOLISM: A THIRD-GRADE EXPERIENCE

Michelle Carey Clark

TEACHER, SHORT HILLS, NEW JERSEY

As an educator I believe that it is my responsibility to empower my students to internalize the world around them. For this reason, we explore symbolism in our world, community, and in literature. Although symbolism and literary images can be difficult concepts for many children, I have found that my students allow their experiences and personal knowledge to guide them in understanding visual and literary imagery.

I feel that it is essential that students are taught to break away from traditional "literal" interpretations. When we begin discussing symbolism, I usually find that my students have very generic responses for visual symbols and few students, if any, can derive symbolism in literature. As we embark upon our exploration of symbols and images I always find it easiest to start the unit with visual, tangible symbols. Symbols such as monuments, safety signs, flags, national symbols, and so forth, are always easiest for the students to recognize. They are able to attach meaning to these common symbols with ease. Once the students become aware of the visual symbols around them in their community, school, home, and so forth, I ask them to create a visual symbol for themselves. I have found that my students come up with very sophisticated and thoughtful "self symbols." For example, one student put a book to display his love of reading, another student drew a heart with animals inside the heart symbolizing her love of animals, and another student drew himself holding hands with a group of people showing the importance of his friends and family in his life.

After a series of activities such as community walks, school searches, "self symbols," and numerous class discussions the children begin to pick up on symbolism in literature. The move from visual to literary symbolism is student driven. It is the student who starts to see beyond the literature. The students naturally take what we have learned about symbols and images and apply it to the nontangible references in literature. I have found that some of my students and classes take it further than others. The class described below took it much further than I had ever anticipated.

For several months my third graders explored the meaning of symbols in our world and symbolism in literature. Many of my students were unaware of the symbols around them and initially had difficulty in differentiating symbolic meaning.

We initially discussed the concept of symbols when we began a unit on people and places in our community. The children actively generated lists of relevant community symbols such as statue, flags, monuments, and safety signs (stop, danger, etc.) The students listed the symbols and went on to connect various meanings to each symbol. The chart remained in the room and as students identified symbols in the community they were added to the list.

Some of the symbols that were eventually added to the list were national symbols, ceremonial symbols, religious symbols, family symbols, and symbols of self. Lisa suggested, "…a symbol gives meaning to something." Tyler contributed, "…a symbol represents something." Thomas added "without symbols things would all be the same." After sharing the responses I asked students if a symbol always means the same thing? After a long pause, Sam stated "…of course not, people are all different, so the way that they think of a symbol will be different."

The students worked in groups to generate webs of different types of symbols. The groups dealt with national symbols, school symbols, and symbols of holidays / celebrations. The students' responses were very sophisticated. (See Figure 59B–1). When the groups shared their responses and interpretations of the symbols it became clear that they had a firm understanding of what supports a symbol. They were realizing that there is meaning behind a symbol!

As we began to explore various themes and images in literature I asked the children to think about symbolism in each novel that we had read. I wanted the children to connect what we had learned about symbols and the literature that we shared.

Using *Sadako and the Thousand Paper Cranes* (Coerr, 1977), we generated a list of symbols that the children had noticed when reading. Brian shared, "the paper crane is a symbol of friendship." Michele added, "…the paper crane becomes a symbol of world peace." Patrick said, "the paper crane is a symbol of courage that brought all the characters

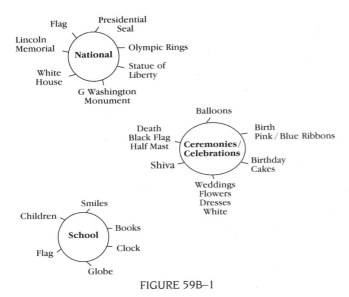

FIGURE 59B–1

together and gave them something in common." Erin reminded the class that "the paper crane was also a symbol of death, because Sadako was dying and hoping to stay alive."

The students discussed the importance of the paper crane and how it became a national symbol of peace, and a constant reminder of the bombing of Hiroshima. This particular story has many "hidden messages," but what struck me was that the children were able to interpret the symbolic meaning of the paper crane in such different ways.

At the conclusion of the discussion the students made paper cranes and wrote their own symbolic interpretations to accompany them. The children shared responses and the cranes were mailed to the Peace Park in Hiroshima as our symbols of peace to be shared on August 15.

Several children reflected upon *A Taste of Blackberries*. (Smith, 1973). Patrick recalled that, "the blackberries are a symbol of everlasting friendship." He went on to explain that without the blackberries, Jamie would have been dead forever. Jamie is kept alive for the narrator through the blackberries. Michele felt that whenever the narrator saw blackberries, he would be reminded of his friend, even in 50 years.

The concept of symbolism and imagery started to come alive for the children. The students began to make connections between symbols and different aspects of literature. For example, Erin and Chris both made the connection that images of color in a story can create the mood or embellish the setting. Chris supported this with an example from: *From The Mixed-Up Files of Mrs. Basil E. Frankweiler* (Koningsburg, 1973). He stated that the images of dark curtains and lighting in the museum create an element of fear and adventure for the reader. Erin elaborated and said that dark colors are symbols of danger and anger.

Monisha brought up a wonderful example from *Molly's*

Pilgrim (Cohen, 1983). Monisha is an English as a second language student who struggles for expressive language. She explained that the pilgrim doll that Molly made is a symbol of her heritage; "The doll that Molly made told us about where she came from. We could imagine what the doll looked like and it told more about the land (Russia) where she was from." This response from Monisha proved to me that she was internalizing and connecting with the literature she read.

When discussing *The Hundred Penny Box* (Mathis, 1975), the class generated many thoughtful responses to symbolism and imagery. The pennies were described as symbols of life, death, friendship, age, fear, past, history, and crying. The students brainstormed the list and had a meaningful example for each symbolic representation. The pennies were seen as symbols of life and death because Aunt Dew claimed that without her penny box she could not live. The pennies symbolized a special friendship between Michael and Aunt Dew. The penny box symbolized history because each year of Aunt Dew's life represented history. Fear and crying are also images associated with the box, because whenever Aunt Dew spoke of losing her box, she cried. The children were very insightful in all their responses to this particular piece of literature. They identified with the dilemma that Aunt Dew and Michael faced and the anxiety that surrounded the hundred penny box.

As a culminating activity, the students designed their own penny boxes and "penny books." They brought in symbols representing each year of their life to put into their boxes. Children brought in pictures, teddy bears, letters, and so forth. The penny book explained why each symbol was important and representative of the child. This particular activity allowed the children to reflect on their own lives and incorporate symbolism in their world.

Gary Paulsen's *Hatchet* lent itself nicely to further investigation of symbolism and imagery. Only a few students read this particular book; however, the whole class benefited from what they shared. The students drew wonderful images of nature and survival from the text. The children saw the hatchet as a symbol of survival. Erin went on to support this: "The hatchet becomes survival for Brian. He uses the hatchet as a symbol of hope that maybe one day he'll get out of the wilderness." John elaborated that "the hatchet is also a symbol of courage."

Jason, a student with enormous learning problems, made a remarkable contribution to the Hatchet discussion when he connected our exploration of art history and remarked that "the statue of David in Florence is also a symbol of courage and bravery."

These are isolated examples of a year-long exploration of symbolism in literature. It is clear from the students' responses and interaction that it is not too sophisticated a concept for children to internalize. My third graders took it much further than I thought they could.

The work with symbolism is some of the most exciting and beneficial that the students do. We do it because it helps us reach a higher level of understanding and thinking in every part of the curriculum.

References

Coerr, E. (1977). *Sadako and the thousand paper cranes.* New York: Dell.

Cohen, B. (1983). *Molly's pilgrim.* New York: William Morrow.

Koningsburg, E. L. (1973). *From the mixed-up files of Mrs. Basil E. Frankweiler.* New York: Dell.

Mathis, S. B. (1975). *The hundred penny box.* New York: Scholastic.

Smith, D. B. (1973). *A taste of blackberries.* New York: HarperCollins.

VOICES FROM THE FIELD: CONSTRUCTING MEANING FROM ILLUSTRATIONS

Richard M. Kerper

MILLERSVILLE UNIVERSITY

Young children in our school classooms bring a wide range of experiences with visual images to the activities in which they engage. They have spent many hours watching programs and commercials on television, viewing images on product labels, and looking at pictures in catalogues. But, how do these experiences prepare children to undetstand the illustrations that they encounter in informational trade books?

As David Considine (1987) states, chidren are "given no guidance in how to read, interpret, and critically evaluate the images and information that they are exposed to" (p. 635). Yet, as a teacher, I often assumed that my students would understand what they saw. The representational nature of pictures in books lured me into complacency. I dealt with pictures as though they conveyed meaning. While my instructional practices demonstrated a belief that young children need guided and supported experiences with print to learn cultural conventions as they became readers, my practices did not treat illustration in the same way. I expected my students to *be* viewers, not to *become* viewers. Now, as I study the ways in which children construct meaning from illustrations, I consider many issues that I did not face early in my teaching.

At home and at school, children learn the language and conventions of print holistically as page after page of words, sentences, paragraphs, and stories are read. Parents and teachers explore their meanings and their stuctures with children. Often these experiences include references to pictures. But are they talked about in the same way? Do parents and teachers possess the language to talk about the conventions of illustration? As an inexperienced teacher many years ago, I did not challenge my students' thinking about pictures because I lacked the language to think about them. My students left my classroom after one academic year with no greater ability to construct meaning from illustration than when they walked through the door on the first day of school.

I fear that my story is not unique. It is one that could be retold by many teachers.

Pliny the Elder states that "the mind is the real instrument of sight and observation" (p. 552). Similarly, Betty Bacon (1981) describes engagement with informational books as "an eye / mind experience that endows the subject with a kind of tangible life" (p. 11). Each focuses on the apperceptive dimension of viewing. For them prior experience frames the meaning that viewers make from illustrations. But, in what ways is viewing a solitary cognitive experience versus a social one? Margaret Meek (1998) contends that children learn through what she calls "private lessons." Through engagement with informational books, children expose themselves to the conventions and implied directions of illustrations. Meek suggests that "understanding ... illustration and iconic interpretation are part of the ontogenesis of 'literary competences'" (p. 10). However, she does not see this activity as a solitary act. It occurs in a social context. Often, the meanings that children construct from what they see are in part someone else's. Interactions with peers and with adults contribute to the meanings made, meanings that are sensed as one's own (Bakhtin, 1986).

In my observations of young children viewing informational books, each child's intentions have been critical to the meanings constructed. These intentions relative to the qualities of the illustrations afford opportunities to make meaning (Heft, 1989). While some children realize the affordance to count and to draw, other children realize opportunities to play and to socialize (Kerper, 1994). These affordances frame the meaning-making process, a process that may be similar in some respects to constructing meaning from print. My observations of children's viewing point to the importance of moving, gesturing, connecting and speculating found by Cox and Many (1992), Hickman (1979, 1981), Hepler (1982), and Harvey (1993) in children's transactions with print. Thus, I wonder about other ways in which meaning making with illustrations and with print are similar and about ways in which each is unique.

The assumption is often made that the illustrations in informational books are intended to communicate facts and that viewers use those pictures to gain information for use in other situations. My observations of children's viewing causes me to challenge this idea. Just as children naturally approach written text with varying purposes, they deal with illustrations in a similar way. Sometimes they will adopt a stance that focuses on information, but at other times they will revel in the virtual reality that the pictues offer (Kerper, 1994). I fear, however, that classroom practice valorizes the former stance over the latter. Teachers may validate what Louise Rosenblatt (1986) refers to as an "efferent stance," a focus on public meaning, and discount the importance of an "aesthetic stance" focusing on personal responses.

In recent years teachers have used and children have explored more and more informational trade books as the integration of instruction has become increasingly popular. This trend may present a real and present danger to children's opportunity to respond aesthetically to illustrations. The potential for subordination of aesthetic experiences to content-based, curricular-driven ones and of visual experiences to verbal ones is clearly present. The pressures of accountability may impel many teachers to focus on the public meaning of print and to ignore the personal meaning of illustrations. My observation of young children points to the impotance of aesthetic experience in their meaning making. Often initial engagement with the virtual reality of pictures leads to children's interest in the more public aspects of meaning, in the content-based information (Kerper, 1994).

As I continue to watch children make meaning with illustrations, I face new questions daily. However, one overarching question about children and book illustrations endures: a question that demands exploration. In varied real-life settings when, if at all, and how do children use illustrations? The answers to this question could provide teachers with valuable information as they plan instruction within their classrooms and as they focus on the often-ignored area of visual literacy.

References

Bacon, B. (1981). The art of nonfiction. *Children's Literature in Education, 12*(1), 3–14.

Bakhtin, M. M. (1986). *Speech genres and other late essays.* In C. Emerson & M. Homquist, (Eds.), (V. W. McGee, Trans.), Austin, TX: University of Texas Press.

Considine, D. M. (1987). Visual literacy and the curriculum: More to it than meets the eye. *Language Arts, 64*(6), 634–640.

Cox, C., & Many J. E. (1992). Reader stance towards a literary work: Applying the transactional theory to children's responses. *Reading Psychology, 13*(1), 37–72.

Heft, H. (1989). Affordances and the body: An intentional analysis of Gibson's ecological approach to visual perception. *Journal for the Theory of Social Behaviour, 19*(1), 1–30.

Hepler, S. I. (1982). Patterns of response to literature: A one-year study of a fifth and sixth grade classroom (Doctoral dissertation, The Ohio State University, 1982). *Dissertation Abstracts International, 43*(5), 1419A.

Hickman J. G. (1979). Response to literature in a school environment, grades K–5 (Doctoral dissertation, The Ohio State University, 1979). *Dissertation Abstracts International, 40*(7), 3764A.

Hickman, J. G. (1981). A new perspective on response to literature: Research in an elementary school setting. *Research in the Teaching of English, 15*(4), 343–354.

Kerper, R. M. (1994). Three children viewing and reading: Transactions with illustration and print in informational books. (Doctoral dissertation,.The Ohio State University, 1994).

Meek, M. (1988). *How texts teach what readers learn.* South Woodchester, Great Britain: Thimble Press.

Pliny, (1967). *Natural history: Vol. III Libri VIII–XI* (H. Rackham, Trans.). Cambridge, MA: Harvard University Press. (Original work published 77 A.D.)

Rosenblatt, L. M. (1986). The aesthetic transaction. *Journal of Aesthetic Education, 20,* 122–128.

WE ARE THE MUSIC MAKERS: HELPING CHILDREN EXPRESS THEMSELVES THROUGH THE MAGIC OF POETRY

Michael R. Strickland

JERSEY CITY STATE COLLEGE

I walk down the hall at Oberlin, Ohio's Prospect School and hear a fourth grader yell, "Here he comes! Let's clap for him." I skip into the large classroom, waving at the students as they cheer, as if I had just been named most valuable player in a sports championship.

I hope that the magic and music of poetry come across to students as soon as I walk into the room. Before the workshop, the students have usually seen my anthologies, *Poems That Sing To You* and *Families: Poems Celebrating The African American Experience* (Strickland & Strickland, 1994). The books have my picture on the inside, back covers. The closest that children usually come to what they consider a "real poet" is seeing his or her picture on the back of the book, but the workshop is "live."

At the end of my 45-minute workshops, students (some with minimal experience with the art form) produce work that includes elements such as: meter, irony, story, humor, and creative stanza forms; rhyme, refrain, onomatopoeia, alliteration, consonance, and other devices of sound; metaphor, hyperbole, personification, and other devices of sense. Many teachers have told me that my methods have produced good writing, including many of these fundamentals of poetry, even from students who have had trouble writing a few sentences in the past. I think that linking poetry and music, utilizing the sound of poetry and its performance, helps students become involved with poetry in meaningful ways.

T.S. Eliot coined the phrase "the auditory imagination" to describe the sound and rhythm of poetry. I tell children that master poets sometimes write and rewrite their pieces 1,000 times before they get the exact pattern of words on a page, and the precise rhythm. The auditory elements of poetry make them like songs. I repeat the phrase "poetry and music have a lot in common and are often one in the same" many

times in my workshops. There are two song lyrics as poems in *Poems That Sing To You*. The book begins with the words to "Dancing in the Street" as recorded by Martha and the Vandellas and ends with Stevie Wonder's "Sir Duke."

To illustrate the power of the link between musical elements and learning, try this experiment: ask a group of students how many of them remember the words of ten poems. See how many hands go up. Then ask them how many remember the words of ten songs. My experience has been that many more hands go up the second time. Tell the students that in the songs, they actually know ten poems by heart.

Poetry is meant to be performed. Any teacher can utilize its oral tradition to engage students in an experience with literature that capitalizes on young people's enthusiasm. All students and teachers are real poets; poetry is a great medium to make them better writers, readers, and speakers as well.

I try through dramatic readings of pieces from the serious to the silly, the ancient to the modern, my own works to those of Walt Whitman, to communicate that poets and poetry are alive. Poets do not have to be dead, or old for that matter. Nor do they have to be people who only live in the forest and write about weeping willow trees .

I use several techniques to create this celebration of language, attempting to help children hear the links between poetry and music. First, variations in inflection, rate, tone, pitch, and volume help make a poem come alive for students. The theme of *Poems That Sing To You* is poetry about music that is musical in its own language. The book includes Eve Merriam's "Advice from a Visiting Poet," in which she says, "Always read a poem twice, once for the words and then for the music of the words."

Using and discussing voice variations, or paralanguage, is another link between poetry and the enjoyment of music. Teachers know how children love to hear works read with expression, and love to be told that they are good readers because they know how to read this way.

Before I have the boys and girls trade off stanzas in a choral reading of Shel Silverstein's "Rock 'n' Roll Band," I perform the piece, saying, "this is an example of how to read with expression." I vary my voice qualities to emphasize the elements of the story in each stanza. A tone of hope enlivens the line, "If we were a rock and roll band / we'd travel *all over* the land (italics added)." Higher volume, quicker rate, and a tone of deep enthusiasm join the second line, "We'd play, and we'd sing and wear spangly things." Giggling and laughing onomatopoetically, I perform the line, "We'd giggle and laugh and sign autographs." Slower rate, lower volume, and a tone of sadness find the line, "but we ain't no Rock 'n' Roll Band." The students are told to listen to their harmony; that "choral" is a form of the word "chorus", and that by reading together they are like the chorus that harmonizes for a piece of music.

The first section of the book is entitled, "Poems That Dance." Kinesically speaking, poems can dance. The kinesics, or body movements that I perform, range from group clapping as I read Eloise Greenfield's "Nathaniel's Rap" to facial expressions of frustration during David Harrison's "Practice." The poem details a child who hates how much his mother makes him play the horn, and I grimace as I say "practice, practice, practice." Poems were meant to be performed over and over with increasing pleasure. When I read "Practice" the second time, the students repeat the refrain in unison, with enthusiasm. In another example, during my composition, "Compact Disk," I pout, sticking out my lower lip at the line "Mom says I'm too young to keep the mall in business, so I only have one."

The visual of a poem is like a symphony that is written in notes on a page; it possesses the potential to come alive when performed. I use free verse poems as visual aids to describe that form of poetry. I show the students the text of a poem to describe a rhyme scheme, saying that one could draw a blueprint for the rhymes in the poem.

The craft of poetry is like building a house. The poet has to visualize the poem, or house, playing with words for a main idea. He or she must lay a foundation on which the structure stands, charting out meter to determine its rhythm and flow. A well-crafted poem looks like a skeletal house structure at first, with words all over the page, being moved, changed, added, deleted, and built upon. Just as a newly built home's bricks, mortar and wood grow prettier and prettier until this construction actually becomes a lovely house the persistent rearranging of words into poetic music involves crafting an architectural vision into a beautiful structure.

On the adjoining page to "Rock 'n' Roll Band" is Nikki Giovanni's "Kidnap Poem." The children see how she wrote a 19-line love poem in one stanza, with no rhyming, no punctuation, and only one capital letter. In the line "wrap you in the red Black green," African-American colors are seen as something to be cloaked in, with a capital "B" for the color of our skin. At the end the students can see how she plays with words: "yeah if i were a poet i'd kid / nap you," and how that visual splitting up of the word kidnap adds a playful, childish tone to the poem.

My responsibility as a teacher is to carry the message that each child is a poet. Each one has a song inside him or her, the child's self-esteem waiting to be expressed. The children write and perform their works at the end of my workshops.

To reinforce the link between poetry and music, I frequently end with this writing assignment: complete the phrase, "When I hear music ...." The students are told to write whatever they think or feel when tunes are played. Writing in this relaxed mode, with no rules, often produces great poems. Children pick up on the musical theme with creativity, alacrity, and pleasure. The student becomes an instant composer and performer. The fun of being a rap artist, rock star, or a modern day Mozart is blended with reading, writing, and oral presentation .

As I engage them, students get in touch with the music inside themselves and express it through writing—painting a verbal picture of their own song and performing it for the class.

Adrienne Gonzalez, while a fourth grader at School 18, Paterson, NJ, wrote:

> When I hear music ...
> I jump up and boggie
> When I hear music
> I pick up a jar of cokkies
> and shake um and eat um
> When I hear music my ears get numb
> When I hear music I jump up and run

Joseph Vogel, while a second grader at Shelter Rock School, Manhassett, NY, wrote:

> When I hear music I think of people,
> famous people, important people. When
> I hear music I think of colors,
> dark colors, bright colors, light colors,
> dull colors. When I hear music,
> I think of books, long books, short books,
> Big books, little books. When I hear
> music I think ....

Michael R. Strickland teaches writing at Jersey City State College, is studying toward his Ph.D. in English Education at New York University, and is a consultant to Scholastic's first core reading program, "Literacy Place."

References

Strickland, M. R. (1993). *Poems That Sing To You*. Honesdale, PA: Boyds Mills.

Strickland, M. R., & Strickland, D. R. (1994). *Families: Poems Celebrating the African American Experience*. Honesdale, PA: Boyds Mills.

·60·

VOICES FROM THE WORLD OF
CHILDREN'S BOOKS

·60A·

THE EYE AND THE EAR

Jane Yolen
CHILDREN'S AUTHOR, *Owl Moon* AND OTHER BOOKS

Once upon a time, a long time ago, there was a child who loved to listen to stories. And one summer night, in a cottage in Maine, the child sat in an audience of other children and adults while a storyteller recounted the history of a Greek hero named Perseus.

And when the storyteller came to the part where the hero held up the head of the gorgon Medusa, she held her own hand aloft. I could have sworn then—as I can swear now that I saw snakes from the gorgon's head curling and uncurling around the storyteller's arm.

At that moment I and all the other listeners around me were unable to move. It was as if we, and not Medusa's intended victims, had been turned to stone.

It could have been a trick of the firelight behind the storyteller. It might have been the hot dogs I had hastily consumed before trotting over from our cottage, my little sandals slip-slapping on the stony beach walk. It might have been the lateness of the hour or my overactive imagination. But I know that it was none of these. It was simply the power of the teller and the tale.

We were there, all of us, caught up in the centrifugal force of the spinning story. And we would not be let go until the teller finished and the tale was done.

Of course the story in the mouth is different from the one on the page. The tale apprehended by the ear is different from the one taken in by the eye.

Critic Jack Schaefer (1968) states baldly: "Literature is a maimed art, crippled by being printed in books." Though it is true that there is a silent intimidation of print that frightens some children and some adults, I would rather say it this way: The *eye* and the *ear are different listeners*.

What sounds well at night by a listening child's bed does not read as well on the page. What lies perfectly formed in Bodoni Bold on the white sheet may stutter on the tongue tomorrow. I could never write down and make a book of the stories of the absurd "Silly Gorilly" which entertained my three children through years of bedtime telling. How can I recapture my own lumbering gallop around the room, the infection of giggles shared, the pauses, the tickles, the rolling

of eyes? On the other hand, how does one deal with sight rhymes like rain / again or wind / kind, rhymes that resonate to the eye but do not work well on a 20th-century American tongue? In bookmaking, one must try to please the ear as well as the eye, but it is often a compromise.

There is a subtle play of text and type, illustrations and design, that can change a story just as surely as a new telling. In science, when one puts a specimen on a slide, there is a change in the specimen. Similarly, putting a tale onto a page and dressing it up with full-color illustrations provokes a transformation.

Some critics, like Bruno Bettelheim (1976), would have us do without any pictures for the fairy tales. But illustrations are well within the tradition of storytelling. Shamans and seers often accompanied their tellings with drawings, dolls, or puppets. In countries where oral tellings still exist, remants of picture tales exist, too. In Brazil, storytellers in villages often hang appropriate pictures on a clothesline to illustrate their story. In Arab bazaars, tale tellers make paintings of colored sand as they recite. And while it is true that pictures can change a listener's understanding of a story, so have centuries of retellers.

How much can an illustration change our hearing of a tale? Just look at three different versions of *Snow White* and it is easy to see.

Randall Jarrell's (1972) retelling of the Grimm story has full-color pictures by Nancy Ekholm Burkert. They emphasize the medieval setting. Her queen is a professional necromancer, a potent potion-maker, whose *grimoire* is filled with evil recipes. The queen's picture is set about with crucibles, tarot cards, hanging herbs. But we never see her face. And so the old prototype of faceless evil is presented to us.

In Burkert's *Snow White*, on the other hand, we see the heroine's full face on the jacket and beyond. She is so fair of face as to be translucent, other-worldly, reminiscent of the Victorian child saints. Yet she is healthy enough, light-footed and sure with the forest animals; housewifely (almost homely) in her turban as she cooks and cleans for the dwarves. She is seen as saint, as child, as homemaker, the three faces of archetypal woman.

The backgrounds are millefleurs tapestries, recalling the wall hangings of the period.

The dwarves are fully human and therefore pitiable in their role as deformed humanity. The prince and Snow White are innocents, with the faces of children but the bodies of adults. The dwarves have adult faces on which the loss of innocence shows, but they are small and childlike, too. They are midway between the full-face innocence of Snow White and the faceless evil of the queen.

No words intrude upon Nancy Burkert's allegorical presentation. The text is set apart by itself: two pages of text, two pages of illustration. It is fascinating bookmaking, capturing the penumbral side of the tale. It asks questions rather than answers them. It enunciates the archetypes.

Trina Schart Hyman's "Snow White" (Heins, 1974), on the other hand, is firmly rooted in humanity. The faces she pictures are real faces: Snow White is her own daughter Katrin. The Queen is an old friend. Hyman is one of the dwarves herself, the others include her ex-husband and her neighbors in New Hampshire. Portraiture is Hyman's forte.

Her prince is bearded, hawk-nosed, strong-featured, in his thirties. He is the only prince in *Snow White* illustrations who looks as though he knows how to run a kingdom and deal with wicked stepmothers, and he is just waiting for his chance. No beardless adolescent this, no sweet-faced youth just out of knickers. The red-hot iron shoes at the end of the story must be *his* idea.

From the opening scene in Trina Hyman's *Snow White*, where the girl is seen in a flash-forward hanging out dwarf-sized shirts to dry on the line, this is a less regal, more human book. Ms. Hyman is fascinated not by archetypes but by the play of light and dark, good and evil in faces. Even the queen's mirror is ringed with them, faces that shift and direct mood for the reader. Hyman's precursors are the Pre-Raphaelites, Wyeth, and Pyle, and she combines sweetness and toughness to offer an illustrated tale. The text, translated by Paul Heins, is incorporated into the pictures.

Hyman's concerns are immediate, human, sensual. The queen radiates a power that is sexual in nature. The story told by Trina Hyman is the Electra story. We can see it in the faces, we can see the palpable sexuality in the form of the mandrake root that hangs symbolically from the queen's wall. The laces that the queen binds around the innocent Snow White bind her into a caricature of a full-bosomed peasant girl and the dwarves look at the sleeping girl, so bound, with a hint of carnality. Quite simply, Ms. Hyman makes you hear the tale anew.

Walt Disney, on the other hand, sentimentalizes everything in his version of the story, flattens out both the text and the illustrations to cartoon caricatures. His wicked queen is neither the faceless sorceress of legend nor the decaying beauty, but a cartoon witch, with nose and chin threatening to meet. She loses depth, motive, individuality, and so never achieves the power of Burkert's herbalist or Hyman's voluptuary, and she does not die but merely disappears conveniently, in a Perils-of-Pauline ending, "into a bottomless gulf."

Similarly, the dwarves lose their power and place in the Disney story by becoming cute, providing that measure of "adorableness" that, as critic Richard Schickel puts it, was the most persistent problem of Disney's work.

With both her nemesis and her collective alter egos robbed of their power and depth, Snow White herself is left with nothing to resound against. Without true evil, there is little excitement, no contrasting background against which to dramatize virtue. The story becomes, in this telling, a hollow tale. The Disney version illustrates with finality folklorist Mircea Eliade's contention that, "Man's concept of the absolute can never be uprooted; it can only be debased."

Disney was a man who believed that we "recognize [good and evil] instinctively…" and he supposed that any retellings of fairy tales could be approached in this simplistic manner (Schickel, 1968). But the power of the tales is that they are not that simple after all. They are as evocative, as sensual, as many-faceted, as disturbing, as slippery as dreams. They offer a moral, they speak to the human condition, but it is not always the condition or the moral that one immediately sees.

That is why a fine artist can bring to an old tale a new approach, a new direction. Nancy Ekholm Burkert's *Snow White* is a different story from Trina Schart Hyman's. And they are both completely different tales from Walt Disney's oversimplification. If a story was rewritten in succession by John Gardener, Isaac Bashevis Singer, and Dr. Seuss how different each story would be.

The eye and the ear are different listeners. Each storyteller has the ability to select: to select those characters that are just right, to select those details that set the stage, to select the glass mountain that must be climbed, the thorny bush that must be passed or the ring or sword or crown to be won. The storyteller is an artist, and selection is essential to art. There are thousands upon thousands of characters, thousands upon thousands of details, thousands upon thousands of motifs. To know which one to choose requires a kind of magical touch, and that is what characterizes the great storytellers.

But the eye and the ear are different listeners. The modern audience is not the same as the ancient one, and for good reason. Ancient man took in the world mainly by listening, and listening meant remembering. Thus humans both shaped and were shaped by the oral tradition. The passage of culture went from mouth to ear to mouth. The person who did not listen well, who was tone deaf to the universe, was soon dead. The finest rememberers and the most attuned listeners were valued: the poets, the storytellers, the shamans, the seers. In culture after culture, community after community, the carriers of the oral tradition were honored. For example, in ancient Ireland the *ollahms*, the poet-singers, were more highly thought of than the king. The king was only given importance in times of war (Moray, 1965).

An anthropologist once observed that people in preliterate cultures that are still more of the ear than the eye say, "hear you" when they mean they understand something. But we say, "I see." We modern listeners see life more clearly through pictures. We trust the picture more than the spoken word. A picture, we are told, is worth a thousand words. In this century we created the moving picture and credit it, more than anything else, with shaping our children's thoughts.

But the eye and the ear are different listeners, are different audiences. And the literary storyteller is one who must try to bring eye and ear into synchronization. But it is a subtle art. Just as the art of typography has been called "the art invisible," subliminal in the sense that it changes or manipulates a reader's perceptions without advertising its own presence, so, too, the art of storytelling in the printed book must persuade and captivate. It must hold the reader as the spoken tale holds the listener, turning the *body* to stone but not the mind or the heart.

References

Bettelheim, B. (1976). *The uses of enchantment: The meaning and importance of fairy tales.* New York: Knopf.

Heins, P. (1974). *Snow White.* Boston: Atlantic Monthly.

Jarrell, R. (1972). *Snow White.* New York: Farrar, Straus & Giroux.

Moray, A. (1965). *A fair stream of silver.* New York: Morrow.

Schaefer, J. (1968). *If stories must be taught, teaching literature to adolescents; Short stories.* S. Dunning (Ed.). Chicago: Scott, Foresman.

Schickel, R. (1968). *The Disney version.* New York: Simon & Schuster.

BOOKS ABOUT ART: A JOYOUS VISION

Jan Greenberg

AUTHOR, *The Painter's Eye: Learning to Look at Contemporary American Art*

Since the 1970s there has been a movement to broaden the base for teaching the visual arts in schools. The ultimate outcome for teaching art appreciation by classroom teachers is to engage the student in developing an appreciation and knowledge of art objects. Along with the established idea of talking about art to stimulate emotion and pleasure, skills of observation and critical judgment are now being emphasized.

Given this new direction in art education in the schools, what kinds of books about art are most effective to enhance this goal? In this chapter the focus will be on identifying recent books about art for young people that go beyond biographies of artists, which focus on anecdotal material rather than the ways in which an artist's life and work intertwine, or art historical surveys, or books that offer ways to make art. These approaches abound in the literature and certainly have value, as children are interested in the many contexts of art. But recent books about art for young people that explore a new realm of perception open the door to a different means of developing response and are now available to the student as well as the teacher.

These books offer students a language to talk about art, a system of looking, which stresses going beyond the psychological response of "I like it" or "I don't like it" to value judgments supported by arguments of evidence. The critical process is examined so that the reader or viewer of the art object engages in an analytic method by which they perceive the work, describe it, become conscious of the formal properties of the work and how it is composed, and finally understand the meaning or expressive content of the art object. It is hoped that they will go on to look at the real works of art in museums and galleries and begin to make aesthetic judgments about the merit of the work. They will become both appreciators, as well as critics, and enjoy a lifelong dialogue with art.

An additional method for teaching art, widely practiced in museum education, involves children with artworks using a multisensory approach. The idea or sensory interaction invites the children to react through their senses and goes beyond descriptive or analytic language to become more metaphoric, poetic and personally expressive, that is, using body movements to parallel the movement in a sculpture. This approach can be appropriate for the primary grades, where language level may not allow for the analytic method. Books that invite children to respond to artworks in terms of sight, smell, movement and touch can also be of interest to teachers and are included in this chapter.

I will begin by discussing my recent books about 20th century art, followed by a bibliography of other titles that lead students to explore art using a descriptive/analytic method and / or a multisensory approach.

In both *The Painter's Eye: Learning to Look at Contemporary American Art* and *The Sculptor's Eye: Looking at Contemporary American Art* (Greenberg & Jordan, 1991, 1993), artworks by 20th century artists are chosen to introduce a system of looking at art based on my research (and others) in arts and education.

In both *The Painter's Eye* and *The Sculptor's Eye* post-World War II American art has been chosen to introduce the basic principles of art for several reasons. An anecdote might serve to illustrate them.

Last year a segment was aired on the television program *Sixty Minutes* entitled "Yes....but is it art?" The program began with Morley Safer attributing the following quote to P.T. Barnum, "A sucker is born every minute." Safer went on to say that most contemporary art is "worthless junk." Shown with a group of school children at the Whitney Museum in front of a painting by graffiti artist Jean Michel Basquiat, Safer asked, "Do you think you could do as well?" Set up in this manner, a boy responded, "I could do better than that." Unfortunately many people share Safer's point of view.

New art, be it sculpture or painting, bewilders and frustrates a lot of people. These books help demystify new art and help viewers come to contemporary works with open minds and an enhanced vocabulary. In addition contemporary art is accessible to young people and is timely in that it refers to what is happening in our own time and culture. In choosing examples for the text, we were guided by principles of clarity, variety, and personal interest. Although the illustrations do not provide a comprehensive view of contemporary art, they suggest a variety of experiences and styles in this period. All of the artists, from the most celebrated to those more recently emerging, have been recognized and exhibited widely in museums. This provides the reader with quality works against which new experiences with art can be tried.

Although the focus in *The Painter's Eye* and *The Sculptor's Eye* is on contemporary art, the same language can be used to talk about most Western art from the ancient Greeks to the present. Many of the artworks in these books concentrate on color, line, shape, and / or texture without reference to a recognizable image, thus highlighting certain points we wanted to make in the text. The elements of color, shape, line, and texture remain constant, and by learning something about these constants the viewer comes to all paintings and sculptures with greater understanding. Interviews with artists concentrating on where they get their ideas were also included. Teachers often ask how to respond to a student who says, "I do not like it" when shown a contemporary artwork, especially one that is abstract.

The answer to that question might be that the artwork is unchangeable but the students' transactions with it are unlimited, filled with variety. It is the teacher's function to help the student understand that his or her response, negative or positive, depends not only on the artwork but on himself/herself. An introduction to modern art is one way to encourage children to be receptive to new ideas. This is especially necessary in the middle grades, where there is so much pressure to conform.

By looking at individual paintings, one part at a time, children begin a dialogue with art. As they learn the language and develop a method of looking at art, they will feel comfortable exploring different styles of both painting and sculpture.

A passage quoted from *The Sculptor's Eye* demonstrates how the language of art is used to analyze or discuss the formal properties of a sculpture.

> This bronze sculpture *Untitled* by Joel Shapiro is abstract; yet we are reminded of a figure balanced precariously in space. How do we know it's a figure? Despite the simplicity of form, the sculpture appears figural with limbs flying out in four directions from the blocky torso. Suspended in motion, he is involved in a struggle, balanced on one leg like an exclamation point. How would you move if you slipped on a banana peel or tripped on a rock? Follow the path of movement with your arms. What sensory words come to mind—*vertical, jerky, explosive, open, jutting, angular?* We have referred to *Untitled* as "he." If Shapiro had wanted this figure to be feminine, might he have chosen different shapes?"

In this passage the reader is encouraged to respond to the photograph of the sculpture metaphorically and physically. Sensory words lead the reader to view the artwork through the five senses—qualities that are vivid in terms of sight, sound, touch, and so on. Questions are asked to elicit an interpretive response based on the form or shape of the sculpture. Art terms such as *abstract* or *balance* have been

introduced in an earlier chapter of the book and are explored further by a discussion of *Untitled*. The organization of the books is cumulative, progressing from the simple to the complex, yet never losing sight of clarity. Repeating many of the same artworks as the information unfolds allows the viewer to build on prior experience.

In my most recent book (Greenberg & Jordan, 1995), *The American Eye: Eleven Artists in the Twentieth Century,* the emphasis is on the ways in which the lives and times of the artists have shaped their art. In this narrative or anecdotal approach, the reader responds to works of art through the stories behind them. We were interested in examining what is American about American art in the 20th century. We chose artists, such as Arthur Dove, Georgia O'Keefe, Romare Bearden, Jackson Pollock an Andy Warhol, whose works contributed to the modern movement in the United States and whose lives offer such a diversity in terms of personal and artistic styles. The book builds on the previous two books by integrating the method of looking at artworks introduced in *The Painter's Eye* and *The Sculptor's Eye*. This gives the series a sense of clarity and consistency.

Finally the goal of the books about art for young people is to help them feel more confident and more open to future interactions with art in museums, galleries, or anywhere else that art is experienced throughout their lives. Art exists as a unique creative endeavor on the part of the artist, as well as an enriching experience that is unique to each viewer.

The following is a bibliography, along with a brief summary, of some recent books for young readers that emphasize aesthetic perception in the visual arts and architecture. Biographies of artists that stress understanding of the artists works are also included.

Beneduce, A. K. (1993). *A Weekend with Winslow Homer.* New York: Rizzoli.

Middle Grades. Through the imagined voice of the artist, this book (part of an excellent series) invites the reader to visit his home and studio for the weekend.

Blizzard, G. S. (1992). *Come Look with Me: Exploring Landscape Art with Children.* Thomasson-Grant. Ages 6–10.

Blizzard, G. S. (1993). *Worlds of Play.* Charlottesuille, VA: Thomasson-Grant. Ages 6–10.

In this series of books about art, the author discusses a number of paintings that prompt a discussion about theme and style of works, both traditional and contemporary.

Boulton, A. O. (1993). *Frank Lloyd Wright, Architect: An Illustrated Biography.* New York: Rizzoli. Ages 12 and above.

A well-designed book that uses drawings, photos, and text to explore the life and work of this major American architect.

Davidson R. (1994). *Take a Look.* New York: Viking. Ages 12 and above.

Theme and style in a variety of artworks are introduced with well-chosen reproductions.

References

Greenberg, J., & Jordan, S. (1991). *The painter's eye: Learning to look at contemporary American art*. New York: Delacorte.

Greenberg, J., & Jordan, S. (1993). *Sculptor's Eye: Looking at contemporary American art*. New York: Delacorte.

Greenberg, J., & Jordan, S. (1995). *The American eye: Eleven artists in the twentieth century*. New York: Delacorte.

Isaacson, P. M. (1993). *A short walk around the Pyrimids and through the world of art*. New York: Knopf.

Ages 10 and above. The writer, also an architect, has chosen a variety of images from art and architecture to inspire an appreciation of the elements of art and the joy of looking.

Muhlberg, R. (1991). *What makes a Monet a Monet?* New York: Viking / Metropolitan Museum of Art.

Ages 10 and above. One in a well-illustrated series of books that explores the themes and styles of individual artists through their works.

Turner, R. M. (1993). *Faith Ringold*. Boston: Little Brown.

Ages 7–10. One in the Portraits of Women Artists series that discusses the story quilts and bright paintings of this celebrated African-American artist.

Walker, L. A. (1994). *Roy Lichtenstein: The artist at work*. New York Lodestar.

Ages 10–12. A delightful visit to this pop artist's studio with photographs and artworks.

Woolf, F. (1993). *Picture this century. An introduction to twentieth century art*. New York: Doubleday.

Ages 8–12. The author traces the development of the twentieth century through a variety of artworks by both American and European artists.

Zhensun, Z., & Low A. (1991). *A young painter: The Life and Paintings of Wang Yani—China's Extraordinary Young Artist*. New York: Scholastic.

Ages 8–12. Beautiful reproductions trace the life and work of a gifted young Chinese artist.

SOUND AND RESOUND

Katherine Paterson

AUTHOR, *Bridge to Terabithia* AND OTHER BOOKS

When the person sitting next to me on the airplane asks politely, "What do you do?" I answer: "I write novels for children and young people." My seatmate rarely goes on to ask me what I mean by such a statement, but if she did, I would answer something like this.

Well, basically, I am a storyteller, but a novel is a special kind of story. It is story with meat on its bones. The novel, as Flannery O'Connor has pointed out, is incarnational art [literally *in flesh*]. A novel is about human experience. Our first experiences as human beings are very sensual. Most human beings can see, hear, taste, touch, and smell. Novels, then, must involve these basic human senses. Human experience also involves thinking, feeling and acting. It involves relationships among human beings and between humankind and nature. Human beings think—they reflect and imagine, they compute and observe. They act, usually rashly and selfishly, but sometimes with extraordinary wisdom and miraculous compassion.

People talk—they use words to make sense of experience and to communicate with others. Sometimes they talk inside their own heads, sometimes they speak with others, but words are always important, even to newborns, who will turn at the sound of their mother's voice and try before too many months have passed to offer a language of their own.

A novel, a story in the flesh, builds a world from words (and in English every word is an arrangement of symbols which we call letters and we have only 26 of these from which to choose. I feel poor sometimes when I compare my meaningless symbols to the rich images that a word written in the picture language of the East instantly conjures up for the Chinese or Japanese reader).

With words the writer attempts to woo the reader into the world she has created in her own mind. She evokes all the reader's senses. She tries to capture the reader's feelings. She must have (or she will utterly fail) the reader's intellectual ability and will to read what she has written. Her story in the flesh will not come to life unless a living reader brings it to life.

When I am talking to children I often ask them how many of them sing or play a musical instrument. Many do, so they understand immediately the difference between a musical score and music itself. The musical score may be magnificent, but even the genius of Beethoven cannot make it music unless living musicians take his score and play it or sing it. Without musicians, the Ninth Symphony is only black squiggles on a white page.

Without readers who are willing to bring their own lives to my story in the flesh, my book will never come to life. It will only be black marks on pages, bound between covers, gathering dust. Although "it's a wonderful feeling when readers hear what I thought I was trying to say... it is even more thrilling for a reader to find something in my writing that I had not until that moment known was there. But this happens because of who the reader is, not simply because of who I am or what I have done" (Paterson, 1981, p. 24).

I am constantly grateful for the readers who bring my stories to life—those who send me pictures of Terabithia, transformed into a turreted castle complete with portcullis and moat, or portraits of a great, smiling Maime Trotter who is unmistakably African-American. When I talk to children about *Bridge to Terabithia*,

> I find that something has happened for which I cannot take credit. They have taken my bare-bones Terabithia and supplied their own fantasies .... I could not count the number of people who have told me that Terabithia is exactly like a magical place they have or had when they were children. But, of course, what has happened is that they have made Terabithia in their own image. I didn't write the book. They did. It's an absolutely wonderful experience for a writer to have people do this. (Paterson, 1981, p. 70)

When people ask me what I like best about being a writer, it is this intimate connection with readers—this sound from the depths of my being which resounds in their hearts and makes a music neither of us has ever heard before.

Reference

Paterson, K. (1981). *Gates of excellence: On reading and writing books for children*. New York: Dutton.

·60D·

AN AUTHOR CELEBRATES THE UNPREDICTABLE WAYS OF THE ILLUSTRATOR

W. Nikola-Lisa

NATIONAL-LOUIS UNIVERSITY

As an author of picture books, I am in the unique position of initiating an idea but not seeing it through to the end. As a writer, I do most of my work at the beginning stages of the publication process. It is the illustrator—working with the editor and art director, rather than directly with me—who brings the elements of my idea to fruition. In this pseudo-collaborative partnership, it is sheer trust in this oddly constructed creative process rather than good communicative skills which propel the relationship forward. But I do not mind. After going through this process now some half dozen times, I have come to marvel at it, especially the unpredictable ways of the illustrator whose job it is to communicate directly—vis-a-vis visual images—with a young and lively reading audience rather than with me.

Illustrators—as the name indicates—bring to a manuscript an entirely different language, a language of visual representation. With a plethora of approaches (as well as a variety of media), illustrators can shape a text in innumerable ways: they can interpret a text literally, or extend it symbolically; they can embellish a text in pleasing ways, or subvert it with unexpected humor. No matter what approach they take, it is still their job to deepen our understanding and appreciation of the text by building a visual plane upon which the text moves. In short, illustrators "see into the text" in ways an author sometimes never imagined.

Although my long-standing interest in the relationship between text and image in the young child's picture book is primarily academic, it is my recent practical experience as an author of picture books from which I presently write. Reflecting upon the picture books I have published in the last several years, one thing repeatedly stands out: over and over again the illustrator brings to the text a fresh perspective, sometimes predictable, sometimes not.

In *Night is Coming* (Nikola-Lisa, 1991) Jamichael Henterly surprised me not with a radically new interpretation, but with his masterful full-color illustrations. His richly detailed images brought to the text a nostalgia for the countryside. Every textual image was brought more sharply into focus to ponder and to reminisce about. And, yet, his personalization of the text was still his own. The Dutch Pennsylvania countryside, for instance, which he renders throughout the book is not an element of my experience; it is, I suppose, a facet of Henterly's own imagination that is at best suggested by the text. What he created visually, however, is not only appropriate, but an incredibly close match to the visual representation of the text I carried in my own head (even down to the Jersey cows queuing up to come home which is a facet of my own childhood experience having grown up in a small ranching community in the south).

In *Storm* (Nikola-Lisa, 1993), although the end result intimates a certain consonance between text and illustrations, the process involved some intervention on the part of editor Marcia Marshall. In the early stages of developing a dummy for the text, illustrator Michael Hays included "sky gods" in the clouds, figureheads that anthropomorphized the story. Marcia rejected such attempts, steering Michael more toward an impressionistic interpretation of the text with an emphasis on the play of light in the sky, trees and land. Ultimately, Michael's atmospheric paintings radiate precisely because of the quality of light he captures. Faces painted in the sky—gods or not—would have detracted from his refined sensitivity to light and lessened the overall effect of his illustrations.

Perhaps the only illustrations I have been totally surprised by have been those for *Bein' With You This Way* (Nikola-Lisa, 1994a). It is easy for me to say this because it is one of the few manuscripts for which I had little or no visual image in the first place. The text evoked in me only the vague image of children dancing. Beyond this, I had no other visual image (which for me is odd in that I am a very visual person). What illustrator Michael Bryant did in creating a cast of multi-cultural characters at play in a city park was brilliant. Not only did he give the text a setting—and a narrator—but he gave the story an appropriate visual representation, keying off the dynamics of the text's upbeat rhythmical structure. When I first saw his illustrations (a year or more after I had finished revising the text, which is fairly standard), I revelled in his interpretation—even though I had no idea what to expect.

In my latest book, *No Babies Asleep* (Nikola-Lisa, 1994b), although the outcome was similar, the process was quite different. For this text I had a very firm sense of what I wanted visually, but illustrator Peter Palagonia saw things differently. Where I saw the beaches of southern California, he saw a neighborhood carnival. Where I saw an extended family on a weekend outing, he saw a nanny taking care of napping infants. Where I saw babies crawling wildly across the sand, he saw babies playing contentedly with animals on carnival rides. Where I had written twelve stanzas, he used only ten. In the end, however, what I saw did not matter because Peter's vision of the text was stronger and—upon reflection—more densely visual.

The fact that the author does not work closely with the illustrator surprises most audiences. (It certainly did me at first.) Viewing a picture book, you would think that the author and the illustrator work in a tight-knit fashion. But in most cases they do not. Whatever the reason, in my experience it seems to work—almost every time now! Several years ago I heard Richard Jackson, a senior editor at Orchard Books,

explaining in convincing terms the separate roles of the author, illustrator and editor. A picture book is truly the product of these three—if not more—personalities, but the process is not necessarily collaborative.

Over time I have come to accept this without consternation because I have come to trust the illustrator (and the editor and art director). A picture book, in the end, is a specialized format somewhat akin to film in that it demands a team of experts (all of whom contribute their specific expertise and sensitivities) to bring it—frame by frame—to fruition. And, like a good film, a picture book communicates on multiple levels (textual, visual, formal, etc.). It is in this way that a picture book is able to reach a wide audience (including nonreaders), for, as a meaningful set of symbols made up of words, images, and formal (i.e., design-oriented) considerations, it offers readers multiple entry points from which to make sense of its closely patterned and carefully-layered meanings.

Such multiple entry points provide readers with structural supports enabling them to weave their own experience, images, and textual ideas into the reading of a book. The role the illustrator plays is crucial to this reading as he provides not only a visual interpretation of the author's textual ideas, but also his own unique lexicon of visual images, which often deepen and extend the author's stated and implied meanings. At the intersection of these two points of view is the reader, who brings to the reading his or her own set of experiences and understandings making the reading of a picture book a truly unique and enjoyable experience.

References

Nikola-Lisa, W. (1991). *Night is coming.* (Jamichael Henterly, Illus.). New York: Dutton.

Nikola-Lisa, W. (1993). *Storm.* (Michael Hays, Illus.). New York: Atheneum.

Nikola-Lisa, W. (1994a). *Bein' with you this way.* (Michael Bryant, Illus.). New York: Lee & Low Books.

Nikola-Lisa, W. (1994b). *No babies asleep.* (Peter Palagonia, Illus.). New York: Atheneum.

THE VISUAL ARTS MADE ACCESSIBLE THROUGH PICTURE BOOKS

Barbara Kiefer

TEACHERS COLLEGE, COLUMBIA UNIVERSITY

In this century picture books have been found largely in the world of the nursery. However, they have a longer history in the world of art. If we imagine an audience sitting enthralled before the cave paintings at Lascaux, picture a group of medieval worshippers entranced by illuminations in a holy manuscript, or share in a young child's pleasure in a favorite picture book, we are considering an aesthetic engagement with a visual art form. In each of these instances the participant is called upon to engage in interchange of intellect and emotion in a context that allows for both individual and communal response.

The importance of this type of visual / verbal experience is no less powerful today because it is mainly experienced by children in Western culture. The long tradition of the picture book grows out of some essential human characteristic that includes an artist's need to convey meaning through visual symbols. Over the centuries this need has resulted in representations of basic aspects of the individual and society through image and story.

Over the course of its long history the content of the picture book and its designated audience has altered as a result of the changing needs of society. In addition, technological advances have allowed the medium of the picture book to expand beyond the wall of a cave or the floor of the desert to reproductions of all manner of original works, bound in paper between the covers of a book. However, the experience that results from engagement with picture books in their many forms is essentially an aesthetic one that engages the viewer in attempts to make meaning from complex emotional, intellectual and critical reactions. Moreover, just as the cave paintings of Lascaux and the illuminated manuscripts of the middle ages are usually the province of art historians, I would argue that today's picture books rely as much or more on visual meaning as they do on verbal meaning. Thus as art objects, rather than literary works, picture books should be subject to analysis that takes into consideration the meaning making potential of visual art.

This meaning making potential can be realized by elements unique to visual art in general and to picture book design in particular. That is, elements of art such as color, line, shape, value, and texture have the ability to convey meaning and evoke emotion—colors can seem cool or warm, convey anger or serenity, lines and shapes carry weight, convey tension or calm. In addition principles of composition such as balance, rhythm, variety and unity can convey feelings of excitement, agitation, comfort, or dignity. Knowing the basic theme of the book, the motifs and moods, the characters, the setting, and the events that are part of the verbal text (if there is one), the illustrator makes choices about how to express meaning using these artistic elements and how to organize them on each page. Then, in addition to choices of original media, for example, oil or acrylic, the illustrator must consider certain technical choices inherent in the reproduction of the work within the covers of a book. These technical choices may also be expressive of meaning and add to or detract from the overall aesthetic experience possible with a given book. The combination of these artistic choices made by an illustrator can provide the essence of the aesthetic experience possible as a result of a good picture book, one that would be fundamentally and profoundly different if the book's meaning were conveyed only in words.

The effectiveness of these artistic choices will determine the book's excellence and also its impact on the audience. Essentially however, the artist's first responsibility in making these choices is to the meaning of the book rather than to some generic child. In being faithful to the book's meaning, the illustrator, in fact, implies the reader / viewer, and the right child will find his or her way to the book. Because artists, editors, and publishers seem to understand this, we find that at the end of the 20th century the picture book appeals to a much wider audience than it did at the century's beginning—a return, I would hope, to a world in which picture books are meant for all, adults and children alike.

As adults who hope to develop and deepen aesthetic understanding for ourselves and for our students, we must consider the range of choices available to the artist in expressing the meaning of a particular picture book. We can look at elements such as color, line, and shape and consider how they add to the meaning and affect our feelings about the book. We can think about principles of composition and ask how these affect our understanding of a given page and how they move us through the book from beginning to end. We can look carefully at the technical choices, such as endpaper design or typeface, and consider their contribution to our emotional and intellectual response. Our evaluation of the picture book as an art object should lie in our awareness of the artist's choices in conveying meaning.

As we deepen our own understanding of the art of the picture book we can invite children to explore picture books in a variety of ways that will help extend their aesthetic response to both art and literature. I do not believe that we have to teach formal methods in art or literary criticism to children. Nor am I overly concerned with children's visual literacy. I believe that, too often, an emphasis on literacies, both verbal and visual, results in scope and sequences of literal, inferential, or critical skills and not in an exploration of the child's aesthetic response to a picture book.

Instead, I believe teachers can create child-centered classroom contexts that will give children opportunities to explore picture books in ways that build upon their feelings as well as their ideas during encounters with picture books. Teachers can collect picture books in many genres and styles and take time to read and talk about books with children. They can help children come back to the books often to look at them carefully and to explore them fully through more talk, writing, and art making. Teachers can ask children to share their reactions and responses with others and consider how these encounters affect their subsequent understandings. They can help children consider the artist as a meaning maker, asking why artists make visual choices and how these choices affect their responses to books. They can explore other art forms with children and encourage them to make connections between the art of the picture book and the art of the wider world. Finally, teachers can help children consider how their experience with a work of art has changed the way they look at and experience their own world.

I am convinced that, given these experiences, children will become visually literate. More important, however, they will grow in their understanding and appreciation of the world of visual and verbal art. In the 21st century children will not leave behind the powerful attachments to picture books that characterize their younger years. Rather the picture book will serve as a lifelong connection to deeply felt experiences with all the arts.

PLAYING AGAINST CONVENTIONS: THE TRUE STORY OF THE STINKY CHEESE MAN

Steve Tozer and Victoria Chou

COLLEGE OF EDUCATION, UNIVERSITY OF ILLINOIS AT CHICAGO

Jon was an elementary school teacher who liked stories. He wrote stories in his Master of Fine Arts program at an eastern university. He told stories to his students. He had his students rewrite favorite fairy tales in their own words. He wrote stories of his own, too, though magazines like *The New Yorker* and *Esquire* did not seem as interested in his stories as his students were. He wrote columns for a sports magazine, but that was not the same as writing stories. Finally, like his students, he rewrote a fairy tale. He tried to have it published but, again, no publishers seemed interested.

Molly liked art, but she was not an artist. She graduated from a midwest university with a liberal arts degree and a road map to New York City. First she worked there as a proofreader for the sports magazine where Jon occasionally wrote. She was not very good at proofreading. She started helping out in the art department, where she learned about designing magazines. Soon, Molly was in charge of the artwork for the whole magazine. Later, she was asked by other big magazines, in sports, fashion, and business, to design for them. She had been a proofreader, but now she was an editorial designer. Soon Molly met Lane, who drew pictures for magazines.

Lane liked art and films, and he was a painter. At art school, he tried to major in film and in illustration. Only one major was allowed at a time, so Lane chose illustration. He made a film anyway. After art school, Lane drew dark, colorful pictures for *The New York Times* and *Rolling Stone* and many other magazines. Just for fun, Lane illustrated each of the letters of the alphabet, and a large children's book company found an author to write some text for the pictures and called the book *Halloween ABC*. The publisher began selling it in November. Since Halloween was over, not too many copies were sold, but it was named by *The New York Times* as one of the Ten Best Illustrated Books of the Year. Still, Lane thought, "Man, I coulda done films."

Soon, Molly the designer introduced Lane the illustrator to Jon the author. Jon had words for a rewritten fairy tale, but no pictures and no publisher. Lane drew pictures to go with the tale, but it still did not get published. Publishers said it was too unusual—people would not buy it for their children. Some publishers did not like the story. Some did not like the artwork. Finally, in 1989, Viking decided to publish the book. Since then, it has sold a million copies and has been translated into seven languages. It is called *The True Story of the Three Little Pigs*. It was so successful that Jon and Lane were allowed to do anything they wanted with their next book. What they wanted was for Molly to design it. And that is a later story.

"OUR BOOKS AREN'T LIKE THE OTHER BOOKS, AND WE DON'T WANT THEM TO LOOK LIKE THE OTHER BOOKS"

Readers of children's books will recognize two of the main characters above as Jon Scieszka and Lane Smith, who have worked together and separately on several unique, usually very funny, and hugely commercially successful children's books. Less readily recognized is Molly Leach, who, in addition to her editorial design career, has designed two books with Lane and Jon, three more with Lane, and another with a group of illustrators. Each of these three established a career outside of children's literature, and each has done significant children's work in his or her own right. The story of most interest here, however, is their collaboration. It is a collaboration in which three people, playing with words and images and getting silly with the creative process itself, effectively resist several prevailing conventions in children's story book publishing. The resulting originality is grounded not only in the considerable individual talents of the three coconspirators, but also in the way in which they work together.

The True Story of the Three Little Pigs (Scieszka, & Smith, 1989) was the first collaborative effort by Jon and Lane, and it presents some of the convention-challenging components that appear in more striking form in their succeeding picture book collaborations, *The Stinky Cheese Man and Other Fairly Stupid Tales* and *Math Curse* (Scieszka, & Smith, 1995). Building on *The Three Little Pigs*, *The Stinky Cheese Man* has added something immediately evident: Molly Leach's approach to design unifies and extends Jon and Lane's pervasive flaunting of children's book conventions with an inventive and irreverent integration of text and illustrations. Her departures from the conventions of children's book design contribute an overall "look" that is as distinctive as are Jon and Lane's departures from conventions in text and pictures. The combined effect of the three collaborators sets their work apart from even the most successful and innovative of children's books that preceded theirs.

While *The Three Little Pigs* is Lane and Jon's book, Molly was not entirely absent from its final design. A difficulty with the publisher arose over the book's cover, which looks like the front page of a newspaper, *The Daily Wolf*, in which the blaring headline THE TRUE STORY OF THE THREE LITTLE PIGS appears over the byline "A. Wolf." In addition to a news-photo style illustration of A. Wolf himself, the front and back of the book are covered with reproductions of actual newsprint.

Overlapping yellowed columns from the Wilson administration, the Nixon administration, and random points in between compete for the limited space on the cover. But the design caused problems the solution to which introduces Molly into the mix as it illustrates something about conventions in children's books publishing. As Lane tells it:

> So with this cover, we fought, and Jon and I said we really wanted a newspaper cover because it fit the book. They just hated the idea and said they did a book a couple of years before that had a newspaper cover which they said bombed, and they showed it to us and we said, "Yeah, but that's a hideous newspaper cover. Of course it bombed; it's ugly." So we thought we'd do a good newspaper cover. They finally said okay, but they weren't sure how it should be done, so I said, "Well, Molly, what'll we do?" She said, "Well, I'll just get you press type and you can glue it on to your painting and paint around it, just give it to them as is. So this cover was a finished piece of art work; all this type is on the art work, not designed by the publisher. So with this cover, we fought, and Jon and I said we really wanted a newspaper cover. And that was one of the reasons we finally got Molly in there.
> ...They said, "Well, we'll make a deal: we have to hire this art director because he's the best there is, and you guys can design your own books. I said "Great."

One obvious feature of this anecdote is its reminder that publishing is a business seeking to minimize risks and maximize profitability. It should be no surprise that Lane and Jon and, as it turns out, Molly, had to prove themselves as a commodity before the publisher would later be willing to grant them relative autonomy in their work.

Less obvious, however, is the conventional publisher's practice of supplying its own design director for each of the books they publish. Again, this minimizes risk: although a good director may apply the same aesthetic and technical sensibilities to 20 or even 40 books in a single year, at least the publisher can be sure that these book designs will fall within the bounds of what works in the marketplace. It is relatively rare for an author and an illustrator to provide their own designer, and when they do, they have to be prepared to deal with the art director anyway. Lane explains:

> In the kids' book industry a big publisher can do like 50 titles each season, or more, and they just have one art director. They all look alike because it's the easiest thing to do to put an image and a square on the cover and throw some type around it and we, Jon and I, thought, "Our books aren't like the other books, and we don't want them to look like the other books because if they look like the other books, then they will be more like the other books." So we got Molly in there, and there was some resistance.... I think a lot of it was budgetary, they just—"why should we shell out money when we have an art director?" And even to this day.... It's kind of like our books, we're always trying to get her to put her name on there bigger if only so that there won't be such a struggle next time.

Why should it make a significant difference in the book if the publisher allows another designer on board? How many options are there, really, once the author and illustrator have done their work? One source of difference is Molly's lack of familiarity with the conventions of the children's book industry. Instead, her approach has been shaped by her work in adult editorial design.

> I never paid attention to kids' books and I think that's another reason our books look different. I just do what I think seems appropriate or right for Jon and Lane's style.... They're always trying to make pages lively and then the story is so silly that if you did something straight it would be, seems to me, completely inappropriate.... I think a lot of the kids' books are designed the way they are because they just have these rules and if you go to school and they tell you this is the way kids' books look and if you get A's for using the little rounded borders and sweet little typefaces, you know.... It just would never occur to me to use those queer little borders and all the things they do. To me, that's just bad design. What I do is like my editorial work. I design to grab people's attention, so each page will be interesting to read or intense in some way. I don't think anything should fade into the background.

"I DON'T KNOW HOW THIS BIG BAD WOLF THING GOT STARTED, BUT IT'S ALL WRONG"

The creators of *The Stinky Cheese Man* are well aware that other artists, too, have challenged conventions within the children's picture book industry. Jon conjectured that part of his own inspiration may have come from the contrast between what he was reading in elementary school in the early 1960s—basal readers with tame, humorless stories and uniform lines of typeface beneath standardized pastel illustrations—and the surprising, colorful, and comparatively goofy Dr. Seuss books. The Dr. Seuss design artists were breaking conventions by splashing their colors and drawings right to the edge of the page, instead of maintaining the even margins that printers prefer, and the resultant design served to integrate words and text in a way that pulled readers headlong into an expansive world in each double-page spread, rather than setting that world apart from the reader by borders and boundaries. Yet, even in Dr. Seuss's *Green Eggs and Ham* (Seuss, 1960), for example, the text is presented in standardized blocks of type against a white background on the page, more like the basal reader than not. It remains today a prevalent way of integrating text with pictures, with the standard variant of blocking the text within the colored backgrounds of the illustrations themselves.

Later in the 1960s and into the 1970s and beyond, author-illustrators like Maurice Sendak challenged conventions by trying to represent the fantasies of children from their own points of view and through illustrations unique in their mood, artistic merit, and dark imagination. With Caldecott Medal Winner *Where the Wild Things Are* (Sendak, 1964) and Caldecott Honor Book *In the Night Kitchen* (Sendak, 1970), however, Harper and Row's designers stuck to standard conventions of uniform text, inset in light background against darker illustrations which were framed in full- or half-page rectangles. The enchanting stories and the broad, rounded characters in surreal settings were consequently much more innovative than the design itself.

While imaginative stories and rich illustrations won critical acclaim and popular audiences throughout the 1970s and 1980s, certain fundamental design features remained largely unchallenged. For example, *Strega Nona* (de Paola, 1975) and *The Garden of Abdul Gasazi* (Van Allsburg, 1979) were both designated Caldecott Honor Books on the basis of the compelling fantasies they built in text and illustration, yet their design followed traditions of rectangular art displays accompanied by standard lines and blocks of copy in adjacent white panels. In the 1980s, in *Round Trip* (Jonas, 1987) and again in *Reflections* (Jonas, 1987), Ann Jonas used the relatively distinctive design feature of a book that is flipped over at its end, which is only the midpoint of the story. The tale continues back to the book's beginning, revealing that the illustrations used in the first pass through the book can now be viewed upside down to illustrate formerly upside down text on the return trip. Both volumes won American Library Association Notable Book awards. Both observe the standard design conventions of uniform typeface in its panel, illustrations in theirs.

More innovative still, a book like *Black and White* (Macaulay, 1990) won a Caldecott Medal in 1990. The bold label WARNING on the title page and dust jacket gives some indication of the design challenge Macaulay created:

"Warning: This book appears to contain a number of stories that do not necessarily occur at the same time. Then again, it may contain only one story. In any event, careful inspection of both words and pictures is recommended." In this book, four panels appear on each double-page spread, and each of the four panels connects directly with its position-mate on the next double-page spread, so that four stories simultaneously unfold throughout the text. While these four stories intertwine, a slightly different typeface and a different art style for each separates one from the other. The design of *Black and White* also challenges conventional separations of illustration and text, integrating them in imaginative ways. Text is written in clouds, balloon letters appear in white against dark panels, puns are made that reflect a self-conscious recognition of the complicated, multiple storyline

approach (as in one illustration of "udder chaos"). Such innovations as words on scraps of paper, drawn fluttering from one story into the next, help the stories intermingle. More than in most other popular books one is likely to see before 1990, the design of *Black and White* becomes a significant part of its message.

It is this self-consciousness about book design that Jon and Lane asserted so irreverently in the text and illustrations of *The True Story of the Three Little Pigs*, and which Molly helped them push to a new level in *The Stinky Cheese Man*. Despite the evident richness of imagination in text and illustrations, nearly all children's books that have passed through the standardizing process of publisher's art directing have emerged with features that most authors and illustrators would not be likely to question in the first place: a title that straightforwardly represents something about the book's content; a title page that presents the author and publisher; a dedication; sometimes a table of contents; a story with characters in a narrative that has a beginning, a middle, and an end; text that stays in its place adjacent to illustrations that stay in theirs; a dust jacket with information about the authors; and so on—standard features that make a book a book, and which only the most juvenile mind would use as a target for spoof and mockery. Or worse, three juvenile minds.

Silliness seems to be the unique root of *Three Little Pigs* that later blossoms in *The Stinky Cheese Man*. The playful humor of *Three Little Pigs* is reflected in the title: this is The True Story, and adults have got it wrong. Kids are being let in on the "true" story at the same time that they are being let in on the joke that such events could have happened at all. They are given credit for being able to understand a pretty sophisticated irony. The familiar conventions of the fairy tale are being contested, while at the same time these familiarities are exactly what allow young readers to appreciate the rebellion. These twists on the familiar draw young readers into the inner circle of *those who know*. As A. Wolf tells them, "I'll let you in on a little secret. Nobody knows the real story (Scieszka, & Smith, p. 1)." And soon after, the storyteller deepens his intimacy with the reader: "I'm the wolf. Alexander T. Wolf. You can call me Al" (p. 2).

Young readers are then treated to "the real story," in which the Wolf concludes, "I was framed." But the evidence in the wolf's own story seems to implicate his guilt, despite his protestations, creating an irony rare among children's picture books. Children are invited to employ disbelief or at least suspicion, on the one hand, recognizing that the narrator has tried to mislead them throughout, while on the other hand they must suspend disbelief to accept the fact that the wolf is narrating at all. To be suspicious of the wolf's story is to accept that he is telling it in the first place, which, of course, is untrue at its own level. The effectiveness of the fantasy, this fundamental suspension of disbelief, is heightened by a diversionary tactic that keeps children busily suspicious about something else.

The illustrations deepen the reader's suspicions about A. Wolf. While he is claiming innocence, the vivid paintings suggest otherwise. He claims to have sneezed at inopportune moments, "huffing and snuffing," until the pigs' flimsy houses fell down, rather than intentionally huffing and puffing them down. Yet the pictures expose a purposeful puffer of a wolf, and his claims of "wolf's honor" seem flimsier than the sticks and straw in the pictures.

The design feature that most integrates the front and back covers with illustrations and text is newsprint. It, too, serves the irony of the story, because it is clearly authentic newsprint that is reproduced, but the wolf uses it in a transparently inauthentic alibi: he was framed by news reporters, who "jazzed up the story with all of that 'Huff and puff and blow your house down.' And they made me the Big Bad Wolf." *The True Story of the Three Little Pigs* is given the verity of a newspaper headline on the cover, but it proves in the end to be more untrue than fairy tales typically are.

With text, pictures, and design, Lane and Jon (and to a lesser extent Molly) began to establish their modus operandi in *The Three Little Pigs*. They challenged the convention of a well-known fairy tale by turning it on its head, presenting it from the villain's point of view. They conspiratorially encouraged rebellion against conventional fairy tale tropes, inviting children in on a secret that others seemed not to know. By appealing to the children's allusionary base, they credited young readers with being able to get the logic of jokes, unexpected twists, and improvisations that were simply the product of adults at play with traditional ideas and images (play which also yields side jokes that only adults are likely to follow, like the newsprint headline, Little Red Riding Hood Settles Dispute Out of Court).

In fact, playful, silly humor permeates *Three Little Pigs*. To say much more than that would require the deconstruction of what is meant by jokes. One is reminded of the film, *Mr. Saturday Night,* in which Billy Crystal's character repeatedly tries to explain what makes a joke work: "First you get 'em going one way, then—you take 'em the other way." For the creators of *The True Story of the Three Little Pigs,* children's familiarity with the traditional story and its conventions is the set-up, and the book itself is the extended punch line—an exercise in "take 'em the other way."

"IT REALLY WAS COLLABORATIVE, CUTTING UP DRAWINGS ON THE BOARD AND CUTTING UP THE TEXT"

The author, illustrator, and designer of *The Stinky Cheese Man* believe that their collaborative working relationship is critical to the uniqueness of the book itself. Molly contrasts this collaboration to the typical book design process, offering her view of the impact of their success on the industry:

> Usually a writer writes the book and then passes that along to an illustrator and a lot of times the writer and the illustrator never get together. Then the designer gets the text and art and there's really not much he can do. But if I'm talking to Lane, and he's sitting right here, I'll say well, let's do a full-page spread and then have copy over on this page. You find you can just look and then when you turn the page, it will be clear whether it works or not. But the industry still works in its usual ways. Our collaboration really hasn't changed things. Most writers and illustrators still don't know each other and never will. I think that's so that the publisher

will have more power to direct things to where they want them to go.

The publisher, of course, succeeds or fails partly on the basis of his ability to predict what will find a market. Molly is not convinced, however, of the value of the industry's techniques for predicting sales success, particularly as these predictions interfere with new ideas:

> They just say such and such didn't sell. Or they get these focus groups that are jazzed that they've paid so much money for and they just destroy all creative, you know, thinking, and it's unbelievable—they make these sweeping comments about stuff and you say, well, okay, then we can't do that.

It is an old marketing story in any field that industry convictions about what sells can stymie new approaches. Lane first saw *The True Story of the Three Little Pigs* after Jon had encountered publishers' resistance to the initial text. Lane felt that the addition of strong illustrations would make publishers take another look.

> I said, "Well, I really like this a lot, let's do it together. I'll do up a book dummy and insert your text and it will look just like a makeshift children's book and I'll take it around for you and we'll get it published, because you're getting rejected." So I took it around and I got rejected everywhere.

Ultimately, Viking saw potential that others did not, and *The Three Little Pigs* went to market. Lane describes how the collaborative process differed for their next book together.

> When we did *The Three Little Pigs,* Jon just gave it to me and I spent a couple of weeks doing all the paintings and then he said, "Oh, that looks good," and then it just came out. But with *Stinky Cheese Man,* it really was collaborative, cutting drawings up on the board and cutting the text up, and Molly would come in say, "Well, wait a second, you have an extra page here", and then Jon would say, "Well, we'll just throw that story out."

Although Jon generates the original story lines and text for their books, he has a great deal of respect for the talents of his collaborators, and he encourages and responds to their editorial judgments. He describes how, after "honing the voice of a story," he makes no effort to influence how Lane will interpret that story in his artwork.

> It's really exciting to see what Lane will do with it. It's sheer brilliance. He has a filmmaker's sense of storytelling with images. I'm a cheerleader at that point. I might goof around with design issues, like whether there's too much text for what Molly wants to do, and I'll say, "Here, I'll rewrite that," and she'll say, "No, let me see what I can do." Molly enhances that dramatic quality of the page-to-page-ness of a story. She gives it its organic quality.

Lane, too, observes the unifying effect of Molly's design work, but in a counterintuitive way. Rather than follow the industry practice of using the same size and style of typeface throughout a book, *Stinky Cheese Man* uses too many to bother counting (in "Jack's Bean Problem," for example, using six font sizes in three words that are being squashed by the giant's boot). In one story, 23 words are blown up large enough to fill an entire page with text, while another story squeezes 25 *lines* of much smaller type onto the page. This move is repeated throughout the text, the variation creating a theme, as Lane explains:

Molly's other concept for the book too, was that on those full pages, no matter how many words, they would fill the page—so if you had a hundred words or if you just had five words, it would fill the page. It's just kind of nice, since the book is so chaotic, that just brought a nice structure to it. It somehow becomes somewhat unified.

Molly confesses to a greater need for such order than either of her partners display. She often portrays them as clowning around while she strives to make sense of the component parts.

Well, in part, that's an organizational thing. You know, I just can't work until I know every little bit of information I have to have it all on the wall, have it all clear and clean in my head, and these guys are just telling jokes.

But the jokes are at the core of what makes *Stinky Cheese Man* work, as Molly knows. Her different sensibilities seem to expand what is possible for the final integration of words and pictures. If each story in *Stinky Cheese Man* presents a different design innovation, each also has a story of its own behind it, usually one involving two or three of the artists solving a problem together. In "Jack's Story," for example, (different from "Jack's Bean Problem"), the Giant tells Jack that when Jack finishes telling him a story, he will grind Jack's bones into flour for bread. So Jack tells the Giant this very story of the Giant's threat, ending with, "Jack cleared his throat, and then began his story." He retells the story, ending with the same line, and so on recursively, in tinier and tinier print, until it simply runs off the page. Molly recalls this story in illustrating why she values the collaborative style of working:

It's just much better having all three of us together, able to work together. Something like *The Stinky Cheese Man* we could never have done separately because half the stuff I don't even get. It's like, what do you mean, Jon, the story never ends? What's that all about? After he explained, Lane said it would be cool if the story went around and around and around, but I thought it'd be better if the text got smaller and smaller and then just went off the page completely, which Jon liked.

Lane recounts another instance of the collaboration adding up to more than the sum of its parts. In this case, as in others, an intended innovation surpassed the limits of what the industry would allow.

Jon and I originally wanted to have the page actually flop and the page actually melting here and do a dye cut and then on the other page have a cow eating that part of the book—but they said it costs too much money. So that was our concession. We ran it to Molly and said, "Ooh, if we do this kind of melting, then can you make the type melting also?" She said, "Well it's a pain in the ass, but..."

But, in effect, let's see what we can do. The collaborative relationship and its striking results, in which a unique designer has become a full partner in the creative process, are nothing less than a triumph over business as usual in the children's picture book industry.

"RELUCTANT READERS WILL LOOK FOR OTHER BOOKS WITH 'CHEESE' IN THE TITLE"

In, *Stinky Cheese Man,* no chance to "take 'em the other way"

goes unexploited. The mockery of convention is almost relentless. Even the subtitle, *And Other Fairly Stupid Tales,* undermines its content. The front dust jacket flap parodies the commercialism of the children's book market and sales pitches in general, proclaiming "ONLY $16.00! 56 action packed pages, 75% more than those old 32-page Brand-X books." A mock seal of approval exhorts: NEW! IMPROVED! FUNNY! GOOD! BUY! NOW! The joke here, as Molly and Lane tell it, is also that they were being urged by the publisher to stay within the standard printers' page-number increments. "Kids' books are either 32 pages, 40, 48 or 64 pages," explains Lane, "and this book is 56, which just isn't done." Adds Molly: "So, if we came through with 56 they really wanted to put something on there to say it was a bigger than usual book so we made a joke out of it—only $16.00 for 56 pages."

Scholarly and popular reviewers have analyzed *Stinky Cheese Man* in terms of its postmodern sensibilities, one approving critic observing that, "The visuals do not merely further interrogate the self-questioning text, but also engage in their own artistic irony and pastiche" (Stevenson, 1992). Perhaps more significantly, and certainly more simply, the mood and moves of *Stinky Cheese Man* are grounded first in Jon's style as a teacher. He first developed his approach to writing such stories in the elementary school classroom, and he believes that the same orientation to children that informed his teaching continues to inform his writing. Not surprisingly, the communication with children is often two-way.

One thing that my writing takes from my teaching is respect for kids, a belief in their intelligence. Another is the play element. As a teacher, I tried to put humor in almost everything we did. By that I mean a joyful humor, not take-it-apart funny. And I think this works for kids in the books. They get it. And I get great letters from kids telling me they do.

Lane, too, believes that the work of Jon the writer is very close to the work of Jon the teacher, and that his ability to arouse the interest of a broad spectrum of children is one of Jon's strengths in both capacities.

Even though they are big crossover books, we do write them with third grade mentality in mind. That was the grade that Jon was teaching when he wrote *The Three Little Pigs* and a lot of the adults who thought the book was too sophisticated hadn't been in a classroom in years. If you go in there and you read them, you know, the little bitty bunny, you're gonna lose 'em. But if you read them *The Stinky Cheese Man,* they're rollin' in the aisles and the reluctant readers will go ahead and look for other books with cheese in the title.

Lane's illustrations, similar to Jon's writing, seem to aim high. They are sophisticated paintings that seem to capture childish fantasy with a decidedly adult, but surreal, technique. Lane describes his approach:

Well, I think it's just not trying to dumb it down for the third graders. The problem with a lot of kids' books in their writing and in their art work is that they, adults, are writing or illustrating what they think kids should read or see, and Jon and I have never felt that way. Even my work for adults was always weird, distorted, and dark, but it was never gratuitously sexual or violent in any way. And then the stuff I do for kids is the same way. If it didn't have the stinky cheese man in it, the background could be exactly the same but have Richard Nixon's head in there and it'd be just fine. So, I mean, I guess I don't really think, "Oh, a third grader would love this." We don't try to water it down. Kids are watching MTV and they're riding these skateboards with all these cool skulls and neon colors on, and then the adults give them these, you know, pink and blue books and they're going, "What are you, crazy?"

Given their combination of a child's sense of play and adult's command of language and images, the collaborators produce a level of humor interesting to children and adults alike. In the middle of one story, Jack the Narrator's premature telling of "Little Red Riding Shorts" leaves the Wolf and Red Riding Shorts in such a snit that they refuse to narrate their tale. The resulting blank page was again an idea not readily welcomed by the publisher. Lane's account of this reveals something of the adult sensibilities at play in the creation of comedy that succeeds with children:

> We got flack early on when the publisher said, "Well, can't we add a squished bug on there or a thumbprint or something?" Jon was real insistent on "No, if we're gonna do the gag, let's do the gag." It's similar to Ernie Kovacs; I heard a story about how he would have his TV show going and then he would just have a marching band march through the stage and then that would be it. And the sponsor would say "we're paying all this money for the marching band, let's bring them back again for the endup," and Ernie would say, "No, just let's do it once and it's funny that way." That was kind of what we thought about the blank page too; if we're gonna do this, then just make it blank. But we're always tempted to sign our names there when people ask us to sign the books.

But here the defiance of convention goes one step further, and it is this step, only foreshadowed in *Three Little Pigs,* that marks the sharpest break from the unexpected: not only does the book challenge storybook traditions, but the characters themselves draw readers' attention to these departures, sometimes lauding them and other times becoming upset by them. After the blank page appears, for example, the Little Red Hen makes an unexpected and unexplained reappearance from earlier in the book:

> Say, what's going on here? Why is that page blank? Is that my page? .... Do they expect me to tell the whole story by myself? Where is that lazy narrator? Where is that lazy illustrator? Where is that lazy author?

By calling attention to format conventions, Little Red Hen is only continuing what started even before the book's title page, which reads, of course, in letters that fill the entire page:

TITLE PAGE
(for The Stinky
Cheese Man & Other
Fairly Stupid Tales)

Before that page, however, the creators have already begun storytelling on the endpaper, dislodging the title page as a marker for a book's beginning. While Little Red Hen tries to try to begin her story, Jack the Narrator struggles to keep order, interrupting her: "Wait a minute. Hold everything. You can't tell your story right here. This is the endpaper. The book hasn't even started yet." Before the book has started, characters are arguing over how the book should begin, and they are doing so in typeface of contrasting size and color (red and black), creating just the "grab your attention" effect that Molly seeks in her design. Before the book has started, the very notion of a book having a beginning is undermined. The young reader, like the characters, is immediately compelled to attend to structural elements of the book, not just to its story and pictures.

The defiance of convention redoubles as the characters begin to discuss it with the reader. The dedication is written upside down in huge typeface, ostensibly on a white sheet of paper held by the narrator against the slim margin of a dark landscape. "I know. I know," snaps the narrator. "The page is upside down. I meant to do that. Who ever looks at that dedication stuff anyhow?" But just so it is not too hostile, the upside down dedication leaves a place for a child to write in a space labeled "your name here," once again including the child in the rebellion against adult conventions.

And so on throughout the book. The Table of Contents, which instead of the proverbial falling sky comes crashing down on Chicken Licken with such force that the page numbers are jarred loose from the story titles and one story title is dislodged from the Table altogether. No matter: pages are not numbered in this book, and the story bumped from the Table of Contents ('The Boy Who Cried Cow Patty') is bumped from the book, too. Even the ISBN number and bar code on the back cover cause trouble. Chicken Licken returns for one last appearance on the back cover, ranting about the intrusion of the ISBN and bar code. Molly's recollection is one more illustration of the collaborative process at work, even if the final words of the book, "blah, blah, blah, blah," may not themselves seem to be the height of creativity:

> We wanted to shrink the ISBN code. On cassettes and stuff, they're just itty bitty little things. But they wouldn't let us, so Jon and Lane decided to make fun of that too. One time we were gonna make it just really big—just fill the whole back cover with it—but they said that would blow up their scanners, so it's the same size and in the same position on the book as all the rest of the books . But we decided since they wouldn't let us change it that we'd have to do something else. So Lane and Jon came up with something about just having the chicken back there saying, "What is this doing here? It's ugly!" But when I positioned the chicken on the page, I didn't have enough copy, so I just wrote in "blah, blah, blah, blah, blah, blah, blah." It's like dummy copy, but then it just stayed there.

Life After *Cheese Man*

Molly, Lane and Jon continue to work independently and together on new projects. In 1994, Molly completed work on the redesign of *Business Week,* perhaps as far from *Stinky Cheese Man* as editorial design can get. In that same year, Viking published *The Book that Jack Wrote,* written by Jon, illustrated by award-winning painter and magazine illustrator Daniel Adel, and designed not by Viking Press but by Jeri Hansen, Jon's wife. And also in 1994, Lane wrote, directed and co-produced *Water Ride,* a half hour film marked by fantasy, surrealism, and humor. Not a mass market film, *Water Ride* has been shown at several film festivals. This work, together with Lane's success in illustration, has led to bigger things:

They're doing a film version of *James and the Giant Peach,* Roald Dahl's story. Disney is distributing it, Tim Burton is producing it and Henry Selleck is directing it. He's the same director that did the *Nightmare Before Christmas,* another Tim Burton film. It's all stop-motion animation except with James it'll start out in live action and then, evolve into the kid—actually sort of metamorphose into this cartoon character. I'm designing all the characters. I just thought it would be a really fun project and then, independent of that, Disney saw my books, *Happy Hockey Family* and *Stinky Cheese* and stuff, and then they also saw a screenplay that I did for my own little half hour film, and then they hired me to write a feature live action film.

Meanwhile, the collaboration continues. Last fall, *Math Curse* was released by Viking. Calling it, "A Stinky Cheese treatment of mathematics," Jon remarks that the trio has resisted the call to produce more parodies of well-known fairy tales. "We've already done that," says Jon. "In *Math Curse,* a girl wakes up and everything she experiences is a mathematics problem, starting with the number of socks in her drawer, and each problem has a multiple-choice answer. We put mathematics into everything we could in *Math Curse,* including its price."

And the collaboration expands. Most recently, the three artists have been experimenting with the possibilities of CD-ROM production of their stories. Lane tells what by now is becoming a familiar story.

Well, the technology was so hard to grasp, we had so many options this time.

I mean, with *Stinky Cheese Man* we were going crazy and Molly kind of came in and said, "Well, listen, you gotta have some structure," so with CD-ROM, it's gone this far for several months with us just going all over the place, and Microsoft hired Molly to sort of put this into shape. They just assigned us some designer person there who had no design background and she just used the same typeface every time, this sort of typewriter type that comes with the computer ("And it just kills all the jokes," Molly interjects. " It's just so flat.") So we got Molly in there to work and they just look at it and said, "Whoa, this is great, this is like an old medicine show circus poster," and we said, "Yeah, that's what we've been telling you."

Just as they had been dissatisfied with many of the conventions of children's books, the team has found that the CD-ROM technology has not yet caught up to what they would like to accomplish. Lane explains:

With kids' books, the only ones we've seen so far have been, basically, they would just put the book on the CD-ROM and then you'd be able to click on this cow and it'd go "Mooooooooo." Or you'd be able to click on the word and it'd go "No," "No," "No." And Jon and I said, "this is boring," and then we flipped a page and it would take forever for the artwork to load up. So, we just decided, well, we're not gonna do any of the books yet. We will, but, you know, the technology is getting closer and closer and better and better, so we're just gonna sit on *Stinky Cheese Man* probably for another couple of years.

And in the meantime, they will not be idle. Jon, Lane, and Molly are continuing to play at the borders of CD-ROM technology, just as they will continue to play with the conventions of children's books. Their work together represents the coming together of three people with remarkable individual talents, who together reach beyond what any one of them can do alone.

References

de Paola, T. (1975). *Strega nona.* New York: Prentice-Hall.

Jonas, A. (1983). *Round trip.* New York: Greenwillow Books.

Jonas, A. (1987). *Reflections.* New York: Greenwillow Books.

Macaulay D. (1990). *Black and white.* New York: Houghton Mifflin.

Scieszka, J. (1994). *The Book that Jack wrote.* New York: Viking.

Scieszka, J., & Smith, L. (1989). *The true story of the three little pigs.* New York: Viking.

Scieszka, J., & Smith, L. (1992). *The stinky cheese man and other fairly stupid tales.* New York: Viking.

Scieszka, J., & Smith, L. (1995). *Math curse.* New York: Viking.

Sendak, M. (1970). *In the night kitchen.* New York: Harper and Row.

Seuss, Dr. (1960). *Green eggs and ham.* New York: Beginners Books, Random House.

Smith, L. (1991). *The big pets.* New York: Puffin Books.

Smith, L. (1991). *Glasses: Who needs 'em?* New York: Viking.

Smith, L. (1993). *The happy hocky family.* New York: Viking.

Stevenson, D. (1992, Winter). "If you read this last sentence, it won't tell you anything": Postmodernism, self-referentiality, and the stinky cheese man. *Children's Literature Association Quarterly, 17*(4), 32–34.

Van Allsburg, C. (1979). *The garden of Abdul Gasazi.* New York: Houghton Mifflin.

·61·

VOICES FROM THE WORLD OF
FILM AND TELEVISION

REFLECTIONS: ARTHUR MOVES TO TV AND CDS

Marc Brown

AUTHOR, *Arthur* AND OTHER BOOKS

Children's books are among the most carefully controlled and highly scrutinized media to reach a child's hands. Gatekeepers selecting books for children care deeply about the quality of what they choose. I create children's books for a number of reasons. First, creating them allows me to use both my theatrical and artistic background. I can write the script, cast the characters, design the sets and costumes, and direct the story. I like to think of my eye as a television movie camera, moving in, watching the scenes progress.

Now Arthur is appearing on TV and interactive CDs. As I think about that I feel like any parent whose child goes off to live a life of his own. I am a bit concerned that he will be on his best behavior and I hope the world is kind to him. Arthur is probably nervous, too, and perhaps a bit intimidated by all the cameras, lights, and technology. He must feel the warmth of children's love and respect, however, because it comes to him in great bundles. I know children must sense the great respect I have for them because they express their love for Arthur through their letters and by reading his books. I know that respect and love for the Arthur books transfer to the television series and the interactive CD-ROMs. As the ways of telling a story change, so must Arthur and I if we want to reach children.

When my three sisters and I were growing up in Pennsylvania, our grandmother Thora told us the most wonderful stories. Back then I never dreamed that one day I would grow up to tell stories of my own. But when my first son, Tolon, was born, I started telling him stories before he went to sleep. One night Tolon wanted to hear about a weird animal and our story was about an aardvark who hated his nose. The aardvark, of course, was Arthur. Later, I took the manuscript to Emilie McLeod, an editor at Atlantic Monthly Press. She saw something in my work and was willing to invest time and energy in me. She gave me direction and showed me how I was stuck with a technique I had learned in art school. When I showed her the manuscript for *Arthur's Nose*, she thought it needed a lot of work, but she was willing to help. The hardest thing for me at the beginning was to learn how to say something in a sentence or in a few words. I thought I needed three paragraphs. Emilie helped me understand how to use the picture and how to use the words to do what the picture could not do.

Even now, when I originate an idea and I am writing a new book, I always struggle with the writing and I mean *struggle*. Writing is a necessary chore for me to get through in order to do the pictures and see the whole idea happen. I will write a story at least 30 times before I show it to anyone. Sometimes I put the book away for a year before I feel I can even finish it. I do not type or use a word processor. I use pencil and paper. I cut up the paper and move things around with scotch tape and make a long strip of these ideas. I then put the ideas into a proper sequence. I am always conscious of the picture possibilities right from the start, thinking about which words I can replace with pictures. Thumbnail sketches sometimes obscure the words on many drafts.

When I feel that I have a text that is solid, I show it to my editor, and she usually reacts to it and will point out areas that are weak or strong. I then do a dummy, and last turn these ideas into full-size drawings. I work hard to make my drawings seem free and effortless.

I want the art to feel light. A very exciting part for me is adding color. At this point, I allow myself to play music. This is the fun part. By this point I feel both elements have come together; it is going to be a book.

The limitations of camera, paper, and printing are constantly in my mind as I create my art. I consider materials that I can and cannot use to get a certain effect. For instance, certain paints, because of their chemical qualities, do not reproduce well. That is something I have learned to accept over the years.

In my Arthur books I am always working for a tone of humor and informality so that children can fall into the books and have fun reading them. I want children to have the opportunity to feel their feelings, and discharge feeling from within them, whether it be fear, grief, hate, or wonder. I feel this as an adult, as a parent, as an author, and as an illustrator. What I try to do in my books is to provide a mirror for children to explore what is inside of them.

The main reason for moving Arthur to TV and CDs is that more children will be drawn to reading. We know that when children see a book dramatized on television thousands go to get the book. Visual media presentations and reading do not compete with each other; they enliven and enrich the other.

For me the most satisfying part of the process is how children feel about these books. They like what I am doing. I never get tired of knowing that.

BRINGING ARTHUR TO TELEVISION

Kathy Waugh

WGBH EDUCATIONAL FOUNDATION

The idea for an ARTHUR television series was born, appropriately enough, in a library. Some years back, our Director of Development, Carol Greenwald, heard Marc Brown speak at the Medford, Massachusetts, public library. Marc Brown's warmth and rapport with his audience, coupled with the sight of enthusiastic children carrying home piles of *Arthur* books, left an indelible impression. So in 1993, when the National Endowment for Children's Educational Television announced its intention to fund new programs for 6- to 8-year-olds, Arthur seemed a natural fit.

Our interest in bringing Arthur to television is predicated on the belief that stories are one of the most effective ways to inspire and educate children. Go to any classroom, any library during story hour, and you will find children riveted by the telling of stories. Aidan Chambers puts it beautifully in his book, *Introducing Books to Children,* (1983, p. 13) observing that children think and feel with the images and ideas that stories offer, holding them in the "museums of their minds," for later use. The more images stored, the greater the number of resources children have to draw on.

Stories also have important instructional applications. Not only has it been demonstrated that being read to helps children in their later efforts to read and write, but stories provide an early introduction to the traditional structure of narratives, the use of fictional characters and events, and such literary conventions as motivation and conflict. Stories can illuminate important values and behaviors, and give children positive role models to follow. Serialized stories, like the *Arthur* books, have the additional advantage of deepening a child's understanding of what it means to be human. As children encounter characters who evolve and grow over time, they learn that people are complex beings—never static and predictable, but wonderfully changeable.

Perhaps most important, stories help instill in children a passion for reading. Children who are read to, who identify with storybook characters, who associate books with pleasure, tend to become lifelong readers. One thing that struck us, as we were researching and writing the first ARTHUR proposal, was how many children credited the *Arthur* books with a new, or renewed, interest in reading. A typical letter to Marc Brown from a 7-year-old named Jonah proclaimed, "I love *Arthur* books. They teach you to like how we look, and like ourselves. I didn't like to read, but when my tetcher (sic) brought your books, I read every one of your books, and joined the fan club."

But as statistics on literacy reveal, too many children never experience the desire to read. Television can help reverse this trend by presenting significant book-based series targeted to young children and their families. The notion that television and books are necessarily at odds, that children who watch TV will not read books, has been disproved by a number of studies showing that reading, and library use, increase when books are dramatized on television. Daniel Boorstein, a former Librarian of Congress recognized this symbiosis when he wrote, "The book made it possible to send messages across the centuries, but television made it possible to send messages across the continent.... Now we should bring these two technologies together to prove that there is not a competition between them, but that each has the power to enrich and enliven the other." (Charren, & Hulsizer, 1990, p. 2.)

But will a televised ARTHUR actually incite children to read? We think so, based on our experience with a previous storybook series, LONG AGO & FAR AWAY, as well as a related literacy outreach program, the Family Literacy Alliance. LONG AGO offered high-quality adaptations of such classic stories as

---

WGBH, Boston's public television station, is bringing an animated version of Marc Brown's (*Arthur*) books to PBS in the fall of 1996.

The Wind in the Willows and *The Man Who Planted Trees*, which were popular with parents and older siblings as well as young children. Book-based programs that encourage such family viewing can lead to an interest in reading, for through them thoughtful discussions on character, motivation, and perspective can be sparked and nurtured. And of course, parents can lead their children to the books on which such programs are based. This, in fact, was the rationale behind the Family Literacy Alliance (FLA), which draws from three book-based series—LONG AGO & FAR AWAY, WONDERWORKS and READING RAINBOW—to motivate family reading. Parents and children who participate in the FLA (now operating nationwide in homeless shelters, prisons, hospitals and after-school programs) watch stories on television, then read the books and engage in a variety of activities—from drawing pictures to writing in diaries—that emphasize the pleasure to be found in books. What the FLA has demonstrated most clearly is that children—and parents—who see wonderful, inspiring, book-based television *want* to recapture that experience in books.

There are several ways in which WGBH is using ARTHUR to affirm this connection between television and books. We are producing a library tag, which will air at the end of each ARTHUR program and remind children and parents that *Arthur* books are as "near as their local library." We are also developing and implementing a strong, literacy-based outreach plan for the series. In addition to posters for libraries and prebroadcast brochures for teachers, we are developing an ARTHUR "story writing kit," which will encourage students to read the *Arthur* books and then create new Arthur stories based on their own experiences. The kits will be sent to 2nd-grade teachers who request them, and contain books, bookmarks, and pencils, as well as strategies and suggestions for age-appropriate writing activities. The culminating activity will be the creation of a classroom story to be sent back to WGBH.

We are also conscious of all the subtle ways in which ARTHUR can help instill a love of language and literature. For example, the ARTHUR characters are often seen reading, or being read to, visiting the library, playing word games, turning to books for advice or information, making up stories, engaging in imaginary play, enjoying school, and using words, instead of fists, to resolve their differences. Marc Brown created this "book friendly" environment in the *Arthur* books; if you look closely at his illustrations, you will notice that Arthur and his little sister, D.W., have bookshelves—and books—in their rooms, that their parents read, and that adults and children alike turn to books when they have questions, concerns or free time.

The ARTHUR television series is building on all these subtle and overt messages to demonstrate that reading and writing are not only pleasurable, but life-enhancing, activities. Books are, after all, the key to understanding one's own life, one's history, one's place in a larger world. Without them children are locked into experiences and perceptions too narrow for real growth and insight. Decrying the growing problem of illiteracy and the lack of stories in too many children's lives, Action for Children's Television in 1990 called upon television producers to send the message that books *matter.* ARTHUR is our answer to that call.

References

Chambers, A. (1983). *Introducing books to children.* London: Heinemann.

Charren, P., & Hulsizer, C. (1990). *TV, books and children.* Action for Children's Television.

·61C·

READING RAINBOW AND THE JOY OF READING

Twila C. Liggett

EXECUTIVE DIRECTOR, READING RAINBOW

Reading Rainbow is a well-established PBS children's series designed to bring the fun of good books, reading and learning for the *sheer joy* of the experience to our young viewers (targeting 5- to 8-year-olds). Centering each theme around a feature book, the programs use on-location segments to engage children in enriching adventures related to the book's theme. Three books are reviewed and promoted by young readers who entice the viewers with more book choices. The series first was aired in 1983.

It has become a cliché to talk about the power of television, but much of the research (Comstock, 1991) indicates that young children, especially in our target age range are mesmerized by television. They implicitly accept and even embrace television's messages, especially visually. Children are always "learning" from television whether it be negative ideas or even dangerous ones, and can either be stimulated mentally or turned into "couch potatoes" (Van Evra, 1990).

Thus, in addition to establishing *Reading Rainbow's* primary goal of conveying the fun of reading and books, we also felt a strong responsibility to present positive role models that were multicultural, nonsexist, and inclusive of the broad range in age and physical abilities in our society. A strong key to positive role modeling was in the selection of our host, LeVar Burton (then best known for his role as Kunta Kinte in *Roots*).

As the *Reading Rainbow* team carefully developed a pilot program, we paid close attention to our evaluators, RMC Research, who gave us helpful feedback regarding these goals as well as that of the technical decisions that influence young children's *understanding* of what they are watching. For example, while the MTV technique of fast cuts and nonsequential images may capture a child's attention, young children have absolutely no sense of *what* occurred or the *why* of what they saw. Therefore, as a result of our work with RMC, in our approach to books and the theme-related "real life" extensions (our on-location segments), we chose to enhance an important element of literacy, that is, the sense of story. Thus, the notion of logical sequence, and the ability to then relate what happened (the beginning of com-

prehension skills) is a key element of *Reading Rainbow's* design.

Has our approach worked? We think so. Based on 10 years of formative research, RMC developed a summary for the project staff of their key findings in five categories: (1) Contributions to literacy; (2) LeVar Burton as host; (3) Book treatments; (4) Outlook on life / primary messages; and, (5) Entertainment value.

Contributions to Literacy

What makes *Reading Rainbow* different from other series is our primary focus on encouraging independent reading for enjoyment and interest and the more subtle message of locating information applicable to one's own life. This focus makes *Reading Rainbow* different from other "literacy" programs such as *Sesame Street,* with its emphasis on the symbol systems that precede reading, *Ghostwriter,* which centers on using reading and writing strategies to interpret information, or instructional programs that focus on how to decode and comprehend. By overtly sending the message to seek and read the books featured, *Reading Rainbow* consistently achieves this goal. Our unique literacy purpose has been affirmed consistently by parents, librarians, teachers and children themselves when they discuss their understanding of the series and identify reasons for wanting to read particular titles.

LeVar Burton as Host

Although a serendipitous outcome, happily, LeVar Burton has become synonymous with the series—and a unique presence in children's television. (Younger viewers often refer to LeVar as the "Rainbow Man.") Children value LeVar's ability to explain complicated issues and to ask the most interesting questions. They relate to his sense of fun in learning and see him as a great teacher. As a learner, LeVar seems to be a role model for all viewers across all cultures;

there is also some evidence that African-American parents value LeVar as a minority role model.

Book Treatments

Much of our research has been about book treatment; that is, how best to present, position, and reference books in ways that children understand that they are accessible, readable, and meaningful. The subtleties of different approaches to feature and review book treatments are documented in every evaluation from the earliest challenges of ensuring that child viewers do *not* mistake the featured book for a cartoon, but understand that what they are seeing is a "real" book—a concept we have come to call the "bookness" of a book. We implement the "bookness" (in part) by beginning each book presentation with the title page, using actual illustrations with slight camera movement ("iconographic" animation), and superimposing the words "The End" at the book's conclusion. As a result, our evaluations show that children definitely understand that what they saw *on* television *is* a real book. This understanding is most often reflected in children's requests to parents, teachers, and librarians for the books they see on *Reading Rainbow* or in their absolute delight in realizing that the very book they are holding is appearing (or has appeared) on the TV screen.

Outlook on Life-Primary Messages.

A fortuitous finding of our evaluations has been that children understand and believe *Reading Rainbow's* positive messages about their capabilities, values, and options. LeVar also contributes to this perception by conveying to children a sense of the limitless potential of the world that can be obtained through curiosity and openness. We have been gratified to find that while our evaluations have included a range of children across ethnic groups, the delivery of key messages / ideas or entertainment value is accessible to all children and is not diminished in any way based on a child's ethnicity or gender. Our evaluators concluded that the series' elements and design have apparently rendered such potential barriers transparent so that all children enjoy *Reading Rainbow* at a number of levels.

Entertainment Value

As part of the evaluation of a given *Reading Rainbow* episode, the evaluators conduct an observation that gives a sense of children's attention. The series has consistently delivered attention rates of 95–100% over as many as 30 discrete segments within an episode. This attention rate has held true for the episodes evaluated since its inception. Analysis of other responses from children indicates that several factors contribute to this high attention rate, including the program's production style, which gives children

time to think, its productive use of "seen and said" in which visual and aural information are closely matched, careful attention to transitions between segments and the affinity that the viewers have for LeVar. The design of *Reading Rainbow* also recognizes that entertainment value and effectiveness of idea delivery are not a function of surface elements such as the use of music or rapid pacing; rather it is a function of how elements are crafted and combined to stimulate opportunities for children to think and respond to information cognitively. RMC'S evaluations have strongly indicated that children are engaged with *Reading Rainbow* when elements are combined to assist and encourage their process of reflecting upon, remembering, and making use of information.

As stated at the outset, careful design and formative evaluation have been and continue to be incorporated into the production of this series. We feel that not only have we achieved the goals we had set originally, but that we also continue to grow. Over the past 10 years, we have created a "science" strand of shows based on delightful science picture books for children; recently we incorporated a "literature-based math" strand to the series. In addition, we find that *Reading Rainbow* is used in classrooms in multiple, interdisciplinary ways. In a recent, informal survey, for example, teachers responded that they were using the series for whole language, storytelling, science, art, social studies, cultural studies, geography, holiday and seasonal topics, parenting workshops, and teacher in-service. One teacher answered, "for pure enjoyment."

And it is this enjoyment factor that tells us that we were achieving our goals, one that is reflected in letters from our young viewers and the adults around them—the true "voices from the field."

> Hi, *Reading Rainbow.* I love your show. Reading is the best thing in the whole world. Say Hi to LeVar for me. When I go to the library, I go to the *Reading Rainbow* part first. I get lots of books there. I even got my own library card. Frank, age 7, Niagara Falls, NY

> Dear LeVar, I am eight years old. I like to read the books ... [and] I also like to watch the story that you show. I really liked when you went to the cave. It is cool when you go to different places. [She then closes with the theme song, "Take a look, it's in a book..."] Kayla, Spokane, WA

> I have discovered another joy of reading—*Reading Rainbow.* You have helped develop my [four year old] son's passion for reading. He watches the show faithfully and we have purchased several of the books.... He astounds his grandparents with his vocabulary, which consists of words like "microscope"—even "embalmed!" The show has increased his creativity and his desire to learn. Mother, Bellflower, CA

> *Reading Rainbow* is one of the best ideas to come along in a long time. In an age of "steady video" kids are encouraged to read ... explore their horizons and expand their world. Librarian, from *Reading Rainbow's* 1994 National Librarian Survey.

References

Comstock, G. with Paik, H. (1991). *Television and the American child*. San Diego, CA: Academic Press.

Van Evra, J. (1990). *Television and child development*. Hillsdale, NJ: Erlbaum.

VISUAL LITERACY GOES TO THE MOVIES

Lauren L. Wohl

DISNEY PRESS AND HYPERION BOOKS FOR CHILDREN

There are six of us in a cozy living room, settled in front of the television set, a big bowl of popcorn for sharing. Five of us are under nine. Five of us have never seen BAMBI before. Five of us have been invited to watch a movie and talk about it. One of us (the one older than nine; the one who has seen BAMBI) is there to test a hypothesis: do children really *read* pictures? Do they apply the same kinds of skills and thinking when they look at images (in a book or on the screen) as they do when they listen to words or read text? Is visual literacy for real?

Now, the six of us are excited—and ready.

I push the play button and the title appears.

"Bambi," Chloe (age 8) reads aloud, so that the younger viewers will know what it says. But, as the rest of the credits appear, she does not bother announcing them. She knows the little kids would not care much what they say.

We watch the opening scene. It is nearly 4 minutes before there is any real dialogue in the film. I push the stop button.

What's going on?

"Robyn (age 4) tells us: "A new baby deer is just born and everyone comes to meet him."

"Because he's a prince," Beth (age 7) adds.

I ask where, when, how?

"In the forest," Robyn knows.

"Early in the morning," Alyson (age 6) says. She can tell because the little mouse washes his face with a dew drop and because the owl is trying to go to sleep.

"And because it's all grey. The sun hasn't come up yet," Chloe points out.

Beth: "The animals know about Bambi because the bird tells them and shows them where Bambi is."

Jason (age 5): "Bambi's mother is proud. And the other animals like Bambi. They know he's the Prince. Like in THE LION KING."

I push play and do not stop the film until the sounds of gun shots chase Bambi and all the animals from the meadow.

Now what's happened?

Jason: "Bambi learned to walk. He kept falling."

Robyn: "And he learned to talk."

Beth: "Bir-d-d-d."

They all laugh.

Alyson: "And he has friends. Thumper and Flower."

Chloe: "And a girlfriend. Faline."

Beth: "It's the summertime. When Bambi falls into the water, he isn't cold."

Jason: "But he looks silly."

Beth: "Hunters are in the forest, and the animals have to run away and hide."

Chloe: "I think the hunters stay and wait for the animals to come back. "

Why do you think that?

Chloe: "Because they didn't kill anyone, and that's why they came. And because Bambi's mother still looks worried."

I push the play button. Leaves are swirling by on the screen.

Alyson: "It's Fall now. The leaves are falling off the trees."

And, a few minutes later, when Winter arrives, before Bambi tells his mother, Jason tells us that Bambi and his mother have run out of food and they are hungry. Jason is the one most relieved when Spring arrives and the deer find new grass to eat.

Chloe: "Why are they going back to the meadow? The hunters could still be there."

Three children cry when Bambi's mother is killed. Alyson climbs on my lap when Bambi and Ronno fight. It is Robyn on my lap during the forest fire. And the six of us applaud at the end of the movie.

There is lots to talk about, and it is soon clear from their questions and comments that these five youngsters have done a lot more than just follow the story line of this classic film.

Walt Disney's *BAMBI* is a 70-minute animated film with no narration and minimal dialogue. Viewers must take their clues from what they see—filling in information based on prior knowledge and experience, imagination, and comparison.

Chloe, Robyn, Beth, Jason, and Alyson have each done just that. On the skills level, they have made inferences, predicted actions and anticipated outcomes. On the comprehension level, they have enriched the plot with details gathered from the images on the screen, discerned character from the action and from the poses that they watched, and realized themes largely from visuals. On the critical level, they have made comparisons. In short—and to my surprise and delight—they've been *reading the pictures* of this movie.

Robyn: "My favorite part was when Thumper and Bambi go skating on the lake."

How did you know it was a lake?

"Robyn: "Because it's frozen, and it's big, and it's in the forest. In winter, lakes get frozen."

Beth: "My favorite character is Flower. He's shy, but he has two best friends."

Jason: "Bambi's mother died because of hunters. And the fire started because of hunters. People should stay out of the forest."

Chloe: "My favorite part was how the forest looked in different seasons. And how the animals had to change in different seasons. No matter what else happened, the seasons changed. Even after Bambi's mother died."

Alyson: "I liked the whole movie. It's my favorite."

Jason: "I like THE LION KING better. It's better to be a king than a Prince. "

I give each child a copy of the Disney Press Illustrated Classic book, BAMBI. They turn to different illustrations, each one remembering the scene pictured. Each tells me just where in the movie the picture came from—what happened before, what happened next—always filling in with some "extras."

Jason: "This is when Bambi meets the skunk. He calls him Flower, and the skunk likes that name. Flowers smell nice and skunks don't. Skunks don't like the way they smell either."

How do you know that?

Jason: "No one likes to smell bad. Besides, when Flower meets his girlfriend, she's hiding in a flower bush, too. So if skunks hang out in flower bushes, it's because they like things that smell nice."

Oh.

This time I am amazed. Jason is 5, and his mother had warned me: he is not much of a talker.

I take the tape out of the VCR player and begin to make preparations to leave. But the children are still settled in. Chloe is reading to them from the book. She does not bother showing the pictures. The words are all the children need to recall the images from the film and to create pictures of their own.

I have come to some conclusions. Visual literacy is indeed real; viewing a movie can be—is!—a terrific literacy exercise, one that can be even further enhanced with a book. For, when a child enjoys a movie, and then the pictures she has "read" on the screen become the paintings and words of a book, she has a new dimension to explore. Because the images are transformed, first by the illustrator and author/adaptor, then by the reading or listening child, the child becomes aware of her importance in the process. She learns that her perceptions and her imagination are vital to the story. She is able to go deeper into the book—not just to enjoy the story and characters again (although this is certainly valuable)—but to test her comprehension, her visions, her memory, and to find new understandings .

The experience is simply twice as good.

"HOOP DREAMS": AN INTERVIEW WITH STEVEN JAMES—PRODUCER, DIRECTOR, CO-EDITOR

Victoria Chou and Steve Tozer

COLLEGE OF EDUCATION, UNIVERSITY OF ILLINOIS AT CHICAGO

This edited transcript is part of a longer text and comes from an interview with Steven James conducted by Victoria Chou and Steve Tozer on January 18, 1995.

I …Tell us about the purpose of Kartemquin films and its structure as well. This is not a big Hollywood film place, is it?

SJ No. Kartemquin films has been around for nearly 30 years producing social issue documentaries. It started as a collective of filmmakers back in the '60s. Kartemquin for 30 years has been making these social issue documentaries and the way in which they have stayed in business was to also, while they were doing those kinds of films, produce industrials, usually for a good cause—educational films, and things of that nature.

Frederick Marx and I, back in '86, approached Kartemquin to serve as the production company for our film because we had both seen their work at festivals and they have a national reputation. We said that we had an idea for this short, half-hour film on street basketball and the dream of success. What we were going to do was take a snapshot of the dream on a playground court in Chicago. We would be there for a few weeks, we would find a young kid, like an Arthur or William, we would find a washed-up player who'd been through the system, like Curtis ends up being in the film, and we would try and get a pro player, like an Isaiah Thomas who came from that neighborhood and succeeded. And we would just try and sort of check these three different vantage points of the dream, from a young kid who has great hope, a person whose dream went awry, and one whose dream happened. Anyway, we approached Gordon [at Kartemquin] with this idea and he liked the idea, so he agreed to take this project on, even though we had no funding. The reason we went to Kartemquin is that Frederick and I had

left graduate school at Southern Illinois University where we'd made films, but we had no real track record to speak of, especially in this kind of documentary filmmaking. And, for us to try and launch a project like this, it made sense to go to an established company that has an established track record and has a similar aesthetic in terms of what they're about, so Kartemquin was a perfect fit.

I And what are some of the kinds of recognition the film has gotten to date?

SJ It started at Sundance in January 1994 in terms of its developing a national reputation. The film was accepted into the Sundance Film Festival, which is probably the most influential film festival in the world, certainly in the United States. It's dedicated to promoting independent filmmaking, started by Robert Redford. So getting *Hoop Dreams* into the competition section of Sundance was a major victory. And then, to go to Sundance and find that the film truly was the buzz of the entire festival, not just the documentary side. It was the one film that everyone said you must see while you're there, and all our shows were sold out. We've gotten an enormous amount of support from the press and it's been reported repeatedly in the press by reviewers and feature writers that they really think *Hoop Dreams* has a shot at Best Picture.

I What's accounting for this success?

SJ What accounts for it? Well, I think a number of things account for what has happened. I mean, *Hoop Dreams* has become a phenomenon. It's no longer just a film. It has defied virtually every bit of conventional wisdom in its success. It is nearly three hours long, it is a documentary, it is about black inner city families, and it was shot on video, not on film, even.

I I didn't know that.

SJ It looks remarkably good for that fact, but that is a

liability. If it had been shot on at least 16 mm, that would have made some distributors more interested at certain stages. So, that right there is four strikes against the film, yet all of this has happened and I think that some of the reasons why is that, number one, it's a very interesting story. The story that we document is extremely interesting; it's dramatic. It has a lot of plot twists and turns. Amy Taubin in the *Village Voice* said something like, "*Hoop Dreams* has more plot twists and turns than any screenwriter would dare. You'd be thrown out of the pitch meeting on your ear if you went in and suggested a story like this from fiction." So, I think that has accounted in some measure for its success, that it's so dramatic. Everyone who sees it who likes it tells us that it sucks them right in and they're on the edge of their seat.

Beyond that, it also is a story that resonates about something I think America is interested in, at least some part of America is interested in, and that is the American Dream itself, which is such a crucial part of our mythology and our everyday experience, both for good and for bad. I think it's also a film about race and it's a film about the lack of opportunities in certain neighborhoods. It's about America as a place of business, but also a place of opportunity. It's about all of these things, and it's all put in a dramatic context in story. The film doesn't beat you over the head with a polemical or political viewpoint and I think that is also part of its appeal. I think it's because the film doesn't pull punches, take cheap shots. It doesn't have an agenda in that kind of overt way that a lot of documentaries have, that turn off a lot of viewers. I think that the film is incredibly emotional. The most successful films in America, unlike Europe, are films that grab at your heart and *Hoop Dreams* seems to do that. People feel like they really get to know these characters in the film, these subjects of our film, and come to care about them.

When you get to that point with an audience member, the fact that the film is real, that it's not fiction, makes it that much more powerful because you don't have the comfort of at least pulling back on some intellectual level and saying, "Oh, it's not real. It's only a movie." In this case you can't, you don't have that comfort, and people have told us that there are times in the film where they forget on some level that it's real, because of the way it's told; for instance, when William goes to the free throw line to shoot those shots that he misses. They don't ever fully forget it, but they get caught up in the drama and then a moment like that happens and it hits them in the gut that this is real life and that Hollywood is not going to rescue them by having him make the free throws.

I   What were you first trying to achieve? Can you talk a little bit about how that changed, how what you wanted to do with the film changed? Your description of your first intention doesn't describe the film any longer, exactly.

SJ   The original intention was to try and get at some of what that game means culturally to players, black players from the inner city and at some of the complexity of how they feel about the game and the dream. That was the initial thrust of what the film was going to be about. It was in a sense almost going to be like an anthropological film by taking a playground and some guys that play there and trying to understand what this game meant to them. And we would deal with the language, the dress, some of the codes, and the rules of a pickup game itself, of a street game. I finally got a small fellowship grant for this film, and we took that $2,000 and a $500 personal contribution by friends of Frederick and instead of shooting film which was our original intention, we shot video because we didn't have any money. And that's where Peter Gilbert entered the picture. We initially pulled Peter in as a cameraman because of his extensive experience shooting documentary films, but also because he was a basketball junkie, to boot.

And so that very first week when we headed out and started to film, the conception of the film changed. When we met Arthur through Earl Smith (just as you see it in the film, that's how we discovered Arthur), and we followed Arthur out to St. Joe's for that recruiting visit, the whole notion of his being recruited was fascinating. We had no intention when we began that we would document that process. We knew of that process, but that wasn't going to be our focus. We were going to stay on the playground, but Arthur left the playground with Earl to go out to this school and we would have been fools not to document that. And when we got out there and Coach Pingatore said, if you work hard at the grades and you work hard at basketball, I can help you get to college. It hit us then that it would be great if we could follow this kid and then later William, when we found out about William from Coach Pingatore—to follow these two kids over time to find out, at the end of four years, if basketball was able to achieve that for them.

Also, it suddenly was much more interesting to us to want to take viewers inside the experience of the dream itself as it's lived, not to have kids report on what it feels like for them, not, as I said earlier, to take a snapshot of the dream, but to make a book about the dream: a long film about the dream where viewers are thrust into their lives day-to-day and see how it changes, how it grows, how it's diminished, whatever happens to the dream. But at that point, the focus was still very much on the dream. Even then, we were going to focus mostly on the dream itself and we expected to encounter some of the realities of inner city life because that's part of the dream; part of the whole attractiveness of the dream is to escape those realities. So, we weren't ignorant to those realities and we certainly expected them to play a role in the film, but we didn't really have an idea just how broad the story was going to carry us. In other words, we didn't, at that time, anticipate that the other family members' stories would become very important to the film and that the film would have a whole other life to document outside of basketball. And that was the thing that happened from a content standpoint. The project grew not only in size, but it grew in scope. Suddenly, more and more of this film seemed to be about the American Dream, not the basketball dream. The more we worked on the film, the more basketball became a metaphor for the plight of families in the inner city, that they face incredible odds, that it takes tremendous determination for them to succeed, and that they don't always succeed. And a lot of times the system is set up for them not to succeed. And so the basketball dream more and more came to be almost a metaphor for that plight than the actual subject of the film itself.

One of the things in the original conception, when Frederick, Peter, and I would talk about the film and what we saw the film looking like, we saw a film that was going to be much more of an aesthetic statement too, as a work. That it was going to have a lot of very interesting camera angles and it would just be a much more overtly aesthetic and crafted kind of piece. We didn't want it to just be a documentary. We wanted it to really be a very interesting film to watch. That changed for me, considerably, and I think you see the result in the film. It's not that kind of film. The more we got involved with filming these stories and involved in these people's lives, the more I felt strongly that we shouldn't try and attempt to make that kind of film, that we should try and make a film that was very direct in its style and approach. And, I think that was a wise decision, because we increasingly felt like that's where the power of this film lay, in telling it through the eyes and experiences of the families and as directly as we could. And I felt, if anything, that it would be presumptuous to try and turn it into some kind of aesthetic statement. It took a long time for that earlier vision of the film to be jettisoned, but finally it was.

I   There's a sense in which one looks at the title and gets the buzz about what the film is about and makes an assumption that the film is about the dreams of the boys.

SJ   Right.

I   But it becomes pretty clear pretty quickly that the film is also about the dreams of many people.

SJ   Right.

I   And that a championship dream for the coach is a different kind of a hoop dream than Curtis' dream of basketball for himself.

SJ   Right.

I   It's a different kind of a dream from Bo's dream about basketball for his son, and so on. One of the things that seemed to come through strongly in the film is the way in which *Hoop Dreams* played a role in so many different ways. Is this something that emerged for you as a group, as the film went on?

SJ   That's an excellent point. There are so many dreams at work in this film and these kids bear the burdens of their family's dreams. And, those dreams are always at some level selfish, but they're not always bad because we all have them. Even the coach. I understand that dream. He's been a successful coach all these years, he's had great teams, he's been very close. I wouldn't begrudge him having that dream. Curtis, too. At one point in the course of the filming, we were feeling pretty critical toward Curtis, as I think a lot of people watching the film did. There's a tendency to want to shake Curtis and say,

"Leave him alone. Just be supportive." At one point during the filming when William blew his knee out and the dream of possibly being the next Isaiah Thomas was cast into serious doubt, we found ourselves, at some level, feeling like Curtis did.

I   When you want to communicate a story, you always have some thoughts about the audience, you always have some assumptions about the audience in terms of their ability to make sense of what you are doing.

SJ   Right.

I   And here in this medium, you've got to have some ideas about the audience's ability to make sense of visual images as well as verbal narration. Can you talk a little about that? What thoughts did the three of you, or you personally, have about the audience you were trying to reach and what you can assume about that audience?

SJ   Audience is always a tough one, in film. I think that from the start, and I think it remained a goal, we saw this primarily as being a film for white America, for white, middle-class America. We saw this as a chance to speak to them about a lot of things that they don't normally listen to. We figured that by having basketball and the drama of basketball be part of the story, that would be a way to speak to that segment of America about much broader things. That basketball would be the hook. And it wasn't all that calculated either. I mean, we love basketball and that part of the story intrigued us too and so it intrinsically had a lot of attraction to us. But we also thought that it would serve as a very good hook to get an audience of sports enthusiasts, for example, that maybe would never watch a PBS documentary, but would watch a sports story. And that remained a guiding principle, really through the entire film. We were always careful in the editing to try and make sure that a white audience would be able to follow what people were saying, so we did shy away from certain scenes where there was a lot of banter that maybe would be very hard for a white audience to understand.

I think our hope was that even though we saw a white audience as the primary audience, a black audience would relate to this in a different way. That a black audience, particularly an inner city audience, would come to this film and they would see, they would identify with the film more. That it wouldn't be as educational for them as it would be for a white audience, it would be more one of identifying, of seeing something of their life and experience on the screen.

I   Confirmation and affirmation.

SJ   Yeah.

I   Let's push the audience question a little bit and then turn to the educational mission of the film, in a sense. What were your assumptions about what the audience could pick up on, what they could follow? You mentioned that you were concerned about audience being able to catch some of the dialogue if in fact it were a certain kind of a dialogue.

SJ   Right.

I   And so you stayed away from some of that. What other concerns did you have about the audience's ability to get what you were putting out there?

SJ This certainly comes up all the time, especially in the editing. You want to strike a balance between giving people enough to get it, but not beating them over the head with it or have them get the wrong thing. I mean, it's almost like there are a number of right things to get out of it, any one of which is fine. There are certain wrong things you don't want people to get the wrong impression about. For instance, when William comes back to practice after having suffered a slight knee injury before his knee really goes out, he's playing, he's running in the drills and stuff and the coach is making them run. That's an example where we were very careful so that the audience didn't get the sense that because the coach made him run, he reinjured his knee, which is what people would have assumed. Your default inference would be, if you see the coach making William run a bunch of sprints, then, of course, that's how he hurt his knee. And that would have been wrong.

So there are certain kinds of wrong things you clearly don't want to communicate, but there's more of a multitude of right things. I think it's been remarkable how many people have "gotten" the film, in that sense. Not only do they understand the story just on a plot level. There's a certain amount of clarity that you need to establish when you're telling a story. But they also seem to get the deeper implications of what the story is trying to address. I've seen it in virtually all the reviews, I've heard it from people at the end of screenings when they come up and talk about what it is that they felt like they got from the film. And that is a rare thing, I think, for filmmakers, because you don't often get that experience where you feel like what this film was about for you, it was about that for the audience as well.

I   I want to get specifically to that in a moment. Before we do, just a technical question in passing. One of the things that helped the audience get what you were after, particularly in terms of mood, I mean—because in the mood of the film, the look of the film, there's a sense in which you want to affect the audience's mood—what helped was the soundtrack.

SJ Sure.

I   Was that a late decision? How did you think about bringing in music to affect mood, to affect your ability to communicate what you wanted to communicate to the audience?

SJ Well, my feeling is that music is an incredibly powerful tool and because it is so powerful you have to be very careful with it if you're going to use it responsibly. So we always were planning to have music in the film. How much is always a question, and I think that we probably ended up with slightly more music than we had originally planned. But we wanted the music to be evocative), not to be the source of the emotion in the scene, but to just try and underscore something that's really there. Too often in Hollywood films, the emotional content of the film is coming almost exclusively from the music. As an audience member I bristle at that and it backfires, because I reject the film if I feel that the music is the source of the emotional content of the film. And, so we just tried to walk that line and it's an aesthetic choice.

I haven't heard any complaints about the music. Most people don't even comment on the music and in many respects, I think that that's good. The music is there, it seems to serve its purpose, but it's not there in such a way that it causes people to go, hey, I really loved the music. If we were getting a lot of comments about the music, I would actually be more concerned because it would mean that it was standing out from the story too much. The same is true with narration. A lot of people, in their recollection of it, don't think of this film as having any narration in it. In fact, it has a lot of narration. It's hardly ever even mentioned that it was narrated. I think that's because its purpose was more functional than the music, the music tended to be more evocative, but they both serve a similar role.

I   What were you counting on your audience to be able to understand or do that you didn't have to then worry about?

SJ One of the things that we did not want to do was to lay out in excruciating detail the poverty of the inner city. We felt like, number one, there's a lot of that. In fact, that's all you hear about. And that stuff is very powerful imagery and we were very judicious about how much of that we wanted to use. If we gave the audience a lot of that it could overpower everything else. And we felt like part of our mission with this film was for it to be a corrective to those stereotypical perceptions about life in the inner city. We did not want to whitewash the inner city, but we felt like it could be put in in judicious amounts to just, in essence, push the buttons that are already there for the viewer about those things.

I   You've made it clear that the film succeeded, and it's clear to anybody who sits in an audience and watches the film, that the film succeeds at an evocative level. It does pull the audience in deep ways. There's another level at which you wanted the film to succeed and that's what might be called the "message level," or the pedagogical level, when you say you are gratified when you see that people got what you wanted them to get. What else did you want people to get out of the film, you might say, in terms of what do you want them to learn?

SJ Well, I think there were a number of things we wanted them to learn. I think some we succeeded at more than others, but I think we succeeded on some level with most of them. One is that I think we wanted people to realize that kids like Arthur and William are not stupid for having this dream. They often hear that in different ways through the media and through teachers, that you'd have to be a fool, you'd have to be "not all there" to believe that you can use sports to get to the NBA. And I think one of the things we wanted to show was that the dream is about a lot more than just getting to the NBA. It's about having a sense of identity in a community where there's so few things for kids to have a positive identity about. It's about having a sense of pride, getting your name in the paper, not because you shot somebody or died, but because you scored the winning basket. It's about living up to the dreams of others, family and otherwise, and being a receptacle for those dreams. It's about getting the advantages of being treated differently in communities where there are so few resources.

Basketball got William to a private Catholic school for an education that he would never have gotten without basketball. He could have gone to St. Joe's if his family had known about St. Joe's and took him out there and sought financial aid, but the reality is it never would have happened. Basketball got him that education, which eventually got him to Marquette. And even though Arthur left St. Joe's, in a public school like Marshall, where the guidance counselor is in charge of 350 students, he stood out among the 350. And not just because he was in a movie, but because he was the starting guard on the basketball team, and so he got more attention. Basketball got William a summer job. Basketball took him out into a larger, white world. Basketball got William's brother off unemployment and got him a job because of his connection to Encyclopedia Britannica and the President. So there's a million ways in which these kids recognize early on that basketball can serve them, that we as a society don't give credence to because we think that all they're focused on is making it to the NBA and that they must be kind of stupid for believing that it can actually do that for them.

I   And yet these two were still singled out?

SJ   And they both got to college, too. So that was one of the messages, I think, that the film tried to convey. Some people, because they have such a knee jerk reaction to the dream as wrong, in fact, miss that. A lot of people say, "Isn't it tragic that these kids want this dream so badly." I say, "No, it isn't." Yes, there is a tragic aspect to it and you see it in Curtis. Curtis was a guy whose greatest moments of triumph in his life were due to basketball and his worst moments of despair were due to basketball. He was like a yoyo to basketball in his life, and that's where you see the tragic dimensions of this. You see it in our kids' stories, too, but I'm saying that it's not all tragedy. If you asked Arthur and William today are they glad they went through that system and did it the way they did it, they would say yes. They would say that yes, they paid some prices and there were some ups and some downs, and they took their lumps, but hey, look at where I'm at. So that was one of the messages.

I think the other sort of big message of the film is, in fact, to give people a much more three-dimensional portrait of life in the inner city and on that one I think it has succeeded swimmingly because we've had more people come up to us and say that they never realized how much they had in common with these kinds of families until they saw this film.

I   With these mothers who wanted the most for their children?

SJ   Exactly, just like what your mom wanted for you and my mom wanted for me and what I want for my kids.

I   What kind of look, visual look were you trying to achieve in the film, and to what degree do you think you achieved it?

SJ   Well, I think that the look we tried to achieve was really one of just a very direct and honest straightforward approach, what you might call an artless style. In other words, I feel about the film visually like I feel about it in terms of the music and all the other components. If people are spending too much time talking about the look of the film, either in person or in print, then that's probably not a good thing. It may be a flattering thing on some level, for me as the director and for Peter who shot the film, but we're more interested in what furthers the story and takes you closer to the subject than anything. There are a lot of great shots that never found their way into the film, but if we were coming at it from that point of view, we would have found a way to put those shots in the film. There are a lot of shots that are marginal that are in the film because they said something to us, and so that became the guiding principle in terms of the look of the film.

·62·

VOICES FROM THE WORLD OF ART AND MUSIC

•62A•

THOUGHTS ON VISUAL LITERACY

Philip Yenawine

METROPOLITAN MUSEUM OF ART

Visual literacy is the ability to find meaning in imagery. It involves a set of skills ranging from simple identification—naming what one sees—to complex interpretation at contextual, metaphoric and philosophical levels. Many aspects of cognition are called upon, such as personal association, questioning, speculating, analyzing, fact-finding, and categorizing. Objective understanding is the premise of much of this literacy, but subjective and affective aspects of knowing are equally important. Visual literacy usually begins to develop as a viewer finds his / her own relative understanding of what he /she confronts, usually based on concrete and circumstantial evidence. It eventually involves considering the intentions of the maker, applying systems for thinking and rethinking one's opinions, and acquiring a body of information to support conclusions and judgments. The expert will also express these understandings in a specialized vocabulary.

Different skills are called upon to construct meaning from the huge variety of images in contemporary culture: a straightforward news photo requires fewer, simpler operations than a psychologically manipulative ad; an illustration engages the viewer differently from abstract painting; a kitchen chair looks different from a 19th-century farm implement, as does a street sign from a road map; a snapshot from television, a building model from a diagram or plan, and so on. Some images are to be understood at face value. Others have greater built-in complexity, including the possibility of symbolic, implied, and mysterious meanings. Presumably, the visually literate person can comprehend at various levels whatever he or she chooses.

There are, however, degrees of visual literacy. For example, a young person can construct meaning from both simple (e.g., comics) and complex (e.g., art objects) visual materials. An older person, having greater experience and breadth of thinking skills in general, may glean more possibilities from the same images—for example, symbols or implications. An art historian will have acquired a factual base and competence at schemes of visual analysis and can additionally place a work in time and categories by technique, style, and iconography.

The literalness and constant presence of some types of imagery builds a certain perceptual and mental development in most people, but it is incorrect to assume that we learn to negotiate meaning in imagery simply by exposure. Increased capacities require both time and broad exposure as well as educational interventions of various sorts. For example, by studying the way in which people respond to art, we see that beginning viewers apply what they have learned from constant exposure to television, newspapers, magazines and books to art, but this preparation only allows them to deal easily with images that follow well-known conventions or are narrative in a traditional sense, not unpredictable ones nor those in which the story is hard to figure out.

There is virtually no instruction in visual literacy either in schools or out, nor even recognition that learning to look is, like reading, a process of stages. There is no accepted system by which to teach it either—that is, strategies sequenced to address the needs and abilities of an individual at a given moment, strategies that eventually allow one to come to terms with complex images.

It is useful to refer to reading to help illuminate what is missing in visual arts instruction that would help build visual literacy. For example, we still need to understand the long period comparable to "reading readiness" that predates skillful construction of meaning from images. We need to find the turning point which might be called "functional literacy." We need to assess the equivalent of "reading for comprehension" and to be able to describe other observable, measurable stages or phenomena, at least for professionals in the field. Reading levels are understood as gradual and slowly evolving, allowing for large and small developmental changes in skills, understanding, and involvement. Visual literacy should be seen as a similarly slow-developing set of skills and understandings that progress unevenly, each step building on earlier ones, each dependent on certain kinds of exposure and instruction.

The concern for the development of visual literacy comes from two main sources—museum educators who daily face audiences admittedly limited in their ability to find meaning in works of art, and others who witness with alarm the uncritical nature of the public-at-large regarding media. As the head of programs for high school students at The Metropolitan Museum of Art in New York, my own use of the term began around 1970 as a result of facing the realities of young people looking at art. Usually relying on art history, various analytical strategies, and many sorts of hands-on activities, my colleagues across the country and I have experimented over the last 3 decades with devices and content intended to advance viewers' aesthetic understandings to the point where complex visual structures are meaningful and pleasurable, but with little evidence of success.

There is, however, reason to expect progress at this point because of the research and theories of Abigail Housen, the most reliable source of data concerning aesthetic development (for more on Housen's research and theories, see Housen, 1987, 1992). For almost 20 years, Housen has conducted and reviewed thousands of open-ended interviews regarding works of art, studying these responses from both statistical and clinical bases. She has field-tested measurement tools and refined a system of drawing conclusions, as well as seen what and how interventions affect change. From this she has developed a very robust theory, applying it to the spectrum of experience with regard to art. Her conclusions are empirical, and given that her theory makes no assumptions except its commitment to the overall notion of cognitive development as a process involving time and exposure, it reliably supports the creation and measurement of actual teaching strategies.

One of the things that she tells us is that individuals at each of five stages of aesthetic development can have a strong connection to art just as people have strong connections to literature regardless of how well they read personally. During Housen's Stage I and much of Stage II, people might be called "pre-literate."

At the earliest stage, viewers' strength can be characterized as storytelling—that is, relating what they see to what they know by strings of personal anecdotal responses. They see things through their own life experiences—and not through a framework of aesthetic associations as experts do. Teaching effectively to this stage involves presenting the viewer with works that encourage a narrative reading, and relate to familiar contexts and activities. Ask them to look and think about what they see, then to look again, and to share and compare their perceptions and responses with others. The viewers can quickly learn to observe more and ground their stories in evidence within the picture rather than simply in their memories or imaginations. This capacity itself represents growth,

essential for moving to later stages.

At Stage II, people begin to distrust their own judgment; if they see something they think is "weird," they do not believe that the answers to "why" are within them. If the work in question is in a museum, it dawns on them that others recognize some value that they do not perceive; they often want an explanation of that value, but, even more, they want to be able to make more informed, less subjective judgments on their own. This is an immensely "educable" stage. They have developed a curiosity and drive that will help make information stick in their memories. At this point, they can add strategies, comparing and contrasting, for example, or breaking down what they see to determine how colors or materials contribute to meaning. They can be taught to ferret out the decisions of an artist—choices artists make in selecting subjects, for example, or ways of creating space.

By the end of the long course of Stage II, people have developed basic skills, learned essential concepts, and have a small information base. They can comprehend much of what they encounter in art—albeit at a simple level, still mostly on their own terms—but they are equipped to pursue further study if they so choose. They can select what art interests them and decide to develop their interest beyond merely "functioning"; in reading terms again, this might be called "functional literacy."

Housen's Stages III, IV, and V (and the transition stages that she has also described) are ones in which visual literacy is in place. In Stage III, the goals are to acquire and retain information about art and to classify it according to the systems of art historical scholarship. Appropriate instruction exists to address the needs and interests of Stage III viewers: the teaching of art history and criticism as well as varied programs teaching studio practices. The final stages—attained by having made art one's major focus in life, usually one's profession—require no intervention from "educators." Further learning is ongoing and self-guided.

In order to advance in aesthetic understandings and the set of skills which broaden them—visual literacy—viewers need long term, graduated support, like that provided to readers. Instruction for the early stages particularly needs attention. But, given experimentation based on Housen's work, there is evidence that learning to interpret and discuss works of art promotes thinking critically and creatively as well. It is also likely that developing this literacy can enhance the development of other meaning-making systems. We can hope that there is, at the very least, more research in this area in the near future.

References

Housen, A. (1987). Three methods for understanding Museum audiences. *Museum Studies Journal Spring-Summer, 2*(4), 41–49.

Housen, A. (1992). Validating a measure of aesthetic development for museums and schools. *ILVS Review, A Journal of Visitor Behavior, 2*(2), 213–237.

"SONGS CAPTURE SOMETHING THAT'S GONE AND MAKE IT INTO SOMETHING TANGIBLE": AN INTERVIEW WITH SONGWRITER CAROLINE PEYTON

Josephine Peyton Young
UNIVERSITY OF GEORGIA

We use words to represent our innermost thoughts, emotions, beliefs, and what we know about the world. They represent our private thoughts and what we choose to make public. Our choice of words, how we put them together, and the intonations we use to express them create images allowing others to interpret our messages and come to know us. We learn and derive pleasure from reading, listening to, and using words. As a literacy educator, I believe in the power and beauty of words. I talked with my cousin Caroline Peyton, who is a songwriter, singer, and guitarist about how she views words and the images she creates with words and melodies when she writes songs.

Throughout our conversations Caroline talked about how she chose song topics and selected words to create the images that would best represent her message. Our discussion of "Happy Home" (Figure 62B–1) illustrates how these are realized. "Happy Home" is a song Caroline wrote for our grandmother, whom we fondly called Gammama.

Josephine   Caroline, you created the images that characterized Gammama's house for me so well and also expressed your own memories in the song "Happy Home." You said, "it's like capturing your childhood or capturing something that's gone and making it into something tangible." How do you do that?

Caroline   "Happy Home" is based on childhood memories, and it's something that I personally experienced. It doesn't work for me to think about how the song's going to affect or draw people. I just

have to do what comes naturally and then maybe someone will find something in it for them, instead of trying to appeal to what you think somebody wants.

Josephine   In "Happy Home" you mention whistle stop, lilacs and Whitehouse coffee. What made you pick those things to characterize Gammama's house?

Caroline   I used "whistle stop" because Crozet is a very small town in the country and a train went through every night. That train was real haunting to me as a child. I'd be going to sleep and I'd hear the train go by. And you know, instead of putting all those words in, you get all that into two words and you say—it's a whistle stop indicating that it's just a small town and that it has a train going through it. The lilac tree is a sort of symbolic of Gammama. Because she loved the smell of lilacs, and she had lilac wallpaper in the bathroom. So that was kind of poetry, kind of an encapsulating thing. But the memories, I got a pad and just jotted down a lot of things that I remembered about childhood visits to Crozet and whatever I could find a rhyme for ended up in the song.

Josephine   Why did you write "Happy Home"?

Caroline   It was for some occasion, I don't remember. Well, actually the thing that sort of inspired that song was a tiny little picture that I keep in

Happy Home

Words and Music by
CAROLINE PEYTON

2. Oh I was more than six months old when
   My Daddy came home from the Marines
   He'd fought the war out in Korea
   And his baby daughter he had never seen.

   So he took me out to get acquainted
   Under the lilacs blooming in the sun
   Mama said a prayer out on the front porch
   "Thank God at last our family is one."

   At Happy Home, Happy Home
   Open your arms my Happy Home
   Daddy's portrait's on the wall
   Grouse and hominy for all
   The living's easy I recall
   At Happy Home.

3. So the years rolled by, two sisters came along
   We grew up too fast and went our separate ways
   Carrying dreams of Old Virginia
   And of heading back to the good old days.

   At Happy Home, Happy Home
   Open your arms my happy home
   Place a flower on the cross
   Have a picnic on the moss
   Love was n'ere an albatross
   At HAPPY HOME!

Chords in parenthesis should be used on the first half of the second verse before repeating first the 16 bars of music.

© Peytunes (BMI)

FIGURE 62B–1

my wallet. It is a tiny little black and white picture. But it's a picture of Daddy out in Gammama's front yard. He is holding me up under the lilac trees which are in bloom. Mama just told me recently that it was probably on my christening day. It is in black and white and you can barely see anything, but it's just this, fuzzy, black, gray and white image that somehow evoked the whole period for me, my whole childhood. And the whole song is kind of built up around that, around him taking me out in the yard and holding me up under the lilacs.

But I find, as hard as writing is, I think it's much harder if you don't pick something that comes out of your own wellspring of experience. And I think when you are writing songs, they come out better if you talk about or write about something that you know about, that's out of your own personal experience rather than an observation or something out of a newspaper. Songs need to come out of you. That's when the best stuff happens. The question is, does that do anything for anybody else outside of your little circle? So, somehow you have to make your own experiences universal.

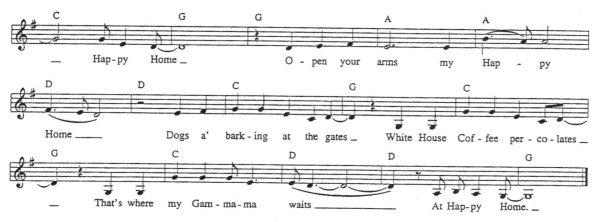

FIGURE 62B–2

Josephine   All the music for your songs is so different. How did you decide what the song, "Happy Home" would sound like?

Caroline   The music for "Happy Home" came out of the poetry, it sort of just flowed out of me. I wouldn't put the words to the song about the hooker to the music for "Happy Home." Different melodies and different chord changes definitely evoke different feelings and emotions in people.

Joephine   How does writing songs make you feel?

Caroline   Expressing yourself through music is extremely gratifying. I've recorded a lot of other people's songs. But when you record one of your own songs, when we start with something really rough, my chords, my melody and my words, and then it comes out really sounding good—it is just the most gratifying thing in the whole world.

"Happy Home" represents Caroline's innermost thoughts, emotions, and memories. Yet "Happy Home" also evokes vivid personal images of feelings, smells, and the happy times that I had with Gammama. For me, Caroline's choice of words and melody was able to " capture something that's gone and make it into something tangible." I am grateful that by listening to "Happy Home" I am able to return to a time I remember fondly and do not wish to forget. Caroline's experiences in writing and performing her songs and the emotions I feel each time I listen to "Happy Home" exemplify the power and beauty of words. The conversations between Caroline and me have renewed my desire to invite students to express their thoughts, feelings, and experiences. By extending this invitation to students, I hope they will discover the power, beauty, and personal satisfaction of reading, listening to and using words.

·63·

VOICES FROM THE WORLD OF PUBLISHING AND TECHNOLOGY

·63A·

JUDGING BY THE COVER: HOW A MAGAZINE PROMOTES COMMUNICATIVE LITERACY

Tamara Hanneman Rubin

EDITORIAL DIRECTOR, SCHOLASTIC MAGAZINE

Don't judge a book by its cover, the old saying goes, but a magazine…

As the editor of *Storyworks,* Scholastic Inc.'s literature magazine for children, I see the cover of our magazine as an invitation to the world of literature. Our cover is the overt but refined communicator of our mission. Open the magazine and appearance also plays a big role. We are enticing children to read, and we have to show them—communicate to them in any and all ways that we can—that reading is exciting, fun, and interesting.

Storyworks has taken on a lofty mission—to turn kids on to the world of literature, to make them critical consumers of what they read and see, to encourage them to be authors and artists of their own creative works, and to inspire in them a lifelong love of literature. The fact is, our mission fails before we begin if our magazine does not look good enough to make a child want to pick it up and read.

Since *Storyworks* is a magazine all about literacy, both visual and verbal, creating a cover and a "look" for the magazine is an experience in what we might call *meta*literacy. When we create a cover or work on the inside of the magazine, we read, think, talk, write, draw, and paint about reading, thinking, talking, writing, drawing, and painting! And we hope we are making it fun and interesting.

We launched *Storyworks* in 1993. The product and the process that creates it are still evolving. However, I am happy to share both how we think about our covers, our content, and the visual presentation of both.

THE MAGAZINE

Each issue of *Storyworks* gives kids a variety of literary genres: fiction, nonfiction, poetry, and plays. The stories and features are written and illustrated by top children's authors and artists working in a variety of genres and styles. We want children to develop knowledge of a variety of literary and artistic styles, an appreciation for what each style can do, and a personal preference for particular styles.

Author interviews and profiles give our readers a behind-the-scenes view of the creative process. But true insight comes from experience. Therefore, the magazine also gives kids easy-to-follow hands-on literary projects that really get them involved in creative writing, illustration, drama, or any other communicative art.

Each issue of the magazine also features news and gossip about books—what books would become movies, what celebrities read, the story behind the publication of a certain book, and other news to make kids feel like literary insiders. Students get a chance to have their opinions heard in our "Reviews by You" column.

The *Storyworks* teacher's edition is full of ideas for using literature to inspire a love of reading, writing, drawing, discussing—communicating—in classrooms. We try to keep teachers in tune with the best literature-based teaching ideas in a timely way, so that they do not have to wait to hear about them in textbooks.

What is in a Name—and a Type Style

When we were launching the magazine and the magazine's identity began to take shape, we asked ourselves: How can we broadcast this identity on our cover? What should the magazine be called? What should it look like, both inside and out?

We created the title *Storyworks* for our magazine because it communicated both the idea of literature, "Story," and the idea of interaction and creation, "works." Some students told us that they read our title and think of a factory where people make stories. We liked that. We knew we had been successful in getting kids to think of the creative process. This is a magazine about creating literature and art and the literature and art that kids create is important.

We designed the magazine's logo to emphasize our interactive identity. "Story" is presented in bold block letters of a common printer's typeface, but "works" is handwritten in stylized letters that suggest action and personal creativity.

We also decided to create covers that were about the overall message and mission of *Storyworks*, as opposed to being connected to one topic or article covered in the magazine. We wanted our covers to be able to express the wide, wonderful, varied, and exciting experiences of reading, writing, and creating.

Over the course of a year, we present a variety of artistic styles on our cover. We try to entice the best from the children's book illustration community to work on our covers. We hope our young readers will come to know and recognize these artists and their work.

When we commission an artist to create our cover, we start by explaining the mission of the magazine. Sometimes we have a specific idea of what we want on the cover, but more often we like to get the artist involved in brainstorming and conceptualizing cover ideas. We tell our artists that we want them to communicate the joy and excitement that reading can bring. We encourage them to show how reading can take you places, how it can open worlds of wonder and surprise, how it is something you can share with others and get excited about—not something that is a solitary, static experience. We might ask an artist to give us a painting that represents or expresses the creative process. We might look for a visual metaphor—a factory, a workshop—that could represent the creative process.

The artists come back to us with sketches and we begin to push ideas around. Together, we come up with a concept that works. Then the artist "goes to final" and presents us with a finished painting. Wow! That is one of the most exciting days on the job!

Cover Art: Start-to-Finish

Our November–December 1994 cover provides a good example of how we conceive of and create our covers. The artist, Kimberly Bulcken Root, also illustrated *Billy Beg and His Bull, Boots and His Brothers, Hugh Can Do,* and *If I'd Known Then What I Know Now.* We love Kimberly's color pallet of rich greens, blues, and reds and her softer yellows and pinks. She uses water colors over black line ink drawings in a style that reminds us of Arthur Rackham, Kate Greenaway and other artists of the turn of the century. We thought this would make a good contrast with our previous cover, which was a highly realistic painting by Wendell Minor, whose credits include *Sierra, Mojave,* and *Heartland.*

We discussed with Kimberly the mission of the magazine and she came to us with a charming sketch of a Florentine village enchanted by books (Figure 63A–1). We loved its fairytale quality and all the different creatures who were involved with books in some way, but we had one small problem. The six main figures in the sketch—four people, a pig carrying one of the people, and a dog—were all of ap-proximately equal size and were lost in their own private relationship with a book. How is the viewer supposed to "get into" this picture? Well, it is hard to get into it. It is rather still and everyone is looking away; no one is inviting you in. Which of these characters would the viewer relate to? Well, it seems hard to relate to any of them since they are all off doing their own thing, and unless you already love reading, you may not be intrigued. No single character seems more important than the others. If one character somehow caught the viewers and hooked them in, then we would have a great cover.

We discussed these concerns with Kimberly and she presented us with a second sketch that became the basis of the finished cover (Figure 63A–2). In the final painting, the girl riding the pig is brought to the foreground and she no longer is reading. As Kimberly puts it, "This girl has just come into this town. She's never been here before. Everybody is reading—even the lizard! The girl's next step would be to try to get a book to see what the attraction is all about. At this second, though, we're catching her awe. Also, I like showing the books as giving delight and surprise. A book is such a treasure that a dog might want to steal and bury it."

This was fantastic. Now, we felt, our readers would relate to the girl. They would wonder: "What is she looking at? What's all the excitement? Why, it's a lizard reading! In fact everyone reads in this town, even the statues!" In other words: Reading is all the rage; it is exciting; it is a treasure. *That* is the message we want to give to our young viewers. A bold cover line, "Discover the Fun" invites our audience to turn the page and begin an adventure in literature.

As an aside, Kimberly told us she wanted to show a girl riding a pig because it is something she had always wondered about as a child. On a school field trip, she had visited a farm. There, she saw big black-and-white pigs that had just been scrubbed clean. "Their big round backs, low to the ground, were strong but less frightening than a horse's. I wondered how many kids could sit on one of those backs. Riding a pig was an idea I carried around for years," she told us. Often, the best inspiration comes remembering what the world looked like when you were a child.

Inside the Edition

We want the inside of our magazine to be as exciting and inviting as the cover. We want the literature and artwork in the magazine to be engaging—to grab young readers' interest and to inspire them. However, we want children to be able to get into the experience comfortably and easily. In other words, the ideas expressed in our stories and artwork should be challenging, but it should be easy to page through the magazine and find something you really want to read or look at.

For example, our September 1994 issue features a short story by Matt Christopher (Figure 63A–3), perhaps the most popular sports fiction writer for children—ever! We knew we could hook some of the most reluctant readers with this story about an exciting baseball game and a young pitcher's struggle with his conscience.

We chose an illustrator for the story who could give us slightly exaggerated expressions to reflect the strain of a close

(Continued on p. 861)

FIGURE 63A–1. Artist Kimberly Bulcken Root's preliminary sketch for a *Storyworks* magazine cover.

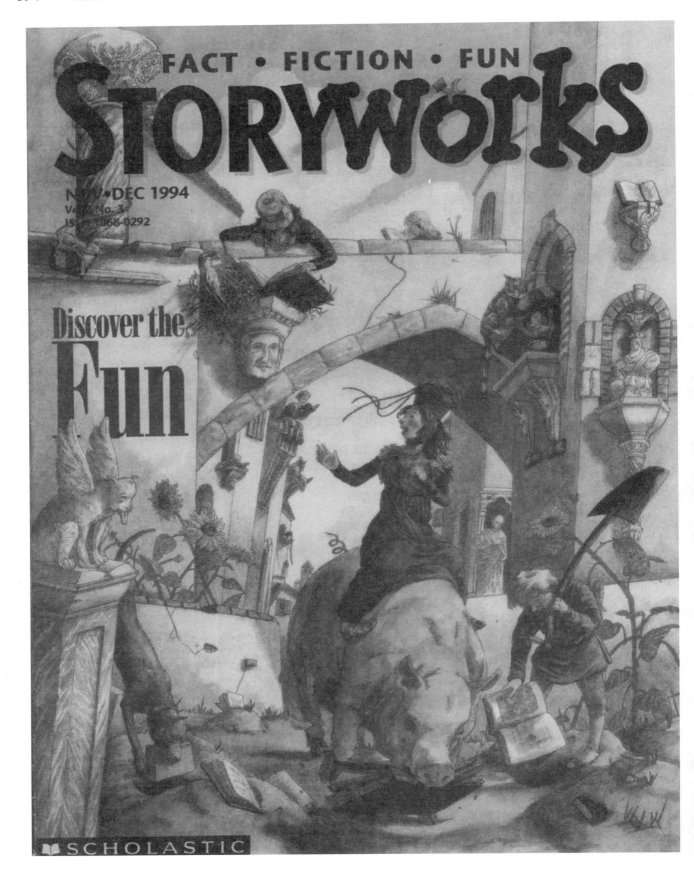

Fiction

Brush 'im Back

BY MATT CHRISTOPHER

Illustrated for Storyworks
by Craig Nelson

THE CHERRY PARK REDBIRDS, JAY'S TEAM, batted first and got lucky. Even Jay, who was twelve and a lefty, had to admit it. Lennie Gross, the Redbirds' shortstop—looking tough in his white uniform with black and red trim—led off and drew a walk. Then Dale Robin, who seldom hit one beyond the infield, poked a skyscraper over the left-field fence for a two-run homer. Redbirds 2, Knights 0.

The Marcellus Knights were one of the most dreaded opponents in the Junior Baseball League for twelve- and thirteen-year-olds. When the Knights were up, power-slugger Marc Wallace came to the plate. He looked more like eighteen than thirteen. The bases were bare so Jay decided he wouldn't throw any inside pitches to him yet. With two outs, Marc couldn't do much damage anyway.

FIGURE 63A–3A.

**Jay was a good Little League pitcher,
maybe even a great one.
But how far would he go to win?**

But he did get a hit. A smashing drive between left and center for a single.

Now to keep him there, Jay thought.

He struck out the next batter and the teams exchanged sides.

The next two-and-a-half innings went by with no runs scored by either team. The Cherry Park Redbirds still led, 2-0. Jay couldn't believe it. Getting ahead of the Knights right off the bat was a feat in itself.

Then, in the fourth, Jay walked the leadoff batter, Marc, and then was pounded for two hits. One was a double, scoring a run. An error on the third baseman gave the Knights another run. An overthrow at first base gave them another, and the inning ended with the Knights going into the lead, 3-2.

"Just like that, they lead us," Jay mumbled half to himself as he headed off the mound.

"Right," said Lennie, as he trotted up beside Jay. "But hang

in there. Just don't let Marc tag onto one."

"Not if I can help it," Jay promised.

Marc Wallace was the Knights' long-ball hitter, a threat every time he stepped up to the plate. Jay wondered if he should try his "brush-'im-back" pitch. Well, he'd see.

It wasn't until the top of the fifth that the Redbirds scored again. Jason Phelps came to bat and stroked a hit over the left-field fence for a home run, tying the score, 3-3. The Cherry Park Redbirds fans went crazy yelling, shouting, and whistling.

The next two batters, Marty Allan and Juke Gillian, flied out, bringing up Jay. So far all he had done at bat was a big fat nothing.

He swung at the first pitch and ➡

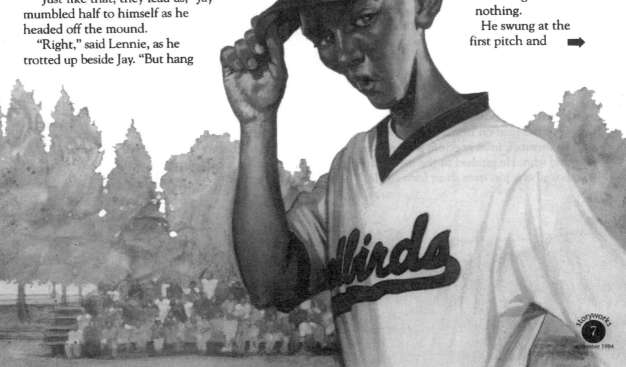

FIGURE 63A–3B.

lined it over third.

"Okay! Send 'im around!" yelled Coach Don Foley from the third-base coaching box.

Lennie, the leadoff batter, was up. He tapped the fat end of his bat against the plate a couple of times, then lifted the wood, snuggled his spikes into the dirt, and waited for Rick McCall's pitch.

Another long clout! But this time it didn't go over the fence. It hit the fence and bounced back. Jay raced around the bases and Lennie stopped on second for a double. Redbirds 4, Knights 3.

The next batter popped up for the third out, and Jay ran out to the mound with a mile-wide smile on his face.

Maybe, he thought, just maybe he wouldn't have to use that brush-'im-back strategy on Marc after all. It wouldn't be necessary, not if the Redbirds remained in the lead.

Then, going into the sixth and last inning, the Knights came up for their last chance to win, and the leadoff batter pulled a fast one. He bunted Jay's first pitch down the third-base line, catching Jay and the third baseman off guard, and made it to first base without trouble.

"Keep your eyes open, Jay!" shouted Coach Foley. "Gary! On the line!"

Gary Marsh, the third baseman, moved up alongside third base and crouched into position. Underneath his lowered hat brim his eyes looked like needle points.

Jay felt the heat on his face. By now he could remember, from previous batters, who followed who. He pitched to the next batter, who poked one just over short for a single. The next batter hit into a double play. Two out!

Jay wasn't out of the woods yet. Another walk, and an error by the shortstop, loaded the bases! And who was up but the mighty Marc Wallace! He filled up his brown uniform like meat filled up sausage skin.

The Knights fans went crazy. "Blast it, Marc!" one cried.

"Out of the lot, Marc!" cried another.

If Marc had never really gotten moral support from his fans before, he was sure getting it now.

"Get 'im outa there, Jay!" third baseman Gary Marsh yelled.

"Strike 'im out, Jay!" Dale Robin cried. "Show 'im you can do it! STRIKE HIM OUT!"

J AY'S HEART POUNDED. SWEAT rolled down his cheeks. All Marc had to do was get a hit, then a run—or maybe two runs—would score, tying the game or winning it.

Jay thought about the brush-'im-back pitch. He stood off the mound, thinking about it. Once, not too long ago, that pitch had been used against him. It not only had brushed him back. It had hit him. That hit had earned him a walk, but it had also forced him to leave the game with a bruised shoulder.

Afterward, all the little-league coaches had warned their players that trying to scare, or even hit, a batter was unsportsmanlike—and dangerous!

FIGURE 63A–3C.

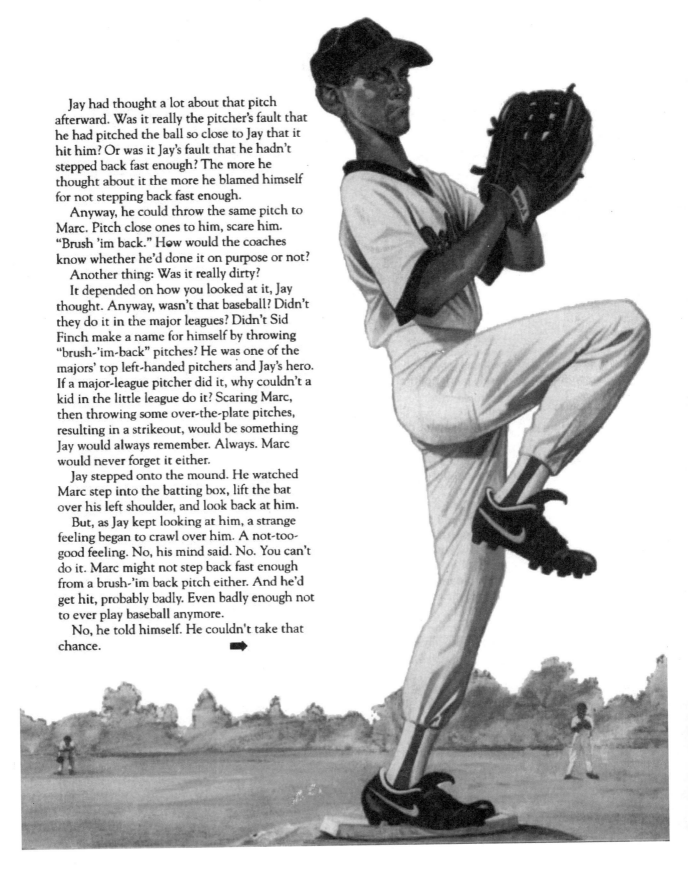

Jay had thought a lot about that pitch afterward. Was it really the pitcher's fault that he had pitched the ball so close to Jay that it hit him? Or was it Jay's fault that he hadn't stepped back fast enough? The more he thought about it the more he blamed himself for not stepping back fast enough.

Anyway, he could throw the same pitch to Marc. Pitch close ones to him, scare him. "Brush 'im back." How would the coaches know whether he'd done it on purpose or not?

Another thing: Was it really dirty?

It depended on how you looked at it, Jay thought. Anyway, wasn't that baseball? Didn't they do it in the major leagues? Didn't Sid Finch make a name for himself by throwing "brush-'im-back" pitches? He was one of the majors' top left-handed pitchers and Jay's hero. If a major-league pitcher did it, why couldn't a kid in the little league do it? Scaring Marc, then throwing some over-the-plate pitches, resulting in a strikeout, would be something Jay would always remember. Always. Marc would never forget it either.

Jay stepped onto the mound. He watched Marc step into the batting box, lift the bat over his left shoulder, and look back at him.

But, as Jay kept looking at him, a strange feeling began to crawl over him. A not-too-good feeling. No, his mind said. No. You can't do it. Marc might not step back fast enough from a brush-'im back pitch either. And he'd get hit, probably badly. Even badly enough not to ever play baseball anymore.

No, he told himself. He couldn't take that chance. ➡

He stretched, delivered, and sent the ball streaking toward the outside corner of the plate.

"Strike!" boomed the umpire.

Jay pegged in another one in almost the same spot.

"Strike two!" the umpire boomed again as enthusiastic shouts exploded from the Redbirds fans.

I can't believe this, Jay thought. But it's true. I guess he's just as nervous as I am!

Two strikes, no balls. Now what?

Jay stood on the rubber, pondering where to try to place the next pitch. All he knew was that he wasn't going to brush Marc back. He just had to find a spot he thought was vulnerable, and hope for the best.

He stretched, came down with the ball, and delivered. A slightly high, outside pitch that Marc probably feared would be a strike.

He swung. He missed! A strikeout!

The fans roared. It was over! The Cherry Park Redbirds won, 4-3! Jay had struck out the mighty Marc Wallace!

He walked off the mound amidst the whistles and cheers. The guys gave him high fives. The coach hugged him.

And there came his mother and father, both smiling, both holding out their arms.

"Pitched like a big-leaguer, son. Just like your hero, Sid Finch," Mr. Miller said. "I'm proud of you."

"No, Dad," corrected Jay. "Pitched just like me, Jay Miller."

What was the most exciting game you ever played in? It could be a baseball game or any other sport or game you enjoy. What happened in the game? Who were the best players? Write a story about the game. Draw pictures that show how the players felt at the most exciting moments.

FIGURE 63A–3E.

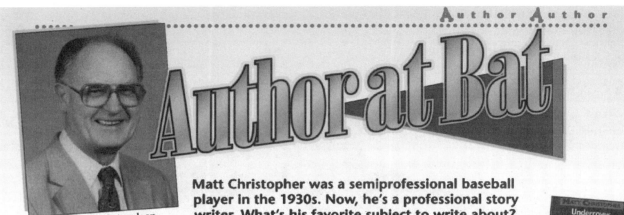

Author Author

Author at Bat

Matt Christopher

Matt Christopher was a semiprofessional baseball player in the 1930s. Now, he's a professional story writer. What's his favorite subject to write about? Sports! He's written more than 93 books. *Storyworks* asked Matt about both of his careers.

How do you start writing a story?

If I'm writing about a baseball game, I always make up a box score before I start. It shows what each character does in each inning. Then I put my box score beside my computer and I work right from that. I'm pretty sure I'd get fouled up otherwise.

For a book about a sport I have never played, I start by doing a lot of research. I talk to kids who play the sport.

Do you rewrite a lot?

Oh yes. I go quite rapidly on the first draft, which is the hardest. Then I set the story aside for two or three weeks. When I go back to it, I can see things that need to be improved.

Matt made up this box score for the Cherry Park Redbirds before he wrote the story "Brush 'im Back."

Why do you like sports?

For me, playing sports has always meant camaraderie—a special friendship with the guys on your team and sometimes with the guys on the other team.

Why do you like to write about sports?

I love writing about exciting plays and the suspenseful moments in close games. Every sport has its own very colorful and inventive slang. It's a real pleasure.

CHECK IT OUT!
Books by Matt Christopher

In *Red-Hot Hightops*, Kelly freezes when she plays basketball in front of a crowd. Then she finds red hightops in her locker. After that, she plays like a star. Are the hightops magic? 148 pages

Return of the Homerun Kid is one of Matt's favorites. It's about a boy who is stuck on the bench until a mysterious ex-baseball player named Cheeko teaches him a few things. Who is Cheeko and where did he come from? 168 pages

Undercover Tailback is about Parker Nolan, a known liar who has to fix his reputation or the whole football season is ruined. 160 pages

11

september 1994

FIGURE 63A–3F. A sports fiction story written by Matt Christopher and illustrated by Craig Nelson, commissioned for the September 1994 issue of *Storyworks*.
Courtesy Scholastic Inc.

game and the stress of the main character's difficult choice between right and wrong. We hope these expressions provoke understanding and empathy. At another level, the Norman Rockwell flavor of the drawings call up ideas of good citizenship and determination, and even a suggestion of American heroism. It was a good match for our main character, who struggles with a moral dilemma and comes out on the side of good.

The designer chose a bold type style for the headline and placed it on a graphic of a team pennant. The type style is repeated throughout the fiction package to give it a unified feel. We use it for the big capital letters or "drop caps" that break the story into easy-to-manage sections and again in the headline of the author interview that accompanies the story. The pennant graphic is used again with the author interview. The choice of color and type style unifies the story and the interview and broadcasts the message: These are sports stories!

However, some parts of this package do not "stand out" in the context of the magazine. They are consistent with the way every other story is treated in the magazine. For example, when you turn to the first page of the story, the "slug" or boldface header at the top clearly labels the piece "fiction." A "deck" or introduction tells kids in a nutshell what to expect from the story. The story itself is printed in a classic, easy to read type face called Goudy. These features are predictable. They give readers a framework or context in which they know they can easily navigate to find a great literature or art experience.

If you were to page through the issue, you would find a photo realistic painting illustrating Nikki Giovanni's poem, "two friends." A combination of children's artwork and photojournalism illustrate excerpts from *Zlata's Diary: A Child's Life in Sarajevo.* A contest based on The Magic School Bus book series borrows artwork and design concepts from those books. Characters talk in speech bubbles and facts and directions are reported in side stories that look like school reports. Finally, still photographs from a movie set illustrate the play, *Black Beauty,* adapted from the classic novel by Anna Sewell and the Warner Brothers film. Each story has its own distinctive typeface in the headlines and subheads, and its own illustration style. However, they all share the consistent elements mentioned above—each is clearly labeled; each has an introduction; the story itself is in the same classic, easy-to-read type.

Getting Readers to See

This explains what goes on in an editor's or designer's mind. But what happens in the minds of the children who read us? That is a much more important question.

At the very least, our readers gain exposure to a wide variety of artistic and literary styles. By seeing *Storyworks* every month, they are beginning to develop their own mental framework for how a magazine works and how pictures and words work together.

Ideally, our readers are talking among themselves about their impressions and opinions as they read the magazine. They are learning what they like and do not like; what they think works and what does not. We know some teachers are leading students down this very important path to literacy. They ask students to describe what they see in the magazine. They ask children to guess why a certain picture was put in the magazine or why a certain headline was made to look the way it does. They ask children to notice the differences between one story and another or one painter's style and another's. Most important, they ask students to judge for themselves whether what they read and see is informative, interesting, or important.

If *Storyworks* sparks these kinds of conversations, then it is going a long way toward achieving its mission. For it is by having these conversations that children begin to incorporate literature and art into their life.

·63B·

WORDS + PICTURES = MAGIC: A DESIGNER LOOKS AT PICTURE BOOKS

Joy Chu
GRAPHIC ARTIST AND BOOK DESIGNER

Recently, people have come up to me and congratulated me on how well I illustrated *Bitter Bananas* (Olaleye, 1994), illustrated by Ed Young. I want to set something straight right now. I am not an illustrator. I am not an artist. I am not a writer. What I am, as a designer, is a *facilitator*. I work directly with the illustrator. I am much like a cinematography film editor. I work with artists to help them pace their books. First, I read a story "inside and out." I get to know the background. I work with the artist in terms of getting the story to fit just right into those 32 pages—and have it flow just right, so that there are not awkward jumps from one scene to another.

The most successful picture books work without words. You do need those words, but they should work just as well without words. It is very much like watching TV: You can turn the sound off and make up a story. If a picture book has that quality, then visually it is a successfully executed picture book. The best kind of manuscript for a picture book has a lot of action, has a strong main character, perhaps dialogue, and a lot of development.

Publishers like to use illustrators *they* select; therefore when a manuscript is accepted, an illustrator is found and the project is assigned to a designer who works with the illustrator and the editor to see the book to completion.

The dummy is the most important stage in the development of a picture book. The dummy is the stage where the artist renders sketches. The text is broken up into sequential pages, with an allowance for the usual front matter, such as title page, copyright, acknowledgements, and dedications. It shows the artist exactly where and how much space the typography will take up. It also serves as the master plan for the overall pacing of the story.

Some books go through several dummies, based on the feedback among the artist, designer and editor. *Bitter Ba-nanas* went through several rough dummies because Ed Young wanted his art to be fully integrated with the text. In the final book, type weaves in and out of nighttime scenes. We made the type large and translucent, echoing the creepy sounds of the rain forest. The text contains repeated refrains, "Oh yes! Oh yes!" and "Oh no! Oh no!" reflecting the emotions of our young protagonist. Ed Young was so enchanted by the sing-song rhythms of the refrains that he wanted to encourage the reader to chant them through the typography. Thus, these phrases are large, and in bright colors to complement the ebullience of Ed's artwork. To capitalize on the visual rhythms created by this, the editor made extra sure that there was an even sprinkling of "Oh yeses!" and "Oh noes!" running throughout the book. The finished book is one of Ed Young's finest achievements, all because he was so inspired by the charm of the written text by Isaac Olaleye, a writer from Nigeria.

It is important to check the pacing of the book dummy. Designers make sure that the scenes move smoothly in and out, as if a camcorder were moving around. Designers also supply illustrators with a template (called a grid) so that they can see the parameters they have in case the text needs to be moved around to make more room for an illustration. Text and pictures should be well-integrated—in other words, the text is reckoned with as part of the overall composition of the illustration. Books should never look like subtitled foreign movies.

Length is usually set at 32 pages, standard for a picture book. Why not 34? The answer is that we are dealing with established trim sizes, and only certain machinery can handle a certain number of pages. Most picture books are 32 pages, and the endpapers are a separate piece of paper. It costs a little bit more to have art on the endpapers.

Special thanks to Leah White, who transcribed much of the above text.

Size is an important consideration. Libraries and book-stores do not have 12-inch shelves. That size is deadly. You want a book to appear face-out or spine-out. When it is too small, it will be placed bottom-edge-out, doomed to anonymity. The tallest we ever go on a picture book is 11 inches. You can fool around with the width a little, but not the height. The designer usually suggests a trim size for the book (the actual size dimensions of the book page) based on the amount of the text, the illustrator's style, whatever suits the subject matter of the book. Sometimes it is best to go with whatever feels right, as long as the costs work out.

When everyone works together the result is a picture book in which text and pictures work together in a seamless whole to produce a picture book that allows readers to make meaning—verbally *and* visually.

·63C·

THE CHANGING FACE OF LITERACY:
A PUBLISHER'S PERSPECTIVE

Roger R. Rogalin

SENIOR VICE PRESIDENT AND PUBLISHER, MACMILLAN / McGRAW-HILL

Publishers as United States citizens have a stake in a literate voter population. Publishing as an industry has a stake in a literate workforce. In addition, publishers have a further compelling reason to appreciate a literate population and thereby ensure an expanded market for their works. Many publishers play an active role in the literary development of the children both for direct commercial opportunity and to facilitate the development of a future population of literate adults. For those who have had a role in developing successful elementary school reading programs, the sheer pleasure of seeing children get excited about reading good books may be motivation enough.

The journey toward developing literate children has taken several directions in prior decades, and one might expect that several more directions will be taken in succeeding decades. Educational trends vary with research findings, the popular promotion of those findings, and the acceptability of those methods to classroom practitioners. The seminal event in the most recent change in the national understanding of English language literacy, from a publishing perspective, was the 1988–89 California Reading / Language Arts adoption.

California, with 11% of the student population of the United States, represents a large market for textbook publishers. Adding to the impact of its large population, California is one of 21 "adoption" states. Adoption states screen submitted instructional materials at the state level and provide funds to the local districts for the purchase of those programs. Local districts across the state often purchase state-adopted materials in a specific discipline in a focused period of time. This results in a large, focused window of opportunity for publishers developing and marketing materials in a specific discipline. In 1988 California accepted bids from publishers for their reading adoption. Programs approved by the state board of education could be purchased with state funds in the summer of 1989 for use in the schools for at least the next 6 years.

Obviously, the California framework for reading / language arts had the potential for profound impact on the form and content of newly published basal reading programs. State Superintendent of Public Instruction, Bill Honig, understood the purchasing power of the state and determined that he would affect reform through instructional materials. His publicly stated intent was to limit the state adopted list to programs that provided an integrated language approach and thereby "encourage" teachers to reform their classroom methodology.

Previously, the dominant approach to teaching reading favored a concentration on discrete decoding skills. Indeed, many reading programs applied these skills in separate worksheets that bore little direct relationship with the recommended literature selections. Selections were abridged and the language was modified to match vocabulary lists that researchers had compiled as developmentally appropriate to particular grade levels. This focus on early reading instruction could be described as "scientific" since it was based on statistically correlated research on the acquisition of deconstructed, discrete skills such as decoding the *schwa* sound.

Around this time, the oppositional philosophy was gaining in favor and, as is always the case in educational practice, threatened to throw the baby out with the bath water. Under Honig's direction, the state framework promulgated an integrated and whole language approach. "Authentic" literature selections, in all their natural richness, were to be included in original and unabridged form. Children would learn the richness of language and the pleasure of reading without being overly concerned about the deconstruction of discrete skills research. In addition, the Framework framers eschewed much of the traditional canon of literature in favor of the politics of inclusion. "Authentic" literature must reflect a diversity of cultures (i.e., written by natives of those cultures).

Phonics, although mentioned, was assigned a weighted value of zero in the state scoring rubric used to evaluate the submitted programs. Therefore phonics was literally without value in consideration of what California's children would use to learn to read. Spelling programs were specifically dismissed in favor of supporting creativity through "invented" spelling. The mechanics of spelling and grammar would be dealt with later in the curriculum. With the exception of bemoaning the loss of revenue from spelling and English grammar books, many publishers embraced the new order and submitted programs that to varying degrees met the basic precepts of the California Framework.

The whole language approach was not unappealing to teachers or parents. How could one argue with the power of great literature in the author's original form? Would not the literacy of our students be enhanced by appreciation of great works that have been tied to the students' own experience? This California adoption, unlike some before or after, was successful in changing the vision of teaching English language literacy held by California educators. The vision spread across the country redefining how literacy would be interpreted. Reading literacy would no longer mean the mere mechanical decoding of word and sound symbols; it would now mean appreciation of meaning and nuance.

The most obvious physical change to commercially available reading programs was the inclusion of "real literature" in the form of trade books. (Trade books are the books you buy in the local bookstore vs. the curriculum-oriented textbooks you find in schools.) It was not enough to include unabridged selections in the basal reading anthologies, the reading packages had to include honest-to-goodness, real-life paperback books.

Not surprisingly, the new approach soon met with resistance. Public schools are paid for by taxpayers. Tax-paying parents have obvious emotional interests in the particulars of what is taught to their children. Two major areas of concern caused parents to question the new approach to teaching literacy to California's school children: social content and the lack of so-called basic skills.

The first backlash came as parents reacted to some of the content in the now unabridged passages. The world was not always "politically correct" as we define that concept today. Mark Twain included racist words and content in his portrayal of 19th-century life along the Mississippi River. Judy Blume described young girls' curiosity about brassieres in novels for middle school readers. The myriad special interests had specific concerns about specific passages or artwork included in programs. These concerns were often in direct conflict with each other, placing publishers squarely in the middle of contentious arguments based on some people's strong personal values and opinions. Although textbook scrutiny and protest had existed for decades before this time, the advent of the requirement for authentic and diverse literature selections opened the door for increased and more highly visible protest.

An equally grave and growing concern of parents was the lack of direct instruction on basic skills like spelling and grammar. The California model eliminated spelling as a separate discipline and suggested that a focus on spelling and grammar rules inhibited creative writing. Children in the early grades were to be evaluated on content and creativity while the technical aspects of spelling, grammar, and syntax would be dealt with in later grades. When parents began to perceive an apparent disregard for spelling and grammar in the wonderfully creative papers that children brought home, the doubts about this new approach began to surface.

The backlash that followed was like a slow pressure cooker. Many parents who were dubious in the beginning but who were willing to accede to the "experts" lost patience when standardized test scores in the state dropped. There were many possible reasons for the drop in reading test scores, including demographics, the newness of the test, and so forth. However, the controversies over the social content in the new test and the existing skepticism about the new framework worked to obscure any mitigating circumstances for the poor results. The change in climate that resulted in the voter revolution of November 1994 fomented political response from the Governor and state legislators that supported the subsequent suspicion of progressive curricula in all disciplines.

Will the current political climate and backlash against progressive curricula result in a new, or even retrograde, view of what constitutes good literacy education? In all likelihood, given past educational patterns, the pendulum will swing back the other way. Are we headed for the "Dick and Jane" approach of the 1950s and 1960s? Not likely. The pendulum swings in educational practice tend to spiral rather than remain in a strictly repetitive path. After all, we do learn, if somewhat imperfectly, from our mistakes. The good news in these events is that parents took interest in their children's literacy. It is possible that this parental interest will lead to behavioral changes at home that would result in more reading and less television.

How will future technologies affect literacy? Broadly defined, "literacy" includes more than the notion of the ability to read and write. It connotes an ability to decode and communicate information in a form that can be decoded and communicated by other individuals in a respective community. Scientific literacy, for example, requires a specific set of decoding, analyzing, and communicating skills. Mathematics literacy demands yet another "language" and thought process. This broader context becomes important when one considers the possibilities for literate communication in the future. Decoding printed words may be only one aspect of the literacy required to "troll the internet" and access appropriate information from the NII (National Information Infrastructure) in coming generations.

Publishers of so-called traditional book materials are redefining their roles as content providers so as to prepare for the digital age. Textbook publishers have long-established expertise in pedagogical literacy and the importance of communicating information in a variety of formats. Determining what to read and when, interpreting diagrams and illustrations in context, and identifying main ideas are as much a part of literacy as decoding word symbols. Although the book is likely to remain a major source of education and entertainment for generations to come, technologies based on visual literacies will provide education and information that print media cannot deliver.

It is said that:

> The sum total of humankind's knowledge doubled from 1750–1900. It doubled again from 1900–1950. It doubled again from 1950–1960. Again from 1960–1965. It is estimated that the sum total of humankind's knowledge has doubled at least once every 5 years since then.... It has been further projected that by the year 2020, knowledge will double every 73 days! (Appleberry, 1992).

How does one remain literate in such an overwhelming tidal wave of information? It will remain for publishers, in one form or the other, to provide a vehicle for sorting the wheat from the chaff, for organizing information in easily retrievable formats and delivering it to people when and where it is needed, for providing education on the use of these systems, for providing peer review... in other words to continue to do what they do so well today.

Reference

Appleberry, J. B. (1992, August 28). *Changes in our future: How will we cope?* Speech presented at California State University, Long Beach, California.

·63D·

NEW DIRECTIONS IN LITERACY INSTRUCTION

Anthony Lucki

SENIOR VICE PRESIDENT AND PUBLISHER, HARCOURT BRACE AND COMPANY

The role of technology in literacy instruction in the United States is rapidly changing. These changes challenge educational publishers to be:

- leaders in developing and integrating appropriate, high-quality technology products with their printed instructional materials.
- responsive to the demand from teachers, administrators, and parents for quality technology that correlates to and genuinely enhances each curriculum area program.

As technology for home and school use grows, it is vital that school publishers meet this demand—not only meet their public's current needs but anticipate their future needs as well. Since audiocassette and videocassette players are found in most schools and homes, publishers continue to provide materials in those formats, often in conjunction with corresponding print materials. With CD-ROM possibly replacing videodisc and videocassette technology, current and future instructional needs will also be affected.

Teachers and parents seek out products that contain activities that are meaningful, exciting, interactive, and fun for children and that address their higher-order thinking skills. The products they demand must go beyond the capabilities of the print medium to expand and enhance instructional opportunities.

Technology has the added advantage of being able to meet many of the individual needs of learners, such as second-language learners, students-at-risk, students with special needs, or gifted and talented students. Products customized to accommodate students with languages other than English promote self-confidence and self-esteem.

Technology is motivating for children. Students are enthusiastic about learning because the activities are engaging. They are less likely to be distracted and more likely to stay on task.

The use of technology helps educators meet special needs. Use of alternate input devices such as the touch screen and mouse enhance children's motor skills. Sound effects provide second-language and at-risk learners with clues to meaning.

Adult set-up options allow for the customizing of products to meet the individual needs of children.

Technology also encourages cooperative learning. Technological products stimulate student–teacher and student–student interaction and provide support for comprehension and learning.

TECHNOLOGY IN THE LANGUAGE ARTS CLASSROOM

What does the presence of advanced technology in the classroom mean to literacy educators? It is interesting to note that both the proponents and opponents of technology in language arts instruction agree on one thing: technology will mean the end of literacy as it is currently defined. Technology in language arts instruction will bring about a whole new notion of literacy—one that gives terms such as "e-mail" or "menu" the same weight as "reader response" or "writing process."

Perhaps one reason that technology and literacy instruction complement one another as well as they do is that our notion of literacy has broadened in the past few years, even for print-based materials. Literacy theorists and researchers have led us—especially over the last decade—to the conclusion that print-based materials are not static. We now use terms such as "negotiate meaning" to describe the process that readers use and "recursive process" to describe writing. It has become widely recognized that the concept of interacting with media is the core to the definition of literacy. The broadening of educators' definitions of literacy is very much in line with the availability of technology.

Take, for example, reading instruction. The notion that print-based books may involve transactions between the writer and the reader—transitions naturally to the concept of "interactive" electronic books. We have only begun to investigate how technology can help reading instruction, and that investigation is yielding rich results.

With existing CD-ROM and laser disc technology, in a matter of seconds a teacher can call up still, video, or animated images of carnivorous plants to show a group of students before they read a difficult expository piece on the topic. Just think of the possibilities for building schema for reading! Minutes later, the same teacher can apply similar technology to help a small group of limited-English proficient students view 10 objects that all begin with the digraph *ch*. At the same time, individual students working on computers may be reading electronic books, having difficult passages read aloud to them or exploring and investigating unfamiliar objects in the art. While it is a natural expectation that technology will provide more access to remediation, it has also proved to be quite useful for increasing students' exposure to enrichment activities.

Writing instruction is also taking on new dimensions. Parallel with the movements toward inquiry-based learning, self-assessment, and cooperative groups, the nature of writing instruction has changed. The use of technology may be the single most significant factor in promoting these aspects of writing instruction and in redefining our perception of the classroom.

Students' research capabilities are infinitely multiplied through their newly found ability to access databases and primary sources outside the confines of the classroom. Immediate access through e-mail to experts in every imaginable field provides a rich resource for student writing. On-line services and e-mail present a whole new universe of publishing possibilities for students. Student "works in progress," still at the drafting stage, look remarkably like published pieces, yet both student and teacher are aware that the content is still malleable. Aside from the obvious advantages of word processing programs in the writing process, technology affords students the opportunity to vary the mode of presentation. Access to images and voice recording technologies has given even the youngest students the tools necessary to produce multimedia presentations. Our students' published pieces will never look the same.

It is interesting that while speaking and listening development were the focus of early technology in the schools (phonographs, cassette recorders, language masters), listening and speaking were not part of initial offerings of digital technology. The initial applications of digital technology to language arts instruction focused first on print media; however, the use of technology to enhance the speaking and listening strands of the curriculum is not far behind. Already we have seen speech become an integral part of electronic books. But that is just the beginning. Text-to-speech technology offers amazing possibilities for individualizing instruction in reading. Even some of today's technology allows students to hear what they write. The modeling of oral language, along with the ability to record students' speaking will provide unprecedented opportunities for promoting oral fluency.

Professional development is one area that has already been significantly affected by technology advances. In these days of shrinking staff development dollars, video technology has become a mainstay of staff development programs. Through video, presenters can model effective techniques in authentic classroom settings. Video has already revolutionized teacher preparation programs, allowing instructors and prospective teachers to review and analyze teaching behaviors. The advent of live teleconferences makes professional collaboration cost effective. On-line services and bulletin boards have made it possible for teachers around the world to share ideas and lesson plans with each other.

The widespread use of technology has also had some unpredicted effects on teaching. The availability and ease-of-use of desktop publishing software has made it reasonable for schools and teachers to produce attractive and effective means of communication with parents. Inexpensive programs give teachers all the tools they need to quickly produce professional-looking banners, posters, and bulletin boards.

The advanced technology that students are being exposed to in the classroom will prepare them for the truly authentic application of their learning—using the technology that will be in place when they enter the workforce. This application may well be the ultimate goal of literacy learned in school.

·63E·

THE CREATION OF A BASAL PROGRAM:

A COLLABORATIVE EFFORT

Susanne Singleton

FORMER VICE PRESIDENT, MACMILLAN / McGRAW-HILL SCHOOL DIVISION

THE PEOPLE

The creation of a basal *program* is a *process* involving hundreds of *people*, working together in a collaborative atmosphere on what is probably close to a three-year timeline. The process is creative in nature, and as is the case with any creative endeavor, it is time-intensive and fraught with rethinking, reflection, and reconsideration. The people involved in the process are program authors, consultants, editors, writers, teacher advisors, student advisors, designers and artists, technology developers, and the publisher's sales representatives and consultants.

Program authors, who are selected based on a variety of criteria—area of curricular expertise, gender, geographical location, and cultural background, for example—bring the research base to the program. They shape the philosophy, provide the rationale, articulate the scope and sequence, and create the program's pedagogical framework. Since balance of viewpoints is critical on an authorship team, it is not unusual for a comprehensive program, such as a reading / language arts program, to have an authorship team of 15–20 members .

Various educational consultants, whose area of expertise may range from multicultural literature to cooperative learning to problem solving to primary sources, contribute to the creation of a basal program by offering advice, resources, and review. Each of the consultants or group of consultants becomes responsible for developing guidelines for and reviewing a particular strand or feature. Editors, most of whom have teaching experience, create prototype units that follow author's suggestions, create guidelines for writers, and hire educational writers to write the program. They also review manuscript to be sure that student material is appropriate for interest and developmental level and that teacher materials are clear and manageable. Educational writers, many of whom are teachers currently in the classroom, write the program under the direction of editors and program authors.

Teacher advisors are crucial to the process and are involved early in program development. Initial, broad-based teacher input may be solicited through questionnaires, which are sent to teachers across the nation at the beginning of the process. Questionnaires seek to elicit information from teachers about such things, for example, as what they like in their current programs, what curricular areas are difficult for their students, what areas of instruction are most important to them, and what new trends and issues are emerging. Publishers also conduct one-on-one teacher visits—sometimes to interview teachers about their thoughts and preferences and sometimes to sit in on classes to observe classroom practices that will inform their decisions about what to publish. Classroom visits are invaluable to publishers for they afford an opportunity for publishers to see how materials are used with children and how children respond to materials.

Student advisors are helpful as reviewers of literature, creators of materials, such as original writing, artwork, and mathematical problems to be used in the programs, and as participants in field testing. Field testing occurs at critical stages during program development to make sure that the materials under development actually work effectively in the classroom.

Designers and artists play an important role in the development of basals, particularly now since the visual is such an integral part of instruction. Students benefit from visual support for the text, improve their visual literacy when exposed to a variety of images, and are motivated by colorful and intriguing illustrations and photographs. Consequently, the work of the designers and illustrators is subject to the same scrutiny and review as the text.

Technology developers work hand-in-hand with the developers of the print program to make sure that technology, such as laser discs, CD-ROMs, and videos are seamlessly integrated.

Finally, a publisher's sales representatives and consultants offer advice and suggestions for program development based on their expertise and involvement with teachers and supervisors across the country. Since they call daily on schools and speak with educators on a regular basis, sales representatives and consultants can offer ongoing input during program development.

THE PROCESS

The identification of the people to be involved in the creation of the program occurs early on in the process. Market research also occurs at this time, although it continues throughout the development process to assure that new issues and trends are addressed in the program. After the people are selected and initial information is gathered through market research, the process to involve the specific requirements of the curricular area under development begins. In reading / language arts, for example, the identification of themes and literature selections would occur at this point. Market research has indicated that teachers today seem to like to teach thematically, and although many choose to select their own themes, sometimes with the assistance of their students, they seem to appreciate the efforts of publishers to organize units thematically. Literature selection is a labor- and time-intensive task involving program authors, editors, teachers, students, and consultants. Literally thousands of books are read and reviewed as a multitude of sources is consulted. Some common sources of quality literature that publishers consult include—

The Horn Book	*School Library Journal*
Publisher's Weekly	*Kirkus Reviews*
The Reading Teacher	Children's Book Council
• Teacher's Choice List	• Best Social Studies Books
• Children's Choice List	• Best Science Books
Newbery and Caldecott Lists	ALA Notable Books
New York Times Reviews	Various State Book Lists
Coretta Scott King Award Books	Reading Rainbow Books

Balance is extremely important in a reading / language arts program; thus, publishers take care to make sure literature is balanced in terms of such things as ethnicity (characters and authors); genre; geographic location (settings); gender (authors and characters); language usage (characters); socioeconomic situation (characters); age (characters); social role (characters); abilities (characters); and family situation.

While the literature search is occurring, the program authors and editors are designing the instructional apparatus around prototypical units of instruction. Prototypes are usually created for a primary unit, an intermediate unit, and a middle-school unit. Units are developed according to the instructional design and philosophy set forth by the program authors and with features suggested by early market research and teacher input. For reading / language arts programs, for example, authors bring to bear the latest research on such topics as emergent literacy, background building, vocabulary and comprehension strategy instruction, reader response, visual literacy, and writing process. Teachers ask for the latest

research translated into manageable classroom practice. They ask for instructional designs that are clear, concise, and easy to follow and for options that allow them flexibility and decision-making power. The publisher's job is to create instructional plans that translate theory into practice effectively.

Once the initial prototypes have been created, it is time once again to involve all the people who are so important to the process. The prototypes are subjected to intensive review and field testing, and the contributions and responses of all the reviewers are evaluated and incorporated. Prototypes are revised and the review process continues until such time as the prototypes are approved. Then program development begins in earnest. On the program timeline, approximately 12–16 months have elapsed at this time.

During the next 9–12 months that it takes for the program to be written, reviewers continue to offer input, and program authors and consultants continue to offer advice. Adjustments are made. Permission might not be granted for a piece of literature, and a substitution must be found. A literature consultant finds a just-published piece of literature that is far superior to one previously chosen. Adjustments are made. A class of 4th-graders says a story is too hard and not very interesting. Adjustments are made. And so it goes.

While the core program is being written, the support materials for the program are finalized, and the creation and review process for them begins. Such components as audiocassettes, posters, transparency sets, practice books, big books, little books, trade book libraries, and sentence strips, to name just a few of the components currently part of basal reading / language arts programs, are developed.

During the 9–12 months that it takes to produce the program—get art designed, get type set, go through various proofing stages and additional review stages, the publisher's marketing department is making plans to package and launch the program .

THE PROGRAM

By the time the program is completed, the publisher has already made extensive plans to launch it. The launch usually occurs at the appropriate national professional convention—IRA, for a new reading / language arts program. The program launch is often surrounded by much celebratory activity as the program is shown for the first time to a larger public audience.

Shortly after the program is finished, the publisher must train the sales representatives and consultants who will sell it. Representatives and consultants must not only be familiar with the program, but they must also know the issues that have informed the decisions that have been made about the philosophy and structure of the program. The program authors are sometimes involved in this training, and they also begin to go out to talk to teachers about the program. Authors support the program by giving workshops, speaking at awareness sessions, and making professional speeches to school districts.

During the first year that the program is out, extensive efforts are made to market and sell the program and to define its place in the marketplace. These efforts involve sales representatives, program authors, editors, and consultants, who present the program to those districts interested in purchasing new materials. Once the program has been purchased by a district, in-servicing begins. It is during in-services that the publisher begins to collect information about how the program is working—what is effective about it and what is not so effective. This user feedback provides the basis for revision plans that the publisher must have since revisions must occur with great regularity to assure that content remains up-to-date and new trends and issues are addressed.

Thus do *people* engage in a *process* to create a *program*. When the process is working effectively, there is a feeling of collaboration that is quite extraordinary, as people with diverse talents come together to produce something they can all call their own.

·63F·

THE ROLE OF COMPUTER GRAPHICS IN LITERACY ATTAINMENT

Barbara Holland Baskin
STATE UNIVERSITY OF NEW YORK AT STONY BROOK

The state of graphic development has accelerated at cometary velocity during the last 30 years, and that speed has generated vast gaps between those who are and are not literate in such environments. In many instances, some youngsters are more sophisticated and comfortable in microworlds than adults, including many of their teachers. Being literate involves bilateral communication and understanding of material in graphic format. It therefore means being able to decode information and encode it, manipulating the material to understand or to shape subtle and / or multiple meanings after the original meanings have been absorbed. It means the acquisition and application of new vocabulary (cyan, pixel, hypercard); alternate meanings for words (primitives, icons); symbols in different contexts and formulations (@, $init); and perplexing new concepts (virtual reality, cyberspace). Some knowledge about semiotics will be required as youngsters translate symbols to operationalize the computer to paint, paste or clip. Even now at the elementary school level, knowledgeable students are able to access and scan a series of images in encyclopedia databases, evaluate their informational content and visual complementarity, select appropriate images, and print them to illustrate their research. Those students with well-equipped technology labs will have access to such resources as Internet and thus be able to connect with print and graphics databases around the world!

Heated arguments are presently dividing the community of professionals engaged in evaluating the impact of the media on learning (Clark, 1994; Kozma, 1994; Ullmer, 1994). This debate revolves around the issue of whether it is the intrinsic quality of the medium itself that impels the learning or whether the context, the curriculum, and use factors are the most important in utilizing technology for cognitive growth. As in the print media, certain picture books have been identified as having extraordinary qualities and may be profitably read independently of an academic context. Yet, excellent teachers can make the literacy experience more potent by dramatizing, pointed questioning and other well-known pedagogical practices. Computer graphics should be similarly assessed. "In the final instructional unit, the strategy and the media are so interdependent it is impossible to separate them" (Morrison, 1994, p. 42).

Nevertheless, serious concerns exist about the quality and applications of computer programs. Will "razzle-dazzle" aspects of these media degrade their educational goals? Will sophisticated visual formats be emphasized to the disadvantage of the instructional content? For example, will some of the new software, which allows the user to "enter" stories and amend them, retard or facilitate literacy, particularly in relation to fiction considered part of the "literary canon"? Will teachers associate graphics solely with games and ignore their classroom potential? How will educational leaders inform staff and train them about the extent of potential applications and instructional power of graphics-aided software?

Technologically "illiterate" staff may not be able to devise circumstances that in turn would promote student opportunities to do complicated research, make useful associations, think analogically, increase vocabulary, undertake innovative analyses, experiment with creative undertakings, readily perceive visual variables, solve problems and participate in other forms of advanced cognitive behaviors related to literacy. Further, how will the educational community bridge the already vast gulf between technologically advantaged schools that have easy access to computers and those that do not? The long-term consequences are serious for children who are already educationally disadvantaged.

Computer graphics, when used judiciously, directly contribute to literacy: A high school science class was recently able to access the same visual database as professional astronomers and could, in real time, use the collision between a comet and Jupiter as an unparalleled science lesson. Graphics can also function instrumentally: These pictorial materials clarify, simplify, and model concepts. They are able to motivate, dramatize, and empower the user. They facilitate tool use, exploration, experimentation, and problem solving. The future possibilities of graphics as learning tools are an unknowable and tantalizing enigma as technological breakthroughs occur at an unbelievably rapid rate, inevitably ahead of awareness of classroom applications.

In conventional schools, faculty can profitably use graphics in virtually every area of the K through 12 curriculum. Health teachers can use graphics to demonstrate bodily processes changing over time, such as gestation or digestion. Math specialists teaching geometry can enrich comprehension as forms under study can be readily rotated, changed in scale, and compared. Graphs take on new meaning as students redraw them to accommodate new data. Graphics in the art curriculum obviously has a central role as students play with color variations or manipulate perspective. Technology teachers are able to use CAD software that controls scale, ratio, and other elements of design as pupils design and construct various objects to meet certain criteria (The State University of New York at Stony Brook, 1994). Extensively illustrated nonfiction, such as Macaulay's masterpiece, has been converted to computer format, also titled *The Way Things Work* (undated).

Science teachers have an incredibly rich body of material to choose from designed by knowledgeable developers. The National Geographic Society has published *Mammals*, (undated), a multimedia encyclcopedia which contains essays, captioned photographs, authentic sound reproductions, maps, and video clips of over 200 animals. Another history program widely used, according to Holtzberg (1994), is *U.S. History* on CD-ROM. Its database of over 100 history books, 1000 photos, numerous maps and tables of historical events can be a powerful resource. Microsoft's *Encarta* (1994), containing maps, pictures, charts and graphs, is another excellent resource for the social studies teacher. After searches for relevant print and graphic material, it is simple for students to retrieve appropriate material and develop their own comprehensive, illustrated report.

These examples of graphics applications are described by discipline but graphics lend themselves particularly well to interdisciplinary study. An old, but excellent example is Liao's *Colortrope* (1983), an interactive program wherein children simultaneously learn art and science concepts by analyzing, experimenting and "making" colors directly on the screen. This program works especially well using cooperative learning approaches: children discuss decisions jointly and share the use of a special ball which acts as a form of prism through which the spectrum can be analyzed.

The teacher may use text and graphics to encourage writing: in a program entitled *The Little Planet Literacy Series* by Applied Learning Technologies (undated), youthful users can compose their own original multimedia books (aided by visual storyboards) and select accompanying sound tracks. Other teachers may wish to introduce Broderbund's *Myst* (1993), facilitating problem solving in a graphics context. Another program with similar objectives is *Thinkin' Things #2*, (Stanger et al., 1993) in which users employ tools to examine depth and perspective. In another one of the five activities, children play with optical illusions and toy with images in three-dimensional presentations.

But what if we hypothesize an unconventional setting in the future? Visualize a classroom where educators do not specify a standard pathway for learning a given subject. What if teachers actually adopted the credo of individualization and student interests and operationalized open-ended learning where individuals or student groups pursued their inquiries through Internet or other resources presently being developed? For example, if students were interested in art, they might access the database of a museum in London and call to their screen such requests as a list or biographies of all the impressionists in the collection, all those born in France, all who used oils, all born before or after a given date, all who used certain themes ... or any inquiry a user wished. The viewer may request an example of a segment of an artist's work, may enlarge it and compare it with that of others all on the screen simultaneously. The user may "play around" pleasurably as new associations and possibilities emerge in this graphic web. As can be imagined, such tools have the enormous potential, not only to revolutionize the classroom and the library, but to radically affect our understanding of the dimensions of literacy.

The response to an old joke about how to make chicken soup is: "First catch the chicken!" Research on computers, especially those with graphics components, has generated reams of results attesting to the power of computers to magnetize children and keep them attending to the stimulus. Multimedia programs with their digitized photos, animation, transferable photos, not to mention excellent vocal narrations and even musical backgrounds are contemporary tools to "catch" youngsters who have grown up in visual environments—heavy television viewers, experienced mall game players, and those who have had exposure to home computers. Increasingly, youngsters entering schools will be at ease in such environments.

Some critics (Sinatra, 1986), have asserted that schools have "eliminated ... experiences which develop youngsters' perceptual, imaginative, and visualizing abilities," (pp. 312). While this is somewhat extreme, it is clear that schools in general have been slow to see the potential of graphics software programs, often using them for motivation or reinforcement, or low-level visual information dissemination. In the distant future, when students enter the world of virtual reality, create sophisticated graphics themselves, or manipulate sophisticated visual data, a revolution will occur in terms of how children "see" their world. Will contemporary educators see how such utilization can make to the literacy goals of the schools? Accepting such innovations could lead to profound educational reform in how and what we teach.

References

Broderbund Software. (1993). *Myst*. Novalo, CA: Broderbund.

Bureau of Electronic Publishing. (undated). *US History on CD-ROM*. Parsippany, NJ: Bureau of Electronic Publishing.

Clark, R. E. (1994). Media will never influence learning. *Educational Technology Research and Development, 42*(2), 21–29.

Holtzberg, C. S. (1994). Kids' play. *CD-ROM World, 9*(4) 54–57.

Kozma, R. B. (1994) Will media influence learning? Reframing the debate. *Educational Technology Research and Development, 42*(2), 7–19.

Liao, T., The National Learning Center and Department of Technology and Society at Sate University of New York at Stony Brook. (1983) *Colortrope*. Cedarhurst, NJ: Queue Associates.

Little Planet Literacy Series. (undated). Nashville, TN: Applied Learning Technologies.

Macaulay, D. *The way things work*. New York: Dorling Kindersley.

Marshall, G. R. (1987). *Computer graphics in education*. Englewood Cliffs, NJ: Prentice-Hall.

Microsoft Corporation. (1994). *Encarta*. Redmond, WA: Microsoft.

Morrison, G. R. (1994). The media effects question: Unresolvable or asking the right question? *Educational Technology Research and Development, 42*(2), 41–44.

National Geographic Society. (undated). *Mammals: A multimedia encyclopedia*. Washington, DC: National Geographic Society.

Sinatra, R. (1986). *Visual literacy connections to thinking, reading, and writing*. Springfield, IL: Charles Thomas.

Stanger, D., Clough, S., Wood, T., Baratt, J., Sinclair, P., Gust, M., Shoemaker, S., Boome, M., Lepisto, S., James, C., Rose, M., Cotichetti, N., & Schottenstein, A. *Thinkin' Things #2*. (1993). Redmond, WA: Edmark.

State University of New York at Stony Brook, Department of Technology and Society. (n.d.). (1994). *Designing technology for people with disabilities*. Melville, NY: NEC of America.

Ullmer, E.J. (1994). Media and learning: Are there two kinds of truth? *Educational Technology Research and Development, 42*(1), 21–32.

Van ErtCasey, H., & Wolf, J. S. (1989). Developing visual literacy among academically able fifth grade students. *Roeper Review, 12*(2), 86–91.

·64·

CURRENT ISSUES AND FUTURE DIRECTIONS

Bertram C. Bruce

UNIVERSITY OF ILLINOIS

The word "literacy" never seems to stand still. It makes its appearance in the discourses of history as well as those of comparative linguistics. It shows up in debates about economics and literature. It mediates interdisciplinary conversations among scholars from history, sociology, anthropology, political science, linguistics, education, literature (Keller-Cohen, 1994). It also participates in public debates about schooling, employment, and public values. It is one of the ways in which we now talk about the visual arts and new electronic media. As it appears in these areas, it assumes different guises and enacts different purposes. The diverse array of meanings and connotations for literacy that we see today provide perverse evidence for Humpty Dumpty's view that a word can mean "just what [we] choose it to mean—neither more nor less."

If we want to survey current issues in literacy, we soon find that any attempt at a fixed definition of literacy quickly becomes enmeshed in larger discussions of language, thought, society, culture, and values. And the situation becomes hopeless when we begin to examine future directions for literacy. Accordingly, in this chapter I will make some working assumptions to keep the word within some bounds, even if it cannot be fully reined in. First, literacy means control over discourses that use and communicate complex forms of knowledge. Since there are many such discourses, there can be multiple literacies. Second, that literacy is so embedded in our daily practices that it can scarcely be conceived as an activity separate from any of them. Third, the changing technologies of literacy provide a window into literacy practices, both because they are the tools through which literacy is enacted and because their construction reveals our conceptions of our basic humanity.

There are five broad areas in which important and dramatic changes are occurring today. The first concerns *democracy*, and in particular, the movement toward univer-

sal literacy; the second relates to *work*, with a focus on changing demands for literacy in the workplace; the third takes us to *social relations*, and especially, the creation of a global society; the fourth concerns *language*, and how our language(s) are evolving; and the fifth relates to *technology*, with an emphasis on the way our literacy practices are becoming immersed in new technologies. Although the areas of democracy, work, social relations, language, and technology cover much ground, I hope to show that trends in these areas exhibit some convergence. Given the many facets of literacy that pervade our lives, these speculations will necessarily be abbreviated, and like all such imaginings, their naiveté will become most apparent as reality actually unfolds.

THE MOVEMENT TOWARD UNIVERSAL LITERACY

Politically, the "literacy crisis," and its cousins, the crises in mathematics and science education, the breakdown of the schools, and so on, serve as a bulwark for arguments from conservative, middle of the road, and liberal perspectives. Some see the lack of literacy skills as an explanation for inequities in the distribution of social power and social goods. They argue that illiteracy accounts for high unemployment or underemployment, and by implication for poverty, crime, substance abuse, and other social ills. After all, they say, if a person does not have the skills demanded by today's employers, how can he or she expect to be hired for a good job?

Others see the lack of opportunities to develop literacy as itself an example of social injustice—an effect rather than a cause of inequities. Class inequities in access to jobs, health care, and housing outside of the school system are reflected in the literacy problems within the schools. One striking

I would like to acknowledge the help of many people in thinking through these issues, including, in an incomplete list, Kevin Leander, Paul Prior, Jim Squire, Cheris Kramarae, Nick Burbules, Gail Hawisher, Jim Levin, Marsha Woodbury, Taku Sugimoto, and Elizabeth Easley.

example is that 40 years after the Brown versus Board of Education decision, which said that separate schooling by race was inherently unequal, many school systems are still effectively segregated, and many of the rest still practice segregation and unequal distribution of resources within schools and individual classrooms.

Interestingly, commentators from all parts of the political spectrum seem to agree that literacy is not what it should be, and that the schools are much to blame. This universal dismal view persists in good economic times and bad. But major long-term trends run counter to it. For example, high school graduation rates in the United States at the turn of the century were around 6–8,%; by the 1920s they had reached 17–29%; and by the 1940s had climbed to 51–59%. For the last 25 years they have remained steady at or above 80%, and are among the highest in the world (Green, 1994; Marable, 1993; National Center for Education Statistics, 1995; White, 1987). Another indicator is the purchase of books and magazines. Annual sales of books and academic journals are at an all-time high in the United States, and are growing (Leslie, 1994; McGuire, 1995). There are also many indications that more people use more reading and writing in their work and leisure than ever before and that the rates are rising despite television (Newman, 1991), alleged inadequate schools, and the so-called breakdown of the social order.

This is not to say that schools should not be improved. There are many schools with inadequate resources and appalling physical conditions. Nearly all could improve their record at providing excellent learning opportunities for all children. And, perhaps most important, what was good education a generation ago may not prove even adequate for tomorrow.

Meanwhile, the students in our schools are changing. More children remain in school, and for most, the consequences of not succeeding may be more severe than ever before. Whether illiteracy causes social distress or is itself a consequence of that distress, it is certainly true that they are closely linked, especially in the inner cities. We are also more aware than ever of the diverse cultures that children bring to school. Although it is debatable how much the degree of cultural diversity within schools has increased compared to earlier periods in our history, there is no doubt that accommodating diversity, and using it as a resource, rather than seeing it only as a problem, is a major concern for future literacy developments.

Developments in technology pose interesting challenges for universal literacy. In principle, new technologies—ranging from crank-up radios to digital video on the Internet—could provide access to texts and tools for writing for all people throughout the world. For example, Project Gutenberg, the On-Line Book Initiative, the Oxford Text Archive, and related projects are making thousands of documents—the complete works of Shakespeare, Beethoven's Fifth Symphony (audio), Supreme Court decisions, the Apollo lunar landing (video)—available through the Internet (Harris, 1994; Krol, 1992; LaQuey, 1994).

Using a $1000 computer system, a classroom anywhere in the world can have access to a library totally unaffordable in conventional print form, one containing resources available to no single library in the world, unless, of course, that library has an equivalent computer system. Moreover, democracy movements in many countries are using fax machines and e-mail in lieu of printing presses hitherto out of reach.

But despite these promising new tools, there are many indications that inequities in access to new technologies are enormous and increasing rapidly. Because of the rapid evolution of information and communication technologies, society is increasingly stratified in terms of "generations" of technology. Even within a single community, people living physically side by side live within different ages of cyberspace. In a country in which the top 1% of families has more wealth than the bottom 90% (Schreibman, 1994), there is little reason to think that information technology resources will be equitably distributed.

This is already evident with computer use in schools. Wealthier countries and wealthier schools within those countries have greater access to new technologies. Moreover, students in wealthier schools more often use computers for open-ended learning activities, such as writing, art, science simulations, and global communication. In contrast, students in other settings, such as inner-city schools, may experience only drill on basic skills (Boruta, et al., 1983). Even within a single classroom there is evidence that the distribution of access to computer tools and information "follows the well-trodden battle-lines of social conflict" (Foucault, 1972, p. 227). Students with computers at home typically become classroom experts, receiving special attention and opportunities. In contrast, students in "remedial programs" fall farther behind when they miss the introduction to the computer because of being pulled out of class (Michaels, Cazden, & Bruce, 1985). There are also large gender inequities. Most Internet users are male, and across wide ranges of computer use in schools, girls have less involvement with new technologies than do boys. The metaphors of use are predominately male, and often, explicitly antifemale (Bryson, & de Castell, in press; Kramarae, & Kramer, 1995; Taylor, Kramarae, & Ebben, 1993). Thus, technological innovations often exacerbate underlying inequities, despite the optimistic visions of change. If "knowledge work" becomes the norm, does that mean that everyone will develop advanced literacy skills?

A similar situation is occurring with the "information highway." This was originally conceived as auguring a new age of two-way communication to empower people of all classes by giving them both information and voice in decision making. But the highway sometimes looks more like a shopping mall or a high-tech medium for the one-way delivery of information. Will the global hypertext mean that for the first time in history all people will have convenient access to all forms of encoded knowledge and the associated empowerment? Or, does it mean that access to knowledge and the use of information tools will become prized commodities, controlled and regimented according to one's wealth and social position?

Will 21st-century literacy be the "the practice of freedom" as Freire says, or will it become commoditized and stratified as never before? Worse still, will the same information tools be used to monitor and control, to imprison us within the technology? As Crawford (1994) says, "The road to freedom via a two-way Information Highway may turn into a one-way Surveillance Street, used to condition people's thoughts and control their behavior." Video surveillance is now so ubiquitous that we may be on television more than we watch it (Patton, 1994).

Events are occurring so rapidly that it is difficult to answer any of these questions. But it is equally clear that discussions of literacy cannot ignore them, because literacy itself cannot be separated from the larger social and political issues. If we are to influence the direction of change, we need to understand the processes better and to grapple directly with the underlying contexts in which decisions are being made. For students of today, universal literacy is dependent upon democratic schooling, and simultaneously, a prerequisite for future democracy.

CHANGING DEMANDS FOR LITERACY IN THE WORKPLACE

In the workplace, literacy is assuming an ever more central role. This is a new kind of literacy, which entails not only basic reading and writing, but the ability to use reading and writing to solve problems and to communicate complex information. It is necessary for "knowledge work," the new modal form of work: "By the end of this century knowledge workers will make up a third or more of the work force in the United States—as large a proportion as manufacturing workers ever made up, except in wartime" (Drucker, 1994, p. 62).

The shift to knowledge work can be seen in more than just a changing proportion of workers who do it. One indication that has a direct bearing on literacy concerns is that there are now tens of thousands of scholarly journals; American libraries alone subscribe to 50,000 of them (Leslie, 1994). No person could ever read all the journals now published, or even all the journals in a major discipline. Sociology, for example, may have 3,000 or more journals. While the need for careful reading does not go away, the sheer mass of writing implies the desperate need for other important reading skills, such as learning how to find materials, how to judge them critically, and how to select from among the abundance available. But, a glance at most published curricular materials shows that they operate on a very different model, one in which students are presented with a few preselected texts, and never given an option to decide that the texts they have been assigned are inappropriate for their needs.

The number of scholarly journals marks more than an issue of quantity: each of these journals reflects a specialized discourse, a way of interpreting the world and making meaning. Control over that discourse means a kind of literacy (Gee, 1990). There are thus thousands of variants in the meanings of literacy reflected in these scholarly journals alone. Moreover, many of these journals correspond to different modes of (knowledge) work, to different ways that literacy is employed in work practices: the way a chemical engineer represents meaning, relates language to the world, and communicates with others is not the same as the way in which a banker does. The proliferation of these multiple literacies is a special challenge for 21st century literacy development.

Along with the profusion of literacies, reflecting the extreme specialization of work, there is a trend toward instability in the characterizations of these literacies. Universities are increasingly finding that the traditional categorization of the disciplines bears little relation to the use of disciplinary knowledge in the workplace. In many work settings, workers must find ways to solve problems in conditions that change rapidly and require collaboration among people with diverse sources of knowledge. This puts a premium on the ability to communicate across differences and to work cooperatively. As an example, faculty in an electrical engineering department have discovered that their graduates rarely need to know how to solve a classic EE problem, which rarely arises neatly in a practical setting. Instead, they need to know how to talk with a physician with whom they are collaborating on a space shuttle project, or with a marketing person about the design of a new piece of software. Ironically hyper-specialization and the technologizing of work has highlighted more than ever the need for the classic liberal arts of tolerance, communication, understanding the perspectives of others, consideration of values, and holistic understanding.

Workers in the 21st century will need to acquire and apply formal knowledge in ways very different from those required in agricultural, manufacturing, and service jobs of the past. They will not be able to get all the information they need from one text or manual but will need to integrate knowledge from multiple sources, most likely obtained in diverse media through electronic resources such as the World Wide Web. There will be too much information for any given task, just the opposite of what has been true in the past. Workers will need to cope with an abundance of information, to select critically considering the source and the relation to what else is known. None of these skills is new, but the 21st century workplace foregrounds them in a way never known before.

Workers will also need to collaborate with others, and to use both oral and written language to facilitate that collaboration. Working together, always an important skill, will become ever more important. The forms of these collaborations may also change. New technologies are creating new social matrices. Many people are already collaborating with others through the Internet and through the use of groupware (multiuser software). In the future, more and more people may collaborate through virtual reality environments. Can we say that a MUD (multiuser dungeons), MOO (MUD object-oriented), or MUSH (multiuser shared hallucination) is only a game, and not a forerunner of the workplace of tomorrow? Even today, there are text-based virtual reality communities. For example, teachers of composition now meet regularly in Media-MOO (at telnet://purple-crayon.media.mit.edu 8888/) to discuss issues related to writing pedagogy. The jargon of the cyber-age is incomprehensible to many, and it changes so rapidly that only an electronic dictionary is of much help in decoding it. I could turn this article into a glossary or I could completely omit technical terms; neither choice seems satisfactory. I chose instead to use a few, hoping that the reader for whom they are unfamiliar will know that the discussion can proceed without every word being fully understood, just as might occur between people who only partially know each other's languages.

These tools are already changing education. For example, the Teaching Teleapprentices Project (Levin, et al., 1994) is a nationally known effort exploring the use of Internet resources, the World Wide Web, and e-mail by children, teachers, future teachers, and university scientists. In this project, electronic communication links children with student teachers, student teachers with their cooperating teachers, university education professors, and scientists. In related projects, experienced teachers engage in reflection on their own practice through an e-mail network (e.g., DiMauro, & Gal, 1994).

Schools have been moderately effective in teaching students how to solve problems that are presented in a familiar, well-structured way. But increasingly, computers are able to solve these well-structured problems, leaving totally untouched the more complex problems that must be addressed in order to get a job done (Spiro, et al., 1992). To take an extreme case, the entire traditional mathematics curriculum from grades 1 through 8 has been dubbed the "$5 curriculum," because most of what was taught could be done by a $5 calculator. But the harder problems of estimating and approximating, selecting which operations are appropriate, relating results to the tasks at hand, evaluating a solution and so on, are left untouched. Other major elements of the standard curriculum, from spel-ling to history dates need to be rethought in the context of new tools. In the workplace of the future, workers will need to be able to find problems, not just solve them, that is, to look at a complex situation and turn it into a structured problem that has a solution.

Perhaps most important, the ability to learn will be not just a helpful, but a necessary condition of productive work. Lifelong learning will become an integral part of more and more careers. Already, spending on industrial training rivals that of the entire public school system. This is but one tangible realization of the adage that schooling is but a beginning to life. In the future workplace, education will be a continuing focus throughout.

THE CREATION OF A GLOBAL SOCIETY

Whether we accept the dismal or the optimistic view of literacy trends, many questions arise regarding what may happen next. We now live in a global society, one that is changing everyday. Increasingly, the work we do, the products we use, and the people we interact with represent languages and cultures throughout the world. What sorts of literacy are needed in this new world? Just as the last remnants of geography are being swept out of schools and universities, it suddenly seems to matter how the rest of the world lives and thinks. Just as high schools, colleges, and universities have all but eliminated foreign language requirements, we begin to understand why it is important to be able to communicate in more than one language and to understand different ways of thinking. Just as we proudly put forth new standards for learning in various subject areas, we begin to see ways in which the traditional concept of the disciplines—English, mathematics, science, social studies may be inadequate for future needs. New standards documents call for more integration of learning across the disciplines, yet they and the corresponding new forms of assessment reify the separateness of the traditional categories. Our plans for literacy development seem to be solving yesterday's problems, while the world is changing around us.

The global society is now a permanent part of our workplaces, schools and neighborhoods. As large corporations become ever more multinational, people may find themselves working with people who inhabit other cultures and speak other languages. For example: A man who has lived his entire life within 10 miles of his birthplace in Texas suddenly finds that his company has been purchased by a company based in Germany. He now needs to learn to speak German, to travel to Germany, and to work with people from Germany. He soon finds, of course, that many of the people he meets in Germany are from yet a third country. Similarly, his children attend a school with children from all parts of the world, something he did not experience. All these changes are but the beginning of a new kind of world in which we will all soon be living at the border.

Among other changes we need to consider is the emergence of the World Wide Web (December, & Randall, 1994; Krol 1992). The Web is a vast sea of documents, including text, graphics, tables of numbers, software, video, and audio. These materials are all linked in a global hypertext (Barrett, 1989). Any information resource that can be put into digital form can be made available to computer users throughout the world. These documents are easily accessible. They are also linked together so that they become, in effect, not just a library, but a single gigantic book, that has been called the "docuverse," or the universe of knowledge.

The World Wide Web started in 1991 at the European Laboratory for Particle Physics (CERN) in Geneva. As the Web began to take shape, easy-to-use interface programs, or web browsers, began to appear, including Mosaic, Netscape, MacWeb, and Lynx. The category of browsers has already become a basic application comparable to word processors, spreadsheets, e-mail, or graphics programs. Today, users can access an amazing array of resources from the home, classroom, or workplace (see Table 64–1). Many people believe that it will become the dominant medium for information exchange in the 21st century.

The growth in the use of the Web is already difficult to comprehend, or even to assess accurately. By the end of 1995, there were over 10 million host computers sharing information through the Web, and several times that many users. Available information resources and information traffic on the Web are now measured in terabytes—trillions of characters—equivalent to millions of books. Commercial on-line services, such as America On-line, telecommunications companies, such as MCI and software makers, such as Microsoft, are all now making substantial investments in the expansion of Web access.

The Web is but a tangible manifestation of the interconnectedness of human knowledge and social practices. Once upon a time, it may have made sense to imagine that we could be satisfied knowing only the history of our region or country, or that our literature was a complete and uncontaminated collection of all the texts we needed to know. In

TABLE 64–1. A Small Sampling of Internet Resources

Activity	World Wide Web Location
See the "Home page" of the White House; listen to Socks the cat meow	www.whitehouse.gov
Get the latest medical information	cancer.med.upenn.edu:3000
Connect with Santa Claus	northpole.net, or www.neosoft.com / citylink
Plan a trip	www.travelweb.com
Look for a job	www.careermosaic.com
Find resources for education	www.ed.uiuc.edu
Attend an art exhibit	gertrude.art.uiuc.edu
Tour the solar system	www.c3.lanl.gov / ~cjhamil / SolarSystem / homepage.html
Obtain government information; read Nelson Mandela's speech to Congress; examine corporate filings before the Securities and Exchange Commission	thomas.loc.gov
View paintings at the Louvre; tour Paris while there	sunsite.unc.edu / louvre
Visit the Electronic Frontier Foundation; become involved with the politics of the Internet	www.eff.org.
Sample the latest music releases	sunsite.unc.edu / ianc / index.html
Read *Wired* magazine; meet with contributors and other readers	www.hotwired.com
Visit the Exploratorium in San Francisco	www.exploratorium.edu

that time, we might also have believed that our religion, politics, social values, language, work, and daily practices could go on without concern for what others "far away" might do. But today, it is evident that everything we know and do is but a small thread in a larger social fabric that we cannot escape, even if we wished to do so. For these reasons, debates about multiculturalism often play out in an imagined past. We worry about whether there will be enough time for Shakespeare if students read Confucius, or whether they should study African history. These are questions about what would happen if we made changes to the curriculum. But the changes *have already occurred.*

This is because the meaning of school practices can never be separated from the larger social life. Ideas that once were at the periphery of educated discourse are now at the center, not by anyone's choice, not by a desire for inclusiveness, not to prepare students for a changing world, but because the world itself is not the same. Formal education, of course, influences educated discourse, but it does not determine it. Confucius, and Mao Tse-tung, are effectively part of the curriculum now, because no study of history, economics, language, politics, and technology can ignore the history of 1.2 billion people. Similarly, African history is part of history. It always was; only in that isolated past could some people

imagine that it was not part of their history.

Reader response criticism provides a case in point. Classic theories (Fish, 1980; Rosenblatt, 1978) of reader response have emphasized the situated nature of response in contrast to the primacy of the text. In so doing, these theories opened the door to a reinterpretation of canonical texts, and to a rethinking of the canon, curriculum, literature, and the act of reading itself. Ironically, though, early reader response theorizing was centered within a Eurocentric and male-dominated domain. Thus, the radical potential of the theories was concealed by the fact that the text examples, the readers, and the interpretive communities were all drawn from one small corner of the social fabric. More recently, response studies have encompassed much more of the fabric. Studies of gender and reading have brought about a reconceptualization of the meaning of many texts, and of the very processes of reading and writing (Flynn, 1988; Flynn, & Schweickart, 1986). Similarly, textual and response studies of African literature have expanded our vision, not only by adding new texts to consider, but by revealing a richness in language and in the processes of meaning making (Gates, 1988).

The emergence of the global society means that literacy is changing. It encompasses more than it ever had before in terms of both content and form. More kinds of knowledge are accessible and more kinds are needed. Discussions of literacy will have to expand to reflect this globalization.

EVOLUTION OF LANGUAGE

Literacy is intimately bound up with language. We need to learn a language before we can become literate users of it and we use literacy as a way to learn other things through language. This connection is so obvious that we often overlook its significance. Often, it is only when reading a text from long ago, such as *Beowulf,* that we become aware of the complex relations between literacy and language. But the evolution of languages will undoubtedly make us much more aware of these relations.

One factor contributing to increased awareness is the changing composition of public school classrooms. In many schools today, students bring not just one or two, but dozens of different languages from their homes. There is now a commitment, to educate students whose home language is other than standard English. This means that the notion of progressing from oral to written language has assumed a significantly new meaning for literacy development. We must consider that students learn not simply a new form for the same language (an oversimplification, even in that case), but new forms and new languages at the same time.

Meanwhile, the definition of English is itself changing. English has always been a paradigm case of an amalgamated language, with roots in Anglo-Saxon and Latin, through French. Speech in English is filled with words from Spanish, Italian, and German, as well as Native American, Scandinavian, Asian, and African languages. But as global communication expands at an exponential pace and as people travel and move from country to country, the mix of language influences on English will undoubtedly increase.

To add to the changes, people all over the world are learning English. There are probably more speakers of English in China today (for most, it is a second or third language), than there are in the United States. There has emerged the concept of world Englishes, to describe the variety of versions of English spoken throughout the world. As more people speak English, and use it in trade, science, and cultural exchange, it will inevitably expand and change to accommodate their experiences and linguistic backgrounds.

Thus, English is no longer the language we thought it was last year, and it will be a different one next year. This cannot but have profound implications for our idea of literacy in English and for promoting literacy development. At the same time, other languages are also changing, many in the same ways that English is changing, and others in very different directions. Hundreds of other languages are dying out as the last speakers themselves die or assimilate into dominant cultures. Many of these languages are being preserved, but only in a curatorial sense, on videotapes and in dictionaries and folklore collections. They thus become accessible for study to everyone at the same time as they become spoken by no one.

In addition, advances in science and technology are producing new words everyday. The ways we describe phenomena in areas of health, communication, transportation, and more, change as we develop new procedures and new understandings. People who market products add to the changes as they strive to develop ever new ways of distinguishing their products or services.

Other technological influences shape the things we can do with language. For example, multimedia systems integrate oral and written language in a hybrid that is causing us to rethink the great dichotomies between oral and literate culture. Also, the ability to manipulate fonts, formats, colors, and other presentational aspects of texts may fundamentally change how we conceive of writing. As everyone who has used e-mail soon becomes aware, dialects of electronic communication are proliferating, with characteristic abbreviations ("BTW" for "by the way") and emotions (such as the smiling face: ":–)").

The nature of publishing is also undergoing rapid changes. Writers are now producing hypermedia texts. For example, Art Spiegelman, the author of *Maus,* and now, *The Complete Maus,* on CD-ROM, says, "I think CD-ROMs imply a new kind of narrative.... Instead of just moving through time, all of a sudden stories now move through space, so that architecture becomes the reigning metaphor" (Voyager, 1994). Academic publishing is also assuming new forms. There are now thousands of electronic journals and newsletters listed in the archives of *NewJour,* itself an active electronic forum for exchanging information about electronic publications, maintained by the Association of Research Libraries. Much scholarly work is now conducted via e-mail and on-line conferences. These trends may fundamentally alter basic aspects of scholarship including copyright laws, academic tenure, concepts of collaboration, the nature of research, and the definition of publishing (Burbules, & Bruce, 1994; Cherniak, et al., 1993).

Meanwhile, e-mail has become a normal part of the daily literacy practice for many people. The Electronic Messaging Association estimates that in 1993 there were 16 million e-mail users in the business sector alone. These users sent the equivalent of 10,000 manuscripts length (not the quality), of *War and Peace,* everyday that year (Leslie, 1993). This indicates two things. First, literacy, at least in the form of reading and writing e-mail, is active and growing rapidly. The advent of computer technology has certainly not eliminated the practice of literacy. Second, the amount of text in the world is astounding. If 10,000 manuscripts length of *War and Peace* appears everyday, the problem may no longer be to finish reading the book, but to find it in the first place. As discussed above, the skills of finding, selecting, and evaluating have become more critical than ever before.

It remains to be seen whether these expanded conceptions of language will lead to better communication. New forms can become obstacles, rather than opportunities. In the final analysis, the human capacity to make meaning and to communicate must take precedence over the characteristics of any medium. We do well to remember Thoreau's (1951, pp. 66, 67) caution, which is more a propos today than when he wrote in the mid-19th century: "Our inventions are wont to be pretty toys, which distract our attention from serious things.... We are in great haste to construct a magnetic telegraph from Maine to Texas; but Maine and Texas, it may be, have nothing important to communicate." Despite this caution, we do have a magnetic telegraph, and much more besides—expanded print publications, radio, video, e-mail, the World Wide Web. As a result, our language has changed, is changing, and will change, perhaps even more rapidly in the future.

These changes raise many questions, with few easy answers: What is English, and what will it become? How do our notions of English literature or of the literatures of the world change in light of the changes in languages and the forms we use for communicating? How do our ideas of the relations between language and inquiry or language and collaboration have to change? What do these changes mean for our concept of literacy? What are the implications for the teaching of writing and reading?

IMMERSIVE TECHNOLOGIES

There has also been an evolution in our views of information and communication technologies for literacy development. If we consider stages in this evolution we can see not only different kinds of hardware and software, but also different visions of literacy and of ourselves. We are now changing our conceptions of literacy further because of our immersion in new forms of knowing and communicating.

In the beginning, we constructed computer technology as an exotic, and marginal, method for teaching. We did this by designing hardware and software to function as an automated tutor for skills and concepts. But we also constructed it in the way we conceived it, as a tool for systematically teaching concepts, presenting problems to solve, and administering drills and practice lessons. In the process, we also constructed our own teaching role as analogous to that of the tutors we designed.

Later, in a second stage, we saw that cybertechnology represents information in new ways. The computer as medium, or cybermedia became our construction. At that time we saw how the computer could offer greater user choice in the presentation of materials, could integrate the text, audio, and video media provided through separate components (slide projectors, audiotapes, television, etc.) in earlier technologies.

Then, in a third stage, we began to understand the information tool potential of cybertechnology; we saw that it provides new tools for learning. Thus, we talked about word processing, desktop publishing, finding information in data bases, making graphs and pictures, and performing calculations in the course of problem solving.

As students began to use cybertools in their own ways for learning, the communication aspect became more central. We moved to a fourth stage, one in which we saw that cybertechnology could do more than represent someone else's information; it could also be a way to share one's own ideas (Bruce, & Rubin, 1993). This naturally led to the view that cybertechnology could create new environments for communication and learning, in which students working together could share their processes of learning (Bruce, et al., 1993). Moreover, they could be connected to a world beyond the classroom, that included experts in every field (Levin, et al., 1987). That view in turn begins to connect with a vision of the augmented human mind and of collective thought whose reach extends beyond that of any individual.

Today, we are entering a fifth stage, in which we merge, for better or worse, with our own inventions. The extent to which this has happened can be seen in the realm of science fiction. Producers of television shows and movies are now using techniques to create science fiction that only a short while ago were the content of sci-fi. Tools such as morphing, in which images are transformed, computer animation, virtual reality, and robotics are current technologies used to create the illusion of a future world in which these very technologies will come into being. Recently, for example, the creator of the television show, *X-Files* used the sci-fi technique of an on-line forum with fans to discuss the direction of the show (Kim, 1994). As Ray Bradbury says, "Science fiction itself has remained the same. We have caught up to it.... We are a science-fiction generation." Science fiction screenwriter Ron Shusett (*Alien, Total Recall*) echoes this sentiment: "We can't think far enough ahead anymore." (Both quotes from Kim, 1994.)

Consider just a few other examples. There is now a commercial music accompaniment system called *Vivace*, which plays along with a student learning an instrument. Like the old *Music Minus One* records, the system plays the other parts of a composition, but it does so responsively. If the student wants to play *allegro*, so will *Vivace*. Moreover, it changes the tempo when he does, *ritards* when he does, and waits when he falters on a note. It learns characteristics of his style and accommodates appropriately at the next practice session. Even its degree of responsiveness can be adjusted, anywhere from the rigidity of a metronome to a humanly impossible total accommodation. Research is underway now on the effects of interacting with systems like this. It is not at all obvious what these will be, but the experience is completely unlike that of the (first-stage) tutor model. Instead of interacting with a device, the student somehow merges with it.

Multimedia software developments present other aspects of the changes underway (see Voyager, 1994). For example, a CD-ROM called *In the Deserts* (Heath, 1995) takes a student on a virtual field trip, starting with a 360 degree panorama of the Sonoran desert. She can click on a plant or animal to see an animation or video segment. Carrying along (a computer simulation of) a computer notebook, she can write about what she discovers and take photographs of anything she sees. She can also access multimedia texts to meet a Native American potter, a storyteller, a naturalist, or other children. Exploratory environments such as this create opportunities for integrated learning through immersion in another world.

Moving a step further, full virtual reality systems (Helsel, 1992; Helsel, & Roth, 1991; Pantelidis, 1993; Pimentel, & Teixeira, 1993) reveal in a tangible way our immersion in technology. Psotka (1994) suggests that virtual reality

> ...provides a fundamentally different mode of communication between computer and person, between symbolic form and mental representation; and between collaborators in conceptual worlds. VR replaces interaction with immersion; it replaces the desktop metaphor with a world metaphor; and it replaces direct manipulation with symbiosis. The magnitude of these changes needs to be experienced to be understood

One of the most sophisticated VR systems is the CAVE (CAVE Automated Visualization Environment). It is a "virtual reality theater" in which several people can share a virtual reality experience, without the need for goggles (users must wear light plastic glasses to perceive the 3-D effect). It is a high-resolution 3-D visual image and audio environment, with correct perspective and stereo projections updated in real time, and images that move with and surround the immersed viewer(s). In one application within the CAVE, the participants feel that they have entered a computer screen saver program, with fish swimming all around them. They can drop pellets for the fish and watch them swim over to eat. One has the feeling of a fundamental shift from spectator to participant. Researchers are only beginning to explore the forms of learning that this technology might enable in areas of mathematics, astronomy, geography, physiology, history, and more.

One other example is an entire new industry, bioengineering. This field hardly existed a generation ago, but has been born of a combination of new technologies. First, there are technologies such as ultrasound, X-ray, EEG, EKG, electron microscopy, fiber optics, and magnetic resonance imaging that have provided new ways to see the human body and its inner workings. These imaging techniques are amplified by the use of laser discs to store images and high-speed networks to distribute them. There are also new kinds of prosthetic devices, such as artificial knees, and new tools, such as microsurgery, for treating dysfunctions in the body. Finally, there are simulation and virtual reality systems to facilitate exploration of our newly constructed knowledge about the body. Together, these tools are creating an entirely new image of our physical existence, one in which we see ourselves through the technologies we have created, modify the functioning of our bodies through other technologies, and express our understanding through yet other technologies. We may celebrate this new world, fear it, or curse it, but what seems unavoidable is that we already inhabit it. We have redefined part of what it means to be human by establishing a symbiosis with new technologies.

Our discourse about technology, including great debates about whether it is good or bad for teaching, is built upon the myth that we can stand apart from technology. As Suchman (1988, p. 174) says, "We are taught to view the political and the technological as separate spheres, the former having to do with values, ideology, power, and the like, the latter having to do with physical artifacts exempt from such vagaries of social life." Thus, we conceive a set of doors into alternate futures, reflecting a free choice among new technologies, and ask "whether" we should pass through.

What we fail to see is that we and our technologies constitute indivisible entities (see Bijker, et al., 1987). We are already cyborgs in the sense defined by Haraway, part fiction, part social reality (1991, p. 149). Our technology part has been constructed out of our beliefs, values, and extant practices, and in turn, it has brought us through the door to the future. Thus, we are already operating within the future that we believe we must prepare ourselves for.

Cybertechnology is not something that some people will choose to adopt; it is already a part of our literacy practices regardless of what we do. One small example: In many libraries, it is not possible to find recent books in the (paper) card catalogue, because only the computer data base is updated. I once tried to find the location of the *Scientific American* collection in the University of Illinois library. The computer told me "No Entries Found", because, as I learned later, it deletes "unimportant words" in a search request, words such as "the", "and", "of" and sadly for me, both "scientific" and "American". Since I could not believe that the university had no subscription to this magazine, I checked the obsolete card catalog, which had not been updated for 10 years, and discovered that there were at least 14 collections of *Scientific American* on the campus. The choice was not whether to use the computer or traditional cards, but whether to use the computer to find a book or not find it at all.

LITERACY ARTIFACTS

Far off in the future, archaeologists interested in literacy might uncover artifacts representative of our literacy practices. Let us consider two artifacts they might find that would call forth contrasting images. The first artifact they might examine is the famous Rosetta Stone. The tablet was discovered in 1799, near the town of Rosetta in the Nile River delta. It was made out of basalt and inscribed with the same text in three different scripts: hieroglyphic demotic, and Greek. It was produced during the reign of Ptolemy V, who ruled Egypt from 205–180 B.C. As this slab had the same text in three scripts, it became a key to deciphering the previously cryptic Egyptian hieroglyphics. It had been preserved for over 2,000 years, and was still readable. Moreover, it provided clues to reading other ancient texts that would enrich our understanding of our cultural past.

This famous tablet would evoke for the future archaeologists the metaphor of "permanence." They would think of ancient hieroglyphics or cuneiform preserved in stone for thousands of years; of monks laboriously copying sacred texts, preserving them for all time; or of a canon of received great literature, to be memorized, studied, and cherished. These thoughts would index the cultural assumptions we hold about connections between literacy and education—our beliefs that education is the process whereby new generations connect with prior human experience; that education is the "means of this social continuity of life" (Dewey, 1966, p. 2); and that literacy gives us access to the permanent record of social life.

The second artifact presents a contrasting image of literacy: there is no stone tablet, not even a book made of paper. Instead, there is a pattern in cyberspace, a string of bits, which could be portrayed on a video screen, printed out on bond paper, or sent through the air as spoken words. The text in this second artifact was constructed collaboratively, by people who lived in different parts of the world and spoke different languages. Individual document pieces are linked to one another and to myriad other texts in the worldwide web of knowledge. Many of these texts contain scripts, like those of the Rosetta Stone, but others have pictures, diagrams, music, voices, and full-motion video. It has holographic images of objects that could be explored from any perspective, with commentary by the creators of the objects and the critics.

This text, like other well-written texts, has a distinctive style, even a voice, that conveys meaning beyond the literal. As do the great classics, it calls for a deep connection between authors and readers, a stretching of horizons. But in contrast to the Rosetta Stone's evocation of history and permanence, this text points the archaeologists toward an image of literacy as a practice enmeshed in change. It suggests radically different ways of thinking and an altered conception of education.

The two artifacts also show the future scientists how our concepts of literacy were inextricable from the literacy technologies we created. The technologies shaped the sorts of literacy we practiced, and in turn, the technologies we created were a function of our evolving conceptions of literacy.

The aspect of change in literacy practices would not trouble the archaeologists; indeed, they would be seeking to understand how the changes in literacy that they knew had actually come about. For people of today the task is more difficult, because we do not know what the literacy artifacts of tomorrow will be. As is the case in many areas of change (Andrews, 1994; Malone, & Rockart, 1991), we will undoubtedly overestimate the short-term effects of current trends, while we underestimate their long-term impact. Nevertheless, the trends described above raise many questions that we cannot afford to ignore regarding literacy development, how to promote it, what it means for schooling and life, and even what literacy is?

Whatever we say about literacy, it is not separable from democracy, work, social relations, language, or technology; instead, these are mutually-constituted practices. As we examine these areas, we see trends and countertrends, major and minor themes, puzzles and contradictions. But there are some consistent, recurring ideas that may help make sense of all the complexity:

1. Future literacy needs will demand a continual rethinking of the purposes of schooling in relation to society, and in particular, an ongoing critical analysis of the ways in which access to societal resources changes in response to changing concepts of literacy.
2. Literacy practices in the future may become highly collaborative enterprises, corresponding to an intensification of emphasis on coordination and communication. The traditional separations among disciplines of study and types of work are in question, implying the need for more integrated conceptions of literacy and literacy development.
3. The globalization of cultural and social relations, is not an option, but a fact in the process of becoming ever more established and articulated. This is inevitably reconstituting and expanding our conceptions of literacy.
4. Literacy is changing along with changes in our languages.
5. Literacy is inextricable from our conceptions and uses of information and communication technologies, including both new technologies, like the Internet, and older ones, like the book. Questions of curriculum are not eliminated by the availability of new tools and greater access to resources, but rather are made much more vital than ever before.

There are basic questions that we once thought we could answer, which need to be asked all over again, among them: What is literacy? What is learning? What is teaching? What does it mean to be human? The issue of who controls the development of literacy technologies and what values are applied in making decisions is critical, but all too often ignored in the discourse about literacy.

It seems inevitable that dramatic changes will occur, have already occurred, in our literacy practices. But whether these changes will lead to a greater access to information and tools, to more liberatory education, to multicultural understanding, to improved social relations, or to a more democratic society remains to be seen. Many forces operate to prevent progressive changes, and we know well that technology alone cannot bring them about. If we are to achieve the possibilities that new literacy holds, we must work to understand both what it is, and what it can be. There is much work to be done.

References

[Note: I have indicated within square brackets any available Internet information for the references cited below.]

Andrews, E. L. (1994, October 30). Changing the wiring takes time. *The New York Times,* The week in review, pp. 1, 4.

Barrett, E. (Ed.). (1989). *The society of text: Hypertext, hypermedia, and the social construction of information.* Cambridge, MA: MIT Press.

Bijker, W. E., Hughes, T. P., & Pinch, T. (1987). *The social construction of technological systems.* Cambridge, MA: MIT Press.

Boruta, M., Carpenter, C., Harvey, M., Keyser, T., LaBonte, J., Mehan, H., & Rodriguez, D. (1983). Computers in the schools: Stratifier or equalizer? *The Quarterly Newsletter of the Laboratory of Comparative Human Cognition, 5,* 51–55.

Bruce, B. C., Peyton, J. K., & Batson, T. W. (Eds.). (1993). *Network-based classrooms: Promises and realities.* New York: Cambridge University Press.

Bruce, B. C., & Rubin, A. (1993). *Electronic quills: A situated evaluation of using computers for writing in classrooms.* Hillsdale, NJ: Erlbaum.

Bryson, M., & de Castell S. (in press). So we've got a chip on our shoulder: Sexing the texts of educational technologies. In J. Willinsky & J. Gaskell (Eds.), *Gender in / forms curriculum: From enrichment to transformation.* New York: Teachers College Press.

Burbules, N. C., & Bruce, B. C. (1994). *This is not a paper.* Manuscript submitted for publication. [http://www.ed.uiuc.edu/EdPsy-387/This-is-not-a-paper.html] .

Cherniak, W., Davis, C., & Deegan, M. (Eds.). (1993). *The politics of the electronic text.* Oxford: Office for Humanities Communication.

Crawford, R. (1994, December 8). *Techno prisoners.* E-mail to Cultural Environment Movement Network. Original in *Adbusters Quarterly,* #11.

December, J., & Randall, N. (1994). *The world wide web unleashed.* Indianapolis, IN: SAMS Publishing.

Dewey, J. (1966). *Democracy and education.* New York: Macmillan. (Original work published 1916)

DiMauro, V., & Gal, S. (1994). Use of telecommunications for reflective discourse of science teacher leaders. *Journal of Science Education and Technology, 3*(2),123–135.

Drucker, P. F. (1994, November). The age of social transformation. *Atlantic Monthly,* pp. 53–80.

Fish, S. (1980). *Is there a text in this class?: The authority of interpretive communities.* Cambridge, MA: Harvard University Press.

Flynn, E. A. (1988). Composing as a woman. *College Composition and Communication, 39,* 423–35.

Flynn, E. A., & Schweickart, P. P. (1986). *Gender and reading: Essays on readers, texts, and contexts.* Baltimore: Johns Hopkins University Press.

Foucault, M. (1972). The discourse on language. In M. Foucault (A. M. Sheridan Smith, Trans.) *The archaeology of knowledge and the discourse on language* (pp. 215–237). New York: Pantheon.

Gates, H. L., Jr. (1988). *The signifying monkey: A theory of African-American literary criticism.* New York: Oxford University Press.

Gee, J. (1990). *Social linguistics and literacy.* Philadelphia: Taylor & Francis.

Green, T. F. (1994, December 22). *Conjecture again.* E-mail to Philosed.

Haraway, D. J. (1991). *Simians, cyborgs, and women: The reinvention of nature.* New York: Routledge.

Harris, J. B. (1994). *Way of the ferret: Finding educational resources on the Internet.* Eugene, OR: International Society for Technology in Education.

Heath D. C. (1995). *Discoveries: In the desert CD-ROM teacher's guide.* Lexington, MA: Author.

Helsel, S. (1992). Virtual reality and education. *Educational Technology, 32,* 38–42.

Helsel S., & Roth, J. P. (Eds.). (1991). *Virtual reality: Theory, practice, and promise.* Westport, CT: Meckler.

Keller-Cohen, D. (Ed.). (1994). *Literacy: Interdisciplinary conversations.* Cresskill, NJ: Hampton.

Kim, A. (1994, December 2). Sci-fi invades Hollywood. *Entertainment Weekly,* No. 251. [http:www.timeinc.com/ew/941202/scifi/251 scifimain.html]

Kramarae, C., & Kramer, J. (1995, February). Net gains, net losses. *Women's Review of Books,* pp. 33–35.

Krol, E. (1992). *The whole Internet: User's guide & catalog.* Sebastopol, CA: O'Reilly.

LaQuey, T. (1994). *The Internet companion: A beginner's guide to global networking.* Reading, MA: Addison-Wesley.

Leslie, J. (1993, March). Mail bonding: E-mail is creating a new oral culture. *Wired, 2*(3).

Leslie, J. (1994, October). Goodbye, Gutenberg: Pixilating peer review is revolutionizing scholarly journals. *Wired, 3*(10), 5–8.

Levin, J. A., Riel M., Miyake, N., & Cohen, M. (1987). Education on the electronic frontier: Teleapprentices in globally distributed educational contexts. *Contemporary Educational Psychology, 12,* 254–260.

Levin, J., Waugh, M., Brown, D., & Clift, R. (1994). Teaching teleapprenticeships: A new organizational framework for improving teacher education using electronic networks. *Journal of Machine-Mediated Learning, 4*(2&3),149–161.

Malone, T. W., & Rockart, J. F. (1991). Computers, networks, and the corporation. *Scientific American, 265*(3),128–136.

Marable, M. (1993). Beyond racial identity politics: Towards a liberation theory for multicultural democracy. *Race & Class, 35,* 113–130.

McGuire, J. (1995). Back to the books. *Home & Away, 16,* 1A–4A.

Michaels, S., Cazden, C., & Bruce, B. (1985). Whose computer is it anyway? *Science for the People, 17, 36,* 43–44.

National Center for Education Statistics, (1995). *The condition of education 1995* (NCES No. 95273, 8/95). Pittsburgh, PA: U.S. Government Printing Office.

Newman, S. B. (1991). *Literacy in the television age: The myth of the TV effect.* Norwood, NJ: Ablex.

Pantelidis, V. S. (1993). Virtual reality in the classroom. *Educational Technology, 33,* 23–27.

Patton, P. (1994). Caught: You used to watch television. Now it watches you. *Wired, 3*(1).

Pimentel K., & Teixeira, K. (1993). *Virtual reality: Through the new looking glass.* New York: McGraw-Hill.

Psotka, J. (1994). *Immersive tutoring systems: Virtual reality and education and training.* [http://198.97.199.60/its.html].

Rosenblatt, L. M. (1978). *The reader, the text, the poem: The transactional theory of the literary work.* Carbondale, IL: Southern Illinois University Press.

Schreibman, V. (1994, December 19). Closing the "values-gap": Communications that block learning. *Federal Information News Syndicate, 2*(26).

Spiro, R. J., Feltovich, P. J., Jacobson, M. J., & Coulson, R. L. (1992). Cognitive flexibility, constructivism, and hypertext: Random access instruction for advanced knowledge acquisition in ill-structured domains. In T. M. Duffy & D. H. Jonassen (Eds.), *Constructivism and the technology of instruction: A conversation* (pp. 57–75). Hillsdale, NJ: Erlbaum.

Suchman, L. (1988, April). Designing with the user: Review of computers and democracy: A Scandinavian challenge. *ACM Transactions on Office Information Systems, 6,*173–183.

Taylor, H. J., Kramarae, C., & Ebben, M. (1993). *Women, information technology, scholarship.* Urbana, IL: University of Illinois.

Thoreau, H. D. (1951). *Walden.* New York: Bramhall House.

Voyager (1994). *3Sixty* [Catalog]. Irvington, NY: Author.

White, M. (1987). *The Japanese educational challenge: A commitment to children.* New York: Free Press.

NAME INDEX

SUBJECT INDEX

893